David Koester

CONCORDIA
SELF-STUDY
COMMENTARY

CONCORDIA SELF-STUDY COMMENTARY

An Authoritative In-Home Resource For Students of the Bible

Old Testament introduction,
notes, and references
by Walter R. Roehrs

New Testament introduction,
notes, and references
and Minor Prophets notes and references
by Martin H. Franzmann

CONCORDIA®

Publishing House
St. Louis

Concordia Publishing House, St. Louis, Missouri

Manufactured in the United States of America

Library of Congress Cataloging in Publication Data

Roehrs, Walter H 1901—
Concordia self-study commentary.

1. Bible—Commentaries. I. Franzmann, Martin H., joint author. II. Title.
BS491.R53 220.7 78-31390
ISBN 0-570-03277-6

FOREWORD

The Concordia Bible with Notes published by Concordia Publishing House in 1947 was a revised edition of the original *Self-Explaining Bible* published by the American Tract Society of New York. This edition proved to be very popular with many Bible students and was therefore sold out within a few years. Unfortunately it was not possible to reprint that edition because the plates were worn out. For this reason and because of repeated requests for such a work we decided to produce an entirely new edition based on the Revised Standard Version.

We asked Dr. Walter R. Roehrs and Dr. Martin H. Franzmann, eminent scholars of the Old and the New Testament, to prepare entirely new notes. The New Testament appeared in 1971.

We herewith present the notes to the entire Bible, under the title *Concordia Self-Study Commentary*.

Although the notes were prepared in reference to the text of the RSV, other versions of the Bible, particularly the King James Version, will be clearly explained by this commentary. The reader will find it helpful to have an appropriate version at hand while using the commentary.

Where words and phrases are quoted from the verses under immediate study, such words or phrases appear in italics. When other related Bible passages are quoted, they are given in quotation marks.

The introductions to the various Bible books have been prepared to present in brief form the background and important features of each book. The introductions will help the reader gain a clear impression of the theme and purpose of the book.

The notes provide in clear, concise language an overview of each section, followed by explanations of passages where further comment was deemed advisable.

The *Concordia Self-Study Commentary* will provide ideal help for the beginner, the advanced student, the teacher, and the Christian family.

The Publisher

CONTENTS

ABBREVIATIONS

OLD TESTAMENT

Gn: Genesis
Ex: Exodus
Lv: Leviticus
Nm: Numbers
Dt: Deuteronomy
Jos: Joshua
Ju: Judges
Ru: Ruth
1 Sm: First Samuel
2 Sm: Second Samuel
1 K: First Kings
2 K Second Kings
1 Ch: First Chronicles
2 Ch: Second Chronicles
Ez: Ezra
Neh: Nehemiah
Est: Esther
Jb: Job
Ps: Psalms
Pr: Proverbs
Ec: Ecclesiastes
SS: Song of Solomon
Is: Isaiah
Jer: Jeremiah
Lm: Lamentations
Eze: Ezekiel
Dn: Daniel
Hos: Hosea
Jl: Joel
Am: Amos
Ob: Obadiah
Jon: Jonah
Mi: Micah
Nah: Nahum
Hab: Habakkuk
Zph: Zephaniah
Hg: Haggai
Zch: Zechariah
Ml: Malachi

APOCRYPHA

1 Esd: First Esdras
2 Esd: Second Esdras
Tob: Tobit
Jdth: Judith
Ap Est: additions to Esther
Wis: Wisdom of Solomon
Sir: Ecclesiasticus, or the Wisdom of Jesus the Son of Sirach
Bar: Baruch
L Jer: Letter of Jeremiah
Ap Dn: additions to Daniel (the Prayer of Azariah and the Song of the Three Young Men)
Sus: Susanna
Bel: Bel and the Dragon
Man: The Prayer of Manasseh
1 Mac: First Maccabees
2 Mac: Second Maccabees

NEW TESTAMENT

Mt: Matthew
Mk: Mark
Lk: Luke
Jn: John
Acts
Ro: Romans
1 Co: First Corinthians
2 Co: Second Corinthians
Gl: Galatians
Eph: Ephesians
Ph: Philippians
Cl: Colossians
1 Th: First Thessalonians
2 Th: Second Thessalonians
1 Ti: First Timothy
2 Ti: Second Timothy
Tts: Titus
Phmn: Philemon
Heb: Hebrews
Ja: James
1 Ptr: First Peter
2 Ptr: Second Peter
1 Jn: First John
2 Jn: Second John
3 Jn: Third John
Jude
Rv: Revelation

OTHER ABBREVIATIONS

cf.: compare, see
ch.: chapter
chs.: chapters
esp.: especially
f.: and the following verse
ff.: and the following verses
KJV: King James Version
lit.: literally
NEB: New English Bible
NT: New Testament
RSV: Revised Standard Version
OT: Old Testament
v.: verse
vv.: verses

THE OLD TESTAMENT

INTRODUCTION

"Put off your shoes from your feet, for the place on which you are standing is holy ground."

So Moses was told when "God called to him out of the bush" which, no different from others he saw, "was burning, yet it was not consumed." (Ex 3:1-6)

The reader of the Scriptures of the OT too should be aware that he has entered into the holy precincts of Him who is "a devouring fire" when "his wrath is . . . kindled," yet also is "merciful and gracious" as His "compassion grows warm and tender" (Dt 4:24; Ps 2:11; Ex 34:6; Hos 11:8). Because the Lord of heaven and earth condescended to make known to the reader "the way of life and the way of death," he humbly prays: "Let me hear what the Lord God will speak." (Jer 21:8; Ps 85:8)

Moses did not inquire why God took a lowly desert shrub, made it "a flame of fire," and from it gave directions for Israel's liberation from Egyptian slavery. So today it would be presumptuous if we were to boggle at the fact that He determined to let His life-giving light shine into our darkness from the pages of the ordinary product of the printing press. As Moses "hid his face" in his encounter with God, so we humbly bow before the miraculous operation by which words spoken, written, and preserved in the form of human communication have been set ablaze with a pervading brilliance of divine truth. As we read and study them, we say gratefully: "Speak, Lord, for Thy servant hears." (1 Sm 3:9)

THE BIBLE OF JESUS

He who was the eternal Word made flesh left us an example of how we are to appraise and use the Scriptures of the OT. It was His Bible, the written Word of God, and invested throughout with authority and power equal to that of the infallible words He uttered.

Jesus demonstrated that He knew His Bible "from cover to cover." We hear Him citing from and alluding to passages found in all its parts. In undergirding His teaching He adduced prooftexts from its sacred pages ranging from Genesis through to Chronicles, the last book in the Jewish arrangement of the canon at the time (cf. Mt 23:35). After His death and resurrection He explained and verified "everything written about" Him in the historical books ("Moses"), in "the prophets," and in the poetic books ("the psalms"; Lk 24:44-49).

A Depository of Ancient History

Jesus confirmed and corroborated what His Bible said took place in Israel's past. In numerous instances He took occasion to attest to the truth of historical data recorded in the OT. What the ancient accounts say had a parallel historical reality in the events and circumstances during His ministry, death, resurrection, and second coming.

The following examples illustrate His use of the Biblical narratives as a depository of recorded facts.

1. The crime against Abel, slain by his brother, and the murder of "the prophets" during all of Israel's past will be repeated and climaxed in Jesus' death. When His enemies kill Him, they will "fill up . . . the measure" of their fathers' guilt incurred "in shedding the blood of the prophets." (Mt 23:29-36; Gn 4:8; 2 Ch 24:21)

2. In "the days of Noah," when the people's "heart was only evil continually," they thought that nothing could change the daily routine of business as usual, "until the flood came and swept them all away." This situation of the distant past will again prevail when a still greater

catastrophe will occur in "the coming of the Son of man" to judge all the nations of the earth. (Mt 24:37-39; Gn 6:5-8)

3. "In the days of Lot" the inhabitants of Sodom are unconcerned about any danger as "they ate, they drank, they bought, they sold, they planted, they built," when suddenly "fire and sulphur rained from heaven and destroyed them all" except Lot and his family. On the day of the Lord history will repeat itself, for it too will come "suddenly . . . upon the face of the earth." (Lk 17:28-30; 21:34 f.; Gn 19:24 f.)

4. The Israelites once "ate manna in the wilderness" which God "gave them . . . from heaven." On this miraculous fact of history Jesus based His claim that the "Father gives . . . bread from heaven" in Him, "the bread of life." (Jn 6:30-35; Ex 16:14 f.)

5. "As Moses lifted up the serpent in the wilderness" to save the people of his day from temporal death, so "the Son of man . . . lifted up" on the cross gives "eternal life" to "whoever believes in him." (Jn 3:14 f.; Nm 21:8 f.)

6. "The queen of the South . . . came from the ends of the earth to hear the wisdom of Solomon." Her search to learn from a wise man put to shame and condemned the people who refused to accept Jesus' teaching even though they had in their very midst "something greater than Solomon." (Mt 12:42; 1 Kgs 10:1 ff.)

7. "The men of Nineveh" who "repented at the preaching of Jonah" were dead and gone. But, says Jesus, they "will arise at the judgment . . . and condemn" His contemporaries on the basis that "to whom much is given, of him will much be required." The heathen in that ancient city accepted the preaching of a foreign prophet; the scribes and Pharisees were granted "something greater than Jonah" when they had the opportunity to hear Jesus' call to repentance. (Mt 12:41; Lk 12:48; Jon 3:5)

A Depository of Doctrinal Truths

He who came from the bosom of the Father adduced prooftexts from His Bible to document and validate what He Himself said about the true relationship of fallen humanity to God.

1. In answer to the question what must man "do" if he expects to "inherit eternal life" Jesus quoted "what is written in the law" of Moses. (Lk 10:25-28; Dt 6:5; Lv 19:18)

2. The rich man's brothers could escape the "place of torment" and instead be "carried by the angels to Abraham's bosom," if they would hear and believe the writings of "Moses and the prophets." (Lk 16:19-31)

3. Jesus established the mission of John the Baptist by quoting what "is written" of him by the prophet Malachi. (Mt 11:2-14; Ml 3:1)

4. Though the disciples did not understand Jesus at the time, He taught them what "is written . . . by the prophets" about the necessity of His impending death and resurrection if the human race was to be redeemed. (Lk 18:31-34)

A Depository to Refute False Doctrines

Teaching "not as" the "scribes" and Pharisees but with "authority" (Mt 7:29), Jesus used His Bible to correct current false teachings and to refute Satan's perversion of Scripture.

1. In order to prove to the scribes and Pharisees that "the tradition of the elders," espoused by them, "made void" what "God commanded," Jesus quoted passages recorded in the Book of Exodus. (Mt 15:1-6; Ex 20:12; 21:17)

2. He accused the Sadducees, who said "there is no resurrection," of knowing "neither the scriptures nor the power of God." Jesus refuted their heresy with a prooftext from His Bible, directing them to read "what was said . . . by God" in Ex 3:6, 16. (Mt 22:23-33)

3. In the Sermon on the Mount Jesus repeatedly took issue with false teachings current at the time. Lest His discussion of legal portions in His Bible be misunderstood, He introduced His pronouncements by saying that He had not "come to abolish the law and the prophets . . . but to fulfil them" (Mt 5:17; cf. Lk 16:17). Throughout His discourse He did not direct strictures against the validity of what was written in the law of Moses but rather inveighed against what His disciples "heard . . . said to the men of old" about its meaning and scope. Again and

again He denounced traditional wrong explanations and limited applications of the divine precepts. In order to correct these aberrations, He revealed how the Lawgiver wanted His words to be understood by declaring: "But I say to you." (Mt 5:21-48)

4. As Jesus upheld the validity of the written word and opposed erroneous views held by people in His day, so He drew prooftexts from His Bible to put to flight "the father of lies," "the ruler of this world" (Jn 8:44; 12:31). Three times He disarmed the devil's temptation with the rejoinder: "It is written." The words He quoted are found in Dt 8:3; 6:16, 13. (Mt 4:1-11)

A Depository of Testimony to Him

Jesus directed His hearers to His Bible to substantiate His claim to be the promised Savior of humanity. The words "written ... by the prophets," He said, "bear witness" to Him and the divine mission He had come to accomplish (Lk 18:31; Jn 5:39). Prophecies of His suffering, death, and resurrection were on record "in all the scriptures" (Lk 24:27). Because "Moses ... wrote of" Him, it is as reprehensible to refuse to believe the written Word as it is to reject His own words. (Jn 5:45-47)

The Word of God

Jesus assigned to His Bible the power and authority of the Word of God.

When He read from it in Nazareth (Lk 4:17), it was not a printed and bound book such as we have. On its sacred pages were "writings" or "scriptures" copied by hand on parchments and therefore introduced so frequently by the formula: "It is written."

Yet what was preserved in written documents was no less the Word of God than when He gave it to His inspired authors. Jesus said nothing to suggest that God's spoken communication with His fallen creatures lost the authority of His infallible Word when it was read in written form. To the contrary, He expressly identified what was recorded in the Scriptures with the Word of God.

1. In Jn 10:35 He equated "the word of God" which "came" to men of old with "scripture" which "cannot be broken."

2. Jesus accused His enemies of "making void the word of God" which could be read in Ex 20:12. (Mk 7:9-13)

3. The words which the Creator Himself spoke were available to anyone who "read." (Mt 19:4-5; Gn 2:24)

4. "The desolating sacrilege spoken of by the prophet Daniel," revealed to him in a vision, was written as a warning for "the reader" of the Scriptures. (Mt 24:15; Dn 9:27)

The identity and synonymous use of the terms Scripture and the Word of God are on record also in Jesus' Bible. "All the words ... spoken" by the Lord to Jeremiah remained no less "the words of the Lord" when they were read from a scroll on which they were written. (Jer 36:1-10)

The Bible of the Inspired Writers of the NT

In instances too numerous and varied to cite here, the authors of the NT followed the example of their Master. They too used the Bible of Jesus as an authoritative depository of historical data, of doctrinal truth, of warnings against false teaching, of prophetic testimony to the person and mission of their risen Lord.

Jesus' equation of His Bible with the Word of God also is repeatedly echoed in their writings. Themselves "taught by the Spirit" and empowered to write "a command of the Lord," they declare "the sacred writings" and "all scripture" to be words "inspired by God" (1 Co 2:13; 14:37; 2 Ti 3:14-16)

1. The Jews were "entrusted with the oracles of God," "God's word" (Ro 3:2; Heb 5:12; cf. Acts 7:38)

2. "The good news" of the risen Christ, "promised to the fathers," fulfilled what "is written in the second psalm" and what God "spoke" in Is 55:3 and "says" in Ps 16:10. (Acts 13:30-35)

3. Paul directed his readers to be instructed by what God "says in Hosea" 2:23 and 1:10. (Ro 9:25 f.)

4. Paul also asserted that "the Holy Spirit was right in saying" the words spoken "through Isaiah the prophet." (Acts 28:25-27; Is 6:9 f.)

5. According to Heb 4:7 God is "saying" what David wrote in Ps 95:7 f.

6. What is written in Ex 33:19 is the word God "says to Moses." (Ro 9:15)

Jesus' Bible: Our Bible

Jesus' Bible is not a museum piece in an antiquarian's collection of ancient literature.

In it are words of "warning . . . written down for our instruction, upon whom the end of the ages has come," lest we too "desire evil" and become victims of "the Destroyer." (1 Cor 10:6-11)

But not only the Law but also the Gospel is found in "the sacred writings," for they "are able to instruct you for salvation through faith in Christ Jesus." (2 Ti 3:15)

Jesus' Bible is not a depository of truth and error. Nothing in it can be ignored as false or discarded as useless, for "all Scripture is inspired by God and is profitable for teaching, for reproof, for correction, and for training in righteousness, that the man of God may be complete, equipped for every good work." (2 Ti 3:16 f.)

It is the writer's hope and prayer that the appended explanatory notes will do in some small degree what Jesus did so perfectly when He "opened . . . the Scriptures" to His disciples on the road to Emmaus.

Walter R. Roehrs

GENESIS

INTRODUCTION

Content

The first book of the Bible, originally unnamed, is known today by the title it bears in the Septuagint, an ancient Greek version of the OT. Genesis is a common noun and denotes a genetic process of coming into being. In the Septuagint it is used to translate the Hebrew word *toledoth* (always in the plural form) that introduces the 10 main divisions of the book. (2:4; 5:1; 6:9; 10:1; 11:10; 11:27; 25:12; 25:19; 36:1; 37:2; cf. 2:4 note; Mt 1:1)

No other book of the Bible is outlined by such clearly marked divisions. These 10 sections in turn have two distinct foci. The first five deal with universal history (2:4—11:26); the remaining half is a record of individuals and their families, the patriarchs whom God chose from the families of the earth to be the bearers of His promise of salvation. (11:27—50:26)

Each of the major parts likewise has a common denominator. As the second part tells of the implementation of God's plan of salvation in the lives of three patriarchs, so the first half revolves about the theme of a thrice repeated crisis in the history of mankind. After time and space, the stage of man's history, had been created (1:1—2:3), man's response to the Creator precipitated three situations that brought him to the brink of catastrophe. But in each instance God's justice is tempered with forbearance. (1) Adam and Eve rebelled against their creature status. However, the sentence of death was not executed immediately and totally. To deliver His fallen creatures from their self-inflicted doom, God promised the coming of the woman's Seed (chs. 2—3). (2) But the human family, begotten of the first parents, was no better than they, even worse. Their "wickedness was great in the earth" to such an extent as to provoke God to "blot out man . . . from the face of the earth." Again total destruction was averted: "Noah found favor in the eyes of the Lord," and the end did not come. God made a new beginning in His covenant with Noah (ch. 6). (3) When the survivors of the Deluge became a family of nations (ch. 10), sin also multiplied. There was national defiance of God, expressed in the building of the Tower of Babel. Man's history seemed to have come to a dead end in the confusion and separation from God that resulted (ch. 11). But His patience still was not at an end. In the Table of Nations there appears the name of a man through whose descendants God had determined to carry forward His plan of saving mankind. The man's name was Shem, the ancestor of Abraham (10:31). So the stage is set for the history of the three patriarchs, recorded in the five "chapters" that constitute the second part of Genesis.

Authorship

From most ancient times Genesis and the four following books have been regarded as a literary unit, called "the Law" by the Jews and known to us as the Pentateuch (a Greek word meaning: having five volumes). The theme of all five books is the creation of the people chosen to be the bearers of God's promise of salvation. Genesis portrays the need of a universal redemption and records the preliminary steps that God took to implement His plan by selecting the patriarchs, the ancestors of Israel. The four books following Genesis tell the story how the ancestral family became that nation, of whom "according to the flesh is the Christ." (Ro 9:5)

The Old and New Testaments ascribe the authorship of the Pentateuch to Moses. While there is no explicit mention of him as the writer of Genesis, the Scriptures refer to passages from Exodus to Deuteronomy as the spoken and written word of Moses (cf., for example, Jos 8:31; 23:6; 2 K 14:6; Ez 6:18; Neh 13:1; Mk 12:26; Lk 2:22; 5:14; Jn 7:23). The terms "law of Moses," "the book of Moses," and others imply that the five books constitute a unit, the writings of Moses, as Jesus called them. (Lk 24:27, 44; Jn 5:45-47)

The Mosaic authorship is denied by most modern OT scholars. Certain literary, historical, and theological phenomena in the present text convince them that these five books are a compilation of several literary strands. Each of these was given written form at various times centuries after the time of Moses. Although there is no agreement on the number of these sources, the time of their composition, and the number of books in which they can be traced, there is a general consensus that the Pentateuch is a fusion of four main documents, still recognizable by their distinctive features and labeled J (Jahwist), E (Elohist), D (Deuteronomic), P (Priestly). Composed separately beginning in the 10th or 9th century B.C., these independent sources were combined with one another in the course of time, the final redaction taking place after the return from the Babylonian Captivity in the 6th century B.C. In more recent times efforts have been made to identify distinctive literary forms within and behind these written sources and to find their origin in oral tradition.

Such an explanation of certain phenomena that are observed in the Pentateuch (difference in vocabulary and style, repetitions, varying religious viewpoints) is admittedly an unproved theory. Its assumptions and conjectures have not been verified historically, leave serious questions unanswered, and raise new ones. Conservative scholars have insisted that these phenomena can be accounted for in a way that does not conflict with the view of a basic Mosaic authorship of the Pentateuch.

OUTLINE

I. 1:1—11:26 History of Mankind

1:1—2:3 Creation of the World: The Stage of Human History

A. 2:4—4:26 History of Heaven and Earth
   1. 2:4—3:24 From "It Is Good" to "Groaning in Travail"
   2. 4:1-26 From Sinful Parents to Sinful Offspring

B. 5:1—6:8 History of Adam
   1. 5:1-32 Adam's Offspring
   2. 6:1-8 The Perversity of Adam's Offspring

C. 6:9—9:29 History of Noah
   1. 6:9—8:19 Noah and the Flood
   2. 8:20—9:29 Noah After the Flood

D. 10:1—11:9 History of Noah's Sons: Shem, Ham, Japheth
   1. 10:1-32 Table of Nations
   2. 11:1-9 Tower of Babel

E. 11:10-26 History of Shem

II. 11:27—50:26 Patriarchal History

A. 11:27—25:11 History of Abraham, Terah's Son
   1. 11:27—20:18 Before Isaac's Birth
   2. 21:1—25:11 After Isaac's Birth

B. 25:12-18 History of Ishmael

C. 25:19—35:29 History of Isaac
   1. 25:19—27:40 Before Jacob's Flight from Esau

2. 27:41—33:20 Jacob's Stay with Laban and Return to Canaan
3. 34:1—35:29 Jacob's Later Family History

D. 36:1-43 History of Esau

E. 37:1—50:26 History of Jacob
1. 37:1—40:23 Before and During Joseph's Degradation in Egypt
2. 41:1—47:31 After Joseph's Exaltation
3. 48:1—50:26 The Blessing of Jacob's Sons and His Death

1:1—11:26 THE HISTORY OF MANKIND

1:1—2:3 Creation of the World: The Stage of Human History

1:1-2 SUPERSCRIPTION: PRIMEVAL ORIGIN OF THE UNIVERSE

1:1 *In the beginning.* The human mind cannot project its thinking beyond this point.—The RSV note offers the alternative translation: "When God began to create." This rendering of the Hebrew text, possible grammatically, implies that Gn 1 does not relate how a nonexistent universe came into being, but what God did to produce cosmological order out of preexistent matter that v. 2 describes as chaotic. The first two verses are regarded as subordinate clauses and depict the circumstances that prevailed when God's creative activity began (3). The first verse, however, is best construed as an independent clause. In keeping with Hebrew usage it serves as a superscription or topic sentence of the entire ch.

Heaven and earth is a comprehensive term to denote everything that we call universe, including the raw materials that God shaped into a cosmos. In the OT the verb *created* is reserved for an action of which only God is the subject. No human activity is analogous to it. Creation produces something that had no prior existence. In some instances God creates by using existing material (man of dust from the ground, 2:7); in others He calls into being something that had no antecedent existence in any form. Sublime in its simplicity, the brief sentence of v. 1 therefore states the eternal truth, comprehended only by faith, that everything, animate and inanimate, came into existence by divine fiat when *in the beginning God created the heavens and the earth.* (Gn 2:4; Jb 38:4; Ps 8; 89:11-12; 90:2; 104; 121:2; 124:8; 146:6; 148:1-6; Pr 8:23; Is 40:26, 28; 42:5; 45:7, 12, 18; 65:17; Jer 51:15; Zch 12:1; Jn 1:1-3; Acts 14:15; 17:24; Eph 3:9; Cl 1:16-17; Heb 1:10; 3:4; 11:3; Rv 4:11; 10:6)

1:2 *Without form and void.* The created materials were unstructured, not as yet "formed . . . to be inhabited" and therefore still destitute of living creatures and vegetation, the final products of the creative process (Is 45:18; Jb 26:7; Jer 4:23). *The earth.* The focus of interest of the following account and of the entire Biblical story is to be man's life on earth in its relationship to the Creator. *The deep.* The watery abyss; Hebrew: *tehom,* a masculine noun; in Babylonian mythology a female dragon, Tiamat, is destroyed by the god Marduk, who divides her body to constitute "heaven and earth."

Spirit of God. RSV alternate reading: "wind" of God; some recent versions: "a mighty wind," eliminating divine involvement and merely describing the turbulence of the "void and empty." As in Greek, the Hebrew word denotes "wind" or "breath," but also has the transferred meaning of "spirit," human and divine. Scripture elsewhere attributes creative activity to the Spirit of God (Jb 33:4; 26:13 [RSV: "wind"]" Ps 104:30). *Moving over,* hovered over, like a bird (Dt 32:11), expressing His power and desire to give form to what was *without form* and to fill the *void.*

1:3—2:3 CREATION OF THE WORLD AND ALL CREATURES

1) 1:3-5 Day One: Light

1:3 *God said.* Putting into effect His will, God commands what was nonexistent (Ps 33:9; Jn 1:3; Heb 11:3; cf. the words of Jesus, Mt 8:3, etc.). *Light.* Its creation meets a prime requisite for life: plant, animal, man (Is 45:7; 2 Co 4:6), as Christ is for spiritual life. (Jn 1:4, 5, 9; 8:12; 9:5; 12:46; Eph 4:14)

1:5 *One day.* The first day, reckoned from *evening* to *morning* according to prevailing custom (Ps 74:16). The six days of creation make up a period of time equal to Israel's workweek. Cf. Ex 20:11 note.

2) 1:6-8 2d Day: Separation of Waters

1:6 *A firmament.* An expanse above and around the earth, acting as an invisible barrier to prevent the merging of the waters "above" and "under" it into the previous chaotic condition, it is also called "spreading out the skies" or "stretching out the heavens"; to the eye it may appear like a "molten mirror," establishing a glistening and yet unbreakably decreed line of demarcation between heaven and earth. (Jb 37:16, 18; Ps 104:2; 148:4-6; Is 42:5; 44:24; 45:12; 48:13; Jer 10:12; 51:15; Dn 12:3; Zch 12:1)

3) 1:9-13 3d Day: Land and Plants

1:9 *Waters . . . dry land.* Conglomerate when created, they are now separated into land masses and bodies of water, thus making the earth habitable for man and capable of sustaining plant and animal life. (Jb 38:8-11; Ps 33:7; 46:2-3; 95:5; 104:9; Pr 8:29-30; 30:4; Jer 5:22)

1:10 *Good.* Like an artisan, God rejoices over the product of His craftsmanship, its beauty and perfection; repeated in vv. 12, 18, 21, 25, 31.

1:11 *Vegetation.* The necessary condition for it having been provided, plant life is made to appear in profusion, endowed with innate fertility *according to its kind.* (Jb 38:27; Ps 104:14; 147:8; Lk 6:44)

4) 1:14-19 4th Day: Sun, Moon, and Stars

1:14 *Lights.* These light-bearers or luminaries are to make for order in a world of space and time and to serve man; the "greater" (the sun) and the "lesser" (the moon) are to signal *seasons* (particularly also the time of festival days) and to calendar the sequence and lapse of *days and years.*

1:16 *The stars.* This includes all the other celestial bodies without differentiating them according to modern astronomical classification. (Dt 4:19; 2 K 23:5; Jb 26:10; Ps 19:1, 4-6; 74:16-17; 104:19-20; 136:7-9; 147:4; Is 60:19-20; Rv 21:23)

5) 1:20-23 5th Day: Birds and Sea Animals

1:20 *Birds.* Presumably they were brought forth from the water like the fish, although it is not explicitly stated.

6) 1:24-31 6th Day: Land Animals and Man

1:24 *Cattle . . . creeping things . . . beasts.* Animal life that moves on the ground is classified in general terms as domesticated (*cattle*), undomesticated (*beasts*), and gliding or crawling creatures (*creeping things;* Gn 1:26; 7:14; Jb 12:7-10). Like the marine animals and the birds (22), they also are made with the inherent power of reproduction *according to their kinds.*

1:26 *Let us.* To call attention to the making of man as the climax of God's creation, He is portrayed as taking this momentous step only after special planning and, as some believe, in consultation with the heavenly court of angels, "the sons of God" (Jb 1:6; 38:7; Ps 29:1; 148:2-3). The plural construction more likely is to indicate that the full power and wisdom of the Godhead (the Hebrew *elohim* has a plural ending) comes into play at this decisive moment. (2:7; 11:7)

Dominion over. Although formed from the ground like the animals (2:7) and sharing some physical features with them, man is made to be superior to them; they are to be subservient to him.

1:27 *In the image of God.* Man's unique status among all other creatures (26, 28) derives from his relationship to the Creator. Not a physical replica of God (Is 40:18; Lk 24:39; Jn 4:24), not an emanation or a part of God, not independent of God, man nevertheless is given features that correspond and relate to the Creator: the capacity to share in His rulership and the responsibility to exercise this partnership in a communion with Him that reflects how God wants him to be and act, and thus bears His "likeness" (26) and imprint. When man subsequently broke this divinely stipulated relationship, dragging all creation with him into frustrating disharmony (Ro 8:20-23), he lost the ability to live and act in harmony with God, as he was intended to do (Gn 3; 5:1-3; Ja 3:9). Christ, "the image of the invisible God" (Cl 1:15; 2 Co 4:4; Heb 1:3), was made man that men might "put on the new nature, created after the likeness of God in true righteousness and holiness" (Eph 4:24; Ro 8:29), "after the image of its creator." (Cl 3:10; 1 Co 15:49; 2 Co 3:18)

1:28 *Be fruitful and multiply.* By the Creator's will and with His blessing man becomes a procreator: a sacred gift and responsibility.

7) 2:1-3 The Sabbath

2:2 *Rested.* The Hebrew *shabath* means to cease working, to rest from work (cf. the noun "sabbath"). Like an artisan who has finished his project, God ended His activity of the six previous days. He had completed what He set out to do: primary or first creation. His creative activity, however, continues in what is sometimes called secondary creation. (Jb 12:7-10; 33:4; Ps 104:30; Pr 22:2; Is 40:26-29; 45:7; Jer 31:35; Jn 5:17; Ro 11:36; 2 Co 5:5; Cl 1:16-17)

Summary: Symmetrical and schematic in structure, approaching poetic form, majestic in its simplicity, this first section of the Bible reveals what human thinking is unable to penetrate: the mystery of the origin of matter and life in their space-time dimensions. Uncluttered by changing scientific terminology, describing "heaven and earth and all that is therein" as phenomena visible to the naked eye of every unsophisticated observer, it sets forth truths that are grasped only "by faith" (Heb 11:3) and are axiomatic for faith in redemption: (1) Matter is not eternal or self-generating; it was given a beginning by God, separate from and transcending it. (2) The universe is not autonomous or "closed," but subject to the Creator's will. (3) Man, like all creation, was made *good,* but in addition *in the image of God,* superior and different from animals; partnership and fellowship with the Creator constitute the prerogative and the requirement of man's humanity; leaving this status makes man inhuman, bestial, rejected of God, and in need of redemption. (4) *The beginning* also points to an end of *heaven and earth.*

2:4—4:26 The History of Heaven and Earth

2:4—3:24 FROM "IT IS GOOD" TO "GROANING IN TRAVAIL"

1) 2:4-7 Condition of Heaven and Earth When Man Was Created

2:4 *Generations.* The Hebrew noun *toledoth* (always in the plural), has connotations that cannot be reproduced by a single English word. Variously rendered in the RSV by "generations," "descendants," "history," "families," it is the equivalent of "genealogical history." Derived from a verb meaning "to beget, bring forth" (children), "to produce" (something: Ps 7:14; Pr 27:1), it denotes a record in terms of antecedents: of persons as begotten of ancestors (descendants) and of happenings as brought forth or issuing from prior circumstances (history). *These are the generations.* This sentence serves as a title or superscription of the 10 "chapter" divisions of Genesis (Gn 2:4; 5:1; 6:9; 10:1; 11:10; 11:27; 25:12; 25:19; 36:1; 37:2). Not a summary of the preceding account of the ultimate origin of all things, as suggested by the division of the verse in the RSV, its purpose in 4 is rather to introduce a "chapter" which relates what developed as a sequel to the creation of heaven and earth: the universal degradation from "it is good" to "groaning in travail" (Ro 8:22), precipitated by man's sin and affecting him and the "whole creation." Ch. 2 sets the stage for the Fall (ch. 3). It tells of the condition of the earth in terms of man's existence, of God's special provision for him, of the scene and circumstances of the Fall, supplementing the terse account of man's creation in ch. 1 with such data only as come into play in the ensuing fatal drama.

Lord. For the meaning of this divine name see Ex 3:15 note.

2:5 *When . . . yet.* Vv. 5-8 set forth the conditions that prevailed on earth in view of man's need when God had "formed man" but before He planted the Garden of Eden. *Plant.* Not vegetation in general is meant, but a "shrub," perhaps the "thorns and thistles" that came as a result of the Fall (3:18). *Herb.* Not herbs with medicinal or pungent qualities but "plants" for which man did not as yet "till the ground" in order "to eat bread" (3:18-19, 23; Ps 104:13-14). *Not . . . rain.* Another not-yet function of heaven and earth.

2:7 *Man . . . from the ground.* In Hebrew this phrase represents a play on words: *adam* from *adamah.* God had proceeded to "make man" (1:26) from the earth like the animals, and like them man became a *living being.* But man is given a uniquely superior status among all creatures by receiving the Creator's own *breath of life* as a constitutive element of his vital being. (Jb 33:4)

2) 2:8-17 The Creator's Provision for Man's Existence: The Garden of Eden

2:8 *Garden.* The Greek translation of the OT renders it "paradise." *Eden.* In Hebrew it means "delight"; here it apparently is a geographic term to denote the area in which the garden was planted and which is further described in 10-14 as a place where a river "divided and became four rivers." Mainly because two of these, the "Pishon" and the "Gihon," remain unidentified, the precise location of *the garden of Eden, in the east* cannot be established. (3:23-24; Is 51:3; Eze 28:13; 31:9, 16, 18; 36:35; Jl 2:3)

2:17 *Tree of the knowledge of good and evil.* The command not to eat of this tree is not a capricious whim on God's part but a sovereign decree, limiting man's status as creature over against the Creator. If man, created with the capacity of a moral choice, arrogates to himself what God has reserved for Himself and seeks to invade the divine prerogative of knowing all things by making himself the judge of what is good or evil, he would thereby vitiate God's intention in giving him life: He would most certainly die. (2 Sm 14:17, 20; Dt 29:39; Eze 18:4; Gn 3:19)

3) 2:18-25 The Creator's Provision for Man's Conjugal Life: Marriage

2:18-25 Again a "flashback" to the sixth day of creation (1:24-31), these verses supply additional information regarding the circumstances that form the background for the main narrative: the account of the Fall, namely, (a) one of the "wild creatures," whose subservience to man is further attested by his naming of all animals, is to play a significant part in depriving man of his original status as God's vicegerent (1:26, 28); (b) the woman is described more fully as *a helper fit for him* (1:27 merely: "male and female") to anticipate the unhelpful role she was soon to play in the Fall, a fit partner in crime and of equal accountability.

2:23 *Woman . . . Man.* A play on words in Hebrew, based on the similarity of sound of *ishah* (woman) and *ish* (man).

2:24 *One flesh.* Woman's nature makes possible a union with man so intimate and complete in every respect as to constitute a merging of themselves into *one flesh.* (Mt 19:4-5; Mk 10:8; 1 Co 6:16; Eph 5:31; 1 Ti 2:13)

4) 3:1-24 Disruption of Man's Relationship to the Creator: The Fall

a. 3:1-7 Temptation to Be Like the Creator

3:1 *The serpent.* One of the "wild creatures," characterized only here as *subtle,* "deceived Eve" (2 Co 11:3), not by its own serpentine cunning but by the diabolical craftiness of the anti-God foe of man, later called Satan, the accuser (1 Ch 21:1; Jb 1:6-9; Zch 3:1; Rv 12:9; 20:2), or the devil. Capable of disguising himself as "an angel of light" (2 Co 11:14), of making man his spokesman or henchman (Mt 16:23; Lk 22:3), of taking possession of human beings (Mt 12:22-27), he here seizes upon the serpent as his device to alienate man from his Creator (Ro 5:12; 1 Co 15:22). *He said.* His conversation with the woman reveals his satanic subtleness: (a) Using the "soft sell" approach, he asks a disarmingly innocent question of information, put in such a way, however, as to kindle doubt in the woman's mind regarding the validity of God's prohibition: was it not in conflict with the previous declaration of His unrestricted kindness ("every tree . . . for food," 1:29)? (b) Although the woman still wants to resist the sly insinuation that a good God could have put a cruel limitation on her, the Tempter gleefully notices that he has succeeded in arousing in her the first indications of bitterness against God as she adds to the stringency of the prohibition: "neither . . . touch it" (3). (c) The Tempter is quick to capitalize on this emerging breach of confidence by denying the validity of the threatened consequences (4) and by brashly asserting that eating of the tree would rather put into her grasp what God was jealously denying her (5). (d) Persuaded by "the father of lies" that the Creator had arbitrarily limited her potential for full self-realization, she regards the fruit of the tree as something that "was to be desired" (6). (e) "Desire when it has conceived gives birth to sin" (Ja 1:15): "she took . . . and ate." (f) Assuming the role of the serpent as the lying spokesman of the Tempter, the woman "gave some" of the fruit "to her husband." Such is the "anatomy" of temptation. (Acts 5:3; 13:10; 2 Co 2:11; 4:4; 11:3; Eph 6:11-16; 2 Ti 2:26; 1 Ptr 5:8; Rv 12:9-12)

3:7 *Naked.* Too late they realized that the Tempter's half-truth was more insidious than an out-and-out lie: their *eyes . . . were opened* indeed, but only to see what brought a hitherto unknown sense of shame (2:25; 3:8). Seemingly only a minor by-product, this result of sin nevertheless epitomizes the catastrophic change in man's entire relationship to his fellow creatures. If sin was capable of tainting even the pure harmony that existed in the most intimate union of man and woman in "one flesh," its corrupting power affects also all other aspects of man's relationship with his fellowmen. (Gn 4:8; Gl 5:19-21; 1 Jn 3:15)

b. 3:8-19 The Creator's Curse and Promise of Redemption

3:8 *Hid themselves.* Sin above all destroyed man's harmonious relationship to his Creator; now it is marked by shame and fear, insolence and defiance. Conscious of his guilt, he attempts to avoid detection; brought to account, he seeks to shift the blame—ultimately on God Himself. (Ex 32:21 note; 1 Sm 13:12 note; 1 Ch 28:9; Jb 31:33; Ps 139:1-12; Pr 28:13; Is 33:14; Jer 17:10; 23:24; Am 9:2-3; Ro 1:20)

3:14 *Cursed.* The punishment of the Tempter, unrelieved by a prospect of a reversal of his fate, is expressed in terms of his instrument, the serpent, in its relationship to *all cattle and . . . wild animals;* to *go upon your belly* (crawl) and to *eat dust* is synonymous with groveling humiliation and defeat. (Ps 72:9; 44:25; Is 49:23; 65:25; Mi 7:17)

3:15 *Bruise your head.* This verse explains how the defeat of the Tempter will ultimately be brought about. Having posed as promoting man's advantage, he is first of all unmasked as the implacable enemy of the woman and her *seed* or offspring. In spite of his initial victory, his enmity and that of his *seed* (his legions) furthermore does not entitle him to lay an uncontested claim on his beguiled victims. Permitted, however, to exploit the evil that he has engendered in man, he will indeed be able to vent his hatred by bruising the heel of the woman and her seed with painful and deadly wounds. But his enmity will also prove to be his undoing. Although no offspring of the woman had been able to overcome him by crushing his head, One, "born of woman" (Gl 4:4) would come "to destroy the works of the devil" (1 Jn 3:8). Mortally wounded in the conflict, He nevertheless inflicted the deathblow on demonic power. Jesus Christ, Executor of God's curse on Satan and man's Champion, enables man to look forward to a victorious end of his strife with his enemy because the "God of peace will soon crush Satan under your feet" (Ro 16:20). The curse on the serpent constitutes the first Gospel, the Protevangel. (Jn 12:31; Acts 26:18; Ro 5:18-19; Heb 2:14; Rv 12:1, 7)

3:16 *Woman.* The painful consequences of sin affect the woman in her role of *childbearing* and in her relationship to her *husband.* (Gn 35:16; Is 13:8; 42:14; Jn 16:21; 1 Co 11:3; 14:34; Eph 5:22-23; 1 Th 5:3; 1 Ti 2:11-14)

3:17-19 *Adam.* For his sustenance man must now engage in wearisome and frustrating *toil* and in unremitting battle against obnoxious products of the *ground,* now *cursed* because of him and made hostile to his efforts to till it. (2:15; 1:29; Ro 8:20; Heb 6:8).

Dust. A final penalty of sin is pronounced: man's earthly existence is to come to an end by the disintegration of his material substance into the lifeless dust of which he was formed. (Jb 34:15; Ps 90:3; Ec 3:20; 12:7; Ro 5:12)

c. 3:20-24 Eve, Mother of All Men, and Man Barred from Eden

3:20 *Eve.* See the RSV note. Without a word of protest, Adam responds to the verdict of "dust to dust" by gratefully acknowledging God's tempering of justice with mercy; instead of imposing immediate and absolute death (2:17), God will let him live to have "living" offspring: "seed" of the woman. (4:1; Acts 17:26)

3:22 *Like . . . us.* Divine self-exhortation had preceded the decision to make man in God's "image" and "likeness" (1:26); now the Godhead contemplates with sad scorn what a grotesque caricature of the perfect design man had made of himself by his ridiculous attempt to be like his Creator in his own rebellious way. (2:7)

Tree of life. Lest man eat of the tree of life and so perpetuate his unhappy existence, God drove him from the garden and posted an angelic guard at its entrance. (Rv 2:7)

4:1-26 FROM SINFUL PARENTS TO SINFUL OFFSPRING

1) 4:1-16 Adam's Sons: Cain and Abel

4:1 *Cain.* RSV note *g* explains the play on words in the Hebrew meaning of the name.

With the help of the Lord. In her son, Eve gratefully recognized a gift of the Lord. According to Luther's translation, "I have the man, the Lord," Eve believed that God's promise of the Crusher of the serpent (3:15) had already been fulfilled in her firstborn; Cain, however, turned out to be a disappointment.

4:2 *Abel.* A common noun in Hebrew, meaning "breath, transitoriness, vanity," befitting one whose life was to be snuffed out prematurely.

4:3 *Offering.* The first recorded worship. Its form is not traced to an explicit direction by God. To express their grateful dependence on Him and to implore the benediction of His grace, men brought gift sacrifices of the best they had to offer.

4:4 *Regard for.* God's reactions were not caused by the material difference in the offerings but by the difference in the motives and attitudes of the two brothers. God sees and looks for more than the outward acts of worship. (Heb 11:4)

4:5 *Very angry.* In some undisclosed way (cf. 1 K 18:31) Cain was made aware of God's displeasure with his sacrifice. But he does not search his own heart for the cause of his rejection. In his sullen anger and downcast mien the inner perversity came to the surface.

4:7 *Couching at the door.* God lays bare the hidden springs of evil in man. With insidious cunning the impulse to sin couches in the subconscious thickets of his thoughts intent upon leaping into action the moment the *door* of opportunity is open. Not God or Abel, not his environment or particular occupation are to be blamed for the fact that Cain has not been *accepted.* If he does not *master* himself and does not *do well,* he is held accountable for it. (6:5; 8:21; 1 Ch 28:9; Ps 7:9; 19:12; 90:8; Pr 4:23, Jer 17:10; Mt 12:34; 15:19; Acts 5:3-4; Eph 6:6; Heb 4:12)

4:8 *Killed him.* No longer in the right relationship with his Creator, man has also no ties with his fellowman that he regards sacred. Social sins run the gamut from not acting as the brother's keeper to spilling his blood in murder.

4:9 *Brother's keeper.* Instead of shedding responsibility, Cain actually incriminates himself with this question. Whoever refuses to consider himself to be under divine obligation to be his brother's keeper has no brother any longer; he has already murderously done away with him. (Mt 5:21; 25:43; 1 Jn 2:9-11; 3:15, 17; 4:20)

4:10 *Your brother's blood.* When Cain silenced the voice of Abel, he set in motion sound waves that shrieked his guilt against his brother's *blood* or life in the ears of its Giver and Protector.

"Abel's blood for vengeance pleaded to the skies;
But the blood of Jesus for our pardon cries."

(Lv 17:11; Ps 9:12; Mt 23:35; Heb 12:24; 1 Ptr 1:19; 1 Jn 1:7; Rv 6:10)

4:11 *You are cursed.* When Adam sinned, not he but the earth was cursed (3:17); now Cain is the direct object of the curse. Because he has desecrated the *ground* with his brother's blood, it will in his case be particularly reluctant to "yield" its "strength" when he tills it. (Dt 11:17)

4:14 *A fugitive and a wanderer.* Sin drives man ever farther from God's *face.* Adam and Eve had been banished from the Garden of Eden, where they had tried to hide themselves from Him. Driven by an evil conscience and the fear of retribution at the hands of fellowmen, Cain "went away from the presence of the Lord" to "the land of Nod" (Hebrew: "wandering") and was thus deprived also of the comfort that comes from mutual trust between man and man. (Pr 14:32; 15:29; 28:1; Hos 9:17; Ro 2:14; Heb 9:14; 10:22)

4:15 *A mark.* As in the case of Adam and Eve, God did not strike Cain dead on the spot but granted him a reprieve and mercifully afforded him protection against a human executioner, an avenger of blood, by a sign of some kind that He put on Cain. *Lest any.* Throughout his life Cain would have to reckon with the possibility that a potential avenger would seek him out.

2) 4:17-26 Cain's Offspring

4:17 *Wife.* The genealogies of Scripture, of which Cain's is the first (17-24), do not furnish a complete list of the members of each family unit. They do not even form an unbroken chain of successive generations (cf. Mt 1:1-17). Since their purpose is to link coming events with the past, they record only the names that are necessary to establish this connection. So in the case of Cain, the name of only one son is recorded. Presumably his wife was his sister, an unnamed daughter of Adam, who became his wife prior to his crime. (3:20; Acts 17:26).

A city. The fugitive and wanderer enclosed his dwellings with a wall, perhaps as a protective measure. No criticism is leveled at urban living as such, although this note may anticipate what developed later when evil men congregated and built a city to "make a name." (11:1-4)

4:19 *Lamech.* The genealogy of Cain runs its degenerate course and ends in further perversion of good into evil: bigamous marriage; metal for murder; instruments of music to accompany lyrics of blasphemy and defiance.

4:24 *Seventy-sevenfold.* What God had devised as His prerogative for Cain's protection (15) is now claimed by Lamech as his right of revenge in grotesque proportions even for minor injuries: "wounding . . . striking." (Mt 18:21-22)

4:25 *Seth.* His name is derived from a verb meaning to "set, put" in the place of his brother.

4:26 *Call upon the name of the Lord.* The account briefly mentions the grandson of Adam to show that not all of his offspring were like Cain, whose genealogy was attached directly to the story of Abel's murder. In sharp contrast with the Cainites who had gone "from the presence of the Lord" (16) to pursue their goals without God and even in defiance of Him, the line of Seth sought communion with God. *Enosh.* A noun meaning "man, mankind," used as a proper noun. Whether or not his very name was to acknowledge his dependence on God, Enosh did express it. He was among those who *began to call upon the name of the Lord,* apparently an act of corporate worship in some form by which men humbly and trustingly committed themselves to God as they knew Him and what He had revealed of Himself (12:8; 26:25; 1 K 18:24; Ps 105:1; 116:17; Jl 2:32; Zph 3:9; Acts 2:21; Ro 10:13; 1 Co 1:2). For the meaning of the divine name *Lord* see Ex 3:15 note.

Summary: What Adam did and came to be is not merely a memory but a sad reality in all men: "sin came into the world through one man and death through sin" (Ro 5:12). There is no exception to the rule: where there is life there is death. But another Adam was to come and bring the good news: where there is death there is life. "The Son of Adam, the Son of God" (Lk 3:38), "the last Adam" (1 Co 15:45), "did not count equality with God a thing to be grasped" (Ph 2:6). He was and remained "the image of the invisible God" (Cl 1:15) and therefore "those who receive the abundance of grace and the free gift of righteousness [will] reign in life through the one man Jesus Christ" (Ro 5:17), for "by a man has come also the resurrection of the dead." (1 Co 15:21)

5:1—6:8 The History of Adam

5:1-32 ADAM'S OFFSPRING

5:1 *Generations of Adam.* The history of heaven and earth (2:4—4:26) told the story how God's good creation was subjected to futility. The next "chapter" (5:1—6:8) traces the developments that had been "generated" by Adam's fall to the point where God resolves to undo creation: to "blot out . . . man and beast" (6:7). The transition to the new "chapter" is furnished by a brief review of the preceding situation: Adam, created in the likeness of God (ch. 1), has a son "in his own likeness" (3), i.e., sinful like himself (Ro 5:12) and subject to death (5). The line of Cain had already demonstrated how wicked the offspring of Adam had become (4:17-24). Now the reader is to learn that even the good line of Seth finally produced offspring whose heart was "only evil continually" (6:5). The mention of the exception at the end (6:8) leads over to the history of Noah. (6:9—9:28)

5:5 *He died.* The biography of man becomes a necrology: a list of the dead (8, 11, 17, 20, 27, 31). Inexorably the bell has tolled the refrain: "dust to dust." (3:19; Ec 8:8; Ro 5:12; 6:23; 1 Co 15:21-22; Heb 9:27)

5:6 *Seth.* Cf. the genealogy from Adam to Noah in 1 Ch 1:1-4 and in Luke 3:36-38.

5:22 *Walked with God.* Reconciled and at peace with God "by faith," Enoch led a life which "pleased God" (Heb 11:5) so that he was spared what Paul calls the dread of being "unclothed"; instead he was "further clothed," what was mortal being "swallowed up by life" (2 Co 5:4; 2 K 2:11). But also those who are not taken by God in this exceptional manner will be raised "a spiritual body" to "inherit the kingdom of God." (1 Co 15:42-50)

5:25 *Lamech.* Some of the descendants of Cain and Seth have the same or similar names. (4:18)

5:29 *Noah.* The name of the last of the 10 descendants of Adam means "rest, repose." It testifies to the longing for *relief* from the restlessness and frustration of human existence after the Fall. Hope was not misplaced in Noah. By the "pleasing odor" (Hebrew: "assuaging fragrance") of his sacrifice after the Flood God was moved to initiate a new era of stability and forbearance, token of the full rest from the *work* and *toil* of sin which a second Noah was to bring. (8:21; Mt 11:28-29; Rv 14:13)

6:1-8 THE PERVERSITY OF ADAM'S OFFSPRING

1) 6:1-4 Degenerate Wickedness

6:2 *Sons of God.* Their marriage with *the daughters of men* (or of Adam) filled the measure of "the wickedness of man . . . in the earth" and provoked God's decree to destroy him. Many believe that *the sons of God* were supramundane creatures similar to those mentioned in Jb 1:6; 2:1; 38:7; Ps 29:1; 89:6 (cf. 2 Ptr 2:4). Their union with *the daughters of men* seeks to destroy the boundary that God had established between heaven and earth, Creator and creature. More plausible: *the sons of God* are the line of Seth, which had hitherto maintained filial relations with God (Ex 4:22-23; Hos 11:1; Jn 1:12; Ro 8:14; 1 Jn 3:1-2). But when they intermarried with those *daughters of men* in whom the seed of Adam's sin had flowered into open defiance of God, as was the case in the descendants of Cain (4:17-24), their offspring also degenerated (cf. Dt 7:4). As a result wickedness became universal and evil was hopelessly ingrained in "every imagination of the thoughts." (5)

6:3 *Shall not abide in man.* KJV: "shall not . . . strive with man." During the long life that God had hitherto granted man, His Spirit's effort to rule in the heart of man had met with growing hostility and a rebellious spirit of self-determination. "God's patience waited in the days of Noah" (1 Ptr 3:20) till the abuse of His grace made Him "sorry that he had made man." (6; Ex 32:14; Nm 23:19; 1 Sm 15:29, 35; Jb 23:13; Jer 26:3; Jl 2:13; Am 7:3; Jon 3:10; Mt 24:38)

6:4 *Nephilim.* KJV: "giants," also in Nm 13:33. Related to and identified with *mighty men* and *men of renown,* they inspired fear by their ruthless fury (like Lamech, 4:23) and reached heights of achievement so that they "made a name" for themselves. (11:4)

2) 6:5-8 Impending Destruction

6:6 *Sorry.* Cf. 1 Sm 15:11 note.

6:8 *Found favor.* The cause of the difference between a good man and the openly wicked is not their natural disposition, but divine favor or grace. The fruits of this grace are piety toward God; integrity, uprightness, benevolence toward men. Although called "a righteous man, blameless in his generation" (9; 7:1; Eze 14:14; Heb 11:7), Noah is still identified with such as have an evil heart by nature (8:21), prone even to shameful deeds. (9:21)

6:9—9:29 The History of Noah

6:9—8:19 NOAH AND THE FLOOD

1) 6:9-22 Righteous Noah Builds the Ark

6:9 *Generations of Noah.* The story of the third "chapter" of Genesis (6:6—9:29) was "generated" from antecedent data. It is a dramatic development of questions raised by the preceding ominous situation: How would Noah find favor in the impending disaster that threatened all his contemporaries (6:1-8)? What part would he play in this upheaval in view of the meaning of his name, "Rest" (5:28)?

6:13 *I have determined.* Having informed Noah of His resolve to *make an end of all flesh,* God continues to reveal to him by what means He will do so ("a flood of waters," 17) and by what device Noah would escape ("an ark," 14).

6:14 *Ark.* From the Latin *arca,* a rectangular "box" or "chest" of various dimensions, translated "basket" in Ex 2:3, but cf. the "ark of the covenant." (Ex 25:10, etc.)

Gopher. A transliteration of the Hebrew word, which occurs only here; not definitely identified, perhaps the cypress, which is resistant to moisture, or some resinous tree; Luther: fir tree.

6:15 *Length . . . breadth . . . height.* If the cubit is reckoned at 18 inches, the dimensions of the ark were 450x75x45 feet.

6:18 *Covenant:* an agreement or pact between men (e.g., 1 Sm 18:3) or between God and man. Although sinful man is in no position to bargain with God, His proposed transaction with man is like a contract in that it stipulates what God, on the one hand, has covenanted or pledged Himself to do in man's behalf, and what man, on the other hand, is to do in response if he is to receive the proffered benefit. In a covenant God extends undeserved mercy to man; man enters it by believing God's promise and expressing that faith in obedience to the terms of the covenant. "By faith Noah . . . constructed an ark for the saving of his household" (Heb 11:7) on dry land; after he "did all that God commanded him," he "went into the ark" (6:22; 7:5, 7). God's covenants usher in a new era or mark a decisive step in carrying out His plan for man's salvation. (9:16; 17:4, 7; Ex 6:4; 24:8; Jer 31:33; Eze 37:26; Mt 26:28; Lk 1:72; Heb 9:15)

6:19 *Two of every sort.* Although "all flesh in which is the breath of life" (6, 17) is to be destroyed and is again to suffer the consequences of man's sin (3:17), God makes provision for the preservation of animal life and its propagation. In the choice of animals to be saved in the ark the basic consideration therefore was to be their ability to function in pairs of male and female. Seven days before the flood began, this general directive was made more specific as to the number of pairs (7:2-3): Noah was to select only one "pair of the animals that are not clean" and "seven pairs of all clean animals" (KJV "by sevens," i.e., three pairs and an additional one for sacrifice). This distinction between animals on the basis of their suitability for offerings that Noah observed in his sacrifice (8:20) was later enjoined upon Israel. (Lv 8)

2) 7:1-5 Noah Fills the Ark

3) 7:6—8:19 Noah Is Saved in the Ark

a. 7:6-24 The Coming of the Flood

7:11 *Fountains . . . windows.* Held in balance by God's ordinance of the second and third days of creation (1:6-7; 8:2), the waters now were permitted to break the established barriers. As they poured upon the earth from above and below, they produced a flood similar to the primeval *deep.* (1:2; Jb 12:15; Ps 104:6; Pr 8:28-29; 2 Ptr 3:6)

7:16 *Shut him in.* God kept His promise to Noah and his family "to keep them alive" (6:19) by making them secure against the raging disaster. When He locks the door to danger, no power in heaven or earth can break it down in order to touch those who have entered "the ark" of His protection. (Dt 33:27; Ps 23:4; 34:7; 37:28; 46:1; 91:9-10; Pr 3:23-25; Is 46:4; Nah 1:7; Lk 12:7; 1 Ptr 5:7)

7:17 *Flood.* In the Septuagint, an early Greek translation of the OT, and in the NT the Hebrew word, occurring only in this account and Ps 29:10, is aptly rendered "cataclysm." (Mt 24:38-39; Lk 17:27; 2 Ptr 2:5)

7:21 *All flesh died.* Covering "all the high mountains under the whole heaven" (19), the flood brought catastrophic destruction: before its onslaught there was no escape for "all flesh in which is the breath of life" (6:17). Only "Noah . . . with seven other persons" was preserved alive. (2 Ptr 2:5; 1 Ptr 3:20; Eze 14:14, 20; Ml 3:17-18)

b. 8:1-12 The Subsiding of the Flood

8:1 *Remembered.* It may have seemed to Noah in the long watches of the Deluge that God had forgotten His promises (6:18; Ps 13:1; 42:9; 77:9; Lm 5:20). But Noah had not been out of God's thought. He *remembered* means, as often in Scripture, that He is about to take action that will show that He has not forgotten His pledged word. (19:29; Ex 2:24; Lv 26:42; 1 Sm 1:19; Ps 105:7-11; 106:45; 111:5; Is 49:15; Lk 1:72)

Subsided. After the waters had increased for 40 days and stood at "flood stage" for another 150 days (7:24), they began their gradual descent: first their stormy turbulence *subsided* or grew calm; then they "receded . . . continually" (literally "coming and going") until they had reached a level where the ark rested on the mountains of Ararat in Armenia (4) and the tops of the mountains could clearly be seen (5); even then a considerable time elapsed before "the face of the ground was dry" again. (3)

c. 8:13-19 The End of the Flood

8:14 *Second month . . . twenty-seventh day.* The flood embraced a period in Noah's life from 2/17 of his 600th year (7:6) to 2/27 of his 601st year. According to a lunar month of 30 days, Noah spent 371 days in the ark. This total number is also the sum of all the days that are mentioned for the various stages in the coming, progress, and going of the flood in chs. 7—8.

8:16 *Go forth.* The long-awaited day of release had finally come; the "night" of watching, hoping, longing must have seemed endless. Even after the ark rested on solid ground (4), liberation from its confining quarters was still to be delayed for months. Three weeks were to pass before a dove did not have to return to the ark for refuge (12). When 29 days later (7:11; 8:13) Noah could remove the "covering of the ark" (13), 57 more days (14) elapsed before the appointed time of liberation came. In spite of appearances to the contrary, God does not forget His own in their need; at His time and in His way He remembers to keep His promise of deliverance. "When through the deep waters" God calls them to go, "the rivers of sorrow shall not overflow." (Is 43:2; see also Ps 25:3, 5; 27:5, 14; 37:7, 9; 40:1; 42:8-9; 69:3, 13; 123:2; 130:5-6; Pr 20:22; Is 8:17; 40:31; 49:23; Ro 8:24-25; Heb 6:11-12; Ja 1:3)

8:20—9:29 NOAH AFTER THE FLOOD

1) 8:20-22 Noah's Sacrifice; God's Assurance

8:20 *Altar . . . burnt offerings.* Both are mentioned here for the first time. Apparently at this time no specific instructions had to be followed in the building of the altar (12:6-8; 26:25; 33:20; Ex 17:15) as was the case later (Ex 20:24-26; 27:1-8). Some distinction evidently had already been made between animals that were suitable for sacrifice (clean) and those unfit for this purpose (unclean). In the Mosaic legislation the division of animals into clean and unclean applied to their use for sacrifice as well as for food (Lv 11; 20:25). Noah sacrificed the animals as *burnt offerings*. The Hebrew word is derived from a verb meaning "to go up" and indicates that the entire animal went up in smoke and fire, leaving nothing for ceremonial feasting.

8:21 *Smelled.* The Lord's reaction to the sacrifice is expressed in terms of human experience and action. Such anthropomorphisms are found throughout Scripture because finite man can only speak about the infinite God by analogies to human emotions, thinking, and modes of action. To say that God smells is no more crude than to say that He hears or speaks. *The pleasing odor,* more lit. "a fragrance that puts to rest," i.e., appeases or assuages anger. Noah was what his name implied: the bringer of rest (cf. 5:29 note). His sacrifice and its acceptance by God brings the story of the flood to a climax: it puts to rest the fear that God would carry out His threat to "blot out man . . . and beast and creeping things and birds." (6:6, 13)

Never again. God's decision never again to *destroy every living creature,* as He had just done by the flood, was not prompted by a basic change in human nature. Man remained what he had been: *evil from his youth,* down to the source of his action and the roots of his thinking (6:5-7; Jb 15:14; Jer 17:9). Nor was God moved to leniency because Noah and his family had atoned for their sins by offering Him in sacrifice what was already His (Ps 50:10-12; Heb 10:4). But "in divine forbearance he . . . passed over . . . sins" (Ro 3:25), reserving full judgment upon "ungodly men" and storing up "the heavens and earth" for fire on the Last Day (2 Ptr 3:5-7). In the meantime those who confess their guilt and plead for reconciliation, as Noah did by his sacrifice, would beomce a *pleasing odor* to God by virtue of a sacrifice that would completely take away "the sin of the world" and make it possible for man to become a new man, "created . . . in true righteousness and holiness." (2 Co 2:15; Jn 1:29; Eph 4:24; Is 54:9-10)

8:22 *Shall not cease.* The renewed world will function in unbroken cycles of order, but only as long as *the earth remains* by His forbearance. (Jer 33:20, 25; Mt 24:34-35)

2) 9:1-7 The World Order for the Future

9:1 *God blessed.* What God had "said in his heart" (8:21-22) is now proclaimed as a blessing upon Noah. Man is to have continued existence in a reconstituted world. "The whole earth" is to be "peopled" (19) by the offspring of Noah and his sons, who will continue to be endowed with the power to *be fruitful and multiply,* first conferred as a blessing upon Adam. (7; 1:28)

9:2 *Fear . . . dread.* In the newly emerging world man is also to continue to have "dominion over" the animals (1:28). But because Adam's sin disturbed his relationship also to creation as a whole, man must resort to instilling fear and dread in animals if he is to hold sway over them. Only when Paradise is regained will full harmony again reign in God's creation. (Hos 2:18; Is 11:6)

9:3 *Food.* In the beginning man was apparently sustained by a vegetarian diet (1:29). At least no reference is made to animals as a source of food until after the flood. But just as their skins had earlier furnished man with clothes (3:21), so no doubt their meat had already previously served to nourish man.

9:4 *Its blood.* Although God was providing stability and the resources necessary for human existence in the postdiluvian world, man is not to presume to be absolute in his lordship over creation. To remind him that all life is a gift of the Creator, God placed a restriction on his use of animals for food. Although he may take an animal's life, he is to acknowledge that his jurisdiction over it is not absolute. As man's eating of the forbidden fruit challenged the Creator's sovereignty, so it would be a denial of God as the source of all life if he savagely ate *flesh with its life, that is its blood.* (Lv 17:10-14; 19:26; Dt 12:23; 1 Sm 14:34; Acts 15:20, 29; 21:25)

9:5 *Your lifeblood.* Shedding of human blood is not merely a crime against a fellow creature but a flagrant invasion of the Creator's domain because He had "made man in his own image" (6; cf. 1:27 note). Murder is a desecration of God's handiwork in man because even after the Fall he remains more highly endowed than all animals and is so constituted that he can be "renewed . . . after the image" of the Creator. (Cl 3:10; 1 Co 11:7)

9:6 *By man.* God "will require" (repeated three times in 5) the penalty for shedding man's blood by deputizing man to be the executioner of the murderer (4:9-16). He grants man the authority to insure the sanctity of human life, but does not at this point specify how man is to exercise this function in His behalf. (Ex 21:23-25; Dt 1:17; Nm 35:19; Ro 13:1-4)

3) 9:8-17 God's Covenant with Noah

9:9 *My covenant.* After God had established a decree to protect man from himself, He also gave him a formal assurance of safety from such disturbances of natural forces as brought about the flood. As He had promised before the flood to keep alive Noah and his immediate family (6:18), so He now gives a pledge to the entire postdiluvian world "that never again shall all flesh be cut off by the waters of a flood" (11). For He established a covenant with Noah and his "descendants" after him, with "the earth," and with "every living creature that is" (8-17). It was a covenant of grace, for man, still "evil from his youth" (8:21), did not have anything to contribute that would move God to enter into this "contract." It represented a bilateral agreement only to the extent that man agreed to accept what God had pledged and to recognize His sovereign right to rule the world according to His will (1-7). Other covenants were to follow (15:18; 17:2 ff.; Ex 24:7 ff.). Each was a promise of redemption, looking forward to a "new covenant" (Jer 31:31; Eze 37:26; Heb 8:8-10; 10:16-17). When it was sealed in the body and blood of Jesus Christ (Mt 26:26-28), all of God's previous promises of salvation reached their goal of fulfillment.

9:12 *Sign.* Like a polychrome signature on a contract, the rainbow is to be the visible pledge that God will never revoke His covenant with Noah. (Eze 1:28; Rv 4:3; 10:1; Ex 31:16-17; Lv 26:42, 45; Dt 7:9; 2 Sm 23:5; 1 K 8:23; Neh 9:32; Ps 106:45; Is 54:9-10; 55:3; Jer 32:40; Eze 16:60; Lk 1:72; Heb 13:20)

9:16 *Look upon it.* When a man sees the rainbow, his eyes, as it were, meet the gaze of God. In this sign of the covenant God is looking back at man whenever clouds are "over the earth" (14) and seem to hide His face.

4) 9:18-29 Noah's Drunkenness;
His Curse and Blessing on His Sons

9:18 *The father of Canaan.* The sons of Noah are mentioned again (6:9) because they play a part in the genealogical history that follows (20-27). And since one of his grandsons (Canaan) is also involved, he is identified in advance as the son of Ham.

9:20 *The first tiller of the soil.* Lit. "Noah, a man of the ground, began and he planted a vineyard." "A tiller of the ground" like Cain (4:2), Noah began to cultivate also the vine. NEB: "Noah . . . began the planting of vineyards."

9:21 *Drunk.* Noah is no exception to the rule that in Adam all have sinned (Ro 5:12-18; 1 Co 15:21-22). Since Noah had in effect now become the progenitor of the human race, he reveals that the flood had not eliminated sin from the heart of man. Nor had the Lord's covenant with him made him immune to the weakness of the flesh. Although "Noah found favor in the eyes of the Lord" (6:8), he is not made out to be a plaster saint, a bloodless ideal of virtue. *Wine,* like every gift of God (27:28; 49:11-12; Ps 104:15; Am 9:14; Mi 4:4), can be —and still is—abused. (Pr 20:1; 23:29 ff.; Is 5:11, 22; 28:7; Hos 4:11; Am 2:8; Eph 5:18)

Uncovered. Wine weakens the grip of self-control, obliterates moral inhibitions, blunts the sense of shame, defaces the sanctity of family relations. Even godly Noah was not strong enough against its sinister powers.

9:22 *Told his two brothers.* No doubt he did not merely report what he had seen, but with ribald jesting took the occasion to exploit his father's weakness for his and—as he hoped—his brothers' amusement (Hab 2:15; Hos 7:5; Ob 12-13). Such a disregard for another's shame is particularly reprehensible if it involves a vulgar flouting of filial respect and obedience (Ex 20:12; Dt 27:16; Gl 6:1; 1 Ptr 4:8). When family relations are not healthy, society as such soon gets very sick.

9:24. *Youngest son.* The order in which the sons of Noah are listed (Shem, Ham, Japheth) suggests that the second is the "younger son" (so KJV), just as Shem is called the "elder brother" of Japheth. (10:21)

9:25 *Cursed be Canaan.* As if to prepare for this turn of events, Ham is twice identified in the preceding account as "the father of Canaan" (18, 22). By his action Ham showed that he was the father of Canaan, who in turn exhibited the nature of his dissolute father. This father-to-son trait and son-to-father likeness will result in the degraded position of the Canaanites in the family of nations, enumerated in the following chapter. (Jos 9:23; Ju 1:30; 2 Ch 8:7-8)

9:26 *Shem.* A blessing is given to those descendants of Shem who worship the Lord, the true God. (Ex 20:1-3)

9:27 *Japheth.* A third segment of Noah's progeny is to be blessed by its contacts *in the tents of Shem* with the worshipers of the true God (Eph 2:11 ff.). *Enlarge.* In Hebrew the word "Japheth" is similar in sound to the form of a verb meaning to "extend, enlarge."

Summary. The big action in this "generation chapter" of Genesis (6:9—9:28) is the Deluge, "begotten" from the parent circumstances of the previous "chapter" (5:1—6:8): "the wickedness of man was great" (6:5); "I will blot out man" (6:7); "Noah found favor in the eyes of the Lord" (6:8).—The God of the Deluge is not a primitive concept of the deity, an "Old Testament God," who gives way to spasms of vindictiveness and snuffs out his creatures like an infuriated ogre. The Father of our Lord Jesus Christ is no less tolerant of sin. What He did to His sinless Son, when He "became a curse for us," demonstrates even more drastically that the severity of His judgment on sin is not inconsistent with His love. In fact, when His "beloved Son" comes again, God's decree to "destroy . . . the earth" (6:13) will go into effect in a cataclysm of which the Deluge was a preliminary type (Mt 24:29-30, 38-39). In the ensuing judgment "the King" will consign those "on his left" to "eternal punishment" (Mt 25:31 ff.). But the NT also tells us just as clearly how the chasm between the holy God and sinful man has been bridged; how all men can find "favor in the eyes of the Lord" (6:8); how the regular cycles of seasons, guaranteed by God's covenant with Noah (8:22), brought the "fulness of the time" and the covenant in the blood of the Lamb of God "to unite all things in him, things in heaven and things on earth." (Eph 1:10; Is 54:9; Mt 28:18; Jn 1:29; Gl 4:4; Heb 13:20)

10:1—11:9 The History of Noah's Sons: Shem, Ham, Japheth

10:1-32 THE TABLE OF NATIONS

1) 10:1-5 Sons of Japheth

10:1 *The generations of the sons of Noah.* This "generations chapter" (10:1—11:9) tells what developed as a result of the blessing to "multiply and fill the earth," bestowed on Noah and his sons (9:1, 7). Mentioned previously in their relationship to their father Noah, Shem, Ham, and Japheth now assume the role of ancestors of the families of nations, from whom "the whole earth was peopled" (9:19). The names of the descendants of Noah's sons therefore represent individuals as well as nations and national territories. Unique among the annals of antiquity, this Table of Nations views the entire human race as united by a common bond in spite of its separation into distinctive units: The blessing of Noah belongs to all, and all remain in need of divine redemption. Ranging over large and widely separated areas, this list is, however, primarily concerned with those national units that were to play a part in the history of the chosen nation.

The terms "son of" or "father of" do not consistently denote an affinity of the same kind. In some instances there was a racial and/or linguistic tie; in others, geographical proximity; in still others, a similarity of political control. None of these criteria remained constant in the course of time: races became mixed; languages could be adopted by peoples of differing racial origins; territories changed hands; political controls took on various forms. Hence the names occurring in this ancient table need not denote peoples or territories identical with those known from later Biblical references or from non-Biblical sources. For example, Havilah is the "son of" Cush (7) and of Shem (21, 29); Elam is listed as a son of Shem (22) although the later Elamites did not speak a Semitic language. Furthermore, not all nations can be identified with historically known peoples.

10:2-4 *Japheth.* Noah's sons appear in the reverse order of their ages. The descendants of Ham and Japheth are mentioned first because they constitute only a historical orientation for the main purpose of the account: to trace the story of mankind's redemption through Shem to Abram, the father of the chosen people (11:10-26). This inverted sequence of the sons of Noah also makes possible a geographical arrangement of the nations, which proceeds from the territories farthest from the Promised Land (Japheth) to those on an inner perimeter (Shem). The descendants of the youngest son appear to have occupied Europe, Asia Minor, areas around the Black and Caspian seas, and the regions to the northeast of them. *Gomer.* Long equated with the Cimmerians, who are known to have occupied territories around and north of the Black Sea, this son of Japheth has been identified also with an ancient people of Cappadocia. *Magog.* In other Biblical references Magog is mentioned in connection with Gog, Meshech, Tubal, and Togarmah and probably denotes peoples of Scythian stock living in the remote northwest areas of Asia Minor (Eze 38:2; 39:6; Rv 20:8). *Madai.* These evidently were the Medes in the distant northeast. *Javan.* It is generally agreed that Javan refers to the Ionians and the peoples associated with the Greeks in the Mediterranean and Aegean seas (Is 66:19; Eze 27:13, 19; Dn 8:21; 10:20; 11:2; Jl 3:6). They had connections with *Elishah* (Cyprus), *Tarshish* (Asia Minor or Spain), *Kittim* (a noun with the Hebrew plural ending; it seems to refer to the coastlands and islands of the eastern Mediterranean, Nm 24:24; Is 33:1, 12; Jer 2:10; Eze 27:6; Dn 11:30), and *Dodanim* (also plural; 1 Ch 1:7 reads Rodanim: perhaps the island of Rhodes). Nothing certain has been established regarding *Tiras, Ashkenaz* (Jer 51:27; in late Hebrew it is the name for Germany), or *Riphath.*

2) 10:6-20 Sons of Ham

10:6 *The sons of Ham.* The *sons of* Noah's second son constitute a circle of peoples and territories in closer proximity to Israel than the sons of Japheth. For this reason they also played a larger role in the history of Israel. The areas involved were Egypt and Africa, the eastern coast of the Mediterranean, the great plains of the Euphrates and the Tigris, and some parts of Asia Minor and Arabia. In some instances "Hamitic" denotes a racial relationship; in others a linguistic affinity; in still others an association in the same general geographical area. *Put.* Although the third son of Ham is mentioned a number of times in the OT in connection with Ethiopia (Jer 46:9; Eze 27:10; 30:5; Nah 3:9), no reference is made to his descendants. This feature among others would indicate that the Table of Nations should not be regarded as a complete tabulation of all peoples of the earth.

10:7 *Cush.* The name of Ham's first son occurs frequently in the OT and designates Ethiopia or Nubia, more distant and therefore less known than other areas of this group (Ps 68:31; 87:4; Eze 29:10; Am 9:7; Zph 2:12; 3:10). *The sons of Cush* are *Seba* (Ps 72:10; Is 43:3; 45:14), *Havilah* (in 10:29 this name is found among the descendants of Shem; in 25:18 it appears to refer to a territory of Sinai and northwest Arabia; cf. also 2:11-12), *Sabtah* (not mentioned again in Scripture), *Raamah* (occurs again only in Eze 27:22 together with his sons *Sheba and Dedan,* North and South Arabia respectively; according to 25:3 "Jokshan was the father of Sheba and Dedan"), and *Sabteca* (otherwise unknown).

10:8 *Nimrod.* While the five sons of Cush listed in 7 seem to have had their patrimony in Arabia, the "kingdom" of this descendant originated in Shinar (10), i.e., Babylonia (11:2; Is 11:11; Dn 1:2). The cities Babel (or Babylon), Erech (or Uruk), and Accad played an important role in the early history of Mesopotamia. The name Nimrod cannot definitely be identified with any of the rulers of ancient Mesopotamia (1 Ch 1:10; Mi 5:6). *A mighty man.* One word in Hebrew; in 6:4 it is used in the plural form to designate the antediluvian men of prowess.

10:9 *A mighty hunter.* Ancient kings hunted ferocious animals in order to display their might and daring. *Before the Lord.* This phrase does not characterize Nimrod as a person particularly devoted to the Lord but was a popular way of expressing the ultimate degree of greatness. So: "Nineveh was a great city to God" (a literal translation of Jon 3:3).

10:10 *All of them.* The same Hebrew consonants (originally not supplied with vowels) may be vocalized to spell "Calneh" (KJV). The RSV rendering seems preferable.

10:11 *Assyria.* The Hebrew has "Asshur" as in 22. The verse can be translated also as follows: "And from that land went forth Asshur and built Nineveh," etc. So rendered, it would reflect the ancient rivalry that developed between Babel (Babylonia) and Nineveh (Assyria). Of the other cities mentioned in this connection, *Calah* is known to have been situated on the Tigris River south of Nineveh, but the others have not been definitely identified.

10:13-14 *Egypt.* The Hebrew word *(Mizraim)* has the plural ending *im,* found also in the names of all the sons of Egypt. The *Ludim* are associated with Ethiopia and Put in an oracle against Egypt (Jer 46:9). The *Pathrusim* occupied Pathros in southern Egypt (Is 11:11; Jer 44:15; Eze 29:14; 30:14). In their migrations the *Philistines,* here related to the unknown *Casluhim,* had contact also with the *Caphtorim,* the people of Caphtor, indentified as the island of Crete (Dt 2:23; Am 9:7; Jer 47:4). The other "sons" remain unidentified.

10:15-19 *Canaan.* When many years later the Israelites took possession of Canaan, it was occupied by an amalgam of peoples of various racial and linguistic characteristics. There were also strong political ties between Canaan and Egypt, one of "the sons of Ham." The areas assigned to the sons of Canaan stretch from the northwest *(Sidon)* and the northeast *(Hamath)* to the shores of the Dead Sea in the south *(Lasha).* From *Heth* came the Hittites, who became a great power in Asia Minor (Jos 1:4) but also held enclaves in Palestine (15:20; 23:3; Dt 7:1; Ju 3:5). The *Jebusites* are named after Jebus, ancient Jerusalem (Ju 19:10-11; 1 Ch 11:4-5; cf. also Nm 13:29; Jos 11:3). The *Amorites* are distinguished from other pre-Israelite inhabitants of Canaan (Nm 13:29; 21:21; Dt 1:7, 19-20), but the term is also used to denote all Canaanites (15:16; Am 2:9-10). A number of descendants of Canaan are known only from later Biblical references: the *Girgashites* (15:21; Dt 7:1; Jos 3:10; 24:11), the *Hivites* (Ex 3:8; Nm 13:29; Dt 8:1; etc.), the *Arvadites* (Eze 27:8, 11). The *Arkites, Sinites,* and *Zemarites* are mentioned only here and in a parallel genealogy in 1 Ch 1.

3) 10:21-32 Sons of Shem

10:21 *Shem.* This "elder brother of Japheth" was the father of "all the children of Eber" although v. 25 does not enumerate all the descendants of Peleg, Eber's son. Among these was Abram, the "Hebrew," i.e., the Eberite. (11:16-26)

10:22-23 *Elam.* The Elamites occupied an area north of the Persian Gulf (14:1; Ez 2:7, 31; Neh 7:12, 34; Is 11:11; Jer 25:25; Eze 32:24; Dn 8:2; Acts 2:9). *Asshur.* Cf. v. 11 note. *Arpachshad.* This son of Shem, mentioned again in his genealogical history (11:10-11), cannot be identified. Some manuscripts of the Septuagint (an early Greek translation of the OT) insert the name "Ca-inan" as a link between Arpachshad and Peleg (25; Lk 3:36). *Lud* may refer to Lydia in Asia Minor, but is not to be confused with the "Ludim, the son of Egypt" (13; Is 66:19; Eze 27:10; 30:5). *Aram.* Aramaea or Syria, to the north and east of Israel, had its later center of power in Damascus. Of Aram's sons only *Uz* is mentioned again in the Scriptures (22:21; 36:28; Jer 25:20; Jb 1:11); the other three remain unknown.

10:24 *Arpachshad.* Cf. 22 note. In an unusually full genealogy his sons are traced to Joktan in the fifth generation, who in turn has 13 sons, one more than Canaan (15-19). Of Joktan's sons, however, the first nine and the last one mentioned remain unidentifiable. Sheba and Havilah (28, 29) occur also in the lineage of Cush (7; cf. also 25:3). While the relationships represented by these names are not clear, Sheba is later known as a territory in Arabia (1 K 10:1 ff.), whose inhabitants engaged in trade (Jb 1:15; Ps 72:15; Is 60:6; Jer 6:20; Eze 27:22). Havilah appears to be a region of Sinai and northwest Arabia (25:18; 1 Sm 15:7). Ophir (29), listed between Sheba and Havilah, was no doubt located also geographically adjacent to them. The land of Ophir became known for its gold, silver, ivory, and precious stones. (1 K 9:28; 10:11 ff.; 2 Ch 9:10)

10:25 *Peleg.* The note added to the mention of the name of this great-grandson of Shem involves a play on the Hebrew verb *p-l-g,* which means to divide, to cleave. The remark that *in his days the earth was divided* may refer to the cleaving of the land by irrigation canals since the common noun "peleg" denotes man-made channels of water (Ps 65:10; Is 30:25; 32:2; Jb 29:6). In 11:17-19 Abram's ancestry is traced from a son of Peleg, Reu, not mentioned in this Table of Nations.

10:30 *Mesha . . . Sephar.* Neither of these names can be identified.

10:32 *The sons of Noah.* The Table of Nations is not designed primarily to furnish anthropological or ethnological information. The concluding verse indicates that its main purpose is to supply a significant link in salvation history. The God who saved Noah also "made from one every nation of men to live on all the face of the earth" (Acts 17:26). As the *sons of Noah* became diverse *nations,* they nevertheless remained one family in their relationship to God. But like all its smaller units in the past, this family of nations would also have a common need, as the verses immediately following this chapter prove. It was unable to free itself from a universal alienation from its Creator. But the next ch. is to tell us also how God was to come to the rescue of *the sons of Noah.* Of all these nations He would choose one to be the channel of worldwide redemption. Abram (11:26) was to be the ancestor of the people of whom it was to be said: "Salvation is from the Jews" (Jn 4:22). When in God's own time the Desire of Nations had come, He would enable all men, whether "Jew or Greek, slave or free" to become one people, "Abraham's offspring, heirs according to promise." (Gl 3:26-29)

11:1-9 THE TOWER OF BABEL

11:1 *One language.* The previous ch. listed the various nations "by their languages," "each with its own language" (10:5, 20). Hence the account of the building of the tower of Babel and the confusion of tongues no doubt reaches back to a time prior to the separation of the peoples. Ch. 11 adds the fact that this movement was in part at least a dispersal that resulted from an act of divine judgment. There are indications that the occupation of other territories did not proceed without friction and attendant evils. Just as individuals in the family of Adam had no regard for fraternal relations (4:8, 23-24), so at least one member of the family of nations added to its domain by violence (10:9-11). The healing of such ruptures of human relationships also awaited the coming of the Offspring of Abraham (Gl 3:16, 19, 29; Acts 2). *Few words.* The Hebrew word is the plural form of "one." In the context it does not stress a paucity in vocabulary but signifies that one word had the same meaning for all people. KJV: "one speech."

11:2 *From the east.* A better translation would be "eastward" or "east" as in 13:11. *Shinar.* The *plain* in the land of Shinar is the Tigris-Euphrates valley east of Mt Ararat. (8:4; 10:10; Is 11:11; Dn 1:2)

11:3 *Come, let us.* This self-exhortation occurs three times; twice to introduce the initiation of human action (4) and once, God's reaction to it. Because no stones were available in this area, clay was dried in the sun or baked in kilns into *bricks. Bitumen,* a black asphalt-like substance, was also readily available.

11:4 *A city and a tower.* In joint endeavors man is motivated by the same perversity of heart that is at the root of his individual estrangement from God. As in the case of Adam and Eve, it is the desire "to be like God"; to ignore the bounds of creaturehood; to be independent of the Creator and, in the final analysis, to replace Him. The postdiluvians exhibited this demonic madness in its crassest form. Deliberately they set out to conspire against God. Instead of "calling upon the name of the Lord" (4:26), they wanted to *make a name* for themselves by building a city and a tower *with its top in the heavens.* (Dt 1:28)

Be scattered. What they sought to accomplish was in defiance of God's will that the descendants of Noah should "spread abroad on the earth" (10:32; 9:1). But God is not mocked. (Lv 26:19; Dt 8:17; Ps 9:20; Pr 6:16-17; Is 2:11-17; Jer 13:9; Eze 28:2, 8-9, Ml 4:1; Lk 1:51; Ja 4:6; 1 Jn 2:16-17)

11:5 *Came down to see.* Serving as a topic sentence, this verse introduces God's reaction to man's presumption and sets the stage for the ensuing action (6-8). It uses anthropomorphic terms in order to let this whole episode appear in its right perspective. "He who sits in the heavens" is not unaware of their nefarious design and "has them in derision" (Ps 2:4). From God's viewpoint their gigantic structure was no more than a tiny molehill that required observation at close range if it was not to be overlooked. (18:21; Ps 37:13; 59:8; Pr 1:26)

11:7 *Let us go down.* Cf. 1:26 note. Unless God curbs wickedness, complete chaos will result. But He will not permit evil, no matter how aggressive or resourceful, to take control of His creation from His hands. He has a way of saying also to the noisiest blasphemers: "Be still, and know that I am God." (Ps 46:10; 76:7-9; 83; 109:29; Is 41:29; 45:16)

Confuse their language. He who endowed man with the gift of intelligent communication can make it also a source of misunderstanding (Ps 55:9). But God is not a God of confusion. When representatives of the nations mentioned in ch. 10 assembled at Jerusalem on Pentecost Day, "each . . . in his own native language" heard "the mighty works of God." The message of what God did to unite heaven and earth, not by a tower of bricks but in Jesus Christ, is intelligible in every language. When accepted, it has the power also to restore harmony among men.

11:8 *Scattered.* What was intended to be a constructive filling of the earth by the increasing descendants of Noah (9:1) became a disruptive dispersion. Sin brought about the fragmentation of mankind and its division into hostile groups.

11:9 *Babel.* The name of the city where the confusion of tongues took place is explained by a play on the similarly sounding verb *balal,* to confuse. It may be designed to dispute the strictly etymological meaning of Babel ("Gate of God") and to say: What men presume to do, as they did at Babel, does not afford entrance to God but results in confusion and alienation from Him. Babel or Babylon is the symbol of anti-God aspirations (Rv 17:18), which God brings to nought by His judgments.

Summary: In the period after the flood the power of sin continued unabated. As it separated man from God (Adam and Eve) and brought deadly strife into an individual family (Cain and Abel), so it impelled men even to join forces in a blasphemous enterprise (Babel). There was no hope that man, individually or collectively, could save himself from this all-pervading poison. But God had a remedy. In the remaining verses of ch. 11 it begins to become clear how He would set out to save the sin-cursed "nations spread abroad on the earth" (10:32). His plan of redemption emerges with the mention of Abram (11:26), of whose "race according to the flesh is the Christ." (Ro 9:5)

11:10-26 The History of Shem

11:10 *Descendants of Shem.* The fifth genealogical "chapter" of Genesis (11:10-26) carries forward the line of descent that ended with Noah (ch. 5). The antediluvian line of descent is given in a framework similar to the one which here spans the period from the flood to Abram. Both are limited to the names of 10 persons; both supply the age of the father at the birth of his son and the total years of his life;

both add the note that each ancestor "had other sons and daughters" in additon to the son whose name appears; in both, the 10th ancestor is a man with three sons (11:26; 5:32). In the Table of Nations some of the descendants of Shem have already been mentioned (10:21-31) together with those of his two brothers, Ham and Japheth. In that context they form a part of the universal family of nations. The genealogy of this ch., however, draws a straight line through the rest of mankind by omitting all names and lines of descent that do not form a direct link between Shem and Abram, the father of the chosen nation.

11:16 *Eber.* The first five generations of the chosen line were mentioned in 10:22-25 (Shem—Arpachshad—Shelah—Eber—Peleg). In 20-26 of this chapter five more are added to conclude with Terah, the father of Abram. Reu, Serug, and Nahor appear only here and in similar genealogical lists. (1 Ch 1; Lk 3)

11:24 *Nahor.* Abram's grandfather and brother had the same name (26; Jos 24:2). A city by this name is mentioned in Gn 24:10.

11:26 *Seventy years.* The age of man decreased considerably after the flood. For a comparison see ch. 5.

11:27—50:26 PATRIARCHAL HISTORY

11:27—25:11 The History of Abraham, Terah's Son

11:27—20:18 BEFORE ISAAC'S BIRTH

1) 11:27-32 Genealogy of Terah, Abram's Father

11:27 *Terah.* Although this "chapter" of Genesis (11:27—25:11) tells the story of Abram, it is called the "generations" or *descendants* of Terah, his father. (See the note on the first of these "chapter headings," 2:4.) *Haran* was the father of Lot and Milcah, the wife of Abram's brother Nahor. The city where Abram and Lot settled before going to Canaan had the same name. (31, 32; 27:43; 2 K 19:12; Is 37:12; Eze 27:23; Acts 7:4)

11:29 *Milcah.* Apparently Nahor married his niece. She gave birth to a number of children (22:20-22). Rebekah was her granddaughter. (24:15)

11:30 *Barren.* Much in the story of Abram is to develop from this rather casual remark. It supplies a note of suspense, when four verses later the reader is told that the husband of a barren wife is to become the father of a "great nation." (12:2; Ps 113:9; Lk 1:36; Gl 4:27)

11:31 *Ur of the Chaldeans.* Stephen apparently identifies "the land of the Chaldeans" with "Mesopotamia" as Abram's point of departure for Haran (Acts 7:2, 4). Because a city with the name of "Ur" is known to have been situated some miles north of Haran, it is tempting to locate Abram's previous home in this area. It is more likely, however, that Ur was the well-known center on the Persian Gulf. No doubt Stephen used the term Mesopotamia loosely to cover not only the land "between the two rivers," the Tigris and the Euphrates, but also the country south of their confluence. At an early time a seminomadic tribe of Chaldeans occupied the territory between the Persian Gulf and North Arabia (15:7; Jb 1:17; Neh 9:7). In the 7th century B.C. they founded the Second Babylonian Empire. (Is 13:19; 23:13; 43:14; 47:5; Hab 1:6-11)

To go into . . . Canaan. Obviously Terah never went there, nor is it necessary to assume that he had set himself this goal. But this is what God had in mind for Abram.

11:32 *Two hundred and five years.* The Samaritan text of the Pentateuch gives Terah's age at 145 years. The lower figure can be more readily reconciled with Stephen's statement that Abram left Haran after his father's death. (Acts 7:2-4; cf. 12:4 and 11:26)

2) 12:1-3 Abram Called and Blessed

12:1 *The Lord said.* The translation "had said" (KJV) assumes that Abram, now at Haran, was at this point obedient to a divine command which he originally had receved in Ur, because 15:7 states that God brought him up from the land of Ur. But the latter remark may merely imply that God's providence already was operative in Abram's life when Terah took his son and "went forth together from Ur of the Chaldeans to go into the land of Canaan." (Cf. 11:31 note)

To Abram. Example of faith though he was, Abram was not a hero who gathered glory by feats of human prowess. No special physical or mental endowments of this hero of faith are mentioned. He was big or small in the measure that he responded to what *the Lord said.* His achievements exemplify what vessels of clay can do—and he had clay feet—when they become conductors of the power of the word that says: "Let there be" (Gn 1). Abram's faith was God's creation. (Ps 84:5; Is 57:13; Jer 17:7; Mt 9:22; Ro 10:9; 1 Co 2:5; 1 Th 2:13)

To the land. Faith is not a leap into the unknown; it is directed to a "land" that is well known to God. Nevertheless obedience of faith ventures into an unseen land of divine promises beyond the material and the tangible: *country—kindred—father's house.*

12:2 *A great nation.* According to the normal course of events, Abram for a long time had prospects of not even one son (11:30; 15:2-3; 16:1; 17:17; 22:12; Ro 9:8; Gl 3:16). No doubt this promise taxed his faith and therefore God repeated it frequently. (15:5; 18:18; 22:17; 28:14; cf. 32:12; 35:11; 46:3)

12:3 *Bless themselves.* The translation suggested as an alternate in RSV note *q* is preferable (18:18; 28:14; also in 22:18 and 26:4, where no note appears). The blessing which *all the families of the earth* will receive and invoke upon themselves was not Abram's to give. But *by* him God had determined to channel His gift of salvation to all mankind. For "when the time had fully come," God "gave his only Son" as "he swore to our father Abraham." (Gl 4:4; Jn 3:16; Lk 1:73; Jer 4:2; Lk 1:55; Acts 3:25; Gl 3:8)

3) 12:4-9 The Promised Land

12:6 *Passed through the land.* Abram held title to the land only by faith (7; 13:15; 15:7; 17:8; 24:7; 28:4, 13-14). During his entire life he *passed through the land* and moved his tent from place to place, always a landless sojourner in occupied territory because "the Canaanites . . . dwelt in the land" (13:7, 18; 15:18-21; 17:8; 20:1; 21:23-24; 23:4). When he needed a few square feet of real estate for a burial plot, he was compelled to acquire it by purchase. (23:17-20)

The oak of Moreh. This tree no doubt had religious significance for the inhabitants and therefore served as a landmark (35:4; Dt 11:30). *Moreh* in Hebrew means "teacher," and the phrase could also be translated: "the teacher's" or "diviner's oak."

Shechem. Recent excavations have called into question the equation Shechem = Sychar (Jn 4:5), although the two sites are not far from one another.

12:7 *Built there an altar.* So far only God had spoken. No words of Abram's response are recorded; he walked the way of obedience in silence. But his compliance with the divine directive was not a grudging, sullen surrender to the power of a nameless fate. At Shechem and Bethel (8) he built altars in order to "call upon the name of the Lord" in prayer, praise, and thanksgiving (cf. 4:26 note). *Bethel.* Cf. 28:19. *Ai.* Cf. Jos 7:2.

12:9 *Negeb.* Lit. "dry," this term denotes a region in southern Palestine.

4) 12:10—13:1 Sojourn in Egypt and Return

12:10 *Went down to Egypt.* Abram's faith was put to the test when he had to evacuate the land which he and his descendants were to possess because *there was a famine in the land.*

12:13 *My sister.* At best a half-truth (20:12; 26:7), this equivocation was a deliberate ruse to mislead the Pharaoh into thinking that Sarah was an unmarried woman. In a temporary lapse of faith, Abram demonstrated the moral impotence of even a believer the moment he loses sight of God (Heb 11:6). By temperament he seems to have been inclined to agree to compromises and to resort to dubious tactics in situations that needed to be faced with fortitude and, above all, with complete reliance on God's help (13:9; 16:4, 6; 20:2). This episode is not an entertaining campfire story to beguile the hearer with a man's cunning and a woman's spirit of ready self-sacrifice. It is written "for our instruction, that by steadfastness and by the encouragement of the scriptures we might have hope" (Ro 15:4) in a forgiving God when we are "overtaken in any trespass." (Gl 6:1; cf. 1 K 19:1-3; 1 Sm 16:2)

12:17 *Afflicted Pharaoh.* We are not told how the Pharaoh became aware that the addition of Sarah to his harem caused the affliction (3; Ps 105:14). *Plagues.* This term may denote a pestilence of infectious diseases but also has more general connotations. (Ex 11:1; 1 K 8:37-38; Ps 39:10)

12:19 *Your wife.* Abram's duplicity is not condoned although no explicit condemnation is recorded. His obedience of faith (1-9) likewise receives no express commendation. The sharp rebuke by the heathen Pharaoh, however, suffices to brand his deed as particularly shameful. When a professed believer sinks below the ethical standards of the unbeliever, he disgraces himself and all children of God.

5) 13:2—14:24 Abram and Lot

a. 13:2-18 Separation of Abram and Lot

aa. 13:2-7 Strife of the herdsmen

13:4 *At the first.* As if to make a new beginning, Abram returned *to the place where he had made an altar.* Here he again *called on the name of the Lord* (cf. 12:8) in order to seek strength for his weakness in renewed communion with God. Although his flight into Egypt became an excursion into the far country of deceit, God stood ready to restore him and to give him continued assurances of His grace.

13:5 *Lot.* A conflict with his nephew could have proved disastrous. The Canaanites could have exploited it to dispossess both Lot and Abram. The riches, acquired in Egypt under false pretenses, turned out to be a source of trouble rather than a blessing.

13:7 *Perizzites.* Not definitely identifiable, these occupants of Palestine are mentioned in lists of other Canaanite peoples, some of which also remain unknown (15:20; Ex 3:8; Dt 7:1; Jos 3:10; Ju 3:5; 1 K 9:20; 2 Ch 8:7; Ez 9:1; Neh 9:8). The combination *the Canaanites and the Perizzites* occurs again in 34:30 and Ju 1:4.

bb. 13:8-13 Lot's departure to Sodom

13:8 *No strife.* Abram's tendency to avoid a crisis had resulted in a compromise of the truth in Egypt. His magnanimous offer to Lot, however, was to serve a good purpose. It brought about a separation between him and Lot, who apparently had joined this adventure of faith merely for material gain.

13:10 *Zoar.* Also called Bela (14:2), this city was in the vicinity of Sodom and Gomorrah.

13:13 *Wicked, great sinners.* Lot's selfish choice of territory "as far as Sodom" (12) was to involve him in the destruction of Sodom and Gomorrah, already hinted at here. (Cf. 10 and ch. 18)

cc. 13:14-18 Confirmation of Abram's blessing

13:15 *All the land.* After Abram had ceded choice territory of Canaan (10) to his nephew, he no doubt needed the emphatic reassurance that God's plan for him had not been changed. Also the land "eastward," where Lot had gone, was to belong to his descendants.

13:18 *Mamre.* At this place, in the vicinity of Hebron, other incidents in the life of Abram were to take place (18:1; 23:17; 50:13). In 14:13 Mamre is a name of an Amorite ally of Abram.

An altar. Abram again sought strength to believe what day by day appeared a greater impossibility. Habitual communication with God is essential to a life of faith and necessary in order rightly to use the blessings, meet the trials, and discharge the duties of life.

b. 14:1-24 Abram's Rescue of Lot

aa. 14:1-12 Lot, prisoner of foreign kings

14:1 *Amraphel.* The land of promise became a battlefield of power politics. Its conquest by the world powers of the day posed a further threat to the promise. None of the five kings mentioned in this verse can be identified with certainty. No record of their invasion of Canaan has been found in extra-Biblical sources, perhaps because it ended in defeat. A suggested identification of Amraphel with the well-known Babylonian king Hammurabi (18th century B.C.) has been quite generally abandoned. *King of Elam.* His land lay east of the Tigris River. *Goiim.* The same word in Hebrew is a common noun, usually translated "nations" (so KJV also here) or "heathen."

14:2 *King of Sodom.* The four invaders under the leadership of Chedorlaomer were met by a coalition of five city-states in the plain of Jordan. Also called *kings,* the rulers of these cities no longer "served" their overlords, that is, they rebelled by withholding tribute.

14:5 *In the fourteenth year.* Apparently Chedorlaomer had subjugated the Jordan valley already before Abram had migrated to Canaan (cf. 16:3). In their punitive expedition the four kings swept down from the north on the east side of the Jordan, penetrating the desert area well below the Dead Sea in a circular motion, and then turned north to defeat the rebels (6-7) in the "Valley of Siddim," a name that occurs only here. (3, 8, 10)

bb. 14:13-16 Liberation of Lot

14:13 *The Hebrew.* To distinguish him from his confederates of a different lineage, Abram is called a *(h)ibri,* as the OT frequently does in such contexts (39:14, 17; 40:15; 43:32; Ex 1:15; 2:11; 1 Sm 14:11; Jon 1:9; also Acts 6:1; 2 Co 11:22). He was a descendant of Shem through the line of Eber (*(h)eber;* 10:21 ff.; 11:14 ff.). In non-Biblical sources frequent mention is made of "habiru," a term that denotes peoples of a lower social or economic status rather than a specific ethnic group. It is quite possible that the early "Hebrews" were regarded by non-Israelites as such nomadic or foreign "habiru," but the equation (h)ibri = habiru remains a debated issue.

14:14 *Three hundred and eighteen men.* Even with the addition of his allies, Abram's army was a small force. Humanly speaking, his attack on the vastly superior hordes of Chedorlaomer was an act of sheer folly. But the man who had cravenly feared for his life in Egypt (12:10 ff.) rose to the occasion in heroic action of faith (cf. Ju 7:1-23). Lot's rescue initiated the fulfillment of God's promise: "I will bless you...so that you will be a blessing." (12:2)

Dan. Its earlier name was Laish. (Ju 18:29; cf. Jos 19:47; Ju 1:34)

cc. 14:17-24 Abram blessed by king of Salem

14:17 *Shaveh.* Evidently in the vicinity of Jerusalem, this valley is mentioned again only in 2 Sm 18:18.

14:18 *Melchizedek.* His name means "the king of righteousness" or "my king is righteousness" and that of his city, "peace." Abram gave this priest-king of Jerusalem a "tenth of everything" (20) because he recognized him as speaking and acting in behalf of the true God, "maker of heaven and earth" (19, 20, 22). The epithet *God Most High* was used as a divine title also by the Canaanites (Nm 24:16; Ps 7:17; 18:13; 46:4). Because Melchizedek was a priest "not according to a legal requirement concerning bodily descent" but prior to "the Levitical priesthood" and because he appears on the scene suddenly "without father or mother or genealogy," he was a type of the eternal and universal priesthood of Jesus Christ. (Heb 7:1-18; 5:6; 6:20; Ps 110:4)

14:23 *Not take a thread.* Abram's refusal to take his share of the booty was not only an act of magnanimity; he also wanted to acknowledge that it was God who had made him a blessing to others. He declined to be enriched in a material way by God's victory; his "reward" was God Himself. (15:2)

6) 15:1-21 God's Covenant with Abram

a. 15:1-6 Abram's Faith

15:1 *In a vision.* Abram's faith must have been sorely tried. The man who was to have descendants "as the dust of the earth" (13:16) still was childless; the land that they were to have as an inheritance still was firmly in the grasp of its occupants. God therefore granted him the extraordinary experience of a vision to assure him that his heirs will outnumber the stars (1-6); in a "deep sleep" (12) he was given a glimpse into the future and enabled to see the Promised Land in possession of his heirs. (7-17)

15:3 *Heir . . . Eliezer.* There was a note of impatience in Abram's reply. So far as he could see, he would "continue childless." To have an heir he would have to resort to the prevailing custom and legally adopt his slave Eliezer.

15:6 *Believed.* Abram's faith was "the assurance of things hoped for, the conviction of things not seen" (Heb 11). His old age and the barrenness of his wife notwithstanding, he said Amen to the divine Word. In Hebrew the verb to "believe" is a form of the same word with which believers have from time immemorial closed their prayers to express their confidence in God's faithfulness. Abram "amen-ed" God, that is, he remained firm and unmovable in his reliance on God's promise. By believing His Word Abram was rooted in God Himself.

As righteousness. Abram's relationship to God was right. He was not righteous in his own right or by his own merit, but because in believing he cast himself unreservedly on divine grace. God accepted this trust as fulfilling His demands for righteousness (Ro 4; Gl 3:16; Ja 2:23). A person who is right with God on such a basis will also seek to do things that are right in His sight. (Dt 24:13; Ps 106:30-31)

b. 15:7-21 The Promise Sealed by a Covenant

aa. 15:7-11 The covenant sacrifice

15:8 *How . . . know.* The text does not indicate how long after the previous episode (1-6) Abram asked for additional assurance that he would inherit the Promised Land. It need not have been a long interval. He who "believed the Lord" (6) must like all believers also say: "Lord, help my unbelief!" (Mk 9:24; Ju 6:17; 2 K 20:8; Lk 1:18)

15:10 *Cut them in two.* The contracting parties

to a covenant performed a solemn rite to symbolize the sacredness of their pledge. Sacrificial animals were halved and placed in such a way as to enable the covenanting persons to pass between the carcasses. By doing so they acted out an oath and declared themselves liable to the fate of the animals should they break the terms of the agreement. (Jer 34:17-20)

15:11 *Birds of prey.* Their appearance was to be expected, for "wherever the body is, there the eagles will be gathered" (Mt 24:28). But they also may symbolize sinister forces, which would attempt to prevent the promise from becoming a reality.

bb. 15:12-21 The covenant promise

15:12 *Deep sleep.* After Abram had passed through the divided animals, he was to see also God binding Himself to the covenant by performing the same ritual. But since physical eyes are incapable of seeing God in action, Abram was given sight of the unseen in a vision of deep sleep. (2:21; 1 Sm 26:12; Jb 4:13)

15:13 *Four hundred years.* What Abram saw in "a dread and great darkness" still remained "the evidence of things unseen." There was to be fulfillment of the promise only in the remote future. After his descendants had endured subjugation in Canaan and Egypt for centuries and after "the iniquity of the Amorites [Canaanites] . . . is complete" (16; 1 K 21:26), only then, "in the fourth generation," would they come into possession of the land. *Four hundred years* is a round figure (Ex 12:40; Acts 7:6; Gl 3:17). In the same way "generation" (16) is used loosely here as the equivalent of a century. Abram was getting impatient awaiting God's time of fulfillment.

15:14 *On the nation.* The RSV does not translate the adverb "also" or "even," which precedes this phrase in the Hebrew text. Also foreign nations are subject to God's *judgment* and must serve His purposes.

15:17 *Fire pot and a flaming torch.* Even in a vision God was seen merely in the symbols of His presence (Ex 3:2; 13:21-22; 19:18; Acts 2:3). To assure Abram once more of His pledged promise, God adopted the current human convention of a covenant. It was a covenant of grace. Abram had nothing to contribute. He could become a signatory to this contract only by agreeing to accept what it offered to him.

15:18 *The river of Egypt . . . to the river Euphrates.* It was not until David's time that the territory of Israel extended from the borders of Egypt to the Euphrates River. (Dt 11:24; 2 Sm 8:3; 1 K 4:21; 8:65)

15:21 *The Amorites.* Mentioned in 16 as a general term for all pre-Israelite inhabitants of Canaan, they appear here as one of nine differentiated groups (Am 2:9; Jos 10:5; 12:2). Some of these cannot definitely be identified. The "Kadmonites" (19) are not mentioned elsewhere.

7) 16:1-16 Abram and His Son Ishmael

a. 16:1-6 Hagar, Ishmael's Mother, Banished

16:2 *Obtain children by her.* Lit. "be built by her," i.e., so as to found a family with descendants. Sarai resorted to a recognized legal procedure of her time. A son born of a union of her husband with her slave could be claimed by a wife as her own (cf. 30:1-6, 9-13). Such concubinage, permissible in ancient society and tolerated in OT times, lacked divine sanction, for "from the beginning it was not so" (Mt 19:4-8). When practiced, it usually resulted in domestic strife and tragedy.

Hearkened. Usually amicable toward others, Abram readily acceded also to this proposal of his wife. (13:8)

16:3 *Ten years.* The events in the life of Abram may not be recorded entirely in their chronological sequence. But this episode has a fitting place in its present setting. Even though Abram "believed the Lord" that "his own son" and not Eliezer should be his heir (15:6-21), he nevertheless was in a hurry to see the promise fulfilled. It seemed impossible that "his own son" could be the son of barren Sarai. His acquiescence in her plan to procure an heir merely "according to the flesh" exhibited the impatience of doubt.

16:5 *Wrong done to me.* Although the unpleasant situation arose as a consequence of what she herself had instigated, she blamed Abram for the fact that Hagar *looked . . . with contempt* on her mistress. (Pr 30:23)

16:6 *In your power.* According to ancient law a slave-mother could not be banished. But it stipulated also that she remain in absolute subjection to her mistress. When Sarai made life miserable for Hagar, *she fled from her.*

b. 16:7-16 God's Rescue of Hagar; Ishmael's Blessing and Birth

16:7 *The angel of the Lord.* Angels are creatures of God and His obedient servants. But the phrase *angel of the Lord* here and elsewhere signifies a manifestation of God Himself. (13; 21:17; 22:11; Ex 3:2, 4; 14:19; Ju 6:11; 13:22)

16:11-12 *Ishmael.* The descendants of Ishmael, listed in one of the later generation "chapters" (25:12-18), were to be Arab tribes who will *dwell over against all his* [Abrahamic] *kinsmen.* Like the *wild ass,* a noble animal of the desert (Jb 39:5-8), they will resist all attempts to deprive them of their bedouin freedom.

16:13 *A God of seeing.* The Hebrew is *el roi.* The second word therefore is identical with the last element of the name given to the well and transliterated Beer-lahai-*roi.* These names are based on a play on words that is difficult to reproduce in translation and may even have been misunderstood by the copyists of the text. The context suggests the translation: "Thou art God who has seen [provided for] me. Have I seen even God and remained alive? Therefore the well was called: 'The well of the Living One who sees [provides for] me'" (32:30; Ju 6:23; 13:22; Ex 3:6; Jb 19:25). Isaac was to dwell there (24:62; 25:11). Located "on the way to Shur" (7) and near Kadesh, it was not too far from Egypt, Hagar's original home. (1)

8) 17:1-27 The Covenant Reaffirmed

ntion of
t into the
e not told
e God had
Abram in the
t it should not
ho "believed the
not wait for the Lord
His own way (ch. 16)
ances lest "he weaken in
refore was not engaging in
n He frequently *appeared to*
to him what He had told him
eds constant nurture. (Ro 10:17;
3:16)

ty. Appearing here for the first
ivine epithet was applied also to
eir worshipers (cf. 14:18). As a name
d of gods it was to remind Abram that
God nothing will be impossible," not even
e birth of a son contrary to human experience.
(Lk 1:37; Gn 28:3; 35:11; 48:3; Ex 6:3)

17:2 *My covenant.* Abram could "walk before" God and "be blameless" only as he remained in the right relationship to God, set forth in His covenant of grace.

17:5 *Abraham.* Every time Abraham heard this name or used it himself, he was to be reminded of the covenanted promise of God to make him *the father of a multitude of nations* (Neh 9:7; Ro 4:17). The new form of his name had this connotation by means of a play on words.

17:7 *An everlasting covenant.* A new feature is added to the promise that Abraham's progeny were to inherit the land of Canaan. His *descendants . . . throughout their generations* were to be also his spiritual heirs (28:13-14; 35:11-12). God pledged Himself to "be their God" (8) as long as they maintained a relationship to Him that was based on the terms of His covenant with Abraham (Ex 6:7; Lv 26:11; Ps 105:8; Jer 24:7; Eze 37:23; Gl 3:17-18; Rv 21:3). When they later proved unfaithful, God pledged Himself to fulfill His promise of salvation in a "new covenant." (Jer 31:31; Eze 37:26; Gl 3:7, 29; Heb 8:8-13; 9:15)

b. 17:9-14 Circumcision: Sign of the Covenant

17:10 *Circumcised.* Circumcision was practiced by other peoples of the ancient world, usually as a puberty rite (Jer 9:25-26). But just as a natural phenomenon like a rainbow had become a sign or pledge of God's covenant, so every male member of Abraham's household was to bear a "sign of the covenant" in his natural flesh (Lv 12:3; Jn 7:22-23; Acts 7:8). It marked him as a willing recipient of God's covenanted mercy. Failure to bear this sign signified refusal to accept the proffered grace of God. Outward compliance with this directive, however, also required a spiritual commitment to the God of the covenant (Dt 10:16; 30:6; Jer 4:4; 6:10; Ro 2:25-29). After Jesus, the Mediator of the new covenant, had come, this sign of the old covenant no longer was a required ordinance. (Acts 15:1; Ro 3:30; 4:9-11; 1 Co 7:18 f.; Gl 5:6; Eph 2:11, 15; Cl 2:11; 3:11)

c. 17:15-21 The Covenant Mother and Child

17:15-16 *Sarah.* Like the new form of Abraham's name ("father of a multitude of nations"), Sarah's name was to signify that she was to become the *mother of nations.* Sarah, meaning "princess," was to be the ancestress of a royal lineage, for *kings of peoples shall come from her*—David's royal line and eventually great David's greater Son, the King of kings. (Mt 1:1)

17:17 *Laughed.* Abraham's behavior disposes of all doubts that he needed the affirmation of God's promise again and again and in ever new and more impressive forms. Although bowing in worship before the majesty of God, he could not suppress the urge to laugh. It seemed ridiculous that at their age he and his wife should become the parents of a promised heir (cf. 18:12). The utter incongruity of his actions demonstrates how severe the struggle of faith can be.

17:18 *Ishmael.* In Ishmael, the heir whom he had provided in his own way (16:1-2), Abraham still saw the only reasonable possibility of a fulfillment of the divine promise.

17:21 *At this season next year.* As the time of fulfillment drew near, God made the promise more precise. The heir was identified by name and the time of his birth was specified (21:2). While Ishmael did not fail to receive a blessing (20; 16:10-12; 25:12-15), all the nations were to be blessed through God's *covenant with Isaac.*

d. 17:22-27 The Covenant Sign Applied

17:26 *Were circumcised.* Overcoming his laughter, "Abraham grew strong in his faith" (Ro 4:30). Without the least delay he put the sign of the covenant on his aged body and that of "the men of his house." By faith every believer is a marked man. (Ro 2:29; Ph 3:3; Cl 2:11)

9) 18:1—19:38 Destruction
of Sodom and Gomorrah

a. 18:1-8 Abraham, Host of Three Men

18:1 *The Lord appeared.* He manifested Himself to Abraham in the form of the Angel of the Lord (cf. 16:7 note). While still at Mamre near Hebron (13:18; 14:13), Abraham bade three approaching strangers to be his guests. Two of these were angels, who later continued their journey to Sodom (22; 19:1; cf. Heb 13:2; 1 Ptr 4:9); the other was the Angel of the Lord, the Lord Himself, who spoke with Abraham and Sarah. (9, 13, 15, 17)

18:2 *Bowed himself.* In Oriental fashion Abraham greeted his unknown guests with appropriate deference.

18:8 *They ate.* Having assumed human form, the Angel of the Lord also partook of the food that Abraham had prepared. (Cf. 32:24; Jos 5:13; Ju 13; Lk 24:41 ff.)

b. 18:9-15 Sarah's Laughter

18:10 *Sarah your wife.* The stranger identified Himself by His knowledge of Sarah's name and of her secret laughter behind the tent door (12, 15). He also repeated the promise that Abraham had previously received from the Lord.

In the spring. Lit. "at the time of life" (so KJV), this phrase may refer to the season of spring, when dead nature returns to life. It may also refer to the "appointed time" (14) required to bring a child to life, i.e., from conception to birth (2 K 4:16). If the latter is the correct meaning, perhaps several months had passed since the birth had been foretold to take place "next year." (17:21)

18:12 *Sarah laughed to herself.* Perhaps her laughter was excusable in view of the condition of her body as long as she did not know who the stranger was. But no doubt like Abraham (17:17) she regarded as ludicrous the fulfillment of the promise if it meant that she was to give birth to a son (11). Isaac's name ("he laughed") was forever after to remind her of her folly to doubt that anything was "too hard for the Lord." (14; 21:6; Nm 11:23; Ps 126:2; Jer 32:17, 27; Zch 8:4-6; Mt 3:9; Lk 1:37)

18:15 *Sarah denied.* Unbelief sets off a chain reaction of sins which usually includes lying (37:29-35; 39:14-17; Ps 36:3). Sarah penitently accepted the reproof and "by faith . . . received power to conceive." (Heb 11:11)

c. 18:16-21 Sodom's Destruction Revealed

18:17 *Shall I hide.* In taking counsel with Himself, the Lord apparently drew the two angels into His deliberations. And as Abraham "went with them"—a final act of hospitality—he also was initiated into what God was *about to do.* Just as God took Noah into His confidence before the coming of the flood (6:13-22), so Abraham's intercession for Sodom (22-32) presupposes that he learned of God's intention to destroy it as he "set them on their way." To Abraham's name the Septuagint (an ancient Greek translation of the OT) adds the apposition "my servant." James calls him "the friend of God." (Ja 2:23)

18:18 *Bless themselves.* Cf. 12:3 note.

18:19 *I have chosen him.* As RSV note *e* points out, the Hebrew text reads: "I have known him." In many instances the Hebrew verb "to know" has a connotation that exceeds mere acquaintance with a person. It is used to mean that two or more people are in personal relationship to one another. When, e.g., a man is said "to know his wife," it denotes that the husband exercises the conjugal prerogative as the expression of the most intimate union of which humans are capable (4:1, 17, 25). God's choice of His people for the purpose of entering a covenant with them is described as His "knowing" Israel. (Am 3:2; Dt 7:6; Hos 2:14-23)

18:21 *I will go down.* The Lord, who "looks down from heaven . . . sees all the sons of men . . . and observes all their deeds" (Ps 33:13-15), did not have to inspect Sodom at close range to *see whether they have done altogether according to the outcry.* God used an anthropomorphic expression to make clear that His judgments are not arbitrary and that there would be no miscarriage of justice in Sodom's case because the judge did not know all the facts (18:25). To let also uninformed men become aware of Sodom's wickedness, they are told of the experience of the two men, the angels, in that city. (19:1-11; cf. Eze 16:49-50)

d. 18:22

18:22

angels p

the Lord

destroying

actually had

dust and ash

relationship gran

"drew near" to Go

tenacity. He did not cea

until he had made six p

As if he were haggling fo

piece of merchandise, he lo

people from 50 to 10 for whose

to be spared. At the end his

shorter and the Lord's replies

Pleading not for his own needs,

believers is not only an example o

others but also of untiring persistence

(32:26; Nm 14:13-18; 16:22; Dt 9:18; 1 S

Ez 9:5; Neh 1:4-6; Ps 55:16-17; 74:10-11, 20,

Is 62:6-7; Mt 15:27; 20:30-31; Lk 11:5-8; 18:1

Heb 10:22)

18:23 *The righteous with the wicked.* God does not dispute Abraham's contention that the righteous should not "fare as the wicked" (25). In fact He "rescued righteous Lot" and his family (19:12 ff.; 2 Ptr 2:7-8; Is 3:9-10; 65:8)

18:25 *The Judge of all the earth.* Abraham conceded that the Lord would *do right* if He destroyed the wicked, and Lot's rescue proved to him that *the Judge of all the earth* does not treat the righteous and the wicked alike. Abraham had no occasion to reflect on instances where no such discrimination was apparent. All Israel, e.g., suffered defeat because of Achan's sin (Jos 7). The destruction of Jerusalem overtook its wicked inhabitants as well as a righteous remnant. All through the ages "acts of God," upheavals in nature, national disasters, wars, have taken the lives of *the righteous with the wicked.* But even in such cases creatures of "dust and ashes" should not presume to impugn the justice of the Judge of all the earth. Without attempting to solve the mysteries of divine providence, people in covenant with God cling to His promise that "in everything God works for good with those who love Him." (Ro 8:28; Dt 24:6; Jb 42:1-6; Jer 31:29-30; Eze 14:12-13; 18; Ro 3:4-6)

e. 19:1-11 Lot, Host of Two Angels

19:1 *Sitting in the gate.* Lot was not sitting in the gate because he expected the angels. In ancient times people gathered at the gates of cities to transact business or to exchange news. (Ru 4:1; 2 Sm 15:2-6; 1 K 22:10; Am 5:10, 12, 15)

19:2 *In the street.* No reason is given why the two men at first declined Lot's invitation to his home but preferred to remain in the open street, where indeed travelers often had to be content to spend the night. But when Lot "urged them strongly" to lodge in his house, out of fear for the safety of the visitors, the wickedness of Sodom is already intimated. The following verses prove that Lot's estimate of his fellow citizens was correct.

19:5 *Know them.* On the meaning of *know*

here and in 8 see 18:19 note. The inhabitants of Sodom, "both small and great," were so "greedy to practice every kind of uncleanness" that the two men were not safe even in Lot's house (Eph 4:19; Lv 18:22; 20:23; Ro 1:24; Jude 7). Sodom's guilt was no longer an "outcry" that had come only to the Lord's attention (13; 18:21) but was a matter of public record. Sodom has become proverbial for the practice of unnatural vice.

19:8 *I have two daughters.* Lot offered his daughters to the lust of the Sodomites. But this attempt to protect his guests was an act of cowardly desperation and cannot be condoned. At the same time it reflects the low status accorded to women by the people of the land as well as by Lot, who was apparently influenced by the prevailing attitude (Ju 19:22 ff.). It is never a God-pleasing solution of a difficulty to commit one sin in order to prevent another.

19:11 *Struck with blindness.* The particular Hebrew word for *blindness* occurs again only in 2 K 6:18, where God inflicted this malady in a similar situation to frustrate the evil designs of men. It was not so much outright loss of sight as a confusion of vision that rendered the victims helpless.

f. 19:12-14 Lot Informed of the Destruction

19:13 *We are about to destroy.* The execution of God's judgment is frequently delegated to angels. (Ex 12:13, 23; 1 Ch 21:15; Eze 9:1-6)

19:14 *To be jesting.* Lot's reaction to the angelic message was far from perfect. He had to be rescued in spite of himself (15-16). But the Sodomites, even Lot's sons-in-law, paid no heed at all to "the judgment's dread alarm." Unbelief scoffs at God's Word to the bitter end. (Jer 17:15; Eze 8:12; Lk 16:14; Acts 2:13; 17:32; Gl 6:7; 2 Ptr 3:3; Jude 18)

g. 19:15-23 Rescue of Lot's Family

19:17 *They said.* As in 21, the Hebrew text reads: "He said." Because the angels were God's representatives and spokesmen, the words spoken by them and by the Lord have identical authority and effect. Similarly the inspired prophets often claimed divine authority for their message by an introductory: "Thus says the Lord" (Am 1:3, 6, 9, 11); but they communicated the Lord's will also without expressly acknowledging their role as His spokesmen. (Am 5:1; Hos 5:1; 6:4)

Do not look back. In contrast with Abraham's prompt obedience to God's directive to abandon everything (ch. 12), Lot had "lingered." He could not tear himself away from his earthly possessions. But God pressed for a decision. Even while fleeing he was not to cast a regretful glance at the destruction of the things he had left behind. (1 Ti 6:10)

19:19 *I cannot flee.* Abraham had negotiated with God in behalf of Sodom; Lot impudently remonstrated with Him in order to improve on His way of saving his own life. But God was patient with Lot's craven fears because He "remembered Abraham" (29) and his intercession for his nephew.

19:20 *Yonder city.* Although Zoar was also marked for destruction, the Lord agreed to exempt it from the fate of the other "cities of the valley" (29) in order that Lot might *escape there.* Because the city was *a little one,* Lot presumed to argue, the crimes committed there would be less in number. Zoar, called Bela in 14:2 and located south of the Dead Sea, is mentioned in the later history of Israel. (Dt 34:3; Is 15:5; Jer 48:34)

19:22 *I can do nothing.* "The prayer of a righteous man has great power in its effects" (Ja 5:16). God let Abraham's intercession, which He remembered (29), bind His hands. (Nm 11:2; Jn 9:31)

h. 19:24-29 Destruction of the Cities

19:24 *Brimstone and fire.* When God miraculously "overthrew those cities" at His appointed time (Lk 17:29), He no doubt commandeered the forces of an earthquake and volcanic eruptions. The latter brought flaming sulphur down on the cities like rain. Fire and brimstone (or sulphur) are frequently mentioned as God's agents of destruction. (Dt 29:23; Ps 11:6; Is 30:33; Rv 9:17; 14:10; 19:20; 21:8)

Sodom and Gomorrah. Besides these two "cities of the plain" two others that shared the same fate are mentioned by name: Admah and Zeboiim (Dt 29:23; Hos 11:8; cf. also Gn 10:19; 14:2). Very likely the site of these cities is now covered by the waters of the Dead Sea.

19:26 *Pillar of salt.* When Lot's wife *behind him* tarried still more to look back, she remained there entombed in salt: a grim memorial to her folly. To all who do not take the Lord's warnings seriously Jesus said: "Remember Lot's wife." (Lk 17:32)

i. 19:30-38 Lot and His Daughters; Moab and Ammon

19:30 *In a cave.* The story of avaricious Lot ends in dismal poverty and disgrace. For the sake of riches he had risked association with the Sodomites (13:10-11). In his old age he had but a cave for shelter. Tricked into a drunken stupor, he was misled into an incestuous union with his two daughters (Lv 18:6-18). "So will the rich man fade away in the midst of his pursuits." (Ja 1:11; 5:1; Pr 28:11; Jer 9:23; Mt 19:24)

19:37 *Moab.* The two sons whom Lot's daughters bore became the ancestors of the Moabites and the Ammonites (38). With these distant relatives the Israelites were to have many encounters. Morally degenerate, they misled Abraham's offspring into the debaucheries of their idolatrous practices. (Nm 25:1-5; Ju 10:6)

10) 20:1-18 Abraham and Abimelech

20:1 *Gerar.* Moving southward around the Dead Sea, Abraham *sojourned in Gerar,* a city in the foothills of the Judean mountains. Here he again palmed off Sarah as his sister, as he had done to avoid harm to himself during his stay in Egypt (12:10-20). Even men of faith repeatedly fall prey to a besetting weakness. Already at the time when God called him "to wander from his father's house," he had agreed with Sarah that "at every place" she was to say: "He is my brother" (13). Though in general similar to the episode in Egypt, his encounter with Abimelech differs in a number of details.

20:2 *Abraham said.* The account of Abraham's life is not a tale of a hero immune to human frailties. In fact whenever he appeared particularly strong in faith, a subsequent incident is added to show how weak he could be when he trusted in himself rather than in God. Soon after implicitly obeying the Lord's command to go into a strange land, he ignominiously surrendered Sarah to the Pharoah (ch. 12). Although "he believed the Lord" that He would carry out His covenanted promise, he submitted to Sarah's scheme of securing an heir in a devious way (chs. 15—16). Not long after he had interceded with the "Judge of all the earth" to spare Sodom, he once again resorted to a dishonest trick in order to insure his safety. Abraham's story glorifies not a man but the Lord, who did not abandon His faltering saint.

Took Sarah. No reason is given why Abimelech added aged Sarah to his harem. About 20 years previously the Pharaoh had done so because she "was very beautiful" (12:14). Abimelech may have been prompted by other considerations. It is also possible that not all events of Abraham's life are recorded in strictly chronological sequence.

20:3 *God came.* The moment had come again when the Lord had to intervene if Abraham, through a son born of Sarah, was to become a blessing to all nations.

20:6 *Kept you from sinning.* God's means of doing so was no doubt the sickness mentioned in 17. (Cf. 12:17)

20:7 *He is a prophet.* Abraham is the first person to be so designated. As mediators between God and men, the prophets transmitted divine messages to people. But they also interceded for them (Nm 11:2; 21:7; Dt 34:10; 1 Sm 7:5; Jer 7:16; 11:14). Abraham *will pray for* the man whom he himself had brought into God's disfavor and who was justified in reprimanding the *prophet* for having done what "ought not to be done" (9). By his deliberate deception Abraham had disgraced himself and God. His action was reprehensible even according to the moral standard of Abimelech, who lived in a land where there was "no fear of God" (11). What an offense to the pagan! "Therefore let any one who thinks that he stands take heed lest he fall."(1 Co 10:12; Ro 11:20)

20:16 *A thousand pieces of silver.* This was a considerable sum of money, if we remember that the price of a slave was 30 pieces of silver.

Vindication, lit. "a covering of the eyes" (so KJV), occurs only here. We would say: It was a "face saving" device to restore Sarah's respectability in the eys of all who were with her. Its rationale was as follows: In the absence of Sarah's father, Abimelech paid her "brother" the customary bride price. Thereby he sought to "cover" her involvement in his harem with the mantle of a legitimate marriage and to "vidicate" her of the charge of harlotry.

21:1—25:11 HISTORY OF ABRAHAM AFTER ISAAC'S BIRTH

1) 21:1-7 Birth of Isaac

21:1 *Visited Sarah.* God enabled her body to function in a way that was no longer possible "according to the flesh," Abraham being 100 years old and Sarah "past the age" of childbearing (Gl 4:23; Heb 11:11; 1 Sm 2:21; Lk 1:68)

21:2 *At the time.* For His reasons and purposes God had delayed the fulfillment of His promise for 25 years (12:4). But when He finally set a definite date, the long-expected moment arrived as "God had spoken to" Abraham the year before (17:21; 18:10). God always does things at the right time.

21:4 *Circumcised his son.* Cf. 17:10 note; also Acts 7:8.

21:6 *Laughter for me.* Isaac's name means "he laughs." Abraham and Sarah had once given way to incredulous laughter at the thought that they were to become parents of a son in their old age (17:17; 18:12). When the impossible happened, Sarah burst out into laughter of joy (Ps 126:2; Is 54:1; Eph 3:20). At the same time she realized that others would *laugh over* her when told that she had *borne . . . a son* at her age. Such a tale would strike them as ridiculous.

2) 21:8-14 Expulsion of Ishmael

21:8 *Was weaned.* Children were weaned after two or three years (1 Sm 1:22-24). The occasion was marked as the first milestone in a child's life and was often celebrated with a *great feast.*

21:9 *Playing.* Ishmael's action is described by a derived form of the same Hebrew verb (to laugh) that occurs in Isaac's name. In 19:14 it is translated "jesting" or "mocking." This rendering is preferable also here (cf. Gl 4:29). Hagar's son followed the bad example of his mother (16:4). This translation furthermore makes it unnecessary to add to the Hebrew text *with her son.* (Cf. RSV note *h*)

21:10 *Cast out.* Sarah demanded a ruthless solution of a problem that she herself had created (ch. 16). She feared that Ishmael would advance some claim to be regarded as Abraham's heir (16:2). Expulsion of the slave woman would be tantamount to a form of legal action. It would be regarded as an official declaration of Ishmael's disinheritance.

21:12 *Be not displeased.* Ishmael's harsh treatment arouses the reader's sympathy. Abraham too had a heart for his son. To expel a slave wife and her son from the parental home was contrary also to recognized custom. But without sanctioning Sarah's heartlessness, God directed Abraham to subordinate his fatherly feelings to His purpose that his *descendants be named . . . through Isaac.* Ishmael would survive this hardship and become "a great nation." But it would be through the "son of promise" that God would bless all nations. (Gl 4:21-28; Ro 9:6-9; Heb 11:18)

21:14 *Along with the child.* Born when Abraham was 86 years old (16:16), Ishmael was now a "lad" (12) of some 17 years. He could not have been put on Hagar's shoulder with the *bread and a skin* (an animal skin as a container) *of water.* The account stresses that Sarah's demand was fully met: Abraham sent Hagar away *along with* Ishmael. Nor need one infer that Ishmael was still a babe in arms when his mother later "cast the child under one of the bushes." (15)

3) 21:15-21 Rescue of Hagar and Ishmael

21:17 *God heard.* Ishmael's name means "God hears." Not a groan, a tear, or a sigh escapes His notice or fails to reach His heart. He hears even "the young ravens" when they "cry" and delights to feed them. (Ps 147:9; 104:27)

Angel of God. When Hagar was still a member of Abraham's household, God manifested Himself as the "Angel of the Lord," i.e., the God of the covenant (16:7). Now the more general term *God* is used to indicate that noncovenant people are not excluded from His providential concern.

21:21 *Paran.* A wilderness of the Sinai Peninsula. (Cf. Nm 10:12; 12:16; 13:3)

4) 21:22-34 Abraham's Covenant with Abimelech

21:23 *Deal falsely.* Abimelech wanted to protect himself against the man who had previously caused him trouble. This mysterious person had wronged him, and yet divine intervention had been on the deceiver's side. (Ch. 20)

21:27 *Made a covenant.* Professing ignorance of his servants' action—no doubt with tongue in cheek—Abimelech formally recognized Abraham's right to the well. Abraham supplied the sheep and the oxen for a ceremonial meal by which the covenant was established. (15:7-11)

21:28 *Seven ewe lambs.* The presentation of a gift in the presence of witnesses was another customary way of "notarizing" the contract. Abimelech expressed surprise that Abraham thought it necessary. The number of lambs was significant. In Hebrew the verb meaning to swear is derived from the numeral seven. To "seven oneself" meant to invoke an oath. Beer-sheba (31) therefore means *Well of seven* or *Well of the oath.*—This bit of real estate, to which Abraham acquired "squatter's" rights, was the first tangible evidence that his descendants would possess the whole land "northward and southward and eastward and westward." (13:14)

21:32 *Philistines.* Associated with the Aegean "Sea Peoples," the Philistines are not mentioned in extra-Biblical sources until they invaded Canaan in force centuries after the patriarchal period. Starting out from a base in Caphtor (Crete; Am 9:7), they ultimately settled along the southern Mediterranean coast of Palestine and became a dangerous enemy of the Israelites. But there is no reason to doubt that smaller contingents of Philistines had infiltrated Palestine even prior to Abraham's time and established themselves in enclaves among the other peoples of Canaan.

21:33 *A tamarisk.* This tree (KJV: "grove") is mentioned again in 1 Sm 22:6; 31:13. It is able to survive even in desert areas like Beer-sheba. Symbolic of a living hope in an unpromising environment, it was a fitting place for Abraham's worship *of the Lord, the Everlasting God.* The next chapter shows that Abraham needed to fortify his faith in the God who is "from everlasting to everlasting"; who loves "with an everlasting love"; who rules over an "everlasting kingdom"; who makes promises "in an everlasting covenant." (Ps 90:2; 145:3; Jer 31:3; 32:40; Hos 2:19)

5) 22:1-24 Trial of Abraham's Faith: The Sacrifice of Isaac

a. 22:1-8 Abraham's Obedience

22:1 *Tested Abraham.* God did not have to come down from heaven in order to discover what was going on in Babel and Sodom (11:5; 18:21). In the same way He did not have to test (KJV: "tempt") Abraham to find out whether he did "fear God" (12). He searches the heart and knows what is in man (Dt 8:2). Nor does He take sadistic delight in the heartaches of His children. When He tests them, He has their interest at heart. He puts their faith to the test in order to "take away the dross from the silver" (Pr 25:4; Is 1:25; Ml 3:3). They must decide whether they regard God as a convenient means to fulfill their wishes or whether they are committed to let God's will be done in full confidence that it is a good and gracious will. God tests each believer according to His wisdom and love—severely or lightly, often or sparingly. But even when He crosses his most cherished plan or deprives him of his dearest possession, the believer will eventually say: "It was good for me that I was afflicted" (Ps 119:71), for "later it yields the peaceful fruit of righteousness to those who have been trained by it" (Heb 12:11; 2 Co 1:6).—So God *tested Abraham.*

22:2 *Whom you love.* Abraham did not have to be told that he loved his son. God knew it also, but anticipated every remonstrance on Abraham's part with this seemingly heartless directive. The words "father" and "son" occur frequently in the account (3, 6, 7, 9) and dramatize the high tension between paternal love and sacred duty.

To the land of Moriah. Solomon built "the house of the Lord in Jerusalem on Mount Moriah" (2 Ch 3:1). Abraham was to offer Isaac as a burnt offering *upon one of the mountains* in *the land of Moriah,* possibly on or near the site where later Israel's altar of burnt offerings stood.

22:3 *Rose early.* Without the least delay Abraham set out to comply with God's instructions. His silence on the way is in marked contrast with the long harangue with which he tried to dissuade God from destroying Sodom (18:22-32). In God's time there was to come a Descendant "of Abraham" who "although he was a Son . . . learned obedience through what he suffered; and being made perfect . . . became the source of eternal salvation to all who obey him" (Heb 2:16; 5:8; Ph 2:8). God "did not spare his own Son [as He did Isaac] but gave him up for us all." (Ro 8:31)

Cut the wood. Because the exact site of the sacrifice was still unknown to him and could be without trees, Abraham took wood with him.

22:4 *On the third day.* Ordinarily it would not have taken 3 days for the journey from Gerar to Mount Moriah, a distance of some 50 miles. No doubt the heavy burden of wood delayed their progress. As a result Abraham had to endure long night watches of agonizing reflection on the impending tragedy. His obedience was not to be the heroic act of an inspired moment but involved him in a protracted struggle with the impulses of his heart.

22:5 *Come again.* Abraham hoped against hope that God, who "was able to raise men even from the dead," would find some way to bring Isaac back alive. (Heb 11:17-19)

b. 22:9-14 Isaac Spared

22:10 *To slay his son.* The descent of the knife would have pierced a father's heart at the same time. But it would have been also the deathblow to every reasonable prospect that God's promise could be fulfilled.

22:12 *You fear God.* To fear God is to acknowledge God's total claim. It requires surrender to Him without reservation; it tolerates no compromise. The testing of Abraham's faith, its pain and heartache, had not been in vain. In the fear of God he "lost" life to "find" it. (Mt 10:37-39; 16:24-25; Jn 12:25)

22:13 *A ram.* God supplied a substitute for Isaac. The practice of human sacrifice by the Canaanites was an abomination in His sight. But this was not the lesson that God wanted to teach Abraham by testing him. The man who feared God indeed acknowledged that as a sinful man his life was forfeit to God. When he sacrificed animals, he confessed his guilt, recognized the need for atonement, and prayed for forgiveness. And God made of this vicarious sacrifice of an animal a sacrament by which He assured the worshiper of his reconciliation with the holy God. Mount Moriah faces toward Golgotha. Here God did "provide himself the lamb" (8) that bore "the chastisement that made us whole." (Is 53:5; Jn 1:29)

22:14 *The Lord will provide.* The name of the place is based on a play on words which uses the verb "to see" in a double sense. Here the Lord "saw to it" that an animal was at hand for the sacrifice by making Himself "seen," i.e., by revealing His will. (16:13-14)

c. 22:15-24 The Blessing of Abraham's Obedience of Faith; Nahor's Children

22:16 *By myself I have sworn.* Human fears stem from uncertainty. Those who fear the Lord are rid of all fears by assurances that are grounded in God Himself. His oath can be trusted as surely as He is God. (Heb 6:13-14)

22:23 *Bethuel.* A list of 12 sons of Abraham's brother Nahor is inserted between the account of Abraham's trial of faith and the story of Sarah's death in the next chapter. This genealogical note serves a good purpose at this point. It reveals how God had been at work for two generations to provide a wife for "the son of promise." God had never intended that he should die on Mount Moriah. Isaac was to marry Rebekah, the daughter of Bethuel (ch. 24). Most of the other sons of Abraham's brother remain unidentifiable. The genealogies of Ishmael and Jacob also list the names of 12 descendants. (25:13; 35:22-26)

6) 23:1-16 Sarah's Death; Purchase of a Burial Place

23:1 *A hundred and twenty-seven years.* Sarah is the only woman whose age at death is recorded in the OT. Almost four decades had elapsed since the birth of Isaac (17:19). This period is passed over in silence in the Biblical account.

23:2 *Kiriath-arba.* Lit. "the city of four," this name preserves an earlier designation for Hebron, located about 20 miles south of Jerusalem. (Jos 14:15; Gn 13:18; Nm 13:22)

Went in to mourn. Abraham entered her tent (24:67) and perhaps sat or lay before the corpse according to an ancient custom of mourning.

23:3 *Hittites.* KJV: "sons of Heth." Cf. 10:15-19 note.

23:4 *Give me property among you.* As a *stranger* and *sojourner* Abraham had been moving from place to place for some 60 years without owning even an acre of the land promised to him and his descendants. The only real estate to which he gained a clear title was a cemetery.

Bury my dead. Abraham was indeed looking for a suitable burial plot for his wife. But it turned out to be more than a place of interment. By his purchase of Machpelah, Abraham was symbolically laying claim to all of Canaan for his descendants. They would have the right to bury their dead throughout its length and breadth. Before his grandson Jacob was "gathered to his people," he requested burial in the same cave. (49:29-32; Ps 105:8-15; Heb 11:9, 13).

23:11 *I give you the field.* The following interchange between the Hittites and Abraham is a good example of Oriental haggling in the transaction of business. Abraham was no stranger to it. He therefore did not take it seriously when the property was offered to him as a gift. In mentioning *the field* Ephron notified Abraham that he could not obtain the cave without purchasing also the real estate adjacent to it.

23:15 *Four hundred shekels of silver.* Feigning sympathy with Abraham's predicament, Ephron pretended that he was giving the former a bargain. Actually the price was exorbitant.

7) 23:17-20 Burial of Sarah

23:18 *Made over to Abraham.* He received the "deed" to the property according to recognized legal procedures. It was to be also his last resting place. (25:9)

8) 24:1-67 Marriage of Isaac

24:1 *Abraham was old.* Before he died, Abraham wanted to make sure that the promise was not jeopardized by Isaac's union with one of "the daughters of the Canaanites," although a marriage alliance with a powerful inhabitant of the land would have proved profitable in a material way. It was customary for a father to provide a wife for his sons through an intermediary. Abraham's trusted "foreman" was to serve in this capacity. No doubt it was Eliezer, mentioned in 15:2.

24:2 *Hand under my thigh.* The same gesture in attesting an oath was demanded by aged Jacob (47:29). Since children are called "the fruit of the loins" or of the "thigh" (see KJV: 35:11; 46:26; Acts 2:30), a hand placed on this part of the body, associated with the power of procreation, was to signify that a man's descendants were thereby empowered to enforce the terms of the oath even after his death. Both Abraham and Jacob did not expect to live long and therefore exacted this kind of oath.

24:4 *To my country.* It was not Abraham's birthplace. He could call it *my country* because there he left behind his "kindred" and his "father's house" to go to a foreign land. (12:1)

24:10 *Camels.* The "ship of the desert," mentioned as part of Abraham's livestock (12:16), is known to have been domesticated by the time of the patriarchs. It appears as a means of transportation only at this occasion and later when Jacab left Laban (31:17). It was employed by the Ishmaelites or Midianites. (37:25)

The city of Nahor. According to 27:43 and 29:4 Laban lived in Haran, here called *the city of Nahor* for the simple reason that Abraham's brother resided there. It may also have come to be known by his name. *Mesopotamia,* lit. "Aram of the Twin Rivers," designates the area between the Tigris and the Euphrates.

24:12 *God of my master Abraham.* The Lord later identified Himself as "the God of Abraham." (26:24; Ex 3:6)

24:14 *I shall know.* The servant's request for a sign was not made in the attitude of the "evil and adulterous generation" of Jesus' day (Mt 12:39). It was a simple prayer for guidance, and God answered it. (Ju 6:17, 37; Is 37:7)

24:15 *Done speaking.* Before his prayer had ended, God's answer was there (Is 65:24; Ps 3:4; 18:6; 22:5; 28:6; 66:20; 107:6; 138:3; Lk 23:42-43; Ja 5:17-18). *Rebekah* was the daughter of Bethuel and the granddaughter of Abraham's brother Nahor (22:20, 23). In 48 the servant calls her the daughter of Abraham's "brother," correctly translated by the RSV with "kinsman" (KJV: "brother").

24:28 *Her mother's household.* Apparently Bethuel was very old and had resigned family responsibilities to his son Laban. The father is not mentioned as engaging directly in the discussion. He did give his consent to the marriage, but not without his son's concurrence. (50)

24:33 *I will not eat.* It was considered a breach of good manners for a guest to decline to eat when *food was set before him.* It was also customary not to broach one's chief concern brusquely but only in the course of the conversation at the meal. But the servant was so eager to discharge his obligation that he ran the risk of offending his host. And he received only the curt reply, *"Speak on."* His own speech, however, was long (34-49). In keeping with the ancient style of story telling, he repeats in detail what the reader already knows.

24:50 *Bad or good.* Convinced that *the thing comes from the Lord,* they refused to consider whether the request was bad or good from their own point of view.

24:54 *Send me back.* It had been so evident that "the Lord had prospered his way" to this point that the servant did not want to do anything that could possibly be an obstruction to divine guidance. Therefore he again disregarded the conventions of hospitality and the comfort of his convenience. He was willing to appear heartless; he insisted that Rebekah sever family ties without delay.

24:58 *Will you go?* This question indicates that Rebekah was not regarded merely as chattel. She was given an opportunity to refuse the marriage proposal.

24:62 *Beer-lahairoi.* Cf. 16:13 note.

24:63 *To meditate.* The Hebrew verb translated *meditate* occurs only here. While Isaac was walking about without a fixed destination, his thoughts also roamed afield, pacing back and forth between the prospects of his coming marriage with an unknown woman. In his meditation he no doubt did not forget to invoke God's blessing upon himself and his bride. Reared in the household of a praying father, the son could be expected to do no less than the servant had done repeatedly (12, 26, 52). Luther did not hesitate to translate: "he prayed."

24:65 *Took her veil.* The veiling of the bride was an ancient marriage custom that is still practiced. In those days it completely hid the identity of the woman. (29:23-25; 38:14, 19)

24:67 *The tent.* Because the addition of the modifier "of Sarah his mother" results in an awkward grammatical construction in Hebrew, the RSV relegates it to a footnote and designates it as a later addition to the text.

9) 25:1-6 Abraham's Descendants
by Another Wife

25:1 *Keturah.* Meaning "the perfumed one" and called a "concubine" (6; 1 Ch 1:32), Keturah evidently was a slave like Hagar. Her sons therefore were not regarded as heirs on an equal basis with Isaac (6). If they were born after Sarah's death, Abraham's "body, which was as good as dead" (Ro 4:19), must have retained its divinely bestowed power of procreation for a considerable time after the birth of Isaac. If events are not recorded chronologically and he *took another wife* during Sarah's lifetime, his example was followed by his grandson Jacob, who had two wives simultaneously in addition to two concubines. (35:22-26)

25:2 *Midian.* The descendants of Keturah lived in the "east country," i.e., in North Arabia. Some of them are well known from later accounts. The Midianites are mentioned in association with the Ishmaelites and the Medanites (37:28, 36; Ju 8:24; see also Ex 2:15b, 21; Nm 10:29; chs. 12—15; Ju 6—8). *Shuah.* One of Job's friends was Bildad, the Shuhite. (Job 2:11)

25:3 *Sheba and Dedan.* Cf. 10:7, 24 notes.

25:6 *Sent them away.* "Born according to the

flesh" like Ishmael, the sons of Keturah were not to "inherit with the son of the free woman" (Gl 4:28-30). According to God's counsel and will the chosen line was to be separated from all other tribal strains, even those emanating from the same father.

10) 25:7-11 Abraham's Death and Burial

25:8 *Abraham . . . died.* When Abraham died at the age of 175 years, there still was no tangible evidence that God was fulfilling His great promises. At his death, the man who was to become a great nation had only one heir; he whose descendants were to possess the entire land of Canaan owned one burial plot.

25:12-18 The History of Ishmael

25:12 *The descendants of Ishmael.* This is the seventh of the 10 genealogical "chapters" of Genesis. Introduced by the usual formula "these are the generations of," it provides a sequel to the previous mention of Ishmael's marriage to "a wife . . . from the land of Egypt" (21:21). This section is short because the descendants of Ishmael did not carry forward the chosen line from which, "according to the flesh, is the Christ" (Ro 9:5). But it is included for a good reason. Salvation history did not take place in a vacuum. God directed the lives not only of the chosen race and their forebears. Alongside and at times intersecting "sacred" history there is the history of peoples like the Ishmaelites. God's power extends also to them, and His plan of salvation is designed to include them.

25:16 *Villages and . . . encampments.* These *twelve princes* (cf. 17:20) lived in northern Arabia (37:25, 27, 28; 39:1; Ps 83:6). It is not possible to identify all their names.

25:17 *Gathered to his kindred.* In Abraham's case the same phrase is translated "to his people" (8).

25:18 *Havilah to Shur.* A general term for the desert area of the Sinai Peninsula. (Cf. 10:7, 24 notes; Ex 15:22 note; 1 Sm 15:7; 27:8)

He settled. Lit. "he fell upon the face of his brethren." The KJV renders: "he died in the presence of all his brethren." Perhaps the meaning is: each Ishmaelite tribe put pressure on its neighbor, even of a kindred tribe, in an effort to enlarge its territory. Thereby the characteristics of their ancestor would show themselves. (16:11-12)

25:19—35:29 The History of Isaac

25:19—27:40 BEFORE JACOB'S FLIGHT FROM ESAU

1) 25:19-28 Birth of Isaac's Twins: Esau and Jacob

25:19 *Descendants of Isaac.* After disposing of the descendants of Ishmael in a short "chapter" (12-18), the account again takes up its main theme: to trace the developments that were "generated" or set in motion by Isaac (25:19—35:29). Although he himself does not play a large part in its action, the plot of the drama revolves about him in his role as the recipient and the transmitter of Abraham's promise.

25:20 *Paddan-aram.* Lit. "the field or plain of Aram," this is another designation for Mesopotamia, called in the Hebrew Aram-naharaim in 24:10.

25:21 *She was barren.* So many situations and episodes in the life of Isaac have parallels in Abraham's history that the son appears to be but a less illustrious copy of his father. Like Abraham's wife, Rebekah was barren (16:1); like Abraham and Sarah, their son and his wife employed devious means to implement God's plan (27:1-40; 16:2-3); like Sarah, Isaac's wife was the instigator of the plot (16:2; 27:5 ff.); as in the case of Ishmael and Isaac, there was friction between Esau and Jacob (21:9; 27:41); like Abraham, Isaac palmed off his wife as his sister (12:10-13; 20:2; 26:6). In spite of these similarities, the circumstances and details are different in each instance.

25:22 *Why do I live?* When *the children struggled together,* Rebekah apparently feared that they would destroy one another. This would prove such a disappointment to her that life would not seem worth living. Under similar circumstances she later asked: "What good will my life be to me?" (27:46)

25:23 *Shall serve the younger.* "Though they were not yet born and had done nothing either good or bad" (Ro 9:11), God "loved Jacob" and "hated Esau" (Ml 1:3). Following Paul's example, we should not try to solve the mystery of divine election or even conclude that it involves an "injustice on God's part" (Ro 9:14 ff.). God desires "all men to be saved" (1 Ti 2:4). Believers can rest assured that He has "destined us in love to be his sons through Jesus Christ, according to the purpose of his will, to the praise of his glorious grace which he freely bestowed on us in the Beloved." (Eph 1:5, 11; Ro 8:28-30; 1 Ptr 1:2, 20-21)

25:25 *Red . . . hairy.* Esau's descendants were called Edomites (36:1). Edom means red (30). The Hebrew word for *hairy* is similar in sound to Esau (27:11). Esau's name and physical appearance characterized the "wild and wooly" nature of his offspring.

25:26 *Jacob.* His name in Hebrew is related to the noun "heel," which in its verbal form means "to supplant, to deceive." Colloquially we use the word "heel" in much the same sense. (27:36; Hos 12:3a; Jer 9:4b)

25:27 *A quiet man.* KJV: "plain"; Luther: "sanft"—soft-tempered. The Hebrew adjective is derived from a root meaning "to be wholesome, upright, peaceful, blameless" and is used to denote the opposite of wickedness (Jb 8:20; 9:20-22; Ps 64:4; Pr 29:10). Despite Jacob's lapses into unethical tactics, he was basically sound in his commitment to God. He believed that the Lord would transmit a universal blessing through the family of Abraham, and that meant through him as the heir of Abraham's son. His *dwelling in tents,* like his shepherd father and grandfather, indicated his desire to conform also to the parental way of life.

25:28 *Loved Esau.* Parental preference of one

child over another is a fruitful source of domestic troubles.

2) 25:29-34 Esau's Birthright Acquired by Jacob

25:31 *Your birthright.* The firstborn son was entitled to greater privileges than his brothers. He received a double share of the inheritance and succeeded the father as head of the family (Dt 21:16-17; 2 K 2:9). No doubt Rebekah had informed her favorite son what God had in store for him (23), and he was quick to seize an opportune moment to wrest the blessing from God's hand. Although it was a crafty maneuver, he felt justified in exploiting his brother's weakness and deceiving his father in order to implement the divine promise.

25:32 *What use is a birthright?* Esau had no sense of values and no sensitivity for things spiritual (Heb 12:16). For the momentary satisfaction of his craving for food he was duped into bartering away a prerogative of lasting value.

25:34 *Went his way.* Having satisfied his appetite for the moment, Esau sauntered off without giving a second thought to the seriousness of what had just transpired.

3) 26:1-5 Isaac's Promise Confirmed During a Famine

26:1 *A famine.* Patriarchal history records how God's providence shaped events to serve His purpose. Dangers were averted; unfavorable circumstances, created by the patriarchs themselves or by others, were controlled to promote the promise that by Abraham and his descendants "all nations shall be blessed" (5). In this chapter a famine again precipitated a situation that induced Isaac, like Abraham, to jeopardize the mother of the promised seed (12:10-16; 20:2, 12-13). If this episode is not recorded in chronological order but rather took place during the 20 years before Jacob's birth (cf. 25:20, 26), Abimelech's appropriation of Rebekah would have prevented the birth of the bearer of the promise.

Abimelech. This need not be the same person that was king of Gerar at Abraham's time (ch. 20). Abimelech, meaning "my father is king," appears to be a title like Pharaoh rather than a proper name. In the superscription of Ps 34 the Philistine king Achish is also called Abimelech. (1 Sm 21:10)

26:2 *Do not go down to Egypt.* Abraham received no such directive when he sought relief from the famine in his day. (Ch. 12)

26:3 *Bless you.* To bolster Isaac's faith, God reminded him of *the oath* that He *swore to Abraham,* his father. It is all the more disappointing that Isaac, with this promise still ringing in his ears, should have failed to entrust himself implicitly to God's protection at the very place to which He had directed him.

26:4 *Bless themselves.* Cf. 12:3 note.

26:5 *Abraham obeyed.* His faith, counted "to him for righteousness," proved its sincerity in obedience to the Lord's will (15:6; 22:16). God did not remember Abraham's foibles against him in view of his faith.

4) 26:6-33 Isaac and Abimelech

26:7 *She is my sister.* Like father, like son (12:13; 20:2, 12-13). Isaac could not even justify his deception with the half-truth that Abraham invoked. (20:12)

26:8 *Fondling Rebekah.* Isaac's intimate caressing of Rebekah revealed that theirs was not a brother-sister relationship. God again intervened to protect His faltering saints. He let Abimelech accidentally discover the true state of affairs.

26:10 *Guilt upon us.* Isaac was rebuked by a heathen Philistine—a most humiliating condemnation of his duplicity! Cf. 20:7 note. Abimelech recognized that desecration of the sanctity of marriage has harmful social results. The guilt of the immediate offenders adversely affects also community welfare.

26:14 *Envied him.* Isaac obeyed the command to "sojourn in this land" (3) and was blessed with good crops. Jealous of the growing wealth of the intruder, the Philistines deprived him of his source of water, an absolute necessity for a sheep owner. The right to use the wells that his father had dug had been a token promise that his descendants would possess the land. But now it appeared that hostile forces would take from Isaac even this tenuous guarantee of future ownership.

26:17 *In the valley of Gerar.* Yielding to force, Isaac moved away from the center of Philistine power and sought to open his father's wells. The right to the first two was challenged and he therefore called them *Contention* and *Enmity* respectively (20, 21). The third remained uncontested. The name *Broad places or Room* expressed Isaac's gratitude to the Lord for success in the venture.

26:23 *To Beer-sheba.* No reason is given for Isaac's move to the place where Abraham had sojourned (21:22-34) and from where he and his father had journeyed to Moriah. (22:19)

26:24 *I am with you.* When God had directed Isaac to stay in Gerar, He had promised: "I will be with you" (3). God had delivered him from a foolish escapade. It was to be added assurance that God was keeping the promise made to his father. Isaac was to continue to be the bearer of that promise if, like Abraham, he responded in faith. And Isaac took the Lord at His word: "he built an altar there and called upon the name of the Lord." (25)

26:26 *Phicol.* The commander of the Philistine army at Abraham's time had the same name (21:22). Like Abimelech, it may be a title rather that a personal name.

26:28 *Make a covenant.* The Philistines were convinced that Isaac was "now the blessed of the Lord" (29) and wanted to be on good terms with him. Although they claimed that they had done "nothing but good" to Isaac, they had previously threatened his existence by cutting off his water supply.

26:33 *Shibah.* This word is another form of the numeral "seven" which as a verbal form means "to swear" (cf. 21:28 note). When the covenant was sealed by an oath on the very day on which water was found, Isaac's experience prompted him to confirm the name *Beer-sheba* that his father had given to the place.

5) 26:34—27:40 Esau and Jacob

a. 26:34-35 Esau's Marriages

26:34 *Made life bitter.* We are not told what the wives of Esau did that caused his parents heartache. No doubt they continued to practice their idolatrous religion with its abominations. In his choice of wives Esau apparently catered to his instincts without any sense of responsibility, as he had done in selling his birthright. (25:29 ff.)

b. 27:1-4 Isaac's Intention to Bless Esau

27:1 *Isaac was old.* Isaac's age at the birth of his twin sons was 60 years (25:26). So he was 100 years old when Esau was married (26:34). Another 80 years were to elapse before he died at the age of 180 years (35:27). Since he *was old and his eyes were dim* when he blessed his sons, this event occurred a number of decades after Esau's marriage but not less than 20 years before his death, since he was still alive after Jacob's return from Mesopotamia. (35:27-29)

27:4 *Bless you.* Isaac's enemies had not been permitted to sabotage God's plan to bless all nations through him and his descendants (ch. 26). In this chapter we see that Isaac's own perverse self-will did not succeed in thwarting the execution of God's will. But Isaac was not the only one guilty of disobedience. Rebekah and Jacob stooped to flagrant deceit. Instead of trusting God to rectify matters in His way, they resorted to their own devious means.

Savory food. The bestowal of the blessing was to be a festive occasion. Esau was directed to prepare game meat to his father's special liking, not necessarily richly spiced as the word *savory* in modern usage might imply. (7, 9, 14, 17, 31; Pr 23:3, 6)

c. 27:5-17 Rebekah's Plot

27:7 *Before the Lord.* This phrase does not occur in the record of Isaac's directive to Esau (4). Perhaps Rebekah added it to impress Jacob with the seriousness of his father's contemplated action. Isaac would assume the role of God's spokesman.

27:13 *Upon me be your curse.* Jacob had no qualms about the deception but feared possible exposure. Rebekah overcame his misgiving. If for some reason the plot were to fail, she declared herself willing to bear the consequences and to exonerate her son.

d. 27:18-29 Esau Deceived; Jacob Blessed

27:20 *The Lord your God.* In effect Jacob made God an accessory to his trickery (Is 48:1). Lies beget lies, even such as are blasphemous. At the same time, the mention of *the Lord your God* increased Isaac's suspicion. Evidently he was not accustomed to hear such pious language from the lips of Esau.

27:27 *Kissed him.* Once enmeshed in the net of dissimulation, Jacob found no way to avoid prostituting the most intimate token of fidelity. (2 Sm 20:9, 10; Mt 26:49)

Blessed him. God indeed wanted the blessing once given to Abraham and Isaac to be transmitted to coming generations (25:23). But it was God's gift and not Isaac's to give at the impulse of his whims. As He will not be mocked by the ungodly, so He will not be deflected from carrying out His determinate counsel by an erring patriarch. Even Rebekah's and Jacob's fraud must serve His purpose. He overruled the disobedient self-will of all participants. (45:5-8; 50:20; Pr 16:9; 19:21)

27:29 *Peoples serve you.* God had made known his intention that "the elder shall serve the younger" (25:23; Zph 2:8-10). *Blessed be everyone.* Isaac is God's spokesman and prophet. Jacob was pronounced the heir of "the fatness of the earth" in the Promised Land. But in his Offspring men will also face the decision of ultimate weal or woe. The fate of mankind depends on its attitude to the Seed of Abraham: "to one a fragrance from death to death, to the other a fragrance from life to life." (2 Co 2:16; Mt 21:44; Jn 9:39; 1 Ptr 2:6-8)

e. 27:30-40 Esau's Chagrin; His Blessing

27:33 *He shall be blessed.* According to popular opinion a word of promise or malediction, once uttered, was like releasing an arrow; it could not be recalled or its flight reversed. However, when Isaac *trembled violently,* he realized that he had propelled God's Word into action; it would irrevocably and unerringly speed to its mark (Ro 11:29). "God breaks and hinders every evil counsel and will which would not let . . . His kingdom come" (Luther). But its coming is not an uncontrollable fate, a machine that operates mechanically once it is set in motion. In His sovereign freedom God makes use of human agents, not puppets, to achieve His purposes. Although this distinction is conferred on them not as a reward for their own achievements or in view of their innate integrity, what they are and do decides their usefulness to Him (25:27; 26:5, 24, 34-35; 27:46; Dt 11:26; 30:15). Esau's "exceedingly great and bitter cry" of remorse and pain was of no avail (34, 38; 28:6-9; Heb 12:15-17). Let no man despair of God's goodness; let no man presume to trifle with it. God is gracious and wants all men to be saved (1 Ti 2:4; Eze 18:23, 32). God is also just (Ro 9:14), far above our criteria or recriminations. (Is 45:9-11; 29:16; Jer 18:6-7; Ro 9:21-22)

27:36 *Supplanted me.* Cf. 25:26 note.

27:39 *Away from the fatness of the earth.* The land of Esau's inheritance will not be as fertile as that given to Isaac's descendants, where *the fatness of the earth* will produce "plenty of grain and wine" (28). On account of its barrenness the Edomites will live "by your sword" (40) and resort to pillage as a means of livelihood.

27:40 *Break loose.* Independent for a time (Nm 20:14), the Edomites were later subjugated by the kings of Israel (1 Sm 14:47; 2 Sm 8:14; 2 K 14:7). As a result of Israel's unfaithfulness to God's covenant, they at times broke loose, regained their independence, and even invaded the Promised Land (1 K 11:14; 2 K 8:20; 16:6; 2 Ch 28:17). In the eighth century B.C. the Assyrians reduced them to a vassal state. Still later Judas Maccabaeus subdued them (1 Mac 5:65). John Hyrcanus incorporated Idumea into the Jewish state at the end of the second century B.C. The Herods were Idumeans.

27:41—33:20 JACOB'S STAY WITH LABAN AND RETURN TO CANAAN

1) 27:41-46 Rebekah's Concern for Jacob

27:41 *Esau hated Jacob.* Esau was incapable of introspection. It did not occur to him that his irresponsible action had contributed to this turn of events. At the same time Jacob and Rebekah were made to realize that their devious behavior had sowed the seed of fraternal strife. Its fruit was parental heartache. God may let sins serve His purpose, but He does not sanction them or relieve the perpetrators of accountability for them. Although a reconciliation was later effected between the two brothers (ch. 33), their descendants were inveterate enemies. (Am 1:11)

27:42 *Comforts himself.* The only way Esau knew to assuage his grief was to avenge himself.

27:45 *Bereft of you both.* In spite of Esau's waywardness, Rebekah was not without compassion for "the son of her womb." If he were to become another Cain (4:8-16), his life would in turn be endangered by the "avenger of blood." (9:6; Nm 35:19)

27:46 *Because of the Hittite women.* Rebekah did not mention Esau's murderous plan to Jacob. With characteristic ingenuity (27:5) she alone had become aware of "what Esau said to himself" (41) and apparently wanted to spare her aged husband additional grief. Esau too showed consideration for his father's feelings (41). In averting a double tragedy, Rebekah at the same time made use of the circumstances to supply Jacob with a wife who would not reject the covenant blessing, as Esau's wives had done. Recognizing the validity of this concern, Isaac instructed Jacob to leave home in order to take as a wife "one of the daughters of Laban" in Paddan-aram. (28:1-2)

2) 28:1-5 Jacob Sent to Laban by Isaac

28:1 *Blessed him.* In his previous blessing of Jacob, Isaac had unwittingly put into effect God's plan. Now he conferred the "blessing of Abraham" on the right person of his own volition. (12:2; 17:8)

28:2 *Paddan-aram.* Cf. 25:20 note; also Hos 12:12.

3) 28:6-9 Esau's Marriage to Ishmael's Daughter

28:9 *Mahalath the daughter of Ishmael.* Apparently Esau's marriage to a woman of Abraham's family was a belated attempt to gain his father's favor and to regain the blessing he had forfeited. The name of this wife does not occur in the genealogy of Esau (36:3). There "the sister of Nebaioth" is called Basemath, also the name of Esau's Hittite wife (26:34). Since Basemath means "the fragrant one," it may be a descriptive term applicable to several women.

4) 28:10-22 Jacob at Bethel

28:10 *Left Beer-sheba.* Jacob's deceitful maneuver to wrest the blessing from God resulted in banishment from his parental home and exposed him to the dangers of a flight through unknown terrain. He did return safely (35:27), but not until he had spent 20 years under the disciplining hand of God. But all the while the "God of Abraham" and the "God of Isaac" (13) was carrying out His plan to make "the seed of Abraham" a blessing to all nations. He continued to be patient with the weaknesses of the bearer of the promise; He kept him wherever he went (15); He brought him back to "this land" in order to give it to him and his descendants (13), through whom "all the families of the earth will be blessed." (14; cf. 12:3 note)

28:11 *To a certain place.* It is not necessary to assume that Jacob arrived there at the end of the first day's journey. The distance from Beer-sheba to Bethel is some 50 miles. Here Abraham's "tent had been at the beginning" (12:8; 13:3). Beyond this point the way to Haran led through less familiar territory. Furthermore, Jacob had to reckon with the ominous fact that "at that time the Canaanites were in the land" (12:6). At the point where he faced the possibility of encountering serious threats to his safety, God calmed his fears by the assurance of His presence.

28:12 *A ladder.* The Hebrew word occurs only here. Some translators prefer to render it "a ramp." A ladder, they suggest, would hardly be wide enough to permit simultaneous ascent and descent of the angels. It is also known that circular ramps led to the top of ziggurats, the temple-towers of ancient Babylonia. On the other hand, scaling ladders were widely used in sieges of a city. But since angels in reality need neither a ladder nor a ramp to execute their role as God's messengers, the specific device that visualized their service to Jacob does not affect the meaning of the dream.

Ascending and descending. One would expect a reverse order of movement by the angels. But Jacob was to be made aware of their presence on his earthly pilgrimage. As they accompanied him, they bore his needs to God's throne and from there, "harkening to the voice of his command," they would descend as "his ministers that do his will" (Ps 103:20; Mt 4:11; 18:10; 26:53). The "heavens were opened" over Jacob in order to let him see and hear that God would not let His plan fail (Eze 1:1; Rv 19:11). In Jesus Christ God completed the bridging between earth and heaven with finality (Jn 1:51). "This was according to the eternal purpose which he has realized in Christ Jesus our Lord, in whom we have boldness and confidence of access through our faith in him" and has "made us sit with him in the heavenly places." (Eph 3:11-12; 2:6, 18; 4:10; Ro 5:2; Rv 21:25)

28:13 *Above it.* The antecedent of the Hebrew pronoun may be the ladder or Jacob. The preposition governing the pronoun may mean "above" or "beside." The alternate reading of RSV "beside him" is grammatically correct. The sentence could also be translated: "God stood above him," i.e., Jacob.

And said. What God said was a repetition of the blessing given to Abraham and Isaac (12:3; 22:18; 26:4). Jacob no doubt knew of it and was aware of his participation in it (25:23; 27:27-29). But apparently this was the first time that God spoke to him directly. His dream had not been a demonic hallucination. Here he was confronted by the God who had through His Word fashioned the lives of his ancestors. His promises activated history. The future would do His bidding.

28:16 *I did not know it.* Jacob learned to know the omnipresent God. He was not a local deity. His authority crossed all territorial borders.

28:17 *How awesome.* Fear gripped him. A look into heaven let him see how presumptuous he, the supplanter, had been in his attempt to play God. Encountering angelic hosts, who delight to execute the will of the transcendent God, he realized how contemptible his self-will had been. At the same time the dream made clear to him that he had nothing to fear, if he feared God and relied on His *awesome* power to accompany him into a fearful future. No night of loneliness will be so dark that the angels of God will not be able to find him; no pit of trouble so deep that the ladder of God's presence cannot reach him. (Neh 4:14; Ps 5:11; 7:1; 18:30; 33:18; 91:11-12; 118:8; 121:3-4; 147:11; Pr 14:26; 16:3; Is 41:10-14; 50:10; 1 Co 2:5; 1 Ptr 4:19)

28:18 *For a pillar.* The same Hebrew word is used to designate the pillars that the Canaanites erected as symbols of the male deity; the Asherah (KJV: "grove"), no doubt a wooden image, represented the mother-goddess. The Israelites were commanded to cut down and to burn these objects of the fertility cult (Ex 23:24; 34:13; Lv 26:1; Dt 16:22). Jacob erected and consecrated a pillar to mark the site where God had manifested Himself (35:7, 14). Later he identified Rachel's grave by such a pillar (35:20). In the OT stones were frequently used to commemorate significant events. (31:45-54; Ex 24:4; Jos 4:1-9; 24:26-27; 1 Sm 7:12; cf. also Rv 3:12)

28:19 *Bethel.* God was not enshrined in the stone in some animistic way. It was the entire *place* that had become a "house of God" by the revelation of His presence there. He chose to use it as a "gate of heaven," removing the barrier between heaven and earth. The portals of prayer were open and permitted traffic in both directions (cf. 11:9 note). Because at Bethel Jacob had become aware of what God meant to him, He was for him "El-bethel," the God of Bethel. (35:7)

Luz. Bethel had been mentioned previously but without any reference to its former name (12:8; 13:3). When Jacob returned from Haran, he reiterated the name he had assigned to it (35:1-15). The Canaanites had no reason to adopt the name Bethel, and it remained known as Luz (48:3). According to Jos 16:2, Luz was the name of a city, while Bethel included the adjacent environs. Eventually the name Bethel was transferred to the city itself. After the division of the kingdom, Jeroboam chose it as one of the centers of calf worship. (Jos 12:16; Ju 1:22-26; 20:18-28; 21:1-4; 1 Sm 7:16; 10:3; 1 K 12:28-29; 2 K 23:15; 1 Ch 7:28; cf. also Am 4:4; 5:5-6; 7:13)

28:20 *Made a vow.* It appears as if Jacob were out to strike a bargain with God on his own terms. But a vow is a pledge to do something over and above ordinary requirements in recognition of a special favor from God. It usually is introduced by a conditional clause. So godly Hannah vowed: "If thou wilt give . . . I will give . . ." (1 Sm 1:11; cf. Nm 21:2; 2 Sm 15:7-8; and the regulations governing vows, Nm 30:2-3; Dt 23:21-23). So Luther, struck to the ground in a storm, vowed to become a monk if God ("Holy Anna") would let him safely reach his home. In an awesome vision Jacob had seen heaven open its resources. It moved him to entrust himself to God to *keep* him. Reliance on his cunning had made him a helpless fugitive. But it was some time before he overcame his besetting weakness—not until he had "striven with God and with men" at Peniel did he "prevail" (32:22-28). We are not told how Jacob kept his pledge to "give the tenth" to God. (Cf. 14:20)

5) 29:1—31:55 Jacob and Laban

a. 29:1-8 Jacob and the Herdsmen from Haran

29:2 *A well.* Cf. 24:11-27; Ex 2:15-21. *The stone . . . was large*—perhaps it was of such size as to prevent one shepherd from removing it and thereby getting more than his share of the water. However, Jacob was able to roll it "from the well's mouth" without any assistance (10). *Three flocks* had already arrived, but the shepherds had agreed to wait until "all the flocks were gathered there."

29:5 *Laban the son of Nahor.* Actually Laban was the grandson of Nahor, Abraham's brother (24:15). But in Biblical usage the terms "son" and "father" have a wider connotation than in English. In 28:13 Abraham is called Jacob's father.

b. 29:9-13 Jacob Meets Rachel and Her Father

29:11 *Kissed Rachel.* She did not object to this intimate greeting; it was customary among kinsmen (13). By weeping Jacob gave further evidence of his emotional nature, although it was quite common for men in his day to express their feelings in this way.

c. 29:14-30 Jacob's Marriage to Leah and Rachel

29:17 *Eyes were weak.* Leah's vision was not impaired. Her eyes merely lacked luster and sparkle. *Leah* means "cow"; *Rachel,* "ewe." (We prefer to give our girls the names of flowers such as Rose, Lily, etc.)

29:18 *Serve you seven years.* Reduced to poverty, Jacob was obliged to earn the "marriage present" that was customarily given to the family of the bride (34:12; Ex 22:17; 1 Sm 18:25; Hos 3:2). It was considered the father's compensation for the loss of his daughter from his household; it also enabled him to provide her with a dowry (24:59, 61; 29:24, 29; 31:15; Ju 1:15; 1 K 9:16). At the same time, this exchange of gifts constituted the legal transaction which validated the marriage agreement. The bride price with which God sealed His betrothal to Israel was "righteousness . . . justice . . . steadfast love . . . mercy." (Hos 2:19)

29:25 *Behold, it was Leah.* The deceiver was deceived. (Cf. also 37:32-36.) The heavy veiling of Leah, the usual oriental wedding gown, made it possible, but it could not have happened without her complicity in the plot.

29:26 *Before the first-born.* Laban's justification of his fraud may have been a glib dodge. But the word *first-born* must have struck home in Jacob's conscience to remind him of his own unscrupulous tactics to achieve that status.

29:27 *The week of this one.* Marriage celebrations lasted a week. (Ju 14:12)

29:28 *Gave him . . . Rachel.* Laban gave her to Jacob "on credit," stipulating, however, that the latter "work off" the marriage price over another period of 7 years. Lv 18:18 forbids a marriage with sisters.

d. 29:31—30:24 Jacob's Eleven Sons and One Daughter

29:31 *Leah was hated.* The meaning is not that Jacob showed hostility to her but that he "loved Rachel more than Leah" (30; see Ml 1:2, 3; also Dt 22:13, 16; 24:3, where the RSV translates "dislikes"; Lk 14:26). His preference for Rachel produced rivalry between the two wives.

29:32 *Reuben.* The names of Leah's four sons expressed her desire to rise in favor with her husband by bearing him children, a prerogative denied to her sister.

29:35 *Judah.* As we see God carrying out His plan of salvation, we notice two recurring features: (1) He passes by the stronger for the weaker vessel, the older for the younger; (2) He overrides human frailties in achieving His purpose. Jacob, the younger, became the first-born, albeit by deception. Unpopular Leah, his wife as a result of Laban's trickery, became the ancestress of the tribe of Judah, of David, "of Joseph the husband of Mary, of whom Jesus was born, who is called Christ." (Mt 1:1-16)

30:3 *Bear upon my knees.* It was customary for a father to acknowledge an infant as his own when the newborn child lay on the knees of its mother (cf. 48:12). Bilhah's children, born on Rachel's knees, were to be claimed by Jacob as though "he had children by" his barren wife (cf. 16:2 note). The children of Zilpah, Leah's maid, were given the same status. (9-11)

30:8 *Naphtali.* Rachel gave Bilhah's children names which, by a play on words, expressed her conviction that God had sanctioned her strategy. Naphtali, "the one obtained by wrestling" in prayer with God, was evidence to her that with His help she had "prevailed" in her contest with her sister. (Cf. 32:22-31)

30:14 *Mandrakes.* The fragrant fruit of the "mandragora," or mandrake, was considered an aphrodisiac and a cure for barrenness (SS 7:13). The Hebrew term contains the consonants of a word for love. Provoked by Jacob's preference for Rachel, the rivalry between the sisters grew so intense that they stopped short of nothing in bargaining for their husband's favor. (14-16)

30:17 *God hearkened to Leah.* As so often in the story of Jacob, human frailty and selfishness served to achieve God's purpose.

30:18 *Issachar.* His name is based on a play on the Hebrew word denoting wages for service rendered (16, "I have hired you"). Leah had given her maid to her husband. She regarded her own son as the Lord's reward for her willingness to let her maid secure offspring for Jacob.

30:20 *Zebulun.* The Hebrew verb involved in this name occurs only here and is translated in the RSV by *honor.* In cognate Semitic languages it has the meaning "bear" or "tolerate." On account of this son, Leah believed, Jacob would bear with her and grant her a more favored status as his wife.

30:21 *Dinah.* Her name is a feminine form of Dan, Rachel's son by her maid Bilhah. (6)

30:22 *God remembered . . . hearkened.* In answer to her prayer God had removed the "reproach" or disgrace of her barrenness (23) and had given her hope for "another son." (24)

e. 30:25-43 Jacob in Laban's Service

30:27 *By divination.* Although Laban worshiped idols (31:19, 32), he attributed his good fortune to *the Lord.* He either regarded Jacob's very presence as a good omen or he had resorted to some form of augury or sorcery that persuaded him of Jacob's value to him. (44:15; Lv 19:26; Dt 18:10; 1 K 20:33; 2 K 17:17)

30:32 *Speckled and spotted sheep . . . and goats.* The wages for Jacob's service must have pleased greedy Laban. He knew that in the majority of cases sheep were white and goats were black. But even Laban was no match for Jacob's cunning. When his wily scheme turned the tables on Laban, he attributed its success to God (31:9). Whether or not Jacob's maneuvers were justified, it was clear that God permitted them to serve His purpose, as He did Jacob's deception of his father.

30:37 *Peeled white streaks.* Jacob acted on the assumption that the color to which the female animals were exposed determined the appearance of their offspring. The results of his strategy do not prove that it is scientifically demonstrable (cf. 31:11-12). This entire chapter, filled with intrigues and unsavory countermeasures, is not recorded to glorify the resourcefulness of clever men. It is a straightforward account of their questionable tactics. God must overcome their unheroic weakness in order to let good come out of evil.

f. 31:1-35 Jacob's Flight from Laban

31:3 *I will be with you.* Several circumstances led to Jacob's departure for the land of his fathers. The change in Laban's attitude to him and the hostility of his sons made further stay precarious. But he did not leave until God had declared that his banishment was to end and had assured him of the same divine guidance on his way home that had spread its protective wings over his flight into an unknown land. (28:15)

31:11 *In the dream.* No doubt Jacob had taken credit for the riches he had acquired. Now he was given to understand that all his scheming would not have succeeded if God had not intervened and made it serve His purpose. (Dt 1:10; 7:13; 8:18; Ps 75:7; 127:1; 78:52 f.; 118:6; Ec 5:19; Acts 5:38-39; Ja 4:15)

31:13 *A vow to me.* Since Jacob had made his vow at Bethel (28:20), he had had ample opportunity to observe how faithfully God had kept His promise in spite of his lapses into self-sufficiency.

31:15 *Sold us.* Laban had *been using up the money given for* his daughters by Jacob instead of providing them with a proper dowry out of the marriage present. He had treated them like saleable chattel. (Cf. 29:18 note)

31:17 *Camels.* Cf. 24:10 note.

31:19 *Household gods.* This RSV translation of the Hebrew word appears only in this chapter. More often it is merely transliterated "teraphim" (Ju 17:5; 2 K 23:24; Eze 21:21; Hos 3:4; Zch 10:2). In 1 Sm 15:23 it is rendered "divination"; in 1 Sm 19:13, "image." Nothing certain is known of the size and shape of these idols or of the precise purpose they served. In this instance they apparently were small enough so that Rachel could hide them by sitting on them (34), but according to 1 Sm 19:13 the "image" seemed to have the proportions of a grown man. Perhaps they had been the means of Laban's "divination" (30:27). Extra-Biblical sources suggest that a husband could claim his father-in-law's possessions as his inheritance if his wife had acquired these idols. If this was the case, Laban's failure to find them would explain his insistence on making "a covenant" with Jacob regarding property rights. (44 ff.)

31:21 *Gilead.* Laban overtook Jacob in the northern part of what is now Jordan. At times Gilead designates the entire territory east of the Jordan down to the Dead Sea.

31:24 *Good or bad.* Lit. "from good to bad." Laban was not to turn from saying words that expressed good intentions to utterances that lead to bad action. Through a dream God confirmed Laban's intuition that Jacob was the recipient of divine favor.

31:28 *Kiss my sons and daughters.* Laban professed affection for his daughters although they felt that he had used them as so much merchandise to enrich himself (31:15). Jacob's fear that he would even now take them "by force" was not entirely unfounded. (31)

31:30 *My gods.* Still a polytheist, Laban distinguished between his *gods* and the God of Jacob's father.

31:34 *Rachel had taken.* She displayed a capacity for deception that matched her husband's craftiness. (Cf. 27:13 note)

g. 31:36-42 Jacob's Defense of His Flight

31:39 *Torn by wild beasts.* A shepherd was not liable for the loss of a sheep if he could produce some remains of the animal as evidence that he had not been negligent in watching over the flock. (Ex 22:10-13)

31:42 *The Fear of Isaac.* This epithet for God appears only here and in 53. The rendering "the Kinsman of Isaac" in some modern versions is based on tenuous evidence. The God to whom Abraham rendered obedience of faith is also the God before whom his father Isaac had stood in reverential fear (28:7; Ps 36:1; 119:120; Is 8:13; Heb 5:7). When men refuse to live in such holy fear of God, they will eventually tremble in fear of His justice (1 Sm 11:7; 2 Ch 17:10; 19:7; Is 2:10, 19-21; Jer 49:5). Jacob acknowledged that he owed all he had to the providential care of this transcendent God. (Ps 32:11; 94:17; 124:1; Pr 16:7)

h. 31:43-55 Covenant with Jacob

31:44 *Make a covenant.* In order to save face, Laban had engaged in swaggering bluster (43). In his heart he was afraid to go counter to the "Fear of Isaac." In a solemn covenant he renounced all his claims. Customary formalities were observed in sealing the contract: a pillar was raised and a cairn of stones was heaped up to "witness" the agreement (cf. 28:18 note). Finally the participants expressed their mutual assent to its terms by partaking of a common meal.

31:53 *God of Nahor.* Besides the God of Abraham, Laban invoked the God of Nahor, the brother of Abraham and the son of Terah. According to Jos 24:2, Terah and Nahor "served other gods." Laban remained a worshiper of these gods and included them in the oath to signify its binding force for him.

31:54 *Jacob offered a sacrifice.* He had reason to do so. God had ended his years of servitude and banishment. He had kept His promise to be with this man of passion, of self-will, of dubious stratagems, of pious fraud.

If Laban had succeeded in incorporating him and his family into an Aramean tribe, God's plan to give the Promised Land to Abraham's offspring and to make them a blessing to all nations would, humanly speaking, have been frustrated. But God had His way. It led to a sacrifice on a hill outside Jerusalem, to a new covenant sealed with the blood of His own Son. Participants in this eternal covenant are free from craven fear, free from slavery to self and every demonic power, free to be heirs of a celestial homeland. (Jn 15:5; 8:34, 36; Ro 8:12-13; 1 Co 6:15)

6) 32:1—33:17 Jacob's Meeting with Esau

a. 32:1-8 Jacob's Meeting with Angels; His Strategy

32:2 *Mahanaim.* Lit. "a twin army." Jacob divided his people into two camps (*mahanoth,* 7). But the name also reflects Jacob's gratitude that "the angel of the Lord encamps around" his family (Ps 34:7; 91:11; 27:3). Though unseen, angelic hosts always "encamp around them that fear" God. Jacob's eyes were opened to see them: at Bethel for his encouragement (28:12); at Mahanaim to impress on him that his own resources were insufficient to ward off annihilation. (2 K 6:14-17; Jos 5:13-14; Ps 33:16)

32:3 *Sent messengers.* The assurance of divine

help does not exempt the believer from using his own ingenuity (cf. also 7, 8, 13-21). In this sense the saying is true: "God helps those who help themselves." "Ora et labora": pray and labor. But if Jacob still had some lingering trust in his own resourcefulness, God deflated it completely, when at Peniel He made him a limping invalid. (22 ff.)

b. 32:9-12 Jacob's Prayer

32:9 *Jacob said.* This is the first recorded petition that Jacob addressed to God. However, it was more than a "foxhole prayer." He humbly confessed that he was "not worthy" of God's "steadfast love and... faithfulness"(10); he held God to His promise ("thou didst say"; also 12); he later lived what he prayed. As long as he had been successful, he had been self-reliant; in his helplessness he was led to see the necessity of calling upon God "in the day of trouble." (Ps 50:15; 81:7; 91:15; 119:71)

c. 32:13-21 Jacob's Presents to Appease Esau

32:13 *A present.* In Hebrew the same word is used to denote an offering that the Israelites brought to God as a gift of reconciliation and allegiance (4:3-5; Ex 29:4; etc.). This present was Jacob's first attempt at a reconciliation with his brother.

32:20 *Appease him.* Lit. "to cover his face." The atoning gift was to act as a blindfold for Esau's eyes and shut out Jacob's offense from his sight, when *I shall see his face.* The same Hebrew verb is used to express the removal of sin from God's face. The sacrifice of atonement served as a "covering of sin" (Lv 16:20-28, etc.). It is a component also of the word translated "mercy seat," the cover of the ark of the covenant in the sanctuary (Ex 25:17-22, etc.). The sacrifices of animals in the OT symbolized the expiating removal of sin from God's face that became a reality when God sent His only Son to be "the expiation for our sins, and not for ours only but also for the sins of the whole world." (1 Jn 2:2; 4:10; Heb 4:14-16; 9:6-14)

d. 32:22-32 Jacob's Wrestling at Jabbok; His New Name

32:22 *Crossed . . . the Jabbok.* It is not clear why Jacob did not leave the protecting barrier of the river between his camp and the approaching Esau. Perhaps he had decided to throw himself unconditionally on the mercy of his brother.

32:24 *Wrestled with him.* The word rendered *wrestled* occurs only here. It denotes an intertwining of the contestants in a hand-to-hand combat. The man is the "Angel of the Lord" in human form. (30; 48:16; Hos 12:3-4)

32:26 *Let me go.* Although Jacob no longer could continue the combat, he clung to his opponent. The latter was not a demon, who according to a popular notion could not endure the light of day. Although Jacob had seen God "face to face," His full glory was to remain shrouded in the darkness of the night, for "man shall not see me [God] and live" (Ex 33:20, 23; 34:29-35; Gn 19:15 f.; Is 6:5). Only when God became incarnate could men behold His glory (Jn 1:14; 14:9 f.; Cl 1:15; 2:9). He entered into deadly combat with the enemy of man and defeated him (3:15). Having given His "life a ransom," He "covered the face" of God's wrath so that everyone who "sees the Son and believes in him should have eternal life," where he will see God "face to face." (Jn 6:40; 1 Co 13:12; 2 Co 3:7 f.; 1 Jn 3:2)

Bless me. God, who crushes man into impotence, lets man "prevail against him" by prayer (29). It is His good pleasure to be vanquished by the stranglehold of faith. (28; 18:23-32; Mt 15:22-28; Lk 11:9; 18:7)

32:28 *Israel.* A name was more than a label of identification. It described the nature and character of the individual so named. God had elicited the confession from Jacob: I am what my name proclaims—a supplanter, a deceiver, a Jacob (25:26; 27:36). Henceforth he would be what the name Israel signifies: "God contends." No longer relying on his own prowess, Jacob would prevail on God to bless him and to fight his battles for him. God did not answer Jacob's question (29) because He had sufficiently revealed His "name" by what He had done.

32:30 *Peniel.* Lit. "the face of God." Jacob had feared to see the face of Esau (20). Instead he had seen the face of God, a catastrophe for a sinner (Ps 34:16; Jer 44:11). But God had made "his face to shine upon him": graciously his *life is preserved* in the face of death.

32:31 *Penuel.* In Hebrew a slight elongation of a letter in Peniel results in a word that means: "God turned his face" (Ju 8:8; 1 K 12:25). When God's face beams on men, there is light in darkness: *the sun rose.* When He "hides his face" and it is dark in our lives, He wants us to "seek his face." (Ps 30:7; Is 64:7; Ps 27:8; 2 Ch 7:4)

e. 33:1-11 Jacob's Reconciliation with Esau

33:1 *He divided.* Cf. 32:3 note.

33:3 *Bowing himself.* In this way a subject approached his king or overlord. Forgiven and blessed by God, Jacob could do no less than to seek reconciliation with his brother by a humble admission of guilt. (Mt 5:23-24; 18:23-35; Mk 11:25)

33:4 *Embraced him.* The high tension of the drama is resolved. We do not know at what point in Esau's "coming to meet" him with 400 men (evidently with hostile intentions) his attitude changed (32:6). God can and does produce a change of heart in people as spiteful and hate-driven as Esau. (31:24)

33:10 *Your face . . . the face of God.* Seeing the righteous God face to face, sinful Jacob could have expected death; instead his life was "preserved" (32:30). Brought face to face with vindictive Esau, he likewise received *favor.*

33:11 *My gift.* Lit. "my blessing." Jacob had sent a "present" to "cover Esau's face" (32:20). Upon Esau's refusal to accept it, Jacob urged him to consider it a token of gratitude and of his willingness to share God's blessing with his brother. Once Jacob had "taken away" Esau's "blessing" (27:35); now he insisted that his brother participate in the benefits of God's overruling providence.

f. 33:12-17 Jacob's Refusal of Esau's Escort

33:12 *Go before you.* Jacob declined Esau's offer to escort him and his entourage, suggesting that the faster pace of the armed force would work a hardship on his family and flocks. The reconciliation seemed too good to be true and Jacob may have harbored some suspicion that Esau might still change his mind.

33:14 *In Seir.* Jacob did not reach Esau's territory, Edom, here called Seir (32:3). Instead he chose Succoth as a stopping place "on his way from Paddan-aram" (18). It was so called because he there erected "booths" *(succoth)* or shelters made of woven branches (Jos 12:7; Ju 8:5; 1 K 7:46). During the Feast of Tabernacles or Booths the people constructed the same kind of temporary dwellings. (Lv 23:33)

7) 33:18-20 Arrival at Shechem

33:18 *Shechem.* Here Jacob established a more permanent residence after buying a piece of property from Hamor, whose father was also called Shechem (12:6-7; 35:1-4). As the subsequent account shows (ch. 34), Jacob would have avoided a calamity if he had not lingered at Shechem but had gone directly to Bethel in order to keep his vow. (28:18-22)

Safely. KJV: "Shalem." The RSV rendering of the Hebrew word as an adverb is to be preferred.

33:20 *Erected an altar.* Having succeeded in acquiring a "piece of land" in the Promised Land, Jacob evidently considered its purchase a token fulfillment of the promise that his new name signified (32:28). In worshiping "God, the God of Israel" he acknowledged his willingness to serve the Lord in the capacity that his new name implied.

34:1—35:29 JACOB'S LATER FAMILY LIFE

1) 34:1-31 Dinah Ravished

34:1 *Dinah.* Reconciled with God and his brother, Jacob could have expected a bright future. But God had His own way of keeping His "Israel" from lapsing into a "Jacob." The next chapters (34, 35, 37 ff.) record a series of bitter tragedies that awaited him. No longer retribution for the evil he had done, these experiences, painful as they were, demonstrated that "the Lord disciplines him whom He loves" (Pr 3:11; Heb 12:6; Jb 5:17; Ps 94:12; 119:71; 2 Co 4:17; Rv 3:19). Even after Peniel the struggle had not ceased in him between the "old man" and the "new man." The strokes of affliction cut deeply; but the rod was in the hand of a concerned Father. All of Jacob's grief arose within his own household. The treachery of his children was a reminder of his erstwhile Jacob-character. It must have deepened his feeling of remorse and made more fervent his prayer that God keep him from straying into old ways (Jn 5:14; Ro 5:3-5; 1 Co 5:1-5; 2 Co 1:4; 7:10-11; 12:7; 1 Ptr 4:1-2). At times God lays a cross on a believer when he least expects it: after a particularly high moment of faith, as when Jacob had "seen God face to face" at Peniel. (32:30)

Dinah, the daughter of Leah (30:21), seems to have invited trouble. Her desire to *visit the women of the land* (lit. "to look at with delight") was more than innocent curiosity, dangerous as that might have been.

34:2 *Hivite.* Cf. Gn 10:17.

34:4 *Shechem.* The son of the Hivite prince sought to make amends for ravaging Dinah. He offered honorable marriage to the disgraced girl and agreed to pay an unlimited amount for the "marriage present and gift" (12; cf. 29:18 note)—evidence that "he loved the maiden." (3)

34:7 *Folly in Israel.* Shechem's sin is branded by the same phrase that was current when Jacob's descendants had become the people of Israel. It denotes a senseless vilification of God and His people. (Dt 22:21; Jos 7:15; Ju 19:23; 20:6, 10; 2 Sm 13:12; Jer 29:23)

34:13 *Deceitfully.* Jacob's sons lured Hamor and Shechem into a deadly trap. They cloaked their unjustifiable treachery with the excuse that it was a means to avenge the treatment of their "sister as a harlot." (31)

34:22 *Become one people.* Jacob's sons were not the only ones to hide their real intentions. When Hamor and Shechem consented to circumcision as a condition for intermarriage between the two groups, they were plotting to disintegrate Jacob's family and in the end to gain possession of "their cattle, their property and all their beasts" (23). The temporary inconvenience and pain would be a small price to pay for the wealth that would accrue to them.

34:25 *Simeon and Levi.* Full brothers of Dinah, they felt particularly entitled to avenge their sister's honor. (1; 29:33, 34; 49:5-6)

34:30 *Brought trouble.* Jacob thought only of threats to their physical welfare. But intermarriage with *the inhabitants of the land* would have canaanized and baalized the seed of Abraham, making them unfit for God's purposes. His intervention again used the evil deeds of men to promote His plan. Events had taken such a turn as to make Jacob realize that he could no longer retain his property among the Shechemites. He was anxious to obey the directive to "go up to Bethel." (35:1)

2) 35:1-29 Isaac's Last Days

35:2 *The foreign gods.* In going "up to Bethel," a considerable climb, Jacob was exposed to attacks by the confederates of Shechem. God intervened again (5). But the mention of Bethel also reminded Jacob that he owed his survival to the God who "appeared to" him at this "awesome place" when he fled from Esau (28:10-22). There at the time of his "distress" he had pledged undivided allegiance to the God of Abraham and Isaac. In the meantime he had tolerated the possession of idols or *foreign gods* in *his household,* such as the teraphim of Laban (31:19, 30-35; Jos 24:2). In God's directive to go back to Bethel he sensed a call to repentance for tolerating the symbols of a divided loyalty (Ex 20:2-3; Jos 24:19-26; Hos 2:13). The change of garments was to symbolize an inner purification. Every true repentance is no less an acknowledgment of the worship of spurious gods; the resolve to *put away* divided loyalty;

the determination to "fear, love, and trust" God from a pure heart. (Mt 6:24)

35:4 *The oak.* Cf. 12:6; Jos 24:26.

35:6 *Luz.* Cf. 28:19.

35:7 *El-bethel.* Lit. "the God of the house of God," i.e., of Bethel. The double mention of God in this name was intended to teach Jacob's household that the transcendent God whom he worshiped had revealed Himself at this very place "when he fled from his brother" and thereby had made it a Bethel, a house of God, a place where His honor dwells (Ps 9:11; 26:8; 74:2). No one "in the land of Canaan" heard Jacob when he first assigned a new name to Luz; now he reiterated it for the benefit of his household.

35:8 *Deborah.* This isolated note about the death and burial of *Rebekah's nurse,* not mentioned previously, may have been included at this point in the account because it deals with another event that happened at Bethel. In point of time it may have occurred sometime after Jacob's return to his home (27-29). The burial of this aged servant-woman is accorded special notice, whereas the death of Rebekah, her mistress, is not mentioned. Devoted and faithful service to God also by people of "low estate," perhaps without acclaim by men, does not go unnoticed by Him. (Lk 1:48; 2 K 5:1-3)

35:9 *Appeared . . . again.* God knows that the faith of men needs the nurture of repeated affirmations of His Word, particularly in days of stress and strain. Jacob's past performance proved that God was not going to unnecessary trouble when He appeared to him again and confirmed that (1) since Peniel he bore the name "Israel" with God's approval and need not be concerned with his unworthiness as a "Jacob," a supplanter (10); (2) there was no change in God's mind since He had appeared to him at Bethel for the first time: Jacob's offspring would become a nation and take possession of the land. (11-12)

35:14 *Set up a pillar.* We are not told what happened to the pillar that Jacob had set up there more than 20 years ago (28:18 note). When God *had spoken with him* at this place, as He had done previously, Jacob was confirmed in his conviction that this was truly "the house of God" and should be so named. A *drink offering* is mentioned here for the first time. (Ex 29:40)

35:16 *Ephrath.* Another name for Bethlehem. (48:7; 1 Sm 17:12; Mi 5:2)

35:18 *Benjamin.* With prophetic vision Jacob called his youngest son "the son of the right (hand)," a harbinger of good things. He was later to be a key figure in effecting a reconciliation between Joseph and his brothers (43:16; 44:12; 45:15). "Rachel died" in childbirth. Once she had said: "Give me children or I shall die." (30:1)

35:21 *Tower of Eder.* Lit. "tower of the flock" and so translated in Mi 4:8; it was located in the vicinity of Jerusalem.

35:22 *Lay with Bilhah.* Since his "conversion" from Jacob to Israel at Peniel, Jacob drank frequently from the cup of sorrows (cf. 34:1 note). This verse records a particularly bitter potion. An outrage under any circumstances, the crime was particularly abhorrent because it was committed by Reuben, the firstborn, supposedly the father's trusted assistant. (49:4; 1 Co 5:1-5)

The sons of Jacob. The birth of the youngest (18) is followed by a list of all the sons of Jacob together with the names of their mothers. Although Reuben, Simeon, and Levi were the three oldest, none of them was to become the bearer of the patriarchal promise. Judah, the fourth in line, was to receive the blessing of the firstborn. (49:1-12)

35:27 *Mamre.* Cf. 23:2 note.

35:29 *Gathered to his people.* Cf. 49:29 note. The weary pilgrim "without a lasting city" in Canaan came to "the assembly of the first-born who are enrolled in heaven . . . to the spirits of just men made perfect." (Heb 12:23; 13:14)

36:1-43 The History of Esau

36:1 *Descendants of Esau.* See the Introduction for the meaning of the term "descendants" in the "chapter" divisions of Genesis.—Almost all the names appearing in this genealogical history remain unknown. Their compilation does not seem to serve the forward movement of the OT toward its fulfillment in the Name of names. We may have the impression that reading this catalog of meaningless names is nothing short of an act of penance. But this chapter too is written for "our instruction." It teaches us that the stream of all history takes its course in the channels of God's making. Salvation history flows from it and back into it. Abraham's line is diverted from the mainstream of the nations (ch. 10; 11:1-9; 12:12; 13:5-12); the offspring of Hagar, the Ishmaelites, branch off from the family of Abraham (25:12-18); Esau's descendants go off in another direction. These records of "secular" history, although brief, are reminders that God has a universal plan of salvation. Not only "Israel after the flesh," but "all the families of the earth" are to be blessed in Abraham's Seed. (12:3; 49:10; Am 9:11, 12; Gl 4:29; Acts 2:21)

Because the genealogical history of Esau has various aspects and purposes (cf. the paragraph titles in the text), some repetition as well as variation of names occurs. Eliphaz, e.g., is mentioned more than once (4, 10, 15). Two of the three wives of Esau seem to have more than one name. (26:34; 28:9; 36:2-3)

37:1—50:26 The History of Jacob

37:1—40:23 JOSEPH'S DEGRADATION

1) 37:1-28 Joseph Sold into Slavery

a. 37:1-4 Jacob's Favoritism Toward Joseph

37:2 *The history of the family of Jacob.* The last and longest "chapter" of Genesis (37:1—50:26) has the same introductory formula as the other nine: "These are the generations of . . ." (cf. 2:4 note). Jacob's history to this point was reported under the heading "the descendants of

Isaac" (25:19). This "chapter" tells of events and persons that were "generated" or came into being by Jacob through his offspring. His favoritism to Joseph provided the impetus that set the drama in motion, and his dying blessing (ch. 49) rings down the curtain. But in the main he played a passive role; he experienced new grief caused by the members of his household. In this respect the "Joseph story" adds another installment to the account of Jacob's chastening (cf. 34:1 note). It also provides continued evidence that God thwarts the evil that men do. The direction of the lives of the patriarchs was a big step toward His ultimate goal: the coming of the Ruler who offers universal peace to men. (49:9-12; Is 9:6; Lk 1:32)

Ill report. No doubt Joseph was instructed to keep his father informed of the behavior of his brothers (12-14). They in turn resented the supervision and hated him for it, refusing even to bid him welcome with the customary greeting: "Peace be with you." (4)

37:3 *Long robe with sleeves.* This rendering of the original ("a tunic of pieces or extremities") appears preferable to the translation "a coat of many colors." The special feature of the garment no doubt was its length, a mark of distinction (2 Sm 12:18-19). Jacob had not learned how foolish parental favoritism to a son is. (25:28)

b. 37:5-11 Joseph's Dreams; Jealousy of Brothers

37:5 *A dream.* Neither of the dreams was the product of Joseph's egotistic thinking. Both were visions of the future, foretelling what was in store for him and his brothers (20:3; 28:12; 31:11, 24). Perhaps in thoughtless naivete, certainly without regard of consequences, Joseph shared their remarkable content with his family.

37:10 *Your mother.* Rachel, Joseph's mother, was dead (35:19). But in his interpretation of the second dream, Jacob recognized her among those who would bow before their son. Perhaps the dreams had occurred earlier and are recorded here in the context of the jealousy of Joseph's brothers.

37:11 *Kept the saying in mind.* Intending to keep Joseph from becoming overbearing, "the father rebuked him." But he sensed that the dreams were more than idle fantasy (Lk 2:19, 51). And he lived to see the day when Joseph, in the role of a mighty potentate, kept him and his family from extinction.

c. 37:12-24 Plot to Kill Joseph; Reuben's Rescue Attempt

37:12 *Near Shechem.* Perhaps the father's anxiety for his sons arose because they had returned to the same area where they had made him and themselves "odious to the inhabitants" by their treachery. (34:30)

37:18 *Conspired against him.* Joseph's persistent efforts to carry out his father's will and his complete lack of apprehension were in sharp contrast with the murderous designs of his brothers.

37:22 *Reuben.* As the firstborn he felt himself responsible for his brother. Not daring to oppose the conspirators directly, he nevertheless persuaded them *to shed no blood.* In the end his compromise with evil played into the hands of his brothers.

d. 37:25-28 Joseph Sold to Slave Traders

37:25 *Ishmaelites.* They were descendants of Abraham and Hagar (16:12); the Midianites (28), of Abraham and Keturah (25:1-6). Related with one another perhaps by marriage and engaged in the same kind of enterprise, this group of traders apparently was composed of people of various family strains. The Ishmaelites and Midianites were closely associated with one another in another undertaking (Ju 8:22-24); the Midianites, with the Amalekites. (Ju 6:1-3)

37:28 *Twenty shekels of silver.* To get rid of their brother, they sold him for 20 pieces of silver, less than the usual price of a slave.

e. 37:29-36 Jacob's Grief

37:33 *A wild beast has devoured him.* The deception had the desired result on Jacob, just as his impersonation of Esau had been equally successful. (Ch. 27)

37:35 *Sheol.* The grave or realm of the dead. (Dt 32:22 note)

37:36 *Sold him in Egypt.* Seemingly the story of Joseph had come to an end. But it had only begun. When "the patriarchs, jealous of Joseph, sold him into Egypt . . . God was with him" (Acts 7:9). The persecution and injustice that was the lot of Joseph and all the other prophets and saints of old was God's way of achieving His gracious purpose in their individual lives. But all the while God was moving toward a greater goal. To the extent that these sufferers were innocent martyrs in His cause, they also "announced beforehand the coming of the Righteous One," who . . . "betrayed and murdered" bore "the iniquity of us all." (Acts 7:52)

2) 38:1-27 Judah's Adultery

38:1 *At that time.* Although Judah had dissuaded his brothers from laying murderous hands on their "own flesh" (37:26-28), his reprehensible behavior, recorded in this chapter, was another link in the chain of Jacob's family trials. For that reason the Tamar episode is inserted at this point before the story of Joseph is resumed in ch. 39. The expression *at that time* is general enough to allow for the possibility of a topical rather than a chronological sequence of the narrative. The dismal account of Judah's excursion into the far country of self-gratification and licentiousness is an unvarnished portrayal of human perversity. But we also learn that God is not diverted from His plan by the evil that men do. The offspring of Judah's incestuous union with his daughter-in-law became a link in the ancestry of Jesus. Tamar, the Canaanite harlot, and Perez, her son, are accorded a place in "the genealogy of Jesus Christ, the son of David, the son of Abraham" (Mt 1:3; Ru 4:18 ff.). *Hirah* was an inhabitant of Adulla, a Canaanite city in the vicinity of Bethlehem. The place name Chezib

(5) remains unidentified.

38:6 *Took a wife for Er.* Judah perpetuated the canaanizing of his family which he had begun by his marriage to Shua. (2)

38:8 *The duty of a brother-in-law.* According to the levirate law it was the duty of the "levir," the husband's brother, to provide his widowed sister-in-law with an heir (Dt 25:5 ff.). The custom was in vogue also among non-Israelites. Onan refused to comply with its demands. (9)

38:14 *Entrance to Enaim.* Lit. "in the opening of the eyes." Perhaps the meaning is "in full view" where no one on his way to *Timnah* would fail to see her. Timnah is mentioned later as a place in the tribe of Judah. (Jos 15:57)

38:15 *Covered her face.* Rather than be left childless, Tamar tricked Judah into fathering her son by posing as a Canaanitish temple prostitute. The latter were veiled to distinguish them from ordinary harlots. Living in a land where such degrading cult practices were common, Judah had no scruples about satisfying his lust by doing in Rome as the Romans do.

38:18 *Your signet . . . staff.* These would later prove Judah's identity. A ring or cylinder, often attached to a cord and worn about the neck, was an engraved seal. With it the owner gave the impress of his signature. Judah's shepherd staff perhaps had his identifying markings on it.

38:24 *Let her be burned.* The Mosaic law required a harlot to be stoned (Dt 22:21; Jn 8:5); if the culprit was the daughter of a priest, she was to be burned. (Lv 21:9)

38:26 *More righteous.* Judah acknowledged that his guilt was greater than that of the woman whom he had condemned to death. While she was motivated by a consuming desire to supply Judah with an heir, albeit by reprehensible means, he did not have even the excuse of good intentions for his part in the crime.

38:29 *Perez.* Esau was the older of the twins, but Jacob was chosen to be the bearer of the promise. Contrary to expectations, Perez too became the firstborn and thereby the ancestor of the Messiah. In the administration of God's kingdom the last often become the first (Mt 20:16). Therefore the purpose of this chapter is not achieved when it has portrayed human depravity. The beams of God's forbearance illuminate its dark pages with hope. If "the firstborn of the dead" (Cl 1:18) did not disdain to have ancestors of this kind, His grace is big enough to make even me His heir, "chief of sinners though I be."

3) 39:1—40:23 Joseph's Degradation in Egypt

a. 39:1-6 Joseph Overseer of Potiphar's House.

39:1 *Potiphar.* His name is very similar to that of Joseph's future father-in-law, Potiphera (41:45). Both contain a reference to an Egyptian deity. *Pharaoh* is a title rather than a proper name. Derived from the Egyptian term for "great house," it was applied to the occupant of the royal residence (cf. our "White House" or the title "His Majesty"). In later accounts some of the Pharaohs are identified by name: Shishak (1 K 11:40), Neco (2 K 23:29), etc.

39:2 *The Lord was with Joseph.* When Jacob had to flee to a strange land, God assured him: "I am with you" (28:15). Not a local or national God, He accompanied also Joseph across the borders of another foreign country. His presence produced results: "The Lord caused all that he [Joseph] did to prosper in his hands." (3)

39:6 *The food which he ate.* The meaning seems to be that Joseph relieved Potiphar of every exertion of effort. Nothing remained for the Egyptian to do but to eat, something no one can do for another.

b. 39:7-18 Temptation to Sin Resisted

39:7 *His master's wife.* Joseph's access to Potiphar's entire domain exposed him to association with his mistress.

39:9 *Sin against God.* Yielding to the woman's seduction would have been a breach of confidence with Potiphar. But above all it was a *great wickedness* because it was no less than a defiance of God's ordinance. He tolerates no compromise with evil; He sees clandestine sins, undetected by men (Ps 90:8; Pr 1:10; 9:17; Ec 12:14; Jer 23:24; Ro 2:16; Eph 5:11, 12). To compromise with sin against God as an expedient adjustment to circumstances is a constant temptation to individuals and the entire church.

39:15 *Left his garment.* His bloody tunic had been presented to his father as proof of his death (37:33); his garment in the hand of Potiphar's wife was designed to be "exhibit A" of his guilt. The conclusion drawn from the evidence in both cases was false.

39:17 *Hebrew servant.* Cf. 14:13 note.

c. 39:19-23 Joseph Imprisoned

39:20 *The king's prisoners.* The victim of gross injustice, Joseph did not know that the choice of his dungeon was not by accident. As its gates shut behind him, God had already made provisions to open them and to make them doors leading to heights of glory. "The Lord was with Joseph" also in prison (2, 21), as He is with all His children when He imposes on them a "prison term" of affliction (Ps 105:16-22; Mt 5:4; Ro 15:4; 2 Co 7:6; 2 Ti 2:12; Heb 12:1-3; Ja 1:12; 1 Ptr 4:12-14; Rv 2:9-10). In the dark loneliness of a Pharaoh's prison their eyes are trained to focus on the radiance of God's face which the shining mirages of prosperity often tend to blot out. All of this is true because God locked His own Son in the prison house of death and then demolished it by raising Him from the dead.

d. 40:1-8 Dreams of Fellow Prisoners

40:1 *Some time after this.* We are not informed how long Joseph was imprisoned (41:1). But the following chs. tell us that God always determines the time when apparently chance circumstances combine to weave the pattern of His good and gracious will. Through the dreams of Pharaoh's baker and his butler God began to set in motion "what he was about to do" (41:25; 20:3-7). The *butler* or cupbearer and the *baker* were not menial servants but important officials of the ancient courts. (Neh 1:11)

40:8 *Belong to God.* Enabled by God to

interpret dreams, Joseph, the "dreamer" (37:19), began his rise to fame (Dn 2:27 ff.). In prison the officers were prevented from securing the services of "magicians" and "wise men" who made it their business to interpret dreams. (41:8)

e. 40:9-15 The Butler's Dream Interpreted

40:13 *Lift up your head.* The same expression occurs in the interpretation of the baker's dream (19). In the first instance it had a symbolic meaning: Pharaoh would act favorably toward the butler (Jer 52:31; 2 K 25:27 KJV). The baker's head was literally to be lifted up to the gallows.

40:15 *Stolen out of the land of the Hebrews.* Out of the land where the Hebrews had settled Joseph had been kidnapped with the connivance of his brothers and so had become a slave. In telling his story he refrains from mentioning those responsible for his plight: his brothers and Potiphar's wife. Although he did not understand the meaning of his misfortunes, he did hope for a turn of events if the butler would "make mention" of him to Pharoah. But nothing happened for another two years. (41:1)

f. 40:16-19 The Baker's Dream Interpreted

g. 40:20-23 Dreams Come True

41:1—47:31 JOSEPH'S EXALTATION

1) 41:1-8 Pharaoh's Dreams

41:1 *Pharaoh dreamed.* The inability of the "magicians" and "wise men" to interpret Pharaoh's dreams reminded the butler of his broken promise. (9-13; Ex 7:11, 22; Is 19:11-13; Dn 2:2; 4:7)

41:7 *It was a dream.* When Pharaoh awoke and realized that what he had seen with his mind's eye had not in reality occurred, he seemed somewhat relieved. Nevertheless "his spirit was troubled" because the dreams appeared to be portents of future calamity.

2) 41:9-13 Joseph Remembered by Butler

41:12 *A young Hebrew.* The butler believed that Joseph personally possessed uncanny powers; Joseph knew better. (16; 40:8; Acts 3:12)

3) 41:14-24 Joseph's Appearance Before Pharaoh

41:14 *Hastily.* It took a long time to let God's plan ripen; it seemed like ages to Joseph. But when the right hour struck, there was prompt action. (Ps 37:19; 113:5-8; Is 60:22; Hab 2:3; Zch 14:7; Acts 1:7-8; 17:31)

Shaved himself. The Egyptians were clean-shaven. Among the Israelites the beard was considered a mark of distinction. Shaving it was a gesture of mourning or disgrace. (2 Sm 19:24; Is 15:2; Jer 48:37)

41:17 *In my dream.* Repeating the dreams almost verbatim (2-7), Pharaoh, however, added a few touches in the description of the "gaunt and thin cows" and of the "thin and blighted" ears. By emphasizing these negative features he underscored the mysterious feature of the dream. Why should strong cows and healthy plants be swallowed up by their weak counterparts?

4) 41:25-36 Pharaoh's Dreams Interpreted

41:25 *Is one.* Both dreams have one and the same meaning. "The doubling of the dream of Pharaoh means that the thing is fixed by God." Pharaoh could not regulate the flow and overflowing of the Nile, upon which Egypt relied for its food supply. It was dependent on "the finger of God." (Ex 8:19)

41:34 *Let Pharaoh proceed.* Convinced that God had spoken through him, Joseph urged Pharaoh to act in order to prevent a national calamity. He did not know then that the Lord of history was making Egypt His instrument for the preservation of His people.

5) 41:37-45 Joseph Made Viceroy

41:41 *Set you over all the land.* Joseph was made the viceroy or vizier of Pharaoh, an official mentioned also in non-Biblical records. The ceremonies of investiture were typically Egyptian: (1) he was given the official signet ring (cf. 38:18); (2) he was robed in the distinctive garment of his position; (3) a golden chain, another mark of authority, was hung about his neck; (4) a royal chariot was put at his disposal.

41:43 *Bow the knee.* The heralds announced the approach of Joseph's chariot by shouting: *Abrek,* a hebraized form of an Egyptian word that may itself be a Semitic loan word. It summoned the crowds in the street to give way before him and to acknowledge his authority.

41:45 *Zaphenath-paneah.* The exact meaning of Joseph's Egyptian name has not been determined. Suggested interpretations are: "Preserver of life," "God says: he is living." The hyphenated phrase may also be equivalent to: Joseph who is called "'Ip'ankh," a common Egyptian name.

Asenath. By his marriage to the daughter of a priest, Joseph, the slave, became a recognized member of the highest caste. Her father had given her a name that expressed his religious convictions: "She belongs to [the goddess] Neit." Nothing is known of her except that she became the mother of Joseph's sons (50-52; 46:20). While Canaanite blood coursed in the veins of Judah's descendants (ch. 38), there was an Egyptian strain in the tribes of Manasseh and Ephraim. The city *On,* as its Greek name Heliopolis indicates, was a center of the worship of the Egyptian sun god Re. It was located a few miles northeast of modern Cairo. *Potiphera* may be the man's name or his title. In either case it has the name of an Egyptian deity as an ingredient. (Cf. 39:1 note)

6) 41:46-57 Joseph Stores Food; His Sons; Joseph Sells Food

41:56 *Thirty years old.* Thirteen years had passed since Joseph's arrival in Egypt—13 years since prison doors, figuratively and literally, had locked him in the dark mystery of suffering. Looking back upon his degradation from the vantage point of his position as prime minister, he realized that he had not been the victim of a cruel fate. God was in control and had shaped events for beneficent results. To the end of his days he may never have understood why in the process God let him walk the way of sorrow. The Joseph story is a partial answer to the question: If there is a good and almighty God, why does He permit evil to happen? It also is a comfort to all crossbearers. They may have to wait until they reach the perspective of celestial heights before they will see why God fashioned their particular cross for them (Ro 15:4; 2 Co 4:16-17; 12:9; Heb 12:11; 13:5-6; Ja 1:12). But in the final analysis the story of Joseph has meaning only because the sinless Son of God willingly went the way of the cross to atone for the sins of Joseph, of his brothers, of all sons of Adam. What Joseph and all OT saints endured was merely a faint foreshadowing of the mystery of Golgotha.

7) 42:1—47:31 Joseph and His Brothers in Egypt

a. 42:1-5 First Journey of Brothers

42:4 *Did not send Benjamin.* The disappearance of Joseph (chs. 37—41) was not to end Jacob's trials. Eventually he would have to give up also Benjamin, at least temporarily. (Ch. 43)

b. 42:6-17 Joseph's Harsh Treatment of Brothers

42:8 *They did not know him.* Only a boy when they sold him, Joseph was now a grown man of 37 years (37:2; 41:46, 53). It is not surprising that the brothers did not recognize him in this potentate, resplendent in the regalia of his position.

42:9 *Remembered the dreams.* In speaking "roughly with them" some feeling of resentment may have arisen in Joseph. But the fulfillment of his dreams reminded him of the fact that God had a hand in shaping his destiny. His continued harsh treatment of his brothers was designed to awaken their conscience: "By this you shall be tested." (15)

Spies. Although the charge was trumped up, the Pharaoh's viceroy could be expected to be on guard against espionage. Egypt's border with Canaan was a particularly vulnerable frontier: "the weakness of the land."

42:15 *By the life of Pharaoh.* The Pharaohs claimed divine descent. However, Joseph did not invoke an Egyptian god in his oath (Jer 12:16; Am 8:14). In order to continue his disguise, he used a formula of asseveration that sounded genuinely Egyptian: "As surely as Pharaoh lives." (Cf. 1 Sm 1:26; 17:55; 2 Sm 11:11; 14:19).

c. 42:18-26 Joseph's Plot to Test His Brothers

42:21 *We are guilty.* Joseph's statement: "I fear God" (18) had assured the brothers that they were not in the hands of an unscrupulous despot. But the fear of God also struck terror into their hearts as they recalled how heinous their "sin against the lad" (22) actually was. Although they admitted their guilt to one another, they were not ready to confess it to others, not even to their father.

42:24 *Wept.* No doubt Joseph's tears were the overflow of mingled emotions. For the time being, however, he held himself in check in order to lead his brothers to a full awareness of their guilt.

d. 42:27-38 Consternation of the Brothers; Report to Jacob

42:28 *God has done.* Joseph's strategy succeeded. Fearing that they were regarded as thieves by the Egyptian ruler, they were concerned about the fate of Simeon, their hostage. Above all, they recognized the disciplining hand of God in their mysterious predicament.

Sack. Three different Hebrew words are used to describe the containers in which the brothers brought their purchases home. The grain was poured into "bags," a term for various kinds of receptacles (25). The money was put into "a sack" that contained the "provender" (26, 27). At the lodging place the money was found "in the mouth of the sack"—another Hebrew term, occurring only in chs. 42—44 of Genesis.

42:31 *Honest man.* The brothers had not lied to Joseph in Egypt. But they withheld the full truth from their father.

42:36 *All this has come upon me.* While Jacob appears to imply that his sons were in some way implicated in his loss of Joseph *(you have bereaved me)*, he accepted his grief as something that had come upon him according to God's direction.

42:38 *Sheol.* The RSV transliterates the Hebrew word, which here has the meaning of grave, the realm of the dead.

e. 43:1-15 Second Journey; Benjamin

43:1 *The famine was severe.* The prolonged famine necessitated a second journey to Egypt. The temporary loss of Benjamin was to be the last of the blows of adversity in Jacob's life. At the end he too realized that in each case "God meant it for good." (50:20)

43:11 *Choice fruits.* To propitiate the severe Egyptian ruler, the sons were to bring him products of Canaan that would be highly prized in Egypt. *Balm,* probably an aromatic resin, was imported into Egypt (37:25). *Honey* was found in the hollows of the rocks in the desert of Judea (Dt 32:13). In the Hebrew text it is not distinguished by an "and" from the next word: *gum,* another resinous substance. Taken as a phrase, the two words may denote a resinous syrup. The same holds true of the next two words: *myrrh* and *pistachio nuts,* which occur only here in the OT. Combined into a phrase, they may refer to an extract made of the bark or the nut of the pistachio tree. *Almonds* grew in Palestine, but probably not in Egypt. A *little* of these products was available in spite of the famine. There was no grain, the staff of life for man and beast.

43:14 *God Almighty.* Cf. 17:1 note. Jacob entrusted his sons to God and resigned himself to His will, even if He should *bereave* him of Benjamin. In fact, this trip to Egypt could have deprived him of all his sons. If they had been convicted as thieves, they could have faced the death sentence.

f. 43:16-25 Audience with Joseph's Steward; Simeon Released

43:21 *Every man's money.* In explaining their predicament, the brothers did not bother Joseph's steward with all the details of the discovery of their money. It began when they *came to the lodging place.* All their money was in their sacks at that time, as they all eventually found out.

43:23 *Rest assured.* Lit. "peace be to you." This common greeting of good will assured the brothers of a friendly reception. All doubts of his good intentions should have vanished, when the steward explained—no doubt on Joseph's instructions—that the God of their fathers had brought about the return of their money. At the same time the statement of the steward should have given them pause to remember that the same God was not unaware that they had taken blood money in selling Joseph. Their "secret sins" had always been in the light of His countenance. (Ps 90:8; Jer 16:17)

g. 43:26-34 Joseph's Banquet for His Brothers

43:26 *Came home.* He returned from his "office" to his private quarters. Although he had difficulty in restraining himself, he maintained his pose as a stranger in order to bring about a complete change of heart in his brothers.

43:32 *By himself.* Joseph observed the restrictions that custom imposed on the Egyptians in their association with foreigners, particularly Hebrews (cf. 14:13 note). Although a Hebrew himself, he had been "naturalized" and made a member of the highest caste.

43:33 *According to his birthright.* Their seating arrangement according to age added to their *amazement.* Was this Egyptian endowed with supernatural knowledge?

h. 44:1-6 Final Testing of the Brothers

44:2 *Put my cup.* Joseph deliberately "framed" his brothers in order to find out whether they would let Benjamin, the innocent victim of the plot, be doomed to death or slavery without any brotherly concern for him.

44:5 *He divines.* The steward was instructed to say that his *lord* used the cup to divine. Later Joseph himself stated: "I can indeed divine" (15). The practice of augury was forbidden in the Mosaic legislation (Lv 19:26; Dt 18:10-14). It is quite possible that Joseph added this fictitious touch to his impersonation of a full-fledged Egyptian. The use of an interpreter was a similar pose. However, if Joseph actually practiced hydromancy (cf. our reading of tea leaves), we would have additional evidence that Scripture does not hesitate to record the weaknesses of its heroic characters.

i. 44:7-17 Refusal of the Brothers to Surrender Benjamin

44:13 *They rent their clothes.* This gesture of grief showed that they had stood the test. They were deeply moved by their brother's plight.

44:16 *The guilt of your servants.* Judah had once persuaded his brothers to sell Joseph (37:26-27). Now as their spokesman he openly confessed what they had hoped to hide: "In truth we are guilty concerning our brother" (42:21). The trumped-up charge of *guilt* convinced them that they were being called to account for a crime to which they could not plead innocent. Judah's offer "to remain instead of the lad" Benjamin (33) proved that he meant to keep his promise to his father at all costs.

j. 44:18-34 Judah's Plea for Benjamin's Release

k. 45:1-15 Joseph's Reconciliation with His Brothers

45:1 *Could not control himself.* Overcome by the sight of Benjamin and the memory of his father, Joseph dropped his posture as a foreigner. His apparent harshness had brought about God-pleasing results. The brothers had not failed to understand that the mysterious concatenation of circumstances was God's way of crushing their hard hearts. So these lying murderers, penitent and forgiven, became the tribal ancestors of God's chosen people.

45:3 *I am Joseph.* The true identity of this Egyptian seemed unbelievable. Joseph had to repeat his statement (4). Then he adduced circumstantial evidence in support of its veracity: (1) he was the same person whom they had "sold into Egypt"; (2) he spoke in their "mouth," i.e., in their language. (12)

45:5 *God sent me.* Joseph meant to allay the fears of his brothers. He would not avenge himself on them for having brought about what God wanted to happen to him. Although he made this solemn declaration four times (5, 7, 8, 9), he did not fully succeed in convincing his conscience-stricken brothers of his sincerity. (50:15)

45:7 *To preserve . . . a remnant.* Here we have the key to the plot of the Joseph story. It is not meant to be an entertaining tale of "poverty to riches." It is recorded not primarily for its moralizing lessons. Its real theme is God's direction of history for His purposes. The designs of wicked men, the weakness of His faltering saints, private plots and international barriers—none of these was able to frustrate the execution of His plan of salvation. The *remnant,* Joseph and his brothers, had escaped starvation in order to develop into Israel, of whom "according to the flesh is the Christ" (Ro 9:5). Such a remnant was never permitted to perish. It survived catastrophic judgments on later Israel and the nations (Ps 80:1; Is 1:9; 4:3; 10:20-21; 11:16; Jer 23:3; Mi 2:12; 5:7). And it still lives on. To the church, beset by dangers from within and without, Jesus said: "Fear not, little flock, for it is your Father's good pleasure to give you the kingdom." "The powers of death (KJV: "hell") shall not prevail against it." (Lk 12:32; Mt 16:18; Eze 34:11-16, 30 f.; Acts 20:28-29)

45:8 *A father to Pharaoh.* God had put Joseph into a position where he gave fatherly advice to Pharaoh.

45:10 *Goshen.* The territory that Joseph selected for his father and brothers was situated in the eastern delta of the Nile. Called "the best of the land," it is also identified as "the land of Rameses" (47:6, 11). Although its exact location and extent cannot be definitely established, it was *near* a center of Joseph's administrative functions, probably Memphis, the capital of the Old Kingdom of Egypt.

45:15 *He kissed all his brothers.* Instead of sentencing them to death, as they had expected, Joseph embraced the confessed culprits. Standing before the bar of divine justice, all men deserve the verdict: "Depart from me, you cursed, into the eternal fire." But the Judge "on his glorious throne" (Mt 25:41, 31) will not be "ashamed to call them brethren" who believe that He became their flesh-and-blood Brother and "delivered all those who through fear of death were subject to lifelong bondage" (Heb 2:11, 14, 15). Acquitted of every guilt by faith in His innocent suffering and death, His brethren are the "children of God" and heirs of eternal life. (1 Jn 3:1-3).

l. 45:16-20 Jacob's Family Invited by Pharaoh

45:16 *It pleased Pharaoh.* Ordinarily shepherds were an "abomination to the Egyptians" (43:32). But Pharaoh readily agreed to the settlement of these foreigners in his domain. In addition, he made provisions for adequate transport of Jacob's family to Egypt. (17-20)

m. 45:21-28 The Brothers Report to Jacob; His Joy

45:24 *Do not quarrel.* Lit. "do not become agitated." Once the long robe of Joseph had fanned the jealousy of his brothers to murderous hate. The special treatment accorded Benjamin (22) could have led to a new feud. But the expression "to become agitated" is a general term; it is used also of excitement to grief or anxiety (2 Sm 18:33). The thought of their guilt could have upset the brothers and agitated their conscience, especially since they were about to confess their shameful deed to their father.

45:26 *His heart fainted.* Lit. it "grew cold." Stunned temporarily, Jacob recovered from the benumbing shock of the news and came to realize that "with God nothing is impossible." (Mt 19:26; Lk 1:37; 24:11, 41)

n. 46:1-7 Jacob's Journey to Egypt

46:1 *Beer-sheba.* No incidents of Jacob's journey from Hebron to Egypt (37:14) are recorded except his stopover in Beer-sheba. Here *he offered sacrifices* to God as he had done at other significant turning points in his life. (31:54; see also 26:23-25; 28:10)

46:2 *Visions of the night.* Jacob had received no divine directive to leave the Promised Land. Once God had forbidden his father to go to Egypt (26:2; see also 1:13). Was his desire to be reunited with his son contrary to God's will? God quieted his fears by visions of the night as He had done once before. (28:12-17)

46:3 *The God of your father.* Cf. 28:13 note. In the last vision accorded a patriarch, God revealed again that His control of history extended beyond international borders. He would go down to Egypt with Jacob (28:15) and in that foreign country fulfill His promise to make his family *a great nation,* shunned by the inhabitants (34; 43:32) and removed from Canaanite influence (ch. 38). But God would not leave them there in default of another promise: to give to Jacob and his descendants the land that they were leaving. Jacob himself would not live to see the day. He would die in Egypt, where Joseph would perform the last rite of closing his eyes in death (49:33). However, his burial in "the cave of... Machpelah" in Abraham's tomb was a token fulfillment of the promise. (50:13; 12:7; 24:7; 25:9-10; 48:4)

o. 46:8-27 Jacob's Family Register

46:8 *The descendants of Israel.* Before the story of Jacob's trip to Egypt continues, a genealogical list of his descendants is inserted. Uninteresting as such statistical registers of names may appear (cf. notes on chs. 10 and 36), they remind the reader that there is a continuity in the historical process that serves God's plan. These "seventy persons" (KJV: "souls") constituted a significant unit, the "remnant" (45:7), a nucleus of peoples and nations involved in God's plan of salvation (Ex 1:5; 24:9; Nm 11:16-17; Dt 10:22; Lk 10:1). No consistent pattern of computation is discernible which would result in the exact sum of 70, the number that occurs frequently to convey the concept of totality or completeness. Presumably Stephen arrives at a total of 75 souls by adding the five sons of Manasseh and Ephraim mentioned in Nm 26:28-37 and 2 Ch 17:14-15. The figure "sixty-six persons" (26) evidently does not include Jacob, Joseph, and the latter's two sons.

p. 46:28-34 Arrival in Goshen; Joseph's Instructions

46:28 *Sent Judah.* Judah continued in the role of leadership that normally was the prerogative of the firstborn. (43:8; 44:18)

46:30 *Let me die.* Jacob did not die "bereaved of" his children," as he had feared (43:14). Having lived to see Joseph, he was strengthened in his conviction that in the past God had shaped the events of his life, inscrutable though they at times had been, to let His good and gracious will be done. Now he could "depart in peace," firmly believing that God in the future would find ways to fulfill all His promises. (3-4; Lk 2:29-30)

46:32 *Men are shepherds.* Not ashamed of his parentage, Joseph did not hesitate to inform Pharaoh that his father and brothers were nomadic *shepherds* and *keepers of cattle,* an "abomination to the Egyptians" (34). Although Pharaoh had offered them "the best of the land" (45:18; 47:6), Joseph wanted them settled in an area where they could continue their way of life. If they had become farmers or craftsmen in close association with the Egyptians, they could more readily have lost their identity. But segregated by their occupation, they were less likely to be Egyptianized.

q. 47:1-6 Goshen Assigned to Jacob's Family

47:6 *In the land of Goshen.* In spite of Pharaoh's offer of *the best of the land,* his consent to let Joseph's family occupy the land of Goshen receives special mention. Ordinarily he would not have been inclined to let Canaanite foreigners hold territory in this strategic borderland, exposed as it was to invasions by other related "Hebrews" (cf. 10:11; 11:14 notes). Through Joseph's bold request and Pharaoh's unexpected compliance with it, God was setting the stage for the Exodus. From Goshen the escaping Israelites could more readily put themselves beyond Pharaoh's reach.

r. 47:7-12 Audience with Pharaoh; Settlement in Goshen

47:9 *Few and evil.* Although Jacob reached an age well beyond the "threescore and ten" years, he acknowledged that "their span is but toil and trouble; they are soon gone, and we fly away" (Ps 90:10; 39:12; Jb 8:9; Heb 13:14). His "sojournings" fell short of the 175 years of Abraham and the 180 years of Isaac (25:7; 35:28). As he looked back upon his checkered career, he recalled its many *evil* days. Some he himself had brought on; in all of them God had purified him of useless dross in order to make him a serviceable instrument in His plan of salvation. (Heb 11:13; Lk 14:27; 1 Co 6:8-9)

47:10 *Blessed Pharaoh.* Where the channel of salvation history runs its course in world history, blessings accrue to those along the way. Every child of God exerts a beneficent influence on his environment. (Mt 5:13-16)

47:11 *Rameses.* See Exodus, Introduction.

s. 47:13-26 Joseph's Administration of Egypt

47:18 *The following year.* Evidently this was the second year after the people had spent their money and sold their cattle to get food during the famine. (14-17)

47:21 *Made slaves.* This translation reproduces the meaning of a single word in the original. The present Hebrew text reads: "he removed" (KJV). By a slight change in the writing of the last consonant, the verb means: "he enslaved." Supported by the ancient versions, the latter reading would relate that Joseph accepted the offer of the people: "we . . . will be slaves of Pharaoh" (19, 25). However, it is also possible that the enslavement of the people involved their removal from hereditary lands to the cities, where they were unconditionally dependent on Joseph's food supply.

47:24 *A fifth.* In effect Joseph gave Pharaoh title to the whole land and reduced the people to the status of tenant farmers. Joseph had no personal interest in enhancing the power of this foreign ruler. No doubt severe measures were necessary, and the people acclaimed him as their rescuer (25). However, once established, this feudalistic government of Egypt remained in power for a long time.

t. 47:27-31 Joseph's Promise to His Father

47:29 *Under my thigh.* Cf. 24:2 note.

47:30 *Lie with my fathers.* Keeping God's promise in mind, Jacob wanted to be buried in the land of the fathers that in God's time was to become the possession of his descendants (46:3-4; 48:4, 21). All who believe that God was at work in the lives of the patriarchs and that His promises to them are fulfilled in Jesus Christ, know that they are foreigners and exiles on their way to the Canaan above. "They desire a better country, that is, a heavenly one." (Heb 11:16; 13:14; Ph 3:20; Cl 3:1, 4; 1 Ptr 1:1-2; 2:11)

47:31 *Bowed himself.* Too weak to prostrate himself on the ground, Jacob stretched himself out on his bed in a gesture of grateful adoration. According to Heb 11:21 he bowed "in worship over the head of his staff." The words "bed" and "staff" are composed of the same Hebrew consonants. The Septuagint, an ancient Greek version of the OT, translated the word as if it were supplied with vowels that compose the noun "staff."

48:1—50:26 JACOB'S BLESSING OF HIS SONS AND HIS DEATH

1) 48:1-7 Joseph's Visit with His Father

48:3 *God Almighty.* Cf. 17:1 note. Joseph, the mighty ruler of Egypt, came to his weak, dying father. Through Jacob the Ruler of the universe was speaking His Word that shapes the destiny of the nations.

Luz. In Canaan, Bethel retained its original name. (35:6)

48:5 *Your two sons . . . are mine.* Jacob gave Ephraim and Manasseh equal rank with Reuben and Simeon, his firstborn sons. They, but not other sons of Joseph (6), were to become the ancestors of two of the 12 tribes of the chosen nation. (Jos 13:7; 14:4)

48:7 *Paddan.* Cf. 25:26 note.

2) 48:8-22 Joseph's Sons Blessed; the Younger Preferred

48:12 *From his knees.* By a symbolic action Joseph surrendered his claim to his sons and declared them eligible for adoption by Jacob. (Cf. 30:3; 50:23)

48:14 *Crossing his hands.* Joseph had placed his sons in such a position before his father as to enable him to extend his right hand upon the older of the two. But Jacob deliberately crossed his hands and gave the younger the status of firstborn. Once the "supplanter" had exploited the blindness of his father to gain preeminence over his older brother Esau (ch. 27). Now blind himself, he acted as God's agent in overruling the natural expectations of Joseph. Once again God disposed what men proposed.

48:15 *Blessed Joseph.* Jacob's name and the names of Abraham and Isaac would "be perpetuated" through Joseph's sons. So God would carry forward His plan of blessing all nations that He had initiated by His promise to make Abraham's "name great" (12:2). Jacob knew the God in whose name he spoke. His (1) Spirit had enabled Abraham and Isaac to walk in the way of faith (17:1; Heb 11:17-20). He was (2) the Maker of heaven and earth whose fatherly providence had *led* him all his life. Acting through His messenger, He had been (3) his Redeemer (Hebrew: "the next of kin") who delivered him from the disastrous consequences of his wrongdoing. (16)

48:19 *Shall be greater.* The tribe of the younger son exceeded Manasseh in numbers and prestige (Nm 1:32, 35). After the division of Solomon's kingdom, all of the seceding tribes in the north were called Israel, but also Ephraim. (Jer 31:9; Hos 5:11-12; 7:11; 11:9)

48:20 *Pronounce blessings.* In blessing others, the Israelites would invoke the God of Ephraim and Manasseh, believing that He could do again what He did for their ancestors.

48:21 *To the land of your fathers.* Joseph showed that he believed the patriarchal blessing by giving similar directives for his burial. (50:25)

48:22 *Mountain slope.* In Hebrew this phrase is one word, identical with the name of the city of Shechem. As a common noun it denotes the shoulder of people or animals. Here it is applied to the topographical characteristic of Joseph's sons' portion. At Shechem Jacob had once bought "a piece of land" but was forced to give it up (33:19). In the future God would make this goodly "portion" (KJV) the permanent possession of Joseph's descendants by driving out the Amorites. (Cf. Jos 24; Gn 14:13 note)

3) 49:1-27 The Blessing of Jacob's Sons

49:1 *Tell you.* What Jacob said with failing breath was the Word of Him who "spoke and it came to be" (Ps 33:9). Therefore what would *befall* his sons *in days to come* (lit. "at the end of days"), whether favorable or unfavorable, would not be brought about by a blind fate. The character of their forebears would live on in the 12 tribes and determine their role in the history of salvation. For in directing the lives of the patriarchs and their descendants God had in view a final fulfillment "at the end of days." His promise envisioned a "fulness of time," "the end of the ages," when His Son would be born of a woman to redeem all nations (Gl 4:4; 1 Co 10:11). It looked to "the end of time" when "every tribe of the sons of Israel" would be gathered about the throne of the Lamb together with "a great multitude . . . from every nation." (Rv 7:1-10)

49:3 *Reuben.* Although he was the firstborn, Reuben had forfeited his right to the prerogatives of his natural birth. (35:22; Dt 27:20)

49:5 *Simeon and Levi.* Sons of the same mother, they had been motivated by "violence," "wantonness," "anger," "wrath" (34:25-30). Apparently incorporated in the tribe of Judah, Simeon is no longer mentioned in Moses' blessing of the tribes (Jos 19:1-9; Dt 33). The descendants of Levi received no tribal allotment of land but were assigned residence in various cities of Canaan. Although not blessed in a material way, the Levites were chosen for priestly functions and served the spiritual needs of Israel.

49:8 *Judah.* The son of Leah, the "hated" wife (29:31), and a sinner like his older brothers (ch. 38), Judah was chosen to be the ancestor of the royal line of David and of David's greater Son (Lk 1:32). The kings of Judah held sway in preparation for the coming of Him "to whom it (i.e., the "scepter" or "ruler's staff") belongs." Identified by such insignia of power, He will establish a kingdom of peace that "passes all understanding" (Ph 4:7); it will be a reign of harmony, reconciliation, and tranquility that transcends everything that men could envision as happening in the realm of nature (10-12). So interpreted, the RSV rendering ("to whom it belongs") of the single Hebrew word *Shiloh* is justifiable. There is good reason, however, for translating this mysterious word with "peace" or "bringer of peace" in view of the description of the rule of peace that this Coming One will set up "among the peoples." (Nm 24:7; Is 9:6; 11:1 f.; Lk 1:32 f., 79; 2:14; Acts 10:36)

49:13 *Zebulun.* His tribe was to have commercial connections with the maritime merchants of Phoenicia. (Jos 19:10-16)

49:14 *Issachar.* Inhabiting a very fertile territory, he will labor like a *strong ass* for material riches. In order to acquire them he will endure physical and spiritual domination by the Canaanites. (Jos 19:17-23)

49:16 *Dan.* Samson, one of the later judges of Israel, was a descendant of Dan. (Ju 13; Gn 30:6)

49:18 *Wait for thy salvation.* Jacob interjected this expression of longing for the "Bringer of peace" before proceeding to reveal what was in store for his other six sons. The next three, Gad, Asher, and Naphthali, receive a brief characterization. Absorbed in the pursuit of earthly welfare, they would be in danger of losing sight of spiritual values. (19-21)

49:22 *Joseph.* In blessing Joseph, Jacob stresses the irresistible power with which his feeble words are charged. His longing for "salvation" (18) is not an idle dream. The promise of a Bringer of peace will not fail because it is the word of "the Mighty One of Jacob," "the Shepherd, the Rock of Israel," "the God of your father," "God Almighty" (24-25). The enmity of men must bow before it (22-24); it commands the forces of nature in "heaven" and in the "deep" (25); it stands firmer than "the eternal mountains" and "the everlasting hills." (26; 2 Sm 23:3; Ps 18:31-34; 21:2-3; 78:3 f.; 80:1 f.; Is 1:24; 40:11; Ro 8:31)

4) 49:28-33 Jacob's Death

49:28 *Suitable to him.* Although in some instances Jacob pointed to unfavorable prospects, all the tribes were destined, whether through weal or woe, to contribute to the one great blessing of salvation that God had set as His goal in the Seed of Abraham. (Gl 3:29; Eph 1:3; Mt 8:11)

49:29 *Gathered to my people.* Jacob's paraphrase of his dying had a positive note. When he "breathed his last," the result was not annihilation but a transfer to another mode of existence. He would share a state of being with such as had already made the change to its new dimensions. (25:8; 35:29; Nm 20:24; Ju 2:10)

49:30 *At Machpelah.* Jacob's desire to be buried at Machpelah was not a matter of sentiment. (Rachel, his beloved wife, would not lie at his side, 35:19.) The field and cave of Machpelah, acquired from the Hittites by Abraham, constituted a token fulfillment of the promise that someday not only the patriarchal burial plot but all of Canaan would be Israel's legacy.

The death and burial of Jacob (ch. 50) closes the first chapter of salvation history. Page by page Genesis presents the unfolding of God's plan of redemption. The first promise is general: the Redeemer will be a member of the human race, the Seed of a woman (3:15). God's next step was to select the descendants of an individual, Abraham, as bearers of His promise. The blessings conferred on the patriarchs move on to the choice of Judah, the ancestor of the King under whose rule of peace "all the nations will be blessed." The NT records the fulfillment of these promises and demonstrates that this Prince of Peace is Jesus of Nazareth. Taking "the chastisement of our peace upon himself" (Is 53), He reconciled man with God. All who believe this are "sons of Abraham." As such they are to bring "the blessing of Abraham" to all men that they might become "Abraham's offspring, heirs according to the promise." (Gl 3)

5) 50:1-14 Jacob Buried in Machpelah

50:2 *To embalm his father.* The mummification of a corpse was a part of the Egyptian cult of the dead. Joseph ordered the physicians to embalm his father because the journey to Canaan necessitated the preservation of his remains.

50:4 *Spoke to the household.* Joseph, the grand vizier, did not appear before Pharaoh, because a person in mourning was considered unclean.

50:10 *Atad.* As a common noun this word means a thorny bush (Ju 9:14 f.; Ps 58:10). It occurs only here to denote the name of a place and remains unidentifiable. Perhaps it derived its name from the abundance of brambles in that area. We are not told why the lamentation took place at this place rather than at Machpelah.

Beyond the Jordan. Cf. Dt. 1:1.

6) 50:15-26 Fears of Joseph's Brothers Allayed; Joseph's Death

50:20 *For good.* Although Joseph had "kissed all his brothers and wept upon them" (45:15), they feared that he had acted friendly to them merely out of consideration of their father (27:41). But Joseph assured them that he would not usurp God's prerogative and avenge their mistreatment of him (19; Ro 12:19). Since they now wanted to be "servants of the God" of Jacob (17), he "reassured them" that he too wanted to let Him have His way in his own life. If God had changed their wicked designs *for good,* any revenge on his part would be a denial of divine providence. All servants of the God of Jacob have the assurance that He *meant it for good* when they suffer injustice. (1 Ptr 1:6-7; 4:12-14; 5:10; Ro 5:3-5)

EXODUS

INTRODUCTION

Content

The second book of the Pentateuch is called Exodus (going out, departure), the name applied to it in the Septuagint, a Greek translation of the OT from the pre-Christian era. It describes its content only in part. In addition to the account of the deliverance of Abraham's descendants, Exodus records how the promise given to the patriarchal families was implemented by the covenant with their offspring, now become a nation. The stipulations of their relationship to God are interspersed with historical narratives. The story of Israel's sojourn in the desert is continued and the covenant legislation is elaborated in Leviticus and Numbers.

The covenant was a formal contract. By ratifying its terms the signatories testified that an agreement had been reached that was satisfactory to the associates in a joint undertaking or to opponents in a dispute. God's covenant with His people was an adaptation of this mode of settling a dispute. Like all analogies drawn from human relationships and concepts, the covenant does not in all respects represent an exact parallel to God's dealings with His creatures. However, it served to express His desire to restore His rebellious people to a reconciled relationship with Himself. Because they were under the just verdict of death, they had no right to bargain with God. Therefore He mercifully took the initiative and established the terms by which He made it possible for man to return to His favor and to a life in harmony with Him. Reduced to their basic requirement, the terms of the covenant stipulated that sin, the cause of the rift, be expiated by atonement, symbolized by the substitutionary sacrifice of animals and other rites of purification. The people had nothing to contribute. They became partners to the covenant by: (1) accepting the unmerited gift of forgiveness; (2) gratefully dedicating every aspect of their lives to their Redeemer's will and commandments. The "old covenant" therefore is a symbolic portrayal of what God intended to make a reality by the "new covenant." The foreshadowing forms and symbols were to give way to their substance in the atoning sacrifice of His own Son.

Authorship

Cf. Genesis, Introduction. At two junctures Moses is expressly commanded to commit proceedings to writing (17:14; 34:27). In another instance, "Moses wrote all the words of the Lord" (24:4) without being told directly to do so.

The Date of the Exodus

As is to be expected, Egyptian records make no mention of the liberation of their slaves. The Egyptian kings of this era are not identified by their personal names in the Biblical account but are referred to by the conventional title of Pharaoh (meaning "Great House"; cf. our use of the term "White House"). These factors, among others, have made the fixing of the date of the Exodus a debated issue. In recent years a preponderant opinion favors the so-called "late date": ca. 1290 B.C. under the Pharaohs of the 19th dynasty. The "early date," in the middle of the 15th century during the reign of the 18th dynasty, is favored mainly because it more readily falls into place in the framework of OT chronological data. One of these is given in 1 K 6:1. This verse states that Solomon began the building of the temple in "the 480th year after the people of Israel came out of the land of Egypt," which coincided with the fourth year of his reign, computed to be 967 B.C. By adding 480 to this date the year 1447 B.C. emerges. If the Exodus occurred 200 years later (the late date), the figure 480 must be regarded as a symbolical number for the completion of an era, i.e., 40 (a generation) multiplied by 12 (the tribes of Israel). Other Biblical references must be dealt with, such as the 430 years of Egyptian servitude and the 300-plus years of the later period of the judges. In arriving at a solution of the problem, philological, historical, and archeological data relating to Egypt and Canaan must be made to fit into the context of the proposed dates. So, e.g., the building of the store-cities Pithom and Raamses (1:11) is urged as one of the main factors supporting the late date, since no Pharaohs were called Raamses prior to the 19th dynasty, beginning ca. 1290 B.C.

The Route of the Exodus

The precise route from Egypt to Mt. Sinai is also difficult to determine. The course taken depends on the identification of the Re[e]d Sea (13:18) and the sites of Israel's encampments such as Succoth (12:37), Baal-zephon (14:2), Migdol (14:2). Cf. the comments in the notes.

OUTLINE

God's Covenant with the Chosen People

I. 1:1—18:27 Birth of the Chosen Nation
- A. 1:1-22 The People Enslaved in Egypt
- B. 2:1—15:21 The People Liberated
- C. 15:22—18:27 The Liberated People Brought to Mount Sinai

II. 19:1—40:38 Constitution of the Liberated People: The Sinai Covenant
- A. 19:1—24:18 The Terms of the Covenant
- B. 25:1—31:18 Directives for the Maintenance of Communion with God
- C. 32:1—34:35 The Covenant Broken and Renewed
- D. 35:1—39:43 Directives for the Maintenance of Covenant Communion Carried Out
- E. 40:1-38 The Dedicated Tent of Meeting Filled with the Glory of God

1:1—18:27 BIRTH OF THE CHOSEN NATION

1:1-22 The People Enslaved in Egypt

1:1-7 GROWTH OF JACOB'S FAMILY TO A PEOPLE

1:5 *Seventy persons.* Cf. Gn 46:8 note. The numbers 70 and 12 play a significant role in the Scriptures (24:9; 15:27; Nm 11:24, 25; Lk 10:1; for 12, see 15:27; 24:4; 28:15-21; Lv 24:5; 1 K 18:31; Mt 10:1; 14:20; Rv 21:12, 14). *Joseph* forms the link between the previous history of Jacob's family and their settlement in Egypt, the stage of a new act in the drama of salvation.

1:6 *Died.* After the death of Joseph and *all that generation* God's plan of redemption for all nations seemed to have been buried with them. For centuries nothing happened—at least nothing is reported—that brought Abraham's descendants back to the Promised Land. On a smaller scale, but just as mysteriously, time seems to drag on indefinitely between our prayers and God's hour of action. "O Lord, how long!" has been the plaintive cry of many whose hour of deliverance never seemed to arrive. (Ps 6:3; 13:1; 35:17; 74:10; 89:46; Hab 1:2)

1:7 *Increased greatly.* All appearances to the contrary, God had not forgotten His covenant. The land of Egypt was the place He had chosen to let the patriarchal family grow into "a great nation." (Gn 17:4-6; 22:17; 35:11; 46:3; Acts 7:17)

1:8-22 OPPRESSION OF THE ISRAELITES

1) 1:8-14 Their Servitude

1:8 *A new king.* Centuries of intervening history are compressed into one sentence. For the identification of the Pharaoh see the Introduction.

Did not know. Joseph, Egypt's former benefactor, was either actually forgotten or the new Pharaoh (perhaps the first of a new dynasty) deliberately reversed the friendly relations of his predecessors with Joseph's family. For the meaning of *know* see Gn 18:19 note. Changes took place also among Jacob's descendants. New generations replaced the eyewitnesses of the mysterious chain of events that had brought them to Egypt (Gn 37—47). Although the divine promises to the patriarchs were no doubt transmitted from father to son by word of mouth, the settlement in this foreign land gradually lost its meaning as a step in the preparation of the chosen people for the role they were to play in God's plan of universal salvation. The "fleshpots" of Egypt were so satisfying that the vision of the Promised Land faded from their view (16:3). But God did not let the history of salvation come to an end in "the cucumbers . . . and the garlic" of Egypt (Nm 11:5). To fashion this people into His instruments, He made Egypt their house of bondage so that their lives were "bitter with hard service" (14). God still knows how to help His children to view life in its proper perspective. He has ways of keeping them from being "conformed to this world," from setting their minds "on things that are on earth" rather than "on things that are above." (Ro 12:2; Cl 3:2; Heb 2:16, 18; 11:16)

1:11 *Pithom and Raamses.* For the identification of these cities see the Introduction.

1:14 *Hard service.* The shepherds and herdsmen were pressed into unaccustomed and—perhaps to them—degrading labor *in mortar and brick, and in all kinds of work in the field.*

2) 1:15-22 The Threat to Their Existence

1:15 *Midwives.* The names of only two women are recorded, hardly enough for the needs of so large a people. No doubt there were many more, but these two distinguished themselves in some special way so that their names lived on in the memory of the people.

1:16 *The birthstool.* Lit. "the pair of stones." In giving birth to a child the mother sat or crouched on a pair of stones or bricks.

1:17 *Feared God.* God is angered by the destruction of the fruit of the womb.

1:20 *Dealt well.* Because the midwives "feared God" rather than man, He blessed them. The explanation of their failure to execute Pharaoh's order was probably true. But even if there was some connivance with the childbearing mothers, shall we presume to "begrudge" God's generosity to the midwives? (Mt 20:15; Ro 9:14-16; Ex 33:19; 2 Ch 19:7) Without sanctioning our weaknesses, God continues to pour blessings on us too in spite of our imperfection.

2:1—15:21 The People Liberated

2:1—3:22 GOD'S CHOICE AND TRAINING OF THE LIBERATOR

1) 2:1-22 Moses' Childhood and Early History

a. 2:1-10 Moses' Birth and Rescue

2:1 *A man from the house of Levi.* The parents of Moses were Amram and Jochebed. (6:20; Nm 26:59)

2:3 *A basket made of bulrushes.* Pharaoh's plot to exterminate the Israelites was not only frustrated but it also served to implement God's plan to liberate His people. A Hebrew mother's ingenuity in circumventing Pharaoh's decree and the impulse of his kindhearted daughter to bathe in the Nile combined—as if by chance—to save the life of a helpless boy and to equip him with a training for his later role as leader of his people. As the adopted son of the oppressor's daughter and at his court "Moses was instructed in all the wisdom of the Egyptians" (Acts 7:22). In the literature of other ancient peoples there are legends which tell how infants of lowly birth escaped death to become national heroes (Sargon, Cyrus, Romulus and Remus). But in spite of some similarities in outward circumstances, these accounts lack the essential ingredient which puts the stamp of reality on the events of the OT. Here we have the record of the Lord of history in action, moving unswervingly toward His announced goal. The Maker of heaven and earth hears even the cry of a child and comes to its help (Gn 21:17). Every believer therefore confesses: "Upon thee was I cast from my birth, and since my mother bore me thou hast been my God." (Ps 22:10)

2:10 *Moses.* Pharaoh's daughter claimed the foundling as her own by calling him *mes*, an Egyptian word for "child," which occurs as a component of the proper names of some Pharaohs (e.g., Thut*mes*). Like a mother she had given him life because she *drew him out of the water.* The Egyptian noun was reminiscent of a Hebrew verb meaning "to draw out." By a play on the sound of the word, his name was made to connote the role that he was to play: *Moses*, the "one who draws out," i.e., who rescues his people from drowning in the sea of slavery. What God did for and through Moses reaches its final goal when, in the name of Jesus Christ, He saves perishing mankind through the water of Baptism. (1 Ptr 3:18-22; Tts 3:5)

b. 2:11-14 Moses' Premature Action

2:11 *To his people.* "When he was forty years old," Moses identified himself with his people (Acts 7:23). Forfeiting his right to be "called the son of Pharaoh's daughter," he chose to "share ill-treatment with the people of God" (Heb 11:24 f.). His renunciation of ease and safety for the sake of solidarity with his suffering brethren is a faint intimation of the sacrifice made by Him who "though he was rich" and "in the form of God," yet for our sakes "became poor," took on "the form of a servant," and "was numbered with the transgressors." (2 Co 8:9; Ph 2:6 f.; Is 53:12)

2:12 *Killed the Egyptian.* Although Moses' sympathy with his people and his zeal to act heroically in their behalf were commendable, his impulsive deed was unjustifiable. In his devotion to a noble cause he crossed the narrow borderline that so often marks the difference between the promptings of human impetuosity and the expression of the obedience of faith. The liberation of His people was indeed God's will. But it was to be achieved in His way and at His direction. Moses refused to await the authorization and the call to act as God's avenger. The means to a good end must be good themselves in God's sight, otherwise an act of heroism is liable to the charge of murder. Therefore Moses' supposition that "his brethren understood" was based on a false premise. (Acts 7:23-25)

c. 2:15-22 Moses' Flight and Marriage

2:15 *Midian.* The Midianites, one of the tribes descended from Abraham and Keturah, occupied territory "eastward to the east country" (Gn 25:1-6), i.e., in southern and eastern Arabia. Never establishing a sedentary way of life, they crossed over into adjacent areas, carried on joint projects with other nomadic tribes and later, individually and with the support of allies, opposed the Israelites (Gn 37:28, 36; Nm 22:4; 25:16-18; 31:1-12; Jos 13:21; Ju 8:28; Is 9:4; 10:26; 60:6). Moses went as far south and east as Mt. Sinai (3:1). Apparently all prospects of Israel's deliverance lay dessicated in the sands of Midian. But the desert was to "blossom" (Is. 35:1). Here Moses, the self-appointed deliverer, would grow into more than a national hero and the founder of a religion. In a training program of 40 years God would let him mature into the stature of leader, attuned to His will and equipped to carry forward His plan of universal salvation (Acts 7:23, 30). Sometimes it may take people a lifetime to realize that they were meant to serve God's purposes and not their own interests.

2:16 *By a well.* Cf. Gn 24:11; 29:2-3.

2:17 *Helped them.* Moses' assistance to these damsels in distress is commendable. But the story is not primarily a lesson in ethical behavior. It demonstrates that God used a good deed to initiate a new phase of His plan of redemption.

2:18 *Reuel.* The father-in-law of Moses is called also Jethro (3:1; 4:18; 18:1). No adequate explanation of this change in names has been discovered. While a number of other persons bore the name of Reuel (Gn 36:4 ff.; Nm 2:14; 1 Ch 9:8) and of Jethro (Ju 8:20; 1 K 2:5; 1 Ch 2:17; 4:17; 7:38), the form Jethro is found only as an alternate for Reuel. This suggests the possibility that Jethro may have been a title of some kind rather than a proper name. In Ju 4:11 Hobab, the son of Reuel (Nm 10:29), is called Moses' "father-in-law," a term used in Hebrew to denote various degrees of relationship by marriage. (4:25, 26; 2 K 8:27)

2:22 *A sojourner.* The meaning that Moses attached to his son's name expressed his feeling of frustration. Cut off from his people and reduced to a menial keeper of animals, he saw no prospect of becoming the liberator of his enslaved brethren in far-off Egypt. But God always selects the right training ground for the servants of His good and gracious will (cf. Jacob's sojourn in Haran, Gn 28—33). A shepherd for 40 years in a *foreign land,* Moses was to play a significant role in God's acts of redemption, culminating in His sending the Good Shepherd, who laid down His life for the sheep. In the obscure town of Nazareth, He spent 30 years as a carpenter's apprentice.

2) 2:23—3:22 God's Appointment of Moses as Liberator

a. 2:23-25 God's Remembrance of the Patriarchal Covenant

2:23 *The king of Egypt.* See the Introduction.

2:25 *God knew.* Having made "a covenant with Abraham, with Isaac, and with Jacob," God was not unaware of the "groaning" of their offspring. Their "bondage" made them responsive to His covenant promise to Abraham. (Gn 15:12-16)

b. 3:1-22 Moses' Call and the Assignment of His Task

aa. 3:1-6 God's appearance in the burning bush

3:1 *Jethro.* Cf. 2:18 note.

Horeb. Derived from a root meaning "to be dry, desolate," this name is used alternately for Sinai. (33:6; Dt 1:2; 1 K 8:9; 19:8; 2 Ch 5:10; Ps 106:19; Ml 4:4; Acts 7:30-34)

3:2 *Angel of the Lord.* Cf. Gn 16:7; 22:11. In the previous events of Moses' life God's providence had been at work. But uninterpreted by His spoken Word, they could have appeared to have been a haphazard chain reaction of natural causes and effects.

Was not consumed. God demonstrates the unbridgeable transcendence of the Creator over His creatures. The latter are all consumed whether by a sudden burst of fire or by the minute-to-minute flames of disintegration, dissolution, dying. God does not come into being nor does He go out of existence. He *is* yesterday, today, forever. (Ps 90:1-4; 102:24-27; Is 41; 1 Ti 1:17; 6:15; Mt 22:31-32)

Bush. In Hebrew this word is similar in sound to Sinai.

3:5 *Holy ground.* Not the courts of a temple or palace but a thorny bush (Gn 3:18) served as the precincts of holiness. Here sinful man encountered God, an unapproachable "flame of fire" (2) to all unholy creatures. What God does to manifest Himself, even in miraculous phenomena, remains a mystery to man unless He adds His revelatory Word. In a gesture of reverence Moses was to take off his shoes, keep his distance, and avoid an unshielded exposure to the holy God.

3:6 *The God of Abraham.* Cf. Gn 12:1-3; 17:1-14; 26:2-5. After a long interval the record of history is resumed. The same God that chose and blessed the patriarchs had not lost control of events. The future would also do the bidding of the Lord of history. (Ps 97:3; 148:3; Is 10:17; 47:14; 66:15; Jer 21:12; Eze 1:4; 10:6; Am 5:6; Ml 4:1; Mk 9:44)

bb. 3:7-12 Moses' hesitation to go to Pharaoh

3:8 *I have come down.* Cf. Gn 11:5; 18:21 notes.

Canaanites. Cf. Gn 15:19-21.

3:11 *Who am I?* When Moses wanted to initiate the liberation of his people (2:11-15), God's hour had not come; when God called him to act, Moses demurred. It had to become clear to Moses that God was not a convenient source of power which he could tap to promote his own ambitions. To be useful to God, Moses had to abandon all self-determination and put himself at the disposal of God's will. Once he had done so, God could transform all his inadequacies into channels of His power. And God was very patient in overcoming Moses' hesitation to surrender his self-will. For every evasive objection He supplied an assuring answer: (a) *Who am I . . .?*—answer: 12; (b) Who are You?—answer: 14; (c) "They will not believe"—answer: 4:3-4; (d) "I am not eloquent"—answer: 4:12; (e) "Send . . . some other person"—answer: 4:14; (f) "I am of uncircumcised lips"—answer 7:1 f. God's later emissaries to His people were no different. The prophets too had to learn not "to confer with flesh and blood" when God claimed them for His service. (Jer 1:6-10; Is 6:1-8; Am 7:14-15; Gl 1:16)

cc. 3:13-22 The "I am"; His will and power to save

3:14 *I am who I am.* This sentence was to be Moses' reply when the Israelites would demand proof that he spoke by the authority of "the God of your fathers" and ask: "What is His name?" In one respect God did not answer the question. He has no name like Osiris, Marduk, or Apollo. No appellation representing human thinking suffices to explain Him. Undefined and undefinable He is different from the idols, whom men could manipulate by using their names in incantations. When men try to comprehend, analyze, dissect Him, they find Him beyond their reach in the simple but inscrutable declaration: I am I (Ex 33:19-20). On the other hand, what God does in revealing Himself in word and deed is His name whereby men know Him. In His self-disclosure He remains the same *I am.* As He had made Himself known to Israel's ancestors, so He would identify Himself to their descendants by fulfilling the patriarchal promise (16-17). He who is before Abraham was, was sending Moses to His people. (Jn 8:58)

3:15 *The Lord.* At the same time, God was to be known by a proper name which differentiated Him from all other gods: *Lord.* It too is a sentence, containing the Hebrew verb "to be." In form it is the third person of "I am." By supplying its four Hebrew consonants YHWH with the vowels of the word for *Lord* (the word that was substituted when God's name later came to be considered too sacred to pronounce), the designation "Jehovah" came into use. The RSV (also Luther) renders the sacred tetragrammaton "the Lord." Scholars conclude that it originally was read and spoken "Yahweh." The "name" of God is mentioned often in the OT to denote the totality of His revelation to the patriarchs and *throughout all generations.* It is to His name therefore that praises are sung (Ps 69:30; 99:3; 113:3). What God said and did in the OT to make Himself known was climaxed when Jesus manifested God's name to men (Jn 17:6, 26; 2:11; 1 Jn 1:2; 3:5, 8; 4:9). In His solemn declarations of "I am" he appropriated the name of God (Jn 14:6, etc.). Because "there is no other [saving] name under heaven given among men," therefore "at the name of Jesus every knee should bow." (Acts 4:12; Ph 2:10)

3:16 *Observed.* KJV: "visited" and RSV in Ru 1:6. The Hebrew verb has the meaning: "to give attention to," "to show concern for," "to attend to." God's observation of men results in action on His part that is redemptive or punitive. (Gn 21:1; Ex 4:31; 13:19; Jer 15:15; 29:10; Lk 1:68; but Ex 20:5; Lk 19:44; in Ps 89:32; Jer 14:10; Hos 8:13; Am 3:2, 14 and other passages RSV translates "punish.")

3:18 *Three days' journey.* God did not at once confront Pharaoh with the demand for the permanent release of His people. If he permitted Israel to "sacrifice to the Lord," Pharaoh would acknowledge Israel's right and his obligation to obey the directions of the Lord. Eventually he might be disposed to set his slaves free for permanent service to their God. (5:2)

4:1-17 THE LIBERATOR EQUIPPED FOR HIS TASK

1) 4:1-9 Power to Do Miracles

4:1 *Will not believe.* God will "smite Egypt with all the wonders" of His destructive power and so force Pharaoh to submit to His will (3:20; 7:14—11:9). In order to give assurance to his own people that "the Lord . . . has appeared" to him (5), Moses was equipped with three wonders. (1 K 18:36-38; Is 7:10-14; Jn 2:11)

4:2 *A rod.* Into the hands of a shepherd God gave the power to overcome demonic resistance embodied in the serpent (cf. Gn 3:11 ff.; Rv 12:3 ff.). In its manifestation as a dragon, the serpent also symbolizes hostile world powers, especially Egypt (Is 51:9; Eze 29:3; 32:2). The instrument of Moses' unpretentious occupation became "the rod of God" (17, 20). It did not turn into a magic wand that coerces deity to do the sorcerer's will. It represented the scepter of a King, who put the resources of His invincible Word at Moses' disposal. Whatever Moses said or did at His command was invested with power by "the rod of His mouth." (Is 11:4; Nm 24:17; Ps 2:9; 23:4; 110:2; Is 10:5; 14:5; 55:10 f.; Rv 12:5; cf. also Num 17:1-11; 2 K 4:29)

4:6 *Leprous.* The second sign assured Israel: "I will put none of the diseases upon you which I put upon the Egyptians; for I am the Lord, your healer." (15:26)

4:9 *Water from the Nile.* The source of Egypt's life, the water of the Nile, was changed into *blood upon the dry ground.* National resources belong to the Maker of heaven and earth and cannot offer resistance to His will.

2) 4:10-17 Appointment of Aaron as His Mouthpiece

4:10 *Not eloquent.* Although there was no end to Moses' excuses, God had not reached the end of His patience. As little as a shepherd's staff could of itself do "wonders" and "signs," so little would the effectiveness of God's Word depend on the eloquence of its human transmitter. Though a man *slow of speech and of tongue,* Moses was to put into action the Word of Him, who "made man's mouth," who spoke all creation into being, who creates history through "the word of His servant" (Gn 1:3 ff.; Ps 33:6; Is 44:24-28; 49:7; Jer 1:9-10). Moses would also know what to say because the Lord would "teach" him (12; 2 Sm 23:2; Is 50:4; Mt 10:19-20; Lk 21:14-15; Acts 4:8). When "the Word became flesh," "every tongue," no matter how heavy, should "confess that Jesus Christ is Lord." (Jn 1:14; Ph 2:11; Jn 16:13; Acts 2)

4:16 *Be to him as God.* Although "the anger of the Lord was kindled against Moses" (14), He made a final concession to His hesitant messenger. His older brother Aaron was to *be a mouth for* him. In the same way the later prophets were the mouth of the Lord when "the word of the Lord came to them." (7:12; Nm 23:4; 12; Dt 5:1; Jer 1:2; 2:1; 7:1; Eze 6:1; 12:1; Hos 1:1; Jl 1:1; etc.)

4:18-31 THE LIBERATOR'S RETURN TO EGYPT

1) 4:18-23 His Leave of Jethro

4:21 *Harden his heart.* While Pharaoh is said to have "hardened his heart" or that "his heart was hardened" (7:13; 14, 22; 8:15; 19, 32; 9:7, 34, 35), we also are told that "the Lord hardened Pharaoh's heart" (4:21; 7:3; 9:12; 10:1; 20, 27; 14:4, 8). God did not in advance resolve to consign Pharaoh to His judgment; He has "no pleasure in the death of anyone" (Eze 18:32; 33:11; 2 Ptr 3:9). On the other hand, it was God who placed before Pharaoh the choice of obeying or rejecting His will. As the stubborn king persevered in his refusal to respond to God, the time came when layer upon layer of disobedience made his heart impervious to God's call and God let him go—yes, made him go his obdurate way to destruction. (Ro 9:17; 11:8; Ps 95:8; Is 6:9-10; Mt 13:14-16; 2 Th 2:11-12; Heb 3:7-8, 15; 4:7)

4:22 *My first-born son.* Pharaoh claimed divine sonship. God adopted a nation of slaves as his first-born. Through this people He set in motion His plan to restore all the sons of men to their original filial relationship with their heavenly Father. As the representatives of this adopted nation those anointed to be kings of Israel were sons of God, holding sway over a "kingdom" of "priests" until the Son of God, "the first-born of all creation" and "the first-born of the dead" became our Brother in order "that we might receive adoption as sons." (Rv 1:5-6; Cl 1:15; Gl 4:5; Ps 2:7; 89:27; Hos 11:1; Mt 2:15; 27:43; Mk 1:1; Jn 1:12; Acts 9:20; 1 Jn 3:1)

4:23 *Serve me.* Pharaoh's serfs were to become God's slaves in a service that frees men from the servitude to the demonic powers of Satan, sin, and self. Israel's liberation was not merely the establishment of a politically independent people among other nations. It would have a right to existence only as it served God's redemptive purpose. Its service to God, imperfect and desultory, was to be fulfilled in Him who "came not to be served but to serve, and to give his life as a ransom for many." (Mk 10:45; Is 42:1; 53:11; Lk 1:74; Ro 6:5-11; 8:14-17)

2) 4:24-26 His Death Averted

4:24 *Sought to kill him.* This encounter of Moses with God was more mysterious than Jacob's at Peniel (Gn 32:22-32). It demonstrated that even God's ambassador had no right to existence unless he himself accepted the status of reconciliation with God that the sign of the covenant of grace provided. His failure to circumcise his son, perhaps in deference to his wife, exposed Moses to the threat of "being cut off from his people." (Gn 17:14; cf. Jos 5:2-15)

4:25 *Feet.* Some interpreters hold that this is a euphemism for genitals. (Also in Is 6:2; 7:20)

A bridegroom of blood. Through the blood of his son's circumcision Moses was restored to Zipporah as if he had again become her bridegroom.

3) 4:27-31 His Reception by the Israelites

4:27 *Mountain of God.* We are not told when this meeting of the brothers took place. (Cf. 3:1; 4:20)

4:31 *The people believed.* Thereby they entered into the covenant relationship with God, as Abraham had done. (Gn. 15:6)

5:1—6:1 THE LIBERATOR'S FIRST ENCOUNTER WITH THE OPPRESSOR

1) 5:1-5 Pharaoh's Refusal to Let Israel Go

5:1 *Thus says the Lord.* In their first appearance before Pharaoh, Moses and Aaron, armed only with the Word of "the God of the Hebrews" (3), met with the contemptuous rebuff: "Who is the Lord?" (2). Claiming divinity for himself, Pharaoh saw no reason for yielding to the "lying words" (9) of a god who could give his worshipers nothing better than the miserable lot of serfdom. When the Word incarnate stood before the representative of imperial Rome, the witness to authoritative truth by this fettered Prisoner elicited a similar disdainful question: "What is truth?" (Jn 18:38)

A feast. Cf. 3:18 note.

2) 5:6-21 Pharaoh's Repressive Measures

5:7 *Straw.* The stalks of wheat and barley, chopped into stubble, were mixed with the clay in order to give it greater consistency. The bricks were baked in the sun.

5:21 *Judge.* At the good news of their liberation "the people believed." But their faith was not strong enough to let God bring about their deliverance in His way (14:11; 15:24). Moses' performance was no better. He shifted the responsibility for the debacle on God (22 f.; Nm 11:11-15; Jer 4:10). From its very beginning the history of Israel and its leader is by no means an epic of heroism. God had to save them in spite of themselves. The way of salvation has not changed nor have God's people changed. In the fullness of time the Prophet, who was obedient unto death, made this requirement for discipleship: "If any man would come after me, let him . . . take up his cross and follow me" (Dt 18:15; Acts 3:22; Mt 16:24; Jn 15:20; 16:33). But His followers, beaten by the rod of affliction, have so often remonstrated: "O Lord, why hast thou done evil to this people?" (22). But if Israel, old and new, "stand firm," they will "see the salvation of the Lord," wrought "with a strong hand." (6:1; 14:13; 2 Ch 20:17)

3) 5:22—6:1 God's Answer to Moses' Complaint

6:2—7:7 DIVINE ASSURANCE OF LIBERATION THROUGH MOSES

1) 6:2-8 Promise of Fuller Manifestation by the Covenant God

6:3 *By my name the Lord.* The account of the patriarchs contains references to God as "God Almighty" as well as *the Lord* (Gn 17:1-2; 28:3; 35:11; 12:8; 49:18). This verse could suggest (especially as translated in the RSV) that *the Lord* as an appellative designation for God was unknown prior to the time of Moses. This interpretation, however, is not necessarily the meaning of v. 3. A translation which gives due consideration to the Biblical connotation of the word *name* (cf. 3:14 note) would read as follows: *I appeared to Abraham, to Isaac, and to Jacob* by the manifestation of myself *as God Almighty but by my name* manifesting myself as *the Lord* (YHWH) *I did not make myself known to them.* This rendering does not preclude the possibility that the patriarchs were familiar with the word *Lord* as an appellation of God. The context supports this interpretation. The following verses stress the fact that in God's dealings with the patriarchs He had not revealed Himself as fully as the God of the "covenant" (4) as He was about to do in fulfilling the promise made to the fathers: "I will take you for my people" (7). By leading them out of Egypt and constituting them as a nation in the land which He "swore to give to Abraham, to Isaac, and to Jacob" (8), He would make Himself known to Israel in actions by which He had not revealed Himself to the patriarchs and which they knew only as promises of the covenant. Centuries later God continued to speak about the revelation of His name in the same way: "They shall know that my name is the Lord" (Jer 16:21). The Book of Ezekiel has the oft-repeated refrain: "They [or you] shall know that I am the Lord." (Eze 6:7, 10, 13; 7:4, 9, 27; etc.)

6:6 *To the people Israel.* The people were assured that God was as powerful to meet their needs as He had been in the manifestation of His name in the lives of the patriarchs. But "they did not listen to Moses." (9)

2) 6:9-13 God's Command in Spite of the Rebuff by the People

6:12 *Uncircumcised lips.* Moses had failed in getting a hearing from his own people, to say nothing of Pharaoh's refusal to heed his message. As a result a feeling of inadequacy again came over him. The thought of his spiritual deficiency rather than a physical deficiency ("slow . . . of tongue") raised new doubts in his mind: Had the Word of God failed to produce results because it had been delivered by a messenger whose lips were unclean, tainted by sin? (Is 6:5-6; Lk 5:8-10). God replied to these misgivings as He did to Moses' professed lack of eloquence. The words of his unhallowed lips, once God had touched them, would be as effectual as if God Himself were speaking them (7:1-2). Whether called by God in a burning bush or set afire by the miraculous spark of a Spirit-kindled faith, every messenger of God's emancipation from the bondage of sin needs to remember, especially in moments of doubt or depression, that his *uncircumcised lips* have been charged with the power to do "signs and wonders" in the hearts of his hearers. But like Moses he must also learn that he cannot automatically turn on that power as if he were pressing an electric light switch. At His time and in His way the high voltage of God's Word will "accomplish that which I purpose, and prosper in the thing for which I sent it." (Is 55:11)

3) 6:14-27 The Ancestry of the Covenant People and Their Leaders

6:14 *Heads of their fathers' houses.* The account of historical events is interrupted by a genealogy of the three oldest sons of Jacob: Reuben (14), Simeon (15), Levi (16-25). The reason for inserting this incomplete genealogical history at this point is stated in 26: "These are Aaron and Moses to whom the Lord said: 'Bring out the people of Israel.'" In addition to these two leaders the list identifies other Levites whose subsequent actions were to become a matter of record: Korah (Nm 16); Nadab and Abihu (24.1, 28:1; Lv 10:1-3); Phinehas (Nm 25:1-15; Ps 106:28-31); Eleazar and Ithamar. (28:1; 38:21; Dt 10:6)

4) 6:28—7:7 Moses' Unclean Lips Vested with Divine Authority

7:1 *As God.* Cf. 6:12; 3:11 notes.

7:3 *Harden Pharaoh's heart.* Cf. 4:21 note.

7:8—11:10 PHARAOH'S HEART HARDENED DESPITE SIGNS AND WONDERS

1) 7:8-13 Rod Changed into a Serpent

7:8 *A serpent.* The Hebrew term is not the same as the one used to designate the reptile that came into being when Moses cast his rod on the ground (4:2 f.). Although the two words are used interchangeably (Dt 32:33; Ps 91:13), the serpentine creature that Aaron's rod produced more frequently has the connotation of a "dragon" (Ps 74:13; Is 27:1; 51:9) or "sea monster" (Gn 1:21; Ps 148:7) and is used figuratively of anti-God powers (Is 27:1; Jer 51:34), specifically of Egypt (Eze 29:3; 32:2). Although duplicated to a certain extent by the magicians, the miracle demonstrated that Pharaoh, apparently autonomous, in reality owed his existence to "the Lord, the God of the Hebrews" (16) because He could also bring it to an abrupt end (12). So every demonic opposition to God's rule for the benefit of His people must go down in defeat. (Ps 2; Rv 12; 20)

2) 7:14-24 First Plague: Water Turned to Blood

7:17 *Strike the water.* Pharaoh's negative reply to the demand to let Israel go was followed by "signs and wonders in the land of Egypt" (3). Known as the "Ten Plagues," these miraculous judgments of God upon Pharaoh grew in intensity until the resistance of his "hardened" heart was crushed. Most of them were disasters that were not unknown in Egypt. "The finger of God" (8:19) made them "signs and wonders." Although phenomena of nature were involved, they occurred at the express command of God; they came to an end in the same way; they affected the Egyptians and left the Israelites untouched (8:22; 9:4, 26), "making a distinction between the Egyptians and Israel." (11:7)

7:20 *Turned to blood.* The Nile, Egypt's "lifeline," turned into bloody sewage. At an abnormally high flood stage it carried with it so many particles of fine red earth and microcosmic bacteria as to render it "foul," undrinkable, and deadly to fish. (21; Ps 78:44; 105:29; cf. Jl 2:30; Rv 16:4)

3) 7:25—8:15 Second Plague: Frogs

8:3 *Swarm with frogs.* This plague too arose out of the Nile. Driven from the putrid shores and "pools" of the river's backwaters and infected with disease, the frogs swarmed into the fields and houses and died there. Not an uncommon scourge in Egypt, they were a sign and a wonder because they came at the Lord's behest and left when He was entreated by Moses. The sorcerers were able to produce this menace, but we are not told that they were able also to eliminate it. (Ps 78:45; 105:30)

8:15 *There was a respite.* As soon as the plague was removed, Pharaoh withdrew his consent to let Israel go. He continued to react in the same way to the remaining plagues with the exception of the final one (19, 25, 28; 9:27-28; 10:17). Later apostate Israel was no less perverse under God's punitive hand until it was finally swept into exile (Am 4:6-12). And "so will it be on the day when the Son of man is revealed" (Lk 17:25-30). In the meantime how quickly men ignore the scourge of wars and of other calamities, return to their evil ways, and so become guilty of "storing up wrath . . . on the day of wrath." (Ro 2:5)

4) 8:16-19 Third Plague: Gnats

8:16 *Gnats.* The first pair of plagues came directly from the Nile. The next two, gnats and flies, had their origin in the decomposed fish and frogs, which became favorable breeding places before becoming dry as dust. The gnats (KJV "lice") may have been the insect known to us as the mosquito. The Hebrew word occurs only here and in Ps 105:31.

8:19 *Finger of God.* Cf. 7:17 note. In spite of their previous feats, the sorcerers were forced to acknowledge that the exercise of their powers was subject to the limitations imposed by Him who "formed man of dust from the ground" and whose "fingers" shaped "the heavens" (Gn 2:7; Ps 8:3; 19:1). This confession of impotence, however, did not persuade Pharaoh and his henchmen to submit to the authority of *the finger of God.* (Ro 1:18-23)

5) 8:20-32 Fourth Plague: Flies

8:21 *Swarms of flies.* The second plague to descend upon the Egyptians through the air was inflicted by another kind of winged insect. Mentioned only here and in Ps 78:45; 105:31, its exact nature remains a matter of conjecture; suggestions: beetles (scarabs) or gadflies.

8:26 *Abominable.* As in India today, so in ancient Egypt many animals were considered sacred. The sacrificial killing of sheep, bulls, or goats would have exposed the Israelites to violence by fanatic mobs.

8:27 *Three days' journey.* Cf. 3:18 note.

8:29 *Deal falsely.* God again removed the plague on Pharaoh's promise to let Israel go. But God will not be mocked (Gl 6:7). His patience can be exhausted by continued obstinacy. Disregarding the warning, Pharaoh abused God's leniency and "hardened his heart this time also." (32)

6) 9:1-7 Fifth Plague: Cattle Disease

9:3 *Plague upon your cattle.* The fifth and the sixth plagues were epidemics of infectious diseases. The first of them affected only animals. The Hebrew word is "pestilence," a general term. It is translated in the KJV as "murrain," i.e., anthrax, a bacterial disease rarely transmitted to man. The cattle *in the field* contracted it when they came in contact with infested carrion—perhaps of the frogs and fish.

7) 9:8-12 Sixth Plague: Boils and Sores

9:9 *Boils.* The second and the sixth plague are not preceded by a recorded statement of God's demand to let His people go (8:16; cf. 7:16; 8:1, 20; 9:1). The victims were both *man and beast.* Called "the boils of Egypt," covering the body "from the sole of your foot to the crown of your head" (Dt 28:27, 35; Jb 2:7; Rv 16:2), it produced an inflammation that broke out in "boils" (10), a word that occurs nowhere else in the OT.

9:11 *Could not stand.* Far from being able to duplicate this sign, the magicians themselves were rendered physically impotent. The "finger of God" (8:19) did not only limit demonic powers, it also inflicted judgment on them and their agents. (Nm 22:1-14; Jb 2:6; Lk 9:1; 1 Co 10:20; Mt 25:41)

9:12 *Hardened the heart.* Cf. 4:21 note.

8) 9:13-35 Seventh Plague: Hail

9:16 *To show you my power.* At the first instance of his disobedience Pharaoh had deserved no less than to be "cut off from the earth" (15). God's delay in executing total judgment was not to be attributed to weakness on His part. He had let Pharaoh suffer the previous plagues in order to give him opportunity to recognize His *power* and to comply with His demands. But because Pharaoh persisted in obdurate disobedience, his final fate would serve as a demonstration that God is able to declare His *name . . . throughout all the earth,* that is, to manifest His power to destroy and to save. (Ro 9:17; cf. 3:14 note)

9:18 *Heavy hail.* In order to convince Pharaoh "that there is none like" the Lord (14), He continued to send plagues which demonstrated that "the earth is the Lord's" (29). A hailstorm, an unusual phenomenon in Egypt (23), was of such severity as to destroy the trees and the crops that were "in the ear" at that time (25, 31) as well as "man and beast" if they had not sought a "safe shelter." (19)

9:27 *I have sinned.* Under pressure of the previous plagues Pharaoh had promised to let Israel go, only to reverse himself as soon as relief came at Moses' intercession (8:8, 15, 30-32). *This time* he even admitted that he was *in the wrong*. But his confession of sin was no more reliable. When he repudiated his repentance and "sinned yet again" (34), a still more impervious shell of obduracy enveloped his hard heart. (Ps 81:11-12; Is 26:10; Jer 15:6; 17:23; Ro 2:4-5; Heb 10:26-27)

9) 10:1-20 Eighth Plague: Locusts

10:2 *Made sport of the Egyptians.* This rendering may suggest that God derived pleasure from inflicting judgments on the Egyptians as we engage in a sport for the fun of it. The meaning is that God would demolish their pompous pretense to power with such ease as to make them appear ridiculous (Ps 2:4-5; 59:18) The *signs* that God performed were to be remembered for generations as a warning to the ungodly and for the encouragement of those who patiently wait for His salvation (Dt 4:3-7; Ps 37:12-13; Ro 15:4; 1 Cor 10:11-12). The signs and wonders, done by God in His final victory over all demonic forces that enslaved the entire world, "are written that you may believe that Jesus is the Christ, the Son of God, and that believing you may have life in his name." (Jn 20:31)

10:4 *Locusts.* Locusts or grasshoppers were and are a much-dreaded scourge. Advancing in such dense swarms as to darken the sun, these insatiable little beasts leave a swath of devastation in their wake. (Jl 1:4-10)

10:10 *The Lord be with you.* These words were spoken in sarcastic dudgeon and were followed by action expressive of their derisive intent. Moses and Aaron "were driven out from Pharaoh's presence." (11)

10:17 *Forgive my sin.* Threatened by *death*, the deified king added a plea for forgiveness to his previous confession of being "in the wrong" (9:27). He pleaded for mercy from a vagrant whose scepter was a shepherd's stick and who had no insignia of power except the innocuously sounding pronouncement: "Thus says the Lord, the God of the Hebrews" (3; Ps 33:10; Is 40:10-11; Mt 11:25-27; Lk 1:51-52; 1 Ptr 5:5). When in God's good time the Good Shepherd came, the eyes of unbelief saw merely "the carpenter's son" of Nazareth. (Mt 13:55; Ro 1:22; 1 Co 1:18-25; 2:14)

10:20 *Hardened Pharaoh's heart.* The hour of God's judgment struck when, after pugnacious disobedience, Pharaoh presumed to manipulate God by a feigned repentance (9:35. Cf. 4:21 note). So he became one of "the vessels of wrath made for destruction, in order to make known the riches of his [God's] glory for the vessels of mercy." (Ro 9:22-23; 9:16)

10) 10:21-29 Ninth Plague: Darkness

10:21 *Darkness.* By this "sign," so dense that it could *be felt*, God eclipsed the delusive brightness of the Egyptian sun-god, who, in the appearance of the solar disk, was regarded as the very epitome of divinity. As the Maker of heaven and earth had commanded the hail (9:23 ff.; Jb 38:22), so He who "brings forth the wind from his storehouses" (Ps 135:7) stirred up a dust storm of such intensity as to immobilize the Egyptians, "but all the people of Israel had light" (23). Darkness presages the coming of "the day of the Lord" (Is 13:10; 24:21-23; Jl 2:10; 3:15; Am 8:9; Zph 1:15; Mt 24:29; Rv 6:12; 16:10). When God's judgment of the world was executed on the Light of the world, there was "darkness over the whole land" (Lk 23:44), but "the darkness has not overcome it." (Jn 1:5; Is 60:19-20; Ml 4:2; Rv 21:22-23; 22:5)

10:24 *Your children.* Although a concession to his previous stipulation (10:10), Pharaoh's demand that Israel's cattle be retained as security was still a refusal to relinquish his slaves.

10:28 *You shall die.* In banishing Moses from the court Pharaoh had in reality pronounced the death sentence on himself. He had deliberately severed the line of communication with God's Word and thereby cut himself off from the only source of life. (Is 30:9-14; Jer 8:9; Am 7:12-17; 8:11-14; Mi 2:6; 3:4; Lk 10:16; Ro 2:4-5; 1 Th 4:8)

10:29 *Not see your face again.* Moses would no longer be available to intercede for Pharaoh. After announcing the final plague (11:4-8), "he went out from Pharaoh in hot anger." (11:8; cf. 12:31)

11) 11:1-10 Tenth Plague Threatened

11:1 *One plague more.* Through "signs and wonders" God had revealed His power over the forces of nature. In a final *plague* He would demonstrate that all life was His to give and to take. Every "first-born," from the deified king down to the lowliest slave "in the land of Egypt shall die" (5), when the Lord will "smite the land of Egypt" (12:13). We are not told what the nature of this *plague* would be. Into every house God would send "his destroyer" (12:30), called "a company of destroying angels" in Ps 78:49. (Cf. 2 K 19:35)

11:2 *Jewelry.* Under the pressure of the God of justice the Egyptians would be persuaded that the Israelites had a just claim to recompense for the many years of unpaid labor. (3:22; 12:35-36; cf. Ez 1:6)

11:3 *Very great.* Because Moses commanded the highest respect among the Egyptians, they were willing to reimburse the Israelites for their services. Small of faith at the time of his call (3:11) and unheroic in the face of resistance (5:22), Moses could claim to be great because he realized that God's "power is made perfect in weakness." (2 Co 12:9)

11:7 *Not a dog shall growl.* Lit. "shall sharpen or move his tongue"; a proverbial way of expressing the absence of all resistance. (Jos 10:21)

11:9 *Wonders may be multiplied.* Cf. 9:16 note.

11:10 *Hardened Pharaoh's heart.* Cf. 4:21 note.

12:1-28 PREPARATIONS FOR LIBERATION

1) 12:1-13 Moses Instructed: Passover Lamb

12:1 *The Lord said.* First Moses and Aaron received directions from the Lord how Israel was to be saved (2-20); then the instructions are repeated, transmitted to the elders of the people (21-27); finally the record states how the Israelites were spared because they acted in accordance with the provisions ordained for their safety (28-36). Repetitious according to our rules of rhetoric, this style of narration is characteristic of the OT (cf. Gn 24:1-27, 34-49; Ex. 25—31; 35—39; 40). It is used to good effect to express how God's Word operates: it originates with Him; is accepted by His spokesmen; is transmitted by them to others; achieves its purpose as it finds "doers of the word."

12:2 *The beginning of months.* Because the liberation from Egypt marked the beginning of Israel's national history, the month in which "the passover to the Lord" (48) was to be commemorated was to be reckoned as initiating a new year. Called Abib ("the ripening of the ears of grain"), it coincided with the equinox of spring (13:4; 23:15; 34:18; Lv 23:15; Nm 9:1-5; 28:16; Dt 16:1). After the exile it was known by the Babylonian name Nisan (Neh 2:1; Est 3:7). Another calendar, according to which the year ended and began in the autumn, apparently was used to fix events of a civil or agricultural rather than a ritualistic nature. (23:16; 34:22)

12:11 *The Lord's passover.* It was to be observed by rites that symbolized what the Israelites needed in the night of the final plague and forever after, if they were to survive the wrath of God. Since His judgment was to strike the firstborn of every household in Egypt, all sinful life was exposed to the "destroyer" (23; Heb 11:28). He would "pass over" or spare only those whose unrighteousness had been removed by a vicarious sacrifice. The Israelites were to confess their need of an atonement and of a sacrificial death in their stead by putting the blood of the slain sheep or goat "on the two doorposts and the lintel" of their homes. (7, 22-23; 13:2, 12; 22:29b; 34:20)

In the night of its institution and on every day of its memorial *the Lord's passover* had as its second purpose a ritual demonstration that reconciled Israel constituted a community that had the privilege and obligation of living in communion with God. This bond of union was symbolized by a communal eating of the animal from which the atoning blood had been secured. Because this meal had "sacramental" significance, any remaining meat was not to be kept for profane usage; it was to be burned (10). For the same reason the lamb "without blemish" was to be "roasted" in its entirety (5, 9). The "unleavened bread" was to remind the Israelites that God liberated them in "haste"; they did not have even as much time to contribute to their deliverance as it takes yeast to raise dough (8, 11, 34; Dt 16:3). The "bitter herbs" were to impress on the Israelites how sweet their life, united with their Deliverer and dedicated to His service, was in contrast with the biting sting of their former slavery.

The deliverance of Israel as a redeemed community through the Passover of the Lord was an important link in the chain of events by which God implemented His plan for the reconciliation of the world to Himself. The atonement of the wrath of God, symbolized by the blood of a slain animal, became a reality in the "departure" (lit. the "exodus," Lk 9:31) of "Christ, our paschal lamb." Because He was a sacrifice, "a lamb without blemish," His blood "cleanses us from all sin" (1 Co 5:7; 1 Ptr 1:19; 1 Jn 1:7; Jn 1:29; 19:36; Heb 7:26; 9:13-14, 26, 28). He who eats His flesh and drinks His blood "has eternal life" (Jn 6:54). Rejoicing in their deliverance "from the dominion of darkness" (Cl 1:13), His redeemed community gathers to "celebrate the festival" in order to "proclaim the Lord's death until he comes" (1 Co 11:23-26). Israel already was taught that the events commemorated by the Passover, great as they were, were merely a shadow of the final redemption to come, which is later described in terms of the first exodus. (Is 41:17-19; 42:7; 48:21; 51:9-11; 52:13-15; 53; Jer 16:14-15)

2) 12:14-20 Moses Instructed:
Feast of Unleavened Bread

3) 12:21-28 The People Instructed by Moses

12:22 *Hyssop.* Branches of a plant of the majoram variety were used in other symbolic purification rites. (Lv 14:4; Nm 19:6, 18; Ps 51:7; Heb 9:19)

12:23 *Destroyer.* Cf. Nm 16:41, 49; 2 Sm 24:16; 2 K 19:35; 1 Co 10:10; Heb 11:28.

12:29-42 ISRAEL LIBERATED AFTER THE TENTH PLAGUE

1) 12:29-36 Firstborn in Egypt Slain;
Israel Released

12:36 *Despoiled the Egyptians.* Cf. 11:2, 3 notes.

2) 12:37-42 Israel's Hasty Departure

12:37 *Rameses.* Cf. 1:11 and the Introduction.

Succoth. The name of the first site reached by the fleeing Israelites (13:20; Nm 33:5-6) may be a hebraized word ("booths, tabernacles") for an Egyptian location, as yet not identified with certainty.

About six hundred thousand. The more exact number for this round figure was 603,550 (without the Levites) according to the census in Nm 1:46. If the women and children were added to this total, the departing Israelites numbered well over two million people. Cf. Numbers, Introduction, "The Numbers in . . . ."

12:38 *A mixed multitude.* It was composed of people of various racial and social affinities (Neh. 13:3: "of foreign descent"; Jer 25:20: "foreign folk"; Jer 50:37: "foreign troops"). We are not told whether they were temporary camp followers or were incorporated into Israel by the rite of circumcision. (Nm 11:4)

12:40 *Four hundred and thirty years.* Abraham had been told that his descendants would be sojourners and slaves "in a land that is not theirs" for a period lasting 400 years (Gn 15:13-14). Paul writes that the giving of the Law "came four hundred and thirty years afterward," the immediately previous incident mentioned by him being "the promises . . . made to Abraham" (Gl 3:16-17). The Septuagint and a Dead Sea manuscript add "and Canaan" to the phrase *in Egypt*. The question whether the 430 years are to be reckoned as beginning with Abraham's sojourn in Canaan or with the arrival of his grandchildren in Egypt is a factor in fixing the date of the Exodus. (Cf. the Introduction)

12:43—13:16 ADDITIONAL ORDINANCES TO COMMEMORATE THE LIBERATION

1) 12:43-51 The Celebration of the Passover

12:43 *No foreigner.* In determining eligibility for participation in the Passover celebration the Israelites were to make a distinction between a *foreigner* (KJV: "stranger"), a "sojourner," a "hired servant," a circumcised "slave," and a "stranger" who has become "a native of the land" by accepting "the sign of the covenant." (44-48; Gn 17:12)

12:46 *Not break a bone.* The sacrificial lamb was not to be treated like an ordinary animal that served as food for a social or national celebration. Left unbroken, whole and undivided, it was to remind Israel of its total commitment to God and the unfractured unity that was to be established between God and His people. What the Passover lamb symbolized and foreshadowed was achieved in the unbroken Sacrifice that hung on Golgotha. (Jn 19:33-36; cf. 11 note)

2) 13:1-2 The Firstborn

13:2 *All the first-born.* In addition to the Passover festival, another "ordinance" (10) was to keep Israel from forgetting that it owed its existence to God's mercy. Because the "destroyer" (12:23) took the life of all Egyptians, represented by their firstborn son, but did not enter the homes of the Israelites, made immune to divine wrath by the atoning blood of the lamb, the life of every firstborn male child was to be regarded forfeit to the Lord unless it too was redeemed by the vicarious sacrifice of the firstborn animal or by the payment of five shekels to the priests (2, 11-16; 22:29; 34:19-20; Nm 18:15-18; Dt 12:6, 17). During the wilderness journey the Levites were consecrated to the Lord for the redemption of the firstborn. (Nm 3:40-41)

3) 13:3-10 The Feast of Unleavened Bread

13:4 *Abib.* Cf. 12:2 note.

13:6 *Unleavened bread.* Two previous instructions for memorializing the deliverance "out of the house of bondage" are repeated and expanded: the eating of unleavened bread (6-10; cf. 12:14-20) and the redemption of the firstborn (11-16; cf. 1). Israel, once it enjoyed prosperity from the rich benefits of the Promised Land, would be prone to forget its origin by the Lord's "strength of hand." (3)

13:9 *A sign . . . and . . . memorial.* Both ritualistic observances were to be so concrete a reminder of the Exodus as if they wore a mnemonic device on their hand (cf. our tying a string to a finger) or between their eyes where they would always be in sight (16; Dt 6:8; 11:18). Interpreted literally, this admonition gave rise to the custom of wearing encased parchments inscribed with the words of Ex 13:1-16; Dt 6:4-9; 11:13-21). Called "phylacteries" in the NT (Mt 23:5) and "Tephilim" (prayers) in Judaism, they are worn at the morning prayers, except on the Sabbath and high festival days. When the "night of watching" (12:42) passed into Easter morning, the Paschal Lamb, slain for our sins and raised for our justification, gave directions to the "witnesses of these things" to preach "repentance and forgiveness in his name to all nations" (Lk 24:44-48; Acts 1:8; 2:32). By their testimony, "in season and out of season," also "gentiles in the flesh" and "strangers to the covenants of promise" are "brought near in the blood of Christ" to be "fellow citizens with the saints and of the household of God" (Eph 2:11-22). In remembrance of Him, the Israel of the new covenant eats His body and drinks His blood and so proclaims "the Lord's death until He comes." (1 Co 11:23-26)

4) 13:11-16 Consecration of the Firstborn

13:17—14:20 FROM SUCCOTH TO THE RED SEA

1) 13:17-22 Choice of the Longer Way

13:17 *The land of the Philistines.* The most direct route along the Mediterranean would have brought the Israelites to Canaan within a few weeks. Because it was heavily guarded, it would have given the Israelites occasion to *see war*. (Nm 14:2-4)

13:18 *The Red Sea.* Lit. "a sea of reeds or weeds." Today *Red Sea* is a comprehensive term to denote the two long arms of water that extend northward around the Sinai peninsula: the Gulf of Suez on its western side and the Gulf of Aqaba east of it. In the OT the Re[e]d Sea also denotes various bodies of water. (1) It is used of the sea that Israel crossed in leaving Egypt, identified by many with the "Bitter Lakes," north of the Gulf of Suez. (2) The encampment at the Re[e]d Sea, mentioned in the later journeyings of Israel, was east of the Gulf of Suez. Its northernmost extension is also considered the sea of the crossing. (3) When the Israelites still later were directed to journey toward "the wilderness by the way to the Re[e]d Sea (Nm 14:25; Dt 1:40; 2:1) and then "set out by the way to the Re[e]d Sea, to go around the land of Edom," the Gulf of Aqaba is meant. (Nm 21:4; cf. 1 K 9:26; Jer 49:21)

13:19 *The bones of Joseph.* Cf. Gn 50:24-25.

13:20 *Etham.* The added remark that it was *on the edge of the wilderness* is not sufficient to identify it with certainty. If it was an Egyptian border fortress, located south of Succoth, the Lord's command "to turn back" (14:1) led the Israelites northward again. Etham may have been fortified because there the sea could easily be forded or because it guarded access to Egypt across a channel between the Gulf of Suez and the Bitter Lakes which had dried up.

The pillar of cloud . . . and . . . fire. The "watching by the Lord" (12:42) was made visible to the Israelites in phenomena of nature which manifested His protecting presence. (14:19; 16:10; 20:18, 24:15-18; 33:10; 34:5; 40:34;

Ps 78:14; 105:39; Mt 17:5; Acts 1:9; 2:2-3)

2) 14:1-4 Change of Directions

14:2 *Piha-hiroth . . . Migdol . . . Baal-zephon.* These sites were *by the sea* that Israel crossed, but their exact location has not been definitely determined. Since Etham was "on the edge of the wilderness," the command to *turn back* brought the fugitives into territory where Pharaoh could more readily reach them. By delivering Israel when it was a certain victim of Egypt's mighty forces, God demonstrated to Pharaoh that He was "the Lord" (4; cf. 7:4-5). The Israelites entrusted themselves to God's guidance in spite of its apparently suicidal consequences (4b). With seemingly cruel deliberation God at times leads all His children into situations so hopelessly desperate that they might learn anew that He is "the Lord," the only Helper "when other helpers fail and comforts flee." Man's darkest hours are God's opportunities to reveal His unfailing power to save. "When the need is greatest, God is always nearest."

3) 14:5-9 Pursuit by the Egyptians

14:5 *Let Israel go.* Cf. 10:7

14:8 *Defiantly.* A prepositional phrase in Hebrew, it is translated "triumphantly" (Nm 33:3); in Nm 15:30 it is rendered literally "with a high hand," indicating defiance of God. The meaning here is that the Israelites moved out under the "high [protecting] hand" of God.

4) 14:10-18 Assurance of Deliverance

14:10 *Cried out.* Their faith severely put to the test by a seemingly inescapable disaster, the Israelites did indeed turn to the only hope for help: "the Lord." But at the same time they voiced their doubt that He really knew what He was doing through Moses (11). Such wavering between trust and doubt has often been duplicated in the lives of God's children. So often they have been tempted to live by sight rather than by faith. When catastrophes appear to engulf them, many a quavering cry to God does not succeed in suppressing the question: Why does He let these things happen? (Nm 11:20; Jb 3:11 ff.; Mt 14:30; Mk 9:24)

14:12 *In Egypt.* Cf. 5:19-21; Ps 106:7-8.

14:13 *Fear not.* The Israelites saw only the threat to their existence. But God is very patient with His people when they are terrified by the trials of their faith. He comes to their aid with the encouraging assurance: "Do not fear, only believe" (Mk 5:36). If they will only *stand firm,* in the "conviction of things not seen," they will without fail *see the salvation of the Lord.* (Heb 11:1; Gn 49:18; Dt 20:3; 2 K 6:15-17; 2 Ch 20:15, 17; Ps 27:1-2; 46:1-3; Is 30:15; 41:10, 14)

14:15 *Go forward.* Standing "firm" and being "still" is a disposition of the heart. It gives evidence of its sincerity by acting on God's word of promise. In the obedience of faith the believer then goes forward in the face of overwhelming odds and apparently insurmountable obstacles.

5) 14:19-20 Israel Obscured by the Pillar

14:19 *Angel of the Lord.* Cf. 3:2. *The pillar of cloud* was the intangible mantle of God's presence, covering Israel's naked helplessness.

14:20 *The night passed.* The RSV translation, based on the Septuagint text, makes sense (Jos 24:7). The Hebrew reads: "yet it lit up the night." While the cloud produced darkness on the Egyptian side, it shone in the light of God's glory for the Israelites. (24; 19:16; 24:15-18; 40:34-35)

14:21—15:21 MIRACULOUS CROSSING OF THE RED SEA

1) 14:21-25 A Dry Path Through the Sea

14:22 *On dry ground.* Marshalling the force of the "strong east wind," the Lord of creation made "the sea dry land." (Ps 106:9; 114:3, 5; Is 63:12-13; cf. Ex 7:17, 11:1 notes)

14:24 *Discomfited.* Pharaoh's disciplined chariotry was thrown into utter confusion by a terrifying spectacle, produced by *the Lord in the pillar of fire and of cloud.* The ensuing panic gave the Israelites time to pass through the sea while the advancing Egyptian rearguard brought the whole army to a standstill.

14:25 *Clogging.* The RSV adopts the reading of the Septuagint text; KJV: "took off."

2) 14:26-31 Destruction of the Egyptians

14:30 *They believed.* When the Israelites "cried out to the Lord," albeit not without recrimination of His guidance (10), He gave them an object lesson that trust in Him is not a hope that deceives. He led them into an impossible predicament in order to do the impossible. If faith is farsighted, as indeed it must be, it will ultimately see *the great work which the Lord did* (Mk 9:23; Jn 11:40; 13:19; 20:31). If by faith we have seen "the salvation of the Lord" (13) in Christ Jesus, for which the Exodus was but a prelude, we may, like Israel of old, often find ourselves between "the devil and the deep blue sea" and "cry out" from the depths of anguished desperation; but if we but "stand firm," we too shall see that when God seemed weakest, He proved to be strongest.

3) 15:1-18 Triumphant Song of Moses

15:1 *Sang this song.* Moses and the people, who in a frenzy of fear had "cried out to the Lord" (14:10, 15), broke out just as spontaneously in a song, praising God for His victory over the forces of evil represented by Pharaoh and the gods in whom he trusted. In graphic figures of speech, characteristic of poetry, the song retells the story of what had happened (1-12) and proceeds to look forward to what lay ahead as its result: the establishment of God's "reign" over the nations and His presence among His redeemed people. (13-18; cf. Cl 1:13)

I will sing. Expressed in the first person singular, the joy of the redeemed individual wells up from his heart in an unabashed effusion of his feelings. He cannot speak of the salvation of the Lord with the impersonal detachment of a spectator. Because he had been doomed to a life of hopeless degradation, because he saw "Pharaoh's chariots and his hosts" advancing upon him, because he was there when the "right hand" of the Lord shattered his enemies, he cannot but say: "*I* will sing . . . praise . . . exalt . . . *my* strength . . . *my* salvation . . . *my* God" (2). His emotional outburst was not a self-induced illusion or an escape mechanism from reality. It arose from the hard facts of God's deed in a hard world of hard enemies. At the same time, he was aware that he was not singing a solo. It was congregational singing by "the people whom" God had "redeemed" and was guiding to His "holy abode." (13)

15:3 *Man of war.* "Terrible in glorious deeds" (11), God showed His love for His people by wielding the fearful weapons of His arsenal to destroy all rebellion against His rule (Ps 24:8; Is 42:3; Jn 3:36; Ro 1:18; Eph 5:6; Cl 3:5-6). This song does not exhibit a primitive concept of God that was gradually outgrown and replaced as men learned of the love of God, revealed in Jesus Christ. The relentless finality with which this "man of war" (3) destroyed His Egyptian "adversaries," the "fury" with which He consumed them "like stubble" (7) is but a preliminary manifestation of the inexorable justice that awaits all His enemies. The King, "majestic in holiness" (11), who will send them "away into eternal punishment" is none other than "the Son of man" whose love they have spurned. (Mt 25:31-46)

15:8 *Blast of thy nostrils.* Poetic for: "the Lord drove the sea back by a strong east wind." (14:21; 2 Sam 22:16; Jb 4:9; Ps 103:15-16; Is 40:7-8, 23-24)

15:11 *Among the gods.* Cf. 20:3 note; also 18:11; Dt 3:23; 1 Ti 6:16.

15:13 *Thy holy abode.* God's presence makes a locality "holy ground" (3:5), a "house of God" (Gn 28:16). Eventually He will bring the Israelites to His "sanctuary" on His "own mountain" in Jerusalem. (17)

15:14 *They trembled.* The news of God's judgment on the Egyptians brought "terror and dread" on other enemies of His people: the Philistines (14), the Edomites, the Moabites, the Canaanites. (15)

15:18 *Will reign.* He has the power to make His "kingdom come" even when "kings of the earth set themselves . . . against the Lord." (Ps 2:2, 48:4-6)

4) 15:19-21 Response Led by Miriam

15:20 *Miriam sang.* Lit. "answered them." Moses' sister led a chorus that antiphonally repeated the opening words of his song (1). To proclaim the words and deeds of God was the function of His prophetic servants. Another such "prophetess" was Deborah (Ju 4:4-5; cf. 1 Sm 2:1; Lk 1:46). On Patmos, John heard those who "had conquered" singing "the song of Moses . . . and the song of the Lamb," while they stood "beside the sea of glass with harps of God in their hands" (Rv 15:2-4). As the redeemed Israelites "were baptized into Moses in the cloud and in the sea," so those who through baptism into Christ were "united with him in a death like his" have been liberated from their "old self" and its demonic driver, leaving them "buried," as dead as the Egyptian hosts in the Red Sea (1 Co 10:2; Ro 6:4-14). Through this "washing of regeneration" they are also "united with him in a resurrection like his," alive to God as men who have been brought from death to life (Tts 3:5; Ro 6:4-14; Cl 2:12). As long as they are still "in the flesh," victorious living, however, requires "that the Old Adam in us should, by daily contrition and repentance, be drowned and die with all sins and evil lusts." (Gl 2:20; Luther's Small Catechism)

15:22—18:27 The Liberated People Brought to Mount Sinai

15:22-27 MARA: WATERS SWEETENED; ARRIVAL AT ELIM

15:22 *The wilderness of Shur.* Cf. 13:18 note. Here Israel's long wandering in various wildernesses began. It was an interim kind of life: no longer under the lashes of relentless exploitation, but not yet enjoying the "rest" in the promised life. It was an existence different from what it had been and would be. Above all, it was a life of faith. Denied the possibility to provide themselves with even the barest necessities by their own labors, they had to rely from one day to the next on God's promise to sustain them. The Israelites did not always measure up to the demand of such a desert-faith. When they followed God's guidance and as a consequence encountered circumstances that brought them face to face with the threat of annihilation, they concluded that they had made a mistake in entrusting themselves to God's promises. They preferred the material security that the "fleshpots" of Egypt had to offer them as slaves to the certainty that comes from "the conviction of things not seen" (Heb 11:1). Refusing to live "by everything that proceeds out of the mouth of the Lord," they failed the test of faith (Dt 8:2-3). The record of their pilgrimage is punctuated with expressions by which they challenged God's trustworthiness: they "murmured" (24); they "found fault" with Moses; they "put the Lord to the proof" (KJV: "tempted the Lord," 17:2). But God did not bring them to the brink of disaster because He was amused to see them squirm like panic-stricken ants. When Israel was helpless to save itself, it had the opportunity to learn how true it was that God was "the Lord, your healer" (15:26), "the Lord your God" (16:12), "the Lord among us" (17:7), "the Lord is my banner" (17:15). Every test of faith was designed to fortify them against the temptation to self-sufficiency, to produce a firmer trust in God's wisdom and powers, in short, to keep the desert-wanderers on His way, the only way to the promised land. Every child of God must learn to say: "Guide me, O Thou great Jehovah, Pilgrim through this barren land." Divine wisdom knows the way; divine love keeps him on the way, if necessary by trials of faith; divine power removes all obstructions from the way. (Jn 16:23; Acts 14:22; Ro 5:1-5; 8:35-39; 2 Co 4:17-18; 1 Ptr 1:6; 4:12-13; 5:10; Rv 2:10; 7:13-17)

15:26 *The Lord, your healer.* Those whom the

Lord has healed will remain in a state of health if they follow the prescriptions of their Physician. By obedience to His *commandments* and *statutes* the vitality of faith is "proved" (John 14:15; 15:10). "The healing of the nations" (Rv 22:2) was accomplished when a tree of bitter pain bore Him through whose "stripes we are healed." (Is 53:5; Ml 4:2)

15:27 *Elim.* At their second stopping place after leaving Egypt the Israelites found a good supply of water. For the numbers *twelve* and *seventy* cf. 1:5 note.

16:1-36 WILDERNESS OF SIN: BREAD AND MEAT SUPPLIED

1) 16:1-3 Murmuring of the People

16:2 *Murmured.* Cf. 15:22 note. This grumbling may seem incredible so soon after Israel's song of the Lord's triumph (15:1-21) and the very recent evidence of His ability to provide them with water (15:25). But its quick drop from high praise to base murmuring is not without parallel in the lives of such as profess trust in the Lord and then—for less reason than Israel's—complain about His guidance.

2) 16:4-12 Promise of Bread and Meat

16:4 *Bread from heaven.* Through a trial of faith God directed their gaze to the source from which all their needs were supplied (Ps 78:23-24; Ml 3:10; Neh 9:20). In the fullness of time there was to come "down from heaven" "the bread of life," the "supernatural food" that "gives life to the world." (Jn 6:32-40; 1 Co 10:3)

Prove them. From day to day they had to rely on God's promise. (Dt 8:3, 16; Mt 6:11)

16:7 *The glory of the Lord.* V. 10 adds the phrase "in the cloud." Cf. 14:19 note.

3) 16:13-21 Quails and Manna

16:13 *Quails.* The name of these small migratory birds, still plentiful in Egypt and Sinai, is derived from a root meaning "to be fat." Overweight and clumsy, they are easily caught.

16:14 *Flake-like thing, fine as hoarfrost.* The "bread from heaven" is later said to resemble the aromatic, grayish-yellow "seed" of the "coriander" plant (31); its appearance was "like that of bdellium" (a precious metal, Nm 11:7-9). A desert bush is known to produce nightly secretions. Found in the morning during certain seasons of the year, these seedlike drops disintegrate in the heat of the sun (21) or are soon eaten by ants. By this bread from heaven, however, Israel was to know "the Lord your God" (12) because it would become evident that He would go beyond the natural processes of nature in making it available. By direct intervention He would (a) endow it with properties that would satisfy each person regardless of the amount gathered (16-18); (b) lengthen the time of its ordinary usefulness every sixth day (19-27); (c) supply it without interruption for 40 years. (35)

16:15 *What is it?* This translation is based on the possibility that *man* is an unusual form of the interrogative pronoun *mah,* "what?" As the RSV note indicates, the Hebrew reads: "*Man* it is." It suggests that the Israelites gave it the name of an object, the meaning of which is no longer known. It was like *man*, but different, for *they did not know what it was.* The Hebrew form, always *man* and at times with the article, appears in the Greek of the NT as *manna* and is so transliterated also in the versions of the OT, ancient and modern. (Nm 11:6-9; Dt 8:3, 16; Jos 5:12; Neh 9:20; Ps 78:24; Jn 6:31, 49; Heb 9:4; Rv 2:17)

16:16 *Omer.* This term denotes a measure that is mentioned only in this chapter (18, 22, 32, 33). It was equal to "the tenth part of an ephah" (36), the latter holding about four gallons, and is not to be confused with a "homer," the equivalent of 10 ephahs. (Lv 27:16; Nm 11:32; Eze 45:13)

4) 16:22-30 Manna for the Sabbath

16:23 *A holy sabbath.* The seventh day was to be observed as *a day of solemn rest* even before the sabbath law was formally promulgated at Mt. Sinai.

5) 16:31-36 Memorial Jar of Manna

16:34 *Before the testimony.* Aaron placed it there after the tabernacle and the ark had been built. The latter contained "the two tables of the testimony, tables of stones, written with the finger of God." (31:18; 25:16, 22; 27:21; Lv 16:13; Nm 17:4; Heb 9:4)

16:35 *To a habitable land.* Cf. Jos 5:12; Neh 9:20-21.

17:1-16 REPHIDIM: THIRST QUENCHED; ENEMIES DEFEATED

1) 17:1-7 Water from the Rock

17:1 *Rephidim.* The last recorded incidents of the journey to Sinai took place at a site that has not been identified with certainty. A more complete "log" of Israel's progress is given in Nm 33:12-14.

17:2 *Found fault.* Cf. 15:22; 16:2 notes. Facing a new test of faith, many a person is prone to mistrust the goodness and power of God although he had repeatedly and quite recently seen His promises fulfilled.

17:6 *At Horeb.* With a slight change in the vocalization of the Hebrew consonants—the original text was not supplied with vowel signs—this phrase could be translated "in dry desolation." This rendering underscores the miraculous element of the incident: the rock was in a place where no natural possibility existed to account for the sudden appearance of water. According to ch. 19 Israel had not yet reached Sinai, for which Horeb is an alternate term. Cf. 3:1 note.

Strike the rock. The demonstrations of God's presence and the repeated manifestations of His saving power in the wilderness are a type or foreshadowing of His life-giving purposes, fulfilled in Christ. (1 Co 10:4; Jn 7:37-38; 4:10, 14; 1 Ptr 2:4)

17:7 *Massah . . . Meribah.* Two names were applied to Rephidim which characterize Israel's attitude. *Massah* is derived from a verb meaning "to test" or *put to the proof.* By their murmuring Israel expressed its lack of faith and demanded proof that the Lord was "among" them. *Meribah* describes Israel's action as a quarrelsome, contentious *fault-finding* with God's providence. When Israel later at Kadesh made similar charges against Him and for the same reason, this site too was designated Meribah and Meribath-kadesh. (Nm 20:2-13; Dt 32:51; Ps 78:15-20; 81:7; 95:8-9; 114:8; 1 Co 10:9)

2) 17:8-16 Victory over the Amalekites

17:8 *Amalek.* Descendants of Esau (Gn 36:12, 16). This nomadic tribe of the Negeb and Sinai tried to block Israel's advance through the territory controlled by it at that time. Because of its attacks on Israel (Nm 14:43, 45; Dt 25:17-18), God decreed to "utterly blot out the remembrance of Amalek." (14; Nm 24:20; Dt 25:19; 1 Sm 15:2-3; 30:1; 1 Ch 4:43)

17:9 *Joshua.* Moses' successor is mentioned here for the first time. The son of Nun, an Ephraimite (1 Ch 7:20-27), he is here called Hoshea (salvation); Nm 13:8; Dt 32:44, but more commonly "Jehoshuah," translated "Jesus" by the Septuagint.

17:10 *Hur.* This member of the tribe of Judah (1 Ch 2:19-20) served again as Aaron's assistant when Moses and Joshua "went up into the mountain of God" (24:14). No other reference is made to him.

17:13 *Mowed down Amalek.* Under Joshua Israel engaged the enemy in the valley with weapons of war; but victory was won by Moses' unarmed hands extended in intercessory prayer to the Lord of hosts. Servants of God may sooner grow "weary" in prayer than in the use of other means. (12; Acts 15:40; 1 Th 5:25; 2 Th 3:1; Heb 13:18)

17:15 *My banner.* As Israel's existence depended on the Lord's intervention when they lacked food and drink, so its extermination by Amalekite swords was averted because its army fought under the banner of the Ruler of the nations. Its rescue was to be put on record "as a memorial" (14) in order that future generations too might be encouraged by faith to lay "hand upon the banner of the Lord" in their battle with enemies, particularly when they would not be "contending against flesh and blood, but . . . against the spiritual hosts of wickedness." (Eph 6:11-18; Ps 20:5; 60:4-5; Is 11:10, 12; Ro 8:37-39)

18:1-27 ARRIVAL AT MOUNT SINAI; JETHRO'S VISIT

1) 18:1-12 Jethro's Arrival and Sacrifice

18:1 *Jethro.* Cf. 2:18 note.

18:2 *Zipporah.* Cf. 2:21; 4:25.

18:3 *Gershom.* Cf. 2:22 note.

18:5 *In the wilderness.* God often chooses the bleakest circumstances for the arena of His saving activity. The rugged peak of a bare rock looked like anything but *the mountain of God.* (Jn 1:46)

18:7 *Did obeisance and kissed him.* He bowed before his father-in-law and embraced him in keeping with the Oriental custom of politeness. (Gn 23:7, 12; 43:26)

18:9 *Rejoiced.* The report of "all that God had done" (1) had brought Jethro to Moses. Upon his arrival he heard from Moses himself *all the good which the Lord had done to Israel.* It moved him to praise the Lord as "greater than all gods." (11; 12:12; 15:11; Gn 14:18-20)

18:12 *To eat bread.* Besides betokening amity between the participants, joining in a meal *before God* expressed communion with Him, signified by offering *burnt offering and sacrifices.* Representing the people, *Aaron . . . with all the elders* ritually demonstrated that Israel sought and received union with the God of the covenant, the terms of which were soon to be set forth (chs. 20 ff.). For other such meals cf. Gn 31:54; Ex 12; 24:11.

2) 18:13-23 Jethro's Suggestion

18:13 *To judge the people.* Moses was the arbiter of disputes. In this judicial capacity he delivered "the statutes of God and his decisions" (16). It also afforded him the opportunity to transmit "statutes and decisions" by which the people were to "know the way in which they must walk" (20) in the future. Since Israel was a religious as well as a political community, regulations of cultic and civic affairs came into consideration.

18:21 *Choose able men.* While Moses remained the sole mediator between God and the people (9), the application of divine principles to individual cases, secular as well as religious and moral, should be entrusted to competent and God-fearing men. Jethro's advice was sound because the burden of Moses' work was so great that he could not "perform it alone." (18)

18:22 *Every great matter.* The difference between it and a *small matter* is not defined. Moses' mediatorship was, however, safeguarded. He would continue to receive directions from God and to intercede with Him in behalf of the people. (Cf. Acts 6:1-7)

3) 18:24-27 Jethro's Advice Heeded

19:1—40:38 CONSTITUTION OF THE LIBERATED PEOPLE: THE SINAI COVENANT

19:1—24:18 The Terms of the Covenant

19:1-25 THE PEOPLE PREPARED FOR THE COVENANT

1) 19:1-9 Divine Decree: Israel a Covenant Nation

19:1 *Wilderness of Sinai.* From this desert area a mountain by the same name was visible (11, 18, 20). The location of this "mountain of God" (18:5) has been a matter of dispute. It is best identified with the rugged peak that is now known as "Jebel Musa" (i.e., mountain of Moses, elevation about 7,400 ft.) in the southern Sinai Peninsula. It is also called Horeb. (Cf. 3:1 note)

19:2 *Moses went up.* Called previously to "serve God upon this mountain" (3:12), Moses now ascended it in order to receive instruction from the Lord *out of the mountain.*

19:5 *My covenant.* In some instances the original word has been translated "testament."

All that God said and did in the "Old Testament" was designed to renew a harmonious relationship with Him, culminating in "the blood of the new covenant," recorded in the "New Testament." Through the revolt in the garden of Eden against the terms that the Creator had established for his creatures, all the sons of Adam, begotten in his image (Gn 5:3), were alienated from God and subject to the penalty of death. But God at once proclaimed His plan to heal the broken ties of fellowship (Gn 3:15). In the covenant with Noah God bound Himself not to "destroy all flesh" (Gn 9:8-17). From all the descendants of Noah He chose an individual, Abraham, to be the bearer of His blessing to all nations. The basis for the reconciliation was set forth in the terms of a covenant (cf. Gn 17:2 note). At Sinai God took another step toward the goal of His plan of salvation. *Among all peoples* He chose to make a covenant with Israel. In it He pledged Himself to make the descendants of the patriarchs His instruments to achieve His purpose: the reconciliation of all men through the Mediator of the new covenant. The remainder of the OT is the record of God's covenant actions and Israel's reactions to it.

My own possession. KJV: "a peculiar treasure." The Hebrew noun has no descriptive adjective and denotes any property to which a person lays claim (1 Ch 29:3; Ec 2:8). Although "all the earth" is the Lord's, Israel was to be His very *own* or "special" possession. Once the serfs of Egyptian owners, the Israelites had been "redeemed, purchased, and won" by the Lord from the power of Pharaoh (4) to be "His own" in a very special way (cf. Luther's explanation of the Second Article of the Creed). But being His property did not subject them to a new bondage; they were to recognize His lordship by a service which set them free to be a "kingdom of priests" and a "holy nation." (Dt 7:6; 14:2; 26:18; Ps 135:4; Ml 3:17; 1 Co 6:19-20; 7:23; Tts 2:14; 1 Ptr 2:9)

19:6 *Kingdom of priests.* Although selected from all nations, Israel was not constituted for lordship over them in a power structure of political kingship. The Israelites, each in his own person and collectively, were to serve in the capacity of priests, mediators of God's salvation to all peoples. (Is 61:6; 1 Ptr 2:5, 9; Rv 1:6; 5:10; 20:6)

A holy nation. Before God entered into a special relationship with Israel at Sinai, Israel is called a *nation*, the Hebrew word used regularly for gentile peoples. Through the covenant it received a status which distinguished it from all other nations. As God is holy by His "otherness" from everyone and everything outside of Him, so Israel was consecrated to a holy task, uniquely distinct from that of any other nation. It was to share in God's holiness to the extent that it dedicated itself to His holy purposes; it was to promote the recognition of God's holiness by obedience to His holy will. (39:30; 1 Ptr 2:9; Lv 19:2; Dt 14:2; 28:9; Eph 1:4; Cl 1:21-23; 1 Ptr 1:15; 2 Ptr 3:11; cf. also Paul's address to "the saints" in the epistles: Ro 1:7; 1 Co 1:2; etc.)

2) 19:10-14 The People Consecrated; Their Approach Prohibited

19:10 *Consecrate the people.* Moses was "to make them holy" by outward ceremonial acts, which symbolized that they were inwardly disposed to act as God's holy people. They were to *wash their garments* to signify the need of a cleansing from "every defilement of body and spirit" (2 Co 7:1; Ex 29:4-5; Is 52:1, 11; Mt 22:11-13; Ja 1:21; Rv 3:18). To "be ready" to meet God the Israelites furthermore were forbidden to "go near a woman" (15). By means of sexual intercourse God creates life. By abstaining from it they were to acknowledge God's claim to life in its very origin. Refusal to comply with this restriction rendered a person ritually unclean. (1 Sm 21:5).

19:12 *Set bounds.* God's choice of Israel to be His "own possession" did not eliminate the unbridgeable chasm that separates the Creator from His creatures. The repeated warnings not to *go up into the mountain* or to "break through to the Lord to gaze" (21, 24) alerted Israel to the danger of a misconception of God that has persisted through the ages. For breaking the barrier between God and man, to be "like God," is at the root of all sin (Gn 3:5). God does not tolerate the pantheistic heresy of reducing Him to a part of nature. Efforts at a mystic fusion with Him are blasphemy. To trespass in any way on God's domain exposes the intruder to the sentence: "You shall die." (Gn 2:17; Ex 3:5; 19:12-13, 21; Ps 18:13; 1 Ti 6:15-16)

3) 19:15-25 God's Terrifying Manifestation; Moses on Mount Sinai

19:16-19 *Thunders and lightnings, and a thick cloud.* In these phenomena of nature God revealed His presence and at the same time concealed Himself because "man shall not see me and live" (33:20). *In thunder* His voice was heard (Ps 29:3-9; 68:33; Jn 12:29; Rv 6:1; 14:2). "Lightning" flashes from His quiver of "arrows" (Ps 77:17-18). "Thick clouds" clothe His mysterious splendor (16:10; 24:15-18; Nm 9:15; Eze 1:4; 10:4; Acts 1:9). *Fire* manifests His blazing glory (3:2; Dt 4:11-12; Eze 1:4, 13; Mt 3:11; Acts 2:3), His protecting presence (13:21-22; 2 K 6:17), and His consuming intolerance of sin (Gn 3:24; Is 66:15-16; Am 1:3-4, 7; 2 Th 1:7-8). *Smoke,* the result of fire, shares its significance. (Gn 15:17; 19:28; Dt 29:20; Ps 74:1; 104:32; Is 4:5; 6:4; 34:10; Jl 2:30; Acts 2:19; Rv 9:2; 15:8)

Quaked greatly. Not a volcanic eruption, but a visible demonstration that "the mountains quake before him." Nah 1:5; Ps 68:8; Mt 27:51)

19:22 *Priests.* Even before the Levitical priesthood had been instituted, sacrifices were offered by persons who served in the capacity of priests. (24:5)

20:1-20 BASIC TERMS OF THE COVENANT PROMULGATED

1) 20:1-17 Epitome of the Covenant: The Decalog

20:1 *God spoke.* The prescriptions for Israel's

preparation "to meet God" and the warning not to "go up into the mountain" (19:7, 12) were the basic negative aspects of the covenant: Rebellious man could not presume even to appear before God, much less wrangle with Him for a peaceful coexistence. In the following *words* God set forth in positive terms on what basis Israel could become and be His "own possession, a kingdom of priests, a holy nation" (19:5-6). If harmony is to be restored, the initiative can be taken only by God: *He spoke.* What He said about Israel's participation in the covenant fills most of the remaining chapters of the Book of Exodus and is the main subject of the books of Leviticus and Deuteronomy. It can be summed up as follows: First of all, Israel was to recognize its complete dependence on God's redemptive mercy and power; helpless in the shackles of slavery, it had not merited divine favor nor had it contributed to its deliverance "out of the house of bondage" (2). It could merely respond to the undeserved grace of God in obedience of faith. No less than an unreserved commitment of its total life to its Savior-God was required (Dt 6:5). By keeping the precepts of the covenant Israel was doing no more than to give evidence of its desire to accept the proffered grace of reconciliation and of its readiness to live in harmony with the will of its Redeemer. To obey the commandments in order to become worthy of a favorable relationship with God was to vitiate the basic intent of the covenant. Israel agreed to the negative and positive provisions of the covenant (19:8; 24:3). When the new covenant fulfilled the old and superseded it by abolishing its provisional regulations, it did not abrogate the basis for a life in communion with God, enunciated at Sinai. Reconciliation with God through "the blood of the new covenant" is a "gift of grace, not of works." The response to it by its recipients calls for a total surrender of self to their Redeemer and an obedience of faith that is no less drastic and no more meritorious than Israel's keeping of the words that God spoke at Sinai. (1 Co 6:19-20; 7:22-23; Eph 2:4-10; Cl 3:12-14; Tts 2:11; Heb 12:22-28; 1 Ptr 1:13; 2:1; etc.)

These words. Because the immediately following words are called "the ten words" (Dt 4:13; 10:4), we speak of them as the Decalog, a term compounded of the Greek for "ten" and "words." Their position at the head of all other precepts indicates that they are a basic epitome of the response that God expects of the participants in His covenant of grace. The profusion of directives of the old covenant—ritual, social, economic—radiate from these central principles. Brief yet comprehensive, simple yet incisively absolute, general yet applicable to every specific situation, these "ten words" are more than a system of ethics or a moral code of outward behavior. They lay claim to man's total being from the hidden stirrings and intentions of the heart to their overt expression in word and deed. It eliminates all assertions of man's self-determination. The new covenant does not minimize but rather sharpens the demands of an uncompromised surrender of self to the Redeemer and the Fulfiller of the Law (see, for example, the Sermon on the Mount, Mt 5—7). The "ten words" are not supplied with numbers from one to 10. Nor does Scripture inform us how many commandments were engraved on each of the "tables of stone." (32:15-16, 19; Dt 10:4-5)

20:2 *I am the Lord your God.* God manifested Himself as the *I am* by electing the enslaved descendants of Abraham to be His covenant people (cf. 3:14 note). By delivering them *out of the house of bondage* He demonstrated His sovereign power to keep His promises and to overcome all demonic opposition to His will. Therefore in the Decalog the *I am* revealed how Israel was to recognize and express its total dependence on God's covenanted mercy.

20:3 *No other gods.* The claim of the "I am" to man's total commitment to Him is ignored and the covenant relationship is broken if man: (a) fails to give Him supreme and undivided allegiance (3); (b) attempts to degrade Him by making "graven images" and thus seeks to capture and impound His incomprehensible majesty in forms that conform to human thinking and subject Him to man's manipulation (4); (c) arrogates to himself the use of divine power that God displays in the revelation of His "name" and invokes it in order to show his contempt of God, to support falsehood, or to exercise functions that God has reserved for Himself (7); (d) refuses to devote a part of God's gift of time to acknowledge his covenant relationship to Him by acts of worship (8); (e) defies the authority that God has vested in His human representatives. (12)

Before me. The first commandment is monotheistic in its intent. It prohibits that the veneration that belongs exclusively to God be extended to any creatures, visible and invisible, or to the figments of the imagination that men designate "gods" and elevate to the status of deity "besides me" (RSV note). Throughout the OT *gods* and "idols" are synonymous terms. Both are declared to be nonexistent as rivals of God's unity. (32:4; Dt 4:28; 32:37-38; Jos 24:14; Ju 10:13-16; 1 K 18:21; Is 42:17; 43:10-11; Jer 2:28; 10:11; Zph 2:11; cf. also Acts 19:26; 1 Co 8:4; Gl 4:8)

20:4 *Graven image.* Material representations of God were regarded as an attempt to reduce the Creator to creature-likeness and make His transcendent nature conform to an image of man's finite conceptions. When man makes God out to be what he wants Him to be, he robs Him of His sovereignty and makes Him subservient to his desires. God is not like any creature *in heaven above* (astral deities or angels; Jer 44:17; Cl 2:18) *in the earth* (plastic or sculptured images; Dt 7:5), or *in the water under the earth.* (Rahab or other marine monsters; Ps 89:10; Is 51:9)

20:5 *Jealous.* Cf. Dt 4:24 note. To *bow down* or to *serve* any man-made caricature of God is not a petty peccadillo. It is the sin of sins. Its perpetrators *hate* God and are subject to His wrath *to the third and the fourth generation of* those who follow in the footsteps of their idolatrous forebears. (Dt 5:9-10; 24:16; Nm 10:35; Eze 18:4, 14-20; Mt 23:31-32; Ro 8:7; Rv 18:4)

20:7 *In vain.* God's name is misused by swearing falsely (Lv 19:12; Hos 10:4; Zch 5:4), by false teaching (Jer 14:14; 23:25-27, 31, 32), by cursing (21:17; Nm 22:6, 12), by invading God's prerogative of doing supernatural feats such as sorcery. (Dt 18:9-11)

20:11 *In six days.* Israel is to follow the Creator's example when He made heaven and earth in 6 days and "rested on the seventh day from all his work which he had done" (Gn 2:2). Some interpreters reverse the comparison and hold that the Sabbath law provided the schematic pattern for the creation account. Because what God did "in the beginning" transcends human comprehension, it is presented in the anthropomorphic form of a sabbatic workweek of six consecutive days, followed by the cessation of labor on the seventh. As Israel was to have surcease from work on the Sabbath, so God is said to have been "refreshed" by resting on the seventh day. (31:12-17; Heb 4:4, 9, 10)

20:12 *Father and mother.* God demands that His rulership be recognized in those to whom He has delegated His authority in the family and in the larger domain of communal life. (21:15-17; 22:28; Lv 19:1-4; Dt 27:15-16; Ro 13:1; Eph 6:5)

20:13 *You shall not.* The remaining commandments require the participants in God's covenant to recognize that injury done to fellowmen is more than a disruption of the social order. Ultimately violations of these laws disregard God's claim to man as the work of His hands, made in His image. The Creator does not want His creatures to suffer any infringement of the "inalienable rights" that He has granted them. They are under His protection against: (a) the loss of life by illegal means—lit. "do not murder" (13); (b) the violation of the sanctity of marriage (14); (c) the seizure of their property (15); (d) the defamation of their character and honor (16); (e) the desire unlawfully to acquire their home, its inmates, and its appurtenances (17). No threats or promises are attached to these prohibitions. They are not necessary if man's relationship to God, set forth in the previous commandments, has been accepted as the basis of God's claim to obedience.

20:17 *Not covet.* The first commandment lays the foundation of all covenant obedience; the last attacks disobedience at its root: longing in the heart for forbidden fruit.

2) 20:18-20 The People Terrified at God's Manifestation

20:21—23:19 COVENANT ORDINANCES: TOTAL COMMITMENT OF LIFE

1) 20:21-26 The Altar

20:22 *The Lord said.* The "ten words" that God had spoken *from heaven* were accepted by the people (18-20). In the following section (20:22—23:19) the basic principles of the Decalog are elaborated. Through the mediatorship of Moses the Israelites received directions how they were to express their allegiance to the Lord (20:22-26; 23:10-19). Furthermore the general rules of the Decalog that were to govern man's relationship to his fellow members in the covenant society are applied to specific life situations (22:1—23:9). If Israel would "hearken to his voice" and "not rebel against him," God pledged Himself to bless His people and give them the promised land (23:20-33). Because Moses read these words of God to Israel from "the book of the covenant," this entire section has been called "the covenant code." Although it contains ordinances, ritualistic as well as ethical, that existed also in the nations of Israel's environment, they differ from them in many respects, primarily in their basic claim to validity and in the motivation for their observance. Amplified in later legislation (chs. 25—40; the Book of Leviticus), these provisions were to govern the religious and communal life of God's people under the old covenant until the Mediator of the new covenant would create the "Israel after the spirit," "a holy priesthood, to offer spiritual sacrifices." (1 Ptr 2:5)

20:24 *Altar of earth.* The simplicity of the *altar,* made of the *earth* that God had created, was to obviate the false notion, prevalent among Israel's neighbors, that man's effort in constructing it merited divine favor. Similarly if for some reasons stones were used, they were to be left "unhewn" (25). Artistic craftsmanship did not contribute to the worshiper's right to appear before God. The altar was not to be ascended "by steps" lest "nakedness" be "exposed." The fertility cult of baalism relied on sympathetic magic for the procreation of man and beast. (26)

In every place. This phrase asserts that God is not a local deity, confined to one place. But it also restricts Israel's worship to such places as He would choose for the revelation of His *name* (cf. 3:14 note). It anticipates that in the course of Israel's wanderings and later history God would appoint a series of sites for worship. (Shechem, Shiloh, etc. Cf. Dt. 12:5 note)

2) 21:1—22:20 Ordinances Regulating Overt Actions of Communal Life

a. 21:1-11 Treatment of Slaves

21:1 *The ordinances.* Although God chose Israel to be His "own possession" (19:5), He did not take it out of the world. He did not create for it a social and economic order that had no parallels among the nations of its time and environment (cf., for example, the Babylonian law code of Hammurabi). However, the regulations for its communal life were not dictated merely by political expediency. Because Israel was to be a "holy nation," the categorical demands of the Decalog are applied to its civic affairs (21:1—23:9). In form these ordinances resemble our case laws. The area of conduct under consideration is introduced by a "when" clause or by a paticipial phrase, followed by "if" clauses which define the more specific situations that may arise in application of the general rule (v. 2 elaborated in vv. 3-6; v. 12, in vv. 13-14). In both instances the verdict on the action is expressed in the categorical form of the Ten Commandments "[he] shall be stoned" (28). At times the law may be stated in a simple declarative sentence. (22:18-20)

21:2 *Slave.* The first group of civic ordinances deals with the treatment of slaves (2-11). Practiced by all nations at the time, slavery in Israel was a comparatively humane institution. "The master" (not: "the owner") was not permitted to treat his "servant" (the same Hebrew word is used of free men) as if he were disposable chattle without any recognition of his personal rights. (See also 20-21, 26, 27)

b. 21:12-32 Sanctity of Human Life

aa. 21.12-17 Capital punishment

21:12 *Strikes a man.* The section (12-17) lists crimes that are punishable by death. When inflicted at God's behest and by authorized authorities, capital punishment did not conflict with the commandment: "You shall not kill" (20:13; Ro 13:4). The extreme penalty was to be exacted of those who deliberately violate God's sole prerogative to give and take life, man's irreplaceable possession. The same punishment was to be meted out to such as vilify and reject those through whom He creates life: parents. (15, 17)

21:13 *Let him fall.* An exception was to be made if God shaped circumstances so that they were the cause of death rather than the action of the victim's known enemy. The latter was to take refuge in a designated place. (Cf. Nm 35:11-34; Dt 4:41-43; 19:1-13)

bb. 21:18-27 Restitutions for unintentional injuries

21:18 *One strikes the other.* In the covenant community God protected His foremost creature also against bodily harm which was not fatal at once or which might result in death, whether the victim be master or slave, whether the perpetrator of the injury be man or beast. (18-32)

21:20 *His money.* The slave represents an investment of the master's resources.

21:24 *Eye for eye.* The so-called "lex talionis" (the law of punishment proportionate to the crime), enforced by the constituted authorities, outlawed personal and excessive revenge (Lv 24:17-22; Dt 19:16-21). In the case of a slave, reparation was to be made by setting the slave free (26, 27). In the new covenant, Jesus requires the sufferer to forego retaliation and to treat the perpetrator of the nefarious deed with forbearance and kindness. (Mt 5:38-39)

cc. 21:28-32 Injury to life by animals

c. 21:33—22:17 Protection of Individual Rights

aa. 21:33-36 Property loss by negligence

21:34 *Make it good.* Besides man's most precious possession, his life and his body, his material property, personal and real, was to be safeguarded against theft and encroachment upon it (21:33—22:17). Restitution was to be made for livestock, whether the loss of it resulted from negligence (33-36) or outright theft. (22:1-3)

bb. 21:37—22:15 Property loss by theft and other causes

22:2 *No blood guilt.* The following section sets forth judicial procedures in more unusual cases of impairment and loss of life and property (1-20). If a person protected his property and killed a thief at night, he was not guilty of murder.

22:5 *A field or vineyard.* If crops were destroyed by the grazing of roaming animals or set on fire, restitution for the loss was to be made. (5, 6)

22:7 *Money or goods to keep.* Provisions were made for the loss of property that had been entrusted to another for safekeeping or that was stolen from the person to whom it had been loaned (7-14). If it allegedly had been taken by an undetected thief or if two people laid claim to the same belongings, the case was to be brought to "God," that is to His representatives (the Hebrew word "God" may here have the meaning of "mighty ones," i.e., the judges; see Gn 6:2; Dt 19:16-19). "Both parties" to the dispute might be required to submit to an ordeal by swearing an "oath to the Lord" (11). The liar incurred the punishment for blasphemy that God imposed on all such as use His "name in vain" (20:7). In other cases "God shall condemn" the actual offender by an oracle which disclosed the truth to the judges. (Cf. Nm 5:16-28)

cc. 22:16-17 The loss of virginity

22:16 *Marriage present.* Cf. Gn 24:53, 59, 61; 29:18, 27; 34:12.

d. 22:18-20 Capital Punishment: Crimes Against God and Man

22:18 *Not permit to live.* In the preceding civil ordinances (21:1 ff.) capital punishment was to be inflicted in cases of murder, the deliberate denial of the Creator's claim to the life of His creature, made in His image. (In Hammurabi's code theft was punishable by death.) The next verses (18-20) enumerate crimes that invade the domain of God's sovereign majesty. Its violators are to "be put to death." This punishment is demanded in the same unconditional form of "you shall not"—"you shall" as in 21:15-17. A *sorceress* desecrates God's holy name (20:7) by using it in the attempt to disclose what He has reserved as the sole prerogative of His revelation. Bestiality (19) transgressed the sanctity of the order governing the use of the mysterious power of procreation with which He has endowed His creatures. Offering "sacrifices to any god" (20) was a transgression of the first commandment. Whoever robbed God of the homage that belonged exclusively to Him was to "be utterly destroyed" (literally "put under the ban"; cf. Dt. 13:13 ff.). All such overt acts against God were to be punished because the old covenant invested Israel with civil as well as religious authority.

3) 22:21—23:9 Divine Retribution for Undetected Offenses

a) 22:21-27 Abuse of the Stranger and the Needy

22:21 *You shall not.* The following section

(22:21—23:9) contains additional covenant legislation. By keeping it the Israelites were to demonstrate that they were "consecrated to" the Lord (31). The categorical demands of both tables of the Decalog are applied to specific aspects of the social, economic, and religious life of the "holy nation" (19:5-6). They differ from the "ordinances" (21:1—22:20) not only in outward form but also in the scope of their demands and in the sanctions for their violation. The former dealt with overt breaches with which the constituted authorities were to deal. Transgressors of the following laws were subject to the Lord's own retributive threat (21, 27; 23:7, 10). They take into account the unseen motivation of a deed and instances of forbidden acts that may elude human detection. The Lord "will not acquit the wicked" (23:7) who in thought, word, or deed (a) are unmerciful to the defenseless and the underprivileged (21-27); (b) refuse to recognize God's claim to their "consecrated" allegiance (28-31); (c) harm any fellowman, even an enemy, by false testimony and injustice whether in or out of court. (23:1-9)

You were strangers. Obedience to these divine demands did not earn God's favor; it was to demonstrate a grateful recognition of God's undeserved and merciful act in delivering enslaved and defenseless "strangers" in Egypt (see the introduction of the Decalog 20:2; 23:12, 15; Lv 19:34; Dt 10:19; 24:18). Because God is "compassionate" (27), He will not tolerate it if His covenant people mistreat such as could easily be deprived of their rights: the stranger, the widow and orphan (22), the poor, and those in financial distress (25). Although not a member of the chosen people, the stranger was not excluded from God's protection. (Lv 19:33; Dt 24:17; 27:19)

b. 22:28-31 Disregard of God's Claim to All Life

22:31 *Torn by beasts.* One of the ways by which the Israelites were to exhibit their complete submission to God (28-31) was not to eat flesh from which the blood had not been drained. Since "the life of the flesh is in the blood," observance of this prohibition honored God, the Creator of all life. (Lv. 17:10-13)

c. 23:1-9 False Witness in and out of Court; Bribery

23:7 *Not acquit the wicked.* In the last verses of the previous chapter (22:28-31) the Israelites were required to be "consecrated" to the holy God. In the opening section of this ch. (1-9) they are held to abstain from unholiness by doing injustice toward their fellowman, whether he is rich or poor, friend or foe, fellow citizen or stranger. God will not acquit those who are guilty of injustice done (a) by malicious gossip or false testimony in court (1-3); (b) by refusing to help an enemy (4-5); (c) by subversion of equity and judicial probity. (6-9)

23:9 *Strangers.* Cf. 22:21 note for the motivation that was to prompt obedience to the requirements of mercy (22:21-27), holiness (22:28-31), and justice. (23:1-9)

4) 23:10-19 Assent to Precepts Demanding Israel's Total Commitment to God

a. 23:10-13 Yearly and Weekly Sabbaths: God's Rest

23:10 *Six years.* The statutes in vv. 10-19 are given in the same apodictic form of "you shall—you shall not" as those in 22:21—23:9 with the exception that the imperative is usually preceded by adverbial phrases (*six years,* "six days," 12; "three times," 14) or by the object of the verb (19). Israel's inner commitment to the Lord was to be manifested by outward "civic" observances at stated intervals. At these occasions it was to acknowledge time as God's gift and to devote certain periods of it to accomplish His sovereign purposes either by abstaining from profitable labors (10-13) or by engaging in activities that honored Him (14-19) to the exclusion of "other gods" (13). Six days in the week and 6 years in 7 were to be retained by Israel in order to reap the benefits that the Creator's blessing lets the soil produce (Gn 1:11). Every seventh day and every seventh year were to be surrendered to Him in order to restore, at least in part, the original order of creation: (a) the restoration of fertility to His good earth and equal opportunity for all to exploit its benefits (10-11); (b) rest for all from wearisome toil that sin had made a hardship (12-13; Gn 3:17-19). Thrice a year Israel was also to take time for the celebration of festivals. On these occasions they were to glorify the Giver of the fruits of their labors (16) and to worship the Lord of history, the Redeemer and Creator of Israel (15; Is 43:14-15). In 15 and 16 brief instructions are given regarding the kind of offerings and rites for the celebration of the festivals. Vv. 18-19 prescribe the procedures to be followed in the worship acts. (Cf. 12:14-20; 34:18-23; Nm 28—29; Lv 23; Dt 16)

b. 23:14-17 Annual Festivals: God's Time

23:15 *Abib.* Cf. 12:2 note.

c. 23:18-19 Offerings: God's Gifts

23:19 *In its mother's milk.* This regulation prohibited one of the superstitious fertility practices by which the Canaanites worshiped Baal. (Dt 14:21)

23:20-33 BLESSINGS OF COVENANT OBEDIENCE

23:20 *An angel before you.* If Israel observed the terms of the covenant, God pledged Himself to accompany it with His blessing and protection and to bring it to the promised land; if it would break the covenant and "rebel against him" (21), He would not let such willful "transgression" go unpunished (20-33). Both promise and threat were to be carried out by *an angel*, called "my angel" in 23. Because God's "name is in him" (21), what he does is a manifestation of the Lord Himself. (On the name of God see 3:13-14; on the angel of the Lord, Gn 16:7)

23:22 *An enemy to your enemies.* As long as Israel lived as God's covenant people, every violator of its divinely established rights became God's enemy. It could appeal to God's pledge to vindicate its cause; it had the right to invoke punishment on its common enemy. This principle was applicable also when an individual was deprived of his covenant rights by a wicked fellow Israelite. It is expressed frequently in the so-called imprecatory psalms such as Ps 35; 69; 83; 109; 149.

23:23 *Amorites.* Cf. Gn 15:21 note.

23:24 *Pillars.* Cf. Gn 28:18 note; Ex 24:4.

23:27 *My terror.* Terror instilled by God. (Cf. Gn 15:12; 35:5; Ex 15:16; Dt 32:25; Jos 2:9)

23:28 *Hornets.* As people flee before a swarm of large wasps, so the Lord's "terror" will put to flight the enemies of Israel. (Dt 7:20; Jos 24:12)

23:31 *Your bounds.* The borders of the Promised Land were to extend from the *Red Sea* (cf. 13:18 note) to the *sea of the Philistines* (the Mediterranean), *from the* (Arabian) *wilderness to the Euphrates.* (Gn 15:18; 1 K 4:21)

24:1-18 COVENANT COMMUNION ESTABLISHED

1) 24:1-8 The Covenant Ratified by Israel

24:1 *Come up.* After Israel had heard the basic provisions of the covenant (chs. 20—23), it still needed to be ratified. Aaron, his two sons, and the 70 elders represented Israel *afar off;* Moses was the mediator between God and the people, the spokesman for both parties of the agreement (3). Therefore he "alone shall come near to the Lord" (2). After Israel had accepted all the stipulations of the covenant (3), it was documented (4) and sealed by the following ceremonial rites: (a) Moses threw a part of the blood of sacrificial animals "against the altar," representing God's presence; it signified that Israel had access to Him only after atonement had been made by the substitionary death of animals (5, 6); (b) the documented covenant was read and formally accepted by Israel (7); (c) Moses threw the remaining blood "upon the people" to attest that Israel's life was protected from the wrath of God by virtue of the vicarious atonement of its sins (8); (d) Israel's mediator and its representatives "beheld God, and ate and drank" in order to symbolize that communion with God, like a blood brotherhood, had been established and was in effect. (9-11)

24:4 *Pillars.* Cf. Gn 28:18 note.

24:5 *Young men.* The official priesthood had not been established.

24:6-8 *The blood of the covenant.* When the old covenant had served its purpose, the vicarious life and death of the Mediator of the new covenant actualized the atonement that the animal sacrifices symbolized and foreshadowed. He summarized man's reconciliation when He said: "This is my blood of the new covenant." (Mt 26:28; Ro 11:27; Heb 8:6-13; 9:11-14; 12:24; Jer 31:31-34; Eze 37:24-28)

2) 24:9-11 Israel's Representatives in Communion with God

24:10 *Saw the God of Israel.* Reconciled Israel's representative "beheld God" (11) in a vision. We are not told how God dimmed the devastating brilliance of His absolute glory and yet made His presence visible (17; 33:20; Is 6:5). The mention of a *pavement of sapphire stone* under His feet suggests that He manifested Himself in a vision similar to Ezekiel's (Eze 1; Rv 4:1-6). God "did not lay his hand" on them (11). The fury of His wrath did not consume them because by accepting the covenanted mercy of God their sins, the cause of death, had been removed from His sight (Gn 15:6). But by this vision Israel was also reminded that the God who had stooped to accept them was the Holy One of Israel, the King of kings, who claims: "Heaven is my throne and the earth is my footstool." (Is 66:1)

3) 24:12-18 The Covenant Mediator in Communion with God

24:12 *Tables of stone.* Moses again ascended the mountain in order to receive *the law and the commandment* in the form of a permanent document *for their instruction.* No doubt the two tables of stone were inscribed by God with the Decalog. Moses himself recorded "all the words of the Lord." (24:4; cf. 20:1 note)

24:18 *Forty days and forty nights.* Cf. 34:28; Dt 9:9; 1 K 19:8; Mt 4:2.

25:1—31:18 Directives for the Maintenance of Communion with God

25:1—27:21 THE TABERNACLE: PLACE OF COMMUNION WITH GOD

1) 25:1-9 The Freewill Offerings for the Tabernacle

25:1 *The Lord said.* In chs. 19—24 we were told how God made a covenant with the descendants of Abraham. Its basic terms were set forth by God and accepted by the people. Then Moses again ascended Mt. Sinai (24:15-17) in order to receive additional covenant promises and stipulations. The chosen people were to be assured of God's abiding presence in their midst and to be instructed how they were to express and acknowledge their covenant relationship with God in rituals and forms of worship. They were to acknowledge their communion with God by: (a) erecting a sanctuary, "the tabernacle." It was a visible pledge of God's invisible presence in their midst (chs. 25—27); (b) designating certain people as priests. Their services were to be a daily reminder of the ongoing need of intermediaries between a sinful people and the "devouring fire" (24:17) of a holy God (ch. 28); (c) instituting sacred rites. These ceremonies were to symbolize their dependence on the mercy of God if their covenant relationship with God was to be maintained (29:1—31:17); (d) accepting the "tables of the testimony," the permanent record of the covenant. (31:18)

25:2 *Offering for me.* The sanctuary with "all its furniture" (9) was to be a concrete token that God, whom "heaven and the highest heaven cannot contain" (1 K 8:27), desired to "dwell in their midst" (8). The materials for it were to be furnished by every person *whose heart makes him willing.* Gifts motivated only by gratitude were the kind acceptable to God.

25:5 *Goatskins.* KJV: "badgers' skins." If the Hebrew term is an Egyptian loanword, it means simply leather. In the cognate Arabic language it denotes a dolphin.

25:9 *Tabernacle.* Literally "a dwelling place."

The "sanctuary" (8) was to be a movable structure, appropriate for the migratory life of the people. It is also called "the tent of meeting" (33:7-11) and the "house of the Lord." (Jos 6:24)

2) 25:10-22 The Ark

25:10 *An ark.* The description of the tabernacle with its "furniture" is given again in the account of its construction (chs. 36—38). Tedious according to our canons of composition, this detailed repetition is characteristic of OT narration. And it is not without effect. It drives home the fact that communion with God is possible only on His terms and according to His express prescriptions. The repetitious monotony is relieved, however, by reversing the sequence in which the parts of the tabernacle are enumerated. The subsequent record begins with the description of the outer tent coverings, whereas here Moses' attention is directed at once to the innermost and most sacred of its "furniture": the ark in the holy of holies. Designated by a different Hebrew word than the one used in Gn 6:14 and Ex 2:3, it was a chest (3¾ x 2¼ x 2¼ ft.) reminiscent of the coffers that the Israelites had seen used by the Egyptians to carry their idol images in processions. In spite of this structural similarity, the ark served an entirely different purpose.

25:16 *The testimony.* Preserved in the ark, the two tables of stone gave permanent testimony to God's demands that Israel be a holy people and abstain from breaking the commandments (24:12; 31:18; 32:15-16; 34:1, 28). Because it served this purpose, it is called "the ark of the testimony." (22; 40:21; for other names see Nm 10:33; Dt 10:8; 1 K 2:26; 1 Ch 15:1; 28:2)

25:17 *Mercy seat.* One word in Hebrew, this term is derived from a verb meaning "to cover." In its literal meaning it occurs only once (Gn 6:14); in a derived verb form it is used exclusively in the transferred sense of covering or obliterating sin by atonement, expiation, propitiation. The high priest sprinkled atoning blood upon the golden lid of the ark to signify that the people's sins against the commandments lying under it had been removed from God's sight. Thus it became the symbolic *seat* or base of God's forgiving *mercy.* Here He would condescend to "meet with" His reconciled people and to "speak with" them of His covenanted grace and of their response to it (22). The *mercy seat* symbolically foreshadowed the actuality: the access that sinful men have to the holy God through the atoning sacrifice of the "holy, blameless, unstained" High Priest, "separated from sinners, exalted above the heavens." (Heb 7:26; 4:14-16; Ro 3:21-25; Gl 3:10-14; 1 Jn 2:2; 4:10)

25:18 *Two cherubim.* Unlike heathen shrines, the sanctuary contained no image of the deity (20:4). In its stead figures of God's angelic creatures faced one another at each end of the mercy seat and acted as its guardians (37:7-9; 1 K 6:23-28). Their "flaming sword" would annihilate any unauthorized intruder into the presence of the holy God. (Gn 3:24; 1 Sm 4:4; 2 Sm 6:2; 2 K 19:15; Ps 80:1; 99:1; Is 6:2; Eze 1:4 ff.)

3) 25:23-30 The Table for the Bread of the Presence

25:23 *A table.* In addition to the ark, the sanctuary was to contain a table (3 x 1½ x 2¼ ft.). On it was to be "set the bread of the Presence" (KJV: "showbread"; lit. "bread of the face"). It symbolized God's communion with His people. He acted as the host who according to Oriental custom prepared a meal for his guests as an inviolate seal of friendship. Consisting of "twelve cakes" (flat loaves), the bread was to be eaten every Sabbath day by "Aaron and his sons" (Lv 24:5-9). His "Presence" as a benign host signified God's covenant relationship with all the tribes of Israel throughout the 12 months of the year. When the Bread of life came, He spread a table with His body given into death and His blood shed for the remission of sins. The guests at the new covenant table receive the seal of their communion with God and proclaim their union with one another. (Mt 26:26-29; 1 Co 10:16-18)

25:31 *A lampstand.* The third piece of "furniture" in the sanctuary was to be a *lampstand* equipped with "seven lamps," symbolizing the light of "the eyes of the Lord, which range through the whole earth" (Zch 4:10b; Rv 5:6). Burning in the darkness of the sanctuary, these lamps assured Israel that in all vicissitudes of its wanderings the light of God's countenance would illumine their way (Ps 32:8; 139:7-12; Am 9:2-4). When He makes "his face to shine upon" His people, they have "peace." (Nm 6:24-26; Ps 80:3, 7, 19)

5) 26:1-30 The Structure of the Tabernacle

a. 26:1-6 The Inner Sanctuary

26:1 *The tabernacle.* The description of the "furniture" of the sanctuary (25:10-40) is followed by directives for the building of its structural parts. Although the instructions are given in some detail and were sufficiently clear to Moses (cf. 25:9, 40; 26:30), the record does not contain specifications in such clarity as to make it possible to construct a modern blueprint. Its overall dimensions were 45 ft. long, 15 ft. wide, and 25 ft. high, half the size of Solomon's temple. (1 K 6:2)

Ten curtains. The account again begins with the innermost part of the sanctuary (1-6; cf. 25:10 note). The space enclosed by these brilliantly colored *ten curtains,* adorned with *cherubim skillfully worked,* constituted the tabernacle in the strictest sense of the term.

b. 26:7-14 The Outer Coverings

26:7 *For a tent.* The sanctuary itself was to be covered by a *tent,* consisting of *curtains of goats' hair.* (7-13)

26:14 *A covering.* The tent in turn was overlaid with another layer of *tanned rams' skins and goatskins.* (For the latter term see 25:5 note)

c. 26:15-30 The Structural Framework of the Sanctuary

26:15 *Upright frames.* Under these layers of curtains and supporting them, a paneled framework was to be erected at the back and the two sides, leaving the front open (15-30). Made to be a portable housing, the tabernacle lacked the structural parts of a permanent temple.

6) 26:31-37 The Veil

26:31 *A veil.* Derived from a root meaning "to bar or prevent access," the Hebrew term used for this hanging is different from the word used for the "curtains" (26:1 ff.). As its name indicates, the veil divided the sanctuary into separate compartments (cf. 1 K 6:16; Mt 27:51). The first, called the "holy place" (33) or "outer tent" and "tabernacle" (Heb 9:6), was restricted to the priests for the performance of their ritual duties. Entrance to it was shut off by a "screen" (36). On the inner side of the veil was the "most holy," literally "the holy of holies," also called "the holy place within the veil" (Lv 16:2; Heb 9:12), the "second" tabernacle (Heb 9:7) or simply "the sanctuary" (Heb 10:19). Into it Moses was to place "the ark of the testimony" (cf. 25:10, 16, 17 notes). Its holy precincts were to be entered once a year by the high priest to make "atonement for himself and for his house and for all the assembly of Israel" (Lv 16:17). Although God had assured Israel of His presence in the sanctuary (25:22), the veil signified that man did not have the right of access to Him who dwells in "unapproachable light" (1 Ti 6:16), unless his sins had been removed by atonement. This veil, barring rebellious man from the devouring wrath of God, foreshadowed the need of Him at whose atoning death on Golgotha "the curtain of the temple was torn in two." (Mt 27:51; Heb 9:11-14; 10:19-22; Ro 5:1-2; Eph 2:13-18; 3:11-12)

7) 27:1-8 The Altar of Burnt Offerings

27:1 *The altar.* The sixth piece of "furniture" (25:9) was a portable *altar* of burnt offering (1-8; 38:1-7) which was to be placed in the outer court, separated from the holy place by a "screen" (26:36). Its hollow framework of *acacia wood,* overlaid with bronze, was perhaps filled—at least partly—with earth (20:24) as its "fireplace." Projecting from its corners were four "horns," symbols of God's power extending into all directions of the compass (29:12; 1 K 1:50; 2:28; Ex 21:14; Ps 118:27). By their sacrifices on this altar the people were to have the privilege to express their worship and adoration of God, who had covenanted to enter into communion with them. While no longer bound by the provisional old covenant forms of worship, the redeemed and reconciled people of the new covenant are enjoined to respond to God's grace in obedience of faith and to present their "bodies as a living sacrifice . . . spiritual worship." (Ro 12:1; 6:12-13; Eph 5:2)

8) 27:9-19 The Outer Court of the People

27:9 *The court.* The outer court in which stood the altar of burnt offering and "the laver" (30:17-21) was an area of larger dimensions, 150 x 75 x 7½ ft. (9-21). All ceremonially clean Israelites could appear here to participate in sacrifices. Here they were also to present "pure" oil, secured by crushing olives, which served as fuel for the "lamp." (25:31-40)

9) 27:20-21 The Oil for the Lampstand

28:1-43 VESTMENTS OF THE HIGH PRIEST, MEDIATOR OF THE COVENANT COMMUNION

1) 28:1-4 Aaron and His Sons, the Wearers of the Sacred Garments

28:1 *Priests.* The tabernacle was to be constructed (chs. 25—27) in order that God would have a place to "meet with" and to "speak with" the Israelites. But communion with "the glory of the Lord," "a devouring fire" to rebellious man, was impossible without atonement for his sins, the basic rationale of OT rites and sacrifices. Performed by authorized intermediaries, these symbolic acts visualized the need of forgiveness and God's willingness to grant it to those who penitently expressed the desire to accept such unmerited mercy. The mediating and atoning function of the priest was visualized also by "the holy garments" which he was to wear (28:1-43). Each part of his prescribed vestments symbolized a particular aspect of the mediating function of his office. His service "for glory and for beauty" (2) was efficacious not by virtue of any merit in his person but solely in his capacity as the bearer of "the holy garments," the visual insignia of God's communion with His reconciled people. The new covenant people, "put on Christ," their High Priest and Mediator. (Gl 3:27; Ro 13:14; Rv 4:4)

2) 28:5-14 The Ephod and Its Shoulder Pieces

28:6 *The ephod.* It is difficult to find adequate English equivalents for some of the parts of the priest's vestments. "Ephod" is merely a transliteration of the Hebrew word. An apron-like, sleeveless outer garment, extending from the breast to the hips, it was to be fabricated of the same materials used to make the "curtains" and the "veil" of the sanctuary. Wearing garb woven of the same "stuff" that housed God's presence, Israel's intermediary was clothed with the materials of a divine viceroy.

28:7 *Shoulder-pieces.* Attached to the *two edges* of the ephod and hanging over it, were two three-cornered *shoulder-pieces.* On them in turn were set "two onyx stones," each engraved with six "names of the sons of Israel" (9). Wearing "their names before the Lord . . . for remembrance" (12), the priest was entrusted with the burden of responsibility for the entire people. At the same time the shoulder-pieces, like epaulets of authority, entitled him to recognition as God's representative to the people. (Cf. Rv 21:12, 19-20)

3) 28:15-30 The Breastplate of Judgment: Urim and Thummim

28:15 *A breastpiece of judgment.* The Hebrew word is used exclusively to describe this pouchlike badge of the priest. Attached at the bottom to the ends of the shoulder-pieces and at the top to their stones, this 9 x 9-inch square pectoral was studded on the outside with 12 precious stones, representing the tribes of Israel. It served also as the receptacle for the "Urim and Thummim," by which Aaron was authorized to "bear the judgment of the people of Israel upon his heart before the Lord continually" (30). The meaning of the words Urim and Thummim, the means of ascertaining God's decision, is not completely clear. Etymologically these transliterated terms may signify: Light and Right, or Right and Wrong, or Curse and Right. It seems evident, however, that these objects, perhaps inscribed stones, were used for casting or drawing lots for the purpose of securing an expression of God's will (Nm 27:21; Dt 33:8; 1 Sm 14:41; 23:6, 9-12; 28:6; Ez 2:63; Neh 7:65). Wearing the breastpiece, the priest bore the names of Israel in intercession when he went "into the holy place." Equipped with the Urim and Thummim, he was authorized to render divine verdicts for the maintenance of justice and order.

4) 28:31-35 The Robe of the Ephod

28:31 *Robe of the ephod.* An armless tunic was to be worn over—some think under—the ephod (31-35). A fringe at its bottom consisted of alternating pomegranates and bells. The tinkling of the latter was to alert the people that their intermediary was ministering in the holy place. It was also to remind him at every step that his service before God was a fearfully responsible task. Its thoughtless or irreverent performance would result in his death. (Cf. Ml 2:1-9)

5) 28:36-38 The Golden Plate on the Turban

28:36-38 *A plate . . . on the turban.* The fifth badge of the high priest was to be a golden *plate* or frontlet, attached to a *turban* and engraved with the words: *Holy to the Lord.* This inscription epitomized the significance of his office. God, as it were, laid His hand on his forehead as if to declare him a sacrificial offering to the Lord (cf. 29:10; Lv 4:4). Furthermore *any guilt* incurred in the holy offering which the people of Israel *hallow* rested on his head. But functioning as a divinely appointed mediator, he nevertheless bore before his eyes the constant assurance that through his mediation the people's offering was *accepted before the Lord.* The High Priest who actualized what Aaron's tiara symbolized wore as His headdress a crown of thorns. (Mt 27:29)

6) 28:29-43 The Inner Robe, Girdle, and Breeches

28:39 *Coat.* This actually was the long undergarment that reached down to the ankles. No special significance seems to be attached to it and the other more incidental accessories: the *girdle* or sash, the cap, the breeches, the latter for modesty's sake (cf. 20:26). The coat was made of white linen similar to the tunic worn by the Roman emperor in a triumphal procession and by "one like a son of man, clothed with a long robe and with a golden girdle round his breast," standing "in the midst of the lampstands," *the* High Priest. (Rv 1:12-16)

29:1-46 PRIESTHOOD: ORDINATION AND SACRIFICES

29:1 *You shall do.* God had given specifications for a place of meeting with His covenant people (chs. 25—27). In the tabernacle, communion with His unseen presence was to be made possible by intermediaries, identified as such by their holy garments (ch. 28). In the next section (chs. 29—31) the Israelites were told what they *shall do* ritually to express their need of reconciliation with God and by what outward rites their communion with Him, granted out of pure mercy, was to be maintained.

Consecrate . . . as priests. The first ceremonial act established the office of mediatorship between God and Israel: the priesthood (1-9). Aaron and his sons were consecrated to this awesome service by a series of symbolic rites: (a) bringing them "to the door of the tent"—God's declaration of their eligibility (4); (b) washing them—the removal of outward impurities to symbolize the inner cleansing of the stains of guilt (4); (c) clothing them with the holy garments—their equipment for the functions of their office (5-6, 8-9); (d) anointing them—God's claim to them for His holy purposes and the imparting of His enabling Spirit (7); (e) filling their hands—their full investiture with the authority of their office, similar to the prevailing custom according to which an earthly overlord put an object—possibly a stone—into the hands of his vassal to betoken the reception of the covenanted rights. (Cf. 22-28)

29:10 *Bring the bull.* The consecration of the high priest as Israel's representative was to be accompanied by a second ritual act: the offering of three animals (1, 10-37). The first was a "sin offering" of a young *bull* (10-14). Its sacrifice signified that Aaron, a sinful man himself, was in need of reconciliation with God if he was to function acceptably as Israel's intermediary. The removal of his sins was to be symbolized by: (a) the laying of Aaron's *hands upon the head of the bull* to signify the transfer to the sacrificial animal of his guilt and the forfeiture of his right to life (10; also 15); (b) the killing of the bull "before the Lord," the substitute of Aaron's forfeited life (11); (c) the smearing of some of the blood on "the horns of the altar" and the pouring of the remainder at "the base of the altar" to symbolize that God accepted the vicarious death of the animal for the atonement of Aaron's sins (12; see 27:1 note; also Lv 17:11; Ex 12:13; Is 53:12; Heb 12:24); (d) the burning of parts of the carcass on the altar and the burning of the rest "outside the camp," where criminals were executed, to indicate that the obliteration of the transferred guilt was complete. (13, 14; Lv 16:27; 24:14, 23; Heb 13:11-13)

29:15 *One of the rams.* The second sacrifice in the consecration of Israel's representative was an "offering by fire" of the first ram (1, 15-18). After procedures similar to the preceding sin offering, the entire animal was to be burnt on the altar, "a pleasing odor" to the Lord, i.e., a fragrance that placated and pleased God (25, 41; see Gn 8:21 note; Lv 1:9; Nm 28:13). Reconciled with God by the sin offering, God declared that ritual acts of veneration, performed by Aaron in Israel's behalf, were acceptable to Him.

29:19 *The other ram.* Cleansed of sin and declared acceptable to God by the sin offering and the burnt offering (10-18), Israel's highpriestly representative was consecrated by a third ordination rite: the offering of the second ram, "a ram of ordination," literally "ram of fillings" (19-35; note 29:1). Part of its blood was to be dabbed on three members of Aaron's body; the rest was to be thrown against the altar, some of it in turn to be sprinkled on the holy garments together with anointing oil. This use of the blood signified that God laid claim to the high priest's bodily faculties and functions: his hearing, the use of his hands, the movements of his feet. At the same time God endowed them with the ability to perform his sacred duties and recognized his garments as authorized insignia of his holy office (19-21). The disposition of the meat likewise had a symbolic meaning (22-28). Most of it was to be burned on the altar; the breast was assigned to Moses in Aaron's behalf after it had been waved "for a wave offering," i.e., thrust forward as a gesture of presenting it to the Lord. Since both God and the officiant (in the initiatory rite, Moses) partook of the meat, this part of the ceremony signified God's sacramental communion with Israel through its representative. By putting the breast into the hands of Aaron, Moses was to entrust him and his sons with the future performance of such sacrifices (cf. Lv 7:29-36). The High Priest whom Aaron foreshadowed consecrated Himself (Jn 17:19) and offered Himself for the sins of the world, a sacrificial atonement that gave substance to the symbolic ministrations of the high priest of the old covenant. (Heb 13:12; Eph 5:2; Jn 1:29; Mk 10:45; Lk 22:15-20; 1 Co 5:7-8)

29:36 *A sin offering for the altar.* In order to make it "most holy," the altar also was to be dedicated to the Lord by a *sin offering for atonement* (35-37). On the consecrated altar a morning and evening "burnt offering" was to be offered "continually" throughout the coming generations (38-46). As a burnt offering made Aaron and his ministrations in the consecrated tabernacle acceptable to God, so He acknowledged the entire people's admission to communion with Him by accepting their offerings as a "pleasing odor." (41; cf Gn 8:20 note; also Nm 28:3-8)

30:1-10 INCENSE ALTAR

30:1 *Burn incense.* The third kind of activity in which Israel was to engage to signify its covenant relationship to God was the burning of incense (1-10). Arising to the throne of God from a special altar "before the veil" of the holy of holies, the clouds of sweet aroma symbolized that He was pleased to accept the prayers, adorations, and oblations of priest and people (Ps 22:3; 141:2; Is 6:4; Eph 5:2; 2 Co 2:15; Rv 8:3-5). Once a year Aaron and his successors were to "make atonement upon" the horns of the altar "with the blood of the sin offering" (10). This was necessary because only such acts of worship were a "fragrant incense" to God as had been cleansed of the taint of sin by atoning blood. For its fulfillment see Eph 5:2; 2 Co 2:15. For "unholy incense" (9) see Lv 10:1-2.

30:11-16 COVENANT MEMBERSHIP

30:12 *The census.* A fourth means to indicate Israel's participation in the covenant was the payment of the *ransom* shekel by every member who had reached his 20th year, the age of mustering for military duty (11-16; Nm 1:3; 2 Ch 25:5; 1 Sm 11:8; 1 K 20:15). As the priest, the nation's representative, had to be consecrated (29:1-37), so each mature male was to "make atonement" (15) for himself if he was acceptable for membership and service in the covenant community. Failure to comply with this demand exposed the offender to the danger of a *plague* (cf. 32:35 note). The gathered "atonement money" was to be used to maintain "the service of the tent of meeting," enabling every "layman" to be represented in the rites performed there and to become their beneficiary. For the wrong motive in taking a census see 2 Sm 24; 1 Ch 21.

30:17-38 BRONZE LAVER, ANOINTING OIL, INCENSE

30:18 *A laver.* Three material objects were to be used as visible means of Israel's sacramental communion with God: (a) *a laver* or large washbasin (17-21); (b) anointing oil (22-33); (c) holy incense (34-38). The washing of hands and feet in the *laver* was an outward ceremony which signified the need of the inner cleansing of the priest if he was to survive in the performance of his awesome duties.

30:25 *Anointing oil.* The persons and objects over which this *anointing oil* of prescribed ingredients was poured were thereby ritually dedicated to God and made visible means and bearers of grace. (22-33)

30:35 *Incense.* The third material which the people were to use in order to express their covenant communion with God was *incense.* "According to its composition" of specified ingredients it was not to be used for any other purpose except to be placed "before the testimony in the tent of meeting," i.e., on the altar of incense in the holy place to be burned there (1-10). For the purpose of this oblation cf. 30:1 note.

31:1-11 SELECTION OF WORKMEN

31:2 *Called by name.* Through Moses the people had been told: "You shall make" the tabernacle with its "furniture" and the holy garments. However, their actual construction and fabrication was assigned to two divinely appointed men: Bezalel of the tribe of Judah and Oholiab of the tribe of Dan (1-11). For their task they were filled "with the Spirit of God." Their highly skillful "ability" and "craftsmanship" was not to be used for the gratification of their vanity but, under Moses' supervision, was to be put at God's disposal for the promotion of His honor (cf. 20:24 note). "Able men," no doubt selected by Moses, were to serve as their assistants.

31:12-17 SABBATH: COVENANT SIGN

31:13 *My sabbaths.* The *sign* of God's presence and communion with His people was the keeping of the Sabbath, already instituted in the Decalog (12-17; cf. 20:8 note). While the other symbolic ties with God required activity by the people, this outward testimony of their "perpetual covenant" relationship with God demanded their surcease from action. Devoting one day out of seven of their Creator's gift of time to Him, they were to be privileged to partake of the rest and refreshment that He Himself enjoys, a foretaste and promise of the "sabbath rest" that "remains . . . for the people of God." (Heb 4:9-10)

31:18 TABLES OF STONE

31:18 *Two tables.* All of God's *speaking with* Moses on Sinai's heights in the "devouring fire" and ominous cloud of His glory (24:12-18) was epitomized and engraved on two *tables of stone.* This miraculously inscripturated Word by *the finger of God* (Lk 11:20) preserved in man's written form of communication what He had revealed in the fading sounds of human speech. (Cf. also 24:4; Mt 5:17-18)

32:1—34:35 The Covenant Broken and Renewed

32:1-6 THE COVENANT GOD DEGRADED

32:1 *Moses delayed.* The basic terms of the covenant had been accepted by the Israelites (24:3, 7, 8). But while Moses received additional instructions on how it was to be acknowledged and implemented (chs. 25—31), the people lost faith and broke it at a crucial point (32:1—34:35). In direct violation of 20:4 they demanded a tangible representation of the deity, fashioned to conform to their notions and subject to their manipulation.

Gods. Although the noun is in the plural form, also when referring to the true God, the singular, "a god," is probably preferable in vv. 1-6 as well as in 1 K 12:28. In spite of their disobedience to a direct command, the Israelites apparently had not lapsed into polytheism, but in a panic of doubt wanted an image of the deity who had brought them up out of Egypt. (4)

The man. Their faith attached itself to a human being and gave him credit for their deliverance rather than to the unseen hand of God. (4)

32:4 *A molten calf.* This masculine noun is more exactly rendered "bullock" since in its feminine form it denotes a heifer. In Israel's environment the bull was a common representation of the virile power of the deity. In the final analysis therefore and despite their protestation of loyalty to the true God, the Israelites had exchanged Him for an idol.

32:6 *Rose up to play.* This was no innocent game. The worship of the molten deity appealed to their senses and degenerated into a sensuous display of their passions. Orgiastic dances frequently were included in the rites of idolatrous worship (25; 1 Co 10:6-8; Acts 7:41; Ps 106:19-23). All deification of perverted human impulses is a surrender to the degrading slavery of bestial instincts.

32:7-14 ISRAEL SPARED AT MOSES' INTERCESSION

32:10 *Consume them.* What Israel did was no peccadillo; in defying God they had "corrupted themselves," lit. made themselves deserving of destruction. Grace received and spurned heightens responsibility and aggravates the punishment of its abuse (Lk 12:47-48; Heb 10:28). Having disposed of the apostate people, God, who could have raised children for Abraham from stones (Mt 3:9), offered to make a new beginning with an individual and to make Moses *a great nation.*

32:11 *Besought the Lord.* It is a mystery, unfathomable as God Himself is, that He should be persuaded by the remonstrances of fallible man to alter His announced course of action and to turn from wrath to compassion. Moses was the great intercessor of the OT (8:9; 9:28; 10:17; Nm 11:2; 14:13-19; 16:22; 21:7; Dt 9:25-29; cf. Jer 15:1; Ps 99:6; 106:23). Affirming his solidarity with the evildoers when God disowned them and called them his ("your") people, he insisted that they still were God's *(thy)* chosen nation. He appealed to God's promise to the patriarchs (13) and His commitment to the former slaves of Egypt. Faith in God's mercy even emboldened Moses to address God in the imperatives later used by the prophets in speaking to recalcitrant Israel: "Turn . . . repent . . . remember." God is not an impersonal principle or inflexible fate. The personal, living God delights to be overcome by the brazen impudence of faith. (Cf. Gn 32:26 note)

32:14 *Repented.* Cf. Gn 6:3 note; also Ju 2:18; Ps 106:45; Am 7:3; Jon 3:10; Jl 2:13; Zch 8:14. The Servant of God, of whom Moses was a type, "poured out his soul to death . . . and made intercession for the transgressors." (Is 53:12; Ro 8:34; Heb 7:25; Lk 23:34; 22:32)

32:15-20 THE APOSTATE PEOPLE REBUKED BY MOSES

32:15 *Went down.* The amnesty that Moses had wrung from God would go into effect only if the Israelites accepted it by penitently turning to God. But Joshua reported that they were still "singing" out their wanton chant of self-gratification.

32:19 *Broke them.* When Moses heard and saw that the people had sunken to such depths of spiritual and moral turpitude, his *anger burned hot* (cf. 9) in such intense indignation that he shattered the "tables of the testimony" (31:18). Thereby he dramatically proclaimed that God's gracious union with the people had been broken and that God's judgment upon them, as sanctioned in the covenant, would take its course.

32:20 *Took the calf.* In order derisively to demonstrate the impotence of this fabrication of human hands, Moses *burnt* the wooden image, overlaid with gold, and *ground* the metal *to powder* (Ps 115:3-8; Is 40:18-19; 44:9-17; 45:20; Jer 10:3-5). By scattering the shattered idol on the water, the absolute necessity for existence in the desert, he furthermore visualized that Israel had poisoned its only source of life, which God's revelation supplied. (Jer 2:13; 14:3; Ps 36:8-9; Jn 4:14)

32:21-24 AARON REBUKED; HIS EXCUSES

32:21 *Said to Aaron.* Moses first of all called to account the appointed guardian of Israel's spiritual purity. While admitting his guilt, Aaron, however, vainly sought to shift the responsibility for the crime to the people and to some uncanny process by which the calf "came out" of the melting pot. (23, 24)

32:25-29 REBELS SLAIN BY LEVITES

32:25 *Broken loose.* Those who were (lit.) "out of control" and therefore incapable and unwilling to cast off the spell of their frenzied delusion were to be slain by such as were willing penitently to return to "the Lord's side." (25-29; Dt 33:9-10; Lk 14:26)

32:29 *Ordained yourselves.* Lit. "filled your hands," i.e., found worthy of being entrusted with "service of the Lord" (cf. 29:24). The Levites were made the recipients of God's "blessing," promised in His covenant with Abraham (Gn 12:2-3) and with the patriarchal descendants at Sinai. (Nm 3:6 ff.; 8:14 ff.; Ml 2:4-5; see also Nm 25:11-13)

32:30-35 MOSES' SELF-SACRIFICE REJECTED; REAPPOINTMENT TO LEAD ISRAEL

32:30 *Atonement.* The Lord "had repented of the evil" of exterminating the entire people (14). But their *sin* (the noun or verb occurs eight times in these verses) demanded atonement. Moses proposed to expiate their guilt at the cost of being blotted out of God's "book," i.e., being cut off from His salvation (Ro 9:2-3). God rejected his offer of self-sacrifice (33; Ps 49:7). The atonement by Moses and all OT intermediaries, themselves in need of forgiveness, remained unsatisfactory and awaited the effectual expiation by the sinless Bearer of the world's guilt. (Is 53:6-12; Jn 1:29)

32:35 *A plague.* Lit. "the Lord smote the people," i.e., He inflicted punishment.

33:1-23 ISRAEL'S RESTORATION TO COVENANT COMMUNION

1) 33:1-6 Former Covenant Promises Repeated and Modified

33:1 *Go up hence.* Although Israel had broken the covenant, God would keep the promise made to the patriarchs: He would give their descendants the land occupied by the Canaanites (1-6; 23:23-31). But Israel's folly had provoked a rift in God's immediate fellowship with His people. He would not Himself "go up among" them (23:20-22) but "an angel shall go before them." (2; 32:34)

33:4 *Mourned.* In order to show the sincerity of their mourning over these *evil tidings* and outwardly to acknowledge their guilt in breaking the covenant, the Israelites were not to wear their "ornaments from Mount Horeb onward."

2) 33:7-11 God's Guidance Restricted to the Mediator of the Covenant

33:7 *The tent . . . outside the camp.* God's withdrawal from their "midst" (25:8; 29:45) was visualized by restricting His communication with Israel to Moses' tent *outside the camp, far off from the camp* (7-11). Here He would "speak to Moses" from "the pillar of cloud," "as a man speaks to his friend." Only through an intermediary could Israel be in contact with God. The way back to God for Israel and all men was not made a full reality until the Mediator of the new covenant came, who was not merely God's "friend," but His own Son. (Jn 10:7-18)

3) 33:12-16 The Mediator's Request for a Visible Manifestation of God's Presence

33:12 *Let me know.* In his conversation with God, Moses remonstrated with Him and sought assurance for his own person that he had *found favor* in God's sight. He wanted to be certain that God knew his name, i.e., had established a personal relationship with him and through him with the people. To dispel his misgivings God was to reveal His "ways": His hidden plan for the future of His people. (Cf. Jn 14:6-11)

4) 33:17-23 The Request Granted but Limited to Human Endurance

33:18 *Thy glory.* Not satisfied with the verbal promise of God's presence (14, 17), Moses pressed on for a visible manifestation of His *glory.* Because Moses was not prompted by idle curiosity, his request was granted to the extent that sinful man can endure to "see" God's "face." God indeed spoke to him "face to face," i.e., as person, but not even Moses could see God and live (20; Acts 9:9; Is 6:2-5; 33:14; Ps 42:2; 17:15; 63:2; 84:7). Reminding His disturbed servant of the revelation of His ongoing "goodness" in His name (I am that I am; 3:13-14), God permitted him to see His "back," i.e., the reflection of His glory that has "passed by" (cf. 1 K 19:11-12). This mysterious experience of Moses reached its fulness when men beheld God's glory, veiled in the human flesh of His Son, and beholding "with unveiled face" the glory of the Lord are "changed into his likeness from one degree of glory to another." (2 Co 3:18)

34:1-35 RENEWAL OF THE COVENANT

1) 34:1-10 New Tables of Stone

34:2 *Come up.* Moved by Moses' intercession, God on Mt. Sinai formally renewed the broken relationship with His people by: (a) writing upon tables, now cut by Moses, "the words that were on the first tables" (1-4; cf. 32:15-16); (b) proclaiming for the fourth time "the name of the Lord," the revelation of His enduring mercy and righteousness (5-9; 3:14; 20:2; 33:19); (c) binding Himself anew to His previous covenant. (10)

2) 34:11-28 Salient Terms of the Renewed Covenant; the Covenant Recorded

34:11 *Observe.* What Israel was told to do in order to maintain its mended relationship with God restated and underscored some of the salient features of the so-called Book of the Covenant (20:22—23:33). The change of the order of the laws and the omissions of large sections of the previously recorded legislation arise from the circumstances of the new situation. Israel's recent perversion of the worship of the only true God necessitated a repeated emphasizing of pertinent aspects of its worship life: (a) a warning against idolatry and the making of "molten gods" (12-17); (b) God's unreserved claim to Israel's entire life, its time and its possessions (18-24); (c) the observance of proper ritual procedure in offering sacrifices (25-26). Israel's later history proved how necessary the repeated inculcation of these requirements was.

3) 34:29-35 God's Glory Reflected on the Face of the Renewed Covenant's Mediator

34:29 *His face shone.* Moses' authority did not derive from his own person. He served merely as the transmitter of God's Word. *Because he had been talking with God* on the mountain, there was an afterglow of light on his face, a reflection of the glory of the divine origin of his message so bright that he covered his face with a veil. He had to do so also subsequently whenever he "went in before the Lord." Paul referred to this covering of God's brightness and asserted that "only through Christ is it taken away." Faith in Him unveils the glory of the "whole fullness of deity" that bodily dwelt in Him. (2 Co 3:12-18; Cl 2:9; Jn 1:14; 2 Co 4:6; 1 Jn 1:1-4; 1 Co 13:12; Rv 1:12-18; Acts 26:12-14)

35:1—39:43 Directives for the Maintenance of Covenant Communion Carried Out

35:1—38:31 THE TABERNACLE

1) 35:1—36:7 Materials Furnished by the People

35:2 *A holy sabbath.* In Moses' vision of the tabernacle on Mt. Sinai, the Sabbath law was the final capstone of God's covenant ordinances (31:14-17); in transmitting the divine directions to the people (4-19), Moses put it at the head of the subsequent instructions (1-3). It was accorded these prominent positions, also in Israel's later history, because it is the alpha-and-omega purpose in erecting a place of God's reconciling dwelling with men. Not a means of meriting God's favor, it rather epitomized symbolically His ultimate design: to redeem creation from its groaning in futility and travail by affording it an opportunity to share in the Creator's Sabbath rest and to restore man to the pristine tranquility of paradise. (Ro 8:22; Heb 4:9-10; Mt 11:28; Rv 21:3)

35:5 *A generous heart.* Cf. 25:2 note. The materials for the construction of the tabernacle were to be furnished by a freewill offering, contributed by "every one whose heart stirred him" (21; cf. 25:2 note). Israel responded generously to the point of superabundance. (20-29)

36:3 *They received.* The gifts of the people, received by the authorized workmen, were "sufficient to do all the work, and more" (2-7). When the hearts of men are moved by the Spirit of God, they overflow with liberality. (Ps 116:12; Cl 2:6-7; 3:15; 1 Co 15:57-58; 2 Co 8:3; 9:13-15; 1 Ti 1:12-14)

2) 36:8-38 Building the Structural Parts

36:8 *Made the tabernacle.* The materials and parts of the tabernacle and the various garments of the high priest are enumerated several times after their specification had been given to Moses on Mt. Sinai. Briefly mentioned in the report of the accumulated materials (35:4-9), they are repeated in greater detail in the following section which records their fabrication. Other summaries appear at various points: shortly before the work was completed (39:32-43); when Moses is directed to erect the assembled parts (40:2-9); when he complied with the directive (40:17-33). Like so many hammer blows these seemingly tiresome repetitions first of all drive home the tireless mercy of God, who deigns to use these profane materials to symbolize His presence and favor. Simultaneously the people are forcefully reminded that the gift of God's gracious and reconciled presence must be apprehended by an unremitting obedience of faith, demonstrated by unceasing labors in the production of the tabernacle. As it gradually emerged in its completed form, "the tent of meeting" gave the people tangible assurance of their access to a gracious God and of their communion with Him. The frequent reiteration of such clauses as "as the Lord had commanded Moses" (e.g., nine times in ch. 39) was to eliminate any doubt that God wanted His grace to flow to the people in channels of His own designing and none other. To tamper with His appointed means of grace or arrogantly to devise others would result in Israel's loss of the state of grace.

Ten curtains. In recording the construction of the tabernacle its parts are listed in the reverse order of their previous enumeration (cf. 25:10 note). Beginning with the outer housing and proceeding to its inner components, the sequence here is as follows: (a) the tent and its coverings (8-19; 26:1-14); (b) the golden inner sanctuary (20-34; 26:15-29); (c) the dividing veil. (35-38; 26:31-37)

3) 37:1—38:20 Making the Furnishings; Constructing the Outer Court

37:1 *The ark.* The structural framework of the tabernacle completed, it was supplied with the necessary furnishing, made by Bezalel: (a) the ark of the covenant (1-9; cf. 25:10-20); (b) the table of the bread of the Presence (10-16; cf. 25:23-30); (c) the golden lampstand (17-24; cf. 25:31-39); (d) the altar of incense. (25-29; cf. 30:1-5)

38:1 *The altar of burnt offering.* The chapter division interrupts the enumeration of the furnishing of the tabernacle begun in the previous chapter. To the preceding list are added: (e) *the altar of burnt offering* and the laver (1-8; cf. 27:1-8; 30:17-21); (f) the outer court. (9-20; cf. 27:9-19)

38:8 *Mirrors.* Before the use of glass was known, *mirrors* were made of polished brass.

4) 38:21-31 Accounting of Expenditures

38:21 *The sum of the things.* The report of the building of the tabernacle is followed by an accounting of the materials which had been "offered by the people" for its construction (21-

31). *Counted . . . under the direction of Ithamar, the son of Aaron,* they were put at the disposal of the craftsmen, Bezalel and Oholiab. The gold from "the offering" (cf. 35:5) was used to embellish the inner "sanctuary" (24); the silver, raised by a poll tax (30:11-16), to cast "the bases of the sanctuary, and the bases of the veil" (25-28); the bronze, also "contributed" (35:5), to make those objects that came in contact with fire, e.g., the bronze altar (29-31). It is difficult to estimate the total value of these metals in view of the changing purchasing power of monetary systems. For one of the sources of this wealth see 12:35-36.

38:26 *Six hundred and three thousand, five hundred and fifty men.* For this total of the census see Numbers, Introduction.

39:1-31 FABRICATION OF PRIESTLY VESTMENTS

39:1 *The holy garments.* After a brief accounting of the metals used to construct the tabernacle (38:21-31), the account proceeds to describe how Bezalel and Oholiab made the sacred vestments of the high priest out of the materials likewise furnished by the people (35:4 ff.): (a) the ephod and the shoulder pieces with the stones bearing the names of the 12 tribes (2-7; cf. 28:5-14); (b) the breastplate with 12 stones "according to the names of the sons of Israel" (8-21; cf. 28:15-30); (c) the robe of the ephod (22-26; cf. 28:31-35); (d) the coats, the turban, the breeches, the girdle (27-29; cf. 28:40-43); (e) the plate of the crown. (30, 31; cf. 28:36)

As the Lord had commanded. Added seven times as the production of the highpriestly garments and equipment proceeded (1, 5, 7, 21, 26, 29, 31), this qualifying clause declared emphatically that the office of the high priest and his mediating ministrations, symbolized by his vestments, had divine sanction. See also 36:8 note. After the High Priest of the new covenant effected reconciliation with God, of which the ministrations of the Aaronite priesthood were but a shadow, the latter's symbolical garb is likewise no longer required. But the new covenant is just as insistent that communion with God depends solely on His forgiving mercy, available to man only by divinely prescribed means of grace. There is no other word of salvation except the Gospel of Jesus Christ; sacramental union with God cannot be effected by rites of human devising but must conform to the imperatives: Baptize!—Do this in remembrance of Me! (Mt 18:18-20; Gl 1:6-9; 2 Th 1:8-10; 1 Co 11:23-26)

39:32-43 THE TABERNACLE AND THE VESTMENTS INSPECTED AND BLESSED

39:32 *Was finished.* The enumeration of the various parts and contents of the tabernacle is bracketed at its beginning (32) and end (43) by the note that the work had been completed *according to all that the Lord had commanded* (cf. 36:8 note). When God reviewed the completed heavens and earth at creation, He saw that they were "very good" and blessed the day when He "rested . . . from all his work" (Gn 1:31—2:2). So Moses, after he "saw all the work" to establish a place where God deigned to dwell in order to give His people His Sabbath rest from sin's turmoil, "blessed" the completed results of their labors.

40:1-38 The Dedicated Tent of Meeting Filled with the Glory of God

40:1-15 COMMAND TO CONSECRATE THE SANCTUARY AND ITS OFFICIANTS

40:2 *On the first day of the first month.* The month of Israel's liberation from Egypt is meant (12:2, 6, 12). After the arrival at Mt. Sinai "on the [following] third new moon" (19:1), Moses had spent two periods of 40 days—almost 3 months—on the mountain (24:18; 34:28). Hence a little over 7 months of the first year had remained for the construction of the tabernacle and the making of the highpriestly garments. Parts of both are once more enumerated. (Cf. 36:8 note)

40:9 *Anoint . . . and consecrate.* Each of these imperatives with slight variations occurs seven times in this section (1-15). Places and objects—profane in themselves—were to be specially marked as outward symbols of communion with the holy God; persons—sinful themselves—were to be designated as fit for the performance of their hallowing office. This consecration was to be accomplished by pouring *anointing oil* over them. It demonstrated visibly that the Holy One had condescended to use these unholy agencies and agents as the means of His saving grace.

40:16-33 PLACEMENT OF FURNISHINGS

40:16 *Thus did Moses.* The report of Moses' compliance with God's command on the appointed day (1-15) contains the last catalog of the objects to be consecrated (16-33). Interspersed with the note that Moses did "as the Lord had commanded," it reiterates in final, concentrated form that a healthy relationship with God is possibly only when He mercifully takes the initiative and when man seeks it in reliance on His enabling Word. For the same reason almost every object "in the tent of meeting," where God's communion with His people was to be realized, is designated, with tireless insistence, as a prescribed component of His "tabernacle," literally His "dwelling" (17, 18, 19, 21, 22, 24, 28, 29, 33). All required preparations were completed for the advent of God's life-giving presence among His people.

40:34-38 THE GLORY OF THE LORD IN THE TABERNACLE

40:34 *The glory of the Lord.* The closing verses of this book record how the Lord's glory entered His dwelling place in the visible form of a cloud which *covered the tent of meeting* (cf. 1 K 8:10; Eze 10:18 ff.; 43:1-4). Reconciled with God by the blood of atonement sprinkled on the mercy seat of the ark of the covenant (25:22; 30:6) and committed to respond in faith by a holy life, summarized on two tables of stone within the ark (25:21; 31:18), the Israelites could once more commit themselves to the guidance of their covenant God "throughout all their journeys." (36; 13:20-22; 33:14-17)

Epilog. The tabernacle was "a shadow of what is to come" (Cl 2:17; Heb 8:5). It was the temporary symbol of the presence of the "Lord of heaven and earth," who "does not live in shrines made by man" (Acts 17:24; 1 K 8:27-30). Implementing His eternal plan of salvation, this preliminary housing of God pointed beyond itself to Him "of whom Moses in the law and also the prophets wrote, Jesus of Nazareth, the son of Joseph" (Jn 1:45). When in the fulness of time "the Word became flesh and dwelt (literally "tabernacled") among us," "the whole fulness of deity dwells bodily" in Him (Jn 1:14; Cl 2:9). "Greater than the temple," destroyed for our transgressions and raised again on the third day for our justification (Mt 12:6; Jn 2:19; Ro 4:25), He is the fulfillment of God's promise: "Here I will meet with you" (25:8; 29:43). Because He dwelt in "the earthly tent we live in" (2 Co 5:1), we not only have access to a reconciled God through His sacrificial life and death but can also be "built into a spiritual house, to be a holy priesthood, to offer spiritual sacrifices acceptable to God through Jesus Christ" (1 Ptr 2:5; 1 Co 3:16; Jer 31:33 f.; Is 54:13). This temple of which He is the "cornerstone" (Eph 2:20-22; 1 Ptr 2:6; Is 28:16), is still in the process of being built (Ro 11:25; Jn 10:16; Jer 3:16-18). When it is completed and the Builder comes "with the clouds of heaven" (Mk 14:62; Acts 1:11; Rv 21:4), "the dwelling of God ...with men" will be consummated no longer in a material symbol of His presence but in "a new heaven and a new earth" in which "the Lord God the Almighty and the Lamb" is the temple (Rv 21:1, 3, 22). Longing for the day of this perfected communion with God and the surcease from the "tears" of their desert pilgrimage, the redeemed of Israel pray for His advent: "Amen. Come, Lord Jesus!" (Rv 22:20)

LEVITICUS

INTRODUCTION

Content

The name given to this book by the Septuagint and the Vulgate is an adequate summary of its contents if the term Leviticus is understood in the wider sense to mean a compendium of ritualistic practices performed and supervised by an authorized personnel of the tribe of Levi. Although every Israelite participated directly or indirectly in the prescribed rites, certain ceremonial functions were reserved for Moses' brother, Aaron, and his sons of the tribe of Levi (Ex 2:1). Some members of this Levitical family were chosen to be priests, one of whom, in turn, became the chief officiant, the high priest. But "all the sons of Levi" were charged with assisting in the performance of ceremonial rites (Ex 32:28-29) and with instructing the people in the law of the Lord. (2 Ch 17:7-9)

The Book of Leviticus is the logical continuation of the Book of Exodus. "The glory of the Lord," which had filled the completed tent of meeting, was unapproachable even for Moses (Ex 40:34-35). How could Israel "stand before" such a God and live in communion with Him? How could Israel be a "holy nation" (Ex 19:6) and meet the demands of a holy life, set forth in the Decalog (Ex 20) and elaborated in the laws of the covenant (Ex 21—23)? Leviticus not only repeats the demand of holiness for covenant fellowship with God (Ex 19:6; Lv 11:45), it also views, in the perspective of holiness, all ordinances and provisions for His dwelling among His people and their meeting with Him. Therefore it is not surprising to find the word "holy" some 90 times on its pages. It also stresses that the means of attaining holiness is atonement (occurring over 40 times). Expiation for sin, symbolized by the vicarious sacrifice of animals, removed the barrier between the holy God and an unholy people. Acceptance of this covenant mercy committed Israel to consecrate all aspects of life to God in accordance with His holy will. It was to respond in holy obedience to standards of moral behavior and a variety of ceremonial regulations.

Leviticus does not record any movements of Israel toward the Promised Land. The setting does not change from the locale of the end of Exodus: at the door of the tabernacle "at (rather than "on") Mount Sinai." (1:1; 27:34)

Since we are no longer required to conform to the outward forms of holiness set forth in Leviticus, we may be inclined to find the reading of these provisions of the old covenant unrewarding. But it should be of more than passing interest for two reasons. In the first place, it plays an important role in the divine plan of salvation. It was God's way of educating His people by concrete object lessons in what they needed to know for their salvation. By a profusion of outward ceremonies He made it unmistakably clear what sin is and why it constitutes the barrier between rebellious men and the holy God. Unless it is removed by vicarious atonement, unholy man cannot appear in God's presence, much less live in a wholesome communion with Him. Making animals the substitutionary bearers and expiators of sin was a symbolic foreshadowing of what was to become a reality through the atoning life and death of that Son of Israel who was also the Son of God.

In the second place, accepting by faith the imputed holiness of Him who died and rose for us constitutes us a "holy nation," consecrated to the will of the Redeemer by a self-abnegation and a surrender of all aspects of life to Him that is as total, unreserved, and uncompromising as the holiness expected of Israel (1 Ptr 2:9; 1 Jn

1:7-9; Heb 9:11-14). Relieved of the outward forms of Israel's ritual, we cannot but demonstrate that we are not our own by heeding the directives: "As he who called you is holy, be holy yourselves in all your conduct; since it is written: 'You shall be holy, for I am holy' . . . conduct yourselves with fear throughout the time of your exile. . . . Offer spiritual sacrifices acceptable to God. . . . Whether you eat or drink, or whatever you do, do all to the glory of God." (1 Ptr 1:15-17; 2:5; 1 Co 10:31)

Authorship

Leviticus does not state explicitly that Moses recorded its contents. It does, however, consistently claim that it is of Mosaic origin. Beginning with the first verse, it asserts some 30 times: "The Lord said to Moses." Its divine authority is underscored by the repeated declaration (some 40 times): "I am the Lord" or "I am the Lord, your God." Adherents of the source hypothesis (see Genesis, Introduction) interpret these statements as attempts to give Mosaic sanction to later legislative developments. Because of stylistic and conceptual peculiarities it is regarded as a separate code, produced about a thousand years after Moses and incorporated into a final compilation of the Pentateuch. Because it is said to represent a Priestly tradition, this strand of the five books of Moses is designated "P." Its threads are traced to material beginning at Ex 25 and continuing to Nm 10. Even parts of the P code are said to have existed at one time as separate pieces of literature, especially the so-called Holiness Code, which comprises chs. 17—26.

OUTLINE

I. 1:1—16:34 Holy Communion Expressed by Holy Rites
   - A. 1:1—15:33 Rites for the People and Their Representatives
   - B. 16:1-34 The Day of Atonement: Sanctifying Rites by the High Priest

II. 17:1—27:34 Holy Communion Maintained by Laws of Holiness
   - A. 17:1—20:27 Precepts for a Holy People
   - B. 21:1—22:33 Precepts for a Holy Priesthood
   - C. 23:1-44 Precepts for Keeping Holy Days
   - D. 24:1-9 Precepts Regarding Sacramental Elements
   - E. 24:10-23 Prescribed Penalties for the Desecration of Holiness
   - F. 25:1-55 Precepts for the Observance of Holy Years
   - G. 26:1-46 Blessings of Holy Communion; Punishments for Its Violation
   - H. 27:1-34 Voluntary Expressions of Holy Communion

1:1—16:34 HOLY COMMUNION EXPRESSED BY HOLY RITES

1:1—15:33 Rites for the People and Their Representatives

1:1—10:20 FIVE OFFERINGS: POSITIVE EXPRESSIONS OF HOLY COMMUNION

1) 1:1—6:7 Participation by People and Priests

1:1 *Called Moses.* After "the glory of the Lord filled the tabernacle" at Mt. Sinai, the people were told through Moses how this fabrication of their hands could serve as a "tent of meeting" with the holy God (Ex 40:34-35; Lv 7:38; 25:1; 27:34; Nm 7:89). Actually God's holiness constitutes an antithesis to fellowship and union; it stresses His separation from everything that is incompatible with His very being: His transcendence over all the works of His hands and His untainted perfection. Because God is holy, communion with a people unholy in sin is as incongruous as mixing fire and water. In the following chapters the Israelites were told that God had made provisions to enable them to become a "holy nation" and so to fulfill the requirements of meeting with Him. (Ex 19:6; Lv 19:2).

1:2 *An offering.* In the NT the Hebrew word used here appears in its transliterated form: "Corban" (Mk 7:11). It is a comprehensive term and etymologically denotes anything that is "brought to" the Lord. In the following chapters five different kinds of "Corbans" are distinguished.

1:3 *Burnt offering.* The term for the first kind of "Corban" literally denotes a "going up" completely in flames and smoke (9; 1-17; 6:8-13; Gn 8:20; 22:22; Ex 10:25; 18:12). It is therefore called also a "whole burnt offering" (Dt 13:16; 33:10). By bringing this sacrifice anyone who presumed to stand *before the Lord* confessed his need of a means "to make atonement for him" (see note on "mercy seat," Ex 25:17). He had sins which necessitated "covering" (atonement) from God's sight; without it his life was exposed to the death that was inflicted vicariously on the sacrificial animal. He had symbolically transferred his sins to the victim by laying his hand upon its head (4; Ex 29:19-21). When his substitute's blood was thrown "against the altar" and its carcass was consumed by "an offering of fire," he was "accepted before the Lord." By this "whole burnt offering" the reconciled offerer at the same time portrayed his total consecration to the holy God. (Ro 12:1)

1:9 *A pleasing odor.* Cf. Gn 8:21 note; also Ex 29:18, 25, 41.

1:10 *Without blemish.* The sacrificial animals had to be male specimens without physical defects. But even "the blood of bulls and goats" without any blemishes did not suffice to "take away sins"; they merely were types of Him "who knew no sin" and was "holy and unstained," but was made "to be sin," "so that in him we might become the righteousness of God." (Heb 10:4-7; 7:26; 2 Co 5:20-21; 1 Ptr 1:18-19)

1:14 *Birds.* The range in cost of the sacrificial animal from cattle down to birds adjusted the requirements of the burnt offering to the economic status of the offerer (cf. 5:7). Even the poorest could afford *turtle doves* or *young pigeons.*

2:1 *Cereal offering.* The Hebrew word for the second kind of "Corban" is simply "a gift." To distinguish it from animal sacrifices, translators have added the modifier "cereal" or "meal." The KJV "meat offering" is misleading in modern English. It has an even wider meaning than "Corban" (cf. 1:2 note) and may be applied to such secular transactions as the giving of tribute (Ju 3:15; 1 K 4:21). As a religious term it is used comprehensively to designate anything presented to the Lord including animal sacrifices (1 Sm 26:19; Gn 4:4). But in its usually restricted meaning it refers to an oblation consisting chiefly of flour. While the burnt offering represented the sacrifice of man's lifeblood, the cereal offering symbolized that also man's "staff of life" and the fruits of his labors were consecrated to the Lord.

2:2 *Memorial portion.* The cereal offering could consist of grain that had not been baked or boiled. A handful of it, mixed with oil and frankincense, was to be taken by the priest and burned on the altar, *an offering by fire, a pleasing odor to the Lord* (cf. Gn 8:21 note). This portion is called a *memorial.* The Hebrew word occurs only in connection with the cereal offering (ch. 2; 6:15; Nm 5:26) and with the bread of the Presence (24:7) and contains a root that normally has the meaning "to remember." If this derivation is correct, the burning of this portion expressed the purpose of this offering: to remind God of His covenant promises and to implore Him to let these tokens of inner consecration be acceptabe to Him. (Ex 2:24; 6:5; Lv 26:42, 45; Lk 1:72; Acts 10:4)

2:4 *Baked.* When the flour was baked or cooked (7), a part of it was likewise to be a "memorial portion" (9) and was to be burned on the altar, "a most holy part . . . to the Lord" (3, 10). The remainder of the cereal offering was for "Aaron and his sons."

2:11 *No leaven nor any honey.* Because food containing fermenting ingredients such as yeast and honey would more readily spoil and become putrid, it was not to be offered on the altar (12). This restriction did not apply to every kind of offering. (23:17-18)

2:13 *With salt.* In order to conteract corruption such as caused by leaven and honey, the cereal offering was to be seasoned with salt, called *the salt of the covenant.* In ancient times a relationship of reciprocated amity was recognized to exist when two or more people joined in eating salt. (Nm 18:19; 2 Ch 13:5)

2:14 *First fruits.* The Hebrew word is different from the one rendered "first fruits" in 12. This section gives additional directions for the treatment of *new grain* that has just been taken *from fresh ears.* Further instructions in this matter are given the priests in 6:14-23.

3:1 *A sacrifice of peace offering.* The word *sacrifice* indicates that this "Corban" required the slaughtering of animals. The phrase *of peace offering* (only one word in Hebrew and usually in the plural) identifies its purpose. The basic meaning of peace is the opposite of every kind of brokenness and incompleteness. Peace supplies what is lacking for wholesomeness of body and soul; it puts together the disjointed pieces of a shattered relationship into a harmonious whole; it may involve compensation or expiation to fill in the disintegrating gaps. A sacrifice of peace offering was the ritual demonstration that the broken relationship between the holy God and unholy Israel had been healed. As was the case in the burnt offering (ch. 1), the prescribed procedure signified first of all that sin, the cause of the disruption, had been removed by (a) transferring it to the animal (cf. 1:3 note); (b) throwing the blood of restitution against the altar. Then Israel was given the privilege of accepting and celebrating its reconciliation with God in a meal of holy communion. God partook of it by accepting the "food offered by fire to the Lord" (11) as "a pleasing odor" (5). The eatable parts of the animal that were not God's portion were Israel's share in this fellowship banquet. (Cf. 7:11-18)

4:3 *A sin offering.* The prescriptions for the preceding offerings spoke only in general terms of the barrier between the holy God and the unholy people that must be eliminated by atoning rites, constituting a "pleasing [i.e., assuaging] odor to the Lord" (1:13; 2:2; 3:5). The next two offerings prescribe what is to be done to establish communion with God when it has been disrupted by specific kinds of "sin" (4:1—5:13) or "guilt" (5:14—6:7). The terms "sin offering" and "guilt offering" denote the violation of the covenant, for which atonement and restitution were to be made, rather than the nature of the offering itself. Because an infraction of God's will by *sin* as well as by *guilt* results in the same consequences, a breach of covenant relations, the terms themselves appear in some instances to be used interchangeably (see, e.g., 5:6). Sin offerings were specifically designed to provide expiation for doing "unwittingly . . . the things which the Lord had commanded not to be done" (2-3, 13, 22, 27; 5:3) in the prescribed ritual of worship. The meaning of the adverb "unwittingly" (literally "in error") is extended to include also such infractions of the law as are not done with "a high hand," i.e., not defiantly but in weakness or without malice or forethought. (5:1-4; Nm 15:30)

4:4 *The bull.* Every sin offering required the slaughtering of a substitutionary animal. But the kind of sacrificial animal and the rites of atonement varied according to specified circumstances. Account was taken of the offender and the kind of misdeed committed. Procedures are therefore given separately for cases involving (a) the priest (1-12); (b) the whole people (13-21); (c) the ruler (22-26); (d) one of the common people (27-35); (e) specific ritual and moral violations (5:1-6); (f) the poor. (5:7-12)

4:5 *The anointed priest.* The priest is not called *anointed* anywhere else in the OT except in this chapter (3, 5, 16). Because he had been especially consecrated to perform holy functions, his failure to conform to all requirements of his office was a very grave offense. It not only disqualified him as God's representative but also brought "guilt on the people" whom he represented. His sin was expiated by rites similar to those prescribed for the burnt offering (1:1-17) and the peace offering (3:1-17). They differed in two respects: the entire animal was not burned on the altar (burnt offering) nor were parts of it to be eaten (peace offering). After the fat and kidneys had been burned on the altar, the rest of the carcass was to be carried "forth outside the camp to a clean place" and there burned "on a fire of wood." (11-12; 6:30; Nm 5:3; 15:35; Heb 13:12)

4:13 *The whole congregation.* Just as the action of the anointed priest affected all the people, so the solidarity of the congregation demanded expiation if one of its members *commits a sin unwittingly*. Therefore "the elders" confessed the corporate sin and transferred it to the sacrificial bull (14-15). The slaying of the animal was to be followed by rites similar to those prescribed in the case of the offending representative of the people.

4:22 *A ruler.* If the person who had committed an unwitting sin was not the "ecclesiastical" head of the people but a "lay" official (Ex 18:21), the offender was required to bring a male goat without blemish for a sin offering.

4:27 *One of the common people.* Although the whole congregation needed expiation for the sin committed by one of its members, the individual "lay" culprit likewise had to atone for an unwitting sin "when it is made known to him." He was required to "bring for his offering" a female goat or a sheep. (28, 32)

5:1 *A public adjuration.* Whereas all preceding sin offerings were for violations of anything in general "which the Lord has commanded not to be done" (4:2, 13, 22, 27), two specific offenses are now enumerated: the abuse of God's holy name in oaths and the contamination that results from contact with unholy things or persons (5:1-6). When the misdeed is "hidden from" the offender (2-4) or if he hears a false oath or utters a "rash oath" and only later "comes to know" and "confesses" the sin (1, 4), a female lamb or goat was to be offered to atone for these unwitting transgressions. Because he is "guilty in any of these" (4:13, 22, 27; 5:5), the sin offering is here called a "guilt offering." (6, 7; cf. 4:3 note)

5:7 *Cannot afford.* The poor were not exempt from bringing a sin offering but were permitted to substitute for the costlier lamb *two turtle doves or two young pigeons*. When even these were beyond their means, "a tenth of an ephah of fine flour" (about 2 or 3 quarts) would be acceptable (11). However, the basic requirement of a sin offering was observed: a certain part was burned on the altar. (10, 12)

5:12 *Memorial portion.* Cf. 2:2 note.

5:15 *Valued . . . in shekels.* The prescriptions for *guilt offerings* had much in common with the regulations for sin offerings (cf. 4:3 note). Three kinds of offenses are listed that require the bringing of guilt offerings: (a) a *breach of faith*, consisting of an unwitting sin *in any of the holy things* (15, 16); (b) unknowingly doing what "the Lord has commanded not to be done" (17-19); (c) "unfaithfulness to God" by "deceiving" one's "neighbor" and unlawfully gaining possession of what rightfully belongs to him (6:1-7). In addition to an offering, required also in the case of a sin offering, the offender was obligated to "make restitution" and pay reparations in specified amounts. The sacrificial animal for all guilt was a ram. (Nm 5:6-8; Lv 6:6; 19:21)

2) 6:8—7:38 Participation
by People's Mediator Prescribed

6:9 *Aaron and his sons.* From the first chapter to this point, participation in the offerings by the offender consisted largely in providing the materials for the sacrifices. The following section (6:8—7:38) stresses functions and duties, privileges and prerogatives that constituted the priestly participation in the prescribed ritual. Partly repeating and partly supplementing directions already given, the instructions for the priests deal again with: (a) burnt offerings (6:8-13); (b) cereal offerings (6:14-23); (c) sin offerings (6:24-30); (d) guilt offerings (7:1-10); (e) peace offerings (7:11-36). With respect to the *burnt offering* the priests were to observe the following points: (a) it was to be *on the hearth upon the altar all night*; (b) the fire on the altar was not permitted to "go out" (12-13); (c) when removing the ashes the priest was to wear only "his linen garments" and "his linen breeches." (Ex 28:39, 42; 29:38-42)

6:14 *The law of cereal offering.* Repeating in general the prescriptions of 2:1-15, this law instructed the priests that the eating of their portion of the people's oblation (2:3, 10) was restricted to the "male" members of their family in a "holy place." Anyone else who touched it became "holy" (18), i.e., it made an unauthorized person subject to the penalty of contamination that resulted from contact with things consecrated wholly to God (16-18, 27; Ex 29:21, 37). Special directions applied to the cereal offering when brought on the day of Aaron and his sons' anointing for their office (19-23; Ex. 29:1-2). At these occasions "the whole of it shall be burned."

6:25 *The law of sin offering.* This law supplements the priestly functions and responsibilities mentioned in connection with the bringing of sin offerings in 4:1—5:13. It emphasizes its *most holy* character requiring the priest to observe special purifying rites with respect to garments sprinkled with its blood and the vessel in which it was boiled. No earthen or bronze container obviously was large enough to hold a bull, required as the sin offering for the priest and the people (4:13-21). The boiling evidently refers to the scalding of the sheep and goats for the purpose of removing the wool or hair—a practice in vogue among the Samaritans to this day.

7:1 *The law of the guilt offering.* This law makes several additions to the previous legislation (5:14—6:7). It specifies what parts of the sacrificial animal were to be burned on the altar as the Lord's portion (1-5). It declares that the priests' portion of the guilt offering was "like [that of] the sin offering." It goes on to enumerate other priestly perquisites: the skin of an animal offered as a "burnt offering" and parts of the cereal offering that accompanied animal sacrifices.

7:11 *The law . . . of peace offerings.* These priestly instructions contain amplifications and refinements of the prescriptions given in 3:1-17. Three kinds of peace offerings are distinguished: those brought (a) for a thanksgiving, no doubt for a special blessing; (b) to fulfill a vow; (c) as a voluntary offering not for any particular reason but from a sense of gratitude and consecration to the Lord. Instead of repeating the kinds of animals suitable for such occasions (3:1, 6, 12), this legislation dwells at some length on the "cakes" of various kinds, leavened as well as unleavened, that were to be brought in addition to the bloody sacrifices. This supplementary feature is mentioned explicitly only in connection with the first of the peace offerings (12, 13) but no doubt may be assumed to apply as well to the others. Only "one cake from each offering" was the Lord's portion. But instead of burning it on the altar, as was to be done in the case of the cereal offering (6:15), it was consigned to His representative, the priest (14). Furthermore the people—at least "all who are clean" (19-21)—were permitted to partake of the meat of this offering. They were entitled to eat what was not offered to the Lord (the fat and the blood; 22-27) or was not assigned to the priests (the breast and the thigh; 31-32). The latter were to be "waved" or "heaved" (RSV: "offered"). These gestures were to signify that also these portions were construed as being given to the Lord although His representatives actually received them (30-36). The priests were also to see to it that the people observed the proper time for eating of the meat. (15-18)

3) 8:1—10:20 Participation by Mediator Initiated

8:2 *Take Aaron and his sons.* The present division of the Pentateuch into "books" to some extent obscures the continuity of transactions recorded in them. Chapters 8—10 of Leviticus tell how Moses obeyed the command to consecrate priestly mediators, given in Exodus, chs. 29 and 40:12-15. The official garments had been provided (Ex 39) according to directions given in Ex 28. The tabernacle itself and its furnishings, built and fabricated according to divine specifications (Ex 25—30), had been dedicated (Ex 40:16-33). Moses proceeded with the ordination of Israel's representatives only after the kinds of service that they were to render in its hallowed precincts had been set forth in the preceding seven chapters. This account therefore presupposes that the reader is acquainted with the priestly regalia described in Ex 28 and the significance of the various kinds of sacrifice. (Lv 1—7)

8:6 *Moses brought.* In accord with his unique position as the mediator of the entire covenant, Moses performed the priestly functions of ordination. Aaron and his sons were passive except that they participated in this special ceremony as the people did when they officiated. (8:31-35)

8:9 *As the Lord commanded.* This clause of approbation occurs 15 times and echoes the sevenfold stress on his obedience recorded in the making of the priestly garments and the building of the tabernacle. (Cf. Ex 39:1 note)

8:10 *Anointing oil.* Cf. Ex 40:9 note.

8:14 *Laid their hands.* Aaron and his sons were required to perform this symbolic act at every sacrifice of their ordination. (18, 22; cf. 1:3 note)

8:18 *The ram.* The use of the definite article in referring to all three sacrificial animals (14, 18, 22) presupposes that they have been identified in the instructions given to Moses. (Ex 29:1, 10, 15, 19)

8:22 *The ram of ordination.* Literally "the ram of fillings." To "fill the hands" was a gesture signifying investiture of rights. It is translated "ordain" or "consecrate" in Ex 28:41; 29:29, 33, 35; Lv 16:32; 21:10 (cf. Ex 29:1 note). Because the offering of this ram was restricted to a special occasion, ceremonial procedures for presenting it were not included in the general instructions in chs. 1—7. Although it is not explicitly so called, the ordination rite resembled the peace offering. (3:1-17; 7:11-36; Ex 29:19-37)

8:34 *As has been done today.* The ordination sacrifices and rites were repeated for seven consecutive days.

9:2 *Take a bull calf.* On the day after Aaron and his sons had been ordained, they assumed their tasks. The first official act was an atonement for the person of the priest by means of a sin offering (8) and a burnt offering. (12)

9:15 *The people's offering.* In addition to a sin and whole burnt offering, the inaugural service of the priest for the people included a cereal and a peace offering.

9:22 *Blessed them.* The blessing was probably bestowed in the well-known formulation called the Aaronic blessing and recorded in Nm 6:22-26.

10:1 *Nadab and Abihu.* As "fire came forth from before the Lord and consumed the burnt offering" (9:24), so divine flames "devoured" the two oldest sons of Aaron (Ex 6:23) because they *offered unholy fire before the Lord.* Just what made it *unholy* is not stated. Literally the word means "strange, foreign, illicit." Perhaps these sons of Aaron arrogated functions to themselves that were reserved for their father, the high priest. Or they kindled their own fire instead of taking it from the burning coals of the altar (16:12; Ex 30:9). Whatever the act of desecration was, the severity of the punishment made it clear that God is not mocked. He will not tolerate worship arbitrarily devised by men in defiance of His holy will.

10:9 *No wine.* Perhaps this prohibition is appended here because Nadab and Abihu had acted so rashly while under the influence of intoxicating drink. A befuddled mind would in general be incapable of distinguishing between "clean" and "unclean" and of teaching the people "all the statutes of the Lord." (10, 11; Eze 44:20-21)

10:16 *Moses diligently inquired.* In the offerings of ordination (ch. 9), the regulations regarding the eating of meat by the other sons of Aaron (17; 6:24-30) apparently had been confused with the directions dealing with ordinary cereal and sin offerings. Since the action was not malicious, Moses accepted the intercession in their behalf by Aaron, who acknowledged having had a share in the mishap. (19)

11:1—15:33 AVOIDANCE AND REMOVAL OF IMPURITY: NEGATIVE ASPECT OF HOLINESS

1) 11:1-23 Abstention from Eating Unclean Animals

11:1 *Said to Moses and Aaron.* The rites, ordained to establish and express Israel's covenant communion with the holy God (Ex 19:6; Lv 11:45), entailed positive action: offerings and sacrifices of atonement and consecration were to be brought to the tent of meeting (chs. 1—6), where the priests acted in behalf of the people (chs. 7—10). But being a "holy nation" (Ex 19:6) also had a negative aspect (Ex 22:31). Everything declared ritually unholy or unclean was to be avoided or, if contamination had taken place, proper measures were to be taken to remove the taint of impurity (10:10). Such impurity was caused by (a) certain animals (ch. 11); (b) childbirth (ch. 12); (c) leprosy (chs. 13—14); (d) human discharges. (Ch. 15)

11:2 *Beasts . . . on the earth.* The animals that were not to be eaten belonged to four groups: (a) quadrupeds (1-8); (b) marine animals (9-12); (c) birds (13-19); (d) flying insects (20-23); (e) swarming things (29-31). The only reason advanced for the differentiation between clean and unclean is simply the declaration that abstention from their meat is required by the holy God of His holy people (45). The acceptable land animals are such as are "cloven-footed" and "chew the cud." This classification was a simple rule of thumb, based on outward appearances. Since also such rodents as the rock badger and the hare can be seen to keep their jaws in motion much like the camel, they are identified as chewing the cud. In Gn 7:2 animals appear to be called clean and unclean from the viewpoint of their appropriateness for sacrifice. (Cf. Gn 9:3)

11:9 *In the waters.* In order to be eatable, creatures of the sea must also have two outward marks of identification: they must have *fins and scales.* Others, such as oysters and eels, were unclean.

11:13 *Among the birds.* All the birds mentioned here have not been fully identified. No general characteristics are mentioned which serve as the criterion for the differentiation; birds of prey and carrion-eating birds, however, seem to predominate among those that are an *abomination.*

11:20 *Upon all fours.* This section deals with the smaller winged creatures that are distinguished from the two-footed birds. The eating of insects is forbidden with the exception of some that have "legs above their feet" such as several kinds of locusts.

2) 11:24-47 Abstention from Contact with Animals

11:24 *Become unclean.* Eating of unclean animals is forbidden. Even contact with them "when they are dead" produced uncleanness.

11:29 *Swarming things.* Vv. 29-31 mention smaller land animals that are unclean. Besides those mentioned in 29-30, the term *swarming things* includes all such animals as fall under the more general classifications given in 42. If contact with the carcass of a clean animal resulted in uncleanness (39), it would certainly be true when the animal was one of the *swarming things*, to say nothing of eating one. (41-42)

11:45 *Be holy.* God's claim to Israel's holiness emanates from His own sovereign holiness. He alone is holy in an absolute sense. Always separate and distinct from man by the unbridgeable gap between Creator and His creatures, He rejects every effort of man to deal with Him on equal terms. His holiness excludes toleration of man's sin and cuts man off from the only source of life. But He also put into operation a plan, conceived in eternity, to let man become holy again and have communion with Him. With power and mercy, which only the holy God can muster and exhibit, He brought *up out of the land of Egypt* a disreputable group of slaves. He gave them rites that in symbolic promise assured them of the removal of the unholy taint of sin. He also gave them guidance how to respond to His goodness. For the simple reason that He is holy they were to abstain from contamination with the designated symbols of uncleanness. When symbolized cleanness and forgiveness became a reality through the unstained life and the vicarious sacrifice of God's "holy Child Jesus" (Acts 4:27), the outward forms of holiness had served their purpose and are no longer necessary "to cleanse ourselves from every defilement of body and spirit, and make holiness perfect in the fear of God." (2 Co 7:1; Lk 11:41; Ro 14:17; Cl 2:16-17)

3) 12:1-8 Removal of the Uncleanness of Childbirth

12:2 *She shall be unclean.* All persons, whether male or female, become ceremonially unclean through bodily discharges (5; ch. 15). The cleansing required of a woman after childbirth falls into this category (12:1-5). "Atonement" was necessary not because procreation itself was sinful (Ps 127:3; 128:3-4). But while the woman was "in the blood of her purifying," she was excluded from participation in rites that required that she "be clean from the flow of blood." The time of ritual confinement after the birth of a son was doubled "if she bears a female child." (5)

12:6 *Burnt offering . . . and a sin offering.* The woman herself was to *bring to the priest* the offerings prescribed for her purification. In cases of poverty less expensive animals could be substituted. (Lk 2:24)

4) 13:1—14:57 Avoidance of the Impurity of Leprosy

13:2 *A leprous disease.* The term leprosy is applied in these chapters to a wide variety of imperfections that appear on the skin of people and on the surface of garments and houses. In all cases they constituted not a sin in themselves but an uncleanness, contact with which had to be avoided. If it was a curable disease in human beings or if garments and houses responded to treatment, ritual procedures had to be followed in order to restore afflicted persons to the "holy nation" and to make the material things usable by its ceremonially clean constituents. In the diagnosis of human diseases the skin was examined for various irregularities that might be the symptoms of the incurable kind of leprosy in its earliest stages (Nm 12:10-15; 2 K 5:27; 2 Ch 26:19-23). Not all symptoms can be definitely identified.

13:11 *Not shut him up.* It was not necessary for him to go to the "isolation ward" for a reexamination.

13:45 *Cover his upper lip.* The actions required of a leper resemble mourning rites for the dead. (Eze 24:17, 22; Mi 3:7; Lm 4:15; Lk 17:12)

13:47 *Leprous disease.* The Hebrew word translated *disease* in this section is derived from a root meaning to "hit, strike, afflict." It is not strictly a medical term but is applicable also to such strokes of affliction as are not in the form of a disease (Ex 11:1; 1 K 8:37-38: "plague"). It occurs frequently in these chapters to denote maladies that consume the flesh of humans and the materials of which garments and houses consist. The kinds of "leprosy" are in all cases distinguished by the manner in which they give evidence of their presence and not according to the bacteriological causes that produced them.

13:51 *Malignant.* This adjective is used again to describe "leprous" houses (14:44). It apparently describes a decaying condition of the material that was not merely on the surface but penetrated deeper and caused disintegrating damage. Perhaps these "leprosies" were comparable to mildew and dry rot.

14:1 *Day of his cleansing.* If the skin abnormality was not pronounced unclean leprousy, the person needed only to wash his clothes (13:6, 34). If, however, a person's disease, diagnosed as unclean, had been healed, he could again become a member of the holy community only after a series of purification rites had been performed (Mt 8:24). The ceremonies, prescribed for the first seven of the eight days, had features and used materials (such as "cedar wood" and "scarlet stuff") that had not been mentioned in connection with the other offerings and sacrifices. No explanation of the rites is given except to state that, if performed, the person could enter the camp; but he was still required to remain outside his tent. (8)

14:10 *Eighth day.* Various kinds of animal sacrifices completed the cleansing ceremony: a guilt offering (12), a sin offering (19), a burnt offering (20). A cereal offering of one tenth of an ephah of flour no doubt accompanied each sacrifice (10; Nm 29:4; Ex 29:40). A *log* is the transliteration of a Hebrew word for the smallest liquid measure: about ½ pint. The use of oil apparently symbolized that the person was again entitled to participate in the offerings prescribed for a holy people. (Cf. 8:12)

14:21 *Cannot afford.* If the leper was *poor*, substitutions for the sacrificial animals were permissible (cf. 5:7, 11; 12:8) with the exception of the *male lamb for a guilt offering*.

14:35 *Some sort of disease.* For the meaning of the word *disease* see 13:47 note. Because the evidence of some damaging impurity appeared on the surface of the houses, as it did on the skin of a person, these defects in buildings are classified also as leprosy. Treatment of such unclean houses varied according to the nature and severity of the *disease.*

14:44 *Malignant.* Cf. 13:51 note.

14:49 *For the cleansing.* This cleansing resembles the rites prescribed for a leprous person during the first 7 days of his purification. (4-9)

5) 15:1-33 Removal of Contamination Through Bodily Discharges

15:2 *Discharge from his body.* Still a blessing of God (Gn 1:28), procreation since the fall produces offspring that are by nature sinful and subject to the curse of death (Ps 51:5). Childbirth (ch. 12) as well as certain male and female sexual discharges results in a ceremonial uncleanness for which atonement must be made (cf. Ex 19:15; 1 Sm 21:4). Discharges that are caused by a physical abnormality (2-15) are distinguished from mere involuntary emissions (16-17) and such as occur when "a man lies with a woman." (18)

15:19 *For seven days.* The rules again made a difference between regular menstrual uncleanness (19-24) and abnormal discharges of blood. (25-30)

16:1-34 The Day of Atonement: Sanctifying Rites by the High Priest

16:1 *The death of the two sons of Aaron.* Nadab and Abihu had suffered the extreme penalty for violating the prescriptions for holy rites (10:1-7). Lest Aaron also die (2), he must not enter "the holy place within the veil, before the mercy seat which is upon the ark" except on the annual "day of atonement[s]" (34; 23:27-28; 25:9; for "mercy seat" see Ex 25:17 note). Although popularly known as "Yom Kippur" (day of atonement), the plural form may indicate that the rites of this day were intended "to cleanse you from all your sins" (30). The unique and climaxing character on this once-a-year atonement is also apparent from the fact that the performance of its rites were restricted to the high priest.

16:4 *Shall put on.* Because it was primarily a day of humiliation and prayer, the high priest did not wear the full regalia of his office (4; Ex 28) until atonement had been made. (23-24)

16:5 *Shall take.* The preliminary instructions (1-5) also designate the animals required for the sacrifices. For himself Aaron was to bring "a young bull for a sin offering and a ram for a burnt offering" (3); for the people, he was to take *two male goats for a sin offering, and one ram for a burnt offering.* (5)

16:8 *Azazel.* This is the transliteration of the Hebrew word. It occurs nowhere else in the OT although the noncanonical Book of Enoch speaks of a fallen angel with the name *Azazel.* The KJV translation "scapegoat" regards the word as compounded of the noun for goat and the verb for departing: "the goat of departure" or "[e]scape goat." The RSV suggests that it is a proper name for a demon of the desert because Aaron was to cast lots to determine which goat was *for the Lord* and which one *for Azazel.* It should be remembered, however, that this goat is to be presented "before the Lord" (10). Furthermore, sacrifice to "satyrs" (lit. hairy goats) is forbidden in the next chapter, v. 7. The preposition preceding this word is the same in all instances although it is translated *for* here but "to" in vv. 10 and 26. Since this preposition is also the sign of the infinitive (like our "to" remove), some have sought to explain this enigmatic word as a verb meaning to take away. Whatever the meaning of the word associated with this goat, its release into "a solitary land" "in the wilderness" clearly symbolized that it vicariously bore all the people's "iniquities," "transgressions," and "all their sins" (21) and removed them from Israel and the sight of the Lord. (Mi 7:19; Ps 103:12; Is 53:6, 11, 12; see also the visionary removal of iniquity from Israel to the far-off land of Shinar, Zch 5:5-11)

16:16 *Uncleannesses of the people.* The blood of the sin offering was to remove from *the holy place* and "the altar" (18) everything done by the people to profane them.

16:20 *The live goat.* It was kept alive in order that Aaron might "make atonement over it" (10) for all of Israel's sins. These were transferred to it when he laid both his hands upon its head and so confessed "over him" Israel's entire guilt.

16:24 *Put on his garments.* After performing the rites in the holy of holies, dressed as prescribed in 4, Aaron concluded the ceremonies after putting on all the garments of his office.

16:29 *A statute . . . for ever.* The other annual festival days are given a fixed date in ch. 23. *The seventh month* on our calendar is September/October. The observance of the Day of Atonement required also that the people *afflict* themselves, i.e., show the genuineness of their repentance by fasting.

16:34 *An everlasting statute.* Although the Day of Atonement was explicitly prescribed *that atonement may be made for the people of Israel once in the year,* there is no reference in the OT to its later observance. Some scholars therefore assume that it originated after the Babylonian captivity. But an argument from silence is always precarious. The writer of Hebrews knew the value of this ritual and expounded its foreshadowing significance. (Heb 9—10)

17:1—27:34 HOLY COMMUNION MAINTAINED BY LAWS OF HOLINESS

17:1—20:27 Precepts for a Holy People

17:1-16 RESTRICTIONS ON KILLING AND EATING ANIMALS

17:1 *The Lord said.* In chs. 1—16 God provided Israel with various rites and ceremonies which symbolized the removal of the barrier between an unholy nation and the holy God. A people whose sin was forgiven and whose uncleanness was removed could gain access to God and enter into communion with Him. Ch. 16 forms not only the climax of these atoning rites but also serves as a transition to the following chapters (17—26) by its insistence that reconciliation and fellowship with God must remain an ongoing process in the lives of the people. Hence the following section of this book contains prescriptions, ordinances, and statutes in which Israel is to "walk" if it is to "live" (18:4, 5), i.e., remain in holy communion with God (26:3 ff.). Because these chapters stress this walking in holiness, they have been called the Holiness Code. (Cf. Introduction, "Authorship")

17:3 *Kills it.* No animals, acceptable for sacrificial purposes, were to be slaughtered except at "the door of the tent of meeting." In this way they became a part of the "sacrifices of peace offerings" (5). This restriction was to prevent the people from slaying animals in "the open field" and offering them to idols, here called "satyrs" (literally "hairy goats"). If Israel was to remain a holy people, it was not to yield to the temptation of joining in the idolatrous worship of demonic powers practiced by others (19:4; 26:1, 30). Here and in many other OT passages such unfaithfulness to the only God is called harlotry (7; 20:5; Ex 34:15-16; Hos 1—3). As long as Israel lived a camp life, it was possible to keep such an ordinance of centralized slaying of animals, but it had to be modified to meet the diffusion of the people after the occupation of Canaan. (Dt 12:5-21)

17:10 *Eats any blood.* Not only the slaughter of animals was restricted to one place; limitations were placed also on the parts of the animal that were to be used for food and on the conditions under which its meat could be eaten. Certain portions of the sacrifice were reserved for God and the priests. But no one was to eat "flesh with its life, that is, its blood" (Gn 9:4). Blood visibly represents the Creator's indispensable gift of animation to all creatures (11, 14). Because God "has given" the life of an animal "to make atonement for your souls" (the plural of the same word twice translated "life" in 11), animal blood was to be regarded as the substitute for man's life, all of which was forfeit to God by his sin. This ordinance was in sharp contrast to the practice of heathens, who consumed blood in order to partake of its life-giving power. Allowance is made for exceptional cases in 15-16.

18:1-30 MARITAL AND SEXUAL PRESCRIPTIONS

18:3 *As they do.* In order to remain God's holy people, the Israelites were not to imitate their neighbors, among whom sexual license and perversion were rampant.

18:6 *Near of kin.* Literally "flesh of his flesh." The nouns in this combination, however, are not identical although they may be used as synonyms. The second word occurs in the sentence: "They become one flesh" (Gn 2:24). Used together in the same phrase, they designate an identity with another person which prohibits conjugal union. This close relationship is to be recognized to exist between blood relatives (e.g., father, sister) and between relatives by marriage (e.g., daughter-in-law).

18:18 *A rival wife.* This translation does not make the relationship of a man to his sister-in-law a barrier to marriage after his wife's death; it does forbid an uncovering of the former's nakedness *while her sister is yet alive.*

18:20 *Your neighbor's wife.* Adultery constitutes not only a ceremonial defilement but is also a moral offense. (Ex 20:14; Lv 20:10; Pr 6:32)

18:21 *Molech.* The sacrifice of children to Molech is mentioned in this context because sexual indulgence under the guise of fertility rites was a part of the worship of this and other idols (Dt 12:31; 2 K 23:10, 13; Jer 32:35; 1 K 11:7). The sacrifice of children was not an uncommon occurrence in later apostate Israel (2 K 17:17; 21:6, 2 Ch 28:3, Eze 16:20-21, 20:26, 31; 23:37, 39). The name of this idol, usually with a prefixed article, "the Molech," has been explained in various ways. Because the consonants *m-l-ch* are identical with the Hebrew common noun for king: "melech" (as in Abi*melech*, Gn 20:2), some believe that the Jews expressed their contempt for this "king" by transferring to him the vowels from the word for shame: "bosheth." Others think that Molech is a technical term for the idolatrous sacrifice itself.

18:30 *I am the Lord.* Israel's obedience was to be a response to *the Lord,* the covenant God to whom it owed everything: its undeserved redemption from Egypt (19:36) and its admission to communion with the holy God by His grace (cf. Ex 20:2, where the keeping of the Decalog is motivated by God's deed of deliverance). If the Israelites were to remain in this relationship to the Lord, they were to discharge their covenant obligation of being a "holy nation," chosen for the express purpose of being separate from "the nations" of Canaan (24). This solemn declaration *I am the Lord* is repeated 15 times in the next chapter. It is the basis for all demands of holiness on the part of the chosen nation.

19:1-37 SUNDRY CEREMONIAL AND MORAL REQUIREMENTS

19:2 *Be holy.* The requirement that was basic for Israel's entering communion with the holy God (11:44-45) is applied in this chapter to a great variety of situations and relationships that come into play if holiness is to be maintained. The random listing of demands for holy living seems designed to give the impression that no aspect of life was to remain unaffected by God's claim. Scattered through the chapters are laws dealing with the proper relationship to God. Some of these are of a moral nature, already enunciated in the Decalog (e.g., 4: idols; 3, 30: sabbaths); some are in the area of ceremonies (e.g., 5-8: peace offerings; 27-28: heathen customs). The majority of the precepts exemplify the comprehensiveness of the demands of the second table of the Law, summarized in the radical command "to love your neighbor [even a stranger] as yourself" (18,

34; Mt 19:19; 22:39; Ro 13:9; Gl 5:14; Ja 2:8). Hate is eradicated from its root: the "heart." (17)

19:3 *Revere.* This is a good rendition of the Hebrew verb usually translated "to fear." Awe of God and of His representatives, the parents, is an attitude of respect that gives evidence of love. (Dt 6:5, 13; Luther's explanation of the Decalog)

19:4 *Idols.* Lit. "nothings." It is a term of derision and declares that any power ascribed to these figments of the imagination by their worshipers is nonexistent. (26:1; Ps 96:5; 97:7; Is 2:8, 18, 20; Hab 2:18)

19:19 *With a different kind.* This prohibition does not use the same word for "kind" that occurs in Gn 1:11, 21, 25. The rationale of this law, as well as the prohibition against wearing garments made of different stuffs, remains unclear. Perhaps they are based on the principle of avoiding mingling of incongruous elements and so negating purity. It is also possible that they are directed against practices that had heathen and magical implications such as those mentioned in 27-28. (Cf. Ex 23:19 note)

19:27 *Hair on your temples.* In 27-28 Canaanite customs of mourning for the dead are forbidden. Disguises and changes of appearance were employed as magical means of warding off the spirit of the deceased.

20:1-27 PENALTIES FOR VIOLATIONS OF HOLINESS

20:2 *Put to death.* Capital punishment is decreed for violations of holy relations with God and for disregard of the sanctity of marriage. *Molech.* Cf. 18:21 note.

20:6 *Mediums and wizards.* Cf. Ex 22:18 note.

20:9 *Curses.* Cf. Ex 21:12 note. Branded previously as violations of God's will, the sins mentioned here and in 6 are repeated from the perspective of their incompatibility with holiness. (7; see also 3)

20:10 *The wife of his neighbor.* The sins for which penalties are decreed in the remaining verses have been enumerated in chs. 18—19 with the exception of bigamous marriage with a wife and her mother. (14; Dt 27:23)

20:15 *With a beast.* Warning against this kind of sexual perversion was necessary. The peoples of Israel's environment attached no stigma to bestiality since even their gods committed it without incurring the least censure.

20:19 *Uncover the nakedness.* This expression for illicit sex relations occurs only in chs. 18 and 20. It describes them as an encroachment on what the Creator wants kept covered or set apart by His decrees of holiness. They constitute a violation of cleanness in the same way that contact with an unclean person or animal (chs. 11—15) profanes His holy name.

20:20 *Die childless.* In this context the penalty of childlessness (also in 21) may be but another way of saying: "They shall [at once] be cut off from among their people," i.e., executed before a child so conceived could be born.

20:23 *Abhorred them.* Death is not decreed for the failure to distinguish between "clean" and "unclean" (25, 26; cf. chs. 11—15). But if Israel was to be "holy to God" (26) and "separated from the peoples" of Canaan (24), it must be different from the latter also in this respect if it is not to incur the same penalty. (22)

20:27 *Man or woman.* The former decree against occultism had not specifically mentioned that the penalty applied also to female practitioners. This verse adds furthermore that the cutting off from among their people was to be by stoning. (6)

21:1—22:33 Precepts for a Holy Priesthood

21:1-15 PERSONAL HOLINESS

21:1 *The priests.* In accordance with the basic principle of holiness, God had "separated" Israel "from the peoples" (20:24) and had bridged their rebellious separation from Him. Another segregation within Israel itself was to serve the same sanctifying purpose. There were to be holy priests, men set aside to perform functions from which the people as a whole were excluded. Because they held the exclusive position of intermediaries of the people and performed sacred rites in their name, they must be "holy" (literally "consecrated") to God (7). They must first of all meet special requirements of personal qualifications and conduct that are exacted only or to a particular degree of them. (1-9)

21:2 *Nearest of kin.* Contact with corpses except those of the priest's *nearest of kin* was completely forbidden. His wife is not mentioned among them. She is more than *kin*, having become "one flesh" with him (Gn 2:24). For the same reason his "virgin sister" was counted among his kin because his married sister had entered a conjugal union with her husband.

21:4 *As a husband.* The original Hebrew text permits an alternate translation: "He shall not defile a husband among his people so as to profane it."

21:5 *Tonsures.* Cf. 19:27 note.

21:10 *Chief.* A final segregation was to be made within Israel, separated from the peoples, and within the priests, separated from the ordinary people. But also this separation was to help maintain the union of sinful man with the holy God. One of the priests was to be *chief among his brethren* (lit. "the greatest of his brethren"). Because of this distinction, even more stringent ceremonial cleanness was required of him than of the other priests.

21:16-24 DISQUALIFYING PHYSICAL DEFECTS

21:17 *A blemish.* The sacrificial animal had to be "without blemish" (Ex 12:5; 29:1; etc.). This ceremonial requirement of physical perfection applied also to the person who was *to offer the bread of his God* and "the Lord's offerings by fire" (21). When THE High Priest came and all who accept His mediating sacrifice have become a "holy priesthood," the ceremonial requirements for the priesthood of the old covenant no longer obtain. But all who constitute this "royal priesthood" have the sacerdotal duty "to declare the wonderful deeds" of Him who made them "God's own people," to "abstain from the passions of the flesh," and to "maintain good conduct" which glorifies God (1 Ptr 2:5, 9-12). This applies particularly to those who have the responsibility of shepherding this chosen people, sanctified by the blood of the everlasting convenant. (1 Ti 3:2-7; Tts 1:5-9; Acts 20:28)

22:1-33 DISCHARGE OF PRIESTLY DUTIES

22:2 *Keep away.* This prohibition is not absolute but applies only if or as long as the priest was ceremonially unclean. He was not to perform the functions of his office as long as the conditions described in 1-9 obtain. While "holy things" (3) is a general term embracing all offerings to God, particular mention is made of those sacrifices during which the priest was permitted to "eat of the holy things." (6)

22:10 *Outsider.* In personal relationships there was "one law for the native and for the stranger" (Ex 12:49; Lv 24:22; see also Ex 22:21; Lv 19:33; Dt 10:19). But the priests were to keep the outsider and any other unauthorized members of the laity from eating "their holy things" lest they "profane" them. (15, 16)

22:19 *To be accepted.* Specific criteria are given by which the priests were to determine what animals qualified to be classified under the general rubric *without blemish* and were acceptable for sacrifice. (1:3; 3:1; 4:3, 28)

22:27 *With its mother.* Two other factors besides physical defects could make an animal ineligible for sacrificial purposes: (a) its age: not before *the eighth day* of its life; (b) the slaughter of the female and her young on the same day (28). The latter provision is similar to the prohibition not to "boil a kid in its mother's milk." (Cf. Ex 23:19 note; see also Ex 34:26; Dt 14:21)

23:1-44 Precepts for Keeping Holy Days

23:2 *Appointed feasts.* Lit. "the meetings," the Hebrew word being simply the plural form of the same noun in the phrase "the tent of *meeting*." In the tabernacle a place had been provided where the holy God would meet in holy communion with a people cleansed from unholiness and hallowed for reunion with Him. This chapter proclaims that there were to be also special days of "meetings" in the tent of meeting. The observance of these recurring weekly and annual days stressed Israel's need of continuing efforts to maintain its status as a "holy nation." Most of these festival days could be kept only after Israel had entered the Promised Land and a settled agricultural economy had been established.

23:3 *Sabbath.* The only day of *holy convocation* that was to be kept more than once a year was *the seventh day* of each week. Its observance required primarily what its name means: *rest. No work* was to be done, while only "laborious work" was forbidden on the annual meeting days. (7, 21, 35; cf. Ex 20:8 note)

23:4 *Holy convocations.* The "passover" festival together with that of "unleavened bread" (6) was the first of the three pilgrimage festivals (Ex 23:14-15). It was the first also on the calendar of Israel's ceremonial or ecclesiastical year. This "first month," called Abib, would coincide with our March/April. It was the month when Israel "came out of Egypt." Why and how it was to be celebrated is recorded in Ex 12:1-20, 43-49 and is later restated in Dt 16:1-8.

23:6 *Unleavened bread.* Closely associated with the Passover, commencing on the day following it and lasting *seven days*, was *the feast of unleavened bread.* (Cf. Ex 12:14-20; 23:14-15; Nm 28:16-25)

23:10 *First fruits.* While the Israelites were commemorating their national beginnings, they were simultaneously to express their dependence on God for the continued preservation of their life. On the second day of unleavened bread they were to bring a token offering of their *first fruits* and "wave the sheaf before the Lord" (Ex 29:24; Lv 8:27). The Hebrew word for *sheaf* is translated omer in Ex 16:16, 18 ff. It was a bowl holding one tenth of an ephah: about 4 pints. As the gathering of these *first fruits* was but the beginning of the full harvest, so Christ, the "grain of wheat" that died, by His resurrection became "the first fruits of those who have fallen asleep." (Jn 12:24; 1 Co 15:20; Ja 1:18; Rv 14:4; Ro 8:23; 11:16)

23:13 *Drink offering.* Translated "libation" in Ex 29:40 and 30:9, this offering consisted of the produce of the field in liquid form. The emphasis of the Hebrew word is on the fact that it was poured out, the only manner in which a portion of this oblation could be presented to the Lord (Ex 30:9; Gn 35:14). It does not appear as an independent offering but accompanied the meal offerings, as here (and in Nm 6:15, 17; 15:24; 29:31), and also the burnt offerings. (Nm 28:7 ff.)

23:15 *Seven full weeks.* This festival is called "the feast of weeks" (Ex 34:22; Dt 16:10, 16) because it was celebrated 7 weeks or sabbaths after the feast of unleavened bread—May/June on our calendar. Since it was reckoned to begin after 49 days, the NT refers to it as Pentecost, the Greek word for "fifty" (Acts 2:1). "A cereal offering of new grain" (16; Hebrew: "a new cereal offering") was to consist of flour, made of the "first fruits" (not the same Hebrew word used in 10) of the final harvest. The "two loaves" brought from the "dwellings" represented the ordinary bread of the Israelites. This token of gratitude for their daily sustenance was therefore "baked with leaven" (17). Leaving some of the harvest "for the poor" was another way of acknowledging that they owed their existence to the Lord (22). It anticipated the words of Jesus. (Mt 25:40)

23:24 *In the seventh month.* As the seventh day of the week was holy to the Lord and 7 weeks of days marked a holy day (15-22), so *the seventh month* (our September/October) of the year had special significance. It was the month of three festivals: the feast of *trumpets* (23-25), the day of atonement (26-32), and the feast of tabernacles (33-36). It brought to a close the agricultural or civic year (Ex 23:16; 34:22), and its first day was therefore a New Year's Day, signalled by the blowing of *trumpets*.

23:27 *On the tenth day*. The only annual festival previously fixed on the calendar was the day of atonement (16:29). The rites to be observed on this solemn occasion did not have to be described because they had been prescribed in detail in ch. 16.

23:34 *The feast of booths*. The third festival during the seventh month derived its name from the kind of structures in which the Israelites were to live during its week-long observance. Consisting only of "branches of palm trees" and "boughs of leafy trees" (40), these huts were to remind the Israelites of their sojourn in the desert when they did not live in permanent houses. The KJV "tabernacles" is confusing. The movable structure that served as Israel's sanctuary is also called a tabernacle, although the Hebrew word is different. The great number of sacrifices to be brought at this feast are more fully described in Nm 29:12-38. It was to be a particularly happy occasion at which the Israelites were to "rejoice before the Lord" (40; Dt 12:12, 18; 16:11; 27:7). The old covenant prescribed many exacting requirements of holiness. But it was not a religion of gloom and servile resignation. Provided with the means of communion with the holy God and cheered by its promises, the Israelites knew the "joy of salvation" (Ps 51:12; 27:6; 33:1; 42:4; 43:4; Is 12:3; 29:19; 35:2, 10; Jer 15:16). Small wonder that the holiness effected by the blood of the new covenant should destroy gloom and produce rejoicing "with unutterable and exalted joy." (1 Ptr 1:8; Ro 5:2; 14:17; Gl 5:22; Ph 1:18; 4:4; 1 Th 5:16)

24:1-9 Precepts Regarding Sacramental Elements

24:2 *Pure oil*. For the construction of the lampstand see Ex 25:31-40; 37:17-24. The people's obligation to supply the oil and the duty of the priests to tend it "from evening to morning" (Ex 27:20-21) are repeated here in a context which emphasizes the need of maintaining holiness *continually*. (4; cf. Ex 30:7-8; 1 Sm 3:3)

24:5 *Twelve cakes*. Instructions for the making of the table of the Presence had been given and carried out (Ex 25:23-30; 37:10-16). Here the bread for the table is described, and its part in the maintenance of holiness is stressed: "a covenant for ever," "a perpetual due" (8, 9). The bread was to be eaten by the priests; but the frankincense, placed next to "each row" or pile of cakes "for a memorial," was to be offered by fire. (1 Sm 21:1-6; Mt 12:4)

24:10-23 Penalties for the Desecration of Holiness

24:11 *Blasphemed the Name*. Israel had been granted the gift of entering into communion with the holy God. But abuse of His holy name not only severed the bonds of peace but also exposed the offender to the consuming fire of His wrath (cf. 10:1-7). This case established the precedent that every blasphemer, "the sojourner as well as the native," "shall be put to death." (16; cf. Ex 12:38)

24:17 *Kills a man*. The holiness of God demands that human life be regarded as His inviolate gift. The penalties for taking life or injuring the body, already set forth in Ex 21:12, 23-36, are here declared to apply also to the "sojourner."

25:1-55 Precepts for the Observance of Holy Years

25:1-7 THE SABBATICAL YEAR

25:2 *The land*. As a holy people the Israelites were to acknowledge that their time belonged to God by consecrating to Him every seventh day of the week as well as other days of the year (ch. 23). They were to recognize furthermore that *the land* was a gift of God by giving it a "sabbath of solemn rest."

25:6 *The sabbath of the land*. "What grows of itself" during that year was not to be harvested like private property but was to provide a source of food for anyone, especially the poor. (Ex 23:10-11)

25:8-55 THE YEAR OF JUBILEE

25:10 *Fiftieth year*. There was to be not only a Pentecost of days (23:15-22) but every *fiftieth year* also was to have special significance for the nation that maintained its relationship of holiness with God. This special year owed its name *jubilee* to the fact that it was proclaimed by the blowing of a ram's horn (Hebrew *yobel*). The trumpet blast summoned Israel to let each *return to his property* and *to his family*. It is therefore called also "the year of liberty" (Eze 46:17). The land was again to lie fallow (11), but the sixth year would be blessed so that its produce would suffice for the sabbatical (seventh) year and the following year of jubilee (20-21; cf. Ex 16:22). Because the land was the Lord's (23), it was never to be sold "in perpetuity" nor become the monopolized possession of a few landed aristocrats (Is 5:8; Mi 2:2). The price of real estate was therefore to be reckoned according to the number of years that remained before the next year of jubilee.

25:25 *Next of kin*. All property automatically reverted to the original owner "in the jubilee." But prior to it the *next of kin* who was charged with maintaining the rights of a family (Ru 4:3-6) could redeem it at a fair price. The previous owner had the same right if meanwhile he had again become prosperous. (25-28)

25:29 *Dwelling house*. The exception to the law of redemption was urban property which was not directly involved in producing the necessities of life. It could become the new owner's possession in perpetuity. The Levites, however, were subject to a special ruling. (32-34)

25:35 *Your brother*. No one was to exploit his fellow Israelite's misfortune by charging him interest (Ex 22:25; Dt 23:19-20) although it could be exacted from a "foreigner" (Dt 15:3), no doubt a different kind of person from the one designated a "stranger." (Ex 12:49; Lv 24:22)

25:39 *Sells himself.* An Israelite who was forced to pay his creditor by selling himself to him was not to be treated like a slave. He was to be declared free of his obligations at the jubilee (40) even if less than 7 years of actual service had been rendered. Strangers, on the other hand, could not be redeemed. (But see also Ex 22:21; Lv 19:33)

25:47 *Sells himself to the stranger.* An Israelite, held for debt by a stranger, could be "redeemed" at a price, prorated according to "the year when he sold himself . . . until the year of jubilee." If such payment was not made by a relative, he "shall be released in the year of jubilee." (54)

25:55 *My servants.* The words "servant" and "slave" are translations of the same Hebrew noun. God had redeemed the Israelites from their former owners, the Egyptians (42). Because He had made them His "own possession among all peoples" (Ex 19:5), He had a claim to expect them to put themselves fully at His disposal.

26:1-46 Blessings of Holy Communion; Punishments for Its Violation

26:1-2 INTRODUCTION: TWO BASIC CONDITIONS OF COMMUNION

26:1 *No idols.* The admission of the Israelites to communion with the holy God required undivided allegiance to the *Lord*. He had granted them the privilege of entering a "covenant" with Him (9, 42, 45) in order that they might be a "holy nation" (Ex 19:6). His claim to their total allegiance to Him was summarized in the commandments of the first table of the Decalog. They were axiomatic for all other required responses of holiness, also for those set forth in the second table of the Law.

26:3-13 BLESSINGS OF COVENANT COMMUNION

26:9 *Confirm my covenant.* The Israelites had deserved that God "abhor" them (11). Instead He had pledged Himself in the covenant to "walk among" them (12) and to bless them with tranquillity and fertility of the soil, reminiscent of the bliss of the Garden of Eden, where perfect peace existed between the holy God and unsullied man. But if He was to be their God and they were to be His people (12), they were expected to respond to this gift of reconciliation by walking in His "statutes" and observing His "commandments."

26:14-39 PUNISHMENTS OF COVENANT DISOBEDIENCE

26:15 *Break my covenant.* God's covenanted grace is free and boundless. But it cannot be abused. Failure to respond to it by a life of consecrated obedience could only provoke God to "execute vengeance for the covenant" (25). The bliss of Paradise would disappear and in its stead the people would suffer: (a) diseases, defeat, and famine (14-20); (b) depredations by wild beasts (21-22); (c) the scourge of war (23-26); (d) complete devastation of the land and exile "among the nations." (27-39)

26:34 *Enjoy its sabbaths.* This description of the exile, repeated in 43, is based on the concept of rest required on the sabbath. Because Israel did not keep the sabbaths (2, 35), the land itself would observe them, i.e., endure a period of rest from occupation and cultivation by its inhabitants. Its lying desolate is payment (RSV note) or making "amends" (41; the same verb in Hebrew), exacted as punishment from Israel for breaking the covenant. (2 Ch 36:21; Jer 17:19-27; Lv 26:40-45)

26:40-46 GOD'S STEADFAST COVENANT

26:42 *Remember my covenant.* In spite of the Israelites' unfaithfulness to their covenant obligations to be a holy people, God would not "destroy them utterly" (44). If they confessed their iniquity and humbled themselves, He would again through them pursue His plan of salvation, set forth in His covenants with the patriarchs (Gn 12:2-3; 26:2-5; 28:13-15) and implemented by the Exodus (Ex 6:6-8). God did not forget His promises. The old covenant was fulfilled in the Mediator of the new covenant. (Lk 1:72; Heb 9:15; 12:24)

27:1-34 Voluntary Expressions of Holy Communion

27:1-8 VOWS INVOLVING PERSONS

27:2 *A special vow.* The previous chapters prescribed the mandatory requirements for establishing and maintaining communion with the holy God. In addition, the Israelites were given the opportunity of expressing their consecration to Him by means of voluntary votive offerings. However, once a vow had been made, its payment became obligatory (Dt 23:21-23) according to the regulations laid down in this last chapter of Leviticus. Such special pledges could be made in petitions for help in times of great stress, as a thankoffering for extraordinary blessings, or simply from a deep sense of devotion (Nm 6:1-21; Gn 28:20-22; Ps 22:25; 66:13). Votive offerings were mentioned incidentally in the preceding legislation (7:16; 22:18-23; 23:38); this chapter determines at what monetary value they were to be computed. For although it speaks of persons, animals, houses, and land that may be vowed to the Lord, it is their *valuation* that actually constituted the substance of their pledge. The price at which these could be redeemed determined the amount of money that was involved in a vow. The *valuation* of a person, e.g., ranged from three to 50 shekels. (3, 6; cf. Nm 30)

27:8 *Too poor to pay.* This verse makes it clear that a "vow of persons" was a way of expressing and computing the value of a special gift to the Lord and did not require that people be offered to Him.

27:9-13 VOWS INVOLVING ANIMALS

27:9 *An offering to the Lord.* In distinction from vows involving persons, certain pledged animals were *holy,* i.e., they could not be redeemed but were themselves to belong to the Lord.

27:14-25 VOWS INVOLVING REAL ESTATE

27:16 *The seed for it.* The size and value of land was to be computed according to the amount of seed necessary to put it into production. Its "money value" in terms of its redemption price was determined furthermore by the years to the next year of jubilee. (25:8 ff.)

27:25 *Twenty gerahs.* The *shekel* was not a coin but an amount of metal of varying weight. The *gerah* is estimated to have amounted to about one tenth of an ounce.

27:26-34 LIMITATIONS ON FREEWILL OFFERINGS

27:26 *Firstling.* The closing verses of this chapter mention persons, animals, and tithes which could not be vowed as a freewill offering and therefore could not be redeemed: (a) ceremonially clean firstlings belonged to the Lord (26, 27; Ex 13:2, 12); (b) anyone or anything "devoted," i.e., under the divine ban of destruction, was forfeit to the Lord (21, 28, 29; Jos 6:17); (c) the "tithes of herds and flocks" remained "holy to the Lord." (30-33)

NUMBERS

INTRODUCTION

Content

The name "Numbers" comes to us from the Septuagint and the Vulgate translations of the OT. It calls attention to a characteristic feature of the book. Counting and totaling of persons, animals, and things play a more prominent role than in other books of the Pentateuch (1:20-46; 3:14-51; 7:10-83; 26:5-51; 28:1—29:38; 31:32-52). However, these numberings are more or less incidental to the main contribution of Numbers to the Pentateuch as a whole. Among the Jews the fourth book of Moses was called "in the wilderness," the fifth Hebrew word of the first verse. This title, though rather general, nevertheless links the contents of Numbers with Israel's earlier march from Egypt to Mount Sinai (Ex 14—18). After the people had remained at the Holy Mount several months in order to enter into a covenant with the Lord (the remainder of Exodus) to be a "holy nation" (Leviticus), they embarked on their journey to Canaan. But instead of going by a direct route and arriving there within a short time, they were permitted to reach their goal only after 38 years of wandering in the desert. Numbers records what happened before their departure from Mt. Sinai and during the wilderness journey until they camped in the fields of Moab with only the Jordan separating them from the remainder of the Promised Land.

During this long desert sojourn the Israelites received additional instructions in covenant holiness. Some of the divine directives are attached to specific events during the journey, as was the case in Exodus and Leviticus. Some of these repeat and amplify previous legislation. A few new legal regulations are introduced to meet communal needs of protracted life in the desert. Others look forward to the occupation of Canaan and the sedentary life within its confines. Numbers looks even further into the future and sees God's purposes accomplished through His chosen people: there will be a scepter out of Judah, wielded by the Messianic King.

Authorship

Moses again dominates the scene, distinguishing him not only from the people but also from all other prophets. God spoke with him "mouth to mouth" (12:8). The recording of the stations in the desert is directly attributed to him (ch. 33). Those scholars who operate with some form of the source hypothesis (see Genesis, Introduction) assign the legal sections as well as some historical material to the P tradition, which reached its present form after the return from the Babylonian captivity in the sixth century B.C. The remaining parts of the book are identified as strands of J and E or a conflation of the two.

The Numbers in the Book of Numbers

A survey of the Book of Numbers should include some comments on the numerical data recorded in it and other parts of the Bible. The following brief remarks are based on two guiding principles. In the first place the numbers of the original text should not be regarded as fanciful inventions and therefore impossible and false. They were meant to represent a counting of persons and items that conformed to the facts in the case. In the second place every effort should be made to determine what the original text actually said and how it came to read now as it does.

It is a known fact that mistakes in numbers are the main source of misprints even in modern publications in spite of copyreaders and editorial scrutiny. The transmission of numerical data in the OT manuscripts was no exception. But the problem was aggravated by factors unique to the recording of figures in the Hebrew language. The writers and copyists did not have Arabic numerals. The word for a number had to be spelled out in consonants without affixed vowels. When abbreviations, consisting of the first letter of the word, came into use, they became an additional source of confusion (a modern parallel: the letter *t* could stand for 2, 3, 10, 20, 1,000). The individual letters of the alphabet were also pressed into service to designate figures, for example, *a* for 1. The first letter of the Hebrew alphabet could also be the abbreviated spelling for the word thousand. Groupings of vertical and horizontal strokes appear in ancient Aramaic documents to specify the number of thousands and hundreds in a given figure. These and similar factors encountered by copyists of the ancient manuscripts may account for many numerical difficulties in the present text.

Discussion has been provoked particularly by figures that appear to be excessively high. For example the census totals in the Book of Numbers are 603,550 and 601,730 men capable of bearing arms (1:46; 26:51). Accordingly the total population of Israel must have been 2½ to 3 million persons. Various attempts have been made to reduce these figures. None of these should be regarded as valid if it is motivated by the attempt to eliminate the miraculous intervention of God in sustaining His people in the desert.

It is apparent that most of the high figures involved the Hebrew word for thousand, *eleph*. However, this word also means family or clan (1:16; 10:4: "heads of the tribes"; see also Jos 22:21, 30). When the same consonants are supplied with different vowels, the word designates "chiefs" (Gn 36:15 ff.; Ex 15:15). It has been suggested, therefore, that in many instances this Hebrew *eleph* did not represent a number, as the later copyists assumed, but referred to an individual: a military leader of thousands, a commander of a large group, an officer, a fully equipped soldier. During the generations when Israel was under foreign domination this military meaning of the word was lost so that the copyists of the text understood it only as a number (a modern parallel would be "fore-men" spelled "four men" and so interpreted).

Taking the word *eleph* in the sense of a commander and the word for hundred to mean a contingent of soldiers, a recent writer suggested that the text of the census figures originally meant to say: 580 leaders of 235 contingents, each of which consisted of some 25 to 100 men. The total fighting force is then estimated at 18,000 men and the entire population at about 72,000. The second census in ch. 26 is computed with comparable results. It should be noted that such a large group of people still was in need of bread from heaven and water from a rock to keep them alive during 40 years of desert wandering. The same writer suggests that besides making unintentional errors of various kinds the later copyists apparently added a zero or two to the original figures (a modern way of expressing it) in order to make the history of Israel more impressive. It is a known fact that Rabbinic teaching glorified the past beyond the limits of the Biblical records. For example, the number of male Levites is given as 22,000 (3:39). By dropping a zero and making the figure 2,200 the result would be in a much better proportion to the total of all male firstborn in Israel, which is put at 2,273 (3:43). Admittedly such attempts to arrive at the intent of the original text rely on assumptions that remain tentative.

OUTLINE

A Generation in the Wilderness
From Sinai to Moab

I. 1:1—10:10 Instructions Anticipating the Wilderness Journey

A. 1:1—4:49 Organizational Provisions
B. 5:1—6:21 Provisions for Purity and Order in Camp
C. 6:22—9:14 Worship Provisions
D. 9:15—10:10 Provisions for Breaking and Making Camp

II. 10:11—21:35 On the March to the Promised Land
A. 10:11—20:13 From Sinai to Kadesh
B. 20:14—21:35 From Kadesh to Transjordan

III. 22:1—36:13 Events in Transjordan; Record of the Past; Provisions for the Future
A. 22:1—25:18 Two Encounters with the Moabites
B. 26:1-65 The Second Census
C. 27:1-11 Provision for Inheritance Through Daughters
D. 27:12-23 Joshua Commissioned to Succeed Moses
E. 28:1—29:40 Directives for Offerings in Canaan
F. 30:1-16 Directives for Vows by Women
G. 31:1-54 Midian Destroyed; Booty Divided
H. 32:1-42 Inheritance East of the Jordan
I. 33:1-49 A Recording of the Itinerary from Egypt to the Jordan
J. 33:50—36:12 Preparations for the Occupation of Canaan
K. 36:13 Conclusion

1:1—10:10 INSTRUCTIONS ANTICIPATING THE WILDERNESS JOURNEY

1:1—4:49 Organizational Provisions

1:1-54 ELEVEN MILITARY UNITS

1) 1:1-16 Census Officials Appointed

1:1 *Tent of meeting.* Erected and dedicated a month earlier, the tent of meeting was the place from which the Lord gave the directions to His people recorded in Leviticus (Ex 40:17; Lv 1:1). The first 10 chapters of Numbers contain the record of the instructions that Moses received *in the tent of meeting.* It differs from the former in that it supplies provisions for the march from Mt. Sinai to the Promised Land. The first chapter tells how the nation was organized into military contingents. On each day's journey the people were to proceed with the order and discipline of an army. The numerical strength of each unit was to be carefully recorded by "a man from each tribe . . . the head of the house of his fathers" (4). *The first day of the second month.* Nineteen days later Israel was to leave Mt. Sinai (10:11). No doubt this mustering could be completed so quickly because a census had been taken months earlier in order to levy the temple tax. (Ex 30:11-12; 38:26)

2) 1:17-46 Tabulation of the Census

1:20 *Reuben.* The tribes are not enumerated in the order in which the census tabulators are listed (5-15). In keeping with the purpose of the mustering they are grouped in threes according to their encampment in military units. Reuben, Simeon, Gad, for example, were deployed on the south side of the tabernacle.

1:46 *Their whole number.* See the Introduction, "The Numbers in the Book of Numbers." The total agrees with the round figure given in Ex 12:37 and with the exact count in Ex 38:26 and Nm 2:32. It is somewhat larger than the sum recorded after the lapse of 38 years (26:51). In both cases the figures for the individual groups add up to the given total.

3) 1:47-54 Exemptions: The Levites

1:47 *Not numbered.* Because the Levites were appointed "over the tabernacle," there was no need to tabulate their manpower in a military census. Their numbers and duties are therefore recorded separately in chs. 3—4.

1:52 *Standard.* This word occurs here and 13 times in the next chapter (only again SS 2:4). Very likely it designates a banner to identify the larger groups, while the individual tribes also had distinctive ensigns of some kind.

1:53 *Encamp.* How the various Levitical families were to *encamp around the tabernacle* is also set forth in 3:21 ff.

No wrath. Every unmediated approach to the

holy God works disaster (see Leviticus, especially 10:1-7). Communion with Him is possible only if men accept the means of grace, instituted in the covenant.

2:1-34 ORGANIZATION OF THE CAMP

2:2 *Facing the tent.* As the next chapter shows, the tribes were stationed quadrilaterally about the tabernacle but did not actually come into contact with it. The space immediately surrounding it was assigned to the Levites on three sides and to Moses, Aaron, and his sons on the remaining side. To make clear their central position the Levites are mentioned after the first two and before the last two military groups. (17)

2:32 *As numbered.* The number of each tribe is repeated as given in ch. 1 and the total also agrees with the figure given in 1:46. While each triad of tribes had approximately the same manpower, the vanguard on the east side was the strongest. (3-9)

3:1—4:49 ORGANIZATION OF LEVI

1) 3:1-4 Distinguished from the Priests

3:1 *Generations.* Cf. Gn 2:4 note.

3:3 *Anointed,* The difference in status between Aaron's sons, the priests, and the other descendants of Levi is indicated by their respective rites of installation. Aaron and his sons were *anointed* and "ordained" to perform "the rites within the sanctuary" (38; Ex 29; Lv 8—9). The Levites "were appointed" to their auxiliary tasks (4:49) at the tabernacle. The Levitical duties are described in general terms in 5-10. In 21-37 and in 4:1-33 each of the three "families" composing the tribe is given a specific assignment.

3:4 *Nadab and Abihu.* Cf. Lv 10:1-7; 1 Ch 24:1-6; Nm 20:25.

2) 3:5-13 Distinguished from the Other Tribes

3:9 *Wholly given.* Exempt from military duties, the Levites were chosen *from among the people* to give full-time assistance to the priests (8:16). Since they ministered to God's ordained representatives, their services, although humble and menial, were in the final analysis devoted to the Lord. God, the sovereign Lord, supplies many talents to some people, to others a smaller number. Not the results achieved by them but the use of them to their full potential is His criterion for bestowing the award of grace. (Mt 25:14-30; 1 Co 4:2; Mt 10:42; Heb 6:10-12)

3:12 *Instead of every first-born.* To remind the Israelites that in their liberation the firstborn in all of Egypt were slain, the *first-born* of Israel were to be considered forfeit to the Lord; in their stead and for their redemption the Levites were given wholly to the Lord (Ex 13:2; 22:29b; Nm 8:17). Animals were offered to the Lord in recognition of the same claim of God to Israel's firstborn. (Nm 18:15-18; Dt 12:6, 17)

3) 3:14-39 Census of All Levites;
Location; General Duties

3:15 *Fathers' houses.* The numbering of the Levites was to follow the pattern set in the census of the other tribes except that *every male from a month old and upward* was to be counted instead of only those that were old enough for military duty (1:17-18). The three "sons of Levi" and their immediate descendants are listed first (17-20). Then the names are repeated as each of the three major groups is (a) counted; (b) assigned a place in the encampment; (c) given its general area of responsibility. Their tasks are described in greater detail in ch. 4. The first group, the Gershonites, were to have "the charge of" the structural coverings of the ark (25, 26); the second, of the furnishing of the sanctuary (31); the third, of the structural framework of the tabernacle. (36)

3:39 *Twenty-two thousand.* This figure is too low for the sum of the three groups since 7,500 plus 8,600 plus 6,200 equals 22,300. It is also out of proportion to the figure for the total firstborn of all Israel, which according to 43 in 22,273. To make the figures for the various groups total 22,000 a scribal error no doubt raised the 300 to 600 in 28, a mistake easily accounted for in the Hebrew writing of the word for three and for six. In order to establish a reasonable ratio of the Levites to the other tribes it is furthermore suggested to lower the total by dropping the accretions of zeros to the original text in each of the individual items (7,500; 8,300; 6,200) making the total of Levite males 2,200 (see the Introduction). The number of Levites between 30 and 50 years would likewise be reduced from 8,580 to 858 (4:48). But the amount of redemption money at 5 shekels per person would then have to be adjusted by raising the amount by two zeros from 1,365 to 100,365. (3:50)

4) 3:40-51 Counted to Redeem All Firstborn

5) 4:1-49 Levites Between 30 and 50 Years

4:3 *Thirty years.* According to 8:24 the Levites were eligible for *work in the tent of meeting* at the age of 25. The difference in the wording of the two passages appears to envisage a different kind of service at the lower age from the full exercise of official duties at the age of 30. The Septuagint reads 25 years in both instances.

4:4 *The most holy things.* Most closely related to Moses and Aaron, the Kohathites had the most sacred assignment. They were to carry "the sanctuary and all the furnishings" after Aaron and his sons "have finished covering" them (15). Therefore they were explicitly warned not to handle or even "to look upon the holy things . . . lest they die." (15, 17-20)

4:11 *Golden altar.* "The altars" (3:31) were the *golden altar* of incense and the altar of burnt offering. (Ex 30:1-3; Nm 4:13)

4:28 *Ithamar.* The Kohathites were under the direct supervision of "Eleazar, the son of Aaron" (16). The other two divisions were *under the oversight of Ithamar,* the other son of Aaron. (33)

4:48 *8,580.* If this sum is to fit into the figures suggested in 3:39 note, the total as well as the individual items (36, 40, 44, 48) would have to be reduced by dropping the last zero. The number of Levites at work on the tabernacle would then be 858.

5:1—6:21 Provisions for Purity and Order in Camp

5:1-4 ELIMINATION OF DEFILEMENT

5:2 *Put out of the camp.* For the march toward Canaan the Israelites had been organized into functional units, surrounding the tabernacle on all sides (chs. 1—4). Next, directives were issued for the maintenance of purity and order within the camp. The first stipulation required that no one be tolerated within its confines who was a *leper*, had a *discharge*, or was *unclean through contact with the dead* (cf. Lv 13:45-46; 15:1-3, 25; 22:4; Nm 19:11-13). These measures were to keep Israel ceremonially clean and no doubt served also as hygienic precautions.

5:5-10 PROTECTION OF PROPERTY

5:7 *Make restitution.* Crowded camp life offered opportunities for acquiring property by unlawful means. Because the theft could easily remain undetected by men it is called "breaking faith with the Lord." *Restitution* was to be made to the rightful owner or his kinsmen according to Lv 6:1-7; in case neither of these could be found, the penalties were to be paid to the priest.

5:11-31 MARITAL PURITY

5:13 *She is undetected.* Close association in a camp furthermore heightened temptations to adultery. The integrity of marital relations, the basis of a healthy social order, was protected by a procedure unique in the OT. A husband, suspicious of his wife's fidelity, brought a cereal offering of remembrance (15). In order to invoke God's judgment upon her, the woman had to undergo an ordeal (16-31). While holding the cereal offering of remembrance and while under an oath of incrimination she was asked to drink "holy water," containing the dust that "is on the floor of the tabernacle." Her guilt or innocence would become manifest by the results that this potion, nonpoisonous or uninjurious itself, effected in her. This method of determining guilt or innocence was no magical process but depended on God's direct intervention. There is no other instance of trial by ordeal in the record of Israel's judicial procedures, and no instance of its application to an actual case is mentioned. Perhaps this "law in case of jealousy" was given to meet the unique social exigencies of camp life.

6:1-21 NAZARITE VOW

6:2 *A special vow.* The fourth provision for maintaining order and purity in the camp regulated the so-called *Nazirite* vow. Although not mentioned previously, it apparently was not an unknown rite of special consecration. Regulations for its practice were introduced at this point in order to take into account the unusual situations of camp life (cf. 9). As the RSV points out, the noun *Nazirite* is derived from a root meaning to "separate, consecrate, abstain." For some unspecified reason, but of his own free will and for a certain period of time, a person could make a special pledge of dedication to the Lord over and above the normal requirements of holiness. This "vow of separation" was to include three elements: (1) abstention from all products of the grapevine, fermented and unfermented (3, 4; cf. Lv 10:9; Am 2:11); (2) letting his hair grow (5); (3) avoidance of all contact with the dead. (6-12; see the priestly regulation in Lv 21:1-4)

6:13 *Has been completed.* When *the time of his separation* had been completed, a special sacrifice was to mark his release from the pledge (14-16). The lifelong dedication to God's cause of Samson and Samuel was not made by these men themselves (Ju 13:3-5; 1 Sm 1:28; see also Lk 1:15). It should also be noted that Nazirite and Nazareth (Nazarene) have a different etymological base, the latter being derived from a root meaning "a shoot, a branch."

6:22—9:14 Worship Provisions

6:22-27 THE AARONIC BLESSING

6:23 *You shall say.* In the following section some additional aspects of Israel's worship life come to the fore. After the tabernacle had been dedicated (Ex 40:1-33) and before Israel began its trip through the wilderness, the Lord had given directions for Israel's communal life (Nm 1:1—6:21). God's gracious attitude to the Israelites was to be expressed in a formula that Aaron was to use when he "lifted up his hands toward the people and blessed them" (Lv 9:22). Echoes of this benediction are found in the Psalms. (Ps 4:6; 67:1; 80:3, 7, 19; 119:135)

6:25 *Make his face to shine.* The blessing of divine protection (24) comes to God's people only because He does not frown upon their sins but graciously lets the beams of His forgiveness and good will stream out upon them.

6:26 *Lift up his countenance.* The same word in Hebrew is used for "face" (25) and for "countenance." When God's favor lights up His gaze upon us, the result is *peace,* well-being, wholeness, the integration of all contrary and disturbing elements of life into a harmonious oneness that has its center in God.

6:27 *Put my name.* The words of the blessing are not merely a pious wish. They actually bestow upon the recipient all the benefits that God's name makes available to man. (Cf. Ex 6:3 note)

7:1-89 GIFTS FOR THE TABERNACLE

7:1 *Finished . . . the tabernacle.* This chapter adds details that were not mentioned in the account of the dedication of the tabernacle and its various parts (Ex 40:1-33). For the transport of the tabernacle "six covered wagons and twelve oxen" were necessary. Out of gratitude for God's mercy these were supplied by "the leaders of the tribes" (2). The report of their offering is inserted here because the time for moving the tabernacle was near at hand. Other gifts "for the dedication of the altar" by each tribal representative are recorded in the same connection. The ceremony had extended over a period of 12 days (11).

7:12 *Judah.* Although the gifts are identical, they are listed individually in the roll call of the various leaders. The reading of this tabulation may prove wearisome. But its repetitiousness stresses the fact that God looks for a response to His goodness from all its beneficiaries. No tribe was an inactive member of the chosen people.

7:89 *The voice speaking.* Adding details of the mode of divine communication, this verse apparently forms the conclusion of what the Lord "said to Moses" (4; Ex 25:21-22). It could also serve as a general introduction to the following series of divine directives, each of which is prefaced by: "the Lord said." (8:1, 5, 23)

8:1-4 POSITION OF THE LAMPS

8:2 *The lampstand.* The "Menorah" or seven-armed candelabrum had been a freewill offering of the people and is described more fully in Ex 25:31-40. It was to "be set up so as to give light upon the space in front of it" where stood the table of the bread of the Presence (Ex 25:37). It was to be Aaron's duty to *set up the lamps* (KJV: "light the lamps") according to the specific directive, given to Moses (see also Ex 27:20-21; 30:7-8). Since the sanctuary was about to leave the place of its construction, this detail is added at this point to indicate that all provisions for its proper use in the future had been completed.

8:5-26 INSTALLATION OF THE LEVITES

8:6 *From among the people.* The duties of the Levites had been delineated in chs. 3—4. Before they began to carry out their assignments, they were formally inducted into office. The command to set them apart for their sacred services came to Moses (5-19) and was executed by him and Aaron (20-26). The rites of installation consisted of (a) ceremonial and physical purification (6-8); (b) the transfer of the people's guilt to the Levites and from them to the sacrificial animals (9-12); (c) the dedication of the Levites as a "wave offering." (11)

8:10 *Lay their hands.* Because the Lord had "taken the Levites from among the people . . . instead of every first-born" (3:11-13), the people's sins were symbolically laid upon them as a substitutionary oblation (Lv 1:4). The Levites in turn laid their hands on the heads of the bulls which were slain "to make atonement for the Levites." (12; Ex 29:10)

8:11 *As a wave offering.* To perform this ritual Aaron no doubt led them to the altar and then drew them back. (Cf. Lv 8:27)

8:19 *To make atonement.* Atoning sacrifices were brought only by the priests. But by their *service for the people of Israel at the tent of meeting* and by their "attendance upon Aaron and his sons" (22) the Levites contributed to the *atonement for the people.*

8:24 *Twenty-five years.* Cf. 4:3 note.

9:1-14 PASSOVER OBSERVANCE ADJUSTED

9:1 *The first month of the second year.* Not all Israelites felt that they were eligible to proceed on the journey which was to begin 20 days after final directions for it had been given (1:1; 10:11). They were aware that a person who had not kept the Passover was to "be cut off from his people" (13). But some of them had been "unclean" and therefore had been excluded from participation in the Passover when it was observed on its regular day, the 14th day of the first month. Their dilemma was presented to the Lord. (8)

9:9-11 *On the fourteenth day.* The Lord permitted such *unclean* persons to observe the Passover 2 weeks later. By taking advantage of this dispensation all Israelites could be prepared to undertake the journey into the wilderness, which was to begin 6 days later. This special provision was to apply also when their *descendants* in the desert had strayed *afar off on a journey* (lit. "on a distant way"). However, the basic requirements of the Passover were not abrogated. (11-12; Ex 12:46)

9:15—10:10 Provisions for Breaking and Making Camp

9:15-23 THE CLOUD

9:17 *Set out; and . . . encamped.* The final directive for the departure from Sinai and the journey in the wilderness gave explicit marching orders. The first of these came from God in the form of a cloud. It had guided Israel on its way out of Egypt (Ex 13:21-22; 14:19-20). When it originally had taken its place over the completed tabernacle the purpose which it was to serve in the future was briefly outlined (15; Ex 40:34-38). It was to signal the breaking and making of camp. This function is here repeated and explained in greater detail because God was about to lead His people by this means on their way to the Promised Land. Israel showed its faith in God's directing their going out and their coming in; they "kept the charge of the Lord," even when He delayed their forward movement for as long as a month or longer. (17-22; cf. Ps 16:11; 27:11; 119:105; 139:3; 142:3)

10:1-10 THE TRUMPETS

10:2 *For breaking camp.* Israel was to follow the guidance of God in an orderly fashion. Like a large military unit it was to be summoned for action by prearranged signals given by *two silver trumpets.* These instruments were straight metal tubes, different from the curved ram's horn, also translated trumpet (Ex 19:16, 19; 20:18; Lv 25:9). At the blast of one trumpet the leaders of Israel "gathered themselves" to Moses (4). At the sound of both "all the congregation" was summoned to the tabernacle (3). The signal to break camp was to "sound an alarm," the sustained blowing of both trumpets (7). The tribes stationed on the east side of the tabernacle were to take the lead and set the pace for the others. (2:3-8; 10:14-17)

10:9 *Go to war.* The trumpets were to be used later when Israel was in its land in time of war and on days of "gladness." (9-10; Lv 25:9)

10:11—21:35 ON THE MARCH TO THE PROMISED LAND

10:11—20:13 From Sinai to Kadesh

10:11-36 FROM SINAI INTO THE WILDERNESS OF PARAN

10:11 *On the twentieth day.* Twenty days after final preparations for the journey had been completed (1:1) Israel broke camp from Mt. Sinai "by stages," that is, according to the prearranged orders of march. The account emphasizes that the prescribed procedure was followed by recording the sequence of the tribal groups and once more listing the leaders, known from ch. 2.

10:12 *Paran.* Moving in a northeasterly direction, the tribes, on signal, settled *in the wilderness of Paran*, perhaps a general name for all the territory comprising the Sinai peninsula. The northern reaches of *Paran* are called the wilderness of Zin (cf. Nm 20:1; 13:26). From there the borders of the Promised Land could have been reached within a short time. The next chapters (10:11—21:35) explain why it took 38 more years before Israel arrived in "the plains of Moab," opposite the river Jordan.

10:17 *The tabernacle.* Those Levites who bore the structural parts of the tabernacle set out with the first contingent of three tribes (4:21-33). The Kohathites, "carrying the holy things" (21; 4:27-32) and thus constituting "the midst of the camps" (2:17), followed along with the next three standards.

10:29 *The son of Reuel.* Cf. Ex 2:18 note. Hobab, the Midianite brother-in-law of Moses, is called his "father-in-law" in Ju 4:11. Perhaps he had in the meantime become the head of his family. Although God was directing the march of the Israelites, they needed help from an experienced man in the ordinary tasks of setting up a camp. Hobab apparently was persuaded to cast his lot with Israel because people identified with him were among the inhabitants of Canaan. (Ju 1:16 note; 4:11)

10:33 *The ark . . . before them.* If taken literally, this sentence would say that the ark of the Lord was carried in advance of the entire marching group contrary to the general rule that it was to be "in the midst of the camps" (2:17). It is possible that such a deviation from general practice was decreed for the first 3 days of the journey (cf. Jos 3:6). But the reference to the ark may merely want to emphasize the fact that the real guide of Israel was not Hobab but the Lord who dwelled above the mercy seat of the ark. He directed the course of the march through "the cloud."

11:1—12:16 ON THE WAY TO KADESH

1) 11:1-3 Murmuring at Taberah

11:1 *Complained.* Although the march to the fields of Moab lasted a whole generation, only comparatively few incidents along the way are recorded. Almost all of them are variations of the same theme: Israel's murmurings and revolts against God's guidance. The story of the chosen people is not an epic of national heroism; it is not the glorious record of a people willing to suffer hardship for the sake of freedom. They *complained* (11:1-3); they "wept" over the food (11:4-35); they rebelled against Moses (chs. 12 and 16); they "raised a loud cry" after hearing the report of the spies (13:1-36); they disobeyed an express command not to enter Canaan from the south (14:39-45); they "contended with Moses" because of lack of water (20:1-5); even after reaching Moab they "spoke against God and against Moses" (21:4-9). And so it had been from the beginning (Ex 14:10-12; 15:22-25; 16; 17). And so it is with us. It is only because "the steadfast love of the Lord never ceases," because "his mercies . . . are new every morning," that we remain His true children and do not turn back to the slavery of self, materialism, and the demonic bondage of evil. (Lm 3:22-23; Ml 3:6)

2) 11:4-35 Murmuring at Kibroth-hattaavah

11:11 *Why hast thou?* The petulant insolence of Israel stretched the patience of Moses to the breaking point and brought words of complaint to his lips that resemble Israel's murmurings and weeping (cf. Jer 20; 1 K 19:4). Because he turned to the Lord in his feeling of insufficiency and frustration his complaint did not degenerate into rebellion. The Lord came to the aid of His weak and distraught servant. He gave him a twofold solution of his problem.

11:16 *Seventy men.* First of all, Moses' task of administering so large and unstable a nation was to be lightened by the appointment of *seventy men of the elders of Israel* who were to "bear the burden of the people with" him. (17). The Lord also removed the immediate cause of Israel's irritating weeping by an oversupply of meat. (18-20)

11:17 *Some of the spirit.* God's Spirit equips the spirit of His servants in various degrees. Moses' assistants were to work in harmony with him in carrying out God's will. Therefore they were to be endowed with the same spiritual gifts that Moses possessed in such an extraordinary measure. At the same time they were not to supplant him as the sole leader of the people.

11:24 *Gathered seventy men.* These *seventy men* could have been the same that were chosen on Jethro's advice (Ex 18:21 ff.; see also 24:1). In that event their office at this time received divine sanction. As evidence of their approbation, "they prophesied." The Hebrew verb to prophesy is here not in the form in which it is usually used to express the mediation of a prophetic message throught the Spirit. The form used here stresses that the Spirit manifested His presence by overpowering a person and producing in him ecstatic phenomena. (1 Sm 10:6; 19:20-24; see also 18:10; 1 K 18:29; 22:10, Acts 2:1-3)

11:25 *Did so no more.* This translation is preferable to KJV "and did not cease." This extraordinary manifestation of divine power took place only in order to validate the authority of the 70 elders. When they left the tent, this miraculous gift was no longer available to them.

11:28 *Forbid them.* For some reason two of the elders were prevented from leaving the camp proper and assembling around the tent. When they too "prophesied," Joshua feared that they were assuming authority in competition with Moses. However, the latter assured him that the Lord gives His Spirit under various conditions for the same purpose. (Lk 9:49-50)

11:31 *Quails from the sea.* Cf. Ex 16:13 note. Moses was at a loss how to provide meat for so large a people (21-22). But the Lord's hand was not "shortened." (23)

11:33 *Anger of the Lord.* God gave the Israelites what they craved. But because of their rebellious attitude He turned the fulfillment of their desires into *a very great plague*. Its victims gave the place its name "the graves of craving." Material things that we insist on having and are acquired at all costs often turn out to be a bane rather than a blessing.

3) 12:1-16 Opposition by Miriam and Aaron

12:1 *Spoke against.* This event took place at the next recorded place of encampment, Hazeroth (11:35). Moses' sister and brother attacked his preeminence. The subterfuge for their claim to equal authority with him was his marriage to *a Cushite woman*. On his flight from Pharaoh Moses had married Zipporah, daughter of the Midianite Jethro (Ex 2:21). After her father had brought her to the Israelite camp she is not mentioned again (Ex 18:1-6). Since the Hebrew word *cush* usually refers to Ethiopia, some think that after the death of Zipporah Moses had entered a second marriage with a woman of that nationality who had left Egypt with the Israelites. The explanatory sentence *for he had married a Cushite woman* seems to suggest a rather recent event. In Hab 3:7 Cushan and Midian are parallel towns. Therefore others believe that the Cushite woman mentioned here was Zipporah, who belonged to a tribe of the larger group called Midianites.

12:3 *Was very meek.* Moses did not vociferously rise to his own defense or resort to repressive measures against his brother and sister. He was humble before the Lord, who quickly acted in his vindication (Hab 2:3). Moses' faults and virtues are mentioned with equal candor. Here his humility motivates God's intervention in his behalf.

12:8 *Mouth to mouth.* Moses held a unique position. God communicated His will through him more directly and intimately than through any other prophet, including Aaron and "Miriam, the prophetess" (Ex 25:22; 33:11; Dt 18:15, 18). He was even granted to see *the form of the Lord*. (Cf. Ex 33:18 note)

12:13 *Heal her, O God.* Only Miriam was punished. Perhaps she was the instigator of the opposition and Aaron only the weak-willed accomplice (cf. Ex 32:1-6, 21-24). Or perhaps his full confession of guilt averted the Lord's anger (11). When Moses interceded for his offending sister without a word of recrimination, he had to be nothing short of "very meek." (3)

12:14 *Seven days.* Cured of her disease, Miriam was nevertheless required to observe the period of isolation prescribed for the cleansing of lepers (Lv 14:8). God was very lenient with her. A daughter who had so disgraced her father that he *spit in her face* deserved public rebuke. Miriam had offended the Lord Himself. Dt 25:8-9)

13:1—20:13 EVENTS IN PARAN AND AT KADESH

1) 13:1—14:10a Exploration of Canaan by Spies

13:3 *From the wilderness of Paran.* After their reconnaissance of the land, the spies returned to Kadesh, which was located in the northern part of a larger area called the *wilderness of Paran* (25; cf. 10:12 note). At Kadesh the Israelites were only some 40 miles southwest of Beer-sheba and the southern border of the Promised Land. But at Kadesh the Israelites so insolently provoked God that He sentenced them to more than 30 years of wandering in the desert. He therefore thwarted their high-handed attempt to penetrate the land at once from the south (14:39-45). According to Dt 1:22 the command of the Lord that spies be sent was His answer to Israel's request for such an exploration of the land.

13:8 *Hoshea.* The 12 men chosen to explore Canaan were not the same tribal leaders mentioned in 1:5-15. Of them only two are mentioned again: Caleb and Hoshea, the son of Nun. Moses had changed the latter's name from Hoshea (salvation) to Joshua (the Lord's salvation). First mentioned in Ex 17:9, this "minister of Moses" had perhaps been renamed by Moses long before his assignment to be one of the scouting parties (11:28). The older name occurs again in an account at the end of Moses' activity. (Dt 32:44, RSV note *h*)

13:17 *Negeb.* Traversing the area of Palestine called *the Negeb* (the dry land) and ascending the central highlands, the spies penetrated as far north as Rehob, in the vicinity of Hamath, on the Orontes River (21; 2 K 14:28). This brief summary of the entire territory explored by the spies is followed by a more detailed account of their experiences in one of the areas (22-24). In the Negeb they were closer to their home base and were able to carry out the assignment "to bring some of the fruit of the land." (20)

13:22 *Anak.* As a common noun this word means necklace. Nothing is known of these people except their reputed great size (cf. Gn 6:4 note; also Dt 9:2). The descendants of Anak are called Nephilim. (KJV: "giants")

13:23 *Eshcol.* This valley is mentioned only in connection with the spying out of the land (32:9; Dt 1:24). The name given to it at that time apparently did not continue to be used.

13:26 *Brought back word.* In their report the spies praised the fertility of Canaan (27). But when most of them maintained that Israel was not able to conquer a land studded with such fortified cities and occupied by so many and formidable peoples, Caleb tried to counteract their discouraging remarks (28-30). Although only Caleb is mentioned in this rebuttal to the other spies, Joshua no doubt joined him. (14:6-10)

13:32 *Devours its inhabitants.* The 10 spies attempted to support their claim that the Israelites were no match for the Canaanites. These *men of great stature* were able to exterminate one another and denude the land of its inhabitants although they had the protection of fortified cities. How could Israel hope to cope with such experienced warriors?

14:1 *The whole congregation.* This outburst of dissatisfaction exceeded previous murmurings. It had the support of *the whole congregation.* Its vehemence was apparent furthermore in the radical decision to "go back to Egypt" (3). The phrase "choose a captain" (lit. "give a head") may also mean: let us be headstrong and insist this time to have things our way. (Neh 9:17: "they stiffened their neck")

14:5 *Fell on their faces.* Moses and Aaron sensed the gravity of the situation and in a posture of abject meekness importuned the people to reconsider their rash decision.

14:6 *Rent their clothes.* By this gesture Joshua and Caleb warned the Israelites that their action was equivalent to blasphemy (Mt 26:65; Acts 14:14). Then they continued to rally them to trust the Lord. If they did so, they urged, He would give them "the land which flows with milk and honey." But the contenders for the Lord barely escaped being stoned by the rioting people.

14:9 *They are bread.* Although the land "devours its inhabitants" (13:32), the Israelites would be able to exterminate them as easily as if they were eating bread.

2) 14:10b-38 Exclusion of a Generation from Canaan

14:12 *Make of you a nation.* Cf. Ex 32:10 note.

14:13 *Moses said.* Moses readily admitted that Israel deserved that the Lord "kill this people as one man" (15). He rested his appeal for divine forbearance entirely in God. His glory would suffer, he argued, if it appeared that He was unable to put into execution what He had clearly announced to the patriarchs. Furthermore the "nations who had heard" His fame would scoff because in their view the defeat of a people was also a proof of the impotence of their gods (13-16; Ex 32:11-12; 9:29; 12:12; Ju 16:24; Is 37:18-20). But Moses knew that ultimately this kind of daring wrestling with God for the life of Israel was valid only if God would "pardon the iniquity of this people" (19). In "forgiving iniquity and transgression" His glory shines most brilliantly. (Ex 34:6-9; cf. Ex 20:4 note)

14:20 *Your word.* A prayer of intercession "has great power in its effects." (Ja 5:16; Gn 18:22-33)

14:22 *Ten times.* This is regarded as a round figure (compare our "dozen times"). Although the number of recorded murmurings approached this total, the measure of Israelite iniquities was full. Their continued "faithlessness' (lit. "whoredoms," 33) had brought about a great turning point in their lives and the lives of their children.—God always forgives penitent sinners, even more than 70 times 70 times. But the natural consequences of disobedience to His will are often not eliminated and serve His purposes in the lives of His people.

14:24 *Caleb.* Cf. 13:26 note. Joshua was to be Moses' successor. He and Caleb were the only ones not to be affected by the Lord's decree.

14:25 *The way to the Red Sea.* This directive did not mean that the Israelites were to return to the sea that they had first crossed in escaping from Egypt. The Red Sea here refers to the northern arm of the Red Sea, now known as the Gulf of Aqaba. (Cf. Ex 13:18 note)

14:34-35 *Forty years.* Two years had elapsed since the liberation from Egypt. During the remaining 38 years of wandering *this wicked congregation* was to *come to a full end.*

14:37 *Died by plague.* Those who lead others into temptation have the greater sin. (Mt 18:6-7)

3) 14:39-45 False Obedience Punished by Defeat

14:40 *We will go up.* Revolting against God's leadership, the people had just said: "Let us . . . go back to Egypt" (4). Suddenly they insisted on giving evidence of their faith but in their own way and in defiance of God's direct command. Despair and presumption are but the obverse sides of the same coin of unbelief. (Jer 17:9; Eph 4:22-23)

14:45 *Hormah.* The name means "complete destruction." The place was so named after the Israelites later defeated the enemies there. (21:3; Dt 1:44)

4) 15:1-41 Provisions of a Renewed Covenant

15:1 *The Lord said.* Only a few chapters (15—21) record what happened during the next 38 years of wandering in the wilderness. Furthermore, none of the events in these chapters is supplied with a definite date. But since Israel had so completely broken its covenant ties and had suffered such a dismal defeat, it may be assumed that it was not long after the debacle recorded in the previous chapter before the Lord assured His erring people that He did indeed "abound in steadfast love" (14:18). The younger generation did not have to abandon hope that they would "come into the land" of Canaan (2, 18). Some of the ceremonies by which the covenant people were to enjoy communion with God were therefore repeated. In some instances additions or adjustments were made.

15:4 *Cereal offering.* The first section (1-6) sets forth how much flour, wine, and oil was to accompany the various animal sacrifices.

15:20 *Coarse meal.* In the land of Canaan offerings of firstfruits were to include *a cake* made of the meal that was ground from the first grain as it came from the threshing floor. (Cf. Lv 2:14)

15:22 *If you err.* The whole nation had been punished for its disobedience and 10 of the spies had "died by plague before the Lord" (14:20-38). But the people were to have no fear that the Lord had changed His covenant policy regarding sin done "unwittingly," whether by the whole congregation (23-26) or by an individual. (27-31; cf. Lv 4:1-5, 13)

15:30 *With a high hand.* The person who committed sins in defiance of God and with malice aforethought removed himself from God's covenant grace and forgiveness. (Cf. Mk 3:28-30; 1 Jn 5:16-17)

15:32 *On the sabbath day.* As a warning against willful sinning a breaker of the Sabbath law was executed (Ex 35:2-3). It had been decreed that such a person was to "be put to death" (Ex 31:14), but the mode of execution had not been specified. Moses and Aaron therefore awaited explicit directions and then had them carried out. (Cf. Lv 24:12)

15:38 *Tassels.* Time and again the Israelites had forgotten the Lord. To help them remember "all the commandments" they were given a mnemonic device. On the *corners* (literally "wings," for example, the sleeves) of their garments they were to fasten a fringe of tassels, fastened by *a cord of blue.* So equipped, they would not be able to engage in any activity without being visibly warned "not to follow after your own heart and your own eyes, which you are inclined to go after wantonly" (39; Dt 22:12). This outward means to help them "be holy" (40) like all others was later abused and made the means of parading empty piety. (Mt. 23:5; see also 6:1)

5) 16:1—16:50 Rebellion by Korah
and Confederates

16:2 *Rose up.* The text does not indicate when during the 38 years of wandering this insurrection raised its ugly head against the mediators of the covenant, Moses and Aaron. One should think that the sad experiences recorded in ch. 14 would not soon have been forgotten. But Israel's repeated murmurings had previously come in rapid succession and within short intervals (Ex 14:11-12; 15:23-24; 16:2-3, 20, 26-28; 17:1-2). Two separate groups joined hands in an attempt to overthrow the divinely established order. Each gave vent to its particular grievance. Dathan and Abiram apparently based their challenge to Moses' leadership on their claim that they were descendants of Reuben, the firstborn of the tribal ancestors. The other group of malcontents was lead by Korah, one of the "sons of Levi" (7). Since these movements arose at the same time, their development and catastrophic end are recorded in an account that deals with both rebellions simultaneously. Although the Levites had been given the distinction "to do service in the tabernacle of the Lord" (9; chs. 3—4), they presumed to "seek the priesthood also," to which God had appointed only Aaron and his immediate family. They went so far as to claim priestly privileges for every Israelite, "for all the congregation are holy." (3)

16:13 *A prince over us.* Aaron was merely the right hand of Moses, against whose leadership the whole movement was ultimately directed. Dathan and Abiram claimed that Moses' divine authorization was false because he had failed to give them the promised "inheritance." They insisted that he had misled them to kill them in "the wilderness," in comparison with which Egypt was a "land flowing with milk and honey." (See this description applied to the Promised Land in Lv 20:24)

16:26 *From the tents of these wicked men.* All who showed their agreement with the rebels by refusing to leave their dwellings "went down alive into Sheol" with "all their goods" (32-33). The earth opened and "closed over them." Members of Korah's immediate family apparently were not involved. (Cf. Nm 26:9-11; also the heading of such psalms as Ps 42; 1 Ch 6:22)

16:37 *They are holy.* The censers of the rebels were to be set aside for a sacred purpose. Hammered into bronze "plates as a covering for the altar," they were to be "a sign to the people of Israel" of the dire consequences of disobeying the divinely established rule of worship.

16:41 *All the congregation.* The people's mind had been so poisoned by the rebellious propaganda that they refused to acknowledge the death of the instigators as God's punishment. They charged that Moses had *killed the people of the Lord.* However, God's threat to "consume them in a moment" was again averted by Moses' intercession. (45)

16:46 *Take your censer.* Ordinarily Aaron offered incense only on the altar in the sanctuary (Ex 30:1-10; Lv 16:12-13). But extraordinary means were required to make atonement for the stricken people. When Aaron ran "into the midst of the assembly" with his censer, "the plague was stopped" (47-48). It was to teach the people that a sacred rite, executed by the divinely authorized person, had a salutary effect while the illegitimate use of it by Korah had resulted in death.

16:49 *14,700.* If the original text is interpreted according to the theory mentioned in the Introduction, the number of the dead amounted to 14 leaders or fully armed men and 700 others.

6) 17:1—19:22 Events and Provisions

a. 17:1-13 Aaron's Status Demonstrated
in the Wake of the Rebellion

17:3 *Write Aaron's name.* Korah, a Levite, and Dathan and Abiram, Reubenites, had asserted equal status for all tribes before the Lord. Their claim was a direct violation of the words that God had spoken through Moses. In order to demonstrate the validity of this ordinance the Lord let Aaron's rod, inscribed with his name, blossom during the night while the staves, representing all other tribes, showed no signs of life. This miraculous sign was to convince the people to "make an end of their murmurings against" the Lord. Aaron's rod was to be placed "before the testimony" (that is the ark of the covenant) and preserved there "as a sign for the rebels." (10; Ex 25:21-22; Heb 9:4)

b. 18:1-32 Status of Priests
and Levites Reaffirmed

18:1 *Bear iniquity.* The recent calamity made it necessary to assure the people that not everyone "who comes near to the tabernacle of the Lord shall die" (17:12). God had not acted arbitrarily. Aaron and his sons still were privileged to "attend to the duties of the sanctuary and . . . the altar" (5). Their particular functions did not have to be itemized again (see for example Lv 6:8-18). At the same time it remained true that their office made them liable to bear the consequences if *iniquity* was incurred *in connection with* the performance or the neglect of their sacred duties. (Ex 28:36, 38)

18:2 *Bring your brethren.* The status of the Levites also remained unchanged. "No one else" besides them was to assist the priest in "all the duties of the tent" (cf. chs. 3—4). But they themselves were excluded from priestly functions in the sanctuary or at the altar. If these regulations were followed, no one would die. (3, 7)

18:8 *A perpetual due.* Occupied with sacred duties, the priests were dependent for their livelihood on *whatever is kept of the offerings* (lit. "the heave offerings"), that is, whatever had not been designated as belonging to the Lord and therefore need not be burned. The gifts of the firstfruits and the "redemption price" of human firstlings was to be another source of income. (15-16)

18:19 *Covenant of salt.* Cf. Lv 2:13 note.

18:21 *Every tithe.* Every Israelite was required to return a tithe to the Lord (Lv 27:30-33). Because the Levites like the priests had "no inheritance" in Canaan, their livelihood was to come from *their service in the tent of meeting. In return for their service* they were to receive whatever part of the tithe was not designated for "an offering to the Lord" on the altar. The main source of their recompense seems to have been the tithe levied on the crops that the other tribes grew on their inheritance (28). Later Moses gave directions how the tithe of "the yield . . . from the field year by year" was to be collected and disbursed once the Israelites were settled in their inheritance. (Dt 14:22-29)

18:25 *Said to Moses.* The first part of this chapter, spoken to Aaron (1, 8, 20), dealt with the priests and Levites and assigned them a unique position. The following verses were addressed to Moses. He in turn was charged with the supervision of the priests and the Levites and their relationship toward one another. The latter were to pay a "tithe of the tithe" to Aaron the priest. (26)

c. 19:1-22 Purification from Contact with the Dead

19:2 *Red heifer.* Contact with corpses or an animal carcass rendered the Israelites ritually unclean (Lv 5:2; 11:24-28; 21:1-4, 10-11; 22:4-7; Nm 6:6-12). The death of many in "the affair of Korah" (16:49) called for special measures of purification. The defilement was to be removed by the application of ritually prepared water. A young cow was to be slain and burned outside the camp. Materials used also in the purification from leprosy were added to the fire (6; Lv 14:4, 6, 49). The ashes were to be kept "for the water [of purification] for impurity" (9). The Hebrew word for impurity is used of the ceremonial uncleanness incurred by a woman's "discharge of blood" (Lv 15:19-35). No reason is given for the requirement that the color of the sacrificial animal was to be red. In addition it had to meet two other requirements: it had to be *without defect*; it was never to have been used as an ordinary draft animal.—All rites to achieve ceremonial cleanness and "the purification of the flesh" would not have spanned the gap between the holy God and sinful mankind if they had not pointed to the only acceptable sacrifice: Christ Jesus, who "offered himself without blemish to God." (Heb 9:13-14)

7) 20:1 Miriam's Death

20:1 *In the first month.* The year in which the death of Miriam occurred is not supplied. No doubt it took place at the end of the 38 years of wandering (cf. 33:36-39), that is, in the 40th year after the liberation from Egypt. For *the wilderness of Zin* see 10:12 and 13:3 notes.

8) 20:2-13 Moses Excluded from Canaan

20:2 *No water.* Soon after the Israelites had left Egypt they had "found fault with Moses" because "there was no water for the people to drink" (Ex 17:1-7). Since that time many of the "brethren died before the Lord." But the younger generation showed no greater trust in the Lord than their elders. At Moses' intercession the Lord gave them additional evidence that He was able to supply all their needs.

20:8 *Tell the rock.* At Rephidim Moses had been commanded to "strike the rock." (Ex 17:6)

20:10 *Shall we bring forth?* "Meek" Moses also had clay feet (12:3). It appears that his endurance and patience were exhausted. Goaded by the repeated murmurings against his person, he succumbed to the thought that he had to assert himself against the *rebels* or at least take some credit for the miraculous supply of water. Instead of letting the Word of the Lord reveal its power (8) he sought to make his contribution to the miracle by striking the rock twice. Thereby he had failed to "sanctify" God "before the eyes of the people." His leadership was to come to an end before he could bring this "assembly into the land."

20:13 *Meribah.* The place where "contention" with the Lord over the need of water had previously occurred was named Meribah (Ex 17:1-7). In order to distinguish the second incident from the one at Rephidim, this place is called Meribah of Kadesh. (27:14; or Meribath-kadesh, Dt 32:51)

20:14—21:35 From Kadesh to Transjordan

20:14-21 PASSAGE THROUGH EDOM DENIED

20:14 *To the king of Edom.* By turning northward from Kadesh the Israelites would have been able to take a direct route to the Transjordan Valley. Athwart this line of march lay Edom. It was occupied by the descendants of Esau, Jacob's twin brother (Gn 25:21-26; 36:1 ff.). Although the Israelites promised their "brother" a peaceful passage through the land, they were forbidden to trespass on Edomite territory (Dt 2:4). According to Ju 11:17 the king of Moab likewise responded negatively to a similar request by the Israelites.

20:16 *An angel.* Cf. Ex 14:19.

20:17 *The King's Highway.* This important caravan route and military road ran northward from Ezion-Geber on the Gulf of Aqaba. It crossed Edomite and Moabite territory and continued east of the Dead Sea and the Jordan as far north as Damascus. Denied the use of this highway by their kinsmen and forbidden to employ warlike measures, the Israelites took a circuitous route around Edom and Moab. (21:4; Dt 2:4-9)

20:22-29 AARON'S DEATH

20:22 *Mt. Hor.* Before the Israelites had gone far from the "border of the land of Edom," Aaron was "gathered to his people" "in the fortieth year after the people of Israel had come out of the land of Egypt, on the first day of the fifth month" (33:38). His death occurred after his son Eleazar had been installed in his place on Mt. Hor (Dt. 32:50). The territory in the vicinity of this mountain is called Moseroth ("chastisements"; 33:31; Dt 10:6). Its exact location has not been definitely established.

21:1-3 THE CITIES OF ARAD DESTROYED

21:1 *The way of Atharim.* Before the Israelites left the area of Kadesh they destroyed the cities of the Canaanite *king of Arad.* He had attacked and defeated the Israelites when they had attempted to move northward into his territory on a road called *the way of Atharim* (14:39-45). The KJV, following the Septuagint and the Vulgate, translates "the way of the spies." For "Hormah" see 14:45 note.

21:4-9 IMPATIENT ISRAEL PUNISHED BY SERPENTS

21:6 *Fiery serpents.* Because the people realized that they were on "the way to the Red Sea" which led them southward away from Canaan, they "became impatient" and once more rebelled against the Lord's guidance. Many of them died when they were bitten by serpents, called fiery no doubt because of the burning pain produced by their poisonous bite.

21:9 *A bronze serpent.* Upon Moses' intercession for the rebels God spared those who accepted the means of rescue that He provided in the form of *a bronze serpent*, set *on a pole.* Healing did not magically emanate from the coiled piece of metal but depended on an act of faith in the power of God's Word. Every victim lived if he accepted God's promise that looking at the bronze serpent would counteract the venomous bite. When at a later time healing power was not attributed to the Creator but to the creature, King Hezekiah destroyed the serpent (2 K 18:4). His action was all the more necessary since serpents were the idolatrous object of veneration among the earliest peoples.—But the rescue from death that God wrought through the bronze serpent was only a type of what He purposed to do when His incarnate Son was lifted to the tree of the cross. When "faith looks up to" Christ crucified, all victims of the fatal venom of sin are saved from eternal death. (Jn 3:14-18, 36)

21:10-20 JOURNEY AROUND EDOM AND MOAB

21:10 *Set out.* Having "set out by the way to the Red Sea" (4), the Israelites had turned eastward and northward. Eventually they reached the territory of the Brook Zered (12), which flows into the southern end of the Dead Sea. Later they came to the area of the Arnon River, which empties into the Dead Sea halfway to its northern shore and forms "the boundary ...between Moab and the Amorites" (13). It appears that at this stage of the journey the Israelites followed a course just east of the King's Highway, skirting and at times crossing into Edomite territory. At certain places some of the Edomite tribes enriched themselves by selling food to the desert wanderers despite their king's command (Dt 2:6). The borders of Edom and Moab may have been somewhat fluid, and central control may not always have been effective. Pressing still farther north, they encamped at "the valley lying in the region" (lit. "the field") of Moab" (18-20). Here they were at a high spot which overlooked "the desert." The RSV note calls attention to the fact that *jeshimon* may also be a proper name (cf. 1 Sm 23:19, 24b; 26:1). The word *pisgah* in 20 (literally "the cleft") always has the definite article in Hebrew. Since it denotes various heights it probably should be translated as a common noun (23:13-14; Dt 3:27; 34:1). In a number of instances the places of encampment, listed here and in ch. 33 and Dt 1—2, cannot be identified with certainty.

21:14 *The Book of the Wars of the Lord.* Nothing more is known of this book. It appears to have been a separate collection of songs celebrating the victories of Israel against opposing forces. There were numerous occasions for such rejoicing over God's help. The song of Moses would be a good example (Ex 15). The quotation from the song is so brief that it merely indicates the joy of the Israelites that they reached the unidentified sites in the *valleys of the Arnon.* (Cf. 17-18, 27-30)

21:17 *This song.* Another poetic expression of joy, known as "the song of the well," was sung because the Lord had led them to a place where they merely had to dig below the surface to find a natural supply of water. The days were over when they traversed dry areas and were dependent for water from a rock.

21:18 *The scepter.* The Hebrew text does not have the connective *and* between the words *staves* and *scepter.* The latter noun at times denotes the insignia of rulers (Gn 49:10; Ps 60:7; 108:8), but it is also rendered "commander" or "ruler" (Ju 5:14; Is 33:22; KJV in Gn 49:10 has "lawgiver"). The meaning here seems to be that the people used their staves to dig below the surface when directed to do so by "the lawgiver" (KJV).

21:21-35 DEFEAT OF TWO AMORITE KINGS

21:21 *Amorites.* These peoples had invaded

territory on all sides of the "fertile crescent." In their thrust eastward they had founded a dynasty in Babylonia of which the king Hammurabi is famous for his law code (about 1750 B.C.). They had also penetrated westward into Canaanite lands east of the Jordan (cf. Gn 10:15 note). Under King Sihon they had "fought against the former king of Moab and taken all his land . . . as far as the Arnon." (26)

21:22 *King's Highway.* On their continued march northward the Israelites sought permission to use this route, previously denied to them in the territory of the Edomites and the Moabites. (Cf. 20:17 note)

21:24 *To the Jabbok.* This river flows into the Jordan about 20 miles north of the Dead Sea (Gn 32:22). The area conquered by Israel north of the Arnon River had been in part owned by the Ammonites before the Amorites seized it. The former had been forced to move east of the Jabbok (Dt 2:37; Jos 12:2; 13:10, 25; Ju 11:13, 22). The Moabites and Ammonites were descendants of Lot, Abraham's nephew. (Gn 19:36-38)

21:27 *Ballad singers.* The defeat of the Amorites in the former Moabite territory called forth a mocking song composed by such as were skilled in this type of poetic proverbial sayings (Hab 2:6). All three songs of this chapter are regarded by some scholars to be intrusions into the narrative account because they appear to interrupt the sequence of events. "Chemosh" was the god of the Moabites. (Jer 48:46; 1 K 11:7; 2 K 23:13)

21:31 *Jazer.* By taking this city the Israelites completed the conquest of the Amorite territory of Sihon.

21:33 *Og the king of Bashan.* Farther north the Israelites penetrated the fertile territory known as *Bashan*, held by another Amorite king of enormous size (Dt 3:1-11). When his two capitals *Edrei* and Ashtaroth, directly east of the Sea of Galilee, fell into their hands, they had control of the entire Transjordan area from the Arnon River to the vicinity of Mt. Hermon (Dt 1:4; 3:8), the source of the Jordan River.

22:1—36:13 EVENTS IN TRANSJORDAN; RECORD OF THE PAST; PROVISIONS FOR THE FUTURE

22:1—25:18 Two Encounters with the Moabites

22:1—24:25 UNSUCCESSFUL PLOT TO CURSE ISRAEL

1) 22:1—22:40 Balak's Negotiations for Balaam's Services

22:2 *Balak.* In obedience to God's command the Israelites did not "harass" the Edomites and the Moabites (Dt 2:9). But Balak "was overcome with fear" lest the same fate was in store for him that had befallen the Amorite kings Sihon and Og. (Ch. 21)

22:4 *The elders of Midian.* Descendants of Abraham and Keturah, the nomadic Midianites moved about in various desert areas, also those east of Moab and Edom (cf. Gn 25:2; 37:25 notes). It has been suggested that Balak himself was a Midianite. If that was the case, he would have been "king of Moab at that time" because he had seized control of former Moabite holdings as the Amorites had done in other territories. (21:26; see also 31:8)

22:5 *Balaam.* The man whom Balak tried to engage to curse Israel is one of the most mysterious and complex characters of OT history. His nationality cannot definitely be determined. In order to hire him, Balak's messengers went to *Pethor, which is near the River* Euphrates far to the north in "Aram," i.e., Syria (23:7; Jos 24:9). *The land of Amaw* (KJV: "his people") is mentioned by the Assyrian records among place names in that area. The account does not explicitly state that Pethor was his original home. Possibly he had gone there because his services had been sought there. When later "he went back to his place," he apparently did not return to the distant north since he remained active among the Midianites and eventually met his death there (24:25; 31:8, 16). Balaam's religious convictions are even more mystifying. On the one hand he acknowledged and obeyed Israel's "Lord" (8, 18; 24:3). But he also persisted in heathen practices. If like Jethro, the father-in-law of Moses, he was a Midianite, he could have had some knowledge of the true God. Perhaps he also shared the prevailing notion that a national deity was expected to protect the people worshiped by them. No doubt he knew that Israel's God had enabled His people "to lick up all that is round about us" (4). This non-Israelite went so far as to speak of the Lord as "my God" (18). But in spite of his professed recognition of the true God he succumbed to his cupidity for rich rewards and repeatedly sought a way to comply with his royal benefactor's nefarious request. The tension between his self-determination and the will of God is a good example of the complexity of human perversity (2 Ptr 2:13-16). But when he attempted to ply his trade as a soothsayer, God put true words of prophecy on his lips (6; Jos 13:22; Jn 11:49-51). The NT refers to the story of Balaam as a warning against the sins of avarice and idolatry. (2 Ptr 2:15; Jude 11; Rv 2:14)

22:6 *Curse this people.* God overruled the plan which according to heathen nations would have harmed Israel. He used the desperate machinations of Balak to demonstrate that His control of history is not affected by the magical incantations of a soothsayer. Even the forces of evil must serve His purposes. At a time when Israel was still separated by the Jordan from full possession of the Promised Land, Balaam became God's instrument to assure His covenant people that a glorious future was in store for them.

22:8 *The Lord speaks.* In the account of Balaam's confrontation with Israel's Protector the general term "God" (9, 12, 20, 38; 23:4) and His proper name "Lord" (8, 13, 18; 23:3, 5) frequently occur side by side, often in successive verses, even in the same verse. (22; cf. Ex 6:3 note)

22:9 *Who are these men?* God did not ask this question to get information. It was designed to alert Ballam that the wicked purpose of the Moabite delegation was not unknown to Him.

22:19 *That I may know.* When Balak's princes appeared a second time, their offer of a greater reward for Balaam's services induced him to pretend that he did not already know what "the command of the Lord" was (12). Because it was God's way of teaching Balaam the consequences of insisting on having his own way in opposition to the known divine will, He permitted the greedy soothsayer to accompany Balak's emissaries. At the same time He made it clear that the expedition served only His purpose.—Balaam is not an isolated example of God's dealing with people who ignore His will in their quest for material gain. He may let them attain their coveted objective and makes it a means of breaking their rebellious self-will. (Cf. 11:33 note; Ps 106:13-15; Is 10:12-14)

22:22 *Anger was kindled.* Balaam still harbored the secret desire somehow to manipulate the permission to "go with them" (20) for his own enrichment. In order to convince Balaam that his impure motives were known to God, He manifested His anger in a most dramatic way. In 35 *the angel of the Lord* is identified with the Lord. (Cf. 20 and Gn 16:7 note)

22:23 *Saw the angel.* Only Balaam's beast of burden was at first enabled to see the heavenly vision. "The princes of Moab" and the "two servants" apparently remained unaware of it. (2 K 6:17; Acts 9:1-7; Jn 12:28-29)

22:28 *She said to Balaam.* By nature animals are not endowed with the ability of rational communication with man. But there can be no doubt that the Creator, who brought them to life from the dumb earth (Gn 1:24), can empower them to utter His message to man when it serves His purpose. (2 Ptr 2:15-16)

22:34 *I have sinned.* Balaam confessed that the Lord who "tried the minds and hearts" had known that he had not changed his intention to use the Lord's permission to "go with them" (20, 34) to gratify his lust for wealth. (Ps 7:9; Jer 11:20; Rv 2:23)

22:35 *That shall you speak.* Balak's plot was to be frustrated by the very agent whom he had chosen to carry it out. At the end of Balaam's journey he was to become the transmitter of a genuine word of prophecy.

22:39 *Kiriath-huzoth.* Literally "city of streets," this site is mentioned only here.

22:40 *Sacrificed oxen and sheep.* In Balaam's honor Balak gave a banquet for which oxen and sheep were slaughtered. The Hebrew word *sacrificed* does not always denote the killing of animals for ritual purposes. (Dt 12:15, 21; 1 Sm 28:24; 2 Ch 18:2)

2) 22:41—24:25 Balak's Plot Thwarted; Balaam's Blessings

22:41 *Bamoth-baal.* Literally "the high places of baal." Superstitious technique seemed to require that the curse be uttered from a place where the soothsayer *saw* his victims. When the attempt failed at this otherwise unknown height, Balak took Balaam to "the top of Pisgah" (23:13-14) and finally to "the top of Peor." (23:28)

23:1 *Seven altars.* Balaam followed the same procedure on the other heights: (a) he sacrificed a bull and a ram on each of seven altars (14, 29); (b) except in the last instance he left Balak and his princes at the altars in order to "meet" the Lord (3, 15); then he returned to them with the word of the Lord. (3-6, 15-17)

23:7 *His discourse.* Balaam uttered his blessing on Israel in the kind of discourse which made a mockery of Balak's sinister intentions (KJV: "parable"). The truth was that God had blessed Israel and would continue to do so in order, through this chosen people, to establish His kingdom among men. Each of the discourses presents new evidence that God's favor rested on the covenant nation and builds up to a climax in the fourth prophecy. The central thought of each blessing and the sentence that summarizes it are as follows: (a) God has made the seed of Abraham into a great multitude: "Who can count the dust of Jacob?" (10); (b) Israel has the assurance of God's unfailing promises: "he has blessed, and I cannot revoke it" (20); (c) Israel will overcome all hostility: "Blessed be every one who blesses you, and cursed be every one who curses you" (24:9); (d) out of Israel God will "in latter days" raise up a Ruler who will let His kingdom come: "A star shall come forth out of Jacob, and a scepter shall rise out of Israel." (24:17)

23:10 *The death of the righteous.* Balaam acknowledged that the Israelites were righteous in God's sight. In His covenant of grace He had declared them acceptable to Him in spite of their sins.

23:14 *The field of Zophim.* Literally "the field of the watchers," an unidentified place. For *Pisgah* see 21:10 note.

23:19 *Repent.* Here this word means: He does not change His mind. (1 Sm 15:29; Ml 3:6; Ro 11:29; Tts 1:2; Ja 1:17)

23:21 *Misfortune . . . trouble.* Israel had deserved and received God's punishment for its unfaithfulness to Him, but cf. 10 note.

23:28 *The top of Peor.* Like Bamoth-baal (22:41), this may have been a high place on which the god Peor was worshiped. (31:16; Jos 22:17; Hos 9:10)

24:3 *Opened.* The Hebrew word occurs only here and in 15. If it is derived from a root meaning to "close" (cf. RSV note), then it means to say that Balaam had been blind to "the vision of the Almighty" (4) until "the Spirit of God came upon him" (2) and *opened* his eyes.

24:7 *Agag.* An Amalekite king bearing this name or title was defeated by Saul and slain by Samuel. (1 Sm 15:4 ff.)

24:14 *I will let you know.* Balaam's discourses end in a grand finale of prophetic utterances. He mentions specific nations whose opposition to the covenant people will be shattered. He envisages the course of actions which God will initiate and pursue so that finally "salvation is from the Jews." (Jn 4:22)

24:17 *A star.* A *star* is the symbol of royalty inasmuch as the king is invested with authority from heaven to wield the *scepter*, the emblem of his power. Here the word *scepter* may also denote a comet or a constellation in the form of a staff that will light up the skies of Israel's future. It arose over Israel's horizon in David's glorious reign. But it reached its full brightness in the Messianic King whom the Wise Men found under the star of Bethlehem. (Gn 49:10)

24:18 *Edom.* David vanquished both Edom and Moab (2 Sm 8:2, 14). The latter is also called Sheth. (17)

24:20 *Amalek.* The first enemy defeated by the Israelites (Ex 17:8-13) will likewise *come to destruction*. (1 Sm 30; 1 Ch 4:41-43)

24:21 *Kenite.* The Kenites were associated with the Midianites (10:29; Ju 1:16; 4:11; 1 Sm 15:6; 27:10; 30:29). "Kain" may be a Kenite tribal name or designate a locality that "shall be wasted."

24:22 *How long.* This question yields better sense when translated: "How long [will it be before] Asshur takes you captive?" *Asshur* is the usual Hebrew word for Assyria. Some commentators believe that here it denotes some other unknown tribe. In 24 it is linked with "Eber," also an unidentified people.

24:24 *Kittim.* The sea peoples from Cyprus and the eastern Mediterranean coast will in turn destroy *Asshur and Eber*. Israel alone will survive.

24:25 *To his place.* Cf. 22:5 note.

25:1-18 MOABITE SEDUCTION SUPPRESSED

25:1 *Play the harlot.* Scripture does not mince words in describing unfaithfulness to God. Idolatry is here and elsewhere branded harlotry (see the Book of Hosea; Is 1:21; Jer 3:1; etc.). However, this ugly word is more than a figure of speech when it refers to the worship of a fertility god such as the Baal of Peor (3). In order to gain a favorable response from him, his devotees engaged in sexual orgies. (6-8)

25:2 *Invited the people.* This enticement came "by the counsel of Balaam" (31:16). When this enigmatic and perverse soothsayer had been unsuccessful in his attempt to curse the Israelites, he devised a scheme which would undo his blessing. By their worship of Baal the Israelites would incur the wrath of God and so destroy themselves.

25:4 *Hang them.* Lest the bad example of *the chiefs of the people* lead the whole congregation astray, they were put to death. God "has no pleasure in the death of any one," but let no one make Him out to be less than a devouring fire when His holy will is flouted. (Eze 18:32; 33:11; Ro 1:18-32; Eph 5:6)

25:8 *Pierced both of them.* In this particularly brazen case of harlotry by an Israelite "head of a father's house" with a Midianite woman of the same social rank (14-15), both offenders were put to death by the grandson of Aaron. Because "he was jealous for his God," Phinehas and his descendants were to serve as high priests, whose foremost function was to make "atonement for the people." (16:46; Ex 30:10, 15; 40:15; Lv 16:29-34)

25:9 *24,000.* If the original vowel pointing of the word translated *thousand* had the meaning of tribal or military leader, then 24 "chiefs of the people" such as Zimri were slain. (Cf. Introduction)

25:16 *Harass the Midianites.* Cf. 31:1-12.

26:1-65 The Second Census

26:1-4 MOSES AND ELEAZAR PUT IN CHARGE

26:2 *Able to go forth to war.* In view of the impending conquest of Canaan by force of arms Moses was to make another tabulation of Israel's military forces. (Cf. ch. 1)

26:5-51 FIGURES FOR EACH TRIBE

26:51 *601,730.* The totals of the census are somewhat smaller than, but comparable in most cases with, those recorded prior to the 38 years of wandering in the desert. At that time the figure stood at 603,550. But while the individual items add up to the new total, some of the tribes show an unusual decrease. For example, Simeon's figure is now given as 22,200 compared with the earlier 59,300 (2:13). Other units registered a disproportionate increase: Manasseh from 32,200 to 52,700 (34; 2:21). Such exorbitant differences in the totals for the individual tribes may be the result of scribal errors in the transmission of the text. For the grand total of 601,730 see Introduction.

26:52-65 CENSUS AND DIVISION OF THE LAND: CENSUS OF THE LEVITES; SUMMARY

26:62 *Every male.* Since the Levites were exempt from military duty, there was no point in establishing how many had reached the age of 20 years (26:2). In their case all those male members were to be counted that had survived the critical 30 days after birth.

27:1-11 Provision for Inheritance Through Daughters

27:1-4 PLIGHT OF ZELOPHEHAD'S DAUGHTERS

27:3 *Our father died.* These women were daughters of a family head who had died but had no male heirs (26:33). They raised the question whether their father's allotment of tribal land would be lost to their family.

27:5-11 DISPOSITION OF THE PROBLEM

27:11 *A statute and ordinance.* The general rule for the division of the land was amended. In such cases the inheritance was to remain within the smaller family unit. No individual was to acquire large estates. This ordinance was in keeping with the provision of the year of Jubilee. (Lv 25:8 ff.)

27:12-23 Joshua Commissioned to Succeed Moses

27:12 *Abarim.* One peak of this mountain range was Mt. Nebo (33:47; Dt 32:49; 34:1). The appointment of Joshua as well as the events recorded in the following chapters took place before "the very day" that Moses complied with the command to *go up into this mountain* to "be gathered" to his people (Dt 32:48-52). The mention of his impending death alerted Moses to the need of appointing his successor.

27:14 *Meribah.* Cf. 20:10-13.

27:21 *Urim.* Cf. Ex 28:15 note. God had communicated with Moses "face to face" (Ex 33:11; Dt 34:10). His successor likewise was to act *at his word.* But the will of the Lord was to be transmitted to Joshua through Eleazar, who *shall inquire for him by the judgment of the Urim.*

28:1—29:40 Directives for Offerings in Canaan

28:1-8 REGULAR DAILY BURNT OFFERING

28:2 *Command the people.* The people who were about to cross the Jordan consisted of an entirely new generation (26:64-65). For their benefit the Lord emphasized that the offerings and sacrifices, prescribed by Him through Moses, were to be brought also after the new leader had taken command in the land of Canaan. The kinds of oblations and the occasion when they were to be brought had been defined for their dead elders (Lv 1—7; 23; Nm 15:1-16). In repeating much of this legislation the Lord made it clear that by regular communing with Him they were assured of His unceasing presence and benediction. The sacrifices and offerings were to be brought in *due season:* (1) daily (3-8); (2) on the weekly Sabbath days (9-10); (3) at the beginning of every month (11-15); (4) on specified days of the year. (V. 16—29:40)

28:7 *Pour out.* The amount of wine had been specified (Ex 29:40) but no direction had been given as to how it was to be offered to the Lord.

28:9-10 OFFERING ON THE SABBATH

28:11-15 REGULAR MONTHLY OFFERING

28:11 *Beginnings of your months.* Cf. 10:10.

28:16—29:40 REGULAR ANNUAL OFFERINGS

28:16 *Passover.* Cf. 9:1-14; Ex 12:6, 18; Lv 23:5.

28:17 *Unleavened bread.* Cf. Lv 23:6-8.

28:26 *Feast of weeks.* Cf. Lv 23:10, 15 notes.

29:1 *On the first day.* Cf. Lv 23:23-25.

29:7 *Tenth day.* Cf. Lv 16:29-34; 23:26-32.

29:12 *Fifteenth day.* The provisions for the celebration of this 8-day festival are expanded (Lv 23:33-36). Directives are added which specify the number and kinds of animals to be sacrificed, together with the required cereal and drink offerings.

30:1-16 Directives for Vows by Women

30:2 *Vows a vow.* The foregoing section had dealt with prescribed offerings but had not repeated previous regulations governing "votive offerings and freewill offerings" (29:39; Lv 5:4-6; 27; Nm 6). The general rule was to remain in force: all vows were to be kept (2, 9). But special provisions are now added for vows by women if they affected relations "between a man and his wife, and between a father and his daughter" (16). In certain instances the head of the household may "make void" the pledge, provided that he makes his objections known "on the day that he hears" of it.

30:3 *Binds herself.* The purpose of the additional regulations was to safeguard marital harmony. The vow to abstain from sexual relations was to be made by women only with the consent of their husbands or the men they were about to marry (cf. 1 Co 7:1-7). However, a widow or divorced woman, who was not bound by family ties, could make vows of any kind. (9)

31:1-54 Midian Destroyed; Booty Divided

31:1-12 DIVINE VENGEANCE ON MIDIAN

31:2 *Avenge.* God was provoked to vengeance on the Midianites becaused they had seduced Israel to harlotry (16; ch. 25). The command to annihilate the entire population does not reflect a primitive concept of God which in the course of time gave way to a more enlightened or humane view. What happened to the Midianites is indeed described here as done at the behest of God. But He still permits catastrophes to wipe out masses of people without discrimination of age or sex. When such wholesale destructions are brought about by human agents, the latter cannot claim direct divine authorization. No modern nation is in the position of God's OT people. But it also remains true that the omnipotent God often does not restrain the military power of nations from inflicting death on thousands of men, women, and children. The OT revelation does not blink the fact that the ultimate cause of disasters rests in God's will and providence. No human speculation about the nature of God should attempt to give any other answer. (Cf. Ps 137:9 note)

31:6 *Phineas.* He, not Joshua or Eleazar, was chosen to direct this campaign, no doubt because he had proved that he was "jealous for his God" (25:6-13). The army, to which each tribe contributed a contingent, was equipped with the insignia of a holy war: *the vessels of the sanctuary* (lit. "the instruments of holiness") *and the trumpets for the alarm* (10:9). Perhaps the connective *and* in this case has the explanatory meaning of "namely."

31:13-24 PURIFICATION RITES FOR THE AVENGERS

31:18 *The young girls.* Virgins, who had not been the cause of Israel's harlotry, were to be spared.

31:23 *Pass through the fire.* Those who had come in contact with corpses were to perform the prescribed purification rites (19, 24; 19:11-22). All material objects of spoil were to be "purified with the water for impurity" (29; 19:9-19). Metals had to pass through fire to *be clean*.

31:25-47 DISPOSITION OF THE BOOTY

31:27 *Into two parts.* All *booty* was to be shared equally by the soldiers and the civilians. The former were required to "take from their half" and to give to the priests "one out of 500"; the noncombatants contributed from their part "one out of 50" to the Levites. The totals, as given in the following verses (32-47), are of immense proportions. The basic figures of the original text may have been raised to corresponding thousands by exuberant scribes or copyists. (See Introduction)

31:48-54 FREEWILL OFFERING BY THE OFFICERS

31:50 *Articles of gold.* When the military leaders saw that they had suffered no casualties, they realized how good the Lord had been. Out of gratitude they brought freewill offerings to Moses and Eleazar.

32:1-42 Inheritance East of the Jordan

32:1-5 REQUEST OF REUBEN AND GAD

32:5 *This land.* The prospect of material gain motivated the request by Reuben and Gad. Selfish interests prevailed over their sense of unity as the covenant people. They were inclined to shirk their obligation to complete the conquest of the Promised Land by joint military action. (Gn 13:10-12)

32:6-15 IMMEDIATE SETTLEMENT DENIED

32:7 *Discourage the heart.* Moses feared that the desertion of the common cause by the two tribes would have the same disheartening effect on the people that the report of the spies had produced and would precipitate a similar judgment by the Lord. (Chs. 13—14)

32:16-27 ASSISTANCE TO OTHER TRIBES PLEDGED

32:21 *Pass over the Jordan.* Moses succeeded in convincing Reuben and Gad to participate in the military campaigns necessary to acquire the inheritance of all tribes (Jos 1:12-18; 4:12-13; 22:1-4). Upon their promise to do so, they were permitted to claim the land between the Arnon and Jabbok rivers, most of which had already been taken from the Amorites (21:21-35). It appears to have been a joint occupation of the entire territory without clearly defined borders between the two tribes. Manasseh was able to get his Transjordan portion by dispossessing the Amorites north of the Jabbok. (39-42)

32:28-32 PROPOSAL ACCEPTED

32:33-42 TRANSJORDAN TERRITORY ASSIGNED

33:1-49 A Record of the Itinerary from Egypt to the Jordan

33:1 *Stages.* Lit. "their breaking camp," this noun is derived from the verb repeatedly translated in this chapter: "they set out."

33:2 *Moses wrote down.* Israel's journeys under Moses' leadership had come to an end. Having brought his people within striking distance of their ultimate goal, he compiled a list of their encampments. For the modern reader this collection of statistical data may be as unexciting as the genealogical tables in Genesis. But each link in this long chain of place names stirred a song of praise in Israelite hearts because a mighty and forgiving God had been with them every step of the way from Egypt to the Jordan. He did not forsake the escaped slaves no matter where they "encamped" or from where they "set out."—Every believer, particularly a senior citizen, needs to hear only the names of the encampments of his pilgrimage to be moved to recount gratefully what God did for him at these junctures of circumstances.

33:5 *From Rameses.* Moses surveyed the people's past from the Exodus (Ex 12:37; 13:4) to their arrival "in the plains of Moab" 40 years later (38, 49). The list contains the names of places recorded in the preceding accounts of their desert wanderings. The journey from Egypt to Mt. Sinai is recapitulated in 5-15 (Ex 12:37—19:2). But this section also contains the names of two sites hitherto not mentioned (12-14). In the remaining verses of the chapter the names of many more sites supplement the sketchy account of Israel's progress from Mt. Sinai which is given in the preceding chapters of Numbers. On the other hand this log does not mention encampments that did appear in the preceding record (21:18-19). The location of some of these stations cannot be identified. Consequently the exact route of the wanderings, particularly during the last 38 years, cannot be definitely established. The schematic pattern of these geographic notes does not preclude the possibility that the Israelites at times broke up into smaller groups. One or several of them may not have been prevented from crossing Ammonite or Edomite territory and encamping at such a site as Punon, which has been identified as situated within the borders of Edom. (41-49; cf. 21:10 note)

33:50—36:12 Preparations for the Occupation of Canaan

33:50-56 COMMAND TO DESTROY THE IDOLATROUS INHABITANTS

33:52 *Drive out.* The tribes were to "inherit the land by lot" (54). The extent of each allotment was to be in proportion to the size of the tribe, which had been established by the census (26:52-56). The Canaanites were to be driven out and their idolatrous symbols and sites of worship were to be demolished (Ex 23:23-25, 32-33). At this time their measure of iniquity was "complete." (Gn 15:16)

33:56 *Do to you.* The Israelites were to know that their God was not a partisan or national deity. If later their disobedience to this command brought about their apostasy from Him, He would punish them as severely as the Canaanites (Dt 8:19-20). Unfortunately the

Israelites disregarded this warning and broke the covenant. God carried out His threat. Through foreign nations such as the Assyrians and Babylonians He took the land away from them. (2 K 17; 25)

34:1-15 SURVEY OF THE BORDERS OF CANAAN

34:3 *Your south side.* The southern border of the Promised Land began at the lower tip of *the Salt Sea* (i.e., the Dead Sea) and swept southward in a semicircle turning northward along the Brook of Egypt and ending at the Mediterranean. (Jos 15:1-4)

34:7 *Mount Hor.* This unidentified mountain must be distinguished from the height where Aaron was buried (20:22-29; 33:37-39). It apparently was a name given to a northern peak of the Lebanon range. From here the northern border was formed by a line drawn eastward to the desert and ending at an oasis named Hazarenan, west of Hamath.

34:12 *The Salt Sea.* The eastern border is traced from its north and west point (Hazarenan) down through some unknown sites to a line that ran westward to the southeastern edge of "the sea of Chinnereth" (i.e., the Sea of Galilee). From here it followed the Jordan to the Dead Sea, the starting point of the survey. (3)

34:16—36:12 DIRECTIVES FOR ALLOCATION OF THE LAND

1) 34:16-29 Tribal Supervision Instituted

34:17 *For inheritance.* Before the Israelites began to take possession of the land, God reminded them that they had no vested claim to it; it was His gift to them. Therefore each tribe would receive an allotment that He would assign to it by lot (13; Jos 14:2; Nm 26:52-56). Ten tribal leaders were chosen to carry out the divine directives for the division of the land west of the Jordan. Reuben and Gad had already received their portion.

2) 35:1-8 Allocaton of Levitical Possessions

35:6 *Forty-two cities.* The Levites were not to have their inheritance in one compact area (18:20-24). Because they were to represent all of Israel by their service in the tabernacle (18:1-7), each tribe, "in proportion to" its size, was to contribute cities and their surrounding grazing grounds in order to provide them with dwelling places and a means of sustenance (Jos 21). Adding *the six cities of refuge* to the 42 Levitical holdings, the number of localities surrendered by all tribes comes to 48.

3) 35:9-34 Appointment of Cities of Refuge

35:11 *Select cities.* Advance instructions for the allotment of Israel's inheritance included the directive to set aside six cities which were to serve the common good in the maintenance of social order. They were to be *cities of refuge* for the protection of a manslayer *who kills any person without intent.* According to ancient custom a slain person's nearest of kin had the right to act as "the avenger of blood." It devolved upon him to take the life of the murderer of his relative (25, 27; Gn 4:9). This means of safeguarding the sanctity of life and of administering justice was to be severely restricted. The old system could have resulted in endless feuds. Henceforth the person who unintentionally or without malice aforethought had caused the death of another could find safety from the avenger in one of the six cities of refuge (Ex 21:13). The "three cities ... beyond the Jordan" were named by Moses (Dt 4:41-43); the "three cities in the land of Canaan" were appointed by Joshua. (Jos 20:1-9)

35:16 *A murderer.* The institution of cities of refuge was not to abrogate the law that "whoever sheds the blood of man, by man shall his blood be shed" (Gn 9:6; Ex 21:12, 14; Lv 24:17). But capital punishment could be inflicted on an accused murderer only "on the evidence of witnesses" to the crime. (30; Dt 19:15)

4) 36:1-12 Restriction on Inheritance Through Women

36:3 *The inheritance of our fathers.* Moses had ruled that daughters were entitled to inherit their father's portion if he had no sons (27:1-11). The leaders of the tribe of Manasseh, to whom the litigant women belonged, foresaw that an unrestricted application of this provision could have led to an obliteration of the established tribal borders. If such an heiress married a member of another tribe, her husband would become the owner of the land within another tribe's *inheritance.* Even "the jubilee of the people" would not restore the property to the original tribe. In the year of the jubilee only such holdings were to be returned to the former owner as had been acquired by financial transactions (4; Lv 25:8-24). In order to keep the borders of the tribal allotments intact, Moses was instructed to decree that heiresses "shall marry within the family of the tribe of their father." (6)

36:13 Conclusion

36:13 *Commandments and ordinances.* This verse summarizes the directives that up to this point Moses had transmitted to the Israelites after their arrival in the plains of Moab. Before his death he had more to say to his people. His final instructions are contained in Deuteronomy.

DEUTERONOMY

INTRODUCTION

Content

The Book of Deuteronomy is a fitting sequel to the first four books of the Pentateuch. It continues the story of how God put into operation His eternal plan to save fallen mankind from the curse of sin. He revealed His gracious intentions in terms which they could understand. As men draw up a contract or treaty and let its provisions constitute a basis for harmony among themselves, so He made a covenant with His rebellious creatures. He pledged Himself to provide a way to bring back the fallen race to a life-giving communion with Himself. (For the terms of the covenant see the Introduction to the Book of Exodus.)

The first book of the Bible relates how God bound Himself to bless all nations through Abraham and his descendants, the ancestors of the Woman's Seed. Exodus records how He implemented His promise to the patriarchs: He created the covenant nation and proclaimed the terms of the covenant at Mt. Sinai. Leviticus contains further instructions as to how the chosen people were to express their covenant relations to Him. The Book of Numbers testifies to the fact that God kept His covenant promises: He brought the second generation of the former Egyptian slaves to "the land of Moab." Only the Jordan separated them from the Promised Land. In this setting the events recorded in Deuteronomy took place.

In the land of Moab a long chapter of covenant history came to an end. With the occupation of Canaan a new stage was to begin. Anticipating the people's needs in their new environment, Moses "undertook to explain this law" which would continue to determine their status as a covenant nation. Each generation was to obligate itself to the same basic principles of the covenant the fathers had entered at Mt. Sinai. Only minor adjustments were necessary to meet the needs of living in occupied Canaan. There the Israelites would no longer be a closely knit community moving from camp to camp. They would have permanent residences situated in widely separated parts of the land.

The historical data only serve to set the stage for the action of the book. Its main happening is the word spoken by Moses. Almost all pages are devoted to a record of the leader's parting message to the people in this transitional period of their history.

The name "Deuteronomy," by which it has come to be known, reflects this characteristic feature of its contents. In the Septuagint, an ancient Greek translation of the OT, it was designated *deuteronomion*, i.e., "a second law." The translators derived this title from their rendering of the phrase "a copy of this law" (17:18). However, the primary purpose of the book is not to promulgate a second or new law. In sermonic form it reiterates and expounds the basic terms of the covenant made at Sinai.

The modern reader may think that there is little in these instructions to an ancient people that is of any value to him. Several factors should change such an opinion. It should be of interest to him, first of all, that through the old covenant God was taking steps to implement His plan to reconcile the world to Himself. Furthermore, no Christian will regard this book as irrelevant if he remembers that the Mediator of the new covenant repeatedly drew upon its words in order to meet His own needs and to instruct His followers in their relationship to God (Mt 4:4, 7, 10; 22:37; see also Acts 3:17-26). Finally, modern man, like Israel of old, lives in a turbulent period of transition. He is faced with changes that drastically affect his mode of living. He must cling to the Word of "the Rock" (32:4) if he is not to be overwhelmed in the raging sea of new uncertainties.

Authorship

Until he passes from the scene, Moses holds the center of the stage of the fifth book that bears his name. His addresses, legislative directions, and parting blessing constitute its contents. He also wrote "this law" (31:9, 22, 24) that he had expounded. Jesus and the NT writers testify to its Mosaic origin (Mt 19:6-8; Mk 12:19; Ro 10:5-8; 1 Co 9:8-9; Heb 10:28). It could be assumed that the account of his death in the last chapter was appended by a contemporary associate, probably Joshua or Eleazar. Some scholars credit the same writer with supplying also the other narrative material that provides the setting of Moses' discourses.

Proponents of the source hypothesis of the Pentateuch (see Genesis, Introduction) maintain that Moses had little or nothing to do with the literary production of Deuteronomy. In their opinion he did not even *speak* "the words of this law." However, their views of the date of its origin are so diverse as to cancel out one another. The assumed settings range from the time of Samuel to the postexilic period, some six centuries later. Some hold that from a basic Mosaic nucleus the book grew by successive accretions and editions during a long span of time. Its author(s) belonged to a school of writers that are called Deuteronomists. Their programmatic view of history, expressed in its basic principles in Deuteronomy, dominates also the books from Joshua to Kings. According to a widely accepted theory Deuteronomy was produced, at least in basic outline, at the time of King Josiah. Its writer(s) sought to promote centralization of worship in Jerusalem and hid the book in the temple. There it was found by Josiah's men in 621 B.C., when he renovated the house of God. However, this theory does violence to the express claims of the book. It also fails to establish a setting for it that is in harmony with the general and specific circumstances that are reflected in the text.

OUTLINE

I. 1:1—26:19 The Future in View of the Past
- A. 1:1—4:43 Covenant History Reviewed and Applied to the Future
- B. 4:44—11:32 Basic Covenant Terms Reviewed and Applied to the Future
- C. 12:1—26:19 Covenant Ordinances Expounded and Adapted

II. 27:1—30:20 The Future in View of Covenant Fidelity
- A. 27:1-26 Assent to Covenant Validity
- B. 28:1-68 Covenant Alternatives
- C. 29:1—30:20 Covenant Terms: Past, Present, Future

III. 31:1—34:12 Transition to New Era: From Moses to Joshua
- A. 31:1—32:47 A Changeless God amid Changing Circumstances
- B. 32:48-52 Moses' Death Summons
- C. 33:1-29 Moses' Parting Blessing
- D. 34:1-12 The End of Moses' Leadership

1:1—26:19 THE FUTURE IN VIEW OF THE PAST

1:1—4:43 Covenant History Reviewed and Applied to the Future

1:1—3:29 SURVEY OF PAST EVENTS

1:1 *Moses spoke.* Filling almost all pages of Deuteronomy, the speeches of Moses were delivered at a major turning point in Israel's history. "In the fortieth year" (3) after leaving the house of bondage, the second generation of former slaves in Egypt had arrived "in the land of Moab" (5). Within a short time they were to cross the Jordan. Life in Canaan would be different. They would no longer move about from place to place, but would receive places of permanent residence. They would no longer have the solidarity of a single camp, but live in widely separated communities. No longer would the only leader they had known be there to direct them. In order to prepare the erstwhile wanderers for this transition to a new social, economic, and civic environment, *Moses spoke* to them primarily of what would not change: the promises and obligations of the Sinai covenant.

The manner in which the setting of Moses' words is given is designed to bridge the dimensions of time and space that separate his hearers from God's first promulgation of the covenant at Mt. Horeb. The intervening 38 years of wandering, Moses insisted, did not affect its validity for the survivors, their children, and all future generations. Nor did the many miles that lay between their present location and Mt. Sinai make any difference. The setting of *the words that Moses spoke* therefore includes a schematic summary of their desert wanderings (1-2). A vertical line is drawn from *the wilderness* (the steppe land) of Moab down to *Suph*, no doubt the Gulf of Aqaba (cf. 1:40; 2:8; Nm 33:5 note). The entire area between these points is called *the Arabah,* the rift valley extending southward from the Sea of Galilee. In a similar schematic pattern a horizontal line is drawn across the map of Israel's desert sojourn: *between* the wilderness of *Paran and Tophel*. The latter was a city in Edomite territory, 16 miles southwest of the Dead Sea. For *Paran* see Nm 10:12 note.

When the Israelites had arrived at "Kadesh-barnea" almost four decades earlier, they could have entered Canaan within a short time after leaving Horeb. The distance between these two points is only "eleven days' journey." Because of their rebellion against God they had been subjected to the long delay which finally came to an end when Moses addressed them in Moab. *Laban, Hazeroth, Dizahab* lie between Horeb and Kadesh-barnea. Of these place names only the second is mentioned previously (Nm 11:35); the other two have not been identified. —In this setting Moses addressed his contemporaries. They were to listen to him as if they heard God speaking to them again from Mt. Sinai and making the covenant with them.

1:4 *Sihon . . . and Og.* Cf. Nm 21:21-31.

1:5 *Beyond the Jordan.* Literally "at the crossing of the Jordan," this phrase denotes territory on both banks of the Jordan. In the narrative portions of Deuteronomy it occurs six times to denote the eastern side (1:1, 5; 4:41, 46, 47, 49). In four instances its double point of reference is clarified by the addition of "in the east" or "on the east side." In Moses' speeches it designates the eastern (3:8) and the western side. (3:20, 25; 11:30; see also Jos 9:1; 1 K 4:24; Is 9:1)

Explain this law. At Mt. Sinai Moses had transmitted God's words to the Israelites. What he said to them 38 years later was also "all that the Lord had given him in commandment to them" (3). Once he had received the Decalog chiseled into stone by the hand of the Lord; now he set out to engrave the teaching of the covenant upon their hearts. Hence the admonition "remember" and "forget not" occur almost 200 times in Deuteronomy. "Law" *(torah)* appears only in the singular. It denotes not only commandments but is used in the more comprehensive meaning of instruction or teaching.

1:6 *In Horeb.* Cf. Ex 3:1 note. Moses began his summary of the past at the point when God had established His covenant with the Israelites (Ex 24:3-8). In spite of their unfaithfulness from the very beginning (Ex 32), God carried out His promises. The first step was to put the chastened and penitent people on the way to "the land which the Lord swore . . .to Abraham, to Isaac, and to Jacob, to give to them and to their descendants." (8; Gn 12:7; 15:18; 17:7-8; 26:4; 28:13)

1:7 *Amorites.* Cf. Gn 10:15-19 note; 15:16. *Negeb.* Cf. Nm 13:17 note; Gn 24:62.

1:9 *At that time.* In the first four chs. Moses summarizes the journey of the Israelites from Horeb to their present location "beyond the Jordan, in the land of Moab." His purpose was not simply to repeat what is recorded in Nm 10—22. He reviewed past event in order to teach his hearers that their response to the covenant would determine their weal or woe also in the future.

1:10 *The Lord your God.* This divine title occurs almost 300 times in Deuteronomy (cf. Ex 3:14 f.). It links the people with God's revelation of the past. He who had chosen them "to be a people of his own possession" (4:20) and had redeemed them "out of the house of bondage" (13:5) was still there to help them. They could rely on this Lord, who never changes, to be faithful to His promises. However, this title was also to remind them of their covenant obligation to "walk in his ways" and to "obey his voice" (26:17-18). The account of their journey from Horeb to Moab was to convince them that this Lord will not tolerate disloyalty to Him. At the same time, He is a God of mercy, ready to forgive when they return to Him in sincere repentance.—The God of the new covenant is no different. We were made His own in baptism, yet we daily sin much. But He who called us into "the fellowship of his Son" "is faithful and just, and will forgive our sins and cleanse us from all unrighteousness." (1 Co 1:8; 1 Jn 1:9; Heb 10:23)

1:13 *Appoint them.* God had made Abraham's descendants "as the stars of heaven for multitude" (10; Gn 15:5). But He did not let them disintegrate into an unorganized rabble. Moses was in command (18). As suggested to him by Jethro (Ex 18:21-27), he in turn delegated authority to *wise . . . and experienced men,* who were to assist him in maintaining law and order. As "judges" they were to be impartial and recognize "the small and the great." All had equal right since "the judgment is God's" (17). Even "the alien" was not to be deprived of justice.

1:19 *We set out.* Assured that the Promised Land was theirs for the taking, the Israelites had moved northward to *Kadesh-barnea* (Nm 10:11). After covering this comparatively short distance (2), they saw their goal not far away. From this *hill country of the Amorites* they were to "go up" and "take possession" of Canaan from the south. But because of their rebellion, almost 40 years were to elapse before they were again within striking distance of Canaan beyond the Jordan.

1:22 *Send men.* Cf. Nm 13:3 note. Passing over the events that happened on the way to Kadesh-barnea (Nm 10—20), Moses drew attention to the sending of the spies from there (Nm 13:1 f.). It eventuated in a great turning point in Israel's history. Faith in God's power to overcome all obstacles, which He had demonstrated in the past, gave way to unbelief and open rebellion against Him. Therefore God swore that "not one of these men of this evil generation shall see the good land" (35). Then began the long years of desert wandering with the command to "turn [southward], and journey [away from Canaan] into the wilderness in the direction of the Red Sea," i.e., the Gulf of Aqaba. (40; cf. Ex 31:18 note)

1:24 *Eshcol.* Cf. Nm 13:23 note.

1:28 *Anakim.* Cf. Nm 13:22 note.

1:36 *Except Caleb.* Joshua, the only other survivor, was destined to "cause Israel to inherit" Canaan as Moses' successor. (38: Nm 14:38)

1:37 *Angry with me.* God's judgment on the older generation brought to Moses' mind his own exclusion from the Promised Land. God is not "partial in judgment"; "the small and the great alike" suffer the consequences of disobedience (17; cf. Nm 20:10 note; Dt 3:25-26; 4:21; 32:51; Ps 106:32). According to human standards Moses' guilt was negligible compared with Israel's flagrant rebellion. But God acts according to the criterion "to whom much is given, of him will much be required" (Lk 12:48; 1 Co 10:11). When Moses told the Israelites that it was "on your account" that "the Lord was angry with me," he did not try to exonerate himself, as did Adam and Eve. He simply reminded them that they had created the circumstances of his own downfall.

1:41 *Easy to go up.* What would have been *easy* with the Lord's help (30) became an act of "presumptuous" futility when the Israelites went *up into the hill country,* relying on their own strength and defying God's will. (Cf. Nm 14:40 note; Jn 15:5)

1:44 *Hormah.* Lit. "a complete destruction," this name may have been applied to various places where such a disaster occurred (cf. Nm 21:1 note; Ju 1:17; Jos 12:14; 15:30; 19:4). Here the city is located *in Seir,* a general designation for the territory occupied by the Edomites. The term *Amorites* occurs at times to denote all the earlier inhabitants of Canaan regardless of racial affinities. (Cf. Gn 15:21 note)

2:1 *Into the wilderness.* After their defeat at Hormah (1:44-46), the Israelites did *as the Lord told* Moses. They began to serve their punitive years in the *wilderness* by turning southward from Kadesh *in the direction of the Red Sea,* on the shores of which were "Elath and Ezion-geber" (8). Moses did not repeat the events of this dismal period. He summarized the *many days* of 38 years as one long detour *about Mt. Seir* (1:44) and compressed all strokes of affliction into one crushing blow: "until the entire generation . . . had perished" (14). The lesson for the future came through loud and clear: "Do not be deceived; God is not mocked" (Gl 6:7). Do not "presume upon the riches of his kindness and forbearance and patience." (Ro 2:4; 1 Co 6:9-10)

2:3 *Turn northward.* The Israelites had suffered the consequences of their unfaithfulness "for many days" and had once more come to Kadesh (Nm 20). Here they received orders for the march toward an entry into Canaan, this time from the east. On their way *northward* they were not to molest their patriarchal relatives: the Edomites (descendants of Abraham through Esau; 4-8), the Moabites and the Ammonites (descendants of Abraham's nephew Lot; 9, 19; Gen 19:37 f.; 25:30; 36:18 f.). The command not to "contend with them" also underscored the fact that the Israelites owed their status as the chosen people entirely to the sovereign and gracious will of the Lord of the nations. They had every reason to respond to "this law," which Moses was expounding, and to remain faithful to the covenant.

2:6 *Purchase food.* Cf. 28 f.; Nm 21:10 note.

2:8 *The Arabah road.* From the compressed review of Israel's itinerary it is difficult to establish the exact route. On their march "northward" they evidently kept to the southeastern border of Edom, crossed the brook Zered (Nm 21:12) by going *in the direction of the wilderness of Moab,* bypassed Moab itself on its eastern side, proceeded northward until they crossed "the valley of the Arnon" and reached the area which the Amorites had taken from the Moabites. (24; Nm 21:13)

2:9 *Ar.* Mentioned as a leading center of Moabite jurisdiction at that time, its exact location has not been determined. (18, 29, Nm 21:15, 28; Is 15:1)

2:10 *Emim.* The following list of largely unidentifiable peoples has a common denominator. By whatever name they were known, these original inhabitants of the land occupied by the sons of Esau and Lot were *great and many, and tall.* But "the Lord destroyed them" and had given their land to the Edomites, Moabites, and Ammonites. Therefore the Israelites should have harbored no doubts that the Lord was able also to give them the Promised Land even though the spies reported that they had encountered "men of great stature" before whom they seemed "like grasshoppers" (Nm 13:33; Dt 9:2; see also Gn 14:5; 15:20). The "Horites," mentioned already in Gn 14:6; 36:20, seem to be distinguished from the other ethnic groups, although the word "also" does not occur in the Hebrew text (12). From extra-Biblical sources they have been equated with the Hurrians, a non-Semitic people who played a significant role in the ancient Near East. For the "Caphtorim" (23) cf. Gn 10:13-14 note. For "Zered" (13) cf. Nm 21:10 note.

2:24 *The valley of the Arnon.* Lit. "the break of the Arnon"; cf. Nm 21:10 note.

2:26 *Sent messengers.* The Israelites had moved northward to *Kedemoth* on the eastern border of the territory which *Sihon,* the Amorite, had taken from the Moabites, about 15 miles east of the Jordan, midway between the rivers Arnon and Jabbok. For *Heshbon* cf. Nm 21:27.

2:30 *Hardened his spirit.* Cf. Ex 4:21 note. Moses impressed on his hearers that they owed their possession of Sihon's land to God, who "gave him over to us." (33)

As at this day. The term *this day* occurs a number of times as a point of reference to the past (4:20, 38; 8:18), to the present (2:18; 15:5; 19:9; 26:16, 18), and to the future (29:28). In all instances Moses stressed that God's faithfulness in keeping His promises and threats should motivate the people to carry out their covenanted obligations. This was the burden of this message when he "undertook to explain this law." (1:5)

2:34 *Utterly destroyed.* They executed upon the cities God's decree that they be banned, i.e., devoted or consigned to complete destruction (cf. Lv 27:28-29 note). For the morality of such wholesale destruction see Nm 31:2 note.

3:3 *Og.* The defeat of this Amorite king was the climax of Israel's campaign "beyond the Jordan" and set the stage for the crossing of the Jordan. (Nm 21:33-35; Jos 9:10; Ps 135:11; 136:20)

3:4 *Argob.* Not found in other sources, this term may be a synonym for Bashan or it may describe the natural characteristic of the land (perhaps "fertile"). It occurs again only in 14 and 1 K 4:13.

3:8 *Mount Hermon.* Over 9,000 feet high and visible from the heights of Moab, this peak in the Anti-Lebanon range marked the northern limits of Israel's conquests (Jos 11:17). A parenthetical note (9) tells of other names by which it was called by the Sidonians and the Amorites.

3:10 *Salecah and Edrei.* The extent of Israel's territory east o the Jordan is defined also by two cities. The defeat of Og at Edrei apparently removed one of the last strongholds blocking Israel's expansion across Gilead to Mt. Hermon. Salecah marked the eastern limits of Bashan. (Jos 12:1-5)

3:11 *His bedstead.* Another parenthetical remark gives additional information about Og the Amorite. Although all of his kingdom was called "the land of Rephaim" (13), he *only* was of their stature (cf. 2:10 note). His *bedstead of iron,* measuring 13½ by 6 feet, very likely refers to a sepulchral structure of basalt, which contained iron. Made *in Rabbah,* the capital of the Ammonites, it remained there after he seized Bashan.

3:12 *I gave.* Moses brought the experiences of his hearers up to date. The recent occupation of Transjordan by two and a half tribes (Nm 32:32-33) had been possible only because God had given enemies of superior resources into their hands. But in these victories there was also assurance for the future. What God had done on the one side of the Jordan, He will be capable of doing "to all the kingdoms into which you are going over" (21 f.).—Moses' words were written for our learning. Confronted by seemingly insurmountable obstacles, God's children of every age need the assurance that "the Lord's hand is not shortened" (Is 59:1; Nm 11:23). God can dispose of the most formidable forces of evil that threaten chaos and annihilation. Above all, the Christian believer has seen his seemingly invincible foes go down in defeat at Golgotha and the opened tomb. "If God is for us, who is against us?" (Ro 8:31 f.; Ps 118:6; Mt 11:28; 17:20; Heb 4:9 f.)

3:15 *Machir.* Jair (14) and Machir represent the tribe of Manasseh.

3:17 *From Chinnereth.* The conquered territory is described as lying between two seas; in the north: *Chinnereth* (Gennesareth or Galilee), in the south: *the sea of the Arabah, the Salt Sea* (the Dead sea). The latter faces *the slopes of Pisgah on the east.* (Cf. Nm 21:10 note)

3:18 *Commanded you.* Cf. Nm 32:1-32.

3:23 *Besought the Lord.* The promise that his people would soon inherit the Promised Land moved Moses to ask God to rescind the decree that he was not to "go over . . . into the good land beyond the Jordan" (cf. 1:37 note). The petition was denied. But God softened the sentence as He gave the aged leader a panoramic view of Canaan from the top of Pisgah.

3:29 *Beth-peor.* Lit. "the house or temple of Peor," a deity also called "Baal of Peor" (4:3; Nm 25:3), it may be a fuller name of the height called simply Peor. (Nm 23:28; 31:16; Dt 4:46; 34:6)

4:1-40 EXHORTATIONS FOR THE FUTURE

4:1 *And now.* These words introduce the burden of Moses' address at this crucial turning point in the lives of the Israelites. He had something important to say to them now that they were about to make the transition from desert wandering and *go in and take possession of the land which the Lord, the God of your fathers, gives you.* This prospect is mentioned some 70 times in Deuteronomy. But in spite of outward changes God's relationship to them would remain unaltered. As in the past (briefly sketched in chs. 1—3), they could expect to "live upon the earth" (10), as long as they remained "a kingdom of priests and a holy nation" (Ex 19:6). God's promises of unmerited blessings were subject to their response to the terms of the Sinai covenant, summarized in "ten commandments" (chs. 4—11) and amplified by ceremonial "statutes and ordinances" (chs. 12—26). For the covenant concept see Exodus, Introduction. Justified through faith in God's grace, as was Abraham, the present and each succeeding generation were also to bear the fruits of faith. (Ro 4:9-22)

4:3 *Baal-peor.* Cf. Nm 25. Obedience is the basis "that you may live" (1); disobedience results in death as *your eyes have seen . . . at Baal-peor.* So it will also be in the future.

4:6 *Your wisdom and your understanding.* If they would *keep* the covenant, God would demonstrate *in the sight of the peoples* how highly favored they were. No other nation was blessed by the revelation of His "righteous" will. They need not fear the future; He was "near" them; they could draw on His help whenever they "call upon him" (7). How grateful they should be that they knew how to order their lives according to this God-given wisdom and understanding. (2 Sm 7:23)

4:10 *At Horeb.* The reminder of their unique blessings was to motivate the Israelites to keep God's statutes and ordinances (5-8). At the same time they were not to forget that their covenant relation with the Lord of heaven and earth was not a matter to be taken lightly. When He "declared His covenant" at Mt. Sinai, they had caught a glimpse of His world-shaking power and His devastating glory (Ex 19:16-19; 20:22). Therefore they and their children were *to fear* the dire consequences of disobeying "the ten commandments" and "the statutes and ordinances" which "he commanded" them to "perform." This admonition is frequently repeated. (6:24; 8:6; 10:12; 14:23; 19:9; 28:58; 31:13)

4:16 *A graven image.* "In the land which" they were "going over to possess" (14) the Israelites would be tempted to *act corruptly* and break the covenant at crucial points. They were not to reduce the transcendent God, who had "no form" (12, 15), to a tangible *form of any figure.* Making a *likeness* of Him would indicate that in their thinking they had constructed a god in their own image, whom they could coerce to do their will. The baals of the Canaanites were such idols.

4:19 *Worship them.* Worship of creatures instead of the Creator is the basic perversion of idolatry. By His almighty Word He had made the heavenly bodies, an act so stupendous that *all the peoples under the whole heaven* were *allotted* the benefits of His cosmic power. Moses may also imply that God gave up to the worship of astral deities such as "did not see fit to acknowledge God." (Ro 1:18-28; 2 Th 2:11)

4:21 *Angry with me.* If the Lord was not indifferent to Moses' breach of faith, which might appear excusable in the circumstances, how much more will God be a "devouring fire" (24) if the Israelites flagrantly defied Him and made an idol of Him. (Cf. 1:37 note)

4:24 *Jealous.* Applied only to God, this adjective does not have the connotation of envy. Heathen gods were feared because they were thought to be jealous of man's good fortune. God's jealousy is His determination to demand undivided allegiance to Him. Anyone who gives His "glory" to an idol or His "praise to graven images" arouses His holy zeal to vindicate His honor. He becomes a *devouring fire* to demonstrate that He is unyielding in His claim to undivided allegiance. (Is 42:8; Ex 20:5; 34:14; Dt 4:3; 6:15)

4:26 *Perish from the land.* God's threats were not empty words. Once the Israelites were "in the land" it would remain theirs as long as they did not "provoke him to anger." If they should break the covenant by "doing what is evil" (25), He would deprive them of their inheritance and scatter them "among the peoples." (27; 28:64-67)

4:31 *A merciful God.* In spite of their unfaithfulness God would not *forget the covenant* if they would "return to the Lord" with "all your heart and with all your soul" (30:1-5; cf. Ex 34:6 f.; Nm 14:18; Ps 103:3-5). In the OT God required the observance of many outward ceremonies. But external rites were to be the expression of an inner attitude of wholehearted devotion to a *merciful God* (6:5; 10:12; 11:13; 13:3; 26:16; 30:2, 6, 10). No matter how "corruptly" the people had violated the covenant, God would *not fail* them if they sought forgiveness with a "broken and contrite heart." (Ps 51:17; 34:18)

4:37 *Loved . . . and chose.* Moses continued to call attention to the recent and more remote past in order to motivate the Israelites to "keep his statutes and his commandments" (40). Loyalty to the covenant was to be their reponse to what God had done for them. They were where and what they were at "this day" only because the only true God had made them beneficiaries of His boundless mercy and of His power "in heaven above and on the earth beneath." They owed the distinction of being His people solely to God's unmerited love for their *fathers.* Purely out of goodness and mercy He *chose* them and *their descendants* to be the objects of His favor. "Out of the midst of the fire" at Sinai He spoke to them through Moses. "By a mighty hand and an outstretched arm" He had broken the chains of Egyptian bondage. He had driven out mighty nations that had obstructed their march to the Jordan. (Nm 10:11—21:35)

4:39 *No other.* Anyone or anything that men may regard as a "god" (33 f.) is "the work of men's hands" (28) or the figment of their perverse minds. Twice Moses declared that "the Lord is [*the*] God" (the Hebrew has the definite article), the only God, and that *there is no other* "besides him" (35). What a privilege to *know* Him! How ungrateful not to *lay it to your heart!*

4:41-43 PREVIOUS PROVISIONS IMPLEMENTED

4:41 *Three cities.* Vv. 41-43 report that at Moses' direction a previously given provision for Israel's future well-being was put into effect as far as the circumstances permitted (cf. Nm 35 notes). In the conquered territory he *set apart three cities* which were to serve as asylums for unintentional manslayers. Three more were to be selected for the same purpose on the west side of the Jordan. (19:2; Jos 20:7-9)

4:44—11:32 Basic Covenant Terms Reviewed and Applied to the Future

4:44—6:25 THE CORE OF THE COVENANT: THE DECALOG

4:44 *The law.* The concluding verses of ch. 4 may summarize Moses' first address and elaborate its setting (1:1-5). They can just as well serve as an introduction to the second and longer exposition of the *law.* (5:1—26:15)

4:46 *Beth-peor.* Cf. 3:29; Nm 25:3; 31:16. *Sihon.* Cf. 1:4; Nm 21:21-25.

4:47 *Og.* Cf. 1:4; Nm 21:31-35.

4:48 *Aroer.* Cf. 2:36; 3:12. *Sirion.* Cf. 3:8 f.

4:49 *The Sea of the Arabah* is the Dead Sea (3:17; Jos 3:16; 12:3; 2 K 14:25). *Pisgah.* Cf. Nm 21:10 note; 23:13 f.; Dt 3:17.

5:2 *A covenant with us.* In his exhortation Moses stresses the continuing validity of the covenant for his contemporaries and all succeeding generations. Contracted many years ago, its validity did not expire with the "fathers" (3). In order to drive home this point, Moses used drastic language. When he declared that the Lord did not "make this covenant" with the fathers, he did not mean to deny their participation in it at Mt. Sinai. In an idiomatic way he was simply emphasizing that God intended the terms of the covenant to apply not only to the former generation but to have binding force as well for "all of us here alive this day." (For similar examples of such absolute statements for the sake of contrast see Ex 6:3; Ps 40:6; 51:16 f.; Is 1:11; Hos 6:6).—In the same way the benefits of the new covenant are available to all generations and not merely to those who stood on Golgotha's hill.

5:6 *The Lord your God.* Cf. 1:10 note. This introductory sentence sets forth the rationale of the covenant. God had abundantly revealed Himself to the Israelites as *the Lord* (Ex 6:6). He had made them His people by bringing them *out of the house of bondage.* Their compliance with the covenant therefore did not earn God's favor; it could only be their grateful response to His deeds of salvation, which they had not merited.

5:7 *No other gods.* The core of the covenant obligations was the Decalog (Ex 20:3-17). Moses not only restated it; He devoted a considerable portion of his address to an exposition of its decisive significance for his hearers (chs. 5—11). On the basis of this constitution he then proceeded to set forth its bylaws, "the statutes and the ordinances" that were to regulate various phases of Israel's religious and communal life in Canaan (chs. 12—26). See the notes on the commandments in Ex. 20.

5:12 *Observe the sabbath day.* In his oral presentation Moses at times deviated from the engraved words of the Decalog recorded in Ex 20. There this commandment reads: "Remember the sabbath day" (Ex 20:8). Its basic intent and purpose remained the same. One out of 7 days was to be *holy,* i.e., set aside "to the Lord" as a reminder that time was put at man's disposal by divine dispensation. Ex 20:11 links the Sabbath observance with God's creative work of 6 days. Here the Israelites were commanded "to keep the sabbath day" in remembrance of the power displayed by the Creator when He freed them from a bondage in which they had been forbidden to use their time for their own benefit.

5:16 *Go well.* In keeping with his hortatory purpose, Moses added this clause to the wording of this commandment in Ex 20:12.

5:21 *Neighbor's wife.* In Ex 20:17 the *house* precedes the *wife.* In anticipation of Israel's agricultural economy, Moses applies the prohibition of coveting to the neighbor's *field,* not mentioned specifically in Ex 20.

5:22 *No more.* God's revelation had not come to an end. But the Decalog, written on "two tables of stone" (4:13; 10:4; Ex 31:18), needed no additions. Distinct from the statutes and ordinances, the Ten Commandments are a complete summary of God's irrevocable will for all men. (Mk 10:17-19; Ro 13:8-10; Ja 2:8-13)

5:24 *God speak.* Moses sought to impress on his hearers that their relationship to God was a matter of life and death. He recalled the appearance of His devastating glory at Mt. Sinai (Ex 19:17-19). When the Israelites heard *his voice out of the midst of the fire,* they could only fear that a confrontation with Him must "consume" them, guilty of rebellion as they were (Ex. 20:18 f.). But the *voice* of the living God sounded forth and they *still lived.* However, it would be a fatal mistake to assume that God was indifferent to their response to His mercy. In the future as in the past "this great fire will consume" them if they break the covenant by disobedience to His holy will. (29; Ex 22:24; Jos 23:16; Is 30:27; Jer 7:20; Ro 1:18; 2:5; Cl 3:5 f.; Rv 6:15 f.)

5:31 *Tell you.* Moses was the "intermediary" of God's covenant with Israel (Gn 3:19). In this capacity he was a shadowy figure of the "one mediator between God and men, the man Christ Jesus," through whom God reconciled the world to Himself. (1 Ti 2:5; Heb 9:15; 12:24; Ro 5:1 f.; 8:34; Eph 2:18; 3:11 f.)

6:1 *Teach you.* Moses had confronted his hearers with the Decalog, the "words the Lord spoke . . . out of the midst of the fire" almost 40 years ago. They constituted *THE commandment,* the quintessence of covenant requirements. In view of their vital importance Moses at once expounded them at some length. He stressed their foremost demand (God alone), the proper motivation in keeping them (love and gratitude), and the decisive effect of their observance for all generations (chs. 6—11). The "statutes and ordinances" (chs. 11—26), regulating all aspects of Israel's life—social, economic, political, religious—were only corollaries of these axiomatic 10 words.

6:4 *One Lord.* The core of the covenant is the Decalog; the heart of the Decalog is allegiance to the only true God. "The Lord your God" is in a category all His own. There is no coexistence "besides Him." Everything else owes its existence to Him. When men have "other gods besides Him," they engage in counterfeiting the *one* genuine coin. The Canaanite baals were the personification of various powers of nature, created by Him. What folly to dress them in the trappings of divinity! But the Lord is *one.* Not divisible into separate forces which man can manipulate by magic, He is the sole source of all natural phenomena and the sovereign director of man's destiny.

6:5 *Shall love.* In spite of man's rebellion against Him, this transcendent Lord of creation desires to be loved by His wayward subjects. He had done so much in the past to elicit this response from the Israelites (4:37; 7:7 f.; 10:15). From the recipients of His unmerited love the Lord expects total commitment to Him, a love that is unalloyed in sincerity *(all your heart),* without reservations *(all your soul),* engaging all faculties to their full capacity *(all your might).* Love of God is "the first of all" commandments (Mk 12:28-31; Mt 22:38; 2 K 23:25). It results in love for fellowmen (Ro 13:10; Jn 15:12; 1 Jn 2:5, 15; 4:16-21). Known as the "Shema," the Hebrew word for "hear" (4), vv. 4-9 (with the addition of 11:13-21 and Nm 15:37-41) remain the primary confession of faith in Judaism. However, the unicity of God does not militate against the doctrine of the Trinity: three Persons in the "one Lord."

6:8 *Bind them.* Cf. Ex 13:9 note.

6:9 *Write them.* In literal obedience to this command loyal adherents to Judaism still fasten a small capsule-like container to the entrance of their homes. Called "mezuzah" (doorpost), it contains a parchment inscribed with the words of 6:4-9 and 11:13-21.

6:12 *Forget the Lord.* Man's failure to love God has its roots in forgetting his debt of gratitude. It is the diabolical perversity of the human heart that the more prodigal God is in bestowing material blessings (10-12) the more prone men often are to neglect "to love the Lord your God with all your heart." Therefore Moses repeatedly warned his hearers not to succumb to this innate depravity of forgetting God when "they have eaten and are full" (8:11-20; 31:20; 32:15). The history of the Israelites records that in Canaan their prosperity led to their defection from God and their ultimate disinheritance (Hos 2:8-13; 13:6-8; Jer 5:7-9). "Love of money" remains "the root of all evils" (1 Ti 6:10; see also Mt 6:19-21; Lk 12:13-21). Almost invariably prosperity has resulted in apostasy from God and the downfall of individuals and whole nations.

6:13 *Fear the Lord.* This command is not inconsistent with the requirement "you shall love the Lord" (5). In the first place, men need the reminder that total commitment to God in response to His mercy is not something that they can neglect with impunity. Failure to love God kindles His "anger." In the second place, there is a kind of fear that is a concomitant of man's love for God. It is an awe-inspired attitude of reverence and adoration, fearful of offending so sublime a Being. Luther begins the explanation of the Ten Commandments with a twofold requirement: "We should fear and love God." When Jesus was tempted by Satan, He repelled His adversary by citing a part of this verse. (Mt 4:8-10)

6:14 *Other gods.* Cf. 4 note.

6:15 *Jealous.* Cf. 4:24 note.

6:16 *Put . . . to the test.* Cf. Ex 17:7 note; also Ps 78:18; 95:8. Covenant faith requires unquestioning trust in God. It is an act of unbelief to prescribe to God how or when He must prove that He has the willingness or the power to keep His promises. Such testing is nothing short of attempting to coerce God to do man's biddings. Tempted by Satan to succumb to such presumption, Jesus quoted the first part of this verse. (Mt 4:7)

6:21 *To your son.* The terms of the covenant, as set forth 4-19, would remain in effect in the future. Therefore fathers owed it to their children to instruct them in "the meaning of the testimonies and the statutes and the ordinances" (20; Ex 13:14). Two basic principles were to be stressed: (a) every generation was to recognize its debt to God for His unmerited goodness (21-23); (b) God would bless obedience which is the fruit of faith. (24 f.)

7:1-26 OBEDIENCE TO CORE COMMANDMENT

7:1 *Into the land.* The Israelites would have occasion to practice the core requirement of the covenant (6:4). If they associated in any way with the idolatrous inhabitants of Canaan, they would be tempted to serve "other gods" (4). The *seven nations* mentioned here represented various ethnic strains. But in the melting pot of Canaan they had all become Baal worshipers. In order to avoid such baalization the Israelites were to (a) "utterly destroy" them and their idolatrous symbols (1-5); (b) rely on "the faithful God" to direct their destiny (6-11); (c) trust "the Lord your God" to supply their physical needs and to shun the fertility rites of baalism (12-16); (d) remember the former display of God's power in their behalf (17-26). For names of the inhabitants of Canaan see Gn 10:15-19 note.

7:2 *Destroy them.* Cf. Nm 31:2 note.

7:5 *Pillars . . . Asherim.* Cf. Gn 28:18 note.

7:6 *Own possession.* Cf. Ex 19:5 note.

Holy. Cf. Ex 19:6 note.

7:9 *Steadfast love.* KJV: "mercy." One word in Hebrew, this term emphasizes the trustworthiness of God's goodness. He displays it as He *keeps covenant* and steadfastly adheres to its terms (12; 5:10; Ex 20:6; Ps 136:1-26; Jer 32:18). It is in marked contrast to man's unfaithfulness in fulfilling his covenant obligations to God and his fellowmen.

7:13 *The fruit of your body.* The Canaanites practiced sympathetic magic. By sacred prostitution and orgiastic rites they sought to induce fertility in man, beast, and soil.

7:20 *Hornets.* Cf. Ex 23:28 note.

7:22 *Little by little.* The defeat of the Canaanites was no less decisive because the conquest extended over a longer period of time. In each encounter there would be no question of the outcome. (9:3)

7:26 *An accursed thing.* Anything liable to the ban of utter destruction. (Cf. 2:34 note; Nm 21:2)

8:1—11:32 RESPONSE TO THE COVENANT GOD

1) 8:1—10:11 Recognize Covenant as His Gift

8:1 *Be careful to do.* Moses expounded *all the commandment* in order to motivate his hearers *to do* it. They would be preserved from disobedience if they bore in mind (a) that God had taught and preserved them "these forty years in the wilderness" (1-10); (b) that their future prosperity was contingent on God's "power to get wealth." (11-20)

8:2 *Testing you.* In the wilderness God taught them how utterly dependent on Him they were, humbling though the lesson was.

8:3 *Bread alone.* God fed them *with manna* from heaven, proving to them that *man lives* solely by virtue of the power that *proceeds out of the mouth of the Lord.* For *manna* see Ex 16:14 f. note. Jesus resisted Satan's temptation to prescribe to God how He must use His power and what kind of sustenance He must provide. For the quotation of this verse see Mt 4:4.

8:17 *My power.* Cf. 6:12 note.

9:1 *Mightier than yourselves.* The Israelites had every reason to give sole allegiance to the Lord their God. They were not a self-made nation. Only because He went before them "as a devouring fire" would they be able to *dispossess* the entrenched inhabitants of Canaan (9:1-3). Their status as the covenant people was a gift of His grace. Possession of the Promised Land was not a reward for their "righteousness" and "uprightness" (4 f.). They deserved that God "destroy them and blot out their name"; they "provoked the Lord . . . to wrath" from the day they "came out of the land of Egypt." At Sinai they "turned aside quickly out of the way" to make a "molten calf" (6-21). During the wilderness journey they "rebelled against the commandment" at various places (22-24). Nevertheless they survived annihilation because God was moved to mercy by Moses' intercession (25-29). He forgave their sins and renewed the covenant. (10:1-10)

9:2 *Anakim.* Cf. Nm 13:22 note.

9:4 *Wickedness of these nations.* The "iniquity of the Amorites" was not "complete" (Gn 15:16; Dt 18:12). But the execution of God's punishment on the Canaanites did not entitle the Israelites to pride themselves on their *righteousness.*

9:5 *Your father.* Cf. Gn 12:7; 13:15; 26:3 f.; 28:13.

9:8 *At Horeb.* Cf. Ex 32:1-6.

9:10 *The day of the assembly.* Cf. Ex 19:17.

9:14 *Destroy them.* Cf. Ex 32:10.

9:22 *At Taberah.* Cf. Nm 11:1-3. *Massah.* Cf. Ex 17:1-7. *Kibroth-hattaavah.* Cf. Nm 11:4-15, 31-34.

9:23 *Rebelled.* Cf. Nm 14:1 note.

9:24 *Knew you.* In Biblical usage the verb "to know" often denotes more than intellectual awareness. It has the additional connotation of entering into a personal relationship with someone. (Gn 4:1; Hos 13:5)

9:25 *Lay prostrate.* Moses continued to drive home the point of Israel's unworthiness to be favored by God. He had interjected a reference to some instances of its refusal to "believe him or obey his voice" after the episode at Horeb (22-24). Now he returned to that critical moment when Israel's worship of the molten calf violated the primary requirement of the covenant. Moved by Moses' plea for mercy, God forgave Israel's rebellion (25-29; 10:10 f.) and renewed the covenant (10:1-10). For Moses' intercession see Ex 32:11 note.

10:1 *Two tables.* The Decalog constituted the basic terms of the covenant. Cf. Ex 19:5 note; 20.

10:3 *Ark.* Moses seems to be telescoping two events: the preparation of the tables and their being placed later into the ark of the covenant (Ex 25:16, 21; 40:20), or he may refer to a temporary chest in which the tables were housed.

10:6 *Journeyed.* Vv. 6 f. provide a logical connection with Moses' preceding and subsequent remarks. Referring to events that happened after Israel's departure from Sinai, they present the evidence that God had indeed forgiven His "stubborn people" and kept His part of the renewed covenant. Israel was permitted to continue its journey under His provident guidance. God did not "destroy" Aaron (9:19 f.), but He reinstated him *as priest* and after his death continued to provide the mediating ministrations of his office through *his son Eleazar. At that time,* i.e., while Israel was at Mt. Sinai, God also had "set apart the tribe of Levi" and assigned to it special functions in the renewed covenant. (8; Nm 1:47-54; 3:5-10)

Moserah. Aaron died on Mt. Hor (Nm 30:22-29). *Moserah* (in the plural form of "Moseroth" in Nm 33:30) means chastisement. It designates the site of Aaron's death as a place of punishment for his unfaithfulness. The other three place names (6 f.) are mentioned in Nm 33:31-33 but not in the same order. No doubt the Israelites stopped at these places more than once, since they were a source of much-needed water.

2) 10:12—11:17 Be Grateful for Unmerited Goodness

10:12 *Require of you.* Moses had demonstrated from the past that the Israelites owed their existence solely to the forgiving mercy of God (8:1—10:11). *And now*—in grateful recognition of this undeserved goodness—they were to respond with wholehearted love toward

God and toward their fellowmen (12-22). However, as in the past, "his mighty hand" would remain "outstretched" to enforce compliance with His will (11:1-7). On the other hand, if the Israelites would "keep all the commandment," He would reward their grateful obedience by giving them "a land flowing with milk and honey" (11:8-12). After they were in Canaan, their welfare would continue to depend on their willingness "to love the Lord" and keep His commandments (11:13-17). See Jesus' summary of the Law. (Mt 22:37; also Mi 6:8)

10:14 *Heaven of heavens.* A Hebrew way of saying: "the highest heaven"; so RSV in 1 K 8:27.

10:16 *Circumcise . . . your heart.* Mere outward observances of rites and ceremonies did not suffice. Obedience must come from the heart, shorn of its natural propensity to self-will. (Jer 6:10; Ro 2:29)

10:17 *God of gods.* Cf. Ex 20:3 note.

10:20 *Swear by his name.* An oath by the name of another was an act of idolatry. (Cf. Ex 20:7 note)

11:1 *Love the Lord.* Moses cannot say it often enough that the Israelites owed the Lord a debt of love. They had received "grace for grace" in their election to be His covenant people (10:14 f.), in their redemption from Egypt (2-5), in the forgiveness for their rebellions (9:6—10:11). In response for this unmerited love they were to *love the Lord* and discharge this obligation by keeping *his charge, his statutes, his ordinances, and his commandments.* See also 10:12 note.

11:6 *Dathan and Abiram.* God had showered His love on the Israelites. But His judgment on Korah, Dathan, and Abiram was to be a grim reminder that He will not tolerate abuse of His grace. (Nm 16:32-33)

11:9 *Flowing with milk and honey.* A figurative description of the productivity of the Promised Land. (Ex 3:8; Lv 20:24)

11:10 *With your feet.* Egypt receives no "rain from heaven." Water for the growing of crops must be supplied by irrigation. Devices for lifting it from the Nile were operated by foot.

3) 11:18-32 Remember the Covenant

11:18 *In your heart.* Obedience to *these words* of the covenant required a commitment to the Lord that sprang from the deepest recesses of *heart* and *soul* and excluded "other gods" (16; 6:5; 10:12). The Israelites were never to lose sight of their debt of total consecration; it was to be a determining factor in every moment and in every situation of their lives. For *frontlets* and "doorposts" (20) see Ex 13:9; Dt 6:9 notes.

11:19 *Your children.* Moses repeatedly emphasized that the covenant, made at Sinai with the fathers, had binding force for the living generation as well as for their descendants. (5:3; 4:9 f.; 6:7, 20-25)

11:24 *Western sea.* The Mediterranean.

11:26 *Set before you.* In their relationship to God there was no possibility of neutrality. The covenant presented the Israelites with unavoidable alternatives: *a blessing and a curse.* After crossing the Jordan they were to remind themselves of this either-or by an antiphonal recital of "the blessing on Mount Gerizim and the curse on Mount Ebal." (29; 27:11-14; Jos 8:33)

11:30 *Beyond the Jordan.* Mt. Ebal and Mt. Gerizim were visible to the Israelites as they looked westward across the Jordan. In *the Arabah,* the rift valley of the Jordan (1:1), lay "Gilgal," where they first encamped "on the east border of Jericho" (Jos 4:19). Across the Jordan also was "the oak of Moreh" at Shechem, where God appeared to Abraham "when they had come to the land of Canaan." (Cf. Gn 12:6 note)

12:1—26:19 Covenant Ordinances Expounded and Adapted

12:1—16:17 WORSHIP OF THE ONE LORD

1) 12:1-32 The Place of Worship

12:1 *Statutes and ordinances.* In the first 11 chs. Moses reviewed Israel's history for the purpose of exhorting his hearers to remain faithful to the terms of the covenant, summarized in the Decalog. In his exposition of the Ten Commandments he confined himself almost exclusively to their foremost and basic requirement: to fear and love the one and only Lord with all their heart. An unreserved commitment to God was basic to the covenant. Observance of the other commandments would follow to the extent that this axiomatic principle was accepted. In chs. 12—26 Moses proceeded to review some of the corollaries of the Decalog. In *the statutes and ordinances* the Israelites were told how to express their covenant relationship to God (12:1—16:17) and then how to regulate their lives as members of the covenant community. (16:18—26:19)

12:5 *Seek the place.* The first statute, defining Israel's relationship to God, required the covenant people to express their unreserved allegiance to the one and only Lord (6:4) by (a) rejecting all worship practices that acknowledge the existence of "other gods before" Him (5:7); (b) worshiping the one sovereign God only at that one particular place where from time to time He *will choose . . . to put His name.* This statute therefore had exclusive as well as inclusive force. It ruled out reducing God to one of the baals of Canaan. He was the Creator and not the composite personification of the various forces of nature, deified by the Canaanites. Such an idol, divisible into several forms of energy, could be harnessed to the wishes of its devotees. They could manipulate him at all places where his services were necessary and where he was thought to be most readily available and susceptible to licentious rites of sympathetic magic. There they erected images and symbols of the reproductive functions which the baals were to supply (cf. Gn 28:18 note). But the true God could not so be impounded by men. He determined where He would accept the worship of His people. They could bring their sacrifices only to the place where He *put his name,* i.e., where He chose to reveal Himself for the purpose of establishing *his habitation* among them and receiving their homage. This first of "the statutes and ordinances" was so basic for Israel's relationship to God that Moses repeated it some 20 times (cf. 11, 14, 18, 21, 26; 14:25; 15:20; 16:7, 15 f.; 17:8, 10; 18:6; 31:11). Rigidly excluding every unauthorized approach to God, it was stated in terms elastic enough to allow for worship "in every place" where in the future God would cause His "name to be remembered" (Ex 20:24). Before His *habitation* came to "rest" in the Jerusalem temple (9; 1 K 8:56), God chose various localities and sanctified them for Israel's response to His presence. (See for example 27:4-7; Jos 18:1; 1 Sm 1:3)

12:8 *We are doing.* No doubt orderly worship procedures had been neglected during the struggles to seize Moab from its occupants. (Nm 21:21-31; 31:1-12)

12:15 *Your towns.* "The place which the Lord will choose" in Canaan would be far from the residence of some people. Therefore an adjustment of the ordinances regarding the slaughter and eating of animals was necessary (cf. Lv 17:3-7). The previous exception that "any beast or bird" taken in hunting such as *the gazelle* and *the hart* need not be brought "to the door of the tent of meeting" was to apply to all animals that were not "holy things," i.e., sacrificial offerings (22, 26; Lv 17:13). Hereafter they could be killed and eaten *within any of your towns.*

12:23 *The blood.* In this adaptation of the law to new circumstances there was to be no relaxation of the basic rule not to *eat the blood.* (Gn 9:4; cf. Lv 17:10 note)

2) 13:1-18 Idolatry Rooted Out

13:1 *A prophet arises.* In Canaan the temptation would arise to follow the example of the inhabitants and to engage in their idolatrous practices "upon the high mountains and upon the hills and under every green tree" (12:2). Hence all symbols and places that might lure the Israelites to do such "abominable" things, including child sacrifice (12:31), were to be destroyed. Similar drastic action was to be taken when the impetus to "go after other gods" came from their own midst by (a) "a prophet" who "taught rebellion against the Lord" (1-5); (b) any one, even the closest relative, who "entices you secretly" (6-11); (c) "the inhabitants of the city" who had been "drawn away" by "certain base fellows" (12-18). None of these was to be shown any mercy.

13:2 *Sign or wonder.* The people were not to be misled even if *the sign or wonder* of a prophet *comes to pass.* If he advocates going *after other gods,* they could be sure that he did not derive his uncanny power from God, but from the "father of lies." To this day a teacher of false doctrines is to be shunned although he may claim the ability to perform miracles. (Mt 24:24; Mk 13:22; Rv 19:20)

13:10 *Stone him.* The Mosaic legislation was very much concerned about domestic and social relationships. Natural affections were not stifled. The integrity of the family was safeguarded. But loyalty to God was to transcend the obligations of the most intimate human ties. The Israelites were not to love father or mother, son or daughter more than God (Mt 10:37 f.). The infliction of capital punishment, harsh though it was, was designed to protect the people against being infected by a sin, the wages of which is eternal death. The Levites had obeyed such a command in similar circumstances. (Ex 32:25 ff.)

13:12 *One of your cities.* Israel was to be purged of a whole community if it had been induced "to serve other gods." Under the OT dispensation the functions of the church and state were combined in what is called a theocratic government. The NT church has no civil authority to enforce obedience to religious requirements.

13:17 *Devoted things.* Cf. 2:34 note.

3) 14:1-21 Restrictions in Customs and Diet

14:1 *Cut yourselves.* The Israelites were to demonstrate that they were *sons of the Lord* by: (a) avoiding superstitious mutilations or markings of their bodies, practiced by the Canaanites (1 f.; cf. Lv 21:5 note); (b) abstaining from eating animals that God had declared "unclean" for "a people holy to the Lord." (3-21; Lv 11:2-45; 17:15; Ex 22:31)

14:7 *The hare and the rock badger.* Cf. Lv 11:2 note.

14:21 *In its mother's milk.* Cf. Ex 23:19 note.

4) 14:22—15:23 Recognition of God,
the Source of All Good

14:22 *Tithe all the yield.* The ordinances in 1-21 required the Israelites to abstain from unholy practices if they were to maintain a holy relationship to God. In the following section (14:22—15:23) the covenant people were directed to express their recognition of the one Lord also in a positive way. In order to betoken their total dependence on Him for (a) the fruits of the field: they were to dedicate a 10th of the produce to Him (22-27); (b) all their possessions: creditors were to cancel debts in the year of release (15:1-11); (c) their redemption from Egyptian bondage: all indentured and bonded servants were to be released (15:12-18); (d) their flocks: the male firstlings were to be consecrated to the Lord. (15:19-23)

14:23 *Eat the tithe.* According to Nm 18:20-27 the Levites received the tithe for their livelihood. Vv. 28 f. seem to prescribe how the tithe was to be collected and made available to the Levites as well as other needy individuals. The Levites were also to be guests at a ceremonial meal at the sanctuary (12:6, 12). For such festive occasions the tithed produce could be brought to *the place which he* (God) *will choose,* or its equivalent amount could be purchased there. However, the detailed procedure in computing and allocating the tithe (or tithes) remains unclear.

14:26 *Rejoice.* Cf. Lv 23:34 note.

15:1 *Grant a release.* The Israelites were to honor the Lord as the source of all blessings by acts of kindness to unfortunate members of His people (cf. 14:22 note). Every seventh year "every creditor" was to cancel his neighbor's unpaid loan (1-11) and remit the debt which a Hebrew man or woman had been paying by working it off. (12-18)

15:3 *A foreigner.* Cf. Lv 25:35, 39 notes; Dt 23:20.

15:4 *No poor. The Lord will bless* the people *in the land* so bountifully if they obey His voice (5) that actually no poverty needed to exist. But by reason of human frailty "the poor will never cease out of the land." (11)

15:15 *Redeemed you.* Moses frequently reminded the Israelites that they were indebted to God for their release from Egyptian bondage (5:15; 9:26; 13:5; 16:12; 21:8). "Bought with a price" and made His "own possession," they had the opportunity to acknowledge their obligation to their Redeemer by forgiving the debts of their fellow redeemed. Israel's emancipation from Egypt was a part of God's plan to redeem all mankind from the slavery of sin. The price He paid was the blood of His own Son (Ro 3:21-25; Gl 4:4-6). Forgiven, the redeemed cannot but forgive their debtors. (Mt 6:12; 18:23-35)

15:17 *Bondman.* Cf. Ex 21:2 note.

15:19 *Firstling males.* Not the baals, as the Canaanites would tell the Israelites, but the Lord multiplied their *herd and flock.* The first perfect male young to which each female gave birth was to be consecrated to God in order to remind the people that they owed also their livestock to divine goodness. (Cf. 14:22 note; 12:6; Nm 18:17-19)

15:22 *Gazelle or hart.* Cf. 12:15 note.

5) 16:1-17 Annual Festivals

16:1 *Observe.* Moses ended his rehearsal of the "statutes and ordinances" that the Israelites were to "be careful to do" with a reminder of the annual pilgrim festivals (cf. 12:1 note). "Three times a year" (16; Ex 23:17) all males were to appear at the sanctuary in order to observe: (a) "the passover," associated with the feast of unleavened bread (1-8); (b) "the feast of weeks" or pentecost (9-12); (c) "the feast of booths" (13-15). Detailed instructions for the observance of these festivals had been issued previously: (a) Ex 12 f.; Lv 23:4-8; Nm 9:1-14; 28:16-25; (b) Lv 23:15-22; Nm 28:26-31; (c) Lv 23:33-36, 39-43; Nm 29:12-40.

16:2 *At the place.* In Egypt the Israelites celebrated the first passover in their homes. During the wilderness journey it was observed in their tents, clustered about the tabernacle. The three pilgrim festivals were to prevent the loss of their covenant solidarity after they had settled in widely separated areas of Canaan. Moses stressed the adjustment of these festivals to the new circumstances (2, 6, 11, 15, 16). Sacrifices for the passover were to be taken *from the flock*: a lamb offered "in the evening" (6; Ex 12:21); for the immediately following festival of unleavened bread, *from the flock or the herd:* "two young bulls, one ram, and seven male lambs." (Nm 28:19)

16:7 *Boil it.* Cf. Lv 6:25 note; Eze 46:24.

16:18—26:9 COMMUNAL LIFE

1) 16:18—17:20 Administration of Covenant Law

16:18 *Judges and officers.* Moses had reviewed the statutes and ordinances by which the Israelites were to express their total commitment to the only Lord (12:1—16:17). But the obligations of the covenant people did not end there. Their entire communal life was also to be ordered according to God's instructions. The following section (16:18—26:19) contains these directives. They deal with the administration of a wide range of religious, civil, and domestic affairs. During the wilderness journey Moses appointed "elders" to serve as lower court adjudicators (1:16; Ex 18:25 f.). However, occupation of the Promised Land required adjustments of the legal system if *righteous judgment* was to be rendered in all cases. The judicial personnel was to be augmented by *officers* (translated "foremen" in Ex 5:6). They were to have jurisdiction *in all your towns* (2 Ch 19:11). Every trial was to be conducted without the least "partiality." (19; 24:17 f.; 25:13-16)

16:21-22 *A tree.* The judges were reminded that the Israelites were first and foremost a religious community. It was to be a prime concern of the constituted authorities to maintain proper relations with God (cf. 17:1-7). For *Asherah* and *a pillar* see Gn 28:18 note.

17:3 *Other gods.* In cases of flagrant idolatry the court was to sit in the "gates" of the city (5). If the crime was established "on the evidence of two witnesses," the verdict of death by stoning was to be imposed on the offender. (Cf. 13:6-18)

17:8 *Too difficult.* Before the settlement in Canaan the local judges brought "hard cases" to Moses (Ex 18:25 f.) and to Joshua (Nm 27:18-21). The same procedure was to be followed when cases *too difficult* later came up *within your towns.* The "priests" and "the judge," no doubt the high priest, were to serve as the court of appeals. Their decision was final. Perhaps it was obtained by consulting the Urim and Thummim (Nm 27:21). Defiance of the verdict of "the judge" was punishable by death.

17:14 *A king.* Allowance is made in advance for the desire of the people to be governed by a king *like all the nations.* However the monarchy was to differ in essential points from that of the Canaanites. It was not to be a repudiation of the Lord as the supreme Ruler (cf. 1 Sm 8:4-9). Only such a person from their "brethren" as the Lord "will choose" was to occupy the throne. In administering his office the king must shun the temptation to self-glorification, avoid putting his trust in the accumulation of "horses . . . silver and gold," resist the impulse to self-gratification by multiplying "wives for himself," and refrain from subjecting the covenant people to Egyptian domination. (14-17)

17:18 *A copy of this law.* Israel's king was not to be an autocratic despot. He was to be subject to God's law, Israel's constitution. From *a copy* of it he was to read "all the days of his life" and to "learn to fear the Lord." *This law* may refer to the Book of Deuteronomy or the entire legislation which Moses was expounding. Unfortunately, however, many of Israel's kings did not comply with these directives. (See for example 1 K 11:1-7)

2) 18:1-8 Livelihood of Priests and Levites

18:1 *Levitical priests.* Moses had previously instructed the *Levitical priests* and the other members of the *tribe of Levi* regarding their respective functions and prerogatives (Ex 28 f.; Lv 8 f.) In his directive to the people he again distinguished between "the priests" (3) and the "Levites" (6) as he had done when he had declared that the Lord is the "inheritance" of Aaron, the priest, and also of the other Levites (Nm 18:20, 24). He made it clear that all priests were Levites but not all Levites were priests. In v. 1 the RSV obscures this difference by inserting *that is* between *the Levitical priests* and *all the tribe of Levi.* The Hebrew text has an unconnected series of appositions: "the priests, the Levites, all the tribe of Levi." Since the distinction between what we would call upper and lower clergy is maintained in the following verses as well as elsewhere, the last appositional phrase cannot be intended to obliterate the difference in status and function between the priests and the other Levites. The KJV distinguishes the two groups by inserting an interpretative "and" before *all the tribe of Levi.*

No portion. As a religious community the Israelites were to provide for those who devoted their time to sacred duties: the Levites and the priests, chosen from this tribe. The clergy was not to become a landed aristocracy, as was the case in Egypt. However, the people were to provide them a dwelling place and livelihood. (1 Co 9:13 f.)

18:8 *His patrimony.* No member of the tribe of Levi was to receive "an inheritance with Israel." But the acquisition of private property was not forbidden. (Cf. Jer 32:6-15)

3) 18:9-22 Divine Disclosure Through Prophets

18:9 *Abominable practices.* Israel was not a secular state. There was no distinction between the profane domain and the sacred. The judges tried offenses against God (16:21—17:7) as well as those committed against fellow citizens (17:8-13). Royal authority was to uphold divine law (17:14-20). The clergy were supported by a divinely imposed federal tax (1-8). In the remaining verses of this chapter the covenant people are forbidden to pry into divine mysteries by occult practices (9-14). What they need to know, God will supply by sending them His spokesmen, authenticated prophets like Moses. (15-22)

18:10 *Burn his son or his daughter.* Cf. Lv 18:21 note.

18:11 *Necromancer.* Lit. "a consultee of the dead" (1 Sm 28:8 ff.). "These abominable practices" of divination persist in various forms to the present day.

18:15 *A prophet like me.* God will not be coerced by magical means to do the will and satisfy the curiosity of men. Nevertheless He would continue to direct His people by putting His Word into the mouth of prophets like Moses. The message of such spokesmen they were to *heed* as if God were again speaking to them directly as He did in the fire *at Horeb.* But Moses and all his successors were to be types of the coming Prophet in whom divine revelation would become incarnate (Jn 1:1-4, 14). Jesus Christ was Himself the Word of God (Acts 3:22; 7:37; Jn 5:46). More than Moses, He sent others to proclaim His Gospel. (Lk 10:16; Mt 28:16-20)

18:21 *Know.* God will let only *the word* of a genuine prophet come true (Jer 28:8 f.; 1 K 22:28). But even if He permits a charlatan to do "sign or wonder," he can be detected as a "presumptuously" speaking impostor if he advocates the violation of the revealed will of God (cf. 13:1, 2 notes; Is 8:20). The NT people of God are confronted with the counterpart of the false prophets in Israel. They too must "test the spirits to see whether they are of God." (1 Jn 4:1-3; Mt 7:15; 24:11, 24; 2 Ptr 2:1-3; Gl 1:6-9)

4) 19:1-13 Sanctity of Life

19:2 *Three cities.* In the communal life of the covenant people the individual was to have protection against: (a) loss of life (1-13); (b) loss of property (14); (c) false incrimination (15-21). For the provisions safeguarding the sanctity of life see Nm 35:11, 16 notes. As the need would arise, "you shall add three other cities [of refuge] to these three" which had been set aside east of the Jordan. (9-10; Nm 35:10-12; Jos 20:7 f.)

5) 19:14 Property Rights

19:14 *Landmark.* The stone slab or simply a heap of stones marked the borders of a man's property. A thief could easily move them, thus reducing his neighbor's "inheritance" to his advantage. Such larceny violated not only the neighbor's rights but also subverted God's order that ownership of real property remain fixed. (Cf. Lv 25:8-28; 1 K 21; Dt 27:17; Hos 5:10)

6) 19:15-21 Trial by Witnesses

19:15 *Any crime.* The ordinance requiring more than one *witness* in a murder case (17:6; Nm 35:30) is here extended to apply to trials for *any crime.* The victim of false testimony had the right to appeal to the highest court: "the priests and the judges" at the sanctuary (cf. 17:8). A perjured witness was to receive the penalty for the crime of which he had falsely accused the defendant (18-21). Punishment was imposed by governmental authority, outlawing personal retaliation.

7) 20:1-20 Conduct of War

20:1 *To war.* Simultaneously a religious and a civil community, the Israelites received theocratic directives in matters of external as well as internal policy. Military campaigns against enemy nations were holy wars because the Holy One of Israel was the Commander in chief of its armed forces. In this role He assured His holy people through the mediator of holiness, "the [high] priest," that He would: (a) annihilate all hostile forces which, like the Egyptians, opposed His holy will (1-4); (b) determine through a draft board of "officers" who was to be exempted from military duty (5-9); (c) give instructions as to how to proceed in the siege and eventual capture of a city. (10-20; see also 21:10-14; 23:10-14; 25:17-19)

20:5 *Officers.* The Hebrew word for these officials suggests that they functioned chiefly as keepers of vital statistics and other records (1:15). They were to excuse from military service such as would suffer hardships or simply were "fainthearted."

20:17 *Utterly destroy.* Cf. 2:34 note; Nm 31:1; Ex 23:23, 33.

8) 21:1-9 Expiatory Rites for Murder

21:1 *Found slain.* In Israel the sanctity of life was not to be an empty phrase. A willful murderer, convicted of his guilt by the authorities, was to die at the hands of "the avenger of blood" (19:11-13). However, if the perpetrator of the crime *is not known,* the city nearest the field in which the corpse was found was to assume the responsibility for the crime, declare its inability to bring the murderer to justice, and purge itself of the "guilt of innocent blood" by an expiatory rite. A heifer, the substitute of the murderer, was executed outside the city to still the blood crying to God for vengeance from the ground. (Gn 4:10)

21:8 *Forgive.* Literally "cover," so that the guilt was no longer exposed to the punitive justice of God. (Cf. Ex 25:17; Gn 20:16 notes)

9) 21:10-21 Marital and Family Ordinances

21:11 *A beautiful woman.* Community stability had its roots in orderly matrimonial and family life. Therefore Moses gave explicit directives regarding: (a) marriage with a captive woman (10-14); (b) the status of the firstborn son (15-17); (c) parental discipline. (18-21)

21:12 *Bring her home.* A female prisoner, taken in wars against enemies other than those mentioned in 20:16 f., was not to be the victim of her captor's sexual whims. After she had undergone ritualistic preparations of a month's duration, he could enter a marriage relationship with her.

Pare her nails. Cf. 2 Sm 19:24.

21:14 *Not sell her.* The marriage, perhaps a concubinage (cf. Gn 16:2 note), could be dissolved if the husband no longer had *delight in her.* Nevertheless, he could not dispose of her by *treating her as a slave.*

21:17 *The first-born.* Disruption of community life was to be prevented by a regulation governing its smallest unit: the family. The ancient *right of the first-born* son was to remain in force. After his father's death he became the head of the family (Gn 25:31 ff.; 27:36 f.) and received a *double portion* of the inheritance. The personal feelings of the father for his wives or his sons was not to change the selection of his heir. (Cf. Gn 29:31 note; 1 Sm 1:5)

21:18 *Rebellious son.* Anarchy in the nucleus of society, the home, was to be rooted out. (Ex 21:15, 17; Lv 20:9; Dt 27:16)

10) 21:22-23 Burial of Criminals

21:22-23 *Hang him.* "Put to death," the criminal was hanged on a tree. The exhibition of his corpse was to demonstrate visibly that he had suffered the consequences of God's curse on his sin. Lest he *defile your land,* he was to be buried *the same day* (Jos 8:29). Hanged on the tree of the cross, the object of God's wrath on the sins of the world, the sinless Son of God "redeemed us from the curse of the law." (Gl 3:13; Jn 1:29; 19:31; Lk 22:37; Is 53:12)

11) 22:1-4 Neighborly Kindness

22:1 *Take them back.* Vv. 1-4 are an elaboration of the law of neighborly concern recorded Ex 23:4.

12) 22:5-12 Miscellaneous Regulations

22:5 *Not wear.* Vv. 5-12 contain a number of unrelated ordinances. Wearing apparel of the opposite sex was an "abomination to the Lord" because it was the vogue among the Canaanite fertility worshipers.

22:6 *Bird's nest.* Humanitarian treatment of birds would at the same time prevent the reduction of their number to the point of extinction.

22:8 *A parapet.* The houses had flat roofs (2 Sm 11:2; Jer 19:13; Mk 2:4)

22:12 *Tassels.* Cf. Nm 15:38 note.

13) 22:13-30 Sexual Integrity

22:13 *A wife.* The ordinances in the remaining verses deal with sexual purity: (a) a husband had the right to expect his wife to be a virgin at the time of her marriage (13-21); (b) degrees of punishment for adultery were to be determined by the kind of person involved and the attendant circumstances. (22-30)

22:17 *Spread the garment.* Bed clothing spotted with blood were *the tokens of virginity.* Embarrassing to our sensibilities, this means of exhibiting proof of premarital virginity was in keeping with the unabashed treatment of sexual matters at that time.

22:19 *A hundred shekels.* Twice the penalty exacted from the violator of a betrothed virgin. (29)

22:22 *Purge the evil.* The penalty for adultery, forbidden in the Decalog and Lv 18:20; 20:10, varied in severity depending on whether the woman was a wife, a betrothed young woman, an unbetrothed virgin, and whether she was violated with or without her consent.

22:23-24 *Neighbor's wife.* After the formal betrothal and the payment of the bridal price (cf. Gn 29:18 note), the woman was accorded the status of a married woman in assessing the punishment for violating the right reserved exclusively for her future husband.

22:30 *Uncover her.* A euphemism for sexual intercourse.

14) 23:1-14 Cultic and Physical Purity

23:1 *Enter the assembly.* Israel was a holy community, a people called and set aside to fulfill God's special purpose (cf. Ex 19:5, 6, 10 notes; Gn 35:2-3). Therefore it was to exclude from participation in its sacred rites all such as did not meet the demands of cultic purity, whether they were from its own midst (1 f.) or from other ethnic groups. (3-7)

23:3 *No Ammonite or Moabite.* The descendants of the incestuous union of Lot with his daughters (Gn 19:36-38) were not to enter the assembly of worshipers *even to the tenth generation,* i.e., forever (Neh 13:1). Moses recalled that Balaam at the behest of the Moabites had attempted to curse Israel. (Nm 22:1-6)

23:7-8 *Edomite.* Descendants of Esau, Jacob's twin brother (Gn 25:24-26), were to be admitted to the assembly after *the third generation* because the Edomite is *your brother.* During the wilderness journey the Israelites had not received brotherly treatment from the Edomites (Nm 20:14-21). The Egyptians were to be accorded the same consideration. During the sojourn of the Israelites in Egypt, slaves though they were, they were able to become a great nation.

23:9 *In camp.* Israel's wars were holy (cf. 20:1 note). The rules of cultic purity and physical cleanliness were to be observed in military camps.

15) 23:15—25:19 More Miscellaneous Laws

23:15 *A slave.* The remaining verses of this ch. and the entire next ch. contain rules that cover a wide range of community concerns. Not codified under topical headings but loosely strung together, they range from the citizen's duty to God to his marital and civic obligations, including even such things as his treatment of dumb animals. Some of these laws had been set forth previously; others appear only here.

23:17-18 *Cult prostitute.* The Israelites were not to tolerate in their midst female or male *(a dog)* harlots. They were *an abomination to the Lord* because they prostituted their bodies in immoral and unnatural cult practices. *Hire* or *wages* for this degrading service were not to be offered in payment of a vow.

23:19 *Interest.* Cf. Lv 25:35 note.

23:21 *Vow.* Cf. Nm 30:2 note.

24:1-4 *Take her again.* Divorce was a concession to their "hardness of heart" (Mt 19:8). It could be granted to the husband if he *found some* sexual *indecency* in his wife. However, he could not remarry her after she had become *another man's wife.* (Mt 5:31; 19:9)

24:5 *Newly married.* Cf. 20:7.

24:6 *In pledge.* The poor, in need of a loan "of any sort," were not to deposit as surety things indispensable to their livelihood or well-being such as a *millstone* or a "cloak." (Cf. 10-13)

24:7 *Stealing.* Cf. Ex 21:16.

24:8 *Leprosy.* Cf. Lv 13:2 note.

24:14 *A hired servant.* Cf. Lv 19:13.

24:16 *His own sin.* Israel's courts were to inflict capital punishment only on the culprit (2 K 14:6). This directive to human judges did not abrogate God's sovereign right to punish offenders according to the standards of His perfect justice. (5:9; Ex 20:5; Jer 31:29-30; Eze 18)

24:19 *Reap your harvest.* The Israelites were not only to accord equal justice to the underprivileged in their community (17) but also to provide them with gifts of charity (Lv 19:9 f.; 23:22). Such acts of kindness to their fellowmen were to be done in recognition of their debt to God's undeserved goodness to them when they were helpless slaves in Egypt. (22)

25:1 *A dispute.* This ch. continues the enumeration of various ordinances begun 23:15. In their communal life under a theocratic government the Israelites were to: (a) be moderate in punishing quarrelsome citizens (1-3); (b) be humane to animals (4); (c) keep ancestral estates within the respective families (5-10); (d) punish indecent acts of women (11 f.); (e) insist on honesty in business transactions (13-16); (f) execute God's judgment on an ancient foe. (17-19)

25:3 *Forty stripes.* Found guilty in court of disturbing the peace, the culprit was not to be the victim of personal revenge; he was to be punished "in his [the judge's] presence" (2). In administering the penalty the authorities later made sure that *no more* than *forty stripes* were inflicted by reducing the number to "forty lashes less one." (2 Co 11:24)

25:4 *Muzzle an ox.* Grain was threshed by driving oxen over the grain. St. Paul argues that if laboring animals should not be deprived of sustenance, then certainly "those who proclaim the gospel should get their living by the gospel." (1 Co 9:9, 14)

25:5 *Her husband's brother.* Cf. Gn 38:8; Lv 18:18; 20:19 notes. For the specious argument of the Sadducees, based on this so-called levirate marriage see Mt 22:23 ff.

25:9 *His sandal.* It is no longer clear what significance was attached to the forceful removal of a person's shoe (cf. Ru 4:7 note). By spitting "in his face" the spurned widow expressed the contempt of the whole community for one derelict in this solemn obligation.—The sinless Brother who atoned for all men's offenses in order that they might have an eternal inheritance did not hide His face "from shame and spitting." (Is 50:6; Mt 26:67)

25:11-12 *Cut off her hand.* Mutilation of offenders was a common form of punishment in other ancient law codes. In Israel it was seldom inflicted.

25:13 *Your bag.* Stones used as weights were carried in a bag (Mi 6:11). Honesty in business transactions (Lv 19:35 f.) became particularly important when the Israelites later engaged in commercial pursuits. (Am 8:5)

25:17 *What Amalek did.* Cf. Ex 17:8 note. All who "did not fear God," whether individuals or nations, were to receive the just reward of their deeds.

16) 26:1-19 Tokens of Gratitude

26:1 *The land.* The covenant community was never to forget that the source of their subsistence, the soil of Canaan, was an outright gift of God. As a reminder of their indebtedness to Him the people were regularly to offer tokens of gratitude for this unearned *inheritance,* promised to the fathers: (a) "some of the first of all the fruit" (1-11); (b) the full tithe of their "produce." (12-15)

26:3 *Go to the priest.* At the central sanctuary (12:11) the worshipers were to set the basket of firstfruits "down before the Lord" (10) to designate its contents as the prescribed offering. The officiating priest in turn accepted them in the name of God and set them down "before the altar" (4), thereby dedicating them for sacred use. (Lv 23:9 f.)

I declare. The offering of their hands was to be accompanied by the sacrifice of the worshipers' lips. In words of abject humility they were to confess that they would have no "fruit of the ground" and no "good" whatsoever if God had not brought them out of Egyptian slavery "with a mighty hand" and given them "this land" in which their patriarchal ancestors had been landless migrants.

26:5 *Wandering Aramean.* Of the three patriarchs, Jacob the father of the 12 tribal ancestors deserved particularly to be called a wandering Syrian. Son of an Aramean mother, he spent many years in Paddan-aram as a shepherd of his wives' father, the Syrian Laban. On his flight thither he was beset by such dangers as to make him feel that he was "ready to perish." (KJV; cf. Gn 28—31)

26:13 *Say before the Lord.* A tenth part of the "produce" was to be given to the Levites and underprivileged (cf. 14:23 note). In making these charitable contributions to "the least of" their brethren, they "did it to" the Lord who had given them "a land flowing with milk and honey" (cf. Mt 25:40). On a pilgrimage to the sanctuary "in the third year" (12) they were solemnly to declare they did not "rob God" (Ml 3:8) by withholding a part of the tithe, diverting it to forbidden purposes or defiling it by ceremonial uncleanness (Nm 19:11, 14). The NT child of God cannot be less grateful to the Father of the Lord Jesus Christ. (Heb 13:15; Cl 3:16 f.; Ja 1:27)

26:16 *Do these statutes and ordinances.* In conclusion Moses once more emphasized the unifying principle of the various *statutes and ordinances* that he had expounded to his hearers (chs. 12—26). All of them stemmed from their covenant relationship to God. Without any merit or worthiness on the part of the people, He had promised to be their God and chosen them "for his own possession" (7:6-16; Ex 19:5 f.). In response to His saving grace they were to be "a people holy to the Lord" and as such "keep all his commandments."

27:1—30:20 THE FUTURE IN VIEW OF COVENANT FIDELITY

27:1-26 Assent to Covenant Validity

27:1-10 RECORDED ON STONES

27:1 *Commanded the people.* In three concluding addresses Moses impressed on his hearers how inescapably their response to the covenant would determine their future weal or woe. First he and his associates gave orders that "all the words of this law" were to be inscribed on stone: a visual demonstration of their ongoing validity on the other side of the Jordan (1-10). Then in a highly dramatic setting the people were to say "Amen" to the covenant and acknowledge its stipulations as the decisive factor of their destiny. (11-26)

27:2 *On the day.* Not the very same day, but "when you have passed over the Jordan" (4, 12). Mt. Ebal was some 20 miles distant from the point of crossing.

27:3 *All the words of this law.* From Moses' record of the covenant provisions they were to be transferred to "large stones," prepared to receive a legible inscription by a coating of "plaster" or lime (8). In the ancient world stones were frequently used to publish official decrees. The entire legal code of Hammurabi (18th century B.C.), containing almost 300 paragraphs, was engraved on an 8-foot-high stela. The stones on Mt. Ebal were to be inscribed with *all the words of this law,* at a minimum the contents of chs. 5—26. (4:44; Jos 8:32)

27:5 *An altar.* As the sanctuary was to be at such places as the Lord would choose "to put his name there" (cf. 12:5 note), so altars were to be erected "in every place where I cause my name to be remembered" (cf. Ex 20:24 note; Jos 8:30-32). Abraham had "built an altar to the Lord" soon after his arrival in the Promised Land (Gn 12:8). Israel was to do likewise.

27:11-26 RECITED ANTIPHONALLY

27:11 *Charged the people.* Moses here gave more detailed instructions how the people were to "set the blessing on Mount Gerizim and the curse on Mount Ebal" (11:29). The tribes were divided according to their maternal ancestry; on Mt. Gerizim: descendants of Rachel and Leah, including the Levites, who did not officiate in the ceremony; on Mt. Ebal: the sons of Jacob's concubines and, to equalize the number of tribes, the sons of Reuben, who had defiled his "father's bed." (Gn 49:4)

27:14 *Declare to all the men.* The tribes on both sides of the valley were to respond antiphonally with an "Amen" to the 12 curses spoken by the Levites. Thereby they acknowledged their liability to divine retribution even for such violations of the covenant which, done "in secret," might escape human detection.

27:26 *Doing them.* Every Israelite had to admit that he was subject to the curse of the Law. He had to admit that he could not *confirm* the demand that he love the Lord with all his heart and with all his soul and with all his might (6:5). When Jesus Christ became "a curse for us" and vicariously suffered its consequences, He atoned for the sins of the world and removed the curse of the Law. (Gl 3:10-13; 4:4-7)

28:1-68 Covenant Alternatives

28:1-14 BLESSINGS

28:2 *These blessings.* The tribes were stationed in equal numbers on the two mountains in order to ratify what the covenant had to say to "bless them" and "for the curses" (27:11-13). Apparently the blessings were spoken from the intervening valley toward Mt. Gerizim and the curses toward Mt. Ebal. It may also be assumed that "all the people" responded with an "Amen" to both kinds of pronouncements, as they are reported to have in 27:15-26 (Jos 8:33-35). The blessings (1-14) were not only a reward of the individual for keeping certain commandments. By Israel's obedience it would remain God's covenant nation "holy to himself" through which His plan of universal salvation was to be put into effect. Conversely the curses (15-68), the result of breaking the covenant, would render the descendants of Abraham useless as bearers of God's promise to bless all nations. (Gn 12:3; Acts 3:25 f.; Gl 3:8 f.; Lv 26)

28:10 *Called by the name.* A Hebraic way of saying that God had chosen Israel to be "his own possession" (7:6; 14:2; 26:18; Ex 19:5 f.). As long as it served His purposes, God would "break and hinder every evil counsel and will which would not let His kingdom come." (Luther)

28:15-68 CURSES

28:20 *The Lord will send.* Vv. 7-14 are an elaboration of the sixfold "blessed shall be" pronounced in 3-6. Similarly 20-68 develop in greater detail the sixfold "cursed shall be" of 16-19.

29:1—30:20 Covenant Terms: Past, Present, Future

29:1-15 BASIS OF THE COVENANT: GOD'S MERCY

29:1 *Words of the covenant.* In a closing exhortation Moses stressed once more the perennial validity of the covenant which he "undertook to explain" to the people *in the land of Moab* (1:5). Its terms had been set forth at Mt. Sinai. With only minor adjustments to the new circumstances of life in Canaan (e.g., 12:15) they constituted an "everlasting covenant" (Gn 17:19). Therefore every new generation must "enter into the sworn covenant of the Lord" (12) as their fathers had done when at Sinai they had agreed to do "all that the Lord had spoken" (Ex. 19:7-9). "This day" and in the days ahead the Israelites were to recognize that their relationship to God was governed by the following unalterable principles: (a) their partnership with God was not something they had merited; it was a gift of God's mercy (1-15); (b) unfaithfulness to the covenant would provoke God's anger and result in their expulsion from the land (16-29); (c) if the people would then penitently "return to the Lord," He would have compassion on them and renew the covenant relationship (30:1-10); (d) the people cannot claim ignorance of God's revealed will (30:11-14); (e) the covenant confronts the Israelites with the alternatives: life or death. (30:15-20)

29:4 *Has not given.* God had made the Israelites His covenant people; He demonstrated it by "signs" and "wonders." But they had thwarted His attempts to prove to them that they owed everything to Him (Jn 20:30 f.). God did not give them "eyes to see or ears to hear" because they made themselves blind and deaf to the revelation of His unmerited mercy. (Cf. Ex 4:21 note; Is 6:9 f.; Ro 11:8; Mt 13:14 f.)

29:7 *Sihon . . . Og.* Cf. Nm 21:21-26, 33-35.

29:16-29 COVENANT DISLOYALTY: GOD'S ANGER

29:16-17 *Idols.* Lit. "round pieces of dung," an expression of utter contempt in the OT for the *detestable things* which *the nations* regarded as deities.

29:18 *Poisonous and bitter fruit.* If they forsook the covenant, "the curses written in this book" (chs. 27—28) would come to fruition as surely as a *root* produces a yield after its kind.

29:19 *Moist and dry alike.* Apparently a proverbial saying denoting the devastation of all soil; "the whole land" would become a waste, described in 23.

29:29 *Secret things.* The quotation marks (25-28) could very well be extended to include this verse. It would then be the concluding remark of what "men would say" when judgment had overtaken the land. It behooved them and their *children for ever,* they would say, to remember what God had *revealed* to them in the promises and threats of His covenant—*the secret things* that they would not have known unless He had deigned to disclose them for their guidance. (Mt 11:25-27; 1 Co 2:6-13)

30:1-10 COVENANT RENEWAL: GOD'S FAITHFULNESS

30:2 *Return to the Lord.* For the context of this ch. see 29:1. Moses repeatedly warned against apostasy. But he foresaw that the spiritually dead Israelites (29:4) would "walk in the stubbornness" of their hearts (29:19), bringing upon themselves "all the curses written in this book" (29:27). However, God would even then let the door of covenant grace stand wide open. He would let them again be His children if they returned to Him with hearts circumcised in true repentance and with the sincere intention to love Him "with all your heart and with all your soul" (2, 6; cf. 10:16 note). Upon their return from the Babylonian captivity many years later, Nehemiah reminded his contemporaries of this promise (Neh 1:9). God's "steadfast love endures for ever" (Ps 118:1-4). He who through His perfect obedience and vicarious suffering reconciled the world to God assured us that our heavenly Father is ever ready to forgive us, although "we daily sin much and indeed deserve nothing but punishment" (Luther), if like the prodigal son we return to His waiting arms (Lk 15:21 ff.; 1 Jn 1:9). At His second coming the Son of man will "gather his elect from the four winds, from the ends of the earth to the ends of heaven." (Mk 13:26 f.)

30:11-14 COVENANT REVELATION: GOD'S CONDESCENSION

30:11 *Too hard.* Lit. "too wonderful." God had revealed "the secret things" (29:29) of the covenant in such a way as to make them readily accessible to every Israelite. No one had an excuse for not observing them. God spoke in simple, straightforward terms, not in abstruse concepts which only the highly intelligent could understand. Initiation into the ancient mystery cults was reserved for such as could penetrate their occult abstractions. Nor did the Israelites have to venture *far off* to learn of God's Word. He had not kept it locked up in His inpenetrable "heaven." He had condescended to bring it "very near" to them, in their own hearing (cf. Ro. 10:6-8). Therefore they could "do it." God's full revelation in Jesus Christ is so simple a Gospel that "the wise and understanding" reject it as "folly." (1 Co 1:23; Mt 11:25)

30:15-20 COVENANT LIFE AND DEATH: GOD'S PROMISE AND THREAT

30:15 *Set before you.* At the close of his address Moses once more reminded his hearers of the crucial alternatives which they faced in the covenant. (Cf. 11:26 note; ch. 28)

30:19 *To witness.* God made His promises and threats in the hearing of a universal audience. *Heaven and earth,* His whole creation, was summoned to testify that He had told His people in advance what the results of their choice would be: it was a matter of *life and death.* (4:26; 8:19; 31:29)

31:1—34:12 TRANSITION TO NEW ERA: FROM MOSES TO JOSHUA

31:1—32:47 A Changeless God amid Changing Circumstances

31:1-8 ASSURANCE OF UNDIMINISHED POWER

31:1 *These words.* Poised for the crossing of the Jordan, the Israelites were about to enter a new social and economic way of life (cf. 1:1 note). In this transition from wandering in the desert to coming to "rest" in their "inheritance" (12:9), they would experience another major change. Moses, the mediator of the covenant, would be replaced by his faithful understudy, Joshua, the son of Nun. But the appointment of a new leader would not break the continuity with the past. The same omnipotent Lord would "go over before" them. Therefore Moses charged *all Israel* (1-6) and his successor (7 f.) "to be strong and of good courage" (1:37 f.; 3:18). At the same time future generations were not to forget the covenant. Lest this happen, Moses put "this law" into written form and commanded the priests to read it "before all Israel" . . . "at the end of every seven years" (9-13).

The new leader was to have the same divine authorization as his predecessor. Both "presented themselves in the tent of meeting" in which God had appeared to Moses "in a pillar of cloud" (14 f.; Ex 33:7-9). Under the new leadership the same basic principles were to be in effect. Moses was to summarize the terms of the covenant in a song (19-21). After he had written it (22) both he and his successor recited it "in the hearing of the people" (32:44). By jointly "speaking all these words to all Israel" the people were to be assured that the Lord had "commissioned Joshua" to take over Moses' responsibility and authority.

Finally there never was to be any doubt what God's immutable will was. After Moses "had finished writing the words of this law in a book," it was to be deposited for safekeeping "by the side of the ark of the covenant." (24-27)

31:2 *Go in and out.* At the age of 120 years Moses' "eye was not dim, nor his natural force abated" (34:7). But he was no longer equal to the exhausting demands of leadership, particularly to the rigors of the military campaigns across the Jordan.

31:4 *Sihon and Og.* Cf. Nm 21:21-31.

31:9-13 REGULAR READING OF GOD'S UNCHANGING WILL

31:9 *This law.* Cf. 27:3 note. For *the priests* see 18:1 note.

31:14-23 ABIDING PRINCIPLES UNDER NEW LEADERSHIP

31:19 *Write this song.* The Hebrew text has: "write ye this song for you" (KJV). Moses composed the song (22) but its content was to represent Joshua's message to the people (32:44). Invested with the same authority, this versified summary of "the law" (26) was to be another "witness against" the people should they break the covenant.

31:23 *Commissioned.* Joshua had been a leader in Israel's military campaigns from the beginning (Ex 17:8-13). Previously invested with some of Moses' "authority" (Nm 27:18-23), he was now given sole responsibility for the welfare of his people. *The Lord* (RSV) does not appear in the original text. The context may suggest that God was the agent of the action (14, 16). In the commissioning God promised to *be with* Joshua, the same words of encouragement that He had given to Moses at the flaming bush. (Ex 3:12)

31:24-29 THE WRITTEN LAW IN A PERMANENT DEPOSITORY

31:28 *Assemble to me.* This command sets the stage for the following chapter. "In the ears of all the assembly of Israel . . . Moses spoke the words of this song" (30) that he had written at God's behest. (19, 22)

31:30—32:47 MOSES' SONG RECITED

32:1 *Give ear.* Moses' song is a poetic recapitulation of what he had said when he "undertook to explain this law" (1:5). After a call for attention to his "teaching" (1-3), he at once struck the thematic chord of the hymn: God was, is, and will remain a "Rock," unmovably dependable, unwaveringly just, and unswervingly steadfast in carrying out His will. By contrast His chosen people were, are, and would be unstable, easily swayed to forsake the "God who had made them" a nation and cared for them "as the apple of his eye" (4-18). In this "witness against" them (31:19, 26) Moses once more served notice that "the Rock," true to His threat, would "make the remembrance of them to cease from among men" if they provoked Him to anger by apostasy (19-33). But His steadfast love also will endure forever. Upon their repentance He will have "compassion on his servants" and destroy the nations which sought to thwart His determinate counsel and will. (34-43)

After Moses had "recited all the words of this song," he added the final exhortation to "lay to heart all the words." The life of the people depended on them. (44-47)

32:2 *Teaching.* Literally "something taken by me." Moses' "doctrine" (KJV) was not of his own making. He had received it from God's Spirit as His mediating spokesman.

32:3 *Name.* Cf. Ex 6:3 note.

32:6 *Your father.* The Israelites owed their national life to God's creative power. Through their deliverance from Egypt He had brought them into existence, nurtured them in the wilderness, and made them His sons. (10-18; Hos 11:1 ff.; Is 44:2)

32:8 *Fixed the bounds.* The sovereign Lord of creation reserved Canaan for Israel's "allotted heritage" (9) when He assigned *to the nations their inheritance.* (Gn 11:8; Acts 17:26)

Sons of God. There is no need to change the Hebrew text. (Cf. RSV note)

32:15 *Jeshurun.* This name for Israel is a derivative of the Hebrew word "straight" or "right," used to describe God in 4. Applied ironically to Israel here, it describes how the chosen nation was to have been; instead it was "crooked" (5; cf. 33:5, 26 for its use as a complimentary title of what Israel by the grace of God could be). In 15-18 Moses projected his vision into the future and described the apostasy of Israel's later generations as if it already were a matter of historical record.

32:17 *Demons.* The "strange" and "new gods" whom Israel learned to know in Canaan were impostors, "no-gods," dressed up in the trappings of divinity. Only the Lord was God, because "there is no god besides me" (39). What the devotees of these strange and new cults sacrificed to their idols, they in reality offered to *demons* and not to God (Ps 106:37; 1 Co 10:20). The battle against such "spiritual hosts of wickedness in the heavenly places" continues to the present day. (Eph 6:12)

32:20 *Hide my face.* The Israelites stood convicted of being a *perverse generation.* God "saw it"; "heaven and earth" testified to their guilt (1; Is 1:2 ff.). The Judge, whose "ways are justice"(4), pronounced sentence on the violators of the covenant; He brought upon them "all the curses written in this book." (28:15 ff.; 29:21)

32:21 *Jealousy.* Cf. 4:24 note; Ex 20:5. By their worship of "no-gods" Israel had *stirred* God to *jealousy.* His punishment would fit the crime. He would *stir them to jealousy;* He would make them the victims of *those who are no people,* i.e., who did not exist for the purpose for which God had chosen Israel (Eph 2:11 f.). The rod of God's punishment would be *a foolish* Gentile *nation,* lacking the wise principles of the covenant with which He had blessed Jeshurun (4:6 ff.). In the course of Israel's repeated defections from God, He used several such nations as "the staff of my fury." Finally the Assyrians and the Babylonians were engaged by Him to "scatter them afar." (26)

32:22 *Sheol.* This Hebrew noun is transliterated by the RSV because it has several meanings in the OT. Here it denotes "the depths" of the earth (Am 9:2). Elsewhere it designates the grave or the realm of the dead (Gn 37:35), where man's ultimate destiny is unalterably fixed. (Is 38:18)

32:27 *Judge amiss.* Israel's conquerors would not recognize that they were but the instruments of God, but would arrogantly presume that they controlled the fate of the nations. (Is 10:13)

32:28 *No understanding.* Through their "Rock" the Israelites could be victorious against great odds (Lv 26:7 f.; Ju 7:1-23). When, however, one or two enemy soldiers would put to flight great numbers of them, this reversal from strength to impotence should alert them to the folly of their infidelity to their only source of strength.

32:31 *Judges.* Even the enemies would have to concede that the power of *their rock* or idol had to vanish before the *Rock* of Israel.

32:34 *Laid up in store.* Nothing could change God's determination to execute vengeance on the perverted and unscrupulous conquerors of His people.

32:42 *Drunk with blood.* Cf. Nm 31:1 note.

32:48-52 Moses' Death Summons

32:50 *And die.* Announced previously, the day of Moses' death had come (Nm 27:12-13). For Mt. Hor see Nm 20:22 note.

32:51 *Broke faith.* Cf. Nm 20:10, 13 notes.

33:1-29 Moses' Parting Blessing

33:1-5 INTRODUCTION:
ISRAEL A FAVORED PEOPLE

33:1 *The blessing.* Dying Jacob had announced the fate of the 12 tribal ancestors. *Before his death* Moses left a legacy to their descendants, now confederated into a covenant nation. The dominant note of his "song" was a warning against unfaithfulness (32:1-43). In his last testament, also poetic in form, he stressed the benefactions that upright "Jeshurun" (32:15) could expect from its mighty Lord who "loved his people" (3). The introduction extols the transcendent majesty of Israel's King (1-5). His coming from His heavenly abode to give the "law" at Mt. Sinai is compared with the radiant glory of a sunrise. (Hab 3:3 ff.)

33:2 *Seir.* Another name for Edom (1:2). For Mt. Paran see Nm 10:12 note.

From the ten thousands of holy ones. From His celestial throne, around which "all the hosts of heaven" constitute His court. (1 K 22:19)

33:5 *King.* The RSV supplies *the Lord* as subject, which does not appear in the Hebrew text.

33:6-25 A BLESSING FOR EACH TRIBE

33:6 *Reuben.* The tribes received their blessing in a sequence different from that followed by Jacob. Leah's and Rachel's sons precede those of their maids, Bilhah and Zilpah (Gn 35:23-26). Moses too begins with the firstborn, Reuben, but then follows a different order. Simeon's name does not appear at all. His tribe was later closely allied with Judah (Ju 1:3). A Septuagint manuscript makes Simeon the subject of the second line of this verse. Jacob linked him with Levi. (Gn 49:5)

33:8 *Thummim and . . . Urim.* Cf. Ex 28:15 note.

Massah . . . Meribah. At these places Moses and Aaron, the foremost members of this tribe, were tested. (Ex 17:1-7; Nm 20:2-13)

33:9 *Father and mother.* Cf. Ex 32:26-29. Jesus requires total allegiance of all His followers. (Mt 10:37)

33:12 *Shoulders.* These parts of the human body are used figuratively to denote slopes or mountainsides (so translated Gn 48:22). On Benjamin's rocky border later stood the temple, the final place to serve as God's *dwelling* among His people. (1 K 8:27-30)

33:13 *Joseph.* His two sons, Ephraim and Manasseh, received Jacob's benediction in a special ceremony (Gn 48:8-22). Moses' parting words echoed what their ancestor had promised Joseph. (Gn 49:22-26)

33:16 *Dwelt in the bush.* An allusion to Ex 3:2.

33:19 *They shall call.* Zebulun and Issachar are given a blessing reminiscent of Jacob's words. (Gn 49:13 f.)

33:20 *He who enlarges.* A circumlocution for God.

33:22 *From Bashan.* The Danites migrated from their original inheritance west of Jerusalem to Bashan in the far north on the east bank of the Jordan. (Jos 19:47)

33:23 *The lake.* Their territory along the Sea of Galilee extended southward from its northern plateau to the plains of that *lake.*

33:24-25 *In oil.* Olives, the source of oil, grew in rich abundance in Asher's allotment. Its inhabitants would have the *strength* to protect their borders so effectively as if the latter were bolted by *bars* of *iron and bronze.*

33:26-29 THE BLESSING CONCLUDED

33:26 *Like God.* The KJV renders the first line of this verse: "There is none like unto the God of Jeshurun." This translation is fully justified. In the conclusion to the blessing of the individual tribes (26-29) Moses glorified the only true, eternal, omnipotent God and reminded Israel of its blessed relationship to Him, as he had done in the introductory verses (1-5). Upheld by "everlasting arms" the covenant people "dwelt in safety." No enemies would be able to rob them of the blessings God had in store for the instrument of His choice to bring salvation to a sin-cursed world. The Prophet like Moses (18:15) and the Mediator of the new covenant promised that "the powers of death shall not prevail against" His Israel, the church, elect of all nations and redeemed by His blood. (Mt 16:18; 28:18-20; Jn 10:28)

34:1-12 The End of Moses' Leadership

34:1-8 MOSES' DEATH AND BURIAL

34:1 *Went up.* For the authorship of this ch. see the Introduction. This verse records that Moses did as commanded (3:27; 32:49). *Pisgah.* Lit. "the cleft," this word probably is a common noun. It always has the definite article in Hebrew and is used to designate various heights and ridges (Nm 21:20; 23:14; Dt 3:27). *Mount Nebo.* In Muslim tradition the site of Moses' death is identified with Jebel Osha, a high peak *opposite Jericho.* From this pinnacle in the Abarim mountain range (32:49) a panoramic view of "all the lands of Canaan" is possible: "Dan" in the north, the land "as far west as the Western [Mediterranean] Sea," the "Negeb and the Plain" (literally "the circle," i.e., the rounded basin of the Jordan) "as far [south] as Zoar." (Cf. Gn 19:20 note; Nm 13:17)

34:4 *The Lord said.* On the Mountain of Transfiguration Moses appeared to the transfigured Christ and spoke to Him "of his departure (lit. "His exodus"), which He was to accomplish at Jerusalem" (Lk 9:31). Israel's deliverance from Egyptian bondage took place under the leadership of Moses, "the servant of the Lord." Albeit not perfect in obedience (32:51), he foreshadowed what God purposed to do through that Servant who was "obedient unto death" (Ph 2:8). By His mediatorship "we have redemption, the forgiveness of sins" and the promise of an eternal "inheritance which is imperishable, undefiled, and unfading, kept in heaven." (Cl 1:12-14; 1 Ptr 1:3 f.)

34:6 *Buried him.* Moses "died there." He was not bodily translated to heaven like Elijah, who appeared with him on the Mount of Transfiguration. His burial by the Lord has been interpreted to mean that his lifeless body was immune to decay. According to Jude 9, "the archangel Michael, contending with the devil, disputed about the body of Moses." (For "Beth-peor" see Nm 23:28 note; Dt 3:29; 4:46)

34:8 *Thirty days.* An equal length of time was devoted to mourning the death of his brother Aaron. (Nm 20:29)

34:9-12 EULOGY

34:9 *Had laid his hands.* God had provided for this change in administration. In this critical period Israel was not left without a leader *full of the spirit of wisdom.*

34:10 *A prophet.* Cf. 18:15 note. *Face to face,* see Ex 33:18 note.

JOSHUA

INTRODUCTION

Content

The Book of Joshua is oriented to the past as well as to the future.

God had promised Abraham: "To your descendants I will give this land" of Canaan (Gn 12:7). Centuries passed. For generations the children of the patriarchs were foreigners in Egypt, far from the Promised Land. Reduced to slavery, they even faced the threat of losing their national identity. But God's plan was not to be thwarted. He sent a deliverer to lead them out of the house of bondage. At Moses' death most of the land east of the Jordan had passed into the hands of the Israelites. The Book of Joshua tells how God continued to keep His promise of old. Moses' faithful assistant and successor defeated the forces that challenged Israel's entry into Canaan west of the Jordan.

But Joshua's accomplishments are linked also with the future. In a series of battles he had broken the backbone of enemy resistance (chs. 1—12). Although he left "yet very much land to be possessed" (13:1), he believed that all of God's promises (1:4) would come true if Israel had the faith to act upon them. He therefore allotted a territory to each tribe which it could claim as its inheritance (chs. 13—21). Then he impressed on his people that they could not expect to possess the land and to survive as a nation unless they committed themselves to "serve the Lord." Moved by his pleading, they vowed allegiance to the covenant once made with their fathers. (Chs. 22—24)

Place in the Canon

In the rabbinic grouping of the OT books, Joshua is the first of a second canonical category following the Pentateuch. Called "the Prophets," it consists of two subdivisions: "the Former Prophets" and "the Latter Prophets." The second subtitle embraces the books from Isaiah to Malachi with the exception of Lamentations; Joshua, Judges, 1 and 2 Samuel, 1 and 2 Kings are called the "Former Prophets." These four historical books record events from the death of Moses to the Babylonian captivity in the 6th century B.C. Although they are a chronicle of the past, the kind of history that they present warrants being called "prophetic." Its inspired writers knew that each link in the chain of cause and effect was forged by the Lord of history. He sees the end from the beginning. He shapes events for His purposes. He announces what He wants them to accomplish through His forth-tellers and fore-tellers, the prophets. Other nations of antiquity recorded data and happenings. But their archivists could not interpret history from the perspective of "the Former Prophets."

Authorship

All four books of "the Former Prophets" are anonymous. Scripture nowhere mentions Joshua as the author of the book that bears his name. Primarily the field officer of the "commander of the army of the Lord" (5:14), he did engage also in literary activity. He wrote the words of the renewed covenant "in the book of the law of God" (24:26). He had a written survey made of the land and used it in apportioning "the land to the people of Israel" (18:1-10). Some sections imply that the writer was an eyewitness of the events (5:6; 14:4). Rahab was still alive when he produced his record. But the book also contains the account of Joshua's death (24:29 f.). It records Israel's faithfulness to the covenant during "the days of the elders who outlived Joshua" (24:31). Such statements indicate that the book, substantially in its present form, was composed not too long after the death of Joshua. Like Luke, its unknown writer undertook "to compile a narrative of the things which have been accomplished" during his lifetime. (Lk 1:1-4)

Some modern scholars apply the source hypothesis of the Pentateuch to Joshua. They find strands of composition in the latter which they have isolated in the five books of Moses. The final redaction of this "Hexateuch" was the work of a postexilic editor (cf. Genesis, Introduction, "Authorship"). A somewhat different theory has gained increasing support. Its proponents link the last book of the Pentateuch with Joshua and the other "Former Prophets." Together they form a record of Israel's past from Joshua to the Babylonian captivity that is called "Deuteronomic" history. Drawing on various traditions, the compiler of this literary complex wrote history from a point of view that is most clearly enunciated in the fifth book of Moses. According to his philosophy of history, good or bad happened as the direct result of Israel's obedience or disobedience to the covenant. He applied this theory so inflexibly that at times he gave a distorted picture of the actual course of events. However, the axiom that God is moved in the shaping of history by man's positive or negative response undergirds the OT message from Genesis to Malachi. The Book of Joshua is only one example that God so lets His "will be done."

Date of the Conquest

The immediate sequel to Israel's 40 years of desert wandering, the events recorded in Joshua depend for their date on that assigned to the Exodus (see Exodus, Introduction). Excavations of Canaanite cities have confirmed most modern scholars in their conviction that the so-called late date is correct. Archaeological findings at these sites indicate that they were destroyed in the 13th century B.C. However, the Book of Joshua does not mention the burning of cities with the exception of Jericho and Hazor. The problem of the date is beset by other difficulties. The correspondence of Canaanite kings, dated ca. 1400—1360 B.C. and found at Amarna in Egypt, mentions that they were threatened by invaders called Habiru. The relationship of the latter to the Hebrews is still a much debated issue.

OUTLINE

Journey's End: Inheritance

I. 1:1—12:24 Battle for Inheritance
- A. 1:1—5:15 Preparations
- B. 6:1—12:24 Battle Joined

II. 13:1—21:45 Division of Inheritance
- A. 13:1-7 Introduction: Allotment Before Full Occupation
- B. 13:8-33 Land East of Jordan
- C. 14:1—19:51 Land West of Jordan
- D. 20:1-9 Cities of Refuge
- E. 21:1-42 Cities for Priests and Levites
- F. 21:43-45 Comprehensive Review

III. 22:1—24:33 Terms of Inheritance
- A. 22:1-9 Charge to East-Jordan Tribes
- B. 22:10-34 No Idolatrous Altars
- C. 23:1—24:28 Joshua's Charges to All Israel
- D. 24:29-33 Close of an Era

1:1—12:24 BATTLE FOR INHERITANCE

1:1—5:15 Preparations

11:1-9 DIRECTIVES FOR JOSHUA

1:1 *The Lord said.* This simple sentence throbs with power. God spoke heaven and earth into existence (Gn 1:3 note; Ps 148:5). History too is His creation. Its events spring to life when He says: "Let there be." His Word had brought Abraham to Canaan (Gn 12:1). It had launched the Exodus from Egypt and wrought the signs and wonders that removed all obstacles from Israel's path. The conquest of Canaan also proceeded "out of the mouth of the Lord" (Dt 8:3). He initiated the action (a) by giving direction to Joshua (1-9) and to the people (10-18); (b) by ordering the reconnaissance of Jericho (ch. 2); (c) by opening a channel through the Jordan (chs. 3 f.); (d) by preparing Israel and its leader spiritually for the grueling struggle. (Ch. 5)

Servant of the Lord. Moses had received this highest of all titles during his lifetime (Ex 14:31; Nm 12:7; Dt 34:5; etc.). For the service he rendered in intimate association with the Lord see such passages as Ex 32:10-14, 30-32; Nm 12:8; 14:11-19; Dt 34:10-12.

Joshua. His earlier name Hoshea ("salvation") was changed to *Jehoshuah*, "the Lord is salvation" (Nm 13:8, 16). The Septuagint renders it with the Greek equivalent for Jesus. The Ephraimite son of Nun gave Israel its inheritance in Canaan and was the foreshadowing type of Jesus, "the Son of God," who provided an eternal rest for His followers (Heb 4). Moses' successor had been appointed to be Israel's new leader before the death of his predecessor (Nm 27:18-23; Dt 31:14 f., 23). For his previous service and devotion to God and His people see such passages as Ex 17:8-13; 24:13; 32:17; 33:11; Nm 13 f.; 26:63-65; 32:28; Dt 31:14 f., 23. The time had come to "arise" and to complete the task left unfinished by his erstwhile mentor (Dt 32:48 ff.). *Moses' minister* was so faithful in carrying out his assignment that he too became worthy of the title *servant of the Lord*. (24:29; Ju 2:8)

1:2 *Am giving.* Canaan was God's gift. The Israelites did not deserve it, nor were they able to conquer it by their military might. The "Lord of heaven and earth," who "determined allotted periods and the boundaries" of every nation (Acts 17:26), granted it to His chosen people because He had promised it to the patriarchs (Gn 15:18 ff.) and to Moses (Dt 11:22 ff.). The past ("I have given"), the present (*I am giving*), and the future (I shall give) merge in the timeless perspective of God's sovereign and gracious will. (Ps 90:4; Ja 1:17; 2 Ptr 3:8)

1:4 *Your territory.* Israel's territory was to extend from *the wilderness* in the south to the *Lebanon* mountains in the north, from "the river Euphrates" in the northeast to "the Great [Mediterranean] Sea" in the west (Gn 15:18; Ex 23:31; Dt 11:24 f.). Under David Israel's possessions approached these boundaries (1 K 5:4). But it never was to occupy the full extent of its territory. God's promises are contingent on man's action in response to them. Israel's later history records how it failed to live up to its covenant obligations. Of the various occupants of Canaan only the *Hittites* are mentioned here (3:10; Dt 7:1; Gn 10:15-19 note; 23:7)

1:6 *Be strong.* This admonition is repeated twice (7, 9; Dt 31:23). It is so important because God's gift comes to those who have the courage of faith to take it. Doing "according to all the law" is the eviden and expression of such faith (7-9). Committed without reservations to God's promise and will, Joshua would become the invincible executor of the oath which God *swore to their fathers*. (Ex 6:8)

1:10-18 DIRECTIVES FOR ISRAEL

1:10 *Joshua commanded.* The chain of command proceeds from God to Joshua (1-9), to *the officers of the people* (Dt 1:13 note), to "the people" (11). The conquest was to be a joint undertaking of all tribes, including those which previously had received their inheritance east of the Jordan. (32; Dt 3?; Nm 32)

1:11 *Within three days.* This phrase may be a conventional way of saying: within a short period of time (Hos 6:2). It is also possible that the account is not arranged in chronological order and that the spies had already left on their mission. In that case the crossing began three days after the return of the spies. (3:1 ff.)

Take possession. The full meaning of this verb is important for the understanding of the relationship of the Book of Joshua to Judges. The Hebrew word has a negative and a positive connotation—to dispossess or drive out inhabitants and to occupy their former possession. God indeed intended the Israelites eventually so to *take possession* of the Promised Land. However, Joshua's defeat of the Canaanite military forces was only the initial phase. The result of his victories is not described as taking *possession of the land.* At the end of his campaigns there was "yet very much land to be possessed" (13:1). The Book of Judges records to what extent the Israelite tribes took full possession of their alloted territories and settled in them.

1:14 *Beyond the Jordan.* Cf. Dt 1:5 note.

1:16 *They answered.* Cf. Ex 19:7 f.; Dt 5:24-27.

2:1-24 RECONNAISSANCE

2:1 *Spies.* Joshua and Caleb had been two of the 12 men whom Moses had sent from Kadesh "to spy out the land of Canaan." The majority report terrified the people. They rebelled against the Lord's direction to enter the land from the south (Nm 13), Joshua sent two men to *view the land, especially Jericho*, one of the "fortified and very large" cities (Nm 13:28). His purpose was to impress on the people that the situation had not changed. They could not rely on their own resources to capture the city. They were to believe that "truly the Lord has given all the land into our hands." (24)

Jericho. The fall of this city, 5 miles west of

the Jordan, was to give Joshua a strategic bridgehead in central Canaan. From there he would be able to strike out to the south and north. The spies left from the last campsite mentioned in Nm 25:1, about 5 miles east of the Jordan. *Shittim*, Hebrew for acacias, probably owed its name to these trees.

House of a harlot. In such a public house, which may also have served as an inn, the presence of two strangers would not attract attention, they hoped. However, this stratagem did not succeed in allaying the suspicion that they had "come to search out all the land." (3)

2:6 *Hid them.* Rahab hid the spies on the flat roof of her house (Ju 16:27; 1 Sm 9:25; Mk 2:4). Here she had been drying flax stalks, which are harvested in March/April. Consequently the crossing of the Jordan occurred in spring, when its waters are at flood stage. (3:15)

2:9 *I know. All the inhabitants* had heard of the signs and wonders that the Lord had done in Israel's behalf. Only Rahab, liar and harlot though she was, turned to the "God in heaven above and on earth beneath" (11; Heb 11:31; Ja 2:25; Dt 4:39; 2 K 5:15; Mt 21:31 f.). Not an Israelite deity, the Lord had a place in His kingdom for Gentile women such as Rahab, Thamar, Ruth. He even accorded them the distinction of being links in the ancestry of Jesus (Mt 1:3-6). God's inexhaustible grace covers the multitude of sins of the most disreputable outcast who says: "God, be merciful to me a sinner." (Lk 18:13)

2:10 *Sihon and Og.* Cf. Nm 21:22-34.

Amorites. Cf. Nm 21:21 note.

Utterly destroyed. Cf. Dt 2:34 note; Lv 27:26 note.

2:15 *Into the city wall.* Built on a separate wall or on the two walls surrounding the city, her house was high enough to enable her to let the spies down *through the window*. (1 Sm 19:12; Acts 9:25)

2:18 *Scarlet cord.* Perhaps it was the "rope" by which she let down the spies. Its color does not appear to have any special significance except that it later identified her house, although it is not mentioned again. (6:22-25)

2:22 *Three days.* Cf. 1:11 note. Used also by robbers, the caves in *the hills* of Jericho afforded good hiding places. (Lk 10:30)

2:24 *Has given.* From a military standpoint the mission of the spies had been futile. They found no weakness in Jericho's defenses; they had no strategy of attack to suggest. But they confirmed the people's need of faith in the Lord to give *all the land* into their hands. What He had done and promised to do made all the inhabitants *fainthearted*.

3:1—5:1 INVASION OF BATTLE ZONE

3:1 *Set out.* Joshua did not hesitate to act on the command: "Go over this Jordan" (1:2). Camp was moved from Shittim (2:1 note) to the river's bank. His officers issued marching orders. He himself commanded the people to commit themselves to the Lord and His promise to "do wonders among" them (1-6). Assured that the Lord would grant success to his leadership, Joshua explained more specifically what miraculous help the people could expect. "The waters of the Jordan shall be stopped from flowing" to enable them to cross it safely and begin the conquest of Canaan. (7-13)

3:2 *Three days.* Cf. 1:11 note.

3:3 *Levitical priests.* Cf. Dt 18:1 note.

3:4 *Two thousand cubits.* About 3,000 feet. In rabbinic legislation this distance marked the extent of travel permitted on the Sabbath.

3:5 *Sanctify yourselves.* The people were to engage in rites by which they declared themselves a holy people, dedicated to the purpose for which God had chosen them. (Ex 19:10 note; Nm 11:18)

3:6 *The ark.* Here God had promised to "meet" the people "from above the mercy seat" (Ex 25:22). It preceded the people, signifying that "the Lord of all the earth" (11, 13) was opening a passage through the Jordan. For the abuse of the ark as a magical device to coerce God see 1 Sm 4:3 ff.

3:14 *Set out.* The account of the crossing is given in a form characteristic of Hebrew narrative style. Harking back to previous commands and statements, it develops the story without observing a strictly chronological sequence of events. The course of action that emerges from the remaining verses of this chapter and from ch. 4 is as follows. *The priests* led the procession (3). When their feet "dipped in the brink of the water," the river bed became dry (11-17). Having proceeded to the middle of the stream, they halted while the people "were passing over on dry ground." Thereupon Moses sent the 12 selected men (12) to "the very place where the priests' feet stood." From there they took up the 12 memorial stones which were to be set up at Gilgal (4:1-3, 8, 19-24). Apparently on his own initiative Joshua had 12 additional stones erected "in the midst of the Jordan" for a second memorial (4:4-9). When "all the people had finished passing over" the Jordan and the priests had carried the ark to shore, the waters of the Jordan again "overflowed all its banks" (4:10-18).

3:15 *The time of harvest.* The crossing took place "on the tenth day of the first month," called Nisan (4:19). At this time the Jordan, fed by late rains and the melting snows of Mt. Hermon, *overflows all its banks*.

3:16 *Adam.* Not mentioned again in the OT, this city has been identified with a hilly site some 15 miles north of Jericho but south of the confluence of the Jabbok with the Jordan. *Zarethan* very likely was located on the former. At *Adam* the waters *rose up in a heap* and *cut off* the flow of the Jordan southward to the Dead Sea. Cave-ins of river cliffs which completely dammed up the Jordan have been reported in this area, one as recent as 1927. When the Israelites needed a passage through the Red Sea, God "drove the sea back by a strong east wind" (Ex 14:22 note; 15:8; Jos 4:23; Ps 66:6). In both instances the Israelites received miraculous help. The Ruler of the winds and the seas commandeered the forces of nature. "Working salvation in the midst of the earth," He used them for His purpose at His appointed time. (Ps 74:12-15)

4:1 *The Lord said.* In 3:12 only the command to select 12 men is recorded. What they were to do is reported in connection with the crossing. (1-7)

4:3 *Priests' feet.* Called Levitical priests in 3:3. Cf. Dt 18:1 note.

4:6 *A sign.* These stones marked the place where "the waters of the Jordan were cut off before the ark" (7). The memorial at Gilgal was to remind future generations that the crossing was completed. Both were tangible testimony that Israel owed possession of the Promised Land to God's miraculous intervention.

4:9 *To this day.* This phrase occurs six times in Joshua. It stresses the enduring character of the actions. The memorial *in the midst of the Jordan* was still there when the book was written. See Introduction, "Authorship."

4:10 *Moses had commanded.* Joshua obeyed Moses' order to "go with this people into the land." (Dt 31:7)

4:12 *Passed over armed.* This parenthetic note establishes continuity with the past. The two and one half tribes kept the promise they had given to Moses. (Nm 32:17)

4:13 *Forty thousand.* See Numbers, Introduction, "The Numbers. . . ." If the calculation suggested there is correct, the men *ready armed for war* of these tribes consisted of 40 "hundreds" or military contingents. (Ju 5:8)

4:20 *Gilgal.* Literally a rolling or circular placement of stones, this name was given to various sites (Dt 11:30; 2 K 2:1). Here it designates a place about 2 miles between the Jordan and Jericho. Cf. 5:9 note.

4:24 *Fear the Lord.* Cf. Dt 6:13 note.

5:1 *Amorites . . . Canaanites.* Cf. Dt 1:7; Gn 10:15-19 note; Nm 21:21 note. The occupants were so convinced that "the hand of the Lord is mighty" (4:24) that *their heart melted.* Therefore they did not molest the Israelites during the events recorded in the remainder of this chapter.

5:2-15 SPIRITUAL REARMAMENT

5:2 *Circumcise.* Before the Israelites and Joshua engaged in military operations, they were spiritually fortified for the conquest. Their occupation of Canaan was not an invasion by another group of land-hungry marauders. The land "flowing with milk and honey" was to become the arena of God's deeds of salvation. Here His chosen people were to become a blessing to "all the families of the earth" (Gn 12:3). They were to recognize their covenant obligation to serve His eternal purpose and plan. "All males" were to bear in their bodies "the sign of the covenant" (Gn 17:11). Circumcision marked them as God's men (2-9). Observance of the Passover (10-12) put them in mind of the Exodus. At that time the "outstretched arm" of God delivered them from the Egyptians. They could expect victory over the superior forces in Canaan only if "the Lord will do wonders among" them (3:5; Ex 13:25-27). Finally in a vision the field officer of Israel's army met his superior, the "commander of the army of the Lord." Joshua was not to rely on his own strategy. His orders came from "holy" headquarters. (13-15)

The second time. Perhaps "all the people who came out [of Egypt] had been circumcised" at one time soon after the Exodus. But the second generation "had not been circumcised" "on the way." The mass observance of the rite was equivalent to a renewal of the covenant.

5:6 *Milk and honey.* A figurative expression to describe the productivity of Canaan (Ex 3:8). Rebellious Dathan and Abiram spoke of Egypt in the same terms. (Nm 16:12-14)

5:8 *Were healed.* The Israelites trusted in God to protect them while, in the obedience of faith, they were incapacitated to defend themselves against a possible attack by the Canaanites. So every believer "abides in the shadow of the Almighty" although he is beset by dangers on every side. (Ps 91)

5:9 *Rolled away the reproach.* In Egypt the Israelites had suffered the shame of slavery. This ignominy ended decisively when they crossed the Jordan. By their circumcision they had placed themselves under God's liberating guidance. They expressed the removal of their former reproach in the meaning they attached to Gilgal. By a Hebrew play on words they called it the place where God rolled ("gilgalled") away their disgrace.

5:10 *The passover.* The Israelites crossed the Jordan on the 10th of Nisan, the day on which the observance of the Passover should have begun (4:19). However, they were able to eat the sacrificial lamb on the designated "fourteenth day of the month" (Ex 12:1-3, 6, 8). "On the morrow after the passover" they ate the prescribed "unleavened cakes and parched grain." (Ex 12:15)

5:12 *Manna.* Cf. Ex 16:14, 15 notes.

5:13 *Behold, a man.* The vision granted Joshua has elements in common with Moses' experience at the burning bush (Ex 3). However, Joshua was given the role of a military leader under "the commander of the Lord's army."

5:15 *Is holy.* Joshua had asked the "Cammander in chief" what he was to do (cf. Acts 9:4-6). The answer he received contained no military orders. But the short, almost enigmatic reply moved the entire war of conquest into its proper perspective. In every campaign Joshua was not standing on his own feet. He occupied a position hallowed by God's appointment. Canaan was to be the holy arena of His mighty acts of deliverance. (Cf. Ex 3:5 note)

6:1—12:24 Battle Joined

6:1—8:35 CAMPAIGN IN CENTRAL CANAAN

1) 6:1-27 First Victory: Jericho

6:1 *Was shut up.* "Fainthearted because of" the Israelites (2:24), the inhabitants of Jericho sought security within its fortifications. But "by faith the walls of Jericho fell down" (Heb 11:30).

Joshua received and transmitted orders for the most unusual siege operations (2-7). The Israelites would never be able to boast that this strategic city succumbed to their ingenuity, military powers, or even some magical spell that they cast about the city. They were to engage in a ridiculous exercise of futility from a human point of view. Acting in "the assurance of things hoped for, the conviction of things not seen" (Heb 11:1), they were to demonstrate their faith in the Lord, "enthroned upon the cherubim" of the ark of the covenant (Ps 80:1). He it was who laid siege to Jericho's ramparts. The fading sound of the priestly trumpets was the earth-shattering blast of His power (Ps 18:8, 15). And the word of the Lord did not return empty (Is 55:11). The Israelites did as directed (8-14), and on the seventh day "the wall fell down flat" (15-21). Because the Lord had given them the city, they were not to enrich themselves with its plunder. "All . . . within it," except Rahab and her family were "devoted to the Lord for destruction" (17); the metals were "put into the treasury of the house of the Lord" (22-25; cf. Dt 2:34 note; Nm 31:1 note). The city was to remain a ruined heap, a mute witness to God's intervention in Israel's behalf and a warning to all who incur His wrath. (26)

6:4 *Seven priests.* The number seven symbolizes fulfillment and completeness. (Gn 2:1-2; Ex 20:11; 12:15, 19; Lv 16:29; 25:2-6, 8)

6:5 *Trumpet.* More exactly "ram's horns of [i.e., used for] the jubilees," called simply "the *yobel*" in Ex 19:13 (cf. Lv 25:10 note). The blowing of the trumpets was not so much a summons to battle as a call to faith in God's presence. "A loud trumpet call" will announce the coming of "the Son of man . . . with power and glory" to "put all his enemies under his feet," including death, "the last enemy." (Mt 24:31; 1 Co 15:25-26, 52; 1 Th 4:16)

6:7 *Armed men.* Joining the procession but not striking a blow, the armed forces could hope for victory with God's help when later they would be called upon to use their weapons.

6:20 *Down flat.* Lit. "under itself," i.e., it crumbled into a heap where it had stood. God "looks on the earth and it trembles" (Ps 104:32). Perhaps He used a "natural" phenomenon, an earthquake, to do His bidding at His appointed moment (3:16 note). According to reports of recent excavations at Jericho all traces of the wall have disappeared by erosion. (See Introduction, "Date of the Conquest")

6:25 *Saved alive.* Joshua kept the promise made by the spies to Rahab (2:8-21). Ceremonially unclean, she and her family were at first placed "outside the camp." Ultimately she was "grafted" into "the olive tree" of Israel (Ro 11:17 ff.). Such infusions of Gentiles into the bloodstream of the chosen people betokened God's purpose to bless "all the families of the earth" in Abraham's Seed. (Gn 12:1-3; Mt 1:2-6)

6:26 *An oath.* Jericho was to remain a demonstration of the ban placed upon it. Whoever removed this grim evidence of God's judgment subjected himself to the curse pronounced upon it (1 K 16:34). "Salvation" came to the tax collector's house in Jericho when Jesus, who bore the curse of the world's sin, entered it. (Lk 19:9)

2) 7:1-26 Defeat at Ai

7:1 *Broke faith.* The conquest of Canaan came to an abrupt halt. Victorious against great odds at Jericho, the Israelites suffered a stunning setback from an enemy that numerically should have been no match for their armed forces. Almost two whole chapters are devoted to the debacle and ultimate victory at Ai (7:1—8:29). All the remaining campaigns are compressed into chs. 9—12. However, the length of the account of this comparatively minor skirmish is not out of proportion to its importance for the central message of the entire book. Its basic concern is to make clear that Canaan is a promised inheritance, God's gift to His chosen people. But when the latter "transgressed the covenant" (10), they closed the channel of grace and stopped up the flow of divine intervention in their behalf. V. 1 gives the key to the entire plot: they *broke faith in regard to the devoted things* taken at Jericho (6:17 f.). Kept and hidden by only one person, this forbidden booty "brought trouble on" the entire camp (25). The resulting military failure unnerved the people (2-5) and brought Joshua to the brink of despair (6-9). Thereupon God disclosed why they had been unable to "stand before their enemies." He also gave directions how the perpetrator of the "shameful thing" was to be detected in order that they might "destroy the devoted things from among" them (10-15). Achan, identified by lot as the offender, confessed his guilt (16-21) and was stoned to death (22-26). Purged of "the devoted things," the Israelites turned defeat into victory. Ai was taken and burned. (8:1-23)

7:2 *Ai.* This place name, in Hebrew always prefixed by the definite article, means "the heap" or "the ruin." It has been identified with a place about 2 miles southeast of Bethel (8:28 note). Excavations at this site indicate that it had remained unoccupied for 1,200 years after a destruction ca. 2200 B.C. However, these findings do not preclude the existence of a settlement at Joshua's time. A population large enough to have its own "king" (8:29) could have served as an outpost for nearby Bethel. The latter was not burned at that time. Its army was routed when it joined forces with Ai.

Beth-aven. No doubt closely associated with Bethel (8:17), *Beth-aven* is mentioned again in 18:12 and 1 Sm 13:5. Later prophets say that by Israel's false worship at Bethel ("house of God"; Gn 12:8; 28:19 ff.) the latter has taken on the meaning of Beth-aven. ("House of nothingness," i.e., of a nonexistent god; Hos 4:15; 5:8; 10:5; Am 5:5)

7:3 *Not all the people.* According to the spies' report Israel's own resources were sufficient to assure victory. No mention is made of the fact that the success of the venture depended on God. How different from the report of the spies sent to Jericho! (2:24)

7:5 *Shebarim.* Literally "the breakings";

perhaps "stone quarries," not mentioned elsewhere. The Septuagint translates: "until they had crushed them."

7:6 *Rent his clothes . . . dust upon their heads.* Gestures of extreme grief. Joshua's despondency was similar to Moses' feeling of frustration. (Ex 5:22)

7:7 *Amorites.* Cf. Gn 10:15-19 note; Nm 21:21 note.

7:9 *Thy great name.* The cutting off of Israel's *name from the earth* was not the prime issue at stake. If need be, God could from "stones . . . raise up children to Abraham" (Mt 3:9). Joshua rather based his appeal on the Lord's *great name.* God had revealed His intention to let Israel be the instrument of His eternal plan of salvation. Would He—so Joshua argued—admit defeat and let Israel's unfaithfulness bring to nought what He had promised to do? (Ex 6:3 note; 32:11-14; Dt 9:25-29; Eze 36:20, 22, 32; 20:44)

7:10 *Arise.* God was not repudiating Joshua's prostration in abject humility. But repentance entails more than an expression of grief. It must lead to appropriate action. The cause of offense, "the devoted things," must be removed.

7:11 *Covenant.* For the meaning of this word see Exodus, Introduction, "Content." For the specific response required of Israel for God's gift of Jericho see 6:18 f.

7:13 *Sanctify.* Cf. 3:5 note.

7:15 *A shameful thing.* The RSV usually reproduces the meaning of the Hebrew noun with "folly" (Gn 34:7 note; Dt 22:21; Is 32:6; Jer 29:23). "Claiming to be wise" (Ro 1:22), Achan had *transgressed the covenant.* Breaking off relations with God is folly compounded with infamy. Willful disobedience to His will amounts to joining the fool in saying: "There is no God" (Ps 14:1). Conversely "the fear of the Lord is the beginning of wisdom." (Ps 110:10; Pr 1:7)

7:18 *Achan . . . was taken.* Identified by lot (perhaps by means of the Urim and Thummim (Ex 20:15; 28:15 note; 1 Sm 14:40-42), Achan *was taken* into custody like a criminal caught in the act.

7:19 *Glory to the Lord.* By his confession Achan was to vindicate the justice of the judgment of *the Lord God of Israel.* From the offender's mouth the entire people were to learn that their defeat was not the act of a capricious deity. It redounded to God's *glory* and *praise* when He carried out the terms of the covenant—its promises as well as its threats.

7:21 *Shinar.* Cf. Gn 10:8; 11:2 notes. Achan had *coveted* the loot because its value was considerable. Actually it was a mere bagatelle in comparison with the total amount of plunder which had been destroyed. But God does not compute guilt by "shekels." The wages of sin whether small or great—qualitatively or quantitatively—is death (1 Jn 3:15; Mt 5:17 ff.). Ananias and Sapphira offended with respect to only "a part" of their property but thereby became "guilty of all of it." (Acts 5:1-11; Ja 2:10)

7:24 *Valley of Achor.* Lit. "the valley of trouble," so called by a word play on the Hebrew verb "to trouble" (*achar*) and Achan's name, the cause of the trouble (26). In the Prophets the name occurs proverbially to designate Israel's sin and retribution. But for a penitent people God would make the valley of defeat into a "door of hope" for a bright future (Hos 2:15; Is 65:10). The next chapter tells how "the Lord turned from his burning anger" (26). Achan "received the due reward" of his deed outside the camp, where the sin offering was burned (Lv 16:27; Lk 23:41). "Made to be sin" for us, He "who knew no sin" "suffered outside the gate in order to sanctify the people through His own blood (2 Co 5:21; Heb 13:11-12). Through His suffering, trouble, and death Christ Jesus opened the door of hope for death-bound mankind. (Ro 5:1 f.; 1 Co 15)

7:25 *Stoned him.* The account implies that "his sons and daughters" shared the father's fate (24; Dt 17:5). It seems unlikely that he could have buried the treasure in his tent without their connivance. Israel's judges were to punish only the guilty. (Dt 24:16)

3) 8:1-29 Victory at Ai

8:1 *Do not fear.* Joshua had reason to *be dismayed.* In their attack on Ai the Israelites apparently had proceeded on their own initiative. They had learned that they could not overcome even a "few" (7:3) by their superior numbers unless God gave the land into their hands, as He had at Jericho. But obedient to God's command and trusting in His promise, they need fear no foe. Doing what *the Lord said* made them the agents of His invincible Word. (Ps 127:1 f.; 121)

8:2 *Booty for yourselves.* This provision appears to be a reversal of the directive for the capture of Jericho (6:21). There the Israelites were to be taught that Canaan and everything in it belonged to God. They were to take only what He gave. Having painfully learned this lesson, they were now assured that God also had ways of providing for their physical needs. (11:14)

8:3 *All the fighting men.* The "commander of the army of the Lord" (5:14) had determined the strategy. The details of its execution are difficult to reconstruct from the brief account. Apparently the whole fighting force was to set an "ambush" against the city, deployed as follows. A large contingent was secretly to move into position "behind [i.e, west of] it," not "very far from the city." A smaller band of commandos seems to have been stationed also "between Ai and Bethel" but closer to the former (12). The deployment of the troops was complete when "the main encampment . . . was north of the city and its rear guard [in ambush] west of the city" (13). It has also been suggested that v. 12 refers to the same ambush as v. 4, the difference in number being the result of a scribal error. In that case this task force is mentioned again as a part of the summary report on the various positions assigned to *all the fighting men* (1, 12 f.). *Thirty thousand* should perhaps be translated "30 picked men." (See Book of Numbers, Introduction, "The Numbers . . .")

8:9 *Spent that night.* Joshua's lodging *among the people* is especially noted. Their "hearts" had "melted" and become "as water" (7:5). No doubt he spent the night with them in order to renew their courage, telling them of the promise of victory that he had received (1-2). V. 13, which summarizes the disposition of the army, also repeats that he had taken his position "in the valley."

8:14 *Toward the Arabah.* In the direction of the plain or valley which is a part of the Jordan depression. It begins at the Sea of Galilee and extends southward to the Dead Sea, also called the Sea of the Arabah. (Dt 3:17)

8:18 *The javelin.* We are not told how this prearranged signal came to the attention of the men in "the ambush." Stretching out the javelin also signified the unleashing of divine power. The uplifted hand of Moses had opened and closed the Red Sea (Ex 14:26 ff.; see also Ex 7:19; 8:16). Joshua kept his spear pointing toward the enemy until victory was complete. (26; cf. Ex 17:11-13)

8:19 *Set the city on fire.* This verse tells how the Israelites attained complete victory. V. 28 mentions the burning of Ai again in a closing recapitulation of the entire campaign.

8:26 *Utterly destroyed.* Executed the ban. (Dt 2:34 note; Nm 31:1 note)

8:28 *A heap.* Hebrew: *a tel.* A site today called simply "Et-Tell" (Arabic for "the heap" or "the mound") has been identified with ancient Ai (7:2 note). Many modern place names have "tel" prefixed to them, e.g., Tell-el-Amarna.

8:29 *Hanged the king.* Cf. Dt 21:22-23 note.

4) 8:30-35 Reconsecration to Covenant Loyalty

8:30 *Mount Ebal.* In the next five verses the scene shifts to the vicinity of Shechem, some 20 miles north of Ai. We are not told whether the Israelites reached this destination in the heart of Canaan without meeting opposition, or if they did, how it was overcome. Nor is a defeat of Shechem at the foot of Ebal and Gerizim listed in the summary of Israel's victory (ch. 10). Not a full account of all encounters, the Book of Joshua records only a selected number of decisive events. Among these the episode described in these verses merits mention. It once more sets forth the basic principle upon which the outcome of all action hinges: Israel's covenant relationship with God. The land could be conquered only as God "gives" it to a people that carried out His purpose. At Ai Israel had "transgressed the covenant of the Lord" (7:10, 15). A reconsecration to its high calling was in place at this juncture. As prescribed by Moses (Dt 27), "all the assembly of Israel" reaffirmed its total dependence on God and acknowledged its covenanted obligation to respond to His undeserved goodness. There was high drama: sacrifices of reconciliation and fellowship with God, writing of the law on stones, antiphonal Amens to blessings and curses (see Dt 27; 28 notes). At the end of his career Joshua once again pledged the people to covenant loyalty. (Ch. 24)

8:31 *Unhewn stones.* Cf. Ex 20:24 note.

8:32 *A copy of the law.* See Deuteronomy, Introduction, "Content."

8:34 *The blessing and the curse.* Cf. Dt 11:26 note.

9:1—10:43 BATTLES AGAINST SOUTHERN CONFEDERATIONS

1) 9:1-27 Precipitated by Gibeon's Deception

9:2 *Gathered together.* Other inhabitants of Canaan reacted to the report of Israel's victories as did the citizens of Jericho: their "hearts melted" (2:11). Most of them feared that they would share Jericho's and Ai's fate unless they joined forces against the invaders. (For Israel's battles against such coalitions see chs. 10 and 11.) The Gibeonites and their confederates felt that even such a maneuver could only end in disaster for them. They tried to save themselves by surrender under the best possible terms. So they pretended to have come "from a far country" where they would not be an obstacle in Israel's path. Their ruse succeeded. Without asking "direction from the Lord," the Israelites made a solemn covenant to "let them live" (3-15; cf. Ex 23:32; Dt 7:2). Three days later the deception was discovered. But "the leaders of the congregation" urged the people not to violate their oath "lest wrath be upon" them. Joshua agreed but consigned the deceivers to menial servitude. (16-27)

9:3 *Gibeon.* The surrender of Gibeon, about 5 miles northwest of Jerusalem, and of the other cities within a radius of some 10 miles, put the Israelites into control of central Canaan.

9:6 *Gilgal.* For the meaning of this place name see 5:9 note. There may have been several Gilgals. According to Dt 11:29 f. there was a Gilgal near Shechem at the foot of Ebal and Gerizim (see also Gn 12:6 note). A modern site known by the Arabic equivalent of Gilgal has been excavated to the east of Shechem. An encampment at this Gilgal is a more suitable location as a base of operations for later campaigns. (See, e.g., 10:9 note)

9:7 *Hivites.* These inhabitants of Canaan are frequently identified with the Horites (Gn 36:20, 21; etc.), known from extra-Biblical sources as Hurrians. The latter played a significant role in territories north of Palestine. Penetrating southward, the Gibeonites and their allies (17) formed a Hivite-Horite enclave among various other peoples that had invaded and occupied Canaan. In 2 Sm 21:2 they are called Amorites, a general designation for all Canaanites. (Jos 24:15; Nm 21:21 note)

9:14 *Partook of their provisions.* A joint meal served to seal the treaty (Gn 31:44 note). *Direction from the Lord* could have been secured from the Urim and the Thummim (Ex 28:15 note; Nm 27:21 note). Joshua too neglected to avail himself of such guidance and ratified the treaty. (15)

9:21 *For all the congregation.* The Gibeonites did not become the personal slaves of the Israelites (8). Joshua and the leaders executed the ban on the deceivers to the extent that they were devoted to menial service rendered to the

Lord by the worshiping *congregation*. (27)

9:27 *The place.* Cf. Dt 12:5 note.

2) 10:1-27 Defeat of Allied Amorites

10:1 *Made peace.* The surrender of Gibeon gave the Israelites a strategic foothold in central Canaan. The *king of Jerusalem* "feared greatly" that from this vantage point they would extend their victories southward. With the help of four other kings he therefore tried to regain control of this "great city" (1-5). Joshua honored his treaty with the beleaguered Gibeonites. The allied forces were routed in a surprise attack (6-11) and completely annihilated while "the sun stood still." (12-15)

Adonizedek. His name—or perhaps better his title—means "my lord is righteousness" (cf. Melchizedek, Gn 14:18 note). It is not certain whether "Zedek" is also the name of a Canaanite deity. The name *Jerusalem* occurs here for the first time in the OT. (Cf. Gn 14:18; Ju 19:10 f.)

10:5 *Five kings.* Adonizedek's allies were the kings of *Hebron,* 20 miles south of Jerusalem, *Jarmuth, Lachish,* and *Eglon,* respectively about 16, 30, and 35 miles southwest of Jerusalem.

10:8 *Do not fear.* Joshua had reason to be fearful. He had never faced such a formidable concentration of military might. But he did not have to rely on his own resources. If he acted in obedience of faith, his ally was God's irresistible Word of promise.

10:9 *All night.* In order to reach Gibeon in one night from Gilgal near Jericho, the Israelites would have had to climb a rise of 3,000 feet for 20 miles. (Cf. 9:6 note)

10:10 *Threw them into a panic.* Through Moses God had promised to "throw them into great confusion" (Dt 7:23 f.). The Israelites were able to chase the panic-stricken enemy westward down a 1,000-foot descent to lower *Beth-horon* and southward toward the lowlands known as the Shephelah, where *Azekah and Makkedah* were located.

10:12 *Sun, stand thou still.* The often heated discussion of this passage proceeds from two opposite viewpoints. Many interpreters find here no miraculous intervention in the regular course of nature. Poetic in form and language, the account is merely a figurative way of saying that the day was long enough to permit Israel to destroy the fleeing enemy. It is similar to Deborah's exclamation: "The stars . . . fought against Sisera" (Ju 5:20). Radically opposed to this contention is the insistence that this day was miraculously prolonged beyond the normal 24 hours. The believer has no reason to doubt that He who created "the heavens and the earth . . . and all the host of them" could control the work of His "fingers" (Gn 2:1; Ps 8:3; Is 34:4). He had the power to stop the vast machinery of the universe with its myriads of interlocking gears. Without denying that "whatever the Lord pleases He does, in heaven and on earth" (Ps 135:6), a third interpretation finds the miraculous element in the fact that God at the right moment commandeered the forces of nature as He did in Egypt and at Jericho (Ex 7:17 note; 8:3 note; 14:21; Jos 3:16; 6:20 notes). At Gibeon He sent a barrage of hailstones. The accompanying storm prolonged the darkness of the night. Under its cover the Israelites had surprised the enemy and then were able to complete the pursuit of the fleeing allies. Accordingly the result of God's intervention was sustained darkness rather than additional hours of sunlight. The meaning of the Hebrew verbs describing the phenomenon is cited in support of this view. *Stand . . . still* has the basic meaning to "be silent" and then by analogy to "cease" or "desist" from a given activity. "Stayed," literally "stand," at times has the same connotation of stopping to function. "Go down," literally "enter," is used of the disappearance of the sun in the west. Used in connection with the preceding verbs it means that the sun did not come into view "for about a whole day." (13)

10:13 *The book of Jashar.* Literally "the book of the upright one," this anthology of ancient Israel (see the meaning of Jeshurun, Dt 32:15 note) has not survived the ages. From time to time other poetic descriptions of events apparently were added to this collection of songs. (2 Sm 1:18; see also Nm 21:14 note)

10:15 *Joshua returned.* This verse is repeated verbatim in v. 43. It may have been inserted into the text at this point as a result of a copyist's error. It seems more probable that the execution of the five kings described in the immediately following verses (16-27) followed immediately upon their defeat.

10:24 *Feet upon the necks.* A humiliating gesture to symbolize that the kings were completely in the power of the victors (Ps 110:5; Ml 4:3). In the battle against "the principalities and powers," Jesus "disarmed" man's mortal enemies, and God "has put all things under his feet." (Cl 2:14 f.; Eph 1:22; 4:8; 1 Co 15:25-28)

10:26 *Hung them.* Cf. 8:29; Dt 21:22 note.

3) 10:28-43 Victory over Other Southern Kings

10:29 *Passed on.* "Because the Lord God of Israel fought for Israel" (42), Joshua extended his victorious march into southern Palestine (29-43). In this campaign he defeated enemy forces coming from as far south as Kadesh-barnea (Nm 13:3 note) and as far west as Gaza on the Mediterranean coast (41). The other cities were situated at intermediate points within these limits.

10:37 *Its king.* No doubt a ruler who succeded the king of Hebron, slain previously.

10:40 *Negeb.* Cf. Gn 12:9 note.

10:41 *Goshen.* Not the region in Egypt where the Israelites lived prior to the Exodus (Gn 47:5 f.), but a city "in the hill country" about 10 miles southwest of Hebron. It was later assigned to Judah. (15:48-51)

10:43 *All Israel.* It should be noted in passing that the Book of Joshua reports victories over Canaanite forces which were the result of a joint venture of all Israel. However, this general softening-up process left "very much land to be possessed" (13:1). None of the cities mentioned in this chapter was burned. After the various battles the army returned to Gilgal without leaving an occupation force to hold them. It was left to the individual tribes, sometimes in cooperation with others, to establish a permanent settlement in their respective inheritances. To what extent their efforts were successful is briefly mentioned in a few instances but is taken up more fully in the Book of Judges. Spiritual warfare likewise is an "already" and a "not-yet." Our faith "is the victory that overcomes the world" (1 Jn 5:4) but it remains necessary to "fight the good fight of the faith." (1 Ti 6:12)

11:1-15 BATTLES AGAINST NORTHERN CONFEDERATION

11:1 *King of Hazor.* Israel's successes in central Canaan (ch. 9) and in the south (ch. 10) reached the ears of the northern kings. They also formed a coalition in a desperate attempt to stem the tide of invasion. The king of Hazor spearheaded the counterattack. *Jabin* may have been his title rather than his name (Ju 4:2). Excavations have revealed the great size of his walled city. Situated about 10 miles northwest of the Sea of Galilee, the whole complex afforded space for an estimated population of 40,000 people. The assembled army represented a motley array of warriors from the north ("under Hermon") plus "the Jebusites in the hill country," possibly contingents that had fled northward after the campaign in the south. (1-4)

11:5 *Merom.* Fed by springs a few miles northwest of Hazor, its waters flowed southward toward the Sea of Galilee.

11:6 *Afraid of them.* Joshua was about to meet an enemy not only vastly superior in numbers but also equipped with most formidable weapons: war chariots.

11:8 *Chased them.* The routed confederates fled as far as *Sidon and Misrephoth-maim*, both on the Mediterranean coast, and as far as *Mizpeh*, perhaps the same as Mizpah (3)—both spellings have the same meaning of watchtower.

11:11 *Burned Hazor.* Besides Jericho and Ai only Hazor was burned by Joshua. Recent excavators fix thetime of its destruction in the middle of the 13th century B.C. It is possible that Joshua burned only the lower part of the city which covered about 175 acres. (13)

11:12 *As Moses . . . commanded.* Cf. Dt 7:2 ff.; 20:16 ff.

11:16—12:24 SUMMARY OF VICTORIES

11:16 *All that land.* There follows a summary of the territory in which Joshua had defeated the enemy (16-23). Some points of reference were not previously mentioned. But they fall into place within the general framework of the terrain extending from the "Negeb" in the south (10:40-41) to the Lebanon valley in the north. (17)

11:18 *A long time.* This remark indicates that the preceding account is not a complete record of all encounters with the Canaanites, as itemized in the next chapter.

11:20 *Harden their hearts.* Cf. Ex 4:21 note.

11:21 *Anakim.* Mentioned particularly perhaps because the spies sent by Moses feared that the Israelites would not be able to defeat these giant Canaanites. (Nm 13:22 note, 33)

11:23 *Took the whole land.* This summary statement of Joshua's victories does not claim that he possessed, i.e., seized and controlled all of Canaan. He *took the whole land* in the sense that *the land had rest from war.* He had broken the power of the Canaanites to undertake aggressive wars against the Israelites. According to chs. 13—22 Joshua allotted the land "for an inheritance to Israel" although very much of it remained to "be possessed" (13:1). Before permanent settlement in every assigned inheritance was possible, many sections had to be wrested from the Canaanites who still occupied them.

12:1 *The kings.* The survey of the territories in which Joshua had been victorious (11:16-23) is followed by a list of 31 defeated *kings.* For the most part they had jurisdiction over only one city and its immediate environs. The large number of such kinglets indicates that Canaan was far from being a unified state. The first list (1-6) records the rulers whom the people of Israel under Moses had vanquished east of the Jordan (Nm 21:21 ff.). Their land was "given for a possession" to the tribes of Reuben, Gad, and Manasseh. (Nm 32:33 ff.)

12:7 *West side of the Jordan.* A second tabulation repeats the names of kings whom Joshua defeated (chs. 2—7) but also adds a considerable number not mentioned previously (7-24). This summary credits Joshua with victories over the Canaanite rulers. It does not claim that he "took possession of their land," as Moses had done east of the Jordan (1; 1:11 second note; 10:43 note). The parenthetic note that *Joshua gave their land to the tribes of Israel as a possession according to their allotments* anticipates the following chapters. He was commanded to take this action although "there remains yet very much land to be possessed" (13:1). This catalog of defeated Canaanite kinglets—for the modern reader a barren statistic of unknown names—is a faint intimation of the shout of victory that will resound when "the kingdom of the world has become the kingdom of our Lord and of his Christ." (Rv 11:15)

13:1—21:45 DIVISION OF INHERITANCE

13:1-7 Introduction: Allotment Before Full Occupation

13:6 *Allot the land.* The promise of eventual ownership of Canaan came to the patriarchs while they were still strangers and pilgrims in it. Joshua apportioned the land before the Israelites had fully occupied it. All of it was the land of promise. Full possession was contingent on Israel's response in obedience of faith. The Book of Judges begins the story of repeated lapses into apostasy. Some areas mentioned in 2-6 did not come under Israelite control before the time of David. Others, like the Phoenician territory of *the Sidonians,* did not become a part even of his empire.

Joshua assigned the inheritance to the tribes in three installments: (a) Presumably while still at Gilgal (10:43), he confirmed the boundaries of the land east of the Jordan, already allotted by Moses to Reuben, Gad, and half of Manasseh (6-32). Here (14:6) he also determined the lot of Judah and of Joseph's sons, Ephraim and Manasseh, on the west side of the river (chs. 13—17). (b) At Shiloh the remaining tribes were given their patrimony, also west of the Jordan (chs. 18 f.). (c) Finally he set aside cities that were to remain "federal domain": cities of refuge and the Levitical cities. (chs. 20 f.).

These chapters contain a complex array of geographical data not always presented in the same schematic pattern. So, e.g., the cities within the boundaries of Ephraim and Manasseh are not listed, as is the case in the report on other tribes. In a number of instances the lines of demarcation are difficult to reconstruct. Some accounts appear to be incomplete. Nevertheless the general picture of the land that emerges fits the situation at this early stage of Israel's history.

The modern reader may find this catalog of ancient and strange place names as unedifying as the genealogies of Genesis. But this account too was written for his learning. The tribal possessions of Israel were the arena chosen by God to put into effect His plan of salvation (21:45). He selected this Palestinian soil with Him in view who promised: "I go to prepare a place for you." (Jn 14:2)

13:8-33 Land East of Jordan

13:8-14 COMBINED TERRITORY OF TWO AND ONE HALF TRIBES

13:8 *Moses gave.* Cf. Nm 32:33-42.

13:15-31 SPECIFIC ALLOCATIONS

13:15 *The Reubenites.* Vv. 8-14 give a survey of the entire Transjordan inheritance of the two and one half tribes. The next verse reports how this entire area was divided among the Reubenites (15-23), the Gadites (24-28), and the Manassites (29-32). Their allotments coincided in general with the boundaries that marked the territory of the dispossessed occupants of the land or with previously defined areas such as Gilead (Nm 32:1, 33-42). Therefore no full description of the individual borders was necessary except in the case of Gad (26 f.). West of the Jordan the situation was different. There the Israelites fell heir to a land pockmarked by more than a score of small city-states (12:7-24). No recognized borders existed. Hence it was necessary to give a more detailed orientation of the inheritances of the nine and one half tribes. (chs. 14—19)

13:23 *Balaam.* More dangerous to Israel than the military might of Og and Sihon (Nm 21) was the temptation to Midianite idolatry. The soothsayer Balaam, previously hired to curse Israel, had suggested this subtle means of destroying the chosen people. (Nm 22—24; 31:1-20)

13:32-33 RECAPITULATION

13:33 *No inheritance.* The Levites received no inheritance within the borders of one defined area. This exceptional provision is noted at various points in the tribal allotments (13:14; 14:3; Nm 18:20). Assigned to bring "the offerings by fire," the Lord God of Israel would recompense them for their priestly services with cities within the territory of all tribes, whom they represented at the sanctuary. (Dt 10:8-9; 18:1; Jos 21)

14:1—19:51 Land West of Jordan

14:1—17:18 FIRST SERIES OF ALLOTMENTS: NINE AND ONE HALF TRIBES

1) 14:1-4 Introduction

14:2 *By lot.* The introduction to the tribal allotments west of the Jordan (1-5) stresses a fact that the Israelites were so prone to forget. This land was theirs not by virtue of what they had done in conquering it. It was an *inheritance*, an unmerited reward; they "received" it from the Lord. He determined *by lot* what each tribe's gift was to be (cf. 7:18 note). "Eleazar, the [high] priest" and Aaron's successor, is mentioned first no doubt because he administered the casting of the lots.

2) 14:5—15:63 Judah

14:6 *Caleb.* The account of the allotment of all the land west of the Jordan begins and ends with the provisions made for two individuals: *Caleb* and *Joshua* (6-14; 19:49 f.). These heroes of faith had lived to see "the assurance of things hoped for" (Nm 13:30—14:30). Within this framework of promise and fulfillment the other tribes too received what the Lord had given long before they set foot on Canaan. Caleb reminded Joshua that 45 years ago he had been assured of a portion among the people of Judah (Nm 13—14; cf. Dt 1:35 f.). He was a *Kenizzite*, a descendant of Esau, who had cast his lot with the Israelites. (Gn 36:10 f.; 1 Ch 4:13-15)

14:12 *Shall drive them out.* Joshua led Israel's combined forces to victory over Hebron's king (12:10). The actual occupation of the allotted inheritance remained the responsibility of the individual tribe or clan. (Chs. 15 ff.)

14:15 *Anakim.* Cf. 11:21 note.

15:1 *The lot . . . of Judah.* Chs. 15—17 report the inheritance of three tribes who received large areas in the heart of Canaan: Judah and the two sons of Joseph, Ephraim and Manasseh. In broad outline the borders of their territories were as follows: (a) *Judah* received the land below a line running east and west between the northern end of the Dead Sea and the Mediterranean. Its southern border began at the southern tip of the Dead Sea, dipped farther south to Kadesh-barnea, then turned northward and ended at the Mediterranean by "the Brook of Egypt" (ch. 15; Nm 34:3 note). (b) Ephraim's territory extended from the Jordan to the Mediterranean. Its southern boundary line, for the most part contiguous with Judah's northern border, ran from the Jordan near Jericho to "the sea" (ch. 16). But between Ephraim and Judah lay an east-west strip occupied by the smaller tribes Dan and Benjamin (cf. 18:11 ff.; 19:40 ff.). (c) Above Ephraim's northern border lay Manasseh's patrimony. It too stretched from the Jordan to the Mediterranean but was bounded on the north by the southern limits of Issachar, Zebulon, and Asher (ch. 17; 19:10-31). The map of Canaan should be consulted for the geographical data in these chapters.

15:14 *Drove out.* Some attempts by individual tribes to appropriate the territory of the defeated Canaanite kings were made during Joshua's lifetime. Caleb and his brother Othniel succeeded in occupying their inheritance (13-19). However, the whole tribe of Judah, even with the help of neighboring Benjamin, "could not drive out [dispossess] . . . the Jebusites, the inhabitants of Jerusalem." (63; Ju 1:8, 21)

15:21 *The cities.* For the people of Judah who were to settle in these cities, this detailed list of their homes was of more than passing interest. They were located in four districts: (1) *the extreme South* or Negeb (21-32); (2) the western "lowland" or Shephelah (33-47); (3) "the hill country," a central ridge (48-60); (4) "the wilderness" along the eastern border. (61 f.)

3) 16:1—17:18 Joseph's Sons:
Ephraim and Manasseh

16:1 *Descendants of Joseph.* In the general survey of the combined inheritance of Joseph's two sons only its southernmost boundary—Ephraim's southern border—is defined (1-3). When the territorial extent of each tribe is later described (4-9; 17:1-11), no list of cities within their borders is attached (see the cities of Judah, 15:20-61). It is possible that such lists followed 16:9 and 17:9 respectively but were dropped from the text in the course of its transmission, bringing with it a dislocation of some verses.

16:5 *Ephraimites.* Substantially repeating the southern boundary of the Ephraimites (1-3), vv. 5-10 add a description of their border with Manasseh to the north. If allowance is made for some scribal confusion, it appears that the dividing lines between the two tribes are drawn not like Judah's (15:1-12) from their eastern and western extremities but from points midway between the Jordan and the Mediterranean: in the south, from *Ataroth-adar* westward and eastward; in the north, from Michmethath eastward and westward.

16:10 *Not drive out.* Cf. 15:14 note.

17:1 *Manasseh.* On the west side of the Jordan Manasseh's territory had a common border with Ephraim to the south. Along Manasseh's northern frontier "by [rather than "in"] Issachar and by Asher" lay a zone of fortified Canaanite cities (11-13). Unable to take these strongholds, "the tribe of Joseph" complained that their territory was limited to "the hill country," covered by "forests." But Joshua, himself an Ephraimite, encouraged them to "clear" the land they already occupied. He also assured them that the territory still held by the Canaanites would become a part of their tribal possession. (14-18)

17:3 *Only daughters.* Cf. Nm 27:3, 11; 36:3 notes.

18:1—19:48 SECOND SERIES OF ALLOTMENTS

18:1 *Shiloh.* Chs. 13—17 relate how five tribes received their inheritance—presumably at Gilgal (14:6). Chs. 18 and 19 record the allotments made to the remaining seven tribes at Shiloh: (1) Benjamin (11-28); (2) Simeon (19:1-9); (3) Zebulun (19:10-16); (4) Issachar (19:17-23); (5) Asher (19:24-31); (6) Napthali (19:32-39); (7) Dan. (19:40-48)

At Shiloh, some 15 miles south of Shechem (cf. 9:6 note), *the tent of meeting* was set up (Ex 25:1 note, 8, 22). It was to remain there during the period of the judges. (1 Sm 4:11; Jer 7:12)

Congregation. The people of Israel are so called to underscore a basic truth. Canaan came into their possession not through their achievements or national preeminence but solely by virtue of their covenant relationship to the Lord. First and foremost a religious community, they were to bring spiritual blessings to all families of the earth.

Subdued. Because of Joshua's victories the people could assemble without fear of an attack.

18:3 *Slack.* The next phase of the conquest was the responsibility of the individual tribes. They were to *take possession of the land* by dispossessing the Canaanites who still occupied their inheritance. Apparently these seven tribes were particularly *slack* in venturing on such an enterprise of faith (Ju 5:16-18). However at Joshua's prodding three men from each tribe surveyed the land "with a view to their inheritances" (2-9). With a written "description of the land" before him, Joshua "apportioned the land to the people." (10)

18:11 *Benjamin.* The last miles of the Jordan before it empties into the Dead Sea formed "its boundary on the eastern side" (20). "On the western side" its lot ended where Dan's territory began. To the north it bordered on Ephraim; to the south, on Judah. The names of 12 places are mentioned in tracing the limits of this comparatively small area "round about" (11-20). Then follows a list of 14 cities that lay within its confines, including such well-known ones as Jericho and Jebus—Jerusalem. (21-27)

19:1 *Simeon.* No boundaries are given for his lot since his inheritance *was in the midst of the inheritance of the tribe of Judah*, whose *portion* was *too large for them* (9). In military ventures Simeon joined forces with Judah (Ju 1:3, 17) and eventually was absorbed by its stronger ally. At Saul's time such cities as "Hormah" (4) and "Ziklag" (5) were under the jurisdiction of "the elders of Judah" (1 Sm 30:26-30). In the list of Simeon's "thirteen cities," "Sheba" appears to be a dittography (scribal repetition) for the immediately preceding "Beer-sheba." (2; see 1 Ch 4:28, where Sheba does not occur)

19:10 *Zebulun.* Manasseh's northern border formed the southern boundary of Issachar and Asher. Between these two tribes, also immediately to the north of Manasseh, lay Zebulun. (17:1 note, 10 f.)

19:17 *Issachar.* With Manasseh to the south, Zebulun to the west, and Napthali to the north, Zebulun's eastern "boundary ends at the Jordan." (22)

19:32 *Napthali.* "Touching Zebulun at the south, and Asher on the west" (34), Napthali's inheritance had for its eastern border the Sea of Galilee and the upper Jordan.

19:34 *Judah on the east.* The meaning of this reference cannot be that Napthali's territory touched Judah far in the south. The Septuagint omits *Judah* and reads: "at the Jordan on the east."

19:40 *Dan.* The last and smallest tribal inheritance was situated within boundaries previously established for its contiguous neighbors. Between Ephraim to the north (16:1-3) and Judah to the south (15:5-12) there lay a corridor running all the way from the Jordan to the Mediterranean. The eastern end of this strip was assigned to Benjamin (18:11-15), leaving its western extension to Dan. In addition to this general delineation of its borders, the names of the cities in 41-46 serve as points that mark its limits.

19:47 *Was lost.* Cf. Ju 1:34; 18:1 ff. In compensation for their loss the Danites occupied a territory far to the north along the sources of the Jordan. The former name of its chief city, *Leshem*, is given as "Laish" in Ju 18:29. In Egyptian records it is called Lus(i).

19:49-50 JOSHUA'S CITY IN EPHRAIM

19:49 *Joshua.* Cf. 14:6 note.

19:51 RECAPITULATION

19:51 *Dividing the land.* In this summary of the division of Canaan the word *inheritances* again puts Israel's possession of the land into its proper perspective. Every piece of ground was purely a gift, its particular limits determined *by lot . . . before the Lord.* No feudal or other centralized system of control was prescribed. The tribes formed a union of 12 "federated states." Their "constitution" was the covenant.

20:1-9 Cities of Refuge

20:2 *Cities of refuge.* Within the tribal inheritances some areas were to become "federal" domain serving the corporate welfare of the nation. Six cities of refuge were set aside lest bloody feuds endanger physical life (ch. 20); the Levitical cities were to provide livelihood for those who served the spiritual needs of the community. (ch. 21)

Through Moses. For the function of "the cities of refuge" see Nm 35:11, 16 notes; Dt 19:2 note.

20:6 *High priest.* The Hebrew text has "the high priest." Eleazar, who served in that capacity at the time, is called simply "the priest" to distinguish him from all others who also performed priestly functions. (19:51; 21:1)

20:7 *Set apart.* Literally "sanctified," i.e., they withdrew these cities from profane or ordinary use and assigned them a divinely assigned purpose. Moses had already set apart three cities east of the Jordan and commanded that this be done also west of the Jordan (Dt 4:41-44; 19:1-10). In the following verses all six cities are mentioned. Their location made them accessible to all fugitives. West of the Jordan, *Kedesh* served the northern region; *Shechem*, the central; *Kiriath-arba*, the southern. East of the Jordan, Bezer was in the south; Ramoth in the center; Golan in the north.

21:1-42 Cities for Priests and Levites

21:1 *The Levites.* The previous account of the division of the land is interspersed with the note that "to the tribe of Levi Moses gave no inheritance" (13:14, 33; 14:3; 18:7). Accordingly the list of their "cities . . . along with their pasture lands" (2) was not made a part of the former tribal allotments. The Levites were to "get their living" from contributions by all tribes. Through Moses God had already so provided for them. (Nm 35:1-8)

21:3 *The following cities.* This list of names may fascinate the modern reader as little as the enumeration of place names in the previous chapters. However, each geographical datum here too adds a brush stroke to a picture with a message for Israel as well as for us. Dispersed throughout the land, the Levites, by their very presence, were a living demonstration that, in the final analysis, it was true of all Israelites: "The Lord . . . is their inheritance." They had not displaced the Canaanites by right of conquest as other nations seized the territory of vanquished peoples. In carrying out their duties before the Lord, the priests and their Levitical assistants acted as the representative intermediaries of a "holy nation," chosen in its entirety to function as "a kingdom of priests" (Ex 19:6; Nm 8:5-26; 18:22 ff.). All Israelites were priests in the sense that they had been given national existence for only one purpose: to serve the Lord and to carry out His purpose. To his environment the NT believer has a similar duty. In the world but not of the world, he is to witness to his fellow sojourners that "here we have no lasting city" (Heb 13:14). A pilgrim and exile himself, he is to point them to an "inheritance which is imperishable, undefiled, and unfading, kept in heaven." (1 Ptr 1:3-4; Ro 8:17)

21:4 *The families.* The settlement of the Levites in widely separated areas did not sever their internal family ties. A *lot came out* for the branches of the tribe, named after the sons of Levi: Kohath, Merari, Gershon. Among the Kohathites the *descendants of Aaron* formed a special group: the priests (Nm 3:10). These four families received a specified number of cities within the inheritance of three clusters of tribes. (4-7)

21:8 *These cities.* The various groupings of the

Levites are followed by a list of cities arranged according to their location in each tribal inheritance (8-42). Some of these were also cities of refuge, e.g., Hebron. (11; 20:7)

21:41 *Possession of the people.* Joshua had allotted Canaan before all of it was actually occupied by the Israelites. The Levitical cities were allocated under the same circumstances.

21:43-45 Comprehensive Review

21:45 *Promises.* God kept His promises in the measure that Israel responded to them in faith.

22:1—24:33 TERMS OF INHERITANCE

22:1-9 Charge to East-Jordan Tribes

22:1 *Summoned.* Joshua had defeated the enemy forces that resisted Israel's entrance into Canaan (chs. 1—12). Although very much land remained to be occupied, he had apportioned the Promised Land among the 12 tribes (chs. 13—21). The three closing chapters (22—24) contain his addresses to the people. In all of them he drove home the fact that Israel's nationhood was not an end in itself. God had created it to be His instrument of salvation to "all the families of the earth" (Gn 12:3). It had a future only if it carried forward His eternal plan (Eph 1:4-10). How the chosen people were to serve His purpose, God had expressed in the form of a covenant (Exodus, Introduction, "Content"). Therefore Israel's title to its inheritance was subject to terms, divinely established and sanctioned by the people. Lest the people forget the role they were to play in the Promised Land—as they were soon to do—Joshua stressed their unique relationship to God at three occasions: (a) when he dismissed the two and a half tribes (ch. 22); (b) when he "summoned all Israel" to a solemn convocation (ch. 23); (c) when he asked "all the tribes of Israel" to pledge themselves to covenant loyalty. (24:1-28)

22:2 *Moses . . . commanded you.* Cf. Nm 32.

22:4 *Given rest.* Israel's covenant obligations were a response to the unmerited gifts of God. (Ex 20:2 note)

22:5 *Love the Lord.* Observance of *the commandment and the law* was to flow from an inner commitment to God. The whole heart and the whole soul was to dedicate its love to Him. (Dt 6:5 note)

22:6 *Sent them away.* Separated by the Jordan from the rest of Israel, the dismissed tribes were not to forget their covenant solidarity with their brethren.

22:8 *Spoil.* Under the OT covenant there was no separation of church and state. Hence regulations for political and social procedures were provided. (Nm 31:27; 1 Sm 30:24)

22:9 *Shiloh.* Cf. 18:1 note.

22:10-34 No Idolatrous Altars

22:10 *An altar.* Reported at some length (10-34), the episode of the altar by the Jordan clearly demonstrates that Israel was well aware of its covenant status and obligations. One of the basic terms of agreement stipulated that the God of Israel was "one Lord." He was not divisible into sundry forces of nature like the baals whom the Canaanites sought to impound by magical rites wherever they determined to do so. Only at the place which the Lord would choose "to make his name dwell there"—at that time it was Shiloh (18:1)—were they to bring their burnt offerings and sacrifices (Dt 12:5 note). The altercation about the altar furthermore showed that the Israelites knew what it meant that they were "the congregation of the Lord." Not merely a political aggregation of loosely federated tribes, but the one "holy nation" and "kingdom of priests," they were accountable for any "treachery" and "rebellion" by their members. (Cf. Eph 2:13-22; Ro 16:17; 1 Co 5:1-13)

22:11 *The land of Canaan.* Here *Canaan* refers to the land west of the Jordan as in 9 and 32 (see also Nm 32:32; 35:14). The altar was "of great size" (10), literally "great for seeing," i.e., capable of being seen at a great distance. Visible from the east side of the river, it was to "witness" (27, 34) to the Transjordan tribes that they too had "a portion in the Lord." In order to express this solidarity with their brethren in *Canaan,* they pledged themselves and "the generations after" them to "worship (literally "to fear") the Lord" (25). Therefore their explanation of the altar's purpose was not a devious equivocation fabricated in a desperate situation. It expressed their original intent.

22:13 *Phinehas.* The issue was in an area of covenant relations that was the special concern of the priests. Therefore not Joshua but the future high priest headed the delegation of "ten chiefs" (Ju 20:28). The people could rely on him not to make any compromises because he had proved his abhorrence of idolatry at a previous occasion. (Nm 25:6-13; see also Dt 13:14)

22:17 *Peor.* Cf. Nm 25. Here open idolatry had been abolished. However, the people had *not cleansed* themselves of their latent tendency to "turn away . . . from following the Lord."

22:19 *Unclean.* They should find *a possession* west of the Jordan rather than engage in forbidden rituals, if they felt that their inheritance, far from the tabernacle, was *unclean.*

22:20 *Achan.* Cf. ch. 7.

22:28 *A copy.* Outwardly a replica *of the altar of the Lord,* it was not intended, they insisted, to be a place *for burnt offerings, nor for sacrifice.*

23:1—24:28 Joshua's Charges to All Israel

23:1-16 COVENANT LOYALTY AND POSSESSION OF CANAAN

23:1 *A long time afterward.* Joshua *was old* when he allotted the land to the tribes (13:1). But before he was "to go the way of all the earth" (14; 1 K 2:2), he "summoned all Israel" and delivered two charges to "their elders and heads, their judges and officers." (2; 24:1)

In both of them he spoke of Israel's future. He warned his hearers that they would retain their inheritance in Canaan only if they remained true to "the covenant of the Lord" (16; 24:25). They "have seen" that God had kept His pledged word to fight for them. He would continue to do so and drive out "those nations that remain" (3-6; 13:2-6). But they could not expect this undeserved favor if they did not respond to it with an uncompromising obedience of faith. In his first address Joshua warned them not to let any association with the Canaanites tempt them to "transgress the covenant" lest they "perish quickly from off the good land" (ch. 23). In his second speech he stressed that covenant loyalty required a personal commitment of every generation to "serve the Lord" and Him alone. (24:1-28)

23:2 *Summoned all Israel.* The exact time and the place of this convocation is not given.

23:3 *God has done.* The Israelites were to "love the Lord," "because he first loved" them (11; 1 Jn 4:19; see also Ex 20:1 note). If they so "cleave to the Lord" (8), this inner compulsion will move them to "do all that is written" (6). The Joshua of the new covenant summons His followers to the same kind of allegiance. (See, e.g., Mt 5—7)

23:6 *Law of Moses.* Cf. 1:7; 8:34; Dt 5:32; 31:9.

23:7 *With these nations.* Cf. Ex 23:32 f.; Dt 7:2-5.

23:10 *One man.* A proverbial way of explaining Israel's victories in battles against great odds when God "fought for them." (3; Dt 32:30; Lv 26:8)

23:15 *Evil things.* Cf. Dt 28:15 ff.

24:1-28 COVENANT LOYALTY: A PERSONAL COMMITMENT

24:1 *Shechem.* Cf. 8:30 note; Dt 27:11-13. The Septuagint has "Shiloh" where Joshua had "set up the tent of meeting" (18:1 note). At this convocation Joshua again confronted "all the tribes of Israel" with the one factor upon which hinged Israel's future in the Promised Land: covenant loyalty. Later history proved that he was not engaging in needless repetitions. As he had done in his previous charge (ch. 23), he set forth the basic terms that determined Israel's relationship to God. But in this address he developed his theme in a wider historical context (2-13), pledged himself to "serve the Lord" (14 f.), and urged the people to make the same unequivocal decision (16-18). Moved by his admonition and his good example, they renewed the covenant, thereby personally committing themselves to serve "the Lord, the God of Israel." (19-28)

24:2 *Says the Lord.* Obedient to God's will as revealed to Moses (1:2-9; 8:30; 11:12), Joshua too became the channel of divine communication. In this dramatic climax of his career, he was empowered to speak what the Lord had to say to His people.

Your fathers. At the convocation recorded in the previous chapter Joshua recalled only what God had done under his leadership. In this new appeal for covenant loyalty he traced the history of the living generation (a) to the separation of the patriarchs from their idolatrous environment (3 f.); (b) to the deliverance from Egypt and the wilderness journey (5-7); (c) to the victories east of the Jordan (8-10); (c) to the crossing of the Jordan, the defeat of the Canaanites, and the allotment of the tribal inheritances (11 f.). Israel was the mystery of the ages, the miracle of God's creation. As it owed its existence solely to His goodness and power, so it had a future as it served His plan to bless all nations.

24:6 *Brought your fathers out.* Joshua's hearers did not personally experience the great events of the Exodus. Its benefits accrued to them as heirs of God's saving acts. Similarly the present-day believer was not "there when they crucified the Lord." Yet by faith he is the beneficiary of the atoning sacrifice made on Calvary more than 19 centuries ago.

24:9 *Balak.* Cf. Nm 22—24.

24:12 *The hornet.* Cf. Ex 23:28 note.

24:14 *Now therefore.* God expected Israel to respond to His goodness. It was to do so voluntarily ("choose"), *in sincerity,* i.e, from the heart (Dt 10:12) and *in faithfulness,* i.e., in undivided loyalty. (23 note; Lv 17:7)

24:15 *As for me.* Joshua practiced what he preached even if it meant to stand alone. (1 K 18:21 f.)

24:17 *Our God.* Joshua's hearers recognized the validity of God's claim upon them.

24:19 *Cannot serve.* Joshua did not want the Israelites to be carried away by a momentary flash of enthusiasm or while they were under the spell of mass hysteria. He urged that they very soberly "sit down and count the cost" of their decision (Lk 14:28). In terms so drastic as to appear contradictory, he brought his hearers up short. Unholy as they were, even their best efforts would not suffice to satisfy the demands of *a holy God.* In every lapse from a perfect obedience they had to reckon with *a jealous God* (Ex 20:5 note; Dt 4:24 note). They could not presume on His good nature to *forgive* their *transgressions* and *sins* as a matter of course.

24:23 *Foreign gods.* Secretly some people still venerated idols. At Shechem Jacob had long ago purged himself and his household of foreign gods. (Gn 35:1-4)

24:25 *Covenant with the people.* Hebrew: "for the people." Recipients of God's mercies in the past, the people of Joshua's time were to share in the blessings and affirm the obligations of the covenant made under Moses (Dt 29:10-15). The *statutes and ordinances* which Joshua made for them restated the terms of Israel's relationship to God, established originally at Mt. Sinai and reiterated at Mt. Ebal (8:30-35). Joshua recorded the proceedings "in the book of the law of God," as Moses had done. (Ex 24:4, 7)

24:26 *A great stone.* Erected *under the oak* (Gn 12:6; 35:4), this stone was to be a memorial of Israel's pledge of allegiance (Lk 19:40; Hab 2:11). The oak was not *in* but "by" *the sanctuary of the Lord.*

24:29-33 Close of an Era

24:29-31 JOSHUA'S DEATH AND BURIAL

24:29 *The servant of the Lord.* At the beginning of his career Joshua was called the "minister" of "Moses the servant of the Lord" (1:1). On his epitaph he was given his predecessor's title. It said in effect: "Well done, good and faithful servant . . . enter into the joy of your master." (Mt 25:21, 23)

24:30 *His own inheritance.* Cf. 19:50.

24:31 *All the days of Joshua.* Repeated Ju 2:7, this verse has ominous overtones. It links an era when "Israel served the Lord" with the following dreary period of the judges when Israel "served the Baals." (Ju 2:11; 3:7; 10:6)

24:32 INTERMENT OF JOSEPH

24:33 ELEAZAR'S DEATH AND BURIAL

24:33 *Gibeah.* These obituary notes at the end of the book bear out the sad truth that even faithful servants of the Lord are not exempt from the verdict: "The wages of sin is death." At the same time their resting places in the soil of Israel's inheritance were mute testimony that "all the good things which the Lord . . . promised . . . have been fulfilled" (23:15). What God did through "the son of Nun" was a step toward His goal in "the fullness of time." Then a Joshua, the Son of God, died the death of sinners. But He rose again and destroyed "the last enemy" of man. For every grave-bound mortal He won an inheritance "kept in heaven . . . to be revealed in the last time." (1 Co 15:26; 1 Ptr 1:3-5)

JUDGES

INTRODUCTION

Content

The Book of Judges resembles the preceding Book of Joshua. Both present a chapter of Israel's history after a great leader had passed from the scene. What happened "after the death of Moses" is recorded in the book known by his successor's name (Jos 1:1). The Book of Judges in turn relates events "after the death of Joshua" (1:1). Both accounts take up approximately the same number of pages: both record only selected incidents of their respective eras; both interpret history from the same point of view. (See Joshua, Introduction)

But there are also divergent features. The first book of the "Former Prophets" (see Joshua, Introduction) surveys the relatively short period of the conquest under Joshua; the second covers a span of time measured by centuries rather than by decades. In the first, the focus of attention is on concerted action by all Israel, in the second there is tribal cooperation only to a limited degree. In the first, prospects for the future seem bright although much of Canaan remained unoccupied at Joshua's death; deep shadows flit across the pages of the second. Failure to act on God's promise left tribal inheritances in the hands of the Canaanites. Covenant loyalty all but vanished. Idol worship flourished. The breakdown of moral and social principles led to anarchy and even civil war. Such apostasy brought divine retribution. Again and again God brought the chosen people under the scourge of foreign invasion and subjugation. It was an era in Israel's history that deserves to be called the dark ages.

But true to His covenant promise God did not let the night of extinction fall on the nation from which, according to the flesh, "the Light of the world" was to come. Whenever "the anger of the Lord was hot against Israel" and they cried: "We have sinned," He "raised up judges for them" (2:14-18). They owed their judicial title to the fact that God delegated to them authority and power to adjudicate litigation on a national as well as an international level. On the basis of divinely established law they presided over court cases within Israel (4:4 f.). In the main, however, they brought divine justice to bear on Israel's disputes with the nations. Through the judges "the Lord, the Judge" of "all the earth" (11:27; Gn 18:25) vindicated the chosen people's right to existence as long as they carried forward His eternal plan to bless all nations through Abraham's Seed. When foreign invaders threatened to frustrate His gracious will, He pronounced sentence on them and the judges executed it: "they delivered" the bearers of the promise "out of the power of those who plundered them" (2:16). For the full realization of God's plan see Mt 19:28.

"The Spirit of the Lord" called the judges to their task and equipped them with the ability to perform it (11:29 etc.). It has become customary to call them "charismatics," i.e., specially gifted men. Other leaders in Israel were so anointed with power from on high: Saul (1 Sm 11:6), David (1 Sm 16:13), the prophets (Is 61:1; Zch 7:12). In spite of this divine endowment, the judges were not always models of moral integrity. The Book of Judges does not gloss over their lapses into sin but lets the reader see the clay feet of these exemplars of heroic faith. (Heb. 11:32)

Authorship

In common with the other "Former Prophets," the Book of Judges is anonymous. Because it contains a historical record that extends over centuries, the unknown author had to resort to sources for information about events that did not happen during his own lifetime. Whether these sources were written or oral, or both, cannot be determined with certainty. In an introduction (1:1—3:6) he supplies the underlying reason why judges appeared on the scene during the centuries after Joshua's death. The main section of the book (3:7—16:31) is an account of the individual judges and their exploits. In the closing chapters (17—21) he relates two stories of Israel's sacrilegious and moral depravity for which "the anger of the Lord was kindled."

But the author is more than a chronicler. He interprets what he records. Events happen in a cause-effect pattern that is as consistent as the Lord of history is unchangeable. Whenever the Israelites "transgressed" the "covenant" (2:20), God carried out its threats of punishment through foreign oppressors; whenever the apostate people penitently "cried to the Lord" (4:3, etc.), He kept His promise to forgive and "raised up judges, who saved them" (2:16). This recurring cycle—sin, punishment, repentance, deliverance—repeated by the author to the point of monotony, has a double effect. The reader cannot help being impressed with the inflexible holiness of God, with which man cannot trifle with impunity. At the same time, every penitent sinner can be sure that God does not turn a deaf ear to his plea for mercy, no matter how vile his crime is, no matter how often he must apply for forgiveness.

According to rabbinic tradition the author of the Book of Judges was Samuel. But there is no reference in the book itself or in other Biblical books to sustain this assertion. Nevertheless it is quite likely that the book was written during or soon after the time when this imposing figure in Israel's history had appeared on the scene. A date in the early reign of David, anointed by Samuel, is suggested by casual remarks about circumstances that prevailed when the author composed the book (cf. 1:21; 17:6 notes). See also Joshua, Introduction, "Authorship."

Chronology

Some 20 references to time appear in the book. Nevertheless it is difficult to arrive at an absolute chronology for the period of the judges. Linked as it is with the conquest of Canaan under Joshua, its beginning and duration depends on the date assigned to the Exodus (see Exodus, Introduction, "The Date of the Exodus"). Addition of the years allocated to the length of each oppression, judgeship, and subsequent period of rest yields a total of some 400 years. This figure is too high for the interval between the Exodus and the time of David and Solomon (1 K 6:1 note). This difficulty is resolved in part if some periods of oppression and deliverance occurred simultaneously in various parts of the land (10:7 note). Furthermore the chronological data are almost invariably given in round figures of 40, its multiple 80, or its half 20. These factors would justify reducing the period of the judges to an actual time span of about 300 years (11:26). The late date of the Exodus (13th century B.C.) allows only 200 years for this era of Israel's history.

OUTLINE

I. 1:1—3:6 Prolog: Why God Raised Up Judges

II. 3:7—16:31 Core Content: What the Judges Did to Deliver Israel

III. 17:1—21:25 Appendix: How Deeply Israel Had Fallen

1:1—3:6 PROLOG: WHY GOD RAISED UP JUDGES

1:1—2:5 Partial Occupation of Canaan

1:1-21 SUCCESSES AND FAILURES OF JUDAH AND SIMEON

1) 1:1-8 Successful Joint Campaigns

1:1 *The death of Joshua.* A new chapter in Israel's history began when the wilderness journey came to an end "after the death of Moses" (Jos 1:1). The post-Joshua era too had its own characteristic features. In an introductory section the author briefly sketches two interlinking causes that produced the dismal period of the judges: (a) the tribes failed "to take possession" of "the territory allotted to" them and made "a covenant with the inhabitants of this land" (1-35); (b) they repeatedly broke their covenant with the Lord. In willful defiance of its basic term, "they served the Baals and the Ashtaroth" the "gods of the peoples who were [permitted to remain] round about them." "In sore straits" when God, provoked to anger, "sold them into the power of their enemies," they "cried to the Lord." "Moved to pity by their groaning," He "raised up judges" who "saved them from the hand of their enemies" (2:6—3:6). Hence these first chapters give the reader the key to the plot developed in the main section of the book. (3:7—16:31)

Inquired. See Nm 27:21 note; Ex 28:15 note; Ju 20:18, 27; Acts 1:24-26.

1:2 *Judah shall go up.* The tribal attempts to occupy the allotted inheritances constitute a significant part of the background of the book. It is therefore quite natural that the author should incorporate some efforts toward that goal which had been mentioned in the Book of Joshua. There are flashbacks to the success and failures of Judah and the Judahite Caleb in 1-21 (Jos 14:6-15; 15:13-19). In the remaining verses of this chapter (22-36) the vicissitudes of Manasseh and Ephraim, as well as those of smaller tribes, likewise mentioned previously, are adduced to round out the general setting.

1:3 *Simeon.* Cooperation by these tribes is explained by the fact that Simeon's "inheritance was in the midst of the inheritance of the tribe of Judah," the former's blood brother. (Jos. 19:1; Gn 29:33, 35)

1:4 *Perizzites.* Cf. Gn 13:7 note; 15:20.

Ten thousand. Cf. Book of Numbers, Introduction, "Numbers . . . ."

1:5 *Adonibezek.* His name means lord of Bezek. A modern site, known as Khirbet Bezqa, is located west and slightly north of Jerusalem. Another Bezek, farther north, is mentioned 1 Sm 11:8.

1:6 *Cut off.* Mutilation, even of prisoners of war, was practiced only rarely by the Israelites. In this particular instance they apparently took recourse to the principle of retribution set forth in Lv 24:19 (cf. Ex 21:24 note). Adonibezek admits that "God has requited" him for having incapacitated his own victims in the same way. The number "seventy" need not be an exact figure. The king very likely meant to say that he had done this thing to his prisoners over and over again.

1:8 *Took it.* Jerusalem lay on the border between Judah and Benjamin. The latter, to whom it had been allotted (Jos 18:21-27), was not able to "drive out" its inhabitants and occupy it permanently (on the meaning of "drive out" see Jos 1:11 note). The Judahites, who apparently had come to the aid of their weaker neighbor, *took it* but they too could not "drive out" its inhabitants (Jos 15:63). The end result was that it remained unoccupied by "the people of Benjamin." (21)

2) 1:9-15 Judahites Caleb and Othniel

1:9 *Negeb, and in the lowland.* Cf. Jos 15:21 note.

1:10 *Hebron.* About 20 miles south of Jerusalem. Cf. Jos 15:14 note.

1:11 *Debir.* Eleven miles south of Hebron. Cf. Jos 15:15-19.

1:13 *Son of Kenaz.* The brothers were descendants of Kenaz, Esau's grandson. Caleb is therefore called a Kenizzite. (Jos 14:6 note)

3) 1:16-21 Judah and Simeon in Other Joint Campaigns

1:16 *The Kenite.* On the name of Moses' father-in-law see Ex 2:18 note. In Nm 10:29 he is called a Midianite. The Kenites were associated with two other nomadic tribes: the Amalekites (1 Sm 15:6) and the Midianites. (Ex 18:1)

City of palms. Jericho, allotted to Benjamin (Jos 18:21), is so designated in 3:13 and Dt 34:3. The Kenite thrust into southern Judah suggests that a city in that area had the same descriptive name. There is a La Grange ("the farm") in almost all states of our country.

Arad. About 5 miles south of Debir (11). Early in their wilderness journey the Israelites had defeated the Canaanites, led by the king of Arad, "utterly destroyed them and their cities," and called "the place" Hormah (Nm 21:1-3; 21:1 note; Jos 12:14). "Zephath" apparently was one of those cities (17). Rebuilt after more than 40 years, it was now "utterly destroyed" (put under the ban) by Judah and Simeon and called "Hormah," i.e., a banned city. (Dt 2:34 note; Nm 31:1 note)

1:18 *Gaza . . . Ashkelon . . . Ekron.* Together with Gath and Ashdod these cities were the centers of the Philistine confederacy, also called the pentapolis. They were situated in "the [low-lying Mediterranean coastal] plain." Although Judah *took* them, he was unable to "drive out" its inhabitants but "took possession [only] of the hill country" (19). The Septuagint reads: "Judah took not Gaza," etc.

1:19 *Could not.* It appears that God was not fulfilling His promises. Through Joshua He had said: "I will myself drive them [the remaining Canaanites] out," "though they have chariots of iron" (Jos 13:6; 23:15; 17:18). But Judah and Benjamin, as well as the other tribes (27-36), *could not drive out* the inhabitants of their allotted inheritances. The answer to this apparent contradiction must be sought in Israel's failure to act in obedience of faith (Jos 23:4-16).

"By faith the walls of Jericho fell down" (Heb 11:30). Likewise *chariots of iron* were no obstacle in Israel's path when it moved forward with complete trust in God's promise (Jos 11:1-9; Ju 4:15). On the other hand, because "Israel has sinned . . . transgressed my covenant," it suffered ignominious defeat at Ai in spite of military superiority over the enemy (Jos 7). Weakness of faith and covenant unfaithfulness brought on a power failure. Joshua already had to rebuke the people for being "slack to . . . take possession of the land" (Jos 18:3). Faith, even if it is like "a grain of mustard seed," can move mountains. (Mt 17:20; 21:21 f.; 9:22; 13:58)

1:20 *Moses had said.* Nm 14:24; Dt 1:36; Jos 14:9; 15:13 f.

Anak. Cf. Nm 13:22 note.

1:21 *To this day.* Jerusalem remained in the hands of the Jebusites until David's time. (2 Sm 5:6-10)

1:22-36 SUCCESSES AND FAILURES OF OTHER TRIBES

1) 1:22-26 Successful Campaigns by House of Joseph

1:22 *House of Joseph.* Individual campaigns by Manasseh and Ephraim failed (27-29), but a joint attack on Bethel was successful. (22-26)

1:26 *Hittites.* Cf. Gn 10:15-19 note. No other reference to the newly built city of *Luz* has been found.

2) 1:27-29 Failures of Manasseh and Ephraim

1:27 *The Canaanites persisted.* The remaining verses of this chapter record the failure of the Joseph tribes and others to *drive out the inhabitants.* Enough instances are cited to afford the reader a sufficiently clear picture of the unfavorable circumstances that obtained when the judges appeared on the scene. Almost all verses are flashbacks to action recorded in Joshua: (a) 27: Jos 17:11 f.; (b) 29: Jos 16:10; (c) 30: Jos 19:15; (d) 33: Jos 19:32 ff.; (e) 34: Jos 19:40 ff. See the notes on these passages in Joshua.

3) 1:30-36 Failures of Zebulun, Asher, Naphtali, and Dan

1:31 *Asher.* The border of his allotted inheritance is given in Jos 19:24 ff. However, there is no previous mention of the cities from which *Asher did not drive out the inhabitants.*

1:34 *Danites.* Their plight was the worst of all. Other tribes were at least partially successful in occupying their territories. *Pressed . . . back into the hill country,* the Danites finally had to leave their inheritance to seek a new home in the far north. (18:1 ff.; Jos 19:47 f.)

Amorites. At times all inhabitants of Canaan are called Amorites. For a restricted use of this name see Nm 21:21 note.

1:35 *Aijalon.* Of the Amorite cities mentioned in this verse the location of only *Aijalon* is definitely known (Jos 10:12). Allotted to Dan (Jos 19:42), it lay south of the border of *the house of Joseph,* more particularly of Ephraim. The latter, by far the stronger tribe, was able to subject it and the other cities *to forced labor.* Whether before or after the Danite migration, whether for a longer or shorter period of time, is not indicated.

1:36 *Akrabbim.* Cf. Jos 15:3; 15:11 note. South of Dan lay the territory of Judah. On their eastern border the Judahites too were hedged in by *the Amorites,* more specifically by the Edomites. Some Septuagint manuscripts actually read "Edomites" instead of *Amorites.*

2:1-5 CAUSE OF FAILURES

2:1 *Angel of the Lord.* Ch. 2 continues to a to the backdrop of the stage on which the judges were to appear. It supplies the reason for the political situation sketched in ch. 1. Why could the tribes not "drive out" the Canaanites from the Promised Land? God would have remained faithful to His covenant with them (Ex 33:1; Nm 14:23; etc.). However, the Israelites flagrantly violated its terms: they made a "covenant with the inhabitants of this land" (Ex 23:32 f.; 34:12-16; Nm 33:55; Dt 7:2, 5, 16; 12:3; 30:16). Their inability to possess the land was not the result of military inadequacy to overcome the superior fighting power of the Canaanites. God manifested Himself in the form of an angel in order to confront the unfaithful people with the debilitating cause of their failures. (Cf. Gn 16:7 note; 22:11; Ex 3:2; 33:18 notes)

Bochim. This revelation took place at a site to which the Israelites attached a name descriptive of their weeping response to God's indictment. *Bochim,* occuring only here as a place name, remains unidentified. Some manuscripts of the Septuagint read Bethel instead of Bochim in v. 1. For *Gilgal* see Jos 4:20; 5:9; 9:6 notes. The occasion for the assembly of "all the people" (4) at this place is not mentioned.

2:3 *A snare.* Joshua had warned against this danger of coexistence with the Canaanites. (Jos 23:13)

2:6—3:6 Apostasy After Joshua's Death

2:6-10 RISE OF NEW GENERATION

2:7 *Great work.* Israel's failure to "know the Lord" (10) was inexcusable. It was not ignorant of the manifestations of divine mercy through "the signs, the wonders, the mighty hand, and the outstretched arm" (Dt 7:19). It sinned against better knowledge. It deserved "a severe beating."—For God's judgment upon rejection of the ultimate revelation of His grace, *the great work* that He did in Christ Jesus, see Lk 12:47 f.; Heb 10:28-30; 2:2-4.

2:8 *Joshua . . . died.* In a history written in terms of great men, Joshua deserves mention as representing a watershed between two eras of Israel's national life. The report of his death not only closes the book that bears his name but also marks the end of the period when "the people served the Lord" (Jos 24:29, 31 notes). The account of his passing appears again in the Book of Judges in order to introduce the reader to the radical change that was about to take place after his influence waned. The rise of "another generation" that "did not know the Lord" explains why the next period was of such a nature as to require the activity of the judges. For the meaning of "know" see Gn 18:19 note; Ex 1:18.

2:11-15 REPEATED IDOLATRY AND JUDGMENT

2:11 *Did . . . evil.* The remaining verses of this chapter offer a condensed preview of what happened with cyclic regularity during the period of the judges. There is nothing artificial in the programmatic description of the events recorded in the following chapters. Each incident will illustrate how the Lord of history rules the universe according to a consistent pattern of principles. As inevitably as sin "provoked the Lord to anger" and incurred punishment, so surely the cry of repentance found God's mercies "new every morning" (Lm 3:22 f.; Ps 57:10); as persistently as men again "turned back and behaved worse than their fathers," so undeviatingly "the anger of the Lord was kindled against Israel" (19-20). The plot of the Book of Judges is so unimaginatively uniform because man is so monotonously rebellious against God. Reading this rhythmic repetition in the history of Israel cannot be wearisome for anyone who day by day kneels before the throne of grace, acknowledging that "we daily sin much and indeed deserve nothing but punishment." (Luther)

2:13 *Forsook the Lord.* The Biblical designation of sin as folly, particularly often in the Book of Proverbs, is fully justified (19:23 note). How absurdly wicked the Israelites were to worship nonexistent phantoms of their imagination, the personified forces with which the Creator of heaven and earth had endowed nature (Is 40:18-26; 44:9-20)! Modern man is no less foolish. The most ridiculous religious "ism" does not fail to attract hordes of gullible followers.

The Baals and the Ashtaroth. The gods and goddesses of fertility, worshiped throughout the ancient Near East. Baal is a common noun meaning "owner," "lord," "husband." The Canaanites regarded every locality as the possession of such a baal. Hence the term frequently became a proper name of a local deity. His devotees ascribed to him the fructifying power that produced fertility in vegetation, animals, and humans. His female counterpart was "Ashtoreth," which usually, as here, occurs in the plural form "Ashtaroth" (not to be confused with Asherim or Asheroth, Gn 28:18 note; Dt 16:21). The worshipers of these personified forces of nature engaged in degrading rites of prostitution, both male and female. "Sacred" sex acts at the local shrine were supposed to function like sympathetic magic, i.e., put the deities under a spell to produce corresponding results: bountiful crops, enlarged herds, numerous human offspring.

2:15 *Against them.* "The anger of the Lord" is not a harmless, self-exhausting tantrum of a child. In righteous indignation He puts into action His threat to punish the offenders of His holy will. His chosen people too did not escape the dire consequences of their violation of the covenant. "They could no longer withstand their enemies" for the simple reason that God refused to "fight for" them (Jos 23:10 note). Instead of giving them the land, He "sold them into the power of their enemies round about" (14). An owner relinquishes claim to property by selling it. So the Lord renounced His "own possession" (Ex 19:5 note). Ironically He used the very people whose gods the Israelites had worshiped as "the rod of [His] anger" (Is 10:5 ff.).—God still reacts to "all ungodliness and wickedness of men" as He did of old (Ro 1:18 ff.). Apostate Christian nations are liable to punishment by enemies who themselves are as heinously corrupt and inhumane as the heathen Canaanites.

2:16-23 DELIVERANCES BY JUDGES; RELAPSES

2:16 *Saved them.* God's steadfast love is the second basic ingredient in the overall plot of the Book of Judges. "Moved to pity by their groaning" (18), He forgave His people no matter how often they "transgressed my covenant" (20). Again and again He *raised up judges* who "saved them from the hands of their enemies." (18)

2:19 *Turned back.* Israel's repeated lapses into unfaithfulnesss explain why the Book of Judges contains the stories of so many judges. In the spiritual realm, thrust and counterthrust, action and reaction, operate as consistently as in the laws of nature. Wickedness has a gravitational pull that inevitably draws down divine retribution; man's perversity is as rhythmic as the throbs of his fearfully wicked heart; the cry of a penitent sinner reaches God's ear as surely and as often as sound travels on the waves that it sets in motion.

2:21 *I will not.* The Hebrew text has: "also I will not drive out."

2:22 *Test Israel.* God reserved the right to give Israel the Promised Land in His own way. He determined to "clear away" the Canaanites "little by little" rather than in one fell swoop (Ex 23:29-30; Dt 7:22 note). Under Joshua the gradual process of conquest had begun, leaving "very much land to be possessed" (23; Jos 13:1, 6 note). In the second place, God would not automatically supply the power necessary to take possession of the land. He would fight for them only as they by faith drew on the resources of His omnipotence. Brief notes in Joshua and in the first two chapters of Judges record how the full occupation of Canaan was delayed for centuries by Israel's failure to respond to God's promises with the required obedience of faith. By breaking the covenant (2) they had created a situation that God in turn used as a proving ground of their loyalty to Him (Ja 1:13 ff.). They could be bearers of His promises to *their fathers* only on the condition that they stood the test of choosing between Him and the baals of the Canaanites. (3:4; Ex 16:4; Dt 8:1-3, 11-20)

3:1-6 ISRAEL'S SEDUCERS

3:2 *Teach war.* Israel's failure to possess the land not only excluded the people from their inheritance (2:11-23); it also involved them in constant warfare. They had to "learn war" if they were to survive. However, in God's providence this evil too served a good purpose. He let it "test" those who "had no experience of any war" under Joshua's leadership. In their battles with "the nations which the Lord left" they would have opportunity to prove whether they trusted their own military prowess or whether they would let the Lord fight for them. (4)

3:3 *The nations.* The introductory section of Judges closes with an enumeration of the nations that "the Lord left" (1) "for the testing of Israel" (4). Most of them are mentioned in the accounts of Israel's futile attempts to dislodge them (1:4; 21, 26, 29, 34). For Sidonians see Jos 13:6 note; for Philistines, Gn 21:32 note.

3:7—16:31 CORE CONTENT: WHAT THE JUDGES DID TO DELIVER ISRAEL

3:7-11 Othniel and the Mesopotamian King

3:7 *Did evil.* In the prolog (1:1—3:6) the author set the stage on which the judges were to play their role. A skeleton outline of the drama too has been announced in advance (2:11 note). Each scene will have its own leading character(s). However in each instance the plot will be as uniform as Israel's wickedness is monotonously repetitious, as God's judgment on sin follows with inevitable certainty, and as His mercy on penitent sinners remains constant. In keeping with the unvarying pattern of the whole drama, the auther uses stereotype formulas to introduce and develop the various acts (3:12; 4:1; 6:1; 10:6; 13:1). For *the Baals and the Asheroth* see 2:13 note.

3:8 *Cushan-rishathaim.* Compressed into four verses, the account of Othniel, the first deliverer, omits all details. Its brevity poses questions that can no longer be answered with certainty. The name of the oppressor does not appear again in Scripture nor is it known from extra-Biblical sources. *Cushan* may be a proper name or an ethnic designation (Hab 3:7). It is unlikely that he called himself "Rishathaim," i.e., "of double wickedness." Very likely this epithet was attached to him by others to describe his character (cf. such names as Ivan the Terrible and Louis the Insane).

Mesopotamia. Literally "the Aram [Syria] between the two rivers," a general term for the area beyond the northern and eastern border of the Promised Land. (Gn 24:10)

3:9 *Othniel.* The location of his patrimony in the extreme south of the Promised Land (1:11-15; Jos 15:13-19) leaves the reader to wonder how many tribes of "the people of Israel" "served" this oppressor: Did he cut a swath across several tribal territories from the far north down to Judah's inheritance along the Dead Sea? Or did Othniel move up from the south to relieve his northern brethren?

3:10 *Spirit of the Lord.* Othniel and the other judges were not heroic figures like Roland or Siegfried, celebrated in national epics for prowess of personal endowments. Nor could Israel's deliverers put God under obligation to share His power with them by means of narcotic intoxication or ecstatic rites such as those in vogue among the Canaanite worshipers of their deities. Of His free and sovereign will the Lord "raised up" a savior, supplying him with the necessary initiative to undertake his task and the strength to carry it out (6:34; 11:29; 13:25; 14:6, 19; 15:14; 1 Sm 10:10; 11:6; 16:13). The recipients of this special gift of grace or charisma have been called charismatics. For the energizing power of the Spirit see Gn 1:26-28; 2:7.

The Lord gave. The Israelites had been victorious under Moses and Joshua because and when the Lord fought for them (Ex 14:14). The judges were able to save them from their oppressors only as the Lord gave the enemy into their hand.

3:11 *Forty years.* See Introduction, "Chronology." *Othniel* brought temporary relief from temporal ills. He and his successors were merely shadows of Him on whom John saw the Spirit "descend and remain" (1 Jn 1:33 f.; Is 11:1-5); who by bearing the sins of the world "disarmed the principalities and powers" (Cl 2:15); who won the battle for us "against the spiritual hosts of wickedness" (Eph 6:12); who secured for us an eternal rest so that no power can "separate us from the love of God" (Heb 4:9 f.; Ro 8:38 f.); who Himself sends "the Counselor . . . the Spirit of truth" (Jn 15:26; Acts 2). *Othniel . . . died,* but He who "sat down at the right hand of the Majesty on high" "shall reign for ever and ever." (Heb 1:3; Cl 3:1; Rv 11:15)

3:12-30 Ehud and the Moabites

3:12-13 CRIME AND PUNISHMENT

3:12 *Eglon.* The Lord was not at a loss to find heathen nations for scourges on His people when they *again did what was evil.* The territory held by Moab was east of the Dead Sea between the River Arnon and the Brook Zered (Nm 21:10, 24 notes). Both descendants of Lot, the Moabites and Ammonites maintained close relations with each other (Gn 19:36 ff.; Nm 21:24 note; 2 Ch 20:1). The Amalekites, associated with the Edomites, were a nomadic tribe whom the Israelites first encountered soon after their escape from Egypt. (Gn 36:12, 16; Ex 17:8 note; Dt 25:17 f.)

3:13 *City of palms.* Jericho is so called in Dt 34:3 (but see Ju 1:16 note). Crossing the Jordan in the vicinity where Israel entered Canaan, Eglon *took possession* of this well-watered and strategically located site. The account does not say that he rebuilt the city on which Joshua had pronounced a curse. (Jos 6:26)

3:14-30 REPENTANCE AND DELIVERANCE

1) 3:14-23 Eglon's Assassination

3:15 *Ehud.* This *deliverer* was a member of the tribe of Benjamin, whose inheritance lay directly in the path of the invaders (Gn 46:21; Jos 18:11 note). The incidental note that he was *left-handed* (Septuagint: "ambidextrous") is important for the plot of the story (21; see also 20:16 note; 1 Ch 12:2)

3:16 *A sword.* The Hebrew word denotes a cutting or stabbing instrument of various sizes and shapes (Eze 5:1). Ehud's weapon was a daggerlike blade about 13 inches long. The Hebrew word translated "cubit" does not occur elsewhere in the OT. Apparently it measured the distance from elbow to knuckles rather than to fingertips, the span of the ordinary cubit.

3:17 *Presented the tribute.* The location of Eglon's residence is not specified. It may have been west of the Jordan, at Jericho or in its vicinity. It is also possible that he set up his headquarters east of the Jordan while his fighting forces were deployed on the other side. If the latter was the case, Ehud proceeded as follows: from his home in Benjaminite territory, west of the Jordan, he crossed the river, *presented the tribute to Eglon,* and returned to "Gilgal" (19), 3 miles northeast of Jericho. From there he "turned back," recrossing the Jordan, for his private interview with the king. After killing Eglon he escaped across the river back to Gilgal and beyond (26). At this point the Israelites "seized the fords of the Jordan" (28), cutting off the retreat of the Moabite army.

3:19 *Sculptured stones.* A single word in Hebrew, it is usually translated "graven images," the symbols of Canaanite worship which the Israelites were told to destroy (Dt 7:5, 25; 12:3; Is 30:22; 42:8). At Gilgal Joshua had erected unhewn stones as a memorial (Jos 4:6, 20 notes). It is possible that apostate Israelites had engraved them with idolatrous figures. KJV: "quarries," the place where stones were cut or hewn. In any event, a well-known landmark is meant.

3:20 *He arose.* Eglon did not hesitate to grant a private audience to one who appeared to be a loyal tribute-bearing vassal. A worshiper of many gods and anxious to hear "the secret message" *from God,* he rose out of superstitious reverence for the bearer of an oracle (Nm 23:18). Because he "was a very fat man" (17) he had some difficulty in getting on his feet. Ehud had time enough to draw his sword and "thrust it into his belly."

3:22 *The dirt.* The Hebrew word occurs only here. RSV and KJV give it the meaning of excrement. It may denote an opening: the dagger penetrated the entire abdomen and *came out* of the vent.

3:23 *Vestibule.* More elaborate than the ordinary dwelling of that day, *the roof chamber* appears to have consisted of two parts or partitions. An outer chamber—perhaps some kind of reception room—could be closed by a double door from the throne room proper and locked from the inside without a key. The word translated *vestibule* occurs only here. It may denote some aperture or opening of the inner chamber through which Ehud escaped while Eglon's servants were waiting in the anteroom.

2) 3:24-25 Ehud's Escape
3) 3:26-30 Annihilation of Moabites

3:26 *Seirah.* Its location remains unknown. Very likely it was some thickly wooded site on the edge of the Ephraimite highlands.

3:29 *Ten thousand.* See Introduction of the Book of Numbers, "The Numbers in Numbers."

3:30 *Eighty years.* See v. 11 note. Eglon's assassination by Ehud was a gruesome act similar to the treacherous acts of violence by modern partisans of underground movements. However, the question arises whether it was ethically justifiable, perpetrated as it was by a deliverer whom "the Lord raised up" (15). Several factors need to be kept in mind. Eglon's deed is merely made a matter of record. In the account there is no explicit approval of what he did. Furthermore, God achieves His goals—here the survival of the chosen people—through human agents who frequently are anything but morally perfect. Other called servants such as Moses and Aaron at times failed to conform to God's will. Finally, Biblical accounts do not hesitate to ascribe everything that happens to the sovereign will of God, even such things as the hardening of the heart (Ex 4:21 note; see also Dt 2:34; Nm 31:17; 1 Sm 16:14; 1 K 22:23; 2 Th 2:11 f.). Exploits by other judges must be viewed in this perspective. (Jael: 4:17 ff.; Samson: 14—16)

3:31 Shamgar and the Philistines

3:31 *Shamgar.* The brief account of this deliverer omits the information usually furnished in stereotype form: the "evil" that Israel did; the oppression; its duration; the "rest" that followed the deliverance. These details are also lacking in the record of Tola and Jair (10:1-5) and of Ibsan, Elon, Abdon (12:8-15). Hence it has become customary to call these six the minor judges.

Son of Anath. Anath was a Canaanite goddess. Shamgar, a non-Israelitish name, is found frequently in extra-Biblical sources. If by birth he was not a member of the chosen people, he may have thrown in his lot with the Israelites in order to stop the encroachment of the Philistines (for the Philistines see Gn 21:32 note). However, *son of Anath* may also be a reference to his birthplace at Beth-anath. (Jos 19:38; 15:59)

Oxgoad. A staff some 8 to 10 feet long. Provided with a metal tip, it became an improvised spear.

4:1—5:31 Deborah, Barak, and the Canaanites

4:1-3 SIN; OPPRESSION BY JABIN

4:1 *Did evil.* The fourth judgeship is cast in the same formalistic cycle of sin, judgment, repentance, deliverance (3:7 note). However, within this general framework there are several features unique to this episode: (a) not men but women hold the center of the stage; (b) Deborah dispensed divine justice in Israel's dispute with a foreign foe, but, unlike most judges, she also rendered decisions in internal litigations; (c) the decisive action took place at the northern limits of the Promised Land; (d) tribal cooperation was more general than in other conflicts; (e) victory was commemorated in a poem charged with emotion.

4:2 *Jabin.* See Jos 11:1, 11 notes. He is called *king of Canaan* (also v. 24). Already before its destruction by Joshua, Hazor "was the head of all those kingdoms" (Jos 11:10). Reoccupied by Canaanites, this strategically situated city again became the center of a coalition of neighboring city-states.

Sisera. If he was a Hittite, as his name seems to indicate, he was a survivor of the Hittites who had combined forces with other peoples at the time of Joshua. Evidently he was the ruler of one of the city-states allied with Jabin. He *dwelt* (perhaps better translated: "occupied the seat of authority" *in Harosheth-ha-goiim,* i.e., Harosheth of the gentiles. Tentative identification of this city places it some 30 miles southwest of Hazor, either near Megiddo or in the vicinity of Mt. Carmel. For the extent of the first coalition under the king of Hazor see Jos 11:1-5.

4:3 *Chariots.* For some unstated reason Jabin put his federated army under the command of Sisera (7). The defeat of the allied forces under this commander in chief was the decisive factor in Israel's liberation. For this reason not Jabin but Sisera plays a prominent role in the subsequent account as well as in Deborah's victory song. Humanly speaking Israel's foot soldiers were no match for his vast array of war chariots—comparable to tanks in modern warfare. This disparity in military strength is mentioned in order to drive home two basic lessons of the Book of Judges: (a) "with God all things are possible" (Mt 19:26; Acts 26:8; Ps 20:7 f.); (b) divine omnipotence can be tapped by a faith such as Deborah's "That, when in danger, knows no fear, In darkness feels no doubt."

4:4-24 LIBERATION BY DEBORAH AND BARAK

1) 4:4-11 Mobilization

4:4 *Deborah.* The Hebrew word for "bee" (cf. Melissa, a Greek word with the same meaning). The Spirit of the Lord enabled her to proclaim God's decisions in lawsuits when "the people came up to her for judgment" (5).. Divinely inspired, she pronounced God's verdict also on Israel's enemies. In her career she resembled Samuel, "the last of the judges," who likewise "judged Israel" and, though not a military leader, invoked God's vindicating justice on the Philistines (1 Sm 7:5-13). In God's economy of revelation other women were chosen to be vehicles of divine revelation: Miriam (Ex 15:20); Huldah (2 K 22:14); Anna. (Lk 2:36)

4:6 *Barak.* The name of Deborah's military leader occurs frequently as a common noun meaning "lightning." Her messengers traveled some 50 miles to communicate with him: from "Ramah and Bethel," a short distance north of Jerusalem, to *Kedesh in Naphtali,* a few miles north of Hazor. No doubt Barak's *tribe of Naphtali and the* neighboring *tribe of Zebulun,* which bore the full brunt of Jabin's oppression, played a decisive role in an opening skirmish with the enemy. Apparently they were joined by neighboring tribes after an initial blow for freedom had been struck at *Mount Tabor* (14). This mountain, south of Hazor, had a pivotal position in relation to territories occupied by the three tribes Zebulun, Issachar, and Naphtali. (Cf. 5:14; Jos 19:10, 17, 24 notes)

4:7 *Kishon.* This river flows in a northwesterly direction, draining the fertile valley of Esdraelon or Jezreel and emptying into the Mediterranean north of the Carmel ridge. Along its southern bank lay such cities as Megiddo and Taanach (5:19). Rains turned the "brook Kishon" (1 K 18:40) into a raging torrent. Overflowing its bed, it inundated wide areas of lowlands where Sisera's chariotry was deployed. In the marshy soil the war wagons bogged down when "the heavens dropped, yea, the clouds dropped water." (5:4)

4:8 *Not go.* At first this hero of faith (Heb 11:32) was reluctant to undertake what appeared to be a suicidal mission without the reassuring presence of the prophetess. For similar hesitation on the part of other men of God see Ex 4:13; Ju 6:15; Jer 1:6.

4:9 *Go with you.* Deborah's promise to go with him gave Barak the courage to lead the attack against an apparently invincible foe. However, because of his initial dallying the *glory* of the victory would not be his alone. Sisera, the grand prize of war, would fall *into the hands of a woman,* namely Jael (17-22). The *woman* may also refer to Deborah herself because she initiated and directed the entire campaign of liberation.

4:11 *Heber.* This verse furnishes the final detail of the setting. It explains how Heber's wife Jael came to take part so *far away* from the hereditary Kenite territory in southern Judah (1:16 note). *Za-anannim* was a border city of Naphtali. (Jos 19:33)

2) 4:12-16 Jabin's Army Defeated

4:15 *The Lord routed.* This terse statement does not explain how the Lord "threw them into a panic," the RSV rendering of the same Hebrew verb in Jos 10:10. Deborah's victory song supplies the answer. In highly figurative language it ascribes the rout to a severe thunder storm (5:4 f., 20 f.). Mired down in the flooded terrain, the chariotry was thrown into an uncontrollable confusion.

3) 4:17-22 Jabin's General Slain

4:17 *Fled away.* Sisera deserted his panic-stricken army, which fled northwestward down the Esdraelon valley. In a calculated attempt to elude his pursuers he turned northeastward, no doubt hoping to find refuge ultimately in Hazor. On his way he passed through Kenite settlements (11). So it was that he come *to the tent of Jael.*

4:18 *Rug.* KJV: "mantle." The exact meaning of the Hebrew word, occurring only here, has not definitely been established. Other possible meanings: "a curtain," used to separate areas within the tent; a material woven like a "net" which protected the sleeper from flies and insects.

4:19 *A skin of milk.* KJV: "bottle." A container made of the skins of goats or sheep.

4:21 *A hammer.* It was a woman's task to pitch the tent. Hence Jael was adept at wielding the wooden mallet with which she had driven the *tent peg* into the ground.

4:22 *Dead.* Jael's deed, gruesome and treacherous as it was, is merely reported as a matter of record. In the song of Deborah she is called "most blessed of women" (5:24). For the ethical issues involved see the note on Ehud. (3:30)

4) 4:23-24 Jabin's Power Ended

4:24 *Bore harder and harder.* Catastrophic though it was, more than the defeat of Sisera, Jabin's general, was necessary to free Israel completely from domination by the *king of Canaan.* The brief statement of this verse implies that the Israelites had to engage in a protracted struggle before they *destroyed Jabin.* Furthermore the phrase *the people of Israel* suggests that it was a concerted effort by a number of tribes. (6 note)

5:1-31 DEBORAH'S VICTORY SONG

1) 5:1-3 Motif: Bless the Lord

5:1 *Sang Deborah and Barak.* This outburst of exuberant thanksgiving for Israel's deliverance is a poetic masterpiece. It throbs with genuine emotion; it is studded with daring figures of speech; its short, abrupt sentences create a highly dramatic effect; its archaic language and imagery is in keeping with its spontaneous fervor. Such superb qualities suggest that it was composed by Deborah. Barak joined her in singing it just as "Moses and the people" sang his hymn of praise (Ex 15:1). It may have been preserved in such anthologies of war songs as "the Book of Jashar" (Jos 10:13 note) or "the Book of the Wars of the Lord" (Nm 21:14 note). The text in its present form is at times difficult to translate. Apparently later copyists no longer understood some of its ancient terms and expressions. (Cf. RSV notes)

5:2 *Bless the Lord.* The first lines of the poem state its theme. It is a call to praise "the Lord, the God of Israel" (3), who by omnipotence (4 f.) raised Israel from the depths of humiliation (6-9). The "triumphs of the Lord" (10 f.) were achieved when the people rallied to Deborah's and Barak's call for action against the oppressor even though some tribes failed to cooperate (12-18; 22 f.). "The kings of Canaan" were swept away by the power of the Ruler of the universe (19-21). Their commander suffered an ignominious death at the hands of a woman (24-27) while his mother waited in vain for his return (28-30). The Lord's victory demonstrated the futility of all opposition to His sovereign will. (31)

2) 5:4-5 God's Power

5:4 *From Seir.* Couched in poetic language, vv. 4 and 5 recall previous demonstrations of the Lord's power: at Sinai and during Israel's wandering in the wilderness. (Dt 33:1, 2 notes; Ps 68:7-9)

3) 5:6-9 Israel's Degradation

5:6 *Shamgar.* Cf. 3:31 note.

5:7 *You arose.* Here and in 12 Deborah is addressed. This fact need not rule out her authorship of the poem. In ancient literature writers at times refer to themselves in this way.

5:8 *New gods.* Disarmed and cowed by the enemy, farmers and merchants feared to venture forth. This humiliation was God's judgment on Israel's acceptance of "other gods besides" the Lord. (Dt 32:17 note; Ju 2:11, 19 notes)

Forty thousand. Cf. Jos 4:13 note.

4) 5:10-11 The Lord's Triumphs

5:10 *Tawny asses.* The nobles and the wealthy who could afford to ride on light-colored animals, saddled with *rich carpets* (10:4 note; 12:14), as well as the less favored *who walk* were to assemble at "the gates" and "repeat," i.e., to sing responsively, their song of thanksgiving.

5:11 *Triumphs.* More literally "righteousnesses" or "acts of righteousness"; other translations of the same Hebrew word in the RSV are: "saving deeds" or "saving acts" (1 Sm 12:7; Is 45:24; Mi 6:5); "righteous acts" (Dn 9:16); "vindication" (Ps 103:6). Through human judges the Judge of heaven and earth restored to His penitent covenant people the right to serve the purpose for which they had been chosen: to bless all nations. (Gn 12:3 note)

5) 5:12-18 Tribal Response

5:13 *The people . . marched.* Deborah and Barak, stirred to action by God's call, were able to arouse at least six tribes to a common venture of faith against apparently insurmountable odds.

5:14 *Machir.* The Machirites, descendants of Manasseh, occupied territory on both sides of the Jordan. (Gn 50:23; Jos 13:31; 17:1-3, 7-9)

5:15 *Searchings of heart. The clans of Reuben* and other tribes are rebuked with biting sarcasm for their failure to discharge their covenant obligations to their embattled brethren.

6) 5:19-23 Futile Opposition to God's Power

5:19 *Taanach . . . Megiddo.* Cf. 4:7 note.

5:20 *From heaven.* How futile it was for "the kings of Canaan" to "rely on horses" and to "trust in chariots" (Is 31:1-3)! The Lord who put *the stars* in *their courses* commandeered the forces of nature, sweeping away the puny might of proud men. Israel's ancient neighbors worshiped the heavenly bodies rather than their Creator. Modern astrologers, who cast horoscopes, have not advanced beyond this primitive idolatry.

5:23 *Meroz.* Tentatively identified with a site about 7 miles south of "Kedesh in Naphtali," Barak's home. A curse was invoked on *its inhabitants,* no doubt because their craven refusal to join their own fellow tribesmen was more resprehensible than the quiet of the other uncooperative tribes. (15-17)

Help of the Lord. This phrase may have the meaning: *help* provided by the intervention *of the Lord.* It may also be a bold way of saying that the Lord had deigned to enlist their aid in order to achieve His purpose. (1 Co 3:9; 2 Co 6:1)

7) 5:24-27 Sisera, Victim of Jael's Guile

5:24 *Most blessed.* For this commendation of her deed see 3:30 note.

8) 5:28-30 Sisera's Mother's Premonition

5:28 *Mother of Sisera.* In the closing verses (28-30) the scene suddenly shifts to the home of the assassinated general. Here his mother's ladies-in-waiting try to soothe her misgiving about his delay in returning. The pathos of the situation is heightened by the fact that they were raising false hopes.

9) 5:31 Jubilant Conclusion

5:31 *Thine enemies.* The epilog of the poem states a universal truth. In God's direction of history, Sisera's defeat is only an example of His determination to "break and hinder every evil counsel and will which would not let . . . His kingdom come" (Luther; Ps 68:2 f.; 82:8; 92:7 f.). Eventually He will destroy "every rule and every authority and power" and "put all things in subjection under" the feet of His crucified and risen Son. (1 Co 15:24-28)

6:1—9:57 Gideon and the Midianites

6:1—8:35 LIBERATION FROM INVADERS

1) 6:1-6 Midianite Exploitation

6:1 *Evil.* The story of the fourth major judge, introduced, developed, and concluded within the general framework of cause and effect established in 2:11-19 (cf. 3:7; 4:1 notes), has its own characteristic features: (a) it is longer than the account of any other judge; (b) an entire chapter records events after the death of Gideon; (c) internal strife and tribal disunity play a part unequalled at any other time; (d) no hero, with the exception of Samson, succumbs to human weakness as often as Gideon.

6:2 *Midian.* God's scourge on "evil" doing Israel was a series of annual raids by seminomadic peoples that crossed the Jordan from the East. For "Midianites" see Ex 2:15 note; for "Amalekites" 3:12 note; Ex 17:8 note; Dt 25:17. "The people of the East" (3) is a general term for various desert tribes.

6:4 *Gaza.* The tribes "brought low" were principally Manasseh and its northern neighbors Asher, Naphtali, Zebulun (35; 8:1). However on their swift "camels" (Gn 24:10 note) the marauders made raids as far as Gaza, the southernmost Philistine city on the Mediterranean coast. (1:18 note)

2) 6:7-10 Call to Repentance

6:7 *Prophet.* In words similar to those of "the angel of the Lord" (2:1-5), an unnamed human spokesman of God exposed the enormity of Israel's "evil." Contrary to an explicit prohibition, the ungrateful nation paid "reverence to the gods of the Amorites" or Canaanites. (1:34 second note; Nm 21:21 note)

3) 6:11-24 Call of Gideon

6:11 *Angel of the Lord.* Cf. 2:1 note. God initiated Israel's liberation by: (1) overcoming the reluctance (11-18) and the fears (19-24) of the selected leader; (b) enlisting support against the common enemy from Gideon's tribe (25-32) and from the neighboring tribes (33-35); (c) granting signs to Gideon in order to remove any lingering doubts of success. (36-40)

Abiezrite. Gideon was a member of a "clan" (15) in the tribe of Manasseh whose allotted territory was west of the Jordan (Jos 17:2). His home town *Ophrah* has not been identified with certainty.

6:12 *Mighty man of valor.* "The least" in his "family," which in turn was the "meekest" in the tribe of Manasseh, Gideon did not consider himself qualified to "deliver Israel," cast off by the Lord and helplessly in the grip of "the hand of Midian." "Greatly troubled at the saying," he asked: "How shall this be?" (Lk 1:29, 34). In his case, as so often in Israel's history (and in the history of the church), "God chose what is weak" "so that no human being might boast in the presence of God" (1 Co 1:27, 29). (For similar evasive answers to God's call see Ex 3:11 note; Jer 1:6)

6:14 *The Lord.* The Creator of the angels appeared in the form of His creatures. (Cf. vv. 22 f.; Gn 16:7; Ex 3:2 note)

6:16 *With you.* Procrastinating Moses received the same promise (Ex 3:12). Weak Gideon too was assured that he could draw on the Lord for the courage and strength to *smite the Midianites as one man,* i.e., as if the enemy, "like locusts for number" (5), were a single individual cut down by one blow.—The incarnate "God with us," the Immanuel, promised His abiding presence to those who accept His victory over sin, death, and devil. (Mt 28:19, 20)

6:17 *A sign.* God granted Gideon's request for proof that the strange visitor and His perplexing message were not the hallucinations of his fevered mind. For other examples of divine patience in similar situations see Gn 17:17-20; Ex 3:2; 4:1-9; 33:18; Lk 1:18-20.—"The carpenter's Son" too did "signs" "that you may believe that Jesus is the Christ" (Jn 20:31). For His refusal to do a miracle see Mt 12:38 f.

6:18 *My present.* Translated "tribute" in 3:15, the Hebrew word is used more commonly to denote gifts brought to the Lord in the form of sacrificial offerings. (Cf. Lev 2:1 note; Ju 13:19, 23)

6:22 *Alas, O Lord God.* Convinced by the miraculous burning of the offering and the sudden disappearance of his visitor that he had *seen the angel of the Lord,* Gideon feared that he had been exposed to the consuming glory of God. (Gn 32:30 note; Ex 33:18 note; Ju 13:22; Is 6:5)

6:24 *Peace.* No longer in the visible form of an angel, the Lord assured Gideon that He had not come to destroy but rather to bring all the blessings capsuled in the Biblical word "peace." For its wide range of meanings see Nm 6:26 note.

4) 6:25-35 Enlistment of Popular Support

6:25 *Altar of Baal.* In order to gain a following in his own clan, he exposed the impotence of the idols of Canaan, as Boniface proved to the heathen Teutons that their sacred oak was only a piece of wood. He pulled *down the altar of* the local *Baal, cut down the Asherah* (3:7 note), and then on an "altar to the Lord" sacrificed his father's bull, which apparently had been reserved for *seven years* for a special offering to the Baal. Why the animal is called *the second* is not clear.

6:32 *Jerubbaal.* Gideon means "the one who sits down." The exact etymological meaning of *Jerubbaal* is: "let Baal grant increase." By a play of words on the verb involved, the challenger of Baal's power came to be called: "let Baal contend," i.e., in defense of his claim.

6:33 *Valley of Jezreel. Crossing the Jordan* from the east, as they had done for "seven years" (1), the invading hordes swept into the fertile valley which slopes southeastward from the city of Jezreel to its junction with the Jordan valley at Bethshean.

6:34 *Took possession.* Lit. "clothed himself with," a figurative expression for which there is no idiomatic equivalent in English (see RSV note at 2 Ch 24:20). As a garment serves its wearer, so Gideon was equipped by the Spirit for the great things for which God had called him (3:10 note). Jesus promised the disciples that they would be "clothed with power from on high." (Lk 24:49)

6:35 *Sent messengers.* Gideon's own tribe, Manasseh, and three tribes north and northeast of Jezreel answered the call to arms. For some reason Issachar, the direct target of the Midianite invasion, is not mentioned.

5) 6:36-40 Signs to Reassure Gideon

6:37 *Shall know.* Gideon was not a hero in his own strength. Nor did endowment with the Spirit turn him into an unthinking automaton. As the hour of decision drew near, his faith was less than heroic. He requested two more signs to "make trial" of God's promise to *deliver Israel by my hand.* (Cf. 17 note; Ps 103:14)

6) 7:1—8:3 Defeat of Midianite Army

7:1 *Encamped.* Chs. 7—8 present the climactic action for which ch. 6 set the stage. The Israelites defeated the Midianites in their entrenched position (7:1—8:3), pursued them eastward across the Jordan, intercepted and destroyed the fleeing enemy at the fords of the river (8:4-21). God granted Israel victory in such a way as to impress on the people and their leader that they could not ascribe their liberation to their own strength. Their army, already outnumbered by the enemy, was reduced to 300 men lest "Israel vaunt themselves" that they were delivered by their "own hand" (7:2-8). At the zero hour of attack God again provided a way to bolster their leader's sagging confidence (7:9-14). Bearing neither offensive nor defensive weapons of war, the small task force was able to rout the enemy because "the Lord set every man's sword against his fellow" Midianite. (7:15-25)

Tribal jealousy and cowardice marred the victory. Ephraim sulked with hurt pride (7:24—8:3). Fearful of reprisals by the enemy, two cities east of the Jordan refused provisions to Gideon's men as they pursued the fleeing Midianites. (8:4-21)

In the end the Israelites failed to acknowledge that they owed their deliverance solely to God. Seeking security in a man, they wanted to make Gideon their king. Although the latter refused to assume the role of rulership that belonged to God, he became the cause of a new outbreak of idolatry in Israel. (8:22-35)

Harod. The opposing armies were barely 5 miles apart. The Israelites were *encamped beside the spring of Harod* at the foot of Mt. Gilboa; the enemy camp was *north of them* across the valley of Jezreel. *The hill of Moreh* was south of Mt. Tabor.

7:3 *Fearful and trembling.* Two thirds of the men took advantage of the exemption from the draft, based on Dt 20:8.

Return home. As the RSV note indicates, the Hebrew text reads "from Mt. Gilead," located far from the battlefield on the eastern side of the Jordan. "Gilead" may be a textual corruption for "Mt. Gilboa." However, to "depart from Mt. Gilead" may have been an idiomatic way of saying: let him hie himself from the place where the action is.

Twenty-two thousand. The Hebrew word translated *thousand* also has the meaning of clan, as in 6:15. (See Introduction to the Book of Numbers, "The Numbers . . .")

7:5 *Laps.* The vast majority knelt *down to drink* directly from the water. Only 300 dipped handfuls of water from the stream, apparently remaining on their feet. *As a dog laps* with his tongue, so they repeatedly brought small quantities of water to their mouths with their hands. In this way they proved that they would remain on the alert under all circumstances.

7:8 *Jars.* The Hebrew word for provisions (KJV: "victuals") here must denote the earthen vessel in which they were carried. Before Gideon dismissed *the people,* he asked them to equip the 300 men with *the* empty *jars* (16) and the *trumpets,* both of which were to be used in the charge against the enemy.

7:13 *Dream.* God used an enemy soldier's dream to give Gideon a final assurance of victory. According to the interpretation by the Midianite's comrade, the demolishing *cake of barley* represented the Israelites, whose grain the nomadic marauder, who lived in a "tent," had been carrying off.

7:16 *Trumpets.* The *trumpets,* made of the horns of animals, were fastened to their person, leaving their hands free to hold the inverted *jars* over the *torches.* At a prearranged signal they removed the jars, letting the light of the torches suddenly burst upon the darkness. With their right hand they could then raise the trumpets to their mouths. The blast from the instruments was interspersed with the shout: "For [the restoral of the reign of] the Lord and for [His chosen instrument] Gideon."

7:19 *Middle watch.* Sentries were posted at 4-hour intervals. The second detachment came on duty at about 10 p.m.

7:22 *The army fled.* The Lord never is at a loss for means to grant victory to those who act "through faith" (Heb 11:32). The surviving Midianites tried to escape by retracing their steps southeastward down the valley of Jezreel and toward the Jordan. Without any semblance of military order some fugitives stampeded across the river, reaching the cities mentioned here. They were pursued by members of the three tribes from which Gideon had selected his 300 men (23). Farther south the Ephraimites intercepted other remnants by seizing the western tributaries and the fords of the Jordan "as far as Beth-barah," an unidentified site. (24)

7:24 *Oreb and Zeeb.* The names of the Midianite princes *Oreb* (Raven) and *Zeeb* (Wolf) became attached to the place where each was slain. (Ps 83:11; Is 10:26; cf. the name of Starved Rock for the site in northern Illinois where many Indians starved to death)

8:1 *Done to us.* Perhaps fearful of a rebuff, Gideon had not included the powerful and proud tribe of Ephraim in his original call to arms (6:35). Rather than to let jealousy lead to serious dissension he gave a self-effacing answer when *they upbraided him violently* for having slighted them (Pr 15:1). For Jephthah's treatment of a similar complaint by the same tribe see 12:1-6. Apparently the pacification of the Ephraimites took place after Gideon had crossed the Jordon in hot pursuit of the enemy, who was fleeing southward in Transjordan (4-12). At any rate, Gideon was "beyond the Jordan" when the Ephraimites "brought the heads of Oreb and Zeeb" to him. (7:25)

7) 8:4-21 Pursuit Beyond Jordan

8:5 *Succoth.* Located along the Jabbok, some 50 miles from the original battlefield in Jezreel, this city and nearby Penuel (8; Gn 32:26, 30, 31 notes) doubted Gideon's ability to inflict a permanent defeat on the enemy. Fearful lest the recuperated Midianites return to avenge their cooperation with the Israelites, the men of Penuel and Succoth refused to *give loaves of bread to* Gideon and his men, who were *faint* yet *pursuing.* (4)

8:7 *Flail.* Gideon threatened to "thresh" them. The punishment was to resemble, or actually to be, a threshing operation. Grain was beaten out with a *flail* or trodden out by oxen or loosened from its stalks by driving threshing sledges over it. (6:11; Dt 25:4; Am 1:3)

8:10 *Karkor.* Gideon pursued the Midianites into their own haunts. Following "the caravan route east of Nobah [unidentified] and Jogbehah" (15 miles southeast of Penuel), he overtook them at *Karkor,* many miles east of the Dead Sea.

8:13 *Heres.* Gideon returned to execute his threats against Succoth and Penuel by an *ascent* that is mentioned only here and remains unidentified.

8:14 *Wrote.* The fact that a nondescript youth, caught at random, recorded the names of 77 men testifies to widespread ability to write.

8:21 *Slew.* Gideon avenged the death of his brothers apparently after his return to his home town of Ophrah. The account does not specify when or how the two Midianite kings had slain them.

8) 8:22-28 Gideon's Refusal of Kingship; His Offense

8:22 *Rule. The men of Israel* did not "return and give praise to God" (Lk 17:18) for their miraculous deliverance *out of the hand of Midian.* Gideon refused the proffered kingship; its acceptance would have abetted the ungrateful people in giving him credit for their victory rather than to the Lord (1 Sm 8:6). The OT is the record that "the Lord will rule over" Israel (23) so that eventually the thorn-crowned "King of the Jews" might establish His eternal kingdom by His victory over mankind's spiritual enemies. (Ph 2:5-11; Mt 25:31 f.; 26:64)

8:24 *Ishmaelites.* This designation is used in a general way to denote the nomadic way of life of these "people of the East" (6:1-3), just as we speak of people as being gypsies. Ethnically the Midianites were descendants of Abraham and Keturah (Gn 25:2); the Ishmaelites, of Hagar. (Gn 16:15)

8:27 *Ephod.* The ephod of the high priest was a garment of precious cloth to which was attached a "breastpiece of judgment," the receptacle of "the Urim and the Thummim" (Ex 28:6, 15 notes; Lv 8:8). Gideon's replica of this sacred vestment apparently was made in the form of a statue since he *put it* (literally "made it to stand") *in his city.* Perhaps he intended it to be a memorial. However, by this unauthorized representation of God's presence he led all Israel astray as Aaron had done. (Ex 32:4)

8:28 *Forty years.* Cf. 3:11 note.

9) 8:29-32 Gideon's Death

8:29 *His own house.* Gideon returned to private life.

8:30 *Many wives.* Cf. Gn 16:2 note.

10) 8:33-35 Israel's Reversion to Apostasy

8:33 *The Baals.* From playing *the harlot after* Gideon's ephod it was but a short step to worship the Canaanite fertility idols. The local representative of this cult was called *Baal-berith,* i.e., the baal of the covenant. His name seems to commemorate a treaty between the Canaanites and the Israelites, a departure from the rule not to "make a covenant with the inhabitants of the land." (Ex 34:12)

9:1-57 CIVIL WAR UNDER GIDEON'S SON

1) 9:1-6 Abimelech's Coup d'Etat

9:1 *Son of Jerubbaal.* The dreary sequel to Gideon's judgeship grew out of circumstances for which he largely was responsible. His ephod paved the way for out-and-out apostasy (8:27, 33); his polygamous marriages sowed the seed of civil war (ch. 9). People who had repudiated their covenant with the Lord would not hesitate to commit crimes against their fellow signatories to that covenant.

Abimelech. "The Spirit of the Lord took

possession of Gideon" (6:34); his son by a Shechemite concubine was victimized by the demon of unscrupulous ambition. In his lust for power he massacred his 70 half-brothers in cold blood (1-6). Jotham, the only survivor, exposed the assassin's true character by means of a fable (7-21). Abimelech succeeded in putting down a counterrevolution, fomented by his own clansmen in Shechem (22-49). However, during the siege of another rebel city he was mortally wounded by a millstone which a woman dropped on him from the wall (50-57). His bloody kingship was, as Jotham had predicted, a bramble fire of short duration. It belied the meaning of his name: "my father is king" or "father of a king."

Shechem. A concubine continued to live with her family (cf. Samson's relations with Philistine women (15:1; 16:4). Hence the Shechemites were readily persuaded to accept their "brother's" proposal to rule over them. For previous events at Shechem see Gn 12:6 f.; 33:18 ff.; 37:13 f.; Jos 8:30-35.

9:5 *Upon one stone.* Like so many animals, slaughtered on a single altar, Gideon's sons were butchered *upon one stone.*

9:6 *Beth-millo.* Literally "the house of filling-in," i.e., a fortified city. Either within or outside its protective walls, the Shechemites had built a "stronghold" or citadel, called "the Tower of Shechem." (46)

2) 9:7-21 Abimelech, the Bramble King

9:7 *Mount Gerizim.* Perched safely in a crag of the mount, Jotham shouted his message to the people below.

9:8 *Trees.* Jotham composed a fable in order to expose the folly of the Shechemites' choice of Abimelech as their king. They acted like trees, he said, which could not get such useful members of the plant family to accept rulership over them as *the olive tree,* "the fig-tree," "the vine," but chose an obnoxious "bramble." Abimelech's promise of a beneficial rule was as ironical as a bramble's boast to provide "shade" under its sparse, thorny branches. Its unfruitful thorns were nothing but a fire hazard. Easily kindled, its flames could "devour" even the noble "cedars of Lebanon." For another example of a fable see 2 K 14:8 ff.

9:9 *Gods.* KJV: "God." The Hebrew noun in the plural form denotes both the true God (Gn 1:26 note) and idols (5:8; 6:10; 10:14). While it is true that oil and wine (13) were used in Israel's worship ritual (Ex 30:25 note; Lv 2:1; Ex 29:40; Nm 15:4 note) Jotham was addressing people who "played the harlot after the Baals" (8:33) and likewise used oil and wine to honor their gods.

9:16 *If you acted.* Jotham did not have to interpret his fable. Its meaning was so evident that he could apply it at once to his distant audience. The future would soon prove, he warned, that he had spoken the truth. (Cf. 56 f.)

3) 9:22-57 Abimelech's Ignominious Death

9:22 *Ruled over.* The verb used is not the usual word to denote the reign of a king. A more adequate translation would be: "he lorded it over Israel," i.e., that part of Israel which submitted to his domination.

9:23 *Evil spirit.* Scripture does not hesitate to trace all events to their ultimate source in God's sovereign will. (Cf. Dt 2:34 note; Ex 4:21; Nm 31:2)

9:25 *Robbed.* Shechem controlled important caravan routes. Abimelech levied toll taxes on the merchants that traveled them. However, the very man who put him into power treacherously deprived him of this source of revenue.

9:26 *Gaal.* The fickle Shechemites *put confidence* in a new demagog, unknown except for his attempt to depose Abimelech.

9:27 *Men of Hamor.* At the festivities of grape harvest, Gaal harangued the Shechemites to repudiate Abimelech and *Zebul,* his deputized governor. He reminded them of their hereditary independence as descendants of *Hamor,* the father of ancestral Shechem (Gn 34: 2, 6). The *son of Jerubbaal,* he implied, should be doing their bidding rather than be lording it over them. The address *men of Hamor* (men of an ass) may also refer to a treaty which the Canaanite inhabitants had ratified by the sacrifice of an ass. (Cf. 8:33 note)

9:31 *At Arumah.* KJV: "privily." Because Abimelech "dwelt at Arumah" (41), RSV changed the reading "with *tormah,*" i.e., "by means of deception," to indicate the destination of the messengers rather than the survey of their mission. The change appears unnecessary. At this stage of the revolt Abimelech's governor had not been deposed. However, the populace was aroused to the point where he did not dare to act openly if his message was to reach Abimelech.

9:36 *Shadow.* At first Zebul tried to convince Gaal that Abimelech's men *coming down from the mountain tops* were merely *the shadow of the mountains.* When they came into full view, he resorted to another stratagem. Shrewdly challenging Gaal to "go out now and fight" (38), he forced him to make good his boast (29) if he did not want to lose face with the people. Gaal's hastily assembled army suffered a crushing defeat. (39 f.)

9:37 *Diviner's Oak.* Cf. Gn 12:6 note; see also v. 6.

9:41 *Arumah.* An unidentified site.

9:42 *Went out.* After the expulsion of "Gaal and his kinsmen" (41), the Shechemites apparently assumed that they could resume their usual farming activities. However, in another surprise attack Abimelech cut down the unsuspecting citizens in the field, "took the city, and killed the people that were in it." (42-45)

9:45 *Sowed it with salt.* Salt makes land sterile and unproductive. To sow a city with salt means that it was reduced to barren waste. It was so thoroughly destroyed that it was like "an uninhabited salt land." (Jer 17:6)

9:46 *Tower of Shechem.* If this stronghold was a part of Shechem's fortification rather than a citadel beyond its walls, the following verses take up v. 45, giving further details how Abimelech "took the city, and killed the people."

El-berith. "God of the covenant," an equivalent for Baal-berith. (8:33 note)

9:48 *Mount Zalmon.* "Mount of shade or darkness," evidently so named because of its dense cover of trees. It has not been identified with certainty.

9:50 *Thebez.* No doubt this city, about 13 miles north of Shechem, had joined the revolt against Abimelech. After he "took the city," "a strong tower within" it still offered resistance. His attempt to "burn it with fire," as he had done to Shechem (46-49), proved to be Abimelech's undoing.

9:53 *Millstone.* In milling grain into flour, a circular stone, 2 or 3 inches thick and about 18 inches in diameter was revolved on another rock slab under it. "Grinding at the mill" was a woman's task. (Mt 24:41; Ex 11:5)

9:54 *Draw.* A man of war considered it a disgrace to suffer death at the hands of a woman or of someone who "was still a youth." (8:20)

10:1-2 Tola

10:1 *Deliver Israel.* At an unspecified time *after Abimelech,* Tola, the second so-called minor judge (3:31 note), "saved" the Israelites "out of the power of those who plundered them" (2:16). The record omits all details, even the identity of the oppressor. The purpose of the Book of Judges is not to glorify man; it bears witness to the fact that God's "power is made perfect in weakness" (2 Co 12:9). What the judges accomplished, whether reported at length or in barest outline, served the plan of the Lord of history to bring salvation to all nations.

Shamir. Tola *lived* in an unidentifiable city in *Ephraim* even though his name appears in the ancestry of the tribe of Issacher (Gn 46:13; Nm 26:23). The verb translated *lived* at times has the meaning of "sit" in the sense of occupying the seat of authority.

10:3-5 Jair

10:3 *Judged Israel.* The account does not specify how Jair as well as the remaining three minor judges (12:8-14) discharged the function of a judge. No foreign oppressor is mentioned on whom they executed judgment. However, the brevity of the record does not preclude the conclusion that they too were the instruments of divine justice in maintaining the chosen people's right to the Promised Land. It is quite possible that they also were judicial arbiters in internal disputes, a function explicitly ascribed to Deborah (4:5) and Samuel. (1 Sm 7:15-17)

10:4 *Thirty sons.* In the exercise of his judgeship, Jair let 30 sons, hardly all the offspring of one wife, administer 30 cities. Riding on *asses* marked them as men of distinction and wealth. (5:10 note; 12:14)

Havvoth-jair. Lit. "the tent-villages of Jair." Located east of the Jordan and south of the Sea of Galilee, these villages were so named when they were taken by Jair's namesake, the son of Manasseh (Nm 32:41). "Kamon," Jair's burial place, was in the same area.

10:6—12:7 Jephthah and the Ammonites

10:6—11:40 DELIVERER FROM FOREIGN OPPRESSION

1) 10:6-9 Ammonite Invasion

10:7 *Philistines and . . . Ammonites.* The next episode in Israel's history again has the three elements that constitute the framework of the stories of the judges: (a) Israel did "what was evil," serving "Baals and Ashtaroth" (6; see 3:17 note; 2:13 notes); (b) *the anger of the Lord was kindled* and *he sold them into the hand of* oppressors (cf. 3:8 note; 4:2; 6:1); (c) when the people repented of their sins (10), "the Spirit of the Lord came upon" a deliverer. (11:29; cf. 3:10 note)

However, at this time God's scourge upon apostate Israel came from opposite directions: the *Philistines* from the west and southwest and the *Ammonites* from the east across the Jordan. Jephthah rescued Israel from eastern invaders; Samson, perhaps at the same time, dealt with the Philistines.

10:8 *Land of the Amorites.* The Transjordan territory between the Arnon and Jabbok rivers. (Nm 21:21, 24 notes)

2) 10:10-16 Israel's Repentance

10:11-12 *Deliver you.* Israel's guilt was compounded. It deserved to "receive a severe beating" as a "servant who knew his master's will" (Lk 12:47 f.) and His repeated past acts of deliverance from such enemies as (a) *the Egyptians* at the time of the Exodus; (b) *the Amorites* under Sihon (Nm 21:21 ff.); (c) *the Ammonites* at the time of Ehud (3:12 ff.); (d) *the Philistines* at the time of Shamgar (3:31); (e) *the Sidonians,* probably confederates of Jabin (ch. 4); (f) *the Amalekites,* allied with the Moabites (3:13) and the Midianites; (g) *the Maonites,* perhaps a reference to the Edomites, in whose territory lay a city called Maon. The Septuagint has Midianites.

10:13 *No more.* The Lord made clear, no doubt through a prophet (6:8), that divine grace is not a cheap commodity available to the whim of man. God is under no obligation to forgive abuse of His goodness whenever the sinner whimpers under the rod of His anger. At the same time, mysteriously diabolical as the power of iniquity over the human heart is, the victory of mercy over justice in God's heart is a mystery as unfathomable as God Himself is beyond human comprehension (Hos 11:8 f.). In this instance too He reversed His decree to deliver *no more* when the people demonstrated the sincerity of their confession by deeds of repentance (15 f.).—Our abuse of God's grace may be as flagrant and frequent as Israel's of old; nevertheless God "is faithful and just, and will forgive our sins and cleanse us from all unrighteousness." (1 Jn 1:9)

3) 10:17—11:40 Deliverance by Jephthah

10:17 *Mizpah.* Also written Mizpeh, the word

means watchtower. Jacob had made a covenant at such a "Mizpah" in Transjordan Gilead. (Gn 31:48 f.)

11:1 *Jephthah.* Information regarding his antecedents is supplied (1-3) in order to explain the circumstances that led to negotiations between him and "the elders of Gilead" (4-11). Son of a man who bore the name of his clan, *Gilead,* and of *a harlot,* he was forced by his legitimate half brothers to leave his "father's house" and to seek refuge in "Tob," at this time a kind of no-man's-land east of the Jordan and north of Gilead. Here he proved himself *a mighty warrior,* leader of a band of "worthless [literally "empty"] fellows" who for some reason had likewise lost their claim to possess something of worth. (1 Sm 22:2)

11:6 *Leader.* The Hebrew word is used of military "chiefs" (Jos 10:24) and of "rulers" in general (Is 1:10; 3:6 ff.). The Gileadites offered to make Jephthah their "head" (8), when "the Ammonites made war against Israel."

11:9 *The Lord gives.* At the very outset Jephthah made it clear that the people were not to ascribe any success to his ability as their "head and leader."

11:11 *Before the Lord.* The assembled "leaders of Gilead" (10:18) called on the Lord to be "witness" (lit. "a hearer") of the conditions under which Jephthah was to "fight with the Ammonites."

11:12 *Messengers.* Jephthah was unable to persuade the king of the Ammonites to evacuate the occupied territory. The invader claimed as "my land" an area of some 50 by 15 miles, bounded by the Arnon (south), the Jabbok (north), the Jordan (west), and the wilderness (east).

11:14 *Again.* In his reply Jephthah set the record straight. In the first place, the king of the Ammonites was falsely claiming ownership of land that had been occupied largely by their kinsmen, the Moabites. Furthermore, when "the Lord" gave it "into the hand of Israel," the disputed territory was not "the land of Moab or the land of the Ammonites" because it had been taken from them by the Amorite king Sihon. (See Nm 21:21, 24 notes)

11:16 *From Egypt.* In order to prove his point, Jephthah outlined the course of Israel's wandering from Egypt (16-18) and then recalled how it got possession of "the territory of the Amorites from the Arnon to the Jabbok" (19-22). For *Red Sea* see Ex 3:18 note; Nm 14:25 note; for *Kadesh,* Nm 13:3 note; for *wilderness,* Nm 20:14, 17 notes.

11:24 *Chemosh.* The national god of the Moabites, whereas the chief deity of the Ammonites was Milcom or Molech (Nm 21:29; 1 K 11:5, 7). Jephthah's messengers taunted the Ammonites with the reminder that Chemosh, the god worshiped by the Moabites, had not been able to prevent "the Lord, the God of Israel" from giving their land first to the Amorites and then to Israel. Those who put their trust in such an impotent idol, they said, should be satisfied with what they believed he was able to give them *to possess.*

11:25 *Balak.* As further proof of the folly of trusting "other gods besides" the Lord, Jephthah's men cited the futile attempt of the *king of Moab* to thwart Israel's advance: Balaam, hired by him to curse the Israelites, blessed them. (Nm 22—24)

11:26 *Three hundred years.* For centuries the Lord had maintained Israel's right to dwell in such cities as *Heshbon* and *Aroer,* formerly occupied by the Moabites. For the duration of the period of the judges see Introduction, "Chronology."

11:29 *Spirit of the Lord.* "Mighty warrior" (1) though he was, Jephthah would have been unable to cope with the situation if God had not equipped him with the power of His Spirit. (3:10 note)

11:31 *Whoever.* The propriety of Jephthah's vow has been justified by translating the Hebrew relative, which does not distinguish genders, with "whatsoever" (KJV), thus allowing for the possibility that an animal or a man would emerge to meet him. In that case it must be assumed also that he contemplated a distinction in the manner of fulfilling his vow. He would consecrate a person that came out to a lifelong service to the Lord, "or" (not *and;* see RSV, Ru 2:20) if it were an animal, he would *offer him up for a burnt offering.* However, it is not necessary to conclude that Jephthah acted on the impulse of the Spirit when he made a vow which did not exclude the sacrifice of a human being. Other charismatic leaders such as Gideon and Samson likewise acted in flagrant violation of God's Law. Hence it is possible that Jephthah too succumbed to the heathen practice of seeking divine favor at all costs, and if need be, by human sacrifice (2 K 3:27). The terse sentence that he "did with her according to his vow" (39) does not help to determine her ultimate fate.

11:35 *Take back.* For laws governing vows see Nm 6:1-21; 30:2; Dt 23:21, 23.

11:37 *My virginity.* Whether consecrated to the Lord for lifetime service or offered as a burnt offering, the daughter would die childless, a fate considered as lamentable as death. Because she was "his only child" (34) and "had never known a man" (39), Jephthah subjected himself to the disgrace of leaving no offspring to perpetuate his name and family.

11:40 *To lament.* This "custom" seems to imply that the daughter suffered a fate more tragic than a living death of virginity.

12:1-6 SUPPRESSOR OF INTERNAL STRIFE

12:1 *Ephraim.* Israel's deliverer from foreign oppression encountered internal hostility. Jealous of its prestige, the powerful tribe of Ephraim took up arms against the Gileadite Jephthah, justifying the action with trumped-up charges: (a) he had not called for its help; (b) Jephthah and his Gileadites were "fugitives of Ephraim," i.e., traitorous renegades "in the midst of [the Joseph tribes] Ephraim and Mannasseh."

12:4 *Smote Ephraim.* Jephthah did not mollify his detractors with "a soft answer," as Gideon had done (8:1 note). He *smote* the Ephraimite forces which had crossed the Jordan to the Gileadite town of "Zaphon." (1)

12:6 *Shibboleth.* The Gileadites "took the fords of the Jordan," thus cutting off retreat to the west side of the river. The "fugitives of Ephraim" were asked to say *Shibboleth,* the Hebrew word for ear of grain or flowing stream. As Peter's "accent" identified him as a Galilean (Mt 26:73), so the dialect of an Ephraimite betrayed him, for he *could not pronounce it right,* but would say *Sibboleth.*

Forty-two thousand. An exceedingly large number, unless the Hebrew word *thousand* is not used in a numerical sense. (See Introduction to the Book of Numbers, "The Numbers . . .")

12:7 JEPHTHAH'S DEATH

12:7 *Buried him.* Beginning with 8:32, the burial place of the judges, also of the minor judges, is noted. Why this information deserves special mention is not clear. Possibly it is added to stress the fact that these leaders maintained their prominence in their area throughout their lifetime. But see 3:11 note.

12:8-10 Ibzan

12:8 *Ibzan.* The next three judges (8-15) complete the roster of the so-called minor judges, the other three being Shamgar, Tola, Jair (3:31; 10:1-5). The brief account of their activity—8 verses—mentions the fact that entitles them to a place in the book: all three *judged Israel* (10:3 note). The name Ibzan occurs only here. *Bethlehem* is thought to be a city in Zebulon (Jos 19:15) rather than the well-known birthplace of the Deliverer of mankind.

12:11-12 Elon

12:11 *Aijalon.* The Hebrew consonants of this city name can be supplied with vowels that spell Elon, i.e., a place in Zebulun named after the judge. At all events it is not the Danite Aijalon, where "the sun stood still" at Joshua's command. (Jos 10:12)

12:13-15 Abdon

12:13-15 *Pirathon.* The burial place of *Abdon* was *in the hill country of the Amalekites.* Apparently this area came to be so named because it was the site of some encounter with these marauding descendants of Esau, who were frequently allied with Israel's enemies. (3:13; 6:3; 7:12; 10:12; Ex 17:8 note)

13:1—16:31 Samson and the Philistines

13:1 ISRAEL PUNISHED BY PHILISTINES

13:1 *Philistines.* Jephthah had delivered the Israelites from the Ammonites (10:6—12:7). Simultaneously with the latter's invasion from the east, the Lord had "sold" the apostate people "into the hand of the Philistines," who encroached on Israelite territory from the west and southwest (10:7 note). Chs. 13—16 record the story of Samson, who was to "begin to deliver Israel from the hand of the Philistines." (5)

Samson, the last of the line of men on record in the book who "judged Israel" (16:31), differs from his predecessors in a number of respects: (a) his birth to a barren mother was foretold by the angel of the Lord; (b) he was dedicated to be a Nazirite from birth; (c) he flagrantly and repeatedly succumbed to the impulses of the flesh; (d) he was not the leader of tribal or national campaigns against the enemy; rather he sought to break the power of the Philistines single-handed (but see 3:31); (e) he died without having achieved a decisive victory over the national foe. Nevertheless Samson's life story is but another chapter in the basic theme that the Book of Judges develops. His accomplishments are not recorded in order to entertain the reader with tales of human prowess. Similar in some respects though his exploits are to those found in the heroic epics of ancient mythology and folklore, they are designed to reveal how God's strength is made perfect in weak vessels of clay. Nowhere is Samson depicted as a superman, endowed by nature with bulging muscles and a huge frame. Quite to the contrary, he "won strength out of weakness" when "through faith"—at times no more than a "dimly burning wick"—"he called on the Lord." (15:18; 16:28; Heb 11:32, 34; Is 42:2; Mt 12:20)

13:2-25 SAMSON'S BIRTH AND YOUTH

13:2 *Zorah.* Mentioned in the allotments of both Dan and Judah, this border town between the two tribes was approximately 15 miles due west of Jerusalem and 20 miles from the Mediterranean seacoast, along which lay the five strongholds of the Philistines (Jos 15:33; 19:41). When the latter moved eastward and northward, Samson's birthplace Zorah and the neighboring towns of "Eshtaol" (25) and "Timnah" (14:1) were some of the first to succumb to the infiltrating enemy.

13:3 *Angel of the Lord.* Cf. 2:1; 6:11 notes.

Barren. Other barren women who became the mothers of great men were Sarah, Hannah, Elizabeth.

13:5 *Nazirite.* For the requirements of the Nazirite vow see Nm 6:2 note. In Samson's case his mother was to have a part in dedicating him to the Lord. Before his birth she was to observe dietary restrictions to which among others her Nazirite son was to obligate himself "to the day of his death." (4, 7)

13:6 *A man of God.* Samson's parents believed God was speaking to them through a human spokesman or prophet as He had done at Gideon's time (6:8). However his mother, who saw something so majestic and awe-inspiring in his whole appearance *(countenance),* had a premonition that he was more than an ordinary messenger, *the angel of God.*

13:15 *A kid.* In keeping with oriental custom, Manoah wanted to prepare a meal for his guest, whom he had not fully recognized as "the angel of the Lord" (16). For similar incidents see 6:17 ff.; Gn 18:3-8.

13:18 *Wonderful.* Manoah was to believe that his barren wife would bear him a son. His strange visitor was the Lord Himself, for whom nothing is "too wonderful" (Gn 18:14). "Too wonderful" for man's comprehension, the Lord makes known "his name" when He "works wonders" (19; see also Gn 32:27-30; Ex 3:14, 15; 6:3 notes).—The fullest revelation of the Lord came through Him whose "name will be called Wonderful Counselor, Mighty God, Everlasting Father, Prince of Peace." (Is 9:6; Ph 2:9 f.)

13:20 *Fell on their faces.* By His flaming disappearance the Angel of the Lord had displayed His power to work wonders. (6:21 ff.)

13:22 *Surely die.* Manoah feared that they had *seen God* in such a way as to expose them to the decree: "man shall not see me and live" (Ex 33:18 note). However, his wife contended that He could not have appeared to them in order to "kill" because He had "accepted a burnt offering and a cereal offering at our hands" (23). Furthermore, she argues, they were sure to survive for the simple reason that the Angel of the Lord had announced "such things" as were to happen to them in the future. God Himself brought peace of mind to Gideon under similar circumstances. (6:22-24; see also Is 6:5-7)

13:24 *Samson.* The unnamed mother gave her son of promise a name containing the Hebrew word for "sun" *(shemesh).* In extra-Biblical records of the 14th and 15th centuries B.C. similar names for sun-worshiping Canaanites are found. It does not necessarily follow that Samson's mother too worshiped the "host of heaven" (2 K 23:5, 11; Jer 8:1 f.). There is good reason to believe that she was expressing her confidence that "the Lord God is a sun and shield" who "bestows favor and honor" on "those who walk uprightly." (Ps 84:11; Ml 4:2)

13:25 *Mahaneh-dan.* Lit. "the camp of Dan." Under Philistine pressure the Danites may have been forced to live in camplike settlements. Under such humiliating circumstances *the Spirit of the Lord began to stir* Samson to "begin to deliver Israel." (5)

14:1-20 FIRST ENTANGLEMENTS WITH PHILISTINES

14:1 *Timnah.* Evidently the Philistines felt themselves so firmly entrenched in their "dominion over Israel" that they did not regard it necessary to impose strict travel restrictions on the Israelites. At any rate, Samson managed to roam about extensively: to *Timnah,* about 5 miles southwest of his parental home at Zorah; to "the rock of Etam," a short distance east of Timnah (15:8); to Delilah's house in "the valley of Sorek," immediately south of Zorah (16:4). He even ventured into two of the chief Philistine cities: Ashkelon (14:19) and Gaza (16:1), respectively about 25 and 40 miles southwest of Zorah.

14:2 *Get her.* Samson's exploits against the Philistines came in the wake of unlawful relations with women, two of them harlots (16:1, 4). Divine prohibitions and parental admonitions did not curb his lust to *get* a woman, in or out of wedlock, if she pleased him (3). For the law against mixed marriages see Ex 34:16; Dt 7:3.

14:4 *An occasion.* The impulse to contract a forbidden marriage came from Samson's disobedient heart and not *from the Lord.* Nevertheless "it was the Lord's doing" (Ex 4:21 note) to let this act of human self-will serve His good and gracious will: He made it *an occasion* to challenge the Philistine "dominion over Israel." He was determined to let His kingdom come despite the repeated apostasy of His chosen people (13:1) and despite the failings of the men whom He chose to deliver the bearers of His promise.

14:6 *Came mightily.* Previous judges became successful leaders in military campaigns when "the Spirit of the Lord came upon" them or "took possession of" them (3:10 note; 6:34; 11:29). Expressed in different terms, Samson's endowment with the Spirit manifested itself in a different way. When *the Spirit of the Lord came mightily upon him* (19; 15:14; 16:28-30), he was enabled to perform prodigious feats of physical strength.

14:8 *The carcass.* The killing of the lion (5c-7) is a backflash which explains why Samson found honey in the dead lion. He had slain the beast when he first "went down to Timnah" (1) and "talked with the woman" who pleased him (7). When *after a while,* accompanied by his parents, *he returned to take her,* enough time had elapsed for the dry carcass to become a beehive.

14:9 *Not tell.* Presumably Samson did not want to let his parents know that he had violated the requirement of the Nazirite vow not to "go near a dead body." (Nm 6:6)

14:10 *The father.* It was the father's prerogative and duty to negotiate the marriage terms. (Gn 24:1 ff.; 38:6)

14:11 *Thirty companions.* These "sons of the bridechamber" (Mt 9:15 RSV: "wedding guests") were selected for Samson by *the people* when they *saw him.* The Septuagint translation ("when they feared him") suggests that the Philistines *brought thirty companions to be with him* as a precautionary measure.

14:12 *Riddle.* Solving riddles was a popular way of entertaining guests. The object was to find the meaning of sayings propounded in ambiguous language. The RSV renders the Hebrew noun as "dark speech" (Nm 12:8); the Queen of Sheba tested Solomon's wisdom with "hard questions." (1 K 10:1)

14:15 *Fourth day.* The RSV adopts the reading of the Septuagint and the Syriac versions in order to establish a sequence with the "three days" of v. 14. Perhaps a better solution is suggested by an ancient Hebrew manuscript which has "seven" in both verses. From the very beginning of the feast the Philistines had tried to win the wager by enlisting the woman's wiles: "she wept before him the seven days" (17). On the last day they became desperate, threatening to burn her and her father's house. So "she pressed him hard" and succeeded in cajoling Samson into telling her the answer.

14:18 *The sun went down.* Sunset of the seventh day was the stipulated deadline of the contest. It also marked the time when, according to prevailing custom, a bridegroom entered his bride's chamber to consummate the marriage. Apparently Samson did not do so, but at once "went back to his father's house" (19). Therefore the woman's father felt free to give her to "his best man" ("the friend of the bridegroom," Jn 3:29).

15:1—16:3 OTHER FEATS OF STRENGTH

15:1 *After a while.* After killing "thirty men of the town" (14:19) Samson delivered three more strikes against the Philistines: (a) when he returned to Timnah to claim his wife (1-8); (b) when his own countrymen tried to hand him over to the enemy (9-17); (c) when the citizens of Gaza tried to ambush him. (16:1-3)

A kid. A token of reconciliation or perhaps the conventional gift for this kind of visit to a wife who continued to live with her family. (8:31)

15:3 *Blameless.* Samson felt his grievance against the Philistines justified him to resort to *mischief* in order to even accounts with them.

15:4 *Three hundred foxes.* The same Hebrew noun designates jackals as well as foxes. A large number of the former could have been caught more readily because they run in packs. However, the figure 300 seems so high as to prompt the suggestion that the actual number received an extra nought in the transmission of the text. (See Numbers, Introduction, "The Numbers . . .")

15:6 *Burned her.* So they had threatened to do (14:15). By their cruel act they seemed to indicate that in their opinion Samson had a valid claim on his wife. At any rate, he in turn made it grounds for bloody vengeance on the Timnites. (7)

15:8 *Hip and thigh.* An idiomatic phrase, perhaps borrowed from terminology to describe a pugilistic contest; cf. our expression "to administer a knockout blow."

Etam. Cf. 14:1 note.

15:9 *Lehi.* The Philistines responded in force to the slaughter of their compatriots. In their search for the culprit they crossed over into Judean territory, sending out raiding contingents from a place in the vicinity of Etam, called Lehi, a Hebrew common noun meaning jawbone. Its cliffs may have had the appearance of a jagged row of teeth. After Samson's slaughter of the Philistines with the jawbone of an ass its name was associated with the weapon he used. (17)

15:13 *Bound him.* This traitorous action of "the men of Judah" was a pathetic demonstration that they had lost all morale. They had given up the will to resist. Preferring comfort and safety, they were ready to submit to a peaceful coexistence with the infiltrating Philistines and eventual absorption by them. But God saved them from being Canaanized, as the Philistines themselves had been. In spite of the people's apathy and Samson's moral weakness, He kept His promise to the chosen nation—the theme of the entire Book of Judges.

15:14 *Spirit of the Lord.* Cf. 14:6 note. Samson's ropes and bands *melted off his hands,* token evidence that God cannot be fettered by puny man when He desires to let His kingdom come. In the ancient collect of the church today's faltering saints can pray with confidence to "Almighty God" for the gift of the "Holy Spirit" that His "Word . . . may not be bound."

15:16 *Heaps upon heaps.* The full effect of Samson's exuberant ditty is difficult to reproduce in English because it is based on a play of words on a Hebrew homonym which means both "ass" and "heap." Moffat's translation is helpful: "With the jawbone of an ass I have piled them in a mass." *A thousand men* very likely is a round figure for a large number. (Cf. our saying: "I have a thousand and one things to do.")

15:18 *Called.* In his distress Samson professed his desire to be a *servant* of the Lord. Frequently disobedient and self-willed though he had been, he was willing to be *the hand* which God deigned to use for His purpose.

15:19 *Lehi.* Not "in the jaw" of the ass (KJV) but in the place called the Jaw (Hebrew: *lehi*). The spring received its name because "there came water from it" when Samson called to the Lord for help.

15:20 *Judged Israel.* The identical statement appears at the end of the Samson story (16:31). Whether or not it was inserted here by a careless copyist, it does serve to provide the reader with the proper perspective on this wild man's career. Intent at the very outset on serving self (14:1-3), he nevertheless was chosen to be the instrument to execute the decrees of "the Judge" of heaven and earth.

16:1 *Gaza.* The reckless adventurer's next encounter with the Philistines took place in one of the five principal cities on the Mediterranean coast, some 40 miles southwest of his parental home at Zorah. Here "the servant" of the Lord (15:18) consorted with *a harlot.*

16:2 *Lay in wait.* The Philistines seemed to be afraid to make a search for Samson at night. However, they wanted to be ready to overpower him in *the light of the morning.*

16:3 *Doors of the gate.* It may appear strange that the Philistines did not seize their quarry at *the gate of the city.* However, in the next episode too "the lords of the Philistines" did not dare to tackle him in broad daylight.

Before Hebron. If *the hill* where Samson deposited his heavy trophy was immediately *before Hebron,* he would have carried it about 40 miles eastward, deep into Judean territory. The Hebrew phrase can mean: "on the hill which is in the direction of Hebron."

16:4-22 VICTIM OF DELILAH'S CHARMS

16:4 *Delilah.* Samson's lust for women had been the occasion for revenge on the Philistines twice before (14:1—16:3). His third illicit affair ended in his undoing. Deprived of the source of his strength, a broken and blinded prisoner of his jubilant enemies, he was able to avenge himself only at the cost of his own life. His fatal temptress may have been a Philistine woman with a Semitic name, *Delilah* meaning either a "devotee" (i.e., of a deity, perhaps Dagon) or "the one with long falling tresses." Samson had to go but a few miles from his home into *the valley of Sorek* to fall into her clutches.

16:5 *The lords of the Philistines.* According to 3:3 they were five in number, each the ruler of a capital city in a confederation known as the Pentapolis. The high price they set on Samson's head, equivalent to several thousand dollars, showed that they considered him such a serious menace to their national welfare as to call for a considerable outlay of money. They made the stakes high enough to induce Delilah to betray her lover into their hands no matter what risk it might involve or how contemptible such a treacherous act might be.

16:6 *Great strength.* Evidently the Philistines believed that Samson was not endowed by nature with the necessary muscle and brawn to account for his superhuman feats of strength. Superstitious as they were, they were convinced that he had a magical amulet or that he knew some formula of incantation by which he could tap a supernatural powerline. He would be "like any other man" (7, 11, 13) if they could solve this "secret of his strength." (9)

16:7 *Bowstrings.* Three times Samson misled Delilah to think that she had cajoled him into divulging the secret. The spell would be broken, he said, if (a) she used *fresh bowstrings* of gut to bind (7-9); (b) she took "new ropes" (10-12); (c) she wove his "seven locks" into the warp of her loom. (13, 14)

16:17 *All his mind.* Samson was not the first nor the last to be so infatuated as to lose his head, figuratively and literally. She "pressed him hard," nagging him "to death" with "much seductive speech" and "smooth talk" (Pr 7:21 ff.). Finally he succumbed to her wiles as he had to the tears of the woman of Timnah. (14:17)

Nazirite. Cf. 13:5. Samson's superhuman strength did not derive magically from his long hair. His seven unshorn "locks" were but the outward token of an inner dedication to God. By breaking his Nazirite vow he had violated his special covenant with the Source of his strength, whose Spirit had "come mightily upon him" in the past. "His strength left him" because "the Lord had left him." (19, 20)

16:19 *Torment him.* Perhaps better translated: "she began to humiliate him" by exposing his weakness.

16:20 *At other times.* On three previous occasions. (9, 12, 14)

16:21 *Mill.* The helpless victim of Philistine abuse, Samson was compelled to grind flour, ordinarily a woman's task. (9:53 note)

16:22 *Grow.* The Philistines did not shave off his growing hair, confident no doubt that his blindness would sufficiently handicap him even if he should regain his strength.

16:23-31 SAMSON'S FINAL REVENGE

16:23 *Dagon.* The name Dagon is related to the Hebrew word for grain *(dagan)* and not to the word for fish *(dag)*. A vegetation deity, known to have been worshiped from the Euphrates to the Mediterranean, Dagon became the baal of the Philistines. In Canaan, their new home, they did as the Canaanites did. The immigrant Israelites were constantly in danger of succumbing to the same Canaanizing process. Samson's exploits were to demonstrate that the Lord and not Dagon ruled the destinies of men.

16:25 *Sport.* They mocked him with the request to put on a strongman act for their amusement.

16:28 *I pray.* When "the people of Israel cried to the Lord" for help after having done "evil in the sight of the Lord," "the Lord raised up judges" (2:11, 16). When Samson, the judge, broke his Nazirite vow, the Lord heard also his penitent plea for the restoral of strength to avenge himself *for* the loss of at least *one of* his *two eyes.*

16:29 *Middle pillars.* Their removal brought the whole structure down in a heap, much as an arch collapses without its keystone.

16:31 *Twenty years.* Cf. 3:11 note. After two decades, liberation from the Philistines merely had begun (13:1 note). In some respects the most colorful and glamorous of the judges was the least effective instrument in the hands of "the Judge" to vindicate the right of His chosen people to remain bearers of His promise. In fact, the Philistine oppresssion grew worse after Samson's death. Nevertheless through him and his fellow judges the Lord carried forward His plan to free mankind from the shackles of eternal bondage. By its very inconclusive ending the story of the judges awaits the perfect obedience and the sacrificial death of Him who was "born of woman" "when the time had fully come." (Gl 4:4-6)

17:1—21:25 APPENDIX: HOW DEEPLY ISRAEL HAD FALLEN

17:1—18:31 Brazen Idolatry and Sacrilege

17:1-13 IN EPHRAIM

17:1 *A man.* Ch. 16 ends the account of the judges and their activities. The closing chapters (17—21) illustrate in greater detail why, "in the days when the judges ruled," "the anger of the Lord was kindled against Israel" (3:8; Ru 1:1). They contain two stories which elaborate the general indictment: "Israel did evil in the sight of the Lord" (3:7, 12; etc). Two observations become unmistakably clear. On the one hand, the evil was comprehensive: the people broke the terms of the covenant that governed their relationship to God as well as to their fellowmen, i.e., both tables of the Law. Furthermore, the evil was not a sin of weakness but openly rebellious and dastardly wicked.

The first of these stories lays bare a blatant disregard of the divine prohibition not to make and to worship man-made images. Even a Levite prostituted his sacred office to become the tribal priest of an idolatrous cult (chs. 16—17). The second narrative is a sordid tale of moral depravity, a sex crime of bestial degeneracy. (Chs. 19—21)

17:3 *Graven . . . molten.* The silver was either cast in a solid block and then *graven* to give it the desired contours, or it was carved of wood and then overlaid with the metal.

17:5 *Ephod and teraphim.* Cf. 8:27 note; Gn 31:19 note.

17:6 *No king.* During the period of the judges *there was no king in Israel* who, charged to enforce the divine law, prevented every man from "doing whatever is right in his own eyes" (Dt. 12:8). Evidently the author lived at a time when he expected the central authority of the monarchy to exercise such restraint on all Israel. (18:1; 19:1; 21:25; 1 K 2:1-4)

17:7 *Judah.* He was not a member of the tribe of Judah but of that family of Levites who received an inheritance within Judah's territory. For the distribution of the Levites among the tribes see Nm 35; Jos 21. Apparently an adventuresome *young man,* he *sojourned* for a time in Bethlehem before going in search of a new place "to sojourn." (9)

17:10 *Father.* A title of respect for his office (Gn 45:8; 2 K 6:21). Micah in turn would provide for the physical needs of the Levite as if the latter were "one of his sons." (11)

17:13 *Priest.* Micah knew that only *a Levite* was to perform priestly functions (Dt 18:1 note). At the same time he was brazen enough to expect the Lord to *prosper* him for hiring a renegade Levite to do what God had threatened to punish (Dt 5:8-9; 11:26-28).—Men still hire ministers to tell them "what is right in their own eyes" rather than the full counsel of God.

18:1-31 IDOL WORSHIP IN NORTHERN DAN

18:1 *Danites.* Micah's idols became involved in the migration of the Danites from their original allotment in the south and their resettlement in the extreme north. A brief summary of their relocation and the reason why *no* permanent *inheritance . . . had fallen to them* is given 1:34 f.; Jos 19:40-48.

18:2 *Zorah . . . Eshtaol.* In these border cities of Judah, the Danite Samson had "judged Israel" (13:2, 25; Jos 15:33). Apparently not all Danites joined the search for a new home "in those days" (1). Therefore in point of chronological sequence the events of these chapters could have preceded the activity of Samson. (Chs. 13—16)

18:3 *Voice.* The Hebrew could have the meaning of dialect (12:6 note). They recognized his southern brogue.

18:5 *Inquire.* In those days even a Levite had no scruples to take the name of the Lord in vain. He used the work of his hands as an instrument of soothsaying, professing to have received a good omen from "the Lord."

18:7 *Laish.* For its location and name see Jos 19:47 note. Absorbed in the pursuit of trade *after the manner of the Sidonians*—the great merchantmen of the day—the *unsuspecting* people of Laish had made no military preparations to ward off invaders. At the same time they were isolated *far from the Sidonians* to the west by the Lebanon mountains. Furthermore, to the east they had no *dealings with any one,* being shut off by Mt. Hermon and the Antilebanon range from such people as the Syrians. By a slight change in one consonant the Hebrew word for *any one* has the meaning of "Syria," a reading adopted by some manuscripts of the Septuagint.

18:9 *Arise.* Compare this glowing report with the majority report of Moses' spies (Nm 13:25 ff.). The Danite scouting party said that their prospects of possessing *the land* were so good that they could be certain that "God has given it into your hands." (10)

18:12 *Kiriath-jearim.* This "city of forests" was one of the chief centers of the Gibeonites with whom Joshua made a covenant (Jos 9:16 ff.). One of the border cities of Judah and Benjamin, it was 9 miles west of Jerusalem. The Danites had traveled northeastward only about the same distance, when they made camp at a place *west of Kiriath-jearim,* which came to be known as "Mahaneh-dan," i.e., the camp of Dan. (Cf. 13:25 note)

18:13 *Ephraim.* Evidently the other tribes granted the migrating Danites free transit through their territories.

18:17 *Took the graven image.* A note of ironic contempt for the "gods" (24) that the Israelites worshiped instead of the living God pervades the account. Their folly is the measure of their perversity. The frequent mention of these ridiculous objects of worship in 14-20 underscores the question: Is it possible that these people could put their trust in silver stolen from a mother by her son, cursed by the mother, cast and graven into a lifeless image, stolen from its owner, manipulated by a Levite for filthy lucre, attended by a kidnapped priest? For a similar exposé of idol worship see Is 40:18-20; 44:9-18.

18:23 *Ails you.* Brazenly brushing aside Micah's claim to the "god," the Danites threatened him for molesting them.

18:25 *Angry fellows.* Among them were "men embittered of soul,"[f] i.e., people with a nasty, short temper.

18:27 *Smote . . . burned.* The sack of the city is described in the same matter-of-fact manner in which the sin of idolatry is reported. The whole episode simply records the fact that "every man did what was right in his own eyes." (17:6)

18:28 *Beth-rehob.* No doubt the fuller name of the northernmost city "near the entrance of Hamath" which was scouted by Moses' spies and called "Rehob" in Nm 13:21. It lay in a valley that today is called simply "El Buqa‘," "The Valley."

18:30 *Moses.* The Hebrew text indicates that

an *n* has been inserted into the proper noun. With the addition of this consonant the word could be supplied with vowels (originally not written) to spell the name "Manasseh" (so KJV). No doubt some scribe did not want the grandson of Israel's founding father to be associated with this idolatrous cult. For the name Gershom see Ex 2:22. This note is additional evidence that the phrase "in those days" (17:6) refers to a period not too long "after the death of Joshua" (1:1). The writer appended this episode in order to demonstrate that during the time of the judges Israel fully deserved "the anger of the Lord." (3:7 f.)

Captivity of the land. Centuries later the Danites shared the fate of the Northern Kingdom. In 722 B.C. the Assyrians carried large segments of the northern tribes into captivity (2 K 17). However, the next verse indicates that an earlier *captivity* is meant here. The graven image remained in Dan "as long as the house of God was at Shiloh," i.e., to the time of Samuel (1 Sm 1—4). During his time Shiloh was destroyed by the Philistines (Jer 7:12, 14; 26:6; Ps 78:60) and the ark of the Lord was "captured" or, as the verb also can be translated, "went into exile" (cf. 1 Sm 4:19 note). Some scholars have suggested that one consonant of the Hebrew word "land" be changed so that the phrase reads "until the captivity of the ark." No explanation is given here or elsewhere as to how or why the destruction of Shiloh about 20 miles north of Jerusalem put an end also to the worship of Micah's image in Dan far to the north of Shiloh.

19:1—21:24 Collapse of Morals and Civil War

19:1-30 WANTON IMMORALITY IN GIBEAH

19:1 *Levite.* A Levite plays a role also in the second episode (19—21), appended in order to give a graphic description of "the evil in the sight of the Lord" that "provoked the Lord to anger" in the days of the judges. Jonathan, the priest of Micah's graven images, epitomized Israel's idolatry, its cardinal sin against the first table of the Law (chs. 17 f.). The story of the Levite who *took to himself a concubine* demonstrates in lurid detail how far the Israelites went in sin against their fellowmen. Not a paragon of virtue himself, this unnamed Levite set the stage for a horror drama of moral degeneracy and social disintegration. The wanton murder of his concubine, raped to death by the men of Gibeah (ch. 19), precipitated civil war (ch. 20). The extinction of the tribe of Benjamin was averted only by recourse to more bloodshed and to devious stratagems. (Ch. 21)

19:2 *Angry.* If she "played the harlot against him" (RSV note), she no doubt fled to escape the prescribed punishment for adultery. (Lv 20:10)

19:3 *Speak kindly.* Whatever prompted her leaving him, the Levite did not use force to *bring her back.* He spoke *kindly to her,* lit. "upon her heart," i.e., in words of endearment with which a lover woos his prospective bride (Gn 34:3). In God's unfathomable love for sinners He speaks tenderly to all who "have played the harlot against him." (Hos 2:14; Is 40:2)

19:9 *Toward evening.* For no apparent reason the Levite insisted on leaving so late in the day after having spent the previous 4 nights with his father-in-law. His departure *toward evening* explains why he got only as far as Gibeah when "the sun went down."

19:10 *Jebus.* Jerusalem did not "belong to the people of Israel" until David's time. (12; 1:21; 2 Sm 5)

19:14 *Gibeah.* A few miles south of *Ramah* and north of Jerusalem.

19:15 *Open square.* The public square just inside the city gates, where court was held and business was transacted. By their failure to extend hospitality to a stranger the men of Gibeah had broken a cardinal principle of social behavior. Such "base fellows," like outlaws, would be capable of any crime against their fellowmen.

19:16 *An old man.* There was not a single decent person in Gibeah except the Levite's fellow Ephraimite.

19:18 *My home.* KJV: "house of the Lord." A Levite on a pilgrimage to the sanctuary would have had a special claim to hospitality. Even though he had not mentioned it previously, he could have intended to stop over on his way to go *home* (9) to thank the Lord for prospering his journey. The RSV rendering makes it unnecessary to suppose that the Levite advanced this additional reason for seeking shelter. It does not involve a drastic textual change. The letter added to the Hebrew word *home* to make it read *my home* is also the first consonant of the sacred name "the Lord," which was often abbreviated.

19:22 *Base fellows.* KJV: "sons of Belial," but "ungodly men" in Ps 18:4. The Hebrew word "son" is used in a wider sense than in English. As a son derives his physical being in the likeness of his father, so in a figurative sense a man is the offspring or product of moral qualities. Rebellion, e.g., begets "sons of rebellion," i.e., "rebels" (Nm 17:10). "Belial" is not the proper name of an ancestor after the flesh but a common noun meaning "worthlessness." Morally and spiritually the men of Gibeah were sired by the kind of wickedness that destroys everything of value. St. Paul refers to "the father of lies" as Belial. (2 Co 6:15)

Know him. A euphemistic expression for sexual relations. (25; cf. Gn 18:19 note; 19:5)

19:23 *Vile thing.* Literally "folly" and so translated by RSV in Gn 34:7; Jer 29:23, but also "wantonness" (20:6), "wanton crime" (20:10), "wanton folly" (2 Sm 13:12), "shameful thing" (Jos 7:15). The added phrase "in Israel," as in 20:6, defines the nature of this folly. Its perpetrator wantonly disregarded what he knew to be an established rule of conduct. An Israelite guilty of such folly disavowed his covenant relationship to God. If such a *vile thing* was tolerated in Israel, the entire nation forfeited its covenant status. (Jos 7; 1 Co 5:1-8)

19:24 *Ravish.* Cf. Gn 19:8 note.

19:25 *Abused her.* The bestial rape of the Levite's concubine is labeled the most heinous crime that was committed since "the people of Israel came up out of the land of Egypt" (30). Centuries later the prophet Hosea indicted his contemporaries by telling them that they had "corrupted themselves as in the days of Gibeah." (Hos 9:9; 10:9)

19:27 *At the door.* After callously sacrificing his concubine to save himself from abuse, the Levite showed no concern for her until he *rose up in the morning* to claim her again.

19:29 *Twelve pieces.* The dismembered body of his concubine was grisly proof of her death as well as a call for united action to avenge it. Possibly the 12 pieces also implied a threat. All who did not respond to his demand for punitive measures were to suffer the same fate. Saul summoned the Israelites to a joint campaign by a similar device. (1 Sm 11:5-7)

20:1-48 RETRIBUTION BY OTHER TRIBES

20:1 *The people of Israel.* The subsequent united action by *all the people of Israel* supports the view that this tragic episode took place not too long "after the death of Joshua" (1:1; 18:1, 2 notes). "In those days" (19:1) the tribes were aware of their solidarity as a federated nation, united by the bonds of the covenant. This sense of unity had all but vanished as time wore on. The judges no longer had the support of *all the people of Israel.* Some tribes failed to cooperate; some engaged in jealous bickering; some openly challenged the authority of the judges (5:15-18, Deborah; 8:1-3, Gideon; 12:1-6, Jephthah.) Furthermore in the course of time tribal territories were occupied by foreign oppressors, making united action by *all the people* difficult if not impossible.

Dan . . . Beer-sheba. From Dan, in the far north, *to Beer-sheba,* 45 miles south of Jerusalem, became a conventional phrase to denote the full extent of Israelite territory. It occurs most frequently in the books of Samuel (1 Sm 3:20; 2 Sm 3:10, etc). Its use in the Book of Judges indicates that the author lived at a time after the migrating Danites had been established in their newly acquired homeland. (Ch. 18)

Mizpah. The allied forces, including those from Transjordanian *Gilead,* encamped at a *Mizpah* (10:17 note) in Benjaminite territory immediately northwest of Gibeah (Jos 18:26; 1 Sm 7:5; 10:17). When "the assembly of the people" heard the Levite's story (2-7), they resolved that the "wanton crime" called for punitive action against Gibeah (8-11). The Benjaminites came to the defense of their fellow tribesmen (12-17). "The people of Israel," led by Judah (18), were defeated in the first two engagements with the rebels (19-28). Victorious in a third attack, "the men of Israel" "put away evil from Israel," exterminating almost all male Benjaminites and burning their cities. (29-48)

20:2 *Four hundred thousand.* The figures for the allied and the Benjaminite armies (15) are enormous for the limited area in which they were deployed. It would have been difficult, for instance, for an ambush of 10,000 men to remain undetected west of the small village of Geba (29, 33). See Numbers, Introduction, "The Numbers . . . ."

20:5 *Kill me.* Evidently the Levite assumed that he would have suffered fatal mistreatment, as in fact his concubine did.

20:16 *Seven hundred picked men.* The Benjaminite army, consisting of men that "drew the sword," was reenforced by a contingent armed with slings. The accurate marksmanship of these men is related to the fact that they were *left-handed* like Ehud. (3:15 note)

20:18 *Inquired.* At this time, "the ark of the covenant" apparently had been moved to Bethel, some 5 miles northeast of the camp at Mizpah (26 f.), where the people received an answer to their question through Phinehas, the high priest. (28; 1:1)

20:28 *Into your hand.* No explanation is given why the Lord had not granted them success in the first two battles. Perhaps the Lord was impressing them with the necessity to "put away evil from Israel" (13) no matter what the cost might be.

20:29 *Ambush.* In their third onslaught on the rebels the federated forces used the strategy of an ambush, as Joshua had done at Ai (Jos 8:3 ff.). Advancing "as at other times" in a frontal attack from the northwest (Mizpah), they lured the Benjaminites, by a feigned retreat, to pursue them, leaving unprotected Gibeah an easy prey for the *men in ambush* who rushed in upon it from the northeast (Geba). The smoke of the burning city was the signal for "the men of Israel," who earlier "gave ground," again to take the offensive. Now attacked from the front and the rear, the Benjaminites "turned their backs," fleeing northeastward to "the rock of Rimmon." Only 600 reached safety there. The rest, unable to break out of the deadly pincer movement, were ground to pieces.

20:31 *Gibeah.* Gibeah and Geba are proper names derived from a noun meaning hill or height. The name of a third city, Gibeon, about 5 miles northwest of Gibeah, has the same etymological root. Only one Hebrew letter differentiates the spelling of these three "heights." In this verse the original text may have read "Gibeon" instead of "Gibeah." The former was on a highway that the men of Israel would take on their simulated retreat from Gibeah toward their camp at Mizpah.

20:33 *Baal-tamar.* An unidentified place.

20:35 *Defeated.* The outcome of the expedition is summarized in 33-36a. These topic sentences are developed in greater detail in 36b-48.

20:42 *The wilderness.* Eastward away from their encounter with the enemy at Gibeah.

20:43 *Nohah.* No such place name is known (cf. RSV note). A more meaningful translation is suggested: "and they pursued them without [allowing them] rest and overtook them opposite Geba." (Instead of Gibeah; cf. 31 note)

20:45 *Rimmon.* About 4 miles east of Bethel.

Gidom is unknown. It may be another scribal error for Geba, which lay on a straight line of flight from Gibeah to Rimmon.

20:46 *Twenty-five thousand.* The Benjaminites had a fighting force of 26,000 + 700 (15). According to v. 35 the exact total of their casualties was 25,100. If 600 escaped, it would leave 1,000 unaccounted for. This problem can be solved if with some Septuagint manuscripts the figure of 25,000 instead of 26,000 is adopted in 15.

20:48 *Smote them.* Personal vengeance for the two previous defeats may have prompted *the men of Israel* to resort to such extreme measures. On the other hand, they may have thought it was their duty to impose the ban of total destruction prescribed for cities which "serve other gods." (Dt 13:12-18)

21:1-24 BENJAMIN'S EXTINCTION AVERTED

21:2 *Wept bitterly.* "The men of Israel" had discharged their covenant obligations: they had "put away evil from Israel" (20:13). However, a vindictive spirit had intruded itself into their righteous indignation. Upon more sober reflection they realized that their rash vow (1) would result in the extinction of an entire Israelite tribe. Weeping bitterly before the Lord at Bethel (20:18 note), they devised two schemes which would enable them to satisfy the formal demands of their oath and at the same time assure the survival of Benjamin. In reality both plans were an ingenious maneuver to circumvent the intent of their avowed threat. They would not give their own daughters in marriage to the 600 refugees at Rimmon but contrive to supply them with wives from other sources. First they spared "four hundred young virgins" when they destroyed the population of Jabesh-gilead for its failure to "come up in the assembly of the Lord" (8-15). The remaining 200 Benjaminites were permitted to carry off "the daughters of Shiloh" when the latter came out to dance in the vineyards during a yearly festival. (16-24)

21:4 *An altar.* Previously the people had brought offerings on an altar at Bethel, where "the ark of the covenant" was (20:26 f.). Altars at places other than at the central sanctuary, such as the one at Mizpah (1), were deemed necessary under the stress of critical circumstances. (1 Sm 7:5-10; 13:8-12; 14:34 f.)

21:8 *Jabesh-gilead.* About 2 miles east of the Jordan and some 40 miles northeast of Mizpah. Its inhabitants had not joined the punitive expedition against Gibeah perhaps because they had close family ties with the Benjaminites through Rachel, patriarchal ancestress of both groups.

21:10 *Smite.* Moses gave similar orders in regard to the Midianites. (Nm 31:1 note, 17)

21:12 *Shiloh.* By the time the task force of the congregation returned from its grisly mission, the Israelites had moved their camp from Mizpah (8), some 13 miles northeast to *Shiloh.* Here Joshua had "set up the tent of meeting" (Jos 18:1). During the campaign against Gibeah and the Benjaminites "the ark of the covenant" had been transferred to Bethel (20:26 ff.). Thereupon Shiloh again became Israel's central sanctuary (18:30 second note; 1 Sm 1:3). The note *which is in the land of Canaan* seems to be superfluous. However in the context of the account it serves to underscore the fact that the unmarried women had been brought safely across the Jordan.

21:18 *Cannot give.* In "their compassion for Benjamin their brother" (6), the other tribes resorted to another subterfuge in order to assure "an inheritance for the survivors" (17). In supplying them with the first contingent of 400 prospective mothers, they had kept the letter of the oath, they reasoned, inasmuch as none of them had given *"his* daughter in marraige" (1). Next they capitalized on the word *give,* professing that they were not bound by their vow to interfere with the remaining 200 Benjaminites if each of them would *seize* "his wife from the daughters of Shiloh."

21:19 *Yearly feast.* Only the part that "the daughters of Shiloh" had in its observance is mentioned. Their dancing "in the vineyards" suggests that it was a harvest festival. Because none of the other tribes seemed to participate, it may have been a local celebration of thanksgiving to *the Lord* rather than one of the national pilgrim feasts. However, the feast of the tabernacles is also called "the feast of harvest" (Ex 23:16). When the tribes moved their camp to Shiloh (12), they may have brought the ark with them on their way through Bethel (20:18). The Book of Judges does not mention the tabernacle, which must have been erected at Shiloh before Samuel's time. (1 Sm 1-4)

21:25 Concluding Summary of Conditions

21:25 *His own eyes.* The book ends on a depressing note. In a final refrain it once more summarizes the religious, moral, and social chaos that blighted this period of Israel's history (17:6; 18:1; 19:1). The two preceding episodes (chs. 17 f.; 19—21) supplied detailed evidence of this lawless state of affairs when every man simply did as he pleased. The judges came and went without effecting a lasting change. "Whenever the judge died," the people "turned back and behaved worse than their fathers" (2:19). Even such kings as David restored order only temporarily. Nevertheless the Lord "bore with" the people of His covenant until He "brought to Israel a Savior, Jesus, as he promised." (Acts 13:16-23)

RUTH

INTRODUCTION

Content

Two books of the OT bear the names of women: Ruth and Esther. They were heroines in dramas not only centuries apart in point of time but also as different in plot as the role played by Ruth contrasts with that of her contemporaries, the judges of Israel. The latter were public figures, tribal and national representatives, arbiters of international disputes. However, Ruth has a niche in the hall of Israel's great because she was found "faithful in a very little" (Lk 16:10), namely in the way she met and overcame domestic crises which frequently arise in the everyday life of an ordinary private citizen. The scenes in Judges are black with crimes against God and man: treachery, brutal war, massacre, cities in ruins. Into these "Dark Ages" of Israel, the Book of Ruth sheds a ray of light: filial piety, marital fidelity, social responsibility, rural tranquility.

History, the OT here demonstrates, is more than a record of battles, dates, and dynasties of kings. It is indeed comforting to know—and the OT furnishes abundant evidence—that "the Judge of all the earth" has the power to direct the destiny of nations even though "the kings of the earth set themselves . . . against the Lord" (Gn 18:25; Ju 11:27; Ps 2:1 f.). However, it is just as comforting to be assured that "he who sits in the heavens" is not so occupied with running the universe as not to be able to be concerned with the vicissitudes of ordinary little people. It is a part of "the secrets of the kingdom of heaven" (Mt 13:11) that an inconspicuous believer—a peasant woman, a convert like Ruth—can achieve the status of royalty. God lets strange circumstances and a resolute obedience of faith on her part combine to make her the great-grandmother of Israel's illustrious king David, and thereby an ancestress according to the flesh of the King of kings. (Mt 1:5)

A key word in the development of the plot is "kinsman." Etymologically this term has nothing to do with blood relationship as such. In its root meaning it refers to the functions which a person was required and privileged to perform by virtue of his ties of blood with another. "Kinsman" is the participle of a verb translated "redeem." It was the privilege and duty of a "redeemer" to (a) save his brother's name from extinction by marrying his widow (levirate marriage; Dt 25:5 note); (b) prevent the land of the deceased relative from being lost to his heirs (Lv 25:25 note). "Redemption" (4:6) of a family name and property provided social stability in the covenant nation through which God promised to raise up that "Kinsman" of all mankind who was to "redeem Israel from all his iniquities," who in the fullness of time did bring "redemption through his blood, the forgiveness of our trespasses," to all who were under "the curse of the law." (Ps 130:8; Gl 3:13; Eph 1:7; Heb 2:14 f.; 1 Ptr 1:18)

Time

"The days when the judges ruled" (1:1) comprised an era extending over centuries (see Judges, Introduction). The last two accounts of Judges describe conditions that prevailed not long "after the death of Joshua" (Ju 1:1; 18:30 note; 20:1 note). However, the events of Ruth's life evidently took place in the final decades of that turbulent age. There was as yet "no king in Israel" (Ju 17:6 note). But only two generations intervened between Ruth and David (4:17). Saul, the first king, was soon to be anointed by Samuel, the last of the judges.

Place in Canon

Ruth does not follow the Book of Judges in the Hebrew Bible. There it appears in the third and last major divison of the OT canon, called simply "the Writings." Following Psalms, Jobs, Proverbs, it precedes the Song of Solomon, Ecclesiastes, Lamentations, Esther, with which it constitutes a special liturgical grouping. Known as "the Rolls" or "the Scrolls," these books were read on designated festival days. Ruth was selected for the Feast of Weeks (Pentecost), also called the Feast of Harvest (Lv 23:15 note), presumably because of the prominence of harvesting activity in the story.

Authorship

There is general agreement that the story of Ruth is one of the "loveliest" literary productions of an "idyllic and epic" nature (Goethe). Among its excellent features is the effective use of dialog—more than half of its verses. Rabbinic tradition has it that Samuel wrote this exquisite short story. However, its author remains unknown. The time of composition too can not be established with certainty. Some scholars posit a date as late as the return from the Babylonian captivity, some five centuries after the events of the story, mainly because they regard the book as a historical novel and not as an account of actual events. Its author concocted the tale in order to counteract the prohibitions against mixed marriages, enforced by the postexilic leaders Ezra and Nehemiah. This view is no more than an assumption. Supporting clues for a late date, drawn from the book itself, can be met by valid counterarguments. There is no cogent reason why Ruth could not have been written during or soon after the reign of David.

OUTLINE

How Ruth "Happened" to

I. 1:1-22 Come to Live in Bethlehem

II. 2:1-23 Meet Her Future Husband

III. 3:1—4:17 Become Boaz' Wife

IV. 4:18-21 Become David's Ancestress

1:1-22 HOW RUTH "HAPPENED" TO LIVE IN BETHLEHEM

1:1-5 Married and Widowed in Native Moab

1:1 *A famine.* Before Ruth enters the plot of the story, a disaster occurred *when the judges ruled* (see Introduction, "Time"). It was the first link in a chain of circumstances that "happened to come" (2:3) by divine providence to shape the heroine's destiny. Brought on by drought, plagues of locusts, or other natural causes, famines were not infrequently the cause of emigration in search of sustenance (Gn 12:10; 26:1; 41:56). In this instance the lack of food could have resulted from raids on the harvest by marauding nomads such as the Midianites and Amalekites (Ju 6:3-6). Certain fields *in the land* may have been hit particularly hard and often.

Bethlehem. The cupboard was bare even in a place called "the house of bread" (its derivation from a Canaanite god Lahmi is not well founded). Still obscure and not yet one of the most renowned places in Israel, it is identified by the phrase "in Judah" to distinguish it from another Bethlehem in Zebulun (Mi 5:2; Mt 2:6; 1 Sm 16:1; Jos 19:15). The older name of the city was Ephrathah, sometimes written Ephrath (Gn 35:16, 19; 48:7). When therefore the Bethlehemites of this episode are called "Ephrathites" (2), the purpose may be to identify them as a prominent family, long established in an ancestral heritage (cf. 19-21). The story of Ruth begins with citizens of Bethlehem and ends with the Bethlehemite David (4:22), in whose house God "raised up a horn of salvation." (Lk 1:68 f.)

Country of Moab. Lit. "the fields of Moab." People in search of food would naturally seek out fertile areas in a country. Moab consisted to a great extent of a plateau, 3,000 feet high and scarred by deep ravines (Is 16:10 ff.; Jer 48:33). In order to *sojourn,* i.e., take up temporary residence, there, the Bethlehemites had to travel from their home, 6 miles south of Jerusalem, around the northern end of the Dead Sea and midway down its eastern shore—some 100 miles.

1:2 *Elimelech.* A name often was chosen to describe a characteristic of its bearer. Elimelech means "my God is king" or "God is king." *Naomi,* derived from a common noun meaning favor, delight, loveliness, beauty, is one who is regarded as having "favor with God and man" (Lk 2:52; Ps 90:17; 27:4). The etymological connotation of *Mahlon* and *Chilion* is not clear beyond doubt. Their names seem to derive from roots meaning respectively to be weak or sickly and to be frail, failing, wasting away.

1:4 *Moabite wives.* The Moabites are not explicitly mentioned among the nations of Canaan with whom the Israelites were forbidden to intermarry (Dt 7:1-3). However, the law decreed that a Moabite shall "not enter the assembly of the Lord even to the tenth generation" (Dt 23:1, 3 notes). Whether in accord with the provisions for Israel's ethnic purity or not, the Lord let the wife of such a marriage become an ancestress of the Savior of all nations. (Eph 2:11-22)

Orpah . . . Ruth. Because so little is known of the Moabite language, it is difficult to determine the precise meaning of the wives' names. *Orpah* is related to the cognate Hebrew word for neck, used figuratively in the phrase "stiff of neck," i.e., stiff-necked or stubborn (Ex 32:9, etc. but see also SS 4:4). *Ruth* appears to be a contracted form of a noun which in Hebrew means "companionship, friendship, fellowship."

1:6-22 Emigration to Israel

1:6 *To return.* It is not necessary to assume that Naomi's sons were married at the beginning of the "ten years" (4) of their Moabite sojourn. Not blessed with children, the marriages no doubt took place not long before their death and Naomi's decision to return home. For *visited* see Ex 3:16 note.

1:8 *Mother's house.* Under their mothers' care and direction the widows would have assumed their premarital status, making them eligible for remarriage. Apparently their fathers—at least Ruth's—still were living.

1:9 *A home.* KJV here and for a synonym in 3:1: "rest." The Hebrew word has a wider range of meanings than relief from tiring labor. It is frequently used to denote the successful attainment of one's striving, the goal of restless activity (parallel with "inheritance," Dt 12:9; Jos 21:43-45; Ps 95:11; "dwellings," Is 11:10).

1:13 *Exceedingly bitter.* The first part of this verse makes good sense if rendered: "For the bitter [fate that has overtaken] me is too onerous for you [to share it with me]." Naomi advanced good reasons why her daughters-in-law had no prospect of establishing a home if they remained with her: (1) she was too old to bear sons whose duty it would be to enter a levirate marriage with them (Gn 38:8 note; Dt 25:5; Lv 18:18 note); (2) even though she were to be married again and were capable of bearing sons, the widowed sisters could not be expected to *wait till they were grown. The hand of the Lord has gone forth,* striking her with such severe blows of adversity as to leave her future bleak with frustrations—why should they want to throw in their lot with her? Naomi humbled herself, perhaps not without some resentment, "under the mighty hand of God," making it the source of all that happens, as does all of Scripture. (21; 1 Ptr 5:6; Dt 2:15; Ju 2:15; 1 Sm 5:9; Is 51:17; Acts 11:21; 13:11; Heb 10:31)

1:16 *Where you go.* Her sister-in-law's compliance with Naomi's directives did not deter Ruth from entrusting her future, dark with forebodings of hardships, to "the Lord," Naomi's and Israel's God. Her reply to Naomi may serve as a wedding text, as it often has, if a daughter-in-law's faithfulness to her mother-in-law is made exemplary for the relationship of husband and wife.

1:17 *The Lord do.* No longer a worshiper of Chemosh, the Moabite national deity (Nm 21:29), Ruth declared her readiness to "renounce all" by invoking the name of Israel's covenant God to subject her to dire consequences in case she should break her vow. For similar oaths in which the formula "so and more also" set no limit to the punishment for unfaithfulness see 1 Sm 14:44; 2 Sm 3:35.

1:20 *Mara.* Before she left, Naomi had been the favored or lovely one (2); she returned a broken, "empty," childless widow. The Almighty had dealt so *bitterly* with her that her present condition would be more aptly described if people called her "Mrs. Bitter." Resigned and yet bewildered to the point of recrimination—how many believers have not shared her perplexity?—she did not realize that in His providence God was linking her name with Him who was to be given a name "which is above every name," because He was to "save his people [including her] from their sins." (Ph 2:9; Mt 1:21)

2:1-23 HOW RUTH MET HER FUTURE HUSBAND

2:1-7 Chance Gleaning in Boaz's Field

2:1 *Boaz.* The first chapter tells how "Ruth the Moabites" came to live in Bethlehem. However, even there she could have remained an obscure widow if she had not come to know her future husband. His name *Boaz,* perhaps composed of a preposition and a noun (like Immanuel), may mean "in him is strength." It occurs again only as the name of the left pillar of Solomon's temple. (1 K 7:21)

Kinsman. At this point in the story Boaz is not yet called a "kinsman" in the technical sense of "redeemer" as in 20; 3:2, 12; 4:3 (see Introduction). The Hebrew word here is a more general term which introduces him as no more than an associate, a relative *of the family of Elimelech*—a skillful use of the element of suspense on the part of the writer.

2:2 *Glean.* "The sojourner, the fatherless, and the widow" were permitted to follow "after the reapers" (3), gathering the stalks of grain which the latter had missed or dropped. (Lv 19:9; 23:22; Dt 24:19)

2:3 *Happened.* Ruth's destiny was shaped by a series of circumstances which appear to happen by chance. However, her story demonstrates that there is no such thing as a blind fate. Designed by "the hand of the Lord" (1:13), even the most insignificant turn of events is providentially intended to give each individual, whether peasant or king, the chance to play a particular role in life. (Lk 10:21; 2 Sm 1:6; Ex 2:14 f.)

2:4 *Behold.* It so "happened" (3) that *Boaz came* upon the scene at the right moment to get acquainted with Ruth, of whom he had heard a good report.

2:7 *For a moment.* The RSV reproduces the intent of the servant's word. The Hebrew text makes sense if rendered: "This [that you see] her [now] sitting in the house [erected as a shelter for the harvesters] has been [only] for a little [time].

2:8-16 Kind Treatment by Boaz

2:8 *My daughter.* Ruth was not disappointed in her hope to find a landowner in "whose sight" she might find favor. Boaz treated her, "a foreigner" (10), like a daughter, commending her for her kindness to her mother-in-law. He declared her deserving of a "full reward" from "the Lord, the God of Israel," under whose protecting "wings" she had "come to take refuge." Implementing that "recompense" himself, Boaz granter her (a) a place close to his maidens; (b) protection against being molested; (c) permission to quench her thirst from his reapers' water supply.

2:11 *Left.* Ruth's leaving her homeland is reminiscent of Abraham, who "by faith . . . went out, now knowing where he was to go." (Heb 11:8; Gn 12:1)

2:13 *Spoken kindly.* Literally "spoken upon the heart," i.e, as tenderly as a lover speaks to the woman he is wooing. (Gn 34:3; Hos 2:14; Is 40:2)

2:14 *Eat.* Boaz accorded Ruth additional privileges, letting her (a) be his guest at lunch (14); (b) "glean even among [better: "between"] the sheaves," no longer "after the reapers" (15, 7); (c) carry off "bundles" the young men were deliberately to "pull out" for her. (16)

2:17-23 Disclosure of Boaz's Relationship

2:19 *The man's name.* Surprised that Ruth brought home almost a bushel of barley, considerably more than the normal yield of a day's gleaning, Naomi concluded that "the Lord" in His "kindness" had directed her daughter-in-law to the field of "a relative." If Boaz would act also in the capacity of a kinsman (see Introduction), this chance meeting held prospects of additional and more permanent help. For the first, Ruth was to keep "close to the maidens of Boaz."

2:22 *Molested.* It is not necessary to give this meaning to the Hebrew verb, which indeed it frequently has. Naomi is concerned that if "they [i.e., some people] meet" her there (KJV), Boaz would be offended upon hearing about it.

2:23 *Barley and wheat harvests.* During the 3 months of April, May, June.

3:1—4:17 HOW RUTH BECAME BOAZ'S WIFE

3:1-5 Marriage Proposal Planned

3:1 *Said.* Naomi now took steps to accomplish what she evidently had in mind from the moment she heard of Ruth's meeting a relative (2:19 note). "Too old to have a husband" herself (1:12), the older widow contrived a way for her daughter-in-law to approach Boaz with the request to assume the role of a kinsman, which meant entering a levirate marriage with her (1-5). Not averse to the proposal, Boaz, however, deferred acting on it until "a kinsman nearer than" he had been apprised of his rights in the matter (6-13). Sending Ruth back to Naomi (14-18), Boaz at once took steps to clear up the situation. When the nearest of kin waived his "right of redemption" (4:1-6), the prospective bridegroom had the fact publicly notarized that he was legally entitled to marry Ruth. At the same time he publicly obligated himself to acquire title to her dead father-in-law's property, no doubt heavily encumbered with debts, in order to restore it to the family of Elimelech.

A home. Cf. 1:9 note.

3:2 *Kinsman.* A more discriminating translation would be: "an acquaintance" (2:1 note). Naomi was hopeful that this distant relative would act in the capacity of kinsman, a redeemer.

3:4 *Lie down.* Naomi instructed Ruth how to let Boaz know that she had not "gone after young men" in search of a husband but was quite willing to have him "do the part of the next of kin," i.e., to marry her. Perhaps the Moabitess daughter-in-law needed specific directions because she was not acquainted with this strange procedure. However, no parallels to it are known to confirm the supposition that it was an accepted custom even in Israel. The circumstances are unusual indeed, requiring drastic measures. Ordinarily marriages were contracted by the male head of the house. In this case a woman without a husband had to find a way for her widowed ward to propose a marriage which the law made obligatory for a kinsman. Boaz did not interpret Ruth's action as a wily attempt to lure him into intercourse with her, thereby putting him under obligation to her. Whether Naomi was prepared to have Ruth take such a course, if necessary, cannot be determined.

3:6-18 Proposal Temporarily Declined

3:7 *Heap.* Taking advantage of an evening breeze, Boaz had been "winnowing barley" (2) on "the threshing floor," which was communal property. He slept there in order to guard "the heap of grain" which he had been unable to transport into his granary.

His feet. The Hebrew word is not the usual noun for *feet.* Outside of this chapter it occurs again only in Dn 10:6 in the phrase translated "arms and legs." The context suggests that Ruth "uncovered the place at his feet," which here need not be a euphemism for male genitals. (Ex 4:25 note)

3:8 *Startled.* The basic meaning of the verb is to tremble, usually because one is "afraid" (KJV). Perhaps Boaz awoke shivering because of the cold. He *turned over* can be translated "he bent forward."

3:9 *Your skirt.* Lit. your "wings." Boaz had commended Ruth for taking refuge under the "wings" of "the Lord, the God of Israel" (2:12; so often of God's protection in the Psalms: 17:8; 36:7; 57:1; 91:4; etc.). Now she asked her kinsman to let her find safety under his "wings." However, she implied more. The same noun is used to denote the wings of a garment, i.e., its skirt. The expression "to spread a skirt over" a woman means to take her in marriage. (Eze 16:8; Dt 22:30)

3:11 *Woman of worth.* A general phrase denoting excellent qualities of various kinds. KJV: "virtuous"; also in Pr 12:4; 31:10, where RSV renders "a good wife."

3:14 *Said.* Evidently in the sense "he said to himself," "he thought." (Gn 20:11)

3:15 *Six measures.* The Hebrew ("six of barley") does not specify what the *measures* were. Whatever its exact weight, the gift was so generous that he *laid it upon her,* i.e., helped her to get it on her shoulder or head.

3:17 *Empty-handed.* The same word translated "empty" (1:21). The Lord was filling her empty hands and heart.

4:1-12 Legal Status Clarified

4:1 *The gate.* Boaz *sat down there* where court was held and business transactions were legalized, "the elders of the city" serving as witnesses, jury, and judge.

4:3 *Kinsman.* The literal translation "brother" (KJV) is preferable (cf. 3:2 note). The term brother does not only denote a member of the same family but also a more distant relative. Lv 25:25 makes provision for a "brother" who has become poor.

4:4 *Besides you.* There is no one who can dispute your claim to be "the next of kin."

4:5 *Buying Ruth.* KJV: "buy it [the field] also of Ruth." Boaz, who fully understood the situation, explained to the prospective kinsman that Ruth too had a claim to the land (9). Its redemption obligated the kinsman *to restore the name of the dead* by marrying the childless widow. Legally the heir to the property, the first son of this marriage would perpetuate Elimelech's son's name.

4:6 *Impair.* The kinsman was financially unable to assure responsibility for property other than the *inheritance* of his immediate family.

4:7 *Custom.* Even though it was no longer in vogue, the writer knew the custom by which a voluntary transfer of property was publicly attested. In cases of a kinsman's refusal to see to it that his obligations were discharged—as they were in this instance by Boaz, a more distant relative—the procedure was quite different. (Dt 25:7-10)

4:10 *Ruth . . . I have bought.* He had acquired the legal right to marry her. The money paid for the field was the equivalent of the usual bride price. (Gn 29:18)

4:11 *Rachel and Leah.* The people invoked upon Ruth the blessing of such fruitfulness as made Jacob's two wives the matriarchs of all Israel, the children of their maids, Bilhah and Zilpah, being reckoned as belonging to their mistresses. (Gn 30:3 note)

4:12 *Perez.* In offering their good wishes to the bridal couple the women mentioned a less-known ancestor of Boaz (18-21) because he was born to Judah of Tamar, who like Ruth had lost her first husband. (Gn 38:1, 8, 15 notes)

4:13-17 Marriage Consummated

4:17 *A name.* It was not customary for the women of a community to name a child. However, the circumstances of Ruth's marriage were very unusual too. Naomi treated her son as if he were hers. *Obed,* meaning "servant," was *born to Naomi* in the sense that through him her husband's name would live on. God moved in a mysterious way to let Ruth, the Moabite peasant girl, become the great-grandmother of Israel's great king David.

4:18-22 HOW RUTH BECAME DAVID'S ANCESTRESS

4:18 *Descendants.* For this term see Gn 2:4 note. As if officially to verify Ruth's status in Israel, alluded to in the previous verse, the book closes with a genealogy, beginning with Perez, the son of Judah, and ending with her famous descendant David. The register of names is not complete. E.g., there must have been intervening links between "Salmon," the husband of Rahab, at the time of the conquest under Joshua (Mt 1:5), and Boaz, living "when the judges ruled." (1:1)

FIRST AND SECOND

SAMUEL

INTRODUCTION

Content

The Book of Judges holds out little hope for Israel's survival. Violating religious, moral, and social principles, the nation appeared to be drowning in a sea of chaos. Family stability, as depicted in the Book of Ruth, could not long escape being drawn into the maelstrom of national dissolution.

However, in His infinite mercy God did not abandon His covenant to bring salvation to all nations through Abraham's descendants (Gn 12:3 note). The books of Samuel record not only how the chosen people were saved from threatening extinction but also how they rose to heights of imperial power. It all happened under King David, ancestor and foreshadowing type of "the King of Israel," "the Ruler of the kings of the earth" (Jn 1:49; Rv 1:5; 22:16; Ro 1:3). His rise from pasture to imperial palace is more than an epic of a national hero. It was the Lord who "established him king . . . and exalted his kingdom for the sake of His people Israel." (2 Sm 5:12)

The change from anarchy to empire status was both gradual and abrupt. Some order was restored by Samuel, the last of the judges (Acts 13:20), after his mentor Eli had left the nation in political and religious shambles. Conditions again improved in the early reign of Saul, the first king. However, at his death Israel appeared helpless to ward off absorption by the Philistines.

But within a few years Israel experienced a complete reversal of its fortunes. Under the leadership of an erstwhile shepherd boy, it embarked on an uninterrupted march from servile degradation to unprecedented—and never again to be attained—glory. By astute maneuvers David united the tribes; in two encounters he freed the land from Philistine occupation; in quick succession one neighboring people after another was brought under his sway.

David "walked with integrity of heart and uprightness" (1 K 9:4; Acts 13:36). Nevertheless this "anointed of the God of Jacob, the sweet psalmist of Israel" (2 Sm 23:1), was "brought forth and conceived in sin" (Ps 51:5). He needed divine pardon no less than all men "made in the likeness and image" of Adam (Gn 5:3). However, "in the house of his servant David," the adulterer and murderer, God "promised beforehand through his prophets" to raise up "a horn of salvation for us" (Lk 1:69; 2 Sm 7:8 ff.; Ro 1:3). Because of the sinless life and vicarious death of David's Son and Lord, the good news comes to every penitent sinner: "The Lord has put away... your sin." (2 Sm 12:13)

Time

The events of the two books of Samuel occurred during a period extending some decades beyond a century. During these years Palestine remained unmolested by the major world powers. Humanly speaking, David's empire could not have become a reality if Egypt had been at its former peak of power or if the Assyrian war machine had appeared on the scene centuries earlier than it actually did. The Lord of history so timed the rise and fall of nations as to give Israel its day of splendor.

Monarchy

For centuries Israel was "a kingdom of priests" without a king. In this respect it was not at all "like all the nations" of its environment (1 Sm 8:4 f.). From time immemorial all states—the Egyptian empire as well as the small Canaanite city-states—were governed by sovereigns wielding absolute power. Furthermore when the monarchy eventually was introduced in Israel, it was to be different from the despotic rule of neighboring autocrats. The man on Israel's throne was to be a theocratic ruler no less than Moses had been. Chosen by God and anointed at His direction, he was king by divine grace in the fullest sense of the term. Far from being free to reign arbitrarily, he was subject to a constitution, drawn up by God Himself, the Mosaic law (1 K 2:1-3). Israel was both church and state. Nevertheless there was to be no royal usurpation of priestly functions.

Authorship

Scripture does not identify the author of the books, now known by the name of the man who bridged the era from judgeship to kingship. Rabbinic tradition that "Samuel wrote the book that bears his name" evidently was not meant to be taken seriously since half of the recorded events happened after his death (1 Sm 25:1). For its grouping under "the Former Prophets" in the Hebrew canon see the Introduction to Joshua.

It is evident that the unknown author had access to existing documents in producing what originally comprised a single volume. Written records are mentioned in 1 Ch 29:29. See also 2 Sm 1:18 note. There are indications that the time of composition was not long after the northern tribes seceded from the "union" at the death of Solomon, David's son. Frequent references are made to the two kingdoms, "Israel" and "Judah." (1 Sm 27:6; 2 Sm 20:14; etc.)

Those scholars who maintain that the five books of Moses are the product of a long process of compilation and editing assert that they can isolate two or more strands in the books of Samuel which have the same distinguishable characteristics as those identified in the Pentateuch (see Introduction to Genesis, "Authorship"). The writer(s) drew on a history of David's reign produced by a chronicler attached to the royal court. From these sources the compiler(s) presumably incorporated some duplicate accounts of the same events, which at times contain contradictory details and viewpoints. However, if properly interpreted, these so-called doublets merge into a harmonious and consistent narrative.

OUTLINE

- I. 1:1—15:34 David's Antecedents
  - A. 1:1—7:17 Samuel, the Last Judge
  - B. 8:1—15:35 Saul, the First King
- II. 16:1—2 Sm 24:25 David's Reign
  - A. 16:1—2 Sm 5:5 How David Became King
  - B. 2 Sm 5:6—9:13 How David Reigned
  - C. 2 Sm 10:1—12:31 How David Sinned
  - D. 2 Sm 13:1—20:26 How Troubles Arose in David's House
- III. 2 Sm 21:1—24:25 Supplementary Accounts of David's Reign

1:1—7:17 SAMUEL, THE LAST JUDGE

1:1—7:2 Birth and Youth in Evil Days

1:1—4:1 PRIESTLY CORRUPTION

1:1 *Elkanah.* The First Book of Samuel bridges the era between the chaotic conditions of the judges, when "every man did what was right in his own eyes" (Ju 17:6; 21:25), and the stable rule of David. The two leading figures of this transitional period were Samuel, the last of the judges, and Saul, the first but ineffective king. The story of Samuel (chs. 1—8) reads like a chapter from the Book of Judges: (a) once again sacrilege and worship of "foreign gods" "provoked the Lord to anger" (Ju 2:12; ch. 17); (b) as He had done at the time of Samson, "the Lord gave them into the hand of the Philistines" (Ju 13:1 ff.); (c) when "the hand of the Lord was against them for evil," the Israelites repented of their sins (Ju 2:15); (d) again the Lord relented and "raised up" a judge "who saved them" (Ju 2:16; 1 Sm 7:15). Samuel's judicial functions too were similar to those of his predecessors: (a) he vindicated the right of the chosen people in their controversy with foreign enemies; (b) he presided at local courts of justice. (Cf. Judges, Introduction, "Content")

Samuel's father, *an Ephraimite,* i.e., a resident *of Ephraim,* was of the lineage of Kohath, Levi's second son (1 Ch 6:22-28, 33-38). His immediate family were descendants of *Zuph* and therefore called *Zophim.* The name of their hometown *Ramathaim* is also a common noun meaning "height." It occurs here in the dual form: "the twin heights." The singular "Ramah" is used in all other references (19; 2:11, etc). It is usually identified with the Ramah 5 miles north of Jerusalem.

1:2 *Two wives.* On polygamy in the OT see Gn 16:2 note. Perhaps Elkanah married Peninnah because Hannah proved to be barren.

1:3 *Year by year.* Three times a year all males were to "appear before the Lord God" (Ex 34:23). It is possible that during the disturbed conditions Elkanah attended only one of the three pilgrim feasts. However, the text may say no more than that once a year he did not make the journey alone but took his wives with him. Also see 21 note.

Lord of hosts. This divine title occurs here for the first time. It is found in more than 270 subsequent passages. The transliteration of the Hebrew word is "Zebaoth." The hosts or armies under God's command are not limited to Israel's fighting forces (17:45). He has the power to direct all created powers, "the heavens and the earth . . . and all the host of them." (Gn 2:1)

Shiloh. Cf. Jos 18:1 note.

1:5 *Only one.* This translation, based on the Septuagint, is to be preferred to KJV: "a worthy portion." Elkanah divided the portions equally among the members of his family. Because Hannah was childless she was not entitled to more than her one share. At these occasions she was particularly conscious of the disgrace of her barrenness. "Her rival" exploited her dilemma "to irritate her" with cutting remarks.

1:9 *Eli.* He was *the priest,* i.e., the high priest. His sons, Hophni and Phinehas, were "priests of the Lord" (3). Because of the father's advanced age they no doubt acted in his behalf in many instances. Seated "beside the doorpost of the temple," the old man still was able to function as adviser and judge. The tabernacle, erected by Joshua at Shiloh, remained there until the Philistines captured the city (4:11; Jos 18:1; Ju 18:31; Jer 7:12). Perhaps it was provided with structural additions such as doorposts. *Temple* and "tabernacle" are used interchangeably (Ex 25:9; Ps 27:4). In 2 Sm 12:20 the tent under which the ark was kept is called "the house of the Lord."

1:11 *All the days.* Dedicated from his youth to continuous service at the sanctuary, Hannah's son was to assume obligations that exceeded the normal Levitical duties (Nm 8:24-26). In addition he was not to cut his hair. For long hair as a part of the Nazarite vow see Nm 6:2, 13 notes.

1:16 *A base woman.* Lit. "a daughter of Belial" (KJV; cf. Ju 19:22 note). Eli thought she was "filled with new wine" (Acts 2:13) because her behavior aroused his suspicion. Instead of rejoicing before the Lord she "wept bitterly," as some drunken people do; she seemed to be mumbling incoherently, moving her lips but not praying audibly as was customary.

1:21 *His vow.* Elkanah's trips to Shiloh for *the yearly sacrifice* may have had the purpose to *pay his vow* which he had made voluntarily over and above the required annual pilgrimages. (Nm 30:2 note.)

1:22 *Weaned.* Women suckled their children from 2 to 3 years. No figure is given for his age when he was left at the sanctuary. (24)

1:23 *His word.* No specific promise by God is mentioned unless Eli's words (17) are vested with divine sanction. The Septuagint reads "your word," meaning: may the Lord help you to keep your vow.

2:1 *Prayed.* Her worship included a hymn that has the thematic strains of Mary's Magnificat (Lk 1:46-55). She praised the Lord besides whom there is no other God (1 f.). With Him nothing is impossible: (a) He shatters all resistance in order to help the needy (3-5); (b) the issues of life and death are in His hands (6); (c) as its Creator He governs the universe; therefore the mighty are not beyond His control and the poor can look to Him for vindication (7 f.); (d) in the future too the Lord will have His way; in spite of all opposition, "the ends of the earth" will recognize the rule of His King, the anointed or Messiah. (9 f.)

2:5 *The barren.* A direct reference to Hannah's cause for thanksgiving.

2:10 *His anointed.* Hannah was given a glimpse of a better future. The period of the judges was coming to an end. Her son was to initiate the kingship, anointing both Saul and David. The latter's illustrious reign was not to be an end in itself but only the shadow of things to come—the everlasting kingdom of God's own Son who was to be "of the house and lineage of David" (Luke 2:4). Jesus was *the* Christ, the Greek equivalent for the Hebrew "anointed one," which in its transliterated form is "Messiah." (Jn 1:41; 4:25)

2:11 *Went home.* Elkanah had accompanied Hannah to Shiloh. (1:25)

2:12 *Worthless fellows.* Lit. "sons of Belial" (cf. 1:16). The times were evil, as they had been under preceding judges (Ju 8:27; 17:7 ff.). Men who should have promoted the true worship of the Lord corrupted it. The high priest did not resolutely restrain his sons' sacrilege of the sanctuary when they (a) "treated the offering of the Lord with contempt" in order to serve "their own appetites" (11-17; cf. Ro 16:18; Ph 3:19); (b) "lay with the women who served at the entrance to the tent of meeting." (22)

2:13 *Custom of the priests.* Eli's sons disregarded the procedures prescribed for offering "a sacrifice," i.e., a meat offering by (a) taking of the meat whatever they could get although they were entitled only to the breast and thigh (Lv 7:34); (b) claiming their share before God's portion was burned on the altar; (c) using "force" to intimidate the worshipers.

2:18 *Ephod.* Unaffected by the bad example of Hophni and Phinehas, Samuel *was ministering before the Lord . . . girded* at the waist *with a linen ephod.* This was not the article of clothing worn by the high priest, made of much more costly material (see Ex 28; 39:1 notes). Although the ephod is not mentioned among the prescribed garments of the priests, its material (linen) or its design distinguished it from loincloths not used for ceremonial purposes. Priests came to be known as people who "wore the linen ephod" (22:18). David danced before the Lord, "girded [only] with a linen ephod" (2 Sm 6:14). Samuel's mother annually provided her growing son with "a little robe," a long outer garment of the kind worn by men of status.

2:25 *Will of the Lord.* When Eli's reprimand made no impression on his sons' hearts, hardened by willful disobedience, God decreed their punishment. He does not lead men into sin in order to have an excuse for taking their lives; at the same time the transgressor's punishment is the inevitable result of His holy *will.* (On the hardening of the heart see Ex 4:21 note; Jos 11:20.)

2:26 *To grow.* The account of the fall of Eli's house is interspersed with notes about Samuel's progress (2:11, 18-21, 26; 3:1, 19). Unknown to men, God had a future leader in training.

2:27 *Man of God.* The end of Eli's priesthood, here announced in detail by a prophet (27-36), was later confirmed when Samuel transmitted God's judgment to his mentor. (3:2-18)

Your father. Eli was a descendant of Ithamar, youngest son of the first high priest, Aaron, to whom God *revealed* himself. (Ex 4:4-16; 29:9; 1 Ch 24:3)

2:31 *Father's house.* Fulfillment of the prophetic word began when Hophni and Phinehas fell in battle against the Philistines. Later Eli's grandson Abiathar was deposed from office by the "anointed" king Solomon (35) and replaced with Zadok, a descendant of Aaron's third son Eleazar. (1 K 2:27; 1 Ch 6:3-10)

2:35 *For ever.* Literally "all the days." Eli's "house" (31) gave way to the "sure house" of Zadok, whose descendants held office for centuries. But his house too came to an end in the Babylonian captivity. However, what every "faithful priest" of the OT did was designed by God to be a promise of a High Priest who needed no successors. By the "single offering" of "his own blood," Jesus Christ "once for all" secured "an eternal redemption." (Heb 9:11-14; 10:11-18)

3:1 *Rare.* KJV: "precious." Before "a man of God" came to Eli (2:27), there was no revelation by *word* or by *vision* since the days of Gideon (Ju 6:11 ff.). This chapter tells how God again transmitted His Word to "all Israel" through Samuel so clearly that everyone knew that he was "established as a prophet of the Lord" (20-21). When at first "the word of the Lord came" to Samuel, he did not realize that "the Lord was calling" him. Because he had not received such a call previously, he "did not yet know the Lord" as the source of the communication (2-9). The first message which the young prophet received briefly confirmed God's intention to reject Eli's house (2-9; cf. 2:27-36). At the latter's request he conveyed the sad news to him. (15-18)

3:3 *Lamp of God.* The seven-branched candelabrum in the sanctuary was to burn "from evening to morning" (Lv 24:1-3; Ex 25:31-40). God's call therefore came to Samuel shortly before dawn. It is not necessary to assume that he was sleeping beside the ark in the holy of holies. God promised to "speak with" Israel from the *ark of God* which was *within the temple.* (Ex 25:22; Nm 7:89)

3:10 *Stood forth.* In addition to calling to Samuel, God revealed Himself to him in a visible form.

3:14 *Not be expiated.* Cf. 2:25 note.

3:17 *More also.* For the meaning of the oath see Ru 1:17 note.

3:20 *All Israel.* How Samuel functioned as an accredited prophet to all Israel is told in ch. 7. The intervening section (chs. 4—6) relates Eli's death and the capture of the ark by the Philistines. In this hour of dire need Samuel "cried to the Lord for Israel, and the Lord answered him" (7:2, 9). For *Dan to Beer-sheba* see Ju 20:1 note.

4:1 *The Philistines.* For their presence in Canaan see Gn 21:32 note. While Eli's sons "were blaspheming God" at the sanctuary (3:13), "all the house of Israel" also provoked the Lord to anger by idolatrous worship of "foreign gods" (7:3 f.). As in the days of Samson, "the Lord gave them into the hand of the Philistines" (Ju 13:1) and the Israelite forces suffered two disastrous defeats (2-4, 5-11). In the second battle the enemy captured the ark of the covenant. The news of the catastrophe had two tragic effects: the death of Eli (12-18) and of his daughter-in-law, the latter dying in childbirth. (19-22)

Ebenezer. "Stone of help"; this site as well as the place where 20 years later Samuel erected a stone, giving it this name (7:12), remains unidentified. The Philistine camp was close by at *Aphek.* Its meaning, "stronghold" or "fortress," accounts for the fact that several places bore this name (Jos 19:30; 1 K 20:26). This *Aphek* was some 20 miles west of Shiloh and about 10 miles from the Mediterranean coast. *Israel went out to battle against the Philistines* in order to check the latter's thrust northward along the seacoast. Perhaps only the northern tribes gave battle because they were directly affected by the invasion. For similar circumstances see Ju 10:7; 13:1 notes.

4:2—7:2 INVASION BY PHILISTINES

4:2 *Four thousand.* See Numbers, Introduction, "The Numbers. . . ." If the Hebrew word for *thousand* here and in 10 does not have a numerical value but denotes fully armed men, the losses would be reckoned in terms of these fallen heroes. The "slaughter" of four and then 30 of such warriors would have been a decisive blow, the others having "neither sword nor spear." (13:22)

4:3 *The ark.* Cf. Ex 25:10, 16, 17, 18 notes. As men have done ever since, the Israelites believed that God was under obligation to do their bidding. They went so far as to think that they had "the Lord of hosts" (1:3 note) enshrined in the ark like a good-luck charm which magically produces desired results. But God is not a puppet of man's manipulation. He is the sovereign God of *the covenant.* Not a device to imprison Him whom "heavens and the highest heaven cannot contain" (1 K 8:27), the ark was the symbol of His gracious condescension to be accessible to a people when they sought His forgiveness and help. For the use of the ark in earlier military ventures see Jos 3:6; 6:6.

4:6 *Hebrews.* The term for the Israelites used by foreigners. Cf. Gn 14:13 note.

4:10 *Was defeated.* After the decisive defeat of Israel's army the victorious Philistines no doubt marched on to Shiloh and destroyed it. (Jer 7:12, 14; 26:6, 9)

4:12 *Clothes rent.* Display of emotions was not considered unmanly. Rending one's clothes and placing earth on one's head was a customary expression of mourning.

4:18 *Judged.* Eli still belonged to the period in Israel's history when the human agent of God's justice bore the title of judge. (For the broad meaning of this term see Judges, Introduction.) He functioned in this capacity for *forty years,* the round figure found frequently in Judges. (Ju 3:11; 5:31; 8:28, etc.)

4:19 *Daughter-in-law.* The news of the debacle killed an old man. It also turned a mother's joy that "a man is born into the world" into fatal pain. Before she died, Eli's daughter-in-law expressed her grief by calling her son "Ichabod," which means "Where is glory?" God had used the ark to manifest His "glory" (Lv 16:2). Its capture betokened the end of God's covenant relationship with Israel. His glory "had departed" (literally "gone into exile"; cf. Ju 18:30 note).

5:1 *Captured the ark.* The previous chapter demonstrates that God cannot be coerced by a magical use of such means of grace as the ark. The next section (5:1—7:2) makes just as clear that neither the Philistines nor His people can profane His glory with impunity. The former suffered disaster when they tried to reduce the Creator to the level of a man-made god such as their idol Dagon. The Israelites came to grief when they debased the holy mysteries by prying into them with sacrilegious curiosity. But there is also a positive side to this story of the ark. In spite of its mistreatment by men, God preserved it, restored it to penitent Israel, and continued to let it testify to His covenant with the people chosen to be the bearers of His promise to all nations.

5:2 *Dagon.* On the Philistine idol see Ju 16:23 note.

5:5 *Threshold.* This superstitious practice was not restricted to Ashdod (Zph 1:9). The threshold was considered the place from which evil spirits exercised their influence on those entering a house. The kind of humiliation suffered by Dagon gave the inhabitants of Ashdod additional reason not to *tread on the threshold* of their idol temple.

5:6 *Tumors.* Dagon's disintegration demonstrated that God will tolerate "no other gods before" Him (Ex 20:3). Lest the Philistines fail to understand this, the Lord *terrified and afflicted them* with an infectious and deadly epidemic of *tumors* (KJV "emerods," i.e., hemorrhoids). Translated "boils" in Dt 28:27, these swellings may have been symptoms of the bubonic plague, spread by rodents. The Septuagint reads in 12: "the land swarmed with mice."

5:11 *Send away.* When in each of the three cities "tumors broke out," the inhabitants connected the outbreak of the plague with the presence of *the ark of the God of Israel.*

6:3 *A guilt offering.* After 7 months the Philistine "priests and diviners" suggested an experiment to test whether it was only a coincidence that the people suffered an epidemic as soon as the ark was brought to their city. If they would "send it to its place" and they would "be healed," it would be proof that there was a cause-effect relationship between the ark and "this great harm" (9). Allowing for the possibility that "the God of Israel" had been offended, they were to return His shrine with a *guilt offering,* the same term used as sacrifices of reparation in Israel's worship. However, the Philistine offering was to achieve its purpose by means of sympathetic magic. It would automatically produce results if it consisted of golden replicas of the tumors and the mice "according to the number of lords of the [five principle cities of the] Philistines." (Cf. 17)

6:6 *Harden your hearts.* The priests cited Pharaoh as a warning example. Even though the Exodus is not mentioned in the Egyptian records, the defeat suffered by the mighty world power of the Nile was not unknown.

6:7 *New cart.* The Philistines took every precaution not to mar the experiment by using inappropriate means. In order to show their respect for the ark, the Israelites later transported it on the same kind of vehicle (2 Sm 6:3). The Philistines contrived two more tests to make certain that their misfortune had not "happened . . . by chance" (9). The heifers which they hitched to the cart were unbroken to the yoke and ordinarily would have balked. Furthermore these *two milch cows* had calves from which they normally would have refused to be separated.

6:12 *Beth-shemesh.* Overcoming maternal instincts, *the cows went straight in the direction of* an Israelite border city, located some 10 miles southeast of Ekron.

6:15 *Levites.* Beth-shemesh was one of the cities assigned by Joshua to the Levites (Jos 21:16). *The great stone* in the field of a certain Joshua served as an altar of burnt offerings and sacrifices.

6:18 *All the cities.* Not only the five principle cities but also others *belonging to the five lords* made contributions of gold.

The great stone. The Hebrew text has "unto Abel," an unknown place (so KJV). Abel and the word for stone (as in *Eben*ezer) are very similar. The RSV reading assumes that a copyist wrote an *l* instead of an *n*.

6:19 *Looked.* God proved to the Philistines that He will not be mocked. When the chosen people presumed to trifle with the symbol of the devouring fire of His holiness, they too learned that He meant it when He said: "They shall not go in to look upon the holy things . . . lest they die" (Nm 4:20). Every transgression of God's will, whether man considers it a mortal or venial sin, exposes the perpetrator to divine wrath. In this connection the words of Jesus are apropos: "Remember Lot's wife." (Lk 17:32; Gn 19:26 note)

Seventy men. The Hebrew manuscripts upon which the KJV is based add another 50,000. This enormous figure no doubt is due to a corruption of the text.

6:20 *Stand.* The ark was not to be touched by unauthorized hands (Nm 1:50 f.; 4:5). But hysterical with fear, the men of Beth-shemesh thought that death awaited anyone who dared to "have charge of the ark." (7:1)

7:1 *Kiriath-jearim.* There is general agreement that it is to be identified with a site 9 miles west of Jerusalem. No reason is given why the men of this particular city *came and took up the ark.* An otherwise unknown citizen, *Eleazar* son of *Abinadab,* was consecrated to guard the ark against further desecration.

7:2 *Twenty years.* It remained there until David brought it to Jerusalem (2 Sm 6). The first *twenty years* of this long interval are gone over in silence. It was a time of apostasy and general disorder, during which the Word of the Lord remained "rare" (3:1). In order to produce a hunger for it, the Lord is often compelled to take it away from those who reject it. The prophet Amos threatened such a "famine . . . of hearing the words of the Lord." (Am 8:11; see also Jesus' directions to His disciples in Mt 7:6)

7:3-17 Samuel's Judgeship

7:3 *Samuel said.* When "all the house of Israel lamented after the Lord" (2), He "raised up for them a deliverer," as He had done so often in the past (Ju 2:16; 3:15). Samuel, the last of the judges, was called to act in a judicial capacity similar to that of his predecessors: (a) he executed God's judgment on the Philistines (3-14); (b) he enforced the law of the Lord in Israel's internal affairs, holding court in various cities (15-17). But he was instrumental also in ushering in a new kind of leadership in Israel. By anointing Saul and David he established the monarchy.

7:4 *The Baals and the Ashtaroth.* Cf. Ju 2:13 note.

7:5 *Pray . . . for you.* Moses welded the 12 tribes into a nation. When Israel was at the point of losing its national identity, Samuel's healing of the threatening disintegration was of such far-reaching significance as to earn him recognition as the nation's second founder. Both men were so successful because they "cried to the Lord for Israel, and the Lord answered" them (9; Ex 15:25; 17:4, etc.). They lived on in Israel's memory as its great intercessors (Jer 15:1; Ps 99:6). The secular or spiritual leader who prays for his people has tapped unlimited resources.

Mizpah. Having penetrated deeply into Israelite territory, the Philistines launched an attack a few miles north of Jerusalem. (Ju 10:17; 20:1 notes)

7:6 *Drew water.* Pouring out water symbolized utter abasement before the Lord.

7:9 *Offered . . . a whole burnt offering.* After the destruction of Shiloh and the death of Eli, Samuel assumed sacerdotal duties.

7:10 *Thundered.* The Israelites could not claim credit for the victory. The Philistine rout resulted from the confusion produced when the Creator commandeered the forces of nature in behalf of His people, as He did on previous occasions. (Ex 9:23 f.; Jos 10:10 f.)

7:11 *Beth-car.* Not mentioned elsewhere, this site remains unidentified. From the context it appears to have been a place close to Philistine territory.

7:12 *Ebenezer.* Cf. 4:1 note. The location of *Jeshanah* is not known.

7:13 *Again enter.* The Philistines were not driven from their fixed base of operation along the Mediterranean coast. Furthermore, there were battles *against the Philistines all the days of Samuel.* However, Samuel put an end to their occupation of Israelite cities. It was not till the days of Saul, when the Israelites again served "other gods" (8:8), that the Philistines were able to renew their inroads into the heart of Israel's territory.

7:14 *Amorites.* At times this term denotes all non-Israelite inhabitants of the Promised Land (Gn 15:21 note). But it is used also of a particular racial group of Canaanites. (Nm 21:21 note)

7:16 *Judged Israel.* At Mizpah Samuel *judged Israel* in their controversy with a national assailant (6). But he *administered justice* also in litigations of one Israelite against another, as Deborah had done (Ju 4:4 note). He held court at intervals in *a circuit* of cities north of Jerusalem. All were within close proximity of Ramah, his birthplace and residence, except Gilgal, which was some 15 miles to the east in the Jordan valley. (Jos 4:20 note)

7:17 *An altar.* Abuse of the sanctuary had brought about the destruction of Shiloh and the disruption of prescribed procedures of sacrifice. However, even in the OT outward regulations of the ritual were secondary to the prime requirement that the people worship the Lord. So altars were erected at Ramah and various other places.

8:1—15:35 SAUL, THE FIRST KING

8:1—10:27 How Saul Became King

8:1-22 ISRAEL'S REQUEST FOR A KING

8:1 *Old.* Samuel did not remain the only appointed leader in Israel. He himself was to be instrumental in vesting God's rule over His people in a king. However, he did not relinquish his prerogative to apply divinely established criteria even to actions by royalty and if need be to condemn them.

Chs. 8—10 record how Saul came to be the first person to occupy the throne. First anointed in private by Samuel (8:1—10:16), he was chosen by lot before the assembled tribes. (10:17-27)

8:4 *Gathered together.* The representatives of the people advanced several reasons why they requested *a king to govern them.* The first was valid: Samuel's sons should not take his place because "they took bribes and perverted justice" (1-3). That they "did not walk in his ways" because he, like Eli, was too permissive is not explicitly stated. Sometimes children go wrong for other reasons. The second reason "displeased Samuel," and rightly so (6). Kingship as such was not a form of government irreconcilable with God's will. Through Moses He had told the people: "You may indeed set as king over you him whom the Lord your God will choose" (Dt 17:14 ff.). But when the people, *like all the nations,* put their confidence in a man rather than in God, they actually rejected Him "from being king over them" (7). Finally the Israelites again were threatened by foreign oppression. When Saul became king, the Philistines indeed were deep in Israelite territory (chs. 13 f.). But instead of repenting of their sins of "serving other gods" (8), they wanted a king to "go out before us and fight our battles" (20), spurning God's promise to "fight for" them. (Ex 14:14; Dt 1:30)

8:9 *Hearken.* At times God lets men have what they demand in order to teach them the folly of their stubborn self-will (18; Ps 106:13-15). When people sacrifice religious and moral principles in order to get what they crave, the fruits of their striving often have a bitter taste (Mt 6:24). But God is able also to bring good out of evil. Under David the monarchy became the type and promise of the Messianic kingdom established by Jesus, "The King of the Jews." (Mk 15:26)

8:1 *Ways of the king.* Kings in Israel's environment made even more autocratic demands on their subjects than those mentioned by Samuel (11-18). Some rulers of the chosen people were to adopt *ways* like those of the kings of "all the nations."

9:1—10:16 FIRST KING ANOINTED BY SAMUEL

9:2 *Saul.* Chs. 9—10 tell the story how Samuel carried out the Lord's command: "Make them a king" (8:22). "All the elders . . . gathered together" before Samuel (8:4) were not to appoint their monarch; they were dismissed "every man to his city" (8:22). God had His own way of letting Saul become king: (a) as if by chance the son of Kish was led to Samuel, who secretly anointed him "to be prince over" Israel (9:1—10:16); (b) to "all the tribes of Israel," assembled at Mizpah, God used the casting of lots to announce who their king was to be (10:17-27); (c) still later the people themselves, in a special ceremony, "made Saul king before the Lord in Gilgal." (11:12-15)

Handsome young man. The Hebrew word for *handsome* is "good," which the remainder of the verse applies to his stature rather than to his features. *Young man,* one word in the original, does not stress youth but denotes a person in the prime of life, particularly his ability to bear arms. When Saul fought against the Philistines, he had a grown son (13:2). The account, highly compressed as it is, does not specify how much time elapsed between Saul's first meeting with Samuel and his actual coronation. It must be remembered too that in a patriarchal society the sons remained under the jurisdiction of their father even after they established their own household.

9:5 *Zuph.* See 1:1 note on Ramathaim zophim. "Shalishah" and "Shaalim" (4) cannot be identified.

9:7 *Man of God.* Somehow Saul's servant heard that in this unfamiliar countryside there was a man who was *held in honor* because *all that he says comes true.* Even though "all Israel from Dan to Beer-sheba knew that Samuel was established as a prophet of the Lord" (3:20), it does not follow that Saul or his servant had ever met this *man of God* or knew where he lived.

Present. Saul took for granted that they could not consult the man without giving him a perquisite. In some instances such a *present* was no more than a bribe to secure a favorable answer (see the "fees" sent by Balak to Balaam, Nm 22:7). In Israel too it was said that its false prophets "divine for money." (Mi 3:11)

9:9 *Seer.* The parenthetic note explains that at that time the term *seer* was a popular designation for the same person later called a "prophet." Hence the fact that Saul and his servant refer to Samuel as a seer does not imply that in their opinion this "man of God" was a soothsayer of dubious character.

9:12 *The high place.* Samuel had "built there an altar to the Lord" (7:17 note). Therefore the sacrifice he offered at this elevated place was not devoted to Baal, whose "high places" the Israelites were to demolish. (Nm 33:52; Dt 12:2)

9:15 *Revealed.* Vv. 15-17 explain Saul's surprise that Samuel not only knew about the lost animals but also made him, the lowly "Benjaminite," the guest of honor at the sacrificial meal (18-24). Once Samuel's initial opposition to the monarchy had been overcome by the divine directive to "make them a king" (8:22), there was no reason why the prophet should not honor the person chosen by the Lord for the royal office.

9:24 *The leg and the upper portion.* The part of the sacrificial animal normally reserved for the priest.

10:1 *Prince.* The Hebrew word does not denote royal lineage but means "one designated" by God to rule *over his people.* Applied to Saul and others, this term sheds light on the kind of monarchy envisioned for Israel (9:15; 13:14; 25:30; 1 K 1:35). The king was not to *reign over the people of the Lord* by usurping power over them to his own advantage. He held office by God's choice and at His direction. At the same time, the *oil . . . poured . . . on his head* symbolized that his office had divine sanction. Anyone who touched such an anointed one or Messiah was guilty of more than a political offense. Jesus was THE Christ, the Greek word for Messiah, because "God anointed Jesus of Nazareth with the Holy Ghost and with power" (Acts 10:38). What the designated incumbents of the various offices that God established in Israel could achieve only imperfectly, was done to the complete satisfaction of His Father by THE Prophet, THE High Priest, THE King.

The Sign. In order to assure Saul that this unexpected and unprecedented turn of events would indeed come to pass, certain unforeseen things would happen: (a) he would be told that the lost asses had been found (2); (b) he would receive bread and wine from three strangers (3-4); (c) the Spirit of the Lord would "come mightily upon" him, causing him to prophesy. (5-7)

10:2 *Rachel's tomb.* On Jacob's return from Mesopotamia his wife Rachel died as "they journeyed from Bethel [in Benjamin] . . . on the way to . . . Bethlehem [in Judea]" (Gn 35:16-20). Marked by a pillar, her tomb was *at Zelzah,* an unidentified site. According to Jer 31:15 (Mt 2:18) "Rachel is weeping for her children . . . in Ramah," 5 miles north of Jerusalem. Therefore the phrase *in the territory of Benjamin* is better translated "in the border of Benjamin." (KJV)

10:3 *Oak of Tabor.* A landmark familiar at that time but unknown today. Perhaps because the tree was unusually tall, it was named after Mt. Tabor.

10:6 *Prophesy.* Saul was to meet and join a "band of prophets." Enabling him to *prophesy with them, the spirit of the Lord will come mightily upon* him. As this action of the Spirit supplied Samson with superhuman strength, so it produced a state of ecstasy in Saul. Although called "prophesying," this manifestation of the Spirit must be distinguished from the power which was bestowed upon men to transmit an inspired message from God. But the men who "moved by the Holy Spirit spoke from God" (2 Ptr 1:21) and the recipients of ecstatic rapture are called prophets, and both are said to prophesy. As there were false prophets of the Word in and about Israel, so there were ecstatics who did not *prophesy* in the name of the Lord, e.g., the prophets of Baal. (1 K 18:29; RSV: "they raved")

10:9 *Another heart.* This is another way of saying that he was to be "turned into another man" (6) when the Spirit of the Lord would come upon him.

10:10 *Band of prophets.* Perhaps this was a group later called "sons of prophets" whom Samuel organized for the purpose of fostering various gifts of the Spirit including the type of prophesying into which Saul was drawn. The person "standing as head over" (19:20) these sons or disciples was called a "father" (12; 2 K 2:11 f.). The prophesying to the accompaniment of musical instruments is mentioned only rarely in the OT. Because some groups who claimed the gift of prophecy evidently had a bad reputation, the people were surprised to find Saul in such company. "A man of the place" therefore wanted to know who their "father" was. If it was Samuel, there was no disgrace attached to Saul's joining them. Nevertheless what happened to the farmer's son was so unexpected that it gave rise to a proverb.

10:14 *Uncle.* Apparently Saul's uncle Ner (14:50) did not know that Kish had sent his son in search of the strayed animals.

10:17-27 SAUL CROWNED PUBLICLY

10:17 *Called the people.* When the people of their own accord had "gathered together" at Ramah to demand a king, Samuel dismissed them (ch. 8). Instructed by the Lord to "make them a king," he now assembled "all the tribes" at Mizpah to make known to them what only he knew, namely that the Lord had chosen Saul to be their "prince." Samuel took occasion to remind them once more that their motive in asking for a king was wrong (8:4-7). But in His providence "the Lord had chosen" Saul in order to bring good out of evil (8:9 note) and to promote His plans for Israel. (9:16)

10:20 *By lot.* Thc Urim and the Thummim, often the means of casting lots, are not mentioned (cf. Ex 28:15 note). However, the procedure resembled that followed in the case of Achan (Jos 7:14 ff.). Somehow it was possible that "Saul . . . was taken" even though he had "hidden himself among the baggage." (22)

10:25 *The rights and duties.* One word in Hebrew as in 8:11, where it is translated "the ways." No doubt the *book* containing them gave more elaborate prescriptions than those set down in advance for a potential king in Dt 17:14-20. It is not clear just when and where Samuel *laid the book up before the Lord.* Shiloh, where the tabernacle had been, was destroyed; the ark was at Kiriath-jearim. (7:2; Ex 16:33; Nm 17:7)

11:1—15:35 How Saul Ruled and Failed

11:1-15 GOOD BEGINNING: DEFEAT OF AMMONITES

11:1 *Jabesh-gilead.* At the beginning of his reign Saul acquitted himself with distinction both abroad and at home. When the Ammonites (Nm 21:24 note) threatened to enslave Jabesh-gilead (Ju 21:8 note), he summoned the tribes to united action and led them to a decisive victory over the aggressors (1-11). His magnanimous treatment of his Israelite detractors brought him the joyous acclaim of "all the men of Israel," gathered at Gilgal for a formal coronation ceremony. (12-15)

11:3 *Seven days.* Confident that the Israelites lacked the strength or the courage to undertake a major military compaign (perhaps because the Philistines threatened them from the west), the Ammonites were certain that the surrender of Jabesh-gilead was only a matter of time. If they waited, no siege operations would be necessary.

11:5 *The oxen.* In carrying out his royal functions the first king had no more administrative resources than the judges. Lacking an income from taxation, he returned to farming for a living. Because there was no standing army, he had to rely on a citizen army, summoned to a joint campaign by a symbolic call to arms (see Ju 19:29). As in the case of the judges, "the Spirit of the Lord came mightily upon Saul" in order to rouse him to action. (10:6 note; Ju 19:29 note)

11:8 *Bezek.* Some 40 miles north of Jerusalem and directly west across the Jordan from Jabesh-gilead. The army consisted of contingents furnished by *Israel* and *Judah,* the names used to distinguish the two parts into which the nation split after Solomon's death. However, a temporary schism between these two segments of the kingdom occurred already at David's time (2 Sm 20). For the number of troops see Numbers, Introduction, "The Numbers. . . ."

11:11 *Cut down.* The inhabitants of Jabesh-gilead did not forget the debt they owed Saul (31:11-13). After his death the people of Gilead remained loyal to his son. (2 Sm 2:8 f.)

11:14 *Renew.* A change of one consonant in the Hebrew verb would result in the translation: "Let us sanctify the kingdom." While this emendation is not necessary, Saul's coronation at Gilgal was in fact a sacred ceremony. Anointed in private by Samuel as "prince" and acclaimed by the people as God's chosen one, Saul was only now "made king before the Lord," i.e, with sacrificial rites. Here the people affirmed for the first time that Saul was not only God's choice but also their own. By offering "peace offerings before the Lord" they invoked God's blessing on the new ruler.

12:1-25 PLEDGE TO COVENANT LOYALTY

12:1 *Samuel said.* When Israel came to the end of its desert wanderings, Moses led the Israelites in a renewal of the covenant (Dt 29:10-15). The people were to understand that new outward circumstances did not affect their relationship to God. The terms of the covenant would remain in effect when the desert wanderers exchanged their migratory for a sendentary way of life.

The monarchy marked another significant change in the commonwealth of Israel. Therefore Samuel, called Israel's second founder, held a convocation in order to affirm that the terms of the covenant had not been abolished with the judgeship. Even the king was subject to them.

This renewal of the covenant had several features in common with its original promulgation at Mt. Sinai. As there, God demonstrated His power to sanction the agreement by commandeering the forces of nature (18; Ex 14:31); gripped by fear, the people asked Samuel to intercede for them (19; Ex 9:28); like Moses, Samuel calmed them with the assurance that they had nothing to fear if they "serve the Lord with all your heart." (20; Ex. 20:19)

12:3 *Testify.* Samuel opened the solemn proceedings as if they represented a court scene. He established his own compliance with the covenant by challenging the people to *testify against* him, the Lord serving as his "witness." (5)

12:7 *Plead.* Continuing the use of judicial terms, Samuel acted as prosecuting attorney, pleading with, i.e., bringing suit against, the people. He drew his evidence from Israel's history, compressed into a few verses (see Moses' much longer view of the past in Dt 1—3). From earliest times to the present day the former Egyptian slaves repeatedly broke the covenant in the face of *all the saving deeds of the Lord* (6-12); for *saving deeds* see Ju 5:11 note.

12:9 *Sisera.* Cf. Ju 4:2 note.

12:10 *The Baals and the Ashtaroth.* Cf. Ju 2:13 note.

12:11 *Delivered you.* Including himself, Samuel mentioned only four leaders from the period of the judges: *Jerubbaal* (Ju 6—8); *Barak* (Ju 4 f.); *Jephthah* (Ju 11). His reference to himself in the third person strikes us as strange, but it was not felt to be incongruous according to ancient custom.

12:12 *Nahash.* His invasion of Transjordan (11:1 ff.) was a part of the whole situation which incited the Israelites to demand a king to "fight our battles." (8:20)

12:14 *Fear the Lord.* In spite of their most recent breach of the covenant—their desire to have a king like other nations—God would not break His covenant promises if they and the king *will follow the Lord.* (13-15).

12:17 *Wheat harvest.* During the summer months of May and June rain was very rare. When a thunderstorm arose in answer to Samuel's request, God voiced His approval of the transaction. At the same time He demonstrated that He, not the fertility gods, was in command of the forces of nature.

12:21 *Vain things.* Literally "the emptiness," this derisive term for idols is used to describe the primeval emptiness of the universe in Gn 1:2. Idols are as void of reality as things before they are brought into existence. (Is 41:29)

12:23 *Pray.* Asked to intercede for them (19), Samuel assured the people that he would continue the prophetic functions of interceding for them and of instructing them *in the good and the right way* even after "the Lord has set a king over" them (13). This supremacy of the prophetic word over the king was unique in the ancient world.

13:1—14:46 PHILISTINE CAMPAIGNS; SAUL'S OFFENSE AND REJECTION

13:1 *Reigned.* In the transmission of the text the numerals were omitted which specified his age at the time of his accession to the throne and the length of his reign (cf. Acts 13:21). In the Septuagint the entire verse is missing. On Saul's age see 9:2 note.

13:2 *Michmash.* Saul had driven off the Ammonite invaders east of the Jordan (ch. 11). With the Lord's help (14:15, 23) he inflicted a defeat also on the more powerful Philistine enemy. Moving eastward from the Mediterranean coast, they penetrated deeply into Israelite territory, occupying such places as Geba and Michmash less than 10 miles north of Jerusalem. However in this encounter with the enemy Saul displayed a bent to disobey divine directives when they interfered with his thirst for power. His attempt to displace God from being king over Israel (12:12) brought about his rejection.

13:3 *Geba.* From the available information it is difficult to reconstruct the details of the maneuvers. Making allowance for scribal confusion of Geba and Gibeah in some passages (cf. Ju 20:31 note), the following general course of action emerges. At first, attack and counterattack centered about Geba and Michmash, heights separated from one another by a deep gorge (14:4 f.). Jonathan took the initiative against the invaders, defeating *the garrison of the Philistines which was at Geba.* Other translations suggest that he smote "the resident representative" or that he broke "the pillar," i.e., the local emblem of Philistine authority. The enemy retaliated with a counterattack in force, driving Saul out of Michmash. Thereupon Saul gathered his dispirited troops at Gilgal in the Jordan valley some 10 miles east of his former position before joining Jonathan at Geba (16). The latter again took the offensive. After scaling the heights of Michmash, he slaughtered the first 20 men he encountered (14:1-15). Terror-stricken by this attack and by an accompanying earthquake, the Philistines fled in a "very great panic." Saul and his men took heart and pursued the fleeing invaders, driving them back to Beth-aven and "beyond." (14:23; 13:5)

13:5 *Thirty thousand.* Evidently the original figure was enlarged in the transmission of the text. Cf. the size of the chariotry of Pharaoh (Ex 14:7), of Sisera (Ju 4:13), of the Ethiopian Zerah. (2 Ch 14:8)

13:6 *In straits.* The Philistine domination had cowed the people; their will to resist had given way to fear and flight. There could be no doubt it was the Lord who "delivered Israel." (14:23)

13:8 *Seven days.* The report of the military action is interspersed with two accounts telling how Saul succumbed to his besetting sin: his lust for power. Driven by an overweening ambition, he attempted to (a) unite royal and priestly functions in his own person (8-15); (b) enhance his prestige by imposing an unnecessary hardship on his troops. (14:24 ff.)

13:12 *Forced myself.* Saul professed that he was constrained to disobey the divine ordinance by force of circumstances: (a) Samuel—for some unstated reason—did not appear at the specified time; (b) before opposing the growing Philistine menace, he felt the need to entreat *the favor of the Lord.*

13:13 *The commandment.* Attached to the "signs," verifying God's choice of Saul (10:1-7), is a note which reports the only explicit directive for the new king. He could do "whatever" his hand "finds to do." However, at Gilgal he was to await further instructions from Samuel. (10:8)

13:14 *Your kingdom.* Committed under extenuating circumstances, Saul's misdeed was but a peccadillo according to human standards. David, whom the Lord appointed "to be prince over his people," was a murderer and adulterer. Nevertheless the Lord established his kingdom forever (2 Sm 7). "Is there injustice on God's part? By no means!" God does not judge as men do. (Ro 9:14-18; Dt 32:4; Ps 145:7)

13:15-18 *Raiders.* Only *six hundred men* had the courage to oppose the raiding Philistines. The others "hid themselves in caves" or sought safety on the east side of the Jordan. From their camp at *Michmash* the enemy terrorized the countryside to the north (*Ophrah*), to the west (*Beth-horon*), and the east (*valley of Zeboim*). Apparently Saul's city of *Gibeah* kept the raiders from moving southward.

13:19 *No smith.* The next verses add a final touch to the picture of Israel's utter helplessness. There appeared to be no prospect of expelling the Philistines if they were able to prevent the Hebrews from making *themselves swords or spears.* The invaders had such a monopoly on metal as to force the Israelites to bring even their farming implements to the Philistines for repair.

13:21 *Pim.* Mentioned nowhere else in the OT, this unit of weight amounted to two thirds of a shekel. Several pims have been turned up by the archeologist's spade.

14:1 *Let us go.* This chapter relates how "the Lord delivered Israel" (23) when it appeared to be beyond help. Demoralized, disarmed, outnumbered, the chosen people seemed doomed to extinction. But God intervened again. When Jonathan overpowered the surprised garrison of the Philistine camp at Michmash, "the earth quaked" and "a very great panic" ensued (1-15). Saul "rallied" his men to do battle with the enemy, fleeing in so great a "confusion" that "every man's sword was against his fellow." (16-23; Ju 7:22)

14:2 *Migron.* Mentioned again only in Is 10:28, its location has not been determined with certainty. It was either south or north of Michmash.

14:3 *Ahijah.* This great-grandson of Eli, erstwhile *the* high *priest* at Shiloh, may have offered the sacrifices at Gilgal when ordered to do so by Saul (13:8 f.). *Ahitub* is mentioned as the father also of Ahimelech, priest at Nob (22:9). For *ephod* see 2:18 note.

14:4 *Garrison.* Not the same word translated *garrison* in 10:5 (cf. 13:3 note). The two rocky crags, *Bozez* (shining one) and *Seneh* (acacia) are no longer known. Somehow Jonathan took advantage of the terrain to take the garrison by surprise.

14:6 *Uncircumcised.* A term of contempt reserved for the Philistines, distinguishing them from other peoples in Israel's environment who practiced circumcision. (Gn 17:10 note; Ju 15:18; 1 Sm 17:26, etc.)

14:11 *Hebrews.* The name applied to the Israelites by foreigners. (Gn 14:13 note)

14:13 *They fell.* Even though the Philistines had seen the Hebrews down in the pass, the men of the garrison did not believe that anyone would dare to climb the steep precipice.

14:14 *Furrow's length.* The plot of ground on which Jonathan cut down *about twenty men* was no larger than half the size of a square which a yoke of oxen could plow in one day. Jonathan's *slaughter* of the enemy was the more remarkable because within such a small area the victims could have come to one another's aid.

14:15 *A very great panic.* Lit. "a panic of God." (Gn 35:5)

14:18 *Ark.* The Septuagint has "ephod." In Hebrew the words for ark and ephod are very similar. Saul did not wait for the drawing of the sacred lots to be completed when he saw the Philistines in headlong flight. (41)

14:21 *With the Israelites. The Hebrews* seem to be distinguished from the Israelites. The former may have been mercenaries, called "habiru" in extra-Biblical sources. (See Gn 14:13 note)

14:23 *Beth-aven.* Cf. Jos 7:2 note.

14:24 *Avenged.* Saul thought only of himself and the satisfaction that the rout of the Philistines gave him. In his egotistic mania he showed no concern for his troops. His senseless order, forbidding his soldiers to take nourishment during the battle, was disobeyed by Jonathan, who did not know that it had been issued (24-30). When the pursuit of the enemy finally ended, the "faint" soldiers were so hungry that they "flew upon" the cattle and the sheep, devouring the meat without observing the ritual prescriptions for slaughtering animals (31-35). While God did not answer Saul's question whether to pursue the Philistines "by night," "Jonathan was taken" by lot as the one through whom "sin has arisen" (36-42). However, the people would not permit Saul to carry out his threat to execute the violator of the intemperate command. (43-46)

14:27 *Bright.* Relief from fatigue was reflected in his eyes.

14:31 *Aijalon.* From Beth-aven (23) Saul's troops drove the marauders farther westward toward the Philistine plain. The mop-up expedition was now about 20 miles from the original battle site at Michmash.

14:32 *The blood.* Cf. Lv 17:3, 10 notes; 19:26; Dt 12:16.

14:33 *Great stone.* Slaughtering the animals on this large stone assured the observance of cultic regulations. Apparently Saul ordered the stone to be converted into "an altar," "the first . . . that he built to the Lord" (35). There is no record of others built by him. (Cf. 7:17 note)

14:41 *Urim . . . Thummim.* Cf. Ex 28:15 note. In the Hebrew text the word *Thummim* occurs without the plural ending *im.* KJV therefore translates: "give a perfect lot."

14:44 *Do so.* For this oath formulation see Ru 1:17 note.

14:45 *Ransomed.* The people made some kind of redemption offering for Jonathan's release. (See the redemption of the firstborn, Ex 13:1 note)

14:47-52 SUMMARY OF SAUL'S REIGN

14:47 *All his enemies.* After giving a lengthy account of Saul's compaign against the Philistines, the author chose to insert at this point a brief summary of the first king's military successes. He "did valiantly" against enemies on all of Israel's borders: (a) in the east: *Moab* and *the Ammonites* (ch. 11); (b) in the south: *Edom;* (c) in the north: the Aramean *kings of Zobah;* (d) in the west: *the Philistines.*

14:49 *Ishvi.* His name appears in various forms. Originally it may have been Eshbaal (fire of Baal; 1 Ch 8:33). In order to register abhorrence for the Canaanite idol it was changed to Ish-bosheth (man of shame) (2 Sm 2:8). The Septuagint spells it Ishyo (man of Yahweh).

14:50 *Abner.* This list of names (49-51) is at the same time a link with the future. *Abner,* the king's cousin and commander in chief, was to play a leading role in the events leading to David's rule over all Israel. Names of women usually do not appear in rosters of this kind. But of the two daughters of Saul one was to be promised to David in marriage; the other actually was to become his wife. (18:17-27)

14:52 *Attached him.* Because of the *hard fighting,* Saul began to recruit a standing army.

15:1-35 SAUL'S SECOND OFFENSE; REJECTION CONFIRMED

15:1 *Hearken.* The war against the Amalekites, already mentioned among others in the summary (14:47-48), is selected for a more detailed account. It is given such prominence not because it was intrinsically more important than others but because it ended in the confirmation of Saul's rejection, announced in the setting of another war (13:1-15). The first king was not the foreordained victim of divine prejudice or caprice. In the Amalekite campaign he demonstrated that his disregard for God's will at Gilgal was a surface symptom of a deep-seated craving for power. To gratify his ambition he presumed to countermand the divine order to "utterly destroy" Amalek (1-9). Confronted by Samuel, he tried to shift the blame on the people (10-16). But through His messenger the Lord declared that Saul had given further evidence of a mania for self-aggrandizement, confirming the justice of the decree that he was "rejected . . . from being king" (17-23; 13:14). By a symbolic act Samuel then visibly demonstrated the divine decision to tear "the kingdom of Israel from" the man "whom the Lord . . . anointed king over Israel" (24-31). Finally Samuel did what the king had been ordered to do: he put to death Agag, the Amalekite king (32 f.). Even though he "grieved over Saul," Samuel cut off relations with the king. (34 f.)

15:2 *Amalek.* Cf. Ex 17:8 note.

15:3 *Destroy all.* Literally "put to the ban"; see Dt 2:34 note; Nm 31:1 note.

15:4 *Telaim.* A place name that occurs only here. It may be the site "in the extreme South" of Judah spelled "Telem" in Jos 15:24. Saul's army was capable of hiding in a "valley" or dried brook bed. For its size see Numbers, Introduction, "The Numbers . . . ."

15:6 *Kenites.* Cf. Ju 1:16 note.

15:7 *Havilah . . . Shur.* Cf. Gn 10:7, 24 notes; 25:18.

15:8 *All the people.* All those settled in this particular vicinity. Large contingents of this scattered nomadic people survived into David's time. (27:8; 30:1, 18)

15:11 *Repent.* To explain God's action He speaks of Himself as if He were a human being. But God is "not a man, that he should repent" (29) as His fallible and sinful creatures frequently must do. "Declaring the end from the beginning" (Is 46:10), He makes no wrong judgments. But He does alter His course of action in accordance with man's changing response to His promises and threats. (Gn 6:6; Ex 32:14; 2 Sm 24:16; Eze 18)

15:12 *Carmel.* A city in southern Judah, a few miles south of Hebron, where later the encounter between David and Nabal took place. (25:1 ff.)

15:17 *Little.* An anointed *king over Israel* should not pretend that he had to defer to the wishes of the people as Saul did. (15, 21)

15:22 *Sacrifice.* No outward ceremony can take the place of obedience, the sacrifice not of things but of the heart on the altar of self-surrender to the divine will. The delusion that men can please God by mechanical motions of religiosity is a universal perversion of religion. Men cling so perversely to this "rebellion . . . and stubbornness" that the prophets resorted to drastic language. In order to rouse their hearers from this coma of self-complacency, they seemed to say that God has no delight in any sacrifice "of bulls, or of lambs, or of he-goats" (Is 1:11-13; Jer 6:20; Hos 6:6; Mi 6:6-8) Jesus, THE Prophet, continued to attack this deep-rooted malady (Mt 9:13; 12:7). To this day people must be told that *to obey is better than* mere outward church attendance.

15:26 *Rejected you.* Samuel's earlier declaration that Saul's "kingdom shall not continue" (13:14) is now confirmed in a more direct charge against the king's personal unfitness for the royal office.

15:29 *Glory of Israel.* A title not again applied directly to God; but see Jer 2:11. More frequently *glory* denotes a manifestation of God. (Ex 16:7; 24:15-18, etc.)

15:32 *Cheerfully.* The Septuagint translates "trembling" and quotes Agag as saying: "If it be thus, bitter is death."

15:33 *Hewed . . . in pieces.* This verb occurs only here. It may not have the gruesome overtones suggested by the translation, but may mean no more than that Samuel had him executed.

15:35 *See . . . again.* The decree to reject Saul was irrevocable. The prophet would not be sent to *see* the king *again* in order to transmit to him a reversal of God's decision. When Saul "prophesied before Samuel" (19:24), the former received no inspired message from his erstwhile counselor (see also 28:6).—The finality of divine judgment on Saul contrasted with fallen David's restoral to God's favor has a parallel in the grim fate of Judas and Peter's reinstatement as an apostle. (2 Co 7:10)

16:1—2 Sm 5:5 HOW DAVID BECAME KING

16:1-13 Secretly Made Saul's Successor

16:1 *Fill your horn.* The remaining chapters of 1 Sm (16—31) relate what happened after Saul's rejection until death ended his tragic career. However, the record of events during his remaining lifetime is not designed primarily to preserve a chronicle of his reign. Its purpose is rather to give an account of the choice of his successor and of the long training by which God prepared the shepherd of Bethlehem for his role as king. After Samuel anointed David in private (16:1-13), the chosen prince served a rigorous apprenticeship (16:14—2 Sm 4) before he finally became the acknowledged ruler of all the tribes. (2 Sm 5:1-5)

16:2 *Kill me.* At previous occasions he had dared to denounce the king regardless of consequences (chs. 13, 15). Perhaps Samuel's concern was the fact that if Saul were to kill him, God's order to anoint a successor could not be carried out. But see Elijah's sudden fear of Ahab's wife Jezebel (1 K 19:1-3). In order to accomplish His purpose the Lord declared that Samuel did not owe the king an enumeration of every reason for his visit to Bethlehem; he was to announce only that he was going *to sacrifice to the Lord.*

16:4 *Trembling.* Samuel was known to have announced divine judgment.

16:5 *Consecrate.* Cf. Ex 19:10 note.

16:11 *Keeping the sheep.* To "shepherds out in the field" of the same Bethlehem angelic choristers were to announce the birth of "the good shepherd," who was to lay down "his life for the sheep." (Jn 10:11)

16:12 *Handsome.* The Lord is not restricted to "outward appearance" in His evaluation of a person (cf. 6). Nevertheless, the Creator's gift of physical attractiveness may be an added asset for more effective service in His cause.

16:13 *Spirit of the Lord.* See Ju 15:14 note; also 1 Sm 10:6 note. The remaining verses of this chapter begin the account of what God did to prepare David for his role as Saul's successor. It was a long and, for the most part, a trying educational program. At times the exact sequence of the incidents is difficult to determine. Evidently the author did not record all of them in a strictly chronological sequence, telescoping some of them from a topical point of view. The account of David's playing at the court (14-23) is a good example. It summarizes a certain aspect of his relationship to Saul which need not conflict with details recorded in connection with subsequent encounters of a different kind, e.g., at the time of the slaying of Goliath.

16:14—31:13 Subjected to Long Training for Kingship

16:14-23 IN SAUL'S SERVICE AT COURT

16:15 *Evil spirit.* Not a permanent victim of demonic possession, Saul was tormented by intermittent seizures of depression and fear, which rendered him incapable of sane judgment and action. For the fact that this malady was *from God* see Ex 4:21 note; Nm 31:1 note.

16:18 *Man of war.* Evidently the courtiers exaggerated David's qualifications in order to persuade the king to accept their suggestion, unless they meant that he had the potential of a warrior.

16:21 *Became his armor-bearer.* Literally "he was to him an armor-bearer," perhaps an honorary title conferred on some members of the king's immediate entourage, just as modern "colonels" are not always military officials.

16:23 *Refreshed.* David's playing had a soothing effect on Saul's disturbed mind. The therapeutic value of music is recognized today.

17:1—18:9 ISRAEL'S CHAMPION AGAINST GOLIATH

17:1 *Philistines gathered.* David's encounter with Goliath is only one in a long series of adventures which brought the shepherd of Bethlehem to the throne. None of these is supplied with a date specifying when or in what sequence they took place. Each episode appears to be a more or less self-contained vignette which portrays a particular feature of the future king's strength and weakness. As the author arranged the material, the slaying of Goliath, portraying David's courage and physical dexterity, immediately follows a section describing his musical ability. But this sequence does not necessarily imply that these events in their entirety followed one another in point of time.

Socoh. After their defeat at Michmash (chs. 13 f.) the Philistines attempted to invade Israelite territory some 15 miles southwest of Jerusalem. The ensuing battle was part of the "hard fighting against the Philistines all the days of Saul" (14:52). Both *Socoh* and *Azekah* belonged *to Judah* (Jos 15:35). *Ephes-dammim,* mentioned only here, has not been identified. "The valley of Elah" (2) was one of several valleys descending into the Philistine plain.

17:4 *Goliath.* Mentioned by name only here and in 23, this giant of some 9 feet was the Philistine *champion.* This term denotes a person who engaged an individual opponent in single combat with the understanding that the outcome of the duel would determine the defeat or victory of the army he represented.

17:5 *Five thousand shekels.* About 150 pounds.

17:7 *Weaver's beam.* Resembling a beam used by weavers in their looms, his spear had so large a shaft that an iron head of 19 pounds could be attached to it.

17:12 *Ephrathite.* Cf. Ru 1:1 note, Bethlehem. Already supplied in the account of his anointing (ch. 16), information regarding David's home and family is now used to set the stage for his encounter with Goliath.

17:15 *From Saul.* At this time Saul was not at court but "in the valley of Elah, fighting with the Philistines" (19). If the slaying of Goliath follows chronologically upon David's appointment as harpist (16:14-23), then the son of Jesse returned home for longer or shorter intervals before becoming permanently attached to the court. The Septuagint omits 12-31, 41, 48, 50-55, 18:1-5, thereby eliminating all questions of sequence. The Dead Sea Scrolls also have a shorter text. However, if all references to circumstances were more fully elaborated, each detail would fall into its proper place.

17:18 *Token.* David was to bring back some evidence that he had found his brothers in good health.

17:28 *Eliab's anger.* Samuel anointed David "in the midst of his brothers" (16:13). His oldest brother either did not understand the full import of the ceremony or he deliberately disregarded it because the youngest was preferred to the firstborn of the family.

17:40 *Sling.* Faith in "the Lord of hosts, the God of the armies of Israel" (45), puts unlimited power into insignificant resources. God is not restricted to save "with sword and spear." (47)

17:49 *His forehead.* David was as accurate as the Benjaminites who "could sling a stone at a hair, and not miss." (Ju 20:16)

17:52 *Israel and Judah.* After Saul's death his son was king for a time over *Israel,* the northern tribes, while David had the support of *Judah* in the south (2 Sm 2:8-11). After Solomon's reign this division into *Israel and Judah* became permanent.

Shaaraim. Literally "gates," apparently a reference to a Y in the road, the northern branch leading to *Ekron* and the southern to *Gath.*

17:54 *To Jerusalem.* David could not have brought his trophy into the city at this time because it was still occupied by the Jebusites (2 Sm 5:7-9). Nob, where Daivd later received Goliath's sword, was very near Jerusalem (21:9). The reference to *his tent* into which David put the giant's *armor* is also at loose ends. We do not know where, when, or how he acquired a tent.

17:55 *Whose son.* Saul thought of his promise which stipulated that the "father's house" of Goliath's slayer was to be "made free in Israel" (25). It should be noted that the king did not ask: "Who is this stripling?" Both he and Abner either did not know or had forgotten who David's father was.

18:1 *Knit to the soul.* One of David's most pleasant experiences in his training for the kingship was the friendship which grew up between him and Saul's son. Not a weakling but a hero in his own right and an inspiring leader himself (chs. 13 f.), *Jonathan loved* David with a love which is the noblest example of the high ideals set forth by Paul in 1 Co 13. But Jonathan too had need of the "friend of tax collectors and sinners" who laid down His "life for his friends" in order that each of them might be "called the friend of God." (Ja 2:23)

18:4 *Stripped himself.* Jonathan, as it were, merged his identity with his friend. Giving David his weapons and his clothes was an outward expression of an inner union. Believers, who in Baptism have "put on Christ," have thereby established a unity with the King's Son which entitles them to "reign in life" through Him. (Gl 3:27; Ro 5:17)

18:9 *Eyed David.* The king kept a jealous and suspicious eye on his courtier. During his seizures by the evil spirit Saul's fear of David burst into irresponsible attempts on David's life.

18:10-11 ESCAPE FROM SPEAR THRUSTS

18:10 *Raved.* KJV: "prophesied." Under the influence of an evil spirit Saul acted in a frenzy similar to the ecstatic effects produced by the Spirit of God on the prophets. (Cf. 10:6 note)

18:11 *Cast.* The Hebrew consonants of the verb can be supplied with vowels which give it the meaning: "he brandished the spear." If this is the meaning, then Saul at this occasion made a threatening motion which later became an actual attempt to pin David to the wall. (19:9 f.)

18:12-16 REMOVAL FROM COURT

18:13 *Commander.* This verse elaborates the general statement that "Saul set him over the men of war." (5)

18:17-30 THE KING'S SON-IN-LAW

18:17 *Merab.* Saul used his daughters as pawns in a plot to eliminate the popular hero. He promised him *Merab* (17-19) and then Michal (20-29) *for a wife* on the condition that he engage the Philistines in combat. If they killed him, he would not have to lay his own hands on him.

18:20 *Loved David.* No doubt Saul gave Merab to Adriel (19) because he wanted to exploit Michal's love for David "to make David fall by the hand of the Philistines" (25). Therefore he set more definite and dangerous conditions than he did in the case of his older daughters. David was required not only to "be valiant for" him against the Philistines in a general way but to furnish proof of having slain 100 enemies.

18:25 *Foreskins.* Because the Philistines were uncircumcised (17:26), it was possible for David to furnish this grisly evidence of their death. For *marriage present* see Gn 29:18 note.

19:1-24 SAUL'S CONTINUING HATRED

19:1 *Kill David.* Foiled in his scheme to bring about David's death through the Philistines, Saul, "more afraid of David" (18:29), ordered his son and his servants *that they should kill David.* Jonathan's intercession for his friend brought a temporary suspension of hostilities. With an oath his father promised that David "shall not be put to death" (1-7). But when "an evil spirit of the Lord came upon him" again, the mad king tried to pin David to the wall (8-10). Saul now began a long series of unsuccessful attempts to track down his fleeing quarry. Hoping that Saul's attack was only a momentary fit of rage, David at first took refuge in his own house. Here Michal contrived to save him from her father's "messengers" (11-17). When Saul pursued the fugitive to Samuel's city of Ramah, the persecutor was rendered incapable of hostile action by the Spirit of the Lord. (18-24)

19:3 *Field.* Evidently Jonathan confronted his father there in order to be in a position more readily to warn David if he failed to placate the king.

19:9 *Evil spirit.* Suffering progressively more severe attacks of his malady, Saul was oblivious of his oath not to kill David.

19:13 *Image.* The Hebrew word is "teraphim." Always occurring in the plural form, it is translated "household gods" (Gn 31:19 note, 34) and "divination" (15:23). Apparently Michal was not entirely free of the superstitious notions associated with these forbidden objects of idolatry, just as some Christians today are not above wearing good-luck charms or putting credence in horoscopes. Michal's *image* must have been as large as a man's torso. In order to make it look like David she put a pillow or quilt or wig of *goats' hair at its head.* According to another suggestion the word "teraphim" here denotes old rags and the *pillow of goats' hair* was an actual old he-goat.

19:18 *Ramah.* Samuel's birthplace and base of operations (1:1 note; 7:17). *Naioth* probably should be rendered as a common noun meaning "abodes" or "dwellings." In these houses "the company of prophets" resided in some form of communal life, Samuel acting as their "father." (10:10 note; 2 K 6:1 ff.)

19:20 *Prophesying.* Cf. 10:6 note.

19:22 *Secu.* Mentioned only here, it remains an unidentified site. Some manuscripts of the Septuagint read the word as a common noun meaning "a bare hill."

19:23 *The Spirit of God.* In some mysterious way Saul was brought under the influence of divine power in order to prove to him that opposition to God's will was futile. Lying half naked on the ground, he was completely immobilized.

19:24 *It is said.* In connection with Saul's previous experience, the proverb expressed surprise (10:12). Now a note of derision is added.

20:1-42 JONATHAN'S FUTILE APPEAL

20:1 *Before Jonathan.* Returning to the vicinity of Gibeah, David wanted to make one more effort to find out whether Saul's attempts on his life were but the impulsive acts of momentary fits of anger or whether the king had resolved not to rest until he had eliminated his enemy. Perhaps he hoped that Saul's encounter with the Spirit of God (19:18 ff.) had brought his persecutor to his senses. Jonathan too seems to have hoped his father could be persuaded to change his attitude toward David. The two friends therefore agreed on a scheme to "sound out" the king (1-11). After they had pledged one another not to let the outcome of the experiment affect their own relationship (12-17), Jonathan made sure he would be able to communicate the results. If need be, he would use the signals which had a coded message (18-23). When, as planned, Jonathan excused David's absence from the court (24-29), Saul transferred his implacable hatred of David to his son (30-34). Going out into the field, Jonathan used the prearranged signals to let David know that he must flee for his life. Convinced that they were not being watched, the two friends openly embraced one another and then parted company.

20:5 *New moon.* At this religious festival, observed with "gladness" (Nm 10:10; 28:11-15; Is 1:13 f.), protocol required that David occupy his seat at the king's table. (18, 25, 27)

20:6 *Bethlehem.* By informing the king of his intention to attend *a yearly sacrifice there for all the family,* David implied that the festivities of *his city* took precedence over the royal banquet.

20:13 *So . . . and more also.* Cf. Ru 1:17 note.

20:15 *My house.* David kept his promise (2 Sm 9:1 ff.). Other kings followed the cruel custom of killing all survivors of the preceding dynasty. (1 K 15:29; 16:11; 2 K 10:7)

20:19 *The matter was in hand.* Literally "on the day of the deed"; perhaps a reference to the procedure adopted in 19:2 ff. "The stone Ezel" (KJV) is an unidentifiable landmark. RSV follows the Septuagint, which reads the word "ezel" as a Hebrew pronominal adjective meaning *yonder.*

20:26 *Not clean.* Ceremonial uncleanness precluded attendance at a sacrificial meal. (Lv 7:19 ff.)

20:30 *Against Jonathan.* Jonathan's previous intercession for David had resulted in a reconciliation with Saul. His outburst against his own son indicated a deterioration in his condition.

20:32 *Cast his spear.* Cf. 18:11 note.

20:41 *Arose.* Assured by the dismissal of the lad that they were unobserved, David left his hiding place to bid his noble friend a sad farewell.

21:1-9 AIDED BY HIGH PRIEST AT NOB

21:1 *Nob.* The next two episodes in David's life are not a credit to his integrity and sound judgment. Fleeing for his life, he embarked on a desperate and injudicious course of action. In his first move he resorted to prevarication. In order to obtain provisions for himself and his followers he gave an untruthful reason for his coming to this village of priests. At the fugitive's request the high priest gave him also Goliath's sword (1-9). Apparently throwing all caution to the wind, he then sought refuge in the Philistine city of Gath, where King Achish's servants recognized him as the slayer of Goliath, their most illustrious citizen. (10-15)

Ahimelech. After the destruction of Shiloh (4:11) the priests took up residence in *Nob,* a few miles north or northeast of Jerusalem (Is 10:32). At this time *the* high *priest* was *Ahimelech,* the son of Ahitub (22:9) and the great-grandson of Eli (14:3). He came to meet David *trembling,* fearing that the coming of the king's son-in-law augured no good.

21:4 *Holy bread.* The bread of the Presence was to be eaten by the priests (Lv 24:5 note). Ahimelech consented to give it to David if he and his men had *kept themselves from women,* thus meeting a requirement of being ceremonially "holy." (Ex 19:14 f.)

21:5 *Vessels.* This word appears to be a euphemism for sexual organs. (1 Th 4:4 in KJV)

21:6 *Gave him.* Cf. Jesus' use of this incident. (Mt 12:3 f.)

21:7 *Doeg.* It is not clear why he was *detained before the Lord.* Perhaps the meaning is that he was not permitted to participate in sacred rites because he was an *Edomite* proselyte or because he was ceremonially unclean at the time.

21:9 *Ephod.* For this part of the high priest's vestment see Ex 28:6, 7 notes.

21:10-15 FLIGHT TO PHILISTINES

21:11 *King.* The Philistines exaggerated David's importance in order to impress the king.

21:13 *Mad.* Because insane people were thought to be the agents of evil spirits, they were considered dangerous. David exploited this superstition to extricate himself from a precarious situation.

22:1-2 ESCAPE TO ADULLAM

22:1 *Adullam.* After his escape from Gath, David crossed and recrossed the hill country of southern Judah. His first hiding place was one of the caves in the vicinity of Adullam, some 12 miles east of Gath and the same distance southwest of Bethlehem. By this time he had attracted a motley band of men who for various reasons had become fugitives from Saul. Their number soon grew from 400 to 600 (23:13). *His brothers and all his father's house* also joined him.

22:3-5 PARENTS TRANSFERRED TO MOAB

22:3 *Moab.* Traveling many miles eastward, David brought his parents to *Mispeh* (watchtower), an unidentified place in the homeland of his great-grandmother Ruth. He remained in a Moabite "stronghold" until the prophet Gad ordered him to return to Judah (5). The location of "Hereth" is unknown.

22:6-23 SAUL'S REVENGE ON THE PRIESTS

22:6 *Saul heard.* Saul complained that he received rumors of David's movements but that no one supplied him with specific information. Currying the king's favor, Doeg disclosed that the fugitive had received aid from Ahimelech (6-11). Mad with anger, Saul ordered the unscrupulous informer to massacre the priests of Nob. (12-19)

The height. "Ramah" (KJV) here is a common noun denoting an unspecified elevated place where Saul held court.

22:7 *Benjaminites.* Saul insinuated that the men of his own tribe (9:1) could not expect fair treatment from *the son of Jesse,* a Judahite.

22:9 *Inquired.* Doeg may have been lying. But it is possible that the high priest rendered David this service even though it is not mentioned in 21:1-7.

22:15 *Nothing.* Ahimelech rejected the accusation that he was involved in fomenting a rebellion against the king.

22:19 *The city.* The ban of extermination was executed on *Nob* as if it had harbored rebels against the Lord Himself. (Lv 27:26 note; Dt 2:34 note)

22:20 *Abiathar.* The only survivor of the bloodbath was able to reach David, bringing "an ephod in his hand." (23:6)

22:22 *Occasioned.* David's prevarication (21:2) had tragic results. Even so-called white lies may lead to disastrous consequences.

23:1-29 SAUL'S PURSUIT OF DAVID

23:1 *Keilah.* David's next adventure brought him to *Keilah,* a city on the border of the Philistine plain about 3 miles south of Adullam. There he "delivered the inhabitants" from Philistine raiders on their food supply, evidently taking enough booty from the enemy to feed his followers at least for a time (1-5). Warned of Saul's intention to trap him within Keilah, David fled to the Wilderness of Ziph, about 3 miles south of Hebron and some 20 miles below Jerusalem (6-14). Here Jonathan came to him once again to exchange pledges of friendship (15-18). When the Ziphites betrayed him to Saul (19-24), the harried outlaw retreated some 5 miles farther south to the wilderness of Maon. Closing in upon him, Saul was about to capture him. "But God did not give him into his hand" (14). News of a Philistine "raid upon the land" prompted the king to give up "pursuing after David" in order to deal with the newly arisen national emergency. Thereupon David sought safety in "the stronghold of Engedi" on the shore of the Dead Sea.

23:2 *Inquired.* Obviously by means of the ephod of the high priest, as explained more in detail in 9-13. No doubt Abiathar had found David before the latter "delivered the inhabitants of Keilah." The Septuagint translates v. 6: "And it came to pass when Abiathar . . . fled to David that he went with David to Keilah, having an ephod in his hand."

23:12 *Surrender me.* Because the answer given by the ephod was either Urim or Thummim ("yes" or "no") to only one inquiry at a time, David had to repeat the first part of his double question (11; cf. 14:41 note). The men of Keilah were willing to *surrender* David either because they feared the superior power of Saul or because they did not want hundreds of men in their vicinity who had to depend on foraging to sustain themselves.

23:15 *Horesh.* Horesh occurs as a common noun meaning "a wood" (2 Ch 27:4 and other passages) and is so translated in KJV.

23:17 *Fear not.* When David in dire straits needed comfort, his selfless friend risked his life to assure the hounded outlaw that God's plan for him would not miscarry, Saul's irrational persecution notwithstanding.

23:18 *Went home.* Never to see David again.

23:19 *Hachilah.* Tentatively identified with a ridge northwest of Ziph. *Jeshimon* means desert and is so translated in Nm 21:20; 23:28. Here and in 24 and 26:1 it may refer in a general way to the region known as the Wilderness of Judah.

23:23 *Thousands.* Here the Hebrew word *eleph* is not a numeral but has the meaning of "clan" as it does in 10:19 and is so translated by RSV in Mi 5:2.

23:24 *Arabah.* A general term to denote the long rift valley stretching from the Sea of Galilee down to the Gulf of Aqaba. (Cf. Dt 1:1 note)

23:26 *Closing in.* The messenger came just in time to save David. The Ruler of the nations still times national and international incidents in order to let His kingdom come. If the Turks had not threatened Europe and occupied the emperor's attention, the Reformation—humanly speaking—would have been suppressed.

23:28 *Rock of Escape.* This translation reproduces the effect of God's liberating intervention. More literally the name is "the Rock of Divisions." When Saul's and David's ways parted at this point, it brought much-needed relief to the latter.

23:29 *Engedi.* David retreated to a better hiding place on the western edge of the Dead Sea. As the names Engedi (spring of the goat) and "Wildgoats' Rocks" (24:2) indicate, this area was cut up by rough and steep crags. Its many caves made it an ideal hideout; its spring provided the necessary supply of water.

24:1-22 PURSUIT RENEWED

24:1 *Returned.* As soon as Saul again had a free hand, he moved in on David's new hiding place. Even though the fugitive had the opportunity to kill his pursuer, David refused to lay hand on the person of the anointed king (1-7). Later—and evidently at a safe distance atop a rock—David showed Saul a piece of cloth from the royal garment to prove that he had been in a position to cut off the crowned head (8-15). Light broke into Saul's benighted mind long enough to wring a confession of guilt from his lips. However, David kept his distance. He knew better than to entrust himself to a man driven by an evil spirit and victimized by homicidal impulses. (16-22)

24:3 *Sheepfolds.* Rows of stones were raised about the mouths of caves, affording the sheep protection during the night.

24:4 *The men of David.* It is self-evident that not all of David's 600 followers (23:13) were in the same cave with him. Those who were with him tried to convince him that the assassination of Saul would be God's way of fulfilling His promise to clear their leader's way to the throne. But David refused to believe that God wanted him to use foul means to achieve a good end. (For Abraham's impatience in a similar situation see Gn 16:2, 3 notes)

24:5 *Smote him.* When Saul "laid hold upon" Samuel's robe, "it tore" (15:27 f.). Perhaps David, on second thought, feared he had performed a similar symbolic act without proper authorization.

24:9 *Words of men.* One such evil-mouthed man was Doeg.

24:11 *My father.* An honorary title like the English "sire." The king addressed David as "my son." (16)

24:13 *Wickedness.* If it had been *wicked,* "out of the heart" of David would have "come . . . murder" (Mt 15:19), as it did later.

24:14 *Dead dog.* David protested that his own person was not worth all the effort which Saul was putting forth to eliminate him.

24:15 *Be judge.* Vengeance, David believed, was God's prerogative (Ro 12:19). He was sure, furthermore, that the Lord would bring about the vindication of his cause. (Ps 35:1; 43:1; Mi 7:9)

24:20 *I know.* Jonathan was convinced that his father was acting against better knowledge in persecuting David. (23:17)

24:22 *Stronghold.* Past experience taught David that he could not risk to take Saul at his word. Therefore he *went up* to an unnamed stronghold, perhaps a place in the Engedi region, which had natural ramparts for its defense.

25:1 SAMUEL'S DEATH

25:1 *Mourned.* Judge, prophet, king-maker, Samuel richly deserved the grateful tribute which Israel once paid its founder (Dt 34:5 ff.). Moses and Samuel remained linked in the nation's memory. (Jer 15:1)

25:2-44 DAVID KEPT FROM BLOODGUILT BY FUTURE WIFE

25:2 *Paran.* After Samuel's death David remained the leader of an outlaw band. Hard pressed to find provisions for his followers, he hit upon the scheme to require owners of crops and flocks to remunerate him for protecting them against loss by raiding parties. Nabal, a wealthy sheep owner, refused to comply with such a demand (2-8). David flew into a rage (9-13) but was kept by the man's wife Abigail from killing her husband as he had threatened (14-35). After Nabal's sudden death (36-38) David married his widow.

The wilderness of Paran was far to the south of Judah (Nm 10:12 note). The Septuagint has "the wilderness of Maon" (23:24 note). *Carmel* was only about a mile north of Maon. Traditionally it was an occasion for festivities and general good will when a man *was shearing his sheep.* (8; 2 Sm 13:23 ff.)

25:3 *Nabal.* His name means "fool," and he acted the part of one in the opinion of his servants and of his wife (25). In Scripture the words "wise" and "foolish" denote more than an intelligence quotient. He is a "fool" who says: "There is no God" (Ps 14:1). For a description of Nabal, the fool, see Is 32:6. For *Calebite* see Jos 14:6 note.

25:10 *Servants.* Adding insult to injury, Nabal insinuated that David was an escaped slave who should be returned to his master.

25:16 *Wall.* The servants upheld David's claim to remuneration for protecting Nabal's flocks.

25:17 *Ill-natured.* Literally "a son of Belial"; see 1:16 note.

25:23 *Bowed.* Abigail proved that she deserved to be characterized as a "woman . . . of good understanding" (3). Humbly taking the blame for her husband's behavior, she nevertheless had the courage to remind David that through her the Lord was restraining him from "taking vengeance" and assuming "bloodguilt."

25:27 *Present.* Literally "a blessing"; the same word is used of the "gift" which Jacob sent to his brother. (Gn 33.11)

25:28 *A sure house.* A permanently established line of successors to the throne.

25:29 *Bundle.* Literally "a pouch" or "a bag." As a person puts a coin or gem into a purse for safekeeping, so the Lord is careful to keep His own among "the living," hiding them "in the day of trouble." (Ps 27:5; 31:20; Is 49:2)

25:30 *Prince.* On the meaning of this word see 10:1 note.

25:37 *As a stone.* Apparently he suffered a paralyzing attack which completely immobilized him. After 10 days he died because "the Lord smote" him, perhaps with a second and now fatal stroke. The OT does not blink the fact that the ultimate cause of disaster rests in God's will and providence. (Cf. Nm 31:1 note; Ex 4:21 note)

25:39 *Wooed Abigail.* Even before he became the acknowledged king of all Israel, David began to imitate the custom of eastern potentates. According to 1 Ch 3:1-3 he had a total of six wives in addition to Michal. On polygamy in the OT see Gn 16:2 note.

25:43 *Ahinoam.* Saul's wife had the same name (14:50). The mother of David's oldest son Amnon came from *Jezreel* near Maon.

25:44 *Given Michal.* Perhaps soon after David became a fugitive. Her new husband *was of Gallim,* a short distance north of Jerusalem.

26:1-25 FINAL ENCOUNTER WITH SAUL

26:1 *Ziphites.* Moving a few miles north of Carmel and Maon, David came again into "the wilderness of Ziph." Because the Ziphites had betrayed David (23:19 ff.) and now feared his vengeance, they reported his whereabouts to Saul, who at once responded to their call. After David's scouts discovered the camp of the enemy (1-5), he and a volunteer companion "went to the army by night," finding the very spot where "lay Saul sleeping." Again he refused to put forth his hand against "the Lord's anointed" (24:6), insisting on letting God choose the time and the manner of removing the rejected king. In order to be able to prove that the latter had been at his mercy, David "took the spear and the jar of water from Saul's head" (6-12). Safely perched "on the top of the mountain," he then displayed his trophies to Saul's general Abner, taunting him for his failure to provide the king with adequate protection (13-16). David also took the opportunity to plead with Saul not to "pursue after" him, "his servant," on whose hands there was no "guilt" (17-20). Admitting that he had "erred exceedingly," the king promised to do his "son David" no harm. But "David went his way," still fearful of the instability of Saul's mind. (21-25; see 24:22)

26:2 *Ziph.* On *Ziph,* Hachilah, and Jeshimon see 23:1, 19 notes. "East of Jeshimon" (literally "beside the face of Jeshimon") makes better sense if translated "before" or "facing" Jeshimon, i.e., the desert.

26:5 *Abner.* Cf. 14:50 note.

26:6 *Ahimelech.* On the Hittites see Gn 10:15-19 note. Of the same nationality as Uriah (2 Sm 11:3), this Hittite is mentioned only here. *Abishai* was the son of David's sister or half sister Zeruiah (1 Ch 2:16; 2 Sm 17:25). Sometime later he and his brother Joab had no compunctions about killing Abner. (2 Sm 3:30)

26:8 *Twice.* Abishai assured David that he would strike Saul with such force as to make a second blow unnecessary.

26:12 *Deep sleep.* A single word in Hebrew, it is used to describe the loss of consciousness which the Lord "caused . . . to fall upon" Adam and upon Abraham (Gn 2:21; 15:12). It is used also in a figurative sense to denote spiritual inability to respond to God. (Is 29:10)

26:19 *Other gods.* Israel's neighbors believed the authority of their gods did not extend beyond the borders of their nation. But the history of the chosen people abounded with evidence that their God was the Lord of heaven and earth. He had demonstrated His unrestricted power in lands where the inhabitants served national idols: in Ur of the Chaldees, in Egypt, in the Sinai Peninsula, in the fields of Moab, in Canaan. If apostate Israelites actually worshiped foreign deities, it would not be surprising if some of them did not share also this heathen view, expressed by the *cursed* men whom David quoted. Their aim was to banish David from *the heritage of the Lord,* i.e., the Promised Land. The expressions used by his enemies do not prove that David believed that the Lord's power was confined to one country or city. There is no evidence that he served Dagon during his exile in Philistia (ch. 27). But he hoped the Lord would not permanently exile him to a foreign land where he could not participate in the prescribed worship in "the presence of the Lord." (20)

26:24 *Deliver me.* Rather than to take matters into his own hands, David preferred to pursue a course of "righteousness and . . . faithfulness," trusting the Lord to fulfill His promises in His own way. The next chapter reveals, however, that David was not completely successful in carrying out his lofty resolve to "be still before the Lord, and wait patiently for him." (Ps 37:7)

27:1—28:2 FLIGHT BEYOND SAUL'S JURISDICTION

27:1 *Land of the Philistines.* The picture we get of David in Scripture is not of an idealized hero of unblemished rectitude. Apparently wavering in his conviction that the Lord would deliver him "out of all tribulation" (26:24), he decided on a desperate expedient. His flight to one of the five capitals of Israel's archenemy did indeed put him beyond Saul's reach (1-4). But it also created serious dilemmas from which he had to extricate himself by resorting to wily cunning and morally questionable tactics. He duped Achish, the Philistine king, into making him governor of one of his cities, Ziklag (5-7). Using this appointment, he continued to hoodwink his trusting overlord. He pretended to make forays against his own people of Judah, whereas in reality he "made raids upon" various tribes which molested Israel. "Lest they should tell about" his deception, he "left neither man nor woman alive" in the communities he raided. (8-12)

27:5 *Found favor.* The Philistine king too was fishing in troubled waters. Aware of Israel's protracted internal strife, he was happy to have the support of the young contender for the throne, particularly since David was no longer a lone fugitive as before (21:10 ff.) but now commanded a formidable task force.

27:6 *Ziklag.* Here, some 20 miles southeast of Gath, David could avoid direct surveillance by Achish. Once assigned by Joshua to Simeon "in the midst of the inheritance of . . . Judah" (Jos 15:31; 19:5), *Ziklag* had been overrun by the invading Philistines. When the books of Samuel were compiled, it *belonged to the kings of Judah.*

27:8 *Geshurites.* The seminomadic tribes upon whom David *made raids* occupied territories with undefined borders in desert areas south of *Shur* (cf. 15:7 note; Gn 16:17; Ex 15:22). "The regions of the Philistines, and . . . of the Geshurites" were adjacent to one another. *The Girzites* remain unidentified. Saul did not extirpate *the Amalekites* in his campaign against them. (Ch. 15; see also Ex 17:8 note)

27:10 *Negeb.* Literally "dry land," the *Negeb* is a general term for the desert area south of the Dead Sea running out into the Sinai Peninsula. It was the home of *the Jerahmeelites,* a Judahite clan, and of *the Kenites,* a Midianite tribe incorporated into Judah. (Ju 1:16)

27:12 *Utterly abhorred.* Achish thought that David had burned all his bridges behind him.

28:1 *Against Israel.* The incursion of Israel's king elect into enemy territory developed into an acute crisis when Achish summoned him to participate in an all-out compaign against the chosen people (1 f.). Before the reader is told how David escaped taking up arms against his own countrymen (ch. 29), the scene shifts to Saul. Unable anymore to consult Samuel (25:1) and denied an oracle in any form from the Lord (6), the frantic king turned to an illegitimate means to ascertain the outcome of the impending battle with the Philistines (3-7). At his request his servants recommended "a medium at Endor." Seeking her out in the dead of night, he requested her to conjure up Samuel. To her astonishment and dismay, the form of the dead prophet appeared (8-14). However, he only confirmed what the Lord "spoke by" him during his lifetime: a Philistine victory would bring Saul's reign as king of Israel to an end (15-19). Saul was so unnerved by this shattering experience that he ate the food prepared for him by the woman only after "his servants, together with the woman, urged him" to revive his strength for his return to the army. (20-25)

28:2 *Bodyguard.* Literally "keeper of mine head" (KJV). David's deliberately ambiguous response to Achish's summons seemingly misled the king into putting the greatest trust in his cunning vassal. It is also possible that he intended to keep him nearby for firsthand observation.

28:3-25 SAUL'S VISIT TO THE MEDIUM AT ENDOR

28:3 *Mediums and wizards.* Saul's attempt to enforce the Mosiac law prohibiting occultism of every kind had driven its practitioners underground (Lv 19:31; 20:6, 27; Dt 18:10 f.). The *mediums* (Hebrew: "skin bottles") claimed to be the vessels which the spirit powers occupied and filled, just as an ordinary container serves to hold its contents (KJV: "familiar spirits"). The word "wizard," in Hebrew a derivative of the verb "to know," denotes a practitioner of divination who purports to possess techniques of supernatural know-how.

28:4 *Shunem.* The Philistine attack was designed to gain control of the strategic and rich plain of Jezreel, also called Esdraelon, where Israel under Deborah and Barak defeated the forces of Jabin, king of Hazor (Ju 4:7 note). *Shunem* was on the northern end and Mt. Gilboa on the southern side of the valley.

28:7 *Endor.* A village a short distance northeast of the Philistine camp. In order to reach it, Saul had to pass through the valley of Jezreel and skirt around enemy-held territory.

28:12 *Cried out.* Ordered by her visitor to "bring up Samuel," the woman went into her usual routine of hocus-pocus by which she had duped her gullible customers. (The Septuagint translates the Hebrew word for medium with "ventriloquist.") To her consternation this seance produced unexpected results. God permitted the practice of forbidden necromancy to bring Saul a message from dead Samuel. However, divine intervention in this particular instance does not sanction attempts by spiritists to penetrate mysteries that God has reserved for Himself. On the other hand, the appearance of Samuel, as well as that of Moses and Elijah on the Mount of Transfiguration, should assure the believer that departed saints remain in God's hands.

Deceived me. During his lifetime Samuel had conveyed God's oracles to the king. Seeing the prophet actually materialize before her at Saul's request gave the medium the clue to the identity of her disguised visitor.

28:13 *A god.* An unearthly figure.

28:15 *Disturbed.* There was no need to bring up Samuel from the dead to repeat what he had said while in the flesh and what Saul already knew: *God has turned away from me.*

28:18 *Amalek.* Cf. 15:1, 2 notes.

28:19 *With me.* Their earthly existence would end, as Samuel's already had. The Septuagint has: "you and your sons with you shall fall."

28:25 *That night.* Saul had to get back to his headquarters before daylight if he did not want to run the risk of capture by the enemy

29:1-11 DAVID RELEASED FROM SERVICE AGAINST ISRAEL

29:1 *Aphek.* This chapter resumes the narrative of David's plight when the Philistine king pressed him into service against Israel (28:1-4). Achish assembled all his contingents at *Aphek* (4:1 note) before taking up an encamped position at Shunem (28:4), facing Saul across the valley of Jezreel. At this point the Philistine commanders angrily voiced their mistrust of David's loyalty to their cause. They were sure that in battle "this fellow" would turn on them in an attempt to "reconcile himself to his lord" Saul (1-5). Reluctantly acceding to the demands of his leaders, Achish sent David back to "the land of the Philistines." (6-11)

29:3 *Hebrews.* For this designation of the Israelites by foreigners see Gn 14:13 note.

29:5 *Sing.* The Philistines feared the prowess of the man whose victories over them had brought him national acclaim. (18:7; 21:11)

29:6 *Lord lives.* In his oath Achish called on David's God to witness to the fact that he had *found nothing wrong* in his Hebrew vassal.

29:10 *Depart.* David had not sought divine guidance for his excursion into Philistia. But the Lord did not permit this action to have disastrous consequences for the man whom He had chosen to play a great role in His eternal plan of salvation. "He who fashions the hearts of them all" (Ps 33:13-15) directed the decisions and actions of the Philistine king and his commanders in such a way as to "provide the way for escape" for David. (1 Co 10:13; Ps 124:6 f.)

30:1-31 DAVID FREE TO PROTECT JUDAH

30:1 *To Ziklag.* Relieved of his obligations to Achish, David arrived at his former base of operations after 3 days of forced marching (27:6). Here more trouble awaited him. His own followers "spoke of stoning him" because during his absence the Amalekites had raided Ziklag, burned it, and carried off the women, including David's two wives (1-5). The dazed and bereaved leader immediately pursued the marauders (7-10). Guided by an abandoned and half-starved slave of the Amalekites (11-15), he overtook the robber band, surprised them as they were "eating and drinking and dancing," and "recovered all that the Amalekites had taken" (16-20). Ignoring the protests of "wicked and base fellows among the men," David did not withhold a fair share of the booty from those who had been "too exhausted to follow David" (21-25). In order to gain the goodwill of the elders of various cities in southern Judah, he sent them some spoils of war, taken from "the enemies of the Lord." (26-31)

Amalekites. Previous campaigns against them by Saul (15:1 ff.) and by David (27:8) had not wiped out this seminomadic tribe. In this instance too 400 escaped on their fleet camels. (17)

30:6 *Strengthened himself.* He renewed his strength by prayerfully entrusting himself to the Lord, his Strength. (Ps 18:1 f.; 27:1; 56:3, 4, 11)

30:7 *Abiathar.* As he had done before he joined forces with the Philistines, David sought the Lord's guidance through the office of the high priest. (23:2 note)

30:8 *Rescue.* The worst had not happened; the captives were still alive.

30:9 *Besor.* Mentioned only here, this brook has not been identified postively. It must have been south of Ziklag.

30:14 *Cherethites.* The whole Negeb (27:10 note) was left vulnerable to Amalekite attack when "the Philistines gathered all their forces," including David's men, at Aphek far to the north. Ziklag was only one of the victims of a raid that extended over a wider area. The *Cherethites* and the Philistines were associated with one another since both migrated from the island of Crete (Eze 25:16; Am 9:7). Later David recruited his bodyguard from the Cherethites. (2 Sm 8:18; 20:23)

30:16 *Dancing.* Certain that no armed forces could be pursuing them, the raiders threw all caution to the wind.

30:20 *David's spoil.* David was given the privilege of disposing of the captured flocks and herds which the raiders had taken from other settlements in the Negeb besides Ziklag. Vv. 26-30 record what he did with the spoil.

30:25 *A statute and an ordinance.* David's ruling in the matter became a permanent decree. Moses and Joshua had required a similar division of booty at specific occasions, however without making their requirements a general *statute and an ordinance.*

30:26 *Present.* Literally "a blessing." It was a gift invoking a benediction on the recipients (25:27 note; Gn 33:11). David assured the elders of southern Judah of his concern for them in spite of his temporary link with the Philistines.

30:31 *Hebron.* Mentioned last in a list of 11 cities, *Hebron* was not the least in importance. David made it his first capital (2 Sm 5:3). All the other sites, some of which cannot be identified with certainty, lay south of Hebron.

31:1-13 PERSECUTION OF DAVID ENDED

31:1 *Israel fled.* After several digressions—Saul's visit to the medium at Endor (28:3-25), David's release from Philistine service (29:2-11), his recovery of the booty from the Amalekites (ch. 30)—this chapter relates what happened when "the Philistines gathered their forces for war, to fight against Israel" (28:1; 29:1). The report on the battle itself is very brief. Without specifying exactly where the opposing forces met or how they were deployed, the account concentrates on the tragic results: the defeat of Israel, the death of Saul and his sons (1-7), and the disposition of Saul's corpse. (8-13)

31:2 *Sons of Saul.* Abinadab is not mentioned in a previous list of Saul's family members (14:49-51). Another son, Ish-bosheth, survived the slaughter because he either eluded the enemy or for some reason did not take part in the battle.

31:3 *Found him.* The archers got him into range of their arrows.

31:4 *Fell upon it.* Rather than let the Philistines *make sport of* him, as they did of Samson (Ju 16:25), Saul took his own life—one of the few instances of suicide mentioned in the OT. (2 Sm 17:23)

31:6 *All his men.* Like the armor-bearer, the men whom Saul had selected for his bodyguard chose to die with their king rather than to seek safety in flight.

31:7 *The other side.* The side north of the valley of Jezreel, where Saul's army had made camp (28:4). Victory at Mt. Gilboa put the Jordan within easy reach of the Philistines. Hence *those beyond the Jordan* were terrified. Actual occupation of Transjordan territory seems to have been limited to some sites close to the river. (Cf. 11)

31:10 *Ashtaroth.* Cf. 7:3; Ju 2:13 note. Apparently *the temple* in which they hung their trophies was a particularly well-known sanctuary. *Beth-shan,* only 4 miles west of the Jordan, controlled access to the valley of Jezreel.

31:11 *Jabesh-gilead.* Some 10 miles southeast of Beth-shan and 2 miles east of the Jordan, this city evidently was not occupied by the Philistines. Grateful to Saul for their rescue from disaster (11:1 ff.), its inhabitants risked their lives to rescue his body and that of his sons from the walls of Beth-shan. They first "burnt" the corpses—evidently so that the enemy could no longer identify them—and then buried the charred remains.

2 Sm 1:1—2:7 David Anointed King

1:1 *Death of Saul.* Saul's death was a significant turning point in David's life. However, he did not become king immediately after his persecutor passed from the scene. The opening chapters of 2 Sm continue the record of events that played a part in his rise to the throne. David was still at Ziklag (1 Sm 30), when an Amalekite survivor of the battle brought him the news of Israel's defeat at Mt. Gilboa. Hoping to ingratiate himself with David, the courier claimed that he had dispatched the mortally wounded king (1-10). However, his report backfired. David had him executed on the testimony of his "own mouth" that he had put forth his "hand to destroy the Lord's anointed." (11-16; 4:10 ff.)

1:10 *Crown.* More lit. "[the insignia of] the consecration." The same word is used of the *crown* of the high priest (Ex 29:16). Possibly it was a jeweled band around Saul's helmet worn as a badge of office like the stars on the caps of our generals.

1:13 *A sojourner.* A non-Israelite who had taken up residence with the chosen people and was therefore subject to the laws of the land. (Ex 20:10)

1:17 *Lamented.* In his elegy, eulogizing the dead king and his son, David nobly called to remembrance only the good features of Saul's reign. His grief over his former persecutor was no less sincere than his pain in losing "his brother Jonathan," both "beloved and lovely." The poem that he composed for the occasion is an artistic gem. It consists of three strophes of diminishing length, each introduced by the refrain "how are the mighty fallen" (19, 25, 27). The last stanza is no more than a choked sob.

1:18 *Be taught.* The Hebrew text has: "to teach the children of Judah the bow." Perhaps the word "bow" designates the kind of poem that David composed. For *the Book of Jashar* see Jos 10:13 note; Ju 5:1 note.

1:19 *How.* This exclamatory interjection, characteristic of this kind of elegy, introduces a sentence which has the sense: how tragic the situation has become now that the mighty are fallen.

1:21 *The deep.* The Hebrew text as translated in the RSV note makes sense. Upon Mount Gilboa there were to be no "fields [productive] of first fruits," i.e., choice fruits, qualified to be used in offerings. Saul's shield, *not anointed with oil,* was left to disintegrate and rust to pieces. (Is 21:5)

1:23 *Not divided.* Linked with one another *in life* in a father-son relationship, they should share the same fate *in death.*

1:24 *Clothed you.* In his earlier reign Saul provided for more than the essential needs of his people.

2:1 *Cities of Judah.* More than 7 years (11) were to pass before David sat on the throne, first occupied by Saul. It was a time of confusion, intrigue, assassinations, and bloody clashes. First God directed David to leave the Philistine-dominated territory and to return to *the cities of Judah* (1 Sm 30:26-31). In *Hebron,* some 20 miles south of Jerusalem, he permitted—no divine guidance is mentioned—the men of Judah to anoint him "king over the house of Judah." From there David sent messengers to Jabesh-gilead, commending them for "loyalty to Saul" (1 Sm 31:11-13). But he also suggested that they accept his leadership, as the house of Judah had done (4b-7). However, Saul's general Abner prolonged the division between the tribes. In a power move he took Ish-bosheth, the son of Saul, and "made him king over . . . Israel," that is, of all the territory north of Judah on both sides of the Jordan. (8-11)

2:8—4:12 Contender in North Eliminated

2:8 *Ish-bosheth.* Cf. 1 Sm 14:49 note. He survived the battle of Gilboa if he took part in it at all. The references to him give the impression that he lacked the physical or mental capacities to take a forceful hand in affairs of state. His improvised capital was at Mahanaim, east of the Jordan and well beyond Philistine control. (Gn 32:1 note)

2:10 *Two years.* His reign ended after David "was king in Hebron . . . seven years and six months." In the confusion following the Philistine victory it evidently took Abner some 5 years to secure the semblance of royal rule for the son of his dead cousin. (1 Sm 14:50 note)

2:12 *Gibeon.* A city on the border between Benjamin and Judah, some 5 miles north of Jerusalem. When the northern and southern forces faced one another there across "the great pool" or reservoir (Jer 41:12), the opposing generals agreed to have chosen men from both sides "play before" them, that is, give an exhibition of their skill with arms in individual combat. The outcome of the contest was to determine which army was victorious (1 Sm 17:8-9). When no champion survived the deadly game, the two armies fought it out in a "very fierce" battle, in which the servants of David emerged victorious. (12-17)

2:18 *Asahel.* This swift-footed brother of David's general refused to let up in his pursuit of the opposing general Abner, who finally turned and killed him (18-23). Joab later avenged his brother's death. (3:27 ff.)

2:24 *Pursued Abner.* After pursuing the retreating enemy all day, Abner finally agreed to a truce, suggested by Joab (24-28). Thereupon the two armies returned to their respective bases, Mahanaim and Hebron (29-31). The location of Ammah and Giah is not known.

3:1 *Long war.* Ch. 2 records the only battle in this protracted struggle.

3:2 *Sons.* Mention of "the house of David" (1) prompted the note of David's family (3-5). While he "grew stronger and stronger" politically, he added also to the numbers in his domestic circle. In addition to Ahinoam and Abigail (1 Sm 25:42 f.) he took to himself four more wives.

3:3 *Absalom.* The mother of the son who was to lead a revolt against David (chs. 13—18) was the daughter of an Aramean kinglet whose domain lay east of the Sea of Galilee. Amnon and Adonijah too were to cause their father grief. (ch. 13; 1 K 1:5; 2:25)

3:5 *Eglah.* The fourth wife, Haggith, and the

fifth, Abital, have no identification beyond their names. It is not clear why Eglah should be called *David's wife* in a list of women who likewise were his wives.

3:6 *Himself strong.* A decisive development in the struggle for the throne was Abner's decision to desert Saul's son and to promote David's cause. Ish-bosheth's charge that his father's general had openly assumed royal prerogatives led to a break in the relations between the two men (6-11). Abner's negotiations with David by messengers were successful; the latter's demand that Michal, his first wife, be returned to him was granted (12-16). Abner secured the promise of the northern tribes to support David (17-19) and then conferred with him in Hebron. (20-21)

3:7 *Rizpah.* It was customary for a king to take over his predecessor's harem. Ish-bosheth accused Abner of making himself Saul's successor.

3:9 *More also.* For this oath formula see Ru 1:17 note. Apparently it was common knowledge that *the Lord has sworn* to "set up the throne of David over Israel and over Judah."

3:10 *Dan to Beer-sheba.* Cf. Ju 20:1 second note.

3:14 *Michal.* No reason is given for David's demand that Saul's daughter be returned to him (1 Sm 18:17-29; 25:44). He may have hoped to gain the support of Saul's followers if he had a close relationship to the dead king.

3:15 *Palti-el.* In 1 Sm 25:44 his name appears in the abbreviated form of Palti.

3:16 *Bahurim.* In the environs of Jerusalem.

3:18 *Save my people.* There is no record of this promise to David. Perhaps Abner invented it in order to gain the support of "the elders of Israel."

3:22 *Not with David.* Learning of Abner's visit with David, Joab accused Saul's general of duplicity (22-25), lured him back to Hebron, and with the help of Abishai killed him to avenge "the blood of Asahel his brother" (26-30). After pronouncing a curse upon the house of the assassins (28 f.), David declared his innocence of the crime and "lamented for Abner." However, "though anointed king," he did not dare to punish the "sons of Zeruiah" because they were "too hard for" him. (31-39)

3:26 *Sirah.* Unknown today, it may have been not far to the north of Hebron.

3:29 *A spindle.* Male descendants who barely had the strength of doing what women did with ease.

3:33 *A fool.* In his elegy David lamented particularly the manner of Abner's death. Only a fool would die without defending himself. But the fallen general, a victim of treachery, was unable to strike back even though he was "not bound" and "not fettered."

3:39 *The Lord requite.* Cf. 1 K 2:5 f.

4:1 *Courage failed.* The death of Abner, kingmaker and strong man in Saul's house, left the northern tribes without effective leadership. Ish-bosheth was incapable of firm action (1-3); Mephibosheth, Jonathan's son, was an invalid (4); left without adequate protection, Ish-bosheth was beheaded "as he lay on his bed." When the assassins brought the dead man's head to David, he "commanded his young men" to execute the slayers of "a righteous man."

4:2 *Benjamin.* The son of Saul, a Benjaminite, fell victim to his own tribesmen, who hailed from Beeroth, a town about 7 miles north of Jerusalem and one of the Gibeonite cities (cf. Jos 9:3-27). No reason is given for the flight of the Beerothites to the unidentified Gittaim. Perhaps they had been affected by Saul's action against the Gibeonites. (21:1 f.)

4:4 *Mephibosheth.* His name was changed from Meri(b)baal (1 Ch 8:34). Bosheth (shame) was substituted for the word "baal" in order to express revulsion for the Canaanite idol. (2:8 note)

4:7 *Arabah.* They followed the rift valley which extends from the Sea of Galilee to the Gulf of Aqaba (Dt 3:17). Abner had traveled this road in the opposite direction. (2:29)

5:1-5 David Made King over All Israel

5:1 *Tribes of Israel.* The death of Ish-bosheth removed the last obstacle to the unification of the divided nation under David's kingship. Already pledged by Abner to support the man whom Samuel had anointed privately (1 Sm 16:13) and Judah had chosen to follow (3:17-19), "all the elders of Israel" came to Hebron and "anointed David king [also] over Israel."

5:2 *Shepherd.* This figurative term to describe the relationship of a king to his people, occurring here for the first time, is frequently used hereafter as a designation of royalty (Eze 34:5, 8, 12, 23). The reign of David and his successors was a part of the divine plan of salvation to be realized in "our Lord Jesus, the great shepherd of the sheep" (Heb 13:20; 1 Ptr 5:4; Mt 25:31 ff.). For the term *prince* see 1 Sm 10:1 note.

5:6—9:13 HOW DAVID REIGNED

5:6-25 Consolidation of Power

5:6 *To Jerusalem.* The remaining chapters of 2 Sm describe the reign of David. In recording what happened, the chronological sequence at times gives way to a topical arrangement. The verses following immediately upon the record of his coronation mention two essential requirements for an effective reign: (1) establishment of a capital (6-10), where Hiram, king of Tyre, "built David a house" for his growing household (11-16); (2) clearing the invading Philistines out of the land. (17-25)

Jebusites. These Canaanites maintained their control of "the stronghold of Zion" despite the efforts of the Israelites to dislodge them (Ju 1:8 note; Nm 13:29). The Jebusites felt so safe in the natural defenses of their impregnable citadel that the efforts of lame and blind defenders, they taunted David, would suffice to ward off an attack.

5:8 *Water shaft.* This cryptic remark suggests that David's men surprised the garrison by climbing through and up the tunnel which extended to a spring beyond the city and supplied it with water.

5:9 *Millo.* The Hebrew word, always with the article, means "filling in" and suggests the building of fortifications at that part of the "stronghold" which was not protected from attack by natural precipices. (1 K 9:15; 11:27; 2 Ch 32:5)

5:12 *Exalted his kingdom.* Not for his own glorification but *for the sake of his people Israel,* from whom was to come great David's greater Son and in whose "Zion" all nations were to find refuge. (Is 2:2-4; Mi 4:2)

5:14 *Solomon.* On polygamy see Gn 16:2 note. How David became the father of Solomon is told later. (11:3 f.; 12:24)

5:17 *Went up.* When *David had been anointed king over Israel,* the Philistines realized that their erstwhile vassal no longer was promoting their interests. David's two defeats of the invaders may have preceded his capture of Jerusalem. *The stronghold* to which he *went down* probably was his earlier base of operation, Adullam (1 Sm 22:1-5). From here he "went up" to "the valley of Rephaim," southwest of Jerusalem. (Jos 15:8)

5:21 *Carried them away.* 1 Ch 14:12 adds that he burned them.

5:25 *Geba to Gezer.* Geba, meaning height, may have been the name of an unidentified place south of Jerusalem and not the site of Jonathan's exploit (1 Sm 41:1 ff.). Gezer was located 19 miles northwest of Jerusalem.

6:1—7:29 Promotion of Religious Life

6:1-23 TRANSFER OF ARK TO JERUSALEM

6:1 *Again gathered.* In addition to measures to establish his reign outwardly (5:6-25), David sought to promote the spiritual unity of the chosen people, constituted not as a secular power but as "a kingdom of priests" (Ex 19:6). The means to express its covenant relationship to God centered in the ark, where "the Lord of hosts . . . is enthroned on the cherubim" (1 Sm 4:4; Ex 37:1-9). After the first attempt to move it to Jerusalem on a cart brought tragic results (1-11), it was carried—the prescribed manner of transporting it—to its new resting place (12-23). David was not satisfied to have the ark of the Lord dwell "in a tent" which he had provided. His plan to build "a house" for it was approved by the prophet Nathan but did not receive divine sanction. (Ch. 7)

6:2 *Baale-judah.* 1 Ch 13:6 has the shorter form "Baalah" and identifies it with Kiriath-jearim, where according to 1 Sm 7:1 the ark had been taken after it was released by the Philistines.

6:3 *Abinadab.* The ark remained in his house during Samuel's and Saul's time, perhaps some 20 years (1 Sm 7:1 f.). Uzzah and Ahio no doubt were his grandsons. Following the example of the Philistines rather than the explicit directives for transporting it, the men *carried the ark . . . upon a new cart.* (Ex 25:14; Nm 4:5, 15, 19 f.)

6:6 *Nacon.* Not known as a place name. Translated as a common noun, it would mean "the fixed or established threshing floor." (1 Ch 13:10)

6:7 *Smote him.* For the severity of the punishment see 1 Sm 6:19, also Heb 10:28-31.

6:10 *Obed-edom.* A member of the Levitical family of Korahites (1 Ch 15:18, 24; 26:1-4), his name (a servant of Edom) may imply that at some time the Edomites had exacted service from him or his family. *Gittite* identifies him as a native of Gath, hardly the Philistine city by that name, but of Gath-rimmon, a Levitical city mentioned in Jos 21:24 f.

6:13 *Bore the ark.* "As Moses had commanded according to the word of the Lord." (1 Ch 15:15)

6:14 *Linen ephod.* Cf. 1 Sm 2:18 note.

6:17 *David offered.* As little as David himself "brought up the ark of God" (12), so little need one conclude that David personally assumed functions reserved for the priests.

6:20 *Uncovers.* Laying aside his royal garments and dancing "before the Lord," clad only in a linen ephod, David, according to Saul's daughter, had so exposed himself as to lose the respect of his subjects, especially of *his servants' maids.*

6:23 *No child.* Evidently her sarcastic remarks brought about a permanent estrangement between David and Michal.

7:1-29 PROPOSAL TO BUILD TEMPLE

7:1 *Rest.* In the text David's proposal to provide a permanent structure for the ark follows immediately upon the transfer of the sacred chest to Jerusalem (ch. 6). In point of time, however, he made this secomd move to foster the religious life of his people only after he had subdued *his enemies round about,* as recorded in ch. 8. Because in these battles he "shed much blood," he was not permitted to carry out his good intentions (1 Ch 22:8; 28:3). While denying the warrior king the privilege to build a structural dwelling place for the divine presence, God at the same time promised to build for David a dynastic "house" of kings whose rule was to continue "forever." Solomon, who built the temple, was to be one of them. But God's prophetic word was looking beyond him and the successors of the Davidic ruling house to that "son of David" (Mt 1:1) who says: "I am the root and the offspring of David, the bright morning star." (Rv 22:16; Jer 23:5; Mt 22:41-45; Lk 1:31-33; Acts 2:29-36)

7:2 *Nathan.* Mentioned here for the first time, this prophet was to be David's adviser and confessor (ch. 12; 1 K 1:11 f.). His personal opinion was overruled when he became the infallible instrument of God's inspired directives. (4 ff.)

7:6 *In a house.* "The tent of witness," erected by Moses, was a movable structure. It was "a habitation for the God of Jacob" in the same way that He whom "heaven and the highest heaven cannot contain" condescended to dwell in the house that Solomon was to build. (Acts 7:44-50; 1 K 8:27)

7:11 *Make you a house.* Even Solomon's temple served only as a temporary habitation of God. It would give way to that "offspring" of David who "dwelt" (tabernacled) among men and in whom "all the fullness of God was pleased to dwell" bodily. (Jn 1:14; Cl 1:19; 2:9)

7:13 *Kingdom for ever.* The Davidic dynasty lasted some 400 years. God did not "lie to David" (Ps 89:35 ff.). His promise to *establish... his kingdom forever* remained in effect until there came to "the throne of his father David" the "Son of God" of whose "kingdom there will be no end." (Lk 1:32-33)

7:18 *Sat before the Lord.* Facing the ark, the ritual throne of the Lord, David sat in deep contemplation of Nathan's mysterious message. He put the innermost thoughts of his heart into words of a prayer which humbly gave all glory to God for bringing him *thus far,* expressed his willingness to let the Lord overrule his plan, and glowed with faith in the prophetic promise regarding his "house for a great while to come." ("For ever": 24, 25, 26, 29)

7:19 *Future generations.* See the RSV note. KJV following the Septuagint makes the clause an interrogative sentence: "And is this the manner of man, O Lord God?" Luther: "That is a manner of a man who is God the Lord."

8:1-14 Expansion into Empire

8:1 *After this.* This phrase does not necessarily denote a chronological sequence with the previous chapter. Here it is no more than a transition to another feature of David's reign (so also in 10:1). After reporting that the king established a strong political home base (5:6-25) and fostered Israel's cohesion as a covenant people under God, the author now proceeds to another topic: the subjugation of nations bordering on Israel: (a) the Philistines—west (1); (b) the Moabites—east (2); (c) the Syrians—north (3-8); (d) the Edomites—south. (13 f.)

Metheg-ammah. David not only drove out the Philistines from his territory (5:17 ff.), but also took the city of Gath, here figuratively called "the bridle of the mother [city]," i.e., the center of control. (1 Ch 18:1)

8:2 *Moab.* David treated the country where he had left his parents for safekeeping (1 Sm 22:4) with unusual harshness. Perhaps some act of treachery on their part provoked him to kill two of every three Moabites.

8:3 *Hadadezer.* On the upper *Euphrates,* north and east of the Sea of Galilee, there were at this time several independent Aramean or Syrian kingdoms, later united under the leadership of Damascus. Still north of the latter lay *Zobah.* The name of its king means "Hadad [the sun god] is [my] help."

8:4 *Thousand and seven hundred.* The number according to 1 Ch 18:4 was "a thousand chariots, seven thousand horsemen." The difference may be the result of faulty transmission of the text.

8:9 *Hamath.* Situated north of Damascus on the Orontes River. The name of its king *Toi* occurs only here and in the form of "Tou" in 1 Ch 18:9.

8:12 *Amalek.* David defeated the Amalekites before he became king (1 Sm 30:16 ff.). No other encounter with these desert tribesmen is recorded.

8:13 *Edomites.* The text has "Syrians" (KJV), obviously a copyist misreading of the text, as is evident from 1 Ch 18:12 and the heading of Ps 60. In Hebrew the words for Syrians and Edomites are almost identical. The one is spelled with an *r* and the other with a *d,* letters which themselves are very similar in form. *The Valley of Salt* was south of the Dead Sea.

8:15-18 Administrative Officers

8:15 *Administered.* The account of David's successes at home and abroad is followed by a list of his officers who were needed to administer so extensive a realm.

8:17 *Ahimelech.* Zadok's associate elsewhere is *Abiathar,* the son of *Ahimelech* (20:25; 1 Sm 22:20). Possibly the names of father and son have been transposed in this verse as well as in 1 Ch 18:16.

8:16 *Cherethites and the Pelethites.* David's bodyguard consisted of *Cherethites* or Cretans and *the Pelethites*, more generally known as Philistines, who likewise immigrated from Crete. The form *Pelethites* for the more common Philistines occurs only in the stereotype phrase: Cherethites and Pelethites.

Priests. The same word is used in 17 and generally of the occupants of the sacerdotal office. Its etymology is not known. Since David's *priests* have just been mentioned, his sons evidently did not perform the same functions but were civic intermediaries, i.e., civic "chief officials." (1 Ch 18:17; 1 K 4:2)

9:1-13 Kindness to Saul's Grandson

9:1 *House of Saul.* Another noteworthy feature of David's reign was his refusal to abuse his power in dealing with the members of Saul's family. In his day the king of a new ruling house usually exterminated all survivors of his rival. However, David "administered justice and equity" (8:15). He not only refused to harm Mephibosheth, Jonathan's son and Saul's grandson, but also provided generously for his needs. The record does not specify the time of this event. At the death of his father, Mephibosheth was 5 years old (4:4); when David brought him to his table he had a son of his own. (12)

9:3 *Kindness of God.* In 1 Sm 20:14 the same phrase is translated "the loyal love of the Lord." As God is lovingly true to His promises, so David wanted to keep the oath that he swore "in the name of the Lord" when he made his covenant with Jonathan. (1 Sm 20:17, 42)

9:4 *Lo-debar.* An unidentified site. But the location of *the house of Machir* apparently was near Mahanaim, the Transjordan center of Ishbosheth's ill-fated reign. (2:8 note, 29; 17:27)

9:7 *The land of Saul.* His land and base of

operation had been at Gibeah. (1 Sm 10:26; 11:4)

9:11 *David's table.* As a precautionary measure David kept Saul's heir to the throne under surveillance at the court. Later Ziba accused Mephibosheth—perhaps falsely—of disloyalty. (19:25 ff.)

9:12 *Mica.* A possible contender for the throne. Jonathan's descendants through Mica are listed in 1 Ch 8:34 ff.

10:1—12:31 HOW DAVID SINNED

10:1—11:27 The Occasion: Ammonite Wars

10:1 *Ammonites.* David's war with the *Ammonites,* briefly mentioned in a previous summary (8:12), is described in greater detail than any other of his military exploits (chs. 10—12) because it marks a turning point in his reign. As in his other campaigns he defeated the enemy, but in this instance he lost the battle against himself. When the war was in progress, he was "lured and enticed by his own desire" to commit adultery and murder (Ja 1:14). This double crime against the sanctity of marrige and human life had tragic results for the remainder of his career.

10:2 *Hanun.* Saul had delivered Jabesh-gilead from the threat of Hanun's father Nahash (1 Sm 11). However, the latter *dealt loyally,* i.e., he observed the terms of a treaty, with David. For some unknown reason the son reversed the father's policy.

10:4 *Shaved off . . . cut off.* Considered a most demeaning insult, violating a Hebrew's sense of propriety.

10:6 *Syrians.* Before David could deal directly with the Ammonites, he had to eliminate their Syrian confederates. His successful encounter with the latter, briefly summarized in 8:3 ff., is here described in greater detail. The *Syrians* whom Hanun *hired* came from several city-states: *Beth-rehob,* near the headwaters of the Jordan north of the Sea of Galilee (Nm 13:17 note; Ju 18:28 note); *Zobah* (cf. 8:3 note); *Maacah,* directly south of Beth-rehob on the border of Transjordan Manasseh (Dt 3:14); *Tob.* (Cf. Ju 11:1 note)

10:8 *The gate.* Of the capital city of the Ammonites, Rabbah. (11:1)

10:16 *Hadadezer.* Cf. 8:3 note. After their defeat at Rabbah by Joab, who was in command of "the mighty men," no doubt David's elite corps of veterans (16:6; 20:7), the Syrians brought in reinforcements from beyond the Euphrates. To meet this new threat David now "gathered all Israel together" and personally led the attack against Hadadezer's general *Shobach.*

Helam. An unidentified site, perhaps in the vicinity of Damascus.

10:18 *Seven hundred chariots.* On the difference between the number of slain Syrians recorded here and that in 8:4 and 1 Ch 19:18 see 8:4 note.

11:1 *David sent Joab.* The account of the war with the Ammonites is resumed because its second phase furnished the occasion of David's fall into sin. The heinous crimes of the "man after his [God's] own heart" (1 Sm 13:14) are not suppressed or minimized. All sordid details are faithfully put on record. This scripture too is written "for our instruction"; for our warning: "let anyone who thinks that he stands take heed lest he fall" (1 Co 10:11 f.); for our comfort: there is forgiveness with God for the most despicable sins if we follow David's example and penitently come to Him in a sincere prayer for forgiveness such as Ps 51.

11:2 *He saw.* From the flat roof of David's house, built on higher ground than that of other buildings, he had a view of those around him. See also his order to Uriah to "go down to his house." (11:8)

11:3 *Bathsheba.* If her father is to be identified with the Eliam who was a son of David's "mighty man" Ahithophel (23:34), she was the latter's granddaughter. In 1 Ch 3:5 she is called "Bath-shua, the daughter of Ammiel." Her Hittite husband's name Uriah (the Lord is light) indicates that his family acknowleged Israel's God.

11:6 *Sent word.* The remaining verses of this chapter describe David's efforts to conceal his adultery. He first contrived to make it appear that Bathsheba had conceived the child by her husband during the latter's furlough from the front (6-13). When Uriah refused the opportunity to have relations with his wife, David sought to cover up his adultery by resorting to murder. In order to make Bathsheba his wife and to pose as the legitimate father of her son, he ordered his general Joab to devise a treacherous maneuver to have the troublesome husband killed in battle. (14-26)

11:8 *Wash your feet.* This may be a euphemistic expression for cohabitation.

11:11 *In booths.* Uriah refused the comforts of his home as long as the army was deprived of this privilege. The ark too had only a tent for a covering. Support for the inference that the ark had been taken into battle is based on such passages as 1 Sm 4:3; 2 Sm 15:24.

11:13 *Drunk.* David did not succeed in breaking down Uriah's inhibitions. He slept in the servants' quarters of his lord.

11:16 *Assigned Uriah.* Joab substituted his own plan for David's order (15). Unconcerned about the lives of "some of the servants of David" (17), Joab did not follow David's scheme to bring about only Uriah's death. He was sure that the king would not charge him with insubordination as long as he could report to him: "Uriah the Hittite is dead." (21, 24)

11:21 *Jerubbesheth.* The reference is to Gideon. His other name, Jerubbaal (Ju 6:32 note), occurs here in a form which substitutes the word for "shame" for the detested term "baal." For the story of the death of *Abimelech,* Gideon's son, see Ju 9:50-54.

11:27 *His wife.* In order to make it appear that Bathsheba's child was legitimately his own, David added her to his wives, as soon as she had observed the custom of mourning for her husband, very likely a period of 7 days.

12:1-25 David's Repentance and Restoration

12:1 *Sent Nathan.* David kept what he "did ...secretly" locked in an impenitent heart for almost a year (12, 14). Among Israel's neighboring peoples his crimes would have gone unchallenged as the prerogative of an absolute king. However, a fearless prophet of the Lord hailed the royal culprit before the bar of justice and pronounced him a criminal worthy of death. David was also assured that God's mercy is big enough to forgive even the most lurid crime if the sinner repents. In his parable Nathan presented a hypothetical case of gross injustice. When David pronounced the death sentence on its perpetrator (1-6), the prophet declared that the king, guilty of a similar and even more grievous outrage, stood convicted by his own verdict.

12:5 *Deserves to die.* The circumstances of the rich man's villainy so outraged David that he imposed a punishment that exceeded legal requirements. (Ex 22:1)

12:7 *The man.* Nathan was as fearless in his denunciation of royal sins as Samuel (1 Sm 15:26), Elijah (1 K 21:17 ff.), John the Baptist. (Mk 6:18)

12:10 *Never depart.* Though forgiven, David's sin against Uriah and his wife produced a train of tragic consequences in the royal family: incest and fratricide, insurrection and violation of his wives by a son, execution of the rebel prince. (13-19)

12:13 *Against the Lord.* David penitently acknowledged the full magnitude of his guilt. Laying hands on one's fellow creatures was in the last analysis a defiance of their Creator and Protector, as Nathan had pointed out. (9; Ps 51:4; 32:5)

12:18 *The child died.* Fasting and lying on the ground, David "besought the Lord" for the recovery of the son who, had he lived, would have been a constant reminder of the father's misdeeds. However, when the child died, David submitted to the Lord's chastisement, cheered by the thought of a reunion with the infant.

12:25 *Jedidiah.* David called Bathsheba's second son Solomon (the peaceful one). The name Jedidiah, occurring only here, means "beloved of the Lord." Formed from the same etymological root from which the name David is derived, it was designed to give both father and son the assurance of divine favor.

12:26-31 Conclusion of Ammonite War

12:26 *Against Rabbah.* The account of the war against the Ammonites is resumed from 11:1, where it was interrupted to tell of David's sin and of Solomon's birth, the latter occurring after the final campaign described in the following verses.

12:27 *City of waters.* After Joab took that part of "the royal city" (26) where the king's residence stood and which also guarded the water supply, the fall of Rabbah was only a matter of time.

12:30 *Their king.* One word in Hebrew, its consonants may be supplied with vowels which spell "Milcom," the name of the Ammonite god (Jer 49:1; Zph 1:5). The captured crown weighed *a talent,* some 100 pounds. Perhaps only the *precious stone* in it *was placed on David's head.*

12:31 *Set them to labor.* The RSV so interprets the Hebrew text, which in its present form reads: "he placed them with saws, etc." The translation "toil at" instead of "pass through" (KJV) requires the change of one consonant in the original.

13:1—20:26 HOW TROUBLES AROSE IN DAVID'S HOUSE

13:1-19 Incest

13:1 *Tamar.* The next six chapters record how David's sin against the sanctity of marriage had tragic consequences in his own family. Members of his own household committed wanton crimes that caused him untold misery. His sons became guilty of incest (1-19), fratricide (22, 28-29), rebellion (chs. 15—20).—Tamar, Absalom's full sister, was ravished by Amnon, her half brother and David's oldest son.

13:2 *Seemed impossible.* Amnon's cousin Jonadab devised a scheme to bring Tamar, kept secluded in the women's quarters, to Amnon's house.

13:13 *Not withhold me.* Marriage with a half sister, prohibited by Israel's law (Lv 18:9, 11), was not uncommon among other nations. Apparently Tamar had first tried to put off Amnon with the suggestion that David would sanction such a marriage. After her assailant nevertheless "forced her," she proposed such a union as less degrading than being abandoned. (16)

13:15 *Be gone.* Amnon's sudden change from passion to revulsion and cruelty is not uncommon in cases of pathological personalities.

13:18 *A long robe.* The same word is used of Joseph's coat (Gn 37:3 note). Her distinctive robe is mentioned because, so clad, all who saw her knew that she was one of *the virgin daughters of the king.*

13:20—14:33 Fratricide

13:21 *Very angry.* David's anger stopped short of punishing Amnon. Perhaps like other parents, he did not feel justified in invoking sanctions of the law for the kind of sin of which he himself was guilty. But his indulgence of one son gave the other an opportunity to plot revenge for his sister.

13:23 *Two full years.* Absalom waited so long hoping that Amnon would think the matter was forgotten. *Baal-hazor* was about 15 miles north of Jerusalem near a place called *Ephraim,* probably another name for Ophrah, a Benjaminite town. (Jos 18:23)

13:32 *Amnon alone.* It seems odd that Jonadab knew of Absalom's plan to kill Amnon *from the day he forced . . . Tamar.* Ostensibly the dead brother's "friend" (3), he may have been Absalom's secret agent in a devious plot to eliminate David's oldest son, normally the king's successor. If so, Amnon's crime and death was the first ruthless step in Absalom's scheme to seize the throne.

13:34 *Horonaim.* The Hebrew text: "from a way behind him" makes sense if taken to mean simply that the *people* approached from a direction opposite the one in which the watchman was looking. The RSV rendering involves a textual change.

13:37 *Geshur.* Absalom was "the son of Maacah the daughter of Talmai king of Geshur" (3:3), ruler of a Syrian kingdom east of the Sea of Galilee. Had David been so minded, he could have demanded that Absalom be extradited. Indulgently failing to punish his unscrupulous son, David only sowed to the whirlwind, as the next chapters prove.

14:1 *Joab . . . perceived.* Prompted either by a false sense of duty to the king or by a desire to advance his own influence at the court, Joab by an ingenious device brought about a partial reconciliation between David and Absalom. He engaged a wise woman to solicit the king's verdict in a simulated case in which she cast herself in the role of the mother of a son guilty of fratricide (1-7). When David's verdict was that no purpose would be served if the "avenger of blood" were to take the life of the culprit (8-11), the woman deftly urged that by "this decision" the king had committed himself to "bring his banished one home again" (12-17). Even though David discovered that Joab had put "these words in the mouth" of the woman "in order to change the course of affairs" (18-20), he let his general bring Absalom home, but confined the troublesome son to "his own house." (21-24)

14:2 *Tekoa.* A town about 6 miles south of Bethlehem; also the home of the prophet Amos. (Am 1:1)

14:11 *Avenger of blood.* The practice of blood revenge by the nearest of kin to a murdered person persisted. (Nm 35:11 note, 19)

14:13 *Convicts himself.* If David set aside the demands of justice in her case, the woman argues, he must also reverse himself and pardon his own son lest he be guilty of injustice.

14:14 *Take away the life.* The RSV adds to the text: "of him who." This translation suggests that a man, in this case David, who *devises means* to recall the outcast will not incur God's displeasure. If God is the subject of both verbs (as in the RSV note), the woman may be subtly reminding the king that God did not *take away* his *life,* guilty of death though he was.

14:20 *The course of affairs.* By his clever move Joab made it possible for Absalom rather than one of the other sons of David to succeed his father.

14:24 *The king's presence.* Banishment from the court was a serious handicap for a person scheming to take over the throne.

14:25 *His beauty.* A description of Absalom's physical attractiveness is inserted at this point because it helps to explain why he gained popular support in his conspiracy against David.

14:26 *King's weight.* Absalom's hair was weighed by standards set by the king. If the correct figure is preserved in the text, its weight was at least 3½ pounds.

14:31 *Field on fire.* Absalom's outward beauty belied the ugliness of his inner self. Informed of the high-handed and unscrupulous treatment of his patron Joab, the reader will not be surprised when told shortly that this treacherous blackguard turned even on his father.

14:33 *Kissed Absalom.* Full reconciliation with the king set the stage for the tragic drama that is to be described in the next chapters: Absalom's rebellion.

15:1—20:26 Revolt by Absalom

15:1-12 SUCCESSFUL CONSPIRACY

15:2 *Beside . . . the gate.* The city's "public square." Perhaps counseled by David's traitorous adviser Ahithophel (12), Absalom proceeded according to a diabolically effective plan of intrigue. His first step was to create disaffection in Israel, the northern part of David's kingdom, which for some time had remained loyal to Saul's house (1-6). After 4 years of agitation under the very eyes of his indulgent father, he felt he had enough support to abandon all pretense. He had himself proclaimed king at Hebron, his birthplace and the city of Judah which had first acknowledged David's rule. (7-12)

15:4 *Judge.* Had Absalom used the term king, he would have been liable to the charge of sedition. However, since the king was the final arbiter of justice, the people could not miss the point of his veiled language.

15:7 *Four years.* KJV, following the Hebrew text, has "forty." RSV adopts the more likely reading of the Septuagint. Apparently David refused to believe that his pampered son was guilty of anything more than making a nuisance of himself.

15:8 *Geshur.* Cf. 13:37 note.

15:12 *Gilonite.* His home was in Giloh near Hebron. (Jos 15:51)

15:13—16:14 DAVID'S FLIGHT

15:14 *Flee.* Because Absalom had cajoled "two hundred men from Jerusalem" to join him (11), David feared that Absalom could rally enough support in the capital itself to make it dangerous to risk a siege of the city. He did not know how many other conspirators were within its walls.

15:18 *Cherethites . . . Pelethites.* Cf. 8:18 note. The Gittites perhaps constituted the nucleus of his original outlaw band who remained loyal to him during his flight to Gath. (1 Sm 23:13; 27:1 ff.)

15:19 *Ittai.* Unlike the veteran Cherethites and Pelethites, this Philistine soldier of fortune had only "yesterday" taken service with David.

Nevertheless Ittai decided to throw in his lot with the king rather than to *stay with the* self-appointed *king* Absalom. David's trust in this untried mercenary was not misplaced. (Cf. 18:2)

15:23 *The brook Kidron.* David fled eastward *toward the wilderness* of the Jordan fords, crossing the brook from which the King of kings was to set out on the "via dolorosa" in order to take upon Himself the guilt of mankind's rebellion against its Creator. (Jn 18:1)

15:24 *Abiathar.* The Hebrew text reads: "And Zadok came up." The RSV assumes that the name of Abiathar, his associate, has dropped out of the text here and in 27. Whatever David's reason was for addressing only Zadok (25), the fugitive king preferred to leave the safety of the ark in God's hands rather than make its mere presence a guarantee of success. For a superstitious trust in the ark see 1 Sm 4:3 ff.

15:28 *Inform me.* Certain that Absalom would not stoop to lay hands on the priests, David recruited them to send him *word* of developments in Jerusalem while he was still *at the fords of the* Jordan *wilderness.*

15:31 *Ahithophel.* Perhaps through messengers sent by the priests, David was told the disconcerting news that Absalom's conspiracy was masterminded by the wily *Ahithophel.*

15:32 *Hushai.* From *the summit* of "the Mount of Olives" (30) David ordered his "friend" to return to Jerusalem. Posing as a defector to Absalom's cause, he was to "turn the counsel of Ahithophel into foolishness" (31). Identified as an *Archite* (Jos 16:2), *Hushai* no doubt was so old as to be a "burden to" the king, hampering the latter's swift movements.

16:1 *Ziba.* Before David reached the Jordan (14), two incidents occurred in which he had to deal with members of "the family of Saul." First *Ziba, the servant of* Jonathan's lame son *Mephibosheth,* accused his master of abetting Absalom's revolution (1-4). A little later Shimei, a distant relative of Saul, cursed David, invoking the Lord's vengeance on the king for having shed "all the blood of the house" of his predecessor. (5-14)

16:3 *Give me.* Ziba risked his future by throwing in his lot with David. But to make the most of his decision, he maliciously exaggerated his master's aspirations to get *back the kingdom of* his *father.*

16:4 *All that belonged.* Taking Ziba's accusations at face value, David promptly rewarded the renegade servant.

16:5 *Bahurim.* A hill east of Jordan. (3:16; 17:17-21)

16:7 *Man of blood.* In his wild rage Shimei made David accountable to the Lord for deaths in the house of Saul, referring perhaps to the blood shed in the "long war between the house of Saul and the house of David" (3:1) or to the murder of Ish-bosheth and his general Abner (3:27; 4:1-3) or to the execution of Saul's seven sons. (21:1-9)

16:12 *Will look.* Even though David countered the rebellion with every means at his disposal, he would let the Lord, to whom Shimei had appealed, dispense justice in His own way. If "the Lord has bidden" Shimei to curse him, he would submit to this *affliction* as divine chastisement for his "iniquity." (Cf. RSV note)

16:15—17:23 ABSALOM IN JERUSALEM; HIS ADVISERS

16:15 *To Jerusalem.* The scene now shifts from the fugitive king at the Jordan to developments in Jerusalem. Once in the capital, Absalom still needed to devise means to complete the seizure of the throne. In choosing the proper course of action, he looked for advice to Ahithophel, whose counsel in the past had proved to be as reliable as an "oracle of God" (23), and to Hushai, who succeeded in allaying all suspicion that he was David's secret agent. (15-19)

16:21 *Concubines.* Absalom's fellow conspirator proposed two stratagems. The first was to claim the throne irrevocably by taking over his father's harem (20-23; cf. 3:7; 12:10 notes). Then he advocated an immediate pursuit of David with a quickly assembled army of chosen warriors. (17:1-4)

17:3 *Only one man.* Once David was eliminated, Absalom would overcome all opposition.

17:7 *This time.* Referring to the sound *counsel* of his rival as *no good,* Hushai was able to persuade Absalom to adopt a plan that gave David valuable time to cross the Jordan and to deploy his forces to his advantage. (5-14)

17:11 *In person.* Hushai knew how to appeal to the rebel's vanity. Skillfully exploiting this weakness, the crafty counselor pictured Absalom—not Ahithophel—at the head of an army representing all tribes *from Dan to Beersheba.* His warning that hastily assembled troops might panic in the suggested night attack gave his advice the ring of truth.

17:14 *Defeat.* In answer to David's prayer. (15:31)

17:16 *Tell David.* Acting on David's order "to inform" him (15:28), the priests had arranged for secret accomplices to relay their message to David. They urged David to cross the Jordan that very night (21) lest Absalom still should change his mind and attack at once. "A maidservant" kept them informed of developments, rendezvousing with them at "Enrogel" (the well of the fuller), a source of water supply south of Jerusalem's walls.

17:18 *Well.* No doubt a dry cistern over which the woman "spread a covering," pretending to use it for drying some kind of crushed "grain."

17:23 *Hanged himself.* No doubt the premonition that Absalom had embarked on a disastrous course prompted the rejected counselor to take his own life lest he die the death of a traitor at the hands of David.

17:24—18:18 REBEL ARMY DEFEATED; ABSALOM SLAIN

17:24 *Mahanaim.* Surprisingly David received full support from the people of Ish-bosheth's erstwhile capital in "Gilead." (2:8-10)

17:25 *Amasa.* Absalom put his cousin, the son of David's sister, in command. In the Hebrew text Amasa's father *Ithra* is called an "Israelite"; in 1 Ch 2:17 he is said to have been an *Ishmaelite.* Perhaps he owed the latter designation to associations with the Ishmaelites, among whom he was known as "Ithra the Israelite."

17:27 *Shobi . . . Machir . . . Barzillai.* Provisions for David's men were supplied by: (1) *Shobi,* whom David evidently had appointed as his governor in *Rabbah,* the Ammonite capital, after Hanun had been deposed (10:1 ff.); (2) *Machir,* Mephibosheth's benefactor (9:4); (3) *Barzillai,* "an aged" but "very wealthy man" from Rogelim north of Mahanaim but south of Lo-debar. (Cf. 19:31-39)

18:1 *David mustered.* Absalom's untried army under an inexperienced leader was no match for the well-disciplined though outnumbered troops directed by the veteran strategist. Persuaded not to "go out" into the front lines at the head of the three segments into which he had divided his army (1-5), David nevertheless took full advantage of the rugged terrain between Mahanaim and the Jordan, called "the forest of Ephraim." On such a cut-up battlefield the rebel army was unable to deploy its numerically stronger forces. Furthermore, once put to flight the forward contingents would throw those to their rear into utter confusion. In the ensuing panic Absalom's forces were wiped out, the "forest" jungle making them an easy prey for the sword of David's men (6-8). Contrary to David's order to "deal gently . . . with the young man Absalom," Joab thrust "three darts" into the body of the rebel hanging suspended in the branches of an oak (9-15) and buried him in "a great pit in the forest." (16-18)

18:7 *Twenty thousand.* A very high figure. Perhaps the Hebrew word for *thousand* here denotes the kind of soldiers slain. (See Numbers, Introduction, "The Numbers . . .")

18:9 *Caught.* Although not mentioned, Absalom's long hair may have made it more difficult for him to extricate his head, which had been driven into a fork formed by low-hanging branches of the oak.

18:14 *The heart.* If *heart* here denotes the vital organ, there hardly would have been any need for Joab's armor-bearers to kill Absalom. Hence *into the heart* may mean no more than that Joab's darts struck home, piercing the body to its inmost parts. (See "heart of the seas," Jon 2:3)

18:17 *Heap of stones.* These stones made the pit a criminal's grave (Jos 7:26). The "pillar" which Absalom had erected for himself remained a monument commemorating his uncontrollable vanity, which proved his undoing.

18:18 *No son.* Either Absalom's three sons (14:27) had died young or he had no hopes that they would do anything noteworthy enough to keep his *name in remembrance.*

18:19—19:8a DAVID'S GRIEF

18:19 *Tidings.* The scene shifts from the battlefield to David, who gave way to such "weeping and mourning" (19:1) at the news of Absalom's death as to prompt Joab to reprimand him for neglecting his duty to the people (19:5-8). Warning Ahimahaz that Joab knew how David would receive the message of his son and that its bearer would not receive a "reward for the tidings" but was apt to incur the king's displeasure, Joab selected a "Cushite," i.e., an Ethiopian mercenary or slave, to be the courier. Regardless of consequences, Ahimahaz insisted that he too be permitted to "run."

18:24 *Alone.* A lone runner was a good omen. For if the battle had been lost, the watchman would have sighted great numbers of David's forces in precipitate retreat. The appearance of "another man running alone" only confirmed David in his expectations of good tidings. (24-27)

18:28 *Well.* Evidently Ahimahaz insisted on being a courier because he wanted to break the shattering news as gently as possible (28-30). Even though he "outran" the Cushite, either because he was swifter of foot or because he chose "the [less rugged] way of the plain" (23), he was not able to complete his report before the arrival of the other runner, who proceeded more directly to announce Absalom's death.

18:33 *My son!* More than the natural grief of a father cut deeply into David's heart. Bitter thoughts of self-incrimination for his own despicable deeds haunted his anguished memory. Absalom was not the last child to break the heart of indulgent parents.

19:5 *Covered with shame.* Though sharing their king's sorrow over his son, the people who had risked their lives for him were chagrined by his lack of concern for them. Joab's harsh words were necessary to remind David of his duty to put the welfare of his kingdom above personal feelings. Resolute action must replace disconsolate weeping.

19:8b—20:26 HEALING OF THE BREACH

19:9 *Tribes of Israel.* It took considerable time and effort to bring order into the confusion caused by Absalom's aborted rebellion. Of their own accord the northern tribes of Israel urged their leaders to "bring the king back" (9b f.). On the other hand, Judah, David's own "kinsmen," consented to "bring the king back to his house" only after he sent them a conciliatory message and even promised to put Amasa, Absalom's general, in command of the entire army "in place of Joab" (11-15). On his way back to Jerusalem, David granted amnesty to Shimei (16-23), restored half of the confiscated land to Mephibosheth (24-30), and permitted the aged Barzillai to decline the invitation to be his honored guest in Jerusalem (31-40). But before David again was in undisputed control it was necessary to put down another uprising in the north.

19:13 *Commander.* David's action assured all

other participants in the rebel army that they would not have to fear reprisals, if Amasa, their general, not only was to go unpunished but even was to be promoted to commander in chief. Infuriated by his demotion, Joab waited for an opportune time to assassinate his less competent successor. (20:9 f.)

19:20 *Sinned.* David did not hesitate to accept at face value Shimei's claim of a change of heart. A refusal to pardon the culprit would have alienated the "thousand men from Benjamin" whom he had gathered about him.

19:27 *Slandered.* In dealing with Ziba's accusations against Saul's grandson (16:1-4), David resorted to a compromising solution. Instead of determining definitely whether Ziba had maligned his master or whether Mephibosheth's protestations of innocence were true, the king only modified the penalty that he had imposed on Jonathan's son. Perhaps he harbored the suspicion that both were not entirely truthful.

19:36 *Recompense me.* David readily acceded to aged Barzillai's request to let "Chimham," perhaps his son, accept the reward to "provide for" him in Jerusalem for having "provided the king with food while he stayed in Mahanaim."

19:41 *Stolen you away.* Petty tribal jealousy held up progress toward national unification under David. "Half of the people of Israel" (40) had accompanied the king across the Jordan to "Gilgal," a city belonging to the north. Here they were met by a large group representing *all the men of Israel,* who charged that the men of Judah had in effect kidnapped the king in order to ingratiate themselves with him (41-43). Judah's intemperate reply so inflamed the tempers of the northern tribes that a demagog, Sheba, was able to persuade them to secede from the union (20:1 f.). Having established himself in Jerusalem (20:3), David dispatched the dilatory Amasa, the recently appointed commander, to put down the rebellion. When the troop had proceeded no further than Gibeon, barely 10 miles northeast of Jerusalem, Joab treacherously killed his rival (4-10a), assumed command (10b-13), pursued Sheba, now deserted by all except his own clansmen, and besieged him in Abel of Beth-maacah, a city about 25 miles north of the Sea of Galilee. Acting on the advice of a "wise woman" in their midst, its citizens "cut off the head of Sheba . . . and threw it out to Joab" (14-28). The long story of the schism and its healing ends with a list of officials in the reconstituted kingdom. (23-26)

20:3 *Concubines.* As Absalom had proclaimed himself king by appropriating them (16:20-22), so David "put them in a house under guard" in order to signify that he again was the sole ruler.

20:6 *Abishai.* The appointment of Absalom's general Amasa (19:13) was an astute political move on David's part. But when the latter proved incompetent, David selected *Abishai* rather than Joab to carry out the order of a speedy mobilization.

20:9 *The beard.* It was customary to draw a person close by his beard in order to kiss him. Joab's despicable use of an intimate gesture to hide his evil intention was more than matched when Judas by a kiss betrayed his Lord.

20:14 *Bichrites.* The RSV's change of the unknown "Berites" of the Hebrew text to "Bichrites" has in its favor the fact that Sheba hailed from the town of Bichri in Benjamin (1). If this reading is correct, Sheba's following had dwindled to his own townsmen.

20:19 *Mother. Abel,* meaning meadow, is further identified by the addition of "Beth-maacah." Apparently in demand for its sage advice of all kinds, the city played the role of a counseling mother to the entire area.

20:24 *Adoram.* A list of David's officials from an earlier period is given in 8:16-18. Besides Joab and other officials listed there, this roster adds the name of an additional administrator, *Adoram,* who supervised *the forced labor,* a form of taxation which the free Israelites resented. (1 K 12:4, 14, 18)

20:26 *Ira.* He replaced "David's sons." (Cf. 8:18 second note)

21:1—24:25 SUPPLEMENTARY ACCOUNTS OF DAVID'S REIGN

21:1-14 Expiation of Saul's Bloodguilt

21:1 *Days of David.* The closing chapters of the book (chs. 21—24) consist in the main of flashbacks to isolated incidents which for some reason are not included in the previous account of David's life. The first of these vignettes is the story of the expiation of *bloodguilt* resting *on Saul and on his house.* It had been incurred by the former king, who had polluted the land with the blood of the *Gibeonites,* whom he killed in violation of a treaty (Nm 35:31-34; Gn 4:10; Jos 9:15). The result was a famine for 3 years. Informed by an oracle of its cause, David ordered the execution of seven of Saul's sons.

21:3 *Bless the heritage.* The expiation of the blood of the Gibeonites would remove the curse on Israel and its promised inheritance and again dispose God to bless the land.

21:6 *Hang them.* Either to impale them or to leave their corpses exposed to view as proof of their death.

21:8 *Merab.* The Hebrew text reads Michal, evidently a copyists error for Saul's older daughter (see RSV note and 1 Sm 18:19). Rizpah's son *Mephibosheth* was not Jonathan's son by the same name (7) to whom David had pledged "kindness." (9:1 ff.)

21:9 *Gave them.* David did not feel constrained to act according to the legal provision that children were not to "be put to death for the fathers" (Dt 24:16) either because the Lord had declared them guilty (1) or because they were in some way accessories to the crime.

Before the Lord. In exhibition of compliance with the divine will (1 Sm 15:33 note). According to the Hebrew text of v. 6 the Gibeonites requested as the site of execution "Gibeah of Saul, the chosen of the Lord." By this designation of Saul the Gibeonites seemed to imply that the crime was particularly heinous because it was committed by one divinely chosen to enforce the law.

21:10 *Harvest.* The end of April or the beginning of May. The mother's pathetic vigil lasted *until rain fell,* usually not before October.

21:12 *Jabesh-gilead.* In order to prove that his motives for executing his erstwhile rival's sons were not personal animosity, David accorded them as well as their father's remains honorable burial. Saul had been hastily buried in Jabesh-gilead. (1 Sm 31:11-13; 2 Sm 2:4b)

21:14 *Zela.* Saul's ancestral tomb was a site in Benjamin which has not been identified.

21:15-22 Heroic Deeds During Philistine Campaign

21:15 *War again.* This appendix (15-22) furnishes some details of David's struggles with the Philistines. It lists four heroic deeds of his men who in the course of several campaigns felled enemy soldiers of a stature similar to that of Goliath.

21:17 *Lamp of Israel.* A figurative expression for David's "house," which was not to be extinguished. (7:12 f.; 1 K 11:36)

21:19 *Goliath.* 1 Ch 20:5 preserves a better reading: "Elhanon the son of Jair slew Lahmi the brother of Goliath." Only minor changes in the Hebrew text are necessary to correct the errors made by the copyists of the Samuel text.

22:1-51 David's Psalm of Thanksgiving

22:1 *Song.* This poetic outpouring of gratitude to God is a fitting supplement to the more matter-of-fact account of David's triumphs recorded in the preceding chapters. With some minor changes it is repeated in the collection of his psalms (Ps 18). In the opening lines David at once states his purpose: "the Lord . . . is worthy to be praised" (1-4). In his dire need (5-7) the ruler of heaven and earth (8-16) delivered him from enemies "too mighty for" him (17-20). This goodness of God was at the same time a reward of grace for keeping "the ways of the Lord" (21-25), who in "perfect" justice rights the wrongs of all innocent sufferers (26-31). Once more acknowledging that God was the source of his victories (32-43), particularly against "foreigners" (44-46), David concludes his song in an exultant burst of praise to the living Lord, who delivered him in the past, continues to give "great triumphs" in the present, and will show steadfast love to "his descendants for ever." (47-51)

22:2-3 *Rock.* The heaping of figurative epithets for God *(fortress, shield, horn, stronghold),* expresses David's confidence in the Lord as his *deliverer* or Savior from dangers.

22:6 *Sheol.* Cf. Gn 37:35; Dt 32:22 note.

22:8 *Earth reeled.* The poetic description of natural phenomena in these verses testifies to the Creator's unlimited power to enforce His will.

22:21 *Rewarded.* The context of the psalm makes it clear that David is not making a self-righteous claim to God's merciful dealing with him but sets forth the reason why the Lord "delighted in" him (20) rather than in his "strong enemy" (18). Even though "conceived in sin" and therefore in need of forgiveness as much as his foes, David gratefully acknowledges that the Lord's "way is perfect," proving "true" to His covenant and promise to grant a reward to those who are "careful to do all his commandments." (Dt 28:1 ff.)

23:1-7 Prophetic Last Words of David

23:1 *Last words.* His last poetic utterance. It is not necessary to assume that David composed this psalm immediately before his death. What he said as his "time to die drew near" is recorded in 1 K 2:1 ff.

23:2 *Spirit of the Lord.* Having identified himself for posterity in 1, David by divine inspiration uttered a prophetic "oracle." No opposition by "godless men" will thwart God in keeping the "everlasting covenant" which He made with his "house" (7:11, 13 notes). The blessings upon David "ruling in the fear of God" are but a token of the benefactions which God will bestow on all men in the reign of "the Prince of Peace," David's Son and Lord.

23:8-39 Roster of Distinguished Warriors; Their Exploits

23:8 *Mighty men.* In fighting his way to the throne and extending his power over neighboring peoples, David commanded a formidable army. The next verses list the names of men who deserve special mention for the role they played. First in order to be recognized for their loyalty and valor was a most distinguished group, the "Big Three" (8-12). Next on the roll of honor were the famous "thirty." Three of them, who perhaps formed another special group besides the first three, risked their lives to quench David's thirst (13-17). The commander of the 30 was Abishai, Joab's brother (18 f.). Besides the exploit by the three unnamed heroes, mentioned in 13-17, there were the daring feats of another "among the thirty," Benaiah (20-23). Then there follows a full roster of the men who won a place in the elite corps of the "thirty." (24-38)

23:18 *Thirty.* If the Hebrew text which here has "three" is correct, then Abishai *was chief of* the trio mentioned in 13-17 who were in a class by themselves though not of the same high rank as the first "three." (23)

23:20 *Ariels.* A transliteration of a rare Hebrew word which in Eze 43:15 is translated "altar hearth." If this is its meaning, Abishai penetrated two Moabite sanctuaries and destroyed their altars.

23:39 *Thirty-seven.* This total is made up of the 31 names listed in 24-38, plus the three of the first group (8-12), plus the three in the second category (13-22). Joab, the commander in chief, is left unmentioned. As some of "the mighty men died," other names were added to the roll of honor called "the thirty." In 1 Ch 11:41-47, 16 more names are assigned to the hall of fame.

24:1-25 Israel's Sin; David's Pride; Punishment

24:1 *Anger of the Lord.* The last appended episode provides another example of the consequences of sin similar to the incident recorded in ch. 21. *Again the anger of the Lord was kindled against Israel.* We are not told why in this instance the people as a whole came under divine judgment. For reasons known to God alone, He chose a sinful act by David as the immediate occasion of national punishment. Motivated by pride or by a lust for power, the king ordered a census of his fighting forces (1-9). Given a choice of chastisements, he selected a "three days' pestilence" (10-14). Because "the Lord repented of the evil," the ravaging plague did not run its full course (15-18). When David built an altar to the Lord on a "threshing floor" which he bought from its Jebusite owner, the plague "was averted from Israel." (18-25)

Incited David. Even though God "himself tempts no one" (Ja 1:13 ff.), He creates situations in which man has the choice of following his evil desires or of overcoming the temptation. It is only natural that Satan should make full use of such circumstances to mislead man into disobedience. (Cf. 1 Ch 21:1)

24:5 *Crossed the Jordan.* All the tribes of Israel from "Dan to Beer-sheba" were to be numbered. Beginning at *Aroer,* a city of Reuben east of the Dead Sea, the census takers moved northward to *Jazer* on the border of *Gad,* continued through "Gilead" to "Dan" north of the Sea of Galilee. West of the Jordan they proceeded southward from "Tyre" and "Sidon" through "all the cities" settled by remnants of "the Hivites and Canaanites" (Ju 1:27; Gn 34:2) until they reached "Beer-sheba" in the "Negeb," the southland of Judah below the Dead Sea.

24:9 *The sum.* The totals, 800,000 *valiant men* of Israel and 500,000 of Judah would presuppose a population of at least five or six million. In 1 Ch 21:5 the figures are 300,000 higher in one instance and 30,000 lower in the other. A lower figure results if the Hebrew word for thousand is not taken in its numerical meaning but denotes fully armed soldiers as differentiated from all men of military age, a distinction which later copyists no longer understood. In addition there is the possibility of a faulty transmission of the figures themselves. Operating with these assumptions, the following computation has been proposed: for Israel 80,000 men of draft age plus 30 men who *drew the sword;* for Judah 40,000 and 70 respectively. (See Numbers, Introduction, "The Numbers . . .")

24:14 *Hand of the Lord.* Because the other options, famine and defeat by foes, involved the possibility of human greed and hostility, David preferred to subject himself to a chastisement inposed directly by the Lord.

24:16 *Angel.* Cf. Ex 12:23. For *the Lord repented* see 1 Sm 15:11 note; Gn 6:6; Ex 32:14 note.

24:17 *Sinned.* This verse explains that the hand of the destroying angel was stayed (16) because the Lord saw that David's repentance was sincere.

24:18 *Araunah the Jebusite.* Before David took Jerusalem, the city was known as Jebus. The name of this original resident, perhaps a Hittite, has the variant Hebrew spelling of Ornan in 1 Ch 21:15.

24:22 *Take.* David knew that this offer of a gift was not to be taken seriously. See Abraham's purchase of land from Ephron in Gn 23:11 note.

24:24 *Fifty shekels of silver.* The Hebrew text of 1 Ch 21:25 has 600 shekels of gold, for which the Syriac translation has "50 staters," the equivalent of 50 shekels. It is possible that David bought the oxen, the wood, and the smaller site of the altar for 50 shekels, but paid the larger sum for the entire area where the temple was to be built.

24:25 *Altar.* The book closes without describing the last days and death of David. But the purchase of the temple site and the erection of an altar there anticipate the building of the temple, recorded in the first chapters of 1 Kings.

FIRST AND SECOND

KINGS

INTRODUCTION

Contents

Abraham's offspring, chosen from Adam's descendants to be the bearers of God's promised blessing to all nations (Gn), became "a kingdom of priests and a holy nation" (Ex 19:5 f.) when at Mt. Sinai the Lord entered into a solemn covenant with the erstwhile slaves of Egypt.

Forgiving their repeated lapses into infidelity, the Lord brought them to the Promised Land (Ex to Dt), settled them within its borders (Jos), and let grace continue to abound when by periodic apostasies they deserved to be abandoned to oppressors. (Ju)

Next, God linked the covenant promises and provisions to the royal house of David, during whose reign Israel rose to unprecedented heights of national glory. (1 and 2 Sm)

The two books of Kings relate how God "cut off Israel from the land" because it persisted in flouting the basis of the covenant: "You shall have no other gods before me." At the death of David's son Solomon the kingdom split into two rival factions, almost always in hostile action against one another. After about two centuries the Assyrians subjugated the 10 northern tribes (Israel), carrying off large numbers into exile. About one and a half centuries later the southern half (Judah) fell a prey to the Babylonian conqueror.

At this point the chosen people should have become extinct, buried under the sands of time, together with its smaller neighbors and even its conquerors. But God did not fail to keep His covenant with David to "establish the throne of his kingdom for ever" (2 Sm 7:13). Out of the root of Jesse and at a time when Israel had no king but the Roman Caesar, God put on "the throne of his father David" that Son of David of whose "kingdom there will be no end." (Lk 1:32 f., 68 ff.)

Purpose

The books of Kings demonstrate that the Lord of history executes the threats and keeps the promises of "his holy covenant."

The destruction of the holy city, the burning of the temple, and the subjugation of the chosen people were not accidents of fate but the lashes of God's scourge on an apostate nation. No longer fit to be the instrument of His eternal plan of salvation, Israel as a political state was discarded.

In spite of this dreary ending, the books of Kings are open to the future. Shining from their pages are repeated references to the reassuring fact that the Word of the Lord does not return "empty" but is able to "accomplish that which" He purposes (Is 55:11). "The holy and sure blessings of David," promising him "a kingdom for ever," were not to be an exception (Is 55:3; 2 Sm 7; Acts 13:34). They too would be realized. God did not lack the good and gracious will nor the power to make His Word come true, all appearances to the contrary notwithstanding. (2 Ch 21:7)

The liberation of the Davidic king Jehoiachin from a humiliating imprisonment, recorded in the last four verses of 2 Kings, is a token of greater things to come. In God's own way and when His time "had fully come," there was to be a Son of David so "highly exalted" that before Him "every knee should bow, in heaven and on earth and under the earth." (Ph 2:9 f.)

Prophetic History

The books of Kings deserve a place in that grouping of he Jewish canon called the "Former Prophets" (see Judges, Introduction). Though in annalistic form, they are in substance a sustained prophetic proclamation that the course of history is determined "according to the definite plan and foreknowledge of God." (Acts 2:23)

Events from an era of four centuries are selected for mention because they illustrate and document the pervading theme: God keeps His covenant, its threats and its blessings.

Political achievement is not the primary criterion in evaluating the reign of about 40 kings. They are assessed and given proportionate prominence on the basis of whether they did "what was right [or evil] in the sight of the Lord."

Religious crises during the reigns of such kings as Ahab or Hezekiah occupy by far more space in the record than the successful statecraft of a king like Omri, who gained international recognition.

About one third of the pages of this sermonic history is devoted o Elijah and Elisha, the contemporary kings being little more than foils for their prophetic activity. (1 K 17—22; 2 K 1—9)

Structure

In the books of Samuel only three men dominate the scene. In the first 11 chapters of 1 K, the center of interest continues to be a single person, Solomon. However, the reader encounters a perplexing array of leading characters in the remainder of the books. After Solomon's deah 19 kings of Israel and 12 of Judah (plus one queen) move on and off stage. To add to the difficulty, some kings in the north and the south have the same or similar names. This mass of information is put into a structured framework by introductory and concluding formulas for each king. Among the regular items of information furnished are (1) the time of accession to the throne in terms of the regnal years of the king's contemporary in the north or south respectively; (2) the age of he new king; (3) the length of reign; (4) an appraisal of the king's character.

In Chronicles there is a parallel account of David and his successors.

Authorship.

As in the case of the other books of the "Former Prophets," the author of the books of Kings is unknown. The rabbinic tradition that it was Jeremiah commends itself for a number of reasons. However, because he was taken to Egypt soon after the fall of Jerusalem (586 B.C.), he could hardly have been in Babylonia to witness Jehoiachin's release from prison, which took place in 561 B.C., the 37th year of his captivity. (Jer 43:5 f.; 2 K 25:27-30)

Most modern scholars claim that the books of Kings underwent at least two redactions or revisions. To a great extent the final product owes its historical viewpoint to an assumed editor, called the Deuteronomist (see Joshua, Introduction), who imposed his philosophy of history on all the books of the "Former Prophets." The theory of a multiple authorship and of a process of recensions is based on unproved hypotheses. There is no reason why these books cannot be the product of one man. Living some four centuries after the events described in the opening chapters, the unknown author indeed had to draw on extant chronicles for data pertaining to eras before his time. Three such sources, which he excerpted for his special purpose, are explicitly cited (1 K 11:41; 14:19, etc.; 15:7, etc.). Other documents were available, such as the historical section in Is 36—39 and the chronicles mentioned in 2 Ch 9:29; 12:5; 13:22.

Chronology

One of the characteristics of the books of Kings is an intricately synchronized system of chronology. Scores of events in each kingdom are dated in relation to fixed points of time in the other kingdom as well as in the reigns of foreign rulers. Any attempt to demonstrate that these figures are consistent with one another—in specific instances and in their sum totals—must establish the prevailing systems of dating on which the figures are based. Once the different methods of computing regnal years, used in the author's sources, have been discovered, most of the apparent inconsistencies disappear. One should be aware also that in the transmission of so many numerical data some errors could have slipped into the text.

OUTLINE

I. 1:1—2:46 Solomon, David's Coregent and Successor

II. 3:1—11:43 Solomon's Reign

III. 12:1—16:28 Divided Kingdom: Period of Hostility

IV. 16:29—2 K 8:29 Divided Kingdom: Cooperation Against Common Foes

V. 2 K 9:1—17:41 Divided Kingdom: Renewed Hostilities to Fall of Israel

VI. 2 K 18:1—25:30 Last Kings of Judah; Babylonian Exile

1:1—2:46 SOLOMON, DAVID'S COREGENT AND SUCCESSOR

1:1-37 Rivalry for the Throne

1:1-4 AGED DAVID'S WANING VITALITY

1:1 *Was old.* The books of Samuel, devoted primarily to the life and reign of David, stop short of recording how the son of Jesse transferred the kingdom to a successor. Drained of vitality (1-4), the aged monarch nevertheless took a firm hand in settling the contest for the throne. (5-37)

1:2 *Bosom.* It was accepted practice to use a young human body to supply warmth to a person whose circulation no longer functioned adequately. Mention of David's ebbing vitality introduces the account of the two contenders for the throne.

1:3 *Shunammite.* The "very beautiful" Abishag hailed from Shunem, where the Philistines encamped when they defeated Saul in the battle of Gilboa (1 Sm 28:4 note). See also the story of Elisha and a "wealthy woman" of Shunem (2 K 4:8 ff.). David's physical condition and its remedy by Abishag is made a part of the record because she became involved in subsequent court intrigue. (2:13-25)

1:4 *Knew her not.* A Hebrew euphemistic way of saying that David "had no intercourse with her" (NEB). Cf. Gn 4:1.

1:5-10 ATTEMPT ON THRONE BY OLDEST SON

1:5 *Be king.* Adonijah either did not know or chose to disregard the fact that David had settled the question of succession (13, 17). Although there was no resort to force, the attempt by the king's oldest son to seize the throne had some features in common with the coup d'etat of Absalom (2 Sm 15:1), whom he resembled also personally ("handsome" and pampered).

1:6 *After Absalom.* David's "first-born" Amnon had been killed by Absalom, the third oldest, who likewise had died a violent death. Presumably the second in line too was dead. (2 Sm 3:2 f.; 13:1 ff.; 18:9-15)

1:7 *Joab.* No reason is given why Adonijah had the support of David's nephew who "was in command of all the army" (1 Sm 26:6; 2 Sm 20:23) and of *Abiathar the priest.* The latter escaped when "Saul had killed the priests of the Lord" at Nob, joined David, and rendered him valuable service before and after he became king. (1 Sm 22:20-22; 23:6, 9; 2 Sm 15:35 ff.; 17:15 f.)

1:8 *Zadok.* Not *with Adonijah* and his conspirators were: (1) Abiathar's associate, *Zadok* (2 Sm 8:17; 15:29); (2) the captain of David's bodyguard, *Benaiah* (2 Sm 8:18); (3) *Nathan the prophet,* who denounced David's crimes but also brought the Lord's promise of a "kingdom for ever" (2 Sm 12:1-14; 7:4-17); (4) two officials, *Shimei* and *Rei.* The former, not to be confused with the man who cursed David (2 Sm 16:5 ff.), may have become one of Solomon's "twelve officers" (4:18). (5) David's *mighty men.* This group consisted of the distinguished warriors listed in 2 Sm 23:8-39. No doubt it also included "the servants" (33) who composed the royal guard, called "the Cherethites and the Pelethites." (44)

1:9 *En-rogel.* Literally "fountain of the fuller," a spring just below Jerusalem where the Kidron Valley and the Valley of Hinnom merge. (Jos 15:7 f.; 18:16)

1:11-17 COUNTERMEASURES IN SOLOMON'S BEHALF

1:12 *Own life.* Nathan initiated countermeasures to Adonijah's plot. He warned Bathsheba that she and her son were about to be liquidated if, upon seizing the throne, Adonijah should follow the prevailing custom of slaying all members of the opposing party. (21)

1:13 *Swear.* No such oath is recorded. However, there is no reason to suspect that Nathan and Bathsheba made aged David believe that he had in fact so committed himself. An opportune occasion for such a promise was the birth of Solomon. (2 Sm 12:24; see also 1 Ch 22:9-13)

1:22 *Came in.* Nathan entered the royal palace and was announced to David. Permitted to appear "before the king," he remonstrated with him for his failure to take decisive steps in the settling of the question of succession. (22-27)

1:28-37 SOLOMON'S SUCCESSION CONFIRMED BY DAVID

1:28 *Call Bathsheba.* She had left the bedchamber when the prophet received an audience, perhaps to avoid giving the impression of using pressure tactics. Nathan likewise withdrew when David recalled his wife to announce his determination to "do this day" what was necessary to assure Solomon's accession (28-31). Giving the lie to any suggestion of senility, he issued precise instructions on how the enthronement ceremonies were to be conducted (32-37). His orders were carried out with dispatch. (38-40)

1:33 *Own mule.* It was a mark of royalty to own and ride a mule (2 Sm 13:29; 18:9). When One "greater than Solomon" entered Jerusalem, riding the same kind of animal, the people expressed their expectations by shouting: "Hosanna to the son of David" (Mt 12:42; 21:9, 15). He claimed indeed to be "a king," he Anointed, the Messiah, but His "kingship is not of this world." (Jn 18:36 f.)

Gihon. Another spring in the Kidron Valley north of En-rogel, from which Hezekiah later dug a tunnel to the Pool of Siloam (2 Ch 32:30). Symbolic considerations may have dictated the choice of a spring for the site of coronations, the perpetual flow of water signifying a stable and resourceful reign.

1:35 *Ruler.* The Hebrew word translated "prince" in 1 Sm 9:16; cf. 1 Sm 10:1 note.

1:38-40 Solomon's Coronation

1:38 *Cherethites and the Pelethites.* Cf. 2 Sm 8:18 note.

1:39 *Horn of oil.* For the preparation of anointing oil see Ex 30:23-32.

1:40 *Split.* A literary hyperbole like our expression: the laughter shook the rafters.

1:41-53 Collapse of Opposition

1:41-48 ADONIJAH INFORMED OF SOLOMON'S ANOINTING

1:41 *Heard it.* Apparently *Adonijah* lacked Absalom's wily ability as well as his perverse determination to seize the throne even if it meant taking up arms against his father. Hearing that "King David has made Solomon king," he did not prolong the contest (41-48). The new monarch promised to spare his rival's life if the latter would "prove to be a worthy man." (49-53)

1:42 *Jonathan.* The son of Abiathar, this *Jonathan* became a secret informant for David. (2 Sm 15:27 ff.; 17:17 ff.)

1:49-53 ADONIJAH SUBMITS AND IS PARDONED

1:50 *Horns of the altar.* The provision that a person guilty of unintentional manslaughter could flee for refuge to the *altar* apparently was extended to apply to other crimes punishable by death. (See Ex 21:12 note)

1:53 *Solomon sent.* He assumed royal functions before David's death. The record does not specify how long the coregency lasted or whether it is included in computing the length of Solomon's reign (cf. 1 Ch 22:6—29:25). Another such coregency is explicitly mentioned in 2 K 15:5. There are indications that a father-son rule occurred in other instances, a factor that helps to solve some of the chronological difficulties that occur in the synchronization of the kings during the divided kingdom.

2:1-9 David's Parting Instructions to Solomon

2:1-4 BASIC PRINCIPLE: KEEP THE COVENANT

2:1 *Charged Solomon.* David's instructions to his son and successor were of a twofold nature: (1) a general admonition to be faithful to the covenant (1-4); (2) directions on how to deal with specific individuals. (5-9)

2:3 *May prosper.* These verses are the key to the understanding of the entire history recorded in 1 and 2 K. The terms of the covenant, *as it is written in the law of Moses,* made it clear that "keeping his statutes, his commandments, his ordinances, and his testimonies" did not merit God's favor. Obedience to the divine will was Israel's response to undeserved mercy. Nevertheless, observance or neglect of covenant obligations was not a matter of indifference, as Moses explained at length in the Book of Deuteronomy. Even the king was not above the law. Solomon's reign too was subject to the curses and blessings of the covenant. *Walking in his ways,* Solomon would prosper; if he and the nation "turned aside," the Lord would "cut off Israel from the land" (9:6 ff.). The books of Kings bear out that God says what He means and means what He says. In His sovereign way—inexorably just, endlessly patient, inexhaustibly gracious—He still directs the course of history according to this basic principle whether men agree or not. (Ro 11:22; 1 Co 2:16; 2 Ptr 2:9; RV 15:3)

2:5-9 SPECIFIC DIRECTIONS: JOAB, BARZILLAI, SHIMEI

2:5 *Joab.* David's general admonition in the four previous verses is similar to God's own charge to Joshua (Jos 1:1-9). However, his orders regarding Joab and Shimei are difficult to reconcile with covenant principles. His instructions to execute the cold-blooded murderer of Abner and Amasa can be justified inasmuch as the curse of bloodguilt needed to be removed (2 Sm 3:27 ff.; 20:8 ff.; 21). In Shimei's case (8 f.), he may have wanted to avoid the impression that the punishment was a matter of personal revenge. However, it cannot be denied that he commanded his son to do what he had sworn not to do, thereby in effect breaking his oath to the offender (2 Sm 19:23). Furthermore, if both evildoers deserved the death penalty, as indeed they did, then there was no reason for Solomon to "act . . . according to . . . wisdom" (6), i.e., as "a wise man" (9) to wait for a good occasion to execute them.

2:6 *Sheol.* Cf. Dt. 32:22 note

2:7 *Barzillai.* For his *loyalty* and David's offer of reward see 2 Sm 17:27 ff.; 19:33 ff.

2:10-12 David's Death

2:10 *Slept.* A circumlocution for dying which often may have referred to burial in an ancestral tomb but which was used also in the more general sense of joining the fathers in the common lot of mortal man. David's life-span did not exceed the three score years and ten. (2 Sm 5:4)

2:13-46 Removal of Former Conspirators

2:13-25 HALF BROTHER ADONIJAH EXECUTED

2:13 *Adonijah.* The remainder of this chapter records how the new king dealt with four men who possibly could pose a threat to his rule. All of them broke the letter of the law, making it legal for him to (1) kill Adonijah, his rival for the throne (13-25); (2) banish the priest Abiathar from Jerusalem (26 f.); (3) slay Joab, who with Abiathar had supported Adonijah (28-35); (4) execute Shimei, an adherent of the rival house of Saul. (36-46)

2:17 *Give me Abishag.* Apparently a foolish rather than an insidious petition. A new king appropriated his predecessor's harem in order to establish his claim to the throne (so Absalom, 2 Sm 16:21 f.; see also 2 Sm 3:7 ff.; 12:8). Actually Abishag was not David's wife or concubine (1:4 note). However, Adonijah's request for a woman associated with the court exposed him to the suspicion of still having designs to become king. Charging the former conspirator with that motive (22), Solomon ordered his execution. (25)

2:18 *Very well.* Adonijah asked Bathsheba to plead his cause because the queen-mother had great influence at court (so Athaliah 2 K 11:1 ff.). She readily consented to *speak for* the hapless suitor, perhaps because she secretly hoped that her son would react as he did.

2:23 *More also.* For this oath formula see Ru 1:17 note.

2:26-27 HIGH PRIEST ABIATHAR BANISHED

2:26 *Abiathar.* Solomon took action against him and Joab, accusing them of complicity in a new plot against him. For their earlier support of Adonijah see 1:7.

Anathoth. A priestly city about 3 miles northeast of Jerusalem (Jos 21:18), the home of Jeremiah. (Jer 1:1)

2:27 *Word of the Lord.* Abiathar was a descendant of Eli, for whose house "a man of God" predicted disaster (1 Sm 2:31-36). Later his descendants were permitted to resume service at the temple. (1 Ch 24:6)

2:28-35 COMMANDER IN CHIEF JOAB PUT TO DEATH

2:28 *Horns.* Cf. 1:50 note. The altar was in *the tent of the Lord,* i.e., the tent which David had made for the ark. (2 Sm 6:17)

2:31 *Strike him down.* A willful murderer was not to be granted sanctuary at the altar. (Ex. 21:14)

2:34 *Own house.* In view of his distinguished services to his people he was granted honorable burial in his ancestral estate *in the wilderness* of Judah, possibly east of Bethlehem.

2:36-46 SHIMEI, PROMOTER OF SAUL'S HOUSE, KILLED

2:36 *Summoned.* In order to keep Shimei under close surveillance, Solomon transferred him to Jerusalem from Bahurim. (8; 2 Sm 16:5 note; 17:18)

2:37 *Kidron.* He would have had to *cross the brook Kidron* east of the city in order to reach his hometown Bahurim. The intent of Solomon's order was that Shimei was not to move from the immediate vicinity of Jerusalem. The Philistine city of Gath, where he went to retrieve his escaped slaves, was some 30 miles southwest. Invoking the announced sentence for the culprit's failure to keep within the specified dounds, Solomon ordered his execution.

2:39 *Maacah.* Perhaps a variant for "Maoch," whose son Achish was king of Gath at David's time. (1 Sm 27:1 note)

3:1—11:43 SOLOMON'S REIGN

3:1-2 Overall Perspective

3:1 *Marriage alliance.* The record of Solomon's reign begins with a short preview of some of his characteristic policies (1 f.). His marriage to an Egyptian princess may not have occurred at the very outset of his regime. But it is an outstanding example of his general practice of multiplying foreign wives (11:1). Other prominent features of his career were his extensive building program and his tolerance in worship practices. Directly or indirectly all of them contributed to his fall, explaining in advance why "his heart had turned away from the Lord." (11:9)

3:3—4:34 Solomon's Wisdom

3:3-15 A GIFT OF GOD

3:3 *Loved the Lord.* In spite of the imperfections of his love for the Lord, Solomon received a special measure of divine grace. Given a choice of gifts, he asked for wisdom to govern his people (3-9). By this request he showed that in his inmost heart he wanted to be motivated by the desire to serve God and his people rather than by the promptings of the flesh for personal gain. God gave him not only "a wise and discerning heart" but also promised him "both riches and honor" (10-14), for all of which he was truly grateful. (15)

3:4 *Gibeon.* No reason is given why Solomon *went . . . to sacrifice* at *the great high place* in Gibeon, about 6 miles northwest of Jerusalem, but see 1 Ch 16:39; 2 Ch 1:3-5. The figure *a thousand burnt offerings* denotes a large number rather than an exact count.

3:5 *Dream.* One of the means of divine revelation (Nm 12:6; 1 Sm 28:6, 15), claimed also by false prophets. (Jer 23:32; Zch 10:2)

3:7 *Child.* A figure of speech to express lack of experience *how to go out or come in,* i.e., how to tackle the problems of administering "a great people" whose sheer numbers were bewildering (8; Nm 27:17; Dt 31:2). Actually Solomon had a child of his own at that time. (Compare 11:42 with 14:21)

3:9 *Understanding mind.* Lit. "a hearing heart." The Hebrew verb "to hear" frequently means "to hearken to, to obey" (so in: "To obey is better than sacrifice," 1 Sm 15:22). In order to act in obedience to God, Solomon wanted to be able to *discern between good and evil.* To be sure, such discrimination required a mind capable of analytic judgments. However, only a heart which listens to the Lord could supply the basis for making correct decisions, the desire to conform to the divine criterion, and the willpower to act accordingly. As used in the OT, wisdom is not an intellectual quality capable of producing a philosophy of life or a norm of behavior. It is the ability to put into action what a sanctified mind, applying God's revealed standard, determines should be done under given circumstances.

3:13 *Give you also.* Cf. Jesus' promise to those who "seek first his kingdom." (Mt 6:33)

3:15 *Ark.* David had brought it to Jerusalem. (2 Sm 6:16 f.)

3:16—4:28 DEMONSTRATIONS OF PRACTICAL WISDOM

3:16 *Then . . . came.* The connection between 3:1-15 and what follows is logical rather than chronological. The remaining verses and all of the next chapter demonstrate that Solomon actually received "an understanding mind": (1) he was able to "render justice" in a difficult case (3:16-28); (2) he displayed executive ability by dividing the country into 12 administrative districts (4:1-19); (3) he "ruled over" a farflung empire (20 f.); (4) he managed a grandiose establishment. (22-28)

4:2 *High officials.* To be "king over all Israel" required administrative machinery. Solomon appointed various officials of cabinet rank, associated with him in Jerusalem (1-6), and 12 regional managers, stationed in their respective districts. (7-19)

The priest. V. 4 lists Zadok and Abiathar as "priests." It seems unlikely therefore that *Azariah the son of Zadok* refers to another incumbent of the sacerdotal office. Cf. 2 Sm 8:18 note, where the term "priest" is applied to David's sons, who according to 1 Ch 18:17 were his "chief officials." In 5 the "king's friend" is also a "priest." Taking "Elihoreph" as a phrase and making a slight change in the text, some scholars suggest the reading: "Azariah, son of Zadok the priest, was in charge of the calendar." (So NEB)

4:5 *Over the officers.* Perhaps over those mentioned in 7-19. The title *king's friend* does not stress this officer's personal friendship with the king as much as the confidential service that he rendered. He was Solomon's trusted counselor as Hushai had been David's. (2 Sm 15:32 note)

4:6 *Forced labor.* Introduced by David (2 Sm 20:4 note), conscription of laborers for work on state projects became so oppressive under Solomon that it was a main factor in precipitating the division of the kingdom (9:15 ff.; 12:4, 11, 18-20). The name of the officer *in charge of* these labor gangs, *Adoniram,* appears in the shorter form "Adoram" and in the variant spelling of "Hadoram." (12:18; 2 Sm 20:24; 2 Ch 10:18)

4:7 *Twelve officers.* Two noteworthy features of Solomon's reign emerge from this detailed list of officers and the areas under their supervision: (1) Even though some of the place names have not been identified with known sites, enough fixed points are mentioned to establish the fact that the three districts east and the nine west of the Jordan did not coincide with the territories allotted to the 12 tribes. This administrative realignment of the borders may have been based on the productivity of the land, since each new district was required to furnish a month's *food for the king and his household.* (2) "One officer," appointed to supervise the project in all tribes, had his headquarters "in the land of Judah." However, Solomon's own tribe apparently was not required to furnish a monthly share of provisions for the royal household. If this was the case, this act of discrimination no doubt added fuel to the discontent among the other tribes which burst into flames after Solomon's death.

4:19 *Sihon . . . Og.* Cf. Nm 21:21, 33 notes; Dt 3:8-10.

4:20 *Happy.* With wealth flowing in from a vast empire (21), the people *ate and drank* enough to make life enjoyable even though they were required to supply enormous provisions for the king's grandiose establishment (22-28). Progressively greater requirements by Solomon finally made his exactions a "heavy yoke." (12:4)

4:22 *Cors.* A dry and liquid measure holding about 30 bushels or 80 gallons. If the figures are transmitted correctly, the collected provisions were adequate to feed at least 1,500 people: the royal family, the officials, the regular troops.

4:24 *Tiphsah.* Located on the upper Euphrates about 200 miles northeast of Damascus. *Gaza,* the Philistine city near the Mediterranean, was the southwest limit of the empire. In 21 the extent of Solomon's empire is mentioned in order to account for the source of his income. Here the reference to distant borders makes clear why his expenditures were so huge.

4:25 *Dan to Beer-sheba.* Israel's territory extending from north to south. (Ju 20:1 note)

4:26 *Forty thousand.* No doubt preserving a better text, 2 Ch 9:25 has: "four thousand stalls," enough to accommodate the horses of "fourteen hundred chariots." (10:26; 2 Ch 1:14)

4:29-34 WISDOM DISPLAYED IN PROVERBS AND SONGS

4:29 *Wisdom.* Solomon gave evidence of his God-given capacities not only by his judicial acumen (3:16-28) and his administrative astuteness but also by the sage maxims which he put into the form of "proverbs" and "songs." He did not engage in a scientific study of botany and zoology. Nevertheless the lessons he drew from plant and animal life (33) surpassed in variety and in profundity of thought "the wisdom of all the people of the east [Babylonians and Arabs], and all the wisdom of Egypt" (30). Only a few of such maxims have been preserved in the Book of Proverbs. (Pr 6:6; 10:12; 30:15 ff.)

4:31 *Ethan.* Evidently the men mentioned in this verse were well-known for their wisdom. Their names apprear in the genealogy of Judah. (1 Ch 2:6)

5:1—8:66 Solomon's Building Enterprises

5:1—7:51 THE TEMPLE PLANNED AND BUILT

1) 5:1-12 Negotiations for Building Material

5:1 *Hiram.* Almost half the account of Solomon's reign (chs. 5—8) is devoted to still another way in which he displayed wisdom: his building enterprises, particularly the construction of the temple (12). Ch. 5 tells of two preliminary steps: (1) successful negotiations with the Phoenician king Hiram for cedar and cypress wood from Mount Lebanon (1-12); (2) conscription of a huge army of workmen in wood and stone to prepare the raw materials (13-18). For evidence that Hiram *loved David* see 2 Sm 5:11. Besides the form *Hiram* the Phoenician king's name occurs in other spellings: "Hirom" in the Hebrew text (10, 18); "Huram" (2 Ch 2). All three may be an abbreviation of Ahiram.

5:6 *The Sidonians.* The ancient Israelites did not excel in architecture or the plastic and pictorial arts.

5:9 *Rafts.* The timbers were towed in floats from Phoenician seaports to Joppa, the only natural harbor on Israel's coast (2 Ch 2:16). From there they were hauled overland to Jerusalem, a distance of about 35 miles.

2) 5:13-18 Conscription of Workmen

5:13 *Levy of forced labor.* The addition of the interpretative phrase *of forced labor* in translating the single Hebrew word *levy* is justified by the context and by the meaning of a cognate equivalent which occurs in non-Biblical literature.

5:15 *Burden-bearers.* They and "the hewers of stone" were remnants of Canaanite inhabitants whom Solomon reduced to permanent slave laborers. (9:20 f.)

5:16 *Chief officers.* 2 Ch 2:18 has 3,600 "overseers" instead of 3,300; 1 K 9:23 lists 550 "who had charge of the people," whereas 2 Ch 8:10 has 250. No doubt the difference of 300 in both instances results from different classifications of these groups.

5:17 *Costly.* The Hebrew adjective could mean simply "heavy" or "massive" (so NEB). The quarrying of such *great . . . stones,* however, made them costly as well.

5:18 *Gebal.* Hiram sent expert stonemasons from *Gebal,* a seaport north of Sidon. They were to work with *Solomon's builders* in the limestone "hill country" (15) of Palestine.

3) 6:1-38 Temple Construction

6:1 *He began.* For *the four hundred and eightieth year* see Exodus, Introduction, "The Date of the Exodus."

6:2 *Sixty cubits.* The description of the temple, detailed though it is in many respects, does not supply all the data necessary to make a complete blueprint of the entire complex. Nevertheless it suffices to make possible a reconstruction of its general features.

If 18 inches are allowed for a cubit, the following ground plan emerges (2-6). The inside dimensions of the temple proper were 90 ft. long, 30 ft. wide, and 45 ft. high (on the height see 2 Ch 3:4). This rectangular *house* consisted of two parts: (1) Occupying one third or 30 ft. of its western end was the "inner sanctuary," also called "the most holy place" or "the Holy of Holies" (16; Ex 26:34; KJV: "oracle"; NEB: "inner shrine"). (2) The remaining 60 ft. of *the house,* here called "the nave," constituted "the holy place" (8:8; Ex 28:29; KJV: "temple"; NEB: "sanctuary"). Only the priests entered the inner sanctuary and the nave.

Extending eastward from the temple proper was a "vestibule" (KJV: "porch"), "equal to the width of the house."

Into the thick walls of the nave and the inner sanctuary (but not of the vestibule) Solomon built "a structure," consisting of "side chambers" in three stories. As the walls grew narrower at the top, the chambers became wider. At each of the three levels were "offsets" (KJV: "rests"; NEB: "rebates") attached to the temple wall on which the "supporting beams" or joists of the chambers rested so that the latter were not an integral part of the temple proper. This structure no doubt contained treasury and storage rooms, possibly also living quarters for the priests during their term of duty.

Above these chambers the house had "windows with recessed frames" similar to clerestory windows.

The discovery of Phoenician and Canaanite sanctuaries having similar ground plans does not disprove the uniqueness of Israel's religion. Already in the OT God did not physically take

His people "out of the world" of their contemporary environment but "chose" them "out of the world" that they might not be "of the world." (Jn 17:16; 15:19)

6:11 *Word of the Lord.* Even before Solomon "finished building the house of the Lord" (9, 14; 9:1), God reminded him that there was no magical power which could impound Him within its walls. He would condescend to "dwell" in this house only for the purpose of blessing king and people according to His covenant promises.

6:15 *Lined the walls.* The sketch of the structural components (2-10) is followed by a description of a predominating interior feature: the exclusive use of wood, ornamented often with gold, so that "no stone was seen" (14-36). Cedar and cypress wood were used for lining floors and walls, for carved ornamentations, and for making an incense altar which was "overlaid with gold."

6:20 *Twenty cubits.* According to this verse, "the inner sanctuary" or "most holy place" (16) was a cube of 20 cubits or 30 feet. However, the overall height of the entire house was 30 cubits or 45 feet. Hence either the ceiling of the house was lowered to the floor or the sanctuary was raised 10 cubits or 15 feet.

6:21 *Chains.* Only mentioned here, these golden chains perhaps served as drawstrings on the veil which separated the inner sanctuary from the nave. (2 Ch 3:14; Ex 26:31-34)

6:23 *Cherubim.* The next interior ornamentation of wood to be mentioned is a pair of cherubim, overlaid with gold (23-28). "Facing the nave" (2 Ch 3:13), they stretched their wings across the entire 20-cubit width of the inner sanctuary's innermost or western wall. On the mercy seat of the ark two more golden cherubim faced one another (Ex. 25:1 note). These celestial beings carried out God's will and epitomized His universal sovereignty (Gn 3:24; 1 Sm 4:4; 2 Sm 22:11; Ps 18:10; Eze 10:18 f.). They were visualized as having various forms. Part human (hands) and part animal (wings), they appear with two as well as four heads, also human and animal. (Eze 1:10; 41:18 f.)

6:29 *The walls.* The wooden walls were ornamented with a frieze of carved figures; the wooden floor was overlaid with gold.

6:31 *Doors.* The last of the interior furnishings of wood to be mentioned were two doors, the one giving *entrance to the inner sanctuary* (31 f.) and the other "to the nave" (33-36). The latter had the ordinary form of a square. The former, rectangular at bottom and triangular at the top, had the shape of *a pentagon.*

6:36 *Inner court.* For the walls of the open-air court, situated immediately before the roofed buildings, wood was used only in part.

6:37 *Ziv.* Also called the second month (Nm 9:11), Ziv corresponds to April/May on our calendar. "Bul" was the eighth month, or October/November. "Seven years" is a round figure which does not take into account the half years between Ziv and Bul.

4) 7:1-12 Royal Edifices

7:1 *His own house.* It took Solomon twice as long to build his royal edifices as it did to complete the temple (6:38). One of them alone was considerably longer and wider than the house of the Lord. However, only 12 verses are devoted to this building program (1-12). From the available data it is impossible to gain a clear picture of the architectural features and the specific function of these buildings.

7:2 *Forest of Lebanon.* The individual structures in the royal building complex were named in part according to their basic features and in part according to their purpose. The first, 60 ft. longer and 45 ft. wider than the temple, required so much cedar wood for its construction as to make it a veritable *Forest of Lebanon.* It served as an armory. (10:17)

7:6 *Hall of Pillars.* The characteristic feature of the second edifice was its colonnaded pillars.

7:7 *Hall of the Throne.* In the third structure Solomon set up his throne, from which he rendered judgments.

7:8 *Like workmanship.* His own royal residence and the palace for the Egyptian princess were similar in structure or material to the Hall of the Throne.

7:9 *Great court.* It appears that this court surrounded all the buildings erected by Solomon, including the temple complex with its smaller "inner court." (12)

5) 7:13-50 Temple Furnishings of Metal

7:14 *Bronze.* After describing the temple's structural features (6:1-10) and its wooden interior (6:14-36), the account goes on in this chapter to list its furnishings and vessels of (1) bronze (13-47); (2) gold (48-50). To do the castings, Solomon commissioned a half-Tyrian *worker in bronze* whose name, like the king's, was Hiram (cf. 2 Ch 2:13 note). *All his work* consisted of producing: (1) two massive pillars (15-22); (2) a large reservoir (23-26); (3) 10 lavers or basins (27-39) (4) a large number of smaller items (40-45). To this list 2 Ch 4:1 adds the great "altar of bronze."

7:15 *Two pillars.* Standing "at the vestibule of the temple" (21), the pillars had an ornamental rather than a structural function. Eighteen ft. high and 12 ft. in circumference, these hollow columns were surmounted by capitals, 7½ ft. high and bowllike in shape. The tracery and embellishments on the latter were so ornate and intricate that it is difficult to reconstruct an exact picture from the text. The main features were chainlike festoons (17), rows of pomegranates (18), and "lily-work." (19)

7:21 *Jachin . . . Boaz.* The name of the first pillar is a verb meaning: "He [God] will establish." Boaz is a prepositional phrase plus a noun: "in Him [is] strength." It is also possible that both names were read as one sentence: "He will establish in strength."

7:23 *The molten sea.* Hiram's second casting was a reservoir so large that it was called a *sea,* a term applied to no other water basin. It always has the definite article because it served a unique purpose (2 Ch 4:6). If the dimensions (circumference, 45 ft; diameter, 30 ft; depth 7½ ft.) are meant to be exact, it was *round*(ed) or slightly oblong with bulging or convex sides.

7:26 *Two thousand baths.* About 10,000 to 12,000 gallons. The text of 2 Ch 4:5 raises the number of baths by 1,000.

7:27 *Ten stands.* More complicated in design than the stationary sea were the 10 movable basins or lavers in which the water was wheeled in order to make it available to "rinse off what was used for the burnt offering" (2 Ch 4:6). Surprisingly detailed for a piece of equipment serving only a secondary function, the description of the *stands* and their vehicular apparatus uses terms for the various parts and their connection with one another in such a way as to make it difficult to reconstruct an exact model.

7:38 *Forty baths.* If the figures for the dimensions of the lavers and for their capacity are correctly transmitted, each held at least 200 gallons.

7:40 *Also made.* In listing all the items of bronze made by Hiram, the three major castings (pillars, sea, lavers) are repeated.

7:46 *Plain of the Jordan.* The molds for the castings were made of Jordan Valley clay which was of a consistency suitable for that purpose. For the location of *Succoth* see Ju 8:5 note. The site of *Zarethan,* spelled Zeredah in 2 Ch 4:17, has not been determined definitely.

7:48 *The vessels.* Much of the wooden interior of the temple was overlaid with gold (6:14-36). These verses contain a list of objects which were made entirely of the precious metal. *The golden altar* was for the burning of incense. For *the bread of the Presence* see Ex 25:23 note; Lv 24:5 note.

6) 7:51 Completion of Temple

7:51 *David . . . dedicated.* Cf. 2 Sm 8:11; 1 Ch 22:14.

8:1-66 DEDICATION OF TEMPLE

8:1 *Assembled the elders.* After Solomon brought *the ark of the covenant* into the finished temple from that part of Jerusalem called "the city of David" (2 Sm 6:16) and all "the holy vessels" were in place (1-11), the rites of dedication began with a hymn of adoration (12 f.), followed by: (1) a blessing and an address (14-21); (2) a dedicatory prayer (22-53); (3) a benediction and admonition (54-61); (4) dedicatory offerings. (62-64)

8:2 *The feast.* Even though Solomon completed the building in the eighth month of the previous year (6:38), he waited 11 months before dedicating it. As an appropriate time for the solemnities he chose *the feast* of tabernacles, which began on the 15th of Ethanim, the seventh month, also called Tishri. (Lv 23:33 ff.)

8:7 *Poles.* Used in carrying the ark (Ex 25:10-15). The significance of the fact that the poles protruded from the holy place escapes us.

8:8 *This day.* The books of Kings were composed after the temple had been destroyed (see Introduction). The author did not delete this note from the source in which he found it.

8:9 *Nothing . . . except.* We are not told how or when the other articles associated with the ark were lost. (Ex 16:33 f.; Nm 17:10; Heb 9:4)

8:11 *The glory of the Lord.* Cf. Ex 20:21; 40:3 note; Nm 11:25; 12:5.

8:12 *Set the sun.* In the hymn of praise with which Solomon opened the dedicatory rites he struck the keynote of the celebration: the condescension of the Creator in accepting the worship of His creatures. Apparently only the opening strains have been preserved. The "thick darkness" in which God dwelled (Ex 20:21) is His transcendental, unbridgeable distance from man. Unapproachable in His holiness for sinful man, beyond comprehension by His finite creatures, the Creator of the universe nevertheless permitted Solomon to build a house for Him where He made Himself accessible to every covenant-keeping worshiper. Lest the Israelites forget that the "inscrutable" Lord (Ro 11:33-36) cannot be manipulated or made to conform to their thoughts, He dwelt invisibily in the windowless Holy of Holies, "in the cloud upon the mercy seat." (Lv 16:2)

8:15 *Has fulfilled.* After blessing "all the assembly" Solomon reminded the people that he built the temple according to the Lord's instruction and promise. (14-21)

8:18 *My name.* For the meaning of *name* as used in the OT see Ex 6:3 note. In the temple the Lord who dwells in darkness chose to reveal Himself in accord with "the covenant" made when He brought the fathers "out of the land of Egypt."

8:22 *Spread forth.* Spoken in the outer court before the great bronze *altar,* Solomon's dedicatory prayer begins with the plea that the "God of Israel" keep what He promised the house of David (23-26; 2 Sm 7:11 ff.). All the other petitions (27-53) ask God to "hear in heaven" when king and people "make supplication to thee in this house." The distinction between God's presence in "this house" and His "dwelling place" in heaven, where He hears prayers, is a refrain repeated in each of the eight requests for divine aid (30, 32, 34, 36, 39, 43, 45, 49). After a general plea that God "hear in heaven" whenever he and the people pray "toward this place" (28-30), Solomon lists seven specific needs for help: (1) vindicate the just cause (31 f.); (2) forgive a chastened people (33 f.); (3) send rain (35 f.); (4) relieve bodily ills (37-40); (5) regard the foreigner (41-43); (6) help in time of war (44 f.); (7) restore the exiled people. (46-53)

8:27 *Contain.* The entire prayer emphasizes the fact that "the Most High does not dwell [is not confined] in houses made with hands" whether it be the man-made, movable "tent of witness in the wilderness" or a stationary house set on a foundation (Acts 7:44-50; Is 66:1).—When "God's Spirit dwells in" men's hearts, they become "God's temple" in all circumstances of life. (1 Co 3:16; 6:19)

8:30 *Forgive.* Man's foremost need is mentioned in almost every petition. (30, 34, 36, 39, 50)

8:46 *Captive.* The threat of exile was a part of

the covenant stipulation. (Lv 26:27-39; Dt 4:27; 28:64)

8:48 *Toward their land.* So Daniel. (Dn 6:10)

8:51 *Iron furnace.* Rescue from exile will in effect repeat Israel's deliverance *out of Egypt.*

8:54 *Knelt.* Solomon "stood defore the altar" (22). Having taken his place there, he assumed a kneeling posture either at once or at some time during the prayer.

8:55 *Blessed.* In his closing words Solomon invoked God's benediction on the people, at the same time exhorting them to "be wholly true to the Lord" (61) who had promised them His covenant blessings.

8:62 *Sacrifices.* Offerings of various kinds proclaimed by symbolic action what Solomon had expressed in words. For "peace offerings" see Lv 7:11 note; "burnt offerings," Lv 1:3 note; "cereal offerings," Lv 2:2; 6:14 notes. The number of oxen and sheep (63), originally perhaps 2,200 and 12,000 respectively, may have accumulated several zeros in the course of the transmission of the text. (See Numbers, Introduction, "The Numbers . . . .")

8:65 *Seven days.* "On the eighth day" of the feast of Tabernacles, which followed the dedication festivities, Solomon dismissed the people. They came from as far northeast as *the entrance of Hamath,* the valley between the two Lebanon ranges (2 Sm 8:9 note) and from as far southwest as *The Brook of Egypt.* (Nm 34:3 note; Jos 15:1 note)

9:1—10:29 Miscellaneous Features and Incidents

9:1-9 TEMPLE GOVERNED BY COVENANT TERMS

9:2 *A second time.* In a second appearance (3:4-15) the Lord made clear that the terms of the covenant applied also to the temple. Its stone and wood would not automatically guarantee the permanency of its builder's dynasty or magically insure the nation's safety. The temple "will become a heap of ruins" if it no longer was the place where the chosen kingdom of priests expressed their undivided devotion to the Lord. King and people will be "cut off . . . from the land" if they thought that the habitation of God's name made them immune to the consequences of sin. (Jer 7:1-4; 22:8)

9:9 *Because . . . therefore.* In God's dwelling with His people there is an inexorable logic of cause and effect. Not the writer of Kings alone, but all of Scripture expresses this principle of God's reaction to man's response to Him. Its rationale is a basic presupposition in the preaching of the prophets (see, e.g., Amos). Jesus applied the same "because—therefore" to Jerusalem and the temple of His day when He predicted their destruction (Mt 23:37 ff.). It still is true that "whatever a man sows, that he will also reap." (Gl 6:7 f.)

9:10-25 ADDITIONAL INFORMATION ON BUILDING PROGRAM

9:10 *Had built.* The remainder of this and all of the next chapter report more or less unrelated incidents and features of Solomon's reign. Vv. 10-25 contain information on his building program, supplementing the account given in chs. 5—8. The reader learns (1) how he paid Hiram for supplying material and services during the "twenty years" when he built the temple (7 years) and the royal buildings (13 years, 10-14); (2) how he recruited laborers and supervisors (15-23); (3) how Pharaoh's daughter occupied her house (24); (4) how he offered sacrifices in the completed temple. (25)

9:11 *Twenty cities.* Solomon was able to pay for Phoenician timber with wheat and oil (5:10 f.). But he reimbursed Hiram for "one hundred and twenty talents of gold" (3½ million dollars) by pawning *twenty* Israelite *cities* which were later redeemed. (2 Ch 8:1 f.)

9:13 *Cabul.* In keeping with the customary practice in trading transactions, Hiram professed dissatisfaction with the exchange value of the cities, calling the ceded territory *Cabul,* which may mean unproductive land or simply something good for nothing.

9:15 *Gezer.* Solomon conscripted *forced labor* under appointed overseers to build not only the temple, his royal edifices, and the walls of his capital but also to fortify strategically located cities "in all the land of his dominion" (19). At the mention of *Gezer,* the account is interrupted (16) in order to report how this city, about 20 miles northwest of Jerusalem, came into Solomon's possession. For *Millo* see 2 Sm 5:9 note; *Hazor,* Jos 11:1 note. At *Megiddo* (Ju 4:7 note) stables for horses have been found at various excavated levels.

9:17 *Lower Beth-horon.* Located about 12 miles northwest of Jerusalem, it guarded an important road from the Mediterranean plain into the hill country of Judah.

9:18 *Baalath.* Apparently the city by that name assigned to the tribe of Dan (Jos 19:44). It controlled another approach into Judah almost directly west of Jerusalem.

Tamar. A note in the Hebrew text has "Tadmor" (so KJV and 2 Ch 8:4), a city located 150 miles northeast of Damascus and later known as Palmyra. *Tamar*—no doubt the better reading—was a site a few miles southwest of the Dead Sea. (Eze 47:19; 48:28)

9:20 *Slaves.* The former inhabitants of Canaan were reduced to slavery. The Israelites too had to labor on state projects without remuneration. Their service was a levy or form of taxation. They worked only till they put in the required number of days (5:13; 11:28). Some of them became officials of various kinds.

9:23 *Five hundred and fifty.* Cf. 5:16 note.

9:24-25 *Own house.* In connection with his building operations, a short note tells of: (1) Pharaoh's daughter's transfer from temporary quarters in *the city of David* to her *own house* which Solomon completed before he *built the Millo;* (2) Solomon's sacrifice in the finished temple.

9:26-28 MARITIME ENTERPRISE ON RED SEA

9:26 *Ships.* With the help of Hiram's experienced Phoenician "seamen," Solomon engaged in maritime enterprises on *the Red Sea,* to which he had access through *the land of Edom,* a vassal state (26-28). From the northern end of the Gulf of Aqaba the fleet of merchantment sailed to "Ophir," known particularly for its supply of gold (Jb 22:24; Ps 45:9; Is 13: 12) but also for other natural resources (10:11-12). Its location has not been definitely established. The following sites have been suggested: The Arabian coast, the Indian coast, the east coast of Africa.

10:1-13 VISIT OF THE QUEEN OF SHEBA

10:1 *Queen of Sheba.* When she *heard of the fame of Solomon* and of the house which he built for *the name of the Lord,* she came from southwest Arabia (Yemen) to Jerusalem, a distance of over 1,000 miles. There she tested him *with hard questions,* the Hebrew word translated "riddle" in Ju 14:12. Overcome by Solomon's wisdom and wealth (1-5), she presented her host with costly gifts (6-10). From his own store of treasures, accruing to him from commercial ventures in Ophir (11 f.), Solomon was able to reciprocate with royal generosity. (13)

10:5 *No more spirit.* What she saw and heard was breathtaking.

10:8 *Wives.* Cf. RSV note. The omission of the first consonant from the Hebrew word for "men" changes it to "women."

10:9 *The Lord.* The queen attributed his wisdom and prosperity to Israel's God, referring to Him by His own distinctive name, as did Hiram (5:7). For the meaning of "the Lord" see Ex 3:14; 6:3 notes

10:10 *She gave.* Very likely the exchange of gifts served in part to ratify a trade agreement.

10:11 *Almug.* An unidentified kind of tree. Therefore the Hebrew noun is not translated but merely transliterated. Some think it was the reddish and fragrant sandalwood. In 2 Ch 2:8; 9:10 the variant form "algum" occurs, suggesting that it was not a Hebrew but a foreign term.

10:12 *Supports.* The Hebrew word, which occurs only here, is in the singular. Derived from a verb meaning to support or to sustain, it could denote some kind of decorative railing or inlaid paneling.

10:14-22 SOLOMON'S LAVISH USE OF GOLD

10:14 *Weight of gold.* The mention of Solomon's wealth, of which he "gave to the queen of Sheba all that she desired" (13), occasions two additional notes: (1) elaborating his source of income and his lavish use of gold (14-22); (2) explaining the acclaim that his riches and wisdom brought him from "the whole earth." (23-25)

10:17 *Shields.* The Hebrew word for *shields* is not the same as the one used in the previous verse. Kept and exhibited in *the House of the Forest of Lebanon* (7:2 note), these shields apparently were carried by a royal honor guard whenever "the king went into the house of the Lord" (14:28). "Six hundred shekels of gold" (about 6 lbs.) went into the larger kind; for the smaller ones *three minas* (about 2 lbs.) sufficed.

10:18 *Ivory throne.* Richly inlaid with ivory, as was Ahab's house. (22:39)

10:22 *Ships of Tarshish.* Ships large enough to sail to Tartessus in Spain (cf. our names for ships such as China clippers, South India men, etc.). However, the word *Tarshish* may be a common noun denoting the smelting of ore. Ships were so designated because they were capable of carrying a heavy cargo of ore or because they sailed to ports where it was exported.

10:23-29 WISDOM AND WEALTH WIDELY ACCLAIMED; PROFITABLE TRADE IN HORSES

10:26 *Chariots.* The miscellaneous information on various features and incidents of Solomon's reign (9:10—10:29) ends with a brief note about his cavalry, of which units were stationed in strategically located *chariot cities* (4:26 note; 9:15 note), and about a related subject: his lucrative trade in horses. (26-29)

10:27 *Made silver.* This verse explains parenthetically that Solomon had the resources to acquire and maintain his chariot divisions.

10:28 *Import.* Not all the details of Solomon's trade in horses are clear. It seems that sitting astride the north-south trade routes, he played the part of the middleman in profitable transactions between *Egypt and Kue* in Asia Minor (KJV "linen yarn" is confusing). To the north and east of Israel was the territory of "the kings of the Hittites and the kings of Syria," with whom *the king's traders* in horses also did a brisk business.

11:1-43 Solomon's Sin and Tragic Last Years

11:1-13 COVENANT UNFAITHFULNESS AND CONSEQUENCES

11:1 *Foreign women.* The closing verses of the previous chapter (10:26-29) report Solomon's "delight . . . in the strength of the horse" (Ps 147:10), violating the divine prescription that the king was not to "multiply horses" (Dt 17:16). This chapter records that this highly favored monarch did not only "multiply wives for himself" (Dt 17:17) but even joined these "foreign women" in worshiping their idols (1-8). Because Solomon had "not kept" one of the basic "statutes" of "the covenant," the Lord announced that He would "tear the kingdom from" him, leaving only the southern part to his successor (9-13). Already during Solomon's lifetime cracks appeared in the imperial structure and in the nation's solidarity. Vassals in the south (Edom) and in the north (Syria) plotted and achieved their independence (14-25). Sanctioned by a prophet, internal disruption found a leader in Jeroboam, who had been in "charge over all the forced labor." (26-40)

11:2 *Into marriage.* For prohibitions against such matrimonial alliances see Ex 34:16; Dt 7:3 f.; Jos 23:6-13.

11:3 *Seven hundred wives.* The largeness of

the harem is evidence of the splendor of his court rather than of sexual excesses. His *wives,* who outnumbered the *concubines,* were *princesses* whom he acquired out of political considerations.

11:4 *Turned away.* Gifts of God, such as wisdom and riches, are not in themselves a guarantee that their recipient will use them to glorify the Giver. Solomon demonstrated how irrational human wickedness is. The temptation to be *turned away . . . after other gods* became greater the more generously God showered him with wisdom and riches (Dt 32:15 note; Mt 19:23; 11:25). However, God will not let "the wise man glory in his wisdom" or "the rich man . . . in his riches" (Jer 9:23 f.). Because "the Lord was angry with Solomon," his empire disintegrated and the nation was torn into two hostile camps. (Cf. Lk 12:21; Ro 1:18)

11:5 *Ashtoreth.* Cf. Ju 2:13 note. The name of the Ammonite idol appears in two forms: "Molech" and "Milcom." (Lv 18:21 note; 2 Sm 12:30 note)

11:7 *Chemosh.* Before entering Canaan, Israel defeated the "people of Chemosh" (Nm 21:29), who sacrificed children to their national idol. (2 K 3:27)

11:9 *Twice.* Cf. 3:5; 9:2.

11:13 *Your son.* Rehoboam precipitated the division of the kingdom. Under his rule Judah "committed [abominations], more than all their fathers had done." (14:22)

11:14-25 CRACKS IN IMPERIAL SOLIDITY

11:14 *Hadad.* This member of the Edomite *royal house* escaped a punitive campaign directed by Joab and Abishai (2 Sm 8:13; 1 Ch 18:12). Smuggled into Egypt by a circuitous way, he "found great favor in the sight of Pharaoh," receiving "the sister of his own wife" in marriage. After David's death he returned to his homeland for the purpose of "doing mischief" (25), very likely by engaging in guerrilla warfare against Solomon.

11:19 *Tahpenes.* Egypt's prestige was at a low ebb. In its better days foreign rulers found it politically expedient to send their noblewomen to the court on the Nile. Now a Pharaoh gave his sister-in-law in marriage to a fugitive prince. (Cf. 40 note)

11:23 *Rezon.* When David crushed the power of King Hadadezer (2 Sm 8:3-12; 10:16-19), the latter's vassal succeeded in making Damascus the capital of an independent domain. Under Rezon and his successors this Syrian state was a perennial threat to Israel in the northeast until, two centuries later, both Syria and Israel were overpowered by the Assyrians.

11:26-40 INTERNAL DISMEMBERMENT: TEN TRIBES TO JEROBOAM

11:26 *Jeroboam.* The man who capitalized on the general discontent with Solomon's demand for "forced labor" and brought about the secession of the north was an *Ephraimite* from *Zeredah,* a village as yet not definitely identified. Because Ephraim and Manasseh were the two most powerful tribes of the 10 which revolted, the northern kingdom at times is called "the house of Joseph" (28; Eze 37:16, 19; Am 5:15). Given "charge over all the forced labor" in this large area, "industrious" Jeroboam fomented resentment against the royal demands. When by some overt act he *lifted up his hand against the king* and "Solomon sought . . . to kill him," he "fled into Egypt" (40), where he bided his time.

11:29 *Ahijah.* Perhaps it was through him that "the Lord said to Solomon" what the consequences of the king's unfaithfulness would be. By a symbolic act, which he at once explained, the prophet now revealed just how the kingdom would be divided into two parts. (For a similar symbolic act see 1 Sm 15:27 ff.)

11:32 *One tribe.* Jeroboam was to receive 10 tribes. Solomon's son was to rule over only one tribe (the small tribe of Benjamin) besides his own tribe of Judah. Benjamin and the tribe of Simeon were virtually absorbed by Judah so that "there was none that followed the house of David, but the tribe of Judah only." (12:20)

11:34 *Ruler.* For the term see 1 Sm 10:1 note.

11:36 *A lamp.* A figurative expression. We would say the line of David was not to be extinguished. (15:4; 2 K 8:19; 2 Sm 21:17 note)

11:39 *Not for ever.* Never again mighty in the political domain, "the house of David" maintained its identity till out of it there came He who was "greater than Solomon." (Lk 2:4; 11:31)

11:40 *Shishak.* The first Pharaoh to be mentioned by name in the OT. Known in the Egyptian records as Sheshonq, he founded the weak 22d or Libyan dynasty about 945 B.C. After Solomon's death he invaded Judah and Israel. (14:25 f.)

11:41-43 SOLOMON'S DEATH

11:41 *Acts of Solomon.* One of a number of unknown sources to which the reader is referred for data not included in the books of Kings. (See Introduction, "Structure")

11:42 *Forty years.* The years during which he was associated with his father may be included in this figure. (1:53 note)

12:1—16:28 DIVIDED KINGDOM: PERIOD OF HOSTILITY

12:1—14:20 Jeroboam, First King of Israel

12:1-24 SEVERANCE OF POLITICAL TIES

12:1 *Made him king.* The predicted division of the kingdom became a reality when negotiations with Solomon's son Rehoboam proved futile. At Shechem the 10 northern tribes, henceforth called Israel, severed political ties with Judah, electing Jeroboam to be their king (1-20). The "word of the Lord" forbade Rehoboam to use force in an effort to restore the union (21-24). Until the northern kingdom was overrun by the Assyrians two centuries later, the chosen people remained a house divided against itself. With the exception of an interlude of about three decades, the separated brethren were so hostile to one another that they engaged in civil war. At times they even sought and obtained foreign military aid against one another.

At *Shechem,* the chief city of Ephraim, some 30 miles north of Jerusalem, Joshua had made a covenant with "all the tribes of Israel" (Jos 24:1 ff.). Nearby were Mount Ebal and Mount Gerizim. (Jos 8:30 ff.)

12:4 *Heavy yoke.* Cf. 4:6 note; 5:13.

12:6 *Took counsel.* The monarchy was still elective to the extent that Rehoboam negotiated with "all the assembly of Israel" (3) for his succession to the throne (1 Sm 10:1 note). For Saul's and David's popular acclamation see 1 Sm 11:14 note; 2 Sm 5:1-3. In deliberating on the request to "lighten the hard service" of his father, Rehoboam received opposite advice from two groups of counselors (6-11). Unfortunately he adopted the hard line, advocated by "the young men who had grown up with him" (10, 12-15). No doubt they argued that the incipient uprising should be squelched by repressive measures. The northern tribes promptly declared their independence, stoned Rehoboam's emissary, and elected Jeroboam as their king. (16-20)

12:11 *Scorpions.* Named after a dreaded animal, these scourges are thought to have had many lashes, each carrying a piece of metal at its end. (Cf. our cat-o-nine-tails)

12:15 *Turn of affairs.* In His sovereignty God gave the negotiations such a *turn* as to *fulfill his word.* Though unseen and often uninvited, the Lord of the nations still is present at councils on all levels of diplomacy. His "hand is not shortened" in directing the world's history. (Is 59:1; 50:2; Nm 11:23)

12:16 *To your tents.* The shout of rebellion, raised by Israel at David's time (2 Sm 20:1). For examples of long-standing differences between the northern tribes and Judah see 1 Sm 11:8; 2 Sm 2:8 ff.

12:18 *Adoram.* Following the advice of his young counselors, Rehoboam flaunted his authority before the people by sending to them the *taskmaster over the forced labor,* the very man to whose office they objected so vehemently (2 Sm 20:24 note). For another form of his name see 2 Ch 10:18.

12:19 *This day.* The record from which the author took the account of the rebellion appears to have been written while both kingdoms still were in existence, i.e., prior to 722 B.C., when the northern tribes became an Assyrian vassal state.

12:20 *Judah only.* Cf. 11:32 note.

12:24 *Not . . . fight.* Heir to his father's military power, Rehoboam quite likely could have forced Israel to submit. The "continual wars between Rehoboam and Jeroboam," mentioned in 2 Ch 12:15, no doubt were more in the nature of border skirmishes.

12:25—14:20 SEVERANCE OF RELIGIOUS TIES

1) 12:25-33 Calf Worship Instituted by Jeroboam

12:25 *Penuel.* On the river Jabbok, east of the Jordan. (Gn 32:26; Gn. 32:30, 31 notes; Ju 8:8)

12:28 *Two calves.* The secession of the northern tribes severed religious as well as political ties. Fearing that worship in Jerusalem would heal the breach, jeopardizing the entire movement and his own life, Jeroboam established two sanctuaries within the borders of the new state. The new religious centers were at "Bethel," not far from Jerusalem, and at "Dan" in the far north, where veneration of graven images flourished at the time of the judges (Ju 18:27-31; cf. Ju 18:30 note). The golden calf or bullock erected in both of these cities was to represent the "gods . . . who brought up [Israel] out of the land of Egypt" (cf. Ex 32:1, 4, 6 notes). Whether regarded as symbols of the divine presence or as actual images to be venerated, the bullocks identified the God of Israel with the objects of Baal worship, reducing the Lord of history to a fertility deity.

12:30 *A sin.* It brought about the destruction of the house of Jeroboam (13:33 f.) and eventually of the entire northern kingdom (14:16). His successors are condemned with the refrain: "he walked in all the way of Jeroboam the son of Nebat." (15:30; 16:7, 19, 26, etc.)

12:31 *From among all the people.* Not from the Levites only. He also arrogated priestly functions to himself. (13:1)

12:32 *A feast.* In order to wean the people from customary pilgrimages to Jerusalem, Jeroboam appointed *a feast* which was to be celebrated a month later than the Feast of Tabernacles. (Lv 23:34)

2) 13:1-32 Destruction of False Altar Predicted

13:1 *A man of God.* Jeroboam's violations of the covenant were condemned *by the word of the Lord* transmitted to him by *a man of God* from Judah. The divine emissary foretold the destruction of the spurious altar. The king's hand withered when he ordered the arrest of his critic, but was healed when the latter "entreated the Lord." However, in obedience to "the word of the Lord," the man of God refused Jeroboam's hospitality, returning home as directed. (1-10)

13:2 *Josiah.* The fulfillment of the prophecy 300 years later was a matter of record when the books of Kings were written. (2 K 23:15-20)

13:8 *Not eat bread.* No reason is given for the prohibition not to partake of food or drink nor for the command to return home by "another way." Perhaps he was to avoid familiarity with the idolatrous people.

13:11 *Old prophet.* Residing in the city where the spurious altar stood but not raising his voice in protest against it, this old man apparently was a prophet of Baal (18:40). We are not told why he tricked the man of God into disobedience. (11-19)

13:21 *Disobeyed.* Because the man of God disobeyed an explicit command, "a lion met him

. . . and killed him" (20-25). His fate serves as a warning not to be misled by men who claim divine inspiration for a message which clearly contradicts the revealed Word of God. On the severity of the punishment see 1 Sm 6:19 note; 2 Sm 6:6 f.; Nm 31:1 note.

13:30 *Own grave.* By his request to share "the grave in which the man of God is buried," the old prophet sought to assure himself that his own corpse would not be desecrated (2; 2 K 23:16).—Men bent on gaining some advantage do not hesitate to pursue their selfish course even over the dead bodies of their fellowmen.

13:32 *Samaria.* By the time the prophecy against Bethel was fulfilled, Samaria instead of Shechem (12:25) was the capital of the northern kingdom.

3) 13:33-34 Jeroboam's Disregard of Warning

13:33 *Not turn.* In spite of the warning by the man of God, Jeroboam brazenly continued in the sin which was to "cut . . . off and destroy" his house, as the next chapter bears out.

4) 14:1-16 Punishment for Jeroboam's Apostasy Announced

14:1 *Fell sick.* When Jeroboam's wife came to the prophet Ahijah to inquire whether their sick child would recover, he recognized her in spite of her disguise (1-6). "Charged with heavy tidings," he predicted: (1) the death of the child; (2) the extinction of Jeroboam's dynasty; (3) the eventual downfall of Israel. (6-16)

14:2 *Disguise yourself.* Because her husband thought he could hoodwink the prophet or because the king wanted to keep her mission to a true prophet a secret. To add to the deception, she was not to take a very costly reward for the prophet but only some food. For such gifts to a prophet see 1 Sm 9:7 note. Ahijah, who had foretold Jeroboam's rise to power (11:29 ff.), remained in the Israelite town of *Shiloh.* Here, less than 10 miles north of Bethel, the tabernacle of the Lord had stood from Joshua's to Samuel's time. (Jos 18:1; 1 Sm 1:3; Jer 7:12)

14:9 *All . . . before you.* As king of Israel, Jeroboam had no predecessors. But he was not the first "leader" (7) over the "people Israel" who had provoked the Lord to anger by evil deeds.

14:14 *Today. And henceforth.* The extinction of Jeroboam's house would take place in the immediate future. However, it would be two centuries hence before *the Lord will raise up for himself a* foreign *king* who shall rule *over Israel,* scattering them "beyond the Euphrates," the land of their Assyrian captors.

14:15 *Asherim.* Cf. Gn 28:18 note; Ju 2:13 note.

14:16 *Sins of Jeroboam.* Almost all the kings of Israel were "like the house of Jeroboam," walking "in the sins which he made Israel to sin." (16:7, 26)

5) 14:17-20 Jeroboam's Death

14:17 *Tirzah.* Tentatively identified with a site a few miles southeast of Shechem (12:1 note) and evidently Jeroboam's summer residence, Tirzah later was the capital of the northern kingdom. (15:33)

14:19 *Chronicles.* Not a reference to the Biblical book by that name. For the records used by the writer of Kings and his principle of selecting accounts from them see the Introduction, "Authorship."

4:21—15:24 Three Successors of Solomon

14:21-31 REHOBOAM OF JUDAH

14:21 *Rehoboam.* From the division of the kingdom and the first king of Israel the account returns to the reign of Solomon's son Rehoboam (21-29) and of two of his successors: Abijam and Asa (15:1-24). In order to synchronize the history of the two kingdoms, the author then resumes the story of five kings who ruled in the north. (15:25—16:28)

Naamah. In the formula introducing the kings of Judah (not of Israel) the name of the queen mother is a regular feature. The part that Bathsheba, Solomon's mother, played in putting her son on the throne (1:11-31) is a good example of the influence wielded by dowager queens.

14:22 *Jealousy.* On this term see Ex 20:5 note.

14:24 *Prostitutes.* Sacred prostitution, both female and male, played a prominent part in the worship of Baal. His devotees expected these *abominations* to have the power of sympathetic magic, automatically putting the deity under a spell to produce fertility in human beings, herds, and crops. On "pillars" and "Asherim" (23) see Gn 28:18 note.

14:25 *Shishak.* On this Pharaoh see 11:40 note. It is hardly accidental that the account of Egyptian invasion, the only incident recorded for Rehoboam's reign, follows immediately on the description of the abominations which provoked the Lord to jealousy.

14:26 *Shields of gold.* Cf. 10:17 note.

14:31 *Slept.* When Lazarus had "fallen asleep," Jesus went "to awake him out of sleep." (Jn 11:11; see also 1 Co 15:13-18)

15:1-8 ABIJAM OF JUDAH

15:1 *Abijam.* The account of his reign is shorter even than that of Rehoboam, his predecessor on the throne of Judah (but see 2 Ch 13:1-22). His name occurs in the variant form "Abijah." (2 Ch 12:16)

15:2 *Abishalom.* Another spelling of Absalom. Cf. 2 Ch 13:2 note.

15:4 *A lamp.* Cf. 11:36 note.

15:6 *Rehoboam and Jeroboam.* Apparently an accidental scribal repetition of 14:30 omitted by the Septuagint, but see Ch 13:2b which reads "Abijah and Jeroboam."

15:9-24 ASA OF JUDAH

15:9 *Asa.* Asa's reign, which was nearly as long as that of wicked Manasseh's 55 years (2 K 21:1), is noted for: (1) his zeal for the true religion (9-15); (2) his appeal to a Syrian king for help against the Israelite king Baasha. (16-24)

15:10 *Maacah.* She retained her influential role of "queen (grand)mother" until Asa deposed her. (13)

15:13 *Abominable image.* Derived from a root meaning "to shudder," this Hebrew word denotes an idol image which produced horror because of its ugliness or obscene representation. It occurs only here and in the parallel account, 2 Ch 15:16.

15:15 *Votive gifts.* Translated "things . . . dedicated" in 7:51, these unspecified gifts were to replace the "treasures" which Shishak "took away." (14:26)

15:17 *Ramah.* A fortress only about 5 miles north of Jerusalem, it was like a dagger aimed at Judah's heart.

15:18 *Ben-hadad.* Perhaps the grandson of Rezon, the founder of the Syrian state with headquarters at Damascus (11:23 note). At least two of its kings bore the name of *Ben-hadad,* which means the son of the storm god Hadad (20:1; 2 K 13:24). By a foreign alliance against the Israelite king Baasha, Asa intensified the civil war.

15:20 *Cities of Israel.* Those listed were on Israel's northern border near the sea of *Chinneroth,* i.e., Gennesaret or Galilee. For *Naphtali's* territory see Jos 19:24 note.

15:21 *Stopped building.* Pressure on his northern frontier by the Syrians forced the Israelite king to "withdraw from" his building operations on his southern border. For *Tirzah* see 14:17 note. Taking advantage of his rival's preoccupation, Asa mobilized "all Judah" to build his own fortified cities with the stones and timbers from Ramah. Geba and Mizpah were a short distance north of Jersualem.

15:12 *His might.* For his military power see 2 Ch 14:8 ff.

15:25—16:28 Jeroboam's Successors in Israel

15:25-32 NADAB OF ISRAEL

15:25 *Nadab.* Synchronizing the history of the two kingdoms, the author interrupts the account of the kings of Judah (14:21—15:24) for a survey of five kings of Israel (15:25—16:28). The reign of the last of these northern kings marked a transition to a period of peaceful relations between the two segments of the divided kingdom.

15:27 *Gibbethon.* Located some 20 miles west of Ramah and originally assigned to the tribe of Dan (Jos 19:44), Gibbethon was under Philistine control. Evidently Nadab's siege was unsuccessful. Twenty-four years later the Israelites were again—or perhaps still—encamped against the same city. (16:15)

15:27 *Conspired.* During the two centuries of its existence Israel was ruled by 19 kings representing nine different dynasties. Conspiracies and regicides were responsible for the frequent changes in ruling houses, of which none lasted longer than four generations. Jeroboam was succeeded only by his son.

15:29 *The word of the Lord.* Cf. 14:10.

15:32 *And there was.* Omitted by the Septuagint, this verse repeats 16.

15:33—16:7 BAASHA OF ISRAEL

15:33 *Twenty-four years.* Of lowly origin in the tribe of Issachar (27; 16:2), the usurper reigned 2 years longer than the founder of the Ephraimite dynasty whom he displaced. For his hostile relationship to his contemporary on the throne of Judah see 16-22.

16:1 *Jehu.* Not to be confused with the later king of Israel by the same name (2 K 10:28 ff.). His denunciation of Baasha was not motivated by political prejudice; he rebuked also a king of Judah (2 Ch 19:2). For his literary activity see 2 Ch 20:34.

16:8-10 ELAH OF ISRAEL

16:8 *Elah.* Baasha, like Jeroboam, had only one successor. After reigning only 2 years he was struck down by Zimri, "commander of half his chariots," "in the house of Arzah," an official who may have abetted or even helped plan the assassination.

16:10 *Zimri.* In the power struggle for the throne of Israel, military leaders played a prominent role. The cavalry commander Zimri had barely proclaimed himself king when the troops "encamped against Gibbethon" made Omri, "commander of the army, king over Israel," who in turn had to eliminate Tibni, another contender. Zimri became proverbial for assassination. (2 K 9:31)

16:11-20 ZIMRI OF ISRAEL

16:13 *Idols.* Lit. "vanities"; cf. Dt 32:21 note.

16:21-28 OMRI OF ISRAEL

16:21 *Tibni.* Supported by "half of the people," Omri's rival maintained his claim to the throne for about 5 years. Then he "died," presumably a casualty of the civil war.

16:22 *Omri.* Founder of one of the more stable dynasties, Omri restored order in the northern kingdom. During the reign of his successors (Ahab, Ahaziah, Jehoram) the relationship between Israel and Judah changed from hostility to peace and cooperation. The former army commander made a wise move when he moved the capital to "the hill of Samaria" (24). Virtually inaccessible on three sides, it was able to hold off the Assyrian army for 3 years. (2 K 17:5)

16:27 *Rest of the acts.* According to extra-Biblical sources Omri achieved international fame. Assyrian records refer to Israel as "the land of Omri" even after his dynasty had vanished from the scene. However, considerations other than military and political interest guided the writer of Kings in the selection of what he recorded in his prophetic history (see Introduction, "Purpose"). Hence he devoted only eight verses (21-28) to this king who appears to have been one of Israel's more illustrious rulers. By contrast the story of Omri's son takes up six chapters (16:29—22:40), more space than is accorded any other king since Solomon.

16:29—2 K 8:29 DIVIDED KINGDOM COOPERATION AGAINST COMMON FOES

16:29—22:40 Ahab of Israel

16:29-34 WICKED HUSBAND OF EVIL JEZEBEL

16:29 *Ahab.* The conciliatory attitude toward the southern king, no doubt fostered by his father, later led to full cooperation of the two kingdoms against a foreign aggressor. (Cf. 22:1-4)

16:30 *Evil.* The history of Ahab bulks so large because under his reign apostasy, the cause of Israel's fall a century later, reached a new high. Without necessarily observing a chronological sequence, the author presents a series of events as evidence of this *evil in the sight of the Lord.* The king's marriage to a Phoenician princess and worship of her national idol, known as Melkart, deserves mention at the very outset to show how far he went to "provoke the Lord . . . to anger." Capable of violating this basic requirement of the covenant, he could be expected to defy other laws of the Lord.

16:33 *Asherah.* Cf. Gn 28:8 note.

16:34 *Built Jericho.* As the king's marriage was symptomatic of his evil bent of mind, so the rebuilding of Jericho was indicative of the people's disregard of the Lord's will. For *the word of the Lord* see Jos 6:26 note. Hiel's loss of his sons from *his first-born* to *his youngest* also forecasts the completeness of the judgment which awaited the nation as a whole. It too would come *according to the word of the Lord.*

17:1—18:46 AHAB, ELIJAH, AND THE DROUGHT

7:1 *Elijah.* To counteract the evils of Ahab's reign God raised up one of the most arresting figures among OT prophets. In "spirit and power" Elijah was to foreshadow one besides whom there was none greater "among those born of women" (Lk 1:17; 7:24-28). As Moses was the type of THE Prophet (Dt 18), so Elijah prefigured the forerunner of the Messiah, John the Baptist. (Ml 4:5 f.; Mk 9:4 f.)

The remaining six chapters of 1 K and the first two of 2 K are not so much the history of Ahab the king and of his successors, but rather a record of Elijah, the prophet. It opens with an account of what he did before, during, and after a severe drought (chs. 17 and 18). After announcing its coming and going into hiding, he was kept alive miraculously (17:1-7). Directed by the Lord, he spent the remainder of the drought in the Phoenician city of Zarephath, where he performed two miracles. (17:8-24)

Tishbite. A native of *Tishbe,* an obscure village in transjordanian Gilead, mentioned only in connection with Elijah. He suddenly appeared on the scene as if coming from nowhere; he vanished from sight even more mysteriously. (2 K 2:11)

17:9 *Zarephath.* A small coastal town of Phoenicia between Tyre and Sidon, referred to by its Greek and Latin name "Sarepta" in Lk 4:26 (KJV; NEB). Jesus' only excursion beyond the borders of Israel was "to the region of Tyre and Sidon," where He too met a Syrophoenician woman of great faith. (Mk 7:24-30)

17:12 *Die.* Evidently the drought was not restricted to Israelite territory.

17:16 *Not spent.* At the brook Cherith ravens brought Elijah food; now he miraculously provided sustenance for the widow and himself. In the religious crisis during the days of Elijah and Elisha more "signs and wonders" witnessed to the power of the true God than in any period since the Exodus (Ex 7:3). The casting out of demons by Jesus proclaimed that "the kingdom of God has come." (Lk 11:20)

17:22 *Hearkened.* Elijah was a "man of God" who by "the word of the Lord" (24) and by intercessory prayer revived the widow's son (see also 2 K 4:34; Acts 20:10). The Word made flesh commanded the dead by virtue of His own authority: "I say . . . arise." (Mk 5:41; Lk 7:14)

18:1 *Send rain.* As Elijah had announced the drought (17:1), so he was to transmit to Ahab *the word of the Lord* which alone could terminate it. The famine was so "severe" during the 3 years—more exactly 3½ years (Lk 4:25; Ja 5:17)—that the king himself with a high-ranking official went in search of grass to "save the horses and mules alive" which he needed for commercial and military operations. (1-6)

18:3 *Obadiah.* True to his name, "servant of the Lord," Obadiah used his position at court to save "a hundred prophets" of the Lord whose lives were threatened by murderous Jezebel. (13; 19:10)

18:12 *Kill me.* Obadiah feared that *the Spirit of the Lord* would suddenly transport Elijah to another hiding place.

18:16 *Ahab.* Swallowing his pride, the desperate king sought out the prophet.

18:17 *Troubler.* Ahab refused to acknowledge that he had brought on the drought because he had "forsaken the commandments of the Lord." Elijah was not the last preacher of "future judgment" to suffer abuse. (See, e.g., Acts 16:20 ff.)

18:19 *Mount Carmel.* In order to prove to the king that he and his "father's house" brought divine judgment on himself and his apostate people, Elijah demanded a convocation of *all Israel* including the *prophets of Baal* on the 15-mile-long mountain range which juts out toward the Mediterranean Sea.

18:21 *Go limping.* In a trial by fire Elijah dramatically demonstrated that: (1) the Canaanite fertility gods were not in control of nature (20-29); (2) the "Lord of hosts," Creator of "the heavens and the earth . . . and all the host of them" (Gn 2:1), was a "jealous" God who did not tolerate divided allegiance (30-40; Ex 20:5 note; Dt 4:24 note; Jos 24:19 note). The names for idols have changed, but the temptation persists to believe that it is possible to "serve God and mammon" (Mt 6:24). Nor is modern worship of newly discovered powers of nature less ridiculous than the ancient cry into the silence of space: "Baal, answer us." (1 Co 8:5)

18:22 *I only.* Elijah alone challenged the false prophets; the other prophets of the Lord were in hiding. (4)

18:26 *Limped.* NEB: "danced wildly."

18:27 *Gone aside.* For a bowel movement. Cutting sarcasm!

18:29 *Raved.* Gashing themselves with knives, they "prophesied" (KJV), i.e., they stimulated themselves into a state of frenzy (cf. 1 Sm 10:6 note). They did not give up *until the time of the offering of the oblation,* very likely "the evening cereal offering." (2 K 16:15)

18:30 *Altar of the Lord.* We are not told at what time and under what circumstances this altar was erected. For worship of God at various places see Dt 12:5 note.

18:38 *Fire.* For other instances of divine manifestation by fire see Ex 14:24; 19:18; Lv 9:24; 1 Ch 21:26; 2 Ch 7.1.

18:40 *Killed them.* In such passages as Dt 13:6-11 and 17:2-7 the death penalty was decreed on those who entice the Israelites to "go and serve other gods" (see also Dt 13:1, 10 notes). For *the brook Kishon* see Ju 4:7 note.

18:45 *Jezreel.* On the king's return to his royal residence in Jezreel, a distance of more than 15 miles, Elijah humbly served as his forerunner.

19:1-21 ELIJAH'S FLIGHT FROM AHAB'S WIFE

19:3 *Afraid.* Unnerved by Jezebel's threat, the hitherto dauntless champion of the Lord's cause *went for his life.* Fleeing the northern kingdom, he did not stop until he *came to Beer-sheba,* the proverbial southernmost city of Judah (1-3; Ju 20:1 note). From there the dispirited prophet continued his journey southward to Mt. Sinai "in the strength" of food supplied by "the angel of the Lord" (4-8). Ordered "to stand upon the mount," Elijah received new instructions from the Lord, who manifested Himself in "a still small voice" (9-18). After he "departed from there," he carried out one of the new assignments: he called Elisha to be his successor. (19-21)

19:3 *Afraid.* For a similar lapse into fear see 1 Sm 16:2 note.

19:4 *Broom tree.* A desert bush that reaches a height of 10—12 ft. The Hebrew text has: "one broom tree," the numeral emphasizing the sparsity of vegetation in that desolate area. Here Elijah wanted to die sharing the fate of his fathers.

19:8 *Forty days and forty nights.* Elijah had experiences similar to those of Moses: (1) on *the mount of God* (Ex 3:1) both men went without food for the same length of time (Ex 34:28); (2) as Moses was in "a cleft of the rock" when the Lord's "glory" passed by, so Elijah stood "at the entrance of the cave" (13; Ex 33:22); (3) Elijah "wrapped his face in his mantle"; Moses "hid his face" at the burning bush. (13; Ex 3:6)

19:9 *Doing here.* The question and answer in 9 and 10 anticipate what is repeated in 13 and 14.

19:11 *Strong wind.* At other times God manifested Himself in phenomena of nature: in wind (Eze 1:14), in an earthquake, and in fire. (Ex 19:18)

19:12 *Still small voice.* Elijah was to resume his prophetic mission not out of fear of the power of God, irresistible though it was. God wanted His servant to respond to His call under no other compulsion than its quiet, undramatic appeal to man's inner self. Once Elijah heard that *still small voice,* no outward circumstance would be able to prostrate him under a broom tree of despair.

19:15 *Return.* In a renewed battle against idolatry Elijah was to anoint (1) *Hazael to be king over Syria* (2) Jehu, "king over Israel"; (3) Elisha, a "prophet," to succeed him. Elijah personally recruited Elisha (19-21), who in turn carried out the commands concerning Hazael and Jehu. (2 K 9:1-10; 8:7-15)

19:16 *Abel-meholah.* Elisha's home was a few miles east of the Jordan and some 20 miles south of the Sea of Galilee.

19:18 *Seven thousand.* Even though many were to die by the sword of Hazael and Jehu, for whose rise to power Elisha was responsible (17), a large number would be found in Israel who did not succumb to the seduction of Baal worship.

19:20 *Done to you.* Elijah granted Elisha's request, explaining that the call to discipleship was not intended to conflict with filial respect for parents. But cf. Jesus' reply to a similar request. (Mt 8:21 f.)

20:1-43 AHAB'S DOUBLE VICTORY OVER THE SYRIANS

20:1 *Ben-hadad.* Not the first Syrian king by that name (15:18 note). Renewing the attacks on Israel, originally made at the request of the Judean king Asa, he besieged Samaria. His army consisted of 32 divisions, each of which was under the command of an allied king or provincial chieftain. Ahab refused his imperious demands for surrender (1-12). Instead he took the offensive. His sally from the city (13-15) surprised the drunken, overconfident enemy (16-18) and drove off the invaders (19-21). As predicted by a prophet (22), Ben-hadad returned "in the spring" with an equally strong force. His advisers persuaded him that the Israelites worshiped "gods of the hills" and not "a god of the valleys." Consequently he chose a battlefield "in the plain" (23-25). However, the Lord gave "all this great multitude" arrayed against Israel's much smaller army into Ahab's hand (26-30a). The Syrian king, locked up in the city of Aphek, surrendered to Ahab, who set him free, making "a covenant with him" (30b-34). Because Ben-hadad, whom the Lord "had devoted to destruction," had been spared, "a certain man of the sons of the prophets" declared Ahab had drawn the released prisoner's sentence upon himself and the people. (35-42)

20:9 *This thing.* When Ahab realized that Ben-hadad's words (3) were not merely a demand for recognition of Syrian overlordship, expressed in bombastic rhetoric, but that the invader meant to carry out these threats literally, he accepted the advice of his elders to refuse the humiliating terms.

20:10 *Handfuls.* The Syrian threatened to demolish Samaria so completely that his men would be able to carry off the remaining dust in their hands. For a similar threat against Jerusalem see 2 Sm 17:13.

20:15 *Governors.* Ben-hadad's invasion of Israel brought all the provincial officials to Samaria for refuge.

20:16 *Booths.* Their temporary barracks. The same Hebrew noun occurs in the phrase "the feast of Tabernacles."

20:23 *Gods of the hills.* The remark of Ben-hadad's servant reflects the notion, prevalent in the ancient world, that a certain deity had power only in one geographic area or in the exercise of only one function.

20:26 *Aphek.* A number of cities bore this name. (See, e.g., 1 Sm 4:1; 29:1)

20:29 *A hundred thousand.* No doubt the Hebrew word for *thousand* here and in 30 is not a numeral but denotes a fully armed soldier or a commander of a detachment. (See Numbers, Introduction, "the Numbers . . . . ")

20:34 *Cities.* Evidently Ahab's father Omri suffered reverses which are not mentioned in the short record of his reign. (16:21-28)

20:35 *Sons of the prophets.* Cf. 1 Sm 10:10 note.

20:38 *Bandage.* Disguised as a wounded soldier, a member of the prophetic guild (2 K 2:3, 5; 4:38) used a parable to trap Ahab into condemning himself, as Nathan had elicited David's verdict upon himself. (2 Sm 12:1-12)

20:39 *A talent.* The penalty for negligence was set at a huge sum. A talent was equal to 3,000 shekels, a hundred times the price of a slave.

20:42 *Let go.* From a political point of view the release of Ben-hadad was a wise move. Cooperation between the two countries was necessary to check the growing menace of Assyrian expansion into Syria and then southward into Israel. Later Ahab and the Syrians did make common cause against the Assyrian king Shalmaneser III. The battle took place in 853 B.C. at Qarqar, some 100 miles north of Damascus.

21:1-29 AHAB'S CRIME AGAINST A PRIVATE CITIZEN

21:1 *Naboth.* Ahab "did evil in the sight of the Lord" by introducing Tyrian idolatry (16:29-34) and by entering a forbidden political alliance (20:31-34). This chapter records still another kind of crime. In order to satisfy a royal whim, he deprived a private citizen of his inalienable right. Chagrined by Naboth's refusal to part with his ancestral vineyard (1-4), the pouting king let his wife Jezebel secure it by an unscrupulous maneuver. After taunting her husband for lack of aggressiveness (5-7), she contrived to have Naboth and his sons put to death on trumped-up charges of blasphemy and treason (8-14; 2 K 9:26). Thereupon she gleefully handed the confiscated property over to Ahab (15 f.). However, Elijah, sent by the Lord, pronounced the doom of extinction on the royal pair for their unparalleled wickedness (17-26). When the king "humbled himself before" the Word of the Lord, the punishment was deferred till "his son's days." (27-29)

21:3 *Inheritance.* Naboth had the law on his side. (Lv 25:25-28; Nm 36:7-12)

21:9 *A fast.* Jezebel insinuated that a crime of such a grave nature had deen committed as to require the calling of a penitential general assembly (Ju 20:26; 1 Sm 7:6). Unsuspecting Naboth was to be accorded a place of honor.

21:10 *Two base fellows.* Literally "sons of Belial." (Dt 13:13; Ju 19:22 note)

21:13 *Stoned him.* The penalty prescribed in Lv 24:13-16.

21:15 *Take possession.* Property reverted to the crown if its owner was executed or if there were no rightful heirs.

21:19 *In the place.* A literal rendering of a Hebrew phrase which also has the transferred meaning of "instead of": "as dogs licked up the blood of Naboth, so dogs shall lick up your own blood." For another example of the phrase in this sense see Hos 1:10 (RSV; NEB). Naboth was killed at Jezreel (13); Ahab, at Samaria (22:38). The corpse of Ahab's son Jehoram was thrown into Naboth's vineyard. (2 K 9:25)

21:23 *Eat Jezebel.* For the fulfillment see 2 K 9:35 ff.

21:25 *Sold himself.* Ahab was soft clay in the strong hands of evil Jezebel, the "Lady Macbeth" of the OT. She did not share his repentance. (27-29)

21:29 *Son's days.* The death of his son J[eh]oram is recorded in 2 K 9:24; the extermination of his house, in 2 K 10:1-11.

22:1-40 AHAB'S DEATH IN THIRD SYRIAN CAMPAIGN

22:2 *Third year.* In a third encounter with the Syrians, Ahab was to lose his life. Apparently Ben-hadad did not return all the cities to Israel as he had promised (20:34). After a lapse of 3 years Ahab, allied with the king of Judah (44), decided to take Ramoth-gilead, an Israelite city some 30 miles southeast of the Sea of Galilee (1-4). Even though his 400 prophets predicted the success of the campaign, the king sent for Micaiah, a man known for unpopular prophecies (5-12). At first he mockingly imitated the hired prophets by repeating their prediction of "triumph." Then he announced the disastrous outcome that he foresaw: "all Israel scattered upon the mountains." At the same time he branded the professional prophets dupes of a "lying spirit" (13-23). Imprisoned for his courageous words, Micaiah foretold that the king would not return alive from the battle (24-28). In an attempt to disprove Micaiah's prediction, Ahab "disguised himself and went into battle." However, an arrow shot "at a venture" by an enemy archer found its way into his vitals. When "at evening" Ahab died, the Israelite soldiers scattered "every man to his city, and . . . country" (29-36). In Samaria, where the king was buried, "the dogs licked up his blood," as "they washed" it from his chariot. (37-40)

22:4 *With me.* The two kingdoms were no

longer hostile to one another, as they had been for a long time after the division. Friendly relations were cemented by the marriage of Ahab's daughter Athaliah to Jehosphat's son Jehoram. (2 K 8:18)

22:7 *Prophet of the Lord.* As the calves at Dan and Bethel were supposed to represent the God who brought the people "up out of the land of Egypt" (12:28), so there were prophets in Israel who professed to proclaim "the word of the Lord" (5).

22:10 *Prophesying.* The same form of the Hebrew verb is translated "raved" in 1 Sm 18:10. (See 1 Sm 10:6; 18:10 notes)

22:11 *Horns of iron.* One of the false prophets supplemented the spoken incantation with an action that was magically to produce the effect which it portrayed. True prophets also acted out or pantomimed their message in order to make it more impressive. (2 K 13:14-19; Jer 27:2; Eze 4)

22:16 *The truth.* Ahab realized that Micaiah's prophecy of "triumph" was intended to ridicule the king's fawning lackeys.

22:17 *No shepherd.* A nation without a leader. (Nm 27:17)

22:22 *Entice him.* What Micaiah "saw" was a visionary portrayal of the fact that when men "refused to love the truth and so be saved," God "sends upon them a strong delusion." (2 Th 2:11; see also the hardening of Pharaoh's heart, Ex 4:21 note)

22:28 *In peace.* Better translated "in safety." (NEB)

22:31 *Thirty-two captains.* The Syrain force apparently was made up of 32 divisions as before. (20:16, 24)

22:34 *At a venture.* "At random" (NEB), without aiming at any particular target. Events that appear to happen "by chance" (Lk 10:31) are not the product of blind fate; each of them has on it the signature of God's providence.

22:38 *Harlots.* When they *washed themselves* by *the pool of Samaria,* as they were accustomed to do, the water was tainted with Ahab's blood. Though not recorded in Elijah's prophecy (21:19), this desecration of his blood added to the disgrace of his death.

22:39 *Ivory house.* Luxuriously inlaid with ivory. The prophet Amos says such houses "shall perish" because they were built by extortion and oppression of the poor. (Am 3:15)

22:41-50 Jehoshaphat of Judah

22:41 *Jehoshaphat.* After devoting seven chapters to events during the reigns of Omri and of Ahab (chs. 15—22) and before continuing the history of Israel (2 K chs. 1—7), the author inserts a brief note of 10 verses about a contemporary on the throne of Judah. Succeeding a father who did not hesitate to call in Assyrian aid against his northern rival (15:16-24), Jehoshaphat "made peace with the king of Israel" (44). This reversal of policy resulted in more than cessation of hostilities. Jehoshaphat fought side by side with two Israelite kings: with Ahab against the Syrians (1-4, 29 ff.) and with Ahab's son Jehoram against the Moabites. (2 K 3:4-8)

22:49 *Not willing.* Even though allied with the northern kingdom, Jehoshaphat retained his independence at least to the extent of refusing Ahaziah's help in a maritime expedition. Its purpose was to retain the trade initiated by Solomon. (10:22 note)

22:51—2 K 2:25 Ahaziah of Israel

22:51-53 SUMMARY OF REIGN

22:51 *Ahaziah.* Summarized in the closing verses of this chapter (51-53), the history of Ahaziah's reign is continued in the opening chapters of 2 K.

1:1-16 AHAZIAH AND ELIJAH

1:1 *Moab rebelled.* This note explains why Ahaziah's brother and successor later undertook an expedition against Moab with the cooperation of Jehoshaphat of Judah (3:4-27). The only incident recorded of Ahaziah is a confrontation with Elijah. When the king sent messengers to "inquire of Baal-zebub" whether he would recover from a fall through a latticed window, a prophet waylaid the delegation to announce that the injury would prove fatal (2-4). The messengers' description of the strangely dressed prophet convinced Ahaziah that they had been intercepted by none other than Elijah (5-8). Sent by the king to arrest Elijah, two captains and their contigents of 50 men were consumed by fire which fell from heaven at the request of "the man of God" (9-12). A third captain pleaded for his life and that of his men. "The angel of the Lord" instructed Elijah to "go down with him to the king" in order to announce in person what he had told the messengers (13-16). The brief notice of Ahaziah's death (17 f.) is followed by the account of the end of Elijah's career and the beginning of Elisha's ministry. (2:1-25)

1:2 *Baal-zebub.* His name originally was Baal-zebul, meaning "Baal is prince" (Mt 12:24 ff.). In order to express disdain for this Canaanite idol, he was called Baal-zebub, "Lord of a fly." At that time *Ekron,* a Philistine city some 40 miles southwest of Samaria, seems to have boasted of a baal with unusual powers of healing.

1:3 *Tishbite.* Cf. 1 K 17:1 note.

1:8 *Garment of haircloth.* The Hebrew phrase is "baal or possessor of hair." Occurring only here, it may mean that his hair including his beard was long or that he wore a hairy garment such as became the characteristic clothing of men who were or claimed to be prophets. (Zch 13:4; Mt 3:4; Mk 1:6)

1:10 *Fire came.* Because the purpose of Jesus' first coming was to "seek and save the lost," He did not perform a miracle of judgment such as Elijah's (Lk 9:51-55). However, at His second coming the Son of Man will consign those who rejected Him to "the eternal fire prepared for the devil and his angels." (Mt 25:41)

1:12 *His fifty.* We are not told whether the men under the command of the captains objected to the royal orders. On such mass punishments in the OT see Nm 31:1 note; Dt 2:34 note.

1:16 *No God in Israel.* Elijah did not concede actual existence to the false gods even though he mockingly encouraged the prophets of Baal to intensify their cry to the unresponsive idol. (1 K 16:13 note)

1:17-18 AHAZIAH'S DEATH AND SUCCESSOR

2:1-12a END OF ELIJAH'S MINISTRY

2:1 *To heaven.* After briefly noting the death of Ahaziah (1:17 f.) and before taking up the account of his successor's reign (3:1 ff.), the author records the end of Elijah's ministry (2:1-12a) and the first deeds of his disciple Elisha (2:12b-25)

2:2 *Bethel.* On a final journey, perhaps to bid farewell to his friends and associates, Elijah went 7 miles south from a place called Gilgal to Bethel and from there some 12 miles in a southeasterly direction to Jericho. Apparently sensing what was to happen, Elisha insisted on accompanying his "father" even though the latter for some reason discouraged him. From Jericho both crossed the Jordan "on dry land" to the east bank, where Elijah "went up by a whirlwind into heaven." Cf. Enoch's translation to heaven. (Gn 5:21-25)

2:8 *Struck the water.* Moses stretched out his rod to open a path through the Red Sea. (Ex 14:21 f.)

2:9 *Double share.* Claiming the inheritance of the firstborn, Elisha requested a "share" of his father's spirit "double" that of the other "sons of the prophets." (Dt 21:17)

2:11 *Chariot . . . and horses of fire.* Elisha later saw the mountains round about hard-pressed Samaria "full of horses and chariots of fire" (6:17), a visible demonstration of divine protection and power. A prophet like Elijah who kept the people in communion with the omnipotent Ruler of heaven and earth deserved to be called "the chariots of Israel and its horsemen." A later Israelite king bestowed this title on Elisha himself. (13:14)

2:12 *No more.* Designed to be a type of John, Jesus' forerunner (Ml 4:5 f.; Mt 11:13 f.; Lk 1:17), Elijah was expected by some people to return in the flesh (Mt 16:14). For his appearance on the Mount of Transfiguration see Mt 17:3.

2:12b-25 BEGINNING OF ELISHA'S MINISTRY

2:13 *The mantle.* After tearing "his own clothes," a common gesture of grief (5:7), Elisha dramatically demonstrated that he had inherited the spirit of Elijah: with his master's mantle he performed the same miracle of parting the Jordan (12b-14). Back on the west side of the river, he convinced the people that "the Spirit of the Lord" had not transported Elijah to a secret place in this world (15-18; cf. 1 K 18:12; Acts 8:39 f.). Embarking on his own prophetic career, Elijah's successor purified a spring (19-22). At Bethel two she-bears "tore" 42 boys whom he cursed because they "jeered at him" (23-25). On such mass punishments in the OT see Nm 31:1 note; Dt 2:34 note.

2:23 *Baldhead.* The boys jeered at baldheaded Elisha's claim to be the successor of bushy-haired Elijah (1:8 note). To prove that he was not an impostor, they demanded that he imitate Elijah and *go up* into heaven.

2:24 *Tore.* NEB: "mauled."

3:1—8:15 Jehoram of Israel

3:1-3 INTRODUCTORY DATA AND APPRAISAL

3:1 *Jehoram.* The record of his reign is interrupted at several points. His succession to the throne after the death of his brother Ahaziah, mentioned in 1:17, is followed in ch. 2 by the story of the ascension of Elijah and of the beginning of Elisha's ministry. Ch. 3 tells the story of his participation in an ill-fated campaign against Moab. The report of his death appears five chapters later (9:14-26), the intervening section containing: (1) accounts of Elisha's activities (4:1—8:15); (2) a brief summary of two kings of Judah (8; 16-29); (3) the story of the seizure of his throne by Jehu, his assassin and successor. (9:1-13)

3:4-27 MOABITE CAMPAIGN

3:4 *Mesha.* He inscribed his version of the conflict with the allied invaders on a stone which was discovered in 1869. Written in a language very similar to Hebrew, this so-called Moabite or Mesha Stone supplements and confirms the Biblical account. Jehoram is called Omri's son rather than his grandson.

3:8 *Edom.* Instead of crossing the Jordan above the Dead Sea and invading Moab from the north, the allied kings agreed on a "circuitous march" around the southern end of the sea *by the way of the wilderness of Edom.* They forced the Edomite king to join the expedition, assuring themselves against a rear attack from the south.

3:9 *No water.* Threatened by disaster, the kings sought out Elisha, who for some reason accompanied the troops (9-12). When "the power of the Lord came upon him," he announced relief from the drought and the defeat of the enemy. The next morning there was an abundant supply of water at hand even though they did "not see wind or rain." (13-20).

3:11 *Poured water.* The service that a person rendered his master or teacher. Jesus washed His disciples' feet. (Jn 13:4 ff.)

3:15 *Minstrel.* Music is seldom mentioned as a means to make a prophet receptive to divine inspiration (1 Sm 10:5). More often *the power* (literally "the hand") *of the Lord came upon* His spokesman without musical accompaniment. So, e.g., on Elijah (1 K 18:46) and on Ezekiel. (Eze 1:3)

3:19 *Every good tree.* In the conquest of the Promised Land, the Israelites were not to engage in this scorched-earth policy. (Dt 20:19 f.)

3:22 *Red as blood.* The reflection of the sun's early morning glow on the reddish cast of the soil gave the water the appearance of blood. From this phenomenon the Moabites drew the false conclusion that the allies had "slain one another." Hoping to find a weak enemy, they attacked but suffered heavy losses in a counterattack by the Israelites. When Mesha and his picked troops were unable to "break through" the enemy lines, the king in desperation sacrificed his "eldest son . . . for a burnt offering upon the wall." Thereupon the Israelites "returned to their own land." (21-27)

3:25 *Kirhareseth.* Identified with modern Kerak some 10 miles east of the Dead Sea and equally distant from its southern end.

3:26 *The king of Edom.* Perhaps Mesha hoped the Edomites would offer less resistance. However, the Hebrew words for Edom and Aram (Syria) are almost identical. If the original text read Aram, as translated in an ancient Latin version, then Mesha tried to break through to the north in an attempt to get help from the Syrians.

3:27 *Wrath upon Israel.* This cryptic remark seems to say that the Israelites "withdrew from" Mesha in order to show their revulsion at the human sacrifice. It is also suggested that the Moabites, inspired by their king's sacrifice, drove off the Israelites who were superstitious enough to believe in the efficacy of the heathen rite.

4:1—7:20 OTHER MIRACLES OF ELISHA

1) 4:1-7 Miraculous Supply of Oil

4:1 *To Elisha.* Elisha's participation in the Moabite campaign (ch. 3) is followed by a longer section telling of other incidents in the life of Elijah's successor (4:1—8:15). Apparently not arranged in chronological sequence, these accounts are more or less independent narratives. None of them is dated. The ruling monarch is not identified by name but simply called "the king of Israel" (5:5; 6:9). Elisha was active during the reign of Jehoram's successors (13:14, 20). Chs. 4—7 record eight miraculous deeds, the first four of which make up ch. 4: (1) a prodigious supply of oil from a small flask (1-7); (2) a Shunammite woman's son restored to life (8-37); (3) poisonous food made wholesome (38-41); (4) 100 men fed with 20 loaves of bread. (42-44)

The creditor. Because the woman's husband was dead, he had the right to demand that the son's labor be impounded to pay the debt. (Lv 25:39; Neh 5:5; Mt 18:25)

2) 4:8-37 Woman's Son Revived

4:8 *Shunem.* Elisha's second deed has two miraculous elements. To a hospitable but childless woman whose husband was old (1 Sm 28:4 note; 1 K 1:3) he announced the birth of a son (11-17). Years later the child died of a sunstroke. Without telling her husband what had happened, the woman hurriedly traveled by donkey to seek out Elisha, who was at Mount Carmel, some 20 miles northwest of Shunem (18-25a). He responded to her "bitter distress" by sending his servant to her home. But she refused to leave until the prophet agreed to accompany her in person. On their journey back to Shunem they met Gehazi, who reported that he had laid his master's staff "upon the face of the child" but produced "no sound or sign of life" (25b-31). However, when Elisha "stretched himself upon him," life returned to the corpse. (32-37)

4:10 *Roof chamber with walls.* Literally "an upper room of a wall." Apparently she suggested that the wall of the house be raised, at least on one side, to make possible the construction of a permanent room on the flat roof.

4:13 *On your behalf.* If she was being mistreated in any way, Elisha offered to intercede on her behalf with the highest authorities, who were known to respect his counsel (3:11 ff.). However, the Shunammite woman had no need for that kind of intervention in her affairs. Her "own people," namely her friends and relatives, kindly shielded her from harm.

4:16 *At this season.* Next year at that time (cf. Gn 18:10 note). The woman regarded the birth of a son impossible.

4:22 *Come back.* Turn right around and come back at once.

4:23 *Be well.* Her hurry perplexed the husband because it was not the time of a religious festival which required her presence at a specified time. Without disclosing the reason for the hasty journey, she parried his questions with the one Hebrew word "peace," meaning to say: "Good-bye, don't worry about the outcome." Later she answered Gehazi's question with the same single word, not wishing to be detained by him. (26)

4:29 *Staff.* Wielded by Gehazi, the symbol of his master's authority failed to produce any results.

4:32 *On his bed.* Elisha's bed is meant.

4:33 *Prayed.* Cf. 1 K 17:22 note.

4:35 *House.* Here the word house has the meaning of room.

3) 4:38-41 Poisonous Food Made Wholesome

4:38 *Gilgal.* He had been there before with Elijah (2:1). The local *sons of the prophets* (1 Sm 10:10 note) suffered the effects of *a famine.* The Hebrew text has "the famine," perhaps referring to the one mentioned in 8:1.

4:39 *Wild gourds.* The fruits of a cucumberlike vine thought to be the colocynth. Although used for medicinal purposes, they can produce deadly effects when eaten in large quantities.

4:40 *While.* Better translated: "when they began to eat of the pottage." NEB: "when they tasted."

4) 4:42-44 A Hundred Fed with Twenty Loaves

4:42 *Baal-shalishah.* Perhaps the same place called Shalisha in 1 Sm 9:4, located about 15 miles north of Gilgal. Recognizing in Elisha *a man of God,* someone from there brought him *the first fruits* which normally were given to the priests. (Ex 23:19)

4:43 *Am I to set.* See the similar remarks by

Jesus' disciples when He fed the multitudes. (Mt 14:17; 15:33)

5) 5:1-27 Healing of Naaman; Disease Transferred to Servant

5:1 *Naaman.* The account of his cure is the longest of the miracle narratives, taking up the entire chapter. Believing the conviction of "a little [slave] maid from the land of Israel" that Elijah could "cure him of his leprosy," the Syrian commander set out for Israel (1-5a). Upon his arrival there "the king of Israel" accused him of espionage even though he had letters from the king of Syria explaining the purpose of his journey (5b-7). Elisha on the other hand insisted that the visit of the foreigner would demonstrate that "there is a prophet in Israel." At first the Syrian was "in a rage" that Elisha did not prescribe some occult procedure or dramatic ritual but—wihout even a personal interview—simply directed him to "wash in the Jordan seven times." But persuaded by his servants to follow the simple instructions, the leper became "clean." (8-14)

When the prophet refused a "present" for healing him, the commander requested "two mules' burden of earth" so that at home he might worship the Lord on Israelite soil. (15-19a)

Victory. The God of Israel was the ruler of all nations. The enemy of Syria whom Naaman defeated probably were the Assyrians. For prescriptions in Israel regarding leprosy see Lv 13:2 note.

5:2 *Little maid.* Taken captive on some Syrian raid in Israel, the slave girl became a foreign missionary.

5:6 *You may cure.* Apparently the king of Syria thought that his commander would be cured by a "prophet" (3) who was attached to the court in Samaria.

5:11 *The place.* The diseased area of his body.

5:12 *Abana and Pharpar.* Both rivers rise north and west of Damascus. In Naaman's opinion they were *better* than the Jordan because they watered fertile fields along their banks. The murky waters of the Jordan, rushing in a deeply eroded riverbed to the Dead Sea, had little irrigation value.

5:15 *A present.* The Hebrew word is "blessing"; see Gn 33:11 note.

5:17 *Burden of earth.* Only recently convinced that "there is no God in all the earth but in Israel" (15), Naaman still thought that he needed to worship God on Israelite soil if his offerings were to be acceptable. The notion prevailed in his day that the domain of a god was determined by national borders. For other instances of this view see 1 K 20:23 note; 2 K 17:16; 1 Sm 26:19.

5:18 *Rimmon.* Another name for the Syrian storm god Hadad (1 K 15:18 note). Naaman's request to *bow . . . in the house of Rimmon* has become proverbial for compromising principle under stress of circumstances. Instead of upbraiding the new convert Elisha dismissed him "in peace." However, of the Israelites, fully indoctrinated by God, Elijah demanded that they stop "limping with two different opinions" (1 K 18:21). Cf. the unequivocal commitment required by Jesus. (Lk 11:23; 16:13)

5:22 *Ephraim.* Such centers of *the sons of the prophets* as Gilgal and Bethel were situated in Ephraim north of Jerusalem. (2:1-3)

5:24 *The hill.* The Hebrew word, transliterated "Ophel" in 2 Ch 27:3; 33:14, is not the usual common noun for hill. Except in this instance it is used exclusively of the Jerusalem temple hill. The definite article indicates that in this case too a well-known Samaritan elevation is meant.

5:25 *Nowhere.* As in the case of Joseph's brothers, lies beget lies in an attempt to cover up fraud. However, dishonesty is only one of the noxious growths that spring from the love of money, "the root of all evils." (Gn 37:31 f.; 1 Ti 6:10)

5:27 *A leper.* According to 8:1-6 Gehazi was not isolated from people. No doubt his intercession for the widow of Shunem, the event recorded there, took place some time before the healing of Naaman. For the sequence of Elisha's miracles see 4:1 note. "The king of Syria" (1) and "the king of Israel" (5) are not identified by name.

6) 6:1-7 Recovery of Sunken Ax

6:1 *Too small.* By divine help Elisha brought relief also in minor emergencies. He recovered a borrowed ax which one of the sons of the prophets under his *charge* had dropped into the Jordan. The accident occurred while his proteges were cutting logs for a larger dwelling. It appears that this prophetic center was at Jericho, from where it was not far to the "jungle of the Jordan." (2:6-8; Jer 12:5)

7) 6:8-23 Syrian Army Captured

6:8 *Was warring.* Elisha miraculously foiled two Syrian attacks on Israel (6:8-23; 6:24—7:20). At some unspecified time when an unnamed king of Syria invaded Israel, the prophet disclosed the foreigner's secret plans to "the king of Israel," likewise unidentified (8-10). Told by "one of his servants" who and where the culprit was, the king of Syria sent a large detachment of his troops to surround the city of Dothan (11-14). "In accordance with the prayer of Elisha," the Lord struck the attackers with blindness, enabling the prophet to lead the helpless victims into the heart of Samaria (15-19). Here "the Lord opened their eyes" to their predicament. However, the king of Israel, who would have been able to "slay them," set them free. (20-23)

6:10 *To the place.* An Israelite reconnaissance party verified the truth of Elisha's disclosures. The information which he furnished was so accurate that the Syrian king was convinced that there was a traitor among his "servants." (11)

6:13 *Dothan.* The invaders encountered no opposition when they moved some 20 miles westward of the Jordan to this city. Controlling a pass through "the mountain" (17) of the Carmel Ridge, Dothan lay on the road from

Syria to Egypt on which the Ishmaelites took Joseph to the land of the pharaohs. (Gn 37:17)

6:17 *Horses and chariots of fire.* Normally unseen by human eyes, "the angel of the Lord encamps around those who fear him, and delivers them" (Ps 34:7). No matter how invincible the forces of evil may appear, they never are a match for the heavenly hosts at God's command. (Mt 26:53; Ro 8:31)

6:19 *To Samaria.* A distance of about 10 miles almost directly south of Dothan.

6:23 *No more.* The very next verses, which record a siege of Samaria by the Syrians, seem to contradict this statement. However, the miracles are not arranged in chronological sequence. *No more* may also be a relative term meaning that the Syrians did not raid Israelite territory as long as a conciliatory spirit lasted.

8) 6:24—7:20 Deliverance of Samaria

6:24 *Besieged Samaria. When the entire army* of Ben-hadad (1 K 15:18 note) laid siege to Israel's capital, its inhabitants resorted to cannibalism to keep from starving. For some reason "the king of Israel" held Elisha responsible for the sad state of affairs, vowing to have his head (24-31). However, he did not carry out the threat when the prophet announced "the word of the Lord" which promised that within a day the food supply in the city would be more than ample (6:32—7:2). Quite unexpectedly relief came from the enemy who was causing the famine. Panic-stricken by the Lord, the Syrians fled so hurriedly that they left all their provisions and possessions in the camp, where four desperate lepers discovered them (7:3-8). After the latter "ate and drank" their fill, they reported the bonanza to the gatekeepers in order to share it with the famished people in the city. The king assured himself that the hasty retreat of the enemy was not a trap. But his scouts found "all the way" to the Jordan "littered with garments and equipment which the Syrians had thrown away in their haste" (7:9-15).The people brought so much booty from the abandoned camp into the city that the price of food plummeted to the level predicted by Elisha. At the same time another prophetic word came true. The king's skeptic captain did not live to see the happy turn of events. In their mad rush to get the food, "the people trod upon him in the gate and he died," as Elisha had predicted. (7:16-20)

6:25 *Ass's head.* Normally scorned as food, it sold at highly inflated prices. Another such commodity was *dove's dung.* It is true that in some sieges the people were driven to seek nourishment from various kinds of excrement. However, *dove's dung* may be the name of a plant which ordinarily was not eaten. In any event the famished people were glad to pay huge sums of money for just a small quantity of it. A *kab* was the equivalent of about 2 pints.

6:29 *Boiled my son.* During the final siege of Jerusalem by the Babylonians "compassionate women . . . boiled their own children" (Lm 4:10; 2:20). For the threat of such dreadful punishment see Lv 26:29; Dt 28:53.

6:31 *More also.* For this oath formula see Ru 1:17 note.

6:33 *The king came.* This very compressed sentence should read: "the messenger came down and [the king who came down immediately behind him] said," etc. The king was not willing to wait any longer for God's intervention, which Elisha apparently had promised.

7:1 *At the gate.* Where business was transacted.

7:2 *Windows.* Coming through the *windows of heaven* (Gn 7:11; 8:2), rain would raise crops and eventually supply food. But the captain doubted that more immediate relief from the famine could be forthcoming.

7:3 *At the entrance.* Excluded from the city, as required in Lv 13:45 f.

7:6 *Come upon us.* If the Hittites came upon them from the north and the Egyptians from the south, the Syrians could be ground to pieces like grain between the upper and the lower millstone. However, the Hebrew word for Egypt is similar to a term which in Assyrian records designates a territory bordering on the land of the Hittites. If the kings from this area are meant, the Syrians fled because they were hopelessly outnumbered by *a great army* of confederates.

7:9 *Not doing right.* To let the people in the city die of starvation when food in abundance was available was a crime for which *punishment* from the king or from God would *overtake* them. Failure to share material or spiritual blessings with others is no less reprehensible today. (Heb 13:16)

7:13 *Will fare.* If the scouting party did not risk death at the hands of the Syrians, they would die of starvation in the city *like the whole multitude of Israel.*

7:14 *Two mounted men.* Literally "two chariot[s] of horses." The number of men assigned to the chariots is not specified.

7:16 *Fine meal.* One word in Hebrew. Ground wheat flour was more expensive than barley.

8:1-6 SHUNAMMITE WOMAN'S PROPERTY RESTORED

8:1 *Elisha had said.* Not an account of another miracle, the next verses (1-6) record what happened as the result of one of "the great things that Elisha" did. When the king saw the son of the Shunammite woman "whom Elisha restored to life" (4:8-37), he granted her request for the restitution of her property. The *famine* during which she went to Philistia for 7 years may have been the same mentioned in 4:38.

8:2 *Philistines.* In their territory Isaac sought survival during a famine in his day. (Gn 26:1)

8:3 *Appeal.* During her long absence, *her house and her land* evidently had been declared forfeit to the king.

8:4 *Gehazi.* This incident took place before he became a leper (5:27). Through him Elisha now spoke on her behalf, as he had offered to do. (4:13)

8:6 *Produce.* The income which accrued from her property.

8:7-15 ELISHA'S INTERVENTION IN SYRIAN AFFAIRS

8:7 *To Damascus.* In the Syrian capital Elisha carried out the task assigned to Elijah: "anoint Hazael to be king over Syria" (1 K 19:15). Acting in accord with divine revelation (9), "the man of God" gave impetus to a revolt against Ben-hadad so that "Hazael became king in his stead."

8:8 *This sickness.* No doubt the king knew that Naaman owed his recovery to *the Lord,* Elisha's God.

8:10 *Recover.* Elisha gave a cryptic answer. The king would recover from his present illness but would nevertheless *certainly die,* namely from another cause.

8:11 *Fixed his gaze.* Elisha's prolonged prophetic gaze proved disconcerting to Hazael.

8:12 *Weep.* Elisha carried out his mission regardless of his personal feelings in the matter. For *the evil* that he foresaw see 10:32 f.; 13:3; 15:16; Hos 13:16; Am 1:3 f.

8:13 *A dog.* Hazael registered surprise that a person of his low status should rise to royal heights. For reference to *a dog* to express contempt see 1 Sm 17:43; 24:14.

8:15 *He took.* Very likely the antecedent of the pronoun is Hazael.

8:16-24 Jehoram of Judah

8:16 *Joram.* In this period the divided kingdom had rulers with the same name. In Israel King Ahaziah had a Jehoram as successor; in Judah the sequence was the reverse: a Jehoram was followed by an Ahaziah. The shortened form *Joram* occurs for the rulers in both kingdoms. The history of the Israelite Jehoram, begun in ch. 3, was interrupted by a lengthy report of Elisha's activities (4:1—8:15). However, before resuming the account of this northern king, the author inserted brief notices of two Judean rulers: Jehoram (16-24) and Ahaziah (25-29). The latter is introduced at this point because the next chapter relates how he and his northern contemporary, Jehoram, came to be killed in a revolt led by the Israelite general Jehu.

8:19 *Lamp.* Cf. 1 K 11:36 note.

8:20 *Revolted.* Earlier Edom was ruled by a Judean deputy (1 K 22:47). "Zair" very likely was a town on the border between Edom and Judah.

8:22 *Libnah.* Joram lost control also of a city on the edge of Philistine territory some 15 miles southwest of Jerusalem where Sennacherib's army was encamped at a later time. (19:8)

8:25-29 Ahaziah of Judah

8:25 *Ahaziah.* His association with the Israelite king (9:16) explains the circumstances of his death, which is reported later.

9:1—17:41 DIVIDED KINGDOM: RENEWED HOSTILITIES TO FALL OF ISRAEL

9:1—10:36 Jehu of Israel

9:1-13 ACCESSION TO THE THRONE

9:1 *Ramoth-gilead.* Jehoram of Israel was fighting against Hazael, king of Syria, where Ahab had opposed Ben-hadad (1 K 22:2 note). While the battle was in progress, Elisha sent "one of the sons of the prophets" to carry out the second task assigned to Elijah: to anoint Jehu "to be king over Israel" (1 K 19:16; 2 K 8:7 note; 9:1-3). "The young man" performed the ceremony privately (4-10). However, Jehu's military associates were suspicious, insisting on knowing the mission of the strange messenger. When they found out what it was, they enthusiastically "proclaimed: 'Jehu is king'" (11-13). His accession to the throne marked the end of the brief period of cooperation between the two kingdoms. (1 K 16:22 note)

Much blood was to flow before the coup d'etat had eliminated all possible sources of opposition. By Jehu's own hand or on his orders the following lost their lives: (1) the king of Israel, Jehoram (14:26); (2) the king of Judah, Ahaziah, who was visiting his brother-in-law Jehoram (27-29); (3) Jezebel, queen mother of Israel (30-37); (4) "seventy sons" of Ahab, Jehoram's father (10:1-11); (5) visiting princes of Judah (10:12-14); (6) Ahab's remaining descendants (10:15-17); (7) a temple full of Baal worshipers. (10:18-27)

9:7 *Jezebel.* Cf. 1 K 16:30 note; 18:4, 13; 19:10.

9:8 *House of Ahab.* Wicked Ahab's like-minded descendants were to *perish* just as previous dynasties had been *cut off.* Jeroboam, Israel's first king, had only one successor (1 K 14:10; 15:29); Baasha, the third king, had none. (1 K 16:3 f.)

9:11 *Mad fellow.* When in the state of ecstasy, prophets appeared to act like lunatics. On this kind of prophesying see 1 Sm 10:6 note. In order to put off his curious fellow officers, Jehu referred to *the fellow and his talk* in a derogatory way.

9:13 *Bare steps.* Literally "the bone of the steps." The phrase suggests that the soldiers put their clothes on the stones much as flesh covers the bare skeleton of the body. When Jesus entered Jerusalem riding on a mule, as Solomon did at his coronation, the people spread their garments before Him, acclaiming "the Son of David" as their king. (1 K 1:32-34; Mt 21:8 f)

9:14—10:17 END OF PREVIOUS REGIMES

9:14 *Against J[eh]oram.* Trusting that the army was of a "mind" to support him, Jehu at once drove some 45 miles west to Jezreel, where King Joram was recuperating from wounds sustained at Ramoth-gilead (14-16). In order to keep his mission secret, he forced the horsemen, sent out from the city to meet him, to "ride behind him." As he drew nearer, the watchman recognized him by his furious driving (17-21).

Apparently not suspecting his commander of unfriendly intent, the king himself rode out. Jehu pierced his heart with an arrow. "In accordance with the word of the Lord" (1 K 21:19) his corpse was thrown on the plot of ground stolen from its former owner Naboth.

9:20 *Furiously.* Literally "with madness." Jehu's fast and furious driving has become proverbial.

9:22 *Harlotries.* By her Baal worship Jezebel "played the harlot after other gods." Biblical writers and Jesus do not mince words in describing unfaithfulness to God. (Ju 2:17; Lv 19:29; Jer 3:2; Hos 2:2 f; Mt 12:39; 16:4)

9:25 *Behind Ahab.* In his retinue.

9:27 *Ahaziah . . . fled.* Warned by his brother-in-law's cry of "Treachery!" (23), the king of Judah escaped southward *in the direction of Beth haggan,* some 7 miles below Jezreel. A little farther south, near *Ibleam* and at an unknown *ascent of Gur,* Jehu's men wounded him. From there he backtracked some 10 miles northwestward to Megiddo. According to 2 Ch 22:9 the fugitive did not die until he made his way back to Samaria, where Jehu killed him. In 27 the Hebrew omits *and they shot him* (RSV note), an indication that in its transmission the text at this point has suffered some kind of dislocation or mutilation.

9:29 *Eleventh year.* A postscript, repeating in part the summary of Ahaziah's reign given in 8:25, according to which his accession occurred in the 12th year. For the different bases of computing the years see Introduction, "Chronology."

9:30 *Painted her eyes.* Eye shadow and other cosmetics were not unknown to women in the ancient world. Groomed in her queenly finery as if she were about to hold court, Jezebel faced her executioners with iron nerve.

9:31 *Zimri.* More than 50 years ago he assassinated Baasha, the third king of Israel (1 K 16:8 ff.). In our country Benedict Arnold has become proverbial for a traitor.

9:34 *A king's daughter.* Her father was the king of Sidon. (1 K 16:31)

9:36 *Word of the Lord.* Cf. 1 K 21:23.

10:1 *Seventy sons.* Challenged by Jehu to oppose him, the guardians of Ahab's 70 sons or grandsons realized that resistance to the conspiracy was useless. To prove that they had transferred their loyalty to the new dynasty, they agreed to send the severed heads of the former king's offspring to Jehu.

10:4 *Two kings.* Jehoram, Ahab's son, and Ahaziah, king of Judah.

10:9 *Struck down.* Pretending to be surprised by the grisly heap of heads, Jehu pointed out to the turncoats that by their execution of "the house of Ahab" they now were irrevocably committed to his cause.

10:10 *Word of the Lord.* Cf. 9:8.

10:13 *Kinsmen.* The next victims of the purge were 42 Judean princes related to King Ahaziah, whose father had married Athaliah, sister of the slain Israelite king Jehoram (8:18, 26). Jehu met them "at Beth-eked," literally "the house of binding," so named because shepherds bound their sheep there at shearing time.

10:14 *Slew them.* As Jehu proceeded to establish himself on the throne, his wholesale executions went beyond the directive of "the word of the Lord." Carried away by personal ambition rather than motivated by "zeal for the Lord," God's appointed avenger of the house of Ahab (9:8) went so far as to provoke the Lord to say: "I will punish the house of Jehu for the blood of Jezreel" (Hos 1:4). The end never justifies the means.

10:15 *Jehonadab.* The descendants of *Rechab,* a Kenite like Moses' father-in-law Jethro (1 Ch 2:55; Ju 1:16 note), were extreme in their opposition to the fertility cult of baalism. They opposed agricultural pursuits, particularly the growing of vineyards (Jer 35:6-10), believing that a return to a bedouin kind of life was Israel's salvation. Jehonadab believed Jehu's revolt was a step in the right direction.

10:18-27 MASSACRE OF BAAL WORSHIPERS

10:18 *Serve him much.* Jehu's treacherous "cunning" in luring the Baal worshipers to their death richly deserved the Lord's rebuke. (Hos 1:4)

10:22 *Vestments.* They identified his victims.

10:24 *Offer sacrifices.* In order to allay all suspicion, Jehu pretended to join in the worship of Baal.

10:28-31 APPRAISAL OF JEHU'S REIGN

10:29 *Did not turn aside.* Jehu does not receive a wholehearted endorsement (28-31). He retained *the golden calves* besides being guilty of excesses in overcoming opposition to his regime. However, the Lord commended him for overthrowing Ahab's idolatrous house.

10:30 *Fourth generation.* The next four kings of Israel were his descendants: Jehoahaz, J[eh]oash, Jeroboam II, Zechariah.

10:32-36 LOSS OF TERRITORY; JEHU'S DEATH

10:32 *Cut off.* Zeal for the Lord did not automatically guarantee outward success. During Jehu's reign the Syrians overran Israelite territory "from the Jordan eastward" and extending southward as far as "Aroer" near "the Arnon," a river which empties into the Dead Sea almost midway between its northern tip and its southern extremity. (Cf. 8:12)

11:1-21 Athaliah, Queen in Judah

11:1-3 PURGE OF ROYAL FAMILY; JOASH'S ESCAPE

11:1 *Athaliah.* Jehu's seizure of the Israelite throne had repercussions in Judah. Here Ahab's daughter Athaliah, the mother of Ahaziah, slain by Jehu (9:27 f.), made herself sole ruler. She almost succeeded in eliminating all possible contenders for the throne, including her own grandchildren. However, Ahaziah's infant son escaped the purge because his aunt Jehosheba hid him (1-3). Six years later Athaliah lost her life in a counterrevolution, masterminded by the priest Jehoiada, husband of the young prince's guardian. Assured of popular support and of cooperation by the temple guards (4-8), "he brought out the king's son, and put the crown upon him" (9-12). When the queen intruded on the coronation scene, "she was slain" (13-16). At the high priest's prompting the new king solemnly pledged to abolish the religious and political abuses which the preceding pro-Ahab regimes had introduced. "All the people of the land" were in accord with the reform program. They demolished the altars of Baal; "they slew Mattan the priest of Baal before the altars." (17-20)

11:4-21 COUNTERREVOLUTION LED BY HIGH PRIEST

11:4 *Carites.* The name suggests that Athaliah's bodyguard was recruited in Caria in Asia Minor. The Hebrew consonants composing the words Carites and Cherethites are very similar. For the latter see 1 Sm 30:14 note; 2 Sm 8:18 note.

11:5 *Off duty.* Not every detail of the plot is clear. However, it seems that Jehoiada planned to have on hand a double detachment of Levites (2 Ch 23:8) and of temple guards. On a certain sabbath day the groups going off duty were to remain to reinforce the contingents coming on duty. By deploying "the two divisions" at strategic places, he isolated the surprised queen from her supporters. He was also able to surround the king with a sufficiently strong bodyguard.

11:6 *Gate Sur.* Its location as well as that of *the gate behind the guards* can no longer be established.

11:12 *The testimony.* A copy of the Law, called "the testimony" in Ex 25:16. The crown and the Law were the insignia of the royal office. (Dt 17:18-20; 1 Sm 10:25; 1 K 2:3)

11:13 *She went.* Without a trace of fear Athaliah faced the crisis as defiantly as her mother Jezebel greeted her executioners. (9:30 ff.)

11:14 *By the pillar.* The place customarily reserved for the king, perhaps on a dais. (23:3)

11:17 *Covenant.* They solemnly pledged to observe the provisions by which God had agreed to constitute Israel as His "own possession among all peoples." (Ex 19:5 note; 2 Sm 5:3)

11:18 *Mattan. The priest of Baal* whom Athaliah had imported from Israel for the promotion of the Phoenician idol worship, which her mother had introduced from her homeland. (1 K 16:31-33)

11:20 *The people of the land.* This recurring expression (vv. 13, 18) seems to refer to a particular segment of the population, very likely the land-owning citizens. Because the revolt had popular support, *the city was quiet* as soon as the power of foreign domination was broken. There was no wholesale bloodshed such as Jehu instituted in the north (chs. 9—10). For other instances when the people of the land played a role see 21:24; 23:30, 35; 25:19.

12:1-21 Jehoash of Judah

12:1 *Forty years.* A boy king of 7 years when he began to reign, J[eh]oash was only 47 when "his servants . . . struck him down" (21). Until the death of Jehoiada the priest, who "instructed him" also after his childhood and youth, the king "did what was right" (2 Ch 24:17 f.). The repair of the temple building, completed at his insistence, exemplifies Jehoash's zeal for the worship of the true God. He had the regular religious taxes and freewill offerings diverted into a special building fund. After 23 years there was no money in that treasury because the priests did not budget the temple income as ordered. More drastic measures were necessary (4-8). From henceforth the priests were to handle only the contributions for their livelihood: "the money from the guilt offerings and . . . the sin offerings." All other "money that was brought into the house of the Lord" was to be put into "a chest" by the donors. This collection system produced the funds to make all necessary repairs. (9-16)

12:2 *All his days, because.* Better translated: "wherein [as long as] Jehoiada . . . instructed him." (So KJV; see 2 Ch 24:2, 17 f.)

12:3 *High places.* Reforms by other kings were likewise only partly successful. (1 K 15:14; 2 K 14:4)

12:4 *Money of the holy things.* A general term for all money set aside for sacred purposes. Among these contributions were the required temple tax and the freewill contributions. (For the religious poll tax see Ex 30:11-16; for regulations regarding voluntary offerings see Ex 35:5; Lv 27:1-8)

12:5 *His acquaintance.* The priests were to collect funds from those laymen with whom they were personally acquainted. According to 2 Ch 24:5 there was a solicitation among "all Israel." If the term *acquaintance,* which occurs only here and in v. 7, refers to a fellow officiant in the temple, the priests were to ask also their associates to contribute to the fund.

12:9 *A chest.* In Jesus' time there was a receptacle in the temple for special contributions called "the treasury" (Mt 27:6). Jehoiada placed the chest *beside the altar* of burnt offering which stood in a courtyard outside the temple proper. (2 Ch 24:8)

12:13 *Not made.* At first all collected money was necessary to make structural repairs. After these were completed, funds continued to come in with which "were made utensils for the house of the Lord." (2 Ch 24:14)

12:16 *Guilt offerings and . . . sin offerings.* For directives concerning these offerings see Lv 4:3; 5:15 notes; Nm 18:8 note.

12:17 *Gath.* In reaching this Philistine city, some 25 miles southwest of Jerusalem, the Syrian king had swept down from the north "throughout the territory of Israel." (10:32)

12:18 *Votive gifts.* Pious king Asa had to resort to the same humiliating expedient. (1 K 15:18)

12:20 *Slew Joash.* A fuller account of the

conspiracy and the assassination is given in 2 Ch 24:20-26.—For *the house of Millo* (Hebrew: "Beth-millo") see Ju 9:6, 20; 2 Sm 5:9 note; 1 K 9:15.—The location of *Silla* remains unknown.

13:1-9 Jehoahaz of Israel

13:1 *Reign over Israel.* Before taking up the reign of Amaziah, the next king of Judah (12:21; ch. 14), the author turns to two contemporary rulers in the northern kingdom: Jehoahaz (1-9) and J[eh]oash (10-25). The first of these followed in the footsteps of Jeroboam (1 K 12:26-33), thus incurring "the anger of the Lord," who "gave them continually into the hand of" Syrian kings. (3)

13:5 *A savior.* Israel was saved from oppression by the Syrians because they had to defend their eastern borders against inroads by the Assyrians. This relief from Syrian pressure was evident particularly under the next two Israelite kings: Jehoash (25) and Jeroboam II. (14:27)

13:7 *Ten chariots.* Israel's military strength had all but vanished. According to Assyrian records, Ahab had once been able to field a cavalry contingent of 2,000 chariots.

13:10-25 Jehoash of Israel

13:10 *Joash . . . Jehoash.* The king of Judah (12:1-21) and the king of Israel had the same name: *Jehoash.* Both are known also by the shorter form *Joash* (12:19). After providing a brief summary of the rule of Jehoash of Israel (1-3; cf. 14:15), the author records three events which took place during this king's reign: (1) a symbolic action by Elisha, promising victory over Syria (14-19); (2) revival of a corpse thrown into Elisha's grave (20 f.); (3) recovery of cities taken from Israel by the Syrians. (22-25)

13:12 *Against Amaziah.* The next chapter reports what happened in the battle between the two kings. (14:8-14)

13:14 *Fallen sick.* Some 50 years had passed since Elisha had helped put Jehu on the throne (9:1-13). Now old and stricken with a fatal illness, he had one more message to deliver. He directed Joash to shoot an arrow "eastward." The flight of the arrow in the direction of Syrian-held Transjordan and of Syria itself symbolized that Israel was going to be able to break out of domination by this inveterate foe. However, the number of Israel's victories was reduced when the king struck the ground with his arrow only three times instead of oftener. (14-19)

13:16 *Upon the king's hands.* This gesture symbolized that the arrow became "the Lord's arrow of victory" because divine power was transmitted to the king. (For other symbolic acts see Jos 8:18 note; 1 K 22:11 note; Jer 19:10 f.)

13:17 *Aphek.* Various sites bore the name which in Hebrew means "fortress" (1 K 20:26 note). This *Aphek* probably was located east of the Sea of Galilee.

13:22 *Oppressed.* Better translated: "had oppressed." The servile condition of Israel under Joash's predecessor is recalled in connection with the liberation effected according to the promise given in v. 19.

13:24 *Ben-hadad.* Cf. 1 K 15:18 note; 20:1 note.

14:1-22 Amaziah of Judah

14:1 *Son of Joash.* This chapter resumes the history of the southern kingdom which had ended in 12:21 with the note that Amaziah succeeded his assassinated father Joash. Exemption of the children of the latter's murderers from punishment is cited as an example of the new king's desire to do what was right. In his war with Edom he demonstrated his ability to lead Judah's forces to victory (1-7). But he overestimated his prowess when he issued a foolhardy challenge to the king of Israel, who crushed him as a wild beast tramples down a thistle (8-14). Apparently this disastrous defeat so enraged his subjects that "they made a conspiracy against him" and "slew him." (15-22)

14:6 *Law of Moses.* See Dt 24:16; also Eze 18:4, 20.

14:7 *Edomites.* They had "revolted from the rule of Judah" some 50 years ago during the time of Jehoram of Judah (8:20-22). By defeating them Amaziah opened the trade routes south to "Elath" on the Gulf of Aqaba (22; for Solomon's use of this port see 1 K 9:26-28). *The Valley of Salt* was a marshy region south of the Dead Sea. *Sela,* meaning "rock," was later known by the Greek name "Petra." *Joktheel,* probably meaning "vanquished by God," remains in use as its name to *this day,* i.e., the time when the record of the Edomite campaign was written which the author of Kings is citing.

14:8 *In the face.* A challenge to meet in face-to-face combat.

14:9 *A thistle.* A similar fable was told by Jothan. (Ju 9:8-15)

14:11 *Beth-shemesh.* Located about 15 miles west of Jerusalem.

14:13 *Ephraim Gate.* A gate on the north side of the city opening on a road to Ephraim. The *Corner Gate* was at the northwestern corner of the city's wall.

14:19 *Lachish.* About 35 miles southwest of Jerusalem.

14:23-29 Jeroboam II of Israel

14:21 *Azariah.* Even though Amaziah and his father were victims of assassination, the Davidic dynasty continued. In the northern kingdom regicides established new ruling houses.

14:25 *Restored the border.* The author devotes only seven verses (23-29) to the long and politically noteworthy reign of Jeroboam II (see Introduction, "Prophetic History"). During his reign both Syria and Assyria were too weak to prevent the extension of his domain as far north as *the entrance of Hamath* (1 K 8:65 note) and as far south as *the Sea of the Arabah,* i.e., the Dead Sea. The prosperity that followed this expansion brought moral degeneracy, social evils, and religious corruption and in turn called forth vehement denunciations and dire threats of punishment by the prophets Amos (e.g., Am 2:6-8) and Hosea. (E.g., Hos 4:1 f.)

14:25 *Jonah.* The international situation which made possible Jeroboam's rise to power was not an accident of history. The Lord of the nations made it known in advance through the same prophet whom He chose to bring a message of repentance to the Assyrians (Jon 1:1).—*Gath-hepher* was an Israelite town a little north of Nazareth.

15:1-7 Azariah (Uzziah) of Judah

15:1 *Azariah.* The long reign of the next king of Judah (52 years), also called Uzziah (13, 30, 34), is allotted no more space than his contemporary Jeroboam in Israel received (14:23-29). In his case too there is no record of his political and military activity even though he extended the borders of Judah so that the territory of the two kingdoms at this time approximated the size of David's empire. (14:22; 2 Ch 26:6-15)

15:5 *A leper.* The account in 2 Ch 26:16 ff. states that *the Lord smote* him with this disease because he usurped the priestly function of offering incense in the temple.

15:8-12 Zechariah of Israel

15:8 *In Samaria.* The next 25 verses (8-31) cover 22 years of Israelite history. During these turbulent two decades, following the vigorous reign of Jeroboam II, no less than five kings laid claim to the throne. One maintained himself only a month; three were assassinated; only one succeeded his father.

15:10 *Struck him down.* Zechariah was the last descendant of Jehu, fulfilling the word of the Lord that the latter's sons were to sit on the throne of Israel to "the fourth generation" (13; 10:30). For *Ibleam* see 9:27 note.

15:13-16 Shallum of Israel

15:13 *One month.* Shallum, Zechariah's assassin, was struck down by another conspirator, Menahem, who put down all resistance with the most barbarous atrocities. (16; Hos 13:16; Am 1:13)

15:16 *Tappuah.* Allotted to Ephraim (Jos 17:8), this city was located some 15 miles south of *Tirzah,* for which see 1 K 14:17 note.

15:17-22 Menahem of Israel

15:19 *Pul.* The Assyrian king Tiglath-pileser (29), known in Babylon as Pul, reigned 745—728 B.C. With his help Menahem was able *to confirm his hold of the royal power,* ending the bloody rivalry for the throne. Six years after Pul's death the Assyrian army was to capture Samaria and crush Israel's independence.

15:20 *Fifty shekels.* In order to make up the required sum of "a thousand talents of silver," more than 50,000 *wealthy men* had to contribute the equivalent of about 30 dollars. But this general prosperity was soon to end.

15:23-26 Pekahiah of Israel

15:23 *Two years.* Conspiracies and infighting continued in the northern kingdom. After occupying the throne for only 2 years, Pekahiah lost his life in another military coup. Pekah, "his captain," who conspired against him, in turn was struck down by Hoshea (30), the last of the Israelite kings.

15:25 *Citadel.* In this part *of the king's house* Zimri, an earlier contender for the throne, also died a violent death. (1 K 16:18)

15:27-31 Pekah of Israel

15:27 *Twenty years.* The chronology of this period presents particularly serious problems. A suggested way to synchronize the two kingdoms is to assume that the data involved several scribal errors, all of which involve the raising of figures by 10s. It is assumed that the original text read 10 instead of 20 in this verse; 7 instead of 17 and 6 instead of 16 in 16:1-2; 5 instead of 25 in 18:2.

15:29 *Captured.* Pekah and his Syrian ally Rezin, whose land formed a buffer state between Israel and Assyria, tried to put a stop to Tiglath-pileser's conquests by forcing Judah into an alliance against their common enemy. In spite of this maneuver, briefly noted in 37 and further explained in 16:5 ff., Tiglath-pileser overran Israelite cities and territories on both sides of the Jordan. Only Samaria and the adjacent area retained some semblance of independence under the next Israelite king, Hoshea, who, however, ruled only by the grace of his Assyrian overlord (17:3). The deportation of inhabitants from invaded territories, initiated by Tiglath-pileser, was designed to break resistance to the conqueror.

15:32-38 Jotham of Judah

15:32 *Jotham.* Before continuing the story of Hoshea and the end of Israel (ch. 17), the author resumes the account of the kings of Judah where he left it at the beginning of the chapter (1-7). Jotham, the first of these, receives the same kind of short notice that is accorded all kings mentioned in this chapter. (32-38)

15:35 *Built.* The *gate* which he repaired may be the one mentioned in 11:19 or in Jer 20:2.

15:37 *Began to send.* Pressure on Judah by this northern coalition began to build up during Jotham's reign; its full thrust came in the days of his son Ahaz. (16:5 ff.)

16:1-20 Ahaz of Judah

16:2 *Kings of Israel.* The record leaves no doubt that Ahaz rivaled the northern kings in wickedness. He engaged not only in all "the abominable practices" of Canaanite Baal worship (1-4) but, after receiving aid from Tiglath-pileser in his struggle against the kings of Israel and Syria (5-9), he also had an Assyrian altar erected in the Jerusalem temple. (10-18)

16:3 *Burned his son.* Literally "made his son

pass through the fire," i.e., as an offering to the idol (RSV note). In the parallel account (2 Ch 28:3) the Hebrew verb "to burn" is used; so also in the account of human sacrifice by the king of Edom (17:31). Ahaz's grandson Manasseh likewise "made his son pass through the fire" (21:6). Moses warned the Israelites not to adopt the practice of the Canaanites who "burn their sons and their daughters in the fire to their gods." (Dt 12:31; cf. Jer 7:31; 19:4 f.; Eze 16:20; 20:31)

16:5 *Wage war.* See 15:29 for the reason of this so-called Syro-Ephraimitic war, which also was the occasion for the Immanuel prophecy. (Is 7)

16:6 *Edom.* So the Septuagint instead of Syria. The Hebrew words for Edom and Aram (Syria), which originally were not supplied with vowels, are composed of consonants which are very similar. For another possible confusion in the text see 3:26 note. Earlier, Uzziah had defeated the Edomites; Elath, the southern port city, had been occupied by Amaziah. (14:7 note, 22)

6:10 *Damascus.* Syria and its capital Damascus lay athwart the conqueror's path into Palestine. Tiglath-pileser therefore "marched up against Damascus and took it" before he overran Israel (15:29 note). He carried the Syrians captive to "Kir," probably a city on the Euphrates where they had sojourned before they migrated farther north and east (Am 9:7). Ten years later Israel's capital Samaria was to suffer the same fate at the hands of the Assyrians.

Model of the altar. Ahaz manifested abject submission to Tiglath-pileser by giving the worship of the Assyrian idol a place in the Jerusalem temple. "The bronze altar," made by Solomon (1 K 8:64), even lost its place of prominence to the replica of "the great altar" of the Assyrian god Asshur, whose worship the conqueror already had established in the former Syrian capital. (14 f.)

16:15 *Inquire by.* Perhaps the apostate king went so far in desecrating the bronze altar as to use it for examining the entrails of sacrificial animals for good or bad omens, a mode of divination used also by the king of Babylon. (Eze 21:21)

16:18 *He removed.* It is not clear why these structural changes were made in the temple "because of the king of Assyria," i.e., in deference to him.

17:1-41 Hoshea; End of Israel

17:1-23 FALL OF SAMARIA

17:1 *Nine years.* The end of Hoshea's short reign also marked the fall of Samaria and the dissolution of the northern kingdom. The brief description of the events leading up to this catastrophe (1-6) is followed by a longer review of the reason why this calamity befell Israel. From the time God brought up the chosen people from Egypt they "despised his statutes and his covenant," "provoking him to anger." The Lord was very patient with His apostate children. "But they would not listen" when again and again He called them to repentance. Finally their measure of iniquity was full. "Very angry with Israel," He "removed them out of his sight," as He had spoken by all His "servants the prophets." (7-23)

17:3 *Shalmaneser.* According to Assyrian records, Hoshea's conspiracy against Pekah succeeded because he accepted support from Tiglath-pileser (15:29 f.). When the latter's son Shalmaneser came to the throne, the Israelite puppet king did not remain a tribute-paying vassal very long. Misled by a promise of help from Egypt which never came, he threw off the Assyrian yoke. Shalmaneser lost no time in putting down the insurrection. Ignoring Hoshea's belated protestations of loyalty, he "shut him up . . . in prison," captured Samaria after a siege of 3 years, and "carried the Israelites away to Assyria."

17:4 *So.* The king referred to cannot be equated with certainty with a Pharaoh known by that name from Egyptian records. If *So* represents a transliterated Egyptian common noun meaning vizier, the sentence would read: "he had sent messengers to the vizier of the king of Egypt."

17:6 *King of Assyria.* In his annals Shalmaneser's successor Sargon (722—705 B.C.) takes credit for destroying Samaria. He claims to have taken 27,280 captives into exile, no doubt the upper social stratum. They were settled in *Halah,* an unidentifiable site; in *Gozan,* a city on the *Habor* river, which empties into the middle Euphrates; in *the cities of the Medes* south of the Caspian Sea. Here the so-called "Lost Tribes" lost their national identity. Most of them were integrated with the population of their new homes.

17:7 *This was so.* The disappearance of the Northern Kingdom and later the fall of Jerusalem (19 f.) were the result of God's direction of world history. Proud, cruel Assyria, unaware that it served His purpose, was His instrument, the rod of His anger on a people who did not keep His covenant. (Is 10:5 ff.)

17:10 *Asherim.* Cf. Gn 28:18 note; 1 K 14:23 f.

17:16 *Host of heaven.* Astral deities, worship of which was forbidden Dt 4:19 note; 17:3.

17:22 *Sins which Jeroboam did.* Cf. 1 K 14:16 note.

17:23 *Until this day.* The time when the record was written on which the author of Kings drew for this account. So also in vv. 34, 41.

17:24:41 FOREIGN SETTLERS IN ISRAELITE CITIES

17:24 *Brought people.* Deportation of the inhabitants and importation of foreigners was designed to break the spirit of nationalism in occupied countries. Intermarriage between the remaining Israelites and the heathen newcomers produced "the Samaritans." (29)

17:26 *God of the land.* Cf. 1 K 20:23 note.

17:29 *Gods of its own.* Even though the repatriated priest taught the immigrants how they should "fear the Lord," they "also served their own gods" whom they had worshiped in their homeland. They came from widely separated places: from "Babylon" south of Assyria to "Hamath" in northern Syria. Their gods too represented a motly assortment, some of whom have not been identified. (30 f.)

17:34 *Fear the Lord.* By their syncretistic religion the new settlers thought "they feared the Lord" (33). In reality it was displeasing to Him as was Israel's agelong failure to have no other gods besides Him. (Ex 20:3)

17:41 *These nations.* After condemning Israel's past unfaithfulness (34b-40), the writer returns briefly to the mixed worship of the Samaritans. By the time of Jesus they no longer "served . . . graven images."

18:1—25:30 LAST KINGS OF JUDAH; BABYLONIAN EXILE

18:1—20:21 Good Reign of Hezekiah

18:1-12 ACCESSION AND SUMMARY OF REIGN

18:1 *Hezekiah.* The fall of the Northern Kingdom occurred in the early part of Hezekiah's reign, the pious son of wicked Ahaz. Six more kings were to occupy the throne of Judah. However, the record of his reign extends over three of the remaining eight chapters (18-20). The first two of these tell at some length what happened when he "rebelled against the king of Assyria," whose vassal he had become after the fall of Samaria.

18:2 *Twenty-five years old.* His father was only 36 years old when he died (16:2). See the suggestion in 15:27 note.

18:4 *Nehushtan.* Hezekiah's reform was more thorough than that of his predecessors. Besides destroying *the pillars* and *the Asherah* (17:10 note), *he removed the high places* which were "not taken away" by such kings as Asa and Jehoshaphat (1 K 15:14; 22:43; see also 2 K 12:3; 14:4; 15:4). He also *broke in pieces the bronze serpent that Moses had made* during a plague in the wilderness but to which the people *burned incense* as if it were an idol, perhaps a symbol of fertility (Nm 21:8 f.). Its name *Nehushtan* is a combination of the Hebrew words for serpent and bronze.

18:7 *Rebelled.* What resulted from his rebellion is told in 18:13—19:37. Actually Jerusalem almost shared Samaria's fate, which is briefly recalled. (9-12)

18:8 *Smote the Philistines.* The events mentioned in the introductory survey of Hezekiah's reign (1-8) are not dated. His campaign against the Philistines may have been an attempt to force the coastal cities to join him in his rebellion against the Assyrians.

18:13—19:37 DELIVERANCE FROM ASSYRIANS

18:13 *Sennacherib.* Sargon, who began to reign in the year that Samaria fell (722 B.C.), was succeeded by Sennacherib in 705 B.C. In his annals he relates how after 4 years he was able to deal with rebellious groups in the west including Hezekiah. *All the fortified cities of Judah* surrendered to the Assyrian, who puts their number at 46. Still safe behind Jerusalem's walls, Hezekiah sent him a huge amount of gold and silver apparently with the understanding that nothing beyond payment of tribute was expected of him (13-18). But Sennacherib demanded more. From his camp in Lachish he dispatched three high officials to Jerusalem who arrogantly and blasphemously demanded the unconditional surrender of the city (19-25). The leader of the delegation harangued the citizens "in a loud voice in the language of Judah." Their only hope of survival, he said, was to rebel against their king and to "come out to" the invincible Assyrian king (28-35). Isaiah the prophet assured terror-stricken Hezekiah (36 f.) that the Lord would not permit the enemy to carry out his threats. (19:1-7)

The Assyrian emissaries reported Hezekiah's resistance to Sennacherib, who in the meantime had moved his headquarters some 10 miles north to Libnah. However, a report that an Egyptian army was advancing against him kept him from marching on Jerusalem. Forced again to rely on diplomacy, he sent his emissaries back to Jerusalem with the same imperious demands (19:8-13). Hezekiah took the letter, brought to him by the Assyrian messengers, and "spread it before the Lord" in a fervent prayer for deliverance (19:14-19). God answered the king through Isaiah, promising that Sennacherib would not even lay siege to Jerusalem, much less take it (19:20-34). The Lord's word did not return void: "the angel of the Lord" slew 185,000 "in the camp of the Assyrians." Sennacherib "departed and went home," where two of his sons assassinated him (19:35-37). For a parallel account of Hezekiah's deliverance see Is 36 f.

Fourteenth year. According to Assyrian records this was the year 701 B.C., which in turn should have been Hezekiah's 28th year, for according to 18:9 f. Samaria's fall (722 B.C.) took place in the sixth year of his reign. Very likely his first 14 years are here reckoned as a period preceding his assuming sole regency.

18:14 *Lachish.* This strongly fortified city, some 35 miles southwest of Jerusalem, guarded the main road from the lowlands up to Judah's capital. Before proceeding to Jerusalem, Sennacherib took time to capture Lachish, not risking to have a center of resistance in his rear.

18:17 *The Tartan.* The article preceding Tartan, Rabsaris, and Rabshakeh indicates that these words are not proper nouns but represent titles of Assyrian officials. A "tartan" was also the commander in chief of Sargon, Sennacherib's predecessor. (Is 20:1)

Conduit of the upper pool. Here, outside the city, Isaiah had tried in vain to persuade Hezekiah's father Ahaz that the Lord was able to avert a threat to Jerusalem (Is 7:3 ff.). A well-known site at the time, it can no longer be identified with certainty. The same holds true of *the Fuller's Field,* a place so called because there clothes were fulled, i.e., washed and bleached.

18:18 *Came out.* Hezekiah sent top-ranking

men of his cabinet to meet Sennacherib's delegation. Such officials aided the king since the days of Solomon. (1 K 4:1-6)

18:21 *Broken reed.* To rely on Egypt for help was as foolish as leaning for support on the crushed stalk of a marsh plant. The last king of the Northern Kingdom learned this lesson too late (17:4-6). Trust in Egypt proved to be a fatal mistake also in Judah's policy. (Is 31:1-3; Eze 29:6)

18:22 *On the Lord.* The Assyrian argued that Judah could not expect divine intervention because Hezekiah had curtailed rather than promoted the worship of the national deity. Later he blatantly "mocked the living God" with the blasphemous claim that even if the Lord should put all His power at the king's disposal, He would not be able to "deliver Jerusalem out of" Sennacherib's hand. (30, 35; 19:4, 10)

18:23 *Set riders.* Even if Egypt supplied the horses, Hezekiah did not have the manpower to set riders on them.

18:25 *The Lord said.* Sennacherib tried to make the people believe that his capture of "all the fortified cities of Judah" (13) had the Lord's sanction.

18:26 *Aramaic.* Aram or Syria did not attain world power by force of arms. However, its Semitic dialect became the language of international diplomacy, understood by government officials but not by the common people. After the Babylonian captivity it replaced Hebrew even on the popular level. A few Aramaic words spoken by Jesus are preserved in the NT. (Mk 5:41; 15:34)

18:28 *Loud voice.* The Rabshakeh tried to convince the people that their only hope of survival was surrender to Sennacherib. Even if they were exiled, life would be agreeable, at least preferable to death by starvation in the doomed city.

19:1 *House of the Lord.* Disaster seemed inevitable. But Hezekiah was a man of faith and prayer. He asked the prophet Isaiah to intercede for him and "the remnant that is left." For his father Ahaz's failure to trust in the Lord see 16:5-9; Is 7:12.

19:2 *Amoz.* Not to be confused with another prophet, Amos.

19:7 *Spirit.* The Lord would set in motion a feeling of fear in his heart by a *rumor,* the Hebrew word usually translated "report" or "news." What Sennacherib was about to hear about the fate of his army would be so terrifying that he would beat a hasty retreat to his own land, where he would *fall by the sword.* (37 note)

19:8 *Libnah.* From here, while awaiting the approach of an Ethiopian (Egyptian) army, Sennacherib "sent messengers again to Hezekiah," still hoping to convince the hard-pressed king of Jerusalem that it would be suicidal to continue the defense of the city.

19:9 *Tirhakah.* The general and brother of a ruling Pharaoh of the 25th (also called the Ethiopian) dynasty, who later became king in his own right (690—664 B.C.). There is no record that the two armies actually met in battle.

19:12 *Gods of the nations.* Sennacherib claimed that the idols of the peoples whom he defeated were no match for the Assyrian gods. The cities and areas mentioned here are in part those cited on the Rabshakeh's first visit to prove how futile it was to resist his master. Some of these have not been definitely identified. *Eden* very likely is a state on the upper Euphrates known in extra-Biblical sources as Bit-'Adinni.

19:14 *Spread it.* Either a symbolic gesture or a figurative way of saying that Hezekiah presented the contents of the letter to the Lord in prayer.

19:15 *Thou alone.* A categorical denial of Sennacherib's assertion that idols, "the work of men's hands," directed the fate of *the kingdoms of the earth.* Hezekiah appealed to the only "living God," the Creator of *heaven and earth,* who had condescended to reveal Himself to Israel, *enthroned above the cherubim* of the ark of the covenant. (1 Sm 4:4; Ex 25:18-22; Nm 7:89; 1 K 8:12, 22 notes)

19:19 *May know.* Jerusalem's deliverance would demonstrate to all kingdoms of the earth that the world conqueror, who had cast the "no-gods" of the other nations into the fire, could not "mock the living God" with impunity. (Ps 83:13-18; 92:5-9; Ex 14:18)

19:20 *Prayer . . . heard.* Since Isaiah's earlier promise of divine help (5-7) the situation had become more desperate. In answer to Hezekiah's continued pleading the prophet again assured him that his prayer had been heard. However, this time "the word that the Lord has spoken" is given, for the greater part, in a literary form of prophetic utterance called a taunt or mocking song (see for example Is 10:5 ff.). Addressing the Assyrian with devastating irony, Isaiah deflates his blasphemous arrogance. "The Holy One of Israel," whom Sennacherib "mocked and reviled," will force the overconfident conqueror to retreat to his homeland, leading him like an animal by a hook in his nose or a bit in his mouth (21-28; Eze 19:4, 2 Ch 33:11). No enemy troops will remain in Judah to interfere with the raising of crops (29-31). Sennacherib will not even be able to attempt a full-scale siege of Jerusalem. (32-34)

19:21 *Wags her head.* A gesture expressing contempt. Jesus suffered the same kind of derision. (Ps 22:17; Mt 27:39)

19:24 *Streams of Egypt.* Sennacherib did not actually invade Egypt. He merely prided himself that he could overcome all resistance also in that land.

19:25 *I planned.* Sennacherib claimed the authority of determining the fate of nations (23 f.). The Lord set matters straight (25-28). Nothing had happened without His foreknowledge and permission (Is 46:8-11). In His divine providence He let the Assyrian king *bring to pass* what He *planned from days of old* (Is 45:7). The "arrogance" of puny man who wants to play God is a delusion of grandeur. Such a dreamer will awaken to a humiliating reality (Is 10:5 ff.).—"Behold, the Lord's hand is not shortened, that it cannot save" also in our day when men wield atomic weapons instead of swords. (Is 59:1; 50:2; Nm 11:23)

19:29 *Sign.* Normal sowing and harvesting in the third year would assure Hezekiah that the siege had been lifted permanently.

19:34 *My own sake.* In order to be true to His promises which He gave to His *servant David.* (20:6; 2 Sm 7:4 ff.)

19:35: *Angel of the Lord.* At the time of the Exodus the Lord sent "the destroyer" into every Egyptian home to smite its firstborn (Ex 12:23 note). *The angel of the Lord* executed judgment at David's time by means of a pestilence (2 Sm 24:15-17). It is possible that he *slew* the Assyrian army by employing the same means.

19:37 *Nisroch.* The name of this idol occurs only here and in the parallel account (Is 37:38). The national Assyrian god was Asshur, whose name may appear here in the strange rendering of Nisroch. Sennacherib's assassination by his sons is mentioned immediately after the report of the disastrous campaign but actually occurred 20 years later. Esarhaddon (681—669 B.C.) pursued his father's murderers north as far as *the land of Ararat,* i.e., southern Armenia, where they found asylum.

20:1-11 HEZEKIAH'S RECOVERY FROM ILLNESS

20:1 *Sick.* The first 11 verses of this chapter tell how the Lord answered Hezekiah's prayer in another matter. He received divine help not only in a national calamity (chs. 18 f.), but also in a personal affliction. His recovery from a fatal illness no doubt occurred before the Assyrian invasion (6, 19). In answer to the king's fervent pleading, the prophet Isaiah announced that the Lord would not permit the illness to run its deadly course, but would let a poultice cure his incurable disease, adding 15 years to his life (1-7). As a sign that "the Lord will do the thing that he has promised," "he brought the shadow back ten steps . . . on the dial of Ahaz." (8-11)

20:3 *Remember.* Wrestling with the Lord in prayer, as Jacob did (Gn 32:22 ff.), Hezekiah holds the Lord to the oft-repeated covenant promise that those will "live long" who "walk in all the way which the Lord . . . has commanded" (Dt 5:33; see also the promise attached to obedience to parents, Dt 5:16). In his song of praise after his recovery, the king confesses his need of forgiveness for "all my sins" (Is 38:17), thus disavowing any self-righteous claim to God's goodness.

20:7 *Figs.* Still used for medical purposes in the Near East.

20:8 *The sign.* Evidently Hezekiah requested the sign before the cure mentioned in the preceding verse took place. Isaiah had rebuked his father Ahaz for refusing to ask for a sign. (Is 7:10 ff.)

20:11 *Back ten steps.* The normal recording of the sun's progress *on the dial of Ahaz* was reversed. Apparently the phenomenon was observed only locally (2 Ch 32:31). The word translated *dial* more commonly has the meaning of "steps" or "stairway" (NEB). An outer stairway may have been built in such a way as to let the sun's shadow appear on various levels as the day wore on.

20:12-19 HEZEKIAH'S DISPLAY OF RESOURCES REPROVED

20:12 *At that time.* As in the case of Hezekiah's illness and cure (1-7), his reception of the Babylonian embassy is not supplied with a definite date. While this incident occurred after *Hezekiah had been sick,* it no doubt preceded the Assyrian invasion (chs. 17 f.). *At that time* Hezekiah had not as yet emptied "his treasure house" of its silver and gold (18:15). Hezekiah's recovery from illness was only diplomatic window dressing for the real purpose of the mission. The Babylonian envoys came to enlist support in the west for a resistance movement against Assyrian domination. Hezekiah displayed the resources which he could contribute to a joint attempt to throw off the Assyrian yoke (12-15). Isaiah reproved the king for pride in his own strength and trust in a foreign alliance. Sennacherib's invasion was soon to teach the vain king the futility of his boasting. Ironically the very nation enlisting his cooperation would someday carry off the treasures and inhabitants of Jerusalem to its land of Babylon. (16-19)

20:18 *Eunuchs.* The Hebrew word translated "officer" in Gn 37:36; 1 K 22:9; 2 K 8:6. In some instances these men were castrates. (2 K 9:32; Est 2:3; Is 56:3)

20:19 *Word . . . is good.* Hezekiah seems to have been grateful that the threatened exile was not to come during his lifetime. Perhaps he also hoped that if God postponed the disaster He could be moved to avert it entirely if the next generation would truly repent.

20:20-21 CLOSING SUMMARY OF HEZEKIAH'S REIGN

20:20 *The conduit.* In the summary of Hezekiah's reign special mention is made of the tunnel which he made through solid rock from the Virgin's Spring or Gihon Spring outside Jerusalem to the Pool of Siloam within the city's walls. More than 1,700 ft. long, this amazing engineering feat was discovered nearly a century ago. On its wall was an inscription telling of its construction.

21:1-18 Wicked Reign of Manasseh

21:2 *Did . . . evil.* Hezekiah hoped in vain for a successor who by wholehearted devotion to God might save Jerusalem from the doom pronounced upon it by Isaiah (20:16-19). The 55-year rule of his son was longer and more wicked than that of any king of Judah. What he and the people did was worse even than *the abominable practices of the nations whom the Lord drove out before the people of Israel* (1-9). Through "his servants the prophets" God announced that Jerusalem fully deserved the fate of the Northern Kingdom (10-15). Nevertheless, a little more than half a century was to elapse before divine judgment engulfed the city. (2 Ch 33:10-13)

21:3 *Rebuilt.* Manasseh's "abominable practices" ran the whole gamut from baalized worship of the Lord on *the high places* to unabashed adoption of the fertility idols of Canaan and the veneration of the heavenly bodies, imported by the Assyrians. On *high places* see Dt 12:2, 5 note; on *Asherah,* Gn 28:18 note; 1 K 14:24 note; on *host of heaven,* 2 K 17:16 note.

21:6 *Burned his son.* Cf. 16:3 note; on *mediums,* 1 Sm 28:3 note.

21:7 *Put my name.* Cf. 1 K 8:29; Dt 12:5 note.

21:11 *Amorites.* The name of a certain national group of pre-Israel inhabitants of the Promised Land which at times is used as a general term for all the various racial groups of Canaan. (Gn 15:16, 21 note)

21:13 *Measuring line . . . and the plummet.* Instruments used in erecting buildings to make them conform to predetermined specifications. Judah will discover that its fate will correspond with measured exactness to the words of threat here uttered (24:3 f.). The end of Ahab's dynasty and the destruction of Samaria were warning examples that the Lord's condemnation of apostasy should not be ignored.

21:16 *Much innocent blood.* Like Jezebel he persecuted the prophets; like Ahab he stooped to judicial murder whenever a Naboth stood in his way. (1 K 18:4; 21)

21:19-26 Short Reign of Amon

21:19 *Two years.* Amon continued his father's policies. After reigning only 2 years he was assassinated. However, his "servants" or courtiers did not succeed in seizing the throne. "The people of the land" (11:20 note) slew the conspirators and perpetuated David's house by making "Josiah his son king in his stead." The account of the new king fills the next two chapters.

21:26 *Garden of Uzza.* For some reason Amon and his father were not buried "in the city of David" with their predecessors but in a private, unidentified tomb. (12:21; 14:20, etc.)

22:1—23:30 Josiah, the Reformer

22:1 *Josiah.* During the years of his minority the boy king of 8 years evidently was under the tutelage of such elders as Hilkiah, the high priest, who taught him "what was right in the eyes of the Lord" (for a parallel case see 11:21; 12:2). During his reign of three decades he vigorously promoted a national return to covenant faithfulness (22:3—23:25). At the age of 20 he ordered that repairs be made with the money which had been "collected from the people" (3-7). As the operations got under way, a book was discovered. The high priest recognized it as "the book of the law" (8-10). Terrified by its condemnation of the prevailing apostasy (11-13), the king sent a delegation to the prophetess Huldah, asking her to "inquire of the Lord" how "all the words of the book" applied to him and the whole nation (14-20). How he reacted to her words is told in the next chapter.

22:3 *Eighteenth year.* 2 Ch 34:3 ff. states that Josiah began his reforms 10 years before he undertook the repair of the temple. In this project he followed procedures adopted two centuries earlier by Jehoash, who likewise came to the throne at an early age. (12:10 ff.)

22:8 *The book of the law.* The book or scroll contained "*the* law," a definite body of legislation of unchallenged authority. Its teaching had existed in written form and was known as "the book of the law of Moses" (14:6; see also Jos 1:8; 8:34). A copy of it survived the religious persecutions of Manasseh (55 years) and of Amon (2 years). Perhaps it lay hidden at the bottom of the treasury chest as 2 Ch 34:14 seems to indicate. Because the king could read "all the words of the book" at an assembly of the people (23:2), the rediscovered scroll may not have contained all the writings of Moses but only that part now known as Deuteronomy. (See Deuteronomy, Introduction, "Authorship")

22:13 *Wrath of the Lord.* "The words of this book" which threatened to "bring evil upon" an apostate city and nation (15) were clearly summarized in such passages as Dt 28:7 ff.; 31:16 ff.; Lv 26:14 ff.

22:14 *Huldah.* The title *prophetess* is conferred also on Miriam, Moses' sister (Ex 15:20), Deborah (Ju 4:4), a woman called Noadiah (Neh 6:14), Isaiah's wife (Is 8:3), and Anna (Lk 2:36). Huldah lived in a sector of Jerusalem called *the Second Quarter* (KJV's "college" is misleading). No reason is given why Jeremiah, who began his ministry in the 13th year of Josiah, was not consulted. (Jer 1:2)

22:20 *In peace.* Without questioning the validity of the book or inquiring about its origin, Huldah proclaimed on its authority that God's wrath against the people would "not be quenched." No doubt Josiah's reforming legislation met only with grudging and outward compliance which by and large left the heart and soul of the people untouched. However, because of the sincerity of the king's repentance Jerusalem would remain intact during his lifetime even though he himself was to be a battle casualty. (23:30)

23:1 *The king sent.* In the hope that the destruction of Jerusalem, predicted by the prophetess, could still be averted if he and the people complied with "the book of the law," Josiah (1) "made a covenant before the Lord to walk after the Lord" (1-3); (2) cleansed the temple and its environs of idolatrous altars, images, and paraphernalia (4-14); (3) destroyed the false altar at Bethel and "all the shrines also of the high places" (15-20); (4) revived the celebration of the Passover festival (21-23); (5) ordered the people to abolish private superstitious practices. (24 f.)

23:3 *The pillar.* Cf. 11:14 note.

This covenant. In a solemn ceremony Josiah and the people pledged themselves "to perform the words of this covenant that were written in this book." For similar renewals of the covenant which God made with Israel at Mt. Sinai see Dt 5:2; 26:16 notes; Jos 24:1, 25 notes.

23:4 *Commanded Hilkiah.* All actions taken by Josiah to cleanse the temple and the land of false worship are enumerated in the next section (4-14). Some of these anteceded the finding of the law book (2 Ch 34:3-7). He assigned supervision of the operations to the high priest, to his deputies and therefore next in rank (25:18), and to *the keepers of the threshold,* the latter identified as Levites in 2 Ch 34:9. For *Asherah* see Gn 28:18 note; 1 K 14:24 note; for *host of heaven,* 2 K 17:16 note. *Bethel* was the site of Jeroboam's illegitimate altar. (15)

23:5 *Idolatrous priests.* One word in Hebrew, this term for officiants in idolatrous worship occurs only here and in Hos 10:5; Zph 1:4. They are distinguished from "the priests of the high places" (9) who professed to worship the Lord but at shrines outside the temple of Jerusalem.

The constellations. Possibly the signs of the zodiac (NEB: "planets"). The Hebrew word occurs again in a slightly different form in Jb 38:32, where RSV transliterates it "Mazzaroth" (NEB: "signs of the zodiac").—In our modern scientific age horoscopes are growing in popularity.

23:7 *Male cult prostitutes.* Cf. 1 K 14:24 note.

23:8 *Geba to Beer-sheba.* Judah's territory extended from *Geba,* a few miles north of Jerusalem (1 K 15:21 note), *to Beer-sheba.* For the expression "from Dan to Beer-sheba" see Ju 20:1 note.

23:9 *Unleavened bread.* Prohibited from officiating at the altar, these demoted priests nevertheless did not have to take up a secular occupation but were allowed to share in the perquisites of *their brethren,* the loyal sons of Aaron. (Nm 18:8-20)

23:10 *Topheth.* A place where children were burned to *Molech,* the Hebrew word for king *(melek)* supplied with the vowels of the word for shame *(bosheth;* see Jer 7:32). Perhaps *Topheth* represents a similar vocalization for a word meaning fireplace. From the Hebrew for "valley of Hinnom" *(ge-hinnom)* comes the NT word "Gehenna." (Mt 5:22 RSV note)

23:11 *Horses . . . chariots.* Equipment dedicated to the sun god for his trip across the sky. The *chambers . . . of the chamberlain* and *the precincts* remain unknown.

23:12 *Ahaz . . . Manasseh.* Cf. 21:1-5.

23:13 *Mount of corruption.* Apparently a reference to a part of the Mt. of Olives. For *Ashtoreth* see Ju 2:13 note.

23:16 *The word of the Lord.* Cf. 1 K 13:2 note.

23:18 *Prophet of Samaria.* Cf. 1 K 13:31 f.

23:21 *The passover.* For a more detailed account of this celebration see 2 Ch 35:1-19.

23:24 *Mediums . . . wizards.* Cf. 1 Sm 28:3 note. For *teraphim* see Gn 31:19 note.

23:26 *Did not turn. The provocations* to God's *great wrath* were so deeply rooted in the people that the official decrees of Josiah did not produce a popular reform.

23:29 *Neco.* Josiah was able to carry out his reforms even in the former Northern Kingdom because for some time Assyria had lost control of Palestine. In 612 B.C. its capital Nineveh was destroyed by the Babylonians and the Medes. In the ensuing contest for world control Pharaoh Neco (609—594 B.C.) marched through Palestine to join surviving Assyrian forces against the rising power of Babylon. The allied army was defeated at Carchemish on the upper Euphrates in 605 B.C. In an attempt to block the Egyptian advance through Palestine, Josiah opposed Neco at Megiddo, one of the most strategic passes through the Carmel ridge (Ju 4:7 note; 1 K 9:15 note; 2 K 9:27). In the battle Josiah lost his life.

23:30 *Dead in a chariot.* Success in mundane ventures was not a matter of course in Josiah's life even though in his efforts to reform the people "there was no king like him." (25; 18:5 f.)

23:31-35 Jehoahaz Deposed by Egyptians

23:33 *At Riblah.* After killing Josiah, Neco proceeded northward beyond Tyre and Sidon to Riblah on the Orontes River *in the land of Hamath.* Here at Nebuchadnezzar's later base of operations (25:6) the Pharaoh deposed Josiah's son Jehoahaz, also called Shallum (Jer 22:11), and *put him in bonds.* No doubt Neco feared that "the people of the land" had made him king because he would follow his father's anti-Egyptian policy.

23:34 *Eliakim.* Neco changed the name of his appointee to the throne in order to impress his vassal with his authority. For a similar action see 24:17. The overlord also exacted tribute which the puppet king paid by taxing "the people of the land." (11:20 note)

23:36—24:7 Jehoiakim, Babylonian Vassal

23:26 *Twenty-five years old.* No reason is given why the people chose Jehoahaz, who was 2 years younger than his brother (31). Jeremiah describes in greater detail the evil that Jehoiakim did in the sight of the Lord. (Jer 7:16-18; 22:18 ff.; 25; 26)

24:1 *Nebuchadnezzar.* Neco's domination of Palestine was short-lived. After defeating him at Carchemish, Nebuchadnezzar pursued him to the borders of Egypt. Jehoiakim had no other choice but to submit to the new world conqueror. On his return to Babylon, Nebuchadnezzar took with him a group of hostages, consisting of members "of the royal family and of the nobility." Among them were Daniel and his associates (Dn 1:1 ff.). When after 3 years the Babylonians suffered serious reverses in a battle with Neco, Jehoiakim *rebelled.* His trust in Egypt was unwarranted (7). Fifteen years later Nebuchadnezzar leveled Jerusalem to the ground.

24:2 *Sent against him.* Nebuchadnezzar was not at once in a position to deal personally and in full force with the rebellion. During this time *the Lord sent against* Jehoiakim the Chaldaean, i.e., Babylonian, occupation troops, stationed in neighboring Syria, Moab, and

Ammon. *Bands* from these countries joined in harassing raids against Judean territory.

24:8-17 Jehoiachin, Prisoner in Babylon

24:8 *Jehoiachin.* Three years after Jehoiakim's rash revolt Nebuchadnezzar was ready to mount a full-scale attack against Jerusalem. In the meantime Jehoiakim, only 36 years old (23:36), had died or had been assassinated. His 18-year-old son, also called Jeconiah and Coniah (1 Ch 3:16; Jer 22:24), could hold out for only 3 months. In the year 597 B.C. he "gave himself up to the king of Babylon," who took him "into captivity from Jerusalem to Babylon." Nebuchadnezzar deported with him the royal family, the palace officials, and a large segment of the population, leaving behind only "the poorest people of the land." Among these captives was the prophet Ezekiel (Eze 1:2 f.). The conqueror also carried off much plunder from the temple and the city. In place of the deposed Jehoiachin he made Josiah's third son king, changing his name from Mattaniah to Zedekiah. (17)

24:18—25:30 Zedekiah, Last King of Judah

25:2 *Was besieged.* A decade after the first capture of the city (24:10 ff.) "the anger of the Lord" burst upon Jerusalem and Judah with unrestrained vehemence. The prophet Jeremiah urged the king to keep his solemn pledge of allegiance to the Babylonian overlord (Jer 27). However, weak-willed Zedekiah yielded to a pressure group in the city which advocated rebellion. Expected help from Egypt proved a delusion (Jer 37:5-11; Eze 17:15 ff.). Nebuchadnezzar's patience too was at an end. He directed the siege of Jerusalem from his headquarters at Riblah (cf. 23:33 note). After about a year and a half the city's fortification began to give way. Zedekiah and his men tried in vain to escape toward the valley of the Jordan, called "the Arabah." Cruel punishment awaited the captured king. Nebuchadnezzar blinded him after killing his two sons "before his eyes" and then "bound him in fetters, and took him to Babylon." (1-7)

25:4 *Way of the gate.* No longer identifiable, this gate seems to have been on the eastern side of the city.

25:8 *Nebuzaradan.* In the year 587 B.C., a month after "a breach was made in the city" (4), Nebuchadnezzar's general carried out his orders to reduce to rubble the temple, the walls, and the other structures of the city. Almost all of the remaining inhabitants were "carried into exile" (8-12). Large quantities of bronze, silver, and gold, taken from furnishings and vessels of the temple, were sent as plunder to Babylon. (13-17)

25:13 *Pillars of bronze.* The two large pillars, named Jachin and Boaz, which Solomon erected at the entrance of the temple. (1 K 7:15-22)

25:21 *Smote them.* Nebuchadnezzar vented his fury not only on the king and his sons; he also executed the religious leaders, the political officials, and "sixty men of the people of the land." The latter were the more prominent citizens who had considerable influence in state affairs. (Cf. 11:20 note)

Into exile. Other nations which suffered the fate of Israel and Judah became extinct. Even the captors of Samaria and Jerusalem, Assyria and Babylonia, disappeared under the sands of time. However, God did not let the ruins of Jerusalem and the Babylonian captivity become the grave of His chosen people. Humanly speaking its hopes of revival were as dead as the dried skeletons in Ezekiel's vision (Eze 37:1-14). But God remained true to His covenanted promise to bless all nations in Abraham's Seed (Gn 12:3). By His "breath of life" (Gn 2:7) He raised the national corpse from its Babylonian tomb. Revived Israel retained its identity so that the Son of David could say: "salvation is from the Jews." (Jn 4:22)

25:22 *Gedaliah.* Judah now was reduced to a Babylonian province. The governor's father *Ahikam* had rescued Jeremiah from mob violence when the prophet urged submission to the Babylonians (Jer 26:24). No doubt Nebuchadnezzar entrusted the son with the governorship hoping that he too would advocate nonresistance. For a more complete account of Gedaliah's ill-fated administration see Jer 40—41.

25:23 *Mizpah.* Gedaliah set up headquarters a few miles north of ruined Jerusalem in a city which an earlier king of Judah had fortified (1 K 15:21 note). Here the governor met with *the captains of the forces* who had eluded the siege of Jerusalem.

25:24 *Officials.* Literally "servants"; no doubt officers in command of Babylonian garrisons.

25:25 *Ishmael.* This fanatic member *of the royal family* acted on the instigation of the king of neighboring Ammon, whither he had fled during the siege and fall of Jerusalem. (Jer 40:13 f.)

25:26 *To Egypt.* Afraid that they were not safe anywhere in Palestine from Nebuchadnezzar's long arm, they fled to Egypt, taking Jeremiah with them (Jer 52:30). Five years later the Babylonian king exiled another contingent from Jerusalem, possibly in reprisal for Ishmael's treachery or in anticipation of another similar incident.

25:27 *Evil-merodach.* The Hebraized name of Nebuchadnezzar's son Amel-Marduk. Jehoiachin had been in prison for 37 years, since 597 B.C. when he "gave himself up to the king of Babylon" (24:12). As if prophetic of a brighter future, the account of Kings ends with the recognition of royalty accorded a dynastic descendant of David. Jehoiachin's grandson was Zerubbabel, who with Jeshua the priest "built the altar of the God of Israel" in Jerusalem for the repatriated Babylonian exiles. (Ez 3)

FIRST AND SECOND

CHRONICLES

INTRODUCTION

Contents

In the books preceding Chronicles there is a historical progression from creation and the age of the patriarchs to the formation of the chosen people (Gn—Dt); from Israel's occupation of the Promised Land to the turbulent period of the judges (Jos, Ju, Ru); from David's and Solomon's days of glory to the fall of Jerusalem and the Babylonian captivity. (1 and 2 Sm; 1 and 2 K)

It may be surprising to learn that the two books of Chronicles traverse the same millennia of the past. The story begins again with Adam and ends at a point only a quarter of a century after the last event recorded in the final chapter of 2 K (the liberation of King Jehoiachin from a Babylonian prison in 562 B.C.). The last two verses of 2 Ch relate that when the Persian King Cyrus became the new world ruler in 538 B.C., he issued a decree of general amnesty, permitting exiles to return to their homeland. No postexilic happenings are mentioned in Chronicles, although a list of people who dwelt again in their homeland appears. (1 Ch 9; see also the descendants of David, 1 Ch 3:10-24)

However, this review of bygone ages is not simply a condensation of the history as it is told from Genesis to Kings. The reader soon discovers that he is not encountering a balanced resumé of Israel's past. While some accounts have a counterpart in Samuel and Kings, Chronicles is not designed to recapitulate the contents of these books.

One obvious indication of the special interest of Chronicles is the large number of pages allotted to some particular phases of history in comparison with others. Of its 65 chapters almost one third are taken up with the account of a single individual: David (1 Ch 10—29). By contrast, the eons preceding his reign are compressed into introductory genealogical lists of names, comprising nine chapters (1 Ch 1—9), the same number devoted to the activities of another individual: David's son Solomon (2 Ch 1—9). Furthermore, the 400 years of the divided kingdom after Solomon's death to the Babylonian captivity are covered in only 7 chapters more than the number accorded the 40 years of David's reign. (2 Ch 10—36; 1 Ch 10—29)

In its review of the past from Creation to Cyrus, Chronicles not only assigns a disproportionate amount of space to David and Solomon—almost one half of its pages—but it also restricts its reports on these two kings almost entirely to a single aspect of their reigns. Their political achievements receive only passing attention; their personal lives go practically unnoticed. Interest centers in what these men, at the pinnacle of Israel's outward glory, did to further the spiritual edification of their people. There are extensive and detailed reports on how they planned, built, and dedicated the temple; how they promoted true worship forms; how they fostered music as a prominent feature of the services; how they were careful to have only authorized personnel officiate in the temple.

Purpose

There is a reason why, in a survey spanning millennia, David's and Solomon's concern for the temple, its services and officiants, bulks so large. Chronicles had something to say from the past to people who barely survived extinction in the land of their Babylonian captors. Even though they again walked the soil of their fathers, they could not blink the humiliating fact that they were "slaves" of the Persian king (Neh 9:36). Prospects of becoming "a light to the nations" appeared to lie buried in the ruins of the temple and the rubble of the holy city. (Is 49:6)

To this dispirited band of immigrants Chronicles recalled history in the perspective of God's "everlasting covenant" with David (Is 55:3). To those who lamented: "Our hope is lost," the reminder of God's "steadfast, sure love for David" proclaimed: "There is hope for your future" (Eze 37:11; Jer 31:17). So, for example, each name in the lists of ancient forebears (1 Ch 1—9) was not just the bare statistical entry of an archivist. The genealogies going back to Adam were a sustained litany, chanted in monotone to be sure, but intoned so persistently as to bring every doubting heart in tune with its message: All appearance to the contrary, you are the people whom the Creator of all mankind has chosen in order to bless all the families of the earth. (Gn 12:1-3)

For the same reason Chronicles goes on to let Israel's glory under David and his son shine into the dark days of the postexilic period. To a people who owed a precarious existence to the grace of a foreign ruler, the past sang out: What these leaders of Israel were able to achieve showed that the Lord of history is able to let His kingdom come according to His determinate counsel and will. Nations rise and fall at His command.

But Chronicles reviews history in its own unique way for another reason. "In great trouble and shame" (Neh 1:3), the postexilic community indeed needed encouragement. But instruction in righteousness likewise was necessary. From the past the chosen people were to learn too that they had no future if they obstinately "sinned against thy [God's] ordinances, by the observance of which a man shall live" (Neh 9:29). The cardinal sin was idolatry. It canceled all covenant promises; it invoked dire curses. Undivided devotion of the heart was to be expressed through rites prescribed by God, by officiants appointed by Him, in the place designated by Him. Therefore the temple, once planned by David and built by Solomon but now in ruins, spoke of what had been and again must be central in the relationship of Israel to God. Here was the heartbeat of the nation; here grace and mercy sustained its life.

By the same token, Israel's history showed that its downfall began when it no longer worshiped God according to His ordinances. Neglect of prescribed forms of worship was the outward symptom of an internal malady. It proved that the people did not love the Lord with all their heart and with all their mind and with all their soul. Ritual disobedience proved to be the spring from which flowed all the foul waters of covenant disloyalty, including the sins against fellowmen.

Authorship

Scripture nowhere identifies the author of Chronicles. Jewish tradition suggests that Ezra wrote it. Many modern scholars hold that it formed a trilogy with the books of Ezra and Nehemiah. All three were composed by an anonymous writer, called "the Chronicler." Much can be said in favor of this view. However, the contents of Chronicles do not require a date of composition later than the last quarter of the fifth century B.C. (Cf. 3:18 note)

Sources

There are more references to sources in Chronicles than in any other OT book. Covering eons of past history, the author was dependent on records for most of his material.

For the five centuries from Saul to the exile, he mentions a large variety of documents to which he was indebted for his data. No doubt he was acquainted with the canonical books of Samuel and Kings, which span the same period. However, for much of his material he went back to sources upon which those Biblical books are based. (See, e.g., 1 K 14:19, 29)

For the detailed lists of names, which make up the first nine chapters and which appear also in other parts, the writer must have had access to statistical records in addition to the genealogical tables preserved in the canonical books.

Name

In the Hebrew Bible these two books have the title "Words [relating events] of the Days." The English name "Chronicles" derives from the Latin word *chronicum,* a term which Jerome, translator of the Vulgate, applied to them. He states that they constitute "a *chronicum* of the entire divine history."

OUTLINE

From Creation to Re-Creation

I. 1:1—9:34 Israel's Ancestral History

II. 9:35—29:30 History of David

III. 2 Ch 1:1—9:31 History of Solomon, Builder of the Temple

IV. 10:1—11:4 Division of the Kingdom

V. 11:5—36:23 Davidic Rulers in Judah

1:1—9:34 ISRAEL'S ANCESTRAL HISTORY

1:1-27 Genealogy from Adam to Abraham

1:1-4 PRIMEVAL ANCESTORS BEFORE THE DELUGE

1:1 *Adam.* The first nine chapters consist almost exclusively of a tabulation of names. The modern reader may feel that such a seemingly endless catalog of proper nouns, for the most part unknown and irrelevant to him, has as much spiritual value for him as he would find in an equal number of pages of a large telephone directory. However, in the Biblical writer's scheme of things each name is like a separate stone in a mosaic. It may have little intrinsic beauty nor bear an identifiable signature. But it is a necessary component in a meaningful picture. In its way and at its place it contributes to the message which the artist wanted to convey by assembling so many little pieces in a certain arrangement. As the reader confronts these first nine chapters as well as other lists of names in Chronicles, he need not stop to identify or ponder each entry in this hoary genealogical mosaic. Yet viewed in the aggregate, these chapters delineate the pattern of God's plan of salvation which has meaning not only for the postexilic community of Israel but also for the present-day believer as he remembers that "salvation is from the Jews" (Jn 4:22). For him too there is more here than a barren compilation of ancient statistics if he views the whole in the proper perspective. In its sheer countless components he will discover a central motif, intended for his "instruction" that he "might have hope" (Ro 15:4). See the genealogies of Jesus, Mt 1:1-17; Lk 3:23-38.

Without an introductory formula of any kind, the opening verses trace Israel's descent from Adam, the "one" from whom God "made . . . every nation of man to live on all the face of the earth" (Acts 17:26). From the very beginning and from all the families of the earth God selected the forebears of the survivors of the Babylonian exile in order that from them in turn was to come universal salvation through "the one man Jesus Christ" (Ro 1:3; 5:17-19). After the Deluge the three ethnic groups of the human race developed out of the one family of Noah. Of his three sons, Shem was to become the ancestor of Abraham, the father of believers (1:27). His son Isaac was chosen to be the bearer of the promise. Of the latter's twin sons it was Jacob who became the progenitor of the 12 tribes of Israel, God's "own possession among all people." (1:28—2:2; Ex 19:5)

With some variations in spelling, most of the names in this chapter appear also in Gn (see notes on chs. 5, 10, 11, 16, 21, 25, 35). However, the lists are not exhaustive. Adam's sons Cain and Abel, for example, are not mentioned in v. 1 since the line of descent proceeded through his other son, Seth.

1:4 *Noah.* A schematic pattern seems to determine the number of names listed for the era preceding the 12 tribes of Israel. The line of the chosen people consists of two ancestral chains, each having 10 links: (a) from Adam to Noah (1:4); (b) from Noah through Shem to Abraham (27). Symmetry rather than completeness appears to be the basis in other instances. Through his three sons (Shem, Ham, Japheth) Noah became the progenitor of 70 ethnic groups (5-23). Chosen from the resulting mass of peoples to be the patriarch of Israel, Abraham likewise sired three branches of descendants. If his son Isaac is counted, the number of his offspring through his other son Ishmael and from his concubine Keturah likewise totals 70 names (28-42). Abraham's line of descent through Isaac and Jacob is listed separately in ch. 2. See the three groupings of 14 names in Mt 1:2-17.

1:5-27 DESCENDANTS OF NOAH TO ABRAHAM

1:11 *Egypt.* In several instances the country or area occupied by various groups is noted rather than their racial relationship. Cf. Gn 10:1 note.

1:28-54 Isaac and Non-Israelite Descendants of Abraham

1:28-33 DESCENDANTS OF ISHMAEL AND KETURAH

1:28 *Abraham.* The writer of Chronicles does not stop to report the history of the patriarchs, assuming that the reader knows it from Gn 12—50.

1:34-54 ESAU AND THE EDOMITES

2:1—7:40 Jacob's Sons: The Tribes of Israel

2:1—4:23 JUDAH: DAVID'S LINE

2:1 *Israel.* In ch. 1 the author draws the line of descent from Adam through an array of families and nations to Jacob (1:34), the immediate ancestor of the people through whom God determined to bless "all the families of the earth" (Gn 12:3). In the next six chapters (2—7) he traces the genealogy of Jacob's 12 sons, from whom derived the tribes of Israel.

2:3 *Judah.* Not the firstborn, Judah is given special prominence. His genealogical history, occupying three chapters (2—4), is the first to be recorded because it leads to David, his dynastic successors, and to such leaders in the postexilic community as Zerubbabel. (3:19)

The Canaanitess. The author makes it a point to mention the non-Israelite strain in Judah's family tree. He likewise does not cover up Judah's incestuous relations with his daughter-in-law Tamar (4; Gn 38).—Jesus, Savior of Jew and Gentile, of harlots and sinners, has in His human ancestry not only the Canaanitesses Tamar and Rahab, but also Ruth the Moabitess, and Bathsheba, wife of the Hittite Uriah. (Mt 1:3-6)

2:7 *Achar.* Achan is here called Achar, *troubler,* because by his selfishness he did "bring trouble on" the Israelites as they began to occupy Canaan. For the word play on his name see Jos 7:24 note.

2:9 *Chelubai.* This name occurs in two other forms: "Caleb" (18, 24, 42, 49; 4:15) and "Chelub" (4:11). It is unlikely that all references are to one and the same person even though "Caleb the son of Hezron" and "Caleb the son of Jephunneh" are said to have a daughter named Achsah (18, 49; 4:15; Jos 15:13, 17). For the story of Caleb, Joshua's associate in spying out the land of Canaan, see Nm 13 f.

2:15 *David.* Telescoping centuries and eons, the author's line of descent from Adam quickly comes to David, whose significance in Israel's covenant relationship to God is the underlying theme of Chronicles. The opening chapters call attention at once to his importance, listing not only his ancestry but also his descendants down into the postexilic period (ch. 3). Of Jesse's eight sons only seven are named here (1 Sm 16:10 f.; 17:12). No doubt one was omitted from this genealogical list because for some reason he left no descendants. Eliab, mentioned here, and Elihu in 1 Ch 27:18 may be variant forms of the same name. For David's ancestry see also Ru 4:18-22.

2:16 *Sisters.* Mentioned here because their sons played important roles in David's reign. The most influential was Joab. (2 Sm 2:18 ff.; 3:26 ff.; 11:1 ff.; 18:9 ff.).

2:17 *Ishmaelite.* Jether or Ithra is called an Israelite in 2 Sm 17:25. Cf. note there.

2:18 *Caleb.* David's lineage from Judah through the second son of Hezron (9) is followed by the genealogy of the latter's other two sons, Caleb and Jerahmeel (18-55). The clans which sprang from these two ancestors were for some time not associated with the 12 tribes until Judah adopted them. The Kenites (55) were a branch of Caleb's family. (Ju 1:16; 1 Sm 27:10)

3:1 *Sons of David.* Not content to give David's tribe first place in the general scheme of his genealogical compilation (2:15 note), the writer of Chronicles accords additional prominence to this illustrious Judahite. Before recording the descendants of the tribe of Judah as such (ch. 4), he gives not only a full list of David's sons but also traces his family history through five centuries to the return from the Babylonian captivity (3:10-24).—As is quite often the case, some persons bear names in Chronicles different from those by which they are known in Samuel and Kings or they appear in slightly different forms. *Daniel,* the son of Ahinoam, is called Chileab in 2 Sm 3:2-5 (cf. note there). "Bath-shua" (5) is a variant of Bathsheba. If Elishama (6) is read "Elishua" as in 14:5 and 2 Sm 5:15, the repetition of the same name in 8 is eliminated.

3:15 *Johanan.* None of Josiah's successors on the throne is known by this name. *Shallum,* so called also by Jeremiah (Jer 22:11 f.), is to be identified with Jehoahaz, Josiah's son, whose reign of 3 months Pharaoh Neco terminated. (2 Ch 36:3 f.)

3:16 *Jeconiah.* The shorter form "Coniah" occurs in Jer 22:24, 28. He is called also "Jehoiachin" (2 Ch 36:9 f.; 2 K 24:6 f.). On the relationship of *Zedekiah,* the last king of Judah, to Josiah see 2 Ch 36:10 note.

3:17 *Shealtiel.* The list of David's descendants goes beyond the exiled Jeconiah or Jehoiachin, mentioned in the closing verses of 2 K. One of the leaders in the postexilic period of reconstruction was Zerubbabel, called "the son of Shealtiel" in Ez 3:2; 5:2; Hg 1:1. The next two verses indicate that the word "son" is used in the broader sense of grandson or successor, as it is in other instances. (Gn 31:55)

3:19 *Sons of Zerubbabel.* It is difficult to determine from the next verses how many generations of Zerubbabel's offspring are to be included in the list. V. 21 mentions his two grandsons and then adds the names of four other descendants. Taking up the last named of these four, 22-24 trace his line of descent into the fourth generation. If this genealogy extends over a minimum of six generations (the Septuagint has 11), Chronicles was not written before 400 B.C. since Zerubbabel was active after the return from the Babylonian captivity in 536 B.C. It seems reasonable therefore to assume that all entries beyond the names of his grandsons in 21 were added to the text later in order to keep the list current.

4:1 *Judah.* In 1-23 this chapter supplements the list of Judahite family groups given in ch. 2 and then goes on to record those of another southern tribe, Simeon (24-43). Some names of Judah's lineage, occurring in ch. 2, are repeated here in different contexts. It is not clear why certain groups are singled out for special mention. In some instances perhaps the site they occupied made them worthy of note as, e.g., Bethlehem. (4)

4:9 *Jabez.* His piety is recorded rather than his family ties. Because his mother was in great pain (*'ozeb*) when he was born, she gave him a name which, by transposing the last two consonants, means: "He gives pain." In answer to his prayer, blessing rather than pain came into his life.

4:11 *Chelub.* Cf. 2:9 note.

4:17 *Daughter of Pharaoh.* This phrase may mean no more than that she was an Egyptian woman, to distinguish her from "his Jewish wife." (18)

4:21 *Shelah.* Mentioned in 2:3. His descendants followed occupations in permanent settlements (linen workers, potters) in contrast to the seminomadic way of the clans mentioned in 11-20.

4:22 *To Lehem.* The Septuagint and Vulgate read "to Bethlehem."

4:24-43 SIMEON

4:24 *Simeon.* His descendants did not play an illustrious role in Israel's history "like the men of Judah" (27). However, they did not lose their identity (1 K 11:32 note; Jos 19:9), even though they were dominated politically by their brethren to the north of them. Four verses suffice to trace Simeon's families (24-27); only six are needed to list their settlements. (28-33)

4:31 *David reigned.* During his reign a census was taken from which the names of the cities just mentioned may have been taken (2 Sm 24:1-9). It is also possible that the administration of these localities changed at David's time.

4:38 *Princes.* The two exploits by Simeonite leaders (39-43) are not mentioned elsewhere. The first was a foray in the direction of Gedor, an unknown site, unless it is a scribal miswriting of Gerar, where Abraham and Isaac lived for a time. (Gn 20:1 note; 26:1)

4:40 *Ham.* A Canaanite people.

4:41 *Meunim.* Defeated also by King Uzziah (2 Ch 26:7), these victims of a later Simeonite attack probably were so called because of their association with Ma'an, an Edomite city southeast of Petra. The phrase *to this day* designates the time the source was written from which the writer took this account.

4:43 *Amalekites.* In another movement of expansion (42 f.) the Simeonites destroyed *the Amalekites that had escaped* to "Mount Seir," i.e., Edom, perhaps at the same time when Saul made war on them. (1 Sm 15:4 ff.; see also Ex 17:8 note; 1 Sm 27:8; 30:1; 2 Sm 8:12)

5:1-10 REUBEN

5:1 *Sons of Reuben.* Ch. 5 contains the ancestral history of the two and one-half tribes located east of the Jordan. It begins with Reuben, whose territory lay mostly along the Dead Sea down to the Arnon River (1-10); above Reuben was Gad's patrimony (11-22); half the tribe of Manasseh occupied an area extending northward from Gad (23-26). Israelite possessions in Transjordan frequently are said to consist of "Gilead" (9 f., 16) and "Bashan" (16, 23), the latter designating the northern section. However, the term Gilead is at times applied to the entire East Jordan area. (Dt 34:1)

Reuben, born of Leah, was the oldest of Jacob's sons (Gn 29:32). *But because he polluted his father's couch,* the double portion of inheritance, the prerogative of the firstborn, went to Joseph's two sons Ephraim and Manasseh. (Gn 29:32; 35:22; 48:5, 14-16; 49:3 f., 22-26; Dt 21:17)

5:2 *A prince.* Even though *the birthright belonged to Joseph,* the royal, Messianic line issued from Judah. On the term *prince* see 1 Sm 10:1 note.

5:6 *Tilgath-pilneser.* A variant spelling of Tiglath-pileser. There is no record of an Assyrian exile of *Beerah,* who also cannot be identified. However, a deportation of Israelite captives by Tiglath-pileser is mentioned 2 K 15:29.

5:10 *Hagrites.* For a fuller account of this campaign see 18 ff.

5:11-22 GAD

5:11 *Sons of Gad.* This list of descendants (11-17) and the war of the Transjordan tribes with their neighbors to the east (18-22) are reported nowhere else.

5:17 *Were enrolled.* The names in the preceding verses came from an otherwise unknown census which was taken after the kingdom was divided. A genealogical tabulation of Gad is given in Nm 26:15-18.

5:18 *Valiant men.* In the figures for them and for the prisoners taken (21), the Hebrew word for thousand does not have an arithmetic meaning. See Numbers, Introduction, "The Numbers in Numbers." The figures for the captured booty must have acquired zeros in the course of the transmission of the text.

5:19 *Hagrites.* Eastern tribes, very likely called Hagrites because they were descendants of Hagar, the mother of Ishmael. Their confederates Jetur and Naphish are listed among Ishmael's sons. (1:31)

5:23-26 MANASSEH, EAST OF JORDAN

5:23 *Manasseh.* Additional genealogical data is given 7:14-19.

5:26 *Pul.* For his name see 2 K 15:19 note. For the place names see 2 K 17:6 note.

6:1-81 LEVI; TEMPLE OFFICIANTS

6:1 *Sons of Levi.* The stress on true worship begins to appear in the space devoted to the genealogy of the authorized officiants in the temple—almost three times the number of verses accorded all three tribes in ch. 5. All descendants of the third son of Jacob by Leah are called Levites, but not all of them had the same functions to perform (cf. Dt 18:1 note). The first 15 verses trace the high-priestly line of the Levite Aaron to the time of the Exile. Supplementing this highly select group of Levi's descendants, the next verses (16-30) resume the genealogy of his three sons: *Gershom, Kohath, Merari.* Both lists are not exhaustive.

6:28 *Samuel.* On his status as a Levite see 1 Sm 1:1 note. On the name of his son *Joel* see RSV note. "Vashni" (KJV) apparently is not a proper name but an adjective meaning "and the second."

6:31 *Service of song.* The descendants of Levi's three sons who "ministered with song" receive special mention (31-47). The writer of Chronicles stresses the service of song with musical accompaniment as an essential element of worship (see, e.g., ch. 25). The names of Heman, Asaph, and Ethan (or Jeduthun) appear in the titles of the Psalms. (88, 89, 50, 62).

6:49 *Made offerings.* "The service of the tabernacle of the house," performed by the Levites (48), is distinguished from *the work of the most holy place,* assigned to those sons of Levi who were sons of Aaron (49-53). The list of high priests ends with Ahima-az, who held office at David's time.

6:54 *Dwelling places.* Because "no portion was given to the Levites in the land," the Lord ordered that they be given "cities to dwell in, with their pasture lands" within the inheritance of the other tribes (Jos 14:4; 21:3; Nm 35:1-8). The 13 cities allotted to the Kohathite priests are named first (54-60). All the tribes contributed territory to the non-Aaronite descendants of Kohath and to the other two branches of the Levitical family—35 cities in all (61-65), some of which are then enumerated. (66-81)

6:57 *Cities of refuge.* On their purpose see Nm 35:11 note. The only city of refuge mentioned here is Hebron. (55; Jos 21:13)

6:77 *Rest of the Merarites.* The meaning is: to the rest of the Levites, namely the Merarites.

7:1-5 ISSACHAR

7:1 *Sons of Issachar.* The genealogies of six (possibly seven) tribes are compressed into one chapter.

7:2 *Days of David.* Very likely the data supplied in these verses was taken from the census which David made. (2 Sm 24:1ff.)

7:6-12 BENJAMIN (DAN, ZEBULUN)

7:6 *Sons of Benjamin.* The tribe of Zebulun, located northwest of Issachar, is not mentioned unless there is scribal confusion in the text at this point. The suggestion that the following verses contain entries from Zebulun's genealogy is supported by the fact that another family tree of Benjamin appears in ch. 8.

7:12 *Of Aher.* The original can also mean "of another." If so translated, it may refer to Dan, who would otherwise receive no notice in the genealogy of the 12 sons of Jacob. The *Hushim* were his sons according to Gn 46:23. Dan may not be mentioned by name because the writer of Chronicles wanted to express his contempt for the tribe which in its earlier years was guilty of the brazen idolatry recorded Ju 17—18.

7:13 NAPHTALI

7:14-19 MANASSEH

7:14 *Manasseh.* Members of his tribe living east of the Jordan were listed in 5:23-26. This tabulation includes residents on both sides of the river. Women are given a prominent place no doubt because they introduced a non-Israelite strain into the tribe.

7:20-29 EPHRAIM

7:20 *Ephraim.* Ephraim, the second Joseph tribe, occupied territory south of Manasseh and north of Benjamin. Its most illustrious son was Joshua. (27)

7:21 *Men of Gath.* Nothing more is known of a raid on the Ephraimites by Canaanites associated with the Philistine city of Gath. If it occurred in the early days of Israel's occupation of Canaan, *Ephraim* (22 f.) is a collective term for the tribe's ancestors.

7:24 *Built.* It is unusual that a woman engaged in building activities. For *Beth-horon* see Jos 10:10 note; 1 Sm 13:15 note. *Uzzen-sheera* remains unidentified.

7:30-40 ASHER

7:30 *Asher.* The inheritance of Asher was west and north of Zebulun. (Jos 19:10, 24 notes)

7:40 *Mighty warriors.* Their total is considerably smaller than the number of fighting men credited to Asher in 12:36 and Nm 1:41; 26:47. Here only the *chief of the princes* are mentioned.

8:1-40 Saul's Benjaminite Ancestry

8:1-28 BENJAMIN

8:1 *Benjamin.* The ancestral history of the small tribe of Benjamin takes up a whole chapter, whereas the genealogies of a number of large tribes are compressed into the previous chapter. The descendants of Jacob's youngest son are given such prominence because of their links with David, the dominating figure of the entire book. Before the exile many Benjaminites, whose territory overlapped with Judah's, lived in Jerusalem, "David's city" and, after the exile, the center of the theocratic community (Ju 1:21; Ez 1:5). Judah, David's tribe, and Benjamin united forces against a common enemy (1 K 12:21). The most illustrious Benjaminite was Israel's first king and David's predecessor, Saul, whose ancestors and descendants are recorded in 29-40. In the scheme of Chronicles, this chapter serves as a transition to the story of David and the "everlasting house" promised him. (Chs. 10—29)

His first-born. There are differences between 1-5 and parallel passages for which no satisfactory solution is known. (7:6 ff.; Gn 46:21; Nm 26:38-40)

8:6 *Ehud.* The judge by that name was the son of Gera (Ju 3:15). The incidents mentioned here and in the next verses are otherwise unknown.

8:28 *Chief men.* The names in the preceding verses (8 ff.) are not recorded anywhere else. None of them is mentioned in the lists of those who returned from Babylon (9:1-9; Neh 11:1-9). Therefore *these dwelt in Jerusalem* before the exile.

8:29-40 SAUL'S ANCESTORS AND DESCENDANTS

8:29 *Gibeon.* A few miles northwest of Jerusalem, where "the tabernacle of the Lord" was and where Solomon worshiped before he built the temple. (21:29; 2 Ch 1:3)

8:33 *Kish of Saul,* In order to make the line of descent complete, the text here and 9:39 should read: "Ner was the father of Abner and Kish of Saul." According to 1 Sm 14:50 f., Ner and Kish were brothers. For the name *Eshbaal* see 1 Sm 14:49 note.

8:34 *Merib-baal.* For his name see 2 Sm 4:4 note.

8:40 *Bowmen.* For their skill in archery see 12:2; Ju 20:15 f.

9:1-34 Repatriated Families in and Near Jerusalem

9:1-9 JUDAH AND BENJAMIN

9:1 *Unfaithfulness.* David's dynastic history, the great concern of Chronicles, is about to begin. Viewed in retrospect, it proved that Israel could be the instrument of God's plan of universal salvation only as it continued in covenant loyalty, expressed above all in worship of the true God according to His ordinances. Because of unfaithfulness *Judah was taken into exile in Babylon.* Israel's ancestry, traced back to Adam (chs. 1—8), on the one hand, and the return from the Babylonian captivity, on the other, constitute the framework within which this historical survey runs its course. In the first part of this chapter, continuity with the past is established. The repatriated "people of Judah, Benjamin, Ephraim, and Manasseh" had the assurance that they were still a part of *all Israel* whose *genealogies* are on record in the previous chapters. "Jerusalem" (3), David's capital and the site of Solomon's temple, was again at the center of things (1-9). Furthermore, worship rites, as "David and Samuel the seer established them," were resumed by the authorized officiants, the priests and their Levitical assistants (10:34). The last verses of the chapter introduce the reign of David by repeating the ancestors and descendants of Saul, his only predecessor. (35-44; cf. 8:29-40)

9:2 *Temple servants.* KJV has "Nethinim," a transliteration of the Hebrew word which means "those who are given or set apart for an assignment." Ez 8:20 explains that they were people "whom David and his officials had set apart to attend the Levites" (see also Ez 2:43, where RSV note has *nethinim).* The designation Nethinim is found only in Ch, Ez, and Neh, postexilic writings. It evidently refers to non-Israelites who were pressed into service at the temple. See the captives mentioned Nm 31:47 and the "hewers of wood and drawers of water" in Jos 9:27. Associated with the Levites, they too had quarters in Jerusalem and lived in Levitical cities. (Ez 2:70; Neh 3:26, 31; 11:21)

9:10-13 PRIESTLY FAMILIES

9:13 *Able men.* The total figure in Neh 11:10-14 is 1,192. The difference may be due to a different basis of calculation.

9:14-34 LEVITICAL FAMILIES

9:17 *Gatekeepers.* Their total of 212 is given as 172 in Neh 11:19.

9:32 *Showbread.* Literally "bread of ordering." It was set in two rows, six loaves (cakes) to a row. In the Pentateuch and elsewhere it is called "the bread of the Presence" (Ex 25:30; Lv 24:5-9; Nm 4:7; 1 K 7:48). On its significance see Ex 25:23 note.

9:33 *Singers.* Chronicles stresses the importance of music and song in the temple worship (see, e.g., 6:31 note). Therefore it seems strange that no names of singers are appended at this point.

9:35—29:30 HISTORY OF DAVID

9:35—10:14 Saul, His Predecessor

9:35-44 GENEALOGY OF ISRAEL'S FIRST KING

9:39 *Saul.* The last verses of this chapter (35-44) furnish another—slightly different—list of Saul's ancestors and descendants (see 8:29 ff.). It serves here to lead over to the story of the death of the first king, which in turn is an introduction to the main theme of Chronicles: the reign of David, recorded in the remaining 19 chapters of 1 Ch.

10:1-7 SAUL'S DEATH IN BATTLE

10:1 *The Philistines fought.* No incidents of Saul's life described in 1 Sm 8—31 are recorded here except the disastrous battle with the Philistines. In the framework of Chronicles, Saul comes into consideration only as David's unfaithful predecessor from whom "the Lord . . . turned the kingdom over to David the son of Jesse" (14). For the circumstances of Saul's death see the notes on the parallel account 1 Sm 31.

10:6 *All his house.* This expression refers to "all his men" (1 Sm 31:6) who constituted his immediate entourage or his bodyguard. The previous chapter lists descendants who survived him.

10:8-12 SAUL'S BURIAL

10:10 *Fastened his head.* For the disposition of his corpse see 1 Sm 31:10 note.

10:13-14 REASON FOR SAUL'S REJECTION

10:13 *Unfaithfulness.* How he proved unfaithful is told in such passages as 1 Sm 13:8-15; 15:1-9; 28:5-19.

10:14 *The Lord slew him.* "Wounded by the archers," Saul took his own life. In the OT the cause of death and disasters is ascribed directly to God even though they are brought on by human agents. (Cf. Dt 2:34 note; Nm 31:1)

11:1—12:40 David, King of All Israel

11:1-3 CORONATION AT HEBRON

11:1 *All Israel.* As the previous chapter contains no record of Saul's persecution of David before the former's death, so here there is no mention of the struggle for the throne which ensued after the battle of Gilboa (2 Sm 1—4) and lasted for 7½ years. It finally ended when "all the elders of Israel" came to Hebron and "anointed David king over Israel."

11:4-9 CAPTURE OF JERUSALEM

11:4 *Jerusalem.* The account of David's acceptance by all Israel (1-3) is followed by the story of the capture of Jerusalem (4-8). For both events see 2 Sm 5:1-10 notes.

11:10-47 DAVID'S MIGHTY MEN

11:10 *Mighty men.* The honor roll of David's military men (10-47) follows at once upon the telling of his accession to the throne and the acquisition of his capital, whereas in Samuel this roster appears as an appendix to the account of his reign (2 Sm 23:8-39). Here and elsewhere a topical rather than a chronological sequence determines the order in which events are reported. The men listed distinguished themselves in David's service not only at the time when all Israel "made him king" but also later *gave him strong support in his kingdom.*

11:11 *Three hundred.* The larger figure of 800 is given in 2 Sm 23:8. This difference no doubt arose through scribal inaccuracy.

11:13 *Barley.* The text in 2 Sm 23:11 has "lentils." A copyist could easily confuse the Hebrew words for these grains because of the similarity in their consonantal structure.

Pas-dammim. A place called Ephes-dammim is mentioned in 1 Sm 17:1. See note there.

11:14 *He took.* Only two of "the three mighty men" are named: Jashobeam (11) and Eleazar (12). The third, Shammah (2 Sm 23:11), apparently is the subject of the verbs here and the main hero of the exploit.

11:15 *Adullam.* For this episode see 2 Sm 23:13-17; 23:8 note. For the location of Adullam see 1 Sm 22:1 note; for "the valley of Rephaim," 2 Sm 5:17 note.

11:20 *Abishai.* His feat (20 f.) and that of Benaiah (22-25) are reported in 2 Sm 23:18-23.

11:26 *Men of the armies.* This roster of mighty men (26-47) is more complete than the list in 2 Sm 23:24-39, where the 16 entries following Uriah's name (40) do not appear. For loyalty to their king, these heroes—many unknown and unidentifiable—belong to history's immortals. Inscribed in "the book of life" are by far more names whose glory will not end when material rolls of honor perish. Subjects of the King of kings by faith in His redeeming power and arrayed in garments of holiness from the royal wardrobe, they are counted worthy to receive "the crown of righteousness," "the unfading crown of glory." (2 Ti 4:8; 1 Ptr 5:4, Ja 1:12)

12:1-40 GROWTH OF DAVID'S MILITARY POWER

1) 12:1-22 Defectors from Saul

12:1 *Came to David.* Ch. 11 reports a number of factors in the rise of Bethlehem's Shepherd lad to Israel's illustrious ruler: he received the pledge of united Israel at his coronation (11:1-3); he administered his kingdom from Jerusalem, his capital city (11:4-9); he had a staff of generals and military leaders of superior ability and of proven allegiance to him (11:10-47). Ch. 12 traces the growth of his military forces from the earliest times (1-22) to their strength at the time of his coronation (23-37). Several contingents of *mighty men* threw in their lot with him while he still was a fugitive of Saul's fury (1 Sm 19—30). Four groups of defectors from Saul are mentioned. They came from: Benjamin (1-7); Gad (8-15); Benjamin and Judah (16-18); Manasseh (19-22).—There is no record of these accretions to David's army in 2 Sm.

12:2 *Saul's kinsmen.* The Benjaminites head the list of those who rallied to David, even though they were not the first to do so in point of time. They joined him when he was "at Ziklag" not too long before Saul's death (1 Sm 27:2-6). However, because the Benjaminites were Saul's kinsmen, their defection to David was particularly noteworthy. Even those who because of ties of blood could be expected to remain faithful to the mad king found his rule so intolerable that they joined the resistance movement against him. For their ambidextrous ability to *shoot arrows and sling stones* see Ju 20:15 f.

12:4 *Thirty.* The *thirty* referred to here and in 18 apparently represented a select group different from the one in the chain of command mentioned in the previous chapter. None of the names listed here appears there.

12:8 *Gadites.* Their territory lay east of the Jordan (5:1 note), where Saul's son Ish-bosheth maintained himself for 7½ years after his father's death. The desertion of Saul by his own tribesmen, followed by that of their immediate neighbors, reveals the extent of the disaffection with his rule. When the Gadites *went over* (literally "separated themselves [from Saul]") *to David,* they burned their bridges behind them. They came to David *at the stronghold in the wilderness,* probably a reference to "the cave of Adullam," where he fled soon after Saul ordered his arrest. (1 Sm 22:1 note)

12:15 *Crossed the Jordan.* The dissident Gadites had no mean obstacles to overcome. For some reason they had to cross the Jordan when it was at flood stage *in the first month* or Nisan, our March—April. In addition they had to *put to flight all those in the valleys,* no doubt their own loyalist tribesmen who tried to prevent their defection to David.

12:17 *In friendship.* These "men of Benjamin," who like the Gadites "came to the stronghold to David," apparently made their move earlier than their tribal compatriots mentioned 1-7, acting jointly with men from adjacent Judah. We are not told why David made sure of the trustworthiness of this mixed contingent. During his flight from Saul he learned that he had to be careful whom he trusted. For his encounter with treacherous people see 1 Sm 23:19 ff.; 26:1 ff.

12:18 *The Spirit.* The text has "a spirit." It may indicate no more than that the otherwise unknown Amasai gave a spirited assurance of their loyalty in lofty poetry. However, for instances where the Spirit clearly provided divine impulse see Ju 6:34; 3:10 notes.

12:19 *Deserted to David.* No doubt this chapter furnishes only a partial list of men who supported David before the death of Saul. No mention, e.g., is made of Ephraimite deserters, whose territory lay between Benjamin (1-7) and Manasseh (19-22). *Some of the men of Manasseh deserted to David* shortly before Saul's death; others joined him already "as he went to Ziklag" (cf. 1 note). David *did not help . . . the Philistines* in the battle of Gilboa because their rulers did not trust him. (1 Sm 28:1 f.; 29).

12:21 *Raiders.* The Amalekites who destroyed Ziklag when David left it unprotected. (1 Sm 30)

12:22 *Army of God.* Like God's host of angels (Gn 32:2; Mt 26:53) David's fighting forces were *a great army,* their number growing as *from day to day men kept coming to David.*

2) 12:23-40 Contingents from All Tribes at Hebron

12:23 *In Hebron.* Before Saul's death and during his son's ill-fated regime, David received growing support from various volunteer groups. When "all the rest of Israel were of a single mind to make David king" at Hebron, he became commander of Israel's national army, composed of *divisions* furnished by the various tribes. (23-40)

12:38 *All these.* The number of "mighty men of valor for war," credited to each tribe, totals 340,600. The figures are given in thousands and hundreds. For the suggestion that these terms are not meant to represent arithmetic figures but were military classifications designating "commanders of thousands and of hundreds" (13:1) see Numbers, Introduction, "The Numbers. . . ."

12:39 *Their brethren.* The people of Judah, in which Hebron lay, assumed the main burden of providing *eating and drinking* for the visitors from other tribes.

13:1-14 Attempt to Bring the Ark to Jerusalem

13:1-4 PROPOSAL APPROVED BY LEADERS

13:3 *The ark.* Written to stress the importance of true worship, Chronicles disregards the chronological sequence in order to highlight David's concern for the ark, the symbolic throne of the transcendent God (6). In effect, the preceding chapters only set the stage, explaining how David was able to undertake the moving of the ark. Wearing the crown of all Israel (10:1—11:3) in the former Jebusite city of Jerusalem (11:4-9) and commanding a national army (11:10—12:40), he was in a position to promote the spiritual life of his people. According to the parallel account in 2 Sm 6:1-11, David did not undertake to make Jerusalem the religious capital before he had cleared the land of the Philistines in two battles (2 Sm 5:17-25), which are recorded in the next chapter of Chronicles (14:8-17). For the neglect of the ark *in the days of Saul* see 1 Sm 5:1—7:1.

13:4 *All the assembly.* The first four verses supply information not found in 2 Sm. *All the people* had a voice in the matter through their representatives.

13:5-8 JOYOUS PROCESSION FROM KIRIATH-JEARIM

13:5 *Shihor . . . to . . . Hamath.* From the southern to the northern border of the land (see 1 K 8:65 note). A more common expression is "from Dan to Beer-sheba." (Ju 20:1 note)

13:9-14 UZZAH'S DEATH; PROJECT ABANDONED

13:9 *Chidon.* Called "Nacon" in 2 Sm 6:6 note.

14:1-17 Consolidation of David's Regime

14:1-17 *Build a house.* As if to allow for the time which elapsed between the stay of the ark "with the household of Obed-edom" (13-14) and its successful transfer to Jerusalem (ch. 15), this chapter intersperses three additional factors, unrelated to one another in subject matter as well as in point of time, which demonstrate that "the Lord had established him [David] king over Israel" (2). Evidence for the stability of his reign is: (1) his building activity with the help of a foreign king, Hiram of Tyre (1-2); (2) conditions permitting domestic tranquillity and growth of his family (3-6); (3) the double defeat inflicted on the Philistines, who threatened the independence of the land (8-17). See notes on the parallel account 2 Sm 5:11-25.

14:4 *Children.* Some are mentioned only here. The names of a few have variant forms in other lists.

15:1—16:43 Transfer of the Ark; Worship Directives

15:1-15 INSTRUCTIONS TO PRIESTS AND LEVITES

15:1 *Place for the ark.* This chapter resumes the story of the ark, interrupted by ch. 14. Because of the prominence of this sacred chest in Israel's worship, the writer of Chronicles fills two chapters with the report of its transfer to Jerusalem and the provisions made for it at its new location (see the parallel account, compressed into eight verses, 2 Sm 6:12-19; 1 Ch 15:25—16:3, 43). The description of ceremonial procedures takes up most of the space: (1) David's instructions to priests and Levites to observe the ritual prescriptions for moving the ark (15:1-15); (2) directives for processional music (16-24); (3) the ceremonies observed as the festive group moved toward Jerusalm (25-29); (4) the worship program established by David after the ark had been moved (16:1-43): (a) appointment of musicians "as ministers before the ark" (16:4-6); (b) the order that "thanksgiving be sung to the Lord" (16:7-36); (c) provisions for services "before the ark" and at the tabernacle at Gibeon. (16:37-43)

15:2 *Carry the ark.* No longer "afraid of God," as he was at the time of Uzzah's death (13:10), David realized that God did not object in principle to the moving of the ark. In its temporary quarters it brought blessings to "the household of Obed-edom" (13-14). Therefore the cause of the disaster must have been the unlawful way in which it was handled. For the prescribed procedure see Ex 25:14; Nm 1:50; 4:5-15; Dt 10:8.

15:4 *Sons of Aaron.* In addition to priestly representatives, of whom only Zadok and Abiathar are mentioned (11), more than 800 Levites were to take part in the procession. The latter came from all three branches of the Levitical families: Kohath (5), Merari (6), Gershom. (7; see 6:1 note)

15:12 *Sanctify yourselves.* Observe the purification rites required of those who engage in holy ceremonies. (Ex 19:10, 14 f.; Lv 11:44)

15:15 *Carried the ark.* In order to stress that this time the ark was moved *according to the word of the Lord,* the carrying is described as already accomplished.

15:16-24 DIRECTIVES FOR PROCESSIONAL MUSIC

15:16 *Singers.* Processional music, vocal and instrumental, was to be offered under the direction of the three Levites: Asaph, Ethan, and Heman (17; cf. 6:31 note). They were to be assisted by "their brethren of a second order" (18), i.e., in a subsidiary position to the three leaders.

15:18 *Obed-edom.* The name of the person in whose house the ark had been left (13:14) occurs frequently (18, 24; 16:5, 38; 26:15). If the same person is meant in all instances, he engaged in several kinds of activity. One of "the gatekeepers of the ark" (24), he had a part also in the service of song during and after the procession.

15:20 *Alamoth.* Lit. "virgins." The meaning of this musical term is no longer certain. It may refer to instruments which produce high notes, suited for accompaniment of female voices. See the heading of Ps 46.

15:21 *The Sheminith.* Literally "the eighth." Another musical term, which probably designates a tonal range one octave lower.

15:25—16:3 DAVID'S PARTICIPATION; SACRIFICES AND FESTIVITIES

15:26 *Seven bulls and seven rams.* These were sacrificed when the procession reached its destination. As it started out, "an ox and a fatling" were offered (2 Sm 6:13). For the section 15:25—16:3 see 2 Sm 6:12-19 notes.

16:1 *Tent.* A temporary shelter, no doubt made of goats' hair (Ex 26:7), which David had *pitched* to provide a covering for the holy chest. The tent or "tabernacle of the Lord" at Gibeon retained its religious significance (2 Ch 1:3). Perhaps it was so impaired by age that it was considered inadvisable to move it.

16:4-43 RITUAL REGULATIONS AFTER TRANSFER OF ARK

16:5 *Asaph.* Most of the men, chosen to provide the ministry of music "before the ark" in its new location, had been appointed "to raise sounds of joy" during the procession. (15:16 ff.)

16:7 *Asaph and his brethren.* There was no way to record the sound of instrumental music (harps, lyres, cymbals, trumpets) which David ordered played before the ark. However, it was possible to preserve some of the words of the hymns which Asaph and his associates sang "to invoke, to thank, and to praise the Lord" (4). Their songs had a sustained note of *thanksgiving,* heard so clearly in those psalms from which the writer of Chronicles excerpted pertinent passages, strung together in 8-36. For 8-22, see Ps 105:1-15; for 23-33, Ps 96:1-13; for 34-36, Ps 106:1, 47 f.

16:37 *Each day required.* The services *before the ark* in Jerusalem followed established procedures just as the "burnt offerings" at Gibeon were made "according to all that is written in the law of the Lord." (40)

16:39 *Zadok.* His associate Abiathar (15:11) may have remained in Jerusalem.

16:41 *Jeduthun.* Presumably he was also known as Ethan (6:31 note). His name appears in the titles of Ps 39, 62, 77.

17:1-27 David's Desire to Build God's House; God's Promise to Build David's House

17:1 *Under a tent.* Lit. "under the curtains." David did not want to continue to leave the ark, the symbolic throne of the King of Israel, under a makeshift shelter (16:1 note) while he occupied regal quarters built of cedar. See Hg 1:4 for a similar situation. Nathan, the prophet, approved of the king's plan to build God "a house to dwell in" (4). But the Lord intervened, reversing the action: He would build David's dynastic house, a structure which was to endure forever. For out of it would emerge the King of kings, Ruler of an eternal kingdom (Rv 22:16; Is 11). See the notes on 2 Sm 7, which with minor variations duplicates the report of this chapter of Chronicles.

18:1—20:8 David, Ruler of an Empire

18:1-13 SUBJUGATION OF FIVE NEIGHBORING PEOPLES

18:1 *David defeated.* Even though not permitted to engage directly in the construction of the temple, David did much to make the deferred project an eventual success. His first contribution to the cause was of a political nature. His son Solomon would be able to undertake and complete building operations because God "cut off" all of his father's enemies (17:8). There would be no interference from neighboring nations which harassed Israel in the past, particularly during the period of the Judges. One after another they were forced to submit to David's overlordship (chs. 18—20). However, David contributed also directly to the building program. He supplied the site for the temple (21:1—22:1) and stockpiled material for it. On how "the Lord gave victory to David" (6, 13) see the notes on parallel accounts in 2 Sm 8.

18:14-17 STATE OFFICIALS

18:14 *David reigned.* A short roll call of David's officials is inserted between the list of the defeated enemies and the longer account of his victory over the enemies, as in 2 Sm 8:15-18.

19:1—20:3 VICTORY OVER AMMONITES AND ALLIES

19:1 *Ammonites.* See notes on the parallel account of the subjugation of the Ammonites in 2 Sm 10—12. However, Chronicles does not report David's fall, which occurred during the Ammonite war (2 Sm 11:1—12:25). His sins against Bathsheba and Uriah indeed had tragic and far-reaching consequences. But mention of these personal defects is not essential to the portrayal of a national setting in which his successor could build the temple unmolested by enemies from without. The writer of Chronicles deletes from the record other data of David's reign such as his kindness to Saul's son Mephibosheth (2 Sm 9:1-8) because they do not contribute to the development of the central theme: the temple and its services.

19:7 *Chariots.* For the difference in figures here and in v. 18 from those given in 2 Sm 10:6, 18 see 2 Sm 8:4 note.

20:1 *Smote Rabbah.* The conclusion of the Ammonite war (20:1-3) is recorded also in 2 Sm 11:1; 12:26-31. Cf. notes there.

20:4-8 PHILISTINE GIANTS FELLED BY DAVID'S MEN

20:4 *Philistines.* Even though driven from Israel's borders in two battles (14:8-17), the Philistines challenged David's supremacy. Cf. 2 Sm 21:15-22 notes.

21:1—27:34 David's Concern for Future Temple and Worship

21:1—22:1 PURCHASE OF BUILDING SITE AFTER CENSUS

21:1 *Number Israel.* Besides bequeathing a politically strong nation to Solomon (chs. 18—20), David made tangible contributions to the temple by (1) providing the building site (21:1—22:1); (2) stockpiling construction material (22:2-5). The account of the census, recorded in this chapter, has the purpose of explaining how it came about that David chose and purchased the particular parcel of real estate where "the house of the Lord" was to be erected (cf. 2 Ch 3:1; Gn 22:2 note). One of the more significant variations between this chapter and the parallel account in 2 Sm 24 is the description of how David was "incited to number Israel." (Cf. 2 Sm 24:1 note)

21:5 *Sum.* For the sum as recorded here see 2 Sm 24:9 note.

21:12 *Three years.* The text in 2 Sm 24:13 has 7 years. See RSV note there.

21:15 *Ornan.* The name of this non-Israelite appears in the form of Araunah in 2 Sm 24:16 ff.

21:25 *Six hundred shekels.* See the amount paid Ornan according to 2 Sm 24:21 note.

21:26 *With fire.* This visible demonstration of divine approval is not mentioned in the parallel account, 2 Sm 24, but for other instances see Lv 9:24 (Aaron's consecration); 1 K 18:38 (Elijah on Carmel); 2 Ch 7:1 (dedication of the temple).

22:2-5 BUILDING MATERIAL STOCKPILED

22:2 *For building.* In addition to paying for the site of the future temple (ch. 21), David assumed much of the cost of the material which went into the building (2-5). For his stockpiling program he recruited *aliens,* i.e., non-Israelites who were compelled to work in forced labor gangs. (2 Ch 2:17; 8:7 ff.)

22:6-16 CONSTRUCTION ENTRUSTED TO SOLOMON

22:6 *Charged him.* Matching the liberality of his financial contributions to the temple (21:1—22:5) was the sincerity of David's moral support for the project which he himself was not permitted to undertake. In no uncertain terms he (1) laid the unfinished business on Solomon's heart, charging him to "be strong, and of good courage" (6-16); (2) urged "all the leaders of Israel to help Solomon his son" bring the ark of the covenant "into a house built for the name of the Lord." (17-19)

22:8 *Great wars.* David here supplies the reason, not previously stated, why he was not chosen to build the temple. (See also 28:2 f.)

22:9 *Man of peace.* For the meaning of the Hebrew word for peace see Nm 6:26 note. The "peace and quiet" necessary for building the temple resulted from David's victories over the neighboring peoples. (Chs. 18—20)

22:14 *Talents of gold.* At the height of his glory Solomon had an annual income of 666 talents of gold. David may be speaking here in figures which are meant to indicate large sums rather than totals based on actual calculations. It is also possible that the original numerals acquired additional zeros in the transmission of the text.

22:17-19 LEADERS ADMONISHED TO COOPERATE

22:19 *Holy vessels.* Utensils and furnishings dedicated for use in the temple.

23:1—27:34 ORGANIZATION OF ADMINISTRATIVE PERSONNEL

1) 23:1-32 Levites

23:1 *Was old.* At the end of his life David had done everything to advance the building of the temple short of its actual construction. He supported the project financially (21:1—22:5) as well as morally (22:6-19). The next four chapters (23—26) report how he anticipated another need. Having made Solomon his coregent, he convened a national assembly at which he organized the temple officiants in such a way as to assure orderly and regular worship services. The descendants of Levi who were not of the priestly line of Aaron were divided into four groups of varying size, each to function in a different capacity (2-6). The first contingent, consisting of representatives of the three Levitical families (7-23), was to "have charge of the work in the house of the Lord" (4, 24, 28, 32). Beginning at the age of 20 and working in 24 "divisions" or shifts like the priests (24:1), these Levites were to "assist the sons of Aaron" in various kinds of "work for the service of the house of God" (24-32). How the other three groups were to function is told later: the musicians in ch. 25; the gatekeepers in 26:1-19; those in "charge of the treasuries," the officers, and judges in 26:20-32.

23:3 *The total.* It is quite possible that the original figures of all Levites and of their various divisions acquired extra zeros in the transmission of the text. When "David assembled all Israel . . . to bring up the ark," the number of participating Levites was 862. (15:1-10; see also Nm 3:39 note)

23:7 *Sons of Gershom.* Members of the three branches of Levi's descendants (6:1 note) received assignments in the first group: Gershom (7-11), Kohath (12-20), Merari (21-23). Their list is supplemented in the next chapter. (24:20-31)

23:24 *Twenty years.* The Levites began to minister at the age of "thirty years" (3; Nm 4:3 note). "By the last words of David" (27) they were to be *registered* for service at the age of 20. (2 Ch 31:17; Ez 3:8)

2) 24:1-19 Priests

24:1 *Sons of Aaron.* As if to underscore the difference between the functions of the Levites and *the sons of Aaron,* "their brethren," the writer of Chronicles at once reports how David organized the priests "according to the appointed duties in their service" (24:1-19) before continuing with the ordinances for the other three groups of Levites, mentioned in 23:4 f. David divided the descendants of Aaron's two sons, Eleazar and Ithamar, into 24 courses or work shifts in order to provide for uninterrupted performance of the prescribed ritual. Within a year's time each group would be on duty for about 2 weeks. Zechariah, the father of John the Baptist, was "of the division of Abijah." (Lk 1:5)

3) 24:20-31 Supplementary List of Priestly Assistants

24:20 *The rest.* This list of the sons of Levi contains entries not included in the previous catalog of those who were to assist the priests (23:7-23) even though it repeats names from there (some in altered form).

4) 25:1-31 Levitical Singers, Musicians

25:1 *Set apart.* The writer resumes the report on the organization of the four levitical groups whose numbers and areas of activity he mentioned 23:4 f. After supplying the priests with assistants (23:7-32; 24:20-31), David ordered staffs of musicians and singers to be on hand regularly *for the service* in the temple. They consisted of *certain of the sons* of Asaph, Jeduthun (or Ethan), and Heman (6:33-47), set apart into 24 choruses or ensembles. Each of these was made up of 12 individuals, for a total of 288 persons (1-8). Every unit, constituted by lot, had members from the three musical families. The order in which they were chosen determined also the sequence in which they were to be on duty in the temple. (9-31)

25:3 *Prophesied.* Singing *thanksgiving and praise to the Lord* with musical accompaniment had much in common with proclamation of the prophetic word (2; cf. 1 Sm 10:6 note). The term seer, a synonym for prophet, is applied to Heman in 5.

25:4 *Hananiah.* His name and the names of the persons following him, when rearranged and slightly altered in form, constitute the words of a short hymn. Hananiah, e.g., means: "Lord, have mercy." Perhaps these sons of Heman came to be known by the title of anthems they rendered. They bear these names also in the longer list 9-31.

5) 26:1-19 Levitical Gatekeepers

26:1 *Gatekeepers.* This chapter lists two other groups of Levites whom David organized into functional units for service in the temple: the gatekeepers (1:19); guardians and administrators of the treasuries (20-28). The first of these had a total of 93 men, recruited from two branches of the levitical families. (1-11; see 16:38, where as many as 68 gatekeepers were put on duty after the transfer of the ark to Jerusalem)

26:12 *Divisions.* The following verses do not supply the names of the individuals making up the 24 divisions but specify the gates to which each of the working units was assigned. (12-19)

26:18 *Parbar.* A transliteration of a Hebrew word of uncertain meaning. It may refer to an open court or a colonnaded enclosure. What seems to be the plural of the same word is translated "precincts" by RSV in 2 K 23:11.

6) 26:20-28 Levitical Treasurers.

26:20 *Treasuries.* David not only provided guards for the approaches to the temple but also put Levites in *charge of the treasuries of the house of God.* Apparently the latter were a subdivision of the assistants to the priests, mentioned in ch. 23. While not engaged directly in the worship or "service of the house of God" (23:28), they were responsible for the treasuries which held the funds needed for building the temple (29:6-9) and for maintaining its services. For the kinds of contributions which flowed into these treasuries see Ex 30:11 ff.; Nm 18:15 f.; Lv 27:1 ff.; 2 K 12:4, 18.

7) 26:29-32 Officers and Judges

26:29 *Outside duties.* The final group of Levites to be mentioned had duties which were not directly connected with the temple. But just as David's victories over the neighboring nations made the temple safe from external enemies, so his appointment of *officers and judges* made for internal order and stability.

8) 27:1-34 Military and Civil Officials

27:1 *The heads.* In David's plans for the temple the tribe of Levi played an important role (chs. 23—26). Even "the officers and judges" who had duties "outside" the sanctuary contributed, though not as directly as the others, to the construction and care of the temple (26:29 note). However, David bequeathed to Solomon a kingdom with other administrative features, designed to let building and maintenance operations proceed smoothly: (1) he created a well-organized army, capable of warding off invasions by the neighboring enemies (chs. 18—20), should they renew their attacks (1-15); (2) he appointed local government officials, responsible to the crown (16-24); (3) he made 12 "stewards" responsible for supervising the income from royal estates and livestock (25-31); (4) he created a small advisory council to assist the king in directing the administrative program. (32-34)

Month after month. The military system devised by David provided for a monthly rotation of duty by 12 *divisions.* If the Hebrew word for *thousand* here is not an arithmetic but a military term, denoting a commander of a unit, then the meaning is that to each division there were 24 commanders. The Hebrew text does not have the word *numbering* as the RSV suggests. See Numbers, Introduction, "The Numbers . . . ." Each of the 24 staffs of *commanders of thousands and hundreds . . . came* on duty *and went* off duty *month after month throughout the year,* i.e., they reported for a month's tour of active duty, perhaps to royal headquarters. The names of the 12 divisional officers (2-15) appear, with slight variations in some instances, also on the roll call of David's mighty men. (11:10-47; 2 Sm 23:8-39)

27:7 *Asahel.* His successor is mentioned because he was slain by Abner while David still was king only in Hebron. (2 Sm 2:18 ff.)

27:16 *Chief officer.* A royal administrator is mentioned (16-24) for every tribe except Gad and Asher. However, in the tribe of Levi there was a special officer for the descendants of Aaron (17). Manasseh, divided by the Jordan, had an officer on the west and on the east side of the river. (20 f.)

27:23 *Twenty years.* At the age of 20, Israelite young men were considered "able to go forth to war." (Nm 1:3)

27:24 *Wrath came.* Apparently a reference to the uncompleted census with which "God was displeased." (21:6 f.)

27:25 *King's treasuries.* These were distinct from "the treasuries of the house of God" (26:20). The source of David's personal wealth was mainly booty taken from defeated enemies. (1 Sm 30:20; 2 Sm 8:6-8)

27:28 *Sycamore.* Not our shade tree but a tree bearing figlike fruit which the prophet Amos cultivated. (Am 7:14)

27:32 *Counselor.* This list includes men like Ahithophel and Hushai who were members of David's inner circle of advisors already at the time of Absalom's rebellion (2 Sm 17). Their names do not occur in a similar catalog of royal dignitaries preserved in 18:14-17 and 2 Sm 20:23-26. A nephew of David called Jonathan is mentioned in 20:7; but an uncle by that name is otherwise unknown.

27:33 *King's friend.* For this term see 1 K 4:5 note.

28:1—29:25 David's Last Official Acts Before Assembled Israel

28:1-8 SUCCESSOR PRESENTED TO LEADERS

28:1 *Assembled . . . the officials.* Before telling how David proceeded when he "made Solomon his son king over Israel" at the assembly of "all the leaders of Israel" (23:1 f.), the writer inserted a digression of five chapters (23—27) which explain who these leaders were, what their duties were, and how they were organized into working units. At the convocation all that David did to promote the building of the temple came to a climax and fitting close when he (1) presented Solomon to the assembly as the man whom the Lord had chosen of all his sons to be his successor and the builder of the temple (1-8); (2) "in the sight of all Israel" entrusted Solomon with the responsibility and the plans to erect the house of the Lord (9-21); (3) supplied additional funds for the project (29:1-9); (4) led the assembly in invoking a divine benediction on their efforts (29:10-22a); (5) made the assembly the occasion for coronation ceremonies with the result that "all the leaders and the mighty men and also the sons of King David pledged their allegiance to King Solomon," the future temple builder. (29:22b-25)

28:2 *Rose.* In his address to the assembly, David reviewed the circumstances which accounted for the action he was taking. Forbidden to build the temple, he was entrusting the unfinished business to Solomon, whom God had chosen of his sons "to sit upon the throne of the kingdom of the Lord over Israel." (1-8; see also 22:6 ff.)

28:7 *Kingdom for ever.* For God's promise of an everlasting kingdom see 2 Sm 7:13 note.

28:9-21 BUILDING OF TEMPLE COMMITTED TO SOLOMON

28:9 *Know . . . God.* At the end of his address to the assembly, David turned to Solomon (8). Then calling him by name, he added words of fatherly admonition and encouragement. He impressed on him first of all that God could use him for His purpose only as his *heart* and *mind* responded wholly and willingly to the great privilege granted him. For the meaning of *know* in the OT see Dt 9:24 note.

28:11 *The plan.* Even though David was not permitted to build the temple, he had the privilege of drawing up the plan for its structure and specifications for its furnishings. As God showed Moses "the pattern of the tabernacle, and of all its furniture" (Ex 25:9, 40; 26:30), so David received divine direction in producing the blueprints for the temple (19). For the description of the temple as built and furnished by Solomon see 1 K 6—7 notes.

28:12 *Had in mind.* The RSV follows the Septuagint. The Hebrew text has: "of all that was with him by [or through] the Spirit," i.e., of God.

28:15 *Each lampstand.* According to 1 K 7:49 there were 10 such lampstands.

28:18 *Chariot of the cherubim.* The text has "the chariot, the cherubim." The second noun is an interpretive apposition explaining that God is pictured as moving about on these celestial beings as on a chariot. (Ps 18:10; Eze 1)

28:19 *All this.* This verse may be addressed to Solomon. If so, David was saying: "All this [I deliver to you] in writing [set down when] the hand of the Lord was upon me [and] gave me wisdom, [namely] all the works of this pattern."

28:20 *Be strong.* After handing the plan to Solomon, David encouraged him to execute it. (20 f.)

29:1-9 BUILDING FUND INCREASED

29:3 *In addition.* Still in the presence of "all the assembly," David gave additional financial aid to the building of the temple, here called "the palace" (1, 19). He supplemented the contributions from other sources (22:3-5) with a huge personal gift and encouraged others to do likewise. (1-5)

29:7 *Darics.* A part of the sum supplied by the leaders is computed in terms of a Persian gold coin which was current when the books of Chronicles were composed. The totals of the donations are so enormous that it is reasonable to assume that the figures acquired additional zeros in the transmission of the text. (Cf. 22:14 note)

29:10-22a DAVID'S PRAYER AT THE ASSEMBLY

29:10 *Blessed the Lord.* The wholehearted response by the assembly to David's proposals moved him to turn to God in prayer (10-19) and then to ask those present to join him in grateful worship. (20-21a)

29:11 *Exalted.* In the first part of his prayer (10-13) David addressed the "God of Israel" as "our father," praising His "glorious name" in words of adoration resembling the closing doxology of the prayer we call the "Our Father."

29:15 *No abiding.* Praise of "the Father of lights with whom there is no variation or shadow due to change" (Ja 1:17) befits those whose *days on the earth are like a shadow* and who have no "hope" of escaping death. (RSV note; Ps 33:1; 147:1)

29:18 *Keep for ever.* Confident that the Lord has the "power and might" (12) to bring their plans to fruition, David went on to plead with *the God of Abraham, Isaac, and Israel* to *direct* the hearts of the people and particularly of his son so that they would persevere in the undertaking committed to them. (14-19)

29:20 *Worshiped.* The assembly followed David's precept and example to bless the Lord (20-22a). As true adoration always is, the worship at this occasion was with "great gladness." (22; Ps 100:2)

29:22b-25 SOLOMON MADE KING

29:22b *The second time.* The contents of chs. 22—29 have no parallel in the history of David as recorded in 1 K. In keeping with his stress on true worship, the writer of Chronicles devotes much space to those features of David's reign which demonstrate his concern for the temple and its services. By the same token, he treats Solomon's accession very briefly. He only alludes to Solomon's coronation without relating the struggle for the throne (1 K 1—2). The question was settled decisively at a *second* ceremony (22b-24). The assembled leaders of all Israel "pledged their allegiance to King Solomon," thus promising him support for his great project, the building of the temple.

29:26-30 David's Death

29:28 *He died.* For fuller accounts of "the acts of King David" the reader is referred to other historical records which, no longer available today, contained "accounts of all his rule." Almost two thirds of the chapters of 1 Chronicles (10—29) are devoted to David's history. However, the focus of interest is his promotion of true worship. Other aspects of his reign receive mention if and to the extent that they furnish background or motivation for the main action: preparations for building the temple. See Introduction, "Contents" and "Purpose."

1:1—9:31 HISTORY OF SOLOMON, BUILDER OF THE TEMPLE

1:1-17 New King Accepted by People; Blessed by God

1:1-6 NATION UNITED IN INAUGURAL WORSHIP

1:1 *Solomon.* In the account of Solomon's reign (chs. 1—9) the first chapter and the last two chapters serve as a framework for the feature of main interest: the building of the temple (chs. 2—7). Ch. 1 sketches the setting, telling how (1) Solomon, *established . . . in his kingdom* and joined with "the assembly," invoked God's blessing on the immense project (1-6); (2) God promised to equip him with wisdom for the task and to provide the necessary riches (7-13); (3) God did bless Solomon with military and financial resources adequate for the uninterrupted pursuit of his goal. (14-17)

1:3 *Gibeon.* Cf. 1 Ch 16:39; 1 K 3:4 note.

1:5 *Bronze altar.* Made of acacia wood and overlaid with bronze. (Ex 27:1 f.; 31:2-11)

1:7-13 PROMISE OF WISDOM AND RICHES

1:7 *God appeared.* For a more complete report of this event see 1 K 3:5-13 note. The writer of Chronicles does not mention how Solomon displayed his wisdom in the lawsuit of the two women, recorded in 1 K 3:16-28.

1:14-17 MILITARY POWER; WEALTH THROUGH TRADE

1:14 *Chariots and horsemen.* Cf. 1 K 10:26-29 notes, where the same information is supplied after the story of the building of the temple has been told. However, see also 2 Ch 9:13-28.

2:1—7:22 Building and Dedication of the Temple

2:1-18 PRELIMINARY STEPS

2:1 *Purposed.* Solomon's first concern was to secure the necessary manpower and materials. His appeal to the king of Tyre for aid met with a favorable reply (1-16). See the notes on 1 K 5—7 for the parallel account of the building of the temple. The writer of Chronicles omits some features and elaborates on others. He makes only a general reference to the *royal palace for himself,* described at greater length in 1 K 7:1-12. However, the exchange of messages between Solomon and Hiram, here called Huram, appears in an expanded form of 1 K 5:1-12.

2:3 *Solomon sent.* He was encouraged to do so after a delegation from Hiram assured him that friendly relations between the two nations were to continue. (1 K 5:1)

2:8 *Algum timber.* Cf. 1 K 10:11 note.

2:11 *Huram . . . answered.* His reference to *the Lord,* "the Lord God of Israel" (12) may be only diplomatic courtesy.

2:13 *Huram-abi.* The first part of his name is identical with the king's. "Abi" means "my father" or "master of," namely, the king's craftsman (so NEB). The mother of this master craftsman, "a woman of the daughters of Dan," apparently also had been a resident of Naphtali. (1 K 7:14)

2:17 *Aliens.* On their identity and number, the latter repeated from 2, see 1 K 5:15, 16 notes. In addition to them "Solomon raised a levy of forced labor out of Israel." (1 K 5:13)

3:1-17 TEMPLE UNDER CONSTRUCTION

3:1 *Mount Moriah.* For the dimensions of the various structural units and the materials used in them (1-14) see the more complete account in 1 K 6. However, only Chronicles makes mention of the location of the temple *on Mount Moriah,* a term which occurs nowhere else in the OT except in the story of Abraham's sacrifice of his son. (Gn 22:2, 4 notes)

3:3 *Old standard.* A different standard for the cubit seems to have been in use at the time when the writer composed Chronicles.

3:6 *Parvaim.* This name occurs only here and has not been identified with certainty. No doubt it refers to the same area more commonly called Ophir. (1 Ch 29:4; 2 Ch 8:18)

3:15 *Two pillars.* See the more detailed description in 1 K 7:15-22.

4:1-22 TEMPLE FURNISHINGS AND EQUIPMENT

4:1 *An altar.* From a description of the building complex (ch. 3) the account moves on to enumerate the interior furnishings, equipment, implements, and ornamentation of the temple (ch. 4). See notes on the parallel section 1 K 7:23-50, where, however, no mention is made of the altar of bronze.

4:3 *Figures of gourds.* The word used to describe the ornamental knobs on the molten sea in 1 K 7:24 is gourds, whereas here their shape is said to resemble "oxen" (RSV note). In Hebrew the words for oxen and gourds are very similar; a copyist could easily confuse them. These decorative symbols were strung around the 30-cubit circumference of the great basin in a symmetric pattern so that there were "ten in [every] cubit." The textual change made by the RSV is not necessary.

4:5 *Three thousand baths.* Cf. 1 K 7:26 note.

4:8 *Ten tables.* Not mentioned in Kings, they seemingly had some connection with the lampstands. (7)

4:9 *Court of the priests.* Restricted to use by priests, it was smaller than *the great court* where the people assembled and where Solomon erected his bronze platform. (6:13)

4:17 *Zeredah.* Cf. 1 K 7:46 note.

4:19 *Tables.* Only one table is mentioned in 13:11; 29:18; 1 K 7:48. In what way 10 tables, referred to also in 1 Ch 28:16, were put to use in exhibiting *the bread of the Presence* is not explained.

5:1 DAVID'S CONTRIBUTIONS DEPOSITED

5:1 *Was finished.* Before dedicating the *finished* temple, Solomon deposited in it *the things which David . . . had dedicated* to the Lord, such as those mentioned in 1 Ch 18:11.

5:2—7-22 TEMPLE DEDICATION

5:2 *Assembled the elders.* The occasion chosen for dedicating the temple was "the feast" of tabernacles, when the elders of Israel were gathered in Jerusalem. The record of the dedicatory rites agrees substantially with the account in 1 K 8:1—9:9. See the notes there. In some instances the writer of Chronicles describes liturgical procedures in greater detail. Ceremonies began with the transfer of *the ark of the covenant* from its makeshift quarters (1 Ch 15:1) into "the inner sanctuary of the house," i.e., the holy of holies (2-14). When the symbol of divine presence was in place, "the glory of the Lord filled the house of God," hallowing it as His dwelling place. (14)

5:11 *All the priests.* In 11b-13a the writer of Chronicles reports two items not found in Kings: (1) *all the priests* and "all the Levitical singers" participated at this occasion, not only those who were on duty in Jerusalem at the time; (2) the theme song of the singers, accompanied by instrumental music, was a liturgical refrain (13b) which David had used. (1 Ch 16:34; see also Ps 118:1-4, 29)

6:1 *Solomon said.* His dedicatory address (1-11) is recorded in almost identical form 1 K 8:12-21. See notes there.

6:12 *Spread forth.* For Solomon's prayer see 1 K 8:22-40 notes.

6:13 *Platform.* The same Hebrew word is used to describe the lavers in 4:6. The rim of Solomon's speaker's dais may have curved upward to resemble a basin. It is not mentioned in Kings.

6:41 *Arise.* The concluding words of Solomon's prayer from 1 K 8:52 f. are not included here. In their place the writer supplies an ending in poetic form, preserved also in Ps 132:8-10 with minor changes.

6:42 *Thy anointed.* Solomon, the anointed king, entreats the Lord to fulfill the promise of a "kingdom forever," made to his father David. (1 Ch 17:1-15; 2 Sm 7; Ps 89:49)

7:1 *Fire came down.* God approved the dedicatory *burnt offering and the sacrifices* with fire from heaven. For similar manifestations of divine approbation see Lv 9:24; Ju 6:21; 1 K 18:38; 1 Ch 21:26. The words with which Solomon "blessed all the assembly" (6:3), recorded in 1 K 8:54-61, are not included in his report by the writer of Chronicles.

7:4 *Offered sacrifice.* For the dedicatory offerings see the parallel account of 1 K 8:62-64. Reflecting his interest in liturgical music, the writer gives the additional information contained in 6.

7:12 *Appeared to Solomon.* Except for the addition of 13-15, God's answer to Solomon's prayer (6:12-42) is recorded also in 1 K 9:3-9.

8:1—9:28 Miscellaneous Ventures and Incidents

8:1-10 CITIES BUILT WITH CONSCRIPTED LABOR

8:2 *Rebuilt.* The building of the temple is the focal point in the account of Solomon's reign. Ch. 1 is in the nature of a prolog, explaining why it was possible for him to undertake the project. The rather detailed report of construction and dedication of the temple is followed by a kind of epilog of 2 chapters (8 f.). These contain a series of more or less unrelated episodes which make the point that under the temple builder's regime it was possible for all Israel to worship in the dedicated sanctuary "according to the ordinance of David" (14). The first to be mentioned is Solomon's control over all Israelite territory and the protection of its borders against possible invaders (1-10). Apparently as the result of negotiations, Hiram returned to him the 20 cities ceded to the king of Tyre to finance the building program in Jerusalem (1 f.; cf. 1 K 9:10-13). After he rebuilt and resettled them, Solomon built "store-cities" and "fortified cities" at strategic locations with a "forced levy" composed of inhabitants of Canaan "who were not of Israel." (3-10; 1 K 9:20 note)

8:3 *Hamath-zobah.* On the northern frontier Solomon had to reassert his sway over a territory which had come under David's control. (1 Ch 18:3-10)

8:4 *Tadmor.* For the location of the cities mentioned in these verses see notes on 1 K 9:17 f.

8:10 *Chief officers.* For their number see 1 K 5:16 note.

8:11 NEW DWELLING FOR EGYPTIAN WIFE

8:11 *My wife.* More accurately translated: "one of my wives." Cf. 1 K 3:1; 7:8.

8:12-16 WORSHIP IN COMPLETED TEMPLE

8:13 *Commandment of Moses.* The dedicatory sacrifices initiated observance of all ritual prescriptions for offerings *as the duty* (literally "the word") *of each day required* (12-16). When "the house of the Lord was completed" (16), worship in it was conducted on ordinary sabbaths as well as on festive days *according to the commandment of Moses.* But Solomon ordered also compliance with "the ordinance of David" (14) which provided for uninterrupted services by priests and Levites.

8:17-18 MARITIME ENTERPRISES

8:18 *Ships and servants.* For Solomon's "fleet of ships," built and manned by Hiram's servants, see 1 K 9:26 note.

9:1-12 VISIT OF QUEEN OF SHEBA

9:1 *Queen of Sheba.* Her visit to the temple builder was evidence that he, in addition to providing safety and peace at home, had amicable and profitable relations with a country as distant and rich in resources as Sheba (1-12). See notes on the parallel account in 1 K 10:1:13.

9:13:21 SOLOMON'S LAVISH USE OF GOLD

9:13 *Weight of gold.* The gold and silver which Solomon lavished on the temple did not exhaust his supply. He had enough of the precious metal for ornaments and "drinking vessels" in his own palace. (13-21; cf. 1 K 10:14-28 notes)

9:21 *To Tarshish.* The meaning is that he had ships capable of going to Tarshish. (Cf. 1 K 10:22 note)

9:22-28 WISDOM AND WEALTH WIDELY ACCLAIMED

9:22 *Excelled.* For the final reference to Solomon's illustrious reign see 1 K 10:23-29.

9:29-31 Solomon's Death

9:29 *Acts of Solomon.* For *the rest of the acts of Solomon* the writer of Chronicles refers his readers to records kept by three prophetic writers (1 K 11:41 note). From these sources, no longer extant today, he selected those accounts which he presented because they served his immediate purpose: to teach the people after the Exile that they cannot be God's people without honoring Him in worship acceptable to Him.

10:1—11:4 DIVISION OF THE KINGDOM

10:1-15 Unfruitful Negotiations with Northern Tribes

10:1-5 REHOBOAM ASKED TO LIGHTEN BURDENS

10:1 *Rehoboam.* Worship in the temple by a united nation came to an end at Solomon's death. At the accession of his son, 10 northern tribes seceded from the union of all Israel. How this schism, never to be healed, came about is told in 10:1—11-4. For notes on the disruption of the kingdom see the parallel account in 1 K 12.

10:4 *Yoke.* "Israel," i.e., the 10 northern tribes, objected particularly to Solomon's conscription of forced labor as described in 1 K 5:6-18; 11:28.

10:6-15 HARSH MEASURES ADOPTED

10:16—11:4 Secession of Northern Tribes

11:3 *All Israel.* The seceding tribes may be called Israel to distinguish them politically from the people *in Judah and Benjamin* (10:3, 16). However, the latter represent Israel, the people of the promise.

11:5—36:23 DAVIDIC RULERS IN JUDAH

11:5—12:16 Rehoboam

11:5-12 CITIES FORTIFIED

11:5 *In Jerusalem.* The remaining chapters of 2 Ch deal with the reigns of the Davidic successors of Solomon. The rulers of the Northern Kingdom receive mention only when relations with the schismatic tribes affect the kings in Jerusalem. The false worship introduced by Jeroboam, the first secessionist king (1 K 12:25-33), was perpetuated as long as the Northern Kingdom existed, a period of about two centuries. Because the writer was intent on recording how true worship survived in Jerusalem in spite of dismal periods of idolatry, he excluded the history of the north, where perversion remained entrenched.

Cities for defense. The king fortified approaches to Jerusalem from the south and southwest. From this direction came an Egyptian invasion (12:1-12). These circumstances suggest that events are not set down in chronological order. Rehoboam may have strengthened these border defenses in order to prevent another attack from the same enemy.

11:13-17 MIGRATION OF LEVITES TO JUDAH

11:13 *Resorted to him.* The border between the two kingdoms remained open. Priests, Levites, and others *in all Israel* who refused to take part in the false worship at Bethel and Dan crossed over "to Jerusalem to sacrifice to the Lord."

11:15 *Satyrs.* Demons thought to be in the form of he-goats. (Cf. Lv 17:3 note)

11:17 *They walked.* The Septuagint reads: "he walked." He "forsook the law of the Lord" (12:1) after 3 years.

11:18-23 REHOBOAM'S WIVES AND SONS

11:18 *Jerimoth.* Not mentioned in the list of David's sons (1 Ch 3:1-8). He may have been the son of a concubine.

11:20 *Maacah.* According to 2 Sm 14:27 Absalom had only one daughter, Tamar. The Hebrew words for son and daughter at times refer to grandchildren.

11:21 *Eighteen wives.* Rehoboam's polygamous marriage relations no doubt accounted for the fact that "he forsook the law of the Lord," just as his father's "wives turned away his heart after other gods" (1 K 11:4). On polygamy in the OT see Gn 16:2 note.

12:1-12 UNFAITHFULNESS PUNISHED BY EGYPTIANS

12:2 *Shishak.* The invasion by the king of Egypt is described in greater detail than in Kings, where it is summarized in three verses. (1 K 14:26-28; see note there)

12:3 *Sukkiim.* Known to have had a part in other Egyptian military operations but mentioned only here in the OT.

12:5 *Shemaiah.* He also recorded "the acts of Rehoboam from first to last." (15)

12:7 *Some deliverance.* Another possible translation: "deliverance within a short time." Because "the princes of Israel and the king humbled themselves" in repentance, God tempered the severity of the punishment, as He did when Moses interceded for the people. (Ex 32:14 note)

12:8 *Know my service.* The invasion was to teach that the alternative to serving the Lord was servitude to *the kingdoms of the countries,* the rod of His anger on apostasy. (Is 10:5)

12:12 *Good.* Prosperity prevailed again after the enemy left.

12:13-16 CONCLUSION OF REHOBOAM'S REIGN

12:14 *Did evil.* Cf. 1 K 14:21-24 notes.

13:1-22 Abijah

13:1-2a INTRODUCTORY SUMMARY

13:1 *Abijah.* The writer of Chronicles supplements the summary of his reign, given in 1 K 15:1-8, with an account of his victory over the northern king, Jeroboam.

13:2a *Micaiah.* This name appears also in the form of Maacah (11:20 ff.). Abijah's mother was "the daughter of Uriel" and the granddaughter of Absalom.

13:2b-22 WAR WITH JEROBOAM

13:2b *War.* Before the battle began, Abijah warned the opponents that they were fighting "against the Lord" (12) because they were rebels against the divinely ordained "kingship over Israel" (2b-7). They could only expect defeat because God's wrath was sure to overtake them because they were guilty of idolatry. (8-12)

13:3 *Four hundred thousand.* If the Hebrew word for *thousand* here is a military term rather than a number, then 400 "valiant men of war" were arrayed against 800 under Jeroboam's command, of whom 500 were killed (17). See Numbers, Introduction, "The numbers . . . ."

13:4 *Zemaraim.* The name of a town about 12 miles north of Jerusalem, mentioned in Jos 18:22.

13:5 *Covenant of salt.* Cf. Lv 2:13 note.

13:7 *Young.* Literally "a boy," with the connotation of inexperience. As Solomon called himself "a little child" (1 K 3:7), so Rehoboam lacked administrative discretion, even though he was over 40 years old (12:13). For the term *worthless scoundrels* see Ju 19:22 note.

13:8 *Kingdom of the Lord.* By warring against Rehoboam, Jeroboam was in effect trying to dethrone God, who had decreed to rule in Israel through *the sons of David.* (1 Ch 28:5)

13:9 *Like the peoples.* When Jeroboam *made priests* in defiance of God's law, the worship they conducted at Bethel and Dan was as offensive as the idolatrous rites of the Gentiles round about Israel.

13:12 *Sound the call.* For this function of the priests see Nm 10:2, 9 notes.

13:13 *Ambush.* The larger northern army, deployed in a clever manner, would have routed Judah if God had not "defeated Jeroboam and all Israel" (13-22). For other instances where "God fought for" those who relied on Him, giving the enemy into their hand, see Jos 10:14, 42; 23:3; 1 Ch 16:12.

13:19 *Took cities. Bethel,* where Jeroboam erected a golden calf (1 K 12:28 f.), was 10 miles north of Jerusalem. *Jeshanah* and *Ephron* were a few miles farther north. But these border towns soon reverted to Israel. Baasha, the next northern king, fortified Ramah, only 5 miles north of Jerusalem. (16:1)

14:1—16:14 Asa

14:1-8 RELIGIOUS ZEAL; PROSPERITY

14:1 *Asa.* The report on his reign fills three chapters, supplementing and expanding the much shorter account in 1 K 15:9-24. The writer treats Asa's history at greater length because it drives home the lesson his readers were to learn from history: the blessing of covenant faithfulness and the dire results of apostasy. Asa's prosperous reign is related directly to his purging the land of idolatry (1-8). He was spared a foreign invasion because "the Lord defeated the Ethiopians" who attacked his southern and western borders. (9-15)

14:3 *Asherim.* Cf. Gn 28:18 note.

14:6 *No war.* V. 1 gives the round figure of 10 years for the period when "the land had rest." Hostilities broke out with the northern king Baasha (16:1-6), who began his reign of 24 years in the third year of Asa (1 K 15:33). In summarizing the relationship of these kings to one another, the writer of Kings adds: "And there was war between Asa and Baasha . . . all their days." (1 K 15:16)

14:8 *Three hundred thousand.* For the size of the army see 13:3 note.

14:9-15 VICTORY OVER ETHIOPIAN GENERAL

14:9 *Zerah.* He may have been a general whom the Pharaoh put in command of Egyptian mercenary troops. Perhaps he was an Arabian chieftain called *Ethiopian* (Hebrew: "Cushite") because he was a descendant of Cush, ancestor of several Arabian tribes. (Gn 10:7 note)

14:13 *Gerar.* Asa confronted the invaders at Mareshah (9), a city some 25 miles southwest of Jerusalem which his father had fortified (11:8). After defeating them in battle, he *pursued them as far as Gerar,* located in the Philistine plain 25 miles southwest of Mareshah.

14:14 *Fear of the Lord.* Cf. 1 Sm 11:7, where the same phrase is translated "the dread of the Lord." NEB: "the Lord had struck the people with panic."

15:1-19 REFORM MEASURES

15:1 *Azariah.* An otherwise unknown prophet admonished the people to seek the Lord if they wanted Him to be with them. He reminded them that when Israel deserted Him in the past, He also forsook them. As a result they suffered "distress . . . no peace . . . great disturbances," civil war (1-7). The prophet's words struck home. Determined to stamp out idolatry "from all the land," he convoked a general assembly at which he prevailed on the people to pledge full loyalty to the Lord in a covenant-renewal ceremony. (8-15)

15:3 *Teaching priest.* Instruction in the Law was a priestly duty (Lv 10:11). For an example of its performance see 17:9.

15:5 *Those times.* The prophet did not say explicitly what era he meant. However, his hearers would realize that he was describing the period of the Judges, the "Dark Ages" in Israel's history.

15:8 *Abominable idols.* One word in Hebrew and so translated in 2 K 23:24; Dt 29:17. See the second reference for its meaning. For "an abominable image," a different noun (16), see 1 K 15:13 note.

15:9 *Simeon.* It is not clear why this tribe, south of Judah and to a great extent absorbed by it, should be mentioned together with the "sojourners" from the northern tribes of Ephraim and Manasseh (11:16; cf. 1 K 11:32 note). Perhaps the Simeonites declared their full solidarity with the Southern Kingdom at this time.

15:12 *A covenant.* King and people solemnly reconsecrated themselves *to seek the Lord,* who at Mount Sinai had pledged Himself to make the Israelites "a kingdom of priests and a holy nation" without any merit or worthiness on their part (Ex 19:5; 20:1, 2 notes). On the covenant concept see Exodus, Introduction, "Content." Deuteronomy contains "the words of the covenant which the Lord commanded Moses to make with the people of Israel in the land of Moab, besides the covenant which he had made with them at Horeb" (Dt 29:1). For other renewals of the covenant see Jos 24:25 ff.; 2 Ch 23:16; 29:10; 34:31.

15:13 *Put to death.* On capital punishment in the OT see Ex 22:18 note; Dt 13:10 note.

15:16 *Queen mother.* For her position at court see 1 K 15:10 note, 12 f.

15:17 *Not taken out.* He "took away . . . the high places" (14:3) to the extent that this could be done by royal decree. In his intentions he was *blameless.* But evidently the people found ways of circumventing his orders so that he did not succeed in eradicating an entrenched custom. His successors fared no better. (17:6, 20:33)

Israel. Not a reference to the Northern Kingdom. Under the Davidic kings of Judah, Israel in the religious sense continued to exist in spite of much unfaithfulness. (11:3 note)

15:19 *Thirty-fifth year.* Cf. 16:1 note

16:1-10 FOREIGN ALLIANCE AGAINST ISRAEL

16:1 *Built Ramah.* Cf. notes on the parallel account in 1 K 15:16-22, where, however, no date is given for this incident. It can be dated *in the thirty-sixth year of the reign of Asa* if the lapse of time is reckoned from the division of the kingdom rather than from his own accession to the throne. According to 1 K 15:33, Baasha ruled 24 years, beginning in the third year of Asa. Hence in the latter's 36th regnal year the northern king was dead for some 10 years.

16:7 *Hanani.* A seer or prophet reproved Asa's appeal for foreign help. If the king had relied on the Lord, he would not have needed to tap forbidden resources. In times of crises men are prone to "trust in chariots . . . and in horsemen because they are very strong, but do not look to the Holy One of Israel or consult with the Lord." (Is 31:1; 30:1 ff.; Eze 17:15; Ps 20:7 f.)

16:10 *Prison.* It seems almost incredible that a man so zealous for the Lord (ch. 15) should be the first king of Judah to persecute God's messenger. Chronicles gives an account of Asa which needs no debunking, a warning to "any one who thinks that he stands [to] take heed lest he fall." (1 Co 10:12)

16:11-14 CONCLUDING SUMMARY

16:12 *Physicians.* Chronicles adds some details to the account of Asa's disease and death in 1 K 15:23 f. As in the national emergency (1-6), so in his personal predicament he *did not seek the Lord.* In his illness Hezekiah "prayed to the Lord" (2 K 20:2), but the physicians (lit. "healers") from whom Asa *sought help* practiced more magic than medicine.

16:14 *Fire.* Lit. "a great burning," not of the corpse but of "spices" (Jer 34:5). His grandson Jehoram was not given such an honorable burial (21:19). For the disposition cf. 1 Sm. 31:11 note.

17:1—20:37 Jehoshaphat

17:1-19 REVIEW OF GOOD FEATURES

17:1 *Jehoshaphat.* The account of his reign is longer by one chapter (17—20) than that of Asa his father (14—16). Of all kings after Solomon only Hezekiah is accorded more space (chs. 29—32). By contrast, Jehoshaphat's reign is compressed into 10 verses in 1 K 22:41-50. Chronicles has a lengthier report because the action and the attitude of this king exemplified the lessons the writer wanted to draw from the past (cf. 14:1 note). The Lord "established the kingdom in his hand" (5) because "his heart was courageous in the Lord" (1-6). He not only abolished idolatry but also introduced a program of mass education in "the law of the Lord" (7-9). God's blessings were evident: he "grew steadily greater" abroad and at home. (10-19)

17:3 *With [him].* No man has the right to demand God's gracious presence. A person who responds to this undeserved gift with a godly life has the kind of mind God blesses with "riches and honor." (5)

17:9 *Book.* Called "the book of the law of the Lord given through Moses" in 34:14. It seems that only one copy was in circulation. After the return from the Babylonian exile, *the book of the law of the Lord* was read at assemblies of the people (Neh 9:3; 8:2-8). The teaching priests (15:3 note) were assisted by Levites. The "princes" or officers of the king served notice on the people that the teaching mission had royal sanction and protection.

17:10 *Fear of the Lord.* As God created panic in the ranks of Israel's attacking enemies (14:14 note), so He let Jehoshaphat's might grow to such proportions as to make the Philistines and the Arabs afraid even to initiate the kind of invasion which his father repulsed (14:9-15). Peace among nations depends on God.

17:14 *Muster.* If the Hebrew word for "thousand" in the following verses has its usual numerical meaning, Jehoshaphat had a standing army of 1,160,000 men. However, see 13:3 note.

18:1—19:3 COOPERATION WITH ISRAEL

18:1 *Marriage alliance.* The marriage of Jehoshaphat's son with Athaliah, daughter of Ahab (21:6), may have been designed to unite the divided kingdom politically and religiously. However, the attempted reconciliation produced nothing good. This chapter records how first of all it led to a military disaster. For an almost identical account of Jehoshaphat's cooperation with Ahab in an ill-fated campaign against Syria see 1 K 22:1-36, where it concludes the history of the northern king.

19:1 *In safety.* Like his father Asa, Jehoshaphat was not a perfect saint, idealized by legend. Disregarding Micaiah's warning, he continued to make common cause with "the wicked" (2). God spared his life. But a prophet made it very clear that by his disobedience he had incurred "wrath . . . from the Lord." Ch 21 tells what happened. Going against God's will is no less evil if it serves what might appear to be a good purpose.

19:4-11 JUSTICE IN COURTS

19:4 *At Jerusalem.* Reproved for going abroad to join Ahab, Jehoshaphat restricted himself to activities he could initiate in Judah with headquarters in Jerusalem. Rather than persecute the Lord's messenger, as his father did (16:10), he renewed his efforts to bring *back to the Lord* all people under his jurisdiction from the southern border at Beer-sheba (45 miles south of Jerusalem) to the northern boundary in the hill country of Ephraim. To that end he personally undertook a campaign to reform the judicial system of the land (4-11). In all cases the judges were to enforce the law of the Lord without fear or favor because in reality they "judge not for man but for the Lord" (6). "Disputed cases" of civil litigation were to come before a superior court in Jerusalem, presided over by "the governor of . . . Judah." "In all matters of the Lord" (11), i.e., in cases involving worship and ritual, the high priest had final authority.

19:7 *Fear of the Lord.* The reform was not a political maneuver or innovation but a restoration of God's rule over His chosen people. The judges were His representatives, appointed to administer legislation which expressed His will. (Cf. Dt 1:17 f.; 16:18-20; 17:8-13)

20:1-30 VICTORY OVER INVADERS

20:1-30 *Against Jehoshaphat.* "The kingdoms of the lands that were round about Judah . . . made no war against Jehoshaphat" (17:10) until after his disastrous alliance with Ahab (ch. 18). Perhaps encouraged by the victory of the Syrians, several tribes west and south of the Dead Sea joined forces in an attack on Judah. The invading forces consisted mainly of Moabites and Ammonites. As they rounded the southern end of the Dead Sea, they were reinforced by *some of the Meunites.* These confederates are later described as coming from Mount Seir, another name for Edom (10, 22), which at this time had no king (1 K 22:47). The invaders pushed northward along the western shore of the Dead Sea. When they arrived at En-gedi, only 15 miles from Jerusalem, Jehoshaphat "proclaimed a fast throughout all Judah." Before an assembly, representing "all the cities of Judah," the king led his people in a fervent prayer for help (5-12). The "Spirit of the Lord," speaking through a prophet, announced the answer to the prayer: the outcome of the impending battle would be "the victory of the Lord" on their behalf. As if the promised deliverance were already a reality, king and people worshiped the Lord, the Levites singing hymns of praise "with a very loud voice" (13-19). Their faith was not in vain. In the ensuing battle they did not have to strike a blow. The Lord so confused the enemy that he destroyed himself (20-23). Jehoshaphat and his people did not forget to be thankful. Laden with booty, they "blessed the Lord" in a nearby village. "Returning to Jerusalem with joy," they came "with harps and lyres and trumpets, to the house of the Lord." (24-30)

20:2 *Edom.* For scribal confusion of Aram (Syria) and Edom see 2 Sm 8:13 note. At En-gedi David once hid from Saul. (1 Sm 23:29 note; 24:1 ff.)

20:3 *Feared.* He had a strong army (17:14 ff.). Yet he knew that all efforts were in vain if the enemy was the rod of God's wrath against them. (19:2; Is 10:5 f.)

20:5 *New court.* Perhaps a newly repaired court.

20:6 *God in heaven.* Reminiscent of Solomon's prayer at the dedication of the temple, which is summarized in part in 9. (Cf. 1 K 8:22-53)

20:7 *Thy friend.* So called because he believed God. (Ja 2:23; Is 41:8)

20:10 *Invade.* For God's command not to invade or harass these "brethren" of the Israelites see Dt 2:4, 9, 19.

20:11 *Thy possession.* Jehoshaphat boldly shifts the responsibility for the safety of the land on God, pointing out that it really belongs to Him—a good example of how to wrestle with God in prayer and prevail. (Gn 32:28)

20:14 *Jahaziel.* Not mentioned otherwise. When the Spirit of the Lord came upon him, his words had divine authority. (20)

20:16 *Ziz.* A few miles north of En-gedi, south of which lay *the wilderness of Jeruel.*

20:17 *Victory of the Lord.* At the Red Sea they likewise saw "the salvation of the Lord" while they stood still and let the Lord fight for them. (Ex 14:13 f.; see also David's encounter with Goliath, 1 Sm 17:45-47)

20:19 *Kohathites and Korahites.* Descendants of Levi who were temple musicians. (1 Ch 6:1, 22, 31)

20:20 *Wilderness of Tekoa.* Tekoa, the home of Amos and of a wise woman, was about 6 miles south of Bethlehem. (Am 1:1; 2 Sm 14:2 note)

Believe . . . be established. In Hebrew these verbs are different forms of the same root, meaning to be firm, stable. Standing unwaveringly on God's Word is faith. Such trust in God gives a firm foundation to life regardless of outward circumstances. (Is 7:9; Hab 2:4)

20:22 *An ambush.* Lit. "liers in wait." We are not told who they were, only that their attack was so unexpected and mysterious that the enemy was completely confused. In the end "they all helped to destroy one another" (23). So God once routed the Midianites at Gideon's time and the Philistines when Saul was king. (Ju 7:22; 1 Sm 14:20)

20:26 *Beracah.* This valley begins its slope near Tekoa and reaches the Dead Sea near En-gedi.

20:29 *Fear of God.* Better: "terror of God," as in 2 Ch 14:14.

20:31-34 SUMMARY OF JEHOSHAPHAT'S REIGN

20:33 *High places.* They *were not taken away* because the royal decree for their removal (17:6) did not have popular support. (See 15:17 note)

20:35-37 MARITIME DISASTER

20:35 *Ahaziah.* After Ahab's death (18:34) his son Jehoram reigned in Israel for 12 years (2 K 3), to be succeeded by Ahaziah.

20:36 *Go to Tarshish.* This phrase explains what kind of ships were built (cf. 9:21 note). The next verse states that they were wrecked even though they were of a size capable of going to Tarshish.

20:37 *Joined.* According to 1 K 22:49 Jehoshaphat refused to cooperate with Ahaziah in a similar expedition.

21:1-20 Jehoram

21:1-7 HIS VIOLENCE AND APOSTASY

21:1 *Jehoram.* The marriage alliance his father made with Ahab (18:1) had more serious consequences than unsuccessful military and maritime ventures undertaken jointly by the two kingdoms (18:2 ff.; 20:35 ff.). For some time Judah came directly under the evil influence of the house of Ahab. Jehoram, no doubt prompted by his wife, the daughter of Ahab (22:3), "slew all his brothers . . . and also some of the princes of Israel" (4). See the parallel account in 2 K 8:16-19.

21:2 *Azariah.* It is not clear why the first and the fourth son have the same name. A scribal error may be involved.

21:8-10 LOSS OF TERRITORY

21:8 *Edom.* See 2 K 8:20-22

21:11-20 RETRIBUTION

21:11 *Unfaithfulness.* Supplementing the account in Kings, the remaining verses of the chapter record the fact that Jehoram's wickedness did not go unpunished (11-15). Judah was invaded (16 f.) and the king died of a horrible disease.

21:12 *Elijah.* Sudden, unannounced appearances were characteristic of his ministry. The arrival of a letter from him seems unusually strange. He had no other known contact with the kings of Judah. His translation into heaven is reported earlier (2 K 2:1). His successor Elisha, on the other hand, accompanied Jehoram's father on the campaign against the Moabites (2 K 3:11). Therefore the suggestion seems justified to assume that a copyist misread Elijah for Elisha. However, Elisha may have begun his prophetic activity during his spiritual father's lifetime. The time of the latter's disappearance from the earth is not clearly indicated.

21:14 *Plague.* The Hebrew noun has the more general meaning of a severe "blow," which may take the form of a disease or epidemic. In 1 Sm 4:17 it is translated "slaughter."

21:16 *Ethiopians.* A similar group of raiders was repulsed by Jehoram's grandfather Asa. (14:9 note)

21:17 *Jehoahaz.* The more common form of his name is Ahaziah (22:1). Both names mean "the Lord took." In the one case the Hebrew verb to take (*'ahaz*) is preceded by the divine name; in the other the verb comes first. A king by this name later occupied also the throne of Israel. (2 K 13:1)

21:19 *No fire.* The people burned no spices "in his honor" as they did "in a very great fire" at his grandfather's funeral. (16:14 note)

22:1-9 Ahaziah

22:1-6 PARTNER TO ISRAEL'S APOSTASY

22:1 *Youngest son. Ahaziah,* the sole survivor of the raid on "the camp" of Judah, met a violent death after he reigned only a year. His mother, daughter of Ahab and granddaughter of Omri, was "his counselor" for evil so that "in doing wickedly" he matched the kings of Israel (1-6). Therefore his downfall by Jehu "was ordained by God." (7-9; see the parallel account 2 K 8:25-29; 9:27 f.)

22:2 *Forty-two.* Several Hebrew manuscripts and the Septuagint have "twenty-two years," no doubt the better reading. His father died at the age of 40. (21:20)

22:7-9 SLAIN BY JEHU

22:10—23:21 Athaliah, Ahaziah's Mother

22:10-12 PURGE OF ROYAL FAMILY EXCEPT YOUNGEST PRINCE

22:10 *The royal family.* Despotic, cruel, iron-willed, Athaliah did not shrink from killing off her own grandsons, fearing that they could challenge her usurpation of power. However, one of them escaped the assassins. "While Athaliah ruled over the land," the year-old survivor, Joash, was kept in hiding for 6 years by his aunt and her husband, the high priest Jehoiada (10-12). "But in the seventh year" a counterrevolution, masterminded by the high priest, put the young prince on the throne. Athaliah was executed (ch. 23). See the parallel account in 2 K 11. The writer of Chronicles adds some details not found there, but omits others.

22:11 *Jehoshabeath.* In 2 K 11 she is called Jehosheba.

23:1-21 COUNTERREVOLUTION BY HIGH PRIEST

23:1 *A compact.* In plotting the overthrow of Athaliah, Jehoiada first gained the support of the military leaders, among whom "the captains of the Carites and of the guards" are mentioned in particular in 2 K 11:4 note.

23:3 *The Lord spoke.* For God's promise to David see 2 Sm 7:12, 16; 2 Ch 6:16.

23:4 *Priests and Levites.* The writer emphasizes the part played by the authorized officiants in the temple, merely alluding to "the captains who were set over the army" (9, 14, 20). The presence of "singers with their musical instruments" likewise receives special notice. (13; cf. 1 Ch 25)

23:18 *Posted watchmen.* Better translated: "he placed the offices of the house into the hands of the priests and the Levites." Both were *organized* by David. According to Mosaic prescriptions, the former were *to offer burnt offerings* while the latter were "gatekeepers at the gates of the house."

24:1-27 Joash

24:1-3 PERSONAL DATA

24:1 *Seven years.* For the reign of Joash as long as he was under the good influence of the high priest see the parallel account of 2 K 12:1-16.

24:4-14 TEMPLE REPAIRS

24:5 *Levites.* Supplementing the account in Kings, the writer of Chronicles makes repeated reference to the *Levites* (6, 11). He adds also other details: (1) the reason for the repair of the temple (7); (2) the explanation that the tax to be collected was levied by Moses (6, 9); (3) the note that the people dropped the tax into the chest under the supervision of the priests. (10)

24:15-24 APOSTASY IN LATER YEARS

24:16 *Among the kings.* Joash was denied burial "in the tombs of the kings" (25), an honor accorded Jehoiada, who was regent while the king was a minor and whose wife was a royal princess. (22:11)

24:18 *Asherim.* For the meaning of the term see Gn 28:18 note.

Forsook. The king's apostasy after the death of Jehoiada is not mentioned in Kings. Swayed by fawning courtiers to serve idols in spite of repeated warnings by God's spokesmen (15-19), he sank so low that he executed Zechariah, the first prophet in Judah to suffer martyrdom (20-22). *Wrath came upon Judah and Jerusalem* through an invasion by the Syrians (23 f.). Discredited and disgraced, the killer of a prophet became the first of Judah to be cut down by assassins. (25-27)

24:20 *Took possession.* Translated: "came upon" in 1 Ch 12:18. Cf. Ju 6:34 note.

24:22 *Jehoiada, Zechariah's father.* Even though Zechariah was not the last whose "righteous blood" was shed, Jesus refers to him in a summary of all martyrs beginning with Abel, whose death is recorded in Genesis, and ending with Zechariah, whose death is recorded in Chronicles, the last book of the Jewish canon (Mt 23:35). One of the best NT manuscripts omits the troublesome phrase "the son of Barachiah." (Cf. Zch 1:1)

24:22 *Avenge.* Lit. "require," i.e., the penalty for having shed "the blood of man" (cf. Gn 9:5-6 notes). The Martyr of Golgotha asked that God forgive His executioners. (Lk 23:34; see also Acts 7:60)

24:25-27 JOASH ASSASSINATED

24:26 *Who conspired.* The mothers of the conspirators were foreigners. It may be for this reason that the names of both mothers and sons appear in somewhat different form in 2 K 12:21.

24:27 *Commentary.* The Hebrew word for this unknown source occurs only here and in 13:22, where it is translated "story."

25:1-28 Amaziah

25:1-4 GOOD BEGINNING OF REIGN

25:1 *Amaziah.* The ninth king to succeed David "did in all things as Joash his father had done" (2 K 14:3), as is evident from the following facts: (1) at the beginning of his reign he "did what was right" according to "the law, in the book of Moses" (1-4) and the words of "a man of God" (5-13); (2) later he rejected censure for idolatry, threatening God's prophet with death (14-16); (3) divine retribution came: he suffered a crushing defeat in battle (17-24) and died at the hands of assassins. (25-28)

25:5-13 EDOMITES DEFEATED WITHOUT ISRAELITE TROOPS

25:5 *Assembled.* Amaziah's victory over the Edomites is reported more fully here than in Kings, where it is compressed into one verse (2 K 14:7 note). In the figures for his army, the mercenary troops from the Northern Kingdom (6), and for the losses sustained by the enemy (11 f.) the Hebrew word for "thousand" very likely does not have numerical meaning but is a military term denoting a fully equipped warrior or leader (for other instances see 13:3 note; 17:14 note) *Those twenty years old and upward* were of legal draft age. (Nm 1:3; 1 Ch 27:23)

25:7 *With Israel.* As other kings learned to their sorrow, cooperation with the apostate Northern Kingdom had dire consequences. (19:2; 20:37)

25:9 *Much more.* It is true in all situations that "better is a little with righteousness than great revenues with injustice." (Pr 16:8)

25:11 *Seir.* Another name for Edom. (20:22)

25:12 *Threw them down.* No reason is given for the massacre of the prisoners. Perhaps it was in retaliation for a crime committed by the Edomites.

25:13 *Beth-horon.* About 16 miles northwest of Jerusalem. Having "returned home in fierce anger" (10), the northern mercenaries started out *from Samaria* to raid a wide band of Judean cities.

25:14-16 LAPSE INTO IDOLATRY REPROVED

25:15 *Deliver.* Worshiping gods who could not protect their devotees was as absurd as it was sinful. All idols are no less ludicrously impotent whether fabricated by hand or in the workshop of human thought.

25:17-24 DISASTROUS WAR WITH ISRAEL

25:17 *To Joash.* For Amaziah's foolish challenge of his contemporary on the throne of

Israel and its disastrous consequences see the parallel account in 2 K 14:8-14.

25:23 *Ephraim Gate.* The gate opening on the road to Ephraim, i.e., the Northern Kingdom, the Damascus Gate of today. The *Corner Gate* was at the extreme west end of the wall, where it formed an "Angle" (26:9) with the wall from the south.

25:24 *With them.* The Hebrew text has only "with Obed-edom." The stolen *vessels* were in "the storehouse" of the temple which Obed-edom and his sons were to guard. (1 Ch 26:15)

25:25-28 SLAIN BY CONSPIRATORS

25:27 *Slew him.* Amaziah's violent death is not mentioned in Kings. Lachish, about 30 miles southwest of Jerusalem, was one of the cities fortified by Rehoboam, Solomon's son. (11:5-12)

25:28 *Upon horses.* The Hebrew text has "the horses," referring perhaps to the animals on which the assassins had come. Hence no particular significance seems to attach to the mode of transporting the king's corpse to Jerusalem.

26:1-23 Uzziah (Azariah)

26:1-5 GOOD BEGINNING OF REIGN

26:1 *All the people.* There was unanimity in the nation that the Davidic succession was to continue even though a conspiracy swept away the previous occupant of the throne. *Uzziah* ("my strength is the Lord"), also known as Azariah ("the Lord helps"; so in 1 Ch 3:12 and in Kings), "did . . . according to all that his father Amaziah [and his grandfather Joash] had done." At first "he sought the Lord" and "God made him prosper." Later he "was false to the Lord." While he did not lose his life to assassins, as his immediate predecessors did, he was forced to hand the reins of government to his son because "the Lord had smitten him" with leprosy. Uzziah's reign of 52 years is summarized in nine verses in Kings (2 K 14:21 f.; 15:1-7). The writer of Chronicles supplies more details both of his prosperity (6-15) and of his punishment. (16-21)

26:2 *Eloth.* Also spelled Elath. For its location and significance see 1 K 9:26 note; 2 Ch 8:18 note.

26:5 *Zechariah.* Perhaps the person by that name who attested Isaiah's message. (Is 8:2)

26:6-15 VICTORY IN WARS; MILITARY PREPAREDNESS

26:6 *Made war.* Judah suffered invasions under his father and grandfather. Uzziah recaptured and fortified cities on the western and southwestern borders. *Gath* had fallen into David's hands (1 Ch 18:1 note). *Ashdod* was about 30 miles west of Jerusalem; *Jabneh,* about 10 miles north of Ashdod.

26:7 *Gurbaal.* Perhaps to be identified with a city near Beer-sheba at the southern border of Judah some 45 miles southwest of Jerusalem.

26:9 *Corner Gate.* Cf. 25:23 note. *The Valley Gate* opened into the Valley of Hinnom, west and south of the city. A tower was built *at the Angle,* literally "at the turning," i.e., where the wall turned in another direction.

26:10 *The soil.* Uzziah made the land productive as well as safe. He promoted agriculture and cattle raising in various parts of the country: in *the Shephelah* or lowlands, where the hills of Judah fall away toward the Mediterranean; *in the wilderness,* the grazing lands south and southeast of Jerusalem; *in the plain,* the tableland east of the Jordan and the Dead Sea; *in the hills* or hill country as well as in the more *fertile lands.* The Hebrew word for the last named soil is *carmel* (KJV: Carmel), which here is not a proper but a common noun, as in Is 16:10 where it is translated "fruitful field."

26:11 *Army.* Uzziah put it under the command of 2,600 "mighty men of valor" or professional soldiers. Their forces could be augmented by calling up a militia for service *in divisions.* The figure for the men under arms no doubt was enlarged in the transmission of the text. At least one zero should be dropped from the total given in 13.

26:15 *Engines.* Devices such as catapults.

26:16-21 PRIDE AND PUNISHMENT

26:16 *Proud.* The writer supplies the reason why "the Lord smote the king, so that he was a leper to the day of his death" (2 K 15:5). Puffed up with pride, he entered the temple wanting to *burn incense on the altar of incense* which stood in the "sanctuary" or holy place. But in Israel not even the king was permitted to assume worship functions, reserved by divine law for "the priests the sons of Aaron" (18; Nm 16:40; 18:7).—Pride, mankind's undoing from the beginning, has not lost its appeal for all children of Adam. (Gn 3:6; Pr 16:18; 29:23)

26:21 *Governing.* The son exercised the functions of government while the father was still alive.

26:22-23 DEATH AND BURIAL

26:22 *Isaiah.* He was called to his prophetic office "in the year that king Uzziah died" (Is 6:1). The writer no doubt drew on what *Isaiah . . . wrote* for details about Uzziah's prosperity and his fall which the writer of Kings did not incorporate.

27:1-9 Jotham

27:1 *Jotham.* The account of his reign in this chapter adds some details to 2 K 15:32-38 and omits others.

27:3 *Upper gate.* Jotham continued his father's building program. He added to the fortifications of Jerusalem and of cities guarding approaches to it. *The upper gate* which he *built* or reenforced gave access to "the king's house" from *the house of the Lord* (23:20). *Ophel* was the southern part of the temple hill.

27:5 *Ammonites.* Jotham completely subjugated the Ammonites, already defeated and made tributary by his father (26:7 f.) A *cor* held about 10 bushels.

27:7 *His wars.* No serious invasion from the

north seems to have occurred during his lifetime. But "in those days the Lord began to send Rezin the king of Syria and Pekah the son of Remaliah [king of Israel] against Judah." (2 K 15:37)

28:1-27 Ahaz

28:1-4 IDOLATROUS ABOMINATIONS

28:1 *Ahaz.* One of the worst of the Davidic kings. The writer of Chronicles supplements the account of his reign given in 2 K 16 and Is 7 by: (1) adding some details to the characterization of Ahaz (1-4; cf. 2 K 16:1-4 notes); (2) giving a fuller description of the losses inflicted on Judah by Rezin of Syria and Pekah of Israel (5-7). "The men of Israel" took very many captives but were persuaded to release a large number of them because they were their "kinsfolk" (8-15). Ahaz was in dire straits, pressed from the north by Israel and Syria, from the south by the Edomites, from the southwest by the Philistines. In desperation he appealed for help to the Assyrians. However, the heavy tribute which Ahaz had to pay Tiglath-pileser only added to Judah's distress (16-21). Instead of turning to the Lord, the king "became yet more faithless." He "sacrificed to the gods of Damascus," desecrated the temple in Jerusalem, and shut its doors. (22-27)

28:3 *Hinnom.* Cf. 2 K 23:10 note.

28:5-7 INVASION BY ISRAEL AND SYRIA

28:5 *Defeated him.* The results of the invasion by Israel and Syria, summarized in one verse in Kings (2 K 16:5), are described more fully here. (5-15)

28:6 *Thousand.* If the Hebrew word for *thousand* here is not a numeral but a military term, then Pekah slew 120 *men of valor* (cf. 25:5 note). The number of captives (8) very likely received zeros in the transmission of the text. A figure of 2,000 would be more in keeping with the circumstances.

28:8-15 CAPTIVES RELEASED BY ISRAEL

28:9 *Oded.* An otherwise unknown prophet, although a man by that name is mentioned in 15:8. Release of prisoners of war was urged also by Elisha. (2 K 6:20-23)

28:15 *Mentioned.* Their names are given in 12.

Palm trees. Jericho is so called also in Dt 34:3; Ju 1:16.

28:16-21 APPEAL TO ASSYRIA

28:17 *Edomites.* They were in a position to even the score with their former Judean overlords because Rezin had taken Elath and driven "the men of Judah from Elath." (2 K 16:6)

28:18 *Philistines.* Ahaz lost control of the cities which his father had taken from the Philistines (26:6 f.), who proceeded to make inroads into *the Shephelah* (26:10 note) and *the Negeb,* the southland of Judah.

28:20 *Tilgath-pilneser.* So spelled also in 1 Ch 5:6. Cf. note there.

28:22-27 PROGRESSIVE RELIGIOUS DECLINE; DEATH

28:23 *Gods of Damascus.* Ahaz added these idols to his pantheon, believing that they helped the Syrians to "distress" him. After the Assyrians took Damascus, he had a replica made of an altar which Tiglath-pileser seemingly had left standing there.

28:24 *Vessels.* Some of them Ahaz mutilated (2 K 16:17; others he "discarded." (29:19)

29:1-2 ACCESSION; PERSONAL DATA

29:1 *Hezekiah.* The account of his reign, filling four chapters (29—32), is longer than that of any other king except David and Solomon. It differs from the three chapters devoted to it in 2 Kings (18—20) in two respects. Political events and Hezekiah's personal adventures are reported more briefly than in Kings. In the space so gained, the writer of Chronicles tells a much more complete story of the restoration of true worship, capsuled in three verses in 2 K 18:4-6. See the Introduction, "Purpose." On the usual introduction (1 f.) there follows at once the story of the religious reform which the son of wicked Ahaz carried out in three phases. Each of these is the topic of a whole chapter telling how he (1) cleansed the temple and rededicated it to the service of the Lord (ch. 29); (2) restored the observance of the annual festival days by keeping the Passover (ch. 30); (3) reinstituted the other services in the temple, also providing for the livelihood of the priests and Levites. (31)

29:3—31:21 HEZEKIAH'S REFORMS

1) 29:3-36 Restoration of Temple and Worship

29:5 *Filth.* After years of neglect, the temple needed a thorough housecleaning. Hezekiah assigned the task to the authorized personnel: the priests and the Levites. First, however, both groups had to make themselves ceremonially clean (3-11). After they "sanctified themselves," the priests brought "the uncleanness" from "the inner part of the house [the holy place] . . . into the court of the house," from where the Levites "carried it out to the brook Kidron." It took 16 days to make the entire temple complex ready for the dedication ceremonies. (12-19)

29:5 *Sanctify yourselves.* Remove all ceremonial defilement. (1 Ch 15:12 note)

29:7 *Burnt offerings.* The paganized sacrifices offered by Ahaz (2 K 16:15) were an abomination to *the God of Israel.*

29:8 *Wrath . . . came.* "The Lord brought Judah low because of Ahaz" (28:16-21), making them an "object . . . of hissing," i.e., of derision, among the heathen nations. The destruction of Jerusalem was the climax of disgrace. (Jer 25:9, 18; Dt 28:25)

29:10 *Covenant.* For other renewals of the covenant relationship see 15:12 note; 23:16; 34:31; Neh 9:38.

29:12 *Levites.* Levi's sons through Gershon,

Kohath, and Merari had special assignments in the transport of the tabernacle (Nm 3:14-37). For "the service" of music in the temple, there were "set apart" the branches of the Levitical family who were descendants of Asaph, Heman, and Jeduthun. (1 Ch 25:1-7; 15:16 ff.)

29:15 *Words of the Lord.* The king's command had divine authority because it was based on God's command laid down in the law of Moses or because it was directly communicated by a prophet. (30:12)

29:16 *Kidron.* Immediately outside the city walls, the valley of Kidron served as the dumping ground for discarded objects of false worship. (15:16; 30:14)

29:20 *Went up.* The temple cleansed and "all the utensils . . . made ready and sanctified" (19), its reconsecration could begin. The ritual of purification consisted of sin offerings and burnt offerings (20-24). While the priests performed these rites, the Levites provided vocal and instrumental music. The king and all others joined in the worship by bowing themselves. (25-30)

29:21 *Sin offering.* Seven goats were sacrificed for a sin offering "to make atonement for all Israel," differentiated as *the kingdom* (the king and his family), *the sanctuary* (the temple and its officiants), and *Judah* (the rest of the people).

29:22 *Blood.* The blood, caught in basins, was thrown *against the altar* as prescribed Lv 1:3-6.

29:23 *Laid their hands.* A symbolic transfer of guilt to the sacrificial animal. (Lv 4:15; 1:4)

29:26 *Trumpets.* At the dedication of the temple, 120 priests sounded the trumpets (5:12). The Levites played on "cymbals, harps, and lyres" (25), *instruments of David.* (Cf. 1 Ch 23:5)

29:31 *The assembly.* The dedicatory service, conducted by the priests and Levites, resulted in a surge of popular enthusiasm for worship. For the total of 3,970 animals offered see 1 K 8:62 note.

29:34 *More upright.* The Levites, who had not come under the influence of the renegade high priest Uriah (2 K 16:16) as directly as the priests, responded in large numbers to Hezekiah's call to sanctify themselves for service in the temple. (3 ff.)

2) 30:1-27 Restoration of Passover

30:2 *Passover.* As soon as possible after the rededication of the temple, Hezekiah restored the observance of Israel's great festivals. The first on the ecclesiastical calendar was the Passover festival, also called "the feast of unleavened bread" (13, 15; Lv 23:4-7; Nm 28:16 ff.; Dt 16:1-8). At its first celebration the former slaves of Pharaoh became God's redeemed community (Ex 12:11 note). Its observance under Hezekiah reestablished Israel's covenant relationship, reconstituting the nation as God's chosen people (29:10). Invitations to participate went out by couriers also to the people of the Northern Kingdom who had "escaped from the hand of the kings of Assyria" (1-9). "Many people came together in Jerusalem" (13) even though "only a few men" of Israel responded (10-12). Some of them were unable to prepare themselves "as prescribed." "Yet they ate the passover" without censure (13-22). After keeping "the feast of unleavened bread seven days," the assembly was so caught up "with great gladness" that they "agreed together" to prolong the festivities for another 7 days. "Great joy" prevailed. The king and the princes provided an abundance of animals "for offerings." "Priests sanctified themselves in great numbers" so that enough of them were at hand to officiate at the sacrifices. (23-27)

30:3 *Its time.* The time stipulated was the 14th day of Abib, the first month (Ex 34:18). Sixteen days of the month had been taken up with cleansing the temple (29:17). However, the Law provided for a later celebration if it was impossible to be ready by the regular date. (Nm 9:10 f.)

30:5 *Beer-sheba to Dan.* A popular expression for the extent of the Promised Land. (Ju 20:1 note)

30:6 *Israel.* Hezekiah reminded the northern tribes, called Israel to distinguish them from Judah, that they too were descendants and heirs of *Abraham, Isaac, and Israel.* But they must repent. Because of their apostasy, God punished them in "His fierce anger" (8). Many had been taken into exile by *kings of Assyria* such as Tiglath-pileser. (2 K 15:29; 16:9)

30:10 *Zebulun.* The northernmost of the tribes mentioned. Apparently the couriers did not get beyond its borders.

30:14 *Altars.* The people followed the king's example, extending the cleanup of the temple to the entire city and making it a fit place to celebrate the Passover. Ahaz had "made himself altars in every corner of Jerusalem." (28:24)

30:15 *Shame.* By their greater readiness to worship, the laity shamed the clergy into action. They *sanctified themselves* for their tasks "in sufficient number." (3)

30:19 *Cleanness.* The worshipers did not "die in their uncleanness" (Lv 15:31) because they did not willfully disregard the ritual prescriptions. The Lord "healed them," i.e., he did not let their uncleanness result in their death. As "the sabbath was made for man, not man for the sabbath" (Mk 2:27), all other ceremonial laws were not an end in themselves.

30:23 *Keep the feast.* The word *feast* is not in the Hebrew text which, in a more literal translation, reads: "they agreed to observe other seven days." For a similar extension of festivities, when Solomon dedicated the temple, see 1 K 8:65 note.

30:24 *Bulls . . . sheep.* All told 19,000 sacrificial animals. Cf. 1 K 8:62 note.

30:25 *Sojourners.* The same Hebrew word translated "stranger" in Ex 12:48, which stipulates that such a non-Israelite could eat the passover if he was circumcised.

30:27 *Priests and the Levites.* The Hebrew text has: "the priests, the Levites." The apposition *the Levites* stresses that the men who pronounced the blessing were rightful priests because they descended from Levi. This needed to be emphasized after Ahaz introduced so many unlawful practices.

3) 31:1 Nationwide Destruction of Idols

31:1 *The cities.* Eradication of idolatry spread from the temple (29:1-17) to the city (30:14) and from Jerusalem to the outlying districts, even to the cities of the Northern Kingdom, of which *Ephraim and Manasseh* were the representative tribes. For *Asherim* see 14:3 note.

4) 31:2-21 Restoration of Regular Worship

31:2 *Divisions.* Hezekiah rededicated the temple (ch. 29) for worshipers, reconstituted as the covenant nation (ch. 30). His next course was to restore regular worship services, suspended by his father (29:7). With that goal in mind he gave several broad directives: (1) he put priests and Levites on duty in the temple and at its gates according to the schedules and *divisions* established by David (1 Ch 23-25) (2) "from his own possessions" he contributed sacrificial animals and required the people to "give the portion due to the priests and the Levites" for their livelihood (3-10); (3) he prepared "chambers in the house of the Lord" for storing "the contributions, the tithes and dedicated things" brought by the people (11); (4) he put officers in charge of these contributions. It was their responsibility "to distribute portions to every male among the priests and to every one among the Levites who was enrolled." (12-19)

31:3 *The law.* Legislation regarding sacrifices for various occasions *is written* in Nm 28—29.

31:4 *The priests.* For their "portion" consisting of "the first fruits . . . the tithe . . . and dedicated things" (5) see Nm 18.

31:5 *Honey.* Its use in meal offerings to the Lord was forbidden. (Lv 2:11 note)

31:7 *Third . . . seventh month.* Contributions of various kinds of produce came in during the harvesting season, which began in *the third month.* In *the seventh month* the feast of tabernacles, also called "the feast of ingathering," marked its end.

31:10 *Azariah.* A person by the same name was "the chief officer of the house of God" (13). Another *Azariah* was high priest during the reign of a king who himself bore that name. (26:17; 2 K 15:1)

31:11 *Chambers.* Solomon built "side chambers" into the walls of the temple. For the temple structure see 1 K 6:2 note.

31:15 *The cities.* In order to make sure that no one was overlooked, an "enrollment of the priests" and "the Levites" was made in the Levitical cities as well as "in the fields of common land belonging to their cities" (19). Vv. 17-18 tell how the two groups were registered.

31:16 *Those enrolled.* Those who were *enrolled by genealogy* and *by their divisions* to serve their term of duty in the temple were certain of support there during the period of their service.

32:1-23 DELIVERANCE FROM ASSYRIAN ASSAULT

32:1 *Sennacherib.* The writer of Chronicles summarizes in 23 verses (1-23) Hezekiah's encounter with the Assyrian king, which is spread over three chapters in 2 K 18—20. See the notes there; also Is 36—38.

32:3 *Planned.* Despite the overall brevity of the account, the description of Hezekiah's defensive maneuvers (3-8) has no parallel in Kings. Before the siege began, he (1) cut off the supply of water *outside the city* (3 f.); (2) strengthened the city's fortifications and stepped up the production of weaponry (5); (3) converted the city into a military camp, setting "combat commanders over the people" (6); (4) bolstered the morale of the defenders, reminding them that the enemy, "an arm of flesh," was no match for the Lord, who would fight their battles. (7 f.)

32:4 *The brook.* No doubt the Gihon. What he did besides closing "the upper outlet of" this brook is mentioned in 30 and 2 K 20:20 note.

32:5 *Millo.* A part of the city's fortification which needed periodic repair. (2 Sm 5:9 note; 1 K 9:15; 11:27)

32:9 *Servants.* Sennacherib's attempt to cajole and frighten Hezekiah and the people into surrender (9:19) is described in greater detail in 2 K 18:14-37; 19:8-14.

32:20 *Prayed.* For the words of Hezekiah's prayer and God's answer to it through Isaiah see 2 K 19:15-34 where, however, the prophet's intercession is not mentioned.

32:22 *Gave them rest.* The Hebrew text has "he led them." RSV follows the Septuagint.

32:24-26 RECOVERY FROM SICKNESS AND PRIDE

32:24 *Sick.* For a more complete report on Hezekiah's recovery from illness see 2 K 20.

32:25 *Wrath.* Hezekiah was tried and found wanting (31). "The pride of his heart" (26) seduced him into showing his resources to Babylonian envoys (31). But as his physical malady was not fatal, so he recovered also from the attack of a spiritual virus. His repentance, said Isaiah, held off the day of wrath. (2 K 20:16-19)

32:27-33 HEZEKIAH'S WEALTH, PROJECTS, TRIAL

32:32 *The rest.* The sources on which the writer drew were "the vision of Isaiah" (see Is 1:1; chs. 36—39) and the last "Book of the Kings of Judah and Israel."

32:33 *Ascent.* There was a rise in the terrain leading to the royal sepulchres. For rites to honor the dead see 16:14; 21:19 notes.

33:1-20 Manasseh

33:1-9 RAMPANT IDOLATRY

33:1 *Manasseh.* His reign of 55 years, longer than that of any other king, set a record also for apostasy. For decades "the abominable practices" of the Canaanites held sway, running the gamut from soothsaying to child sacrifice. The situation is described in almost identical words in 2 K 21:1-9.

33:6 *Sons.* In 2 K 21:6 the text has "his son." For *the valley of . . . Hinnom* see 28:3; 2 K 23:10 note.

33:10-13 IMPRISONMENT, REPENTANCE, RESTORATION

33:10 *Spoke.* What the Lord "said by his servants the prophets," as recorded in 2 K 21:10-15, bore no fruit. However, Manasseh "humbled himself greatly" when the Lord inflicted distress on him through the Assyrian king. Brought to Babylon in fetters (10-13), the reprobate king did not seek forgiveness in vain. God "brought him again to Jerusalem" (13), where he proved the sincerity of his repentance by destroying false altars and idols and commanding Judah "to serve the Lord, the God of Israel." (14-17)

33:11 *King of Assyria.* The Assyrian empire was at the peak of its power in the days of Manasseh. While his name appears in the records of two of its mightiest kings, neither of them mentions the episode recorded here. However, an Egyptian vassal prince received similar treatment when he became involved in machinations against his overlord.

33:14-17 BUILDING PROJECTS; IDOLS REMOVED

33:14 *Gihon.* See 32:30; for *Ophel,* 27:3. The *Fish Gate* in the north wall very likely was so named from its use by fish merchants.

33:17 *High places.* Manasseh's reformation, coming at the end of his life, failed to eradicate worship *at the high places.* But by every act of sacrifice contrary to God's ordinance the people heaped up wrath for themselves (Jer 15:4). Even the king's son remained unregenerate. (21-25)

33:18-20 CONCLUDING SUMMARY

33:18 *Prayer.* The apocryphal book called "The Prayer of Manasseh" purports to have preserved the words he spoke, a claim which cannot be substantiated.

33:21-25 Amon

33:21 *Amon.* His short, disastrous reign is recorded also in 2 K 21:19-26 which, however, does not contain the note that "he did not humble himself before the Lord, as Manasseh his father had humbled himself." (23)

34:1—35:27 Josiah

34:1-7 EARLY REFORM MEASURES

34:1 *Josiah.* The two chapters devoted to Josiah (34 f.) complement the account in 2 K 22 f. Both accounts contain the main features of his reign. However, the writer of Chronicles again takes occasion to emphasize how important true worship is (see Introduction, "Purpose"). He fills the greater part of ch. 35 (1-19) with a description of the Passover celebration, which is summarized in three verses in 2 K 23:21-23.

At the beginning of Josiah's reign, idolatry was as entrenched in Judah as it had been at his grandfather's time if not more so. Following in Hezekiah's footsteps, the young king initiated a campaign to destroy the images and altars of heathen worship (1-7). "When he had purged the land and the house," he went on "to repair the house of the Lord" (8-13). In the process, "Hilkiah the priest found the book of the law of the Lord given through Moses" (14-18). Terrified by its contents (19-21) and by the condemnation of Judah's apostasy by the prophetess Huldah (22-28), he called an assembly of the people, read to them "all the words of the book," and renewed the "covenant before the Lord," demanding that "all who were present . . . stand to it" (29-33). After an intensive purge of the "abominations," now extended to "all the territory that belonged to the people of Israel" (33), he reconsecrated himself and the people to the Lord by celebrating the Passover. (35:1-19)

34:3 *Eighth year. While he was yet a boy* of 16 and again at the age of 20, Josiah *began to seek the God of David his father.* The writer of Kings does not mention these early efforts *to purge Judah and Jerusalem.* Later he gives a more complete description of the "abominations" which the king "took away." (2 K 23:4-20)

34:6 *In their ruins.* If this translation is correct, the reference is to the devastation inflicted by the Assyrians. The Septuagint has: "and in the [open] places round about," i.e., the villages.

34:8-28 DISCOVERY OF BOOK OF LAW

34:8 *Repair.* See the notes on the parallel account of 2 K 22:3—23:3.

34:11 *Buildings.* The same Hebrew word translated "houses" (1 Ch 28:11) and "the house." (1 Ch 29:4)

34:12 *Levites.* As he does in other instances, the writer of Chronicles takes special note of the part played by the Levites.

34:20 *Abdon.* In 2 K 22:12 he is identified as "Achbor the son of Micaiah."

34:22 *Tokhath.* In 2 K 22:14 Huldah's husband is called "the son of Tikvah, son of Harhas."

34:29-33 COVENANT RENEWAL

34:30 *Levites.* 2 K 23:2 reads "prophets" instead of *Levites* although some Hebrew manuscripts agree with Chronicles.

34:32 *Stand to it.* "All the people joined in the covenant," says 2 K 23:3.

35:1-19 PASSOVER CELEBRATION

35:1 *Passover.* One of the highlights of Hezekiah's reformation was likewise a memorable observance of the Passover, described at length in 30:1-27 but left unmentioned in Kings. Josiah's celebration too is reported in greater detail (1-19; cf. 2 K 23:21-23; see also 2 Ch 34:1 note). The king did more than merely issue the order to "kill the passover lamb . . . according to the word of the Lord by Moses" (1-6). He himself provided sacrificial animals in great numbers (7-9). The priests and Levites carried out his orders, performing their duties according to the prescribed ritual (10-15). As a result, "the passover at that time" was kept on a scale which eclipsed even Hezekiah's grand celebration. (16-19)

35:3 *Ark.* The command to return it to *the house* suggests that it was removed from its sacred place during the upheavals under the reigns of Manasseh and Amon. However, no such sacrilegious act is reported. Therefore it is possible that Josiah meant to say no more than that the Levites should now *serve the Lord* as assistants to the priests in the temple because they *need no longer carry* the ark on their shoulders as their forebears did on the way to the Promised Land.

35:4 *Directions.* Literally "the writing." Solomon "appointed the divisions of the priests ... and the Levites ... according to the ordinance of David" (8:14); cf. 1 Ch 23—26

35:7 *Thirty thousand.* For the figures of the sacrificial animals (7-9), totaling 41,400, see 30:24 note; 1 K 8:62 note.

35:11 *Killed the ... lamb.* The next verses describe the rites observed in the killing of the Passover lamb as well as "in offering the burnt offerings" of oxen. The latter were "holy offerings" or peace offerings which were partly burned on the altar and partly eaten by the worshipers, "as it is written in the book of Moses" in Lv 3:6 ff.

35:13 *Roasted.* The Hebrew text here has the same verb translated "boiled" in the next verses. The Passover lamb was roasted (Ex 12:8 f.) after its wool was removed by seething the animal. (Cf. Lv 6:25 note)

35:15 *Asaph.* The service rendered in various ways by the Levites receives special mention, a characteristic touch of Chronicles. For the three divisions of singers see 1 Ch 25.

35:20-27 JOSIAH'S DEATH IN BATTLE

35:20 *Neco.* For Neco's unsuccessful attempt to play a decisive role in the power politics of the day see 2 K 23:29 note.

35:21 *The house.* The emerging Babylonian world power.

35:22 *Words of Neco.* Neco claimed divine sanction for his campaign. No doubt he referred to an oracle which he ascribed to his own deity. However, in this instance it expressed also the will of the true God concerning Judah. In effect, Josiah was "opposing God" in his attempt to deflect the threatened judgment on the apostate nation. (34:24 ff.)

35:24 *Second Chariot.* Literally "the chariot of the second," which may mean the second in command or "next in authority" (28:7). Josiah died on the way to Jerusalem. (2 K 23:30)

35:25 *The Laments.* This dirge, *uttered* by Jeremiah, existed in written form *to this day,* i.e., the time of the writer of Chronicles. It is not our book of Lamentations.

36:1-4 Jehoahaz

36:1 *Jehoahaz.* He is the first of four kings to rule within the short interval of two decades, the remaining years before the fall of Jerusalem. For Jehoahaz' removal from the throne and the appointment of his older brother Eliakim or Jehoiakim see 2 K 23:33, 36; 24:1, 2 notes.

36:3 *In Jerusalem.* Neco deposed him in Riblah "that he might not reign in Jerusalem." (2 K 23:33)

36:5-8 Jehoiakim

36:6 *Bound him.* The binding of Jehoiakim at Nebuchadnezzar's behest is not mentioned in the parallel account in 2 K 24:1 ff. Apparently the plan *to take him* in fetters *to Babylon* was not carried out. However, "part of the vessels of the house of the Lord" were brought to the conqueror's "palace in Babylon," as reported also in Dn 1:2.

36:9-10 Jehoiachin

36:9 *Jehoiachin.* For a more complete account of his reign see 2 K 24:8-17 notes. No doubt he was not eight but 18 years old when he began to reign (2 K 24:8), the number in Chronicles being a copyist's error.

36:10 *Brother.* Zedekiah was his brother in the broader sense of "relative." Strictly speaking, he was Jehoiachin's father's brother. (2 K 24:17; 1 Ch 3:15)

36:11-23 Zedekiah; Babylonian Exile

36:11-14 APOSTASY; REBELLION

36:11 *Zedekiah.* Rather than dwell on the events of Jerusalem's last days, as given in 2 K 24:18—25:21, the writer of Chronicles takes pains to make clear why the city was doomed. Zedekiah "did not humble himself before Jeremiah," but he and the people followed "all the abominations of the nations," just as previous generations had rejected "the messengers of God, despising His words." God was longsuffering. But finally there came a point when His wrath "rose against his people, till there was no remedy" (11-16).—Let no one deceive himself to think that mocking the messengers of God, despising His words, and scoffing at the threat of punishment is a less offensive crime than it was when Jerusalem received the wages of sin. (Gl 6:7)

36:12 *Jeremiah.* For rejection of his message by Zedekiah and the people see Jer 34:8 ff.; 37:1 f.

36:15-21 JERUSALEM DESTROYED, PEOPLE EXILED

36:21 *Sabbaths.* For the description of the Exile as a sabbath see Lv 26:34 note. *Seventy years* is a round or a symbolic figure, which, however, is also a very close approximation of the actual duration of the Exile. Some captives were carried off 20 years before the city fell in 586 B.C. (Dn 1:1-6). In 536 B.C. the first exiles were permitted to return. For *the word of the Lord by the mouth of Jeremiah* see Jer 25:11; 29:10.

36:22-23 EXILE ENDED BY CYRUS

36:22 *Cyrus.* The last two verses duplicate the opening verses of Ezra (Ez 1:1-3a). They were appended here to assure the reader that the chosen people did not remain buried in the Babylonian captivity. See the same intimation of hope at the end of Kings. (2 K 25:27 note)

EZRA AND NEHEMIAH

INTRODUCTION

Content

The books of Ezra and Nehemiah record how the Babylonian captivity, the tomb of Israel's national identity, became the womb of its rebirth.

The nation from whom, "according to the flesh," the Christ was to come (Ro 9:5), was God's special creation from the beginning. From Abraham's body, "as good as dead," and "the barrenness of Sarah's womb" came the son of promise, born "according to the Spirit" (Ro 4:16 ff.; Gl 4:21 ff.). The offspring of the patriarchs, shut up in the dungeon of Egyptian slavery, seemed destined for oblivion. But God spoke His mighty "come out" (Jn 11:43), and a young nation, "a holy nation," "a kingdom of priests" sprang into being (Ex 19:6). It turned out to be a disobedient nation, unfaithful to its high calling. Now the end had come. Its capital and temple in ruins, its land scorched and occupied by the enemy, its population decimated and carried into exile, Israel seemed destined to share the fate of all vanquished peoples of antiquity. In the normal course of events it was doomed to extinction, the victim of attrition and absorption by the conqueror. But God once more spoke a life-giving word. There was a resurrection of Israel's "dead bones" (Eze 37:1-14). There was a second exodus, as foretold by the prophets. In the Promised Land the seed of Abraham continued to be the people by whom the Lord of the nations was to bless "all the families of the earth." (Gn 12:3)

There are two phases in the story of Israel's rehabilitation. Though reported in separate books, each stage consists of a construction program in wood and stone followed by a reestablishing of moral and spiritual foundations. Ezra records the building of the temple (Ez 1—6); Nehemiah, the erection of Jerusalem's walls (Neh 1:1—7:73a). Ezra the priest alone initiates the first reform (Ez 7—10); in the second he has the support and collaboration of Nehemiah the layman (Neh 7:73b—13:3) who, however, takes action also independently. (Neh 13:4-31)

The drama of Israel's restoration opens 60 years before Ezra appears on the scene. In 536 B.C., when Jerusalem had been in ruins for half a century, a large contingent of exiles returned to the homeland. Prominent figures in that early period were the two governors Sheshbazzar and Zerubbabel, and Jeshua, the high priest. It took 20 years before the returnees were able to complete the building of the temple (516 B.C.). The next recorded events are Ezra's return to Jerusalem almost 60 years later (458 B.C.) and his vigorous compaign against mixed marriages. After another interval of 12 years, Nehemiah received permission from the Persian king to investigate reports that the repatriated exiles were "in great trouble and shame" (Neh 1:3). On his arrival in Jerusalem (445 B.C.) he at once set to work to make the city safe against attacks from the outside. Overcoming serious difficulties, he built the walls of the city, organized watchmen to guard them, and increased the population in all areas enclosed by them. In the spiritual rearmament of the people which followed he yielded initiative to Ezra. Apparently recalled by the king, Nehemiah left Jerusalem in 433 B.C. When after some time he returned, he found it necessary again to correct abuses which had crept in during his absence.

Their contributions to Israel's reconstruction made, both Ezra and Nehemiah vanish from sight as abruptly as they appear on stage.

Time

Israel's rehabilitation in the Promised

Land, as reported in Ezra-Nehemiah, did not materialize overnight. The dates in the above resumé make clear that more than 100 years elapsed between the arrival in Jerusalem of the first exiles (536 B.C.) and the reforms carried out by Nehemiah on his second visit to the city (433 B.C.). This century coincided almost exactly with the first half of the existence of the gigantic Persian empire, which stretched from the Indus River through Asia Minor to the Mediterranean and down through Palestine to the waters of the Nile. Its turn to be buried under the sands of time came 100 years later. In 331 B.C. Alexander the Great became the next world conqueror.

In both books events are synchronized with the regnal years of the following Persian rulers: Cyrus, 539(550)—530; Cambyses, 530—522 (not mentioned); Darius, 522—486; Xerxes, 486—464 (mentioned only in passing); Artaxerxes, 464—424. Five more kings held the throne in the following century. There was another Xerxes; two were called Darius and two Artaxerxes.

Daniel (in part, Cyrus) and Esther (Xerxes) were contemporary with events in Ezra-Nehemiah, but are not mentioned because they were not involved in the reconstruction program in the homeland.

Authorship

Scripture does not make direct statements on the authorship of the books in which Ezra and Nehemiah have a leading role. According to a widely held theory, they form a literary unit with Chronicles, produced by an unknown person and therefore conveniently called the Chronicler. Some propose Ezra as the author of the trilogy. There are enough similarities in the three books to suggest that they are the composition of the same writer. However, there are also factors which favor individual authorship. Rabbinic tradition, counting Ezra-Nehemiah as one book, holds that "Ezra wrote his book" but adds significantly that Nehemiah "finished it." If this is true, then the first person accounts, found in both books, would not be memoirs, incorporated by a compiler, but autobiographical notes by Ezra and Nehemiah themselves. Both writers present statistical materials, based on documents current at the time. Only Ezra contains sections written in Aramaic, at that time the language of international diplomacy (Ez 4:8—6:18; 7:12-26). One of the reasons advanced for a date of authorship a century after the time of Ezra and Nehemiah is the genealogy of the high priestly line. See Neh 12:1-11 notes.

OUTLINE

Rebirth of a Nation

I. Ez 1:1—10:44 Israel's Revival: First Phase
  - A. 1:1—6:22 Rebuilding the Temple
  - B. 7:1—10:44 Renewal of National Integrity

II. Neh 1:1—13:31 Israel's Revival: Second Phase
  - A. 1:1—7:73a Rebuilding Jerusalem's Walls
  - B. 7:73b—10:39 Spiritual Rededication
  - C. 11:1—13:31 Various Measures to Promote Rehabilitation

1:1—6:22 REBUILDING THE TEMPLE

1:1—2:70 Restored Community of Temple Builders

1:1-4 CYRUS' DECREE FREEING EXILES

1:1 *Cyrus.* The Most High God, whom "heaven and the highest heaven cannot contain" and who "does not dwell in houses made with hands" (1 K 8:27; Acts 7:47), deigned to take up His abode in a temple which was to replace the one destroyed by the Babylonians some 60 years ago. As once Pharaoh's might could not prevent the birth of Israel, His chosen nation, so the imperial power of Persia served as midwife at its rebirth. So also Caesar Augustus when "the Word became flesh" (Jn 1:14; Lk 2). The first chapter of Ezra tells how through a second exodus a new community of temple builders came to life in Judah. It was not an accident of history that the king of Persia *made a proclamation* permitting every captive Israelite to "go up to Jerusalem . . . and rebuild the house of the Lord." God had planned the end of the Exile, announcing it in advance *by the mouth of Jeremiah* (Jer 29:10-14; 25:13 f.). Nor was it by chance that Cyrus was able and willing to liberate the captives. Before anyone knew the name of this world conqueror and his rise to power, He who "made the earth" and "stretched out the heavens" "anointed" him to "fulfill all my [God's] purpose" (Is 44:28; 45:1, 12 f.). The Lord, from whom came the impulse and power to "subdue nations" in order to rule over "all the kingdoms of the earth" (2), now *stirred up the spirit of Cyrus,* directing him to promote the kingdom of heaven. (Is 41:2, 25; Jer 50:9; 51:1; for the expression *stirred up* see also Ez 1:5; Hg 1:14)

1:2 *Charged me.* It is reasonable to assume that *the Lord, the God of heaven,* stirred Cyrus to action through a prophet, although He used dreams to communicate with such kings as Nebuchadnezzar and Belshazzar (Dn 2 and 7). Cyrus was tolerant of all religions, letting conquered peoples retain their national gods. Accordingly he allowed also any Israelite to serve "his God" who, as he thought, "is in Jerusalem." (3)

1:3 *Go up.* Up to this point, the first three verses are essentially identical with the closing verses of 2 Ch. (36:22 f.)

1:4 *Men of his place.* Neighbors were to assist the surviving Israelite *in whatever place* he may have been settled by the captors. For a similar arrangement at the exodus from Egypt see Ex 3:21 f.

1:5-11 RETURN UNDER SHESHBAZZAR

1:7 *Vessels.* Nebuchadnezzar had "carried off all the treasures of the house of the Lord" (2 K 24:13; 2 Ch 36:7; Jer 27:19-22). For their desecration see Dn 5:3.

1:8 *Sheshbazzar.* The first governor of the returning exiles to be appointed by the Persian court. Apparently he died soon after he brought to Jerusalem the sacred vessels entrusted to him and "laid the foundation of the house of God" (5:14-16). It devolved on his successor, Zerubbabel, to complete the building of the temple (Hg 1:1, 14). If Shenazzar (1 Ch 3:18) is but another form of his Babylonian name, Sheshbazzar was the fourth son of King Jehoiachin and therefore the uncle of Zedekiah, the last king of Judah (1 Ch 3:18 f.). The proposal that Sheshbazzar and Zerubbabel are variant names of the same person has not gained general acceptance.

1:9 *The number.* The items listed in these verses add up to 2,099, whereas v. 11 gives a total of 5,400. Not all vessels may have been itemized, or the discrepancy may be the result of a mistake by the copyist of the text.

2:1-70 REGISTER OF RETURNEES

2:1 *Returned.* The list of those *who came up out of the captivity* appears again with minor variations in Neh 7:6-73. It was an important document, representing a kind of charter of the newly founded *province* of Judah. No doubt new names and numbers were added from time to time to keep the record current. Seven groups are distinguished: (1) the leaders (1, 2a); (2) "the men of the [common] people" by families and cities (2b-35); (3) priests (36-39); (4) Levites (40-42); (5) temple servants (43-54); (6) descendants of Solomon's servants (55-58); (7) groups without certified family ties (59-63). For the significance of such lists for the modern reader see 1 Ch 1:1 note.

2:2 *Zerubbabel.* Most of the leaders who head the list are unknown (Neh 7:7 adds a 12th name). Zerubbabel was to become governor of Judah (Hg 1:1; 2:2). The probable meaning of his Babylonian name is "Seed of Babylon." The next chapter tells how he and the high priest Jeshua or Joshua (Hg 1:1) finished building the temple after the project had to be abandoned for many years. The third person mentioned, Nehemiah, bore the same name as the governor who arrived in Jerusalem some 90 years later. (Neh 1:1)

2:21 *Bethlehem.* In 21-35 a count is given of the people according to the cities they occupied. All of these clustered about Jerusalem within a radius of some 20 miles. If the list is complete, the reclaimed area was considerably smaller than the territory of pre-exilic Judah. The immigrants were hemmed in on all sides by various racial groups. (Neh 4:7 note; 13:23)

2:40 *Levites.* The total number of Levites was 341, while that of the priests was 4,289. Normally these two groups of temple officiants would be in a reversed proportion to one another. The prospect of again serving as assistants to the priests may have kept the Levites from leaving Babylon, where they were on an equal footing with their countrymen. At a later date Ezra found "none of the sons of Levi" in the group which volunteered to return to Jerusalem with him (8:15).—To serve in a supporting role, often without acclaim in the church, requires a full measure of consecration.

2:43 *Temple servants.* Cf. 1 Ch 9:2 note.

2:55 *Solomon's servants.* Cf. 1 K 9:15, 20 note.

2:63 *The governor.* KJV transliterates "the Tirshata," a word probably of Persian derivation, which designates the men appointed by Persian kings to administer affairs in the restored community of Judah (Neh 7:65, 70; 8:9; 10:1). There is general agreement that the term does not denote the function of a governor but is a title of respect similar to our "His Honor" or "His Excellency."

Urim and Thummim. Cf. Ex 28:15 note.

2:64 *Whole assembly.* The total given for the entire assembly is far larger than the sum of the individual contingents recorded in the previous verses. When these are added, the figure is only 29, 818. Not all groups may be listed separately, or the larger figure may be due to a misreading of the numerical signs which were used in earlier manuscripts (see Numbers, Introduction, "The Numbers. . . ."). However, the same total is given in Neh 7:66 whereas the individual entries there add up to 31,089. Jeremiah notes that all the persons carried away under Nebuchadnezzar were only 4,600 (Jer 52:28-30). However, Sennacherib, the Assyrian king, claims to have exiled over 200,000 from 46 Judean cities which he captured in 601 B.C.

3:1-13 Temple Construction Begun

3:1-7 ALTAR BUILT; SACRIFICES RESTORED

3:1 *Seventh month.* The first two chapters set the stage for the events which were to culminate in the rebuilding of the temple. In the seventh month of the first year of their repatriation those who had availed themselves of Cyrus' proclamation (ch. 1) and had formed a registered community (ch. 2) erected an altar on which sacrifices were resumed (for a similar use of an altar without a temple see 2 Sm 24:25). But intent on restoring the full worship ritual, they hired workmen to build "the temple of the Lord" and contracted for cedar wood for its construction (1-7). Already in "the second year" work got under way under "the oversight" of "the priests and the Levites" (8 f.). Soon "the foundation . . . was laid" with fitting ceremonies. (10-13)

3:2 *Zerubbabel.* He and the high priest Jeshua *arose* to take charge of the construction work for which Sheshbazzar had been commissioned (1:8-11). Because the whole venture was under the latter's immediate jurisdiction, the enemies later held him responsible also for initiating the program, reporting to the king that he "laid the foundations of the house of God" (5:14-16). Sheshbazzar does not seem to have outlived the interruption of construction which was soon to follow (ch. 4). At any rate, when the work could be resumed after a stoppage of 15 years, Zerubbabel had succeeded him as governor. (Hg 1:1; 2:2)

Son of Shealtiel. According to 1 Ch 3:19 he was the son of Shealtiel's brother Pedaiah. It is possible that Zerubbabel's status as his uncle's legal heir is put on record in the genealogical registry of Chronicles, where, however, the Septuagint reads also "the son of Shealtiel."

Jeshua. A variant form of Joshua (Hg 1:1), a popular name at this time. The Jeshua mentioned in 9 was not the high priest but the head of a levitical family. (2:40)

Altar. Earlier attempts to continue worship in Jerusalem after its destruction were not successful. (Jer 41:5)

Law of Moses. Nm 29:1-6 decreed that the first day of the seventh month be observed by special ceremonies. Regular "burnt offerings morning and evening" (3) were prescribed Ex 29:38 and Nm 28:3 ff.

3:3 *In its place.* More lit. "upon its base," i.e., the site where it formerly stood.

Fear. The new immigrants wanted the altar built in order to have a place where they might gather to implore God's help against *the peoples of the lands* round about them. It soon became evident that their fears were not unfounded (ch. 4). Their prayer, though not answered for a long time, did not go unheard. (Ch. 5)

3:4 *Feast of booths.* This feast, celebrated from the 15th to the 21st day of the seventh month (our October), was the last of the three annual high festivals. For the prescribed ritual see Lv 23:33 ff. and Nm 29:12 ff. No doubt circumstances permitted only a token observance of its elaborate festivities. The first complete celebration came after the temple had been built (Neh 8:17). For other events hallowed by this festival see 1 K 8:65 note and Neh 8:14-18.

3:5 *After that.* "They began to offer burnt offerings . . . from the first day of the seventh month" (6), but it was only after the celebration of the feast of the booths that the cycle of the special feasts could be inaugurated.

3:7 *Sidonians . . . Tyrians.* For a similar agreement with them by Solomon for building material see 1 K 5:10 and 2 Ch 2:15 f. Costs were defrayed out of *the grant . . . from Cyrus.* (6:4)

3:8-9 BUILDING OVERSEERS APPOINTED

3:8 *Second year. In the second month* (our April/May) of the following year they *made a beginning* in putting building plans into operation under *the oversight* of the Levites, among whom were Jeshua and Kadmiel (2:40) and Henadad. (Neh 10:9)

3:10-13 FOUNDATION LAID, DEDICATED

3:10 *Foundation.* For features similar to this celebration see the dedication of Solomon's temple. (2 Ch 5:11-14; 7:3)

Directions of David. Cf. 1 Ch 25:1; 2 Ch 6:4-6.

3:12 *Old men . . . wept.* Their memories went back 50 years to the grandeur of *the first house,* built with the resources of Solomon's empire. Now Israel was dependent on the good will of a foreign overlord and had to fear intervention by petty neighboring adversaries. No doubt some of the tears were salted with remorse over the folly which had destroyed temple and nation. The glory had "departed from Israel" (1 Sm 4:21) because their great guilt "mounted up to heaven" (9:6). "Given into the hand of the kings of the lands, to the sword, to captivity, to plundering, and to utter shame," they had been "receiving the due reward" of their evil deeds. (9:7; Lk 23:41)

4:1-24 Construction Hindrances

4:1-5 WORK ON TEMPLE HALTED BY SAMARITANS

4:1 *Adversaries.* Cyrus conquered the world of his day, thereby fulfilling the Lord's purpose: the rehabilitation of the chosen people (Is 44:24-28). It may seem strange then that hostile "people of the land," Palestinian vassals of the same king of Persia, should be permitted to frustrate the building of the temple, a project which by divine guidance he himself had initiated (1:1-4). But Israel was to learn that by its own strength it could not cope even with minor obstacles. God's dealings with His people were all the more mysterious because their very refusal to compromise the worship of the only God caused the adversaries to launch a campaign of intrigue by which they succeeded in stopping construction on the temple for some 15 years (1-5, 24). By means of the same tactics they were also able to delay the rebuilding of Jerusalem's walls for about 90 years. (6-23; Neh 2:1 ff.)

4:2 *Build with you.* "The people of the land" who became "adversaries" when their proffered cooperation was rejected came to be known as Samaritans because they occupied territory of which Samaria was the capital since the days of the division of the kingdom, following Solomon's death (1 K 16:24). About two centuries later the Northern Kingdom succumbed to the Assyrians. They deported many of their new vassals, replacing them with settlers from foreign provinces. This pacification measure continued to be standard policy even after the fall of Samaria in 722 B.C. (2 K 17:24), practiced by such kings as Esarhaddon (681—669 B.C.) and his successor Ashurbanipal, called Osnappar in v. 10. The result was a mixture of racial strains and a blend of religious beliefs (2 K 17:25-33). The returned exiles, fearing they would commit themselves to a blurring of the difference between right and wrong, refused the offer of these neighbors to make the building of the temple a joint project.

4:5 *Frustrate.* The Samaritans and other enemies persuaded Cyrus to reverse himself. Not only he but also his successor Cambyses (530—522 B.C.) stopped construction on the temple. The returnees had to wait till the second year of the third Persian king, Darius (522—486), before they were permitted to resume the project—a delay of some 15 years.

4:6-23 WORK ON WALLS HALTED BY SAME TACTICS

4:6 *Accusation.* The next verses (6-23) do not continue the story of the temple but record how attempts to build the walls of Jerusalem were also frustrated by "the adversaries of Judah and Benjamin" even after the temple had been completed for about 70 years. As they "hired counselors" who persuaded the Persian kings to forbid the erection of the temple, so they filed written accusations at the imperial court charging the Jews with seditious intent in fortifying the city with walls.

Ahasuerus. The first king to whom they wrote came to the throne in 486 B.C., 30 years after the dedication of the temple. Ahasuerus is the Hebrew version of his Persian name. The Greeks called him Xerxes. Esther became his queen. (Est 1:1; 2:16 f.; Dn 9:1)

4:7 *Artaxerxes.* By their machinations the enemies were able to convince also Xerxes' successor of the evil designs of "that rebellious and wicked city" Jerusalem (12). A decree that "this city be not rebuilt" (21) remained in effect for the first 20 years of his reign (464—424 B.C.). Finally Nehemiah persuaded him to reverse himself. (Neh 2:1 ff.)

Aramaic. For the use of Aramaic, like Hebrew a Semitic language, in international diplomacy see 2 K 18:26 note. This entire section (4:8—6:18), which contains several communications of an official nature, is preserved in Aramaic, as is also 7:12-26.

4:8 *Rehum.* In their letter to Artaxerxes the writers mentioned in 7 refer to a previous communication by two Persian officials, Rehum and Shimshai, and then add the names of the latter to a list of others who also signed the accusation (9 f.). Because there was no reply to the original letter, they enclosed a copy of it, the content of which is cited 11-15. A concluding note (16) stated that the purpose of their writing was to reiterate the validity of the charges made by Rehum and his associates. The latter then received written authorization from the king to stop the building of Jerusalem's walls lest its inhabitants presume to declare their independence. (17-22)

4:9 *Associates.* The signatories represented various national groups. *Erech* was a Babylonian city; *Susa* was the capital of Elam, east of Babylon.

4:10 *Osnappar.* Cf. v. 2 note.

4:11 *Beyond the River.* For administrative purposes the Persian empire was divided into 20 districts, called satrapies. The fifth of these was known as *Beyond the River* because it was made up of territory beyond or west of the Euphrates. Its governor or satrap was responsible to the king for Syria, Palestine, and Cyprus. "The province of Judah" (5:8) constituted a smaller unit of control within his satrapy.

4:24 NO BUILDING FOR 15 YEARS

4:24 *House of God.* In a modern history 6-23 would appear in a footnote stating that opposition to the rehabilitation of Jerusalem was not confined to interference with the building of the temple but carried over into a later period when attempts were made to build the walls. V. 24 leads back to the mainstream of the narrative, where v. 5 had left it. Work on the temple ceased for the remainder of Cyrus' reign (539—530), during the entire rule of Cambyses (530—522), and for 2 years after Darius came to the throne. (522—486)

5:1—6:22 Building Resumed and Completed

5:1-2 RESUMPTION URGED BY PROPHETS

5:1 *Now.* The Aramaic text has "and," connecting the sequel with the second year of Darius (4:24). At that time the prophets Haggai and Zechariah roused the people to renew their efforts to build the temple (Hg 1:1; Zch 1:1). Zerubbabel and Jeshua again directed the project (3:8). This time they were successful even though the Persian satrap investigated the project (3-5) and sent a letter of inquiry to the Persian king (6-17). When the original decree of Cyrus, authorizing the erection of the temple, was found "in the house of the archives" (6:1-5), Darius ordered the officials to "let the work on this house of God alone" (6:6-12). Five years later the temple was finished (6:13-15). A month after it had been dedicated (6:16-18), the Passover festival could be celebrated. (16:19-22)

5:3—6:12 PERMISSION TO PROCEED GRANTED

5:3 *Tattenai.* The *governor* of the large satrapy called *Beyond the River* (4:11 note). At this time Zerubbabel was "the governor of Judah," a province under the jurisdiction of Tattenai. (Hg 1:1; cf. Ez 3:2 note)

5:7 *A report.* The satrap, not remiss in his duty, took note of a major undertaking in his bailiwick. However, he did not interfere with the project on his own authority. Aware that the governor of Judah was appointed by and directly responsible to the Persian king, he did not want to countermand a royal directive. He therefore reported the matter to Darius as objectively as possible, requesting confirmation of the claim that Cyrus some 20 years earlier "made a decree that this house should be rebuilt." (6-17)

5:14 *Sheshbazzar.* Cf. 1:8; 3:2 notes.

6:1 *House of the archives.* Lit. "house of books." Such libraries or despositories of documents have been uncovered by archaeologists. The search for the decree was begun *in Babylonia,* where the exiles had been released. However, the document was found "in Ecbatana," capital of Media and summer residence of Persian kings almost 300 miles northeast of Babylon. Cyrus is known to have spent some time there during the first year of his reign.

6:2 *A record.* The oral "proclamation" of Cyrus' decree, as the exiles heard it from his heralds, is recorded in 1:2-4. Fortunately he "also put it in writing" (1:1). Filed away in the archives, this written memo of the decree preserved the essential points of his edict.

6:3 *Sixty cubits.* No figures are given for the length of the building. The dimensions of Solomon's temple were 60 cubits long, 20 wide, and 30 high (1 K 6:2). Cyrus' secretary did not transcribe his master's dictation correctly or the copyist of the Biblical text did not transmit the complete specifications.

6:6 *Governor.* For the relationship of "the governor of the Jews" to the *governor of the province Beyond the River* see 5:3 and 5:7 notes.

6:8 *A decree.* In the following verses Darius issues specific orders, implementing the original directive by Cyrus.

6:10 *God of heaven.* For references by Persian rulers to the true God see 1:2 note.

6:13-15 CONSTRUCTION COMPLETED

6:14 *Artaxerxes.* This verse lists three kings who took action benefiting the temple. Even after the temple was completed early in the reign of Darius, sorely needed funds for its maintenance were contributed by his successor Artaxerxes, as recorded in the next chapter. (7:12-26)

6:15 *Sixth year.* Darius began to reign in 522 B.C. *Adar* is the equivalent of our February/March.

6:16-18 TEMPLE DEDICATED

6:16 *Dedication.* It was only natural that ceremonies at the dedication of Solomon's temple were duplicated as much as possible (1 K 8). The difference in the case of "this house" (7) as compared with the earlier one was particularly in reduced resources, as reflected, e.g., in the smaller number of sacrificial animals. (1 K 8:5, 63)

6:17 *All Israel.* The sin offering of 12 he-goats represented a declaration of the reconstituted solidarity of the chosen people, again consisting of "the twelve tribes of Israel" as it did at Solomon's time.

6:18 *Moses.* The restored community observed the Mosaic regulations governing the eligibility of priests and Levites for service in the temple (Ex 29; Lv 8; Nm 3 and 8). The authorized personnel served *in their courses* or working units as stipulated by David. (1 Ch 23 f.)

6:19-22 PASSOVER CELEBRATION RESUMED

6:19 *The Passover.* The first observance of the Passover in Egypt marked the birth of Israel as a nation; its celebration after the Exile proclaimed its rebirth. The regular day for its observance came in the month following the completion of the temple. (15)

6:20 *Fellow priests.* Lit. "their brethren the priests." The Levites who killed the Passover lamb and the priests who sacrificed it were descendants of Levi. But not all sons of Levi were priests. (2 Ch 30:27 note; Dt 18:1 note)

6:21 *Separated himself.* Those who *had returned from exile* were joined by those who had not been carried away into captivity. The latter were admitted to the Passover if they renounced the false worship of *the peoples of the land* such as that of the Samaritans. (10:11; Neh 9:2; 10:28)

6:22 *King of Assyria.* Darius is meant. The Persian kings who replaced the rulers of the Assyrian and the Babylonian empires not only reversed the flow of captives from Israel but also aided the exiles in establishing themselves in their homeland.

7:1—10:44 RENEWAL OF NATIONAL INTEGRITY

7:1—8:36 Ezra's Return to Jerusalem

7:1-10 PERSONAL DATA

7:1 *After this.* This brief phrase spans an interval of more than five decades: from the dedication of the temple in the sixth year of Darius (522—486) to "the seventh year of Artaxerxes" (464—424). The Biblical record at this point passes over in silence the remaining years of Darius' long reign and all the years of his successor Xerxes (486—464), the king at the time of Esther. The events recorded in the remaining chapters of Ezra and in the entire book of Nehemiah all transpired in the reign of Artaxerxes. Soon after his accession to the throne "the adversaries of Judah and Benjamin" duped him into forbidding the building of Jerusalem's walls. (4:7-24)

Ezra. A half century after the temple of stone and wood was erected, it was apparent that a rebuilding of their moral integrity was needed if the rehabilitation of the chosen people was not to end in national dissolution. The man who cleared away the rubbish of abuses and laid new spiritual foundations was Ezra. After his return to Jerusalem at the head of a group of exiles (chs. 7—8), he attacked the threatening disintegration at its roots: mixed marriages. (Chs. 9—10; Ml 2:11)

Son of Seraiah. In order to certify Ezra as a priest, his genealogy is traced from Seraiah, high priest when Jerusalem was destroyed (2 K 25:18), to "Aaron the [first] chief priest." However, not all ancestral links are supplied in 1-5.

7:6 *Scribe.* The same Hebrew term, applied to a court official in the days of the Davidic kings, is translated "secretary" (2 Sm 8:17; 1 K 4:3; 2 K 18:18; cf. our use of the title secretary for the men in the President's cabinet). However, as a man of letters, Ezra "set his heart to study the law of the Lord . . . and to teach his statutes and ordinances" (10). He may have had official recognition at the Persian court in his capacity as "the scribe of the law of the God of heaven" (12). A long line of scribes down to and beyond NT times claims him as the founder of their guild, devoted to copying, preserving, and interpreting the sacred writings.

Hand of the Lord. The king reached his decision prompted by God's providential direction (27), as once "the Lord stirred up the spirit of Cyrus" to release the exiles (1:1). The "good hand of his God" also gave success to Ezra's and Nehemiah's efforts. (V. 9; 8:18, 22, 31; Neh 2:8, 18)

7:7 *Seventh year.* Some scholars believe that the text originally read "the thirty-seventh year." This emendation is part of the assumption that, arranged in a strictly chronological sequence, Ezra's return to Jerusalem came 17 years after Nehemiah's in the 20th year of Artaxerxes (Neh 2:1). Some factors in the narrative seem to favor such an inversion. However, the text as it stands does not pose insurmountable difficulties.

7:11-26 COMMISSION AUTHORIZED BY KING

7:11 *Letter.* Written in Aramaic (cf. 4:7 note), this document authorized Ezra (1) to visit Jerusalem accompanied by other volunteers and to deliver various donations "for the service of the house of . . . God" (12-20); (2) to draw on provincial treasuries for additional aid in money and materials (21-24); (3) to effect conformity to the divine law through appointment of judges and magistrates. (25 f.)

7:12 *To Ezra.* The salutation of the letter ends with a word equivalent to our *et cetera.* It indicates that amenities, usually appearing in greetings, have been abbreviated. (Cf. RSV note)

7:14 *Seven counselors.* An intimate circle of advisers who "sat first in the kingdom." (Est 1:14)

7:17 *With all diligence.* This phrase stresses scrupulous compliance rather than fast or zealous action. The money was not to be used for any other purpose than for the specified items. (Also in 21)

7:19 *Vessels.* Ezra delivered very costly bowls and vessels to the proper authorities in Jerusalem. (8:26 f.)

7:22 *Talents.* The limits *up to* which Ezra could draw on the provincial treasuries involved huge sums. The weight of a *talent* was about 75 pounds. A *cor* held some 7 bushels; a *bath* about 6 gallons.

7:23 *His wrath.* Persian kings thought it wise to placate the national gods of the peoples incorporated in the empire.

7:24 *Temple servants.* All personnel serving the temple should be exempt from taxation, including the servants or Nethinim. (2:43; 1 Ch 9:2 note)

7:25 *Wisdom.* A reference to the law of God which Ezra "had in his hand." (14)

7:26 *Judgment.* Ezra's commission gave him powers fully equal to the authority of a governor, even though it is not explicitly said that he held this office. Not only murder but also such crimes as idolatry and adultery were capital offenses according to the law of Moses. (Ex 22:20; Lv 20:10)

7:27-28 GRATITUDE FOR COMMISSION

7:28 *To me.* The short doxology (27 f.) uses the first person, as does the narrative in chs. 8 and 9.

8:1-14 LIST OF RETURNING FAMILY HEADS

8:1 *Father's houses.* Mention in the previous verse of "leading men," whom Ezra gathered "to go up" to Jerusalem with him, occasioned the insertion at this point of a list of the heads of families (1-14). The same *fathers' houses,* mentioned here, were represented in the group which returned from Babylon some 80 years earlier (ch. 2). Not breathtaking reading at our time, this list verified the bona fide citizenship of these latecomers. Their number was considerably smaller: all totaled about 1,500 men. (Cf. 2:64)

8:15-30 FINAL PREPARATIONS FOR JOURNEY

8:15 *I reviewed.* As this group of "leading men" (7:28), whose genealogical status was on record (1-14), gathered at an encampment, Ezra insisted on recruiting more "ministers for the house of . . . God," both "sons of Levi" as well as "temple servants" (15-20). Before setting out on the long journey of 4 months, he "proclaimed" a fast, committing himself and his fellow travelers to God's protection rather than to a proposed military escort (21-23). Finally he appointed guardians of the treasures, of which he made a complete inventory. (24-30)

Ahava. An unidentified river or canal, perhaps near Babylon.

8:17 *Casiphia.* Apparently there was a considerable settlement of Levites at this site, which remains unidentified. For reluctance on the part of Levites to return to Jerusalem see 2:40 note.

8:21 *Straight way.* Not a direct but an unimpeded and safe way.

8:22 *Soldiers.* Ezra, who had committed himself prayerfully to God's protection, believed that it would be a humiliating reflection on his faith if he now accepted a military escort. However, Nehemiah demonstrated that taking such a precautionary measure need not be evidence of lack of trust. (Neh 2:7, 9)

8:26 *Talents.* If the figures in the text have been transmitted correctly, the total value of the gifts amounted to millions of dollars.

8:27 *Darics.* For this monetary standard see 1 Ch 29:7 note.

8:31-36 SAFE ARRIVAL IN JERUSALEM

8:31 *Jerusalem.* Taking the long way—about 900 miles—around the northern end of the desert, the emigrants arrived safely in Jerusalem. There "the silver and the gold and the vessels" were delivered to the temple authorities (31-34). Mindful that "the hand of . . . God was upon" them, the newly arrived exiles "offered burnt offerings" to express their gratitude. Continued success of their venture seemed assured when the Persian officials Beyond the River "aided the people and the house of God" in accord with "the king's commissions." (35-36)

8:33 *Fourth day.* According to 7:9, the expedition was underway from the 12th day of Nisan (March/April) to the first day of Ab (July/August). As soon as possible after their arrival, the appointed priests and Levites (24) complied with Ezra's directive to transfer the treasure to the temple.

8:36 *Commissions.* The orders issued by the king (7:21-24) to his highest representatives, the *satraps,* and his minor officials, *the governors.* For the administration of the Persian empire see 4:11 note.

9:1—10:44 Mixed Marriages Dissolved

9:1-5 SHOCKING PREVALENCE OF ABUSE

9:1 *Separated themselves.* Sent "to make inquiries about Judah and Jerusalem according to the law of . . . God" (7:14), Ezra soon discovered that even though the temple had been rebuilt, the structure of Israel's life as the chosen people was in danger of collapse. He was "appalled" to learn from the leading men that amalgamation by intermarriage with *the peoples of the land with their abominations,* abetted by "the officials and chief men," threatened to canaanize the nation and to baalize their religion (1-5). Turning to God in fervent prayer, Ezra confessed that by its "faithlessness" the "remnant that . . . escaped" extinction in Babylon deserved to have divine justice "consume" them (6-15). His words, spoken in the hearing of a large gathering of people, awakened them to the gravity of their guilt. They were willing to "take oath" to give Ezra a free hand in any corrective action "according to the law" (10:1-5). The next morning he summoned "all the returned exiles" to assemble at Jerusalem (10:6-8). His demand at the convocation that they separate themselves "from the peoples of the land and from the foreign wives" met with almost unanimous approval (10:9-15). As authorized by the assembly, Ezra appointed "heads of fathers' houses" to enforce the reform in "every city" (10:16-17). In doing so, they made it a point to record the names of all men who had contracted a mixed marriage. (10:18-44)

Canaanites. The various "peoples of the land" enumerated here were those with whom the Israelites came in contact when they took possession of Canaan under Joshua. Marriage with their descendants, themselves of mixed stock, posed the same threat to Israel which prompted laws against these alliances in the days of Moses (cf. Ex 34:11-14; Dt 7:1-3). Exceptions and deviations from the ordinance did not abrogate its general intent or its validity. (Dt 21:10-14; Ru 1:4; 2 Sm 3:3; 1 K 3:1; 11:1 f.)

9:2 *Holy race.* Intermarriage with Canaanites worked at cross-purposes with God's design. He Himself had "separated" the Israelites "from the peoples" that they might be a "holy nation," i.e., a people set aside from others to put into operation His eternal counsel and will through them. (Lv 20:26; Ex 19:6 note, Dt 7:6)

9:3 *Pulled hair.* Besides tearing his inner and outer garments, Ezra expressed his grief by a gesture not mentioned otherwise. Shaving off the hair was less drastic. (Jb 1:20; Is 15:2; Jer 16:6; Eze 7:18; Am 8:10)

9:5 *Spread out . . . hands.* For other instances of the same posture in prayer see Ex 9:29, 33; 1 K 8:22; Is 1:15.

9:6-15 UNRESERVED CONFESSION OF GUILT

9:6 *Our iniquities.* Throughout the prayer Ezra identified himself with the people for whom he was interceding.

9:7 *Days of the fathers.* The *guilt* and the *iniquities* which Ezra confessed take on a deeper hue when seen in the light of God's dealings with Israel. He did not let *the kings of the lands* such as Assyria and Babylonia exterminate "the holy race," but rather moved "the kings of Persia" such as Cyrus and Artaxerxes to let a "remnant" again get a "secure hold within his holy place," Jerusalem (6-9). When the very people who had experienced this undeserved rescue broke God's "commandments again," He would be "just" if now He were to "consume" them "so that there should be no remnant, nor any to escape" (10-15). For purposes of instruction Moses likewise reviewed Israel's recent past in Dt 1—3; see also Neh 9:6-38; Dn 9:4-19.

9:11 *Prophets.* What Moses, called a prophet in Dt 18:15; 34:10, commanded in the Law and what had been reiterated by later spokesmen of God is summarized in 11 f. All through its past, Israel's prophets warned against being spiritually "mismated with unbelievers" (2 Co 6:14) and thus becoming one with them in their "abominations," "uncleanness," and "pollutions." After the Exile economic advantages made the temptation particularly great to "intermarry with the peoples who practice[d] these abominations." (Mal 2:11 ff.)

10:1-17 REFORM MEASURES ADOPTED

10:1 *Ezra.* The preceding section, beginning at 7:27, is autobiographical.

10:2 *Shecaniah.* Ezra's confession (9:6-15) awakened the people to the seriousness of their guilt. The name of their spokesman is mentioned in the list of the returned exiles (8:3), while his father's name, "Jehiel," appears among those who had married foreign women. (26)

10:6 *Jehohanan.* A man with his father's name *Eliashib* was high priest at the time of Nehemiah (Neh 3:1; 13:4, 7). According to Neh 12:10 f., Eliashib had a grandson named Jonathan, supposedly a variant form of Jehohanan, who appears in an Aramaic document as high priest during the latter part of the reign of Darius (424—405 B.C.). If he is the Jehohanan mentioned here, then Ezra's lodging place may be identified by its later occupant. It is also possible that there was a younger son of Eliashib, not necessarily a high priest, who had a chamber in the temple, as Tobiah the Ammonite did at Nehemiah's time (Neh 13:4-9). Among the returned exiles several people had the name Jonathan or Jehohanan. (8:6; 10:15, 28)

10:7 *Proclamation.* The same word used of the Persian king's decree. (1:1)

10:9 *Ninth month.* Our November/December. Ezra now had been in Jerusalem 4 months (7:9). Perhaps he allowed ample time for the proclamation to reach everyone and for the people to arrange to come, attendance being compulsory.

Heavy rain. The ninth month normally was "the time of heavy rain." Its unusual severity seems to have been regarded as a sign from heaven affirming Ezra's condemnation of their misdeeds in *this matter.*

10:14 *Fierce wrath.* In his confession Ezra had declared that a "just" God had every reason to "consume" the ungrateful remnant, leaving none to escape (9:14). In order that such a disaster "be averted," "all the assembly answered with a loud voice" that the evil be rooted out by "the elders and judges of every city."

10:15 *Meshullam.* Mentioned in the appended list of offenders. (29)

10:16 *Examine.* It took the *heads of fathers' houses,* appointed for the task by Ezra, over 3 months to conduct the investigation, from the 20th day of the ninth month (9) to "the first day of the first month" of the following year.

10:18-44 LIST OF OFFENDERS

10:18 *Were found.* The book closes abruptly with a list of those who had contracted mixed marriages (18-44). However, the report of Ezra's career does not end here. He engaged not only in the remedial action recorded in the book bearing his name, but he also made a positive contribution to the spiritual upbuilding of the postexilic community (cf. Neh 9—10). Some 12 years elapse before he reappears on the scene, this time in the company of Nehemiah. It is not clear what he did during this time. He may have been recalled to the Persian court after his commission in Judah expired. At any rate, all attempts to rebuild the walls of Jerusalem during this interval remained unsuccessful. (4:6-23)

The persons who "married the daughter of a foreign god" (Ml 2:11) are grouped according to a customary classification (2:2, 36, 40; 9:1). There were 17 priests, 10 Levites, 86 sons of Israel or laymen, for a total of 113 men. In comparison with the total population this number may not appear alarming. However, the danger of assimilation by the peoples of the land was very real in view of the fact that "in this faithlessness" the clergy, "the officials and chief men," were "foremost" (9:2). When even "the sons of Jeshua," high priest in Zerubbabel's day (2:2), set the fashion, the whole populace could be expected to follow their example. As it was, repeated efforts were necessary to eradicate the evil. (Cf. Neh 13:15 ff.)

10:44 *With their children.* The concluding words add the note that separation took place even if children were involved. The disruption of family ties must have caused grief and hardships. However, some measure of support no doubt was provided so that innocent victims of the reform were not left to shift for themselves. Even today convicted criminals inflict disgrace and suffering on their families.

1:1—7:73a REBUILDING JERUSALEM'S WALLS

1:1—2:10 Nehemiah's Journey from Susa

1:1-3 REPORT OF JERUSALEM'S PLIGHT

1:1 *Nehemiah.* The Book of Nehemiah records the second phase in the rehabilitation of postexilic Israel. (For introductory helps see Ezra, Introduction.) Supplementing Ezra, it too tells the story of a material reconstruction, the fortification of Jerusalem (chs. 1—7), and of a moral and spiritual rebuilding through reform and covenant renewal (chs. 8—12). The walls of the holy city rose on ancient foundations under the leadership of a highly resourceful and deeply religious layman, who held high office at the Persian court. Hearing there of "the trouble and shame" of defenseless Jerusalem (1-3) and invoking divine blessing on his decision to help (4-11), Nehemiah requested and received permission from the king to take charge personally of his proposal "to seek the welfare of the children of Israel" (2:1-8). His coming to Jerusalem for that purpose incensed Persian officials in adjacent areas (2:9 f.). Aware of their opposition, he secretly surveyed the damaged city wall "with its gates burned" (2:11-16) before he revealed his intentions even to his compatriots (2:17-20). Within a short time construction operations were under way (ch. 3). Overcoming machinations by hostile neighbors (ch. 4), dissension in his own ranks (ch. 5), and even attempts on his life (6:1-14), Nehemiah completed the project in a crash program. (6:15-19)

Twentieth year. Of the reign of Artaxerxes (464 424 B.C.). Some 12 years intervene between the end of the Book of Ezra and the opening verses of this chapter. (Cf. Ez 10:18 note)

Susa. The capital of ancient Elam, some 200 miles east of Babylon, which Persian kings used as a winter residence. (Est 1:2; Dn 8:2)

1:2 *Hanani.* Not necessarily a member of Nehemiah's immediate family, this "brother" (7:2) was one of a group which brought a firsthand report of conditions in "Judah," called a "province" (3) of the Persian empire. (Ez 2:1; 5:3 note; translated "district" in 1 K 20:14)

1:3 *Trouble and shame.* It was about 140 years since the Babylonians had *broken down* the wall and *destroyed* the gates *by fire.* Perhaps efforts had been made to refortify the city. If so, hostile neighbors saw to it that they ended in disaster. However, the *trouble* may refer more generally to the great need of protecting the temple against marauders and the *shame* to the humiliating interference with their previous attempts to build the walls. (Ez 4:7-23)

1:4-11 PRAYER FOR FORGIVENESS AND HELP

1:4 *Sat down.* The usual posture of people when they *wept and mourned* (Jb 2:13; Ps 137:1; Ez 9:3). In abject humility Nehemiah implored *the God of heaven* in a prayer similar to Ezra's (Ez 9:6-15). Even though a layman and not a scribe or priest, he was able to couch his prayer in phrases and sentences from Scripture, particularly from Deuteronomy. See, e.g., the phrase "great and terrible God" in Dt 7:21; cf. v. 5 with Dt 7:9; v. 9 with Dt 30:2-4; v. 10 with Dt 9:29.

1:5 *God of heaven.* This address to the Ruler of nations was appropriate because his prayer dealt with an international situation, as did Abraham's many centuries earlier (Gn 24:7; see also Ez 1:2; Is 66:1 f.). For the expression *steadfast love* see Dt 7:9 note.

1:6 *We.* Nehemiah, a high-ranking political figure, did not disdain solidarity with his downtrodden people; so also Ezra. (Ez 9:7)

1:8 *Moses.* The *word* which Nehemiah attributed to the ancient lawgiver (8-11) is not a quotation of a specific section from the Pentateuch. Nehemiah knew how to summarize Mosaic teaching of such passages as Lv 26:33-45; Dt 4:27-31; 30:1-4.

1:11 *Fear thy name.* On the meaning of *fear* see Dt 4:10 note; on *thy name,* Ex 6:3 note. The success of Nehemiah's venture depended primarily on the submission of *this man* Artaxerxes to divine guidance.

Cupbearer. Nehemiah was more than a wine steward at the royal table. The cupbearer was one of the most influential officials of the court. The king relied on him for protection against assassination by poisoning. (Cf. Gn 40:21; see also the reference to Solomon's "cupbearers," 1 K 10:5)

2:1-8 TRIP GRANTED BY KING

2:1 *Nisan.* Nehemiah did not bring the subject of Jerusalem's plight to the king's attention from "Chislev" (November/December) when the Jerusalem delegation arrived (1:1), till *Nisan* (March/April). Another cupbearer may have been on duty during that time. More likely Nehemiah was waiting for an opportune moment to risk broaching a matter to the king for reconsideration on which he had ruled not too long ago (Ez 4:21). Moreover, no one spoke at the Persian court unless spoken to by the king. Failure to observe this rule could have jeopardized the cause Nehemiah was about to champion. It even could have ended his career. By the time the 4 or 5 months of waiting were over, Artaxerxes was completing the first half of "the twentieth year" (1:1) of his reign, reckoned here as beginning in the sixth month, called Tishri.

2:2 *Sad.* Literally "bad." Apparently the king thought that Nehemiah was not succeeding in hiding "badness of the heart," i.e., some evil plot against him. The cupbearer therefore had every reason to be *very much afraid* that he might be put to death on the suspicion of harboring thoughts of a rebellion.

2:3 *Fathers' sepulchres.* Jerusalem's enemies branded it a hotbed of "rebellion and sedition" (Ez 4:19). Nehemiah did not even mention it by name but very diplomatically referred to it as an ancestral burial place which needed to be preserved from desecration. (5; 3:16)

2:4 *Prayed.* He had time to send heavenward only a quick sigh for help. When conditions permitted it, he communed with God at length (1:4-11). All through his career he remained a man of prayer. (4:4; 5:19; 6:9, 14; 13:14)

2:5 *Rebuild.* Assured by prayer that "the good hand of . . . God was upon" him (8), Nehemiah dared to ask Artaxerxes to reverse himself (Ez 4:21). It was a risk because the king still could be convinced that rebuilding Jerusalem's walls was the first step in a conspiracy to end Persian control. Judged guilty of promoting intrigue against the throne, the hapless cupbearer was in danger of losing everything: position, wealth (5:14 ff.), his very life.

2:6 *Queen.* Mention of the first lady of the king's harem suggests that she was to some extent responsible for the king's favorable reply. For the influence wielded by women at the Persian court see the Book of Esther. Officials, especially those whose duties gave them access to the royal quarters, were eunuchs (Est 4:4). The record neither affirms nor denies that Nehemiah too was a eunuch.

2:7 *Beyond the River.* For the administrative divisions of the Persian empire see Ez 4:11 note.

2:8 *Forest.* The Hebrew equivalent for paradise or park. The forest of Lebanon, which supplied lumber for Solomon's buildings as well as for structures at the Persian court, may be meant. However, the speed with which the walls were erected (6:15) suggests a source of wood closer to Jerusalem.

Hand of . . . God. For this figurative expression, denoting providential direction of events, see Ez 7:6 note.

2:9-10 ARRIVAL IN JERUSALEM; HOSTILE NEIGHBORS

2:10 *Sanballat.* "Letters" from the king (7) did not make Nehemiah immune to underhanded maneuvers by jealous and suspicious men who saw their power or prestige somehow threatened if Jerusalem, again fortified, were to become the center of a separate province, headed by a special appointee of the Persian king (10:1). Listed first among them is a man with the Babylonian name Sanballat. He is known from extra-Biblical sources to have been the Persian satrap of Samaria (19; 4:7; 6:1). Ordinarily the governor of Judah was under his jurisdiction, but Nehemiah had orders directly from the king. Sanballat is called a *Horonite,* perhaps because he was a descendant of the foreigners settled by the Assyrians in Beth-horon, a city located in the former Northern Kingdom some 15 miles northwest of Jerusalem. (2 K 17:24, 29-31; 2 Ch 25:13 note)

Tobiah. A Hebrew name meaning "The Lord is good." The appositions, *the servant* and *the Ammonite,* are intended to identify him but no longer serve that purpose. He may have been Sanballat's assistant or a former slave who had become governor of Ammonite territory east of the Jordan.

2:11-20 Preliminary Steps

2:11-16 SECRET SURVEY OF RUINED WALLS

2:13 *Valley Gate.* Not all places and gates can be identified with certainty. However, it appears that Nehemiah made a full circuit of the city on his secret inspection of the walls, leaving by the Valley Gate and again entering by it at the end of the tour (15). It was called the *Valley Gate* because it opened into the Hinnom Valley, which rounds the southwestern corner of the city (2 Ch 26:9 note). Proceeding eastward, he passed the *Jackal's Well* or Well of the Dragon, a landmark no longer known. At the *Dung Gate* at the eastern end of the wall he turned northward to the Fountain Gate, no doubt so called because of its location near a spring, perhaps En-rogel (1 K 1:9 note). As he progressed beyond the King's Pool, apparently another name for the Pool of Siloam (2 K 20:20 note), the path close to the ruins grew so impassible that he was forced to continue "by the valley," i.e., the Kidron Valley. At this point he "turned back" (15), not retracing his steps but making his way around the city also along its northern and western walls and back to the Valley Gate.

2:17-20 DISCLOSURE OF PLAN DESPITE OPPOSITION

2:19 *Geshem.* As soon as Nehemiah disclosed how he intended to "seek the welfare of the children of Israel" (10), the opponents accused him and his supporters of *rebelling against the king.* In this maneuver Sanballat and Tobiah had the support of Geshem, chieftain of desert tribes in northern Arabia who were on friendly terms with the Persians.

2:20 *No portion.* Zerubbabel had rejected the Samaritan offer to help build the temple. (Ez 4:1-3)

3:1-32 Construction Assignments

3:1 *Built.* Details describing the parts of an ancient wall and lists of people building them do not make for exciting reading. It is particularly difficult to maintain interest in a compilation of workers' names which come to us from the distant past and in addition are otherwise unknown. Furthermore, some of the gates and landmarks along the walls cannot be identified with any certainty. However, enough of the topography is known to establish that the walls on the four sides of the city are described in the following order: (1) north wall (1-5); (2) west wall (6-12); (3) south wall (13-14); (4) east wall (15-32). Some observations emerge from this welter of information which make also this chapter "profitable for teaching" (2 Ti 3:16). The systematic manner in which the project was organized reflects the stature and character of Nehemiah. A man of recognized administrative ability, he did not hesitate to put his "ten pounds" (Lk 19:13) to work in the Lord's cause, undaunted by jeers from associates in high places. Deserving recognition too is the way the people who shouted enthusiastically: "Let us . . . build" (2:18) showed they actually "had a mind to work" (4:6). Scattered through the chapter are references to various groups who though not carpenters or masons by trade did not hesitate to accept their building assignments: the high priest and the priests (1), the goldsmiths and perfumers (8), the ruler of a district (14), Levites (17), temple servants (26), merchants (31). Some were willing to do double duty. (21, 27)

Sheep Gate. Sheep to be sacrificed were driven through this gate, located near the temple in the northeast corner of the city. The survey of other sections of the wall begins here and proceeds in a counterclockwise direction around the city, ending where it began (32). For the location of other gates, towers, and landmarks consult a Bible dictionary.

4:1—6:14 Obstacles Overcome

4:1-23 HOSTILITY BY FOREIGNERS

4:1 *Building.* Though well planned (ch. 3) and enthusiastically undertaken (2:68; 3:10), the project encountered such serious interference from without and within as to threaten its completion. Hostile leaders of neighboring areas mounted a double attack: (1) they resumed their campaign of vilification, hoping by a constant barrage of taunts to break down the morale of the builders (1-5; 2:19 f.); (2) they forced the overburdened workers to protect themselves against attacks by force (6-23). Finally Nehemiah had to foil a Samaritan plot to assassinate him (6:1-14) before "the wall was finished." (6:15-19)

4:2 *Army.* Not necessarily the imperial militia of the province. The Hebrew word is a general term denoting strength, which may be in the form of a military contingent as well as in concentrated wealth or political power. NEB has "garrison."

4:4 *Hear.* Nehemiah's prayer, quoted without an introductory statement, puts the ridicule of the adversaries into sharp contrast with his trust in God. Opposition to work enjoined by God is defiance of His will. Men of strong faith do not shrink from using strong words as they ask God to "break and hinder every evil counsel and will which would not let . . . His kingdom come" (Luther's explanation of the third petition of the Lord's Prayer; see also Jer 18:23; Ps 69:27 f.). Nehemiah's unequivocal espousal of God's cause commends itself as a remedy to a Christianity gone flabby for lack of convictions.

4:6 *Joined.* As the assigned sections, though still not of the required height or width, were linked with one another, the wall formed an unbroken circuit about the city.

4:7 *Ashdodites.* Jerusalem was surrounded by enemies on all sides: on the north by the Samaritans; on the east and south by the Ammonites and Arabs; on the west by the inhabitants of the Philistine city of Ashdod.

4:8 *Fight.* Very likely by guerrilla attacks. They hardly would have risked open warfare in defiance of "the king's letters." (2:9)

4:9 *Prayed . . . and set.* A good illustration of the Latin proverb: *Ora et labora* (pray and work).

4:10 *Strength . . . failing.* What follows (10-23) reveals how the success of the venture depended on Nehemiah: his tenacity of purpose, his courage against odds, his resourcefulness, his firm, contagious faith. When the strength of the workers was taxed to the breaking point and fear of threatening raids all but paralyzed them, he devised such an effective system of protection against the enemies as to "frustrate their plan" of attacking the city. At the same time he bolstered the sagging faith of the people, reminding them that they could meet every challenge if they put their trust in the "great and terrible" Lord. (14, 20; 1:5 note)

4:13 *Behind the wall.* Nehemiah *stationed the people . . . in open places* behind it, where there was space between it and adjacent buildings. It afforded some protection even though not built to its full height or thickness. (6)

4:16 *Servants.* Lit. "young men," perhaps Nehemiah's personal guard. Half of them were on full alert to prevent a surprise attack on the city's defenses. The other half took over sentry duty at night. (21)

4:18 *Trumpet.* A bugler stood by ready to "rally" reinforcements to the point of attack from other sectors. (20)

4:22 *Within Jerusalem.* Nonresidents capable of bearing arms were ordered to *pass the night within Jerusalem* in order to keep the defenses at full strength.

4:23 *Weapon.* The last three words, as translated literally in the RSV note, evidently are meant to describe another feature of instant readiness on the part of those on guard duty.

5:1-19 INTERNAL DISSENSION

5:1 *Outcry.* Social and economic inequities, tolerated for some time (7) but aggravated by the additional strain of building the walls, worked such a hardship on the poor people, who were "many," as to bring them to the point of mutiny. Exorbitant interest rates charged on mortgages and debts by "the nobles and the officials" forced the borrowers to sell their children into slavery and brought them to the brink of starvation (1-5). Nehemiah was as courageous and resolute in attacking this internal evil as he was in dealing with dangers threatening from the outside. At "a great assembly" he minced no words in confronting the wealthy culprits with their sins of oppression. He so impressed the hardhearted creditors with their guilt that they promised under oath to restore what they had acquired by unlawful means (6:13). Nehemiah himself set a good example of restraint and forbearance, shaming the greedy landowners. He did not "demand the food allowance of the governor" from the heavily burdened immigrants, to which he was entitled, lest "the work on this wall" be impeded. (14-19)

5:4 *Tax.* The same Aramaic word translated "tribute" in Ez 4:13; 7:24. It was levied on subjugated peoples by the Persian conqueror.

5:7 *Interest.* For the injunction against taking interest see Lv 25:35 note.

5:8 *Bought back.* In the Exile the Jews set free their enslaved brethren by redeeming them from their foreign masters.

5:10 *Lending.* Nehemiah gained the goodwill of the assembly by admitting that loans at some rate of interest were made under his administration.

5:11 *Hundredth.* Perhaps the monthly interest rate, which would amount to 12 percent per annum. Payments were made in *money* or in *grain, wine, and oil.*

5:13 *Shook.* Nehemiah's explanatory words underscored the obvious meaning of the gesture. For other instances of symbolic action see 1 K 22:11 note; Jer 27:2; 28:10.

5:14 *Twelve years.* Apparently Artaxerxes did not want to be without the services of his trusted cupbearer for a long time (2:6). However, he must have granted petitions to extend his leave of absence. Nehemiah's ability to pay the maintenance of his official household makes him out a man of considerable personal wealth. He was willing to run the risk of losing it in the promotion of the right cause.

5:19 *Remember.* Nehemiah made this or a similar request repeatedly (13:14, 22, 29, 31). For its intent see Hezekiah's prayer 2 K 20:3 note; also Gn 8:1 note; Ps 25:7; Lk 23:42.

6:1-14 ATTEMPTS ON NEHEMIAH'S PERSON

6:2 *Meet together.* Nehemiah frustrated attempts of foreigners to sabotage the building project (ch. 4). Nor did he let internal dissension bring about a breakdown of operations (ch. 5). Now the enemies resorted to plots against his own person. However, Nehemiah outmaneuvered them: (1) he refused to be lured into a deathtrap by would-be assassins (1-9); (2) he foiled a subtle attempt to discredit his integrity and undermine his leadership. (10-14)

Ono. Some 20 miles northwest of Jerusalem. It was obvious to Nehemiah that the meeting was only a ruse to get him to leave the protecting walls of Jerusalem and its armed citizenry.

6:7 *A king.* The conspirators tried to convince Nehemiah that it would be advantageous to *take counsel together.* The ostensible purpose of the meeting was to counteract the rumor, "reported among the nations" and also "to the king" of Persia, that the governor had himself proclaimed *king in Judah,* an obvious act of rebellion. During Nehemiah's time such prophets as Haggai, Zechariah, and Malachi arose to proclaim their message. But they were not *set up* by Nehemiah to make him king.

6:9 *O God.* As indicated in KJV, this address to God is not in the Hebrew text. Some ancient versions read: "Yet I made my hands strong."

6:10 *Shemaiah.* The foreign adversaries were able to enlist fifth-columnists among the Jews in a new plot against Nehemiah. "Prophets" and a "prophetess" whom "God had not sent" were willing to be "hired," i.e., bribed, in a scheme to undermine and eventually to eliminate his leadership. For earlier false prophets see 1 K 22:7 note. Prominent among these traitors was an otherwise unknown Shemaiah. He had Nehemiah come to his house because he himself was *shut up,* i.e., confined there by circumstances which are not specified. He may have been "debarred from going to the house of the Lord" by some ritual impurity (Lv 13:4 f.; Jer 33:1; 36:5). Or he may have feigned fear of walking the streets lest as a friend of Nehemiah he too would be a marked man. Professing to speak by divine inspiration, Shemaiah tried to make the situation appear so desperate that the injunction against desecration of the temple by unauthorized personnel would not apply. Access to the Holy Place was restricted to priests on pain of death. (Nm 3:10; 18:7)

6:14 *Noadiah.* An otherwise unknown woman who like her male counterparts claimed to receive and transmit divine revelation. However, not all prophetesses were deceivers. (2 K 22:14 note)

6:15-19 Walls Finished in Spite of Intrigue

6:15 *Elul.* August/September on our calendar. The wall was finished in such a short time because enough of the old foundation was left to carry the superstructure. At the same time, the speedy completion of the project is a tribute to Nehemiah's courageous and resourceful management and to the devotion of the people. In the final analysis success was possible only "with the help of . . . God." (16)

6:16 *Afraid.* See RSV note. The Hebrew verbs to see and to fear are very similar.

6:18 *Shecaniah.* The mention of the reaction by the opponents to the completed wall (16) is followed by a final example which, but for Nehemiah's acumen and alertness, could have defeated the project. Tobiah, the ally of the Samaritan governor Sanballat, had married into a prominent family of returned exiles. His father-in-law Shecaniah was the son of "Arah," head of a clan (Ez 2:5; Neh 7:10). There were family ties also with "Berechiah," supervisor of a contingent of workers on the wall (3:4, 30). These relatives were Tobiah's channels for a campaign of propaganda and intimidation.

7:1-73a Further Provisions to Make City Safe

7:1-4 SECURITY MEASURES PRESCRIBED

7:1 *Built.* Nehemiah realized that if the completed walls were to make life in the city safe, it would be necessary (1) that they be manned by enough guards, and the gates remain open only in full daylight (1-4); (2) that the population of the city be increased in order to raise the number of potential defenders. However, those who were to be moved into the city from the countryside were to be screened carefully lest subversive elements destroy the city from within. Nehemiah was about to take a census to determine "by genealogy" who the bona fide members in "the province" were, when he came upon "the book of the genealogy of those who came up [out of exile] at the first" (5), namely at the time when Cyrus issued the decree about 90 years ago authorizing the Jews to return to their homeland. This roster of registered families was considered so vital for the future welfare of the city that it was made a part of the record, duplicating the list in Ez 2 (6-73). The report of the repopulation itself is deferred to ch. 11.

Gatekeepers. Ordinarily they guarded the approaches to the temple (1 Ch 26:12 ff.; 2 Ch 8:14). Nehemiah recruited them for guard duty on the wall, adding *the singers, and the Levites* to their ranks. (43-45)

7:2 *Hanani.* He and "certain men out of Judah" had alerted Nehemiah to the "great trouble and shame" of Jerusalem (1:2 f.). Now the security of the city, probably divided into two districts (3:9, 12), was entrusted to him and a companion with the very similar name *Hananiah.* However, the phrase *and Hananiah* can be translated also "namely Hananiah," explaining that the name of Nehemiah's brother was current in two forms. The word *governor* is better translated "commander," to avoid confusion with the position held by Nehemiah.

7:3 *Guards.* During the night the regular sentries were to be reinforced. Residents of the city were to stand guard at points adjacent to their homes.

7:4 *Few.* Reference to the sparse population serves as a transition to the account of Nehemiah's efforts to remedy the deficiency.

7:5-73a LIST OF RETURNEES: BASIS FOR REPOPULATION

7:6 *The people.* The following list contains essentially the same names appearing in Ez 2:1-70.

7:66 *Whole assembly.* For the totals given in these verses see Ez 2:64 note.

7:70 *Gave.* The contributions, summarized in Ez 2:68 f., are enumerated here according to the various donors. (70-72)

Five hundred. The text of Ezra suggests the reading "five hundred minas of silver and thirty priests' garments."

7:73 *Seventh month.* The last part of this verse leads over to the second major division of the book. The first seven chapters record the external fortification of Jerusalem, the building of the walls; the next section (chs. 8—10) records a spiritual rearmament of the people. Nehemiah, layman and builder in stone, yielded leadership in matters of heart and soul to Ezra, priest and scribe. At two convocations the latter led his people to reaffirm their allegiance to God on the basis of "the law of Moses" (8:1; 9:3). The first assembly responded to the reading of the Law (8:1-8) and the exhortation to comply cheerfully with it (8:9-12) by celebrating the feast of tabernacles "according to the ordinance" (8:13-18). The climax of a second gathering 24 days later was a formal renewal of all provisions of the covenant (chs. 9—10).—The restoration of the physical temple and the rebuilding of its living stones, the people—both on old foundations—got under way at meetings held *when the seventh month had come* (Ez 3:1), the "first day" of which was observed as New Year's Day. (Lv 23:24 note)

7:73b—10:39 SPIRITUAL REDEDICATION

7:73b—8:18 First Assembly

7:73b—8:8 LAW READ AND EXPOUNDED

8:1 *Ezra.* Not all of his history is recorded in the book bearing his name. For his appearance on the scene at this time see Ez 10:18 note. He is not mentioned among the builders of the wall (Neh 3). Perhaps he was too old for strenuous physical work.

Water Gate. Also mentioned in 3:26, it probably owed its name to its location near the spring of Gihon. (1 K 1:33 note)

The law of Moses. Identified with "the law of the Lord" (9:3). Ezra, "a scribe skilled in the law," had it "in hand" when he set out to regulate the social and religious life of the returned exiles. (Ez 7:6, 14)

8:3 *From it.* Ezra had to limit himself to selected portions of "the law of Moses which the Lord has given to Israel." The time *from early morning until midday* would not have permitted reading the entire Pentateuch. To judge by the response of the people, he chose selections which were particularly pertinent. According to Dt 31:11, Moses required that "this law" be read "before all Israel in their hearing."

8:4 *Pulpit.* Literally "a tower of wood," i.e., a wooden dais or elevated platform. Other details are given in 4-8: the names of people who supported the reading (4); the respectful attention given the reading from the moment Ezra "opened," i.e., unrolled the scroll (5); the invocation and response (6); the help given by the Levites to "the people to understand the law." (7-8)

8:8 *Clearly.* The Levites repeated the words loudly and clearly for all to hear or they paraphrased in Aramaic what Ezra read in Hebrew for those who no longer understood the language of the fathers.

8:9-12 PEOPLE EXHORTED TO REJOICE

8:9 *Governor.* The original has "the Tirshata," as in Ez 2:63 note. In the entire report of the religious activities (chs. 8—10) Nehemiah's name occurs only here and in 10:1.

8:10 *Grieved.* Evidently what the people heard Ezra read made them realize that they had cause to "mourn or weep" in repentance, as their forebears did under similar circumstances (2 K 22:11, 19). Grief over breaking the law was in order, and the proper time to express it was to come (ch. 9). However, that particular day was *holy to our Lord,* i.e., set aside for the purpose prescribed by Him. According to the law of Moses it was to be a day of rejoicing with blowing of trumpets (Lv 23:24; Nm 29:1). The completion of the walls a few days earlier was to make this New Year's Day a particularly joyous one.

8:13-18 FEAST OF TABERNACLES CELEBRATED

8:13 *Came together.* As the leaders of the

community continued to study the Law, they found that another joyous festival was to be observed in the seventh month, the feast of booths or tabernacles (from the 15th to the 22d day; Ex 23:16; Lv 23:33-36; Nm 29:12-38; Dt 16:13-15). The day of atonement, which fell on the 10th day of the seventh month, is not mentioned.

8:15 *It is written.* The words in quotation marks, while not a verbatim citation of any passage, nevertheless give the intent of the way the feast was to be observed.

8:16 *His roof.* It was flat.

Gate of Ephraim. Cf. 2 K 14:13 note.

8:17 *Had not done so.* The festival had been observed (e.g., Ez 3:4), but not with the same degree of fervor and awareness of its meaning. Once upon a time the fathers were welded into a nation when they lived in temporary dwellings at the time the Lord "brought them out of the land of Egypt" (Lv 23:43). The memorial celebration of the feast after Jerusalem was safe behind walls was particularly joyful because it marked the reestablishment of the chosen people, freed from the Babylonian house of bondage and planted securely in the Promised Land.

8:18 *Day by day.* Fuller indoctrination *from the book of the law of God* had the beneficial results recorded in the next chapter.

9:1—10:39 Second Assembly

9:1-5 PENITENTIAL GRIEF

9:1 *Twenty-fourth day.* Two days after the feast of tabernacles (8:13 note) *the people of Israel were assembled* again. Already at the first convocation "the people wept when they heard the words of the law" (8:9). Continued reading (8:18) made them so aware of "their sins and the iniquities of their fathers" that they penitently sought forgiveness and renewal (1-5). Ezra put into words what needed to be said. In a long intercessory prayer he (1) praised God's acts of mercy to Abraham and his descendants (6-15); (2) confessed the nation's sins from its very beginning to the Babylonian captivity (16-31); (3) pleaded for continued mercy (32-37). Upon their confession the people promised to amend their sinful life. To that end they renewed the covenant, pledging to respond to God's grace with total consecration to His will. (9:38—10:39)

9:2 *Separated themselves.* Those who participated in the day of humiliation and prayer recognized that allegiance to God required severing compromising ties with evil. To be God's people they had to "separate . . . from the peoples of the land and from the foreign wives." (Ez 6:21 note; 10:11)

9:4 *Stairs.* Either the ascent to the platform mentioned in 8:4 or the raised dais itself.

9:5 *Levites.* It is no longer clear why the two groups of Levites (4 f.) were composed as they were or why five of the eight who "cried . . . to the Lord" (4) joined others in exhorting the people to "stand up and bless the Lord." (5)

9:6-38 EZRA'S INTERCESSORY PRAYER

9:6 *And Ezra said.* These words, not in the Hebrew text, are supplied from the Septuagint. The prayer (6-37) is so saturated with Biblical references and allusions as to suggest that it must have been a "priest and scribe" (8:9), immersed in the Scriptures as Ezra was, who composed it. The opening words gratefully attribute the origin of Israel to the Creator of the universe and the Lord of history. In sovereign majesty He (1) chose Abraham, making him the progenitor of the chosen people and the father of all believers (6-8; Gl 3:8, 29); (2) demonstrated His power in the exodus from Egypt and revealed His holy will through Moses on Mt. Sinai (9-15).—Moses too reminded the people of the exodus (Dt 29:2-4) before asking them to renew the covenant (Dt 29:10-15). See also Jos 24; Ps 78; 106; Ez 9:6-15.

Their host. A more modern translation is "army" (Gn 2:1). *The host of heaven* includes angelic creatures. (1 K 22:19; Ps 103:21)

9:8 *Canaanite.* Cf. Gn 15:21; 13:7 notes.

9:10 *A name.* Cf. Ex 9:16; 6:3 notes.

9:14 *Sabbath.* The only individual commandment mentioned. Keeping the sabbath was a distinguishing mark of a Jew; breaking it was a capital offense. (Ex 31:13 note; 35:1-3)

9:16 *And our fathers.* The *and* is better translated "namely." The response of the fathers to the material and spiritual blessings grew more disappointing as God's favors kept mounting. But for His "great mercies" (19) they should have been left to perish for such callous disobedience in the face of undeserved mercies on their way to the Promised Land. (16-25)

9:17 *Return.* Cf. Nm 14:1-4.

9:20 *Good Spirit.* Probably a reference to the special endowment of the 70 elders whom Moses chose to be his assistants (Nm 11:16 ff.). In this survey of the past all action is attributed directly to God. There is no mention of Israel's great men, not even of Moses, "the servant of God" (10:29), or of David, founder of Israel's greatness.

Manna. For the meaning of the term see Ex 16:14, 15 notes.

9:22 *Sihon . . . Og.* Cf. Nm 21:21-35 notes.

9:26 *Prophets.* Israel's continued disobedience in the Promised Land deserved to be labeled willful rebellion (26-31). God's chastisements, e.g., at the time of the judges, made no lasting impression. Prophets, spokesmen of His "Spirit" (30), were ignored or even killed. (1 K 19:10; Jer 26:20 ff.; 2 Ch 24:20 ff.; Zch 7:12)

9:27 *Saviors.* A reference to the judges. (Ju 3:9, 15)

9:29 *Shall live.* Israel did not earn the right to live by *observance* of the ordinances. Escape from death, the wages of sin, was solely a gift of God's grace offered and bestowed in the covenant. Obedience to commandments was to flow from grateful acceptance of this unearned mercy. (Lv 18:5; Eze 20:11; see the meaning of covenant in Exodus, Introduction, "Content."

9:31 *Great mercies.* "Where sin increased" throughout Israel's history "grace abounded all the more" (Ro 5:20). God's great mercies were not exhausted. In the wilderness (17), during the occupation of Canaan (27), even in the Babylonian exile He did not *make an end of them,* as they fully deserved. For "the great and mighty and terrible God" (32) is at the same time *a gracious and merciful God.* The plea for continued mercy and the pledge of covenant faithfulness (32-38) could be made without fear of rejection.

9:32 *Steadfast love.* One word in Hebrew. For its meaning see Dt 7:9 note.

Kings of Assyria. Israel's *hardship,* begun by the Assyrians (e.g., the captivity of the Northern Kingdom in 722 B.C.), culminated in the Babylonian exile, where now the chosen people were "slaves" to a new world power, the Persians. Even those who had returned to the land of the fathers were not an independent community.

9:38 *Covenant.* At Mt. Sinai the people entered into covenant with God after they received the Law through Moses. The people at Ezra's time felt the need of renewing their pledge of loyalty to the same covenant after hearing "the law that the Lord had commanded by Moses." (8:14)

10:1-39 COVENANT RENEWAL

10:1 *Their seal.* This chapter brings a fuller report on the renewal of the covenant. It had the support of the secular and religious leaders. A list of those who endorsed the written agreement with some identifying mark or seal is made a record in 1-27. "The rest of the people" gave a solemn oath to "do all the commandments of the Lord . . . his ordinances and his statutes" (28 f.), some of which are then enumerated. (30-39)

Nehemiah. The list of signatories is headed by the name of "His Excellency" the governor (Ez 2:63 note). Ezra's name does not appear among the priestly signers (2-8). It is quite likely that he acted as mediator of the covenant as Moses did originally. Nehemiah's name is followed by that of an unknown *Zedekiah,* perhaps a member of the royal house of David.

10:2 *Seraiah.* Some of the names of the 21 priests (2-8) occur again in 12:1-3. Perhaps they were representatives of priestly families, such as the heads of families mentioned in Ez 2:36 f.

10:9 *Levites.* A list of 17 Levitical family representatives (9-13) is followed by a roster of 44 "chiefs of the people." (14-27)

10:29 *Curse and an oath.* The whole assembly was willing to "enter a sworn covenant of the Lord" (Dt 29:12). Under oath they invoked a curse on themselves should they break their pledge. (See Ru 1:17 note for an oath formula.)

10:30 *Will not.* The general pledge "to walk in God's law" (29) included areas of social, economic, and religious life in which, at the time, there was a pronounced tendency to be unfaithful (30-39). Therefore the people vowed specifically: (1) to refrain from intermarriage with foreigners (30; cf. Ez 9:1; Neh 13:23 ff.); (2) to observe the sabbath and the ordinances of the sabbatical year (31); (3) to contribute to the maintenance of the temple and its worship services. (32-39)

10:31 *Seventh year.* For the law "given by Moses" on this subject see Ex 23:10 note; Lv 25:1-7; Dt 15:1-3.

10:32 *Third part.* A half shekel was required by law (Ex 30:13; Mt 17:24). If computed according to Persian currency, the *obligation* which the people laid on themselves perhaps was equal in value to the required tax.

10:33 *Showbread.* Cf. 1 Ch 9:32 note.

10:34 *Wood offering. Written in the law* was the ordinance that "fire shall be kept burning upon the altar continually" (Lv 6:12 f.). The people agreed how they were going to supply the wood necessary to meet this requirement. (13:31)

10:35 *Obligate ourselves.* They pledged to make various contributions. Some were prescribed; some were freewill offerings.

10:36 *Sons.* For the redemption of *first-born* sons see Nm 18:15 f.

11:1—13:31 VARIOUS MEASURES TO PROMOTE REHABILITATION

11:1—13:3 During Nehemiah's First Visit

11:1-36 REPOPULATION OF JERUSALEM

11:1 *Cast lots.* The last three chapters of the book record additional measures which under Nehemiah's leadership contributed to the rehabilitation of the people. Some provided physical security; others strengthened the moral and spiritual life. Some were introduced during his first visit to Jerusalem (11:1—13:3); others on his return to the city some years later (13:4-31). First on the list of his achievements is the repopulation of Jerusalem (ch. 11). Because "the people within it were few and no houses had been built" (7:4, 73), there were not enough residents to protect the city, even though it now had a wall. Nehemiah remedied the deficiency by bringing people from *other towns* into *the holy city* (1 f.). The "book of genealogy" which he found no doubt served as a checklist. (7:1 note)

11:3 *In Jerusalem.* Reference to the population of the city is followed by a list of those *who lived in Jerusalem* (3-24) and of "the villages" where the people settled (25-36). The city directory has almost the same names found in 1 Ch 9:2-34. It is arranged under five categories: "Israel," i.e., laymen (3-9); priests (10-14); Levites (15-18); gatekeepers and temple servants (19-21); officials responsible to the king (22-24).

11:14 *A hundred and twenty-eight.* For the total number of priests and gatekeepers see 1 Ch 9:13, 17 notes.

11:23 *Provision.* This "overseer" administered the king's provisions for the support of the temple. For the interest of the Persians in this matter see Ez 6:9 f.; 7:22 f.

11:24 *King's hand.* Negotiations *in all matters concerning the people* were handled at the Persian court by an adviser, appointed by the king.

11:25 *Villages.* Apparently many people

preferred to live in unwalled towns *with their fields* rather than in the close quarters of fortified Jerusalem. The villages mentioned here were in territories occupied by Judah and Benjamin before the captivity.

11:30 *Beer-sheba.* The southernmost end of the area where they encamped, about 45 miles south of Jerusalem. *The valley of Hinnom* skirted Jerusalem. (2 K 23:10 note)

11:31 *Geba.* North of Jerusalem, as were the other Benjaminite towns.

11:36 *Joined to Benjamin.* Some divisions of Levites changed their residence from Judah to Benjamin.

12:1-26 LIST OF PRIESTS AND LEVITES

12:1 *Priests and the Levites.* Lists of them appear also in Ez 2:36 ff. and in Neh 10:3-9. Some names appear on all of them. But there also are different entries. The reason for the variation is no longer clear. In some instances names may have been added in order to keep the roster up to date. The genealogical table beginning at 11, which appears to trace generations beyond the time of Nehemiah, may have been appended to his book at a later date. According to other calculations Nehemiah may have lived long enough to complete the list in its present form.

12:22 *Jaddua.* A high priest by this name is said by Josephus, an ancient Jewish historian, to have held office at the time of Alexander the Great. For that reason many commentators do not identify the *Darius* of this verse with the king so named in Ez 4:24 but with a Darius Codomanus whom Alexander defeated in 331 B.C.

12:27-43 WALLS DEDICATED

12:27 *Dedication.* This event is recorded as one of the last achievements during Nehemiah's first visit to Jerusalem. The report of the completion of the wall appears much earlier (6:15). Notice of its dedication may be inserted at this point because it marked the capstone of the governor's labors in behalf of the struggling community. However, no date is given for this happy occasion, leaving the possibility open that in reality it occurred earlier. A twofold ceremony gave expression to the "great joy" (43) which prevailed: (1) priests and Levites performed purifying rites by which the city's defenses were hallowed to the service of God (27-30); (2) the assembled "princes of Judah" marched around the entire city on its newly erected wall, gratefully acknowledging that building operations were complete. The triumphant processional divided itself into "two great companies." One, led by Ezra, began the circuit along the south side of the city (31-37); the other, led by Nehemiah, started off in the other direction. Both groups converged on the temple where "great sacrifices" were offered. (38-42)

12:28 *The circuit.* Priests and Levites from the countryside *round Jerusalem* were summoned for the occasion. *Sons of,* i.e., members of, the guild of singers are noted particularly because the festivities called for jubilant vocal and instrumental music.

Netophathites. Netophah, the head of their family, is mentioned in Ez 2:22; see also 1 Ch 9:16.

12:30 *Purified themselves.* Purification rites for Levites are described in Nm 8:5 ff., 21 f. Ceremonial cleanness of priests is demanded in Lv 21:1-9; 22:1-9; see also Ez 6:20; Neh 13:22. Removal of uncleanness was required of the people (Nm 19:11-22). When the temple was reconsecrated at the time of Hezekiah, Levites who had sanctified themselves "brought out all the uncleanness" from the sanctuary. (2 Ch 29:12-16)

12:31 *The right.* As a person faced east, south was to his right and north to his left (38). Not all walls, towers, and landmarks along the path of the two groups can be located with certainty. Some are mentioned also in tracing Nehemiah's secret tour of the walls. (2:11-16)

12:44-47 APPOINTMENT OF TEMPLE OFFICIALS

12:44 *That day.* A general term, not necessarily the day of dedication (cf. 13:1). The walls assured safekeeping of contributions and dues, *required by the law* to be brought to the temple. Within the fortified city the sacred rites could be performed safely. The proper personnel could carry out their prescribed duties without hindrance (44-47). However, as they did in earlier days, the people were soon to neglect the opportunity to worship under such favorable circumstances. (13:10 ff.)

12:45 *Purification.* It was the duty of the Levites "to assist the sons of Aaron" in "the cleansing of all that is holy," i.e., set aside for sacred use. (1 Ch 23:28)

David and his son. David's organization of the temple officiants (1 Ch 23—26) was put into operation by his son Solomon. (2 Ch 8:14)

12:46 *Asaph.* Cf. 1 Ch 15:16 f.; 16:5.

12:47 *Zerubbabel.* Under his governorship the temple was built (Ez 5:2; 6:14 f.); Nehemiah surrounded it with protecting walls. *All Israel* responded gratefully to both events, but in each instance devotion soon waned.

13:1-3 THOSE OF FOREIGN DESCENT BANNED

13:1 *Found written.* The preceding section (12:44-47) records the institution of worship by authorized officiants. The next verses report action taken in a related concern: restriction of worshipers to those eligible to *enter the assembly of God,* as required in *the book of Moses.* (13:1-3; Dt 23:3 note)

13:2 *Balaam.* For his story see Nm 22—24.

13:3 *Separated.* According to 9:2, the people who renewed the covenant "separated themselves from all foreigners" to demonstrate their desire to serve the true God. Further instruction prompted them to exclude *all those of foreign descent* from participation in worship.

13:4-31 Reforms During Second Visit

13:4-9 TOBIAH EXPELLED FROM TEMPLE

13:4 *Before this.* The closing verses of the book list several reforms which Nehemiah carried out during a second term of office in Jerusalem. After serving as governor of Judah for 12 years, he "went to the king" (6). No reason is given for his return to Persian headquarters. Perhaps he was recalled to give a personal report of his administration. It is also possible that the king felt that a change in administrators was desirable. Officials had a way of using their position to promote their own interests, especially if they occupied a post for a long time. Nehemiah must have given a good account of his stewardship. When he "asked leave of the king" to return to Jerusalem, his request was granted. His absence of "some time" (6) was long enough for abuses again to infest the sacred community. The evils he found were not too different from those he had coped with once before. "Very angry" (8) at these unexpected relapses, he proceeded against the offenders in high dudgeon. He took drastic action first against desecration of the temple by Tobiah (4-9). Eliashib, the high priest (28; 3:1; 12:10) or a supervisory priest by that name, had permitted him, an Ammonite (2:10) and Nehemiah's archenemy (4:3, 7 f.; 6:1), to occupy space "in the courts of the house of God," reserved for sacred purposes. For the location of *the chambers* see 1 K 6:2 note.

Connected with. By marrying into a prominent family, Tobiah established ties with such men as Eliashib. (6:17-19)

13:6 *King of Babylon.* This title, one of many claimed by the Persian kings, was particularly meaningful to the Israelites because they had been exiles in Babylon.

13:10-14 SUPPORT FOR TEMPLE OFFICIANTS RESTORED

13:10 *Portions.* Nehemiah "remonstrated with the officials" on this matter with good cause. At the renewal of the covenant the people had solemnly pledged to make all the contributions necessary for the maintenance of the temple and its worship (10:32-39). But their devotion was "like the dew that goes early away" (Hos 6:4). The Levites, deprived of their income, *had fled each to his field* in order somehow to make a livelihood. Within a short time Nehemiah "set them in their stations" in the temple. Again supported by the restored influx of tithes, they could resume their assigned tasks. He also appointed "faithful" supervisors so that the donations were distributed equitably.

13:14 *Remember.* Cf. 5:19 note.

13:15-22 SABBATH LAWS ENFORCED

13:15 *Sabbath.* Its desecration was the third evil to be corrected. As if it were a heathen city, it was business-as-usual in Jerusalem on the sacred day of rest. In order to put a stop to the forbidden traffic, Nehemiah ordered the city gates closed on the sabbath. He also threatened to proceed against foreign merchants who brought their merchandise to the immediate environs of the city, tempting citizens to violate the law.

13:16 *Tyre.* The Phoenician city of Tyre was a center of world trade. For its commercial fame see Eze 27:12-36; 28:16.

13:18 *Fathers.* Rejection of warnings against *profaning the sabbath* had brought God's wrath on the city and was certain to do so again (Is 56:4, 6; 58:13; Jer 17:21-23; Eze 20:12, 20; 44:24). The punishment could be expected to be even more severe. (Ez 9:14; 10:10)

13:23-29 RENEWED ACTION AGAINST INTERMARRIAGE

13:23 *Saw.* Relapse into the evil of mixed marriages so infuriated Nehemiah that he resorted to violent measures (for a previous attempt to suppress it see Ez 9—10; see also Ml 2:11-16). He not only lashed out at the offenders in a tirade, declaring them liable to God's judgment; he also inflicted severe physical punishment on them. (23-29)

13:24 *Ashdod.* One of the Philistine cities, about 35 miles west of Jerusalem. Its inhabitants, no doubt already "a mongrel people" (Zch 9:6), were among those who had tried to prevent the building of the walls (4:7 ff.). The language spoken there as well as in transjordanian Ammon and Moab very likely was a mixture of dialects similar but also different from *the language of Judah.*

13:26 *Solomon.* For the story of how "foreign women made even him to sin" see 1 K 11. If a person called Jedidiah, i.e., beloved of the Lord (2 Sm 12:25 note), did not escape divine retribution for "marrying foreign women," the present generation, forwarned by his example, could expect punishment of the same, if not greater, severity.

13:28 *Sanballat.* It seems incredible that the inveterate enemy of the people (2:10; 4:1; 6:1) could infiltrate the family of the high priest. Breakdown of integrity in high places demonstrated the threat posed by such marital alliances. The common people would follow the bad example of the leaders. Not only would Israel lose its national identity; it also would render itself unfit to be the bearer of God's promise to all nations.

13:30-31 SUMMARY OF REFORMS

13:31 *Remember me.* The book closes with Nehemiah's oft-repeated prayer (5:19 note). Here the curtain falls also on his career. He and Ezra drop from sight as suddenly as they appeared on the scene of action. What they did to promote the kingdom of God is a matter of record, "written down for our instruction" (1 Co 10:11). Their full life's story is known only to God. He has inscribed their names in the book of life, making them citizens of "the holy city Jerusalem" which John saw "coming down out of heaven from God." (Rv 21:9 ff.)

ESTHER

INTRODUCTION

Content

The Book of Esther does not pick up the thread of history where the two preceding books left it but supplements the record of the same century of postexilic Israel spanned by Ezra and Nehemiah (see Introduction to Ezra). It tells of events which happened after the rebuilding of the temple (515 B.C.; Ez 1—6) but before Ezra's arrival in Jerusalem (458 B.C.; Ez 7—10). However, it does not furnish a continuous chronicle of this half century. The account is limited to a series of connected episodes during the early part of the reign of Ahasuerus or Xerxes (486—464 B.C.), referred to only in passing in Ez 4:6.

Esther is complementary to Ez-Neh also as far as the place of action is concerned. The scene shifts from the newly established community in Jerusalem to provinces within the Persian empire where many Jews chose to remain rather than return to the homeland. The court of Xerxes is the focus of attention.

The first three chapters introduce the chief actors of a drama full of suspense and sudden reversals. The first to appear on the stage is the Persian king. The fate of the Jews, threatened with extinction, is subject to the whims of this all-powerful ruler (ch. 1). Esther, who became his queen, is the heroine; her cousin and guardian, Mordecai, is the hero (ch. 2). The villain is Xerxes' grand vizier, Haman. His plot to destroy the Jews, even though sanctioned by the king (ch. 3), is foiled by courageous countermeasures. The tables are turned. Not Mordecai but Haman is executed. Not the Jews but their enemies are slain (chs. 4—9). In the closing scene an annual festival called the Purim feast is established to commemorate the happy turn of events.

Esther and Ez-Neh complement one another most strikingly by their respective portrayals of divine providence. In the latter all that happens is ascribed directly to God's action. He "stirred up the spirit of Cyrus" (Ez 1:1); His "good hand . . . was upon" Nehemiah (Neh 2:8). In Ezra's review of history there is no mention of the part played by the great men in Israel's past; they were but channels through whom God governed the universe (Neh 9:6-37). Some passages in the OT appear to make God responsible even for evil (Nm 31:1 note; Am 3:6). Esther seems to go to the other extreme. Here there is only one vague reference to divine providence. God even goes unmentioned throughout the book except for a veiled allusion (4:14 note). In this scheme of things, people do not express their dependence on Him. There is no prayer for help when disaster threatens (but see 4:3 note); there is no song of thanksgiving when deliverance comes; only action, as if everything depended on human courage and resourcefulness. This feature of the book was felt so strongly at a later time that apocryphal additions to Esther were composed in which lengthy prayers are placed on the lips of Mordecai and Esther and the deliverance of the Jews is repeatedly attributed to God.

However, even without these apocryphal additions, God's guiding hand is clearly present in the book. Despite their noblest efforts hero and heroine would have gone down to defeat had it not been that favorable circumstances made success possible. At crucial points coincidences beyond their control converged to produce situations which spelled the difference between life and death. Joseph, e.g., had seen the same power create the chance happenings which determined his life. In both cases it was not a blind, capricious force; "in everything" it deliberately let "God work for good with those" for whom it shaped events (Ro 8:28). It could not be stymied by forces of evil even if they represented the resources of a world empire. It established a universal tribunal of justice where right and wrong have their day in court. What this often unnamed power does, proclaims: "This is the finger of God." (Ex 8:19; Lk 11:20)

To those tempted to misunderstand the workings of God's providence, the Book of Esther says: "Again it is written" (Mt 4:7) that He expects men to work out their own salvation even though He bestows it. He lets men reap the fruits of their labor even though He makes them grow. He lets men rejoice in their accomplishments even though their reactions are not always blameless.

Authorship

The writer remains unknown. Only general information about him can be gleaned from the book. He composed it sometime after the death of Xerxes (464 B.C.) because he refers to the king's biography, "written in the Book of the Chronicles of the kings of Media and Persia" (10:2). He had access also to records kept by Mordecai (9:20, 32). At the same time he draws on his personal acquaintance with Persian life to put events into their proper setting. His incidental descriptions of the palace in Susa, the royal court, its protocol and customs, have been found to be so accurate as to suggest that he was a contemporary of the events he records. A person so intimately acquainted with the details of the story is not apt to commit blunders in major historical references, as charged by many scholars. From the opening clause: "Now it came to pass" (1:1 KJV, as in Jos, Ju, 2 Sm) to the closing reference to documentation (10:2) he purports to write what actually happened and not what his fancy produced in the form of a historical novel.

Place in Canon

In our English Bible, Esther is the last of the historical books; in the Hebrew Scriptures, it is the last of the five festival scrolls, so called because they are appointed for public reading on festival days (see Introduction to Ruth). The feast of Purim, whose origin the book describes, comes at the end of the Jewish ecclesiastical year.

OUTLINE

I. 1:1—3:6 Introduction to Principal Characters
- A. 1:1—2:4 Xerxes, Persian King
- B. 2:5-23 Heroine and Hero
- C. 3:1-6 Villain: Haman, Enemy of Jews

II. 3:7—4:3 Plot to Liquidate Jews
- A. 3:7-11 Haman's Wicked Proposal Sanctioned
- B. 3:12-15 Extermination Ordered by King
- C. 4:1-3 Distress of Jews

III. 4:4—8:17 Counterplot to Save Jews
- A. 4:4-17 Esther's Cooperation Enlisted
- B. 5:1—8:17 Esther's Successful Intervention

IV. 9:1-19 Countermeasures Carried Out
- A. 9:1-15 Enemies Slain
- B. 9:16-19 Rejoicing on Third Day

V. 9:20-32 Deliverance Commemorated:
- A. 9:20-22 Festival Instituted by Mordecai

B. 9:23-28 Name Explained; Future Observance Ordered

C. 9:29-32 Celebration Promoted by Esther

VI. 10:1-3 Epilog: Peace Under Mordecai's Administration

1:1—3:6 INTRODUCTION TO PRINCIPAL CHARACTERS

1:1—2:4 Xerxes, Persian King

1:1-22 REJECTION OF VASHTI, HIS QUEEN

1:1 *Ahasuerus.* In an introductory section (1:1—3:6) the author brings on stage the chief characters of his highly dramatic story. He provides background information about them which the reader needs to know in order to understand their respective roles. First to make his appearance is the Persian king, because the outcome of the issues depends on his decision. For his name see Ez 4:6 note; for his capital Susa, Neh 1:1 note; for the administration of the Persian empire, Ez 4:11 note.

Xerxes' domestic affairs rather than his military exploits furnish the setting of the account. His rejection of one queen and selection of her successor precipitate the action and to a great extent determine the course of events. At a banquet for the men of high office (1-9), the king, deep in his cups, ordered Queen Vashti to display "her beauty" to those in attendance. She refused to comply with his wishes (10-12). Thereupon his guests, as befuddled as he, advised him not only to depose Vashti but also to issue a pompous decree throughout the empire that "every man be lord in his own house." (13-22)

India to Ethiopia. The territory and resources of the Persian kings exceeded those of previous empires. Men did his bidding from the Indus River to Ethiopia, south of Egypt. If forces of evil should be favored by such a potentate, they would appear to be invincible.

Provinces. The number of smaller administrative units may have varied from time to time. (Cf. Dn 6:1)

1:3 *Third year.* The ancient historian Herodotus reports a gathering of Xerxes' mighty men in 483 B.C., two years before the ambitious king set out on an ill-fated campaign to conquer Greece.

1:4 *Many days.* No doubt the king did not entertain all of his guests for the entire period of half a year ("one hundred and eighty days"). Continuous festivities were in progress as various groups of imperial representatives had their turn at the court of "Persia and Media." In the early days of the empire, the Medes supplied the leadership until Cyrus gave their cousins, the Persians, the dominant role.

1:8 *Compelled.* By *law* or special decree the king set aside a rule of etiquette governing royal banquets. Ordinarily guests were required to drink only as the king raised his goblet or as the master of ceremonies gave the appropriate signal. At these drinking bouts such restrictions did not apply. *As every man desired,* he could imbibe to his heart's content.

1:9 *Vashti.* A Persian word meaning beautiful. The only queen of Xerxes known from an ancient extra-Biblical source is called Amestris. However, enough information on the king's character is available to warrant the conclusion that more than one beautiful woman was favored to become the first lady of his harem.

1:10 *Seven eunuchs.* Cf. Neh 2:6 note. Their names as well as those appearing in 14 are otherwise unknown.

1:12 *Refused.* No reason is given for her defiance of a royal order, officially transmitted to her by the eunuchs (10, 12, 15). Perhaps the queen too had imbibed too freely at the "banquet for the women" (9) or she may have felt revulsion against being exhibited as nothing more than another piece of ornamental property reflecting the "pomp of his majesty." (4)

1:13 *The times. The wise men* were experts either in the pseudo-science of astrology (Is 44:25; Dn 5:15) or in the interpretation of law, based on precedent (1 Ch 12:32). Persian kings relied on "seven counselors" for advice in making important decisions (Ez 7:14 note). They "saw the king's face" at regular intervals, being admitted to his presence on a standing order of *procedure.*

1:18 *Contempt.* The noblemen either humored the king or they engaged in mock heroics engendered by imaginary fears which the wine had conjured up in their fevered minds. The decree they recommended was ridiculous at a time when women had no choice but to "give honor to their husbands."

1:19 *Altered.* A royal decree, issued officially and publicly announced, could "not be revoked." (8:8; Dn 6:8, 12, 15)

1:22 *His people.* To assert himself as *lord in his own house* a man could demand that his wife, if she was not of his nationality, adopt her husband's language.

2:1-4 SEARCH FOR NEW QUEEN

2:1 *Remembered.* The record does not reveal whether "the anger of King Ahasuerus" decreed only that Vashti be deposed or whether he ordered her executed. In a more sober and calm moment he realized, perhaps with some twinges of regret, that a search for a new queen was necessary because of his rash act. (2:1-4)

2:5-23 Heroine and Hero

2:5-18 ESTHER

2:7 *Esther.* Next in the cast of characters to be introduced is the heroine (1:1 note). Her appearance on the scene is a natural sequel to the state of affairs created by an ill-tempered, autocratic ruler (1:1—2:4). Before the main action gets under way, the reader learns how she came to be in the eye of the hurricane. An orphaned Jewess and ward of her cousin, Esther rose from a favored position in the royal harem (2:5-11) to a place at Xerxes' side as his queen. (2:12-18)

Hadassah. A derivative of a common noun in Hebrew meaning myrtle. As did other exiles, she acquired a foreign name (Dn 1:6 f.). Esther is an adaptation of the Persian word *stareh*, meaning star, or a variation of the name of a goddess known in Babylonia as Ishtar and in Canaan as Ashtoreth (Ju 2:13 note; 1 K 11:5). Secular history has no record of a Jewish queen of Xerxes by any name. (1:9 note)

Mordecai. Very likely an adaptation of the common Babylonian name Mardukaia, i.e., a devotee of the god Marduk. (Ez 2:2)

Adopted her. Because *her father and her mother died,* Esther is introduced as the *beautiful and lovely* cousin of an exiled Jew who became her guardian. Both of them were in exile because their common grandfather Kish "had been carried away . . . with Jeconiah" (also known as Jehoiachin) by Nebuchadnezzar in 597 B.C., more than 100 years ago. (2 K 24:8-16)

2:9 *Pleased him.* Esther began to rise from obscurity when, "taken into the king's palace," her charm captivated the keeper of the royal harem.

2:10 *Not made known.* A possible reason for concealing "her people or kindred" was the fear of prejudicing her chances of advancement. In this connection the question arises how she was able to keep her nationality a secret without compromising her religious beliefs. (Cf. Dn 6:10)

2:12 *Turn came.* Esther had to undergo a prescribed regimen of *beautifying,* lasting a year, before she was considered ready for admission to the king. Then she faced the prospect of every maiden in the harem to spend only one night with the king unless he "delighted in her and she was summoned by name" (12-14). As it turned out, Esther won a permanent place in the palace because "the king loved Esther more than all the women . . . and made her queen instead of Vashti." (15-18)

2:14 *Second harem.* Lit. "the second house of the women," where those unfortunate women were confined for the rest of their lives who had the privilege of indulging the king's desires for one night. In the normal course of events Esther would have joined them.

2:16 *Seventh year.* Esther became queen 4 years after Vashti's rejection (1:3) and 1 year after Xerxes' defeat at Salamis (480 B.C.), where his expedition against Greece foundered. The month "Tibeth" corresponds to January/February on our calendar.

2:19-23 MORDECAI; KING'S ASSASSINATION FOILED

2:19 *Mordecai.* He not only remains behind the scene of action as Esther's guardian but also has an independent role to play. In addition to the information about him already available to the reader (5-7, 10 f.), the writer reveals an incident in his life which explains his contribution to later developments. He saved the king's life by exposing a plot to assassinate him. (19-23; see 6:1 ff.)

Second time. It seems the search for virgins to be added to the harem did not end when Esther was chosen queen.

2:20 *Her kindred.* Esther's well-kept secret worked also to Mordecai's advantage (10 note). If it had been common knowledge that he was the queen's cousin, the king's enemies would have been doubly careful to keep their mouths shut in his presence. "The king's gate" (19) was the place where exchange of gossip and rumor filled the air.

3:1-6 Villain: Haman, Enemy of Jews

3:1 *Haman.* The last of the principal characters to be introduced is the villain. Haman, the grand vizier of Xerxes, was a formidable opponent. Anyone who incurred his displeasure would find it difficult to survive. He was also ruthless and cruel. "Filled with fury" over Mordecai's refusal to "bow down" before him, he "sought to destroy all the Jews." (1-6)

The introduction (1:1—3:6) supplied the reader with the necessary background for the high drama which he is about to witness. The lines of combat are drawn. Hero (2:19-23) and heroine (2:5-18) must match wits with a man bent on murdering an entire people (3:1-6). "On earth is not his equal" in power unless it be the ruler of the empire himself. (1:1—2:4)

Agagite. It is tempting to think that this epithet links Haman genealogically with Agag, king of the Amalekites, against whom Saul, "the son of Kish" (2:5; 1 Sm 9:1 f.), waged war (1 Sm 15). It is also possible that it is a geographical term. Reference to a Persian district called Agag has been found. Haman's name is Persian, as are the names of his father and 10 sons. (9:7-10)

3:2 *Bow down.* Because "he was a Jew" (4), Mordecai refused to accord Haman the honor he expected. It would appear to have been needlessly foolhardy and provocative for a member of an exiled people to offend the king's fully accredited representative unless the particular act of homage implied a violation of religious principles. Ordinarily a Jew did not need to withhold reverence from kings and rulers. (Gn 43:26; 2 Ch 24:17)

3:7—4:3 PLOT TO LIQUIDATE JEWS

3:7-11 Haman's Wicked Proposal Sanctioned

3:7 *Twelfth year.* The main action of the book is precipitated by Haman's plot to kill all Jews

(3:7-15). It was 5 years after Esther became queen (2:16) that he initiated his vicious program. The villain planned carefully. Before getting the king's approval, he cast lots to make sure what day would be auspicious for his venture. Then he proceeded to obtain the king's approval. To get it he had to tell a big lie. He represented Jews as detrimental to the state because they refused to be assimilated, being different from all other peoples. He suggested furthermore that his proposal would be financially profitable inasmuch as the property of the executed criminals was forfeit to the crown (7-11). Duped by his vizier, the king sent out official notices ordering that the Jews "in every province" be executed on the day agreed upon. (12-15)

Pur. This word reproduces the sound of a common noun, found in Assyrian records. It designates the kind of pebble used in throwing dice. In its plural form, Purim, it was to become the name of the festival which commemorates the fact that divine providence overruled this casting of lots. (9:26)

Adar. Beginning with Nisan, the first month, and ending with Adar, the last on the calendar, they took up "month after month," casting lots on each in turn in order to determine a propitious date. They repeated the process to find the right day of the month, proceeding *day after day.*

3:8 *Different.* Living among *every other people,* the Jews had to resist amalgamation with them and absorption into a mixture of races if they were to observe the religious, social, and dietary regulations which were known to them from "the law of Moses" (Ez 7:6, 10). However, their distinctiveness did not demand that they refuse to *keep the king's laws,* as Haman claimed. (Jer 29:7)

3:9 *Ten thousand.* More than half the amount which annually accrued to the imperial treasury. Haman may have exaggerated the value of the property to be confiscated in order to make the suggested action appeal to the king's greed.

3:10 *Signet ring.* See 8:2 note; also Gn 38:18 note; 41:42.

3:11 *Given to you.* Haman knew that the king did not mean to say that his grand vizier was to keep the money for himself.

3:12-15 Extermination Ordered by King

3:12 *First month.* Eleven months were to elapse before the execution of the decree (13). No doubt it was the date determined by lot. The delay would make sure also that the order reached every corner of the empire. No Jew was to escape.

Satraps. For the administration of the Persian empire see Ez 4:11 note.

4:1-3 Distress of Jews

4:3 *Mourning.* Mordecai and his countrymen expressed consternation over their impending doom by wailing and other customary rites of mourning (Gn 37:34). Fasting usually was associated with prayer; lying in sackcloth and ashes, with repentance. (4:16; Ez 8:23; Neh 1:4; Is 58:5; Jon 3:5 f.)

4:4—8:17 COUNTERPLOT TO SAVE JEWS

4:4-17 Esther's Cooperation Enlisted

4:4 *Told her.* Drastic action was required if Haman's wicked designs (3:7-15) were to be foiled. Mordecai promptly set in motion a counterplot by enlisting Esther's cooperation (4:4—8:17). Reluctant at first, she agreed to risk her life "to go [unbidden] to the king to make supplication to him and entreat him for her people" (4-17). Her charm gained her an unusual audience with the king. However, she did not present her request to him at once. Only after he was her guest at two banquets did she find the opportune moment to make her appeal. The result was that the tables were turned on the villain and the decree to kill the Jews was neutralized by another edict which permitted the Jews to defend themselves. (Chs. 5—8)

4:5 *Called for.* Kept secluded in her quarters, Esther had to rely on the eunuch, *appointed to attend her,* to establish communication with her cousin (2:11). Mordecai's refusal to put on the garment she sent him and his insistence on wearing the sackcloth of mourning "in the open square of the city" alerted her to the fact that the cause of his grief was not a personal bereavement but a calamity of national proportions, for lamentation for one's private distress was not made in public.

4:8 *Her people.* Circumstances now demanded that Esther make "known her people or kindred" (2:10). Had she identified herself with the condemned race earlier, access to the king could have been jeopardized if not ruled out entirely.

4:11 *One law.* The penalty for entering *the inner court without being called* applied even to the queen. She did not seek an audience through the proper channels apparently because she feared a rebuff. For *thirty days* the king had not been disposed to see her, either because, for some reason, she was in disfavor with his capricious highness or because she was the victim of court intrigue. She had no other choice but to take the calculated risk of an unauthorized appearance before the king.

4:14 *Another quarter.* Literally "another place." Mordecai believed that *deliverance will rise for the Jews* whether through Esther's intervention or in some other way. In the final analysis, however, more than human effort was necessary if the forces of evil were to be overcome. Help would come from "the place." This word came to be a designation for God, as "heaven" was used to denote Him who dwells there (Mt 5:34; Lk 15:18, 21; cf. "the kingdom of heaven" interchange with "the kingdom of God" in Mt 3:2; 6:33; etc.). God's presence made "the place" where Moses stood "holy ground." (Ex 3:5; Jos 5:15)

To the kingdom. Esther was to realize that her

position as queen carried with it responsibilities commensurate with its distinction. Her willingness to live up to them at the risk of losing both honor and life has encouraged people in key positions to put their resources and influence in the service of a righteous cause, come what may. (Neh 2:5 note)

4:16 *A fast.* Cf. 3 note. As there is only an indirect reference to God in 14, so there is no explicit mention of an appeal to Him for help. See Introduction, "Content."

I perish. The heroic words with which Esther declared her determination to take the offensive in a fight to the death against an entrenched power of evil have found an echo in the hearts of all who had the courage to take what appeared to be suicidal action.

5:1—8:17 Esther's Successful Intervention

5:1—7:1 FIRST DAY OF BANQUET

1) 5:1-8 King and Haman Invited

5:1 *King's hall.* Remains of such an audience chamber have been uncovered by archaeologists. The only hope of counteracting Haman's plot was to get through to the king. Fully aware that the prospects of saving her countrymen and her own life were at stake, she entered the royal court in defiance of a rigid protocol. However, instead of incurring the king's displeasure, she "found favor in his sight." Nevertheless she did not divulge the purpose of her intrusion at once even though he promised to give her "to the half" of his kingdom if she had a special request to make. Biding her time, she chose to make certain that she was firmly established in his good graces. She made sure also that the villain would be present when the time came to expose him. Therefore she invited the king and Haman to a banquet (1-7). The latter was jubilant to be the only other quest at such an exclusive function. Confident that he could count on the queen's support in his revenge on his enemy, he had gallows erected on which to execute Mordecai. (9-14)

5:3 *Request.* The king rightly surmised that Esther dared to act "against the law" (4:16) because she needed his help in a matter of grave concern to her. Anticipating a costly request, he used the stereotyped formula *even to the half of my kingdom* to indicate that he was willing to grant even such a favor. For a similar pompous promise see Mk 6:22. When therefore Esther asked for nothing more than his and Haman's presence at a banquet (4), he pressed her for her real "petition" by repeating his earlier question (6). Esther agreed to "do as the king" wished only after he was her guest at "the dinner" for him and Haman. (8; 7:2)

2) 5:9-14 Haman Confident of Royal Favor

5:9 *King's gate.* At the news that Esther had consented to intervene with the king, Mordecai removed his sackcloth (4:1). Dressing as decorum demanded (4:2), he returned to the vicinity of the palace (2:19), where he was more apt to keep himself informed about developments.

5:10 *Restrained.* Haman did not dare to proceed without royal authorization. However, the invitation to dine with the king and queen made him so sure that he could obtain orders for Mordecai's immediate execution that "he had the gallows made" in advance.

5:13 *No good.* Indignation over Mordecai's insult rankled so painfully in Haman's vain heart that it spoiled his enjoyment of the many good things which had come his way.

5:14 *Gallows.* Literally "a tree" and so translated in Gn 40:19; Dt 21:22 f.; see also Acts 5:30; Gl 3:13; 1 Ptr 2:24. In his rage Haman wanted Mordecai hanged so high—over 80 feet—that all people would take warning not to insult the grand vizier.

3) 6:1-14 Events During Night Before Banquet

a. 6:1-11 Mordecai's Belated Reward

6:1 *Not asleep.* Esther acted more wisely than she could know when she decided to take her time in bringing her concern to the king's attention. Her delaying action permitted a chain of circumstances to develop into a situation which made the king favorably disposed to her countryman "Mordecai the Jew" (10) and paved the way for the failure of Haman's plot against him and all the Jews. It so happened that during the night before the banquet the sleepless king was reminded of his failure to reward Mordecai for exposing a coup d'etat against his royal person. The villain too could not sleep. He came to the court in order to get Mordecai's death warrant at the earliest possible moment. However, when he did get summoned before the king, he got orders to bestow on Mordecai the honor and public acclaim to which he thought he was entitled (1-11). It suddenly became evident to him that in his controversy with Mordecai the king had taken sides against him. "His wise men and his wife" confirmed his fears that his doom was only a matter of time (12 f.). When the king's eunuchs arrived to escort him "to the banquet that Esther had prepared" (14; 7:1), he was anything but "joyful and glad of heart." (5:9)

6:2 *Had told.* For the plot against the king's life see 2:21-23.

6:4 *Just entered.* Anyone not reckoning with divine providence would have to account for the sequence of events in this chapter as the result of very lucky coincidences. To all appearances it was entirely "by chance" (Lk 10:31) that: (1) the king spent a sleepless night; (2) he chose to relieve his boredom by having the royal annals read to him; (3) he hit upon the account of Mordecai's unrewarded deed of loyalty; (4) Haman came to the court at the moment the king was about to pay his debt to Mordecai; (5) all this happened in the night before the banquet.

6:8 *Royal crown.* Ornamental turbans, resembling crowns, were placed on the heads of the king's horses.

6:9 *Proclaiming.* Joseph was honored by similar acclaim. (Gn 41:42 ff.)

6:10 *The Jew.* The explicit mention of Mordecai's race at this point seems to imply (1) that Haman's dispute with him was quite generally known; (2) that his refusal to bow down before the grand vizier was dictated by a principle peculiar to a Jew.

b. 6:12—7:1 Haman's Premonition of Doom

6:12 *Head covered.* A gesture of mourning. (2 Sm 15:30; Jer 14:3 f.)

6:13 *Wise men.* "His friends" were wise only by hindsight. Actually they gave him very foolish advice. (5:10, 14)

7:2—8:2 SECOND DAY OF BANQUET; TABLES TURNED

1) 7:2-10 Haman Sentenced to Die

7:2 *Second day.* Esther let the first day of the banquet (7:1) pass without complying with the king's request to tell him what she intended to ask of him that was so urgent that she risked an unannounced audience with him (5:3). When the king *again* pressed her for an answer on the second day of the banquet, she decided she had nothing to gain if she postponed the moment of decision any longer. As straightforward as necessary and as diplomatically as possible she presented her case. The result was a dramatic and drastic reversal of fortunes: (1) not Mordecai but Haman was hanged on the gallows (2-10); (2) Haman's position of grand vizier was entrusted to his intended victim. (8:1-2)

7:3 *My people.* The die was cast. Esther identified herself with a people under sentence of death by royal decree. As she quoted the edict almost verbatim (4; 3:13), the king could not fail to conclude that she was a Jewess.

7:4 *Loss to the king.* Esther seems to make two points. On the one hand, she makes clear how desperate the situation was. If her and her people's *affliction* were not a matter of life and death, she would not have brought it to the king's attention. On the other hand, she intimates that the king would sustain a great loss indeed if he were to let the decree be executed.

7:6 *Haman.* Esther brought the interview to a climax. She pointed her finger at Haman. He was the man who "would presume to" murder "my people." From this accusation the king could gather that she was speaking of Haman's plot to kill all Jews and that she, a Jewess, would share their lot.

7:7 *Beg his life.* When the king stormed out of the room in a fit of anger, Haman had reason to expect the worst. As a last resort the exposed villain pleaded with the Jewess to intercede for him. However, this humiliating appeal only helped to seal his fate. The enraged king accused the hapless grand vizier of attempted rape because he found him at Esther's feet when he returned (2 K 4:27; Mt 28:9). During the king's absence from the room she remained on the "couch" on which guests at a banquet were accustomed to recline. The man who brought unjust charges against the Jews (8) was himself falsely accused by the king.

7:8 *They covered.* The attendants at the court used this gesture to indicate that in their opinion Haman's crime was so abhorrent that he should be given no consideration or mercy. The ancient Greeks and Romans covered the face of a criminal about to be executed. In the OT shame or dishonor is said to cover one's face (Ps 69:7; Jer 51:51). A person covered his face to express humiliation or grief. (2 Sm 19:4; 15:30)

7:10 *Prepared for Mordecai.* He fell "into the hole which he . . . made." (Ps 7:15 f.; 9:15 f.; Pr 11:5 f.; 26:27)

2) 8:1-2 Mordecai Made Grand Vizier

8:2 Signet Ring. The king invested Mordecai with the full authority of a grand vizier. He was soon to make use of the right to affix the royal seal, engraved on the king's ring, to an official document. (3:10 note; 8:8)

8:3-14 DECREE TO KILL JEWS NEUTRALIZED

1) 8:3-8 Request to Rescind Decree Denied

8:3 *Evil design.* The villain would no longer harm the Jews. However, the decree "to destroy the Jews," masterminded by him, was still in effect. Even the king's hands were tied. He could not "revoke the letters devised by Haman," as he reminded Esther when she pleaded with him to countermand the order. The best he could do was to let a proclamation go out in his name which would neutralize the effects of the original edict without canceling it (3-8). The new grand vizier acted at once. He issued a decree supplementing the earlier one. The new directive authorized the condemned people to "defend their lives." If they were "to slay, and to annihilate any armed force . . . that might attack them" and "plunder their goods," they would not be liable to the charge of murder and theft. (9-14)

8:4 *Scepter.* Apparently Esther "spoke again to the king" (3) "without being called" by him (4:11). Signaling with his scepter as before (5:2), he granted her another audience, even though she violated the rules of the court.

8:6 *My people.* Esther no longer had to mention herself (7:3). She could rely on the king's protection, who now knew that his queen was a Jewess.

2) 8:9-14 Decree with Opposite Effect Issued

8:9 *Third month.* The new decree went out more than 2 months after Haman's was published. (3:12)

8:11 *Plunder.* When the Israelites left the Egyptian house of bondage, God allowed them to "despoil the Egyptians" (Ex 3:22; 11:2 f.). The liberation from the Babylonian captivity too is described in terms of the Exodus in such passages as Is 48:20 f.; 49:8-10; 50:2 f.; etc.

8:15-17 JOY OVER PROSPECT OF DELIVERANCE

8:15 *Rejoiced.* Fear for their lives gave way to joy among the Jews "wherever the king's command and his edict came" (15-17). In Susa the populace greeted the new grand vizier with loud acclaim as he emerged from the palace dressed in robes of blue and white, the national colors of Persia, and decked out with royal insignia.

8:17 *Declared themselves.* Mordecai's prestige made identification with Jews so attractive for "many from the peoples" that they "joined them" (9:27) as proselytes.

9:1-19 COUNTERMEASURES CARRIED OUT

9:1-15 Enemies Slain

9:1-10 IN ALL PROVINCES

9:1 *Changed.* As the tables were turned on Haman (7:10), so the new edict, issued by Mordecai, effected a reversal in the fate of the Jews. Allowed "to avenge themselves upon their enemies" (8:13), they got *the mastery over their foes,* laying "hands on such as sought their hurt." In "all the provinces" they turned on those "who hated them." In Susa alone they "slew and destroyed five hundred men" (1-10). At Esther's request, the king granted the Jews in the capital a second day on which they had a free hand to destroy their enemies (11-15). On the third the Jews gathered in Susa for feasting and gladness. (16-19)

9:3 *Fear of Mordecai.* All Persian government appointees realized they would have to reckon with the grand vizier if they harmed his countrymen. This "fear of the Jews" (8:17; 9:2) overcame not only the officials but spread to all people throughout the empire.

9:5 *Smote.* According to 8:11 the Jews were allowed to "defend their lives" against those "that might attack them." It appears that they went beyond protecting themsleves against attacks. The account simply records the fact of the *slaughtering* without condemning or approving it from a moral standpoint.

9:11-15 IN THE CAPITAL ON TWO DAYS

9:12 *The capital.* If the Hebrew word, used here and in 6, has the more restricted sense of citadel or fortress (Neh 7:2), Esther requested permission to extend the purge of their enemies to the entire city of Susa.

9:15 *Plunder.* This feature of the operation is mentioned twice (10) as if to make the point that the Jews were not guilty of Saul's disobedience to God's command when he waged war against the Amalekites (1 Sm 15:3, 19; see note on Haman "the Agagite," 3:1). However, their refusal to take spoils may be emphasized because it was in contrast to the action of the Israelites at the time of the Exodus. (Cf. 8:11 note)

9:16-19 Rejoicing on Third Day

9:16 *Seventy-five thousand.* No doubt the king was not aware that so many of his subjects would be affected by Mordecai's decree. On his ill-fated campaign in Greece he sacrificed the lives of many more thousands. Nevertheless a figure of 7,500 would appear to be more realistic. All the figures for the slain victims, also in 6 and 15, may have acquired an extra zero in the course of the transmission of the text. See Numbers, Introduction, "The Numbers. . . ."

9:19 *Fourteenth day.* This verse explains a difference in the custom of observing the deliverance from Haman's plot. *The Jews of the villages* begin *feasting and holiday-making* one day earlier than their brethren who live in cities like Susa where the original festivities were preceded by two days of bloodshed rather than only one.

9:20-32 DELIVERANCE COMMEMORATED: PURIM FEAST

9:20-22 Festival Instituted by Mordecai

9:20 *Sent letters.* Mordecai called on *all the Jews* to make the days on which they "got relief from their enemies" occasions for annual celebrations (20-22). Queen Esther lent her prestige to her cousin's ordinance (29-32). The name which the newly ordained festival acquired was a reminder how close the "wicked plot" came to being successful. All that remained for "the enemy of all Jews" and his cohorts to do was to await the day set for the execution. They felt they could not fail because they selected the date by casting what they called "Purim," i.e., lots (cf. 3-7 note). At the annual "commemoration of these days" the Jews were to rejoice that they were not helpless victims of a blind fate (23-28). The NT may refer to this festival in Jn 5:1

9:23-28 Name Explained; Future Observance Ordered

9:24 *Plotted.* The events which were the basis for Purim are briefly summarized in 24 f.

9:28 *Commemoration.* Present-day observance of the festival includes the reading of the Book of Esther.

9:29-32 Celebration Promoted by Esther

9:29 *Second letter.* Esther added her endorsement to the kind of letter sent out by Mordecai in his own name.

10:1-3 EPILOG: PEACE UNDER MORDECAI'S ADMINISTRATION

10:3 *Next in rank.* The book concludes with a brief sequel to the story. The Jews did not have to fear a repetition of Haman's threat to their lives for some time. They were safe everywhere at least as long as Mordecai was the highest official of a king whose "power and might" stretched across "the land" from the Indus River (1:1) to "the coastlands of the [Mediterranean] Sea." The record of Mordecai's administration, "written in the Book of the Chronicles of the kings of Media and Persia," has not been discovered. The "chronicles" referred to in 6:1 likewise remain buried in the ruins of the Persian empire.

JOB

INTRODUCTION

Content

In our English Bibles the Book of Job follows Esther, the last of the historical books. Yet a wide gulf of contrasts lies between them. It is difficult to find two Biblical books which are so different from each other.

In Esther it is quite obvious that "in everything God works for good with those who love Him" (Ro 8:28). In Job sinister forces of evil inflict endless misery on "a blameless and upright man, who fears God." (1:8)

In Esther divine providence comes to the rescue of people without explicit reference to their spiritual life. The question of Job's relationship to God constitutes the central theme of the book.

Esther records the deliverance of the Jewish nation. Job is universal in scope. It demonstrates the need of salvation of all mankind, represented by "a man in the land of Uz" (1:1) beyond the confines of the commonwealth of Israel. The hero's inability to respond to his Creator with unreserved devotion is the fatal predicament of all sons of Adam. The best of them cannot achieve a relationship with his Maker that is unmarred by the sin of self-love.

In Esther deliverance is a matter of recorded history, commemorated by an annual festival. In Job the healing of mankind's separation from God still rests on promise. That Servant, in whom God was well pleased, was still to come.

The two books are equally divergent in style and manner of presentation. Esther is straightforward narrative. Job, four times as long, is almost entirely poetic in form.

The Book of Job develops its theme on a grand scale. The scene alternates between heaven and earth. The conflict is between the Creator of heaven and earth and "the ruler of this world," "the prince of the power of the air" (Jn 14:30; Eph 2:2). God's voice is heard coming "out of the whirlwind" (38:1). The destiny of man, the crowning glory of God's handiwork, is at stake.

Satan precipitates the conflict. He declares that man no longer fulfills the purpose for which the Creator made him. Even such a man as Job, he contends, does not "fear God for nought" (1:9). He does not love God for His own sake. He is loyal to God because serving Him pays off. Making Job a test case, the old evil Foe sets out to prove that God must give up His claim to His creature. If Job yields to selfish impulses, he is in reality obedient to Satan's unholy promptings and repudiates his allegiance to God.

At first Job passes the test. Loss of everything—wealth, children, health—is not able to separate him from the love of God. He rejects his wife's suggestion to "curse God, and die." (2:9)

But Satan does not give up. His frontal attacks repulsed, he resorts to more subtle maneuvers. Disguising himself as "an angel of light" (2 Co 11:14), he approaches Job through his pious friends, turning their good intentions to help him into a diabolical trick. They try to make Job understand why he is suffering. The reasons they advance have the form of truth. As Satan himself did in his temptation of Jesus, they too could have claimed: "It is written" (Lk 4:9-10). Actually what they say is only half the truth. They have some pieces of a jigsaw puzzle which indeed have a place in the pattern but they put them where they do not fit and leave distorting gaps in the overall picture. The result is a caricature of God and His dealings with mankind in general and with Job specifically.

This probing into the why of Job's

suffering by his friends and the insinuating answers they give achieve what the blows of adversity themselves failed to do. The thinly veiled accusation that he is suffering much because he sinned much elicits a defense from him which lets Satan make his point: Job does not serve God "for nought." From the hidden recesses of the crushed sufferer's heart there emerge thoughts which did not come to the surface before. As he puts them into words, they reveal that he cannot prevent selfish motives from desecrating his love of God. Fight against it as he will, he does succumb to the big lie that his piety deserves a reward. When God withholds it, he calls Him to account, challenging Him to vindicate His justice.

Job's discussion with his friends constitutes the bulk of the book (chs. 3—37). Only such as have not sat where Job sat will find it a harangue wearying by its length, tiresome because of its needless repetitions, artificial in its emotional appeal. Every perplexed child of God knows how true to life this sheer endless battle of words is. Their fury is the echo of conflicting emotions that surge back and forth in his own heart. Dazed by sudden and savage blows of affliction, numb with pain, blinded by tears, he wants to hold on to his faith that God is good. But he finds himself in the grip of contrary thoughts, arising from black depths of his heart where the prince of darkness still agitates. The ensuing struggle is literally heart-rending. He is torn between the determination to let God have His way and the diabolical suspicion that God is either not good or not all-powerful or neither. As in the debate between Job and his friends, there is skirmish after skirmish in the long night watches of doubt and despair. Unholy thoughts mount not only a persistent attack; they seek entrance also in an endless variety of formulations and approaches. At times faith asserts itself (19:25). But its voice fades out in the din of battle. Job's cries of anguish are not the contrived sounds of stage play. They arise from every tortured soul when all that gave meaning to life threatens to sink into an ocean of meaninglessness.

The question of suffering indeed bulks large in the Book of Job. However, it is not the writer's purpose to present a treatise on this topic, much less to solve the mysteries of pain in human life. Job receives no answers to his persistent whys. His friends advance reasons for the misery inflicted on him which are unacceptable to him and only intensify his grief. Neither do God's thunderous words (chs. 38—41) give a rational explanation of Job's plight. In fact he is told not to expect to understand God's ways with man. It ill becomes Job to subject the Creator and Preserver of the universe to a trial in the court of human reason. (40:2)

Left unexplained, Job's suffering nevertheless makes a major contribution to the primary objective of the book. It is the means of uncovering the tragic truth that even Job is no exception to the verdict: "The children of men . . . are all alike corrupt, there is none that does good, no not one" (Ps 14:2-3). In the crucible of pain, fired white-hot by Satan's fury, the impurity of Job's love comes to the surface. His piety turns out to be disguised self-love. And because it is not possible to serve God and self (Mt 6:24), all his "righteous deeds are like a polluted garment" (Is 64:6), an attempted but futile camouflage of his real self.

Tested and found wanting, condemned out of his own mouth, Job throws himself on the mercy of God. His only hope of escaping Satan's claim on him is to "repent in dust and ashes" and to plead for pardon (42:6). And God does forgive and restore His prodigal servant, not imputing to him his unholy thoughts and rebellious words and remembering only his saying "what is right." (42:7 ff.)

So ends the Book of Job. However, whatever its particular characteristics, it is like all other OT books in this respect that it is not God's last word to His lost creatures. It is open-ended to the future. As in Adam all men are doomed to separation from God in outer darkness (Ro 5:12; 1 Co 15:21-22), so Job furnishes the evidence that no son of Adam can reestablish communion with his Creator. Someone must come to do it for him. In Job, Satan won a battle; in Jesus Christ he lost the war. For the sake of Him, "smitten by God, and afflicted" (Is 53:4), yet "obedient unto death . . . on a cross" (Ph 2:8), "the Lord accepted

Job's prayer" (42:9), forgave his sins and let him bask in the sunshine of His grace.

Job needed a Savior. In the fullness of time God sent His son to atone for the sins not only of "a man in the land of Uz" but to be "the expiation . . . for the sins of the whole world." (1 Jn 1:7; 2:2)

Corollaries

The 42 chapters of Job explode the big delusion that fallen man has enough good in him to gain God's approval. Corollaries growing from the root of this humbling truth are equally distasteful to human pride.

(1) From the discussion between Job and his three friends (chs. 4—28) it becomes clear that God is far beyond the reach of man's mind. In their attempt to explain why Job is suffering, they can do no better than to reduce the eternal "I am" (Ex 3:14 note) to an impersonal principle of justice which operates by a rule of thumb of their own making. It is true that God rewards piety and punishes wickedness, for He said He would. But when they insist that He does so on their terms and to their satisfaction, they make of the Ruler of the universe no more than a puppet who goes into action when they pull the strings.

Elihu, Job's fourth visitor (chs. 32—37), does not do much better. God, he says quite correctly, knows what He is doing; He has a purpose in chastising a man. But he too subjects divine providence to the law of cause and effect. "For according to the work of a man He will requite him" (34:11). Job's suffering is so severe because the wrongdoing of which he is to be purged is no less grievous. The correction fits the crime. If Job confesses and repents of his sin, there will be a corresponding reaction in God. He will remove the thorn in his flesh. (2 Co 12:7)

(2) God, above the reach of human thinking, reveals Himself to man. But what He manifests of Himself does not make Him more accessible to man's reason or sense perceptions. Job hears God speaking out of the whirlwind. What he hears is not an answer to his question but a call to entrust himself unquestioningly to the Creator and Preserver of the universe (chs. 38—41). Faith in His wisdom and power is not merely dull resignation to an inescapable fate, imposed arbitrarily on a helpless victim. Forgiven and restored, Job is assured that God, in absolute control of his destiny, is as infinitely kind and gracious as He is mighty and wise.

Job and Scripture

In the Book of Ezekiel, Job is given a place of honor beside Noah and Daniel as a righteous man. (Eze 14:14)

James reminds his readers of Job's "steadfastness" (Ja 5:11). A better example of a tenacious faith would have been hard to find. Under the blows of adversity, the like of which few if any experience, he did not let go of God. He relaxed his hold at times. He strayed into the path of doubt. He stumbled into the mire of defiance and rebellion. But in the end neither torment of body and soul nor taunt of wife or friend could separate him from the love of God.

Job's example is not only a challenge to go and do likewise. When doubts and satanic thoughts arise in his troubled heart, let every child of God think of Job and be comforted. For he too weakened under the strain. But "the Lord, compassionate and merciful," did not reject His bungling servant. With Him there is "plenteous redemption." (Ps 130:7)

From the story of Job comes furthermore the reassuring reminder that God "will not let you be tempted beyond your strength." Satan cannot "harass" Job beyond endurance. In His own way and at His own time, God provides "the way of escape." (1 Co 10:13; 2 Co 12:7-10)

The NT believer has advantages over Job. The Gospel of fulfillment proclaims that man's need, demonstrated in the Book of Job, has been met in the perfect obedience and innocent suffering of Jesus Christ. However, he cannot do without a Job-like faith. He too is asked to believe that "in everything God works for good with" him, no matter how bad things look. His trials may be even more baffling than Job's. He may be tempted to ask whether a God who claims to love him so much that He gave His Son to die for him should not have exempted him from suffering.

Nor is the present-day believer more immune to the temptation to serve God for selfish reasons even though he has received fuller revelation regarding life eternal.

Instead of thinking of heaven as a gift of grace, he remains susceptible to the satanic suggestion that God is under obligation to reward his virtues in the world to come. Furthermore, the promise of reigning with Christ may fail to satisfy him when he looks for relief from distress in the here and now.

Authorship

By common consent the Book of Job ranks as one of the world's greatest literary masterpieces. However, it remains anonymous. No attempt to identify the unnamed author has achieved general acceptance. Known authors of other Biblical writings such as Moses and Jeremiah have come to mind. An unknown wise man is suggested. But the time when he supposedly lived ranges from the era of Solomon deep into the intertestamental period.

Attempts to find clues to an author in the setting of the recorded events have led likewise to widely differing theories. To some scholars the incidental references to certain circumstances suggest the age of the patriarchs. Others believe that internal evidence points to a time as much as a millennium later. It is proposed, e.g., that the action took place in Arabia (modern Saudi Arabia) shortly before the end of the Babylonian captivity. Support for this view is found in recently discovered Babylonian records as well as in the strong influence of the Arabic dialect on the Hebrew of the book.

The book itself furnishes an account of events in the life of Job which constitute its message. The setting is briefly set forth in a prose introduction (chs. 1—2) and epilog (42:7-17). The intervening chapters (3—41) reproduce, in poetic form, a long discussion of Job's fate precipitated by four of his associates and ended by the Lord Himself.

OUTLINE

I. 1:1—2:10 Job's Love of God Tested
- A. 1:1-22 Steadfast in Loss of Possessions and Children
- B. 2:1-10 Steadfast in Loss of Health

II. 2:11—37:24 Job's Self-love Exposed
- A. 2:11—26:14 In Discussion with Three Friends
- B. 27:1—31:40 Self-love Manifest in Discourses
- C. 32:1—37:24 Self-love Exposed by Elihu

III. 38:1—42:6 Job's Lack of Trust Reproved by God
- A. 38:1—40:5 First Speech: Trust the Creator's Transcendent Wisdom!
- B. 40:6—42:6 Second Speech: Trust the Creator's Limitless Power!

IV. 42:7-17 Job's Restoration
- A. 42:7-9 Reinstated as Servant
- B. 42:10-17 Blessed in Latter Days

1:1—2:10 JOB'S LOVE OF GOD TESTED

1:1-22 Steadfast in Loss of Possessions and Children

1:1 *A man.* A member of the human race who was to demonstrate that every son of Adam without exception had to look beyond himself for a Savior from Satan and from his own demonic self. If anyone could be expected to pass the test of unalloyed love of God, it would be *a man* considered *blameless and upright, one who feared God.* Job was no godless reprobate. His devotion to God was not hollow pretense. When Satan challenged the sincerity of his piety, neither the loss of wealth or of his children (ch. 1) nor the torture of physical pain (ch. 2) could induce him to "sin with his lips" or to "charge God with wrong" (1:22; 2:10). Yet before Satan is through with Job, it will be evident that even the best of men fails to love God "for nought," i.e., solely for His own sake and expecting nothing in return. (1:9)

Uz. Job lived among "the people of the east" beyond the borders of the Promised Land (3; Ju 6:3; Is 11:14; Eze 25:4). However, a more exact location of his homeland remains a matter of dispute. Suggested are (1) a territory known as the Hauran, northeast of Canaan; (2) an area under Edomite control, south and east of the Dead Sea; (3) a settlement in that part of Arabia known today as Saudi Arabia. Job's friends are identified by place-names linked with Edom. (2:11 note; Jer 25:20; Lm 4:21)

Job. Derived from a Hebrew root, his name means "one exposed to hostility"; an Arabic etymology suggests the meaning "one who returns or repents." Job emerges from mankind's past as an unidentified figure. No information is available on his ancestry, his racial or national affiliation, the time when he flourished in terms of contemporary history. His story is more than the biography of an individual. It sets forth the universal plight of mankind.

1:4 *His day.* Job's children were the more precious to him because they were on such good terms with one another. The seven sons could afford to entertain one another and the three sisters every day of the week, each brother taking his turn on *his appointed day.* However, the expression *his day* may refer to the birthday of the sons. The recorded number of children is not only a statistical note. The total 10, the sum of seven and three, suggests a family circle complete in all respects.

1:5 *Burnt offerings.* In patriarchal times the head of the family performed priestly functions (Gn 12:7; 35:1). The Jews in the Babylonian captivity refrained from animal sacrifices. It is therefore suggested that Job lived before the promulgation of the Mosaic law which made the offering of sacrifices the exclusive privilege of the sons of Aaron. (But see Ju 6:24)

1:6 *Before the Lord.* The reader is to know from the very outset that not blind fate but divine providence is responsible for Job's testing (6-12). God, who "knows the secrets of the heart," is about to teach Job a vitally important lesson (Ps 44:21; 139:1 f.; Jer 17:10). The loss of "all that he has" (10) will give him pause to examine the basis of his relationship to his Creator. He will be confronted with the question whether he "fears God and turns away from evil" (8) for no other reason than to please and honor Him or whether his piety is polluted at its roots by hidden motives of self-love. God's educational method, however severe, is necessary to expose man's delusion that he has any claim to God's favor. For glimpses of action in "the presence of the Lord" (12) granted to others see 1 K 21:19 ff.; Is 6; Eze 1:1; Rev 4:1.

Satan. Transliteration of a Hebrew word used (1) to denote various human antagonists or adversaries (1 Sm 29:4; 2 Sm 19:22; 1 K 5:4; 11:14; Ps 109:6); (2) to designate the archenemy of man who did not keep his own position among the celestial hosts (Jude 6), here and elsewhere called "sons of God" (38:7; Gn 6:2 note). By prefixing the definite article to the Hebrew noun, the OT stigmatizes him as "*THE* enemy" of man (so 14 times in Jb and in Zch 3:1-2, but not in 1 Ch 21:1). In the heavenly court he plays the role of prosecuting attorney. But he is not intent on vindicating God's honor. He is out to "destroy" Job (2:3), claim him as his subject, and demand that he share his fate in outer darkness. In his cruel attacks on his human victim, he has at his disposal the forces of nature (16, 19). Relentless in pursuit of his quarry, he appears nowhere else as diabolically bold and cunning except when he tempted Jesus.

1:9 *For nought.* Expecting nothing in return.

1:10 *A hedge.* Protection against threats to his well-being.

1:11 *Curse.* The Hebrew verb, normally meaning to bless, is used to avoid even expressing the abhorrent idea that man should invoke a curse on God (so again in 5; 2:9; 1 K 21:10, 13). If Job renounces God in such blasphemous terms, Satan is sure of his prey.

1:13 *A day.* In four almost simultaneous blows Satan stripped Job of his herds, flocks, and herdsmen, his material wealth, his servants, and his children. (13-19)

1:15 *Sabeans.* A nomadic tribe of the Arabian desert.

1:16 *Fire of God.* See 2 K 1:12.

1:17 *Chaldeans.* At an early date they occupied territory stretching eastward from southern Babylonia into the desert (Gn 11:31 note). Later they became masters of Babylonia and heirs of the Assyrian empire. Nebuchadnezzar was a Chaldean.

1:20 *Rent his robe.* Following customary mourning practices, Job tore his outer mantle and shaved his head. (2 Sm 15:32; Eze 9:3; Jer 7:29; Mi 1:16)

1:21 *Blessed.* Other children of God have repeated the words of this verse, humbly acknowledging God as the Giver of all that accrued to them in this life (cf. 1 Ti 6:7; Ec 5:15). However, only such as have shared Job's heartaches know the inner turmoil to be overcome before they could say with quivering lips: "Blessed be . . . the Lord."

1:22 *Wrong.* This word occurs again only in Jer 23:13, where it is rendered "unsavory thing." Job said nothing to indicate that God had become offensive to him; the sweet odor of divine goodness had not taken on a vile odor.

2:1-10 Steadfast in Loss of Health

2:1 *Again.* In a second audience with God Satan asked permission to intensify the severity of the test. If Job loved God "for nought" (1:9), loss of his most precious possession, his health, should not affect his attitude toward God (1-6). Reduced by disease to a loathsome heap of flesh and bone (7-8), Job still uttered no recrimination against God, even when his wife became Satan's spokesman, urging him to "curse God." (9-10)

2:4 *Skin for skin.* Satan used a proverbial saying to insinuate that Job was willing to pay the price of external losses if thereby he could ward off threats to his own person. Godliness, he said, still was a bargain if it assured man health and well-being.

2:7 *Loathsome sores.* In Hebrew a singular noun: "a grievous inflammation," translated "boils" or "boil" (Ex 9:9-11; Dt 28:27, 35; 2 K 20:7), associated with leprosy (Lv 13:18-20, 23). From Job's description of his disease many scholars conclude that it was elephantiasis. (7:5; 19:17, 20)

2:11—37:24 JOB'S SELF-LOVE EXPOSED

2:11—26:14 In Discussion with Three Friends

2:11-13 FRIENDS ARRIVE TO CONDOLE WITH JOB

2:11 *Friends.* Satan's frontal attack failed; "Job did not sin with his lips" (10). Undaunted, the tempter resorted to more insidious strategy. He drafted Job's three friends into his service. Sincere and well-meaning, they actually throw a volley of diabolical darts into his already crushed and lacerated heart. The half-truths with which they think to comfort him bear the brand of the father of lies. In their long discussions with Job (2:11—26:14) they cause him spiritual agony beyond his endurance. Tortured by their insinuation and even blunt accusation that the intensity of his suffering is the consequence of a proportionately grievous guilt, he reveals that in his godliness there lurks a latent profit motive. His love of God is disguised self-love. He does not serve God "for nought" but for what he expects in return. Satan succeeds in making his point.

His own place. Job's visitors likewise are "people of the east" (1:3) though seemingly not from his immediate vicinity. Their names and the descriptive adjective following each of them give some clues as to the location of their residence. Esau, the ancestor of the Edomites, had a son called *Eliphaz* (Gn 36:4), who in turn headed a clan called Teman (Gn 36:11; 1 Ch 1:36). In other passages Teman occurs as the name of a site occupied by Edomites, whose jurisdiction at some time extended eastward into Arabia (Jer 49:7; Eze 25:13; Am 1:12; Ob 9). The description of the other two friends yields even less positive identification. *Bildad* may have been a descendant of Shuah, Abraham's son by his concubine Keturah and presumably a founder of a desert tribe related to the nomadic Midianites (Gn 25:2; 1 Ch 1:32). The only Biblical reference to Naamah to be associated with *Zophar* is the name of the Ammonite mother of king Rehoboam (1 K 14:21). Her people had holdings east of the Jordan.

2:13 *Sat.* Job's three visitors were not fair-weather friends. At the news of his calamity they agreed that the least they could do was to express their sympathy in person, hoping thereby to afford him some comfort. No doubt their silent presence at his side for a whole week let Job feel how deeply his misery touched their hearts. A warm handshake still may be a more effective expression of shared grief than a torrent of words. It was when Job's friends tried to "condole with him" that they became "miserable comforters." (16:2)

3:1-26 FIRST SIGNS OF RESENTMENT IN JOB'S LAMENT

3:1 *Opened his mouth.* Job's friends must have arrived some time after Job was stricken. When he opened his mouth in their presence, they no longer heard words of quiet resignation such as he uttered when the storm first broke over his head (1:21; 2:10). Unrelieved agony of body and soul built up emotional pressure to the point of explosion. Bursting all bonds of restraint, he gave vent to his feelings in a sustained shriek of pain. In words so poignant as to pierce the hardest heart he (a) wishes he had not been born (1-10); (b) longs for relief in death (11-19); (c) recoils at the thought of continued existence in misery (20-26).

In his outcry there is no rebellion against God, no repudiation of His sovereignty, no threat of suicide. However, from the deep recesses of his soul the insidious question of why comes to the surface (11, 20) and with it the first inkling that he expected piety to be rewarded by good days. His friends pick up the subject. They insist that they know why he is suffering. He in turn contests their explanation that there is a direct correlation between the intensity of his pain and the enormity of his sin. However, in refuting their incriminations, he also makes statements which clearly reveal what he only intimates in his lament in this chapter, namely that he does not serve God "for nought."—The author reproduces Job's wail in highly poetic language.

3:3 *Perish.* Bewildered by undeserved persecution, the prophet Jeremiah likewise cursed the day of his birth. (Jer 20:14-18)

3:4 *Seek it.* In almost endless variations of figures of speech Job wishes that the day which ushered him into existence had never dawned. If only its place in the flow of time had been a blank! If only it were not one of the days with which God is concerned!

3:5 *Deep darkness.* KJV: "Shadow of death"; so translated by RSV in Ps 23:4. "Blackness of day" is an eclipse of the sun.

3:6 *Number of months.* His birthday and its anniversaries are to be deleted from the calendar.

3:7 *Joyful cry.* The "joy that a child is born into the world." (Jn 16:21)

3:8 *Curse it.* In heaping desecrations on the day which ultimately led to his misery, Job uses imagery borrowed from current superstitions. Sorcerers claimed the ability to put a spell on certain days, making them unlucky.

Leviathan. KJV: "their mourning." The same consonants, supplied with other vowels, spell the word for the monster mentioned again in 41:1; Is 27:1; Ps 74:14; 104:26; Eze 29:3-5. In the mythological thinking of the day this untamed monster was the enemy of cosmic order in the universe. If it had been roused to bring back a void and empty chaos (Gn 1:2), his birthday would not have occurred in the orderly sequence of time.

3:9 *Eyelids of the morning.* A poetic description of dawn.

3:11 *Die at birth.* As there would have been no trouble for Job, had he not been born, so he would "have been at rest" (13) if he had died at birth. (11-19)

3:12 *Receive me.* See Gn 30:3 note.

3:13 *Slept.* Death held no terrors for Job. He longed for the relief it brought. Because it ends the earthly activity and consciousness of all men, whether good or bad, small or great, slave or free, he would have been spared all subsequent pain if he could *have lain down and been quiet.*

3:14 *Ruins.* Death is no respecter of persons. It cuts down even kings who have resources to rebuild ruined places.

3:20 *Light.* To his unfulfilled wish never to have been born or at least to have died at birth, Job adds the question why God now prolongs his miserable life. (20-26)

3:23 *Hedged in.* For the first time Job makes God directly responsible for his plight. He no longer is "a hedge about him" to afford him protection (1:10 note), but uses its rows of thorns to prevent his escape from the prison of life (Rv 9:6). His question why God prolongs his misery has overtones of resentment. He believes he has a right to expect better treatment. This implicit challenge of God's justice opened an issue the three friends were eager to discuss. In sheer endless variations they contend that Job's suffering is the just reward for his unconfessed guilt. Their attempt to answer Job's why and his rebuttal of their explanation make up the bulk of the book. (chs. 4—26)

4:1—5:27 ELIPHAZ' CONTENTION: ONLY THE WICKED PERISH

4:1 *Answered.* Job's three friends are ready to take up the question raised by him: Why must I suffer? (3:11, 12, 20). Their answer precipitates a long discussion, resembling a debate. The issue can be phrased: "*Resolved,* that Job suffers much because he has sinned much." The friends alternately assert the affirmative. Job defends the negative, replying in turn to each speaker in the three rounds of the debate. However, in the ensuing battle of words there is no logical development from one point of contention to the next. Rather than progressing vertically from A to B to C etc., the movement of thought is circular. Each speaker draws concentric circles of argumentation about the central topic, repeating the issue and elaborating proof and rebuttal from various points of view. To our way of thinking this kind of reasoning may appear repetitious and tiresome. Yet it is very effective in the total impact it produces. —In his attempt to disprove the false charges made against him, Job proves Satan correct in his claim that no man serves God purely out of love for Him.

Eliphaz, the first affirmative speaker, puts forth the axiomatic proposition that no one who is "innocent" or "upright" is ever "cut off." He asserts that this is a truth (a) with which Job himself comforted others (1-6); (b) which is attested by experience (7-11); (c) which was revealed to him in a vision (12-21); (d) which applies to all cases without exception (5:1-7); (e) which is the hope of the downtrodden (5:8-16) and comforts those undergoing chastening. (5:17-27)

4:3 *Instructed.* Job was upright and blameless not only in that he feared God (1:8) but also in his love for his fellowman. Eliphaz reminds him that he "upheld him who was stumbling" by comforting him with what he himself believed, namely that the sufferer's "fear of God" and his "integrity" should be the source of his "confidence" and "hope." Job should not be "offended" or become "impatient" if his friend now asks him to apply this truth to his own situation. (2-6)

4:7 *Perished.* Eliphaz quickly comes to the basic contention which he and his companions will maintain throughout the discussion. In his opening words (2-6) he only intimated it. Now he states it very bluntly. If Job "perishes," as he wished he could (ch. 3), it is not because he was *innocent* or *upright* but because he was only reaping what he sowed. There is a direct ratio between the intensity of a man's suffering and the severity of God's judgment on his sin. No one escapes "the blast of his anger" even if he pretends to be as fierce as a lion. (7-11)

4:12 *Brought to me.* Eliphaz asserts that the doctrine of divine retribution he enunciated is a truth confirmed to him by revelation. As a thief enters *stealthily,* so a vision stole over him in "deep sleep." It filled him with "dread" and "trembling" so that his hair bristled. (Gn 15:12)

4:15 *A spirit.* Hebrew: "a wind," a word also denoting immaterial beings. Here no doubt an angelic messenger is meant (Ps 104:4; Heb 1:7). "It" or he stood still but Eliphaz could not discern "its appearance" or face. (16)

4:17 *Mortal man.* The voice coming out of the

vision affirmed man's innate depravity. This axiomatic truth established the basis of Eliphaz' charge that Job is suffering the consequences of sin. Man, who quickly returns to "the dust" from which he came, is "without wisdom" if like Job he pretends that *before God,* i.e., from God's viewpoint, he is *righteous* and *pure* and therefore exempt from the wages of sin. (17-21)

4:18 *His servants.* Even his *angels,* God's immaterial creatures, fall short of the perfection of divine holiness. In His presence they cover their face and feet with their wings. (Is 6:2)

4:19 *Houses of clay.* Man's transitory existence, the result of sin, is graphically portrayed. Formed of perishable clay, his life-span is that of a *moth.* (33:6; Ps 90:5, 6; Is 40:6-8)

4:21 *Tent-cord.* Human life collapses as suddenly as a tent falls in a heap when its guy rope is cut (cf. 2 Co 5:1). Death overtakes men even though they do not have the *wisdom* to realize that their "days are like an evening shadow." (Ps 102:11; Jb 14:1-2)

5:1 *Call now.* After appealing to his vision to validate his doctrine of man's sinfulness (4:12-21), Eliphaz cites examples of God's fearful retribution on the wicked. Turning directly to Job, he challenges him to prove that he is an exception to the universal rule that "affliction" and "trouble" are the result of one's inborn depravity (1-7). If Job were to appeal for comfort to *any one* among his fellowmen or even to the "*holy ones,* i.e., the angels, he would get no better solution of his problem. (4:18; 15:15; Zch 14:5; Dn 4:13; 8:13)

5:2 *Kills the fool.* Eliphaz again cites examples from his own experience (4:8-11) to prove his point that disaster inexorably overtakes everyone who in his folly acts as if he were not accountable to God for his deeds.

5:3 *Cursed.* Even though the fool prospered for a time, Eliphaz declared him deserving of God's curse on the wicked which effectually ends his prosperity (Pr 3:33; Ps 37:35-36). Another translation suggests a continuation of the thought expressed in the first line of the verse: "but suddenly his stalk rotted."

5:4 *Gate.* Where courts of justice were held. (31:21; Dt 25:7)

5:5 *Thorns.* The thought suggested by this verse seems to be that intruders penetrate even a hedge of thorns to eat the harvest or that they consume everything, even what grew up among thorns.

5:6 *From the dust. Affliction* does not arise from causes outside man.

5:7 *Sparks.* Lit "sons of a flame." Because evil is intrinsic in man's nature, he should not be surprised if *trouble* eventuates as inevitably as sparks emanate from a heated iron when it is struck.

5:8 *Seek God.* Rather than complain to men and angels (1) Job is advised to come to terms with his Maker. God is able and willing to come to the aid of such as are brought low by "the devices of the crafty," "the schemes of the wily," "the hand of the mighty." Lurking in this comforting assurance is an insinuating sting of rebuke. Job can commit his cause to God for vindication if he is suffering "injustice" at the hands of evil men. If, however, he himself was guilty of crimes such as those mentioned, divine justice turned the tables on him, delivering his innocent victims from his greedy and cruel hands. (8-16)

5:11 *Lowly.* This thought is echoed in Hanna's song and Mary's magnificat. (1 Sm 2:7; Lk 1:51-52)

5:13 *Craftiness.* The only quotation of Job in the NT is from this verse. Paul is warning his readers against "the wisdom of this world." (1 Co 3:19)

5:17 *Reproves.* Eliphaz advances another reason why Job should "seek God" (8). Divine providence "smites" men in order to "heal" them. Job should be *happy* to know that God's *chastening* rod inflicts pain on him in order to warn him not to continue on a path leading to destruction. When the Almighty has achieved His disciplinary purpose, He again protects His penitent children from evil and showers every kind of blessing on them (17-27). What Eliphaz proclaims is true (Dt 32:39; Ps 94:12; Hos 6:1; Ja 1:12 Heb 12:5-11). However, he implies that God, always acting in direct proportion to man's guilt, had to apply drastic chastening in Job's case because he went so far astray.

5:17 *Almighty.* Cf Gn 17:1 note. Job's friends do not refer to God by his covenant name, the Lord (Ex 6:3 note). The title *Almighty* occurs some 30 times, almost twice as often as in all other books of the OT.

5:19 *Six . . . seven.* the progression from a number to the next higher one is a literary device to denote items of the same category by way of example rather than for the purpose of offering an exhaustive list (Pr 6:16). Other sets of numerals, e.g., "three . . . four," are used in the same way. (Pr 30:18)

5:21 *Scourge of the tongue.* Slander.

5:23 *In league.* Eliphaz holds out the prospect of paradisiacal fertility and peace. Cleared of stones, a field could produce a maximum yield. (Is 5:2)

5:24 *Miss.* Preferable to KJV: "sin." The basic meaning of the verb is to fail to reach the object one seeks or aims at. Usually it denotes missing the mark of the Law and hence is a common synonym for sin.

6:1—7:21 JOB'S REPLY

6:1 *Answered.* In his reply to Eliphaz Job (a) cries out again in pain (1-13; see ch. 3); (b) turns to his friends, expressing his disappointment with them (6:14—7:6); (c) remonstrates with God, pleading for surcease from torment. (7:7-21)

6:3 *Rash.* Eliphaz' speech brought Job no comfort because it lacked understanding of the enormity of his "vexation" and "calamity" even though he cried out in words sounding rash or wildly incoherent.

6:4 *Arrows of the Almighty.* His suffering is unbearable because he endures not only physical pain but also spiritual and mental anguish. He is sorely wounded by the thought that God causes his pain, so contrary to his expectations.

6:5 *Bray.* Job's wailing is not a stage act. As famished beasts howl out their pain of starvation, so he is reacting to real aches gnawing at his vitals.

6:6 *Tasteless.* Eliphaz' attempts to comfort him are as unpalatable to him as unsalted food is insipid. The *purslane,* a plant sometimes used for salads, needs condiments to give it any taste.

6:9 *Crush me.* His suffering exceeds the ability of his friends to alleviate it by their words of comfort. It is beyond his power of endurance. Only a quick death would bring him "consolation." (8-13)

6:10 *Not denied.* Job does not know how much longer he can be "patient" (11). If his end came quickly, he could die knowing that he made no statement in outright opposition to God's declared will. He had reason to doubt his constancy. Soon his friends were to hear him challenge God's justice.

6:14 *Friend.* After bewailing his lot in a kind of monolog (2-13) Job addresses himself more directly to his friends (14-30). He defends himself against their insinuations by (a) charging them with lovelessness (14-23); (b) challenging them to produce proof of his wrongdoing. (24—30)

6:15 *Treacherous.* The Hebrew text of 14 has lent itself to various translations. What he intended to say becomes clear in the section following it where Job illustrates and applies its meaning. He did not experience "kindness" as he had every right to expect "from a friend." His *brethren* disappointed him as sadly as parched travelers are "confounded" when they eagerly search out a stream only to find out that it dried up in the heat of summer.

6:19 *Tema . . . Sheba.* Located in the Arabian desert.

6:22 *Gift.* Job did not presume on their friendship. All he looked for was a kind word.

6:24 *Erred.* Job challenges his friends to prove that there is "any wrong on my tongue" (30). "Honest words," wrung from "a despairing man," should not be held against him but should be regarded as of no more might than "the wind." People who would charge that he erred would be cruel enough to sell an orphan or a friend into slavery.

6:28 *Look at me.* With one hand Job thrusts his friends from him; with the other he draws them to him, hoping that somehow his "vindication" would result if they listened to him. They can rely on his ability to "taste" or "discern" the difference between right and wrong.

7:1 *Hard service.* Job injects another cry of pain. His life, futile, hard, and restless like all human existence, is made unbearable by a loathsome, fatal disease. (cf. 2:7 note)

7:7 *Remember.* In the remaining verses of this chapter Job for the first time speaks directly to God though still without addressing Him by name. He first continues his gloomy reflections on the transitoriness of human life. It is swifter than a "weaver's shuttle" (6), fleeting as a *breath,* evanescent as a "cloud" which fades and vanishes (7-10). The thought of his own insignificance then prompts him to "complain in the bitterness of . . . soul" to God that He bothers to scrutinize His frail creatures so mercilessly. Rather than to hold them to strict account it would be more in keeping with His vast superiority to overlook and pardon their "transgression" and "iniquity." If God cannot let him alone, he would sooner die than live. (11—21)

7:9 *Sheol.* Cf. Gn 42:38 note.

7:10 *No more.* Man has but one life to live on earth (10:21; 14:7-22; Ps 103:15-16). Even Christ's victory over the grave has not made death less final as the termination of our earthly sojourn. (1 Ptr 1:24; Heb 9:27)

7:12 *Sea monster.* The mighty waves of the sea and the untamed monsters of the deep frequently are represented as God's formidable enemies, threatening to plunge His ordered universe into primordial chaos. (9:8; 38:8-11; Ps 46:2-3; 65:7; 74:13-14; 89:9; 93:4; Pr 8:29; Is 27:1; 51:9))

7:14 *Dreams.* Wracked by pain and fever, he even is deprived of refreshing sleep by hallucinations and nightmares.

7:15 *My bones.* He would prefer to choke to death rather than to continue to suffer in the "earthly tent," whose supports are the framework of his bones. (2 Co 5:1)

7:17 *What is man.* Rather than thank God for man's superior status among His creatures (Ps 8) and for His constant watchfulness and concern for his welfare (Ps 139), Job complains that the transcendent "watchers of men" (20) should *make so much* of His lowly handiwork as to keep him under observation "every moment" (18), intent on discovering petty infractions of His divine ordinance.

7:19 *Swallow . . . spittle.* A proverbial saying. God does *not look away* from Job any longer than it takes to swallow one's saliva.

7:20 *Why . . . ?* Unwittingly Job's friends played Satan's game. Desiring to help him by their insistence on the absolute and unerring administration of divine justice, they provoked him to the edge of declaring himself in rebellion against God. He tried to refute the principle advocated by them that suffering is punishment befitting the crime. As a result he remonstrates with God for making him the *mark* or target of cruel, undeserved retribution. God could readily have overlooked the kind of "transgression" he may have committed.

8:1-22 BILDAD EXTOLS GOD'S JUSTICE

8:1 *Bildad answered.* His Shuhite friend (2:11 note) is the second to try to be helpful to Job. He prescribes the same remedy recommended by his companion (chs. 5—6). Job must realize that whereas piety brings blessing without fail, suffering is always the consequence of sin. For God's justice is inflexible in reacting to man's behavior. Without sparing Job's feelings,

Bildad (a) states bluntly that man gets precisely what he deserves (1-7); (b) cites the experience of "bygone ages" to substantiate this truth (8-10); (c) warns not to be misled by the apparent successes of the godless (11-19); (d) promises Job "laughter" for his tears if he proves himself "a blameless man." (20-22)

8:2 *Great wind.* His words are as blustering but also as empty as a gust of wind. (15:2; 16:3)

8:3 *Pervert justice.* In his answer to Eliphaz Job did not accuse God of injustice in so many words. However, Bildad insists that Job's defiant complaint of harsh treatment (7:20) is at bottom a charge that God does not "render to every man according to his works." (Ro 2:6; 3:5; 2 Ch 19:7)

8:4 *Sinned.* Bildad, the self-appointed physician, feels he must cut deeply into a grieving father's heart if he is to effect a cure. Painful though the process may be, Job must be brought to his senses. The death of his children, says Bildad, demonstrates that sin by its very nature is relentles in exacting its toll.

8:5 *Seek.* In his last words to Eliphaz (7:21) Job said that God could no longer "seek" him out to rain more blows on him, once he were dead. In rebuttal Bildad urges Job to *seek* God, imploring His grace in *supplication.* As automatically as punishment followed sin, so surely God "will rouse himself" (Ps 7:6, 35:23) in his behalf, prolong his life, and in his "latter days" let him reap the rewards of being "pure and upright."

8:8 *Bygone ages.* Eliphaz claimed a vision to validate the doctrine of divine justice (4:12 ff.); Bildad insists that it is supported by more evidence than he accumulated in his lifetime. It is based on incontrovertible evidence of past generations.

8:13 *Forget God.* The fate of the godless cannot be cited to disprove the unfailing justice of God (Ps 37;73). They may seem to flourish for a time, but inevitably judgment overtakes them. Bildad adduces three analogies illustrating the certainty of their ultimate and disillusioning collapse: (a) they "wither away" like the reed on the edge of a "marsh" when the water recedes depriving them of indispensable sustenance (11-13); (b) their achievements have no more stability than "a spider's web" (14 f.); (c) they "thrive" for a short time only like a luxuriating plant which must be pulled up because in its rocky soil it could not find enough moisture for continued growth.

8:17 *Lives.* KV: "seeth the place of stones." In Hebrew the verbs "to live" and "to see" are almost identical in form.

8:18 *Never seen.* The wicked is destroyed, pulled up by his roots. No trace remains of what he considered "the joy of his way" (19). No one misses him as he is replaced by others.

8:21 *Laugher.* God's judgment on "evildoers" is inexorable. A "blameless man" can be just as certain of a reward for his piety. Bildad even implies that if Job would "seek God" (5) and repent of the heinous sin for which he received such severe punishment, his tears would change to laughter as surely as God is God. (Cf. 5:17 note)

9:1—10:22 JOB CHALLENGES GOD'S JUSTICE

9:2 *It is so.* Job agrees with the previous speakers that a man cannot win a case against God (4:17; 8:3). Tried in God's court of justice, he never emerges as *just,* that is, as the vindicated part of a lawsuit. However, the veiled accusation that Job is suffering what he deserves irritates him to the point that he denounces the fairness of the trial and the principles by which it is conducted. He insists there can be no equitable settlement of his case because (a) God cannot be haled into court to answer charges (1-12); (b) God uses His power to destroy both "the blameless and the wicked" (13-24); (c) God will not let a disinterested arbiter prove Job's innocence. (25-35)

9:3 *Contend.* In a law suit man would be no match for the wisdom of God. Challenged to justify His actions, He could confuse man *a thousand times* with questions so that he could not "answer back to God." (Ro 9:20)

9:4 *Strength* God is also so powerful that no one has *succeeded* in defying Him. How can puny man enter a contest with him who "removes mountains," who "commands" the sun, the stars and the heavenly constellations, doing it all without letting man see Him at work? (5-12).

9:6 *Pillars.* As in other poetic descriptions of the universe and natural phenomena, the earth as well as the heavens are pictured as resting on pillars (26:11; 1 Sm 2:8; Ps 75:3). However according to 26:7 God "hangs the earth upon nothing."

9:9 *Bear.* The constellations, designated by our names for them, are mentioned again 38:31; Am 5:8. *The chambers of the south* may refer to stars or a constellation in the southern hemisphere.

9:13 *Helpers of Rahab.* God overcomes all opposition as decisively as Rahab, a female monster representing chaos in the Babylonian creation myth, and her cohorts are depicted as having *bowed* in defeat to the superior strength of Marduk, the hero of the epic. (26:12; Is 51:9)

9:15 *Appeal.* Even if Job could "summon" God to appear in court with him (19), justice would not prevail. Instead of being acquitted, he would be so overwhelmed and confused by the divine presence that he would enter a plea of guilty and beg for mercy.

9:22 *Destroys.* Protesting his innocence and caring not whether he pays for it with his own miserable life, Job utters the blasphemous charge that God does not differentiate in His treatment of *the blameless and the wicked.* At this point Job did "charge God with wrong" and "sin with his lips" (1:22; 2:10). Satan had proof that even this "upright man" did not serve God "for nought." (1-9)

9:25 *My days.* All attempts during Job's short span of life to establish his innocence are of no avail (25-26). It is useless (a) to affect cheerfulness in suffering (27-28) (b) to engage in purifying ceremonies, signifying purity of conscience (29-31); (c) to seek trial before a neutral "umpire" (32-33); (d) to hope for an opportunity openly and fearlessly to profess his conviction of innocence. (34-35)

9:31 *Abhor me.* No matter how much Job would "labor" to make himself acceptable, God would reject him as unclean as if he were covered with such putrid filth as makes a person objectionable even to the clothes he wears.

9:33 *Umpire.* God supplies Job's and all mankind's need through Him who is the "Mediator between God and men, the man Christ Jesus, who gave Himself as a ransom for all." (1 Ti 2:5-6; Heb 9:15)

9:35 *In myself.* Job is convinced of his innocence.

10:1 *Complaint.* Weary and despairing of life (7:11), Job continues to raise charges against God, accusing Him of dealing unfairly with him (9:2 note). Now addressing his complaints directly to Him, he (a) protests that God should "oppress" Him ostensibly in search for sin, all the while knowing that he is "not guilty" (1-7); (b) asserts God takes pleasure in destroying man, created and nurtured by Him for the very "purpose" of reducing him "to dust again" (8-13); (c) claims God tracks down "the wicked" and "the righteous" alike as if He were "lion" hunting (14-17); (d) declare himself entitled to a brief respite before death overtakes him as it should have at his birth. (18-22)

10:2 *To God.* Job has no choice but to turn to God himself because no "umpire between" them is available. Stunned and perplexed though he is, he does not "curse God, and die" by his own hand (2:9). He still looks to God for a solution of his problem.

10:4 *Eyes of flesh.* Man, whose vision and insight are imperfect, often errs in judging others. Or he may wrong them because for lack of time he acts too hastily. But "The Lord sees not as man sees" (1 Sm 16:7) and therefore should know that Job is "not guilty."

10:8 *Made me.* His suffering does not drive Job to atheism. He acknowledges that he owes his existence and preservation to God's creative power and watchful care. But he dishonors his Creator by concluding that He fashioned him for the express "purpose" of destroying him.

10:10 *Pour me out.* The origin of life in the womb is described in poetic language. (Cf. Ps 139:13-16)

10:14 *Mark me.* Job sinks deeper into the mire of despair claiming that his experience confirms his statement about God's intention in creating man (13). God will not be deterred from his purpose of destroying Job whether he admits his sin or whether he stands with head erect, professing innocence (15-16). Like a hunter, out to bag irrational game, God uses His power to "work wonders" in order to bring down His quarry.

10:20 *Let me alone.* It would have been an act of kindness if he could have been carried from the womb to the grave (18-19; 3:11 ff.). But because he has only one short life to live on earth, God is unjust and cruel to make it such a torture.

10:21 *Not return.* The last two verses of the chapter stress the finality of death as the end of earthly existence. The Prince of life urged His followers to "work . . . while it is day" because "night comes, when no one can work." (Jn 9:4; cf. Jb 7:10 note)

11:1-20 ZOPHAR REBUKES JOB

11:1 *Zophar.* Job's *Naamathite* (2:11 note) friend underscores what his two companions said about God's absolute justice. However, he is more direct and blunt in bringing this doctrine to bear on Job's situation. He believes he must not mince words if he is to set Job right and thus keep him out of his predicament. Without wasting his breath on words of sympathy he castigates his hapless friend for challenging God's providence, insisting that (a) Job has no reason to complain because he is being beaten with fewer stripes than he actually deserves (1-6); (b) God's justice, beyond puny man's cavil, never lets "worthless men" escape retribution (7-12) while rewarding such as set their "heart aright" when chastised. (13-20)

11:3 *Mock.* Job's "doctrine" that God was punishing him even though he was innocent of any crime (4; 9:21; 10:7) was not only a "great wind" of nonsense (8:2) but in reality a direct insult to God. Job may be able to hoodwink and *silence men.* But God's "understanding" penetrates and exposes what to human wisdom are dark "secrets." If He were to speak, He could prove that He more often was overlooking Job's sins than punishing him as he deserved.

11:7 *Deep things.* Job conceded that God's power and wisdom were beyond human comprehension or explanation (9:4 ff.). Zophar reminds him that these divine attributes are guarantee that no "worthless men" are so devious or so mighty as to slip through His hands.

11:12 *Colt.* Apparently Zophar is citing a proverbial saying to the effect that the prospects that Job's empty head will be filled with understanding are as remote as the possibility of an ass producing offspring endowed with human intelligence.

11:13 *Aright.* As inexorably as God punishes the wicked (7-12), so unfailingly will he receive Job back into favor if he repents of the sin for which he has been disciplined so severely. In still more glowing terms than those of Eliphaz (5:17 ff.) and of Bildad (8:20 ff.) Zophar describes the reward of godliness as a veritable paradise on earth. No man need serve God "for nought."

11:15 *Lift up.* Once he has cleared his conscience of the blotch of guilt, he need not fear to walk with his head high.

11:17 *Life.* His span of life will be much longer than he expected. (7:6; 9:25 ff.; 10:20)

11:18 *Is hope.* Zophar contradicts what Job said (7:6) and would repeat 13:15.

11:20 *Wicked.* As a final word of warning Zophar reminds Job that all the wicked have to hope for is a timely end of their miserable existence.

12:1-25 JOB EXCORIATES FRIENDS

12:2 *Wisdom will die.* Job begins his answer to Zophar's supercilious harangue by rejecting the claim to superior wisdom made by all three friends. In words barbed with sarcasm he brushes aside their diagnosis of his case, asserting that (a) their pearls of wisdom only added insult to injury (1-6); (b) they lectured him learnedly about things which a quick glance at nature makes obvious (7-12); (c) they pretend to say something new when they declare God's wisdom to be unfathomable and His power irresistible, whereas everybody knows from experience how He shatters the resistence of even the mightiest of men and exposes the most cunningly devised plot. (13-25)

12:4 *Laughingstock.* Instead of affording him sympathy the friends made him the butt of ridicule. He feels the sting of disgrace so keenly because formerly no one made derogatory remarks about him. In answer to his prayer God granted him the reputation of *a just and blameless man* and people respected him.

12:5 *At ease.* This verse seems to be the equivalent of our saying that a bully enjoys hitting a man when he is down.

12:6 *God in their hand.* The friends are wrong in claiming that God does not let the crimes of "worthless men" go unpunished (11:10 f.). They rob their fellowmen with impunity; they enrage God but are not disturbed. Another group of unmolested sinners are idolators who have a god they can carry about, or who know no other god than power symbolized by their hand.

12:7 *Teach you.* Job's friends are pompous proclaimers of the most obvious and widely recognized facts. For God's "eternal power and deity has been clearly perceived in the things that have been made" (Ro 1:19 f.; Ps 19:1-6). Any one who can distinguish sounds or can taste the difference in foods (11) is wise enough to make the observations they palm off as mysteries.

12:12 *Aged.* Perhaps better translated as a question, this verse lampoons the impression created by the friends that their rhetoric represented the distilled wisdom of ancient sages.

12:13 *Wisdom and might.* Job goes to some length to show that he too is well aware of God's absolute control of man's destiny (13:1 f.). He cites example after example to illustrate the fact that no man or nation is strong or clever enough to escape a divinely decreed fate. However, Job and his friends draw different conclusions from this truth. They argue Job is no exception to the rule that calamity is the consequence of sin. He should not try to conceal the sin for which God's mighty hand is heavy on him. Job, however, insists that he is not guilty of a crime for which he deserves to be crushed. There can be only one explanation of his situation. The omniscient and omnipotent God wields His power indiscriminately. Consequently He "destroys both the blameless and the wicked." (9:22)

12:22 *Deeps.* Intrigues plotted in deepest secrecy.

12:23 *Destroys them.* Job fears that as God creates the individual for the purpose of undoing him (10:13) so He lets whole nations flower only to cut them down.

13:1—14:22 JOB DESIRES ANSWERS FROM GOD

13:3 *The Almighty.* Job wants to speak to God Himself because his friends are of no help to him. What they have to say about God's power and wisdom he knew all the while (12:7—13:2). And when they apply these generally known truths to him they in fact misrepresent God (3-12). Come what may, he is determined to argue his case in a divine court of appeals (13-16), confident of being vindicated (17-19) unless God terrifies him so that he cannot talk freely (20-22). He would begin with an interrogation, demanding to know what he did to deserve being hounded to death. (23-28)

13:4 *Whitewash.* Job cannot get a fair hearing from his friends because they cover up the inequities of God's government. They "show partiality toward him" (8,10) because they curry favor with Him. All the while they are hiding their own guilt for which God ought to terrify them if He is as intolerant of wickedness as they claim.

13:5 *Keep silent.* Even a fool may be considered wise as long as he keeps his mouth shut. (Pr 17:28)

13:12 *Defenses.* Their mouthing of platitudes, dusty with age, is as worthless as a fortification made of such crumbling material as mud and ashes.

13:14 *Flesh.* The second line repeats the same thought. We would say: I am ready to take my life in my hand (Ju 12:3; 1 Sm 19:5; 28:21). In desperation Job is willing to risk everything to get redress. As it is, life is not worth much anyway.

13:15 *No hope.* KJV: "Though he slay me, yet will I trust in him." Job once expressed such tenacity of faith in the face of overwhelming disaster (1:21; 2:10; see also Hab 3:17-18). However, the text and context do not warrant such a robust affirmation of trust at this point. Here Job is in a defiant mood. He is prepared to defend his record if need be at the cost of his life. For other expressions of desperation see 7:6; 11:8; 14:7; 17:15-16.

13:16 *Godless man.* Job is so confident he can prove his innocence, if given a fair trial, that he is willing to risk death in the attempt.

13:20 *Grant.* What Job asks of God constitutes *two things* in the sense that there is a negative and a positive aspect to his request: let up on your stranglehold on me so I have the full use of my faculties; do not confuse me with a terrifying display of your powers of destruction (21; 9:15 note; 9:34 f.). If God will agree not to take unfair advantage of him, other court procedures are of no great concern to him. God may "call," i.e., act as prosecutor, or he may "answer," i.e., play the role of a defendant in the case.

13:23 *My sins.* If Job could hope for a fair trial,

he would demand to know, first of all, why God is meting out such severe punishment to him. He may have been indiscreet in his "youth" (26), but he is being hounded and crushed as if he were the worst kind of criminal (23-28).

14:1 *Man.* If Job were to "speak to the Almighty" (13:3), he would claim that he was being punished personally for crimes he did not commit (13:23-28). His next move would be to challenge God's harsh treatment of him as a member of the human race, so pitifully short-lived, so helplessly prone to make mistakes. How can God justify making man's brief stay on earth so miserable, holding him to account for being what he is by nature? (1-6). Why does God make man suffer the consequences of sin in this life if in the life to come He is going to waive all punishment for penintent sinners? (7-17). Why does death so inevitably and with such finality put an end to man's hope for joys this side of the grave? (18-22)

14:2 *Flower . . . shadow.* Frequently used in figurative language to describe man's transitory existence. (Is 40:6 ff.; Ps 90:5 f.; 103:15; Ec 6:12; 1 Ptr 1:24; Ja 1:9-11

14:4 *Clean thing.* It is unreasonable for God to keep man under constant surveillance, ready to pounce on him for every misstep (3). For it is as impossible for man to rise above his hereditary tendency to evil as it is to expect something *unclean* to produce something *clean.* (Ps 51:5; 53:3; Pr 20:9; Jn 3:6; Ro 5:12; Eph 2:3)

14:6 *Look away.* God inflicts enough punishment when he cuts short man's life. As a hired laborer is dismissed after a day's work, so swiftly man's allotted tenure on earth is terminated. Therefore he should be let to *enjoy* it undisturbed while it lasts. (7:19 note)

14:7 *Sprout again.* A tree, *cut down,* may renew its life by sending up new shoots from its roots. But once man is dead, "he will not awake" to continue life on earth. But if God's wrath does not pursue the sinner after his "release" from this earth, granting him full pardon, why does God inflict such severe penalities on man in this life? This inconsistency on God's part is particularly grievous because after death it is impossible to return to a more pleasant life on earth.—Present-day believers have the assurance that Jesus Christ conquered death and brought life and immortality to life. But they too have trouble at times finding comfort in the promise of a bliss hereafter when God lays heavy burdens on them in the here and now. Godliness, they had hoped, would guarantee them a this-worldly paradise.

14:13 *Sheol.* The realm of the dead. See Dt 32:22 note.

14:14 *Shall he live?* Job puts in the form of a question what he later affirms unconditionally (19:25 note). He compares the time till God would "call" him from his "sleep" (12, 15) with a period of *service* required of a soldier.

14:16 *Then.* If the Hebrew adverb has its more usual meaning of "now," as translated in KJV, Job is reverting to his complaint that God does not remit the penalty of sin in this life.

14:20 *For ever.* Because God inevitably and permanently terminates man's brief life on earth (1, 2), death ends participation in the joys and sorrows of fellowmen, even of his own children. Nor can anyone share with another the "pain" and grief which death inflicts on an individual and so ease the burden. (22)

SUMMARY. A diagram of the first round of speeches (chs. 4—14) would resemble six concentric rings of a tree trunk. The three speeches by his friends and Job's reply to them represent a series of circles not only because the discussion has revolving motion. This does not mean that the participants avoid coming to grips with the issue. In ever new formulations and from different angles, they draw lines aimed at the same central question like so many radii from a perimeter. The three friends insist Job is concealing a great sin because God's punishment always fits the crime. Job denies that his suffering is the measure of his sin. However, baited by his accusing friends, Job supplies Satan with evidence that even such a blameless man as he does not serve God "for nothing" (1:9). Hurting in body and soul, Job lets it be known that he expects godliness to pay dividends.

In chs. 15—21 the four participants in the dispute complete another cycle of six speeches, each again encircling the topic under discussion. Each speaker takes the opportunity to develop what he said before. His voice is shriller than before and his words take on a more cutting edge. Job continues to cling to God with one hand while raising the other in protest against Him for not treating him as he deserves. So Satan scores again.

15:1-35 ELIPHAZ' SECOND SPEECH

15:1 *Eliphaz . . . answered.* No longer with any concern for his friend's feelings as before (see ch. 4), Eliphaz unlooses a vehement tirade on Job. The latter is to know that by his bombastic attempt to conceal his guilt he (a) was subverting the basis of true religion and at the same time incriminating himself (1-6); (b) was claiming to be wiser than the "consolations of God," transmitted to him by his friends (7-11); (c) was raging against God's holiness (12-16); (d) was making himself liable to the horrible fate decreed by divine justice on every one who "stretches forth his hand against God." (17-35)

15:2 *Wise man.* A sarcastic reference to Job's boast of being wise. His words of wisdom had as much substance as the wind. Not only were they "unprofitable" but also destructive as the scorching sirocco "east wind" blowing in from the desert.

15:4 *Fear of God.* If Job's words were true, there no longer would be any point in urging men to lead a God-fearing life (as he formerly did; 4:3-6) or to turn to God in prayerful meditation. (Ps 119:97, 99)

15:6 *Condemns you.* Rather than proving to be a defense of his innocence, Job's attacks on divine justice were evidence that he was concealing his guilt. What his *mouth* and "crafty" tongue uttered had its source in the "iniquity" he was hiding.

15:7 *First man.* Eliphaz continues to ridicule Job's pose as "a wise man" (2). Matching Job's sarcastic remarks about his comforters (12:2 ff.), the Temanite asserts that Job talks as though he had the wisdom of primordeal man before it was impaired by sin, or as if he were endowed with superhuman wisdom, which existed "before the mountains had been shaped" (Pr 8:22-31; Jb 38:4, 7). Does he claim a monopoly on wisdom because he had the unique privilege to attend a heavenly "council"? (8; 1 K 22:19 ff.; Jer 23:18). Does he pretend to know more than the accumulated wisdom of the ages? (9 f.). Why is he so haughty as to reject "the consolations of God," transmitted "gently" to him by Eliphaz? (11). For the latter's claim to inspiration see 4:12 ff.; for his avowed purpose to help Job see 5:17-27.

15:13 *Such words.* Job let himself be carried away. His eyes flashing wildly, he scorns not only God's spokesmen but turns even *against God* Himself.

15:14 *Clean.* Eliphaz maintained earlier and Job agreed that no man is guiltless before God (4:17-18; 14:4). Those who are as "abominable and corrupt" as Job evidently must be, deserve to be punished severely.

15:15 *Holy ones.* See 4:18 note.

15:17 *Show you.* There is no truth in Job's claim that "the earth is given into the hand of the wicked" (9:24) (4:12 ff.). On the strength of what he has "seen" in his night vision and of what "wise men" have told him, Eliphaz states categorically that no one goes unpunished who "stretched forth his hand against God." (25)

15:19 *Alone.* The distilled wisdom, stored up for generations, was kept from being contaminated by false notions, imported from foreign sources.

15:20 *Writhes.* Even while seemingly successful, *the wicked man* is not at peace. Pangs of conscience and forebodings of catastrophe do not let him get rid of the torturing fear that "a day of darkness is ready at his hand" (23; Is 48:22; Lv 26:36)

15:23 *Wanders abroad.* His dread of the future is so intense that he visualizes his impoverishment as an accomplished fact.

15:25 *Bids defiance.* Eliphaz goes to considerable length to describe the wicked. They run "stubbornly" against God as if they could ward off divine retribution as effectively as soldiers absorb the arrows of the enemy with a heavily embossed shield (26). They are "fat" with arrogance (27; Jer 5:28). They live in cities marked by God for permanent destruction (28). They may accumulate "wealth" but it has as little stability as a plant exposed to fire. (29 f.)

15:31 *Emptiness.* All appearances to the contrary, the good fortune of the "godless" turns out to be as deceptive as a mirage. Therefore the "upright" and "pure in heart" should not be "envious" when they see "the prosperity of the wicked" (Ps 37; 73). Of course Eliphaz' discourse on the inability of criminals to slip through God's primitive hands is not meant to cheer Job but to break down the hard shell of his impenitence. There is hope for him only if he makes a clean breast of his guilt. Because the friends find no evidence of repentance, they fear his doom is sealed. In the second cycle of speeches they therefore do not continue to portray the blessings awaiting Job's return to God. (Cf. 4:17-21; 8:20-22; 11:13-20)

16:1—17:16 JOB'S SECOND REPLY TO ELIPHAZ

16:1 *Job answered.* Everyone whose faith has been shaken to its foundation by a crushing calamity, who has battled against cynicism, who has been irritated by hollow words of sympathy, will not be surprised at the abrupt changes of mood displayed in Job's fourth speech. After letting fly some stinging words of sarcasm aimed at his friends for their heartless kind of comfort (1-5) and after bitterly questioning God's right to torture him (6-17), he suddenly appeals to God to vindicate him (18-22), only to lapse again into a lament (17:1-3), into recriminations against his friends (17:4-5), into a dull stupor of resignation. (17:6-16).

16:2 *Miserable comforters.* Comforters causing misery instead of assuaging his grief.

16:3 *Windy words.* Not he (15:2) but the friends are windbags. The charge, echoing through their speeches, that he is a criminal has no more substance than a gust of air.

16:4 *In my place.* Continuing his caustic remarks, Job asks his friends how they would feel if the roles were reversed, if they were in trouble and he consoled them with the hypocritical twaddle they unloaded on him. He too could string together sanctimonious phrases and shake his head to imply that their pain would go away if they repented.

16:7 *God.* Job's friends reason that he must be guilty of a heinous crime to judge by the intensity of pain inflicted on him. His suffering, it is true, beggars all description. In an effort to tell what he is asked to bear, he resorts to lurid figures of speech. God, he says, acts toward him like a wild beast (9), like a bone-crushing monster (12), like an archer, whose rain of arrows finds its target in him, like a death-dealing swordsman (13), like an enemy soldier breaching the wall of a besieged city (14). Yet as he sits in his "sackcloth" and weeps "in deep darkness," he protests there is no "violence in my hands" for which he deserves to be punished.

Desolate. His children are dead; his wife is estranged; his friends deserted him. (19:13 ff.)

16:9 *Hated.* The Hebrew verb, related to the word for Satan (1:6 note), has the connotation to bear a grudge, to cherish enmity, to persecute (so translated Ps 55:3; Jb 30:21).

16:10 *Gape.* Job's outcry of pain and forsaken loneliness anticipates and typefies the lament of that Sufferer who bore all our iniquity including Job's. (Is 53; Ps 22)

16:13 *Kidneys . . . gall.* God tore open his vitals.

16:18 *My blood.* Innocent Abel's blood cried to

God for justice "from the ground" (Gn 4:10; see Eze 24:7; Rv 6:9 f.). Job does not want the earth to let his blood be silenced until God acts on his plea for a favorable verdict. In his appeal to "a witness in heaven" (19) Job contradicts himself. Dazed and confused to the point of declaring God his "adversary" (9), he nevertheless pours "tears" at His feet in humble supplication, frantically holding on to Him as his only friend. Earlier he felt the need of an "umpire" to represent him in his trial before God (9:33). Now he confidently asks that God Himself plead his cause in the heavenly court of justice. If God, his Advocate, "vouches for" him, God, the Judge, is sure to rule in his favor.—This longing for an advocate before God, who Himself is God, became a reality when "in Christ God was reconciling the world to himself" so that "we have an advocate with the Father, Jesus Christ the righteous" (2 Co 5:18 f.; 1 Jn 2:1 f.)

16:22 *Few years.* Job's days are numbered, he fears. If he is to be vindicated in this life, God must act promptly.

17:1 *Broken.* Job's declaration of trust in God (16:18-22) quickly gives way to renewed complaint and lament, as he faces the stark reality of his suffering, unrelieved by God's intervention. He is not the only one to cry: "O Lord—how long?" (Ps 35:17; 74:10)

17:2 *Mockers.* While God delays, not only does his distress go on unabated, but he also continues to be the target of the cutting taunt that relief was within easy reach if he confessed and repented of his crime.

17:3 *Pledge.* God must give a token of confidence in him if his mockers, with minds "closed" by Him (4), are to be silenced.

17:5 *Will fail.* V. 5 apparently is a proverbial saying. Job quotes it to condemn his detractors. They deserve the punishment which a person deserves who denounces his friend in order thereby to enrich himself.

17:6 *He.* Without mentioning Him by name, Job again declares God responsible for the mockery heaped on him by his acquaintances. Because God tortured him to the point of death, they feel they have good reason to subject him to ridicule and defamation.

17:8 *Appalled.* His hypocritical friends, posing as *upright* and *innocent,* are aghast at the fate which overtook him, the *godless* one. If he were "righteous," he would instead be growing "stronger and stronger." (9)

17:10 *A wise man.* If they *again* make their false charges, he is prepared to dispute their claim to being wise as he did once before. (12:2)

17:12 *Night.* The friends hold out the hope that the night of Job's suffering will change into a day of sunshine and delight, even as the light of dawn comes when it is darkest. All he has to do is follow their simple advice.

17:13 *Sheol.* Job despairs of relief during his lifetime. He is about to experience death and its ravages as intimately as he knew the members of his immediate family. (14)

17:15 *Hope.* Death will not permit him to regain his former "ease" (16:12), thus depriving him of the opportunity to let others *see* the reward his piety really deserved.

18:1-21 BILDAD'S SECOND SPEECH

18:1 *Shuhite.* Cf. 2:11 note. Bildad, impatient, blunt, and inconsiderate as in his first speech (ch. 8), declares that Job's flamboyant rhetoric betrayed how puffed up he was with his own importance. But his angry bluster would not be able to render inoperative the principle of retribution, established by God as immutably as the laws of nature (1-4). Even if he were to "hunt for words" (2) to prove his innocence until he exhausted his entire vocabulary, he could not prove that he was an exception to the universal rule: the wicked do not escape the punishment they deserve. The certainty of their doom should bring Job to his senses. (5-21)

18:2 *Consider.* Rather than accuse them of lacking understanding (17:4) to the point of being stupid as "cattle" (3), Job himself ought to think before he speaks and listen to them.

18:4 *The earth.* His boisterous raging is sheer nonsense. It is as impossible for him to be right as it is unthinkable that God should abolish the laws of nature and let the universe slip back into chaos.

18:5 *Put out.* In the following verses Bildad takes up Job's claim that "those who provoke God are secure" (12:6). It is an established fact that the doom of the wicked is inevitable and horrible. Its graphic description implies that Job too is suffering the consequences of his wickedness. For Bildad's earlier insinuation of Job's guilt see 8:11-19.

18:8 *His own feet.* Ps 9:15.

18:12 *Hunger-bitten. Calamity* seeks to devour him as eagerly as a hungry person craves food; it is ready to pounce on him the moment it sees him *stumbling.*

18:13 *First-born of death.* The kind of disease which ranks first in the number of victims it had to its credit. No doubt a reference to Job's dread malady.

18:14 *King of terrors.* Among the terrors besetting man, death reigns supreme.

18:15 *Brimstone is scattered.* As on Sodom and Gomorrah. (Gn 19:24 note; Dt 29:22 f.)

18:20 *West . . . east.* The news of the wicked man's ultimate fate creates consternation from one end of the world to the other.

19:1-29 JOB'S FIFTH RESPONSE

19:1 *Job answered.* He opens his reply to Bildad by underscoring what he said previously. His friends are not comforters but tireless tormentors. They refuse to believe that God is wronging him (1-7) by assaulting and degrading him (8-12) so that he has become a social outcast, shunned even by his own family (13-19). In the second part of the speech there is a change of attitude towards his friends and to God: (a) he no longer exchanges recriminations and insults with his visitors, but pleads with them at least to have pity on him in his misery (20-22), leaving it to future generations to pass judgment on his case (23 f.); (b) he no longer calls God to account for inflicting undeserved punishment on him, demanding restitution in this world, but confidently looks for deliverance from all evil when he sees God in the life beyond the grave. (25-29)

19:3 *Ten times.* An idiomatic expression like our "at least a dozen times." Job is compelled to "hunt for words" (18:2) because his friends persist in tormenting him with reproaches.

19:4 *With myself.* Job insists that any *error* which he possibly committed should be none of their concern. Their unsympathetic and insulting manner made him forget that brotherly admonition is required by the law of love. (Gl 6:1)

19:7 *No justice.* No one listens to his protestations of innocence because his "humiliation," imposed by God "without cause," is considered proof of his guilt.

19:9 *Crown.* He considered his reputation for righteousness and justice his crowning glory. (29:14)

19:11 *Adversary.* God acts like an enemy commander who sends wave after wave of "fresh hosts" (10:17) against a city which he wants leveled to the ground. (16:9, 14)

19:19 *Intimate friends.* Humiliated and discredited by loss of status, repulsive because of his loathsome disease, he is snubbed by his servants, bombarded by catcalls from juveniles, rejected by his most intimate friends and associates including his brothers and his wife. He on whom God laid "the iniquity of us all" was not spared the disgrace of being rejected of men and the torment of being forsaken of God. (Is 53:1-6; Ps 22:1; Mt 27:46)

19:22 *My flesh.* To eat someone's flesh was an idiomatic expression for slander. To the affliction from "the hand of God" (21) they add their insatiable urge to tear his reputation to bits.

19:24 *For ever.* Job does not expect to receive justice during his lifetime. Therefore he wants his case to become a matter of indelible record, confident that coming generations will side with him against his friends.

19:25 *I know.* The "dimly burning wick" of Job's faith (Is 42:3; Mt 12:20) suddenly bursts into a bright flame only to have it all but extinguished, smothered by doubts and despair. He abruptly turns from his complaints against God to commit himself to Him in a climactic declaration of unreserved trust in His power and will to deliver him. Rising above his request for an "umpire" (9:33 ff.) and his appeal to God to be his advocate (16:18 ff.), Job exults in the hope of full restoration after death. (25-27)

The Hebrew text in its present form presents some difficulties. However, Job's words have been preserved clearly enough for the following meaning to emerge: (a) He expects to be in God's presence; (b) God will no longer afflict him but be his Redeemer; (c) he expects God to appear in his behalf even though he has returned to the dust of the ground from which he and all were made (Gn 2:7); (d) he will have eyes to see God even though nothing remains of his flesh, covered with skin as it is now; (e) in this new mode of existence his identity will be preserved.

Job's faith in deliverance from all evil after death was indeed "the conviction of things not seen" (Heb 11:1). He did not live to see God's victory over death, man's "last enemy," become a reality in His Son's resurrection. However, even after Easter the promise of the resurrection of the body still is "an assurance of things hoped for." By what process "the mortal puts on immortality" remains a mystery not to be understood by reason but to be accepted by faith (1 Co 15:51 ff.). Job already said what needs to be known: he will be with his Redeemer and will see "whom he believed." (Ph 1:23; 2 Co 5:8; Rv 1:7; 22:4; Mt 24:30; 2 Ti 1:12)

Redeemer. In Hebrew this noun is derived from a verb denoting various kinds of action beneficial to a person who cannot help himself. A man acts as a redeemer of his fellowman when, as his next of kin, he (a) redeems him from slavery (Lv 25:25); (b) prevents the extinction of his kin's name by marrying his widow (Ru 2:20); (c) avenges the death of a murdered nearest of kin (Nm 35:12, 19-28). God's redeeming action too is undeserved kindness to men inasmuch as they are victims of forces from which they cannot extricate themselves. He redeemed Israel when the chosen nation faced extinction in Egyptian slavery and later in the Babylonian exile (Ps 77:15; 78:35; Is 43:1, 14; 49:7, 26). God's redemption comes to the rescue of orphans and widows, of the downtrodden and persecuted, of those in death's grip (Pr 23:11; Gn 48:16; Ps 69:18; 119:154; 103:4). Job is persuaded that God's redemptive power does not stop short at the grave. He commits himself to the care of Him whose mercy is from everlasting to everlasting even though he does not understand why his life in this world has become such a nightmare.

At last. He who is the First and the Last, the Alpha and Omega, is not affected by the passing of time. (Is 41:4; 44:6; 48:12; Rv 1:17; 2:8; 21:6; 22:12 f.)

19:26 *From my flesh.* The RSV footnote is misleading. Job again has bodily flesh (27), from which his eyes look out to *see God.* Justified by faith and restored to communion with God, Job has no fear to "behold his face" and "shall understand fully" the riddle of his suffering. (Ps 11:7; 1 Co 13:12)

19:27 *On my side.* More lit. "for me." God will be his "adversary" no longer. (11)

Not another. The person at peace with God after death will be none other than the same individual who now suffers and laments.

Faints. To try to comprehend what all this means is so overwhelming as to leave him exhausted and limp.

19:28 *Pursue him.* Convinced of eventual redemption, Job warns his friends that they will have to answer for persecuting him. If they persist in their false charges, the "sword" of divine justice will overtake them as surely as a root, though hidden from view, sends stalks or stems to the surface. (Ps 7:12; Is 31:8; 34:6)

20:1-29 ZOPHAR'S SECOND SPEECH: THE WICKED PERISH

20:1 *Naamathite.* Cf. 2:11 note. In the second cycle of speeches Zophar is again the last to take the floor (ch. 11). Indignant at Job's insulting replies, he vigorously defends his previous contention that when a man is wicked, God's punishment does not fail to overtake him. Evil doers may triumph momentarily, but their "exulting is short" (1-11). Their pleasures fail to bring them lasting satisfaction (12-19). Terrors dog their steps until destruction overtakes them (20-29). Zophar, though not referring to Job by name, is pointing him out as a clear case in point.

20:2 *Therefore.* Because Job insulted him (19:2, 29), Zophar has been chafing at the bit to put him in his place with an answer he had ready for some time.

20:3 *A spirit.* He claims to have received a special revelation (4:12 ff.) or at least to speak only after due deliberation so that he makes sense whereas Job's words were nothing but "a great wind." (8:2; 11:2 f.; 15:2)

20:8 *Vision.* The successes of the wicked have no more substance than the phantom creations of a dream. (Is 29:8; Ps 73:20; 90:5)

20:10 *Favor of the poor.* His children will be forced to go begging.

20:12 *Sweet.* Pleasure derived from sinful gains is deceptive. What at first seems as sweet as a piece of candy, which the taste buds savor as long as possible, turns out to be as bitter as "the gall of asps." (14 Pr 20:17; 23:31 f.)

20:15 *Vomits.* God forces the wicked to give up their spoils as poison makes a person disgorge what he has eaten.

20:17 *Rivers.* Struck down suddenly as if bitten by "a viper" (16), he will no longer feast his eyes on the irrigated canals which turned his acres into "a land flowing with milk and honey." (Ex 3:8)

20:20 *No rest.* His greed was insatiable; everything fell a prey to it.

20:22 *In straits.* At the height of enjoyment, sudden ruin will squeeze him to the wall.

20:23 *To the full.* As he filled his belly to bursting with the fruits of wickedness, so God *will send His fierce anger into him* in overflowing measure. It will penetrate his innermost being, wounding him "in his flesh." (RSV: *as his food)*

20:24 *Arrow.* Should he escape an iron spear, the bronze tip of an arrow, shot into his vitals, will bring on him the "terrors" of death.

20:26 *Not blown upon.* The fire which will *devour him* is not started and fanned by man. It is the hot flame of God's devastation.

20:27 *Heavens.* Job sought vindication from a "witness" in heaven and wanted the "earth" to testify to the injustice done him (16:18 f.). Zophar counters that heavenly justice stirs earthly agencies to *rise up* to deliver "the wicked man's portion from God." (29)

21:1-34 JOB'S SIXTH SPEECH: THE WICKED FLOURISH

21:1 *Job answered.* Zophar and his two companions held doggedly to their verdict that Job's suffering was divine retribution for unconfessed crimes. Punishment for sin as well as reward for virtue was God's automatic reaction to man. Hence there could be only one explanation for pain and misery. In this chapter Job attacks this basic rationale of his comforters. He asks them to listen to him and to face the facts even though the true state of affairs leaves him and them with a riddle as frightening as it is insoluble (1-6). For experience proves beyond doubt that the wicked, even blasphemers, reach "old age and grow mighty in power" (7-16). There is no evidence that virtue or wickedness determine the kind of life in store for man (17-26). For it is a known fact that "the wicked man" not only dies unavenged but also receives an honorable funeral and is eulogized as a hero deserving emulation. (27-34)

21:2 *Your consolation.* Instead of bringing him "consolations of God," as they professed (15:11), they turned out to be "miserable comforters." The only consolation they can afford him is to listen to him while he unburdens himself of his complaints.

21:3 *Mock on.* After Job is through speaking, they may not be inclined to continue making him the butt of their ridicule.

21:5 *Appalled.* What he has to say is not a "complaint against man" (4) but concerns divine providence. Therefore the facts in the matter, about to be presented by him, are as shocking to him as they must be to them. Confronted with the prosperity of the wicked, they will shut their mouth in awe (40:4; Mi 7:16). The riddle of God's inscrutable ways must produce "shuddering" and trepidation.

21:7 *Why . . . ?* This question is directed ultimately to God, for it is He who grants the wicked not only joy "for a moment" (20:5) but also the enjoyment of good things to a ripe *old age.* They have and keep everything Job lost: health, children (8), safety from fear (9), growing herds (10), happy family gatherings (11 f.), a painless, peaceful death. (13)

21:9 *Safe from fear.* The friends' statements were not true to facts. (15:28; 18:14; 20:28)

Rod of God. Job felt its blows. (9:34)

21:13 *In peace.* A quick easy death and not after a disabling and painful illness like Job's.

21:14 *They say.* The recipients of all these good things do not only ignore God, they also are in open rebellion against Him, blatantly declaring their independence of Him and claiming that their prosperity is not God's doing but the product of "their hand." (16; 34:9; Ex 5:2; Dt 8:17; Ps 73:8 f.; Ml 3:14 f.)

21:16 *Far from me.* Job does not want their godless behavior to affect him.

21:17 *How often . . . ?* Job questions the validity of the statements that "the light of the wicked is put out" (18:5 f.), that "calamity is ready for his stumbling" (18:12), that "God will send His fierce anger into him (20:23), that the wicked will be "swept away" "like straw before the wind." (18; 15:30)

21:19 *Stores up.* If the friends would point out that the wicked may escape punishment themselves but that God nevertheless inflicts it on his sons, Job would counter that justice is not done if the evildoer is not the first to "drink the wrath of the Almighty." (20; Ex 20:5; Ps 75:8; Is 51:17; Jer 25:15; Rv 14:10)

21:22 *Teach God.* Job accuses his friends of presuming to tell the transcendent God how to administer justice, forgetting that he was guilty of the same rebellious behavior inasmuch as he complained about God's dealing with him. See Job's complaint 9:22-24.

21:27 *Your thoughts.* Job lets the friends know he realizes that their description of the horrible fate of the wicked was aimed at him. They *wrong* him with their insinuations that he is getting what he deserves. As proof that God's justice cannot be reduced to a mechanical formula of action and counterthrust, he demands evidence for their claim that crimes do not go unpunished in this life.

21:33 *Follow after him.* The wicked is accorded every honor at death. His mourners hear his praises sung. They are told to model their lives after his illustrious career.

21:34 *Empty nothings.* Their arguments, when tested, vanish into thin air. It was false *comfort* to tell him his suffering would end if he repented of the sin for which he was being punished.

22:1-30 ELIPHAZ' THIRD SPEECH

22:1 *Temanite.* Cf. 2:11 note. Eliphaz, the first to speak in the two previous discussion cycles (4:1; 15:1), again takes the floor to open the final round of speeches. The point at issue remains the same. Job, he says again, brought on his calamity himself; it is God's punishment for some unconfessed sin. However, the debate has become increasingly vehement in tone. No effort is made to spare Job's feelings. The more or less veiled insinuations of guilt give way to a direct indictment with an attached bill of particulars. Ignoring Job's pleas of innocence, Eliphaz bluntly asserts that divine justice finally has caught up with his friend's "wickedness." There is no other way to explain his suffering (1-5). Eliphaz confronts Job with a list of the kind of "iniquities" of which he must be guilty to be punished as he is. For "sudden terror overwhelms" anyone who exploits his defenseless fellowman even though he deludes himself into thinking that God "does not see it" (6-11). Job cannot escape the fate God decreed on "wicked men" in the past (12-20). His only hope of averting doom and of attaining former bliss is to "return to the Almighty," penitently confessing his guilt and sincerely resolving to "remove unrighteousness far from his tent." (21-30)

22:2 *Profitable to God.* In high dudgeon, Eliphaz blurts out some questions to prove how logical his conclusion is that "there is no end to your [Job's] iniquities." Everyone will readily agree that God is not concerned with human response to Him because man's behavior adds to or detracts from the perfection of His being. He does not punish sin because He is dependent on man's "righteous" or "blameless" behavior to make up a deficiency in Himself.

22:4 *Fear of him.* For the meaning of *fear* see 1:6 note; Dt 6:13 note. It is true that God does not need man. However, it does not follow that He is indifferent to virtue or vice (see Is 64:5; Lk 17:10). Acting from moral principles, he simply rewards or punishes man according to his deeds. Job's suffering only can be God's "judgment" on his great "wickedness." (5)

22:6 *Exacted pledges.* Eliphaz enumerates certain heinous crimes against fellowmen of which Job must be guilty to be punished as severely as he is. He could be a pitiless creditor (Ex 22:26; Dt 24:6, 17; Am 2:8), a man untouched by human misery (7; Is 58:7; Eze 18:16; Mt 10:42), an unscrupulous, land-hungry baron (8; Is 5:8; Mi 2:2), an exploiter rather than a supporter of the helpless. (9; Ex 22:22-24; Dt 10:17 f.; 27:19; Jer 7:6 f.; 22:3)

22:13 *You say.* Job sinned against the laws regulating society. He also degraded God claiming that He does not see whether man keeps His commandments or not. In making this charge Eliphaz is misquoting Job. He did indeed say that God treats the good and evil alike (21:23-26) but not that He is unconcerned with earthly affairs. For *deep darkness* and "thick clouds" which "wrap him" (14) see Ex 20:18; 1 K 8:12; Ps 18:11.

22:15 *Old way.* Job is on the pathway of ungrateful (18) blasphemers. In the past it led to sudden and complete destruction. The language used to describe the acts of God's judgments suggests that Eliphaz is thinking of such disasters as the flood (16) and the destruction of Sodom. (20)

22:18 *Far from me.* Eliphaz disassociates himself from their wicked way of life as insistently as did Job. (21:16)

22:21 *Agree with God.* If Job's estrangement from God (1-14) is not to be his undoing (15-20), he must recognize his suffering as God's visitation on his sins, repent of them, seek forgiveness, and so be *at peace* with God and accept his guidance.

22:24 *Gold in the dust.* Job's past action was motivated by love for gold. If we would regard this precious metal no higher than the *dust* on the street or *stones* on a river bed and would rather make God the "gold" and delight of his heart, he would again enjoy bliss and prosperity.

22:28 *Be established.* Urging Job to serve God so that "good will come" to him was playing into Satan's hands. The latter was out to prove that even such a "blameless" man as Job did not love and serve God "for nought." (1:9)

22:29 *The proud.* Cf. Pr 3:34; Mt 23:12; Ja 4:6; 1 Ptr 5:5.

22:30 *The innocent.* The Hebrew text, cited in the RSV note, declares that God delivers even a man like Job, who is not innocent, if he admits his faults and repents of them.

23:1—24:25 JOB'S SEVENTH SPEECH

23:1 *Job answered.* He resents Eliphaz' accusation that he is guilty of unconfessed crimes. In rebuttal he insists that God is inscrutable in his treatment of him individually (ch. 23) and of mankind in general (ch. 24). As far as his own case is concerned, Job is certain that God could not convict him of wrongdoing in a court of justice (1-7). But God remains inaccessible, refusing to grant him a fair trial (8-17). His is not an isolated case. Injustice prevails on a wide scale. For God "pays no attention" when the underprivileged are reduced to an animal existence (24:1-12). Criminals, operating under cover of darkness, are not apprehended and punished (24:13-17). Contrary to the claim of the friends, the good life of the wicked is not cut short (24:18-20) because God condones and even rewards evil. (24:21-25)

23:2 *Today also.* Even now after listening to his friends' weary efforts to comfort him, he is in a *bitter* or defiant mood, unable to restrain his *groaning.*

23:3 *Find him.* Pleas for an answer to the riddle of his suffering go unanswered. If only he could reach God to summon Him to trial, he would have so good a "case" to plead that he would be "acquitted" of the charges made by his friends (7). At least God would have to "answer" and explain why He treats His creature as He does.

23:6 *Greatness of his power.* As at previous occasions, Job expressed misgivings that God would meet him on equal terms, fearing to be overwhelmed by a show of terrifying power. (9:4 note; 13:13 f.)

23:8 *Go forward.* Probing in all directions of the compass, Job encounters only silence.

23:10 *Gold.* The trial would not act as a purifying fire. There is no dross of wickedness in his behavior which needs to be removed.

23:12 *Commandment.* What more than compliance with His commandments could God expect?

23:13 *Unchangeable.* God is unique in this that no one can force him to deviate from a course He has taken, terrifying to man as "such things" (14) may be as He decrees. Shrouded in "thick darkness," Job trembles at the thought of not knowing what to expect.

24:1 *Times of judgment.* God is responsible for letting crime inundate society. Lawlessness would soon end, if without delay He were to arraign the villains before a court of justice. *Those who know him* and take Him at His word have a right to expect such action. But *his days* of prosecution and judgment never come. For "the days of the Lord" as a term denoting an appointed time of judgment see Jer 46:10; Jl 1:15; 2:1 f.; Am 5:18-20.

24:2 *Landmarks.* Cf. Dt 19:14; Is 5:8; Hos 5:10.

24:5 *Wild asses.* The poor are treated like animals. Exploited, cowed into submission, forced into slavery, they sustain themselves with "fodder" (6:5), the food thrown to cattle in the field.

24:6 *Glean.* Dispossessed of their own land, the poor have nothing to harvest except the stray leavings in the field and vineyard of *the wicked man.*

24:10 *Carry the sheaves.* Desperately in need of sustenance, they dare not prepare food from the sheaves they are harvesting. Nor are they permitted to have any of the oil they are pressing from olives or any of the wine they tread from grapes.

24:12 *Their prayer.* The prayer of the downtrodden. If the consonants of the Hebrew noun are supplied with the same vowels as in 1:22, a word meaning "guilt" or "reprehensible behavior" results. Then Job is saying God *pays no attention* to the deplorable situation just described.

24:13 *Against the light.* As God does nothing about the open and flagrant degradation of the poor (1-12), so crimes of violence such as murder, adultery, and burglary, committed in secrecy, are allowed to go undetected and unpunished. (13-17; Jn 3:19)

24:14 *Dark.* The Hebrew text has "at the light," i.e., as the light is about to give way to darkness or at "twilight." (15)

24:18 *You say.* In 18-20 Job sarcastically quotes his friends who persist in saying that the kind of evildoers just described *are swiftly carried away* like a piece of driftwood floating "on the face of the waters" (8:18; 15:29 f.; 18:16-20; 20:4-29). The introductory words *You say,* not in the Herew text, are added to alert the reader that these lines were spoken in an ironic tone of voice. Some commentators believe that verses 18-25 are the misplaced conclusion of Bildad's otherwise very brief speech (25:1-6) or that they constitute Zophar's final comment.

24:21 *Childless woman.* Just the opposite of what the friends maintain is true. God comes to the aid of such despicable people as take advantage of a helpless woman who has no sons or a husband to support her.

24:24 *A little while.* They may not exceed the average lifespan of mankind but they depart life peacefully. Death is not preceded by prolonged torture as in Job's case.

25:1-6 BILDAD'S THIRD SPEECH

25:1 *Shuhite.* Cf. 2:11 note. Bildad is the last of the three friends to contribute to the discussion initiated at 4:1. He has very little to say. Zophar has nothing to add. Apparently they consider it useless to elaborate once more on their oft-repeated line of argument. Their rhetoric is exhausted. It is also possible that they came to the conclusion that they were "in the wrong," as Elihu tells them later. (32:3)

25:2 *Dominion and fear.* A fear-producing rulership. Bildad remonstrates with Job for charging God with tolerating gross inequities in directing the affairs of man. Man, the creature of a day, is so inferior to God in power and moral perfection, says Bildad, that criticism of divine providence is as meaningles as the squirming of "a worm."

Peace. God has unchallenged control of celestial powers. (21:22; Is 24:21)

25:3 *His light.* Everything lies bare before His scrutiny, including hidden sin. (Ps 90:8)

25:5 *Not clean.* Cf. 4:18 note; 15:15

26:1-14 JOB'S EIGHTH SPEECH

26:1 *Job answered.* After a sarcastic swipe at Bildad's supercilious display of "wisdom" (2-4), Job again insists: "What you know, I also know" (13:2). To prove it he enlarges on Bildad's portrayal of God's irresistible power and absolute control over the entire universe from top to bottom (5-14). However, Job's problem begins at this point. God, he has been saying, does not use His omnipotence discriminately, subduing the wicked and rewarding those "who know Him." (24:1)

26:4 *Whose help.* Continuing in an ironic vein, Job ridicules the impression the friends give that they are dropping pearls of unsurpassed wisdom whereas he has every reason to ask: "Who does not know such things as these?" (12:3)

26:5 *Shades.* Some scholars believe that 5-14 have become dislocated from their original place in the text. If inserted after 25:6, they would form a fitting close to Bildad's dissertation on God's transcendent majesty. But when this subject came up at other junctures of the discussion, Job not only agreed with the assertions of his comforters but also elaborated on them as he does here (9:1-12; 12:13-25). God's control, he adds, extends to the depths of the sea, the underworld, and the realm of the dead (5 f.). The *shades* of the dead are in "Sheol" (Dt 32:22 note), also called "Abaddon." Pr 15:11; Rv 9:11)

26:7 *Void.* The word so translated Gn 1:2; rendered "chaos" Is 45:18.

Upon nothing. In the figurative language of the OT the earth is said also to rest on "pillars" or "a foundation" just as the heavens are sustained by "pillars" (11; 9:6; 38:4, 6). Creation is a sovereign, effortless act of God, not the result of a conflict between forces of nature, personified and deified as the ancient myths claimed (3:8; 7:12; 9:13 notes). The *north* was considered the primordial home of the gods. (Is 14:13; Eze 1:4)

26:9 *Moon.* In Hebrew the words for throne and moon are very similar. The reading "throne" can be retained. "The Lord has established his throne in the heavens," inaccessible to human eyes. (Ps 103:19)

26:12 *Rahab.* Cf. 9:13 note. Called a "fleeing serpent" in 13.

SUMMARY. The only winner of the long debate (chs. 4—26) between Job and his friends was Satan. The comforters helped him prove his point: no man, even "blameless" Job, serves God "for nothing" (1:9). Stung by their insinuations and accusations that God was punishing him for some black, unconfessed crime, Job was baited into revealing hidden motives of selfishness. At various points in the discussion it became evident that he expected a reward for his piety. The tempter won his case. In the final analysis man does his bidding. If God must buy man's virtue, His claim to his creature's love no longer holds good. In the lengthy discourses by Job (chs. 27—31), he continues to maintain that he deserves better treatment than he received.

27:1—31:40 Self-Love Manifest in Discourses

27:1-23 DISCOURSE ON GUILT AND PUNISHMENT

27:1 *Discourse.* Ch. 26 records Job's last direct reply to his friends. What he has to say now (chs. 27—31) is more in the nature of a dissertation than a challenge to continued dialog (see his lament in ch. 3 preceding the exchange of views with his visitors). The miserable comforters still are addressed in passing (5, 11, 12). It is also clear that the discourse is provoked by points made in the conversation. But the debate is over. It failed to solve Job's problem. He still is "bitter" (2). Under oath he declares the friends were not "right" (5) when they claimed that his suffering only could be the wages of sin (1-6). The "godless" (8) indeed deserve the terrible fate which they have seen befalling him (7-12). However, when God's judgment overtakes the wicked, as it eventually must, it does not follow that his misery likewise is evidence of guilt, deserving the same kind of punishment. (13-23)

27:2 *As God lives.* Reeling under furious blows of misfortune, badgered by "miserable comforters," Job gave way at times to remarks bordering on repudiation of God. Anyone who has staggered through a night of numbing grief knows how readily resentment and frantic determination to cling to God keep surging through his inmost being like successive waves of the sea. Job too is tossed back and forth by conflicting thoughts. What he says at this point has no logical consistency. He acknowledges the sovereignty of God by taking an oath in His name while, almost in the same breath, he accuses Him of being an unjust arbiter of his *right.* (34:5)

27:5 *Are right.* Job cannot be charged with "deceit" (4) in declaring his innocence.

27:7 *Enemy.* Job elaborates his claim that his "heart does not reproach" him (6). A person who because of his wickedness is abhorrent to God is His enemy for the same reason. Not one of "the godless," he does not deserve the retribution God has in store for *the unrighteous.*

27:11 *Teach you.* The friends are "altogether vain," i.e., empty-headed, to insist that *the hand of God* was heavy on him in punishment which "they have seen" God impose on the wicked and which he is about to describe in detail.

27:13 *Portion of a wicked man.* The thoughts expressed in the remaining verses of this chapter appear to be at variance with Job's previous pronouncements on the fate of the wicked (cf. 14 with 21:8; 15 with 21:32). He took issue with his friends when they insisted that divine justice overtakes the criminal without fail. Now he does not hesitate to repeat the very expressions used by Zophar (cf. 13 with 20:29; 20 with 20:23). It has been suggested therefore that 13-23 constitute the final speech of Zophar which through a dislocation of the text came to stand in the wrong context. If, however, the sequence of thought is as suggested in notes on 1 and 7, a textual rearrangement is not necessary. Job at times appropriated the words of his friends (24:18 ff.). He also reversed himself, charging God with injustice and yet trusting Him implicitly. (19:25-27)

27:18 *Spider's web.* No more permanence than a moth's cocoon. (4:19)

27:19 *No more.* Either his wealth disappears overnight, leaving nothing to be gathered in the morning, or during the night his "soul is required of" him. (Lk 12:20)

27:21 *East wind.* Cf. 15:2 note.

28:1-28 DISCOURSE ON TRUE WISDOM

28:1 *Surely.* The Hebrew word is also the conjunction "for." If so translated, it establishes a connection with the foregoing chapter. Calamity is the eventual "portion of a wicked man with God" (27:13) because he spurns the "wisdom" to fear God and the "understanding" to "depart from evil" (28). Rejection of this wisdom is a fatal mistake, no matter how ingenious man may be in other matters. He may develop techniques to make the earth yield its hidden treasures so that "his eye sees every precious thing" (1-11). But he cannot discover the priceless gem of wisdom even though he probes for it in the vast reaches of creation and even though he is willing to pay any price for it (12-19). God alone has the key to mysteries of the universe because He called it into being and knows how to control it. Man, himself the product of that creative wisdom, is truly wise only as he accepts "the wisdom from above" (Ja 3:15-18). It is not an intellectual achievement or a construct of abstractions but a way of life, centered in the all-wise God. In all issues He is the undisputed and exclusive point of reference. His will determines every choice of action. (20-28)

28:2 *Out of the earth.* Man has inventive capacities far superior to the instinct of animals (7). He may be able to sink "shafts" into the earth (4) to uncover all kinds of mineral deposits and costly stones. But no technological breakthrough gives access to the one thing needful: the wisdom to live in harmony with the Creator resulting in "the peace of God, which passes all understanding." (Ph 4:7)

28:13 *Land of the living.* Mines may yield every precious thing (10). But wisdom is the "one pearl of great value" (Mt 13:46) which eludes man's search no matter where in the universe he searches and which he cannot acquire no matter how rich he is.

28:16 *Ophir.* Cf. 1 K 9:26 note.

28:22 *Abaddon.* Cf. 26:5 note. You may scale the heavens like "the birds of the air" or dig deep into the earth to the underworld; wisdom will remain "hid from the eyes of all living."

28:23 *Knows its place.* Only God knows where to acquire true wisdom because it has its source in Him. Witness thereof is the creation and preservation of the universe. (1 Co 1:21; 2:7; Ro 11:33 ff.)

28:28 *He said.* Man is dependent on God for instruction if he is to be able to order his life in a way which alone deserves to be called wise. He remains a fool who does not let *the fear of the Lord* motivate and direct all he thinks and does. Oriented in this wisdom, he moves beyond slavish fear to accord his Creator the awe, respect, veneration, and trust He deserves (Dt 6:13 note; Ps 111:10; Pr 1:7; 9:10). The negative aspect of this *understanding* is the determination to *depart from evil.*

Identifying godliness with wisdom accentuates Job's problem. He professed to fear the Lord and depart from evil. Yet God did not treat him as his living in accord with wisdom and understanding deserved. In his discourse, recorded in the next chapters, he again proves Satan right; he does not serve God "for nought." (1:9)

29:1—31:40 FINAL DISCOURSE: REVIEW OF LIFE'S RIDDLE

29:1 *His discourse.* In principle Job subscribed to the doctrine he just propounded that "the fear of the Lord . . . is wisdom" (28:28). However, he cannot understand why a God-fearing way of life did not continue to be rewarded by the benefits he once received in such abundance. Again lapsing into a monolog similar to his lament preceding the discussion with his friends (ch. 3), he gives a final review of his mysterious experiences (chs. 29—31). Only a short time ago fellowship with God and kindness to fellowmen paid high dividends in his life (ch. 29). In favor with God and men, he had every reason to expect a long, peaceful existence on this earth. "But now" he has lost everything: honor among men, physical well-being, fellowship with God, peace of mind (ch. 30). He cannot explain why when he "looked for good, evil came" (30:26). He did not incur guilt in thought, word, or deed, making him liable to punishment. If he could argue his case in a court of justice, his plea of innocence would be upheld. But God does not answer him (ch. 31). To Satan's delight the underlying principle with which Job operates bears out the tempter's contention that his love for God is in reality self-love. His "fear of the Lord" failed to yield the wages of a good life. Profit, not love, motivated his piety.

1) 29:1-25 Former Godliness and Resulting Bliss

29:2 *Months of old.* Only recently Job basked in the sunshine of God's favor. (Nm 6:25)

29:3 *Darkness.* The light of God's countenance guided him through perplexities besetting his path. (Ps 139:12; Mi 7:8)

29:4 *Autumn days.* As crops and fruits reach the stage of maturity in fall, so Job attained full manhood, enjoying the blessings of a close fellowship with God. The Hebrew word for *friendship* has the connotation of intimate and confidential association. It is translated "council" (15:8), "intimate [friends]" (19:19), "[sweet] converse" (Ps 55:14).

29:6 *Washed with milk.* A figure of speech denoting an overabundance of resources. Canaan is described as "a land flowing with milk and honey" (Ex 3:8; cf. 20:17). *Streams of* olive *oil* are said to pour forth from infertile rocks.

29:7 *Gate.* God-fearing and God-protected (1-4), the head of a happy family (5), a man of uncounted wealth (6), Job commanded the respect of young and old, of prince and pauper (7-10, 21-25). When the council of elders met or when court was held in *the gate of the city* (Dt 22:15; Ru 4:1), everyone deferred to his opinion, acclaiming him "the greatest of all the people of the east." (1:3)

29:11 *Blessed.* The respect paid Job was not fear of reprisal. He did not climb to the top by exploiting the misfortunes of others. He earned everyone's esteem by acts of kindness. He used his wealth and influence to help the poor and to right wrongs inflicted on the downtrodden.

27:17 *Fangs.* Job did not hesitate to incur the hostility of *the unrighteous* in order to rescue their innocent victims from imminent disaster at their hands. (Pr 30:14)

29:18 *I thought.* He expected his fellowship with God and his social righteousness to guarantee him security for the rest of his days. He would live to a ripe old age as comfortably and snugly as a bird in its *nest.*

29:20 *Bow.* Nourished like "a tree planted by streams of water" (Ps 1:3), his *glory* or renown among men would "not wither" nor would the *bow* of his strength loose its tautness. (Gn 49:24; Ps 18:34)

29:21 *Listened to me.* The first misfortune Job is about to mention is the loss of the high respect accorded him by his fellowmen (30:1-15). In order to heighten the contrast between then and now, he describes once more how men formerly hung on every word he uttered.

29:22 *Dropped.* His word refreshed drooping spirits as rain revitalizes parched ground. (Dt 32:2; Pr 19:12)

29:24 *I smiled.* No matter how dejected people were, his smile restored their confidence.

29:25 *Their way.* When he suggeted a course of action, people followed his advice.

2) 30:1-31 Complete Reversal of Status

30:1 *But now.* Occurring again in 9 and 16, this phrase frames the content of the chapter. Job's present situation is the very opposite of what he once was and had. Gone is the esteem of the noblest; now the dregs of society dare to heap indignities on him (1-8), vilifying and taunting him in droves (9-15). Gone is health of body, peace of mind, friendship with God; now even plaintive cries for mercy go unheeded (16-23). Gone is the sound of cheering music; now discordant wails of grief fill the air. (24-31)

Younger. Formerly honored by the aged and the young, by princes and nobles (29:8-9), Job now has no standing in the community. No one comes to his defense when the impudent young or even the most disreputable and degenerate characters open their vile mouths to *make sport of* him. In the next verses Job goes to some length to describe this "brood" of detractors as the scum of society in order to bring out the stark contrast between his present degradation and the former admiration he received from the best who treated him "like a king." (29:25)

30:3 *Gnaw the . . . ground.* Reduced to drawing sustenance from the most unfertile soil, they eke out a precarious existence.

30:4 *mallow.* A herb growing in salt marshes, also called salt wort.

30:7 *Bray.* Their behavior is more animallike than human.

30:9 *Song.* Job is the subject of their taunt and ridicule. (Lm 3:14)

30:11 *Loosed my cord.* He no longer has the strength to pull his bowstring taut enough to shoot an arrow to ward off assaults. (cf. 29:20)

30:12 *Cast up.* As enemy troops raise siege works against a city, so they close in on him intent on his destruction.

30:14 *Wide reach.* Once besiegers have breached the wall of a city, they pour in through the opening, overrunning the population.

30:16 *Poured out.* In lamentation.

30:18 *Garment.* Perhaps a figurative allusion to his skin disfigured by disease. The second line of the verse seems to say that his tunic fits him tightly because his body is swollen.

30:19 *God.* What makes Job's suffering unbearable is the fact that God, who is responsible for his misery, pays no attention to his cries. (20)

3:23 *The house.* The paths of *all living* meet eventually at death's door.

30:24 *Heap of ruins.* The RSV translation of this difficult verse suggests Job appealed to God as desperately as a man threatened with the total collapse of his world or as frantically as a drowning person stretches out his hand for help. But all his attempts to "seek God," as his friends advised him to do, were in vain. (5:8)

30:25 *Weep.* If God only were as sympathetic to him as he was to those who needed help in distress!

30:26 *Looked for good.* In view of his integrity Job felt he had every reason to expect a pleasant and bright future (29:18-20). However, now his days are evil and dark.

30:28 *Blackened.* Job is referring to the blackness of mourning engulfing his soul or to the discoloration of his skin caused by his disease. (30)

30:29 *Jackals . . . ostriches.* His "cry for help" (28) is no longer an articulated plea. It resembles the howls of jackals and the strident shriek of the ostrich.

30:31 *Lyre . . . pipe.* The gay sound of musical instruments has gone out of his life, leaving it to be filled with mourning and weeping.

3) 31:1-40 Suffering Not Provoked by Guilt

31:1 *How . . . could I.* Job is at a loss to account for the catastrophic changes in his life, portrayed in the two previous chapters. However, he is certain of one thing. All accusations of his friends to the contrary, there is no hidden sin in his past. If there were, God would be aware of it and would have just cause to let the kind of "calamity befall" him which overtakes "the workers of iniquity" (2-4). To prove his innocence, Job subjects himself to a thorough self-examination. He probes his conscience for any possible offense down to the stirring of evil thoughts in his heart. His eyes did not *look upon a virgin* to lust after her (1; Mt 5:28). God knows he maintained "integrity" in dealing with fellowmen (5-8). No charge of adultery can be brought against him (9-12). His treatment of his servants will stand up under God's scrutiny (13-15). The poor, the widows, the orphans testify to his compassion for them (16-23). No idol was permitted to take the place in his heart claimed by God (24-28). Kindness to fellowmen extended to enemies and strangers (29-34). If only an "indictment" of specific wrongdoing were drawn up! Then he could disprove the charge publicly and display the document as proof of his innocence (35-37). As he closes his monolog, one more kind of transgression comes to mind which, if on his record, could account for his suffering: the unlawful acquisition and use of land. If this charge were made, he would disprove it too, declaring his innocence under oath. (38-40)

Made a covenant. He had as it were a contract with his eyes not to act as purveyors of temptation. (Mt 6:22)

31:7 *From the way.* Prescribed by the law of love for his neighbor (23:11). He did not let his heart covet what his eyes saw but could come into his possession only by "falsehood" and "deceit."

31:8 *Let me.* Job is willing to invoke a curse on himself to prove the truth of his words. See the oath formula in Ru 1:17 note.

31:9 *Lain in wait.* For an opportunity to ravish the neighbor's wife.

31:10 *Grind for another.* Let her become another's slave, forced to grind meal and to yield herself to her master's sexual desires. (Ex 11:5; Dt 28:30)

31:11 *By the judges.* Cf. Dt 22:22

31:12 *Abaddon.* Cf. 26:5 note.

31:15 *Made me.* Job did not treat his servants like chattel but like fellow human beings, aware that he as well as they were the handiwork of the same Creator. (Ml 2:10; Eph 3:9; Cl 4:1; Pr 14:31; 22:2)

31:16 *To fail.* To grow dim in disappointment.

31:20 *Loins . . . blessed me.* In gratitude for supplying them with clothing.

31:21 *Help in the gate.* Job did not use his influence with the judges (29:7 ff.) to win favorable action against orphans. For a miscarriage of justice see 1 K 21:8-14.

31:24 *My trust.* He did not try to "serve God and mammon." (Mt 6:24; cf. Mk 10:25)

31:26 *Sun . . . moon.* Worship of heavenly bodies, prevalent in the ancient world (2 K 21:3-5; Jer 44:17-18; Eze 8:16), has survived in superstitious trust in horoscopes.

31:27 *Kissed my hand.* He did not raise his hand to his mouth as a gesture of veneration. (Cf. 1 K 19:18; Hos 13:2)

31:28 *Iniquity.* Reference is to a crime punishable by death. (Dt 17:2-7)

31:29 *Hated me.* Cf. Ex 23:4 f.; Pr 24:17; 25:21.

31:31 *Who is there . . . ?* Members of his household knew of no one turned away hungry.

31:33 *Concealed.* Job had no *transgressions* to hide which, if known, would have exposed him to the wrath of the "multitude" (34). He did not fear to walk about tall and fearless in his community.

31:35 *Signature.* Job once again challenges God to submit to a court of justice (9:32; 13:22; 23:3 f.). Such a trial could produce no evidence of crimes on his part of the kind enumerated in the preceding verses or of any other kind. Unafraid of being proved a liar and perjurer, he would sign an affidavit attesting his innocence. He wants the *adversary* or prosecutor to prefer charges against him. He would prove the absurdity of such an *indictment* so convincingly that he would display it in public as a badge of his rectitude.

31:38 *Cried out.* In a final declaration of good conscience Job calls on the *land* to rise up in testimony against him if he had no legal right to it and its "yield."

SUMMARY. In his discourses (chs. 27—31) Job arrives at no solution to his problem. However, his speeches are marked by more moderation. He is able to suppress the rebellious thoughts which came to the surface in the earlier stages of his struggle with unbelief, aggravated as it was by his "miserable comforters." He is also more positive in declaring his determination to come to terms with God. However, there still is clear evidence that his "fear of the Lord" is polluted with selfishness. Satan is right. He does not serve the Lord "for nought" (1:9). Before the Lord sets him right (chs. 38 ff.), Elihu, a fifth speaker, gives a new direction to the discussion, which he hopes will calm the tempest raging in Job's soul (chs. 32–37). The latter will have nothing to say in reply to the new speaker. "The words of Job are ended" (31:40) except for a brief acknowledgment of his sinful presumption in challenging God's way with him. (40:3-5; 42:1-6)

32:1—37:24 Self-Love Exposed by Elihu

32:1—33:33 ELIHU'S FIRST SPEECH

32:1 *Ceased.* Job's three friends let his extended discourse (chs. 27—31) go unchallenged. When "no answer" was forthcoming from them, a young man named Elihu stepped forward from the circle of listeners to improve on the efforts of his elders. With youthful vigor and self-reliance he undertook to prove Job "in the wrong" (3) to claim that *he was righteous* and that God was "in the wrong" (40:8). Before taking up the issues, he exhorts both his seniors and Job to heed his words, even though he is their junior. The three friends, he says, will realize when he gives his "opinion" that their age itself did not guarantee them wisdom superior to his (6-14). It is evident that "they have not a word to say" while he is "full of words" (15-22). Turning to Job, he assures him that he need not fear to hear what he has to say. His words express the sincere concern of a human being for his fellow creature (33:1-7). Preliminaries over, Elihu proceeds to the fallacies in Job's case against God. He attaches his remarks to the point he just heard Job make: "There is no iniquity in me." (Ch. 31; 33:9)

Elihu's speeches (chs. 32—37) are aimed at correcting the basic flaw in Job's relationship to God which came to light in the discussion with the three older friends. He did not serve God "for nought" (1:9). Because he expected a reward for his piety, he ranted against God's administration of justice. Before God Himself appears on the scene (38—42), Elihu plays the role of His defense attorney. He has "something to say on God's behalf" in order to "ascribe righteousness to" his Maker (36:2 f.). In defending divine providence he operates in part with the principles advocated by the elder speakers. However, he does not attempt to relate them primarily and directly to Job's situation, as they did, but rather urges him to see himself in the perspective of God's absolute perfection. God, he points out, is just for the simple reason that He is God, the almighty Creator of the universe and the omniscient Ruler of heaven and earth. Unaffected in His being by the behavior of puny men, God nevertheless is concerned about the destiny of the work of His hand. According to His good and gracious will, He uses affliction to correct and purify them.

32:2 *Rather than God.* Job's complaint of suffering in spite of his innocence (ch. 31) was an attack on God's justice.

32:8 *Spirit.* Growing older does not always make a person wise (7). Man gets true wisdom as the Spirit of God supplies it.

32:13 *Beware.* A warning against conceit. Because they failed to refute Job, they should not conclude that no one else can do so.

32:14 *Your speeches.* Elihu will not have to present their warmed-over arguments for the simple reason that he is not going to follow their untenable line of reasoning.

32:18 *Constrains me.* Elihu feels the same inner compulsion to speak which moved the prophets to proclaim their message. (Am 3:8; Mi 3:8; Jer 20:9; 2 Ptr 1:21)

32:21 *Partiality.* He has no ax to grind, no favors to seek. If he did, he deserves to be silenced by God.

33:1 *O Job.* Elihu's approach is conciliatory and more intimate in tone than the formal and more aloof style of the three friends, who did not address Job by name.

33:6 *Piece of clay.* Elihu tries to put Job into a receptive mood for his message. He is sincere and has no ulterior motive (3; cf. Job's impression of his friends 6:25). Furthermore, he will not be able to "crush" him with a display of unearthly power and superhuman wisdom such as Job feared God might resort to in order to "terrify" him (9:16-17, 34-35; 13:20-22). Elihu is in the same relationship "toward God," the Creator, as Job.

33:9 *Clean.* Promising Job an honest man-to-man talk (1-7), Elihu launches into his first defense "on God's behalf" (36:2). He finds it necessary to "ascribe righteousness" to his Maker (36:3) because he heard Job repeatedly claim that God treated him like a criminal even though he was "without transgression" (8-11). In fact Job had just held forth at length on his innocence (ch. 30). The young defense counsel, wiser than the three older friends, does not become involved in a discussion of Job's alleged virtues, as they did to no avail. He prefers to build his whole case on God's integrity. He begins with a refutation of Job's charge that man is kept in total ignorance of God's will and purposes. Elihu is prepared to produce evidence to the contrary. It is an established fact that God does communicate with man by means of dreams (12-18). Let it be known too that he uses sickness "to declare to man what is right for him" (19-28). Can Job deny that "God does all these things?" (29-33)

33:12 *God is greater.* At the very outset Elihu states the basic thesis he is going to develop in his attempt to set Job straight. All he has to say will illustrate or support this topic sentence. Job, he contends, would no longer want to be "righteous in his own eyes" (32:1) if he let God be God, dwelling "in unapproachable light" (1 Ti 6:16), all-wise in His loving concern for His creatures, all-powerful to execute His will. Elihu is not misrepresenting his divine Client. Speaking for Himself "out of the whirlwind," God brings Job to his knees to repent "in dust and ashes" for presuming to "contend with the Almighty." (Chs. 38—42)

33:13 *My words.* Job complained of God's refusal to supply him with answers to his questions. (9:16; 19:7; 23:5)

33:14 *In one way and in two.* An idiomatic way of saying "in several ways." (See also in 29)

33:15 *Dream.* For dreams as a means of divine revelation see Gn 20:3; 1 K 3:5; Jb 4:13 ff.; Mt 1:20; 2:13, 19; 27:19.

33:19 *Pain.* Job may not have had the kind of dream just described. However, it is quite likely that God is speaking to him by another means He uses to communicate with man: a serious illness. His purpose is to chasten, correct, purify.

33:23 *A mediator.* One who mediates by interpreting a foreign language (Gn 42:23) or what is otherwise unintelligible. Man may misunderstand the purpose of God's chastening. Elihu says *an angel,* of whom there are myriads, stands ready to come to the sufferers' asistance.

33:24 *Deliver him.* The angel also intercedes on man's behalf. He points to *a ransom,* an expiation of guilt. He *found* it. Neither he nor man produced it. At Job's time the full ransom as yet had not been paid. The "one mediator between God and men," "superior to angels," was still to come "to give his life as a ransom for many," redeeming "those who draw near to God through him." (1 Ti 2:5; Mt 20:28, 1 Ptr 1:18 f.; Heb 1:4 ff.; 7:25)

33:26 *Prays.* What the person prays *with joy* and "sings before men" (26-28) proves that the chastisement achieved its purpose. He is drawn closer to God. "His salvation" is something he wants to make known to others.

33:29 *These things.* God has not withdrawn Himself into distant silence, as Job complained. He has His own ways of speaking to men and uses them not once but repeatedly.

33:32 *Justify you.* Elihu wants Job to speak out freely if he has *anything to say* to maintain his complaint against God, as he did in the discussion with his three older friends. His silence now is to be taken as acquiescence.

34:1-37 ELIHU'S SECOND SPEECH: GOD'S JUSTICE

34:1 *Elihu said.* After pausing for a possible reply to the point he made in 33:12-28, Elihu continues to speak "on God's behalf" (36:2). When piety brought Job misery rather than the expected reward, "he justified himself rather than God" (32:2). Elihu now proceeds to tell Job he is "not right" to insist on his righteousness at the expense of God's justice. As he did in his first speech, he builds his case on the axiom: "God is greater than man" (33:12). Both Job and his friends disregarded the truth of this fact. In effect they sought to dethrone God: he, when he accused God of "taking away" his right (5-6); they, when they presumed to dictate to God how, according to their principles of justice, He must deal with "evildoers" (7-9). However, it remains true that God's justice is as much above human criticism and as far beyond man's understanding as the Creator is more than the creature. Because he called "the whole world" into being, there is no reason to doubt that He is endowed with the ability also to deal justly with the work of His hands. Injustice and the divine nature are as incompatible as fire and water (10-15). Furthermore, the way God has ruled on a worldwide scale is proof that he is "righteous and mighty." His justice is not thwarted by the mightiest of men; nor is it bent in favor of the rich (16-20). Finally no miscarriage of divine justice is possible because the omnipotent Creator and just Ruler of the universe is also omniscient. Evildoers cannot hide their crimes from Him. Sooner or later judgment overtakes them (21-30). Therefore when fallible man undertakes to dictate to God when or how He must act in a given case, he must be charged with "rebellion." (31-37)

34:2 *Wise men.* In his opening statement Elihu presents the views held by the three wise friends and by Job. The latter is quoted 5-6. Vv. 7-9 reproduce the conclusion reached by the other three.

34:9 *Profits . . . nothing.* Job is not quoted verbatim. However, he did state quite clearly that his piety did not pay the dividends he expected. (9:22, 31 f.; 10:3; 21:7 ff.)

34:10 *Hear me.* Elihu is going to oppose both parties to the dispute. He is in full agreement with the premise that God recompenses man "according to his ways" (11). However, he does not undertake to demonstrate how this principle applies in a cause-and-effect ratio to Job. When the friends did so, they only embittered Job, Elihu shifts the discussion from man to God and His transcendent Being. To say that God is not just is to deny that He is God, who of His own free will created the universe, assumes responsibility for all His creatures, and knows what they are doing. Elihu's reasoning makes sense only to those who accept the existence of God.

34:17 *Shall one . . . govern?* Among earthly rulers it may happen that a person governs who *hates justice.* However, the Creator made men in order to govern them justly.

34:20 *At midnight.* Suddenly and expectedly. (Ex 12:29; Lk 12:20)

No human hand. Cf. Lm 4:6; Dn 2:34; 8:25.

34:22 *Deep darkness.* No man can hide from God. (25; Ps 139: 2; Am 9:2 f.)

34:23 *Appointed a time.* God does not need to set a date for a trial or to conduct an "investigation" (24) to establish a man's guilt.

34:29 *Quiet.* God may not act at once or according to human criteria. At times it appears that *He hides his face* so that no one can fathom His ways in dealing with nations, individuals, rulers.

34:31 *Any one.* God is just. However, no one should presume to administer justice for Him or "make requital to suit" his particular notion of equity (33), as Job's friends presumed to do.

34:34 *Men of understanding.* Addressed previously in 2 and 10. Elihu now quotes them in the remaining verses of the chapter (not only in 35 as in RSV). They professed to know all along what caused Job's suffering. He deserved it for "his sin" to which he added "rebellion," charging God with injustice.

34:37 *Claps his hands.* A gesture similar to our thumbing the nose at someone.

35:1—37:24 ELIHU'S THIRD SPEECH: GOD'S GREATNESS

1) 35:1-16 God the Perfect Disciplinarian

35:3 *Advantage.* Elihu now takes up Job's charge that God cannot be just if "it profits a man nothing that he should take delight in God" (34:9). This problem too is out of focus, he insists, unless it is viewed in the proper perspective. Because "God is greater than man" the question is, in principle, out of order. Elihu exposes its false premise by asking counter questions. Can man's piety or wickedness add to or detract from the perfection of God's being? If not, as is obviously the case, what should provoke God to injustice if he owes the good man nothing or is not injured in his God-head by the bad man? This is not to say that "wickedness" and "righteousness" are of no consequence to "a man like" Job. The transcendent God does concern Himself with man. "For according to the work of a man he will requite him" (34:11). Confining himself to the one point at issue, Elihu makes no mention of other aspects of God's relationship to man such as His yearning for man's fellowship.

35:4 *Friends.* Job's friends too needed to be set

right. They, it is true, also asked him: "Can a man be profitable to God?" (22:2-5). However, they drew the wrong inference from a correct premise. In effect negating the principle itself, they presumed to know how God must react to Job's behavior. His suffering had to be divine punishment, incurred by the vilest of crimes. (22:6-11)

35:9 *Cry out.* Related to the question of unrequited piety is the problem of unanswered prayer (9-16). Why God tolerates a *multitude of oppressions* at all is not the point at issue, and Elihu does not discuss it. However, he does assert "the cry of the afflicted" does not go unheeded (34:26-28; 33:26). But he is equally insistent that it must arise from a truly humble and God-fearing heart. If it is no more than a vocal reflex to pain or a shriek such as "the beasts of the earth" instinctively give forth when hurt, it is not surprising that God does "not answer" such "an empty cry."

35:10 *Songs in the night.* An acceptable prayer comes from the firm conviction that God can and will dispel the darkest gloom (Acts 16:25). The plea for help turns into a song of thanksgiving.

35:14 *Not see him.* Cf. Job's complaint 13:24; 23:8 f.; 30:20.

35:16 *Empty talk.* To say that God is indifferent to "oppressions" because He does not answer all prayer for their removal has no more substance than a whiff of air.

2) 36:1-23 God, the Great Teacher

36:1 *Continued.* Elihu had devoted one sentence to Job's charge that God did nothing to curb oppression. He branded the complaint as vapid ranting (35:16; cf. 21:7 note; 24:12). In his last speech he has "yet something to say on God's behalf" (2) which will serve to substantiate his previous short declaration (1-4). In order to vindicate his Maker's "righteousness," he observes that God has a purpose in all His dealings with his creatures. He is the incomparable "Teacher" of men (22), "mighty" enough to enforce His will, wise enough to apply discipline when, where, and how needed. His program of education does not tolerate disorder or injustice (5-7). He uses "affliction" as a teaching and testing device. Its ultimate design is to bring men back to Him when they are in danger of "behaving arrogantly." Sad to say, there are such as "do not hearken" to the warning to "return from iniquity." Closing their minds to "knowledge," they perish in their sins (8-12). Lest Job share their fate, he should regard his "adversity" as God's way of keeping him from taking the way "that leads to destruction." (13-23)

36:3 *From afar.* As he did in his first speech (32:16 ff.), Elihu confidently claims to be transmitting *knowledge* passing human understanding. It has its source in Him "who is perfect in knowledge." (4; 37:16; 1 Co 2:12 ff.)

36:6 *The wicked.* Elihu presents a carefully developed case in God's defense. The disciplinary purpose of God's ways with man, about to be described by him, would be subject to questioning if Job's claim that the wicked go unpunished were true (12:6; 21:7 ff.; 24:1 ff.). Therefore God's advocate once more lays down the basic truth that "the Almighty will not pervert justice." (34:9-12, 21-28)

36:10 *Instruction.* Because the Hebrew noun has overtones of correction, it is frequently translated "discipline" (Pr 5:12, 23; 6:23, etc). In 5:17 it is rendered "chastening."

36:11 *Serve him.* Elihu has no quarrel with the principle, enunciated by Job's three friends, that God uses suffering to purify men's hearts (5:17 ff.; 11:13 ff.; 22:21 ff.). However, in their application of this truth to Job they reduced God to an ethical, legal system, which operates in a standardized framework of cause and effect. Elihu, on the other hand, stresses the necessity of man's change of heart if God's chastening instruction is to be beneficial.

36:16 *You.* Vv. 16-22 fit the context best if understood as addressed by way of example to a person who in spite of his exalted status "with kings" (7) was not immune to divine correction by affliction. "God is mighty" (5) and "great" (26) enough to be his Teacher. Let him take warning not to "turn to iniquity" (21) again as soon as God ends his *distress.* Let him "beware" of sins to which a person with royal prerogatives is particularly prone.

36:17 *Seize you.* A judge, while pronouncing *judgment on the wicked,* may himself deserve to have divine *judgment and justice seize* him.

36:18 *Wrath.* Wielding great power over men, he may be tempted to feel justified to be angry with divine providence. He may also be tempted to accept a *ransom* or bribe. (1 Sm 12:3; Am 5:12)

36:20 *The night.* Do not resort to deeds of violence done under the cover of darkness.

36:21 *Chosen.* If he had accepted the discipline of affliction, he would not have turned again to iniquity.

36:22 *Like him.* God, *exalted in his power,* is *a teacher* who disciplines even the mightiest of men and who makes no mistakes of judgment. (23)

3) 36:24—37:24 God, the Lord of Creation

36:24 *Extol.* Elihu closes his speech by reminding Job who the "teacher" disciplining him is. *Remember* how cosmic forces of nature spring into action at His beck and call. If He directs the course of universe, "who are you, a man, to answer back to God?" (Ro 9:20). Reflection on *his work,* incomprehensible in grandeur and magnitude, must drive man to his knees in adoration and praise. All grumbling complaint will cease. Practicing what he preaches, Elihu does not pretend to explain the "unsearchable" and "inscrutable" providence of God (Ro 11:33-36). His only answer to Job's why is: Don't ask it! A just, loving, omniscient, almighty God is in full control. He makes no mistakes. Trust Him!

36:27 *Draws up.* Elihu speaks of the phenomena of nature as they appear to an unsophisticated observer. We still say we can see the sun drawing water.

36:29 *Pavilion.* It would do Elihu an injustice

to squeeze a literal meaning out of his highly poetic and figurative language.

36:30 *Roots of the sea.* A figurative expression for the depths of the sea, the hidden, inexhaustible reservoir replenishing the clouds with moisture.

36:33 *Jealous.* The RSV translation of this textually difficult verse takes it to mean that while the thunderstorm "gives food in abundance" by furnishing necessary moisture (31), it also proclaims the vehemence of His *anger against iniquity.* For the term *jealous* as applied to God see Dt 4:24 note.

37:2 *Voice.* Thunder is called the voice of God in poetry (Ps 18:13; 29:3 ff.; 46:6; 104:7). Elihu's "heart trembles" because by "His majestic voice" (4) God lets men get some inkling of what to expect when He comes in judgment.

37:4 *After it.* "His lightning" is followed by thunder.

37:5 *Great things.* Eliphaz said something very similar (5:9; 9:10). Elihu agrees with him in principle but differs widely from him in the conclusion to be drawn from this observation. Job's older comforter professed to know how God uses His power in dealing with a man like Job. Elihu takes the opposite view. Because "God is great, and we know him not" (36:26), it behooves man not to second-guess Him. However, Job does not have to resign himself to being a plaything of a capricious and unprincipled monster. God is as good and kind as He is mighty.

37:7 *Seals up.* Ice and snow force men to stop working and "the beasts" to look for shelter. (8)

37:9 *Its chamber.* A figurative way of speaking of God's control of nature, repeated 38:22; Ps135:7. Cf. 36:29 note.

37:12 *His guidance.* The irrational forces of nature respond to laws designed by their Creator to carry out His will.

37:17 *Hot.* The last of "the wondrous works of God" (14), testifying to His power, is stifling heat under a cloudless sky, spread overhead like a "mirror" of molten metal. (18; Dt 28:23; Gn 1:6 note)

37:22 *Golden splendor.* As Elihu speaks of God's greatness, manifested in nature, a shining cloud from the north draws near. God, *clothed with terrible majesty,* is about to speak "out of the whirlwind." (38:1)

37:24 *Fear him.* At the approaching storm Elihu quickly concludes his speech with a brief summation. To the very end he did not attempt to solve Job's problem from the viewpoint of human reason. When the three friends tried to do so, they only infuriated him. Elihu pointed Job to God. Because He is "great in power and justice, and abundant [in] righteousness," Job is ill-advised to rebel against Him.

38:1—42:6 JOB'S LACK OF TRUST REPROVED BY GOD

38:1—40:5 First Speech: Trust the Creator's Transcendent Wisdom

38:1-3 GOD SPEAKS OUT OF WHIRLWIND

38:1 *The Lord answered.* In his dialog with his friends, Job repeatedly demanded the opportunity to interrogate God (13:3, 22; 23:3-9). He was confident of proving a miscarriage of divine justice in his case. Even though God did not owe him an explanation, He graciously condescends to speak to His complaining creature. However, He gives no direct answer to the question what right or reason He had for letting grief and pain come into Job's life. Instead He inundates His cross-examiner with a flood of questions of His own, designed to convince Job that He who is shaping his life (a) knows what He is doing (chs. 38—39) and (b) is fully able to do whatever in His concern for man needs to be done. (chs. 40—41)

How foolish of Job to instruct God as to what course his life should take if he cannot begin to comprehend how the Creator put the universe together and keeps it in running order (34-38)! Would he want to offer advice to Him who (a) designed the structure of the earth (4-7); (b) let "the dry land" emerge from "the waters under the heavens" (Gn 1:9 ff.) and does not let it sink back into a sea of chaos (8-11); (c) daily turns on earth's light of day (12-15); (d) knows what goes on in the far-flung areas of creation, in its depths as well as in its heights (16-21); (e) regulates the forces of nature producing snow and hail (22-24), rain (25-27), and frost (28-30); (f) gives orders to heavenly bodies (31-33) and such celestial phenomena as torrential rain, produced by clouds and acccompanied by lightning (34-38). Furthermore the Creator and Manager of the inanimate cosmos and its functions displays such a knowledge of and solicitude for the animal world as to make Job realize how absurd it is for him to question the wisdom of God's way in caring for him. (38:39—39:30)

Whirlwind. God is not an abstraction of human thinking; He speaks person to person. He is not a genial crony with whom one exchanges pleasantries; He is clothed with might and majesty. For other manifestations of His glory see Ex 19:16; 2 K 2:1; Is 6:4; Eze 1:4; Lk 2:9.

38:2 *Darkens counsel.* Job's *words* were *without knowledge* because they made "the definite plan and foreknowledge of God" (Acts 2:23) appear to be a dark, impenetrable jumble of contradictions.

38:3 *Gird up your loins.* We would say: Roll up your sleeves and get ready for action (Ex 12:11; 1 K 18:46). It will take heroic efforts on Job's part to supply the required answers. He is soon to realize how foolish and brash he was to request an opportunity to match wits with God (13:22). He scores zero on his test to explain how God directs the universe and provides for the beasts of the field (38:4—39:30). Because he is unable to understand God's mysterious workings in the vast realm of nature, Job realizes he should not attempt to advise his Maker how to order his little life.

38:4—39:30 WONDERS OF CREATION BEYOND COMPREHENSION

38:4 *Foundation.* Cf. 26:7 note.

38:7 *Morning stars.* A celestial chorus was "telling the glory of God" in a burst of song (Ps 19:1-6). At the dawn of creation the stars echoed the Creator's praise, sung by *the sons of God,* the angelic hosts. (Gn 6:2 note; see note on Satan, 1:6)

38:11 *No farther.* Satan too is on God's leash. He cannot go beyond "prescribed bounds" (10) in his attacks on Job. (1:12; 2:6)

38:14 *It.* The antecedent is "the earth." When "the dawn" illumines its most remote regions, called "skirts," the light lets its contours stand out clearly, as a seal stamped on a blank piece of clay produces clearly defined forms.

38:15 *From the wicked.* The *light* during which they work as if it were day is the night. Under its cover their arm is *uplifted* to commit crimes. (24:16 f.)

38:16 *The deep.* The word used in Gn 1:2. Job is reminded of the unexplored vastness of the universe. Modern man has done no more than to cross its threshold.

38:21 *You know.* The disparity between the limitless reaches of God's domain and the beggarly range of Job's experience is brought home to him by the ironic side remark that, of course, he was at hand to witness how the wonders of creation took shape. (15:7 f.)

38:23 *Time of trouble.* God commandeers hail in *the day of battle and war* in order to defeat the enemies of His people (Jos 10:11 ff.; Is 30:30; Eze 13:11, 13; 38:22)

38:26 *Desert.* God's use of the forces of nature is not determined by man and his needs. It benefits areas *in which there is no man* to reap what grows there.

38:31 *Pleiades.* Pleiades, Orion, and the Bear (32) are names by which we designate these constellations (9:9). The individual stars of the first two are said to be held in place by *chains* or *cords;* those making up the Bear are called its "children."

38:32 *Mazzaroth.* A transliteration of a Hebrew feminine plural noun. It is left untranslated because it is not certain what configuration of stars is meant.

38:33 *Ordinances.* The course of the stars in *the heavens* is regulated by a timetable not devised by Job. Their scheduled movements in their respective hemispheres constitute *the rule* which determines the change of seasons *on the earth,* as the sun was made "to rule the day" and the moon "to rule the night." (Gn 1:16)

38:37 *Waterskins.* Hides of animals were used as containers of liquids.

38:38 *Into a mass.* After a downpour *dust* and *clods* congeal into a solid mass.

38:39 *Hunt the prey.* After a lesson in the wonders of the inanimate universe (4-38), Job is asked next if he would know how to supply the needs of living creatures, equip them with the necessary instincts, and endow them with physical powers and widely differing skills. Several animals are mentioned by way of example. If Job is not competent to provide for brute beasts in the Creator's great animal kingdom, how can he claim to know better than God what course his little life should take?

38:41 *The raven.* The lion, terror of the jungle, and the least cherished of the birds, the raven, "look to" God to give them "their food in due season." (Ps 104:27; 147:9; Mt 6:26)

39:2 *Number the months.* God not only supplies His animals with food (38:39-41), He also implanted in them the capacity to reproduce after their kind. The wonders of the propagation of wildlife are not man's invention or his concern.

39:7 *Scorns.* If man cannot bring under control the stampeding denizens of "the steppe," should he in his two-by-four mind attempt to corral God?

39:9 *Wild ox.* Not "the unicorn" (KJV) but an animal related to the bison. Man cannot harness the strength God gave it.

39:18 *Laugh at.* The ostrich may not be endowed with enough sense to incubate her eggs as carefully as other birds do. She may lack "the wisdom" to care for her young (Lm 4:3). Yet even this odd creature has not been forgotten by the Creator. He has endowed it with the ability to outrun *the horse and* his *rider.*

39:22 *Laugh at fear.* The magnificent description of the war-horse—its beauty, speed, strength, fearlessness—was to remind Job that this splendid animal was designed, structured, and animated by a Creator whom he did not credit with enough wisdom to direct his affairs satisfactorily.

39:26 *By your wisdom.* Job is to look up at *the hawk* and "the eagle" soaring high over his head. The wisdom of Him who teaches and enables them to defy the law of gravity passes all understanding of earthbound clods. These birds are able to spy out prey from remote heights. He who gave them such "eagle eyes" does not have to strain His vision as He "looks down from heaven [and] sees all the sons of men." (Ps 33:13)

40:1-5 JOB ACKNOWLEDGES GOD'S WISDOM

40:2 *Contend.* Once Job found fault with divine providence, repeatedly clamoring for an opportunity to argue his case with God in an impartial court of justice (13:3; 23:4; 31:35-37). However, brought face to face with his Maker, he has not a word to say. What he knows is "of small account" in comparison with God's superior wisdom. There is no longer any outward manifestation of resentment or recrimination. However, the divine "teacher" (36:22) does not end the course of instruction at this point. He does not rest until Job confesses to an inner change of heart.

40:6—42:6 Second Speech: Trust the Creator's Limitless Power

40:6-9 AGAIN SPEAKING FROM WHIRLWIND

40:6 *The Lord answered.* Continuing His instruction "out of the whirlwind" (38:1), God reproves Job for his failure to trust his Creator's omnipotence. He should recognize that he does not have "an arm like God" because: (a) he cannot "tread down the wicked" on the face of the earth so that law and order might prevail everywhere (9-14); (b) he cannot make brute animals do his bidding. If he cannot domesticate Behemoth and Leviathan, it behooves him not to criticize but to stand in awe of the God to whom they owe their creature strength. (40:15—41:34)

40:8 *In the wrong.* Job took exception to God's administration of justice in general as well as in his own particular case. (9:22-24; 34:5)

40:10—42:6 ABSURDITY OF QUESTIONING DIVINE GOVERNMENT

40:14 *Acknowledge.* If Job were able to eliminate all injustice on a worldwide basis, he would deserve to receive the veneration given God by His worshipers. What a ludicrous spectacle Job presents! Sitting on a throne of ashes, barely able to hold his head erect, he presumes to tell the Ruler of the universe how to use His power.

40:15 *Behemoth.* A transliteration of the plural form of the Hebrew feminine noun *behemah,* the ordinary word for animal, cattle, beasts (Gn 1:24). In 15-24 it is construed as a masculine singular noun. The description seems to fit the hippopotamus. However, because some of the features are said not to belong to the monster of the Nile, it is suggested that the plural form of the noun beast is used (in a Hebrew idiomatic usage) to express the highest degree of bestiality. Behemoth is not to be regarded so much as a particular kind of animal but as the epitome of untamed animal life, the sum total of everything wild.

Made you. The purpose of the reference to Behemoth is made clear at the very outset. Job, critical of God's use of power, is to realize how ridiculous his judgment in the matter is. He has undertaken to advise the Creator when he cannot master his fellow creatures.

40:19 *First of the works.* Another translation reads: "the beginning of the ways of God." Behemoth stands at the head of the line of animals with respect to size and strength, much as "the fear of the Lord" is said to be "the beginning of wisdom" (Ps 111:10; Pr 1:7). Behemoth is so ferocious that only his Maker can approach him with a *sword.*

40:23 *Jordan.* Better rendered "a Jordan" or "a Jordanlike stream," i.e., a river flowing as rapidly as the well-known one in Palestine. In Hebrew usage the proper noun Jordan always has the definite article affixed to it. In this verse and in Ps 42:6 the article is missing.

41:1 *Can you . . . ?* God illustrates His incomprehensible power by pointing to another fearsome beast. Like the word "Behemoth" (40:15), *Leviathan* too is the transliteration of a Hebrew word. But unlike Behemoth, it is mentioned in other passages of the OT (cf. 3:8 note). As described in this chapter, Leviathan has many features in common with the crocodile. However, 31 suggests a sea monster. The language used to portray Leviathan is sprinkled with figures of speech drawn from mythological lore, the substance of the myth fully demythologized (cf. 7:12; 9:13; 3:8 notes). A portrait of this creature "without fear" is held before Job's eyes to drive home the same lesson which Behemoth was to teach. (40:15 note)

41:5 *Play with him.* A bit of sardonic humor.

41:10 *Before me.* If man is wary of meddling with Leviathan, how much more should he hesitate to enrage Him who created both beast and man? To make demands on God is an insult to His majesty and sovereignty. Job insisted that God "repay him" (11) for his piety whereas He owes man nothing. (Cf. Ro 11:35; 1 Co 10:26; Ex 19:5; Ps 24:1; 50:12)

41:14 *Doors of his face.* His mouth.

41:18 *Eyelids of the dawn.* Cf. 3:9 note.

41:32 *Hoary.* The wake he leaves behind him is topped with white as if it were the head of an old man.

41:34 *Sons of pride.* Translated "proud beasts" in 28:8.

42:1 *Job answered.* He does not reply in order to take issue with the Lord's speeches from the whirlwind (chs. 38—41). He realizes how wrong he was to doubt the wisdom, power, and goodness of his Creator. He is truly sorry that he sat in judgment on God, impugning His motives and questioning His justice. The change is complete. He turns from overweening pride to "despise" himself; from sinful self-assertion to "repent in dust and ashes." (1-6)

42:2 *All things.* Job still does not understand why pain and anguish had to come into his life. Even God did not explain why He let it happen. But now Job no longer asks Him to give an account of Himself. It is enough for him to know that He who can *do all things* is in charge also of his life. He is content to let Him whose *purpose* cannot be *thwarted* carry out His good and gracious will in His own way, devious and inscrutable though it so frequently is from man's point of view. (2 Co 12:8-10)

42:3 *Who is this . . . ?* This question and all of 4 were addressed by God to Job (38:2-3; 40:7), who repeats them here as a part of his confession. God was right in charging him with ignorance and in demanding intelligent answers from him.

42:5 *Sees thee.* God came to the aid of His bewildered servant in a way granted to men of such stature as Moses and Isaiah (Ex 33:11; Is 6:1). What he learned about God from others *by the hearing of the ear* came to his consciousness much more directly and convincingly when the Lord appeared visibly to him. God's self-revelation reached its culmination when "the Word became flesh and . . . we have beheld His glory." (Jn 1:14; 12:44 f.; 14:9)

42:6 *Repent.* Satan proved his point. Even Job, "blameless and upright" like none other "on the earth," had to admit that he failed to serve God "for nought" (1:8-9). He had to repent because his devotion to God was tainted with self-love. He was devout not out of love for God but out of a profit motive. When God did not pay according to his wage scale, he condemned his Creator's policies. "As sin came into the world through one man [Adam] and death through sin," so Job represents all mankind's failure to avoid the wages of sin (Ro 5:12). But what Job could not do even for himself, God did when "the grace of that one man Jesus Christ abounded for many." (Ro 5:15; 1 Co 15:21-23)

42:7-17 JOB'S RESTORATION

42:7-9 Reinstated as Servant

42:7 *To Job.* No words of absolution are recorded. The closing verses of the book (7-17) document God's readiness to forgive every sinner if he repents in dust and ashes. When the prodigal comes home from the wastelands of profligate living, his father does not hesitate to speak of him as "my son"; after Job returns from wanderings into the "never-never" land of doubt and rebellion, God calls him "my servant" three times as if nothing had happened since He first so named him. (7, 8; 1:8; cf. Jer 31:34; Ps 25:7). He remembers only what Job said that was "right," expunging from his memory all that was wrong.

Wrath is kindled. The three friends sinned against God and Job. They reduced the transcendent God in their thinking to their puny stature, demanding that He act according to their standard of justice. By their false doctrine they misled Job into questioning divine justice.

42:9 *Job's prayer.* God *accepted* the intercession of His forgiven servant for his comforters who became his tormentors. The Suffering Servant who needed not to "offer sacrifices . . . for his own sins," "made intercession for the transgressors" and continues to do so at the throne of God. (Is 53:12; Heb 7:24-28; Lk 23:34)

42:10 *Restored.* God often tests men's faith by depriving them of what is most precious to them in this life. But He will not let men be tempted beyond their strength. When trials have served their purpose He provides "the way of escape." Job received again all his children and double the value of his earthly possessions. God can shower these blessings on him, for he will not again consider them wages earned by piety.

42:10-17 Blessed in Latter Days

42:11 *Brothers and sisters.* During his dark days they shunned him (19:13-15). The *piece of money* and the *ring of gold* they presented to him were tokens of esteem for their host.

42:13 *Seven sons and three daughters.* Not double the original number. Children are not counted like so many sheep or oxen.

42:14 *The name.* The daughters received names which expressed the father's tender love for them: Jemimah=Dove; Keziah=Cinnamon Blossom; Keren-happuch=Horn of Eye Shadow.

42:15 *Among their brothers.* According to Mosaic law a man's daughters were eligible for inheritance only if they had no brothers (Nm 27:1-11). However, Job let his daughters become property owners in their own right, thus preserving the family circle intact.

42:17 *Full of days.* At peace with God and himself, Job reached the ripe old age of the patriarchs whom he resembled in death (Gn 25:8; 35:29; 50:23). St. James reared an epitaph to his memory, inscribed with the words: "You have heard of the steadfastness of Job."

PSALMS

INTRODUCTION

Content

The Book of Psalms is a prayer book.

It is written for us who do not know "how to pray as we ought" (Ro 8:26). Here saints of the old covenant talk to God because they heard Him speak to them. They thank and praise Him, they cry for help, they plead for forgiveness, they groan and sigh in troubles, they seek relief from doubt, they revel in revealed truth, they celebrate the manifestations of divine goodness and power, they delight in the kingdom of heaven and its Messiah. When present-day believers turn to the Psalter, they find every spiritual need anticipated whether at the moment their heart leaps for joy, whether they are depressed by burdens, whether their faith is groping for assurances, whether their spirits are willing to worship but their flesh is weak.

Jesus prayed the psalms (Mt 27:46; Lk 23:46; Mt 26:30 note). He also interpreted them, teaching that "everything written about" Him in "the psalms must be fulfilled" (Lk 24:44). The NT writers draw heavily on the Psalter to establish the continuity of the old and the new covenant. They quote directly from 40 psalms, referring indirectly or alluding to almost all of them.

The Book of Psalms is a songbook.

Its prayers rise to God's throne on winged words of poetry. To beauty of language was added the voice of song and the sound of music. However, the psalms are not subjective outpourings of fancy-free feelings. Their composers are inspired and informed by God's revelation in word and deed. They are moved to respond to what He has said or done.

We call this collection of poems psalms. This name is derived from the Greek term used to translate the Hebrew noun which in the superscriptions designates a certain kind of poetic composition. Etymologically the Hebrew as well as the Greek word denotes a song sung to the accompaniment of a stringed instrument. (See "Types" below)

Divisions

In our Bibles the psalms are divided into five "books" of unequal length: 1—41; 42—72; 73—89; 90—106; 107—150. Each of them is marked by a final doxological verse, Psalm 150 as a whole closing the book with a shout of praise. This arrangement represents an ancient Jewish tradition. Apparently it was thought that the Pentateuch, God's Word to man in five books, should be balanced by man's response in a corresponding number of sections in the Psalter.

Within each of these five divisions there are other groupings, consisting of psalms strung together on the basis of characteristic features. In the course of successive collections, psalms were arranged in series, determined in part at least by such distinguishing factors as the particular divine name employed and authorship.

In Book I (1—41) the covenant title "Lord" is used almost exclusively (see Ex 6:3 note). In Book II (42—72) the more general title "God" predominates. In Book III (73—89) the use of the two titles is almost exactly even. In Books IV and V "Lord" is found 339 times while "God" occurs only seven times.

Classification according to authors played a part in some groupings. Book I with the exception of Psalm 1 is a solid block of Davidic psalms; also Psalms 51—72. Psalms 42—49 are assigned to the sons of Korah; Psalms 73—83, to Asaph. However, psalms of David are found in all five books. In Book V he is the only author mentioned besides Solomon.

Other unifying elements are: (1) the

occasion when the psalm was to be used: the Psalms of Ascent (120—134); (2) an opening Hallelujah (Praise the Lord), in Psalms 146—150; (3) the subject matter; in Psalms 93—100 it is God's limitless kingdom.

In many instances the principle determining the sequence of psalms is not recognizable.

Types

The titles distinguish nine different kinds of psalms. The basis for differentiating these categories is no longer clear. We fail to understand why some 60 of the poems are called "a psalm" in distinction from others; why about 30 are labeled "a song"; why only five are under the rubric of "a prayer"; why only one (Ps 145) is said to be a "song of praise" (whereas the Jews called the entire Psalter "the Book of Praises"); why about 25 are left unclassified.

A solid block of 15 psalms (120—134) each bears the name "A Song of Ascents," usually assumed to indicate suitability for recitation or singing as pilgrims went up to Jerusalem.

In three instances even the meaning of the Hebrew words defining the category cannot be established with certainty. In transliteration these terms are: "Maskil" (13 times), "Miktam" (6 times), "Shiggaion" (Ps 7 only).

Modern scholarship seeks to categorize the psalms by establishing the life situation out of which they arose and by determining the liturgical purpose they were to serve. This investigation has proved to be of value in some instances. However, it is forced to operate with unverifiable assumptions. Its results remain dubious.

From the viewpoint of purpose and content, only two general classes of psalms need be distinguished. They either express a plea because of some need or they offer thanksgiving and praise to God for some benefit. Some psalms even combine these two features.

Praise of God includes a rehearsal of what He has done. At times the descriptive element consists of a poetic rehearsal of a message or oracle received by inspired prophets. There are promises of a universal and eternal kingdom of God (e.g., Ps 47; 93) under the rulership of His Son, the coming messianic King. (Ps 2; 45; 72; 89; 110; 132)

In other psalms the response to God consists in a grateful review and a meditative appreciation of His revelation in deeds and words (Ps 19; 78; 119; etc.) or in an edifying contemplation of a God-pleasing life. (Ps 15; 52; etc.)

Punishment is invoked on enemies in the so-called imprecatory psalms (Ps 58; 59; etc.). The rationale of these prayers is the conviction that hostility to a person consecrated to God's cause is in the final analysis an attempt to frustrate His good and gracious will. Because their persecutors are God's enemies, the psalmists pray that "God would break and hinder every evil counsel and will which would not let His kingdom come." (Luther)

Superscriptions

All but 34 psalms have titles or superscriptions. In Book III all psalms bear such a heading, whereas 28 of the 34 untitled or "orphan" psalms are found in Books IV and V. They supply such data as (1) authorship; (2) the setting; (3) the type of poetry represented (see "Types" above); (4) liturgical and musical directives.

It is not known how long after the composition of the psalms they were prefaced with these notes. They were hoary with age when they were translated into Greek in the Septuagint, begun in the third century B.C. The rendition of some terms proves that their meaning was no longer known at that time. Modern translations resort to transliteration of Hebrew words (e.g. "according to The Sheminith," Ps 6; "according to The Gittith," Ps 8). Phrases like "according to The Hind of the Dawn" (Ps 22) and "according to Lilies" (Ps 45) seem to indicate the melody according to which a psalm is to be sung. However, no one knows what these tunes were or why they were so called. The meaning of the Hebrew word translated "choirmaster" in 55 superscriptions, seems assured. The transliterated word "Selah," occurring 71 times within and/or at the end of 39 psalms, seems to be another musical notation. What it signified can only be surmised.

Authorship

Almost a third of the psalms are left anonymous. The superscriptions ascribe about half of the psalms to David. Book I is almost solidly Davidic. However, psalms by David are found in all divisions of the psalter. In 13 titles the occasion is mentioned when "the sweet psalmist of Israel" (2 Sm 23:1) composed a particular psalm.

The phrase "by David" can be translated also "to David" or "for David." It is therefore suggested that it need not refer to authorship in all 73 instances where it occurs. However, this interpretation dare not contradict the statements of Jesus and of New Testament writers who assert that David wrote Pss 16 (Acts 2:25-28); 32 (Ro 4:6-8); 69 and 109 (Acts 1:16-20; Ro 11:9 f.); 110 (Mt 22:41-45; Mk 12:35-37; Lk 20:42-44; Acts 2;34); 95 (Heb 4:7). Ps 2, which has no tttle, is quoted as spoken "by the mouth of . . . David . . . by the Holy Ghost." (Acts 4:25 f.)

Other authors are mentioned. There are 12 Psalms "of Asaph" (50, 73—83); two of Solomon (72, 127); one each "of Heman" (88), "of Ethan" (89), "of Moses." (90)

Archaeological discoveries prove that poems of similar structure and form as the psalms existed in written form centuries before David's time.

Poetry

Hebrew poetry is similar to our classical verse in its use of choice language, figures of speech, and rhetorical devices. However, the psalms and other poems in the OT do not depend on rhyming words and a strict metrical pattern to achieve cadence. Phonic balance and a regular beat of accented and unaccented syllables gives way to a rhythmic arrangement of thought patterns. What is said in one line is "rhymed" in the following one with a similar or related thought. Such balancing of ideas is achieved by repeating the first statement in other words, by expressing it antithetically, or by completing it in various ways. Because two or more lines complement one another in this fashion, the distinguishing characteristic of Biblical poetry is called parallelism.

However, the words expressing these parallel thoughts are not arranged without any thought of the effect produced by their sequence. While there is no rigid pattern of metrical feet, there is a conscious effort to align words so that the accented syllables of a line occur at measured intervals and produce a rhythmic beat. The number of unstressed syllables, preceding or following the stress, may vary, resembling our blank verse. Furthermore the lines of the same psalm need not have the same number of accented syllables.

Grouping of smaller units into strophes or stanzas is recognizable in some psalms. In a few instances clusters of verses are marked by a refrain. (Ps 42:5-11; 43:5; 46:7-11)

The most structured device of poetic form is found in a number of acrostic psalms. Retaining parallelism of thought and rhythmic stress, they have the additional feature that the first word of each verse or group of verses begins with a letter in the order in which it occurs in the alphabet (e.g. Ps 34). In Ps 119 there are units of eight verses, each of the latter beginning with the same letter in alphabetic sequence. It is virtually impossible to translate these psalms in such a way as to reproduce their acrostic arrangement.

Psalm 1

1:1-6 *Blessed.* The first psalm is a well-chosen gateway into the holy precincts of prayer and praise. If the psalter is the Bible in miniature, as Luther said, then the opening six verses are the portal leading into a treasure-house of communion with God. The inscription over the entrance reads *Blessed is the man.* It promises a "pearl of great value" to those who seek it here. All who live in and by the psalms will lack nothing to make them happy. There are no restrictions. The invitation to be blessed goes out to all sons and daughters of men—whoever, whatever, wherever they may be. The happiness offered is unqualified, unlimited, unaffected by circumstances.

Happiness is a blessing bestowed by God. There are those who accept it and live accordingly both negatively and positively. Avoiding a way of life advocated by men who offend and mock God (1), they ponder with delight and rehearse untiringly what God has made known for their instruction (2). So oriented and anchored, their lives have an unshakable stability and an unfailing source of satisfying accomplishment (3). Unfortunately there are also those who refuse to live such blessed lives. Whatever happiness they appear to enjoy is an illusion. Inevitably it disintegrates in the storm of God's judgment, in which the wicked are swept away like chaff before the wind (4-5). There are no alternatives and no exceptions. All men are either *righteous* and *blessed* or they are *wicked* and *perish.* (6)

Ps 1 is the first beatitude of more to follow in the psalter. Again and again its pages will light up with the benediction *blessed is.* As the blessing is repeated, its features stand out more clearly. Happiness (1) is the product of God's initiative (65:4); (2) is made possible by God's forgiving mercy (32:1); (3) is guaranteed by the never failing power of God (2:12; 34:8-9; 40:5; 146:5 f.); (4) grows out of a total commitment to God (84:5, 12; 112:1; 128:1); (5) finds fulfillment in doing what God commands (41:1; 106:3; 119:1-2); (6) expresses itself in praising God (84:4); (7) is a serene confidence in God's goodness even in days of pain (94:12); (8) is shared in the family circle and extends to a whole nation (127:5; 33:12; 89:15; 144:15); (9) anticipates God's vengeance on the enemies of His cause. (137:8-9)

1:1 *Walks . . . stands . . . sits.* Entanglement with evil advances by stages: from going along with wrong suggestions to letting false principles become a standing rule of procedure to a deep-seated antagonism to God. Each downward step descends to a lower level of perversity. First there is agreement with *the counsel of the wicked,* people whose tendency to wrongdoing has become apparent; then comes commitment to *the way of sinners,* people whose course of action runs afoul of the law; finally a feeling of kinship develops in the company of *scoffers,* people who take demonic pleasure in mocking and ridiculing God.

1:2 *The law of the Lord.* Spurning man-made philosophies of life, whether concocted by the ungodly or fashioned from "the imagination . . . of his heart" (Gn 6:5), he relies on what God has to say. The Hebrew word translated *law* is a comprehensive term. It regularly denotes the commands or prohibitions of a legal code. However, it embraces also all instruction expressing God's will for man's happiness, set forth in His covenant of grace (on the meaning of "covenant" see Exodus, Introduction, "Content"). To live in and by this law is a *delight,* not a hated burden, not a hindrance to enjoyment of life. (19:8; 112:1; 119:24, 77, 97, 143, 165, 174)

Meditates. Untiring in his determination to learn the will of God ever more thoroughly, he rehearses to himself over and over again the recorded words of divine revelation (Dt 4:5 ff.; Jos 1:8; Mt 4:4). His meditation is not a meritorious exercise, done to be rewarded. It can only appropriate undeserved blessings, provided by God's goodness.

1:3 *A tree.* For the same figurative description of a tree rooted in God see Jer 17:7 f.; Ps 92:12 f. Once there was perfect bliss when "the Lord God planted a garden in Eden" and filled it with trees "pleasant to the sight and good for food," watered by "four rivers." (Gn 2:8-10)

Prospers. Nourished by unfailing *streams of water,* a "sound tree bears good fruit" (Mt 7:17) without fail and in spite of drought and scorching winds. So an unwithering fruitfulness marks the life of a man in the measure that he draws into himself the vitalizing and energizing power channeled to him in the Word of God (Is 55:10 f.; Eze 47:12). He prospers even in fires of affliction and amid outward failure, disturbing though painful experiences may be. (Ps 37; 73; the Book of Job)

1:4 *Chaff.* The contrast between *the wicked* and "the righteous" is the difference between a firmly rooted, fruitful tree and worthless, unstable grain hulls and bits of straw, thrown into the air from an ancient threshing floor so that the wind might carry them away.

1:5 *Not stand.* Cut off from the benefits offered and dispensed *in the congregation of the righteous, the wicked* and *sinners* are anything but happy. They have forfeited the blessings of forgiveness and communion with God guaranteed to His covenant people. Exposed to divine wrath, they face "a fearful prospect of judgment" (Heb 10:27). The chaff will be burned "with unquenchable fire." (Mt 3:12; 13:30)

1:6 *Knows.* For the meaning of the Hebrew verb "to know" beyond intellectual awareness see Gn 18:19 note; Dt 9:24 note.

Righteous. Is it possible to expect to be "blessed" if "there is no righteous man on earth" and "all our righteous deeds are like a polluted garment" (Ec 7:20; Is 64:6)? God made it possible because His "righteous . . . servant" caused all to "be accounted righteous" when "the Lord . . . laid on him the iniquity of us all" (Is 53:6, 11). Ps 1 is predicated on the coming of "the Righteous One," who pronounced blessings in His own name. (Acts 3:14; 1 Ptr 3:18; 1 Jn 2:1; Mt 5:3-11; 11:6)

Ps 1 ends on a note of serene assurance: (1) God determines the fate of all men; pray with confidence in His unlimited power; (2) God is deeply concerned with "the way of the righteous"; pray trusting His inexhaustible goodness; (3) God knows what makes a man "blessed"; pray relying on His perfect wisdom to choose what is good for you.

Psalm 2

2:1-12 Ps 2 is a prophecy of the reign of Jesus Christ, "anointed . . . with the Holy Spirit and with power" "to be King of kings and Lord of lords" (Acts 10:38; Rv 19:16; 17:14). In winged words, coming from "the mouth of . . . David . . . by the Holy Spirit," the four strophes of this dramatic poem envision the fulfillment of the promise brought to David by Nathan the prophet (Acts 4:25-27; 13:33; 2 Sm 7:14-16). But David was not only the inspired mouthpiece of divine words; he himself was a prophetic figure. As God carried out His eternal plan of salvation, He made him "a type of the one who was to come" and his kingdom "a shadow of what is to come" (Ro 5:14; cf. Jer 23:5; 30:9; Eze 34:23;

37:24; Cl 2:17; Heb 10:1). The significance attached to David's person and the features of his reign were designed to point forward to a Successor "greater than Solomon" (Mt 12:42). Items of correspondence between the lesser and imperfect that was, and the greater and perfect that was to be, are the woof and the web in a tapestry of regal splendor exhibited in the psalm.

David was king of Israel by the grace of God, ruling as His earthly vicegerent on "the throne of the Lord as king" (cf. 1 Ch 28:4-7; 29:23); Jesus, David's son, was David's Lord. (Mt 22:43)

By virtue of his coronation to govern Israel, God's adopted "son" (Hos 11:1; Dt 32:18), David ranked as His "firstborn" (Ps 89:20-27); Jesus, "the only Son from the Father," was God incarnate. (Jn 1:14, 18; 3:18; Ph 2:6 f.; Heb 1:5; 5:5; 2 Ptr 1:17)

David held sway over an empire from Jerusalem and the "holy hill" of Zion; Jesus, "Ruler of kings on earth," is enthroned in "the heavenly Jerusalem," "far above all rule and authority and power and dominion." (Rv 1:5; Eph 1:20-23; Heb 12:22-24)

David subdued nations threatening Israel's borders (2 Sm 8); before Jesus will "be gathered all the nations" after He has destroyed "every rule and every authority and power" so that "the kingdom of the world has become the kingdom of our Lord and of his Christ, and he shall reign for ever and ever." (Mt 25:31 ff.; 1 Co 15:24 f.; Rv 11:15; Mi 5:4; Zch 9:10)

The psalm is more than a proclamation issued to rebellious subject nations by a king of Israel. It speaks for and in the name of the Messianic King. Opposition to *the Lord and his anointed,* though worldwide in scope (1-3), is as futile as a child's temper tantrum. It cannot unseat the *king on Zion* (4-6), the Lord's Son and Heir of *the ends of the earth* (7-9). Therefore let the earth's great *serve the Lord with fear;* let those who *take refuge in him* know how *blessed* they are (10-12). Other Messianic psalms are 8, 16, 22, 45, 69, 72, 89, 110, 132.

2:1 *Why . . .?* The question is not prompted by anxiety over the outcome of the conflict. It expresses astonishment at the stupidity of a plot destined by its very nature to be *in vain.*

The nations. In the Hebrew text there is no definite article preceding the nouns denoting the plotting groups and their leaders. They are left undetermined as to number and unspecified as to circumstances. Whenever and wherever *nations, peoples,* "kings of the earth," "rulers" (2) launch movements against the kingdom of heaven, they are doomed to disaster.

2:2 *Kings of the earth.* Earth-kings, no matter how formidable they may appear, are as effective in their struggle against Him who "sits in the heavens" (4) as dogs baying at the moon can alter the course of the celestial bodies. For instances of enmity against Israel, God's chosen nation, see Ps 83.

Anointed. A translation of a Hebrew word transliterated "Messiah." Its equivalent, derived from the Greek, is "Christ" (Jn 1:41; 4:25). In Old Testament times ceremonial oil was applied to the head of a person to symbolize his consecration to the sacred office of a priest or a prophet or a king (Ex 28:41; 1 K 19:16; 1 Sm 10:1). Because they acted in God's behalf, their position made their person inviolate. (1 Sm 24:6; 2 Sm 19:21; 1 Ch 16:22)

2:4 *Laughs.* In order to impress on the mighty of the earth how totally "in vain" it is for them to raise a clenched fist against the Lord, He is portrayed as meeting the challenge as men would react to the telling of a joke by a comedian. See also 37:13; 59:8.

2:5 *Then.* At a time determined by Him. Sometimes it may appear that the conspiracy is not a laughing matter because He delays to take note of it.

2:6 *Zion.* Jerusalem was "his holy mountain" because God chose "to make his name dwell there" (Ps 48:1 f.; Dt 12:5 note, 11). It became "the city of David" (2 Sm 5:9). In Jerusalem "everything that is written of the Son of man by the prophets . . . [was] accomplished" (Lk 18:31). John saw "the holy city, the new Jerusalem, coming down out of heaven from God." (Rv 21:2)

2:7 *My son.* Declared God's adopted son when elevated to "the throne of the kingdom of the Lord" (1 Ch 28:4-7), David foreshadowed that "Son who was descended from David according to the flesh and designated Son of God according to the Spirit of holiness by his resurrection from the dead, Jesus Christ our Lord" (Ro 1:3-4; Mt 3:17; 17:5; Heb 1:5; 5:5). His dominion extends beyond "the ends of the earth" (8) because to Him "all authority in heaven and on earth has been given" (Mt 28:18). He will let His subjects reign with Him. (Rv 2:26 f.)

2:9 *A potter's vessel.* He shatters all opposition as easily and decisively as an iron bar smashes a piece of pottery. (Is 11:4; 45:9; see also Lk 20:18)

2:11 *Serve . . . with fear. Trembling* before His "wrath" (5), lest they "perish in the way" of rebellion, "rulers of the earth" can escape disaster if they "come in fear to the Lord and to his goodness." (Hos 3:5; Mt 10:28; Heb 10:31; 12:28 f.; 2 Co 5:11; Ph 2:12; cf. Dt 6:13 note)

2:12 *Kiss his feet.* This translation is the result of a rearrangement of the consonantal text and a different vocalization of its component parts. The traditional rendering ("kiss the son") is declared suspect mainly because it is based on a reading which has the Aramaic noun for son *(bar)* rather than the Hebrew word *(ben)* which occurs in 7. See the proper names Bar-Jesus (Acts 13:6) and Benjamin. Kissing the king or his feet was a gesture of homage and submission (1 Sm 10:1; Is 49:23). The psalm consistently demands that equal obedience and honor be accorded "the Lord and his anointed" (2). The Lord's "king" (6) is His "son." (7)

Blessed. Ps 1 opens with a blessing on "the righteous," the fate of "the wicked" serving as its foil. Ps 2 pronounces doom on God's enemies, contrasted in a closing beatitude on those who *take refuge in Him.* Believers at all times need the assurance, so dramatically set forth in this psalm, that the course of the universe is firmly in the hands of "the Lord and his anointed," all appearances to the contrary notwithstanding.

Psalm 3

3:1-8 For the occasion which prompted this *Psalm of David* see 2 Sm 15—18. The passing of ages has not outmoded its usefulness. It is written to sustain the faith of all who face a conspiracy of hostile forces, intent on turning life into chaos. Whatever the crisis may be, here they (1) can learn that they need not hesitate to tell their troubles to the Lord (1-2); (2) are led to calm their fears by casting all their cares on Him who cares for them (3-6); (3) are emboldened to rouse God into action in their behalf (7); (4) are reminded that they too share in the *blessing* pronounced on the whole *people* whose union with God is guaranteed by His sworn covenant. (8)

3:1 *Many.* The prayer for help begins by informing God how desperate the situation is. It takes for granted that He wants to be told what is happening as if He did not know that the enemy is on the march in great numbers (*many* three times in 1-2) and so confident of victory that even God could not prevent it. (2)

3:3 *Shield.* Declared useless (2), prayer nevertheless rises on the wings of unwavering confidence in God's ability to deflect the deadly missiles of adversity against which armor of human contrivance is inadequate. For other examples of divine protection described as a shield see Gn 15:1; Dt 33:29; Ps 18:2; 28:7; 84:11; 119:114.

Glory. God demands that the glory due Him not be given "to another" (Is 42:8; 48:11; Jer 2:11; Ps 29:1 f.; 96:7 f.). But He is the glory of those who trust in Him also in the sense that He guards them against suffering shame and disgrace (34:4 f.; Is 49:23; 50:7; Ro 9:33; 10:11). He is a *lifter* of heads bowed by grief and anxiety. (Cf. the Aaronic blessing, Nm 6:26)

3:4 *Holy hill.* Jerusalem. See 2:6 note.

3:5 *Wake.* When He who neither slumbers nor sleeps (121:2-4) is the shield of defense, worry need not cause sleepless nights. "Sleep will be sweet" (Pr 3:24) when the eyes of faith have seen "horses and chariots of fire round about" the camp of those whom *the Lord sustains.* (2 K 6:17)

3:7 *Arise.* Prayer moves from trust in God's power and willingness to help (3-6) to a bold plea for deliverance, echoing an ancient battle cry of God's people. (Nm 10:35)

Break their teeth. The *enemies* are compared with ferocious beasts with fangs bared against their victims. (7:2; 10:9; 17:12; 22:20 f.; 58:6)

3:8 *Thy people. Deliverance* which God alone brings about is a *blessing* which the individual can make bold to claim because God has covenanted to bestow it on the entire community of believers.

Psalm 4

4:1-8 For *choirmaster* see "Superscriptions" in the general introduction to the psalms. The heading does not specify the circumstances which gave rise to this *Psalm of David.* However, in content it is similar to the plea for help voiced in Ps 3. The same firm conviction that God hears prayer animates both psalms. The cry for deliverance, compressed into one verse as in 3:7, takes for granted that God will respond to it as He did when called upon in a previous emergency (1). The certainty of being heard is expressed in the form of an admonition to two groups of people, addressed as if they were present to hear what God's unfailing intervention should mean to them. First those who made it necessary for *the godly* to *call to* God for help should realize that they will be exposed for what they are. Their entire case of trumped-up charges will collapse as inevitably as God's vindication of the falsely accused is sure to materialize. The futility of opposing the Lord should induce them to abandon all wicked plans and to turn to Him in trust and obedience (2-5). On its positive side, a firm faith breaks out in a word of encouragement to the despondent and dejected. They are bidden to share the *joy* of knowing they are safe if they entrust themselves to God. (6-8)

4:1 *God of my right.* God can be trusted to render a verdict vindicating the right of the falsely accused. (17:2; 37:6)

Room. In colloquial language we would say: You have helped me out of a tight spot.

Gracious. Every time God hears a prayer, it is an act of undeserved mercy.

4:2 *Vain words.* In David's case the *honor* of the king was besmirched by Absolom's slanderous campaign of lies (2 Sm 15:2 ff.). But the rebel's charges were not only untrue, they initiated a movement which was deceptive also in its results. Even before deliverance from this "distress" has come, the leading *men* are warned that their efforts are an exercise in futility. For other examples of a direct address to the wicked as part of a prayer see 6:8; 52:1-4; 62:3; 119:115.

4:3 *The godly.* The Hebrew term used here denotes a person who lives in a covenant relationship with God. Having accepted God's pledge of steadfast love, he responds to it by an unwavering determination to please God in thought, word, and deed. In other instances the same word is translated "loyal" (18:25), "faithful" (50:5; 89:19; 149:1), "saints." (30:4; 31:23, etc.)

4:4 *Be angry.* The basic meaning of the Hebrew verb is to tremble or to quake (said of the earth, Ps 18:7); of *the heavens* (2 Sm 22:8). Applied to persons, it denotes an emotional agitation, produced by various causes: fear (Is 32:11), awe (Ps 99:1), grief (2 Sm 18:33), joy (Jer 33:9). In their aroused state of mind let the enemies consider whether they contemplate the kind of action which incurs the wrath of God because it is sinful (Ex 20:20; Eph 4:26). Let them probe privately into their conscience and stifle every impulse to lay wicked plans.

4:5 *Right sacrifices.* Only sacrifices offered in the right attitude are "acceptable to God" (51:17). All others are an abomination. (Is 1:13)

4:6 *Some good.* In order to demonstrate that a favorable answer to the plea for deliverance is expected as confidently as if the desired change were an accomplished fact, the psalm adds a word of encouragement to such as do not "trust in the Lord" (5) as they should (6-8). They are downhearted because what they consider *good* has not materialized. It appears to them that the benefits promised in the Aaronic blessing are still outstanding. (Nm 6:26)

4:7 *Joy.* Communion with God in prayer lights up the heart with joy even in the darkest hour.

4:8 *Sleep.* Those who entrust themselves to the Lord are assured of a peace "which passes all understanding" (Ph 4:7). There need be no waking hours of solitary anxiety between lying down and falling asleep. At every eventide as well as at the close of life's day they close their eyes knowing that they *dwell in safety.*

Psalm 5

5:1-12 For some unknown reason *the choirmaster* is directed to render this *Psalm of David* to the accompaniment of wind instruments ("pipes," 1 K 1:40) and not "stringed instruments" (Ps 4). The superscription does not indicate what life situation occasioned its composition. Nor does the psalm itself provide the necessary details to pinpoint the particular hour of trouble or the enemies causing it. Its lack of specifics suggests that it was designed to be adaptable to the need of *all . . . the righteous* (11 f.) whenever their adversary, the devil, and his flesh-and-blood henchmen are on the prowl "seeking some one to devour" (1 Ptr 5:8). At such a time the first and most urgent thing to do is to ask for a hearing in the court of justice presided over by *my King and my God* (1-3). Vindication and deliverance are certain. *Evildoers* need not even try to get a hearing for their *lies.* The Judge not only sees through their *wickedness* but also uses His power to destroy *deceitful men* (4-6). Quite the opposite is true of those who entrust themselves to the safety assured them by God's *righteousness.* Appealing to His pledge of *steadfast love* and humbling themselves in adoration of His awesome majesty, they are certain to receive a favorable verdict. It will affirm their right to pursue a God-pleasing *way* of life (7-8). It will also have a negative effect on those defying this royal restraining order. Because of their diabolical persecution of God's subjects for their loyalty to Him, they are declared guilty of rebellion against the King Himself. Inasmuch as God's people are the immediate target of the attacks, they need not hesitate to ask Him to take whatever measures are necessary to "break and hinder every evil council and will which will not let His kingdom come" (9-10; see Luther's explanation of the Third Petition of the Lord's Prayer). When in answer to such a prayer God comes to the rescue of *all who take refuge in* Him, they will *sing for joy.* (11-12)

5:1 *Groaning.* The Lord can be counted on to listen to prayer whether expressed in articulate *words* or in "sighs too deep for words." (Ro 8:26)

5:2 *My King.* Not an earthly potentate of limited power but a King "sitting upon a throne, high and lifted up" who is God, Creator and Ruler of heaven and earth (Is 6:1 ff.; Mt 19:26). It is of the very nature of faith to claim Him as *my* King and *my* God. It is also an undeserved privilege.

5:3 *Morning.* Not an afterthought or a last resort, prayer raises its *voice* heavenward as soon as danger rears its head. For the attitude of expectant waiting see Mi 7:7; Hab 2:3.

5:5 *Boastful.* Translated "arrogant" in 73:3. They are not harmless windbags but insolent braggarts of their wickedness (75:5). Therefore they "will not stand in the judgment." (1:5 note)

5:7 *Steadfast love.* A hearing is not to be granted on the basis of merit. Sinful man cannot appear before God except on appeal to His mercy pledged in His covenant of grace (Ex 34:6; Nm 14:18; Dt 7:9 note; Ps 69:13). To Israel He deigned to be present enthroned on the mercy seat, the lid of the ark of the covenant (Ex 25:17 note; Ps 99:1). It was His *house* and His *temple* even before Solomon built a structure of stone for it. (27:4, 6; 1 Sm 1:9; 2 Sm 6:17)

5:8 *Lead me.* There is no request for material blessings; no desire for personal revenge. Only one concern: to be assured of protection under God's *righteousness* so that the *way* of life pleasing to Him is *straight,* i.e., not beset by obstacles. (Is 40:3-4; Ps 25:4, 5, 12; 27:11; 86:11)

5:9 *Sepulchre.* What they say has a deadly effect. Their appetite for victims is not sated, as if they were a grave always *open* and ready to draw more victims into its maw.

5:10 *Transgressions.* They are not charged with harmless peccadillos or sins of weakness. The connotation of this Hebrew term for sin is contained in the parallel statement: *they have rebelled against* God. They demonstrate their defiance of God by seeking to harm those "who take refuge" in Him. So Paul persecuted Christ. (Acts 9:4 f.)

Psalm 6

6:1-10 This is the first of a group of psalms known by their usage in the church as the "Seven Penitential Psalms," the others being 32, 38, 51, 102, 130, 143. The notation *A Psalm of David* appears in all superscriptions except 102 and 130. Only the heading of 51 specifies what occasion prompted the outpouring of a penitent heart.

Ps 6 contains neither an explicit confession of sin nor a plea for forgiveness. However, it pulsates with an aroused sense of guilt and a shattering dread of God's retributive justice. Yet it is not a morbid indulgence in self-pity. Nor does it end in blank despair. Appeals to God's mercy calm the raging storm of fear. In the end, faith triumphs. Exulting in the assurance of peace with God, it defies all attempts to undermine this conviction.

The change from debilitating agitation to a healthy frame of mind is described briefly but graphically. Severe affliction and painful chastening were taken to be evidence of the unquenchable fire of God's wrath on sin. Frenzied terror seized the soul and drained the body of strength (1-3). Life itself seemed to be ebbing away. There was hope only if God would listen to an appeal to His *steadfast love,* promised in the covenant (4-5). In order to move God to compassion, more details of the pitiful state of affairs were called to His attention (6-7). Relief came in a surge of confidence that the Lord heard the *supplication,* as He did in previous instances. The newly found communion with God was so precious as to prompt the desire that all threatening to disrupt it be *put to shame.* (8-10)

Sheminith. A transliteration of the ordinary Hebrew word for "eighth," left untranslated because its point of reference is no longer clear. Apparently it is the equivalent of our musical term octave, prescribing a lower setting or an instrument with a lower tone.

6:1 *Chasten.* God disciplines His own "as a man disciplines his son" (Dt 8:5). It is not unusual for the chastened one to give way to the terrifying thought that God's wrath "rests upon him." (Jn 3:36; Ps 27:9; 38:1, 2, 5)

6:2 *Heal.* The *bones* as well as the "soul" (3) were *troubled.* Torture of conscience and pain of body frequently react to one another. Whether in this particular instance physical sickness produced mental anguish or the reverse was the case, it is clear that the whole man was affected and needed restoration to health. (38:3 f.; 51:8; 103:3; 147:3)

6:5 *Sheol.* Cf. Gn 42:38 note. To *praise* God in *remembrance of* His "steadfast love" is the sole object and obligation of mundane existence. In desperation the sufferer made bold to remind God that an early death would make it impossible to devote the usual span of earthly life to singing His praises. The OT saint may have known less about the mode of life after death than we do, little as our comprehension of it actually is. But firmly believing that God's power did not end at the grave, he entrusted himself to his Maker and Redeemer at the end of life's day. (Ps 139:8; 31:5; Am 9:2; Lk 23:46)

6:6 *Flood.* The language used to describe his suffering is highly figurative rather than literal in meaning. We too say: he drowns himself in his sorrow.

6:7 *Foes.* They either rejoiced over his misfortune or charged that it was so severe because it was well-deserved punishment for unconfessed crimes, as, e.g., Job's friends did.

Psalm 7

7:1-17 It is no longer possible to determine what distinguishes a *Shiggaion* from the more ordinary designation "A Psalm of David." Appearing only here, the Hebrew word for the former is reproduced in a transliterated form because its meaning has been lost. A *Shiggaion* seems to be a kind of composition which was different because David *sang* it, a feature not mentioned in the description of the ordinary psalm. The person concerning whom David sang it is also unknown. The Biblical record makes no mention of *Cush, a Benjaminite.* However, during his flight from Saul (1 Sm 20—26), David repeatedly encountered experiences which could have evoked the words recorded here. For other psalms assigned to this period of his life see 34, 52, 54, 56, 57, 59, 142.

The appeal to God for rescue from vicious men, hounding their intended victim to death (1-2), takes on the form of a lawsuit in a court of justice. The accused declares under oath that he is the innocent party (3-5). A just verdict can be expected. No one can disregard the summons to appear before "the Judge of all the earth" (Gn 18:25), who will also in this instance rule in favor of *righteousness* (6-8). Justice will not be hampered by lack of knowledge. The Judge knows all the facts in the case, including undisclosed thoughts and unexpressed desires (9). But because the suppliant is *upright in heart,* he has nothing to fear (10-11) whereas *the wicked man* will be sentenced to suffer the *mischief* and the *violence* which he intended to inflict on his victims (12-16). Victory is so certain that the prayer for deliverance turns into a doxology. (17)

7:1 *Take refuge.* The *pursuers* will overtake their victim unless God supplies a protective covering against their deadly attacks. For the same thought see the opening verse of Ps 11, 16, 31, 57, 71. There is no doubt that God can supply the needed safety or that He is minded to do so. The plea for help is addressed to the *Lord,* who brought His people out of Egypt and pledged them His steadfast love in a solemn covenant. (Ex 20:2; Dt 5:2; 29:14)

7:3 *If I.* In the theocratic commonwealth of Israel legal procedure specified that certain cases be tried in the temple, the priests acting as judges (Dt 17:8 ff.). The parties to the cases were required to swear an oath before the altar asking God to expose the liar and to vindicate the truth (1 K 8:31 f.). Accused of crimes by his friends, Job made a similar declaration of his innocence. (Jb 31:1 note)

7:6 *Arise . . . awake.* To the person experiencing the *fury* of heartless enemies, it appears that He who does "neither slumber nor sleep" is not aware of what is going on and must be aroused to *anger* over the wicked.

7:8 *Righteousness.* The accused makes no pretense to moral perfection or absolute *integrity.* Nor does he claim to deserve consideration because he tried to do what is right. However, in the issue at hand he pleads innocent of any wrongdoing.

7:9 *Minds and hearts.* Lit. "hearts and reins or kidneys." The latter were regarded as the seat of emotions (so still in Rv 2:23). God no less than His incarnate Son "knew what was in man" (Jn 2:25). Therefore He "judges righteously." There will be no miscarriage of justice because man's whole inner life is an open book before Him. (26:2; Jer 11:20; 12:3; 17:10; 20:12)

7:11 *Every day.* As yet God has not arisen in His anger to let "the wicked come to an end" (9). But this does not mean that He indulges man in his wickedness.

7:12 *Man . . . God.* As the RSV note indicates, the Hebrew text says: "he does not repent" and "he will whet his sword" and in v. 14 also reads simply "he conceives evil." In all three cases the antecedent of the pronoun "he" must be supplied from the context.

His sword. God is pictured as proceeding against the wicked as if He were a soldier, equipped to inflict mortal wounds. (Dt 32:41; Ps 21:12)

7:14 *Conceives evil.* Prayer restores confidence in a moral world order. Because "God is a righteous judge" (11), evil cannot triumph. Conceived and born in a lie, it has no more substance than a delusion. It deceives itself. It destroys itself. The hurt it intended for others brings about its own downfall. (Jb 15:35; Is 59:4; Ps 9:15 f.; 37:14 f.; 57:6; Pr 26:27)

7:17 *Most High.* See Gn 14:18 note.

Psalm 8

8:1-9 This *Psalm of David* is a call to worship the mystery of what God once did in man's creation and of what, according to His "plan for the fulness of time" (Eph 1:10), He was to do in man's redemption. It bids us praise the wonders of God's condescension in giving *dominion over the works of* His hands to man, formed from a handful of dust and ashes. How small he is in comparison with the vast expanse of the *heavens* from where *the moon and the stars* shine down on him! Measured against the ages of their allotted existence, how frail and fleeting is his life! How weak he is in comparison with the forces of nature put at his disposal!

However, there is still greater cause for amazement and adoration. God was so *mindful* of His fallen creatures' need that in His Son He became "the man Christ Jesus" (1 Ti 2:5). "Born of a woman," "he humbled himself and became obedient unto death" (Gl 4:4; Ph 2:8). So it came about that He who came "down from heaven" was exalted at the right hand of the Father "in the heavenly places" (Jn 6:38; Eph 1:20). The *glory and honor* with which God crowned "those who are of the dust" foreshadows the exaltation of that *son of man* through whom all men can become "a new creation" (1 Co 15:48; 2 Co 5:17). The NT proclaims that God has fulfilled in the "man Jesus Christ" what He promised in Ps 8. (Heb. 2:6-8; Mt 21:16; 1 Co 15:27; Eph 1:22)

In the superscription, *Gittith* is left untranslated because its meaning is no longer known. It could be a derivation of the name of the Philistine city of Gath, in which case it seems to denote a musical instrument or a melody originating there; or it could be the melody of a song sung at the grape harvest. Two other psalms have the same musical notation. (81; 84)

8:1 *Name.* Not only the words used to address Him, such as God or Lord, but everything He does and says to let man know who He is and what "His eternal power and deity" is. (Ro 1:19 ff.; cf. Ex 6:3 note)

8:2 *Babes and infants.* As translated and punctuated in the RSV, the first verses say that God's "glory" is so firmly established *above the heavens* that the prattle of children constitutes a bulwark strong enough to ward off and silence all opposition (Is 40:22-24; Mi 1:3 f.; Hab 3:12 f.; cf. 1 Co 1:27). Jesus appropriated these words when His enemies objected to the song of children hailing Him as Messiah. (Mt 21:16)

8:4 *Son of man.* The word used for *man* in this phrase is also the proper name "Adam," so called because he was taken from the ground (Hebrew: *adamah).* Because after the fall into sin all sons of Adam "return to the ground" (Gn 3:19), the term *son of man* expresses mankind's susceptibility to death and decay. Jesus referred to Himself some 70 times as "the Son of man," thereby calling attention to His solidarity with mortal man in His suffering and dying but also asserting His divine, eternal nature hidden in His human person. (Cf., e.g., Mt 9:6; 25:31; Lk 18:31-33)

8:5 *Less than God.* God "crowned" Adam, made of the dust of the ground but also in His image, king "over the works of" His hands. As God's vicegerent he was responsible to no superior except the Creator Himself. The writer of Hebrews quotes these words in the version of the Septuagint, the Greek translation of the OT. He refers to Christ's brief stay in human form as being made "lower than the angels," ministering spirits in heaven who communicate God's will to man (Heb 2:5-8; 1:14). The *glory and honor* bestowed on "the first man Adam" reaches a climactic fulfillment in the exaltation of "the last Adam" in "the world to come." "King of kings and Lord of lords," he rules at God's "right hand in the heavenly places." (1 Co 15:27, 45 ff.; Eph 1:19-23; 1 Ti 6:15; Rv 17:14)

8:9 *Our Lord.* The hymn, framed by a refrain (1), issues a call to worship.

Psalm 9

9:1-20 In ancient versions (Septuagint and Vulgate) as well as in some Hebrew manuscripts Ps 9 and 10 are not divided into separate compositions. Similarity in form, vocabulary, and content suggest that they constitute a unit. The poetic device known as an alphabetic acrostic is recognizable (only in Hebrew) in both (see Introduction, "Poetry"). Only six other psalms have this feature (25, 34, 111, 112, 119, 145). Furthermore, Ps 9 arranges the first half of the Hebrew alphabet to form the acrostic, while Ps 10 continues with the remainder. Even though some letters are not used to introduce a verse and some are out of sequence, there is enough regularity to give the impression of two parts designed to complement one another. It should be noted also that Ps 10 has no superscription. However, separating or combining the two psalms does not affect their meaning. Each contributes to the development of a common theme.

Ps 9 issues spontaneously from a heart throbbing with thanksgiving for past deliverance in time of need; bursting to tell others of God's mighty deeds; undaunted by doubts about His ultimate victory. The exhilaration is irrepressible. It erupts into exclamations and declarations uninhibited by formal considerations of presentation. Situations and scenes change and merge; personal and national concerns overlap; past, present, and future blend into a timeless hymn of adoration. The opening words are a burst of wholehearted gratitude addressed in the first person to the *Most High* (1-2) for His *righteous judgment* which brought about the defeat of personal enemies (3-4). But this is not all. Seen in proper perspective, this deliverance betokens God's protection of all of Israel against *nations* who were *wicked* because they attempted to keep His chosen people from serving His purposes. *The peoples* of *the world* are not autonomous. Not strength of arms or superior numbers but what the eternal and righteous Judge of heaven and earth decrees determines the course of the universe (5-8). *In times of trouble* therefore all *oppressed,* whether on the international or domestic level, have a *stronghold* to protect them if they *put their trust in* the Lord (9-10). Past experience and confidence in the future should prompt them to join in singing *praises to the Lord* (11-12). Whatever their particular extremity may be or however desperate it may be, a plea for God's gracious intervention in their behalf changes lamenting into rejoicing (13-14). In order to substantiate this assertion the scene shifts back to God's wonderful deeds as Lord of the nations. Because He executes *judgment,* the evil men do has implanted in it the seed of destruction (15-16). *The wicked* pass away, whereas those who recognize their helplessness and let God be their stronghold need not despair (17-18). Boldly taking God at His word, faith proceeds to rouse Him to action, prodding Him to demonstrate how futile opposition to His will by puny man is (19-20). This seemingly impudent demand that God do what He promised is repeated in 10:12. *In times of trouble* (9:9; 10:1) it may appear as if *the needy* and *the poor* are to be oppressed *always* and *forever* (9:18). Ps 10 speaks to this problem at greater length.

The superscription directs *the choirmaster* to render this *Psalm of David* according to the melody of a song entitled *Muth-labben.* The meaning of the words is "death to the son," but a musical composition by that name is no longer known. The same holds true of the transliterated term *Higgaion* at the end of v. 16.

9:1 *Whole heart.* Without reserving any credit for himself for his escape from evil men (Dt 6:5; Ps 111:1; 138:1). To bring it about God did *wonderful deeds* such as He performed in Israel's past (Ex 3:20; 34:10; Jos 3:5; Ju 6:13) and as are mentioned frequently in other psalms. (26:7; 40:5; 71:17; 72:18, etc.)

9:2 *Name.* See 8:1 note.

9:4 *Just cause.* The defeat of the enemies is represented as resulting from a conviction of crimes in a court of law. When God passes a sentence of *righteous judgment,* He also sees to it that it is carried out.

9:5 *The nations . . . the wicked.* These terms are used interchangeably 15, 16; 10:15, 16. Nations and individuals incur God's wrath when they seek to destroy God's covenant people or violate the rights of its members.

9:8 *World.* It may appear that not all *peoples* need fear the Lord. But they must all appear before "his throne for judgment" in this world and the next. (96:13; Acts 17:31; 2 Co 5:10)

9:10 *Know.* For the meaning of *know* in a wider sense than intellectual awareness see Gn 18:19 note; Dt 9:24.

9:11 *Zion.* See 2:6 note.

9:12 *Avenges.* As God will not permit the shedding of innocent blood to go unpunished (Gn 4:10; 9:5), so *the afflicted* who "put their trust in" Him (10) can call on Him for redress of any injury.

9:13 *Be gracious.* Perhaps vv. 13 and 14 are a direct quotation of "the cry of the afflicted" (12). While the petitioner has a "just cause" for complaint, he also knows that it will be an act of undeserved mercy if God comes to his aid.

9:15 *Pit.* Any one making a plea for mercy such as uttered in vv. 13 and 14 is assured that God will hear it, for "he has executed judgment" in the past (see 5 f.). Evil cannot triumph. *Nations* are made up of "men," mere "grasshoppers" in God's sight. (20; Is 40:22; Ps 7:14 note)

9:17 *Sheol.* For the meaning of this term see Dt 32:22 note. The wicked are swept through "the gates of death" (13) to which they had brought their victims. (55:15, 23; 63:9 f.; see also Mt 16:18)

9:18 *Needy . . . poor.* Occurring frequently in the Book of Psalms, these terms denote not only such as are reduced to economic poverty, but also such as in their need have no spiritual resources to commend themselves to God. Because they have nothing of any value to God, they rely on His mercy and goodness for deliverance.

Not always . . . for ever. For reasons known to Him, God may at times delay to answer prayer so long that *the needy* and *the poor* appear to *be forgotten* and left to *perish.* Faith so tried gets impatient. It feels it must rouse God to action. Confused by God's delay to judge "with equity" (8), it confronts Him with the demand to know why. He continues to "stand afar off" (10:1). Ps 10 takes up this problem at greater length.

Psalm 10

10:1-18 For the relationship of this psalm to the preceding one see the introductory remarks to Ps 9. As a continuation of the latter, Ps 10 elaborates a subject briefly broached in 9:18: the strain on the faith of "the oppressed" (9:9) when they seemingly have to wait "for ever" before God does something to end their misery. As a separate composition, it takes its place alongside such psalms as 73, 37, 13, devoted expressly to the same problem (see also the Book of Job). Ps 10 too laments what appears to be a glaring contradiction in divine providence. Contrary to His promises, God looks the other way when *the poor* and *the meek* (17) call for help. The situation reaches grotesque proportions when those who blatantly blaspheme God and exploit their fellowmen unmercifully are able to boast that their crimes pay rich dividends (1-11). Their faith shaken by such observations, the *hapless* victims must not let go of their hold on God. Instead His delay to answer should prompt them to throw themselves into His arms with renewed "importunity," saying: *Arise, O Lord* (cf. Lk 11:8; Ps 9:19). For it remains true that the *king* of the nations has not only the power *to do justice* but also the good will to *hear the desire of the meek.* (12-18)

10:2 *Let them.* Perhaps better translated: "They [the poor] are caught in the schemes which they [the wicked] have devised."

10:3 *Curses.* The Hebrew text has "blesses." RSV translates as in Jb 1:5, 11; 2:5, 9. If the verb is understood in its usual sense, the meaning is that the greedy man, while hypocritically blessing God with his lips, denounces Him with his crimes.

10:4 *No God.* If there is a God, His "judgments are on high" (5), too far removed to be concerned with the affairs of men. (13; 14:1; Jer 5:12; Zph 1:12)

10:5 *Puffs.* Scoffing at God, he sneers contemptuously at the possibility of human opposition.

10:8 *Hapless.* This word to describe the helpless victims occurs two more times in this psalm (10, 14) but nowhere else.

10:11 *Forgotten.* All appearances to the contrary, it should be noted that "the needy shall not always be forgotten." (9:18)

10:12 *Thy hand.* God's power is able to "break . . . the arm of the wicked." (15; Mi 5:9)

10:15 *Find none.* No *wickedness* is so diabolically clever or so firmly established as to go unpunished.

10:16 *King.* The Lord is the "Most High" (9:2), whose judgment overtakes the evildoer in Israel as well as the wicked *nations* threatening His chosen people. (Cf. 9:15-18)

Psalm 11

11:1-7 This short psalm is not a prayer. It speaks of the Lord in the third person. Nevertheless it enriches devotional life by its assertions of unqualified confidence in the final victory of good over evil. It is the nature of faith to accept no other guarantee for security except the Lord's promises. It will hear of no substitute even when the entire structure of meaningful existence threatens to sink into chaos (1-3). Faith has its own reasons for its unshakable trust in divine providence. It knows for a fact that (a) the Lord, enthroned in heaven, is not unconcerned with what *the children of men* do on earth (4); (b) He subjects all of them to a test, based on absolute criteria (5); (c) those found *wicked* cannot escape their ultimate doom; those counted *righteous* bask in the light of His countenance (6-7).—"Why are you afraid, O men of little faith?" (Mt 8:26)

11:1 *Take refuge.* Cf. 7:1 note. A bird can escape the hunter by fleeing to hiding places in *the mountains.* However, the hunted believer resents the advice to look solely to natural resources for safety rather than to "the Lord, who made heaven and earth." (121:1 f.; 44:6 f.; 118:8 f.; Is 31:1)

11:2 *Upright.* The targets of *the wicked* are innocent of crimes against their persecutors. (7:3 note)

11:3 *Foundations.* When crime undermines the basis of community life, *what can the righteous do* to escape the collapse?

11:4 *Test.* Originating *in heaven,* divine surveillance has all men in full view; even what man thinks in the most secret chambers of his heart does not go undetected. (33:13-15; 94:9; 139:1-18; Jb 28:24)

11:6 *Cup.* What God allots to man is figuratively portrayed as something to be drunk from a cup. It is filled with "salvation" for some (116:13; 23:5); for others there is "a cup of wrath" (75:8; Is 51:17; Jer 25:15). See also Jesus' reference to His impending suffering and death. (Mt 20:22; 26:39)

11:7 *His face.* Not swept away by the storm of divine wrath, *the upright* remains in God's presence, where there is "fulness of joy" (16:11; 17:15; 27:8 f.). See Jesus' blessing on "the pure in heart" (Mt 5:8). The NT adds the assurance: "Your life is hid with Christ in God." (Cl 3:3)

Psalm 12

12:1-8 There is a good reason for the frantic cry *Help* with which this psalm begins. Truthfulness in communication, one of "the foundations" (11:3) of human existence, has all but disappeared (1-2). As a result the *godly* and *the faithful* are threatened with extinction unless the Lord puts an end to deception and doubletalk (3-4). In contrast with the duplicity of men, *the promises of the Lord* to rescue *the needy . . . are pure,* unalloyed by deceit (5-6). Even though *the wicked* still *prowl . . . on every side,* the Lord can be trusted to hear the plea for protection. (7-8)

12:1 *Godly.* Cf. 4:3 note. Elijah once felt that he alone remained of those "faithful" to the Lord. (1 K 19:10; see also Is 57:1; Hos 4:2; Mi 7:2)

12:2 *Double heart.* We say a man is "two-faced"; the Indian, that he speaks with "a forked tongue"; James speaks of "a double-minded man" (Ja 1:8). For harm done with the tongue see Ja 3:5-10.

12:4 *Master.* As they "smite . . . with the tongue," they are a law unto themselves. (Jer 18:18; Ps 10:4)

12:5 *Poor . . . needy.* Called "godly" and "faithful" in v. 1. Cf. 9:18 note. Their *groan* is not in vain. God, as it were, rouses Himself to action in their behalf. (9:19; 10:12; Is 33:10)

12:6 *Furnace.* Molten metal flowed from pottery crucibles into receptacles in or *on the ground.*

12:7 *Generation.* Here this word designates people who had a certain characteristic in common rather than a period of time when they lived. (Dt 32:5; Ps 14:5; cf. Mt 12:39; 16:4)

Psalm 13

13:1-6 It may take a lifetime to learn to pray this short *Psalm of David.* It tells of the triumph of faith over despair. Victory is not easy. It leaves battle scars. When misery drags on, the heart cries out in anguish: "How much longer must I wait before God helps me in answer to my prayer?" (1-2). Though sorely tempted to wallow in self-pity or even to "curse God and die" (Jb 2:9), the child of God is encouraged to tighten his hold on God in renewed prayer (3-4). There is relief. Into the prison of doubt and dereliction comes the strength to sing "songs in the night." (5-6; Jb 35:10; Acts 16:25)

13:1 *How long . . .?* The question, repeated four times, was prompted by a desperate situation. Not a passing discomfort, the affliction was so severe and so unrelenting that hope of survival had all but faded (3). This impassioned—almost impertinent—complaint of God's delay in answering prayer reechoes through many psalms and has been pressed from anguished hearts throughout the ages. (6:4; 35:17; 74:10; 80:4; 89:46; 94:3; 119:84)

13:2 *Bear pain.* The translation "holds council" makes good sense. In his *soul* the sufferer has conflicting thoughts as he tries to reason out the mystery of his suffering.

13:3 *Lighten.* Grief and pain make eyes lose their sparkle. (6:7; 38:10; Jb 17:7)

Sleep. Scriptures speak of death as sleep. (Jb 3:13; Dn 12:2; 1 Co 15:51; 1 Th 4:14)

13:4 *Rejoice.* When a person trusting God to protect him against his *foes* is overwhelmed by them, His honor suffers. (25:2)

13:5 *Steadfast love.* Cf. Dt 7:9 note; Ps 5:7 note.

13:6 *Sing.* Confidence in "salvation" has returned. There is rejoicing as if it were a reality.

Psalm 14

14:1-7 Laments over the breakdown of law and order are not a modern phenomenon. In this ancient *Psalm of David* the root of the problem is exposed: the universal corruption of mankind. By nature all men act as if there were no God. Flouting all authority, they satisfy every selfish impulse arising in their *corrupt . . . heart* (1). However, the Judge of heaven and earth is fully aware of their depravity (2-3). He sits in judgment on their crimes against their fellowmen: He notes their refusal to acknowledge their obligation to Him (4). He will not let their lawlessness go unpunished. Those who have "no fear of God" (36:1) will experience *great terror* (5); those trusting to find a *refuge* in Him can confidently await His deliverance (6-7). Ps 53 is almost identical with this psalm.

14:1 *Fool.* The wrong thinking *in his heart* expresses itself in a morally bankrupt way of life. Jesus, who "knew what was in man," describes the products of this folly (10:4 note; Jn 2:25; Mk 7:21-23). Cf. St. Paul's quotation of this psalm in Ro 3:10-12.

14:2 *Looks down.* Man's foolish claim to autonomy and the right to unrestrained self-assertion does not alter the fact that he is accountable to an all-seeing Observer of his "abominable deeds." (Gn 6:5, 12; 11:5; 18:21; Ps 33:13; 92:6-8)

14:4 *Eat up. Evildoers* satisfy their voracious appetites at the expense of others without any qualms or inhibitions. (Mi 3:2 f.; Eze 22:27)

14:5 *There.* In situations where they thought they could act with impunity. (Is 33:14)

Generation. Cf. 12:7 note.

Righteous. Though "no man living is righteous" before God (143:2), "the poor" who depend solely on His grace and mercy will know what it means that *God is with* them. (Cf. 9:12 note)

14:6 *Confound.* Cf. 7:14 note.

14:7 *Would come.* Though oppressed and victimized, the true *Israel* confidently expects the day *when the Lord restores the fortunes of his people.* (126:1 ff.; Zch 2:11 f.; 2 Th 1:5-10; Rv 21:1-5)

Psalm 15

15:1-5 Under the old covenant worshipers participated directly or indirectly in an elaborate system of ceremonies. This *Psalm of David* guards against formalism. Rites, performed merely mechanically, do not effect communion with God. Least of all are the ceremonies magical formulae which automatically force God into action. He who would appear in God's presence needs to ask whether his worship is going to be acceptable (1). The answer is that a profession of devotion is mockery and blasphemy unless coupled with the sincere intent to think, speak, and act in a God-pleasing manner (2-5a). Coming in such a frame of mind, the worshiper stands on solid ground: he can count on the blessings assured him in God's covenant of grace. (5b)

15:1 *Dwell.* Not take up a permanent residence in the sanctuary but be a welcome guest on regular visits to the *tent* and *holy hill* hallowed by God's promise to be a gracious Host to wayfarers of life who entrust themselves to His keeping.

15:2 *Blamelessly.* This verse lists basic principles molding the attitude and character of an acceptable worshiper. He is determined to be blameless in conduct (Gn 17:1; 6:9), is governed by righteousness (Ps 1), and is motivated by sincerity (12:3). Such a person shuns acts enumerated by way of example in the following verses.

15:3 *Slander.* The sins mentioned in 3-5 have two characteristics: (1) temptation to commit them arises between visits to the sanctuary as the worshiper has day-by-day dealings with his fellowmen; (2) the offender could avoid detection and escape prosecution in the courts of justice.

15:4 *Change.* He does not break his oath even though it is to his disadvantage to keep it.

15:5 *Interest.* See Ex 22:25; Lv 25:35 note; Dt 23:20 f.

15:6 *Never be moved.* His house, founded on a rock, stands firm in the storms of life. (Mt 7:24 ff.; Is 26:3-4; Ps 61:4; 16:8)

Psalm 16

16:1-11 David revels in an unreserved commitment to God in life and death. Acknowledging Him as the covenant *Lord* in a short prayer, he claims Him as his highest and only *good* (1-2). His unqualified devotion to God affects his relationship to his fellowmen positively and negatively. He is in wholehearted accord with like-minded *saints;* he will have no truck with worshipers of *another god* (3-4). In words of exuberant faith he goes on to describe the bliss of his fellowship with God. His lot in life is always *pleasant* because the Lord is all he needs and wants to make him happy (5-6). Grateful that the Lord has taught him this satisfying way of life, he seeks further guidance in continued meditation on the divinely given *counsel.* As he does so, his trust in the Lord grows, making him unafraid of anything the future may bring (7-8). Even death holds no terrors for him. Because God's power does not stop at the grave, it cannot sever his ties with the living Lord. *Pleasures for evermore* are in store for him (9-11).—The exultation of David's faith is prophetic. The hope he expresses became a reality because and when it was realized in the life, death, and resurrection of Him "who abolished death and brought life and immortality to light" (2 Ti 1:10). Paul and Peter, quoting from the Septuagint, testify to the fulfillment of this psalm in David's greater Son. (Acts 2:25-28; 13:35-37; cf. Ps 2:1-12)

16:3 *Saints.* Lit. "holy ones," i.e., such as are mindful of the Lord's demand of those set apart to be His people: "You shall be holy, for I the Lord your God am holy." (Lv 19:2)

16:4 *Libations of blood.* This term may refer to the blood of sacrificial animals poured at the foot of the altar, although human sacrifice was practiced in the ancient world and even within Israel's borders. (2 K 23:10; Jer 7:31; Is 57:5)

16:6 *Lines.* A *heritage,* consisting of real estate, was assigned by lot. Its location and size were determined by measuring lines. To the Levites, who received no land of their own, God said: "I am your portion and inheritance." (Nm 18:20)

16:10 *Sheol.* Cf. Dt 32:22 note.

Godly one. David, a sinner, was *godly* because he looked to God for His forgiving mercy. Jesus was the "Holy One" of God "who was put to death for our trespasses and raised for our justification." (Acts 2:27; Ro 4:25)

16:11 *Fulness of joy. The path of life,* directed by God, leads to His *right hand,* where *pleasures* satisfy all human yearning for happiness.

Psalm 17

17:1-15 This *Prayer of David* is cast in the form of a plea in a court of justice (cf. 7:1-17 note). The plaintiff asks frantically for a hearing (*hear—attend—give ear* [1-2]). He expects a favorable verdict because he has taken "pains to have a good conscience" (Acts 24:16). The all-knowing Judge Himself has examined his record with respect to the charges brought againt him (3-5). He is confident of redress too because the Arbiter to whom he appeals has pledged Himself to be the *savior* of those taking refuge in Him *from their adversaries* (6-9). The latter, however, take pride in their unscrupulous and deadly assaults on their fellowmen (10-12). Because they are about to move in for the kill, it is necessary to plead for swift justice. And because they cannot be deterred from their vicious plan, the judgment rendered must impose on them and their kind the full penalty *stored up* for such crimes (13-14). The embattled cry for relief ends in a calm and firm assertion of faith. Whatever the outcome of the immediate struggle for survival, there will be full justification of the litigant and satisfaction of all his wants when he awakes to behold God's face (15).—Four other superscriptions bear the title *A Prayer* (86; 90; 102; 141; cf. the end of "Book II," Ps 72:20). It is not apparent what distinguishes them from other psalms which likewise contain fervent supplications.

17:1 *Free of deceit.* Evidence of truthfulness is submitted in 3-5. There is no fear of a verdict based on what is "right."

17:3 *By night.* The wicked "plots mischief while on his bed" (36:4; 4:4). However, the cry for "vindication" comes from a *heart* which, when God probes into its deepest recesses, is found to harbor no thoughts of *wickedness* later manifest in what is said and done.

17:4 *Violent.* The Hebrew word is translated "robbers" in Jer 7:11; Eze 18:10.

17:7 *Steadfast love.* The *savior* who in His covenant of mercy promised to be the *refuge* of His people (Dt 7:9 note) is not at a loss to bring about *wondrously* what they desire.

17:8 *Apple of the eye.* As a man automatically flicks his eyelids to protect the pupil of his eye, so God can be trusted to react without fail when "deadly enemies" threaten harm (Dt 32:10; Pr 7:2; Zch 2:8).—Young birds seek cover under the mother bird's wings. (36:7; 57:1; 61:4; 63:7; 91:4)

17:13 *Arise.* Cf. 7:6 note. To deliver *life* from *the wicked* God is asked to strike before they do and to *overthrow them.* (Cf. 1 K 8:31 f.)

17:14 *The world.* The enemies are crass materialists, whose "god is their belly." (Ph 3:8-9; 1 Jn 2:15-17)

Stored up. They are to experience the accumulated measure of God's wrath. This part of the verse can be translated as an added characterization of carnal-minded people who refuse to recognize God as the Giver of all good things. They are men "whose belly Thou fillest with Thy hid treasure," whose desire for children is satisfied, who have enough to bequeath to their infants (cf. KJV). They are not only unprincipled in their relationship to their fellowmen (10-12) but also utterly unresponsive to God's goodness.

17:15 *Face . . . form.* Though God is faceless and formless, He may appear in human form (Nm 12:6 ff.). However, satisfaction of all human longing will be complete when men *awake* from the sleep of death to the beatific vision and to "pleasures for evermore" at God's "right hand." (16:11; Jb 19:25 f.; Dn 12:2; 1 Jn 3:2; Rv 22:4)

Psalm 18

18:1-50 Cf. 2 Sm 22, where this psalm, with minor variations, appears in its historical setting.

Psalm 19

19:1-14 This *Psalm of David* is a prayerful and grateful meditation on "the things" God tells man "that make for peace" (Lk 19:42). "Praise befits the upright" (33:1) at the thought that "training in righteousness" is furnished by the Maker of heaven and earth (2 Ti 3:16). He speaks in the cosmic *handiwork* of *the heavens.* What goes on there makes no audible sounds, yet is highly eloquent. To anyone who has ears to hear, it keeps declaring the power and wisdom necessary to devise and issue celestial ordinances for the maintenance of order and continuity in the universe (1-4a). When the sun follows his prescribed circuit, *the glory of God* echoes and reechoes through the skies (4b-6). No less *perfect* is the spiritual guidance provided for the rational inhabitants of the earth. Because they too are the Creator's handiwork, He knows what they need to think and do if they are to be at peace with Him and with themselves. As little as the celestial bodies are left to plot their own courses, so little can man be a law to himself if he is to avoid deadly collisions. However, following the path of divine direction does not prove to be an irksome yoke. *The law of the Lord* affords satisfactions which nothing on earth can provide (7-10). Pondering this priceless treasure leads to the humbling admission that man fails to comply with its provisions as he should. Prone to commit *errors* of which he may not be aware, he needs to pray for forgiveness for *hidden faults.* He may be tempted to let even *presumptuous sins . . . have dominion over* him and thus end in open rebellion against his Maker (11-13). Lest this come to pass, the psalm closes with the plea that this *meditation be acceptable in* God's *sight.* (14)

19:1 *Firmament.* Cf. Gn 1:6 note.

19:4 *Voice.* KJV gives the usual meaning of the Hebrew word: "line" or measuring tape. The thought is that to compute the distance transversed a line would have to be stretched *through all the earth.* In the Septuagint, which Paul quotes in Ro 10:18, the Hebrew word is rendered *voice* or sound. In Is 28:10, 13, "line" denotes the sounds heard in prophetic utterance, rejected by scoffers. (Cf. also Ro 1:19 ff.)

In them. In the heavens.

19:7 *Law.* The Hebrew word *torah* is not restricted in meaning to legal demands. It has the more general connotation of "instruction." God, the Creator and Ruler of the material universe (1-6), is also *the Lord* who condescended to enter into covenant with Israel (cf. Ex 6:3 note), pledging the chosen people His steadfast love. Israel's response to God's overtures of grace is laid down in *the law,* for which several synonyms are used in 7-9. For *testimony* see Ex 25:16, 21. For a sheer endless song of gratitude for *the law* see Ps 119. (Cf. Ro 7:12, 22)

Simple. Not deficient in mental acumen but aware of the need for guidance and willing to accept it.

19:9 *Fear of the Lord.* The attitude of reverence and worship engendered by "the law." (Cf. Dt 6:13 note)

19:13 *Presumptuous sins.* Not done in ignorance or weakness, but against better knowledge; also said to be committed "with a high hand" (Nm 15:30 note). When such sins *have dominion over* a man (Gn 4:7), he is guilty of *great transgression,* i.e., out and out rebellion.

19:14 *Redeemer.* For the meaning of this title for God see Jb 19:25 note.

Psalm 20

20:1-9 This *Psalm of David* provides the people with an intercession for their king. Pleading for *help* in *the day of trouble,* it springs from the conviction that God, who promised to dwell in their midst, would respond favorably to *offerings* and *sacrifices* brought as tokens of full dependence on His goodness and might (1-3). Because the king seeks divine guidance in his *plans,* the people pray confidently that the Lord fulfill all his *petitions* for success (4-5). Trusting the Lord's "right hand" (17:7) to do battle for them and His *anointed* representative, the people *boast* of their security against attacks by enemies armed only with earthly weapons (6-8). All will be well if the Lord answers their call for help. (9)

20:1 *Name.* As used three times in this psalm (1, 5, 7) and frequently elsewhere in the OT (Ps 44:5; 54:6; 118:10; 124:8; Pr 18:10), this term does not denote primarily the proper noun by which God is addressed (such as *the Lord;* cf. Ex 6:3 note) but comprehends all He has said and done to reveal His transcendent Godhead to man. The prayer is based on such manifestations of His power to save as *Jacob* experienced. (Gn 35:3; Ps 46:7, 11)

20:2 *Sanctuary.* Though God dwells in "his holy heaven" (6), the ark of the covenant on Mt. Zion (3:4) was the hallowed symbol of His gracious presence for the people of the old covenant. (Ex 25:8, 22; Nm 7:89; 1 Sm 4:4; 1 K 8:27 ff.).

20:3 *Remember. Offerings* and *sacrifices* were visible forms of prayer by which the worshiper expressed his allegiance to God and pleaded for His help.

20:6 *Now.* After recalling the king's wholehearted commitment to the Lord and after praying for him, the people, individually and collectively, are as certain of the requested deliverance as if it were an accomplished reality. For *anointed* see 2:3 note.

20:7 *Chariots . . . horses.* Formidable fighting machines of the day, considered as decisive in ancient warfare as those in modern arsenals are prized for their destructive power.

We boast. As David did, facing Goliath. (1 Sm

17:45; cf. also Dt 20:1; Ps 33:16 ff.; Is 30:15 ff.; 31:3; Zch 4:6)

Psalm 21

21:1-13 The first part of this psalm sings thanksgiving and praise to *the Most High* for granting the king *the request of his lips,* such as the one uttered in v. 4. Thanksgiving was in order because it was the Lord who granted the king success; praise was elicited by the magnitude of the *goodly blessings* bestowed on him (1-7). The second part expresses the confidence that enemies *will not succeed* in overthrowing the Lord's rule, administered by His earthly representative (8-12). To Him be all praise and honor (13).—In God's eternal plan to bless "all nations" (Gn 12:3; 22:18) the kingdom granted the chosen people of the old covenant was the shadow of greater things to come (cf. Ps 2). Victory over all man's foes down to the "last enemy" came to great David's greater Son when Jesus Christ was raised from the dead to be "crowned with glory and honor" (Ro 6:9; Heb 2:9; 1 Co 15:25 f.). No one can snatch His subjects out of His hand (Jn 10:28). They can look forward to the time when "the kingdom of the world has become the kingdom of our Lord and of his Christ" or Anointed One (Rv 11:15), who will consign all rebels to "eternal fire." (Mt 25:41; Rv 20:15)

21:3 *Set a crown.* God added luster to the symbol of royalty.

21:4 *For ever.* The customary acclamation of the king was: "May the king live forever!" (1 K 1:31; Neh 2:3; Dn 2:4; cf. also 1 K 3:14)

21:7 *Steadfast love.* Cf. the promises of God's covenant with David in 2 Sm 7:4-16. (Ps 89:24, 28, 33; Is 55:3)

21:8 *Your hand.* The Hebrew text permits vv. 8-12 to be construed as a prayer to God: "May thy hand find out," etc. What the king does as the Lord's instrument merges in thought with action of God's *right hand.* The change to the third person in v. 9 is not unusual; it occurs also in v. 7.

21:9 *Blazing oven.* All "enemies" will be consumed like chaff in the fires of divine judgment. (Is 30:27; 33:11 f.; Ml 4:1; Mt 3:12)

Psalm 22

22:1-31 Frequently called the Passion or Good Friday Psalm, this *Psalm of David* was written to "be accomplished" when Jesus Christ died on the tree of the cross and rose to "enter into his glory" (Lk 18:31; 24:25 f.; Jn 19:24). The suffering and the resulting victory, described in this prophetic "scripture," are of such a nature as to point beyond the experience and achievement of OT saints to the "man of sorrows . . . smitten by God and afflicted . . . for our transgressions" and raised again for our justification (Is 53; Ro 4:25).—The psalm begins in woe and ends in triumph. From dark perplexity and anguished cries for deliverance (1-21) it rises to a song of jubilation over universal salvation (22-31).—Suffering, unrelieved in spite of fervent prayer, is so intense as to produce fear of being forsaken by God (1-2), a dread all the more mysterious because in the past God did not fail to *deliver them* who trusted in Him (3-5). Adding to the agony, a leering mob gathers to scoff at reliance on divine help (6-8). Yet the fact remains that there is *none to help* if not the God who gives life and sustains it from infancy (9-11). The situation is truly desperate: (a) the enemies are strong as *bulls* and fierce as lions (12-13); (b) strength to endure the strain is fast ebbing away (14-15); (c) *evildoers* like a pack of wild dogs *gloat over* the effect of their cruelty, certain that the spoils of their murderous scheme would be theirs to share (16-18). Suddenly light dispels the gloom. Now prayers arise from a conviction so certain of deliverance as if they were already answered (19-21). Anticipation of being heard prompts the resolve to sing the praise of God in the hearing of those *who fear the Lord* so that they too might join the jubilation over the accomplished salvation (22-24). For its blessings accrue to all who seek . . . the Lord (25-26). There are no restrictions of place or time. *All the ends of the earth* (27-28) and a *people yet unborn* will benefit from the *deliverance* which God *has wrought.* (29-31)

22:1 *Forsaken me.* Sinful mankind deserves to be abandoned by a righteous God. The sinless Son of God, bearing the sins of the world, endured the agony of estrangement from His heavenly Father as He spoke the opening words of this psalm. (Mt 27:46)

22:3 *Praises of Israel.* The grateful acclaim of God's goodness by the faithful in Israel, so strong and constant in the past, is portrayed figuratively as bearing aloft the throne of His majesty. To symbolize His gracious presence He is said to be "enthroned upon the cherubim" on the ark of the covenant. (80:1; 99:1)

22:6 *Worm.* No longer resembling a *man* but "marred beyond human semblance." (Is 52:14; 53:2)

22:7 *Mock.* Forsaken by God, Jesus was scorned by those He came to save. (Mt 27:39-44; Mk 15:29-32)

22:9 *From the womb.* There is "none to help" if the Creator of life does not sustain it.

22:12 *Bashan.* Cattle raised in the grazing lands east of the Sea of Galilee were proverbially *strong.*

22:14 *Poured out.* Mental and physical exhaustion, produced by suffering, is described graphically in 14 and 15. Courage and ability to bear up are as unstable as spilled water (Jos 7:5; Jb 30:16; Eze 7:17); bodily coordination fails as if the *bones* were dislocated; the *heart* is like *wax* exposed to heat. (Jos 2:11; 2 Sm 17:10)

22:16 *Pierced.* The RSV note notwithstanding, the Hebrew text admits of the traditional translation. "Like a lion" yields no sense in the context. The reference to Jesus' crucifixion is obvious.

22:18 *Divide my garments.* Jesus' executioners did so "to fulfil the scripture." (Jn 19:23 f.)

22:21 *Afflicted soul.* The translation in the

RSV note, "Thou hast answered me," is to be preferred. It serves as a transition to the second part of the psalm (22-31), which exults over the deliverance prayed for in 1-22. See also Heb 5:7.

22:22 *Name.* Cf. 20:1 note.

22:23 *Praise him.* What God did in answer to prayer is told gratefully in the midst of those *who fear the Lord,* because sharing in the benefits they have every reason to *glorify him.*

22:25 *Vows.* The thanksgiving to be rendered is expressed in terms of OT worship. Praise is as much in order as sacrifices of thanksgiving were called for in the keeping of vows (Lv 7:11-17; Ps 50:14; 61:8; 66:13; 116:14). Such offerings were a communion service. Fellow worshipers partook of the consecrated food (26). As vv. 27-31 make clear, the limitations of OT ritualistic forms were to be superseded by an unrestricted invitation to the great Messianic banquet described in Is 55; 25:6. Cf Lk 22:30; Rv 2:7; Lk 14:15-24.

22:27 *Ends of the earth.* Those who will be mindful of the Lord's victory over the forces of evil and *turn to* Him for their own salvation will come from *all the families of the nations,* thereby establishing the universal kingdom of God.

22:29 *Go down.* Every mortal man *who cannot keep himself alive* indefinitely, including "a people yet unborn" (31), is eligible to "serve" the Lord because of the "deliverance . . . that he has wrought."

Psalm 23

23:1-6 In spite of its imagery of a bygone day, the "Good Shepherd Psalm" is the source of renewed strength and abiding comfort to which children of God down to the present day have turned more often than to any other except for the petitions formulated by the incarnate Good Shepherd Himself. There is an esthetic appeal in the charming cadence of its poetic simplicity and sturdiness. However, it is more than a masterful combination of pretty words and phrases depicting an idyllic scene of rustic tranquility. It faces the grim realities of life with unflinching candor. Human ingenuity and resources are unable to cope with them. However, trust in the Lord's power, wisdom, and goodness can bring light and hope into a dark and meaningless existence. Commitment to His guidance and providential care affords a serene peace of mind. Nothing can happen that is an *evil.* This outlook on life is not the stolid determination to bear the inevitable blows of a blind fate with composure and dull resignation. For peace and security faith depends on a sympathetic and thoughtful Good Shepherd who takes a personal interest in every sheep in His flock. He knows and can supply their individual needs (1-3). He is ever at their side to calm all their fears even, as a well-known hymn has it, "when other helpers fail and comforts flee" (4). No harm can come to them if they turn to Him for protection. There is no end to the joy over the *goodness and mercy* that His presence guarantees (5-6).—When the NT believer prays this psalm, he hears ringing through it the voice of the Good Shepherd who said: "I lay down my life for the sheep." (Jn 10:11 ff.; Rv 7:17; 1 Ptr 2:24 f.)

23:1 *My shepherd.* The pronouns *I, me, my,* occurring in almost every line, express the conviction that the "Shepherd of Israel" is concerned with and supplies the wants of each individual in His flock. (Cf. 80:1; 74:1; 77:20; 78:52, 70-72; 79:13; 100:3)

23:3 *Restores my soul.* A good shepherd does not drive his sheep through arid wastelands where food and drink are hard to find. He knows how to lead them to places where they can rest themselves from exhausting marches, while foraging in meadows of lush growth and quenching their thirst with wholesome water. So the Lord is able to provide what His children need if they are to be at rest. He supplies the means necessary to renew vitality and to reanimate flagging spirits. For *name's sake* see 8:1 note.

23:5 *Table.* The Lord is able not only to avert "evil" (4) but also will not let *enemies* interfere when He dispenses the good things in life. (78:19 f.)

Oil. Guests were supplied with oil for their heads as a gesture of hospitality (92:10; Am 6:6; Lk 7:46). For *cup* see 11:6 note.

23:6 *Follow me.* The supply of blessings does not give out. They overtake and accompany every footstep along the way. For *mercy* see Dt 7:9 note.

House of the Lord. Not self-reliance but perennial communion with God is the source of strength. Blessed is the man who resorts to it *all the days of* his *life.* (27:4 f.; 52:8 f.)

Psalm 24

24:1-10 This *Psalm of David* dramatizes instructions for God-pleasing worship (cf. Ps 15 for similar directives). The superscription does not state whether it was acted out at a specific occasion such as David's transfer of the ark of the covenant to Jerusalem (2 Sm 6). Nor is there any record that it was recited antiphonally as bands of pilgrims approached *the hill of the Lord* (3) to observe the prescribed festivals (cf. the Psalms of Ascents, 120 ff.; also 68:24 ff.). Whatever its historical origin or setting, it sets forth in lively dialog form basic ingredients of acceptable communion with God. As if from ethereal heights comes the reminder of the transcendent majesty of Him to whom rites and ceremonies are directed: He is the omnipotent Creator of the universe; all it contains is already at His disposal according to His good pleasure (1-2; 136:4-8; Is 6:1). The question therefore arises what kind of people dare to appear in His exalted presence expecting to receive a *blessing?* The answer is: only those who "strive for . . . holiness" in thought, word, and deed (3-6; Heb 12:14). Because "the high and lofty One who inhabits eternity" (Is 57:15 f.) deigns to be present among His people, it behooves them to be aware how "awesome" is *His holy place* (3; Gn 28:17). In order to impress on them what it means for *the King of glory* to *come in* and dwell among them, the *gates* are ordered twice to raise their beams and vaults for His entry. Each directive to the gates is followed by a question and answer designed to underscore His eminence. The worshipers are to have an audience not with an earthly potentate but with *the Lord of hosts,* unlimited in power, invincible in battle, unsurpassed in glory (7-10).—God's condescension to have His glory enshrined in Israel's sanctuary made by hands was worthy of praise and adoration. But when the "King of kings and Lord of lords" "was manifested in the flesh" and tabernacled among His creatures in "the form of a servant, being born in the likeness of men," "great indeed, we confess, is the mystery of our religion" (Rv 19:16; 1 Ti 3:16; Ph 2:7). At Adventtide we welcome Him anew into our lives in the words of this psalm.

24:2 *Upon the seas.* The dry earth, separated from the waters at creation, is kept from returning to chaos. For other figurative expressions to denote God's way of establishing and maintaining a stable universe see Jb 26:7 note; 38:6.

24:3 *Hill of the Lord.* Cf. 2:6 note.

24:4 *Hands and . . . heart.* As in Ps 15, no ritual or ceremonial requirements are mentioned. Not unimportant under the old covenant, outward forms of worship were not a mechanical or magic device which automatically coerced God into granting a "blessing." Sacrifices were an abomination (Is 1:13) unless the heart was cleansed of impure motives and the hands were restrained from doing wrong. (Jer 7:9 f.)

Lift up his soul. The Lord searches "the minds and hearts" also for undivided loyalty to Him (7:9; 26:2). The worshiper is to have no reservations when he professes: "To thee, O Lord, I lift up my soul" (25:1; 86:4; 143:8). For the true God will not share His honor with *what is false,* i.e., with idols, which are "no-gods" (Dt 32:21 note; 1 K 16:13 note; Jer 5:7; 18:15; Ps 31:6). To *swear deceitfully* takes the holy name of God in vain. (Ex 20:7 note)

24:6 *Generation.* Cf. 12:7 note.

24:10 *Lord of hosts.* Cf. 1 Sm 1:3 note.

Psalm 25

25:1-22 Though composed in the artistic sequence of an acrostic poem (cf. Ps 9), this *Psalm of David* is not a stilted or contrived exercise in devotional writing, but vibrates with feelings arising from a real-life experience. Reflecting spontaneous reaction to a distressing situation, motifs erupt, are repeated, and become intertwined with one another, uninhibited by concerns for strict logical progression. In the first section (1-7) a prayer for deliverance, an appeal for guidance to understand the Lord's *ways,* and a plea for forgiveness are interlaced with expressions of trust in God's mercy. As if to bolster confidence in Him, His *steadfast love and faithfulness* toward *the man that fears the Lord* are called to mind in a hymn of praise, interspersed with a second prayer for forgiveness (8-15). The psalm closes with a prayerful summation of the items of concern already presented, including a third petition for removal of sin. (16-22)

25:1 *Lift up my soul.* Cf. 24:4 note.

25:2 *Put to shame.* Importunity in prayer makes bold to confront God with the suggestion that if He does not answer the prayer of those "that wait for" Him, His honor too is at stake. *Enemies* would be entitled to gloat over the futility of trusting His promises.

25:4 *Ways . . . paths.* Coupled with the cry for deliverance is the repeated plea for guidance through life's perplexities (5, 8, 9, 10, 12). Two things are needed: first, rejecting "the way of sinners" (1:1), it is imperative to strive for a better understanding of and a fuller compliance with the orientation of life as set forth in God's covenant; second, one must have implicit confidence that God's choice of paths "for those who fear him" (14) is always determined by His "steadfast love and faithfulness" (10; Ex 33:13; 1 K 2:3; Ps 5:8; 23:3; 27:11; 86:11; 119:35).—God's concern for man's welfare culminated in the coming of Him who is "the way, and the truth, and the life," granting us "newness of life." (Jn 14:6; Ro 6:4)

25:6 *Steadfast love.* Cf. Dt 7:9 note.

25:7 *For thy goodness' sake.* "The man that fears the Lord" (12) and "keeps his covenant and his testimonies" (10) has not merited the granting of deliverance, guidance, and forgiveness. He dares to ask for them only because he can appeal to the mercy and grace of God (6, 16; Ex 34:6 f.), which "have been from of old." (6)

25:10 *Covenant.* For its meaning see Exodus, Introduction, "Content."

Testimonies. Cf. 19:7 note.

25:11 *For thy name's sake.* Cf. 8:1 note.

25:13 *In prosperity.* Lit. "in good." Because He is "good" (8), He keeps the promises attached to the covenant. (Dt 4:40; see also Mt 5:5)

25:14 *Friendship.* The personal, intimate relationship established by the covenant.

25:21 *Preserve me.* The repeated plea for forgiveness comes from a sincere heart, intent on doing "what is right" (9) in the future and looking to God for help to stay on a path of *integrity and uprightness.*

25:22 *Israel.* God lets "none that wait for" Him "be ashamed" (3). He is to come to the aid of all "who keep his covenant" (10) when they bring their individual or collective *troubles* to Him.

Psalm 26

26:1-12 The situation reflected in this *Psalm of David* is similar to the setting of Ps 7 (cf. 7:1-17 and 7:3 notes). Charged with a capital crime, the accused appeals for a verdict of vindication to the Lord who can *test . . . heart and . . . mind* (1-3). The defendant asserts his innocence (4-7) and renews his plea for rescue (8-10), confident of acquittal. (11-12)

26:1 *Walked in my integrity.* Not a self-righteous boast of moral perfection but a disclaimer of willful acts of crime. (Cf. 7:8 note)

26:2 *Test.* Lit. "smelt" or "refine" like metal to analyze ingredients hidden within (17:3; Is 1:25; 48:10; Jer 6:29; 9:7). For *heart* and *mind* see 7:9 note.

26:4 *False men.* Lit. "men of falsehood or vanity," i.e., such as are devoted to "what is false" (24:4 note). People who *consort* with "evildoers" and "sit with the wicked" forfeit God's blessing. (Ps 1)

26:6 *Wash my hands.* A symbolic gesture to profess innocence (Dt 21:6 f.; Ps 73:13; Mt 27:24) or indicate ceremonial cleanness (Ex 30:17-21). A worshiper would only increase his guilt if he appeared at the *altar* harboring known and unconfessed sin.

26:8 *Thy glory.* Cf. Ex 40:34 note.

26:9 *Sweep . . . away. Sinners* cannot "stand in the judgment" (1:5 note)—Jesus, crucified between malefactors, "was numbered with the transgressors." (Is 53:12; Lk 22:37)

26:11 *Redeem . . . be gracious.* Certain of being cleared of alleged crimes and determined to avoid them by walking in *integrity* as before, the suppliant knows nevertheless that he has not earned the right to claim God's intervention on his behalf. Divine help is an act of pure grace.

Psalm 27

27:1-14 At the core of this *Psalm of David* is a fervent appeal to the *God of my salvation* for deliverance from *enemies* and *adversaries* who defame and *breathe out violence* against His *servant* (7-12). As if to assure himself that he is not whistling in the dark, the suppliant introduces and closes his petition with bold declarations of faith in God's power and willingness to come to his rescue (1-6 and 13-14). In the opening verses (1-3) he asserts his conviction that, with the Lord as his *stronghold,* he is not *afraid* even though battalions of *foes* assault him. He goes on to say that this sense of absolute security comes from seeking and maintaining constant fellowship with God. Worship in His *house* is like entering a *shelter in the day of trouble.* Certain of the defeat of his enemies, he vows to *sing* songs of thanksgiving (4-6). The note of confidence dominates the prayer which follows (7-12). The last two verses are like an Amen, spoken in imperturbable confidence. (13-14)

27:1 *Light.* God disperses the enervating gloom of perplexity, helplessness, and loss of meaning in life (36:9; 43:3; 97:11; Is 10:17). He whose name means *salvation* is "the true light that enlightens every man." (Jn 1:9; Is 49:6; Jn 8:12).

27:2 *Uttering slanders.* The phrase "to eat up my flesh" (RSV note) is used figuratively in Aramaic to describe the havoc wrought by "false witnesses" (12). Here, as elsewhere in the psalms, the point of comparison is the ferocity of wild animals intent on devouring their victim. (7:2; 14:4; 17:12)

27:3 *A host.* If the Lord is on his side, what can men do even if thousands attack in serried ranks? (118:6; 3:6; Ro 8:31)

27:4 *Beauty.* The promised presence of the Lord in His "tent" or tabernacle (5-6) makes this sanctuary built by hands *his temple* or heavenly palace (Jos 6:24; 1 Sm 1:9 note; 3:3). Here "the favor of the Lord" was to be sought and found (90:17). To "behold his face" is a daily obligation and privilege. (11:7 note; 23:6 note)

27:6 *Make melody.* Cf. 33:3; 107:22; Nm 10:10.

27:8 *My heart says.* God's directive to seek Him where He is to be found prompted the decision to confront Him with His promise to "be gracious" and to "answer" the prayer for deliverance. (7; 24:6; Dt 4:29)

27:10 *Have forsaken me.* Better translated: "even though my father and my mother forsake me," as in Is 49:15.

27:11 *Thy way.* Cf. 25:4 note.

27:13 *I believe.* Confidence in the Lord as the only hope in a desperate situation is expressed more forcefully if the verse is translated as an incomplete sentence: "If I had not believed." The principal clause expressing the result of facing life without God is omitted as too horrible even to contemplate.

Psalm 28

28:1-9 Though similar in setting and content, this *Psalm of David* begins with a prayer and ends in praise, thus reversing the sequence of thought followed in Ps 27 (cf. vv. 1-14 there). Here the opening verses raise *the voice of . . . supplication* for deliverance from sharing the disastrous fate deserved by *workers of evil* (1-5). Misgivings that the Lord will remain *silent to* the plea for intervention give way to the conviction that *he has heard* (6-7). All of *his people* can trust *their shepherd* to *save* and *bless* them. (8-9)

28:1 *Deaf.* God's children grow impatient when He appears to turn a deaf ear to prayer and needs to be importuned not to remain *silent* (35:22; 39:12; 83:1; 109:1). The situation seems to be so desperate that further delay is equivalent to letting the embattled sufferer *go down to the Pit,* i.e., the grave. (30:3; 88:4 ff.; 143:7)

28:2 *Sanctuary.* The Hebrew word translated "inner sanctuary" (1 K 6:5, 16; 2 Ch 4:20; 5:7, 9) denotes the Holy of Holies, where God was enthroned above the ark of the covenant (Ex 25:22). The lifting of hands was a gesture of worship. (63:4; Neh 8:6)

28:4 *Requite them.* Uttered not in a spirit of vindictiveness but animated by the concern that the principles of justice, established by God, become operative and manifest, lest moral chaos prevail (see the note on "imprecatory psalms" in the introductory remarks to the Book of Psalms).

28:8 *His people.* Belonging to God's covenant people, *anointed* or set aside to be "a kingdom of priests" (Ex 19:6), gives each member the privilege of finding *refuge* in His *strength.* Therefore a closing prayer (9) pleads with the "Shepherd of Israel" (80:1; 74:1; 79:13; 95:7) to continue to keep His *heritage* in loving care. (Dt 9:26, 29; Mi 7:14)

Psalm 29

29:1-11 This *Psalm of David* is a magnificent hymn in praise of God's awesome power which is (a) worthy of adoration by angelic hosts (1-2); (b) fearfully demonstrated when unleashed in a thunderstorm (3-9); (c) beneficent in affording *peace* to His people. (10-11)

29:1 *Heavenly beings.* God is not the personification of the forces of nature like the storm gods of the heathen pantheon but the sovereign Creator of "the heavens and the earth . . . and all the host of them" (Gn 2:1; Ps 33:6). His celestial creatures are enlisted to join the voices "from the earth" in paying humble homage to His *glory and strength.* (148:1, 7; 89:6; 1 K 22:19; Jb 38:7 note; Is 6:1-5)

29:2 *In holy array.* As mundane priests were to appear before the Lord vested in "holy garments," so the ethereal worshipers should be adorned with holy reverence. (Ex 28:2; 2 Ch 20:21; Ps 96:9)

29:3 *Voice of the Lord.* The omnipotent Word of *the God of glory* by which He spoke heaven and earth into existence (33:6, 9; 148:5) still resounds in the ominous voice of the storm (18:12 f.; Jb 37:1-5). Like rolling claps of thunder *the voice of the Lord* reverberates in vv. 3-9, echoed and reechoed seven times. Issued from the heavens (68:33 f.), it roars out over the "thick clouds" dark with *many waters.* (18:11)

29:6 *Sirion.* Mt. Hermon, the highest peak of Palestine (Dt 3:9). The power generated by the storm breaks "all the cedars of Lebanon," symbols of "all that is proud and lofty" (Is 2:12 f.), and convulses the crags in which they are anchored.

29:7 *Flames of fire.* Forked lightning.

29:8 *Wilderness of Kadesh.* The earthshaking power of the storm hits also the flatlands such as the wilderness through which Israel passed on the way to Canaan. (Nm 13:26; 20:16)

29:9 *The oaks.* The Hebrew words for *oaks* and "hinds" are spelled with the same consonants. The translation in the RSV note suggests that the storm, as it *strips the forests bare,* affects the female deer, causing them to "calve" prematurely.

Glory. In *his* heavenly *temple,* high above the raging storm, *all* angelic hosts (1 f.) respond to the voice of thunder with a *gloria in excelsis.* (148:1 f.; 150:1; Is 6:3)

29:10 *Over the flood.* The *king* whose "throne is in heaven" (11:4) and whose "voice goes out through all the earth" (19:4) is "mightier than the thunders of many waters" (93:4). As He once "opened the windows of the heavens" and let "the fountains of the great deep burst forth" to execute judgment on a corrupt world, so He reigns *forever,* serenely enthroned above all cosmic forces. (93:2)

29:11 *Peace.* God's voice of thunder (3-9) need not awaken dread in *his people.* It is to assure them that His Word is no less powerful to *bless* them with all they need for their well-being and *peace* of mind. If they appeal to Him, He is able to command life's raging storms "Peace! Be still!" (Mk 4:39).—When "the Word became flesh" (Jn 1:14), "a multitude of the heavenly hosts" sang "Glory to God in the highest and on earth peace among men." (Lk 2:13 f.; cf. Jn 14:27)

Psalm 30

30:1-12 This *Psalm of David* is a song of gratitude for a twofold deliverance. Praise is offered (a) for preservation of physical life; deliverance from the brink of death is acknowledged publicly as a gift of God's *favor* (1-5); (b) for recovery of spiritual health; adversity, God's antibiotic against pride and self-sufficiency, produced the cure (6-10). The change from *mourning* to *gladness* produces the vow to *give thanks* to God's mercy *for ever.* (11-12)

In the Hebrew text the superscription reads: "A Psalm—a Song at the dedication of the Temple—of David." The appositional insertion dividing the phrase *A Psalm of David* may be a scribal addition reflecting the appropriation of the psalm for liturgical use at a later time such as at the Jewish Feast of Dedication (Channukah), which was observed to commemorate the reconsecration of the temple after its desecration by Antiochus Epiphanes. (1 Mac 4:54 ff.; 2 Mac 10:1 ff.; Jn 10:22)

30:1 *Drawn me up.* The Lord is exalted in words of praise because He pulled up the sufferer as he was sinking into the "Pit" of death, like a bucket of water drawn up from a well. Had he not been rescued, the enemies would have gloated over his disaster as punishment for crimes.

30:2 *Healed.* Ordinarily this verb refers to restoration from sickness. However, it is used also in a transferred sense to denote alleviation of other painful distresses inflicted by the Lord's rod of affliction. (Is 19:22; 30:26; 53:5; 57:17-19; Jer 30:17; 33:6 f.; Hos 6:1; 14:4)

30:3 *Gone down.* Better translated: "those who go down to the Pit" as in 28:1.

30:4 *Saints.* Cf. 4:3 note. For similar grateful proclamations to others of God's favor which turns a brief night of weeping into bright joy (5) see 9:11; 31:23 f.; 40:10; 116:14.

30:6 *Prosperity.* The Lord has a remedy for self-confidence which forgets that a carefree life depends on His favor: He shakes the "strong mountain" of stable security which He alone can provide (7; Dt 8:10 ff.; 32:15 ff.). The resulting dismay produces prayer to the only "helper" (8-10) and the resolve to recognize dependence on Him "forever." (11 f.)

30:9 *What profit.* Cf. 6:5 note.

30:11 *Sackcloth.* The garment of *mourning.* (35:13; 69:11; Gn 37:34)

Psalm 31

31:1-24 This *Psalm of David* is not a dispassionate, logically organized treatise on the need of prayer. It throbs with the irregular beat of a heart aquiver with emotional strain. In both parts (1-8 and 9-22) fear and confidence come and go; trembling supplication alternates with rejoicing and thanksgiving as if deliverance already had come. The opening prayer, seeking *refuge* in the *strong fortress* of God's *righteousness* (1-2), is followed by an affirmation of unreserved committal to a *faithful God* whose demonstrations of redeeming and *steadfast love* in the past give assurance that a song of gladness and thanksgiving will replace the anguish of *adversities* (3-8). No one panic-stricken in a shattering catastrophe will find it unrealistic or tiresome when the second part of the psalm (a) again entreats God to *be gracious* (9-10) in view of hostile forces arousing *terror on every side* (11-13); (b) reiterates trust in God's ability and readiness to come to the rescue of *the righteous,* assailed by wicked *enemies and persecutors* (14-18); (c) breaks out anew in more sustained strains of praise in anticipation of finding safety *in the covert* of God's *goodness* and in the *shelter* of *his steadfast love,* earlier misgivings and doubts notwithstanding (19-22). The last two verses recommend to all beset by similar trials to *take courage* and confidently *wait for the Lord.*

31:1 *Refuge.* Cf. 7:1 note. The suppliant's appeal to God's *righteousness* expresses the conviction that he has a just cause and has every reason to expect vindication from that Judge who never fails to "judge the peoples with equity" (67:4; 7:11; 96:10; Jer 11:20; 1 Ptr 2:23). An unfavorable verdict would *put to shame* everyone who relies on His promise and ability to maintain justice.

31:3 *Thy name's sake.* On God's name see 8:1 note; 23:3.

31:4 *Net.* The enemies "hid their net" to trap their victim as a hunter sets concealed snares for his quarry. (35:7; 7:15; 9:15; 140:5)

31:5 *Commit my spirit.* Words hallowed in a special way when spoken by Jesus as "he breathed his last" (Lk 23:46) and repeated by His first martyr. (Acts 7:59)

31:6 *Vain idols.* Cf. 24:4 note. The reading "I hate" (cf. RSV note) affirms the suppliant's *trust in the Lord* by his abhorrence of idol worshipers.

31:7 *Adversities.* Lit. "distresses of my soul." For *steadfast love* (also in vv. 16 and 21) see Dt 7:9 note.

31:8 *Broad place.* No longer hemmed in by pressures from the enemy. (Cf. 4:1 note under "room")

31:10 *Misery.* The Hebrew words "iniquity" (RSV note) and *misery* have the same consonantal components.

31:11 *Acquaintances.* Cf. Job's complaint (Jb 19:13-15); also Ps 38:11; 88:8.

31:15 *My times.* The *hand* into which everything has been committed (5) controls the timing of life's every moment. Nothing happens too soon or too late; there is no accidental tragedy and no delayed blessing. (139:5; Is 33:6; Mt 10:29)

31:16 *Face shine.* Cf. Nm 6:25 note; Ps 4:6.

31:17 *To Sheol. The wicked* are implacable; only death can end their persecution.

31:21 *Besieged city.* The clause *when I was beset as* is added by the RSV as an interpretation of the phrase *in a besieged city* (lit. "in a city of siege"). The meaning may be simply: the "covert" and the "shelter" (lit. "booth") provided by God's *steadfast love* proved to be as safe as a city fortified to resist a siege. (Nah 1:7)

31:22 *In my alarm.* The first hasty reaction to the impact of so dreadful a disaster was to panic with fear and despair.

Psalm 32

32:1-11 In this second penitential psalm (cf. Ps 6:1-10), "David," says St. Paul, "pronounces a blessing upon the man to whom God reckons righteousness apart from works" (Ro 4:6). And indeed David claims no merit or worthiness, entitling him to absolution; even his penitential tears and abject remorse do not produce anything deserving consideration. Giving all glory to God, he revels in sharing the happiness which is bestowed out of pure grace on *the man to whom the Lord imputes no iniquity* (1-2). His gratitude grows as he recalls the agony of mind and body he endured (3-4) before he unburdened his conscience in honest confession and God forgave the iniquity of his sin (5). Appreciation for what he received prompts him to urge fellow sufferers to follow his example and make the Lord their *hiding place* when assailed by *trouble* (6-7). If they will not be obstinate but let the Lord *instruct* and *counsel* them, they will not experience *the pangs of the wicked* but will rejoice as *steadfast love surrounds* them (8-11).—For the occasion of the psalm see the superscription of Ps 51.—The meaning of the transliterated Hebrew word *Maskil* cannot be determined with certainty. (Cf. introductory notes to the Book of Psalms, "Superscriptions")

32:1-2 *Blessed.* Cf. 1:1-6 note; 103:1-5. To describe what brought him bliss, the poet uses a variety of synonyms. The cause of man's misery is *transgression* (willful disobedience), *sin* (missing the mark), *iniquity* (guilt in wrongdoing). God eliminates what separates man from the source of health and life when *transgression is forgiven* (lifting of a crushing burden), when *sin is covered* (removal from sight and remembrance), when He *imputes no iniquity* (declaration of pardon and cancelation of guilt) and so produces a *spirit* purged of unholy *deceit.*

32:4 *Dried up.* The Hebrew word translated *strength* occurs again only in Nm 11:8, where it describes "cakes baked with oil." Apparently using an unusual metaphor, David describes himself as being drained of body fluid as if he were fried on a griddle (cf. 22:15). One Hebrew manuscript has "my heart was dried up."

32:6 *Godly.* Cf. 4:3 note. The RSV emends the Hebrew text quoted in the footnote. However, left unchanged, the transmitted wording makes good sense. If the godly does not delay but prays at the time when the Lord "may be found" (Is 55:6), it is not at all possible for the waters of distress to reach and overwhelm him. (For an example of the adverb "only" intensifying a verb with "not" see Gn 24:8.)

32:7 *Deliverance.* Safe in God, his *hiding place,* he can turn in every direction and find occasions for "shouts of deliverance." (RSV note)

32:8 *I will instruct.* In order to reinforce his advice that also others "offer prayer to" God when in need of a "hiding place," David intersperses his words with a short declaration from the Lord Himself, expressed in the form of a divine oracle. (Cf. 25:8; 33:18)

32:9 *Horse.* Cf. Ja 3:3.

32:11 *O righteous.* A man must trust "the steadfast love" of the Lord if he is to escape "the pangs of the wicked." (10)

Psalm 33

33:1-22 This *new song* of praise proclaims in 22 verses (the number of letters in the Hebrew alphabet, as in Ps 38) what the "righteous" should and can say when summoned to "rejoice . . . and shout for joy" (32:11). The opening verses (1-3) give six directives how this is to be done. There is to be no grudging muttering, no halfhearted mumbling, no reciting of empty words, but a spontaneous, full-throated outburst of jubilation, accompanied and stimulated by the strains of music. Then (4-19) the psalm spells out the reasons why *praise befits the upright* (1). They cannot but break out in song if they ponder: (a) that the Lord can be trusted to exercise also in their behalf the power of His Word by which He *commanded* heaven and earth to emerge into existence (4-9); (b) that His people need not fear *the counsel* and *plans* of men because He is able to frustrate all evil designs (10-12); (c) that nothing that men do or even think escapes His all-seeing eye or eludes His control, so that trust in their *great strength* turns out to be a *vain hope* (13-17); (d) that the watchful *eye of the Lord,* just described, never loses sight of *those who fear him* when they are in need of help (18-19). This rousing call to worship the omnipotent, omniscient, gracious Lord produced results. It moved those who heard it to *trust in his holy name* and to pray for the continued manifestation of His *steadfast love.* (20-22)

33:1 *Righteous.* For the qualifications of acceptable worshipers see 1:5, 6; 15:2-5; 24:3-5; 32:11; 118:19 f.

33:3 *New song.* Composed specifically in response to every act of God's mercies which "are new every morning" (Lm 3:22 f.; Ps 40:3; 96:1 f.; 98:1; 144:9; 149:1). For the new song by the redeemed in the new heavens and the new earth see Rv 5:9; 14:3.

33:4 *Word of the Lord.* It is *upright,* making known "the truth" and declaring "what is right" (Is 45:19). The Lord faithfully carries out in *all his work* what He has said He will do.

33:5 *He loves.* By His Word the Lord reveals His nature and the kind of rule He establishes. He speaks in order to maintain a moral world order, based on *righteousness and justice,* as well as to keep the covenanted promises of his *steadfast love.* (11:7; 18:50; 37:28; 100:5; 103:6; 119:64; 136; Ex 20:5 f.; Dt 32:4; Jer 32:17 f.)

33:6 *The heavens.* "In the beginning" "he spoke" and there "came to be" (9) what did not exist (Ro 4:17): *the heavens . . . and all their host* (Gn 1:1, 16; 2:1) and the earth, separated from "the waters of the sea" (7; Gn 1:6). Cf. also 8:3; 19:1; 148:5 f.; Is 40:26; 48:13.

33:7 *Bottle.* KJV: "as an heap" (cf. Ex 15:8; Ps 78:13). The Hebrew words for a heaped-up mass and for a container of liquid, made of an animal skin, are very similar. RSV follows the ancient versions in adopting the reading *bottle.* For similar figurative terms to denote the Lord's control of the forces of nature see 135:7; Jb 38:22; Jer 10:13.

33:11 *Counsel of the Lord.* As heaven and earth did not come into existence by chance, so nothing contrary to His will and plan can evolve in the course of world history. "Nations" and "peoples" could not frustrate His determined counsel to make Israel "his heritage." (Dt 4:7, 20, 32 ff.; Is 8:10; 14:24; 40:22 f.; 46:10)

33:15 *The hearts.* From His heavenly throne of sovereign majesty the Lord *observes* not only what "the sons of men" do but He also peers into their hearts and controls their thinking. (7:9)

33:17 *War horse.* A "great army," equipped with most dreaded weapons, is doomed to defeat unless it marches under the banner of the Lord of hosts. (20:7; Pr 21:31; Is 40:23 f.)

Psalm 34

34:1-22 In this *Psalm of David* the resolve to *bless the Lord* at all times and the exhortation to others to do likewise (1-3) grow out of an actual experience of deliverance in answer to prayer (4-6). For what the Lord did in one instance should encourage all listeners to *fear* Him and to *taste and see that the Lord is good* (7-10). However, they need to remember that *the fear of the Lord* requires that they prove its sincerity by striving to avoid what is *evil* and to do what is *good* in life's every day (11-14). Then two reasons are advanced why total commitment to God makes a difference in life: (a) the Lord hears the cry of *the righteous* and *delivers them* whereas He is *against evildoers* (15-18); (b) even when the Lord permits His *servants* to suffer *many . . . afflictions,* they can be sure that He will not chasten them beyond what they can endure, whereas *the wicked . . . will be condemned* and slain by the very *evil* they do (19-22).—For the occasion of the psalm mentioned in the superscriptions see 1 Sm 21:10-15. It has the same acrostic form as Ps 25.

34:2 *Boast.* The vow to "rejoice in the Lord always" (Ph 4:4) disavows reliance on human wisdom, might, and riches. (Jer 9:23 f.; Ps 49:6; 1 Co 1:31; 2 Co 10:17)

34:3 *Magnify.* Praise cannot add to the stature of God; its sole purpose is to acknowledge and extol His greatness of which the revelation of *his name* gives overwhelming proof. (69:30; Dt 32:3; for the meaning of *name* see Ex 6:3 note)

34:5 *Look to him.* The transmitted text reads: "they look to him." It expresses a general observation: the face of those who expect help from the Lord will beam with *radiant* joy (Is 60:5; Jer 31:12), a truth verified in the experience of one "poor man." (6)

34:7 *Angel of the Lord.* Cf. Gn 48:15 note; Ex 14:19 note.

Encamps. The Lord's angel, one of legions at His command (Mt 26:53), provides a protective ring of armed might, always on the alert and capable of warding off all attacks (Gn 32:1 f.; 2 K 6:15-17; Ps 35:6; 91:11; Dn 6:22)

34:8 *Taste.* Find out by personal experiment as food is savored by tongue and palate. (1 Ptr 2:3)

34:9 *Saints.* Lit. "holy ones," i.e., such as share in the blessings of God's holy nation and strive to be holy as He is holy. (16:3; Ex 19:6 note; Lv 19:2 note)

34:10 *Young lions.* As the king of the animal world often goes hungry in spite of his strength and agility, so man's resources cannot be relied on to supply needs essential to human welfare. (35:17)

34:11 *Fear of the Lord.* Cf. Dt 6:13 note.

34:12 Vv. 12-16a, quoted in 1 Ptr 3:10-12, make clear that "the fear of the Lord," while it cannot claim divine favor and protection as wages, nevertheless by its very nature must motivate the kind of life which will "strive for peace with all men, and for . . . holiness." (Heb. 12:14; Is 1:16 f.; Mt 5:9; Ro 14:19)

34:15 *The eyes of the Lord.* Those who fear the Lord can be sure that He has the will and the power to enforce principles of just retribution toward "evildoers" as well as to let mercy prevail toward "the brokenhearted" and "the crushed in spirit."

34:19 *Many . . . afflictions.* The lot of *the righteous,* depicted so far, may appear to run counter to the hard realities of life. However, the Lord's promise to deliver them "out of all their troubles" (17) is not proved unreliable when their prayers for relief from heartbreaking disappointments and black nights of misery seemingly go unanswered. Afflictions do not happen because the Lord cannot or will not deflect them. They are an essential feature of a wise educational process, aimed at drawing "his servants" closer to His fatherly heart of goodness. Assured of this, they can "bless the Lord at *all* times" (1) even when they "meet various trials" (Ja 1:2; Lk 6:22 f.). No matter how crushing the blow or how long it hurts, He never lets the situation get to the point where He cannot deliver them in His own way.

34:20 *All his bones.* The promise that there is a limit beyond which "afflictions" are not allowed to go was fulfilled in a unique way in the suffering of our Lord, the only truly righteous and holy One. (Jn 19:36; see also Ex 12:46)

Psalm 35

35:1-28 For some unknown reason the superscription in the transmitted text does not contain the designation *A Psalm* but has only *of David.* It is made up of three appeals to God's *righteousness* (24) for a favorable verdict, exonerating the victim of criminal charges, which were brought against him by *malicious* (11) and ungrateful perverters of the truth. Unless curbed and *confounded* (4), they are about to gloat and *rejoice over* (24) the success of their vicious plot to destroy an innocent, god-fearing person. Anyone who has faced a threatening catastrophe, devised by sinister forces *too strong for him* (10), will recognize how true to life it is when the cry for help is uttered not once but three times (1-10, 11-18, 19-21). By the same token he will not find it strange that in each plea the Lord is told how desperate the situation is. However, if he prays this psalm, he can learn to pray with confidence, as he notes that each petition includes the vow to *rejoice in the Lord* (9) in anticipation of the expected deliverance.

35:1 *Contend.* Plead his "cause" (23) as his advocate, representing him in a lawsuit. For an appeal for deliverance presented in terms of trial in court see Ps 7:1-17 note.

35:2 *Shield and buckler.* All doubts of God's power to come to the aid of the "weak and needy" (10) vanish in recalling that He is "mighty in battle," "the Lord God of hosts." (24:8; Ex 14:14, 25; 15:3; Dt 1:30; 20:3 f.; Is 42:13; Jer 50:25)

35:4 *My life.* The situation is a matter of life and death, requiring that the attackers be *turned back and confounded.* They are so obsessed by demonic hatred that they will not desist unless they are removed from the scene "like chaff before the wind" and made to fall into the pit which "they dug" for their intended victim (5; 7 f.; 1:4; 83:13; Is 17:13; Ps 7:15; 9:15; 57:6). See also the note on imprecatory psalms in the introduction to the Psalter, under "Types."

35:5 *Angel of the Lord.* Cf. 34:7 note.

35:10 *All my bones.* Every fiber of his being.

35:11 *Malicious witnesses.* Lit. "witnesses of violence," i.e., such as intend their false testimony to subject the accused to violence.

35:12 *For good.* He had not provoked their dastardly attack. Rather than injuring them, he had prayed for their recovery from sickness as fervently as he would for members of his own family, proving the sincerity of his sympathy by wearing "sackcloth," the garment of mourning and penitence, and by "fasting," an expression of deep grief. (13 f.)

35:13 *Head bowed.* The RSV translation suggests another gesture of humility in prayer. The reference is to persistent intercession if the last line of the verse is construed as a subordinate clause introducing v. 14: "When my prayer returned [unanswered for a time] to my bosom . . . I went about," etc.

35:16 *More and more.* The Hebrew text, as translated in the RSV note, makes sense if "mockers of a cake" designates professional jesters or buffoons at banquets who stoop to ribald witticisms.

35:21 *Aha, aha!* They break out in shouts of hurrah, certain of attaining their "heart's desire." (25)

35:23 *Bestir thyself.* Cf. 7:6 note.

35:24 *Vindicate me.* Translated "judge me" in 7:8.

35:27 *My vindication.* Or "righteousness," i.e., a verdict of "not guilty" as charged rendered in the court of God's "righteousness."

Psalm 36

36:1-12 This *Psalm of David* ends in a confident prayer for defense against *evildoers* (10-12) prefaced by two reasons why God cannot fail to intervene: (a) the *wicked* are guilty of arrogant blasphemy and of devious crimes against man (1-4); (b) the *mischief* they plot by day and night cannot succeed because God faithfully keeps the promises of His *steadfast love* made to those who walk in the *light* of His revealed will and because His worldwide *judgments* cannot fail to establish His rule of *righteousness.* (5-9)

36:1 *Speaks.* The life of the wicked is not oriented by an "oracle" of the Lord, usually translated: "Thus says the Lord" (e.g., Am 2:4, 6); the demon of *transgression* (willful, rebellious sin) inspires their thinking, persuading them that they can perpetrate "iniquity" and "deceit" with impunity and that, if there is a God, He is unable to "call to account" anyone deliberately and defiantly choosing "a way that is not good." (10:4, 11, 13; 14:1; Jer 5:12)

36:6 *Righteousness.* As God is not hampered in the exercise of His "steadfast love" toward "the upright of heart" (10) by anything under the heavens, so the execution of His justice on "evildoers" is as unshakeable as *the mountains* and as inscrutable as *the great deep* of the sea.

Beasts. Cf. 104:14, 21, 27 f.; 147:9; Mt 6:26.

36:8 *Abundance of thy house.* "The children of men" can experience how "precious" God's steadfast love is as they worship in His house. Communion with Him gives assurance of protection "in the shadow of [his] wings" (17:8; 57:1; 63:7) and access to an inexhaustible source of true happiness and unfading *delights.* (Eph 3:17-19)

36:9 *Thy light.* It shone most brightly when "the light of the world" came to tabernacle among men in order to dispel their darkness (Jn 1:4, 9; 8:12; 9:5; 12:35 f.). He is also *the fountain of life* which becomes "a spring of water welling up to eternal life" when men drink of it. (Jn 4:10-13; 6:35)

36:10 *Know thee.* For the meaning of *know* see Gn 18:19 note; Dt 9:24 note.

36:12 *Lie prostrate.* God's judgment on the evildoers is as certain as if executed already, even though He may seem at times to delay too long. (See the next psalm.)

Psalm 37

37:1-40 God's "servants" may be tempted to question God's righteousness when they suffer many "afflictions" (34:19-22). This *Psalm of David* deals with another experience of life which may disturb the faith of *the righteous.* They may *fret* themselves and even register *anger* (8) when, as they think, God lets *wrongdoers* prosper and does nothing to stop them from carrying out their *evil devices.* However, God is not to be charged with injustice. The fault lies in man. Shortsighted and impatient, he cannot wait *a little while* for God to intervene, whereas He has His own way and time of administering justice. Though grown *overbearing* (35), the wicked will not go unpunished because *his day* of judgment *is coming* (13) eventually, inexorably. It causes only anguish to presume to play God. However, trust in Him allays all fear that evil can triumph, all appearances to the contrary notwithstanding. Therefore the call to implicit, sustained faith, sounded throughout the psalm (3, 4, 5, 7, 9, 34, 39), is its theme. It is not developed in logical sequence from point to point. Pertinent observations and facts repeatedly cluster about the central concern like so many concentric circles (for this way of reasoning see Jb 4:1 note).—To recognize the acrostic form of the poem one must have access to the Hebrew text.

37:1 *Fret not.* A colloquial equivalent would be: Don't get hot and bothered (Pr 24:19). To do so is not only useless; it "tends only to evil" (8), making yourself miserable as well as guilty of sinful doubt. Cf. also Ps 49; 73; Jer 12:1 f.; Ml 2:17; 3:14 f.; the Book of Job.

37:2 *Soon.* Though at times not soon enough in man's opinion, God's judgment on the wicked is never too late to destroy them as quickly and devastatingly as grass withers before fire. (90:5 f.; 103:15; Jb 14:1 f.; Ja 1:10 f.)

37:3 *Do good.* The "righteous" (16) is not entitled to receive "the desires of his heart" by faithfulness in doing good. However, doubting God's justice and goodness, he may be tempted to act as if he did not owe Him obedience to His will. (27, 30)

37:5 *Commit.* Cf. 28:8 note.

37:9 *Possess the land.* God will not permit a reign of terror to dispossess those who "trust in him" of their heritage, thus nullifying His solemn pledge to let the covenant people "dwell in the land which the Lord swore to your fathers" (Dt 30:20). This basic assurance is given repeatedly. It is like a charter of rights, assuring the righteous that they will not be deprived of the privilege of pursuing godliness and enjoying its fruits. (3, 11, 22, 29, 34; 25:13; see also Is 57:13; 60:21; Mt 5:5)

37:11 *Prosperity.* Lit. "peace," i.e., well-being or welfare as in 35:27.

37:13 *Laughs.* Cf. 2:4 note.

37:16 *A little.* Cf. 4:7; 84:10; 1 Ti 4:8.

37:25 *Forsaken.* Experience proves that God does not abandon the righteous to the power of the wicked (33). Evil men cannot frustrate His good will to give "the poor and needy" (14) their daily bread or to bless them with an abundance of this world's goods which He wants them to have.

37:31 *In his heart.* Because "his delight is in the law of the Lord" and he "meditates" on it "day and night," the righteous has his heart set on guarding *his steps* from slipping into the way of sinners. (1:2; 40:8)

37:33 *Brought to trial.* When unjustly accused

of crimes, "his saints" are assured of vindication from the Lord who "loves justice." (28; see Ps 7 and 35)

37:34 *Will look.* If they *wait for the Lord,* the righteous will see the day when *the destruction of the wicked* is an accomplished fact.

37:35 *Cedar of Lebanon.* The Hebrew text: "spreading himself like a native green [tree]," i.e., like a luxuriant tree growing in its native soil.

37:39 *Refuge.* The last two verses summarize the lesson of the psalm: though the righteous may encounter a *time of trouble,* they are not to fret themselves but "wait for the Lord" (34) to keep His promise to save them.

Psalm 38

38:1-22 This *Psalm of David* begins and ends with a prayer for deliverance from the misery brought on by the debilitating effect of sin (1-2 and 21-22). Framed by this plea to the God of *salvation* are unreserved confessions of guilt and a graphic description of the pitiful wretchedness produced by the awareness of having offended the holy God and incurred His wrath. Pangs of conscience cause a *tumult* (8) in the heart. The pain is no less real and enervating than aches resulting from a combination of disabling diseases attacking every part of the body (3-8). Relief cannot come to the sufferer from friends who do not understand his plight and desert him (10-11) and much less from enemies who are out to destroy him but to whose abuse he does not reply (12-14). Only God can help (9, 15). And He will because (a) He will not let enemies take advantage of his miserable condition to bring him to fall (16-17); (b) He graciously pardons everyone who confesses his sins and repents of them (18), whereas human adversaries continue relentlessly to render evil for good. (19-20)

Though not an acrostic, the psalm is composed of 22 verses, the number of letters in the Hebrew alphabet. (Ps. 34)

For the memorial offering is an interpretive rendering of the Hebrew infinitive: "to call to remembrance," suggesting that the psalm was meant to be recited while the priests offered the memorial sacrifice. (Cf. Lv 2:2 note)

38:1 *Rebuke.* Ps 6 has the same opening verse.

38:2 *Arrows.* A figurative way of describing God's reaction to sin (Dt 32:23; Jb 6:4; Eze 5:16). For the punitive *hand* of God see 32:4; 39:10.

38:3 *No soundness.* Repeated in v. 7. Ill health *because of . . . sin,* as portrayed in the following verses, has the combined symptoms of almost every known physical ailment, described in such realistic terms as to suggest that actual bodily suffering is meant. (Cf. 6:2 note)

38:4 *Over my head.* Despair overwhelms him as if waves of high tide were breaking over his head (69:2, 15; 124:4 f.; Ez 9:6). In the same breath he speaks of his iniquities as a crushing weight or *burden.* (Cf. Mt 11:28)

38:9 *Known to thee.* Telling God what He already knows is not a superfluous part of prayer.

38:11 *Plague.* The Hebrew noun is translated variously: "stroke" (39:10); "scourge" (89:32; 91:10); "assault" (Dt 17:8; 21:5); "plague" (Ex 11:1), frequently associated with leprosy (Lv 13:2 note). Friends and close relatives leave the hapless sufferer in the lurch. They have no remedy for the pain eating at his vitals. Like a leper he is left to his own devices.

38:13 *Open his mouth.* Conscious of his offense against God, he does not defend himself against those who hate him "wrongfully" (19).—The sinless "man of sorrows," "wounded for our transgressions," "opened not his mouth" "when he was reviled." Deserted by friends, forsaken of God, He stood alone under "the chastisement that made us whole." (Is 53; Lk 23:49; Mt 26:56; 1 Ptr 2:22 f.)

38:16 *Rejoice.* Cf. 13:4 note.

38:19 *Without cause.* The Hebrew text does not require a change if translated: "my foes are alive [and] strong" or "my mortal foes are mighty."

Psalm 39

39:1-13 This *Psalm of David* is another example of the struggle of faith to subdue fretting over afflictions (Ps 37; 73). Under a shattering *stroke,* inflicted by the chastening hand of God (9 f.), fires of bitterness and doubt are kindled, fanned by the observation that *the wicked,* seemingly unmolested and prosperous, heap *scorn* and ridicule on those faithful to the Lord. Smouldering under the surface for a time (1-3), the flames of discontent burst out in a complaint that God makes life, so short and unsatisfying, still more miserable (4-8). Faith, sorely tried, however does not lose hold on God as the only *hope* in life. Harangue gives way to an ardent *prayer* that God may let *gladness* brighten the remaining days of a *passing guest* on earth (12 f.).—For *Jeduthun* see 1 Ch 16:41 note.

39:1 *In my presence.* If the wicked heard him questioning divine providence, they would gloat over his predicament and ridicule trust in God (13:4; 35:26; 38:20). Job likewise "did not sin with his lips" when calamity first struck. (Jb 2:10; 1:22)

39:2 *To no avail.* Lit. "from good," i.e., he suppressed the urge to remonstrate with God even though his situation was far from being good.

39:4 *Let me know.* Even though in the form of a prayer, the words erupting from his "hot" heart give vent to an ill-concealed, almost sarcastic recrimination against God for what He is doing to shorten his life, a *fleeting* "breath" of useless "turmoil" as it is. (Jb 14)

39:5 *Breath.* A puff of wind. (62:9; 90:10; 94:11; 103:15; 144:4; Ec 1:2 f.)

39:7 *My hope.* Trust in the Lord gains the upper hand in the embattled soul. Life has meaning only as man resolves to *wait* for the Lord to "remove" the chastening when, in His good pleasure, it has served its intended purpose. (62:1 f.)

39:8 *Fool.* He is a fool because he says: "There is no God." (14:1 note; 10:4 note)

39:11 *A moth.* God can destroy what man considers precious and beautiful as a moth eats holes into the best garment. (Is 50:9; Hos 5:12; Jb 13:28)

39:12 *Passing guest.* The psalm ends in a tearful plea that God "look away from" the suppliant, passing him by rather than inflicting more chastisements so that the few days of his sojourn may again be bright and cheerful. (Jb 10:19 f.; 14:6; Ps 119:19)

Psalm 40

40:1-17 This *Psalm of David* combines a *song* of praise for God's *wondrous deeds* of deliverance in the past (1-10) with a plea that His *steadfast love* provide protection from *evils* which still pose a threat to life and well-being (11-17). There was abundant reason for an outburst of joy: God heard the prayer of *the man who makes the Lord his trust* when disaster seemed unavoidable (1-5). Gratitude was heartfelt. It was not a matter of merely speaking words of thankfulness or of participating in outward forms of worship. It expressed its sincerity as a living sacrifice, offering to God cheerful obedience to His *will* as laid down in His *law* (6-8). It was only natural that a man so richly blessed would want to tell *the glad news of deliverance* to all within the reach of his voice (9-10). However, because life remains full of evils *without number,* praise turned into an appeal for the continuation of God's *steadfast love* and *faithfulness* (11-12). Such help would *put to shame* those more intent on doing deadly harm and at the same time prompt *all who seek* the Lord to *rejoice and be glad* (13-17).—With only slight changes vv. 13-17 appear as Ps 70.

40:2 *Desolate pit.* There seemed to be no hope of survival. The catastrophe is described figuratively as unavoidable and horrible as the slow but certain death of a person left to die in a gruesome dungeon or to drown in a *miry bog.* (Gn 37:23 f.; Jer 38:6; Ps 69:2, 14)

40:3 *New song.* Cf. 33:3 note.

40:4 *False gods.* Lit. "a lie"; so translated Am 2:4.

40:5 *Toward us.* The individual experienced God's help as a member of the covenant people. Israel's history records more *wondrous deeds . . . than can be numbered. To proclaim and tell of them* requires an endless song of praise. (Dt 4:34 ff.; Ps 92:5; 106:2; 139:17 f.)

40:6 *Not desire.* Sacrificial offerings of various kinds were required by the "law" of Moses. Because he delights to do "the will" of God (8), the thankful believer has no intention of disregarding the statutes prescribing formal worship. However, he does declare emphatically that his thanksgiving is not an outward performance of ritual. He is at the same time laying on God's altar the sacrifice of self-will and the offering of wholehearted consecration. For other categorical statements for the sake of contrast see Dt 5:2 note; 1 Sm 15:22 note; Ps 51:16 f.; Is 1:11-13; Jer 6:20; 7:22; Hos 6:6.

40:7 *Lo, I come.* I enter the sanctuary to offer sacrifices. Quoted in Heb 10:5-7 according to the Septuagint, vv. 6 f. attain their ultimate meaning when spoken by Jesus of Himself, whose voluntary self-sacrifice on the altar of the cross removed once and for all the barrier of sin between God and man.

40:12 *Iniquities.* Praising God is not a meritorious deed. He is aware of deserving the consequences of sin of which he is guilty in spite of efforts to avoid them.

40:15 *Aha, aha!* Cf. 35:21 note.

40:16 *Great is the Lord.* Cf. 34:3 note; 35:27.

Psalm 41

41:1-13 Several psalms call those truly happy who are in covenant relationship with God: Their transgression is forgiven (32:1 f.); they can take refuge in God (34:8; 46:1); they worship Him (65:4); they delight in His law (1:2). This *Psalm of David* pronounces a beatitude on those who "honor" their "Maker" by being compassionate with their fellowmen (Pr 14:31). The opening verses (1-3) state the general principle which Jesus affirmed when He said: "Blessed are the merciful, for they shall obtain mercy" (Mt 5:7). The validity of this axiom is borne out by a personal experience, related in the following verses (4-10). It may appear that *trouble* instead of happiness awaits the benefactor of *the poor.* And indeed there was a time when he was on the brink of disaster. Gloating enemies seized on his misfortune as proof of his depravity; a trusted friend turned against him. However, though well aware of his sinfulness, he pleaded with God graciously to prove him innocent of the criminal offenses brought against him. His prayer was not in vain. God *upheld* his *integrity.* Cleared of false charges and relieved of his suffering, he continued to experience the blessing of God's *presence for ever.* The benediction pronounced in vv. 1-3 remains true (11-12). V. 13 is a doxology, marking the end of "Book I" of the psalter. See "Divisions" in the introductory notes to the Book of Psalms.

41:3 *All his infirmities.* The Hebrew text (RSV note) makes sense if translated: "Thou changest all his lying abed in his illness," namely into the opposite state of well-being. Sickness, one of the afflictions of "the day of trouble" from which God "protects him," is at times used figuratively to denote pain of various kinds resulting from a prostrating blow of adversity. (6:2 note; 30:2; Dt 32:39; Jer 6:14; 15:18; Hos 5:13; 6:1)

41:4 *Heal me.* Lit. "heal my soul."

41:9 *Lifted his heel.* Lit. "made big a heel against me," i.e., to trip me or to kick with his heel like a horse or mule. What a treacherous "bosom friend" did to a kind benefactor who himself was a sinner (4) foreshadowed the betrayal of the sinless Son of Man by His disciple. (Jn 13:18)

41:10 *Requite them.* He says nothing about repaying evil for evil. All he desires is to be able to hurl back their charges when God vindicates his "integrity."

Psalm 42

42:1-11 Ps 42 and 43 belong together though for some unknown reason they appear as separate units in almost all Hebrew manuscripts as well as in the ancient versions. Cast in the same poetic form and drenched with tears of the same emotional stress, they complement each other also in content. The refrain which marks the two component parts of Ps 42 occurs again at the end of Ps 43. The latter has no superscription to identify it as an independent composition whereas every psalm of "Book II" (42—72) is so marked. When combined, the two psalms form a trilogy of three cycles revolving about a common center: intense yearning for God and communion with Him in the holy precincts of the temple (1-5; 6-11; 43:1-5). This theme is developed in each of the three parts by means of concentric circles composed of laments over circumstances preventing participation in temple worship, expressions of fear of being forsaken by God, impatient questions of *why,* self-exhortations to hope in God, and appeals for divine intervention to remove the obstacles preventing access to the holy hill and its altar.—For the term *Maskil* see Ps 32:1-11. For *the Sons of Korah* see 2 Ch 20:19 note.

42:1 *Flowing streams.* To describe his unfulfilled yearning to worship in "the house of God," the author compares himself with a deer which frantically seeks out flowing streams only to find that "the water brooks are dried up." (Jb 1:20; see also Ps 63:1; 84:2; 119:20; Is 55:1)

42:2 *Living God.* Not an idol of lifeless metal or wood (Is 40:19 f.), the Lord of life is a never-failing "fountain of living waters," the only source from which man can quench his thirst for true happiness. (Jer 2:13; 17:13; cf. Jn 4:10; 7:37 f.)

Behold the face. Three times a year all male Israelites were to "appear before the Lord God" in corporate worship (Ex 23:17). Prevented from doing so for some unspecified reason, the psalmist longs for the time when he again can join the "multitude keeping festival." (4)

42:3 *Where is your God?* Eating "the bread of tears" (80:5), the frustrated worshiper has to hear *men* ridiculing his desire to pay homage to God, who, they claim, does nothing to help His devotees (10; 79:10; 115:2; Jl 2:17). These taunting "adversaries" (10) seem to be "an ungodly" foreign "people" who seized him in a raid and forced him to live in the land of "the enemy." (43:1 f.)

42:4 *I went.* As he grieves over his plight, he would remember the happy experiences of the past to bolster his hope that God again would make it possible to worship Him in compliance with His directive.

42:5 *Why . . . ?* As if in conversation with his *soul,* he reproaches himself for moaning and encourages himself to *hope in God.* The same soliloquy comes at the end of two more outbursts of grief (11; 43:5). Every tried soul knows that the battle with doubt is not won in one skirmish.

42:6 *The land of Jordan.* The prayers arise in some unnamed land beyond the borders of the Promised Land, where the Jordan has its source in the Hermon mountain range. *Mount Mizar,* lit. "Hill of Littleness," no longer can be identified.

42:7 *Cataracts. Waves* and *billows* of grief rush over him with the sound and fury of the Jordan cascading over waterfalls and producing thunderous noises in the sustained rhythm of successive waves of the *deep.*

42:10 *Deadly wound.* He feels the taunt of the *adversaries* as if he had received a bone-crushing blow.

Psalm 43

43:1-5 Cf. Ps 42:1-11.

43.1 *Vindicate.* Even though the author still raises the question "why" God lets him go "mourning" (2), he clings to God in prayer, asking Him to espouse his *cause* against the *deceitful and unjust men* who have deprived him of his sacred privilege to "go to the altar of God." (4)

43:3 *Light and . . . truth.* In order that the gloomy thought of being cast off by God might turn to joy, the latter is to let the light of His countenance and His unfailing faithfulness be his constant companion and guide. (36:9; 25:10)

Psalm 44

44:1-26 This psalm records a cry for deliverance when "the afflictions of the righteous" were permitted in God's providence to assume the proportions of a national calamity (34:19; Ps 7). Here the chosen people, stunned and bewildered by blows of a disastrous chastisement, raise their collective voice in supplication to the Lord of nations. What happened was a deep mystery. *In the days of old* God established Israel's fathers in the Promised Land in spite of enemy opposition (1-3). For generations He came to the aid of their descendants so that they *boasted continually* of His faithfulness and power (4-8). Now, however, trust is severely shaken. The armies of the Lord of hosts suffer humiliating defeats at the hands of merciless foes who loot, kill, and take prisoners (9-12). As a result the nation, chosen by God to glorify Him, must endure *the derision and scorn* of godless neighbors (13-16). The catastrophe is the more baffling because they have been intent on keeping the *covenant* which God made with them (17-19). Because He knows that they are not guilty of such vile sins as idolatry, they conclude they are *slain all the day long* for His *sake,* i.e., for no other reason than that they are His people (20-22). *Bowed down to the dust* under the weight of grief, the nation makes its corporate plea for relief with the same importunity and boldness with which individuals pray for rest from their personal burdens (23-26; 7:6 ff.).—For the term *Maskil* and *the Sons of Korah* see Ps 42.

44:1 *Told us.* In obedience to God's command, the fathers saw to it that each new generation knew how miraculously God delivered the 12 tribes from Egypt and gave them the land of promise. (Ex 10:2; Dt 6:20 f.; 32:7; Jos 4:6, 21; Ps 77:11 f.; 78:3 f.)

44:2 *Plant.* The young nation was settled in its new homeland as firmly as a plant anchored by its roots in the soil. (80:8 f.; Ex 15:17)

44:3 *Thou didst delight.* They owed their good fortune solely to God's unmerited goodness and the power of His *right hand.*

44:4 *My God.* As spokesman for the nation, the author at times lapses into the first person singular. (6, 15)

Ordainest. The *victories* of the sons of Jacob were God's deeds of salvation. The RSV note points out that in the Hebrew text the verb "ordain" or "command" is in the imperative form. If this reading is adopted, the psalmist already at this point injects a short prayer which he expands in the closing verses.

44:8 *Boasted.* Cf. 20:7 note; 33:16; 34:2. For the *name* of God see Ex 6:3 note.

44:10 *Turn back.* The *enemies* who routed the "armies" (9) are not identified, making it uncertain when this disaster occurred in the history of Israel.

44:12 *Sold.* God's punitive action in the days of the Judges is described as selling His people "into the power of their enemies" (Ju 2:15 note). However, in the present situation God seemingly made a bad bargain, bartering them away without getting anything in return which would profit His honor. On the contrary, "the derision and scorn" heaped on His people by ungodly neighbors (13-16) brought dishonor on His name.

44:17 *Not forgotten thee.* As the afflicted individual denies the accusation that he is guilty of criminal offenses (7:3 note), so the nation as a whole rejects the charge of outright apostasy. For verification of its faithfulness it appeals to God Himself, who "knows the secrets of the heart." (21)

44:22 *For thy sake.* God afflicted them and gave the enemy occasion to ridicule their trust in Him. They suffer on His account in the sense that it is He who was chastising them for reasons known to Him alone. Therefore submitting to His inscrutable will, they plead with Him to deliver them for the sake of His "steadfast love." (23-26; cf. Ro 8:35-39)

Psalm 45

45:1-17 This psalm enlarges the scope of the Messianic prophecy recorded in Ps 2 (cf. vv. 1-11 there and 2 Sm 7). The Davidic kings, sitting "on the throne of the kingdom of the Lord" (1 Ch 28:4-7; 29:23), were chosen not only to establish the kingdom of God in their day, but also to let their reign foreshadow the fulfillment of the divine plan of salvation unfolding in Israel's history and culminating in the Messiah. The *glory and majesty* of the earthly ruler (2-3), his victory over *enemies* (4-5), the stability of his throne, his righteous and benevolent reign and the glory of his court (6-9) are portrayed in terms designed to arouse expectations that One "greater than Solomon" was to come, who, though in the form of a servant, "reflects the glory of God and bears the very stamp of his nature." (Mt 12:42; Heb 1:3, 9)

To this vision of the future the psalm adds another feature. It goes on to describe the *queen* (9) standing at the *right hand* of Israel's king (10-15). United with her *lord* with intimate ties of marriage, she too came to occupy a position of honor and glory which in its fullest sense became a reality when "Christ loved the church and gave himself up for her . . . that he might present the church to himself in splendor" (Eph 5:25-27; 2 Co 11:2; Rv 19:7 f.; 21:2). The psalm closes with an expectant look to future generations when God's promises to Israel's king will be fulfilled (16-17).—*According to Lilies* may refer to a melody according to which the psalm was to be sung. For *Maskil* and *the Sons of Korah* see Ps 42. *A love song* is a translation of the Hebrew phrase "a song of lovelinesses."

45:1 *Overflows.* The *heart* of the writer bubbles over with thoughts on the *theme* (lit. the "word") of the *verses* (lit. the "work") he is about to compose. They are dedicated *to the king,* whom, however, he does not name. The portrait which he draws with *the pen of a ready scribe* (Ez 7:6) has the features of the Davidic ruling house rather than of any individual monarch.

45:2 *Fairest.* Cf. Is 33:17; Ps 50:2. He is favored by God also with a charming flow of words.

45:3 *O mighty one.* One word in Hebrew, it occurs as a modifier in the Messianic title "Mighty God." (Is 9:6)

45:4 *Dread deeds.* Acts inspiring awe, as he defends the cause of the poor against the strong and crushes all opposition to his rule.

45:6 *Your divine throne.* This translation and the first offered in the RSV note address these words to the Davidic king in keeping with the context. Divinely appointed to occupy the throne of the kingdom of the Lord, he is truly a prophetic type of Him to whom the Father delegated "all authority in heaven and on earth" (Mt 28:18; Cl 1:15 f.). In quoting these words, the author of Hebrews, adopting the Septuagint version (see second translation in RSV note) and living after the prophecy was fulfilled, leaves behind the provisional and preliminary aspects of the promise in order to focus directly on its final intent: a proclamation of the deity of the Messiah. (Heb 1:8 f.)

45:7 *Anointed.* The oil poured on the king as a coronation ceremony (1 Sm 10:1; 16:13) not only gave him a status above all others but also betokened the overflowing gladness which in regal splendor he was to derive in the exercise of his royal powers. (Is 61:1, 3)

45:8-9 *Ladies of honor.* Robed in perfumed garments, the king held court in *palaces* inlaid with ivory. His beautiful consort, herself a "princess" (12), sat beside him. Adding to the splendor of his throne room were ladies-in-waiting who too were *daughters of kings.* For *gold of Ophir* see 1 K 9:26 note.

45:12 *The people of Tyre.* As she pays homage

to her "lord" and king, the "queen" shares the prestige and riches of her royal husband. The Phoenician city of Tyre, renowned in the ancient world for its wealth, represents the worldwide acclaim and favor accorded the wife of the king. All this was but a shadow of things to be fulfilled when the King of kings espoused His followers from "all the families of the nations" (22:27) as His bride, showering her with the priceless treasures of His kingdom of grace. In expectation of reigning with Him in glory, "the Spirit and the Bride say: 'Come.'" (Rv 22:17; 21:2, 9; see also Is 60:4-7)

Psalm 46

46:1-11 Paraphrased by Luther in his "Battle Hymn of the Reformation," this heroic hymn of faith offers a potent antidote to fear in threats of the most dire disaster. The child of God is reminded that God does not lose control, whatever the circumstances may be. Because He has all menacing powers firmly in hand, there is no reason why those who seek *refuge* in Him should not be serene and calm though ominous clouds of disaster darken the sky. Should the universe itself appear to *change* in a cataclysm, causing the mountains to *tremble* and be swallowed up in roaring tidal waves, He still would stand—a bastion of *strength* towering over the seething chaos (1-3). The might of the Creator proves to be *a very present help* also against "rulers of the earth" (2:10) when they try to annihilate *the city of God,* chosen to be His *holy habitation.* Though they *rage,* they cannot dry up the *streams* of His mercy which *make glad* its citizens (4-7). However, not man-built walls, not armaments, chariots, and horses (20:7) make Jerusalem impregnable. It is *the Lord of hosts,* who in the past *wrought desolations* in destroying the enemy and who still is able to make *wars cease to the end of the earth.* Let *the nations* take warning to desist from their futile attempts to thwart His will to be *exalted in the earth* (8-11). The word *Selah* marks the end of the three sections at vv. 3, 7, 11. The last two of these contain a concluding refrain which, however, is not found at v. 3 as could be expected.—*Alamoth,* lit. "virgins," may be a melody, proposed as suitable for the singing of the psalm. (See "Superscriptions" in the introductory notes to the Psalter.)

46:1 *Very present help.* Lit. "a help in troubles found [reliable] very much."

46:2 *Sea.* Lit. "seas." "The mountains tremble," shaken to their foundations, as if they were to disappear into waters of primeval chaos. (Gn 1:2)

46:4 *River . . . streams.* God's presence in the midst of *the city* in which His temple stood was the source of gladness as once "a river flowed out of Eden to water the garden." (Gn 2:10; see Ps 36:8; Is 41:18; Jer 2:13; Zch 14:8; Eze 47:1 ff.)

46:5 *Right early.* Lit. "at the turning of the morning," i.e., when night turned into day (90:14). The morning of God's miraculous help dawned on Israel at the Red Sea and on embattled Jerusalem at Hezekiah's time. (Ex 14:27 f.; 2 K 19:35)

46:7 *The Lord of hosts.* For this title of God see 1 Sm 1:3 second note; Ps 24:10. For *God of Jacob* see 20:1 note; 75:9; 76:6, etc. The phrase *with us* constitutes the first part of the name "Immanuel." (Is 7:14)

46:9 *Wars cease.* Peace is achieved not by military superiority or by man's ingenuity. It comes when "the works of the Lord" (8) destroy the war-making capacity of His people's enemies.

46:10 *Be still.* Lit. "desist," i.e., from your attempts to defy the Lord of the nations.—The church of Jesus Christ, as long as He "is in the midst of her" (5), need "not fear though" (2) assailed by "the powers of death." (Mt 16:18; Jn 10:27 ff.)

Psalm 47

47:1-9 Finite man is compelled to ascribe human terms and concepts to God (such as Father, Judge, Maker) if he is to have some inkling of what God is and does. In this psalm and several others (93; 96—99) He is pictured as *a great king over all the earth* (2), seated *on his holy throne* from which He *reigns over the nations* (8). *All peoples* (1) are summoned to recognize that He is "exalted in the earth" (46: 10). Because His dominion is universal, He shapes world history for His sovereign purposes. Two examples are cited to demonstrate that He carries out His plan of salvation for the benefit of all mankind (each introduced by the conjunction *for* in vv. 2 and 7). (1) *Songs of joy* are called for to commemorate Israel's victory over "nations greater and mightier than" they, when He gave His chosen people their *heritage,* the land of Canaan promised to the fathers (1-5; Dt 4:38; 32:8-14). (2) *Praises* should be sung to *the king of all the earth* because, as Israel's *King* in a special way, He is keeping the promise made to *Abraham* that by him "all the families of the earth" shall be blessed. (6-9; Gn 12:3 note; 17:6; 35:11)

47:1 *Clap your hands.* Israel acclaimed her kings with loud applause and blasts of the trumpet. (2 K 11:12; 9:13; 2 Sm 15:10; 1 K 1:34)

47:4 *Pride of Jacob.* The chosen people had reason to be proud of their *heritage,* "the most glorious of all lands." (Eze 20:6; Is 58:14)

47:5 *Gone up.* Israel's neighbors observed an annual festival to celebrate the renewed enthronization of their deified king. There is no concrete evidence that a similar ritual was enacted in Jerusalem every New Year's Day. God is pictured here as returning to His heavenly throne after having come down to set mundane things in order. For other examples of this figurative way of describing how the transcendent God comes down to intervene in human affairs and then goes up to resume His place in heaven see Gn 11:5, 7; 17:22; 35:13; Ju 13:20; Is 31:4.—So Jesus Christ, having fulfilled His mission on earth, returned to the right hand of the Father; from thence He will come to judge the quick and the dead. (Eph 1:20; Cl 1:16; Rv 5:13; 19:16)

47:7 *A psalm.* A special kind of psalm called a "Maskil" (RSV note), a term found in the superscriptions of some psalms such as 42, 44, etc.

47:9 *Gather. The princes of the* non-Israelite *peoples* are seen in joint worship with *the people of the God of Abraham,* the father of all believers. (Is 2:2-4; 60:10 f.; Gl 3:6-14; Ro 9:24)

Shields of the earth. The princes, so called because they were to protect their subjects. (84:9; 89:18)

Psalm 48

48:1-14 The people of God are safe in *the city of . . . God* (Ps 46), "the king of all the earth" (Ps 47), because, says Ps 48, as long as *the great King* is *within her citadels,* He makes it *a sure defense.* Selected to be His royal residence, it becomes "the perfection of beauty," *the joy of all the earth* (2; Lm 2:15); *Mount Zion* on which it is founded becomes a *holy mountain.* (1-3).—Attempts by "kings of the earth" (2:2; 76:12) to destroy the base of His kingdom are in vain. It is as if at the mere sight of the city their armed forces disintegrated, panic-stricken and shattered like a ship battered to pieces by the wind (4-8; Is 29:8). Such protection, provided by God's *right hand,* calls for joyous contemplation of His *steadfast love* (9-11). As the liberated people view the fortifications of the city standing intact, they are to see to it that *the next generation* too knows that they have such a God as their *God for ever and ever.* (12-14; 102:18)

48:2 *In the far north.* Geographically Mount Zion constituted the northern extremity of the city complex. However, the phrase may be a figurative way of proclaiming Jerusalem the undisputed and unrivaled capital *of all the earth.* It rejects the notion current among neighboring peoples that "the seat of the gods" on a mountain *in the far north* was the center of the universe (Eze 28:2; Is 14:13). As Israel's God is "a great King above all gods" (95:3) which, however, exist only in the minds of their devotees (Ps 24:4 note; 31:6), so "the hill of the Lord" (24:3), chosen to be His earthly throne city, was the place from which world affairs were administered.

48:4 *The kings.* They are not identified by name or nationality. The suddenness of their crushing defeat recalls what happened in one night to the Assyrian king Sennacherib (2 K 18 f.; Is 36 f.), who claimed the title "the great King" (2; cf. 2 K 18:19, 28) and whose commanders were themselves kings (2 K 18—19; Is 36—37). All "rulers of the earth" should "be warned" not to attack "the city of the Lord of hosts." (8; 2:2, 10; 46:6, 10)

48:7 *Ships of Tarshish.* Cf. 1 K 10:22 note; 2 Ch 20:36 f.; Jn 1:3. The *east wind,* feared in particular for its withering effect on the crops (Is 27:8; Jer 18:17; Eze 17:10), is at God's command to *shatter* the pride of man's achievement, symbolized by the ships of Tarshish. (Is 2:16)

48:10 *Thy name.* The manifestations of God's glory and power elicit praise *to the ends of the earth.* For the *name* of God see Ex 6:3 note. God's *victory* (lit. "righteousness") is apparent in His "judgments," executed on Zion's enemies.

48:11 *Daughters.* The OT frequently refers to the towns clustering about a city as daughters. (97:8; translated "villages" in Nm 21:25; Jos 17:16)

48:14 *For ever.* When "the glory of the Lord went up from the midst of the city" of Jerusalem (Eze 11:23) because of its unfaithfulness, it fell a prey to its enemies. But what God had begun in the Zion of old, He continued in the Jerusalem of the new covenant to be completed at the end of time. (Eph 2:19-22; Mt 16:18; Heb 11:10; Rv 21:10—22:5)

Psalm 49

49:1-20 The large number of alternate translations offered in the notes of the RSV indicate that in several verses the meaning of the transmitted text is not easily determined. However, the clarity and the thrust of the psalm are not affected by individual variant readings. It resembles Ps 37 and 73 in grappling with the *riddle* of unequal distribution of this world's goods, aggravated by the observation that the wicked use their wealth and power to oppress the poor. The solution offered here stresses the transitory nature of earthly possessions. They fade out of existence at death whereas God's power to redeem His own does not stop at the grave. This *wisdom* and *understanding* is proclaimed to *all peoples* by one who has a receptive ear for a divine oracle (1-4). Even though his message is in poetic form, it is based on the facts of life. Those whose god was "mammon" (Mt 6:24) have used their wealth to make also this life miserable. But in such *times of trouble* (5-6) it is comforting to know first of all that the oppressors cannot buy immunity from death with all the riches of the world (7-9). Even wisdom, more precious than gold or silver, cannot ward off the inexorable fate which awaits these men and the brute beasts alike (10-12). However, though men of wealth and wisdom cannot resist being herded into the grave like dumb driven sheep, those who like the psalmist commit themselves into the hands of the living God should know above all that He can and *will ransom* their soul from the power of Sheol, making them partakers of His unending life (13-15). By contrast, to the man whose life consisted only "in the abundance of his possessions," death is the negation of life because he cannot carry away the "good things" of this life. (16-20; Lk 12:15; 16:25)

49:1 *All peoples.* As in Ps 46—48 the subject to be discussed concerns *all inhabitants of the world,* where, however, they remain for a brief "lifetime" only. (39:5)

49:4 *Proverb.* What he was about to propound in the poetic form of proverbial sayings came to his *ear* by divine inspiration.

49:7 *Truly.* The RSV takes the Hebrew word for brother to be an exclamation rather than a noun, as in Eze 6:11 (for the KJV translation see RSV note). In some instances the law of Israel allowed a man to pay for "the redemption of his life"; in others, no *ransom* was to be accepted (Ex 21:30; Nm 35:31). But whether paid by himself or by another for him, the amount that would "suffice" to pay the penalty of sin and to redeem man's life from death so that "he should continue to live on for ever" cannot be found in the coffers of even the wealthiest.

49:14 *Straight to the grave they descend.* This translation does not require very drastic changes in the traditional Hebrew text. The latter, followed by KJV (cf. RSV note), makes sense as an interjected statement anticipating the difference in the death of the wicked materialist and "the upright."

49:15 *Receive me.* The ransom no man can raise to redeem his soul (7), God Himself has a way of paying, freeing His dying creature to share His glory (73:24; 16:10). The verb translated *receive* is used also of God's action when He "took" Enoch and Elijah. (Gn 5:24; 2 K 2:3, 5)

49:17 *Go down after him.* Namely into death. (Jb 1:21; 1 Ti 6:7)

Psalm 50

50:1-23 Participants in any kind of formal worship may be tempted to "heap up empty phrases" and to go through the symbolic motions of adoration and devotion while "their hearts are far from" God (Is 29:13; Mt 6:7). Because they had so many rites to perform, the people of the old covenant had to be alerted constantly to the danger of lapsing into a purely mechanical observance of the prescribed ritual. Ps 50 is a scathing exposé of external religiosity, indicating hypocrisy as a degrading affront to God and a cloak to hide wrong done to fellowmen. It is so serious and despicable an offense that God is envisioned as appearing in person to hold court. He prefers charges against all who pretend to be *faithful ones* and pronounces them guilty of so heinous a crime that He threatens to *rend* them *and there be none to deliver* (22). There is no refusing the summons issued by the Judge. His jurisdiction extends *from the rising of the sun to its setting* (1-2). His robes of authority are *a devouring fire*; His bailiffs, *a mighty tempest. The heavens* and *the earth* are put on the witness stand to testify to the justice of the verdict pronounced on those whom He has chosen of all nations to be *his people* (3-6). They are perverting the purpose of *sacrifices* and *burnt offerings* if they think they can put God under obligation to them by giving Him what He already owns (7-11). Furthermore, *the flesh of bulls* and *the blood of goats* do not take effect like magical paraphernalia, automatically bending God to grant their wishes. Sacrifices compound the sin of the worshiper unless they are brought in the right attitude. They are intended to be nothing more than an outward means of acknowledging the unpayable debt of gratitude due God, of expressing unreserved dependence on His goodness for help *in the day of trouble,* and of discharging the obligation to *glorify* Him (12-15). People who make a pretense of their devotion to God in their acts of worship have no scruples either in outwardly mouthing the *statutes* of His *covenant* and at the same time flouting them by association with criminals and giving their *mouth free reign for evil* even against the members of their immediate family (16-21). At the end of the confrontation God threatens to punish all *who forget God,* exhorts every one of them to change *his way,* and promises *salvation* to those who honor Him with sincere thanksgiving (22-23).—*Asaph* was one of the men appointed by David to provide music for the temple services. (1 Ch 15:16 f., 19; 25:1; 2 Ch 29:30)

50:1 *The Mighty One.* The heaping of divine names in v. 1, occurring again only in Jos 22:22, makes clear from the outset that the Judge cannot be ignored when He *speaks and summons the earth.* As Israel's *Lord,* the covenant God, He has a grievous complaint to make against His unfaithful people. (Ex 3:15 note; Am 3:2)

50:2 *Out of Zion.* The Lord's coming from Jerusalem, "the city of the great King" (48:2 note), is as awe-inspiring as when He "came down upon Mount Sinai." (Ex 19:18, 20; 20:18 f.; Dt 33:2)

50:4 *He calls.* For a similar subpoena issued to all creation to appear as witnesses when He testifies against His people see Dt 31:28; 32:1; Is 1:2.

50:5 *Faithful ones.* Cf. 4:3 note. The sin of hypocrisy is not committed by out-and-out unbelievers and scoffers. It is an act of unfaithfulness to a professed loyalty to God, a pretending to be in *covenant* with Him, once made *by sacrifice* and ever after kept in effect, by outwardly engaging in the required worship forms. (Ex 24:5-8)

50:7 *Testify.* God acts as prosecuting attorney as well as judge.

50:8 *Not reprove.* The charge against His people is not that they have neglected to offer sacrifices and burnt offerings or that such rites are repugnant to Him, as the next verses seem to suggest. For similar denunciations not of the use but of the abuse of the prescribed worship forms expressed in categorical terms see 40:6 note; 51:18 f.; Hos 6:6; Am 5:21-26; Is 1:11-15; Jer 7:21-23.

50:14 *Sacrifice of thanksgiving.* Slain animals are an insult to God unless the sacrifice is motivated by a grateful heart, itself offered to Him in humble recognition of total dependence on His unearned mercy (Hos 14:2; Ro 12:1). The payment of *vows* (Lv 7:16) likewise is a token of gratitude.

50:16-17 *Recite.* Men may be able to rattle off the *statutes* and the creed of *the covenant* and yet refuse to accept divine *discipline* in their lives, turning their backs on the *words* of God to which they profess allegiance (Jer 5:3; 7:27). Such people are *wicked* indeed.

50:21 *Like yourself.* They show their contempt

for God by making Him out to be as tolerant of evil as they are, interpreting His delay to act to be indifference.

Psalm 51

51:1-19 Anyone crushed by a guilt feeling or tortured by an awakened conscience can find relief and healing if he approaches God in the words of this fourth and most highly treasured of the so-called "penitential" psalms (cf. Ps 6:1-10). The obverse also is true. Anyone insensitive to the consequences of sin will become aware of what a fearful thing it is to offend the holy God and incur His wrath, if he prays this psalm. Its opening verses (1-2) are an anguished cry for mercy. All that follows is based on this appeal to *sola gratia,* grace alone. No other course is possible. There is no denying the reality of sin. *Transgressions,* outgrowth of a deep-rooted wickedness within, are not only known to the perpetrator but above all are in full view before God who, to be God, cannot but pass a *sentence* of doom on everything *evil* (3-5). The sinner has nothing to offer in his defense—no excuses, no extenuating circumstances, no ignorance of the Law. If he is to live in harmony with his Creator and have peace of mind, *joy and gladness* within, God must act not according to the demands of justice but according to His *abundant mercy.* Two gifts of pure compassion are necessary: (1) God must cancel the guilt of revolt against Him and *blot out all . . . iniquities* (6-9); (2) as forgiveness is His sole prerogative, so He alone can generate the desire and ability to do what is pleasing to His *holy Spirit* (10-12). Equipped with a *clean heart* and a *new spirit,* the pardoned sinner has the compulsion to do two things: (1) he wants to share with fellow sinners the joy he has found, urging them to *return* to God; (2) he wants to sing songs of praise to God, offering Him not mere words or only outward rites but the sincere gratitude of *a broken and contrite heart* (13-17). The psalm closes with a prayer for Zion and its worshipers (18-19).—For the occasion of this *Psalm of David,* alluded to in the superscription, see 2 Sm 11 f.

51:1-2 *Transgressions.* Various aspects of disobedience to God's will are expressed by three synonyms: *transgressions—iniquity—sin.* For their connotations see 32:1-2 note; also Ex 34:6 f. Each of these, in turn, is associated with a different kind of action denoting its removal: (1) *Transgressions* are an ugly blotch on a page or an entry of a debt which must be blotted out, i.e., expunged from the record (Is 43:25; Ps 109:14; Nm 5:23; Acts 3:19; Cl 2:14). (2) *Iniquity* is like a filthy garment which must be washed *thoroughly.* In ancient times this required vigorous action. Clothes were beaten on flat stones in a stream or were trampled to loosen the dirt. For the washing of garments to achieve ceremonial cleanness see Ex 19:10. (3) *Sin* is a stain which "lye" and "much soap" cannot remove (Jer 2:22); it yields only to God's cleansing action. The blood of animals was applied to the altar to symbolize that it was hallowed "from the uncleannesses of the people of Israel" (Lv 16:19). But what the blood of bulls and goats did not have the intrinsic power to do became a reality in the blood of Jesus, God's Son, which "cleanses us from all sin" and from "all unrighteousness." (Heb 10:14; 1 Jn 1:7, 9)

51:4 *Against thee.* Wrong done to fellowmen is more than social injustice; it offends their Creator. To reach their victims the murderer and the adulterer tear down the walls of safety and well-being which the Lawgiver has built around them for their protection. Joseph and David were well aware that every sin, whether against the first or the second table of the Ten Commandments, was a repudiation of God's holy will. (Gn 39:9; 2 Sm 12:5)

Justified. Cf. Ro 3:4.

51:5 *Conceive me.* The action of husband and wife which initiates life is not itself sinful. Nor can a person offer his innate propensity to evil as an excuse for his wicked deeds. Recognizing the true nature of sin, the penitent sinner knows that it is not only what he occasionally does wrong that he must confess. The evil act brings to the surface what he is in the deepest recesses of his being. (Gn 8:21; Jb 14:4; 15:13; Ps 58:3; Is 6:5; Jer 17:9)

51:7 *Hyssop.* A branch of a bush with fragrant leaves used in ritual sprinklings. (Ex 12:22; Lv 14:1-9; Nm 19:4-19)

Whiter than snow. Even when sins "are like scarlet," God can *wash* away their stains completely. (Is 1:18; Rv 7:13 f.)

51:8 *Bones.* A "broken . . . heart" and a "broken spirit" (17) can make a person feel broken-up all over. (Cf. 6:2 note)

51:10 *Create.* Only God can do what this verb describes. As He called "the heavens and the earth" into existence, "formed man of dust from the ground, and breathed into his nostrils the breath of life," so the coming into being of a clean heart, animated by *a new and right* (steadfast) *spirit,* requires the word of the Creator: "Let there be." (Gn 1:1, 3, 27; 2:7; Jer 24:7; 32:39; Eze 36:26; Jn 3:3; 2 Co 5:17)

51:14 *Bloodguiltiness.* The plural of the Hebrew word for blood is used at times to denote the guilt incurred by shedding it. (Dt 19:10; 1 Sm 25:26, 33)

51:16 *No delight.* On the apparent rejection of all sacrifices to emphasize the necessity of sincerity in acts of worship see 40:6 note; 50:8 note.

51:18 *Rebuild the walls.* The Hebrew text says simply "build . . . the walls" (KJV). The RSV translation is interpretative, suggesting that this verse was written after Jerusalem had been destroyed by the Babylonians. However, the closing prayer of the psalm may just as well reflect the thought that whereas sins such as David's "set a city aflame" and cause it to be "overthrown," "righteousness exalts a nation." (Pr 11:11; 14:34; 29:8)

Psalm 52

52:1-9 When a *mighty man* uses *the abundance of his riches* to oppress his fellowmen and even *boasts* of the *destruction* he is *plotting, the godly* may be tempted to ask whether God cares. This *Maskil of David* assures those who *trust in the steadfast love of God* that justice will prevail, all appearances to the contrary notwithstanding. It differs from other psalms having the same purpose (e.g., Ps 10) in that it does not first call God's attention to the lamentable state of affairs and ask Him to intervene but at once denounces the workers of iniquity (1-4) and announces the judgment which inevitably will sweep away *the man who would not make God his refuge* (5-7). By contrast, *the righteous,* secure *for ever* under God's protection, will *thank* Him that He *is good* (8 f.).—For the meaning of *Maskil* see Ps 32. For the record of Doeg's villainy see 1 Sm 21:1-9; 22:9-23.

52:1 *O mighty man.* Evildoers are addressed directly also in 4:2; 6:8; 119:115. For warnings against reliance on earthly resources see 49:5 f.; Jb 31:24-28; Jer 9:23.

Against the godly. The Hebrew text need not be changed. It reads: "Why do you boast of mischief, O mighty man? The steadfast love of God is all the day" (i.e., forever). The second sentence tells the mighty man how empty his boasting and futile his plotting is because his intended victims can count on the covenanted promises of God to protect them.

52:4 *Words that devour.* Slander and false accusations destroy a man as if they had "swallowed him up." (35:25; 27:2 note)

52:6 *Laugh.* Those who respond to God's forgiving grace by striving to be *righteous* in their conduct will be filled with awe when they *see* the fearful judgment executed on the wicked (40:3). They *laugh,* not in vindictive glee that the "enemy falls" (Pr 24:17; Jb 31:29) but in the joyous assurance that God frustrates the evil designs of the "worker of treachery" (2) who boasts that his riches enable him to defy and deflect divine judgment. (Rv 18:20; 19:1 ff.)

52:8 *Green olive tree.* Well-being under God's providence is compared with a sturdy tree drawing sustenance from the streams which issue from *the house of God.* (46:4 note; 1:3; 92:12-15)

52:9 *Godly.* Cf. 4:3 note.

Psalm 53

53:1-6 This psalm is substantially identical with Ps 14. Cf. the notes there. In vv. 2, 4, 5, 6 the divine name "Lord" is replaced by the term *God.* In v. 5 the content of 14:5 f. is recast. The superscription is more elaborate. *Mahalath* may denote a musical setting or melody (cf. "Superscriptions" in introductory notes to the Book of Psalms). For *Maskil* see Ps 32.

Psalm 54

54:1-7 This psalm can serve as a model in a situation when disaster seems too imminent to allow time for "many words" (Mt 6:7). Its few verses are hardly more than a shriek of anguished concern. It bursts into an ejaculation for help (1-2) from *ruthless men* and their murderous design (3), followed by a compressed affirmation of faith in God as *Helper* (4-5) and a vow to *give thanks* for His deliverance *from every trouble* (6-7). For the situation in David's life referred to in the superscription see 1 Sm 23:19 ff.

54:1 *Thy name.* God's name is more than the word by which men address Him. It is the sum total of the manifestations of His Godhead (8:1 note; 20:1 note). Prominent among His revealed characteristics is His *might.* (66:7; 71:18)

54:3 *Insolent men.* This translation is based on some Hebrew manuscripts and the ancient versions. The word for "strangers" (KJV) is very similar in spelling. These men are identified as refusing to acknowledge God and ruthlessly seeking the life of those faithful to Him. (10:4; 14:1)

54:6 *Freewill offering.* A token of gratitude not required by law (Ex 35:29; 36:3-5; Lv 7:16). It is pledged as confidently as if the deliverance were an accomplished fact.

54:7 *Looked in triumph.* Cf. 52:6 note.

Psalm 55

55:1-23 Betrayal by a trusted friend or intimate associate is one of life's most bitter experiences. When treachery by a traitor wins popular support and threatens to subvert moral and civic order, fervent prayers for divine intervention ascend to God. Such was the case when David's son Absalom led an uprising against his father. The coup d'etat seemed destined to succeed. Ahithophel, David's counselor and confidant, joined the conspirators. Jerusalem became such a hotbed of intrigue as to force the king to seek safety in the open country beyond the Jordan (2 Sm 15). The opening verses of the psalm are an appeal to God for relief from *the oppression of the wicked* (1-3), which has unnerved the intended victim to the point that he wishes he could *fly away* from *the raging wind and tempest* whirling about him (4-8). However, this is only an idle dream. If there is to be an end to *violence and strife,* God must bring confusion into the ranks of the wicked plotters (9-11). Even something more drastic is necessary. The *familiar friend,* turned traitor, and those misled by him can be stopped only by sudden death (12-15). Because they refuse to fear God, He must grant protection against their murderous designs (16-19), especially in view of the villainy of the promoter of the plot (20-21). The conviction that God will not let *men of blood and treachery* win out is so strong that everyone is encouraged to *cast* his *burden on the Lord.* (22-23)

55:3 *Bring trouble.* Cf. RSV note. KJV: "they cast iniquity upon me."

55:6 *Like a dove.* "Fear and trembling . . . and horror" produce the plaintive cry for escape from reality on the wings of a bird which can *fly away and be at rest* "in the clefts of the rock. in the covert of the cliff" (SS 2:14; Jer 9:2). In the following verses such wishful thinking gives way to the only realistic relief from disaster: refuge in God. (Cf. 11:1 note)

55:9 *Confuse their tongues.* God once frustrated the attempt to build "a tower with its top in the heavens" when He confused the language of its builders and "scattered them abroad over the face of all the earth." (Gn 11:1-9)

55:10 *They go.* "Violence and strife" stalk about in the city.

55:13 *My equal.* Lit. "a man like my rank." The traitor had access to the thoughts and secrets of his benefactor. See Jesus' pained greeting to Judas (Lk 22:48), but also the woe pronounced on His betrayer. (Mk 14:21)

55:15 *To Sheol alive.* A reference to the sudden death which swept away rebellious Korah and his associates. (Nm 16:31-33)

55:19 *Keep no law.* The Hebrew text, translated in the RSV note, makes the point that the villains refuse to change their ungodly way of life and to *fear God* instead. Their murderous intention cannot be curbed unless God destroys them.

55:20 *My companion.* This noun is supplied from the context. The text has only: "He stretched," etc. It is only natural that a prayer uttered in a frenzy of emotions should revert to the dastardly deception perpetrated by a false friend who *violated his covenant* of trust.

55:22 *Burden.* The Hebrew word so translated occurs only here in the OT. The RSV note suggests a derivation from the verb to give. The resulting translation contains the comforting thought that while God's wisdom and love determine what happens in life, He does not let a situation develop for which He does not also supply the strength to "be able to endure" "what he has given." (1 Co 10:13; Ps 37:5; 1 Ptr 5:7)

Psalm 56

56:1-13 This *Miktam of David* (cf. Ps 16) anticipates Paul's heroic statement of faith: "If God is for us, who is against us?" (Ro 8:31; see also Heb 13:6). Twice the refrainlike challenge punctuates the psalm: *What can flesh/man do to me?* (4, 11). This antidote to fear is not a theoretical abstraction. It is a triumphant shout of defiance, preceded in both instances by a realistic description of an impending calamity (1-3 and 5-7). The basis of confidence is the simple declaration: *In God I trust* (4, 10), amplified in 8 f. The certainty of being heard transforms the prayer into a closing vow to *render thank offerings* to God for the anticipated deliverance.—*The Dove on Far-off Terebinths* seems to be a melody or musical setting appointed for the rendition of the psalm (cf. "Superscriptions" in the introductory notes to the Psalter). For the incident in David's life referred to see 1 Sm 21:10 ff.

56:1 *Be gracious.* One word in Hebrew, translated "Have mercy on me" (51:1) and "Be merciful to me" (57:1). It makes clear at the very outset that the granting of the prayer is an act of undeserved goodness on God's part.

Men trample. Better rendered: "pant after," i.e., in hot pursuit, or "snap at" (so also in 2 and 57:3).

56:2 *Proudly.* KJV: "O thou most High." The noun occurring here is best construed adverbially to describe the haughty action of the enemy rather than as a divine epithet, for which a different Hebrew word is used in 57:2 and otherwise.

56:4 *Word.* Faith is grounded on what God said He would do. To *praise* these promises is to confess joyous trust that His Word will "not return to me empty" (Is 55:11). Such confidence is not whistling in the dark. For *flesh,* i.e., mortal, puny man, must wither like grass "when the breath of the Lord blows upon it." (Is 40:6-8; Ps 118:6)

56:7 *Recompense them.* The Hebrew text yields sense if translated as in KJV: "Shall they escape by iniquity?" Cf. RSV note.

56:8 *Tears in thy bottle.* Nothing escapes God's watchful eyes. Nor is He indifferent to tears shed by His children. It is as if he collects every one of them in a container for liquids, which in ancient times was the skin of an animal (Gn 21:14 f.; Ju 4:19), and keeps a record of them in a book. (Ml 3:16; Ps 139:16)

56:12 *Thank offerings.* Cf. 50:14 note.

Psalm 57

57:1-11 This psalm is similar to the prayer voiced in the immediately preceding *Miktam of David.* Repeated wrestling with God in prayer will not appear superfluous to a person face to face with threatening calamity. There is some formal resemblance with Ps 56. The opening words are identical. A refrain occurs in the middle and at the end (5, 11; cf. 56:4, 11). However, there is no monotonous sameness. Intensity of feeling is expressed by repetition of words in vv. 1, 3, 7, 8. More pronounced than in Ps 56 is the note of thanksgiving in vv. 7-11, which in turn occurs again in Ps 108:1-5.—*Do Not Destroy,* here and in the next two psalms, indicates the melody or the musical setting to be used in the rendition of the psalm. *In the cave* refers to an episode in David's flight from Saul, either the one recorded 1 Sm 22:1 or the one described 1 Sm 24:3-7.

57:1 *Shadow of thy wings.* Cf. 17:8 note.

57:4 *Lions.* Evil men, ferocious as wild beasts and "aflame" (RSV note) with animal hunger for prey, are in relentless pursuit of their victim. (Cf. 3:7 note)

57:6 *Have fallen.* Faith in God's "steadfast love and . . . faithfulness" (3) sees the desired deliverance as an accomplished fact. (Cf. 7:14 note)

57:8 *Awake the dawn.* "Joy comes with the morning" after a night of weeping (119:147; 30:5). But this song of joy begins so early as to open "the eyelids of the morning." (Jb 3:9 note)

57:11 *Be exalted.* When God proves to be a "refuge" from "the storms of destruction" (1), His *glory* will be recognized *over all the earth.*

Psalm 58

58:1-11 This *Miktam of David* is another plea for redress similar to the two preceding psalms so designated in the superscription. It too arises from a crisis produced by hostile forces so formidable that human efforts can not cope with them. The appeal for divine intervention is made with the high degree of confidence animating the other calls for help. It differs from them in the circumstances from which relief is sought. Here a demonic perversion of the courts of justice threatens the existence of *the righteous,* i.e., the innocent party. The language is unusually vivid and picturesque. The 11 verses of the psalm are ablaze with graphic comparisons and daring figures of speech. It begins in a defiant mood. Those who do not judge *uprightly* but use their authority to *deal out violence* are summarily haled into the supreme court of divine justice (1-2). Charges are preferred against the culprits in a bitter denunciation of their ingrained wickedness (3-5). Turning abruptly from them to "the Lord, the righteous judge" (2 Ti 4:8; Heb 12:23), the advocate of the helpless victims calls for a penalty for their despicable deeds in terms as fiercely realistic as their crimes are outrageously ghastly (6-9). When the sentence is carried out, as it is sure to be, confidence in a just world order will be restored (10-11).—For *Do Not Destroy* see the superscription of Ps 57.

58:1 *Gods.* The Hebrew noun, so translated, occurs again only in the superscription of Ps 56, where it is rendered "terebinths" or oaks. If it is derived from a root denoting inability or failure to speak, the meaning would be: "Do you by silence decree what is right?" implying the charge that the judges do not open their mouths to "maintain the rights of the poor and needy" (Pr 31:8 f.). Spelled with different vowels and a slight consonantal change, the noun is the plural form of *el,* the regular word for God, but which is used also of idols, the "no-gods" (Is 31:3; Dt 32:21; Dn 11:36). If *gods* is the correct reading, the thought would be that the judges act as they do because they are possessed by a spirit of perversity as demonic and immoral as the idols of popular worship. The same word, so vocalized, also has the meaning given in the RSV note (2 K 24:15; Eze 17:13). The KJV translation "congregation" is based on rabbinic tradition. For a similar indictment of unjust judges see Ps 82. The prophets cry out against the same outrage (Is 1:23; 5:23; 10:1 f.; Jer 5:28, etc.) For the grief resulting from miscarriage of justice see Jb 24:1-12.

58:8 *The snail.* It leaves behind a trail of quickly drying *slime.*

58:9 *Green or ablaze.* The kind of judgment to overtake the judges is depicted figuratively. It is to be as sudden and complete as a gust of wind sweeps away the thorns, used as fuel, before all of them have caught fire.

58:10 *Vengeance.* Retribution is not self-administered, but left in the hands of Him who says: "Vengeance is mine." (Dt 32:35; Ro 12:19; Heb 10:30)

Bathe his feet. The OT is not squeamish in its use of graphic language. The rejoicing of *the righteous,* however, is not satisfaction of a thirst for blood. God's victory over the forces of evil and His restoration of "righteousness" are a legitimate cause of joy. (Rv 18:20; see also Rv 6:10; 19:2, 17-18)

Psalm 59

59:1-17 The fourth in a series of psalms called *A Miktam of David* is another desperate cry for relief from impending disaster. Any person unable to extricate himself from a tight web of circumstances spun by evil forces will not grumble about repetitiousness if he finds more than one prayer to send to the throne of mercy in the dark night-watches of anxiety. Nor will he consider it strange if the psalm lacks a consistent sequence of thought. He knows how true to life it is that fears may subside as he tells God his troubles only to haunt him anew and provoke supplications as fervent as those with which he began. In the first half of Ps 59 (1-10) there is (1) a fourfold cry for deliverance (1-2) from insidious and *fierce men* who, without provocation, *lie in wait for* their victim (3-4a); (2) an impassioned plea that God take note of and *punish* all who *treacherously plot evil* (4b-5); (3) a scathing denunciation of bloodthirsty men, vicious as a pack of wild dogs and blatantly blasphemous (6-7); (4) an affirmation of trust in God's power to confound the enemies (8-10). But the struggle for peace of mind goes on. In the second part of the psalm (11-14) the frantic search for security in God's *might* and *steadfast love* begins all over again.

59:4 *No fault of mine.* The deadly plot is wholly unwarranted. (7:3 note)

Rouse thyself. Cf. 7:6 note.

59:5 *God of hosts.* Cf. 1 Sm 1:3 note; Ps 24:10; 46:11. The plea for help is not directed to an impotent idol. The *God of Israel,* powerful enough to destroy wicked nations (9:5 note; 10:16 note), is able to execute justice on a handful of men as perverse in their opposition to His rule as the godless heathen. This thought is repeated in v. 13.

59:7 *Snarling with their lips.* In this verse the enemies are not compared with dogs as in v. 6. Therefore the Hebrew text makes sense if translated: "They pour forth [words] with their mouths; swords are in their lips." (For "pour out" see 119:171; 145:7; for "swords," 55:21; 57:4)

Who . . . will hear us? What they say is an impudent denial of accountability to God (10:13; 14:1; 64:5; 94:7). But for "the words of their lips" they will "be trapped in their pride." (12)

59:8 *Laugh.* Cf. 2:4 note; 37:13.

59:10 *Look in triumph.* Cf. 52:6 note; 54:7.

59:11 *Slay them not.* If God were to "consume them" (13) instantaneously, the lesson of His retributive justice could soon be forgotten. This would not so easily be the case if they were destroyed one by one in a series of judgments. (Is 26:10)

59:16 *In the morning.* "Weeping may tarry for the night, but joy comes with the morning." (30:5)

59:17 *O my Strength.* Prayer can turn agitation and dread into a song of *praises,* anticipating the demonstration of God's *steadfast love.*

Psalm 60

60:1-12 This *Miktam of David* is a prayer that Israel, defeated in battle, be granted victory over inveterate enemies and so be enabled to live up to its high privilege to be the covenant nation, chosen to be God's instrument of universal blessing. Relief from frenzied consternation, resulting from military disaster (1-5), is sought in (1) recalling the promises which *God has spoken* and in granting Israel possession of the land in spite of all opposition (6-8); (2) turning prayerfully and confidently to God for *help against the foe* (9-12).—The superscription refers to military expeditions by David and his general Joab. These are not mentioned in the summary of victories recorded 2 Sm 8 and 1 Ch 18.—*Shushan Eduth* is a transliteration of the Hebrew words "Lily of Testimony," no doubt denoting the melody or musical setting prescribed for the rendition of the psalm. "Lilies" are mentioned also in the superscriptions of Ps 45, 69, 80.

60:1 *O God.* The psalm expresses faith in God's control of the destiny of nations. It also acknowledges and laments the fact that He has found reason to be *angry* with Israel and has used its enemies as a scourge of "hard things." (44:9 f.; 74:1; 89:38 f.)

60:2 *Land to quake.* The feeling of dismay is described in highly emotional figures of speech. It is as if the very foundations of existence were about to give way.

60:3 *Wine to drink.* When God punishes sin, He is said to make men drink "the cup of his wrath." (Is 51:17; Jer 25:15 f.; cf. Ps 11:6 note)

60:4 *A banner.* Instead of issuing a command to rout the enemy, God, as it were, ran up the signal for retreat (Jer 4:6). The words for *bow* and "truth" (RSV note) have the same consonants in Hebrew. Still claiming to be God's "beloved," the people pray that flight may be turned into victory.

60:6 *In his sanctuary.* The translation in the RSV note is to be preferred. God's promises are made with an oath by His "holiness" (89:35; Am 4:2). The next lines remind Him of what He said. The chosen people were to occupy the Promised Land, its full extent being represented by the territories mentioned. Neighboring nations would not be able to offer resistance. (Gn 15:18 ff.; Jos 1:2-6)

60:8 *Washbasin.* God's power to overcome all opposition is described in highly anthropomorphic figures of speech. Moab, adjacent to the Dead Sea, is said to be no more than a basin in which God washes His feet. To Edom, situated nearby, He casts His *shoe* as a master assigns the task of cleaning it to his slave (but see also Ru 4:7-9, where the shoe plays a part in acquiring property).

60:9 *Who . . .?* A rhetorical question, confessing that there is no hope of launching a counterattack on Edom's *fortified city* unless God, who had rejected His people, grants "help against the foe." (11)

60:12 *With God.* With this motto inscribed on their banners, "those who fear" God (4) are armed to take up the struggle with foes of every kind and description.

Psalm 61

61:1-8 This *Psalm of David* pleads for an end of banishment and for a return to the reassuring communion with God provided by participation in temple worship (1-4). The prayer, spoken in full confidence (5), goes on to invoke blessings on *the king* to whom God entrusted the maintenance of order necessary for Israel's religious life. (6-8).

61:2 *The end of the earth.* Separation from the sanctuary in Jerusalem is felt so keenly that the location of the exile might as well have been in the most distant part of the world. (Cf. 84:1-4, 10)

Higher than I. "Refuge" beyond the reach of hostile forces cannot be provided by human resources. (18:2; 27:5; 62:7)

61:4 *Tent.* Cf. 15:1 note; 27:4 note. For *shelter of thy wings* see 17:8 note; 57:1.

61:5 *Heritage.* The Promised Land or the people living in it. (Ex 6:8; Ps 111:6; 94:5)

61:7 *Enthroned forever.* For Messianic promises given David see 2 Sm 7; 1 Ch 17:16-27. Note David's reference to himself in the third person. (Jer 30:8 f.; Eze 34:23 f.)

Psalm 62

62:1-12 In this *Psalm of David* the little word *only* has the sound of trumpets, making the heavens ring with strong notes of trust in God, the immovable *rock* of *salvation,* and of calculated defiance of bad men, fleeting as a puff of wind. Its clarion call somewhat muted by a variety of translations ("alone," "but"), this adverb introduces six of the twelve Hebrew verses with the flourish of a herald's bugle. In vv. 1, 2, 5, 6 it bids frightened souls to calm their fears because they can take refuge in God, the only *fortress* in which they can feel safe.

In vv. 4 and 6 it calls attention to the dangers against which God alone can provide protection. On the one hand, there is no blinking the fact that there are monsters of iniquity who have no compunctions in crushing their victim (3 f.); on the other hand, it is just as true that puny, strutting men, armed though they be with the might and resources of wickedness, are nothing more than "the dust on the scales" of God's justice (Is 40:15), a *delusion* of grandeur when the *power* that *belongs to God* sweeps them away. (9-12)

62:1 *In silence.* God's children may have trouble at times to "be still before the Lord and wait patiently for him" (37:15). It is therefore not without reason that vv. 1 f. are repeated in 5-7. (Cf. 42:5, 11)

62:3 *All of you.* Men who "only plan to thrust . . . down" others will not hesitate to combine forces in pursuit of their cruel aims.

62:8 *O people.* The person who by pouring out his heart before God has found solid ground under his feet is compelled to recommend this cure of gnawing fears to others.

62:9 *They go up.* Ancient scales consisted of two pans which were balanced against one another (Jb 31:6). Weighed by God, men, "both low and high" (49:2) are *lighter than a breath.*

62:11 *Once . . . twice.* An idiomatic way of saying "repeatedly." (Jb 33:14 note; 40:5).

62:12 *Requite.* Cf. Jer 17:10; Ro 2:6; Cl 3:25; Rv 2:23.

Psalm 63

63:1-11 To pray this *Psalm of David* is putting life's priorities into proper perspective. Because God's *steadfast love is better than life,* longing for communion with Him in His *sanctuary* and the desire to praise Him *with joyful lips* (5) should dominate all other emotions of the heart (1-4). It is only natural that the *soul,* its inmost needs satisfied, also *clings to* His *right hand,* confident of protection against cruel enemies (5-8), who are doomed to an ignominious death because of their opposition to God (9-11).—For the episode in David's life referred to in the superscription see 2 Sm 15:23, 28; 16:2, 14; 17:16

63:1 *Thirsts.* The need to have God supply the needs vital to the soul is felt like the physical craving for water *in a dry and weary land.* (42:1 f.; 143:6)

63:2 *Looked upon thee.* In worshiping His *power and glory* and contemplating His "steadfast love," God becomes very real to the eyes of faith. (3; 27:4 note)

63:3 *Better than life.* Man's most precious earthly possession. (Cf. 36:7 f.; 73:26)

63:5 *Marrow and fat.* Fat was considered the choicest part of meat. (Gn 45:18; Lv 7:23, 25)

63:11 *The king.* Cf. 61:7 note.

Psalm 64

64:1-10 Though similar to other cries for help in dire need, this *Psalm of David* will be of comfort particularly to anyone confronted by insidious plots, spun with demonic cunning. After a brief plea for deliverance (1-2), the *complaint* is taken up against the *scheming . . . evildoers,* who are *laying snares secretly* and *without fear* of being called to account (3-6). However, *God will shoot his arrow at them* before their *arrows* and *swords* (3) can strike home (7-9). *What God has wrought* in maintaining a just world order will fill the heart of *all men* with *fear* (9) but prompt all who *take refuge in Him* to *rejoice.* (10)

64:3 *Their tongues.* The harm they intend to inflict is as deadly as an assassin's weapons. (55:21; 57:4)

64:5 *Who can see us?* It is difficult to determine how much of vv. 5 and 6 should be put into quotation marks, for which Hebrew writing has no equivalent. But whether quoted directly or indirectly, these verses describe the fanatic determination with which the wicked *hold fast to their evil purpose.* No one, not even God, they boast, can do anything to stop them. (10:4 note; 14:1 note; 59:7 note; 94:7)

64:7 *His arrow.* When God shoots His "fiery shafts" of judgment (7:12 f.), their "arrows" (3) become harmless. The mischief their tongues were to do is made to be their own undoing.

Psalm 65

65:1-13 When Paul wrote to the Colossians: "Sing psalms and hymns and spiritual songs with thankfulness in your hearts," he could have had in mind also this *Psalm of David* (Cl 3:16; Eph 5:19 f.; Ph 4:6; 1 Th 5:18). Here the hallowed precincts of the sanctuary and flowered meadows, spiritual refreshment and fructifying raindrops, blessings of the soul and a bountiful harvest of the fields—all so easily taken for granted—are woven into a high song of jubilant thanksgiving to God. *Praise is due* Him for (1) the privilege of gathering as His covenant people in His *house* to be satisfied with the *goodness* which comes from communion with Him in His *holy temple* (1-4), (2) His control of world-history unshaken by *the tumult of the peoples* (5-8); (3) fields, softened by *showers* and made to bear a bumper crop. (9-13)

65:2 *All flesh.* The first and foremost reason why "praise is due" God is His mercy in blotting out "sins" and "transgressions" which corrupt *all flesh,* including the people whom He chose to be in covenant with Him. (4; Hos 14:2)

65:3 *Prevail.* For the crushing weight of unconfessed and unforgiven sin see 32:3 f.; 38:4.

65:4 *Be satisfied.* For the blessings of fellowship with God and of worship in His *house* see 36:8 note.

65:5 *Dread deeds.* God can answer prayer because He has the awe-inspiring power to bring about *salvation* to *the ends of the earth.* His acts of righteousness determine the destiny of peoples to "earth's farthest bounds." All opposition gives way to fear before the "strength" which "established the mountains." (Cf. 66:3-5)

65:7 *Roaring of the seas.* Cf. Is 17:12.

65:8 *Outgoings.* The farthest reaches from east to west touched in the "circuit" of the sun. (19:6)

65:9 *Visitest.* Not for a social call but to put into effect His purposes. (Ex 4:31; 13:19; 32:34; translated "punish" in Ps 59:5; 89:32)

The river of God. God's supply of rain is like a constantly flowing river from which irrigating channels carry water to a field.

65:11 *Crownest.* In the poetic language of the psalm the year is personified and the rich harvest becomes a crown of gold on its head. (Cf. 103:4)

Tracks of thy chariot. One word in Hebrew; translated "paths" by RSV in all other instances (17:5; 23:3, etc.). It is as if God passed through the land enriching the soil to produce the best of yields. For "fatness" see 63:5 note.

Psalm 66

66:1-20 One of the blessings often taken for granted is membership in the communion of saints and the privilege of participating in public worship. An Israelite, born into the chosen people, was prone to forget to thank God for creating and establishing a nation whose citizens had a share in these benefits, pledged to it in a covenant of mercy and grace. In this psalm, called a *Song,* an unidentified writer offers an antidote to this kind of ingratitude. He is so stirred by the thought of the unique place and function God assigned Israel in world history that he calls on *all the earth* to recognize and sing praises to His *glory* and *power* (1-4). The author's thoughts go back to *what God has done* to demonstrate these attributes when *he turned the* [*Red*] *sea into dry land,* enabling Israel to escape from Egypt (5-7). Mindful of belonging to this favored nation, the psalmist goes on to speak of *our God,* who to make them "His own possession among all the peoples" (Ex 19:5) *tested us* with *affliction* and *kept us among the living* to that very day (8-12). But what God did for the nation as a whole, He did also for the author when he *was in trouble.* As the latter brings the thankofferings he promised, he wants all to hear what the God of Israel has done for him and stands ready to do for all *who fear God* and trust *his steadfast love.* (13-20)

66:3 *How terrible.* Cf. 65:5 note.

66:5 *Dry land.* Cf. Ex 14:21; Jos 3:17.

66:10 *Tested us.* As silver is refined by smelting out the impurities from the ore, so God puts His people into the furnace of afflictions to purify them of the dross of infidelity. During the time of the Judges God had at hand nations "to test Israel by them." (Ju 3:1)

66:12 *A spacious place.* One word in Hebrew. It occurs again only in 23:5, where it describes overflowing abundance. By changing one Hebrew letter, it becomes a noun denoting a place of unrestrained freedom of action.

66:13 *I will come.* Besides the blessings which the psalmist had in common with all the members of the chosen people, he has good reason to invite all "who fear God" to praise Him for "what he has done" for him in particular when he "was in trouble" and "cried aloud" for help.

66:18 *Cherished iniquity.* If he had had impure motives or if he had asked for something sinful, God *would not have listened* to his prayer.

Psalm 67

67:1-7 The refrain of this *Song* (vv. 2 and 7) underscores its missionary motif. It is concerned with the purpose God had in mind when he elected Israel to be the covenant nation. He showered material and spiritual gifts on the descendants of Abraham not for their enjoyment alone. He chose them in order that through them His *saving power* might be made known also *among all nations.* However, to be a blessing to *all nations,* they needed God's grace to live and act in such a way as to make *the peoples* realize that they were the grateful beneficiaries of the God of salvation.

67:1 *Face to shine.* Words from the Aaronic blessing. (Nm 6:24-26)

67:2 *Way.* Evidence of the Lord's continued dispensations of goodness and mercy. For the use of *way* in apostolic times see Acts 9:2; 18:25; 19:9, 23.

67:6 *Yielded its increase.* Crop failure would have indicated unfaithfulness to the covenant, making Israel "a reproach among the nations." (Jl 2:17, 19; see also Lv 26:3-4; Jer 33:9)

Psalm 68

68:1-35 It requires serious effort to join in singing this *Psalm of David,* frequently hailed as a hymn of rare grandeur. It is composed in a high key of soaring figures of speech. There are kaleidoscopic changes of scenes. There are cryptic allusions to events in the dim past of an ancient people. Past, present, and future merge and come apart again. The establishment of Jerusalem as the center of God's kingdom on earth and His dwelling in the temple as His royal residence and court are celebrated as the culmination of God's triumphant march through centuries of history. But at the same time these peaks of achievement become the vantage point from which the summit and goal of God's direction of history come into view: the salvation of all nations of the earth. However, the prime requisite for reaching the high notes of praise of this *Song* is a heart bursting with rapture at the thought of God's transcendent greatness and condescending mercy. This psalm fills a need in the life of a child of God when the inclination to thank Him for what He is and does is only a smoldering wick and needs to be fanned to a bright flame of adoration and worship.

The opening verses (1-4) announce the theme of the psalm. *The righteous* have every reason to *exult before God.* When He arises to act in their behalf, all opposition by *the wicked* disintegrates *as wax melts before fire.* He who has the forces of nature at His beck and call and is enthroned in *his holy habitation* in the heavens deigns to champion the cause of the victims of injustice and oppression (5-6). In order to substantiate these statements of invincible power in the service of righteousness, several flashbacks from Israel's past are introduced (7-18). In scintillating colors they depict (a) how, shaking heaven and earth, God brought His chosen people through the wilderness and into the land flowing with milk and honey (7-10); (b) how then and thereafter *the kings of . . . armies* could not rob Israel of its heritage (11-14); (c) how after the conquest of the Promised Land, God in sovereign choice made *the high mount* of Zion the earthly seat of His reign, even though loftier mountain peaks were close at hand. This marked a decisive point in world history. Here the execution of God's eternal plan of salvation reached a new plateau from which to look for still greater things to come. Here was high drama, described in highly imaginative language and bold human analogies (15-18). What the *God of salvation* did in the past, and does *daily,* assures the continuation of His victorious and beneficent rule in the future (19-23). Again God's coming to dwell in a house built with hands is flashed on memory's screen with the spotlight shifting from the celestial *chariotry* of His triumphal entry (17) to the jubilant reception given Him by *the great congregation* assembled from all tribes of Israel (24-27). Next comes a short prayer that God achieve the purpose of making the *temple at Jerusalem* His headquarters on earth. Let His *might* and *strength* proceed from there to overcome the most powerful opposition (28-31). Because *the God of Israel* is not a tribal deity, confined to a *sanctuary* in Jerusalem, but *rides in the heavens* and lets the thunder of *his mighty voice* proclaim *his power . . . in the skies,* the *kingdoms of the earth* are exhorted to worship and *sing praises to the Lord.* (32-35)

68:1 *Let God arise.* "Whenever the ark set out" on a day's journey through the wilderness, Moses said: "Arise, O Lord, and let thy enemies be scattered" (Nm 10:35). The echoes of this ancient war-cry were to rouse the righteous to be joyful, reminding them that when God goes into action on their behalf *those who hate him* cannot frustrate Him.

68:4 *Rides upon the clouds.* A daring figure of speech to describe the unlimited power at God's command (36:5; 45:4; 57:10; Dt 33:26). The translation offered in the RSV note gives an alternate meaning to two Hebrew words, used in this sense in Is 40:3. For the meaning of *name* see 8:1 note.

68:5 *Holy habitation.* From celestial heights (Dt 26:15) He reaches down into earthly affairs, protecting the weak and the wronged and destroying "the rebellious." (10-14)

68:8 *Poured down rain.* The poetic imagery, glorifying God's power to harness the forces of nature, is similar to outpourings of feelings in Deborah's victory song. (Ju 5:4 f.; cf. Ex 19:18)

68:9 *Rain in abundance.* Either to be understood literally of the rainfall in Canaan (Dt 11:11) or figuratively of the showers of blessings bestowed upon His *heritage* and "flock." (61:5 note)

68:11 *The command.* Lit. "the word." The Lord needs only to speak to get the desired result (33:9; 148:5; Is 48:13; 55:11). *Those who bore the tidings* (one word in Hebrew, with a feminine ending) are the women, who stayed at home "among the sheepfolds" and upon the return of the army celebrated the victory in song and dancing. (Ex 15:20; 1 Sm 18:6)

68:14 *Zalmon.* Lit. "Black Hill," mentioned again only Ju 9:48. There is no record of a battle which *scattered kings there.* The verse seems to be another highly figurative way of describing how God came to Israel's rescue. The defeat of powerful armies had the effect of bright snow falling on the dark slopes of a mountain.

68:15 *Mountain of Bashan.* Mt. Hermon, its triple peaks soaring much higher than Zion, "the mount which God desired for his abode" (cf. 132:13 f.), overlooked Bashan, a territory to the east and north of the Sea of Galilee.

68:17 *From Sinai.* God is represented as coming directly from the thunder and lightning of Mt. Sinai to dwell on Zion even though centuries intervened between these events. (Cf. Dt 33:2)

68:18 *Ascend.* God's victorious march through Israel's past, culminating in establishing His rule in Jerusalem, had as its ultimate goal and fulfillment Christ's triumphant entry into the heavenly Jerusalem to rule as Head and Protector of His church. (Cf. Eph 4:8)

68:21 *Hairy crown.* The enemy soldiers had "long-haired heads" (Dt 32:42) because they had sworn not to cut their hair until they had won the battle.

68:22 *Bring them back.* There is no escape or hiding from God. (139:7 ff; Am 9:2-4)

68:23 *Bathe your feet.* Cf. 58:10 note. For the reference to *dogs* see 1 K 21:19; 22:38.

68:24 *Solemn processions.* One word in Hebrew; the adjective *solemn* is interpretative addition. The procession which comes to mind took place when David brought the ark, symbol of God's presence, into the city of Jerusalem. (1 Ch 13:5-8; 15:25-28)

68:26 *Of Israel's fountain.* The 12 tribes came forth from Jacob's loins.

68:27 *Benjamin.* All Israel was represented. *Benjamin* (Saul's tribe) and *Judah* (David's tribe), both situated in the south, were joined by *Zebulun* and *Naphthali* from the far north and by all *princes* from the intervening territories.

68:29 *Because of thy temple.* Perhaps better translated "from thy temple" and linked with the preceding line.

68:30 *Beasts . . . among the reeds.* Egypt, described as a crocodile or hippopotamus (cf. Jb 40:15 note; 41:1 note), is symbolic of Israel's enemies. *The herd of bulls* are hostile rulers; their *calves* are their dependents. Though the precise meaning of some words in this and the following verse escapes us, the general thought is clear: The most formidable enemies must give way before the Lord and the extension of His kingdom.

68:33 *His mighty voice.* "Heaven and the highest heaven cannot contain" the God worshiped by Israel in Jerusalem (1 K 8:27). His voice is the thunder, reverberating through the heavens; He manifests "his power . . . in the skies." (Cf. 29:3-9; 19:1-6)

Psalm 69

69:1-36 This *Psalm of David* has two noteworthy features: (1) it is quoted more frequently in the NT than any other psalm except 22 and 110; (2) it asks for the execution of divine justice on godless persecutors in terms matched for vehemence only in such psalms as 35, 109, 137. Not all details of the situation can be determined. However, it is evident that here there is a zealous *servant* of God (17) who (1) is *afflicted* by God (26, 29); (2) as a result is falsely accused of crimes; (3) therefore fears for his survival. Panic-stricken and distraught, he bursts into God's presence shouting: *Save me* (1) and then intermittently repeats and elaborates his cry for help (6, 13-18, 29). Interspersed between these recurring appeals are (1) a tearful description of the desperate state of affairs (1 b-4; 7-12; 19-21); (2) a frank confession of his sinfulness in God's sight (5); (3) an ardent plea that God vindicate the cause of *those who hope in* Him by letting His *burning anger overtake* those who persecute His saints (22-28). The closing verses show how prayer changed things. The frightened soul grows calm, certain that *the Lord hears the needy.* Praise for anticipated deliverance replaces frenzy and despair (30-36).—*According to Lilies,* appearing also in the superscription of Ps 45, may refer to the melody according to which the psalm was to be sung.

69:1 *Neck.* The Hebrew word is the oft-occurring noun usually translated "soul" or "life." Cf. Is 8:8, where a different word for neck is used. The growing threat to life is described in similar terms in 14 f.; cf. also 40:2; 88:6 f.; 124:4 f.

69:4 *Without a cause.* Innocent of the crime of stealing, as accused (4), he nevertheless pleads guilty of wrongs in God's sight (5; cf. 35:19; 59:3 f.; see also Lv 6:4). The undeserved hatred of men which he endured was designed to be a type, foreshadowing the persecution and suffering of that righteous Servant who had no sins to confess, having offended neither God nor man. (Jn 15:35)

69:5 *Folly.* To commit sin is the worst kind of foolishness (38:5); to attempt to hide it from God is still greater folly.

69:7 *For thy sake.* The enemies persecute him because they hate God and anyone who is godly (44:22 note; Jer 15:15). Successful defiance of God would try the faith of all who trust His promises.

69:9 *Zeal for thy house.* Promoting God's cause resulted in grief and insult rather than in blessings. See the NT references to this verse in Jn 2:17 and Ro 15:3.

69:11 *Sackcloth.* The garment of mourning and penitence. (Gn 37:34; 2 K 19:1; Ps 30:11; 35:13)

69:12 *In the gate.* Where men gathered to exchange news and conduct business.

69:13 *Acceptable time.* When in God's good pleasure a favorable answer to the prayer could be expected. (Is 49:8)

69:18 *Redeem me.* Not zeal for God's house but His unmerited mercy is the basis of the prayer. See the note on "Redeemer," Jb 19:25.

69:19 *Thou knowest.* Prayer tells God the sins which He already knows (5). It offers opportunity also to throw into God's lap one's troubles, which He knows too.

69:21 *Vinegar.* Jesus was offered "wine . . . mingled with gall" (Mt 27:34); in answer to His cry "I thirst" He was given vinegar to drink. (Mt 27:48; Jn 19:29)

69:22 *Table.* Men who were their guests were to turn against them and ensnare them in a treacherous plot.

Sacrificial feasts. See RSV note. The Hebrew text makes good sense if translated: "And to those who are at peace [i.e., feel secure] may it [i.e., the table of hospitality] become a trap." See Paul's use of vv. 22 and 23 in Ro 11:9 f.

69:25 *A desolation.* See Peter's reference to this verse in Acts 1:20.

69:26 *Smitten.* God has afflicted him with a chastisement which is left undefined. The enemies add insult to injury by their claim that God is punishing him for unconfessed crimes. See the same kind of argumentation on the part of Job's friends in Jb 4:1 ff.

69:28 *Book of the living.* See Ex 32:32 f.; Is 4:3; Rv 3:5; 13:8; 20:12, 15; 21:27. For the imprecation on the enemies see 35:4 note; 58:10 notes.

69:31 *Horns and hoofs.* Animals acceptable for sacrifice had to be mature (horns) and be classified as clean (cloven hoofs, Lv 11:3). See notes on 40:6; 50:8; 51:16

69:34 *Heaven and earth.* When God's "salvation" comes to an individual, all who "seek God" are asked to join in praising God for they can expect Him to come also to their rescue. All of creation reflects His glory.

69:35 *Rebuild.* See 51:18 note.

Psalm 70

70:1-5 Except for a change in the divine name and for other minor variations, this psalm duplicates 40:13-17. Cf. the notes there.

Psalm 71

71:1-24 People whose life's *strength is spent* (9) often are lonely and sad. To someone with *gray hairs* (18) who in addition to the ordinary maladies of *old age* (9, 18) has an unusually grievous burden to bear, this psalm offers comfort as well as a good lesson in godliness. The unknown author did not spend his youth in riotous living nor his manhood worshiping creature comforts rather than the Creator. *Taught* by God (17) from a child, he walked in His ways. He knew by heart many a song sung by the congregation in worship. Snatches from various psalms (such as 31 and 22) came to him as he put together verses expressing his own feeling. The result of his efforts was not a scintillating masterpiece of poetic artistry. It lacks even logical progression of thought. Declarations of confidence in God, prayers for deliverance, and vows to thank God for the anticipated help flow in and out of one another at random. These diverse elements are strung together in vv. 1-11 only to be woven into one another again in vv. 12-24 with the slight difference that in the second half there is more sustained emphasis on the praises to be sung. Yet in spite of such stylistic shortcomings the rhetoric of faith comes through loud and clear. Instead of letting this godfearing man live out his remaining years in peace, the Lord made him *see many sore troubles* (20) which his enemies—*wicked, cruel, unjust* (4)—exploited to threaten his life. But he is not a disillusioned, bitter old man, ready to "curse God and die" (Jb 2:9). He entrusts himself to the Helper on whom he has depended from birth; he prays: *Deliver me and rescue me* (2); he still has a mission in life: to witness to God's power and goodness.

71:1 *I take refuge.* The first three verses are an echo of 31:1-3.

71:3 *Strong fortress.* The Hebrew text makes sense if translated: "Be thou to me a rock of dwelling to which I might come always [and which] thou has appointed to save me."

71:6 *From my mother's womb.* Cf. 22:9 f.; Is 46:3.

71:7 *Portent.* A word frequently occuring in the combination translated "signs and wonders" (Ex 7:3; Dt 6:22, etc.) The thought here is that the heavy affliction God let come to a person who professed to be upright in his devotion to godliness was taken by his enemies to prove that he was suffering well-deserved punishment for concealed crime.

71:13 *Accusers.* A participle of the verb from which "Satan" is derived. (Jb 1:6 second note)

71:15 *Righteous acts.* Praising God for what He has done times without number in the cause of "righteousness" and *salvation* encourages the aged sufferer to "hope continually" that he too will have occasion to "shout for joy" over such an act of vindication and deliverance in his own case.

71:16 *I will come.* To "enter his gates with thanksgiving and his courts with praise." (100:4)

71:18 *Might.* Lit. "arm"; see Ex 6:6; Dt 4:34; 26:8; Is 40:10; 51:5; 52:10; Jer 27:5.

71:20 *Revive.* God can help even if the persecuted victim is as good as dead and buried in *the depths of the earth.*

71:21 *My honor.* Lit. "greatness." God's intervention would silence the "accusers" and detractors and restore to him the respect due a servant of God.

71:22 *Holy One of Israel.* This title of God is appropriate in a song of praise (78:41; 89:18) because it recalls that the sovereign, transcendent Lord of creation entered into covenant with a people whom He had freed from slavery.

Psalm 72

72:1-20 Whether the superscription is translated *A Psalm of Solomon* or "A Psalm for Solomon" (KJV) does not affect the intent and meaning of this hymn. In either case, it expresses a longing and hoping for the blessings of absolute justice and universal peace. This projected ideal is cast in the mold of the promises made to David and his house (2 Sm 7). However, neither his rule nor that of any of his successors was more than an imperfect anticipation of what was expected in answer to the petitions and the desires heard in this psalm (cf. Ps 2 notes). The worldwide era of "peace on earth" (Lk 2:14), foreshadowed by the reign of those who sat "upon the throne of the kingdom of the Lord over Israel" (1 Ch 25:8), was ushered in when the Son of David, "greater than Solomon" (Lk 11:31), came to occupy "the throne of his father David" (Lk 1:32). But His *dominion . . . to the ends of the earth* (8) still "is not coming with signs to be observed" (Lk 17:20). Until "the Son of man comes in his glory" to "sit on his glorious throne" as Judge of "all the nations" (Mt 25:31 f.), His church, assailed from within and from without, pleads: "Come, Lord Jesus!" (Rv 22:20). Hence we devoutly take our place beside the OT saints as we say, in the words of their psalm: "Thy kingdom come." This prophetic poem of the ancient past portrays what the king of Israel needed to be and do as a type of the Messianic King: (1) His reign of righteousness results in *prosperity for the people* and lets *peace abound* (1-7); (2) his *dominion* incorporates *all nations . . . to the ends of the earth* (8-11) who receive the benefits of his rule, no less than his own people (12-14); (3) his universal reign will *endure forever,* producing an endless array of blessings. (15-17)

72:1 *Thy justice.* Because "the judgment is God's" (Dt 1:17), His representative on the throne of Israel was to be the executor of divine justice, righting the wrongs of "the poor," "the needy," the oppressed (cf. 2 Sm 8:15; 1 K 3:6-9). See such Messianic promises as Is 9:6 f.; 11:1-5; Jer 23:5; 33:15.

72:5 *May he live.* The Hebrew text (cf. RSV note) expresses the thought that the people will "fear" God (Dt 6:13 note) for the blessings accruing to them through His vicegerent, the king. The wish that the king may live long is voiced in 15. (See also 89:36 f.; 1 Sm 10:24)

72:8 *From sea to sea.* Universal *dominion* is expressed in geographic terms used to denote worldwide extension (Zch 9:10). The *River* is the Euphrates. (Gn 15:18; Ex 23:31)

72:10-11 *Tarshish.* Cf. 48:7; 1 K 10:22 note. For *Sheba* see 1 K 10:1 note; for *Seba,* Gn 10:7 note; Is 43:3. For the homage paid by "all kings" to the Messiah see Is 45:14; 49:23; 60:1 ff.; Mt 2:1, 11.

72:14 *Precious is their blood.* Not cheap and expendable, but highly valued and protected from being shed by *oppression and violence.*

72:16 *Abundance of grain.* V. 16 and 17 perhaps should be put into quotation marks to indicate that they are the words of the "prayer . . . made for him continually" (15). Undreamed-of fertility of the soil and a teeming population are ascribed figuratively to the Messianic age. (Am 9:13; Jl 3:18; Is 30:23 ff.; Zch 10:10; Is 49:19-21; 54:1-3)

72:17 *Bless themselves.* See the promise made to Abraham (Gn 12:3 note; 22:18).

72:18 *Blessed be the Lord.* A similar doxology is found at the close of "Book I" (Ps 41:13). Cf. the introductory notes to the Psalter, "Divisions."

72:20 *Ended.* This verse is a note to indicate that in this collection of psalms no more "prayers of David" are included. In "Book III" (73-89) only Ps 86 is attributed to David.

Psalm 73

73:1-28 This *Psalm of Asaph* (cf. Ps 50) is the story of an *almost*—how a believer *well nigh* lost his faith in God's goodness, but emerged from his bout with doubt more firmly convinced than ever that God is never anything but *good to . . . the pure in heart* (1). For the benefit of all who may be tempted for similar reasons to question whether *it is good to be near God* (28) he goes on to tell what it was that all but made him lose his hold on God and what brought him back to cling to Him for guidance in life and for hope in death. He had come to the brink of unbelief when he *saw the prosperity of the wicked* which they achieved by *malice* and *oppression* and in blatant defiance of divine retribution. The situation became utterly confusing when, on the one hand, God did nothing to curb their arrogant violence, even sparing them the ordinary troubles of human existence, and, on the other hand, let His scourge of affliction rain heavy blows on him, innocent of their crimes though he was (2-14). He did not solve his problem by rationalizing it, by philosophic submission to the inevitable, by consoling himself with the thought that virtue is its own reward. Discarding all considerations of merit, he found the key to a satisfying, radiant, victorious way of life when he *went into the sanctuary of God.* In the holy precincts of eternal wisdom he *perceived* things in their true perspective. It was shortsighted to be disturbed by the passing success of the ungodly when in God's time *their end* was but *a moment* away (15-20). He became aware too how *stupid and ignorant* his sense of values had been. It came to him that *nothing upon earth* mattered except to be *continually with* God. To rely on His *counsel* to *guide* him was to know that nothing on life's way could harm him, come what may. God's designs go beyond time's horizons: His ultimate purpose is to *receive me to glory,* when *my flesh and my heart . . . fail* (21-26). In view of all this, there is no reason to doubt whether *it is good to be near God.* (27-28).

73:1 *To the upright.* This translation rather than "to Israel" (KJV; RSV note) is based on a different division and punctuation of the traditional Hebrew text. The change is not necessary if "Israel" is understood to refer to all who are upright in maintaining their relationship to God, established by His covenant with the chosen people.

Pure in heart. All who comfort themselves with the axiomatic thesis of the psalm that *God is good* should know that He searches "the minds and hearts" for unfeigned devotion to Him (7:9, with note; Mt 5:8). Note the repeated references to the *heart* in vv. 7, 13, 21, 26.

73:3 *Envious.* The psalmist was not the first nor the last to be troubled when he saw that God appeared to be good to *the wicked* rather than to "the pure in heart" (Mt 5:8). (Ps 37; 49; 94; Jb 21:7-16; Jer 12:1 f.)

73:6 *Necklace.* They display their *pride* and *violence* as if it were a piece of jewelry, worn for adornment.

73:10 *Praise them.* The graphic description of the influence of the wicked on others is retained if the verse is translated: "Therefore his people turn thither and waters in abundance are drained from them" (cf. RSV note). Admiring crowds seek them out, eager to saturate themselves with prescriptions for success that stream from the lips of men who have made it rich.

73:11 *Can God know?* "The arrogant" (3) challenged God to stop them. Such unpunished blasphemy made it seem incredible that He maintains a moral world order. (10:4 note)

73:13 *Washed my hands.* Cf. 26:6 note.

73:15 *Generation.* Cf. 12:7 note.

73:17 *Sanctuary.* The Hebrew word, also in the plural form, occurs in 68:35; Eze 28:18. In order to solve what appeared to be glaring inconsistencies of life, the disturbed doubter went to seek out what the holy God had revealed on the matter.

73:20 *They are like a dream.* Cf. RSV note. The Hebrew text makes sense if the verse is translated: "As a dream [vanishes] on awakening, so, O Lord, thou dost despise their [shadowy] semblance, when thou dost bestir thyself." For other references to man's phantomlike existence see 39:5 note; 39:6; Jb 20:8; for God's awakening, see 7:6 note; 35:23.

73:24 *Receive me to glory.* "Neither death nor life" can separate the believer from his God. (Ro 8:38 f.). Cf. 49:15 note.

Psalm 74

74:1-23 This psalm will rise as fervently from the hearts and lips of God's *congregation* as it did in ancient Israel, whenever and wherever ruthless anti-God forces threaten to reduce all that is holy to *perpetual ruins,* making shambles of sanctuaries and suppressing worship. When this lament and prayer was first uttered, the temple in Jerusalem lay in ruins, burned to the ground by the Babylonian conqueror. For a long time there were no *signs* and no words of a *prophet* that the rule of terror would end. In this dark night of distress one of "the sons of Asaph" (2 Ch 35:15) cried out to God to save His holy *name* from mocking and reviling by the *impious* (18-22). His opening appeal (1-11) begins and ends with the question of *why* God has surrendered the people whom He once "redeemed" into the hands of scoffers (1, 11). As he presents his supplication, he takes occasion to call God's attention to the complete desecration of His *holy place* (4-8). Then acting as the spokesman of the people, the psalmist turns abruptly to a declaration of faith in God's power. The catastrophe did not happen because He could not prevent it, for He is the Creator of heaven and earth and the Lord of history (12-17). To this omnipotent Ruler of the universe the embattled believer makes a final plea, importuning Him to subdue His blasphemous *adversaries,* as He pledged Himself to do in His *covenant* with the chosen people, now *downtrodden, poor and needy* (18-23).—For *Maskil* see Ps 32:1-11 note.

74:1 *Why?* The same question regarding God's mysterious dealing with individuals (10:1; 22:1) here becomes a lament in behalf of an entire nation, called *the sheep of* His *pasture* (79:13; 95:7; 100:3; Jer 23:1; Eze 34:31). Because for decades no reversal of the calamity was in sight, it seemed to the stunned "congregation" that God had cast them off *forever* and that the "sanctuary" was doomed to lie in "perpetual ruins" (3; cf. Is 58:12; 61:4). Similar outpourings of grief and supplication are found in Ps 79 and in the Book of Lamentations.

74:4 *Their own signs.* Emblems and standards

raised by the Babylonians to signify absolute control of God's "dwelling place."

74:5 *They hacked.* The text of this verse, though "uncertain" (RSV note), yields sense if rendered: "It made it seem as if men were swinging axes in high strokes in a wooded thicket."

74:6 *Carved wood.* Cf. 1 K 6:29 ff.; for a description of the demolition of the temple see 2 K 24:13; 25:9, 13-17.

74:8 *Meeting places.* The same word translated "holy place" in v. 4. It is used in the plural form here to denote the several parts of the temple (cf. 73:17 note) or call to mind how often God had met there with His worshiping people (Ex 25:22; 29:42, etc.). The translation "synagogues" (KJV) is wrong.

74:9 *Signs.* God "wrought his signs ... and his miracles" when He "redeemed" His people (78:42b-43). After Ezekiel was carried off to Babylonia and Jeremiah to Egypt, there was *no longer any prophet* to answer the question *how long* the enemy would be allowed to revile God's name. (Cf. Lm 2:9; Eze 7:26)

74:11 *In thy bosom.* The second line of this verse is an impetuous cry for an end to God's inaction: "Destroy [the scoffers by taking] thy right hand from thy bosom," where it rests unflexed.

74:14 *Leviathan.* Cf. Jb 3:8 note; 41:1 note; Ps 68:30 note.

74:15 *Cleave open springs.* The "King" of creation used His power over the things and forces He had made when He worked "salvation" (12) for Israel: He divided the Red Sea; He provided water from a rock; He dried up the overflowing waters of the Jordan. (Ex 14:21; 17:5 f.; Jos 3:13)

74:19 *Thy dove.* Cf. 68:13; Is 38:14; 59:11.

74:20 *Dark places.* Even hiding places did not assure safety from the heartless conquerors.

74:21 *Poor and needy.* Cf. 9:18 note.

Psalm 75

75:1-10 This *Psalm of Asaph* in effect supplies a rejoinder to the question "Why?" raised in the preceding psalm. Here a prophetic word of God gives assurances which in Ps 73 the individual received when he "went into the sanctuary of God" (73:17). *The boastful* and *the wicked* cannot defy the Creator's moral government. *At the set time* His sovereign power will establish *equity* (2-5; cf. Acts 17:31). Furthermore, *the wicked of the earth* cannot escape His judgments no matter where they turn for protection (6-8). Trust in the promise that "the Judge is standing at the doors" (Ja 5:9) is so firm that the psalm begins and ends with thanksgiving and rejoicing (1, 9-10).—For *according to Do Not Destroy* see Ps 57:1-11 note.

75:1 *Call on thy name.* This translation (cf. RSV note) requires a correction of the text which if left unchanged may be rendered: "for near is thy name which thy wondrous deeds declared." For the meaning of *name* see 8:1 note.

75:3 *Pillars.* Cf. Jb 9:6 note; 26:7 second note.

75:4-5 *Horn.* Because animals such as steers rely on their horns, the latter are frequently used as symbols of strength. (V. 10; 89:17; Lk 1:69)

75:8 *Cup.* Cf. 11:6 note. The wine is *well mixed,* i.e., strongly fortified with additives to increase its intoxicating effect. (Cf. 60:3)

75:10 *He will cut off.* The Hebrew text "I will cut off" (RSV note) supplies another word of the Lord, added without an introductory formula, as in 2-5, or it records the psalmist's grim determination to act as God's instrument of retribution.

Psalm 76

76:1-12 Confidence in God's power to establish justice on earth (75:10) bursts into *A Song* of exultation in this *Psalm of Asaph.* It celebrates the rout of *the men of war* who lifted up their "horn" (75:4) in an attack on Jerusalem, earthly *abode* and royal residence of the heavenly "King" (1-6; 74:12). His victory over powerful enemies in the past inspires a hymn in praise of His declared purpose and incontestable ability *to save all the oppressed of the earth* wherever and whenever they are threatened by *the wrath of men,* be they *princes* or *kings.* (7-12)

76:2 *Salem.* Ancient name of Jerusalem, embodying the consonants of the Hebrew word for peace. (Gn 14:18 note; Cf. Ps 122:6-9)

76:3 *There.* Using His "dwelling place in Zion" as a base of operations, He issued His "rebuke" of the enemy forces which resulted in their complete defeat. Though not explicitly mentioned, the incident commemorated very likely is the destruction of Sennacherib's army at the time of King Hezekiah. (2 K 18:13—19:37)

76:10 *Wrath of men.* When God frustrates the evil designs of men, the hollowness of their claim to willful self-determination will be so apparent that the intended victims of their wrath will have every reason to praise Him. Every victory over *the residue of wrath,* i.e., every bit of attempted antagonism, shines like a jewel with which He adorns Himself. (Cf. Gn 50:20; Ex 9:15 f.; Ro 9:17; Jer 13:11)

Psalm 77

77:1-20 The specific time and circumstances of the distress which gave rise to the perplexed wrestling with God in prayer recorded in this *Psalm of Asaph* are not clearly indicated. The emphasis is on the anguished struggle of faith to hold on to God when there was no longer any evidence of His *steadfast love* because *he in anger shut up his compassion* (8 f.). The psalm offers comfort and instruction to children of God tortured by sleepless nights of *grief.* The first thing to note is that the psalmist, though bewildered and dazed, did not stop praying *in the day* and *in the night* (1-2). Even though God seems not to hear, he insists on remonstrating with Him, asking Him to explain why He has *forgotten to be gracious,* as He so manifestly was in *the days of old* (3-10). As he prays, he suddenly sees the past in an encouraging perspective. He recalls the *mighty deeds* and *wonders* of the Lord which He did when He delivered His helpless people from the bondage of Egypt. And there the psalmist lets the matter rest, content to know that he and his people still are in the hands of the *holy* God and almighty Creator of the universe. (11-20)

77:6 *I commune.* Cf. RSV note. The moaning of the psalmist appears in sharper contrast with his former gay mood if the text is left unchanged and translated: "At night I recall my music of stringed instruments." (Cf. Lm 5:14; Ps 42:8; Jb 35:10)

77:10 *Has changed.* As the questions in 7-9 indicate, the embattled psalmist thinks the explanation of his predicament can only be the refusal of *the Most High* to use His *right hand* of power "to be gracious," as He did in the past in accord with His "steadfast love" and "promises." However, the very thought that God could change seemingly brings him to his senses. Rather than charge the Holy One with inconsistency, he turns his lament into a song in praise of the undeserved goodness and the irresistible power which God manifested when He redeemed His people from slavery and led them "like a flock."

77:13 *Like our God.* Cf. Ex 15:11 note; 20:3 second note.

77:16 *The deep trembled.* "Mighty deeds" and "wonders" took place at the time of the exodus from Egypt because the Redeemer of Israel had at His disposal the unlimited might of the Creator of the universe and could harness the terrifying forces of nature. There is a scintillating blending of motifs in the dramatic figures of speech with which the poet describes the cosmic power at God's command when He led His "people like a flock by the hand of Moses and Aaron."

Psalm 78

78:1-72 In the immediately preceding psalms a look into the past serves to dispel doubt that God is willing and able to promote and safeguard the welfare of His children, collectively and individually. Ps 78, the second-longest in the psalter, dips into Israel's history for a different purpose. It paints a picture of bygone days in black and white; the dark, mysterious power of wickedness over man and the bright beams of God's long-suffering mercy. The contrast is not only as absolute as night and day, but the respective opposite features are also so extreme as to defy comprehension. It is impossible to plumb the depth of man's depravity; God's patient goodness passes all understanding. Far from being an epic of heroic achievements, Israel's history from its very beginning is a dismal record of sniveling ingratitude for God's miraculous help and of open rebellion against His will. But the Lord, who chose Israel to be His "own possession among all peoples" (Ex 19:5), was not a national god like the idols in and about Canaan, dependent on human worshipers and bound to the fate of their devotees. When the Israelites broke the covenant, *the anger of God rose against them* (31) to punish and to destroy. However, the riddle of Israel's irrational infidelity was matched by the wonders of God's ineffable patience and mercy. If He had not been "abounding in steadfast love and faithfulness . . . forgiving iniquity and transgressions and sin" (Ex 34:6 f.), there would not have been a history of Israel to record.—The story of ancient Israel in a distant land, written for our learning, is repeated in miniature in every believer's life. There too is found the daily rhythm of grace abused and sin forgiven. (1 Co 10:1-11; Heb 2:1-4; 3:7-9)

In the opening verses the psalmist issues a summons to his contemporaries to heed the *teaching* of history which he is about to present, lest they *forget the works of God* and be as *stubborn and rebellious* as their forefathers were so often (1-8). He has no intention of furnishing a chronological survey of the entire past. Instead he lifts out episodes from various eras in order to demonstrate how irrationally and persistently perverse Israel as a nation had been. Over and over again the people forgot what God *had done and the miracles that he had shown them* when He delivered them from Egypt, supplied their wants on the wilderness journey, and settled them in the Promised Land. In righteous *anger* God *slew the strongest of them* in the desert. When *they repented and sought God earnestly . . . he, being compassionate, forgave their iniquity* (9-39). Yet *how often they rebelled against him in the wilderness* when the *signs* and *miracles* of the plagues inflicted on the Egyptians should have been fresh in their minds! Always ready to forgive, God eventually *brought them to His holy land,* driving out *nations before them* (40-55). However, the attitude of the people did not change. Settled in the Promised Land, they promptly *rebelled against the Most High God* by worshiping the *graven images* of the Canaanite baals. *Full of wrath,* God let enemies burn *Shiloh* and carry off the ark, which had been housed there. But again *the Lord awoke as from sleep* and *put his adversaries to rout* (56-66). He ushered in a new era when He let *the tribe of Judah* provide *upright* leadership under *David his servant* and under Solomon *built His sanctuary* on *Mount Zion* (67-72). Here the author's review of Israel's past comes to an end. We know that even this new beginning did not bring permanent results. Finally God did not hesitate to let the Assyrians carry off the northern half of the kingdom and to give Jerusalem and the temple into the hands of the Babylonians, as the next psalm laments. Yet after a few decades He brought back a remnant from captivity and a new chapter of salvation history began.

78:2 *Parable . . . dark sayings.* Translated "proverb" and "riddle" (49:4; Pr 1:6). The psalmist is about to explain a dark mystery by adopting a form of instruction which imparts wisdom by means of analogies and examples. The "teacher come from God" (Jn 3:2) brought this teaching device to a level of perfection unprecedented in the past and unattainable ever after. (Mt 13:34 f.)

78:5 *Testimony . . . law.* The ordinance that one generation tell the next of "the works of God" was so vitally important that it is repeated again and again. (Ex 10:2; 12:26 f.; 13:8, 14; Dt 6:4-25)

78:9-10 *Ephraimites.* The descendants of Joseph's sons Ephraim and Manasseh were the two strongest tribes which seceded from the house of David after Solomon's death. Because of their earlier position of leadership, the Ephraimites are cited as examples of disappointing infidelity. Because they failed to *keep God's covenant* and *to walk according to his law,* they are compared with soldiers who, though armed for combat, shirk their duty *on the day of battle.*

78:12 *Fields of Zoan.* The territory in the vicinity of a city located in the Delta region of the Nile, known in Greek as Tanis, and destined to become a capital of Egypt (43; Is 19:11, 13; 30:4; Eze 30:14). *In the land of Egypt* God *wrought marvels,* the ten plagues (Ex 7—12). Other "miracles" were to follow: the passage through the Red Sea (13; Ex 14:16, 21; 15:8); guidance "with a cloud and . . . a fiery light" (14; Ex 13:21; Ps 105:39); water from a rock. (15; Ex 17:6; Nm 20:11; Ps 105:41)

78:18 *Tested.* Translated "put the Lord to the proof" Ex 17:2, 7 note; Ps 95:9; 106:14 (cf. 1 Co 10:9; Heb 3:9). The Israelites had a "craving" (30) only for the satisfaction of their physical needs. (Cf. Ex 16:2 f.)

78:23 *Yet.* The greatest miracle in Israel's history was God's patience with an incredibly stubborn people, impervious both to acts of kindness and of judgment. And yet He remained "compassionate" and "did not destroy them." (38; Ex 34:6 f.)

78:24 *Manna.* Poetically described as *the grain of heaven* and "the bread of the angels." Cf. Ex 16:15 note.

78:27 *Winged birds.* Cf. Ex 16:13; Nm 11:31.

78:31 *Slew the strongest.* Cf. Nm 11:33.

78:33 *Vanish like a breath.* They were to end *their days* in the wilderness. (Nm 14:28-30, 35; 26:63-65)

78:36 *They lied.* Even when God's scourge inflicted wounds on them, and the people "repented" (34), they merely *flattered him with their mouths* in order to move Him to end the punishment.

78:43 *Signs in Egypt.* Seven of the ten plagues, alluded to briefly in vv. 11 f., are enumerated. (44-51)

78:50 *Plague.* Cf. Ex 11:1 note.

78:51 *Ham.* Ancestral name for Egypt. (Gn 10:6; Ps 105:23, 27; 106:22)

78:60 *Shiloh.* At that time the Israelites suffered invasions by the Philistines. Shiloh, where the tabernacle was for some time, was destroyed (Jer 7:12; 26:6); the ark of the covenant, here called God's "power" and "glory," was captured; the sons of Eli, the high priest, were killed (1 Sm 4:10 f.); the "fire" of God's wrath cut down the "young men," robbing "maidens" of prospective husbands.

78:64 *No lamentation.* Conditions were such as to make it impossible to perform the customary funeral rites. (Jb 27:15)

78:65 *Awoke.* Cf. the oft-repeated prayer that God awake or bestir Himself (7:6 note; 35:23; 44:23; 59:4). The Philistines were defeated under Samuel, Saul, and David. (1 Sm 7:5-14; 14:47; 2 Sm 5:25)

78:67 *Tent of Joseph.* A new chapter in Israel's history was to begin when God "chose David . . . to be the shepherd of Jacob, his people" (70 f.). The ark was not returned to Shiloh in the territory of Joseph's tribes. It was brought to Jerusalem in "the tribe of Judah," where Solomon built the temple.

Psalm 79

79:1-13 It should not surprise us to find another fervent prayer for deliverance from the same disaster out of which Ps 74 arose (cf. notes there). If God should seem to *be angry forever* (5) because He let our world crash about us and let us stand tear-blinded in the ruins of our hopes, we would understand why Israel sent more than one cry of anguish to the throne of mercy when all that was meaningful and holy was shattered and defiled. The Babylonians destroyed the holy city, burned the temple, and carried all but the poorest inhabitants into exile. These shattering disasters seemed to have extinguished all the stars of promise with which God had studded the heavens of Israel's future. Out of this black night comes the wail of pain, telling God of the deadly wounds inflicted by the enemy (1-4). But because in the final analysis *the heathen* who *devoured Jacob and laid waste his habitation* were but the instruments of God's *wrath,* the psalmist turns to Him and His *compassion* for relief and redress (5-13). His prayer is not a dispassionate exercise in verse making. It comes hot from a soul seared by the admission of past and present sins but also incensed by the disgrace which the defeat of God's cause has heaped on His honor. *The glory of* His *name* is at stake. To restore and maintain it requires *the avenging of the outpoured blood of* His *servants.* (9-10)

79:1 *Thy inheritance.* Israel is so designated frequently. (Dt 4:20; 9:26; Ps 74:2)

79:2 *Saints.* Cf. 4:3 note.

79:3 *Bury them.* Cf. Dt 28:26; Jer 7:33; 14:16. It was considered a great calamity if a corpse was not buried properly. Even a criminal was to be buried immediately after his execution. (Dt 21:22 f.)

79:5 *How long?* Cf. 13:1 note. For *jealous* see Dt 4:24 note.

79:6 *Pour out.* Cf. Rv 16:1. For the meaning of *know* to connote a personal relationship see Gn 18:19 note; Dt 9:24 note.

79:9 *Our sins.* Though "the iniquities of" their fathers (8) brought on the destruction of Jerusalem (Jer 25:1-14), their sons did not pretend to be any better. They have no merit on which to base consideration of their plea.

79:10 *Why should the nations say?* For similar boldness in prayer see Ex 32:11 note; Nm 14:13

note. *The avenging* is left in God's hands. (58:10 notes; Dt 32:43; Neh 4:4 note; Rv 6:10)

Psalm 80

80:1-19 The person or community of believers intent on heeding the prescription to "pray constantly" (1 Th 5:17) will welcome another psalm pleading for help in a trying crisis of life. The cry *come to save us!* (2) arose in ancient Israel because God *fed them with the bread of tears* (5). Dark days of calamity had replaced the bliss of former times when God's people basked in the sunshine of His goodness. Hence the burden of the psalmist's prayer is a return to God's favor, underscored by the refrain: *Restore . . . let thy face shine!* (3, 7, 19; cf. also 14: *turn again).* Confident of the concern of the *Shepherd* for His *flock* and of the *might* of the *God of hosts* to bring about the desired reversal (1-3), he describes how desperate the situation has become (4-7). He illustrates the contrast between the past and the present by comparing the chosen people with a vine transplanted from Egypt into the Promised Land. There under divine husbandry it became a vineyard covering the length and breadth and height of the land. Now, however, God has *broken down its walls* with the result that *the boar from the forest ravages it* (8-13). Continuing in figurative language, the author pleads that God again *have regard for this vine* and drive off those who *have cut it down.* Gratitude for the anticipated rescue prompts the vow never to *turn back from* their Deliverer (14-19).—For *according to Lilies* see Ps 60.

80:1 *Shepherd of Israel.* While this divine title occurs only here, the relationship of God to His people is described frequently as that of a shepherd to sheep. (Gn 49:24; Ps 74:1; 78:52; 79:13; Is 40:11; Eze 34:11 ff.; Mi 7:14; Ps 23:1-6)

Enthroned upon the cherubim. Cf. 1 K 6:23 note; 1 Sm 4:4; 6:2; Ps 99:1.

80:2 *Ephraim and Benjamin and Manasseh.* Because only tribes holding territory north of Jerusalem are mentioned, it appears that the occasion for this psalm was an invasion of that part of David's kingdom which seceded after Solomon's death (cf. 78:9-10 note). After suffering repeated inroads by foreigners, this so-called Northern Kingdom was destroyed by the Assyrians in the year 722 B.C. "Rachel," mother of Benjamin and grandmother of Ephraim and Manasseh (Joseph's sons), had reason to weep "for her children." (Jer 31:15)

80:4 *Lord God of hosts.* Cf. 1 Sm 1:3 note.

Angry. The question *how long* God's anger is going to "smoke against the sheep of" His pasture (74:1) is at the same time an admission of guilt. The people confess that they had "tears to drink" because their sins provoked God to wrath.

80:6 *Scorn.* There is no need to emend the Hebrew text (RSV note). God let Israel become an object of "strife" in as much as *neighbors* quarreled with one another, each claiming it as a possession.

80:8 *Vine.* For other instances where Israel is compared with a single grape plant as well as with a vineyard see Is 5:1-7; 27:2-6; Jer 2:21; 12:10; Hos 10:1. Like branches growing luxuriantly in all directions, so Israel came into full possession of Canaan from "the sea [the Mediterranean] . . . to the River [Euphrates]."

80:15 *Stock.* Lit. "the son" (RSV note). By a blending of related figures of speech, Israel, the vine cutting propagated and brought to full growth by God, is said to be His son. (Cf. Ex 4:22 f.; Jer 31:20; Hos 11:1)

80:17 *Man of thy right hand.* As in 15, the people are referred to collectively. The nation can prosper only if God's *right hand,* which gave it life and strength in the past, will make it strong also in the future. The parallel term *son of man* emphasizes how dependent the Israelites, made of the dust of the ground, are on the creative and sustaining power of God. (Gn 2:7 note; cf. Ps 8:1-9; Eze 2-3)

Psalm 81

81:1-16 Meditation on this *Psalm of Asaph* will prove helpful in avoiding hazards connected with ceremonies of worship. The call to *shout for joy* (1-5b) is needed when service in God's house is in danger of degenerating into a melancholy performance of duty or an unspiritual mouthing of forms. The second part of the psalm (5c-16) is a necessary reminder that "to obey is better than sacrifice" (1 Sm 15:22 note). Outward ceremonies are an abomination unless they represent the offering of a living obedience, brought in grateful response to God's unmerited acts of salvation.—For *Gittith* see Ps 8.

81:2 *Raise a song.* Though its forms were rigidly and minutely prescribed by "statute," "ordinance," and "decree" (4-5), worship in Israel was not to be a sullen observance of regulations. The annual festivals especially were designed to give the people occasion to "rejoice before the Lord" (33:1-22; 66:1 f.; Dt 12:12, 18; 16:11; 27:7; Ez 3:11). The "feast day" mentioned in v. 3 very likely refers to a particularly joyous event, the feast of tabernacles. (Cf. Lv 23:34 note)

81:5 *I hear.* As the next verses show, the speaker is about to present an oracle having divine sanction. It does not represent a message that he had known because it originated in his own thinking.

81:7 *Secret place of thunder.* Cf. 18:11 f.; Ex 13:21; 14:9 f.; 24:15-18.

Meribah. Cf. Ex 17:7 note; Ps 95:8.

81:9 *No strange god.* The First Commandment is cited as embracing everything to which Israel was to "listen." (Vv. 8, 11, 13; cf. Ex 20:3 notes; Dt 5:7 note)

81:12 *Gave them over.* God does not turn man into a mechanism which automatically responds when the electric current is turned on. He lets *stubborn hearts follow their own counsels* if they refuse to "walk in" His "ways." (V. 13; Dt 29:18 f.; Acts 7:42; Ro 1:24, 26, 28)

81:15 *Him.* The antecedent is Israel.

8:16 *Honey from the rock.* Cf. Ex 3:8; Dt 32:13 f.; Ps 147:14.

Psalm 82

82:1-8 In ancient times courts of justice were frequently corrupt, as they still are today. This *Psalm of Asaph* assures faithful Israelites and all believers of God's concern for the rights of the individual. Here He Himself indicts and condemns venal and unjust judges, as His spokesmen and prophets did in His name (Am 5:10-12; Mi 3:9 ff.; 7:3; Eze 45:9; see also Ex 22:22; 23:6 ff.; Lv 19:15). Perversion of justice was a particularly heinous crime in Israel. The laws of the land were more than a social contract. They, no less than the Decalog, were divine legislation, given by God Himself and administered by those whom He appointed to "judge . . . for the Lord" (2 Ch 19:6 f.). Because "the judgment is God's" (Dt 1:17), a case brought before Israel's judges was in a real sense a trial "before God" (cf. Ex 21:6; 22:7 note). In this psalm He calls the administrators of His laws *gods* and *sons of the Most High* (1, 6). In view of His repeated statements entrusting legal authority in Israel to human agents and making them responsible for the enforcement of His laws, it is only reasonable to conclude that He is also here confronting men of flesh and blood (cf. 58:1 note). According to the united testimony of the OT all gods besides the Lord exist only in the imagination of their devotees. It is inconceivable that the holy God should invest a *council* of such "no-gods" with the right to dispense justice on earth as His vicegerents (cf. 24:4 second note; 31:6). The author of Ps 82 draws on the language and features of such a mythical council to create a highly dramatic condemnation by the true God of His appointed judges in Israel. (Cf. Jn 10:34 f.)

82:1 *Council.* Usually translated "congregation." Israel is called "the congregation of the Lord." (Nm 27:17; 31:16; Jos 22:16 f.; Ps 74:2)

82:5 *Foundations.* Cf. 11:3 note.

82:8 *Arise.* Cf. 7:6 note.

Psalm 83

83:1-18 God's children do not stop praying even when He appears to *keep silence* (1). This psalm is another impassioned plea for protection against an expected attack by a coalition of evil forces. The specific time when Israel was so terrorized is not clearly indicated. However, there is no doubt as to the diabolical and deadly intent the enemies had in mind. There were *crafty plans* afoot *against* God's *people,* designed to *wipe them out as a nation* and to obliterate *the name of Israel* from the annals of history (3 f.). The danger is depicted as if a confederacy of inveterate enemies were converging *with one accord* on the covenant nation from all points of the compass. After calling God's attention to the critical situation (1-8), the psalmist goes on to make his plea for deliverance in the framework of history: Let God do again what He did in times past when His enemies tried to thwart His plans for His chosen people. (9-18)

83:1 *Hold thy peace.* Troubled and fearful hearts get impatient and seek to prod God into action. (Cf. 7:6 note)

83:2 *Thy enemies.* It is not from nationalistic pride that the Israelites identify their foes as being also God's enemies. They relied on their status as His "protected ones." He promised to hide them "in the covert" of His presence because He chose them to carry out His eternal plan of blessing all nations through them. (31:20; 27:5; Ex 19:5 second note)

83:6 *Edom.* Ten peoples are listed as making "a covenant" (5) against God's covenant nation. Attacks are to be launched from all directions: Edom, Moab, Ishmaelites, Ammon, Amalek, Hagrites, Gebal from the south and east; Philistines and inhabitants of Tyre from the west and north; Assyria from the north and east. From the latter area comes support for "the children of Lot," i.e., tribes associated with the Moabites and Ammonites already mentioned (Gn 19:37 note). So God's followers are "hated by all nations." (Mt 24:9)

83:9 *Midian.* Cf. Ju 6 to 8; for *Sisera* and *Jabin* see Ju 4 and 5. Endor was a town near the scene of battle against Sisera and Jabin. (Jos 17:11; Ju 5:19 ff.)

83:11 *Oreb and Zeeb . . . Zeba and Zalmunna.* Midianite princes and kings. (Ju 7:25 note; 8:4-21)

83:17 *Let them perish.* God is to do what is necessary to restrain rebellious men from frustrating His plans of salvation. If they can be shamed to "seek" and reverence His "name," well and good (16); if not, let God destroy them. (58:10 note; 79:10 note; Ju 5:31 note)

Psalm 84

84:1-12 Because God's "steadfast love is better than life" (63:3), there should be no higher delight than to commune with Him in worship. It may indicate a need to examine what the Lord means to us if the yearning for fellowship with *the living God* (2), expressed in this psalm (1-4), appears to be a bit of pompous rhetoric or if the rhapsodic portrayal (5-12) of the bliss, fulfillment, and ultimate satisfaction to be derived from a visit to *the courts of the Lord* (2) does not seem to ring true. The OT believer reveled in the privilege of coming into the presence of God in His *dwelling place* of stone and wood. The NT worshiper cannot be less exuberant in praising the *Lord God of hosts* who in the Word made flesh "dwelt among us, full of grace and truth" (Jn 1:14).—For the term *Gittith* see Ps 8; for *Sons of Korah,* 2 Ch 20:19 note.

84:3 *A home.* If even the birds that built their nests in the walls of the temple felt secure there, these holy precincts would prove to be a refuge from the storms of life and a haven of serene peace for those who gathered there as "the household of God." (Eph 2:19)

84:6 *Baca.* It remains unknown as the name of a site traversed by pilgrims on their way to Jerusalem. The Hebrew word, meaning a balsam tree (2 Sm 5:23 f.), is similar to a root meaning to weep (cf. Bochim, Ju 2:1 second note). From the two following lines of the verse it is evident that a dry, barren place is meant. It appears to be used in a figurative sense. All who make fellowship with God the goal of life's "highways" find the strength to march through dreary stretches of earth's pilgrimage as if they were verdant paths.

84:7 *Will be seen.* To the worshipers who "seek" the "face" of the Lord, He "will appear," i.e., be present to "lift up his countenance upon" them and give them peace. (27:8; Lv 9:4; Nm 6:26)

84:8 *My prayer.* The psalmist interrupts the description of the bliss of worship with a short prayer, asking God to let services in the temple continue undisturbed.

84:9 *Thine anointed.* The king, on whom the welfare of the nation depended. (28:8; 61:6 f.; 63:11)

Psalm 85

85:1-13 A break with a regrettable past and a resolve to start life over again may fail to produce expected quick results. Sins are forgiven; determination to walk in God's ways is sincere; initially all goes well. But then misfortunes come rather than blessings, disappointments rather than successes. In such a situation it will prove helpful to turn to this psalm. It was composed at a time when Israel, its unfaithfulness forgiven, had returned from the Babylonian captivity to make a new beginning in its own land (1-3) but soon was in such deplorable circumstances as to plead with God not to prolong His *anger to all generations* (4-7). The fearful saints are reminded that God never fails to *speak peace to his people* (8-9). When His *salvation* (9) becomes a full reality, there will be nothing to mar the bliss He bestows. (10-13)

85:1 *Favorable.* By means of the Babylonian captivity God's wrath overtook His rebellious people. Their restoration therefore was an act of His forgiving mercy. (Cf. 44:3 note; 147:10 f.; 149:4)

85:6 *Revive.* Translated "give us life" (80:18). Adverse conditions threatened to strangle the life out of the newly born community. For its troubles see Ez 4:4 f., 24; Neh 1:3; Hg 1:5-11.

85:8 *Let me hear.* In his plight of unfulfilled hope the author as a member of the covenant people wants to let God *speak* to the situation (73:17 note). It will make "firm the feeble knees" (Jb 4:4) to hear what He has promised "those who fear him."—For the meaning of *saints* see 4:3 note.

In their hearts. The warning sounded in the Hebrew text (RSV note) that God's goodness is not to be abused is very much in place. Social and religious evils were again on the increase.

85:9 *Glory.* God's presence in the temple. (1 K 8:11; Ex 40:34 note; Eze 43:4; Ps 63:2)

85:10 *Will meet . . . kiss each other.* The "salvation" God will ultimately bring about is described in entrancing figures of speech. It will be as if the dreary countryside, which the harassed and impoverished inhabitants knew, were transformed into a veritable paradise of well-being and fertility. Not crime, want, and oppression will stalk through the land, but God's *love and faithfulness,* His *righteousness and peace* will walk serenely over the landscape and have sweet, undisturbed converse with one another. At the same time, these divine manifestations and the blessings attending them will produce their counterpart in the lives of men. Responding to the benedictions from above, people too will practice *steadfast love and faithfulness;* they too will embrace *righteousness and peace.* To bring about such idyllic conditions God will "create new heavens and a new earth" (Is 65:17 ff.; 2 Ptr 3:13; Rv 21:1). The latter will "yield its increase" (12) in superabundance. (Hos 2:21 f.; Am 9:13; Is 30:23 f.)

Psalm 86

86:1-17 No details are given of the threatening catastrophe out of which this psalm arose except to say that *ruthless men* had designs on the *life* of an innocent victim (2, 14). Hence anyone in *trouble* (7) can appropriate this *Psalm of David* and let it tell God of his particular fears and needs. It will appeal, moreover, because it is made up to a great extent of words, phrases, and expressions occurring in other psalms and OT books. Though not original in language and phrases, it originates in the kind of attitude of heart which nevertheless makes it a model to be copied and emulated. The suppliant is exemplary in assessing himself in his relation to God. He prays because he is *godly* (2), i.e., he makes the most of the privilege of appealing to God, granted him in the covenant; he is *poor and needy* (1), not self-sufficient and the master of his own destiny; he *trusts* God for help; he is God's *servant* (2, 16) or slave, totally committed to his Master, the Lord. In spite of his sins he dares to come into the presence of the holy God because he believes Him to be also *good and* [disposed to be] *forgiving* (5); in spite of his own lapses into covenant unfaithfulness he is confident that God is *abounding in steadfast love and faithfulness* (15).—The structure of the psalm too is worth noting. Interspersed between the opening *cry of supplication* (1-7) and its resumption in 14-17, there are two elements easily omitted when praying in dire straits: (1) praise and adoration of the Creator and Ruler of the universe (8-10); (2) gratitude and the promise of undivided dedication of life to the Deliverer. (11-13)

86:2 *Godly.* So translated, the Hebrew word may give the impression that the psalmist feels entitled to pray because of his virtuous life. For the meaning of the word see 4:3 note.

86:5 *Forgiving, abounding.* The author here and in v. 15 holds God to his word, asking to be the beneficiary of those divine traits which the Lord Himself professed to have when He entered into covenant relations with Israel. (Ex 34:6 f.; Nm 14:18)

86:8 *Among the gods.* Cf. Ex 15:11; 20:3 note; Dt 3:24.

86:11 *Unite my heart.* More lit. "make my

heart one," i.e., let nothing divert me from making the one aim of life to *walk in thy truth* so that Thy name may be hallowed. (Cf. Jer 32:39; Eze 11:19; Ps 73:25)

86:16 *Son of thy handmaid.* A parallel term for *servant,* translated "son of . . . bondmaid" in Ex 23:12.

86:17 *A sign.* God's help against "a band of ruthless men" should put them *to shame,* making them *see* clearly that they cannot harm him whom God protects.

Psalm 87

87:1-7 This short psalm reminds us of the wonders of God's kingdom and of our belonging to it even though we cannot claim descent from the covenant nation of the OT (Ro 11:17-24). It will help us not to take our membership in God's people as a matter of course, if we enter into the amazement and excitement with which the psalmist of old looked forward to the time when "all the nations . . . shall come and bow down before" the Lord (86:9). He envisions the glorious things to come in the perspective of Israel as the center of God's worldwide dominion. *Zion,* the *city of God,* founded by Him to become the capital of an international commonwealth of nations. (1-3)

Foreigners from far and near were to be eligible to claim birthright and citizenship in it (4-6) and so share in the jubilation of having every need supplied (7). For other prophecies of God's universal kingdom with Jerusalem as its center see Is 2:2-4; 56:3-8; 60:1-3; Mi 4:1-4; Zch 8:20-23; for their fulfillment see Gl 4:26; Eph 2:11-22; Heb 11:10; 12:22-24; Rv 7:9; 15:4; 21:10-14.

87:4 *Know me.* God is the speaker. For the meaning of *know* in a wider sense than acquaintance see Gn 18:19 note; Dt 9:24; Ps 9:10; 36:10. The five non-Israelite nations, mentioned as having the privilege of one born to citizenship in Jerusalem, are representative of God's global dominion: *Rahab* is proud Egypt (Is 30:7); *Babylon,* the land of great empires; *Philistia,* a smaller neighboring state, often a thorn in Israel's flesh; *Tyre,* the Phoenician center of maritime commerce; *Ethiopia,* a remote, uncharted land on the African continent.

87:6 *He registers.* The Lord is pictured as keeping a record of *peoples* granted the privilege of citizenship.

87:7 *Singers and dancers.* They are jubilant because out of Jerusalem flow *springs* and streams of blessing which satisfy every want they may have. (46:4 note; Zch 14:8; Is 12:3)

Psalm 88

88:1-18 It is natural that this psalm will make the reader sad. Here a soul, *full of troubles* and on the brink of death (3 ff.), raises a pitiful cry for help, as he did so often before, only to be left to weep *in darkness* (18). However, for that very reason this *Maskil* (cf. Ps 32) is a shining example of a tenacious faith wrestling with God in prayer and refusing to let go (Gn 32:26). There was ample need for prayer. The suppliant, afflicted from youth by a dreadful disease which caused his *companions to shun* him, feels he is *close to death* (3, 4, 8, 15, 18). *By day, in the night,* and *every day* (1, 9) he called for relief to Him whose *wrath* lay *heavy* on him and made him *a thing of horror* (7 f.). But there was no let-up of *dread assaults* surrounding him *like a flood* (16 f.). However, in the face of all rebuffs he did not "curse God and die" (Jb 2:9). Undaunted He prayed once again, confident that the Lord sometime and somehow would prove to be the "God of my salvation" (v. 1 RSV note). Verily, O ancient sufferer, "great is your faith" (Mt 15:28).—The term *Song* in the superscription seems inappropriate unless it merely calls for a vocal rather than a spoken rendition. *Mahalath Leannoth* are transliterated Hebrew words, suggesting perhaps a mournful melody for the *Song.* A man by the name of "Heman" was among those appointed by David to supervise the instrumental music in the temple (1 Ch 15:17, 19), but *Heman the Ezrahite* remains unidentified.

88:5 *Remember no more.* For death as ending man's earthly relationship with God see 6:5 note; 30:9; 31:12; Jb 10:21 note; Is 38:18.

88:8 *Shun me.* In Israel lepers were cut off from society.—Friends and "acquaintances . . . stood at a distance" from Him who, bearing the curse of the world's sin, hung on the cross forsaken of God. (Lk 23:49)

88:10 *Praise thee.* Further evidence that the sufferer did not lose his faith is his desire to declare God's steadfast love and faithfulness to his fellowmen. By means of several questions (10-12) he boldly reminds God that with death "night comes when no one can work." (Jn 9:4)

88:11 *Abaddon.* Another term for death. (Jb 26:5 note)

88:15 *I am helpless.* The Hebrew word so translated occurs only here.

Psalm 89

89:1-52 In the preceding psalm an individual continues to wrestle with God in prayer even though from his youth he pleaded in vain for relief from a disabling and disfiguring malady. In this psalm it is a national calamity which sorely tries Israel's faith in God's power and willingness to keep His promises. More than the survival of an ancient people was at stake. God's plan to make the offspring of Abraham a blessing to "all the families of the earth" (Gn 12:3) seemed to have gone awry. For a *long* time (46) such a distressing situation prevailed as to prompt the question whether God was not failing to honor His sworn pledge to David that *his line shall endure forever* (36). How could the universal, eternal kingdom of the Messiah spring from the house of David when his dynastic successor was defeated *in battle* and his *throne* cast *to the ground* (38-45; cf. 2 Sm 7:8-16; Ps 2:1-11)? Though no longer able to see where God's *steadfast love of old* is (49), the psalmist continues doggedly to appeal to Him for redress (46-51). Determined not to relax his hold on God, he prefaces his brief prayer with a magnificent song extolling precisely the divine attribute which appeared to have ceased functioning: God's *steadfast love* and *faithfulness* (1). All appearances to the contrary notwithstanding, he will not give up the conviction that God is willing and able to keep His word, specifically His oath *sworn to David* (1-18). Therefore he reminds God at length of how He obligated Himself by His *holiness* (35) not to remove His *steadfast love* from *David* and *his children* even if the latter would forsake His law (19-37). He leaves it to God to reconcile the dismal facts of reality with the promised vision of future glory (38-45).—Trust in God's promises was not misplaced. His "steadfast, sure love for David" held firm in "an everlasting covenant" (Is 55:3). At His own time and in His own way He "raised up a horn of salvation for us in the house of his servant David," for "of this man's posterity God has brought to Israel a Savior, Jesus, as he promised" (Lk 1:69; Acts 13:23; cf. 15:16). Given "the throne of his father David," He rules in a kingdom of which "there will be no end," either in time or territorial jurisdiction (Lk 1:32 f.; cf. Rv 1:5).—*Ethan the Ezrahite,* mentioned in the superscription, remains unidentified. Very likely he had some relationship to the Ethan whom David together with Heman (Ps 88) put in charge of the temple music. (1 K 4:31; 1 Ch 2:6)

89:1 *Steadfast love . . . faithfulness.* Synonyms denoting the same divine attribute, these words carry the theme of the psalm (1, 2, 5, 8, 14, 24, 33, 49), bringing various aspects of its concern into focus. What they predicate of God is the basis of the psalmist's faith. He prays because he trusts God to be true to His word (5-18). Even when it appears to him that God has "renounced the covenant with" David, His "servant" (19-45), he appeals to Him to "remember" what He promised. (46-52)

89:3 *Covenant with . . . David.* The first four verses announce the theme of the psalm: The faithfulness of God as manifested in general (1, 2, 5-18) and as required in particular in view of His pledge to David. (3, 4, 19-37)

89:4 *For ever.* For this aspect of the covenant see 2 Sm 7:13 note; Ps 45:6 note.

85:5 *The heavens.* In singing of God's faithfulness the psalmist first of all removes any misgivings that the "Lord of hosts" (59:5 note) lacks the power to do what He promised. Praised and worshiped by angelic characters and celestial beings, He commands obedience from the forces of nature. They are at His disposal because they are a part of the universe created by Him. (5-13)

89:6 *Heavenly beings.* Cf. 29:11 note.

89:10 *Rahab.* Cf. Jb 9:13 note; 7:12 note; 3:8 second note; Ps 74:13.

89:12 *Tabor and Hermon.* Lofty mountain peaks in Canaan.

89:14 *Righteousness and justice.* God is not an arbitrary, capricious potentate who uses his power to wrong his subjects.

89:15 *Blessed.* A corollary to the axiom of faith in God's unlimited power and unfailing justice is the conviction that those who trust Him will have ample reason to exult in His "name" (16), i.e., in what He does to manifest His care for them. (8:1 note)

89:18 *Shield . . . king.* Israel is guaranteed safety because its *king* is the appointed representative of *the Holy One of Israel.* (71:22 note)

89:19 *In a vision.* What God let Nathan see with prophetic eyes, recorded in 2 Sm 7 and briefly summarized in vv. 3 f., is here retold in the artistic profusion of the poet. (19-37)

89:27 *First-born.* As the entire nation was God's "first-born" (Ex 4:22), so in a special sense also *the highest of the kings of the earth* because he sat on "the throne of the kingdom of the Lord." (2:7 note)

89:32 *Punish their transgressions.* The Books of Kings record how often God's punishing *rod* came down heavily on David's "children" and heirs. Finally people and king reached a stage of disobedience where they no longer served the purpose of God's covenant, forcing Him to resort to a different way to put into effect His plan of salvation.

89:43 *In battle.* The military defeat which cast the Davidic "throne to the ground" (44) may refer to the capture and destruction of Jerusalem by the Babylonians. One of the last kings of Israel, Jehoiachin, was removed from the throne in "his youth." (45; 2 K 24:8-13)

89:47 *Measure of life.* The Hebrew text, in highly compressed syntax, echoes the thought of 39:5: "My lifetime is as nothing in thy sight." (Cf. Jb 7:6-8; 9:25 f.)

89:52 *Blessed.* This verse is the doxological note ending the Third Book of the Book of Psalms. See the introductory notes on the Psalter, "Divisions."

Psalm 90

90:1-17 This *Prayer of Moses* is an abiding source of strength and comfort especially in times of bereavement. It brings light and warmth into the cold darkness of human existence. The concluding plea for relief from a period of sadness, described only in general terms, and for a return to joyous, satisfying times (13-17) is prefaced by a frank recognition of the reasons why mortal man needs to implore God's *steadfast love* (14) if life on earth is to be more than a bit of shimmering foam cresting for a moment and inevitably sinking into a sea of futility (1-12). It is only too true that the *children of men* (3) take but a few quick breaths before they return to the dust of the earth from which they came (Gn 3:19). They may profess stolidly that the end of a heartbeat comes as a matter of course in the rhythm of nature. The psalmist is not taken in by such sophistry. He knows that life instinctively abhors death. Yet while recoiling from the ugly grim reaper, he is equally convinced that turning *back to the dust* (3) is not a dissolution into an impersonal void. For life *fades and withers* at the summons of its Creator. It stays in the hands of Him who is *from everlasting to everlasting* (1-6). At the same time, the certainty of death is a call to repentance. Men die after a short life of *toil and trouble* because they are *consumed* by God's *wrath.* Death is the wages of sin (7-10; Ro 6:23; 5:12). Those whom God gives *a heart of wisdom* consider *the power of* His *anger* (11-12). Truly penitent, they turn to Him, imploring Him to *have pity* on those whom He has *afflicted* and in His mercy to bless their weakness with His *glorious power* (13-17).—Moses is called *the man of God* in Dt 33:1; Jos 14:6.

90:1 *In all generations.* When in life's storms every earthly shelter and human contrivance for shelter collapses, the Lord remains man's *dwelling place,* towering over the wrecks of time and standing firmly even "though the mountains shake in the heart of the sea." (46:2 f.; cf. 71:3; 91:9; Dt 33:27)

90:2 *Mountains.* They represent what in man's experience is permanent and immovable (Dt 33:15; Ps 65:6; 104:5-9; Hab 3:6). In a daring figure of speech the Creator is said to have ushered them into existence as a woman gives birth to a child. For similar poetic descriptions of the origin of the world and its inhabitants see Jb 38:8; 15:7; Dt 32:18.

90:3 *To the dust.* In sharp contrast with Him who is not subject to the corrosion of time, men "dwell in houses of clay, whose foundation is in the dust, who are crushed before the moth" (Jb 4:19; cf. Ps 104:29). In heaped metaphors the brevity of human life is compared to a splash of raindrops in a sweeping downpour; to "a dream" which flits across the mind; to "grass" which "fades and withers" after flourishing for only a day; to a "sigh," a breath of air drawn in and expelled in one quick movement. (5, 6, 9, cf. Jb 14:1 f.; Ps 37:2; 73:20; 103:15 f.; Is 40:6 ff.; Ja 4:14)

90:4 *A watch.* The night was divided into three periods of four hours, each constituting a watch.

90:10 *Toil and trouble. The years of our life,* few and fleeting though they are, are no longer spent in the Garden of Eden but amid the "thorns and thistles" of sin's curse (Gn 3:17 ff.). This appraisal of life is not dull resignation to an irrational fate; not the wail of morbid pessimism; not the futile shriek of a helpless victim, crushed by a monstrous ogre. While it faces facts squarely and realistically, it does not stop in negation and hopelessness, as the remaining verses of the psalm proclaim.

Span. The Hebrw text has "pride" (RSV note). The very achievements in which man takes pride turn out to be disappointing. What *toil and trouble* produced *are soon gone,* slipping out of his grasp as power of body and mind *fly away.*

90:12 *Teach us.* By his own reason and strength mortal man cannot see himself in the perspective of Him who "alone has immortality" (1 Ti 6:15 f.). Only if God grants *a heart of wisdom* does His sin-blinded creature know enough tó acknowledge "the power of" His "anger" (11) and then to flee to His "steadfast love" (14) for redemption. (Dt 5:29; 32:29; Ps 39:4-6; Hos 14:9)

90:13 *Return.* On the basis established in the first part (1-12), the psalmist calls God's attention to his particular needs and those of his fellow *servants.* They ask Him to let the sunshine of His "favor" light up their days, made so sad by hard blows of affliction.

Psalm 91

91:1-16 Ps 90 is realistic in facing the specter of death; this psalm seems to be blind to dangers which threaten to snuff out man's existence. The unknown author looks out serenely on life's vicissitudes from behind walls of a *fortress* which assures him of absolute security. Having by faith taken *shelter* in the *Almighty* (1-2), he summarily defies every hostile and hurtful force to harm him (3-8). Within this impregnable *refuge* God's *angels* are on permanent guard duty, preventing every kind of accident (9-13). The psalmist, anxious to share his blithe outlook on life with others, says to everyone: You too can be carefree if you cast "all your anxieties on him" who "cares about you" (1 Ptr 5:7). To substantiate that claim the writer lets God Himself proclaim His promise of unfailing deliverance to everyone who *cleaves* to Him (14-16). This closing oracle of God prevents drawing false conclusions from the psalm. Faith in Him does not transport a person into a never-never land of pure delights, as every believer well knows. There are indeed times when he too is *in trouble* and has need to call on God to *deliver* and *rescue* him (14 f.). Nevertheless *he who dwells in the shelter of the Most High* (1) can rest assured that there is no mishap or disaster which He cannot deflect. If He so wills it, *no evil* can befall him and *no scourge* can come near his *tent.* (10)

91:1 *Shadow.* Escape from the scorching sun (Is 25:4). See also the phrase "shadow of thy wings" (17:8 second note) and the reference to "refuge" "under his wings" in v. 4.

91:3 *Deadly pestilence.* More literally: "a pestilence of destruction." The consonants of the Hebrew term for pestilence, when supplied with other vowels, spell also the usual noun for "word." According to 38:12 the enemy lays "snares" for his unwary victims because he "speaks of ruin," i.e., he trumps up charges against them in a court, hoping they will be sentenced to death. (Cf. 5:9 note; Ps 64:1-10 and v. 3 note)

91:5 *Night . . . day.* When you trust Him who neither slumbers nor sleeps (121:4), *you* need *not fear* whether an attack comes treacherously under cover of darkness or brazenly in broad daylight. (Cf. 11:2; 64:3)

91:6 *Pestilence . . . destruction.* Deadly diseases are communicated *in darkness,* i.e., by an unseen, mysterious process. *At noonday* there was danger of sunstroke (121:6). The author may be simultaneously rejecting superstitious notions, current at the time, that sickness was the result of demonic activity. (Cf. Is 34:14; Lv 17:3 note)

91:7 *A thousand . . . ten thousand.* God let His own survive the catastrophe of the Flood (Gn 8:18), the destruction of Sodom and Gomorrah (Gn 19:29), the slaughter of uncounted Egyptians at the time of the exodus (Ex 12:12 f.). They lived to "see the recompense of the wicked." (8)

91:10 *No evil . . . no scourge.* God will not let anything happen which does not work "for good with those who love him" (Ro 8:28), hard as it may be at times for them to believe it when they are "in trouble" (15) and their eyes red with weeping. (6:6; 42:3)

91:11 *Guard you.* Jesus gave us a key to the meaning of this psalm. On the one hand, He rejected Satan's attempt to make it an excuse to experiment with God's promises of protection (Lk 4:9-12). On the other hand, He subtracted nothing from the absolute assurance of God's power to save His disciples even if they should encounter enemies as strong as a "lion" and as deadly as an "adder." (13; Lk 10:19)

Psalm 92

92:1-15 "Praise befits" (33:1) the writer of this psalm because the *Most High* has rescued him from enemies (9, 11), letting them fall into the pit they dug for their intended victim (9:15 f.; 7:15 f.; 35:8). However, in calling for "a joyful noise to God" (66:1; 81:1 f.; 95:1 f.; 98:4) he mentions his own reason for rejoicing only in passing (10-11). He wants *to give thanks to the Lord* not only for what He did to make him glad but above all for the *steadfast love* and *faithfulness* of which all His *works* are evidence (1-4). To *dull* and *stupid* people it may appear that God has lost control or is inconsistent when He lets *evildoers flourish.* Their prosperity may have made also the author "envious of wrongdoers" (37:1; 73:2 f.). But now he realizes that God's *thoughts are very deep.* In spite of superficial and momentary appearances to the contrary, *the wicked* are God's *enemies, doomed to destruction forever.* After serving His purposes they *perish* and are *scattered* (5-9). Furthermore, while *the works* of God demonstrate that *evildoers* cannot mock Him, they prove also that He is *upright* in keeping His promises to *the righteous.* To their song of praise the psalmist adds his own voice (12-15).—It is not clear why this psalm is more appropriate *for the Sabbath* than other hymns of thanksgiving, as the superscription stipulates.

92:1 *Name.* By His "works" (4) God reveals who He is. (8:1 note; Ex 6:3 note)

92:10 *Horn.* Cf. 75:4-5 note.

92:11 *Have seen.* The "salvation" (91:16) of "the righteous" (12) by the Lord entails *the downfall* of His and their "enemies." (V. 9; cf. 52:6 note; 54:7)

92:13 *House of the Lord.* Cf. 52:8 note.

92:15 *No unrighteousness.* Blessing the righteous and destroying the wicked necessarily complement one another in God's moral world order. (Cf. 7:14 note)

Psalm 93

93:1-5 If man is to praise God, who dwells "on high for ever" "in unapproachable light" (92:8; 1 Ti 6:16), he must resort to thinking of Him in terms of human relations (cf. Ps 47:1-9). This psalm bids us bow in humble adoration before the King whose throne is in heaven and who carried out His royal designs on earth by making Jerusalem "the city of the Great King" (48:2; 24:8; 29:10; Is 24:23; Zch 14:16). The more fully His subjects are impressed with His majesty, the more often they want to appear in His court singing hymns of praise such as follow one another in Pss 93—100. The first of these briefly introduces some of the themes to be developed in a sheer endless effusion of poetic eloquence: (1) the eternal sovereignty of the King's reign (1-2); (2) His disdain of all challenges by hostile powers (3-4); (3) the unfailing success of His holy *decrees.* (5)

93:1 *The Lord reigns.* Ruling "from everlasting" (2) and "for evermore" (5), He needs no man-made pageantry or ceremony to enthrone Him, nor can any human scheme dethrone Him. He is not like the idols whom Israel's neighbors subjected to such indignities. (47:5 note)

93:3 *Floods.* For the sea as representing hostility to God see Jb 7:12 note; 9:13 note; 3:8 second note; Ps 89:10; 104:5-9.

93:5 *Decrees.* What He declares to be His holy will is *sure* to go into effect. *House* may refer to the temple where He chose to be symbolically "enthroned upon the cherubim" (80:1; 99:1; Ex 25:22) or to the King's dynastic house as in 2 Sm 7:16.

Psalm 94

94:1-23 Even *the righteous* (15, 21) may doubt at times that "the Lord reigns" and that His "decrees are very sure" (93:1, 5). This psalm allays such migivings. It upholds the sovereignty of the King by asserting that He is the *judge of the earth* (2; cf. also 50:4; 96:10, 13; 98:9; Gn 18:25; 1 Sm 2:10). No one is beyond the borders of His royal domain; no one can escape being haled before His court of justice. Because the King-Judge is committed to right wrongs, His loyal subjects boldly summon Him to *rise up* against *the wicked* and *render to the proud their deserts* (1-3). Delay of divine retribution is puzzling especially in view of the heinous crimes committed with devilish glee against such helpless people as widows, orphans, and nonresident strangers (4-7). Addressing *the evildoers,* the psalmist proceeds to expose the folly of thinking that their brazen flouting of the Law goes undetected. They behave like irrational animals if they think that *He who planted the ear does . . . not hear* what they say or that *He who formed the eye does . . . not see* what they do (8-11). Next the writer turns to those whom these bestial criminals have plunged into dark *days of trouble.* He pronounces them *blessed* if they let the Lord teach them that (1) He uses the ungodly to chastise *the righteous;* (2) the situation never gets out of control. When He has achieved His purpose, He sees to it that *a pit is dug for the wicked* (12-15).

Finally the author of the psalm adds his own testimony to the validity of the principles he has enunciated so confidently. He too was in dire need of help against those who *band together against the life of the righteous;* he too felt the apparent incongruity between God's promises and His failure to prevent *wicked rulers* from tyrannizing *the innocent.* Though brought to the verge of despair, he nevertheless continued to rely on the Lord's *steadfast love.* And it proved trustworthy. God became his *stronghold* and *refuge.* (16-22)

94:1 *God of vengeance.* "The King whose name is the Lord" is also "a God of recompense" (Jer 51:56 f.). Victims of malice and injustice are not to avenge themselves but to "leave it to the wrath of God" (Ro 12:19; Lv 19:18; Dt 32:35, 41, 43; Heb 10:30). However, because He has assured them a moral world order, they need not hesitate to appeal to Him to *shine forth* as "an avenger of . . . wrongdoings." (99:8; Jer 11:20)

94:5 *Heritage.* Cf. 61:5 note.

94:6 *The widow.* The wicked "exult" (3) because they were able to *slay* and *murder* such victims as often had no defense except the explicit warning of the Lord not to "wrong" or "afflict" them. (Ex 22:21 f.)

94:7 *Does not see.* Cf. 10:4 note; 14:1 note.

94:10 *Chastens the nations.* If the Creator of man's sense perceptions also determines the destiny of whole nations, can individual citizens be so dull as to think that they, nothing "but a breath" (11; 39:5), can act with impunity against members of God's "people"? (5)

94:12 *Blessed.* Cf. 119:71; Pr 3:11 f.; Jb 5:17; Heb 12:5 f. For man to understand the mystery of suffering, he must let the Lord *teach* him its meaning out of His *law,* i.e., His revealed instructions.

94:16 *Who rises up . . . ?* A rhetorical question answered in the following verses.

94:20 *Wicked rulers.* Lit. "throne of destructions." The King of righteousness cannot share His throne of authority with those who *frame mischief by statute,* i.e., pervert justice under the pretense of legality.

Psalm 95

95:1-11 This psalm combines a rousing call to *worship* (6) the *great King* of creation (1-5) and the Shepherd of His chosen people (6-7a) with the solemn warning that *songs of praise* (2), if they are to be acceptable, must come from the lips of such as *hearken to his voice* and do not disobey it as the Israelites did during their 40 years of wandering in the desert (7b-11). Cf. Ps 81 for a similar blending of motifs.

95:1 *O come.* Known as the "Venite," the Latin translation of the first word, the first part of the psalm serves as an "Invitatory" in churches using ancient liturgies.

95:3 *Above all gods.* Cf. 24:4 second note; 48:2 note; Ex 20:3 notes; Dt 10:17.

95:7 *Today.* Delay in responding to the offer of salvation often is disastrous (Lk 19:42). For the reference to "Meribah" and "Massah" (8) see notes on Ex 17:7 and Nm 20:13. For the heightened responsibility of those who know of the salvation in Jesus Christ, of which God's "work" (9) in the old covenant was a promise, see Heb 3:7—4:13.

Psalm 96

96:1-13 The thought of the King whose "throne is . . . from everlasting" and whose "decrees are . . . for evermore" (93:2, 5) inspires one *new song* after another in praise of *his marvelous works.* In the first part of this psalm a summons is issued to Israel, who had the benefit of *his salvation* and knew how *greatly to be praised* and *feared* He was, to broadcast *his glory among the nations* (1-6). At hearing the good news, all the *families of the peoples* are to *come into his courts* rendering Him *the glory due his name* (7-9). A still greater panorama comes into view. Acclaim of the past and present exercise of dominion by the Creator-King turns into jubilant expectation of His eventual coming to *judge the world with righteousness and the peoples with His truth.* Then it will be evident that His kingdom has achieved its ultimate purpose. Man and the universe he lives in will join "the morning stars" in an ever-new song with the theme and refrain: *The Lord reigns* (10-13; Jb 38:7; cf. also Rv 5:9; 14:3). Found with but minor variations in 1 Ch 16:23-33, this hymn of exuberant joy is made up largely of phrases, strains, and motifs occurring in other psalms and in chs. 40—66 of the Book of Isaiah.

96:1 *A new song.* Cf. 33:3 note; 40:3; 98:1; 149:1; Is 42:10.

96:2 *Name.* Not merely the title by which He is addressed but everything He did to manifest Himself by "his marvelous works." (3; 8:1 note; Rv 15:3 f.)

96:5 *Idols.* Lit. things of nought, devoid of reality; translated "worthless idols" in 97:7. *All the gods of the peoples* exist only in the imagination of their worshipers. (Lv 19:4 note; 26:1; Is 2:8, 18, 20; 10:10 f.)

96:6 *Before him.* The courtiers in attendance about the King's throne and representing His character are the personified qualities of *honor and majesty . . . strength and beauty.* (Cf. 89:14)

96:7 *Ascribe.* Cf. 29:1 f., where "heavenly beings" are summoned to render the Lord the homage of worship.

96:11 *Be glad . . . rejoice.* Those entrusting themselves to the King need not fear the day when "he comes to judge the earth" (13). It will be an occasion for rejoicing because "redemption is drawing near." (Lk 21:28)

96:12 *Trees . . . sing.* Long "subjected to futility," "the creation itself will be set free" to testify to the glory of its Creator in the restored perfection of "a new heaven and a new earth" (Ro 8:19-25; Rv 21:1; Is 44:23; 49:13). The bliss resulting from peaceful relations between man and his Maker is described in terms of primordial harmony in the animal world and of paradisaical productivity of plants in such passages as Is 11:6-9; 35:1-10; 55:12 f.; Am 9:13.

Psalm 97

97:1-12 This royal psalm takes on special meaning at times when it seems hard to find evidence of "righteousness" and "truth" in the Creator-King's government, so confidently asserted in 96:13. Once again the unqualified proclamation is issued: *The Lord reigns.* Lest anyone doubt the worldwide validity of this claim, it is followed by a declaration of the Judge's irresistible power to execute *righteousness* and *justice* (1-5). *The heavens . . . and all the peoples* will become aware with what inevitable finality His *judgments* are enforced. Attempts to thwart His decrees by trusting in gods "besides" Him (Ex 20:3 RSV note) will be *put to shame;* Mt. Zion, "the city of the great King" (48:2), and all worshipers of the *Lord . . . most high over all the earth* will *rejoice* when He carries out the unchanging principles of His reign (6-9). What a comfort to know that this transcendent Ruler of the universe is not too occupied with directing national and international affairs to be concerned with the needs of individual *saints* who are *righteous* and *upright in heart.* (10-12)

97:2 *Thick darkness.* The portrait of the "Lord of all the earth" (5) is a composite of passages used to describe past manifestations of His ethereal grandeur, particularly at the time of Israel's exodus from Egypt. (77:16 note; Ex 19:16-18; 20:21; 24:17; Dt 4:24; Ju 5:4 f.; Ps 46:6; 50:3 f.; 114:3-8; Mi 1:3 f.; cf. also Is 10:7; 2 Ptr 3:10-12)

97:7 *Worthless idols.* Cf. 96:5 note.

97:10 *Saints.* For the basis of this title see 4:3 note.

97:12 *Rejoice.* In confident anticipation that in His way and at His time "he delivers them from the hand of the wicked." Present-day "saints" too may be tempted to doubt that "the Lord reigns" when the wicked seem to control their destiny. But they have all the more reason to *rejoice in the Lord* because they have the added assurance that God "will judge the world in righteousness by a Man whom He has appointed" on "the day of Jesus Christ." (Acts 17:31; Ph 1:6; Ro 2:16; 1 Co 1:8)

Psalm 98

98:1-9 Repeating the opening and closing words of Ps 96, this *Psalm* (so designated in the superscription) is another variation on the theme "The Lord reigns" (93:1). Only "the dull man" (92:6) will find it tiresome to sing yet another song in praise of His royal honor. *A new song* (96:1 note) is called for as often as *the house of Israel* ponders the *marvelous things* done in faithfulness to His covenant promises and in demonstration of His power over *all the ends of the earth* (1-3). The *vindication* of His chosen people *in the sight of the nations* should move *all the earth* to participate in joyous acclamation of *the King, the Lord* (4-6). Even inanimate nature is invited to give a thunderous welcome to its Creator when *He comes to judge the earth.* (7-9)

98:1 *Marvelous things.* One word in Hebrew, translated "wonders" in Ex 3:20; Jos 3:5; Neh 9:17 to underscore the miraculous acts necessary to create the covenant people; "their own arm" (44:3, cf. note there) did not give them the victory.

98:8 *Floods.* Cf. 93:3 note.

Psalm 99

99:1-9 Another anthem in praise of the King, "the Lord of all the earth" (97:5), this psalm develops a cardinal aspect of His sovereign rule mentioned in a passing reference to "his holy name" (97:12). The characteristic ascribed to Him by this adjective lifts His reign to a level of perfection high above all human concepts of rulership (Lv 11:45 note; 19:2 note). Because the Lord who reigns is holy, there never is an arbitrary or capricious use of His power. His holiness manifested itself in the past when He *executed justice and righteousness* among the nations in accord with His promises to Israel (1-5). However, this transcendent Ruler of the universe did not remain in a holiness of disdainful silence. He chose men to communicate His will to His fallen creatures. And when *He spoke to them,* they faithfully transmitted and *kept his testimonies* (6-7). All the while His unholy subjects were "able to stand before the Lord, this holy God" (1 Sm 6:20) only because He was *a forgiving God to them.* But let those who presume to abuse His grace know that He is the unfailing *avenger of their wrongdoings.* (8-9 f.)

99:1 *Upon the cherubim.* The Lord before whom "the peoples tremble" (Ex 15:14 note; Dt 2:25) condescended to be present "in Zion" and there to receive the homage of a people chosen to let His kingdom come. (48:2 note; 80:1 second note)

99:3 *Holy is He!* The theme of the psalm is underscored by the refrainlike repetition in vv. 5 and 9 of the ascription to the King of a quality which, as Isaiah saw and heard, makes flaming seraphim break out into an ecstatic song of praise. (Is 6:1-3)

99:5 *Footstool.* To depict His ethereal majesty, the King's *footstool* is said to be the entire earth (Is 66:1; Mt 5:34 f.), Mt Zion (Lm 2:1), the temple. (Ps 132:7)

99:6 *Priests.* As the appointed officiants in the temple acted as mediators between the holy God and the sinful worshipers, so three prominent leaders in Israel's past interceded with the King in behalf of His people. For *Moses* see Ex 14:15; 17:11; 32:31 f.; Nm 14:13-19; for *Aaron,* Nm 16:44-48; 17:10 f.; for *Samuel,* 1 Sm 7:8-10; 12:16-23; see also Jer 15:1.

99:7 *Pillar of cloud.* Cf. Ex 33:9-11; Nm 12:5 1 K 8:10 f.

Psalm 100

100:1-5 Known in its English versified form as "Old Hundreth," this psalm is a fitting finale for the series of hymns celebrating the universal significance of the proclamation: "The Lord reigns" (93—99). Once more the faithful are summoned to appear in His audience chamber, there to kneel *with gladness* in their hearts and *a joyful noise* on their lips as they pay homage to their Creator-King (1-3). Their worship can be only a spontaneous outburst of jubilation because there are endless royal benefactions for which they ought to *give thanks to him.* (4-5)

100:1 *All the lands.* The translation "all the land" (RSV note), i.e., all residents of the Promised Land, is to be preferred because the entire psalm calls upon "his people and the sheep of his pasture" (74:1 note) to "enter . . . his courts with praise."

100:3 *Made us.* His people are to *know* (cf. Dt 9:24; Gn 18:19 note) *that the Lord* alone *is God* (Dt 4:35, 39; Jos 24:15, 18, 21; 1 K 18:39), for He provided them not only with physical life but by a creative "let there be" called them into being also as His chosen nation. (Gn 1:3; Dt 7:6-11; 32:6-15; Is 43:1, 21; 44:2)

100:5 *The Lord is good.* Always and invariably, even when He lets the eyes of those who serve Him brim with tears. Cf. the refrain in Ps 136.

Psalm 101

101:1-8 In this Psalm *David,* the earthly administrator of "the kingdom of the Lord" (1 Ch 28:4-7), the Lord praised in Pss 93—100 with a "joyful noise," vows to rule according to the principles which are the "foundation" of his heavenly liege-Lord's "throne" (89:14). To achieve this goal the occupant of "the throne of the Lord" (1 Ch. 29:23) in Israel pledges (1) to live a *blameless* life himself (2-4); (2) to establish a regime in which *he who walks in the way that is blameless* has full protection of the law (5-8).—Even David, "a man after his [the Lord's] own heart" (1 Sm 13:14), fell short of the personal and the administrative ideal set forth in the psalm. Perfect justice will not prevail until "the root and the offspring of David," Himself "holy, blameless, unstained," "comes into his glory" and "as a shepherd separates the sheep from the goats" (Rv 22:16; Heb 7:26; Mt 25:31 f.). Nevertheless, all who are "made . . . guardians to feed the church of the Lord" are charged to "take pains to have a clear conscience toward God and toward men." (Acts 20:28; 24:16)

101:1 *Loyalty.* The Hebrew word for this attribute of God is translated "steadfast love" in almost every other instance. For its meaning see Dt 7:9 note. In v. 1 the recipient of the undeserved distinction of acting as the Lord's vicegerent praises Him for His steadfast love in entrusting him with the exercise of divine *justice* (89:1-4, 49; Is 55:3; Ps 72:1) and then proceeds (vv. 2-8) to promise to perform the delegated duties in a way pleasing to his Superior. (Cf. Dt 17:18 ff.; 1 Sm 8:11-18; Ps 122:3-5)

101:2 *When wilt thou come . . .?* This interjected question may refer to a specific situation in David's life (e.g., the delay in bringing the ark to Jerusalem, 2 Sm 6:6-11) or it may reflect his longing for a fulfillment of the promise given his house in 2 Sm 7.

Psalm 102

102:1-28 The fifth of the seven "Penitential Psalms" (cf. 6:1-10) displays a bold venture of faith in the way it prays for God's gracious deliverance from the pain inflicted by the shattering blows of His *indignation and anger* (10). After pleading for a hearing at the throne of mercy (1-2) and calling attention to his pitiful condition in language and terms used by petitioners in similar prayers (3-11), the embattled sufferer adopts an unusual strategy in wrestling with the Lord in prayer. He confidently claims for his own person what God has promised to do for His chosen people as a whole. As *the appointed time* is sure to come when He who is *enthroned forever* will *arise and have pity on Zion,* rescuing it from threatening national extinction, so He is bound to relieve him, the individual member of the covenant community, of his personal agony as soon as it has served its intended purpose (12-17). From reveling (18-22) in the assurance of the miraculous revival of Israel's "dry bones" (Eze 37:1-14) the suppliant turns again to his own plight. Though his life still hangs by a hair (23-24), he has no misgivings about entrusting himself into the hands of the almighty Creator of heaven and earth and the eternal Guardian of His *servants* (25-28).—This psalm should teach the NT believer to apply to himself individually what Jesus Christ, "the same yesterday and today and forever," has promised His church when He said: "The powers of death shall not prevail against it." (Heb 13:8; Mt 16:18; see also 1 Jn 2:17)

102:1 *Hear my prayer.* The Lord does not demand novelty of expression in prayer. The introductory invocation (1 f.) is composed of stereotype phrases, occurring in other psalms. (Cf., e.g., 18:6; 31:2; 39:12; 56:9; 59:16; 69:17)

102:3 *Like smoke.* In 3-11 the sufferer tells of his distress as if the Lord were unaware of it. Pains of body, mind, and spirit gnaw at his vitals. If relief does not come, life will be over as quickly as smoke disappears in a gust of wind (37:20; 68:2; Is 51:6) or as grass withers when the wind passes over it. (4; 37:2; Is 40:6-8)

102:6 *Vulture.* So translated in Zph 2:14; but "pelican" in Lv 11:18; Dt 14:17; "hawk" in Is 34:11. Whatever other characteristics this bird may have had, it was a proverbial symbol of melancholy loneliness.

102:8 *Curse. Enemies taunt* him in his misery, interpreting it as well-deserved punishment for concealed crimes, as Job's friends did. They are so sure of their diagnosis that they invoke a fate like his on other evildoers. (Cf. Jer 29:22; Is 65:15; see also Nm 5:21, 27)

102:12 *Enthroned for ever.* Human life—at best precarious and fragile, always transitory and moribund—has meaning only when committed to the safekeeping of Him who was there to "lay the foundation of the earth" (25), whose "years endure throughout all generations" (24; Is 41:4), who is "the same," unaffected by the flux of eroding time. (27; Is 34:4; 51:6; Mt 24:29; Heb 1:10-12)

102:13 *Arise.* Cf. 7:6 note. Faith is so impertinent as to tell God that *the appointed time* for action on His part *has come.* For the time announced when "the Lord will build up Zion" (16) after the Babylonian exile see Jer 25:11 f.; 29:10; Is 40:2.

102:22 *Peoples . . . and kingdoms . . . worship.* Cf. 22:26 f.; 96:7-9; Is 2:2-4.

102:23 *In midcourse.* Having lived out only half of the normal days of human life. (Cf. 55:23)

Psalm 103

103:1-22 Ps 102 is an agonizing cry for alleviation of personal distress, based on God's promise to "have pity" (102:13) on His chosen nation as a whole. In this *Psalm of David* there is jubilant thanksgiving for benefactions of divine goodness which the individual shares with all members of the covenant people. Foremost among the blessings received, and essential to his entire well-being, is a gift of pure grace: the granting of forgiveness by a *holy* God to His offending creature (1-5). The people of Israel, one and all, would have perished long ago if the Lord had not pardoned their iniquities but had dealt with them as they deserved. From their very beginning under Moses they were dependent on His *steadfast love.* It is as wondrously boundless as the vast reaches between heaven and earth; it grants full and irrevocable amnesty, putting all acts of rebellion as far out of sight as the eastern horizon remains distant from the western; it is as tender as the compassion of a *father* for *his children* (6-13). He who formed man of the *dust* of the ground knows how much His transitory handiwork needs His *steadfast love.* As generations of men come and go, "His mercies never come to an end"; no matter how many *children's children* tap their supply, "they are new every morning" (14-18; Lm 3:22 f.). Constant and inexhaustible, this *steadfast love* is not impotent sympathy. He who *is merciful and gracious* (8) is none other than the Lord whose *throne* is *in the heavens,* whose *kingdom rules over all,* whose word of command is carried out by armies of *angels.* These mighty *ministers that do his will* are to add their voices to the chorus of praise coming from human lips, even as *all his works* echo His glory. (19-22)

103:1 *Bless.* Men bless God as they kneel before Him (95:6) in order humbly and gratefully to acknowledge the "benefits" bestowed by Him.

103:2 *Forget.* Beneficiaries of God's goodness are prone to take some of His most precious gifts for granted because He dispenses them so bountifully, regularly, and unobtrusively. There is danger that even spectacular help in time of great need such as Israel's deliverance from Egypt may be forgotten. (Dt 4:9, 23; 6:12; 32:18)

103:3 *Iniquity.* If God were to manifest "his holy name" (1), renegade man would be consumed in the fires of His wrath. However, the forgiven sinner need no longer be afraid. His *iniquity* pardoned, he seeks out his Benefactor, bringing to Him an offering of thanksgiving which expresses his innermost feelings.

Diseases. Recovery from sickness, the consequence of sin, and deliverance from death, the wages of sin, also are undeserved gifts of "steadfast love and mercy." (Cf. Dt 29:22; Ex 15:26; 2 Ch 21:18; Jer 16:4; Ro 6:23)

103:5 *As long as you live.* The traditional Hebrew text reads: "who satisfies with good your ornament," i.e.,"your soul." Cf. 16:9, where a literal translation reads: "my glory [i.e., my soul] rejoices"; so also 7:5; 57:8; 108:1.

Like the eagle's. For the eagle as a symbol of vitality and sudden bursts of energy see Is 40:31.

103:6 *Vindication.* This word for God's intervention in behalf of His people is translated "triumphs" (Ju 5:11), "saving deeds" (1 Sm 12:7), "righteous acts" (Dn 9:16), "saving acts." (Mi 6:5)

103:8 *Merciful and gracious.* An echo of the compassionate words transmitted to Israel by Moses in Ex 34:6 f.

103:9 *Anger forever.* Cf. 30:5; Is 57:16.

103:11 *Fear Him.* Cf. Ex 20:6; Dt 7:9-11; Lk 1:50.

103:14 *Frame.* What came into being when "the Lord . . . formed man of dust from the ground" (Gn 2:7 note). For an impassioned plea for mercy based on man's fragile nature see Jb 7.

103:15 *Like grass.* For similar comparisons with man's fleeting existence see 90:5; Jb 14:1 f.; Is 40:6; 1 Ptr 1:24.

103:17 *Steadfast love . . . from everlasting to everlasting.* Salvation was by God's grace for those who kept "his covenant" (18) in the days before "the goodness and loving kindness of God . . . appeared" in "our Savior," Jesus Christ. (Tts 3:4; cf. Eph 2:4-10)

Psalm 104

104:1-35 The last verse of the preceding psalm contains a brief summons to "all his works" to "bless the Lord." This psalm lists what the Creator still does in the universe that is "telling the glory of God" even though "there is no speech nor are there words" (19:1-6; cf. 148:1-9). When the universe sprang into being, "all the sons of God shouted for joy," for "behold, it was very good" (Jb 38:7; Gn 1:31). The psalmist declares that the reason for their jubilation is apparent in the enduring excellence of the finished product. Therefore he conducts a tour through the wonderland of natural phenomena. At various points he asks the reader to stop and listen. If he has ears to hear, he will be entranced by the stereophonic sounds of music and song converging on him from all directions. In the very court of creation's King the splendor of His handiwork proclaims His *honor and majesty:* The *light* He made at the beginning is His royal *garment;* His palace consists of *chambers* founded in the "firmament" (Gn 1:7 f.) *on the waters;* the courtiers and servants attending His majesty are *the clouds, the winds,* the flashing lightning (1-4). When God "let the dry land appear" (Gn 1:9), the habitable earth which emerged still exists because He kept it from being inundated again by the primordial waters of the deep (5-9; Jer 5:22). But the Creator does not only preserve the earth from becoming a chaos. Songs of praise arise from it also because He supplies it with what is indispensable for the existence of plant and animal life: perennial *springs* of water and rain from His *lofty abode* (10-13). So watered, the soil can produce fodder for animals and *food* and *wine* for *man* (14-18). Again praise of the Creator reechoes through the vaulted heavens where the lights He set in the firmament never fail to do His bidding (19-23), "to rule over the day and over the night and to separate the light from the darkness" (Gn 1:18). A hymn to the infinite wisdom and power of the Creator rises also from the *creatures* which still fill the earth and the *living things both small and great* with which the sea *teems* (24-26). Awe-inspiring too is the vast storehouse of provisions which He maintains *to give them their food in due season* (27-30). If God's material and brute creation sings His praises, should not man, endowed with capacity for *meditation* on His *works* and given a voice to *sing to the Lord,* exhort his *soul* to *bless the Lord* in a manner pleasing to his Maker? If he does not *rejoice in the Lord,* he aligns himself with *the wicked* who have forfeited the right to existence. (31-35)

104:1 *Bless the Lord.* These are the opening and closing words of this psalm and of Ps 103. For their meaning see 103:1 note.

104:3 *Beams of thy chambers.* Cf. Jb 26:7 second note; Ps 24:2 note; 33:6 note.

Ridest. Cf. 68:4 note.

104:7 *Rebuke.* Cf. Jb 7:12 note.

104:14 *For man to cultivate.* Lit. "for the service of man." The meaning also may be: "plants which serve man's need."

104:15 *Wine.* Cf. Ec 10:19; Ju 9:13.

104:16 *Trees of the Lord.* So designated because they owe their growth to the Lord. The modifying phrase may be restrictive, referring to trees not planted by human hands.

104:18 *Badgers.* In Lv 11:5 they are classified as unclean.

104:19 *The moon . . . the sun.* In the mythological poetry of Israel's heathen neighbors the sun is the deified force of creation. Though there are similarities in language and form between these ancient hymns and the psalm, there is also a fundamental difference. The psalmist does not worship nature or any part of it. He glorifies the Maker of "the heavens and the earth . . . and all the host of them," including the sun and the moon. (Gn 2:1)

104:23 *Man.* The psalm does not recount how God created man and the animal world. It looks out on an existing universe and its cosmic clockwork so regulated that both "the beast of the forest" (20) and human beings can pursue their activities on an unchanging schedule.

104:26 *Leviathan.* See Jb 3:8 second note; 41:1 note; Ps 74:14; Is 27:1. If *in it,* the last two words of the verse, are translated "with him," i.e., with Leviathan, then the thought is that even the largest sea monster is something for the Lord to "play with" as with a pet animal. (Jb 41:5)

104:30 *Spirit.* The same word is translated "breath" in 29. The cycle of life and death is not maintained by an inherent law of nature. Breath, essential to all creatures, comes as the Spirit of God animates them; life ceases when He takes "away their breath." This is true in a higher sense of man, into whose "nostrils" God "breathed . . . the breath of life." (Gn 2:7; cf. Ec 12:7; Ps 31:5; Eze 37:9)

104:35 *Be consumed. Sinners* and *the wicked,* making raucous noises of rebellion and blasphemy, have no place in a world designed to praise its Creator.

Praise the Lord! In its transliterated form this exclamation is the well-known word "hallelujah," found also at the end of the next psalm.—Modern penetration into the expanse and the intricacies of nature's amazing wonders, undiscovered in the writer's day, has not outmoded this psalm. On the contrary, every new discovery is but an additional reason to join in this hallelujah chorus from a deeper feeling of adoration.

Psalm 105

105:1-45 Ps 104 bids the reader listen to the "honor and majesty" (104:1) ring out from the marvels produced by the Maker of heaven and earth. This psalm issues a call to *give thanks to the Lord* and to *glory in his holy name* for *wonderful works* and *miracles* of another kind. For the omnipotent King of Creation is also the Lord of history. With unlimited power and incomprehensible wisdom He directed the course of earth's peoples with a fixed purpose in mind: to create and preserve Israel, the nation He chose to bless all nations. The *offspring of Abraham* and the *sons of Jacob* therefore should rouse themselves to *sing praises to him* (1-6). How can they fail to do so if they but *remember the wonderful works that He has done* since the days of their ancestral fathers: Abraham, Isaac, Jacob? Having promised that He would *give the land of Canaan* to them, "the Judge of all the earth" (Gn 18:25) let *no harm* come to them even though they remained migrant *sojourners in it, wandering from nation to nation* (7-15). He chose His own way of keeping His covenant with them. He used the envy of Joseph's brothers to bring him to Egypt, where he rose from slavery to be the second in command to the Pharaoh (16-22). Next He *summoned a famine* to bring Joseph's father, brothers, and their families to Egypt. However, when their offspring increased in such numbers as to arouse the fears of the Egyptians, the latter resorted to repressive measures designed eventually to exterminate the Hebrews (23-25). But faithful to His covenant, God came to the rescue. Empowered by Him, Moses and Aaron wrought *signs* and *miracles* which finally loosened the grip of the oppressors (26-36). Led out of the house of bondage "with a mighty hand and an outstretched arm" (Dt 26:8), the freed slaves would have been overwhelmed by the pursuing Egyptian army if God had not come to their aid with another miracle. In the desert beyond the Red Sea they would have perished if God had not provided for their sustenance with water from a rock and with *bread from heaven* (37-42). At long last *he gave them the lands of the nations,* the territories in the Promised Land formerly occupied by a variety of peoples. The Israelites did not deserve what God did for them. However, if they were to be the people of the covenant and serve His purpose, they were to respond in gratitude for unmerited grace with a wholehearted endeavor to *keep his statutes and observe his laws* (43-45).—The prose account of God's covenant faithfulness, which covers many pages of recorded history beginning with Gn ch. 12, is here compressed into a few verses of poetry. The artistic treatment of the subject matter is evident in the poet's language, his selection and omission of incidents, and the sequence in which they are presented.—The first 15 verses of this psalm appear again in 1 Ch 16:8-22, where they are cited as representative of David's thanksgiving at the time when the ark of the covenant was brought to Jerusalem.

105:1 *O give thanks.* The opening words also of Ps 106, 118, 136. Worshipers comply with this directive as they *call on his name,* better translated "proclaim His name" (cf. Ex 33:19). On the meaning of "name" see 8:1 note; 33:21; Ex 6:3 note.

105:7 *Judgments.* In order to be "mindful of his covenant" and keep it, God executed punitive "miracles" on all who threatened to frustrate His good and gracious will. Particularly noteworthy were the plagues inflicted on the Egyptians and described in some detail in vv. 26-36.

105:9 *Covenant.* On the meaning of this significant term see the introductory notes to the Book of Exodus entitled "Content." For the covenant with Abraham see Gn 12:1-3; 15:7-18; 17:2-14; with Isaac see Gn 26:1-5; with Jacob see 28:10-15.

105:12 *Sojourners.* In a land occupied by many "nations" (v. 44) the patriarchs remained a nonresident minority, at times forced to "wandering from nation to nation." (Cf. Gn 12:10; 26:1; 28:10)

105:14 *Rebuked kings.* Such as Pharaoh and Abimelech. (Gn 12:17; 20:3)

105:15 *Anointed ones.* Ceremonial oil poured on the heads of priests and kings symbolized that they were set apart for functions specifically assigned to them by God. Hence their persons were sacrosanct (2 Sm 1:14, 16). His "sworn promise" (9) to the patriarchs made them His special appointees whom no man was to *touch* (cf. Gn 26:11). Like the *prophets* in Israel's later history, the patriarchs made known by word and deed what God was about to do. (Gn 20:7; cf. Ex 7:1 f.)

105:17 *Sent a man ahead.* Joseph explained the mystery of God's strange dealings with him when he told his brothers: "God sent me before you to preserve life." (Gn 45:5)

105:18 *Neck.* The bare statement that Joseph's Egyptian master "put him into the prison" (Gn 39:20) is embellished for artistic effect. The Hebrew word "neck" is the same noun more commonly translated "soul" or "person."

105:19 *What he had said.* As he told his dreams. (Gn 37:5-11)

105:22 *Instruct.* If "bind," the reading of the traditional Hebrew text (RSV note), is retained, the meaning would be that Joseph had the authority to imprison even *princes,* better translated "chiefs" or "officials," such as "the chief butler" and "the chief baker." (Gn 40:9, 16)

105:23 *Israel.* The patriarch called "Jacob" in v. 10.

105:25 *Turned their hearts.* As a result of God's blessing His people became "very fruitful." This in turn made the Egyptians hate them, fearing that immigrants from Canaan were becoming "too many and too mighty" for them. (Ex 1:9 f.)

105:26 *Moses . . . and Aaron.* The psalmist cites some of the Egyptian plagues to illustrate the kind of "signs" and "miracles" which God empowered them to do. The poet feels at liberty to change the order of their occurrence in the prose account. At times he adds realistic touches not found in the record of Ex 7—12.

105:27 *Land of Ham.* Cf. 78:51 note.

105:28 *They rebelled.* If the traditional Hebrew text ("they did not rebel," RSV note) is retained, the reference is to the obedience of Moses and Aaron. However, it is possible that the final effect of the plagues on the Egyptians is anticipated: They no longer refused to let Israel go. (Cf. v. 38; Ex 12:33)

105:37 *Silver and gold.* Cf. Ex 12:35 f.

105:39 *Covering.* The *cloud* provided a protective shield by "coming between the host of Egypt and the host of Israel." (Ex 14:19 f.; cf. Is 22:8)

105:40 *They asked.* For the rebellious spirit prompting their request see 78:18-31 and the next psalm.

105:45 *Praise the Lord!* One word in Hebrew and known in its transliterated form "hallelujah." People of the new covenant have every reason to join in ancient Israel's hallelujah chorus. For if they are Christ's, they are also "Abraham's offspring, heirs according to the promise" (Gl 3:29; Ro 4:16; 9:7 f.). They too are the beneficiaries of what "the God of Abraham and the God of Isaac and the God of Jacob" did "to perform the mercy promised to our fathers and to remember his holy covenant." (Mk 12:26; Lk 1:72)

Psalm 106

106:1-48 Ps 105 praises God's "wonderful works" and "miracles" with which Israel's history is studded. However, Ps 106 points out that His goodness is the more amazing and praiseworthy in view of the fact that He did not cease to keep His covenant promises even though He was rebuffed by ingratitude and rebellion. After issuing a call to give thanks for *the mighty doings of the Lord* and pleading for a personal share in the *favor* shown to Israel as a whole (1-5), the psalmist lets God's faithfulness shine in full splendor against the black backdrop of Israel's shameful past. Without regard for chronological sequence he turns to a number of pages in Israel's dismal record of base ingratitude. He first calls to mind seven instances of disloyalty from the time of the exodus and the subsequent wandering in the wilderness: (1) distrust of *his mighty power* to deliver them before crossing the Red Sea (6-12; Ex 14:10-12); (2) putting *God to the test* by their demand for water and meat (13-15; Ex 15:24; 16:2 f.; Nm 11:4 ff., 31-34); (3) revolt against *Moses and Aaron* (16-18; Nm 16; Dt 11:6); (4) worship of the golden calf at Mt Sinai (19-23; Ex 32; Dt 9:8-21); (5) refusal to believe *his promise* to give them land after they heard the spies' report (24:27; Nm 13 f.); (6) succumbing to the degrading worship of the Moabite *Baal of Peor* (28-31; Nm 25); (7) murmuring because there was "no water to drink" at Meribah (32-33; Nm 20:2-13). Moreover, the Israelites did not leave their perversity behind in the desert. If anything, it reached a lower level after God brought them into the Promised Land: *They sacrificed to the idols of Canaan* (34-39). God's goodness cannot be abused with impunity. As happened in the desert, His *anger . . . was kindled against His people.* At His instigation and His direction, *their enemies oppressed them.* Nevertheless, from *the abundance of his steadfast love,* He delivered them *many times* when they cried to Him (40-46). The psalmist ends with a plea that God continue to be the forgiving Savior of His people also in his day (47). The doxology (48) closes the fourth book of the psalter. (See the Introduction, under "Divisions.")

106:1 *Praise the Lord!* See 105:45 note. For *steadfast love* see Dt 7:9 note.

106:2 *Who can utter . . . ?* If man will only stop to think, he will discover that the "wondrous deeds" of God are even "more than can be numbered," to say nothing of praising them adequately. (40:5 note)

106:5 *Chosen ones.* God's choice of Israel to be "his own possession" was an act of undeserved love. (Dt 4:20, 37; 10:15)

106:6 *And our fathers.* More literally: "We have sinned with our fathers." The psalmist does not claim to be any holier than the fathers whose disgraceful record of perversity he is about to document. For the opposite attitude see Eze 18:2.

106:7 *Most High.* This translation is based on a slight change in the traditional Hebrew text which reads: "but they rebelled by the sea, [namely] at the Red Sea." For their rebellious words before crossing the sea see Ex 14:11 f.

106:9 *Desert.* Better translated "meadow" (cf. 65:13). God *led them through the deep* as a shepherd guides his sheep across a grazing place.

106:12 *Believed.* (Ex 14:31)

106:13 *His counsel.* They refused to wait for God to carry out His plan in His own way. (Cf. 33:11; 73:24; 107:11)

106:14 *Test.* Cf. 78:18 note.

106:16 *Holy one.* Aaron was holy, i.e., set apart to serve God in the sacred office of the priesthood. All priests are called holy. (Lv 21:6-8)

106:17 *Dathan . . . Abiram.* The third ringleader, Korah, is not mentioned here or in Dt 11:6.

106:19 *Horeb.* Another name for Sinai. (Ex 3:1 second note)

106:20 *Glory of God.* Lit. "their glory," i.e., God, who revealed His glory to them. (Jer 2:11; Ro 1:23)

106:22 *Land of Ham.* Cf. 78:51 note.

106:23 *Breach.* God's consuming wrath was about to advance on Israel as enemy soldiers, pouring through an opening in the wall, devastate a city. Moses' intercession closed the gap, and destruction was averted.

106:24 *Despised the pleasant land.* They preferred certainty of existence as slaves in Egypt to trusting the Lord's promise that He would lead them into Canaan, "a land flowing with milk and honey." (Ex 3:8, 17; Jer 11:5; Eze 20:15)

106:27 *Disperse.* This rendering is based on the text of Eze 20:23.

106:28 *Dead.* Instead of worshiping "the living God" (Jer 10:10) they joined the Moabites in sacrificing to *Baal of Peor,* a lifeless, inert construct of their own making (115:4-8). For the story of Phineas see Nm 25.

106:32 *On their account.* Provoked by the repeated murmurings of the people to utter "rash" words, Moses forfeited the right to lead them into the Promised Land. (Nm 20:10 note; Dt 1:37; 4:21)

106:34 *The Lord commanded.* Cf. Dt 7:1 6; 20:16-18.

106:37 *Their sons.* Cf. 2 K 3:27 note; 16:3 note; 23:10. For "demon" worship see Dt 32:17 note.

106:39 *Played the harlot.* Unfaithfulness to God is described frequently as the attitude and action of an adulterous wife and a promiscuous harlot. (Ex 34:16; Jer 2:33; 3:1; Eze 16:15-34)

106:41 *Gave them into the hand.* A statement occurring in the Book of Judges at regular intervals. (Ju 2:14; 3:8; 4:2; 6:1; etc.)

106:47 *From among the nations.* God carried out His threat to scatter disobedient Israel "among the nations" (Lv 26:33; Dt 28:64). However, He also answered the prayer to "grant them compassion in the sight of those who carried them captive" (1 K 8:46-53).—Paul warns the Israelites of the new covenant to take heed lest they regard themselves immune to the temptations which brought about the downfall of Israel according to the flesh. (1 Co 10:1-13; Ro 11:17-22)

Psalm 107

107:1-43 "Book V" contains several series of psalms grouped according to readily distinguishable features. They are known as the "Hallel Psalms" (113—118), the "Songs of Ascents" (120—134), and the "Hallelujah Psalms" (145—150). Chosen to head the list in the last major collection of the psalter, Ps 107 at the same time serves as a sequel to Ps 106. There the Israelites pray the Lord of history to "gather" them "from among the nations" (106:47); here *the redeemed of the Lord* (2) are exhorted to *thank the Lord for his steadfast love* (15) in hearing their prayer. In the first three verses this summons is issued to all whom *the Lord . . . gathered in from the lands.* In vv. 4-32 they are reminded how truly thankful they ought to be in view of their deliverance from the threat of national extinction in the Babylonian captivity. The danger they faced is described graphically by comparing it with four life situations in which men are faced with imminent death. The returned exiles needed help as desperately as people saved from (1) death from hunger and thirst in a trackless desert (4-9); (2) life imprisonment with *hard labor* (10-16); (3) illness leading *to the gates of death* (17-22); (4) foundering in a storm at sea (23-32). These four highly poetic word-pictures are framed by a double refrain. The first records the fact that *they cried . . . and he delivered them* (6, 13, 19, 28); the second is the reminder that after such a miraculous rescue they should not forget to *thank the Lord* (8, 15, 21, 31). In a second section (33-43) the psalm points out that *the steadfast love of the Lord* (43) to which the exiles owe so much is not an impotent feeling of good will. He who was so kind to them also has the power to harness nature and to direct the doings of men to serve His good and gracious will so that they are truly *wise* who *give heed to these things.* (43)

107:2 *The redeemed of the Lord.* So designated also in Is 62:12; the Israelites are called upon to remember that they cannot take credit for their deliverance from oblivion in the Babylonian exile. It came about not because they deserved it but only because "the Lord . . . is good," not because they were so strong but only because "his steadfast love endures for ever."

107:4 *Some.* This word has no corresponding equivalent in the Hebrew text. It represents an interpretative translation which assumes that four distinct groups assembled in the temple, each having been rescued from a different threat to their lives. The same holds true of vv. 10, 17, 23. The Hebrew text says simply: "they wandered in desert wastes" or "wanderers in desert places." It supports the view that all "the redeemed of the Lord" are meant. In the exile they were like lost travelers dying of hunger and thirst whom the Lord led to safety "by a straight way." At the same time the description of the disaster facing the captives in exile recalled the "wonderful works" by which the Lord kept the young nation of freed slaves from actually perishing in the desert after their escape from Egypt. There also may have been individuals from time to time who had reason to thank God for keeping them from perishing in the desert.

107:10 *In irons.* For redemption depicted as release from prison see Is 42:7; 45:2; 49:9.

107:11 *Rebelled.* The Babylonian exile was Israel's punishment for rejecting God. (Is 63:10; Zch 1:4)

107:17 *Sick.* Cf. RSV note. Sickness is the result of sin, which in turn is called folly (Pr 1:7; Ps 38:5; 69:5 note; see also Jb 33:19-28). For the Babylonian captivity described as a consuming disease see Lm 1:13 f.; for forgiveness and restoration as healing see 6:1 f.; 41:4; Hos 6:1 f.; 11:3; Is 19:22; 57:18; Jer 33:6.

107:23 *Down to the sea.* In the Babylonian exile the Israelites were like sailors who "were at their wits' end" (27) because they could do nothing to escape an inevitable death at sea.

107:31 *Let them thank.* The last element in the fourfold refrain (8, 15, 21, 31) underscores the theme of the psalm, stated in its opening words. This reminder is not superfluous. Even "the redeemed of the Lord" (2) are prone to forget the Redeemer's "wonderful works to the sons of men." (8)

107:33 *Rivers into a desert.* There are reasons for giving thanks to God besides the one just mentioned in vv. 4-32. The restoration of Israel was but one demonstration of the exercise of power by Him who can harness the forces of nature to do His bidding (33-38). Furthermore, as He shaped the fate of nations at that time, so He can be trusted to direct all the doings of men for the benefit of the "upright" (39-42). The God of creation and history is described in language containing allusions to mighty deeds of the past as well as to promises of blessings still to come. For rivers turned into a desert see 74:15; Ex 14:21; Jos 3:16 f.; for fruitful land changed to salty waste see Gn 13:10; 14:3; 19:24; Dt 29:22 ff.; Jer 17:5 f.; for vv. 36-38 see Dt 7:13; Is 41:18-20; 49:19 f.; 65:21; Eze 36:30, 33-36.

107:41 *The needy.* Cf. 1 Sm 2:8; Ps 113:7-9; Jb 21:8-11.

107:43 *Wise.* As sin is folly (17), so "the fear of the Lord is the beginning of wisdom." (111:10; Pr 9:10; cf. Ps 64:9; Hos 14:9)

Psalm 108

108:1-13 This psalm combines extracts from Ps 57 and Ps 60, both ascribed to David. Vv. 1-5 repeat 57:7-11; vv. 6-13 duplicate 60:5-12. It is not clear what occasioned the combination of these two components, the one praising the goodness of God (1-5), the other pleading that He keep His promise to help (6-13). See the notes on these sections in their earlier settings.

Psalm 109

109:1-31 This *Psalm of David* arises out of the same kind of desperate situation from which relief is sought in Pss 35 and 69. The suppliant faces court proceedings. If convicted of the hideous crimes with which he is charged, he loses everything: reputation, possessions, family, even life itself. Fearing the worst, he frantically appeals for vindication to Him who "judges the world with righteousness" (9:8). He does so with a good conscience and full confidence because in charging him his accusers speak *with lying tongues.* All this is the more reprehensible and perverse because he showed them every kindness in the past (1-5). In order to dispel any possible doubt of their vicious intent he puts their indictment of him (6-20) on record from their own *wicked and deceitful mouths* (2). The prospect of being found guilty of these dastardly misdeeds and of suffering the penalties imposed by the law on the offender made a physical and mental wreck of him. He knows no other defense than to pray for divine intervention in his behalf (21-25). God's verdict, declaring him innocent, at the same time will let his *assailants be put to shame* (26-29). As he prays, he is so certain of being heard that he pledges to *give great thanks to the Lord* after being delivered. (30-31)

109:1 *God of my praise.* He is certain that the God whom he praised for blessings in the past will come to his rescue also in this deadly threat to his existence (Jer 17:14). For the plea *Be not silent* see 83:1 note; 7:6 note.

109:4 *Prayer for them.* By their "words of hate" they are returning "evil for good" because he spoke words of prayer in their behalf (cf. 35:12, 13 notes). Jeremiah invoked God's punishment on people who "dug a pit" for his life even though he sought to shield them from divine wrath by interceding for them. (Jer 18:20-23)

109:6 *Appoint.* Though not formally introduced as direct speech, this verse and the following ones are summarized in v. 20 as representing the words of "those who speak evil against" the defendant. Supplied with quotation marks and the introductory word "saying" (as, e.g., in 2:2 f.; 52:6 f.), they repeat the charges brought against the defendant and attach to them the punishment which awaits him upon conviction.

An accuser. A judicial term similar to our "prosecutor." He stood at the right hand of the defendant in court (cf. RSV note) in order to "accuse," i.e., prosecute him (6, 20, 29). The Hebrew is transliterated "Satan" when man's accuser before God is meant. (Jb 1:6 second note; Zch 3:1)

109:8 *Goods.* The Hebrew word almost without exception has the meaning "appointed charge" or "office," so translated by the Septuagint and quoted by Peter with reference to Judas. (Acts 1:20)

109:16 *Pursued.* Instead of using his position to promote the welfare of *the poor and needy* as Job did (Jb 29:11-17), he enriched himself by exploiting them. Punishment for oppression of the helpless was indeed severe. (Ex 22:23 ff.)

109:20 *May this be the reward.* This verse is best taken as summarizing the bill of particulars offered in court by the accusers. So understood, it should be translated: "This is the work of my accusers." They assert arrogantly and hypocritically that their efforts will be crowned with success because they have support and sanction *from the Lord.*

109:21 *But thou.* After describing the horrible fate awaiting him if he is convicted (6-19), the harried defendant asks God to clear him of the trumped-up charges for His *name's sake.* (Nm 14:13 note; Ex 32:11 note; Ps 79:9, 10 note)

109:22 *Poor and needy.* He finds himself sharing the lot of those whom he supposedly "pursued . . . to their death." (16)

109:23 *Like a locust.* He has no firmer hold on life than an insect has on a garment. By a flick of the finger it can be *shaken off.* His enemies apparently point to his broken health as proof "from the Lord" (20) that he is guilty as charged. Job's friends insisted that his sickness was divine punishment for serious, unconfessed crimes.

109:28 *Let them curse.* What they said is recorded in vv. 6-19. It will be offset when God blesses His *servant* by vindicating him. The second line of this verse can be translated: "When they rise up, let them be put to shame, but let thy servant rejoice."

109:29 *Be clothed with dishonor.* If God proves the accused innocent, His intervention cannot but expose the wickedness of the accusers to their shame and disgrace. For the question whether it is justifiable to invoke such a result on an enemy even though "indeed God deems it just to repay with affliction those who afflict you" (2 Th 1:6) see 58:10 notes; 35:4 note.

Psalm 110

110:1-7 Quoting from it no less than 17 times, the New Testament bears unequivocal testimony to the prophetic intent of this psalm and to its fulfillment in that Son of David whom God "raised . . . from the dead and made . . . sit at his right hand in the heavenly places" (Eph 1:20). Jesus Himself challenged His enemies to disprove the fact that "in the Book of Psalms" "David, inspired by the Spirit," identified David's Son and David's Lord (Mt 22:43 f.; Mk 12:36; Lk 20:42; see also Mt 26:64; Acts 2:34; 7:55; Ro 8:34; Cl 3:1; Heb 1:13; 8:1; 10:12; 1 Ptr 3:22). The cited passages and others let the bright rays of Messianic glory break through the preliminary forms of ancient kingship and priesthood. In seven mysteriously sublime verses the psalm hails the coming of (1) a king from the house of David to whom God will entrust worldwide sovereignty (1-3; 2 Sm 7); (2) a mediator who though *after the order of Melchizedek* yet will be unlike that priest-king of old in that he will be *a priest for ever* (4-7). Each function is assigned by a solemn declaration of the Lord (vv. 1 and 4), followed by a brief description of the circumstances that will prevail (2 f. and 5-7). See Ps 2 notes for the Davidic kingship as a type of the Messiah.

110:1 *The Lord says.* For the name *the Lord,* also in vv. 2 and 4, see Ex 6:3 note. What the Lord *says* is expressed in the original by the noun "oracle," i.e., a divine communication or revelation which the prophets transmit to their hearers with the introduction: "Thus says the Lord." (2 Ch 34:26)

My Lord. The Hebrew noun denotes a respected or superior person. It is used as a title in addressing kings and other dignitaries (Gn 19:2; 23:6; 1 Sm 22:12; 2 Sm 13:32). The king *to* or "concerning" whom this prophetic oracle speaks is by that very word of God made to be the "King of kings and Lord of lords" (Rv 19:16).

His elevation to the *right hand* of power is to coincide with the defeat of enemies, reduced to serve as a *footstool* (Jos 10:24; 1 K 5:3). For the fulfillment of this promise see Acts 2:25; 1 Co 15:25; Heb 1:13; 10:13.

110:3 *Upon the holy mountains.* The words of the traditional Hebrew text "in holy array" (RSV note) occur also in 29:2 note; 96:9. Here they indicate that the people who *offer themselves freely* (lit. "are freewill offerings") do so with decorum befitting "a kingdom of priests." (Ex 19:6 first note)

Your youth. The young volunteers constituting the royal *host* are described in highly figurative language. They are as numerous as myriads of dewdrops to which the dawn gives birth; as each morning produces a fresh supply of dew, so there always will be replacements on hand to fill the ranks of the royal army.

110:4 *Sworn.* For solemn pledges given to David see 89:3 f., 35; 132:11. For *Melchizedek* see Gn 14:18 note; Heb 5:6, 10; 7:1 ff.

110:5 *At your right hand.* The performance of royal and priestly functions will not be frustrated by opposing forces of evil. God will provide the power to *shatter kings on the day of his wrath.* For other references to God's right hand see 18:35; 20:6; 118:15 f.; 139:10.

110:6 *Chiefs.* Lit. "head" (RSV note), a singular noun used collectively of hostile leaders as in 68:21.

110:7 *He will drink.* What the Lord does at the King's right hand in executing judgment "over the wide earth" merges into an accomplishment by the King. The latter is like a warrior who in pursuit of the enemy stops at a brook to refresh himself only to drive on and to *lift up his head* in complete victory (3:3; 27:6). Jesus receives "authority to execute judgment" but also acts as sovereign Judge. (Jn 5:27; Mt 25:31 ff.; Acts 10:42)

Psalm 111

111:1-10 Ps 111 and Ps 112 constitute two movements in an oratorio of high praise. The first of these sings of perennial streams of blessing, physical and spiritual, which flow from the past into the lives of each new generation; the subject of the second aria is the blessedness of "the man who fears the Lord" (112:1). Both psalms are cast in the mold of an acrostic poem, a feature recognizable only in the Hebrew text. After an introductory "hallelujah" (104:35 second note) the first words of all lines begin with letters in the sequence of the Hebrew alphabet (see introd. notes to Ps 9). In Ps 111 the poet bursts into song *in the company of the upright* at the thought of *the works of the Lord.* As they are *studied* and *remembered,* the reasons for rejoicing multiply. They are not only *great* and *wonderful* in themselves; they also reveal God's *honor and majesty,* His nature to be *gracious and merciful . . . ever mindful of his covenant . . . faithful and just.* What He did has meaning for all times. Because He *sent redemption to his people* and *commanded his covenant,* His *precepts* too were meant to be *established forever.* Therefore living in *the fear of the Lord* is not only an opportunity to *give thanks to the Lord* (1) for His *wonderful works* (4) of redemption, it is also *wisdom* of the highest order, providing *all those who practice it* with true and abiding blessings, as the next psalm will declare.

111:1 *Whole heart.* To "love the Lord . . . with all your heart" (Dt 6:5) cannot but fill it with an irresistible compulsion to *give thanks to the Lord.*

111:4 *Remembered.* Israel's great festivals were to be memorials of the wonderful works God did in making the former slaves of Egypt His "own possession" and at the same time to make all succeeding celebrants aware of their continuing status as members of the covenant people. (Ex 19:5 f.; 12:14; 13:8; 23:14-17)

111:5 *Food.* The psalmist is thinking primarily of the miraculous feeding during Israel's wandering in the desert.

111:6 *The heritage of the nations.* Canaan was occupied by many nations before Israel took possession of it. (Ex 3:8, 17)

111:9 *Redemption.* The descendants of the patriarchs were not a self-made people. Nor did they deserve deliverance from the Egyptian house of bondage and a *covenant* relationship with God. For the covenant concept see the introductory notes to the Book of Exodus, "Content."

111:10 *The fear of the Lord.* To act out of reverence and awe of God's "wonderful works" (4) by abstaining from what He abhors and doing what pleases Him must be the axiomatic starting point if human existence is to be meaningful, satisfying, rewarding. Any philosophy of life which does not have its *beginning* in such a relationship to God is not *wisdom* but folly of follies. (Pr 9:10; 1:7).

Psalm 112

112:1-10 This psalm is a sequel to the preceding one (see the introductory notes there). The man who takes "pleasure in" "the wonderful works" of God's "redemption" and "covenant" faithfulness (111:2, 4, 5, 9) also *greatly delights in* [*doing*] *his commandments* (112:1). As "the fear of the Lord" (111:10 note) motivates and controls his thinking and doing, he cannot but sing another "hallelujah" in view of the streams of bliss flowing into his life.

112:1 *Blessed.* The first word in the Book of Psalms (Ps 1 introductory note). By contrast, the wrath of God awaits those for whom "the Word of the Lord is . . . an object of scorn" (Jer 6:10 ff.).—The beatitude pronounced on *the man who fears the Lord* is elaborated in the remainder of the psalm. The list of blessings is not exhaustive. Nor is it to be regarded as a blanket guarantee that God will not let "the upright" be saddened by "evil tidings" of disaster (7) or let "the righteous" (6) sit bewildered "in the darkness" of grief and pain (4). For the role of suffering in such instances see the Book of Job and Pss 37 and 73.

112:3 *His righteousness.* Because God's "righteousness endures for ever" (111:3), His saint likewise is "firm" (7) and "steady" (8) in doing what is right.

112:4 *The Lord.* An unnecessary addition to the text (cf. RSV note). The godly person attempts to be Godlike: *gracious, merciful, and righteous* (cf. Ex 34:6). And in the measure that he succeeds, he channels divine blessings to his fellowmen. Because the God-fearing man is the subject of discussion throughout the psalm, the verse should read: "He sends forth bright beams in darkness, [acting as] a light to the upright [because] he is, etc."

112:8 *Sees his desire.* Cf. 92:11 note.

112:9 *Horn.* Cf. 75:4-5 note.

Psalm 113

113:1-9 Echoing Hannah's song of praise and anticipating Mary's Magnificat (1 Sm 2:1-10; Lk 1:46-55), this psalm calls on "servants of the Lord" at all times and in all places to laud and magnify His glorious name (1-4). No one is excluded. No one should think that the Lord, enthroned *above the heavens* in transcendent majesty, is too preoccupied to be concerned with petty problems of human existence. On the contrary, it is precisely "those of low degree" (Lk 1:52), the little people, the underprivileged, those without prospects of fulfillment in life, who have every reason to call the sublime Ruler of *the heavens and the earth* (6) *our God* (5). Because "the high and lofty One who inhabits eternity" (Is 57:15) stoops down to raise *the poor from the dust* and to let a hitherto barren life produce supreme satisfactions, the summons to *praise the Lord* should meet with wholehearted response (5-9)—In the course of time Pss 113—118 were combined into a liturgical unit called the "Hallel," i.e., the song of praise prescribed for the celebration of Israel's great festivals. In observing Passover, Pss 113—114 are sung before the meal and Pss 115—118 after eating it. No doubt they constituted the "hymn" sung by Jesus and the disciples at the occasion of His last Passover. (Mt 26:30)

113:1 *The name of the Lord.* For the comprehensive meaning of this phrase, repeated in the two following verses, see 8:1 note; Ex 6:3 note.

113:7 *Raises the poor.* Vv. 7 and 8 are taken almost verbatim from Hannah's hymn. (1 Sm 2:8)

113:9 *Barren.* A woman who like Hannah was unable to bear children considered herself doomed to one of life's most cruel disappointments. (1 Sm 1:2, 10)

Psalm 114

114:1-8 This brief "Hallel" psalm (see introductory note to Ps 113) cites memorable events in Israel's history as evidence that the Lord is not lacking in power to lift "the needy [nation] from the ash heap" of slavery and to let "the barren woman," destined to national extinction in "the house of bondage," become "the joyous mother of children" (113:7, 9; Ex 20:2; Is 54:1). In sprightly language of poetic imagery the poet recalls (1) how the Creator of the universe marshaled the forces of nature to give the children of Israel dry passage through the Red Sea and the Jordan (3; Jos 4:23); (2) how Mt Sinai "quaked greatly" at the giving of the Law (4; Ex 19:18); (3) how God brought "water out of the flinty rock" to keep the desert travelers from dying of thirst. (8; Dt 8:15; Ex 17:6; Nm 20:11)

114:2 *His sanctuary.* From degradation in "the dust" (13:7) of servitude to a foreign master God raised the chosen nation, later divided into *Judah* and *Israel,* to be "a kingdom of priests and a holy nation," the hallowed "throne" and center of His *dominion* (Ex 19:6; Jer 3:17).—What God did to redeem the descendants of Abraham was a part of His plan to save all mankind from the slavery of sin and the tyranny of Satan.

Psalm 115

115:1-18 "Wonderful works" (111:4) such as God did in the past (Ps 114), not to reward good behavior but solely to *give glory* to *His name,* give a later generation of Israelites the courage and confidence to ask Him to act also in their behalf. They too make no claim to merit; they too can hope to persuade God to intervene only because His honor is at stake. After their return from the Babylonian captivity the people, chosen to bring blessings to the ends of the earth, remained the butt of ridicule among *the nations.* The latter attributed the degradation, still dogging the returned exiles, to the impotence of the Lord to make good His promises of future splendor. Sorely tried by the apparent truth of such mockery, the disconsolate community is directed to appeal to God to vindicate His honor *for the sake of* His *steadfast love and . . . faithfulness* (1-2). This bold maneuver of faith is based on the conviction that the true and living God *does whatever he pleases,* whereas *all who trust in* power ascribed to *idols* are doomed to disillusionment and disgrace (3-8). However, because as yet nothing has happened to change the distressing situation, three calls to *trust in the Lord* are issued, each bolstered by the assurance that He will not fail to be *their help and their shield* (9-11). Such confidence is not misplaced. *The Lord . . . will bless* those who trust Him because He *has been mindful of* them in the past (12-13). With His benediction resting on them (14-15), they have every reason to *bless the Lord from this time forth and for evermore* (16-18).—Jesus summed up this psalm for His followers in the words: "Fear not, little flock, for it is your Father's good pleasure to give you the kingdom." (Lk 12:32)

115:2 *Where is their God?* Cf. Eze 36:6, 20; Ps 42:10; 79:10 note.

115:4 *Idols.* For similar satires on the folly of worshiping false gods see Dt 4:28; Is 44:9-20; Jer 10:1-16.

115:9 *O Israel.* The summons to "trust in the Lord" alternating with the identical reason for doing so (9-11) lends itself to antiphonal recitation or singing. Cf. Ez 3:10 f.; Neh 12:40; also Ps 118:2-4; 135:19 f.

115:11 *You who fear the Lord.* This epithet is applied to those who wholeheartedly commit themselves to God's power and love, whether of Israelite or Gentile extraction (Ex 18:21; Ps 31:19; 40:3; 60:4; 66:16; 1 K 8:41-43; Ml 3:16; Acts 10:1 f.; Rv 19:5). Trust and fear are not incompatible ingredients in a believer's relationship to God.

115:17 *The dead.* Cf. 6:5 note; 88:5 note.

Psalm 116

116:1-19 Though this psalm records what an individual said and did to thank God for snatching him from the jaws of death, it is not inappropriately included in the "Hallel" psalms, sung at the Passover celebration (cf. Ps 113 introductory note) to commemorate a national deliverance. Furthermore, the psalmist is so occupied with praising God that he does not specify how he was brought to the brink of disaster or what God did to spare his life. Consequently anyone who for any reason had a close brush with the grim reaper can pray this psalm as fervently as its ancient author. The latter did not calmly compose a well-organized dissertation moving logically from point to point. Apparently his experience was so recent and so frightful that he has not regained *rest* of mind (7). There still is a tremor in his voice and some disarray in the sequence of his presentation. He is convinced that the Lord will accept his hallelujah even though he lacks poetic originality and must interlard his song with snatches from hymns composed by other sacred singers.

116:1 *I love.* He does not presume to ask why God let him suffer *distress and anguish* (3). His first impulse is to declare that as a result of his ordeal he is closely knit to the Lord with ties of love. (5:11; 18:1; 40:16)

116:3 *Snares of death.* Vv. 3 and 4 are an echo of 18:4-6.

116:6 *Simple.* Cf. 19:7 second note.

116:10 *Kept my faith.* He said nothing prompted by unbelief. Quoting the first line of this verse from the Septuagint translation, Paul broadens its scope to include all speaking impelled by faith. (2 Co 4:13)

116:11 *Vain hope.* He lost faith in men because they proved to be liars (12:2; 78:36). Perhaps their lies were responsible for the author's plight.

116:13 *Cup of salvation.* The wicked drink from God's cup of wrath (cf. 11:6 note). Because God filled the writer's cup with a blessing, he lifts this symbol of his redemption on high for all to see, i.e., he wants all to hear what God has done for him. For the use of wine in the worship rites of the OT see Ex 29:40 f.; Nm 28:7.

116:15 *Precious.* The life of *his saints* (4:3 note) is a matter of great concern to the Lord. (72:14 note)

116:16 *Son of thy handmaid.* Cf. 86:16 note.

Psalm 117

117:1-2 Confined to two verses, this shortest of all psalms has an unlimited range of vision. It dares to issue a summons to an assembly composed of *all nations* and *all peoples.* They are to *praise the Lord* for blessings available to them because in *steadfast love* and *faithfulness* He kept His promises to the covenant nation. St. Paul quotes this psalm together with other passages from the OT to proclaim that God's plan of universal salvation became a full reality in Christ Jesus. (Ro 15:9-12; see also Gl 3:28; Cl 3:11)

Psalm 118

118:1-29 The last of the "Hallel" psalms (cf. 113 introductory note), it very likely concluded also the "hymn" sung by Jesus and the disciples in observing His last Passover (Mt 26:30). The author gives his song of thanksgiving the framework of a high festival. In spirit he joins a pilgrim throng, greeted by an invitational chant to *give thanks to the Lord* (1-4). Obeying the summons, he emerges from the group to assume the role of its soloist. He sings his own thanks to God. But he does so in such a way as to allow fellow worshipers to think of their personal deliverance as well as of their gracious preservation as members of the chosen people (5-18; for another such song in the first person see Is 12:1 f.). As the author visualizes the approach of the festive group to the temple, he requests that its gates be opened, because he is aware that only *the righteous* can expect to enter the Lord's presence to thank Him for His *salvation* (19-21). At this point the author again joins the worshipers, now assembled in the court of the temple. He sings along with them as they rejoice over *the Lord's doing* and ask to be *blessed . . . in the name of the Lord* (22-27). In closing the psalmist vows to continue to *give thanks to* God in response to the well-known litany of praise which in v. 1 served as the introit to his service of thanksgiving. (28-29; 136:1, 26; Jer 33:11)

118:4 *Fear the Lord.* Cf. 115:11 note.

118:7 *Look in triumph.* Cf. 92:11 note.

118:8 *Confidence in man.* Cf. 40:4; 56:4, 11; Jer 17:5-8; Heb 13:6.

118:10 *All nations.* Spokesman for a festive gathering, the psalmist moves his and their deliverance into the perspective of Israel's victory over national enemies.

118:12 *Blazed.* The Hebrew "were extinguished" (RSV note) makes sense. The assault by the enemy was like a brushfire which flared only for a brief moment.

118:13 *I was pushed.* If the Hebrew (RSV note) is retained, "thou" refers to the Lord who "chastened" (18) His people *hard* (cf. Dt 8:2-5; Is 54:8) or to the hostile nations who are addressed as the collective threat to Israel's existence.

118:19 *Gates of righteousness.* In the temple God deigned to be present to hear Israel's prayer and to execute righteous judgment. (20:2 note; cf. Jer 31:23; also Pss 15 and 24)

118:22 *Head of the corner.* Either the cornerstone in a foundation, which supports and binds together the walls of a building (Is 28:16), or the keystone of an arch, without which the structure collapses. The "righteous" in Israel were despised by the wicked; Israel as a nation was the laughingstock of its neighbors. What God did to honor those whom *the builders rejected* was prophetic of the exaltation of Jesus Christ, "despised and rejected by men" (Is 53:3), to be "the head of . . . the church" and "of all rule and authority." (Cl 1:18; 2:10; Mt 21:42; Mk 12:10; Lk 20:17; Acts 4:11; Eph 2:20; 1 Ptr 2:7)

118:25 *Save us.* This cry in its transliterated form "Hosanna!" was taken up by the multitudes to hail Jesus as the Messiah as He entered Jerusalem on Palm Sunday. (Mt 21:9; Mk 11:9; cf. Lk 13:35; 19:38)

118:27 *Bind.* The exact meaning of this liturgical directive escapes us. Apparently it was a call to the worshipers to leap and dance about the altar waving palm branches (cf. Lv 23:40). *The horns of the altar* were vertical projections on its corners. (Ex 29:12; Lv 4:7, 18)

Psalm 119

119:1-176 The length of this psalm results from the author's grandiose design for his poem. He set himself the task of producing an acrostic on a grand scale (see introduction to the Psalms, "Poetry"). Poets using this structural device usually were content to have the first word of every verse begin with a letter in alphabetic sequence (e.g., Ps 34). In this psalm eight successive verses begin with the same letter. The 22 letters of the Hebrew alphabet yield a total of 176 verses. In addition, the author determined to have each verse of the 22 sections contain a noun denoting God's means of communicating with man, such as law, word, precept, testimony, etc. In endless variations the author proclaims the blessing of "those who hear the word of God and keep it" (Lk 11:28). The heaping of verse on verse is to convey the magnitude of God's condescension in revealing to His estranged creature what he needs to know to be reunited with his Maker. The reiteration of words and phrases simulates the language of a lover who does not tire to intone the same "I love you" into the ear of his beloved.

The hard and fast mold into which the author cast his poem restricts him in the use of features and conventions associated with poetry. Parallelism, the basic characteristic of Hebrew verse, plays a minor role. Figurative language and vivid imagery give way to repetitious formalism. It is difficult to discern a progression of thought from one section to the next. Even within an alphabetic unit, the order of the verses can be reversed without seriously changing their thrust. Rules of rhetoric and canons of poetry can be dispensed with if only all lines, like so many arrows, point directly to the object of contemplation: the incomprehensible and unspeakable goodness of divine revelation. In his own way the unknown psalmist has created a magnificent piece of devotional literature. All who share his gratitude to God will be delighted to sing along with him. It also should help to rekindle the dying embers of devotion in the hearts of those whose love for the Word of God is in danger of growing cold.

Of the more than 12 synonyms used to designate what God made known to man, the term "law," occurring 25 times, needs clarification. It is not antithetic to "Gospel" but embraces all manner of instruction given for man's benefit (cf. 1:2 note). But even when reference is made to "precepts" and "statutes," as these are found written in the law of Moses, such prescribed responses to God's goodness are not regarded as a burdensome yoke. To know what pleases God and to do it is the author's greatest delight. God's Word in its written form is not a dead letter but a life-giving dynamic. It sustains the writer when ridiculed and persecuted. It supplies him with everything to make life meaningful and satisfying.

119:1 *Blessed.* In the first three verses the author pronounces a benediction on all who share his attitude to *the law of the Lord* which he describes in the remainder of the psalm.

119:37 *Vanities.* Cf. 24:4 second note; 31:6 note.

119:51 *Do not turn away.* Here and in v. 55 the psalmist does not claim moral perfection. Different from the wicked who flout the Law, he is determined to treasure and obey it. In his attempt to keep it he is dependent on God, who must "graciously teach" him if he is to avoid "false ways" (29, 26, 73).

119:83 *A wineskin.* Skins of animals were used as containers of liquids. Such a "bottle" (AV) could become brittle and shriveled if left hanging *in the smoke* of the hearth-fire for a longer period of time.

119:97 *Meditation.* Cf. 1:2 second note.

119:109 *My life.* In spite of his godliness, the writer must cope with threats to his life.

119:130 *Unfolding.* Literally: "door" or "opening." Through God's *words* light enters man's dark world of confusion and frustration.

119:132 *As is thy wont.* Lit. "according to judgment." God is to turn to him according to His decision, announced in His word, to bless those who love His *name.*

Psalm 120

120:1-7 The next 15 psalms (120—134) bear the superscription *A Song of Ascents* (AV: "Degrees"). Because the Hebrew word translated *ascents* is used frequently to denote the steps of a staircase, Rabbinic tradition took the word to refer to the risers said to have led from the Court of the Women to the Court of the Israelites. The Levites were stationed on these steps as they provided vocal and instrumental music for the great festivals. According to a widely accepted explanation, the Songs of Ascents constituted a special little hymnbook, consisting of various kinds of short psalms (only Ps 132 has more than 9 verses) which pilgrims found appropriate to sing as they were "going up to Jerusalem" to observe the three high feasts (Mt 20:18; Jn 7:8). However, on what basis these psalms were selected is no longer clear. Some of them do not appear to be particularly apropos.

Ps 120, which heads the list, is a case in point. Here an individual gratefully testifies that the Lord answered his prayer when he was *in . . . distress* (1). The words he addressed to God at the time (2) and to his tormentors (3-4) indicate that he almost succumbed to the *sharp arrows* of slander. He shudders as he thinks back to his *dwelling among those who hate peace,* whereas he is all *for peace.* (5-7)

120:1 *I cry.* The situation described in the psalm requires the first verse to be translated: "I cried . . . and you answered."

120:3 *What more.* The sufferer invokes retribution on his persecutors "who whet their tongues like swords" (64:3) with the oath formula: "The Lord do so to me and more also." (Ru 1:17 note; 1 Sm 3:17)

120:4 *Broom tree.* A bush reaching a height of about 12 feet. It furnished intense heat.

120:5 *Meshech . . . Kedar.* Meshech was a son of Japheth, and Kedar of Ishmael (Gn 10:2; 25:13). Their descendants occupied areas in Asia Minor and the Arabian desert respectively. The author uses their names metaphorically, suggesting that his enemies acted like the most barbaric heathen.

Psalm 121

121:1-8 Many wayfarers on their pilgrimage to the heavenly Jerusalem have turned to this *Song of Ascents* (cf. Ps 120 introductory note) to find strength and courage to march on even though the road ahead seemed to lead straight into dark ravines or insurmountable barriers. On the way to and from Jerusalem the ancient traveler could see the road beset by *hills* or "mountains," as the Hebrew word is translated in 125:2; 133:3. He pauses for a moment to consider from whence he can expect help to provide safe passage through them. But then all fear vanishes as he commits himself without reservation or doubt into the strong hands of *the Lord, who made heaven and earth* (1-2; 124:8; 134:3; 146:5 f.). He goes on to assure himself that (1) the "Shepherd of Israel" (80:1) *will neither slumber nor sleep,* so that each individual is safe in His keeping whether *by day* or *by night* (3-6); (2) heavenly guardians are deployed along the way, ready and able to *keep . . . all evil* away from the beginning to the end of the journey. (7-8)

121:5 *Shade.* For its benefits see 91:1 note.

121:6 *Moon.* Certain maladies were thought to be caused by the moon. Without passing judgment on this belief, the psalm proclaims that God, ever watchful and all-powerful, affords protection against all manner of afflictions, regardless of their origin or cause.

121:8 *Going out . . . coming in.* Cf. Dt 28:6; 31:2.

Psalm 122

122:1-9 This *Song of Ascents* (cf. Ps 120) can help to prevent our meeting together for worship (Heb 10:25) from degenerating into a hollow formality or a wearisome drudgery. The attitude exhibited in this psalm *of David* reveals what a thrilling experience and sacred privilege it was for an attendant at one of the great festivals of Israel to *go to the house of the Lord* (1-2). Within the holy city he sensed the elation of communion with *the tribes of the Lord* as they joined *to give thanks to the name of the Lord* (3-5). Grateful to God for establishing *Jerusalem* to be His dwelling place, he prays that its holy precincts be preserved for all who seek *the peace* it affords. (6-9)

122:4 *Decreed for Israel.* Cf. Ex 23:17; 34:23; Dt 16:16. For *the name of the Lord* see 8:1 note; Ex 6:3 note.

122:6 *Peace of Jerusalem.* In the original this phrase represents a word-play. In Hebrew the word for peace and the last part of the city's name, "Salem," are composed of the same consonants. Cf. 76:2 note. For Jerusalem of old as a shadow of things to come see Heb 12:22 ff.

122:9 *The house of the Lord.* The psalm ends where it begins (v. 1), in the place where God's honor dwells.

Psalm 123

123:1-4 This *Song of Ascents* would be appropriate on the lips of a pilgrim to Jerusalem (cf. Ps 120) who relies on God, *enthroned in the heavens* (1; 2:4; 11:4; 115:3, 16), to vindicate His "saints" (97:10) who look expectantly to Him to put an end to the *contempt* and *scorn* heaped on them for a long time by their prosperous and proud neighbors. (3-4; see also 17:10 f.; 35:19-26; 44:13-16; 69:8; 102:3-11; Neh 2:19; 4:1 ff.)

Psalm 124

124:1-8 Pilgrims on their way to Jerusalem found in this *Song of Ascents* (Ps 120) a fitting expression of their festive mood. They sang praises to God for averting a catastrophe which threatened their national existence. Though the occasion for celebration is not identifiable, the description of their rescue is so graphic as to give the impression of a recent event. As if it happened only yesterday, the onslaught of the enemy is recalled. It would have *swallowed up* and *swept . . . away* Israel if the Lord had not come to their aid (1-5). Freed at the last moment like *a bird from the snare of the fowlers,* grateful Israel blesses *the name of the Lord,* at the same time entrusting its future to Him *who made heaven and earth.* (6-8)

124:1 *Now.* The Hebrew word does not denote time but is a particle expressing urgency. For other exhortations to praise see 118:2; 129:1. For a similar acknowledgement of failure if the Lord had not been on the *side* of an embattled pilgrim see Gn 31:42; also Ps 94:17; 119:92; 124:2.

124:2 *Men.* Defiance of men, made of the dust of the ground, is based on trust in the Creator of "heaven and earth." (8; 56:11; 118:6)

124:8 *Our help.* This verse has a prominent place in the worship of the Israel of the new covenant, beset by hateful enemies (Mt 24:9; Jn 15:18 ff.; 16:1 ff.) It too has the Lord "on our side." (Mt 10:31; 16:18; 18:20; 28:20)

Psalm 125

125:1-5 Singing this *Song of Ascents* (cf. Ps 120), pilgrims on the way to Jerusalem fortified their faith in God's unfailing protection of *those who trust in the Lord* (1) and who express their allegiance to Him by being *good* and *upright in their hearts* (4). Even when *evildoers* take control, tempting also *the righteous . . . to do wrong, the scepter of wickedness* (3) will hold sway only as long as He permits. Hence *his people* (2) can pray confidently for the overthrow of those on *crooked ways* so that there may be *peace . . . in Israel.* (5)

125:1 *Like Mount Zion.* As "the city of God . . . shall not be moved" though "nations rage" against it (46:4-6), so the bulwarks of protection with which God surrounds His embattled people are as unmovable as *the mountains . . . round about Jerusalem.* (2; 78:69; 87:5; see also Zch 2:5; 2 K 6:17)

125:3 *The land allotted.* Cf. Nm 26:55; Jos 18—19.

125:5 *Lead away.* Cf. 104:35 note; Pr 2:21.—God's people of the new covenant have the assurance of *peace* to the end of time even though "the powers of death" assail His church. (Mt 16:18; 28:18-20; Gl 6:16)

Psalm 126

126:1-6 For the situation reflected in this *Song of Ascents* (cf. Ps 120) see the notes on Ps 85. The *shouts of joy* and the peals of *laughter* which rang out when God delivered His people from extinction in the Babylonian exile gave way to *tears* and *weeping* after they returned to their homeland. There unexpected hardships and disillusioning suffering tested their faith in God's promise to restore *the fortunes of Zion* (1-3). Resorting to prayer for relief, they comforted themselves with the assurance that in His wisdom God may let His children *sow in tears* in order that at harvest time they may *come home with shouts of joy* (4-6).—Travelers beset by "many tribulations" on the way to "the kingdom of God" have found in this psalm the courage and strength to continue their pilgrimage. (Acts 14:22; cf. Ps 30:5; Lk 6:21; Rv 7:17)

126:1 *Dream.* What God did seemed too good to be true.

126:2 *They said.* The nations no longer said: "Where is their God?" (79:10 note; 115:2 note)

126:4 *Negeb.* Arid areas in southern Palestine. As dry stream beds there suddenly can become raging torrents, so the Lord is to let a flood of blessings pour into the desert of Israel's hopes.

Psalm 127

127:1-5 In this *Song of Ascents* (cf. Ps 120) pilgrims to Jerusalem call to mind the blessings God bestows on their homelife. They acknowledge gratefully that without His benediction their efforts to provide the necessities of life would be *in vain.* They are dependent on Him if they are to succeed in building a house, protecting their city, toiling for daily bread (1-2). The children in their homes too are His gifts, which He can grant or withhold. (3-5; cf. Gn 20:17 f.; 30:1 f.)

127:1 *The house.* The Hebrew text has "a house," i.e., any house and not necessarily the house of the Lord as the phrase "Of Solomon" in the superscription would lead one to believe.

127:2 *For he gives.* A better translation of the last line of this verse is as follows: "So [much as is adequate] He gives His beloved while he sleeps." This is not an endorsement of sloth and idleness. It emphasizes that God's blessings come so silently, so unobtrusively, so graciously as if man does nothing but sleep.

127:3 *Heritage from the Lord.* Children, like so many "arrows" in a warrior's "quiver," made for security and prosperity in Old Testament society.

127:5 *In the gate.* Cf. 69:12 note; Jb 5:4 note.

Psalm 128

128:1-6 In this *Song of Ascents* (cf. Ps 120) the pilgrims remind one another, as they did in Ps 127, that domestic bliss and the success of their daily labors are gifts of God's goodness. Two thoughts are given prominence: (1) Everyone who *fears* Him and *walks in his ways* can rely on His promise to make him *happy* (1-4; see 1:1 note); (2) individual well-being and its permanence require that God, who dwells in *Zion*, grant national *prosperity* and give *peace* to all of *Israel.* (5-6; 125:5)

128:1 *Fears the Lord.* Cf. 111:10 note; 112:1 note.

128:2 *It shall be well.* In His wisdom, God makes exceptions to the rule. Cf. Pss 37, 73; the Book of Job.

Psalm 129

129:1-8 As is the case in Ps 124, Israel here (1) looks back gratefully on its deliverance from wicked and heartless tormentors (1-4) and then (2) looks forward expectantly to God's continued intervention so that the designs of *all who hate Zion* will wither like plants in shallow soil. (5-8)

129:1 *From my youth.* From Israel's earliest beginnings as a nation. (Hos 2:15; 11:1)

129:6 *On the housetops.* Plants growing in a thin layer of dirt on the flat roof of a house are "blighted" by the hot sun and die without bearing fruit. (Is 37:27; Ps 37:2)

129:8 *The blessing of the Lord.* Reapers in the harvest fields greeted one another with a blessing. (Ru 2:4)

Psalm 130

130:1-8 Pilgrims going up to Jerusalem to observe a festival take occasion in this *Song of Ascents* (cf. Ps 120) to (1) remind themselves how blessed they are that God hears their prayers for *forgiveness,* thereby lifting them out of the abyss and misery of their separation from Him into the sunlight and bliss of His favor (1-4); (2) encourage one another to continue to *hope in the Lord* to supply the most precious gift of His *steadfast love: redemption* from the curse of their *iniquities* (5-8).—Ps 130 is the sixth of the

"Seven Penitential Psalms," for which see Ps 6:1-10.

130:1 *Depths.* Sin hurls man into a chasm from which he cannot by his "own reason or strength" (Luther) climb back to God and life. If divine mercy does not bridge the gap, sinners remain in deep trouble: haunting fears of retribution, torments of an aroused conscience, physical and mental suffering as a foretaste of an eternal suffering in outer darkness. (40:2; 69:2, 14; Is 59:2)

130:3 *Mark iniquities.* If God would not erase them from our record, we would be unable to *stand* trial in His tribunal of justice.

130:4 *Be feared.* God's forgiving mercy is not a cheap commodity. If "supplications" for it come from a truly penitent heart, the recipient, realizing what a horrible offense against the holy God sin is, will resolve not to incur His wrath and outrage "the Spirit of grace." (Heb 10:29; see also Neh 1:4-11; 1 K 8:38-40; Ro 2:4)

Psalm 131

131:1-3 A person who confesses that his very existence depends on the mercy of God (Ps 132) also wants to overcome the compulsion of overweening ambition and sinful pride. He no longer strives for *things too great and too marvelous* for his God-given endowments, because to attain such goals he must resort to illegal means and resources. Not a sluggard, unwilling to exploit to the fullest his potential, he nevertheless has "learned . . . to be content" in "whatever state" God grants him success. (Ph 4:11; see also Ps 18:27; 37:5; 101:3; 138:6; Ja 4:6; 1 Ptr 5:5)

Psalm 132

132:1-18 This psalm, the longest *Song of Ascents* (cf. Ps 120), gave the pilgrims going up to Jerusalem an opportunity (1) to recall how the city of David came to be God's *dwelling place* (1-10) and (2) to assure themselves of His solemn covenant to make it His *resting place for ever* (11-18). What David *swore to the Lord* (2) and what *the Lord swore to David* is reproduced in the imaginative form of dramatic impersonation. In 3-5 David is introduced as speaking; in 6-10 he is joined by the people at the time the ark was transferred to Jerusalem; in 11-18 the Lord appears on the scene to repeat in poetic language what He said of the glorious future of David and his descendants as His *anointed* representatives and of *Zion,* chosen to be the earthly residence of the heavenly King and the administrative base of His eternal kingdom. These promises seemed to fail of fulfillment when Jerusalem was leveled with the ground and the Davidic dynasty came to a shameful end. But the expectations and longings expressed in this psalm were fulfilled in "Jesus Christ, the Son of David," in whom "the whole fulness of deity dwells bodily" and of whose "kingdom there will be no end." (Mt 1:1; Lk 1:32-33, 68-79; Cl 2:9)

132:2 *He swore.* David's resolve to build the temple (2 Sm 7:2) and the Lord's answer (2 Sm 7:4-16) are not introduced by an oath formula. By saying that they *swore,* the poet wants to underscore the sincerity of David's vow and the absolute certainty that God "will not turn back" from His pledged word. For *the Mighty One of Jacob* see Gn 49:24; Is 1:24; 49:26; 60:16.

132:6 *Ephrathah.* Cf. Ru 1:1 second note; 1 Sm 17:12 note. Here the term may refer to a district in which *the fields of Jaar,* i.e., Kiriath-jearim, was located (1 Sm 6:10—7:2), from which David transferred the ark to "the tent which David had pitched for it" in Jerusalem. (2 Sm 6:17)

132:8 *Arise.* Cf. 2 Ch 6:41 note.

132:10 *Anointed one.* Cf. 2:3 note.

132:11 *On your throne.* Cf. 2 Sm 7 notes.

132:17 *Horn.* Cf. 75:4-5 note; Lk 1:69. The Messianic King is said to be a "branch" or "shoot" from the "stump of Jesse," David's father (Is 11:1; Jer 23:5; 33:15; Zch 3:8; 6:12). for the figurative meaning of *a lamp* see 1 K 11:36 note.

Psalm 133

133:1-3 Pilgrim bands on their way to celebrate their communion with their heavenly Father sang this *Song of Ascents* to express their delight over the ties that bind them to one another. As *brothers* of the same community but above all as members in the family of God, they rejoice in their *good and pleasant* relationship of concord and cordiality. This gift of peace and goodwill is hailed and underscored by two comparisons which have an ancient setting: (1) the perfumed oil dropping down Aaron's *beard* onto his high-priestly vestments, in which he acted as Israel's representative before God (Ex 29:7; 30:31; Lv 21:10); (2) *the dew of Hermon,* supplying parched fields with needed moisture. (Gn 27:28; Hos 14:5; Zch 8:12)

Psalm 134

134:1-3 The last *Song of Ascents* (cf. Ps 120), sung perhaps by the homeward-bound worshipers, exhorts the officiant remaining at the sanctuary to *bless the Lord* by *night* and day (cf. 1 Ch 9:33; 23:30; Is 30:29) and invokes a parting blessing on the dispersing congregation from *Zion,* the dwelling place of Him *who made heaven and earth.* (Cf. Nm 6:22-26; Dt 21:5)

Psalm 135

135:1-21 The writer of this psalm gathered pretty blossoms from the garden of his Scripture and tied them into a bouquet, lovely to behold and fragrant with the "aroma" of thanksgiving and praise (2 Co 2:14 f.). His selections from the Bible of his day are held in place by an opening and closing "hallelujah" (vv. 1 and 21). In a call to *praise the name of the Lord* he briefly announces why "it is good to give thanks to the Lord" (1-4; 92:1; 147:1). In the main part (5-18) he takes up and substantiates the suggested reasons: (1) God, the Creator, rules supreme in nature (5-7); (2) God, the Lord of history, shapes the destiny of nations for the benefit of *his people Israel* (8-12) and will continue to do so *forever* (13-14); (3) God, the living Lord, never fails to act, as do the lifeless *idols of the nations* (15-18). Therefore a rousing summons is issued to the officiants in the temple and to all *that fear the Lord* to join in praising Him for the blessings flowing to them *from Zion.* (19-21)

135:1 *Servants of the Lord.* The author's first verse echoes 113:1.

135:4 *His own possession.* God's choice of Israel to be His "peculiar treasure" (AV) was an act of unmerited divine goodness (Ex 19:5 second note; Dt 7:6 ff.; 14:2; 26:18). This same holds true of "God's own people" of the new covenant. (1 Ptr 2:9)

135:5 *Above all gods.* Cf. Ex 20:3 notes; 15:11; 18:11; Dt 3:24; 10:17; Ps 84:7.

135:6 *He does.* For a similar description of God's control of the forces of nature see 33:7; 115:3; Jb 38:8-11.

135:8 *He it was.* For the allusions to events in Israel's past from the exodus to the conquest of Canaan in vv. 8-12 see Ex 7—15; Dt 4:38; 7:1 f.; Nm 21:21-35.

135:13 *Thy name . . . endures.* For the meaning of *name* see Ex 3:15 note; 6:3 note; Ps 8:1 note.

135:15 *Idols.* Vv. 15-18 reproduce 115:4-8; see also Dt 4:28; Is 44:9 ff.; Jer 10:3 ff.

135:20 *That fear the Lord.* Cf. 115:11 note; 118:4.

Psalm 136

136:1-26 Often called the "Great Hallel" (cf. 113:1-9), this psalm is similar to Ps 135 in purpose and content. It too issues a call to *give thanks to the Lord* (1-3) and then gives much the same reasons why the chosen people owe a debt of gratitude to the *God of gods* and *Lord of lords.* It was the Maker of heaven and earth (4-9) who created Israel by (1) liberating the descendants of Abraham from mighty Pharaoh of Egypt (10-16); (2) overcoming the kings who opposed His plan to give to them the Promised Land as their heritage (17-22); (3) rescuing them from foes threatening their national safety, and supplying their physical needs (23-25). However, this song of praise differs in structure not only from Ps 135 but also from all other psalms. It is cast in the form of a litany in which the second line of its 26 verses consists of the identical refrain: *for his steadfast love endures for ever.* If these recurring responses are omitted, the first lines of every verse tell events of Israel's past in historical sequence.

136:1 *Steadfast love.* For the meaning of this key word see Dt 7:9 note.

136:2 *God of gods.* Cf. the references in the note to 135:5.

136:5 *By understanding.* The created world reflects the ability of its Builder and Architect, which exceeds human comprehension. (Pr 3:19; Jer 51:15)

136:6 *Earth upon the waters.* Cf. 24:2 note; Is 42:5; 44:24.

136:7 *Great lights.* Vv. 7-9 echo Gn 1:14-16.

136:11 *Brought Israel out.* Events in history did not happen by accident. Nor did Israel's courage or prowess determine its fate. It is the Lord who makes and breaks nations.

136:19-20 *Sihon . . . Og.* Mentioned also in 135:11.

136:26 *God of heaven.* Transcending everything mundane, Israel's God "is in the heavens" and "does whatever he pleases." (115:3; see also Ez 1:2; Neh 1:4; 2:4; Dn 2:18; Jon 1:9)

Psalm 137

137:1-9 An unknown poet declares his love for God, His temple, and His people in an emotional outburst of unequaled fervor. It pained him to tears when he and his fellow exiles in Babylonia were denied the privilege of worshiping in Jerusalem and were ridiculed by their *captors* for their inability to serve the Lord as they were required to do (1-3). For him and every member of God's people to *forget . . . Jerusalem,* his *highest joy,* would be a crime for which he deserved to be punished severely (4-6). Enemies, such as Edom and Babylon, who try to frustrate God's kingdom, are consigned to Him for total destruction. (7-9)

137:1 *Waters.* The two main "streams" (RSV note) of Babylonia were the Tigris and the Euphrates. In addition, a network of irrigation canals supplied the land with water. (Cf. Eze 1:1; 3:15)

137:2 *Willows.* Not our weeping willows but trees belonging to the poplar (cf. RSV note) family.

137:3 *Songs of Zion.* Jerusalem and the temple lay in ruins. In jeering *mirth* the *tormentors* asked the captives to sing of the glory of Zion as they did in such psalms as 46 and 47. In effect they were asking: "Where is your God?" (42:3; 79:10; 115:2)

137:7 *Edomites.* The descendants of Esau, Jacob's brother, were Israel's inveterate enemies down to *the day of Jerusalem,* i.e., the day of its destruction, when they cheered on the Babylonians to *rase it . . . to its foundations.* (Ob 8-15; Am 1:11 f.; Is 34:5 ff.; Jer 49:7 ff.)

137:8 *Daughter of Babylon.* In the Book of Revelation, Babylon is the symbol of all anti-God powers. "Saints and apostles and prophets" are invited to rejoice over the downfall of the "mother of harlots and of earth's abominations." "A great multitude in heaven" is heard singing praises to God because "he has avenged on her the blood of his servants." (Rv chs. 17, 18, 19)

You devastator. Better translated: "You who are destined to be devastated."

137:9 *Little ones.* The psalmist invokes God to keep His threat to "requite Babylon . . . for all the evil that they have done in Zion" (Jer 51:24; Rv 18:6). God said also that "their infants will be dashed in pieces before their eyes" (Is 13:16). In the ancient world this kind of cruelty was not uncommon (2 K 8:12). Children are still among the victims of modern warfare. To pray God to inflict the kind of punishment on His and His people's enemies which He Himself threatened and then executed offends against the law of love if it is motivated by a desire for personal revenge. (Cf. Nm 31:2 note)

Psalm 138

138:1-8 In this "Psalm of David" thanksgiving is offered for an answer to an urgent prayer in a time of crisis. What God granted was such a remarkable demonstration of His *steadfast love and . . . faithfulness* as to call for ringing praise of His undisputed power and for humble adoration of His goodness (1-3). Not only the immediate beneficiaries but also *all the kings of the earth* should be moved to acknowledge His *ways* of exalting *the lowly* and debasing *the haughty* (4-6). God's unfailing protection in the past is full guarantee that in the future too He *will fulfil his purpose for me.* (7-8; 57:2)

138:1 *Before the gods.* Praise of the only God is to be regarded as a disavowal of objects of worship falsely called *gods.* (See also 29:1 note; 48:2 note; 82 introductory note; 95:3 note; 96:5 note; Ex 20:3 second note)

138:2 *Thy name and thy word.* The Hebrew text (see RSV note) suggests the following meaning: In keeping this particular *word* of promise God exceeded previous demonstrations of His *name.* (Ex 6:3 note)

138:4 *Kings of the earth.* Cf. 102:15; 2:2 note, 10.

Psalm 139

139:1-24 The thematic center of this *Psalm of David* is the word *search.* The plea: *Search me, O God* (23) has its counterpart in the declaration: *O Lord, thou hast searched me* (1). The prayer recorded at the end of the psalm (19-24) arose out of a desperate situation. A defendant in a court trial was accused of a capital crime. (For a similar predicament see notes on Pss 35, 69, 109.) Declaring himself innocent of a *wicked way* (24), punishable by execution, he submitted his case to "the Judge of all the earth" (Gn 18:25), appealing to Him to render a verdict according to His declared principles of justice. He called on God to *slay the wicked,* a fate he himself must share if found guilty as charged. This cry for divine intervention is preceded in the psalm by a touching confession of faith affirming God's undisputed control of human destiny (1-18). The suppliant tells the Lord why he entrusts himself into His care. Nothing harmful can happen because (1) God knows everything, even the unexpressed thoughts of the mind (1-6); (2) God is at hand no matter where in the universe the need for help arises (7-12); (3) God is at work from life's embryonic inception and reads a man's completed biography before he is born. (13-18)

139:2 *From afar.* God knows man's intentions before they enter his mind.

139:5 *Beset me.* Nothing escapes God's omniscience. It encircles man as completely as a besieged city is hemmed in by enemy forces.

139:7 *Whither shall I go?* The questions in this verse are not motivated by a desire to get beyond God's control. As the following verses make clear, His omnipresence gives assurance to the suppliant that he is always and everywhere in easy reach of God's helping "right hand."

139:8 *Sheol.* Cf. Dt 32:22 note; Jb 26:6; Am 9:2-4.

139:13 *Knit me together.* For a similar poetic description of God's activity in forming life see Jb 10:10 f.; Jer 1:5.

139:14 *Fearful and wonderful.* The Hebrew text (cf. RSV note) yields sense if translated: "I am made to be wonderful in a most awesome way."

139:15 *Depths of the earth.* What goes on in the *secret* of the womb is hidden from sight as if it were in the dark recesses of the earth.

139:16 *Unformed substance.* As God sees and forms the embryo before birth, so He also knows all the days of a person's life before any of them have dawned and become a part of history. For other references to God's *book* of records see Ex 32:32; Ml 3:16; Dn 7:10.

139:18 *When I awake.* The Hebrew verbs "to awake" and "to come to an end" are similar in form (RSV note). The meaning of the verse is either: "When I come to the end" [of my counting the precious thoughts of God] or "when I awake" [after being overcome by sleep from the exertion], "I would still be with thee [enumerating thy great deeds]," so vast is their number.

139:20 *Lift themselves.* The Hebrew text (cf. RSV note) can be retained if translated: "They speak wickedly of thee."

139:24 *Wicked way.* Hebr: "a way of pain," i.e., a way of life which deserves to be punished by painful consequences. (1:6)

Psalm 140

140:1-13 See notes on Ps 64, to which this prayer for aid against insidious intrigue is very similar. Cf. also Ps 58.

140:10 *Burning coals.* The wicked cities of Sodom and Gomorrah were destroyed by a rain of fire and brimstone (Gn 19:24; Ps 11:6; 120:4). The reference to *pits* may be an allusion to the fissures of the earth which swallowed up the rebellious tribe of Korah. (Nm 16:32)

Psalm 141

141:1-10 In this psalm help is sought against enemies as crafty as those described in Ps 140. These *evildoers* pose a double threat. They set "traps" and *snares* for innocent victims (8-10). But they are dangerous too because the success of their *wicked deeds* and the luxurious living they can afford tempt the faithful to follow their bad example. Not trusting his own strength to resist the allurement to "be conformed to this world" (Ro 12:2), the psalmist turns to the Lord in prayer (1-2). He asks Him to stand *guard* over the words of his *lips,* the thoughts of his *heart,* and the *deeds* of his hands (3-4). At the same time he vows to accept the admonition of *a good man* lest he share the doom awaiting the wicked. (5-7)

141:2 *Evening sacrifice. Prayer,* the *sacrifice* of the lips, is to be as welcome to the Lord as the "pleasing odor" of *incense* and burnt offerings (Ex 29:18, 25; Lv 23:18; Gn 8:20 f.). Israel was required to bring morning and evening sacrifices. (Ex 29:39-41; Nm 28:4; cf. Dn 9:21)

141:4 *Dainties.* They "feasted sumptuously every day" on "the bread of wickedness" and "the wine of violence." (Lk 16:19; Pr 4:17)

141:5 *Rebuke me.* It is difficult to determine the exact meaning of vv. 5-7. They appear to refer in idiomatic terms to circumstances which are no longer clearly discernible. However, the basic thrust evidently is the determination not to "throw in" his "lot" with those who must ultimately come to grief. (Pr 1:14)

Psalm 142

142:1-7 This *Maskil of David* bears witness to the power of prayer to change things even when no outward change in a calamity is within sight. Here a *supplication to the Lord* tells Him of *trouble* which He already knew about (1-3a; Mt 6:32; Ps 1:6). Ruin seems unavoidable. No one *takes notice; no man cares* what happens (3b-4). But prayer banishes the feelings of loneliness and helplessness. No one is alone in suffering; no one is beyond hope. To the turbulent heart comes the assurance that, whatever the future may hold, it must bring occasion to *give thanks to* the Lord for what He did in the hour of trial and through it (5-7).—For "Maskil" see Ps 32. For the situation in David's life indicated in the superscription see Ps 57.

142:1 *With my voice.* The situation is so alarming that prayer is not confined to unuttered sighs but bursts out in audible words.

142:4 *To the right.* Where the advocate stood in a court trial. (16:8; 109:31; 121:5)

Psalm 143

143:1-12 Anyone driven by pressure from without and turbulence from within to turn to the Lord in the words of the foregoing psalm will welcome the opportunity to continue to press his suit before the heavenly mercy seat in this *Psalm of David.* Here too there are frantic *supplications* for the divine Helper to *make haste* if *life,* already *crushed . . . to the ground* by enemies of God, is not to *go down to the Pit* of death (1, 3, 7, 11, 12). However, this plea for deliverance is very explicit in confessing that God must act "purely out of fatherly, divine goodness and mercy" (Luther) because *no man living is righteous before* Him (2). Because of this confession of sinfulness Ps 143 has been included in the "Seven Penitential Psalms" (cf. Ps 6). Penitent awareness of past failures to meet God's demands of holiness also recognizes how necessary it is that the *good spirit* of the Lord *teach* and *lead* His *servant* to do His will. (10, 12)

143:1 *In thy righteousness.* Repeated in v. 11. If God does what is right in *faithfulness* to His covenant of mercy, the answer to the prayer will be "vindication" and "deliverance" of those who "trust" His "steadfast love" (8; 51:14; 98:2; 103:6; Hos 2:19). On that basis they dare to plead: "Judge me." (7:8 note; 35:24 note; 43:1; cf. 143:2)

143:2 *No man . . . is righteous.* If God were to bring men to trial for their sins, no one would escape the sentence of death. (14:3; 51:5; 130:3; Jb 4:17-19; 9:2; 15:14; 25:4; Jn 8:7; Ro 3:9, 30; Gl 2:16)

143:8 *In the morning.* Cf. 30:5; 59:16; 90:14; 130:6.

143:10 *Thy good spirit.* Cf. Neh 9:20; Ps 51:11 f. For a *level path* see 25:4 note; 26:12; 27:11.

Psalm 144

144:1-15 This psalm consists of prayers by and for king (1-11) and people (12-15). In a variety of popular metaphors the nation's ruler pays homage to the "great king over all the earth" (47:2) as the unfailing source of national blessings (1-2). And because even a royal person is but a fleeting *breath* and *passing shadow* like every *son of man* (3-4), he sends petitions to the heavenly throne for protection *from on high* against treacherous foes (5-8) and vows a song of gratitude, confident that the plea for deliverance will be heard (9-11). Safe against foreign aggression, the citizens turn to internal needs, invoking on themselves the blessings of a happy family life and an abundant supply of physical necessities (12-15). Thought and language of this psalm have much in common primarily with Ps 18 but also with Pss 33, 102, 103, 104.

144:3 *What is man . . . ?* Man's evanescent existence is mentioned repeatedly in the OT. Cf. 8:4; 39:4 f., 11, 62:9; Jb 7:16; 8:9.

144:6 *Them.* The enemies.

144:8 *Right hand.* Raised in giving an oath.

144:10 *Thy servant.* David is called God's servant in 89:3.

144:12 *Corner pillars.* As ornamental pillars beautify a palace, so may daughters adorn a household.

144:15 *Happy the people.* Cf. 33:12.

Psalm 145

145:1-21 This is the only psalm bearing the title *A Song of Praise.* One word in Hebrew, this term in its plural form "Praises" came to be applied to the entire psalter. It derives from the same root contained in the call to adoration "Hallelujah" ("Praise the Lord"), issued in the opening and closing verses of the five remaining psalms (146—150). This concluding series of hymns bears out what the *saints* (145:10; 148:14) and the "faithful" (149:1) should say to God above all, as they commune with Him. They may indeed cry to Him for help when stricken by disaster and grief; they may plead for pardon for sin and relief of doubts. But if they are what they claim to be, their ultimate desire and constant delight will be to "sing to the Lord a new song" (149:1) of praise and thanksgiving. If repeated exultation in their Maker, Provider, and Redeemer, as it echoes and reechoes through these psalms, seems to be wearisome, it should give them pause to think about their relationship to God. Ps 145 is like a flourish of trumpets initiating the "joyful noise to God" (66:1) heard in Pss 146—150. It revels in the greatness and the goodness of God, the Preserver and Ruler of the universe. Cast in the form of an alphabetic acrostic and sprinkled with conventional Biblical phrases, it nevertheless has artistic appeal. There is an effective progression in an ever-widening circle of those summoned to praise the Lord. In vv. 1-3 the psalmist exhorts himself to extol *God,* the *King.* Then successive generations are to glorify His *mighty acts* (4-7) and His *compassion* (8-9). Next *all . . . saints* are gratefully to acknowledge *the glorious splendor of* His *kingdom* (10-13). In vv. 14-20 *all who are falling* and *all who call upon him* are to recognize His faithfulness and grace in hearing their prayers. The psalm ends in a climactic call to *all flesh* to *bless his holy name.* (21)

145:1 *Thy name.* Men get a glimpse of God's "unsearchable" greatness (3) as He discloses it in "mighty acts," "wondrous works," "terrible acts," "mighty deeds." (4, 5, 6, 12; cf. 8:1 note; 20:1 note; Ex 6:3 note)

145:10 *Saints.* Cf. 4:3 note.

145:13 *Everlasting kingdom.* To God belongs "the kingdom and the power and the glory for ever and ever." (Ex 15:18; Jer 10:11; Dn 4:3, 34; Matt. 6:13 RSV note)

145:15 *The eyes of all.* This and the next verse are often used as a prayer before meals. (104:27 f.; 136:25)

145:21 *All flesh.* All earthly praise will come to a climax in "a new song" sung by "every tribe and tongue and people and nation" to the enthroned Lamb, once "slain" to "ransom men for God." (Rv 5:9)

Psalm 146

146:1-10 The last five psalms are in the nature of a response to the summons to "speak the praise of the Lord and . . . bless his holy name" (145:21). Known as the final "Hallel" (cf. Ps 113 introductory note), they sing "Hallellujahs" in untiring variations and reiterations of the proposed theme. After an introductory self-exhortation to *sing praises . . . to God* till life's last breath (1-2; 104:33), the author of Ps 146 exults in the Lord as the only basis for hope in human existence. It is useless to *put . . . trust in princes* because even the most powerful men are but mortal earthlings, crumbling into the dust from which they came (3-4; Gn 3:19; Ps 104:29; 118:8 f.). But the Lord always is able to keep *faith* and maintain a moral world order because the might of the Creator is inexhaustible (5-7a; 121:2; Ex 20:11). Furthermore He is as good and merciful as He is powerful. He champions the cause of the underprivileged and brings relief to those deprived of well-being (7b-9). There never is a time when He is not in control: for *the Lord will reign for ever.* (10; 145:21)

146:1 *Praise the Lord.* Cf. 105:45 note.

146:5 *The God of Jacob.* Cf. 20:1 note.

146:9 *Sojourners.* Resident aliens in Israel. (94:6)

146:10 *O Zion.* Cf. 99:1 note; 102:15 f., 21 f.; Is 52:7.

Psalm 147

147:1-20 The medley of thoughts running through this Hallelujah-Psalm is held together by a double theme of praise: (a) There is exultation in view of the Creator's *abundant . . . power* and *understanding . . . beyond measure* (5). To compose a hymn in adoration of the limitless might and unsearchable knowledge of God is not a grudging concession or unpleasant duty. *It is good to sing praises to our God* (1; 92:1). (b) Nor is it terrifying to realize that one's fate is determined by such an all-powerful God. For He is not a cruel, heartless despot. *Praise is seemly* above all because *He is gracious* (1). Divine greatness and goodness serve as melody and counterpoint in the three stanzas of the psalm, each introduced by a summons to join in the song: (1) He who *determines the number of the stars* controls history for the benefit of His chosen people: He *builds up Jerusalem,* destroyed by the Babylonian conqueror, and *gathers the outcasts of Israel* (1-6; cf. Neh 12:27-43). (2) He who supplies the *food* for all creatures *takes pleasure in those who fear him* (7-11). (3) He whose command brought the universe into existence and who issues directives to the forces of nature *declares his word to Jacob,* teaching *Israel* by *statutes and ordinances* how to live in covenant harmony with Him. (12-20)

147:4 *Their names.* Cf. Is 40:26.

147:9 *Their food.* Among Israel's neighbors the forces of nature were deities who had to be appeased if grass was to "grow upon the hills."

147:10 *Strength of the horse.* God is not pleased if trust is placed in the might of the war horse and in armed men rather than in Him, who supplies all energy and resources.

147:11 *Who fear . . . who hope.* In man's response to God, awe of His greatness and fear to offend Him are coupled with implicit trust *in his steadfast love.*

147:15 *His word.* God's word never fails to produce what He wills should be done or known. (33:9; 148:5; Is 48:13; 55:10 f.)

147:20 *Any other nation.* The choice of Israel over other nations is a mystery of divine wisdom and mercy. Cf. Dt 4:8, 32-38; 7:6 ff.

Psalm 148

148:1-14 The chorus summoned to praise the Lord in this psalm is so vast that it needs the dome of the universe for its concert hall. Its ranks are made up of all animate and inanimate creatures existing in the sheer endless reaches of celestial space (1-4) as well as in the terrestrial world from the *monsters* of the ocean's depths to the *fruit trees* on the hilltops (5-10). A special section is made up of human choristers embracing *kings of the earth and all peoples,* whether male or female, young or old (11-14). As if they should instinctively know the text of their song, the reason why they are to *praise the name of the Lord* is mentioned only in passing. Voiceless and speechless, sun, moon, and stars nevertheless have much to say to glorify Him who *commanded and they were created* and who *fixed their bounds* (5 f.; 19:1). On earth, *fire and hail, snow and frost . . . all hills . . . and all cedars* are eloquent in proclaiming the glory of their Maker (8 f.). However, *his people* and *his saints* have more for which to worship Him than the wonders of their creation. He whose *glory is above earth and heaven* condescended to single out *the people of Israel* for a special gift of grace. He let them draw *near to him* in a covenant relationship, and when they seemed destined for extinction, *raised up a horn* for them, i.e., restored them to national vitality. (13 f.; 89:17, 24; 92:10; cf. Luke 1:69)

148:2 *Host.* The armies of "the Lord of hosts" consist of *his angels* as well as of celestial luminaries (46:7 note; 29:1 note; 103:19 ff.; Neh 9:6; Jb 38:7 note). The latter are not independent deities but messengers obedient to Him who said: "Let there be lights in the firmament." (Gn 1:14)

148:4 *Highest heavens.* Translated more literally "the heaven of heavens" in Dt 10:14, cf. note there; Neh 9:6; but see 1 K 8:27; 2 Co 12:2.

148:7 *Sea monsters.* Cf. Gn 1:21; Ps 68:30 note; 74:14 note.

148:13 *Name.* Cf. Ps 8:1 note.

148:14 *Saints.* Cf. 4:3 note.

Psalm 149

149:1-9 A *new song* of vociferous praise is to be rendered *in the assembly of the faithful.* God, who made *the sons of Zion* into a nation and agreed to be *their King,* intervened in behalf of *his people.* Humbled and shamed in defeat by enemies intent on dethroning "the Lord and his anointed" (Ps 2:2), they have evidence that *the Lord takes pleasure* in them, as *he adorns them with victory* (1-4). However, it is in the nature of the case that salvation of *the faithful* and advancement of God's kingdom cannot be achieved unless hostile forces are eliminated. To save His people He enabled them *to wreak vengeance on the nations* and *to execute on them the judgment written. High praises* are due God also for this aspect of His rule on earth. (5-9)

149:1 *New song.* Cf. 33:3 note; 96:1 note; Rv 14:3.

149:2 *Maker.* Cf. 100:3 note. For *Zion* as the earthly outpost and base of operations of the *King* see 48:2 note; 99:1 note.

149:9 *The judgment written.* As God chose "the sons of Zion" to be His instrument of salvation to "all the families of the earth" (Gn 12:3), so He also solemnly pledged that the bearers of His promise would "wreak vengeance on the nations," should they attempt to frustrate Israel's mission to the world (Dt 32:40-42; Is 41:15 f.). However, the fact that God once executed judgment through Israel does not authorize the people of the new covenant to take "two-edged swords in their hands" (6) in promoting the kingdom of heaven even though they too "will judge the world" on the last day. (1 Co 6:2; Mt 19:28; Rv 2:26 f.; see also Rv 18:20; 19:1 ff., 11 ff., 19 ff.)

Psalm 150

150:1-6 Whether or not written expressly as a concluding doxology for the entire Book of Psalms, Ps 150 brings the praise of God to a resounding finale (cf. the doxologies at the end of the four preceding "Books": 41:13; 72:18 f.; 89:52; 106:48). A massed chorus is gathered in God's *sanctuary* on earth and is joined by angelic voices *in his mighty firmament* (1). With the help of a full orchestra it shakes the rafters of the universe with the sound of music. Nothing more is necessary to motivate this thunderous outburst of acclaim than to call attention to God's *mighty deeds* and *his exceeding greatness.* (2)

PROVERBS

INTRODUCTION

Purpose

The Book of Proverbs is designed to teach wisdom. In pursuing this avowed goal it proceeds on the basis of two unargued axioms.

(1) It operates with the undisputed assumption that man can be taught because he can think and benefit from the thinking of his fellowmen. Even though tainted and handicapped by innate sin, the sons and daughters of Adam are equipped by the Creator with rational powers. They can learn to do things well (Gn 41:39; Ex 31:3). They are born with the capacity to reason from cause to effect, to benefit from their experiences and those of others, to formulate principles of conduct in the interest of individual and social well-being.

In the ancient cultures surrounding Israel these natural endowments of mankind were exploited to a remarkable degree. Men of keen intellect delved deeply into the mysteries of human existence. Sages gave guidance for the attainment of satisfaction and happiness in life. The accumulated prudence of generations circulated widely in the form of popular sayings.

Much of this wisdom, produced by human intelligence, expresses valid truths. The Book of Proverbs, too, contains maxims which are the result of man's reasoning power. They commend themselves for the simple reason that they are reasonable, logically and experientially.

(2) The second presupposition underlying the wisdom which the Book of Proverbs teaches is the axiom of man's total dependence on and responsibility to God.

At his best man is neither autonomous nor infallible in his thinking.

He is truly wise only if "the fear of the Lord is the beginning of wisdom." (1:7; cf. Ps 111:10 note; Pr 14:26 f.; 3:5; 16:3; 18:10)

By his own sagacity man is not able to determine the course of his life because "a man's steps are ordered by the Lord." (20:24; cf. 16:9, 25; 19:21)

At every move he makes he must be aware that "the Lord weighs the heart" and "the spirit." (21:2; 16:2)

There is no aspect or detail of life which is secular in the sense that it is immune to the holy will of God. To do wrong is not only an offense against society but "an abomination to the Lord." (3:32; 6:16; 15:8-9, 26; etc.)

The laws of God's moral world-order cannot be broken with impunity, for "the Lord's curse is on the house of the wicked" and "an evil man will not go unpunished." (3:33; 11:21)

Form

The English word "Proverbs" appearing in the title of the book may be misleading.

The Hebrew noun so translated does indeed denote a brief, pithy truism such as our proverb: "A stitch in time saves nine." (Cf., e.g., Gn 10:9; 1 Sm 10:12; Eze 16:44; 18:2)

But it is not restricted to this meaning. In other contexts and in the headings of other pronouncements it is rendered "discourse," "allegory," "byword," "taunt," "taunt song." (Num 23:7, 18; Jb 29:1; Eze 17:2; Jer 24:9; Is 14:4; Mi 2:4)

This variety of literary forms has a common denominator in the etymology of the Hebrew term. Derived from a root meaning "to be like" or "to resemble," it came to be applied to any composition involving a comparison or the drawing of inferences from points of similarity.

To a great extent the Book of Proverbs is made up of short sententious sayings resembling our proverbs. However, in keeping with the wider range of meanings of the Hebrew term, it embodies also extended discourses on various aspects of wisdom and its application to life. Dissertations of this kind are found particularly in the opening and closing chapters. (1—9; 30—31)

Both epigrams and essays are cast in the form of parallelism, the basic feature of Hebrew poetry (see Introduction to Psalms, "Poetry"). Proverbial maxims consist almost exclusively of two lines, whereas the praise of a virtuous woman is sung in an acrostic poem of more than 20 verses. (31:10-31)

The literary artistry adorning these teachings of wisdom indicates that individuals of poetic skill were responsible for their final form. There was in Israel a profession of "wise" men (22:17; 24:23) concerned, among other things, with the application of general principles "made known . . . to Moses" (Ps 103:7) to the complexities of everyday living. As God's people were troubled by false prophets, so there also were counselors disseminating spurious wisdom. (Is 5:21; Jer 8:8; 18:18; Eze 7:26)

Authorship

The title "The Proverbs of Solomon" applies specifically to 17½ of the 31 chapters. The section making up 10:1 to 22:16 has the heading "The Proverbs of Solomon"; chs. 25—29 contain "proverbs of Solomon which men of Hezekiah... copied out" of a larger collection of his wise sayings. For references to Solomon's wisdom see 1 K 3:9, 12; 4:29-34; 5:12. Unnamed "wise" men produced 22:17—24:34. Chs. 30 and 31 contain the contributions of Agur and Lemuel, both of whom remain unidentified. The introductory chs., 1—9, preserve a series of versified discourses which usually are regarded as another collection of anonymous writings. Some proverbs occur more than once, no doubt because they were "copied out" from several collections made in the course of time.

Value

The NT affirms and sanctions the wisdom propounded in the Book of Proverbs by quoting it and adopting its expressions (see, e.g., Ro 12:20; Heb 12:5 f.; 1 Ptr 5:5; 2 Ptr 2:22). The NT also proclaims that the personification of wisdom (especially in ch. 8) was to be more than an illustrative figure of speech. Its ultimate design was to be fulfilled in Him "in whom are hid all the treasures of wisdom and knowledge," through whom "all things were created," "the first-born of all creation." (Cl 2:3; 1:15-17; cf. Jn 1:1-3, 10; 1 Co 1:30; Heb 1:1 ff.; Rv 3:14).

The religious value of the Book of Proverbs can be challenged only by demanding that it answer questions which are not pertinent to its specific purpose. It limits its purpose to illustrating the workings-out of a divinely ordained moral world-order. At all points in his life man is subject to an absolute and universal standard of right and wrong which he disregards only with dire results.

Having unequivocally established this basic, comprehensive truth, the Book of Proverbs is content to leave other questions of man's relationship to God to be answered elsewhere in Scripture. Such questions are: What should motivate the pursuit of virtue? Why is the reward of virtue not always evident? Is there any hope for the man who breaks God's law? Is God's reward of virtue restricted to man's mundane existence?

OUTLINE

The Book of Proverbs touches on a great variety of subjects without, however, arranging them in a topical sequence or in logical units. Therefore an outline can do no more than isolate certain outward groupings of content.

I. 1:1—9:18 Introductory Poems Teaching the Nature and Value of Wisdom

II. 10:1—22:16 Proverbs of Solomon, a Mosaic of Maxims Consisting of Two Lines

III. 22:17—24:34 Two Groups of Instructions Incorporating "the Words of the Wise"

A. 22:17—24:34 The Main Group

B. 24:23-34 An Appendix

IV. 25:1—29:27 Proverbs of Solomon, Added by "the Men of Hezekiah," King of Judah Some 300 Years After Solomon

V. 30:1—31:31 Four Additional Compositions Extolling and Commending Wisdom

A. 30:1-14 The Words of Agur

B. 30:15-33 Five Numerical Proverbs Interlaced with Warnings Against Folly

C. 31:1-9 The Words of Lemuel

D. 31:10-31 An Acrostic Poem in Praise of the Virtuous Woman

1:1—9:18 INTRODUCTORY POEMS TEACHING THE NATURE AND VALUE OF WISDOM

1:1-33 The title of the book (v. 1) is expanded into five verses (2-6) which, in heaped synonyms and parallel reiterations, state the purpose of these collections of proverbs: to inculcate wisdom. There is no need to search for and determine what is wise. It begins and ends in a given datum: *the fear of the Lord* (7). The only requisite for learning is a personal relationship of total commitment to the Lord. Achievement is more than academic mastery of facts. Progress in wisdom is determined by the degree that the fear of the Lord permeates and controls a person's life-style in all its ramifications. No one finishes the course, no matter how long he tries; no one scores a perfect grade, no matter how hard he tries.

Immediately following the introductory statement of purpose, the course gets under way. The remaining verses (8-33) and chs. 2—9 present versified units of instruction. They are not proverbs in our sense of the term but poems of varying length praising wisdom and urging everyone to pursue it. The individual lessons are not clearly marked off. They treat a variety of subjects, using the pedagogical principle of repetition. The address "my son" may often be regarded as indicating chapter headings. It is used 13 times for this purpose. (1:8; 2:1; 3:1, 11, 21; 4:1, 10, 20; 5:1; 6:1, 20; 7:1, 24)

Ch. 1 issues wisdom's warning against enticement into robbery by evil companions and their promise of easy money (8-19). To counteract this allurement into ruin, wisdom "cries aloud," begging for acceptance of good counsel and warning against the dire consequences of not living in "the fear of the Lord." (20-33)

1:1 *Proverbs of Solomon.* For the meaning of the Hebrew term *proverbs* see Introduction, "Form." For *Solomon's* contributions to the Book of Proverbs see Introduction, "Authorship."

1:2 *Wisdom.* In the contexts in which this key word occurs on almost every page of the book (37 times) it denotes prudent behavior and wise action rather than the abstract and theoretical wisdom of the philosopher. The synonyms in the immediate context of its first occurrence (2-6) lead to the same conclusion. Man's intellect comes into play. However, it does not produce wisdom. Its function is to apply acknowledged criteria in choosing the right course of action in the complexities of life. "The simple" as well as "the wise" face this challenge every day.

1:4 *Simple.* Not lacking intelligence, but open and susceptible to suggestion. Such inexperienced and immature people are easily "tossed to and fro . . . with every wind of doctrine." (Eph 4:14; Ps 19:7 second note)

1:6 *Proverb . . . figure . . . riddles.* Wisdom is going to be taught in parabolic forms which are designed to arouse interest, but which also require concentrated and unprejudiced thinking if their content is not to remain enigmatical (Mk 4:13; Lk 8:10). In a *figure* the reader or hearer must sense the element of scoffing and satire (Hab 2:6, "taunt"). For *riddles* see Ju 14:12; Eze 17:2; also translated "hard questions" (1 K 10:1), "dark sayings" (Ps 78:2), "dark speech." (Nm 12:8)

1:7 *Fear of the Lord.* The indispensable ingredient of our knowledge. For the meaning of this phrase see Ps 111:10 note; 147:11 note; Jb 28:28 note.

1:8 *My son.* Imparting wisdom begins with a *father's instruction* and a *mother's teaching,* the duty of both parents (10:1; 15:20; 19:26; 20:20; 23:22, 25; 30:17). "The wise man" addressed also his pupil as "my son."

1:12 *Sheol.* Death personified as in Is 5:14. For the term itself see Dt 32:22 note.

1:16 *Run to evil.* This verse, occurring also in Is 59:7, supplies Paul with a description of man's natural depravity. (Ro 3:15)

1:17 *In vain.* The meaning of this verse seems to be that birds go into a net even though they see the fowler spread it, but those who "consent" when "sinners entice" them are even more stupid in that they themselves set the trap in which they are caught.

1:20 *Wisdom.* A feminine noun in Hebrew, wisdom is personified as a woman. For other examples of this rhetorical device see chs. 8 and 9.

1:21 *On the top of the walls.* The Hebrew text makes sense if translated: "at the head of noisy [streets]," i.e., where streets, filled with the noise of heavy traffic, fan out in all directions.

1:26 *Laugh.* Once committed, an act of folly mocks all attempts to make it undone and to evade its dire results.

1:28 *Not answer.* It is too late to seek "counsel" when one is suffering "calamity" and "distress" caused by one's choice of action contrary to "the fear of the Lord."

1:31 *Fruit of their way.* The laws creating and governing a moral world order are inflexible. It is built on an absolute standard of right and wrong. If it is to function at all, good and bad deeds must inexorably have opposite consequences. However, God is not a set of ethical principles; not a computer automatically turning out programmed data. He is a Person, the Law-Giver who reserves for Himself the right how and when to punish wickedness, how and when to grant a reward of grace to piety.

2:1-22 The second part of the previous chapter (vv. 20 ff.) catalogued hurtful consequences of disobeying wisdom's call, ending on the positive note that "he who listens . . . will dwell secure . . . without dread of evil" (33). In ch. 2 a teacher of wisdom tells his *son* and pupil more about the kind of life all are assured who seek wisdom *like silver and search for it as for hidden treasures* (1-4). Rich benefits await them for (a) they *will understand the fear of the Lord* and thereby be preserved from evil on life's way (5-8); (b) they will know how to choose a just course and find pleasure in doing so (9-11); (c) they will know how to avoid becoming entangled with wicked men (12-15) and how to withstand the fatal wiles of an adulterous woman (16-19); (d) they will not lose their heritage of covenanted blessings. (20-22)

2:4 *Hidden treasures.* Wisdom, which has its beginning in the fear of the Lord, remains undiscovered if man relies on his own ingenuity to uncover it. Even when "the Lord gives wisdom" (6), man can and does reject it. Furthermore, to *seek it* and *search for it* remains a lifelong quest for perfection never fully attained.

2:8 *Saints.* Cf. Ps 4:3 note.

2:16 *Loose woman.* She is "strange" or "foreign" (RSV notes) because as she "forsakes the companion of her youth," i.e., her lawful husband, she invades territories of intimacy where she has no right to be. Warnings against sexual sins fill whole chapters. (See chs. 5 and 7; also 6:20-35; 9:13-18)

2:17 *Covenant of her God.* Unfaithful to her husband, "the loose woman" disrupts relations also with God, who will not tolerate marital infidelity. (Ex 20:14; Ml 2:13-16)

2:18 *Shades.* The sage of old knew that life does not end at *death.* "The dead" (9:18; 21:16) live on in a mysterious existence which is shadowy because bodily vitality has ceased. (Ps 88:10; Is 14:9; Jb 26:5)

2:21 *Inhabit the land.* Cf. Ps 37:9 note.

3:1-35 The course in wisdom continues in three units of instruction, each headed by a call from the teacher to his *son* (1, 11, 21). The lessons have interlocking content. A threefold admonition not to *forget, despise,* or *let escape* what is taught is followed by (a) assurances of blessings resulting from observing wisdom; (b) individual maxims to be followed. Yet each section also develops a different aspect of the subject: in 1-10 there is an exhortation to *trust in the Lord* and not to be *wise in your own eyes;* in 11-20 the son is told to accept *the Lord's discipline* as proof of His fatherly love; He makes no mistake in applying *reproof,* having manifested His wisdom in the creation of the universe; 21-35 stress how to be wise in dealing with one's *neighbor.*

3:2 *Welfare.* Usually translated "peace," the Hebrew word denotes everything that makes for wholesomeness, completeness, fulfillment.

3:3 *Loyalty and faithfulness.* God exhibits these attributes perfectly. The first word is often translated "steadfast love" (Gn 24:27; 32:10; Ex 34:6; Ps 85:10; cf. Dt 7:9 note). In his relations to God and his fellowman the wise person is to cultivate these divine qualities. (14:22; 16:6; 20:6)

Bind them. Never lose sight of them. (Ex 13:9 note; Dt 6:8; 11:18)

3:4 *Good repute.* Translated "good understanding" (RSV note) in 1 Sm 25:3; Ps 111:10.

3:8 *Flesh.* This translation, based on the Septuagint, requires the addition of one letter to the Hebrew word for "navel."

3:9 *First fruits.* The Israelites were to *honor the Lord* as the Giver of their *substance* by offering to Him *the first fruits* of field and herd. (Ex 23:19; Nm 28:26; Dt 18:4; 26:2; 15:19)

3:11-12 *The Lord's discipline.* Quoted according to the Septuagint in Heb 12:5 f.; see also Dt 8:5; Jb 5:17; 33:16 ff.

3:18 *Tree of life.* An allusion to Gn 2:9, occurring repeatedly in the Book of Proverbs. (11:30; 13:12; 15:4)

3:19 *Founded the earth.* Cf. Ps 24:2 note; 104:24; 136:5 note. The part assigned to wisdom in creation is treated more fully in 8:22-31.

3:27 *Do not withhold.* What the son is to do to

"keep sound wisdom and discretion" (21) is exemplified by five specific "Do not's" in his relationship with his fellowman (27-31), followed by a series of declarations telling him that the kind of life he chooses brings him either the Lord's curse or His blessing. (32-35)

3:32 *Confidence.* Translated "friendship" in Ps 25:14; see note there.

3:35 *Get.* The Hebrew verb makes sense if translated "carry off disgrace" as the reward of folly.

4:1-27 A wise father delivers three more lectures to (a) impress on his *sons* and pupils how crucial it is that they *get wisdom* (1-9); (b) urge them to choose *the paths of uprightness* rather than the ruinous *path of the wicked* (10-19); (c) plead with them to go straight without swerving *to the right or to the left.* (20-27)

4:2 *Precepts.* Translated "learning" in 1:5, the Hebrew word derives from a root meaning to take, to receive. It is not untried, theoretical *teaching* that is being offered; it has stood the test of long experience, having been transmitted from father to son for generations.

4:7 *Get wisdom. Wisdom* does not just happen. To *get* it requires determined effort, which begins with a deliberate choice of action.

Whatever you get. More literally: "with all you possess." Wisdom is a "pearl of great value"; a person would make a good investment if he "sold all that he had and bought it." (Mt 13:45 f.; Pr 23:23)

4:10 *Years . . . be many.* Length of life has a prominent place among the promised rewards of walking "in the paths of uprightness." (3:2, 16; Ex 20:12; Dt 5:16; Ps 21:4; 91:16)

4:14 *Path.* A man's life-style is often called a *path* or *way.* (Ps 1:1, 6; 25:8; 119:101)

4:23 *Springs of life.* As water gushes from an underground spring, wise action originates in inner convictions and drives. Unless one loves the Lord with all one's *heart,* the potential for evil is not eliminated at its source. (Dt 6:5 f.; Ps 119:2, 10; Mt 12:34; Mk 7:21; Lk 6:45)

4:25 *Directly forward.* It is not enough to make a beginning in getting wisdom (7). There must be a sustained, undistracted effort to stay on course. (Ph 3:13 f.; 1 Ti 6:12 ff.)

4:26 *Take heed.* The rare Hebrew verb may be derived form a root meaning to level a path for a straight course or from a root meaning to weigh, evaluate, examine. RSV adopts the latter here and in 5:6, 21.

5:1-23 As in our day, temptations to sin against the divinely ordered sex life lured many in Israel into "the path of the wicked" (4:14). Recognizing the seductive attractiveness of sexual immorality, especially to the young, the Book of Proverbs again and again speaks out in unvarnished terms against its deceptive pleasures. Already mentioned in 2:16-19 and shortly to be repeated in 7:5-27, violations of the rules of chastity are the topic also of two lessons of instruction which make up ch. 5 (see also 22:14; 23:27 f.; 29:3; 30:20; 31:3). Each unit is introduced by the conventional call to *be attentive* or to *listen to* the words of wisdom (1, 7). In vv. 1-6 the teacher warns his *son* against the fatal mistake of succumbing to the wiles of *a loose woman;* in a longer section (7-23) he first continues to plead with his *sons* to stay *far from her* because consorting with her brings only ruin and remorse (7-14) and then goes on to recommend a wholesome alternative to licentiousness and promiscuity: satisfaction of the natural sex drive in the love life of marriage. (15-23)

5:2 *Guard knowledge.* Keep the *lips* from saying the thing that is wrong and foolish.

5:3 *Loose woman.* Cf. 2:16 note.

5:4 *Wormwood.* The bitter taste of this plant is used figuratively to describe what *in the end* results from being deceived by the honeyed words of the "loose woman." (Jer 9:15; see also Ps 55:20 f.)

5:5 *To Sheol.* Marital infidelity is not a harmless lark or a trifling peccadillo. It has deadly consequences. (2:18; 7:27)

5:6 *Take heed.* On the two meanings of this verb in Hebrew see 4:26 note.

5:9 *To others.* The husband of the adulteress will be *merciless* in exploiting the opportunity for blackmail and extortion until nothing remains of what it took the victim *years* to accumulate.

5:12 *How I hated.* Ruined financially, broken physically, disgraced socially, the philanderer regrets remorsefully that he did not "listen to the voice of my teachers." (13)

5:14 *Utter ruin.* In Israel adultery was a capital offense. (Lv 20:10; Dt 22:22; Eze 18:10-13)

5:15 *Drink water.* In uninhibited and rapturous words, reminiscent of the unabashed language of the Song of Solomon, the sage advocates the "delight" of legitimate sexual relations. The *cistern, well,* and "fountain" from which sensuous satisfaction is to be derived, is "the wife of your youth," i.e., the wife the husband married in his youth. (Cf. SS 4:12, 15)

5:16 *Your springs.* Your offspring.

5:21 *Eyes of the Lord.* The standards of chastity and marital fidelity are not set by society. Nor does consent to do wrong make it right. What a man does sexually, comes under the scrutiny and judgment of Him who made man "male and female" (Gn 1:27). For admonitions in the NT see 1 Co 6:18; 2 Ti 2:22; 2 Ptr 1:4.

6:1-35 In this chapter the *son* receives two more lessons in wisdom. The first (1-19) consists of four prescriptions in separate but related areas of prudent living illustrating the "great folly" (5:23): (1) Do not risk the loss of all you own in speculative investments (1-5); (2) instead of dallying with easy get-rich-quick schemes, learn from *the ant* to be industrious and so provide for the future (6-11); (3) do not incur the penalty meted out to character assassination and *sowing discord* (12-15); (4) avoid harming your fellowmen in any way exemplified by *seven* offenses *which are an abomination to* the Lord (16-19). In the second unit of instruction the *son* is entreated ever to be mindful of the *father's commandment* and the *mother's teaching* not to fall prey to a seductive *adulteress,* a folly by which he *destroys himself.* (20-35)

6:1 *Become surety.* Obviously the *son* is not taught to "refuse him who would borrow from you" or to ignore the injunction to lend to someone in need even without interest (Mt 5:42; Ex 22:14; Lv 25:35 f.). The kind of *surety* meant seems to refer to a contract with professional lenders or "dealers in merchandise" (Eze 27:27) by which an investor underwrote a business venture. The Book of Proverbs repeatedly warns against such hazardous transactions. (11:15; 17:18; 20:16; 22:26 f.; 27:13)

6:3 *Hasten.* Swallow your pride and importune him to release you from your obligation.

6:6 *Go to the ant.* In some respects man is more stupid than the animals (Jb 12:7 f.; see also Pr 30:24-28; 1 K 4:33). If he is to be *wise,* he must be warned against indolence many times over. (10:26; 13:4; 15:19; 19:24; 20:4; 21; 25; 22:13; 24:30-34; 26:13-16)

6:10 *A little sleep.* There is irony in the voice of the teacher. The sluggard always needs a little more rest when called upon to work. His idle excuse is repeated 24:33 f.

6:13 *Scrapes.* A gesture in vogue at the time, pointing in an insinuating way to the maligned person.

6:15 *Broken beyond healing.* "There is a God who judges" (Ps 58:11) also slanderous talebearing which destroys a man's reputation.

6:16 *Abomination.* The sins mentioned are offenses not only against society but also *things which the Lord hates.* For the numbers *six* and *seven* see Jb 5:19 note.

6:24 *The evil woman.* She is an unfaithful "neighbor's wife" (29). The son will not be misled by her *smooth tongue* and beauty, enhanced by facial makeup, if he remains obedient to parental teaching.

6:26 *Loaf of bread.* As the RSV note indicates, the sentence may be translated: "On account of a harlot a man is reduced to a loaf of bread," i.e., to a pauper's existence. Both versions make the point that sexual relations with "a man's wife" have more disastrous consequences than consorting with a *harlot,* whose honor no one will defend. The adulterer robs the husband of a prized possession, for which "he will accept no [monetary] compensation" (35) as he would in the case of a theft of property.

6:30 *A thief.* "If he is caught," he must pay the full penalty of his crime even though he may have been driven to steal by hunger. "He who commits adultery" (32) does not get off so easily. He may "multiply gifts" but will not appease the husband's "jealousy." (34 f.)

7:1-27 The entire chapter is devoted to another warning against adultery (cf. ch. 5; 6:20-35). It is not superfluous. Committed in the name of *love* (18), immorality has a particularly deceptive appeal to *the simple* and *the youths* (7; cf. 1:4 note). If the *son* is not to be lured by *smooth words* into the clutches of a *loose woman* (5), he must embrace and cling to the teachings of *wisdom* (1-5). In order to fortify him against falling prey to this insidious temptation, the wily strategy and enticing charm of the temptress are exposed in a dramatic presentation of an encounter between her and a naive victim (6-23). The moral to be drawn by the *sons* is summed up in a brief appeal not to *stray into her paths* on which *many a victim* has been destroyed. (24-27)

7:2 *Apple of your eye.* Cf. Ps 17:8 note; Dt 32:10.

7:8 *Taking the road.* As he saunters through the town, he happens upon the road to her house.

7:10 *Dressed as a harlot.* Cf. Gn 38:14 f. She is *wily of heart* or more literally "guarded of heart," i.e., she keeps her designs hidden by deceptive words and actions.

7:14 *Offer sacrifices.* Pretending to be religious, she baits the trap with the promise of preparing a fine meal with the meat of a sacrifice which was to be eaten at home without delay. (Lv 7:15)

7:20 *A bag of money.* The husband would not surprise them. He left "on a long journey" on which he had much business to transact.

7:22 *All at once.* On a sudden, thoughtless impulse. The verse goes on to compare the duped youth with a victim going *to the slaughter.* There is no resistance to the impending doom, nor any possibility of escaping it.

8:1-36 Here instruction in prudent living reaches a climax. In soaring flights of poetic imagery wisdom is given the form of an ethereal woman of noble qualities (1:20 note), the antithesis to the coarse "loose woman" depicted in ch. 7. In contrast to the whispered seductions to any wanderer, wisdom *cries aloud* from the rooftops into the crowded town square, hoping to reach the largest possible audience (1-5). The immoral woman, lurking in the shadows, is devious and deceptive; *there is nothing twisted or crooked* in the *noble things* wisdom speaks (6-9). To frequent the house of the adulteress was nothing short of "going down to the chambers of death" (7:27); those who love wisdom, as exemplified in the rule of good *kings,* attain *enduring wealth* (10-21). There is no doubt that wisdom can produce *fruit . . . better than gold* (19). She is God's primordial creation, a mysterious cosmic principle by which He planned the universe, let it emerge from chaos, and keeps it from disintegrating (22-31). Because wisdom operates as unfailingly and unerringly as the laws of nature, she entreats the *sons* not to neglect her teachings if they are to be *happy* (32-36). For the prophetic intent of wisdom personified see Introduction, "Value."

8:4 *Men . . . sons of men.* Translated "low and high" in Ps 49:2. Attainment of wisdom is not restricted to an exclusive circle of philosophers.

8:5 *Simple ones.* Cf. 1:4 note.

8:12 *Dwell in prudence.* The by-product of close association with wisdom is "that prudence may be given to the simple." (1:4)

8:13 *Fear of the Lord.* Cf. 1:7 note; 2:5.

8:14 *Counsel . . . insight* (understanding) . . . *strength.* The Messianic King is equipped with these gifts of *wisdom,* enabling Him to reign "with righteousness" and "with equity." (Is 11:2-4)

8:18 *Prosperity.* The Hebrew word ordinarily has the meaning of "righteousness," as in v. 20 and 10:2. If so translated here, it would assert that the promised *wealth* need not be acquired by unrighteous means.

8:19 *Fruit.* Wisdom is called "a tree of life" in 3:18; see also 8:35.

8:22 *Created me.* Not the usual word in Hebrew to denote the creative activity of God, it is used in the title "Maker of heaven and earth" (Gn 14:19, 22; cf. Dt 32:6; Ps 139:13). The wisdom advocated in the Book of Proverbs is not the concoction of fallible men. She derives her validity from Him who produced nothing that was not "very good." She is as reliable as the laws of nature because she is the instrumental embodiment of the principles which were in operation when the Creator "founded the earth . . . [and] established the heavens" (3:19; Ps 104:24; 136:5; Jer 10:12).—For the poetic terms describing the origin of the universe see Jb 38; Ps 104.

8:26 *Dust.* A plural noun in Hebrew to denote the countless particles that make up the substance of the habitable world. (Is 40:12)

8:27 *Circle.* Translated "vault" in Jb 22:14; but see Is 40:22.

8:28 *Established.* The Hebrew text makes sense if translated: "when the fountains of the deep were strong," i.e., in their threat again to inundate the dry land.

8:30 *Workman.* The alternate reading "little child" (RSV note) suggests that God took *delight* in the perfection of His handiwork as one does in a frolicking child. What He did "by wisdom" (3:19) was the source of rejoicing.

8:32 *And now.* Wisdom, operative in the physical world, is no less a determining force in the moral world order, which one neglects to reckon with at the cost of one's life.

9:1-18 The last chapter in the first major division of the Book of Proverbs (see Introduction, "Outline") is in the nature of a true-false test, concluding the poetic units of instruction in wisdom (chs. 1—8). One of two opposite ways of life is to be chosen. Both are figuratively represented as women, each of whom issues the same invitation to passers-by to *turn in* and to partake of a meal ready to be eaten (4, 16). The first to compete for guests in *her house* is Dame Wisdom (1-6). To eat and drink what she has to offer prolongs life (11). Her rival is Dame Folly. She can offer only *stolen water* and *bread* which must be *eaten in secret.* At first her fare is deceptively *sweet* and *pleasant;* in the end it proves to be lethal poison (13-18). A group of proverbs which have a bearing on the choice to be made separates the calls of the two hostesses. It is a useless, thankless act to appeal to the *scoffer* to accept the right invitation, whereas the *wise man,* motivated by *the fear of the Lord,* welcomes every opportunity to become *wiser.* Each individual must decide on his course of action. (7-12)

9:1 *Seven pillars. Wisdom,* her perfection and many facets indicated by the plural form of the Hebrew noun (as in 1:20; 24:7), is not the personified cosmic figure of the previous chapter. Here she is a wholesome woman dwelling in a stately *house.* It has a courtyard supported by *seven pillars,* i.e., meeting the requirements of a spacious, comfortable dwelling.

9:5 *Come.* The invitation by wisdom's "maids" is heard again in Jesus' parable of the marriage feast. (Mt 22:1-14; Lk 14:15-24)

9:7 *Scoffer.* He deliberately and maliciously flouts wisdom, heaping *abuse* on anyone who *corrects* or *reproves* him. (15:21; 21:24; Ps 1:1)

9:10 *Fear of the Lord.* Cf. 1:7 note.

9:13 *Noisy.* The characterization has overtones heard in the description of the vulgar woman in ch. 7. (Cf. 7:11)

9:17 *Stolen water.* For man's sinful nature there is a demonic lure in the enjoyment of what is *stolen* or what must be *eaten in secret* because it is forbidden fruit. (20:17)

9:18 *The dead.* Cf. 2:18 note.

10:1—22:16 PROVERBS OF SOLOMON, A MOSAIC OF MAXIMS CONSISTING OF TWO LINES

The section beginning here and ending at 22:16 consists of 375 proverbs in our sense of the term, i.e., short maxims and pithy sayings (see "Outline"). In most instances they are the distillation of shrewd observation gained from experience. However, they are more than common sense rules of what is profitable in life. The nine preceding chapters of short essays on wisdom give them a setting which obliterates the distinction between the secular and the sacred. What is good has its norm and motivation in "the fear of the Lord" (1:7; 9:10). People commit the greatest folly and destroy themselves when they do what is "an abomination" (3:32; 6:16; 8:7); they are truly wise when they "honor the Lord" (3:9 f.). This order of things is always in operation, even when it may appear that wisdom for a time goes unrewarded and folly unpunished.

The Book of Proverbs also disposes of the notion that an Israelite needed to do no more to be right with God than to go through the motions of ritual ceremonies. The detailed Levitical laws of worship have a complementary counterpart in the requirements of sanctified daily living, hammered home in the pedagogical form of proverbial sayings. They leave no doubt that whatever a man thought, said, and did every day and moment of his life was either holy or unholy, an act of covenant faithfulness or of rebellion. As stated categorically in the Decalog, the one kind of behavior had the promise of blessing; the other incurred a curse.

Wisdom, so defined, is the strand on which select pearls of instruction are strung. No attempt is made to group them in a systematized sequence of topics. However, in form they are alike. Each is cast in the literary mold of the same kind of poetic parallelism, consisting of two lines, of which the second almost invariably rhymes with the first by repeating it in an antithetic statement.

10:1 *Proverbs of Solomon.* See Introduction, "Authorship."

10:4 *Makes rich.* Wealth is a blessing of God. It is evil only when "gained by wickedness" or made the object of false trust. (vv. 2, 22; 3:16; 11:4, 18, 28; 13:22)

10:6 *Conceals violence.* Repeated in v. 11. The wicked do not divulge their evil designs, in order to take their victim by surprise.

10:8 *Prating fool.* Lit. "one foolish of lips." The line is repeated in v. 10, where the RSV substitutes the reading of the Septuagint.

10:10 *Winks.* Indicating duplicity.

10:12 *Love covers.* Cf. 17:9; 1 Ptr 4:8; 1 Co 13:7; Ja 5:20.

10:13 *A rod.* Fools must be restrained by "flogging." (19:29; 26:3)

10:15 *Strong city.* Repeated 18:11. As walls of a fortified city provide safety against invasion, so *wealth* is protection against the hardships resulting from *poverty.*

10:18 *He who conceals.* This verse is one of few in this section of the book where the second line completes the thought of the first in a positive and not an antithetic assertion.

10:21 *Feed many. The righteous* satisfy the need of others for sound counsel.

10:22 *Adds no sorrow.* The translation in the RSV note makes the point that man's "toil" does not make rich unless God blesses it.

10:23 *Sport. To do wrong* affords the *fool* amusement.

10:26 *Vinegar . . . smoke.* Causes of irritation.

11:1 *Abomination . . . delight.* Almost all proverbs deal with human relations. But right and wrong are not determined merely by social contract. How a man treats a fellowman is either an *abomination* or a *delight* to Him who has set absolute standards of behavior also in the area of community life (11:20; 12:22; 15:8 f., 26, etc.). The Lawgiver, however, is not a helpless observer, delighted when man's actions are good, chagrined when they are bad. He executes penalties for infraction of His laws and rewards compliance with them. A veritable blizzard of proverbs swirls about these truths. Proliferation and reiteration are necessary for several reasons: (1) Men are so prone to act as if in secular affairs there were no regulations and sanctions which derive validity from the almighty Maker of heaven and earth. (2) This notion is so hard to eradicate because so often the wicked seem to be blessed with the good things in life whereas the righteous languish in degradation, poverty, and weakness. It takes hundreds of proverbs to keep reminding short-sighted men that God does maintain a moral world order, all appearances to the contrary notwithstanding. (3) Men so often think they have reason to doubt the equity of God's government because they presume to dictate to Him how, when, and where He is to administer justice. He has reserved for Himself the right to determine the proper manner, time, and place to bless "those who hunger and thirst for righteousness" (Mt 5:6) and, conversely, to let the wicked come to grief. (4) There is such a profusion of proverbs, furthermore, to make clear that the principle of right and wrong applies to all phases of human activity.

False balance. Lit. "scales of deceit." Explicitly forbidden by law and denounced by prophets (Lv 19:35; Dt 25:15; Am 8:5; Mi 6:11), dishonesty in business deals was a temptation as attractive in the long ago as it is today. (16:11; 20:10, 23)

11:4 *Riches.* Cf. 10:4 note. No matter how great, wealth cannot buy immunity from retribution. (Cf. Lk 12:16-21; 16:19-31)

11:8 *Trouble.* The fact that *the righteous* are allowed to get into distressing circumstances and need to be *delivered* does not disprove the justice and benevolence of divine providence, as the Book of Job and such Psalms as 37 and 73 make clear in greater detail.

11:15 *Surety.* Cf. 6:1 note.

11:16 *A gracious woman.* The praise of a good woman is sung at length in 31:10-31 but see also 12:4; 18:22; 19:14; 21:9; 25:24. Here her quiet charm by which she attains honor is contrasted with the tactics of brute force by which *violent men get riches.* The Septuagint adds three lines to the text which are incorporated in some English translations.

11:19 *Will live . . . die.* The terse Hebrew text has only "to life" and "to death," i.e., the righteous and the evil pursue a course leading respectively to life and death.

11:22 *Gold ring.* Worn by women on the finger but also in the ear and nose (25:12; Gn 24:22; Is 3:21), jewelry is as incongruous in a *swine's snout* as a lack of good taste and refinement is in *a beautiful woman.*

11:25 *One who waters.* A comparison based on the use of irrigation. The more water is applied, the greater the harvest.

11:28 *Green leaf.* Cf. Ps 1:3; 92:12 ff.

11:29 *Servant.* In spite of the *fool's* miserliness his treasury is left filled only with *wind.* In the end he is forced to eke out his livelihood in the service of the *wise.*

11:30 *Lawlessness.* The Hebrew text (RSV note) yields sense if translated: "He who is wise takes souls," i.e., gets people under his influence, thereby becoming to them *a tree of life.* (3:18; 15:4)

12:1 *Discipline.* The kind of "instruction" is meant (1:2, 7, 8; 4:13, etc.) which reproves and corrects wrong behavior for the purpose of restraining the tendency to continue in it. In 16:22 it is rendered "chastisement."

12:4 *A good wife.* See Ru 3:11, where the same phrase is translated "a woman of worth." An evil woman destroys a man as surely as *rottenness,* i.e., a deadly disease, eats away the very marrow of his *bones.* (Cf. 14:30; Jb 13:28)

12:8 *Good sense.* Necessary in deciding on the right course of action.

12:9 *Plays the great man.* By putting on a false front. The clause *works for himself* may be translated "who has a servant." The meaning then is that a man in modest circumstances may have someone working for him; but if he is wise, he will not give lavish displays of wealth which he does not have.

12:10 *Beast.* Domestic animals are meant such as the ox (Dt 25:4). The *mercy,* here better translated "feelings," of the wicked are cruel.

12:11 *Worthless pursuits.* Repeated almost verbatim 28:19. Honest labor is advised rather than some get-rich-quick scheme which ends in bankruptcy. (Cf. 6:1 note)

12:12 *Stands firm.* Cf. RSV note. The verse becomes intelligible if translated: "The wicked desires what evil men seek to capture, but the root of the righteous bears [fruit]." The contrast is between what the *wicked* covet by crafty and violent means and the good things which grow naturally out of the lives of the *righteous.*

12:21 *No ill.* Cf. Ps 91:10 note.

12:26 *Turns away from evil.* Without conjectured correction, the Hebrew text yields the translation: "A righteous person is better off than his neighbor" whose fate is described in the next line.

12:27 *Catch.* The Hebrew verb occurs nowhere else in the OT. The sluggard does not bestir himself to get what he needs. The second line of the verse states the contrast: "To be industrious is a man's precious asset."

12:28 *Leads to death.* An alternate translation reads: "And its pathway is marked 'no death.'" *Righteousness* does not end in *death.*

13:8 *Means of redemption.* In the Hebrew text the last words of this verse are identical with the close of v. 1: "does not hear rebuke." The meaning could be that the rich man is the victim of blackmail or kidnapping because he is able to pay a *ransom* to his tormentors who, however, do not find it profitable to make threatening demands of *a poor man.*

13:9 *Rejoices.* As the face of a happy man is said to beam brightly, so *the righteous* are a *light,* burning lustily and spreading joy all about them. (4:18 f.; Jb 29:2 f.; Ps 18:28; 97:11; 112:4)

13:11 *Wealth hastily gotten.* Lit. "wealth from vanity." Men who get rich overnight by means of speculative schemes can become paupers just as quickly. *Little by little* (lit. "by a hand") denotes the more gradual accumulation of wealth by hard work or sound investments.

13:12 *Hope deferred.* Failure or delay in realizing one's aspirations makes one heartsick. Fulfillment, on the other hand, has the invigorating effect of eating from the *tree of life.* (3:18 note)

13:13 *The word.* Disregard of God's revealed will results in disaster. To spurn it is to incur liability to a debt which, at the cost of life itself, must be paid to "the last penny." (Mt 5:26)

13:15 *Is their ruin.* This phrase replaces a word in the Hebrew text meaning "constant, perpetual." Cf. RSV note. *The way* of those unfaithful to wisdom does not bear the fruit of *favor* among men but remains unchanged, i.e., barren, unproductive.

13:24 *Spares the rod.* Spare the rod and spoil the child (19:18; 22:15; 23:13 f.; 29:15, 17). Modern educators may advise other methods of restraining a child. But the fact remains that parents do their children a loving service if they provide a training based on firmness and the principle of discipline.

14:1 *Wisdom.* As in ch. 9, wisdom is personified. There Dame Wisdom is contrasted with Dame Folly, who emerges from her house to lure the unaware to their doom. Here wisdom is compared with the lady of the *house* who enhances the well-being of her household, whereas *folly . . . tears it down.*

14:3 *A rod.* Because of their succinct, compressed form some proverbs are not easily understood. If in this verse the original text is left unchanged, the following interpretative translation suggests itself: "In the mouth of a fool there is a shoot [growing out] of pride, but the lips of wise ones preserve them [from arrogance]." The Hebrew word for "shoot" occurs again only is Is 11:1, where it is said to "come forth . . . from the stump of Jesse."

14:6 *In vain.* There is no *wisdom* to be found by the person who mocks God, because he rejects "the fear of the Lord," "the beginning of knowledge." (1:7)

14:12 *Death.* The plural form "deaths" in Hebrew implies there are many paths leading off the one straight road which all end in disaster.

14:13 *Joy . . . grief. Laughter* and tears, delight and pain often follow one another in quick succession.

14:17 *Discretion.* The Hebrew word is used in a good sense in 1:4; 2:11; 3:21; 8:12. But in other contexts it can denote also cogitation aimed at doing what is wrong. If here it has the meaning of "evil devices" (as in 12:2; 24:9), then the verse points out that the short-tempered person *acts foolishly* and the man plotting evil "is hated."

14:22 *Loyalty and faithfulness.* Cf. 3:3 note.

14:24 *Their wisdom.* The unchanged text of this verse reads: "The crown of the wise is their riches, but the folly of fools [remains] folly." Apparently one of the "riddles" employed to teach wisdom (1:6 note), it yields meaning if explained as follows: Riches crown the efforts of the wise, whereas folly is productive of nothing but folly.

14:30 *The flesh.* Mental and bodily health interact. A detrimental *passion* frequently mentioned is jealousy. (6:34; 27:4)

14:31 *His Maker.* Kindness to fellowmen is not only a humanitarian act. Human relations are the concern of Him who made all men, the *poor* as well as the rich. (Jb 31:13 ff.; Pr 17:5; 19:17; 22:2; Mt 25:34-40)

14:33 *Not known.* Without the negative which the RSV has supplied from the Septuagint, the verse describes a contrast between *a man of understanding* and *fools* expressed in a number of other proverbs (10:14; 12:23; 13:3): Wisdom remains quietly at work in the former whereas the latter prattle about what they regard as wisdom.

15:2 *Dispenses.* The verb in the Hebrew text

declares that *the wise* put their *tongue* to good use in disseminating *knowledge* in contrast with *the mouths of fools* which *pour out folly.* (vv. 7, 23; 16:21)

15:4 *Gentle tongue.* More lit.: "When it heals, a tongue is a tree of life." The word for *perverseness* is translated "crookedness" in 11:3.

15:7 *Minds.* Lit. "the heart," which determines the kind of words *the lips* utter.

15:8 *Sacrifice.* Outward ceremonies as such are not *an abomination to the Lord.* However, a warning is in place against using them as a cover for wickedness.

15:10 *The way.* The same word is translated "path" and defined as "the path . . . of life" in 12:28.

15:11 *Sheol . . . Abaddon.* Cf. Jb 26:5 note; see also Ps 139:8; Pr 27:20.

15:16 *A little.* Cf. 16:8; 17:1; Ps 37:16.

Trouble. When great treasure is gotten by dishonest and oppressive tactics, the despoiled victims will raise a disturbing outcry against the outrage.

15:17 *Herbs.* Not necessarily having medicinal qualities. Any dish of greens or vegetables is meant. (Dt 11:10; 1 K 21:2)

15:25 *Widow's boundaries. Widows* represent the kind of people whom *the proud* can easily dupe or rob of their possessions. (22:28; 23:10 f.; Dt 19:14; Ps 94:6; 146:9)

15:26 *Words of the pure.* The Hebrew text reads: "but clean are words of pleasantness." As offerings of only ceremonially clean animals were acceptable to the Lord, so "pleasant words" (16:24) please Him whereas *the thoughts of the wicked are an abomination to* Him.

15:30 *The light of the eyes.* A bright, cheerful look sends beams of joy into the hearts of others.

15:33 *Humility.* One must first learn to bow under the Lord's "discipline" if one is to have the right attitude to receive *honor* from others.

16:1 *Plans of . . . man.* The first nine verses of this chapter cluster about a core fact: Man proposes, but God disposes. At the very outset it should be remembered that even the capacity to think and the ability to express thought in words *belong to man* only because he has received them *from the Lord.*

16:4 *Even the wicked.* God does not create a man for the purpose of destroying him (cf. Ex 9:16 note; Ro 9:17). However, nothing happens by chance or at cross-purposes to divine providence. Hence also the wicked are not masters of their destiny. Inevitably there will come a *day of trouble* when ordained retribution will overtake them. See also Gn 50:20; Is 10:5 ff.

16:6 *Atoned for.* See 10:12; 17:9. *By loyalty and faithfulness* a man is to make amends for the harm done to his fellowman. Doing such an *evil* will be avoided from the outset if *the fear of the Lord* controls the heart.

16:10 *A king.* In Israel he was to rule as God's representative (cf. notes of Pss 2; 110). When he lived up to that responsibility, he was the exponent, administrator, and guardian of wise living. His decrees had the validity of a prophetic oracle; his decisions fostered divine justice. Unfortunately the kings of Israel fell short of this ideal. (28:15; 29:12; 31:3-5)

16:16 *Better than gold.* How much better wisdom is than *gold* or *silver* is set forth in the next verses.

16:21 *Persuasiveness.* Translated "learning" (1:5) and "precepts" (4:2). When wisdom is advocated by *pleasant speech,* men will more readily be convinced of its value.

16:25 *Death.* See 14:12 note.

16:26 *Works for him.* Man is so constituted by nature that hunger drives him to exert himself if he is not to starve to death. This observation confirms wisdom's warnings against sloth. (6:6-11; 24:30-34)

16:30 *Winks.* Be on guard against the man whose facial expressions betray wily scheming to bring *evil to pass.*

16:31 *A hoary head.* God crowns *a righteous life* with "length of days." (3:2; 10:27; 11:19, etc.)

16:33 *The lot.* It *is cast* by human hands but God determines *the decision* it is to effect. On the use of lots see the note on Urim and Thummim Ex 28:15; also Nm 26:55; 33:54; Pr 18:18.

17:1 *Feasting with strife.* Literally: "sacrifices with strife." Sacrificial meat which was to be eaten in the home made the meal a festive occasion because meat was in very short supply. Only a rich man could afford to have *a house full of* it.

17:2 *Will rule. A slave who deals wisely* could expect to be freed by his master and given authority to overrule *a son who acts shamefully.* For examples of servants who earned the esteem of their superiors and were rewarded by them see Gn 15:2; 24:2; 39:2-6; 2 Sm 16:4.

17:3 *Crucible.* As *silver* and *gold* are purified of dross, so the Lord tests the minds and *hearts* of men for the metal of unalloyed devotion. (27:21; Ps 7:9; 17:3; 66:10; Jer 6:27; 9:7; 1 Ptr 1:7)

17:6 *Glory of sons.* It is truly gratifying if sons can boast of their father's character and achievements.

17:7 *Fine speech.* One should not expect discourse excelling in wisdom on the lips of a *fool.* Still more out of place is deception on the lips of a noble character.

17:8 *Magic stone. A bribe* works like magic on recipients branded as "wicked" in v. 23.

17:14 *Letting out water.* A hole in a dike must be plugged up while it is small if it is not to become the channel of a devastating flood. So strife, if not stopped in *the beginning,* grows in vehemence and destructiveness.

17:16 *Buy wisdom.* Wisdom cannot be acquired by an impersonal investment of money. Only an inner desire for it is acceptable coin when one sets out to buy it.

17:17 *For adversity. A friend,* if indeed he is one, will be ready at all times to act as a buffer against *a brother's adversity.*

17:18 *Pledge.* Cf. 6:1 note.

17:19 *His door high.* To live high and ostentatiously makes others jealous and courts ruin.

17:23 *Bosom.* The folds of the garment serving as a pocket. (6:27)

17:27 *Has a cool spirit.* Not hot-headed.

18:1 *Is estranged.* The verse makes a point of common experience if translated: "He who separates himself [from others] seeks gratification of his [own] desire (10:24; 11:23); he breaks out in a rage against all sound wisdom." Anyone who declares himself independent of communal restraints is out to give free rein to selfish drives and, as a result, makes peaceful relations with others impossible.

18:2 *His opinion. A fool* does not know enough to hide his lack of discrimination by silence. He reveals his stupidity by talking nonsense.

18:8 *Inner parts.* Choice bits of slander, eagerly gobbled up, leave a deep-seated impression.

18:11 *Strong city.* Cf. 10:15 note. When *a rich man* puts his trust in *wealth* rather than in the Lord (10), the protection he seeks may turn out to exist only "in his imagination." (RSV note)

18:12 *Humility.* Cf. 15:33 note.

18:14 *Can bear.* A man can stand up under physical suffering; but once his *spirit* is *broken,* he collapses.

18:16 *Makes room.* A generous person makes friends. The good will he creates opens avenues for his advancement.

18:18 *The lot.* Cf. 16:33 note.

18:19 *A brother helped.* The Hebrew text yields another meaning if translated: "A brother wronged is more difficult [to win] than a fortified city; contentions [between brothers] are like a bar on the gates of a city." It is a verifiable observation that reconciliation gets more difficult the closer the parties to a feud are related to one another.

18:20 *Satisfied.* We reap what our words sow. (12:14; 13:2; 18:21)

18:24 *Friends.* There are people who will cut a friend to pieces if it is to their advantage. Such an experience, however, should not lead to cynicism. It is possible to find a friend who will remain loyal, cost what it may. (17:17; 1 Sm 18:1-3)

19:1 *A poor man.* The poor man who refuses to violate *his integrity* in order to get rich is a *better* character than the person who stoops to deception. The latter *is* also *a fool* to think that ill-gotten gain brings happiness.

19:4 *Wealth.* Cf. 14:20.

19:6 *Generous man.* One word in Hebrew, translated "prince" and "nobleman" (8:16; 17:7, 26; 25:7). He can buy *favor* and allegiance with *gifts.*

19:7 *Hate him.* Because he constantly implores them for help.

He pursues V. 7 consists of three lines whereas all proverbs in this section of the book are limited to two. *But does not have them* may be rendered: "But they are not," i.e., they *go far from him* in order to escape his persistent begging.

19:10 *Live in luxury.* Affluence would not become him because it would only afford him the means to make a more flamboyant display of his folly. It is even less likely that *a slave* who unthinkingly obeyed orders would know how to use administrative authority in regulating the affairs of *princes.*

19:13 *Continual dripping.* A leaking roof makes for disagreeable living. (27:15; Ec 10:18)

19:18 *On his destruction.* A father in effect signs his son's death warrant if he fails to *discipline* him. Or the meaning may be: the father is not to let up on discipline thinking that the son can no longer be dissuaded from a life of crime which sooner or later will cost him his life.

19:19 *Do it again.* A man with a bad temper is incurable. *If you deliver him* from the bad consequences of his *great wrath,* he will only get into trouble again.

19:22 *A liar.* Even though *a poor man* lacks the resources to prove his desire to help, he *is better* to have as a friend than the person of means whose promises of aid prove to be lies.

19:23 *Leads to life.* Though printed in three lines in English, this verse consists of two parallel statements. The second and third lines form a single statement, explaining how *the fear of the Lord* affects the person committed to it: he goes to sleep well-fed and without fear of *harm.*

19:24 *Bring it back.* A touch of ironic humor: a *sluggard* is too lazy even to put food into *his mouth.* (26:15)

19:25 *Will learn.* Struck by blows of retribution, *a scoffer* "rages against the Lord" (3), but *the simple* (1:4 note) takes warning from the fate of the wicked to live prudently.

20:1 *A mocker.* "Those who tarry long over wine" (23:29-35) show its stupefying effect in their mockery of God and their brawling among themselves.

20:5 *Draw it out.* Some people may use dissembling language in order to keep their real intentions hidden in deep secrecy, but *a man of understanding* knows how to uncover them by probing beneath the surface of the schemer's words.

20:6 *Proclaims.* Professions of *loyalty* to others are plentiful, but people *faithful* to their promise to give help are rare.

20:9 *Who can say. . .?* The self-evident answer is: no one. This confession of universal human failure to keep the *heart clean* of *sin* applies also to "a righteous man who walks in his integrity." (7; see also Ps 14:3; 51:5 note; Jb 14:4 note)

20:11 *Even a child.* The kind of character training the individual needs is apparent at an early age.

20:12 *Hearing . . . seeing.* These senses with which the Creator has endowed man are to be used to become aware of the way of life which conforms to God's revealed will. (Jer 5:21; Eze 12:2)

20:14 *Boasts.* It was not uncommon for a *buyer* to pretend to find imperfections in the wares offered for sale in order to get them at a reduced price only to brag later of his cunning in getting a bargain.

20:16 *Garment.* The outer garment was deposited by the borrower as security for a loan

(Ex 22:25 ff.). For the kind of business transaction referred to here see 6:1 note. This proverb seems to say with subtle irony that once a person has made a speculative investment with *foreigners* all he can do is vainly to hold them to their contract, which very likely will prove worthless.

20:18 *Are established.* If "plans" are not to "go wrong," they should be reviewed by "many advisers" (15:22; 11:14), as the disastrous results of an ill-advised *war* demonstrate on a large scale. (Lk 14:31)

20:25 *"It is holy."* If in a momentary rapture of emotions a person makes a rash vow in sacred things, he may find himself caught in the predicament of being unable to pay or do what he has pledged.

20:26 *Winnows drives the wheel.* In administering justice the king acts like a farmer who sifts out the grain from the chaff or drives "a cart wheel" over the stalks to thresh out the kernels. (Ps 1:4; Jb 21:18; Is 28:27 f.; Am 1:3)

20:27 *Spirit.* "The breath of life" God breathed into man's nostrils distinguishes him from all other creatures (Gn 2:7 note). It penetrates, illumines, and energizes every human faculty.

20:30 *Blows that wound.* Cf. 13:24 note. In educating His adult children the heavenly Father also resorts to deeply cutting *strokes* of adversity in order to *cleanse away evil* entrenched in *the innermost parts* of their being.

21:1 *A stream of water. In the hand of the Lord* even a *king's* thoughts are like water in an irrigation canal which a farmer can divert into the channels he selects.

21:3 *Sacrifice.* Cf. 15:8 note; Ps 40:6 note; Is 1:10-17; Am 5:21-24.

21:9 *Corner of the housetop.* Where he is lonely and cramped for space. This verse is repeated 25:24. See also 19:13; 21:19; 27:15.

21:11 *A scoffer.* Cf. 19:25 note.

21:12 *Righteous.* God, the righteous Judge, may be meant. If a man of good character is meant, the proverb may say to him: If you take cognizance of a stately house built with the earnings from crime, don't forget that there is Someone who topples *the wicked* into *ruin.* (3:33; 14:11; 15:25)

21:14 *Bosom.* Cf. 17:23 note.

21:16 *The dead.* Cf. 2:18 note.

21:18 *Ransom.* When *the righteous* is delivered from trouble and *the wicked* gets into it instead, the penalty exacted from the latter is, as it were, a ransom which sets *the upright* free from suffering his fate. See Is 43:3, where the catastrophes inflicted on the Egyptians are said to be the ransom which freed Israel from slavery.

21:20 *Precious treasure.* Because a wise man does not squander his money on "pleasure" (17), he always has on hand a store of things his family desires for its keep and comfort. "Oil" (RSV note), a staple in an oriental household, also served to make life pleasant. (Ps 104:15)

21:25 *Desire.* Because the *sluggard* desires always to be at ease, he dies of privation. (6:6 ff.; 19:24; 26:13 ff.)

22:1 *Favor.* A good reputation is necessary if one is to have the good will and respect of his fellowmen.

22:2 *Maker.* Cf. 14:31 note; 17:5; 29:13.

22:3 *The simple.* Cf. 1:4 note; 14:16; 27:12.

22:8 *The rod of his fury.* When well-deserved *calamity* overtakes the sower of *injustice,* he will no longer be capable of inflicting blows on his innocent victims.

22:9 *Bountiful eye.* Lit. "he who is good of eye," i.e., a person whose eyes let his benevolent character shine like a "lamp" (Mt 6:22). An evil eye betrays a "stingy," "miserly" man. (23:6; 28:22)

22:12 *Keep watch.* The Lord sees to it that *knowledge* provides an enduring way of life but *overthrows* the declared intentions of the wicked.

22:13 *A lion.* The sluggard is the butt of ridicule as in 19:24; 26:13 ff. He makes the most preposterous excuses for his indolence.

22:15 *In the heart of a child.* A child's innate tendency to evil should be curbed by stern discipline. (13:24; 22:6; 29:15, 21)

22:17—24:34 TWO GROUPS OF INSTRUCTIONS INCORPORATING "THE WORDS OF THE WISE"

22:17—24:22 The Main Group

22:17 *Hear the words.* This verse introduces another group of wise sayings similar in form as well as content to "the words of the wise" (1:6) found in chs. 1—9. The intervening "proverbs of Solomon" (10:1—22:16) are a miscellaneous collection of pronouncements on wise living, each limited to a verse of two lines. In 22:17—24:22, as in the first section of the book, there are larger units dealing with a given topic. Here too the purpose is not to offer tried maxims—proverbs in our sense of the term—but to address advice and admonition to the "son" or pupil in wisdom's school, pleading with him not to stray from a God-pleasing conduct of life. Because he is so easily misled, warnings against dangers along the way, previously sounded, are repeated and restated.

22:20 *Thirty sayings.* The traditional Hebrew text here has only one word which means "three days ago," "some time ago." It would represent the attempt of the wise man to underscore the importance of his instruction; he is once more urging acceptance of the *admonition and knowledge* supplied some time ago in written form. A marginal note in the Hebrew text recommends reading a word which looks very much like the above adverb but means "officers" or "captains" and is taken to mean things of high rank, "excellent things" (KJV) or "noble things" as in 8:6. Supplied with other vowels, the consonants of the marginal reading spell the numeral *thirty.* This rendering is widely accepted because it provides a link with an ancient Egyptian document, entitled "The Instruction of Amen-em-Opet," which is dated variously from 1300 B.C. to 300 B.C. In this treatise on wise living the writer calls on the reader to "see these thirty chapters" written on the subject. Furthermore a goodly number of exhortations in chs. 22—24 of the Book of Proverbs are similar to prescriptions offered by the Egyptian sage. For the possibility and the significance of a proposed interdependence of the two documents see the Introduction, "Purpose and Content."

22:26 *Give pledges.* Cf. 6:1 note.

22:27 *Bed.* Foreclosure by unscrupulous creditors may well deprive you of a place to sleep.

22:28 *Ancient landmark.* The marker at the property line sometimes consisted only of a heap of stones. Cf. 23:10; Dt 19:14; 27:17.

23:2 *A knife to your throat.* Restrain yourself as if your life depended on it.

23:3 *Deceptive food.* The host may be deceiving you if you believe he is wining and dining you out of friendship for you.

23:7 *Inwardly reckoning.* If his undivulged calculations were known, it would be evident that he does not mean what he says when he plays the part of a generous party-giver.

23:8 *Pleasant words.* As you become aware of his true character, the food nauseates you and you realize that the exchange of pleasantries was a waste of breath.

23:11 *Redeemer.* Cf. Jb 19:25 second note; Ps 19:14; Is 41:14, etc.

23:13 *Will not die.* Not a premature criminal death. See also 19:18 note; 13:24; 22:15; 29:15.

23:15 *Glad.* Nothing will please the master more than to see the *son* walk the way of wisdom.

23:21 *Drowsiness.* Stupor brought on by too much drinking and eating.

23:23 *Buy wisdom.* Cf. 4:7 note.

23:27 *Adventuress.* The Hebrew word is so translated in 6:24, but "loose woman" in 2:16 (cf. note); 5:20; 7:5. Having relations with an adulteress is like falling into a deep, narrow pit from which there is no escaping.

23:29 *Complaining.* Those "who tarry long over wine" fancy themselves victims of assault and battery.

23:30 *Mixed wine.* Cf. Ps 75:8 note; Pr 9:2.

23:34 *Top of a mast.* The meaning of the verse seems to be that to an intoxicated person everything under and about him seems to rise and fall like the waves of the *sea.*

23:35 *They struck me.* In this verse the drunkard speaks as he begins to sober up. He vaguely remembers having been in a brawl but has no recollection of feeling any pain, anesthetized by alcohol as he was. An addicted inebriate, he wants to *awake* from his stupor only enough to get *another drink.*

24:1 *Envious.* Cf. vv. 19 f.; 23:17; Ps 37:1 note.

24:3 *A house.* The prosperity of evil men rests on shifting sands whereas life *built* on *wisdom* is like a house having solid foundations (Mt 7:24 f.). Its "rooms" are a safe depository for "riches" accruing from prudent living.

24:5 *Mightier.* The Hebrew text (RSV note) may simply say: "A wise man is powerful; a man of knowledge has formidable strength," letting the next verse explain why, contrary to appearances, these statements are true. (20:18 note)

24:7 *In the gate.* Because *wisdom* is beyond the reach of a *fool,* he has nothing to contribute to the deliberations of the elders of a city when they meet at its gate, the town hall of those days. (Dt 21:19; 22:24)

24:10 *If you faint.* The verse seems to say: to be of any value, your *strength* must be able to stand the test of *the day of adversity.*

24:11 *Rescue.* "A truthful witness saves lives" (14:25). To keep silence in the trial of a person accused of a capital offense, pretending not to know anything about the case, and thus to contribute to a miscarriage of justice, is a crime which does not go undetected and unpunished by the Lord "who weighs the heart." (12; 21:2; 1 Sm 16:7)

24:13 *Eat honey.* Wisdom is just as *good* and *sweet.* For the same comparison see 16:24; Ps 19:10; 119:103.

24:16 *Falls seven times.* God helps *a righteous man* back on his feet no matter how often he falls (Ps 37:23 f.), but a single *calamity* is enough to lay *the wicked* low because he fails to seek forgiveness and deliverance from the Lord.

24:18 *Turn away.* Self-righteous gloating over an enemy's fall incurs even greater guilt and punishment than the crime for which the Lord struck him down.

24:21 *The king.* In Israel he was to rule as God's vicegerent. The Hebrew text of the second line (RSV note) can be retained. It makes the point that association with those who have a change of heart and no longer fear God and the king makes the son liable to share their disaster and ruin.

24:23-34 An Appendix

24:23 *Sayings of the wise.* Vv. 23-34 represent an appendix to "the words of the wise" introduced in 22:17.

24:26 *Kisses the lips.* To tell the truth when questioned about someone is an act of friendship worthy of the token of the most intimate love.

24:30 *A sluggard.* This comparatively long tirade against indolence (30-34) is not the first nor the last warning issued against this vice in the Book of Proverbs. The last two verses are an echo of 6:10 f. See also 10:26; 13:4; 15:19; 19:24; 20:4; 21:25; 22:13; 26:13-16.

25:1—29:27 PROVERBS OF SOLOMON ADDED BY "THE MEN OF HEZEKIAH"

25:1 *Solomon.* See Introduction, "Authorship." (Chs. 25—29 are a collection of maxims which *the men of Hezekiah* excerpted from a larger compilation of Solomonic wise sayings. In the first three chapters a topical grouping of subject matter is evident, whereas in chs. 28 and 29 no logical sequence is observed, as is the case in the first collection of the Proverbs of Solomon (chs. 10—22). It will also be apparent that chs. 28 and 29 consist almost entirely of brief, one-verse maxims, similar to proverbs in our sense of the term and those in chs. 10—22, whereas in chs. 25—27 sage advice is offered in longer literary units. The first seven verses of ch. 25, e.g., focus on thoughts dealing with the king.

25:2 *Conceal things.* Because He is God and not man, God remains beyond human comprehension even when He reveals Himself to men (Dt 29:29; 1 K 8:12; Is 40:13 f.; 45:15; 55:8 f.; Ro 11:33; 1 Co 2:7). Therefore it behooves them to glorify Him. Kings, however, are to be honored if they use their wisdom and judicial authority *to search things out* which need to come to light if their throne is to "be established in righteousness" (5). At the same time, they too may proceed on occasion in a way which is "unsearchable" (3), i.e., keeping their plans and maneuvers a deep secret.

25:8 *Into court.* Hasty litigation may be a boomerang. Try first to settle a dispute with a brother out of court, telling him his faults "between you and him alone." (Mt 18:15; Ro 12:18)

25:11 *Fitly spoken.* The right *word* spoken "in season" is "a joy to a man" (15:23), beautiful and precious as *gold* cast in the shape of *apples* and set off in *silver* filigree.

25:13 *Cold of snow.* On the hot days of harvesttime workers in the field would be refreshed by a snow-cooled drink and so avoid a sunstroke. (2 K 4:18 f.)

25:15 *Persuaded.* Not an angry outburst but *patience* and "a soft answer" (15:1) may mollify a peevish and arbitrary prince. Gentle persuasion can *break* down resistance, hard as *a bone* though it be.

25:16 *Honey.* Honey is a wholesome delicacy. But when a person consumes it in large quantities, its sweetness has a cloying effect. Just so, says v. 17, friendliness and neighborliness, if carried to tactless extremes, become an offensive intrusion into privacy.

25:20 *Songs.* A display of lighthearted gayety is offensive when people are not in the mood for it. To pour *vinegar* into a pot of "lye" (RSV note) is a silly waste of resources.

25:26 *Muddied spring.* To see *a righteous man* succumb to wicked influences is as saddening and dismaying as coming upon a clear stream or *spring* which trampling feet have muddied and *polluted.*

25:27 *Be sparing.* The Hebrew text (RSV note) complements the first line of the text if rendered: "neither [is it good] to seek honor upon honor."

26:1 *Like snow.* The next 12 verses, except v. 2, have something uncomplimentary to say about the *fool.* Here the point is made that for a fool to hold a responsible position which men regard highly is an incongruous situation.

26:2 *Causeless. A curse* uttered without provocation by "a prating fool" (10:8) will have as little effect as birds *flitting* about aimlessly but never settling anywhere.

26:3 *A rod.* Cf. 10:13 note.

26:4 *Answer not.* Treatment of a fool may vary with circumstances. As a general rule it should be taken for granted that it is pointless to engage him in debate in order to convince him of his *folly.* At times, however, it may be advisable to "answer" him, as v. 5 states, if for no other reason than to keep him from thinking that he is "wise" because he hears no rejoinder.

26:8 *Binds the stone.* It defeats the purpose of a *sling* to fasten a stone into it so tightly that the missile cannot be released.

26:10 *Like an archer.* It is no longer clear with whom the fool is compared here. A suggested translation of the verse, more in keeping with the traditional Hebrew text, is as follows: "A master craftsman goes through with every [task], but he who hires a fool is like a person hiring whoever happens to come along." A workman so chosen at random evidently will not be qualified to do the job; in fact he may do more harm than good.

26:12 *In his own eyes.* The most hopeless of fools is the supercilious person: his self-conceit makes him impervious to suggestions intended to help him overcome his ignorance. (5; 3:7; Is 5:21; Ro 1:22)

26:13 *A lion.* Vv. 13-16 are directed against the folly of sloth. For similar strictures, barbed with sarcasm, see 22:13 note; 6:6 note.

26:16 *Seven men.* Here, as in other instances, seven is not a numeral but denotes a round number of persons or things, their total being ample to illustrate the point under consideration. (25; 6:16; 9:1)

26:17 *A passing dog.* Dogs were not domesticated in ancient Israel. Whoever seized one of these wild animals *by the ears* was sure to be bitten.

26:22 *Delicious morsels.* Cf. 18:8 note.

26:23 *Glaze.* "Silver of dross" (RSV note) is the metallic residual after the silver was removed from the ore. Words of ardent love, spoken by a hypocrite, are like the shiny finish made of this substance and applied to pottery to hide the base material underneath it.

27:3 *Provocation.* What a fool says or does to annoy and nettle others.

27:4 *Jealousy.* Nothing appeases an outraged husband. (6:30 note)

27:6 *Profuse. A friend,* because he is faithful to his avowal to be a friend indeed, will inflict *wounds* of rebuke but only sparingly and as needed. A deceitful *enemy,* however, will shower a profusion of importunate *kisses* on a person to express pretended friendship.

27:9 *By trouble.* The second line of the verse may be translated so as to make the good counsel of a friend produce the same pleasing effect on *the soul* which oil and perfume have on the body (RSV note). The verse then reads: "As oil and perfume make the heart glad, so a man's friend is sweet by reason of the counsel of the soul," i.e., counsel given from the heart, in all sincerity.

27:10 *Brother's house.* Because the next of kin may be too *far away* to render aid in a sudden emergency, don't hesitate to appeal to a nearby friend, trusting him to stick "closer than a brother." (18:24 note)

27:11 *Reproaches me.* The *wise* conduct of the pupil will refute the contention that the teacher instills wrong principles or is ineffective in inculcating what is right.

27:13 *Surety.* Cf. 6:1 note; 20:16 note.

27:14 *Blesses his neighbor. Loud* and profuse mouthing of salutations prompts the *neighbor* who senses their insincerity to respond with a curse.

27:15 *Continual dripping.* Cf. 19:13 note; 21:9, 19.

27:16 *Restrain her.* The person who tries to shut up a garrulous, "contentious woman" might as well try to impound *the wind;* his *right hand* touches oil, i.e., it is as useless as attempting to keep something as fluid and smooth as oil from slipping through one's fingers.

27:17 *Iron sharpens iron.* If you associate long enough with a person, some of his traits will rub off on you no matter how different you and he are in character. (13:20; 22:24 f.)

27:20 *Sheol and Abaddon.* Cf. 15:11 note.

27:21 *Silver . . . gold.* Cf. 17:3 note. To appraise a man's character, take note of the people or things he praises or of the people who *praise* him.

27:23 *Flocks . . . herds.* A shepherd who day in and day out cares for his animals may not overnight amass great "riches" or wear a "crown" of renown (24), but he can be assured of having enough to feed and clothe his family; gradually he may even be able to increase h s landholdings. See 6:1 note for a warning against speculating in get-rich-quick schemes.

28:2 *Many rulers. A land* cannot prosper when rulers come to power only to be toppled in turn by new regimes. It is also true that the more officials a land has the greater is the burden of taxation to support the bureaucracy.

28:3 *A poor man.* An impoverished official or landholder who makes heartless demands on his subordinates is like a cloudburst which washes away everything, leaving the victims destitute of the necessities of life.

28:4 *The law.* The Hebrew word here and in vv. 7 and 9 lacks the definite article. In 3:1; 4:2; 7:2 the instructor in wisdom uses the same term to denote his "teaching." People who reject the precepts here set forth thereby sanction and promote the life-style of *the wicked,* which is an abomination to the Lord.

28:9 *An abomination. Prayer* is blasphemous hypocrisy if the petitioner does not at the same time make a sincere effort to live according to the teaching of wisdom. (15:8 note)

28:11 *Find him out. A poor man* may not have an abundance of worldly graces, but if he *has understanding,* he is able to expose the *rich* man's claim to wisdom as sham and self-conceit.

28:17 *A fugitive.* According to Israel's law "the avenger of blood" could track down and execute a "murderer" (Nm 35:19 ff.). *No one* was to obstruct justice by helping the criminal to escape.

28:18 *Into a pit.* The Hebrew words for "pit" and "one" are the same except for one letter. If left unchanged, the traditional Hebrew text points out that "he who is perverse in his ways will come to grief on one" of them; i.e., though his duplicity goes unpunished for some time, sooner or later one of his crimes will trip him up.

28:20 *Hastens.* He determines to get *rich* regardless of the tactics he must use.

28:24 *Companion.* Anyone who by violence or deceit gets control of parental property and then adds insult to injury by brazenly denying having done anything wrong is so degenerate that he will not shrink from wholesale bloodshed, taking as many lives as "the destroyer" who slew the firstborn in all Egypt. (Ex 12:23, 29; see also 2 Sm 24:16)

29:4 *Gifts.* Contributions in the form of taxes or payments exacted in return for political favors.

29:9 *An argument.* If brought to court, *a fool* exhibits his lack of understanding by alternatingly acting the part of a madman and of a clown, causing endless confusion.

29:10 *The wicked.* If the Hebrew text is retained (RSV note) the meaning is: "the upright show concern for his life," i.e., for the *life* of the *one who is blameless.*

29:13 *Meet together.* Though different in many respects, *the poor man and the oppressor* have a most precious gift in common: their eyesight, bestowed on them by the same Maker who also is not indifferent to what happens to the poor at the hands of the oppressor. (22:2; 14:31 note; 17:15)

29:15 *Left to himself.* Cf. 13:24 note.

29:16 *Their downfall.* At His time and in His way God will put an end to the triumph of wickedness.

29:18 *Prophecy.* Communicated by revelation, divine rules of behavior are designed to keep men from acting like uninhibited animals. To "break loose" (Ex 32:25) from such *restraint* brings dire consequences.

29:19 *By mere words.* More than verbal castigation is required if a sullen slave is to be taught to do things right. Corporal punishment, however, was to be kept in bounds. (Ex 21:2-11, 20, 26 f.; see also Dt 5:14 f.; 15:12-18; 23:15 f.)

29:21 *Hei-.* This Hebrew noun occurs only here. If one letter were written slightly different, it would spell the word for "head shaking," pointing out that the servant would turn out to be obstinate and disobedient.

29:24 *The curse.* Anyone who shares in a thief's loot and consequently fails to identify him when a public adjuration to testify in the matter is made, is his own worst enemy.

29:25 *Fear of man.* To be afraid to live wisely because fellowmen might take exception to it does not make for tranquillity of mind. Nor does deference to human reaction solve problems but increases the risk of getting trapped in situations which threaten not only self-respect but life itself. Resolutely doing what is right and entrusting the consequences to the Lord, on the other hand, lifts to heights of serenity unreached and unmarred by life's vicissitudes.

30:1—31:31 FOUR ADDITIONAL COMPOSITIONS EXTOLLING AND COMMENDING WISDOM

30:1-14 The Words of Agur

30:1 *Agur.* "The wise" men whose "words" are found in 22:17—24:34 and "the men of Hezekiah" who "copied" chs. 25—29 are left unnamed. The last two chapters of Proverbs are virtually anonymous also, even though Agur and Lemuel (31:1) are mentioned as authors. No other references to these men can be found. The only clue to their identity may be contained in the word *Massa.* It appears, e.g., in the titles of some prophets (Nah, Hab, Ml), where it is translated "burden" (KJV) and "oracle" (RSV). If, however, it is a proper noun, the name of one of Ishmael's sons (Gn 25:14; 1 Ch 1:30), we would know only that they were related in some way to an Edomite or Arabian tribe. For a similar situation see the note on the land of Uz (Jb 1:1). The name *Jakeh* is completely unknown, as is also *Ucal. Ithiel* is on record as the name of a Benjaminite (Neh 11:7). Perhaps the latter two were the sage's pupils or followers.

The man says. Lit. "the oracle of the man," as in Nm 24:3; 2 Sm 23:1.

30:2 *Too stupid.* Agur disavows having "learned" the "wisdom" or acquired the "knowledge" necessary to fathom "the Holy One" (3) because he has to admit that he is unable even to comprehend his fellow human beings—their physical, mental, emotional capacities—even if others may claim to be able to do so (cf. Ps 73:22; 92:5 f.). Vv. 2 f. are an echo of the lesson Job learned (Jb 42:1-6; cf. ch. 28) after God spoke to him "out of the whirlwind." (Jb 38—41)

30:4 *Ascended.* God is beyond the reach of man's puny investigative power. He can't be brought down into the laboratory of human thought processes to be dissected, analyzed, classified. Knowledge of Him becomes available only as He condescends to let it *come down* from *heaven.* "The only Son, who is in the bosom of the Father, he has made him known." (Jn 1:18; 3:13)

30:5 *Word.* When God discloses Himself to men, He is said to be speaking to them. A word is the means of human communication of thought; produced by a rational mind, it transmits signals which his fellowmen can decode and understand. What God discloses to His creatures is reliable, redemptive, holy, adequate. (Dt 4:2; 12:32; Ps 18:30; 19:7-10; 33:4; 56:4, 11; 107:20; Rv 22:18 f.)

30:7 *I Ask.* Trusting what he has heard through the "word of God," Agur prays for lifelong help to overcome *two things* in particular: the temptations to deception and those incidental to great riches (arrogant self-sufficiency) and extreme poverty (stealing).

30:10 *Slander.* The prohibition against character assassination applies also when the victim is a lowly *servant.* Because his master is apt not to believe what he says in his self-defense, he is driven to invoke punishment on the slanderers by uttering a *curse* on them.

30:11 *There are those.* Vv. 11-14 mention four classes of people who undermine family and community life: wicked children (11), those blind to "their filth" (12), the arrogant (13), the merciless, rapacious destroyers of "the poor." (14)

30:15-33 Five Numerical Proverbs Interlaced with Warnings Against Folly

30:15 *Three things . . . four.* In vv. 15-33 wisdom is advocated by the rhetorical device of raising a given numeral to the next higher one. Its purpose was to indicate that enough data could be offered to sustain the validity of a stated fact (Jb 5:19 note; Pr 6:16). There is no reason to doubt that Agur was familiar with this ancient form of literary composition. The first thing to be discussed is greed. Insatiable as a *leech,* it is *never satisfied* by what it consumes, as little as the examples to be cited ever cease to demand more: "Sheol" or the grave, its maw always open for new victims; a "barren womb," ever requiring fertilization but never producing a child; "the earth," never permanently saturated by moisture; "fire," its existence depending on ever new supplies of fuel.

30:17 *Mocks a father.* As it is in the nature of some things to be "never satisfied" (15 f.), so conversely it is unnatural for children to treat their parents shamefully. Here the punishment is graphically portrayed which children deserve who do what v. 11 says.

30:18 *Too wonderful.* The sage, wise though he may be, finds himself baffled by mysterious phenomena in nature which testify to the superior wisdom of Him whose "let there be" produced them: an eagle's ability to mount the wind and ride the air; the serpent's mode of locomotion without feet; the ship's passage through the sea without leaving a path; man, created "male and female" and endowed with the power of procreation.

30:20 *An adulteress.* Another perplexing riddle is how the prerogatives of holy matrimony can be prostituted to such a bestial level as to regard promiscuous intercourse as nothing more than the natural satisfaction of a physical appetite.

30:21 *Earth trembles.* It creates an intolerable situation if: an uncouth, wholly incompetent person should be entrusted with royal power (19:10 note); a boorish churl has the means to live sumptuously; a woman is unloved by her husband (Gn 29:31 note); a maid lords it over her mistress. (Gn 16:4)

30:24 *Small . . . wise.* Though not impressive for size or strength in the animal world, these *four* irrational creatures can teach human beings some big lessons in wise living: "the ants," which lay by winter's store in summer (6:6 ff.); "the badgers" or "rock badger" (Lv

11:5), a kind of marmoth which builds homes in the safety of steep cliffs (Ps 104:18); "the locusts," which are virtually irresistible in attack because of disciplined, unified strategy; "the lizard," which is resourceful enough to gain entrance into places usually heavily guarded such as "palaces."

30:29 *Stately. Three things* are chosen from the animal world to serve as examples of the kind of bearing becoming "a king." The Hebrew word translated "cock" on authority of the Septuagint occurs nowhere else in Scripture. The suggestion that it is a poetic term for a warhorse is attractive.

30:32 *Exalting yourself.* If you foolishly have put on airs, aping the demeanor of a king (29-31), restrain your vanity as you should your impulse for *devising evil.*

30:33 *Pressing.* The results of three kinds of action, expressed by the same verb, are cited. The first two are analogies from observable cause-and-effect situations, adduced to demonstrate the validity of a principle in human behavior. As surely as constant stirring of milk produces *curds* and continued pressure on the nose causes it to bleed, so surely will *strife* break out if you let *anger* go on agitating your mind.

31:1-9 The Words of Lemuel

31:1 *Lemuel.* There are no clues to his identity. For *Massa* see 30:1 note. His mother wanted him to be a good *king* and earnestly exhorted him to avoid: sexual immorality (3); drunkenness (4-7); neglect of the helpless (8); judicial partiality (9). Instruction by both parents is presupposed by such passages as 1:8 note; 6:20. However, a mother's teaching is on record only here.

31:2 *Vows.* Cf. Hannah's vow (1 Sm 1:11). The son's name "Lemuel," meaning "to God," seems to indicate that the mother promised to dedicate him to God.

31:4 *To desire.* If the word in the Hebrew text is to be read "where" (RSV note), it is part of a direct quote, the introductory formula being understood: "It is not for kings to say: 'Where is strong drink?'"

31:6 *Give.* While overindulgence in alcoholic drink is to be shunned (20:1; 23:29-35), its use is recommended to deaden the pain of those *perishing* and to "gladden the heart" of those *in bitter distress.* (Ps 104:15; Mt 27:34, 48; 1 Ti 5:23)

31:8 *The dumb.* They have no voice in pleading their cause.

31:10-31 An Acrostic Poem in Praise of the Virtuous Woman

31:10 *A good wife.* The first letter of the opening word is also the first of the 22 letters of the Hebrew alphabet. Each verse hereafter begins with a word whose first letter is next in alphabetic sequence. See The Book of Psalms, Introduction, "Poetry."—Economic and social conditions have changed since this poem was penned. However, the principles of virtue, expressed here in terms of a bygone culture, are not out of date. A modern housewife will be the better spouse and mother if she emulates her ancient sister. Such a good wife, lit. "a woman of worth" (Ru 3:11 note), may be hard to *find* but she is worth the search; she surpasses the value of precious jewelry (cf. 3:15; 12:4; 19:14). As a helpmeet and homemaker she exhibits the opposite traits of the women so roundly denounced in the Book of Proverbs. (2:16-19; chs. 5 and 7; 11:22; 19:13; 21:19; 22:14; 23:27 f.; 25:24; 27:15 f.)

31:14 *From afar.* Her modern counterpart goes to great lengths in shopping for bargains.

31:16 *Buys it.* Her astute management of resources makes it possible for the family to increase its landholdings. In order to engage in such business activities, women at that time must have had considerable freedom.

31:20 Then as now, women were active in charitable pursuits.

31:21 *Snow.* In wintertime her family was warmly dressed. She could afford to buy *scarlet* and "purple" (22) material even if it was not cheap. (2 Sm 1:24; Jer 4:30)

31:23 *In the gates.* Where the council of elders met. Far from being a hindrance to *her husband,* she helped him acquire a position of honor in the community.

31:24 *Girdles.* Men of distinction wore broad belts or sashes which were expensive because they were ornately embroidered.

31:25 *Time to come.* Because of her *strength and dignity* of character there was no need to be apprehensive of the future.

31:30 *Deceitful.* A beautiful face may mask an ugly character (11:22). *A woman who fears the Lord* has an essential quality which wrinkles and disfiguring disease cannot mar.

ECCLESIASTES

INTRODUCTION

Purpose

Both Proverbs and Ecclesiastes—close together in our English Bible but separated in the Hebrew canon—give counsel on practical issues of everyday life. However, they do not duplicate but rather complement one another.

Ecclesiastes warns against concluding from the teaching of Solomon and the other sages that living in the fear of the Lord magically changes this vale of tears, "subjected to futility" as it is (Ro 8:19-22), into a heaven on earth. To expect wise living to produce the unmarred bliss of the Garden of Eden is to live in a fool's paradise.

In effect Ecclesiastes says to those who misinterpret the Book of Proverbs: "Again it is written" (Mt 4:7). In order to jar his readers out of a dream of utopian bliss the author makes statements which appear to be irreconcilable:

- He negates life, yet affirms it.
- He finds life meaningless, yet urges piety.
- He deprecates wisdom, yet counsels wise living.
- He deplores the futility of life, yet considers it a good thing to be alive.
- He finds no evidence of a moral world order, yet warns against irresponsible behavior.

However, Ecclesiastes knows also how to reconcile these inconsistencies. In order to bridge the logical gap between them, one needs only to remember his relationship to God and some resulting corollaries:

- If life is the gift of the almighty Creator of heaven and earth, it bears on it the stamp of His design.
- If the vicissitudes of life come at His direction, nothing that happens is meaningless.
- If wisdom begins and ends in the fear of the Lord, it ill behooves the creature of dust and ashes to dictate to his Maker how or when He is to fulfill His promises and execute His threats.
- If He governs the universe, no one need doubt that the laws of a moral world order are in effect.
- If He controls the outcome of man's labors, it is presumptuous to complain about the futility of life.

Authorship

The title of the book gives us no clue to the identity of its author. Ecclesiastes is not a proper noun. Nor is it found anywhere else in Scripture. However, the root from which it is derived occurs frequently in the verb meaning to assemble, convoke a meeting, and in the noun denoting an assembly or convocation. On analogy of similar Hebrew noun formations, the word "Koheleth" (1:1 RSV note) is correctly translated by the Greek derivitive "Ecclesiastes," i.e., one competent or authorized to address a gathering of people. The English equivalent "The Preacher" may be misleading. He was not primarily a pulpiteer but rather a teacher about whom people gathered to be instructed in wisdom.

Luther was among the first to suggest that the reference to the Preacher as "the son of David" who was "king over Israel" (1:1, 12) is not necessarily intended to make Solomon the author of the book. The writer wants to suggest that a man as wise, as rich, as experienced in worldly affairs as Solomon would confirm the conclusions reached in this treatise. There is even some indication that the author wanted the book to be understood as a faithful summary of the Preacher's teachings rather than his own.

Publication date of this Solomonic wisdom is not indicated by references to known historical events. The description of prevailing social and economic conditions is also too general to pinpoint a particular time in Israel's history.

Because of the author's way of developing his theme, the sequence of thought does not lend itself readily to topical divisions. Rather than detract from its impact on the reader, this style of composition has a persuasiveness all its own. The whole is like a piece of tapestry which cannot fail to attract attention. Its woof is as black as night; woven back and forth into it are threads of a bright hue. The lines so created form no regular pattern, but the abrupt change in color makes the contrast more impressive. The notes on the text point out how various sections contribute to the overall design.

1:1-3 AUTHOR AND THEME

1:1 *The Preacher.* See Introduction, "Authorship."

1:2 *Vanity of vanities.* The author boldly states a thesis the universal validity of which he is going to demonstrate in the subsequent discussion. The area of inquiry is unlimited in scope: "*All* the toil" (3) of men everywhere is going to be examined for the profit it yields. The conclusion drawn from his observations is summed up in an absolute pronouncement: *All* is vanity. There is no exception to the rule. Let men toil at whatever they will, there is only one thing they can gain from it: vanity. This doleful word occurs some 30 times in the book. It proclaims the end result of man's search for satisfaction to be as fleeting as an exhaled breath, as elusive as a handful of air, as unreal as yesterday's puff of wind. It is not disappointing only to a certain degree; it is vanity of vanities, the emptiness of emptiness. There is not a drop of reality to be squeezed out of it. A similar idiomatic doubling of nouns to express the superlative degree is found in such expressions as "the heaven of heavens" (Dt 10:14), the "King of kings" (Rv 17:14), the "Song of Songs," the Hebrew title of the Song of Solomon.

1:3 *Under the sun.* This prepositional modifier occurs only in Ec and there almost as frequently as the word "vanity" (27 times). It underscores the universal range of the Preacher's inquiry. As there is no one on whom the rays of the sun do not fall, so the judgment of vanity applies to all mankind without exception. At the same time, this phrase delimits the basis on which a pessimistic evaluation of human existence depends. It is when viewed solely from a materialistic, humanistic perspective that life on earth must be judged to be a riddle of negations. Light from an uncreated Source, higher than the observable phenomena of nature, must break in on man's darkened soul if he is to discover a meaningful relationship to the universe. The Preacher says it over and over again: Don't look *under the sun* for satisfying values in life. In order to prove this, he subjects man's mundane existence to a merciless scrutiny, laying bare every area *under the sun* where lasting happiness might be found.

1:4-11 A TREADMILL OF FRUSTRATIONS

1:4 *Goes and . . . comes.* The first disappointing feature of living "under the sun" to be noted is the unescapable imprisonment in a universe which man cannot stop from going its own independent and predetermined way. Willy-nilly he is caught up in a closed circuit of unalterable circumstances. Life is nothing but going in circles. It reaches no new goals, no matter how many generations try to change things. Tomorrow is going to be like today as surely as the sun rises and sets (5), as inevitably as the wind changes direction (6), as inexorably as rivers flow into seas to be recycled. (7)

1:8 *Utter it.* Carried along like flotsam on life's swiftly flowing stream, man only tires himself if he tries to explain what he sees and hears along the way.

1:11 *No remembrance.* If something seems "new under the sun," it is only because people forget "what has been." (9)

1:12—2:26 SOLOMON'S SEARCH FOR HAPPINESS

1:12-18 Experimentation with Wisdom

1:12 *King over Israel.* Though not mentioned by name, "the son of David" (1) who was in a position to test "everything that is done under the sun" (14) as a source of happiness was Solomon. Speaking in his name, the Preacher is anything but an atheist. God has so constituted man, he asserts, as to implant in him the urge "to search out by wisdom" (13) what life is all about (3:11). At the same time, God lets this quest for answers to crucial questions turn out to be "an unhappy business" (13) and "a striving after wind" (14). Stopped short of attaining self-sufficiency by his own ingenuity, man is reminded of his creatureliness and its limitations. The more he finds out about himself and his environment, the greater is his "vexation" and "sorrow" (18) when he cannot straighten out glaring inconsistencies or find the pieces to fit the jigsaw puzzle of life.

1:17 *Madness and folly. To know wisdom* should enable one to distinguish it from its opposite. But in the final analysis he *perceived* that the difference between the two was of no great significance.

2:1-11 Experimentation with Pleasure and Wealth

2:1 *A test.* The next area "under heaven" to be explored for human fulfillment was indulgence in pleasures which are not out of reach of "folly" because "wisdom" is not necessary to enjoy them. However, in order to get the full benefit of the experiment, Solomon would let his "mind" be guided by wisdom to the extent that he would avoid excesses. Besides "wine" "to cheer" his "body" he had everything to make life enjoyable: "houses," "gardens," wealth, servants.

2:8 *Concubines.* According to 1 K 11:3 Solomon had 300 concubines. The Preacher does not pass judgment on this feature of the royal court. He only makes the point that the king's experiment in happiness included also this kind of pleasure. However, it should be noted that he does not use the usual Hebrew term for concubine, occurring also in 1 K 11:3. The noun so translated here by RSV is not found elsewhere in Scripture. It may denote women or ladies in general, regarded as *man's delight.*

2:11 *Nothing to be gained.* It turns out to be sheer madness to expect "laughter" and "pleasure" (2) to result in true happiness. Gratification of the senses leaves life as void of satisfaction as does the exhilaration derived from achievements of the mind.

2:12-17 Wisdom and Death

2:13 *Excells folly.* The question is: If wisdom is not necessary to gratify the senses (1-12), is there an advantage in being wise rather than foolish? The answer is: It is undoubtedly true that wisdom lights a candle, dispelling some of the darkness of human existence, but its rays cannot penetrate the ultimate issues of life. Death, mysterious and inexorable, enshrouds both the wise and the fool. If therefore "one fate comes to all," whether wise or foolish, there is nothing "under the sun" to make life worthwhile.

2:18-23 Death Destroys the Fruits of Wisdom

2:18 *Leave it.* The advantage of wisdom over folly is to be questioned because death cuts down all men alike (12-17). This gloomy fact brings to mind two disillusioning corollaries. No matter how much the wise achieves in life, he must leave it all behind as if he had been foolish and accomplished nothing (Ps 49:16-20; Jb 1:21). In the second place, what a person accumulates by wisdom and toil falls into the hands of a survivor who has not labored for it and may not have the wisdom to profit from it. In Solomon's case, the man who came "after the king," his son Rehoboam, was a good example of a person who lacked the capacity to become wise; he only repeated the folly he had "already done." (12; 1 K 12)

2:24-26 No Satisfaction Apart from God

2:24 *Nothing better.* Introduced by this translation, the closing verses of this chapter let a glimmer of light into the gloomy assessment of life "under the sun." Man can *eat and drink and find enjoyment in his toil* if he keeps in mind (1) that even the bare essentials of day to day living come *from the hand of God;* (2) that He does make a distinction between "the man who pleases Him" and the man who is a willful "sinner." However, it is another exercise in vanity to try to understand how and when God makes this difference apparent (3:12, 22; 5:18; 8:15; 9:7; 11:9). —However, the Hebrew text does not have the usual form to express the comparative *better,* but says simply "good." So translated, the verse reads: "There is nothing good residing in man that he should be able to," etc. Man, created to be a rational being, seeks to understand himself and his world. But his innate capacity to think is no "good" when he tries to explain the most elementary facts of life (3:11). He must conclude that the simplest things he does as well as his highest attainments (1:12—2:17) are not worth the effort. Only as he looks beyond himself and realizes that all he is and has and can do comes *from the hand of God,* the Creator and Judge of all men, can he "eat and drink and take pleasure." (3:13)

3:1-15 MAN AND THE TIMING OF EVENTS

3:1 *A season.* In 1-9 the Preacher notes another frustrating feature of human existence if the range of view is restricted to observations *under heaven.* Man is not only carried through life like a package on a cosmic conveyor belt which he did not set in motion and which he cannot stop (1:4-11), but even during the short duration of his stay on earth he must await the arrival of propitious circumstances for everything he sets out to accomplish. To begin with, he has nothing to do with setting the time when he is to arrive on the scene and when he is to depart (2). And between his first and last breath he must depend on situations to develop which determine what he can or ought to do (2-8). The "gain" of such a state of affairs can only be fatalism, dull resignation, bitterness (9). However, when man raises his sights above what he sees "under heaven" and lets Him come into the range of his vision who "has made everything" (11), man no longer need consider himself the victim of accidents of time and circumstance. What the Creator of "seasons" (Gn 1:14) lets happen is always "beautiful in its time" (11) so that there is a right *time for every matter* (1). Man is indeed able "to be busy with" thoughts about the meaning of life because "God has given to the sons of men" the capacity to think. When He breathed into man's "nostrils the breath of life" (Gn 2:7), He also "put eternity into man's mind," i.e., an awareness that life is more than things material, temporal, and transitory (cf. Lk 12:23). However, it is also true that man, broken by sin, cannot fulfill the inborn desire to understand why "everything" God does is "beautiful in its time" (11; 8:17). Hence it behooves man to "fear before" God (14) rather than try to "be like God" (Gn 3:5). Nevertheless the assurance that not a blind fate but "God," who sees things "from the beginning to the end" (11), decides what every moment should bring His creature lifts the curse of vanity from human existence. Accepting this "gift" of God, man does not "eat and drink" merely to stay alive in a meaningless world but has reason to "take pleasure in all his toil" (13). Short as the span of their lifetime may be, men can "be happy and enjoy themselves." (12)

3:2 *A time.* The writer is not only a profound thinker but also a skillful poet. As if he were tolling a bell, he lets the word *time* ring out over human existence at the beginning and in the middle of 14 consecutive lines. In 14 pairs of examples man's subjection to a scheme of things not of his choosing or making rings out over everything he does. Each line in turn fills in pertinent details, ranging from one kind of action to its opposite pole.

3:16-22 INJUSTICE UNEXPLAINED

3:16 *Wickedness.* Everything does not appear to be "beautiful in its time" (11) when one tries to explain why "the wicked" hold sway over "the righteous," leaving victims of injustice unable to regain their rights (4:1). To have to wait for God's appointed time to "judge the righteous and the wicked" (17) and not be given any reason for His delay to act makes human existence as irrational as the fate which overtakes "the beasts" (19). From a purely biological point of view man is no different from the animal. Both are "from the dust and turn to dust again" (20; Gn 1:24; 3:19; Ps 104:29). Furthermore no physical data can be found to determine "whether the spirit of man goes upward and the spirit of the beast goes down to the earth" (21). Oriented by observations *under the sun,* man likewise does not know "what will be after him." The best he can do under such conditions is to try to "enjoy his work" (22) during his short stay on earth.

3:21 *Who knows . . . ?* For the Preacher's answer see 12:7.

4:1-16 MORE UNSOLVED INEQUITIES

4:1 *Again I saw.* From a world view rising no higher than human horizons the Preacher observed man "striving after wind" because he cannot escape the evils of society. To make his point he lists several examples: There are men in a community who can make their fellowmen so miserable that death is preferable to living (1-3); there are those whose motive for success is "envy" and rivalry (4-6); a miser is not "satisfied with riches" acquired in a lonely pursuit of material things (7-12); a ruler's acclaim and esteem comes and goes as cheers turn to jeers. (13-16)

4:2 *More fortunate.* For the same preference of death to living see 6:3; 7:1; Jb 3:11 ff.; Jer 20:14 ff.

4:5 *Eats his own flesh.* A fool destroys himself by his failure to provide the necessities of life (Pr 6:6 ff.; 10:4 f., etc.). Indolence is no remedy against envy. A partial solution of the problem is offered in the next verse: contentment with little.

4:9 *Two are better.* In vv. 9-12 the Preacher adduces three proverbs to demonstrate that man should be able to benefit from joint endeavors. Association and cooperation with others should make life at least relatively more rewarding.

4:13 *Old and foolish king. A poor and wise youth* who like Joseph rises to power from obscurity may ride the crest of popularity for a time. But "this also is vanity," to discover that "those who come later" will turn from him too, forgetting all the reason they had to "rejoice in him." (Cf. Ex 1:8)

5:1-9 HOW TO WORSHIP GOD AND BEAR OPPRESSION BY MAN

5:1 *Guard your steps.* Turning from negative observations on human existence, seen from the low vantage point "under the sun," the Preacher provides positive directives to be observed in man's relationship to God (1-7) and then adds a bit of advice on how to cope with a bad situation created by his fellowmen (8-9). In dealing with God it is imperative to be aware with what holy awe and fear man "upon earth," made of its "dust and ashes" (Gn 18:27), should undertake to commune with Him who "is in heaven." It is a *sacrifice of fools* to engage in outward rites of worship without the heartfelt intention of conforming one's life to God's will (1; 1 Sm 15:22; Ps 50:7 ff.; Pr 21:3; Is 1:11 ff.; Am 5:22 ff.). It is also a foolish mistake to think God hears prayers offered in the sanctuary simply because many words are recited. Few words, sincerely spoken, are much more acceptable than a mechanical mouthing of meaningless litanies (2-3). Vows should not be made frivolously (Pr 20:25); but once made, should be kept (4-5; Dt 23:21-23). Do not try to minimize your sin, calling it an unwitting "mistake" when you appear "before the messenger," i.e., God's priest in the temple (6-7; Lv 4; Ml 2:7).

5:3 *A dream comes.* Even in earthly affairs this proverbial saying holds true; as much worry results in disturbed dreams which do nothing to solve the problem, so nothing is gained by listening to the senseless chattering of a fool.

5:7 *Fear God.* The Preacher has been testing attempts to find meaning and satisfaction in human existence evaluated from a viewpoint "under the heavens." A relentless investigation of the best man can do confirms his initial verdict: "vanity of vanities" (1:2). This negative appraisal, however, does not plunge him into agnosticism, atheism, nihilism. In the face of it all he makes two comprehensive statements of faith, "the conviction of things not seen" (Heb 11:1). Beyond the range of physical sight there is a God, he asserts. Unaffected by the ravages of time, He remains in full control of everything He made and lets happen in heaven and on earth. To this axiomatic fact he appends a corollary defining man's relationship to Him who is "from everlasting to everlasting" (Ps 90:2). It is the brief but comprehensive directive:

Fear God. Even if fools deny His existence, acknowledge His right to determine the course of your life; even if you would rather go a different way, believe that He knows where He is leading you; even if He at times seems to succumb to forces of evil, stand in awe of His power to overrule all opposition.

5:8 *Amazed.* Do not be shocked and lose faith in God's management of the world if you encounter oppressive and corrupt officials on all levels of human government.

5:9 *A king.* If an earthly monarch is meant here, his subjects are advised that in spite of oppressive bureaucrats they must make the best of the king's aim to rule over *a land with cultivated fields.* For he will not allow exploitation to become so oppressive and confiscatory as to make the country unproductive of revenues. A greater *advantage* would be indicated if the *king* refers to the King of kings, to whom all earthly potentates must given an account.

5:10—6:12 ENJOY WHAT GOD GIVES

5:10 *Not be satisfied.* "Wealth and possessions and power" do not make man happy unless he recognizes whatever he has—whether much or little—as "the gift of God" (19). To view riches only "under the sun" and to make them life's highest goal without considering their Giver lets life end in *vanity.* The Preacher points out not only why the pursuit and amassing of material things fails to satisfy human yearning for fulfillment but also why their possession is attended by evils which the poor man is spared: (a) *he who loves money* never gets enough of it; he is like a man drinking salt water to quench his thirst (10); (b) the rich man has to fight off beggars and parasites (11); (c) overindulgence in food results in indigestion and sleeplessness (12); (d) riches, hoarded "by their owner to his hurt" rather than spent for his enjoyment, may be lost "in a bad venture" or investment, leaving a "father" no more to bequeath to his "son" than he had when "he came from his mother's womb" (13-17; Jb 1:21; Ps 49:17; Lk 12:20). However, wealth in itself need not be an evil because everything "God has given" is good. Accepting it from God's hand, the rich man can "find enjoyment in his toil" no less than the poor man whose "lot" it is to have only enough to "eat and drink" to sustain him "in all the toil." (18-20; 2:24; 3:12, 22; 8:15; 9:7)

5:13 *A grievous evil.* Wealth can waste away for various reasons just as the tissues of the body can be destroyed by an insidious disease.

5:20 *Occupied.* The person who is content with what God gives him does not have morbid worries about the number of *the days of his life.* God lets him occupy his time with thoughts and activities designed to put *joy in his heart.*

6:1 *An evil.* Vv. 1-9 continue the discussion of the limitations of riches in man's quest for happiness. God, the Giver of "wealth, possessions, and honor," must also bestow the "power to enjoy them." A man may get "all that he desires," he may be blessed with a family of "a hundred children" to share his fabulous resources, he may be accorded a lifetime of "a thousand years twice told" in which to take advantage of his countless blessings, yet if God does not also provide him with the right disposition or set of mind to "enjoy life's good things" at his disposal in such profusion, such a person is no "better off" than the dead who have nothing anymore or the child born dead who will never acquire anything (1-6). What is true of money applies also to "all the toil of man" which he spends on earthly things. He can labor to acquire much rich food "for his mouth" and strive hard to get everything to gratify his physical craving, but the more he stuffs himself the more insatiable his "desire" becomes (7-9). "To dispute" this ordained order of creaturely existence results in "more vanity" "the more words" are wasted on the subject. Man sees things from a very restricted perspective. It does not allow him to conclude "what is good for" him even during "the few days of his vain life," to say nothing of determining by observations "under the sun" "what will be after him," i.e., after he dies. (10-12; cf. Jb 42:1-6)

6:9 *Better.* This verse is a proverb similar to our popular saying: A bird in the hand is better than two in the bush.

6:10 *Named.* Before man arrives on the scene, God has *named,* i.e., ordained, *what man is* and what his limitations are to be.

7:1-25 WISE CHOICES

7:1 *Better.* Even though no one can conclude from happenings "under the sun" "what is good for man" (6:12), the Preacher nevertheless insists that one attitude or action in a given situation is better than its opposite (see the "better . . . than" maxims in Pr 16:19; 21:9, 19; 25:7, 24). The person "who fears God" (18) will make the right choice without demanding that God first "make straight" what He appears to have "made crooked" (13). Nor will he refuse to distinguish between right and wrong because his Creator does not let him "find out" how a "day of prosperity" spoiled by a "day of adversity" makes sense in an eternal scheme of things (14; 3:18). Content to accept all circumstances, whether good or bad in his opinion, as "the work of God" (13), he is willing to follow prescribed directives in coping with life's problems.

Day of death. It "is good for man" (6:12) to look realistically at death and what it does to such highly prized possessions as a good reputation. Though *better than* perfumed *ointment* (cf. Pr 22:1), it too is something man must leave behind with his mortal remains. If he had not been born, he would not have toiled to acquire something as transitory as everything else under the sun. (4:3; 6:3-5)

The Preacher proceeds to advise what one is to think and do in a world in which death terminates even such a noble achievement as *a good name.* Because life comes "from the hand of God" (2:24), it makes sense (a) to give serious thought to its brevity (1-8); (b) to submit humbly to His providence (9-14); (c) to avoid self-righteousness as well as uninhibited wickedness (15-19); (d) to acknowledge universal human depravity (19-22); (e) to recognize that there are things which are beyond human comprehension. (23-25)

7:2 *Mourning.* In this chapter the Preacher dwells at some length on man's mortality. He is not advocating a morbid, debilitating preoccupation with death, which would contradict his repeated exhortation that man "should eat and drink and find enjoyment in his toil" (2:24; 3:12, 22; 5:18; 8:15). His purpose is to warn against the "fool's" attempt to escape the hard, ugly fact of the inexorable *end of all men.* It is silly to try to forget it by *feasting,* by "laughter," by "mirth." (Cf. Ps 39:4; 90:12; 102:11)

7:6 *Crackling of thorns.* Foolish hilarity may make boisterous noises similar to the sound of burning thorns. But *the laughter of the fools* is also as short-lived as a brush fire.

7:10 *Former days. It is not from wisdom* to demand to know *why* God lets *days* come which seem bad in comparison with *better* ones in the past.

7:11 *Wisdom . . . with an inheritance.* Even though wisdom cannot stave off death, there is *an advantage* in possessing it if it is allowed to determine what one does with material things, particularly those one has received without having labored for them. (2:18 f.)

7:12 *Preserves . . . life.* If *money* is used with discretion, it can make life more tolerable than existing in dire poverty. However, true *wisdom* has *the advantage* over possessing material things because it is essential for a happiness that satisfies. (Pr 3:18, 21 f.; 4:13; 10:17; 13:14)

7:13 *Crooked.* What happens in life often does not seem to make sense (15; 1:15; 3:16; 4:1). However, leave it to God to decide what is good or bad for you at a given time. You can do so with confidence because He is not shortsighted as you are but sees everything "from the beginning to the end." (3:11; cf. Jb 1:21; 2:10)

7:16 *Overmuch.* In this and the following verse the Preacher is not advocating lowering the standards of ethical behavior. What he says is rather a warning against two opposite attitudes, both of which incur God's anger. The one is making a scrupulous observance of the Law the basis of a self-righteous claim on God's favor, as Job did when he expected better treatment in view of his good record. No less an abomination to God is the man who thinks it does not matter how wicked he is. "He who fears God shall come forth from" (18) the dangers of both hurtful views. He will not insult God presuming to put Him under obligation by an outwardly respectable life; nor will he defy the divine Lawgiver by flouting all decency.

7:19 *Gives strength. Wisdom* is a greater asset than the defenses provided by any number of *rulers that are in a city.* (9:13-18)

7:20 *Not a righteous man.* Wisdom, rooted in the fear of God, perceives mankind's true nature (1 K 8:46; Ps 19:13; Jb 15:14 f.). Because there is no one *who does good and never sins,* nobody is justified in telling the holy God what is "straight" and what is "crooked" in His management of earthly affairs (13). Nor should anyone get angry when he hears "all the things that men say" about him. His own "servant" may have good reason to curse him. (21f.)

7:23 *Far from me.* Human wisdom grants advantages over folly (2:13 f.; 7:11, 19). However, it cannot solve the mysteries of human existence. To understand completely "that which is" remains a distant, unattainable goal and an unplumbed depth (24; Jb 11:7; ch. 28; Ro 11:33 f.).

7:26—9:17 EVILS UNCOVERED BY WISDOM

7:26-29 Mankind No Longer Upright

7:26 *Bitter.* In his attempt to comprehend the meaning of life the Preacher came up against mysteries and inconsistencies which wisdom could not solve. However, as he applied his "mind to all that is done under the sun" (8:9), he became wise enough to reach the following negative conclusions: (a) human nature, created "upright," has become degenerate and succumbs to evil "devices" (26-29); (b) civil authority can be expected to be despotic and arbitrary (8:1-9); (c) the fate "the wicked" deserve is suffered by "the righteous" (8:10-15); (d) even "a wise man" "cannot find out" God's purpose in "all the work . . . done under the sun" (8:16-17); (e) death is the lot of all men regardless of their character (9:1-10); (f) the most skillful and strong are not safe from the accidents of "time and chance." (9:11-17)

Snares and nets. The "loose woman" is described in similar terms in Pr 2:16 ff.; 5:3 ff.; 7:25 ff.

7:27 *The sum. Adding one thing to another* did not give him a total which accounted for the sinister perversity of the bad woman and the folly of "the sinner" who succumbs to her wiles.

7:28 *Among a thousand.* Wisdom is hard to find among men and, according to a proverb current at the time, one must search even wider to find a wise woman (Pr 31:10). The Preacher is not a woman-hater (cf. 9:9). His point here is: mankind, both male and female, are no longer "upright," as they were when God made them. Now "they are all alike corrupt" (Ps 14:3; Ec 7:20). Driven by a mysterious, demonic power, they devise ways to corrupt what was made to be a blessing, such as the relationship between man and woman.

8:1-9 Man Debased by Fellowmen

8:1 *The wise man. A man's wisdom* may fail to give a satisfying *interpretation of a thing* (cf. 7:23 f.). Yet it gives him enough discretion to avoid a head-on collision with a despotic ruler who "lords it over man to his hurt" (9). Instead of acting precipitously, he awaits the appointed "time and way" to bring him relief from his "trouble" even though it "lies heavy upon him" and he does not know how long he will live. (6-8)

8:10-15 The Evil of Delayed Punishment

8:10 *I saw.* Another stultifying observation making human existence an irrational "vanity" (14) is the honor accorded *the wicked* to the end of their lives and their escape from retribution. Such a state of affairs encourages others to follow their example. Left without an explanation for this apparent breakdown of a moral world order, man can only cling to the assurance that somehow and sometime God will make a difference between "those who . . . fear before Him" and those who do not.

8:15 *Enjoyment.* Seen in the limited perspective of human wisdom, *man has no good thing under the sun.* Nevertheless he need not give way to cheerless pessimism or dull resignation. He is not the plaything of a blind fate. Because *the days of life* in which he toils are what *God gives him,* the Preacher can *commend enjoyment.* For the same advice see 2:24 note; 3:12, 22; 5:18-20; 9:9; cf. 5:7 note; Pr 16:9; 20:24; 21:2.

8:16-17 God's Mysterious Providence

9:1-10 Death, the Fate of Good and Evil Alike

9:1 *Examining it all.* The Preacher continues to test whether "by wisdom" (7:23-25) he can understand "all that is done under the sun" (3, 6). In this chapter he records his discovery of two other unsatisfying situations. He notes first of all that whereas *the righteous and the wise . . . are in the hand of God,* the same fate "comes to all . . . the good and the evil" alike: both "go to the dead." Hence if man is to judge by the way God's providence operates, he does not know whether he is the object of divine "love or hate" (1-6).

9:4 *Living dog.* Human nature rebels against the prospect of death. To be alive, even if it be a dog's life, is considered better than to be the corpse of the mightiest potentate, lionized by many during his lifetime.

9:5 *Know nothing.* Once man is dead, mundane aspirations and activities come to an end.

9:9 *Portion.* As when facing other problems defying a solution, so the Preacher does not let his inability to rationalize death induce him to declare life empty of all meaning (cf. 8:15 note). To offset the gloomy thought of death he appends several verses explaining how God wants man to *enjoy life.* (7-10)

9:10 *With your might.* Because life must end, it behooves man to apply himself to his appointed task with enthusiasm and all the energy given him before "night comes, when no one can work" (Jn 9:4). For the meaning of *Sheol* see Dt 32:22 note.

9:11-17 Accidents, the Bane of the Wisest and the Strongest

9:11 *Again I saw.* In a final observation on disappointing facts of life the Preacher notes that the best efforts, the highest skills, and the noblest attitudes offer no protection against "an evil time when it suddenly falls upon them." (12)

9:12 *His time.* Man does not determine when it is his "time to die" (3:2). Death may take him by surprise, trapping him like a fish in a net and a bird in a snare.

9:13 *Example of wisdom. Wisdom under the sun* cannot answer all questions. Nevertheless, "the words of the wise," though often "despised," can do more to save a city "than weapons of war." (13-18)

10:1—11:10 WISE MAXIMS

10:1—11 Be Alert to Occupational Hazards

10:1 *Wisdom.* The Preacher's answer to the vanity of making sense of the nonsense observed "under the sun" (5) is summed up in two words: "fear God" (5:7) —believe there is a God; tremble in His presence because He "will judge the righteous and the wicked" (3:17); trust the superior wisdom of His providence, confident that "he has made everything beautiful in its time" (3:11). In chs. 10 and 11 the Preacher applies these axiomatic principles of revealed religion to concrete situations as they arise in everyday life. It does make a difference, he insists, how a person reacts to circumstances confronting him. In the form of proverbial sayings, similar to the practical directives of the Book of Proverbs, he points out positive values in being wise, touching on the following topics: (a) dangers to be avoided (1-11); (b) the effects of wise words and foolish chatter (12-15), (c) good and bad government (16-20); (d) courage in making investments (11:1-8); (e) the freedom and responsibility of "youth." (11:9-10)

Evil odor. Even *a little folly* is enough to make what should be a delightful experience *give off an evil odor.* The wise man knows how to make the best of what is obnoxious or dangerous to begin with. If he is a government official, he will act with composure and patience when exposed to "the anger of the ruler" who is likely to make "an error" because he is capable of nothing more than "folly" (4-7). If one makes his living in other occupations, "wisdom helps one to succeed" in doing the job without getting hurt and without wasting energy. (8-11)

10:4 *Deference.* Submission to a despot's outbursts of undeserved *anger* rather than vehement denunciation of his folly is counseled also in 8:2-9; Pr 16:14; 15:1, 18.

10:6 *Rich.* Those possessing a wealth of wisdom. (Cf. Pr 19:10 note)

10:8 *A pit.* Not necessarily one to trap an enemy as in Ps 7:15 f.; Pr 26:27. Here the thought is that in the pursuit of various callings "men of skill" (9:11) must be on their guard against accidents.

10:10 *Blunt.* The use of properly prepared instruments is required if one is to expend energy wisely and profitably.

10:11 *Serpent bites.* This proverb makes the point that even such a highly specialized skill as a snake charmer may have is of no value if it is not used at the proper time.

10:12-15 Shun Foolish Prattle

10:12 *Consume him.* For similar warnings of folly's disastrous consequences see Pr 10:14; 14:3; 18:7.

10:14 *After him.* The *fool multiplies words* about things which even the wisest person does not claim to know.

10:15 *The way to the city.* The *fool wearies* himself by talking incessantly although he does not know the most obvious things such as how to follow the well-marked road to the city.

10:16-20 Count the Blessings of Life Under a Good King

10:16 *A child.* Immature because lacking in experience or undisciplined like a willful youth. Such a *king* and his *princes* are not concerned about the welfare of their subjects. Their only interest is unrestrained self-indulgence. They begin to *feast* already *in the morning* and end the day in "drunkenness." (17; Pr 31:4; Is 5:22 f.)

10:17 *Free men.* Not born a slave who has no training in leadership. (Pr 19:10 note)

10:18 *Sinks in.* This proverb of the consequences of slothful neglect in domestic affairs is adduced to assert what happens to the *house* of state when a playboy king neglects his duties.

10:19 *Bread . . . wine . . . money.* This verse gives the reason why an irresponsible king and his courtiers act as they do. Their only aim is to exploit the good things in life to satisfy their inordinate craving for sensual pleasures.

10:20 *A bird.* It is dangerous to *curse* such a *king* and his *rich* princes because he has spies lurking in the most unexpected places. Cf. our proverb: The walls have ears.

11:1-8 Banish Worry of Failure

11:1 *Cast your bread.* The Preacher continues to give counsel on wise living, begun in the previous chapter. In a world in which "time and chance" (9:11) may sabotage a carefully planned project, it is nevertheless foolish to refuse to engage in ventures for fear of sustaining losses. V. 1 cites a proverb which, though more specific and graphic, is the equivalent of our saying: Nothing ventured, nothing gained. It gives the example of a merchant engaged in trade *upon the waters* of the sea. A storm could sink his ships and his fortune. But this possibility does not deter him from investing huge amounts in a risky business. The truth expressed in this maxim is often applied to charitable endeavors. The point is that deeds of mercy and kindness are not a bad investment. Like ships sent out to sea they return laden with rich dividends though it may be *after many days.*

11:2 *Portion.* The proverb in this verse urges a caution in making investments. Because *evil may happen on earth,* it is wise not to put all your eggs into one basket, as our saying has it.

11:3 *Clouds.* The outcome of man's enterprises depends on circumstances beyond his control such as the havoc caused by the forces of nature. He cannot keep clouds from emptying themselves nor direct the course of the wind which fells a *tree* where *it will lie.* Nevertheless, it is foolish not to "sow" because "the wind" could blow it away or not to harvest a ripe crop because it might rain. (4)

11:5 *Do not know.* Man, who does not even know how he comes into existence *in the womb of a woman,* should not wait to understand *the work of God who makes everything* before he launches a project which may or may not prove profitable. Because it is God's world, it is good to be alive (7). If He grants "many years," let man "rejoice in them all," making the most of the opportunities they afford before old age brings "the days of darkness" which bring home the fleeting vanity of life. (8; 2:24 f.; 3:13; 5:18; 8:15; 9:7-10)

11:9-10 Rejoice but Remember

11:9 *Youth.* Nothing should restrain the exuberance and vitality surging through young people except two sobering facts: (1) they too are accountable to God for all they do (9; Pr 16:2); (2) they dare not delay living life at high flood of vigor because the zest for living ebbs quickly away. The brevity of youth is part of the "vanity" of human existence (10), as the first verses of the next chapter will make painfully clear.

12:1-8 YOUTH FADES; LIFE ENDS

12:1 *Remember . . . your Creator.* The modern chapter division of the text obscures the close connection between these verses and those immediately preceding them. Here the Preacher goes on to elaborate two reasons he gave only in passing, advocating positive, enterprising living in the fear of Him "who makes everything" (11:5): (a) "the days of darkness," crippling vigorous *youth,* are not only "many" (11:8); they come quickly, inevitably, and irreversibly. Therefore, "O young man," "rejoice" (11:9) now *before* the debilities of old age make life a burden. Note that the conjunction *before* appears three times—vv. 1, 2, 6. (b) There is no avoiding the "judgment," just mentioned in 11:9. The Judge to whom the young man too must answer for the way he rejoiced in life is none other than the Creator. Because the creatures made for blissful communion with Him rebelled against Him, they languish under an inescapable sentence of death. Their bodies deteriorate until they return to the dust of which He made them. Their "spirit returns to God who gave it" (7). He who gives and takes life "has appointed a time" when He "will judge the righteous and the wicked" (3:17; 12:14; Ro 14:10; 2 Co 5:10). Lest a young man fail to remember that he cannot "escape the judgment of God" (Ro 2:3), the Preacher paints a dismal but true picture of "the days of darkness" (11:8) which come as surely as night follows sunset. Nothing can prevent physical decay. Dried out and weather-beaten, the house of clay crumbles and finally collapses into a heap of rubble. (Jb 4:19; Is 38:12; 2 Co 5:1 f.; 2 Ptr 1:13 f.)

12:2 *Darkened.* The "evil days" of old age are the winter of life: bleak and gloomy, cold and stormy.

12:3-4 *In the day.* Skillful poet that he is (3:2 note), the Preacher tells the sad story of bodily deterioration and the dulling of the senses by using an array of graphic figures of speech describing a household which has fallen on evil days. Translating picture language into prose, we understand him to say: a man's arms (*the keepers of the house*), once firm and taut with muscle, *tremble* uncontrollably; his legs (*the strong men*) are *bent* and misshapen; his teeth (*the grinders*) *cease* to be able to chew his food; eyesight (*those that look through the windows*) is *dimmed;* the ears (*the doors on the street*) *are shut* to sound so that familiar noises (*the sound of the grinding*) seem *low* and indistinct; sleep, no longer sound and restful, becomes fitful and short so that *one rises* at early dawn (*at the voice of a bird*); music (*the daughters of song*) is *brought low*, its happy melodies hardly perceptible.

12:5 *Afraid.* When strength is gone and the senses are dull, as just described, the slightest elevation seems too *high* to take in stride. Now too *terrors are in the way* which one once walked without fear. These disabilities are irreversible. The winter of life does not pass into a rejuvenating spring, as winter does in the yearly cycle of seasons. Trees like *the almond* may bloom again and creatures like *the grasshopper* may again appear on the scene, but this renewal in nature passes the aged by. His *desire fails;* there is nothing to revitalize him and revive his zest for life. For the time has come when he must leave his fleeting abode in an eroded body and enter "his eternal home," an existence of unending duration. His survivors stand by helplessly. They can only give him a fitting funeral by hiring *mourners,* as was customary at the time. (Jer 22:18; 34:5; Am 5:16; Mt 9:24)

12:6 *Silver cord.* As the Preacher marshaled intriguing similes to describe "the evil days" which herald man's steady progress to the grave (2-5), so he now uses striking comparisons to depict the irreparable damage which death inflicts, robbing man of his most precious possession on earth (6-8). The candle of mundane life, once snuffed out, cannot be lit again. A *silver cord,* torn to shreds, cannot be mended; a *golden bowl, broken* into bits, defies restoration to beauty; a *pitcher,* shattered *at the fountain,* no longer can supply man with water, life's indispensable commodity; when *the wheel* used to draw water from *the cistern* is *broken,* man is left without an absolute necessity.

12:7 *Dust returns.* At death man leaves behind what "is perishable" (1 Co 15:42; Gn 3:19; Ps 103:14); what God breathed into a clump of clay to give it life is not subject to decay but *returns to God who gave it.* (Gn 2:7; cf. Ps 104:29)

12:8 *Vanity of vanities.* No one will deny the Preacher's claim to have demonstrated the truth of the thesis stated so boldly at the outset: "all is vanity" (1:2). In his search for something to still man's restless spirit and to make him truly happy he has tested everything "under the sun." However, he found nothing there to fill this need. The worst and the best man can do, have, or think has no more substance or stability than the breeze which cools his hot brow for a moment.

12:9-14 SUMMATION: FEAR THE LORD

12:9 *Being wise.* The Preacher was a competent, reliable, and resourceful instructor. Endowed by his Creator with the capacity to be wise, he did not isolate himself in an ivory tower, selfishly delighting himself with abstruse philosophical musing. What he knew he made accessible to *the people* in carefully selected *proverbs.* He was not only determined to write "words of truth" but was also concerned to make his teachings attractive in form. (10)

12:11 *Sayings of the wise. Collected* in written form for ongoing study, instructions by sages such as the Preacher have two commendable traits: (1) They are *like goads.* As a sharpened stick was used to drive animals forward (Acts 26:14), so the pointed sayings of the wise prod the careless to give serious thought to the meaning of life. (2) They are *like nails.* As a peg driven into the ground held a tent in place, so the words of the wise nail down the truth so *firmly* that no passing wind of opinion can blow it away. However, in order to be stimulating in the right direction and to promulgate unshakable principles of action, they must be *given by one Shepherd.* The authority and reliability of a teacher of wisdom do not depend on his own creative thinking but on his readiness and faithfulness to pass on to the flock entrusted to him what the "Shepherd of Israel" gives him to say. (Ps 80:1; 74:1; 78:52; Is 40:11)

12:12 *Beware.* The wise sayings, given by "one" Author, are contrasted with *many books* by many authors and with *much study* by hosts of researchers. Any study to determine what man is and should do which does not begin and end with his relationship to his "Creator" (12:1) and with the "words of truth" "given by one Shepherd" (10 f.) will bear out the Preacher's verdict: "In much wisdom is much vexation, and he who increases knowledge increases sorrow." (1:18)

12:13-14 *The end.* The search for something which conceivably could fill man's longing for happiness and fulfillment has been completed. Everything "under the sun"—wealth, pleasure, youth, intellectual pursuits, wisdom, folly—*all has been heard* and found wanting. However, the Preacher does not advocate ending this purposeless existence by suicide. Life does have meaning, but only when light is shed on what is "without form and void" by Him who "let light shine out of darkness" (Gn 1:2 f.; 2 Co 4:6). Two words suffice to sum up the only satisfactory philosophy of life: "Fear God" (cf. 5:7 note; also 3:14; 7:18; 8:12 f.). It will only be natural for a person so oriented to *keep his commandments.* But with an unreserved commitment to one's Creator comes also the possibility to "find enjoyment in his toil," to have "a merry heart," and to "rejoice" in youthful vitality (2:24; 3:13; 5:18; 9:7-10; 11:9). Furthermore, inequities—the prosperity of the wicked and their oppression of the righteous (8:10 f., 14; 4:1-3)—no longer need engender resentment. For *every deed,* even when it is a *secret thing,* is known to "the Judge of all the earth" (Gn 18:25). No one can escape being brought *into judgment* before Him.

SONG OF SOLOMON

INTRODUCTION

Interpreters agree on but one feature of this book. By common consent it is what its title (1:1) claims for it: "The Song of Songs," i.e., poetry of superlative excellence.

Beyond this estimate of its artistic quality, opinions differ in all directions as to its form and meaning. In this lyrical gem emotion explodes with such force, moods change so quickly, flights of fancy soar so high that scarcely two commentators explain in the same way how it all hangs together and what it is designed to say.

Form

Some exegetes regard the Song as a series of poems reveling in the mysterious, compulsive attraction of the sexes to one another as it manifests itself in the innate drive in a man and woman to become "one flesh" (Gn 2:24) in nuptial union.

However, there are a variety of views regarding the number of identifiable units or episodes and regarding the contribution each of these makes to the exposition of the theme. Some scholars hold that there is no structural connection between its component parts. According to them the book is a compilation of erotic poems and wedding songs—perhaps as many as 30—which originated independently of one another. Others find larger groupings or cantos, each a variation on the subject of human love.

Opposed to the theory of a more or less disjointed composition is the view that its units are linked by an overall scheme. The author, it is held, developed a central theme in a quasi-dramatic structure. Not designed to be a stage-play in the usual sense of the word, the poem nevertheless has features commonly associated with a drama: a cast of characters, dialog from beginning to end, a plot, a resolution of conflict.

There are no preliminary scenes leading up to the crisis. The very first words come from the stage of a fully developed collision of interests. As the actors speak their lines, they reveal their involvement in the plot: a perplexing dilemma facing the heroine, a comely, unsophisticated farm girl, called the Shulammite (6:13). Brought against her will to the king's court to become a lady in the royal entourage, she must choose between accepting a position of prestige and glamor or remaining true to her affianced lover, a country bumpkin. The conflict is resolved when love triumphs over the lure of material advantages. Because the battle takes place in the heart of the Shulammite, evidence of her victorious struggle comes to the surface in her dialog with the king, in her monologues and soliloquies, in her fancied conversations with her lover.

Though dramatic in structure, the Song need not be based on an actual happening. The plot and characters may well have been created by a skillful poet. He let sharply profiled actors appear on the stage of a play, casting them in roles designed to produce the desired effect of his poem.

However, the portrayed situation was true to life at the time. Kings like Solomon did have a court, graced by scores of concubines and ladies-in-waiting (1 K 11:3). Royal scouts no doubt scoured the countryside in quest of women qualified to fill the ranks of such a harem.

In the appended notes the Song is treated as a literary unit, resembling a drama to the extent that the author conveys the message of his poem by having persons appear on the scene and letting them play appropriate roles in a recognizable plot. What they are given to say rather than what they do on the stage constitutes the dramatic thrust and counterthrust.

Meaning and Purpose

As a part of the inspired canon the Song too was "written for our instruction" (Ro 15:4) even though the name of God is not mentioned (cf. the Book of Esther). The author nowhere tells us in so many words what lesson is to be drawn from his poem. He simply lets it speak for itself, trusting that the mood of high principle, created in counterpoint to base aspiration, makes direct, prosaic instruction superfluous.

Because of the absence of an explicit statement of purpose, opinions differ as to the meaning and application of these lyrical outpourings of emotion. Divergence of views arises mainly in answer to the question whether the poet is describing the marital bond uniting a son and daughter of Adam or whether he is speaking figuratively of a divine-human relationship.

In approaching the problem, two basic rules of Biblical interpretation need to be recalled: (1) Scripture must be allowed to interpret itself without contradicting itself; (2) a book or its parts must be understood in a literal sense unless a clash with passages of undisputed clarity results.

Applying these principles to the Song, it should be noted that exulting in the marvels bestowed on His foremost creatures by their Maker is not forbidden but rather encouraged (see, e.g., Pss 8; 139). The mystique of sexuality is no exception. The physical and spiritual attraction of a man to a woman is by the Creator's design (1 Ti 4:3; Ro 14:14). When the desire for union is consummated in marriage, the rapture of fulfillment has divine sanction (Gn 1:28; 2:24). However, it is no longer "very good" (Gn 1:31) but rather becomes something dirty and shameful when men and women prostitute their capacity to love and be loved, reducing it to the level of an animal instinct to be satisfied like the craving for food and drink.

There is of course a way of speaking about male and female relations which is offensive and degrading. However, there are no smutty remarks or salacious jokes in the Song. Its language is unabashedly descriptive, but not lewd; sensuous, but not vulgar; amorous, but not obscene. It avoids both Victorian prudery as well as modern verbal and pictorial exhibition of the purely physical as an end in itself.

A second feature to be noted in the Song is its high doctrine of marriage. In spite of its realism there is an idealistic strain pervading it. The espoused couple envisions life together as approaching the ecstatic bliss experienced by the man and woman whom God Himself united in the Garden of Eden. According to the pristine ordinance of wedlock, there is only one to whom each partner will cleave to the exclusion of all others. It is a holy estate they hope to enter, kept sacred by a vow of undying faithfulness.

Though not applied directly in the Song, matrimony, the most intimate and exclusive relationship of which human beings are capable, is used figuratively in Scripture to describe God's solemn covenant with fallen mankind. His pledge of undeserved, redemptive love is to awaken and motivate the nuptial response of total, undivided devotion to Him. In the OT Israel's idolatrous and apostate behavior frequently is portrayed as marital unfaithfulness and shameful fornication. Betrothed to God "for ever" by a vow of "steadfast love," she is said to play the part of an adulterous woman and a promiscuous harlot (see, e.g., Hos 1—3; Eze 16). The prophetic messengers do not use pretty words to describe the ugly crime of Israel's spiritual whoredoms.

In the NT the incarnate Son of God is cast in the role of the heavenly Bridegroom. Having, with his own blood, cleansed His bride, the church, of every "spot or wrinkle," He adorns her with shining garments of righteousness, the wedding dress of salvation. (Eph 5:25-33; 2 Co 11:2; Mt 22:2-14; 25:1-13)

The marriage bond is used figuratively in Scripture to symbolize not only an existing status in a human-divine relationship but also to prefigure events and developments still outstanding in God's plan of salvation.

In the OT the union of man and wife in matrimony takes on the contours of a prophetic type of greater things to come in Messianic times, when God would fulfill what He promised to do to make all things new. Then Paradise Lost would become

Paradise Regained. Mankind would not have to be afraid of the Creator as were the first spouses after they "knew that they were naked" (Gn 3:7, 10). He would remove the shame of their disobedience, re-create man and woman in His image, pronounce them "very good," worthy to live in harmonious communion with Him. See such passages as Hos 2:14-23; Jer 33.

The NT records the fulfillment of these prophecies in the life, death, and resurrection of Jesus Christ. On its pages the marriage symbolism in turn foretells the paradisiacal bliss awaiting His "chaste" bride, the church. He will come to make her His own at the "marriage of the Lamb." Longing for her Bridegroom, she prays: "Come, Lord Jesus!" (Rv 14:4; 19:7; 22:20)

In the Song's idealistic description of the espoused pair and their anticipation of supreme bliss one detects not only reminiscences of the perfection which once existed in the Garden of Eden but also hears overtones of a yearning for its return in "the world to come." (Heb 2:5; 6:5)

Authorship

The heading, prefixed to the opening words of the text and now incorporated in it as its first verse, entitles this book "The Song of Songs" and declares it to be "Solomon's."

This superscription is of ancient origin. Found in all ancient manuscripts, it suggests that the poem is one of the "thousand and five" "songs" composed by the versatile and wise son of David (1 K 4:32). It assumes, furthermore, that when Solomon is named (no less than six times, 1:5; 3:7, 9, 11; 8:11, 12) he is referring to himself in the third person.

However, these references to him as well as other features in the Song are better explained if he is not regarded as its composer. His name is invoked to make the point that even a king like "Solomon in all his glory" (Mt 6:29) was not able to entice the Shulammite to forsake her betrothed for a life of ease at the court. The writer's aim was to sing of the beauty and power of love. Though tempted by wealth such as a Solomon could offer her, a poor girl remains faithful to her shepherd lover. The Shulammite is a "Solomon-ess," a queen of virtue and marital integrity.

Other books of the Bible do not quote the Song or ascribe its origin to Solomon. The language in which it is composed also points to an era later than his. The title in our English Bibles "The Song of Solomon" is not found in the manuscripts.

Outline

As one would expect in a drama, the Song of Songs consists entirely of direct discourse. However, it lacks all stage directions. The speakers are not introduced as they are in the Book of Job (And Job said . . . Then Eliphaz answered . . . Then Job said . . .). Their identity must be deduced from what they say.

In the appended notes the plot is assumed to develop as follows. The Shulammite holds the center of the stage and has the most to say. She responds to the king's tempting proposal as well as to remarks made by the ladies of the court. In spirit she communes with her absent lover. Borne to his side on the wings of reverie, she extols his manliness and virtues as she in turn hears him praise her beauty. Reveling in the prospect of reunion with him, she visualizes herself returning to her betrothed in order to give him her zealously guarded wedding present: her virginal love.

1:1 *Song of Songs.* For other examples of nouns in this combination to express the superlative degree see Gn 9:25; Ex 29:37 (lit.: the holy of holies); Eze 26:7; Rv 17:14, etc.

1:2 *Kiss me.* The drama opens with the frenzied outcry of a distraught girl brought to the king's chambers to become his concubine. Her first words betray her excited, almost hysterical state of mind. Beginning with an ardent appeal to her faraway shepherd lover to soothe and strengthen her with his caresses, sweeter *than wine* (2-4), she turns abruptly to the ladies-in-waiting at the court (5-6) only to revert as suddenly to the one her "soul loves." Bewildered and perplexed, she fancies that he only would have to tell her where he has moved his flocks to enable her to tryst with him (7). She even hears him giving her the desired directions. (8)

1:5 *Daughters of Jerusalem.* The king's ladies-in-waiting. Introduced again 2:7; 3:10; 5:8, 16, their function approaches the role played by the chorus in Greek drama.

Dark. Tanned and darkened by constant exposure to "the sun," her complexion is "swarthy" in comparison with that of the pale ladies at court. The tents of nomadic tribes like those of *Kedar* were made of black goats' hair. (Gn 25:13; Ps 120:5 note)

Curtains of Solomon. In spite of the dark pigment of her skin, she compares her beauty with richly embroidered draperies such as Solomon had. For the reference to his name see Introduction, "Authorship."

1:8 *Follow.* Interpreted above as spoken by the shepherd, this verse may be the sarcastic reply of the daughters of Jerusalem, urging the unsophisticated country girl to go back to her lowly occupation.

1:9 *I compare.* The king woos her with flattery and the promise of precious jewelry (9-11). We would not compliment a lady by comparing her with *a mare.* Every culture has its own concept of beauty.

My love. Both the king and the shepherd address the Shulammite with this term of endearment, occurring only in the Song (1:9, 15; 2:2, 10, 13, etc.). It is the feminine form of the masculine noun for friend (2 Sm 13:3; 1 K 4:5; 16:11; 2 Ch 20:7). She in turn calls the shepherd "my beloved" (1:13; 2:8, etc.). In its plural form this word is used in the Song and elsewhere to denote the caresses and embraces of lovers. (1:2, 4; 4:10; 5:1; 6:1; 7:13; Pr 7:18; Eze 16:8; 23:17)

1:12 *Couch.* A circular divan on which the king ate in a reclining position. While he is feasting, she drinks in the *fragrance* of her beloved, wafted to her on the winds of memory. The thought of him is perfume as sweet as *nard* (Mk 14:3), "myrrh" (Mt 2:11; Mk 15:23), and the flowers of the "henna" shrub, so called because its leaves when crushed furnished a red dye. "En-gedi" is a spring-fed ravine west of the Dead Sea.

1:15 *Beautiful.* Delirious with the aroma of his fancied presence (12-14), the Shulammite lets also the sound of his voice entrance her. She hears him whisper his admiration for her (15) and then repeats the compliments she paid him in an enchanted bower of verdant carpets and arching cedar and pine. (16-17)

2:1 *Rose of Sharon.* Not the kind of flower we call a rose but a crocus which grew profusely in Sharon, a plain along the Mediterranean Sea. Countering the king's proposal to make her a fixture of artificial court life, she regards herself as a wild flower which should not be transplanted (1). The mention of *a lily* reminds her how her shepherd had whispered to her that, in comparison with her, all other "maidens" were "brambles" (2). To her he stands out "among young men" as "an apple tree"; its "fruit" excels "the trees of the wood" (3-4). Turning again to the "daughters of Jerusalem" (cf. 1:5), she asks them to supply her with the nutriments capable of keeping alive and healthy her devotion to her shepherd lover (5) and to cease their efforts to "awaken love" in her for anyone else, even the king. (7)

2:4 *Banqueting house.* Lit. "house of wine." The "delight" her lover afforded her in the garden of love (3) was as intoxicating as wine.

2:5 *Raisins . . . apples.* According to popular opinion these fruits were regarded as possessing the power of erotic stimulation similar to the mandrake. (7:13; Gn 30:14 note)

2:7 *Gazelles . . . hinds.* Graceful yet easily aroused, these animals in the Shulammite's countryside symbolize the beauty and excitability of love (Pr 5:19). Because it is something sacred, she adjures the ladies in its name, as Jonathan gave David an oath "by his love" (1 Sm 20:17). She exacts the same solemn pledge from the ladies in 3:5 and 8:4.

2:8 *He comes.* The Shulammite steels herself against the king's blandishments by conjuring up her beloved. In her mind's eye she pictures him coming in search of her. Refusing to let the ladies "awaken love" in her for the king, she envisions her shepherd wooing her amid the stimulating delights of a spring day (8-14). At his request to hear her voice, she sings a popular ditty about "foxes" and "vineyards" which perhaps gives him a hint where to look for her (15). Brought back to the reality confronting her, she declares that she and her beloved pledged themselves to one another to the exclusion of all others (16; repeated 6:3). She therefore longs for his coming amid the cooling breezes of the evening. (17; cf. 4:6, 16)

2:12 *Turtledove.* A migratory bird (Jer 8:7), its return to the northern climate announced the arrival of spring.

2:15 *Catch us the foxes.* She had a coy, sly way of letting her "gazing" and "looking" (9) shepherd know where to find her. She sang a verse of a popular song mentioning *vineyards,* where her brothers put her to work as a "keeper." (1:6)

2:17 *Rugged.* The Hebrew word seems to be derived from a verb meaning to cut to pieces, to cut up.

3:1 *By night.* Distress over her separation from her lover and gnawing fear of having lost him whom her *soul loves* disturb the Shulammite's sleep. She dreams she must search him out on the strange streets of Jerusalem. After several unsuccessful attempts, she finds him. She "would not let him go" until she could claim him as her own in her "mother's house" (1-4). Cheered by the happy ending of her imaginary quest for him, she again adjures the daughters of Jerusalem not to tempt her to give her love to another. (5; 2:7 note)

3:3 *Watchmen.* Mentioned also in Ps 127:1; 130:6; Is 21:11 f.; 52:8.

3:6 *Coming up.* Lest anyone doubt what a tempting proposal the poor peasant girl has to cope with, the poet lets the Shulammite visualize the luxury and acclaim she could share if she joined the daughters of Jerusalem at the court of a king as magnificent as Solomon. She sees herself among spectators who describe the splendor of a royal procession and the homage paid its central figure. She hears, as it were, the king saying to her: "All these I will give you" (Mt 4:9) if you will forget your troth to your impoverished shepherd. (6-11)

3:7 *Litter.* As the word "palanquin" (9) indicates, the king's conveyance was not a simple stretcher but an ornate symbol of wealth and royalty. Its splendor was of the kind for which Solomon had become proverbial. (See Introduction, "Authorship.")

3:11 *Go forth.* The maidens in Jesus' parable hear the cry: "Behold, the bridegroom! Come out to meet him" (Mt 25:6). In ancient times the dowager queen, the king's *mother,* wielded considerable influence. (1 K 1:11-31; 15:10 note)

4:1 *You are beautiful.* In vv. 1-6 the royal suitor may be the speaker. He woos the Shulammite by praising her physical charms. It seems preferable to assume that she seeks to overcome the temptation to riches and ease, so vividly portrayed in 3:6-11, by envisioning her lover at her side and repeating the sweet things he once whispered to her (1-5). He is so real to her that she blurts out a promise to rendezvous with him amid the "myrrh" and "frankincense" of nature's fragrance (6; 2:17). Quickly realizing the impossibility of such a flight to him, she contents herself with thinking she hears him assuring her that she has captured him by her ravishing beauty and pure character (7-15). She cannot suppress a cry of delight at the thrilling thought. She hails him to "come to his garden" and to gather the "choicest fruits" of love (16). As if he hears her, he responds eagerly to her invitation. (5:1)

4:2 *Shorn ewes.* The figures, employed to extol the various features of physical beauty, are based on comparisons which seem strange and rather uncomplimentary to us. (1:9 note)

4:4 *Arsenal.* The Hebrew word occurs only here. It may be related to a root describing *the tower* as built in courses of stone.

4:8 *Come with me.* To be able to join her betrothed, the *bride* would have to escape the royal court, which is described figuratively as mountain heights. There she is beyond his reach. There too she must ward off temptation as dangerous and insidious as wild beasts lurking in the cliffs. *Amana* is part of the double-spurred *Lebanon* range from which the peaks *Senir and Hermon* rise to great heights. (Dt 3:8 note)

4:12 *Garden locked.* Her virgin love is compared to a walled garden to which no stranger has gained access and to *a fountain sealed,* its waters kept for the refreshment of none but its rightful owner. See v. 16, where the Shulammite refers to her chastity as "his garden," kept exclusively for her betrothed. Though inflexible in her resolve to keep it intact for him, she is deliriously uninhibited in anticipating the rapture of marital union.

5:1 *I come.* The first verse of this chapter is the shepherd's reply to the Shulammite's passionate invitation to "come to" his "garden" (4:16). In agreeing to come he visualizes their wedding festivities in full swing. He, "the bridegroom," "rejoices greatly" (Jn 3:29), calling on his guests to be happy with him.

5:2 *Slept . . . awake.* Yearning for her absent lover and fearful of losing him, the Shulammite again finds her sleep disturbed by a dream (cf. 3:1-4). Her heightened agitation and frustration are reflected in its nightmarish ending. In her feverish mind she heard him knocking at her door late at night after she had gone to bed. But when, all aglow with excitement at the sound of his voice, she opened the door, he had vanished. Her search for him "in the city" was futile. It brought her only humiliation and a beating at the hands of "the watchmen" (cf. 3:3 note), who mistook her for a loose woman (1-7). Turning to the "daughters of Jerusalem," she pleads with them to tell him she is not angry with him but "sick with love" (8). They taunt her with a question suggesting that she's foolish to be enamored of him to the exclusion of "another beloved" (9). Her answer to their disparaging insinuation is a fervid description of his entrancing physique and masculine charms. (10 16)

5:10 *All radiant.* The features of male beauty which the Shulammite finds so "desirable" (16) are described in superlatives of poetic figures of speech. Some of them may not appeal to our ideas of beauty, but they all express her fascination in terms meaningful to her.

5:12 *Doves.* The eyes of the Shulammite are likewise said to be like doves (1:15; 4:1). The pupils immersed in the white of the *eyes* are compared with doves bathing in milk. The phrase *fitly set,* more literally "sitting on fulness," may refer to an abundant supply of *water* in the *springs* or to the setting of the eye in the center of the eyeball.

5:14 *Gold . . . sapphires.* His physique is more attractive to her than the costly jewelry of the royal court.

5:16 *My friend.* The masculine form of the noun so frequently applied to the Shulammite and translated "my love." (1:9 second note)

6:1 *Seek him.* The daughters of Jerusalem continue their snide remarks (cf. 1:8 note; 5:9). The Shulammite has just described her lover so vividly as if he were standing before them (5:10-16). Reminding her that he was nowhere to be seen and that she has enlisted their help in finding him (5:8), they pretend to be sympathetic with her plight, inquiring where they might search for him. They know full well that in her answer she again must refer to his lowly occupation as a shepherd, so far beneath the position she might share with them at the court. (2-3)

6:4 *You are beautiful.* The Shulammite's temptation to forsake her lover reaches a climax when the king, like a lovelorn swain, heaps fulsome praise on her beauty, hoping to break down her resistance (6:4—7:9). However, the royal suitor discovered in this *comely* maid a strength of character as formidable *as an army.* (Cf. 6:10)

Tirzah . . . Jerusalem. For a time the capital of the Northern Kingdom (1 K 16:15, 23), Tirzah was considered to be so charming as to merit a name which in Hebrew means "delightful." Jerusalem was "the perfection of beauty." (Ps 50:2; Lm 2:15; Ps 48:2)

6:5 *Turn away.* The king was so smitten with love that he could not bear her glance, which overpowered him like an army conquering a fortified city.

6:8-9 *Queens . . . concubines.* Among the glamorous ladies at the court there is none to compare with the Shulammite.

6:10 *Who is this . . . ?* The king repeats what the "queens" and "concubines" said when the beautiful girl was brought to the court.

6:11 *I went down.* The Shulammite interrupts the king to explain how she came to be the center of attraction at the court. She did not come there intent on seeking her fortune. To the contrary, while sauntering through her native countryside, she suddenly found herself face to face with a royal scouting party. There was no need to relate what the obvious sequel of this encounter was.

6:12 *Before I was aware.* The verse is translated and interpreted in various ways. The meaning seems to be that unwittingly her *fancy* or impulse to examine blossoms and buds on a spring day (cf. 2:10-13) landed her in the princely chariot.

6:13 *Return.* In the Hebrew Bible this verse opens ch. 7. To show her lack of interest in the king's flattering words, the displaced shepherdess apparently turned away from her royal suitor. He begs her to hear him out.

Shulammite. This term is the only clue to her identity. It may indicate that she hailed from a town called Shulam, as "the Gileadite" tells the reader that Jephthah was a native of Gilead (Ju 11:1; so also Elijah the Tishbite, 1 K 17:1; Abishag the Shunammite, 1 K 1:3). However, because the name Shulam is not mentioned in Scripture, it is thought to be a variant spelling of Shunem, a village in the Esdraelon Valley (Jos 19:18; 1 Sm 28:4; 2 K 4:8). According to another explanation the word Shulammite contains the same consonants composing Solomon's name plus a feminine ending (cf. 2 Sm 12:25 note). The nobility of character displayed by this peasant girl entitles her to be called a Solomon-ess, the queenly counterpart of the monarch ruling in Israel's golden age of peace.

A dance. The second part of v. 13 apparently is the Shulammite's indignant response to the king's request to let him feast his eyes on her beauty. She refuses to cheapen herself as if she were displaying her charms like a dancing girl. *A dance before two armies* may be the name of a well-known dance, as the RSV note suggests.

7:1 *How graceful.* Undaunted by the maiden's negative reaction, the king continues to try to win her by extolling her beauty. Her charms are again described by comparisons which strike us as strange.

7:4 *Heshbon.* A city in a well-watered region about 20 miles east of the northern end of the Dead Sea (Nm 21:25-30). *Bath-rabbim* is unknown. Lit. "daughter of multitudes," it seems to refer to a city with a gate through which large numbers of people passed.

7:5 *Carmel.* A promontory-like peak facing the Mediterranean Sea. Used as a common noun, it is translated "fertile lands," "fruitful field," "fruitful land." (2 Ch 26:10; Is 16:10; Jer 4:26)

Tresses. Her "flowing locks" are thought of as strands enmeshing a man in the net of love. Even *a king is held captive* by them.

7:8 *Palm tree.* In an outburst of sensual imagery the king declares his burning desire to *climb the palm tree and lay hold of its branches,* i.e., to have her share her ravishing charms with him in a passionate embrace.

7:9 *Kisses.* Lit. "palate," i.e., mouth. As "the scent" of her "breath" (lit. "nose") is said to be "like apples" (8), so her mouth is intoxicating *like the best wine,* which *goes down smoothly* (cf. Pr 23:31) as it moistens the "lips of sleepers" (RSV note), arousing and stimulating them to pleasurable sensations.

7:10 *My beloved's.* At this point the battle of clashing forces has reached its climax. The king's wooing of the Shulammite, culminating in a crescendo of emotional outpouring (1-9), also marks the turning point of the drama. The heroine's response is true love's song of victory, won over vehement assaults of temptation. She begins by repeating her declaration of total and exclusive commitment to her beloved (10; cf. 6:3). Then dreaming of the day when she can invite him to go out with her into the sensuous fragrance of springtime's "blossoms," she longs for the time when she can give herself into his caressing arms. (11-13)

7:13 *Mandrakes.* Cf. Gn 30:14 note.

8:1 *Like a brother.* In her reverie the Shulammite harks back to the days when maidenly decorum would not allow her to make a public spectacle of her love. If her beloved had been her brother, she could have taken the initiative, invited him into the family circle and served him the best "wine" and "juice" (2). Now untrammeled by inhibitions, she unblushingly speaks of her yearning to surrender herself into his embrace (3; 2:6). Once more she turns to the daughters of Jerusalem, telling them how futile any attempt would be to "awaken love" in her for anyone else. (4; 2:7 note; 3:5)

8:5 *Leaning upon her beloved.* In the closing verses of the Song, the Shulammite envisions herself released from the court by a defeated king. As she sees herself returning to her rural home, she hears the villagers expressing their surprise to see her united with her beloved (5a). The happy couple passes *the apple tree* where his *mother* gave him birth and where his love for his beloved came to life (5b). She goes on to ask him to accept her vow of undying devotion as if it were a signet ring, worn by him to betoken and seal their mutual pledge. There is no doubt in her mind that his love like hers "is strong as death" and immune to all temptations to break the bond (6-7). Next she visualizes a meeting with her brothers. She assures them that she has retained her chastity (8-10) even though it meant resisting the alluring offer to become a king's concubine (11-12). Proud of her victorious battle against royal blandishment, her beloved is anxious for her to tell him and his "companions" of her sensational experience at the court (13). As the final curtain drops on the drama, the Shulammite calls to her beloved to "make haste" to make her dreams come true. (14)

8:6 *A seal.* Engraved seal-cylinders, often worn as ornamental pendants or signet rings, were pledges of a contractual responsibility and emblems of personal probity (Gn 38:16-18; 41:42; Jer 22:24). The lovers' exchange of vows was to be attested publicly.

8:7 *All the wealth.* The Shulammite's refusal to barter away her *love* for a life of riches and ease exemplifies how invincible true love can and should be.

8:8 *A little sister.* As in thought the Shulammite returns home, she meets her brothers. She recalls how, even before she reached the age of maturity, they were concerned to keep her chastity unblemished. They hoped she had remained a strong "wall," capable of resisting all attempts to violate her virtue. But if she had opened the "door" to unwarranted intrusion, they would fence her in "with boards of cedar" to prevent further molestation (9). Above all she could meet the gaze of her beloved and receive his praise for having kept her honor intact (10). For she had rebuffed a proposal to let her live in the Solomonic luxury of the king's fabulous income, pictured as "fruit" yielded by an enormous "vineyard" (11). Nothing could induce her to give up her "vineyard," the domain reserved solely for her lover. (12; 4:12 note)

8:11 *Baal-hamon.* An unidentified place name. As its meaning (owner of a multitude) indicates, it may be a figurative expression of the vineyard's enormous size: it required armies of keepers to tend it.

Solomon. For the significance of his name see Introduction, "Authorship."

ISAIAH

INTRODUCTION

Personal Data

Prince among OT prophets, Isaiah left almost no space in his book of 66 chapters for information about himself. Except for his father's name Amoz (not Amos, the prophet of Tekoa), we are left without a clue to his antecedents. Unidentified beyond being called "the prophetess," his wife is mentioned because she bore sons whose names epitomize the double-pronged message of threat and promise he was given to proclaim (7:3; 8:1-4). His own name, meaning "Salvation of the Lord" or "The Lord Saves," indicates that the preaching of the Law is designed to pave the way for the comfort of the Gospel, presented so effectively—particularly in the second part of the book—that he has been called the evangelist of the Old Testament.

His call to the prophetic office too is not so much informative autobiography as a solemn declaration of his accreditation by "the Lord of hosts" (ch. 6). What he has to "say to this people" is not the ranting of a gloom peddler nor the pipe dreams of a deluded optimist. Though himself "a man of unclean lips" and useless until his "guilt is taken away," he is authorized to transmit the words of "the King" which never return empty (55:11), so that "the whole earth is full of His glory." (6:3)

His ready access to the earthly monarchs of his day has been interpreted to indicate that he was of noble birth. Whatever his social status may have been, there is no doubt regarding the regal quality of his literary style—his mastery in adapting rhetorical forms to varying content, his skill in combining words and phrases to produce the mood appropriate to the occasion. When he denounces sin, the thunder of doom rolls from one sentence into the next; when he brings the comfort of the Gospel, it is as if the birds make sweet melody after the storm has passed.

Historical Setting

Embedded in the book are references and allusions to political events and religious circumstances which form the background of Isaiah's message. Pertinent sections in 2 K (chs. 14—21) and in 2 Ch (chs. 26—33) supply additional information. Ancient secular records confirm and supplement the Biblical accounts.

From these sources it is evident that Isaiah held prophetic office over a long period of time. Called in 740 BC, the year King Uzziah died (6:1), he was active during the reign of at least three successors to the throne (1:1). The last of these, Hezekiah, died in 687 BC, five decades after Isaiah began his ministry. Manasseh, Hezekiah's son and successor, became sole regent after his father's death One of Israel's most wicked rulers, he not only sanctioned and promoted idolatry of every kind but also persecuted the true worshipers (2 K 21:1-9; 2 Ch 33:1-9). Isaiah does not mention Manasseh by name. However, some of the prophet's most vehement denunciations of degenerate religious rites appear in his reaction to the wickedness prevailing during this period. For his fearless reproof of these abuses Isaiah suffered a martyr's death, if an ancient Jewish tradition is true. He is said to have been "sawn in two." (Heb 11:37)

God would not be mocked. Nor was He at a loss how to execute judgment on His apostate people. At His beck and call stood the world powers of the day. All He had to do was to "whistle" (7:18) to one empire after another to do His bidding.

The first to be summoned were the Assyrians. Eighteen years after Isaiah was commissioned to preach, they invaded

Palestine, captured Samaria, capital of the Northern Kingdom, and carried off the 10 tribes of Israel into exile. Judah, with Jerusalem its capital, escaped disaster by paying tribute to the conqueror. When in the course of time it was withheld, the Assyrian king Sennacherib besieged Jerusalem but was not permitted to take it, as Isaiah assured king Hezekiah.

By prophetic vision Isaiah also foresaw the end of Assyrian rule some 70 years before it came. In 612 BC the city of Nineveh fell into the hands of a nation destined to become the new masters of the world, the Babylonians. They were to be the next rod of God's anger on His faithless people. So said Isaiah a century before their king Nebuchadnezzar destroyed Jerusalem in 586 BC and took a large segment of the population captive to Babylonia. Anticipating the spiritual needs of the exiles, Isaiah had much to say to them of God's unbroken resolve to bring salvation "from the Jews" (Jn 4:22). As He used the kingdoms of this world to chastize and purify them, so He would summon still another foreign power to bring them back to their homeland in order to reconstitute them as bearers of His promise.

Two centuries were to pass before Isaiah's words came true. God's servant and anointed instrument of liberation was Cyrus, a king of the Medes and Persians. Their home territory lay east and north of Babylon and Nineveh. In Isaiah's day no political observer would have guessed that they, vassals of the Assyrians at the time, would become a world empire, embracing not only Assyria and Babylonia but also all the lands along the Mediterranean coast from Asia Minor down through Palestine into Egypt. Unforseeable too was Cyrus' humane and tolerant treatment of subjugated peoples such as the Jews. His decree permitting them to return to Palestine and to rebuild the ruined cities formed the setting to which Isaiah addressed himself as confidently as if it all were recorded history.

The return from the Babylonian captivity, however, was not the end of prophetic penetration into the future. God let Isaiah see what was to happen in a setting which was to become history in the fullness of time. When Rome ruled the world, a virgin gave birth to the Prince of Peace. He founded a universal kingdom not by force of arms but by love. He died to free all His subjects from the slavery of the prince of this world. Justified by His vicarious death and victorious rising on the third day, they are free to live blissfully under His reign of grace. Because He is God's Son, there will come a time when all opposition will cease. Sitting "on his glorious throne" at the end of time, "before him will be gathered all the nations" in a final judgment scene. The outcome of His verdict will be either "eternal life" or "eternal punishment." (Mt 25:31-46)

Content

Isaiah's forthtelling and foretelling were not the product of his own keen observation and shrewd interpretation of the signs of the times. The title of his book calls his message a "vision" (1:1). God let him see things as He sees them. Therefore his assessment of the existing state of affairs was valid beyond dispute. His portrayal of the future was as true as God is true. His picture of coming events, however, is not a flat portrait, but rather like images projected on a series of successive transparencies. As the light of revelation illumines them, intervals of time merge only to appear again as separate eons. Contours and colors of events in the more immediate future are superimposed on scenes which were to materialize in remote ages to come. Unhampered by the dimensions of time and space, the prophet's vision ranges back and forth on a line stretching from his day to the final consummation of all things temporal and terrestrial. He is granted a perspective which allows him to see the past, the present, and the future not in a mundane sequence of events but in the divine light of an eternal now.

Composition

Isaiah brings us God's revealed truths according to a rhetorical scheme differing from our system of composition. Committed to Aristotelian logic, we arrange our facts in a line of progression from one set of data to the next. After one aspect of the issue has been exhausted, we proceed to the next unit pertinent to the discussion. Isaiah and his fellow prophets are not bound by our literary canons. They develop their messages in a circular movement of thought. Rather than elaborating subject matter vertically, completing point "A" before advancing to "B," they draw a series of concentric circles around a given topic. In order to drive home a point they take it up again and again, encircling it with additional reasons, observations, and illustrations. The result is not tedious repetitiousness but an effective teaching device which has not lost its appeal to readers of all ages.

Authorship

Until two centuries ago Christian interpreters regarded the 66 chs. of the book as the literary deposit of "the vision of Isaiah, the son of Amoz" (1:1). Today a majority of Biblical scholars deny large segments of the book to the prophet named in the superscription. Chs. 40—66 are attributed to writers living at least two centuries later. Chs. 1—39 do not fare much better. Large and smaller sections are declared spurious, notably chs. 27—29 and 32—35. When critical excising has run its course, the authentic remainder amounts to no more than 1/5 of the book. Refusal to accept these "assured results" invites the stigma of obscurantism or the charge of stubborn disregard of patent facts.

All proponents of this decimation of the ancient document admit that their case rests entirely on internal evidence, that is, on inferences drawn from the book itself as interpreted by them. Only a multiple authorship, they contend, can explain the lack of uniformity they find in three areas: literary style and vocabulary, theological concepts, and the historical standpoint of the writers.

There is no external, objective evidence in ancient literature, religious or profane, to validate this theory. No manuscripts or ancient documents, including the Dead Sea Scrolls, support divisions of the book into Deutero-Isaiah (40—55) and Trito-Isaiah (56—66). The New Testament knows of only one Isaiah. Quotations from all parts of his book, chs. 1—39 as well as 40—66, are cited as spoken "through Isaiah the prophet" (Acts 28:25-27; Jn 12:37-41). Rejection of this testimony must assume a theory of inspiration which makes the New Testament writers subject to error. Products of their day, they could not know the results of scientific scholarship. To say that Jesus too accommodated Himself to a traditional but erroneous view conflicts with what the Scriptures teach about the person of God's Son.

OUTLINE

I. 1:1—5:30 Introductory Development of Twofold Theme: Threat of Judgment and Promise of Redemption

II. 6:1-13 Isaiah Cleansed and Commissioned to be God's Messenger

III. 7:1—12:6 Immanuel: His Messianic Kingdom

IV. 13:1—23:18 Judgment Pronounced on Foreign Nations and Apostate Jerusalem

V. 24:1—27:13 Consummation of History: The Day of the Lord

VI. 28:1—33:24 Jerusalem to Be Destroyed and Restored

VII. 34:1—35:10 V-Day in God's Kingdom

VIII. 36:1—39:8 Jerusalem Delivered from Assyrians, Destroyed by Babylonians

IX. 40:1—66:24 The Way of Salvation Through Forgiveness to Glory
  A. 40:1—48:22 The Way of Deliverance
  B. 49:1—57:21 The Way of Forgiveness Opened for All Sinners by the Sinless Servant
  C. 58:1—66:24 The Way to Glory

1:1—5:30 INTRODUCTORY DEVELOPMENT OF TWOFOLD THEME: THREAT OF JUDGMENT AND PROMISE OF REDEMPTION

1:1 *Vision.* The superscription informs the reader how the author came to issue the contents of the book (see also 2:1; 13:1). It does not contain his own assessment of the state of affairs or his interpretation of the signs of the times (cf. Jer. 23:16). God miraculously opened his mind's eye enabling him to see things from His unerring point of view and to envision coming events in the perspective of His eternal plan of salvation (see Nah 1:1 for the same term applied to an entire book; also Ps 89:19 note). What the prophet *saw* was not the fantasy of an emotionally disturbed visionary. He was a seer who was given insight into the hard facts of reality.

Isaiah. The man whose inspired forthtelling and foretelling is on record here bore a name suggestive of his high calling. Composed of Hebrew nouns, it spelled out what the ultimate purpose of his mission was to be: to proclaim "the salvation of the Lord."

Amoz. His father's name gives us no clue as to Isaiah's ancestry or social standing, since it occurs only in the stereotype formula: *Isaiah, the son of Amoz.* As the spelling indicates, he was not related to the prophet Amos. What matters is not who or what Isaiah was but what the vision enabled and compelled him to say. His recorded words make clear that he did not have tentative proposals to suggest which might be worth considering. Nor did he issue but a single statement, couched in the ambiguous language of a Delphic oracle. Confronting his hearers with unequivocal alternatives, he expounded them so clearly and so repeatedly that only the deliberately obstinate could fail to understand what was at stake.

Judah and Jerusalem. The people who heard Isaiah's voice lived in the area of the Promised Land which remained loyal to the Davidic dynasty when the northern tribes seceded after Solomon's death some two centuries before the prophet began to teach. What he saw concerned Judah and Jerusalem in the role they were to play in God's plan to bring salvation to all the nations of the earth. The vision made the wickedness of the chosen people appear in the lurid colors of its despicable guilt. Judgment had to come. However, God was not to be foiled. Chastened and brought home from the Babylonian exile, a remnant was again to be the bearer of His promise of universal redemption. All coming events would be shaped to bring about what Isaiah had to say *concerning Judah and Jerusalem* so that in the fullness of time "salvation" came "from the Jews" (Jn 4:22). To the end of time God's redeemed would constitute a spiritual Israel, gathered from all nations, protected against "the powers of death," sustained by faith in the coming from heaven of a "new Jerusalem." (Mt 16:18; Rv 3:12; 21:2, 10; Gl 4:26)

1:2-31 *Rebelled.* Isaiah's messages are not arranged in strictly chronological order, as is evident from ch. 6, which records his authorization to proclaim what *the Lord has spoken.* Ch. 1 no doubt owes its position in the book to considerations of its contents rather than to its priority in point of time. The sermons are given first place because they afford a preview of the entire volume. They introduce the two basic topics, elaborated in all subsequent chapters: God's wrath consumes impenitent sinners—God's mercy offers penitent sinners redemption and salvation. The first ch. makes clear also that both the threat of death and the promise of life are not idle speculation or wishful thinking. Behind them stands *the Holy One of Israel* (4), the title of God characteristic of Isaiah's messages from beginning to end.

Without preliminaries, the first words let loose a full-scale barrage against sin, blasting away all camouflage of respectability and laying bare how offensive and unnatural Israel's life-style is. In turning against the fatherly goodness of God the people sink to a level lower than the brute animal (2-4). Blind and obstinate, they *continue to rebel* even though their shameful behavior brought on them *bruises and sores and bleeding wounds* (5-6). To bring them to their senses God let their land become the prey of *aliens* who all but made it as desolate as *Sodom* and *Gomorrah,* the cities God destroyed by fire from heaven (7-9; Gn 19:24 f.). What made Israel's sin all the more obnoxious and insulting to God was the attempt to coerce Him to do their bidding by going through the outward motions of worship forms (10-17). Nevertheless God stood ready to be rconciled with perpetrators of the vilest of crimes if they but sought His pardon and gave evidence of true repentance in their lives (18-20). However, lest anyone consider this offer of grace unnecessary, Isaiah quickly reverts to an indictment of the once *faithful city.* It is a lamentable fact that the rebellion against God is evident in the flagrant, heartless way His laws of social justice are flouted (21-23). Let no one presume to think that *the Mighty One of Israel* will let *murderers . . . thieves,* and exploiters of widows and orphans make a mockery of His demands for civic righteousness. As a refiner does not hesitate to *smelt* ore to purify it of worthless *alloy,* so *the Lord of hosts* will purge away the corruption in the fire of His *wrath.* What is left will again *be called the city of righteousness* (24-26). There will come a time when *Zion* will have to be *redeemed* as Israel was from Egyptian slavery (Ex 15:13). Divine *justice* and *righteousness* will rescue and ransom the chosen people from the Babylonian exile. True, *rebels and sinners shall be destroyed,* but a "remnant" (10:20 ff.) will be brought back to the homeland. Dedicated to justice and devoted to righteousness, they will be counted worthy to carry forward God's plans to redeem all mankind. (27-31)

1:2 *Hear, O heavens.* Israel is summoned to stand trial in court. To uphold the validity of the charges against the defendants, God calls on His handiwork in nature to testify in the case (Dt 4:26; 32:1; Ps 50:4). Hoary with age, heaven and earth had been spectators of what went on in Israel. They were witnesses to how God *reared and brought up* sons with a father's most tender care only to have them repay His goodness by rebelling against Him. (Dt 32:6, 18, 20)

1:4 *Holy One of Israel.* This title for God occurs 39 times in the Book of Isaiah and only five times in all other books of the OT. It serves as a key to understanding everything Isaiah has to say. The basic ingredient in the meaning of "holiness" is the concept of separation (cf. Lv 11:45 note). All attributes of perfection which distinguish God from His creatures are bound up in the word "holy." He is not tainted by moral blemishes. He transcends human comprehension in wisdom, power, and majesty as the heavens are higher than the earth. Prompted by love, which defies rational explanation, this *Holy One* condescended to enter a covenant relationship with *Israel.* No power on earth would be able to keep the chosen nation from carrying out His program to save fallen mankind from "the wages of sin" (Ro 6:23), as long as it was a faithful instrument of His saving grace. If, however, it became a *sinful nation, a people laden with iniquity,* it would not be spared the rod of His holy wrath.

1:7 *Desolate.* During Isaiah's lifetime Judah suffered destructive raids at the hands of several enemies. The most extensive desolation resulted from an invasion by the Assyrian king Sennacherib (cf. 2 K 18:13 note). The nation resembled a person beaten to a pulp and wounded from head to foot. (Cf. Dt 28:35)

1:9 *Sodom . . . Gomorrah.* The only *survivors* of these cities were Lot's family (Gn 19:24-29). "The Holy One of Israel" is capable of punishing transgression, for He is "the Lord of hosts" (1 Sm 1:3 second note; Ps 24:10; 46:7). In v. 24 He is called "the Mighty One of Israel."

1:11 *Sacrifices.* The heathen "men of Sodom were wicked, great sinners against the Lord" (Gn 13:13). The chosen people were as bad if not worse. Given acceptable rites and ceremonies to worship the true God, they used them to cloak their crimes with sanctimonious hypocrisy. God *had enough* of such blasphemous abuse of sacrifice and prayer. On the emphatic rejection of outward formality without inward participation see 1 Sm 15:22 note; Ps 40:6 note; 50:8 note; 51:16 note; Jer 6:20; Am 5:21-24; Mi 6:7.

1:18 *Reason together.* Israel, haled into the court of divine justice (v. 2), accused of *scarlet* and *crimson* crimes, stands convicted as charged. Instead of passing sentence on the convicted culprits, the Judge proposes to them a full pardon for their offenses. Actually there is no alternative to discuss, as if escape from paying the full penalty were possible on any other basis than a declaration of undeserved amnesty. The only question that remains is whether the accused are willing to throw themselves unreservedly on the mercy of the court (Ro 4:5; 11:6). If they are, they cannot but prove the sincerity of their plea for forgiveness by being "obedient" sons (19) and no longer rebellious and corrupt "evildoers." (4)

1:24 *My enemies.* It grieves the Holy One of Israel to see how every virtue expected of "the faithful city" has given way to its corresponding vice: undivided commitment to God to the harlotry of idolatry; purity of devotion to contamination with polluting elements; civic equity to political exploitation (21-23). However, God's lament is not a helpless wringing of hands over a situation beyond His control. When men rebel against Him, they become His *enemies* and *foes* who expose themselves to His *wrath* and cannot escape his avenging retribution.

1:27 *Be redeemed.* As inflexible as was God's determination to smelt away the "dross" and "alloy" from His unfaithful people (25), so irrevocable was His resolve not to let the Babylonian empire swallow up the nation from whose midst the promised Redeemer of all mankind was to come. Not some accident of history but the exercise of divine *justice* and *righteousness* would bring about the rescue of the remnant helplessly facing extermination (6:13; 10:20 ff.; 11;11, 16). These "ransomed of the Lord shall return . . . to Zion" (35:10; 51:11; Ps 25:22). Jerusalem was to be again the earthly outpost of a heavenly kingdom until it would become the spiritual capital of an Israel composed of "all . . . nations." (2:2; 27:13; 66:18-23; Ps 2:6 note; 48:2 note; Heb 12:22 f.)

1:28 *Be destroyed.* Lest *sinners* presume they can continue to be *rebels* with impunity because "Zion shall be redeemed," Isaiah hastens to reiterate the warning of their inescapable doom.

1:29 *Oaks.* The people sank so low in their rebellion against God that they engaged in the immoral rites of Canaanite nature worship, carried on in *gardens* and groves of trees. (57:5; 17:8; 2 K 16:4; 17:10; see also the note on "pillar" Gn 28:18).

2:2 *In the latter days.* Lit. "in the end of days."

Translated "in days to come" (Gn 49:1; Dt 31:29), this phrase points to a future time which brings to completion what God set in motion in the history of the chosen people (Nm 24:14; Dt 4:30; Jer 23:20; 30:24; Hos 3:5). However, it envisions also the end results which God promised to bring about in the fulness of time down to the very end of time. (Eze 38:16; Dn 10:14; Mt 13:40; Acts 2:17; Heb 1:1 f.; 9:26; 1 Ptr 1:20)

The highest of the mountains. Isaiah and Micah (4:1-4) use figurative language to describe what God will accomplish *in the latter days* of the Messianic era. They are not speaking of a physical reshaping of the universe and its mountains or of the formation of a political world empire. The Jerusalem God promises to create is constructed of "living stones," "built upon the foundation of the apostles and prophets, Christ Jesus himself being the cornerstone" (28:16; 1 Ptr 2:4-8; Eph 2:19-22). Its citizens constitute the church of Jesus Christ, against which "the gates of Hades shall not prevail" (Mt 16:18). Not a geographic point on the globe, this Jerusalem has no earthly limits. It embraces "strangers and sojourners" from *all the nations* as they become "fellow citizens with the saints and . . . the household of God" (Eph 2:19) and learn "his ways" and to "walk in his paths" (3). The blessings they find in their citizenship are not won or retained by force of arms. Though composed of "every tribe and tongue and people and nation" (Rv 5:9 f.), this citizenry has the basis for perfect harmony. Once naturalized, those enrolled from one nationality will live in peace with those coming from a different nation. For a description of the Jerusalem "in the end of days" see Rv 21:9-27.

2:4 *Plowshares.* The spiritual benefits available to "all the nations" in the "Jerusalem" of "the latter days" are pictured in Isaiah as the restoration of the bliss of the Garden of Eden: undisturbed peace, harmony in the animal world, paradisiacal fertility of the earth. (11:1-9; 32:15-20; 65:17-25)

2:6 *Thou hast rejected.* Isaiah turns to address God. He is fully justified in withholding His favor from a people chosen to be the bearer of the promises just enumerated (2-4) but now guilty of sins prevalent in heathen nations: soothsaying and divining (Dt 18:10; Lv 19:26, 31); trust in alliances with *foreigners,* worship of idols, "the work of their hands" (8, 18, 20). For a more extended expose of the folly of bowing down to the product of carpenter and smith see 40:18-20; 44:9-20; Jer 10:1-16.

2:10 *Enter into the rock.* The pride of self-sufficiency will vanish when men will vainly seek refuge from *the terror of the Lord.* (19, 21; Lk 23:30)

2:12 *A day.* Judgment cannot be averted. Judah will not escape punishment by insisting that God must preserve His chosen people regardless of their behavior (Am 5:18-20; Mt 3:7-10; 23:33). Nor is anyting *proud and lofty* in nature or in human attainment capable of warding off humiliation when "he rises to terrify the earth" (19, 21). In Isaiah's description of the hurricane before which "the pride of men shall be brought low" (17) there are overtones of the universal and final judgment to come when "heaven and earth pass away" (Mt 5:18). This day of wrath is described more fully in chs. 24 and 34.

2:13 *Bashan.* Used here as a parallel to Lebanon, Bashan designates the territory lying east of the Jordan and extending northward to Mt. Hermon. (Dt 3:3 note)

2:16 *Tarshish.* Cf. 1 K 10:22 note.

2:20 *Idols.* For the meaning of the Hebrew term see Ps 96:5 note.

2:22 *Breath.* If God were to take it back, "man would return to dust" (Jb 34:14 f.). In a concluding call to repentance, Isaiah urges his hearers to *turn away from man* who "fades and withers" within a day (Ps 90:5 f.; 103:15 f.) and therefore is of no *account.* To put trust in a creature, formed of "dust from the ground" (Gen 2:7), rather than in the Creator is certain to end in disaster.

3:1-26 *Taking away.* The Lord's "day" of judgment (2:5-22) will not bring only slight inconvenience or a minor dislocation of life. Law and order will collapse like a building deprived of its supporting pillars. Unprincipled and inept officials will produce civic chaos (1-5). No one will have the will or the resources to assume leadership in the existing state of anarchy (6-8). Those posing as leaders are *oppressors* and do all they can to create confusion (9-12). *The elders and princes,* responsible for justice, fatten themselves with *the spoil of the poor* (13-15). The breakdown of society will be apparent in a debased womanhood. Parading in every *finery* of the current fashion and *glancing wantonly with their eyes,* the insipid ladies will hasten the day when, stripped of every glittering ornament and violated by cruel invaders, they will be forced to adorn themselves with the *sackcloth* of mourning. (16-26)

3:2 *Diviner.* The persons to whom the people vainly looked to maintain stability included the interpreter of omens, "the skillful magician" and "the expert in charms." The practice of sorcery and soothsaying was forbidden under stern penalties. (Ex 22:18 note; Dt 18:10-12)

3:6 *Mantle.* In their frantic search for a *leader* to restore a semblance of order and justice the people will resort to finding a man who owns only the necessary "covering" against the elements (Ex 22:26 f.). But even he has "neither bread nor mantle." (7)

3:7 *Healer.* The wounds on the body need the binding up of a physician if they are not to prove fatal.

3:9 *Partiality.* Literally: "the look of their faces." A glance at their facial expressions reveals that they flout all decency as insolently as did the people of *Sodom.*

3:10 *The righteous.* The "woe" pronounced on "the wicked" (9, 11) does not apply to the godly. Amid the terrors of judgment "it shall be well with them." (2 Ptr 2:9; Lk 21:28)

3:17 *Scab.* A disease of the scalp producing baldness.

3:18 *Finery.* The wardrobe of the fashion plate of the day consisted of some 20 articles of attire and accessories. It did not concern the wearer that these expensive articles were acquired "by grinding the face of the poor." (15)

3:24 *Shame.* The ancient manuscript referred to in the RSV note is one of the Dead Sea Scrolls. The traditional Hebrew text may be translated: "instead of beauty, branding," i.e., the mark of slavery.

3:26 *Her gates.* The change from "festal robes" to "sackcloth" will come when the daughter of Zion, Jerusalem, is ravaged by war and her "mighty men" fall in battle. Then the male population will be so decimated that the once-proud women will endure the "reproach" of childlessness unless they degrade themselves by becoming concubines. (4:1)

4:1 *Seven women.* This verse concludes the section of judgment begun at 3:16. Cf. 3:26 note.

4:2 *In that day.* The day of judgment (2:11, 12, 17, 20) is necessary to cleanse away "the filth of the daughters of Zion" (4). However, its "burning" (4) blasts are the means to a constructive end. Through *the survivors of Israel* God will carry forward His plan of universal salvation, as described in 2:1-4. In 4:2-6 the blessings to be bestowed are described again in figurative language. At that time "The Lord God will cause righteousness and praise to spring forth before all the nations," "as the earth brings forth its shoots" from ground no longer encumbered by the curse which caused it to produce "thorns and thistles" (61:11; 27:6; Gn 3:17 f.; cf. also Am 9:13; Zch 9:16 f.). In Jeremiah (23:5; 33:15) and Zechariah (3:8; 6:12) the Messiah Himself is called the "Branch." See also Is 11:1, where He is said to be "a shoot from the stump of Jesse."

4:3 *Holy.* As the descendants of Abraham were chosen to be a "holy nation" (Ex 19:6 second note; Lv 11:45 note), so "all the nations" constituting Israel "born according to the Spirit" (2:2; Gl 4:29; 1 Ptr 2:9) will be called and dedicated to "serve him without fear, in holiness and righteousness." (Lk 1:4 f.)

4:5 *Cloud . . . smoke . . . fire.* Though still exposed to the forces of evil, those "recorded for life" (3) will have the presence, guidance, and protection God once manifested "in a pillar of cloud" and "a pillar fire" when Israel of old wandered through the desert to the Promised Land. (Ex 13:21 f.; 14:19 f.; Ps 99:7; Ph 4:3; Rv 21:27)

5:1-30 *Vineyard.* In vv. 1-7 Isaiah uses a skillfully developed parable to make clear Israel's failure to carry out the purpose for which God chose and blessed it as a nation: the salvation of all nations as envisioned in 2:1-4 and 4:2-9. The opening lines resemble the kind of happy song his hearers would be delighted to hear as they rejoiced over a bountiful grape harvest. Its lyrical charm is enhanced by strains reminiscent of *a love song* (lit. "a song of my beloved"; cf. SS 1:9 second note). Suddenly at the end of v. 2 the note of joy turns into a lament. In spite of the tender care given the vines, they did not *yield grapes* but rather *wild grapes* (more lit. a stinking, rotten mess). The application begins with v. 3. The Lord, the Owner of the vineyard, tells what kind of fruit He had a right to expect from the *inhabitants of Jerusalem* in return for the unstinted nurture and blessing He had bestowed on them. As any owner of a vineyard producing nothing but putrid, unusable fruit is fully justified in destroying and abandoning the very site of *his pleasant planting,* so the Lord will let *the house of Israel* become a desolate *waste.* (5-7)

No longer speaking in a parable, Isaiah goes on to catalog the *wild grapes* which came to fruition from Israel's root-sin: ungrateful rejection of God's goodness. In a series of denunciations, introduced by the exclamation *woe,* the prophet offers a bill of particulars, indicting the apostate nation on six counts: (1) robbing small landowners of their family estates (8-10); (2) drunken debauchery (11-17); (3) cynical scoffing at God's power to call them to account for their malicious indulgence in wrongdoing (18-19); (4) flouting standards of right and wrong (20); (5) arrogant self-will (21); (6) perversion of justice by venal judges *who are heroes at drinking wine* (22). In the first two "woes," sentence is pronounced immediately upon the declaration of guilt (9 f.; 3-17), whereas announcement of impending disaster, introduced by *therefore,* follows the last four in a separate and longer section (24-30). Because *they have rejected the law of the Lord of hosts,* the fire of His *anger* will consume them (24 f.) when He will summon *a nation afar off* to execute judgment on them. (26-30)

5:2 *Wine vat.* In anticipation of a good harvest of grapes, the owner hollowed out a rock which would serve as a winepress.

5:5 *My vineyard.* For other examples of God's relationship to His people described as vines under His care see 3:14; 27:2-5; Jer 2:21; 12:10; Ps 80:8-13. See also Jesus' parable of the Vineyard. (Mk 12:1-9)

5:7 *A cry.* Namely for help.

5:8 *House to house.* By usury, extortion, and shady deals big moneymen gained title to houses and farms until *no more room* was left for the small landowner to call his own. (Am 5:10-13; Mi 2:2)

5:10 *One bath.* The land would become unproductive. The yield is given in ancient terms of liquid and dry measures. A *bath* and an *ephah* held about 6 gallons. Ten ephahs equaled a *homer.* (Cf. Ex 16:16 note)

5:12 *Deeds of the Lord.* In their drunken stupor the revelers gave no thought to "the miracles" and "marvels" God did in their history. (Ps 78:11 f.)

5:13 *Go into exile.* The prophet sees the punishment as an accomplished fact.

5:14 *Its appetite.* Death is compared to an insatiable beast. For *Sheol* see Dt 32:22 note.

5:16 *Exalted.* The execution of *justice* redounds to the glory of *the Holy God.*

5:17 *Kids.* See RSV note. The traditional Hebrew text has "aliens," i.e., nonresident people seeking pasturage for their flocks. By a slight change of one letter the Hebrew word spells *kids,* so translated also by the Septuagint.

5:18 *Draw iniquity.* The people defy God to do something about their indulgence to sin, to which they are addicted as firmly as if they were dumb animals harnessed by *cords* and *ropes* to draw a *cart.*

5:25 *His anger is not turned away.* The last two lines of this verse are a refrain with which Isaiah punctuates his message of doom in 9:12, 17, 21; 10:4.

5:26 *A signal.* The Hebrew word is translated also "ensign" and "standard" (11:10, 12; 13:2; 18:3; 30:17; 31:9; 49:22; 62:10). "Assyria, the rod of" God's "anger" (10:5), is able to inflict total destruction. Its soldiers, mustered and united for action under a national banner, are described in the following verses as irresistible.

6:1-13 ISAIAH CLEANSED AND COMMISSIONED TO BE GOD'S MESSENGER

6:1-13 *I saw.* "The vision of Isaiah" (1:1 note), epitomized in chs. 1—5 (1:2 note), transmits a message from "the Lord of hosts." In order to make the prophet and his hearers aware of its validity, he is given a glimpse of the glory of *the King* (5) in whose name he is to speak (1-4; cf. Jn 12:41). However, Isaiah, a son of Adam with *unclean lips* and subject to sin's curse, is doomed if he as much as comes into the presence of "the Holy One of Israel" (5:19; cf. Ex 33:18 note), to say nothing of presuming to act as His messenger (5). Only after his *guilt is taken away* by *a burning coal . . . from the altar* (6-7) is the forgiven sinner emboldened to volunteer his services as God's ambassador (8). The Lord accepts Isaiah's offer to be His mouthpiece. Serving in that capacity, the prophet is not to express his own opinions. For that reason God puts on his cleansed lips the very words he is to *say to this people.* The communication assigned to him is not a pleasant one. He is to proclaim to an apostate nation that their *land* will become *utterly desolate.* Because they will refuse to heed the call to repentance, only a *stump* will remain standing when Israel, the *oak* of the Lord's planting (cf. Jer 11:16 f.), *is felled* by the axe of divine judgment. (9-13)

6:1 *King Uzziah.* For the account of this king's reign, also called Azariah, see 2 K 15:1-7; 2 Ch 26. Human monarchs come and go, but there is never a time when *the Lord* is not *sitting upon a throne, high and lifted up,* from which He governs the universe He created. (66:1; 1 K 22:19; Ps 9:7; 29:10; Eze 1:26 ff.)

His train. Earthly kings wore a robe with a long flowing *train* or skirt. The royal garment in which the King of kings appeared to Isaiah was so long and wide that it *filled the temple.* The Hebrew word for *temple* denotes also "the king's palace" and is so translated in Dn 1:4; Pr 30:28.

6:2 *Seraphim.* A transliterated Hebrew plural noun which occurs only here and in v. 6 as a name for celestial things. Derived from a verb meaning to burn, the same word is used of serpentine creatures, translated "fiery serpents" (Nm 21:6, 8; Dt 8:15) and "flying serpents" (Is 14:29; 30:6). For the order of angels called cherubim see 1 K 6:23 note. Appearing to Isaiah with features resembling a man with *six wings,* the seraphim perform two functions. They praise God in an antiphonal hymn with thunderous, unearthly effects (3-4). Then one of them engages in a symbolical act; he cauterizes Isaiah's "unclean lips" with "a burning coal" taken "from the altar" (5-7). Atonement for "sin" and "guilt" (7), typified by sacrificial offerings in the Old Testament, was made by "the Lamb of God" on the altar of the cross. (Jn 1:29; 1 Ptr 3:18; 1 Jn 1:7)

6:8 *For us.* God, who "is one Lord" (Dt 6:4), speaks in the first person plural. (Gn 1:26 note; 3:22 note)

6:10 *Lest they see.* The result of Isaiah's preaching and its purpose are viewed together. "Due to their hardness of heart" (Eph 4:18; Mk 6:52). God's warning of judgment to come will be rejected by *this people* and seal their doom. (Mk 4:12; Acts 28:26 f.; Ro 11:8; cf. also Ex 4:21 note)

6:13 *Seed.* Though the threatened devastation will overtake the apostate people as a nation, there will be a nucleus which is *holy,* i.e., declared worthy to carry out the purpose for which God chose Israel. (4:3 ff.; Ex 19:5 f.)

7:1—12:6 IMMANUEL: HIS MESSIANIC KINGDOM

7:1-25 *Wage war.* This ch. offers a glaring example of the hardness of heart on the part of Isaiah's hearers which God said would not let them "turn and be healed" (6:9-13). King Ahaz is told to *believe* if he is to *be established* rather than be struck down by the combined attack of Rezin of Syria and Pekah of Israel (1-9). Masking his unbelief with sanctimonious excuses, he refuses the offer of a miraculous *sign* which would demonstrate God's power to deliver him (10-12). Even though Ahaz rejects the proposal, the Lord gives the *house of David* a sign of His own choosing: the sign of *Immanuel* (13-17). The Syrian and Israelite campaign will fail in its objective. However, because of the people's continued apostasy, God will summon another nation, the Assyrians, to devastate the land, reducing it to *briers and thorns.* (18-25)

7:1 *Ahaz.* For the account of his reign see 2 K 16; 2 Ch 28. For *Jotham* see 2 K 15:32-38; 2 Ch 27. For *Rezin* see 2 K 15:29 note. For *Pekah* see 2 K 15:25-31.

7:3 *Shear-jashub.* Given a name meaning "a remnant shall return," Isaiah's older son was a living proclamation of Israel's survival. Though decimated by war and carried into exile, a nucleus of the chosen people would remain the instrument of God's plan of universal salvation (11:11, 16; 37:4, 31 f.; 46:3), whereas He will cut off "name and remnant" of the nations seeking to frustrate His good and gracious will. (14:22, 30; 15:9; 16:14)

Fuller's Field. Cf. 2 K 18:17 second note.

7:6 *Tabe-el.* No person with this name is known. In its Hebrew form it may express derision: "a good for nothing." See the expression "sons of Belial," translated "base fellows." (Ju 19:22 first note; 1 Sm 1:16 note)

7:8-9 *The head of Syria.* What the two enemies plan "shall not come to pass" (7) because *Syria* and *Ephraim* have at their head frail human beings, residing in man-made capitals. They cannot destroy Jerusalem contrary to the will of the King of kings, who "dwells on Mt. Zion" (8:18), the base of His earthly operations. (2:3; Ps 46:1-11)

Sixty-five years. Even the inhabitants of the Northern Kingdom who were not carried off into exile by the Assyrians would *no longer be a people* of unmixed nationality because imported foreigners were to be made a part of the population already after the fall of Samaria (2 K 17:24) and again during the reign of the Assyrian king Esarhaddon (681—669 BC), six decades after Isaiah began his ministry.

Believe . . . be established. Faith and its effect on life are combined in a word-play for which there is no equivalent in English. A different form of the same Hebrew verb is used to describe what it means to believe and what results from believing. Underlying the OT conception of faith is the determination to take one's stand firmly and unconditionally on God's promises. As long as he remains steadfast and unmovable in this stance of trust, the believer—and he alone—can be confident that he will *be established.* He has solid ground under his feet, "though the earth should change, though the mountains shake in the heart of the sea." (Ps 46:2; Mt 24:29)

7:14 *A young woman.* The NT establishes the ultimate meaning of the *Immanuel* sign. It was given to foretell that God would let His Son be born of the Virgin Mary by the operation of His Holy Spirit. "Born of woman," one who had "no husband," the incarnate Son of God was indeed *Immanuel,* "God with us," for He came to "save his people from their sins," their greatest enemy. (Gl 4:4; Lk 1:34; Mt 1:21 [cf. Mt 1:18-25 note])

The context of the prophesied virgin birth of the Savior provides for a preliminary fulfillment of the sign: deliverance from the "two kings" (16) threatening the destruction of Jerusalem. Within the nine months that a young woman of marriageable age who was presumed to be a virgin before her wedding (cf. Dt 22:13-21) conceives and gives birth to a child, it will be so evident that God was with His people to deliver them that she will call her son *Immanuel,* i.e., "God is with us." By the time he "knows how to refuse the evil and choose the good," i.e., the age of discretion, the enemy not only will have given up his design of conquest but his own "land . . . will be deserted," laid waste by the emerging Assyrian empire (15 f.). See Hos 11:1 (Mt 2:15) for another example of God's direction of Israel's history in such a way as to let the event foreshadow what He would do in the life of His incarnate Son.

7:15 *Curds and honey.* It would be some time before the land would recover from the ravages of war. Instead of living on the products of agriculture such as grain and meat, the survivors of the invasion would sustain themselves with food derived from a pastoral way of life: curdled milk and honey gathered from trees in the woods. (Vv. 21-25).

7:18 *Whistle.* Summoned by God, the executors of His judgment will descend on Israel like swarms of flies and bees, infesting every nook and cranny. Palestine would become the battleground of the Assyrians and the Egyptians, both determined to annex it to their respective empires.

7:20 *Shave.* Assyria, the nation Ahaz foolishly *hired* to ease the pressure from Syria and Israel and now described as a *razor,* will denude the land from one end to the other. (2 K 16:7 ff.)

8:1-22 *Write.* Chs. 7 and 8 have several features in common. Both address themselves to the same situation (cf. 7:1 note). As the name given Isaiah's older son foretold the failure of the enemies to conquer Jerusalem (7:3 ff.), so the meaning of the younger son's name was a prophetic proclamation that Damascus, capital of Syria, and Samaria, capital of the Northern Kingdom, would be overcome and sacked by *the king of Assyria* (8:1-4). To this promise of relief from immediate disaster, Isaiah again attaches the announcement of Israel's eventual doom: the Assyrian forces will overrun the length and breadth of Ahaz' land like an irresistible deluge (5-8; cf. 7:17 ff.). A godless nation such as the Assyrians may serve as the Lord's "rod" to chasten His chosen people (10:5). However, any attempt by earthly rulers to frustrate His sovereign will *will come to nought* (8:9-10). Therefore what should instill *fear* and *dread* is not a *conspiracy* of impotent men such as the plot of Syria and Israel against Judah; what will prove fatal is the refusal to stand in holy awe of *the Lord of hosts.* All who commit themselves to Him will find in His *sanctuary* a refuge, "a very present help in trouble" (Ps 46:1); to those in *both houses of Israel* who dishonor Him and "put confidence in man" (Ps 118:8) He will be *a rock of stumbling* causing them to *fall and be broken* (11-15). Firmly convinced that what *the Lord spoke* through him will not fail to come true, Isaiah directs his disciples to keep on file the written and sealed record of his *testimony* and *teaching* (16-17). His own name (the Lord saves) and the names he gave his sons also will be living *signs and portents* of what the future will bring as predicted by him (18). To listen to the hokum of soothsayers rather than to the revealed *teaching and . . . testimony* of God will bring a people only *the gloom of anguish* and *thrust* it into the *thick darkness* of despair (19-22).

8:1 *In common characters.* Placarded in large letters of ordinary script, the name was to be read and its meaning understood not only by those skilled in orthography but by the general reading public.

Maher-shalal-hash-baz. Cf. the RSV note for the translation of this long and strange-sounding name. The message it is to convey every time it is used to address the boy is given in v. 4.

8:2 *Uriah.* A priest by this name is mentioned in 2 K 16:10, 11, 15. The other witness, *Zechariah,* cannot be identified. He is not the prophet bearing that name.

8:6 *Waters of Shiloah.* The stream, arising from the Spring of Gihon (1 K 1:33 second note), flowing gently along the southeastern wall and emptying in a reservoir within the city (the Pool of Siloam; cf. 7:3), symbolizes the quiet assurance of divine providence which faith accepts in calm confidence (Ps 46:4 note). Having *refused* God's promise of safety "in fear before" the threatening enemy, "this people" ultimately will suffer foreign invasion, pictured as flooding "waters of the River," i.e., the Euphrates, which flows through territory held by the king of Assyria.

Melt in fear. This translation is based on the substitution of one Hebrew "s" sound for another. See RSV note.

8:8 *O Immanuel.* The inhabitants of the land are so addressed because they would remain unharmed if they would only "believe" (7:9) and express their faith by saying, "Immanuel," i.e., "God is with us." (10; 7:14 note)

8:13 *Sanctuary.* The temple of "The Lord of hosts, who dwells on Mount Zion" (18), was designed also to offer asylum to persons having unintentionally committed manslaughter. (Ex 21:13 note; 1 K 1:50 note; see also Eze 11:16)

8:18 *I and the children.* Quoted in the NT. Cf. Heb 2:13 note.

8:19 *Mediums . . . wizards . . . consult the dead.* To resort to various occult means of unlocking the unknown rather than to *consult their God* was rejection of the Lord and a lapse into crass paganism (cf. Dt 18:10-12; Lv 19:31; 1 S 28:3 note). Practitioners of divination and spiritism are said to *chirp and mutter,* i.e., make their voices sound mysterious and unearthly.

9:1-21 *No gloom.* As light burst in on primordial darkness (Gn 1:3), so 9:1-7 lets a flash of prophetic vision break in on "the gloom of anguish" (8:22) "to give light to those who sit in darkness and in the shadow of death" (Lk 1:79). Undaunted by the unfaithfulness of the chosen people, *the zeal of the Lord . . . will do* (7) what was required so that men everywhere might "inherit the kingdom prepared for [them] from the foundation of the world" (Mt 25:34; Eph 1:4; 1 Ptr 1:20). *To establish it and to uphold it* a child is to be born to *the throne of David* (7) on whom titles are conferred which no earthly ruler has a right to claim. He is not only David's son but also his Lord (Mt 22:42-45). The Messiah's reign of justice, righteousness, and peace began when angelic hosts announced the birth of *a son* (6) "wrapped in swaddling cloths and lying in a manger" (Lk 2:10 ff.); it will reach its culmination when He "comes in his glory, and all the angels with him" (Mt 25:31; see also Lk 1:68 f.; 2 Sm 7:12-29). The *great light* of promise is like a flash of lightning blazing across Israel's skies; it quickly gives way to the *deep darkness* about to engulf the people of Isaiah's day. In the remaining verses (8-21) he again announces the doom which must overtake and purify the chosen nation if it is to be bearer of the salvation held out in vv. 1-7. Unbowed by earlier chastening blows of adversity, *the people will know* from sad experience how fatal self-reliance in defiance of God is (8-12). The refusal to *turn to him who smote them* is not restricted to an isolated few or to a single stratum of the population; *head and tail*—from the highest to the lowest levels—*everyone is godless* (13-17). Such unrestrained indulgence in sin is self-destructive; it ends in anarchy in government, in chaos in society, and in individual self-gratification so ruthless that *no man spares his brother* and yet so unsatisfying that they *are still hungry.* (18-21)

9:1 *Zebulun and . . . Naphtali.* The hereditary lands of these two tribes constituted Israel's northern border west of the Jordan. *Beyond the Jordan* to the east lay the region called *Galilee* (i.e., circuit or district) *of the nations.* Through these areas ran *the way of the sea,* an east-west road ending at the Mediterranean. Because the invading enemy came from the north, these outlying districts would be the first to fall victim to the conqueror's might and the last to be freed from his domination.

9:4 *Midian.* In the days of the Judges, Gideon freed Israel from *the yoke* of marauding "Midianites . . . Amalekites and the people of the East" (Ju 6:2 f. note; ch. 7; Is 10:26; Ps 83:9). Their defeat by a handful of Israelites is cited as evidence that mighty foes must fail when they oppose the kingdom God promises to establish.

9:5 *Fuel for the fire.* The symbols of subjugation and all traces of bloody conflict will vanish. (Ps 46:9 note; Eze 39:9)

9:6 *His name.* Four sets of two Hebrew nouns describe the person and the work of the Messianic King. All are titles ascribed to God Himself. The wisdom of His counsel and providential ordering of events is apparent when He does wonders and miracles for which the Lord receives praise (Ex 15:11; Is 25:1; Jer 32:18). No mere human deserves to be called "Mighty God" (Ex 15:11; Ps 89:8). Though born of a woman, He is the *Everlasting Father,* ruling and governing all things "from this time forth and for evermore" (7). He is the *Prince of Peace* who provides healing of the fatal dissension between God and man, "bringing the hostility to an end" through His cross, so that the fallen sons of Adam need no longer be at odds with their Creator, with themselves, and with their fellowmen. (Cf. notes on 2:2, 4; also 11:1 ff.; Eph 2:16).

9:7 *Zeal of the Lord.* As God jealously prohibits having other gods before Him (Ex 20:3 second note, 5 note; 34:14; Dt 4:24 note; Ps 78:58; 79:5; Eze 16:38), so those who trust Him are assured that no opposition can thwart His ardent desire *to establish* and *to uphold* His kingdom *for evermore.* (37:32; Is 63:15; 2 K 19:31)

9:10 *Bricks have fallen.* In this verse Isaiah records a proverb which the people quote to express their perverse determination to pursue their wicked course in spite of the reverses by which God was calling them to repentance.

9:11 *Adversaries.* Cf. RSV note. "The adversaries of Rezin," the Syrian king, were the Assyrians, who overran Syria before proceeding southward to destroy the Northern Kingdom. Before Rezin and Pekah, king of Israel, united forces against Judah, the Southern Kingdom, several Syrian kings had made serious inroads into Israelite territory. (2 K 10:32 f.; 13:22)

9:12 *His anger.* The last two lines of this verse are a concluding refrain, found again at the end of v. 17, v. 21 and 10:4. Cf. 5:25 note.

9:14 *Head and tail, palm branch and reed.* From the highest echelons down to the lowest levels of society, the nation stands condemned as "godless," richly deserving the punishment dealt by God's "hand." (17)

9:15 *The prophet.* Instead of assuming leadership by giving moral direction to governing officials, men who profess to be God's spokesmen become boot-licking lackeys. We would say: The tail wags the dog.

9:20 *Devours.* When men act solely out of selfish motives, they injure not only their fellowmen but ultimately destroy themselves as they in turn become victims of the law of the jungle.

10:1-34 *Woe.* This chapter begins with an accusation against the covenant nation similar to the charges recorded in 9:8-21. The first four verses declare that the *wealth* accumulated with the help of unjust judges and at the expense of *the poor* and *widows* will vanish on the day of punishment. While this section constitutes a strophe, marked by the concluding refrain which is found also in 9:12, 17, 21, it is set off from the preceding denunciations by an introductory *woe,* a formula introducing a lament as in 5:8, 11, 18, 20, 21, 22. In this way the last in a series of threats against Israel is linked with the "woe" (translated *Ah*) pronounced against Assyria in the following verses (5-19). God did indeed call on a cruel, rapacious nation to be *the rod* with which, in His righteous *anger,* He was about to rain devastating blows on His chosen people. They deserved the full *fury* of His wrath because they had sunk to the level of *a godless nation,* alienated from the Lord by a way of life as depraved as that of a heathen community.

The instrument chosen by God to be His avenger was well equipped to carry out the assignment. Nation after nation fell before the Assyrian war machine as it approached Jerusalem (5-11). However, the Scourge of God (as Europeans later called Attila the Hun) had *in his mind to destroy* kingdoms and nations to satisfy his own imperialistic ambition.Arrogantly he claimed credit for his victories, ascribing his successes to his *strength* and *wisdom* (12-14). But this mighty conqueror too had to remain but an instrument in the hand of the Ruler of nations. He who had fashioned it would destroy it when it no longer served His purposes. (15-19)

At this point Isaiah's vision of coming events went beyond the fall of the Assyrian empire, which took place a full century after he spoke (612 BC). He saw *that day* in the still more distant future when, after another century had passed, a small surviving *remnant* of God's people *will return* to their homeland. Chastened by adversity and exile, they will again *lean upon* Him who will not deceive them as did the Assyrians to whom they appealed for help. (20-23)

After providing a glimpse into a coming era, the prophet lets his contemporaries see what lies ahead in the more immediate future. God will not let the Assyrians capture Jerusalem even though they will be allowed to advance to the very gates of the city (24-32). The army of the invader, proud of its victorious march and disdainful of any possible opposition, will be destroyed as swiftly and completely as a forest of trees as *majestic* as the cedars of *Lebanon* is leveled by a storm of *terrifying power.* (33-34)

10:5 *Staff of my fury.* God was about to use the Assyrians as an instrument of punishment. They were to wield it as His agents. At His behest they were to pour out His fury on the apostate people.

10:7 *So intend.* The Assyrian conqueror refused to think of himself as doing what God commanded him. He took orders from no one. He had no other thought than to satisfy his lust to *destory,* to *cut off* many *nations,* and to replace their kings with his commanders. He defied what he called the "idols" of Jerusalem (11) to protect the city against the army he had made invincible.

10:9 *Calno . . . Damascus.* The cities mentioned in this verse were captured by the Assyrians in their march southward against Jerusalem. The southernmost of these was Samaria, capital of the Northern Kingdom, and the most distant was Carchemish, more than 300 miles to the north. The other cities lay between these two points.

10:12 *Will punish.* Even before the Assyrian king finishes his tirade of *haughty pride* (cf. 13 f.), a reminder is inserted that the Lord has him firmly in leash. Not impotent and nonexisting as the idols of the conquered kingdoms, the Lord will let the blasphemous boaster do no more than the specific task assigned to him.

10:14 *Chirped.* The Assyrian hordes conquered and plundered peoples with as little effort as it takes to *gather eggs* from a nest forsaken by the mother bird. She does not dare to move *a wing* to defend it or ever to open her *mouth* in a screeching protest against the robbery.

10:15 *Not wood.* Wood and iron remain inert and passive even when made into implements. As such tools did not determine how they were to be shaped, so they cannot dictate to the sovereign will of their maker when and how he is to use them. God, having fashioned the

Assyrians into instruments of judgment, will destroy them if they refuse to be of service to Him.

10:17 *The light of Israel.* God is like a *flame* of fire, shining benignly on His faithful people and at the same time destroying His enemies as irresistibly as a forest fire devours everything in its path whether lofty "trees" (19) or lowly *thorns and briers.* (27:4; 29:6; 30:27)

10:18 *Soul and body.* The destruction of the forest of Assyrian pride and presumption will be as thorough as if the two components of man were wiped out.

10:20 *Remnant.* Occurring again in the next two verses this term drives home the meaning of the name of Isaiah's older son (7:3). It contains a message of hope: The chosen people will not become extinct. But it also predicts severe losses of population: "Only a remnant" will survive the "destruction . . . decreed" by "the mighty God." (21 f.; cf. 9:6)

10:23 *Full end.* The Lord will carry out to the full what He has *decreed,* proving His power to determine the destiny of *all the earth.*

10:26 *A scourge.* Because the Assyrians abused the assignment to be God's "rod" and "staff" on Israel (5), they themselves will be dealt lashes inflicted by the anger of the Lord. Two incidents from the past are cited to illustrate this fact. A little band under Gideon's command, armed only with torches and trumpets, crushed the dreaded Midianite hordes (Ju 7; cf. also 1 Sm 14:6). All Moses had to do to destroy Pharaoh's army was to stretch *his rod . . . over the sea* at God's direction. (Ex 14:16-29)

10:27 *From Rimmon.* The RSV translation of the last line of v. 27 is based on changes in the traditional Hebrew text. If left unaltered, the words make sense if translated: "and the yoke will be shattered in view of fatness." As oxen grow so fat and strong as to shake off their yoke, so Israel will have the strength to free itself from the burdensome oppression.

10:28 *Aiath.* Vv. 28-32 trace the advance of the enemy through towns situated immediately north of Jerusalem. Though some of the localities cannot be identified with certainty, it may be assumed that they too are points along the same route. It ends at "Nob" (32), which lies between "Jerusalem" and "Anathoth" (30), the latter only 2½ miles north of the object of the campaign. Some of the place names seem to be mentioned because they make possible a play on words, which cannot be reproduced in a translation. By this dramatic and highly poetic description of an envisioned line of march, so direct and unimpeded, Isaiah seeks to convince his hearers of the reality of God's threat to use such a cruel nation as the Assyrians as the rod of His anger.

10:33 *Lop.* When the Assyrians have served the purpose for which God hired them (10:5 note), He will "cut down" their blasphemous pride.

11:1-16 *A Shoot.* In this chapter prophetic vision ranges farther into the future than the fall of Assyria, just predicted in figurative language. A century was to elapse before this great empire, standing as "lofty" and "great in height" as the cedars of "Lebanon," was to be "hewn down" (10:33 f.). Now Isaiah sees what was to happen several decades later. The axe of divine judgment would cut down to a *stump* also the kingdom established by David, the son of *Jesse.* However, this disastrous state of affairs in Israel's history is but the point at which a long-range projection across centuries and aeons begins. Isaiah beholds a king, growing out of the *roots* of Davidic stock, whose rule was to affect human history to the end of time. Emerging as a *Branch* out of the lineage of Jesse, this Son of David is greater than Solomon and all kings of human origin (Mt 12:42). He is the promised Messiah, permanently endowed by *the Spirit of the Lord* with such perfect personal traits and with such unlimited executive capacity as to assure Him accomplishments far exceeding those of the most enlightened and capable monarch (2-3a). He dispenses justice with absolute *righteousness.* The verdict He renders is carried out throughout *the earth* (3b-5). He makes it possible for His subjects to enjoy an inner "peace . . . which passes all understanding" (Ph 4:7). A dramatic change takes place in their lives. It is a transformation no less radical than the reversal from prevailing hostile instincts in the animal world to the harmony which prevailed in the Garden of Eden before man's sin turned all of creation into an arena of conflict. (6-9; 65:25, cf. note on "Prince of Peace," 9:6; also Ro 8:19-23)

The Messianic King is capable of making all things new and of calling into being "a new creation" (2 Co 5:17) because He, *a shoot from the stump of Jesse,* is at the same time *the root of Jesse,* the life giving Source of the royal lineage of David. Furthermore, whereas an earthly ruler such as David was able to incorporate a few neighboring states into his empire, the King of *that day* has sway over a domain unlimited by territorial borders and unaffected by the passing of time. *The peoples* (regardless of racial diversities) and *the nations* (regardless of geographic location) will not cease flocking to Him as loyal troops, of their own accord, rally about *an ensign* or flag, the symbol of their allegiance. (10)

The concluding verses of the ch. (11-16) round out the prophetic picture of the new Davidic kingdom. Old Testament allusions and analogies again serve as types of the greater things to come. The universality of the Messiah's reign, announced in general terms (10), is graphically portrayed by comparing what God once did with what will happen when He acts *yet a second time.* At the dawn of Israel's history God called the chosen nation into being by redeeming the enslaved and outcast sons of Jacob from one country, Egypt. *In that day* the new Israel will be composed of people summoned *from the four corners of the earth.* The prophet envisions this international ingathering under the *ensign* of the Messiah in terms of what God would do *to recover the remnant . . . of his people* after David's kingdom had become a *stump* (1) and *the remnant* of its citizens were dispersed into the countries surrounding Palestine (11-12; see the cosmopolitan makeup of the assembly on Pentecost, Acts 2:8-11). Other features of the Messianic kingdom, also cast in Old Testament molds, will be (a) internal harmony (13); (b) victory over foes from without (14); (c) its establishment by divine control of nature and history. (15-16)

11:1 *A branch.* This term is used to designate a human king in Dn 11:7. In Is 60:21 the people under the Messiah's rule are called "the shoot of" God's "planting" (cf. also 4:2). A synonym of the Hebrew word appears as a Messianic title in Jer 23:5; 33:15; Zch 3:8; 6:12. (Cf. also Rv 5:5; Acts 13:22 f.)

11:2 *Shall rest.* "The Spirit of the Lord came upon" men in the past for a limited time and for a particular purpose (Ex 35:31; Nm 11:25; Ju 3:10; 6:34; 2 Sm 23:2; 2 Ptr 1:21). There will be no end to the flow of the Spirit's gifts equipping great David's greater Son with every trait and ability to make Him a perfect Ruler (42:1; 61:1-3; Jn 1:32; Acts 10:38; Rv 1:4; 3:1; 4:5). The six royal endowments, arranged in three pairs, echo the meaning of the same number of names given the King in 9:6. For the meaning of "knowledge" see Gn 18:19 note; Dt 9:24 note; for "the fear of the Lord" see Dt 6:13 note.

11:4 *Rod of his mouth.* Cf. 49:2; Hos 6:5; Rv 1:16.

11:6 *The wolf . . . with the lamb.* The cessation of hostilities between men used in 2:1-4 to describe the kind of peace to be enjoyed by the King's subjects is here extended to include the elimination of fear between animal and animal and between man and animal as it has existed since the disruptive intrusion of sin into the bliss of Paradise. (Cf. 65:25)

11:9 *Holy mountain.* Cf. 2:2 second note.

11:10 *Root of Jesse.* Cf. Ro 15:12; Rv 5:5; 22:16.

11:11 *Assyria . . .* Egypt. Two world empires, which approached Palestine from the north and south respectively. *Pathros* and *Ethiopia* were Egyptian territories along the upper Nile. Elam was situated at the head of the Persian Gulf. *Shinar* is a Biblical term for Mesopotamia (Gn 10:10). *Hamath* marked Israel's northernmost boundary (Nm 34:8; Jos 13:5; Am 6:14). *The coastlands of the sea* are the islands and shorelands of the Mediterranean.

11:13 *Ephraim . . . Judah.* For the strife between the northern and southern divisions of David's kingdom see 7:17; 9:21. Dissension and rivalry will vanish to the extent that people come under the sway of the Prince of Peace. Even those of different national and racial origins can expect to enjoy His blessings. (Gl 3:28 f.; Cl 3:11)

11:14 *Shoulder.* Seen from the Judaean hill-country, the territory occupied by the Philistines resembled the shoulder of a man.

11:15 *Utterly destroy.* The Lord will eradicate all obstacles hindering access into the Messianic kingdom, as once the Red Sea had to give way at His command before "Israel when they came up from the land of Egypt" (16; Ex 14:15 f.). Before the power which the Lord stands ready to use in behalf of "the remnant . . . of His people" all opposition must disintegrate. He can not only open a path through the sea; He can eradicate the entire *tongue of the sea of Egypt* (perhaps the Gulf of Suez is meant). He needs only to *wave his hand* and the Euphrates, known simply as *the River,* will be reduced to a trickle. See the words of Jesus about His church, Mt 16:18.

12:1-6 *Give thanks.* The six verses of this chapter are a sequel to the preceding chapter. There the subject is the blissful, universal reign of "the Root of Jesse" to be established "in that day" (11:10 f.); here those who share in the *salvation* provided *in that day* would praise God, individually and collectively, for its blessings and vow to *make known his deeds among the nations* that they might *be known in all the earth.* The subjects of the Messianic King have every reason to be grateful. Though they have deserved the wrath of God, He is no longer *angry with* them. They need not *be afraid* of Him but can *trust* Him to be their *strength.* The songs of salvation sung by the new Israel have the form and content of OT hymns. For similar strains see Ex 15 (the song of Moses); 1 Ch 16:8-36; Ez 3:11; Ps 105:1-6; Is 35:10; 40:1 f.; Jer 33:10 f.; but see also the "new song" of the "saints" in Rv 5:8-14; 14:3; 15:3 f.

12:3 *Wells of salvation.* God is the only source of "living water." (Jer 2:13; Jn 4:10; 7:37 f.)

12:6 *Holy One of Israel.* Isaiah's characteristic title for God. (1:4 note)

13:1—23:18 JUDGMENT PRONOUNCED ON FOREIGN NATIONS AND APOSTATE JERUSALEM

13:1—14:27 Babylon

13:1-22 *Isaiah . . . saw.* Because he was a man "who hears the words of God, who sees the vision of the Almighty . . . having his eyes uncovered" (Nm 24:4), he had more than normal sight. In chs. 7—12 he records a preview of the Messianic King arising "from the stump of Jesse" (11:1) and holding sway to the end of days. Continuing to look across vistas of time in chs. 13—23, he makes sketches of what happens when "kings of the earth set themselves . . . against the Lord and his anointed" (Ps 2:2). Though different characters are depicted, the pictures are designed to teach one and the same lesson: No power on earth can prevent the coming of the prophesied kingdom, or destroy it once it is established. In order to convince Isaiah's contemporaries of God's absolute control of history, he portrays the inevitable doom of nations who tried to keep the chosen people from carrying out their assigned role in the divine plan of universal salvation. However, in the range and perspective of prophetic vision, scenes are blended as one is superimposed on another. Israel's enemies of old and their fate become transparencies through which the light of divine revelation penetrates and illumines even the most remote age of the future. Over the desolations of ancient Babylonia, Moab, Philistia, etc., there flash the lightnings of God's judgment on *the arrogant* and *the ruthless* (11) of all times, culminating in the cataclysm of that *day of the Lord* (6, 9) when "the earth and the works that are upon it will be burned up." (2 Ptr 3:10)

Therefore what Isaiah has to say about ancient kingdoms and distant empires buried under the sands of time is of interest not only to the historian and archaeologist. It concerns today's member of the kingdom of God as vitally as it did the citizen of Jerusalem seven centuries before the Prince of Peace appeared. Under all circumstances and at all times "it is better to take refuge in the Lord than to put confidence in man" (Ps 118:8; 40:4; Jer 17:5). No one at any time need fear a breakdown of the moral world order. The Maker of heaven and earth will not succumb to the forces of evil, no matter how diabolical their design, no matter how much power they generate. Through Isaiah God has already pronounced sentence on them. And He will carry it out as surely as He did in the case of the nations flourishing at the prophet's time.

13:1 *Oracle.* The term introducing the doom pronounced on foreign nations is not the word occurring over 300 times in the phrase "oracle of the Lord," which the RSV translates "says the Lord" (e.g., 14:22). Derived from the verb meaning "to lift, to raise," the noun used here is rendered "burden" in the KJV (so also by the RSV in Jer 23:33 ff.). So interpreted, it describes what the prophet has to say as imposing a load on those addressed and crushing them under its weight. This connotation is found in the content of the messages so introduced. In many instances the words which follow are heavy with denunciation of sin and threat of punishment. However, the term may be associated with the Hebrew idiom "to lift up the voice." In that case, it denotes simply a message spoken with a raised voice. This more general meaning seems to be indicated when it is used in titles of entire books (Nah 1:1; Hab 1:1; Ml 1:1; cf. also Pr 30:1 both notes). Chs. 13—23 represent a collection of 11 oracles. With the exception of ch. 22, all of them are directed against heathen nations. For similar groupings of prophecies against these nations see Jer 46—51 and Eze 25—32.

Babylon. The nation which was to destroy the holy city and carry its inhabitants into exile is the first to be arraigned. In the Book of Revelation, Babylon is used symbolically as the embodiment of hostility to God and His people. (Rv 14:8; 16:19; 17:5; 18:2, 10, 21)

13:2 *Cry aloud.* In vv. 2-16 the doom later to be proclaimed specifically on Babylon (17-22) is first seen in the larger perspective of a final, universal "day of the Lord" (6, 9, 13). When "the Lord of hosts" gathers His army, recruits come in uncounted numbers "from the end of the heavens" (2-5). It is impossible to escape "destruction from the Almighty" (6-8); "in the day of his fierce anger" He makes "the earth a desolation" by ordering the universe to return to primordial chaos (9-16). Because it is in His jurisdiction and power to "punish the world for its evil" (11), His sentence of guilty on "the splendor and pride of the Chaldeans" (19) too will be carried out so inexorably that "its days will not be prolonged." (17-22)

13:3 *Consecrated ones.* Selected by God to carry out His holy will. (Ex 19:6 second note)

13:6 *The day of the Lord.* Cf. 2:11 note; Jl 1:15; 2:1-11; Zph 1:7, 14-18.

13:12 *Ophir.* Cf. notes on Gn 10:24; 1 K 9:26.

13:17 *Medes.* "The wrath of the Lord of hosts" has no trouble finding agents to lay low "the pride" and "the haughtiness" of men "in the day of his fierce anger" (11, 13). At His beck and call they come from the mysterious and "distant land" (5) of Media. Located below the Caspian Sea and along the high Zagros mountain range, Media to the Israelites meant the ends of the world. Its warriors *have no regard for silver,* i.e., they reject all offers of bribes.

13:19 *Chaldeans.* At the time of Isaiah, Babylonia was a province of the Assyrian empire. Revolts against foreign domination were instigated by leaders whose base of operations was in Chaldea in southern Babylonia (Gn 11:31 note; Jb 1:17 note). King Hezekiah, likewise chafing under Assyrian control, was asked by a Chaldean rebel king, called Merodachbaladan in the OT, to join forces in a war of liberation (ch. 39: 2 K 20:12-19). Isaiah opposed the foreign alliance because it was motivated by a trust in men rather than in God. The folly of the proposed political maneuver was soon to become evident. The Assyrian king Sennacherib destroyed Babylon and massacred its inhabitants. Furthermore, the very Babylonians who asked for an offensive treaty were to capture and destroy Jerusalem a century later (586 BC). For in the meantime the Assyrian empire has run its course, as predicted in 10:12 ff. It was "hewn down" (10:33) in 612 BC by a revived Babylonia, aided by the Medes. However, a half century after the fall of Jerusalem, Babylonia too came under the judgment of the day of the Lord. Incorporated in the Medo-Persian empire of Cyrus in 538, it never regained its independence. Eventually it disappeared entirely from view until the spade of the archaeologist dug up its ruins from the sands of the desert.

13:20 *Arab.* It will be too desolate even for Bedouin tribes.

13:21 *Satyrs.* Isaiah adopts the language of popular lore, according to which demonic creatures in the form of hairy he-goats roamed about in the desert.

14:1-27 *Compassion on Jacob.* Seen in the perspective of "the day of the Lord" (13:6, 9, 13), divine interventions in mundane affairs appear to take place within the measure of time we call a day. However, prophetic vision leaps across all barriers of chronology, ranging back and forth between scenes separated by centuries and millennia of human computation. Each manifestation of "the wrath of the Lord of hosts" (13:9, 13) at a given point in history foretells the dawning of a final day when He will "make the earth a desolation and . . . destroy its sinners from it" (13:9). Ch. 14 presents the obverse side of God's judgment on those who oppose the coming of His kingdom. When they are eliminated, *the house of Jacob,* purified in the fires of exile, can again assume the role assigned to it in God's plan of universal salvation. (1-2)

Jubilant over the termination of *hard service* under *the king of Babylon,* the redeemed burst into a song of defiance, addressed to their *oppressor.* With biting sarcasm they make him the butt of their ridicule for his silly attempt to dethrone the Creator of the universe (3-21). As if to affix the signature of *the Lord of hosts* to this superb satire on human pride, the next two verses introduce Him as speaking words of doom on the arrogance of Babylon, where Israel's hopes for survival seemed buried forever (22-23). Finally, the Lord enforces His declaration with a solemn oath, swearing that no power on earth can *annul* what He has *purposed concerning the whole earth.* As a guarantee that in every age enemies such as Babylon cannot cross His plans, He foretells a deliverance from a foreign invader which Isaiah's hearers were to experience in the near future. He will *break the Assyrian,* who had overrun the land and threatened to capture Jerusalem (24-27). For the fulfillment of this prophecy see chs. 36—37.

14:2 *Peoples.* The return from Babylon, likened to the rescue of enslaved Israel from Egyptian bondage (cf. 40:3-5), serves, in turn, as a type of the subjection of "all rule and authority and power" to the Redeemer of all mankind. (Eph 1:21)

14:4 *Taunt.* Derived from a root meaning "to be like, to be similar," this term is translated "parable" or "allegory" (Ps 78:2; Eze 17:2; 24:3); when such comparisons illustrate generally accepted truths, they come under the category of "proverbs" (Pr 1:1; Ps 49:4; Eze 12:22 f.); when the point to be made in a parable or proverb is mockery, the Hebrew word is rendered "taunt song" or simply "taunt" (Mi 2:4; Jer 24:9; Hab 2:6). The ode beginning at v. 4 unleashes a torrent of vitriolic ridicule on God's enemies. Line after line of highly imaginative verse cuts down the pretensions of arrogant men. They are such ludicrous figures because they must leave all their "pomp" behind as they go down to the grave and its decay (4-11). In vv. 12-21 the futility of death-bound men wanting to "be like God" (Gn 3:5) is made graphic by a parable drawn from a pagan tale about a celestial deity. Not content to be a brilliant star in the sky, who determined the destiny of earthly kingdoms, he aspired to make himself "like the Most High" only to be "cut down to the ground." Denied even a "burial," his corpse is "trodden under foot."—This magnificent satire has the force of a proverb. It applies whenever anti-God powers set out to defy and to destroy the kingdom of heaven. At every age there will be heard "glad songs of victory in the tents of the righteous" (Ps 118:15). They rejoice because "the old evil foe . . . can harm us none; he's judged."

14:9 *Sheol.* For the meaning of this transliterated Hebrew word see Dt 32:22 note. On *shades* see Pr 2:18 note.

14:12 *Day Star.* The Hebrew word, occurring only here, means "shining one." The translation "Lucifer" (light-bearer) in the KJV is derived from the Latin name for Venus. This identification fits the appositional phrase *son of Dawn,* i.e., morning star. In Babylonian and Canaanite mythology celestial bodies became personified deities. See the NT description of the defeat and fall of Satan, the Lucifer who became the archenemy of God and His people. (Lk 10:18; Rv 9:1; 12:9)

14:13 *Mount of assembly.* Pagans thought their gods resided on a high mountain *in the far north.* Here they held council.

14:19 *Untimely birth.* One word in Hebrew, it is translated "shoot" in 11:1 and 60:21. A sprout, snapped off before it grows into a sturdy oak, is considered of no value. So the oppressor will be *cast out* on the rubbish heap. He will be so *loathed* for his crimes that he will not be granted burial in a *sepulchre,* a fate considered very degrading. (Jer 22:19; 36:30)

14:27 *Who will turn it back?* Faith in this promise moves the believer to pray "that God would break and hinder every evil council and will which would not let His kingdom come." (Luther)

14:28-32 Philistia

14:28-32 *Ahaz died.* When Ahaz died in 715 BC, it was six years since Samaria, capital of the Northern Kingdom, had been captured by the Assyrians. The Philistines, still occupying territory on the Mediterranean seacoast, likewise became tributary to Assyrian kings. At some time when the *rod* of foreign domination seemed *broken,* Philistine messengers came to Jerusalem proposing joint action against the common enemy. *This oracle* (cf. 13:1 second note) is directed against foreign entanglements. If the chosen people trust in the alliance with their Lord and keep His covenant, no army of men can harm *Zion,* which *the Lord has founded.* The Philistines, on the other hand, can expect the Assyrians to come *out of the north* in successive waves, each more terrifying than the former, until not even a *remnant* remains in their land.

15:1—16:14 Moab

15:1-9 *Concerning Moab.* The third oracle (cf. 13:1 second note) pronouncing doom on foreign nations (chs. 13—23) is directed against the descendants of Lot, Abraham's nephew (Gn 19:30-38). When the Israelites were on their long journey from Egypt to the Promised Land, they were denied passage through Moabite territory, which lay east of the Dead Sea (Nm 21:10—24:25; Dt 2:8 f; Jos 24:9; Ju 11:15-18). In a poetic outburst of denunciation and woe Isaiah describes the inevitable destruction decreed by the Lord on this unbrotherly neighbor of the chosen people. Moving in spirit from place to place, the prophet hears wailing *round the land of Moab* (8). It is so pitiful that his own *heart cries out* in compassion for the victims (5; 16:9). The words *concerning Moab* overflow into ch. 16. For other pronouncements against the same enemy see Jer 48; Eze 25:8-11; Am 2:1-3.

Ar . . . Kir. Isaiah lists cities and sites from every part of the doomed nation. The exact location of some places can no longer be determined.

15:9 *A lion.* We are not told by whom judgment on Moab is to be executed. Subdued by various invaders, it vanished from the face of the earth.

16:1-14 *Sent lambs.* In the first part of this ch. (1-5), prophetic vision is able to see Moab as one of the heathen nations seeking salvation in the Messianic kingdom, here called *the tent of David* (5). There is hope for *the outcasts of Moab* (4) if they seek refuge on *the mount of the daughter of Zion* (1), where "a shoot from the stump of Jesse" rules in *justice* and *righteousness* (5; 11:1-5; 9:7). This view of the distant future quickly fades as Isaiah returns abruptly to the Moab of his day. Divine judgment will overtake it, he says, because it is guilty of *pride* and *insolence* (6-7). The thought of its impending doom provokes another expression of grief (8-12), similar in tone and content to the lament echoing through ch. 15. The oracle closes with a brief note declaring that the threat against Moab spoken also *in the past* will go into effect without delay. (13-14)

16:1 *Sela.* The Hebrew word is at times used as a proper noun to designate one of Edom's chief cities (2 K 14:7; in its Greek form: "Petra"). If it has this meaning here, the context intimates that fugitives from ravaged Moab fled to the Edomite stronghold. But even in this naturally fortified citadel "the outcasts of Moab" did not feel safe; their emissaries turn to *mount . . . Zion* for "refuge . . . from the destroyer" (4).—However, the Hebrew word transliterated "Sela" occurs very frequently as a common noun meaning "rock" (e.g., 22:16; 32:2). Hence it could here refer to the rocky terrain of the Moabite plateau, which rises to a height of 3,000 feet.

16:6 *Pride.* The sin at the root of rebellion against God. (Gn 3:5; Is 25:11; Jer 48:29; Zph 2:10)

16:7 *Raisin-cakes.* The vineyards and fields which produced the ingredients of these delicacies will be destroyed (SS 2:5; 2 Sm 6:19). In Hos 3:1 "cakes of raisins" are associated with idol worship, in which the Moabites too indulged. (12)

16:14 *Three years.* As a *hireling* is engaged for a time not more and not less than the term of service specified in a contract, so the Lord has fixed a day when *the glory of Moab* will be no more.

17:1-14 Syria and Israel

17:1-14 *Damascus.* The capital of Aramaea or Syria, the next nation to be the target of *an oracle* (13:1 second note). Because the Northern Kingdom, also called *Ephraim* and *Jacob* (3-4), threw in its lot with its neighbor to the north (ch. 7), both states were to share the same fate (1-9). In 732 the Assyrians captured Damascus. Ten years later Samaria, capital of Israel, fell before the same invaders. The desolation left in their wake is described in vv. 4-6. Isaiah then adds the reason why this segment of the chosen people was punished so severely. They were guilty of the same idolatry practiced in heathen countries (10-11). In the closing verses (12-14) Syria's and Israel's doom is moved into the larger perspective of the judgment awaiting all insurgents against God's kingdom.

17:3 *Fortress.* Damascus acted as a bulwark against the Assyrian advance southward into Israel.

The glory. Syria, subjugated and disgraced, is ironically called *the glory of the children of Israel.*

17:5 *Valley of Rephaim.* A fertile valley southwest of Jerusalem mentioned Jos 15:8; 18:16; 2 Sm 23:13.

17:8 *Asherim.* Cf. 1:29 note; Gn 28:18 note.

17:9 *Hivites . . . Amorites.* Inhabitants of Canaan dispossessed by Israel. (Gn 10:15-19 note; 15:21 note)

17:10 *Pleasant plants.* The heathen cult, adopted by Israel from its neighbors, was dedicated to the mysterious forces of fertility in man, beast, and vegetation. Rites in honor of this personified nature-god included the growing of "pleasant plants." Their blossoming symbolized the deity's return to life after winter's cold had killed him. Isaiah warns that "a day of grief and incurable pain" (11) will come as inexorably as flowers are certain to fade.

17:12 *Roar.* For a similar hymn exulting in God's victory over the combined forces of evil see Pss 46 and 76. The destruction of Syria and Israel "in that day" (4, 7, 9) is put into the framework of divine judgments culminating on the Last Day, when all opposition to Him will be "no more." (Cf. 13:1-16)

18:1-7 Ethiopia

18:1-7 *Ethiopia.* In ch. 17 Isaiah exposed the folly of putting confidence in an alliance with Israel's northern neighbor rather than trusting in "the God of . . . salvation" (17:10). The object of combining forces was to stem the Assyrian invasion. Now he warns against making a defensive pact for the same purpose with a nation far to the south of Judah's border. In Isaiah's time the Ethiopians, whose territory lay along the upper (i.e., the southern) Nile, overthrew their northern overlords, the Egyptians. Founding the so-called 25th dynasty, they not only controlled the land of the Pharaohs for 60 years but also played a role in international politics (2 K 19:1; Jer 46:9; Is 20). The prophet directs the foreign *ambassadors* to return to the land of *whirring wings,* of swarming gnats (1-2). Neither the Ethiopians nor any other nation can do anything to change the course of history as plotted by the Lord. *All . . . inhabitants of the world* must *hear* when He calls them to account (3-6). *At that time* peoples from such distant lands as Ethiopia will acknowledge *the Lord of hosts* as King (7). In the language of fulfillment *Mount Zion* represents the rule He exercises over His worldwide church. (2:2 second note)

18:1 *Rivers of Ethiopia.* The "canals" and "branches" (19:6) which constitute the Nile.

19:1—20:6 Egypt

19:1-25 *Concerning Egypt.* The warning against an alliance with Ethiopia, the dynasty in power at the time in the Nile valley (ch. 18), has as its sequel an *oracle* (cf. 13:1 second note) directed against Egypt, the more comprehensive term by which the land of the Pharaohs was known. In the first part of the ch. (1-15) Isaiah foretells the judgment of God to overtake this mighty nation. When the Lord comes to Egypt *riding on a swift cloud* (Ps 68:4 note), *the idols* (Ps 96:5 note) will not be able to prevent the outbreak of a ruinous civil war. In spite of frantic activity by *the sorcerers and the mediums and the wizards,* the people will be forced to serve *a hard master* (1-4). The doom of Egypt is sealed when *the Nile will be dried up.* Without its irrigating waters there will be no food to eat and no textiles to weave (5-10). The king's *counselors, wise men* though they be, will *become fools,* unable to fathom what is happening. (11-15)

The second part of the ch. consists of six prophecies, each projected to be fulfilled *in that day* (16, 18, 19, 21, 23, 24). By means of this significant phrase, prophetic vision ranges through coming aeons, bringing into view the purpose for which God chose Abraham's descendants and intervened in world history in their behalf. What He does in Egypt becomes the symbol of His design for all nations. His judgments are to fill the hearts of men *with fear* (16-17). In lands formerly as hostile as Egypt there will be *cities* and communities swearing *allegiance to the Lord of hosts* (18; 65:16). Idolatrous people like the Egyptians will *cry to the Lord* to *defend and deliver them* in time of trouble. Because they *will know the Lord* (Cf. Gn 18:19 note), they will bring Him acceptable offerings. He in turn will treat them as He did Israel of old, *smiting and healing* them in order to keep them loyal to Him (19-22). Worship of the true God will be the link uniting nations as far apart in miles and as mutually antagonistic as Assyria and Egypt (23). *In that day* the promise given to Abraham will materialize that by him "all the families of the earth shall be blessed" (Gn 12:3 RSV note), whether they be *Israel, Egypt,* or *Assyria.* (24-25)

19:4 *A hard master.* When the Assyrians invaded Egypt, they treated the conquered land with their accustomed harshness.

19:11 *Zoan.* A capital city in the Delta of the Nile. "Memphis" (13), another administrative center, was situated a few miles to the south. Here the *counselors of Pharaoh,* renowned for their wisdom (1 K 4:30; Acts 7:22), rendered service at the court. However, they gave *stupid counsel* when they tried to prevent or explain the terrible disaster, because they did not know what "the Lord . . . has purposed against Egypt." (12; cf. 41:20; 44:25; 47:12-15)

19:17 *The land of Judah.* The Lord's earthly base of operations, from which He brought *terror to the Egyptians.*

19:18 *Language of Canaan.* The Hebrew language, used by Israel to worship *the Lord of hosts.*

City of the Sun. Probably a reference to the city of On, a famous center of sun worship near Cairo, which the Greeks called Heliopolis. KJV, following the traditional text, translates "city of destruction." The Hebrew words for sun and destruction are almost identical. If a play on words is intended, the name of one of the cities indicates that when its citizens swore *allegiance* to the Creator of heaven and earth and all its hosts (45:12), veneration of the sun was abolished. For this reason it received special mention among the cities given in a round figure as *five.*

19:20 *A savior.* At the time of the Judges, God let foreign invaders punish the backsliding Israelites. When the latter repented, He "raised up a deliverer." (Ju 3:9, 15)

20:1-6 *Ashdod.* Isaiah transmitted the will of God to the people not only by word of mouth but at times also by visual demonstration. They could see him act out in pantomime what they heard him say in spoken oracles (cf. 8:18; Jer 2:2 ff; Eze 4—5). Unsandaled and dressed only in a loin cloth, he impersonated Ethiopian and Egyptian *captives* of war, carried into exile by *the king of Assyria.* Isaiah did not live long enough to see the scene he enacted become a fact of history. However, only three years later he could point his audience to the fate of Ashdod as a preview of what was in store for all who sought *to be delivered from the king of Assyria* by joining forces with Egypt. For in 711 BC the inhabitants of this Philistine city only 35 air miles west of Jerusalem had to surrender to the "Tartan" (KJV) or *commander in chief* of an Assyrian king. The Egyptians made no attempt to come to the aid of the stricken city as they had agreed to do. *Naked and barefoot for three years,* Isaiah was not only an object lesson but also *a sign and a portent* of the disaster which was to overtake the Egyptians themselves. Therefore the offer of an alliance made by the "ambassadors" from the land of "the Nile" should be rejected (18:2). Apparently King Hezekiah heeded the prophet's warning, for the Assyrians did not mount an attack on Jerusalem at this time.

20:1 *Sargon.* Mentioned only here in Scripture, the name of this Assyrian king vanished from other ancient records until the ruins of the empire he helped build were unearthed by archaeologists. He began to reign in 722 BC, the year in which Samaria, the capital of the Northern Kingdom, became a victim of the Assyrian war machine.

21:1-10 Babylon

21:1-10 *Oracle.* This ch. contains oracles concerning three foreign nations. The first is directed against Babylon. At Isaiah's time "Merodach-baladan . . . king of Babylon, sent envoys with letters and a present to Hezekiah" (39:1). Ostensibly their mission was to congratulate the latter on his recovery from his illness. However, the real object was to draw the king of Judah into an alliance against Assyrian domination. When "ambassadors" from "the Nile" (18:2) came to Jerusalem for the same purpose, Isaiah warned against the proposed treaty. The Egyptians, he said, would not even be able to defend themselves against their common enemy (chs. 18—20). It is just as foolish, he now declares, to join hands with Babylon. For it too is destined to become a prey of the Assyrian *plunderer* and *destroyer.* The prophet does not hesitate to make this dire prediction, because it is not based on his own fallible calculations. As *whirlwinds,* unprovoked and uncontrolled by man *sweep on* in the desert of southern Canaan, so he was caught up in a *vision.* Gradually a dramatic scene takes shape before his mind's eye. He sees an aggressor, as yet unnamed, urging his satellites, *Elam* and *Media,* to *go up* and *lay siege* to a city (2). The prospect of the horrible carnage that is bound to ensue fills the prophet with pain as severe as *the pangs* of childbirth (3-4). He has all the more reason to expect the worst because the victim of the attack, also not as yet identified, is blissfully unaware of the coming storm (5). In order to get a better view of what is happening, Isaiah is told in the vision to play the part of a *watchman* who from a lofty perch can survey a wide field of operations (6-7). After standing *upon a watchtower* for what seemed a long time, he was able to make out *horsemen* and beasts of burden laden with military material. Finally the whole scene moves into focus. The city under attack is *Babylon.* And the outcome is announced: *Fallen, fallen is Bablyon.* (8-10)

21:1 *Wilderness of the sea.* The Euphrates River traversing the flat plains of Babylonia is called a sea. The same Hebrew word, translated "river," is used to designate the Nile in 19:5.

21:5 *Oil the shield!* Unaware of the approaching enemy, the Babylonians are summoned to arms from a banquet. Oiling or anointing the shield may have been designed to give it magical power to ward off deadly blows. Or the surface of shields may have been greased simply to make them slippery so that the weapons of assault could be deflected more easily.

21:9 *Babylon.* Repeated attempts to gain independence from Assyrian domination failed. In 689 Sennacherib captured and sacked the rebel city. However, some 70 years later it became the center of the empire which was to swallow up also the land of Judah. In the NT, Babylon is symbolic of hostility to God. (Rv 14:8; 18:2)

21:10 *Threshed and winnowed.* Isaiah's vision is to assure his people, the victim of severe blows by foreign powers, that *the God of Israel* is *the Lord of hosts* who controls the destiny of nations. (cf. v. 17).

21:11-12 Edom

21:11-12 *Seir.* This brief *oracle* (13:1 second note) is directed against Edom, for which *Seir* is a synonym (Gn 36:8; Nm 24:18). *Dumah* is not known as a place name. The Hebrew word occurs as a common noun meaning silence (Ps 94:17; 115:7). It may be used figuratively here to denote the ultimate fate of Edom. After alternating periods of *morning* following *night,* it will end up silent as the grave.

21:13-17 Arabia

21:13-17 *Arabia.* The next *oracle* is *concerning* the nomadic peoples whose main base of operations was the Arabian peninsula along the Red Sea (13:20; Jer 3:2). The *Dedanites* and *the sons of Kedar* carried on trade as far north as Tyre (Eze 27:20 f.). *Tema* was an important caravan center.

22:1-25 Jerusalem

22:1-25 *Valley of vision.* This cryptic designation for Judah and its capital Jerusalem points to the reason why an *oracle* concerning them (13:1 second note) is included in a series of pronouncements against foreign nations. The chosen people lived in a land blessed more richly than any of its neighbors. God condescended to reveal Himself here through Isaiah and other prophets (1:1 notes). However, its inhabitants proved to be no better than the heathen. In fact, they acted as if God did not exist. Isaiah alludes to two occasions when they manifested such perverse ingratitude and such detestable conceit as to incur irrevocable sentence of *destruction* (vv. 4, 14). When the Assyrian king Sennacherib massacred the troops trying to stop his advance on Jerusalem and executed the fleeing leaders (2b-3), the city's *choicest valleys were full of chariots* and *horsemen took their stand at the gates* (5-8a). The citizens *looked to* and improved the defenses against the besieging enemy, as they could be expected to do. However, they *did not look to him who* long ago *planned* this *day of tumult* (8b-11, 5). And when God's angel drove off the invader, they again acted like pagans. They celebrated with *shoutings* from *the housetops* (1b-2a). But it did not occur to them that the devastation of the countryside and the siege of the city was God's call to repentance. So instead of *weeping and mourning* over sin (12), they compounded their guilt by riotous banqueting; instead of committing themselves to God's providence, they wanted to live by the atheistic principle of fatalism. Satisfaction of physical appetites became the professed goal of life (13). *This iniquity will not be forgiven* because it is the kind which wants no forgiveness (14). Isaiah refuses to join revelry. Alone and inconsolable, he can only *weep bitter tears.* (4)

22:6 *Elam.* Cf. 11:11 note. *Kir* is mentioned in the history of the Syrians (Am 1:5; 9:7). Used as a common noun, the Hebrew word means city. Possibly more than one place was so named.

22:8 *Covering of Judah.* At the time of the exodus God supplied Israel with a cloud covering for its protection.

House of the Forest. Cf. 1 K 7:2 note.

22:9 *Lower pool.* It and "the old pool" were used in a new system of supplying the city with water. (Cf. 2 K 20:20 note)

22:15 *Shebna. This steward,* a high official responsible directly to the king, was a glaring example of the self-seeking pride of which Isaiah accused the people in the preceding verses (1-14). "Thrust . . . from . . . office," he will not be buried in "a tomb on the height," a memorial to his greatness. When he dies, not fame but disgrace awaits him. His corpse will lie unburied in a "wide land" (15-19). His successor, "Eliakim" (mentioned with Shebna in 2 K 18:18, 26, 37; 19:2; Is 36:3, 11, 22; 37:2), was thought worthy of the title "servant" of the Lord. But he too failed to live up to expectations. Favor-seeking relatives and friends brought about his downfall. (20-25)

22:22 *Key of the house of David.* Power to determine the eternal destiny of mankind was to be vested in great David's greater Son. (Rv 3:7)

23:1-18 Phoenicia

23:1-18 *Tyre.* Phoenicia, called *Canaan* (11), owed its title of *merchant of the nations* (3) to the maritime trade, flowing in and out of Tyre and Sidon, its two great port cities. The last *oracle concerning* a foreign nation (13:1 second note) announces their impending doom, portrayed as high drama on the far-flung stage of the Mediterranean Sea (1-14; see also Eze 26—28). Crews of returning merchantmen, making a final port call at the nearby island of *Cyprus,* are told to *wail* because *Tyre is laid waste* (1-4). From here the news spreads *to Egypt* and to remote Phoenician colonies, producing cries of *anguish* wherever it is heard (5-14). No ships will sail the sea for *seventy years,* i.e., not until the decreed period of judgment has run its course. Then the outcome of renewed commercial ventures, depreciatingly called the *hire* of a *harlot, will be dedicated to the Lord,* from whom comes "every good endowment and every perfect gift" (15-18; Ja 1:17).—Tyre and Sidon, victims of several ancient invaders, long have played no role as maritime trade centers

Ships of Tarshish. Cf. 2:16; 1 K 10:22 note.

23:3 *Shihor.* A synonym for the Nile, and so translated in Jer 2:18.

23:4 *The sea has spoken.* The sea, personified mother of Sidon, laments the disappearance of ships as if she had never given birth to them.

23:10 *Daughter of Tarshish.* The destruction of Tyre and Sidon set their colonies free from the *restraint* imposed on them by their Phoenician masters.

23:13 *Chaldeans.* The Babylonian ruling class, which brought on the destruction of their capital as the result of rebellions against Assyrian domination (cf. 21:9 note). The same kind of disaster awaits Tyre. The text of the verse need not be changed if translated: "Behold the land of the Chaldeans! This is the people which is no more. The Assyrians appointed it for beasts of the wilderness. They erected . . ." etc.

23:15 *Seventy years.* A round figure for the lifetime *of one king* and of all men (Ps 90:10) as well as for the duration of the Babylonian exile. (Jer 25:11 f.; 29:10; Zch 1:12; 7:5)

24:1—27:13 CONSUMMATION OF HISTORY: THE DAY OF THE LORD

24:1-23 *Lay waste the earth.* In chs. 24—27 "the vision of Isaiah" (1:1 first note) becomes broader in scope. The focus in chs. 1—12 is on the chosen people. Chs. 13—23 deal with individual nations that played a part in Israel's history. Now the whole world of nations comes into view. However, the seer's eyes are opened not only to take in a wider scene of action but also to peer deeply into the future—to the very end of time. What every "day of the Lord" (2:11 note) was to effect—whether judgment or deliverance—will reach a decisive climax *on that day* (21; 25:9; 26:1; 27:1, 2, 12, 13) when all nations will cease to be because heaven and earth will pass away. The defeat of all evil forces will be undeniably manifest. There will be no sorrow or death to mar or end the bliss of those who inherit the kingdom of God. This cataclysmic consummation of history is announced by authority of the Creator of the universe, who is capable of "declaring the end from the beginning." (46:10)

The form in which God's spokesman tells what is to happen *on that day* is called apocalyptic, i.e., revelatory (cf. the NT book "The Revelation to John"). As his gaze penetrates the ages still to come, it passes through transparencies tinged with the colors of contemporary scenes, institutions, and events. Past, present, and future merge in a kaleidoscopic perspective. He gives his hearers some understanding of existence beyond the dimensions of time and space by using terms and concepts that are meaningful to them by way of comparison. So, e.g., *Mount Zion* in *Jerusalem* is the throne from which *the Lord of hosts will reign.* The *elders* of Israel constitute the worshiping congregation gathered about the celestial throne (23; Rv 4:4, 10; 5:6, 8, 11, 14; 7:11; 11:16; 14:3; 19:4). "Moab" represents the enemies of God, "trodden down . . . as straw . . . in a dung-pit." (25:10)

Chs. 24—27 are like a documentary film of the eternal kingdom of God which will be initiated after all things temporal are gone. The very first verses of ch. 24 envision a time when *the Lord will lay waste the earth* so *utterly* that all social and economic institutions cease to function (1-3). This universal desolation is the result of sin; its *curse devours the earth* (4-13). From all corners of the universe shouting and jubilation greet *the God of Israel,* undisputed Victor over the forces of evil (14-16a). However, the prophet has not yet arrived at the point where he can join in these songs of praise. He can still see *the treacherous deal treacherously* for some time to come. Because they succeed with apparent impunity, he breaks out in a lament (16b). All the same, he knows that their eventual doom is inevitable. They will be able to avoid the *terror, and the pit, and the snare* of retribution as little as the people of Noah's time escaped death when *the windows of heaven* were *opened* (17-20, Gn 7:11). *On that day* the demonic powers of *heaven* and *earth,* permanently *shut up in a prison,* will no longer contest or interfere with the ultimate goal of *the Lord of hosts.* When *sun* and *moon* and the entire material universe have vanished at His command, He will usher in a kingdom for which His *reign on Mount Zion* was but a symbol and a promise. (21-23; 60:19-22)

24:5 *Covenant.* God agreed to be gracious to the sinful sons of Adam. In grateful response to this undeserved goodness they were to keep *laws* and *statutes* governing their behavior to Him and their fellowmen. A covenant, or pact, based on these terms, existed since the time of Noah and was to remain in effect for all times to come. (Gn 9:1-17)

24:10 *Chaos.* The Hebrew word is translated "without form" when it is used to describe the earth's primordial emptiness and confusion (Gn 1:2). Every *city,* once an organized community of great throngs of people, will be a heap of ruins.

24:21 *Host of heaven.* Cf. 1 Sm 1:3 second note.

24:23 *Mount Zion.* Cf. 2:2 second note.

25:1-12 *Exalt thee.* The defeat of all opposition to the coming of God's eternal kingdom brings "songs of praise" from the lips of those who, gathered "from the ends of the earth," surge about the heavenly throne of glory (24:14-16). The first verses of this ch. record their theme song. It is a hymn of thanksgiving for the *wonderful things* God did to provide *a shelter from the storm . . . of the ruthless.* Destroyed according to *plans formed of old* and carried out faithfully as promised, the enemies can no longer terrorize *the poor* and *the needy* (1-5). The bliss evokes endless rounds of songs at a banquet to which *all peoples* are invited. The food is rich, the wine *well refined.* The mood of the guests is serene and gay. The pall of grief which had been hanging *over all peoples* is gone. *Death,* prime cause of lamenting, is swalled up *for ever* (cf. 1 Co 15:54-57). Nothing remains which could bring tears to their eyes. They will no longer suffer *the reproach* which their enemies heaped on them when God seemed to turn a deaf ear to the prayers of His children (6-8). Reflection on "pleasures for evermore" (Ps 16:11) leads to renewed singing (9). The celebration need never stop. Every foe is *cast to the ground, even to the dust,* as *Moab,* Israel's inveterate enemy, went down to the pit of oblivion. (10-12)

25:2 *The city.* Cf. 24:10 note.

25:6 *Fat things.* Considered delicacies.

Wine on the lees. Left on its fermented sediment to improve its strength and flavor.

25:8 *Swallow up death.* John quotes this verse in describing "the marriage supper of the Lamb" which will take place after "the former things have passed away." (19:9; Rv 21:1-4)

25:10 *Moab.* Cf. 16:1 notes. In 34:5 ff. and 63:1 ff. the hostile forces that need to be overcome are represented by Edom, also related to Israel.

26:1-21 *Salvation.* The strains of rejoicing echoing through ch. 25 are taken up anew. *This song too is sung in that day* when *perfect peace* prevails (3). *The poor* and *the needy* have no one to fear. Every foe has been *brought low.* Even death, "the last enemy," has been swallowed up (25:8; 1 Co 15:26). *The land of Judah,* once Israel's land of promise, has become the land of fulfillment for all nations (1-6). From this vantage point in God's eternal kingdom, reflections revert to the time when the redeemed walked by faith and not by sight. To *wait for* God and to commit all of life to Him was not in vain even though doubts may have arisen when His *chastening was upon them* (16). No one should ever doubt God's undeviating desire and unlimited power to *make smooth the path of the righteous* (7-9). If the wicked do *not learn righteousness but continue their attempts to frustrate God's plan to ordain peace,* His fires of judgment will *consume them* (10-15). *In distress* the thing to do is look to God, because human efforts to save are abortive (16-19). Until *the Lord is coming forth . . . to punish the inhabitants of the earth,* the *people* are urged to be patient. (20-21)

26:11 *Let the fire . . . consume.* For this kind of prayer see notes on Ps 35:4; 58:10; Neh 4:4.

26:13 *Other lords.* Foreign rulers whom they were forced to serve.

26:14 *Will not arise. Dead* and gone, *they will not live* on earth again to enslave its inhabitants.

26:18 *Wind.* A woman in the pangs of childbirth is rewarded by the emergence of new life. The "chastening" they suffered was as painful but seemed unproductive of anything desirable.

26:19 *Dead shall live.* God's power does not stop at the grave. At His command the corpses of individuals come to life. Therefore He can order also the resurrection of a whole nation, apparently entombed forever in exile. (Eze 37:1-14)

Shades. Cf. 14:9; Pr 2:18 note.

27:1-13 *He will slay.* This ch. adds more prophetic glimpes into the kingdom which God will usher in *in that day* (1, 2, 6, 12, 13) when everything temporal and mundane has passed away and every domestic *dragon* of resistance has been slain (1). The focus is not so much on the bliss of the celestial "feast" (25:6-8) but rather on the way God carried out "plans formed of old" (25:1) to establish His reign of "perfect peace" (26:3) over subjects gathered "from the ends of the earth" (24:16). He did "wonderful things" (25:1) in and for a people chosen to be instruments of His sovereign will and gracious design. However, in the perspective of apocalyptic vision, the history of Israel is at the same time the record of God's dealings with all who "sit at table with Abraham, Isaac, and Jacob in the kingdom of heaven" (Mt 8:11). He is as concerned about them as a *keeper* of a *pleasant vineyard* is alert to *guard it night and day* (2-5). He expects the vineyard "to yield grapes" (5:2, 4) because He wants to *fill the whole world with fruit.* When the children of Israel produced the "wild grapes" (5:4) of revolt, He would not blindly continue to *show them . . . favor.* In order to chasten and purify them, He gave them into the hands of foreigners. But they were not *slain as their slayers were slain,* never to rise again. They repented and disavowed all false gods. God forgave them and permitted them again to *take root* in their homeland (6-11), no matter how widely they had been scattered (12-13). So *in that day* the redeemed of God will stream into the Jerusalem above from all corners of the earth, grateful for the providential care and the fatherly discipline that brought them there.

27:1 *Leviathan.* Cf. Jb 41:1 note; Ps 74:14; 104:26; also Jb 9:13 note; Is 51:9; Rv 12:9; 20:2.

27:4 *No wrath.* But if He were to find *thorns and briers* there, he would *burn them up together.* The wicked will not escape the fires of divine wrath unless they "make peace with" God (5).

27:7 *Who smote them.* The nations God used as a chastening rod on "Jacob" and "Israel" did not revive after their downfall.

27:8 *Measure by measure.* The Hebrew prepositional phrase is better rendered "by a frightening sound," the kind which scares up animals from their hiding place. God drove Israel into exile as one shoos a flock of chickens out of the yard.

27:9 *Expiated.* God did not destroy His people. A temporary exile was all the chastisement needed to produce repentance in Israel. For *Asherim* see Gn 28:18 note; Is 17:8.

27:10 *Fortified city.* As in 24:10; 25:2, the permanently destroyed center of hostility is meant, on which God will "not have compassion." (11)

28:1—33:24 JERUSALEM TO BE DESTROYED AND RESTORED

28:1-29 *Woe.* In chs. 13—27 "the vision of Isaiah" (1:1 first note) ranged beyond the borders of the Promised Land. As one foreign nation after another came under review, the prophet beheld the failure of foreign opposition to the coming of God's kingdom. In chs. 28—33 the focus of attention returns to the chosen people. As in chs. 1—12, Isaiah denounces the shameful abuse of their high calling. The Holy One of Israel will not tolerate their apostasy (28:1; 29:1, 15; 30:1; 31:1; 33:1). However, the fires of destruction are designed to purge silver of dross. God will not abandon His plan to save all mankind. There will be a faithful *remnant* (28:5; 7:3 note). Descendants of Abraham, they will continue to be channels of His grace to "all the families of the earth" (Gn 12:3). However, the promises of mercy, at times introduced abruptly, do not soften or abrogate the threats of judgment. The doom of impenitent sinners is inevitable. The first to be arraigned and sentenced is *Ephraim,* the Northern Kingdom, also called Israel (1-6), for dissolute self-indulgence. Judah, the Southern Kingdom, is no better. Its degenerate spiritual and civic leaders may scoff at prophetic warning as childish prattle (7-10). But when they will *be broken, and snared, and taken,* they will realize that *the word of the Lord* is no laughing matter (11-13). It is sheer folly to devise means of their own to ward off destruction. They will prove to be a *refuge* of *lies* and a *shelter* of *falsehood* (14-15). Only *he who believes* in God's promises of salvation has solid ground under his feet. All others will find out in *sheer terror* that *a decree . . . from the Lord of hosts* cannot be countermanded. (16-22)

However, God has "no pleasure in the death of any one" (Eze 18:32). When His purpose is to bring back to Him the erring and the straying, He chastizes no longer or more severely than is necessary to achieve the desired result. He acts like a farmer, endowed by his Creator with *wisdom* to work purposefully and discriminately. In the spring he does indeed tear up the ground with a plow and pulverize it with a harrow. But he stops as soon as he has prepared the soil adequately to receive the seeds which are to produce the desired crops. At harvest time he does thresh and flail the stocks in order to free the kernels from the stems. But he chooses threshing instruments which will do so without injuring the various kinds of produce. Even when using the heaviest equipment, he proceeds with care lest he crush the grain. So God does not cut furrows across men's lives because He delights in wounding them. Nor does He inflict heavier blows of adversity than are necessary to achieve salutary results. (23-29)

28:1 *Crown of the drunkards.* Samaria, capital of *Ephraim,* rises above *the rich valley* surrounding it on all sides. But like *the fading flower* which reveling drunkards twine into chaplets to adorn their heads, *its glorious beauty* "will be trodden under foot." (3)

28:2 *Mighty and strong.* The Assyrians were the instrument which *the Lord has* ready to execute His threat. Cf. 17:1 note.

28:4 *First-ripe fig.* As a person finding the first fruit of the season *eats it up* with gusto, so the conqueror will satisfy his appetite for conquest without delay.

28:5 *In that day.* In vv. 5 f. a flash of light penetrates the impending gloom, giving Isaiah a snapshot view of a bright scene which was to emerge from the threatened destruction. God's judgment is designed to preserve a *remnant of*

His people who will not be drunk with self-trust but to whom *the Lord of hosts will be a crown of glory.*

28:7 *These also.* Isaiah now points an accusing finger at the disgusting spectacle of drunken *priest* and *prophet* in Jerusalem.

28:10 *Precept upon precept.* The debauched leaders make a ribald joke of the prophet's message. It is an insult, they say, to be taught as if they were gullible children. They mockingly suggest that his words sound like a nursery rhyme, composed (in the original) of repeated monosyllables.

28:11 *Strange lips.* Because the people rejected words of warning, spoken plainly in their own tongue, *the Lord will speak to* them in a way they cannot fail to hear even though they will not understand the language of the foreign conqueror.

28:12 *Rest.* They could have avoided catastrophe if they had heeded God's proposal to give them *repose* and safety.

28:15 *Covenant with death.* Reliance on their own devices for protection made them feel as secure as if they had reached *an agreement* with death itself to grant them immunity from *Sheol* (cf. Dt 32:22 note). Anticipating the day when they will realize their foolish bravado, Isaiah lets them speak with prophetic irony of their maneuvers as taking *refuge* in *lies* and seeking *shelter* in *falsehood.* Cf. his own words in v. 18.

28:16 *Foundation.* Faith in God, not in human resources, provides the only solid basis for hope. He will indeed carry out His threat to destroy Jerusalem. But He will not give up His plan to build an indestructible *Zion,* made up of "living stones" and founded on *a precious cornerstone.* The NT proclaims the fulfillment in Jesus Christ and His church. (1 Ptr 2:4-6; Ro 9:33; Eph 2:20)

Believes. Cf. 9:7 note.

28:20 *Too short . . . too narrow.* This verse may be a proverbial saying which Isaiah quotes to illustrate his point that all human efforts to defy God will prove to be disappointingly ineffective.

28:21 *Perazim . . . Gibeon.* At these places God once intervened to give Israel victory over foes (2 Sm 5:20; 1 Ch 14:11; Jos 10:9-14). Now He will be on the side of the enemy and thus inflict punishment for the breaking of His law, no matter how *strange* it may appear and how *alien* it is to His original gracious intentions.

28:25 *Dill . . . cummin.* Small seeds used as spices.

28:27 *Threshing sledge.* A heavy wooden sled, spiked with iron, which was drawn across the grain on the threshing floor. In Am 1:3 it refers to an instrument of war.

29:1-24 *Ho.* The Hebrew word usually translated "woe" as in v. 15. It introduces a pronouncement of doom on the city of David (cf. next note). Contrary to popular opinion, it was expendable even though throngs of people gathered there to keep prescribed *feasts* and offer sacrifices. Ritual observances are an abomination to the Lord if they do not express sincere repentance, a plea for mercy, and a total surrender of the heart to His holy will. God will not be mocked when people desecrate His means of grace, making them insulting devices to coerce Him to favor them regardless of blatant disobedience. Their false sense of security will give way to *moaning and lamentation* when He brings on them the horrors of a besieged city and turns it into a vast altar on which enemies will slaughter its inhabitants as if they were sacrificial animals (1-4). Nevertheless *all the nations . . . that fight against Mount Zion* will be disillusioned if they think they can frustrate the establishment of God's kingdom (5-8). However, Israel cannot serve His purpose either if the people persist in their willful rebellion against Him. *Drunk* with the wine of self-delusion and staggering in a blind stupor of pride, they give God no other choice but to give them up to their delusions, pouring out on them *a spirit of deep sleep,* "lest they see with their eyes and hear with their ears." (9-12; 6:10 note; 2 Th 2:11; Ro 11:8; Ex 4:21 note)

So ingrained is the false notion that worship forms, *learned by rote* and mouthed mechanically, produce and maintain a favorable relationship with the Lord that He has more to say about people who *draw near with their mouth* but whose *hearts are far from* Him. If they thought they could conceal their lack of *fear of* Him by pious cant, they will discover to their grief that the God who once did astounding "wonders" to deliver His people from Egyptian bondage (Ex 3:20) will *again do marvelous things,* but now to execute horrifying judgment on their insolent offenses against His majesty. (13-14)

A third *woe* is provoked by a similar fatal mistake about the nature of God. Those who direct the affairs of state act as if the Lord is unaware of their devious maneuvers, planned *in the dark* of secret *counsel.* This arrogant and ridiculous assumption turns *upside down* their creaturely relation to their Maker. He remains in control of their lives as surely as a *potter* who designed and formed a vessel out of *clay* can dispose of the work of his hand (15-16). However, because *the Holy One of Israel* is the Maker of heaven and earth, He is able not only to execute His threats of *woe* on the obdurate *scoffer* but also to bring to full consummation what He promises *the meek* and *the poor among men.* They will inherit the kingdom *in that day* when He creates "new heavens and a new earth in which righteousness dwells" (17-21; 2 Ptr 3:13; Is 65:17; 66:22; Rv 21:1-8). The *house of Jacob,* chastened and purified, will again serve *the God of Israel* as He implements His promise to make *Abraham* and his descendants a blessing to all the families of the earth. (22-24)

29:1 *Ariel.* A compound noun consisting of the Hebrew words for "hearth" and "of God." In Eze 43:15 f. it is translated "altar hearth." Jerusalem, conquered by David, is so named because God established it as a center of worship in which the altar of burnt offerings played a prominent part. Because the sacrifices offered on it were thought to obligate God to make the city unconquerable at all costs, He will punish such a mockery of His holy name. All of Jerusalem will be to Him an *Ariel,* a fireplace of His consuming wrath. (2)

29:4 *Deep from the earth.* Shouts of jubilation, customarily heard as crowds observed "feasts," will turn into "moaning" resembling the ghostly sounds made by those who professed to consult the dead. (Cf. 8:19 note)

29:6 *Visited.* As *the Lord of hosts* fought against His people with irresistible power (28:2), so He will move heaven and earth when the time comes to intervene in behalf of "Ariel." (7)

29:8 *Not satisfied. Mount Zion* may seem an easy prey to *the multitude of . . . nations* arrayed against it. But they will be able to satisfy their lust for conquest as little as a dream can provide a man with the food and drink he craves.

29:10 *Deep sleep.* The kind that God caused to fall on Adam (Gn 2:21). Because they "blind" themselves, prophetic preaching will make them totally insensitive to God's call to repentance. Isaiah was told to expect this reaction to his ministry. (6:9 f.)

29:13 *Mouth . . . lips.* Jesus quoted this verse to expose the hypocritical recitation of religious formulas. (Mt 15:8 f.; Mk 7:6 f.; see also Eze 33:31)

29:14 *Wise men.* Cf. 1 Co 1:19.

29:16 *Potter.* The same comparison is used to define the relationship to the Creator in 45:9; Jer 18:1-11; Ro 9:20-23; see also Is 10:15 note.

29:17 *Lebanon.* God, who can transform wooded heights into *a fruitful field,* is able also to effect changes resulting in conditions of perfect bliss for those who entrust themselves to His grace and power. The next verses illustrate what is in store for them.

29:22 *Abraham.* God *redeemed* him when He led him out of "Ur of the Chaldeans," where his father "served other gods" (Gn 11:27-32; Jos 24:1-3). "With a mighty hand" He later redeemed the patriarch's descendants from the Egyptian house of bondage. (Dt 9:26)

30:1-33 *Rebellious children.* The fourth *woe* (cf. 28:1-29 note) adds two features to God's indictment of His people contained in the two previous chs. (1) It identifies Egypt as the nation with which secret negotiations were under way. An alliance with the Pharaoh, it was hoped, would make the inhabitants of Judah as secure against Assyrian conquest as if they had "made a covenant with death" (28:15 note). (2) Isaiah diagnoses this act of disobedience and all of Israel's misdeeds as symptoms of one and the same disease. Its name is unbelief: refusal to trust God's promises and rejection of His principles of conduct. This perverse orientation of their lives, moreover, is also basic in determining God's attitude to them. It compels Him to treat them as rebels. Their pretense to be His children only adds *sin to sin* and therefore aggravates the severity of punishment awaiting them. To *make a league* with Egypt is contrary to God's *plan* and *spirit*; to trust men rather than His promises *brings neither help nor profit, but shame and disgrace* (1-5). *Riches* and *treasure* sent to the Pharaoh to curry his favor will produce results as *empty* as a mirage of the desert encountered on the hazardous way to Egypt. (6-7)

But whereas these machinations are an exercise in futility, the word spoken by Isaiah will stand the test of time. He need not fear to *inscribe it in a book.* The written record will prove to be *a witness forever,* bearing out the prophet's warning that *rebellious people* and *lying sons* cannot escape the judgment he predicted. For their negotiations with Egypt were not merely a miscalculation, a wrong move in the game of international politics, but a deliberate act of defiance, an expression of their contempt for *the Holy One of Israel* and for the *word.* They will hear from Him. He will not let their crime go unpunished. Sudden destruction and total devastation will overtake them (8-14). How sad it all was! To *be saved* from the Assyrians they needed only to commit themselves *in quietness and in trust* to *the Lord God.* But because they *would not,* preferring instead to rely on the *swift steeds* of Egyptian chariotry, they will flee before their *pursuers* in headlong flight (15-17). It cannot be otherwise. Because the Lord is confronted with such heinous crimes, *therefore* He cannot but act at this time as *a God of justice* though He always desires *to show mercy* and *to be gracious.* Hence it is also true that *all those who wait for him* need not fear that He has abandoned His plan to establish His kingdom. *Affliction* and *adversity* are educational means employed by the divine *Teacher* to discipline waywardness and to produce willing obedience to His instruction. (18-22)

For the strengthening of the faithful, Isaiah appends a glowing description of the perfect bliss awaiting them at the consummation of the promised Messianic reign. Paradise lost will become paradise regained (23-26). No enemies will be able to thwart His good and gracious will; they will discover no defense against the *devouring fire* of *his anger* (27-28). Isaiah's contemporaries will have proof of His power to protect His people against overwhelming odds. The Assyrian war machine, against which all resistance seemed useless, would be no match for the weapons in the Lord's heavenly arsenal. *When he smites with his rod,* the biggest and best-equipped army becomes dry firewood, set ablaze by *a stream of brimstone.* Miraculously delivered, Jerusalem burst into *a song* to the sound of *timbrels and lyres.* (29-33)

30:4 *Zoan.* An administrative center in the Nile delta. *Hanes* may be the name of another city in the same area or an Egyptian term for the Pharaoh's royal palace. In either case, the point seems to be that negotiations with official representatives of the Pharaoh were actually in progress.

30:6 *Oracle.* For the meaning of this term see 13:1 second note. *The Negeb* is the desert south of Judah, where the caravans bearing tribute to Egypt would have to be prepared to cope with dangerous beasts. Perhaps this route was chosen rather than the open highway along the Mediterranean coast in order to avoid detection.

30:7 *Rehab.* Cf. Jb 9:13 note; 3:8 second note; 7:12 note; Ps 87:4; Is 51:9. Egypt makes the noises of a raging monster. But it is all bluster. This ferocious beast lacks the strength even to move.

30:8 *Write.* Isaiah received a similar directive in 8:1.

30:10 *Smooth things.* Things to their liking. The people clamored for visionaries who did not see what is true and for *prophets* who proclaimed *illusions,* knowing full well that these impostors were not teaching them "the way" and "the path" revealed to them by "the Holy One of Israel."

30:13 *A break.* The disaster provoked by *this iniquity* will come as unexpectedly as when *a high wall* with nothing but a crack suddenly bulges and collapses in a heap. The resulting demolition will be as crushing as if one "smashed" "a potter's" earthen "vessel" into bits so small as to be completely useless.

30:15 *In returning.* To *be saved* a change of heart was necessary, a turning from defiant self-will to trusting self-surrender to God, from frantic search for help "in the strength of the horse" and "in the legs of a man" (Ps 147:10) to a calming *trust* in the Lord (32:17). The *quietness* which faith bestows is not irresponsible inaction or unrealistic pacifism, but the imperturbable tranquility of mind which knows that nothing can go wrong with any enterprise planned and carried out in the fear of God. For similar calls to faith see 7:4; 28:16.

30:20 *Teacher.* God will bring down the rod of *adversity* and *affliction* on His erring people in order to recall them to "the way" they were to walk. When they again "dwell at Jerusalem" after exile in Babylonia, they will realize why they were disciplined. Their lesson learned, they will resolve to act at every turn of their lives as if God were standing "behind" them directing them to choose the course of action pleasing to Him.

30:23 *Rich and plenteous.* The unearthly bliss to come is described in earthly terms not only in vv. 23-26 but also in such passages as 35:5-7; 60:17-22; 65:17-25; Jl 3:18; Am 9:13-15; Rv 21:23; 22:5.

30:27 *The name of the Lord.* "In the day of the great slaughter" (25) ending all attacks on His kingdom, the Lord will manifest the irresistible power at His disposal. His *lips* issue commands which reverberate through the heavens in roaring thunder; the *devouring fire* of lightning responds to orders issued by His tongue.

30:31 *The Assyrians. At the voice of the Lord* "the angel of the Lord went forth and slew a hundred and eighty-five thousand in the camp of the Assyrians." (37:36; 2 K 19:35 note)

30:33 *A burning place.* A single word in Hebrew and only slightly different in spelling from "Topheth" (RSV note), the name of the site in the Hinnom Valley south of Jerusalem where children were burned in sacrifices to an idol contemptuously called "Molech" (RSV note; 2 K 23:10 note; Jer 7:31 f.; 19:6, 10-15). God's judgment is described as a sacrifice in 34:6; Jer 46:10; Eze 39:17-20; Zph 1:7 f.

31:1-9 *Egypt.* As in ch. 30, Isaiah pronounces *woe* on *the house of the evildoers* who rely on Pharaoh's *horses* and *chariots* (1-3) and pleads for a penitent return to faith in *the Lord of hosts,* who alone can save them from the Assyrian menace. (4-9)

31:2 *Yet he is wise.* The scheming politicians may think they are clever. But they cannot outsmart the Lord. *His words* will make fools of them. It is a fatal mistake to act as if mortal "men," such as the "Egyptians," were not subject to "God," who made them from the dust of the ground, and as if the "flesh" He gave to short-lived "horses" could affect the course of history contrary to His eternal "spirit."

31:4-5 *A lion . . . birds.* Isaiah uses two illustrations from the animal world to demonstrate how unnecessary it was to "go down to Egypt for help" (1). God is like *a lion* that cannot be scared from carrying off its prey—nothing can deter the Lord from His determination *to fight upon Mount Zion.* He is like mother *birds* that spread their wings over nestlings—so the Lord *will protect Jerusalem.*

31:9 *Rock.* The Lord of hosts is Israel's unmovable Rock (Ps 18:2; 31:3; 71:3; Is 33:16). The Assyrian king and the god he trusts will prove to be deceptive quicksand when soldiers and officers are forced to flee *in terror* and *in panic.*

32:1-20 *In righteousness.* In vv. 4-9 of the previous ch. Isaiah foretells the destruction of the Assyrian army threatening to destroy Jerusalem. The unexpected deliverance of the besieged city was not a fluke of chance. Brought about by divine intervention, it was a link in a chain of events that took place "according to the definite plan and foreknowledge of God" (Acts 2:23). For centuries a long-range program was under way. The opening and closing verses of ch. 32 record Isaiah's vision of God's ultimate purpose (1-8; 15-20). No military might, such as represented by the Assyrian war machine, and no perversity in Israel, such as exhibited by the frivolously *complacent* women (9-14), will deflect the Lord of history from achieving His goal: to establish His Messianic kingdom and to make its blessings available to all people. Those who let the King, portrayed in 9:6 f. and 11:1-5, hold sway in their hearts are described as an ideal commonwealth. Its leaders, righteous and just, provide security (1-2); the subjects, once blind and deaf to the truth, live by high ethical standards (3-4) and no longer only pretend to be good and wise (5-8). This transformed community will not come into existence because mankind will eventually rise to higher levels of spiritual insight. It is a communion of saints, whose hearts have been changed because God's *Spirit is poured upon* them. (15)

32:3 *Eyes . . . ears.* The reversal of the blindness and deafness to result from Isaiah's preaching. (6:10 note)

32:4 *Stammerers.* People who hesitate to

enunciate their convictions clearly because they are confused or because they are afraid to reveal what is in their minds.

32:9 *At ease.* The *women,* denounced for their love of luxury (3:16-26), are warned that their false sense of security will vanish when, "in little more than a year," they face the stark reality of total disaster.

32:15 *The Spirit.* The Spirit, who will "rest" on the Messianic King (11:2 note), will be "poured upon" the people, moving them to accept Him as their Lord. See also Eze 39:29; Jl 2:28 f.; Acts 2:1-21.

32:19 *The forest . . . the city.* Figurative language to describe the defeat of forces hostile to the coming of the Kingdom. "The city" appears as the center of opposition. (24:10; 25:2)

33:1-24 *Woe.* The sixth and last of Isaiah's sermons introduced by the exclamation *woe* reiterates the message which is central to the five preceding it (28:1-29 note). The theme developed in all of them is the unargued axiom of God's absolute control and unerring guidance of history. Everything that happens or will happen is either the execution of His threat or the fulfillment of His promise. Both implement His plan to provide redemption for all mankind. There are to be people who will escape the deadly consequences of their rebellion against their Creator because they "will be forgiven their iniquity." (33:24)

However, while ch. 33 reinforces this overarching thesis, it also has some distinctive features. An alien *destroyer* is the target of the *woe* pronounced in the first verse and not the wicked within Israel as is the case in the other opening announcements of judgment (28:1; 29:1, 15; 30:1; 31:1). In chs. 28—32 threats of destruction and promises of deliverance follow one another abruptly. In ch. 33 the changes are more frequent. Here unannounced speakers follow one another and hold forth as if they are characters in a drama. In v. 2 the people of Jerusalem appear on the stage uttering a prayer for *salvation in the time of trouble.* Next the prophet takes the floor to assure the suppliants that the God at whose *thunderous* command *nations are scattered* still is able to give *Zion* all it needs to be safe (3-6). The people in turn respond with a lament, pointing out how sorely they need the help for which they just prayed (7-9). Now God Himself takes part in the dialog. The fiercest opposition, He declares, is just so much *chaff* and *stubble* in the *fire* of His wrath (10-13). The flaming presence of the Lord strikes terror into *the godless* in Israel. They raise the point whether anyone can escape *the devouring fire* of a holy and righteous God. The prophet answers their question. *Everlasting burnings,* he informs them, are in store only for those who reveal their lack of love for God by their loveless mistreatment of their fellowmen (14-16). Those, on the other hand, who *wait for* (2) the Lord can be just as certain that their tribulations will cease at His direction. In the new Jerusalem of the Messianic kingdom there will be no enemies to harass them; sickness and death, the wages of sin, will not make them miserable; their iniquity forgiven, they are blessed forever. (17-24)

33:1 *Treacherous one.* The attack on Zion was unprovoked. The enemy is motivated by a wanton lust for conquest. However, God has him in leash. He can go only so far as God needs him as "the rod" of His "anger" (10:5-19). There will come a time when the *destroyer . . . will be destroyed* (Hab 2:1-15). "But he who endures to the end will be saved." (Mt 10:22)

33:4 *Caterpillar . . . locusts.* When a swarm of these dreaded insects descends on a field, they devour everything of value (Jl 1:4). So "peoples" and "nations" will have nothing left after the Lord lets their despoilers pounce on them.

33:6 *Your times.* Isaiah's hearers lived to see Jerusalem delivered from the Assyrians. The believer has *stability* because he knows his times are in God's hands. (Ps 31:15 note)

33:7 *Valiant ones.* The word, occurring only here, is translated by KJV and RSV as if it were composed of the nouns "lions of God," i.e., fearless warriors. Its consonantal components are almost identical with those spelling the name "Ariel" and suggest the alternate translation "people of Ariel." (Cf. 29:1 second note)

33:8 *Witnesses.* A slight change in one Hebrew consonant of this word spells the noun for "cities" (RSV note). In his advance on Jerusalem, the Assyrian king Sennacherib captured "all the fortified cities of Judah" (36:1). Hence, he had only contempt for the possibility that they would come to the rescue of Jerusalem.

33:9 *Lebanon . . . Carmel.* The most fertile areas of Palestine (35:2). For *Sharon* see SS 2:1 note; for *Bashan,* Nm 21:33 note; *Carmel* is translated "fruitful field" (Is 16:10), "garden land." (Mi 7:14)

33:11 *Conceive.* What the enemy plans and produces is of no more enduring substance than *chaff* and *stubble* when thrown into *a fire.*

33:14 *Who . . . can dwell.* For the same kind of answer to a similar question see Ps 15 and 24 and the notes there.

33:17 *In his beauty.* The *king* in the Messianic commonwealth of nations will not wear the "sackcloth" of mourning as King Hezekiah did (37:1; cf. also Ps 45); His domain is not limited to a walled city but extends to *a land that stretches afar,* beyond national borders.

33:18 *Mind will muse.* Every fear and humiliation the citizens of Jerusalem once knew will be but a memory. There will be no *tribute* to pay; they will not encounter arrogant conquerors whose foreign language they do not understand (19); there will be no need to worry about the city's fortifications. (20)

33:21 *Rivers and streams.* The protection provided by the Lord is compared with a moat deep enough to hold off an attack by land but not navigable for hostile warships. (Cf. Ps 46:4 note; Eze 47:1-12)

33:23 *Tackle hangs loose.* Israel's ship of state was not a seaworthy vessel when Isaiah spoke to his people.

34:1—35:10 V-DAY IN GOD'S KINGDOM

34:1-17 Vengeance on the Wicked

34:1-17 *O nations.* As the prophetic sentence pronounced on individual foreign nations in chs. 13—23 is followed in chs. 24—27 by a vision of a "day" at the end of time when all evil will cease and unmarred bliss will reign (24:21; 25:9; 26:1; 27:1), so the six exclamations of "woe" on the wicked (28:1; 29:1, 15; 30:1; 31:1; 33:1) have a counterpart in a universal *day of vengeance* (8) as envisioned in chs. 34 and 35. When it dawns, there will be no more history to record. For the world of heaven and earth, where *all the nations* staged their little drama, will pass away (1-4). All who like the Edomites of old were the enemies of God's people—and therefore His enemies—will receive fearful *recompense* (8) for their crimes. No one will put up resistance or escape. When the *sword* of divine justice *descends for judgment,* evildoers will have as little prospect of survival as animals waiting to be slaughtered at *a sacrifice* (5-6). Their land, once a well-watered garden, will be transformed by a cataclysm of fire and brimstone into a howling desert as desolate and barren as the *confusion* and *chaos* (11) which existed before the Creator said. Let there be fertile fields and a habitable world. (5-17)

34:4 *Host of heaven.* The host or army of "all the nations" (2) is no match for "the Lord of hosts" (1:24). At His command heaven and earth will disintegrate just as He once ordered them into existence. (13:10; 24:21, 23; 51:6; Mt 24:29; 2 Ptr 3:10; Rv 6:13 f.)

34:5 *Drunk its fill.* The "hard and great and strong sword" (27:1) of the Lord's wrath is personified. It acts like a man drunk with fury. When it *descends for judgment,* it will execute the ban of total destruction once declared on Jericho. (Jos 6:21, 24)

Edom. The descendants of Esau, Jacob's brother, are the symbol of continuous hostility to God's people (Ps 137:7 note; Is 63:1, Eze 25:12-14; Am 1:11 f.). In 25:10 it is Moab, related to Israel through Abraham (see also 11:14); in the Book of Revelation it is Babylon (Rv 16:19; 17:5; 18:10). For the use of historical peoples, events, and scenes in Isaiah's vision of the end-time see 24:1 note.

34:6 *Sacrifice.* For other instances of God's judgment compared with the "slaughter" of sacrificial animals see 30:33 note; Jer 46:10; 51:40; Eze 39:17-20; Zph 1:7 f. The realistic portrayal of a bloody massacre, inflicted by the sword of divine justice, offends only such as refuse to believe that "is is a fearful thing to fall into the hands of the living God" (Heb 10:31). Cf. the horror resulting from "the wrath of the Lamb" (Rv 6:16)

34:8 *Vengeance.* God does not indulge in revenge as people do when they get even with an enemy. He acts as a judge who imposes the penalty the convicted criminal deserves. In a court trial He sees to it that "Edom" receives just "recompense" for offenses against *Zion* (35:4; Eze 25:14, 17; Ps 94:1). Cf. Jesus' sentence of "eternal punishment" on those who were not kind to "the least of" His "brethren." (Mt 25:31-46)

Day. Though the wicked may for a time avoid the wages of sin, God has a date fixed on His calendar when they will receive the due reward of their deeds. (2:12; 61:2; 63:4; Jer 46:10; 51:6; Acts 17:31)

34:11 *Confusion . . . chaos.* The Hebrew words so translated are rendered "without form and void" in Gn 1:2. (Cf. Is 24:10 note)

34:14 *Satyr . . . night hag.* Cf. 13:21 note; Lv 17:3 note; 2 Ch 11:15 note. The word translated *night hag,* occurring only here, may be a bird which like the "owl" (15) frequents waste places. In Rabbinic lore it is the proper name of a female demon.

34:15 *Kites.* Birds of prey.

34:16 *Book of the Lord.* What the prophet spoke in the name of the Lord will become a written record which will enable future generations to compare prophecy and fulfillment.

35:1-10 Victory of the Redeemed

35:1-10 *Be glad.* The "day of vengeance" (34:8) on God's enemies, typified by the Edomites (ch. 34), will be at the same time a day of *everlasting joy for the ransomed of the Lord* (10), prefigured by Israel's return from captivity to the Promised Land. Let *the redeemed* (9) *be strong* (4) in faith! For the bliss awaiting them passes understanding. Isaiah describes it as a renewal of the woes brought on by mankind's rebellion against the Creator. What was a wilderness in nature will again be a fertile paradise; disease and physical ailments, the consequences of sin, will no longer mar human existence; whatever caused *sorrow and sighing shall flee away* (10).—This ch. is the OT lection for the last Sunday of the church year.

35:2 *Glory of Lebanon.* For the reverse see 33:9 note.

35:4 *Vengeance . . . recompense.* Cf. 34:8 note.

35:5 *Eyes . . . opened.* Quoted by Jesus (Mt 11:5). See also Is 29:18; 30:20 f.

35:8-10 *Highway.* For similar descriptions of the Messianic age and its consummation at the end of time see 11:6-12; 40:1-11; 41:17-19; 43:14-21; 48:20 f.; 65:17-25.

36:1—39:8 JERUSALEM DELIVERED FROM ASSYRIANS, DESTROYED BY BABYLONIANS

36:1—37:38 *King Hezekiah.* Chs. 36-39 combine history and prophecy. They record the destruction of Sennacherib's mighty army at the gates of Jerusalem. This unforeseen turn of events did not come about by accident. It demonstrates that the word of promise spoken by Isaiah in the name of the Lord can be trusted to come true. However, in the course of events, King Hezekiah played a role which in turn prompted prophetic proclamation of dire things to come. A century later, Isaiah announced, God will summon the Babylonians to do what He did not let the Assyrians do: destroy Jerusalem and exile its inhabitants.

Chs. 36 and 37 tell the story of prophecy fulfilled; chs. 38 and 39 relate how attendant circumstances gave occasion for renewed projections into the future. Together these historical accounts furnish a connecting link between the two major divisions of the Book of Isaiah. In chs. 1—35 he speaks in the first place to his contemporaries, faced by the Assyrian invasion. In 40—66 he envisions the needs of his people primarily after the Babylonians have destroyed Jerusalem as foretold by him.

The story told in chs. 36—39 is almost identical with the account found in 2 K 18—20. See the notes there on the historical data of the period.

For Isaiah's activity as a writer of history see 2 Ch 26:22; 32:32.

38:1—39:8 *In those days.* The events recorded in chs. 38 and 39 took place before the siege of Jerusalem by the Assyrians. Cf. 2 K 20:1 note.

38:9-20 *A writing.* By changing one letter in the Hebrew word it spells "Miktam," the title occurring in Ps 16 and Pss 56—60. The prayer of Hezekiah resembles these psalms in structure and content. The healed king recalls the anguish which seized him when his illness threatened to cut short his days *in the land of the living* (10-13). Now he knows that his fervent prayers have been answered (14-15). He realizes too that because it is God who sustains and orders his life by the *things* He says and does, even his recent *great bitterness* was designed for his *welfare.* There can be no doubt about God's gracious purpose because He has cast all of Hezekiah's sins behind His back to be remembered no more. Therefore he *thanks* God *this day* and will continue to do so all the days he is permitted to remain among *the living* (16-19). He will encourage not only his children to do likewise but will ask the entire congregation, assembled for worship *at the house of the Lord,* to join him in singing praises to God. (20)

Hezekiah's prayer after his rescue from death can serve also those who, still in the grip of dire calamities, turn to God in supplication firmly believing that "those who sow in tears" will "reap with shouts of joy" (Ps 126:5; cf. also Pss 56—60).—This hymn is not found in the account of 2 K 20. As the RSV notes indicate, the translation of the text is beset with difficulties.

38:11 *See the Lord.* As He reveals His power and goodness. (Cf. Ps 38:10)

38:12 *Dwelling.* Hezekiah compares his life with *a shepherd's tent* which can be dismantled very quickly and with the finished product of *a weaver* which he is about to sever *from the loom.*

38:16 *These things.* When "the word of the Lord" (4), spoken by Isaiah, prolonged the king's life, the latter understood that "man does not live by bread alone, but . . . by everything that proceeds out of the mouth of the Lord." (Dt 8:3)

38:18 *Cannot thank thee.* For the thought that "inhabitants of the world" (11) cease to praise God when they *go down to the pit* see Ps 6:5 note.

38:21 *Cake of figs.* Vv. 21 f. append narrative details which in the account of 2 K 20 are added immediately to the promise that the king's life-span is to be extended.

40:1—66:24 THE WAY OF SALVATION THROUGH FORGIVENESS TO GLORY

40:1—48:22 The Way of Deliverance

40:1—44:28 ISRAEL'S LIBERATION FROM BABYLONIAN SLAVERY, A STEP TOWARD THE FREEING OF ALL MANKIND FROM THE BONDAGE OF SIN

The title "The Vision of Isaiah" (1:1) aptly describes the contents of chs. 1—39 and of chs. 40—66, commonly regarded as the two major divisions of the book. In both parts the prophet declares what became visible to him by more than physical sight or mental perception.

God's messenger was equipped, in the first place, with unerring insight into human nature. What he discovered is not a pretty picture. The deadly malignancy of sin shows up in every son and daughter of Adam. The prognosis is death. However, there is a remedy for this universal malady, and God licensed His spokesman to prescribe it. No human physician concocted it. It is the miracle drug of divine forgiveness. The cure is complete. Sins "red like crimson" become "white as snow" (1:18) because the Lord "laid . . . the iniquity of us all" on a Servant whose atoning blood was untainted by the virus of disobedience. (53:6)

In the second place, the kind of seeing which accounts for the message of the entire book was television—far-vision, unhampered by the barriers of time and space. Happenings in remote lands materialized before the seer; events in the distant future became present realities. The prophet's gaze ranged from scenes of his immediate future to those of our own era and beyond it to a point when heaven and earth, the stage of all human activity, will cease to exist (34:1-4; 66:22-24). Along this line of time prophetic vision moved forward and backward with bewildering ease. Intermediate developments came into focus only to merge in a perspective which extends to the consummation of all things temporal and terrestrial. What happened and will happen to Israel is in the foreground, but simultaneously it is the background of what is to come. It is at the same time history and prophecy, fact and preview, of God's eternal plan of universal salvation. The events by which He directed the destiny of the chosen people constitute outline and contour of final acts of redemption and judgment.

However, while the same kind of insight and foresight produced "the vision of Isaiah" (1:1) in its entirety, there is a difference in perspective and emphasis in the two major divisions of the book. In both parts, events are foretold which in part await fulfillment in our day. But in chs. 1—

39 the point of departure is the more immediate future of Isaiah's contemporaries, whereas in chs. 40—66 projections of things to come proceed from a setting when the Babylonian exile was ending, about two centuries after the prophet began to preach. Chs. 1—39 stress the wages of sin; chs. 40—66 have more to say about deliverance from sin's fatal consequences. Escape is possible, says Isaiah here, because there is a way of forgiveness.

It is the way Israel was to go out of Babylonian slavery and the way all mankind can go to freedom from the bondage of sin. (Chs. 40—48)

It is the way opened by the sinless Servant of the Lord, who died to atone for the sins of every disobedient servant and who rose again to share His victory with His redeemed. (Chs. 49—57)

It is the way on which penitent and pardoned sinners ultimately enter the bliss of a new heaven and a new earth. (Chs. 58—66)

In each section of the above outline there is overlapping of the various aspects of the central theme. As is the case generally in prophetic composition, the movement of thought advances in a series of concentric circles rather than in a vertical progression from one subtopic to the next. In such a convoluted development of his thesis the writer, as it were, walks round and round his topic in order to examine it from every possible point of view.

40:1-31 *Comfort, comfort.* The good news of forgiveness is to be proclaimed repeatedly, vigorously, clearly, fearlessly, unreservedly. The order to broadcast it to forlorn sinners is issued by the highest authority, for so *says . . . God.* It is significant that the bearers of the divine message are not named. And they need not be. For their number is unrestricted and their identity of no importance. Because the comfort of release from sin's deadly bondage is needed at all times, an endless succession of ambassadors is commissioned to announce it. Their names may change but what they are to say is always to be: "Take heart, my son; your sins are forgiven" (Mt 9:2). Furthermore, the plight brought on by sin will never be so hopelessly beyond redemption that God's spokesmen will turn out to be "miserable comforters" (Jb 16:2) because they have no consolation to bring that is worth hearing. No relief from the consequences of sin seemed possible in the situation envisioned in these verses and in subsequent chs. The people of Jerusalem were to be carried off into Babylonian exile. Here they would lose their national identity if they shared the fate which overtook other enslaved peoples.

However, even when circumstances would give rise to despair, God's spokesmen need not hesitate to tell those in need of consolation that their *iniquity is pardoned* (1-2). In order to substantiate the validity of this good news, *a voice cries,* announcing God's determination not to let any obstacles scuttle His eternal plan for mankind's salvation even though the people He chose to be the bearers of His promise seemed destined to be swallowed up by a hostile world power (3-5). The same *voice* orders the prophet to *cry* that not only the Babylonian empire but all opposition to the coming of God's kingdom will be futile. The worst that creatures of *flesh* can do *withers* like *grass* and *fades* like a *flower, when the breath of the Lord blows upon it.* On the other hand, nothing can undo what *the mouth of the Lord* (5) says will happen (6-8; 1:20; 58:14; 1 Ptr 1:24 f.). At His command *Zion, Jerusalem,* and *the cities of Judah,* when reduced to ruins as threatened by Isaiah (3:24-26; 5:5 f.; 6:11 f.; 32:12 ff.; 39:6), would nevertheless become the abode of the chosen people resurrected from the grave of the exile in order to carry forward God's plan to bless "all the families of the earth" through Abraham's descendants (Gn 12:3). However, in prophetic perspective these geographic locations take on the contours of a worldwide spiritual community of redeemed sinners. They are to hear the *good tidings* that their own *iniquity is pardoned* (2) and then become *heralds* of that same comforting evangel to all their fellowmen. He who gave His life in order to make this news authentic explained that prophetic Scriptures were fulfilled when He charged "that repentance and forgiveness of sins should be preached in His name to all nations, beginning from Jerusalem." (9-11; Lk 24:44-47; cf. also Mt 28:19; Acts 10:34:43).

No one need *fear* (9) that the promised redemption will not materialize. Neither the Babylonian empire nor *all the nations*—anywhere, at any time, in any combination—can determine the course of history any more than a particle of *dust* can tip *the scales* or *a drop* clinging to the outside of *a bucket* can be of any consequence. What human ingenuity and might attempt to do becomes *less than nothing and emptiness* when opposed to the wisdom and power of Him who made the vast universe to be the stage on which His creatures act out their little drama (12-17). No cast of characters can put on a play if its plot does not have the approval of the Director *who sits above the circle of the earth.* All attempts to reach Him in order to manipulate or control Him fall far short. Finite minds cannot even conceive of anything big enough to correspond to the infinity of His deity. It is still more ridiculous to construct Him in the *likeness* of a material idol, fashioned by a *goldsmith* or a *craftsman.* To this incomparable, transcendent God not only ordinary *inhabitants* of the earth *are like grasshoppers,* but at His command also *princes* and *the rulers of the earth* come *to nought* and become *as nothing.* All of them without exception are *like the flower of the field* (6) which *scarcely has . . . taken root in the earth* when He sends *the tempest* that turns it into withered *stubble.* (18-24)

However, the comforting message to be brought to God's people is also positive in content. Let it be known that *the Creator of the ends of the earth* and of the myriads of luminaries in the sky, who destroys all flesh obstructing His plan of salvation, uses *the greatness of His might* no less to establish and promote His kingdom of grace. There may come times when control of history may seem to have slipped from His hands, as when *Jacob* and *Israel*, the nation chosen to serve His purpose, seemed destined to vanish from the face of the earth. It is then particularly that His ambassadors are to obey the command: *Comfort, comfort my people* (v. 1). The latter's doubts that God is aware of their distress and their complaint that He is not doing right by them is to be met with the assurance that (1) there never is or will be a time when *the everlasting God* will become *faint* or grow *weary;* (2) they can trust Him to know what He is doing even though *his understanding is unsearchable* for their puny minds; (3) *they who wait for the Lord* will never be disappointed, for He is able to *renew their strength* when all human resources are exhausted. (25-31)

40:2 *Speak tenderly.* Not harshly and menacingly as rebels against the King of heaven and earth should expect, but in the tone of winsome pleading with which a lover seeks to touch the heart of a maiden he is courting (Hos 2:14; Gn 34:3; Ju 19:3). So Joseph spoke to his conscience-stricken brothers (Gn 50:21). Jerusalem, too, did nothing to deserve tender words of comfort. Her redemption would be an act of divine mercy without any merit or worthinesss on her part. For God promised to (1) cut short the time of "hard service" (14:3) in the exile even though justice required that suffering for sin should never be *ended;* (2) consider the penalty of *her iniquity* paid even though she could do nothing to make amends for the debt she incurred; (3) let her receive *from the Lord's hand* good things in *double* proportion to the punishment she deserved for all her sins. (61:7; Jb 11:6)

40:3 *A voice cries.* According to His eternal plan, *the way of the Lord* has as its predestined goal the redemption of all mankind through His Son Jesus Christ. All obstacles will be cleared from His *highway* of salvation. His chosen people will come forth from the grave of the exile and survive the rise and fall of empires in order that the Savior might be born "of the house and lineage of David" (Lk 2:4) as foretold. However, there would be also spiritual roadblocks which must be cleared away if *the way of the Lord* is to gain entrance into the hearts of men. Therefore John the Baptizer was to be commissioned to "go before the Lord to prepare his ways" (Lk 1:76-79). He did so when he preached repentance "in the wilderness of Judea." (Mt 3:1-3; Mk 1:3; Lk 3:4-6; Jn 1:23)

40:5 *All flesh.* As the following verses explain, all mankind is meant. When *the glory of the Lord* was *revealed* in His incarnate Son, His purpose was not to destroy sinners but to bring the light of salvation to all peoples of the earth (6:8; 52:10; 60:1-3). However, there will also come a time when "the Son of Man comes in glory" to judge "all the nations." (Mt 25:31 ff.)

40:10 *His reward . . . his recompense.* The Lord is not like a workman who reaps no benefits from his labors. Because He *comes with might,* the efforts He puts forth bring the desired results. (59:16; 62:11)

40:11 *Like a shepherd.* Even though He is ruthless when He must "put down the mighty from their thrones," those who "hear his voice and . . . follow him" can depend on Him to be kind and generous in caring for them, be they ever so helpless and weak. (Ps 23:1; Lk 1:52; Jn 10:3 f.)

40:12 *Who . . .?* The answer to the questions in these verses is: no one but He whose "handiwork" the vast universe is. (Ps 19:1; 104; Jb 38—39; Is 48:3)

40:16 *Lebanon.* If one were able to place all the stately trees from its wooded heights as *fuel* on an altar and then were to sacrifice all the *beasts* inhabiting its glens and crags, the resulting *burnt offering* would not *suffice* to express the veneration and homage God's transcendent glory deserves.

40:19 *Idol.* The Hebrew word is usually translated "graven image" or simply "image" (so in v. 20; 10:10; 44:15). Other terms, also translated simply "idol," express biting sarcasm for "other gods" very trenchantly by their etymological meaning (cf. Dt 29:17 note: "dung"; Ps 96:5 note: "nonentity"). Here the process of manufacturing an "image" (20) shows how ridiculous men are to worship what they themselves fabricate out of lifeless, inert material. For the same kind of satire see 41:6 f.; 44:9-20; 46:1 f.; Jer 10:1-16.

40:21 *Not known.* There is no excuse for the folly of idolatry. Not only could God's "eternal power and deity" be "clearly perceived in the things that have been made," but He also revealed Himself "by the mouth of his holy prophets, which have been since the world began." (Ro 1:20; Lk 1:70 KJV)

40:23 *Nothing.* Translated "emptiness" (17), "chaos" (24:10 note; 45:18), "void." (Jb 26:7)

40:26 *Their host.* The stars are like a huge army which appears overhead as if created anew every night, and then marches across the sky in unbroken ranks. *Not one* of them fails to take its assigned place. (Ps 147:4)

40:27 *Right is disregarded.* God's promises to His chosen people seemed meaningless. However, their complaint was a lack of faith which is reproved and challenged by God's question: *Why do you say* such things?

41:1-29 *Listen . . . in silence.* In this ch. the comforting message that "the way of the Lord" to redeem sinful mankind is on a "straight" course to its goal (40:3) takes on the form of a summons to a lawsuit. A call to appear for trial is issued by "The Judge of all the earth" (Gn 18:25) to *the peoples* and their *molten images* (29; for God's case against His own people see 1:2 second note; 3:13-15; Ps 87:1-7; Mi 6:1-5). As they *draw near for judgment,* they are challenged to prove their claim that they can *renew their strength* from their own resources so that they can nullify the divine promise that "they who wait for the Lord shall renew their strength"

(40:31). The verdict rendered lets no doubt that "all the nations are . . . less than nothing" and that their handcrafted gods "will not move" to help them (40:17, 20). The idols do not determine events, for "the Creator of the ends of the earth" is also the Lord of history. (40:28)

The immediate case in point is the meteorlike march of conquest by Cyrus the Persian from his base in *the east* to the *coastlands* of the Mediterranean Sea. *Generations* before he appeared on the scene the great *I am* planned his rise to power. It was to be an important milestone on the highway of universal salvation, for this new master of the world was to free the chosen people from the Babylonian exile (1-4). Because the nations in the conqueror's path cannot account for their plight except to conclude that they are victims of a blind fate, they *are afraid.* Joint action and mutual encouragement cannot allay their fears. Nor will it help to refurbish their idols, because these themselves must be kept from falling apart *with the hammer* and *with nails.* (5-7)

At this point in the proceedings the Judge takes time to "speak tenderly" (40:2) to the people of Israel. They need not fear that they too will be swept out of existence by the hurricane engulfing the world. However, their survival will not come about because they are "more in number" or because their virtue entitles them to special treatment (Dt 7:7; Eze 36:22, 32). They have a future only because God has chosen them, *the offspring of Abraham,* to be His *servant* in carrying out the gracious promises made to their ancestors (cf. Gn 12:2). Though they proved to be unworthy and disobedient servants, they had not been *cast . . . off* (8-10). If they are faithful in serving God, all opposition will be *as nothing at all* (11-13). *The Holy One of Israel* will not allow *Jacob* to be trodden under foot like a defenseless *worm.* Though on the verge of being crushed to death by the Babylonians, the *men of Israel* will be empowered by their *Redeemer* to overcome all enemies (14-16). For He who says *Fear not* is not an impotent idol. He has at His disposal all the resources of the universe. When, therefore, *the poor and needy* seek relief in a contrite and humble spirit, they will never "wait for the Lord" in vain (57:2; 66:2; 40:31). Whatever help they need will be *created* by *the hand of the Lord* as surely as "the world was created by the word of God." (17-20; Heb 11:3)

Resuming the trial of the nations, the Judge turns directly to their gods. They are to state their *case.* Can they produce *proofs* that they can foretell *what is to happen?* Is it not true that they cannot explain the *outcome* because they did not understand the meaning of *former things?* Because their silence is evidence that they are unable to know *the things to come* or affect the course of history for good or evil, they stand condemned as a fabrication of *nothing.* Anyone who *chooses* them is branded *an abomination* (21-24). The *King of Jacob* (21), on the other hand, is the Lord of history and the arbiter of human destiny. For He not only *stirred up* Cyrus to do His bidding, He also *declared* the coming of Zion's liberator from the exile long before anyone had any inkling of who he would be. (25-29)

41:2 *One from the east.* Cyrus is mentioned by name in 44:28; 45:1. After becoming king of Persia and Media, he marched in a westerly direction to Lydia on the Mediterranean coast, subduing it and all intervening peoples. In campaigns "from the north" (25) he conquered Babylon. Thereby Jerusalem and Judah, also south of his northern supply lines, automatically became a part of the Persian empire.

41:3 *Not trod.* The conqueror's advance was so swift that *his feet* did not seem to touch the *paths* leading to his victims.

41:4 *I am He.* As His name indicates, the Lord antedates the beginning of history and will continue to exist after *the last* of temporal things has ceased to be (43:10-13). For the meaning of His name see Ex 3:14 note; 3:15 note; 6:3 note.

41:8 *My servant.* It was an unmerited distinction for *Abraham* and his *offspring* to be *chosen* of all families of the earth and to be given a role in God's eternal plan of salvation. However, in spite of spiritual and material blessings conferred on *Israel,* that nation turned out to be a disobedient servant—so "deaf" to God's guidance and so "blind" to His goodness that "he poured upon him the heat of his anger" (42:18-25). Chastened, forgiven, redeemed from the Babylonian exile, Israel would again render service necessary for the coming of that Servant of the Lord who would be obedient to death and by dying and rising would atone for the sins not only of Israel but of all sons and daughters of Adam. (52:13—53:12)

My friend. Abraham is given the same title in 2 Ch 20:7 note; Ja 2:23.

41:10 *Fear not.* So God spoke to His servants of old (Gn 15:1: Abraham; 26:24: Isaac; Jos 1:5-9: Joshua). Because faith is hesitant to believe that there is nothing whatsoever to fear if God says: *I am with you,* He must say again and again: *Fear not,* as He does in 41:13 f.; 43:1, 5; 44:2; 51:7.

41:14 *Redeemer.* Occurring more than 10 times in the following chs., this comforting title of God describes what He must do to rescue His helpless people. For its meaning see Jb 19:25 second note.

41:15 *Threshing sledge.* Every obstacle in "the way of the Lord" (40:3) will be dissipated as if it were a bundle of grain which a farmer threshes and winnows. Cf. 28:27 note.

41:18 *Open rivers.* There are no limits to the help "the poor and needy" can expect. Nature springs into action at God's command. (Ps 107:33 note)

41:23 *That you are gods.* Unless the idols can interpret history ("the former things") and foretell the future (*what is to come hereafter*), their claim to deity is a fraud.

41:25 *Call on my name.* In his proclamation permitting the exiled Israelites to return to their homeland, Cyrus said: "The Lord, the God of heaven, has . . . charged me to build him a house at Jerusalem." (Ez 1:2)

41:28 *Among these. There is no one* among those considered gods who could have "instructed" the Creator. (40:13)

42:1-25 *Behold . . . I uphold.* Introduced by *"Behold,"* the last verse of the preceding ch. exposed idols as "a delusion." Now the same exclamation points to the only true God, who *created the heavens and . . . the earth* (5). While they remain impotent, He is directing the course of history "from the beginning" (41:4) to a fixed and well-defined goal. It was He who "stirred up" Cyrus (41:25). However, the founding of the Persian empire and Israel's return to Palestine were but preliminary steps in a long-range program. Its purpose was to create a worldwide kingdom. Not ushered in and maintained by force of arms, it was to be a rule assuring every subject pardon and peace.

Behold, says God, *my servant* whom I have *chosen* to establish this spiritual realm and to extend it to *the nations* wherever they may be *in the earth* (1-4). Because of who the Servant is and what He will do, God will ratify *a covenant* obligating Him to cancel the sins of the world and to free mankind from the consequence of its rebellion against Him. *The people* of Israel and *the nations* of heathen will share alike in the spiritual benefits, as if they constituted one global community (5-9). These *new things,* foretold to take place when *the former things have come to pass* as decreed by the Lord (9), will bring such joy as to evoke *a new song* of praise (cf. Ps 33:3 note). Because nations far and wide are the beneficiaries of salvation, voices singing *glory to the Lord* are to be heard *from the end of the earth.* (10-13)

For reasons known to Him alone, the Lord did not set the stage earlier for the appearance of the Servant-Redeemer. But as *a woman in travail* cannot delay the birth of a child, so He will let nothing hold up the coming of His kingdom when the appointed time comes (14-17). For a time it seemed He had made a wrong move. Israel, chosen of all nations to be His *servant* in a special task, proved unreliable and unworthy of that honor. The people refused to be the kind of community God wanted them to be if *a light to the nations* (6) was to shine out of their midst. They spurned *his law* so flagrantly and refused so obstinately to *walk* in His *ways* that He let them *become a prey* of the Babylonian conqueror. *With none to rescue* them from *prisons* and exile far from home, the service for which God called them into being (41:8 f.) seemed to have ended forever (18-25). However, as the opening verses of the next ch. make clear, God's mercy was not exhausted. He would not let His promises of a universal Savior from sin go by default. Israel was to be freed in order again to serve His gracious purposes.

42:1 *My servant.* God chose to call many individuals His servants. The service they rendered carried out a wide variety of assignments. Honored by this title were Abraham (Gn 26:24; Ps 105:6), Moses (Nm 12:7 f.), Caleb (Nm 14:24), David (Is 37:35), Isaiah (Is 20:3), prophets in general (2 K 17:13; Is 44:26), Eliakim (Is 22:30), Zerubbabel (Hg 2:24), even such heathen kings as Nebuchadnezzar (Jer 25:9) and Cyrus (Is 43:10). It occurs also as a corporate name for all Israelites to indicate the reason for their existence as a nation (Jer 30:10 and frequently in Is 40—66). However, no individual(s) or Israel collectively can qualify as the Servant described in vv. 1-9 of this ch. and in the so-called "Servant Songs" (49:1-13; 50:4-9; 52:13—53:12). In these passages it becomes progressively clear that "the prophet" is not speaking "about himself or about some one else" among his fellow Israelites but is proclaiming "the good news of Jesus" (Acts 8:30-35). In Him alone God's *soul delights* without ever finding fault, as "a voice from heaven" declared at His Son's baptism and transfiguration (Mt 3:17; 17:5). By contrast, see what God says about His servant Israel in the closing verses of this chapter of Isaiah. Because the Israelites, even the best among them, were in need of forgiveness, they could not save themselves, much less atone for the guilt of their companions in crime throughout the world. But God was promising a sinless Servant who could redeem not only disobedient servant-Israel but also all *the nations.* The NT validates this interpretation of vv. 1-4 by quoting them as fulfilled in Jesus Christ. (Mt 12:18-21; see also Acts 3:13, 26; 4:27, 30; Ph 2:7-9)

My Spirit. The Servant is divinely authorized and empowered to carry out His assigned mission (cf. also 11:2; 61:1). However, He will *bring . . . justice to the nations* not by forcing His will on the world by military campaigns as Cyrus did, treading down "kings" and "rulers" "as the potter treads clay" (41:2, 25). There will be no noisy, flamboyant victory marches "in the street" (2). Yet He will bring it about that even the weakest in His worldwide dominion will have a rightful claim to the benefits He bestows. —All three Persons of the Trinity are mentioned in this OT verse.

42:3 *Bruised reed.* Cf. 40:29; 57:15; 61:1-3.

42:4 *Not fail or be discouraged.* The last "Servant Song" makes it very clear how the Servant will establish "his law" "in the earth" (52:13—53:12). Here it is only intimated that it will entail suffering to the point of failure. However, though He may become weak and exhausted by "the travail of his soul" (53:11), He will not give up the struggle.

42:6 *A light to the nations.* Paul and Barnabas justified their bringing "the light of the world" (Jn 8:12) to the Gentiles by referring to this verse and to 49:6. (Acts 13:47; see also Simeon's words Lk 2:30-32)

42:8 *My name.* Cf. 41:4 note.

42:11 *Kedar . . . Sela.* Cf. Ps 120:5 note and Is 16:1 second note.

42:13 *His fury.* Translated "zeal" (9:7 note) and "jealous wrath." (Ps 79:5 second note; Dt 4:24 note)

42:14 *Gasp and pant.* In His battle with His enemies, God is cast in the role of "a mighty man . . . of war" (13). An even more daring anthropomorphic comparison describes Him as a pregnant woman who, when the time of delivery comes, can only *cry out* in pain but cannot delay the birth of her child. Though He *restrained* Himself for a long time, nothing can prevent Him from keeping His promise to open the way of forgiveness for fallen mankind. In order to put to utter shame those "who trust in graven images," He will do deeds greater even than those He did when He redeemed Israel from Egyptian bondage. (15-17)

42:21 *Magnify his law.* Israel had no excuse for its failure to perform its assigned service It was a "servant who knew his master's will but did not . . . act according to his will" (Lk 12:47). *The Lord was pleased* to reveal His saving will and to give instructions in profusion and *glorious* clarity. Yet the people maliciously stopped their ears to His voice and willfully closed their eyes to His guidance.

43:1-28 *But now.* Justice demanded that Israel, the "deaf" and "blind" servant just described (42:18-25), pay the full penalty of his criminal abuse of God's goodness. The disobedient people could expect the worst. It was for a good reason that they had to be told so often *Fear not* (1, 5; 41:10 note), because they faced the dreadful prospect of paying the wages of sin in full. *But now . . . says the Lord . . . I have redeemed you.* And these welcome words were not an idle tale. *The Holy One of Israel,* who justly poured out "the heat of his anger" on the transgressors (42:25), is also moved by a boundless mercy to forgive them and to cancel the punishment of sin. Let no one doubt that He is willing and able to do this miracle of grace. For the *Savior* of His people is none other than He who *created* them a nation when they were nothing but slaves and who *formed* them out of the clay of the 12 sons of Jacob. However, Israel's redemption from Babylonia and restoration to national life were to be but one more step in creating a people of God much greater than the offspring of Abraham according to the flesh. Gathered from the four corners of the earth, this universal community of the redeemed will include *every one who* has as his goal to live to the *glory* of his Redeemer. (1-7; cf. 2:2 notes, 11:11 f.)

Blind and *deaf,* but now chastened and forgiven, Israel will live on in order to testify to *all the nations* that *there is no savior* besides the Lord. The gods of *the peoples,* on the other hand, could not foretell how *former things* were designed to produce a revived Israel and eventually a worldwide salvation. There will be those in the redeemed people on whom God can call to be *witnesses* to His mercy, which has no bounds, and to His power, which no opposition *can hinder.* They will speak from conviction because from experience they *know and believe . . . and understand* that He who says of Himself *I am He* (10, 13, 25) can save and will do so *also henceforth* (8-13). To achieve His purpose God *will send to Babylon* its appointed destroyers. Again let no one doubt His word. For He who says *Thus says the Lord* has proved His might as *the Creator of Israel.* He once did signs and wonders as He called into being a nation whose *King* He wanted to be. He still can commandeer the forces of nature as He sets out to do *a new thing.* It will be a miracle of such a marvelous nature as to cause *the former things* to fade from memory. For the re-creation of His chosen people of old is not an end in itself. It in turn is prophetic of the future. For there will be a day when He will have a people to be gathered from *the end of the earth* (5 f.) and to be freed *that they might declare my praise.* (14-21)

What God is about to do, however, is not a reward for Israel's excellence but an undeserved gift. Instead of pleasing the Lord, it had *burdened* Him with *sins* and *wearied* Him with *iniquities.* Even its worship only added insult to injury (22-24). Israel was forced to admit that it had a record of sin from the very beginning. Its best and noblest representatives transgressed against the Lord. It deserved the *utter destruction* which God decreed on the cities of Canaan at Joshua's time (Dt 2:34 note). There was hope only if God would blot out transgressions for His *own sake* without any merit or worthiness on its part. (25-28; Ps 51:1, 9)

43:2 *Waters . . . fire.* Even though God's people go "through fire and through water" in time of adversity, He will not permit the heat or floods of judgment to destroy them. (Ps 66:12; 32:6; 42:7 f.; 124:4 ff.; Dn 3:26 f.)

43:3 *Your ransom.* God restructured the whole ancient world for the sake of a small people apparently sinking into oblivion in a foreign land. Their liberation is described as if the Persians were to be compensated for giving the exiles freedom by conquest of Egypt including related Ethiopia and Seba.

43:7 *Called by my name.* Belonging to Him. (44:5)

Bring forth. Israel and "all the nations" are summoned to appear in a court of law (41:1 note). When the worshipers of idols can produce no "witness" to vindicate their gods, the Lord calls to the stand His "witnesses," His "servant" Israel, to testify that as He "declared" in advance, He saved His people and thereby "proclaimed" their dependence on Him, who alone is God. (12; cf. 44:8)

43:12 *Strange god.* Only the true God can claim to have been active in Israel's history.

43:14 *Chaldeans.* For this name for the Babylonians see 13:19 note. The last two lines of this verse yield sense if translated: "and I will cast down all of them as fugitives, also the Chaldeans who exult in ships."

43:18 *Remember not.* The meaning cannot be that God's people should erase from memory *the former things* by which He revealed Himself earlier (46:9). The nation, created to be His servant, did not have only a past. It was not to be buried in Babylon. It had a still more glorious future. It could expect "a new thing," a miracle so marvelous as to eclipse *the things of old.* (Cf. Cl 2:17)

43:23 *Burnt offerings.* Israel's worship

degenerated into a mechanical performance and an exhibition of hypocrisy. God refused to accept it as something offered to Him, but rejected it as an insulting abomination. For a scathing denunciation of such hallow mockery see 1:11 note.

43:24 *Sweet cane.* The "aromatic cane" or reed used in the preparation of holy anointing oil (Ex 30:23). *Fat,* considered a choice part of the sacrificial animal, was burned on the altar because it "is the Lord's." (Lv 3:14-16)

43:27 *Your first father.* Adam was the father of all men; Abraham, of the Israelites (51:2; Jos 24:3). The *mediators* were those appointed to intercede in behalf of Israel, such as prophets and priests.

44:1-28 *Fear not.* Because Israel was "delivered . . . to utter destruction" for its sins (43:28), it had every reason to be afraid. There was no instance on record to show that a conquered, exiled people could hope to avoid national extinction. Anyone facing annihilation knows how welcome and necessary it is to be told again and again: Fear not. In order to dispel Israel's doubts and to strengthen its faith, it too needed to hear these comforting words spoken over and over again. For that reason they are repeated also in this ch. (8; cf. 41:10 note)

Furthermore, to "speak tenderly to Jerusalem" (40:2) is not to raise false hopes. He who says *but now hear* (1; cf. 43:1) is none other than the Lord who chose and created this people to be His *servant* from their infancy. They will not perish but have *descendants* on whom He will pour streams of spiritual blessings (1-5). The frightened prisoners are to remember, too, that this *Redeemer* and *King of Israel* is *the Lord of hosts.* No one antecedes Him; and when heaven and earth have vanished, He remains untouched by time and age. The people of Israel are His *witnesses* to His power to do *the things to come* as *announced from of old* by Him. (6-8; cf. 43:10-13)

Finally, if the enslaved Israelites are to cast out fear, they must refuse to believe the reason for their plight advanced by their masters. It was evident, the latter insisted, that their gods had vanquished and immobilized the God worshiped in Jerusalem; did not the hard facts prove how true this conclusion was? The next verses deal with this false reason for fear, exposing the folly of trusting idols in a satirical tirade more trenchant even than previous denunciations (9-20; cf. 40:18-20; 41:5-7, 21-24). The real cause of fear has been removed. God has *swept away* the *transgressions* and the *sins* for which His *servant* Israel deserved all it suffered and more (21-22). So great and glorious is the Lord's redemptive goodness that the *heavens* and the *earth,* from its *depths* to its *mountains,* are invited to *break forth into singing* (23). For because Israel has as its *Redeemer* the Creator of the universe, nothing His prophetic *messengers* promised will fail to materialize. So in order that Jerusalem might be *built* and *inhabited* again, as foretold, He has chosen *Cyrus* to lead His people home and to *fulfill all* His *purpose.* (24-28)

44:2 *Jeshurun.* "Upright," poetic name for Israel.

44:4 *Spring up.* The blessings of the Spirit are described as having the effect of showers of rain on "thirsty land" (3; cf. Jl 2:23-32; Acts 2).

44:5 *This one . . . another.* Among the "descendants" (3) of the new Israel there will be those who cannot claim sonship by natural birth. They will give oral and written testimony of their desire to be *the Lord's* and enjoy the blessings of membership in His people.

44:7 *Set it forth.* Again in a courtroom setting (cf. 41:1 note), God orders the devotees of a god "besides" Him (6) to act as "witnesses" (9) in behalf of their idol. They are to give an account of instances in which the object of their veneration foretold what the future would bring or what the past meant.

44:9 *Nothing.* For the meaning of this word see 24:10 note; 40:23 note. Idol worshipers entrust themselves to a delusion, whereas the Lord is a "Rock" (8) so strong and firm as to stand unmoved in the worst storms of life. (Cf. Ps 18:2, 31, 46; 27:5; 92:15, etc.)

44:11 *Fellows.* Associated with the manufacturing and veneration of idols.

44:12 *Becomes hungry.* If the idol-maker himself gets hungry and tired, can he produce something less dependent on sustenance?

44:15 *Warms himself . . . bakes bread.* It is so preposterous to pray to something made of the same substance that serves as heating and cooking fuel. A primitive god carved out of a "block of wood" (19) is no less ludicrous than the most sophisticated idol that a man "shapes" (12) with the tools of his mind. It can be nothing more than "the figure of a man" (13), a likeness and projection of himself, as fallible, unreliable, and impotent as he is.

44:18 *He has shut.* Better translated: "their eyes are blinded." But see also Ex 4:21 note; Is 6:10 note.

44:21-22 *Remember these things.* It will rid the people of their fear that idols of the nations determine their destiny if they keep in mind the comforting truths dinned in their ears: There is only one true God; you are His *servant;* He has blotted out *your transgressions* (43:25); He has *redeemed you.*

44:26 *His messengers.* What spokesmen proclaim in the name of Him who "made all things" (24) and whom the forces of nature obey (27) will come true, whereas fortune-telling "diviners" will prove to be "liars." (25)

44:28 *Cyrus.* The one whom God "stirred up from the east" (41:2 note) is here mentioned by name and again in the next verse (45:1). His worldwide conquests were a part of God's scheme of things. The service he was to render the chosen people was the kind of concern and guidance a *shepherd* provides for his flock.

45:1—48:22 CONTINUED ASSURANCES THAT DELIVERANCE IS ON THE WAY

45:1-25 *Says the Lord.* Infinitely merciful and

patient, God does not tire to repeat Himself. Again and again He promises to deliver His fallen creatures who cannot free themselves nor deserve to escape the fatal wages of sin. Then he goes to great lengths in persuading doubting and fainthearted souls to accept and believe the proclamation of their liberation. To Israel, doomed to extinction in the Babylonian exile, the comforting news of restoration to national life was contrary to reasonable expectations. History and experience taught that absorption into the stream of conquering and conquered nations was inevitable for an exiled people.

Still more irrational was the way this incredible turnabout was to take place. For even if the Persian *Cyrus* was to overthrow the Babylonian regime, the enslaved Israelites would only exchange one master for another. So it was when the previous Assyrian empire was succeeded by the Babylonians. No, says the Lord, Cyrus is but His "shepherd" (44:28), entrusted with the care of His people. And then to rouse even the most dispirited exiles, He startles them by surnaming the heathen king His *anointed,* a title reserved for Israelites who were consecrated to hold positions of high trust such as priests, prophets, and kings. Even though Cyrus did *not know* the Lord as the chosen people did, he was singled out to play a significant role in implementing God's plan to bring about mankind's salvation. For as Assyria was "the rod of" God's "anger" (10:5), so the Persian ruler, firmly in His *right hand,* was to "prepare the way of the Lord" (40:3) by letting His *servant Jacob* again become the bearer of His promises. In carrying out his assignment, Cyrus was to overcome all resistance because *all these things* which shape world history were ordered by the only true God (1-7). He who lets showers of rain fall *from above* to water the earth and make seed spring forth and bud, also will let *the skies rain down righteousness* and *cause righteousness to spring up.* (8)

However, let no one presume to dictate to the Creator of the universe how He is to go about saving fallen mankind whom He "formed . . . of the dust of the ground" (Gn 2:6). Anyone guilty of such brazen insolence not only forfeits the proffered deliverance but also provokes God to pronounce a fearful *woe* on him. Furthermore, in spite of silly objections, the divine plan of salvation remains unchanged. The Gentile king Cyrus will carry it forward, for God *aroused him in righteousness* to set Israel free. (9-13).

At the same time, Israel's liberation from physical bondage, important as it was, only set the stage for the eventual drama toward which God was directing world events. It was His purpose to create a spiritual Israel, a worldwide communion of saints. Nations such as those incorporated in the Persian empire *(Egypt, Ethiopia, the Sabeans)* would seek citizenship in this commonwealth in order to participate in the *everlasting salvation* found nowhere else (14-17). This glorious vision of the future is not a mirage. For the Creator of heaven and earth will not let the direction of history slip out of His hands and let the world sink into *a chaos* of confusion (18-19). Certain of the fulfillment of His promises, the Lord issues an invitation to *all the ends of the earth* to forsake their useless idols and to turn to Him, for only in Him can they *triumph and glory. (20-25)*

45:1 *Anointed.* One on whose head oil was poured in a ritual of consecration. Cf. Ex 30:25 note; 1 Sm 10:1 first note.

Ungird the loins. Figurative way of saying that the kings were to be deprived of power, just as to "gird" (5) someone strengthened him.

45:7 *Weal and . . . woe.* Nothing happens without the Lord's knowledge and permission. He is the cause of well-being, but He also inflicts retribution. (12:3; 60:21; Am 3:6)

45:13 *Not for price or reward.* The exiles had nothing to contribute to their emancipation. They could not produce their own ransom money or gain Cyrus' favor with costly gifts. Their undeserved deliverance envisions the spiritual liberation of all nations, held "in chains" (14) of Satan's bondage and ransomed "not with . . . silver or gold, but with the precious blood of Christ." (1 Ptr 1:18 f.)

45:19 *Not . . . in secret.* Though God determines in sovereign holiness how He will save His fallen creatures, He proclaims His good and gracious will to carry out His plan "from the beginning." (46:10; 48:16; Acts 3:18, 21)

45:23 *Every knee shall bow.* For the fulfillment see Ro 14:10 ff.; Ph 2:10.

45:24 *Of me.* That is: of the Lord.

46:1-13 *Their idols.* God is not needlessly repetitious when he urges *transgressors* (8) over and over again to accept the message of salvation. Aware that the sons and daughters of Adam are *stubborn of heart* (12), He does not give up on them after one attempt to break down their resistance and to overcome their doubts. He has His prophet fill ch. after ch. with the same urgent pleas and admonitions to believe the glad tidings of their redemption. As is so often the case, faith in God's promises at the time of the Babylonian exile ran counter to the hard facts of reality. It was undeniable that Israel was a crushed and dying nation. There was nothing even to suggest that it could survive. It also seemed to be a valid conclusion, drawn from experience, that the gods of the victorious army simultaneously reduced the God of Israel to impotence, rendering Him inoperative in national affairs. In order to refute this popular claim, the Lord once more exposes the folly of worshiping idols, the symbols of a man-made philosophy. (For previous denunciations of this delusion see 40:18-20; 41:21-29; 44:9-20; 45:20 f.)

The Babylonian gods *Bel* and *Nebo* are no exception. Their images, customarily paraded about in festive processions, will be loaded on beasts of burden to be carted off as spoil by the victorious invaders of the city. Each of them in effect *bows down* and *stoops* in abject submission to these captors (1-2). The God of *the house of Israel,* far from being manipulated by His worshipers, has *borne* His people from the birth of the nation and *will bear* and *carry* them even when they are hoary with age (3-4). Who, therefore, in his right senses would *compare* the Lord of history with the product of a *goldsmith,* which *cannot move from its place* no matter how much *gold* and *silver* its devotees *lavish* on it? (5-7) The fainthearted and skeptical in Israel need only *consider* and *remember the former things of old* to be persuaded that God will bring about their deliverance as He has *spoken* and *purposed.* For *from ancient times* He never failed to *accomplish* what *from the beginning* He planned and promised to do. Therefore the exiles have no reason to doubt that Cyrus, whom He is *calling* like *a bird of prey . . . from a far country,* will *bring . . . to pass* (8-11) their *deliverance,* whose time is *not far off.* (12-13)

46:1 *Bel . . . Nebo.* The chief gods in the Babylonian pantheon. Bel, the equivalent of Baal in Hebrew and a component in Belshazzar, is known also as Marduk (spelled Merodach in Jer 50:2). Nebo, his son, appears in the name Nebu-chadnezzar.

46:11 *From the east.* For Cyrus' rise to power see 4:12 note.

46:12 *Stubborn of heart.* In 45:9 ff. a woe is pronounced on those who think they can dictate to God how He is to let righteousness prevail.

47:1-15 *Come down.* The Babylonian gods will "go into captivity" when the city and the empire they were to protect will succumb to an invader called by the Lord "from a far country" (46:2, 11). Because the only true God has "spoken" and "purposed" "to bring it to pass" (46:11), the doom of the imperial city comes into prophetic view so clearly that Isaiah composes the kind of oracle rendered at a funeral. However, while in the form of a dirge, it does not express grief and sympathy but taunts the fallen victim in view of the complete reversal of fate, brought about by the *vengeance* of *the Holy One of Israel.*

Personified as a *virgin daughter,* Babylon receives an epitaph which reads: From *mistress of kingdoms* (5), pampered, *tender and delicate,* to a slave, clad in scant rags, degraded to menial drudgery, exposed to gross indignities (1-4). She suddenly came to *sit in the dust* rather than on a throne because she arrogantly assumed to be *mistress for ever* in defiance of the Lord of hosts. Given the task to chastize His people, she acted out of personal hatred and *showed them no mercy* (5-7). She became so infatuated with power as to refuse to acknowledge any authority on earth or in heaven *besides* her; she felt so *secure* in her *wickedness* as to claim that *no one sees* her or has the right to call her to account (cf. 29:15; Ps 52:7). She indulged in this delusion of grandeur and self-idolatry because she was *led . . . astray* by the *enchantments* and *sorceries* practiced by renowned soothsayers and astrologers (8-11). Poetic irony is honed to a keen edge as the doomed lady is encouraged to persist in relying on the *counsels* of these charlatans (12-13). They cannot ward off disaster. It will come with the devastating power of a *fire* which consumes everything in its path *like stubble.* (14-15)

47:1 *Virgin daughter.* Hitherto not ravished by hostile invaders.

Chaldeans. For this name for the Babylonians see 13:19 note. It came to designate a class of people famous for their "wisdom and . . . knowledge." (10; Dn 2:2, 4, 5, 10; 4:7)

47:2 *Grind meal.* The task of female slaves. (Ex 11:5)

47:3 *Take vengeance.* Nations are not autonomous in spite of superior resources and armaments. There is a moral world order governing the rise and fall of empires.

47:6 *Profaned my heritage.* Chosen to be God's "own possession," "a holy nation" (Ex 19:5 second note, 6 second note), the Israelites, at God's direction, became the prey of a profane people because "they would not walk" in His "ways." (42:24)

47:8 *Lover of pleasures.* In the Book of Revelation, Babylon is the symbol of wickedness. (Rv 14:8; 18:2 ff.)

Besides me. Babylon arrogated to herself the claim made repeatedly by God: "I am the Lord . . . there is none besides me." (45:5 f.; 43:11; 44:6, 8; 46:9)

47:9 *Loss of children . . . widowhood.* The queenly city would no longer have a king; her population would be decimated.

47:11 *Atone . . . expiate. Disaster,* like an untamable monster, cannot be placated by magic and incantations.

47:13 *Divide the heavens.* Astrology is not a modern invention. The ancient Babylonians already grouped stars into constellations and zodiacal signs for the purpose of casting horoscopes and predicting future events.

48:1-22 *Hear this.* In this ch. God continues to urge the exiles in Babylonia to act on His repeated declarations that His plan of salvation, seemingly aborted, was on its way to fulfillment. Renewed admonition was necessary because the descendants *of Judah* did not *confess the God of Israel . . . in truth or right,* though they outwardly professed allegiance to Him. It seemed so unrealistic to have full confidence in God in view of His apparent inability to protect them against a nation boasting of the help of superior idols. (1-2)

However, if these *obstinate* and hardheaded pragmatists would but examine the record, they would find overwhelming evidence that the Lord of hosts was indeed the Lord of history. They need only to recall how *former things . . . came to pass* in the past exactly as *declared* by Him *of old* and *announced* long beforehand. No *idol* or *graven image* had anything to do with planning and then guiding the course of events (3-5). Because the doubters *see all this* and must *declare it* to be true, there is no reason why they should not believe that *new things* and such as are still *hidden* from view will not happen *from this time forth* when foretold by the same Lord. (6-8)

As for the exile, neither chance nor Babylonia's idols imposed this *affliction* on them. God brought it on because He wanted them *refined* of the dross of disobedience. Yet as severely as He *tried* them, He did *not cut* them *off* in His *anger* as they deserved (9-11). Designed and put into operation by the Creator *of the earth and . . . the heavens,* the purifying process will also come to an end at His direction (12-13). He therefore asks the nations to *assemble . . . and hear* what He will do to carry out His eternal resolve to redeem all sons and daughters of Adam. Long before any empire of men appeared on the scene, He had *called* Cyrus to overthrow Babylon. Freed and reconstituted, Israel was to continue to be the bearer of His promise to redeem mankind from the slavery of sin. Though still removed by intervening centuries, this universal deliverance too is as sure as if it were an accomplished fact. To prove it, He who was to effect this deliverance speaks of Himself as already *sent* by *the Lord God . . . and his Spirit* to carry out His mission. (14-16)

Meanwhile the exile was a necessary interlude. Because the chosen people refused to go *in the way* they *should go,* they suffered severe chastisement. Nevertheless God did not destroy them, leaving them without *offspring* and *descendants* (17-19). But now the time had come to *go forth from Babylon.* They can do so *with a shout of joy,* for the God who brought their fathers out of Egypt into the Promised Land can protect them in the same miraculous way. There is no alternative. Those who remain slaves of sin will have *no peace.* (20-22)

48:1 *Swear.* It was still customary to use oath formulas invoking the Lord to vindicate the truth of statements made by a witness (Dt 10:20 note). Thereby they outwardly identify themselves as former citizens of "the holy city" Jerusalem.

48:6 *You have heard.* The people of Israel knew from experience that "former things" (3), pronounced by God's prophets long in advance, did not fail to materialize as foretold. For that reason they should not hesitate to believe that *new things,* which as yet they *have not known* as actual events, would happen as Isaiah predicted more than a century ago. However, though the prophetic words of a coming exile reached his hearers on audible sound waves, they "never heard" them, for their "ear has not been opened" to receive them in penitence and faith but they have scoffed at them instead. (8; 5:19; for the verb *hear* used in the sense of hearken or obey see 1 Sm 15:22 note)

48:9 *For my name's sake.* Though Israel deserved the full brunt of His *anger,* God saved them from extinction to preserve His honor. He would not let it "be profaned" (11) by the claim that He could not carry out what He promised to do through His chosen people.

48:10 *Not like silver.* If God in a refining process had subjected Israel to heat in a crucible as intense as is required to free silver ore of dross, He would have found very little worth saving.

48:12 *I am He.* The *I am* has no beginning and no end. (41:4 note).

48:14 *Loves him.* As the Lord "set his love upon . . . and chose" (Dt 7:7) the children of Israel to be "his servant" (20) though they did not deserve this distinction (Dt 4:37; 7:6 ff.), so He let Cyrus experience His favor for the purpose of liberating the chosen people. (45:1-6)

48:16 *In secret.* Cf. 45:19 note.

And now. At this point the Servant who was sent "to seek and to save the lost" (Lk 19:10) suddenly speaks a sentence. Made flesh in the fullness of time, the eternal Word has more to say in the opening verses of the next chapter and in 50:4 ff. (Jn 1:1, 14; Gl 4:4)

48:18 *O that.* Cf. Jesus' lament over Jerusalem. (Lk 19:42)

48:19 *Like the sand.* Abraham, Israel's ancestor and the father of all believers, was promised countless offspring. (Gn 13:16; 15:5; 17:5 f.; 22:17; Ro 4:16; 9:6 ff.; Gl 3:29; cf. Is 44:5 note)

48:20 *Go forth . . . flee.* A complete and permanent severance from "the way of sinners" and "the seat of scoffers" is required. (Ps 1:1; see Lot's flight from Sodom; also Rv 18:4 f.)

49:1—57:21 The Way of Forgiveness Opened for All Sinners by the Sinless Servant

49:1—52:15 THE SERVANT'S PROCLAMATION OF UNIVERSAL SALVATION CONFIRMED

49:1-26 *Listen to me.* The Speaker, unannounced as in 48:16, is the *servant* (3, 5, 6), who now explains why "the Lord God has sent" Him (48:16 note; cf. 42:1 second note). Predestined and equipped for a worldwide mission, He boldly demands the attention not only of Israel but also of *peoples from afar,* for He has a message of vital concern to them. Though for a time it seemed to Him that He *labored in vain,* He receives the necessary *strength* to carry out His assignment to be *a light to the nations* far and near and to bring *salvation . . . to the end of the earth.* (1-6)

The Lord immediately corroborates the words of the Servant, addressing Him and promising Him that even the mighty of the earth will pay Him homage, *deeply despised* and *abhorred* though He was when, "taking the form of a servant," He "humbled himself and became obedient unto death" (7; Ph 2:7 f.; cf. also Is 53:2 f.). Despite appearances to the contrary, the Lord's *day of salvation* will make evident that the Servant was *helped* and *kept* from failure so that for His sake God could agree to *a covenant,* pledging Himself to redeem *the nations* from the force of demonic *darkness.* The liberated *prisoners* will be reinstated in their *heritages* which seemed lost and destroyed forever. They will encounter no obstacles which the Lord cannot remove. For He is as powerful as when He miraculously supplied the needs of His people traveling to the Promised Land from their imprisonment in Egypt. In order to *have compassion on his afflicted,* He will do wonders so great that even inanimate nature—*heavens, earth, mountains*—is summomed to *sing for joy* (8-13). It is strange therefore that God must go to great lengths to convince Israel and the nations of their restoration to freedom, as He does in the remaining verses of the ch. Tirelessly merciful and wondrously eloquent, He gives solemn assurances of His unfailing love and His irresistible power to make His promises come true. (14-26)

"The vision of Isaiah" (1:1), here as elsewhere, presents a view of coming events which resembles a snapshot produced by a double exposure. At times there seem to be two pictures. Israel's return from the Babylonian captivity has distinguishable contours as a distinct event in fulfillment of God's promise. At the same time, its features are absorbed into the portrayal of a redemption of which it was but a preliminary model and anticipatory type: the salvation of all mankind from the bondage of sin. Israel punished for its sins and unable to save itself or its fellow sinners represents the plight of the world under the curse of God. Israel forgiven and restored prefigures what God will do to welcome home all prodigal sons and daughters who have strayed into the far country of rebellious self-will. Israel once again populating its rebuilt cities is a token of the vast throngs streaming into the established kingdom of God from every corner of the globe. Israel recreated by God's command to earthly potentates is a prophetic miniature of the redeemed of all times living in a world of kingdoms and empires directed by the Lord of lords and King of kings. In prophetic perspective scenes may merge and appear again in separate profiles. Divine revelation is not bound to the dimensions of time and space. There is no temporal or geographic distance between what is near and what is far away. Isaiah foretells Israel's return from the exile but can describe it also as an accomplished fact. The Servant can tell the nations of the world how He succeeded in His labors to redeem them from the wrath of God, and yet centuries were to elapse before He appeared on the scene and carried out His mission. Seen through the stereopticon of faith, promised fulfillment and fulfilled promise are in perfect focus.

49:1 *From the womb.* As God's spokesmen, such as Jeremiah, John the Baptizer, and Paul, were chosen for their task before they were born, so the Servant was *called* and equipped to bring His own message of salvation to a worldwide audience before He became incarnate in a virgin's womb. (Jer 1:5; Lk 1:15; Gl 1:15)

49:2 *A sharp sword.* Dwellers on distant "coastlands" and "peoples from afar" (1) are alerted to a message which determines their destiny. What they hear from the *mouth* of this Speaker has the cutting edge of *a sharp sword* and hits its mark with the penetrating force of *a polished arrow* (Jer 1:10; 23:29; Heb 4:12). Nothing can blunt these words, for God's *hand* keeps them *hid* in His scabbard and *his quiver.* The Servant Himself is God's "Word," hid from eternity "with God" until He "became flesh." (Jn 1:1, 14)

49:3 *My servant.* God redeemed Israel, His disobedient servant, from the Babylonian exile in order to "be glorified" (44:23; 60:21; 61:3). When He forgave His rebellious sons (1:2) and moved empires to reinstate them in His service, He displayed mercy and power worthy of praise and honor. Yet if God was to be glorified in mankind's redemption from the shackles of sin, He needed a sinless Israelite, a Servant who "according to the flesh" was of the race of Israel (Ro 9:5) yet was "separated from sinners" (Heb 7:26). Nothing but the perfect service and obedience God demanded but Israel could not render would suffice to rescue a world of sinners, including Israel, from the prison house of outer darkness. To the Servant, capable of this deliverance, God said: "You are my son." (Ps 2:7)

49:4 *Labored in vain.* Redemption came by way of suffering and agony so intense that the Servant "in the days of His flesh . . . offered up prayers and supplications with loud cries and tears" (Heb 5:7; Mt 26:39; 27:46). An angel appeared to assure Him of the justice of His cause and the certainty of *recompense.* (Lk 22:43; cf. Is 40:10 note)

49:6 *Too light a thing.* God promises the Servant success in a task of worldwide scope. He is to be *a light to the nations* and not only to *the tribes of Jacob;* He is to effect a *salvation* benefiting not only *the preserved of Israel* but extending *to the end of the earth.* Paul quoted this verse as he brought the message of "the light of the world" (Jn 8:12) to the Gentiles. (Acts 13:47; cf. Acts 26:23; Lk 2:32)

49:7 *Despised.* He who was to be "a light to the nations" was *abhorred by the nations* (cf. 53:3). But "the darkness has not overcome it" (Jn 1:5). What the Lord did through His *chosen* Servant is "the victory that overcomes the world" (1 Jn 5:4). Even *kings* and *princes* will be found among His subjects, humbly prostrating themselves before "the Kings of kings and Lord of lords." (1 Ti 6:15; Is 52:15)

49:8 *Answered.* The Servant did not spend His "strength for nothing and vanity" (4). From the vantage point of eternal heights God sees the outcome of the deadly struggle as a thing of the past. The time of humiliation has become *a time of favor;* the day of agony has turned into *a day of salvation.* And as the Servant's suffering was vicarious (53:5 f.), so His victory disposed God to extend favor and salvation to *the people* of Israel and to all "prisoners" (9) held by Satan in the Babylonian dungeon of sin and death. (42:1-25 note)

49:10 *Hunger or thirst.* Restoration to God's favor by the Servant is portrayed in terms of physical safety and of satisfaction of bodily needs. (40:11 note; Rv 7:16 f.)

49:12 *Land of Syene.* Modern Aswan on the first cataract of the Nile. However, the meaning of the Hebrew word "Sinim" (RSV note), occurring only here, is not certain. A proposed translation is "land of the Chinese."

49:14 *Zion said.* The deliverance of Israel and the nations, described as a certain reality (1-13), is now viewed from the human standpoint of a promise to be believed (14-26). The Lord therefore pleads tenderly for faith in His tireless love and His limitless power.

49:18 *Ornament.* The ransomed, coming from all directions of the compass, adorn Zion like jewels on the dress of a *bride.*

49:19 *Too narrow.* Zion, seemingly "bereaved and barren" (21), will become the mother of offspring so unexpectedly large as to overcrowd the once *devastated land* of Palestine. However, Israel's restored population is only the preview of a spiritual commonwealth. Composed of peoples ransomed by the blood of the Servant, it spreads across every national boundary. (Cf. 1:27 note; 44:5 note; 48:19 note; 54:1-3; Gl 4:26; Rv 5:9 f.)

49:22 *Lift up my hand.* The Lord needs but to give a *signal* to the *nations* and their rulers to secure their readiness to promote the welfare of His *sons* and *daughters.* (5:26 note; 18:3; 62:10)

49:26 *Eat their own flesh.* Opposition to God's people is self-destructive. He will "set every man's sword against his fellow" (Ju 7:22; cf. Is 9:19 f.; Zch 11:9; Rv 16:4-7). The mighty of this earth are no match for *the Mighty One of Jacob.* (1:24 note)

50:1-11 *Says the Lord.* What He says is not essentially new. As in ch. 49, the Lord exhorts His doubting and despairing people to believe His promises of deliverance. Though not expressly named, the Servant again appears in His role as Redeemer of Israel and of the nations (cf. 49:1 ff.), speaking of His mission in the timeless tense of prophecy. His task, assigned to Him before time began, has been successfully completed even though centuries of history were to intervene before His coming became an event in human chronology. Israel's liberation from the Babylonian exile and repatriation in its homeland continue to be in the forefront of Isaiah's vision, only to become the token of the salvation of mankind from the curse of sin and the pledge of the restoration of all nations to communion with their Maker.

However, this ch. also makes its own contributions to the theme under discussion. In the opening verses the message of hope is developed by means of two comparisons drawn from human relationships. The exiles, though punished and *put . . . away* for their *iniquities* and *transgressions,* are not like a woman irrevocably rejected by her husband after he has obtained a *bill of divorce.* Nor are they like children whom a father sold into slavery in order to pay his *creditors.* If the gracious and omnipotent God agrees to renew the bonds broken by infidelity and disobedience, it is strange indeed that there is no response to His announced intention to *redeem* and to *deliver* the outcasts (1-3). Forgiveness, says the Servant, is a reality. The way back to God is open. He can transmit this *word* of relief to every *weary* captive of fear and despair in view of His perfect obedience to God's will and His willingness to be the innocent victim of pain and shame. God vindicated Him, declaring Him innocent. The guilt He assumed is expiated (4-9). Yet the Servant's offer of release from the powers of *darkness* is not a matter to be treated with indifference. The bright beams of *light,* if rejected, turn into a destroying *fire.* (10-11).

These truths, presented in logical sequence, are linked also by a unifying literary device. Each significant assertion is introduced by the exclamation *behold* (1, 2, 9a, 9b, 11). Each declaration so highlighted is in turn the answer to an immediately preceding question (1, 2, 8, 10). The contents of the ch. can be summarized as follows: Behold, sinners need not despair; behold, their sins are atoned for; behold, the danger of refusing forgiveness.

50:1 *Bill of divorce.* For the regulation in divorce procedures see Dt 24:1-4; Mt 5:31; 19:7. For sin described as marital unfaithfulness see 54:4-8; Jer 3:8; Eze 16; Hos 2:1-5.

Sold you. For instances of creditors doing so see 2 K 4:1; Neh 5:1-5; Mt 18:25.

50:2 *The sea . . . a desert.* Cf. Ps 107:33 note.

50:4 *Me.* The speaker can only be the Servant, identified by name in 42:1; 49:6.

Wakens my ear. While rebellious Israel turned a deaf ear to God, Jesus could claim to "speak as the Father taught" Him (Jn 8:27-29). Therefore *a word* from Him sufficed to *sustain . . . him that is weary* and to give rest to "all who labor and are heavy laden." (Mt 11:28)

50:6 *Gave my back.* For the fulfillment see Mt 26:67; 27:28-31, 39-44.

50:7 *Face like a flint.* Cf. Jesus' determination to fulfill "everything . . . written . . . by the prophets." (18:31; 24:44)

50:9 *Declare me guilty.* Charged with the sins of the world yet vindicated and acquitted when He "was raised from the dead," He "is at the right hand of God," defending the imputed innocence of all who appeal to Him for justification. (Ro 8:31-34)

51:1-23 *Hearken.* We should think that God has spoken enough words of comfort through His prophet (40:1; 49:13). However, God knows how "slow of heart to believe" (Lk 23:25) even those are *who seek the Lord* (1), whom He calls *my people* (4) and who *know righteousness* (7). Those who tire of reading another chapter of encouragement and reassurance do not know how tirelessly patient God must be if He is to overcome the doubts of His despairing children and persuade them to believe the promise of *salvation* (6, 8). Therefore in this chapter He again pleads for faith in His power to redeem.

Though the message is the same, it is not a monotonous repetition of identical phrases. He makes the invitation attractive by ever new variations on the theme. Here He calls for attention by a triple call to *hearken* and to *listen* to Him (1, 4, 7). The descendants of *Abraham,* seemingly doomed to extinction in the Babylonian exile, are to be convinced from their past that there is not "anything too hard for the Lord" (Gn 18:14). It was only by a miracle of power and grace that they became a great nation. For their ancestor and his wife *Sarah* remained childless to their old age (Gn 16:2; 17:17; 18:11-14). So the Lord's "hand" is not "shortened" (50:2) as He promises to restore burned Zion and to let its *waste places* resound again with *joy and gladness.* (1-3)

At the same time, Israel's rehabilitation is suffused with the light of a universal salvation, benefiting *the peoples* and *the coastlands* far beyond Palestine's borders and enduring *for ever* (4-6). This *deliverance* cannot be thwarted even though those who long for it suffer *the reproach of men and . . . their revilings* (7-8). In their distress they are to join the prophet in praying boldly to the Lord, asking Him to *awake* and to *put on strength* as He did in *the generations of long ago.* They can do so with the assurance that no frail *son of man who is made like grass* need be feared. For He has entrusted *the ransomed of the Lord* with the proclamation of His Word, in which He pledges to consummate His plan of salvation in a new heaven and a new earth (9-16; 59:21; 65:17). The enslaved people are to *rouse* themselves too from the stupefying despair of God's willingness to forgive their sins. True, He will not be mocked, as they well know, for they *have drunk . . . the cup of His wrath . . . to the dregs.* However, as certain as He is to execute His threat of punishment, so trustworthy is His promise that they *shall drink no more* of *the cup of staggering.* When He *pleads the cause of his people,* their *tormentors* will taste the wine of *his wrath* with the same paralyzing effect. (17-23)

51:1 *Rock . . . quarry.* Israel did not create itself. It came into being like stones *hewn* and *digged* from a rock vein in a quarry.

51:2 *But one.* Abraham, "as good as dead," became "many" when "by faith Sarah . . . received power to conceive." (Heb 11:11 f.; Acts 7:5)

51:5 *Coastlands.* In 42:1-4 the task of worldwide salvation, here ascribed to God, is assigned to the Servant. The NT too says that Jesus "rose from the dead" and that He "was raised" by the Father. (Acts 10:41; Ro 6:4; 1 Co 15:4)

51:6 *Will vanish.* The material world is transitory, but the word of the Lord "will not pass away." (Mt 24:35; 5:18)

51:7 *Know righteousness.* They were not only informed how and why they were to be right with God, but this *law* or teaching was also in their *heart,* motivating and shaping their lives. For the wider meaning of *know* in Scripture see Gn 18:19 note; Dt 9:24 note.

51:9 *Awake.* To the petitioners, long the helpless victims of oppression, it appears that the Lord is asleep, insensitive to their calling. (Ps 7:6 note; 44:23)

Rehab . . . dragon. Cf. 30:7 note; 27:1 second note.

51:11 *Ransomed . . . shall return.* The answer to the prayer of "the redeemed" (9 f.) comes "while they are yet speaking" (65:24). The entire verse is almost identical with 35:10.

51:16 *My words in your mouth.* In 49:1 ff. the Servant's "mouth" is "made . . . like a sharp sword" as God's spokesman. He is also promised divine protection. It is only natural that the Servant-Redeemer and Israel, the servant to be redeemed, both play a part in God's plan of salvation, inasmuch as both are given the title servant. However, they do not render the same service (49:3 note). God redeemed and preserved Israel so that the Servant could say: "Salvation is from the Jews" (Jn 4:22). The message of that salvation was kept alive in Israel and was spread from Jerusalem and Samaria "to the end of the earth." (59:21; Acts 1:8; 13:47)

51:17 *Cup of his wrath.* Cf. Ps 60:3 note.

51:23 *Pass over.* Conquerors stepped over the prostrate bodies of their victims.

52:1-15 *Awake, awake.* Asked by fainthearted saints to "awake" from apparent unconcern for His people (51:9), the Lord, in turn, directs them to "rouse" themselves from the stupor of despair (51:17) and to *awake* from the nightmare of hopelessness. All appearances to the contrary, God will carry out the purpose for which He chose them from "among all peoples" (Ex 19:5) to be "a holy nation" (Ex 19:6 second note) and Jerusalem to be *the holy city.* They can be certain of deliverance, for He who called their oppressors to be "the rod of" His "anger" (10:15) can as easily disarm them. He will not stand idly by when His *name is despised* by the Babylonian *rulers* who assert: "These are the people of the Lord and yet had to go out of their land" (1-6; Eze 36:20; Ro 2:24). If His people have the ears of faith, they can now already hear the *good tidings* of Zion's *peace* and *salvation* proclaimed from the tops of *the mountains;* if they have the eyes of faith, they can *see the return of the Lord to Zion,* announced to them by the *watchmen* from their lofty lookouts. Joy knows no bounds. Even the *waste places of Jerusalem,* certain of being rebuilt, are bidden to *break forth together into singing,* jubilant of the renewed proof that *God reigns.* Israel's return from the exile was to be an important step toward establishing the Messianic reign of the "shoot from the stump of Jesse" "upon the throne of David" (11:1; 9:7). It will be a universal kingdom, for *all the ends of the earth shall see the salvation of our God* (7-10). It is up to the exiles to implement the divine plan. If they act on His promises and respond in the obedience of faith, they can be sure of the same kind of protection God provided for the slaves He delivered from Egyptian bondage. (11-12; cf. Ex 13:21 f.; 14:19 f.; Nm 10:34)

However, God's worldwide rule will not come by force of arms or military conquest. It will be effected in a way contrary to human calculations. He will let His Servant *prosper* and *be very high* through suffering so intense that He was *marred beyond human semblance.* His victory, though it appeared to be a defeat, will be decisive. *Many nations* and *kings* will stand in awe once they learn of it (13-15). The last three verses of this ch. are a bridge between it and ch. 53. They introduce the fourth and last of the "Servant Songs," to be developed fully in the following ch. At the same time these verses are linked with the *good tidings* (7) proclaimed in an earlier section of the ch. In answer to the question how God will keep His promise to provide *salvation* to *all the ends of the earth* (10), He presents His Servant-Redeemer.

52:1 *Uncircumcised . . . unclean.* The exile came about when Jerusalem was entered and destroyed by the Babylonians, who did not observe the rites provided by God in His covenant with Israel.

52:3 *For nothing.* This phrase, though not identical in Hebrew, occurs again in each of the next two verses. It underscores God's sovereign control of history as well as the unmerited goodness of His redemption of His people. When He "sold" them (50:1), their masters had no claim of their own to their prey. Therefore when the enslaved captives are to "be redeemed," it will be a transaction "without money." God owes the oppressing nations no compensation for their loss, as surely as their victims have nothing to offer their Redeemer for their release. They are saved by grace alone. (Ro 3:23 f.)

52:4 *The Assyrian.* He destroyed and exiled the 10 tribes of the Northern Kingdom in 722 BC. (2 K 17)

52:5 *Here.* In Babylon, the scene of Israel's disgrace.

52:6 *My name.* Not only the appellation "Lord" but what the great "I am" did and said to reveal Himself (Ex 6:3 note; 3:14 note). To "know" that name is to acknowledge and to accept the way of salvation revealed by Him. (Gn 18:19 note; Dt 9:24 note)

52:7 *How beautiful.* St. Paul quotes from this verse to point out the necessity of proclaiming the Gospel if it is to be of any benefit. (Ro 10:15)

52:8 *Eye to eye.* As clearly as when a person looks squarely into the eyes of another. (Nm 14:14)

52:10 *All the nations.* Also called "all flesh." (40:5; 49:26; 66:16, 24)

52:11 *Vessels.* Cyrus permitted the exiles to take with them "the vessels of the house of the Lord which Nebuchadnezzar had carried away from Jerusalem." (Ez 1:7)

52:15 *Not . . . in haste.* The return from the Babylonian exile, reminiscent of the deliverance from Egypt, also was quite different in many ways. (Ex 12:39; Dt 16:3)

53:1-12 FORGIVENESS ASSURED BY THE SERVANT'S SACRIFICE AND VICTORY

53:1-12 *Has believed.* When "the ransomed of the Lord" (51:11) ponder the words of the fourth and last of the "Servant Songs" (42:1 note), they feel constrained to take the shoes from their feet, for here they stand on "holy ground" (Ex 3:5) and in the holy of holies of salvation's temple. For NT believers this "vision of Isaiah" (1:1) says what they feel when in spirit they stand at the foot of Golgotha's cross: penitent sorrow for their part in the wounding of the *man of sorrows;* humble gratitude that *the Lord has laid on him the iniquity* for which they should have endured the torments of hell.

The events of Good Friday and Easter constitute such a mysterious interaction of divine justice and mercy as to raise the question in the minds of the proud and self-righteous whether *the arm of the Lord* has revealed itself in this way (1; Jn 12:38; Ro 10:16; for the phrase "the arm of the Lord" see 40:10; 51:9; 52:10; 63:12). For, judged by human standards, the Servant appeared to be the most unlikely agent of a heavenly mission, *despised and rejected by men* as He was (2-3). The mystery is solved and at the same time heightened when the reason for His ghastly torture is made known. His *griefs, sorrows,* and *stripes* are not "the due reward" of His deeds, for "this man has done nothing wrong" (Lk 23:41). *Wounded for . . . transgressions* He did not commit and *bruised for . . . iniquities* of which He was not guilty, He endured *the chastisement* and the *stripes* which fallen mankind deserved and could not escape. Because *the Lord has laid on him the iniquity of us all,* the guilty can go scot-free (4-6). While vicariously *smitten by God and afflicted* (4), the Servant *opened not his mouth* to protest the injustice of the punishment or to complain of the severity of the ordeal (Mt 26:63; Acts 8:32; 1 Ptr 2:22 f.). Nor did sympathetic crowds cheer Him on. The opposite was true. His patient and voluntary obedience to death became a burden harder to bear because the people of *his generation* failed to realize His innocence (cf. Jn 1:10 f.). Subjected by them to undeserved *oppression* and condemned in their court of *judgment* to be *cut off out of the land of the living,* He was about to receive the ignominious burial of a convicted criminal when *a rich man* named Joseph of Arimathea was allowed to provide Him an honorable resting place. (7-9; Mt 27:57-60)

After the prophet in vv. 7-9 has approved what the community of believers had to say about their redemption (1-6), he goes on to recall that the Servant made *himself an offering for sin* because *the will of the Lord* had resolved in an eternal plan to let mankind's redemption be *the fruit of the travail of his soul* (Acts 2:23; 4:28; Mt 26:24; Mk 8:31; 9:12). And as if to endorse the words of His spokesman, the Lord Himself, as in 42:1, affirms His full satisfaction with the vicarious suffering of *my servant.* Because He, *the righteous One, bore the sin of many, transgressors,* no matter how *many,* can stand in the presence of the holy God and *be accounted righteous.* Even *the great* and *the strong* of this earth will be *a portion* and *the spoil* of His victory over the powers of evil. (10-12; cf. 49:23)

53:2 *Young plant.* Not a sturdy, deeply rooted tree, but a weak sapling. God let His Son grow up in vulnerable human flesh. The Servant was indeed "a shoot from" "the root of Jesse" (11:1, 10). However, the outward kingdom of David's house had been cut down, and in the *dry ground* of the Roman empire there was no prospect of its revival.

53:4 *Our griefs.* Illness and disease are the consequences of sin. (Mt 8:16 f.; 1 Ptr 2:24)

53:7 *A lamb.* John the Baptizer called Him "the Lamb of God" (Jn 1:29, 36). See also Acts 8:32-35; 1 Ptr 1:18 f.; Rv 5:6, 8, 12, etc.

53:10 *Offering for sin.* One word in Hebrew, translated "guilt offering" in Lv 5:15 f. Its purpose in the ritual was to "make restitution" for the wrong done and thus to satisfy the demand for holiness. Because the Servant paid the full penalty incurred by the sin of the world, *his days* did not end in death. By dying and rising again He became the source of life in spiritual *offspring* without number. (1 Ptr 1:3 f., 23; 1 Jn 5:1)

53:11 *By his knowledge.* The Servant knew and did the will of God so perfectly that, for the sake of His obedience, disobedient humanity is entitled *to be accounted righteous* (Jn 17:25; Ro 5:18). It is also true that by knowing and accepting the Servant sinners are justified in God's sight. (Lk 1:77; Jn 17:3; 2 Co 4:6)

54:1—57:21 BENEFITS OF THE SERVANT'S VICARIOUS ATONEMENT

54:1-17 *Children.* The vicarious atonement, made by the Servant (ch. 53), opened the way for sons and daughters of Adam, in turn, to become *servants of the Lord* (54:17). Redeemed, forgiven, and accounted righteous by virtue of the Servant's expiation for their sins, they are designated "his offspring" (53:10). They partake of His life when they are "born anew . . . through the living and abiding word of God." (1 Ptr 1:23)

In ch. 54 this spiritual posterity is described as the children of a *barren* woman who miraculously gives birth to so many *descendants* that they overflow the boundaries of their native land. All of one and the same family, they nevertheless constitute a community composed of *the nations* (1-3). There never will be a time when the mother will have to bear the *reproach* of being a childless widow. For her *husband,* who is also her *maker,* will care for her with *compassion* and *everlasting love.* The wrath she deserved will be shortened to *a brief moment* (4-8). For as He kept His oath not to send another deluge to destroy the earth (Gn 9:8-17), so His *steadfast love* will not fail to put into effect the universal *covenant of peace* mediated by the Servant. (9-10; 42:6; 49:8)

In a final passage (11-17), the Servant's offspring is thought of as a city built of precious stones and bathed in heavenly splendor. Within its walls all its citizens have the assurance of full security against everyone who forges a *weapon* to destroy it. No one can rob them of their *heritage.* The Servant's "offspring" (53:10), here delineated in extended imagery and seen in the prophetic perspective of the completed "will of the Lord" (53:10), is the holy Christian church, the new Jerusalem composed of all the saints on earth and "built upon the foundation of the apostles and prophets, Christ Jesus himself being the cornerstone" (Eph 2:19-22; Gl 4:27). Though *afflicted* and *storm-tossed* (11), those happy to be "fellow citizens with the saints" are comforted with the vision of "the holy city Jerusalem coming down out of heaven." (Eph 2:19; Rv 21:10 ff.; 3:12)

In the foreground of this picture of the future is Israel's deliverance from the Babylonian exile. Though not mentioned by name as in 52:1, "Zion . . . the holy city," destroyed and uninhabited, is cast in the role of a woman, long *barren* and *desolate* (1; cf. 50:1). Contrary to all expectations, she will be blessed with *children,* filling her *tent* to overflowing. However, the repopulation of Judah's *desolate cities* (3) was not an end in itself but rather the means to an end. It was designed to pave the way for the spread of the Servant's "offspring" to all corners of the earth. "He shall see" spiritual sons and daughters, "born not of blood . . . nor of the will of man, but of God," constitute a "chosen race" incorporating "every tribe and tongue and people and nation." (53:10; Jn 1:13; 1 Ptr 2:9; Rv 5:9)

54:1 *Barren one.* As Sarah, childless to the age of 90 years, did not expect to give birth to an heir (Gn 17:17), so there was no prospect, according to human calculations, for Jerusalem to become alive with citizens. The promise of a child put a strain on Sarah's faith. Ch. 54 is a call to believe in the rebirth of Israel so that by it "all the families of the earth shall be blessed." (Gn 12:3)

54:3 *Possess the nations.* Not by political or military subjugation but by a conquest of people's hearts and minds. (49:7; 66:23; Gn 22:17f.; Mt 5:5)

54:4 *Shame of your youth.* The humiliation of Egyptian slavery when Israel first became a nation (Jos 5:9). The Babylonian exile was her *widowhood,* inasmuch as she, now mature, bore the *reproach* of a childless woman. (1 Sm 1:5 ff.; Gn 30:1)

54:8 *Overflowing wrath.* A momentary outburst of anger rather than an endless outpouring of wrath, the full wages of sin.

54:10 *Mountains may depart.* For other assurances of the absolute reliability of God's promises see 51:6; Ps 89:33 f.; Mt 24:35.

54:11 *Antimony.* Used by women as eye-shadow (2 K 9:30; Jer 4:30). The same word denotes one of the items stockpiled by David for the temple. (1 Ch 29:2)

54:12 *Carbuncles.* Rubies.

54:13 *Taught the Lord.* Jesus quotes these words to characterize those who become His disciples. (Jn 6:45)

54:15 *Stirs up strife.* Antagonism to the Messianic Jerusalem does not originate with God. Efforts to destroy what He has built cannot succeed (41:11-16), for every human "smith" who "produces a weapon" designed to destroy it is dependent on Him, his Creator, for each new heartbeat. For His use and control of godless powers as "the rod" of His anger see 10:5, 12.

55:1-13 *Ho . . . come.* Attendance at salvation's banquet, prepared by the Servant (ch. 53) contrary to human calculations, is not restricted to the socially and financially elite. As if He were a town crier, shouting loudly to get the attention of all citizens, God broadcasts the invitation: "Come, for all is now ready" (Lk 14:17). Everyone can afford to respond, for there is no *price* to pay for admission. Yet while it costs the guests no *money,* only this feast can offer them the kind of sustenance that their *soul may live.* Nothing else can save them from dying of spiritual hunger and thirst. No matter how much they *labor* to find their own nourishment and no matter how much they *spend* for the concoctions dished up by others, they will find out that everything produced by the hands or minds of dying mortals lacks the nourishment necessary to sustain immortal life. All of it is "food which perishes" and not "food which endures to eternal life" (Jn 6:27). This invitation to *eat what is good* is no hoax. It is guaranteed to all and for all times by *an everlasting covenant.* God pledged to keep His promise of *steadfast, sure love for David.* From "the root of Jesse" will come that Son of David who "will establish" His "throne . . . forever" (11:1-10; 9:6 f.; 2 Sm 7:12-16). His reign will embrace *the peoples*—unqualified as to number, race, or time in the world's history. He will *call nations* far beyond the borders of Israel. (1-5)

No one is forced to obey the summons. However, those who disregard it must reckon with the possibility that they have heard it for the last time (49:8; 2 Co 6:2; Jn 12:35). Furthermore, while all are invited, there is no room in the kingdom of grace for *the wicked* who refuses to *forsake his way* or for *the unrighteous man* who has *thoughts* of his own righteousness and feels insulted by God's offer to *abundantly pardon* his sins. Let no one presume to come on his own terms because he cannot comprehend God's *ways* and *thoughts* to save fallen mankind. (6-9)

Though His plan of salvation may not make sense to the self-righteous, it cannot fail to materialize. His *word,* ordering His course of action, is not an empty, meaningless sound. Once spoken, it unleashes the power necessary to *accomplish* what He has in mind as surely *as the rain and the snow* which He lets *come down from heaven* is empowered by Him to make the dry earth produce vegetation (10-11; 9:7; Ps 107:20; 147:15 ff.). Therefore Israel's going out from Babylon is not a doubtful venture. It will be an occasion of *joy* and *peace* anticipating a salvation so glorious that all of nature is summoned to rejoice. (12-13; Ps 98:7 ff.)

55:2 *Not bread.* "Man does not live by bread alone"; and water, drawn even from Jacob's well, cannot *satisfy.* (Dt 8:3; Jn 4:10-14; 6:27; Ps 42:1 f.; 63:1; Pr 9:4-6; 1 Ptr 2:2)

55:3 *Love for David.* The illustrious reign God graciously granted him was in turn a prophetic guarantee of the eternal kingdom to be established by David's Son and David's Lord, as Paul proclaimed in Acts 13:34; cf. also Ps 21:7; 89:34-37; Jer 30:9; Eze 34:23 f.

55:4 *A witness.* God's testimony *to the peoples* through Israel's king reached full clarity in "Jesus Christ the faithful witness, the firstborn of the dead, and the ruler of kings on earth." (Rv 1:5; Jn 18:37)

55:7 *Abundantly pardon.* There is no limit to God's readiness to forgive. He will *pardon* and *have mercy* on every penitent sinner no matter how much sin is "increased" (Ro 5:20). All others remain *wicked* and *unrighteous* in His sight, be they ever so respected by their fellowmen.

55:10 *Return not thither.* Before *the rain and the snow* are again drawn up into the sky as mist (Jb 36:27), they achieve the purpose for which they were sent. So God's "word" does "not return" as an "empty" echo devoid of results. It always brings about what He wanted done. (45:23; 46:10 f.; Ps 33:9; Jer 1:9 f.; Heb 4:12)

55:13 *Thorn . . . cypress.* Cf. 35:1 note.

56:1-12 *Keep justice.* According to ch. 55 nothing a person has or can do entitles him or her to attend God's banquet of salvation. Money cannot buy an invitation; exhausting labor does not open the door. The bread and the water of life are offered free of charge to all "who hunger and thirst for righteousness" (Mt 5:6; Is 55:1-5). It is possible, however, to exclude oneself from the feast of mercy and pardon. No one will be admitted who insists on doing what is "wicked" and "unrighteous" (55:7; cf. Mt 22:11-13). The first two verses of ch. 56 give positive directions for the kind of behavior by which those who accept the gift of salvation will prove the sincerity of their resolve to "return to the Lord" (55:7). Responding to undeserved mercy and goodness, they find happiness in doing what is right toward their fellowmen *(righteousness)* and toward God *(the sabbath).*

Lest prescriptions for holy living be misunderstood to mean that a sinner becomes worthy of redemption by doing good deeds, the immediately following verses (3-8) hold out the blessings of salvation to two classes of people who, according to Israel's laws, were not eligible to join the congregation in its services of worship: (a) *the eunuch* (3-5), who was declared ritually unclean because he had been emasculated by those who put him in charge of women's quarters (Dt 23:1 f.; 2 K 9:32; 2 Ch 18:8 [translated "officer"]; Jer 29:2; 38:7; Acts 8:27); (b) *the foreigners* (6-8), i.e., not members of the chosen people by birth. They were denied the right *to minister to* God in the temple and were allowed to join the worshiping congregation only after their families had been in Israel for several generations. (Ex 12:43 ff.; Dt 23:3-7)

While no one needs to fear that there are physical or racial standards which must be met in order to qualify for membership in God's family, it needs to be added at once that He will not tolerate abuse of His goodness. Membership in Israel and even holding positions of trust in this highly favored nation will not afford immunity from God's wrath. His judgment will overtake those who do not yield the fruits of repentance and instead flout His holy will. In the remaining verses of the ch. (9-12) God uses scathing language to denounce those appointed to watch over the spiritual and national welfare of His people. Israel's *watchmen* and *shepherds* have excluded themselves from the blessings of divine favor by neglect of their sacred duties, their lust for personal gain, and their surrender to the appetites of the flesh. In the next ch. the nation as a whole is indicted because it is no better than its leaders.

56:2 *The sabbath.* Observing the sabbath was a part of the sanctified life, prescribed in God's covenant with Israel. Of all ritual requirements it was singled out for special promise from the very beginning. "Throughout their generations" it was to be "a sign" of Israel's "perpetual covenant" with the Lord (Ex 31:12-17; Eze 20:11 f.; Is 58:13 f.). Breaking the sabbath was punished by stoning the culprit (Nm 15:32-36). Through Jeremiah God threatened to destroy Jerusalem for failure to "keep the sabbath day holy" (Jer 17:19-27). After the exile Nehemiah warned that "profaning the sabbath" would "bring more wrath upon Israel." (Neh 13:15-22)

56:3 *A dry tree.* A *eunuch* could not expect to have offspring of his own to perpetuate his name. Yet God promises him spiritual blessings "better than sons and daughters." (5)

56:7 *Burnt offerings and . . . sacrifices.* The worship of all peoples, here described in Old Testament forms, will be acceptable to God. For Jesus declared that the temple "shall be . . . a house of prayer for all the nations." (Mk 11:17; see also 1 K 8:41 ff.)

56:8 *Outcasts of Israel.* Cf. the notes on Is 11:11-16 and 44:5; also Jn 10:16.

56:10 *Watchmen.* Prophets were to warn Israel of spiritual dangers (Eze 33:1-9; Jer 6:17). Because they were like "dumb dogs" which do not "bark" to alert the people, "the beasts of the field" have an open invitation, as it were, to "devour" the land.

56:11 *Shepherds.* For similar denunciations of Israel's officials see Jer 23:1-4; 25:32-38; Eze 34.

57:1-21 *Perishes.* As the raucous drinking song (56:12) fades into the distance, the somber sounds of a dirge fill the air. It bemoans the death of *devout men.* Their lives were cut short (Ec 7:15) because "blind" "watchmen" and "dumb" "shepherds" (56:10 f.) were too drunk to see and too wicked to proceed against insufferable evils in society. These devastating practices were tolerated so long that *no one lays it to heart* when one *righteous man* after another *perishes* and *is taken away* (1-2). However, the absence of popular protest against a reign of unprincipled politicians indicates that the people themselves were as bad as their leaders. They are summoned to *draw near* to hear their indictment. Abuse of their fellowmen is a symptom of a deep-seated malady: a ruptured relationship with the Creator and the rejection of His laws (Pr 14:31). "They have forsaken the Lord" (1:4), the Maker of heaven and earth, preferring to worship the forces of nature with which He endowed His creation. When they indulged in "the abominable practices" for which God drove out the Canaanites before them (Dt 18:9-14; 9:4 f.), they in effect opened their *mouth wide* and stuck out their *tongue* in defiant mockery of Him who *made the breath of life* (16). One of the most degrading religions of the ancient world, baalism was a fertility cult which included such rites as sacred prostitution (male and female) and child sacrifice (3-6). The people at Isaiah's time did not lapse into this horrible idolatry only occasionally or in a moment of weakness. They were ardent devotees, living up to its prescriptions so religiously that they *wearied* themselves. Yet in their perverse zeal they did *not faint* and give up their shameful practices. (7-10)

Because the Lord *held* His *peace, even for a long time,* they did not *fear* Him. However, patient and long-suffering though He may be, He will not be mocked. Their false claim to *righteousness,* their foolish doings and their trust in a whole *collection of idols will not help* or *deliver* the wicked on the day of reckoning when *the wind will carry them off* like chaff. This prophetic word was not an empty threat. A century after it was spoken, Jerusalem was destroyed and its citizens were led into exile. Yet even these dire predictions were not the Lord's last words. Attached to them is the assurance that He will not abandon His promise to give Israel a role in His plan of universal salvation. Anyone *who takes refuge in* Him will again possess the land of promise and have the privilege to worship on the *holy mountain.* (11-13)

In order to let Israel continue to be the bearer of blessings to "all the families of the earth" (Gn 12:3), orders will be issued to "remove every obstruction" standing in His *people's way* and preventing their return to the homeland. No one will be able to countermand these directives. For He who gives them is *the high and lofty One,* untouched by the changes and ravages of time and unaffected by opposition to His holy will. At the same time, this transcendent Lord will condescend to be with anyone *who is of a contrite and humble spirit* (cf. Ps 34:18). Though He does not tolerate *iniquity,* He will not *always be angry;* rather, He will *revive the spirit of the humble and . . . the contrite* (cf. Ps 51:17). Those who were *mourners* because He *smote* them for their *iniquity* are assured that He will *requite* their penitent sorrow with the *comfort* of His pardoning grace. *The fruit of their lips* will no longer be a lament but a song of gladness and praise for the *peace* and tranquility with which He *will heal* their broken, troubled lives. However, while He offers this blessing to everyone, whether he be *far* or *near,* there are those who forego it because they insist on remaining *wicked.* Like the waves of the *tossing sea* which *cannot rest,* they are caught up in a relentless ebb and tide of pursuits producing only *mire and dirt.* (14-21)

57:2 *Enters into peace.* The perfect peace in the presence of God awaiting those *who walk in their uprightness* in "a contrite and humble spirit." (15; Ps 49:15 note; Jb 19:25 note)

57:3 *Sons . . . offspring.* Sorcery, the practice of magical arts, was strictly forbidden because spells and incantations, in effect, presume to coerce God and to repudiate His lordship over human life (Ex 22:18 note; Lv 19:26; 20:6, 27; Dt

18:9-12). Adultery and harlotry, despicable crimes when committed physically, described the spiritual degeneracy of Israel's union with idols (Hos 1—3; Jer 3:1-3; Eze 16:1-52). The people, guilty of these crimes, have a depraved nature. They are called also "children of transgression, the offspring of deceit" (4) and "offspring of evildoers." (1:4)

57:5 *Burn with lust.* Israel's spiritual adultery expressed itself in the lascivious rites of the Canaanite fertility cult. During the reign of King Manasseh, which ended less than 40 years before the fall of Jerusalem, it was practiced with unchecked abandon (2 K 21:1-17). For the reference to *oaks* see 1:29 note; for the phrase *under every green tree* see Dt 12:2; for *burn* see 2 K 16:3 note; 23:10 note.

57:6 *Smooth stones.* Upright stones, worn smooth by brooks which flowed when fed by rains, were heathen cult objects (Gn 28:18 note). Idolators foolishly gave up the living Lord for an inanimate rock as their *portion* and *lot.* (61:7; Ps 16:5 f.; 73:26; 119:57; 142:5)

57:8 *Set up your symbol.* Instead of putting the prescribed words of allegiance to the Lord on the doorposts (Dt 6:9 note), they placed an inscription or a figure within their homes that dedicated them and their occupants to an idol.

Looked on nakedness. Lit. "gazed at a hand." In a context of lewd acts, "hand" may be a euphemistic term for the male organ. (Eze 23:20)

57:9 *Molech.* Cf. Lv 18:21 note.

Sheol. Cf. 28:15 note; Dt 32:22 note.

57:15 *High and lofty One.* Cf. 40:22; 66:1; 1 Ti 6:15 f.

57:17 *Covetousness.* The root *iniquity* of Israel's *backsliding* was materialism, "the love of money." (1 Ti 6:10; 1 Sm 8:3; Ps 119:36; Is 33:15; 56:11; Jer 22:17)

57:19 *Far . . . near.* See 43:5-7 introd. note; 44:5 note; ch. 49 introd. note.

57:21 *No peace.* This verse is almost identical with 48:22.

58:1—66:24 The Way to Glory

58:1—59:21 OPEN TO ALL WHO WALK THE WAY OF REPENTANCE AND FAITH

The way to glory is not the high road of human attainments leading to ever higher plateaus of moral perfection; not a path to a social and economic paradise charted and paved by a more enlightened mind and by a growing sense of ethical responsibility. Left to their own devices, all sons and daughters of Adam cannot help themselves from rushing headlong down "the way . . . that leads to destruction" (Mt 7:13). If there is to be a way to glory, God must provide it. And He did, says Isaiah. He rescued the captives of sin, unable to pay its wages of death or to produce the ransom for their release. The way to glory is constructed on the solid roadbed of God's redemptive mercy and power to save His fallen creatures (chs. 40—48). They can walk the way to glory because they do not have to suffer the penalty of their rebellion against their Creator. The Servant, His own Son, paid it for them by suffering and dying in their stead (chs. 49—57). The way to glory, open to all who repent and accept the vicarious atonement for their sins, stretches far into the future. It extends from Israel's triumph over national extinction in the Babylonian exile into the era of a new covenant. It gives access to the priceless blessings of the Messiah's spiritual kingdom. It leads to vistas under "new heavens" and on "a new earth" (65:17; 66:22). It brings into view "the glory that is to be revealed" after "the sufferings of this present time" have passed. (Ro 8:18)

In "the vision of Isaiah" (1:1) this way "from one degree of glory to another" (2 Co 3:18) stands complete before the seer's mind. Prophetic perspective enables his gaze to range back and forth unhampered by the dimensions of time or place. Scenes of the immediate future and the end of time alternate and merge with one another. For the benefit of his contemporaries he describes distant scenes of glory in terms and concepts they could understand. Israel's liberation from Babylonian bondage, though itself only a promise at the time, provides the words and the coloring to depict mankind's emancipation from the slavery of sin. Jerusalem envisioned as rebuilt and the Promised Land again populated and prosperous serve as types for the founding and expansion of a new Israel after the Spirit, gathered from all nations. The descriptions of the blessings to be enjoyed by the citizens of an international Zion have the contours of the resources and the grandeur of an earthly empire extending from Jerusalem to the ends of the earth. The resumption of peaceful relations with the Creator is portrayed as the return of the harmony and bliss which once prevailed in the Garden of Eden. (For a similar use of ancient history and institutions as a preview and shadow of greater things to come see the notes on 2:2 and 11:6, and the introd. remarks to ch. 40.)

The reader may be puzzled to find the promises of a glorious future, recorded in the closing chs. of the book, interspersed with harsh denunciations of sin and dire threats of judgment. Condemnation of ungodly behavior may seem to be out of place amidst assurances of salvation. However, God knows how necessary the unremitting preaching of Law and Gospel is because the human "heart is deceitful above all things and desperately corrupt" (Jer 17:9). By nature it has the perverse tendency to respond to God in two diametrically opposite ways. It either sinks into dull despair or it is puffed up with overweening pride. The Book of Isaiah is intended to counteract both of these extremes. Words of comfort and encouragement are repeated so often as to appear monotonous (cf. 45:1 note). At the same time, stern warnings are sounded again and again against the delusion that God will be merciful to those who willfully flout His holy will. It cannot be said often enough, especially when describing the blessings of His kingdom, what the last verses of the previous chapter summarized in one sentence: "There is no peace . . . for the wicked" (cf. also 48:22). In support of this declaration two facts are stressed: (a) it is an insult to God's redemptive grace if people pretend to honor Him by going through outward forms of worship while they remain wicked at heart and in their lives; (b) God's goodness cannot be trampled underfoot with impunity. Not peace but outer darkness and gnashing of teeth await those who follow the impulses of their wicked heart.

58:1-14 In ch. 58 the prophet is instructed to *cry aloud* against hypocritical observance of two religious rites: (a) For people *to draw near to God* by fasting and prayer while they sneer at His command not to exploit their fellowmen is an abomination to Him and will not cause their *voice to be heard on high.* If, however, they abstain from food and humble themselves in *sackcloth and ashes* to prove the sincerity of their devotion to God, they will not refuse to undo the *wickedness* done to *the oppressed . . . the hungry . . . the homeless . . . the naked* (1-7). Then *the Lord will answer* and pour out streams of blessings on them (8-12). (b) The same holds true of the way the sabbath is observed. (13-14)

58:2 *Seek me.* Cf. 1:11 note; Hos 6:6.

58:3 *Fasted.* Refraining from eating was to give outward expression and demonstration of inner grief or heartfelt penitence. It was part of the ritual prescribed for the day of atonement (Lv 16:29-31; 23:27-32). Individuals or the whole community chose to fast at other times when they felt the need to "afflict" themselves. (Lv 16:29; 2 Sm 12:22; Ps 69:10; Jl 1:14; cf. also Zch 8:19)

Your own pleasure. What was to be an occasion for self-denial became an opportunity for self-advancement at the expense of others.

58:4 *Quarrel.* Fasting only put them in an ugly mood.

58:5 *Bow down.* Cf. Jesus' words about "practicing . . . piety before men in order to be seen by them." (Mt 6:1, 16-18)

58:7 *Your own flesh.* People having the same parents or ancestors. (Gn 29:14; 37:27; 2 Sm 5:1)

58:8 *Then.* Repeated in 9 and 10. When the sincerity of their allegiance to God is evident in abstaining from mistreating their fellowmen, He will lead and protect them as He did on their trek to Canaan from Egypt. (Ex 14:19; Is 52:12 note)

58:12 *Rebuilt.* The city of Jerusalem was to lie in *ruins* for *many generations.* It would be rebuilt because God would be moved to resume His plan of universal salvation through a penitent remnant of the chosen people.

58:13 *The sabbath.* Cf. 56:2 note.

58:14 *Heritage of Jacob.* Cf. Gn 28:13 second note.

59:1-21 Isaiah adds another ch. on the theme announced in 57:21 and developed in ch. 58: "There is no peace . . . for the wicked." It should be self-evident that communion with God is possible only for *those . . . who turn from transgression* (20) and that "the unrighteous will not inherit the kingdom" (1 Co 6:9). However, the prophet is not beating a dead horse. Human nature is irrational in its defiance of the Creator. It even attempts to bully Him into tolerating the most repugnant criminal behavior in His very presence. Israel's experience is an object lesson. What happened was "written down for our instruction . . . not to desire evil as they did" (1 Co 10:6, 11). God chose the descendants of Abraham to play a significant role in His plan to blaze a way to glory for mankind, helplessly swept along on a course to everlasting shame and disgrace (cf. introductory note to chs. 58—66). Isaiah foresaw that it would be impossible for God to move forward through history on a straight road to His goal. Israel's behavior necessitated a detour. It refused to be "a kingdom of priests and a holy nation" (Ex 19:6). Instead corruption and crimes flourished with such brazen, unchecked abandon as to make their partnership with God impossible. Their *iniquities . . . made a separation between* Him and them as fixed and impenetrable as the firmament created between the waters under and above it. (1-8; Gn 1:6)

Without God in their midst, their doom was sealed. It was not long before Jerusalem was destroyed and its inhabitants carried off into exile by a heathen king. However, God's plan of salvation was not to dead-end in Babylonia. The rod of His anger bruised deeply. Isaiah heard the enslaved, crushed people *moaning like doves* in the *gloom* of their despair. Nevertheless, the hard blow of affliction was also to have a salutary effect. Throwing themselves unreservedly on God's mercy, the chastened survivors acknowledged their guilt and made a full confession of the wrongs done to God and their fellowmen. (9-15a)

Isaiah reports as past events what God would do to carry out His plan of universal salvation (cf. the past tenses in ch. 53). When *he saw . . . that there was no one to intervene* and set His people free, He Himself did battle with their enemies. Prophetic vision enabled Isaiah to look beyond events which were to happen some 2 centuries later. Israel's redemption from Babylonian slavery was to initiate a program to extend God's reign to the end of time. All enemies of His kingdom go down in defeat so that His *name* and *glory* can be honored in *the coastlands,* in *the west* and in *the rising of the sun.* The *Redeemer of Zion* pledges Himself in a solemn *covenant* to sustain with His *spirit* and *words* those *who turn from transgression . . . from this time forth and forevermore.* (15b-21)

59:3 *Hands . . . lips.* Human nature is so depraved and insolent that the bodily members which are used to "make many prayers" (1:15) are also the instruments of murder and deceit.

59:5 *Adders' eggs . . . spider's web.* Two comparisons taken from the world of animals describe these monsters of iniquity. They are a "brood of vipers" (Mt 3:7). Their machinations are like a net spun by a spider which is designed to catch other insects and has no constructive purpose.

59:7 *Feet.* Cf. Paul's use of vv. 7 f. in Ro 3:15 ff.

59:9 *Justice . . . righteousness.* God's people expect Him to act in judgment on evildoers and to bring "salvation" (11, 17) to those who appeal to Him. In v. 14 this pair of nouns denotes the principles which are to govern the administration of justice in human courts of law. In Israel cases were heard "in the public squares."

59:16 *Wondered.* God is described as a person looking in vain for someone to solve a serious problem. In the following verses He is cast in the role of an ancient warrrior preparing himself for battle. Eph 6:13-17 speaks of the believer's equipment for spiritual warfare.

59:17 *Fury.* Frequently translated "zeal," the Hebrew word denotes ardor prompted by jealousy. (9:7 note)

59:20 *Redeemer.* This title for God occurs frequently (41:14; cf. 13:1, 4). For its meaning see Jb 19:25 second note.

To Zion . . . in Jacob. In Ro 11:26-27 Paul quotes vv. 20 f. according to the ancient Greek translation, called the Septuagint. Reading "from Zion" and "from Jacob," this version retains the intent of the prophetic passage and stresses its scope. Through the restoration of physical Zion and the redemption of the bodily descendants of Jacob it was to come about that "salvation is from the Jews" (Jn 4:22). And from this one nation the "good tidings" of "peace" (52:7) were to be published for the salvation of "all Israel" (Ro 11:26), a spiritual commonwealth of nations made up of Jewish and Gentile believers and called the church. The next chs. of Isaiah develop the theme of bright and glorious things to come.

60:1—63:6 THE WAY OUT OF DARKNESS TO THE LIGHT OF GLORY

60:1-22 The way to glory is the transfiguration of mankind's gloom and despair into the radiance of salvation which God, out of His great mercy, shined into a world of sinners doomed to a death-march into "outer darkness" (Mt 22:13). In the two previous chs. Isaiah declared "the way of peace" (59:8) barred to all who choose to love wickedness more than the Redeemer. In ch. 60 the road out of estrangement with the Creator to blessed communion with Him is bathed in "the light of the knowledge of the glory of God in the face of Christ" (2 Co 4:6). Unlike rays from man-made illuminating devices, the beams of prophecy grow brighter the farther they shine into distant eons until they are absorbed into the bright hues of heavenly brilliance, the *everlasting light* which will replace the *sun* and *moon* (19). This highway of lights is to emerge, after a brief detour, out of Israel's liberation from Babylonian slavery and the rebuilding of the city of David. At the same time these events, real and needed though they were to be, serve Isaiah like a prism in which the rays of divine glory are refracted into the iridescent splendor of the Messianic kingdom to be revealed *in its time* (22). What was to happen in Israel in the sixth century BC is more than history; it, in turn, is the promise and shadow of greater things to come. (Cf. the introd. remarks to chs. 58—66)

Jerusalem can arise out of the shadow of death only because *light has come* to it *and the glory of the Lord has risen upon* it from beyond its wretched plight. So *darkness shall cover the earth and gross darkness the peoples* until "the sun of righteousness shall rise with healing in its wings" (Ml 4:2). And it did. It shone in midday brightness in "the light of the world" who brought "the light of life." (1-3; Jn 8:12)

Jerusalem, to be rebuilt, *shall thrill and rejoice* as it again becomes the national home of its citizenry, dispersed into foreign lands by wars and invasion. However, the city built of stones and mortar after the exile is to be a pledge in miniature of "the heavenly Jerusalem" (Heb 12:22). For this spiritual community is to be "a light to the nations . . . to the end of the earth" (49:6 note). "A city set on a hill" (Mt 5:14), it will attract to its peace and bliss not only the sons and daughters of Abraham but also uncounted throngs from every nation under the sun. Delighted and grateful to share in its blessings, its spiritual citizens will freely offer the *gold and frankincense* of their devotion. (4-9)

Through the Babylonian captivity God in His wrath smote Israel. Jerusalem did not deserve to be rebuilt. Nevertheless, because God had mercy on the penitent people, there was to be again *the City of the Lord* and *the Zion of the Holy One of Israel.* At God's direction foreigners such as Cyrus, the Persian king, will contribute to its rehabilitation. These mighty acts of God are not an end in themselves. They furnish Isaiah the prophetic coloring and design of the founding of a spiritual Jerusalem, rebuit by the mercy of God out of the wreckage of a sin-cursed world. Composed of living stones, the communion of saints will be the center around which the rise and fall of nations will revolve. Lords of this earth, even some who for a time *oppressed* "the city of the living God" (Heb 12:22), will *come bending low,* humbly seeking entrance and contributing to its welfare. Its *gates shall be open continually* to admit anyone who wants to share in the priceless *peace* within its walls. (10-18)

Jerusalem rebuilt after the Babylonian exile was a significant milestone on God's way to shed the light of His glory on His benighted creatures; but when all earthly cities like Jerusalem will pass away, when "the sun will be darkened and the moon will not give its light," He will be the everlasting light in "the holy city, new Jerusalem, coming down out of heaven" (Mt 24:29; Rv 21:2; 22:5). Its residents will swell to a multitude, "numbering myriads of myriads and thousands of thousands" (19-22; Rv 5:12). The opening verses of this chapter serve as the epistle lesson on the Feast of the Epiphany of our Lord.

60:1 *The glory of the Lord.* For flashes of its light in previous chs. see 4:5; 9:2; 24:23; 30:26; 40:5, 9-11; 46:13; 49:14-21; 51:3; 52:7-10; 54:11-17.

60:4 *From afar.* For the worldwide pilgrimage to Zion see 2:2 notes; 11:1-16 note; 49:18; 55:5; 66:18.

60:6 *Midian and Ephah.* The nations mentioned here and in v. 7 have ancestral ties with Israel. (Gn 25:2 note, 4, 13; 1 K 10:1 note; Gn 10:7; Ps 120:5 note; Is 21:13 note; 42:11)

60:7 *Rams . . . on my altar.* Worship is expressed in terms of sacrifices, required by the law of Moses but abrogated in the new covenant.

60:9 *Coastlands.* Delivered from the power of darkness, the redeemed of the Lord will come by land and sea, from the east (6 f.) and the islands of the west (11:11 note), bringing tributes of gratitude on camels and on ships "that fly like a cloud" (8). For *Tarshish* see 1 K 10:22 note.

60:12 *Shall perish.* "This is the judgment, that the light has come into the world and men love darkness rather than light." (Jn 3:19; Is 2:11, 17; 13:11; Zch 14:17)

60:13 *Place of my feet.* Cf. Ps 99:5 note; 132:7.

60:16 *Suck the milk.* "The affluence" of the nations (Dt 33:19) will nourish and sustain the worshipers in God's "glorious house." (Vv. 6 f.; 49:23)

60:17 *Overseers . . . taskmasters.* In the city, protected by walls of "Salvation" and entered through gates of "Praise" (18), *peace* and *righteousness* will replace oppression and violence.

61:1-11 The glory to be revealed in the Messianic age is announced by a Messenger, anointed with *the Spirit of . . . God.* His proclamation is not empty cant. He not only has prophetic authority to speak for God (Mi 3:8; 1 K 19:16), but He Himself made the promise come true (Lk 4:18 f.; cf. also Ps 45 notes; Acts 4:27; 10:38; Heb 1:9). What He did is identical with the mission assigned to the Servant and successfully carried out by Him (42:7; 49:8. f; 53:5; 42:1 second note). It is mankind's redemption from sin and its dire consequences. Israel's deliverance from national extinction in Babylon again serves as predictive analogy of the worldwide release of all prisoners languishing hopelessly under sentence of eternal death (cf. 60:1-22 note). The *good tidings* (cf. 52:7), extravagant and utopian when restricted to Israel after the flesh, do not exaggerate the priceless treasures of restored communion with God, promised to Israel after the spirit. Because "the peace of God . . . passes all understanding" (Ph 4:7), human language must resort to comparisons and figures of speech drawn from external experiences and concrete situations as it attempts to describe the internal bliss of "rest for . . . souls." (Mt 11:28 ff.)

Without a formal introduction (cf. ch. 49), the Messenger proclaims the good news of *the Lord's favor* and its liberating, gladdening effects (1-7). In vv. 8-9 the Lord, as it were, affixes His name to the emancipation proclamation in *an everlasting covenant* (cf. 55:3; 59:21). In vv. 10-11 the beneficiaries of the edict are moved to exult over *garments of salvation* and *the robe of righteousness,* to be theirs as surely as the earth lets vegetation grow at the Lord's direction.

61:2 *Vengeance of our God.* Jesus did not include this aspect of the prophecy when, in Nazareth, He declared "this scripture . . . fulfilled" in His person. Final judgment on the wicked and simultaneous vindication of the righteous are to take place when He will be seen "coming on the clouds of heaven with power and great glory." (Mt 24:30; cf. also Is 34:8 note)

61:3 *Oaks of righteousness.* The redeemed of the Lord, rooted by faith in His promises, are "like a tree . . . that yields its fruit in its season and its leaf does not wither" even in the scorching blasts of life. (Ps 1:3; Is 60:21)

61:5-6 *Aliens . . . foreigners.* "The City of the Lord," protected by "walls" of "Salvation" and entered by "gates" of "Praise," is a spiritual commonwealth (60:14, 18). Its citizenry includes converts to faith in Jesus Christ, hailing from every nation under the sun. Having become "fellow citizens with the saints" (Eph 2:19), they willingly dedicate their labors and their riches to the common good of "the household of faith" (Gl 6:10; Is 60:21; Ro 15:27). The mediating services of the tribe of Levi will no longer be needed. All the people of God will be *priests of the Lord,* consecrated to offer themselves as "living sacrifices" and authorized to teach all nations the way of salvation. (Ro 12:1; 2 Co 2:15; Mt 28:19 f.)

61:7 *Double portion.* Cf. 40:2 note; 54:4.

61:9 *Their descendants.* The promise made to Abraham will be fulfilled. (Gn 12:3)

62:1-12 The light of salvation (ch. 60) shines its cheering, liberating beams into the dismal prisonhouse of sin (ch. 61). In the "thick darkness" of Satan's dungeon the eyes of his captives, blinded by a film of unbelief and despair, do not see "the glory of the Lord" (60:1 f.; cf. 2 Co 3:14-16). Infinitely kind, the Lord does more than to say: "Let there be light" in the night of mankind's hopelessness. He stands ready to grant also the vision of faith, enabling the blind prisoners to see the door to liberty unbarred. Ch. 62 is proof of His willingness to send His enlightening Word into the benighted souls of people again and again (cf. e.g., 51:1—52:12 for a similar message). As in previous chs. the way to glory is presented as leading via Israel's release from the Babylonian exile to a salvation *proclaimed to the end of the earth* (11). The reversal of fate from extinction to national independence in the Promised Land furnishes the color scheme on the prophetic canvas portraying the world's rescue from Satan's dominion and revealing the blissful state of a restored communion with God. The envisioned scene is a panoramic view of a new Jerusalem. Its walls of salvation encircle the entire globe. Citizenship is not restricted by human distinctions. "There is neither Jew nor Greek . . . slave nor free . . . male nor female" but all are "one in Christ Jesus . . . Abraham's offspring, heirs according to promise." (Gl 3:28 f.; Ro 10:12)

Through His inspired spokesman God addresses words of comfort to all "looking for the consolation of Israel" (Lk 2:25). He assures them He will not give up on His plan of salvation. He *will not rest* until He has provided *vindication* for those rejected and disgraced for their sins. Adulterous and vile, *the daughter of Zion* (11) deserves to *be termed Forsaken* and *Desolate*. But when His promised *salvation . . . goes forth,* her name will be Hephzibah *(My delight is in her)* and Beulah *(Married)* (1-5). He will *set watchmen* on Jerusalem's *walls*. They are to keep the inhabitants alert to foes eager to invade and harm them and, at the same time, to give *the Lord . . . no rest,* putting Him *in remembrance* of His *sworn* promise to protect them against their *enemies* (6-9). All that is necessary to be *the redeemed of the Lord* is to act on His promises and to *go through the gates* of *salvation* open to *the peoples,* wherever they may come from. (10-12)

62:2 *Vindication.* The Hebrew word, translated "righteousness" in 58:8, denotes a quality or condition which is unattainable unless God provides it (54:17). Zion becomes "the city of righteousness" (1:26) only because *the mouth of the Lord will give* it this new name.

62:4 *Forsaken . . . Desolate.* If God had not taken pity on His fallen creatures, their fate would have been like that of an unfaithful wife, abandoned by her husband to live out her days amid the ruins of her wrecked life. However, the Servant lived and died to effect a reconciliation. Because "the Lord . . . laid on Him the iniquity" (53:6) of all spiritual adulterers, they can again become worthy of a relationship to their Maker as intimate and holy as the marriage bond. (Cf. 50:1-11 notes; 54:4)

62:5 *Sons marry you.* The Hebrew verb used here has the etymological meaning to take possession of a woman in marriage. This idiomatic connotation, lost in translation, says in effect: There will be surviving sons of Israel who again will claim Zion and the Promised Land as their rightful possession.

62:6 *Watchmen.* Prophets, sent by God to be spiritual guardians of Israel's destiny and also intercessors in the nation's behalf, are said to stand "upon a watchtower" as they carry out their commission. (21:8, 11-12; 52:8; Jer 4:17; Eze 3:17; cf. also Is 56:10)

62:10 *Through the gates.* In order to benefit from the proffered salvation, the liberated slaves must believe that they are free to escape through the opened prison doors (48:20 note; 52:11). The way to freedom, however, is not restricted to only a few. It is to be made a *highway* for *the peoples* responding to the Lord's proclamation *to the end of the earth* and marching under the *ensign* or banner of "the root of Jesse." (11:10; 49:22 note; cf. also 40:3 ff.)

62:11 *Reward . . . recompense.* Cf. 40:10 note.

63:1-6 When from "the end of the earth" "nations shall come" to "Zion," "the city of the Lord," on which "the glory of the Lord has arisen," they need not fear the loss of the "liberty" and "gladness" it provides even though its "gates shall be open . . . day and night" (60:1-3, 11; 61:1-3; 62:11). Vv. 1-6 of ch. 63 assure "the holy people, the redeemed of the Lord," that no enemy is able to rob them of their "salvation" because their redemption would simultaneously usher in *the day of vengeance* on all hostile, demonic foes (62:11 f.; 59:17; 61:2). As Israel's rescue from Babylon's clutch and the restoration of Jerusalem initiate and at the same time symbolize what the Creator would do to allow His estranged and enslaved creatures again to become citizens in His kingdom, so ancient *Edom,* Israel's inveterate enemy, is the figurative epitome of forces aligned against God and His people (cf. notes on ch. 34). The battle is over, the Victor returns, *marching in the greatness of His strength.* Asked who He is and why He has crimsoned garments, He answers that as one *that treads in the wine press* is spattered with the juice of the grapes, so His *apparel* is stained with the lifeblood of His defeated antagonists. He had to destroy them *alone.* There was *no one* to help Him because no one else had the kind of weapons necessary for this fray. The decisive battle took place on Golgotha (Jn 12:31 f.; 16:11; cf. the Easter hymn by Thomas Kelly, *The Lutheran Hymnal* 209.) The final execution of judgment will come when the *peoples* and kingdoms of this world will appear before the throne of the ascended Lord. (Rv 14:18-20; 19:13; Jl 3:13)

63:2 *Red.* The Hebrew word Edom, when supplied with different vowels, spells the adjective "red."

63:4 *Vengeance.* Cf. 34:8 note; 61:2 note.

63:5 *I looked.* For the same observation see 59:16.

63:7—64:12 A PLEA FOR RESTORATION

63:7—64:12 God has opened a way out of mankind's darkness to the light of His glory. It is a freeway in every sense of the term. "An ensign over the peoples" (62:10) beckons all alike to seek access to it. There is no toll to pay for its construction or use. Everything has been done to "clear it of stones" (62:10) which might prove a hazard to the traveler. No one will be waylaid. All highway robbers are defeated and dead, drained of their very "lifeblood" (63:6). Strangely enough, many refuse to take the open road to salvation, preferring to stay on "the way . . . that leads to destruction" (Mt 7:13). Equally baffling is the folly of many who, once on "the way . . . that leads to life" (Mt 7:14), turn from it, beguiled by the false swamp lights of self-determination. Misled to think they are wise enough to find and to strike out on a path to happiness of their own devising, they fancy themselves free to follow their own instincts. But to their dismay they will discover that every way of life not paved by the forgiving mercy of their Creator and not hedged by His directives ends in "outer darkness" where "men will weep and gnash their teeth." (Mt 8:12)

Isaiah devotes the remainder of his book to correct two misconceptions his hearers and readers are prone to harbor about the way God wants to lead them to glory. It is a fatal mistake, on the one hand, to think they can "go limping with two different opinions" (1 K 18:21), to walk with God with one foot and with the other to stalk through the open sewer of sin. It is just as big a mistake, on the other hand, on the part of those who have strayed from the path of righteousness to doubt God's willingness to take them back if they repent and plead for mercy. Isaiah had to set Israel straight on both counts. He foretold certain disaster for a "sinful nation, a people laden with iniquity" and so depraved as to dare to lift "hands . . . full of blood" to the Lord in a pose of prayer (1:4, 15). A century and a half later the Babylonian army carried them off into exile. The prophet foresaw also how quickly arrogance and impudence can turn into hopelessness and despair under heavy blows of chastening. Instead of lecturing the grief-stricken people on the just and holy will of God, Isaiah leads them in a prayer based on faith in the promise that though their "sins are like scarlet, they shall be as white as snow." (1:18)

Speaking in behalf of his people but also as one of them, the prophet casts his intercession in the form of a psalm which praises the Lord for *the great goodness to the house of Israel* from the very beginning (7-9; cf. Ps 89; 111; 145—150). Though they soon *rebelled and grieved his holy Spirit,* the Spirit of the Lord gave them rest in the Promised Land, making for Himself *a glorious name* (10-14). Encouraged by the record of God's willingness to bear with His erring people in the past, the petitioner makes bold to ask that the same divine *zeal, might,* and *compassion* come to their rescue again. Unless God does so, it will appear that His *servants,* a faithful remnant, trusted His promises in vain. (15-19; 65:8 f.)

The suppliant continues his wrestling with God in the next ch. In vv. 1-4 he asserts his conviction that if God would only *rend the heavens and come down,* He could overcome all opposition because even *the mountains quaked at* His *presence* (Ex 19:18). However, the salvation of His people is an act of pure grace. Because they all *sinned* and their *righteous deeds are like a polluted garment,* they deserve to *fade like a leaf* which the *wind* sweeps away (64:5-7). They can only plead that God will *remember not iniquity forever* and hope that He will not *afflict* them more than He has. (64:8-12)

63:8 *Sons.* They disappointed the Lord. Showered with favors, they nevertheless rebelled against Him. (10; 1:2)

63:9 *He was afflicted.* This translation accepts an ancient correction of the Hebrew text (cf. RSV note). It expresses the comforting fact that God is not a heartless, sadistic tyrant. It does not afford Him pleasure when He must inflict affliction, but He feels its pain in His own heart. In Jesus Christ we have "a high priest" who is able "to sympathize with our weaknesses." (Heb 4:15)

Angel of his presence. Cf. Ex 23:20 note.

63:10 *Grieved.* Cf. Paul's warning. (Eph 4:30)

63:15 *Zeal.* Cf. 9:7 note; 42:13 note.

63:16 *Our Father.* A prayer using this term for God is a humble confession of dependence and a fervent appeal for help. As children need a father to come into being, so Israel owes its existence as a nation to the Lord (Ex 4:22 f.; Hos 1:1); as children must rely on their father to keep them alive, so Israel pleads with the Lord to be their Redeemer. Though their physical ancestors, the patriarchs, are dead and gone, the Lord's fatherly love and power to redeem are constant through the ages.

63:17 *Make us err.* The importunity of the supplication grows so daring as to complain that God is treating His people as if their perverse, obdurate resistance to His mercy has provoked Him to *harden* their *heart* as He did Pharaoh's. (Ex 4:21 note; Ro 1:24, 26, 28)

63:18 *A little while.* If the sanctuary is to remain destroyed forever, the period during which Israel worshiped in it was short indeed.

See the introductory notes on 63:7—64:12 for the connection of this ch. with ch. 63.

64:1-2 *Rend the heavens.* God appears to have withdrawn His presence from the people crushed by adversity and bereft of hope. They feel that to see their plight, He must "look down from heaven" (63:15); to help them, He must *come down* out of His distant seclusion. However, there is no doubt in their minds what His intervention in their behalf can accomplish. *Mountains* will *quake* and *nations* will *tremble* as surely as *fire kindles brushwood and . . . causes water to boil.*

64:4 *No eye has seen.* Paul uses this verse to marvel at the incomprehensible wisdom "God has revealed" in the Gospel of salvation. (1 Co 2:9 f.)

64:5 *Thou meetest.* To bless.

Be saved. Whether translated as a statement (KJV), a question, or a wish (cf. RSV note), the last clause of this verse points to the underlying cause of all distress: *We sinned.*

64:7 *Delivered us.* More literally: "Thou hast melted us by reason of our sins" as wax disintegrates before a flame.

64:8 *Our Father.* Cf. 63:16 note.

Potter. God created and shaped the destiny of the chosen people as an artisan fashions clay into a crock. (29:16 note)

64:10 *Wilderness . . . desolation.* Isaiah foretold the destruction of the *cities* of the holy nation (Ex 19:6) and of their "holy and beautiful house" of worship (5:5 ff.; 6:11). Foreseeing too what effect this catastrophe will have on the people, he anticipates their need of the comforting message of forgiveness. Though they have every reason to expect national extinction, He assures them there is hope for survival and restoration if they humbly and penitently ask the Lord to "restrain" Himself and not to "afflict" them more "sorely" (12). However, Isaiah's words were designed to benefit not only the exiles in Babylonia more than a hundred years after his death. They were "written" for the "instruction" also of people laid low by adversities to "the end of the ages" in order that they "might have hope." (1 Co 10:11-13; Ro 15:4)

65:1—66:24 GOD'S ANSWER: THE COMING GLORY

65:1-25 The last two chs. of the book constitute the Lord's answer to the cry out of the depths recorded in 63:7—64:12. His message is marked by sharp distinctions. He gives renewed assurances of redemption to those who *have sought* Him (10); He repeats the threats of judgment He will inflict on *those who did not seek* Him (1). See the introductory note to ch. 58 for (1) the reason why both Law and Gospel are proclaimed so often; (2) the vision of world history to its consummation; (3) Israel's redemption from Babylonian servitude in this grand view of the future.

God declares what moves Him to violent anger. It *burns all the day* when He sees how a rebellious people deliberately choose to *walk in a way that is not good.* For, ignoring His persistent pleas for undivided allegiance to Him, they *provoke* Him by giving the honor due Him alone to idols of their own choosing (1-7). However, there are also some "that have not bowed to Baal" (1 K 19:18). For these *servants' sake,* He will *not destroy them all* (cf. Gn 18:26 ff.). Rescued out of the doomed mass of perdition, they will escape into the promised land of God's never-changing favor. Lest those *who forsake the Lord* presume to think that they can insult Him and somehow also share in the promised bliss, He hastens to add in the same breath how fearful their punishment will be (8-12). In order to encourage the obedient servants to remain faithful and to warn the disobedient of the horrors awaiting them, the Lord once more depicts the joy and the misery which will result when He "separates the sheep from the goats." (13-16; Mt 25:31 ff.)

From the rebuilding of Jerusalem by the liberated Babylonian exiles the way to glory soars to a *Jerusalem* not built by human hands but which God will *create.* In it will be room for uncounted myriads to *be glad and rejoice forever.* It will not have a geographic location in this world, for the Lord will *create new heavens and a new earth.* Human thought and imagination, strained to their limits, cannot comprehend or express what mortals can expect to find in paradise regained. If they are to have some inkling of what awaits them there, sacred writers resort to negatives, saying what *no more shall be heard in it* and what *no more shall . . . be in it.* The *former things* which made mundane existence sad and painful will not even *come into mind.* Time will not have an aging effect; no longer will anyone *labor in vain;* children will not be born to die; hostile animals will not *hurt or destroy.* (17-25; cf. Rv 21:1-4; 2 Ptr 3:11-13)

65:1-2 *A rebellious people.* Quoting parts of these verses from the ancient Greek translation called the Septuagint, Paul widens the scope of their application (Ro 10:20 f.). When Israel of old turned a deaf ear to the Lord's repeated calls to faithfulness, insisting instead on following their own devices, they, the chosen people, sank to the level of the heathen who likewise *did not seek* Him. After the Jews of Paul's day rejected the Gospel, the time had come for him to "turn to the Gentiles" who previously *did not ask for* the Lord. (Acts 13:46)

65:3 *In gardens.* Cf. 1:29 note; 17:10 note; 66:17. Isaiah lashes out at pagan rites and forms of divination of which Israel was guilty from the days of their fathers (7; see, e.g., Ju 2:11 ff.). Under King Manasseh, Hezekiah's successor, sacrileges of the grossest kind were the order of the day. The indictment of these detestible practices described in this and the following ch. is too vivid, concrete, and detailed to warrant the view that they are but a figurative condemnation of insincere formal worship. God did "not keep silent" (6). He let the Babylonians destroy the unfaithful nation. After the exile the prophets did not find it necessary to accuse their contemporaries of lapsing into "their former doings" (7), though they were called to upbraid them for other wrongs.

65:4 *Sit in tombs.* For the purpose of engaging in occult forms of divination such as consulting the dead (cf. 8:19). For the prohibition against eating *swine's flesh* see Dt 14:8; Lv 11:2 note.

65:5 *Set apart.* Claiming to be holy by their contact with divine powers, they arrogantly regard themselves charged with supernatural forces which could prove hurtful to the uninitiated.

65:8 *Do not destroy.* Cf. Ps 57:1-11 note for the use of these words to prescribe the musical rendition of Pss 57—59. Apparently the title of a well-known vintage song is meant (cf. 16:10). The owner of the vineyard is told not to discard an entire cluster of grapes if some of them are dried up or rotten, because there are enough good ones left to produce excellent wine. So, says Isaiah, the Lord will not cast out the whole nation and *destroy them all,* because there still are faithful *servants* in its midst through whom He can achieve the purpose for which He created the chosen people.

65:10 *Sharon . . . Achor.* For these sites, one on the western and the other on the eastern border of the Promised Land see 33:9 note; SS 2:1 note; Jos 7:24 note; Hos 2:15.

65:11 *Fortune . . . Destiny.* The names of pagan deities. Their devotees appealed to them in ritual eating and drinking to grant them good luck and an auspicious fate.

65:15 *A curse.* The names of those destroyed by God's wrath will be used in an oath formula when a judgment just as severe is invoked on subsequent enemies of God and of His *chosen.* The second line of the verse may preserve the wording of the imprecation if translated: "So may the Lord slay you" (Jer 29:22; Nm 5:21). *His servants,* on the other hand, will be given *a different name* from those deserving to be cursed. Each of them will be entitled to "bless himself" by praying to "the God of truth," of whose Amen to their petitions they can be certain.

65:20 *A hundred years.* Time will no longer have its aging effect on those who formerly were under the fatal curse of sin.

66:1-24 In the last ch. of the Book of Isaiah the Lord amplifies His response to the praying faithful begun in ch. 65 (cf. 65:1-25 note). He continues to drive home a two-pronged message, insisting that *the hand of the Lord is with his servants and his indignation is against his enemies* (14). Let the faithful take heart; let the wicked be warned. This contrasting theme is developed in much the same way as in the previous ch. Passages of threat and of promise follow one another abruptly. Blessings and curses are projected to take effect over a wide span of time ranging back and forth between the more immediate future and the end of history. The burning of Jerusalem by the Babylonians becomes a small-scale model of the conflagration by a *fire* which shall not be quenched when the Lord will *execute judgment . . . upon all flesh* (16, 24; see Mt 24, where Jesus moves almost imperceptibly from the destruction of Jerusalem to His second coming). Conversely, the return of captive Israel to Jerusalem and to the Promised Land becomes the prophetic symbol of a universal movement when, *from all the nations* (20), *all flesh shall come to worship before* the Lord. They will gather on the holy mountain Jerusalem which *shall remain* when God *will make . . . the new heavens and the new earth* (22 f.; 65:17 ff.). However, while the Lord's spokesman repeats the same basic principles which determine the destiny of those whose *soul delights in their abominations* (3) and of those *who tremble at his word* (5) he submits also new points to consider, driving them home with striking figures of speech.

In the opening verses Isaiah exposes the delusion, popular in his day and prevalent down to our own time, that forms of worship have a magical effect on God, putting a spell on Him and coercing Him to overlook the crimes even of those whose "hands are full of blood" (1:5). *All these things* they would use to neutralize Him are His to begin with because His *hands . . . made* them. Enthroned in *heaven* and resting His feet on the *earth* as if it were a *footstool,* He cannot be locked up within the walls of the kind of house built by His mortal creatures. Because they deliberately *have chosen* to mock the Lord with what was evil rather than to "listen" to His call (65:12), they should know that in His uninhibited sovereignty He *will choose affliction for them.* Yet "the high and lofty One who inhabits eternity" and whom "heaven and the highest heaven cannot contain" condescends to be enshrined in the heart of every one *that is humble and contrite in spirit* (57:15; 1 K 8:27) Cf. Jeremiah's tirade against making the temple a good luck charm (7:1-15) and Stephen's warning against the same folly (Acts 7:49 f.). It may be true that those *who tremble at his word* will be persecuted for His *name's sake* and bear the taunts even of *brethren* (cf. Mt 24:10 ff.), but it is the latter who *shall be put to shame* (1-5). The Lord is not a prisoner behind man-made walls. *From the temple,* considered indispensable to Him and inviolate, *the voice of the Lord* thunders His determination to render *recompense to His enemies.* (6)

However, while "the day of vengeance" is inevitable, "the year of the Lord's favor" too is sure to come (61:2). Not only will Jerusalem be restored by liberated exiles but there will be a *Zion* not of brick and stones but populated by a spiritual community born as miraculously as if a woman should bring forth *a nation . . . in one moment* and *before her pain came upon her* (7-9; Jn 1:13; 1 Ptr 1:23). The new *Jerusalem* will also be like a mother whose *consoling breasts* supply the nourishment necessary for contentment and growth. (10-14)

Let no one suppose, however, that there is room in "the City of the Lord" (60:14) for enemies. All who arouse *his anger* by flagrant disobedience *shall come to an end together.* For when *all nations and tongues* shall be gathered to *see* His *glory,* He will *execute judgment* on those who insisted on defying Him by their wicked *works* and *thoughts.* (15-18)

But there will be also those who will rejoice at the revelation of His glory. Their history begins with the return from the Babylonian exile. There will be *survivors* when the Lord *will set a sign among them* announcing their release. From and through them the call to share in salvation will go out to a worldwide circle of *nations* which were ignorant of the Lord's *fame* and *glory.* The results of making known His glory *among the nations* is pictured in terms of Israel's return from Babylon. What would happen at that time is but a shadow of far greater things to come. The distinction between Jew and Gentile will disappear. Old Testament ordinances in *the house of the Lord* will be abrogated. No longer will only Levites be eligible to become priests. Israel after the flesh is but a type of *all . . . brethren,* united not by physical family ties but by bonds of a spiritual fraternity (2:2 ff.). By virtue of this sacred relationship they themselves become *an offering to the Lord,* replacing the *cereal offering* required by the old covenant (cf. 2 Co 2:14 f.). In the end everything old will exist no longer. The universe of the first creation will give way to *the new heavens and the new earth,* where *all flesh shall come to worship before* the Lord (19-23). As their adoration will not cease, so the *fire* to which those *that have rebelled against* the Lord are condemned, *shall not be quenched.* (24)

66:3 *Slaughters . . . kills.* The use of prescribed offerings *(ox, lamb, cereal, memorial)* as a magical device to immobilize the Lord is as abhorrent to Him as sacrificing human beings or unclean animals such as dogs and swine.

66:5 *Be glorified. Brethren who hate* those *who tremble* at the Lord's word are so degenerate that they blasphemously challenge Him to vindicate His honor and to bring *joy* to those suffering for His *name's sake.* For a similar defiance of God see 51:8 note; 28:10 note.

66:7 *She was in labor.* Vs. 8 identifies the woman as "Zion," who plays the same kind of role in 49:19 note; 54:1-17 note; Gl 4:26.

66:12 *Wealth of the nations.* Cf. 61:5-6 note.

66:17 *One in the midst.* Either the person leading the initiation rites or the goddess to whom they devote themselves. For gardens see 65:3 note. *Mice* were unclean animals. (Lv 11:29)

66:19 *The nations.* Those mentioned to symbolize the worldwide gathering of the redeemed were on the outer perimeter of ancient Israel: *Tarshish* to the west (1 K 10:22 note); *Put and Lud* in Africa (Jer 46:9); *Tubal and Javan* to the north (Eze 27:13); Javan is translated "Greece" in Zch 9:13; cf. Gn 10:2-4 note.

66:20 *All your brethren.* Cf. Ro 11:25 ff.

66:24 *Worm . . . fire.* Jesus used these terms to describe the torment of hell. (Mk 9:43-48)

Abhorrence. Rendered "contempt" in Dn 12:2. A threatening note may not be a pleasant way to conclude a book, but Jesus too ended parables with the grim prospect of "weeping and gnashing of teeth" for all who did not have ears to hear.

JEREMIAH

INTRODUCTION

Setting

In Jeremiah's day Israel's existence as a nation became so critical that he has been called "the prophet of the eleventh hour." However, the time of his ministry is not measured by minutes and hours but by decades. Commissioned to transmit the Lord's Word while still a youth, he discharged his prophetic duties during the reign of five kings of Judah. For 40 years he tried to divert his people from the suicidal course of apostasy. His pleas and warnings went unheeded. As he predicted, the day came when Jerusalem and the temple lay in ruins. Though his prophetic words came true, a group of refugees, left behind by the Babylonian conqueror, persisted in ignoring his advice and took him to Egypt, where he vanished from sight.

God commandeered the great world powers of Jeremiah's time to implement the threat of judgment pronounced by His spokesman. When the young prophet began his career in 627 BC, the Southern Kingdom, called Judah, was nominally a vassal state of the Assyrians, the empire nation God called a century earlier to destroy Samaria, the capital of the Northern Kingdom. Fifteen years after Jeremiah's call to office, Nineveh, the Assyrian capital, fell and the Babylonians set out on a march to world conquests. In 605 BC the Babylonian general Nebuchadnezzar defeated Pharaoh Necho at Carchemish 400 miles north of Jerusalem. Having thus eliminated the contender for control of Palestine, the victorious Babylonians moved southward and reduced Judah to a province of their newly emerging empire. When a few years later Jehoiakim withheld the pledged tribute, Nebuchadnezzar, now made king, put down the insurrection. In an unexpected display of restraint he did not destroy Jerusalem but was content to take Jehoiachin, Jehoiakim's successor, with him to Babylon, together with a stratum of citizens. However, when Zedekiah, whom he appointed king, eventually rebelled, his patience gave out. What Jeremiah foretold came to pass. Jerusalem and the temple were leveled to the ground, and almost the entire population was carried into exile.

Religious Conditions

At the beginning of Jeremiah's ministry there was some prospect of a religious renewal. In 622 BC, five years after his call to the prophetic office, King Josiah (640—608 BC) issued a decree abolishing idolatrous worship, tolerated and sanctioned by his two predecessors on the throne. The results were disappointing. While there was outward and temporary compliance, the official order did not produce a popular reformation. Under Josiah's successors widespread defection set in. To the very end the people and their leaders remained obdurate in resisting correction. Even after the destruction of Jerusalem the fugitives in Egypt attributed their misfortune to the fact that they "left off burning incense to the queen of heaven," one of several deities worshiped by them. (44:18)

Sacrifices and ceremonies still flourished in the temple. But they too were an abomination. Jeremiah condemned the sacred rites because, performed mechanically, they were regarded as magical incantations coercing God to favor the worshipers regardless of their sin against Him and their fellowmen. A broken relationship with God went hand in hand with social evils. "Heaping oppression upon oppression, and deceit upon deceit," the people were "all adulterers, a company of treacherous men." (9:6, 2)

Personal Data

One should expect God to choose a man temperamentally suited to the unpopular, frustrating task assigned to Jeremiah. However, he seemed to possess none of the psychological traits which, one could expect, would make it less burdensome to carry out his assignment. A young man of about 20 years at the time of his call, he had no desire to engage in public debate in the marketplace or to confront the high officials of state and church. He would have been happy to remain an unheralded member of a priestly family in his hometown Anathoth, a few miles north of Jerusalem. He could not deliver the oracles of God without being emotionally involved. The words he had to speak to his wayward, doomed people did not come from his lips in the form of detached announcements. They pierced his heart. Torn between a burning love for his compatriots and the unrelenting obligation to tell of their certain undoing, he became greatly disturbed. In moments of intense anguish he cursed the day of his birth, invoked judgment on his opponents, and blamed God for their resistance to his message.

It is an injustice to him, however, to call him "the weeping prophet." Men of sterner stuff have broken under less intense emotional strain. It needs to be said that he did not allow his personal feelings or preferences to determine his actions and words. Relying on divine assurance of support, he found the fortitude to deliver the entrusted message in the face of ridicule, social ostracism, physical suffering, and threats of death. To kings, princes, priests, and hostile rabble he spoke revealed truth without diluting it with his own opinion or toning it down with cowardly double-talk. And if tradition is correct, he suffered a martyr's death, the supreme penalty for courage in the battle against evil.

God made unusual demands also on Jeremiah's private life. In carrying out his difficult task he was to remain unmarried and forego the simple joys of family living. He was to shun even social gatherings, whether at occasions of rejoicing or mourning. His relatives disowned Him. His countrymen charged him with treason. Isolation from the people he loved reached a climax when he was forbidden to intercede for them.

There was nothing to sustain this lonely prophet in his staggering task other than the conviction of faith that God had chosen him to be His mouthpiece. He had to rely for strength on the meaning of his name, Jeremiah, variously translated "The Lord casts," "The Lord exalts," "The Lord establishes," "Assigned by the Lord."

Though Jeremiah would no doubt fail to pass a modern personality test in applying for a public-career position, his book is undeniable proof of great literary skill. It is to be expected that a man "of the priests who were in Anathoth" (1:1) should be able to deliver prosaic instructions in the law. But this educator expresses himself in poetic passages of superb beauty and strong emotional appeal. He knows how to use rhetorical devices of various kinds to good effect. He displays remarkable versatility, treating the same subject matter over and over again but in ever new variations. It is surprising that, active over 40 years, he does not repeat himself except in a few brief passages.

Composition

The way Jeremiah's messages were put into written form has no parallel in the composition of Biblical manuscripts. The scroll containing the record of his prophetic activity during more than 20 years was burned in the fourth year of King Jehoiakim (608—597 BC). "At the dictation of Jeremiah" Baruch, his secretary, made a new copy of "all the words of the Lord" contained in the original. In the course of time "many similar words were added to them" (36:4, 32). As Baruch transcribed them, he gave them the form of an autobiography but also referred to his master in the third person.

The collected writings of Jeremiah, as we have them, are not arranged according to a consistent pattern. Some oracles, apparently originating at various times, are grouped according to subject matter. In other instances a chronological sequence is observed. However, neither a logical nor a chronological principle determines the overall order in which the chapters follow one another, as the appended outline demonstrates.

OUTLINE

I. 1:1-19 Introduction: Personal Data and Call

II. 2:1—20:18 Prophetic Threats and Promises Occasioned by Circumstances and Events Before the Fall of Jerusalem

- A. 2:1—6:30 Introductory Summary and Theme: Denunciation of Apostasy—Hope for Those Who Penitently Return
- B. 7:1—13:27 Sustained Indictment of Apostasy Delivered in a Dramatic Setting and Supported by Symbolic Action and a Brief Parable
- C. 14:1—15:21 Irrevocable Judgment on an Incorrigible Nation Despite Assurances by False Prophets and Despite Jeremiah's Intercession and Grief
- D. 16:1—17:27 Certainty of Disaster Dramatized by Jeremiah's Unconventional Life-Style, Provoked by Israel's Ingrained Perversity, and Affirmed by God's Right and Power to Determine Mankind's Fate
- E. 18:1—20:18 Jeremiah, Imprisoned and Beaten for Calls to Repentance, Acts Out His Message with the Help of Earthenware Jars; His Deep Despondency and Bitter Complaint

III. 21:1—38:28 Prophetic Threats and Promises Occasioned by Israel's Leaders

- A. 21:1—23:8 Rejection of the Ruling House of David; Bliss of Messianic Rule
- B. 23:9-14 Arraignment of Spiritual Leaders: Prophets and Priests
- C. 24:1—25:38 True Prophecies: Israel's Future and World History Symbolized by Two Baskets of Figs and the Cup of the Lord's Fury
- D. 26:1—29:32 True Prophecies of Judgment Contested by False Prophets
- E. 30:1—33:26 True Prophecies of Future Bliss in the Face of Apparent Hopelessness
- F. 34:1—36:32 Prophecies of Doom Provoked by Kings and the People as a Whole
- G. 37:1—38:28 Uncompromising Prophecies Proclaimed in Private to a Weak King

IV. 39:1—45:5 Prophecies After the Fall of Jerusalem

- A. 39:1—42:22 The Word Spoken to the Remnant in Palestine
- B. 43:1—44:30 The Word Spoken to Fugitives in Egypt
- C. 45:1-5 The Word Promising Protection to Baruch

V. 46:1—51:64 Prophecies Concerning the Nations
  A. 46:1—49:39 Egypt and Several Lesser Nations
  B. 50:1—51:64 Babylon

IV. 52:1-34 Historical Appendix: Prophecy Fulfilled

1:1-19 INTRODUCTION: PERSONAL DATA AND CALL

1:1-19 Serving as a preface to the book, the first three verses supply information about the prophet: his name, parentage, birthplace, and the era of his activity. In the remaining verses of the chapter Jeremiah presents credentials for his authority to speak and for his claim to be heard. He is the ambassador of the *Lord God,* who shapes the life of individuals and determines the destiny of *nations and . . . kingdoms.* Consecrated to the prophetic office *before* he was *born,* this *youth* was not a wide-eyed visionary nor a self-appointed rabble-rouser. He was commissioned to speak *words,* charged with the power *to destroy and to overthrow* whatever opposes the kingdom of God and *to build and to plant* what promotes its coming. (4-10)

It was only natural for the timid, sensitive, inexperienced young man from a country town to stand aghast at the worldwide results his ministry was to produce. The Lord therefore reveals to him that all he is to do is to announce what is to happen. The responsibility for bringing about what he threatens and promises is not his concern. It is the Lord who is *watching over* His *word to perform it;* it is He who is calling *all the tribes of the kingdoms* to do His bidding (11-16). Furthermore, the prophet did not have to rely on his own word or endowments and endurance in carrying out his difficult assignment. There will be violent opposition. But all attempts to intimidate or silence him will prove as ineffectual as arrows shot against *a fortified city, an iron pillar, and bronze walls.* (17-19).

1:1 *Anathoth.* A village about three miles northeast of Jerusalem, assigned to the Levites (Jos 21:18). *Hilkiah,* Jeremiah's father, very likely was a member of the clan associated with Abiathar, the high priest whom Solomon banished to Anathoth (1 K 2:26). The high priest, also named Hilkiah, who held that office during the reign of King Josiah and therefore was Jeremiah's contemporary (2 K 22:4-14) belonged to a different Levitical family.

1:2 *Josiah.* For the account of his reign see chs. 22 and 23 of 2 K and the notes there.

1:3 *Jehoiakim . . . Zedekiah.* Cf. 2 K 23:36—2 K 25:26 and the notes there. Only three of the five last kings of Judah are mentioned because the other two reigned only three months respectively: Josiah's son Jehoahaz, called Shallum (22:11), was deposed by Pharaoh Necho; Jehoiakim's son, Jehoiachin, called Coniah and Jeconiah (22:24; 24:1), was removed from office and taken to Babylon by Nebuchadnezzar (2 K 23:31-33; 24:12).

Eleventh year . . . fifth month. On the seventh day of that month Jerusalem was destroyed (2 K 25:8). From the time the word of the Lord first came to Jeremiah in the 13th year of Josiah's reign (640—608 BC) to this tragic point in Israel's history (586 BC) more than 40 years elapsed. When dating of events by the regnal years of a king was no longer possible, *the captivity of Jerusalem* served to indicate the setting of Jeremiah's ministry (41:1). However, no dates are supplied to establish how long he served the refugees who took him to Egypt. (43:5 ff.)

1:5 *Prophet to the nations.* For words directed specifically to them see chs. 46—51; for the international scene at Jeremiah's time see Introduction, "Setting."

1:6 *A youth.* Lacking the date of his birth, we may assume that he was about 20 years old. God overcame the young man's hesitation to assume his task as He did in the case of others called to His service. (Ex. 3:1—4:17; Ju 6:11-17; cf. also 1 Sm 17:33, 42; 1 K 3:7; 1 Ti 4:12; Gl 1:15 f.)

1:9 *My words in your mouth.* A simple statement of fact which faith accepts at face value. It is a false theory of the miracle of inspiration which advances the explanation that the message of the God who "formed" (5) Jeremiah became tainted with errors when His spokesman proclaimed it. No allowance is made for the possibility that "the word of the Lord" (4) was no longer true in all respects because it was transmitted by a fallible intermediary. Jeremiah insists over and over again that what he says is what "says the Lord" (8, 19; 3:1; 4:1; 5:22, etc.).

1:11-12 *A rod of almond.* The Lord gave His prophet two object lessons to afford him additional assurance that the words put in his mouth would come true because they were *the word of the Lord* (11-19). An ordinary tree and a boiling pot serve to give him visionary experiences not unlike those accorded the prophet Amos (Am 7:1-9; 8:1). In the first instance the message is conveyed by means of a word-play on the noun for "almond" (*shaked*) and the participle "awaken" (*shoked*). As the almond tree is made to awaken and blossom early in spring, so the Creator of the universe will from the very beginning be *watching* to *perform* His *word.* (12)

1:13 *A boiling pot.* Because the fire under it was fanned by a wind *facing away from the north,* it was to be from that direction that "evil shall break forth upon all the inhabitants of the land" (14). Jeremiah lived to see the threat fulfilled. The Babylonian invaders, entering Palestine from the north, inundated it, as he was ordered to prophesy. (4:6; 6:22; 25:9)

1:19 *Fight against you.* The Lord did not

commission His prophet under the illusion that his task would win him popular acclaim. The violent opposition he was to encounter was a type of the hostility which *the* Prophet of Nazareth had to endure.

2:1—20:18 PROPHETIC THREATS AND PROMISES OCCASIONED BY CIRCUMSTANCES AND EVENTS BEFORE THE FALL OF JERUSALEM

2:1—6:30 Introductory Summary and Theme: Denunciation of Apostasy—Hope for Those Who Penitently Return

2:1-37 No date is given when this *word of the Lord came to* Jeremiah. Not necessarily the first discourse he delivered, it apparently was given a leading position in the record of his prophetic activity because it provides the reader with an epitome of his preaching. (For the literary arrangement of his book see "Introduction," *Composition;* for the circular, rather than the logical, development of the theme see Isaiah, "Introduction," *Composition.*)

Ch. 2 points out that Israel's apostasy had a long history. At the very beginning, the nation's *devotion* to the Lord was like a short honeymoon. Hardly had the *fathers* been *brought . . . up from the land of Egypt . . . into a plentiful land* when they *defiled* it. They committed two evils. They forsook God, *the fountain of living waters,* and worshipped Baal-gods who proved to be *broken cisterns.* Such senseless unfaithfulness had no parallel among heathen people, who remained true to their ancestral idols even though they were *no gods.* (1-13)

Further evidence of defection was trust in foreign alliances rather than in Him by whom all nations are "accounted . . . as less than nothing and emptiness" (Is 40:17). This foolish policy had likewise been in vogue for a long time. But God would not be mocked. A century before Jeremiah's time Israel, the Northern Kingdom, became a prey of the Assyrians, to whom King Ahaz earlier had appealed for help (2 K 16:5-9). They made the *land a waste,* reduced the cities to ruins, and made *Israel a slave.* Negotiations with Egypt too would be as disastrous as they had been in the past. For *the men of Memphis and Tahpanhes* were opportunists, eager to exploit the international situation for their own advantage. The struggle for supremacy between the world powers, represented by *the Euphrates* in the north and east and by *the Nile* in the south and west, would end in the subjugation of Palestine no matter which of them would emerge the victor. (14-19)

Israel's refusal to trust and *serve* the Lord expressed itself in brazen worship of Baal which began *long ago.* Reveling shamelessly in the seductive fertility rites of this idol, the chosen people became *degenerate* (20-22). Like female animals in heat, they could not be restrained from seeking to gratify their insatiable lust. (23—25)

Too late they will realize how futile it was to *have turned their back to* the Creator and to have entrusted their fate *to a tree . . . and to a stone,* the symbols of impotent gods. Inevitably there will come a *time of . . . trouble* when, like *a thief* caught in the act, they will be *shamed* to admit that the idols they *made for* themselves cannot *save* them. (26-28)

When disaster does overtake them, they will have no reason to complain against the Lord. He tried *in vain* to warn them. But they refused to accept correcton and chastizing. Nor did acts of kindness keep them from insisting to be *free* to go their own wicked way. For them to *forget* all He did for them was as abnormal and irrational as if *a bride* were not to think of putting on her wedding *attire.* (29-32)

Callous to kindness and deaf to admonition, they *lightly . . . gad about* gratifying their passion in sensuous idol worship and satisfying their greed by squeezing the *lifeblood* from the *guiltless poor.* Though guilty of these heinous crimes, they have the impudence to profess to be *innocent* of wrong-doing. However, they cannot escape divine *judgment.* For the nations *in whom* they *trust* will themselves be rejected. (33-37)

2:2 *Love as a bride.* Jeremiah is not idealizing the past. Though the Israelites at the time of their espousal to the Lord murmured and sinned against Him, as He led them through the *wilderness,* they remained His covenant people to whom He gave the Promised Land. For the use of the marriage bond to symbolize God's relationship to His people see Hos 2; Rv 21:2.

2:3 *Holy to the Lord.* He protected Israel, chosen to be the bearer of His promise, as a man guards choice *fruits* and declares *all who ate of* them *guilty* of theft.

2:4 *All the families.* Jeremiah draws on the history of both kingdoms, the northern called *Israel* or *Jacob* and the southern consisting mainly of the tribe of Judah. In 3:6-10 the guilt of the two "sisters" is compared.

2:5 *Worthlessness.* A derisive term for idols translated "false gods" in 14:22 and "false idols" in 2 K 17:15.

2:8 *Priests . . . rulers . . . prophets.* Though they knew the law of God, the religious and civil leaders deliberately perverted it and so misled the people. See chs. 20—38 for Jeremiah's protracted conflict with those in authority.

2:10 *Cyprus . . . Kedar.* The Lord charges His people with a faithlessness not found even among the heathen nations from the Mediterranean Sea in the west (Cyprus) to the nomadic people in the east such as Kedar. (Is 21:13 note; 60:7; Jer 49:28)

2:11 *Their glory.* Cf. Ps 106:20 note.

2:12 *O heavens.* Cf. Is 1:2 note; Dt 32:1.

2:13 *Living waters.* Cf. Is 55:1-13 note; Ps 36:9 note.

2:14 *Homeborn servant.* Born of a bondwoman and therefore destined to permanent slavery.

2:16 *Memphis and Tahpanhes.* Egyptian cities. The first was the capital of North Egypt; the second, a stronghold on the border to which Jeremiah was taken after the fall of Jerusalem. (43:7)

2:18 *What . . . gain?* Their "wickedness will chasten" them (19) no matter to which foreign nation they turn for relief. At Carchemish in 605 BC the combined forces of Egypt and Assyria could not repulse the Babylonians from their march into Palestine. Revolts against domination by the latter, inspired by promises of help from Egypt, also proved futile.

2:20 *Broke your yoke.* Israel refused to be restrained from wickedness by the terms to which it had agreed in the covenant. Worshiping Baal *upon every high hill and under every green tree,* the Lord's "bride" (2) became a *harlot,* both spiritually and physically.

2:21 *Choice vine.* Cf. Is 5:1-30 note.

2:22 *Wash yourself.* The *guilt* of sin is an inner stain which cannot be removed by outward ceremonies.

2:23 *In the valley.* Children were sacrificed to Molech, another name for Baal, in the Valley of Hinnom south of Jerusalem. (7:31; 19:5; 2 K 16:3 note; 21:6; 23:10; 2 Ch 33:6)

2:25 *Going unshod.* As slaves were forced to do.

2:27 *A tree . . . a stone.* A wooden pillar, called "ashera," represented the mother-goddess, and a pillar of stone, called "mazzebah," the male deity.

2:30 *Devoured your prophets.* For verification of the charge see 1 K 18:13; 2 Ch 24:20 f.; Neh 9:26; Jer 26:20-23; Mt 23:29-36.

2:34 *Guiltless poor.* They were innocent of a crime such as *breaking in* to steal or rob.

3:1-25 In the first five verses God continues to press charges against His apostate people. As in ch. 2, He likens their sin to the incorrigible perversity of a profligate woman who commits *vile harlotry* promiscuously with her many lovers. Rejecting admonition, they *refused to be ashamed* of *all the evil* they did. God cannot *be angry for ever* and must tolerate their infidelity, they assert, because He once chose them to be His "own possession among all peoples." (1-5; Ex 19:5)

However, these opening verses not only add an indictment to the bill of particulars recorded in ch. 2, but they also introduce the motif to be developed in the immediately following verses. Though the unfaithful people deserve to suffer the dire consequences of their heinous crimes, it is not too late to avert the impending doom. "Abounding in steadfast love and faithfulness" (Ex 34:6), God will even now forgive *all the adulteries* if only they *return* to the Lord (1, 7, 10, 12, 14, 22; 4:1). At the same time, the history of *Israel,* the Northern Kingdom, should prove to *Judah,* the southern *sister,* that the call to repentance cannot be ignored with impunity. Because *that faithless one, Israel,* did not respond to the Lord's pleading, He had sent her away into Assyrian exile a century ago. False Judah, doubly guilty for obdurately reveling in the same monstrous sins, will not escape a similar fate. (6-13)

On the other hand, if the *faithless children* do return with their *whole heart* and not *in pretense* only (10), the Lord will not only pardon their offenses but also restore them and assign to them again the role in His plan of universal redemption for which He chose Abraham and his descendants (14-18; Gn 12:3). Yet to His disappointment God must observe that the people at Jeremiah's time continued to act like disobedient sons and *a faithless wife* (19-20). The concluding verses portray *the weeping and pleading* God expects from His *faithless sons* when he calls them to *return* to Him. (21-25)

3:1 *Divorces his wife.* The law of Moses did not allow a man to remarry his divorced wife after her marriage to another (Dt 24:1-4). The point is that, according to human standards, God could not be expected to let Israel return after she *played the harlot with many lovers.* But forgiveness is not only a possibility; God pleads with sinners to accept it.

3:2 *Like an Arab.* As a desert marauder is on the alert for his victims, so Israel sat *by the waysides* eagerly seeking every opportunity to debauch herself with *lovers.* (Gn 38:14 f.; Pr 7:10-12)

3:4-5 *Father.* Fatherly chastisements in the form of drought did not keep Israel from plunging into *all the evil* they *could.* They profess filial love. But what they have *just now . . . spoken* is refuted by what they *have done* immediately afterward.

3:6 *Josiah.* In the 13th year of his reign the word of the Lord first came to Jeremiah (1:2). The next dated ch. (21) mentions Zedekiah, the last of the kings of Judah.

3:7 *Sister Judah.* After Solomon's death the ten northern tribes, called Israel, seceded from the Davidic kingdom. The two remaining tribes constituted Judah. The term Israel, however, continues to be used as a general designation for the covenant nation (20, 21). See Eze 16 for a graphic description of the adultery committed by both sisters.

3:14 *Faithless children.* Jeremiah's preaching of repentance was in vain, and the disaster he predicted overtook the apostate nation. "Out of the north" came the Babylonians, destroyed the land, and took captive its inhabitants (1:14 f.; 4:6; 6:22-24; see ch. 52). But even then the way to *return* to the Lord will remain open. God's forgiveness will wipe the record clean. Through a surviving remnant, brought back *to Zion,* He will usher in "those days" and "that time" when not only the descendants of Abraham but "all nations" can become full-fledged citizens in the Messianic kingdom.

In this worldwide spiritual community, called the church in the NT, the Lord has His "throne," as His "presence" was symbolized by His enthronement over "the ark of the covenant" and as His glory was enshrined in the temple at Jerusalem (16-18; Ex 25:22; 1 K 8:10 f.). For ancient Jerusalem and restored, united, flourishing Israel as types of the "Jerusalem above" and of "Abraham's offspring" "born according to the Spirit" (Gl 3:29; 4:26, 29) see Is 2:2 note; 60:1-22 note; 61:1-11 note; 62:1-12 note.

3:19 *My sons.* Nations besides Israel.

3:21 *Bare heights.* Where they played the harlot. (2)

3:24 *Shameful thing.* A synonym for Baal (Hos 9:10), translated "shame." (Jer 11:13)

4:1-31 Ch. 4 has more to say about the need for repentance. As in chs. 2 and 3, this crucial topic is the thematic center around which pertinent aspects are developed like concentric circles drawn about a given point. In the recurring cycle of admonitions to *return,* vv. 1-4 underscore the necessity of a radical change of *hearts,* demonstrated *in truth, in justice, and in uprightness,* if Israel was to escape disaster and again promote the extension of God's kingdom among the *nations.*

The remaining verses of the chapter (5-31) revolve anew about the dire consequences of impenitence, enlarging on the threat "that it is evil and bitter . . . to forsake the Lord" (2:19). As clearly as if it were an accomplished fact, prophetic vision lets Jeremiah see what *the fierce anger of the Lord* will do when He brings *evil from the north and great destructon* on the land of Judah (5-8). Fright unmans the civic and religious leaders. The fleeing inhabitants seek refuge in vain even in Jerusalem. For *besiegers come from a distant land* to destroy it, the last of *the fortified cities.* (5, 9-18)

At the sight of *disaster . . . on disaster* falling on the *land* and the people he loved, Jeremiah cannot refrain from expressing the *pain* he feels in his innermost being (19-21), only to be reminded by the Lord that the *foolish, stupid,* people deserve the decreed punishment (22). Again contemplating the *desolation* to come, Jeremiah is horrified to see how complete it is. It *looked* to him as if the universe was again *waste and void* as it was before God changed the primordial chaos into a habitable world (23-28). Jerusalem will discover too late how useless it is to play the coquette with foreign nations as if they were *lovers* to be seduced by female charms and wiles. Her false paramours will only *despise* her and *seek* her *life.* Jeremiah hears the anguished *cry of the daughter of Zion* at the approach of her murderers. (29-31)

4:2 *Swear.* God's people are admonished to invoke the name of the Lord instead of swearing by false gods, which is idolatry. (Dt 10:20 note; Ex 20:3 note)

In Him. In the true God. When Abraham's offspring by whom all the families of the earth were to *bless themselves* (Gn 12:3) worshiped *abominations* (1) and seemed doomed to extinction for their apostasy, the name of God was "blasphemed among the Gentiles." (Ro 2:24; Is 52:5 note; Eze 36:20-23)

4:3 *Fallow ground.* If a farmer wants to raise crops, he cannot sow seeds on the hardened surface of soil left uncultivated or scatter them where *thorns* will choke them. So the fruits of "truth," "justice," and "uprightness" (2) cannot grow out of a heart encased in the impervious shell of impenitence and overgrown with the weeds of sinful desires. (Hos 10:12; Mt 13:7, 22)

4:4 *Circumcise.* Mere outward compliance with the law requiring the physical removal of the *foreskin* is no insurance against the *wrath* of God. To be more than a meaningless formality, the "sign of the covenant" must remove the inborn self-will from the *hearts* and render them responsive to the Lord. (Gn 17:11; Dt 10:16; 30:6; Cl 2:11)

4:6 *Standard.* Signposts to guide the refugees to "the fortified cities" as they *flee for safety* from the open country.

4:8 *Sackcloth.* Put on to express grief or dismay. (6:26; 48:37; Gn 37:34; Is 15:3; 37:1)

4:10 *Deceived.* Jeremiah is not a disinterested spectator of the horrible scene unfolding before his prophetic eyes. Here and in 19-21 he injects exclamations of horror and pain as he beholds the invasion and destruction of his beloved country. He cannot repress an impassioned outcry at the thought that the chosen people became so hardened and reprobate, refusing "to take correction" and making "their faces harder than a rock" (5:3), that God determined to send "upon them a strong delusion to make them believe" what lying "prophets prophesy falsely" saying: "No evil will come upon us" (5:12, 31; 2 Th 2:11). For other instances of the judgment of obduration see Ex 4:21 note; 1 K 22:22 note; Eze 14:9 f.

4:12 *For this.* For the purpose just mentioned, namely "to winnow or cleanse" the wheat of chaff on the threshing floor (Ps 1:4 note)

4:15 *Dan . . . Ephraim.* The invading foe has advanced southward from Israel's northernmost city to the hills on Judah's border 10 miles above Jerusalem.

4:18 *Reached your very heart.* A death-dealing blow.

4:20 *My tents . . . curtains.* Destruction of the nation's towns and villages is like a personal blow. It is as if Jeremiah were a Bedouin whose shelter was swept away.

4:23 *Waste and void.* Translated "without form and void" in Gn 1:2.

4:27 *A full end.* A ray of Gospel light: God will not let the chosen people become extinct or lose their national identity by being absorbed by other nations. A remnant will survive and again become His instruments to bless all races. 3:14 ff.; 5:10, 18; Is 6:13 note; Am 9:8)

5:1-31 Jeremiah draws another sermonic circle around the theme which was at the center of his preaching recorded in the preceding chs.: the inevitable wages of sin (cf. 4:1-31). Warnings of impending judgment are supported by evidence of nationwide guilt. Crimes against God and fellowmen are committed by *the great* as well as *the poor.* God cannot *pardon* such heinous deeds as though they were sins of weakness. He must *punish . . . a nation* for doing *these things.* (1-9)

In order to execute the sentence pronounced on His *utterly faithless* people, He will no longer protect them as a highly prized vineyard (Is 5), but will call on a destroyer to *go up through her vine-rows and . . . strip away her branches.*

When this devastation comes, it will prove that the prophets who predicted it were not windbags. God's *words* in Jeremiah's *mouth* too will prove to be *a fire* devouring the apostate nation like so much *wood.* For in spite of protestations to the contrary, the Lord of hosts is commandeering *a nation from afar* to *eat up,* like a monster, not only the food supply but also the inhabitants as well. Those who escape will be carried off captive to a foreign land. (10-19)

What Jeremiah said so often and with such urgent importunity should have made his hearers *fear* the Lord and *tremble before* Him. Yet the prophet is ordered to continue to *declare* and *proclaim* how *foolish and senseless* the *people* are to think that God will *not punish* them for the unchecked flow of evil from *a stubborn and rebellious heart.* For while inanimate nature does not exceed the limits set by the Creator, His rational creatures *know no bounds in deeds of wickedness.* They respond to the material blessings He supplies by exploiting the *fatherless;* they become *great and rich* at the expense of the *needy.* The situation is all the more *appalling and horrible* because false *prophets* and unscrupulous *priests* confirm the people in their lawlessness, refusing to warn them that at *the end* they cannot escape the wrath of God. Lulled to sleep, the *people love to have it so.* (20-31)

5:1 *Run . . . search.* For the sake of no more than 10 "righteous" persons God once was willing to spare the city of Sodom. (Gn 18:23-33; cf. also Eze 22:30; Zph 1:12)

5:2 *Swear falsely.* They use the Lord's name in solemn oath formulas to swear to an untruth.

5:5 *The yoke.* Cf. 2:20 note.

5:7 *To the full.* Moses foresaw how Israel, having "waxed fat" and "sleek," would repay God's bounty by turning to idols *who are no gods* (Dt 32:15). Jeremiah does not hide the ugliness of their sin by using polite language. He brands it *adultery,* as in 2:20 ff.

5:12 *Do nothing.* In effect they join hands with the "wicked" and the "fool" who say: "There is no God." (Ps 10:4, 14:1)

5:13 *Thus.* Jeeringly they suggest that if disaster is to come, it will strike only those who predict it.

5:14 *Lord . . . of hosts.* For the meaning of this term see 1 Sm 1:3 second note.

5:15 *Language.* Cf. Is 28:11 note; also Jer 1:15.

5:16 *Open tomb.* Their arrows bring death to their targets. (Cf. Ps 5:9)

5:18 *Full end.* Cf. 4:27 note.

5:21 *See not.* Cf. Is 6:10 note.

5:22 *The bound for the sea.* Cf. Ps 104:9; Jb 3:8 second note; 7:12 note; 9:13 note.

5:27 *A basket.* A wicker cage.

5:29 *Not punish.* A refrainlike repetition of v. 9.

6:1-30 In this ch. the call to repentance is at the center of another cycle of indictments and threats of dire consequences. Continued rounds of pleading and warning may strike the reader as wearisome repetition. However, tireless reiteration in prophetic preaching, far from being meaningless multiplying of words, testifies to God's patience and goodness and on the other hand to the perversity of human nature. For 40 years Jeremiah pleaded with his people to repent, only to be rebuffed again and again by insolence and scorn. Yet as this ch. again demonstrates, the proclamation of the same message is not a monotonous rehash of trite phrases. The prophet knows how to vary the form of his discourses with an array of rhetorical and poetic devices.

In the first 8 verses he dramatizes the certainty of the *great destruction* to be inflicted on the impenitent people. In spirit he sees the invading enemy *out of the north* making frantic preparations to lay siege to Jerusalem. Formerly recommended as a refuge for people from open towns and villages (4:6), it is about to be destroyed. Hence its citizens are told to *flee for safety . . . from the midst of* it. As the enemy troops await orders to attack, God Himself is heard rallying them to *cast up a siege mound against Jerusalem . . . the city which must be punished* because wickedness keeps gushing out of her like *water* from a spring-fed *well.*

Corruption is not restricted to a small minority or to a single stratum of society. Therefore the wrath of the Lord is about to be poured out on every one, *from the least to the greatest . . . and from prophet to priest.* In order to make sure that no offender is missed, *the Lord of hosts* is heard giving another order. The enemy soldiers are to act as if each of them were a *grape-gatherer* who passes his *hand again over* the *branches* for fruit he may have overlooked. (9-15)

Execution of annihilating judgment is not an unjustifiable temper tantrum on the Lord's part. Not only did He instruct the people in *the good way* from the very beginning, but throughout their history He also *set watchmen over* them to warn them against deserting *the ancient paths* which alone lead to *rest for* their *souls* (cf. 7:25). But willfully disobedient to His *words* and *law,* they only added insult to injury by engaging in hypocritical acts of formal worship. (16-21)

The Lord has an instrument of retribution capable of carrying out His orders. *Coming from the north country . . . a great nation* will be brought to ravage the land and to spread *terror . . . on every side* (22-26). Like a summation by the prosecution, the Lord authorizes Jeremiah to expose the pervasive and unalterable nature of Israel's wickedness. The people are like a piece of ore from which no precious metal can be smelted because it is composed of nothing but *bronze* and *iron* and worthless *refuse silver.* (27-30)

6:1 *Benjamin.* The tribes of Judah and Benjamin composed the Southern Kingdom. *Tekoa* was located about 11 miles south and *Beth-haccherem* about 6 miles west of Jerusalem.

Out of the north. Cf. 1:13 note.

6:3 *Shepherds.* The invading armies, directed by their chiefs of staff, will denude the country as grazing flocks of sheep leave a pasture bare. (2:8 RSV note)

6:4 *Woe . . . lengthen.* As supplied with quotation marks in the RSV, these words are spoken by the besieged people of Jerusalem, as they see the darkness of disaster engulfing them. It is possible also to regard these 2 lines as expressing the disappointment of the besiegers that nightfall is cutting their attack short. V. 5 suggests their determination to continue "by night."

6:10 *Closed.* Cf. RSV note; also 4:4 note.

6:11 *Pour it out.* When *the wrath of the Lord* inundates the city, all its inhabitants from *the children* to *the very aged* will become war casualties. (Is 13:16; Ps 137:9 note)

6:14 *They have healed.* The false prophets refused to tell the people how sick they were. Saying all is well, they put a Band-Aid on the cancerous wound of the nation. The Biblical term *peace* denotes more than absence of war. Its wider meaning is reflected when translated "welfare" or "prosperity," as in 29:11; 33:9.

6:16 *Stand by the roads.* Arriving at a crossroads, travelers must decide in which direction to go. They have the choice of taking "the way . . . that leads to destruction" or to walk in *the good way* on which they will *find rest for* their *souls.* (Cf. Mt 7:13; 11:29)

6:18 *Congregation.* The assembly of *nations* called to witness the "evil" God is about to bring upon His people.

6:20 *Sheba.* In southwest Arabia (Is 60:6). Aromatic *cane* was used in preparing incense (Ex 30:23). Ceremonies which do not express commitment of the heart are an abomination to the Lord. (1 Sm 15:22 note; Is 1:11 note)

6:21 *Stumbling blocks.* God will see to it that the road of rebellious self-will ends in disaster. (Is 8:14; Eze 3:20; 14:3 f., 7)

6:22 *Farthest parts.* The Babylonians came from a country far removed from Israel. (25:32; 31:8)

6:26 *Sackcloth.* Cf. 4:8 note.

6:29 *Bellows blow.* To fan the fire which was to smelt the ore in a refining process. *Lead* was used to separate the silver from the base metals. Israel has resisted purification. It remains a solid block of "refuse" not worth saving.

7:1—13:27 Sustained Indictment of Apostasy Delivered in a Dramatic Setting and Supported by Symbolic Action and a Brief Parable

The essential elements constituting the burden of Jeremiah's preaching are to be found in chs. 2—6. Apparently selected from various periods of his ministry, the discourses assembled there represent the nucleus of all his preaching. Its theme was: Return to the Lord. Sermon follows sermon in an arrangement resembling a series of circles drawn around a common center. As the rings in a tree indicate how old it is, so every new attempt to get Israel to respond proclaims how patient and gracious God is. And some 40 more chs. are to follow. Various points along the circumference of the cyclic exposition of chs. 2—6 become, in turn, centers of concern around which rotate expanded warnings and elaborated promises.

In chs. 7—13 the call to repent is broadcast to the people thronging the temple for worship; the dire results of impenitence are visually demonstrated by a spoiled waistcloth; a parable about a wine jar makes the same point.

7:1-34 In ch. 7 Jeremiah lays bare the enormity of Israel's sin. Standing in the gate of the Lord's house, he charges the assembled people with acting as if the structure they had built could imprison Him whom "heaven and the highest heaven cannot contain" (1 K 8:27). They have reduced Him to an impotent idol whom his devotees will not allow to leave his dwelling-place or to destroy it, no matter what they do to dishonor him. In their minds the *house* where the Lord's name was to be revered was no more than a cave were *robbers* could flee for safety between raids on their hapless victims. There was no excuse for the blasphemous heresy that the *temple* guaranteed immunity from the consequences of evil deeds. For the Lord spoke *persistently* against this desecration of His holiness through His *servants the prophets.* (25)

The culprits should have recalled too what the Lord *did to Shiloh.* In this city only 17 miles north of Jerusalem the ark of the covenant was enshrined for a time. But when the sacred chest was degraded to a good-luck charm, it was captured by the Philistines and the city was destroyed (1 Sm 4; Ps 78:60 ff.). Furthermore, *Ephraim,* the Northern Kingdom devastated by the Assyrians a century earlier, should serve as a warning example that God will not forever tolerate the abuse of His goodness. (3-15)

For *Judah* too the time of grace had elapsed. Because the hour of judgment was at hand, Jeremiah was no longer to *pray for them.* For their only response to his pleading for a change of heart was blatant, unrestricted worship of *the queen of heaven,* an astral deity and goddess of fertility. (16-20)

Their false sense of security stemmed not only from the notion of an inviolate temple but also from a perversion of the purpose of the ceremonies performed there by divine decree. Firmly entrenched in their hardened hearts was the pernicious theory that the rites of *burnt offerings* and *sacrifices,* mechanically performed, put God under a spell, forcing Him to overlook their refusal to *walk in all the way* of moral behavior He had commanded. Though Jeremiah used drastic language to dislodge this heathen distortion of worship forms, he was no more successful than his predecessors, whom God sent *persistently* to His stiffnecked people from the very beginning. (21-28; Is 1:11; Am 5:21)

Therefore they have become *the generation of His wrath,* people whose measure of iniquity is full to overflowing (29; Mt 23:32; 1 Th 2:16). Without the least qualms they *have done evil* as detestable as placing their abominable idols into the Lord's house and as loathsome as sacrificing their children to idols. There can be no doubt that the Lord has every reason to carry out His threat that *the land shall become a waste.* (30-34)

7:2 *Stand in the gate.* A shorter but similar sermon was delivered "in the court of the Lord's house" according to 26:1-6. False trust in the security of the temple was one of the basic causes of Israel's downfall. A second warning, delivered on the very site which gave rise to this fatal heresy, would not have been superfluous. It is also possible that ch. 26 gives a resume of Jeremiah's dramatic preaching in order to provide the circumstances of the prophet's brush with death described in the immediately following verses but not appended to ch. 7.

7:4 *The temple of the Lord.* A slogan of defiance repeated over and over again.

7:10 *We are delivered.* They think they can escape punishment for crimes against God and their fellowmen if they use the temple as robbers take refuge in a cave only to emerge from hiding for fresh adventure.

7:11 *Den of robbers.* Hypocrisy in worship, which brought these words to Jesus' lips, continues to be one of Satan's masterpieces of deception.

7:16 *Do not pray.* Repeated 11:14; 14:11; cf. Ex 32:10.

7:18 *Queen of heaven.* For the trust put in this idol see 44:15-19, 25.

7:19 *Is it I . . . ?* Their idolatry does not harmfully affect the transcendent Lord, but because it moves Him to punish them for insulting Him, they will suffer injury.

7:22 *I did not speak.* Jeremiah is not denying the divine origin of Israel's sacrificial rites. But in order to arouse his hearers to the danger of attributing magical power to a mechanical offering of sacrifices, he resorts to a daring way of speaking. The point he categorically denies is the notion that God prescribed ritual worship as a substitute for keeping His commandments. For similar emphatic rhetorical emphasis on the pronouncement that God did not make a covenant with Israel's fathers see Dt 5:2 note.

7:21 *Eat the flesh.* All the meat of the animals sacrificed in *burnt offerings* was to be consumed by fire. But because the sacrifices as offered by the people were an abomination to the Lord, it was of little consequence whether or not they refrained from eating what was prohibited by law.

7:27 *They will not listen.* Isaiah's preaching likewise was in vain. (Is 6:9-10)

7:31 *Topheth.* Cf. 2 K 23:10 note. For *Hinnom* see Jer 2:23 note.

7:32 *Valley of Slaughter.* Where they butchered their children, they themselves will be slaughtered and buried.

7:33 *Dead bodies.* Desecration of corpses was considered a grievous calamity.

8:1-22 While continuing to foretell that "the days are coming" when lament over unburied dead will silence "the voice of gladness" (7:32-34), the opening verses of this ch. add two features to the picture of the tragic events *at that time:* (1) not only will "the dead bodies of this people" (7:33) receive no honorable burial, but their *bones* will *be brought out of their tombs* by the looting enemies searching for treasure; (2) exposed to *the sun and the moon and all the host of heaven,* the desecrated skeletons bear ironic testimony to the folly of having *worshiped* these astral deities. (1-3; cf. 7:18)

The cause of this horrible fate awaiting the people is, as ch. 7 put it, "the stubbornness of their evil hearts" (7:24). Their *perpetual backsliding* is contrary to human experience and common sense. Even migratory birds, acting purely by divinely implanted instinct, are more responsive to their Maker than His rational creatures. Holding *fast to deceit,* they obstinately refuse to be guided by *the ordinance of the Lord.* (4-7)

All the while they smugly claim to be *wise,* claiming to be automatically safe from misfortune because of the physical presence of *the law of the Lord* in their midst. Propagated by the very men assigned to be the custodians and teachers of divine revelation (the *scribes,* the *wise men,* the *prophet,* the *priest*), this preposterous *wisdom* has *rejected the word of the Lord,* subverting its most basic principles. Such false doctrine about man's relationship to God inevitably undermines social stability. The situation has degenerated to the point where *every one deals falsely . . . from the least to the greatest* without feeling *ashamed* in the least. (8-13)

So inevitable is the threatened retribution for all this wickedness that Jeremiah already hears the victims of the invasion calling to one another in a vain search for a place of safety. But flight even to *the fortified cities* will be in vain (14-15). Jeremiah, acting as God's spokesman, proclaims the devastation of the whole land by a foe as deadly as *serpents* and *adders which cannot be charmed* and made harmless. (16-17)

The vision of the coming calamity, granted Jeremiah, is so vivid that his *heart is sick within* him. Israel's self-inflicted wound is incurable. The best *balm in Gilead* and the ablest *physician* cannot heal the fatal malignancy. The end is at hand because the Lord is *not in Zion* anymore to preserve a people who have *provoked* Him *to anger with their graven images.* (18-22)

8:1 *The bones.* Repeated five times in this verse like the tolling of the nation's death knell.

8:6 *Given heed.* The Lord waited in vain for them "to return" from holding "fast to deceit." (5; cf. Ps 14:2 note)

8:8 *The scribes.* Men capable of using a *pen* in writing, and responsible for the preservation and exposition of *the Law of the Lord,* "deal falsely" (so the last line of this v. is translated in 6:13). They are not accused of falsifying the content of the documents. As v. 11 indicates, they pervert the revealed truth by saying: "'Peace, peace,' when there is no peace." (Cf. 6:14 note)

8:10 *Wives to others.* Vv. 10-12 are a refrainlike repetition of 6:12-15.

8:13 *I gave.* Because the Lord looked for *grapes on the vine* of faith, He will deprive them of the bodily sustenance He has provided for them in the past.

8:14 *Have sinned.* After it is too late and *God has doomed* them *to perish,* the people realize how wrong they were to have "looked for peace" when they deserved "terror." (15; cf. 14:19)

8:20 *Harvest is past.* Apparently a proverbial saying which Jeremiah hears the people in exile apply to their despair of deliverance.

8:22 *Balm in Gilead.* The territory east of the Jordan (Dt 2:36) was famous for producing and exporting a gum or spice prized for its healing qualities. (46:11; Gn 37:25; Eze 27:17)

9:1-26 His "heart . . . sick within" him over his terminally ill people and their refusal to accept the remedy able to restore them to "health," Jeremiah continues to give vent to his overwhelming anguish as he did in 8:18-22. His own wailing and his call for *mourning women* (17), as if death had already occurred, was not a cheap publicity stunt. Even his emotional outbursts are a part of a sustained attempt to bring his hearers to their senses. Consequently we find lament interspersed with renewed charges of guilt; cries of woe alternate with threats of inescapable retribution. Devotion to country and love for his people do not blind him to the unrestrained crimes which have destroyed the very foundation of communal living. *Falsehood, iniquity, evil, oppression, deceit* have made the citizenry *a company of treacherous men.* The lawlessness is so revolting that he would rather be *in the desert,* where he would not have to see it. (1-6)

But the Lord sees it and has no choice but to *punish them for these things* (7-9). More lamentation is in order because in His wrath God *will make the cities of Judah a desolation, without inhabitant* (10-11). And if anyone later thinks he is *wise* but fails to understand why the land is *laid waste like a wilderness,* let him know that the Lord warned the worshipers of *the Baals* in advance what they must expect for having flagrantly *followed their own hearts* rather than His *law* and *voice.* (12-16)

When the Lord carries out His threat, the people who *have left the land* to serve their foreign masters will feel so pained that they are told to engage professional *mourning women,* as was customary at funerals. For *death has* indeed *come up into* their national home. (17-22)

The ch. closes with the warning not to trust in human resources or in the outward performances of ceremony. Neither of these can avert the day of reckoning. (23-26)

9:2 *Adulterers.* Infidelity to God was the root cause of the catalog of crimes against fellowmen listed in the following verses. (2:2 note; 2:20 note)

9:3 *Know.* For the meaning of this verb to denote more than mental awareness see Gn 18:19 note; Ju 2:10.

9:4 *Supplanter.* Israel reverted to the deceptive nature of its ancestor Jacob. For the word-play on the meaning of his name see Gn 25:26 note; 27:36.

9:7 *Refine them.* Of the dross of sin, as described 6:27-30.

9:10 *Take up.* If the reading of the Hebrew text is retained (RSV note), Jeremiah speaks these words and then quotes the Lord in the next verse.

9:15 *Wormwood.* Cf. Pr 5:4 note.

9:17 *Skilful women.* Trained to lead the mourning at funerals. (Mt 9:23)

9:19 *Left the land.* God's inspired spokesman not only predicts the Babylonian captivity but also anticipates how *utterly shamed* the exiles will be after they have been *ruined.*

9:21 *Into our windows. Death* is personified to dramatize the wholesale slaughter by the enemy. (Cf. 15:7-9; 18:21)

9:25 *Yet uncircumcised.* Though physically marked by the "sign of the covenant" (Gn 17:11), the people were no better than the heathen.

9:26 *Corners of their hair.* A heathen custom forbidden. (Lv 19:27)

10:1-25 "Chosen . . . out of all the peoples that are on the face of the earth" to be "a kingdom of priests and a holy nation" (Dt 7:6; Ex 19:6), "the house of Israel is uncircumcised in heart" and therefore no better than its heathen neighbors (9:26). Time and time again Jeremiah had to charge his apostate people with adopting the crassest kinds of idol worship (2:10 f., 27 f.; 4:1; 7:17 f., 30 f.; 8:19; etc.). This ultimate insult to the *King of the nations, the true God, the living God* (7, 10) was not only the depth of depravity but also the height of folly, as Jeremiah repeatedly pointed out.

The first 16 verses of this chapter record his longest and most scathing exposé of trusting what *the hands of a craftsman* produced out of *a tree from the forest* and fastened *with hammer and nails* (3 f.). Similar in tone and content to Isaiah's satires on idolatry (Is 40:18-20; 41:7; 44:9-17; 45:20; cf. also Ps 115:3-8; 135:15-18), Jeremiah's ironic tirade has on it the stamp of his own individuality (cf. the notes below). The stupidity of imitating *the way of the nations* (2) will have dire results. *Slinging out the inhabitants of the land,* God is about to drive them out of the city after it has been *under siege* by the enemy. (17-18)

The prospect of certain disaster is so real to Jeremiah that he utters words of lament with which the exiled people will bemoan their *affliction.* It will appear to them as *grievous* as a *destroyed . . . tent,* never again to be *set up* (19-21). In spirit the prophet also hears the *great commotion* created by the onslaught of the enemy *out of the north country.* (22; cf. 1:13 note)

Speaking in the name of the people, Jeremiah goes on to ask that justice be tempered with mercy in view of the innate weakness of human nature (23-24; cf. Jb 14:1 note). However, *upon the nations,* which have wantonly *devoured Jacob* to satisfy their own lust of conquest, God is to *pour* His *wrath.* (25; cf. Ps 79:6 note)

10:2 *The way of the nations.* The term "way" in the transferred meaning of conduct or lifestyle is one of Jeremiah's characteristic expressions (2:36; 3:13 [translated "favors"]; 3:21; 4:18; 5:4; 6:27; 7:3, 5, 23; etc.). Even before the Israelites entered Palestine, God warned them not to "learn to follow the abominable practices of those nations." (Dt 18:9)

Signs of the heavens. Eclipses of the sun and moon were considered omens of disaster. Superstitious idol worshipers were *dismayed* at them but did not "fear" (7) Him who "stretched out the heavens." (12)

10:3 *False.* A Hebrew noun denoting something as fleeting, empty, insubstantial as a puff of air, used by the Preacher for the word "vanity" (Ec 1:2). One of Jeremiah's favorite terms for idols, it occurs again in v. 15 (translated "worthless"), in 2:5 ("worthlessness"), in 8:19 ("foreign idols"), in 14:22 ("false gods"), 51:18 ("worthless"). Isaiah does not use it in this sense.

10:7 *All the wise ones.* A sarcastic allusion to the superhuman knowledge attributed to the idols (cf. Is 44:7 note). There were so many of them that they were ranked according to authority and power so as to constitute *kingdoms* or hierarchies.

10:9 *Tarshish.* Cf. 1 K 10:22 note; Eze 27:12.

Uphaz. Mentioned again in Dn 10:5, this locality remains unidentified. Perhaps it is the same as Ophir, renowned for its *gold.* (1 K 9:26 note)

10:11 *Gods . . . shall perish.* The entire verse is composed not in Hebrew but in Aramaic, the language of international diplomacy already at the time of Isaiah (2 K 18:26 note) and later the popular language of Palestine. Jeremiah anticipated the needs of the people in exile which he described so graphically. If the Israelites transported to Babylonia would say these words to their captors who there tempted them to worship idols, their answer in Aramaic would be understood.

10:12 *It is he.* Vs. 12-16 are repeated in 51:15-19.

By his wisdom. Cf. notes on Pr 8:22.

10:13 *Storehouses.* Figurative language found also in Ps 33:7 note; 135:7; Jb 37:9 note; 38:22.

10:15 *A work of delusion.* Found again in 51:18 but nowhere else in the Old Testament, this phrase was minted by Jeremiah to brand idols as objects of derision.

10:17 *Bundle.* The exiles would be allowed to take with them only a few personal belongings as they set out on the trip to Babylonia.

10:19 *Affliction.* Lit. "a sickness." Recovery from it did not come as quickly as the afflicted at first thought.

10:20 *Tent.* Cf. 4:20 note. In Is 54:2 the same figure of speech is used for the promise of restoration.

10:21 *Shepherds.* Translated "rulers" in 2:8.

10:24 *In just measure.* Restrained by pity. (30:11; 46:28)

11:1-23 Constantly devising different modes of expressing Israel's need to repent if it is not to destroy itself, Jeremiah in this chapter tries to rouse his hearers from their fatal complacency by labeling their apostasy a *revolt* against God. Their unfaithfulness was not the sin of a weak moment, but a deliberate conspiracy to defy God's claim to their loyalty. Nor could they profess ignorance of wrongdoing. For at Mt Sinai God had made a solemn pact with them. According to *the words of this covenant* He would be their God and they His people if in response to this undeserved gift of grace they would *obey* His *voice* and keep His commandments. But *in the stubbornness of his evil heart* and in the face of persistent warnings Judah repudiated the sacred pledge of obedience. Hence the curse pronounced on disobedience in the covenant will go into effect. Chosen to be God's *beloved* (15; 12:7), the covenant nation faces imminent destruction. Jeremiah's prayer in its behalf and its hypocritical ceremonial observances in God's *house* cannot *avert* its *doom.* (1-17)

It is not surprising that rebels, conspiring to dethrone God, should also plot to silence His messenger. After the Lord revealed to Jeremiah that his own townspeople of Anathoth *devised schemes* designed to *cut him off from the land of the living,* they openly threatened him with death if he were to continue to *prophesy in the name of the Lord.* These wicked machinations too would not go unpunished, for in reality they were but another revolt against God Himself. In answer to Jeremiah's appeal for God's *vengeance* on those who persecuted His ambassador, *the Lord of hosts* authorized him to announce the *evil* to come *upon the men of Anathoth.* (18-23)

11:2 *Covenant.* Occurring four more times in the next eight verses, this term contains everything essential to the relationship which the Lord established with His people. For its use as a synonym for Biblical religion see the notes on Gn 6:18; 17:2, 10; Ex 24:6-8; Dt 29:1. The book found "in the house of the Lord" early in Jeremiah's career was called "the book of the covenant." (2 K 22:8; 23:2)

11:3 *Cursed be.* The rebels against God's lordship made themselves liable to the threats of punishment clearly stated in Ex 20:5; Dt 27:15-26; 28:15-68.

11:14 *Not pray.* Cf. the introductory note to 7:16-20.

11:15 *Sacrificial flesh.* Offered in various kinds of rites.

11:20 *Thy vengeance.* There was no desire for personal revenge in *the heart and the mind* of Jeremiah. He would have given his life to save his people. Nevertheless, as God's spokesman his *cause* is also God's cause. Those who say to him: "Do not prophesy" are in effect telling God He has no right to impose His will on them. Therefore God does not reject Jeremiah's prayer as arising out of impure motives. On the contrary, He vindicates His prophet's jealous zeal for his Lord by ordering him to declare to the men of Anathoth that they "shall die by the sword" and "by famine" (22 f.). Jesus pronounced woes on His adversaries, declaring them liable to "being sentenced to hell." (Mt 23:33)

12:1-17 Though Jeremiah committed his "cause" to the Lord for adjudication, he was perplexed by the tardiness in the administration of divine justice. He wanted to "see . . . vengeance" carried out on his and God's enemies (11:20). Yet nothing happened. Instead they as well as *the wicked* and the *treacherous* in the nation continued to *thrive* and to *prosper*. He could not reconcile the facts of life with his firm conviction that God was *righteous*.

Jeremiah's *case* was summarily thrown out of court. The plaintiff, said the judge, had neither competence nor jurisdiction in determining how or when convicted criminals were to be punished. Put in his place, Jeremiah is told to trust the omniscient, omnipotent God to know how to deal with those who *have dealt treacherously with* him and when "the year of their punishment" (11:23) is to begin. For he will have even greater mysteries of God's government to cope with. (1-6)

In the meantime he can rest assured that the wicked people will not go unpunished. For in the eyes of Him who is not hampered by the dimensions of time the destruction of His *house* and the desolation of the *land,* chosen to be His *pleasant portion,* are already accomplished facts. Though His *fierce anger* demands that He abandon *the beloved* nation into *the hands of her enemies,* it pains Him to see how *wild beasts,* though commandeered by Himself, have made His *vineyard* into *a desolate wilderness.* (7-13)

The *evil neighbors* who ravished His *heritage* will be subjected to the same judgment in store for *the house of Judah.* Yet they too are included in the worldwide salvation to be mediated by Abraham's Offspring (Gl 3:16). If they accept *the ways* God taught Israel, they will *be built up in the midst of* a people of God constituted to be a spiritual community without racial distinctions or geographical boundaries. (14-17)

12:1 *Why . . . ?* Jeremiah was not the first nor the last to raise the question whether the prosperity of the wicked could be harmonized with God's justice. See the Book of Job (e.g., 21:7); Hab 1:5-13; Pss 10; 37; 73; 94.

12:2 *Near in their mouth.* Cf. Is 29:13-14 for a similar judgment on hypocrisy.

12:4 *He will not see.* The pronoun refers either to God (He does not shape our destiny) or to His prophet (he will not live to see his predictions of our death come true).

12:5 *Raced with men.* God does not owe nor does He give Jeremiah a direct answer to his question of "why?" (1). The problem would not exist if he had a firm, unquestioning faith in God's superior wisdom and limitless power to do the right thing at the right time. Instead of interrogating God, Jeremiah should trust God's management of affairs more implicitly if he is going to be able to survive even more severe tests of faith in the future.

Jungle of the Jordan. The banks of the Jordan were a dense jungle and haunt of lions. (49:19; 50:44)

12:7 *Beloved of my soul.* It grieved God to see the love He showered on His chosen people abused so maliciously that He had to "hate" (8) them for their open rebellion against Him.

12:9 *Speckled bird.* As a bird easily recognizable by its brilliant plumage is set upon if it strays into a strange flock, so Israel will be torn to pieces by foreign enemies.

12:10 *Shepherds.* Cf. 6:3 note; 23:1.

12:16 *Swear.* Cf. 4:2 first note.

Built up. Paul uses the image of "a wild olive shoot" grafted into "the olive tree" to explain how God was then fulfilling His promise to incorporate members of Gentile nations into a spiritual Israel. So all believers, whether they be Jew or Gentile, will be saved. (Ro 11:13-26; cf. also Is 2:2 notes; Jer 16:19)

13:1-27 God did not let Jeremiah give up on His people. This ch. records how He has His prophet make the threat of certain judgment unmistakably clear by means of a visual demonstration (1-11) and an illustrative parable (12-14). In each teaching device the point of comparison is made plain and its meaning applied. *A linen waistcloth* provided the material for the dramatized object lesson. This piece of a man's clothes, worn directly on the loins, symbolized the close relationship God wanted but could no longer have with the chosen people. Like the loin cloth, *spoiled* by contact with the soiling and disintegrating elements, they were *good for nothing.* As a useless garment is thrown on the refuse heap, so *this evil people* had reached the point of spiritual decay where they were not worth saving from their enemies. The parable contains the same threatening lesson. The prophet was directed to call attention to the simple, undisputed fact that a *jar* or earthen vessel, when empty, could *be filled with wine.* So the Lord *will fill with drunkenness all the inhabitants of this land,* rendering them unable to distinguish friend from foe and dooming them to die without *pity* or *compassion.*

The remaining verses of the ch. are an urgent appeal to *hear and give ear* to the warnings issued in the symbolic action and in the parable. *Twilight* has already settled on the nation's fortune. If the people in their *pride* will not listen to the appeal to give glory to the Lord, the *darkness* of such a crushing disaster will engulf them as to make Jeremiah *weep bitterly* at the very thought of it (15-17). *The king and the queen mother* will be stripped of their royal insignia; the cities from the north to the *Negeb* south of Jerusalem will be *shut up* by besieging invaders; the inhabitants of Judah will be *wholly taken into exile.* (18-19)

As they see the storm overtaking them *from the north,* they will be made to realize that the disgrace and the *violence* they suffer are not an accident of history but the unfailing execution of divine justice on *the greatness of* their *iniquity.* God could not do otherwise, for depravity was no longer eradicable from their nature. It had so saturated their very being that they could no more change their behavior than *the Ethiopian* can become white-skinned or *the leopard* can get rid of *his spots.* Therefore they are to know that the dreadful *lot* in store for them, though apparently due to the superior might of the enemy, will be determined and dealt them by the Lord because He will tolerate their *abominations* and *lewd harlotries* no longer. (20-27)

13:4 *The Euphrates.* The great river on which Babylon was located. In order to reach it, Jeremiah had to travel some 400 miles. There is no reason to doubt that he could have made the long round trip twice, as directed. However, the lesson to be taught by the waistcloth remains the same if the Hebrew word for Euphrates *(Perath)* is taken to refer to Parah, a town mentioned in Jos 18:23 and situated only a few miles north of Jerusalem. For another symbolic act carried out in full view of the people see 27:2; 28:10. Cf. also Eze ch. 4.

13:13 *Drunkenness.* The execution of divine judgment is described as the stupefying result of having "drunk at the hand of the Lord the cup of his wrath." (Is 51:17; cf. Ps 60:3; Is 51:21; 63:6; Jer 48:26; 49:12; 51:7)

13:18 *The king and the queen mother.* Jehoiachin (Coniah) and his mother are threatened again in 22:26. For the fulfilled threat see 2 K 24:8-17; Jer 29:2. For the influence wielded by the dowager queen see 1 K 2:18 note.

13:20 *The flock.* The kings are called shepherds in 10:21; 23:1-4.

13:22 *Lift up your skirts.* So apparently a harlot was humiliated in public. (26; 2:20 note; Ho 2:10; Nah 3:5)

13:25 *Lies.* The word used for false gods in 10:15.

13:27 *Neighings.* Cf. 5:8

14:1—15:21 Irrevocable Judgment on an Incorrigible Nation Despite Assurances by False Prophets and Despite Jeremiah's Intercession and Grief

14:1-22 Because the people proved to be so "accustomed to do evil" that they were incorrigible (13:23), total disaster *by sword, by famine, and by pestilence* (12) must overtake them. The Lord tried to discipline and correct them. When He chastized them by a devastating drought (1-6), they indeed professed sorrow for their *iniquities* and *backslidings* (7-9). Yet they still *loved to wander* on the paths of *iniquity.* Therefore failing to heed also this call to sincere repentance, they should not expect the Lord to do otherwise than to *punish their sins* (10; cf. 2:27; 4:10 note). For He will not be swayed from His decree to *consume them* by Jeremiah's intercession in their behalf nor by their meaningless ceremonies. (11-16)

This horrible fate is so certain to overtake them that, at its prospect, Jeremiah is to shed bitter tears as if the grievous blow had already fallen (17-18). He also in advance hears the humbled people confess their guilt, reject *the false gods,* plead for *healing,* and affirm their *hope* in the true God. (19-22)

14:1 *Drought.* Hebrew "droughts." The plural may indicate the severity and unusual length of the dryness. Apparently it occurred within memory of Jeremiah's contemporaries.

14:2 *Gates.* Figurative expression for the inhabitants within the walled cities.

14:3 *Cover their heads.* So did David to express his grief. (2 S 15:30)

14:7 *For thy name's sake.* Cf. Is 48:9 note; also Eze 20:9, 14, 22, 44.

14:10 *Wander.* Stray from "the ancient paths where the good way is." (6:16 note)

14:11 *Do not pray.* Though told explicitly that intercession could no longer avert his people's punishment (7:16), Jeremiah continued to wrestle with God as Abraham once did in behalf of doomed Sodom (Gn 18:22-33). He dares to approach the divine Judge again because he has a new argument to present. He pleads for leniency for the masses, mislead by false prophets (13). However, "the people to whom they prophesy" (16) have no excuse for rejecting the doctrines which the Lord "persistently" taught them (7:13; 25:3; 35:14). For denunciations of heretical teachers see 5:12; 6:14; 8:11, etc.

14:17 *Virgin daughter.* God promised to keep His chosen people inviolate for His holy purposes.

14:19 *Looked for peace.* Perhaps a popular saying expressing the disillusionment of trust in a false security. (8:15)

14:21 *Glorious throne.* In the temple. (17:12)

15:1-21 God turned a deaf ear to prayers in behalf of the people (14:11), but not because Jeremiah was unacceptable as a mediator. Men of the stature of *Moses and Samuel* would have fared no better. Their intercessions in crucial periods of the past did indeed save Israel from threatened destruction. Yet because of the impenitence of the nation in Jeremiah's day they would be no more able to dispose the Lord *to turn toward this people* than the prophet from Anathoth. Therefore Jeremiah was to continue to announce that, banished from God's *sight,* they were doomed to *go* the way of relentless judgment by *pestilence, the sword, famine, captivity.* Even *the kingdoms of the earth* beyond Israel's borders would be filled with *horror* at the merciless slaughter of *young men* and the massacre of the *rest* by *their enemies.* (1-9)

In the remainder of this ch. Jeremiah bares his troubled soul to God, who reproves, corrects, and rehabilitates His disenchanted servant. If the reader is inclined to be bored by the record of sheer endless warnings, delivered over and over again to an impenitent audience, he will have a slight inkling why the preacher of these useless sermons went to pieces under the emotional strain of his frustrating assignment. True, he at no time lacked the courage to confront even his nation's highest spiritual and civil authorities with an unequivocal denunciation of their misdeeds. Yet tired and disillusioned, he was ready to say with Elijah, the famous contender for the true religion: "It is enough; now, O Lord, take away my life" (1 K 19:4). In a delirium of pent-up anger he utters words of such strong protest against God as to make him liable to the charge of blasphemy. No longer "an iron pillar" (1:18) but a broken reed, he resented God's way of administering justice. His faith hangs by a thread. But he does not take his place "in the seat of scoffers" (Ps 1:1). Nor does he act on the advice Job's wife gave her sorely tried husband: "Curse God and die" (Jb 2:9). Though ranting against God, he still turns to Him for an answer to his problem. (10-18)

God does not fail to come to the rescue of His blustering, blundering spokesman. Without explaining the mystery of divine providence (as in Job's case), the Lord beckons to him to *return* from the wasteland of doubt to an implicit trust in the promise made when he was called to be "a prophet to the nations" (1:5). If he will again be the *mouth* of the Lord, he will be no less *a fortified wall of bronze* than before, against which all attacks will be futile (cf. 1:18 f.). It will not be a life of ease, for evil men will continue to *fight against* him. Yet the Lord will *save* and *deliver* him. (19-21)

15:1 *Moses and Samuel.* For their successful intervention in behalf of penitent Israel see Ex. 17:11; 32:11 ff.; Nm 14:13 ff.; 1 Sm 7:9; 12:19 ff.; Ps 99:6.

15:4 *Manasseh.* The grandfather of Josiah, the king during whose reign Jeremiah began his ministry (1:1 f.). For the wicked reign of Manasseh see 2 K 21; 2 Ch 33.

15:6 *Weary of relenting.* As at the time of the deluge (Gn 6:5-7), God would no longer allow His mercy to be abused.

15:7 *Winnowed.* Scattered them as worthless chaff was carried off by the wind during threshing operations. Cf. 4:12 note; Ps 1:4 note.

15:9 *Bore seven.* The number seven was used proverbially to express many sons (1 Sm 2:5; Ru 4:15). Mothers so blessed would see their sons struck down "at noonday"; i.e., in the prime of life.

15:10 *Woe.* Job twice cursed the day of his birth. (Jb 3:3 note; 10:18 f.; cf. Jer 20:14 ff.)

Lent . . . borrowed. Jeremiah's associates might have had a reason to curse him if he had taken advantage of them in financial transactions.

15:11 *So let it be.* Textually difficult (cf. RSV notes), this verse makes good sense if translated as follows: The Lord answered: "Verily I will set you free for good; verily I will bring it about that the opponent [will no longer curse you but] will importune you in the time of trouble," etc. For requests by Jeremiah's enemies to intercede for them see 21:1 f.; 37:3; 42:1 ff.

15:12 *Break iron.* The Babylonian invader *from the north* would have an unbreakable grip on his victim.

15:15 *Take vengeance.* Cf. 11:20 note.

15:16 *Ate them.* As food is assimilated by the body, so God's *words* were not an impersonal message, spoken without feeling, but they permeated his innermost being, bringing him *joy* and *delight.* (Eze 3:1 ff.)

15:17 *Thy hand.* What Jeremiah had to say was not of his own concoction; he spoke impelled by divine commission and authority. For the same claim see Is 8:11; Eze 3:14; 8:1.

15:18 *Why . . . ?* God does not answer the question. His children "walk by faith, not by sight." (2 Co 5:7)

Deceitful brook. Jeremiah is tempted to think that "the fountain of living waters" (2:13; 17:13) has become as "treacherous as a torrent-bed" (Jb 6:15) which quickly runs dry.

15:20 *Wall of bronze.* The Lord did not promise to make his ministry any easier but simply repeats the promise made when He called him to be "a prophet to the nations." (1:5; 18 f.; cf. also 12:5 note)

16:1—17:27 Certainty of Disaster Dramatized by Jeremiah's Unconventional Life-Style, Provoked by Israel's Ingrained Perversity, and Affirmed by God's Right and Power to Determine Mankind's Fate

16:1-21 When Jeremiah complained that he "sat alone" (15:17), ostracized by the people angered by his message, the Lord did not promise to lighten the burden of his ambassadorship. The opening verses of this ch. tell of even greater demands on his personal life. In order to be a living "sign" (Eze 24:24) of the fearful disaster announced by the spoken word, he was asked to make three drastic changes in the customary pattern of social behavior: (1) forego marriage, because whole families would be wiped out *by the sword and by famine;* (2) refuse to observe the amenities expected at funerals, because death would be so widespread that no one would survive to perform the customary mourning rites; (3) reject invitations to a house where *feasting* was going on to celebrate a joyous occasion, because there would no longer be any reason for *mirth* and *gladness* (1-9). Asked by brazen observers *why . . . all this great evil* was to happen, he was to answer that the Lord would *show . . . no favor* to a generation which had *done worse* in going *after other gods* than their *fathers.* (10-13)

At the same time, the coming disaster was not to be the end of the Lord's plan of universal salvation. For He would bring the chastened exiles *back to their own land* in order to fulfill His covenant promises (14-15). *First* (RSV note), however, worship of *detestable idols* must be rooted out. All who *have polluted* the land *with their abominations* will pay the full penalty of their sin. The executioners of divine judgment will *catch them* with the ease that *fishers* fill their nets; they will *hunt them* as *hunters* track down their quarry. (16-18)

Looking into the future, Jeremiah implored the Lord to be his *refuge in the day of trouble.* But he also rejoiced to see the time coming when *nations . . . from the ends of earth* will reject their man-made idols and worship the only true God (19-20). Jeremiah's vision was not an empty dream. For the Lord assured him that the manifestation of His *might* and *power* will bring these multitudes to *know* Him. (21)

16:6 *Cut . . . make bald.* Heathen practices in connection with funerals contrary to Mosaic law. (Cf. Lv 19:27 note, 28; 21:5; Dt 14:1)

16:7 *Cup of consolation.* At a meal prepared by friends of the bereaved family the guests drank from a common cup of wine to express their sharing in the grief.

16:14 *Days are coming.* For other brief bursts of Messianic sunlight breaking through the lowering skies of darkest gloom see 3:14, 18 f.; 4:27; 5:10, 18; 27:22; 30:3; 31:31 ff.; 32:37 ff.; 33:14 ff.

16:18 *Doubly.* To the punishment inflicted on the people in their homeland the Lord would add a second, unprecedented feature: captivity in a foreign land.

Carcasses. Idols, as helpless and lifeless as dead bodies, *polluted* the land in the same way a person became ceremonially unclean by contact with a corpse. (Nm 19:11-22; cf. also Ho 6:10)

17:1-27 The reason "why . . . the Lord pronounced all this evil against" His people is clearly stated in 16:10-13. In this ch. Jeremiah adds still more serious charges to the indictment. The wrongdoing for which the people were to be exiled was not an isolated instance or a sin in a moment of weakness. It stemmed from a heart deeply etched with lines of habitual wickedness. The pattern of evil was *engraved* by habit as deeply as an inscription chisled into stone or steel (1-4; cf. Jb 19:24). Furthermore, the offenders could not profess ignorance about how God reacts to the promptings of the heart. They needed only to be reminded of the established principles of divine government, reduced to two simple alternatives: deify *man* and be *cursed,* or trust *in the Lord* and be *blessed* (5-8). Let it be known too that it is impossible to hide from God what goes on in a *deceitful* and *corrupt* heart. There is no escaping retribution for *ways* and *doings* motivated and shaped by base desires. (9-11)

These words of judgment, which Jeremiah was authorized to address to the wicked in general, gave him courage to plead his own case before the *glorious throne* of *the hope of Israel.* He felt the need to be *healed* of the wound his heart sustained as he did battle in the Lord's cause. What sorely tried him was God's failure to *put to shame* those who openly scoffed at *the day of disaster* which he had been told to announce. The insults and hatred he suffered hurt all the more because he would not have uttered prophecies of doom if he had not been ordered to do so. In the final analysis, therefore, God's honor was at stake if He allowed His ambassador to be discredited. Because his enemies persecuted him not for personal reasons but in his capacity as the Lord's spokesman, he prayed that He *destroy them with double destruction.* (12-18)

God's response to His impatient servant's plea for vindication was not a reprimand nor a discharge from prophetic office. Instead he was commissioned to speak *the word of the Lord* to the largest possible audience. He was to confront *the kings of Judah* and *all the inhabitants* at *the gates* of Jerusalem as they would enter and leave the city. As they thronged the public square, he was to illustrate how *cursed* self-deification or *blessed* trust in the Lord (5-8) expresses itself in overt action. The concrete example Jeremiah was to cite was the way the keeping or the breaking of the sabbath law made manifest whether the Lord or sinful greed ruled in the heart. Unreserved commitment to God assured the naton His continued presence in its midst; flagrant repudiation of His claim to obedience would kindle the fires of destruction in the *gates* and in *the palaces of Jerusalem.* (19-27)

17:1 *Horns of their altars.* The blood of sacrificial offerings, applied in a purely outward ritual of expiation, could not erase *the sin of Judah.* Only penitent worshipers were assured of forgiveness, symbolized in the ceremony. (Lv 4:7; 16:18; Ex 27:1 note)

17:2 *Asherim.* Cf. Gn 28:18 note; Jdg 2:13 note; Jer 2:20 note.

17:5 *His arm.* Because "all flesh is grass," trust in human resources is foolish idolatry. (Is 40:6; Ps 103:15 f.)

17:8 *Tree planted by water.* For the same figurative language see Ps 1.

17:9 *Desperately corrupt.* One word in Hebrew, translated "incurable" in 15:18; 30:12.

17:11 *The partridge.* Having hatched eggs which another kind of bird had laid, she would soon discover that the strange brood would desert her.

17:19 *Benjamin Gate.* Though a gate by this name is mentioned 20:2 and 37:13, the Hebrew text here could well refer to an entrance available to "the sons of the people" (cf. RSV note), i.e., a gate to be used by all, whether prince or pauper, layman or priest.

17:21 *The sabbath day.* For the keeping of this commandment as a touchstone of obedience see Is 56:2 note. The forbidden *burden* consisted of articles to be offered for sale by greedy merchants. (6:13; 22:17)

18:1—20:18 Jeremiah, Imprisoned and Beaten for Calls to Repentance, Acts Out His Message with the Help of Earthenware Jars; His Deep Despondency and Bitter Complaint

18:1-23 Sent *to the potter's house,* Jeremiah was to receive an object lesson in the principles of divine government according to which God makes and keeps both His promises and threats. What he would see the human workman do when *the vessel he was making of clay was spoiled* was to be a dramatized parable of the way the heavenly Potter deals with the clay He formed into sons and daughters of Adam. However, the point of comparison is expressly limited to only one feature in the procedure of the man *working at his wheel.* As he did not at once discard the clay when it did not become a satisfactory product but *reworked it into another vessel,* so the Lord reserves for Himself the sovereign right to let the *house of Israel* or any other *nation* marred by *evil* escape being cast on the refuse heap of history if the clay of human hearts proves pliable, i.e., not hardened and resistant to the call to turn *from its evil.* The converse also holds true. God's promise to *build and plant* a nation does not go into effect automatically. If the people of Israel do evil, *not listening* to His demand that they *amend* their *ways and . . . doings,* He *will repent of the good* He *intended to do* and instead shape *evil against* them. (1-11)

The negative answer Jeremiah received to this solemn declaration was evidence that the hearts of his hearers, hardened by *stubbornness* and self-will, were not malleable for reworking (12; cf. the same verdict in 7:24; 9:13 f.; 11:8; 13:10; 16:12; 23:17). What Israel did to provoke the Lord to devise *a plan against* them was not a slight deviation from ideal behavior. Its evil deeds stemmed from a depravity so irrational and so unnatural as to have no parallel even *among the nations.* Therefore the punishment will fit the crime. *In the day of their calamity* He will make *their land a horror* to the amazement of *every one who passes by it;* He *will scatter them before the enemy,* driving them into exile (13-17). This searing indictment only increased Israel's resistance to be *reworked* (4). Hostility to God's messenger grew from passive *stubbornness* (12) to the making of *plots* designed to silence him forever. (18)

For protection against the wicked leaders and their *plotting to slay* him, Jeremiah turns to the Lord who had promised to make him "a fortified city . . . against the kings of Judah, its princes, its priests, and the people of the land" (1:18). In an impassioned plea for vindication he asks God to carry out the threats of pitiless punishment on his persecutors which he had been sent to announce as the word of the Lord in vv. 15-17 and repeatedly on other occasions (cf., e.g., 4:6 ff.; 5:6 ff.; 9:20 ff.; 13:24 ff.; 15:7). The degree to which his hearers have hardened their hearts, he argues, has brought them to the point which requires that the Lord *forgive not their iniquity.* (19-23)

18:8 *Repent.* The verb ordinarily used to describe human regret for sinful action is applied to changes in God's action in view of the way people respond to His promises and threats. (Cf. Gn 6:6 f.; Ex 32:14; Nm 23:19 note; Jer 26:3)

18:9 *Build and plant.* Here and in v. 7 God uses language He used in calling Jeremiah to be His ambassador. (1:10)

18:13 *The virgin Israel.* Cf. 14:17 note.

18:14 *Sirion.* Snow-capped Mt. Hermon (Dt 3:8 note). This verse contrasts the constancy in brute creation with the unnatural turning by Israel to "false gods" (15). This meaning emerges also without textual changes. (Cf. RSV notes)

18:17 *East wind.* Cf. 4:11; 13:24.

18:18 *The priest . . . the wise . . . the prophet.* The spiritual leaders rejected Jeremiah's claim that they were deceiving the people by proclaiming: "'Peace, peace,' when there is no peace" (8:8-12; 4:9 f.; 14:13 ff.). Rather than *heed any of his words* they agreed to use them against him on trumped-up charges as the opponents of *the* Prophet were to do when they sought "to entrap Him in His talk" and then accused Him of "perverting our nation." (Mk 12:13; Lk 12:53 f.; 23:2)

18:20 *Stood before thee.* Jeremiah interceded for his people until forbidden to do so. (7:16; 11:14; 15:1)

18:21 *Their children.* Lit.: "their sons." The punishment God threatened to inflict (and later did) was no less gruesome: "Famine and sword" were to consume "their wives, their sons, and their daughters (14:16). Cf. also Ps 137:9 note.

18:23 *Forgive not.* There comes *the time of . . . anger* when God will no longer *blot out their sin.* (2 Co 6:1 f.; Heb 3:7 ff.; Ps 95:8 ff.)

19:1-15 Obedient to a second divine directive, Jeremiah acted out the threatened punishment of Judah in another dramatized parable (cf. 18:1 ff.). The point of comparison was again to be furnished by *a potter's earthen flask.* Taken outside the city's wall, it was to be smashed into pieces so thoroughly that it could *never be mended.* Before and after Jeremiah carried out the command, he explained the meaning of his dramatic action. It was an object lesson of the way Jerusalem and Judah would be reduced to ruined bits.

In order to anticipate objections that the chosen people had no reason to expect such a dire turn of events, Jeremiah prefaced the symbolic action with a scathing denunciation of his people's heinous crimes. The very place where they heard him and were to see the breaking of the flask was mute yet strident testimony of the depths of depravity to which they had sunk. For there in *the valley of . . . Hinnom* and at the place called *Topheth* they stood accused not only of *burning incense . . . to other gods* but of going so far as *to burn their sons in the fire as burnt offerings to Baal.* The punishment would match their despicable deeds. The horrors of war would overtake them, forcing them to practice cannibalism. Destruction would extend not only to the site outside the city where these abominations and atrocities had been committed, but the Lord would *break this people and this city as one breaks a potter's vessel.* (1-13)

Jeremiah wanted this oracle of doom to reach the largest possible audience. Therefore he returned *from Topheth* and *stood in the court of the Lord's house,* where he could repeat it *to all the people.* (14-15; cf. 7:2 note)

19:2 *Potsherd Gate.* Very likely another name for the Dung Gate, which led to the city dump in *the valley of . . . Hinnom* southeast of Jerusalem. (Neh 2:13; 3:13 f.; cf. Jer 2:23 note)

19:4 *Innocents.* Children who did not deserve to be executed.

19:6 *Topheth.* Cf. 7:31 f.; Is 30:33 note.

19:8 *Hissed at.* This verse is almost identical with 18:16.

19:9 *Eat the flesh.* Predicted in Dt 28:53; fulfilled according to Lm 2:20; 4:10.

19:13 *Host of heaven.* Cf. 7:18 note.

20:1-18 When Jeremiah "stood in the court of the Lord's house" (19:14), Pashhur the *priest* used his authority as *chief officer in the house of the Lord* (Acts 4:1; 5:24) to punish him for daring "to speak words against this holy place" (Acts 6:13). After flogging him for his blasphemy, he locked him overnight in a kind of pillory, hoping to ridicule and discredit this sacrilegious babbler. However, unbowed by physical pain and uncowed by official opposition, Jeremiah announced the threat of the apostate nation's doom more emphatically and pointedly than before. He identified the destroyer "from the north" (4:6; 6:22; 10:22) as *Babylon.* He singled out Pashhur as one of the victims of war and exile (1-6). In this episode Jeremiah proved to be "an iron pillar" (1:18), unbending and unbent by opposition.

However, he was not a self-made hero. In the remaining verses of the ch. he reveals how desperately He needed God to fortify him with spiritual stamina for the task which was so distasteful to him. He remonstrates with the Lord for having given him an assignment for which he was temperamentally unsuited. He had a natural aversion to being *a laughingstock all the day.* He did not like controversy, yet had to *shout: "Violence and destruction!"* He even tried to ignore the divine impulse to speak as an inspired prophet. He was filled with *terror* by the *whispering* even of former *friends,* plotting to *take . . . revenge on him.*

In order to overcome his frustration and fear he had to remind himself that because the Lord had promised to be with him "to deliver" him (1:8), his persecutors could not overcome him. Impatient at the delay in his vindication, yet confident of divine intervention, he asked to *see* God's *vengence upon them* (1-12). Prayer not only quieted his fears but also gave him the boldness to *praise the Lord* as if He had already *delivered* him *from the hand of evildoers* (13). However, the moment he took his eyes off the Lord and became introspective, he slipped back into dark brooding over his fate. Because he was destined to *see toil and sorrow and . . . shame* in the service of the Lord, he wished he had never been born. (14-18)

The sudden change of mood from praise to God (13) to deep melancholy (14-18) will not surprise anyone who has wrestled with God in the night watches of doubt. For he knows from experience that it is not impossible to relapse into self-pity and rebellious complaint at the very moment when he thought his faith had a strong grip on God's promises.

20:1 *Pashhur.* Several priests and officials were so named. (21:1; 38:1; Neh 7:41; 10:3)

20:2 *Benjamin Gate.* Apparently the name of two gates: one in the city wall and the other in the temple precincts. Both faced north. (37:13; 38:7; cf. 17:19 note)

20:3 *Terror on every side.* By a play of words on his name, Pashhur was himself to be the embodiment of the threat of doom he declared blasphemous. For other names as living messages see Is 7:3; 8:3 f.

20:6 *Prophesied falsely.* Jeremiah did not hold out for personal revenge for his mistreatment by Pashhur. His tormentor was to be exiled and die in Babylon because he contradicted the word of God spoken in His name by Jeremiah. For the words of the false prophets see 8:11; 14:13; 23:17.

20:7 *Deceived me.* The basic meaning of this Hebrew verb is to persuade a person to take a certain course of action. Usually it denotes an inducement to do wrong. So a woman may be persuaded to commit adultery or fornication (Ex 22:16). But the same verb is used also when a man allures a woman to become his wife by speaking tenderly to her (Ho 2:14). Jeremiah declares here that he did not become a prophet of his own volition. He had to be prevailed upon to assume an obligation which brought him nothing but anguish and pain. For the deception of false prophets see 1 K 22:22 note; Eze 14:9.

20:9 *A burning fire.* While Jeremiah confesses his natural disinclination to be a prophet, he also bears witness to the psychological mystery of divine inspiration. By the miraculous working of God he became the instrument for the transmission of infallible truth.

20:10 *Whispering.* Cf. 11:19; 18:18.

20:12 *Thy vengeance.* Cf. 11:20 note.

20:14 *Cursed be the day.* The same vehement denunciation of the kind of existence to which he was destined by birth came from Job's lips. (Jb 3:2-19; 10:18; for Elijah's desire to have death end his misery see 1 K 19:4)

20:16 *The cities.* Sodom and Gomorrah. (Gn 19:24 f.)

20:17 *He.* The antecedent is the Lord, mentioned in v. 16.

21:1—38:28 PROPHETIC THREATS AND PROMISES OCCASIONED BY ISRAEL'S LEADERS

21:1—23:8 Rejection of the Ruling House of David; Bliss of Messianic Rule

The next larger section of Jeremiah's book (chs. 21—38) contains a collection of oracles arising out of the prophet's confrontation with Israel's unfaithful leaders. Kings, prophets, priests subvert rather than promote God's plan of universal salvation. Pestilence, sword, famine, and exile await all of them as well as the entire misguided people. However, the Lord of the nations will so direct world history that out of chastened and restored Israel a "righteous Branch" will spring up in the person of the Messianic King, Prophet and Priest. His rule, word and sacrifice will provide an escape for all mankind from the curse of sin.

Another distinctive feature of this section is that in almost all instances the reader is informed at what time or under what circumstances each "word of the Lord came to

Jeremiah" whereas in the preceding chapters hardly any historical data are supplied. Nevertheless, events are not arranged exclusively according to their chronological sequence. So, for example, ch. 21 records an incident which happened in the closing years of Zedekiah, the last king of Judah. Ch. 25, on the other hand, tells what Jeremiah said during the reign of Jehoiakim, who came to the throne more than 10 years before his brother Zedekiah.

21:1-14 In Zedekiah's time the Babylonian king *Nebuchadrezzar* was *making war against* Jerusalem. His troops had begun the siege of the city (2 K 25:1). A delegation, sent by Zedekiah, requested Jeremiah to *inquire of the Lord* whether *perhaps* He could be moved to do another of His *wonderful deeds* like the miracle He did to defeat the Assyrians in the days of Hezekiah (2 K 19:35). The answer from *the Lord, the God of Israel,* sealed the fate of the city. Instead of coming to the aid of its defenders He *will fight against* them with *pestilence, sword, and famine.* The king and those surviving the horrors of the siege He will deliver *into the hand of Nebuchadrezzar king of Babylon* (1-7). The only alternative to facing death was to surrender to the enemy and become *a prize of war.* (8-10)

Even though Zedekiah was a descendant of the *house of David,* with whom God had made a solemn covenant (2 Sm 7:21 ff.), he would have no successors. Kings of Israel were not to be arbitrary despots. If they ignored the demand to *execute justice,* they incurred the burning, unquenchable wrath of God. The royal city and palace, though situated on a *rock* towering over the surrounding *plain,* will not offer protection. (11-14)

21:1 *Pashhur.* Not the same person mentioned in 20:1.

Zephaniah. Mentioned again in 29:25; 37:3. The Zephaniah referred to as "the second priest" in 52:24 may not be the same person.

21:2 *Nebuchadrezzar.* A variant spelling is Nebuchad*n*ezzar. (2 K 24:1; etc.)

21:4 *Chaldeans.* Cf. Jb 1:17 note.

21:8 *Life and . . . death.* The choice of crucial alternatives is represented as a fork in the road also in Dt 30:15, 19.

21:9 *Surrenders.* Deserters did save their lives. (38:2; 39:9; 52:15)

21:12 *In the morning.* Justice was urgent business to be transacted without delay.

21:13 *Inhabitant of the valley.* Jerusalem, rising out of the lower surrounding landscape, appeared to be an impregnable *rock.*

22:1-30 According to ch. 21 Jeremiah was sent to announce divine judgment to Zedekiah, the last king of Judah, and then was authorized to denounce the entire ruling "house of David" (21:12). In this ch. the order of prophetic pronouncements is reversed. First exhortations and warnings are issued to an unnamed king, representing all *who sit on the throne of David.* If they fail to *heed these words* of admonition, *this house* shall become a desolation. (1-9)

Then three kings who immediately preceded Zedekiah are dealt with in chronological order, each one's fate demonstrating how the threat uttered against the whole dynasty would affect the lives of its individual members. Their combined reigns added up to barely a decade. Two of them were sons of Josiah, in whose 13th year Jeremiah was inducted into office (1:2); the third was a grandson of the same godly king. The first, *Shallum,* also called Jehoahaz, was to be lamented *bitterly* because he was not again *to see his native land* after Pharaoh Necho deposed him and brought him to Egypt (10-12; cf. 2 K 23:31 ff.). *Jehoiakim,* appointed by Necho to rule in his brother's place, was not to go unpunished *for shedding innocent blood and for practicing oppression and violence* in order to *compete* with Solomon's building program. At his death, circumstances were to be such as to make a decent burial for him impossible (13-19; 36:30; cf. 2 K 23:36—24:6). *Coniah,* better known as Jehoiachin, ruled only three months before he and his mother were taken to Babylonia, where they died. (20-30; cf. 2 K 24:8 note)

22:1 *Go down.* From the temple area to the royal palace, situated on a lower level.

22:3 *Do justice.* For the same instructions given to the house of David see 21:12.

22:3 *Innocent blood.* Even that of a prophet of the Lord. (26:20 ff.)

22:6 *Gilead . . . Lebanon.* Even though *the house of the king of Judah* was as precious to God as the rich grazing territory of Gilead and the wooded heights of Lebanon were prized by the people, He would not hesitate to let it "become a desolation" like *a desert* or *an uninhabited city.* (Cf. RSV note)

22:7 *Choicest cedars.* As stately trees were felled on Mt. Lebanon, so God would cut down the prominent men of state.

22:20 *Go up.* The city of Jerusalem is addressed. Its citizens are to have reason for shouting their laments far and wide: from the heights of *Lebanon;* from Mt. Hermon, rising out of *Bashan;* from *Abarim,* from which Moses had a glimpse of the Promised Land (Nm 27:12 note; Dt 32:49). Misled by false leaders, called "shepherds," they will wail like "a woman in travail" as they suffer the consequences of their "wickedness." (22 f.)

Lovers. Denoting idols in 3:1 and foreign allies in 4:30 and 30:14, this term occurs as a parallel to "shepherds" in v. 22.

22:23 *O inhabitant of Lebanon.* The king and his nobles felt themselves as secure as birds in their nest high in *the cedars* of Lebanon.

22:30 *Childless.* In his genealogical record no descendant would bear the royal title, though he was to have children (1 Ch 3:17 f.) and his grandson Zerubbabel was to play a prominent role after the Babylonian exile. (Ez 3; Hg 1:1; 2:2)

23:1-8 The arraignment of the wicked shepherds (ch. 22) extends into the opening verses of this ch. God will attend to them as they deserve for neglect of their duties and for their *evil doings* by which they *have scattered* and *driven . . . away* the *flock* entrusted to them by the Lord (1-2; Ps 80:1; 95:7). However, God will not let their wickedness frustrate His announced purpose to let Abraham's descendants be instrumental in blessing "all the families of the earth" (Gn 12:3 note). In order to pursue His plan of universal salvation (16:19), He will first bring back a *remnant* from the Babylonian captivity. (3-4)

Then He will shape the course of history so that *the days are coming* when He will establish His Messianic kingdom on earth. From the root of David's lineage He will let spring forth a *Branch* or Descendant. Unlike Israel's kings He is *righteous* in His person (Zch 3:8; 6:12; cf. also Is 4:2; 9:7; 11:1 note). As indicated by His name, His subjects will also derive a unique benefit from His reign. He will make it possible for them to call Him: *The Lord is our righteousness.* For claiming His merits before the judgment seat of God, they, unrighteous sinners though they are, will be declared righteous (5-8; Ro 3:21-26). God kept His promise "in Jesus Christ, whom God made our wisdom, our righteousness and sanctification and redemption." (1 Co 1:30)

The language and concepts of the prophecy range back and forth between preliminary and final fulfillment, between "shadow" and "the substance of what is to come" (Cl 2:17). Israel and Judah, reunited to become one nation, are a pledge of the spiritual unity of the Messianic kingdom. *Saved* from extinction in Babylonia and permitted to *dwell securely* (6) in its homeland, Israel after the flesh foreshadows the perfect bliss awaiting Israel after the Spirit. The rule of good *shepherds* reaches its fullness when Jesus Christ will *deal wisely* as He effects *justice and righteousness* (5) for those who stand condemned under the Law.

23:4 *Shepherds.* For an expanded prophecy of the Good Shepherd see Eze 34; for its fulfillment see Jn 10:1-18.

23:6 *The Lord is our righteousness.* If the King's name is translated as a sentence (RSV) and not as a combination of two nouns in apposition to each other: "the Lord our righteousness" (KJV), the context requires the interpretation that He bears this title because it is He through whom we become righteous in God's sight.

23:9-40 Arraignment of Spiritual Leaders Prophets and Priests

23:9-40 Not only the kings (21:1—23:8) but also the men to whom God entrusted the spiritual welfare of "the people of His pasture" (Ps 95:7) desecrated their sacred office by false teaching and immoral living. On numerous occasions Jeremiah exposed them for what they were (2:8, 26; 5:31; 14:13-16; 27:9 f., 16-18; 32:32). In the remaining verses of this ch. he develops a full-scale denunciation of their criminal perversion of divine truth and announce their doom *in the year of their punishment* (12). The *holy words* of the Lord the prophet must proclaim are so frightful that he reels *like a drunken man* under their impact, (9-12)

He must speak thus because the prophets of Jerusalem lack every requirement of spokesmen of the Most High: (1) Instead of being an example of godliness to the flock, *they strengthen the hands of evildoers* by committing such heinous crimes as *adultery* (13-15); (2) Instead of reproving sinful behavior, as they would if they had *stood in the council of the Lord* and had *given heed to his word,* they confirm the people in *the evil of their doings* by assuring them that *"No evil shall come upon you"* (16-22); (3) Instead of standing in awe of the Lord of *heaven and earth,* from whom no man can *hide himself,* they glibly mouth each other's *lying dreams* and *the deceit of their own heart* rather than speaking God's *word faithfully,* which by contrast is *like fire . . . and like a hammer which breaks the rock in pieces* (23-32); (4) Instead of truthfully telling the people what *the burden* or message is when they ask, *"What has the Lord answered?"* they *pervert the words of the living God.* If they continue to use the term *"the burden of the Lord,"* even though it is merely every man's own word, they themselves will become a burden to the Lord which He will cast off to their *everlasting reproach and perpetual shame.* (33-40)

23:11 *In my house.* Idols were placed even in the temple. (2 K 21:5; Eze 8:6 ff.)

23:15 *Wormwood.* Cf. 9:15 and Pr 5:4 note.

23:17 *It shall be well.* For other examples of their irresponsible coddling of evildoers see 4:10; 6:14 note; 14:13; Is 30:10.

23:18 *In the council of the Lord.* They were not in intimate association with the Lord as were those prophets to whom He entrusted the task of "revealing his secret." (Am 3:7)

23:19 *The storm of the Lord.* The same threat is found in 30:23 f.

23:20 *In the latter days.* For the meaning of this phrase, occurring frequently in Jeremiah, see Is 2:1 second note.

23:25 *I have dreamed.* God used dreams to reveal Himself (Gn 28:12 f; Nm 12:6; Jl 2:1; Mt 1:20; 2:12, 19). However, the false prophets deceived the people with "lying dreams" (32) fabricated in "the deceit of their own heart." (26)

23:27 *Forget my name.* Prophets who taught contrary to the doctrines revealed by God were to be branded imposters. (Dt 13:1 f. notes; 18:21 note)

23:33 *Burden of the Lord.* The Hebrew word "burden" ordinarily denotes a weight or load carried by man or beast of burden (17:21; 2 K 5:17). It has also the transferred meaning of message or utterance (Is 13:1 second note). In vv. 33-40 Jeremiah plays on its double meaning. When the people mockingly ask: *"What is the burden* (oracle) *of the Lord?"* they are to be told: You are a *burden* to the Lord which He will carry no longer though He once "bore you as a man bears his son." (Dt 1:31)

24:1—25:38 True Prophecies: Israel's Future and World History Symbolized by Two Baskets of Figs and the Cup of the Lord's Fury

24:1-10 Because, unlike the false prophets (ch. 22), Jeremiah "stood in the council of the Lord" (23:18), he was given a vision of the true course of events in Israel's future. The Lord showed him *two baskets,* the one containing *very good figs* and the other *very bad figs.* These commonplace things become object lessons of revealed truth. The Lord will *regard as good* figs *the exiles* whom *Nebuchadnezzar . . . had brought . . . to Babylon* when he removed *Jeconiah* (Jehoiachin) and the skilled *craftsmen* from Jerusalem (22:24 ff.; 2 K 24:10-16). Chastised, humbled, sincerely penitent, they will no longer refuse to let the Lord *give them a heart* so that He can set His *eyes upon them for good* and *bring them back* to their homeland. The bad figs are the people in Jerusalem who escape captivity. Because they remained self-righteous and impenitent, *they shall be utterly destroyed from the land.* (Cf. Dt 28:37)

24:1 *The Lord showed me.* Other ordinary objects that were given parabolic meaning were an almond tree (1:11), a boiling pot (1:13), a potter's vessels (chs. 18 and 19), a yoke. (27:2)

24:2 *First-ripe figs.* Considered a delicacy (Is 28:4; Hos 9:10). Perhaps they were offered as firstfruits (Ex 23:19). If the bad figs, also "placed before the temple of the Lord," were meant to serve the same purpose, they would have been a blatant expression of contempt for the Lord. Sacrificing "what is blemished" was an abomination to Him. (Ml 1:6-14)

24:7 *A heart to know.* For the Biblical meaning of "to know" as denoting more than intellectual awareness see Gn 18:19 note; Dt 9:24 note.

24:8 *In the land of Egypt.* Those who were taken there by Pharaoh Neco (22:10 ff.; 2 K 23:31-34) or who fled there to escape the invading Babylonians.

25:1-38 From the beginning of his ministry "in the thirteenth year" of Josiah (1:2) to *the fourth year of Jehoiakim . . . twenty-three years* later, Jeremiah spoke *the word of the Lord . . . persistently* to *all the people of Judah.* As summarized in vv. 1-7, what he said was diametrically opposed to the untruths propounded by those who spoke "not from the mouth of the Lord" (23:16). Whereas these impostors duped their hearers into believing that "it shall be well with" them (23:17), Jeremiah declared unequivocally that total disaster would overtake them if they did not turn from provoking the Lord by going *after other gods.* But the people had *not listened to* the truth, preached by Jeremiah for more than two decades and by *all His servants the prophets* whom God *persistently* sent in the past.

The Lord of hosts would be mocked no longer. He had at hand a *servant* to whom He assigned the task of executing justice on His apostate people and on the *nations round about* them. It was Nebuchadnezzar, *the king of Babylon.* At that very moment he was setting out on his march southward from Carchemish on the upper Euphrates, where he had defeated Pharaoh Neco in 605 BC (46:2; 2 K 23:29). Eventually this scourge "from the north" (1:14; 4:6) would turn the land into *a ruin and a waste,* forcing its inhabitants to serve him *seventy years.* Then the Babylonians, also called *the Chaldeans,* would in turn be punished *for their iniquity* (8-14). For *the Lord, the God of Israel,* at whose command Jerusalem, the city called by His name, was to be destroyed, will see to it that also *all the nations* will *not go unpunished* (29). The *desolation* awaiting them is described frequently as brought about by a *cup of the wine of wrath,* which Jeremiah, acting as divine cupbearer, will force them to drink. No nation, whether world powers like Egypt and Babylon or one of the lesser states of the ancient world, will be able to *refuse to accept the cup from* his *hand.* (15-29)

Lest anyone think the fate of kingdoms and empires, mentioned by way of example, is merely an accident of history, Jeremiah is instructed to elaborate on the causes of their downfall. The doom not only of the people of *his fold* but also of *all the inhabitants of the earth* is sealed because the Lord insists on *entering into judgment with all flesh* according to unalterable laws of justice. No resistance is possible. For He issues thundering commands *from on high* which *resound to the ends of the earth.* (Am 1:2; Jl 2:11; 3:16) Scornful of any attempted opposition, He has ample reason to *shout like those who tread grapes* in a winepress (30-31). The *great tempest* of judgment will be so devastating that there will be no survivors to bury *those slain by the Lord* (32-33). So certain are *slaughter and dispersion* to materialize as threatened that the prophet can call on the *shepherds* or kings to *wail . . . and cry* as if they and their *flock* had already suffered the pain of *the fierce anger of the Lord.* (34-38)

25:6 *Work of your hands.* Idols (1:16; 10:3 f.).

25:9 *My servant.* So called again in 27:6; 43:10. For the application of this term to various persons see Is 42:1 second note.

25:10 *The millstones and . . . the lamp.* Deathly stillness and unrelieved darkness will replace *mirth* and *gladness.*

25:11 Seventy years. For the computation of this time span see 2 Ch 36:21 note; Is 23:15 note.

25:13 *In this book.* The record of all the words God spoke to Jeremiah until the fourth year of Jehoiakim were burned by the king, necessitating the writing of another scroll by Baruch at Jeremiah's dictation (ch. 36). The phrase "as at this day" (18) may have been incorporated in the later edition.

25:14 *Of them.* Of the Babylonians.

25:15 *This cup . . . of wrath.* Cf. 13:13 note.

25:17 *All the nations.* In the following verses they are listed according to their location in a line running from south (southeast and southwest) to north (northeast and northwest). For the oracles addressed to them all see chs. 46—51, which in the Septuagint, the ancient

Greek translation, are found following the words "written in this book" in v. 13 of ch. 25.

25:26 *Babylon.* The Hebrew text reads "Sheshach" (also in 51:41), a cryptogram which uses a coded way of spelling. Known as Athbash, the last letter of the alphabet was substituted for the first and the second last for the second, etc.

25:30 *Roar.* Cf. Am 1:2; Jl 2:11; 3:16.

26:1—29:32 True Prophecies of Judgment Contested by False Prophets

26:1-24 Denunciation of false security, propagated by lying demagogs, brought Jeremiah not only verbal abuse but resulted in threats against his life. When standing *in the court of the Lord's house* he confronted the assembled worshipers with *all the words* the Lord commanded him to speak; he did *not hold back a word* but boldly announced God's decree to destroy the temple and Jerusalem because of *their evil doings.* Complete disaster was inevitable unless they heeded the urgent call to repentance required by God's *servants the prophets.* (1-6)

A mob consisting of *the priests and the prophets and all the people* demanded that he be executed for uttering blasphemy against God's holy habitation (7-9; Dt 18:20). They pressed their charges before *the princes of Judah* who held court in a gate of the temple (10-11). Defending himself before this tribunal, Jeremiah again unflinchingly insisted that they repent of their *ways* and *doings.* By putting him to death, he added, they would only add to their guilt since they would be shedding innocent blood (12-15). The judges, however, did not impose the *death* sentence, basing their verdict of not guilty on a precedent which occurred over a century ago. At that time King Hezekiah did not put the prophet Micah to death when he spoke similar threats against Zion and Jerusalem. (16-19)

Jeremiah's life had indeed hung by a thread, as a recent incident showed. For *another man* by the name of *Uriah,* who *prophesied . . . in words like those of Jeremiah,* was put to death on orders from Jehoiakim. Because the king regarded the Lord's spokesman guilty of treason, he went to great lengths to seize the accused. When Uriah fled to Egypt, he had him extradited and then executed him like a common criminal (20-23). Jeremiah escaped a similar fate because a man at the royal court by the name of *Ahikam* intervened in his behalf. (24)

26:1 *This word.* On the relationship of the brief sermon recorded here and the longer address also spoken in the court of the temple see 7:2 note.

26:3 *Repent.* For the use of this expression applied to God see 18:8 note.

26:6 *A curse.* Jerusalem's destruction will become proverbial. When uttering a curse, *all the nations* will say: Let Jerusalem's fate overtake you.—For *Shiloh* see 7:12.

26:10 *The New Gate.* Known perhaps also as "the upper Benjamin Gate." (20:2 note)

26:18 *Micah . . . said.* The elders cited verbatim the words spoken by him and recorded in 3:12 of the Book of Micah.

26:20 *Uriah.* Unknown except for the reference here to his tragic fate. At his home in *Kiriath-jearim,* a few miles north of Jerusalem, the ark of the covenant was lodged during Samuel's time. (1 Sm 7:2)

26:22 *Elnathan.* A member of the delegation sent to Egypt to bring Uriah back, he later gave good advice to the king (36:12, 25)

26:23 *Fetched Uriah.* Because favorable diplomatic relations with Egypt existed at the time, the requested extradition was granted.

Burial place. The executed criminal was not accorded a resting place in a family sepulcher but was thrown into a common grave. (Cf. 2 K 23:6)

26:24 *Ahikam.* His father *Shaphan* was a trusted official of King Josiah (2 K 22:12, 14). His son Gedaliah, appointed governor by Nebuchadnezzar, respected Jeremiah. (39:14; 2 K 25:22)

27:1-22 Chs. 27 and 28 record another confrontation between Jeremiah and the purveyors of false teachings (cf. ch. 26). Again prophet was pitted against prophet, Jeremiah's word against a rival claim also asserting, "Thus says the Lord of hosts" (28:2). The conflict had an international setting. Emissaries from five neighboring states came to Jerusalem to enlist Judah's cooperation in a plot to throw off Babylonian domination. At the time Zedekiah was on the throne in Jerusalem. However, he was only a puppet king ruling by the grace of Nebuchadnezzar. In 597 BC the latter had conferred the royal title on him after deposing and exiling his predecessor Jehoiachin.

At the Lord's command Jeremiah employed a visual aid to demonstrate the futility of the proposed joint action. He appeared before the foreign delegates wearing *thongs and yoke-bars* of the kind used to harness oxen to a plow or wagon. This device of animal servitude was to symbolize the subjugation of *all these lands* to the will of Nebuchadnezzar. All efforts to shake off this yoke would end in disaster. For the Babylonian king himself was a *servant* (25:9 note), employed by the Creator of the universe to shape the destiny of nations according to His sovereign will. The Babylonian empire too would exist only until it had served His purpose. Then it, in turn, would become the *slave* of *many nations and great kings.* (1-11)

Lest the king of Judah follow the advice of prophets who urged him and the people not to put their necks *under the yoke of the king of Babylon,* Jeremiah turned to Zedekiah warning him *in like manner* of the catastrophe in store for any nation which will *not serve the king of Babylon.* (12-15)

Finally Jeremiah *spoke to the priests and to all this people* who were inclined to believe the *lie* that the Babylonian power was about to disintegrate. For lying prophets predicted that the sacred furnishings of the temple, which Nebuchadnezzar had taken a few years earlier, *will now shortly be brought back from Babylon.* Jeremiah countered this delusion with the warning that rebellion against Nebuchadnezzar would make *a desolation* of the city of Jerusalem. After its fall *the rest of the vessels* still left in it would likewise *be carried to Babylon,* where they would stay until the Lord determined to *give attention to them.* (16-22)

27:1 *Zedekiah.* The reading "Jehoiakim" is a scribal error, as vv. 3 and 12 demonstrate. See the RSV note.

27:7 *Son and . . . grandson.* It was suicide to oppose the might of Nebuchadnezzar. The Babylonian empire would dominate the ancient world for a period of three generations. Then a coalition of *many nations* under the leadership of the Medes and the Persians and their *great kings* was destined to make a *slave* of the lordly nation.

27:16 *Vessels.* For a description of the furnishings of the temple see 1 K 7:15-39.

27:20 *Jeconiah.* Also called Jehoiachin. (2 K 24:14-16)

27:22 *Carried to Babylon.* For the fulfillment of the prediction see 52:17-20; 2 K 25:13-17. For the promised return see Ez 1:2-7; 7:19.

28:1-17 Jeremiah's dramatized demand for submission to Nebuchadnezzer, God's "servant" of judgment on His apostate people, was not to go unchallenged by prophets who likewise claimed the right to say, "Thus says the Lord of hosts" (27:4; 28:2). Their spokesman was a certain *Hananiah . . . from Gibeon,* a few miles northwest of Jerusalem (Jos 9:3; 21:17). Before the same audience of priests and all the people before whom Jeremiah spoke (27:16), the impostor declared that the Lord already had *broken the yoke* of Babylonian servitude. As a result *all the vessels of the Lord's house* together with *Jeconiah* (Jehoiachin) . . . *and all the exiles* taken *to Babylon* would be brought back to Jerusalem *within two years.* (1-4)

Jeremiah's response was marked by restraint. Nothing would please him more than to be able to say *Amen!* to the prediction of an immediate deliverance of the people he loved so dearly. Nevertheless, he did not retract what he had said. The future would demonstrate whether *the Lord* had *truly sent* him or Hananiah. For *from ancient times* true prophecies, whether of weal or woe, always came true (5-9). Enraged by Jeremiah's calm assurance of vindication, Hananiah broke *the yoke-bars* which the former wore to symbolize his message of doom. Though no doubt the mob cheered to see him humiliated, no one laid hands on him, so that he *went his way* unharmed. (10-11)

As a true prophet he did not make his own reply to his tormentor but waited until *sometime* later *the word of the Lord came* to him instructing him what to say. The divine message he was given to proclaim put an end to Hananiah's career. Because the latter *made this people trust in a lie,* he would not live the *two years* (3) within which his prediction was to have come true. And so it was. Already two months after his confrontation with Jeremiah *the prophet Hananiah died.* (12-17)

28:1 *Hananiah.* Except for the part he played in this incident, nothing is known of him.

28:9 *It will be known.* For criteria of true prophecy see Dt 13:2 note; 18:21 note.

28:12 *Sometime after.* Jeremiah did not refute Hananiah on his own authority but waited for a divinely inspired rebuttal, as he did on a later occasion. (42:7)

28:16 *Rebellion.* Teaching false doctrine is not a trifling misdemeanor but a heinous crime because it misleads people to defy the will of God. Dire punishment awaits such perverters of the truth. (29:21 f.)

29:1-32 Jeremiah's prophecies of certain disaster if the people did not repent met with opposition and ridicule not only at home but also in Babylon, where King Jehoiachin, the influential people of Judah, and the skilled craftsmen were exiled prisoners of Nebuchadnezzar. An early release, as predicted by Hananiah (ch. 28), was confidently asserted also by false prophets in their own midst. Three of them bore the name *Ahab, Zedekiah,* and *Shemaiah* (21, 24). In order to expose their teaching as heresy Jeremiah addressed a *letter . . . to the elders of the exiles, and to the priests, the prophets, and all the people.* It was sure to reach them because he was able to dispatch it by the same couriers who bore an official communication from King Zedekiah to Nebuchadnezzar. (1-3)

Jeremiah warned his readers not to believe the self-styled prophets who in the name of God promised them imminent liberation, for they were peddling a brazen *lie.* Instead of letting themselves be duped by these impostors whom God *did not send,* the exiles were to engage in activities which anticipated a prolonged sojourn on foreign soil, such as building houses, planting gardens, and founding families. The continued welfare of the Babylonian state would determine their own well-being so directly that he urged them to *pray to the Lord on its behalf* (4-9). There was indeed *a future and a hope* in God's plans for the exiled people. However, only after many years would the chastisement produce the desired change in their lives. When they would again turn to the Lord with all their heart, He would keep His promise to bring them back to their homeland. (10-14)

From this brief assurance of eventual *welfare* Jeremiah abruptly reverts to a denunciation of the prophets who, at home and abroad, deny the necessity of repentance to avert God's judgment on an apostate nation. For the benefit of his readers he first reiterates what he had said to their *kinsmen who did not go . . . into exile* with them. Their escape did not disprove his contention that they were "bad figs" (24:2 f., 8), destined to be thrown on a rubbish heap. For contrary to the word of false prophets, they too would eventually suffer the ravages of *sword, famine, and pestilence* (cf. 24:10). In the same way the exiles will find out that the false hopes raised by *Ahab* and *Zedekiah,* who in Babylon claimed to speak in the name of the Lord, would turn out to be *lying words.* For their adulterous lives and their blasphemous fraud the Lord will *deliver them into the hand of Nebuchadrezzar,* who will *slay them before* their *eyes.* (15-23)

In reply to Jeremiah's letter another impostor, named *Shemaiah,* wrote from Babylon reproving those who had *charge in the house of the Lord* for not silencing the *madman* who prophesied that the *exile will be long* (24-28). After *Zephaniah the priest* read the letter in Jeremiah's hearing, the latter sent word *to all the exiles* saying that Shemaiah and his descendants would not live *to see the good* the Lord will do to His people after the exile had run its course. (29-32)

29:1 *The elders.* The Hebrew texts reads "the rest of the elders" (cf. RSV note). Some of them no doubt succumbed to the rigors of the forced march from Jerusalem.

29:2 *Queen mother.* Cf. 13:18 note. The Hebrew word for eunuchs is translated "officers" in 39:3 and "leaders" in 41:16.

29:3 *Zedekiah . . . sent . . . to Nebuchadnezzar.* Perhaps he was sending tribute to Babylon or the delegation was to assure Nebuchadnezzar of Zedekiah's refusal to support the plot instigated by the neighboring states (27:1-7). The bearers of the letter seem to have sided with Jeremiah. *Elasah* may have been a brother of Ahikam, who befriended the prophet (26:24). *Hilkiah,* the father *Gemariah,* probably was the high priest during the reign of Josiah. (2 K 22:4, 8)

29:7 *Pray.* Cf. 1 Ti 2:1 f. for a similar injunction.

29:10 *Seventy years.* Cf. 25:11 note.

29:16 *The king.* At the time Zedekiah sat *on the throne of David.* Jeremiah personally delivered the same threat to the king. (27:12-15)

29:21-22 *Ahab . . . and Zedekiah.* Nothing more is known of them except this prophecy of their execution by fire. For this mode of punishment see Dn 3:19 f.

29:23 *Folly.* Denoting more than an indiscretion, this term designates wanton crimes. (Gn 34:7 note)

29:24 *Shemaiah.* Not mentioned elsewhere.

29:29 *Zephaniah.* Cf. 21:1 note.

30:1—33:26 True Prophecies of Future Bliss in the Face of Apparent Hopelessness

30:1-24 Impelled by the divine necessity laid on him, Jeremiah pronounced inexorable judgment on a nation in defiant rebellion against the Lord of hosts. He carried out his unpopular assignment even though men pretending to speak in the name of the same God ridiculed and opposed him (chs. 26—29). However, he was commissioned not only "to destroy and to overthrow" but also "to build and to plant" (1:10). As documented in chs. 30—33, he was authorized to elaborate God's "plans for welfare" briefly outlined in vv. 10-14 of the previous ch. and elsewhere. (16:14 note)

The vision of future blessings accorded him ranges in scope and time from Israel's national restoration in the more immediate future to mankind's liberation from spiritual bondage in the Messianic age. He need not fear that time will prove him wrong. The Lord ordered him to *write in a book all the words* of his prophecy, for they will stand the test of ages to come. The vantage point in time from which the vision proceeds is the exile. The dispersion of the chosen people had not only occurred, as predicted, but was also about to end, as he said it would, after achieving its chastening purpose. (1-3)

The convulsion attending the overthrow of the Babylonian empire fills the exiles with terror. They fear this international upheaval will bring them a worse fate. However, in this *time of distress* the Lord will shape the event so that they *shall be saved out of it.* For He will use it to initiate *that day* when He will raise up a *David* whose universal kingdom will have no end. (4-9)

Turning directly to the people still in the land of their captivity, Jeremiah assures them of God's power and will to direct the course *of all the nations* so that the descendants of *Jacob* will not vanish from history as their oppressors will. Justly chastened but graciously returned to *quiet and ease,* the survivors of the exile will again be accorded the status of God's *servant* and entrusted with the role for which He chose them. (10-11)

From a human viewpoint they indeed seemed doomed to extinction. For the *wound,* inflicted on them for their *flagrant* sins, seemed *incurable.* Nevertheless, He who made them *cry out over* their *hurt* is able to *restore health to* them. For He will deal a fatal blow to the *foes* who made it appear as if *no one cares* for *Zion.* (12-17)

Then Jeremiah is granted a view of the results of God's intervention in behalf of His stricken people. Brought back to their homeland, they will rebuild *the city* of Jerusalem, raise *songs of thanksgiving* for their restored fortunes, and become an established *congregation.* However, their physical and national well-being is not to be an end in itself. Again in covenant relationship with their God, they would be His instrument to mend mankind's broken fellowship with its Creator. For out of their midst there was to *come forth* a Prince and a Ruler who alone will have the credentials to *approach* the throne of justice as intermediary for a sinful world (18-21). *In the latter days* it will be evident that resistance by *the wicked* to *the intents* of God's *mind* will be swept away by the *whirling tempest* of His *wrath.* (23-24)

30:2 *A book.* For other references to a written record of Jeremiah's words see 25:13 note; 36:2.

30:3 *Days are coming.* They begin with the day of Babylon's overthrow and extend into "the latter days" of the Messianic era. (8, 24; 23:5, 7; 31:31; 16:14 note)

30:6 *Hands on his loins.* Men will cry out as if

experiencing the pangs of a woman in childbirth. (4:31; 6:24)

30:7 *Jacob.* The promise of restoration is made not only to the ten tribes of the Northern Kingdom, often called Jacob or Israel, but to "Israel and Judah." (3; 3:7 note)

30:9 *David.* The "righteous Branch" to arise from David's lineage here bears the name of His royal ancestor. (23:5; Eze 34:23; 37:24; Hos 3:5; Lk 1:32 f.)

30:11 *In just measure.* Cf. 10:24 note. Vv. 10-11 appears again in 46:27 f.

30:14 *Lovers.* Allies. Cf. 22:20 note.

30:21 *Approach me.* The high priest of the old covenant dared not, on pain of death, draw near the holy God by virtue of his own authority and character. The Ruler and Prince to come, combining royal and priestly functions, will have access to the divine throne without sacrificing first for His own sins, for He had none. (Heb 7:26 ff.)

31:1-40 In 40 verses of another ch. Jeremiah says again that "days are coming" when the Lord "will restore the fortunes" of His people (30:3). Reiterated assurances of God's unmerited blessings are not a waste of space. For mankind's heart, "deceitful above all things and desperately corrupt" (17:9), is as reluctant to accept gifts of divine mercy as it is prone to ignore insistent calls to repentance.

Mindful of this human weakness, the Lord lets Jeremiah speak again and at length of *that time* when *all the families of Israel,* though dispersed and enslaved for their apostasy, will once more be united in their homeland and join in worship on *Zion.* The deliverance from *the wilderness* of their exile will be a miracle of grace as once their ancestors were freed from Egyptian bondage only because they "found favor" in God's sight (Ex 33:12-16). For only *everlasting love* and unchanging *faithfulness* is capable of regarding Israel as a *virgin* after she had "played the harlot with many lovers" (1-6; 3:1). So astounding is the fact that *the Lord has saved his people* that the world of nations is called upon to *sing aloud with gladness for Jacob.* The redeemed themselves will *come and sing aloud on the height of Zion* because not even the most distant prisoner and the physically handicapped will be left behind. (7-14)

All this demands faith in God's promises. There was nothing on the contemporary scene even to suggest such a reversal of history. For if *Rachel,* ancestor of Benjamin and some northern tribes, were still alive, she would be heard *weeping for her children,* slain, dragged into captivity and gone for good. However, the Lord would also tell her to dry her tears, for her offspring would *come back from the land of the enemy.* (15-17)

The Lord has heard them *bemoaning* their past behavior, acknowledging that they acted *like an untrained calf* which resists disciplining. Now *chastened* and *ashamed,* they implore the Lord to *be restored* to fellowship with Him (18-19). He hears their penitent pleas, He holds introspection with Himself. His readiness to treat them again as a dear son and a darling child in spite of their insolent waywardness is a mystery of love which defies rational explanation (20). Yet it is true that He is about to summon the reclaimed *virgin Israel* to set out at once on the journey to her own *cities.* By failing to respond properly she would again prove herself a *faithless daughter,* unwilling to believe that the Lord has *created a new thing.* (21-22)

In order to overcome misgivings and unbelief, the Lord graciously lets Jeremiah repeat the promise of redemption over and over again. In five more oracles, filling the remainder of the ch., the fainthearted and the doubting are given renewed assurance of a glorious future: (1) Jerusalem will once again be hailed the *habitation of righteousness* (23-26); (2) The land of Israel and Judah will be repopulated and made prosperous, each citizen recognizing his individual responsibility in the community (27-30); (3) The Lord will create also the kind of spiritual reconstruction necessary if they are to be His people and He their God. Because *they broke* the *covenant* made with *their fathers,* He will not only renew it but also instil the inner motivation to keep it. Response to the *new covenant* will be a spontaneous compulsion to keep His *law,* which He will *put . . . within them* and *write . . . upon their hearts.* It will remain a covenant of grace. If they fall short of perfect obedience, He *will forgive their iniquity and . . . remember their sin no more* (31-34); (4) The revival of the chosen people cannot fail to materialize. For the promise to bring it about is made by the same God who set the universe in motion and keeps it from falling into chaos (35-37; 33:20 f.; Is 54:9 f.); (5) In a closing vision Jeremiah is made to see Jerusalem rebuilt tower by tower and gate by gate. (38-40)

31:1 *All the families of Israel.* Restored to favor with God, the chosen people will no longer be torn by strife among themselves as they were since the death of Solomon. The healing of the breach between the Northern Kingdom (Israel, Ephraim, Samaria) and the Southern Kingdom (Judah) was to reestablish joint worship "on the height of Zion" (12). The restored unity of faith also foreshadowed the common bonds of fellowship by which God would link all believers with one another in a communion of saints, redeemed from the bondage of sin by His Son. (Jn 10:16)

31:7 *Chief of the nations.* Israel owed its preeminence solely to its choice by the Lord to be His instrument in blessing all nations. This undeserved distinction accounts for similar titles of honor: "my first-born" (9; Ex 4:22 note), "dear son," "darling child." (20)

31:14 *Feast the soul.* From a restored prosperity the people will be able to supply the sustenance *of the priests* as required, e.g., by Lv 7:34.

31:15 *Ramah.* Five miles north of Jerusalem. Here Rachel died in childbirth when she and her husband Jacob were on their way to Bethlehem (Gn 35:16; 1 Sm 10:2). Weeping from her grave over the loss of her descendants to a ruthless conqueror, she will shed bitter tears again when the mothers of Bethlehem lament the death of their infant sons killed by Herod. (Mt 2:17 f.)

31:16-17 *Your work.* Her pains in childbirth and her labors in rearing sons will not be in vain, for a "remnant of Israel" (7) will survive and *come back to their own country.*

31:18 *Bring me back.* The Hebrew verb, occurring twice in this sentence, frequently denotes a turning back to the Lord in repentance (3:12, 14, 22). Restoration, whether physical or spiritual, is possible only if the Lord brings it about.

31:22 *Protects a man.* The result of the creative act of God is *a new thing* which did not exist before. The restoration of Israel will have unprecedented results. No longer will strong men be necessary to ward off intruders. Women will suffice to surround their husbands with adequate defense.

31:26 *I awoke.* The revelation accorded Jeremiah was like a pleasant dream. So Jacob "awoke from his sleep" in which he was granted a dream-vision (Gn 28:16)

31:27 *Seed of man and . . . of beast.* The human population and herds of animals will increase as if springing up from seed scattered over the land by the Lord.

31:29 *Sour grapes.* If people wanted to claim to be the victims of a miscarriage of justice, they would quote a proverb about children whose teeth were made to feel dull whereas not they but their fathers had actually eaten *sour grapes. In those days* of their restoration to God's favor (32:38) the redeemed would no longer quote this saying to shrug off personal responsibility for their misdeeds (Dt 24:16; Eze 18). The decree that "every one shall die for his own sin" (30) was not at variance with God's threat to visit "the iniquity of the fathers upon the children to the third and the fourth generation." (Ex 20:5 note; Jer 32:18)

31:31 *A new covenant.* For use of the term covenant to describe God's gracious way of entering again into a blissful relationship with rebellious mankind see Gn 9:8 note. What God agreed to do to enable Israel and all sinners to become "my people" (33) became a reality in that new covenant sealed with the blood of the only Mediator between God and man. (Ex 24:8 note; Lk 22:20; 1 Co 11:25; Heb 8:8-13)

31:33 *Upon their hearts.* God's creative and transforming inscription of His will on the people's spring of action was necessary because the root of their sin lay in their perverse and stubborn will to "follow their own evil heart," as Jeremiah pointed out so often. (3:17; 4:4, 14; 5:23; 7:24 etc)

31:34 *Know me.* Not merely an intellectual knowledge but an acknowledgement of a sacred relationship (24:7 note). The new covenant creates a conviction of fellowship with God which is self-authenticating and available *from the least . . . to the greatest.*

31:38 *Rebuilt.* Before Jeremiah's mind's eye the holy city rises out of its ruins. For *the tower of Hananel, the Corner Gate,* and "the Horse Gate" see Neh 3:1, 28; 2 K 14:13. "Gareb" and "Goah" cannot be identified. The "valley of the dead bodies" is the Hinnom Valley. (2:23 note)

32:1-44 Here the promise of redemption, proclaimed in two previous chs., is highlighted by a visual demonstration of what it means to act on faith's conviction that "nothing is too hard for" the Lord (17, 27). Jeremiah is called upon to practice what he preached. According to vv. 1-5 the event took place when according to human calculations it was sheer folly to hope for Israel's survival. Within months Jerusalem, ringed by Nebuchadnezzar's *siege mounds* (24), would be leveled with the ground. Jeremiah's efforts to avert the tragedy by calling the king and his people to repentance were repaid by imprisonment *in the court of the guard.*

Yet when his *cousin* came to him urging him to buy a family plot of land in his hometown of *Anathoth* (1:1 note), already overrun by the enemy, Jeremiah *weighed out the money to him* and *signed* and *sealed* the *deed of purchase.* Ludicrous as the transaction might appear, he recognized in it God's call to let his action proclaim, louder than his words, how certain it was that *houses and fields and vineyards* would again be occupied by the people seemingly doomed to extinction. (6-15)

As under other trying circumstances, Jeremiah acted in obedience to the impulse of *the word of the Lord.* Nevertheless, on this occasion he revealed how faith had to do battle with doubt even in a prophet's heart. But he also showed how to win. He discussed his problem with the Lord. He knew and could recite an array of Biblical truths to support the proposition that he should not question God's power, wisdom, justice, and goodness. However, the application of the doctrinal axioms to the difficulty at hand was not so easy. He could not understand why it made sense to *buy the field . . . though the city is given into the hands of the Chaldeans.* (16-25)

The Lord came to the aid of His mystified servant. Jeremiah's trouble, He said, was his failure to act also in this case in full reliance on the basic principles of faith which he enunciated in his prayer. If he fully lived up to his bold confession that "nothing is too hard for" the Lord (17, cf. 27), he would no longer ask whether the purchase of the property in conquered territory had any meaning for the future. In order to drive home the inconsistency of Jeremiah's misgivings, the Lord went on to preach almost verbatim what Jeremiah himself had said about the wonder of judgment and grace to take place in Israel's future. *The God of all flesh,* who commandeered the world-conqueror *Nebuchadrezzar* to execute His wrath on His people because they *have done nothing but evil,* could likewise be trusted to *rejoice in doing them good* precisely as Jeremiah had said He would (26-41). Therefore the purchase of property in Anathoth was but a token of the restoration of all the land to its rightful owners. (42-44)

32:1 *In the tenth year.* "In the fourth month"

of the next year "a breach was made in the city" by the Babylonians. (39:2)

32:2 *The court of the guard.* How Jeremiah came to be *shut up* there is told in chs. 37 and 38.

32:5 *Visit him.* Depending on circumstances, God's action described by this verb is a promise of deliverance or a threat of punishment. (5:9; 29:10)

32:7 *Right of redemption.* For the legal provisions in the case see Lv 25:25 note; Ru 4:5 note.

32:8 *Came to me.* The cousin got through enemy lines during a lull in the siege when Nebuchadnezzar had to fight off an Egyptian army. (37:11 f.)

32:9 *I bought the field.* In the New Testament the purchase of this field and the 30 shekels paid in wages to Zechariah (11:12 f.) are cited as prophetic foreshadowing of the acquisition of the potter's field. (Mt 27:9)

32:14 *Sealed deed . . . open deed.* One copy of the contract was rolled up and sealed to prevent its opening. The other remained unsealed for ready reference.

32:17 *Too hard for thee.* God began His answer to the prayer by restating Jeremiah's assertion in the form of a rhetorical question (27). So He asked Sarah (Gn 18:14).

32:28 *Thus says the Lord.* What He said about Israel's sin and punishment echoed the inspired words spoken by Jeremiah. See, e.g., ch. 7.

32:35 *Molech.* For this derisive name for Baal see Lv 18:21 note.

32:40 *Covenant.* The same comprehensive term Jeremiah used to describe the relationship God will establish with His chastened people (31:31 note). It will be *an everlasting covenant* because He will never cease to supply the strength for a wholehearted commitment to His will, here as elsewhere called *the fear* of the Lord. (Dt 6:13 note)

32:44 *Places about Jerusalem.* To the north *in the land of Benjamin;* to the west in *the Shephelah* or coast plain; to the south in *the Negeb.* (Gn 12:9 note; Jos 15:21 note; Jer 17:26)

33:1-26 This is a fitting close to the prophecies of future blessings arranged to follow one another beginning with ch. 29. *The word of the Lord* which *came to Jeremiah a second time* while in prison (32:2) may appear to be unnecessary duplication of the good news proclaimed so often and so clearly that no one could fail to understand it. Yet if Jeremiah needed to hear again the *great and hidden things* which he himself proclaimed (cf. ch. 32), then it should be evident that the Gospel of unmerited salvation has to be repeated over and over again if it is not only to overcome mankind's innate opposition to it but also to keep faith in it from wavering. (1-3)

It is not surprising, therefore, to find nothing essentially new in the prophecy recorded in this ch. Contrary to the false optimism proclaimed by lying prophets, there is again no minimizing of God's wrath on sin and the severity of judgment on the unrepentant sinner (4-5). But Jeremiah also speaks anew of Israel's and Judah's restoration to peace and prosperity after *their sin and rebellion* has been forgiven. (6-13)

Furthermore, as in previous revelations of God's eternal plan for mankind, Jeremiah's vision of good things to come is not limited to the return of the chosen people from exile but penetrates to *those days* and *that time* when the Messianic *Branch,* sprung from David's lineage, will establish His universal kingdom of grace. In describing it Jeremiah here elaborates more on the benefits to be derived from His reign than he did in 23:5 f. The subjects of the King will not only be able to call Him "The Lord is our righteousness" but, by virtue of His righteousness imputed to them, they themselves will bear the holy name *The Lord is our righteousness.* They will have full access to the throne of God through His mediation, prefigured by the *sacrifices* offered by Israel's *priests.* These long-range promises too will be fulfilled as certainly as God lets day and night follow one another. (14-26)

33:2 *His name.* For the proper noun "Lord" see Ex 3:15 note.

33:4-5 *Houses . . . torn down.* Jerusalem's last days are sketched in terse language suggesting the frantic efforts to save the city. Houses were wrecked for material to replace gaps in the walls (Is 22:10). This desperate maneuver too was in vain. The site where the buildings stood would be filled with *the dead bodies* of the defenders.

33:9 *Name of joy.* No longer will the nations "be horrified . . . because of all its disasters" (18:16; 19:8)

33:11 *The voice of mirth.* Reversal of the chaos and grief when the cities suffered the consequences of sin threatened in 7:34; 16:9; 25:10 f.

33:15 *A righteous Branch.* Cf. 23:1-8 note and 23:6 note.

33:17 *Never lack a man.* Zedekiah was the last of David's successors to rule in Jerusalem. The throne of the Messianic King "shall be established forever" (cf. notes to 2 Sm 7:1, 6, 13). He will grant royal status to His subjects. They will "reign with Him" "for ever and ever." (2 Ti 2:12; Rv 22:5; 3:21; cf. also Mt 25:34)

33:18 *Levitical priests.* Priests from the tribe of Levi (Dt 18:1 note). The promise of "a perpetual priesthood" (Nm 25:13) will become a reality, for the Messianic Branch will be also "a priest forever . . . able for all time to save those who draw near to God through him" (Heb 7:21-28). The unnumbered host of those reconciled to God by His perfect sacrifice will constitute "a holy priesthood to offer spiritual sacrifices acceptable to God." (1 Ptr 2:5, 9; Rv 1:5 f.; 5:9 f.)

34:1—36:32 Prophecies of Doom Provoked by Kings and the People as a Whole

34:1-22 The advice which Jeremiah gave to Zedekiah to submit to the Babylonian invaders (chs. 27 and 28) went unheeded. When, as a result, Nebuchadnezzar and his allies *were fighting against Jerusalem and all of its cities,* the prophet was sent again to warn the king that continued resistance could only end in the capture of the holy city and its destruction by *fire.* Zedekiah himself would be brought *face to face* with the Babylonian king for sentencing. Though allowed to die a natural death, the prisoner was not to escape severe punishment. (1-7; 32:4; 52:9-11)

But not only the king was deaf to divine instruction. *The princes . . . and all the people* (19) were so contemptuous of the ordinance regulating the rights of their fellowmen that they will be given *into the hand of those who seek their lives.* At the king's urging everyone had agreed to *set free his Hebrew slaves* (9), presumably because free men would be more apt to help defend the city. However, when Nebuchadnezzar lifted the siege in order to meet the challenge of an Egyptian army, the slaveholders broke their solemn pledge and *took back* the *male and female slaves* (16). For such wanton violation of their covenant with God *their dead bodies shall be food for the birds . . . and the beasts.* (8-22)

34:5 *Burn spices.* It was customary to burn spices at a king's funeral. (2 Ch 16:14 note)

34:7 *Lachish and Azekah.* The two remaining fortified strongholds southwest of Jerusalem did not hold out much longer. Potsherds found in the ruins of Lachish tell the story of the hopeless struggle against the Babylonian war machine.

34:9 *Hebrew slaves.* No Hebrew man or woman, sold into slavery for debts, was to be deprived of freedom for more than six years. (Ex 21:2 note; Dt 15:1 note)

34:17 *Liberty to the sword.* Punishment for the crime, which "profaned" God's name though actually committed against fellowmen, is ironically called a liberation. Freedom from serving God is an independence which foregoes His protection.

34:18 *The calf.* In making (lit. "cutting") a covenant the contracting parties passed between two halves of a slain calf, thereby declaring that they deserved to be cut to pieces if they broke the contract. (Gn 15:10 note)

35:1-19 The incident recorded here took place some 10 years earlier than the events described in ch. 34. Though not in chronological sequence, it is documented here because, like the previous ch., it furnishes further evidence that God was fully justified in threatening to destroy His rebellious people. Their unfaithfulness to Him is here made to appear in sharp contrast with the fidelity to a man-made ordinance strictly observed by a group known as the *Rechabites.* For centuries this Kenite clan had not deviated from the austere, seminomadic way of life prescribed by their ancestor Jonadab (cf. 2 K 10:15 note; Ju 1:16 note; Nm 10:29). At this time they were forced by the Babylonian invasion to take refuge in Jerusalem. Before a large audience, gathered in front of *one of the chambers* of the temple court, they demonstrated their obedience to one of their ancestral rules of conduct. For when Jeremiah set before them *pitchers full of wine,* they refused to drink any of it. (1-11)

Then Jeremiah turned to the *men of Judah.* What they had heard and seen was an object lesson of the enormity of their sin of disobedience. For (1) they broke the law of God, who gave them the Promised Land, and not merely a rule of unproved merit issued by a fellowman; (2) they violated the divine demand not to *go after other gods;* (3) they did this not once but many times over; (4) they could not claim ignorance of God's will, for He *persistently* sent them His prophets to instruct them and call them to repentance. Such deliberate, obstinate wickedness would not go unpunished, whereas the kind of unwavering fidelity displayed by the Rechabites will always be an example of acceptable service to God. (12-19)

35:3 *The son of Jeremiah.* This otherwise unknown person bore the same name given to the prophet.

35:4 *Maaseiah.* Also mentioned in 21:1. As the *keeper of the threshold* he was a high-ranking official in the temple. (52:24; 2 K 25:18; 12:9 f.)

35:19 *Stand before me.* The bodily descendants of the Rechabites no longer constitute an identifiable group. Yet their clan is legion. For the loyalty they displayed lives on as the approved hallmark of countless numbers who dedicate themselves to walk before the Lord.

36:1-32 The episode recorded here is the third in a series of incidents documenting Israel's wanton impenitence which provokes *the anger and wrath that the Lord has pronounced against* them (7; cf. chs. 34 and 35). In a climactic display of calculated impudence King Jehoiakim cut the written word of the Lord to shreds and burned it piece by piece. How he came to do it is told in vv. 1-19. Jeremiah was to make another effort to persuade the house of Judah to turn from its *evil way.* Because he could no longer appear in the precincts of *the house of the Lord* (5), God instructed him to write on a scroll *all the words* he had spoken for 23 years since *the days of Josiah* (1:2). The actual writing was done by his secretary Baruch at Jeremiah's dictation. When, after several months, the manuscript was completed, Baruch was ordered to *read the words of the Lord from the scroll* to a large audience assembled in the temple to observe *a fast day.* (1-10)

A temple official named *Micaiah* reported what he heard there to *all the princes,* assembled for a cabinet meeting in the chamber of the secretary of state. Anxious to hear the contents of the scroll, they had Baruch read the entire document to them. They were so perturbed by what they heard they impounded the scroll in order to bring it to the attention of the king. (11-19)

At Jehoiakim's command it was taken *into the court* and read to him by one of his counselors, named *Jehudi.* Whenever the latter finished reading *three or four columns,* the king cut them from the scroll and threw them *into the fire in the brazier* until every hated word was destroyed. No doubt Jeremiah and Baruch would have shared the fate of Uriah (26:20-23) *but the Lord hid them.* (20-26)

The king's infantile attempt to silence the Word of God failed. At Jeremiah's dictation Baruch rewrote the scroll, embodying in it also the prophecy of *all the evil* pronounced for their iniquity on *Jehoiakim . . . his servants,* and *the inhabitants of Jerusalem.* As time went on *many similar words were added,* completing the book which by divine providence lies before us. (27-32)

36:5 *Debarred.* Jeremiah was not in prison at this time. It appears he was prevented by the temple authorities from appearing there after his clash with them recorded in 20:1-3 and 26:1-11.

36:6 *Fast day.* Observed no doubt in view of the threat of Nebuchadnezzar's advance toward Jerusalem after he defeated the Egyptian army at Carchemish. Cf. 25:1-38 note; also 46:2.

36:22 *A fire.* Need for warmth in the ninth month, our December.

36:30 *None . . . upon the throne.* For Jehoiakim's punishment see 22:1-30 note.

37:1—38:28 Uncompromising Prophecies Proclaimed in Private to a Weak King

Chs. 37 and 38 record Jeremiah's unwavering firmness in proclaiming the inspired Word during the last two years before the fall of Jerusalem. In three private interviews with Zedekiah he did not hesitate to announce the fearful fate awaiting the king, the city, and its inhabitants. Nor did scourging, jailing, and threat of death by the princes cow him into deviating from the truth.

He was called to his first discussion with the king when Nebuchadnezzar lifted the siege of Jerusalem to engage an army under Pharaoh Hophra (44:30; cf. also 32:1-15). Asked to pray that the Babylonians be forced to *stay away* permanently, he announced their inevitable return to *burn* the city *with fire* (1-10). Taking advantage of a lull in the fighting, the prophet of Anathoth undertook a trip home in order to claim his share to some family property. He got as far as one of the city gates, where a sentry arrested him on charges of deserting to the enemy. Without further ado the princes *beat him* and imprisoned him in an underground cell, located *in the house of* a certain *Jonathan.* (11-15)

After he was *there many days,* during which the siege was resumed, Zedekiah had him brought to the palace *secretly* for another consultation. The frenzied king, seeing no prospect of relief by ordinary means, clung to the vain hope that Jeremiah might have a *word from the Lord* that the crisis somehow would pass. However, Jeremiah only repeated the threat that nothing could save Zedekiah from falling *into the hand of the king of Babylon* (cf. 34:2 f.). Because the predictions of popular prophets had proved false whereas he spoke the true Word of God, he pleaded not to be sent back to the same dungeon, where he would be sure to *die.* Afraid to expose him to possible harm by the princes, the king placed him into protective custody in *the court of the guard* and ordered provisions for him. (16-21)

37:3 *Pray.* Jeremiah was forbidden to intercede for people intent on opposing God's will. (7:16; 11:14; 14:11; 15:1)

37:13 *Benjamin Gate.* Cf. 20:2 note.

37:21 *Bakers' street.* Each trade and craft usually occupied the same street.

38:1-28 In "the court of the guard," where he was put by Zedekiah (37:21), Jeremiah availed himself of the more relaxed confinement to tell *all the people* who *came* by that only he who went *out to the Chaldeans* could possibly escape with his bare life. Brought before the king by the infuriated *princes,* Jeremiah was accused of treasonably demoralizing the soldiers. In a tragic display of cowardly fear Zedekiah surrendered the courageous prophet to his enemies. Though they did not put him to death publicly, they *cast him into the cistern* owned by one of them. In the *mire* of this subterranean pit the prisoner was sure to die of exposure and starvation. (1-6)

However, their murderous plot was to fail. Help came from an unexpected quarter. The man who saved the doomed prophet was not an Israelite but an *Ethiopian* named *Ebedmelech* and employed *in the king's house.* When he appealed to Zedekiah's conscience not to let an innocent man suffer a lingering death, the weak but well-intentioned king not only agreed to the rescue operation but also ordered a contingent of men to carry out the project. So it came about that Jeremiah, drawn from the pit by ropes, again *remained in the court of the guard.* (7-13)

From there he was brought before the king for a third and final interview. Wracked by indecision, Zedekiah turned once more to Jeremiah, hoping to hear of a last-minute escape out of his dilemma (14-16). But Jeremiah confronted him with the same unpleasant alternative. He could choose to *surrender to the princes of the king of Babylon;* if he did not, the city would be destroyed, leaving him in the hands of the irate victors. As the next ch. tells us, the king ignored *the voice of the Lord* (17-23). At the end of the meeting Zedekiah gave further evidence of his craven fear of the princes. He pleaded with Jeremiah not to divulge everything they discussed but to mention only his request not to be sent back to the underground cell in *the house of Jonathan.* Jeremiah promised to do so and was permitted to remain *in the court of the guard.* (24-28)

38:1 *Gedaliah.* After the fall of the city a man with the same name was made governor by Nebuchadnezzar. (39:14; 40:5)

38:2 *Goes out to the Chaldeans.* The number of those who followed Jeremiah's repeated advice (21:9) apparently was large enough to make the king afraid of them. If he too were to desert to the enemy, he feared they would "abuse" him for having brought on the city's destruction. (19; 39:9)

38:7 *Ebed-melech.* How he came to be "the

king's servant"—the meaning of his nondescript name—is not known. For his reward see 39:15-18.

38:10 *Three men.* All Hebrew manuscripts except one give the number as 30. The larger contingent may have been necessary to prevent interference with the mission.

38:14 *Third entrance.* Perhaps the king's private entrance to the temple, mentioned 2 K 16:18.

38:21 *The vision.* The Lord enabled His prophet to describe so graphically what lay ahead as if he were a witness of the tragedy. He hears the women of the king's court taunting him with a ditty, mockingly lamenting the fact that his *trusted friends* had left him in the lurch. (22)

39:1—45:5 PROPHECIES AFTER THE FALL OF JERUSALEM

39:1—42:22 The Word Spoken to the Remnant in Palestine

39:1-18 "The word" of the Lord "that came to Jeremiah" from now on (40:1), such as the one recorded in 42:9 ff., was delivered in a setting of fulfilled prophecy. As foretold so often and so clearly in chs. 1—38, *Jerusalem was taken* by the Babylonian army, Zedekiah the king was taken *in fetters* to Babylon, and the citizens of Jerusalem and Judah were *carried into exile* with the exception of *some of the poor people.* (1-10)

However, God did not only carry out His threats; He also kept His promise to be with His prophet "to deliver" him (1:8; 15:20 f.). Imprisoned by the leaders of his own people, he was taken *from the court of the guard* by order of Nebuchadnezzar issued to *Nebuzaradan* his commander-in-chief and relayed to his *chief officers.* The king's men obeyed the command to *do him no harm* and *entrusted him to Gedaliah,* the newly appointed governor. So it came about that *he dwelt among the people* left in Palestine and continued his prophetic ministry in their midst. (11-14)

Deliverance from the sword was to be the reward also of *Ebed-melech,* who rescued Jeremiah from the pit (38:7-13). The pledge of safety given him at that time is no doubt inserted here to show that God did not fail to do for an Ethiopian what He did for His prophet. (15-18)

39:3 *Jerusalem was taken.* Cf. the notes on 2 K 25, which in the main tells the same story of the city's fall, repeated once more in the last ch. of Jeremiah's book.

Princes. Nebuchadnezzar's commanders and officials listed here are not mentioned in 2 K 25. Two of them apparently bore the name *Nergal-sharezer. Rabsaris* and *Rabmag* are titles of offices in Nebuchadnezzar's administration. Cf. 2 K 18:17 note.

39:12 *Look after him well.* Informed by Israelite deserters of Jeremiah's repeated advice not to resist the invaders, Nebuchadnezzar considered the persecuted prophet an advocate of a pro-Babylonian policy.

39:14 *Dwelt among the people.* Jeremiah's favorable treatment by the Babylonians, not mentioned in the two other accounts, is recorded here and in the following chs. to provide the setting for his continued ministry among the people left in Palestine by Nebuchadnezzar.

39:18 *A prize of war.* Preserved alive as was Jeremiah, Ebed-melech shared in "a prophet's reward." (Mt 10:41)

40:1-16 The skeleton outline of Jeremiah's fate during and after the capture of Jerusalem, consisting of the two verses in 39:13 f., is fleshed out in this ch. Vv. 1-6 record events after his initial release from the court of the guard, which eventually made it possible for him to proclaim *the word . . . from the Lord* as he *dwelt . . . among the people* under Gedaliah's governorship. Free to mingle with the surviving population of the doomed city, he was picked up and *bound in chains* by soldiers who evidently did not know him. When his contingent of prisoners *being exiled to Babylon* reached the general assembly point at *Ramah,* 5 miles north of Jerusalem, *Nebuzaradan the captain of the guard . . . let him go* after learning his identity. Obeying his king's command to "look after him well" (39:12), the Babylonian commander-in-chief gave Jeremiah the choice to go on with him to Babylon and safety or end his travels and *return to Gedaliah.* Jeremiah threw in his lot with the latter, whose headquarters were at *Mizpah,* a few miles north of Ramah.

For a time everything went well as the governor brought a semblance of order into the land (7-12). However, *Ishmael,* the captain of a guerilla band which had eluded the Babylonians, plotted to kill Gedaliah though he and others like him had accepted the governor's leadership. Gedaliah refused to be warned of the treachery (13-16) that resulted in the events related in the next ch.

40:2 *Your God.* For similar words by a heathen acknowledging the power of Israel's God to shape the destiny of His people see Ez 1:3 f.; 6:1-12; Jer 22:8 f.

40:8 *Ishmael.* It appears that this man "of the royal family" (41:1) was jealous of Gedaliah, who was not a descendant of David, or he may have acted out of hatred for a collaborator with the Babylonians.

40:14 *Baalis.* The king of Ammon, east of the Jordan River, evidently was fishing in troubled waters. He hoped to gain some advantage from the disorder which would follow the overthrow of a central government in Judah. After the Babylonian exile another Ammonite, Tobiah, tried to prevent the rebuilding of Jerusalem. (Neh 4:1-9)

41:1-18 Refusing to be warned by Johanan and other loyal captains (40:13-16), Gedaliah was cut down by Ishmael, one of his trusted lieutenants. The Jews and the Chaldean soldiers who were with the governor at his headquarters in Mizpah suffered the same fate. The assassin caught his victims off guard. They did not expect a man who *ate bread together* with his commander to break the sacred trust of hospitality (1-3). Next this fiendish villain massacred all but 10 of 80 defenseless pilgrims who were on their way to present *cereal offerings and incense* at the ruins of the temple in Jerusalem. (4-8)

Fearing reprisal for his senseless bloodbath, the murderer *took captive all the rest of the people who were in Mizpah . . . and set out to cross over* the Jordan to his confederates, *the Ammonites* (9-10; cf. 40:14). He got only as far as *Gibeon,* three miles south of Mizpah, where *Johanan* and his fellow captains overtook him and freed the kidnapped prisoners. Ishmael escaped with eight of his men. The leaders, however, did not take the rescued people back to Mizpah, fearing that the Chaldeans would regard them too as rebels. Consequently they moved the entire group southward to the vicinity of *Bethlehem, intending to go to Egypt* for asylum. (11-18)

41:1 *Seventh month.* If this incident took place in the year of Jerusalem's fall (39:2), Gedaliah was governor in Mizpah only three months. It seems a longer period of time would have been necessary to achieve the restoration described in 40:7-12. Perhaps the punitive measures Nebuchadnezzar took four years later were in retaliation for Gedaliah's murder. (52:30)

41:5 *Bodies gashed.* This mourning rite, by which the pilgrims expressed their grief over the destruction of Jerusalem, seems to have been adopted from their heathen neighbors. (16:6 note)

41:9 *King Asa.* Cf. 1 K 15:22.

41:10 *All the rest.* Though not mentioned specifically, Jeremiah evidently was among the people taken captive.

41:12 *Great pool.* Cf. 2 Sm 2:13.

41:17 *Geruth Chimham.* An inn or khan named after the son of David's friend Barzillai. (2 Sm 19:36 note)

42:1-22 The first six verses continue to furnish the setting for "the word that came to Jeremiah" (40:1) after the murder of Gedaliah (chs. 40 and 41). "Intending to go to Egypt," the survivors of Ishmael's unsuccessful coup d'etat reached the vicinity of Bethlehem (41:17). Here they prevailed on Jeremiah to obtain divine sanction for their momentous decision to leave the Promised Land.

As on a previous occasion (28:11), Jeremiah did not presume to give his own opinion in the matter but waited *ten days* until he could say: *Thus says the Lord.* The answer he was authorized to give consisted of: (a) the advice to *remain in this land,* where God would protect them from the Babylonians (7-12); (b) the warning that certain death awaited them in Egypt (13-17). Sensing the people's resolve to continue on their predetermined course, Jeremiah pleaded with them not to reject the guidance they requested and received from the Lord. (18-22)

42:10 *Build . . . up and . . . pull . . . down.* The epitome of the message Jeremiah was commissioned to proclaim. (1:10; 18:7-9; 24:6; 31:4, 28; 33:7)

42:19 *Know for a certainty.* God will not be reduced to a rubber stamp for human aspirations.

43:1—44:30 The Word Spoken to Fugitives in Egypt

43:1-13 *The insolent men* carried out their resolution to disobey "the voice of the Lord" (42:21). Defying His explicit directive and disparaging His prophet, they *took all the remnant of Judah,* including Jeremiah and Baruch, to *Tahpanhes,* a border city of Egypt (1-7; 2:16 note). Here the exiled prophet foretold the punishment awaiting the rebellious fugitives: They would perish in the land where they thought they would be safe from the Babylonians. For Nebuchadnezzar would also here act as God's *servant* in conquering and pillaging Egypt. In order to dramatize the certainty of this prophecy, Jeremiah was directed to lay *large stones . . . at the entrance to Pharaoh's palace,* symbolizing the Babylonian king's throne and undisputed dominion in Egypt. (8-13)

43:5 *From all the nations.* Moab, Ammon, and Edom are mentioned as some of the countries from which people returned during Gedaliah's governorship. (40:11 f.)

43:10 *My servant.* Cf. 25:9 note.

43:11 *Smite the land.* A fragment from a Babylonian chronicle records Nebuchadnezzar's invasion of Egypt in 567 BC.

43:13 *Obelisks.* Lit. "pillars." *Heliopolis* was situated a few miles south of Cairo.

44:1-30 In the land from which the Lord once delivered enslaved Israel, Jeremiah delivered his last recorded oracle and probably suffered martyrdom for it. The occasion was *a great assembly* of Jews who at one time or another had fled to various parts of Egypt (15). They had learned nothing from the past. In spite of repeated warnings against idolatry by God's *servants the prophets* and in spite of *all the evil* He *brought upon Jerusalem and upon all the cities of Judah* because of this cardinal sin, they went right on provoking Him to anger by *burning incense to other gods in the land of Egypt* (1-10). However, they did not elude divine jurisdiction by going to a foreign country. God will punish them in Egypt as He *punished Jerusalem.* All with perish *except some fugitives.* (11-14)

The assembly's response to the threat of judgment reveals the grotesque mystery of human perversity. The idolatrous rabble not only *vowed* to *burn incense to the queen of heaven* as before but also attributed all past disaster to their neglect in *pouring out libations to her* (15-19). Jeremiah countered this blasphemous interpretation of history by insisting that it was precisely their worship of this mother-goddess which caused them to *become a desolation and a waste and a curse* (20-23).

Patient to the end, Jeremiah continued his efforts to dissuade them from their suicidal course. In a final address he made a specific prediction. Punishment would overtake them, he said, after the Lord delivered *Hophra,* the reigning *Pharaoh, into the hands of his enemies.* (24-30)

44:1 *Migdol.* On Egypt's northeastern border. For *Memphis* see 2:16 note. *Pathros* was the territory on the upper Nile as far south as Aswan. (Is 11:11 note)

44:4 *Persistently sent.* Jeremiah was not the first prophet to warn the people of the judgment to come. (7:25; 25:4; 26:5)

44:11 *All Judah.* No one was to think that escape from God was possible even though "few in number" would survive and "return to the land of Judah." (14, 28)

44:15 *Great assembly.* The purpose of the large gathering possibly was to observe a festival in honor of the queen of heaven, an astral deity and goddess of fertility. (Cf. 7:18)

44:17 *Had plenty.* During the reign of King Manasseh, who promoted "the abominable practices of the nations" (2 K 21:1-9). After his grandson Josiah abolished idolatry (2 K 23:4-20) everything went wrong, they claim. A world view which does not reckon with the Lord of history misinterprets the cause of prosperity and of calamity.

44:19 *Without our husbands' approval.* The women, who apparently played a major role in honoring the mother-goddess, had the full support of their husbands. Cf. Nm 30:2 note, 3 note.

44:25 *Confirm your vows.* Spoken ironically.

44:30 *Hophra.* Mentioned by name only here, this Pharaoh tried to come to Jerusalem's aid during Nebuchadnezzar's siege of the city (37:5). As predicted by Jeremiah, he was slain in an uprising by his enemies.

45:1-5 The Word Promising Protection to Baruch

45:1-5 This ch. is in the nature of a footnote. It explains how it came about that *Baruch,* Jeremiah's faithful secretary, survived the destruction of Jerusalem and was able to be with his mentor to the end. As recorded by himself, he owed his life as *a prize of war* to God's promise, delivered to him 15 years before Jerusalem was destroyed. It was at the time when he wrote and then rewrote all the words spoken to him by the Lord. (36:1 f., 27 f.)

45:3 *Woe is me!* The honest scribe admits that he shared Jeremiah's anguish over a painful yet futile task (8:18 ff.; 12:1 ff.; 15:15-21; 20:7 f.). However, his grief is but a faint token of God's sorrow as He must break down what He has "built" for centuries. (Hos 11:1-9)

45:5 *Great things.* Whoever would be great in God's kingdom must surrender selfish ambitions. (Mt 20:26-28)

Prize of war. Cf. the same promise given to Ebed-melech. (39:15 ff.)

46:1—51:64 PROHECIES CONCERNING THE NATIONS

The Creator and Lord of the Universe made known the course of ancient world history through Jeremiah, whom He called to be "a prophet to the nations" and to whom He gave authority "over nations" (1:5, 10). The oracles declaring their destiny are grouped in consecutive chs., as they are also in Isaiah (13—33), Ezekiel (25—32), and Amos (1:3—2:3). What Jeremiah "prophesied against all the nations" in 25:13-28 is expanded in chs. 46—51. The ancient Greek translation of the OT, called the Septuagint, appends these fuller denunciations of the foreign powers to 25:13 and arranges them in a different sequence.

46:1—49:39 Egypt and Several Lesser Nations

"The word of the Lord . . . concerning the nations" recorded in the first four chs. of this section proclaims the defeat of Egypt by the Babylonians and their supremacy over lesser states stretching from the land of the Nile into the distant northeast. Chs. 50 and 51 in turn envision the destruction of the Babylonian empire according to "the word which the Lord spoke . . . by Jeremiah." (50:1)

46:1-28 The setting of the first word concerning the nations was Egypt's attempt to dispute world dominion with the Babylonians after the liquidation of the Assyrian empire in 612 BC. Pharaoh Neco did indeed succeed in reducing Palestine to a vassal state for four years after defeating and killing King Josiah at Megiddo. However, the ambitious Egyptian conqueror was no match for *Nebuchadrezzar king of Babylon.* Vv. 1-12 exult in Neco's crushing defeat in 609 BC *at Carchemish* on the *Euphrates* some 300 miles north of Jerusalem. Jeremiah's language is highly dramatic. Calls to do battle (3 f., 7-9) are followed abruptly by announcements of the defeat and dispersal of the proud Egyptian forces (5 f., 10 ff.). The outcome, however, was not by chance. *The Lord God of hosts* was holding *a sacrifice,* and Egypt was the selected victim.

The Babylonians followed up their victory. Nebuchadnezzar's invasion of the land of the Pharaohs, announced briefly in 43:10-13, is the subject of a second scintillating poem (13-24). A few lines in prose take up the story and report how the effects of the invasion were felt as far as *Thebes,* some 400 miles up the Nile (25-26). The ch. closes with a reminder that God's world-government has a set goal. He lets nations rise and fall in order to establish His kingdom through a chastened, restored "servant": "Israel". (27-28)

46:9 *Ethiopia . . . Put . . . Lud.* The Egyptians recruited "hired soldiers" (21) from these countries. Ethiopia was situated on the upper Nile south of Aswan. Put and Lud were African territories west of the Nile delta. (Is 66:19 note)

46:10 *A sacrifice.* See Is 34:6 note.

46:11 *Gilead.* Famed for its *balm.* (8:22 note)

46:14 *Migdol . . . Memphis . . . Tahpanhes.* See 43:7; 44:1 note.

46:15 *Apis.* The Hebrew word is translated "mighty ones" (Ps 103:20) and "bulls" (Is 34:7; Ps 22:12). Apis is the name of the sacred bull worshiped in Egypt. In v. 25 the god Amon is mentioned.

46:17 *Noisy one.* Pharaoh's pompous declaration of military prowess turned out to be empty braggadocio.

46:18 *Tabor . . . Carmel.* As these mountains tower over the Palestinian countryside, so the Babylonian conqueror would be superior to all opposition. (2 K 18:21; Is 36:6)

46:27 *Fear not.* Vv. 27 f. are found also in 30:10 f. In this context of threats to the nations they reiterate that God's plan to preserve Israel will not come to nought in the upheavals of international politics.

47:1-7 Athwart the Babylonian invasion of the Nile Valley (ch. 46) lay the city-states of the Philistines in the southwestern part of Palestine. The conquering forces *out of the north* would inundate Egypt like a *torrent,* leaving devastation in its wake.

47:1 *Smote Gaza.* Before the Babylonians defeated the Philistines, Gaza, one of their southernmost strongholds, had succumbed to an unidentified Pharaoh.

47:4 *Tyre and Sidon.* Phoenician allies of the Philistines.

Caphtor. Very likely the island of Crete, from which the Philistines migrated to Palestine. (Am 9:7)

47:5 *Anakim.* The unchanged Hebrew text reads: "the remnant of their valley," i.e., of the entire Philistine plain along the Mediterranean. The Septuagint translates "Anakim," the original inhabitants of Palestine. (Nm 13:22 note)

48:1-47 From the southwestern border of Israel (ch. 47) the storm of God's judgment moves to the ancestral territory of the Moabites, situated along the eastern shore of the Dead Sea. Descendants of Lot, Abraham's nephew (Gn 19:37 note), the Moabites played a role in the history of the chosen people from the very beginning (cf. Nm 22—24). At Jeremiah's time "bands of Moabites" ravaged Judah after Nebuchadnezzar invaded Palestine (2 K 24:2). A little later emissaries of "the king of Moab" tried to involve Zedekiah in a plot against the Babylonians (27:1 ff.). The oracle *concerning Moab,* surpassed in length only by the threat against the Babylonians (chs. 50—51), may consist of denunciations spoken at various times and then assembled to form a unit. Poems in highly figurative language are interspersed with sections written in prose. Another feature of the extended arraignment of this foreign nation is Jeremiah's frequent adaptation of earlier prophetic words to formulate his own message. He is indebted especially to Isaiah, chs. 15—16.

The 47 verses of the ch. make up a series of concentric circles revolving about a double central theme: (a) the *desolation and great destruction* (3) to be visited on Moab; (b) the causes of its undoing. In 1-27 the first of these foci is prominent; in 28-47, the second receives stress. Neither topic is developed without reference to the other. If the modern reader is inclined to tire of such a long tirade against an ancient, forgotten people, it should be noted that its repeated warnings have been ignored down through the ages. Pride, trust in self, ungodliness are the downfall of nations to this very day.

48:1 *Nebo . . . Kiriathaim.* A number of the cities are mentioned on the Moabite or Mesha Stone found over a century ago (2 K 3:4 note). A few, such as "Madmen" (v. 2) are not found anywhere else in Scripture and remain unidentified.

48:7 *Chemosh.* The god of the Moabites. (Nm 21:27 note; 1 K 11:7 note; 2 K 3:22 note)

48:10 *Cursed.* When *the work of the Lord* is being executed on evildoers, those refusing to be His appointed instruments invoke His wrath also.

48:11 *At ease.* For a long time Moab escaped the deportations inflicted on Israel and Judah. As a result it *has settled on* its *lees* like wine left undisturbed on its fermented sediment to improve its quality (Is 25:6 second note). The change to be effected by the Babylonians is expressed by the same figure of speech in 12. They will *tilt* the wine jars, empty them, and even break the *vessels.*

48:13 *Bethel.* Where Israel worshiped idols as impotent as Chemosh. (1 K 12:28 f.)

48:20 *Arnon.* The river bisecting Moab and emptying into the Dead Sea.

48:26 *Make him drunk.* For the same figurative language see 13:13 note; 25:15.

48:29 *The pride of Moab.* Jeremiah drew heavily on Isaiah's denunciation of Moab. Compare 29 with Is 16:6; 31 with Is 16:7, 11; 33 with Is 24:7 f.

48:37 *Head . . . shaved.* For similar practices to express grief see 16:6 note.

48:45 *Sihon.* An Amorite king of Moab. Vv. 45 f. reproduce Nm 21:28 f.; 24:17. Cf. notes on Nm 21:26-30.

48:47 *In the latter days.* In the Messianic age Moab will be among the "many peoples" (Is 2:3) constituting the redeemed of the Lord. (Is 2:2 second note)

49:1-39 In this ch. four more national groups of the ancient world are told of the dreadful fate awaiting them. When added to the indictments against Egypt, Philistia, and Moab (chs. 46—48), the numbers of oracles "concerning the nations" (46:1) reaches a total of seven, the number often suggesting completeness. "The Judge of all the earth" (Gn 18:25) determines the rise and fall of human power-structures in all places and at all times. From Moab (ch. 48) the decreed judgment moves to the two neighboring states: Ammon, directly northeast (1-6), and Edom, directly southeast (7-22), then on to Syria in northern Palestine (23-27), and from there to Kedar and Hazor to the southeast (28-33) and to Elam, many more miles south and east. (34-39)

49:1 *Ammonites.* Descendants of Lot and therefore a people related to Israel. (Gn 19:38; Dt 2:19)

No sons? When the Assyrians carried the East-Jordan Israelites captive, the Ammonites moved in and occupied the territory allotted to the tribe of *Gad,* claiming that they and not *Israel* were its *heir* (2 K 15:29). For earlier hostile acts against Israel see Ju 3:13; 1 Sm 11:1; 2 Ch 20:1. After the fall of Jerusalem the king of the Ammonites plotted the death of Gedaliah (Jer 40:13 f.). Their god was *Milcom* (1 K 11:5 note); their capital "Rabbah."

49:3 *Heshbon.* According to 48:34 it was a city in Moab. Perhaps it was captured by the Ammonites or there were two cities by this name. *Ai* remains unidentified as a site in Ammon though a place by that name in Israel is well attested. (Gn 12:8; Jos 7 and 8)

49:7 *Edom.* Descendants of Jacob's twin brother Esau (Gn 36:1), the Edomites were the inveterate enemies of Israel (Am 1:11). Their ancestral home was south of the Dead Sea. Some of their chief cities were *Teman,* "Dedan," and "Bozrah." In the ancient world they had the reputation of excelling in *wisdom.* (Jb 2:11; 15:18; Ob 8)

49:12 *Did not deserve.* If nations not guilty of such unbrotherly crimes as Edom committed will be punished, then certainly Edom deserved to *drink the cup* of divine judgment.

49:14 *Heard tidings.* In ch. 48 Jeremiah quoted from Isaiah (Jer 48:29 note). Here vv. 14-16 are almost identical with Ob 1-4. There are striking similarities also in 7, 9, 10 with Ob 8, 5, 6.

49:23 *Damascus.* The capital of Syria, some 60 miles northeast of the Sea of Galilee. *Hamath* was some 100 miles north of Damascus; *Arpad,* some 100 miles north of Hamath. For earlier invasions of Israel by Syrian kings see 2 K 10:32 f.; 13:3, 7, 22.

49:27 *Kindle a fire.* The verse is almost a verbatim quotation from Am 1:4.

49:28 *Kedar and . . . Hazor.* Settlements and villages in the desert southeast of Syria, such as Kedar, were occupied by bedouin descendants of Ishmael, Abraham's son by Hagar. (Gn 25:12 f.; Jer 2:10 note)

49:32 *Cut . . . their hair.* Cf. 9:26 note.

49:35 *Elam.* Located 200 miles east of Babylon. Its city Susa was to become one of the capitals of the Medo-Persian empire. (Dn 8:1 f.)

49:39 *Restore.* Cf. 48:47 note. Elamites were a part of the multitude in Jerusalem on Pentecost. (Acts 2:9)

50:1—51:64 Babylon

50:1—51:64 *The word . . . concerning Babylon,* recorded in chs. 50 and 51, is only 11 verses short of the number devoted to the seven national groups in chs. 46—49. The length of this oracle is proportionate to the important role the Babylonian empire played in the destiny of the chosen people. The downfall of this mighty world power was a major turning point in the history of redemption. God's proposal to bring universal salvation through Abraham's descendants seemingly ended in failure when Nebuchadnezzar destroyed the holy city and denuded the Promised Land of its inhabitants. In the normal course of events exiled Israel would have lost its national identity as it was gradually absorbed in the melting pot of ancient racial strains. If salvation was to be "from the Jews" (Jn 4:22), the conqueror's fatal grip had to be broken. Enabled by the Spirit of God, Jeremiah foresaw this momentous event. In two long chs. he described it as an accomplished fact even though Babylon at the time stood at the pinnacle of imperial might.

However, even though the reader realizes how crucial the subject matter of these chs. is, he may boggle at the way it is presented. The 110 verses may strike him as a disjointed and repetitious assembly of words. In order to let this apparently diffuse literary production exert its full impact, it is necessary to remember that Hebraic rhetoric is not subject to our Western rules of composition (see the Introduction to Isaiah, "Composition"). While we demand a vertical progression from one logical aspect of a topic to another, the ancient poet constructed cycles of words around a theme. Each of them contributed a feature or an emphasis relevant to the matter under discussion. In chs. 50 and 51 Jeremiah draws concentric circles around a central topic: the destruction of Babylon, the necessary preliminary to the restoration of exiled Israel.

Line after line glows with poetic fervor and scintillating drama. Imagery and figurative language light up verse after verse. Though removed from them by miles and decades, Jeremiah addresses the Babylonians, the enemies and destroyers of Babylon, and the liberated exiles as if he were speaking to them face to face. There are poems in which inanimate objects such as a hammer and a sword become active agents of destruction. A burst of irony strikes home. At the end a symbolical action accentuates the spoken words.

According to 51:59 Jeremiah announced the grim fate of the Babylonians five years before they captured Jerusalem. He could do so confidently. In prophetic vision he looked far beyond these events in the comparatively near future to the founding of the Messianic reign centuries after his day. What he says here about Babylon's fall is but an elaboration of briefer prophecies uttered at various times (cf. 25:12-14, 26; 27:7; 29:10). He had in clear view also the purpose of the Babylonian collapse: the return of exiled Israel to its homeland (cf. 23:1-8; 24:6; 30:3, 8; 33:6 ff.). From this vantage point in the future, Jeremiah spoke in retrospect of the destruction of Jerusalem and the temple as an event which happened in the past and was foretold by him in advance. As if it too were already recorded history, he likewise proclaimed: *Babylon is taken* (50:2; 51:8). God's *vengeance* will destroy the Babylonians as His fierce anger sent "sword, famine, and pestilence" into the cities of Judah. (50:28; 51:11; 24:10).

All this was not an accident of history. The exiles, brought to repentance by their enslavement (29:12 f.), were again to serve God's plan of salvation. When earlier they refused to respond to chastisement, Jeremiah wrote them a letter informing them that the Babylonian exile would not end for a long time because it had not brought them to their knees (ch. 29). The Babylonian empire too was subject to God's eternal purpose and will. It emerged on the scene when He needed a "servant" (25:9; 27:6; 43:10) to punish His apostate people. It sank beneath the sands of time because it *sinned against the Lord,* pursuing its own selfish interest and thus hindering the coming of the kingdom of God. (50:14)

50:2 *Bel . . . Merodach.* Trust in idols was in vain. For *Bel* see Is 46:1 note. *Merodach,* the Hebrew spelling for the Babylonian Marduk, appears in the names Merodach-baladan and Evil-merodach. (2 K 20:12; 25:27)

50:3 *Out of the north.* Babylon, the foe "from the north" (1:13 note), was to become the victim of invaders coming from the same direction. The Medes (51:11, 28) hailed from an area northeast of Babylonia. After the fall of Assyria (612 BC) they extended their conquests as far west as Asia Minor. Though deprived of leadership by their kinsmen the Persians, they were an integral part of the Medo-Persian empire. The city of Babylon, left intact by Cyrus at the time of its capture, was later reduced to desolation.

50:5 *Everlasting covenant.* For the meaning of this term see 32:40 note.

50:7 *Not guilty.* This claim of innocence is refuted in 2:3.

50:12 *Your mother.* The city of Babylon.

50:13 *Hiss.* Jeremiah earlier used the same expression to describe Jerusalem's doom. (18:16; 25:9)

50:17 *King of Assyria.* Cf. 2 K 17:6.

50:19 *Carmel . . . Bashan.* Territories in Israel, famous for their fertility and luxuriant growth.

50:21 *Merathaim . . . Pekod.* Puns on the names of localities in Babylonia. Cf. RSV note.

50:28 *Vengeance for his temple.* The Israelites brought about its destruction when they made it a magical charm granting them license to sin at will (cf. 7:2 note). Babylonia's guilt was the arrogant claim that the destruction of the temple proved Marduk's superiority over the Holy One of Israel.

50:30 *Young men shall die.* Jeremiah is repeating words he spoke in announcing the doom of Damascus in 49:26.

50:34 *Redeemer.* For the overtones of this term as applied to the Lord see Jb 19:25 note.

50:38 *Drought.* The Hebrew words "sword" and "drought" are spelled with the same consonants.

50:39 *Wild beasts.* Vv. 39 f. echo Is 13:19-22.

50:41 *A people comes.* Vv. 41-43 adapt the threat of doom addressed to Judah (6:22-24) to the Babylonians. In 44-46 Jeremiah does the same thing with the words he uttered against Edom in 49:19-21.

51:1 *Thus says the Lord.* The oracle against Babylon is continued from ch. 50.

Chaldea. The Hebrew text has "the heart of my opponents," which serves as a cryptogram for the alternate name for Babylonia. Cf. RSV note and 25:26 note.

51:2 *Winnowers.* For this figurative designation for destroyers see 15:7 note; 4:12 note.

51:3 *Not . . . bend his bow.* In the first two lines of this verse the defenders are told that resistance is in vain, whereas in the following lines the attackers are called upon to prove it. The Hebrew text may also be translated as giving positive directives to the enemy throughout: "Let the archers bend the bow," etc., similar to 50:21, 26 f.

51:6 *Flee.* Addressed to the exiles, as also v. 45 and 50:8.

51:7 *Golden cup.* For divine judgment portrayed as a cup of wrath see 13:13 note; 25:15. Babylon, God's instrument of punishment on *the nations,* is said to be golden because of its imperial might and splendor.

51:8 *Take balm.* Spoken ironically to Babylon's sympathizers and confederates. In the next verse they admit her wound was incurable. Therefore they are to abandon her to her fate.

51:10 *Our vindication.* So the exiles will speak gratefully of their deliverance in view of their position in God's scheme of salvation.

51:11 *Kings of the Medes.* Leaders of various tribes united in the attack on *Babylon.*

51:13 *Many waters.* The Euphrates River was diverted into a network of irrigation canals.

51:15-19 *Who made the earth.* The impotence of idols is described in identical words in 10:12-16. The warning against trusting *a work of delusion* (18) rather than the Creator of the universe, needed to describe Israel's folly, was pertinent also when the Babylonians relied on their god Marduk to defend them against *the Lord of hosts.* (19)

51:20 *My hammer.* As the Assyrians earlier were "the rod" of God's anger (Is 10:5-11), so the Babylonians were to *break nations in pieces* in their appointed rise to empire status. Both rod and hammer were thrown on the rubbish heap because they came to be instruments of self-aggrandizement harmful to God's kingdom.

51:25 *Mountain.* Babylon was located in a flat plain. Figuratively it rose to towering eminence by its conquests.

51:27 *Ararat, Minni, and Ashkenaz.* Districts in Median territory.

51:31 *Meet another.* Messengers of disaster will come and go in quick succession.

51:34 *Me.* Israel is speaking of the *delicacies* or treasured possessions removed completely by the Babylonians.

51:36 *Her sea.* The Euphrates, its canals and reservoirs.

51:38 *They shall roar.* The Babylonians acting like ravenous young lions "inflamed" with feverish craving for prey, will be served food by the Lord which will stupefy them into "a perpetual sleep" and change them from predatory beasts into domestic victims of "the slaughter."

51:41 *Babylon.* Cf. 25:26 note and RSV note.

51:42 *The sea.* Wave after wave of enemies will inundate Babylon.

51:46 *Heart faint.* Rumors of political convulsions in the ancient world could have made the exiles *fearful* lest their lot in a foreign country become even worse.

51:48 *Heavens and . . . earth.* As the whole universe is called upon to witness God's charges against His people, so it is summoned also to join in celebrating the defeat of His enemies. (Dt 4:26; 30:19, Is 44:23; 49:13)

51:50 *You . . . go.* Having *escaped from the sword,* the exiles are to consider their liberation God's signal to return to *Jerusalem.*

51:55 *Waves roar.* The attack by the enemy will be like the irresistible force of the sea and its deafening roar.

51:59 *Jeremiah . . . commanded.* A written copy of the words spoken "concerning Babylon" were to be taken to Babylon, tied to a stone, and cast "into the midst of the Euphrates" to symbolize that "thus shall Babylon sink, to rise no more" (59-63). For other symbolic acts see 19:1 ff.; 27:1 ff.; 32:1 ff.; 43:8 ff. The projected action was to be executed by *Seraiah,* brother of Jeremiah's secretary Baruch (32:12), as he accompanied Zedekiah on the latter's journey to Babylonia in the fourth year of his reign. It is quite possible that the king of Judah, who ruled by the grace of Nebuchadnezzar, undertook the trip in order to assure his suzerain lord that he did not encourage the rebellious agitation in Jerusalem (cf. ch. 28). Earlier a delegation was sent to Babylon apparently for the same reason. (29:3 note)

51:61 *See . . . read.* Seraiah was to seek out the proper time and place to carry out his assignment. No audience is mentioned. It may be assumed that the reading was done in private.

51:64 *Thus far.* The next ch. contains a record of Jerusalem's fall appended to *the words of Jeremiah.*

52:1-34 HISTORICAL APPENDIX: PROPHECY FULFILLED

52:1-34 The last ch. of the Book of Jeremiah serves as an affidavit verifying his claim that he spoke the word of the Lord (1:11 etc.). What he foretold became historical fact. The story begins with the reign of Zedekiah, the last king of Judah (1-3), describes the fall of Jerusalem and the vandalizing of the temple (4-27), tabulates the deportations to Babylon (28-30), and ends by relating how Jehoiachin, imprisoned by Nebuchadnezzar, was released from confinement and treated with dignity by *Evil-merodach,* a later Babylonian king (31-34). Except for minor omissions and additions, the account of these events appears also in ch. 39 and in 2 K 24:18—25:30. (cf. the notes there)

52:12 *Tenth day.* According to 2 K 25:8, Nebuchadnezzar's general *Nebuzaradan* arrived at Jerusalem three days before he ordered the temple to be pillaged and burned.

52:13 *The house of the Lord.* The temple ornaments and the sacred vessels are described in greater detail than in the parallel account of 2 K 25:13-17. (cf. 2 K 25:13 note)

52:28 *Seventh year.* No doubt a copyist's mistake for 17. The dating here as well as in v. 12 is based on one system of counting the regnal years of a king, whereas 2 K 25:8 is based on another equally acceptable way of computing them. See Introducton to the Books of Kings, "Chronology."

Three thousand and twenty three. This number apparently refers only to the Jews taken captive in the city of Jerusalem. The figure 10,000 in 2 K 24:14 represents the total of all prisoners, counting also the 4,000 mentioned in v. 30 here.

52:30 *Carried away.* This deportation is not mentioned in the parallel accounts.

52:31 *Jehoiachin.* This incident also ends the account in 2 K 25, thus concluding on a hopeful note.

LAMENTATIONS

INTRODUCTION

Content

The book following the writings of Jeremiah and preceding those of Ezekiel does not contain oracles of the kind found in these or other prophetic books. Here the reader comes upon a collection of odes which he could expect to find in the Book of Psalms. However, while the lyrical compositions in the Psalter express feelings aroused by a variety of circumstances and experiences, each of the five poems recorded here is an outburst of grief caused by a single tragic event: the fall of Jerusalem. Teardrops stain line after line; choked-up sobs and unrestrained wailing echo and reecho from stanza to stanza. Sustained laments and almost endless cries of pain over an incident in ancient history and in a far-off land may not appear too meaningful to the modern reader. Yet anyone whose native land has suffered the cruel ravages of war or whose life lies in shambles will have no trouble agreeing that this part of Scripture too "was written for our instruction." (Ro 15:4)

Structure.

The first four chs. of Lamentations are cast in the mold of an alphabetic acrostic. For the use of this poetic artistry see the Introduction to the Book of Psalms, "Poetry," and the notes on Ps 119. Limited by the numbers of letters in the Hebrew alphabet, chs 1, 2, and 4 have 22 stanzas. In the third ch. three successive lines begin with the same Hebrew letter, raising the total to 66 verses. Ch. 5, while not conforming to the acrostic pattern, has 22 verses, suggesting coverage of the subject "from A to Z."

Authorship.

In the Hebrew Bible the 266 lines of this book have no caption except the exclamatory adverb "How," the first word of the text, which introduces also chs. 2 and 4. The designation "Lamentations" is a title affixed to these five poems in the ancient Greek translation called the Septuagint. To this superscription the Septuagint adds the note: "And it came to pass, after Jeremiah was taken captive and Jerusalem laid waste, that Jeremiah sat weeping and lamented with this lamentation over Jerusalem and said . . ." This ancient tradition lives on in the title "The Lamentations of Jeremiah." According to 2 Ch 35:25 the prophet of Anathoth did indeed compose the kind of literature called a "lament." However, there is no Biblical statement which ascribes authorship of the dirges in this book to the man often called "the weeping prophet." Arguments based on such internal criteria as vocabulary, literary style, and viewpoint are not cogent enough to prove or disprove Jeremianic composition of these litanies of grief. From the way they are expressed it is evident only that the writer was a contemporary of the tragic events he bewails. If these poems must remain anonymous, they are not, for that reason, less authoritative—just as little as psalms of unknown origin are inferior to those whose writers are named.

In weighing considerations of authorship it may be significant to note the place assigned to this book in the Hebrew canon. There it does not follow the prophecies of Jeremiah but is listed as a part of the third major division of the OT books, called simply "The Writings." In this collection of various literary types it in turn is one of five books designated "The Scrolls" and chosen to be read on special days of the liturgical calendar. The Book of Lamentations served, and still serves, to commemorate the destruction of the temple, observed on the 9th of Ab (July-August).

1:1-22 In the first lament Zion, the destroyed holy city, is personified as a humiliated, deserted widow. In 1-11 her piteous plight is rehearsed. In 12-22 she mounts the poet's stage to bewail the misery of her widowhood. Minor deviations from this general framework occur: v. 11 records a word of prayer uttered by her; in v. 17 she is spoken of in the third person. Both parts have characteristic elements in common with one another as well as with the other four chapters. Nowhere is there any evidence that the shattering blows of affliction caused the victims to give way to a stolid, sullen resignation to the inevitable. For the relief they give, tears are allowed to flow freely and openly; weeping is loud and unabashed. Unsuppressed sobbing rends the air as the bliss of former days is contrasted with the present nightmare of shame and destitution.

At the same time, sustained lamentation does not become an exercise in morbid self-pity. Nor is the tragedy attributed to a cruel fate that blindly and capriciously determines human destiny. The stricken mourners repeatedly confess that the Lord was justified in letting the Babylonians destroy Zion, for she had *sinned grievously* and *become a filthy thing* (8, 17). Nevertheless as undeniable as is *the multitude of her transgressions* (5), so certain it is that penitent cries for restoration will be heard. *The day* (21) will come when God again can use the chastized, forgiven nation as an instrument of His gracious and good will.

1:1 *Widow.* A woman bereft of her husband faced great hardship in ancient Israel, in spite of explicit legislation for her protection. (Ex 22:22; Dt 10:18; cf. Ps 94:6; 146:9)

1:2 *Lovers.* Israel's trust in foreign nations such as Egypt is described as harlotry. (19; Jer 3:1; 4:30; 30:14)

1:12 *Is it nothing?* Though the Hebrew presents difficulties, as the RSV note indicates, it is clear that passersby are hailed to *look and see* how great Zion's *sorrow* is. In the liturgy of Good Friday, Israel's grief is regarded as typical of the suffering of Jesus Christ when *the Lord inflicted . . . his fierce anger* on the Bearer of the world's sin.

1:14 *Bound into a yoke.* Israel could not extricate itself from the consequences of its *transgressions.*

1:21 *Let them be.* Because Zion's persecutors were also God's enemies by their "evil doing" (22) in opposing His kingdom, prayer for their defeat is justified. *The day* of the Lord brought Zion's punishment for her sins (Am 5:18-20; Jer 39:15 f.). When it dawns again she will be restored and her enemies destroyed. (Jer 46:10; 47:4; 50:27)

2:1-22 The same elegiac motifs that compose ch. 1 encompass the tragic theme in ever new circles of poetic artistry. Particularly heavy lines underscore the painful realization that the national catastrophe came about because *the Lord in His anger . . . has cast down from heaven to earth the splendor of Israel. In his fierce indignation* He did not even spare His *footstool,* the temple (Ps 99:5; 132:7). He *poured out His fury* on the entire holy city, all of the land and its rulers, thereby bringing *to an end in Zion appointed feast and sabbath* and all functions of theocratic government (1-10). The severity of divine judgment is dramatized as the daughter of Zion bewails the *infants and babes* fainting and dying of starvation. (11-12)

The poet is at a loss to *comfort* the stricken *daughter of Jerusalem.* He cannot point to others who have suffered a worse fate. Nor can he exonerate her from guilt in permitting lying *prophets* to confirm her in her *iniquity* with *oracles false and misleading* (13-14). She need not expect sympathy either from those who once considered *the city . . . the perfection of beauty,* and still less from her *enemies.* (15-16)

Because it is the Lord who *has demolished without pity,* relief must come from Him. Fervent, incessant prayer alone offers hope (17-19). Responding to this exhortation, the daughter of Zion again appears on the stage and importunes the Lord to be moved to mercy by the horrors suffered by His people. (20-22)

2:4 *The tent. The daughter of Zion* once resided in Jerusalem.

2:6 *His booth.* In the storm of divine wrath the massive structure of the temple disintegrated like a flimsy hut made of leaves and branches.

2:7 *Clamor.* The festive shout of joyous worshipers has been replaced by the raucous cries of invaders.

2:8 *Marked . . . by the line.* Demolition of the wall was carried out with the precision builders use in erecting an edifice. (2 K 21:13; Is 34:11)

2:9 *No vision.* In the destroyed city no provisions of *the law,* civil and religious, were in force. Nor could *prophets* receive and transmit inspired guidance *from the Lord.* After Jeremiah was carried away to Egypt (Jer 40 ff.), no prophetic voice was heard in Palestine for decades.

2:12 *Faint.* For conditions in Jerusalem during the siege see 2 K 25:3; Jer 52:6.

2:14 *Prophets.* For Jeremiah's tirades against purveyors of *false and deceptive visions* see Jer 14:13 ff.; 26:7 ff.; 27:10, 15; 28:5-16; 37:18 f. Those who are misled by religious charlatans share the guilt of their deceivers.

2:15 *Perfection of beauty.* Jerusalem had the distinction of being "the city of the great King." (Ps 48:2; 50:2)

2:19 *Watches.* Prayer was to continue into the night, which was divided into three periods called watches.

2:20 *Eat their offspring.* Cf. 4:10; Lv 26:29; Dt 28:53 ff.; Jer 19:9. "It is a fearful thing to fall into the hands of the living God." (Heb 10:31)

3:1-66 Flanked by two chs., the 66 verses of this lament rise like a cresting wave over a sea of tears. Poetic form reaches a new level of artistic versatility. The acrostic pattern is tripled. Each Hebrew letter in alphabetic order is positioned at the beginning of three verses as if to nail down the thought with as many hammerblows. Within the confines of this framework, elements of various types of poetry have free course, following one another in an almost bewildering freedom of movement. Some groups of verses resemble the kind of psalm in which a sorely tried individual pleads for relief from his pain and grief. In another part the strains of a collective or national lament are prominent. Submission to God's will and confident trust in His mercy at times sound like the psalms expressing a triumphant faith. Advice on how to bear chastisement reads like a page from Proverbs or Job. The grieving nation speaks in the singular "I" and "me" as well as in the plural "we" and "us." Dramatic vividness is achieved by interspersed dialog and soliloquy. The crushed people are personified as a *man who has seen affliction* and also as *the daughter of my people.* (1, 48)

As is the case in the other lamentations, a wail out of the depths of grief emanates from the opening verses. The crushing nature of the blows causing the cries of pain is described in a scintillating array of figures of speech. It is all so frightening that the victim feels himself locked into a dark, tightly sealed horror-chamber (1-9). It seems as if the Lord is tearing at him like a wild beast or has shot arrow after arrow into his flesh. Instead of receiving sympathy, he has become the laughingstock of his fellowmen (10-15). As a result, he is at the point of declaring *expectation from the Lord* a hopeless delusion. (16-20)

Yet he does not drown in despair. He reminds himself of a truth of which he will not let go. All appearances to the contrary, it is an incontrovertible fact that *the steadfast love of the Lord* cannot come to an end (21-24). From this premise it must follow that *the Lord is good to those who wait for him,* also when they have a *yoke* to *bear* in a national disaster (25-27). In this connection there comes to mind what those who have endured affliction have to say about the meaning and goal of trials. They agree on two axioms: (a) it affords the Lord no pleasure to *grieve the sons of men;* (b) he is ready to *have compassion* as soon as the chastisement has served its purpose (28-33). Therefore it is also true that He will not tolerate injustice and oppression which serve only to satisfy the greed and lust of evil men. For no matter how mighty the wicked may be, their punishment is inevitable because He has the power to execute it. (34-39)

However, hope in God cannot be based on human merit. Sins cannot be expiated by suffering. A full confession of guilt and an unreserved plea for pardon are needed if there is to be an escape from the consequences of having *transgressed and rebelled* against the Lord. Because in the past the people refused to *return to the Lord,* He poured out His *anger* on the rebellious nation. The *devastation and destruction* will end only when *the Lord from heaven looks down and sees* a change of heart (40-51). At the same time, let there be no doubt that God can be moved by a penitent appeal to His mercy to forgive and to heal the wounds He inflicted. Deliverance is as certain as if it had already come to pass. In order to awaken faith in God's promises, the poet lets an unnamed person appear on the scene and testify how the Lord heard his cry *from the depths of the pit* (52-57). Convinced that in espousing his *cause* God's honor is at stake, he is bold enough to insist that the Lord *pursue . . . and destroy* his *assailants.* (58-66)

3:1 *Rod of his wrath.* For a similar outburst of pain caused by the Lord see Jb 16:6-17; 19:8-22; Ps 38; 88; 109; 143.

3:6 *In darkness.* Physical sight is terminated by death. (Ps 6:5 note)

3:15 *Wormwood.* Cf. Pr 5:4 note; Jer 9:15.

3:16 *Grind on gravel.* He had stones to chew rather than bread. (Cf. Mt 7:9)

3:18 *Gone is . . . my expectation.* Other sufferers too were tempted to give up hope. (Jb 21; Ps 73:12-14)

3:24 *My portion.* He can claim God for himself as confidently as an heir asserts his right to his heritage. (Ps 16:5; 73:26; 119:57; 142:5)

3:26 *It is good.* Trials are sent by God for a wholesome purpose and should be borne with patient submission to His superior wisdom. (Jb 5:17 f.; Ps 37:7 f.; Pr 3:11 f.)

3:33 *Not willingly.* God has no sadistic delight in making His creatures miserable. He may indeed *grieve the sons of men* as described in vv. 1-18, but His "compassion" and "steadfast love" (32) determine that the pain does not last longer than necessary. (Ps 103:9; 30:5; Jer 3:12; 31:20; Hos 11:8 f.)

3:38 *Good and evil.* Cf. Is 45:7 note.

3:42 *Not forgiven.* Unless those who *have transgressed and rebelled* against the Lord seek His pardon, their sins remain unforgiven, creating a fatal separation between themselves and God. (Is 59:2 ff.)

3:53 *Into the pit.* Though Jeremiah was thrown into a pit (Jer 38:7-13), he would have died there of starvation rather than by drowning. The sufferer speaking here graphically describes the depths of the deadly disasters from which God delivered him.

3:64 *Requite them.* For Jeremiah's prayers for vindication see the introductory notes on Jer 17:12-18 and 18:23 note. Cf. also 2 Ti 4:14.

4:1-22 Another lament over the fall of Jerusalem is not a contrived exercise in emotional display. Shattering grief often causes more than one night of weeping. Submission to God's leading may come only after a prolonged battle against resentment and bitterness. The poet indeed lets cries of anguish have free reign because they are to serve a positive purpose. The intensity of pain is to call to mind how grievously the nation sinned against God if He dealt them such severe blows. Penitent realization of having offended a loving God is not in vain, for restoration to favor will follow when *the punishment . . . is accomplished* (22). This ch., too, is an acrostic.

The first two verses bewail the nation's total loss of status. Formerly prized as *gold, the precious sons of Zion* are as worthless as a clay jug cheaply produced by *a potter's hands.*

Evidence of this degradation is heartrending. Infants die of *thirst* because their mothers lack the strength to nurse them. *Children . . . lie on ash heaps,* dying and dead, for want of *food.* Compared with *Sodom,* the chosen people received a more "severe beating" (3-6; Lk 12:47). That *the Lord gave full vent to his wrath* is apparent also in the fate of the adult population. Robust specimens of manhood *pined away,* dying a lingering death of *hunger.* Otherwise *compassionate women* tried to stave off starvation by eating *their own children* (7-11). As even the heathen acknowledged, none of this would have happened if the Lord had not permitted the enemy to *enter the gates of Jerusalem.* Yet He did so because the crimes of the *prophets* and *priests* could not go unpunished (12-16). Kings and political leaders too were guilty of rejecting the Lord, *watching vainly for help* from *a nation which could not save,* such as Egypt. (17-20)

However, there is still hope for the future. If *the punishment* will bring *the daughter of Zion* to her senses, God will let her again play her assigned part in His eternal plan of universal salvation, while His and her enemies such as *Edom* will perish. (21-22)

4:3 *Ostriches.* Proverbial for abandoning their young. (Cf. Jb 39:13-16)

4:6 *No hand.* The punishment of *Sodom,* destroyed *in a moment,* was less severe because it did not suffer the horrors of a long siege and the cruelties perpetuated by human agents. For Israel's guilt, which provoked God to deal more harshly with His chosen people, see Jer 23:14; Eze 16:48.

4:10 *Boiled their own children.* Alluded to in 2:20 and foretold in Jer 19:9.

4:12 *Did not believe.* Defended by the Lord, *Jerusalem* was impregnable against even such mighty conquerors as Sennacherib (Is 36 f.). Promise of divine protection gave rise to the false sense of security denounced by Jeremiah in chs. 7 and 26.

4:13 *Shed . . . blood.* The religious leaders misled the people by their false teaching and so were accountable for the bloodbath which took place when the city fell. But they were also more directly involved in murderous plots against *the righteous* (Jer 26:7, 20-23).

4:15 *"Away! Unclean!"* In the end popular revulsion against the lying prophets and priests grew so strong that they were shunned like lepers even after their dispersion *among the nations.* (16; Jer 29:21 f.; Lv 13:45)

4:17 *We watched.* The people confess that they ignored Jeremiah's warning against the folly of trying to ward off the threatened punishment by alliances with Egypt and other nations. (Jer 2:18, 36 ff.; 27:3; 37:5-10)

4:20 *The Lord's anointed.* As long as a king, God's theocratic representative, occupied the throne in Jerusalem, the people felt that their existence *among the nations* was assured. But their trust in kings, considered as essential to their well-being as *the breath* of their *nostrils* was to physical life, was shattered when King Zedekiah was trapped like an animal by the Babylonians (Jer 52:8-11). Jeremiah predicted that Zedekiah's irresponsible administration of the royal office would have tragic results. (Jer 37:17 ff.)

4:21 *Edom.* The inveterate foe of Israel is chosen to exemplify the fate awaiting all who attempt to thwart the coming of God's kingdom. No hostile power, great or small, can escape draining *the cup* of divine wrath which renders the drinker as helpless and weak as a drunkard. For other denunciations of Edom see Ob 11-14; Jer 49:7-13; Eze 25:12-14; Ml 1:2-5.

5:1-22 The last lament resembles the preceding chs. in form only to the extent that it has the same number of verses as there are letters in the Hebrew alphabet, the acrostic pattern being dropped. However, the content again is predicated on the conviction that God will not disdain to listen to a tearful recital of troubles, that He accepts a sincere confession of guilt, and that He can be moved to answer humble appeals to His mercy. As if He did not know or failed to *remember,* the people who remained in the land after Jerusalem's fall din their woes into His ears. The pain, they say, smarts all the more when they recall the freedom, peace, and splendor of bygone days and contrast them with the oppression, harassment, and degradation they now endure.

Interspersed in this review of their pathetic situation are frank admissions that in fact they deserve nothing better. They cannot deny the long record of national sins from the time of the *fathers* down to themselves (7, 16). Penitential grief is particularly poignant at the thought that *Mount Zion,* where they had the privilege of drawing near to God in worship and prayer, *lies desolate* (1-18). The plea for the return of *days as of old* boldly asserts that God cannot possibly have *utterly rejected* them. Because they believe that His *throne endures to all generations,* they count on Him to *restore* them to Himself so that His heavenly kingdom may manifest itself on earth through them. (19-22)

5:6 *Egypt and . . . Assyria.* Extending *the hand* of friendship and alliance to the Nile and Euphrates world powers was a national policy dating back, as v. 7 declares, to the days of the "fathers." Prophets warned repeatedly against this rejection of God's promised protection. (Is 30:2 f.; 31:1; Jer 2:18, 36; Eze 16:28; 23:5, 12; Hos 5:13; 7:11; 12:1)

5:7 *We hear.* V. 16 shows that the suppliants did not accuse God of punishing them for sins they did not commit, as some of their contemporaries did by quoting a blasphemous proverb (Jer 31:29 note). While the *fathers* did not live to see the threats of divine judgment come true, their own generation was as guilty as they. (Ex 20:5; Dt 5:19; Jer 15:4; 16:11-13; 32:18). Even "the righteous" (4:13) who share the fate of the wicked in the disaster do not complain of unjust treatment.

5:8 *Slaves.* Servile lackeys of the Babylonians "lorded it over the people." (Neh 5:15)

5:9 *Sword in the wilderness.* Bedouin raiders

threatened them as they eked out an existence in the outer limits of the land.

5:11 *In Zion . . . in the towns.* Among the ruins of Jerusalem and other cities of Judah crimes of all kinds could flourish.

5:21 *Restore us.* Sinners cannot *be restored* to a favorable relationship with God by their "own reason or strength" (Luther). They need to pray for the Spirit's enabling initiative and power.

5:22 *Hast thou . . . rejected us?* The impassioned pleading in five chs. seems to end in an interrogation mark of uncertainty and doubt rather than in the exclamation point of firm trust and joyous anticipation. However, the question in effect boldly challenges God to be true to Himself. If He is "merciful and gracious . . . abounding in steadfast love," as He has declared Himself to be (Ex 34:6) He cannot refuse to pardon and restore His wayward but penitent children. This confidence in God's forgiving mercy is expressed positively in 3:31-33.

EZEKIEL

INTRODUCTION

Historical Setting

The words of Ezekiel are marked with more exact chronological data than any other prophetic book. The anchor date is 597 B.C., the year of "the exile of King Jehoiachin" (1:2). Fourteen events are dated by year, month, and day with reference to this punitive campaign of Nebuchadnezzar which accounted also for Ezekiel's forced stay "in the land of the Chaldeans by the river Chebar" (1:3). Here he was called to prophetic office in the fifth year of his captivity (1:2). The word of the Lord to which he attached the latest date came to him "in the twenty-seventh year" of the exile (29:17). It was evident that he noted the exact time of certain significant events in his career such as his ordination, the arrival of the news of Jerusalem's fall, the grand vision of restoration (1:2; 33:21; 40:1). However, we fail to understand why the words addressed to the foreign nations (chs. 25—32) were of such importance as to account for half of the 14 dates.

The only date difficult to compute on the basis of Jehoiachin's exile appears in the very first verse. "The thirtieth year," mentioned there, most likely gives the prophet's age. If that is the case, then a review of these three decades will bring to mind how fateful these years were in Israel's history. In the year of his birth, 100 years had passed since the Assyrians carried off the ten northern tribes and destroyed Samaria, their capital. When he was 10 years old (612 B.C.), the Assyrian empire collapsed and the Babylonians became the masters of Israel's world. As a boy of 15 years he heard how Nebuchadnezzar defeated Pharoah Necho at Carchemish in northern Palestine, where the Egyptians challenged Babylonian supremacy. On his way back to Babylon, Nebuchadnezzar took with him a number of hostages from Jerusalem, among whom young Daniel was to become famous. Ezekiel was 25 years old when the same Babylonian king came to Jerusalem to put down a rebellion against foreign domination. As a warning against future insurrections, Nebuchadnezzar took Jehoiachin and the upper stratum of the population to Babylonia. Among them was "Ezekiel the priest" (1:3). At the time he was about to begin doing service in the temple, but the Lord had other plans for him. Called to be His spokesman, he carried out his prophetic duties before and after Jerusalem was destroyed. Apparently he did not live to see Israel's return from exile, which he foretold with unshaken confidence. More than three decades were to elapse from the 27th year of his captivity—the last date recorded in the book (29:17)—to the time when Cyrus the Persian issued the decree of liberation.

Person

Ezekiel was endowed with so wide a range of mental and emotional qualities that people of more limited capacities may find it difficult to concede the likelihood of such contrasting characteristics in one and the same person. He was able to produce imaginative, highly artistic poems as well as prose accounts weighted down with tiring, pedestrian minutiae. Pedantic and absorbed in detail, he could also soar to magnificent heights of literary beauty. Because he also displayed diverse and opposite traits of character, he has been made out to be a split personality. Some critics have found him subject to paranoid schizophrenia. This mental abnormality, they charge, was accompanied by epileptic seizures.

However, Ezekiel was not physically or mentally sick. He acted in obedience to "the word of the Lord." When it came to him, it shaped his message and directed his actions. He did not engage in self-induced trances. Always it was "the hand of the Lord" that lifted him into ecstatic visions. If he appeared stern or even heartless, it was because the Lord made his "face hard against" the "hard forehead" of an impenitent people. (3:4-11)

God's demand that Ezekiel surrender himself totally in service to Him is apparent also in the unusual, oft-repeated form of address: "son of man." Only once did God call him by his name (24:24). More than 90 times He used a phrase which can be translated also: "son of Adam." Highly favored by visions and honored to speak divine truth, God's messenger is reminded that, like the first man, he too was formed of clay and would return again to dust and ashes. There is nothing in Ezekiel's words or behavior to show that he needed this admonition to be humble on an average about two times per chapter. Nevertheless, everyone called to the public ministry of the Word realizes that the temptation to pride is a dangerous occupational hazard. When our Lord spoke of Himself so often as "the Son of man," He thereby declared His solidarity with those He came to save. But He used the same title to claim that He came "with the clouds of heaven" and "was given dominion and glory and kingdom . . . which shall not pass away." (Dn 7:13 f.)

Authorship

The early critical dismemberment of the Scriptures left the Book of Ezekiel intact. About 50 years ago, however, a whirlwind of negative criticism descended on it. Radical scholars left only 251 authentic verses out of a total of 1,273. Ezekiel's presence in Babylonia was declared a literary fiction. In more recent years the pendulum has swung to a more moderate position, though whole sections (such as chs. 40—48) are frequently assigned to another author.

Content

The message of Ezekiel falls naturally into three main sections. Chs. 1—24 contain threats of judgment on impenitent Israel; chs. 33—48 bring promise of restoration; the intervening part (chs. 25—32) announces doom on seven neighboring nations in order to allow for the revival of the chosen people. The purpose of Law and Gospel preaching is summed up in the brief statement: "They (you) shall know that the Lord is God," which is found more than 60 times in the book.

OUTLINE

I. 1:1—24:27 Israel, a Rebellious House, Will Fall
- A. 1:1—3:27 God Sends His Spokesman to the Rebellious House
- B. 4:1—24:27 Ezekiel Foretells the Doom of the Rebellious House

II. 25:1—32:32 Foreign Nations, Hostile to God and His People, Will Perish
- A. 25:1-17 Ammon, Moab, Edom, Philistia
- B. 26:1—28:26 Tyre and Sidon
- C. 29:1—32:32 Egypt

III. 33:1—48:35 Chastened Israel Will Be Restored, and the Promised Kingdom of God Will Come
- A. 33:1—39:29 The Message of Restoration
- B. 40:1—48:35 The Visions of Restoration

1:1—24:27 ISRAEL, A REBELLIOUS HOUSE, WILL FALL

1:1—3:27 God Sends His Spokesman to the Rebellious House

1:1-3 PREFACE: WHEN, WHERE, AND THROUGH WHOM GOD SPOKE

1:1-3. Information on the time and place is important for understanding the messages God transmitted to His people through a man who as *the son of Buzi,* a *priest,* normally would have been privileged to assume priestly duties in Jerusalem. The high regrad paid the sacred profession explains why *Ezekiel* was among those from the upper stratum of society whom Nebuchadnezzar carried off to Babylonia in 597 BC (2 K 24:10-16; Jer 24:1). After he spent five years *among the exiles* settled by a large irrigation canal called *the river Chebar,* the drab routine of the prisoner suddenly ended. The change was not of his own making. *The word of the Lord came to* him, propelling and enabling him to assume the crushing responsibility of watching over his people's destiny.

1:1 *Thirtieth year.* The time of the prophetic commissioning is given here according to a chronological reckoning different from that found in the next verse and in all subsequent dates of the book (cf. Introduction, "Time"). The undetermined 30th year and the specified fifth year can be equated without textual changes if the former figure is regarded as supplying the prophet's age at the time of his call. Though the usual Hebrew idiom to express age ("the son of 30 years") does not appear here, it is absent also in computing the "year of Noah's life" in Gn 7:11.

The heavens were opened. Ezekiel did not climb to ecstatic heights on the ladder of self-induced hypnosis. Nor did he presume to indulge in supersensory intoxication simply because he wanted it and asked to have it made available when and where he pleased. The limitations to human perception were removed at the time and place of God's choosing. Ezekiel *saw visions of God* when it pleased the Creator to command that the heavens be opened.

1:3 *The hand of the Lord.* This anthropomorphic expression occurs frequently to explain that God enabled Ezekiel to do what he would not or could not do of his own strength (3:14; 22; 8:1; 33:22; 37:1; 40:1). For other instances in which the phrase "the hand of the Lord" denotes divine propulsion or endowment with miraculous power see 1 K 18:46; 2 K 3:15; Is 8:11; Jer 15:7.

1:4-28 GOD APPEARS IN A VISION TO EZEKIEL

What God enabled Ezekiel to see was so awesome and overpowering that he "fell" on his "face" in a faint (28). Miraculously opened, his eyes beheld: (a) an approaching fiery storm cloud (4), out of which emerged (b) four unearthly creatures (5-14), propelling (c) a four-wheeled chariot (15-21), bearing (d) a celestial platform (22-25), on which was enthroned (e) the glory of the Lord (26-27), framed by (f) the bright colors of a rainbow (28). Perhaps Ezekiel did not fully understand the significance of every detail of the fantastic vision. He heard and saw "things that cannot be told" (2 Co 12:2-4). In his attempt to describe them he repeatedly says that they had "the likeness of" or looked "like" some phenomenon observable by normal sight. At times it seems he goes back to take a second look at a feature he has described before and speaks of it again. Yet the spectacle was not to be a stupendous but meaningless exhibition of pyrotechnics. All through his ministry Ezekiel drew from this vision what he needed to make him strong when he preached of judgment to come (3:23; 8:4) and to give him confidence when he spoke of Israel's restoration and the founding of the Messianic kingdom (43:3). Other servants of God were also accorded visions (Moses: Ex 3:2 ff.; Micaiah: 1 K 22:19; Isaiah: Is 6:1 ff.). Described only briefly, their encounters with God took place but once in their careers. Ezekiel's vision reappears at crucial points in his ministry to sustain and inspire him.

The circumstances under which Ezekiel was called to the prophetic office may explain why the glory of the Lord appeared to him so dramatically and frequently. When he saw it the first time, the world seemed full to the brim with the ignominy and defeat of the God of Israel. A few years later the holy city and the temple were leveled with the ground. The Babylonian conquerors boasted that their god Marduk had taken over control of the world. The faithful in Israel—perhaps even Ezekiel himself—were tempted to doubt the Lord's promise that "all the nations shall flow" to a Jerusalem which no longer existed. (Is 2:2 f.)

At a time when all the stars of hope in the chosen people's skies were eclipsed by the brilliance of brutal, unrestrained force, "the heavens were opened" (1:1). He whom "heaven and the highest heaven cannot contain" (1 K 8:27) let His glory burst upon the mundane scene in such blinding light and cosmic color as to rouse the most dispirited from his gloomy stupor. He is not an idol locked up within the walls of a shrine. He can appear even in the heartland of the conqueror's domain to assert worldwide dominion. The inanimate forces of nature are at His disposal. At His beck and call stand messengers endowed with the power of all animate creatures, both human and bestial. Chariots of fire, geared to move instantly in any direction, are poised and ready to take off to the four corners of the earth. When Ezekiel "told the exiles all the things that the Lord had showed" him (11:25), no one should any longer have doubted the power of the God of Abraham, Isaac, and Jacob to execute His threats and keep His promises.

1:4 *Out of the north.* It is the Lord who can "bring evil from the north" (Jer 4:6; 1:13 note) and not the heathen gods whose primordial home was believed to be in mountains of the mysterious north.

Wind . . . brightness . . . fire. The exiles knew these phenomena of nature as media of divine revelation in times past (Ex 14:24; Dt 4:24; 1 K 19:11 f.; Ps 104:1 ff.; Is 10:17; Nah 1:3). They were not to be misled by the Babylonian myths of Marduk, the lord of the storm, and Shamash, the god of light.

1:5 *Living creatures.* When in a subsequent vision these multi-faced beings appeared again, Ezekiel realized that their features were basically no different from those of the heavenly emissaries called "cherubim" (10:15). The Israelites knew of them from history (Gn 3:24; 1 K 6:23-28; 7:27, 29). They were told that in the temple the Lord was "enthroned above the cherubim" (Is 37:16; 1 Sm 4:4; 2 Sm 6:2; Ps 80:1; 99:1; cf. also Ps 18:10). Ezekiel hesitated at first to call these bearers of divine glory cherubim because they had four faces and four wings whereas they usually were described as appearing with two faces and two wings (cf. the appearance of the cherubim in Ezekiel's temple of the future, 41:17-20). However, the four-ness of their faces and wings underscored the unrestricted lordship of God over all creatures and flesh "in which is the breath of life" (Gn 6:17; Ps 150:6). The number four suggests totality and completeness also when noted with respect to other features of the vision.

The form in which heaven's "ministering spirits" (Heb 1:4) became visible to Ezekiel was no doubt designed to teach the exiles in their heathen environment that similar composite creatures, part human and part animal, to which their captors described magical powers, did not determine the course of human events. Whatever happens to individuals and nations is exclusively the result of God's directive issued to His servants whom He has endowed with the combined intelligence and strength of all living creatures.

In Christian art the four faces of the cherubim represent the variety of form by which the four evangelists record one and the same Gospel.

1:16 *Wheels.* A "chariot of fire" and "of victory," known from previous manifestations of divine power, was at God's disposal also in the land which its citizens claimed as the domain of the god Marduk (2 K 2:11; Hab 3:8; Dt 33:26; Ps 68:17; Is 66:15; Dn 7:9). It was equipped with wheels, each of which was constructed *as it were a wheel within a wheel.* If each bisected the other at right angles, the celestial conveyance was able to move in all four directions without turning.

1:18 *Full of eyes.* Bizarre in our world where the animate and the inanimate are separated categories, this feature of the angelic vehicle seems to give additional assurance of full compliance with God's will. Agencies carrying out divine commands do not take an unexplored road where obstacles impede or wreck the mission.

1:21 *The spirit . . . in the wheels.* The mysterious energy which animated the living creatures supplied the power to propel the wheels.

1:22 *Firmament.* Borne aloft by the living creatures was what had the appearance of a level surface on which rested what had "the likeness of a throne." (26)

1:26 *As it were . . . a human form.* Ezekiel takes great pains not to give the impression that the infinite God can be impounded in a human body. Even in a vision a mortal, sinful prophet cannot come face to face with Him who "dwells in unapproachable light" (1 Ti 6:16; Ex 33:20). As if he had to shield his eyes with three protective lenses, which filtered out the rays of the Creator of light, he says he saw (1) "the appearance of (2) the likeness of (3) the glory of the Lord." (28)

1:28 *The bow . . . in the cloud.* The "stormy wind" and the "great cloud" (1:4) of national disaster had to come. But above and beyond the darkness God's light of forgiving mercy would shine on as brightly as before. The blessings to come, later to be proclaimed by Ezekiel, are diffused with the unextinguishable brilliance of the rainbow, "the sign of the covenant" which will not be broken "for all future generations." (Gn 9:8-17)

I heard. The *one speaking,* identified in a visual manifestation of His glory, needed to communicate verbally with Ezekiel if he was to know why God appeared to him as He did. Cf. the spoken directives to Moses and Isaiah after they saw flashes of God's glory. (Ex 3:10; Is 6:8 ff.)

2:1—3:27 GOD ENTRUSTS HIS WORD TO EZEKIEL

2:1—3:3 Ezekiel was not to bask in the afterglow of the vision (ch. 1) or to spend time privately meditating on its meaning. What he saw was to motivate him for service to his people. However, if he was to take his stand in the Lord's cause and to serve as His spokesman, he needed the vitalizing "Spirit" infused into his prostrate form (1-2; cf. Gn 2:7 for the way Adam, "dust from the ground," became "a living being" after God "breathed into his nostrils the breath of life"). But fortified by divine inspiration, he was equipped to speak God's words to *the people of Israel* though they were *a rebellious house* obstinately resolved to act like *briers and thorns* and *scorpions* in resisting his message (3-7). Further, his assignment was unpleasant because the message he was handed to transmit would produce *lamentation and mourning and woe.* But he was not to let this distasteful aspect of his task deter him. In the end he would have a deep inner satisfaction as if he had eaten the scroll inscribed with the bitter words and it became in his *mouth as sweet as honey.* (2:8—3:3)

2:1 *Son of man.* The first sound Ezekiel was to hear was not his name but a phrase by which God would address him more than 90 times. For its meaning see Introduction, "Person."

2:5 *They will know.* The roll of distant thunder reverberates in this prediction. The destruction of Jerusalem, foretold by the *prophet among them,* will prove that God will not be mocked. (Cf. 33:33)

2:8 *Be not rebellious.* God uses strong language to warn the candidate for the prophetic office against being disobedient and thus becoming no better than the *rebellious house* whose doom he is to announce. But God also encourages His prospective ambassador by a visionary experience. If he would "eat" (3:1) God's words, as Jeremiah did, they would become "a joy" of which no outward circumstance could deprive him. (Cf. Jer 15:16 note)

3:1 *He said.* The mysterious "hand" offering Ezekiel the scroll (2:9) came to him at the instigation of the same "voice" (1:28) he heard ordering him to "stand upon" his "feet." (2:1)

3:4-11 The newly commissioned prophet is not to think his task will be any easier because he is not being sent *to a people of foreign speech* but to *the house of Israel,* with whom he can readily communicate in his and their language. For though they will understand very well what he will tell them *with . . . words* supplied by God, their *hard forehead* and *stubborn heart* will not let it disturb their conscience and affect their will. Therefore God not only sends out His prophet without false illusions of easy success, but He also equips him with a mental and spiritual fortitude *like adamant harder than flint.* It will take great courage to say: *Thus says the Lord God* even though he will be speaking *to exiles* who already were suffering the consequences of not heeding prophetic admonition.

3:12-15 As the sight and sound of *the glory of the Lord* were withdrawn from Ezekiel, he felt the impulse of the *Spirit,* which had set him on his feet (2:2), moving him to the people he was to serve. However, the vision left him not only physically weak. He also lacked the emotional and spiritual stamina to rise to the occasion in a joyous mood. Instead he *went in bitterness* and *heat of . . . spirit.* Having arrived among the exiles, he *sat there overwhelmed among them seven days,* unable to cope with conflicting feelings and clashing opinions. He may have had to battle with his own notions of what needed to be done to promote the welfare of God's kingdom. It seemed that the need of the hour was not a mission to his enslaved people but rather a directive to appear at the Babylonian court with the demand: "Let my people go" (Ex 5:1). Both anger and grief at the thought of speaking to the rebellious house without any prospect of being heard may have increased *the heat of* his *spirit.* For reluctance to enter the Lord's service by other candidates of the prophetic office see Ex 4:2 ff.; Jon 1:3; 4:1. But the Lord overcame also Ezekiel's natural disinclination, *the hand of the Lord being strong upon* him.

3:15 *Overwhelmed . . . seven days.* Cf. Acts 9:9, where Paul tells of a similar experience. For the place name *Tel-abib* see the Introduction, "Setting."

3:16-21 The preceding verses make it clear that Ezekiel still needed instruction and motivation if he was to assume and carry out the duties of a prophet. In 16-21 God impressed on him how crucial it was for his hearers that he speak to them and do it properly. His message to the rebellious house was to be as clear and unambiguous as the clarion call of a watchman's alert. If not, he would be charged with the sinner's death. However, in comparing Ezekiel with a sentry God also relieved him of the responsibility for the success of his preaching. God demands that His spokesmen issue an unequivocal warning to the sinner, but they are not accountable for his refusal to *turn from his . . . wicked way.*

3:20 *A stumbling block.* God has "no pleasure in the death of any one" (18:32; 33:11). However, He brings people face to face with circumstances which demand a decision for or against Him. What is hidden in their hearts will express itself in open actions when they must choose between God and such things as money (7:19), idolatry (14:3), immorality (18:30), false gods (44:12). Cf. also Is 8:14 f.; Jn 9:39.

3:22-27 From the foregoing it would appear that God had said and done everything necessary to prepare Ezekiel for his task. No other candidate for the prophetic office received such an intensive and extensive orientation course. Yet the final verses of this ch. record that God gave him additional instruction and also a directive which no other prophet was required to observe. Until such a time as God will determine, he is not to *go out among the people* to talk to them about general topics of interest, nor is he to *reprove them* as he sees fit or in words of his own choosing. Only when God provides the message to be relayed is he to *open* his *mouth* and speak. Apparently to prepare Ezekiel for this order to surrender his own judgment and to forego disseminating his private opinions, the directive came to him to go *into the plain,* where he was given to see the same vision he *had seen by the river Chebar.* Though he again fell on his face, overwhelmed as before, he no longer gives way to bitterness.

3:27 *I will open.* It was not until Jerusalem had fallen that God lifted the restrictions on Ezekiel's mouth. (24:27)

4:1—24:27 Ezekiel Foretells the Doom of the Rebellious House

4:1—5:17 FURIOUS JUDGMENT PORTRAYED BY FOUR SYMBOLIC ACTIONS

4:1-3 When Ezekiel began to transmit to the rebellious house of Israel what he received in his "heart" and heard with his "ears" from the Lord (3:10), he was instructed to act out the doleful message as other prophets had done (cf., e.g., Is 8:1 ff.; 20:1 ff.; Jer 13:1 ff.; 16:1 ff.; 19:1 ff.). The first symbolic act was to impress on the spectators that nothing could move God to lift an impending siege off Jerusalem once He had let it get under way in full force. After the prophet had sketched the city *in a state of siege* on a soft clay tablet, he was to place *an iron plate* between himself and the menaced city. It was to be *a sign* that cries for deliverance would fail to penetrate and change the immutable decree of judgment issued by Ezekiel, God's representative.

4:4-8 A second dramatized sermon was to make clear that the threatened doom of the rebellious house would not be an accident of history or the chance happening of blind fate. It was ordered by God, who had every reason to inflict it. What the chosen people, composed of *Israel,* the 10 Northern tribes, and of *Judah,* the Southern Kingdom, did so kindled the wrath of the holy God that they would *bear their punishment* for many days to come. In acting out the divine word, Ezekiel was to play the role of the apostate nation. As if crushed to the ground under a heavy burden, he was to lie on his *left side . . . three hundred and ninety days* and then on his *right side . . . forty days,* bearing the punishment of Israel and Judah respectively.

4:5 *A number of days.* Each day was to represent the lapse of a year. The total number of 430 (390+40) days was symbolic of the long period of time during which they would *bear the punishment* of servitude in a foreign land. See Ex 12:40, according to which Israel spent 430 years in the Egyptian house of bondage, and Gn 15:13, where the duration of the sojourn "in a land that is not theirs" is foretold in the round figure of 400 years.

4:8 *Put cords upon you.* A figurative way of describing the restrictions God put on Ezekiel during the symbolic actions (3:25 f.). Evidently he did not have to spend all his waking hours in a prone and rigid posture, for the next verses depict him engaging in activities demanding considerable freedom of action. We may therefore assume that he let the people see him lying on one side and then another long enough to teach the desired lesson. Furthermore, if the total of 390+40 was symbolic rather than an actual count of years, the time required to portray this long but undefined period of history may not have been a literal, arithmetic figure. However, the reason for the breakdown of the total into the disparate components of 390 and 40 remains a matter of conjecture, though their figurative meaning may have been clear to Ezekiel and his audience.

4:9-17 A third series of symbolic actions was to simulate the physical and spiritual suffering the rebellious house would endure during the siege (1-3) and the ensuing exile (4-8). In order to portray how they would *lack bread and water,* Ezekiel was to live on food weighing no more than 8 ounces, and drink only about a pint of water. Next the dough, consisting of an assortment of coarse ingredients, was to be baked on a fire fueled by *human dung.* The defilement resulting from this offensive procedure was to foretell the ritual uncleanness of which the people would unavoidably become guilty because of conditions during the siege and in the exile. Ezekiel, from his youth a meticulous observer of the ceremonial laws, recoiled at the thought of such a repugnant contamination even though it would come about in carrying out a divinely ordered object lesson. Moved by Ezekiel's objection, the Lord let him substitute *cow's dung,* widely used for fuel in place of wood.

4:14 *Defiled myself.* The Israelites were not to eat *what died of itself or was torn by beasts,* i.e., meat of a carcass from which the blood was not properly drained (Ex 22:31; Lv 17:11 ff.; 22:8, 31; Dt 14:21). *Foul flesh,* translated "swine's flesh" in Is 65:4, could also refer to meat which worshipers were forbidden to eat in a sacred meal if it was allowed to become three or more days old. (Lv 7:18; 19:7)

5:1-12 In this ch. the audiovisual instruction, begun in ch. 4, reaches a climax. A fourth series of symbolic actions tells the highly favored but apostate people how "furious" the Lord's "chastisements" (15) will be because their *abominations* have kindled His "anger" and roused Him to "fury" (13). The media of this grisly object lesson were *a sharp sword* honed to a razor's edge, the prophet's *hair* cut from his *head* and shaved from his *beard,* a pair of *balances* or scales to divide the hair into three heaps, and *the skirts* or folds of his *robe.* The hair represents the people; Ezekiel demonstrates what God will do to them. One segment of the population will perish during *the siege;* a second contingent will be slaughtered by the enemy; a third will be uprooted and scattered abroad in the exile. Only *a small number* of these groups will survive. For the *fire* of divine judgment will pursue and overtake them in the land of their captors.

5:1 *Your head and your beard.* God would not hesitate to make the sword of the enemy destroy His people even though He chose them to be what men regard as their pride and joy: a strong crop of hair and a long beard. Loss of these symbols of manliness expresses mourning or disgrace. (2 Sm 10:4 note; Is 15:2; Jer 48:37)

5:2 *Unsheath the sword.* Repeated in v. 12 and in 12:14; cf. also Lv 26:33; Jer 9:16; Am 9:4. Though some of the people would perish in the exile, a remnant would survive, as promised in 6:8 and 12:16.

5:4 *From there.* Conditions in the exile would prove fatal to many.

5:5 *Jerusalem.* Many in Ezekiel's audience may have hoped he was pantomiming the fall of Babylon and Israel's release from captivity. However, though God had designed Jerusalem to be *the center* from which salvation was to radiate to *the nations,* He had to discard her for her rebellions against Him. For the spiritual Jerusalem in the future see Is 2:2 notes.

5:7 *Have acted.* The reading "have not acted" (RSV note) declares Israel's conduct more offensive than that of *countries round about her.* The chosen people, though they had God's "ordinances" and "statutes," did not reach even the level of moral uprightness practiced by the heathen, as charged in 16:47 ff. (Cf. also Jer 2:10 f.; Lk 12:47 f.)

5:10 *Eat their sons.* For the horrors of cannibalism see Lv 26:29; Dt 28:33; 2 K 6:28 f.; Jer 19:9; Lm 4:10.

5:13-17 The people "of a hard forehead and of

a stubborn heart" (3:7) would not be able to say that the meaning of the symbolic action was not made clear. Ezekiel goes on to describe the disasters to come when the Lord, His *anger* and *fury* aflame, sets out to *bring the sword upon* the rebellious house.

5:13 *They shall know.* This solemn declaration of God's sovereign power and determination to execute threatened judgments and to keep covenanted promises occurs 4 times in the next ch. and some 60 times elsewhere in the book. It repeats the words spoken to the covenant nation from the very beginning. (Ex 6:2-8; 7:5, 17; 10:2; 14:4, 18; 16:12; 29:45 f.)

My jealousy. For the meaning of this divine attribute see Ex 20:4 note; Dt 4:24 note.

Spend my fury. Drastic language is necessary to dispel the notion that God is a harmless idol of wood or stone whose nose can be tweaked with impunity. In a more sophisticated age wise people may try to insulate themselves against His burning hatred of sin by fashioning Him in their imagination, making Him out to be incapable or unwilling to punish those who offend His holiness. At all times it is true that "it is a fearful thing to fall into the hands of the living God" (Heb 10:31), but when divine anger spent itself on Him who was "made . . . to be sin" for us, He could say: "It is finished." (2 Co 5:21; Jn 19:30)

5:15 *Furious chastisements.* The agents of judgment (vv. 16 f.) mentioned again in 14:21 and Jer 15:2 f., appear also in Rv 6:7 f.

6:1—7:27 JUDGMENT PROCLAIMED BY WORD OF MOUTH

6:1-7 Continuing to drive home the baleful meaning of the symbolic actions (chs. 4—5), Ezekiel spoke *the word of the Lord* as it *came to* him and through him to the people. They were to *know* that the Lord was about to "execute judgments . . . in anger and fury" for very good reasons. They were guilty not only of defiling the "sanctuary" in Jerusalem with "detestable things" (5:11, 15; cf. ch. 8; 2 K 21:7) but also of committing abominations throughout the land on *the mountains and the hills* and in *the ravines and the valleys.* Here they worshiped the forces of nature rather than the Creator. The punishment will fit the crime. *The slain* idolators will be found strewn among the ruins of the *cities* and the *incense altars.*

6:3 *High places.* For these sites of worship see Dt 12:5 note.

6:8-10 God will *do this evil* not simply for judgment's sake. Its ultimate aim is to *leave . . . alive* a purified and chastened remnant through whom He will achieve the purpose for which He chose the descendants of Abraham. (12:16; 14:22; Is 10:20 ff.)

6:9 *I have broken.* The Hebrew text reads: "I have been broken," meaning that He was broken-hearted over Israel's refusal to respond gratefully to all the favors He showered on them.

Their idols. Related etymologically to the noun "dung" (4:12), the Hebrew word expresses the contempt and revulsion with which false gods were to be regarded. Ezekiel uses this term 38 times, whereas it occurs only about 10 times in all other books.

6:11-14 Lest some hearers draw false conclusions from the promise of a remnant, the closing verses of the ch. repeat the threat that God will *make the land desolate and waste, throughout all their habitations.*

6:11 *Clap . . . stamp.* Gestures calling for attention and expressing aroused emotions. (25:6)

6:14 *Riblah.* (Cf. RSV note.) The Hebrew letters "r" and "d" are very similar. Riblah was a well-known site in northern Palestine (2 K 25:6, 20). Disaster will overtake the entire land *from the wilderness* in the south to its northernmost border. Cf. the more conventional expression "from Dan to Beersheba." (Ju 20:1 second note)

7:1-13 When "the word of the Lord came to" Ezekiel anew (6:1), directing him to speak in the name of *the Lord God to the land of Israel,* the message given him to transmit warned his hearers not to think of the threatened judgment as only a vague or distant possibility without serious consequences. The curtain of time drawn from his eyes, the prophet sees the disaster as an accomplished fact. He stands, as it were, in the ruins of the nation and laments its fall in short, convulsive sentences resembling the repeated, uncontrollable sobs of one mourning the death of a loved one. The dirge is punctuated with the refrain: *The end has come. The day* of wrath will not bring a glancing blow or a temporary setback. *Behold, it comes* with all the finality of the word *end.* And it will not fail to come because their *ways* and *abominations* will not go unpunished by *the Lord, who* [is determined to] *smite* in holy anger. (Cf. the lamentations in ch. 19 and Am 5:1 ff.)

7:6 *Awakened.* The words for *end* and *awaken* are similar in Hebrew. See Am 8:2 for another such play on words.

7:7 *Doom.* The Hebrew word is used in the ordinary sense of "diadem" or crowning wreath. Here and in v. 10 it has the transferred meaning of a circle which revolves like a wheel of fortune and stops to indicate whose turn it is to win or lose.

7:10 *The day.* The disasters awaiting Israel are tinged at times with the colors and configurations of the final day of judgment which will bring "the end of all things." (1 Ptr 4:7, 17)

7:11 *Violence.* God counts Israel's crimes against members of the covenant people as "abominations" and as punishable as idolatry.

7:12 *The buyer . . . the seller.* Because all business transaction will cease, people will no longer rejoice over getting a bargain or regret selling at a loss. The next verse adds that there will be no year of "jubilee," when all property was to revert to the original owner according to Lv 25:10 ff.

7:14-27 In the remaining verses of the ch., Ezekiel resumes and elaborates the warning that what *the day* brings is the *end* in the full sense of negation and cessation: no strength or courage to defend the city; no escape from *the sword,* the *famine and pestilence;* no joy; no business as usual; no help from religious and civic leaders.

7:19 *Stumbling block.* Love of silver and gold tempted them to fall into sin. (Cf. 3:20 note)

7:22 *My precious place.* The temple was the Lord's treasured place because He chose to dwell there.

7:23 *Make a desolation.* The verb in the Hebrew text is in the imperative mood and reads: "Make the chain" (RSV note). The brief interjected command is a dramatic way of saying that fetters and captivity await the perpetrators of *bloody crimes* and *violence.*

8:1—11:25 JUDGMENT REVEALED IN A VISION

Ezekiel brought God's message to the apostate people, dramatizing it by symbolic action (chs. 4—5) and proclaiming it by word of mouth (chs. 6—7). Yet the "watchman for the house of Israel" (3:17) was to sound the alarm by still another means of revelation and communication. Fourteen months after he was commissioned to the prophetic office "the hand of the Lord God fell" on him again (cf. 1:3 note) as he sat in his "house with the elders of Judah." "In visions of God" he once more beheld "the glory of the God of Israel" enthroned over the cherubim and the celestial chariot. When it apeared to him "in the plain" (8:3 f.; 1:28; 3:22 f.), it was to let him see his task in divine perspective. Now it came for the benefit of his hearers. And so, mindful of his duty to "say to them, 'Thus says the Lord'" (2:4), he "told the exiles all the things that the Lord . . . showed" him. (11:25)

What he had to say to them derived meaning and validity from the vision. He therefore described its features as he did at its first appearance. The piercing light of the glory of the Lord penetrated into the dark recesses of His people's hearts and laid bare their blatant idolatry as "abominations" of the most heinous and revolting nature (ch. 8). The divine enthronement over animate and inanimate forces revealed not only the folly of worshiping creatures rather than the Creator but also declared His ability to execute judgment on the rebellious and to deliver the faithful (ch. 9). Manifesting this sovereign power, He ordered the burning of Jerusalem (10:1-7). The description of the mobility of the heavenly conveyance on which the four living creatures transported the Lord served to demonstrate His freedom from spatial limitations. (10:9-22)

However, while already standing "over the cherubim" and poised for flight (10:18), the Lord once more presented evidence that the threatened disaster was not an arbitrary burst of wrath. Ezekiel heard an assembly of the "princes of the people" blatantly declare their immunity from divine justice (11:1-12). The folly of their defiance became evident when Ezekiel while he "was prophesying" saw one of the leaders die (11:13). Horrified at the thought that what he saw and heard meant a "full end" of Israel's national identity, Ezekiel was assured by "the word of the Lord" that the exile was not to be the grave of the chosen people. They would indeed be "scattered . . . among the countries" after the destruction of Jerusalem. But a chastened remnant would survive. They would let the Lord "put a new spirit within them" so that they could again become a blessing to all nations. Bringing them back out of captivity, He would again "give" them "the land of Israel" as He once did when He delivered their ancestors from the Egyptian house of bondage. However, first the day of judgment had to come to cleanse them of their "detestable things" and their "abominations" (11:14-21). The doom of Jerusalem was sealed when Ezekiel saw "the glory of the Lord" leave the city. (11:22-25)

8:1 *The hand of the Lord.* For the meaning of this phrase see 1:3 note.

8:2 *The appearance of a man.* For Ezekiel's studied avoidance of representing God in human form see 1:26 note.

8:3 *Lifted me up.* The Spirit enabled Ezekiel not only to transcend the barriers of future time but also granted him ecstatic television-sight into distant scenes. He felt himself transported between heaven and earth and brought *in visions of God* to far-off Jerusalem. In describing a similar experience, Paul says he did not know whether he was "in the body of out of the body" (2 Co 12:2 f.; cf. also Rv 1:10-16; 4:1 f.). Bodily translocation took place in the ministry of Elijah (1 K 18:12; 2 K 2:16 ff.). What Ezekiel saw in the trancelike projection through space was a series of scenes portraying Israel's fearful wickedness and a symbolic enactment of impending judgment.

The image of jealousy. The first envisioned proof of Israel's repudiation of the Lord was an idol figure. Its devotees ascribed to it the granting of fertility and therefore worshiped it by engaging in lascivious rites exciting lust. Shamelessly defying the command not to "act corruptly by making a graven . . . figure" (Dt 4:16), the apostate people assigned the abomination a *seat* or location at *the gateway of the inner court* of the temple. For the same brazen desecration of the house of the Lord see 2 K 21:7; 2 Ch 33:7. However, as the image aroused the lower passions of its worshipers, it also provoked the Lord to jealousy. (Ex 20:5 note; 34:14; Dt 4:24)

8:10 *Creeping things and loathsome beasts.* Not content to defy the Lord with idolatrous practices which flourished in Canaan, "the elders of the house of Israel" (12) imported cults from other lands. The veneration of animals, including crocodiles, snakes, and bugs, was characteristic of Egyptian worship. In Jerusalem this idolatrous folly was perpetrated "in the dark." Only the initiated had access to the secret chambers of horrors. It took some effort for Ezekiel to find the "door" leading to the place where the "vile abominations" were practiced. (8 f.)

8:11 *Seventy men.* The number seems to

indicate unanimous participation by the elders. Moses was given 70 men to assist him (Nm 11:16 ff.; cf. also Ex 24:1, 9). The Sanhedrin at the time of Jesus also consisted of 70 men. *Jaazaniah* is otherwise unknown unless his father *Shaphan* was Josiah's faithful officer. (2 K 22:3)

8:12 *Room of pictures.* It appears that these elders had a similar chamber on a smaller scale in their homes. They justified their actions by asserting that the Lord had broken the covenant and had *forsaken the land.* (Cf. Zph 1:12)

8:14 *Tammuz.* Worship of this god of vegetation, mentioned by name only here in the OT, was widespread from Assyria-Babylonia to the eastern Mediterranean. Women *sat . . . weeping* in ritualistic mourning over his death, which caused all plant life to die in the fall of the year. For an allusion to this cult see Is 17:10 note.

8:16 *Worshiping the sun.* The fourth abomination visualizing Israel's guilt was also the most abhorrent; (a) it took place *at the door of the temple,* where fervent prayers should have been directed to the Lord (Jb 2:17); (b) it was committed by *about twenty-five men* who as priests had access to these sacred precincts; (c) turning *their backs to the temple of the Lord,* they demonstrated total rejection of the God of Israel; (d) worshiping the sun (perhaps the Babylonian god Marduk), they defied Him whose word "Let there be" made the heavenly bodies shine in the skies (Gn 1:14). For an instance of solar worship in Israel's past see 2 K 23:11 note.

8:17 *Branch to their nose.* The meaning of this cultic gesture is uncertain. Suggesting that it was an obscene act, some scholars believe the words should be translated: "They send forth stench into My [the Lord's] nose."

9:1-11 *Executioners.* The scene from the visionary drama presented in this ch. was to make clear that while God does *not spare* any evildoers, His wrath does not rage indiscriminately. Because Israel's guilt was *exceedingly great* (9), as demonstrated beyond all doubt in ch. 8, Ezekiel heard an order for a citywide massacre issue from *the glory of the God of Israel.* But before it was carried out by *six men,* each *with his weapon for slaughter in his hand,* a seventh angelic figure was summoned to *put a mark upon the foreheads* of those not guilty of *the abominations that are committed.* Those so identified were not to be slain with the offenders. When the Lord smote the firstborn of Egypt, the Israelites whose houses were marked with blood were safe from "the destroyer" (Ex 12:23). In the final judgment those bearing the sign of the Lamb will escape eternal death. (Rv 22:4; cf. Rv 20:4; 3:1-6)

9:6 *Slay . . . outright.* When *old men . . . young men and maidens, little children and women* perish in wars and catastrophes of nature, no apparent distinction is made between the wicked and the righteous. Yet God "knows those who are His" and preserves them to eternal life. (Nm 31:2 note; 2 Ti 2:19 note)

10:2 *Burning coals.* The slaying of Jerusalem's inhabitants (ch. 9) was not to be the end of divine retribution. It would be followed by the burning of the city. Ezekiel saw it in a symbolic act performed by *the man clothed in linen* (cf. 9:2). Filling his hand with fiery *coals* received *from between the cherubim,* he went out to *scatter them over the city.* The result would be as disastrous as when "the Lord rained on Sodom and Gomorrah brimstone and fire." (Gn 19:24)

10:4 *Went up.* The Hebrew verb can be translated "had gone up." Ezekiel wanted it noted that the command to destroy the city came from the same place from which the inhabitants were ordered slain: *the threshold of the house,* the deserted temple (cf. 9:3). The throne (10:1) still was unoccupied by *the glory of the Lord,* which "went forth from the threshold" only after the command to burn the city was issued. (18)

10:12 *Rims . . . spokes.* Cf. the RSV notes. As in ch. 1, Ezekiel found it difficult to describe the bewildering vision without mentioning some of its features a second time. (Cf. 1:4-28 note)

10:13 *Whirling wheels.* One word in Hebrew, it occurs also in vv. 2 and 6 but not in ch. 1. It is used here to call special attention to a feature of the wheels which was soon to be exhibited. They were able to rotate instantly in all directions when the glory of the Lord was ready to leave the city. (11:22 f.)

10:14 *The cherub.* In this ch. Ezekiel not only identifies the celestial attendants collectively as "cherubim" (20) but also calls the individual living creature "the cherub" (v. 7, where the Hebrew text has the definite article as here in 14). However, it is not clear why one of the four faces is here said to be that of *the cherub* rather than that of "an ox" as in 1:10. Note too that the faces are not mentioned in the same order as in ch. 1.

10:18 *From the threshold.* From there the command had come to slay the inhabitants (9:3 ff.) and to burn the city. (10:4 ff.)

11:1-12 Still in a vision, Ezekiel saw and heard *twenty-five men,* representing the *princes of the people,* furnish additional proof of an obdurate refusal to let the threats of divine judgment move them and the people to repent of the abominations exposed in ch. 8. In spite of repeated warnings, they insist that the walls of Jerusalem are like a *caldron* in which *flesh* or meat is safely stored. So they urge that business-as-usual be the order of the day. Ezekiel is ordered by *the Spirit* to set matters straight. Jerusalem, he declares, is not inviolate because the Lord chose it as His habitation. The city is indeed a caldron filled with *the slain,* victims of the wicked policies and crimes of the leaders. But it does not offer protection from the Lord. For He will bring them *forth out of the midst of it. . . . and execute judgments upon* them by *the hands of foreigners.*

11:1 *Jaazaniah . . . Pelatiah.* Both otherwise unknown. The former is not the same person mentioned in 8:11.

11:13-21 The death of the leaders and the threat that all of them would "fall by the sword"

(10) frightened Ezekiel to ask *with a loud voice* whether the Lord was about to *make a full end of the remnant of Israel,* leaving none to implement the promise made to Abraham and his descendants (Gn 12:3). In answer *the word of the Lord* did not rescind the sentence of judgment on those whom Ezekiel saw going *after their detestable things and their abominations* (21). They would perish even though they pointed presumptuously to Ezekiel and his fellow prisoners as deserving their lot whereas they would remain in permanent possession of *this land.* However, *says the Lord God,* among those who were *removed . . . far off among the nations* a chastened, purified remnant would survive. Brought back to *the land of Israel,* they would continue to be the covenant people through whom the plan of universal salvation would move toward its goal. For similar assurances of restoration uttered by Ezekiel even while predicting the doom of the wicked city see 5:3; 6:8 f.; 12:16; 16:60. (Cf. also Jer 23:3; 24:7; 29:14)

11:16 *A sanctuary.* "God, who made the world," is not dependent on "shrines made by man" (Acts 17:24). During the time the exiles were *scattered . . . among the countries* they could be certain of His presence and worship Him even though the temple was destroyed.

11:19 *Stony heart . . . heart of flesh.* A heart transplant by the operation of God's Spirit would motivate the exiles to respond to His saving grace by walking in His "statutes" and keeping His "ordinances." (18:31; 36:26; 1 Sm 10:8; Jer 32:39)

11:20 *My people . . . their God.* These words were spoken when God first made His covenant with the former slaves of Egypt. (Ex 6:7; cf. Ex 19:5 f.; 29:45; Jer 7:23; Eze 14:11)

11:22-25 In the final and most ominous scene of the vision Ezekiel saw the inevitable doom of Jerusalem as *the glory of the Lord* left it and thereby consigned it to the forces of destruction.

11:23 *The mountain . . . east . . . of the city.* The Mount of Olives, where Jesus wept over the impending destruction of the Jerusalem of His day. (Lk 19:37, 41)

12:1—14:23 INEVITABLE DOOM PORTRAYED BY SYMBOLIC ACTS; FALSE HOPES OF SECURITY SHATTERED

12:1-16 The symbolic acts (chs. 4—7) and the report of the envisioned destruction (chs. 8—11) did not penetrate Israel's "hard forehead" and "stubborn heart" (3:7). The *rebellious house* (vv. 1-3) clung to the fatal illusion that, because they were the chosen people and their king was a descendant of David, the Lord was obligated to protect them regardless of their attitudes and actions. In order to shatter this unholy pride *the word of the Lord* instructed His prophet to give two more visual demonstrations of divine judgment, to be executed as threatened. In the first symbolic action Ezekiel impersonated the disillusioned people, with their *prince* at their head, leaving all behind except *an exile's baggage* and setting out into the night of homelessness. Covering his face so as not to see, he dramatized the blinding of the king's eyes by his captors and the latter's removal to Babylon, where he would die without having seen the land of his captivity.

12:3 *Perhaps.* As instructed when he began to preach (3:4 ff.), Ezekiel was not to cease proclaiming the Word of God even when his task seemed a waste of effort. (Cf. Jer 26:3; 36:6 f., 2 Ti 2:25)

12:5 *Dig through the wall.* Houses in Babylonia were built of dried clay.

12:12 *The prince.* As foretold by Ezekiel in pantomime, King Zedekiah was intercepted on his flight from Jerusalem by the Babylonians who "put out" his "eyes . . . and took him to Babylon." (2 K 25:1-7; Jer 39:4-7; 52:4-11)

12:17-20 The second symbolic act added a feature already depicted in ch. 4 to the predicted plight of Jerusalem's inhabitants. Not only would they have to subsist on meager rations, but while eating *their bread* and drinking their *water* in short supply, *fearfulness* and *dismay* would seize them at the prospect of worse things to come.

12:21-28 In answer to Ezekiel's dramatized warnings (1-20), his hearers quoted flippant sayings to the contrary. Prophets like Ezekiel, they said, had cried "Wolf! Wolf!" for a long time but nothing had happened and nothing would (21-25). At best *the vision* of a coming disaster could come true only in *times far off* and leave them unscathed. (26-28)

12:22 *This proverb.* In 18:25 ff. Ezekiel took issue with another popular saying.

12:24 *False vision or flattering divination.* The skepticism and smug complacency exhibited by the people grew out of listening to lying prophets and fake soothsayers. When "the word of the Lord" spoken by Ezekiel "will be performed" (26, 28), their predictions of continued well-being will be exposed as empty delusion. For other instances of ridiculing unbelief when God delayed judgment for a time see Is 5:19; Zph 1:12; Ml 2:17; Mt 24:48-51; 2 Ptr 3:3-13.

13:1-16 The people had a false sense of security (12:21-28) because they let themselves be misled by *prophets who see delusive visions and who give lying divinations* (9), proclaiming *"Peace," when there is no peace* (10, 16). Ezekiel lashes out against these imposters who pretend to speak the Word of the Lord whereas in reality they *follow their own spirit and have seen nothing* (3). Instead of providing the nation with a protective *wall* of truth, they *daub with whitewash* an illusion of safety behind which their hearers hide. *A deluge of rain* and *great hailstones* pouring forth from the wrath of God will demolish this painted fabrication of lies (10-16). For denunciations of false prophets by Jeremiah, Ezekiel's contemporary, see Jer 23 and 29.

13:3 *Foolish prophets.* The folly of which they are guilty is more than an error in thinking. It originates in a perverted mind which promotes "shameful things," as the Hebrew noun for folly is also translated. (Jos 7:15 note)

13:4 *Like foxes.* As these furtive animals frequent uninhabited places, so the false prophets will end up standing *among* the *ruins* of the false hopes they raised.

13:5 *Into the breaches.* They did nothing to fortify Israel against destruction by replacing the gaping holes of apostasy with protective stones of repentance.

13:6 *Divined a lie.* The people should have refused to be misled by liars and charlatans. Self-styled prophets who saw the abominations flourishing openly in Jerusalem and tolerated them by crying "Peace" proved thereby that *the Lord* had *not sent them.* For this simple test of a false prophet see Dt 13:1-5; cf. also Mt 24:4 f.; 2 Ptr 2:1-3; 1 Jn 4:1 ff.

13:17-23 The false prophets not only condoned every form of idolatry but also did nothing to stamp out witchcraft and sorcery, explicitly forbidden in the law of Moses (Lv 19:26; Dt 18:10; cf. 1 Sm 28:9). Occult forms of magic were openly performed by *women* who likewise claimed the gift of prophecy. Adding insult to injury, they invoked the name of the Lord over their incantations and thus *profaned* (19) Him among the people.

13:18 *Magic bands . . . veils.* The exact nature of these paraphernalia as well as the significance attached to their use can no longer be established with certainty. Apparently they cast a voodoolike spell on the designated victim which was to produce injury or death.

13:19 *Handfuls of barley.* They plied their nefarious trade for a mere pittance.

13:22 *The righteous . . . the wicked.* As long as they were paid their fee, the sorcerers disregarded principles of morality and justice.

14:1-11 *The word of the Lord,* here spoken by Ezekiel, is the message the false prophets and prophetesses (ch. 13) should have proclaimed instead of confirming their hearers in their sins. The occasion for his renewed call to *repent and turn away from . . . idols* (6) was a visit which *certain . . . elders* paid him (cf. 8:1; 20:1; 33:30 f.). They *sat before* him hoping he would *inquire* (8) of the Lord. Apparently they expected to be told they would soon return to their homeland. However, while they drew near to the Lord "with their lips," they retained their idols in "their hearts" (Is 29:13). He who tries "the minds and hearts" (Ps 7:9) has but one answer for those guilty of such insolent hypocrisy: He will *destroy* them *from the midst of* the *people* (9). This verdict will be executed even if a prophet who purports to speak in the name of the Lord tells dissembling clients what they want to hear. Because he deceives himself and his inquirers, both will *bear their punishment.* (10)

14:4 *The stumbling block.* Their choice to serve other gods rather than to give undivided allegiance to the Lord brought about their downfall. (Cf. 3:20 note; 7:19 note)

14:7 *Strangers.* Cf. Ex 12:48; 20:10.

14:9 *I . . . have deceived.* God punishes the deliberate and persistent rejection of His Word by letting the hardened sinner be deceived by delusion and destroy himself. (Cf. Jer 4:10 note; Ro 1:24, 26, 28)

14:12-23 Not only can hypocritical lip service and deceptive prophecy not ward off the wrath of God (1-11), the abominations in Israel have reached such a stage as to overrule specious objections to the justice of total destruction. National doom is inevitable. It will do no good to protest the presence of righteous persons in the city. Even if saints like *Noah, Daniel, and Job* were there, *they would deliver but their own lives by their righteousness* when the Lord brings on the land His *four sore acts of judgment, sword, famine, evil beasts, and pestilence, to cut off from it man and beast* (21). Those who survive these agents of death will join Ezekiel's associates in exile and share their disgrace and hardships. Their arrival will prove beyond doubt that God did not act *without cause* (23) when He destroyed Jerusalem.

14:13 *Staff of bread.* Cf. 4:13.

14:14 *Noah.* "A righteous man, blameless in his generation" (Gn 6:9), he survived the flood with his family. However, when God rains fire and brimstone on Jerusalem, "neither sons nor daughters" (16) will be spared on account of the *righteousness* of their fathers.

Daniel. Taken to Babylon 13 years before Ezekiel arrived in Telabib, the prophet Daniel achieved national fame at the royal court when he risked his life in a test of loyalty to the Lord (Dn 1:1 ff.; 6:1 ff.). In Canaanite mythology a king by the same name was hailed as a righteous judge. However, it would seem strange if Ezekiel, a fierce contender for undivided loyalty to the God of Israel, should hold up a heathen king as an example of righteousness.

Job. "Blameless and upright" (Jb 1:1, 8; 2:3), he emerged from severe trials without losing hold on God.

14:16 *These three men.* Jeremiah declared God's decision to destroy Jerusalem irrevocable even if Moses and Samuel were present to intercede for the doomed city. (Jer 15:1 note)

14:21 *Much more.* Each of the *four sore acts of judgment* would have devastating results, as the foregoing verses insist like a refrain. Combined, they produce total disaster. (5:15 note)

14:22 *Be consoled.* The survivors of Jerusalem's capture by the Babylonians would help those already in captivity to understand that no hostile forces could have been victorious if the Lord had not permitted them to punish the apostate people for *their ways and their doings.* The escaped remnant also would be living proof of God's mercy in giving them another chance to repent.

15:1—17:24 JUDGMENT AND MERCY PROCLAIMED BY MEANS OF PARABLE AND ALLEGORY

15:1-8 Using the teaching device of a parable, Ezekiel reinforced his sermon about Israel's guilt in "acting faithlessly" and God's justice in punishing it (14:13; 15:8). The chosen people, he said, were like a *vine* planted for one purpose:

"to yield grapes" (Is 5:1 ff.; cf. also Dt 32:32; Ps 80:8-13; Jer 2:21; Hos 10:1). Because God looked in vain for the fruits of repentance and righteousness, they have become as worthless to Him as *the wood* of a *vine branch* which, even when it is not *charred,* cannot be *used for anything* and therefore is *given to the fire for fuel.*

15:3 *Both ends . . . the middle.* The worthless vine is reminded of what has already happened. It was *charred* at both extremities when the Assyrians ravaged the Northern Kingdom and the Babylonians swept through the territory of Judah in the south. Jerusalem, the center of the nation, was scarred when Nebuchadnezzar carried off its king and many of its people. Useless even "when it was whole" (5), "the wood of the vine" is about to be consigned to the "fire" which "shall yet consume" it completely.

16:1-43a. The parable of the worthless vine (ch. 15) exposed Israel's failure to fulfill the purpose for which God chose the descendants of Abraham. What the highly favored nation did instead of bearing "the fruit of the Spirit" (Gl 5:22 f.) is now spelled out in an allegory which, in lurid detail, brands the apostate nation a lewd, adulterous wife. It is not a pretty picture that emerges as Ezekiel obeys the command to *make known to Jerusalem her abominations* (2). Her infidelity was not a reaction to mistreatment by her husband. She owed her life to him from the very moment of her birth (1-7). After their marriage he supplied her not only with the necessities of life but also with the costliest fineries and brought her to *regal estate.* (8-14)

She did not stray from rectitude in a weak moment of temptation, but deliberately abused her husband's goodness and wantonly *played the harlot* with sordid abandon (15-22). She did not have but one secret lover, but *prostituted* herself *to any passer-by* and *at the head of every street* (23-29). She was even *different* from ordinary harlots. For while they charged their clients, she bribed her lovers with gifts *to come to* her *from every side.* (30-34)

Her punishment will fit her crime. Her *lovers,* also those whom she came to loathe, will turn against her and expose her, stripped and naked, to the public disgrace accorded slaves. Finally she will be sentenced to death as prescribed in the law for *women who break wedlock and shed blood.* (35-43a; Lv 20:10-12; Dt 13:10)

The prophet does not hide the ugliness of these *abominations* (2, 22) by using prudish euphemisms in condemning them. His frank, unabashed language will offend only those who fail to realize what a dirty thing their sin is in God's sight. Throughout the ch. Israel is pictured as *a brazen harlot* (30). Yet at times allegory gives way to nonsymbolical language and factual description of events and situations.

16:3 *Origin and . . . birth.* Jerusalem's and Canaan's earlier occupants are personified as constituting Israel's ancestry. The point of comparison is first of all geographic and historical. Palestine was originally *the land of the Canaanites,* who were in part of *Amorite* and in part of Hittite extraction (Gn 10:15 note; 15:19 note). However, Jerusalem's *birth* of pagan parentage did not account only for her geographic location. By her apostasy she also became a spiritual descendant of her idolatrous forebears. (Cf. vv. 44 f.)

16:5 *Cast out.* In the ancient world unwanted children—especially daughters—were exposed to die. Because they were not to live, such hapless infants were not given the customary hygienic care.

16:8 *Spread my skirt.* Cf. Ru 3:4 note; 3:9 note. *Plighted my troth.* At Mt. Sinai God formally established a relationship with the fledgling nation which was to be as exclusive, intimate, and inviolate as the estate of holy matrimony (Ex 24:7 f.). When Israel chose to have other gods before Him, she broke the marriage *covenant* and became guilty of "harlotries." (15; cf. also Hos 2:2 f.; Is 1:21; Jer 2:20; 3:1-3; for the relationship between Christ and His church see Eph 5:25-33; Mt 22:2-14; 25:1-13; Jn 3:29)

16:13 *Regal estate.* Israel's golden age during the reigns of David and Solomon.

16:17 *Images of men.* The resources God gave His people were used to make idols.

16:21 *Slaughtered my children.* For the despicable practice of child sacrifice see 2 K 23:10 note; Jer 2:23 notes.

16:25 *Lofty place.* Apparently a kind of dais raised at street intersections, on which she offered herself promiscuously *to any passer-by.* In verses 24 and 31 her brothel is called a "vaulted chamber."

16:26 *With the Egyptians.* Israel committed adultery not only in the gross form of idolatry (15-22) but also by calling on foreign "lovers" rather than obeying and trusting the Lord (Hos 2:5; 8:9; Is 57:7 ff.; Jer 2:18 f.). For negotiations with the Egyptians see Is 30:1-3; 31:1; with "the Assyrians" (28) see 2 K 16:7 ff.; with "Chaldea" see 2 K 20:12 f.

16:27 *The Philistines.* Not completely dislodged from the coastal plain of Palestine, these ancient enemies were always ready to take advantage of a situation when God through a foreign invader *diminished* the land *allotted* to the 12 tribes.

16:40 *Bring . . . a host.* According to Mosaic law, those guilty of spiritual or physical adultery were to be haled before the assembly of the people and put to death (Lv 20:10 f.; Dt 13:10; 22:22 ff.; Jn 8:5). Jerusalem will stop "playing the harlot" (41) when the inhabitants are cut to pieces and the houses burned by the enemy.

16:43a *Not remembered.* It is with deep regret that God must take note of Israel's shameful infidelity in spite of all the blessings He showered on her since the days of her *youth.* Moved to "jealousy" and "fury" (42) by her wanton ingratitude, He will indeed let His wrath burn like a consuming fire. Yet He "will no more be angry" when the inflicted chastisement has moved her to repentance.

16:43b-58. The fate of two sister cities is cited to let the enormity of Jerusalem's sin appear in its true light. For divine justice assesses guilt and imposes retribution in proportion to the goodness and mercy shown to the transgressor and spurned by him. *Samaria,* capital of the Northern Kingdom destroyed more than a century earlier, and *Sodom,* the notoriously wicked city annihilated by fire and brimstone, fully merited the recompense meted out to them. Jerusalem, granted a greater measure of grace for a longer period of time, *acted more abominably than they* and so made the *sisters appear righteous* in comparison. Because *more corrupt than they,* Jerusalem is certain to be declared worthy of dire punishment.

16:44 *Like mother, like daughter.* Israel not only acquired the land of the Canaanites from its previous Amorite and Hittite occupants (3) but also absorbed their heathen religion and immorality, much as a daughter derives characteristics from her mother.

16:46 *Elder sister.* The Northern Kingdom, of which Samaria was the capital, was larger in territory and population than Judah. The smaller settlements around a city are called its *daughters.*

16:47 *More corrupt.* Cf. 5:7 note.

16:50 *Haughty . . . abominable.* Steeped in unnatural vices, the Sodomites were "great sinners against the Lord" (Gn 13:13). In the wake of sexual perversion came oppression of "the poor and needy." (49)

I saw it. Cf. Gn 18:21 note.

16:54 *A consolation.* Restored to communion with God, self-righteous, hypocritical Jerusalem will *be ashamed* as she realizes that she was in need of the same forgiving mercy extended to sinners as wicked as "Sodom" and as guilty as "Samaria." Conversely these despised sisters have the comforting assurance that they are not beyond redemption if God restored Jerusalem to her "former estate" of covenant grace though in His sight she "committed more abominations than they." (51)

16:57 *Edom.* Some manuscripts read "Aram," i.e., Syria (KJV). Pagan neighbors gloated over the *reproach* Jerusalem suffered at the hands of victorious invaders.

16:59-63 The two sister cities, Samaria and Sodom, are introduced into the drama not only to let Jerusalem's sin appear in its heinous nature but also to add luster to God's abundant mercy and grace. When the call to repentance is heeded, He stands ready to "restore . . . the fortunes" (53) of all members of sinful mankind in a renewed fellowship with Him whether they be in wicked Sodom, in rebellious Samaria, or in perverse Jerusalem (Is 1:18; Ro 5:20). Through the chastened and penitent people of Israel He will carry forward His plan of worldwide salvation as set forth in the covenant He made with them in their *youth.* Though they broke it, He will bind Himself to His promises in *an everlasting covenant.* According to its terms, not only Israel but all her sisters (and brothers) in sin can become sisters (and brothers) in a spiritual community of saints. (37:26; Jer 31:31-34; Jn 4:22 f.; Eph 1:3-13; 2:11-22; Heb 8:6-13)

16:61 *Not on account.* As God's *covenant* with Israel in her youth was not based on her merit but solely on grace, so His everlasting covenant provides fellowship with Him only because He agrees to "forgive . . . all that" was done to deserve death rather than life. (63; cf. Dt 4:37; 7:6-8; 10:15)

17:1-21 The parable of Jerusalem the adulterous wife (ch. 16) is followed by an allegory denouncing the royal house of Judah (1-10). Lest his hearers fail or refuse to understand its meaning, Ezekiel translates the figurative language into a factual account of past and future events (11-21). The *great eagle* is the king of Babylon. The *topmost* twig of the cedars of Lebanon, broken off by the eagle, is King Jehoiachin, whom Nebuchadnezzar removed and took *to a land of trade,* i.e., Babylonia. *The seed of the land,* planted by a foreign overlord in the *fertile soil* of the deposed king, is Zedekiah. This *twig* or offspring of the Davidic house was granted a measure of independence and growth in his native soil. However, Zedekiah broke the oath of allegiance to Nebuchadnezzar, sworn in the Lord's name, and turned for help to *another great eagle,* the Pharaoh of Egypt. Such treachery and abuse of God's name would not go unpunished. When besieged by the Babylonian army, the rebel king of Jerusalem would look in vain for relief and rescue by an army from the Nile. Nebuchadnezzar would take him captive and carry him off to Babylon after defeating *the pick of his troops* and scattering *the survivors . . . to every wind.*

17:2 *A riddle.* The Hebrew term so translated is also rendered "dark speech" and "dark saying" (Nm 12:8; Ps 78:2). This *allegory* is in the nature of a riddle because the correspondence between metaphor and reality is not as obvious as in the parable of the adulterous wife. For another example of the kind of literary device in which trees represent human beings see Ju 9:8 note.

17:6 *Branches turned toward him.* As long as Zedekiah maintained a pro-Babylonian policy, as he promised "under oath" (13), he prospered though he remained *a low spreading vine* and never attained the height of a "cedar." (3)

17:15 *Ambassadors to Egypt.* For Zedekiah "to go down to Egypt . . . to take refuge in the protection of Pharaoh" was doubly reprehensible (Is 30:1-3). He not only put his trust in a foreign alliance rather than in the Lord, but he also became guilty of "treason" (20) because he broke the sworn covenant he had made with Nebuchadnezzar.

17:19 *My covenant.* Breaking the treaty with Babylon was also a repudiation of the Lord because it was sealed by an oath in His name.

17:20 *Judgment with him there.* Zedekiah was sentenced to lifelong imprisonment in Babylon. For the punishment inflicted on him before he arrived there see Jer 52:9-11.

17:22-24 All appearances to the contrary, God's plan of universal redemption was not to fail when Jerusalem fell and its last king died in exile. In terms of the same allegory which he used to predict inevitable judgment (1-21), Ezekiel goes on to prophesy that God, not Nebuchadnezzar, *will take a sprig from . . . the cedar* of Judah's royal stock and *plant it . . . on the mountain height of Israel* (cf. Is 2:2 second note). This *tender* twig will never be uprooted. Grown *noble* as a *cedar,* it will *bear fruit* and its boughs will offer refuge and shade to birds and beasts *of every sort.* This figurative promise became a reality when God gave to Jesus of Nazareth "the throne of his father David" and established His universal, eternal Messianic kingdom (Lk 1:32; Rv 11:15). For similar prophecies see Is 11:1; Jer 23:5; 33:14 f.; Eze 34:23 ff.; 37:24 ff.; Mi 4:1 ff.

17:24 *Bring low . . . make high.* Cf. Lk 1:51 ff.

18:1-32 JUDGMENT AND MERCY UPHELD CONTRARY TO A POPULAR PROVERB

18:1-21. The validity of Ezekiel's allegories, driving home the demand that Israel repent if it was to escape inevitable doom (chs. 15—17), was challenged by a parabolic saying propounded in the form of a cynical proverb. His hearers quoted it to challenge God's justice although Jeremiah had already refuted its blasphemous charges (Jer 31:29 note; Lm 5:7 note). Ezekiel goes to greater length in unmasking the hypocritical self-righteousness hiding behind this proverb. He states categorically that in God's dealings with *all souls* He does no one an injustice. Each individual is accountable to Him only for the kind of response to His covenanted goodness which he or she expresses in obedience to His will. He punishes no one for another's sin; nor can anyone claim the reward of grace earned by someone else. He never fails to "requite a man according to his work" (Ps 62:12; Jer 17:10). *If a man is righteous,* it is always true that *he shall . . . live* (5-9); his wicked son *shall not live* because he had a righteous father (10-13); nor will a wicked father live because his son is righteous. (14-20)

18:4 *All souls are mine.* This sentence should have ended the dispute about God's justice. For in reality the sovereign Creator owes no accounting to the "dust from the ground" into which He "breathed . . . the breath of life" (Gn 2:7 note; Jb 42:3, 6; Is 10:15 note; 45:9; Ro 9:20 f.). Yet He condescends to justify the way He determines the ultimate issues of life and death for His fallen creatures.

Shall die. More than the end of earthly existence is involved in this decree. For all sons and daughters of Adam are sinners and, without exception, must die because "the wages of sin is death"(Ro 6:23). Yet some mortals "shall not die" but "shall surely live" (9, 17; Ro 8:6). This gift of life is theirs because they are not charged with sin but are accounted "righteous," inasmuch as they appeal to the abundant mercy of God to blot out their transgressions and then prove the sincerity of their repentance by doing "what is lawful and right" (5; Ps 51:1). Restored to unbroken fellowship with their Maker, they are assured "pleasures for evermore" at His "right hand." (Ps 16:11 note; 17:15 note; 49:15 note; 73:24 note)

18:5 *Eat upon the mountains.* Ceremonial eating on high places in honor of idols. For the "statutes" and "ordinances" (9) which the righteous is held to observe in dealing with his fellowman see Ex 20:14; Lv 15:24; 18:19 (adultery and impurity); Ex 22:20 ff. (oppression); Dt 24:10 ff. (pledges); Lv 19:13 (robbery); Ex 22:24 (usury); Jb 31:16 ff.; Is 58:7 (charity); Ex 23:1 ff. (justice).

18:21-32 God not only holds the individual responsible regardless of his pious or wicked parentage (5-20), but He also takes into account the changes that occur in a person's own lifetime. When *a wicked man turns away from all his sins,* no matter how grievous they were, *he shall surely live,* no less than the person not guilty of his crimes. On the other hand, when a person, *righteous* to a certain point in life, *does the same abominable things that the wicked man does, he shall die,* his earlier righteousness notwithstanding (21-24). Ezekiel therefore rejects, in principle, the people's charge that *the way of the Lord is not just* whenever He forgives the penitent sinner and punishes the righteous turned criminal. His justice must take its inexorable course unless sinners *repent and turn.* At the same time, all apostates have the assurance that the way to life is always open if only they get *a new heart and a new spirit,* because the Lord has *no pleasure in the death of any one.* (25-32; cf. ch. 33)

18:24 *He shall die.* The finality of this verdict is the answer to apparent injustice in God's providence when (a) He seems to promote "the prosperity of the wicked" whereas the righteous complains that he is stricken and chastened every morning (Ps 73:3 note, 14; 37:35 note; Jer 12:1); (b) no outward distinction is made between the righteous and the wicked in a national disaster such as was to overtake the entire *house of Israel.* (31; 6:11 ff.)

18:25 *Not just.* When God visits "the iniquity of the fathers upon the children to the third and the fourth generation," He does so because the descendants also "hate" Him and therefore does not deviate from the principle of individual responsibility. (Ex 20:5 note; Dt 5:2 note; cf. 2 K 21:10 f.; Mt 23:35)

18:31 *A new heart and a new spirit.* They can *get* the motivating power for an inner transformation and a redirection of life because God stands ready to supply it. (11:19; 36:26)

18:32 *No pleasure.* The repentance Ezekiel preached so untiringly is evidence that God desires that even the most obdurate sinner *turn and live.* When *the death of any one* is averted, He rejoices as did the father of the prodigal son, who said: "This my son was dead and is alive again." (Lk 15:24; cf. also 1 Ti 2:4; 2 Ptr 3:9; 1 Jn 5:11 f.)

19:1-14 JUDGMENT AND MERCY EXPRESSED FIGURATIVELY IN A DIRGE

19:1-14. Ezekiel continues to issue a call to repentance in figurative and parabolic form, as he did in chs. 15—18. In this ch. he composes the kind of poem appropriate for a funeral and therefore called *a lamentation.* In mournful cadences and metaphorical language he mourns the last *princes* or kings of Judah, described as offspring of *a lioness* (1-9) and the *strongest stem* growing on *a vine* (10-14). All of them perish. The two *young lions* attain maturity only to be brought *to the land of Egypt* and to *Babylon* respectively. The *stem* of the vine *was plucked up* and *transplanted in the wilderness,* where *the east wind dried it up.* The two parts of the elegy describe the fate of historical individuals and thus exemplify the truth, stated axiomatically in ch. 18, that God judges "every one according to his ways" and not according to the "wickedness" or "righteousness" of another member of the family.

Two of the kings who are mourned were sons of the same father; the third was a grandson. Though they are not expressly named, their identity emerges from allusions to circumstances in their lives. The first was king Josiah's son Jehoahaz (1-4). How he came to be brought captive to Egypt is told in 2 K 23:31-33 The second was Jehoiachin, the son of Jehoiakim and nephew of Jehoahaz (5-9). How this grandson of Josiah became a prisoner of the king of Babylon is recorded in 2 K 24:8-15. The third and last to hold *a ruler's scepter* in Judah was Zedekiah, another son of Josiah (10-14). When he died in Babylonian exile, the royal house of David became defunct. (Jer 52:1-11)

19:3 *Devoured men.* Said also of the next king (6). During the regime of both rulers many people lost their lives. (22-25)

19:5 *Was baffled.* The Hebrew "had waited" (RSV note) implies that the first lion disappointed the mother in her expectations.

19:7 *Ravaged their strongholds.* If the Hebrew "knew his widows" (RSV note) is to make sense, it means that, because of the king, many wives lost their husbands.

19:8 *Set . . . snares.* The Hebrew can be translated: "Nations gave forth a loud cry against him from provinces all around." (Cf. 2 K 24:2)

19:10 *In a vineyard.* "In your blood," as the KJV translates (RSV note), suggests the organic affinity of the "stem" (11) to the *vine.*

19:14 *Fire . . . from its stem.* The king brought on his and the monarchy's downfall by his treachery. (17:11-21; cf. also 15:1-8)

Has gone out. The lamentation over Zedekiah may have been written by Ezekiel after the fall of Jerusalem. However, a dirge may also be prophetic of a future calamity, as is the case in Am 5:1 ff.

20:1—22:31 THREATS OF JUDGMENT BY FIRE AND SWORD JUSTIFIED IN VIEW OF ISRAEL'S PAST AND PRESENT ABUSE OF GOD'S GOODNESS

20:1-4. A third visit by *the elders of Israel* (cf. 8:1; 14:1) showed that Ezekiel's unrelenting, impassioned preaching continued to be deflected by the "hard forehead" and the "stubborn heart" of the "rebellious house" (2:6; 3:7). It may be wearisome to read more of the same kind of sermons. Yet the repetitiousness in Ezekiel's preaching also testifies to the infinite patience of God. Because He has "no pleasure in the death of any one," He lets His prophet plead over and over again with the most perverse sinners to "turn and live" (18:32). After serving as "a watchman for the house of Israel" from "the fifth year of the exile" to *the seventh year,* he had to tell the inquiring elders that they still have not removed "their idols" from their hearts but insist "to this day" on worshiping "wood and stone" (1:2; 3:16; 14:3; 20:31-32). Instead of granting the kind of favorable answer they sought, Ezekiel is instructed to *judge* them, pronouncing them guilty of the same *abominations* committed by *their fathers.*

20:1 *Came to inquire.* For the information they wanted to hear see 14:1-11 note.

20:5-32 From its very beginning and at every stage in the nation's history, God would have been fully justified if He had poured out His *wrath* and spent His *anger* on the people's scurrilous rebellions against Him. They escaped destruction solely because God did not want His holy name to *be profaned in the sight of the nations* (14, 22). For it would appear that He was unable to keep His sworn promises of universal blessings through the people He chose to be His "own possession" for that purpose (Ex 19:5 f.). The elders are reminded that before their ancestors left Egypt they defiled themselves *with the idols of Egypt* (5-8). Their deliverance from slavery by the mighty hand of God did not change things. For *in the wilderness* they *rejected* His *ordinances* and *their heart went after their idols* (9-17). Though the first generation was doomed to die in the wilderness, *their children* took no warning but set their eyes *on their fathers' idols* (18-26). Still not destroyed, and brought into the land of promise, they *blasphemed* God by worshiping Canaanite idols on *any high hill* and under *any leafy tree* (27-29). Ezekiel's contemporaries had learned nothing from the distant or immediate past. Unbowed, self-righteous, and hypocritical, they presumed to come to God's prophet while thinking in their *mind* to imitate the idol worship of their captors. (30-32)

20:7 *Idols of Egypt.* In the account of the exodus no mention is made of a lapse into idolatry. Yet the patriarch Jacob already had to tell his household to "put away the foreign gods that are among you" (Gn 35:2). And when the 12 tribes entered the Promised Land, Joshua admonished them to "put away the gods which your fathers served beyond the River and in Egypt." (Jos 24:14; cf. also Ps 106:6 f.)

20:9 *For the sake of my name.* Mentioned frequently as the reason for Israel's survival, the honor of God's name is cited also by Isaiah and Jeremiah as motivating Him to restrain His anger. (Is 48:9 note; Jer 14:7; cf. also Ex 32:11 f.; Nm 14:15 f.; Dt 9:27 f.)

20:11 *Shall live.* Cf. Dt 4:40; Jos 1:7 f.; Lk 10:28.

20:12 *Sabbaths.* For the keeping of Sabbath days *as a sign* of covenant faithfulness see Is 56:2 note; Jer 17:21.

20:15 *Not bring them.* Cf. the account in Nm 14:26-32.

20:23 *Scatter them.* For this early threat of the exile see Dt 4:27; 28:64.

20:25 *Statutes . . . not good.* The laws God gave that "man shall live" (11) can also become "a fragrance from death to death" (2 Co 2:14, 16). When executing judgment on willful, hardened sinners, He sends them "a strong delusion" so that they are "deceived" into perverting wholesome ordinances and making them an excuse for committing the most detestable crimes (2 Th 2:11; Eze 14:9 note). A case in point was the statute requiring that the firstborn be ransomed from the Lord (Ex 22:29; Nm 18:15 ff.). It did not require that parents "offer by fire all their first-born" (26), because this inhuman atrocity was expressly forbidden (Lv 18:21; 20:2-5). Yet the Israelites pretended that the law allowed them to follow the example of the Canaanites who sacrificed their infants to Molech. (Jer 7:31; 32:35; 2 K 23:10 note)

20:32 *Be like the nations.* The exiles of Ezekiel's day hoped for favorable treatment from the Babylonians if they adopted their idols.

20:33-44 As in the past, God would also in the future not "make a full end" of the unfaithful people, because the honor of His name was still at stake (17, 39, 44). *With a mighty hand and an outstretched arm* He would *manifest* His *holiness . . . in the sight of the nations* by doing again what He did at the time of the exodus from Egypt. At that time He *entered into judgment with* their *fathers,* subjecting them to long wandering in the desert. So He brought their descendants into the Babylonian exile, which by analogy He calls *the wilderness of the peoples.* During their forced sojourn in a dreary captivity He *will purge out the rebels from among* them, as He once did in Moses' day. Threatened by extinction in Babylonia as their ancestors were in Egypt, the chosen people will again be set free and become the bearers of His promises. He will bring a chastened remnant *into the land of Israel.* In their homeland once again, the redeemed people should respond to God's mercy by bringing all the required *sacred offerings* as tokens of their gratitude and devotion.

20:37 *Under the rod.* As a shepherd wields his staff to exclude strange sheep from his flock, so the Lord will "bring . . . into the bond of the covenant" (RSV note) only those on whom the exile had a purifying effect and who desire to acknowledge Him as their "king." (32; cf. Lv 27:32; Jer 33:13)

20:41 *Manifest my holiness.* Israel's misdeeds and punishment gave the heathen occasion to blaspheme the holy name of God (Ro 2:24). Restored to their status of His covenant people, they will no longer be the object of ridicule.

20:43 *Loathe themselves.* Ashamed of their misdeeds. (6:9; 16:61; 36:31; Hos 5:15)

20:45-49 Lest the glowing promise of restoration (33-44) be taken to mean that the chosen people can mock the Lord with impunity, Ezekiel is immediately directed to *preach* and *prophesy* that *the blazing flame* of divine wrath will devour *the forest land* of southern Palestine called *the Negeb* (cf. 6:11-14 note). Only a few years later God did indeed *kindle a fire* in Judah when He sent Nebuchadnezzar to burn Jerusalem to the ground and devastate the surrounding territory. However, the delegation of elders shrugged off also this fiery threat, calling the prophet an entertaining but unconvincing *maker of allegories.* In the Hebrew Bible vv. 45-49 are the opening section of the next ch., in which Ezekiel continues his efforts to convince his calloused hearers of inevitable judgment to come.

20:47 *Kindle . . . devour.* For other instances of the figurative use of the fire of divine wrath kindled to consume Israel as its fuel see Is 10:17 f.; Jer 21:14; 44:6; Am 2:5.

21:1-17. When Ezekiel's hearers said he spoke in riddles when he warned of "a fire" and a "blazing flame" about to consume "the forest land" of Judah (20:45-49), the "watchman for the house of Israel" (3:16) did not cease sounding the alarm. In this ch. he describes the coming judgment as executed by a sword drawn for a *great slaughter.* Though developed in highly poetic language, this metaphor of destruction was not likely to be misunderstood as an entertaining conundrum. The people in his audience knew what the sword of the Lord did when wielded against their enemies (Ju 7:20; Is 27:1; 31:8; 34:6; 66:16; Jer 47:6; 50:35; Zph 2:12). They could be expected to recall also that the prophets Amos and Jeremiah foretold that God would no longer fight for His apostate people but would let His unsheathed sword work His vengeance on them. (Am 4:10; 7:9; Jer 14:12, 15; 44:27)

Ezekiel furthermore leaves no possibility of misinterpreting who the victims of the sword are to be. They are identified at the very outset as *Jerusalem* and *the land of Israel* (2). The grim reality of the spoken word is brought home as Ezekiel is directed to dramatize it: to *sigh with breaking heart and bitter grief before their eyes* (6). It appears that he also gesticulated menacingly with a brandished sword as he spoke. The abrupt, disjointed character of what he said to accompany his frenzied actions reflects the high pitch of excitement and aroused emotions of the prophetic actor. The RSV seeks to interpret his impassioned utterances by adopting numerous changes of the text.

21:3 *Both righteous and wicked.* In catastrophes of nature and national disasters there is no distinction in the outward fate which overtakes an entire community. (18:24 note)

21:9 *A sword, a sword.* In this "Song of the Sword" the instrument of death is personified. Jeremiah too addressed it as a self-determining entity and invoked it to slaughter the Babylonians. (Jer 47:6 f.; 50:35-38)

21:10 *Make mirth?* The meaning of this unexpected question and its cryptic answer seems to be that, at the mention of the *sharpened* and *polished* sword, Ezekiel's hearers still were tempted to think it was drawn to destroy their enemies. Turning quickly and directly to them, he unmasked their hypocritical pose with a terse but trenchant statement of the facts in the case. God was resorting to punish them with a murderous weapon of metal because they ignored His previous, more gentle chastisements, inflicted by a *rod* which, in comparison with a sword, is far less deadly because it consists of *wood.*

21:12 *Smite . . . upon your thigh.* A gesture to express anguish and despair.

21:13 *Not . . . a testing.* God must deliver to the sword a nation which He chose to be "my people" (12), because chastisements with a *rod* did not bring them to their senses.

21:17 *Clap my hands.* Not to express applause or satisfaction as we do by this gesture. (Cf. 6:11 note)

21:18-27 The sword of the Lord is more than a figure of speech. It has already been "given into the hand of the slayer" (11). Nebuchadnezzar, chosen to serve God as His executioner (cf. Jer 25:9 note), is well under way on a march of conquest. Having moved his army northward around the desert to the west of Babylonia, he has arrived at Riblah in northern Palestine (2 K 23:33 note). Here he stands *at the head* or fork of *two ways.* Ezekiel is directed to diagram the situation on the ground. From a given point he draws two diverging lines. The one represents the road to Jerusalem; the other, the route to *Rabbah of the Ammonites,* capital of Israel's neighboring state east of the Jordan. Relying on omens, secured by three methods of *divination,* the king of Babylonia decides to move his siege equipment against *fortified* Jerusalem. When the people within its walls are *captured* by him, they are to know that he is divinely commissioned to bring *their guilt to remembrance* even though he may act out of selfish motives. For his treasonable breaking of a sworn covenant the *prince of Israel* will be disgraced and dethroned (cf. 17:14-21). Nothing will remain of his kingdom but *ruin, ruin, ruin.*

21:20 *Ammonites.* For the role they played in Israel's history and their ultimate fate see Jer 49:1 note, 2 note, as well as vv. 28-32 of this ch. of Ezekiel and 25:1-7.

21:21 *Divination.* Nebuchadnezzar did not reach a decision until he received favorable omens from three different kinds of augury: (1) *Arrows,* marked to indicate divergent options, were shaken in a quivver. When the king drew out one of them with "his right hand," "the lot for Jerusalem" emerged. (2) *Teraphim,* carved or sculptured images in human form, were consulted (Gn 31:19 note). How they were manipulated to foretell the future is no longer clear. (3) Professional soothsayers were engaged to examine the *liver* of slain animals. The coloring and the lines of the organ were interpreted to indicate whether a contemplated action would succeed or not.

21:23 *To them.* The people of Jerusalem believed that Nebuchadnezzar's favorable omens would prove to be *a false divination.*

Sworn solemn oaths. Lit. "oaths of oaths are to them." They were so sure that Nebuchadnezzar was being deceived that they swore oath upon oath. The Hebrew noun for oaths may denote "weeks." If translated "weeks of weeks are to them," the meaning is that the people are saying: "It will not be for ages, if ever, that the divination will come true."

21:27 *Whose right it is.* When Zedekiah, the last "prince" of royal lineage, dies in disgrace, the house of David will become defunct until the Messianic King establishes His rule. (Gn 49:10 note; Is 9:6-7; Lk 1:32, 69)

21:28-32 The *sword* of the Lord, deflected from *the Ammonites* for a time, will in due course be *drawn for the slaughter* also of Israel's *unhallowed wicked* neighboring nation. Its inhabitants, slain by *brutal men . . . in the midst of the land,* will *be no more remembered.*

21:28 *Concerning their reproach.* When their "day has come" (29), the Ammonites will no longer rejoice over Jerusalem's ruin.

21:30 *Return it.* If addressed to Ezekiel, the command is God's directive to cease brandishing the sword, symbolizing the execution of divine wrath. If addressed to Ammon, it is an ironic summons to give up the fight because all resistance is in vain.

22:1-16 The *day* (4) of Jerusalem's calamity was at hand. Nebuchadnezzar was about to begin the siege of the city, which was to result in a "great slaughter" of its citizens and was to reduce every structure to rubble (21:14, 27). These tragic events were not an accident of history which God, either out of caprice or impotence, failed to prevent. In this ch. He makes it clear that it was by His sovereign, just decree that the horrors of war and defeat would be inflicted on the city of David.

Acting as God's prosecuting attorney, Ezekiel hales the inhabitants of Jerusalem into court, indicting them for committing *abominable deeds.* In his opening statement he summarily charges them with criminal offenses against both God and their fellow citizens, to wit: Jerusalem is *a city that sheds blood . . . and makes idols to defile herself* (1-5). Then in a bill of particulars he cites example after example of flagrant violations of the Mosaic legal code (6-12). The accused do not deny their evil deeds or plead ignorance of the law. Guilty and convicted, they will no longer have the *courage* to defy "the Judge of all the earth" when He executes sentence on them and disperses them *among the nations.* (13-16; Gn 18:25)

22:2 *The bloody city.* Jerusalem is as "infamous" (5) in God's sight as Nineveh, the notoriously wicked capital of Assyria, against which the prophet Nahum uttered the execration: "Woe to the bloody city!" (Nah 3:1; cf. Eze 24:6). The crimes committed in Jerusalem are so heinous that the charge of shedding blood is repeated six times in the next 11 verses.

22:7-12 *Treated with contempt.* The wrongs here enumerated were prohibited by legislation well-known to the accused. They knew what the law said about *father and mother* (Ex 20:12); *the sojourner, the fatherless, the widow* (Ex 22:21 f.; Dt 14:29; 16:11, 14; 24:19-22); *holy things* (Lv 10:10; 11:47; 20:25); *sabbaths* (Ex 20:8 f.; cf. Is 56:2 note); eating *upon the mountains* (cf. Eze 18:5 note); *lewdness* and sexual impurity (Lv 18:8-20; 20:10-20); *bribes* (Ex 23:8; Dt 16:19); usury. (Ex 22:24; 25:36; Eze 18:6)

22:12 *Forgotten me.* "Abominable deeds" (2), which wrong fellow human beings, are regarded as offenses against God Himself.

22:13 *Strike my hands.* To express aroused feelings of indignation. (Cf. 21:17 note)

22:14 *Courage endure.* Till now they had put on a bold, brazen front, confident that the Lord could not destroy the holy city. (Cf. Jer 7:4)

22:17-22 When God consumes "the filthiness out of" the people (15), the walls of Jerusalem will not offer them security. For God will turn the city, filled with refugees, into a smelting *furnace* in which the fire of His wrath will *melt* them into a heap of slag.

22:18 *Become dross.* For the process of refining metal see Jer 6:27-30 note; 6:29 note. If the word *silver* is left to stand at the end of the sentence (RSV note), then Ezekiel is saying that Israel is not worth saving. It is like ores which when melted down leave no valuable residue of silver but only worthless dross. (Cf. 11:1-12 note)

22:23-31 God is justified in melting Israel in a furnace "as silver is melted" (22) because the entire population has "become dross" (Is 1:22). The religious and civic leaders have turned the sacred office entrusted to them into an opportunity for crime and fraud (25-28). *The people of the land,* i.e., the rank and file citizens, *practiced extortion and committed robbery* (29). The nation, in which all classes of society are incurably bent on defying God, leaves Him no choice but to *destroy it.* And His resolve to do so is as certain to be carried out as if He had already *consumed them with the fire of* His *wrath.*

22:24 *Not . . . rained upon.* If not blessed by rainfall, a land is a worthless desert, unable to sustain life. (Jer 14:2-6)

22:25 *Princes.* There is a difference of only one letter between the Hebrew words for "prophets" and "princes" (RSV note). Members of the royal family rather than prophets would be in a position to commit the crimes mentioned in this verse. The Hebrew word for "princes" in 27 very likely refers to "high officials," as in 1 K 4:2.

22:28 *Daubed.* Cf. 13:1-16 note.

22:30 *Stand in the breach.* A few righteous individuals such as Noah, Daniel, and Job would no longer avert the doom of a nation in which all strata of the citizenry were addicted to a wanton life of crime (14:13 f.). God tried in vain to find someone to gain popular support for a reform movement and so to *build up the wall* which alone could protect the city. Jeremiah, sent *among them* to preach repentance, was rebuffed, ridiculed, and persecuted.

23:1—24:27 GUILT AND DOOM PORTRAYED AGAIN BY ALLEGORY AND SYMBOLIC ACTION

23:1-10 Ezekiel tries to break through the hard resistance to his preaching of repentance by confronting the rebellious house with an allegory as shocking to their self-righteous sensibilities as the one recorded in ch. 16. In language even more realistically indelicate he again declares that their unfaithfulness to God is as vile in His sight as wanton adultery. Indulgence and persistence in this detestable sin by Ezekiel's contemporaries was all the more reprehensible because they knew that God did not let it go unpunished in the past. In order to make this point, Ezekiel reviews the history of the chosen people from the time their ancestral tribes still were in Egypt. Welded into a nation by Moses, they remained united until the reign of Solomon. After his death the kingdom was divided into two sovereign states. The capital of the seceding northern tribes came to be Samaria, while Jerusalem remained the seat of government in the south. The blood relationship of the two separate kingdoms is expressed in the allegory by calling them *daughters of one mother.* As sisters they have also the same family name, the older being surnamed *Ohol*-ah and the younger, *Ohol*-ibah.

23:2 *Played the harlot.* For other instances where having other gods besides the Lord is branded harlotry see Jer 2:20; 3:7 ff.; Hos 2:5; 3:3. It was an endemic disease in the sisters. While still in Egypt, they allowed their virginity to be defiled. (3; cf. 20:7 note)

23:4 *Oholah . . . Oholibah.* The common element in the names is the Hebrew word for tent: *ohel.* Its figurative significance derives from its use to designate Israel's place of worship before the temple was built, called "the tent of meeting" (Ex 29:42; 33:7; Nm 11:24, etc.). The older sister's name is Oholah, i.e., "her tent," because the northern tribes established sanctuaries of their own in opposition to the only legitimate worship center. The younger sister is called Oholibah, i.e., "my tent is in her," because God's approved place of meeting with His people remained in Jerusalem.

Became mine. A figurative way of saying that the covenant made by God with the entire nation was like the marriage vow of a bride and groom, which is to be kept inviolate.

23:5-10 Oholah came to a tragic end when the very *lovers* with whom *she defiled herself* turned against her and *slew* her.

23:5 *The Assyrians.* The Northern Kingdom made overtures of alliance to them. These diplomatic maneuvers deserve to be called "harlotries." In effect they were acts of illicit love. They violated the relationship of total trust and unreserved dependence which the people pledged to maintain exclusively with God. The felony was compounded by the fact that treaties with heathen nations required adopting the worship of "all" their "idols." (Cf. 16:8 note; 2 K 15:19; 17:4; Hos 5:13; 7:11; 8:9; 12:1)

23:10 *Judgment.* Samaria is called "the elder"

of the sisters because it was destroyed more than 100 years before Ezekiel spoke this allegory.

23:11-21 Instead of taking warning from the fate of her elder sister, Oholibah was *more corrupt* than she, *doting* on *her paramours* with the insatiable abandon of a slatternly slut.

23:12 *The Assyrians.* For an example of adultery with them see 2 K 16:7-9.

23:14 *Chaldeans.* They constituted the ruling house of the Babylonians. For dealings with them see 2 K 20:12 note; 24:1.

23:17 *Disgust.* For desire turned to revulsion see 2 Sm 13:15 note.

23:19 *Egypt.* Driven by vulgar, uninhibited lust, Oholibah *increased her harlotry* with them to exceed what she did in *the days of her youth.* (Cf. 17:15 note; 2 K 21:20 ff.)

23:22-35 In these verses God speaks the inevitable *therefore* of judgment on incorrigible Oholibah. Introduced in each case by a solemn *thus says the Lord,* the fourfold sentence passed on her provides the same kind of punishment her wicked sister received: (1) her *lovers* will become her executioners (22-27); (2) they will leave her denuded of resources, *the fruit of* her *labor* (28-31); (3) the rapacious men who will do her in will act at God's command, for He has prepared and filled the *cup of horror and desolation* she will have to drain (32-34); (4) convicted of *lewdness and harlotry,* she will *bear the consequences* of her deeds. (35)

23:23 *Pekod . . . Shoah . . . Koa.* The Babylonian army will be composed in part of Aramean tribes located east of the Tigris River. Their names appear on Assyrian records.

23:24 *From the north.* The Hebrew word, occurring only here, is so translated by the Septuagint, the ancient Greek version of the OT.

23:31 *Her cup.* Cf. Jer 13:13 note.

23:34 *Pluck out your hair.* The Hebrew "gnaw its sherds" (RSV note) makes sense if interpreted as an act of insane delirium produced by the content of the cup.

23:36-46 The abominable deeds and punishment of destroyed Samaria and the *adultery* and still-impending judgment of Jerusalem merge into a single picture of guilt followed by punishment. In the perspective of God's unchanging justice what will happen has already happened, and what has happened must happen again. The wages of sin never go unpaid.

23:38-39 *On the same day.* Adding insult to injury, the idolators having sacrificed their children have the defiant effrontery to enter the temple on a sabbath with the blood of the ghastly crime still on their hands. (Cf. Lv 18:21 note; 2 K 23:10 note)

23:40 *Paint your eyes.* In order to enhance their beauty. (Cf. 2 K 9:30 note; Jer 4:30)

23:42 *Drunkard.* As the RSV notes indicate, some features of the revelry and debauchery cannot be determined with certainty from the transmitted text—not a great loss.

23:43 *Commit adultery.* The meaning of the text seems to be that she was a woman of habitual, unrestrained lewdness. She did not yield to temptation in a weak moment, but permitted men to commit adultery with her as readily as a professional harlot plies her trade.

23:45 *Righteous men.* Though the Babylonians and Assyrians were no better than their victims, they executed righteous judgment because they carried out the sentence which God's holy law demands.

23:47 *Stone . . . and dispatch them.* Cf. Lv 20:10; Dt 21:21.

24:1-14 For four years God's appointed watchman over Israel sounded the alarm in vain (v. 1; 1:2; 3:7). Informed by *the word of the Lord,* he announces that, as he now speaks, the king of Babylon is no longer in far-off Riblah (21:18-27 note) but *has laid siege to Jerusalem this very day* (1-2). Any lingering, desperate hope that God will intervene and miraculously save the city as He did a century earlier (2 K 19:35) is dispelled as Ezekiel is directed to *utter an allegory to the rebellious house.* Jerusalem, surrounded by the enemy, is like a *pot* or cauldron and its inhabitants like *pieces of flesh* and *choice bones,* held helplessly within it and cooked through and through over a blazing fire (3-5; cf. 11:3, 7, 11). After the seethed meat and bones have been taken out *piece after piece,* the cauldron itself will *be melted* because it is pockmarked with ineradicable *filthiness* and corroded with *rust.* So God will deal with the *bloody city.* Its surviving inhabitants indiscriminately taken into exile, it will be left a charred ruin. (6-14)

24:1 *Ninth year.* Ezekiel previously noted the year, month, and day of his call and of two visits by the elders (1:1 f.; 8:1; 20:1). The same exact date for the beginning of the siege is recorded also in 2 K 25:1 and Jer 52:4. After the exile the day was observed annually by fasting. (Zch 8:19)

24:4-5 *Choice bones.* The upper stratum of the citizenry will share the same fate as the rank and file. In order to make sure that the bones too are thoroughly boiled, they are to be placed under the meat and the water is to be brought to a high boiling point. (RSV notes)

24:6 *The bloody city.* For its criminal record see 22:1-12.

24:7 *On the bare rock.* Blood was shed so brazenly and openly that no attempt was made to *cover* the crime or to bring the murderer to justice. Therefore the blood, like Abel's, cries to God for vengeance. (Gn 4:10; cf. Jb 16:18; Is 26:21; Ps 32:1; Ro 4:7)

24:12 *Wearied myself.* Translated "she has wearied me," the thought is that God's previous chastisements were wasted efforts because they failed to produce repentance and so cleanse the city of her "filthy lewdness." (13)

24:14 *I will do it.* God will allow the Babylonians to complete the siege.

24:15-27 Ezekiel was directed to dramatize *the word of the Lord* communicated in the form of an allegory in 1-14. The symbolic action he was to perform was no doubt the most difficult assignment he received, because it required that he suppress deep personal feelings. When his wife, *the delight of* his *eyes,* died suddenly, he was to give no outward expression to his grief and to refrain from observing the customary mourning rites. His highly unconventional, unnatural behavior prompted the people to ask what *these things* meant. He explained that he was acting out *a sign.* For when *a fugitive will come . . . to report . . . the news* that Jerusalem, *the delight of* their *eyes,* had ceased to exist, they too will be laid too low to engage in ceremonial mourning. Realizing finally that *the Lord God* will not be mocked, they will be able only to *groan to one another* as they *pine away* in their iniquities.

24:15 *The delight of your eyes.* Contrary to appearances, Ezekiel was not devoid of tender love, as this term of endearment for his wife shows. God's uncompromising ambassador of judgment, he surrendered his own feelings to his divine assignment so unreservedly that he appeared to be cold, austere, unfeeling. For a different kind of personality in God's employ as prophet see notes on Jer 20:7-18.

24:17 *Sigh.* According to prevailing funeral customs the mourner was expected to: (1) engage women to lament *aloud* (Mk 5:38); (2) take off the *turban* and go barefoot (2 Sm 15:30; Is 20:2); (3) pull down a head-covering over his face to his *lips* (Mi 3:7); (4) eat *the bread of mourners,* prepared by relatives and friends. (Jer 16:7; Hos 9:4)

24:21 *The pride of your power.* For devotion to the temple and the holy city see Ps 27:4; 137:6; Lm 2:4.

24:26 *On that day.* Ezekiel is not saying that *a fugitive* leaving Jerusalem "on the day" of its capture (25) could arrive in Babylonia within 24 hours. In prophetic perspective the tragic event and the arrival of the report are telescoped into a single view. For the fulfillment see 33:21.

24:27 *No longer dumb.* For the fulfillment see 33:22. For the nature of the prophet's temporary dumbness see 3:22-27 notes.

25:1—32:32 FOREIGN NATIONS, HOSTILE TO GOD AND HIS PEOPLE, WILL PERISH

Though not arranged in chronological order, the next 8 chs. are grouped to form a topical unit, In all of them the word of the Lord is addressed not to the rebellious house of Israel but to seven heathen nations. In the overall scheme of the book this collection of oracles serves as a literary interlude. It leaves the reader in suspense whether a fugitive would come to report that Nebuchadnezzar's siege of Jerusalem was successful, as Ezekiel predicted in the last two verses of the preceding ch. At the same time, the doom of extinction pronounced on the foreign nations constitutes a prelude to the third and final section of the book. In chs. 33—48 Ezekiel will prophesy that no nation will be able to thwart God's plan to use the descendants of Abraham in bringing salvation to the ends of the earth (Gn 12:3). For whereas the hostile nations are destined to remain buried under the sands of time, Israel, purified and redeemed, will once again play its assigned role in establishing the kingdom of the Messiah, embracing peoples of every racial strain and making them "fellow citizens . . . of the household of God." (Eph. 2:19)

For similar collections of oracles against Israel's enemies see Is 13—23; Jer 46—51; Am 1:1—2:3. For the relevance these oracles against ancient peoples have for the modern reader see Is 13:1-22 note.

Six of the condemned nations border on Israelite territory: Ammon east of the Jordan, Moab east of the Dead Sea, Edom to the south, Philistia to the west (ch. 25), Tyre and Sidon to the northwest (chs. 26—28). The seventh is Egypt, contender for the control of all Palestine. (Chs. 29—32)

It is hardly accidental that the indicted nations add up to a total of seven and that the seventh is condemned by seven words of the Lord that came to Ezekiel on seven occasions (29:1, 17; 30:1, 20; 31:1; 32:1, 17). As in other instances, the number seven no doubt denotes completeness. Every earthly power structure, whether mentioned or not, must go down to defeat if it seeks to hinder the coming of God's kingdom. It may seem strange that Babylonia is not included in this list of foreign nations challenging God's control of world history. Two reasons for the omission suggest themselves. At the time Ezekiel spoke these words the Babylonian king was not obstructing the purposes of God. Though acting out of selfish motives, he was carrying out a divinely assigned task when he destroyed Jerusalem. In the second place, Ezekiel was trying desperately to combat the notion that God could not surrender His chosen people into hostile hands. A prophecy of Babylonia's downfall would no doubt have confirmed his hearers in their false hope.

25:1-17 Ammon, Moab, Edom, Philistia

25:1-7 For Ammonite relations with Israel see Jer 49:1 second note.

25:8-11 For Moabite relations with Israel see Is chs. 15 and 16 notes; Jer 48 notes.

25:12-14 For Edom's inveterate enmity against Israel see Is 21:11 note; Jer 49:7, 12, 14 notes; Am 1:11.

25:15-17 For Philistine relations with Israel see Is 14:28 note; Jer 47 notes.

25:17 *They will know.* This statement of God's ultimate purpose occurs frequently in sermons addressed to Israel. When it appears repeatedly also in these oracles, it holds out hope that peoples of heathen origin too will be led to come to the knowledge of saving truth vouchedsafed in God's everlasting covenant of grace. (25:7, 11, 14; 1 Ti 2:4)

26:1—28:26 Tyre and Sidon

26:1-14 Some 35 miles northwest of the Sea of Galilee lay the port city Tyre, "mighty on the sea" (17). Together with her sister city Sidon, about 25 miles up the Mediterranean coast, these Phoenician cities established a commercial empire unrivaled in their day. Their ships brought the merchandise of the nations into their storehouses and filled their coffers with treasures (cf. Is 13 notes). However, the amassed riches of the world did not put them beyond God's control. On five occasions *the word of the Lord came to* Ezekiel to announce their doom (26:1; 27:1; 28:1, 11, 20). Befitting her greater prominence at the time, Tyre bears the brunt of the denunciation. In this ch. her false sense of security is shattered by a threefold *thus says the Lord* (7, 15, 19). In executing judgment on her He *will bring up many nations against* her who will make her a *bare rock* (3 f., 14). One of the Lord's agents of destruction will be the *king of Babylon.*

26:1 *The eleventh year.* Because Jerusalem was captured in the same year, the news of its fall must have quickly reached Tyre, where it was greeted with malicious glee.

26:2 *The gate of the peoples.* Situated astride the corridor between the Mediterranean Sea and the desert, Jerusalem was in a position to control the overland trade routes between the nations of antiquity and to levy taxes on wares in transit through its territory.

26:6 *Her daughters.* Phoenician towns of lesser prominence.

26:7 *Nebuchadrezzar.* An alternate spelling for Nebuchadnezzar. After the capture of Jerusalem, he besieged Tyre for 13 years. Though he destroyed the city on the mainland, its island defenses, one-half mile off shore, held out and were not demolished until 332 B.C. by Alexander the Great. Before he could take the fortified rock, he had to build a causeway into the sea and out to it. For Tyre's resistance to Nebuchadnezzar see 29:18 note.

26:15-18 Tyre's satellites and maritime colonies will be *appalled at* the sudden fall of an apparently invincible power structure. Their spokesmen, called *princes of the sea,* will *raise a lamentation over* the wreckage as if it were a corpse.

26:19-21 The dirge over Tyre's demise is appropriate because as the dead cannot return from *the Pit* to *the land of the living,* so the city *will never be found again.*

27:1-9 Ezekiel is directed to *raise a lamentation over Tyre* as mourners were wont to over someone brought "down to the Pit" (26:20). The prophetic elegy opens with a eulogy customarily spoken over the deceased (cf. David's lament over Saul and Jonathan, 2 Sm 1:17-27). Tyre is compared with a magnificent ship, *perfect in beauty,* sturdily built, excellently equipped, lavishly arrayed, and manned by experienced *mariners.*

27:5 *Senir.* The lofty peak in the Anti-Lebanon Range better known as Mt. Hermon. (Cf. Dt 3:8 note)

27:7 *Elisha.* Tentatively identified as a city on Cyprus.

27:8 *Arvad.* An island 100 miles to the north, associated with *Zemer* also in Gn 10:18.

27:9 *Gebal.* A seaport south of Arvad, also called Byblos.

27:10-11 The Tyrian luxury liner could sail confidently to distant ports because its home base was protected by mercenaries assembled from far and wide.

27:10 *Lud and Put.* Territories on the African coast west of the Delta. (Jer 46:9)

27:11 *Helech . . . Gamad.* Unidentifiable place names.

27:12-25a The Tyrian ship of state boasted of such splendor and opulence because of lucrative trade in choice wares obtained from nations in all parts of the ancient world.

27:12 *Trafficked with you.* The list of countries with which Tyre had profitable commercial relations constitutes a veritable map of antiquity. "Javan" (13) denotes Greece; "Tubal and Meshech" were in Asia Minor; "Beth-togarmah" (14) was the territory later known as Armenia; "Rhodes" (15), the well-known island off the coast of Asia Minor: "Edom" (16), south of Judah; "Damascus" (18), the capital of Syria; "Helbon," north of Damascus; "Uzal" (19), a trading center in southern Arabia; "Dedan" (20), in central Arabia; "Kedar" (21), in northern Arabia; "Sheba and Raamah" (22), at the southern end of Arabia; "Haran, Canneh, Eden," in Mesopotamia; "Asshur" is Assyria; "Chimad" remains unidentified.

27:25 *Ships of Tarshish.* Vessels capable of carrying heavy cargoes and going great distances. (Cf. 1 K 10:22 note)

27:25b-36. Suddenly the same sea on which the ship brought riches to port also became its undoing. Wrecked by an *east wind,* the proud liner sank *in the heart of the seas* with the loss of all cargo and all men aboard. *The inhabitants of the coastlands,* who witnessed the catastrophe from *shore,* took to *lamentation,* aghast that the mighty fell so quickly and so permanently.

27:27 *Your riches.* Tyre typifies godless self-sufficiency and self-determination. Every such anti-God power structure will share its fate. So St. John makes Babylon the symbol of opposition to God and in Rv 18 describes its downfall in terms reminiscent of Tyre's shipwreck.

28:1-10 Tyre's sin is epitomized in the pride of the chief of state, *the prince.* Ezekiel condemns him out of his own mouth, quoting him as saying: *I am a god* and *sit in the seat of the gods.* He succumbed to self-deification because he regarded himself *wise as a god* so that by his *wisdom in trade* he *gathered gold and silver* and enormous wealth. However, this arrogant delusion of grandeur will come to an end when, invaded by *the most terrible of the nations,* he will go *down into the Pit* like all mortals.

28:3 *Wiser than Daniel.* Nebuchadnezzar said to him: "No mystery is difficult for you" (Dn 4:9; 1:20; cf. Eze 14:14 note). The king of Tyre lacked "the fear of the Lord," without which the most highly endowed intellect is prone to work havoc. (Pr 9:10; 3:7; 26:12; Is 5:21; Jer 9:23 f.)

28:7 *Most terrible of the nations.* The

Babylonians are given this distinction in 30:11; 31:12; 32:12.

28:10 *Death of the uncircumcised.* Circumcision was the sign of the covenant with God (Gn 17:10-14). In contrast to his claim to royal honor, the king will die the shameful death of the "uncircumcised Philistine" slain by David and left unburied on the field of battle. (1 Sm 17:26, 36, 51).

28:11-19 The defeat and death of the king are so certain to come to pass that Ezekiel is told to *raise a lamentation over* him in anticipation of his funeral. He will share the fate of all who rise against their Maker in rebellious pride, the primordial sin which destroyed God's perfect creation. The elegy Ezekiel composed scintillates with figurative allusions to Adam's fall *in Eden* (13) and to Satan's expulsion from heaven *to the ground* (17). As in 1-10, the poet borrowed descriptive details from the corrupted mythical accounts of primeval events with which the king of Tyre was acquainted.—Pride therefore is not a slight misdemeanor but a radical anti-God orientation of life. It is also an insidious sin, for it beguiled God's creatures when they were *perfect in beauty* and *blameless* in their *ways.* (11, 15)

28:12 *Signet of perfection.* When properly handled, the seal makes an accurate copy of the pattern engraved on it. So the king was a paragon of wisdom and beauty. He exhibited these traits so perfectly as if he were a living facsimile of them in their ideal form.

28:13 *Every precious stone.* The nine jewels listed were also set in three rows on the breastplate of the high priest (Ex 28:17-20). The ancient Greek translation called the Septuagint adds three more, bringing the total to 12, the number prescribed for the priestly vestment. Ezekiel continues to draw on the Canaanite myth. The proud monarch claimed to "sit in the seat of the gods" (2). In this *Eden* he was covered with precious stones and walked amid "the stones of fire" (14), perhaps the stars of ethereal heights (cf. Is 14:12 note, 13 note). In the Biblical account *the garden of God* was an earthly paradise of luxurious trees, to which Ezekiel refers in 31:9, 16, 18; 36:35.

28:14 *An anointed guardian cherub.* This translation, based on the Septuagint, makes an angelic being the companion and protector of the prince *on the holy mountain of God* or the gods. However, after the king "sinned," the same cherub drove him out from his celestial abode and God cast the sinner down to earth (16 f.; cf. ch. 10). The translation adopted by the KJV interprets the text as saying that the prince himself is the cherub who is addressed as the guardian of the garden both here and in v. 16.

28:16 *Your trade.* The figurative language momentarily gives way to a factual description of Tyre's source of wealth, the basis of its pride.

28:18 *Your sanctuaries. By the multitude of . . . iniquities* he *profaned* the sacred precincts "on the holy mountain." (14)

28:20-23 Situated about 25 miles north of Tyre, *Sidon* will share the fate of her sister city.

28:24-26 In marked contrast to Tyre and Sidon, *the house of Israel* has a glorious future. The chosen people will survive captivity, return *from the peoples,* and *dwell securely in . . . their own land.* So God's plan of universal salvation, seemingly thwarted by the exile, will again get under way. Rescued from sin's bondage, a spiritual Israel will be gathered from all nations under the blissful rule of King Messiah, described in chs. 33—48. (Cf. Is 43:1-28 note; 52:1-15 note; 58—66 introductory note; Jer 23:1-8 note; 33 notes)

29:1—32:32 Egypt

29:1-5 These verses introduce oracles against *Egypt,* the seventh foreign nation to be haled into God's court of judgment (cf. 25—32 introductory note). Seven times *the word of the Lord came to* Ezekiel to announce the coming downfall of the proud land of the Pharaohs. Although Israel had dealings with other peoples, the seven nations indicted and condemned in chs. 25—32 represent the totality of worldly powers answerable to God's direction (cf. Dt 7:1). No concentration of human might, whether specifically mentioned or not, is able to obstruct God's plan of salvation. At various times in the past down to the present day it may have appeared that anti-God forces have thrust Him from His throne and overthrown His kingdom. On such occasions the victims of demonic oppression may have been on the brink of despair. It therefore is not a waste of space when Ezekiel fills eight chs. (25—32), one-sixth of the entire book, with sorely needed assurances that it was, is, and always will be the Father's good pleasure to give the "little flock" the Kingdom (Lk 12:32), even though some "Edom," "Tyre," or "Egypt" seeks to prevent it.

It is also significant that half of these chs. are devoted to a sevenfold prophecy against Egypt. Unlike the six other nations cited, Egypt had achieved the status of a world empire and thus could be considered a formidable obstruction to God's government. As Ezekiel wrote his denunciations of the *Pharoah,* the latter was challenging Babylonian supremacy in the ancient world. The outcome of the contest between these two giants hung in the balance for some time. Unbelieving Israelites, at home and abroad, looked to Egypt to break the Babylonian siege of Jerusalem and thus prove Ezekiel's prophecy of its fall to be in error. Yet it was not a shrewd assessment of the signs of the time but the certainty of divine inspiration which gave Ezekiel the insight and courage to announce, without any trace of equivocation, that the battle for world dominion would end in disaster for Egypt. The armies from the *Nile* would not be able to prevent Nebuchadnezzar from doing the task assigned to him by God: the capture of Jerusalem and the chastening of the chosen people in exile. In this role as God's rod of punishment on Israel, the Babylonian king would initiate divine judgment on the land of the Pharaohs, reducing it to "the most lowly of the kingdoms" (15). Prostrate and decadent, it would not be able to interfere with Israel after the return from exile when the descendants of Abraham would once again serve as the bearers of promises to all mankind.

Ezekiel underscores the miracle of Israel's survival among hostile nations and empires by noting the exact date when he received seven of the oracles directed against them, thus accounting for half of the dated passages in the entire book (26:1; 29:1, 17; 30:20; 31:1; 32:1, 17). The word of the Lord recorded in the opening verses of ch. 29 came to him after the siege of Jerusalem had begun. (Cf. 24:1)

29:3 *Dragon.* The kind of marine animal appropriate to describe the ruler of the Nile valley is the crocodile. Because God created "the great sea monsters" (Gn 1:21), they cannot begin to dispute His control of them, for He can dispose of them as readily as He called them into being (Ps 148:7; 74:13 f.). Opposition to God is at times represented by a dragon, identified as Rahab or Leviathan. (Cf. Jb 41:1 note; 9:13 note; Is 30:7 note; 51:9)

29:4 *The fish.* Satellites dependent on Egypt.

29:6-12 Egypt's overthrow will be as complete as if its fertile land along the Nile had become *an utter waste and desolation.* (10)

29:6 *A staff of reed.* Zedekiah found out that to rely on Egypt for help was as foolish as leaning one's weight on one of the many stalks or reeds growing on the banks of the Nile. (Jer 37:6 f.; 44:30 note; cf. also 2 K 18:21; Is 36:6)

29:10 *From Migdol to Syene.* The entire north-south length of the land from the area in the delta to the far south, modern Aswan.

29:11 *Forty years.* A symbolic number to indicate the full duration of the imposed punishment. (Cf. Nm 14:33 note)

29:12 *Scatter . . . and disperse.* Egypt's surrender to foreign domination will be as complete as when Israel was dragged into exile.

29:13-16 Egypt's revival is also described in terms of Israel's return after the exile "from the peoples among whom they are scattered" (28:25). However, God will make the Egyptians *so small that they will never again rule over the nations.*

29:14 *Pathros.* Situated in upper, i.e., southern, Egypt where the Pharaohs once held sway from the ancient capital of Thebes.

29:17-21 Egypt's humiliation will begin when Nebuchadnezzar will *despoil it and plunder it.* According to a fragment of a Babylonian chronicle, he invaded Egypt in 567 B.C. (cf. Jer 43:11 note). When he did so, he *worked for* God, who did not want Egypt to interfere with Israel's restoration.

29:17 *Twenty-seventh year.* The latest date attached to a word of the Lord received by Ezekiel. It came to him in 571 B.C., 15 years after the fall of Jerusalem.

29:18 *Anything from Tyre.* No doubt the Tyrians removed their treasures to the off-shore island, which Nebuchadnezzar was not able to conquer (cf. 26:7 note). The riches of Egypt were to be "the wages for his army" and his own "recompense."

29:21 *A horn.* A frequent symbol of strength (Ps 89:17, 24; Jer 48:25; etc.). When Christ was born, God "raised up a horn of salvation . . . in the house of his servant David." (Lk 1:69; Ps 132:17)

Open your lips. After the fall of Jerusalem they were unsealed (3:27 note; 24:27). He received special eloquence to proclaim Israel's and the world's redemption.

30:1-4 In an undated word of the Lord, Egypt's inevitable and imminent doom is described as a catastrophe precipitated by *the day of the Lord* which will overtake not only Israel but also *the nations.* (Cf. 7:10 note; Is 2:12 note)

30:5-9 The destruction of Egypt's power will have widespread and serious consequences. *Those who support her will fall* also.

30:5 *Put and Lud.* Frequently mentioned together, these place names seem to refer to territories situated in Africa west of the delta. (27:10; Jer 46:9)

Arabia. The Hebrew noun is best vocalized to be read: "the mingled people," meaning, as in Jer 25:20, groups of mixed racial and social affinities which were associated with the Egyptian army or the citizenry.

Libya. The Hebrew text has "Cub," an unidentifiable place name. A change of one consonant yields the word "Lub," Libya.

30:10-12 God *will bring desolation upon the land* of the Nile *by the hand of Nebuchadrezzar king of Babylon . . . the most terrible of the nations.* (Cf. 28:7; 29:17-21)

30:10 *Wealth.* The same Hebrew word is translated "multitude" in 31:2.

30:13-19 No area of Egypt will be spared. On city after city in every part of the land God *will execute . . . judgment.* Located in the region of the delta are *Zoan, Pelusium, Pibeseth,* and *Tehaphnehes;* up the Nile lie *Memphis* and *On* (Heliopolis); in southern Egypt is the area called *Pathros,* in which was the city of *Thebes* (Karnak)

30:20-26 Uttered about 4 months before the fall of Jerusalem, this oracle proclaims the defeat of the Egyptian army under Pharaoh Hophra, the "reed" on which Israel leaned in vain for support (Is 36:6; cf. Jer 37:5 ff.; 2 K 24:7). Because the Pharaoh's *arm* was *broken,* his land lay defenseless before *the king of Babylon.*

30:24 *My sword.* Though "put . . . into the hand of the king of Babylon" (25), it is God's weapon which decides the fate of nations.

30:26 *Scatter . . . and disperse.* Cf. 29:12 note.

31:1-9 Egypt's fall from imperial glory to disgrace and servitude will be like the sudden crashing to earth of a magnificent *cedar.* So Assyria (cf. v. 3 RSV note), only 3 decades earlier, went down to oblivion from heights of world dominion. Egypt too attained *great height,* dwarfing all rivals. The question is whether Assyria's fate will be a warning to *Pharaoh king of Egypt* that "pride goes before destruction." (Pr 16:18; cf. also Tyre's fall, described as the sudden sinking of a proud ship in ch. 27)

31:1 *In the third month.* Two months after Ezekiel received the word of the Lord in 30:20-26.

31:3 *Liken you to a cedar.* The Hebrew text, which reads: "Assyria was a cedar of Lebanon," can be retained (cf. 31:1-9 note above). The Assyrian empire "towered high above" the nations like *a cedar in Lebanon.* But when it stood at the pinnacle of glory, it suddenly disappeared from sight as if it were a tall tree felled in its prime. Egypt, like it "in its greatness" (7), would be like it also as it topples into irreversible ruin.

31:8 *In the garden of God.* Not even "the trees of Eden" were the cedar's equal in beauty and stature.

31:10-14 Because the cedar refused to acknowledge that God "made it beautiful" (9) but *was proud of its height,* He *will cut it down and leave it* to decay. Figurative personification of a nation as a tree at times gives way to a description of actual aspects of a human being. Thus the cedar is said to have a proud *heart* and to go down *to the nether world* like all *mortal men.* For the transient nature of all human achievements see Is 40:6 ff.; Ps 90:5 f.; 103:14 ff.

31:11 *A mighty one.* Nebuchadnezzar is called the king of "the most terrible of the nations" in 30:11.

31:15-18 The cedar's fall from towering strength to helpless impotence is like a cosmic upheaval, affecting *the deep, its rivers and many waters, Lebanon, all the trees of the field, the nations* without exception. The fate decreed on the proud tree is as irreversible as it is impossible for *those who go down to the Pit* to return to their former scene of activity. Death cuts down all mundane attainments, whether great or small. People who have not become cedars of success *will be comforted* to know that humanity's greatest too must end where they do—in the grave. *Pharaoh and all his multitude* will be no exception to this axiom of the Creator's decree.

31:15 *Sheol.* Cf. Dt 32:22 note.

31:19 *Uncircumcised.* Cf. 28:10 note.

32:1-16 A year after the fall of Jerusalem, Ezekiel is directed to proclaim *the word of the Lord* in the form of *a lamentation over Pharaoh.* The dirge he was to compose was not to express pity or sadness over the king's impending inglorious end but to mock his pretensions to be *a lion among the nations,* frightening them into submission by his roaring. He will not be safe even in his homeland. For he is *like a dragon in the seas,* i.e., a crocodile in the Nile, which God will haul up in a *dragnet, cast . . . on the ground,* and let *the beasts of the whole earth* gorge themselves on (2-6; cf. 29:3-5). The judgment to be executed on him is certain to materialize, for it will overtake him with the force of the day of the Lord whose commands are obeyed by the *stars, the sun, the moon,* and *all the bright lights of heaven* (7-8; cf. Is 2:12 note; Jl 2:10 f.; Am 8:9). When the land becomes *desolate* and *all who dwell in it* are struck down, *the daughters of the nations* will play the part of professional mourning women and *chant* this doleful lament. (9-16)

32:2 *A dragon.* Egypt is described as a crocodile also in 29:3-5.

32:3 *Throw my net.* Forced submission to God's power is asserted by the same figure of speech in 12:13; 17:20. The following description of the monster's disposal resembles the language of an ancient myth in which a god in the heathen pantheon establishes supremacy by slaying a rival dragon. Defeat of God's enemies is at times expressed by similar terms—though there is a vast difference in substance. The sovereignty of the Lord of hosts is never in question. He has only to speak His omnipotent word to have men, angels, and devils do His will. The forces of nature are at His beck and call.

32:17-31 In the seventh and last oracle against Egypt, Ezekiel brings to a climax his portrayal of the utter futility of all attempts to interfere with God's plans and decrees. He wails *over the multitude of Egypt* by conjuring up a scene from *the nether world* surpassing Dante's Inferno for unearthly grandeur. When Egypt is doomed to go the way of mortal flesh, *the mighty chiefs* who earlier have *gone down to the Pit* are there to welcome the new arrival. Though Egypt claimed to *surpass in beauty* those *who spread terror in the land of the living* (23), it too must go down to the mass grave of all human ambitions. It shares the same fate with such stalwarts as *Assyria* (22), *Edom* (29), and *the princes of the north* (30). As *Pharaoh* joins them, he can *comfort himself* only with the thought that others fare no better than he. (31)

32:17 *In the first month.* Omitted in the Hebrew text and supplied from the ancient Greek translation of the OT called the Septuagint.

32:21 *Uncircumcised.* Cf. 28:10 note.

32:22 *Assyria.* The mighty empire disappeared from the face of the earth in 612 B.C., less than 30 years before Ezekiel spoke this elegy.

32:24 *Elam.* Occupying territory east of Babylon, this nation was a formidable power in the ancient world until it was subjugated by the Assyrians.

32:26-27 *Meshech and Tubal.* Peoples in Asia Minor, mentioned in 27:13; 38:2. They *do not lie* with heroic warriors who were granted a funeral with military honors.

32:28 *You.* Pharaoh is addressed.

32:29 *Edom.* Cf. 25:12-14 note.

32:30 *Princes of the north.* North of Judah and Israel were Syrian states and Phoenician cities. Of the latter *the Sidonians* are specifically mentioned.

33:1—48:35 CHASTENED ISRAEL WILL BE RESTORED, AND THE PROMISED KINGDOM OF GOD WILL COME

Chs. 33—48 constitute the third major division of Ezekiel's prophecies. Leaving the foreign, hostile nations buried and forgotten (chs. 25—32), these final oracles proclaim that Israel, apparently also doomed to extinction, will rise from the grave of the exile to serve God's plan of universal salvation. In carrying it forward He will, as it were, begin where He left off. The chosen people will experience a new exodus into the Promised Land and again enjoy the special care of the Lord of the covenant. However, its restoration is not an end in itself. It serves at the same time as a blueprint or model of what God ultimately will do through the descendants of Abraham to bless all nations in a restored fellowship with Him.

The glorious future appears in the perspective of prophetic vision. The new covenant is described in terms of the old provisions. The immediate future and the more distant scenes of the Messianic kingdom merge in a single panoramic view of God's accomplished salvation to the ends of the earth. What God will do for His people and what He will do in the fullness of time to the very end of time is depicted in lines making up one glorious picture of the future. There will always be an Israel of God. It will consist not only of Abraham's offspring according to the flesh but of all who "have been born anew, not of perishable seed but of imperishable, through the . . . word of God" (1 Ptr 1:23). Gathered from all nations and tongues, the royal priesthood of believers will worship the Redeemer in spirit and in truth. Though no longer in force, the myriads of legal prescriptions governing every phase of Israel's political, social, and ritual life are to impress on the redeemed in the Messianic era that the measure of their devotion and consecration is to be no less comprehensive, unreserved, and wholehearted. As Israel of old was safe under the mighty hand of the Creator of the universe, so the combined forces of the fiercest foes will not be allowed to harm the people of God of the new covenant. The kingdom of great David's greater Son will not be confined to the borders of the Holy Land, promised and given to the 12 tribes of Israel. Its blessings will flow in ever-growing streams of living water to all parts of the sin-cursed world.

33:1—39:29 The Message of Restoration

33:1-9 Before the news of Jerusalem's capture by Nebuchadnezzar arrives in the land of the Chaldeans, Ezekiel is prepared for his new assignment: to be the preacher of restoration. The instructions he receives are, in effect, a recommissioning to the prophetic office. Such a basic orientation was necessary. Because the message of redemption was radically different from the threat of the wrath of God, delivered to the "rebellious house" in chs. 1—24, he might have concluded that the good news could be proclaimed on a different basis. Therefore *the word of the Lord came to* him to make it very clear that he remained *a watchman* (1, 7) also when dispensing the Gospel. It still is a matter of life and death. The task is still fraught with the greatest responsibilities both for the preacher and the hearers. The salvation to be announced is no group insurance. Each individual must be told as clearly as the clarion sound of a trumpet that unless he personally accepts the proffered escape from impending death, he will not *have saved his life* (5). For Ezekiel's previous appointment as a watchman whose first and primary duty it was to rouse his hearers to the mortal danger of impenitence see 3:16-21 note.

33:10-20 Ezekiel, the preacher of restoration, has to cope with two kinds of negative responses which, though the very opposite from one another, are but the two sides of the same coin of unbelief. The first is despair. When his fellow prisoners came face to face with the consequences of *transgressions* and *sins*, as predicted by Ezekiel, they stoically resigned themselves to *waste away because of them*. In order to counter this illusion of fatalistic hopelessness, the watchman is to sound out the message that the Lord has *no pleasure in the death of the wicked*. The door of salvation stands wide open. It is, however, necessary that each person receive the gift of life personally and then retain it, for it can be lost by a relapse into the ways of sin (10-16). For the principle of individual responsibility see also ch. 18 notes. The second obstacle to acceptance of redemption encountered by Ezekiel was the presumptuous claim that God does not deal justly when He judges the individual *according to his ways*. (17-20; cf. 18:25 note)

33:21-22 The news that *the city has fallen* marked a new epoch in Ezekiel's ministry. Not only did he become the prophet of restoration but in preaching redemption he was no longer to be restricted in communication as before. (Cf. 3:22-27 notes; also 24:27)

The twelfth year. It took the fugitive 1½ years to elude the Babylonian occupation forces and to make his way to the exiles. Some Hebrew manuscripts and the ancient versions read: "The eleventh year," thus reducing the interval to six months.

33:23-33 Another essential feature of the preaching of restoration is that it does not eliminate the necessity of repentance if the blessings of redemption are to be bestowed. Ezekiel had to confront two different groups with the demand that they change their attitude and conduct. The first of these were the inhabitants of the *waste places in the land of Israel* who escaped massacre and captivity when Jerusalem fell. Unbowed by the national disaster, they arrogantly claimed to be the eventual heirs of the holy land once promised to Abraham even though they persisted in the same sins which the people of Judah committed before the fall of Jerusalem (23-29; cf. 18:6-13; 22:6-12). The second group to be told that the Gospel is not a cheap commodity were Ezekiel's fellow prisoners. They thought his preaching to be like the singing of *love songs* to which they could listen to their amusement yet without committing themselves to *do* what his message required of them. Unmoved by what they heard, they remained *set on their gain*. (30-33)

33:24 *Abraham . . . one man.* The impenitent survivors of the fall of Jerusalem made the arrogant claim that they would have *possession of the land* simply because Abraham, who received it by promise, was only one individual whereas they *are many.* But they will find out that willful perpetrators of crime will not inherit the kingdom. By their impenitence they excluded themselves from its blessings even though Ezekiel, the prophet of restoration, offered these blessings to all people.

34:1-10 Oriented in the principles governing the proclamation of restoration (ch. 33), Ezekiel proceeds at once to speak promises of redemption into a situation marked by defeat and enshrouded in black pessimism. Previously a few rays of hope flashed through the lowering gloom of dire judgment (cf. 11:16-20; 16:60; 20:40-44; 28:25 f.; 29:21). These brief glimpses into a bright future gave him and his hearers assurance that God's plan of universal salvation did not lie buried in the exile. Now the sun of redemptive grace is allowed to break out from the clouds and shed bright rays of hope on a sin-darkened world. The brilliance of divine revelation shines into coming centuries. Beams of light bring into focus the redeemed of God, safe and happy under the protection and rule of a "servant David," the Messianic "prince," who negotiates and puts into effect "a covenant of peace." (23-25)

Ezekiel sees this transformation from doom to delight in the perspective of prophetic vision. Past, present, and future merge into a single dimension of timeless fact. In the portrait he paints, the colors of symbol and reality flow into one another and then separate again into their characteristic hues. The old covenant blends into the new covenant only to resume its ancient contours.

However, seen from the vantage point of projected fulfillment, Ezekiel's kaleidoscopic and surrealistic picture of the coming kingdom of God has clearly recognized features which the Scriptures describe also in the matter-of-fact prose of historical reality. After an apparent delay, God's eternal plan for mankind's redemption got under way again when He gathered the ancient Israelites, scattered like lost sheep on the hills, and brought them back from exile to their homeland. Out of their midst arose a Prince "of the house and lineage of David" (Lk 2:4). Not an earthly king of limited authority like his human predecessors, He founded a spiritual kingdom. Though not of this world, it is worldwide in compass. His subjects represent every racial and national affiliation. They can draw on the inexhaustible resources of royal grace so that even the poorest and the weakest have all they need for time and eternity. Finally the injustice and suffering of a sinful, heartless world will be left behind when the King says: "Come, O blessed of my Father, inherit the kingdom prepared for you from the foundation of the world" (Mt 25:34). He has the gift of life to bestow because He is the Good Shepherd who laid down His life for the sheep. (Jn 10:1-18; Heb 13:20 f.; 1 Ptr 2:25; 5:4)

In the opening verses of this ch. Ezekiel points out how the ravages of sin pervert human relations and institutions. Israel's past is cited as evidence. For some time *the shepherds* (i.e., the political and religious leaders) have exploited and fleeced *the sheep* (i.e., the people) instead of providing for their welfare. As a result of their selfish, rapacious rule the flock was *scattered over all the face of the earth* (6), exiled into foreign lands.

34:2 *Shepherds.* For similar denunciations of Israel's leaders see Jer 10:21; 23:1-4; Eze 22:25-30.

34:5 *No shepherd.* Cf. Jesus' lament over the people at His time. (Mt 9:36)

34:6 *My sheep.* Because God chose the offspring of Abraham to serve His plan of salvation, they are called "the people of his pasture and the sheep of his hand" (Ps 95:7; 74:1; 79:13; 100:3). The sheep who hear the voice of the Good Shepherd and follow Him are safe, for "no one shall snatch them out of" His hand. (Jn 10:27-29)

34:8 *My shepherds.* God had a right to expect them to rule as His representatives.

34:11-16 It would do no good for God to replace the bad shepherds with other earthly rulers. Human society cannot lift itself out of the quicksand of pervasive corruption by its own bootstraps. God Himself must come to the rescue. He has not only the power to do so but also the compassion to *seek the lost,* to *bind up the crippled,* and to *strengthen the weak.*

34:11 *Search for my sheep.* The tender, loving care for His miserable fallen creatures, described in these verses, demonstrates that the God of the OT is not a monstrous ogre delighting in crushing helpless victms. He is the Father who sent His Son "to seek and to save the lost." (Lk 19:10)

34:16 *Watch over.* If the Hebrew word "destroy" is retained (RSV note), it would serve to introduce the thought developed in the following verses: God's threat to execute *justice* on those who prey on the weak.

34:17-22 Man's inhumanity to man was not limited to the shepherds' abuse of the flock. Among the *sheep,* the *rams,* and the *he-goats* there were stronger and *fat* ones who oppressed and injured the weak and *lean ones.*

34:23-24 If God is to break the power and reign of sin, He must send into this world His own vicegerent, His *servant David.* This human-divine *Shepherd* and *Prince* will not destroy the sheep but *feed them* with "the bread from heaven." (Jn 6:32-40)

34:23 *One shepherd.* The 12 tribes of Jacob were divided into two kingdoms after Solomon's death. Under great David's greater Son there will be "one flock, one shepherd" (Jn 10:16). No one will occupy the throne after Him, for He will be "prince forever" (37:25). For His human ancestry from royal David's house see 2 Sm 7:11-16; Is 9:5 f.; 11:1 f.; Jer 30:9.

34:25-31 The spiritual blessings to accrue to His subjects when God's "servant David" is "prince among them" (v. 24) are the result of *a covenant of peace.* God pledges Himself to bring back the harmony and bliss He once provided in an unmarred paradise. His flock will know "the peace . . . which passes all understanding" (Ph 4:7). Israel's restoration is the rescue from estrangement from God. He will welcome the redeemed into the eternal "kingdom of His beloved Son," where there "are pleasures for evermore." (Cl 1:13; Ps 16:11)

34:25 *Covenant of peace.* It heals and makes whole again the brokenness of human existence. Man can be at peace with God and with himself. Because its provisions will never be abrogated, Ezekiel calls it "an everlasting covenant." (16:60; 37:26; cf. Is 24:5; 55:3; 61:8; Jer 32:40)

34:26 *Showers of blessing.* For the bliss of restored communion with God described as Paradise Regained see Is 2:4 note; 11:6 note.

35:1-15 God promised great things in ch. 34. Will He be able to carry out His plan? In this ch. He declares that *Edom* (v. 15), which *cherished perpetual enmity* against the chosen people, will not be able to prevent the restoration of Israel. All attempts to seize the Promised Land would fail, even though Jerusalem lay in ruins and the whole country was open to invasion and conquest. Instead the land of the enemy will be reduced to *a waste and a desolation* (1-9). Edom's unholy glee over Israel's desolation by the Babylonians will change to grief. Thus the wicked design to *devour* what once was the *two nations* of Judah and Israel would end in dismal failure (10-15).—Edom, already denounced in 25:12-14, is not only the epitome of hostility to the ancient people of God but also typifies every evil counsel and will which He must hinder and break if His kingdom is to come. (Cf. Ps 137:7 note)

35:2 *Mount Seir.* Though mentioned by name only once in this ch., Edom is immediately identified by the mountain range which traverses its territory south of the Dead Sea.

35:10 *The Lord was there.* For a time it seemed that God had abandoned the Holy Land, when He let the Babylonians desecrate and denude it. Yet it was to remain the land of deliverance and hope. For in it the promises of mankind's freedom from spiritual tyranny would begin to be fulfilled. When "the inheritance of the house of Israel" (15) no longer would have geographic boundaries and Jerusalem would be the spiritual mother of the redeemed from all nations, it would be said: "The Lord is there." (48:35; cf. Gl 4:26)

36:1-15 In order to implement His plan of mankind's redemption, seemingly halted by the exile, God will reserve and preserve the Promised Land for Israel's return from captivity, repopulate it, and shower blessings on it. He makes these promises very dramatic by addressing them directly to *the mountains of Israel.* With a solemn oath (7) He assures them that their fate will be different from that of "Mount Seir," destined to become "a perpetual desolation" (35:1, 9). For He is *against the . . . nations and against all Edom,* which thought to give His *land to themselves as a possession with wholehearted joy and utter contempt* (5). In His *jealous wrath* He will turn the tables on the greedy, malicious predator. When His *people Israel . . . will soon come home,* the Holy Land will again *be their inheritance.*

36:2 ff. *Because . . . therefore.* The unbreakable sequence of cause and effect in God's direction of history is highlighted by a fivefold reiteration of the divine *because-therefore.* (3, 4, 5, 6, 7)

36:5 *Jealousy.* For the meaning of this emotion as applied to God see Dt 4:24 note.

36:8 *Soon.* In God's measure of time "the day is at hand" even though decades were to elapse before the exile was to end. (Ro 13:12; Hab 2:3; 1 Ptr 4:7; Rv 1:3; 22:10)

36:12 *Bereave them.* The ravages of "sword . . . famine, and . . . pestilence," inflicted on Israel as punishment, devoured young and old. (6:11)

36:16-38 Israel could not save itself and return to its homeland. Enslaved in a foreign country, it was about to lose its national identity. However, the exile was no accident of history. God designed it and brought it about because the people *had defiled* the land *with their conduct and their deeds,* for which He *poured out* His *wrath* on them. He made them *go out of His land* even though their defeat and humiliation prompted *the nations, wherever they came,* to profane His *holy name.* The victors attributed Israel's disgrace to the Lord's inability to protect His people and to make them His instruments of worldwide blessings (16-21; cf. Nm 14:15 f.). Such heathen blasphemy was to stop because it defeated the purpose for which God called Israel. By intervening in the course of history and bringing Israel back from extinction, He would through them vindicate *the holiness of* His *name* so that *the nations will know that* He is *the Lord.* (22-24).

But if the exiles were to be worthy bearers of God's promises, He must not only give them back their homeland but also provide cleansing of their *uncleannesses* and give them *a new heart* and *a new spirit.* So spiritually equipped and empowered, they will respond to His goodness by walking in His *statutes* and observing His *ordinances.* The sincerity of their repentance and changed attitude will manifest itself as they *loathe* themselves for their past *iniquities* and their *abominable deeds* (25-32; 6:9; 20:43 note). The restoration of the land from *desolation* to well-populated cities and the inner transformation of the chastened people will so impress *the nations that are left round about* that they will acknowledge that it was the Lord who made it all come to pass. (33-38)

36:22 *Holy name.* God's name is a capsule-word for everything He is and has revealed about Himself (Ex 6:3 note; Ps 8:1 note). Its essential characteristic is "holiness," i.e., transcendence above all limited human concepts, definitions, and comprehension. If, as He says here, His prime motive in rescuing Israel from exile is "concern for" His holy name (21), none of His fallen, rebellious creatures should presume to dictate to Him that His first consideration in saving them should be love and compassion (cf. ch. 20). Moreover, through His prophet Ezekiel He reveals that, when acting *for the sake of* His *holy name,* He is constrained also to play the part of the Good Shepherd who graciously condescends to "seek the lost," "bind up the crippled," and "strengthen the weak" if they are to be saved (34:11-16). It is not accidental that Jesus instructed His followers to let their first petition be: "Hallowed be Thy name," followed by two requests to vindicate His name—by letting His kingdom come and by executing His will. (Cf. also Ps 115:1)

36:26 *A new heart . . . a new spirit.* For these spiritual blessings of the new covenant see Jer 31:31 note, 33 note, 34 note.

36:35 *The garden of Eden.* A return to the luxuriant fertility and undisturbed tranquility of paradise will become a reality in the spiritual bliss and peace of the promised kingdom of God. (Is 2:2 note; 2:4 note; 35:1-10 note; 55:13)

37:1-14 After deflating the pride and self-conceit of his hearers (ch. 36), Ezekiel had to overcome their reluctance to accept the Gospel of restoration, a reluctance stemming from the opposite end of the spectrum of human emotions. Because the heart of the exiles too was "deceitful . . . and desperately corrupt" (Jer 17:9), they did not greet the glorious promise of redemption with jubilation but with the doleful lament of despair: "Our hope is lost; we are clean cut off" (11). However, the Good Shepherd does not hesitate to seek out also the sheep which have strayed into the desolate country of sullen doubt and bleak hopelessness. He granted Ezekiel a vision which was to convince his hearers that their despair grew out of their refusal to believe in a Creator who "calls into existence the things that do not exist" (Ro 4:17; Dt 32:39; Ps 33:9). True, humanly speaking, Israel's hopes for survival appeared dead and buried in the exile. Prospects of national revival were as unlikely as it was to expect a vast array of skeletons, dried and dismembered, to come to life again. Yet at God's command, spoken by His prophet, death must surrender its victims. The bones, arranged according to their former function and position, are covered with sinews and flesh. Finally, "breath came into them," enabling them to function as living beings.

This vision was to remind the exiles that He who promised to revive their dead nation was the same God who "formed man of dust from the ground and breathed into his nostrils the breath of life" (Gn 2:7). They were to remember that He who promised: "I will . . . raise you from your graves" (12) had, through His prophets, demonstrated His power to force death to give up its victims. (1 K 17:17-24; 2 K 4:18-37)

The revelation of God's power to raise the dead sends beams of light into the future beyond Israel's rescue from death in the Babylonian graveyard. A revived Israel is but the earthly clay which He will use to call into being a Spirit-filled people of all nations, once "dead through the trespasses and sins" but made "alive to God in Christ Jesus" (Eph 2:1; Ro 6:11). Finally He who is "the resurrection and the life" will awake those who "sleep in the dust of the earth, . . . some to everlasting life, and some to shame and everlasting contempt" (Jn 11:25; Dn 12:2; cf. Jn 5:25-29). For other Old Testament glimpses of unending life with God see Jb 19:25 note; Ps 49:19 note; 73:24 note; Is 26:19 note.

37:1 *The hand of the Lord.* For the same kind of supernatural influence on Ezekiel see 1:3 note.

The Spirit. The same Hebrew word denotes "breath" (5, 6, 8, 9, 10) and "winds." (9)

The valley. Apparently the same "plain" (RSV note) where the Lord appeared to Ezekiel earlier in his ministry. (3:22)

37:15-28 Israel restored will serve to initiate the coming of God's kingdom. According to ch. 34 it will be unlike any earthly dominion in that there will not be a succession of rulers but only one Shepherd or King: God's "servant David." In the second part of ch. 37 another aspect of His uninterrupted, unending rule is delineated. It will be a universal sovereignty, claiming the allegiance of all nations the world over. He in whom this prophecy was fulfilled combined these two features of His Messianic reign when He spoke of the prospect of "one flock, one shepherd." (Jn 10:16; cf. Gl 3:26-29)

As Ezekiel in his early ministry was directed to dramatize the judgment about to overtake Israel (4:1 ff.; 5:1 ff.), so he also used a symbolic act to portray the promises of the Gospel. The instruments of instruction were two ordinary sticks of wood. The action was simple too. The name of *Judah,* as the southern part of Solomon's divided kingdom was called, was inscribed on the one rod; the other was made to represent *Joseph* or *Ephraim,* the name often given to the 10 tribes which seceded and constituted the Northern Kingdom. Then he enclosed the ends of the sticks in his fisted hand, giving them the appearance of having become a single rod. The pantomimed healing of this ancient political rupture was to visualize the *one nation,* God's cleansed and sanctified people of all races, and the *one king* who will *be their prince for ever,* ruling in accord with *an everlasting covenant* of *peace.* (Cf. Jer 33:14-26)

37:23 *Idols.* The "one king" will bestow on the "one nation" (22) such blessings as will enable His subjects to overcome the temptation to *defile themselves* with *backslidings* into the abominations of idolatry. (Cf. 36:17, 27)

37:24 *My servant David.* The Messianic King is so designated in 34:23.

37:26 *Covenant of peace.* For its purpose see 34:25 note.

37:27 *My dwelling place.* God will be present wherever and whenever His people worship Him "in spirit and truth." (Jn 4:19-26)

37:28 *My sanctuary.* Before Ezekiel elaborates on the homage and service rendered by the new covenant people to their Redeemer and King (chs. 40—48), he assures them in advance that no enemy will be able to silence their song of praise or to prevent the extension of the Kingdom.

38:1-23 Chs. 38 and 39 have a logical place in the sequence and arrangement of the Book of Ezekiel. It is their function to answer the question, provoked by the immediately preceding promise of unalloyed bliss: Will God's "servant David," the "one king" of "one nation," actually rule "for ever" and put into effect "an everlasting covenant" (37:22, 24-26), or will sinister forces combine to destroy His reign of peace?

In order to allay fears for all time, prophetic vision peers into ages to come and to the very end of time. Israel's restoration to its homeland again is the model of a projected worldwide redemption. The seven heathen nations denounced in chs. 25—32 did not prevent the rehabilitation of the Babylonian exiles in the Promised Land, where they *dwell securely* under God's protection. Proceeding from this point of fulfilled prophecy, Ezekiel envisions the era when Israel is no longer the name of a nation but the symbolic title of a spiritual fellowship open to all races and peoples. In these "latter days" (16) of the Messianic age, demonic attempts will indeed be made to destroy the kingdom of the Prince of peace, which is not of this world and therefore seems to be an easy prey of its enemies. But, says Ezekiel, it will come to pass even then that, when "the kings of the earth set themselves . . . against the Lord and his anointed," He will "dash them in pieces like a potter's vessel" (Ps 2). Their doom is sealed by the sevenfold: *Thus says the Lord God* (38:3, 10, 14, 17; 39:1, 17, 25; cf. 29:1-5 note). As the attack is to come in the remote future, so those who launch it are likewise described as hailing from the farthest borders of Israel's ancient world.

The ringleader of this confederacy of evil is *Gog of the land of Magog*. His name occurs nowhere else as the head of a foreign state. His base of operations must be inferred from the location of his allies: *Meshech and Tubal, Gomer* and *Beth-togarmah*. Mentioned in Gn 10:2 f. as descendants of Japheth, they represent peoples living in *the uttermost parts of the north* (15; 27:13 f.; 32:26). Allied with these attackers from the north are *Persia* in the east and *Cush and Put* (Egypt) in the south. The highly figurative presentation of the enemy, his attack and defeat, yields an assurance of a fact in human affairs which is not fanciful: God will protect His spiritual kingdom, the church, so that "the powers of death shall not prevail against it" (Mt 16:18). Gog appears also in the New Testament prophecy of Rev. 20. The setting is the same. His attack comes after the Messianic reign has been established, and his defeat is just as disastrous. This assurance of God's enduring kingdom of grace, carved in rich symbolism, has been literally fulfilled in the preservation of the holy Christian church.

A literalistic interpretation of such apocalyptic prophecies which identifies the foes with individual nations on the historical scene is not only highly speculative but also does violence to Biblical imagery. It usually posits an earthly reign of Christ, an assumption which runs counter to clear statements of Scripture.

38:4 *Turn you about.* God gives free reign to the "evil scheme" (10) and base human motives, but overrules them and makes them serve His purposes. So He used the lust for power of the Assyrians and the Babylonians. (Is 10:5; Hab 1:5 ff.; cf. also 2 Sm 24:1 note)

38:8 *The latter years.* For the meaning of this term, also found in the form "the latter days," see Is 2:2 note.

38:11 *Unwalled villages.* Gog expects little or no resistance in conquering and plundering cities which have no protective *bars or gates* (Zch 2:4). This feature of the prophecy looks beyond the physical defenses of restored Israel. Soon after the return from Babylon, Nehemiah enclosed Jerusalem with a wall. (Neh 1—7)

38:12 *The center of the earth.* Cf. 5:5 note.

38:13 *Sheba.* Mentioned as trading with Tyre (27:22). *Dedan* is associated with Edom (25:13). For the term *Tarshish* see 1 K 10:22 note.

38:16 *Vindicate my holiness.* Cf. 36:22 note.

38:17-23 The assault on Israel is no sneak attack. God knew about it before it was even conceived. His *servants the prophets* spoke about it *in former days*.

38:17 *Prophets . . . prophesied.* Though they did not mention Gog by name, they foretold the defeat of God's enemies who, like Gog, rise up against Him.

38:18 *On that day.* The judgment to be executed is described in the cosmic dimensions of the last "day of the Lord" as found in Is 24:18-20; 29:5-8; 66:15 ff.; Jl 2:30—3:16; Am 5:18-20; Zph 1:14-18; Zch 14:1-5.

38:21 *Every kind of terror.* The Hebrew text which reads: "I will call to a sword to all my mountains" (RSV note) need not be changed. The sword, together with pestilence and famine, is frequently mentioned as a divine implement of punishment. (5:1, 12, 17; 6:3; 11:8, etc.)

39:1-16 In accord with a Hebrew literary convention, the onslaught and defeat of Gog are repeated (1-6) in a brief summary of ch. 38 in order to dwell more at length on features previously mentioned more or less in passing. The point to be stressed now is what an easy prey the redeemed would have been had the Lord not acted for the sake of His *holy name* (7-8) and rescued them from a foe capable of destroying them. The army of Gog and the "many peoples with" him was indeed "a great host . . . like a cloud covering the land" (38:15 f.). Just how vast their numbers were is evident from these facts: (a) after their defeat their discarded weapons provided Israel with firewood for 7 years; (b) their corpses filled a valley; (c) an organized effort over a period of 7 months was necessary to search out and bury all the enemy dead. (9-16)

39:11 *Valley of the Travelers.* So named because it was the valley on the route of those who passed over from Israel to the territory *east of the* [*Dead*] *Sea*. Burial of *Gog and all his multitude* was to be made beyond the borders of the Holy Land.

Hamon-gog. Cf. RSV note. According to v. 16 a city called "Hamonah," i.e., a multitude, likewise derived its name from the mass burial in that area.

39:12 *Cleanse the land.* Unburied corpses made the land ceremonially unclean. (Dt 21:23; cf. Nm 9:6; 19:11; 35:33 f.)

39:17-24 A second thought from ch. 38 to be elaborated here is that in judgment God shows His "greatness" and "holiness" and so makes Himself known "in the eyes of many nations" (38:23). By the horrible outcome of their sinister plan, Gog and every likeminded enemy of the Lord are to know how futile it is to try to destroy His kingdom. Instead of dethroning Him they end up becoming a *sacrificial feast,* helplessly slaughtered like the animals offered on Israel's altars, their *flesh* eaten and their *blood* drunk by *the birds* and the *beasts of the field* (17-21). Judgment on *the nations* will contribute to His *glory* in this way also that they will *know that the house of Israel went into captivity* not because heathen gods were mightier than He (36:20) but because He *gave them into the hand of their adversaries* as punishment for *their uncleanness and their transgressions.* At the same time the exiles will be made to know that they do not deserve to be delivered from their captors.

39:17 *Sacrificial feast.* For the fate of God's enemies compared with the slaughter of sacrificial animals see Is 34:6 note.

39:18 *Bashan.* A trans-Jordan grazing area, known for producing herds of *fatlings.* (Nm 21:33 note)

39:20 *Horses and riders.* The best-equipped and mightiest *warriors* will not escape becoming the prey of the birds and the beasts, invited to the feast at the *table* set for them by the Lord.

39:25-29 Though Ezekiel foretold things in ages to come, the vindication of God's *holiness* (27) is not a utopian dream never to come true. It will begin *now*—in the deliverance from the Babylonian captivity. When He who *sent them into exile* will have *gathered them into their own land,* they *shall know* that they are again to be bearers of His promise to all peoples. Physical resettlement in their homeland will be followed by spiritual renewal when He pours out His *Spirit upon the house of Israel.* (Cf. 36:26 note)

39:26 *Forget.* A rendering of the Hebrew text which fits the context better is: "They shall bear their shame." For this recurring thought see 6:9; 16:61; 20:43; 36:31.

39:28 *Leave none.* Although some exiles did not want to return, God made it possible for all to do so.

40:1—48:35 The Visions of Restoration

In "visions of God" Ezekiel was enabled to see the fulfillment of what he proclaimed in chs. 33—39.

Restoration of the exiled Israelites to their homeland and their rehabilitation as a national unit, as miraculous as the return of the dead to life (37:1-14), is in turn the pledge of greater things to come in the Messianic age. God is again under way implementing His plan to have salvation arise "from the Jews" (Jn 4:22). In due time there will come that "one king" who will rule over "one nation," composed of peoples the world over (37:15-28). Demonic forces as vicious and powerful as Gog and his satanic allies will not overthrow His kingdom (chs. 38—39). The blessings which the subjects of God's "servant David" will enjoy are summed up in the prospect that He will mediate and establish "a covenant of peace" (34:23-28) which provides for a healing of relations with God, broken by the rebellion of sin.

No son or daughter of Adam need hide when they hear the voice of their Creator if by faith they accept and claim the atonement for their guilt, provided by the Prince of peace Himself. For He banishes fear and bestows "the peace . . . which passes all understanding" (Ph 4:7). Reconciled with God and declared a communion of saints, the former servants of sin and self bring to their Redeemer the sacrifices of praise and the offerings of a sanctified life. They need not worry that the supply of royal gifts will give out, for they flow from the throne of grace in streams which grow rather than diminish in abundance. Nor will there ever be a moment when the gracious, protecting presence of the Shepherd-King in His flock will be in doubt, for it will always be true that "the Lord is there." (34:23 f.; 48:35)

Because Ezekiel was to "declare all that" he saw in the vision to his immediate audience (40:4), he describes the coming covenant of peace in terms of the Old Covenant: its place and form of worship, the ordinances governing the religious and civic life, its locale in the Promised Land. The modern reader therefore must be aware that all that was provisional and temporary in the Old Covenant serves as a transparency, illuminating and tracing the abiding configuration of the New Covenant.

However, Ezekiel did not see a mirage without body or substance. We who live in the age which he foresaw rejoice to be the benefactors of his fulfilled prophetic vision: restoration to communion with God through "the offering of the body of Jesus Christ once for all" (Heb 10:10), our "worship in spirit and truth" (Jn 4:24) as "a living sacrifice" (Ro 12:1), our fellowship in the holy Christian church which will endure to the end of time. When St. John had a vision designed to give us a prophetic glimpse of what awaits us when on judgment day the kingdom of grace leaves everything transient behind and becomes the kingdom of glory, he was constrained to portray its perfect bliss in the very same shadowy figures of the Old Covenant we find in Ezekiel. (Rv 21:9—22:5)

40:1—46:24 RESTORATION OF FALLEN MANKIND TO FELLOWSHIP WITH THE HOLY GOD

1) 40:1—43:12 The Temple, Symbol of God's

Presence Among His People, Restored to His Favor

a. 40:1-5 Date and Circumstances of a Grand Vision

40:1 *The twenty-fifth year.* The vision was granted Ezekiel when the Jerusalem temple, destroyed for 14 years, seemed destined to remain a heap of ruins. As in previous instances, prophetic flight through time and space is made possible by *the hand of the Lord* (1-3 note).

40:2 *Like a city.* The *structure* which appeared before his mind's eye was of such a size and complexity as to resemble not a single unit but a series of buildings which make up an entire city. The vantage point from which he surveyed the imposing scene was *a very high mountain,* no doubt Mt. Zion. (Ps 48:2 note; Is 2:2 second note)

40:3 *A man.* An ethereal being, appearing in human form, was to be Ezekiel's companion on a tour of the site and its structures. Ezekiel is to "look," "hear," and "set" his "mind upon all that" he will be shown. The services of the angelic guide are mentioned seven times in ch. 40, twice in 41, once in 43, twice in 44 and 46, and four times in 47. The repeated references to him not only connect the diverse elements of the vision but also affirm that what Ezekiel heard and saw was not a delusion of his fevered imagination.

40:4 *Declare all.* Ezekiel's report *to the house of Israel* would reverse what they got to hear when, on a previous occasion, he "told the exiles all the things that the Lord had showed" him (11:25): the Lord's departure from Jerusalem and the burning of the city and the temple. (Chs. 8—11)

40:5 *A wall.* Upon closer look the "structure like a city" turned out to be *the temple area.* The wall surrounding it was not designed to protect but to isolate it from the profane world all around it. At this point the man with a *measuring reed* began to provide specific dimensions of the various structural elements. The profusion of figures which he compiled may make for wearisome reading, but the exact specifications of all parts should remind present-day saints that their worship too dare never be slovenly, disorderly, haphazard. Yet detailed as the measurements are, they are not complete enough to serve as an architect's blueprint. Such items as the height of the structure and the material to be used are not listed. Moreover, a builder's drawing is not necessary, for Ezekiel was introduced to an existing completed temple. Human masons and carpenters had not erected it. Some of the data were not transmitted correctly by the ancient copyists of the manuscripts. Yet the overall, distinctive feature of the plan is obvious. There is symmetry and balanced arrangement of all its parts, symbolizing the perfection required of a holy habitation of the Lord.

b. 40:6-27 Through the Outer Wall into the Outer Court

Another device to impress the worshiper that he is approaching the transcendent Lord is a series of "steps" leading to ever higher levels from "outside of the temple area" to the outer court (6), to an inner court (31), and finally to the temple itself (49). There were also steps rising to the top of the altar (43:17). "Going up" the first of these stairways, Ezekiel was led through a huge "gateway" in the eastern wall. As he walked across "the threshold," he saw "side rooms" on either side of the massive entrance. In these rectangular niches, separated from the passageway by barriers (perhaps low walls), the temple guards stood watch. Before emerging into the outer court, he passed through a "vestibule" with "jambs" or decorative pillars (6-16). Entering the outer court, he saw "thirty chambers" built onto the three walls (north, south, east). These rooms very likely were at the disposal of worshiping visitors to the temple. They faced a pavement which, though higher than the ground outside the gate, was lower than the surface of the inner court (17-19). On the north and the south side access could be gained to the court through gateways similar to the one Ezekiel had used. (20-27)

c. 40:28-47 The Inner Court and Its Furnishings

Continuing up a flight of 8 steps and through another gateway in a wall, Ezekiel stepped into an inner court. This entrance, directly opposite the one through the outer wall, was duplicated on the north and the south side (28-37). Within the inner court stood 12 tables needed for the preparation of the sacrifices (38-43). Along the north and the south wall he observed rooms reserved for the officiating priests (44-47). In the very center of this court stood an altar, described in 43:13-17.

40:46 *Sons of Zadok.* For their privileged status see 44:15-31.

d. 40:48-49 The Vestibule of the Temple

Climbing 10 more steps and passing between two pillars, Ezekiel arrived at an enclosure which served as a narthex to the temple proper. For the pillars in Solomon's temple see 1 K 7:15-22.

e. 41:1-4 The Nave and the Inner Room

The vestibule or "porch" (KJV) was the entrance to a walled area, containing "the nave" or holy place, and beyond it "the inner room" or "holy of holies." Only the heavenly guide went into the latter.

f. 41:5-15a Walls, Platform, Chambers

On the north, the south, and partly on the east side, the temple proper was surrounded by an outer paved platform and a double wall. From the paved area, entrances on the north and south side led to a space between the walls where Ezekiel found "side chambers" built above one another "in three stories." In each of these were 30 rooms or cells which were probably used for storage of equipment and provisions. Between the two walls there was also "a raised platform" or terrace (8). Its purpose is not indicated. Alongside it and the rows of chambers on the north and south side was a "breadth of twenty cubits" (10) which served as "temple yard" or passageway. To the west and abutting the outer wall of the temple complex was a structure simply called "the building." (12)

41:13-15a The measurements of the temple, all adding up to *a hundred cubits,* testify to its symmetrical perfection.

g. 41:15b-26 Ornamentation

The ornamental feature of the temple consisted of carved and engraved "cherubim and palm trees" (18). The only furnishing of the holy place mentioned was "something resembling an altar of wood," identified as "the table which is before the Lord" (22). Very likely it was to be set with "the bread of the Presence." (Ex 25:23 note)

41:18 *Two faces.* The cherubim which Ezekiel saw bearing up the glory of the Lord had four faces (1:10; 10:21). Perhaps only "the face of a man . . . and . . . of a young lion" came into Ezekiel's line of vision. The cherubim in the tabernacle and in Solomon's temple are not described as multi-faced. (Ex 25:18-22; 1 K 6:23 ff.)

h. 42:1-14 More Chambers

North and south of "the inner court" and still within the area enclosed by the wall separating it from "the outer court" were two series of "chambers" in addition to those mentioned in 41:5 ff. The one row of rooms faced inward to the temple yard. Here the priests were to "eat the most holy offerings" and store them (13). Separated by *a passage* (4) and built *in three stories,* the second row of chambers faced the outer court. In them the priests were to leave *the garments in which they minister* and *put on other garments* before mingling with the people. (14)

i. 42:15-20 Dimensions of the Temple Area

The overall dimensions of the entire temple area are as symmetrical as those of the temple proper. The totals are 500 cubits, compared with 100 cubits for the interior structure (41:13 ff.). The four sides form a perfect square. If the holy God is to take up residence in this place, it must be devoid of anything uneven, incomplete, incongruous, unharmonious. (Cf. Rv 21:15 f.)

j. 43:1-12 The Holiness of the Temple

The kind of sanctuary described in chs. 40—42 is deemed worthy of God's presence. Through "the gate facing east," through which Ezekiel was guided into the temple complex (40:5-19), he now saw "the glory of the God of Israel" enter and fill the temple. The invisible God appeared to him in a "vision" as He did when at "the river Chebar" He commissioned the prostrate son of man to be His prophet and when He came to abandon and "destroy the city" (chs. 1—2; 8—11). "Out of the temple" then came a voice "speaking to" Ezekiel, promising him that God would dwell in it forever (cf. 1:28 note). However, it must remain undefiled (6-9; cf. 1 K 6:13; 8:10-13, 27; Ps 99:5; 132:7; Jer 3:17; 17:12). No desecration was to touch any part of the entire temple area "upon the top of the mountain," for "the whole territory round about" was to be as inviolate as the "most holy place" (41:4). This was "the law of the temple" Ezekiel was to proclaim to "the house of Israel." (10-12)

43:7 *Harlotry and . . . dead bodies.* Two ways in which the temple, now lying in ruins, had forfeited God's presence and protection are cited: (a) the people were guilty of idolatry, often described as marital unfaithfulness (Is 54:5 f.; Jer 3:6 ff.; Hos 2:2 ff.; cf. also 2 K 23:6 f.); (b) kings contaminated the temple when they were buried too near to the holy precincts and when they erected secular structures "with only a wall" separating the profane from the holy. For ceremonial uncleanness resulting from contact with the dead see Lv 21:1; 22:4; Nm 5:2; 6:6; 9:10; 19:16.

2) 43:13—46:24 The Purpose of God's Restored and Abiding Presence: To Receive the Grateful Worship of the Redeemed Communion of Saints

Ezekiel's temple had some features in common with Solomon's building, and the services to be rendered in it resembled, in some respects, the ritual prescribed in the Mosaic legislation. Yet there were significant differences. They were not accidental, for they fit into an overall pattern like the pieces of a jigsaw puzzle.

First of all, there is no mention of the ark of the covenant, which played an indispensable part in the symbolism of Israel's worship. The lid of the ark, called the mercy seat, had to be sprinkled with animal blood to signify that no one should dare to approach the holy Presence without a propitiating sacrifice for his or her sin. Furthermore, as will become evident in 43:12—46:24, the function of a high priest, who alone was permitted to enter the holy of holies and to bring the mediating offer, will no longer be necessary. For the same reason there will no longer be a need to observe the Day of Atonement, the annual high festival when this sacrificial act was performed.

Ezekiel envisions worshipers who have been restored to God's favor. They have been reconciled to Him by that High Priest who "entered once for all into the Holy Place taking . . . his own blood, thus securing an eternal redemption" (Heb 9:12). The redeemed need not fear to come into God's presence, because He "imputes no iniquity" to them but rather "reckons righteousness" to them. (Ps 32:2; Ro 4:6-8)

However, this communion of saints still lives in a fallen world. Its members too succumb to temptations and lapse into unholy thoughts, words, and deeds. Therefore they daily bring a "sin offering" and a "guilt offering," confessing their wrongs to God and pleading for pardon and forgiveness (40:39; 42:13; 44:29; 46:20). But they also "enter his gates with thanksgiving and his courts with praise" (Ps 100:4). Everything they think, say, and do becomes "a living sacrifice, holy and acceptable to God." (Ro 12:1)

a. 43:13-17 The Dimensions of the Altar

Under the Old Covenant an altar was an absolute necessity. Mentioned in passing in 40:47, it is now described in characteristic detail. Its overall structural feature gives it the appearance of a symmetrical step-pyramid. The topmost level, where the sacrifice is burned, rises above the "base" by means of squares or blocks of graduated size. The officiating priests need "steps" (17) to reach a height far enough removed from the profane earth below.

43:15 *Altar hearth.* The Hebrew word, so translated here, is left in the transliterated form of "Ariel" in Is 29:11 (cf. second note there). For the significance of the *horns* of the altar see Ex 27:1 note; 21:12-14; 29:12; 1 K 1:50 note.

b. 43:18-27 Consecration of the Altar: Its Ordinances

If an altar built of earthly material, by sinful hands, was to serve its sacred purpose, the priest was to "cleanse . . . and make atonement for it" by dedication rites similar to those carried out in former days (Lv 8; 1 K 8:62-66). Only descendants of the high priest "Zadok" (19) were to minister at the altar. For the banishment from the high priestly office of Abiathar's family see 1 K 2:26 note.

43:19 *Levitical priests.* All priests were Levites but, as the next ch. makes clear, not all Levites were priests. For this differentiation see Dt 18:1 note.

43:27 *Burnt offerings and . . . peace offerings.* They symbolize the worshipers' unreserved gifts of gratitude to God and sacramental communion with Him who restored them to His favor.

Accept you. Outward rituals, carefully and minutely prescribed for Israel's sanctuary, symbolize what even now constitutes service pleasing to God. a heart totally dedicated in holy obedience to Him who rescued the worshiper from death and restored him to fellowship with his Creator.

c. 44:1-3 Closure of the East Gate

After the glory of the Lord entered the temple through this gate in the outer wall, Ezekiel found "it was shut" and was told that it was to "remain shut." This ordinance was to signify that only God Himself can open the way that leads to communion with Him. When rebellious sons and daughters of Adam arrogate to themselves the right to come into His presence, they insult and profane "the glory of the Lord" which "filled the temple." (4)

d. 44:4-8 The Ordinance Governing Admittance

The kind of worship acceptable to the reconciled Lord continues to be defined in the forms and regulations prescribed in the Old Covenant. As "foreigners, uncircumcised in heart and flesh," were to be excluded from the sanctuary in Jerusalem, so only those who by repentance, faith, and a sanctified life are entitled to membership in the communion of saints have any right to appear before the throne of God. (Cf. notes on Ps 15; 24; Jer 4:4)

e. 44:9-31 The Ordinance Governing Levites

With what holy awe reconciled sinners are to regard the privilege of worshiping the Lord is underscored by the prescription regulating those who perform sacred acts in the envisioned temple. In the first place, not all members of the tribe of Levi, Aaron's ancestor, are permitted to "come near . . . the things that are most sacred" (13). Those who earlier "went astray" and "ministered to . . . their idols" were permitted only to engage in menial tasks (9-14). Next, the faithful Levitical sons of Zadok (43:19 note), who perform priestly functions, must observe strict ceremonial regulations, many of which are found in the law of Moses (15-27). Finally, the distinctive character of their holy office was to be reflected also in the provisions for their livelihood. They were not to have permanent title to land, as did the other tribes, and were to sustain themselves on food offerings brought to the temple. (28-31)

44:10 *Far from me.* For evidence of idol worship in Israel's past see the reforms which King Josiah had to carry out (2 K 23:4 ff.). Those assuming leadership in such abominations "became a stumbling block . . . to the house of Israel," aggravating their guilt. (12)

44:18 *Sweat.* Priestly vestments were to be made of lightweight linen rather than of wool, which tends to make the wearer perspire. The resulting body odor would render him ceremonially unclean.

44:19 *Communicate holiness.* This translation of the Hebrew verb, more commonly rendered "hallow" or "keep holy" (as in v. 24), suggests that holiness could be transmitted by physical contact. The thought to be expressed seems rather to be that if the priests were to mingle with the people in their sacred vestments, it would tend to obliterate "the difference between the holy and the common" (23) which they were to teach the people. The latter would be led to lose respect for the holy office of the priesthood. (Cf. Hg 2:12 ff.)

44:28 *No inheritance.* The priests' office and their God were to constitute their inheritance. (Dt 18:1 f.; but see also Eze 48:8 ff.)

f. 45:1-12 The Holy District

In order to insure acceptable worship within the temple complex, the area immediately beyond and surrounding the outer walls must not be allowed to become the scene of disorderly operations. For that reason "a portion of the land" was to be set aside "as a holy district." It had the shape of a square which was divided into three parallel strips. In the center of the middle zone stood the sanctuary, and about it clustered the residential portion of the priests. The upper strip of the square was reserved for the Levites, while the lower and smaller one was to be occupied by "the city" and city land. On the sides of the sacred square were two rectangular territories which were assigned to the prince, the one extending westward to the Mediterranean Sea and the other eastward to the Jordan River. Worship was to go on without hindrance and hardships. Therefore the price was not to tolerate "violence and oppression" but promote "justice and righteousness."

g. 45:13-25 Offerings and Festivals

After providing the temple with a peaceful setting, ordinances were issued to regulate the worship services within the holy precincts. The people were to "give" an "offering to the prince," who in turn was to provide everything needed for the sacrifices (13-17). Next, three annual festivals were to be observed. The second of these is identified by name as "the passover"

(21). The other two are known in Mosaic legislation as New Year's Day (18-20) and the Feast of Tabernacles. (25)

45:15 *Make atonement for them.* Though reconciled to God and admitted into fellowship with Him, the redeemed community must plead guilty of committing sins and depend on God's mercy to cover them from His sight. (Dt 21:8; Ps 51; Is 44:22; Acts 3:19)

45:20 *Atonement for the temple.* "The difference between the holy and the common" (44:23) was to be marked by dedicatory rites which would make expiation for the profane nature of a building and render it a sacred dwelling place. (Cf. Lv 14:53)

h. 46:1-10 Ordinances Governing Sabbaths, New Moons, and Daily Offerings

In his capacity as head and representative of the restored people of God, the prince was to have special obligations and privileges when sacrifices were to be offered "on the sabbath day" and "on the day of the new moon." He was to provide various offerings also for these minor festivals (45:17). On these occasions he was to be permitted to pass through "the gate" leading into "the inner court" but was to stop "at the threshold" of the sanctuary, which only priests and Levites were allowed to enter. From this vantage point he was able to observe the priests bringing the specified offerings. Then the gate was to be closed during "the six working days" preceding the next sabbath. No reason is given for this procedure. Presumably it was to prevent unauthorized persons from entering the inner court when the prince was not standing guard in the gate. The people were to remain in the outer court. In order to keep the assembly orderly, those worshipers who entered "by the north gate" were to leave "by the south gate" and vice versa. On the six working days, when the prince did not represent the people, he too was to observe this ordinance.

i. 46:11-15 Additional Ordinances for Worship

They specify (a) the size of "the cereal offering" to supplement the animal sacrifices on "the feasts and the appointed seasons" (11); (b) the exception to the rule laid down in v. 1: the east gate is to be opened when the prince provides "a freewill offering," i.e., a voluntary gift not required by law (12); (c) the kind of daily offering to be brought "morning by morning." (13-15)

j. 46:16-18 Ordinance Governing the Prince's Land

Only his sons were to inherit gifts of real estate and hold them in perpetuity. "Servants" were to return such grants to the family estate in "the year of liberty" (cf. Lv 25:10; Jer 34:8-17). As the inheritance of the prince was not to be diminished in size, so it was not to be increased by dispossessing the people and acquiring their property in any kind of transaction. For the abuse of royal power by Ahab see 1 K 21.

46:16 *The prince.* Mentioned 8 times in this ch. and often in other chs. (44:3; 45:7, 17, 22; 48:21), this individual had an unusual but significant relationship to the restored community. He did not, in the first place, exercise royal functions of a civic or political nature. His main responsibility lay rather in promoting worship. Though not granted priestly status and the authority to offer sacrifices, he nevertheless personified the privilege of a reconciled people to commune with God as well as the obligation to bring Him continual sacrifices in an orderly, sanctified way. In this person, unique among the functionaries of the Old Covenant, we see embodied everything the spiritual Israel of the New Covenant may and should do to praise, extol, and glorify God for redemption from Satan's dominion and from the curse of sin.

k. 46:19-24 Facilities to Prepare Sacrifices

After Ezekiel learned about the kinds of sacrifices to be offered and the laws governing them, he finally was shown the "kitchens" (24) in which the offerings were to be cooked and baked by the priests and Levites. He had been led to the immediate vicinity of the first of these "holy chambers" when his angelic guide showed him the priests' chambers in the inner court (42:1-12), for the kitchens were located "at the extreme western end of them" (19). Facilities to be manned by Levites for the same purpose were provided in the 4 corners of the outer wall (21-24).

46:20 *Communicate holiness.* Cf. 44:19 note.

47:1—48:35 RESTORATION TO LIFE AND TO AN INHERITANCE MADE IMPERISHABLE AND UNFADING BECAUSE "THE LORD IS THERE"

1) 47:1-12 The River of Life

Originating in the temple, it flowed from its "south side" until it eventually emptied into the Dead Sea. In its course it grew in depth and width. Yet it was not fed by tributaries. This miraculously increasing supply of water irrigated and fructified ever-widening banks and turned them into a paradise of trees bearing "fresh fruit every month" (12). The river's purifying power was not impaired or neutralized by obnoxious elements. The Dead Sea, rightly so called because its salt kills vegetation and marine life, was able to sustain life when the river flowed into it, overcoming its deadly properties. However, nothing else can bring about this transformation. The "swamps and marshes," untouched by the river, "will not become fresh." (11)

47:1 *Water . . . from . . . the temple.* Water is the symbol of life-giving blessings flowing in the channels of divine grace (Ps 46:4; 65:9; Is 33:20 f.; 43:20; Jl 3:18). When, as here, it emanates from the temple where the reconciled God resides, it prefigures the restoration to life of those who were "dead in trespasses and sins" and are made alive again by Him who "died" and is "alive for evermore" and has the "keys of Death and Hades" (Eph 2:1-10; Cl 2:13-15; Rv 1:18; Jn 4:14; 7:37 f.). The flow of this water never stops. Beyond the grave "the river of the water of life" produces the fruits of eternal bliss. (Rv 22:1-5)

47:8 *Arabah.* Desert land including the area of

the Dead Sea and extending southward from it. (1 Sm 23:24 note)

47:10 *En-gedi and En-eglaim.* For their location see 1 Sm 23:29 note. *The Great Sea* is the Mediterranean.

2) 47:13-23 The Boundaries of the Land

Restored Israel will always have ready access to the temple and its life-giving communion with God. He has established the borders of the Promised Land, within which the liberated community will "dwell securely" (38:11), unhampered in their desire to worship their Redeemer and uncontaminated by foreign influence. The northern limits extended from the Mediterranean Sea near Tyre to the vicinity of "Damascus," once the capital of Syria. "The Jordan" and the "eastern" or Dead Sea formed the eastern border. The latter was also the point marking the southern extremity, which cut across westward to "the Brook of Egypt," a stream emptying into the Mediterranean (cf. Nm 34:3 note). "The Great Sea," i.e. the Mediterranean, was the western border.

As the next ch. will confirm, these borders are not realistic geographical lines of demarcation for an actual, physical homeland. The idealized Promised Land, which they define, is the prophetic symbol of a place in time in which the worship described in the previous chs. will be possible. The time is the era of the holy Christian church; the place is the redeemed, restored community of saints, gathered from every nation and race on earth.

47:13 *Joseph.* Because Levi's inheritance is in the temple area (45:5), the number 12 of the tribes is maintained by allotting a portion to Ephraim and Manasseh, the sons of Joseph blessed by Jacob. (Gn 48:15 ff.)

47:15 *Hethlon.* This place as well as others in this section remains unidentified. For *the entrance of Hamath* see 1 K 8:65 note.

47:18 *The land of Israel.* The land beyond the Jordan, where 2½ tribes had been located, was no longer to be a part of restored Israel.

47:21 *Divide . . . land.* How it was done is on record in the next ch.

47:22 *Aliens.* Peoples of heathen ancestry were to have an inheritance among the descendants of Abraham. (Lv 19:33 f.; Gl 3:7-9)

3) 48:1-29 Tribal Allotments

In these verses two aspects of restoration to God's favor are highlighted: (a) all the redeemed share alike in its privileges and obligations; (b) the blessings bestowed are a permanent possession. The 12 tribes of Israel and the land they receive for an inheritance foreshadow what is in store for all among whom God is pleased to dwell.

In the vision, tribal territories were assigned to the north as well as to the south of the zone from the Mediterranean Sea to the Jordan which was reserved for holy purposes and contained the temple and the city (45:1-7). Because this holy district was south of the line dividing Palestine into two equal parts, seven allocated areas were north of it and only five south of it. All of them were rectangular strips bounded by the borders established in 47:13-23. Immediately north of the sacred corridor was the territory of Judah, followed by areas assigned to Reuben, Ephraim, Manasseh, Naphtali, Asher, and Dan (1 7). Before listing the inheritances in the south, "the holy portion," the allotment for "the city," and the property of "the prince" are described once more (8-22). The first territory below this well-defined area was assigned to Benjamin. The portions of Simeon, Issachar, Zebulun, and Gad followed in that order. (23-29)

For geographic and topographic reasons such a schematic division of the land into parallel strips of equal width and length was an idealistic rather than a realistic program. It could not serve as a surveyor's blueprint for a physical occupation of the Promised Land such as followed its conquest by Joshua (Jos 14—21). As Ezekiel's temple was not built by human hands, so the land of inheritance did not need to be acquired by weapons of war. It is God's to give to a people restored to His favor. It is a prophetic assurance to all members of the holy Christian church that they share "in the inheritance of the saints in light." (Cl 1:12-14; Acts 20:32)

4) 48:30-35 The Gates of the City

As all the tribes receive a portion of land, so they all have access to the holy city—through 4 gates, each of which is assigned to 3 tribes. The city is not an earthly Jerusalem. Its name is: "The Lord is there." Revered and worshiped in His sanctuary, God's presence will also hallow the labors and lives of all redeemed, reconciled sinners. And He will always be "there" until in the "new Jerusalem, coming down out of heaven," "death shall be no more, neither . . . mourning nor crying nor pain." (Rv 21)

DANIEL

INTRODUCTION

Contents

The Book of Daniel provides two kinds of subject matter. In chs. 1—6 the author, writing in the third person, relates what happened to him and three companions at the court of Nebuchadnezzar and of Belshazzar, the last Babylonian regent, and during the reign of Cyrus, the first Persian king.

In chs. 7—12 Daniel, speaking in the first person, tells of visions he was granted. They are four in number. The first two appeared to him in the Babylonian period; the last two, after the Persian Empire was founded.

Form

Because the future was revealed to Daniel by means of visions and dreams, prophetic utterance is cast in the form of symbolic imagery. The animals which cross the pages of the book are not to be thought of as actual zoological specimens of a given era but as representing peoples, kings, and kingdoms. The huge statue, composed of various kinds of metals, will not appear at a point in time, but signifies a succession of earthly centers of power. Numbers, describing the beginning or the duration of envisioned action, are not to be computed mathematically but have figurative, nonnumerical significance. Prophecy cast in this form is called apocalyptic. It had numerous imitators among the writers of non-Biblical literature current in the intertestamental period. In the New Testament book "The Revelation to John" this type of predictive symbolism is a dominant characteristic.

In the Book of Daniel chs. 2—7 are not written in Hebrew but in the related language Aramaic. A fully satisfactory explanation of this phenomenon has not been discovered by Biblical scholars.

Author

The book claims to be the composition of a writer named Daniel, who was brought to Babylon by Nebuchadnezzar in 606/5 BC. Jesus quoted from it and said the words were spoken by "the prophet Daniel." (Mt 24:15)

In the face of these positive assertions, it is a widely held hypothesis that the book was written by an unknown person in the second century BC. The author wanted to encourage his contemporaries to remain faithful to the true religion as they suffered persecution by a king named Antiochus Epiphanes (175—163 BC). In order to achieve his purpose and at the same time avoid direct reference to the cruel regime, he resorted to a literary device. He presented past examples of heroic steadfastness as prophecy. Previous and contemporary events were put in the cryptic form of predictions of the future.

This negative view is supported by alleged internal and external evidence. The account of events, particularly those of the distant past, contains historical inaccuracies, it is said. The validity of some of these charges is challenged in the appended notes.

Argument in favor of a spurious authorship is advanced also on the grounds that the Book of Daniel was written so late that the Hebrew canon of prophetic books was already closed and it therefore had to be incorporated in the third and final collection of sacred Scripture, called the Writings. However, a different reason for its position in the Hebrew listing of books can be advanced. Daniel was not called to the prophetic office, as were previous and later spokesmen of divine truth. While he was granted the gift of prophecy, he was and remained a statesman and counselor of kings.

OUTLINE

I. 1:1—6:28 Daniel, Adviser and Official of Kings in Babylon
   - A. 1:1-21 Arrival in Babylon and Education at Nebuchadnezzar's Court
   - B. 2:1-49 Interpretation of Nebuchadnezzar's Dream
   - C. 3:1-30 Miraculous Rescue in a Test of Faith
   - D. 4:1-37 Nebuchadnezzar's Second Dream: A Futile Warning Against Pride
   - E. 5:1-31 Punishment for Wanton Sacrilege
   - F. 6:1-28 Daniel's Rescue from the Lions

II. 7:1—12:13 Daniel, the Seer of the Messianic Kingdom
   - A. 7:1-28 A Vision Revealing the Passing of Earthly, Transient Kingdoms and the Coming of the Heavenly, Eternal Kingdom of the Son of Man
   - B. 8:1-27 A Second Vision and Its Interpretation
   - C. 9:1-27 The Vision of Redemption by an Anointed One, a Prince
   - D. 10:1—12:13 The Vision of the Latter Days

1:1—6:28 DANIEL, ADVISER AND OFFICIAL OF KINGS IN BABYLON

1:1-21 Arrival in Babylon and Education at Nebuchadnezzar's Court

1:1-7 DANIEL AND THREE OTHER HOSTAGES SELECTED FOR SPECIAL TRAINING

1:1 *The third year.* Jeremiah reports this campaign as taking place in the fourth year of Nebuchadnezzar (Jer 25:1; 46:2). The apparent discrepancy is solved if it is noted that two systems of computing the length of a king's reign are involved. According to the Babylonian method, only the full initial calendar year (from new year to new year) was recorded as the king's first year whereas any part of his reign before his first new year's day in office was reckoned as his accession year. When the latter, as in Jeremiah, is counted as the first regnal year, a difference of one year results in the tabulation. (Cf. the Introduction of 1 and 2 Kings, "Chronology")

Besieged it. The presence of Nebuchadnezzar, who was pursuing the defeated Pharaoh Neco back to Egypt, and the threat of a siege were enough to induce Jehoiakim to capitulate. For the latter's wicked reign see 2 K 23:34—24:6; Jer 36:9-31.

1:2 *Vessels of the house of God.* For their desecration see ch. 5; for their return see Ez 1:7ff.

Shinar. Ancient name for Babylonia. (Cf. Gn 10:10; 11:2 note; Is 11:11 note)

1:4 *Chaldeans.* Chaldea was an earlier name for the southern part of Babylonia. Therefore *Chaldeans* came to be a synonymous designation for all Babylonians. In Daniel's day the term had also a restricted meaning, being applied to a group of Babylonians specially trained in their traditional lore: the wise men, enchanters, sorcerers, priests, astrologers. (2:2, 10; 4:7; 5:7; cf. Is 13:19 note; 47:1 note)

1:7 *Belteshazzar.* The Babylonian names given to the exiled youths replacing their Hebrew names were to signal the demand for total subservience to their captors. Daniel, meaning "God is my judge," was changed to "May [the god] Bel protect his life." Azariah ("Helped by the Lord") was called "Servant of Nebo," the god venerated also in *Nebu*chadnezzar's name. The meaning of the other two Babylonian names is not certain. All of them sought to encourage the youths to blend into their new environment even if it meant to surrender religious beliefs and convictions.

1:8-16 PERMISSION TO ABSTAIN FROM A DEFILING DIET SOUGHT AND GRANTED

1:8 *Defile himself.* Daniel had the courage to refuse to eat the *rich food* and to drink the *wine* which was brought to him from the king's table, because they were served after being consecrated by offerings to idols. Furthermore he had no assurance that the proper dietary rules had been observed, particularly in the preparation of the meat. (Cf. Gn 9:4 note; Lv 17:10-16)

1:16 *Vegetables.* Daniel was not to be disappointed in believing that God would let them thrive on simpler, ritually undefiled fare if they would but trust in Him.

1:17-21 PROMOTION TO ROYAL SERVICE AND HIGH HONOR

1:17 *Learning and skill.* In mastering Babylonian *letters and wisdom,* the youths learned also to distinguish between what was useful in this lore and what was heathen superstition practiced by "the magicians and enchanters." (20)

Visions and dreams. Daniel received a special endowment. He could interpret visions and dreams which God used to reveal what was to be. Because he had *understanding* in these matters, he was not misled by "lying dreams," told by "prophets who prophesy lies" (Jer 23:23-32). For Joseph's interpretation of Pharaoh's dreams see Gn 41.

1:21 *Continued.* This note is not intended to say that *the first year of King Cyrus* ended Daniel's services at the royal court but points out the unusual fact that he held high office not only during the reign of Nebuchadnezzar and his successors but also after the Persian king had replaced the Babylonian government with his own. For corroboration of Daniel's continued service in the Persian era see ch. 10.

2:1-49 Interpretation of Nebuchadnezzar's Dream

2:1-11 EXECUTION OF WISE MEN ORDERED FOR FAILURE TO DISCLOSE AND INTERPRET THE KING'S DREAM

2:1 *Second year.* Daniel's "understanding in all visions and dreams" (1:17) was soon to be put to a severe test. His and his friends' program of studies, which was "to be . . . for three years" (1:5), was barely completed when the king demanded to know what he had dreamed during a certain night of his second regnal year, which coincides with the third calendar year of Daniel's stay at the court. (Cf. 1:1 note)

Had dreams. The king's sleep was disturbed by the mysterious phenomenon called having dreams. One of them in particular had *troubled* him. For God's use of dreams as a means of revelation see Gn 20:3; 31:24; 40:9-19; 41:1-36.

2:4 *In Aramaic.* This phrase, placed in a footnote by RSV, alerts the reader that not only the immediately following response to the king by the Chaldeans but also speeches by others and the record of events from this point to the end of ch. 7 are not recorded in Hebrew but in Aramaic, a cognate Semitic language which had become the medium of international communication (2 K 18:26 note; Is 36:11). No satisfactory reason has been found to explain why this particular section of the book has not come down to us in Hebrew.

2:9 *Tell me the dream.* After awakening, the king apparently no longer was able "to know the dream" (3) and recall its contents. It is possible also that he was suspicious of the magical powers claimed by the enchanters and astrologers. If they really had superhuman skills, they would have to demonstrate them in a test in which he could verify the results.

2:12-16 DELAY OF EXECUTION SOUGHT AND GRANTED

2:14 *Prudence and discretion.* Exhibiting tact and proper decorum, Daniel was able to persuade the king's chief officer, who was to carry out the execution order, to appeal to the king "to appoint him a time" (16) for further reflection on the matter, noting, at the same time, that the "decree" was "severe." (15)

2:17-23 THE MYSTERY REVEALED TO DANIEL; HIS HYMN OF THANKSGIVING

2:18 *Seek mercy.* Whereas the Chaldeans despaired of getting help from their "gods" (11), Daniel and his friends did not hesitate to seek the gracious intervention of *the God of heaven.* They knew they could rely on Him to be attentive to their needs. They were convinced, too, that He had the power to come to their aid. For he created the heavenly bodies to which the astrologers falsely assigned providential direction of human destinies. For the use of the title *the God of heaven* to distinguish the Creator of heaven and earth from gods who were a delusion see Gn 24:7; Ez 1:2; 6:10; 7:12, 21; Neh 1:4; Ps 136:26 note; Jon 1:9.

2:20 *Blessed be.* Daniel did not forget "to return and give praise to God" (Lk 17:18) in a song of gratitude in which he drew on the psalms and hymnody of Scripture. For the meaning of *the name of God* see Ps 8:1 note; 113:1 note.

2:21 *Changes times and seasons.* The God of heaven is the Lord of history, who determines the sequence and duration of world events. (Acts 1:7; 1 Thess 5:1 ff.)

2:24-35 THE KING'S DREAM RECALLED

2:24 *Bring me in.* No doubt Daniel observed proper protocol to gain an audience with the king as he did when he "besought the king." (16; cf. Est 4:11)

2:27 *No wise men.* Daniel included himself among those whose wisdom could not solve the mystery. He assigned credit for divulging the dream solely to "a God in heaven who reveals mysteries" (28). Joseph made a similar confession in Gn 41:16.

2:28 *In the latter days.* They begin with the "hereafter" of Nebuchadnezzar's time and include "what is to be" (29) in the future eon which completes God's eternal plan: the Messianic age extending to the end of all created things. (Cf. Gn 49:1 note; Is 2:2 note)

2:31 *A great image.* The same Hebrew noun is used to denote likenesses representing idols (Eze 7:20; 23:14, etc.). At times it connotes something as transient and unreal as "a shadow" or "phantoms" (Ps 39:6; 73:20 note). The image, though appearing to be *mighty and of exceeding brightness* so as to be *frightening,* is exposed at the very outset for what it really is. It symbolizes the monstrous attempts of puny creatures to be like God and, at the same time, reveals the lack of substance and permanence in every anti-God movement. As the image is composed of various parts of the human body, so the refusal to promote God's cause may express itself in different ways and at sundry times. Yet in reality every attempt to frustrate divine purposes is one and the same image of futility. All of them end "like . . . chaff" which "the wind" drives "away." (35; Ps 1:4)

2:34 *No human hand.* Man-made power structures, symbolized by the image, are not strong enough to escape being "broken in pieces" when *a stone* is released to descend on them from a source of power which is not of this world. When this force of superhuman origin *smote the image on its feet,* the whole colossus crumbled *in pieces* and disappeared from sight.

2:35 *The whole earth.* The force unleashed by the *stone* permeated and dominated the whole world to the exclusion of any rival power.

2:36 *We will tell.* Daniel may have wanted to give some credit to his three friends who joined him in prayer for divine enlightenment. (18)

Its interpretation. What "God has made known to the king" (45) by means of the dream is announced only in broad outline which is elaborated in Daniel's visions (chs. 7—12). Nevertheless, the meaning of some basic features of the dream becomes clear.

The four anatomical parts of the image, each of a different metal, represent successive kingdoms. The ruler of the first of these world powers is Nebuchadnezzar, "the head of gold" (38). His Babylonian empire will be followed by three others, each "inferior" in some way to its immediate predecessors.

Whatever it is that makes each successive regime of lower rank, the general trend of mundane history is not left obscure. It is obvious, in the first place, that the world does not move in recurring cycles drawn by chance circumstances or a blind fate. Each era is a well-defined segment of a straight line to a goal. Each has a predetermined allotment of time to fulfill its assigned purpose. In the second place, though kingdom follows kingdom, there is no upward progress to a golden age. Human society and cultures tend to deteriorate. The last of the four regimes, made of iron, may be able to "break and crush all these" which preceded it, but it cannot make a lasting contribution to a better world because it too is "brittle" as "miry clay." (40-43; cf. Mt 24:12)

2:43 *In marriage.* The combined ingenuity and effort of all races cannot achieve results which will *hold together.*

2:44 *Will set up a kingdom.* Though a fifth kingdom will arise at a point in time, it will be radically different from its metallic, materialistic predecessors: (1) It will not be another in a series of power structures put together by force of arms or skillful social engineering. (2) It will not be "of this world" because it exists independently of mundane resources such as gold, silver, bronze, iron (Jn 18:36). (3) It will not give way to another kingdom but *it shall stand for ever.* (4) It will overcome and *break in pieces* all opposition to it. (5) It will not share *its sovereignty* with a dynasty of rulers from *another people.* (6) It owes its existence to *the God of heaven,* whose "Let there be" created the very stage on which "the kings of the earth" (Ps 2:2) appear and act out their dramas in quickly alternating scenes.

In the days of those kings. This phrase specifying the time when God will set up an eternal kingdom is also a key to the identity of the three unnamed empires following the Babylonian era of Nebuchadnezzar. For when Jesus Christ revealed that He was the "stone . . . cut from a mountain by no human hand" (45), He spoke in the days of those earthly kings of iron and clay who reigned the world from Rome (Lk 20:21 ff.). It follows then that the silver and the bronze parts of the image represent the two intervening kingdoms: the Medo-Persian, which replaced the Babylonian regime, and the Alexandrine-Hellenistic, which succumbed to Roman imperialism a few decades before the King of kings proclaimed: "The kingdom of heaven is at hand." (Mt 4:17)

Bring . . . to an end. The kingdom set up by *the God of heaven* will be not only worldwide but also indestructible, inviolate, and eternal (35). Dominions and empires fashioned of such transitory stuff as gold, silver, bronze, and iron are subject to change and decay. Eventually there will come a time "in the latter days" (28) when the succession of mundane authorities will cease, for the earth itself and everything terrestrial will disintegrate and "be burned up." (2 Ptr 3:10; cf. Mt 24)

2:46-49 THE AFTERMATH: DANIEL'S PROMOTION

2:46 *Offering and incense.* Nebuchadnezzar recognized the working of supernatural power in Daniel's disclosure and interpretation of his dream. We are not told whether the latter permitted the king's servants to pay him the homage, normally reserved for the deity (3:5-7), or whether, like Peter and Paul, he objected to these gestures of deification (Acts 10:25 f.; 14:11-15). Perhaps he accepted them as a tribute to the "God in heaven who reveals mysteries" which neither he nor any wise man "can show" (27 f.) and who revealed Himself to the king through a chosen instrument.

2:47 *God of gods.* Nebuchadnezzar did not accept Daniel's God to the exclusion of other gods. Still granting the existence of a variety of divine beings, he was moved, however, to recognize a manifestation of power unequaled by the deities in his pantheon.

2:48 *Ruler . . . chief prefect.* His functions in these high offices are not specified except that they required his presence "at the king's court," where he could be consulted when his counsel was desired.

3:1-30 Miraculous Rescue in a Test of Faith

3:1-7 THE COMMAND TO WORSHIP AN IDOL

3:1 *Made an image.* For the meaning of the word "image" see 2:31 note. The incident recorded in this ch. assures those who refuse to have "other gods before" the God of heaven (Ex

20:3) that their trust in Him is not in vain. He can protect them when earthly kingdoms such as those envisioned in the previous ch. demand the kind of allegiance which relegates Him to a secondary place in their lives.

Of gold. The size of the image would preclude that it was of solid gold. No doubt it was gold-plated. So "the golden altar," mentioned in Ex 39:38; 40:5, was not made of the precious metal but, as Ex 37:25 f. states, was "overlaid" with gold.

Sixty cubits and . . . six cubits. If the dimensions are transmitted correctly by the copyists of the ancient manuscripts, the image was 90 feet high and 9 feet wide. There is no valid reason to doubt that a structure of such size could be erected. No doubt it rose, like an obelisk, from a tall base or elevation which was included in the figure of its overall height. It may have been surmounted by a statue of an idol, or the colossus as such was to represent deified imperial power. At all events, it was clear to Daniel's three associates that "to fall down and worship the golden image" (5) made them guilty of idolatry. The king himself equated its worship with serving his "gods." (14)

Dura. Because this word, meaning "an enclosing wall," was used to designate various places, the exact location of *the plain* has not been determined more closely.

3:3 *The officials.* Some designations of their office, such as *satraps,* are derived from Persian words. They were current already in the Babylonian administrative structure. It is also possible that Daniel, recording the incident during Cyrus' regime, listed Nebuchadnezzar's functionaries in terms of Persian officialdom.

3:5 *Every kind of music.* Some of the instruments, such as the *symphonia,* translated *bagpipe,* had Greek names. This is not surprising because music transcends cultural barriers down to modern times. Notations such as "allegro," "lento," etc., do not indicate the national derivation or the age of the score. Instruments from the Aegean world could have been imported for some time because Nebuchadnezzar had conscripted Greek mercenaries for his armed forces.

3:6 *A . . . furnace.* Fire as a means of execution was not unknown in Babylonia. (Jer 29:22)

3:8-23 DANIEL'S THREE FRIENDS SENTENCED TO DEATH FOR DISOBEDIENCE TO THE ROYAL PROCLAMATION

3:8 *Accused the Jews.* Perhaps the *Chaldeans* suggested this test of loyalty to Nebuchadnezzar because they were jealous of the Jewish foreigners "appointed over the affairs of the province" (12) and hoped they had found a scheme to eliminate them. For some reason they did not include the Jew Daniel in their plot. However, if he had been affected by the king's order there is no question what he would have done, as ch. 6 proves conclusively.

3:15 *If you are ready.* The king gave them another chance to obey, assuming that their noncompliance was not intentional.

3:16 *No need to answer.* The three men had no defense to offer *in this matter* which would move the king to exonerate them or make an exception in their case.

3:17 *Able to deliver.* They did not question God's ability to keep them alive in *the burning fiery furnace.* "But if" in His providence He should determine not to do so (18), they would let His will be done even though they did not understand why obedience to His command not to serve other gods should result in their death. (Cf. Jb 1:21 note; Ps 27:1-3; 118:6-9; Hab 3:17 f.)

3:19 *Seven times.* An idiomatic expression denoting intensity or an indeterminate but large number. (Cf. Lv 26:18; Jb 5:19; Pr 6:16; Mt 18:21 f.)

3:22 *Slew those men.* The executioners who threw the three men into the fire from the open top of the kilnlike furnace succumbed to the backlash of the flames.

3:24-25 MIRACULOUS PROTECTION IN THE FURNACE

3:24 *Astonished.* Nebuchadnezzar could peer into the furnace through an opening at the bottom.

3:25 *A son of the gods.* The king regarded the fourth person in the furnace as a being who, according to pagan lore, had divine as well as human parentage. Later he called the mysterious apparition an "angel" sent by "the God of Shadrach, Meshach, and Abednego." (28)

3:26-30 NEBUCHADNEZZAR'S TRIBUTE TO GOD; THE THREE MEN AND THEIR RETURN TO OFFICE

3:26 *The Most High God.* The king did not renounce polytheism (cf. 2:47). Yet he granted the three men the right to worship "their own God" (28), conceding that He deserved to be called *the Most High God.*

3:30 *Promoted.* In order to obviate a misunderstanding, the Hebrew verb would be better translated: "he promoted the welfare of" the three men whom he previously had advanced to high office. (Cf. 2:49)

4:1-37 Nebuchadnezzar's Second Dream: A Futile Warning Against Pride

In this ch. the story of how God punished the Babylonian king because he acted "in pride" (37) is told for the most part by Nebuchadnezzar himself. In a manifesto "to all peoples, nations, and languages" (1) he reports how he was cautioned against arrogance by a dream, interpreted for him by Daniel (1-27), and how he recovered from a degrading mental disease inflicted on him because he ignored the warning. An intervening section, written in the third person, tells how he gave way to brazen self-glorification and how the threatened retribution reduced him to the status of a brute beast. (28-33)

4:1-3 THE SALUTATION OF THE EDICT

4:2 *Signs and wonders.* Issued after the events took place which were to be made a matter of record, the proclamation began by praising *the Most High God,* whose "decree" (24) Daniel had made known to him. The king expressed himself in such glowing terms as to suggest his conversion to monotheism (cf. Ps 145:13). Yet the miracles did not persuade him to relinquish his "god" (8). He still held that "the spirit of the holy gods" enabled Daniel to interpret the dream. (9, 18; cf. 5:11, 14)

4:4-27 THE SUBJECT MATTER OF THE EDICT: THE KING'S DREAM AND ITS INTERPRETATION

4:5 *Afraid.* The king had a premonition that the dream foreboded nothing good.

4:7 *Could not make known.* For an earlier failure of their claim to wisdom see 2:10 f.

4:8 *At last.* Perhaps the king turned to Daniel as a last resort because he had hoped to get along without him and his Jewish God.

4:10 *A tree.* Not an ordinary tree but one of such dimensions as could grow only in "the fancies" of a dream (5). For a tree symbolizing boasted greatness destined to be brought low see Ps 37:35 f.; Eze 17:22-24; 31:3-18.

4:13 *A watcher.* Lit. "one awake," i.e., a being not in need of sleep and therefore called *a holy one,* one transcending human nature. The king thought that such "watchers" and "holy ones" carried out "the decree" and "the decision" of "the Most High." (17)

4:15 *Leave the stump.* The tree was not to be uprooted, so as to make regrowth possible.

4:16 *Seven times.* A period of time left unspecified in length except that the number *seven* symbolized a duration long enough to complete the envisioned events. So also in 23 and 25; cf. 3:19 note.

4:19 *Dismayed.* Daniel did not delight in telling Nebuchadnezzar that the dream, as he would interpret it, betokened evil which should befall his *enemies* rather than the king.

4:25 *Like an ox.* The king's overweening boast was to be deflated by a mental derangement which made him feel, act, and appear like an animal. Similar cases of this form of insanity, called lycanthropy or boanthropy, are on record in medical history

4:26 *Heaven.* This synonym for "the God of heaven" (2:18) occurs only here in the OT. In the NT it appears in the phrase "the kingdom of heaven" as an equivalent for "the kingdom of God." (Mt 3:2; 4:17, etc.; cf. also Mt 21:25; Lk 15:18)

4:27 *Break off your sins.* The king was to make a radical change in the administration of his royal office. Henceforth it was to be benevolent and just and no longer marred by *iniquities* if he wanted his *tranquillity* and peace of mind to continue. (Cf. Jon 3:10; Jer 18:7 ff.)

4:28-33 THE WARNING OF THE INTERPRETED DREAM IGNORED; ITS THREAT FULFILLED

4:30 *Great Babylon.* God will not be mocked by the mightiest of earthly potentates who claim independence from Him and assert their defiance of Him. He proved it long ago when He disrupted the building of the tower of Babel (Gn 11:1-9; cf. also Is 10:12 ff.; 47:7 ff.; Eze 28:2 ff.; 29:3 ff.). In the New Testament, Babylon is the epitome of rebellion against God. (Rv 14:8; 16:19; 18:2, 10, 21)

4:34-37 THE KING'S RESTORATION TO SANITY AND HIS PRAISE OF "THE MOST HIGH"

4:34 *Lifted my eyes.* Humans are endowed with *reason* and intelligence in order to acknowledge their Creator as the Giver and Sustainer of life and the Director of their destinies. When they refuse to acknowledge that everything on "earth" and in "heaven" happens "according to his will" (35), they sink to the level of "an ox" (33)

4:36 *Was added.* He no longer claimed *greatness* as his own achievement but as something bestowed on him.

4:37 *King of heaven.* Nebuchadnezzar exalted God's "dominion" and "kingdom" in language which gives the impression that he had been converted from his pagan religion. Yet he nowhere disavowed his polytheistic beliefs.

5:1-31 Punishment for Wanton Sacrilege

5:1-4 SACRED VESSELS DESECRATED AT A WILD BANQUET

5:1 *Belshazzar.* His name, not to be confused with Daniel's Babylonian name "Belteshazzar" (1:7), means "Bel [a national god], protect the king." Before more recent discovery of ancient records shed additional light on this period of history, some Biblical scholars denied the existence of a king by this name. They charged the Book of Daniel with creating a fictitious character for the purpose of teaching that God will not be mocked. While some features of Belshazzar's life and authority still need clarification, the known facts are not at variance with the role he plays in the ch. It can no longer be denied that he was the son of Nabonidus, the third and last successor of Nebuchadnezzar, to whom the father entrusted the kingship during the latter's prolonged absence. Before Nabonidus returned, Babylon fell into the hands of the Persians. Belshazzar lost not only the throne but also his life. The extra-Biblical sources do not specify what powers and functions were delegated to him. As a result, the title "king," applied to him here and elsewhere, is still regarded as unhistorical. By the same token, however, there is no evidence that the coregency did not invest the son with the governmental authority which the father would have exercised had he been present. He may not be called king in the official list of kings. However, it is not incongruous for Daniel to refer to him as "the Chaldean king" and to date the years of his reign (5:30; 8:1), for the coregent Belshazzar determined his destiny with the absolute power of a royal potentate.

5:3 *Vessels. Taken out of the temple . . . in*

Jerusalem by Nebuchadnezzar. (1:2; Jer 52:17-19)

5:5-9 FAILURE OF THE CHALDEANS TO GIVE MEANING TO ENIGMATIC WRITING INSCRIBED ON THE WALL BY A MYSTERIOUS HAND

5:6 *Alarmed him.* Because the hand doing the writing was not attached to a person, the king's frivolity gave way to panic. Inability to make sense of the words added to his fear.

5:7 *The third ruler.* The person who understood the meaning of the writing was to become one of three in a triumvirate of rulers, the chain of command being: Nabonidus, Belshazzar, and the new appointee.

5:10-16 DANIEL SUMMONED TO SOLVE THE RIDDLE

5:10 *The queen.* Because the king's wives were already present (3), the queen-mother must be meant. She could have been Nebuchadnezzar's widow and Belshazzar's grandmother. For influence exerted by dowager queens in ancient times see the role played by Bathsheba. (1 K 2:13 ff.; cf. also 1 K 15:13; 2 K 10:13; 24:15).

5:11 *Your father.* The words "father" and "son" often do not refer to a first-generation relationship. Strictly speaking, Belshazzar's father was Nabonidus. His grandfather or ancestor was Nebuchadnezzar.

5:17-28 DANIEL'S INTERPRETATION OF THE MYSTERIOUS WRITING

5:17 *Read the writing.* It consisted of three words, the first of which appeared twice, perhaps for euphonic reasons. All of them are passive participles of Aramaic verbs, meaning respectively to number, to weigh, to divide. The interpretation, supplied by Daniel, disclosed in what context the action of the verbs was to take place and who or what was to be affected by it.

MENE: "numbered"—the time allotted to Belshazzar's kingdom had run out.

TEKEL: "weighed"—in the scales of God's criteria the king was found lacking in acceptable qualities.

PERES: "divided"—the kingdom will not be allowed to remain intact but will be decimated and made a part of the domain of "the Medes and Persians." The plural form PARSIN which appeared in the writing may have had a double meaning since it could be read also as the word "Persians," the founders of the coming world power.

5:29-31 DANIEL REWARDED; BELSHAZZAR SLAIN

5:31 *Darius the Mede.* The Babylonian regime came to an end when Belshazzar "was slain" by the Persians, who unexpectedly gained entrance into Babylon by diverting the course of the Euphrates, normally flowing through the city from north to south. The person who *received the kingdom* bears a name which does not occur outside the Bible. Many Biblical scholars regard the title Darius the Mede as evidence of historical inaccuracy. The writer of the Book of Daniel, it is said, reflects the false notion that a Median kingdom preceded the Persian empire after the fall of Babylon. The rule of a Median king is out of the question because Cyrus, the Persian, dethroned the last Median king, Astyages, and placed Media under his sovereignty. It is also pointed out that a king by the name of Darius did not come to the throne until some 25 years later (Ez 4:5; Hg 1:1).

These and similar alleged errors are in turn used to undergird the assumption that the Book of Daniel was not written by a contemporary of the events recorded by him, but by an author who lived four centuries later and no longer knew the facts.

However, to conclude that a person is unhistorical merely because he has not been found mentioned in extra-Biblical sources available at a given time has proved to be a procedure fostering error. For a long time the name of Sargon was known only from Is 20:1 (cf. second note there). Belshazzar was regarded by some as a legendary figure until recent years. (Dn 5:1 note)

In the prevailing absence of information from secular records, positive attempts to identify Darius the Mede are therefore warranted. One proposed solution suggests the possibility that this puzzling name was the title conferred on a Median, otherwise called Gubaro, whom Cyrus appointed governor of Babylonia and entrusted with the authority to administrate the newly acquired kingdom. No explanation can be found why a Median official should be given the name of later Persian kings unless it were to symbolize his sovereignty to rule as the vicegerent of the new world-conqueror. For another suggested identification of Darius the Mede see 6:28 note.

6:1-28 Daniel's Rescue from the Lions

6:1-5 DANIEL'S PROMOTION TO HIGH OFFICE; HIS JEALOUS ASSOCIATES

6:1 *Darius.* For questions of his identity see notes on 5:31; 6:28; 9:1. According to Est 1:1 a later Persian king divided his far-flung territory into 127 districts. The jurisdictional territory assigned to each of the *hundred and twenty satraps* whom Darius appointed is not stated. It does not necessarily follow that every one was made the head of an administrative area of the emerging empire. However, a large corps of officials was necessary so that the king's interests "might suffer no loss." The chain of command proceeded from them to "three presidents" or chief ministers who, in turn, were answerable to the king.

6:5 *Any ground for complaint.* In the discharge of his office Daniel was not guilty of wrongdoing or malfeasance. If his fellow officers were to destroy him, they would have to *find* or trump up charges against him.

6:6-9 THE KING TRICKED INTO SIGNING AN ORDINANCE DESIGNED TO BRING ABOUT DANIEL'S DEATH

6:7 *All the presidents.* The conspirators evidently were lying because Daniel, one of the presidents, certainly was not consulted. It may also be assumed that not all the various officials they claimed to represent had agreed to the plot.

Petition. A prayer to a *god* or formal request to a *man.*

Den of lions. The Persians executed criminals by throwing them into a pit or a cavelike enclosure filled with lions. Apparently open at the top, it had a barred "mouth" or aperture at the bottom. (17)

6:8 *The law of the Medes and the Persians.* The legal code, which owed its origin to the unification of two national groups under one king, was in force from the very first year of Darius. It was the law of the land when Esther was brought to the Persian court. (Est 1:19; 8:8)

6:9 *Signed.* The corrupt politicians cajoled the king into issuing the ordinance because it flattered his ego. He had not intended to launch a religious persecution. When he later realized that compliance with the *interdict* required Daniel to compromise his faith, he "was much distressed" and even committed him to the God whom Daniel served, hoping that He would somehow "deliver" him. (14, 16)

6:10-18 DANIEL THROWN INTO THE LIONS' DEN FOR DISOBEDIENCE TO THE NEW LAW

6:10 *Daniel knew.* It was not senseless bravado that motivated Daniel to disobey *the document.* Nor did he invite martyrdom by making a public spectacle of himself. Yet though fully aware of the consequences, he prayed where and how and how often it was his custom to do so. The *upper chamber* was a latticed space on the house's roof (Ju 3:20; 1 K 17:19; Acts 9:37, 39). For the posture of kneeling see 1 K 8:54; for the direction he faced see 1 K 8:30; for "three times a day" see Ps 55:17.

6:17 *A stone. The mouth of the den,* closed by bars or a gate, was made tamper-proof. A stone was placed in front of it *that nothing might be changed* without breaking the *signet* with which it was *sealed.*

6:19-24 DANIEL'S FAITH IN GOD VINDICATED; THE CONSPIRATORS EXECUTED

6:20 *The living God.* After witnessing Daniel's miraculous deliverance, the king conceded that this maligned official's God was not a dead, impotent idol.

6:22 *Blameless.* If Daniel had "done . . . wrong" in disobeying the king, God would not have come to his aid.

6:23 *Taken up.* Hauled up through the open top of the den. Daniel's rescue from a horrible death proved that "nothing is too hard for" an almighty God (Jer 32:17). The experience of his three friends taught the same lesson. Both accounts must record actual life situations if they are to offer a basis of hope to others when they are tempted to doubt God's power and goodness. Those who have endured severe trials of faith are cheered to read of two instances when God did not forsake His own in dire extremities.

6:24 *Those men.* It need not be assumed that all the officials mentioned in v. 7 were *cast into the den of lions.* No doubt only those *who had accused Daniel* were executed. According to the law of the land, *their children and their wives* had to suffer the same fate.

6:25-28 THE KING'S TRIBUTE TO "THE GOD OF DANIEL"

6:26 *A decree.* The king did not revoke the ill-advised law but rendered it inoperative by an edict which superseded it. For praise of God in similar language see 4:37 note.

6:28 *Darius and . . . Cyrus.* The linking of these two names may be a clue to the identity of the elusive figure of Darius the Mede (cf. 5:31 note). The Hebrew connective, normally translated *and,* can also equate two items and place them in apposition to one another. If this usage is applicable here, *the reign of Cyrus the Persian* is an explanatory modifier of *the reign of Darius* and the latter would turn out to be none other than the well-known Cyrus. An exact parallel of the apposition rather than the additive meaning of the Hebrew "and" is found in 1 Ch 5:26. Here two names, joined by "and," refer to one and the same person. The translation interprets the connective particle as explanatory. "Pul king of Assyria" is not to be distinguished from "Tilgathpilneser king of Assyria" but must stand in apposition to the latter.

This idiomatic use of the Hebrew "and" to express identity is found also in a number of other passages in the Book of Daniel. Nouns, separated by "and" in the original, appear in translation as in apposition to one another (4:13, 23: "a watcher, a holy one"; 4:17 in the plural). In 4:19 "and" is replaced by "or"; in 1:3, by "both . . . and."

If Darius is indeed but another name for Cyrus, the explanatory title "the Mede" may call attention to the fact that the successor to the Babylonian empire had previously consolidated the Medes and the Persians into one kingdom and so gained the right to rule "according to the law of the Medes and the Persians" (6:8, 12). The modifier "the Mede" may also reflect the circumstance that his mother was the daughter of the king of Media whom he replaced as king of the Medes. "Darius," an old Persian name which his grandson also took, may have expressed his claim to royal ancestry. It may be in keeping with these considerations that the name "Darius the Mede" appears only in those chapters which record events during his first year (6:1; 9:1; 11:1), whereas later events are dated by the more familiar name Cyrus (10:1). For the puzzling statement that he was "the son of Ahasuerus, by birth a Mede," see 9:1 note.

7:1—12:13 DANIEL, THE SEER OF THE MESSIANIC KINGDOM

7:1-28 A Vision Revealing the Passing of Earthly, Transient Kingdoms and the Coming of the Heavenly, Eternal Kingdom of the Son of Man

This ch. constitutes a transition from the narrative part of the book (chs. 1—6) to a record of visions granted to Daniel (chs. 7—12). The first of these underscores and elaborates the revelation disclosed in Nebuchadnezzar's dream, which Daniel recalled and interpreted for the king (ch. 2). The four successive kingdoms (Babylonian, Medo-Persian, Greek-Hellenistic, Roman) symbolized there by different metal parts in a human image are now represented by four fierce animals which "came up out of the sea" (3). In both instances the transient dominion of rising and falling world empires gives way to the eternal, universal reign of God. In ch. 2 "a stone . . . cut out by no human hand" "broke . . . in pieces" the man-made structures and established a kingdom which "filled the whole earth" (2:34 f.). In ch. 7 "a son of man" appears to whom "was given dominion" unrestricted by the dimensions of time and space (13 f.).

Other features of the promised Messianic reign, not disclosed in ch. 2 but developed in ch. 7, are, on the one hand, the antagonism to it on the part of demonic forces and, on the other hand, the intimate relationship between the heavenly Ruler and the people of His kingdom, called "the saints of the Most High" (18, 22, 27). Though the latter are not divine and do not appear on the scene "with the clouds of heaven" (13), they are destined to "inherit the kingdom" and to "sit on thrones" exercising royal functions. (Mt 19:28; 25:34; Lk 22:28-30; Ro 8:17; 2 Ti 2:11 f.; Rv 3:21; 5:10; 20:4)

Ch. 7 complements ch. 2 also in this respect, that the reason for the demolition of the earthly kingdoms is made more explicit. They are inherently bestial in nature.

The basic interpretation of the vision, "made known to" Daniel (16 ff.), leaves several attendant circumstances undefined. In seeking their meaning, their symbolic character must be kept in mind. As the animals are not zoological specimens which will appear in future historical settings, but represent human rulers and dynasties, so their particular features have figurative rather than literal significance. The number four denotes comprehensiveness and universality (Eze 1:5 note). Other numerals likewise are not to be assigned their usual arithmetic value but are to be taken as descriptive symbols. Chronological data are no exception. Numerical specifications which they provide do not compute time in terms of months and years but conform to the pattern of visionary symbolism.

7:1-14 THE VISION AS DANIEL SAW IT

1) 7:1-12 Four Beasts, Coming Out of the Sea, Are Destroyed

7:1 *Belshazzar.* The visions contained in chs. 7—12 have the same historical setting and chronological sequence as the events in the narrative part of the book (chs. 1—6). Both sections record happenings which begin in the Babylonian period and continue into the time of the succeeding Medo-Persian empire. For the identity of Belshazzar see 5:1 note.

A dream. It is defined by an explanatory *and* as consisting of *visions* of which he became aware not by physical sight but by the mental perception of his *head.*

7:2 *The great sea.* When "its waters roar and foam," they represent the violent yet unsuccessful raging by hostile forces against "the Lord and his anointed." (Ps 2:2; 46:3; cf. also Is 17:12-14; Rv 13:1; 17:1, 15; 21:1)

The four winds. A storm coming simultaneously from all four directions is not a natural phenomenon. Daniel was to be impressed with the vehemence, the universal prevalence, and the singleness of purpose which characterize the rebellion against God by fallen, perverted mankind.

7:3 *Four great beasts.* They represent successive waves of concerted agitation against God. At the same time they typify the sum total of anti-God maneuverings to the end of time. It is hardly accidental that after the four beasts vanish from the scene no fifth demonic representative appears attempting to frustrate God's good and gracious will.

Out of the sea. The beasts spring into being full-grown. Though they are land animals, they are the product of the sea, stirred by tempest and tumult. Because of their this-worldly origin they are described also as arising "out of the earth" (17). Hence they are as different from "a son of man" coming "with the clouds of heaven" as the heaven is higher than the earth. (13)

7:4 *A lion.* Interpreted in v. 17, "these four great beasts are four kings" or kingdoms. *The first* of them corresponds to the head of gold in the image and represents Nebuchadnezzar and the Babylonian empire (2:38). It was only *like* a lion because, in addition to great strength, it had the speed provided by *eagles' wings.* Along the main street of Babylon Daniel saw statues of winged lions, designed to stand guard over the city. The combined features of the king of beasts and the king of birds appear in prophetic books of Scripture as figurative representations of Babylonia. (Jer 4:7; 50:17; Eze 17:3; Hab 1:8)

As I looked. What happened to the lion recalls the strange incident reported in 4:28 ff. Shorn of power and bereft of rationality for a time, Nebuchadnezzar received again *the mind of a man,* enabling him to function as a human being.

7:5 *Like a bear.* The second beast, corresponding to the "breast and arms of silver" in the image (2:32), symbolized the Medo-Persian empire.

Raised up on one side. This feature of the bear would seem to refer to the dual origin and composition of the empire founded by Cyrus and to assert Persian preeminence over the subjugated and absorbed Medes.

Three ribs. Several remnants of the devoured prey in the mouth of the beast attest to the inevitable fate of any animal (i.e., nation) tempting its voracious appetite.

7:6 *Like a leopard.* The third beast symbolized the Greek empire of Alexander the Great and his successors. Its figurative counterpart in the image was the "belly and thighs of bronze" (2:32). The leopardlike animal was equipped with *four wings* to carry it over the face of the earth with the speed of a bird. Its *four heads* betokened total, unrestricted supremacy when *dominion was given to it.*

7:7 *A fourth beast.* The Roman empire, envisioned here, is represented by the "feet . . . of iron and . . . clay" in the image (2:33) This creature was so *different from all the beasts* that no other animal could be named which has at least basic, comparable features. How *terrible and dreadful and exceedingly strong* this monster was became apparent as Daniel saw it appearing, from the very beginning, with an equipment of *ten horns.* This large number testified to its unusual strength. For horns as symbols of solidity and strength see Ps 75:10; 112:9; Lk 1:69.

7:8 *Another horn.* Out of the ten horns with which the beast emerged from the sea there appeared *a little one.* It grew so strong as to dislodge and replace as many as *three* of its companions.

Eyes . . . and a mouth. The little horn was different from the others in a most extraordinary way. It had human eyes and the ability to communicate with *a mouth speaking great things.* What it said is later described as "words against the Most High." (25)

7:9 *Thrones were placed.* Daniel was to see that a limit is set to the roaring of the sea and its beastly offsprings (Ps 104:5-9; Jer 5:22; Jb 41:1 note; Is 27:1). He beheld a heavenly courtroom equipped with thrones, emblems of royal authority. Proceedings were conducted by *one that was ancient of days.* God is so called here in order to assert that He exercised judicial authority long before the beasts appeared on the scene. His jurisdiction was unchallenged, for *his throne was fiery flames.* His verdict was carried out against all resistance, for "a stream of fire . . . came forth from before him." His domain was unlimited, for the throne had *wheels* of *burning fire,* capable of moving it wherever justice needed to be dispensed.

7:10 *Books were opened.* The Judge did not proceed arbitrarily or without the necessary evidence. He had access to a complete record of those arraigned before Him. (Rv 20:11-15)

7:11 *Slain . . . destroyed.* The trial over, sentence was carried out on the beast while the horn was still speaking *great words* of blasphemous boasting.

7:12 *Rest of the beasts. Their dominion* too was cut short although the influence of each extended *for a season and a time* into the succeeding era. However, when the fourth beast was judged, all demonic agitation came to a complete end. (Cf. 2:44 third note)

2) 7:13-14 The Son of Man, Coming with the Clouds of Heaven, Is Given an Everlasting Kingdom

7:13-14 *A son of man.* This designation of the new figure appearing in the vision is clarified by Him who said: "No one has ascended into heaven but he who descended from heaven, the Son of man" (Jn 3:13). Jesus' divine nature is prophetically proclaimed by features ascribed to the Son of man: (1) He did not "arise out of the earth" (17) but was seen coming *with the clouds of heaven* as He shall appear again "coming on the clouds of heaven" when a new heaven and a new earth will replace the sin-cursed world (Mt 24:30; 16:27 f.; 25:31; 1 Co 15:47-49; Rv 21:1; for the celestial conveyance in the OT reserved only for God see Ps 18:10-12; 97:2-4; 104:2-4; Is 19:1; Eze 1; Nah 1:3); (2) He *was given dominion and glory and kingdom* so unlimited in extent and so absolute in authority as to befit only Him in whom "all things were created, in heaven and on earth" (Cl 1:16); (3) His lordship will be acknowledged by *all peoples, nations, and languages* in obedience to the command: "You shall worship the Lord, your God, and him only shall you serve" (Mt 4:10; Dt 6:13); (4) In *an everlasting dominion* divine honor will be bestowed on Him who is "the Alpha and the Omega, the first and the last" (Rv 22:13; 21:6); (5) His kingdom is not merely a continuation of an earthly empire; yet He who embodies infinite power and incomprehensible glory appeared to Daniel not in a devastating burst of fire but *like a son of man.* For He who was born of Mary by the Holy Spirit was like us "in every respect," "yet without sin" (Heb 4:15), in order to be mankind's substitute.

The Ancient of Days. This divine title, occurring only here in Scripture, expresses the profound contrast between God's unchanging permanence and the instability of all human power structures. The mightiest kingdoms come and go, but His throne "is established from of old . . . from everlasting." (Ps 93:2; 90:2; Is 63:16)

7:15-27 THE VISION AS INTERPRETED TO DANIEL

1) 7:15-18 The Beasts Explained as Kings

7:16 *One . . . told me.* A celestial interpreter, no doubt chosen from the "ten thousand times ten thousand" who "stood before" the Ancient of Days (10), came to Daniel's aid. For a similar service rendered by an angel see Zch 4:1 ff.

7:17 *Four kings.* The power of the four beasts was exercised by a succession of men who assumed royal titles and prerogatives. They are here said to *arise out of the earth,* the mundane sphere of their activity. They are not independent from but subject to Him who came "with the clouds of heaven" (13). When v. 3 states that they "came up out of the sea," their hostility to the Most High is stressed. For the sea is the symbolic matrix of all who conspire and plot "against the Lord and his anointed." (Ps 2:1 f.)

7:18 *Saints of the Most High.* The Son of man was given "an everlasting dominion" (14) for the eternal benefit of His subjects. They are reckoned holy because by faith in His atoning sacrifice their sins are canceled. Moved by this undeserved gift of grace, they are intent on leading saintly lives. (Ps 16:3 note; 34:9 note; cf. Rv 8:3; 11:18; etc.)

2) 7:19-27 The Nature and Fate of the Fourth Beast

7:19 *To know the truth.* Because the fourth beast *was different from all the rest* in its hideous appearance and wanton ferocity, Daniel requested more information about it from his angelic interpreter.

7:21 *Made war.* The career and destiny of the fourth beast, summarized in this and the following verses, is described in greater detail in vv. 23-27. Partly bestial and partly human, it did not only look vicious. It used its demonic resources against "the saints of the Most High." While it *prevailed over them* to the extent that some of them became its victims, its reign of terror was permitted to last only "for a time, two times, and half a time" (25). Sentenced in the court of the Ancient of Days (9-11), it vanishes without leaving a trace. No successor is to arise to carry on its anti-God hostility. The vision therefore looks forward to the day, "fixed" by God, when "He will judge the world in righteousness by a man whom he has appointed" (Acts 17:31; Jn 5:22). The era beginning with the Roman empire was to be marked by persecution of the saints which would be so severe that if these days were not "shortened, no human being would be saved" (Mt 24:22). Diabolic perversion of the truth would "lead astray if possible, the elect" (Mk 13:22). St. Paul foretold the coming of "the man of lawlessness . . . who . . . takes his seat in the temple of God, proclaiming himself to be God" (2 Th 2:3 ff.). Opposition to the kingdom of the Son of man is called the spirit and work of the antichrist. (1 Jn 2:18, 22; 4:3; 2 Jn 7)

7:25 *Wear out the saints.* There is a very intimate relationship between them and the Son of man. Jesus Christ called them His brothers (Mt 25:40) and promised that they will "also sit on twelve thrones, judging the twelve tribes of Israel" (Mt 19:28). They are even members of His body (Ro 12:4 f.; 1 Co 10:16 f.; 12:12 f.; Cl 3:15). Yet they are not to be identified with Him. The beast is able to wear out the saints, whereas the Son of man receives an everlasting dominion without being *given into his hand.* The kingdom is His to bestow on "the people of the saints of the Most High" (27; Mt 25:34). The Son of man came from eternal heights "with the clouds of heaven" (13); they will rise from the grave, and those alive at His coming will "be caught up . . . in the clouds to meet the Lord in the air." (1 Th 4:16 f.)

Change the times and the law. Subvert everything basic to established order, resulting in confusion and anarchy.

A time, two times, and half a time. The horn will be allowed to do his satanic work for 3½ periods of time. It will be cut short before it reaches a total of four, the number symbolizing universality.

7:28 THE EFFECT OF THE VISION ON DANIEL

7:28 *Alarmed.* To see future developments on such a large scale was an unnerving experience for Daniel. The severe persecution of the saints may have caused him particular grief. (Cf. Jer 4:19; 8:18-22)

8:1-27 A Second Vision and Its Interpretation

To Daniel, the seer, God revealed additional features of two coming eras, symbolized in broad outline by the silver breast and bronze thighs of the image in ch. 2 and by the bear and the panther in ch. 7.

The first of these was the period of the Medo-Persian empire. Though irresistible in its day, it was shattered by Alexander the Great. His phenomenally rapid rise to power was cut short by his death at the age of 33 in 323 BC. The world he conquered came to be divided among his four generals. Palestine eventually became a part of the area subject to the successors of Seleucus, called the Seleucids. The eighth of these was Antiochus IV, surnamed Epiphanes, i.e. [god] manifest. (175—163 BC)

In an effort to consolidate his reign, he took drastic measures to hellenize or nationalize his subjects not only politically and socially but also religiously. The sacred writings of the Jews were banned. The temple in Jerusalem was profaned. A heathen altar was erected in its sacred precincts. Nonconformity was severely punished. Sacrifices, prescribed by Mosaic law, were forbidden. The high priestly office was desecrated. This pogrom produced casualties and defections in the ranks of the true believers. But it too would not succeed in obstructing the kingdom to be founded by the Son of man (ch. 7). Daniel was assured that this regime of evil "shall be broken" (8:25). This sad yet reassuring picture of coming events came to Daniel again by means of a vision.

8:1-14 THE VISION AS DANIEL SAW IT

1) 8:1-8 A Ram and a He-Goat

8:2 *In Susa.* One of the *capital* cities of the Persian empire, situated on or near *the river Ulai,* which emptied into the Persian Gulf. It is not necessary to assume that Daniel was at the scene in person. No doubt he was transported there on wings of the vision as "the Spirit lifted" Ezekiel and brought him "in visions of God to Jerusalem." (Eze 8:3 note; 40:1 f.)

8:3 *A ram.* As v. 20 explains, this animal represented the kings of Media and Persia. The smaller horn, Media, was surpassed by *the higher one,* Persia, which *came up last.*

8:4 *Charging.* The campaigns of conquest moved in all directions except into the wild, mysterious East.

8:5 *A he-goat.* It symbolized "the king of Greece" (21), known in history as Alexander the Great. He sped *across the face of the whole earth* with such speed as to make it appear that he moved *without touching the ground.* The spectacular achievements of the he-goat are indicated by the appearance of but a single *conspicuous horn between his eyes* rather than the usual two beside or above the eyes.

8:7 *Struck the ram.* Alexander *trampled upon* Persian resistance in 331 B.C.

8:8 *The great horn was broken.* When Alexander the Great died, his empire, extending to *the four winds of heaven,* was not overrun by hostile forces but was bequeathed intact to *four conspicuous horns,* growing out of his own regime, namely his four generals.

2) 8:4-14 An Evil Horn

8:9 *A little horn.* In ch. 7 the little horn developed out of the 10 horns of the fourth beast, the Roman empire (7:7 notes). Here it refers to Antiochus (cf. 8:1-27 introductory material), whose domain was to include *the glorious land* of Palestine.

8:10 *The host of heaven.* The horn assumes the grotesque proportions of a human monster. *The stars . . . cast down . . . and trampled upon* by it, represent the ludicrous heights of its rage against the Lord, *the Prince of the host* and "the Prince of princes" (11,25). It presumed to subvert the course of nature. According to v. 12, "the host" refers also to God's spiritual creation, His chosen people, whom it deprived of the right of worshiping the Creator.

8:12 *Through transgression.* The horn was the instrument of God's "indignation" (19) on His apostate people. The phrase can also be translated "in transgression." The meaning then is that in the place of rightful sacrifices iniquitous offerings were brought on the heathen altar erected in the temple by Antiochus Epiphanes.

8:13 *For how long . . . ?* This question arises whenever God permits the people of His kingdom *to be trampled under foot* by forces of evil. (Cf. Ps 6:3; 13:1 f.; 35:17; 74:10; etc.)

8:14 *Two thousand and three hundred.* Attempts to give this figure an arithmetic or literal meaning lead to no date in history which fits the events and circumstances described. It too is a symbolic feature of the vision. The total of 2,300 days falls short of making up seven years, the number denoting successful completion of an undertaking (4:16 note). Applied to the attempts to destroy God's "host," it proclaims that they will not be allowed to reach their goal but must fail before complete success is attained. For "the time of the end" has already been decreed. (17, 19)

8:15-26 THE VISION AS EXPLAINED BY GABRIEL

8:16 *Gabriel.* In order for Daniel "to understand" the vision (15), an angel is directed to be his interpreter by a *voice* to which only celestial beings respond. Yet it spoke in *a man's voice* so that Daniel too could understand what was said. Gabriel is one of two angels mentioned by name in the Old Testament, the other being Michael. (10:13; cf. Lk 1:11-20, 26-38; Rv 12:7)

8:19 *The latter end of the indignation.* As God's indignation, poured out over Israel in the Babylonian exile, came to an end after it achieved its purpose, so the chastisement under Antiochus Epiphanes has a firmly fixed termination. But God's decree, effecting cessation of evil, applies also to "the time of the end" (17) of all things. For Antiochus Epiphanes is the epitome and the type of hostility to God's kingdom which St. Paul saw as preceding "the coming of our Lord Jesus Christ" (2 Th 2:1 ff.; cf. Rv 13:1-10). These final onslaughts by demonic forces too will not achieve their objective but will "be broken" (25) at *the appointed time of the end.*

8:25 *No human hand.* The adjective *human,* though not a part of the Hebrew text, underscores the fact that the course of world history is not directed by kings and emperors but solely by the Lord. He may use human agents; they succeed or fail as He permits. (Cf. 2:34 note)

8:24 *The people of the saints.* Cf. 7:25 note.

8:26 *Seal up the vision.* Because the vision *pertains to many days hence,* Daniel was to see to it that it be preserved for use in the future. (Cf. Rv 22:10)

8:27 THE EFFECT OF THE VISION ON DANIEL

8:27 *Was overcome.* Cf. 7:28 note. Though Gabriel explained the general meaning of the vision, much of it would be understood only as the prophecy was fulfilled.

9:1—27 The Vision of Redemption by an Anointed One, a Prince

9:1-19 THE OCCASION FOR THE VISION

Daniel's third visionary experience came to him as he pondered "the word of the Lord to Jeremiah the prophet" concerning "the end of the desolations of Jerusalem." Very likely he had before him such passages as Jer 25:11 and 29:10. Though the Babylonians, who had destroyed the holy city, were no longer the dominant world power, Jerusalem still lay in ruins. (1-2)

Concerned lest the promise of Israel's restoration be delayed or even negated by impenitence, Daniel sought "by prayer and supplications with fasting and sackcloth and ashes" to move the Lord to "forgive," to "act," and to "delay not" (19). He freely admitted his own guilt while confessing the nation's abuse of God's grace. He had no excuse to offer for the wrongs done. They were willful rebellions against "commandments and ordinances" promulgated by the Lord and expounded over and over again by His "servants the prophets." Furthermore, "the calamity" of the exile had to come because God is "righteous." He could not fail to execute "the curse" which He pronounced against disobedience "in the law of Moses." The plea for deliverance therefore rested solely on God's "covenant" and "mercy." If He was to rescue the enslaved people, He had to act for His "own sake" and His own honor because Israel was identified with Him by His name. (3-19)

9:1 *Darius.* His identity is not clarified but made more mysterious by the appositional phrases *the son of Ahasuerus, by birth a Mede.*

If, as suggested in 5:31 note, Darius is the name of the official whom Cyrus made to rule in his stead over that part of the empire which constituted *the realm of the Chaldeans,* it must be assumed that he had Median ancestry. Extra-Biblical sources likewise shed no light on his claim to be the son of Ahasuerus. A Persian king by that name, identified as Xerxes, reigned much later (485-465 BC; cf. the Book of Esther and Ez 4:6). If, as suggested in 6:28 note, Darius is but another name for Cyrus, it may call attention to his rightful appropriation of an ancient dynastic title of royalty which later Persian kings adopted as a proper name. The added information that he was by birth a Mede could point to the fact that his mother was a Median princess.

9:11 *Curse.* For the dire consequences of breaking God's covenant *written in the law of Moses* see Lv 26:14-39; Dt 28:15-68.

9:14 *Kept ready.* Because God "watched over" the course of history, He had at hand *the calamity* which disobedient Israel deserved. (Jer 1:12; 31:28; 44:27)

9:18 *Great mercy.* Daniel relied on God's promise of the covenant to forgive the people's unfaithfulness if they "entreated the favor of the Lord . . . turning from . . . iniquities and giving heed to . . . truth" (13; cf. Ex 34:6 f.). For similar confessions of national guilt and pleas for pardon see 1 K 8:22-53; Ez 9:6-15; Neh 1:5-11.

9:20-23 THE VISIONARY APPEARANCE OF GABRIEL

While Daniel "was speaking and praying," the angel Gabriel appeared to him again (cf. 8:16 note). He had "a word" of divine revelation to transmit and to expound. The message came in the form of "a vision" because the things he was about to disclose exceeded the scope and the ability of natural sight.

9:21 *The man Gabriel.* The prophetic word that "went forth" from the Lord was made intelligible to Daniel when the angel, whose name in Hebrew means "Man of God," assumed visible form and spoke to him in a human language.

9:23 *Greatly beloved.* By "confessing . . . sin" and "presenting . . . supplication" on his own and his people's behalf he was accorded a special reward of grace: he was deemed worthy to act as God's highly desirable intermediary as he received and transmitted what he was to see and hear in *the vision.*

9:24-27 THE WORD OF THE LORD EXPOUNDED TO DANIEL

In this vision Daniel was given a prophetic glimpse of redemption as an accomplished fact. It envisioned not only Israel's deliverance from the Babylonian exile but also the rescue of all mankind from the bondage of sin and death. Beyond the rehabilitation of the chosen people and the rebuilding of the holy city there came into view the renewal of peaceful relations of all the rebellious sons and daughters of Adam with their Creator. Their restoration to a blessed fellowship with Him was to be brought about by "an anointed one, a prince." There was to be no doubt about it. Therefore "a word went forth" through Gabriel (23) to assure Daniel that God was shaping the course of history for the express purpose of ushering in and establishing the Messianic kingdom.

In the vision the fulfillment of this promise is not portrayed by an image composed of various metals (ch. 2) or by the successive appearance of strange beasts (chs. 7 and 8), but by the use of the number "seven," the sacred symbol of completeness and successful attainment of objectives. As God rested on the seventh day of the creation week because He had "finished his work," so the "seventy" sevens or "weeks" signify the certainty, to a multiplied degree, that He will not cease "from all his work" until the world's salvation is a created reality (Gn 2:2). It is as if God at the same time were sealing this promise with a tenfold oath, inasmuch as the literal meaning of the Hebrew verb to "swear" is to "seven."

The temptation to assign to this figure of "seventy weeks" an equivalence in terms of 490 years or their parts must be avoided for the same reason that the image and the beasts cannot be expected to appear in the future in those material or actual forms. To calculate a symbolical number as if it were meant to measure chronological years violates a basic principle of Biblical interpretation and makes of Scripture a collection of conundrums. The view taken in these notes does not regard the vision as offering a timetable of dated events but as a figurative and dramatic affirmation that, in spite of appearances to the contrary at Daniel's time, the Creator of heaven and earth and the Lord of history can be trusted to keep His promise to reconcile the world to Himself.

9:24 *Of years.* This phrase in the RSV translation is not a part of the Hebrew text but an interpretative addition to it. The *seventy weeks* or their parts are nowhere defined as consisting of years. *Weeks* or sevens symbolize the assured fact that God was about to do what He had promised, beginning with His decree *concerning* the *holy city* and the chosen *people.*

However, God would not carry out His plan of universal salvation at once or even in the immediate future. Therefore the seventy weeks are broken down, in vv. 25-27, into unequal stages or segments of "seven," "sixty-two," and "one" weeks. This division of the symbolical total gave assurance that the redemption of mankind would take place in a historical setting but not before two distinguishable eras had run their course. The first seven weeks were God's pledge "to restore and build Jerusalem." But the vision enabled Daniel to look beyond his immediate concern. The 62 weeks to follow affirmed that the rebuilt city would continue to function as Israel's religious center when the Messianic age was to begin. The final week would bring the consummation of all things which "are decreed" and preceded it: (1) the death of "an anointed one, a prince" *to atone for iniquity;* (2) the ratification of a covenant with abrogated sacrifices and offerings; (3) the destruction of rebuilt Jerusalem, no longer a holy city but filled with abominations.

Your people and your holy city. God would indeed reconstitute the chosen people in their homeland. However, Israel's revival from the grave of the Babylonian captivity was not an end in itself but another mighty act of God in implementing His plan to bring salvation to "the ends of the earth" (Is 52:10). This ultimate goal is announced in the remainder of the verse by means of six verbs in the infinitive form. The first three aim at eliminating the cause of man's enmity against God: *transgression . . . sin . . . iniquity;* the last three point to positive aspects of redemption.

While there may be a difference of opinion regarding the meaning of one or the other of these objectives, it is clear beyond doubt that they cannot be attained by a human being, himself helpless in the clutches of sin. Only "the precious blood of Christ, like that of a lamb without blemish or spot" could *atone for iniquity* and "put away sin" by the sacrifice of Himself (1 Ptr 1:19; Heb 9:26). *To bring in everlasting righteousness* into a world of people whose "righteous deeds are like a polluted garment" is a gift which only a divine Redeemer can bestow. (Is 64:6)

Vision and prophet. What "many prophets and kings desired to see . . . and did not see" was fulfilled and ratified in Jesus Christ. (Lk 10:24)

A most holy place. The word *place* does not occur in the Hebrew text, which reads "a holy of holies." In the OT "the holy of holies" frequently denoted the most sacred, inner part of the temple, where the Lord dwelled "enthroned upon the cherubim" and where the high priest was allowed to appear in His presence once a year (Ps 80:1; 99:1; Heb 9:7, 25). Jesus Christ, in whom "the whole fulness of deity" dwelt "bodily" as He tabernacled "among us," was anointed "with the Holy Spirit and with power" (Cl 2:9; Jn 1:14; Acts 10:38). The NT speaks also of sanctified believers as "God's temple" and "a dwelling place of God in the Spirit," "poured out even on the Gentiles" (1 Co 3:16 f.; Eph 2:22; Acts 10:45). Because the redeemed are the beneficiaries of all the other projected goals, it is not unreasonable to conclude that the founding of the holy Christian church is envisioned in this final objective.

9:25 *An anointed one.* A transliteration for the Hebrew word *anointed* is "Messiah." Jesus Christ combined in His person the royal (*prince*) and the priestly office. Holders of both offices were anointed in the Old Testament.

Troubled time. During the intertestamental period Jerusalem and the Jewish nation fell short of the prosperity and independence of an earlier day.

9:26 *Have nothing.* When the *anointed one* hung on the cross, He was forsaken even by His Father.

The people of the prince. The legion of the Roman Titus destroyed Jerusalem and the sanctuary in A.D. 70.

Its end. The *desolations* to be visited on Jerusalem will be as destructive as a raging flood, so that "there will not be left here one stone upon another" (Mt 24:2). Though there is no mention of an event which will terminate the last "week," the fall of Jerusalem dramatically heralded the permanent passing of everything necessary for a continuation of Old Covenant provisions. As Jesus predicted the destruction of the city, His gaze simultaneously moved beyond it to the end of all things at "the coming of the Son of man." (Mt 24:3-28)

9:27 *With many.* Those for whom the Messiah will fulfill and confirm what the Old Covenant foreshadowed will not be a select few but multitudes in the absolute sense of *many*, because He "bore the sin of many." (Is 53:11 f.).

Half. The word in Hebrew also has the meaning of midst or middle and is so translated in Ex 12; 2 Sm 10:4; Jer 17:11; Ex 12:29; etc. Within and during the final *week* everything was fulfilled that was required to abrogate the sacrifices and offerings of the OT foreshadowing ritual. That they were to cease was proclaimed when the curtain in the temple was torn from top to bottom at Jesus' death.

Upon the wing of abominations. This phrase supplies the reason why "the city and the sanctuary" will be destroyed. In Mt 4:5 the Greek word for *wing* denotes "the pinnacle of the temple." *One who makes desolate,* i.e., the Roman prince, will pour out *the decreed end* on the temple because it no longer was God's holy habitation but was filled to the brim with *abominations* so detestable as to provoke Him to righteous indignation.

The desolator. This translation declares that the *one who makes desolate* does not determine the course of history. He is God's instrument and will be discarded at the proper time. The Hebrew word may denote also those made desolate. The point then is that the catastrophe will not come to an end until it has produced complete annihilation.

10:1—12:13 The Vision of the Latter Days

The fourth and final vision resembles earlier revelations granted Daniel in that it enabled him to see "days yet to come" (10:14), both in the more immediate as well as the more remote future. Yet it also had features unique in divine disclosures.

No other prophecy deals at such length and in such detail with events which were to take place between two Gentile nations. Thirty verses (11:5-35) are devoted to describe the sordid drama of battles, intrigues, assassinations, cruelty, and duplicity which was to begin some 200 years after Daniel's time and to last for about a century and a half. From extra-Biblical sources we know that the antagonists were two generals of Alexander the Great and their descendants who, after his death in 323 BC, came to hold sway in Eygpt and Syria-Asia Minor respectively.

In the land of the Nile six kings bearing the

name of Ptolemy ruled that part of Alexander's former empire. Their rivals to the north were named either Seleucus or Antiochus. The vision does not identify them by their proper names but refers to them by the general designation of kings of "the south" and kings of "the north."

However, the events predicted in the vision were not intended to provide a preview of secular world history. They are mentioned because they were to affect the Israelite people, bearers of God's promise to redeem all nations. By its geographic location the Promised Land became the bone of contention and battleground of the kings of the south and of the north, as they sought to enlarge their territories at their rival's expense. Ground between the upper millstone (Syria) and the lower (Egypt), the covenant people were in danger of losing their national identity. In addition, a determined effort was made to eradicate the true religion. Persecution of the Lord's worshipers grew particularly severe under the Seleucid king Antiochus IV, also called Antiochus Epiphanes, who ruled from 175 to 163 BC (cf. 8:9 note). But what happened was no accident of history. In the vision, Daniel was given to understand that it was to be a time of testing and purification. The gold of faith was to be refined in the fires of affliction. By the same token, the course of world events would not get out of hand. "The time of the end" (11:35) for the reign of evil was appointed by the Creator of heaven and earth.

The assurance of divine control of history and the accompanying admonition to be faithful in trials were intended not only for the benefit of the people of the Old Covenant. These revealed truths are valid and useful at all times and especially during the tribulations preceding the final day of judgment. In 11:36-45 the light of the vision penetrates into that distant era. What was to happen two centuries after Daniel's day would in turn be prophetic of the end of time. Then the archenemy of God and His people, prefigured by Antiochus Epiphanes, would make a final, monstrous effort to wrest the kingdom from His son. The New Testament would have more to say about him, calling him "antichrist" and describing his insidious character. (1 Jn 2:18, 22; 4:3; 2 Jn 7; 2 Th 2:3 ff.)

Another unique feature of the vision is the appearance of an angelic "prince" doing battle with the demonic "prince of the kingdom of Persia." The latter is defeated with the help of "Michael, one of the chief princes" in the celestial world of spirits. (10:13, 20)

Finally it is to be noted that the account of this vision is unusually long. A whole ch. (10) is taken up with an introductory description of attending circumstances. Ch. 11, containing the prophetic message itself, is one of the longest in the book. It, in turn, is followed by an epilog occupying another ch. (12), the last in the book.

10:1—11:1 INTRODUCTORY DESCRIPTION

The final climactic vision was accorded Daniel "in the third year of Cyrus king of Persia" (536/5 BC), after the aged prophet had been observing penitential rites "for three weeks." At the time he was not in Babylon, situated on the Euphrates, but in a place near "the great river, that is, the Tigris" (1-4). The unsolicited appearance of an unnamed divine emissary so unnerved him that he fell "in a deep sleep" with his "face to the ground" (5-9). The prostrate figure recovered enough to be able to understand what he was to hear about "days yet to come" only after the celestial messenger touched him three times, assuring him on each occasion of the benevolent purpose of the visit. The first attempt to resuscitate Daniel set him "trembling on . . . hands and knees." When in this crouching position he heard himself called a "man greatly beloved" and chosen to hear what the angel was sent to tell him, he "stood up trembling" (10-14). He still faced "toward the ground" and remained dumb until "one in the likeness of the sons of men"—no doubt the angel—touched his lips. All he could say, however, was that he had neither the "strength" nor the "breath" necessary to talk with "my lord" (15-17). It was not until "one having the appearance of a man touched" him a third time, entreating him to "fear not," that he "was strengthened" enough to request the angel to speak the message intended for him. The heavenly speaker then assured him that he was about to receive reliable information, for it was "inscribed in the book of truth" even though it consisted of events which were to happen in the future. (18-21)

10:1 *The third year.* No reason is given why Daniel did not return to the Promised Land when Cyrus allowed his fellow exiles to do so in the first year of his reign (Ez 1:1 ff.; cf. Dn 1:21 note). The *word* of the Lord which came to him at this time was essentially a prediction of *a great conflict* which would engulf the people of God in Palestine a few centuries later and reach even greater intensity in the tribulations of "the latter days" (14) of the world's history. Daniel *understood* what was revealed to him in *the vision* even though at first he was bereft of his senses.

10:5 *In linen. A man* similarly clothed was seen by Ezekiel (9:2; cf. also Dn 12:6 f.). In the next verses his appearance is described as effulgent with the same celestial brilliance emanating from "the likeness of the glory of the Lord." (Eze 1:28; cf. also Rv 1:12 ff.)

God of Uphaz. Cf. Jer 10:9 second note.

10:7 *A great trembling.* The men accompanying Paul on the road to Damascus were similarly affected when "a light from heaven flashed about him." (Acts 9:3, 7; cf. also 2 K 6:17)

10:9 *Deep sleep.* Cf. 8:18.

10:11 *Greatly beloved.* Cf. 9:23 note.

10:13 *Prince of the kingdom of Persia.* His eyes opened to behold scenes ordinarily withheld from human sight, Daniel was afforded a glimpse into a world where evil forces such as "the prince of the power of the air" and "the ruler of this world" (Eph 2:2; 6:12; Jn 12:31) do battle with such spiritual powers as the "commander of the army of the Lord" (Jos 5:14;

cf. 23:10; Is 24:21; Rv 12:7). It is comforting to be told that the rise and fall of worldly empires is contested and fought by unseen armies before soldiers of flesh and blood are brought into the fray. The demonically inspired attempt to use the kingdom of Persia in order to thwart God's plan for His people ended in failure when *Michael* came to the help of the angel clothed in linen (cf. Jude 9). After the defeat of "the prince of Persia," the battle against "the prince of Greece" would have to be fought. (20)

I left him there. The Hebrew text, which reads: "I was left there" (RSV note), makes sense if interpreted to mean that the angel carried the day and, after dispersing the enemy, maintained his position of control over Persia.

10:14 *The latter days.* This term envisions eras of history extending into and through the Messianic age. (Cf. Is 2:2 note)

10:20 *Do you know?* Daniel was so bewildered that the angel made sure that the purpose of his coming, announced twice before (12, 14), was finally understood.

10:21 *Book of truth.* The events in "days yet to come" (14) were destined irrevocably to happen, because in divine perspective they were already a matter of written record (cf. Dt 32:34 f.; Ps 139:16; Ml 3:16). There is also a "book of life" bearing the names of the redeemed. (Dn 12:1; Ph 4:3; Rv 3:5)

11:1 *Strengthen him.* The antecedent of the *him* is Michael, mentioned in the last verse of the preceding ch. Before the "man clothed in linen" (10:5) drew the curtain from the future for Daniel, he added an incident in which he came to the assistance of Michael as the latter had come "to help" him (10:13). For the identity of *Darius the Mede* see 5:31 note; 6:28 note.

11:2-45 THE PROPHETIC MESSAGE

11:2-4 The Persian empire, flourishing in Daniel's time, was to give way to *the kingdom of Greece,* formed by the *mighty king* whom we know as Alexander the Great. This realm in turn was to be *divided . . . but not to his posterity,* i.e., his descendants.

11:2 *Three more kings . . . a fourth.* The fourth Persian ruler after Cyrus was Xerxes (485—465 BC), called Ahasuerus in the Book of Esther. Though others were to succeed him, his unsuccessful attempt to conquer *the kingdom of Greece* made him the symbol of the extent of Persian imperial expansion. An invasion of Europe by Persia failed. Instead "a mighty king" (3) from that continent would put an end to the empire once ruled by Cyrus and Xerxes. When Alexander the Great died in 323 BC and his vast domain came to be divided among his generals, the stage was set for the events described in 5-35.

11:5-20 Israel would suffer in the struggle for power which would develop between Alexander's successors in Egypt, known as the Ptolemies and here called the kings *of the south,* and those in Syria-Asia Minor, known as the Seleucids and here called the kings *of the north.*

11:5 *Strong . . . stronger.* Rivalry arose when a *prince* of Ptolemy I (323—285) established himself in Syria and ruled as Seleucus I (312—280 BC).

11:6 *An alliance.* The attempt *after some years* to foster peaceful relations by royal intermarriage failed. *The king of the south,* Ptolemy II (285—246), gave his daughter Berenice to *the king of the north,* Antiochus II (261—246 BC), who already had two sons by his wife Laodice. When the bartered bride's father died, she lost her status as queen to Laodice. The latter adopted ruthless measures in order to secure the throne for her son. She poisoned her errant husband and engineered the death of her rival and her child.

11:7 *From her roots.* Berenice's brother, Ptolemy III (246—221 BC) raided the land of the north though it boasted to be a *fortress.*

11:9 *The latter shall come.* In retaliation for the incursion into his territory, Seleucus II (246—226 BC) tried to invade Egypt but had to *return into his own land* without achieving success.

11:10 *His sons.* They were Seleucus III (226—223 BC) and Antiochus III (223—187 BC). The latter's conflicts with his counterpart in Egypt, Ptolemy IV (221—203 BC), are described in 11-19.

11:14 *Men of violence.* Apparently some of Daniel's *own people* thought they could somehow *fulfil the vision* of things prophesied by making common cause with Antiochus against Egypt.

11:16 *The glorious land.* Palestine.

11:17 *The daughter of women.* In order to incorporate Egypt in his realm, Antiochus III gave his daughter Cleopatra in marriage to Ptolemy V (203—181 BC).

11:18 *A commander.* A Roman official, Scipio, turned back Antiochus' encroachment on *the coastlands* of the Mediterranean, claimed by Rome.

11:20 *An exactor.* The successor of Antiochus III, Seleucus IV (187—175 BC), had to pay the Romans heavy tribute. In order to raise the money, he sent out a special tax collector who robbed the temple treasury.

11:21-35 The prolonged rivalry between the kings of the south and the kings of the north furnishes the backdrop for the "great conflict" (10:1) which was to plunge God's people into fiery trials. For the next Seleucid king, Antiochus IV (175—164 BC), would not only continue to subject them to the sufferings of warfare (25-30) but would also attempt to stamp out the worship of the Lord, the God of Israel. (31-35)

11:21 *Contemptible person.* Antiochus acted despicably from the very beginning. He usurped the throne *by flatteries* and intrigues from the rightful successor to *royal majesty.*

11:22 *The prince of the covenant.* In his rise to power the contemptible Antiochus did away with a high-placed individual with whom he had a treaty of peace. It may have been the high priest or some political rival. He engaged in the same kind of treachery in dealing with nations with whom he had "an alliance." (23)

11:25 *Stir up his power.* Antiochus launched a large-scale campaign *against the king of the south,* who at the time was Ptolemy VI (181—145 BC) The latter was *not* able to *stand* and repulse the invader because men in whom he had implicit trust undermined him with treason and *plots.*

11:27 *Speak lies.* Professing friendship and promotion of mutual interests, the two kings deceived one another even though it meant violating the sacrosanct trust of hospitality as they ate together *at the same table.* In spite of the appearance of a peaceful settlement, the conflict would continue because the divinely *appointed* time for its termination had not come.

11:28 *The holy covenant.* The land and the people set apart for a sacred purpose by God's election and His promised protection.

11:29 *He shall return.* A subsequent incursion by Antiochus *into the south,* which took place *at the time appointed* by God turned into a fiasco because of the intervention by the Romans.

11:30 *Kittim.* This proper name refers to the island of Cyprus, and it is so translated in Is 23:1, 12 (cf. Nm 24:24 note). Here it is used to denote the naval power exercised by Rome over the entire Mediterranean coast.

'Forsake the holy covenant. In his attempt to supress the true religion, recorded in the following verses, Antiochus ascertained the attitude of apostate Jews in order to be sure he could rely on them for support or at least for nonintervention.

11:33 *Shall fall.* Antiochus did not only promote idolatry but also put to death those who refused to "violate the covenant" (32) God made with Israel. The persecution would be allowed to go on *for some days* for the purpose stated in v. 35. An account of the atrocities committed by Antiochus is given in the apocryphal books called 1 and 2 Maccabees.

11:34 *A little help.* Relief from oppression came when the Maccabees revolted against Antiochus. Though the tvrant's power was broken and a period of comparative tranquility followed, lasting and complete redemption from the ravages of sin would not be effected by force of arms but by the vicarious suffering and death of the Son of God.

11:35 *The time of the end.* This phrase alerted Daniel to the fact that the vision from this point forward would no longer deal with the more immediate future of the Seleucid and Ptolemaic kings, culminating in the persecution by Antiochus Epiphanes, but would now turn its gaze to a "conflict" (10:1) to which God's people will be exposed at the very end of time.

11:36-45 The blasphemer of God and the persecutor of His people predicted in these verses is "the man of lawlessness . . . the son of perdition" whose coming is foretold in 2 Th 2:3 f. What Antiochus would do to destroy God's kingdom would in turn be prophetic of the raging of the Antichrist at "the time of the end" (35). His demonic character and tactics exceed what is known of Antiochus' person and deeds in the measure that the antitype is greater in fulfillment than its preliminary type. Yet this final archenemy too is on God's leash. For *he shall come to his end* at the divinely appointed time (45). The redemption in store for those whose names are "found written in the book" is described in 12:1-3.

11:36 *Above every god.* Though Antiochus claimed to embody divinity, as did other kings of the ancient world, he did not go the extent of "proclaiming himself to be God" (2 Th 2:4) but did in fact give "heed to the gods of his fathers." (37)

11:37 *Beloved by women.* This rendering of the Hebrew phrase seeks to identify the deity referred to with Tammuz (Eze 8:14 note). A more literal translation is: "the desire of women," i.e., the attraction men have for women. This "king" (36) of the end time would be devoid of normal human sensibilities.

11:38 *The god of fortresses.* Calloused to religious emotions, he would make the taking of fortresses and such warlike endeavors his idol, devoting himself to this "foreign god" with unprecedented fervor. (39)

11:40 *King of the south . . . king of the north.* The final onslaught on God's kingdom *at the time of the end* is depicted as a continuation of the battles between the Ptolemies and the Seleucids. The ravages inflicted by the Antichrist are symbolized by a successful invasion of Egypt via "the glorious land," i.e., Palestine (41). The allies of the aggressor are the enemies of ancient Israel: "Edom and Moab . . . the Ammonites" (41), while the satellites of Egypt are "the Libyans and the Ethiopians" (43). The southern allies are unable to ward off the looting of their "treasures" and "precious things." Yet having advanced with apparent impunity, the victor is forced by "tidings from the east and the north" to retreat through the Holy Land (44). How he is to "come to his end" is left a mystery except to state that it would be the result of a catastrophe "with none to help him." (45)

11:45 *Between the sea and the glorious holy mountain.* The destroyer's last campsite will be betwen the Mediterranean Sea and Jerusalem or Mt. Zion. Here, in the land of the people whom he will seek to destroy, the report of his career ends. The scene of the decisive battle at the end time between the forces of evil and good is laid in Jerusalem and its environs also in Eze 38—39; Jl 3:2, 12 ff.; Zch 14:2 ff.

12:1-13 CONTINUATION AND SEQUEL

In 1-4 the angelic visitor lets Daniel see the eventual outcome of the challenge to God's reign "at the time of the end" (11:40) which he has described in the closing verses of ch. 11. "At that time," specified three times in 12:1, all those who are fellow citizens with Daniel in spiritual Israel and those whose names are "written in the book" of life will be completely and permanently delivered from all evil, for they shall awake from the earth "to everlasting life." Those of them who "turn many to righteousness" will receive speical honor and reward. The wicked, on the other hand, will be condemned to suffer "shame and everlasting contempt." Because much time will elapse "until the time of the end," Daniel is to preserve the prophetic words in permanent written form.

The remainder of the ch. reports the answers given by "the man clothed in linen" to two inquiries regarding the time "till the end of these wonders" which were described in ch. 11. The question is asked first by one of "two others" of his angelic companions (cf. 12:6 note) and then is repeated by Daniel in a similar form. The replies do not give a mathematical computation of time but use numbers to symbolize that no matter how severe or long the predicted tribulation will be, the anti-God forces will not carry their evil designs to destroy the faithful to full and complete success. For Daniel in particular it is not important "to know times or seasons which the Father has fixed by his own authority" (Acts 1:7). He need only cling to the promise that if he faithfully goes his "way till the end" (13), he will be included in "a sabbath rest for the people of God" (Heb 4:9). "At the end of the days" he too will "stand" and inherit his "allotted place" in everlasting life.

12:1 *Michael.* The heavenly guardian and champion of the godly will carry out the command to deliver them at *a time of trouble* of unprecedented vehemence. (Cf. 8:16 note; 10:13 note)

12:2 *Many.* This adjective is descriptive rather than restrictive. There will indeed be many who will *sleep in the dust of the earth.* "All" of them, says Jesus, "will . . . come forth" (Jn 5:28 f.; cf. also Is 26:19; Ro 5:19)

12:4 *Run to and fro.* Frantic search for truth will end and *knowledge shall increase* only because reliable instruction will be found in *the book* which Daniel is to preserve so that it will be availabe *until the time of the end.*

12:6 *I said.* The Hebrew text which reads "he said" need not be changed (cf. RSV note). The two angels which became visible to Daniel at this point were not afforded access to the mysteries of God's revelation as was *the man clothed in linen.* There are indeed "things into which angels long to look" (1 Ptr 1:10-12). One of the two acted as the spokesman for both.

12:7 *His right . . . and his left hand.* In giving an oath usually only one hand was raised. The angel calls Him to witness to the truth of his words who said: "I live for ever." (Dt 32:40)

A time, two times, and half a time. For the meaning of this symbolic reference to time see 7:25, third note.

12:10 *Purify themselves.* The purpose of the tribulation, stated already 11:35, is repeated for emphasis. When the hour of trial comes, those being *refined* will need to be told more than once what the meaning of suffering is in their case.

12:11 *A thousand two hundred and ninety days.* The total number of days amounts to 3 years and 6½ months. Verse 12 adds 45 days to this sum, resulting in 3 years and 8 months. The symbolic significance of both figures is found in their failing to add up to 4 years, the number 4 signifying completeness and universality. So interpreted, they contain a truly comforting assurance. Afflictions and trials may seem to last an infinitely long time. But they never reach the point where they will "make a full end" of those who remain steadfast "till the end." (Jer 4:27; 5:18; Dn 12:13)

HOSEA

INTRODUCTION

According to the superscription (1:1) Hosea lived and worked during the brilliant and opulent reign of Jeroboam II (783—743 BC, 2 K 14:23-29), king of Israel (the northern kingdom); but as the dates of the kings of Judah in the superscription and the content of his book suggest, his ministry extended far into the hectic and catastrophic days after Jeroboam, when Israel was careening toward the fall of Samaria (her capital city) and the end of the northern kingdom in 721 BC (2 K 15:8—17:18). The Book of Kings diagnoses the disease of which Israel died with the words, "They went after false idols, and became false" (2 K 17:15). It was from this disease that the Lord, the Healer (7:1; 11:3; 14:4), strove to deal through His servant Hosea.

"They went after false idols." Hosea's words are one long and vehement protest against the apostasy of Israel. The people had deserted the Lord for Baal; or went "limping with two different opinions," as in the days of Elijah (1 K 18:21)—which was worse, since they could lull their conscience with the idea that they were still worshiping the Lord, though in a modified form, when they paid their devotions to the calves of Samaria (8:5; 10:5; 13:1-2) and baalized their worship of the Lord. The prophet wrote his indictment of his people's idolatrous harlotry and adultery with his own blood; he was called upon to enact in his own life, in his own marriage, the agony of the God of love at the infidelity of His people and to experience in his own heart the costliness of a love that forgives, seeks, chastises, and restores. (Chs. 1—3)

"And became false." The life falsified at its heart by idolatry became false in all its manifestations. Hosea indicts priest, prophet, and king for their total failure as guides and leaders of the people (4:4-5; 5:1-2). Lies, murder, adultery, theft, and robbery mark private life (4:1-2); public life is disfigured by anarchy, intrigue, and the killing of kings, politics without principle, and policy without consistent purpose. (7:3-11; 8:4, 7-10; 10:7; 12:1; 13:10-11)

"Therefore the Lord was very angry with Israel," the Book of Kings goes on (2 K 17:18); the Book of Hosea contains some of the most passionate denunciations and threats that the OT knows (e.g., 13:7-8, 15-16). But the distinctive note in Hosea is his portrayal of the God who loves when all possibility of loving has rightly ceased, the God who loves "again" (3:1), the injured Husband who forgives the unforgivable (chs. 1—3), the Father whose "heart recoils within" Him, whose "compassion grows warm and tender" (11:8) for the wayward child whom He led with cords of compassion in his youth (13:3-4), the Healer who hurts in order to restore with compassionate skill and with a love that does not die, simply because it is the love of God and not of man (7:1; 11:3; 14:4; cf. 5:13; 6:1). It is wholly natural that Jesus should answer those who objected to His divine Physician's love with a word from Hosea: "I desire mercy, and not sacrifice" (Mt 9:10-13; Hos 6:6). This love, which loves a world in satanic revolt and in love with the lie (Jn 3:16), will always be a scandal to the right-thinking people who want all moral accounts accurately balanced; it is this love, which Hosea proclaims, that makes a scandal of the cross on which Christ died for us "while we were enemies." (Ro 5:10)

1:2—2:1 HOSEA'S CHILDREN: JEZREEL, NOT PITIED, NOT MY PEOPLE

1:2—2:1 The marriage of Hosea takes place at God's command; not only his mind, heart, will, and word but his whole life, down to its most personal and private aspects, is to be in the service of the Word of the Lord; this is plenary inspiration indeed. His marriage mirrors the history of the unfaithful people of God (2); the names of his children are prophetic, declaring the consequences of Israel's apostasy: Israel's *kingdom* shall end; the *bow* of its military strength shall be broken (4-5); the Lord's *pity* and forgiveness for His people is at an end, as far as Israel is concerned—Judah's future is not yet cut off (6-7); the existence of Israel as God's *people* is at an end—the covenant is annulled (8-9). And yet, into this unrelieved darkness of a kingless, pitiless, nameless future a light does shine. In a future which is left completely undefined, there shall again be innumerable sons raised up for Abraham (10), a people called sons of a living God, a people united under one King and in a common worship; there shall be a day when God sows and there will be a great harvest, a day when names of doom shall be transformed into names of blessing. (2:1)

1:2 *Harlotry* is a key term in Hosea for Israel's infidelity to the Lord, the God of the covenant. It emphasizes the personal character of the bond which Israel is violating and the abhorrent form which the people's apostasy took, that of participation in the licentious fertility cult of Baal, in which sacral prostitution played a vital role (cf. 2:5; 3:3; 4:10, 12, 13, 14, 15, 18; 5:3; 9:1). Whether Gomer (3) was actually a harlot in the ordinary sense is not necessarily said. She was a wife of harlotry in that she, like the rest of her people, participated in the fertility rites of Baal worship; perhaps she submitted to some sort of bridal initiatory rite to insure fecundity for her coming marriage.

1:4-5 *Jezreel* is a border town in the territory of the tribe of Issachar (Jos 19:17-18), a royal residence of king Ahab. It was there that Noboth was killed, by the machinations of queen Jezebel, in order that his vineyard might be added to Ahab's palace gardens (1 K 21). The Word of the Lord by Elijah which predicted that the blood of Naboth would cry out from Jezreel for the blood of Ahab (1 K 21:19) was fulfilled when Jehu slew Joram (Ahab's son and successor) and Jezebel and cast their bodies on the blood-marked plot of ground in Jezreel; and it was to Jezreel that the basket containing the heads of Ahab's 70 sons, murdered at Jehu's request, was sent (2 K 9:1—10:11). God willed and commanded the end of Ahab's line, and Jehu was His chosen instrument (1 K 21:19; 2 K 9:1-10), but God did not will the massive brutality with which Jehu executed his commission. Jehu's house will be punished *for the blood of Jezreel.* It is the history of bloodshed that gives *Jezreel* its sinister tone here. The name itself has a more auspicious sound, for it means "God sows," and to this sense the prophet alludes in 1:11 and 2:22.

1:10 When the people of God, by their guilt, have destroyed every possibility of the fulfillment of God's promise, then the promise made to Abraham will be fulfilled: "I will multiply your descendants . . . as the sand which is on the seashore" (Gn 22:17; cf. 32:12). The pure gratuity of the promise, which Paul was to stress so strongly over against the merit of "works of the law," finds one of its strongest expressions here. Since the fulfillment of the promise is given to *Not my people,* to men who had forfeited utterly the right to the title *Sons of the living God,* Paul can apply this utterance of Hosea's to the inclusion of the Gentiles in the people of God. (Ro 9:25-26)

The word *(it shall be said)* of the *living God* will give the reunited people the gift which they had perversely sought from Baal: life.

1:11 The *one head* probably refers to the Messianic King of the people. Cf. 3:5, where it is said that the repentant people of God "shall return and seek the Lord their God, and David their king" (cf. Eze 34:23-24; 37:15-28). The term "king," which one might expect here, is probably avoided because the recent history of Israel had given kingship an evil connotation. (Cf. 1:4; 7:7; 8:4; 10:3, 7, 15; 13:10-11)

The words *they shall go up from the land* most probably refer to a common pilgrimage of the united people to the House of God in Jerusalem. At the time of the division of the kingdom, the first king of Israel (the northern kingdom), Jeroboam, had set up shrines at Bethel and Dan to rival Jerusalem, lest his "people go up to offer sacrifices in the house of the Lord at Jerusalem" and be weakened in their loyalty to himself. (1 K 12:25-33)

The greatness and wonder of the change produced by the redeeming grace of God is mirrored in the transformation which the word *Jezreel* undergoes: the ill-omened *blood of Jezreel* and the *valley of Jezreel* as the scene of God's judgment (1:4 5) are replaced by the *great . . . day of Jezreel* on which "God sows," that is, recreates His lost and doomed people. (Cf. 2:22-23)

2:1 *Say* is a plural imperative. The people are told to greet one another with the terms that express the end of God's judgment and the renewal of His grace; thus they express their newfound unity in a common confession in praise of the mercy of their God.

2:2-23 THE LORD AND HIS UNFAITHFUL SPOUSE: THROUGH JUDGMENT TO RESTORATION

2:2-23 Between the utter rejection of 1:2-9 and the *Yet* of 1:10 there lies an unanswered question: How can these things be? How can the doomed *children of harlotry* become *sons of the living God*? Ch. 2 answers that question, not in the sense that it "explains" the mystery of the triumph of God's love but in the sense that it shows how that inexplicably persistent love pursues its ends. Not one whit of the judgment is retracted; the adulterous wife who has played the harlot is to be rejected (2), degraded (3), *slain with thirst* (3), and *no pity* will be shown to the *children of harlotry* (4). But a series of three astonishing *therefore's* (6, 9, 14) makes clear that the judgment visited upon spouse and children is not the blind fury of an outraged man; God's judgment is disciplinary and restorative. God will block every way for the wayward wife except the way that leads her back to Him (6-8). He will take from her all the gifts in which she wantonly luxuriated and forgot the Giver (9-13). And then (here the picture of the wife and the literal reality of Israel's history merge), when Israel has returned to the beggary of her beginnings in the wilderness, He will begin her history anew; He will *allure her* with the blessings of the covenant in the wilderness and return her, now restored to the fidelity of her *youth,* to the fruitful land of promise and give her a future and a hope. (14-15)

The content of that hope is pictured in three passages, each beginning with *in that day* (16, 18, 21). God will make all things new; Israel will be given a new and faithful heart (16-17). God will make a new *covenant* and enter a new *betrothal* on that day and bind Israel with bonds of blessings: her life on the earth (*beasts of the field,* etc., 18), her life in history (*bow, sword, war,* 18), her life with her Lord (19-20)—all will be sound and secure; *she shall know the Lord* (20). The primal harmony between God and creation and between man and creation will be restored. When God and His people are at one, then all's right with the world. (21-23)

2:2 *Plead* (or "contend"). The children of Israel are to appeal to mother Israel; the individual members of the people are to call the people as a body to repentance.

2:3 *Strip her naked.* For public degradation as punishment for infidelity cf. Eze 16:37-39.

2:5 *Lovers,* the Baals (cf. 12-13), spoken of in the plural because the fertility god was worshiped at numerous shrines under many local variations of his name.

2:7 *Return* is the characteristic term for repentance. For the thought cf. Lk 15:17-19.

2:8-9 For *grain, wine,* and *oil* as typical blessings of the covenant cf. Dt 7:13; 11:14; 28:51. Her punishment is that she will lose the very things which she sought to obtain by her devotion to Baal.

2:14 For the *wilderness* days as a time of particular untroubled intimacy between the Lord and His people cf. Jer 2:2.

2:15 *And there,* literally "and from there," Israel's history will begin anew, and there will be a new entry into the land of promise with its pleasant *vineyards. The Valley of Achor* (the name means "trouble"), scene of Achan's crime and punishment (Jos 7, especially vv. 24 and 26), will no longer be a place with an ill-omened name but the entrance into a new land and a better day. (Cf. Is 65:10)

Answer, respond to the love of the Lord, cf. 16, 19, 20.

2:16 *Baal* is both a proper noun and a common noun meaning "lord" or "husband." Israel will no longer combine and confuse the worship of the Lord with the worship of Baal as she has done in the past.

2:18 Cf. Lv 26:6; Is 11:6-8; Eze 34:25, 28.

2:19-20 God will make a new beginning, a beginning so wholly new that the harlot and adulteress will be treated as a virgin bride *(betroth),* her sins forgiven and forgotten by the *mercy* of the Lord. He will give bridal gifts for her (cf. Gn 24:53), and these gifts all speak His covenant love and covenant fidelity towards undeserving Israel, the *righteousness, justice, steadfast love, mercy,* and *faithfulness* of God all take their color from the idea of the covenant—the *righteousness* and *justice* of God are His fidelity in maintaining the covenant which He has initiated—and all say: "I will be your God, and you shall be my people" (cf. 23) And all shall *know* the Lord, the God of covenant; in mind and heart and will they shall be one with Him. Cf. Mt 11:27, where Jesus describes His unique oneness with the Father, whom He loves and obeys, in the words: "No one *knows* the Father except the Son." For the whole passage, cf. Jer 31:31-33.

2:21-22 *Answer* has the sense of "respond willingly." When the people of God (*Jezreel,* God sows), planted by God in their land (23), look for *grain, wine, and oil,* the material blessings of the covenant (cf. 8-9), those blessings will be at hand, for the *earth* will supply them; the earth will be able to supply them, for the *heavens* will give their rain; and they will give their rain because the *Lord* commands a blessing.

3:1-5 HOSEA'S ADULTEROUS WIFE

3:1-5 The story of Hosea's marriage, symbolizing the Lord's relationship to his people, is told twice. In the first chapter it is told of Hosea in the third person, with the chief emphasis on the children of that ill-omened union. In the third chapter it is told briefly once more, by Hosea himself in the first person; the idea of deprivation and discipline with a view to the restoration of the adulterous wife, so richly developed in chapter two, is stated briefly once more (3); and what the symbolic action expressed is translated into the literal terms of Israel's history. (4-5)

3:1 *Cakes of raisins* were used as offerings in the cult of fertility goddesses. (Cf. Jer 7:18; 44:19)

3:2 Whether the payment, partly in money *(shekel)* and partly in kind *(barley),* is for the purchase of a slave or the payment of the bride-price, cannot be made out. The *homer* is a dry measure, perhaps about four bushels; the *lethech,* mentioned only here, is calculated at from 1.9 to 3.26 bushels.

3:3 *So will I also be to you,* that is, there will be no connubial intercourse. The prophet's love, like the Lord's, goes the way of harsh self-denial for the good of the spouse.

3:4 The Lord will take from His people all that contributed to their apostasy. Israel will be deprived of her national existence for a time *(without king or prince)* and will live without the legitimate forms of religion which priest and people have abused *(sacrifice, ephod)*. And, of course, the pagan institutions that have become part of Israel's religious life will be removed also *(pillar, teraphim)*. The meaning of *ephod* is not altogether clear; apparently it was a priestly garment (Ex 28:28-29), somehow associated with the obtaining of oracles which declared the will of God. The *pillar* (or *massebah*) is the sacred pillar found in Canaanite places of worship and in Israelite shrines corrupted by Canaanite influence; it is a sign of the presence of a deity. The Bible mentions such pillars in connection with other idolatrous cult objects (Ex 34:13; Lv 26:1; Dt 7:5; 12:3; 16:21-22; 1 K 14:23; 2 K 3:2; 17:10; 18:4; 23:14; Hos 10:1-2; Mi 5:13). The *teraphim*, occurring in close connection with *ephod*, are probably idol figures used as a means of divination. (Cf. Eze 21:21; Zch 10:2)

3:5 The people disciplined by the chastisement of God will be a penitent people; they will *return* and *come in fear* to the Lord. They will be a united people, under one head (cf. 1:11), namely *David their King*, the Messiah whom God in His *goodness* will give to His people *in the latter days* (cf. Jer 30:9). For the color of *latter days*, which designates God's ultimate future (the end of days), cf. Gn 49:1; Nm 24:14; Is 2:2; Jer 23:20; 30:24; 48:47; 49:39; Eze 38:16; Mi 4:1; Dn 10:14.

Note. Chs. 4—14 constitute one long commentary on the infidelity of Israel portrayed in chs. 1—3; the prophet denounces the concrete manifestations of that infidelity in the life of the nation, traces its history, and threatens unfaithful Israel with its consequences. Only at two points is the darkness relieved by the vision of a distant brighter day, in the unforgettable picture of God's love for Israel in ch. 11 and in the song of repentance and promise with which the book concludes, ch. 14.

4:1-19 WITH YOU IS MY CONTENTION, O PRIEST

4:1-19 The heart of the chapter seems to be the indictment of the priests (4-10). The opening verses (1-3) depict the prevalent universal corruption of the people of Israel; the covenant is being outrageously violated and the covenant God ignored. In 4-10 the responsibility for this corruption is laid at the door of the irreverent, neglectful, and greedy priesthood. And 11-19 picture the consequences of the neglect of the priests in the life of the people: drunkenness (11), magic and idolatry (12-13), sexual immorality (13-14), stubborn persistence in sin and apostasy (16-19). A demonic *spirit* (12) of apostasy possesses the people; they are swept on by a tempest (*wind*, 19) of idolatry. The accusations are followed by threats of punishment (5, 6, 7, 9, 10, 14, 19); and Judah, the southern kingdom, is warned not to follow in the apostate footsteps of Israel. (15)

4:1 *Controversy*. For similar indictments of the people pictured as a trial scene, in which God is Accuser and Judge, cf. Is 3:13-15; 5:3-7; Jer 2:4-13; Mi 6:1-8.

Faithfulness and *kindness* are the qualities needed to maintain the life of the covenant in which each person loves his neighbor as himself; the word rendered *kindness* denotes that sense of solidarity which grows out of the appreciation of the blessing of the covenant (God's "steadfast love," cf. 2:19) and meets the person-to-person obligations of the covenant by loving and loyal action. *Knowledge of God* is both knowledge and acknowledgement of Him, of His active grace and the claim which His grace makes on people. (Cf. 2:20; 4:6; 6:3, 6; 8:2; 13:4)

4:3 All creation is struck by humanity's sin (cf. Gn 3:17), just as it shares in the blessing of forgiveness and restoration (2:18, 21-22; cf. Ro 8:19-22).

4:4 *Let none accuse*. Put the blame where it belongs, on the priest.

4:5 As translated in the KJV, *stumble* means "fall, come to ruin," cf. 5:5; Is 31:3, but perhaps the verb should be in the present tense, to describe the erratic course, of no help to the people, pursued by *priest* and *prophet*.

I will destroy your mother. Obscure. Perhaps *mother* means the nation. Some scholars emend the text to read "You have destroyed your people," which makes good sense in the context.

4:6 *My people*. God is jealous for His own. (Cf. 1 Co 3:17)

Rejected knowledge. The failure of the priests is not due to pardonable ignorance but to deliberate suppression of known truth. For the true priest as instructor of the people, cf. Dt 33:10; Ml 2:6-7.

Forget your children. The hereditary priesthood will come to an end, like the kingship. (Cf. 1:4; 3:4)

4:7 *Their glory*, the honor of the priestly office.

4:8 *Feed on the sin of my people*, etc. They are greedy for the priest's portion of the sin offering, Lv 6:26; 7:7. Thus "religion" flourished while knowledge of the Lord and His law languished. (Cf. v. 6)

4:9 *Like people, like priests*. Both will be punished.

4:10 The curse of sin appears even in the sinning, not only in the subsequent punishment of it. Their greed remains unsatisfied, and the fertility rites which they practice *(play the harlot)* do not produce fertility.

4:11-19 The example of the priests has a ruinous effect on the people.

4:11 *Wine*. Alcoholic excess was a part of the fertility cult, as an expression of gratitude to the god or gods who gave the wine and to induce religious frenzy.

4:12 Divination by means of wooden rods replaces true knowledge. (6)

Spirit of harlotry. Sin is a personal power that possesses and inspires them.

4:13-14 *Brides*, daughters-in-law. God punishes their sin by giving sin free reign in their families; the license they want (in their participation in the fertility cults) becomes a license they do not want (in the ruin of their families and their people). Parents are hurt and shocked when their children become as delinquent as they. For the punishment of sin by sin cf. Ro 1:24, 26, 28. ("God gave them up.")

4:15 The example of *Israel* is to be a warning to *Judah. Gilgal,* near Jericho, is the site of an Israelite shrine (cf. 9:15; 12:11; Am 4:4; 5:5). *Beth-aven* ("house of iniquity") is a bitterly ironic reference to Bethel ("house of God"), another Israelite sanctuary. (Cf. 1 K 12:26-33; Am 5:5)

As the Lord lives. This is in itself a legitimate oath, but as it was used by Israelites who frequented Gilgal and Bethel (where worship of the Lord was abominably corrupted) it had become a mockery of the living God who will tolerate no other gods besides Him.

4:16 Israel is not only guilty but *stubborn* in her guilt; perhaps Hosea is alluding to his people's disregard of his warnings. Cf. 9:7, where he depicts Israel as calling the prophet a "fool and a madman." To such the Lord cannot manifest Himself as the Good Shepherd.

4:17 *Let him alone.* God delivers *Ephraim* (Israel) up to his sin as punishment for his sin. (Cf. vv. 10, 14)

4:18 *Their glory* is, apparently, the God of Israel; *their shame,* the wild excesses of their idolatrous worship.

4:19 Israel is caught and carried onward in her sin as if driven by a mighty *wind* or "spirit," as the same word is translated in 12; her infatuation with idolatrous worship *(altars)* can end only in shame.

5:1-7 THE GUILT OF THE GUARDIANS OF JUSTICE

5:1-7 The priests are again addressed (cf. 4:4), but now as part of a group to whom the administration of justice is entrusted (priesthood, elders of the community, and the royal court). Judgment, ordained to guarantee freedom, peace, and security to the members of the covenant people, has in their hands become the very opposite; the guardians of justice have become hunters of men who entrap *(snare, net, pit)* those whom they should guard and preserve. The God of judgment will punish them (1-2). There is no hope of escaping this punishment; the all-knowing and all-seeing God knows and sees the sin of Israel (3). Hope of escape by repentance *(return)* is cut off, for they are trapped in their sins by the *spirit of harlotry* which obsesses them; they are *proud* of the deeds (4, 5) that make them guilty—how shall they turn from them to God? Their flourishing "religious life" will not deliver them from judgment either; for they *seek the Lord* with offerings *(flocks and herds)* but not with their hearts, which have been *faithless* to the Lord. The Lord *has withdrawn* from them; and their religious observance *(new moon)*, apostate and idolatrous, will not save but destroy them. (6-7)

5:1 *House of Israel* probably here means the elders of the various communities in their capacity as administrators of justice. For judicial functions of elders, cf. Dt 19:12; 21:2-20; 22:15-18; 25:7-9.

5:1-2 The allusions to *Mizpah, Tabor,* and *Shittim* remain obscure. Perhaps these places had been scenes of signal perversions of justice.

5:3 *Ephraim* and *Israel* are used interchangeably as designations for the northern kingdom.

5:4 *Their deeds do not permit them.* Cf. 7:2 and Jn 3:19-20. Returning to God means coming to the light in which men's deeds are exposed for what they are, and man resists that exposure.

For *spirit of harlotry,* cf. 4:12; for *know not the Lord,* cf. 2:20; 4:1, 6; 6:6.

5:5 *Pride of Israel,* the cultural, political, and "religious" successes and attainments of which Israel was proud. (Cf. 7:10)

Judah will not heed the prophet's warning (4:15) and shall share Ephraim's fate. (Cf. v. 10)

5:7 *They have borne alien children.* Since they have broken the covenant *(dealt faithlessly)*, their children do not come under the blessings of the covenant; they are "Not my people," no longer "sons of the living God." (Cf. 1:9, 10)

5:8—6:6 THE WAR NOBODY WON: THE GUILT OF BOTH ISRAEL AND JUDAH

5:8—6:6 In this section Judah is mentioned, with a frequency unusual in Hosea (6 times in 14 verses), along with the northern kingdom. If we look for a historical situation during Hosea's time in which both Israel and Judah were guiltily involved, it would be that of the Syro-Ephraimite war (735—734 B.C.). King Pekah of Israel had formed an alliance with Rezin of Damascus in order to be rid of the overlordship of Assyria which both had previously acknowledged. This anti-Assyrian coalition had a chance of success against the able and aggressive king Tiglath-pileser III of Assyria only if a majority of neighboring states could be persuaded, or forced, to participate in it. The Syro-Ephraimite war was the attempt made by the joint forces of Rezin and Pekah to force Judah into the coalition (2 K 16:5-9; Is 7:1-17). They besieged Jerusalem; king Ahaz of Judah saved himself by submitting to Tiglath-pileser and becoming his vassal. Tiglath-pileser intervened successfully on his behalf; he captured Damascus and devastated its territory and stripped Israel of all its land except the capital Samaria and the immediately surrounding territory. The words of Hosea (5:8-11) suggest that Judah at this time aided the Assyrians by launching a campaign against Israel from the south, thus forcing Israel to fight on two fronts. The result of all this intrigue and power politics: Damascus reduced to the status of an Assyrian province, Israel stripped of lands and independence, Judah a vassal of Assyria. Nobody won, both Judah and Israel added to their guilt by relying on foreign alliances rather than on the Lord (5:13; cf. Is 7:9) and by their fratricidal strife.

5:8 The alarm is sounded in Israel; an enemy is approaching from the south. *Gibeah, Ramah, Beth-aven* (Bethel, cf. 4:15), and *Benjamin* all lie on the route of an invader approaching from the south. The invader is the brother nation Judah; the time is that of the Syro-Ephraimite war. (735—734 B.C.)

5:9 The *desolation* of Ephraim (the northern kingdom) at the hand of Tiglath-pileser, aided by Judah, is deserved *punishment,* a foretaste of the *day of punishment* awaiting Israel in the fall of Samaria and the end of the kingdom in 722/721 B.C.

5:10 The fact that Israel's punishment is deserved does not clear *Judah* of guilt. In invading his brother's territory (and perhaps annexing part of it) Judah comes under the curse of Dt 27:17: "Cursed be he who removes his neighbor's landmark." (Cf. Dt 19:14)

5:11 The *vanity* pursued by *Ephraim* is his reliance on political maneuvers and machination to secure his national existence. (Cf. 13)

5:12 What both Ephraim and Judah forget is that, for all their maneuverings, they cannot evade the Lord their God; He is at work in judgment upon them, imperceptibly but surely, like *moth* and *dry rot.*

5:13-14 Both *Judah* and *Ephraim* seek the cure for their disease in the wrong place, in the visible and palpable power of *Assyria*; they will not have Him for their Healer; they shall have Him for their Judge (*lion,* 14).

5:15—6:6 The Lord waits in His heavenly abode *(place)* for the repentance of Ephraim and Judah to which He can respond with His healing grace (5:15). In a depressed post-war mood they do repent, after a fashion; in a hauntingly beautiful penitential liturgy they express their desire and determination to *return to the Lord* and find *healing* (6:1) and *life* (6:2)in Him. But the heart of the matter is missing: they do not acknowledge their *guilt* (5:15; cf. 14:2, where Israel does acknowledge his guilt). The Lord cannot respond to this penitential mood, a mood quick to disappear, like the morning *cloud* and *dew* (6:4). They have not yet responded to the trenchant and clear Word of God uttered by the prophets (6:5); they still use the apparatus of worship *(sacrifice, burnt offerings)* to evade the essential life of worship, the spiritual worship of *steadfast love;* for all their expressed desire to *press on to know the Lord* (cf. 6:3), they do not know and acknowledge the God of love in their communal lives, which is the genuine essential *knowledge of God.* (6:6)

6:3, 6 For the organic connection between *knowledge of God* and a life lived to God, cf. 2:20; 8:2-3; and Jer 31:33-34, where knowledge of God is put in parallel to the inscribing of God's Law upon the heart.

6:7-11a ISRAEL'S GUILT FROM OF OLD

6:7-11a Israel is found guilty in its internal life (5:1-7) and in its external politics (5:8—6:6). Now a third item is added to the indictment: Israel's guilt is of long standing. From the entry into the Promised Land onward (7), the history of Israel is one of faithlessness and violence. (6:7-11)

6:7 *At Adam* the waters of Jordan "stood and rose up" while "the people passed over" into the land of promise (Jos 3:16). From the beginning Israel responded to the wonder-working grace of the Lord with infidelity.

6:8-9 Nothing certain is known of the events at *Gilead* (here a *city* while elsewhere it is a land or a mountain) or at *Shechem* to which Hosea is alluding. The extent to which Israel is corrupted is indicated by the fact that even the *priests* are involved in bloodshed.

6:11 *Harvest.* They shall reap as they have sown. For *harvest* as a picture of judgment, cf. Is 17:4-5; Jer 51:33; Jl 3:13; Rv 14:18-19.

6:11b—7:16 THE INCURABLE CORRUPTION OF ISRAEL

6:11b—7:16 God wills to *restore* (6:11b) and to *redeem* (7:13) Israel; but the efforts of the *healer* (7:1) serve only to *reveal* how incurable the disease of His people is. Private life is corrupted by *false dealing, thievery,* and *robbery* (7:1). Life at the royal court is corrupted by *treachery* (7:3), *adultery* (7:4), drunkenness (7:5), and *intrigue* (7:6) which leads to the assassination of *their kings* (7:7). On the international scene, *Ephraim* assimilates himself to pagan powers (*peoples,* 7:8) and loses his individuality (7:8), his strength, and his youth all unawares (7:9). He pursues a senseless and inconsistent foreign policy, fluttering from one great power to another (7:11); having forsaken his one great true Ally, he is as *silly* and *senseless* as a *dove* (7:11). Worst of all is the complete absence of repentance; *none of them call* on the Lord amid the series of regicides that deface Israel's history (7:7); they do not *return to the Lord their God* although drained and desiccated by their assimilation to alien powers (7:10). When they do *cry* to the Lord, they *do not cry from the heart* (7:14). They ignore the remembering Witness of *their evil works* (7:2); with *insolent tongue* (7:16) they *speak lies* against the God who could heal them (7:13); they *devise evil* against the God who made them great (7:15). If Israel is to be healed, it can only be by the radical surgery of divine judgment. (7:12, 13, 16)

7:1 For God the Healer, cf. 5:13; 6:1; 11:3; 14:4. *Samaria,* capital of the northern kingdom.

7:2 *Their deeds encompass them,* like a circle of accusing witnesses in the presence *(face)* of God.

7:3 Not only do *king* and *princes* fail as administrators of justice (cf. 5:1); they actually encourage and promote *wickedness* and *treachery.*

7:4 The picture of the *heated* baker's *oven* seems designed to portray the furious, unflagging vitality with which the *adulterers* carry on their amorous intrigue; one might paraphrase: "They are like a heated oven which retains its heat even when the baker has ceased to stir the fire while kneading and leavening the dough."

In 6 a similar image is applied to political intrigue.

7:5-7 The interpretation of 5 is uncertain; perhaps the reference is to a carouse by the king and his courtiers on a festive occasion, which ends in wild mockery of God. Such an atmosphere of dissolute irreverence would naturally lead to the palace intrigues and the palace revolutions which were so marked a feature of the history of the northern kingdom. Cf. 1 K 15:25-30; 16:8-10; 16:15-19; 2 K 15:8-10, 14, 25, these last three within one decade during the lifetime of Hosea. See also Hos 8:4.

7:8 A *cake* baked on hot ashes would burn on the underside if *not turned;* the damage would not be noticed. Cf. "he knows it not," 9.

7:10 *The pride of Israel.* Israel is proud of having become a nation among the nations, taking cultural and religious color from them and losing his individuality as the chosen people of God. Israel's "success" is purchased at the cost of infidelity to Israel's God; this witnesses against him, marks him as guilty.

7:12 The picture of the "dove" in 11 leads to the picture of God the avenging Fowler.

7:14 *Do not cry to me from the heart.* Cf. 6:1-3 and the comment there. *They gash themselves,* as the devotees of Baal do (cf. 1 K 18:28), to reenforce their petitions; but even in this they are not seeking God (cf. 10) but their own advantage *(grain and wine).* To attempt to use God as a means toward an end is to *rebel against* Him.

7:16 *They turn to Baal,* instead of to the Lord. (Cf. 10)

A treacherous bow. The word translated *treacherous* could also be rendered "slack, loose." In either case, a bow which is useless to its wielder is meant. For the people of God as a weapon in God's hand, used to execute His will, cf. Zch 9:13.

Insolence of their tongue. Cf. the princely "mockers" of 5.

Derision in the land of Egypt. They will be laughed at in the land whose favor and support they tried so hard to gain. (11)

8:1-14 THEY HAVE BROKEN MY COVENANT

8:1-14 *They have broken my covenant, and transgressed my law* (1). These words are the burden of the indictment and indicate the reason for the impending judgment in this chapter. The people have withdrawn from their God and have opposed His will; and by this alienation and opposition they have falsified their whole life. Their confession is false; they profess to *know God* and yet *spurn the good* which a genuine confession involves and produces (2-3). They have false *kings* and false gods. Their kings are not by the grace of God kings (4), and though their first king, Jeroboam, had pointed to the golden *calves* which he had made and said "Behold your gods, O Israel, who brought you up out of the land of Egypt" (1 K 12:28), the *calf of Samaria* is an idol, not the Lord their God, *made* by a *workman* (6), not the *Maker of Israel.* (14)

Their false kings pursue a false policy, fruitless and disastrous, of reliance upon *allies among the nations,* whose favors they must purchase (7-10), instead of relying upon the Lord, as they could and would if they really *knew* Him (cf. 2). Their worship is false worship; their many altars are *altars for sinning* (11). They delight in sacrifice and its joyous feastings (13); but the steadfast love (cf. 6:6) which God's *law* enjoins is something they do not know; the Law has become *a strange thing* to them (12). Their confidence is a false confidence; they have *forgotten* their *Maker* and put their trust in the trappings of political power, *palaces, fortified cities,* and *strongholds;* and in this *Judah* is as guilty as Israel (14). Over all this falsity the judgment of the true God impends. (1, 3, 6, 7, 10, 13, 14)

8:1 *A vulture,* or eagle, both carrion-eating, unclean birds, here probably referring to the Assyrian power (cf. 3, "the enemy") preparing to swoop down on Israel. Cf. Dt 28:49; Is 8:8.

House of the Lord, the holy land. Cf. 9:15; Jer 12:7; Zch 9:8.

8:2 For the claim to knowledge of the Lord, without basis in fact, cf. 6:3, 6. See also 4:1, 6, for the connection between knowledge of God and living according to His will. For profession without practice, cf. Is 29:13; Mt 15:8-9.

8:4 *Kings . . . idols.* The connection between kingship and idolatry was always close. Alliances with foreign powers concluded by kings usually involved concessions toward the religion of the ally. In Israel the connection was particularly close, for Jeroboam had set up golden calves and established shrines at Bethel and Dan in order to wean his peoples away from worship in Jerusalem, 1 K 12:25-33. Cf. also 3:5, where a return to the Lord and to the Messianic king is spoken of as one act, and the note on 1:11.

8:5 *Pure,* that is, cleansed of the taint of idolatry and serving the Lord with a whole heart. (Cf. Ps 26:6; 73:13)

8:7 For retribution in terms of *sowing* and *reaping* cf. Pr 22:8; Jb 4:8; Gl 6:7.

Israel *sows* a vain, godless course and will *reap* destruction. The sown *grain yields* no food, or what little it yields becomes the booty of the enemy.

8:8 *Swallowed up.* Israel had by this time probably already suffered huge losses in territory. (Cf. 2 K 15:29)

Useless vessel, disregarded and cast aside.

8:9 *Wild ass, wandering alone.* The animal separated from the herd is probably a figure for Israel stripped of most of its territory and no longer playing a role in international politics.

Gone up to Assyria, for assistance.

Hired lovers, as a man buys the favors of a harlot; alliances obtained by gifts and concessions are meant. (Cf. 10)

8:10 *Gather them up,* to carry them off into exile.

Cease . . . from anointing king. Cf. 1:4; 3:4.

8:11 The *altars* have become *altars for sinning* because the cultus has become a substitute for religion rather than an expression of it (cf. 12) and because the cultus itself was corrupted with idolatrous accretions.

8:13 Cf. 6:6.

Return to Egypt, not literally; Egypt is figurative for "house of bondage." (Cf. 11:5-7)

8:14 For *cities* and *strongholds* as expressing a sinful will to autonomy, cf. Mi 5:11.

9:1-17 THEY SHALL NOT REMAIN IN THE LAND OF THE LORD

9:1-17 Some, if not all, of these words were probably spoken at a harvest festival, celebrated to give thanks for the good gifts of the good land which the Lord had given to the fathers. The prophet interrupts the wild noise of *rejoicing* and *exultation* (1) with grim words of accusation. Their exultation is a pagan exultation (*like the peoples* (1), he tells them, not a faithful spouse's pure joy in her Husband but the drunken delight of a *harlot.* They are not thanking the Lord but Baal, and therein they are following in their fathers' footsteps (10). And they have persisted stubbornly in their sin, despising, hating, and persecuting the prophet whose warning voice called them back to God (7-8); the *princes* are as rebellious as the people (15). *Every evil is theirs* (15). Therefore the Lord *will love them no more* (15), will *depart from them* (12), will *punish* (9). In the coming *days of punishment* and *recompense* (7) He will take from them the fruitfulness and fecundity which they sought from Baal; deprivation (2), desolation (6, 11), sterility (11, 14), and bereavement (12, 13, 16) shall be their lot. In all this terrifying vocabulary of doom one motif is prominent and persistent: the punishment of exile. The people will be expelled from the land which has been the occasion and the scene of their sin (3, 4, 6, 15, 17). The delightful *festivals* which they have perverted and corrupted shall cease. (4-5)

9:1 The terms here translated *rejoice* and *exult* are frequently found as expressions of religious joy, especially at sacrifices (with their feasts) and festivals (cf. Dt 12:7, 18; 16:11; 27:7; Ps 9:14; 13:5; 14:7; Jl 2:21, 23; Hab 3:18). Hosea probably uttered these words at a harvest festival.

Harlot's hire. For the image, cf. 1:2 and the note there. Israel thinks of the harvest as a reward given her by her lovers (cf. 2:5, 13), the Baals to whom she devotes herself in licentious rites.

9:3 *To Egypt,* the house of bondage. The *food* of a pagan land like Assyria would be *unclean* since it was not consecrated to the Lord by the offering of the first fruits. (Lv 29:9-14; Eze 4:13)

9:4 *Mourners' bread,* made "unclean" by being in the same house with a dead body. (Cf. Nm 19:14-15)

Not come to the house of the Lord, i.e., in the first fruits which consecrates the whole to God. (Cf. Lv 23:9-14)

9:6 *Gather,* for burial. *Memphis,* chief city of northern Egypt. *Nettles* and *thorns* will grow on the sites of their luxurious living and richly appointed worship.

9:7 *Shall know it,* that is, encounter it, experience it. In Jer 26:21 the Lord says that the nations shall know His power (literally "His hand"), that is, they shall feel it.

The prophet is a fool, etc. These words should probably be set off by quotation marks; this is the popular estimate of the prophet who foretold defeat and exile at a high festival; it is the *iniquity* of the people and their *hatred* (cf. 8) for the truth that makes them speak so.

9:8 For the prophet as the *watchman* who alerts his people to danger, cf. Eze 3:17; 33:1-9; Mi 7:4. A perverse people rewards the *watchman's* service with secret plottings against him *(fowler's snare)* and with open *hatred* even there where God's Word should be welcomed and heeded, *in the house of his God.*

9:9 *Gibeah.* The reference is probably to the outrageous crime of the men of Gibeah recorded in Ju 19—21, a deed so terrible that all Israel arose to avenge it and all but exterminated the tribe of Benjamin, to which Gibeah belonged. (Cf. 10:9)

9:10 *Grapes* found on an oasis *in the wilderness* would be highly prized, and *the first fruit on the fig tree* was a desired delicacy. As such God prized and loved the fathers.

Baal-peor. The fathers rewarded God's early love with an early crass apostasy, even before their entry into Canaan. For the story, see Nm 25.

The thing they loved, the god of Baal of Peor, to whom Israel "yoked himself." (Nm 25:3)

9:11-14 Ephraim has forfeited his *glory,* his position as God's chosen people. The people who sought the blessing of fertility from Baal and not from the Lord are fittingly punished with sterility (11, 14) and bereavement. (12, 13; see also 16)

9:14 Some take this verse as an intercession on the prophet's part: He asks that the Lord would let the race die out rather than face the fate in store for it. Perhaps the prophet begins an intercession but finds that he cannot intercede for so sinful a nation and concludes by urging the Lord to execute the decreed sentence upon them.

9:15 *Gilgal.* Cf. 4:15; Am 4:4; 5:5, where Gilgal is the site of an idolatrous sanctuary. But the reference here seems to be to some specific event, which cannot be identified.

My house, the holy land (cf. 8:1). *I will love them no more.* To this 14:4 is a wondrous commentary.

9:17 *Wanderers among the nations.* (Cf. Dt 28:65-67)

10:1-15 THEIR HEART IS FALSE; THEY MUST BEAR THEIR GUILT

10:1-15 The oracles of this chapter are loosely clustered, rather than organized, about two agricultural images, *Israel* as *a luxuriant* (or degenerating) *vine* (1) and *Ephraim* as a *heifer* that *loved to thresh* (11). The chapter continues a theme touched on in 6:7 and more explicitly stated in 9:9-10, the idea that Israel's sin has a long history; the present evil is the continuation of an evil past (9; cf. 11:1). This theme persists in chs. 11—13.

10:1-10 The Dengenerating Vine

10:1-10 Israel, a *vine* planted by the Lord on good land (cf. Is 5:1-2, 7), has yielded fruit—but it is degenerate fruit from a degenerating vine. Israel's history is the history of failure. Religion became idolatry (1, 5, 6, 8). Kingship has degenerated to the point where the king's subjects consider him a futile nonentity (3); his *words* are meaningless, his *oaths* and *covenants* worthless, his administration of justice *(judgment)* a deadly perversion of justice (4). The ancient *days of Gibeah* (9) are the beginning of a history which can end only in judgment upon Israel, upon Israel's altars and idols (2, 5, 6), upon Israel's king and the idolatry which royalty fostered (7-8), upon the *wayward people* who have continued in the pattern set by the *days of Gibeah.* (9-10)

10:1 *Pillars,* the sacred pillars of Canaanite places of worship, denoting the presence of a deity, taken over by the Israelites.

10:2 *Heart is false,* divided between the Lord and Baal. (Cf. 1 K 18:21)

10:3 *For we fear not the Lord.* The people recognize the judgment of God in the fact that they are cursed with a chaotic succession of degenerate kings (cf. 7:7). But instead of repenting they drift into a cynical doubt as to the value of any kingship.

10:4 *Judgment . . . like poisonous weeds.* (Cf. Am 6:12)

10:5-6 *Tremble for.* They have not "feared the Lord" (3); now they have a god they must be fearful for, an *idol* which becomes a tribute paid to the Assyrian overlord, a god to *be ashamed of.*

Calf of Beth-aven. Cf. 8:5 and 4:15; 5:8.

10:7 *Samaria's king,* whipped about by the maelstrom of power politics, will *perish.*

10:8 The cultic sites *(high places)* established and fostered by the royal house (cf. 1 K 12:31) which led Israel into idolatry *(sin)* will perish with the king.

Aven means "wickedness" and probably is figurative, referring to the sanctuaries at Dan and Bethel, which "became a sin" (1 K 12:30; cf. 2 K 17:7-18). Some take it as a way of referring specifically to Bethel, called Beth-aven in 4:15; 5:8; 10:5.

Mountains, Cover up. Cf. Lk 23:30; Rv 6:16; and Is 2:10, 19, 21.

10:9-10 *Gibeah.* Cf. 9:9. Gibeah may also include a reference to the beginnings of kingship is Israel; Saul's home was in Gibeah (1 Sm 10:26), and various events of his selection as king and his reign are associated with it (1 Sm 10:5, 10, 26; 15:34; 22:6; 23:19). The *double iniquity* would then mean that Israel both became guilty of gross unheard-of immoralities (Ju 19:30) and denied its true existence under God the King (Ju 8:23) and demanded a king to govern them "like all the nations" (1 Sm 8:4), thus becoming a *wayward people.*

10:11-15 The Heifer That Loved to Thresh

10:11-15 The *threshing heifer* is permitted to eat her fill (11; cf. Dt 25:4). Israel delighted in receiving the good gifts of the Lord, the blessings of the covenant, but withdrew *her fair neck* from the obligations of the covenant. When the prophets called upon her to *seek the Lord* by *sowing righteousness* and *reaping steadfast love* (12), she *plowed iniquity, reaped injustice,* and lived on *lies* (13), entrenching herself in her wrong with the power of *chariots* and *warriors* (13). She may not, therefore, look for the *rain of salvation* (12); she must expect the *storm* of God, which shall *cut off Israel's king* and bring the utmost horrors of *war* upon the people. (14-15)

10:14 The identity of *Shalman* is uncertain and the event referred to is unknown. *Beth-arbel* was a town in Gilead.

11:1-11 GOD'S UNQUENCHABLE LOVE FOR HIS WAYWARD CHILD

11:1-11 Once more the prophet looks back to the beginning of Israel's rebellious history. He has previously traced that history back to the dark days of the judges (Gibeah, 10:9; cf. 9:9), to the time of Israel's entry into the land of promise (at Adam 6:7), and to the time of the wanderings (Baal-peor, 9:10). In 12:3 he will go even further back to the ancestor who gave Israel his name, the patriarch Jacob. Hosea sees his contemporaries as "filling up the measure of their fathers," as Jesus said of His contemporaries (Mt 23:32). Now he looks back to the Exodus (1) and portrays Israel's history as one long revolt against the Father's love, disobedience to the voice of love that gave them freedom and nationhood (2), the voice of Him who patiently taught His child to walk and took him up in His everlasting arms, when he grew weary and stumbled, the voice of the Healer of all his diseases (3), the voice of the compassionate Plowman who *eased the yoke* and *bent down to feed* the kine who served Him. (4)

The logic of law, of crime and punishment, calls for retribution, and injured love can rightly react to contempt and rejection with wrath (5-7). The people who have *turned away from* (7) their Liberator shall return to the yoke (7), to the house of bondage in Egypt (5); the people who would not have the Lord reign over them (cf. Ex 15:18) shall have the harsh Assyrian overlord for *their king.* (5)

But God is love, not logic (8-9), and His heart is larger than law. *Because* He is *God and not man,* the *Holy One* separate from sinners, His love surpasses human measure and is not trapped in the causalities which control human love; it persists where human love must fail and cease. Therefore He will not *execute* His *fierce anger,* to *destroy Ephraim.* (9)

God in His holiness will not destroy; neither can His love merely overlook and tolerate man's rebellion. His love will deal effectively with man's sin. With the *roar of a lion* the Lord will declare both His inexorable wrath against sin and His inextinguishable love for His children; and at that roar His wayward children will at last *come trembling* home to Him (10-11). That roar was ultimately heard at Calvary, and all history since then is the history of the homecoming of mankind.

11:1 *Called my son.* Cf. Ex 4:22-23. Matthew sees this word "fulfilled" when God called His Son Jesus out of Egypt (Mt 2:15) and restored Him to the "land of Israel" (Mt 2:21). The redeeming love of God, which called His child out of Egypt and persisted through all Israel's disobedience, was "fulfilled," that is, reached its full measure, when He called the Son, driven to Egypt by the indifference of His people and the enmity of the king (Mt 2:3-14), back to His people and His land to fulfill by His ministry and death the promises given to the fathers and to manifest mercy to the Gentiles. (cf. Ro 15:8-9)

11:3 *Healed.* For God the Healer, cf. 7:1; 14:5; Dt 32:39; Is 6:10; 19:22; 30:26; 57:18-19; Jer 3:22; 17:14; 30:17; 33:6.

11:4 *Yoke on their jaws.* This may refer to release from bondage to another nation. (Cf. 7; Jer 27:8; 28:4; Dt 28:48; Is 47:6)

11:8 *Admah, Zeboiim.* "Cities of the valley" which were destroyed along with Sodom and Gomorrah. (Gn 19:24-29; Dt 29:23)

11:10 *Come trembling.* Cf. "come in fear to the Lord and to his goodness in the latter days," 3:5.

11:12—13:16 THE HARD ROAD TO REPENTANCE

These two chapters are probably the most difficult in Hosea. Apart from difficulties in detail, it is hard to discover the definite structure and the consistent line that one readily finds, for example, in chs. 11 and 14. It may be well, therefore, to work back from what appears to be the close and climax of the book, from the prayer of repentance which Hosea puts on the lips of the penitent people in 14:1-3. According to these verses, three things are essential to true repentance: (a) An absolute and radical honesty that calls sin by its name and confesses it ("iniquity," 14:1-2), not a facile recital of man's need (cf. 6:1-3) but a full confrontation with the Lord, the Judge and Forgiver. Only lips that have so confessed are fit for praise (14:2). (b) A renunciation of the idolatry which divides and destroys the loyalty of faith ("work of our hands," 14:3). (c) A renunciation of the will to autonomy, political (Assyria, 14:3) or military ("horses," 14:3), the willingness to appear before God as an "orphan," a claimant of His "mercy" purely (14:3), with no thought of human champions and guarantors of one's security. The road to repentance leads hither. Israel's *lies* and *deceit* (11:12), Israel's idolatry, and Israel's will to autonomy are three mighty roadblocks in the way, and the prophetic word strives passionately to remove them.

First, the life of Israel is a lie. Their religion is a complex of lies and deceit, a worship ostensibly offered to the Lord but in reality devoted to Baal (11:12; cf. 13:1-2). Their political life is marked by ever-increasing *falsehood* (12:1). The fitting symbol of their commercial life is *false balances* (12:7). They are true descendants of cunning Jacob who overreached his brother (12:3). And since deceit never succeeds in avoiding the open clash which it seeks to evade, *violence* (12:1), oppression (12:7), and *bloodguilt* (12:14) are also registered among Israel's sins.

Second, Israel sacrifices at doomed *altars* (12:11), for Israel's worship is idolatrous and a *bitter provocation* of the wrath of God (12:14; 13:2). Israel is *dead* in the sin of idolatry. Israel has *forgotten* the Lord, their *God from the land of Egypt* (13:4, 6); *Baal, molten images, silver idols, calves* (13:1-2)—these are the objects of their devotion and the focus of their loyalty.

Third, they are *rich,* they have *gained wealth for* themselves (12:8; *fed to the full,* their *heart is lifted up,* and they forget the God who fed them (13:6). They have demanded kings for themselves that they might be "like all the nations" and have gotten them, little knowing that it was the *wrath* of God which gave them this prop to their feeling of autonomy (13:10-11). They have *rebelled against their God.* (13:16)

Thus the prophet exposes the triple sin that impedes the repentance of his people. And he threatens his countrymen with God's just and fearful retribution (12:2, 11-12, 14; 13:3, 7-9, 12, 13-14, 15-16). But he does not only threaten: he also urges and woos them to repentance. If they are now like Jacob the usurper (12:3), they can become like the *Jacob* who *wept* and *sought favor* of the angel; the *Lord God of hosts* may yet *speak with* them in gracious promise as He spoke to Jacob at Bethel (12:4-5). They can yet *by God's help return to their God* and *wait continually* for Him, holding fast to *love and justice* as they walk humbly with their God (12:6; cf. Mi 6:8). The God with whom they have to do when confronted by the prophetic Word (that great gift of God to them, 12:10, 13) is the God whom they have known *from the land of Egypt* (12:9; 13:4), the only God, the *savior* who *knew* and loved and tended *them in the wilderness,* where no human help was found (13:4-5). If He makes them *dwell again in tents,* as in the wilderness days, He will do so in order to make a creative fresh start (12:9). With this God all things are possible, even the miracle of dead Ephraim's rebirth. (13:1, 13)

11:12 *Judah . . . Holy One.* The text and translation of this half-verse are very uncertain. According to the rendering of the RSV, Judah is contrasted with Ephraim and commended for fidelity *to the Holy One.* This seems strange in the light of 12:2, where both kingdoms come under the same indictment. Cf. also 5:5, 12, 13, 14; 6:4, 11; 8:14; 10:11, where Judah is seen in an unfavorable light. Various corrections of the text have been proposed; one that does not involve very radical alterations gives the reading: "And Judah strays from God and attaches himself to cult prostitutes."

12:1 *Herds the wind . . . wind.* The figure points up the pointlessness and futility of Israel's foreign policy of seeking alliances with now one major power *(Assyria)* and now another *(Egypt). Oil is carried,* as tribute.

12:3-4 For the sin of Israel viewed in historical retrospect, cf. 6:7; 9:10; 10:9; 11:1; 13:4-6.

12:3 *Took his brother by the heel.* Cf. Gn 25:26; 27:36.

12:4 *Strove with the angel.* Gn 32:22-31. Genesis does not say that Jacob *wept and sought God's favor;* but Hosea's words are an authentic interpretation of Jacob's words in Gn 32:26, especially in view of Jacob's subdued and humble temper on that night. (Cf. Gn 32:10)

Met God at Bethel. Cf. Gn 28:10-19.

12:6 *By the help of your God, return.* For repentance *(return)* as God's working and gift, cf. 1 K 18:37; Jer 31:18; Lm 5:21.

Love . . . justice . . . wait for God. Cf. Mi 6:8.

12:8 *Ephraim* interprets his prosperity as a proof of God's approval of his ways.

12:9 *The appointed feast,* the Feast of Booths, or Tabernacles, when the Israelites were reminded of their past in the wilderness by dwelling in tents 7 days. (Cf. Lv 23:42-43)

12:10-14 If Israel's life is a lie (11:12; 12:7), the lie is deliberate. Israel cannot plead ignorance, for God has from the beginning of Israel's history shed the light of the prophetic revelation on his way (12:13 and 10); from the time of Moses to the present God has *multiplied visions* and *given parables through the prophets* (10). Israel is responsible, and Israel will be punished. (14)

12:10 *Parables.* The prophets speak the vivid, impressive, and unforgettable language of images and figures. Their speech has the persuasive power of poetry.

12:11 *Gilead.* Cf. 6:8. The reference is obscure. *Gilgal,* scene of idolatrous worship; cf. 4:15; 9:15.

12:12 The point of this renewed reference to *Jacob* (cf. 2-4) is not easy to see. Perhaps the prophet recalls this inglorious episode (Gn 28:5 ff.) in the life of the patriarch to remind Israel that the greatness of his history does not lie in heroic human achievements but in the grace of the God who filled it with His revelation. (Cf. 4, *there God spoke with him*)

12:14 *Reproaches.* Israel's conduct has been an insult to Israel's God.

13:1 *Guilt through Baal and died.* Cf. 8:4. For being dead in sin in the midst of life, cf. Eph 2:1; Cl 2:13; Lk 15:24. The people sought life in the fertility cult—and found death.

13:2 *Kiss calves.* For the calves of Samaria, cf. 8:5, 6; 10:6. For the *kiss* as an expression of religious homage, cf. Jb 31:26-27; 1 K 19:18.

13:3 *Mist, dew, chaff,* and *smoke* are all unsubstantial and transitory. The *window* was an unglazed opening by which smoke escaped.

13:4 It was in the exodus from Egypt that God manifested Himself as the God of radical deliverance, deliverance out of a humanly hopeless situation, the God of Salvation, the Savior. (Cf. Ex 15:2; 14:13)

13:5 *Knew you:* loved you and provided for you.

13:6 Cf. Dt 32:15-18.

13:9-11 When God proceeds to execute His judgment, no human helper can avail, not even the *king* whom Israel once demanded of the Lord (1 Sm 8:5, 19), to make them a powerful nation among the nations (1 Sm 8:20). That demand had in itself been rebellion against the Lord (1 Sm 8:7). He had given them a king *in his anger* (11). And the history of kingship in Israel proved to be the chronicle of God's *wrath* (11; cf. 2 K 17:7-8), a chronicle which concludes with the end of kingship. (11; cf. 1:4; 3:4)

13:12 *Bound up . . . kept in store,* like a scroll, rolled, tied, and put in safekeeping, to be produced in evidence against Ephraim at the judgment. (Cf. Dt 32:34-35)

13:13 There is still opportunity for Ephraim; he can repent and be reborn. But he is *an unwise son* who cannot or will not recognize the signs of the time *(pangs of childbirth),* and so is in danger of missing his opportunity.

13:14 There is much to be said for translating the first half of the verse as a statement: (*I shall ransom . . . I shall redeem* and taking the questions that follow (*where are? . . .*) as expressions of a divine triumph over the *plagues* and *destruction* of *Death* and *Sheol.* In that case the word translated *compassion* would be rendered "repentance," in the sense of Ps 110:4, where it is said that the Lord has sworn and will not repent of it, i.e., "will not change His mind." So here, God's will to grant new life (13) by deliverance from death is said to be His firm and irrevocable will; He desires repentance, not the death of the sinner. (Cf. Eze 18:23, 32)

13:15 *East wind,* the withering sirocco.

14:1-9 REPENTANCE AND RESTORATION

14:1-9 There is only one way to rebirth and new life (13:13-14), and that is the way of repentance. The prophet pictures true repentance in the words which he places on the lips of his judged and humbled people *returning to the Lord their God* (1). Unlike the prayer of 6:1-3, which the Lord cannot accept, this prayer is not silent concerning *iniquity* (1, 2); it does not skirt the sin of idolatry and rebellious self-will. It renounces dependence on political power *(Assyria,* 3), military power (*horses*, 3), or idols (*work of our hands*, 3) and expresses the will to live in dependence on God's *mercy* alone (*orphan,* 3). This prayer is confession and adoration (2, *fruit of our lips*). To this the vigilant mercy of God can respond with *healing,* with spontaneous *love* (4), and with blessing (5-

8). God will no longer be the blasting east wind (13:15) to His people but *dew* (5), shade from the searing sun (7), perpetual *fruit* to refresh and sustain them (8). One last warning against idolatry is inserted in the promise (8)—the God who *loves freely* (4) loves with a holy and jealous love. And a sober admonition to hear and heed the prophet's word which has in it the issues of life and death closes the book.

14:2 *That which is good,* that is, the only good we can offer, *the fruit of our lips,* our thanks and praise.

14:3 For the *horse* as symbol of military power, cf. Ps 20:7; Is 31:1; Eze 17:15. In the light of the last two passages one may see here a reference to alliances with Egypt. (Cf. 12:1)

14:6 *Lebanon.* Referring to the aromatic cedars of Lebanon. (Cf. SS 4:11)

14:7 *Wine of Lebanon,* apparently famous, like the cedars.

JOEL

INTRODUCTION

Joel, son of Pethuel, is known to us only by his prophecy. The dates assigned to his prophetic activity on the basis of evidence in the book itself range from about 800 BC to about 400 BC. The later date is favored by most scholars today. No king is mentioned, priests and elders appear as leaders of the community. The temple is standing, and priesthood, ritual, and offerings are prominent. Many of the people are still scattered in exile. The Greeks appear as a far-off people to whom Jewish slaves were sold, not yet as the conquering people whom the Jews knew from the days of Alexander the Great. All this seems to point to a date after the Exile and after the reforms of Ezra and Nehemiah and before the time of Alexander. The evidence is not absolutely conclusive, and some scholars favor the traditional earlier date. The place of Joel's prophetic activity was probably Jerusalem.

The occasion of Joel's prophecy is clear. A plague of locusts of unprecedented severity has come upon his land. There can hardly be a doubt that he is speaking literally, of a real plague of locusts. The accuracy of his description, down to details, is confirmed by eyewitness accounts both ancient and modern. There is no warrant for taking Joel's portrayal of the invasion of locusts as an allegorical description of an invading army or of the enemies of Israel, as has been done.

But Joel, enlightened by the Spirit, does give more than a surface description of the plague; he interprets it in depth, as a meaningful act of the God of judgment and salvation. He bids the people look beneath the surface of devastation and despair and see in the plague, first an indication (or predictive token) of the coming great Day of the Lord, which bids them cry to the Lord (1:1-20); second, by using the suggestive term "the northerner" for the locusts (2-20), he bids his people see in them the inception, or dawn, of God's approaching last judgmental visitation, which bids men return to the Lord and find deliverance in Him (2:1-27); and, third, his prophetic vision, no longer fixed on the present plague merely, pierces into the future, and he gives a full-scale depiction of the approaching Day of the Lord, the portents that herald its approach, the standard by which its divine decisions will be made, and the finality of these decisions for good or ill. (2:28—3:21)

Joel's prophecy is taken up into the texture of the Revelation to John, as so much of OT prophecy is, in one way or another. It is his prophecy of the outpouring of the Spirit in the latter days (2:28-29) that is quoted by Peter and explicitly marked as fulfilled in the wondrous and startling event of Pentecost (Acts 2:14-21). Peter retains (and indeed, intensifies) Joel's emphasis on the fact that the outpouring of the Spirit is the beginning of the end (Acts 2:17, "in the last days") and is a gift of God designed to work repentance "before the day of the Lord comes." (Acts 2:20, 38, 40)

Joel's prophecy of the Spirit will do its wholesome work in the church if the church allows itself to be reminded by it that the gift of the Spirit is a last-days gift, to be employed in sober, last-days responsibility, that to "live by the Spirit" means "*to walk* by the Spirit" in disciplined and orderly ranks (Gl 5:25). In so doing the church may avoid the self-centered intoxication by the "Spirit" which Paul so sternly rebuked in the Corinthian church, and may become, in virtue of its sober and responsible hope, a powerful instrument in the hand of God, such as the apostolic church once was and may again come to be.

OUTLINE

I. 1:1-20 The Plague of Locusts: Predictive Token of the Day of the Lord
   - A. 1:1-14 The Prophet's Summons: Cry to the Lord
   - B. 1:15-20 The Response of the People: The Cry of the Penitent

II. 2:1-27 The Coming of the "Northerner": The Dawning of the Day of the Lord
   - A. 2:1-11 The Invasion of the "Northerner"
   - B. 2:12-17 Return to Me, Says the Lord
   - C. 2:18-27 The Removal of the "Northerner" and the Restoration of Life

III. 2:28—3:21 The Valley of Decision: The Coming of the Day of the Lord
   - A. 2:28-32 Portents of the Day of the Lord
   - B. 3:1-8 The Standard of Judgment
   - C. 3:9-21The Judgment

1:1-20 THE PLAGUE OF LOCUSTS: PREDICTIVE TOKEN OF THE DAY OF THE LORD

1:1-14 The Prophet's Summons: Cry to the Lord

1:1-14 The coming Day of the Lord is heralded by predictive tokens which bid the people of God be alert to it and respond to its coming. Of these the plague of locusts is one; it bids men *cry to the Lord* (1:14, 19). The community is addressed four times in its representatives (*old men*, 2-4; *drinkers of wine*, 5-7; *tillers of the soil*, 11-12; *priests*, 13-14) and once as a whole with the poetic designation *virgin* (8-10). The response demanded is that all inhabitants of the land *cry to the Lord,* who is hastening toward His day of judgment and deliverance. (14-15)

1:2-4 The *aged men* represent the people *(all the inhabitants).* As the men of memory, guardians of the people's traditions who constitute a bridge between the generations, and as men of authority whose word has especial weight in the community, they are told to *hear* and *tell.* They are to mark the unprecedented character of the plague (comparable only to the eighth plague of the Exodus, Ex 10:14) and to preserve the memory of it, not as just another piece of history but as a speaking act of God which points to the end of history and His judgment upon it.

1:4 The various names for locusts may be names for several varieties of locusts or for the locust in various stages of its development; or, as seems more likely, they may be simply a poetic way of suggesting how completely destructive the hordes of locusts are. Each successive swarm destroys what the previous one has left.

1:5-7 *Drunkards* are told to *awake* to the significance of the plague and therefore to *weep* and *wail.* They are addressed as an extreme case of a tendency in the people as a whole; they represent all *drinkers of wine,* those who "enjoy life" in leisurely relaxation and so are in danger of remaining deaf to what the Lord is telling them concerning His Day (cf. Lk 21:34). The Lord is taking from them the lesser gift of wine that gladdens the heart of man (Ps 104:15) in order to implant in them the need and desire for the greater gift of repentance and salvation.

1:6 The vast numbers and the disciplined organization of the locusts (cf. 2:7) suggest the comparison with a *nation* (cf. 2:2; Pr 30:25). The phrase *come up against* is often used of an invading army. (Cf. 2:5)

1:8-10 Here, in the center of the fivefold appeal (preceded by the word to "aged men" and "drunkards" and followed by the address to "tillers of the soil" and the "priests"), the people are addressed corporately, as a *virgin* lamenting the death of *the bridegroom of her youth.* In form the address is only a comparison *(like a virgin)*, but the lamenting virgin is more than a comparison. It is a designation of Israel, whom the prophets often picture as a *virgin,* especially in portraying her hours of failure and distress (Is 37:22; Jer 14:17; 18:13; 31:4, 21; Lm 1:15; 2:13; Am 5:2). Similarly her covenant relationship to the Lord is pictured as espousal or marriage (Jer

2:2; Hos 1—3). In this hour of her history, when the plague has put an end not only to the blessings of the covenant *(grain, wine, and oil)* but also to the worship in the temple *(offering, house of the Lord, priests)*, the covenant itself is being called into question; Israel is indeed the virgin bride who is burying her hope. It is time to "cry to the Lord."

1:9 For the daily burnt offering, accompanied by the *cereal and drink offering*, cf. Ex 29:38-46; Nm 28:1-10. The cessation of these offerings meant that the divinely ordained normal relationship between the Lord and His people (cf. Ex 29:42-46) was being interrupted. Thus the plague brought not only physical misery but religious distress as well. The "joy and gladness" of assured communion with God within the covenant are cut off "from the house of our God." (16)

1:11-12 If the *tillers of the soil* are *confounded*, this means that the creaturely life, the economic existence, of the whole people is threatened. When they *wail, gladness fails from the sons of men*, and it is time for all to "cry to the Lord."

1:13-14 In the address to the priests, the agony and the imperative of the hour become completely clear. Nine imperatives are directed to them, bidding them recognize the hour and make the assembled people recognize it too. When the heavy visitation of God cuts off the very means of worship, there is but one thing to do: The people must put on the garments of sorrowing repentance *(sackcloth)* and utter the cry of repentance. God's speaking action says: *Cry to the Lord* (14, 19). They must cry as Israel once cried from the house of bondage in Egypt (Ex 2:23-25; Nm 20:16; Dt 26:7; 1 Sm 12:8), as Israel cried from the deeps of her sin and desperation in the days of the judges (Ju 3:9; 4:3; 6:6, cf. 6:1; 10:10-14; 1 Sm 12:10; 1 K 8:52; Neh 9:26-27), and so reach out for the ready compassion of their God (cf. 2:13) before the coming Day cuts off all crying.

1:13 *Sackcloth* is the badge of sorrow, often of the sorrow of repentance. (Cf. 1 K 21:27-29; 1 Ch 21:16-17; Is 22:12; Jer 4:8, cf. 4:1-4; Dn 9:3-5; Jon 3:5-9; Mt 11:21)

1:15-20 The Response of the People: The Cry of the Penitent

1:15-20 The quick and powerful prophetic word has done its work. The cry evoked from the people is a lament for the havoc wrought by the locusts. But it is more than that: the lament is religious, expressive of sorrow over the broken relationship with God, grief at the cessation of the *joy and gladness* of worship in His *house*. (16). And, above all, there is in the cry the recognition that this havoc is a visitation of God, the cast shadow of the coming *Day of the Lord, destruction from the Almighty* (15), with an inescapably demonstrative power (*before our eyes*, 16). Perhaps even the unexpected reference to *fire* and *flame* in 19 and 20 is also an indication that the people are recognizing the disaster as a visitation of God's wrath, for *fire* is one of the commonest OT symbols of the wrath of God: "The Lord our God is a devouring fire" (Dt 4:24; cf. Ps 89:46; Jer 4:4; 15:14; 21:12; Lm 1:13; 2:3; Eze 22:31; Zph 3:8; Is 66:24). And the recognition leads to repentance; the lament becomes a penitent cry for mercy: *Unto thee, O Lord, I cry*. (19)

2:1-27 THE COMING OF THE "NORTHERNER": THE DAWNING OF THE DAY OF THE LORD

2:1-27 In ch. 2, which opens with the command to *blow the trumpet* and to *sound the alarm* in the holy city, the prophet makes a fresh start in his interpretation of the plague of locusts. The locust is still in the picture but is expressly mentioned only once, late in the chapter and almost incidentally (25). The plague has become the occasion of his prophecy rather than its theme; it is seen, not so much as an announcement of the Day of the Lord as the inception of it, as the beginning of God's movement toward that dreadful Day, as something present which has in it the germ of the future. The locust is given a new and suggestive name, *the northerner* (20; see 2:1-11 note), which marks him as part of the whole sweeping judgmental activity of God which leads to, and culminates in, the Day of the Lord. All that has been pictured in the first chapter appears now in higher relief: the Day of the Lord (not mentioned in ch. 1 until v. 15) now appears at the very beginning; the call to repentance is more explicit and is more fully developed (12-17); and the Lord's promise of renewal and restoration is correspondingly richer and fuller. (18-27)

2:1-11 The Invasion of the "Northerner"

2:1-11 The term "northerner" does not occur until 20, in the Lord's promise of restoration. But this loaded term (all the more striking because locusts usually came from the east or southeast) is prepared for by the preceding description of the locusts' devastating approach. To the Israelite, "northerner" would have an ominious sound, for the north is the region from which Palestine was invaded by the great world powers; and from the north, according to the prophets, the judgment of God comes upon Israel (Jer 1:14; 4:6; 6:1; 13:20). The north is the quarter of disaster; from thence, according to Ezekiel, will come the mysterious Gog, who heads up the last concentrated attack of the hostile nations upon God's people (Eze 38:15). "Northerner" can then suggest all God's judgmental visitations, natural and supernatural. In calling the locusts the "northerner," Joel is a aligning them with all the judgmental instruments of God who not only herald but usher in the Day of the Lord.

The locusts are, accordingly, described as an invading *people* (2) of unprecedented and incomparable power, whose coming brings with it a *darkness* mysterious and deep (2). They are a cavalry host whose scorched-earth policy makes the *land* a *wilderness* (3-5), an army whose uncannily disciplined and unswerving advance turns the faces of all *peoples* pale with anguish (6-8). At the coming of this host, the very cosmos is convulsed—*earth, heavens, sun, moon, stars* are shaken (10-11). And no wonder, for this is the Lord's own *army;* His is the *voice* in command; and they *execute* His omnipotent *word* (11). They usher in the *great and terrible Day of the Lord* before which no man can stand.

2:1 *The trumpet,* signal of imminent danger, is associated with the coming Day of the Lord in Zph 1:16 also. Compare also the trumpets of Rv 8—9, where the sounding of the fifth trumpet introduces a plague of monstrous locusts. (Rv 9:1-7)

2:12-17 Return to Me, Says the Lord

2:12-17 Who can endure the coming of this host, the dawning of this Day? Only the Lord can create the possibility of escape. Hope of escape, according to His sure Word (12), lies only in repentance, in *returning* to Him—*returning with all* one's *heart* (12) to Him whose ancient promises reveal Him as the God with a great and compassionate heart (13). He can restore to His penitent people the blessings of the land and of renewed worship (*cereal and drink offering,* 14). To Him the afflicted people are to turn corporately, in *solemn assembly* (15), led by the priests, who appeal to the covenant by which the Lord has graciously bound Himself to His people *(thy people, thy heritage,* 17).

2:13 The description of the Lord as *gracious,* etc., is, as it were, a quotation from Israel's catechism. (Cf. Ex 34:6; Ps 86:15; 103:8; Jon 4:2)

2:14 The hoped-for *blessing* is, of course, the blessing of a good harvest and renewed fertility generally (cf. Dt 7:13-14; 16:15-17). But this material blessing is not an isolated aspect of life; it is acknowledged as a good gift of the Creator in the *cereal offering* and *drink offering for the Lord* and as such is an integral part of a whole life lived to God. (Cf. 26-27: *eat . . . praise . . . know)*

2:16 To *sanctify the congregation* is to summon the people to an assembly for sacred purposes.

The mention of the *bridegroom* shows how all-inclusive the call to *repentance* is. The bridegroom was exempted from military service, "to be happy with the wife whom he has taken" (Dt 24:5); he is not exempted from this corporate act of repentance.

2:17 For the location of *vestibule* and *altar* see 2 Ch 8:12. The priests are probably pictured as standing with their backs to the altar of burnt offerings and facing the sanctuary, the abode of God.

For the taunt, *Where is their God?* cf. Ps 42:3, 10; 79:10; 115:2; Is 36:19; 37:13; Mi 7:10. The taunt implies that the God of Israel is powerless to help. The priests appeal, as it were, to God's concern for His honor.

2:18-27 The Removal of the "Northerner" and the Restoration of Life

2:18-27 The great reversal of fortunes is the Lord's doing and His alone (18-20). His holy zeal *(jealous)* for His honor as Israel's God and His *pity* for His people, in quick response to their penitent pleading, restore the ruin wrought by the invader and cast out the northerner, who *has done great things* as God's executioner and has had his day (cf. 11, 21). Because *the Lord has done great things,* the ravaged *land* (21), the famished *beasts* (22), and the starving sons of *Zion* (23) are called upon to cease from fear and to *rejoice* (23). The *years* that the locusts have made blank periods of ruin will be *restored* (24-25). The Lord of life is bestowing life, full life, on His people. They shall *eat* of His bounty, *praise* His name, and *know* that He is their God and is the only God. Life will be one harmonious whole, where man's economy, his liturgy, and his theology will make one music to the glory of God. (26-27)

2:23 *For your vindication.* The taunt, "Where is their God?" can no longer be leveled at them.

2:28—3:21 THE VALLEY OF DECISION: THE COMING OF THE DAY OF THE LORD

2:28—3:21 The locust plague now disappears altogether. For all its terror, it was but a whisper that heralded and prepared for the day when the Lord will *roar from Zion* (3:16). The last section of the Book of Joel (2:28—3:21) deals with the actual coming of the Day of the Lord, with the portents that herald the coming judgment to the church and to the world (2:28-32); with the standard of the last judgment (the place of the people of God in it, 3:1-8); and then with the execution of the last judgment, portrayed as war (3:9-12), as a harvest (3:13), and as definitive decision and division. (3:14-21)

2:28-32 Portents of the Day of the Lord

2:28-32 The first portent is the outpouring of the *Spirit* upon *all flesh,* with the result that all *prophesy* (28-29). The people of God as a whole will become for mankind what the Spirit-empowered prophet has hitherto been for Israel: the declarer and the interpreter of the will and work of God. Thus Israel prepares the way for the judgment on the Day of the Lord; for prophets force a decision and create a division, as the example of Elijah on Mount Carmel shows (1 K 18:21). The Spirit exposes human sins and is the potent Convicter (Mi 3:8; cf. Jn 16:7-11). Under the afflatus of the Spirit the prophets call humanity to repentance, as Peter did when Joel's prophecy found its last-days fulfillment. (Acts 2:14-40)

God will speak through a nation of prophets; He will also warn and woo the nations by *portents in the heavens and on the earth* before His *great and terrible day comes* (30-31). A tottering universe will warn all people of their doom and point them (this is the major emphasis) to the means of their deliverance, to the Lord who *calls* them. The *survivors* will be those who have heeded His call and, in obedience to it, *call upon the name of the Lord* (32). The key signature before Joel's stern music of judgment is the word concerning the Lord who "is Lord of all and bestows his riches upon all who call upon him." (Ro 10:12)

2:28 In quoting this passage at Pentecost, Peter substitutes "in the last days" for Joel's *afterward* (Acts 2:17); he is being true to the intention of the text in paraphrasing it thus, for the outpouring of the Spirit is in Joel closely connected with the last days, the coming of the Day of the Lord (31). And we find the outpouring of the Spirit associated with the ultimate manifestations of God's creative grace in the other prophets also. (Cf. Is 32:15; 44:3-4; Eze 36:26-27; 37:1-14; Zch 12:10)

3:1-8 The Standard of Judgment

3:1-8 The people destined to be God's messenger to the nations looms large in the picture of the judgment. As this people has been the hidden axis on which all history revolves, so it will be the manifest center of God's last judgment. The goal of God's judging is the redemption of His people (1); and men's fate in the judgment will depend on how they have dealt with God's people (2). As they have done to Israel, so it shall be done to them. "The saints will judge the world" (1 Co 6:2). It is noteworthy that the Lord identifies Himself with His people (*are you paying me back?* 4), just as Jesus identifies Himself with the least of His brethren in His portrayal of the last judgment. (Mt 25:40, 45)

3:2 *Jehoshaphat,* meaning, "the Lord will judge," is a symbolic, not a geographical name. The same valley is called the "valley of decision" in 14.

The judgment rendered will be the final fulfillment of the promise made to Abraham: "Him who curses you, I will curse." (Gn 12:3)

3:3 The fact that men *cast lots* for Jewish captives, sold a boy slave for the price of a *harlot's* hire, and a girl slave for the price of a drink of *wine,* indicates the brutal contempt with which the nations treated the people of God. (Cf. 19)

3:4-5 *Tyre, Sidon,* and *Philistia* are cited as typical cases, like Egypt and Edom in 19. The contemptuous violence with which they treated God's "people" and "heritage" (2-3) and the treasures of His temple (5) indicates that they are animated by a secret grudge against the true God; they are paying Him *back for something,* though He had never done them harm or wrong.

3:6-8 The judgment will be strictly according to the law of requital, an eye for an eye, a slave for a slave, deportation for deportation (cf. Ex 21:23-25). The *Greeks* are mentioned as a people who were, for Jewish feeling, particularly *far off.* The *Sabeans* were another such *far-off* people, a trading nation living in the southwest corner of the Arabian peninsula.

3:9-21 The Judgment

3:9-21 The judgment is pictured in three ways. It is a great *war* (9-12); the world's *mighty men* are summoned to prepare themselves and appear in battle array against the Lord. Thus the rebelliousness of sinful man, his revolt against God, is made clear. Strangely enough, the expected battle is not pictured at all. The Lord *will sit to judge* (12) in quiet sovereign majesty, and that is the sudden end of all rebellion against Him.

Second, the judgment is pictured as *harvest* (13): thus the deliberate character of God's judgment is accented. The judgment is no freakish outburst of fury but the long-prepared-for, long-due, deliberate settling of accounts.

Third, the judgment is portrayed as ultimate decision and division (14-21), with a strong stress on the positive outcome of the judgment for God's people. God has permitted and overcome the last concentrated assault against Him (9-12); He has in long patience allowed the grain and the weeds to grow up together until harvest (13, cf. Mt 13:24-30, 36-43). Now, on the Day of the Lord, the time for final separation has come. The noisy multitudes are gathered in the *valley of decision* (14). Their noise, which has filled the pages of history, is silenced by the voice of the Lord *roaring from Zion,* the place where His glory dwells (16; cf. Ps 26:8; 76:2; 132:13-14). The roaring of that voice will shake the universe (15-16) and will pronounce a doom of desolation on peoples like *Egypt* and *Edom,* oppressors and enemies of His people (19). But for His people that voice speaks everlasting peace: the Lord their *refuge* and *stronghold* (16), their city established for ever in security (17, 20), their land a land of paradisial plenty (18) and, above all, unbroken communion with their God: *You shall know that I am the Lord your God.* (17)

3:10 In Is 2:4 and Mi 4:3 the very opposite of the expression used here occurs ("They shall beat their swords into plowshares," etc.) in a description of the peaceful paradise of the "latter days." Joel (if he is later than they) is using a well-known expression ironically, to indicate that the enemies of God may expect the very opposite of paradise. If Joel is earlier, Isaiah and Micah are using an expression which Joel has made familiar to express the idea that the new age will put an end to the unnatural agony of war.

3:14 The Hebrew word for *multitudes* suggests both numbers and noise.

3:18 The *valley of Shittim* cannot be certainly identified. *Shittim* means acacias, which grow on dry soil; the meaning may be that even lands now arid will be well-watered.

3:21 For the triumphant tone of the words *the Lord dwells in Zion* cf. Is 24:23 and the beautiful words which conclude Ezekiel's vision of restored Jerusalem: "And the name of the city henceforth shall be, The Lord is there." (Eze 48:35)

AMOS

INTRODUCTION

Amos prophesied, chiefly if not exclusively, in the northern kingdom, Israel, during the long reign of Jeroboam II (784—746 BC). Those were great days. Israel's northern neighbor Damascus had been crushed in 805 BC and posed no threat; a succession of weak kings in Assyria could not trouble Palestine. Until the accession of Tiglath-pileser III of Assyria in 745 BC, at the least, Israel was free to expand her territory, to dominate the trade routes passing through her land, to develop a prosperous merchant class and a rich material culture, and to worship her God at numerous shrines with a rich and beautiful ceremonial. Priest and professional prophet gave their blessing to the status quo. (Cf. 2 K 14:23-29)

Politically successful, materially prosperous, culturally advanced, and religiously active, Israel did look like a basket of lush and lovely summer fruit (Am 8:1). But the fruit was full of worms and rottenness. In their power and prosperity the Israelites violated both of the twin commandments of love. They did not love the Lord their God with all their heart; their worship was deadened by formalism and shot through with vicious elements adopted from their pagan neighbors. They did not love their neighbors as themselves; the new class of the influential and powerful rich exploited and oppressed the poor and created bitter divisions within the family of the people of God. Since the members of the prophetic guild were silent, God raised up a farmer from Tekoa in the south to speak His annihilating no to all that. That farmer was Amos. (Am 7:14-15)

He spoke God's no so bluntly, so incisively, and so explicitly that the priest of Bethel, watchful over the royal interests and careful for the king's security, forbade him the land (Am 7:10-13). The priest Amaziah was not the last to find Amos' message oppressively negative. It is still dangerously easy to overlook the fact that Amos' no to the false religious and political complacency of Israel, to the cultus, to the sleek prosperity of the upper classes, to Israel's easy hope, and to the tame household prophets is a mighty yes to God in the glory of His Godhead; that he cannot speak his great words of promise until he has shaken sinners out of the encrusted complacency which insulates them against the call to repentance and faith; that, Israel's answer to his God being what it was, he could only picture the new people of God as arising, by a miracle of grace, from the wreckage of the old.

The NT does not often quote, or even allude to, the words of Amos. Stephen quotes Am 5:25-27 in his last appeal to Israel (Acts 7:42-43). James cites Am 9:11-12 at the apostolic council, in his plea for the free inclusion of the Gentiles in the church (Acts 15:15-18). And of course there are echoes from Amos in the Revelation to John, the NT book of prophecy in which all the ancient prophetic voices are heard again (Rv 8:3; 10:7; 11:18). But the message of Amos lives on mightily in the NT nevertheless. His no to all the human falsehood and sin which profanes God's holy name is heard again in John the Baptist, who has been rightly called a latter-day Amos; in our Lord's unsparing call to repentance; in Paul's proclamation of the exceptionless wrath of God on all ungodliness and wickedness of man, even "religious" man; in the evangelist John's unqualified antithesis between darkness and light; in James' volcanic denunciation of the rich—in short, wherever the NT Gospel asserts and bows before the verdict of the Judge to whom all flesh must come and wherever it insists on the unbreakable tie between worship and life. And in the nativity narratives of Matthew and Luke we see clothed in the flesh and blood of history Amos' promise that God would raise up the fallen house of David from its hopeless ruins and give mankind its hope. (Am 9:11-12)

OUTLINE

I. 1:1-2 Superscription

II. 1:3—2:16 God's Judgment on All Nations

III. 3:1—6:14 Oracles on the Guilt and Doom of Israel
- A. 3:1-2 What Does the Election of Israel Mean?
- B. 3:3-8 The Lord God Has Spoken
- C. 3:9-12 Let the Pagan Powers Assemble to Behold the Guilt of Samaria
- D. 3:13-15 The Judgment of God Strikes the Worship of Israel
- E. 4:1-3 Against the Sleek Ladies of Samaria
- F. 4:4-13 Israel's Vain Worship and the Lord's Fruitless Call to Repentance
- G. 5:1-3 A Dirge over Fallen Israel
- H. 5:4-17 Seek the Lord and Live
- I. 5:18-20 Against False Confidence in the Day of the Lord
- J. 5:21-27 Against False Confidence in the Cultus
- K. 6:1-14 They Have Become Futile in Their Thinking

IV. 7:1—9:6 Five Visions of Judgment: The End Has Come
- A. 7:1-3 First Vision: The Plague of Locusts
- B. 7:4-6 Second Vision: Judgment by Fire
- C. 7:7-9 Third Vision: The Plumb Line in the Hand of the Lord
- D. 7:10-17 Amos' Encounter with the Priest of Bethel
- E. 8:1-3 Fourth Vision: Basket of Summer Fruit
- F. 8:4-10 Against the Greedy Oppressors of the Poor
- G. 8:11-14 The Famine of Hearing the Words of the Lord
- H. 9:1-6 Fifth Vision: The Command to Destroy the Sanctuary

V. 9:7-15 A Word of Promise and Hope

1:1-2 Superscription

1:1-2 Amos prophesied during brilliant reigns, both in the southern (Uzziah) and the northern kingdom (Jeroboam II). In the northern kingdom, the scene of his ministry, the reign of Jeroboam II represents the last great political and cultural flowering of Israel. But the *words of Amos* speak a no to that morbid brilliance; his words are not words of human criticism but of divine judgment. In them the Lord, God of the covenant, roars His devastating verdict, at which His creation, rich meadow and tree-covered mountain, stand aghast.

1:3—2:16 God's Judgment on All Nations

1:3—2:16 The shepherd-turned-prophet invites Israel to behold the Judge of the nations at work. In a sweeping panorama of condemnation the Lord pronounces doom on the surrounding nations: Damascus to the northeast, the Philistine cities (Gaza, Ashdod, Ashkelon, Ekron) to the southwest, Tyre to the northwest, Edom to the south, Ammon to the east, and Moab to the southeast—a fearfully monotonous indictment of international brutality and cruelty. The people of Israel no doubt took deep satisfaction at the sight; perhaps they even joined in the recurrent intonation of *for three transgressions . . . and for four.* But they were soon to learn that no one, not even the chosen people, can be a mere spectator at God's judgment. Perhaps they began to be uneasy when they heard Judah, too, come under judgment for her disobedience and idolatry (2:4-5); certainly they were jolted out of spectator-complacency when the prophet ended his survey with the *three and four transgressions of Israel* (2:6)—and they were confronted with the fact that the rapacity and cruelty for which the Lord condemned the nations were part of their national life, at work between brother and brother in Israel (2:6-8); the fact that their corrupt life stemmed from a corrupted worship (2:7-8); the fact that their whole existence was one piece of rank ingratitude toward the God who had delivered them from Egypt, planted them in their land, and had given them the gift of Nazirite and prophet for the furtherance of their faith (2:9-12), and that they faced God's crushing (2:13) and inescapable judgment. (2:14-16)

Paul's proclamation of God's wrath upon all ungodliness and wickedness of men in Romans similarly proceeds from the rank and obvious sins of the Gentiles (Ro 1:18-32) to the less obvious sin of the one who judges others (Ro 2:1-16) and then to the indictment of the privileged Jew. (Ro 2:17—3:20)

1:3 *For three . . . and for four.* This use of increasing numbers for mounting effect is found also, e.g., in Ps 62:11; Pr 6:16; 30:15, 18, 21, 29; Is 17:6. The nations have gone on and on to fill up the measure of their sins.

Gilead, a region of Israel east of the Jordan, lay on the border between Israel and Syria (Damascus). The *threshing* with *sledges of iron* refers to some act of inhuman cruelty inflicted on Gilead by the Syrians.

1:4 *Hazael* and *Ben-hadad* were kings of Syria, Hazael founded the then-ruling dynasty. There were several kings named Ben-hadad.

1:5 The *bar* is the bar which secures the gate of the city. The *valley of Aven, Beth-eden,* and *Kir* cannot be certainly identified; Kir is mentioned in 9:7 as the original home of the Syrians. In 732 BC the Assyrians carried the people of Damascus captive to Kir. (2 K 16:9)

1:6 From the hostile neighbor to the northeast (Syria) the prophet turns to the hostile neighbor to the southwest, Philistia, represented by four of the five cities which formed the Philistine confederation (Gath is not mentioned but would be included in the "remnant of the Philistines," 8). Syria and Philistia are grouped together in 9:7 also.

The crowning transgression in this case is the carrying into exile of the total population of a vanquished enemy.

1:9 The offense of *Tyre* (representing Phoenicia) is similar to that of Philistia. The *covenant of brotherhood* may refer to the treaty between Solomon and King Hiram of Tyre (1 K 5:6), although that event seems rather remote.

1:11 The offense of *Edom* (descendants of Esau) is his inveterate enmity towards *his brother* Israel, which broke out again and again (e.g., 1 K 11:14 ff.; 2 K 8:20) and is frequently referred to in the prophets. (Is 34:5 f.; 63:1 ff.; Jer 49:7 ff.; Eze 25:12 ff.; 35:1 ff.; Ob 8 ff.)

1:12 *Teman* (a clan and district within Edom) and *Bozrah* (an impregnable fortress city in north Edom) are both used to designate the Edomites generally. Cf. for Teman: Jer 49:7; Ob 9; Hab 3:3; for Bozrah: Is 34:6; 63:1; Jer 49:13, 22.

1:13 The guilt of *Ammon* is, again, cruelty in war, and the scene is *Gilead,* Israelite territory to the north of Ammon.

1:14 *Rabbah,* also called Rabbath Ammon, the capital city.

2:1 The remarkable thing about *Moab's* offense is that it was committed, not against Israel but against Israel's archenemy, Edom. The Lord, God of Israel, is no mere national deity but Lord of all, whose wrath strikes all ungodliness and wickedness everywhere. The three doxologies of Amos (4:13; 5:8-9; 9:5-6) stress this universality of His reign. The *burning of the bones to lime* was intended to degrade the dead and to make him suffer even in death.

2:2 *Kerioth,* a city in Moab (cf. Jer 48:24), presumably its capital.

2:4 *Judah's* sin is disobedience and idolatry: for *lies* as a designation for idols, cf. Ps 40:4 (translated "false gods"); Is 44:9-20; Jer 10:14; Hab 2:18; Ro 1:25.

2:6-16 The indictment of *Israel* has been the goal of Amos' proclamation and is its climax. It is fuller and more detailed than all the rest. The prophet dwells on the guilt of Israel (6-8), expatiates on it as their ungrateful and unnatural response to the blessings with which the Lord had showered them (9-12), and in vivid language depicts the inescapable judgment that will overtake them. (13-16)

2:6-8 The sin of Israel is social injustice in an affluent society, the exploitation and oppression of the *needy,* the *poor,* and the *afflicted* by the rich and powerful. But Amos' indictment is more religiously pointed than "social injustices." The victim of injustice is the *righteous* (6), the Israelite living under the blessing and the claim of the covenant which the Lord has made with Israel. This covenant is being violated, and so God's *holy name* is being *profaned*, that is, His manifestation of Himself as the God of love and righteousness is being disregarded and flouted. The corrupted covenant life is the counterpart and result of their corrupted worship; worship of the Lord is combined with the licentious practices of the fertility cults, in which *a man and his father* consort with the same cult prostitute (7). This indictment of social injustice is a recurrent theme in Amos.

2:6 The rich sell the poor into slavery for trifling debts *(a pair of shoes)*. This may have been within the letter of the law (cf. Ex 22:3) but not within the favor of the God of the covenant, the compassionate.

2:7 *Turn aside the way of the afflicted,* that is, "They thrust the poor off the road" (Jb 24:4), so that they never reach their goal or obtain their rights. (Cf. 5:12; Ml 3:5)

2:8 "You shall rejoice before the Lord your God" (Dt 12:12); joyous feasting was a part of Israel's worship and sacrifice, prescribed by the Law. But the Israelites were reclining to feast *upon garments taken in pledge,* as security for a debt; the law enjoined that such garments should be returned to the debtor at sundown—"In what else shall he sleep? And if he cries to me, I will hear, for I am compassionate," the Lord said (Ex 22:25-27). And they drink wine purchased with fines exacted unjustly from the poor. They are not rejoicing before the compassionate Lord of the covenant; they have in effect made themselves a god of their own, an idol (*their god,* 8).

2:9-12 The God of the covenant who asks love and righteousness of His people is the gracious and mighty Deliverer of His people (cf. Ex 20:2). His mighty deeds attest Him and His will; the words of His *prophets* are a perpetual reminder of that will, and the consecrated *Nazirites* whom He has *raised up* (cf. Nm 6) are a walking embodiment and proclamation of that total devotion to the Lord which should characterize the life of the whole covenant people (11). But the Israelites have closed their eyes and ears to this; they have, by their luxurious and wanton lives, created a climate in which the Nazirite vow cannot be kept and have silenced the wholesome witness of the prophets. (12)

2:9-10 *The Amorite,* the pre-Israelite inhabitants of Canaan. (Cf. Gn 15:16)

2:13-16 Under the judgment of God the brilliant progress of the politically successful and commercially prosperous nation will grind to a halt (13). The picture of the unwieldly farm cart, overloaded with sheaves, halted and stuck where it stands, is in sharp contrast to the gifts of speed and power (all of them unavailing) pictured in 14-16. Before the God of judgment the swiftest and strongest are as helpless as a collapsed wagon.

3:1—6:14 ORACLES ON THE GUILT AND DOOM OF ISRAEL

3:1—6:14 The oracles of chs. 3—6 are a massive elaboration of the indictment and condemnation of Israel found in 2:6-16. Chs. 3, 4, and 5 all begin with the same formula, *Hear this word,* indicating a grouping of oracles, but there does not seem to be any regular progression of thought in the section. It is probably best to take each unit more or less by itself; the oracles are, of course, held together by a common presupposition and a common theme, and this shall be borne in mind.

3:1-2 What Does the Election of Israel Mean?

3:1-2 This oracle is probably designed to meet an objection made against Amos' oracles of doom. "We are God's chosen people," the Israelites would say; "How dare you threaten us thus? God will not deny Himself and forsake His elect, to whom He has pledged Himself." Amos' answer is that election is not only privilege, certainly not a magical protection against all evil; election establishes a personal bond between God and His chosen ones and involves responsibility. "Every one to whom much is given, of him will much be required" (Lk 12:48). The punishment which threatens Israel is not a contradiction of her election but a consequence of it (*therefore,* 2).

3:1 *Whole family.* Apparently both Judah and Israel are addressed; both could take refuge in the idea of election and so evade the prophetic word. But in the following, Samaria (the northern kingdom) alone is prominent. (3:9, 12, 14; 4:4; 5:5, 15; 6:6, where Zion and Samaria occur together)

3:2 The Hebrew verb for *to know* is stronger than its English equivalent. *Knowing* involves a personal connection and communion between the knower and the known and so often involves the idea of election, or choosing. Cf. Gn 18:19, where RSV rightly translates "chosen"; Dt 9:24; Jer 1:5; Hos 13:5; and in the NT, Ro 8:29.

The *therefore* must have been startling for Israelite ears; for the religious complacency of the chosen people cf. 5:18; 6:1; 9:10; Mi 3:11; Jer 7:10. John the Baptist attacked this same complacency in his day, Mt 3:9.

3:3-8 The Lord God Has Spoken

This oracle, too, meets an objection: "Who are YOU to threaten Israel with doom? By what authority do you say these things?" Amos' answer is that he is a prophet and speaks by God's authority (3:8). He leads up to his answer with a series of rhetorical questions which make the point that there is no effect without a cause (3:3-5) and no cause without an effect (3:6-8). In his case the cause is the Lord God and the effect is his (Amos') prophetic speech, however harsh and unwelcome it may be.

3:7-8 V. 7 interrupts the sequence of questions and seems, at first glance, to interrupt the argument. But is it essential to the thought.

Amos' hearers would agree that it is the Lord who sends misfortune *(evil)* on a *city* (6); they would also agree that the Lord God announces the coming disaster through His servants the prophets (7). Surely, then, the prophetic word which the prophet MUST speak (as surely as a man instinctively fears when he hears the lion's roar) has God's authority for it even if it be a word of disaster and doom. (8)

3:9-12 Let the Pagan Powers Assemble to Behold the Guilt of Samaria

3:9-12 The great pagan powers, Assyria and Egypt, are summoned to the high citadel of Samaria to behold the *oppressions, violence,* and *robbery* stored up within that splendid capital; even pagan morality will be shocked by the sight and will assent to God's judgment upon Samaria's defenses and strongholds (9-11). That judgment will be total destruction; Israel dare not dream of a "rescue." There will be just enough "rescued" from destruction to testify to Samaria's death by violence. (12)

3:10 The treasures *stored up* in Samaria are called *violence* and *robbery* because they have been acquired by violence and injustice. (Cf. 2:6-8; 4:1; 5:11-12; 6:12; 8:4-6)

3:12 The word *rescued* seems to be used ironically. According to Ex 22:13, a man entrusted with his neighbor's sheep was not held to make restitution for the animal if it was "torn by beasts" and if evidence of such death by violence could be produced, such as *two legs, or a piece of an ear.* So what is left of Samaria after God's violent judgment will be just enough to attest to His judgment. The words *with a corner of a couch,* etc., are obscure. The attempts to explain them are ingenious rather than convincing.

3:13-15 The Judgment of God Strikes the Worship of Israel

3:13-15 Those bidden to *hear and testify* seem to be the mighty and rich in Israel, who dwell in luxurious *winter houses, summer houses,* and *houses of ivory* (15). They will, in their persons and fate, be witnesses to the fact that their "religion," assiduously practiced at shrines like that at *Bethel,* will not shield Israel from the wrath of God. His wrath will shatter both the *altars* (14), monuments to their hollow worship, and their *houses* (15), monuments to their rapacity and luxury.

3:13 The word translated *against* might perhaps be better translated "in" or "within."

3:14 *Bethel,* one of the major religious centers in the northern kingdom. (Cf. 1 K 12:29-30)

3:14 *The horns of the altar* would be grasped by a man seeking sanctuary, cf. 1 K 1:50. The Israelites shall not have this benefit of asylum.

3:15 *Winter house,* cf. Jer 36:22. King Ahab's house *of ivory* receives special mention in 1 K 22:39. Excavations at Samaria have recovered quantities of ivory-inlay material.

4:1-3 Against the Sleek Ladies of Samaria

4:1-3 The ladies of Samaria are addressed as *cows of Bashan,* high-bred cattle of a fertile land. They luxuriate in bovine thoughtlessness on the profits of their successful husbands and prod them on, as good wives of successful men do, to greater efforts. They drink their cocktails with no thought and no heart for the poor, and so share in the guilt of their husbands, who *oppress the poor* and *crush the needy* (1). And, so the *Lord God has sworn,* they shall share in the punishment; they shall be caught like a fish on a hook and shall pass through the *breaches* of the walls of their ruined city and shall go, like driven cattle *(every one straight before her)* into exile. (2-3)

4:1 *Bashan,* a district east of the Jordan famous for its cattle. (Cf. Ps 22:12)

4:2 *With hooks.* This is not merely a figure of speech; captives were actually dragged off *with hooks.* (Cf. 2 Ch 33:11)

4:3 *Harmon.* Unknown. Some scholars suggest the reading "toward Mount Hermon," i.e., to the region (Bashan) from which they came.

4:4-13 Israel's Vain Worship and the Lord's Fruitless Call to Repentance

4:4-5 "Religion" was flourishing in Israel; the people of Israel *loved* (5) their pilgrimages to Bethel and Gilgal; they "felt good all over" when they sacrificed and tithed (4) and gave due publicity to their *freewill offerings* (5). Why should a dour prophet like Amos denounce their religion so scathingly, saying in effect: Your Sundays are Sindays and you ring the church bells to rebel (4)? Because they did not come to meet their God in Bethel and Gilgal (cf. 4:12); they did not turn to Him (4:6, 8, 9, 10, 11) and they did not really seek Him (5:4, 6, 14). In their worship they sought themselves, their own security, the continuation of the present rotten order of things.

4:4 *Bethel* was "the king's sanctuary and . . . a temple of the kingdom." (7:13)

Gilgal, situated in the Jordan valley near Jericho, was an ancient sanctuary with a long tradition. (Jos 4:19-24; 5:8-9; 1 Sm 11:12-15)

4:4 For the law concerning *tithes* cf. Dt 14:22-29. The Israelites, like the Pharisees of Jesus' day, apparently went beyond the requirements of the Law in tithing and, like them, "neglected the weightier matters of the law, justice and mercy and faith." (Mt 23:23)

4:5 *That which is leavened.* This was actually forbidden by the Law, Ex 23:18; Lv 2:11; extravagant religious zeal and disobedience coexist in strange fellowship.

Proclaim . . . publish. Cf. Mt 6:2.

4:6-13 Israel has not sought the Lord, but the Lord has been seeking Israel. His love spoke a stern language when it cried, *Return to me* (6, 8, 9, 10, 11). It spoke the language of famine (6), drought (7-8), *blight, mildew,* and *locusts* (9), of *pestilence* and war (10), and of great disasters comparable to the overthrow of *Sodom and*

Gomorrah (11). But it was the language and the work of love; the Lord's anguished cry, *Yet you did not return to me,* recurs in Jesus' cry over Jerusalem: "How often would I have gathered your children together as a hen gathers her brood under her wings, and you would not!" (Mt 23:37). Israel has refused to meet her Deliverer; she shall have to meet her God as Judge (12) in all His fearful majesty as *God of hosts.* (13)

For a prophetic poem of similar thought and similarly structured, with a solemn refrain, cf. Is 9:8—10:4.

4:6 *Cleanness of teeth,* famine. The *teeth* are *clean* because they have nothing to bite on.

4:7 At *three months to the harvest* rain is essential for the maturing of the grain. The partial character of the visitation made it plain that the Lord was not minded to destroy His people but was seeking to rouse their conscience and recall them to Himself. Cf. the partial visitations (one fourth, one third) in the Book of Revelation. (Rv 6:8; 8:7, 9, 10, 11, 12)

4:10 *After the manner of Egypt,* like the plagues with which God visited the Egyptians before the Exodus. (Ex 7—12)

The stench of your camp, caused by the many corpses lying unburied there. (Cf. Is 34:3)

4:11 *Brand plucked out of the burning.* Figurative for a last-minute unexpected deliverance from a desperate situation.

4:12 *Thus* hints mysteriously at the terror of the ultimate judgment to come; God's previous visitations have given Israel a hint of it, but only a hint. What the people of God must face when they *meet* the God whose love they have repeatedly rejected is indescribable.

4:13 The closing doxology praises the God of Israel as Creator, Revealer, Lord of all happening, exalted over the earth; who can escape the omniscience and omnipotence of the Lord who has innumerable *hosts* of heavenly servitors at His command?

5:1-3 A Dirge over Fallen Israel

5:1-3 The Lord sorrows over His obdurate people (2:6-11); His servant the prophet sorrows too. In a "limping" sort of rhythm, peculiar to laments over the dead, he intones a dirge over the virgin Israel, whose doom is so certain that he can speak of it as already accomplished (*fallen,* 2). The *land* in which the Lord promised to give her rest (Dt 12:10) will be her grave, her resting place in a tragically different sense (2). The city will be decimated, the *house of Israel* shall mourn 900 sons for every *thousand* that go forth to war. (3)

5:2 The term *virgin* is used frequently to personify communities such as Jerusalem (Is 37:22; Lm 2:13), God's people (Jer 14:17), Judah (Lm 1:15), or foreign nations (Jer 46:11; Is 23:12; 47:1). Here the term is peculiarly fitting, since it suggests the untimeliness of her death; she dies before her life is crowned with motherhood.

5:3 For the thought of decimation, with its suggestion of hope for a remnant, however slight, cf. Is 6:13.

5:4-17 Seek the Lord and Live

5:4-17 These verses all develop the theme announced in 4: *seek me and live* (cf. 6, 14). The theme is developed negatively, in warning and rebuke (which confront the hearers with the harsh realities of their situation before God and cut off all other possibilities of seeking security) and in repeated threats of divine judgment. The Israelites may not seek life on the paths of their accustomed and comfortable piety which take them on pilgrimages to *Bethel* and *Gilgal* or even so far south as *Beer-sheba* in Judah; that way leads to *exile* and nothingness, not life (5). They must face, honestly and radically, the deadly wrongness of their present ways and turn from them wholly; they dare no longer *seek evil* (14); they dare not *turn* the wholesome life-giving draught of *justice* into the bitter *wormwood* of injustice or *cast down to earth* the *righteousness* which should walk upright and patrol the peaceful paths of the people of God (7). They must give up the luxury which they have purchased, at the expense of the exploited poor (11), with *transgressions and sins,* with bribery and the perversion of justice (12). They dare no longer silence the voices which *reprove* their wickedness and speak the *truth* of God, and thus create a climate, an *evil time,* in which silence is the only recourse for the *prudent* (10, 13). The time has come when they must listen, if they would live, to the prophetic voice that threatens their present way with God's judgment, with *exile* (5), with consuming *fire* (6), with *destruction* that *flashes forth against the strong* (9), with a mass dying that fills the public squares with *wailing* and *mourning* and *lamentation* (16), with a plague like that of the fearful night when the Lord *passed through* the land of Egypt and smote the firstborn in the land. (17, cf. Ex 12:12)

The theme, *seek me and live,* is also developed positively, in exhortations and promises that mark this as one of the brightest and most hopeful passages in the whole somber message of Amos. The seeking which the prophet urges is not a desperate search after an unknown God; it is a turning to the revealed Lord, to the gracious God of the covenant (15), whom Israel knows from of old. Seeking Him is no vague mystical quest after absorption into the life of the deity; it is knowing and doing His revealed will, *hating evil and doing good,* in simple, concrete acts like *establishing justice in the gate* (15). The promises are the miracle of God's covenant love, persisting in the face of His people's disobedience and apostasy. In the light of that stubborn disobedience the prophet can utter the promise only as a "perhaps": *It may be that the Lord, the God of hosts, will be gracious to the remnant of Joseph* (15). But from God's side the promise holds, bright and sure: The Lord of hosts in His illimitable power (8) will be with them (14), and His presence means life (4, 6), life to the full: "For with thee is the fountain of life; in thy light do we see light." (Ps 36:9)

5:4 *Seek* (cf. 6 and 14) is here used in a comprehensive sense to describe the way of repentance and faith. Cf. Dt 4:29; Jer 29:12-14; Hos 3:5; 5:15; Zph 1:6; and Jesus' word, Mt 6:33; the sequence of the imperatives is instructive; only by *seeking the Lord* (4, 6), the gracious God of the covenant, does one find the strength to *seek good, and not evil,* to "bear fruit that befits repentance," as John expressed it. (Mt 3:8)

5:5 *Bethel* and *Gilgal* were northern, Israelite shrines, *Beer-sheba* lay in Judah, far to the south; a pilgrimage to it would indicate a strenuous religious zeal, ready to do extra work for extra credit, as it were.

5:8-9 The doxology to the Lord of creation and of history indicates how inescapable His judgment is (6, 9) and what it means to have this God "with you" as Guarantor of life. (14)

5:8 *Pleiades, Orion.* Cf. Jb 9:9; 38:31.

5:10 The *gate* (or the space inside the gate) of a city was the scene of the administration of justice. (Cf. 15; Dt 21:19; Ru 4:1-6, 11; Is 29:21)

5:14 *As you have said,* i.e., as you now claim He is, in your false sense of security (cf. 9:10; Mi 3:11). What is now a groundless boast can become, if Israel will repent, a living reality.

5:15 The term *remnant,* designating those who survive the divine judgment upon the people of God and constitute the germinal nucleus of the new people to whom God's redemptive future belongs, occurs here for the first time in prophecy; the idea itself is older (cf. 1 K 19:18). For Amos, cf. 5:3; 9:8-10; for the idea in subsequent prophecy, cf. Is 4:2-3, 6:13; 7:3; 10:20-22; 28:5-6; 37:4, 31-32; Mi 4:7; 5:3; Zph 2:7, 9; 3:12-13.

Joseph designates the northern kingdom, Israel (cf. Ps 80:1; Eze 37:16) or the whole people of God. (Cf. Ps 77:15; 81:5; Ob 18)

5:16-17 The dread alternative to seeking the Lord and finding life in Him is pictured as a visitation by God Himself (17) which fills the whole land with *wailing, mourning,* and *lamentation.* The professional mourners *(skilled in lamentation)* are not sufficient for the task; the *farmers,* hitherto despised and oppressed, are summoned too. The common disaster unites the oppressors and the oppressed. (16)

5:18-20 Against False Confidence in the Day of the Lord

5:18-20 The Israelites felt secure: They looked back on God's election of Israel and "put far away the evil day" (6:3), certain that God could not reject the people whom He had chosen. Amos had already shattered their complacency in that respect (3:2). But they had another prop for their complacency, their confident expectation that the *day of the Lord,* the day when the Lord would manifestly take up His power and reign, would mean light and triumph for His people and darkness and doom for their enemies. Amos now removes that prop too. The day of the Lord will reveal the Lord as the righteous enemy of all unrighteousness, including the unrighteousness of His own people. His judgment will come unforeseen and inescapably: a man may flee from it as a man flees from a *lion,* only to find it blocking his path as a *bear;* he eludes the bear somehow, runs home and leans panting against the wall—and the judgment of God finds him there, like a *serpent* dropping from the rafters to bite him (19). For a people secure in its sin and deaf to God's call that *day* will be *darkness, and not light.* (20)

For the *day of the Lord* cf. Zph 1:7 note.

5:21-27 Against False Confidence in the Cultus

5:21-27 Between election and the day of the Lord, the Israelites rested comfortably in the cultus, the apparatus of worship. So long as the appointed feasts were celebrated, the *solemn assemblies* duly held (21), the sacrifices *(burnt offerings, cereal offerings, peace offerings)* properly offered (22), and the liturgy properly conducted with the *noise of songs* and the *melody of harps,* they felt sure that Israel stood right with God and all would be well (23). This cultus was ordained by the Law and was among the good gifts of God to His people; but it was not designed and given to be a substitute for the salutary *waters* of *justice* and the *everflowing stream* of *righteousness* which alone can preserve and foster life within the covenant. When God's people so misuse it and corrupt it with idolatrous addition (26), it becomes an abomination to the God who ordained it. His people are offering Him the husk and withholding the grain; and He *hates* and *despises* it (21). There was a time, in the *wilderness,* when the covenant life grew and flourished without the elaboration of the cultus (25); and there will be a time, in the *exile* (27), when Israel, stripped of the cultus and of her false gods (26), will again be reduced to the ancient and essential simplicities of life and worship.

5:26 *Sakkuth* and *Kaiwan* were Assyrian star deities associated with the planet Saturn. *You shall take up* is a grim commentary on the impotence of these idols, in sharp contrast to the mighty God of hosts. (27)

6:1-14 They Have Become Futile in Their Thinking

6:1-14 Paul says of those who knew God and yet did not honor Him as God that "they became futile in their thinking and their senseless minds were darkened" (Ro 1:21). The futility and senselessness of the thinking of those who have removed God from the center of their existence is the note common to all the denunciations of this chapter, which addresses both the southern and northern kingdoms (both *Zion* [Jerusalem] and *Samaria* are addressed in 1, and the extreme northern and southern limits of the territory covered by both are mentioned in 14). The *notable men of the first of the nations* live on *at ease* and *secure* (1) under the sorry delusion that they are the great exception to the judgment of the just God (2), futilely thinking that they can *put far away the evil day* of His judgment by ignoring it (3). They fill the vacuum left in their lives by the removal of God with exquisite furniture, choice meats (4), choice music (5), choice wines in quantity, and choice unguents (6), studiously and stupidly ignoring the fact that the body of which they are members is sick unto death (6). They cannot, or will not, see that their perversion of justice is as futile and senseless as attempting to scale cliffs with *horses* or plowing *the sea with oxen* (12). They exult over their puny conquests as if they were lords of the world, with only themselves to thank for their victories. (13)

This impiously futile thinking invites the judgment of God, who will not be mocked. The *notable men* of the *first of the nations* who think to put off the *evil day* are bringing near the *year* (cf. 3 note) *of violence* which shall destroy them; they *shall . . . be the first to go into exile,* their revels ended (7). Their *pride* and the monuments which they have built to their pride shall be brought low (8). The time will come when the few survivors of the judgment will be afraid to mention the *name of the Lord* (which they might once have invoked for their salvation, Jl 2:32), lest the Lord track them down in their covert and destroy them (10). The Lord will *raise up against them a nation* which shall oppress them throughout the territory which the successes of Jeroboam II have rewon for Israel. (14; cf. 2 K 14:25)

6:1 *To whom the house of Israel come,* to pay court to them or to get their advice, to obtain favors or to obtain legal aid.

6:2 The general sense of this difficult verse seems to be: Are you, Zion and Samaria, any better than cities of Syria *(Calneh, Hamath)* or of Philistia *(Gath)*, doomed to be destroyed by the Assyrian conqueror? Have you any reason to believe that you are automatically exempt from God's judgment? The thought would be similar to that of 1:2—2:8: The evenhanded justice of God executes judgment on all injustice in all nations—or cf. 9:7-8. But the last line of the verse remains obscure.

6:3 A slight change in one letter of the Hebrew word translated *seat* would give a word meaning "year," which fits excellently as a parallel and contrast to the word *day,* while *seat of violence* does not seem to make much sense.

6:6 *Not grieved,* lit. "ill." They lack all sense of solidarity with their sick nation, the feeling which Paul has described in 1 Co 12:26; cf. Eze 9:4, where those who "sigh and groan over all the abominations committed in" the city are exempted from judgment, and Jesus' beatitude upon the mourners, Mt 5:4.

6:9-10 The picture, sketched in a few strokes, is this: The Lord has "delivered up the city" as He threatened (8). So many are the dead that, contrary to normal custom, they are cremated. The kinsman who arrives to perform the last rites finds no one in the house except one hidden in a far corner, so completely demoralized by the terror of the plague that he is afraid to mention the name of the avenging Lord—pronouncing the name of God may betray his presence to God and bring down upon himself, too, the judgment that has emptied his family's house (so his poor, half-crazed mind reasons).

Cremation was not the customary form of burial in Israel; the burning of the mutilated bodies of Saul and his sons was exceptional. (1 Sm 31:12)

6:12 Cf. 5:7.

6:13 *Lo-debar and Karnaim* are names of towns east of the Jordan, apparently captured by the Israelites. They are singled out by the prophet because their names lend themselves to grim word-play. The foolish pride of Israel exults in the capture of *a thing of naught (Lo-debar)* and in the manifestation of its power—*Karnaim* means horns, which are a symbol of victorious strength. (Cf. Ps 132:17-18)

6:14 The city of *Hamath* marks the northern limits and the *Brook of Arabah* marks the southern limits of Israelite territory. (Cf. 2 K 14:25)

7:1—9:6 FIVE VISIONS OF JUDGMENT: THE END HAS COME

7:1—9:6 The Lord God reveals His secret to His servants the prophets in a great variety of forms (3:7); the prophets speak "in many and various ways" (Heb 1:1). The plastic pictorial form of the vision impresses vividly on both prophet and people the quick and living character of the divine Word, reenforcing and driving home the message already given in speech. The five visions of Amos all repeat his message of imminent judgment; but they are not a mere repetition, an unbroken and undifferentiated series.

After each of the first two (the vision of the *locusts,* 7:1-2, and of *judgment by fire,* 7:4) the prophet intercedes for his people (7:2, 5) and the Lord God repents! (7:3, 6). Prophet and people are reminded that their God is no relentlessly mechanical fate but a Person with a will and a heart, who does not desire the death of the sinner, with whom "the prayer of a righteous man has great power." (Ja 5:16)

The third vision, that of the *plumb line* in *the hand of the Lord* (7:7-9), which cuts off intercession, is followed by the narrative of Amos' encounter with Amaziah the priest of Bethel (7:10-17). The story of the prophet silenced by the priest and ordered out of the land makes clear why intercession is no longer possible; a people which consciously rejects the Word of God is dooming itself, is committing the sin unto death (1 Jn 5:16), and is removing itself from the intercession of man.

After the fourth vision of the *basket of summer fruit,* which portends the end of the *people Israel* (8:1-3), a series of oracles once more hammers home the guilt and condign punishment of the greedy and dishonest oppressors of the poor (8:4-10) and points to a form of divine retribution hitherto not spoken of in Amos: God will punish the people's neglect and rejection of His Word by giving them the agony of a Wordless life, by sending *on the land a famine . . . of hearing the words of the Lord.* (8:11-14).

The fifth and final vision, which pictures the Lord ordaining the destruction of His desecrated sanctuary and those assembled in it (9:1-4), expands on the inescapability of His judgment (2-4) and is followed by a doxology in which the prophet bows before the majesty of the omnipotent Judge whose speaking has compelled him to prophesy. (8:5-6; cf. 3:8)

7:1-3 First Vision: The Plague of Locusts

7:1-2 For the devastating effect of a plague of locusts, cf. Jl 1:2-20.

7:1 *After the king's mowings.* Apparently the king had a claim on the first mowing, for the support of the royal cavalry (cf. 1 K 18:5), although nothing is known of this from other sources. In any case the *latter growth* was essential for the survival of the people.

7:2 The intercessions here and in 7:5 are an indication of what it cost Amos the man and Israelite to take his place on God's side, against his people.

He is so small that he cannot hope to survive the overpowering might of his Judge. (Cf. 9:5-6)

7:4-6 Second Vision: Judgment by Fire

7:4 *Fire* appears frequently in the prophets as a picture of God's consuming judgment (cf., e.g., 1:4, 7, 10, 12, 14; 2:2, 5). *The great deep,* the subterranean waters, Eze 31:4.

7:7-9 Third Vision: The Plumb Line in the Hand of the Lord

7:7 For the *plumb line* as expressing the judgment of God, cf. 2 K 21:13; Is 28:17; 34:11; Lm 2:8.

7:8 *The people Israel* are measured and found untrue, and so there can be no further suspension of judgment *(I will never again pass by them),* no more intercession by the prophet. Cf. "Weighed in the balances and found wanting," Dn 5:27.

7:9 Both the religious *(high places, sanctuaries)* and the political (*house* or dynasty *of Jeroboam*) life of the nation come under judgment.

7:10-17 Amos' Encounter with the Priest of Bethel

7:10 Amaziah wants to silence Amos, not because his words are false, but because they are against the national interest *(the land is not able to bear all his words)* and threaten the security of king (10) and kingdom (*it is the king's sanctuary . . . a temple of the kingdom,* 13).

7:11 For the threat of exile, cf. 5:27; 6:7; 9:4. Amaziah's report does not exaggerate.

7:12 Amaziah implies that Amos' motives are mercenary; *eat bread* means "make a living."

7:14-15 Amos' reply meets both Amaziah's insinuation and his command to be silent in Israel. He need not prophesy for a living; he has a livelihood as *herdsman and dresser of sycamore trees.* And he can take orders only from the Lord who has called and commissioned him as prophet.

In saying *I am no prophet, nor a prophet's son* Amos is simply saying that he is not a professional prophet, a member of the prophetic guild, who might reasonably be suspected of self-interest (for this technical sense of prophet's son, cf. 1 K 20:35). The immediate context (*prophesy,* 15) makes it clear that he does claim prophetic authority, and his oracles show that he sets a high value on the institution of prophecy. (2:11; 3:7-8)

7:16-17 The marks of the true prophet are on Amos' words to the priest; he has the authority and courage to make bitterly unwelcome and, at that time, fantastically improbable predictions: Amaziah shall see his wife assaulted by the soldiery of the invader, his children slain, and his property divided (*parceled out by line,* 17) and shall himself die in exile in a pagan *(unclean)* land, along with his people

8:1-3 Fourth Vision: Basket of Summer Fruit

8:1-3 *A basket of summer fruit* might seem an eminently fitting symbol for the northern kingdom during the reign of Jeroboam II, bright, colorful, beautiful. But *summer fruit (qayits)* has an ominous ring in Hebrew; it is close, in sound and spelling, to the word for *end (qets),* and to this the prophet attaches his prediction of *wailing* in the *temple* and the *silence* of death in the street.

8:3 *Silence.* Men will be so overwhelmed by the disaster that the usual lamentations (5:16) will be omitted. (Cf. 6:9-10)

8:4-10 Against the Greedy Oppressors of the Poor

8:4-10 The "basket of summer fruit" (1) is filled with rotten fruit; it is filled with "extortion and rapacity" (4; cf. Mt 23:25). As at the beginning (2:6-8) so here at the end once more the greedy oppressors of the poor are indicted. The holy days *(new moon, sabbath)* are too long for them in their eagerness to get back to business, crooked business with short measure *(ephah small)* and long prices *(shekel great),* inferior goods *(refuse of the wheat)* and false weights (5-6). The God in whom they boast (*pride of Jacob,* 7; cf. Ro 2:17) is the remembering Witness of their deeds (7) and will visit them upon the doers' heads. The earthquake shall make the ground under their hurrying feet as unstable as the flooding and receding *Nile,* and all the dwellers in the land shall *mourn* (8). *Daylight* will become darkness, *feasts mournings, songs lamentations,* the mourning will be as bitter and as hopeless as *the mourning for an only son;* the day of greedy business will end as *a bitter day* indeed. (9-10)

8:5 *Ephah,* a dry measure. *Shekel,* a weight (of silver paid as a price), later a coin.

8:6 *Buy the poor,* etc. Cf. 2:6.

8:7 *The pride of Jacob* probably means the Lord Himself; cf. 6:8, where He swears by

Himself, and 4:2, where He swears by His holiness.

8:9 For darkness as a symbol of judgment and disaster, cf. Amos' description of the day of the Lord in 5:16-20; for the eclipse as predictive token and accompaniment of "the great and terrible day of the Lord," cf. Jl 2:31; 3:15.

8:10 For *baldness* as a sign of mourning, cf. Mi 1:16.

8:11-14 The Famine of Hearing the Words of the Lord

8:11-14 The judgment of God is never so terrible as when He gives guilty people what they want, as their punishment. Those who refuse to see the Light are condemned to blindness (Jn 9:39); those who will not accept the gift which God has placed in their hands are stripped of even what they have (Mt 13:12). Those who want to have done with God and go their way, He gives up to the way which their heart desires; He plunges them into degradation, perversion, and senseless mutual malice. (Ro 1:24, 26, 28)

It is this kind of judgment which hangs over the heads of the Israelites, who say to their prophets, "You shall not prophesy" (2:12), who abhor him who speaks God's truth (5:10), who send uncomfortable prophets packing from the royal sanctuary (7:10-13). They will not hear; they shall not hear. There will be a *famine* more terrible than that of *bread* and *water;* people will hunger and thirst for the *words of the Lord* (11), will seek them the wide world over and not find them (12). Even the youngest and strongest will be unable to endure this drought (13). Those who deserted the clear regions of the divine Word for the murky world of myth and fertility cult *(Ashimah)* shall stumble in that dim world and fall, never to rise again. (14)

8:14 The name *Ashimah* (found also in 2 K 17:30) is probably an intentional corruption of Ashera, the name of the Canaanite mother goddess. It means "guilt" and would be the prophet's way of naming the goddess and condemning her worship in one breath. To *swear* by a deity is to acknowledge its reality and power.

The god of *Dan* would be the golden calf set up in Dan by Jeroboam I. (1 K 12:28-29)

The meaning of *the way of Beer-sheba* is obscure. Beer-sheba was an ancient and legitimate shrine and so not on the same level with *Ashima* and the *god of Dan.* Perhaps Amos is castigating an idle oath *(as . . . lives)* which expresses a superstitious belief in the saving efficacy of a pilgrimage to Beer-sheba. Moslems still swear by the way to Mecca.

9:1-6 Fifth Vision: The Command to Destroy the Sanctuary

9:1-6 The prophet beholds the Lord standing *beside the altar* in the sanctuary, perhaps at Bethel, and hears Him ordering its destruction. Therewith the last refuge of the people is cut off, and utter destruction ensues (1). The sanctuary cannot be their refuge, for they have desecrated it; they have resorted to it, not in order to seek the Lord and live (5:4, 6), but to transgress (4:4-5), they have lain down beside the altar on garments of oppression and have drunk the wine of extortion at their sacrificial feasts (2:8). They have corrupted the cultus with idolatrous admixtures (2:7; 5:26; 8:14); they have made it an abomination in the eyes of the Lord (5:21-23). Him they must now prepare to meet (4:12). His wrath they cannot hope to escape, neither in the depths nor in the heights of heaven and earth (2-3). Even in *captivity* they shall not be quit of Him; His *eye* will find them, and His *sword* will *slay them* (4). For Hs is *God of hosts,* in sovereign control of heaven and earth (5): His Word that once poured the *waters* of judgment *upon the earth* has power to overtake the guilty still. (6)

9:7-15 A WORD OF PROMISE AND HOPE

9:7-15 The Book of Amos closes with the miracle of a promise and a hope where all human possibilities of hoping are cut off, where all apparent possibilities of fulfillment are gone or will go. The apostasy of Israel has canceled the covenant; Israel has forfeited her favored place (cf. 3:2) among the nations and is now on a par with the remotest nation *(Ethiopians)*, on a par with her traditional enemies, the *Philistines* and the *Syrians* (7), a *sinful nation* destined for destruction (8). The *house of Israel* is bound for exile, to be *shaken* and sifted among the nations, and the *sinners* of God's *people shall die by the sword* (9-10). The house of David, bearer of the Messianic promise, will become a broken and dilapidated hut (*booth,* 11). The *cities* of Israel will be *ruined cities.* (14)

The remnant of Israel that emerges from the shaking and sifting of God will learn to seek the Lord, Him alone and Him wholly, and live (cf. 5:4-6); people will again learn to believe as Abraham believed, in hope against hope, in the God "who gives life to the dead and calls into existence the things that do not exist" (Ro 4:17-18). For the promise is His, and He alone will bring in the fulfillment. HE will remember the promise to Jacob (cf. Gn 28:14-15) and will not *utterly destroy the house of Jacob* when He destroys the *sinful kingdom,* that useless vessel unfit for His purpose (cf. Jer 18:1-11). He will raise up and rebuild the fallen *booth of David* and bring in His Messiah when the Messianic hope seems lost, to reign over the *remnant of* now hostile *Edom* and over *all the nations* whom He claims as His. His is the potent Word of promise, and the fulfillment is His deed (*says the Lord who does this,* 12). He *will restore the fortunes of Israel* and *plant* His people in their land in perpetuity (14-15), in a renewed, transfigured world where the seasons compete with one another to bestow their blessings and the once barren *mountains* flow with festive *wine.* (13)

9:7 *Caphtor.* Crete, the original home of the Philistines. *Kir,* cf. 1:5.

For the unfaithful *people of Israel* the exodus from Egypt can no longer be, what it once was, the ground and basis of their confidence; *for them* it is just another movement in history, which is all under the governance of God.

9:8 *The eyes . . . are upon.* Cf. 9:4.

The *kingdom,* the nation as such, goes down in destruction; the faithful in the *house of Jacob* will be preserved, to be used in God's fresh start.

9:11-12. Cf. Acts 15:16-18. Here as in Isaiah (Is 9:1-7; 11:1-10) and in Micah 5:1-6 the bright figure of the Messiah emerges from the darkness of judgment.

9:9 *No pebble shall fall.* When God sifts the sand of His people, not one of the *sinners of his people* (10) shall escape His judgment.

9:12 To be *called by* someone's *name* means to belong to him. Cf. Is 4:1, where it is used of a woman belonging to a husband, and Jer 14:9, where it designates Israel as God's property.

9:13 Such is the fertility of the soil and the benignity of the climate that plowing and harvest, grape-gathering and planting, follow one another in quick succession.

9:14 *Vineyards . . . wine . . . gardens . . . fruit,* cf. 5:11. The curse of senseless futility, which rests on life under judgment, will be removed.

OBADIAH

INTRODUCTION

All roads, of men and nations, lead to the judgment throne of God. The Lord, whose Word secretly governs all history (1, 18), shall have the last word concerning the history of men and nations. All days of history are therefore a movement toward, and prelude to, the Day of the Lord, the Day on which He will do openly and once for all what His Word has been doing throughout history; He will judge men and nations. All days of spite and cruelty (10-14) will be weighed and rewarded on that Day.

The prophet Obadiah (whom we know only from his little book) sees the impending judgment on Edom (kinsman, neighbor, and enemy of his people Judah) in this perspective; the word "day" runs like a scarlet thread through the first part of his prophecy, which announces the doom of Edom and the reason for its doom (1-14); and "Day of the Lord" is the heading of the second part (15-21). And the last sentence of his prophecy gives the judgmental Day its place in the whole sweep of God's activity: God's judgment clears the way for the final coming of His kingdom; it is the negative aspect of the establishment of His royal reign.

God's sovereign Word had told Esau: "You shall serve your brother" (Gn 27:40). The history of the nation descended from Esau (Edom) is a history of rebellion against the Word which assigns to men their place in history. Edom, established in its impregnable mountain fortress in the land south of the Dead Sea, had achieved nationhood and power while Israel was still the wandering people of God. When, on the march to Canaan, Moses asked for peaceable passage through the land of Edom, the king of Edom bluntly refused (Nm 20:14-21). The Edomites' first confrontation with their brother nation is typical of the relationship between the two in subsequent centuries. David incorporated Edom into his kingdom, but by about 850 B.C. Edom was independent once more and continued on its ancient course. The strong language used against Edom by the prophets of Judah witnesses to the inveterate enmity between the brother nations (Is 34:5-17; Jer 49:7-22; Lm 4:21-22; Eze 25:12-17 and ch. 35; Am 1:11-12; Ml 1:2-5). In 586 BC, when Jerusalem fell to the Babylonians, the Edomites filled up the measure of their fathers. They not only "stood aloof" on the day of Jerusalem's misfortune; they were like one of the strangers and foreigners who entered Jerusalem to sack it; they gloated, rejoiced, and boasted over the disaster of God's people, joined in the looting, and cut off and delivered to the enemy the surviving fugitives of Jerusalem (10-14; cf. Ps 137:7). Obadiah proclaims that for this violence done to a brother, Edom shall be visited with shame and destruction: "As you have done, it shall be done to you" (15). The judgment on Edom will be a token and prediction of the ultimate universal judgment on the Day of the Lord; then He will, in judgment and deliverance, establish His manifest and eternal royal reign. (15-21)

1-14 THE GUILT AND DOOM OF EDOM

1-14 These verses are practically identical with Jer 49:7-16. The relationship between the two remains an unsolved problem.

1 The nations are represented as speaking *(we)*, planning to attack Edom *(her)* in obedience to the command of the Lord. In 2-14 the Lord Himself speaks.

3 The Capital of Edom was Sela, which means *rock*.

5-6 The comparison with *thieves* and *grape gatherers* points up how completely devastating God's judgment on Edom will be. The past tenses in 6 and those in 7 are prophetic: Edom's doom is so sure that it is viewed as already accomplished.

7 The *allies* do not provide asylum for Edom's fugitives. Since the Edomites had a reputation for wisdom, *there is no understanding* how they could have been so thoroughly deceived in their allies. Their blindness is a part of God's judgment on them. (8)

8 *Mount Esau* is the mountainous country of Edom.

9 *Teman,* name of one of the clans descended from Esau and of the territory which they occupied, is used by the prophets as a parallel expression for Edom.

10-14 This description of Edom's behavior at the fall of Jerusalem is so vivid and dramatic that most scholars see in it the recollection of a recent event and believe that Obadiah prophesied not long after 586 B.C.

15-21 THE DAY OF THE LORD IS NEAR

15 The Lord will visit the deeds of the Edomites upon their heads. This just requital is a token and an anticipation of the great and final "day of wrath when God's righteous judgment will be revealed" and He "will render to every man according to his works" (Ro 2:5-6). For *the day of the Lord,* see Zph 1:7 and the note there.

15-16 The *you* in 15 is singular and refers to Edom; the *you* in 16 is plural and refers to God's people.

16 For *drinking* from a cup as an expression designating suffering under the judgment of God, cf. Ps 11:6; 75:8; Is 51:17, 22; Jer 25:15; 49:12; Hab 2:15-16; Eze 23:31-33; Zch 12:2; Mt 20:22; Jn 18:11; Rv 14:10; 16:19.

17 There is a hint here that God's people shall be both delivered from their enemies and cleansed of their sins. Mount Zion *shall be holy,* no longer disfigured by the people's sins but wholly devoted to the Lord. (Cf. 21)

18 *The house of Jacob* signifies the southern kingdom; *the house of Joseph,* the northern kingdom. A reunited people will serve God's purposes.

19-20 The southern Israelites *(Negeb)* will possess Edom; the western Israelites *(Shephelah)* will occupy Philistia; the rest *(Benjamin)* will occupy the territories of Ephraim and Samaria to the north and Gilead (east of the Jordan). A united people (17), augmented by the returning exiles (20), will overflow the borders of the land promised to the fathers.

20 *Halah* is a city, or district, of the Assyrian Empire to which captives of the Ten (northern) Tribes were deported in 722 B.C. (2 K 17:6; 18:11)

Zarephath is a Phoenician city situated between Tyre and Sidon; it represents the northern limit of the restored people's expansion into Phoenician territory. The identity of *Sepharad* is uncertain.

21 This verse is most important for an understanding of the prophecy of Obadiah, which is sometimes criticized as breathing a spirit of narrow and vengeful nationalism. First, the term *savior* marks the judgment on Edom as God's business and the deliverance of Israel as God's work; for *savior* is used in the OT for those deliverers whom the Lord raises up, empowers with His Spirit, and leads to victory, against all human probabilities, when Israel in desperation and repentance "cries to the Lord" (Ju 3:9, 15). The story of Gideon, with its emphasis on God's initiative, God's enabling presence, God's Spirit, and success in the face of staggering odds is a good illustration of what is meant by *savior* (Ju 6—7). Second, the closing statement *(the kingdom shall be the Lord's)* gives all glory to God. His is the triumph, not Israel's, and His is the kingdom and the power and the glory for ever and ever. And we can see, however dimly, beyond the *saviors* who shall rule over Edom, the figure of the Savior in whom the kingdom of God was incarnate on earth (Mt 12:28), the Lord to whom homage shall be paid by "every tribe and tongue and people and nation" (Rv 5:9). And the church of the NT can learn of Obadiah to believe in, to assert, and to pray for the coming of the Kingdom as Obadiah did in the days of the Exile, days as dark and as hopeless as any that the NT church has yet come to know.

JONAH

INTRODUCTION

Other prophetic books of the OT contain narratives (e.g., Is 7:1-17; 36—39; Am 7:10-17); the Book of Jonah is all narrative, and the prophetic message of the book is in the narrative. It is unfortunate, and misleading, that the narrative has come to be known as the story of Jonah and the whale. The whale, or "great fish," appears only in one episode, and that not the most important one, for a total of three verses (1:17; 2:1, 10). And the story is, strictly speaking, not Jonah's story either; it is the story of God the compassionate dealing with His servant Jonah the prophet. God is the chief actor in the drama; His "word" initiates and carries on the action (1:1; 3:1, 3). He "hurls" the "great wind upon the sea" (1:4), cutting off His prophet's flight and confronting the pagan sailors with the "Lord, the God of heaven, who made the sea and the dry land" (1:9). He "appoints a great fish to swallow up Jonah" (1:17) when the lot which reveals the divine will falls on him (1:7, 14) and marks him as the guilty one. He "speaks" and Jonah is returned to the land of the living (2:10; cf. 2:6). His Word spoken by the prophet works repentance in Nineveh (3:2-9; note especially 2 and 3); He spares that wicked city (3:10). He "appoints" the "plant" (4:6), the "worm" (4:7), and the "east wind" (4:8) which force the angry prophet to face and answer the question of God with which the story closes. (4:10-11)

The story is God's story. It is a story without a hero; Jonah is like the chief figure in some novels, an "anti-hero." He is a "Hebrew" who "fears the Lord" and can and does confess Him as Lord, the omnipotent and omnipresent "God of heaven, who made the sea and the dry land" (1:9), and yet he attempts to flee from His presence (1:3). He knows, as he prays from the deep, that "deliverance belongs to the Lord" (2:9); and he confesses that the Lord is "a gracious God and merciful, slow to anger, and abounding in steadfast love," a God who "repents of evil" (4:2). And yet he would rather die than see God's long suffering and mercy in free and full operation (4:3). He is put to shame by the behavior of the pagans to whom he begrudges God's mercy. A pagan ship's captain summons the sleeping prophet to prayer (1:6). Pagan mariners "row hard" to save his forfeited life (1:13) and with reluctance obey his command to throw him overboard (1:14, 15); their conscience is tenderer than his. They "fear exceedingly" and "offer sacrifice" to, the "Lord" (1:16) whose word and will Jonah disregards. The men of wicked Nineveh repent in sackcloth and ashes and "believe God" when His prophet threatens the overthrow of their city (3:5-9) and find in Him a merciful God (3:10), while the prophet in a suicidal rage protests against the undeserved compassion of God (4:1-5), the very compassion to which he owes his life. (Ch. 2)

The story is God's, and it ends with God's question: "Should not I pity Nineveh?" (4:11). Jonah's answer is not recorded, but the story leaves no doubt as to how God wanted Jonah to answer it, or how all readers of the Book of Jonah are to answer it. That question of God's is renewed in Jesus' parable of the workers in the vineyard, when the generous owner asks the workers who are growling at grace bestowed on others: "Is your eye evil because I am good?" ("Do you begrudge my generosity?", Mt 20:15; cf. 18:33). OT and NT unite to pose the question designed to be perpetually disturbing to smug men or smug churches who claim God's unlimited mercy for themselves and yet would limit it for others. The story of

Jonah reminds us that these "ethical" protests against mercy for scoundrels stem from an unethical root, from disobedience to the Word of our gracious God.

OUTLINE

I. 1:1-17 A Prophet Flees from the Presence of the Lord

II. 2:1-10 The Prophet Prays out of the Belly of Sheol

III. 3:1-10 The Prophet Obeys and Nineveh Is Spared

IV. 4:1-11 The Prophet's Anger and God's Question

1:1-17 A PROPHET FLEES FROM THE PRESENCE OF THE LORD

1:1-17 The prophet Jonah, whose call compels him to stand before his God (cf. 1 K 18:15), alert and ready to do His will, seeks to evade by flight into a far country the unwelcome commission to *go and cry against that great city Nineveh* (2). But he cannot escape his God by flight (3), nor by sleep (5), nor by drowning (12, 17). The mercy of God which seeks out even wicked Nineveh will not be thwarted, and God will not let His prophet go.

1:1 *Jonah the son of Amittai,* cf. 2 K 14:25.

1:2 *Nineveh,* capital of Assyria, situated on the east bank of the Tigris river, representing the pride and power and brutality of the kingdoms of this world at their worst, was the scourge of nations and the bitterest enemy of the people of God. For a picture of Assyrian arrogance, cf. Is 10:5-19; for the feeling of dread and hatred which this power inspired, cf. Nahum, especially 1:11; 2:12; 3:1, 4, 7, 19.

Cry against it, cf. 3:4.

Their wickedness has come up before me (cf. Jer 51:9; Rv 18:5). It is so great that the justice of God cannot pass it by.

1:3 *Tarshish,* probably Tartessus in southwestern Spain, for a Hebrew "the ends of the earth."

Joppa, the harbor city on the Mediterranean coast.

Flee . . . from the presence of the Lord. The prophet knows in his heart of hearts that he cannot escape Him, cf. Am 9:2-4; Ps 139; but disobedience is blind because it does not want to see. The motive for Jonah's flight is not stated until 4:2; it is not so much the unheard-of character of the mission (he is the only prophet who is commanded to go to an alien and hostile power) with its difficulties and dangers. Rather, Jonah knows that the announcing of judgment is at the same time a call to repentance and so a proffer of mercy (cf. Jer 18:8), and he begrudges Nineveh the possibility of the divine mercy which he as a member of the Lord's convenant people has himself experienced.

1:5 *Fast asleep.* Cf. the disciples in Gethsemane, who shut out the agonizing reality of the hour by sleeping, when the imperative of the hour is "Watch and pray" (Mt 26:41). There is a terrible irony in the fact that a pagan captain must summon the prophet (whose office is to intercede) to prayer.

1:7 For the ascertaining of guilt by *lot,* cf. 1 Sm 14:40-42; Pr 16:33.

1:11, 13 The pagan sailors are reluctant to kill the prophet; they exert themselves to save the man who would not exert himself to save pagan Nineveh.

1:14 *Thou, O Lord, hast done as it pleased thee,* because He had, through the casting of lots, pointed to Jonah as the guilty one.

1:16 What Jonah had sought to avoid by his flight is accomplished by his flight: the Lord is "found by those who did not seek" Him. (Is 65:1)

1:17 Jonah had tried to escape from the Lord in death (1:12). He does not succeed; the prophet who refused to pray (1:5) is forced to cry to the Lord "out of the depths." (Ch. 2; Ps 130:1)

2:1-10 THE PROPHET PRAYS OUT OF THE BELLY OF SHEOL

2:1-10 In the belly of the fish, in the depths of the sea, Jonah again learns to pray; his prayer rises *out of the belly of Sheol* (2), from the abode of the dead. Three things are to be noted concerning this prayer. First, the psalm-like content of ch. 2 is no simple transcript of what Jonah uttered then and there. His prayer is seen retrospectively, from the vantage point of his *deliverance* (9), and both his past petition and his present thanksgiving are recorded. Thus the whole span of Jonah's experience, from his plunge into the waters (1:15) to his return to dry land (2:10), is recorded in a highly economical way.

Second, the prayer concentrates on the inner, religious realities of Jonah's situation, with practically no stress on the physical aspects of his deliverance through being swallowed up and vomited out by the great fish. The *waves* and *billows* which *pass over* him are God's, His judgmental action (3). He feels himself consigned to the Pit, to Sheol, shut out from light and life (6, 2); and the utmost depth of his misery is that he is *cast out from the presence* of God (4)—he finds that what he once sought by his flight (1:3) is unendurable agony. Twice he recalls the *temple,* the sign and embodiment of God's presence among His people in the land from which he had fled (4, 7). Four times he speaks the name of the Lord, the covenant God of Israel; he *calls* to Him (2), *remembers* Him (7), thanks Him for his deliverance from the *Pit* (6, 9), and confesses Him as Author of all *deliverance* (9), to whom all *loyalty* is due. (8)

Third, it is important to note what the prayer (for all its eloquence and sincerity) does NOT say. Jonah does not mention his disobedience, except perhaps indirectly in 8 (where *vain idols,* lit. "lying vanities," could refer to his self-sought way). He utters not a syllable concerning his unfulfilled commission; his thoughts are all of Jerusalem and the *temple* (4), not of Nineveh. He is now, perhaps unconsciously, evading by his silence what he had once evaded by flight. The Lord has brought His servant a long way, but he is not yet prepared to answer God's great question in God's way. (4:11)

2:2 *Sheol,* the underworld, land of the dead.

2:6 *Roots of the mountains.* The earth and its mountains are conceived of as having their foundations in the waters. (Cf. Ps 24:1-2; Jb 38:4-11)

Bars, that is, bars of a gate. The land of the dead has gates which open to receive the dead but do not open to release them.

The Pit, dwelling place of the dead. (Cf. Job 33:18, 30; Ps 16:10; 30:9; 49:9; Is 38:17)

2:7 *Remembered.* Remembering is more than intellectual recall; when the Lord is remembered, He becomes a living Presence in the mind and the heart; faith is revived, and confident prayer becomes possible (cf. Ps 42:4-8). "Remember" runs like a red thread through Deuteronomy; Moses bids Israel remember God (Dt 8:18), His mighty deeds (Dt 7:18; 8:2; 24:9; 11:2-3), the former days (Dt 32:7), their former condition as slaves in Egypt (Dt 15:15; 16:12; 24:18, 22). This remembering is to shape and govern their life under the covenant.

2:8 *Forsake their true loyalty,* forsake Him to whom their loyalty is due.

3:1-10 THE PROPHET OBEYS AND NINEVEH IS SPARED

3:1-10 A straightforward narrative recounts the miracle of Jonah's undeserved second chance (1-2), the fulfillment of his mission (3-4), and its consequences. Nineveh *believes* (5) God and repents; king and people, man and beast, unite in a municipal act of penance; all *cry mightily to God* (8). The vigilant compassion of God *saw what they did,* and *God repented of the evil . . . and he did not do it.* (10). God's servant the prophet has been taught to submit to God's will of mercy. One question remains: Has he learned to love that will?

3:1 For a second chance after failure and forfeit, compare the history of Simon Peter (Jn 21:15-19); Peter's experience taught him to call God "the God of all grace." (1 Ptr 5:10)

3:4 The second half of this verse is the whole of Jonah's prophetic utterance; his *story* is the message of the book that bears his name.

Overthrown. The same word is used of the destruction of Sodom and Gomorrah, Gn 19:25.

3:5-6 *Fasting* (cf. Jl 2:12, 15), *sackcloth* (cf. Jl 1:13), and *ashes* (cf. Jb 42:6; Dn 9:3; Mt 11:21) are the regular manifestations of sorrow and repentance.

3:8 *Violence . . . in his hands,* possessions obtained by violence.

3:9 Cf. Jl 2:14.

4:1-11 THE PROPHET'S ANGER AND GOD'S QUESTION

4:1-11 The final encounter between God and His servant Jonah glaringly exposes the evil root from which sprang the disobedience which had expressed itself first in the flight (ch. 1) and then in the ominous omissions of his prayer (ch. 2). That root is self: self-love, self-assertion, self-pity. Twice he is *angry, angry enough to die,* and asks for death (1, 3, 8, 9), first because the Lord has been too gracious, gracious to the undeserving; he is like the sullen elder brother in the parable of the prodigal son, who views his father's lavish welcome for his undeserving brother as an insult to his deserving self (Lk 15:28-30). He is angry because he is hurt in his self-esteem, where all good men are most easily hurt. In his furious self-assertion he actually dares to reproach God with all that constitutes the glory of His name as the Lord, the covenant God of Israel (2). Then again he is *angry* because the Lord is not gracious enough—to himself. In overwhelming self-pity he asks to die when the gracious discipline of God removes his sunshade. (6-9)

By contrast, the love of God is luminously revealed. The words which the angry prophet hurls at God as a reproach set Him forth as the God who inhabits the praises of Israel, *a gracious God and merciful, slow to anger, and abounding in steadfast love,* the God who loves without limit and punishes only when He must, and therefore a God who *repents of evil* (2). His prophet is quick to anger, but He is slow to anger even in the face of that sullen selfishness; He will not let His willful servant die and clothes His rebuke in a patient, twice-repeated question (4, 9). And a third question (10-11) confronts the prophet with the mystery before which all people must bow in adoration, the mystery of the love of God, His love for Nineveh, the rebel and the enemy, the love of the Creator for the creatures whom He has made and fostered (*labor . . . make . . . grow,* 10) and will not let go. We cannot understand this love, for God is God and not man (Hos 11:8-9), and His love goes far beyond the utmost reach of human love (Ro 5:7-10). But we can, and must, bow before it and adore it; and it is for this obedient adoration that God's last question to His prophet asks. (11)

4:2 Cf. Ex 34:6; Ps 86:15; 103:8; 145:8-9; Mi 7:18; Lm 3:33; Jl 2:13.

4:3 *Take my life from me.* Other servants of

God longed for death too; Moses, because he found the burden of his office intolerable (Nm 11:10-15); Elijah, because his mission had apparently failed (1 K 19:4, 14); similarly Jeremiah (Jer 15:10; cf. 20:14-18). But Jonah wants to die because his mission has been successful, against his expectations and desire.

4:5 The shelter of the *booth* made of leafy boughs would soon be insufficient, when the leaves withered and fell, and so the shelter of the plant would be welcome.

4:8 *East wind,* the hot and withering sirocco. (Cf. Is 27:8; Jer 4:11; Eze 17:10; Hos 13:15)

4:11 *Not know their right hand from their left.* The immature and ignorant, yet penitent, pagans are under the mercy of God, who will not leave them in their ignorance. (Cf. Is 2:1-4; Mi 4:1-5)

And should not I pity Nineveh? Whatever Jonah's answer may have been, in the fulness of time One greater than Jonah (Mt 12:41) appeared who spoke the whole answer with His whole heart and wrote it with His blood. The reproaches of those who, like Jonah, reproached God for His free mercy fell on Him (Lk 15:2; Ro 15:3), who was in person God's quest for the lost sheep, God's search for the lost coin, God's welcome for the penitent prodigal (Lk 15). He, the wholly obedient, went willingly on the mission to which God's pity for all Ninevehs appointed Him, into greater depths than disobedient Jonah knew, and was raised again by the God who would have all men to be saved. He who spoke God's mercy to the full uttered His ultimate call to repentance, lest that mercy be received in vain. (Mt 12:40-41)

MICAH

INTRODUCTION

Micah of Moresheth, a small village to the southwest of Jerusalem, was a contemporary of Isaiah (742—701 BC). See the Introduction to Isaiah for the political conditions of the time. He has one passage in common with Isaiah (Mi 4:1-3; Is 2:2-4), and other passages of Micah show a marked affinity to passages in Isaiah (Mi 1:10-16; Is 10:27-32; Mi 2:1-5; Is 5:8-12; Mi 5:10-14; Is 2:6-22). But whereas Isaiah moves in the world of courts and kings, where the Lord speaks through him to the great political events and the crucial political decisions of the day, Micah's word concentrates more exclusively than Isaiah's on the internal conditions of his people and the judgment that Judah's social sins and religious corruption will bring down upon Judah and Jerusalem. Here his denunciations are unsparing, his announcement of judgment uncompromising, and his call to repentance incisive and moving. In his vision of God's future for His people and mankind, beyond the inevitable judgment, he is again at one with Isaiah; both prophets speak of the future universal reign of God and the advent of the Messiah from David's line in high poetry and with the inspired exaltation that makes their words a marked and signal part of the OT's thrust of promise toward the fulfillment in the New.

1:1 SUPERSCRIPTION

1:1 The introductory verse states the source of the prophet's authority and the historical setting of his prophetic activity. See the Introduction.

1:2-7 THE LORD COMES FORTH FOR JUDGMENT AGAINST HIS PEOPLE

1:2-7 Micah's first word is a proclamation of the impending judgment of God against the capital cities of Israel and Judah (5-6). Wherever the judgment of God may strike, it concerns everyone: He is the God with whom all humankind has to do. His wrath is revealed as a judgment on ALL ungodliness and wickedness (Ro 1:18), wherever it is revealed, especially when it is revealed in judgment upon His people (1 Ptr 4:17), whose history is the beating heart of His dealing with the human race. Therefore all "peoples" (2) are summoned to hear the prophet's annunciation of the God of judgment. He will manifest Himself on the earth; all creation will quail before the terrible majesty of His presence (3-4). So fearful a thing is the sin of His people, sin concentrated and focused in the capitals, Samaria and Jerusalem. Samaria shall be the first to feel the heavy hand of the God against whom she has rebelled: That proud and beautiful city shall be brought low—she shall reap the bitter harvest of her harlotrous idolatry.

1:2 For the thought that judgment upon the people of God involves and concerns all mankind cf. Zph 1:2-4; 1 Ptr 4:17.

1:2-3 The *holy temple* and *place* of God here signify His heavenly abode. Cf. Hab 2:20; Is 63:15.

1:4 *The mountains will melt . . . like wax; the valleys will be cleft . . . like waters poured down a steep place,* splitting into many cascades as they fall.

1:5 In the bold poetry of prophecy the capitals of Israel and Judah are called *the transgression* and *the sin* of the respective countries, since they are the center and focus of national life, where the responsible leadership is found, where national sin is concentrated, and from which it is disseminated. So in the NT Jesus' lament over the sin and doom of His people is a lament over the capital "city." (Lk 19:41-44)

1:6 *A heap,* of ruins. Cf. 3:12, where the same threat is leveled at Jerusalem.

Pour down her stones. Samaria, which King Omri had made the capital about 880 BC, had a magnificent high situation (Isaiah calls the city "the proud crown of the drunkards of Ephraim," Is 28:1, 3); the building activity of Omri and his son Ahab had made it a place of beauty and of military strength: It withstood the Assyrian forces, the most powerful army of its time, for 3 years before it fell in 722/21 BC.

1:7 Here the "transgression" (5) of Israel is

defined as idolatry *(images, idols)*. Rehoboam, the first king of the northern kingdom, had deliberately introduced and fostered a fusion of the pagan fertility cults with the worship of the Lord, in order to wean his people away from the temple and worship in Jerusalem (cf. 1 K 12:25-30). The *images* probably refer to the two golden calves which Rehoboam made and set up for worship ("Behold your gods, O Israel, who brought you up out of the land of Egypt," 1 K 12:28).

Hires and *hire of a harlot* describes Israel's infidelity to the covenant God with an image much used by Hosea, the prophet of the northern kingdom and an older contemporary of Micah (cf. Hos 1:2; 2:5; 3:3; 4:10, 12, 13, 14, 15, 18; 5:3; 9:1). It emphasizes both the personal character of the covenant bond which Israel is violating and the abhorrent form which the people's apostasy takes, that of participation in the licentious fertility cult of Baal, in which sacral prostitution played a vital role. The *hires* destined to *be burned with fire* are probably the adornments of the sanctuaries purchased with the money earned by the sacral prostitutes. The whole apparatus of idolatry was *gathered* from Israel's harlotrous devotion to Baal; the conqueror who sacks Samaria will scoop it up and use it for his idolatry. *From the hire of a harlot... to the hire of a harlot:* as it was gathered, so it shall be spent—a dirty and degraded business from beginning to end; the form which God's punishment takes impresses on Israel how low the people have sunk.

1:8-16 THE PROPHET'S LAMENT

1:8-16 God does not desire the death of the sinner (Eze 33:11). His Son wept over doomed Jerusalem (Lk 19:41-44); His prophet laments the lot of wounded Samaria (8) and beholds in agony a like fate threatening his own land, Judah, and its capital, Jerusalem (9). He sees the invader moving from the southwest toward Jerusalem and city after city succumbing to his power. Succumb they must, for this evil has come down upon them from the Lord (12, 15). Walls, chariots, warriors are of no avail; their lot is waiting in anxiety for good that does not come (12), rolling in the dust in despair (10), wailing (11) and exile (11, 16). The prophet bows before this judgment of God; yet he cannot but sympathize with his people's agony. Sadly he bids Jerusalem put on the insignia of mourning for her lost children, the conquered cities. (16)

1:8 To go *stripped* (barefoot) and *naked* is both an expression of sorrow and an anticipation of the garb of captivity (Is 20:2-4). The wailing howl of the *jackal* is referred to only here in the Bible; the night cry of the *ostrich* has been described like "the hoarse lowing of an ox in pain." (Cf. Jb 30:27-29; Is 13:21-22)

1:10-16 The general drift of this passage is reasonably clear. An invader is approaching Jerusalem from the southwest. City after city falls before him and Jerusalem itself is gravely threatened (12). This would correspond to the situation of 701 BC, when Sennacherib captured 46 walled cities of Judah and besieged Jerusalem (2 K 18:13—19:37). A full appreciation in detail is made difficult by the fact (a) that not all of the cities can be identified; and (b) that the Hebrew abounds in wordplay which cannot be reproduced in English; for example, *Beth-le-aphrah* (10) means "house of dust" and the misery of its inhabitants is therefore expressed in the command, *Roll yourselves in the dust.* Moreover, the text has suffered in transmission; many scholars resort to conjectural emendations in order to solve the difficulties.

1:10 *Tell it not in Gath* is probably a proverbial expression derived from David's lament over Saul and Jonathan (2 Sm 1:20). The general sense is: "Do not betray our desperate situation to our enemies, either by report or public lamentation, lest they gloat over our misfortunes."

1:11 *Pass on your way,* that is, into captivity. The inhabitants of *Zaanan* seek security by shutting themselves up within their fortifications. The last two lines of the verse are scarcely intelligible; perhaps the meaning is: "Do not hope to take refuge in Beth-ezel; the wails of its inhabitants show that it has fallen and cannot offer you any protection."

1:13 *Lachish* may have been one of King Solomon's "chariot cities" (1 K 10:26), center and symbol of military power. The city would thus be the *beginning of sin* and the home of *the transgressions of Israel* because the possession of horses and chariots made men trust in them rather than in the Lord (cf. Ps 20:8; Hos 14:3). See also 5:10-11, where the purification and restoration of the people of God is effected by cutting off horses, chariots, cities, and strongholds.

1:14 *Moresheth* is similar in sound to the Hebrew word for "betrothed woman," who is given *parting gifts* when she leaves her father's house. *Moresheth* will be lost to Judah as a departing bride is lost to her family. Achzib (from a root word meaning "to lie, deceive") will be a *deceitful thing* (like a brook that dries up in summer) because it disappoints the hope that it may be a defense against the invader.

1:15 The *glory of Israel* probably means the soldiery, or the nobility; cf. 1 Sm 4:21; Is 5:13, where RSV translates the same Hebrew word with "honored men." If they come to *Adullam,* the meaning probably is: They will return to the poor and unpromising beginnings of Israel's history as a kingdom. David took refuge from Saul in a cave near Adullam (1 Sm 22:1-2). Israel will be like the hunted outlaw David, with only the promise and hope of a kingdom to live on. This would be in harmony with 5:2, where the future Messianic ruler is said to come not from Jerusalem but from "little" Bethlehem, the place of insignificant beginnings.

1:16 *Zion* (cf. 13) is being addressed. For *baldness* as a mark of mourning, cf. Is 3:24 and Amos 8:10, where it is associated with sackcloth.

2:1-5 WOE TO THE LAND-HUNGRY RUTHLESS RICH

2:1-5 Those who do not love the Lord their God with a whole heart (ch. 1) cannot love their neighbor either. The heart which has been emptied of God is filled with greed. This greed is a restless evil; at night, when they should commune with their own heart on their beds and be silent before their God (Ps 4:4), the land-hungry rich commune with their greed, busily planning and devising schemes of more-having (1). It is a ruthless evil; what the greedy plan at night, they execute in the morning. What they have the power to do, they do, without regard for their victims or for the God of Israel, who has allotted to everyone his inheritance (1-2). They *devise* wickedness (1), God *devises* (3) their punishment: The ruthlessly land-hungry shall be landless; the invading captors shall possess the fields which they have schemed and sinned to get (3-4). Never again shall they have part in the land of promise. (5)

2:1 Cf. Is 5:8-10. They *work evil upon their beds* in the sense that they "work out plans" for it.

2:3 The nation is called *this family,* a group in which ties of blood count as a power that unites people; the ruthless disregard of these ties invokes the divine judgment.

2:4 God *changes the portion* of His people when He gives the land which is their inheritance to their *captors.*

2:5 There is an allusion to the original division of the Promised Land among the tribes by lot (Nm 26:55; Jos 14:2, etc.). When the time of restoration comes (cf. 12-13), the ruthless exploiters of the poor will be excluded from the reapportionment of lands.

2:6-11 "DO NOT PREACH"

2:6-11 Brutal disregard for the rights of one's fellowman (2:1-5) and a cynical disregard for the Word of God go hand in hand (2:6-11). The patricians of property want a windy preacher who will pronounce a blessing on their cocktails (11), not a disturber of their pleasant security who threatens them with disgrace (6). They forget that they have to do with the Spirit of the Lord when the prophet speaks to them (7). Under the impulse of the Spirit the prophet must declare to them their transgression and sin (8-9) and must announce the punishment that awaits them. (10)

2:6 For the protest against unpalatable prophecy cf. Is 30:9-10; Am 2:12; 5:10; 7:16. For the complacent sense of security cf. 3:11.

2:7 This difficult verse is variously interpreted. The RSV translators take it as the prophet's reply to his critics, and the sense seems to be: "Is this how members of God's people should reply to the voice of God speaking through His prophet? Is your impatience with my message a product of the Spirit who inspires my message (cf. 3:8)? Are these your ruthless deeds and your reckless words *his doings,* that is, is the Lord of the covenant the Author of your covenant-breaking? My words, severe though they may be, *do good* to him who receives them in a good and honest heart and repents."—The phrase *Is the Spirit of the Lord impatient?* could also be rendered "Is the Spirit of the Lord too short?" that is, "unable to achieve its goal of exposing and correcting sin (cf. 3:8)—is my accusation false?"

2:8 *Strip the robe,* i.e., take it as security for a debt, without regard for the compassionate injunction of the Law, Ex 22:26-27.

2:9 *My glory,* the possessions with which the Lord has honored them.

2:10 *Arise and go,* into exile. The land in which the Lord promised to give them *rest* (Dt 12:9-10) can no longer harbor them; the threat of Lv 18:28 will be fulfilled: "Lest the land vomit you out, when you defile it, as it vomited out the nation that was before you."

2:12-13 THE PROMISE FOR THE REMNANT OF ISRAEL

2:12-13 The inspired words of the prophet "do good to him who walks uprightly" (2:7). Therefore the word of judgment is not the only word nor is it the last word which the prophet has to speak. However much Israel may fail, the Word of God will not fail, and the covenant-will of God will create a new future where the self-seeking will of man has cut off all hope. The Good Shepherd will gather His flock (12); the downtrodden, leaderless poor shall have a Leader who leads them into freedom and life, and the Lord shall be their King. (13)

2:12 For the abrupt transition from threat to promise, cf. the end of ch. 3 and the beginning of ch. 4; Is 4:2; 9:1-2; Jer 30:16; Hos 1:9-10; 2:14; 11:7-9; 13:16; 14:1-7.

The Lord, the Shepherd King, will gather His flock and restore His sheep to their home pasture; the exile foretold in 1:11, 16; 2:4, 10 is presupposed. *All of you* and *remnant of Israel* are used synonymously; the *remnant* (those who survive the judgment) is the whole true Israel. The remnant is a germinal remnant, a "holy seed" (Is 6:13), and becomes *a noisy multitude of men.*

2:13 The exile is pictured as an imprisonment. *He who opens the breach* is the divinely appointed Leader who leads the people of God into liberty, such as Moses had been and Christ was, in a higher sense, to be. When the leader of the downtrodden and leaderless poor has done his work, then the Lord is King, God's Kingdom comes.

3:1-4 DENUNCIATION OF THE UNSCRUPULOUS RULERS OF THE HOUSE OF ISRAEL

3:1-4 "Those who devise wickedness and work evil upon their beds" (2:1) are not an isolated phenomenon in the life of the people; the very structure of government is corrupted. The *heads* and *rulers* of *Israel,* who should know justice, that is, understand it and administer it, so that each member of the covenant people might enjoy the security and the blessings of the covenant—they are the ones who *hate the good and love the evil;* their whole attitude is the antithesis of justice. And their deeds are an expression of their attitude: They brutally exploit and ruin *God's* people (*my people,* 2-3). Justice becomes a means to their ends; they ignore God when they do not need Him. They shall not find Him in the evil time when they do need Him; He will not answer their cry, and the Lord whose face once shone in blessing on His people will hide His face from them. (4)

3:4 Cf. Pr 1:28; Is 1:15.

3:5-8 DENUNCIATION OF THE FALSE PROPHETS

3:5-8 Those who administer God's justice have forfeited their right to exist and have separated themselves from God; the prophets, the bearers of God's Word to God's people, also have abdicated. They know what side their bread is buttered on and confer the divine sanction on the hand that feeds them (5). They have become the kind of prophet that the people want (2:11); but God cannot use them. The sun of revelation shall go down, and the darkness of God's silence shall shroud them in shame (6-7). The misused and desecrated gift is withdrawn; "from him who has not, even what he has will be taken away" (Mt 13:12). Micah can oppose himself, emphatically, to the false prophets as the true prophet; for he derives his power, not from those whom he flatters but from the God whom he serves. The creative Spirit of the Lord and His even-handed justice give him the power to oppose and expose the sins of people. (8)

3:5 For the mercenary, self-seeking character of the prophets, cf. 11. *Declare war,* lit. "sanctify war," that is declare a holy war, threatening men with the vengeance of the Lord Himself.

3:7 *Disgraced . . . put to shame,* because their past predictions and assurances are proved false by the event (cf. 12) and because they now have *no answer from God.* The last days of Saul provide a grim and tragic commentary on the words *no answer from God* (1 Sm 28:6, 15-19). For *cover their lips* as an expression of the shame of being ostracized and of sorrow, cf. Lv 13:45; Eze 24:17, 22.

3:8 The similarity between this self-portrait of the inspired prophet and that of the Messiah in Is 11:2-4 has often been noted. Our Lord, the fulfillment of all prophecy and THE prophet of the last days (Acts 3:22), has the same features of high prophetic self-consciousness and fearlessness in the exposing of man's sin, cf. e.g., Mt 23. For the Spirit as the Exposer of man's sin, cf. Jn 16:7-11. For the apostolic counterpart to this prophetic integrity and fearlessness, cf. 2 Co 2:15-17; 4:1-6.

3:9-12 BRIBED JUDGE, HIRED PRIEST, BOUGHT PROPHET: DESTRUCTION OF JERUSALEM

3:9-12 Micah prefaces the announcement of the destruction and desolation of Jerusalem (12) with a final comprehensive indictment of the responsible leadership of Judah, those who have made Jerusalem "the sin of the house of Judah" (1:5). They have built Zion (10), made it splendid with winter houses and summer houses, houses of ivory, and houses of hewn stone (cf. Am 3:15; 5:11). But they have built it with *blood* and *wrong;* the city is a monument to their *abhorrence of justice* and their *perversion of equity* (9), which have exploited and ruined the poor (cf. 2:1-2, 8-9; 3:2-3). All the salutary orders given for the preservation of the people of God (the administration of justice, the instruction of the priest, the prophetic Word) have had to serve their self-seeking purposes (11). And they have crowned their sins with the sin of blasphemy. They invoke the Lord as Guarantor and Preserver of the corrupt national life which they have created (11). Therefore they have not built Jerusalem but destroyed it. God is not mocked: "The holy God shows himself holy in righteousness" (Is 5:16). Therefore Jerusalem must fall; its place shall know it no more.

3:11 *Lean upon the Lord.* Cf. Jer 7:1-15; Mt 21:12-13.

3:12 The *house* is the house of the Lord, the temple (4:1). Perhaps Micah is pointedly calling it simply *the house,* to indicate that God is abandoning the desecrated Temple: it can no longer be truthfully called His. Cf. Eze 10:18-19; 11:22-23, and Mt 23:38, where Jesus calls the temple, soon to be destroyed, not God's house but "your house," i.e., the house of those who have invoked upon it the judgment of God.—This prophecy of Micah's was long remembered in Judah; a hundred years later it saved the life of Jeremiah when he took up Micah's message of judgment on Jerusalem (Jer 26:16-19).

4:1-5 THE FUTURE UNIVERSAL KINGDOM OF RIGHTEOUSNESS AND PEACE

4:1-5 God will wipe clean the slate of Zion's tainted history, but His almighty hand will write anew. Ruined and depopulated Mount Zion is not the last scene in the drama of God's dealings with His people and, through them, with all of humanity. The Lord is Lord of the future, and in the *latter days,* whose date He alone knows and determines, the *mountain* of His *house* shall loom up wondrously in a new-created world (1). Not only pious Israelites will make their way to it; Zion and Jerusalem will be the object of the pilgrimage of all nations, drawn thither by the power of the Word of the Lord (2). With that Word the Lord will *judge:* He will make His righteous will prevail and will establish an eternal order of righteousness and peace; the instruments of war and the science of war will become obsolete, and the long, sad history of war between nations will end (3). Everyone will enjoy God's creation, the *vine* and the *fig tree,* without fear forever (4). That golden future is certain, however remote it may be, for *the mouth of the Lord of hosts has spoken* (4). The prophet therefore leads his people in an Amen of faith, in response to the revelation of His future reign: "Whatever gods may claim the loyalties of nations now, the future belongs to *the Lord our God,* to Him alone; and in the light of His revelation (*name*) we will walk until His kingdom comes." (5)

4:1-3 These verses are practically identical with Is 2:2-4. The question of whether one prophet is dependent on the other and, if so, which one, has been much debated without profit.

4:1 For the eschatological term in *the latter days* cf. Gn 49:1; Nm 24:14; Jer 23:20; 30:24; 48:47; 49:39; Eze 38:16; Dn 10:14; Hos 3:5. For the pilgrimage of the nations to Jerusalem cf. Is 66:18-23; Jer 3:17; Zch 8:20-23.

4:3 For the positive sense of *judge* as the establishing of a reign of righteousness and peace cf. Ps 96:10-13, where all creation is bidden to rejoice at the advent of the divine Judge, who is the Savior.

4:4 For the expression, probably proverbial, *under his vine and under his fig tree* cf. 1 K 4:25; 2 K 18:31; Zch 3:10

4:6-8 THE GATHERING OF THE EXILES AND THE RESTORATION OF THE FORMER DOMINION

4:6-8 In the sweeping universalism of the future kingdom of righteousness and peace, the *daughter of Zion* (the ancient people of God, 8) is not forgotten, nor is her role in the establishment of the kingdom negligible. The Lord will gather the strayed and scattered members of His flock and make of them the *remnant,* the vital nucleus of the *strong nation*, His universal people of the latter days, and He will *reign over them* in the new city of God *for evermore* (6-7). The promise made to David (2 Sm 7:11-16) and renewed by the prophets (e.g., Is 9:5 ff.; 11:1 ff.) will not be forgotten either. The *former dominion,* the everlasting reign of great David's greater Son, will come to the daughter of Zion (8). When the Christ, the anointed Son of David, appears (8), the kingdom of God (7) shall be at hand. (Mk 1:15)

4:6 *The lame,* lagging behind and shut out from the communal life of the flock, are a fitting picture of the exiled Israelite, deprived of national life and the community of worship at the temple. (Cf. Zph 3:19-20)

Whom I have afflicted. The exile is not a sad accident but the judgment of God. The promises of chs. 4—5 do not ignore the judgment announced in chs. 1—3 but presuppose it. (Cf. 10, 11; 5:1, 3, 10-14)

4:7 For the idea of *the remnant*, that portion of the community which by the commission of God survives His judgment and therefore is the hope for the continuation of the life of the people of God and the salvation of the human race cf. 2:12-13; Is 4:2-4; 7:3; 10:20-22; 11:10-16; 28:5-6; 37:31-32; Jer 23:3; 31:7; Zph 2:7, 9; Zch 8:6, 11-12; 9:7; Ro 9:27; 11:5. This important idea plays a significant role even where the term is not found, as in the story of Noah (Gn 6:5-8; 7:1, 23), Lot (Gn 19:1-29), Joseph (Gn 45:7), and Elijah (1 K 19:13-18).

4:8 The *tower of the flock* is the tower from which the Good Shepherd watches over His flock; God will again make His abode among His people on His holy hill and give them an anointed King.

4:9-13 THROUGH TRAVAIL TO TRIUMPH

4:9-13 The glory of the latter days is not yet; the way to glory leads through agony so intense that the *daughter of Zion* must *writhe and groan like a woman in travail*; without a *king* to protect her, with no *counselor* to guide her, she shall have to leave the *city* of her delight and traverse the long miles of *open country* into the land of her exile (9-10). But the suffering of *travail* is suffering for a purpose and in hope; out of the deepest depths of her suffering, *there,* the *Lord* will *redeem* her from the hand of her enemies. His will be the victory, and His the glory of redeeming love (10). The enemies of Zion, who have attacked Zion's God in their attack upon her (11), shall receive their due reward. They shall be *gathered as sheaves to the threshing floor,* and God's people shall become an ox with *hoofs of bronze* to *thresh* them out. This will be no personal, national triumph on Zion's part: The spoils of victory *(their gain)* will be *devoted* to the Lord who has, in redemption and judgment, manifested Himself as *the Lord of the whole earth* and given the victory. His will be the glory. (12-13)

4:9 *King* and *counselor* are parallel, denoting the same person. Cf. Is 9:6, where "Wonderful Counselor" is the first of the four names given to the Messianic King. What the loss of the King meant for Israel can be gathered from Lm 4:20, where the king is called "the breath of our nostrils . . . he of whom we said 'Under his shadow we shall live among the nations.'"

4:10 Since Assyria, not *Babylon*, was the world power which threatened the existence of Israel in Micah's day, the mention of *Babylon* presents a difficulty. The difficulty is historical rather than theological; that is, the message of Micah for us in our day is not affected by it. It may be that *Babylon* was inserted into the text by a later believing generation that applied the prophecy to themselves when Assyria had fallen and Babylon became the executor of God's judgment upon His unfaithful people.

4:11 *Let her be profaned,* desecrated, removed from the right relationship to her God. Their enmity is directed toward Israel's God; they want to demonstrate that the "holiness" (consecration to God) of the city is of no avail. *Gaze upon Zion,* gloat over her.

4:13 *I,* the Lord. The *horn* is a symbol of strength. Cf. Dt 33:17; 1 K 22:11; Ps 132:17. *Hoofs.* For the threshing ox cf. Dt 25:4.

For *threshing* as a picture of judgment cf. Is 21:10; Mt 3:12.

To *devote,* or consecrate, the spoils of victory to the Lord indicates that the cause and the victory are the Lord's. This devotion of spoils to the Lord (by utter destruction) is a constant feature of the holy wars of Israel. (Nm 21:2-3; Dt 13:13-19; Jos 10:28-40; Ju 1:17; 1 Sm 15:3)

5:1-15 THE RULER FROM LITTLE BETHLEHEM AND THE RENEWED PEOPLE OF GOD

5:1-15 The oracles of this chapter all deal with the great deliverance of "the latter days," the days of the Messiah. The chapter begins (1) and ends (10-15) with the judgment of God which must precede that deliverance. The two central sections deal with the Ruler and Deliverer from little Bethlehem and David's little clan of Ephrathah (2-6) and the "remnant of Jacob" under the beneficent reign of the Messiah. (7-9)

5:1-6 The Ruler and Deliverer from Little Bethlehem

5:1-6 As in the prophecy of Isaiah, so in Micah the bright figure of the Messiah arises out of the darkness of divine judgment upon the people of the promise (cf. Is 9:2; 11:1, "stump of Jesse"—the royal David's line has been cut back to its humble beginnings). The Israel of the prophet's time is unpromising soil—what promise can grow on it? Its capital is besieged, its king is impotent, insulted, and degraded (1). The Messianic future cannot be a development of potentialities that lie in Jerusalem or in the Davidic line; God will make a creative new beginning. He will go back to the village and clan of David (the word of Nathan will be fulfilled, 2 Sm 7:16), where he once chose young David over his strapping brothers (1 Sm 16:1-13). There, in a place and a clan too little to be statistically significant, He will raise up a Ruler after His own heart (*for me*).

This Ruler will be more than any son of David, more than David himself; his *origin is from of old, from ancient days*—he belongs to a primordial order that antedates David and the tragic decline of David's line, an order that will endure and triumph when David's line has failed (2). The judgment of God must run its course before He appears: God *shall give up*, surrender to judgment, His people until the time of His birth. His father is left mysteriously unnamed; human paternity, so significant in historical human kingship, does not signify here. Only the mother is mentioned, in the vaguest of terms (*she who is in travail*). There is a great mystery about the person of the Ruler. But there is no doubt about what His coming shall mean: a reunited people of God, a reign of a Shepherd King which is an incarnation of the strength of the covenant God (*Lord*) and of His majestic revelation (*name*), a reign which spells security for His people, a universal reign, *to the ends of the earth* (3-4). His reign is a reign of peace; no invading world power shall ever trouble Israel again. Under the blessing of His reign His people shall be invincibly strong and easily victorious. (5-6)

5:1 The situation is probably that of 701 BC, when Sennacherib besieged Jerusalem, 2 K 18:13—19:37; Is 36—37.

5:2 *Ephrathah* is the name of a clan in Judah, to which David belonged, *Bethlehem* the town in which the clan dwelt (Ru 1:2; 1 Sm 17:12). The two terms can therefore be used synonymously, as here and in Ru 4:11.

Micah's word concerning the Deliverer from *Bethlehem* is cited by Matthew in Mt 2:6 as fulfilled by the birth of Jesus in Bethlehem. He (or the scribes who answer Herod's question) interprets as he quotes, as was frequently done in Jewry; his "by no means least" is in keeping with the intention of Micah, according to whom Bethlehem was not *too little* in God's eyes. Neither Micah nor Matthew is interested in Bethlehem merely as a place; for both little Bethlehem stands in contrast to great Jerusalem, the humanly "likely" birthplace of the Messiah. For both evangelist and prophet *little Bethlehem* signifies that "God chose what is weak in the world to shame the strong . . . so that no human being might boast in the presence of God." (1 Co 1:27, 29)

5:3 For the birth of the Messiah as a child of mysterious parentage (with mention only of the mother) and connected with the return of the remnant (*the rest of his brethren*) cf. Is 7:3, 10-17.

5:5 *Assyria* as the world power threatening Judah in Micah's day; in a passage oriented toward the undefined Messianic future the *Assyrian* becomes a symbol of all hostile powers.

For the proverbial use of cumulative numbers (*seven, eight*) cf. Is 17:6; Am 1:3; Pr 6:16; 30:15.

5:6 *Nimrod* is founder of Babylon, and the whole of the Babylonian-Assyrian empire is thought of as his territory. (Cf. Gn 10:8-12)

Sword . . . drawn sword. Vv. 10-11, which indicate that the renewed people will be stripped of all *military* power, indicate that language like this (as well as that of 8-9) is picture language for might and victory, not to be taken literally.

5:7-9 The People of God As a Blessing and a Curse Among the Nations

5:7-9 Under the Ruler from Bethlehem the people shall be blessed; and they shall be a blessing to *many peoples*, as great a blessing as life-giving dew and rain. This blessing is theirs to impart, not by virtue of any national genius or a natural talent for religion but because they have become an instrument of blessing in God's hand. They shall be *like dew from the Lord*, which man can neither produce nor control; it is strictly His free and sovereign gift. (7)

They shall be a blessing; the promise to Abraham shall be fulfilled in them (Gn 12:2). Since they are God's own blessing and since man opposes God's blessing, they shall also be a curse among the nations: "Him who curses you, I will curse," the Lord said to Abraham (Gn 12:3). The same *remnant* (cf. 2:12; 4:7) which has been called *dew from the Lord* is now called devouring *lion* (8), an invincible nation triumphant over its *enemies*. (9)

5:7 For the people of God as a blessing upon mankind cf. Jesus' word concerning His disciples as salt of the earth and light of the world. (Mt 5:13-16)

5:10-15 God's Purifying Judgment on His People

5:10-15 The nation which the prophet has indicted so harshly (chs. 1—3) is not yet a people prepared to receive and impart the blessing of God, and it cannot be trusted to be the occasion and instrument of His curse. Before it can become a blessed dew from the Lord or the lion of His judgment, it must itself be purged by His judgment. And purged it shall be; the Lord will cut off from it all the devices by which men seek to secure themselves and assert themselves, apart from God, whether they be political (*horses, chariots, cities* and *strongholds*) or "religious" (*sorceries, soothsayers, images, pillars,* man-made idols, *Asherim, cities*). Before Israel can be blessed and become a blessing, she must be taught to walk humbly with her God. (Cf. 6:8)

5:10-14 Cf. Hos 8:14; 10:13; Is 2:6-8; 30:15-17; 31:1-3.

5:13 The *pillars* are the sacred stone pillars, signs of the presence of a deity, especially Baal, found in pagan shrines and taken over by Israel.

5:14 The *Asherim* are wooden pillars representing Asherah, the goddess of fertility often associated with the fertility god Baal. *Pillars* and *Asherim* are mentioned and denounced together in Dt 12:2-3.

Cities are mentioned both in the list of the political devices of man's self-assertion, together with "strongholds" (11) and here, among the "religious" devices of human autonomy, since *cities* are both centers of political-military power and centers of corrupted worship. (1:5; 3:9-12)

6:1—7:20 THE ROAD BACK TO GOD

6:1—7:20 The first three chapters of the Book of Micah are almost entirely condemnation and threat; chs. 4—5 are almost entirely promise. In chs. 6—7 these two motifs recur, but here threat and promise are more closely interconnected. The Lord's controversy with His people (1-5), recalling His saving acts from of old, opens the door of repentance (6-8). The voice of the Lord which indicts the city and threatens it with destruction and shame (9-16) is introduced with a sentence which hints, at least, that it is a voice that can be heard and heeded ("It is sound wisdom to fear thy name," 9). The prophet's lament over the sad total degeneracy of his people and the fearful consequences thereof (7:1-6) ends with the prophet's confession of trust in the God of salvation (7:7), a confession in which the remnant would join. And the section concludes with a wondrous liturgy of repentance, promise, prayer, and praise, which does not ignore the impending judgment (7:9) but can look beyond it because it praises the God whose incomparable glory is that He is the God who pardons iniquity. (7:8-20)

6:1-8 The Lord's Controversy with His People

6:1-8 The prophetic indictment now takes the form of a *controversy* (2) in which the Lord and His people are parties of the first part and the second part in a courtroom scene. The ancient *mountains* and the *enduring foundations of the earth* (2), in whose presence the whole drama of Israel's election and deliverance has been played, are witnesses. What right has God's people to be *weary* of the God of the covenant, to ignore Him and His covenant claim on them? Their "weariness" is rank and wrong ingratitude; the Lord has not wearied them but carried them on everlasting arms out of the house of bondage into the rest and freedom of the Promised Land, providing them with prophetic, priestly, and charismatic leadership, converting the curse of their enemies into blessing. His *saving acts* (5) prove His covenant fidelity and are an accusation leveled at His people's infidelity (3-5). The people have no answer to that accusation. They can only ask, "What is the way back to God whose covenant we have violated? Is it by way of extravagant offerings, measureless libations, or inhuman human sacrifice?" (6-7). The fact that they ask the question thus is in itself a damning indication that they have grown "weary" and forgetful of their God. For the Lord has *showed* them *what is good;* His law has made clear His covenant will for His creature man; and His prophets have called on them, in vain, to turn and do that will. Amos has bidden them *do justice*; Hosea has taught them, in words written with his own tears, *to love kindness*; and Isaiah has called upon them *to walk humbly with their God.* (8)

6:2 For the controversy between the Lord and His people cf. Is 3:13-16; 5:3-4; Hos 4:1; 12:2. In Jer 25:31 the Lord's controversy is with all nations.

God's creation (the hills and foundations of the earth) endures; it is preposterously unnatural that His people (also His creation, cf. Is 43:1, 6, 7, 15; Ml 2:10) should fail Him.

6:4 *Aaron* and *Miriam* are mentioned only here in the prophets. That their names should occur in connection with the Exodus is natural enough. (Cf. 4:14-16, 27-31; 15:20-21)

6:5 For the story of *Balak* and *Balaam* see Nm 22—24, especially 22:6, 18, 38; 23:8, 11, 12, 20.

Shittim was the Israelites' last halting place to the east of the Jordan before the entry into Canaan, *Gilgal* the first encampment on the west bank (Jos 3:1—4:20). To *know the saving acts of the Lord* is to encounter them as living realities in one's life and to act in accordance with the will of the covenant God revealed in them, namely, *to do justice,* and *to love kindness,* and *to walk humbly with God* (8). Cf. Is 1:2-3, where "Israel does not know" means that Israel does not act in accordance with the fact that God has reared him as His son; and Hos 4:1-2, where "no knowledge of God" means "swearing, lying, killing, etc."

6:7 Human sacrifice was not, of course, a part of the sacrificial system prescribed by the Law; instances that occur in Israel's history (2 K 16:3; 21:6) are branded as a pagan "abominable practice."

6:8 *He has showed you.* Cf. Mk 10:19.

Do justice. Cf. Am 5:24.

Love kindness. Cf. Hos 6:6

Walk humbly. Cf. Is 29:19.

This passage seems to have been in Jesus' mind when He spoke of "the weightier matters of the law" (Mt 23:23).

6:9-16 The Voice of the Lord Against the Greed, Dishonesty, and Violence of the City

6:9-16 The Lord is heard again, not now as a pleading party to a suit at law but as Accuser and Judge. He addresses the merchants and traders, shrewd, clever, and successful men, who operate with *scant measure* (10), *wicked scales, deceitful weights* (11), and *deceitful tongue* (12) and resort to *violence* (12) where craft fails. The God of "justice" and "kindness" (8) cannot *forget* their wrong or acquit the wrongdoer. *Therefore* (13) He is punishing them in their sinning; He condemns these sensible and successful men to a life that makes no sense and knows no real success (14-15). And He will punish them for their sins. They walk in the ways of *Omri* and *Ahab*, those unscrupulous and brilliantly successful monarchs of Samaria, whose "success" ruined the splendid city which they built (1:6-7); as they have walked, so they shall fare—their city, too, will become disgraced and desolate. (16)

6:10-11 Concerning false weight and measures cf. Dt 25:13-16; Pr 20:10; Am 8:5-6.

6:16 Nothing is known of any specific *statutes of Omri* which would fit the present context, the *statutes of Omri,* like *the works of the house of Ahab,* are descriptive of the temper and methods of these powerful and successful but irreverent kings. (1 K 16:21—22:40)

For the meaning of *hissing* as "object of contempt," cf. Jer 25:9; 51:37; Lm 2:15-16; Eze 27:36.

7:1-7 The Prophet's Lament over the Degeneracy of His People

7:1-7 The prophet in search of a *godly man* (2) among his people stands frustrated and disappointed, like someone standing among the fruit trees and the vines after the gleaners have brought in the last fig and the last cluster of grapes (1). The *godly man* (who loves kindness and walks humbly with his God, 6:8) and the *upright man* (who does justice, 6:8) are no more: It is man against man, brother against brother (2). *Prince* and *judge* and *great man* in their intense and unscrupulous self-seeking constitute an intermeshing network of evil, a hedge of thorns that entraps and injures the unwary (3-4). The *day of their punishment,* which *their watchmen,* the prophets, have foretold, the day of *their confession,* is no longer a far-off event; it is *at hand* (4). They taste the bitterness of its doom already, in a society where all the ties that bind people together are broken and no one can trust anyone (5-6); this is the end-result of the ruthless individualism which they have made their rule of life. For this society there is no human hope; the prophet, and those who heed his word, must *look to the Lord, the God of their salvation;* only he can answer their prayer for a better people and a better day, beyond the present day of judgment. (7)

7:4 For the prophets as *watchmen* over God's people cf. Is 21:6; Jer 6:17; Eze 3:17.

7:5-6 Cf. Ro 1:28-31 for a similar instance of God's judgment; God gives people up to the social hell which their "base mind" has created. Our Lord uses the language of Micah to depict the agony of division which His coming produces. (Mt 10:34-36; Lk 12:53)

7:7 Cf. Is 8:16-18.

7:8-20 A Liturgy of Repentance, Promise, Prayer, and Praise

1) 7:8-10 Repentance

7:8-10 However bleak the present prospect, the prophetic word, spoken in the Spirit of the Lord (3:8), will not have finally been spoken in vain. There will yet be a remnant of God's people who will in penitence assent to God's judgment upon a sinful people and will in faith look for deliverance to the God who justifies the ungodly. Fallen, in darkness, bearing the indignation of the Lord against whom they have sinned (the remnant consists not of sinless saints but of believers), they know that the Lord will be their light, that the God who is now hiding His face from them will lead them to life and victory.

7:8 *My enemy.* One may think of a neighboring people such as Edom, notoriously vindictive toward Israel (cf. Is 34:8 ff.; Ps 137:7; Ob 10-15). The enemy's exultation over Israel is a mockery of Israel's God (cf. 10) and so invites His judgment.

7:9 For the assent to God's judgment in repentance, cf. Ps 51:3-5; Ro 3:4. See also Lk 7:29, where it is said of sinners that they "justified God" in accepting John's baptism of repentance.

Deliverance, lit. "righteousness." The language of this passage is part of the OT background of Paul's use of "righteousness of God" and "justification by faith." Ro 1:17; 3:21-31.

2) 7:11-13 Promise

7:11-13 To a penitent people the unlimited promise is given. The walls of the ruined city shall be rebuilt, and the boundaries of the people of God shall be enlarged, to contain people of all nations (11-12), who come to the city of God and escape the judgment that desolates a sinful world.

7:11 For the extension of the boundaries of the holy land in the age to come cf. Is 26:15; Am 9:12; Ob 19-20; Zch 2:4; 10:10.

7:12 As the climax (*sea to sea,* etc.,) shows, the aim of the verse is to show the universal extension of the boundaries of the people of God.

7:13 *The earth,* i.e., all that is not within the hallowed precincts of the holy land. (Cf. Rv 22:15)

3) 7:14-15 Prayer

7:14-15 A people with such a promise to live on can pray with new fervor and confidence. They pray to the Shepherd of Israel to lead His people back to the green pastures of the Promised Land (14). And their prayer is heard; they shall witness again the wonders of the day when the Lord led His people out of Egypt. (15)

7:14 *Bashan and Gilead,* good lands east of Jordan which once belonged to Israel, Jer 50:19.

For God and Christ the Good Shepherd cf. 2:12; 4:6; Ps 23:1; 80:1; Is 40:11; Jer 23:1-6; Eze 34:11-24; 37:24-28; Zch 9:16; 10:3; Mt 18:10-14 (Lk 15:3-6); Mk 6:34; Jn 10:11-18; Heb 13:20.

4) 7:16-17 Promise

7:16-17 They shall behold more marvelous things than their fathers saw when they came out of Egypt. The nations shall not only tremble in terror and dread as they did at the Exodus when they saw the mighty arm of Israel's God laid bare (Ex 15:14-16); *they shall turn in dread to the Lord* and join in Israel's holy fear of the redeeming God.

7:16 *Lay their hands on their mouths,* i.e., be reduced to silence, Jb 21:5; 29:9.

7:17 *Turn in dread to the Lord,* in repentance and holy fear. (Cf. Hos 3:5)

5) 7:18-20 Praise

7:18-20 The Book of Micah ends with one of the greatest doxologies of that highly doxological book, the OT. It is song in praise of the incomparable Forgiver. He forgives gladly and freely, *because He delights in steadfast love* (18). He forgives compassionately and therefore wholly; He *treads iniquities under foot* and *casts* His penitent people's *sins into the depths of the sea,* never to rise up and accuse again. The God who blessed Abraham and made him a blessing to all the families of the earth (Gn 12:1-3) and was faithful to Jacob (Gn 28:13-15) and bound Himself to blessings with an oath (Gn 22:15-18) will not be turned from blessing by the sin of Abraham's seed or the transgressions of Jacob's sons. He, the Judge, can and will be the Deliverer who will deal with transgression and sin, radically and definitively. With that, the luminous shadow of the Cross falls across the last page of the ancient Book of Micah.

7:18 It is in God's power to deal with the hopeless tragedy of man's sin that His incomparable greatness impresses itself most on man: "There is forgiveness with thee, that thou mayest be feared." (Ps 130:4)

7:20 Cf. Lk 1:55.

NAHUM

INTRODUCTION

Nothing is known of the person of Nahum; even the location of his home, Elkosh, is uncertain. The time of his prophetic activity lies between the fall of Egyptian Thebes, 663 BC, which he recalls (3:8-9), and the fall of the Assyrian capital, Nineveh, in 612 BC, which he predicts. His message, expressed in some of the most powerful and impassionate poetry that the OT knows, can be summed up in the good news of 1:15: "Keep your feasts, O Judah, fulfill your vows, for never again shall the wicked come against you, he is utterly cut off." The centuries-long pressure exerted by the ruthlessly successful Assyrian empire on the whole Near East, the Assyrian triumph over the northern kingdom, Israel, in 722 BC, the Assyrian overlordship over Judah, and the infiltration of Assyrian ideas and idols into the life of the southern kingdom—these were not merely a matter of national concern to the people of God. It was not merely that their patriotic pride was hurt. Their *faith* was shaken as they watched the triumphant progress of this kingdom of this world. When they saw the land which the Lord had given to their fathers falling into the hands of a power which ignored and derided His Lordship, they were a people walking in darkness and dwelling in a land of deep darkness. Where was their God? Had He forgotten His people? Had He abdicated?

Nahum was empowered to speak God's answer to this dark agony of His people, to pronounce His Word of judgment on the "unceasing evil" (3:19) of Assyria's imperial pride and His Word of promise to His suffering people. If there is irony and taunt in Nahum's word, that is not the expression of Judah's national pride or of human vindictiveness. It is, rather, an expression of faith in the sovereign, unshaken superiority of Judah's God: "He who sits in the heavens laughs; the Lord has them in derision" (Ps 2:4). The church can, in her dark hours, draw courage from this laughter of God and can learn to hope confidently for the day when He shall set His King upon a holy hill that is higher and more enduring than Mount Zion.

1:2-11 HYMN TO THE LORD, THE AVENGER AND PROTECTOR

1:2-11 The *oracle concerning Nineveh* begins with a hymn which is very general in its adoration of the jealous wrath, the avenging might, and the reliable goodness of the Lord. Not until v. 11 does the Assyrian power come into view. The hymn is also markedly traditional in its language and imagery; almost every turn of its powerful poetry can be paralleled from the prophets and poets of Israel. It is as if the prophet were drawing on the hymn book of his people, as men of the church turn to the "Te Deum," or "A Mighty Fortress" or "Our God, Our Help in Ages Past" on great occasions, using the language of their fathers to express the prayer and praise of today's faith. This general, traditional introduction to the song of triumph over the impending fall of Nineveh serves a purpose; it fixes men's eyes on the God of their fathers, on His wrath, His mercy, His might, and so blocks the all-too-human impulse to consider the triumph of God as one's personal triumph, filled with personal spite and selfish pride. It makes men say: "Not to us, O Lord, not to us, but to thy name give glory" (Ps 115:1). Thus the prophet helps his people to respond to the summons to keep their feasts and fulfill their vows with a joy tempered by holy fear.

1:3 The phrase *slow to anger* makes clear that the divine wrath is no mere freakish fury but is the deliberate judicial action of the God who *will by no means clear the guilty.*

1:3-5 The *great might* of God, manifested in

nature, is such that all nature trembles and is undone at His approach.

1:4 The drying up of the *sea* and *rivers* recalls the mighty acts that accompanied the exodus from Egypt (Ex 14:21; 15:19) and the entry into the land of promise. (Jos 3:13-17; 4:23)

Bashan (famed for its fertility and its mighty oaks), Mount *Carmel* (whose slopes are praised in the Bible for their beauty and fertility), and *Lebanon* (noted for wine, cedars, and cypresses)—not even these choice portions of God's creation can stand before the annihilating presence of the jealous and avenging God.

1:6-11 The hymn closes with three challenging questions (6, 9, 10), all designed to show how irresistible the wrath of God is.

1:6-8 First question: No one can resist the divine indignation, which comes as inescapably as fiery lava and the earthquake. Only one course is open to man: to *take refuge in Him.* Whoever does so, finds Him *gracious,* a *stronghold in the day of trouble;* and more than that: God *knows* man, that is, enters into personal relationship with man, makes him His own, has regard for him. For this sense of *know* cf. Ps 1:6; 37:18; 1 Co 8:3; Gl 4:9 and, for the negative, "not knowing," Mt 7:23.

1:9-10 Second question: Perhaps Nineveh, or Assyria, is being addressed. There will be no need of taking vengeance twice, for the first judgment will be final. This proved literally true of Nineveh; she never rose again after her overthrow. The *entangled* (or interwoven) *thorns* are probably an allusion to the strong defenses of Nineveh.

1:11 Third question: This seems to be an allusion to the taunting and deceptive words of the Rabshakeh (general) sent by the Assyrian King Sennacherib to demand the surrender of Jerusalem in 701 BC. Cf. Is 36:1-22, especially vv. 16-20 for *counseled villainy.*

1:12-15 PROMISE OF FEASTS AND FREEDOM: THREAT OF DESTRUCTION

1:12-15 The hymn is followed by three oracles, all closely connected with the coming catastrophe of the fall of Nineveh. The first (12-13) is a promise of deliverance addressed to Judah. The second (14) is addressed to Nineveh and predicts the end of her name, her gods, and her life. The third (15) is a joyful cry announcing the coming of a Messenger who proclaims the good news to Judah.

1:12 Nahum is sometimes faulted because he does not, like the other prophets, deal with his people's sins. He does so here; the verb used here for *afflict* is often used of God's punishment of His people for their sins: 1 K 8:35; 11:39; 2 K 17:19-20; Is 64:12; see also Is 53:7, where it is used concerning the Servant who suffers for the sins of His people. For Assyria as God's instrument for disciplining His sinful people, "the rod of his anger," cf. Is 10:5 ff.

1:15 The first half of the verse is found also in Is 52:7; it contains, and helps define, two terms which became central in the NT proclamation: *good tidings,* the Gospel, as news of God's action which delivers people from a desperate situation; and *peace,* in the sense of divinely willed and divinely created soundness, wholeness, health, well-being. Nahum's words are therefore one of the countless fingerposts that point to the Christ, whose coming meant peace on earth (Lk 2:14), who "*is* our peace" in person. (Eph 2:14)

Judah, in keeping her *feasts* and fulfilling her *vows,* will be offering praise and thanksgiving to the God who has cut off her oppressor (*the wicked*). The feasts of Israel commemorate God's saving deeds (e.g., the Passover) and the fulfilling of a vow is, as the psalter teaches us, the expression of thanksgiving to God. (Cf. Ps 22:25; 50:14-15; 61:8; 65:1)

2:1-13 VISION OF THE FALL OF NINEVEH

2:1-13 In staccato style the prophet pictures, in a series of dramatic flashes, the impending fall of the city: The city hears the enemy approach and braces itself to meet his attack (1); the enemy appears in terrifying magnificence and exuberant military vigor (3-4); defense proves futile (5); there is panic and flight in the palace and the city (7-8); the enemy plunders Nineveh's limitless treasures (9). The result is a scene of desolation, ruin, and anguish (10), which is in stark contrast to Nineveh's former proud, aggressive, brute strength and secure enjoyment of her loot (11-12). The closing Word of the Lord (13) marks the fall of Nineveh as God's judgment on Nineveh and provides the transition to ch. 3.

2:1 The enemy is left unnamed; he is identified only by his effect on Nineveh (*shatterer*). In the last analysis God Himself is the *shatterer.* The commands (*man the ramparts,* etc.) are addressed to the rulers and people of Nineveh.

2:2 This parenthetic word makes clear that *the Lord* is at work here and that the dreadful judgment about to be proclaimed is not an end in itself. God is never merely *against* something or somebody; His judgment serves His purpose of salvation, the restoration of His oppressed and exploited people, who now resemble a tree with bare and broken branches, stripped of leaf and fruit.

2:5 It is the king of Assyria, apparently, who *summons his officers* to supervise a last desperate defense of the city. They rush to the wall, stumbling in their haste, only to find that they cannot drive back the enemy, since the attackers are protected by a *mantelet,* a movable structure which shields them against any missiles hurled upon them from the wall.

2:6 The *river gates* may be gates that open toward the river, or sluice gates that are opened to drain the moat and so allow the enemy to enter the city. In any case, the opening of the gates seems to be the decisive moment in the taking of the city; panic, flight, and pillage ensue. (6b-9)

2:7 The queen of Nineveh and her ladies face captivity; they are degraded and carried off. The word translated "palace" in 6b can also mean "temple"; some interpreters therefore take *mistress* to mean the statue of Ishtar, the Assyrian goddess of war and of fertility; the *maidens* would then be the sacral prostitutes in her service. This interpretation seems the more probable, since the *mistress* says nothing and does nothing (natural in a statue), while the *maidens* lament and beat their breast.

2:8 The image of the drained pool pictures the headlong flight of the masses of soldiery, who in their panic are deaf to the commands of their officers. (*Halt!*)

2:9 The invaders are pictured as urging one another on as they plunder the city.

2:10 Devastation and despair are left in the wake of the sacking of the city. The *loins,* thought of as the seat of man's strength (cf. 2:1), are the place visibly affected by affliction (Ps 66:11) and *anguish.* (Is 21:3)

2:11-12 The prominence of the lordly and ferocious *lion* in Assyrian religion and art may have suggested the picture here used to contrast Nineveh's proud and secure enjoyment of the fruits of her brutal military conquests with the desolation and ruin that awaits her now.

2:13 The judgment of God will effect the fall of Nineveh, not merely a combination of political and military factors; *God,* not merely the nations that rise to shatter her tyranny; God, the God of justice, is against her. The *messengers* are the Assyrian envoys and officials who represented the political power of Assyria in the empire, as the *chariots* represent her military strength.

3:1-7 VISION OF THE JUDGMENT OF GOD UPON NINEVEH

3:1-7 This second vision covers, briefly, much the same ground as the first. But there is an emphasis on the guilt of Nineveh, prepared for by 2:13 and touched on in 2:2 ("plunderer") and 2:11-12 ("lions' den") but not yet fully spelled out. Here Nineveh is branded as the city of *blood, lies,* and *booty* (1) and as the *harlot* of *deadly charms,* the imperial power that combined brute military power with deceitful diplomacy to bring down upon itself the hatred of all who became its victims; there is none to bemoan the fall of Nineveh. (7)

3:2-3 Again the attack upon Nineveh is pictured—in a series of exclamations. The emphasis on *hosts of slain* is new.

3:4 The *harlot* is here the picture of malicious seduction and deceit. For an example of Assyria's *deadly charms,* see the words of the Rabshakeh sent by Sennacherib to demand the surrender of Jerusalem in Is 36:13-20, especially 16-17.

3:5-6 Nineveh's punishment is pictured in terms of the public degradation meted out to harlots or adulterous women. (Cf. Eze 16:35-43)

3:8-13 ARE YOU BETTER THAN THEBES?

3:8-13 To predict the fall of Nineveh must have seemed to Nahum's contemporaries, perhaps even to Nahum himself, a piece of folly or, at best, wishful thinking: How was this tight-knit imperial organization, with its vast political and military resources, and this city, with its impregnable fortifications, to be overthrown? The answer is given to all men of little faith in these words: God the Shatterer has shattered invincible cities before; Egyptian Thebes (No-amon), as strategically located as Nineveh (8), supported by powerful auxiliaries (9), capital of a proud empire, had within recent memory (663 BC) fallen before the Assyrian king Ashurbanipal and had suffered the cruel fate of a captured city (10). The cup of God's judgment which Assyria held to the lips of Thebes shall be drunk by Nineveh now. (11-13)

3:8 Thebes was not situated on the *sea,* but the broad waters of the Nile protected her so effectively.

3:9 An *Ethiopian* dynasty ruled Egypt at the time of the capture of Thebes. *Put* is probably Somaliland on the Red Sea. The *Libyans* lived to the west of Egypt.

3:10 *Lots were cast,* to determine whose slaves they were to be. (Cf. Jl 3:3; Ob 11)

3:11 The wrath of God is frequently pictured as a cup from which the enemies of God must drink, to their confusion and downfall. (Cf. Ps 75:8; Is 51:17, 22; Jer 25:15-29; Lm 4:21; Eze 23:32-34; Hab 2:16)

3:13 *Woman* describes the men grown fearful and weak. The *bars* are bars which make fast the gates of the city.

3:14-17 YOUR PREPARATIONS FOR YOUR DEFENSE ARE ALL IN VAIN

3:14-17 In a series of ironic commands Nineveh is told to do her utmost to defend herself, to look to her water supply (necessary in the event of a siege, 14), strengthen with new masonry her already monumental fortifications (14), increase the personnel of economic exploitation and political and military administration of conquered territory (15b-17a). It will all be in vain; the fire and sword of the enemy will devour everything before him, like a swarm of locusts (15a), and the swarm of officials will disappear as suddenly and mysteriously as a cloud of locusts. (15a, 17b)

3:15 For a vivid portrayal of the devastation produced by the locust see Jl 1:4—2:11.

3:17 The *scribes* probably were officials engaged in the collection of taxes in subject countries. The point of comparison with the *grasshoppers* and *locusts* is the mysterious suddenness of their disappearing.

3:18-19 LAMENT FOR THE DEAD CITY

3:18-19 A short poem is the style of a lament for the dead, stressing the finality of Nineveh's doom, brings the book of the vision of Nahum to a somber and impressive close.

3:18 *Shepherds* (i.e., leaders) and *nobles* sleep the sleep of death, leaving a leaderless and impotent people, like a scattered flock, behind them.

3:19 Nineveh's doom is irrevocable; God has struck a fatal blow. And among all the millions of men over whom Assyria once ruled there is none to mourn her fall; all *clap their hands* in wild and vindictive delight at her ruin. That is the harvest reaped by men who have sowed *unceasing evil.*

HABAKKUK

INTRODUCTION

It was the prophetic task of Habakkuk to interpret for the people of Judah the significance of the rise of the Babylonian world power which succeeded Assyria as conqueror and dominator of the nations of the Near East. Nineveh, the capital of Assyria, fell before the Babylonians in 612 BC. The fall of the Assyrian overlord gave rise to the hope that there might again be an independent and powerful people of God, a hope which King Josiah of Judah strove to realize. When Josiah was killed in battle by Pharaoh Neco in 609 BC, that hope died with him. Judah came under Egyptian overlordship. And when Egypt was defeated by the Babylonian Nebuchadnezzar in 605 BC, the Babylonian power loomed up as the next threat to the freedom and to the very existence of Judah. Jehoiakim, the evil successor of good king Josiah, became a vassal (albeit an unfaithful one) of Babylon, and his land suffered from repeated incursions of Babylonian troops (2 K 24:1-2). It is into this period, between 605 and 597 BC (the date of the first siege and surrender of Jerusalem), that the prophetic activity of Habakkuk can be most naturally fitted. The promising days of Josiah, the reformer of the religious life of his people and the restorer (as was hoped) of the Davidic kingdom, have given way to the days of Jehoiakim, who "did what was evil in the sight of the Lord" (2 K 23:37); evil is rife in the land, and the threat posed by the Babylonian is no longer a cloud the size of a man's hand but a huge storm cloud, big with disaster.

Habakkuk gives the lie to the quaint but still widespread notion that the prophets were naturally gifted, independent interpreters of God's purpose in history. To Habakkuk history is a series of agonizing questions to which he cannot of himself find answers. He needed revelation, an "answer" from God, to enable him to understand and interpret what he saw in the history of his own people and the nations. He saw, in his own people, how the will of Judah's covenant God was being flouted—and how God looked on without apparently heeding the prophet's cry of "How long?" (1:2-4). When God finally answered the prophet's remonstrance, He pointed him to the history of the nations, to the Chaldeans (Babylonians) whom He was rousing up to be the scourge of His disobedient people (1:5-11). The prophet accepts the Lord's answer, in faith (1:12); but the answer of God raises more questions than it answers: How can God permit, and even promote, evil in order that good may come of it? How can His pure eyes look upon this monstrously cruel and successful nation that makes its might its right and deifies its own power (1:12-17)? In tense expectancy the prophet awaits the Lord's answer to his renewed complaint. (2:1)

The Lord's answer is not a diagram which makes clear the mystery of the divine governance of history; the answer itself says that it can be understood fully only from the vantage point of the *end,* the goal and conclusion of God's dealings with humanity (2:3). It gives to *faith* a light to walk by and to live in, for it confronts each person with a question, whether he or she is a member of God's people or not, the question: How do you stand before the God whose ways you cannot understand—do you depend on yourself, or do you rest in Him (2:4)? The fate of the individual *whose soul is not upright in him* but is inflamed by wine and filled with arrogance and greed (2:4-5) is portrayed in the fivefold *woe* pronounced upon him, threatening him with retribution from the Lord before whom all the earth must keep silence (2:6-20). To the person of faith, humbled by the sobering answer of God, there appears the vision of God going forth as of old, *for the salvation of His people* (3:1-15). Faith now knows that in Him alone there is life. The prophet, shaken and trembling, has unlearned his impatient questioning and *can wait quietly* till the vision has reached its appointed time (3:16; cf. 2:3) and can face a future about whose grim realities he has no illusions, *rejoicing* in the God of his salvation. (3:17-19)

The question asked by Habakkuk had a particular historical occasion; and the answer he received was to strengthen his faith and his people's in their particular situation. But Habakkuk's question is perennial, and the Lord's answer is valid beyond its first occasion. In this century of accelerated and intensified communication, which pours all the world's disasters into our ears every hour on the hour, the question that plagued Habakkuk is bigger and more insistent than ever before: Why does not God *do* something? And we still labor under the presumptuous delusion that God's ways (even after the great and mysterious revelation of His love in the Cross) must somehow be made transparent to us. The divine answer given to Habakkuk tells us that it is enough if those ways be luminous; that there are questions which we have no right to ask and answers which we have no right to expect; and that God *is* doing something all the while—that, above all, He is doing something to us which is of critical and everlasting importance to each of us. We are being asked whether we are content to lay our hand in His and walk with Him towards His goal; whether amid the dark and threatening uncertainties of the world's future and our own we shall let ourselves be taught by Him to speak the resolute Yea to His ways which our Lord Jesus Christ has spoken before us and to echo Habakkuk's final song: "Yet I will rejoice in the Lord, I will joy in the God of my salvation."

1:1-4 HABAKKUK'S REMONSTRANCE: THE LAW IS SLACKED

1:1-4 Habakkuk protests to the God of the covenant (*Lord*), the Giver of the *law* (4) and the Guardian of its operation (*justice*), that the covenant will of God is being violated within the covenant people. Why is the God of justice deaf to his cry and, apparently, indifferent to *violence* (2), *wrongs, trouble, destruction* (3), and the triumph of the *wicked* over the *righteous*? (4)

1:2 *Violence,* the breaking of the Law and violation of justice, is a recurrent word in Habakkuk. (Cf. 1:3, 9; 2:8, 17)

1:4 The verb translated *is slacked* means, literally, "grows cold." The Law is like a frozen hand which cannot come to grips with wrong. The expressions which the prophet uses (*strife, contention, law, justice*) make it unlikely that he is referring to conditions within Judah rather than, as some interpreters think, to violence on the international scene.

Habakkuk's cry is a cry of faith, a troubled, groping faith, but still faith. He cries out just because he is convinced that God is the God of justice and the Guardian of the covenant and has the will and the power to intervene.

1:5-11 THE LORD'S REPLY: "I AM ROUSING THE CHALDEANS."

1:5-11 The Lord's reply is an answer to the prophet's remonstrance. Wrongs and violence in Judah shall not go unpunished; the Chaldeans will be His scourge for chastising Judah (cf. 1:12). But the very terms with which He describes this scourge indicate that the Lord's answer is one which, far from being a demonstration of His justice that makes faith unnecessary, calls for the assent of faith which believes even where it cannot see. For the work which the Lord is undertaking is an *astounding* work, an unbelievable work (5). He will do His work with a rusty tool, a *bitter and hasty* nation (6), swift to swallow up in conquest, comparable only to beasts of prey (*leopards, wolves, eagle,* 8), scornful of every established authority (*kings, rulers,* 10), undeterred by any obstacle in their way (10). Indeed, they are, according to the Lord's own depiction of them, the very embodiment of what they are designed to punish: *Violence* is the end and object of their being (9); their might is their right (7), and their *might is their god* (11). *Guilty men* (11) are the instruments of divine justice.

1:5 The verbs *look, see,* etc., are plural; through the prophet the whole people, including both the wrongdoers and the faithful, is being addressed.

1:6 The *Chaldeans* are the Babylonians. For God's use of pagan nations as instruments of His justice see Is 10:5-27; Jer 25:1-13; 51:20-23. God can even refer to Nebuchadnezzar king of Babylon as "my servant." (Jer 25:9; 27:6; 43:10)

1:9 *Like sand,* that is, in countless numbers. (Cf. Gn 22:17)

1:10 Instead of beaching the wall of a fortress, these conquerors build a ramp of earth beside the wall and so scale it.

1:12-17 HABAKKUK'S SECOND REMONSTRANCE: THOU CANST NOT LOOK ON WRONG

1:12-17 The Lord's answer to the prophet's first remonstrance called for faith; and the prophet responds in faith. He recognizes the divine purpose of using the Chaldeans as *judgment* and *chastisement* upon Judah and clings to the Lord *(my God, my Holy One, O Rock)* in the assurance that to part from Him is death (*We shall not die*, 12).

But his faith cannot come to terms with the repugnant reality of the way which God is actually going. He still feels that he dare question that way, and he challenges God to give an account of Himself: Can God, dare God, use as His instruments men who are guilty of the very thing which they are to punish (13, cf. 4)? Can He who created humanity in His image reduce people to the level of *fish* and *crawling things* (14) by permitting the ruthless Chaldean fisherman to gather everyone in his seine (15)? Dare God encourage and foster the self-glorifying idolatry of the conqueror who worships his *net* and his *seine,* the instruments of his conquest? (16). Is this merciless international fisherman to succeed forever—will judgment never come? (17)

1:12 *Rock* designates God as a reliable, sure refuge. (Cf. Dt 32:4, 18; 1 Sm 2:2)

2:1-5 THE LORD'S SECOND REPLY: "LIVE BY FAITH"

2:1-5 These five verses constitute the heart of Habakkuk's prophecy. The Lord's second reply is marked as the decisive climax of His conversation with the prophet by the picture of the prophet's tense expectancy as he mounts his watchtower to await the Lord's reply (1), by the divine command to inscribe the prophecy and so to perpetuate it (2), by the command to wait for the fulfillment, and the assurance that the fulfillment will come (3), and finally by the fact that *faith,* which has been the unuttered burden of Habakkuk's remonstrances and the Lord's reply, is now mentioned by name. (4)

All that has preceded has led up to this, and what follows—the fivefold woe upon the individual *whose soul is not upright in him* (2:6-20) and the overpowering vision vouchsafed to *faith* of the majesty and mercy of God as He goes *forth for the salvation* of *His people* (3:2-15)—is an unfolding of the terms employed in the declaration of God's prophet in v. 4. That declaration does not divide us humankind into Chaldeans and Judeans but draws the line between the person *whose soul is not upright* (4), who is inflamed by *wine,* puffed up with *arrogance,* driven on by *greed,* the autonomous satisfier of himself (5), and the person who is *righteous,* that is, living before the God of the covenant on the terms of the covenant. The one *shall fail* in the midst of his doing, his active and energetic *gathering-in* and *collecting* for himself; the other shall *live* and shall live by *faith,* by holding firm in, and clinging to, the God whose ways he cannot understand but can accept, by *quietly waiting for the day* (cf. 3:16) when the conclusion of all God's ways will make their salutary rightness clear.

2:1 Habakkuk's stance is still the stance of faith; he is wholly dependent on God for revelation, and he is willing to accept correction if the Lord rejects his *complaint.*

2:2 The inscribing of the vision in such a way that even the hurrying passerby can read it serves two purposes: the whole people receives the Word; and it is impressed on men that the Lord is ready to stand by His Word and will surely bring it to pass. (Cf. Is 8:1-4; 30:8)

2:3 The *vision* is a living and active power; it *awaits its time, hastens, comes, will not delay.* (Cf. Is 55:10-11)

2:4 For Paul's use of this statement in Ro 1:17 and Gl 3:11 see the note at the end of ch. 3.

2:5 For *treacherous* intoxication, essentially in opposition to God, see the story of Belshazzar, Dn 5.

Sheol is the abode or land of the dead, here personified as an insatiable monster who swallows up *nations* and *peoples.* The very fact that the greed of the intoxicated, *arrogant man* is compared to *Sheol* and *death* indicates how negative and futureless this self-centered *(for himself, as his own)* bent of mankind is.

2:6-20 HE SHALL FAIL: FIVEFOLD WOE UPON THE MAN WHOSE SOUL IS NOT UPRIGHT

2:6-20 The doom of the intoxicated, arrogant conqueror is pictured in the *taunt* raised against him by the violent *nations* and *people* who have suffered at his hand. The five *woes* picture the divine retribution which overtakes him.

2:6-8 *First woe,* against him who *heaps up what is not his own.* The harsh creditor becomes the trembling debtor; the plunderer is plundered.

2:6 The *pledge* is some valuable piece of personal property given to the creditor as a guarantee that the debtor will repay. The conqueror *loads himself with pledges* when he puts the conquered peoples in the position of having to pay him tax and tribute.

2:9-11 *Second woe,* against him *who gets evil gain for his house.* The key word here is *house;* note the terms *nest* (9), *house* (10), *stone, wall, beam, woodwork* (11). *House* seems to be used in a double sense, that of a dwelling and that of a dynasty (cf. "House of Hanover"). The conqueror strives for a strong and glorious dynastic position, which finds expression in a royal palace of stone and wood. The stone and wood, obtained by violence, all witness against him (11), and *shame* (10) will blot out his glory.

2:12-14 *Third woe,* against him *who founds a city on iniquity.* The power and prestige of a state and its royal house is focused and expressed in its capital city, where its political, economic, and religious life is centered. This too shall *fail,* since it is built on bloodshed (12) and the forced labor of conquered and enslaved *peoples* (13); *the Lord of hosts* has decreed (13) that such a city will come to naught and will be destroyed by the *fire* (13) of His judgment (cf. Am 1:4, 7, 10, 12, 14; 2:2,

5). The goal of God's ways is that *the earth will be filled with the knowledge of the glory of the Lord.* (14). When that goal is reached, when He is known, adored, and confessed as Lord by all, there will be no room on earth for cities founded on iniquity and built to the glory of man.

2:15-17 The *fourth woe,* against *him who makes his neighbors drink.* The language of drunkenness seems to be figurative, designed to portray the conquering power as using craft as well as might to overcome opposition and delighting in the degradation of those whom they overcome. Divine retribution will deal with them as they have dealt with others; the cup of God's judgment (cf. Is 51:17, 22; Jer 25:15-16; Lm 4:21) will be theirs to drink, and the *contempt* and *shame* (16) which they have heaped on others will come upon them.

2:17 The *violence done to Lebanon* refers to the felling of its cedars for building purposes by the conqueror (cf. Is 14:8; 37:24). The *destruction* of the beasts may refer to hunting expeditions in the region. The conqueror expresses his contempt for the conquered by exploiting his land as a timber yard and a playground, which he has acquired by violence. (Cf. 8)

2:18-20 *Fifth woe,* against the maker of idols. The first four woes are pretty obviously all unfoldings of the description of the man whose soul is not upright, as given in 5. The fifth woe is not similarly indicated there, for there is no mention of idols. Perhaps this last woe is intended to round out and sum up the picture of autonomous man given in the preceding woes: The self-impelled, self-willed, self-seeking individual who gets his own gain (6-8), establishes his own dynasty (9-11), founds his own city (12-14), and craftily and cleverly feeds his own pride (15-17), also makes his own gods (18-19). His gods are merely a projection of himself (cf. 1:11, 16) and their dumb impotence is the grimmest sort of commentary on the futility and fatuity of the way of the autonomous person. If these be his gods, he shall fail indeed.

2:18 Cf. Is 40:18; 44:9-20.

2:18-20 *Can this give revelation?* The main point in Habakkuk's indictment of idols is that they cannot give the revelation, the Word, on which faith feeds. The idol is a *teacher of lies* (18) because it can say only what is already in its maker's lying heart; it is *dumb* (18, 19), with *no breath in it* (lit. "no spirit")—it cannot *inspire* true prophecy, as the true God can. In contrast, the Lord, before whom all voices fall silent (20), is the God who speaks and answers (2:1), gives visions that will not lie (2:2-3), imparts knowledge of His glory (2:14), and can make known His mighty work (3:2). *He* is a God in whom people can believe; though He may be enthroned in silence in His *holy temple* now, the hour will come when He will plainly speak and act. (Cf. ch. 3)

The five woes are asking the prophet and his people to "walk by faith, not by sight" (2 Co 5:7). The doomed world power did not appear doomed when Habakkuk wrote his vision; rather, it was at the apex of its power and glory. And the following years were to bring further demonstrations of the astonishing success of the self-centered way of the individual whose soul is not upright in him; in 597 BC Babylon subjected Jerusalem, and in 586 BC Jerusalem was destroyed.

3:1-19 HE SHALL LIVE: VISION OF THE GOD OF SALVATION

3:1-19 It is characteristic of Biblical thinking that Habakkuk contrasts the evil person under the fivefold curse (2:6-20) not with the righteous, believing *man* but with the vision of the *God* of salvation (3:3-15). So Paul does also in Romans, where the dreadful picture of mankind under the wrath of God (Ro 1:18; 3:20) is followed by the proclamation of the righteousness *of God* in action (Ro 3:21-31; cf. Eph 1:1-3 and 4-10). This emphasizes the fact that faith is not a virtue in us but, first and foremost, a receiving from God, a being-dealt with by the God of salvation.

The heading, *the prayer of Habakkuk* (2) is an indication of what follows rather than a description thereof. The prayer, or supplication, of Habakkuk occupies only one verse (2). This is followed by the vision of God going forth for the salvation of His people, which is the Lord's response to his prayer (3-15), and the chapter closes with the prophet's reaction to the vision. (16-19)

3:1 *According to Shigionoth* is probably a musical direction for the use of the prayer in worship. *Shigionoth* is thought to indicate a sort of ecstatic, wandering music. Note also the musical direction at the close. (19)

3:2 In his prayer Habakkuk recalls the former *work* of the Lord, His great acts of deliverance for His people (of which the Exodus was chief), and implores the Lord to act thus and manifest Himself thus now, *in the midst of the years,* to *remember* His ancient covenant *mercy* in the midst of His *wrath,* which the sinful people so richly deserve. (Cf. 1:2-4)

3:3-5 Habakkuk is vouchsafed a vision of God, coming from Sinai as He did of old when He brought His people through the land of Edom (*Teman, Mount Peran,* 3) into the Promised Land, clothed in splendor *(glory, praise, brightness, rays,* 3-4) and armed with terrifying power to destroy (*pestilence, plague,* 5).

3:3 *Teman,* the northern district of Edom and *Paran,* a mountain in Edom, to the southeast of Palestine, mark the route of the Lord advancing from Sinai towards Palestine.

3:6-7 The Lord's coming shakes the world (*earth, mountain, hills,* 6) and overawes the nations (*Cushan, Midian,* 7). *His ways are as of old,* when nations trembled at the report of His mighty act on His people's behalf. (Ex 15:13-18)

3:6 *Measured the earth,* that is, claimed it as His own.

3:7 *Cushan* seems to be an old poetic name for *Midian,* a nomadic people to the south who felt themselves threatened by the approach of the God of Israel. The *curtains* are the cloth of which these nomads' tents were made; they are personified and pictured as filled with fear, as the inhabitants of the tents are.

3:8-10 The waters, too (*rivers, sea, water, deep*), are pictured as quailing before the furious onset of the divine "Man of war." (Cf. Ex 15:3)

3:10 The uplifted *hands* of the *deep* are the whipped-up billows that reach upward.

3:11 Like the earth and the water, the heavens are aghast at the furious splendor of Him whose *arrows* and *spear glitter* with a light that makes the *sun* and *moon* turn pale.

3:12-15 Here at last the purpose of God's coming (2) becomes unmistakably clear; it is to fulfill the purpose proclaimed in the vision and inscribed upon tablets, awaiting its time (2:2-3). When God *bestrides the earth in fury, tramples the nations in anger, crushes the head of the wicked,* conquers the ruthless conqueror of the *poor* (13b-14), and puts an end to the powers of chaos (*sea, waters*), then what was *made plain upon tablets* (2:2) will be made plain in the judgment: *He whose soul is not upright in him shall fail* (2:4). And *then* those who have walked by faith and not sight *shall live* (2:4), namely, when God *goes forth for the salvation of His people, for the salvation of His anointed,* those who are marked and consecrated as His own. (13)

3:13 For *anointed* as a designation of the people of God, cf. Ps 28:8. A reference to the Messiah is possible; then the meaning would be that God, in saving His people, would vindicate His anointed King. (Cf. Zch 9:9; Is 52:13-15; 53:10-12)

3:16-19 The prophet's response to the vision is one of holy fear; he is shaken to the very depths of his being. He sees now: This is a God whom one must fear, and a God whom one dare not question. He knows now that he can make no answer when challenged concerning his "complaint" (2:1). But this fear is not incompatible with faith. This is a God whom one can trust to keep His Word, a God in whom one can find rest, no matter how hard the enigmas and agonies of history press upon one: *I will quietly wait* (16). More, this is a God whom one can love. To hold to Him in faith is to *rejoice* in Him, to find in Him a joy which is independent even of His good gifts and depends on Him alone: "There is nothing upon earth that I desire besides Thee." (Ps 73:25)

3:19 *Hinds' feet* are quick and sure, even on difficult terrain.

God treads on the *high places* of the earth (cf. Am 4:13; Mi 1:3) in triumphant majesty, and He will take His own with Him on His triumphant way. (Cf. Dt 32:13; 33:29; Ps 18:33)

Note: The word *faith* occurs only once in Habakkuk (2:4); but his whole prophecy is a word of faith, faith agonized, questioning, seeking, finding repose in God, and jubilant, finally, in the assurance of God's love, and all this in the face of the obstacle to faith posed by God's scandalously mysterious governance of history. When Paul quotes 2:4 in his thematic statement of justification by faith in Ro 1:17, it is only fair to assume that he is quoting with a consciousness of this original context of faith in Habakkuk. For Paul, as for Habakkuk, faith is confronted by an action of God which is offensively enigmatic, namely, the weakness and foolishness of the Cross; for both Paul and Habakkuk faith is faith without works, for both it is "quietly waiting" for God to do His saving work. For both, faith is not one aspect of man's existence before God but the whole of his relationship to Him.

ZEPHANIAH

INTRODUCTION

After the end of Micah's prophetic activity (about 700 BC) there is a long silence in recorded prophecy. It is not until about 630 BC that the voice of prophecy is heard again, in the words of Jeremiah, Nahum, Habakkuk, and Zephaniah. This 70 years' silent interim corresponds roughly with the reign of Manasseh (687—642 BC). His reign was marked by the introduction of idolatry on a grand scale and by injustice and cruelty (2 K 21:1-18; 23:26; 24:3-4); he lives in Judah's history as the worst of her kings. There were, no doubt, prophets who protested, but Manasseh, who "shed very much innocent blood" (2 K 21:16), succeeded in silencing their protest, for a time at least. Things were no better during the short reign of his son, Amon (642—640 BC; 2 K 21:19-26). In the reign of the good King Josiah (640—609 BC; 2 K 22:1—23:30) the Word of God came to be heard and heeded once more, when Josiah (who was only 8 years old at his accession) in the 18th year of his reign trembled at the words of the Law (2 K 22:11-13), inquired of the Lord (2 K 21:13), and zealously undertook long-needed reforms.

Zephaniah's prophecy has on it the imprint of his time, the earlier years of the reign of Josiah. The legacy from the days of Manasseh rests heavily on Judah, poisoning the life of the people of God. Zephaniah confronts this with an uncompromising threat of judgment. His words concerning the Day of the Lord are among the most powerful words of judgment that the OT knows. But the time is marked also by the presence of a king whose "heart was penitent," who humbled himself before the Lord when he heard the Word of the Law and rent his clothes and wept for his guilt and the guilt of his people (2 K 22:19). Zephaniah has words of comfort and hope for the repentant, the "humble of the land" (Zph 2:3; 3:12-13); and he is given a vision which looks beyond the guilt incurred by Manasseh, even beyond the reforms of Josiah (ineffectual in the long run), to the day when God the King takes up His power to give victory to His trusting servants and to renew them in His love. (Zph 3:14-20)

In speaking the salutary word of judgment and deliverance to his generation, Zephaniah is *renewing* the voice of prophecy. The major themes of previous prophecy recur and are united in him; motifs from Amos, Hosea, Isaiah, and Micah live on in Zephaniah's words. Bucer, one of the men of the Reformation, calls Zephaniah a "brief compendium of the oracles of the prophets."

Zephaniah therefore belongs to the goodly fellowship of those who bear witness to Christ. Christ is the hidden center of Zephaniah's proclamation of radical judgment and radical deliverance; His cross, which is the judgment of God on man's sin and God's acquittal of man in one act, is the final answer to the question raised by Zph 3:8-9, that abrupt transition from inexorable judgment to inexplicable grace and salvation. In Christ, the one wholly humble and lowly Israelite, the One who, at every step of His human way, sought refuge in the name of the Lord (Zph 3:12; cf. Mt 4:1-11)—in Him the judgment against His rebellious and defiled nation was executed and "taken away" (Zph 3:15); He died for that nation, and not for that nation only, "but to gather into one the children of God who are scattered abroad." (Jn 11:51-52) Zephaniah is salutary reading in a day when the proclamation of judgment in the church is less frequent and less urgent than it was in the words of prophets and apostles, to waken both the holy fear and the whole trust which is the mark of those who await the day of which Zephaniah spoke, the day we have come to know as the day of our Lord Jesus Christ.

1:1-18 HE HAS FIXED A DAY IN WHICH HE WILL JUDGE THE WORLD

1:1 *Hezekiah* may be King Hezekiah (2 K 18—20). This would account for the fact that the list of ancestors is longer than for any other prophet. Not that it matters greatly; the divine message is more important than the messenger; Zephaniah lives in history and is significant for us because *the word of the Lord came to him.*

1:2-3 This sweeping threat of judgment recalls the Word of the Lord on the eve of the Flood: "I will blot out man whom I have created from the face of the ground, man and beast and creeping things and birds of the air" (Gn 6:7); man and the world created for him are judged together. The wrath of God strikes "*all* ungodliness and wickedness of men" (Ro 1:18). No one can hope to escape, least of all Judah (4), the favored people of God. (Cf. Ro 2:9, 17-29)

1:4 *This place* is Jerusalem.

1:4-6 The "ungodliness" of Judah, her dark heritage from the reign of Manasseh, is here described: worship of the Canaanite fertility god Baal, worship of the stars (introduced from Assyria), and the idolatrous compromise between the Ammonite god Milcom and the Lord God which invokes (and so acknowledges) both in one oath. (2 K 21:1-9)

1:4 The worship of Baal will be rooted out utterly; not even a trace, not even a *name* will be left of it. For this sense of *remnant* and *name* cf. Is 14:22.

1:6 To *seek the Lord* and to *inquire of him* means to consult priest (Ml 2:6-7) and prophet (2 K 22:13-14) in order to obtain through them the guidance of God's Word. (Cf. Is 8:19 20)

1:7 *The day of the Lord* (also called the "great day of the Lord" in 14, "the day of the wrath of the Lord" in 18 and 2:2-3, and simply "that day" in 10 and 3:11) is a motif that runs all through the prophecy of Zephaniah. "Day" occurs in a loaded sense 17 times in his book. The idea of the day of the Lord is found in the prophetic books from Amos in the eighth century to Malachi in the fifth. It signifies the day when the Lord will rise up to manifest His righteousness in a final and fearful way, in judgment on His enemies and for the deliverance of those who submit to Him and seek refuge in His name (Zph 3:12). The prophets take the colors with which they depict that day from the holy wars of Israel's past, the faith-inspiring days of the Exodus, the entry into the Promised Land, and the time of the mighty deliverers of which the Book of Judges tells, when the Lord fought for His people against overwhelming odds, with miraculous manifestations of His power both in nature (darkness, earthquake, etc.) and in man (panic, fear). The story of Gideon is a classic example (Ju 6—7; cf. Is 9:4). With these colors the prophets picture the ultimate holy war, now on a universal scale. God's onset strikes not only one historical enemy of His people; it affects all men, all nations, all creation. The cosmos is shaken by the fury of God's judgment. For this is God's ultimate day of reckoning, THE crisis in His dealing with the nations—and with His people. Israel is not automatically exempt; the Day of the Lord is "against all that is proud and lofty" (Is 2:12). The prophetic proclamation of the Day of the Lord therefore shatters all complacent security on the part of the elect people and purifies their hope by purging away all self-centered and self-seeking dreams of a purely national triumph. In other words, it makes their hope a religious hope, centered in the righteousness and compassion of the Lord, "who alone will be exalted in that day" (Is 2:17). The proclamation at the Day of the Lord is a powerful and moving call to repentance. The NT takes up this thought with great vigor, centering it in Jesus Christ. Jesus Himself speaks of the day of the Son of Man (Lk 17:24; Mt 25:31 ff.), and the apostles proclaim the day of the Lord Jesus Christ as the day of definitive judgment and final deliverance (Acts 2:20; 1 Co 1:8; Ph 1:6, 10; 2:16; 2 Th 1:5-12). The chief OT passages dealing with the Day of the Lord are: Is 2:12-22; 13:6-16; cf. 22:5-14; Jer 46:10-12; Eze 7:14-27; Jl 1:15; 2:1-11; 2:28-32; 3:14-31; Am 5:18-20; Ob 15-21; Zph 1:7-18; 2:2-3; 3:11-13; Zch 12—14.

For the picture of God's judgment as a *sacrifice* cf. Is 34:6-7; Jer 46:10; Eze 39:17-20. Here, Judah is the intended victim; the *guests consecrated* for participation in the sacrifice are probably the foreign powers employed by God to punish His people. There is sad irony in the fact that sacrifice, God's gracious gift to His people, given "to make atonement" for their souls (Lv 17:11), becomes the picture for the execution of His judgment against His people. The misused and slighted grace of God becomes, at last, a stored-up treasury of wrath. (Ro 2:4-5)

1:8 The *king's sons* are members of the royal family, kinsmen of Josiah and influential at his court. Josiah himself was probably still a minor at the time of this prophecy and is therefore not mentioned. (Cf. 3:3)

Foreign attire is censured because it is part of the wave of foreign influence, including the worship of alien gods, which swept the court and country under Manasseh and the early days of Josiah.

1:9 *Leaping over the threshold* may refer to some pagan superstition (cf. 1 Sm 5:5) or, more probably in view of the second half of the verse, to some act of *violence and fraud,* such as obtaining another's house by sharp practice and forcible seizure.

1:10-11 *The Fish Gate* (Neh 3:3; 12:39), *Second Quarter* (2 K 22:14), *the hills, the Mortar* (probably a bowl-shaped valley) were landmarks or localities in Jerusalem, well known to Zephaniah's contemporaries. They cannot now be certainly identified.

1:12 To *search with lamps* is to search thoroughly, as the woman looking for her lost coin searched (Lk 15:8), so that nothing escapes the searcher's eye.

Thickening upon their lees, an image taken from wine-making, is used to describe people who have settled into religious indifference, do not reckon with God's presence and power, and make all decisions without a thought of Him. They resemble wine resting on its sediment, thick and heavy and unchanging.

To say in one's heart is the Hebrew way of saying "to think." (Cf. Is 14:13; 47:8, 10; 49:21)

1:14 The *day of the Lord* is described as *hastening fast.* One cannot calculate its coming and dare not contemplate it as if from afar. Its coming calls for fear and repentance, for it is *near* at every moment—in Zephaniah's day, in Jesus' day (Mt 24:34), in the day of the Seer on Patmos (Rv 1:3), and in ours.

1:18 Some see here an allusion to the Scythian invasion of western Asia (ca. 630—625). Pharaoh Psammetichos bought off these hordes of invaders from southern Russia when they threatened Egypt. There is considerable uncertainty about this, but it is certain that the Lord on His Day cannot be bought off. "The Lord your God is . . . the great, the mighty, and the terrible God, who is not partial and takes no bribe." (Dt 10:17)

2:1—3:13 HOW HE COMMANDS ALL MEN EVERYWHERE TO REPENT

2:1-3 The *shameless nation* is usually taken to mean Judah, and certainly Judah deserves the indictment (cf. 3:5, 7). But the suggestion that Philistia (as representing the nations indicted in ch. 2) is meant, while Judah is addressed in *you humble of the land,* is attractive. Then the address to the nations is taken up with 4 ff. ("for") and the address to Judah in 3:1 ff., with both threat and promise in each section. The structure of 2:1—3:13 would be as follows:

Repent, O Philistia (1-2), for judgment comes upon the nations (4-15). Yet there is hope for the nations too. (11; cf. 3:9)

2:1 *Hold assembly,* to meet your Judge.

2:3 These *humble of the land* are the opposite of those who have turned from the Lord and do not seek Him (1:6), the opposite of the indifferent who thicken on the lees, ignoring God (1:12). They seek first the Kingdom and His righteousness. (Mt 6:33)

2:4 The cities enumerated are the four major cities of the Philistines. Gath, the fifth member of the original Philistine federation, had been reduced to insignificance by the time of Zephaniah. (2 Ch 26:6)

The enemies of *Ashdod* will be so sure of victory and so superior in strength that they can attack *at noon,* in broad daylight, without need of stealth or stratagem.

2:5 The Philistines are called *Cherethites* (Cretans) because they had originally come from Crete.

To have *the Word of the Lord against you* spells sure destruction, for there is no more potent force, for good or ill, than the Word. (Cf. Is 9:8-12)

2:7, 9 The mention of the *remnant* of *Judah* here, in the midst of threats to Philistia, picks up the promise of v. 3. The *humble of the land* shall inherit the earth.

2:8-15 From the Philistines in the west, the prophetic Word moves eastward, to Moab and Ammon (9-10), then southward to Ethiopia (12), and then northward to Assyria. (13-15)

2:11 The gods of the earth will be *famished* because their worshipers will no longer bring them the offerings which were thought of as sustaining the life of the deity.

2:12 *Ethiopia* may be a derisive term for Egypt, which was long ruled by an Ethiopian dynasty.

2:13 For the character of *Nineveh* and the feeling which this "bloody city" inspired in subject nations, see especially the prophet Nahum.

2:14 The *capitals* are the capitals of columns of the abandoned and ruined temples and palaces. For *cedar work* as a mark of wealth and luxury see Jer 22:14-15.

2:15 Nineveh is deifying herself; the words *I am,* etc., are found on the lips of God in Is 45:6. Compare the boast of the king of Babylon in Is 14:14. It is the political form of man's primal sin, the will to be "like God." (Gn 3:5, 22)

Shaking the fist is not, as with us, a threatening gesture but expresses malicious exultation at the downfall of an enemy.

3:1-7 Jerusalem is addressed. Any hope for forgiveness and renewal in Judah lies with the "humble of the land" (2:3), for the capital, Jerusalem, where power and influence are concentrated is *rebellious* and corrupt (*defiled*). The rebelliousness of Jerusalem is elaborated in 2, 6, 7. The corruption is elaborated in the description of the rapacious *officials* and *judges,* the irresponsible *prophets,* and the irreverent *priests* (3-4: cf. 5 and 7), whose character and actions are in glaring contrast to the pure and constant justice of the *Lord,* who claims Jerusalem as His city (5). Where official and judge follow their own self-seeking bent and neither prophet nor priest has the conscience and courage to protest, the city of God becomes *the oppressing city.*

3:3 Again, the king himself is not mentioned. See 1:8 note.

3:5 The *justice* of the Lord is His activity in maintaining the covenant with His people. His judgments on the nations, designed to awaken His people to a sense of their covenant duties and calling, is one example of such divine *justice.*

3:8-13 *Therefore* (1) introduces the announcement of universal judgment. Judgment shall strike both the nations (8) and Israel (11-13). The miracle of it is that in both cases judgment serves God's saving purpose and has a positive outcome. The speech of the nations is made pure, as Isaiah's once was (Is 6:6-7), and the Gentiles break out into the unanimous adoration of the Lord (9). In the case of Israel, the positive outcome of divine judgment is stressed so strongly that it almost overshadows the thought of judgment. But there will be judgment on Israel too: the *suppliants* must be brought back from the exile that was their punishment (10), the proud and haughty will be *removed* (11), and only the humble remnant *left* (12); and there is more than a hint of judgment in 15 and 18 also. It is for the glad outcome that the Lord bids His faithful servants *wait.* (8)

3:8 For the idea of God as *witness* (as well as Judge) of man's sin cf. Ml 3:5.

3:9 God's *name* means God's revealed character and purpose; to *call on the name of the Lord* is to respond to this revelation in faith and adoration. (Cf. Gn 12:8; Ps 75:1; 79:6; Is 65:1; 1 K 18:24-26, 36-37)

3:10 *Daughter of my dispersed ones* means "My dispersed people," as "daughter of Zion" means "the people of Zion."

3:11 Judah-Jerusalem is addressed.

3:12 Jesus reaffirmed and made universal this promise in His beatitudes on the poor in spirit, the mourners, and the meek (Mt 5:3-5). He not only spoke these beatitudes; as God's Servant and obedient Son, He lived them and so made them full reality in the faith and life of believers.

3:13 The last words of the verse are, significantly, introduced by *for.* The new life of faith, righteousness, and truth pictured in 12-13 is made possible by God's saving action; the renewing love (17) of the Good Shepherd creates the new people of God.

3:14-20 REJOICE, O DAUGHTER OF JERUSALEM!

3:14-20 The concluding summons to rejoice centers in the figure of the covenant God as King (15), in whom majesty and mercy are united. He is Judge (15), Warrior (17), Lover (17), and Shepherd (19-20) for His people.

3:15 Where God *takes away the judgments against* someone, that person stands justified, and no one can terrify or accuse him. (Cf. Ro 8:31-34)

3:16 *Let not your hands grow weak,* from terror or despair. (Cf. Is 13:7; Jer 6:24)

3:19 The *lame* are exiles who (like lame sheep who cannot keep up with the flock) have lost contact with their community; the Good Shepherd restores them to communal life and communal worship. (Cf. Mi 4:6-7)

HAGGAI

INTRODUCTION

In 538 BC the great and improbable event foretold by Jeremiah (Jer 25:12-14; 29:10-14; 33:7-13) took place: "That the word of the Lord by the mouth of Jeremiah might be accomplished the Lord stirred up the spirit of Cyrus king of Persia" to issue a proclamation permitting the exiled Jews within the Persian Empire to return to their land and rebuild the house of the Lord (Ez 1-4). The story of the return from exile is told in the Book of Ezra. It is not a very splendid story, this story of the 79,000 returning Jews and their attempt to resettle the land and to rebuild the temple. It is a story of frustrations and dispiriting difficulties and delays; the new temple was not dedicated until 516 BC (Ez 4:24). It is a story of a mounting sense of disappointment and apathy on the part of the returning remnant. The only splendor, really, which the story possesses is the triumph of the Word of the Lord in that "day of small things" (Zch 4:10). In this triumph the prophets Haggai and Zechariah play their part. Through them the Word came to Zerubbabel, representative of the Messianic line, to Joshua, the high priest, and to the remnant of the people (Ez 5:1-2; 6:14). The Word gave them all, leaders and people, eyes for the greatness of the day of small things, a hope for the future which God was opening up for them and mankind, and new courage to set their hands to the task which this their day asked of them. "The elders of the Jews built and prospered, through the prophesying of Haggai the prophet and Zechariah the son of Iddo. They finished their building." (Ez 6:14)

The time when our Lord walked the earth was a day of small things; He Himself called it a day of the planting of the tiny mustard seed (Mt 13:31-32). He lived and died in that day, with the serene courage which shames all other sons of men, in continuous converse with the prophets (cf. Lk 9:30-31) in whose Word He heard His Father's voice. The church learns of Him to listen to the prophetic Word and can learn to see in her day of small things the day when God is preparing to shake the earth and the heavens; thus the church learns to hold fast to that which cannot be shaken and shall remain when God ushers in the day of great things, the day of Our Lord Jesus Christ. (Heb 12:25-29)

1:1-15 HAGGAI'S FIRST WORD: AGAINST SELF-CENTERED APATHY

1:1-11 Whose House Comes First, Yours or the Lord's?

1:1 The superscription gives the date of the prophecy (520 BC), states the authority of the prophet *(the word of the Lord came),* and indicates the persons addressed. The content of the message makes it clear that the people are being addressed in the persons of their leaders. Cf. 2:2, where the "remnant of the people" is expressly mentioned.

1:2-11 With a reproach (2-4), an admonition (5-6), and a command which takes up the reproach once more (7-11) Haggai sets straight the priorities of life: the obvious and forgotten fact that God comes first, that the state of our life depends wholly on our relationship to Him. "Seek first his kingdom and his righteousness, and all these things shall be yours as well," Jesus said. (Mt 6:33)

1:2 The expression *this people* has a note of reproach in it. (Cf. Is 6:9)

1:4 The people dwell in *paneled houses.* In Solomon's temple the most holy place was "lined . . . with boards of cedar" (1 K 6:14-18). Now the people's houses are lined with cedar, while God's house is bare.

1:5-6 and 9-11. A vivid description of the emptiness and futility of the self-seeking life which forgets God. One is reminded of Jesus' parable of the rich fool (Lk 12:16-21), told to show that "a man's life does not consist in the abundance of his possessions" (Lk 12:15), that "he who lays up treasure for himself and is not rich toward God" (Lk 12:21) is indeed putting his money into a bag with holes and can find no storehouse so secure that the blasting breath of God will not blow his gathered stones away. Jesus remains the one true Israelite in this as in all respects. He determined to live by the Word of God and not by bread alone (Mt 4:4); though He had no paneled house which He could call His own (Mt 8:20), He was consumed by zeal for God's house (Jn 2:17), even though that zeal cost Him His life. (Jn 2:21)

1:8 The hill country round Jerusalem was well-wooded in Haggai's day and could supply the needed timber. There was no need to gather stones; Lamentations speaks of the "holy stones" which lay "scattered at the head of every street" in fallen Jerusalem. (Lm 4:1)

1:10 *Dew* is most important for agriculture in the rainless summers of Palestine.

1:12-15 The People's Response to the Prophet's Word: Obedience and Fear

1:12 The word *remnant* has strong religious overtones; it indicates the survivors who have in repentance turned from their sin and their attempts to find security in alliances with world powers and now "lean upon the Lord . . . in truth," thus returning not only to their homeland but also to "the mighty God" (Is 10:20-21) whose judgment has swept away the impenitent mass of the nation.

Obeyed and *feared* express the outer and inner side of the same action. To "fear" God is to take Him with radical seriousness as God, to submit to His Word in complete trust, as Abraham did when he was ready to offer up Isaac: "Now I know that you *fear* God, seeing you have not withheld your son, your only son, from me." (Gn 22:12)

1:13-14 To His penitent, obedient people God renews the ancient promise, given to Isaac, Jacob, Moses, Gideon: "I will be with you." (Gn 26:24; 28:15; Ex 3:12; Ju 6:12, 16)

2:1-9 HAGGAI'S SECOND WORD: AGAINST DISILLUSIONMENT AND DISCOURAGEMENT

2:1 The date, the 21st day of the seventh month, is significant, for this would be the last day of the Feast of Booths (or Tabernacles), cf. Lv 23:33-43. This festival recalled the deliverance of God's people from Egypt. The Law said: "You shall dwell in booths for seven days . . . that your generations may know that I made the people of Israel dwell in booths when I brought them out of the land of Egypt" (Lv 23:42-43). The people's heart and mind would on this day be attuned to the prophet's allusion in 5.

2:2-9 When leaders and people remembered the mighty promises of restoration given through Jeremiah, Ezekiel, and Isaiah (Is 40—55) and now saw what actually had come of them—a temple which, compared with the first temple, appeared as "nothing" in their eyes—disillusionment and discouragement overcame them. To this mood the Lord responds with a strong word of encouragement: "Take courage! Fear not! This is MY word and MUST succeed; all the power that is Mine as Lord of Creation and of all history is at work here, and the end result will be more glorious than anything you can remember from the past."

2:4-9 Three waves of promise roll in: The first (4) is a repetition of the promise made in 1:13; but is it reinforced now (5) by the recollection of the Exodus, the mighty work of God with which the history of Israel as a nation began. The word *made* in the phrase, *the promise that I made you* is the word usually used to designate the establishment of a covenant. One could translate: "The covenant-word that I spoke to you." Thus the whole, spontaneous love of God's covenant with His people is recalled for their encouragement now. (Cf. Dt 7:6-9)

The second wave of promies, *My Spirit abides among you* (5b), is an intensification of the first. The express mention of *Spirit* makes clear that the Lord's presence among His people is an active and creative working presence. The OT speaks of the Spirit as active in Creation (Gn 1:2) and active in history, empowering great deliverers like Moses (Nm 11:17) and Gideon (Ju 6:34), coming upon the anointed king (1 Sm 16:13), empowering the prophet to speak God's judging and redeeming Word (Mi 3:8). The promised Messiah of David's line and the promised Servant-Messiah are to do their redeeming work in the power of the Spirit that rests on them (Is 11:2; 42:1). The Spirit of the Lord is to cleanse and renew His people at the end of days (Eze 36:26-27; Jl 2:28-29); all creation will be transfigured by the creative power of the Spirit. This presence of God is to be a continuing presence, according to the promise given through Haggai; the Lord will hold to His gracious purpose.

The third wave of promise (6-9) shows this active and abiding presence at work. Once before, at the Exodus, the Lord had shaken heaven and earth (the 10 plagues and the cleaving of the waters) and had shaken the kingdom of Pharaoh in order to set His people free; now *once again* this Lord is about to lay bare His arm, but now on a worldwide scale; *all nations* are to be shaken. The rumblings of revolt which ran through the Persian empire at that time and made Israel anxious for the future need not trouble them; all these *shakings* are under the Lord's control and serve His purpose. The purpose now is that He may have His abode among men and reign over them in a concrete place (the temple) where His grace may be focused and concentrated: *In this place I will give prosperity*. The word translated *prosperity* is often translated "peace"; it signifies wholeness, completeness, soundness, health—the normal state of things which the Creator intended for man and his world. The blessing of God upon His people ends with *peace* (Nm 6:26)—*peace* can sum up all that the faith of the covenant people look to God for, all that a gracious covenant Lord can bestow.

The promise harks back to the Exodus and the establishment of the covenant with Israel. It also looks forward; it opens a window toward the NT. The Letter to the Hebrews reminds us that God's shaking of heaven and earth and of all kingdoms has not yet reached its climax (Heb 12:25-29); the Word of the Lord which came by Haggai is still at work.

The promise given through Haggai (*I am with you*) is fulfilled and lives on in Immanuel and in Immanuel's promise of "Lo, I am with you" (Mt 1:23; 28:20). Haggai's vision of the greater temple, enriched by the treasures of all nations, filled with the glory of God's presence, has become history in Him who is more than the temple of wood and stone, in whom all nations are united in one worship (Eph 2:19-22). His promise of peace is fulfilled, and moves toward greater fulfillment, in Him who "is our peace" (Eph 2:14). Our Lord took up the prophet's promise of the abiding Spirit and climaxed it with its NT fullness when He told His disciples: "He [the Spirit] dwells with you, and will be in you" (Jn 14:17).—"We have the prophetic word made more sure." (2 Ptr 1:19)

2:10-19 HAGGAI'S THIRD WORD: TO A DEFILED PEOPLE, "I WILL BLESS YOU"

2:10-19 A month before this time Zechariah had uttered his first call to repentance: "Return to me, says the Lord of hosts, and I will return to you" (Zch 1:3). The third word of Haggai reinforces that call. The people are to know and remember that the great future opened up for them by the Word of the Lord is purely the Lord's creative doing and His giving. By His grace this people, tainted by their dead past and by the deadness of their response to God's promise, have a future and a hope and may look for a blessing. The inherent defilement of the people and the uncanny power of the defilement is pictured in an image taken from the ceremonial law: What is ceremonially holy (e.g., sacrifical meat, *holy flesh,* 12) does not communicate its "holiness" to what it touches indirectly, while ceremonial uncleanness spreads out to infect even what comes into direct contact with it. *So it is with this people* (14); they are themselves unclean, and their uncleanness infects all that they undertake, even the offering of sacrifices. The promised blessing will be a light shining into darkness.

2:15-17 The immediate past is evidence of the people's inner taintedness; they had been woefully slow to undertake the building of the Lord's house, and He had to break through this encrusted impenitence *(yet you did not return to me!)* with repeated chastisements of scarcity and disaster.

2:18-19 Now that chastisement and promise have done their work, a new day dawns. The last seed remaining in the barns has been sown, in faith and hope; and that hope will not put to shame. The trees, too, shall yield their fruit. *From this day on I will bless you* (19). The blessing which God placed on Creation (Gn 1:22, 28), the blessing which He laid on Abraham for all the families of the earth (Gn 12:2-3), the blessing which the sons of Aaron laid on the people of God, which pronounced and gave the light of the Lord's countenance on them (Nm 6:22-27), that potent Word is now freed to do its work. The Word speeds on toward the day when Peter tells the people at the Beautiful Gate about Jesus, God's final Word of blessing: "God having raised up his servant, sent him to you first, to bless you in turning every one of you from your wickedness." (Acts 3:26)

2:20-23 HAGGAI'S FOURTH WORD: TO ZERUBBABEL, BEARER OF THE MESSIANIC PROMISE

Like the preceding promise of blessing upon the people, the promise given to Zerubbabel is pure grace; it derives its power and any likelihood of being fulfilled solely from God's freely choosing love (23). For Zerubbabel is not a likely candidate for greatness; he is not king in Israel but merely *governor* of Judah, and David's kingdom is a subordinate province of the Persian Empire. The promise made to David seems to have withered and died. Moreover, Zerubbabel is grandson of King Jehoiachin, against whom Jeremiah had uttered that terrible curse:

> Write this man down as childless,
> a man who shall not succeed in his days;
> for none of his offspring shall succeed
> in sitting on the throne of David,
> and ruling again in Judah (Jer 22:30).

Jeremiah had, in fact, used the very figure of the *signet ring* in his curse (Jer 22:24). Only the divine Word of promise can overcome that curse. The Lord now promises to make Zerubbabel *like a signet ring.* The signet ring, especially a king's, was a prize and jealously guarded possession; with it the king impressed his seal on documents and marked them as official business of the king. With Zerubbabel the Lord of hosts will put His mark on history and mark it as the king's business. The shaking of the heavens and the earth and the overthrow of kingdoms shall serve the establishment of His reign. He will establish His kingdom in His own way; it shall be a kingdom "not of this world" (Jn 18:36). The Messianic promise of Haggai has the same thrust as that of Zechariah: "Not by might, nor by power, but by my Spirit, says the Lord of hosts" (Zch 4:6). Both found their fulfillment in Jesus, the meek King of God's choosing who came to the royal city without horses and chariots, with only the Word of the Lord of hosts for His strength.

ZECHARIAH

INTRODUCTION

Zechariah came of a priestly family (Neh 12:4) and is himself numbered among the priests in Neh 12:16. His prophetic activity is closely associated with that of Haggai (Ez 5:1-2; 6:14). Haggai's utterances are all dated 520 BC; the dated utterances of Zechariah indicate that he was active until 518 BC (Zch 7:1). How much longer he may have continued to prophesy after that is not known. (For the problem of the date of chs. 9—14 see the note at the beginning of ch. 9.)

The situation to which Zechariah addresses the Word of the Lord (chs. 1—8) is therefore the same as that addressed by Haggai. And his message reinforces and supplements that of Haggai. The difference between them is one of accent and form; where Haggai urges, Zechariah encourages, and sets forth the content of the divine promise in a series of strangely magnificent visions. In saying "Repent, for the kingdom of God is drawing near" both connect the drawing near of the kingdom with Zerubbabel, the representative of the Messianic line and the vehicle of the Messianic hope. Both tie the fulfillment of the promise in with the rebuilding of the temple as the place in which and from which the Lord will act for the salvation of His people and all mankind.

Some have found this emphasis on the rebuilding of the temple disappointing and speak of it as a regrettable limitation on the part of these prophets. But, even apart from the fact that they were commissioned and empowered to speak just THIS word to their people and presumably understood the will of their Lord better than we can, one might ask: What would have happened if the temple had not been rebuilt, if this embodiment of God's presence and token of His promise had not taken shape in 516 BC? Or, if it had become an amiable and leisurely community project in which believers and half-believers joined (cf. Ez 4:1-3), and not an urgent act of faith and hope, done in the power of the Spirit of God? The Lord has a preference for the singular and the concrete. As in the days of Isaiah, so in the days of Zechariah and Haggai, His will concerning His promise is: "If you will not believe, surely you shall not be established" (Is 7:9); and believing is always believing in and acting on a particular and concrete promise of God, as Abraham did (Ro 4:17-22). In 520 BC this promise was centered in the temple, and believing the promise meant rebuilding the temple.

The church can only be grateful for a Word such as Haggai and Zechariah have spoken, a Word which both intoxicates us with visions of a great future and sobers us with the realization that we must, if we believe, lay hold of that future in concrete, perhaps highly mundane, brick-and-mortar action NOW.

OUTLINE

I. 1:1—6:15 The Eight Visions in the Night: Return to Me!
- A. 1:1-6 Introduction to the Eight Visions: The Call to Repentance
- B. 1:7—6:8 Eight Visions of Hope
- C. 6:9-15 The Conclusion of the Visions: The Coronation of Priest and King

II. 7:1—8:23 Your Fasts Shall Become Feasts
- A. 7:1-3 The Inquiry Concerning the Observance of Fasts
- B. 7:4-6 The True Meaning of Fasting
- C. 7:7-14 Why Feasts Become Fasts
- D. 8:1-23 How Fasts Become Feasts

III. 9:1—11:17 His Kingdom Rules Over All
- A. 9:1-8 His Royal Word Rules over All
- B. 9:9-10 Your King Comes to You
- C. 9:11-17 God's Reign Delivers from All Evil
- D. 10:1-2 God the King as Giver of Daily Bread
- E. 10:3—11:3 The Kingdom as the Reign of the Good Shepherd
- F. 11:4-17 The Kingdom of God Suffers Violence

IV. 12:1—14:21 Inherit the Kingdom
- A. 12:1-9 The Victory of the People of God
- B. 12:10—13:6 The Inner Renewal of the People of God
- C. 13:7-9 The Stricken Shepherd and the Scattered Sheep
- D. 14:1-21 The Lord will Become King over All the Earth

1:1—6:15 THE EIGHT VISIONS IN THE NIGHT: RETURN TO ME!

1:1-6 To the remnant returned from the Babylonian exile the prophet renews the old prophetic cry: Repent! Their fathers learned repentance from God's wrath, from the destruction of city and temple and the long captivity; the present generation is invited to learn repentance from God's kindness, which is meant to lead us to repentance, as Paul says (Ro 2:4). Whatever form the call to repentance takes, we dare not trifle with it; for in the prophetic Word we have to do with a divine Word, which *overtakes* us (6) and lives and works on even after the prophets who spoke it are dead and gone. (v. 5)

1:1 The dating of a prophetic oracle underscores the fact that God's Word addresses us concretely and confronts us in a specific situation with an inescapable claim.

1:3 *Return* is the word regularly used by the prophets to describe repentance, which is a radical reversal (effected by God, cf. Lm 5:21; Jer 31:18; 1 K 18:37) from self and sin to God, in trust and obedience.

1:6 *They repented,* after the judgment of the exile had struck them and convicted them. The words of v. 4 *(they did not hear or heed me)* describe their attitude before the exile.

1:7—6:8 Eight Visions of Hope

1:7—6:8 The eight visions portray in manifold images how the kindness of God works to lead sinners to repentance; they are a pictorial commentary on the Word: *I will return to you* (1:3). The first and last visions are independent units; visions two to seven are arranged in pairs.

1:7-17 THE FIRST VISION: THE LORD IS ON THE MOVE

Haggai had foretold that the Lord would shake heaven and earth and kingdoms and so usher in the new age (Hg 2:6, 21-22); the revolts in the Persian Empire during the first years of the reign of Darius had seemed to be ushering in the fulfillment of his prophecy. But now all was quiet again; the revolts had been crushed, and all the earth remained at rest (11). God was, apparently, doing nothing; His wrath of 70 years' standing seemed to be hanging over His people still. Zechariah's vision says that this is appearance only; in reality God is taking action. His patrols are already ranging the earth. He is jealous for Jerusalem and angry with the nations who were, to be sure, the instruments of His just judgment on His people but have exceeded their commission in their cruelty and violence toward God's people. The purpose of God is alive and active in the *gracious and comforting words* (13) which Zechariah is permitted to hear, and these words will be translated into deed; Jerusalem shall be built and be the object of God's elective love.

1:7 The visions are described as the *word of the Lord;* the actions beheld by the prophet are speaking actions and are, moreover, interspersed with interpretive words.

1:8-11 Details of the vision (the myrtle trees,

the various colors of the horses) are not interpreted by the angel who spoke with the prophet (11); they do not seem to have any independent significance.

1:12 *Seventy years* is a round figure for the time elapsed since the fall of Jerusalem in 586 BC. Jeremiah had predicted a 70 years' captivity. (Jer 25:11; 29:10)

1:14 God's *jealousy* (or zeal) has two aspects; it is both His passionate concern of love for His covenant people and His passionate fury at all attitudes and actions on the part of men or nations which impede His covenant purpose for His people.

1:16 The past tense *(I have returned)* is significant; the promise of 3 is already being fulfilled. Jesus, too, describes God as meeting the penitent more than halfway; in the parable the waiting Father runs down the road to meet the returning prodigal son. (Lk 15:20)

1:18—2:5 THE SECOND AND THIRD VISIONS: THE FOUR HORNS AND THE MAN WITH THE MEASURING LINE

1:18-21 The second vision is a pictorial commentary on the Lord's words in 15: "I am angry with the nations." It pictures God's workmen (the *four smiths*) preparing to destroy the powers which have depopulated the land of Judah. *Horns* (18) are a symbol of power (cf. Ps 132:17; Dn 7:7; Rv 5:6; 12:3; 13:1); here they designate the brutal power of the nations who "furthered the disaster" (15) of God's people when God used them as instruments of His judgment upon His faithless people.

2:1-5 The third vision is a pictorial commentary on the words of the Lord in 1:14: "I am exceedingly jealous for Jerusalem and for Zion." In the heavenly world the first step (*measuring,* 1) is already being taken toward realizing God's purpose for His city. But the restoration will not be a political one; the city will have no walls, though walls were indispensable for the security of an ancient city. The Lord Himself will be the wall of Jerusalem, a wall of fire, flexible enough to contain her multitudes and powerful enough to defend her from all harm.

2:5 *Glory* expresses the overpowering manifestation of God in the splendor of His Godhead; it is God's "weight" (the basic meaning of the Hebrew term for *glory*) as it impresses itself on man. Is 6:1-9 is the best exposition of this important term; Isaiah's vision of the enthroned King expresses both the annihilating effect of God's glory, on the seraphim and especially on sinful man (Is 6:1-5); it expresses also the glory of God's grace (Eph 1:6), which reaches out to forgive and cleanse the sinner and to take him into God's service (Is 6:6-9; cf. Zch 2:8). Christ the Reconciler and the Judge of the quick and the dead is called the reflection of God's glory in Heb 1:3.

2:6-13 HO! ESCAPE TO ZION

Direct speech interprets the message of the second and third vision. The Jews still residing in Babylon are summoned and encouraged to return to Zion, assured of the Lord's love for them (*the apple of his eye,* 8) and of His determination to punish their oppressors (9). All the ancient promises will find a new fulfillment (*dwell in the midst of you,* 10: *inherit Judah as his portion,* 12; *choose Jerusalem,* 12). The direct speech adds two new features to what has been said in the visions: (a) The prophet, with his seemingly extravagant promises, will be vindicated (9, 12); and (b) God's grace to Israel is seen as the beginning and means of His grace to all men: *many nations shall join themselves to the Lord . . . and shall be His people.* (11; for this universal note in Zechariah, cf. 8:18-20; 9:6-7, 10; 14:9, 16)

2:13 The prophet sinks down in awe at this universal prospect and bids *all flesh* (man in his infinite frailty) be silent in adoration before the God who is on the move to execute His purposes.

3:1—4:14 THE FOURTH AND FIFTH VISIONS: PRIEST AND KING IN THE NEW AGE

3:1—4:14 A new temple, a new Jerusalem, a new Zion—these are unthinkable without priest and king. The prophet is shown that they are ready to hand in the planning of God and will be fitted for their high offices by the Lord Himself.

1) 3:1-10 The Fourth Vision: The High Priest of the New Age

What man of flesh and blood dare serve as priest, appearing before God as representative of a sinful people? Certainly not Joshua, the then-functioning high priest. Satan has every right to accuse him, and he does. Only the Lord Himself can silence the accusation, for His grace has chosen Jerusalem despite all Jerusalem's sins. He has plucked the dry wood from the fire of His judgment (the exile). He can remove the *filthy garments* (symbol of Joshua's and his people's guilt) and can clothe him in pure priestly garments and make him a faithful priest to rule over God's house. He can even give Joshua access to God such as the angels have. The Messianic age is dawning; God's Servant, *the Branch* (Messiah, cf. Jer 23:5; 33:15) is to come, and that means the removal of man's guilt, the justification of the ungodly, and it means idyllic peace and prosperity.

3:1 For Satan as *accuser* cf. Jb 1:6-12; 2:1-6; Rv 12:10.

3:5 The *turban* is part of the high-priestly vestment (Ex 28:4). Ex 28:38 connects it with the atoning office of the priest, and it is mentioned among the holy garments worn by the priest on the Day of Atonement (Lv 16:4). The express mention of it is therefore fitting in this context of forgiveness and reconciliation.

3:7 *Those who are standing here* are the angels who stand in God's presence (cf. 5 and Is 6:2). Zechariah has a strong sense of the gulf which separates man from God; an angel mediates the divine revelation which he receives (e.g., 1:12-14). It it therefore a strong expression of the fullness of God's forgiveness that a human being should have direct access to God. This is an anticipation of the world to come, where we shall be "like angels." (Mt 22:30)

3:8 The *friends* of Joshua are most likely the

priests who serve under him, the high priest. Since the restoration of the priesthood, like the rebuilding of the temple, is to usher in the new age, they are *men of good omen;* they point to the coming Messiah, the *Branch* of whom Jeremiah had spoken (Jer 23:5-6; 33:15-16; cf. Is 4:2). Zechariah refers to Him again in 6:12, in connection with the building of the temple.

3:9 The significance of *the stone . . . set before Joshua* is not clear; perhaps an ornament on the priestly turban is meant. (Cf. Ex 28:36)

3:10 The expression *under his vine and . . . fig tree* connotes a time of peace and happiness. (Cf. 1 K 4:25; Mi 4:4)

2) 4:1-14 The Fifth Vision: King and Priest, the Two Anointed

The anointed king of the dawning new age is no mere political figure; he performs his task in the power of the Spirit of the Lord (6). He is a religious figure and is therefore closely associated with the priest. Together the anointed priest and the anointed king *stand by the Lord of the whole earth* (14). The elaborate imagery of the golden lampstand with its seven lamps and 49 flames and the two olive trees beside it seems to indicate that under the watchful eye of the omniscient Lord these divinely instituted and empowered leaders will be the means by which the grace of God (*oil*, 12) is supplied to the people of God, for life in the new Jerusalem and for worship in the new temple.

4:7-10 The structure of the account of this vision is as follows. There is, first, a detailed description of the vision (2-3). Second, a declaration of the general significance of the vision: Zerubbabel shall carry out his assigned task in the power of the Spirit; not even the most imposing opposition (*great mountain*) can thwart him; the capstone shall be set upon the new temple amid general rejoicing (4-10). And third, there is given a more detailed interpretation of the vision, which adds the significant detail (12) of the golden pipes from which the golden oil is poured out. (11-14)

4:6 *By my Spirit* emphasizes the fact that the power and the triumph in this undertaking are the Lord's and His alone.

4:10 The *plummet* will be seen *in the hand of Zerubbabel* as he aligns the capstone of the structure and sets it in place.

5:1-11 THE SIXTH AND SEVENTH VISIONS: THE REMOVAL OF SIN FROM THE NEW JERUSALEM

1) 5:1-4 The Sixth Vision: The Flying Scroll

The thief and the perjurer are struck by the curse of God's Law, pictured as a huge scroll (30 by 15 feet). Thus the new Jerusalem is made fit for the new life.

5:2 For the picture of God's counsels as a written document cf. Eze 2:8—3:3; Rv 5:1; 10:8-10. The intentions of God are written down and are therefore permanent, not to be revoked or evaded.

5:3 The thief and the perjurer are mentioned as special objects of the curse. There were probably many disputes concerning property when the returning exiles claimed their ancestral possessions (cf. Jer 32:6-15). Those who had remained in the land and occupied the property retained it unlawfully and swore a false oath to back their claim to it. This interpretation is confirmed by the fact that the punishment strikes the guilty man's "house," the object of his thievery and the reason for his perjury.

2) 5:5-11 The Seventh Vision: The Woman in the Ephah

Not only are individual sinners exposed and condemned; Jerusalem is to be delivered from all evil. Evil *(iniquity)* is symbolized by a woman seated in a vessel shaped like a grain measure *(ephah)*; in it she is imprisoned and transported to *Shinar* (an ancient name for Babylon, Gn 11:2), where she has a dwelling and a place of honor; here evil is not only tolerated but is worshiped.

5:6 The *ephah* is a grain measure containing three eighths to two thirds of a bushel. The point of similarity is evidently the shape of the measure, not its size.

6:1-8 THE EIGHTH VISION: GOD'S SPIRIT REACHES THE EXILES IN THE NORTH

The four winds, the chariots of God, go forth to execute His will in all the earth. God's will is one of salvation for all people. But He will bring salvation to all by way of Israel ("Salvation is from the Jews," Jn 4:22). Therefore interest is centered on the chariot which goes to the *north country*, to Babylon, where the remainder of the exiles are. Thither the chariot brings the Spirit of God, to incite the exiles to join their brethren in Jerusalem, the city of the promise, the seedbed from which God's future will grow and spread.

6:8 Many take the expression *set my Spirit at rest* to mean that God's jealous anger against Babylon is satisfied. This is possible. But the verb *set at rest* means basically "to cause to settle down" or "to lay," "to deposit"; the idea of "rest" is not necessarily expressed. And it seems more likely that the last of the visions of hope should sound a positive note of hope, as a climax to the series.

6:9-15 The Conclusion of the Visions: The Coronation of Priest and King

6:9-15 The visions of hope are followed by a Word of the Lord which bids the prophet perform an action of hope; he is to take the silver and gold brought by a group of returning exiles and to make crowns of them for Joshua and Zerubbabel. (The coronation of Zerubbabel is not told in so many words, but the fact that the Hebrew text speaks of crown*s* and that Zerubbabel is here, as in 3:8, designated by the Messianic title Branch seems to indicate that he too is to be crowned.) The action takes place privately, *in the house of Josiah* (10), and the crowns are not to be worn as yet but are to be kept in the temple *as a reminder* (14). The action is symbolical, pointing to the future, and the full fulfillment of the Messianic prophecy is left indefinite and open-ended. The main point is: Now, in the building of the temple, the beginning of the new age is to be made, and in this the priestly and the royal power are to work together harmoniously (13); and the people, joined by the many exiles who are still to return, are to join in, obeying the voice of the Lord their God. (15)

Since this oracle is undated, in contrast to both the preceding and the following (7:1) utterance, it seems best to take it as the conclusion, or epilog, to the eight visions.

6:11 The reading of the Hebrew text, *crowns* (plural), seems preferable to the singular adopted by the RSV. It is remarkable how closely priesthood and kingship are connected both here and in the visions of the investiture of Joshua and of the Two Anointed (3:1-10; 4:1-14). The prophecy found its final fulfillment in our Lord, who is both priest and king. (Heb 6:20—7:2; cf. Ps 110. 4)

6:15 The last phrase, *if you will diligently obey,* etc., reminds us that the promise of God is a personal Word, which evokes a personal response, the obedience of faith.

7:1—8:23 YOUR FASTS SHALL BECOME FEASTS

7:1—8:23 A delegation from Bethel inquires of the priests and prophets of Jerusalem concerning the observance of the fasts which commemorated the burning of the temple in 586 BC. Need the fasts still be observed, now that the temple is being rebuilt? (7:1-3). The prophet's answer goes deeper than the inquiry. It treats, first, of the true meaning of fasting and all ritual worship (7:4-6). Then, looking back on Israel's history, the prophet recalls why their feasts had become fasts, why their joy had been turned into mourning (7:7-14). And third, the prophet proclaims how their fasts will become feasts again, by the redeeming will and work of God, and what this involves for the conduct of the people of God (8:1-23). It is in this last section of exuberant promises that the direct answer to the inquiry is given. (8:18-19)

7:1-3 The Inquiry Concerning the Observance of Fasts

7:1 The date is 518 BC, and progress has been made toward the completion of the temple, accomplished in 516 BC; the question from Bethel was natural enough.

7:3 The burning of the temple took place in the *fifth month.* (Jer 52:12; 2 K 25:8)

7:4-6 The True Meaning of Fasting

7:5 The fast of the *seventh month* probably commemorated the murder of Gedaliah, appointed governor over the cities of Judah by the king of Babylon after the fall of Jerusalem (2 K 25:22-26; Jer 41:1-3). His death at the hand of Jewish nationalist fanatics proved a grievous blow for the people who remained in the land.

7:5-6 The rhetorical question concerning Israel's fasting implies the same judgment as that which Jesus passed on the fasting of the Pharisees (Mt 6:16-18); it lacked sincerity and integrity. Fasting, which was meant to be an expression of sorrow for sin and of urgency in prayer, had become a self-centered piece of piety. Israel's feasting (*eat* and *drink*) was vitiated by the same basic fault; their self-centeredness robbed all worship of its content and meaning.

7:7-14 Why Feasts Become Fasts

7:7-14 Why did Israel's history become for 70 years, a history of fasting and mourning? Because, in her prime when her territory was intact (7), she did not listen to the voice of the prophets but resisted the Spirit who spoke through the prophets (7, 11-12). She had no ear for a word like Micah's which set before her a simple and unforgettable picture of true worship: "To do justice, and to love kindness, and to walk humbly with your God" (Mi 6:8). The people of Israel would not listen to the Lord when He called to them through the prophets, and so the time came when He would not listen to them. Their conversation with God ended, and the wrath of God scattered them and left their land desolate.

7:8 This *word of the Lord* to Zechariah sums up what the Lord had told His people "by his Spirit through the former prophets," that is, before the exile.

8:1-23 How Fasts Become Feasts

8:1-23 What brings the great reversal in Israel's fortunes? How can fasts become *seasons of joy and gladness, and cheerful feasts* (19)? Not by any act of Israel's but by the mercy of her merciful and mighty covenant God, the Lord of hosts. Zechariah pours out a flood of "gracious and comforting words" (cf. 1:13) to depict His restoring mercy and might. Ten words of promise, each introduced by the formula: *Thus says the Lord of hosts,* picture the opening of the floodgates of His love. In the course of these promises the query concerning fasts receives its answer (18-19). The renewed temple (9) and Israel's acceptable worship (a whole life lived to God in love for one another, 16-17) are to be Israel's response to the Lord's faithful covenant love (*Therefore love truth and peace,* 19). Thus, by the Lord's creative mercy Israel may become a light to lighten the Gentiles. (20-23)

8:6 The Hebrew word here rightly translated *marvelous* is used of the birth of Isaac in Gn 18:14. ("Is anything too hard for the Lord?") The birth of Isaac, child of the promise, to aged parents "as good as dead" (Ro 4:19) and the restoration of Israel in the new age are both sheer miracles of grace and call for faith.

8:9 The response of faith to the great divine promises is the concrete act of building the temple.

8:13 God holds to the promise which He made long since to Abraham *(you shall be a blessing).* (Cf. Gn 12:2)

8:19 Here *the fast of the fourth month* and *of the tenth* are added to the list of fasts. The walls of Jerusalem were first breached "on the ninth day of the *fourth* month" (2 K 25:3-4; cf. Jer 39:2). Zedekiah, the puppet king installed by the king of Babylon, rebelled against the Babylonian conqueror "in the *tenth* month" (2 K 25:1). These events may have given rise to the practice of fasting in the month during which they occurred.

8:23 We Gentiles dare never forget the debt we owe to the Jew; we came into the Kingdom by laying hold of the robe of the Jew. Paul's warning to the complacent Gentile Christians of his day is still needed. (Ro 11:17-24)

Introductory Note: The first eight chapters of the Book of Zechariah mention the prophet by name and date his utterances; the historical situation in which the prophetic word is spoken can be reconstructed with reasonable certainty. In the last six chapters the name of the prophet is not mentioned, none of the oracles are dated, and the specific historical themes of the first half of the book (such as the rebuilding of the temple) do not recur. The style and tone of these chapters differs considerably also. Some scholars account for this difference by assigning these chapters to a later period in Zechariah's life, when conditions had changed. Others assign them to another nameless prophet or other prophets. Among those who believe these six chapters to be the work of someone other than Zechariah, there is little agreement as to the date and the historical background of the prophecies. Some scholars date portions of them as early as the eighth century BC. Others assign all or most of them to the fourth or third century.

Whether these words are the utterances of nameless prophets or are Zechariah's is not a question of first importance. The NT witnesses to the abiding value and the high authority of what God has here caused to be written for our learning, especially concerning the significance of our Lord's passion and death. Cf. Mt 21:1-5 (Zch 9:9); Mt 26:28 (Zch 9:11); Mt 9:36 (Zch 10:2); Jn 10:12 ff. (Zch 11:4 ff., 15 ff.); Mt 26:15 (Zch 11:12); Mt 27:9-10 (Zch 11:13); Jn 19:37 (Zch 12:10); Mt 26:31 (Zch 13:7); Mt 21:12 (Zch 14:21).

The uncertainty concerning the historical setting does create some difficulties for the understanding of these living oracles, to be sure; some of the problems are insoluble. But like all the words of God, these words are greater than their first occasion and can be profitable for teaching, for reproof, for correction, and for training in righteousness even when the original historical setting lies beyond our ken. The last six chapters of the Book of Zechariah can be profitably studied as a vivid commentary on the Kingdom for whose coming the church prays in the Lord's Prayer.

9:1—11:17 HIS KINGDOM RULES OVER ALL

9:1-8 His Royal Word Rules Over All

9:1-8 God's royal reign (Ps 103:19) is the working of His powerful and creative *word* (1; cf. Is 9:8; 55:10; Ps 107:20). When there is a "shaking of nations" (cf. Hg 2:7, 21-22), His Word is shaking them. The Lord is not a local god, competent only in his own territory. His Word runs through the world and does His will in Syria *(Aram)* as much as it does in Israel. Great cities like Tyre, rich, shrewd, and mightily fortified, fall when He brings them low (3-4). The Philistian cities, too (*Ashkelon, Gaza, Ekron, Ashdod,* 5-6), come under His dominion. His universal dominion aims at universal salvation; when He makes *an end of the pride of Philistia,* He does so in order that He may incorporate the *remnant* of Philistia into His people and thus become the Guardian of all those gathered in His *house* (6-8). He sees, and He acts (8); He speaks, and it is done.

It is not certain which historical event occasioned this proclamation of God's universal kingship. Some think of the time when Alexander the Great, having defeated the king of Persia in the battle of Issus (333 BC), proceeded southward on the victorious march that was to lead to the capture of Tyre and the conquest of all Palestine; others suggest the time of the Assyrian conquests (eighth and seventh centuries). The essential thing is that this "shaking of the nations" to the north and west of the Holy Land is interpreted as being the Lord's work and as serving His purpose.

9:5-7 The Philistines are terrified at the fate that has befallen their neighbor Tyre, since they must look forward to sharing that fate.

9:6 The people of *Ashdod* will become a *mongrel people* because they will be mixed with alien colonists settled there by their conquerors.

9:7 The *blood* and *abominations* refer to the eating of sacrificial meat with the blood, which the Mosaic law forbade. The "unclean" Gentiles shall be made clean and fit for incorporation into the people of God, just as the non-Israelite *Jebusites* (the original inhabitants of Jerusalem) had been incorporated into Israel in the time of David. (Cf. 2 Sm 5:6-10; 1 Ch 11:4-9)

9:8 *House* is here used to designate the inhabited land, as in Jer 12:7; Hos 8:1; 9:15.

For God's effectual *seeing* cf. Ex 3:7: "I have seen the affliction of my people."

9:9-10 Your King Comes to You

9:9-10 The kingdom of God is not merely a reign OVER history. His kingdom "comes"; His Word becomes flesh and enters history. His reign will be a reign IN history, and that incarnate reign means blessing for all nations. The King who comes to Zion is the opposite of the "pride of Philistia" (6); He comes in humility, riding upon an ass, and looks to God for vindication and victory *(triumphant, victorious),* not to any human or secular power. His kingdom is "not of this world"; His only weapon is the Word, which speaks peace to all mankind. It puts an end to all armaments *(chariot, war horse)* and to the horror and agony they create. This Servant King, this King of Peace, shall be God's last Word in history, for His dominion has no limits. In Him God will have conquered His world and made it His own.

The NT points to the fulfillment of this prophecy in Jesus' entry into Jerusalem (Mt 21:4-5, Jn 12:14-16). There, as He comes, unarmed and riding on an ass, the animal of peace, to manifest Himself as Jerusalem's King, we see in utmost concentration the will of meekness which characterizes His whole ministry. This was the will which He manifested in His determination to live by every word which proceeds from the mouth of God (Mt 4:4), in His beatitude upon the poor and the meek (Mt 5:3, 5), in His gentleness and lowliness of heart (Mt 11:29), in His refusal to let His followers fight for Him or to summon legions of angels to His defense (Mt 26:51-53; Jn 18:36), in His unshakable confidence that His Father would make His enemies His footstool and set Him at the right hand of the heavenly throne (Mt 22:41-45; 26:64). Thus He created and gave a peace which the world cannot give.

9:10 *Ephraim* and *Jerusalem,* the northern and southern kingdoms, divided since the tragic days of Rehoboam (1 K 12:1-20; cf. 11:26-40), shall be united again in the days of the Messiah, whose peaceful reign will unite all nations under a worldwide *(sea to sea)* dominion.

9:11-17 God's Reign Delivers from All Evil

9:11-17 The Word of God shakes the nations, for their ultimate salvation, and sets before Israel the promise of a Prince of Peace. God has a Word for the dark present too, for His people's present distress in their captivity. He has not forgotten the covenant ratified with atoning *blood* (Ex 24:1-8); He remembers the *blood of* His *covenant* (11), by which He said: "I will be your God"; and He will deliver His people from all evil. He will set the captives free; the prisoners are *prisoners of hope,* assured of deliverance and of double recompense for their sufferings (12). The Lord Himself will fight for His people and give them victory over all enemies (13-15). In His almighty hand His people shall become a warrior's *bow* and *arrow* and *sword* (13). He will set His people free and bless them with the fruitful plenty of the Promised Land. (16-17)

9:11 *Waterless pit* suggests the dry hopelessness of life in exile.

9:12 *Stronghold* probably refers to the fortified home city of the captives, Jerusalem. The *double* recompense is victory over their enemies (13-15) and a blessed and secure existence in their homeland. (16-17)

9:13-15 The battle will be a holy war, in which God Himself is the Warrior: Bowman, Spearsman, *(Brandish,* 13), Swordsman, and Trumpeter.

9:13 What particular Greek power, if any, is meant by *Greece,* can hardly be determined. (Cf. 9:1-8 note)

9:15 The wild imagery of *drinking blood,* being filled with blood like a *bowl* used in sacrifice, or *drenched* like the altar against which the blood of sacrificed animals was poured out (Ex 24:6) suggests the fearfulness of the carnage and the decisiveness of the victory.

10:1-2 God the King as Giver of Daily Bread

10:1-2 Israel was constantly tempted to forget that the God whose kingdom is over all (Ps 145:13) is also the God of everyday needs, the God who gives men their food in due season (Ps 145:15). They forgot the Creator and turned to idols and diviners for help and advice in the critical matter of the *spring rain,* so essential for the maturing of the crops (1). This ignoring of God avenges itself—or, rather, God avenges it; men who will not look to the Good Shepherd are doomed to be a leaderless and afflicted flock. (2)

10:2 The *teraphim* are idols used as instruments of divination. (Cf. Eze 21:21)

10:3—11:3 The Kingdom as the Reign of the Good Shepherd

10:3—11:3 *The Lord of hosts cares for his flock* (3). *The house of Judah* is a flock that desperately needs caring for. The people are not only without shepherds of their own (cf. 2); they are under the domination of alien shepherds, foreign tyrants who oppress them. The Lord of hosts will therefore intervene for them and make the helpless victims mighty victors (3-6). He will provide them with genuine leaders from their own ranks (4), who will lead them to triumph against superior foes *because the Lord is with them* (5). A reunited people (*Judah* and *Joseph,* 6) shall be filled with strength for battle and with the joy of victory. A repentant people, they shall be brought home, freed from the domination of alien powers (10, 11). The wonders of the Exodus shall be repeated (11) and the people shall exult in the strength given them by their God (12). The pride and power of the kingdoms of this world shall be brought low, like proud *cedars* and *oaks* felled and consumed by fire. (11:1-3)

10:3 The *shepherds* and *leaders* (literally "he goats," cf. Dn 8:5-8, 21) are here foreign overlords (cf. Jer 25:34) who exploit the flock, unlike the *Lord,* who cares for His flock.

10:4 The promised Messianic Ruler is compared to a *cornerstone,* which determines the structure of the whole house; to a *tent peg,* whose firmness ensures the stability of the tent; and to a *battle bow,* which provides for the defense of the people. The Ruler shall *come out of them,* that is, be a member of their own people. (Cf. Dt 17:15)

10:6 The lord *will answer* their prayer.

10:8 *Signal,* lit. "whistle." (Cf. Is 7:18)

10:9 For *remember* in the sense of "remember and repent" cf. Dt 30:1-2.

10:10 *Egypt* and *Assyria* are cited as examples of the foreign powers (the *shepherds* of 3) who have afflicted the people of God. As the Lord once delivered His people from their tyranny, so He will again. The returning exiles will be so numerous that even the boundaries of David's great kingdoms *(Gilead, Lebanon)* will not be able to contain them.

10:12 The reading of the Hebrew text *(walk in his name)* is perhaps to be preferred. The reestablished people will be an inwardly renewed people; they shall *walk* (that is, lead their lives) by the light of the revelation *(name)* which the Lord grants them.

11:1-2 For *cedars* and *oaks* as symbols of proud power cf. Is 2:12-13, 17; 10:33; Eze 31:2-3, 10.

Lebanon and *Bashan* are as localities famed for their trees.

11:3 There is a grim irony in the fact that the foreign overlords are called *shepherds* and *lions* in one breath. It is because they are not true tending shepherds but devouring lions that they lose their *glory* and their place *(jungle).*

11:4-17 The Kingdom of God Suffers Violence

11:4-14 In this age the reign of God works against obstacles and opposition; it strikes sparks of conflict when it encounters the pride of Philistia (9:6), the haughty wisdom of Tyre and Sidon (9:2), the oppressors of God's people (9:11-12), the power of Assyria, and the oppressive scepter of Egypt (10:11). It must consume in flame the towering cedars and oaks of the kingdoms of this world (1-2). Even in the midst of God's people, God's reign must struggle to overcome superstition and idolatry (10:2). But the most grievous opposition to the kingdom is that offered by the ingratitude and contempt of the flock to whom the king sends His Good Shepherd.

11:4-14 THE GOOD SHEPHERD REJECTED BY HIS PEOPLE

It is this that the prophet is called upon to portray when he, at the Lord's command, portrays the role of the Lord as shepherd to His people. This section of Zechariah is admittedly one of the most difficult in the OT, and many details which were, no doubt, clear to the prophet's contemporaries remain obscure for us. But this much, at least, is tolerably clear: 1. The people of God, the flock, are desperately afflicted; they are betrayed and exploited by outsiders and by their own leaders (5, 7); they have shepherds whom God must destroy if the flock is to be saved (8). They are a flock doomed to die (4, 7). 2. To this doomed flock, "harassed and helpless" (Mt 9:36), the Lord sends the Shepherd of His choice. He is authorized by his God (4) and equipped for his task with the twin staffs of God's *Grace* and divinely given *Union* (7). He executes God's judgment on false shepherds (8) and faithfully tends the sheep (7). 3. His shepherd ministry is a tragic failure; God's people *detest* the Good Shepherd, and the Shepherd becomes *impatient* with them (8). The doomed people is left to die of its sins (9). The grace that protected them from the *peoples* is withdrawn (10). The people are once more confronted with a decision concerning God's Shepherd when the shepherd asks for his pay. They pay him, but the payment is an insult (15)—30 shekels of silver, the indemnity paid to a slave-owner if his slave was accidentally killed (Ex 21:32). The shepherd is commanded to throw the money *to the potter* (probably a gesture of contempt, 13), and the other gift of God, *Union* (brotherhood in the people of God), is also withdrawn.

11:4 For symbolic actions as a means whereby the prophetic message is vividly impressed on the prophet and his people cf. Hos 1 and 3; Is 20:2-6; Eze 4:4-17. In the present case the action is probably not carried out but is inwardly experienced by the prophet and its content conveyed by the word, as in the case of Ezekiel's vision of the dry bones. (Eze 37:1-14)

11:5 Those who *buy* are probably foreign exploiters of the people, while those who *sell* are those who collaborate with them—they piously thank the Lord, the covenant God of Israel, for traitorous profits. The shepherds are the leaders who ought to protect their people.

11:6 The connection *(for)* between this and the preceding is obscure. *This land* could also be translated "the earth" or "the world." Then the meaning would be: The Lord is sending His shepherd to His people as an offer of mercy before He unlooses the terrible forces of tyranny and destruction as His judgment on mankind.

11:8 The *three shepherds* cannot be identified; they represent a false leadership which impedes the work of the Good Shepherd. The *one month* probably indicates a short period of grace.

For the *impatience* of the good shepherd cf. Jesus' words in Mt 17:17.

11:10 God will no longer prevent the nations *(peoples)* from overpowering His people.

11:11 The Shepherd's action is recognized as being the Lord's *word,* i.e., it expressed His will. According to the Hebrew text, the "poor of the flock" were *watching* the shepherd's action. This would mean that there were those, however poor and insignificant, who responded in faith to the shepherd's ministry. If *traffickers in the sheep* is read, the meaning is that the exploiters of the people recognized the divine authority of the Shepherd's mission and yet resisted it.

11:12 *Thirty shekels of silver* is the indemnity money, paid for the killing of a slave (Ex 21:32). There is a hint here that the shepherd perishes in his ministry, a thought which finds fuller expression in 12:10 and 13:7-9.

11:13 *Lordly price* is ironic. The Hebrew text, *throw it to the potter* is probably to be preferred to *cast it into the treasury. To throw to the potter* seems to mean: to treat with contempt, perhaps because the potter made cheap and perishable ware. More significant is the fact that the action takes place in the temple, *the house of the Lord;* the Lord is witness to the ingratitude of the people and will call them to account for their contemptuous treatment of His Shepherd.

This prophecy of the 30 pieces of silver was fulfilled in a mysterious way when Judas betrayed the Good Shepherd and cast the money into the temple treasury, whence it found its way to the potter—as the price paid for the Field of Blood. (Mt 27:3-10)

11:15-17 THE WORTHLESS SHEPHERD

When God's gifts of Grace and Union are rejected, the result is not a void. The place which they formerly occupied is filled by the judgment of God. Those who refuse the good shepherding of God come under the ruthless rule of the worthless shepherd; and this is God's doing, God's act of judgment. The prophet who enacted the Good Shepherd is commissioned to portray the worthless shepherd too, the shepherd who is the embodiment of all that a shepherd should NOT be (cf. Eze 34:2-10). But even when God permits and uses the evil that people do for His purposes, they remain responsible for their evil; the curse of God strikes the hand which did not wield the shepherd's protecting staff and the shepherd's eye which did not look after the flock.

12:1—14:21 INHERIT THE KINGDOM

12:1—14:21 Chs. 12—14 are in some ways parallel to chs. 9—11; the theme here, too, is the coming of the kingdom of God. But there is a new emphasis on the inner renewal and purification of God's people (12:10—13:6); a broader and fuller portrayal of the inclusion of the Gentiles in the Kingdom of the last days (14:9, 16-19); and, above all, the figure of the humble and lowly King (9:9-10) and the Good Shepherd (11:4-14) emerges with greater clarity in the Pierced One (12:10) and the Smitten Shepherd (13:7-9) and stands beside the Suffering Servant of Is 53 as one of the clearest and profoundest interpretations of Him who is the Kingdom of God in person in all His words and works, not least in His suffering and death.

12:1-9 The Victory of the People of God

12:1-9 The mission of the Good Shepherd has ended in failure, and the people of God have been delivered into the hands of the worthless shepherd. If the people of God are to have a future and a history, only a *creative* act of God can make it possible. It is the God who created the heavens, earth, and the human spirit who will give His people strength and victory. His initiative in the Word is stated at the beginning, and His activity is stressed throughout, in every verse of the section.

12:1 For God the Creator as the omnipotent actor in history and the sure source of deliverance cf. Is 40:12-31; 42:5-9; 51:12-16.

12:2 The *cup of reeling* (or intoxication) pictures Jerusalem as something which is eagerly sought by the nations and proves to be their downfall. For *cup* and intoxication as a picture of the wrath and judgment of God cf. Ps 75:8; Is 51:17, 22; Jer 25:15, 17, 28; 49:12; Eze 23:31-35; Hab 2:16. The words *it will be against Judah also* seem to indicate that there will be opposition to Jerusalem, the city of God, from within the people of God itself. In 5 Judah is pictured as repenting and recognizing Jerusalem as the very city of God, and in 7 Judah even has preeminence in the victory given by the Lord.

12:3 Jerusalem is pictured as a *stone* on which the nations try their strength and come to grief. The church is an anvil that has worn out many hammers.

12:4-6 The Lord will *open His eyes,* that is, regard with favor the house of Judah; the gracious and effectual seeing of God (cf. 9:8; Ex 3:7) is in sharp contrast to the blindness and impotence of His enemies. God's kindness leads Judah to repentance (5; cf. Ro 2:4), and Judah becomes His blazing instrument of judgment (like a pot of live coals or a torch amid dry combustible materials).

12:7 Judah came late to the battle, with a bad record of previous enmity, and yet is the first to enjoy the gift of victory. This marks the victory as purely God's grace and His gift, not a human attainment; not even the royal house or the holy city can claim personal credit. The last shall be first.—So Micah beheld the Messiah coming not from Jerusalem but from little Bethlehem and ruling not in the strength of the royal house in the royal city but "in the strength of the Lord" (Mi 5:2-4)

12:8 *Like David,* the mighty warrior king. God will make all members of His people kings (cf. Rv 1:6; 5:10). *The Angel of the Lord* is a form in which the invisible God makes His presence known to people. Cf., e.g., Gn 22, where "angel of the Lord" (Gn 22:11, 15) alternates with "God" (Gn 22:12) and "Lord" (Gn 22:16). The *house of David* will be like God as He manifests Himself to people in history. There is a hint here of the Incarnation.

12:10—13:6 The Inner Renewal of the People of God

12:10—13:6 The Lord will not only give His people victory over their enemies; He will, by His Spirit, create a clean heart within them.

12:10-14 THE OUTPOURING OF THE SPIRIT OF COMPASSION AND SUPPLICATION

12:10-14 Moved by the *Spirit* which assures them of God's compassion and inspires their supplication, the people repent of the deadly wrong they have done to the Lord in the person of whom they, in their rebellion against the Lord, have put to death.

12:10 The word here translated *supplications* is used frequently for the cry to God "out of the depths" (Ps 130:1-2; cf. Ps 28:2, 6; 31:22; 86:6; 116:1; 140:6; 143:1; Jer 3:21; 31:9; 2 Ch 6:21). It is a penitent cry. The Hebrew text reads: *When they look on Me,* that is, God Himself; then the meaning would be that the one *whom they have pierced* was so closely identified with God that the attack on him was an attack on God Himself. Whatever reading is adopted, the people's relationship with God is deeply affected by their attack on him for whom they now mourn. That person is here left unnamed; it is natural to think of the Good Shepherd of 11:4-14, authorized by the divine Word and equipped with divine gifts for the people of God, whom the people then "detested" (11:8). There is a hint in 11:12 ("thirty shekels of silver," indemnity for a *killed* slave) that the Good Shepherd met with death. This hint is taken up and made explicit here in the words *whom they have pierced;* and this is further explicated in 13:7-9, where it becomes clear that the Shepherd's death is the death of one smitten by God (cf. Is 53:5-6, 10). This too is the witness of John, who applies the prophetic word to Jesus in his Gospel (Jn 19:37) and alludes to it in Rv 1:7.

12:11 *The mourning for Hadadrimmon* perhaps makes the point that the mourning is *intense* by comparing it with the wild ritual lamentation for a pagan vegetation God on the plain of Megiddo; or it emphasizes the *universality* of the mourning by comparing it with the mourning for the good King Josiah, who was slain in the plain of Megiddo in 609 BC. According to 2 Ch 35:24-25, "all Judah and Jerusalem mourned for Josiah. Jeremiah also uttered a lament for Josiah; and all the singing men and singing women have spoken of Josiah in their laments to this day."

12:12-14The mourning is universal, so ordered and arranged that all can participate. Thus it takes on the character of a public confession of common guilt and becomes an expression of universal repentance.

13:1-6 THE FOUNTAIN TO CLEANSE THE PEOPLE OF GOD FROM SIN AND UNCLEANNESS

The effectual cleansing of God will produce a people pure in heart, a people upon whom idols have no hold, whom no false prophet can deceive.

13:1 The *opening of the fountain* is parallel to the outpouring of the Spirit in 12:10. For the use of cleansing by water as a picture for spiritual cleansing cf. Eze 36:25, where it is also associated and combined with imparting of the Spirit. (Eze 36:27)

13:2 The result of God's cleansing: The *idols* will no longer have any significance *(name)* for the faithful and will exercise no influence over them *(be remembered)*. And the *prophets* who are inspired not by the Spirit of God (Mi 3:8) but by the *unclean spirit,* who *speaks lies in the name of the Lord* (3), will be eradicated.

13:3-6 People will so abhor the false prophet that even parental feeling will not keep them from dealing ruthlessly with the false prophet, as the Law commanded (Dt 13:1-5). No one will claim the office or wear the *hairy mantle* which identifies the prophet (cf. 1 K 1:8; Mt 3:4). A man who has previously been a prophet and bears on his body the scars of his self-woundings (such as the prophets of Baal performed, 1 K 18:28) will invent a story discreditable to himself rather than admit the truth. He received the *wounds,* he will say, *in the house of his friends,* that is, in a brawl while carousing with his cronies.—There is no mention of the continuation of true prophecy; perhaps the idea is that prohecy, as a separate institution, will cease in the new age because the Spirit, poured out on all flesh, will make all members of the people prophets. (Jl 2:28-29; Acts 2:17-21)

13:7-9 The Stricken Shepherd and the Scattered Sheep

13:7-9 Jesus applied Zechariah's word concerning the stricken Shepherd and the scattered sheep to Himself and His disciples (Mt 26:31). And indeed the shepherd can only be the Good Shepherd; the Lord calls Him *my Shepherd* and *the man who stands next to me* (7), a term which Leviticus applies repeatedly to one united with another by a close and binding tie, the "brother," the "neighbor," fellow member of the covenant people (Lv 19:15; see also 6:1; 18:20; 19:11; 24:19; 25:14, 15, 17). He is, then, God's Good Shepherd, God's gift given to His people, detested by the people, valued at 30 shekels of silver (11:7-14); He is the Pierced One for whom the people will one day mourn, when the Spirit works repentance in them. (12:10)

Before the blessing of victory and renewal by the Spirit can come, the Shepherd must die (cf. Jn 7:39; 16:7). His death is not an accident but the deliberate judicial action of God (*sword,* 7; cf. 11:17). Zechariah speaks darkly of what Is 53 tells more plainly: The divinely willed atoning death of One on whom the Lord has laid the iniquity of us all (Is 53:5-6). This is the mystery of the Cross, the mystery of God's reckless love. Mysterious, too, is the sequel: The result for the flock is not immediate bliss, but a time of trial that sifts and separates (8-9a), tests and purges the people of God until they become the pure gold that the Great Refiner desires. Not until then is His heavy hand withdrawn; THEN He answers His people's confession and praise with the beatific words: *They are my People* (9b). Jesus knew this aspect of His mission on earth; and He spoke His full assent to the will of God when He asserted that He had come to bring the dividing sword and to cast a purging and refining fire on earth. (Mt 10:34; Lk 12:49)

14:1-21 The Lord will Become King over All the Earth

14:1-21 The last chapter sums up the message of chs. 9—13 by portraying on a broad canvas and in monumental style the coming Day of the Lord, when the Lord Himself comes to establish His kingdom by delivering His holy city from the final massed attack of the nation (1-5), by transfiguring the whole earth under His reign (6-11), by smiting with a fearful plague all the peoples who refuse His reign (12-15), by uniting the survivors of all nations in a common worship (16-19), and by abolishing the distinction between "sacred" and "profane," consecrating *everything* to His own use and glory. (20-21)

14:1-5 THE LORD WILL GO FORTH AND FIGHT

14:1 For *day of the Lord* see Zph 1:7 note.

14:1-3 The victory is marked out clearly as the Lord's and His alone. He intervenes when (*then,* 3) all is, apparently, lost (2), His sovereign control of history appears in the fact that it is He who *gathers all the nations against Jerusalem* (2); even the enemies of God do not escape from His control.

14:4-5 The *splitting of the mountain* portrays the overwhelming might and majesty of the victorious Lord (cf. 1 K 19:11; Ju 5:4-5; Hab 3:6). The resulting *valley* provides a place of refuge for God's people.

The first half of 5 remains obscure. The memory of the *earthquake in the days of Uzziah* remained a vivid one for Israel; cf. Am 1:1. The *holy ones* who accompany the coming Lord are His heavenly hosts of angels.

14:6-11 THE TRANSFIGURED WORLD

14:6-11 The old order of successive seasons and alternate night and day will pass (6). Living waters, symbols of divine life freely implanted, will flow from God's city as they once flowed out of Eden (10; Gn 2:10). Every mountain and hill will be made low; only the mountain and city of God shall be exalted (10; cf. Is 2:12; Mi 4:1); the day when the ban of destruction could still threaten its existence will be forever past. (*Curse,* 11)

14:8 The explanation that the rivers will *continue in summer as in winter* is not superfluous for the people of Palestine, where most streams cease flowing in the dry season of summer.

14:9 The Lord will reign supreme and reign alone; the First Commandment *(one)* and the Second *(name)* will be written on people's hearts.

14:10 *Geba* marks the northern boundary of the kingdom of Judah and *Rimmon* the southern boundary. Cf. 2 K 23:8, where Beer-sheba, some 10 miles southwest of Rimmon, marks the southern boundary.

14:11 For the *curse,* or *ban* of destruction, the terrible judgment of utter destruction upon a city and all its dwellers cf. Dt 13:13-19 and Jos 10:28-40.

14:12-15 THE PLAGUE UPON THE ENEMIES OF JERUSALEM

14:12-15 The judgments of God are as terrible as His blessings are splendid. Those who have shut themselves out from His life shall suffer the plague of living death (*rot . . . rot . . . rot,* 12). Those who have refused His peace shall taste His terror (*panic,* 13) and shall suffer the agony of continued and unreasoning conflict (13). Those who have made their wealth their god shall be stripped of their wealth (14); all that they have will be smitten by the plague. (15)

14:14 For *Judah* as joining the enemies of Jerusalem cf. 12:2. But the phrase could also be translated: "Judah, too, will fight in Jerusalem," i.e., against the attackers of Jerusalem.

14:16-19 THE PILGRIMAGE OF ALL NATIONS TO JERUSALEM TO KEEP THE FEAST OF BOOTHS

14:16-19 As God is King over all (cf. 9), so He will be worshiped by all; the survivors of all the nations will join with His people in *keeping the feast of booths* (or tabernacles). This was "the feast of ingathering at the year's end" (Ex 34:22), fitting symbol of God's great ingathering of all nations at the end of days, a feast, moreover, in which Israel remembered the Exodus, the prototype of all God's acts of deliverance, and recalled how the Lord made them dwell in booths when He brought them out of Egypt (Lv 23:42-43), a time when the covenant was remembered and renewed (Dt 31:10-13; Neh 8:13-18) and the Lord's kingship over His people was vivid in their minds (cf. Ex 15:18; Dt 33:3-5). In keeping the feast of booths, the nations join Israel in grateful homage to their Creator, Deliverer, and gracious King.

14:17 Those who refuse homage to the Giver of rain will be punished by having the rain withheld from them. They have excluded themselves from the Creator's blessings.

14:18 The sentence is somewhat unclear. The meaning seems to be that Egypt too, watered by the Nile and not dependent on rain, will be punished for failure to keep the feast of booths.

14:20-21 ALL LIFE HALLOWED

14:20-21 God shall be all in all; the distinction between "sacred" and "profane" will be set aside because it is no longer needed; God will have brought all things home to Himself and will make them all serve His glory. The *horse* once stood for military might, often enough the might of men in contrast or opposition to the power of God (Ps 20:7; Is 31:1, 3); now the *bells* on the horses' bridles bear the same inscription as the golden plate on the turban of the high priest (Ex 28:36-37). The earthenware pots in the temple will be on a par with the metal bowls, and all the kitchen pots of Jerusalem and Judah shall become sacred vessels; Sunday and everyday will have met and merged. And so there will be no room for the commercialization of religion anymore. (20; cf. Jn 2:16)

MALACHI

INTRODUCTION

All that we know of Malachi is his name and his book. His oracle is not dated, but the nature of the "oracle of the word of the Lord to Israel by Malachi" (1:1) enables us to determine the time and situation for which he wrote with considerable preciseness. The exiles have returned and are living in their homeland under a governor, most likely Persian (1:8). The temple has been rebuilt, and the temple services have been resumed. The prophet speaks to grave abuses that have developed in the life of God's people, and these are the abuses which were dealt with by the reforms of Ezra (458 BC) and Nehemiah (445 BC). Thus a date after 516 BC (the rebuilding of the temple) and before 458 BC seems probable, about 465—460 BC.

Malachi speaks to specific abuses, such as the failure of the priesthood in both sacrifice and instruction, divorce and marriage with pagan women, laxity in tithing; and he speaks very pungently, in a dialog form that buttonholes the hearer and will not spare him the agony of a decision and an answer. But he speaks also to the underlying cause of the specific abuses, to the religious apathy which is, at best, a weary question concerning the profit in serving the Lord and, at its worst, a denial of God's presence on earth and His judgment upon the deeds of men: "Where is the God of justice?" (2:17) But in all this, Malachi is a *prophet,* not merely a demanding reformer; his rebukes and threats are bracketed by an eloquent reminder of God's covenant love for His people (1:2) and the bright promise of the Sun of righteousness which shall arise with healing in its wings for those who fear the name of the Lord. (4:2)

A church in which people's worship, their marriages, and their morals are all in perfect order, a church which can boast of a live sense of the presence of God in all aspects of human life, à church which feels no need of a returning Elijah to lead its members to repentance and reconciliation—such a church may dispense with Malachi. The rest of us will find his oracle, with its strong Gospel and its unsparing exposure of our sins, a disquieting and a salutary word, a gift from Him to whom all the prophets testify.

1:2-5 PROLOG: I HAVE LOVED YOU

1:2-5 Israel, the people of God's choosing, needed to be reminded of the Lord's elective love for her. That love was the origin and basis of Israel's existence (Dt 7:7-8) and the driving power of her checkered career (Hos 11:1). On this love everything depends. If this peg loosens, everything falls: Israel's history loses all meaning, her worship becomes a formality, her faith has no object, and her hope no basis. In the middle of the fifth century BC, this dejected and disillusioned people, under Persian domination, stood in special need of assurance of the Lord's love for her. No appeal for true worship and right action could be made to her unless this conviction of God's love held firm. Malachi appeals to his people as Paul does to the church, "by the mercies of God" (Ro 12:1). This note runs through all his rebukes, admonitions, and commands.

Here, at the beginning, he illustrates the love of God by contrasting the lot of the nation Israel, the descendants of Jacob, with the fate of the nation Edom, the descendants of Esau, who had occupied the neighboring high hill country to the south of the Dead Sea. The judgment of God lay heavy on that bitter and vindictive enemy of Israel (cf. Ob; Ps 137:7; Jer 49:7-22; Eze 35; Am 1:11-12). The high fortress-land lay waste; and, above all, Edom had no future. No bright Messianic hope lightened her dark sky. The fate of Edom points up the fact that the Lord who loves Israel has the power to implement His love: *Great is the Lord, beyond the border of Israel!* (5)

1:3 Probably an allusion to a recent disaster,

the invasion of Edom by the Nabatean Arabs, who expelled the Edomites from their land.

1:6—2:9 THE FAILURE OF THE PRIESTHOOD

1:6—2:9 The note sounded in the Prolog (2-5) rings on in this oracle; God's *love* is speaking. It is the fatherly love of Israel's God, who told Pharaoh: "Israel is my first-born son, and I say to you, 'Let my son go that he may serve me'" (Ex 4:22-23). This is a personal love, the love of a father who looks for a response of love in his son. That response, like all responses in personal communion, does not remain abstract and general but comes in concrete particular acts of obedience and service such as the Law prescribed for priest and people. The priests, representatives of the people before God and *messengers of the Lord of hosts* (2:7) to the people, are unnatural sons and unfaithful servants when they grow slack and careless in their duties: They despise their Father's *name,* that is, God as He has revealed Himself to them. He has revealed Himself in the *covenant with Levi,* an act of love which bestowed *life and peace* (2:5) and was designed to evoke *fear,* an awe-filled holy obedience. That is why Malachi, speaking for his God, is so vehement about the quality of the animals offered to God in sacrifice. He is not concerned merely about ritual correctness; he is concerned about man's response to the love of God. To offer this *great King* (14) less than one would offer the Persian *governor* (8), less than the best, is to commit the sacrilege of despising and profaning the covenant love of Israel's Father and calls down His *curse.* (14)

1:8 The Law prescribed that the choicest animals should be offered in sacrifice. (Lv 22:20-22; Dt 15:21; 17:1)

1:9 *Entreat the favor of God* is, of course, ironical: Give God what no political overlord would accept; HE will be pleased.

1:10 Sacrifice which is not a genuine expression of a son's love and a servant's devotion is an abomination to God (Cf. Is 1:12-17; Hos 6:6)

1:11 These words are to be understood in their setting. The bored and careless worship of Israel makes the darkened and groping adoration of the Gentiles look good by comparison; it is *pure* compared with Israel's "polluted" (7) offerings. Hebrew has a way of making absolute contrasts where our way of speaking would make a relative contrasts, cf. Gn 29:30-31, where in v. 31 "Leah was hated" picks up what was expressed in v. 30 as "he loved Rachel more than Leah." For the thought of a universal worship of God evoked by this general revelation see Acts 17:26-27; for the ultimate estimate on such worship see Ro 1:19-23.

1:14 The guilt of the priests is increased by the fact that the layman is misled by them.

2:2 To *give glory to* God's *name* is to let His revelation count supremely in every particular of worship and life.

The *blessings* of the priests are probably the perquisites of their office.

2:3 A brutally forceful expression of the thought: "As you have profaned *My* name, so I will 'profane' you."

2:4 For God's *covenant with Levi* (his election to the priesthood), cf. Dt 18:1-8; 33:8-11.

2:5-7 This luminous picture of the blessing on the priest and of the blessings that come through the true priest constitutes the contrast to the dark picture of the corrupted and corrupting priesthood of vv. 8-9. This latter picture contains an indictment not mentioned before: The priests curry favor with the great and rich, yet succeed only in winning the contempt of all.

2:10-16 AGAINST MIXED MARRIAGE AND DIVORCE

2:10-16 The God who loved Israel is the Father who called into being *(created,* 10) a nation whose members were to be a family living together in love, love for God and love for brother in unbroken unity. When the one love is violated, the other one is violated too. When Israelites are *faithless to one another,* they *profane the covenant* which God made with their fathers (10), that is, they do not respect the holiness of the family life which their covenant God has created for them. Divorcing the wife of one's youth is a violation of covenant love; and so is marrying a foreign woman.

The prophet's violent reaction to mixed marriages is not a piece of nationalistic exclusiveness; his concern is not nationalistic or ethnic but religious. The Law (Dt 7:3-4; 17:17) and the example of King Solomon (whose love for foreign women turned his heart from its pure devotion to the Lord, 1 K 11:1-13) both made it plain that the danger in mixed marriage is the temptation to idolatry which is involved. The foreign wife is *daughter of a foreign god* (11); her existence is determined by her god, and union with her alienates the husband from worship of the true God. Thus he *profanes the sanctuary of the Lord* (11); it is for him no longer the sanctuary of the one God who claims his whole worship with a jealous love. A man who violates God's love, by divorce and remarriage to a foreign woman, falls under the curse of losing the very thing he sought in marriage: sons to support him in court *(to witness or answer)* and to intercede for him in the temple *(bring an offering,* 12).

2:11 The Bible uses the expression "son of" or "daughter of" to express what is characteristic of a man or woman. As a daughter derives her life and character from her father, so *the daughter of a foreign god* has her existence determined by her god.

2:13-16 As marriage with an alien profanes the sanctuary, so divorcing the wife of one's youth *covers the Lord's altar with tears* (13). Men who have despised the love of Him who created marriage, who is the remembering witness to every marriage covenant (14) and hates the violence of divorce (16), cannot leave the altar with the glad assurance that God has accepted their sacrifice. Instead of the peace which that assurance gives, there are the *tears* and *weeping and groaning* of men haunted by the fear that the

Lord *no longer regards the offering or accepts it with favor* (13). The fear is well-founded; they stand before Him as men whose *garments are covered with violence* (16)—this quiet, civil, and civilized business of divorce is in His eyes a vicious and violent thing. (Cf. Is 1:15)

2:14-15 This reproach contains one of the warmest and tenderest descriptions of marriage to be found in the whole OT. The sanctity of the selfless commitment of love under the witness and blessing of the Lord *(covenant)*, the fervor of young wedded love *(wife of your youth)*, the enduring companionable affection of later years *(your companion)*, the *godly offspring* with which the Creator blesses the union—all are there.

2:17—3:6 WHERE IS THE GOD OF JUSTICE?

2:17—3:6 Even when he is calling to account those who question God's justice, Malachi confronts them with the God of love. It is, in fact, God's love that makes human beings stumble at Him and "presume upon the riches of his kindness and forbearance and patience" (Ro 2:4; cf. Ps 50:21). They judge God by their petty, vindictive selves and cannot conceive of a love that exceeds all human measurement or comparison (cf. Hos 11:9) and therefore can in steadfastness be patient and longsuffering with the sinner: *I the Lord do not change; therefore you, O sons of Jacob, are not consumed* (3:6). But this love is not simply a slack toleration of evil; people may *weary* the Lord for a long time with their idle talk that misinterprets His loving patience as an approval of the sinner (2:17); but the day is coming when the God of love will be a *swift witness* against all lovelessness (3:5). But even then His wrath is not a blind, destructive fury; God is the *Refiner* and *Fuller* (3:2-3) who would restore His people to an unalloyed devotion and a clean and holy fear, so that their worship and life may become a genuine service to their Father and Master. (cf. 1:6)

3:1 Jesus Himself pointed to John the Baptist, the forerunner of the Christ, as the final fulfillment of this promise (Mt 11:10-11). Then *the Lord whom you seek* and *the messenger of the covenant* are both designations of the Messiah and find their fulfillment in Jesus; *He* ushers in the last judgment (Jn 9:39), and in Him God's covenant-will of love is expressed to the utmost. (Mt 26:28)

3:2a Those who ask, "where is the God of justice?" have not considered how terrible His coming will be for them, who have despised His goodness.

3:2b The *fuller* is the craftsman who cleanses newly shorn wool and newly woven cloth of their natural oils. The alkali used for this purpose was strong and biting.

3:5 The *widow, orphan,* and *sojourner* are singled out in the Law as prime objects of the Israelite's love. They need help most and are least able to repay; THERE is scope for genuine love. Cf. Dt 10:17-19; 14:28-29; 16:11, 14; 24:19, 21; 27:19. For the *hireling* see Dt 24:14-15.

3:6 Many scholars take this verse with the following section, as the RSV. But it seems to fit eminently well as a conclusion to this section.

3:7-12 RETURN TO ME!

3:7-12 The God of the covenant reproaches His people for their long history of rebellion (*you have turned aside*, 7). The rebuke is stated harshly: *Man robs God* (8). This presumptuous sacrilege is *cursed with a curse* (9). The payment of the full tithe is, of course, not the whole answer to this fearful situation; the Father is, in His compassion for a wayward son, asking His son to take one little step toward Him in obedience to the Father's voice, to make one concrete gesture of response to his Father's love. And His promise is free and generous: He will turn to the returning son, like the father in the parable of the prodigal son (Lk 15:20) and will shower the prodigal with an *overflowing blessing.* (10)

3:7 *Turn,* or *return*, is the term regularly used by the prophets to express the idea of repentance. Cf. 4:6, where Elijah is pictured as a preacher of repentance: "He will turn the hearts."

3:10 The *tithe* (the annual contribution from the produce of the land), provided for the support of the Levites who served in the temple; therefore the expression, *that there may be food in my house.*

3:12 *Land of delight* might also be translated, "the land in which I [the Lord] delight," and this would fit well in the context. (Cf. Is 62:4)

3:13—4:3 "IT IS VAIN TO SERVE GOD"

3:13—4:3 The theme of this section is similar to that of 2:17—3:6; the same question is asked: Is there a God who governs and judges? But the emphasis here is on the effect which the question has on *those who fear the Lord* (16); it makes them waver in their faith. It is the question raised in Ps 73:2-3, 13, where the psalmist cries " . . . as for me, my feet had almost stumbled . . . For I was envious of the arrogant, when I saw the prosperity of the wicked. . . . All in vain have I kept my heart clean and washed my hands in innocence." The answer is the same as in Ps 73; the faithful are assured: There IS a God who governs, and it is the God who has said, "I have loved you" (1:2). None who serves him with a son's love and servant's fear is forgotten by Him; their names are all written in His unforgetting book (16). The words which He spoke at the Exodus (Ex 19:5) and at the entry into the Promised Land (Dt 7:6) are not withdrawn; His faithful shall be His *special possession* on the day when He shall judge the world. His compassion will *spare* them (17) on that day when the difference between those who *serve God* (14) and those who do not becomes terrifyingly clear. The wicked shall know that day as a consuming fire; for the righteous there will be quite another light and heat on that day: there will be the bright healing warmth of the sun of God's salvation (*righteousness,* 4:2) for them. With the exuberant vitality of a herd of *calves* released *from the stall* they shall live and leap, while the wicked are as ashes on the ground.

3:16 For the *book of rememberance* cf. Ex 32:32; Ps 56:8; 139:16; Is 4:3; Dn 12:1; Ph 4:3; Rv 3:5; 13:8; 17:8; 20:12, 15; 21:27.

4:2 The *righteousness* of God referred to is His faithfulness to the covenant, which spells salvation for His people; the Lord is a RIGHTEOUS God and a savior" (Is 45:21). Cf. Paul's use of "righteousness" as God's redeeming action, Ro 3:21.

4:4-6 EPILOG: THE LAW OF MOSES AND THE RETURNING ELIJAH

4:4-6 These last words of Malachi seem to indicate that it was given the prophet to foresee that his was to be the last voice of prophecy for centuries to come. And so, in closing, he points his people to the Law, the enduring foundation of their existence as God's peculiar people. Their way into the great future promised to them (2; cf. 3:17) is to be a way under the Law; the Law is to be their "custodian," to bring them to Christ (Gl 3:24). Therefore the first of Malachi's two concluding words points backward: *Remember the law of my servant Moses* (4). The other concluding word points forward, to the day which will be a *great* day for the Lord's obedient sons and servants but a *terrible* day for those who are impenitent and unprepared. Israel may expect a large last gift from the Lord who loves her; that day will not come upon Israel unaware. There will be a prophetic voice which will "in the spirit and power of Elijah" (Lk 1:17) prepare men for that day. That voice will work repentance in the people, restoring harmony between the generations, and so "make ready . . . a people prepared" (Lk 1:17). In hearing and heeding that voice Israel can escape the ban of destruction which threatens those who refuse the ultimate proffer of God's love.

Malachi's word prepared for and made possible the reforms of Ezra and Nehemiah. His inspired word helped to produce those patient and pious hopers who meet us in the first chapters of the Gospel According to Luke, men and women like Zechariah, Elizabeth, Simeon, and Anna, who "walked in all the commandments and ordinances of the Lord blameless" (Lk 1:6), immersed in the Scriptures and devoted to the temple, while they awaited the consolation of Israel (Lk 2:25). His word of hope reached its fullness when God sent His Son and Servant to fulfill all righteousness and to be in person the Sun of Righteousness with healing in His wings for His nation and all nations; in Him God's call to repentance reached its fulness in the Baptist's urgent summons to flee from the wrath to come (Mt 3:7). Moses and Elijah, the men of God to whom Malachi pointed his people, appear beside Jesus on the mount at His transfiguration (Mt 17:3). All who call Jesus Lord will have ears for them and for the oracle of Malachi.

THE NEW TESTAMENT

INTRODUCTION

The New Covenant, Commonly Called the New Testament, of Our Lord and Savior Jesus Christ is not, strictly speaking, one book at all: it is a collection of documents of different literary types, of varied provenance, and of different dates. And yet we rightly give these documents a common title and treat this collection as one book, for all the varied and diverse witnessing voices heard in it unite to say that which we can say only by the inspiration of the Holy Spirit: *Jesus is Lord* (1 Co 12:3). From The Gospel According to Matthew to The Revelation to John the New Testament is one great adoring acclamation of Jesus of Nazareth as Lord, an anticipation of that day when every knee shall bow to Him and "every tongue confess that Jesus Christ is Lord, to the glory of God the Father." (Ph 2:10-11)

"Lord" has become for us a rather pale and colorless term; to hear it today as the writers of the New Testament want it to be heard, we need to recall what made just this title one that could inspire the ultimate loyalty of believers, so that for them life became a life to be lived to the Lord and death for His sake became a crowning glory. For the writers of the New Testament there was no other title which so comprehensively and compellingly expressed all that Jesus signifies for faith as "Lord." "Lord" clothed Him in His proper glory. The angel who announced the Savior's birth to shepherds proclaimed Him as "Christ the Lord" (Lk 2:11); at Pentecost Peter asserted that the God who had vindicated the Crucified and had exalted Him to glory at His own right hand, to pour out thence the Spirit upon the new people of God, had "made him both Lord and Christ" (Acts 2:36). Paul can sum up the church's confession to Jesus as Son of David and Son of God in the words, "Christ Jesus our Lord" (Ro 1:4) and "the word of faith" which the apostles proclaim says: "If you confess with your lips that Jesus is Lord . . . you will be saved" (Ro 10:9). The church awaiting His return prays, "Come, Lord Jesus!" (Rv 22:20); and "Lord" shall be the word which hails the Son and Servant of God at the end of days. (Ph 2:11)

A word that in its ordinary usage ran the gamut from respectful address ("Sir") to acknowledgment of deity thus became the New Testament church's first creed. By it believers acknowledged and committed themselves to Jesus as One who by virtue of His redeeming life and death had won the right and power to rule over all times, all history, and all life, the One in whom alone they could find life and salvation, the only name given under heaven whereby we must be saved. (Acts 4:12)

When the writers of the New Testament looked (with eyes of the heart enlightened by the Spirit) to the past, they beheld His Lordship there. They saw Him, at the beginning, present and active in creation, being in person the Word of God that spoke life and light for all (Jn 1:3-4; Cl 1:15-17). They knew that all history had moved toward His coming and His Lordship as toward its judgment and conclusion (Acts 17:30-31), that all God's dealing with us, every manifestation of His righteousness, climaxed in His cross (Ro 3:25-26). The Lordship of Jesus gave them the key to the understanding of the history particularly lit up by the light of God's revelation, the history of Israel prophetically recorded and interpreted in the Old Testament; they recognized their Lord as the as-yet-hidden center and heart of the history that began with the calling and blessing of Abraham. Wherever God dealt graciously with His people, their Lord was there; if God's mercy gave His people water to drink in the wilderness, the Rock from which that water sprang was Christ (1 Co 10:4). His Spirit moved Israel's prophets to utterances that intended Him (1 Ptr 1:10), so that the witness of all the prophets is witness to Him (Acts 10:42 to 43), and He is the Yes of all God's promises from of old (2 Co 1:20). Whatever tokens of God's favor had made bright Israel's way through her history, they all foretokened Him, the ultimate Son of David, God's Anointed, the Christ; *the* Prophet (Acts 3:22; 7:37); *the* Passover Sacrifice that sets God's people free for the final exodus and the last deliverance (1 Co 5:7); *the* Priest-King who offers Himself as the final perfect Sacrifice and inaugurates the new and eternal covenant. (Heb 7—10)

However far back they might look, wherever they looked in the past, they saw the approaching glory of their Lord. The Spirit of whom Jesus had promised, "He will glorify me" (Jn 16:14), opened their eyes to see His glory also in the immediate past, in the servant's form of His ministry in the days of His flesh. They saw in John the Baptist the one sent by God to "make straight the way of the Lord" (Jn 1:23). The little sentence with which Luke introduces the raising of the widow's only son at Nain might serve as a caption over all the synoptic gospels: "The Lord . . . had compassion" (Lk 7:13); and the crowning utterance of the fourth gospel is Thomas' confession to the crucified and risen Jesus: "My Lord and My God!" (Jn 20:28)

The Spirit taught them to see the glory of His Lordship even in His Passion, just there. They saw Him as Lord "on the night when he was betrayed," when He gave Himself in self-sacrificing majesty to His own (1 Co 11:23). The "rulers of this age" who crucified Him crucified "the Lord of glory" (1 Co 2:8). Once the promised Spirit had come, they could see His whole life only in the light of His resurrection, as the glory of the Lord who went into the depths of guilt and death for humanity, the glory of Him who was "designated Son of God in power according to the Spirit of holiness by his resurrection from the dead." (Ro 1:4)

The Son of God in power is Lord of the present, "the head over all things for the church" (Eph 1:22). Those who by God's grace have become "his body, the fulness of him who fills all in all" (Eph 1:23) can and must say, "*Our* Lord reigns." He, the Lamb that was slain, is the Lord who controls all history; He and only He can take the sealed book of God's counsel from God's hand, break the seals, open the book, and speed on their way the horses that make havoc and history and so, whether they know and will it or not, carry out God's bright designs and work His sovereign will (Rv 5—6): for the Lamb that was slain is "Lord of lords and King of kings." (Rv 17:14)

In the world all must obey Him, and all things must serve His ends; in the church we are privileged and permitted to serve Him. Here His rule and Lordship are acknowledged, proclaimed, and praised. Here Jesus is Lord to the exclusion of all other lords, whatever other lords may lay claim to lordship over us (1 Co 8:5-6); here He is all and in all (Cl 3:11). Here His Word dwells richly, and His peace rules in grateful hearts (Cl 3:15-16). Whatever His children may do in word or deed is done "in the name of the Lord Jesus" (Cl 3:17), so done that He is known and acknowledged as the Author of every good will and work.

Nothing can call in question this His comprehensive Lordship. Suffering cannot dim its glory for those who call Him Lord. "We rejoice in our sufferings . . . we also rejoice in God through our Lord Jesus Christ" (Ro 5:3, 11). Not even the last and mightiest enemy, before whose onset all other loyalties to lordship cease, not even death can end His reign: "If we live, we live to the Lord, and if we die, we die to the Lord; so then, whether we live or die, we are the Lord's. For to this end Christ died and lived again, that he might be Lord both of the dead and of the living." (Ro 14:8-9)

To Him we live; all living in thankfulness to Him and accountability to Him. Whatever the problems and agonies of a church may be, Paul brings them all under the judicature of the crucified Lord (1 Co). Not even the most casual action is a matter of indifference under this Lordship. James reminds his churches that where a person is seated in church, how poor and rich are treated in the house where Jesus is called Lord is a matter of paramount and eternal concern for those who "hold the faith of our Lord Jesus Christ, the Lord of glory." (Ja 2:1-13)

"Jesus is Lord," His Lordship shines forth from the past, and it illumines the present. But above all, He is Lord of the future. Under His Lordship, by the power of the Spirit bestowed by Him, the Word of the Lord grows on the thorn-infested soil of this world and brings forth fruit destined to fill the garners of God eternally (Acts). Frail earthen vessels, maligned, persecuted, dying messengers carry abroad the eternal treasure (2 Co 4:7-17) that outlasts all opposing powers and all human wisdom. The Book of Acts closes with the picture of imprisoned Paul "teaching about the Lord Jesus, quite openly and unhindered" (Acts 28:31) at Rome, the portal of the Gentile world and the gateway to the future. To this Lord the future belongs; the Caesars of Rome who are acclaimed as "lord" by fervid subjects have no future comparable to His. Therefore the church, the people of God gathered under His Lordship, is animated by one hope (Eph 4:4), by the living, confident, and trusting expectation that her Lord will return to manifest and exercise His Lordship in open glory. When the people of the church gather to eat the bread and to drink of the cup given them by the Lord as the sign and means of His unbreakable communion with them, they do so with their eyes fixed on the future; they "proclaim the Lord's death *until he comes*" (1 Co 11:26). They pray, "Come, Lord Jesus!" (1 Co 16:22; Rv 22:20); they pray rejoicing, for they know that "the Lord is at hand" (Ph 4:5); they know that waiting for His day is a waiting "for the mercy of the Lord Jesus Christ unto eternal life." (Jude 21)

They can pray confidently and with rejoicing for their Lord's coming, for the future. For the future is no longer a dim and distant prospect; the opaque and ominous wall that separates the present from the future has grown, for them, thin and translucent. For they have received the Spirit; and the Spirit is the guarantee, the firstfruits, and the foretaste of the world to come (Eph 1:4; 2 Co 1:22; Ro 8:23). They have become "partakers of the Holy Spirit"; they "have tasted the heavenly gift . . . and have tasted . . . the powers of the age to come" (Heb 6:4-5). "Through the Spirit, by faith," they scent the fresh and eternal air of God's new world and can in that air live the life of faith working through love.

Martin Luther has caught this primal note of the New Testament witness and has expressed it with characteristic geniality and vigor in his Large Catechism:

> If you are asked, "What do you believe . . . concerning Jesus Christ?" answer briefly, "I believe that Jesus Christ, true Son of God, has become my Lord." What does it mean to "become a Lord"? It means that He has redeemed me from sin, from the devil, from death, and all evil. Before this I had no Lord and King but was captive under the power of the devil. . . . Jesus Christ, the Lord of life and righteousness and every good and blessing . . . has snatched us . . . from the jaws of hell, won us, made us free, and restored us to the Father's favor and grace. He has taken us as His own, under His protection, in order that He may rule us by His righteousness, wisdom, power, life, and blessedness.

"He has made us free . . . He has taken us as His own." Life under Jesus' Lordship is not slavery. When this Lord takes us as His own, He sets us free. He gives us the only genuine freedom that a creature of God can find. For God has created us for Himself, and our heart is restless until it finds rest in Him. We of the late 20th century are people of restless heart, and we dwell amid a nation and in a world filled with people of restless heart. We shall find no rest (and therefore no freedom) until we find rest in God, under the Lordship of His Son Jesus Christ. If we call Him Lord, we shall have Him for our Lord and shall be able to cease from the futile effort to go it on our own, able to lay our lives in His almighty and compassionate hands. We shall live under Him and work for Him with a purpose and meaning that reaches beyond our little today. For our Lord will hear our prayers, and He will come; history will not end with a meaningless bang nor with a despairing whimper but with the revelation of our Lord Jesus Christ.

It is the purpose of these comments to

help people hear the witness of the Holy Spirit in the New Testament more clearly, that they may be moved to heed the invitation to call Him Lord and serve Him in the obedience of faith and the steady buoyancy of hope. This has dictated the manner of interpretation (interpretive paraphrases of larger units rather than verse-by-verse exposition) and the selection of matter. Much that is in its own way interesting and instructive has been omitted or scantily noticed, not merely to save space but primarily to leave room for the New Testament's own major concern: that people may hear the words of Spirit-filled writers who bid them call Jesus Lord.

Martin H. Franzmann

MATTHEW

INTRODUCTION

The written gospels belong under the heading of apostolic "teaching." They are the written result of that "apostles' teaching" which Luke speaks of (Acts 2:42) as the first and basic formative element in the life of the first church. The gospels are not primarily the apostolic kerygma (proclamation of the Gospel) as we see it reflected in the sermons of Peter in the Book of Acts or summarized in Pauline passages like 1 Co 15:1-8, proclamations of the basic facts that summon men to the obedience of faith; they are the expansions of that kerygma, the apostolic teaching that builds up the church already called into being by the kerygma.

They are rightly called gospels, good news (and not "teaching") nevertheless. For they of course include all that the kerygma includes: the sending of the Messiah by God in fulfillment of His promises, the Messiah's ministry to men, culminating in His death for the sins of men, His resurrection and His exaltation and the promise of His return. They have the same basic historical outline, as a comparison between Peter's sermon in the house of Cornelius (Acts 10:34-43) and the Gospel According to Mark shows at a glance. Their content is not a biography of Jesus but the Way of the Messiah from the time that John the Baptist prepared the way before Him to the time when God raised Him from the dead; and they have the same basic intention, namely, to lay bare the redemptive meaning of the Way of the Messiah.

The goal of the apostolic kerygma is, then, that men in faith call Jesus "Lord" in all the fullness of meaning that the word had for the apostles and for the first apostolic church. The goal of the apostolic "teaching" is that this faith may be in every sense the *obedience* of faith, that men may (as Jesus Himself put it) both call Him Lord and do what He tells them (Lk 6:46). The apostolic teaching was from the first, therefore, the natural and necessary extension of the missionary Gospel, an organic growth of the growing Word of the Lord. As our gospels show, this teaching took the form of an ever fuller recital of the words and deeds of Jesus, a filling in of the outlines of the kerygma with the concrete details of what Jesus taught and did. This teaching thus satisfied the natural desire of the believing and hoping church to have a distinct and rounded-out picture of Him who was the object of her faith and hope; but the satisfaction of the historical interest was not the primary concern of this teaching. If it had been, one would expect the accounts to be much fuller, more nearly complete. As it is, the accounts are anything but complete; John in his old age was able to supplement the first three gospels from his own recollections, and even he makes plain that there is much that remains unwritten (Jn 20:30; 21:25). Likewise, if the historical interest were primary, we should expect the accounts to be more detailed; as it is, they are sparse and terse even in Mark, the most dramatic narrator of them all, while Matthew cuts away everything that is not *religiously* essential. And in all the evangelists much that is invaluable from a historical point of view (the exact sequence of events, for example) is disregarded. The basic interest of the teaching is religious; its aim is to confront men with the Christ (Mt 1:1; Mk 1:1), to preserve and strengthen men's faith in Him (Jn 20:31), and to bring men into a disciple's total obedience to Him. (Mt 28:20)

The gospels are genuinely historical; they record facts, and their account of Jesus' words and deeds follows a historical sequence common to the first three gospels (ministry in Galilee, a period of wanderings, last days and death and resurrection at Jerusalem). But their interest and intent are not merely historical; they do not aim merely at reconstructing a piece of the past. For them history is the dress in which the Messiah of God is clothed in order that He may be revealed and may enter men's lives as the present and powerful Christ. The gospels reflect both halves of Jesus' last words to His disciples, both the command which looks backward, "Teaching them to observe all that I *have commanded* you," and the promise which marks Him as perpetually present, "Lo, I am with you always." (Mt 28:20)

The Gospel According to Matthew

The religiously didactic character of the gospels is very apparent in the Gospel According to Matthew. Within a generally chronological framework that is common to the first three gospels, the arrangement of the deeds and words of the Christ is topical rather than chronological. The facts are massed and marshaled in impressive and easily remembered units of three, five, and seven. Thus we have in Matthew three major divisions in the genealogy of Jesus with which the gospel opens (Mt 1:1-17), three illustrations of hypocrisy and pure piety (Mt 6:1-18), three parables of planting and growth (Mt 13:1-32). Jesus' words are presented in five great discourses (chs. 5—7, 10, 13, 18, 23—25), and in the Sermon on the Mount Matthew records five examples that illustrate the full intention of God's law (Mt 5:21-48). Jesus in this gospel pronounces seven woes on the scribes and Pharisees (Mt 23:13-36), and the great parable chapter (Mt 13) contains just seven parables. This topical arrangement is not absolutely peculiar to Matthew; Mark, for instance, twice gives a grouping of five disputes between Jesus and His Judaic adversaries, once in Galilee (Mk 2:1—3:6) and again in Jerusalem (Mk 11:27—12:44). But it is found in Matthew in a fuller and more highly developed form than in any of the other evangelists.

Another feature that illustrates the didactic character of the first gospel (again not wholly peculiar to Matthew) is Matthew's use of what one may call the "extreme case" method; that is, Matthew illustrates the bent of Jesus' will by means of words and deeds that indicate the extreme limit to which Jesus went—as we illustrate a man's generosity, for instance, by saying, "He'd give you the shirt off his back." The first discourse of Jesus in Matthew begins with the beatitude on the "poor"; Jesus promises the Kingdom and all its blessings to the beggar, to the poor in spirit (Mt 5:3); this removes every limitation from the grace of God and makes it as wide and deep as the need of man. In Matthew's account of Jesus' miracles the first three are extreme-case miracles, which illustrate the lengths to which the compassion of Jesus will go (Mt 8:1-15). Jesus heals the leper whom the Law cannot help, but must exclude from the people of God; He helps the Gentile who is outside the pale of God's people; and He restores to health the woman whom Judaism degraded to the rank of a second-rate creature of God. Now men can take the measure of the potent grace of God present and at work in the Christ. And men can measure the greatness of the divine forgiveness which Jesus brings by another extreme case, by the fact that Jesus calls a tax collector (whom the synagog branded as sinner and excluded) to be His disciple, apostle, and table companion. (Mt 9:9-13)

How rigorous and all-inclusive Jesus' call to repentance is can again be seen by the extreme case: Jesus calls the righteous to repentance; more, He imposes the call to repentance also on the men who have become His disciples (Mt 18:1-4). When Jesus bids His disciples love their *enemies,* He has removed every limitation from their loving (Mt 5:44). When He threatens Peter, the disciple who was ready to forgive seven times, with the wrath of the divine King if he will not forgive without limit, the fullness of the fraternal charity which Jesus inspires in His disciples and demands of them is spelled out in unmistakable clarity. How completely Jesus binds the disciple to Himself can be seen in the fact that Jesus makes His own cross (the climax of His life of ministry) the impulse and the standard of the disciple's ministry. (Mt 10:38; 16:24; 20:25-28)

Still another feature prominent in

Matthew's evangelical teaching is the use of contrast. In the genealogy of Jesus, Matthew marks Jesus as the son of Abraham and son of David, the crowning issue of Israel's history (Mt 1:1-17). The immediately following section is in sharp contrast to this: Here it is made plain that God gives to Israel what her history cannot give Israel; the Messiah is not the product of Israel's history, but God's creative intervention in that history of guilt and doom; Jesus is conceived by the Holy Spirit (Mt 1:18-23). Jesus in the Beatitudes promises to His disciples all the blessings of the kingdom of the heavens, all the glory of the world to come (5:3-9)—and put them under the yoke of persecution "for righteousness' sake" (5:10-12). The Christ miraculously multiplies the loaves and fishes and sets a table for thousands in the wilderness (15:32-39)—and yet refuses to show a sign from heaven when the leaders of Judaism demand one (16:1-4). The woman who spent her money lavishly to anoint the dying Christ is put in close and sharp contrast with the disciple who betrayed Him for money (26:6-13; 26:14-16). The Messiah who in sovereign grace gives Himself, His body and His blood, to His disciples and goes freely into death to inaugurate the new covenant is set side by side with the Messiah whose "soul is very sorrowful, even to death" in Gethsemane (26:26-29; 26:36-46). The Son of Man who claims a seat on the very throne of God and proclaims that He will return on the clouds of heaven (26:64), on the cross cries out, "My God, my God, why hast thou forsaken me?" (27:46). These contrasts are a sort of chiaroscuro in narrative, similar to that process in the pictorial arts which creates its impression not by the clearly drawn line but by the skillful blocking out of figures and features by means of contrasting areas of light and shade. Thus the Christ is portrayed by portraying the absoluteness of His grace for men and the absoluteness of His claim on men, by recording both His claim to an absolute communion with God, which strikes His contemporaries as blasphemous, and His full and suffering humanity, which makes Him a stumbling block to His contemporaries. It is the historical Jesus of Nazareth who is being portrayed, but He is in every word and work portrayed and proclaimed as the Christ, the Son of God: He is *the* Son who alone of men gives God the glory that is due Him, who alone does battle with Satan and overcomes him, who alone gives His life a ransom for many. He is not a sage, so that His significance for men can be told in His words alone; He is not a hero whose deeds alone can signify what He means in history. He is the Christ, and His whole person, His words and works as a unity, must be recounted if men are to know Him, believe in Him, and have eternal life in His name.

The deep interest in the disciples of Jesus displayed by all the gospels and the amount of attention devoted to them are further testimony to their "teaching" character. In all the gospels Jesus' first Messianic act (after His baptism and temptation) is the calling of disciples; in all of them the story of Jesus' ministry is told in terms of the widening cleavage between Jesus and Israel on the one hand and the deepening communion between Jesus and His disciples on the other. And in all the gospels the supreme revelation of the Messiah, the appearance of the risen Lord, is vouchsafed to the disciples alone. But Matthew gives us the fullest account of the creation of the disciples—how Jesus called them, how He trained them, how they failed in the face of the cross, and how the risen Lord forgave and restored them. The five discourses of Jesus, which determine the structure of Matthew's Gospel, are all addressed to disciples; and the last word of Jesus in Matthew's record of Him is, "Make disciples" (28:19). The thought which is in all the gospels, that Jesus sought nothing and found nothing in the world except the men whom the Father gave Him, His disciples, comes out with especial force and clarity in Matthew. As God is known by His works, so the Christ becomes known to men by His disciples, by the men whom He called and molded in His own image.

Author of the First Gospel

Who is the author of this massive and carefully organized work? The book itself does not name its author. The ancient church, which from the first read and used the first gospel more assiduously than any other, is unanimous in attributing it to Matthew. No other claimant to authorship is ever put forward by anyone. Little is known of Matthew. Matthew, Mark, and Luke all tell us that he was a tax collector at Capernaum and therefore a member of the outcast class publicly branded by the Jewish community as "sinners." Mark and Luke call him Levi (Mk 2:14; Lk 5:27), the son of Alphaeus; only the first gospel calls him Matthew. It may be that he was originally called Levi and that Jesus gave him the name Matthew (which signifies "Gift of God"), just as He named the sons of Zebedee Boanerges and gave Simon his significant name Peter. Or he may have had two names to begin with. At any rate, we may assume that Matthew was the name by which he was best known in the Jewish Christian community and thus became the name attached to the gospel attributed to him.

Matthew is not prominent in the New Testament record of the 12 apostles. All three of the early evangelists tell the story of his call and of the feast he gave to celebrate this turning point in his life, and all three record that he was among the Twelve; but they tell the story of his calling (the only one recorded after the calling of the first four disciples) not as a part of the record of a prominent apostle but as a testimony to the supreme grace of the Christ, who called into His fellowship and made His messenger one whom Judaism expelled and degraded (Mt 9:9-13; Mk 2:13-17; Lk 5:27-32). As a tax collector, either under the Roman government or under Herod Antipas at Capernaum, he would be a man of some education, skilled in numbers, speaking both Aramaic and Greek, and a man of substance. Early tradition has it that he first preached the Gospel to his countrymen in Palestine, originally wrote his gospel in their tongue, and later went abroad as missionary to other nations. The tradition concerning his later career is relatively late, tends to be fantastic and legendary in character, and often confuses Matthew with Matthias, so that it offers little or no basis for constructing a reliable history of Matthew the evangelist.

Theological Character of the First Gospel

The surest thing we know about Matthew is that Jesus called him as a tax collector. Like Paul, he therefore experienced the call of Jesus under circumstances which marked it most vividly as the absolute divine grace that it was. Matthew no doubt deserved the title the synagog gave him—he was a "sinner." He had, in becoming a tax collector, turned his back on the promise and the blessing given to Israel and had expressed his indifference toward the Law; he had turned to a life whose basic note was a self-seeking materialism. Jesus' call therefore meant for him a radical break with a sinful past; repentance was for him a complete 180-degree turn from sin and self to the grace of God that confronted him in Jesus. Matthew's own experience had given him an unusually keen awareness of how completely and hopelessly man's sin can separate him from God and had impressed on him with unforgettable sharpness the fact that only the grace of the Christ can recall man from that separation into fellowship with God. This gave Matthew a keen perception of two significant features in the words and works of Jesus, features prominent in his gospel.

First, Matthew clearly saw and recorded with emphasis the fact that Jesus' call to repentance is an absolute call demanding the whole man wholly. His gospel is marked by a stern and unsparing opposition to any compromise with evil, whether that compromise be a Jewish or a Christian one. He makes it clear that the call to communion with the Christ is a call to a never-ending struggle against the evil in man that is perpetually threatening this communion. It is no accident that the words of Jesus which impose on the disciple the duty of correcting and winning the sinning brother are peculiar to Matthew and that the necessity of perpetual forgiveness toward the errant brother is reinforced by one of the most powerful of Jesus' parables, again peculiar to Matthew. (Mt 18:15-35)

Second, Matthew saw that the way to obedience can only be the way of faith, faith that is purely the attitude and action of the beggar who receives the grace of

God. Jesus' call had taught him: "One there is who is good" (Mt 19:17). Only One is good, namely God; and no man dare make his own goodness count before Him. But God the Good is surely and wholly good; no man may therefore doubt His goodness and come to God with a divided heart or serve Him with half a devotion. That was the sin of scribe and Pharisee; and Matthew's Gospel is therefore the severest indictment of them in the New Testament. But Matthew indicts the scribe and Pharisee not out of personal animus but on religious grounds. He knew the hollowness and falsity of a religion that could and did degrade the sinner and thus hold him fast in his sin but could not help him by forgiving him. Scribe and Pharisee had shut up the Kingdom before him; Jesus had called him into the Kingdom.

If the call of Jesus set Matthew free from all the authorities that were leading Israel to her doom (ch. 23), it did not separate him from the Old Testament or from the God of Abraham, Isaac, and Jacob. Jesus made a true Israelite of him: His gospel is marked by a rich and constant use of the Old Testament, the fullest of any of the gospels. He sees in the Christ the consummation of Israel's history and the fulfilling of the Old Testament prophecy. Of the 29 Old Testament prophecies recorded in the first gospel, 10 are peculiar to Matthew. And the influence of the Old Testament is not confined to the direct citation of the Old Testament. The Old Testament constitutes the ever-present background and the all-pervasive atmosphere of the gospel. For example, the grouping of the words of the Christ in five great discourses is no doubt intended to recall the five books of the Law and the five divisions of the Psalter. The Gospel According to Matthew is fittingly placed at the beginning of our New Testament, for it constitutes the New Testament's most powerful link with the Old.

Matthew is the most austere of the gospels, stern in its nay to evil, uncompromising in spelling out the inexorable claim of God's grace on the disciple, almost fearfully conscious of how precarious man's hold on that grace is, summoning men to a sober and responsible adoration of the Christ. The austerity of the message is reflected in the sober, restrained, almost colorless style. A monumental quiet seems to brood over the work. The artistry of the gospel is almost entirely confined to the symmetry of its structure. It is as if Matthew had said: "We cannot embellish the Christ with words; we cannot make His grace speak more eloquently by making it speak more beautifully. Let the facts be marshaled and built up into a clear and cleanly articulated whole; let the Christ Himself appear and call men as He once called me. Let the church see how this Jesus of Nazareth once confiscated men by His gracious call. Let the church hear the call of the Christ as I once heard it, and let our human words be but the colorless and transparent vehicle of that call, and the church will remain the church of the Christ." Luke's Gospel has been called the most beautiful book in the world, the Gospel According to Matthew has been termed the most powerful book ever written. A comparison of the parable of the prodigal son, peculiar to Luke (Lk 15:11-32), and the parable of the merciless servant, peculiar to Matthew (Mt 18:23-35), serves to confirm both judgments. The parable peculiar to Luke portrays God's saving act in a warm and moving way, as the act of a father who welcomes home the errant son, and concludes with an appeal to the righteous elder brother to give his glad assent to this free forgiveness of the father. The chief emphasis is on the gratuity of the grace which has appeared in Jesus Christ, a grace offensive to the Pharisee. The parable peculiar to Matthew records God's saving act as the sovereign grace of the king who restores his indebted servant to life and freedom, and the parable is told in order to impress on the disciple what this freedom means for him: God has set him free for his fellowman, in order to forgive as freely and fully as he has been forgiven. The holy obligation which the grace of God imposes, the holy fear in which forgiven man must live by the divine Word of forgiveness in his relation to his fellowman, that is the chief emphasis here. Without the peculiar emphasis of Matthew in the gospel, the church is always in peril of becoming careless and callous, of ceasing to be church. It is no wonder that the gospel which was first written for Jewish Christians and is the most Judaic of them all became also the prime gospel of the Greeks.

Content of the Gospel

The gospel is symmetrically constructed, built up around the five great discourses of Jesus, each marked at its conclusion by the recurrent formula, "When Jesus had finished these sayings" (7:28; 11:1; 13:53; 19:1; 26:1). The five discourses are preceded by an introductory section and followed by the culminating conclusion of the death and resurrection of Jesus. Each of the five discourses is introduced by a recital of deeds of Jesus which prepare for the following discourse and are in turn interpreted by the discourse. Thus there are seven major divisions.

OUTLINE

Behold, Your King Is Coming to You

I. 1:1—4:22 Introduction: Jesus the Messianic Fulfiller
The genealogy and seven fulfillments of prophecy.

II. 4:23—7:29 First Group of Messianic Deeds and Words
The present kingdom and the call to repentance.

III. 8:1—10:42 Second Group of Messianic Deeds and Words
The compassionate Shepherd-King commissions His apostles to seek the lost sheep of the house of Israel.

IV. 11:1—13:52 Third Group of Messianic Deeds and Words
The contradicted Messiah conceals the Kingdom from those who have rejected it (those who "have not," 13:12) and further reveals it to those who have accepted it (those who "have," 13:12).

V. 13:53—18:35 Fourth Group of Messianic Deeds and Words
Toward the new Messianic people of God, the church: The Messiah separates His disciples from the mass of old Israel, deepens His communion with His own, and shapes their relationship to one another.

VI. 19:1—25:46 Fifth Group of Messianic Deeds and Words
The Messiah gives His disciples a sure and responsible hope.

VII. 26:1—28:20 Conclusion and Climax
The Passion, death, and resurrection of the Messiah complete and crown His ministry. The risen Lord in the perfection of His grace and power gives His disciples their universal and enduring commission as His apostles.

1:1—4:22 INTRODUCTION: JESUS THE MESSIANIC FULFILLER

1:7-17 The Genealogy of Jesus Christ

1:1-17 The genealogy of Jesus is hardly meant to be merely proof that Jesus is a son of David. If that were the case, Matthew had no need to go back as far as Abraham. Neither would such proof amount to much; there were thousands of sons of David in Israel, and to prove that a man is a son of David does not demonstrate that he is THE promised Son of David, the Messiah.

Rather, Matthew is linking his story of the Christ with the history of God's dealings with God's people; he is tracing the story of God's blessing, which begins with the free grace of His blessing on Abraham (Gn 12:1-3)—in the face of the accumulated curses on man (Gn 3—11)—and is to end when the Son of Man shall say: "Come, O blessed of my Father" (Mt 25:34). The genealogy is a terse summary of the OT portion of that history.

Matthew is proclaiming the Christ as the climax of the history of God's mercy to His people (cf. 1:21). God has been in control of that history; Matthew points that up by the symmetrical form of the genealogy (3x14 generations, 1:17). God, the Lord of history, is as much in charge of Israel's generations as God, the Creator, is in charge of the 14 days of the waxing and waning of the moon. Israel's history is the history of His mercy; it rises from Abraham to the splendor of David's reign (v. 6) but then goes downward to the *deportation to Babylon* (v. 11), God's signal punishment upon His people's unfaithfulness, and ends in obscurity—Joseph is a nobody and his wife Mary an unknown.

The presence of four women in the genealogy emphasizes that this is the history of God's mercy, His free blessing. Women do not usually appear in Judaic genealogies, and these four are strange claimants of a place in this history. They are not the famous mothers of the race (Sarah, Rebecca, Rachel, Leah), but women who came by strange ways into God's people. Tamar, Rahab, and Ruth were not born Israelites; perhaps even Bathsheba, "the wife of Uriah" the Hittite, did not have a clear title to a place in Israel. Nor were they all unblemished characters. Matthew's reference to "the wife of Uriah" recalls Bathsheba's adultery; Rahab was a harlot; and Judah's words concerning Tamar ("She is more righteous than I," Gn 38:26) say more about Judah's guilt than about the innocence of hapless Tamar. These women appear, moreover, at key points in the history of Israel: Tamar beside Judah, head of the tribe of the Messianic promise (Gn 49:10); Rahab at the entry into the Promised Land; Ruth in the history of the house of Jesse, father of King David; and Bathsheba beside David as mother of King Solomon. The ancestry of the Christ tells the story of Israel's failure and of God's mercy for both Jew and Gentile. When THE Son of David appears, men can only cry, "Have mercy on us, Son of David." (9:27; 20:31)

1:1 *Book of the genealogy.* Literally "book of the generations" or "history of the origin," as in Gn 5:1, and may be the title for the whole gospel; Matthew is writing the new Genesis, the history of the new creation. (Cf. 4:15-16 and the note there)

1:3-6 For the genealogical material available to Matthew cf. Ru 4:18-22; 1 Ch 2:1-15.

1:3 *Tamar.* Cf. Gn 38.

1:5 *Rahab.* Cf. Jos 2 and 6.

Ruth. Cf. the Book of Ruth.

1:6 *David the king.* To David's house the promise of the anointed King (the Christ) was made. (Cf. 2 Sm 7:4-29; 23:1-7)

Wife of Uriah. Cf. 2 Sm 11:2—12:25.

1:11 *Deportation to Babylon.* Cf. 2 K 24—25.

1:17 *Fourteen generations.* The last unit (vv. 12-16) contains only 13 generations. Perhaps one generation was lost in the copying of the text; or perhaps Matthew is hinting that there is still one generation to come—the generation of those who become free sons of God (17:25-26) through THE Son (cf. Jn 1:12-13 and Ro 8:29), the church.

1:18—4:22 The Seven Fulfillments of Prophecy

1:18—4:22 Both the beginning and the end of Jesus' way on earth proved a stumbling block to the faith of His people. They looked on His obscure beginnings and said, "Is not this the carpenter's son? . . . Where then did this man get all this?" (Mt 13:55-56). They looked on His crucifixion, remembered the curse of Deuteronomy (21:23) upon the executed man, and said, "Jesus be cursed" (1 Co 12:3). Matthew proclaims that Jesus is the Christ according to the will and Word of God and cites the OT most richly just at the beginning and the end, he is saying that just here and in just this way the redeeming will of Israel's God is at work, that just here His Word is reaching the full measure of its utterance and effect. His Word is being fulfilled.

Matthew's quotations from the OT are usually very brief; but they seem to be designed to recall (for readers immersed in the OT) a larger context. One is well advised, therefore, to turn to the OT and read Matthew's quotations in their original context.

1:18-25 FIRST FULFILLMENT: IMMANUEL

1:18-25 The promise made to David (cf. 1:6) is fulfilled; by the mysterious and creative operation of His *Spirit,* God implants in the house of David what the ruined and guilty house of David could not of itself produce, the anointed King who dawns on men like the morning light (cf. 2 Sm 23:4). The fulfillment of the promise is so great and wonderful that *Joseph, son of David,* is overwhelmed and dazed by it. He must be compelled to accept the gift of the Deliverer from sin.

The Deliverer is *Emmanuel,* "God with us" (Is 7:14). In 734 B.C. God had sent His prophet Isaiah to Ahaz, king of Judah, when he was beset by enemies from the north and was willing to barter away his freedom and the future of the people of God by subjecting himself to the Assyrian world power in return for Tiglath-pilezer's assistance in the threatening war. Isaiah sought to turn him from this suicidal course in vain. Ahaz would not believe, and so he was not "established," not held and sustained in the purposes of God (Is 7:9). Isaiah then spoke of a sign given by the Lord Himself, a sign which spelled judgment on unbelief and a blessing to faith. Ahaz might fail, but God would not; He would raise up a Deliverer for His people to fill the place left vacant by unbelieving Ahaz, a Deliverer named *Emmanuel.* Where Ahaz and all Ahaz's successors had failed, there Jesus appears; in Him God's redeeming Word reaches full measure. He is *God with us* for the defeated, hopeless people of God. (Cf. Is. 7:1-25; 2 K 16:5-8).

1:18-19 *Betrothed . . . divorce.* With the betrothal the marriage bond was legally established; therefore divorce proceedings were necessary to annul the bond. Cf. Dt 22:22-24, where the violation of a betrothed virgin is punished as adultery.

1:19 *Quietly.* Without the usual public exposure of guilt.

1:21 *Jesus* is the Greek form of the Hebrew name Joshua (full form Jehoshua), which means: "Yahweh (the Lord, God of the covenant) is salvation." (Cf. Ps 130:7-8)

1:23 *Virgin.* Thus the Jewish translators of the Old Testament rendered the "young woman" of Is 7:14. The Hebrew word in Isaiah means "the sexually mature girl." However, the OT authors never use the term for a married woman, and in Isaiah the fatherhood of the Child is wrapped in mysterious silence—and that too in a chapter where practically every male person is identified by his descent on the father's side (Is 7:1, 2, 3, 4, 5, 6, 13, 17). Isaiah's contemporary, Micah, similarly speaks of a Deliverer of mysterious parentage (Mi 5:3). The OT is open-ended toward the virgin birth of Jesus; the NT proclaims it here and in Lk 1:25-38. In both gospels the emphasis is on "conceived by the Holy Ghost," God's creative action. Matthew calls Mary "virgin" only in the quotation from Isaiah.

1:25 *Knew her not.* Did not have intercourse with her. (Cf. Gn 4:1)

2:1-12 SECOND FULFILLMENT: RULER FROM BETHLEHEM

2:1-12 In the eighth century B.C., when Jerusalem was threatened by the Assyrian power, God through His prophet Micah promised His people that He would raise up a Ruler and Deliverer for them to give them assured freedom and lasting peace (Mi 5:1-14). He turned His people's eyes away from Jerusalem, the royal residence, center of political power; deliverance was not to come by a development of potentialities present in the people. God would make a fresh beginning in little Bethlehem, the place of small beginnings (cf. 1 Sm 16:1-13). He would bring forth from there a new David, the Messiah, and create a new order for His chastened and restored people. He opened up the future and gave His people a word of hope which could carry them through not only the Assyrian threat but also the time of all threatening world powers, Babylonian, Persian, Greek, or Roman. *Bethlehem* is not merely a place name; it marks the divine, supernatural character of the Deliverer and the deliverance; the Deliverer would save His people from their sins (Mt 1:21; Mi 5:11-12), and not only His people—He was to "be great to the ends of the earth." (Mi 5:4)

Micah's word finds its fulfillment in Jesus; and the fulfillment is attested in a strangely wondrous way. Israel's scribes (2:4-6) are compelled to point it out to the non-Jewish King Herod and to Gentile wise men from the ends of the earth. Israel remains indifferent to the promised Ruler from Bethlehem; Israel's Idumean King Herod seeks Him out in order to destroy Him; only Gentiles, alerted by His star in the East, guided by the prophetic word and led by His star, seek Him out to worship Him. The story of the wise men is both fulfillment of prophecy (Is 60:3) and a prophecy of things to come: "Many will come from east and west . . . while the sons of the kingdom will be thrown into the outer darkness." (8:11-12)

2:1 *Herod the king,* the powerful, politically adroit, passionate, and ruthless king of the Jews called "the Great" by the Jewish historian Josephus, ruled 37—4 B.C. The events recorded by Matthew fall in his last troubled years, when his suspicion and brutality were at fever pitch.

Wise men. The term used, magi, originally designated a priestly class of the Medes and had come to be used generally of Eastern sages versed in knowledge of the stars.

2:2 *King of the Jews,* the Messiah, the Christ, 2:4. (Cf. Jer 23:5; Zch 9:9; Mt 27:11; Jn 1:49)

His star. Cf. Nm 24:17. The wise men were miraculously led (cf. v. 9); whether or not God employed a regular though rare conjunction of Jupiter and Saturn for this purpose is a minor question.

2:6 The quotation of Mi 5:2 is free (*in the land of Judah* replaces the original "Ephrathah," name of David's clan), and the scribes interpret as they quote, as was customary; *by no means least* replaces Micah's "little" but gives the sense of the prophecy exactly. Bethlehem was "little" in men's eyes but not in God's. The last line *(who will govern,* etc.) is either a free reproduction of Mi 5:4 or taken from 1 Ch 11:2, where the Lord says to David: "You shall be shepherd of my people Israel, and you shall be prince over my people Israel." (The word translated *govern* is literally the verb for playing the shepherd.) Micah also has "clans of Judah": the reading *rulers of Judah* may be due to a difference in the Hebrew text employed by Matthew or the translation from which he quotes.

2:11 *Treasures . . . gold and frankincense and myrrh.* The richness of the gifts and the recollection of passages like Ps 72:10, Is 49:7, 60:10 probably gave rise to the tradition that the wise men were kings (Kaspar, Melchior, Balthasar). In Matthew the story is not that splendid. The gifts are the traditional treasures of the East. (Cf. Is. 60:6; Jer 6:20; Eze 27:22)

2:13-15 THIRD FULFILLMENT: SON CALLED OUT OF EGYPT

2:13-15 Two things are worth noting concerning this "fulfillment." First, what is here being "fulfilled" is a past event and is spoken of by the prophet referred to (Hosea) in the past tense. While we confine the idea of "fulfilling" to the fulfillment of a command or a word of promise, Matthew's use of the word goes beyond these possibilities. He sees the will of God which was expressed in the act of the Exodus *(out of Egypt)* and articulated in the 8th-century prophetic word as reaching its full measure in the coming of the incarnate Son of God to effect the final exodus, the final full deliverance of His people; that is the meaning of *fulfil* here. Second, Matthew reproduces these few words of Hosea with a full consciousness of their original context and evidently expects his readers to recall it. The context (Hos 11:1-11) speaks of the Lord's love for His people with a fervor and a boldness unparalleled in the Bible:

"When Israel was a child, I loved him,
And out of Egypt I called my son." (Hos 11:1)

In the words of Hosea, Israel's unfaithfulness rouses the anger of the Lord, who has loved so tenderly and lavishly, and He resolves to visit His wrath upon them; but His heart recoils within Him and His compassion grows warm and tender (Hos 11:8); He will not execute His fierce anger, "for I am God and not man, the Holy One in your midst" (Hos 11:9). Because God's love is God's, it is invincible and it is creative; therefore there remains for Israel a future in which the Lord sees His repentant children come trembling home to Him (Hos 11:10). It is this lavish and holy love which must punish but will save that is reaching its full measure in the sending of the unique Son, a love that will triumph though Israel's alien King Herod may oppose it and Israel's priests and scribes remain at best indifferent to it. (Cf. 2:5-6)

2:16-18 FOURTH FULFILLMENT: RACHEL WEEPING

2:16-18 The thought of the Bible is much less individualistic than ours; a man and his ancestors, a man and his people, feel and know themselves to be one, united in their weal and woe. Thus it was no mere flight of fancy when Jeremiah heard the mother of the race, *Rachel,* weeping from her grave when Israel went into captivity (Jer 31:15). Rachel wept then; and Matthew hears her weep again, now at the climax of Israel's history of guilt and tears. Rachel weeps now when once again the redeeming purposes of God collide with man's selfish will and the mothers of Bethlehem weep for their children. Again Matthew quotes with a consciousness of the original context. Jer 30 and 31 constitute a Book of Comfort of God's people in the depths of their sorrow; it overflows with promises for a better day, hope for God's great future. Rachel is cheered with the words:

"Keep your voice from weeping,
and your eyes from tears . . . .
There is hope for your future." (Jer 31:16-17)

For all His wrath, the Lord yearns for His "darling child," His people; and He holds out the promise of the new covenant with a people whom He has renewed by forgiving their iniquity and remembering their sin no more (Jer 31:20, 31-34), the hope for a time when the history of God's people would no longer be a history for tears.

2:16 *Tricked by the wise men.* This is of course Herod's point of view. The wise men had actually obeyed God rather than man. (Acts 5:29)

2:18 The town *Ramah* (1 Sm 10:2) lay to the north of Jerusalem; tradition, however, located Rachel's tomb south of Jerusalem near Bethlehem, where a monument to her memory existed at least as early as the fourth century after Christ.

2:19-23 FIFTH FULFILLMENT: CALLED A NAZARENE

2:19-23 The Christ, the King of the Jews, lives in small and obscure Nazareth, a town mentioned neither in the OT nor in Judaic writings. This, too, is part of God's design; His Word is being fulfilled. The prophets who had foretold the coming of the Messiah had spoken of His obscure beginnings. Amos had promised that the Lord would "raise up the booth of David that is fallen" (Am 9:11). In Is 9 the Child with the wondrous names ("Wonderful Counselor, Mighty God, etc.," Is 9:6) arises out of deep darkness (Is 9:2) to rule on the throne of David. It is a "shoot from the stump of Jesse," a scion from the judged and ruined royal house who ushers in the time of righteousness and paradisal peace in Is 11. Zechariah had promised his people a humble king, "humble and riding on an ass" (Zch 9:9). The Servant Messiah of Is 53:2 comes "like a root out of dry ground." All this is fulfilled in Jesus' obscure youth in insignificant Nazareth.

2:20-21 *Land of Israel.* This designation for Palestine occurs only here in the entire NT; it has an archaic ring—the ancient promises of God concerning Israel (cf. Eze 11:17; 20:42; 36:6 ff.; 37:12) are to be fulfilled in this Child in whom "all the promises of God find their Yes" (2 Co 1:20). The Child coming from Egypt enters His own, the promised land of Israel. (Cf. Jn 1:11)

2:22 *Archelaus,* son and principal successor of Herod the Great when Herod died in 4 B. C. Joseph's fear of him was shared by his countrymen and justified by the history of Archelaus' short and violent reign. He was banished by his Roman overlord A. D. 6.

Galilee was governed by Archelaus' brother, Antipas.

2:23 *Called a Nazarene.* Some scholars see a reference here to Is 11:1, where the Hebrew word for shoot *(nezer)* bears some resemblance to the word Nazarene. But how were Greek-speaking readers to catch this? And why is a plurality of *prophets* referred to?

3:1—4:11 SIXTH FULFILLMENT: VOICE IN THE WILDERNESS

3:1—4:11 In Is 40 the prophet hears God pronouncing pardon to His people, still captive in Babylon, to all seeming doomed to be forever in captivity to the power of the kingdoms of this world (40:1-2). Then he hears a voice, mysteriously undefined, giving the command that a way be prepared in the wilderness for the triumphant return of Israel's God, with His people, to Israel's land, that all flesh might behold the revealed glory of Him whose word will stand when all flesh fades and withers, whose coming spells good news for His people—He comes as triumphant Victor, as the Workman who has finished His task and brings His reward with Him, as the Shepherd who will tend His flock with a strong and gentle hand (40:3-11). This ancient voice achieves its full utterance—*Prepare!*—now, when in the face of Israel's utter failure and man's despair a voice is heard in the wilderness announcing the advent of the *kingdom of heaven,* proclaiming the coming of the *mightier* One in whom the Kingdom is to become a reality on earth; bidding men *repent,* to turn toward the God who is turning to them with His renewing Spirit and the dread alternative of fiery judgment on those who refuse His supreme gift. John the Baptist is that voice (cf. Jn 1:23); he *baptizes* men *for repentance,* with a baptism that confers the repentance God demands. He prepares for and ushers in the Son and Servant of God (3:17) who identified Himself with the fallen manhood of Israel by submitting to John's baptism in order to *fulfil all righteousness* (3:15) and meets and conquers the Tempter in the *wilderness,* making good the failure of His people by loving His neighbor as Himself and loving the Lord His God with all His heart. (4:11)

3:1 *Wilderness of Judea.* The southern reaches of the Jordan valley, where John baptized, were wilderness.

3:2 *Repent.* John, last and greatest of the prophets (11:9-11), renews the cry of OT prophecy. The OT prophets conceived of sin as a personal, total turning away from God; they therefore conceived of repentance as a personal and total turning to God (the usual word for repentance in Hebrew is simply "to turn"). They deprecated any merely ritual ceremony of repentance ("Rend your hearts and not your garments," Jl 2:13) and demanded that man turn personally to God in obedience, trust, and radical aversion from self and sin. This turning is God's work in man; He creates the clean heart (Ps 51:10). This last note is particularly clear in John: *Repent, for*—turn to your God, not in order to make Him turn to you but because He has in His grace turned to you. (Cf. Ro 2:4)

Kingdom of heaven. Heaven signifies God; it is one of a number of expressions current in Judaism as a reverential substitute for the divine name. *Kingdom of heaven* summed up for Judaic ears the God of Israel as the OT prophets proclaimed Him, King of creation, Lord of all history, whose kingship over His chosen people found a partial and preliminary "incarnation" in the reign of the Davidic kings. The prophets had foretold that this real but hidden reign of God would one day become manifest and universal; God would lay bare His arms finally and definitively to lead all history to its goal, to triumph over all who refused His royal mercy and to bring home to Himself His people gathered from among all nations. "The Lord will become king over all the earth." (Zch 14:9)

3:4 *Garment of camel's hair,* the traditional garb of the prophet (Zch 13:4), particularly of Elijah (2 K 1:8), whose return Malachi had foretold for the last days. (Ml 4:5)

Locusts and wild honey. Locusts were commonly eaten (cf. Lv 11:21-22), as they are by Bedouins to this day. Both the rough garb and the readily obtainable wild food of the Baptist indicate that he, like the apostles after him, did not seek his own but imparted the Word of God "without pay" (10:8). For John's austere mode of life cf. 9:14; 11:18.

3:7 *Pharisees and Sadducees* represent the religiously elite in Judaism. The Pharisees, under the tutelage of the scribes, were the scrupulous pietists of the Law; the Sadducees represented the priestly aristocracy interested in the temple and the priestly interpretation of the Law. These two parties were in opposition to each other on many points. (Cf. Acts 23:6-8)

Brood of vipers. Brood in the sense of "offspring." Their venomous, vicious character is hereditary, in the blood; they boast of being Abraham's children (3:9) but are in reality no true sons of his. For the expression cf. Mt 12:34; 23:33. For the thought cf. Jn 8:39-44, where Jesus tells the sons of Abraham that they are in reality the children of the devil, the liar and killer.

The wrath to come. Like the prophets before him (e.g., Zph 1:2-18) and like Paul after him (Ro 1:18—3:20), John proclaims the impending wrath of God, His annihilating reaction against all ungodliness and wickedness of man. Not even the religious elite of Israel are exempt; man as man is threatened.

3:9 *Abraham as our father.* See note on 3:7, and cf. Gl 3:6-9; Ro 4:16;17.

Raise up children to Abraham. God's promise to Abraham (Gn 12:1-3) will not fail, even if Abraham's descendants fail; He will raise up children for Abraham from among the Gentiles to inherit His blessing.

3:10 For the *axe* as a symbol of divine judgment cf. Is 10:15; Mt 7:19.

3:11 *Baptize you with the Holy Spirit and with fire. Baptize* means to bestow in fullness (cf. Acts 1:5; 2:33). The *you* is plural; those who repent and believe will receive the promised blessing of the last days from the Coming One; those who disbelieve will forfeit salvation, and the wrath of God (symbolized by fire) remains on them. (Cf. Jn 3:36)

3:11-12 The Mightier One who follows John is nothing less than divine. John is not worthy to perform even the lowliest service for Him *(carry* His *sandals);* the *Holy Spirit* is His to bestow; He executes divine judgment, eternal judgment *(unquenchable fire);* the gathered *wheat* (the redeemed and renewed people of God) is His possession.

3:13-15 These verses make it clear that Jesus, in accepting the baptism of John, is freely identifying Himself with men under the wrath of God. His baptism is the first step toward the cross. Cf. Mk 10:38 and Lk 12:50, where "baptism" clearly refers to the Passion and death of Jesus.

3:15 *Fulfil all righteousness,* the purposes of God. Since this word is spoken against the background of John's proclamation of the wrath of God on all men, *righteousness* probably has the sense of "the redeeming activity of God" familiar to the Jew from the OT (e.g., Ps 103:17; Is 45:8) and familiar from Paul's proclamation (Ro 1:16-18; 3:21). For this sense in Matthew cf. 5:6; 6:33; 21:32.

3:17 *My beloved Son, with whom I am well pleased.* The wording brings to mind two OT passages, one addressed to the anointed King whom the Lord will set on His holy hill to rule over nations to the ends of the earth (Ps 2:6-8), the other addressed to the Servant whom God the Lord gives as a covenant to His people and a light to the nations (Is 42:1, 6), the Servant whose ministry carries Him into a vicarious death for the sins of many and beyond death into life and triumph (Is 52:13—53:12). God's approval rests on the Son and King as He makes Himself one with sinners, the Servant who is to die for all.

4:1-11 In the temptation Jesus is revealed as the obedient Son that Israel was to be (Ex 4:22-23) and never was. The devil appeals to Him as the unique *Son* whom the voice from heaven had attested at His baptism (3:17) and bids Him exploit a Son's privilege (4:3). Jesus takes His stand as man simply, as the obedient son (Israel) addressed in Dt, and wills to *live by every word that proceeds from the mouth of God* (4:4; Dt 8:3), whatever the words may impose on Him, even suffering and death (cf. 26:54). This same will, which is the theme of Dt, refuses to invert the relationship between God and man by tempting God, putting Him to the test, experimenting with Him, manipulating Him, trying to make God live by the word that proceeds from the mouth of man (4:7; Dt 6:16), but gives God a whole worship and an unquestioning service (4:10; Dt 6:13). Thus the upward-reaching satanic will is thwarted (cf. Ph 2:6), the Law is written on the heart of man (Jer 31:33) in this representative Man, and the fulfillment of all righteousness (3:15) is carried another step forward.

4:1 *Led up by the Spirit.* The confrontation with the devil comes by God's will, not by any free initiative of the devil.

4:2 *Forty days and forty nights.* The inclusion of *nights* marks the extraordinary character of this fast; the Jew ordinarily fasted only from sunrise to sunset. *Forty* is commonly used in the Bible as a round number, e.g., to indicate the usual length of a critical period. (Gn 7:4; 8:6; Ex 24:18; Nm 13:25; 1 Sm 17:16; 1 K 19:8; Eze 4:6)

4:4 *It is written.* Ps 91:11-12.

4:7 *Again it is written.* Only Scripture can speak against Scripture, to prevent its misuse and to interpret it rightly. The light shed by Dt 6:16 on man's basic relationship to his God lets him understand Ps 91 rightly and keeps him from confusing the confidence of faith with self-willed and self-seeking presumption.

4:9 *Fall down and worship me.* The devil asks a little compromise, one act of obeisance to himself, and in return promises that He shall reign as anointed King without struggle and pain.

4:11 *Angels came and ministered.* The Greek word for *ministered* suggests service at table; the Father gave His obedient Son the bread which He would not seek for Himself. (Cf. 6:33)

4:12-22 SEVENTH FULFILLMENT: THE GREAT LIGHT

4:12-22 In 734 and 732 B. C. the Assyrian king Tiglath-pileser waged two campaigns against Israel and incorporated into his empire large northern tracts of the Promised Land (2 K 15:29). To Israel it seemed that the promises of God were failing; if the God of Israel "brought into contempt the land of Zebulun and the land of Naphtali" (Is 9:1), what would the end be? Where was the hope and the future of God's people? To this Isaiah replied that the promises of God hold, however great the guilt of His people and the severity of His judgment might be; the God who brought the land into contempt, even He, would "in the latter time . . . make glorious the way of the sea, the land beyond the Jordan, Galilee of the nations" (Is 9:1). And the great reversal of grace would begin just there where His judgment had first struck; in *Galilee,* contemptuously called *Galilee of the Gentiles* because of its mixed population, the *great light* of His new creation would shine. A new "Let light shine" would usher in a new epoch of salvation; for a Son, a Child, would be given to the people, a Child with names that speak the blessing of His reign on the throne of David ("Wonderful Counselor, Mighty God, Everlasting Father, Prince of Peace"), a reign of peace and justice without end, a reign established and eternally guaranteed by "the zeal of the Lord of hosts" (Is 9:2-7). This word of Isaiah is now fulfilled, now when Jesus appears, just in *Galilee of the Gentiles,* after the voice of John has been silenced by his imprisonment, to renew John's cry of the Kingdom at hand, to gather the new people of God, the first of the disciples and apostles. This is the dawn of the new creation; these called apostles could say with Paul: "The God who said, 'Let light shine out of darkness' . . . has shone in our hearts to give the light of the knowledge of the glory of God in the face of Christ." (1 Co 4:6)

4:12 *John . . . arrested.* Cf. 11:2; 14:3-5.

4:14 *Spoken by . . . Isaiah.* Is 9:1-2. Matthew is conscious of the whole Messianic context in Isaiah. (9:1-7)

4:16 *Great light,* not a mere glimmering on the horizon but the full light of the new creation.

4:17 Jesus' announcement of the coming of the *kingdom,* directly and logically *(for)* connected with the call to *repentance,* is identical with John's (3:2); but Matthew makes clear the distinction between the two by means of the Scripture cited to illumine each. John's call is preparatory (3:3); Jesus' announcement is word and act in one.

4:18-22 The calling of the first four disciples-apostles is the first item under the rubric "the kingdom of heaven is at hand." This is divinely royal grace in action, creating the nucleus of the new Israel. The disciples do not choose their teacher as was usual in Judaism; Jesus chooses them (cf. Jn 15:16). And there is no stress on the disciples' qualification for the call. The emphasis is on Jesus Himself, who calls with the sovereign freedom of God to Himself alone. He lays on men His gentle yoke of obedience and renunciation and promises them a life of ministry as *fishers of men* (19). The great light has fallen on men; the new people of God is coming into being, and the last great age of God has begun.

4:18 *Called Peter.* For the significance of the name cf. 16:18 note.

4:21 *Called.* As God once called Abraham (Is 51:2) and His people Israel. (Hos 11:1)

4:23—7:29 FIRST GROUP OF MESSIANIC DEEDS AND WORDS

4:23—7:29 The account of the Messianic deeds that precedes the discourse is very brief in this unit (4:23-25). There is a sketch of Jesus' characteristic activity, just enough to identify Him as the Christ, the kingdom of heaven in person (cf. 12:28). The authority with which He teaches (7:29) is that of the One who proclaims the Kingdom, heals every disease, overcomes the powers of the devil *(demoniacs,* 4:24). His Word is a Messianic word that bestows the blessings it pronounces and moulds men in the image of the Christ. (Chs. 5—7)

4:23-25 Jesus' Ministry in Galilee

4:23 *Teaching in their synagogues and preaching the gospel of the kingdom.* For a vivid account of such teaching and preaching see Lk 4:14-21.

4:25 *Decapolis.* A loose federation of 10 (or more) cities, centers of Greek culture, most of them lying to the east of the Jordan. Decapolis serves to point out how far east (and north) the influence of Jesus had reached.

5:1—7:29 The Sermon on the Mount

5:1—7:29 The Sermon on the Mount is the record of how Jesus moulds the will of His disciple, leading the disciple to live a life wholly drawn from God the King as He is revealed in these last days in His Son, a life which is therefore wholly lived for God the King. The gift of the Kingdom and the claim of the Kingdom (the call to repentance) are to shape the disciple's whole existence.

5:1:12 THE BEATITUDES

5:1-12 Jesus' first words mark Him as the Giver. The word *blessed* indicates that God has acted or is acting or will act for man's good (cf., e.g., Ps 32:1-2; 65:4; 84:12; Dt 33:29; Rv 14:13; 19:9). In Matthew *blessed* is always associated with God's action in Jesus Himself (11:6; 13:16-17; 16:17; 24:46). Jesus' Beatitudes therefore declare what He is and gives; they are a Messianic self-attestation.

5:3 *Poor in spirit.* To the beggarly, those whose state is such that they must look to God for everything and whose disposition is such that they do look to God for everything (the repentant), Jesus' potent Word gives the *kingdom of heaven.* God in His grace is their King; and they are permitted to enjoy and share in His reign. That reign is present *(theirs is)* for them in Jesus. The promise of the first (5:3) and the eighth Beatitude (5:10) is the promise of the Kingdom and is in the present tense; the promises of the other Beatitudes are in the future and portray the ultimate, future blessings of the Kingdom, the final fruit of Jesus' royal ministry. (Cf. 25:34)

5:4 *Those who mourn* are "those who mourn in Zion" (Is 61:3); their mourning is the expression of their intense longing for Him who is the Comfort (Is 61:2) of the afflicted and the brokenhearted. God will comfort them (the passive verb *be comforted* indicates God's action, as often), and God's comforting is Jesus, "the Lord's Christ." (Cf. Lk 2:25-26)

5:5 Jesus' promise to the meek is practically a quotation from Ps 37:11. That psalm pictures the meek as those who trust in the Lord, commit their way to Him, are still before Him, wait patiently for Him confident that He will bring forth their vindication as the Light, will help them, deliver them, and save them because they take refuge in Him. Jesus Himself will go that way of meekness (11:29; 21:5) into death and victory. As the triumphant Messiah He will fulfill the promise of Isaiah "and decide with equity for the *meek* of the earth" (Is 11:4). Those who are His will *inherit the earth* with Him who shall have authority in heaven and on earth. (28:18)

5:6 Those who long for *righteousness*, knowing that they must die without it *(hunger and thirst), shall be satisfied*—God will give them righteousness and life. Jesus is that righteousness in person, the fulfillment of Jeremiah's promise of a Messiah whose name was to be "the Lord is our righteousness" (Jer 23:5-6). Cf. Mt 3:15 and the note there. In 5:10-11 Jesus Himself indicates that suffering for righteousness' sake and suffering for His sake are one and the same.

5:7-10 The first four Beatitudes are a unit; the persons are the same and the promise and gift of Jesus is one. Jesus is giving to those who have nothing and need everything that which answers their every need—comfort, the earth, righteousness, the Kingdom. The last four Beatitudes also are a unit. The promises bring into view the Last Judgment and the new world

God the King will create. And the promises are made to men who have tasted the powers of the world to come in God's present reign, in Christ, and are manifesting that new world in their actions even now.

5:7 *The merciful* have learned mercy from Him whom Jesus revealed as their Father (5:44-48), who desires mercy and not sacrifice (9:13; 12:7). The life they drew from God made them merciful. To them Jesus promises *mercy* in the Judgment. Cf. 25:34-40, where Jesus bestows the blessing of the Father and the inheritance of the Kingdom on the merciful.

5:8 The *pure in heart* are the men of single-hearted, pure devotion, men who have learned from the Son to live by every word that proceeds from the mouth of God to give God that obedience of faith and pure adoration which Jesus made possible by His overcoming of the Tempter (4:1-10) and His obedience unto death. They *shall see God* at the end of days. The vision of God is for Biblical thought not a mystical experience but an eschatological one. In this age men hear God's Word; they shall see His face in the world to come. (1 Co 13:12; Rv 22:4)

5:9 The *peacemakers* are those who follow in the train of the Messianic Prince of Peace (Is 9:6), who have learned peacemaking from the meek King who speaks peace to the nations (Zch 9:10) and have by word and deed brought His peace to men (10:13). God said "This is my beloved Son" of Him who became Prince of Peace by a ministry that bound Him to men in their guilt (3:17). He will *call* those men His *sons* who witness to and serve the Son.

5:10 *Persecuted for righteousness' sake.* Jesus, God's Son and Servant, goes the way through contempt, rejection, and dying to glory and royal reign (Is 53); all sons and servants are called on to follow Him on that way: "We suffer with him in order that we may also be glorified with him" (Ro 8:17; cf. 1 Ti 2:12). To be on the path of suffering is to be on the road to the Kingdom; and the assurance of this is blessedness even now. (Ro 5:2-5)

5:11-12 To find blessedness in suffering does not come naturally to men; Jesus therefore reinforces the last Beatitude. His disciples are not merely to accept persecution and endure it stoically. They are to speak a glad and resolute yea to it and find in it the assurance that thus, in communion with the Servant Christ, they stand in the succession of the *prophets* and can look forward to a great reward.

5:13-16 SALT, LIGHT, CITY ON A HILL: GOOD WORKS

5:13-16 The last four Beatitudes have already indicated that the coming of the Kingdom changes and ennobles the lives of men. The poor in spirit can only receive from God; but they do receive, and God's giving makes them merciful. The present section makes clear that this must happen. *Salt* must by its very nature be salt, *light* must shine, a *city on a hill* is inevitably seen. If a disciple refuses to function as a disciple, he has ceased to be a disciple and involves judgment on himself; he has become saltless salt which can only *be thrown out* (13; cf. Jn 15:2, 6). As sons of God the disciples naturally so live and work that their Father is *glorified*—is known, acknowledged, and adored by men. (16; cf. 1 Ptr 2:12)

5:17-20 JESUS THE FULFILLER: THE NEW RIGHTEOUSNESS OF THE DISCIPLE

5:17-20 In the solitary hour of His temptation (4:1-10) Jesus had overcome Satan with three words from Deuteronomy; He had thus implicitly spoken His assent to God's ancient Word, the OT Scriptures. He now speaks this assent to the *law and the prophets* explicitly and publicly. Moreover, He marks His whole Messianic mission as determined by the entire OT Scriptures; every claim of the Law will be satisfied by Him, every condemnation of the Law will be executed upon Him (cf. Gl 3:13), every prophetic promise of God will be fulfilled in Him (cf. 2 Co 1:20). God's new last-days act, the coming of His kingdom, is witnessed by the Law and upholds the Law (cf. Ro 3:21, 31). For the disciple the way to the new righteousness (which takes the "just requirements" of the Law more seriously than the scribe and Pharisee ever did) is through Jesus, the Fulfiller of Law and prophets. (Cf. Ro 8:3-4)

5:18 Cf. 24:35, where Jesus claims for His own Word more than He here asserts of the Law.

5:19 *The least.* Since Jesus has the written page before His mind's eye (iota . . . dot, 18), He is probably referring to basic commandments, which are least on the page, such as the Fifth Commandment, three syllables in Hebrew.

5:20 *Scribes,* the professional interpreters of the Law, and *Pharisees,* men devoted to the scrupulous fulfillment of the Law and the "tradition of the elders" (15:2), represent the apex of Judaic piety.

5:21-48 THE NEW RIGHTEOUSNESS: FIVE EXAMPLES

5:21-48 With five examples Jesus illustrates the nature of the new "exceeding" (20) righteousness. His mighty *But I say to you* reveals that He is the end of the Law (Ro 10:4); His treatment of the intention and will of the Law shows that He is the end because He is the Fulfiller and ushers in the new age.

5:21-26 The new righteousness (which "exceeds" purely legal corrections of conduct) exemplified by the Fifth Commandment. The disciple sees the protecting hand of God extended not only over his brother's physical life but over his whole life, which is threatened by this fellowman's angry thought and slighting word as well as by his murderous hand.

5:22 *The council,* the supreme Jewish court, presided over by the high priest, composed of high priests, elders, and scribes.

5:24-25 *First be reconciled . . . make friends quickly.* All days since the coming of the Christ are last days (Heb 1:1) and are filled with last-days urgency. No act of worship dare delay reconciliation with the injured brother, for all roads lead to the judgment throne of God, who will punish, inevitably and severely, all loveless action (cf. 18:32-35). If God's royal favor has not made the disciple merciful (5:7), he may not look for mercy in the Last Judgment. (Ja 2:13)

5:27-32 The new righteousness exemplified by the Sixth Commandment. God is witness to the marriage covenant and "hates divorce" as much as bloody violence (Ml 2:14-16). He keeps a jealous and all-seeing watch over marriage, which is violated by the lustful look and by divorce as well as by overt adultery. From this God the disciple draws his life, and he lives his life before Him as his Father; he therefore keeps his *eye* and *hand* under iron discipline (29, 30), lest he look and lust and reach for forbidden fruit and be separated forever from his God and Father *(hell,* 30).

5:29-30 *Eye . . . hand.* In Biblical thought the various parts of the body are the expressive instruments of man's will and may stand for the whole man in action ("Turn your foot away from evil," Pr 4:27). To *pluck out* the *eye* or to *cut off* the *hand* therefore signifies resolute repression of sinful desire, however painful the effort may be.

5:31 The Law conceded divorce and prescribed the *certificate of divorce* (Dt 24:1-4) because the Law could not overcome man's "hardness of heart" (19:8). But God's intention at creation was life-long indissoluble union between man and woman (19:3-6). This divine intention Jesus is now reasserting and inscribing on the heart of His disciple.

5:32 *Except on the ground of unchastity.* Judaism in general interpreted the Mosaic prescription concerning divorce very liberally, and a man could divorce his wife for almost "any cause" (19:3). Jesus championed the cause of woman, left helpless and without honor by this procedure, but she can no more violate marriage with impunity than the husband can.

5:33-37 The new righteousness exemplified by the Law concerning oaths (Lv 19:12; Nm 30:2; Dt 23:21). Jesus applied the Fifth and Sixth Commandments to His disciples with radical rigor; in this case (as in the following, 38-42) He with Messianic authority sets aside the prescription of the Law entirely. He does so, however, in order that the intention of the Law may be fully realized. The Law prescribed the oath with the intention that man be reminded, on occasion at least, that he is speaking in the presence of his God. Jesus removes the oath in order that His disciple may speak his every *Yes* and *No* as in the presence of God.

5:34-36 The Jew tended to evade the seriousness of the oath by artificial distinctions between binding and nonbinding oaths (23:16-22). Jesus sweeps away all such sophistry.

5:37 *From evil.* The reading of RSV note *l (the evil one)* seems preferable. It is the influence of the devil, the "father of lies" (Jn 8:44), which makes the oath a necessity in law.

5:38-42 The new righteousness exemplified by the law of retaliation (Ex 21:24; Lv 24:20; Dt 19:21). The Law cannot remove the desire for vengeance from man's heart; it can only, as it were, regulate revenge, setting a limit to it *(eye for an eye).* Jesus removes the impulse of revenge from His disciples' hearts and bids them live, as He Himself lived, in a love that recklessly exposes itself to the lovelessness of the world and the need of men.

5:43-48 The new righteousness exemplified by the law of love. The Law enjoined love for the neighbor; legalism (the attempt to find favor with God and to stand in His judgment by way of works of the Law) raised the question, "Who is my neighbor?" (Lk 10:29) and sought to limit the imperative of love by finding scope for lovelessness and hate. Jesus removes every limitation from the law of love by enjoining love for the enemy. The highest "righteousness" is love. Jesus went this way of love for the enemy before His disciples and for them; He joined Himself, in love, to men under the wrath of God when He was baptized; He loved the enemy in order to "fulfil all righteousness" (3:15). That way of love took Him to the cross, "so that in Him we might become the righteousness of God." (2 Co 5:21)

5:45 *Be sons,* literally "become sons," that is, "show yourselves to be, evince yourselves as" sons of the God who loves spontaneously and freely without regard for the worthiness of the objects of His love. Sonship involves both: getting one's life from the Father and living a life of love in communion with Him.

5:46 *Even the tax collectors,* hated and despised by good Jews because of their connection with the Roman rule and their greed and dishonesty. (Cf. Lk 3:13; 19:8)

5:48 *Perfect,* in love without reservation or limit, the kind of "perfection" which Jesus held before the rich young man when He bade him sell all his possessions and give them to the poor. (19:21)

As your heavenly Father. For this use of *as* to indicate not only the pattern but also the power for right action see 20:28: "Even as the Son of man came . . . to serve." It is the Gospel of the Father who loves His enemies and the Son who serves that makes men capable of obeying the Law and glorifying their Father in heaven.

6:1-18 THE PIETY OF THE DISCIPLE

6:1-18 The new righteousness brings with it a new piety, which Jesus illustrates by the familiar Judaic triad of *almsgiving* (2-4), *prayer* (5-15), and *fasting* (16-18). As the new righteousness of the disciple is the expression of a life derived from the Father and lived for the Father, so the new piety is distinguished by the same purity of heart, by selfless and unalloyed devotion to the Father. The Father-child relationship gives this piety its characteristic color; the phrase *your Father* occurs nine times in these 18 verses. Since the Father *sees in secret* (4, 6, 18), self-consciousness and display and applause seeking disappear from this piety. Since it is the Father who *rewards* (4, 6, 18) His child with a Father's generous and forgiving love, the disciple does not strain for merit and reward, nor does he seek his reward from men. Thus Jesus takes over the Judaic idea of reward and transforms it; the truth that lives in the idea—that man is set before God in his actions and is responsible to Him—is retained; but man no longer works in order to obtain the favor of God—he works because he is in the sunshine of God's favor.

6:2 *Hypocrites* attempt to divide their heart between God and man. Unable to trust God as their Father for His reward, they seek the reward of men's approval and admiration.

Sound no trumpet. Figurative for "Do not publicize."

6:3 *Left hand know.* Do not let your left hand point to the right hand to call attention to the act of giving.

6:4 *Sees in secret.* The Father knows the hidden deed and its hidden motive.

6:7 *Heard for their many words.* Their prayer is a "magical" prayer; the petitioner attempts to manipulate the Godhead and make Him subservient to his own desires. The Father-child relationship (8) makes such prayer impossible.

6:9 *Hallowed be thy name.* God will hallow His name when He acts in judgment and mercy to reveal Himself finally and forever as the one good (19:17) God that He is (cf. Eze 36:22 ff., esp. 23: "vindicate the holiness of my great name").

6:10 *Thy kingdom come.* The royal reign of God "is at hand" in Jesus' Word and work (4:17; 5:3; 12:28); His coming is the beginning of the end. But the kingdom is still to "come with power" (Mk 9:1) at the end of the End, when Christ returns and bids His own inherit the kingdom prepared for them. For that day the disciple longs and prays and lives.

Thy will be done on earth. The first three petitions are really one prayer that God may fulfill His gracious purposes and come. The third petition adds the all-important idea that man is not a mere spectator of God's great act; God draws man into it and graciously employs men to achieve His purposes. Paul calls his fellow missionaries his "fellow workers for the kingdom of God." (Cl 4:11)

6:11 *Daily.* Cf. RSV note *m.* The exact translation of the rare word used in the Greek is uncertain, but it is certain that the prayer for sustenance is a modest one: "Keep us alive one day at a time."

6:12 *Debts . . . debtors.* For sin pictured as a debt cf. 5:26; 18:23-35.

As we also have forgiven. The disciple as son of God lives by every word that proceeds from His mouth; that word is the word of forgiveness, and the disciple must needs live by it in relationship to his fellowman. (Cf. 14-15 and note)

6:13 *Lead us not into temptation.* This is the prayer the disciples forgot when they failed their Lord in Gethsemane (26:36 ff.). The glad confidence of the disciple that God's name will be hallowed and His kingdom will come is mingled with a holy fear that he may fail to hallow God's name, and he trusts only in God's kindly control of his history to bring him through his encounters with the Evil One.

Deliver us from evil. The disciple knows that he is dependent on his heavenly Father for ultimate deliverance; only He can rescue him from every evil and bring him safely into the heavenly kingdom (2 Ti 4:18). And so his prayer ends as it began with the petition that God break forth in majesty and put an end to all that opposes God and endangers God's sons.

The doxology with which we close the Lord's Prayer is not part of the original text but is thoroughly in keeping with the spirit of the prayer, which seeks first God's kingdom and His righteousness, makes the petitioner dependent on God's grace, and so gives God the glory. (Cf. Ro 4:20)

6:14-15 Jesus commented on the last Beatitude (5:11-12), since man finds it difficult to find blessedness in persecution. So here he reinforces the Fifth Petition, particularly the "as we also have forgiven"; for at this point our discipleship is put to the test again and again, and endless forgiving does not come easy. For a dramatic commentary on the Fifth Petition see the parable, Mt 18:21-35. The alternate translation of RSV note *n (the evil one)* is very probable; the sense of the petition is not essentially changed thereby.

6:16 *Fasting* undertaken voluntarily by individuals was considered a meritorious religious exercise (Lk 18:12). Since fasting is an expression of sorrow for sin and urgency of prayer and therefore speaks to God of a penitent heart, making a display of it is only a piece of religious showmanship.

6:19-34 THE DISCIPLE AND HIS PROPERTY

6:19-34 Property poses a double threat to purity of heart; it tempts to avarice (19-23) and gives rise to anxiety (25-34). Whether a man seeks wealth (19) or anxiously strives for mere security (25), he is dividing his loyalty and is no longer whole-souled in his devotion to God. The avaricious man is giving his *heart,* which belongs to his God, to his *treasures;* the anxious man forgets the God who created him, the Father who will clothe and feed him—his faith shrinks *(little faith,* 30) and atrophies. To this Jesus opposes His warning: You cannot be a slave *(serve,* 24) in full-time, single service to God and property; you dare not cleave your *heart* (21). But He does more than warn; He lets God the Creator and Father grow great before His disciples' eyes (26-30) and bids them *seek first* (33) the given gift of His kingdom (5:3) and His saving righteousness (5:6) and to trust Him who feeds the birds and clothes the lilies for all the rest. He bids His disciples go the way of the obedient Son who would not seek bread (4:3-4) but sought to let God reign in His life—God's angels set a table for Him in the wilderness. (4:11)

6:23 *The light in you,* the eye of the *heart* (21), center of man's desiring, willing, and thinking. If man's inner eye is darkened, he is blinded with a blindness more fatal than any defect of the physical eye, the *lamp of the body.* (21)

6:24 *Mammon,* a word taken over from Jesus' mother tongue (Aramaic); it means "property," "money," "wealth."

6:27 *Cubit,* about 18 inches.

6:30 *Oven.* The Palestinian oven, made of burnt clay, was heated by building a fire INSIDE it. *Grass* was commonly used as fuel.

6:34 The Fourth Petition with its request for "daily bread this day" provides the best commentary on this verse. We live one day at a time under God's care.

Trouble. Jesus does not idealize or gloss over the hard economic realities of life; they are there, and they are no fun. But our King and Father can help us deal with them.

7:1-29 THE DISCIPLE IN AN ALIEN WORLD

7:1-29 The disciple as moulded by Jesus is a new sort of man. Endowed with a new righteousness whose crowning characteristic is unlimited love—love for His enemy (5:17-48), living in a childlike piety that looks only for the Father's reward (6:1-18), freed from the compulsion of both avarice and anxiety and seeking first the reign and saving righteousness of God (6:19-34)—the disciple emerges as one set off from both Gentile (5:47; 6:7, 32) and Jew (5:20), a new third race in a world of alien men. How is he to confront them? What shall his attitudes and actions toward them be?

1) 7:1-14 The Disciple and the Sinner

7:1-14 In a world where the law condemns the wrongdoer and the synagog metes out the discipline of the 39 lashes (cf. 10:17; 2 Co 11:24), where the natural bent of man is to judge the other man (Ro 2:1), the disciple will be tempted to ascend God's judgment throne and condemn the sinner (7:1). This he dare not do, for he lives purely of God's forgiveness (6:12; 18:21-35), and he can only be the voice of God's forgiveness to his fellowman. If he judges, he loses God the Forgiver and will have God against him as his Judge. He wishes to win the sinner (18:15), but he can do so only by calling him to repentance, offering the forgiveness which he, the disciple, has himself received. He must, by repenting, clear his own eye of the *log* of his own sin before he can see clearly to remove the *speck* from the eye of his *brother.* (4-5)

The disciple is not authorized to execute God's judgment (Ro 12:19); neither can he play God in forcing salvation on men, exposing *what is holy* to the malice of men who refuse and resent it (6). Jesus will not permit him to desecrate the precious thing *(pearls)* entrusted him nor to endanger himself needlessly. This does not, however, leave him helpless; he can pray in the rich assurance that his Father will hear and heed his prayer (7-11) and in the strength of the Father's good gifts employ the whole power of love. (12)

7:1 *Be not judged.* By God in the last judgment.

7:6 *What is holy.* Sacrificial meat. (Lv 22:14-16)

7:11 *You . . . who are evil.* In Jesus' eyes man at his best, man who can give his children *good gifts,* is still at bottom evil.

7:12 *This is the law and the prophets.* When men love their fellowmen as naturally, as constantly, and as instinctively as they act to protect and preserve themselves, then they are perfect, as their heavenly Father is perfect (5:48, cf. 45); then His will as proclaimed by the Law and the prophets (the OT) is being done and His kingdom comes.

7:13-14 In this world grown alien to him the disciple will be confronted with an alien majority, a mass of men indifferent to him and pursuing a course which is easier than and the exact opposite of his own. He can find the strength to resist the pressure of this majority only in the Word of his Lord; His word of threat and promise determines the value and the outcome of the two opposing ways. In the power of His Lord's Word the disciple can go through the *narrow gate* down the *hard way that leads to life.*

2) 7:15-23 The Disciple and False Prophecy

7:15-23 The disciples stand in this alien world as successors to the prophets of old (5:12), bearers of the Word of God. They will be confronted by competitors, by *false prophets,* similar to the true prophets, distinguishable from the true only by their *fruits,* their output. The disciples will recognize them as men destined for judgment by the fact that their words do not lead men to Christ and the Father but bind men to themselves. The voice of false prophecy will be raised by men who call Jesus *Lord* and can validate their message with *mighty works.* The disciples will recognize them for what they are, men who will be disowned by Christ *on that day* of judgment, by the fact that they do not do what the Lord Himself did, fulfill *the will of my Father,* the will of love. (Cf. 1 Co 13:2)

7:15 *Sheep's clothing . . . ravenous wolves.* The destroying enemies (Jn 10:12) of the flock (Lk 12:32), the people of God, will appear in disguise as members of the flock. (Cf. 2 Co. 11:12-15)

3) 7:24-29 The Disciple Under the Word of Christ

7:24-29 How shall the disciple attain to this higher righteousness (5:20), this pure piety (6:1), this single devotion to God and freedom from mammon (6:19), this clear-eyed wisdom that can resist the persuasion of the majority (7:13) and the lure of false prophecy (7:15)? Only by remaining under the Word of Jesus. Only by *hearing* and *doing* that Word can he build a house of life which will come through the storm of divine judgment upright and unshaken. Only he who takes Christ at His word and lives of His Word (all of it, the words that confer the gift of Christ and words that make His claim on man) will fully know what the *crowds* sensed, how great is the *authority* of this Teacher; year by difficult year he will be more and more *astonished at his teaching.*

7:25 *Rain, floods, winds.* For the storm as a description of God's judgment cf. Eze 13:10-15.

8:1—10:42 SECOND GROUP OF MESSIANIC DEEDS AND WORDS

8:1—9:34 Ten Deeds of the Messiah

8:1—9:34 Ten, number of completeness (cf. ten commandments, Ex 20; ten plagues in Egypt, Ex 7—11). With an account of TEN deeds Matthew records a comprehensive revelation of the authority and compassion of the Messiah and also of the twofold reaction (faith and praise, opposition and blasphemy) which that revelation provokes. With this Messianic *authority,* authority in the service of compassion (10:1, 7, 8), Jesus will send out the Twelve to the "lost sheep" (10:6); and His Word prepares them for the same twofold reaction (10:12-15, 25, etc.) Matthew punctuates the series of miracles with two accounts of nonmiraculous words and deeds which likewise illustrate Jesus' compassionate authority as it confronts men.

8:1-17 THREE DEEDS: THE COMPASSIONATE SERVANT

8:1-17 The first three deeds illustrate the Beatitude on the poor (5:3); Jesus brings the power and the grace of the Kingdom to persons in their extreme need: to the *leper* whom the Law could only shut out from the people of God, to the Gentile *centurion* excluded by Law from Israel, to the woman whom Judaic opinion considered a second-rate creature of God. He triumphs over the power of *demons* (16) who oppose and attack the work of God, but He triumphs as the Servant whose ministry takes Him into the depths of human misery. (17)

8:2 *Leper.* For the lot of the leper under the Law cf. Lv 13—14.

8:4 *Say nothing.* Cf. 12:15-21, where Jesus is pictured as the Messiah who is the meek Servant of God, who will not call attention to Himself or assert Himself but does His merciful work for the crushed and hopeless in order that God's cause ("justice") may prevail. Jesus did not want to instigate a "popular movement" that hung on Him; He wanted men to see God at work in His deeds, to repent, and accept the royal reign of God (4:17). The Son of God takes on servant form and does His servant work "to the glory of God the Father." (Ph 2:11)

For a proof, that He came not to abolish but to fulfill (5:17), that in restoring the leper to the people He was fulfilling the law which willed that God's people be clean and whole.

8:5 *Centurion,* an officer in charge of 100 soldiers. Whether a Roman or a mercenary in the service of Herod, he would be a Gentile.

8:9 *A man under authority.* The centurion is saying: "If even I, a subordinate, can bring about effective action by my word, how much the more can You whose authority is so much greater than mine."

8:11 Again Jesus fulfills the Law and prophets; the believing Gentile is brought into the people of God which began with *Abraham;* God is raising up children to Abraham. (3:9)

8:12 *Sons of the kingdom,* Israelites called into being by God their King to be "a kingdom of priests." (Ex 19:6)

8:17 Cf. Is 53:4. Matthew is recalling the Servant of the Lord promised in Isaiah, the Servant who goes the downward way of a ministry for the broken and despairing into an atoning death for the sins of "the many." Is 53:4 speaks of that vicarious death; Matthew sees this ministry-unto-death as already beginning in Jesus' deeds of healing. And one can see why, for Jesus uses His power only in service to others, never to assert Himself (8:4; 9:30). He will not let Himself be proclaimed as Messiah until He has by His self-sacrifice revealed Himself as the Messiah of the God of all grace. The miracle forces a decision upon men; it both fosters faith and makes unbelief congeal into deadly opposition (9:3, 34; Jn 11:47-48). This opposition Jesus refused to overwhelm or destroy miraculously. His deeds of mercy are therefore steps toward the cross. His life of serving and His ransoming death are an organic whole. (20:28)

8:18-22 FIRST INTERLUDE: THE CLAIM AND GIFT OF THE SON OF MAN

Jesus' response to the volunteers for the discipleship *(I will follow you,* 19) reveals the *Son of man* (destined to have universal, eternal, indestructible "dominion and glory and kingdom," Dn 7:14) going the way of Servant ministry with such restless devotion that He *has nowhere to lay his head.* He claims men for that kind of ministry, and His claim overrides every other claim, even that of filial piety toward a *father* (21-22). His claim is so high because His gift is so great; with Him is life, the only life in a world of the *dead* (22). His miracles all proclaim what this word says: "With Me is life."

8:19 *Scribe,* interpreter of the Law; the scribes were the theological leaders of the Pharisaic party.

8:22 *The dead.* Cf. Eph 2:1.

8:23—9:8 THREE DEEDS: AUTHORITY OVER THE SEA, THE ENEMY, AND SIN

8:23—9:8 The majesty and mercy of the Lord, the God of Israel, are manifested in the deeds of Jesus; in Jesus men can behold the Lord who is Master of the dreaded chaotic sea and rescues men from its terrors (23-27; Ps 107:23-32); the Lord who stills the enemy (Ps 8:2), before whom His enemies are scattered (Ps 68:1, 21), even *the* enemy whose demonic underlings distort and torment His creature, man (28-34); the Lord who forgives iniquity and heals diseases (9:1-8; Ps 103:3; 107:17-22), whose power over sin reveals Him as the God to be feared (9:8; Ps 130:4). Just here, where the arm of the Lord is revealed in His compassionate Servant (Is 53:1), the opposition of men is provoked. The disciples may bow before the *man* whom *winds and sea obey* (8:27), and the crowds may *glorify* the *God* who has given the *Son of man authority on earth to forgive sins* (9:6, 8), but the Gadarenes will have nothing to do with a *Son of God* who costs them pigs (8:34), and the *scribes* accuse the *Son of man* of blaspheming. (9:3)

8:26 *Little faith.* Faith is little when the object of faith grows little, when the stormy sea seems greater than Jesus (cf. 14:30-31); the great faith of the Canaanite woman saw a God great enough for the needs of all. (15:28).

8:28 *Gadarenes,* citizens of Gadara, a city of the Decapolis, about 5 miles southeast of the Sea of Galilee; the *country of the Gadarenes* extended to the shore of the Sea of Galilee.

8:29 *Before the time.* The demons recognize the *Son of God* and know that He is destined to overthrow them at the appointed *time,* at the end of days (Rv 20:10; cf. 19:20). They are startled and terrified to find that the future time of God's victory projects into the present in the person of Jesus. Both the devil and the demons always recognize Jesus for what He is (4:3; Mk 1:24), the divine Victor of the last days. (Jn 12:31; 14:30; 16:11)

8:32 *Perished.* Jesus thus unmasks the power of Satan and his demons as the absolute negation of created life; Satan is THE killer. (Jn 8:44)

9:1 *His own city,* Capernaum. (Mk 2:1)

9:3 *Blaspheming.* Unless Jesus is what His deeds reveal Him to be, the scribes are in the right; because they refused to accept that revelation, they finally condemned Him to death. (26:63-66)

9:5 *Easier to say.* Both healing and forgiveness by the effective word alone are divine actions, impossible for men; but a man can speak forgiveness without authority and escape being exposed; but the word of healing will either expose him or vindicate him because the result will be verifiable now, *on earth.*

9:8 *Men.* Matthew's comment looks forward to the apostolic church, where the word of forgiveness will be spoken with divine validity (Mt 18:15, 18-20). Forgiveness will no longer be an uncertain, far-off event of the Last Judgment but an on-earth present reality.

9:9-17 SECOND INTERLUDE: JESUS IS CALLER, PHYSICIAN, BRIDEGROOM

9:9-17 The mighty deeds of Jesus are all refractions of the one "great light" (4:16) which Jesus is. The sheer unmerited grace of His call is brilliantly evident here, where He *calls* the tax collector Matthew to be His disciple and apostle (9; 10:3; cf. 4:18-22; 1 Co 15:9-10). He is the Caller of *sinners* (13). The wholeness and the efficacy of His forgiveness appear in His table fellowship with sinners; He is the Lord their Healer (cf. Ex 15:26; Hos 11:3) who does not ignore their sin but deals with it effectually. His presence is the presence of the God who *desires mercy* even as He bestows mercy (13; Hos 6:6). He is the *bridegroom* (Jer 31:32) whose presence puts an end to the night of weeping and ushers in the morn of festal song (15). His coming is the dawn of the new age and brings "new things" (Is 48:6). He is not a *patch* that can be sewn on the old garments of Judaic piety; He is *new wine* that will break the old *wineskins,* the old forms that cannot contain Him—e.g., the temple will pass away because "something greater than the temple is here." (12:6)

9:10 *Tax collectors and sinners.* Notorious sinners are meant, men separated from the *righteous* (13) by the rigorous discipline of the synagog. Tax collectors were classed with them; the tax-farming contracts under which they worked gave ample opportunity for fraud, which they generally exploited. (Lk 3:13; 19:8)

9:14 *Fasting* expressed sorrow over sin and intensity of prayer. The presence of the forgiving Healer and Bridegroom puts an end to such sorrow and is God's answer to longing prayer.

9:15 *Taken away,* a first hint of Jesus' Passion (Is 53:8) and death and His return to His Father. In the days when the church awaits and longs for the return of her Lord, the sobriety and vigilance of her waiting may express itself in fasting.

9:18-34 FOUR DEEDS: DAVID'S SON AND LORD

9:18-34 Here, for the first time in Matthew, Jesus is addressed as *Son of David,* the Messiah (27; cf. 1:1-17). His deeds reveal Him as both David's Son and David's Lord (22:45), for He does what only divine authority can do: He "gives life to the dead" (18-26; Ro 4:17). He responds with healing to the unuttered petition of the woman who *suffered from a hemorrhage* (20-22). He opens *blind* eyes (27-31) and unseals the lips which Satan has sealed (32-34). He is the object of *faith* (22, 28, 29; cf. 8:10; 9:2). Opposition to Him necessarily takes the form of blasphemy; the *Pharisees* can seek to discredit Him only by calling diabolical what must otherwise be confessed as divine. His deeds cannot be explained away in human terms. (34; cf. 12:24)

9:20 The *fringe* (or tassel) on a garment was prescribed by the Law; it was to serve as a reminder of obedience to the Law (Nm 15:38-40). Jesus is "under the law." (Gl 4:4)

9:22 *Your faith,* not the touch or the fringe of the garment. Jesus purges her faith of traces of superstition as He responds to it.

9:23 *Flute players.* Lamentation for the dead was highly formal, involving the service of professionals; the flute was the preferred instrument of lamentation. (Jer 48:36)

9:35—10:42 The Commissioning and Sending of the Twelve

9:35—10:42 The Messiah of compassionate authority commissions and sends His 12 apostles to Israel to speak His message, to do His deeds, to share His sufferings, and to find their life by losing it for His sake.

9:35-38 THE MOTIVE FOR THE APOSTOLIC MISSION

9:35-38 Jesus' motive is His *compassion* (36). His people are like *sheep without a shepherd* (36), a people without a king to lead them and care for them. Man's need is God's opportunity; the *harassed and helpless* crowds are standing fields of grain to be reaped by God's mercy (37).

It is God's harvest; the apostle is apostle "by the will of God" (1 Co 1:1); God, the *Lord of the harvest, sends* him, and he undertakes and carries on his work with prayer to God. (38)

9:35 Cf. 4:23, where the same general description of Jesus' activity precedes Jesus' teaching; there it precedes His sending. The apostles are men whose will the Messiah has moulded (Mt 5—7), who must speak of what they have seen and heard. (Mt 8—9)

9:36 For the picture of the people of God as a flock and the Messiah ("David") as their Shepherd-King cf. Eze 34:22-24; 37:24.

10:1-4 COMMISSIONING OF THE 12 APOSTLES

10:1-4 Jesus equips the *apostles,* His authorized emissaries, with His own compassionate *authority.* The number *twelve* is emphasized (1, 2, 5). Twelve is the number of Israel, the twelve tribes; in sending out just twelve apostles Jesus is making it clear that He is offering the gift of the Kingdom and uttering the call to repentance to all Israel (4:17), to the whole people of God and through them to the whole new people of God that is to be. (Cf. Rv 7:4-8)

10:4 *Judas . . . who betrayed him.* The twofold reaction of Israel to the Messiah is reflected in the circle of the Twelve; one proves unfaithful and turns traitor.

10:5-15 THE APOSTOLIC MISSION: ITS SCOPE, CONTENT, SPIRIT, AND OUTCOME

10:5-15 The SCOPE (5-6) of the apostolic mission is determined by the scope of Jesus' own mission (cf. 15:24); Jesus goes the way that God has gone, through *Israel* to the Gentiles. The Gospel comes "to the Jew first" (Ro 1:16). When Jesus has fulfilled (to the death) His ministry to Israel (Ro 15:8), the apostolic mission becomes universal (28:19); when the Seed has fallen into the ground and died, the hour of the Gentiles has struck; lifted upon the cross the Son draws all men to Himself (Jn 12:20-24, 32). The CONTENT (7-8a) of the mission is likewise that of Jesus' own: the proclamation of the *kingdom* at hand in word and deed. The SPIRIT of the mission is the spirit in which Jesus worked—no small-souled care for self *(gold, silver, bag,* etc., 9-10) but His confident dependence on God, the Lord of the harvest, who will provide *food* (10) for His workmen, who give freely what they have freely received *(without paying,* literally "as a gift." The OUTCOME (11-15) of their mission is again like that of Jesus' own (chs. 8—9): faith and unbelief, acceptance and rejection, houses that are *worthy* (because they accept) and *houses* and *towns* that are *not worthy* (because they refuse), the *peace* of God and at the end the judgment of God. Such is the scope, content, spirit, and outcome of the mission.

10:12 *Salute it.* The common Jewish greeting was "Peace!" (Cf. Lk 10:5). That term is filled, when Jesus or His apostles pronounce it, with its full and true OT sense of soundness, wholeness, health, all's-well-between-God-and-man. (Cf. Nm 6:26)

10:14 *Shake off the dust,* as a sign that all communion with them is broken off. (Cf. Acts 13:51; 18:6)

10:15 *Sodom and Gomorrah.* The fate of these cities lived in men's memories as a signal instance of God's judgment on the wickedness of man because of his unbelief. (Cf. 11:24; Jude 7; Gn 18:16—19:28)

10:16-42 THE APOSTLE AND HIS LORD

10:16-42 The rest of the discourse makes plain and emphasizes what was implicit in the preceding words: the apostle is the living extension of his Lord. Through the apostle Christ works "by word and deed, by the power of signs and wonders, by the power of the Holy Spirit" (Ro 15:18-19; cf. 2 Co 13:3). The apostles' sufferings fill up the measure of "Christ's afflictions" (Cl 1:24); and they shall share in the vindication and triumph of the afflicted Christ. Whoever receives them, recieves Him and the Father who sent Him.

10:16-23 *I send you out* (the *I* is emphatic); the defenseless Servant Christ, 12:19 ("he cannot save himself," 27:42) sends them and they can expect to repeat His history: persecution (18), betrayal (21), hatred (22) await them. But suffering will no more frustrate their mission than it frustrated His. Persecution will enable them *to bear testimony* before kings (18), and the *Spirit* given them by their *Father* will inspire their words (20). They must *endure to the end,* but in the end they *will be saved* (22); the *Son of man* will *come* and put an end forever to their life of persecution and flight in the fulfillment of their mission to Israel. (23)

10:17 *Flog you in their synagogues.* Cf. 2 Co 11:24, where Paul speaks of the 39 lashes which he received five times "at the hands of the Jews."

10:20 *Spirit . . . speaking.* Cf. the promise of the Spirit as Counselor, Jn 15:26; 16:7-11.

10:22 *Saved,* in the Last Judgment. (Cf. Ro 5:9)

10:23 As an indication of the time of Jesus' return this verse is enigmatic, for Jesus Himself declared that time to be a total mystery, known only to the Father (24:36). But three things are clear: (a) Jesus makes the mission to Israel a perpetual obligation of the apostles and the apostolic church; (b) the apostles need not expose their lives needlessly but are to be *wise as serpents* (16; cf. 7:6) in this too (cf. Paul's flights as recorded in Acts); (c) the coming of the Son of Man is the hope that sustains the apostle in his difficult and dangerous mission.

10:24-33 *Disciple* and *teacher.* The enmity that met Jesus did not shrink even from blasphemy; men called His divine work the work of "the prince of demons" (9:34); they identified Jesus with *Beelzebul* (25). Jesus therefore prepares His disciples for the worst; and He arms them with the best, the triple armor of His *have no fear* (26, 28, 31). As they are members of the *household* of Christ and bear the reproaches of Christ, so they shall share in His vindication and victory. When their proclamation shall have made the *hidden* Christ *known* (26) and the time of judgment comes, Christ will *acknowledge* them before the *Father* (32) and lead them to glory. They will triumph over death; their enemies, who *kill the body but cannot kill the soul* (28), shall find that Christ and the Father are mightier than death. Christ will *deny* those who denied Him, and He who *can destroy both soul and body in hell* (28) will be their Judge.

10:25 *Beelzebul,* the prince of demons (9:34), Satan. (12:24, 26)

10:34-39 *Not peace, but a sword.* Christ is the Prince of Peace (Is 9:6). He brings peace indeed; but it is God's peace, which separates men from evil. And since men cling to their evil and refuse God's peace (cf. 12-15), the coming of the Kingdom in Christ means for them judgment, the *sword* (34) which divides and separates. The Kingdom cuts across the closest ties (35-36) and claims the sacrifice of kin (37), of honor and life *(cross,* the criminal's death, 38). For only in Christ is *life* to be found, real life, everlasting life (39; cf. 8:22); to cling to the life of this world, the doomed and forfeited life of man dead in his sins (Eph 2:1), means losing the only real life there is.

10:37 *Not worthy,* because he has refused the gift of Christ. (Cf. 13)

10:40-42 *He who receives you receives me.* Christ identifies the disciple with Himself, and Himself with God *(him who sent me,* 40). Christ, *prophet, righteous man, disciple*—these are all servants of God; God watches over His servants zealously (cf. 30) and will reward even the slightest and most effortless kindness shown to them *(cup of cold water,* 42). The apostles go forth in the consciousness that they shall scatter blessings as they go.

11:1—13:52 THIRD GROUP OF MESSIANIC DEEDS AND WORDS

11:1—13:52 The contradicted Messiah conceals the Kingdom from those who have rejected it (those who *have not,* 13:12) and further reveals it to those who have accepted it (those who *have,* 13:12). The disciples are taught to recognize the Messiah in the contradicted Servant and to understand the *secrets* of the Kingdom. (12:18-21; 13:11)

11:1—12:50 The Contradicted Messiah

11:1—12:50 When Jesus sent out the Twelve as His representatives, He taught them to expect the contradiction and enmity of man (ch. 10). In this section the root of man's contradiction is laid bare: man wants to master God. In one way or another all Jesus' contemporaries try to impose their will on Him: *John* the Baptist (11:2-3), this *generation* generally (11:16-19), *the wise and understanding* (11:25-30), the *Pharisees* (12:1-14; 12:22-32), *scribes and Pharisees* (12:38-42). Against this background of questioning, offense, and opposition the Christ looms up in fearful majesty—to oppose Him is to invoke the judgment of God both now and hereafter (11:6, 19, 20-24, 25; 12:27, 30-32, 33-37, 42, 43-45). And the greatness of the divine work which He has come to do becomes all the more apparent in the face of man's doubts and opposition. (Cf. 11:5 note; 11:11 note; 11:21, 23, 25-27; 12:6, 8, 18-21, 28, 41-42)

11:1-15 JOHN'S QUESTION FROM PRISON

11:1-15 John's question is the mildest example of man's attempt to impose his will on God. Even he, imprisoned now and helpless, wavers concerning *the deeds of the Christ* (2) and his question (3) suggests that Jesus ought to fulfill John's prophecy of the Mightier One who comes with Spirit and fire and executes judgment NOW when John expects it and as John expects it (3:11-12). On the other hand, John's question is addressed in faith to Jesus Himself; and if Jesus is not the Comforting One, John is willing to wait *(shall we look for another?).* He is still willing to submit to a Christ who does not fulfill his expectations at once. And so Jesus warns him gently (6) and answers his question. Jesus' answer (4-5) is couched in the language of the OT (Is 29:18-19; 35:5-6; 61:1), which indicates that the *deeds of the Christ* are in reality the acts of God and God's Servant which God has promised for the last days. God is present in Jesus, and Jesus is indeed *he who is to come.* (2)

John is therefore still one who has, and to him more is given (13:12). Jesus vindicates the Baptist (7-15) by reproaching the crowds for treating him as a mere spectacle to *behold* (7), a great man to *see* (8) instead of hearing and obeying his prophetic word. John is *more than a prophet,* Jesus tells them (9); he is truly the fulfillment of OT prophecy, the *messenger* and the returning *Elijah* whom the Lord had promised to send before "the great and terrible day of the Lord," the Day of Judgment (Ml 3:1; 4:5; cf. Mt 17:11; Lk 1:17). John is the greatest among those *born of women;* he heralds the advent of the Kingdom. (11-12)

11:2 *In prison.* Cf. 14:3-4.

11:3 *Who is to come.* Cf. 3:11.

11:5 The diseases listed are those which excluded a Jew from the official temple services. Jesus in restoring men to health restores them to the fellowship of the worshiping community.

11:6 *Takes no offense,* by refusing to believe or by falling away.

11:9 *To see a prophet.* God's prophets are to be heard.

11:11 *Least.* Literally "less," "smaller." This is usually interpreted to mean that even the least of those who live to see the Kingdom come are more highly privileged than John. But it seems preferable to see in the word a reference to Jesus Himself: He who is an *offense* (6) in His littleness (as the Servant who uses His power in the service of mercy to others) is greater than John, for in Him the Kingdom itself is present. (Cf. 12:28)

11:12 *Kingdom . . . has suffered violence.* John is in prison, doomed to die (14:10); the apostles go out "as sheep in the midst of wolves" (10:16); the Pharisees blaspheme Jesus' work (9:34) and plot to destroy Him (12:14). But the fact that the

Kingdom suffers violence is evidence that it is no longer a hope but a present reality.

11:14 *Elijah.* Cf. 17:10; Lk 1:17.

11:15 *He who has ears.* Cf. 13:9, 43. This solemn injunction, thrice repeated in this section, marks the seriousness of the hour, when he who will not *hear* (in the full sense of hearing, heeding, and obeying) will become as one who has not. Then God's judgment will take from him *even what he has.* (13:12)

11:16-19 THE PETULANT CHILDREN

11:16-19 Jesus pictures His contemporaries as children who want to call the tunes and feel snubbed when their partners do not dance to them. So they are towards God, dissatisfied with the prophet John because he is too stern, and censorious toward Jesus because He is too forgiving. They want to impose their will on God. The divine *wisdom* which sent both the austere prophet of repentance and the freely forgiving *Son of man* will be vindicated *(justified)* by the outcome of *her deeds,* the results, when those who have heeded both John and Jesus shall enter into the Kingdom. (Cf. 21:31-32)

11:20-24 WOE UPON THE CITIES OF THE LAKE

11:20-24 *Capernaum,* Jesus' "own city" (9:1), and the neighboring towns of *Chorazin* and *Bethsaida* were highly favored; in Jesus' *mighty works* God was wooing them, seeking to lead them to repentance (cf. Ro 2:4). They have not accepted God's proffered gift; they shall lose even what they have and be visited by a judgment more severe than that of those notoriously wicked ancient cities, *Tyre, Sidon,* and *Sodom.*

11:23 *Hades,* realm of the dead. Jesus uses the language with which Isaiah had denounced the godless and insolent king of Babylon. (Is 14:13, 15)

11:25-30 THE SON WHO KNOWS THE FATHER

11:25-30 Jesus *knows* and is known by the Father (27); since "knowing" in Biblical usage involves personal communion between the knower and the known, Jesus here claims for Himself a unique, mutual, total communion with the *Father,* the *Lord of heaven and earth* who has *delivered all things* to Him (27)—the healing of all disease, victory over death, the Good News, the gracious inbreaking of God's kingdom. In the strength of this communion He thanks His Father for so disposing His revelation that His *gracious will* (26) is made manifest in it; the simple and unskillled *(babes)* can and do receive it, though the wisdom of the wise makes them stumble over it (they too would master God, 25). The *wise and understanding* are opposed to the Son; if scribe and Pharisee are turned against the Son, that means that He will "fail" and perish. Jesus, the obedient Son and Servant, *thanks* God for that "failure" and continues steadfast on the course which will bring Him death. He chooses still to reveal the Father; He invites men struggling under the burden of the Law and their sin to come to Him for *rest* (28), to find rest and peace for their muddled lives under the beneficent discipline of His *easy yoke,* to take up the *burden* which is *light* because He has borne it before them and for them (29-30). In the midst of contradiction Jesus reveals Himself as "God of God . . . for us men and our salvation came down from heaven . . . incarnate by the Holy Ghost . . . made man."

11:29 *Yoke.* The rabbis spoke of the "yoke of the Law"; Jesus with His yoke is the "end of the law." (Ro 10:4)

12:1-21 LORD OF THE SABBATH AND SERVANT OF GOD

12:1-21 In the face of contradiction the Christ looms large in His merciful majesty. Reproached by the *Pharisees* for letting His disciples "thresh" (1) on the sacred *sabbath,* He recalls the example of *David's* freedom over against the temple-cultus—if David, the man after God's heart (1 Sm 13:14), had this freedom, how much more THE Son of David (1:1), the Messiah (1-4)? Jesus claims even more for Himself: He is *greater than the temple* (6), a higher and fuller presence of God among His people than God's house has been; and if His disciples do work on the Sabbath as they attend upon Him, they no more *profane* the Sabbath than the *priests* who offer the burnt offering on the Sabbath at God's command (Nm 28:9-10). If the Pharisees had an ear for the God who desires *mercy* more than *sacrifice* (Hos 6:6), they would not condemn the *guiltless* disciples, who attend Jesus on His mission of mercy (7), and they would not be offended at the *Son of man* who is *lord of the sabbath* (8) and uses His divine authority *to do good* on the Sabbath (12), while those who carp at Him plot *to destroy him* on the Sabbath which they guard so jealously. (14)

Jesus uses His authority solely in the service of mercy; He will not destroy His destroyers but withdraws before their enmity (15). He will not even capitalize on His deeds of mercy to achieve fame (16), for He is the selfless Servant of the Lord who goes His way of quiet ministration to the hopelessly distressed *(bruised reed . . . smoldering wick,* 20) and waits for God to give Him *victory* (20). That victory means that by the power of the *Spirit* (18) the cause and revelation of God *(justice,* 18, 20) shall prevail and shall avail for all men *(Gentiles,* 18, 21).

12:3 *What David did.* 1 Sm 21:1-6.

12:4 *Bread of the Presence.* The 12 loaves of unleavened bread placed fresh every Sabbath on a table in the Holy Place of the temple as an offering. The old loaves were eaten by the priests (Ex 25:30; Lv 24:5-9)

12:5 *In the law.* Nm 28:9-10.

12:7 *I desire mercy.* Hos 6:6; Mt 9:13.

12:18-21 Is 42:1-4. This is the first of the so-called Servant Songs in Isaiah, which portray a Deliverer sent by the Lord whose quiet, obedient ministry takes Him through contradiction, suffering, and rejection down into an atoning death for the salvation of both Israel and the Gentiles. Is 42:1-9; 49:1-7; 50:4-9; 52:13—53:12; some would include 61:1-4 also.

12:22-37 ULTIMATE CONTRADICTION OF THE CHRIST

12:22-37 Jesus' power over the *demons* moves the *people* to recognize in Him the Messiah *(Son of David,* 23). The Pharisees meet this dawning recognition with blasphemy; they assert that Jesus is in league with *Beelzebul;* they call the divine satanic (24). Jesus in His mercy seeks to win them still. "Your charge," He says, "is folly; Satan will not willingly destroy his own *kingdom* (25-26). Your charge is a self-contradiction; for your *sons,* pious men of your own group, cast out demons too, and you do not call their deeds satanic but works of piety. These *sons . . . shall be your judges* (27); they will testify that only the power of God can overcome the kingdom of Satan. You must recognize that in My deeds the *Spirit of God* is at work, not the unclean spirits of Satan; in My deeds *the kingdom of God has come upon you* (28). God is establishing His reign, promised for the last days, among you now. My power over demons is the fruit of My victory over Satan in the Temptation; I have broken the power of Satan and am plundering Satan's house." (29)

Jesus meets their contradiction with an urgent call to repentance; there is no room for contradition; there is not even room for neutrality (30); a man must either gather the flock, the new people of God, with the Shepherd Messiah (cf. 9:36 note), or else he *scatters* the sheep of God (30). If a man contradicts the Messiah working in the power of the Spirit, he is in danger of committing the ultimate sin of *blasphemy against the Spirit,* the sin which *will not be forgiven* because it makes repentance impossible (31-32). There is still room for repentance, and so Jesus renews the Baptist's call to repentance (33-37; cf. 3:7-10). They can still become *good trees* bearing *good fruit* through God's gift of repentance if they will accept the gift; they can cease being a *brood of vipers* and become *good men* bringing *good* words out of the *good treasure* of their repentant *hearts.* But the hour is the critical hour, for every *careless* word spoken by men against the Messiah will come under God's scrutiny in the impending *judgment.* (33-37)

12:24 *By Beelzebul.* Cf. 9:34; 10:25. The form given here is to be preferred to the more familiar Beelzebu*b* as a designation for Satan.

12:31-32 The *blasphemy against the Spirit* is conscious, stubborn, malicious opposition to divine revelation which becomes unpardonable because it cuts off the possibility of repentance. Notice that just here, when Jesus issues this most terrifying of warnings, He stresses the fullness of God's forgiveness. Paul spoke many *a word against the Son of man* when he persecuted the church; had he persisted in this after the risen Lord appeared to him, he would have been guilty of the unpardonable sin. (Cf. 1 Ti 1:13, 16)

12:33 *Tree . . . fruit.* Cf. 3:10.

12:34 *Brood of vipers.* Cf. 3:7.

12:38-42 DEMAND FOR A SIGN; THE SIGN OF JONAH

12:38-42 At least some of the *Pharisees* and their theological leaders, the *scribes,* remained unmoved by Jesus' warning. Their demand for a sign is a mark of their unwillingness to repent; they are an *adulterous generation* (39), men who will not commit themselves unreservedly to God's love and so come to repentance and faith in God's Messiah on God's terms. They will not accept the given revelation of Jesus' triumph over Satan and demand a special revelation, an overwhelming *sign* (cf. 16:1, "sign from heaven") which will make repentance and faith unnecessary. They are like their fathers in the wilderness who put God to the proof even though they had seen His work (Ps 95:9). They seek to master God, to dictate to Him. And Jesus, who rejects no petition, rejects their demand; no sign shall be given them except the *sign of Jonah,* no sign except the Servant Messiah who goes into death for His people's sins *(in the heart of the earth,* 40), no sign that will relieve them of the need to repent (41). The *men of Nineveh* and the *queen of the South,* who acted on the revelation given them in their day, will appear in the Last Judgment to bear witness against the men who refused the revelation given them in One who is a *greater* Spokesman for God than Jonah and a *greater* King than Solomon, with a *wisdom* far surpassing Solomon's.

12:40-41 Jon 1:17; 3:5.

12:40 *Three days and three nights.* Not intended as a prediction of the exact length of time that Jesus would be in the grave. After three days visible corruption set it (cf. Jn 11:39); God will not let His "Holy One see corruption." (Acts 2:27)

12:42 *Queen of the South.* 1 K 10:1-10.

12:43-50 RETURNING DEMON AND FAMILY OF JESUS

12:43-50 No neutrality is possible (cf. 12:30) over against Jesus. These two brief sections present the alternatives which confront men in Him. Those who would remain uncommitted *(this evil generation,* 45), accepting the benefits of His works but refusing to repent and believe, are like a healed demoniac; their heart is an empty house that invites the return of the augmented powers of evil, and their *last state . . . becomes worse than the first* (45). Man is never so open to the power of Satan as when he has been touched by the Christ but has not been filled by Him. Those *who do the will of my Father in heaven* (50), who accept the Christ and become good trees bearing good fruit (33) by God's planting (15:13)—for them the door of the Father's house is opened wide; they become the true *brothers* and *sisters* of Jesus, no less. (Cf. Ro 8:29)

12:43 The *unclean spirit* exists only to destroy God's handiwork; when driven out from man, the spirit is desolate and restless.

12:50 *Sister.* Woman has her place of undiminished honor in the family of God. (Gl 3:28)

13:1-52 The Secrets of the Kingdom

13:1-52 The parables of Jesus are plain, utilizing materials familiar to every Galilean. The people were familiar with the parable form of teaching; their rabbis used this form. And yet Jesus' parables serve to conceal as well as reveal (11-15). They conceal the *secrets of the kingdom* (11) from those who have rejected the Kingdom as revealed in the words and works of Jesus the Servant, from those who do not hold and treasure *(has not,* 12) what God has given them already in the OT, in John the Baptist, in Jesus' plain words and eloquent acts. The parables are unintelligible to them because they have thrown away the key to them, Jesus. Because they refuse to see in Jesus the coming of the Kingdom (12:28), they cannot (and by God's judgment on their unbelief shall not) see that He is sowing the Word of the Kingdom (13:3-9), that He is the Sower of God's *good seed* (37), the *treasure* of all treasures (44). Isaiah's word that hardened Israel in her unbelief finds a fresh fulfillment in them (14). On the other hand, those who *have* (hold and treasure) what God's previous revelation has given them are enriched by the parables; *more* is *given* them, and they have in *abundance.* (12, 51-52)

13:1-9 THE PARABLE OF THE SOWER

13:1-9 As Jesus' own interpretation (18-23) makes plain, the Kingdom comes in the unspectacular and vulnerable form of the *word* (19), which can be *devoured* (4), *scorched* (6), and *choked* (7). But this "failure" of the Word indicts the soil, not the sower or the seed. Man is responsible when confronted by God's Word and guilty when he fails to use it. Therefore the stern warning at the close. (9)

13:10-17 TO HIM WHO HAS . . . FROM HIM WHO HAS NOT

13:10-17 See note on 1-52 at beginning of chapter.

13:11 *Secrets.* The same word is also sometimes translated as "mysteries." See note on Cl 1:26-27.

13:14-15 Is 6:9-10. Both in Isaiah and here these words are not an eternal decree which predestines some men for salvation and dooms others to unbelief; they describe God's reaction to man's unbelief. What man has refused to hear for his salvation, he is doomed to hear for his hardening and condemnation.

13:16 *Blessed . . . your eyes . . . your ears.* Not hearing and unbelief are man's guilt; hearing and believing, however, are not merit on man's part but God's grace to him.

13:18-23 EXPLANATION OF PARABLE OF THE SOWER

13:23 *Understands,* comprehends, makes his own, so that his will and action are controlled by it. (Cf. Cl 1:9)

Hundredfold . . . sixty . . . thirty. God's seed thrives on good soil but not with a chemical uniformity; the response is personal and individual, for God "apportions to each one individually as he wills" (1 Co 12:11), and each man is individually responsible.

13:24-30 PARABLE OF THE WEEDS AND THE WHEAT

13:24-30 See Jesus' explanation, 36-43. God's action in establishing His kingdom provokes the counterthrust of the Evil One, who sows weeds where God sows His wheat, weeds that look like wheat. The disciples' task is not to institute an inquisition to destroy the weeds but to remember Jesus' words, "Judge not!" (7:1), and to await the hour of God's judgment and to look forward in patience to the time of their own glory. (43)

13:25 *Weeds,* probably bearded darnel, which looks like wheat until grown.

13:26 For the idea that the satanic appears in the guise of the divine cf. 16:22-23; 2 Co 11:3-5, 13-15. In the temptation of Jesus the Tempter quotes Scripture. (4:6)

13:31-33 PARABLES OF MUSTARD SEED AND LEAVEN

13:31-33 The homely language of garden and kitchen is used to warn men against being offended at the slight beginnings of the Kingdom as present in Jesus (cf. 11:6). The *seed* and the *leaven* have in them God's creative power and will achieve God's purposes of full growth and total penetration; the end is potentially present in the beginning. On this kingdom men may confidently fix their faith and hope.

13:32 *Becomes a tree,* etc. Jesus' language here is an echo of certain OT passages in which the tree is a symbol of worldwide dominion. (Eze 17:23; 31:5-6; Dn 4:9-12, 20-22)

13:33 *Three measures.* A large mass of dough, each measure being about 3 gallons.

13:34-35 "I WILL OPEN MY MOUTH IN PARABLES"

13:34-35 Ps 78:2 is quoted as being fulfilled. In Matthew the word *fulfil* covers a much wider range of meaning than what we connect with it (a prediction, promise, or command is "fulfilled"). Here the connection seems to be this: Ps. 78 recounts the history of Israel as the history of Israel's persistent rebellion against the ever-renewed manifestation of God's grace, a rebellion which makes that history an enigma and is marked as such by the psalmist *(parable* can also mean puzzle, enigma). That history of ungrateful revolt is climaxed in Israel's rejection of Jesus, in the people's unbelief which provokes the judgment of Jesus' speaking to them in parables (13). And so the word spoken by the psalmist reaches its full utterance, is "fulfilled," now when Jesus speaks in parables which doom the impenitent and unbelieving.

13:36-43 EXPLANATION OF PARABLE OF THE WEEDS

13:36 *Went into the house.* The rest of the discourse is spoken to the *disciples* alone.

13:37 *Son of man.* Jesus portrays Himself in terms of divine majesty; the *Son of man* owns the world (38), is Lord of the angels (41), and executes the Last Judgment (41-42); yet He remains the Servant and obedient Son who does all "to the glory of God the Father." (43; Ph 2:11; cf. 1 Co 15:28)

13:44-46 PARABLES OF THE HIDDEN TREASURE AND THE ONE PEARL

13:44-46 This pair of parables has particular significance for Jesus' disciples. They have left all to follow Him (4:22), and they can see ever more plainly that following the contradicted Christ will involve painful renunciation. Is this renunciation worth while? Jesus' answer is: The gain of the Kingdom is so great that repentance and renunciation become a *joy.* (44)

13:47-50 PARABLE OF THE NET

13:47-50 The coming of the Kingdom is to bring both grace and judgment; the Christ is to work with both Spirit and fire (3:11). Lest His disciples grow doubtful about the reality of the Kingdom and impatient for the judgment which will *separate* (49) the evil from the righteous (as John the Baptist was tempted to do, 11:2-3), Jesus reminds them that God's judgment will come *at the close of the age* (49), after the nets of His grace have swept all waters and have *gathered fish of every kind.* (47)

13:51-52 THE SCRIBE TRAINED FOR THE KINGDOM

13:51-52 The disciple will be the *scribe* for the new people of God who call Jesus Lord; he will expound God's Word and will for men. And for this his sufficiency is from God. What the parables have given him will be part of his treasure, from which he can draw at need. And since he "has" that, more will be given him; when his ministry grows broader and more complex, he will ever and again find riches of revelation for his need. The theological riches of the NT writings are evidence that Jesus kept this promise to His own, as He did with all His promises.

13:53—18:35 FOURTH GROUP OF MESSIANIC DEEDS AND WORDS

13:53—18:35 Toward the new Messianic people of God, the church: The Messiah separates His disciples from the old Israel, which is rejecting Him, deepens His communion with His own, and shapes their relationship to one another in the fellowship of the church.

13:53—14:21 THE REJECTED, COMPASSIONATE MESSIAH

13:53—14:21 Jesus is rejected in *his own country* and becomes an object of superstitious fear at the court of Herod, who senses that the *powers* which he had attempted to destroy in executing John the Baptist threaten him anew in Jesus. What is happening in the village and the palace is symptomatic of what is happening in all Israel: the men of Israel are rejecting their Messiah. Jesus the unresisting Servant (12:19) *withdraws.* But even now He demonstrates His unbroken will of *compassion* for His people; He *heals the sick* and invites men to the fellowship of His table.

14:1 *Tetrarch* originally meant the ruler of the fourth part of a region, then came to be used more generally as title of a petty dependent prince such as *Herod* Antipas, who succeeded his father Herod the Great as ruler over a part of that monarch's kingdom, namely Galilee. (Lk 3:1)

14:3 *Philip,* not the tetrarch of Lk 3:1 but Philip's half brother Herod, who is not called Philip in other ancient records. Perhaps the reading given in RSV note *l (his brother's wife)* is to be preferred.

14:13 *Heard this,* namely Herod's reaction to His fame. For the threat posed by this reaction on the part of the man who had executed John cf. Lk 13:31.

14:15-21 Matthew records the miracle of the feeding of the 5,000 as well as that of the 4,000 (15:32-38) in a section which culminates in Jesus' discourse on fellowship (ch. 18). The common meal was more significant for the man of the ancient East generally, and for the Jew particularly, than it is for us; it established fellowship, and to violate this bond was the grossest kind of infidelity (cf. Jn 13:18; Ps 41:9). The Pharisees' objection to Jesus' association with sinners made a point of the fact that He ate with them. (9:11; Lk 15:2)

14:16 *You give them.* Here and in the feeding of the 4,000 the disciples for the first time assist in the creative deed of Jesus; they are being taught the ministry of fellowship.

14:22-36 JESUS COMES ACROSS THE WATERS

14:22-36 Though the fellowship of the meal comes to an end, Jesus' fellowship with His own does not end. He comes to them across stormy waters and responds to the prayer of the faith that seeks Him with His enabling command, *Come.* Only *little faith* (which loses sight of the greatness of the commanding Christ) interrupts fellowship with Him. Even little faith can cry to Him and be *saved;* He is the *Lord, the Son of God,* ready to hear and mighty to save. He will be with them "always to the close of the age" (28:20). And as He is to His own, He is ready to be to all; all may *touch* His healing, seamless dress and be *made well.* (34-36)

14:25 The *fourth watch* was the last of the four periods into which the *night* was divided.

15:1-20 THE TRADITION OF THE ELDERS: WHAT DEFILES A MAN?

15:1-20 Jesus separates His disciples from the *tradition of the elders,* which interpreted and expanded the Law, often in such a way that it enabled a man to *transgress the commandment of God* with a show of legality. Jesus leads His own beyond this hypocrisy, even beyond the whole legal conception of cultic purity, to a worship in purity of *heart:* Not what a man eats (cultically unclean food) but what a man thinks, desires, and speaks *defiles a man* and makes him unfit for worship and fellowship with God and his fellowman. Jsus is here transcending the dietary laws of the OT (Lv 11; Nm 19; Dt 14) but is at the same time affirming the will of the Law: that there be a pure, undefiled people of God to worship Him.

15:2 *Tradition of the elders,* the body of interpretation of (and additions to) the Law which had grown up around the Law in the Jewish schools. It enjoyed a prestige and authority practically equal to that of the Law itself. (Cf. Gl 1:14).

15:4 Ex 20:12; 21:17.

15:5-6 *Given to God.* A son might declare that the property which he was in duty bound to use for the support of his parents had been dedicated by him to God and was not therefore available for secular uses. The sacredness of such a vow was utilized to withhold support from parents, even if the property was not actually given to God. Thus a pretext of religion served to *make void the word of God.*

15:8-9. Cf. Is 29:13-14, which threatens divine judgment on the teachers of the people. For Jesus' full indictment of Pharisees and scribes see Mt 23.

15:13 For the picture of the true man of God as a *plant planted* by the *Father* cf. Is 60:21; Jn 15:2; Cl 2:7, "rooted . . . in Him" (Christ).

15:15 *Parable,* the pointed saying of v. 11.

15:21-28 THE CANAANITE WOMAN: GREAT IS YOUR FAITH

15:21-28 Jesus remains faithful to Israel even when Israel proves unfaithful to God by rejecting the Christ (cf. Ro 15:8). He upholds Israel's prerogative over against the Gentiles (24, 26). He oversteps the limitations of His mission only in response to *faith.* His help and healing is available "to everyone who has faith," whether Jew or Gentile (Ro 1:16). Such incidents as these point forward to the command to make disciples of all nations (28:19) and to the universal church.

15:28 *Great . . . faith.* Her faith is great, for she submits wholly to God and assents wholly to His way (through Israel to the world, 27), sees that the table which God set for Israel is rich enough to supply all nations (27), and is willing to accept God's grace on the lowest terms of beggary—she can pray from under the table.

15:29-39 UNFAILING MERCY OF THE MESSIAH

15:29-39 Again (cf. 14:14, 34-36) Jesus heals the sick and suffering members of His people to the glory of the *God of Israel.* Again (cf. 14:15-21) He invites thousands to the fellowship of the common meal—*in the desert,* where the Lord once fed His people with manna. In Jesus God, the Healer of Israel, the Lord who cared for Israel in the wilderness, is present for the salvation of His people.

15:39 *Magadan,* place of uncertain location on the Sea of Galilee.

16:1-28 YOU ARE THE CHRIST: I WILL BUILD MY CHURCH

16:1-28 Jesus separates His disciples from all Judaism. He separates them from the Pharisees and Sadducees who, for all their differences, unite in demanding from Jesus *a sign from heaven;* they ignore God's given revelation and demand a special revelation for themselves, thus disclosing themselves as an *evil and adulterous generation.* The Christ cannot give Himself to their evil and divided hearts (1-4). Jesus warns His disciples against the *leaven . . . of the teaching of the Pharisees and Sadducees;* that teaching might otherwise insinuate itself into their hearts and corrupt their faith. (5-12)

To those who do not demand a sign but live by the given revelation of God, the supreme revelation is given; the Father *reveals* to them *the Christ, the Son of the living God.* And they hear from the lips of the Christ His promise concerning the new people of God *(my church)* which shall triumph over death. In the building of this church the disciples are given a fundamental place as believers in and confessors of the Christ. (13-20)

The confession binds the disciples to the Servant Christ who goes in hiddenness (cf. 20) and shame to His *cross* and resurrection in obedience to God's will; to oppose His way to the cross is satanic opposition to God. Jesus makes His cross the pattern of life for all who are united in His fellowship: The disciple is to *find his life* by *losing* it for the sake of the Christ, who will return in glory to *repay every man for what he has done.* (21-28)

16:3 *The signs of the times,* the words and works of Jesus which reveal that God's kingdom has drawn near.

16:4 *Adulterous,* unfaithful to God. Cf. Hos 1—3; Ja 4:4.

Sign of Jonah. Cf. 12:38-40.

16:5-12 The story of the forgotten bread remains obscure for us in detail, but the main point is clear. The disciples are preoccupied with the food for their bodies, even after seeing how Jesus' mighty grace can supply loaves in abundance. Jesus is concerned about the food for their faith, which the *leaven . . . of the teaching of the Pharisees and Sadducees* would corrupt.

16:13 *Caesarea Philippi* marks the northernmost limits of Jesus' ministry in Galilee; from here His course will be southward toward Jerusalem and the cross. Now Jesus binds His disciples to Himself as the Christ who must die. (Cf. 16:21; 17:22; 20:17-19)

16:14 Jesus separates His disciples not only from those who oppose Him but also from those whose "appreciation" of Him falls short of confessing Him as the Christ. They can see in Him One whose coming prepares for the

Kingdom, but not the Christ in whose person the Kingdom comes.

John the Baptist. Cf. 14:2.

Elijah. Cf. Ml 4:5; Mt 11:14; 17:10-13.

16:17 *Bar-Jona,* son of Jonah. Simon's flesh-and-blood father could not reveal the Christ to him.

16:18 *Peter . . . rock.* As the RSV notes indicate, Jesus is playing on the sense of the name *(rock)* which He gave Simon (Mk 3:16; Lk 6:14; Jn 1:42). In the building which the Christ rears, Peter (and the disciples for whom he speaks in his confession) will have a fundamental position; the apostles constitute the foundation of the structure (cf. Eph 2:20; Rv 21:14). This position signifies not lordship but ministry; the apostles serve (2 Co 1:24; Mt 20:26; 1 Co 3:5; Cl 1:25). The Father reveals; the Christ builds the church, gives the promise of life, and bestows authority. The apostles remain strictly subordinate to the divine action which takes place through them (Ro 15:18); Peter is a rock because the Christ employs him as foundation stone.

Powers of death (gates of Hades). The gates of the world of the dead which do not open to release the inhabitants of Hades will not be strong enough to hold back those whom the Christ calls; the followers of Jesus will lose their life for His sake (25), but they shall find their life in the resurrection of the dead.

16:19 *Keys,* symbols of authority. (Cf. Is 22:21-22; Rv 1:18; 3:7)

Bind . . . loose. The apostolic witness to Christ, the Gospel, will be a divinely valid word *(in heaven).* Those who reject it will be *bound* by it, held fast under the judgment of God; those who accept and believe it will be set free *(loosed)* by it for the eternal liberty of sons of God (17:26; cf. 2 Co 2:14-17; Jn 20:23). The apostles receive this authority not as something to be held exclusively by them but in order to bestow it on the church. (Cf. 18:17-18)

16:20 *Tell no one.* The action of God will at His time and in His way proclaim and glorify the Christ. (28:18; Ph 2:9-11)

16:23 *Satan.* In his attempt to dissuade Jesus from going the Servant's way to the cross, Peter has become the voice of the Tempter (4:1-10), a *hindrance* to Jesus on His way of obedience to the Father.

On the side of God. God wills man's redemption; *men* seek their own ease and advantage. In Jesus' judgment this self-seeking will of man is satanic (Cf. Ja 3:15)

16:24 *Cross* is to be taken literally: loss of honor and life for the sake of Christ and the Gospel.

16:28 *See the Son of man coming in his kingdom.* Peter, James, and John had a foretaste of this when they beheld Jesus' transfiguration. (17:1-8)

17:1-27 TRANSFIGURED BEFORE THEM

17:1-27 The disciples did not demand a sign from heaven; they believed in the Christ, the Son of the living God, on the basis of the revelation which the Father GAVE them. To them the sign from heaven is freely given. They are privileged to behold the Son of the living God in His heavenly splendor (2), to see the Christ whom His people reject receiving the witness of the Law and the prophets *(Moses, Elijah,* 3), to hear the voice from the *bright cloud* attest the *beloved Son* and Servant (5, cf. 3:17). They learn, too, that the Christ "must suffer" (16:21); they cannot hold Him on the mountain of His glory (4). Jesus descends to resume His hidden way to the cross (9), to the world in which the contradiction of the scribes awaits Him (10), where the fate of *Elijah (John the Baptist)* is a prediction of His own end (11-13). He must face and deal with the agony of demon-ridden man and His disciples' littleness of faith (14-21). *The Son of man is* destined *to be delivered into the hands of men* (22). His disciples are *distressed* at that (23); but He goes in free obedience to His death, as the free Son who sets all *sons free* (26). He frees His disciples from the old doomed Israel by freeing them from the temple tax imposed on all adult members of the people (24-27)

17:3 *Moses and Elijah* appear together in the last chapter of the last prophet of the OT, Ml 4:4-6. The disciples see confirmed Jesus' claim that He is Fulfiller of the Law and the prophets. (5:17)

17:4 *Make three booths.* Peter deemed it natural that the glory of this vision (9) should continue, that the Christ remain *transfigured,* not that He descend and resume His way to the cross. (Cf. 16:22)

17:5 *Bright cloud,* symbol of the gracious presence of God. (Cf. Ex 40:34)

My beloved Son. Cf. 3:17 and note there. *Listen to him* marks Jesus as THE Prophet foretold in Dt 18:15-19. (Cf. Acts 3:22-23)

17:9 Cf. 16:20 and the note there.

17:10 *First Elijah must come.* According to Ml 4:5-6, Elijah was to come before "the great and terrible day of the Lord comes" and prepare the people for His coming by leading them to repentance. The *scribes* argued that Jesus could not be the Messiah, since Elijah had not yet appeared. In response to this, Jesus repeats His assertion of 11:14 that the prophecy concerning Elijah has been fulfilled in John the Baptist. (Cf. Lk 1:17)

17:20 *Little faith . . . faith as a grain of mustard seed.* Faith is little when its object is small—as here, where the disciples could not envision an absent Christ strong enough to overcome a present demon. Even the most limited *(grain)* faith can lay hold of the whole power of God and *move mountains.*

17:24 *The tax.* The term used in the Greek makes it plain that the temple tax is meant. This tax was exacted from every male Jew, whether living in Palestine or abroad, from his 20th year onward. If the disciples are free of this, their freedom from Judaism is complete.

17:27 *Not to give offense.* A Jew who refused to pay the temple tax would appear to his countrymen as an outright atheist and could never hope to gain a hearing for the Gospel; therefore the disciples, though "free from all men," are to pay the tax, becoming "to the Jews . . . as a Jew, in order to win Jews" (1 Co 9:19-20). The Book of Acts shows that the first Christians of Jerusalem were obedient to their Lord in this. (Acts 2:46-47; 3:1)

First fish. Their Father will provide the money they need for the payment of the tax, for also the sea is His.

18:1-35 THE FELLOWSHIP OF THE FORGIVEN

18:1-35 The voice at the Transfiguration bade the disciples listen to Him (17:5) who went the way of ministry to the little, the lost, and the guilty. HIS Word shapes the fellowship of the disciples. He breaks the will to greatness in them and bids them *turn* (repent) *and become like children* in order to enter the *kingdom of heaven* (1-4). He identifies Himself with the childlike *(one such child)* and gives His disciples eyes to behold the Christ Himself in the *little ones* who need their help (5). No punishment is too great for those who *cause one of these little ones to sin* (6); no sacrifice is too costly to avoid harming these little ones (7-9). No one in the church dares to *despise one of these little ones,* whose angels are jealous guardians over them and have constant access to the *Father* (10-11). If *one* of them is *lost,* the *Father,* the Seeking Shepherd, *goes in search* of that *one* (12-14); the church can do no less than use her word, her witness, and her prayer to that same end—to *gain* the brother (15-20). The church is made up of men who have received the extravagant forgiveness of their King. They LIVE by the Word that proceeds from His mouth, and that Word is forgiveness. If they will not live by it, they shall die by it; the wrath of the King and Father will deal with them unless they will to give the forgiveness as extravagantly (70x7) as it has been given to them. (21-35)

18:15 *Tell him his fault.* The Greek word used here is employed by the NT authors to convey the idea of confronting a man with his sin IN ORDER TO TURN HIM TO REPENTANCE. The *telling* attempts to *gain* the *brother.* (Cf. 1 Co 14:24-25, "convicted"; Rv 3:19, "reprove")

18:20 *Gathered in my name,* that is, Christ is the reason for their coming together.

18:23 *Servants.* In an Oriental court even the highest officials entrusted with large sums would be accounted *servants,* or slaves, of the king.

18:24 *Ten thousand talents.* A fantastically large sum; the annual income of Herod the Great is estimated at 900 talents. The talent was the equivalent of $1,000 but had a much higher purchasing power.

18:25 *Ordered . . . sold.* For enslavement for debt cf. Lv 25:39-46; 2 K 4:1.

18:38 *Denarii.* The denarius had a monetary value of about 20 cents.

19:1—25:46 FIFTH GROUP OF MESSIANIC DEEDS AND WORDS

19:1—25:46 The Christ is the future of mankind; He is the breaking-in of the new creation (4:17), the only Life in a dying world (8:22; 16:25); and before Him all men must come to receive from His judgment the final blessing or the final curse of God (16:27; 25:34, 41). (a) His Word therefore determines the hoping disciple's relationship to the orders of this passing world (marriage, children, property, 19:1—20:16). (b) His way to the cross and into life (the way of ministry, mercy, and meekness) determines the way of those who are His and would follow Him into life eternal (20:17—21:11). (c) His call to repentance, addressed to Jerusalem in its most appealing and poignant form, remains as the salutary warning to all who would escape the doom of Jerusalem and the temple (21:12—23:39). (d) His interpretation of all history as a history moving toward His return and serving as the sign that points the hope of men to His return will preserve His disciples in a hope which keeps them steady, faithful, and unafraid while they perform their mission in the world. (24:1—25:46)

19:1—20:16 Hope Within the Orders of This World: Marriage, Children, Property

19:1-12 MARRIAGE

Marriage is the Creator's primal ordinance for His world *(beginning,* 4, 8). Man may not violate its sanctity by *divorce;* even what *Moses allowed* because of men's *hardness of heart* has become a thing of the past, now that Jesus is ushering in the new age in which God's primal will holds. Neither may man arbitrarily renounce marriage because he deems it *expedient* to avoid the high claim that marriage imposes on him; celibacy is a gift at God's disposal (cf. 1 Co 7:7, 17), granted to some *for the sake of His eternal kingdom.*

19:3 *Divorce . . . for any cause?* There were differences among the rabbis on the interpretation of Dt 24:1-4, which permitted divorce (cf. 7); a considerable number held that the husband could divorce his wife *for any cause* however slight.

19:5 Cf. Gn 1:27; 2:24.

19:12 *Eunuchs.* Jesus in this statement uses the word eunuch in three senses, all of them referring to men capable of forgoing marriage: (a) men born with feeble sexuality; (b) the normal sense, castrated males; (c) men of resolute will who can renounce marriage *for the sake of the kingdom,* i.e., to be able to devote all their time and energies to the service of God their King.

19:13-15 CHILDREN

What Jesus had said about the child in illustration of the nature of the fellowship of the church (18:3 ff.) is repeated here in the context of the hoping church. He who is Lord of the future has a heart and blessing for the child.

19:16—20:16 PROPERTY

1) 19:16-26 The Peril of Possessions

Where man is husband and father, the

question of property is serious and unavoidable. Possessions can impede a man in his hope and keep him from the way to *eternal life* (16). Since only God is good, a man must do the impossible: turn from all other goods and *follow* Him who is the present Good. Only the grace of the good God, with whom *all things are possible,* can *save* men from the clutch of possessions.

19:17 *Why . . . ask me about what is good?* Jesus will not permit any one to seek the good anywhere but in God and in His Word. (Cf. Mi 6:8)

19:21 *Perfect,* as the Father in heaven is perfect in a whole and perfect love. (Cf. 5:48)

19:25 *Astonished* is a weak translation; the Greek word connotes a mixture of amazement and fear. The disciples feel struck by this word; if property has such a hold on man, no man can consider himself "safe."

2) 19:27—20:16 The Peril of Renunciation

There is peril also for those who do renounce property for the sake of the hope of eternal life. Jesus' promise to them is one of lavish generosity; they shall reign with Him *(throne) in the new world* and shall find recompense for all they have abandoned in the generous fellowship of the church (29). But these *first* recipients of His grace can lose their favored place if they question His generosity toward others who receive that same generous grace. It is as dangerous to try to keep God's grace to oneself as it is to keep possessions to oneself.

19:28 *Judging* here probably has the broader sense of "ruling." Cf. Ju 2:16, 18, where the "judges" are leaders rather than judges.

19:30 *First will be last.* The parable of 20:1-16 is designed to explain this enigmatic statement. To work in the vineyard is privilege and the pay is pure grace; to question that grace for others is to lose it for oneself.

20:17—21:11 The Way of the Christ: Ministry, Mercy, Meekness

20:17—21:11 Jesus' third prediction of His Passion and death concludes, as do the previous ones, with the assurance that *he will be raised on the third day* (19); the way of the Christ leads to life.

20:17-28 THE WAY OF THE CHRIST: MINISTRY

Jesus quells the will to greatness in His disciples by inverting all human standards of greatness; the greatness of man is the greatness demonstrated by the Son of Man, ministry to the full, self-expending love as seen in Jesus' vicarious suffering and death.

20:17-19 The third and most detailed of the predictions of the Passion and resurrection (cf. 16:21; 17:22-23). New are: the delivering of the Son of Man to the Gentiles, the mockery and scourging, and death by crucifixion.

20:22 *Drink the cup.* The cup is a frequent OT symbol for suffering, especially suffering under the judgment of God. (Ps 11:6; 75:8; Is 51:17, 22)

20:28 *Ransom for many,* the price paid for the release of all men—*many* is here used in the inclusive Semitic sense of "all." (Cf. 1 Ti 2:5-6; 1 Ptr 1:18)

20:29-34 THE WAY OF THE CHRIST: MERCY

The way of the *Son of David,* the Messiah, is the way of *mercy*, which opens the blind eyes of men and enables them to *follow Him* into eternal life.

21:1-11 THE WAY OF THE CHRIST: MINISTRY

Jesus comes to Jerusalem to die as the meek King foretold by Zechariah (see note on 21:5). The way of meekness has the promise of eternal victory.

21:1 *Bethphage,* a village not far from the descent of the Mount of Olives. When Jesus reached this point, His approach could be seen from Jerusalem.

21:5 *Your king is coming to you,* Zch 9:9, with the introductory phrase *(Tell the daughter of Zion)* supplied from Is 62:11. Jesus fulfills the promise which the Lord gave through Zechariah: The people of God will be saved by a God-given King who comes without the trappings of power, depending on God for victory, with no weapon but the word which speaks "peace to the nations" (Zch 9:10). His coming signifies peace for all nations, not only for Israel. The fact that He comes mounted on an ass points up His humility; He rides not the horses and chariots of the warrior but the ordinary man's peaceful beast of burden.

Humble, literally "meek," which emphasizes the total dependence on God which gives a man the strength to endure in the confidence that God will vindicate him. See Ps 37 for a portrait of the meek man.

21:9 *Hosanna,* literally "save now." From its use in the liturgy of the Feast of Tabernacles, the words of Ps 118:25-26 seem to have become a word of acclamation and associated with the Messianic hope. But it is possible that *Hosanna* retains its original sense of "save" and that the words are a prayer to God to vindicate (save, give victory to) His Messiah from heaven above *(in the highest).*

In the name of the Lord. His coming is under the authority of the Lord, to accomplish His will. He is the LORD's Anointed.

21:12—23:39 Jesus Calls Jerusalem to Repentance

21:12—23:39 Three temple incidents (21:12-22), three parables (21:23—22:14), three disputes (22:15-40), Jesus' Messianic manifesto (22:41-46), and Jesus' sad and vehement indictment of the hollow piety of scribe and Pharisee (23:1-39) spell out for the last time the message of Jesus to His people: "Repent, for the kingdom of heaven is at hand." (4:17)

21:12-22 THREE TEMPLE INCIDENTS: REPENT

21:12-22 Jesus' cleansing of the temple is an indictment of His people's externalized and commercialized worship which has made of the *house of prayer a den of robbers* (12-13). The temple authorities are *indignant* at the *wonderful things* Jesus did for the *blind and the lame* in the temple precincts and would have Jesus silence the praises of the *children;* Jesus' words point them to the God of the OT who brings forth *perfect praise out of the mouth of babes* (14-17). The blasting of the *fig tree* symbolizes Jesus' judgment on a piety that supports a costly temple and a great ritual but produces no fruit for the Messiah of mercy, ministry, and meekness (18-19). To this hollow piety the *faith* which can move mountains and has Jesus' promise stands in sharp contrast. (20-22).

21:13 *House of prayer.* Cf. Is 56:7. In its context the word of Isaiah, like that of Zechariah, has in it a promise for all nations. (Is 56;6-8)

Den of robbers. Jer 7:11. As robbers use their den to escape arrest and plan new misdeeds, so the men of Israel use the temple and its cultus to escape the consequences of their sins and to plan new sins.

21:16 *Out of the mouth of babes.* Cf. Ps 8:2. The opening verses of the psalm express the psalmist's adoration of the mighty Creator who can assert His will, execute His purposes, and silence His enemies with the slightest of means, the words of children (cf. 1 Co 1:27-29). Jesus sees His Father's almighty hand at work in the cries of these children; God, Jesus is certain, is leading the Son of David to victory.

21:23—22:14 THREE PARABLES OF REPENTANCE: TWO SONS, VINEYARD, MARRIAGE FEAST

21:23—22:14 In the parables Jesus spreads out before the men of Israel all the riches God has given them and still offers them. They are by God's grace God's *sons,* God's trusted tenant workmen, and God's *invited* guests. He therefore bids them give God a son's obedience and the fruits of the vineyard which the *tenants* owe the owner, to come to the *marriage feast* of their King without delay, without excuses, and dressed in the festal *garment* of obedience to His Word. God's kindness is wooing them; but if they will not learn the seriousness of the hour from His kindness, they will learn it from His wrath (21:41, 43; 22:5, 6, 13), that wrath which cuts off all hope forever.

21:25 *From heaven,* i.e., from God. *Heaven* was a Judaic designation for God; cf. kingdom of heaven=kingdom of God.

21:27 *Neither will I tell you.* If they will not acknowledge John as the voice sent by God to call them to repentance and to offer them forgiveness, Jesus cannot tell them of His *authority;* that authority is revealed in ministry and mercy to men who know and feel their need of mercy.

21:32 *In the way of righteousness,* i.e., the way that offered salvation. For *righteousness* in this sense cf. 5:6; 6:33.

21:33 *Planted a vineyard.* For the vineyard as a picture of God's people, the object of His love and care, cf. Is 5:1-7.

21:36-37 *Servants . . . son.* The prophets (cf. Am 3:7) have made their plea; now the Son is making His. It is the final hour.

21:42 *Stone which the builders rejected.* Ps 118:22-23. The psalm gives thanks to the Lord who has given victory to one (probably the king) who fought against overwhelming odds and triumphed solely by the help of the Lord. Perhaps Jesus recalled also the words which preceded the ones He quoted:

"I shall not die, but I shall live,
and recount the deeds of the Lord." (17)

21:46 *Tried to arrest him.* Cf. 22:15. Jesus' pleading call to repentance falls on deaf ears; the impenitent are cutting off their future and their hope.

22:11 *Wedding garment.* The guest is invited by the free grace of the King; he need not earn his invitation, which goes out to *bad and good.* But to come without the *wedding garment* is to despise the grace of the King and desecrate it; this invites judgment. The man without the festal garment is like salt that does not salt and is therefore cast out (5:13). Where grace is received and yet not allowed to shape man's conduct, it is received in vain. (2 Co 6:1)

22:14 *Many . . . called . . . few . . . chosen.* God's call, His invitation, goes out to all Israel (3), to all men, bad and good (10); but God's love working through His Word achieves its goal only in the *few,* whose response to God's call marks them as God's *chosen,* His elect.

22:15-40 THE CALL TO REPENTANCE IN THE THREE DISPUTES

22:15-40 Jesus utilizes even the attempts *to entangle him in his talk* (15) to press home His call to repentance. He bids the Pharisees (who put Him to the test with the question concerning *taxes paid to Casear)* do what the parable of the vineyard enjoined on them: *give God the things that are God's* (15-22), as He was doing when He went to the cross.

When the *Sadducees* attempt to cast doubt on the *resurrection* with their calculated question, He seeks to turn them to the *scriptures* which He obeyed to the death (cf. 26:54) and to give them eyes for the *power of God* which He trusted to raise Him on the third day. (23-33)

He directed the *lawyer* who tested Him with his question concerning *the great commandment in the law* to the overriding and unifying will of God in the Law: *love* for God and man in unbroken unity; obedience to that will took Jesus to the cross in obedience to His Father and as a ransom for all men. (34-40)

22:16 The presence of the *Herodians* is explained by the nature of the question put to Jesus. The question is designed to test His Messianic claim and to confront Him with a dilemma. If He permits payment of *taxes to Caesar,* He will discredit Himself as Messiah—for would not the Messiah put an end to the hated Roman domination? If, however, He forbids payment of the taxes, He will put forward a Messianic claim that makes Him politically suspect. The Herodians, partisans of the Herods who depended on Roman rule, would be quick to inform the Roman authorities. In either case Jesus would be disposed of by men who considered Him dangerous.

22:17 *Lawful.* The question is religious: Could the people of God help maintain an alien pagan power without proving disloyal to their God? Some in Israel answered that question with a violent no and fomented rebellion against Rome (the Zealots).

22:21 Jesus' answer implies that there need be no clash of loyalties; they can pay the coin minted in Rome to the Roman emperor and still give *God the things that are God's:* a son's obedience, a workman's service, an invited guest's response. (21:28—22:14)

22:23-28 The Sadducees' question implies that the *resurrection,* by assigning one woman to seven husbands, contradicts the Law and cannot therefore be a true belief.

22:24 *Moses said.* Dt 25:5.

22:30 *Marriage.* The Sadducees attributed to Jesus the Pharisees' conception of the life of the world to come as merely a more splendid continuation of this present life. Jesus rejects this conception.

22:32 *I am the God of Abraham,* etc. Ex 3:6.

22:40 *Depend,* literally "hang"; take away the basic command of love and the whole OT *(the law and the prophets)* collapses.

22:41-46 JESUS' MESSIANIC MANIFESTO

22:41-46 Jesus calls *the Pharisees* to repentance by showing them how their conception of the *Christ* falls altogether short of the OT promise of the Christ. They hope for a *son of David,* great and powerful, who will deliver them from Roman rule and make them great. Jesus uses Ps 110 to give them a really religious conception of the Christ. Jesus looks not to Jerusalem, Mount Zion, and the throne of David but to heaven and the throne of God; the greatness of the Christ is not that He is *son of David* (that is His humiliation) but that He is David's *Lord,* before whom all *enemies* will be brought low. It was for this Messianic claim that Jesus was called blasphemer and condemned to die. (26:63-66)

23:1-39 WOE TO YOU, SCRIBES AND PHARISEES

23:1-39 Jerusalem and the temple are like a fig tree rich in leaves and devoid of fruit (21:18-19), hopelessly doomed. The false and empty piety that doomed them was the piety of the *scribes and the Pharisees;* they shaped and influenced the religion of Judaism more than any one else. Jesus' last call to repentance is therefore a last indictment of their piety. Their will is at every point a contradiction of the will of Christ. Christ comes to fulfill the Law and the prophets, and His whole life is determined by the Word of God (cf., e.g., 26:54, 56); they *sit on Moses' seat* as the guardians and interpreters of the Word of God and *preach, but do not practice* (3). Christ comes in merciful ministry and gives the heavy-burdened rest (11:28-29); they *lay heavy burdens on men's shoulders* but *themselves* will not lift a *finger* to *move them* (4). Christ comes in meekness and goes the way of the Servant (11:29; 12:18-21); they *do all their deeds to be seen by men,* cultivate their own greatness, and forfeit the reward of God by seeking their reward of men (5-7; cf. 6:2-3)—they are the very opposite of what Jesus is and what His followers are to be (8-12). Christ opens the Kingdom to the poor and the child (5:3; 18:3; 19:14); they *shut the kingdom of heaven against men* (13). Christ the Son makes His followers children of the Father, free sons (5:45; 17:26); they make their convert *(proselyte) a child of hell* (15). Christ is the Light (4:16) and the Shepherd who guides and tends the harassed and helpless flock (9:36); they are *blind guides* who lead their followers into destruction (cf. 15:14) with their frivolous teaching concerning the oath (16-22), whereas Christ made His disciples' simple yes and no an oath, words spoken in the presence of God, the remembering Witness (5:37). For Christ the *weightier matters of the law* (23) loomed large—He held firm in His God even unto death *(faith,* 23) and served Him who desires *mercy* (9:13), in order that He might bring God's *justice* to victory; they are punctilious in *tithing,* as they ought to be, but withdraw from the pressure of the Law when it lays claim to their hearts, their love (23). The Christ is a clear cup filled with the goodness of God, the Giver who gives freely to all, unposed in His transparent goodness; they have hearts that belie their fair appearance, hearts filled with *rapacity* and *iniquity* (25-28). For Christ the word of the prophets was a word to live and die by (5:17; 26:56); they disclaimed connection with the *fathers* who *shed the blood of the prophets,* but they no more obey the prophetic word than their fathers did (29-31). Thus they unite themselves in guilt with their fathers (32-33), will continue in the ways of their fathers (34), and will suffer the judgment that concludes the guilty history of their people. (35-36)

Harsh as these words of Jesus are, they are still a part of His call to repentance. His is the voice of the *hen* that *gathers her brood under her wings,* concerned and compassionate (37). The temple will be abandoned by God; the house of God which they have made *their house* and a den of robbers (21:13) will be *forsaken and desolate.* But when the Christ returns, there will be men of Israel among those who hail His coming. (39)

23:2 *Sit on Moses' seat.* They are recognized expositors of the Law.

23:3 *Whatever they tell you.* After what Jesus has said of the tradition of the elders in 15:3-6, this can hardly include all the additions to and corruptions of the Law which were embodied in that tradition; but the word of Moses remains sacred.

23:5 *Phylacteries,* amulets, bands worn on the arm or forehead; they contained verses of Scripture. The purpose in wearing them was to remind man of the law of the Lord (Ex 13:9; Dt 6:8); by making them *broad* the scribes and Pharisees used them to advertise their piety.

Fringes, or tassels, enjoined by the Law as a reminder of "the commandments of the Lord" (Nm 15:38-41), were made long to call attention to the wearer's piety. Jesus Himself wore the fringe on His garment, in the sense intended by the Law. (9:20)

23:7 *Rabbi,* title of respect, means literally "My great one."

23:23 *Justice, mercy, faith.* For a similar summary of God's claim upon His people see Mi 6:8.

23:33 *Serpents . . . brood of vipers.* Cf. 3:7; 12:34.

23:35 *Abel . . . Zechariah.* The first (Gn 4:8) and the last (2 Ch 24:21) murder of an innocent man recorded in the OT. 2 Chronicles was the last book in the Jewish arrangement of the OT.

Son of Barachiah. The Zechariah *murdered between the sanctuary and the altar* was the son of Jehoiada (2 Ch 24:20-22). The prophet Zechariah was son of Barachiah (Zch 1:1). The confusion here may be the result of a well-intentioned but mistaken note made by some copyist of the text.

23:38 *Your house,* the temple. Cf. Jer 12:7; possibly, however, "your land and people" is meant.

24:1—25:46 The Sign of Christ's Coming

24:1-31 ALL HISTORY THE SIGN OF HIS COMING

24:1-31 Jesus does not answer the question, *When will this be?* (3). He will not permit His disciples to speculate concerning His return; instead He shapes their hope as a vigilant and responsible expectation by teaching them to read in all history the *sign* of His *coming* and *the close of the age.* All history is the sign; they are to see in all history, with its false hopes (5), its wars and disasters, and its apparently meaningless *sufferings* (8), the work of God carrying out His will *(must,* 6) as He moves toward final judgment. (1-8)

The history of the church is the sign. God will be at work in His persecuted, stumbling church manifesting His strength in her weakness. The task of the church will be accomplished; the *gospel* will be universally proclaimed, and then the *end will come.* (9-14)

All history alerts the disciple for the end of history. In that history the fall of Jerusalem has a unique place; in Jerusalem the drama of God's offer of His grace in the Son and man's rejection of that grace, with the resultant judgment, are a miniature of the close of the age. Jesus has separated His own inwardly from the doomed city, and they need not share its fate; they are to flee. (15-20)

Jesus' words on the close of the age are anything but a precise forecast of events; the line between the fall of Jerusalem and the end is left indistinct; the *great tribulation* (21) which the kindly providence of God will shorten *for the sake of the elect* (22), the false and fevered Messianic hopes which mark that time of tribulation (23-26)—these might refer to either event or both. But there will be no room for doubt about the *coming of the Son of man* when He comes; it will be manifest and universal, like *lightning* that emblazons the whole heaven (27), sudden as the appearance of *vultures* where a carcass is (28), accompanied by cosmic convulsions (29) at which *all the tribes of the earth will mourn* (30) and His *elect* will rejoice as at the fruition of their long and strenuous hope. (31)

24:5 *In my name,* claiming the authority of the Christ.

24:6 *This must take place.* Cf. Rv 1:1: The whole Book of Revelation is the inspired commentary to these words of Jesus, tracing even in the most fearful and diabolical disasters the working of God toward His end.

24:8 *Birth-pangs.* The pains of a travailing mother have an end and a purpose. The sufferings are no whim of fate; rather in them God is working out His purposes toward a happy end.

24:12 *Men's love will grow cold.* The bitter disillusionment which comes when men *betray* their brothers in the faith (10), the harsh necessity of exposing *false prophets* and separating the church from them (11)—these things, together with the constant pressure of being *hated by all nations* (9), put a strain on Christian love that threatens to destroy it. (Cf. Rv 2:2-7)

24:15 *The desolating sacrilege.* Cf. Dn 9:27; 11:31; 12:11. The first reference of Daniel's prophecy was probably to the action of Antiochus Epiphanes (168 B.C.), who erected a pagan idol and altar in the temple, thereby desecrating it so that no Israelite could worship the Lord there; this made the holy place desolate (cf. 1 Mac 1:54). Jesus warns His disciples that a similar desecration would foretoken the fall of Jerusalem. Some see the fulfillment of this word in the Roman emperor Caligula's attempt (A.D. 38) to set up a statue of himself (as deified) in the Jerusalem temple, an attempt that horrified all Jewry. Luke 21:20 speaks of the presence of (pagan) armies surrounding Jerusalem as foretokening "that its DESOLATION has come near," and this is probably the nearer reference. Roman emperors, with their claim to divine honors, will be God's instrument in turning the splendor of the temple into the forsaken and desolate house of which Jesus had spoken. (23:38)

Let the reader understand. Let him read the word of Daniel and take it to heart as a word that speaks to him in his situation.

24:19 Flight would be especially difficult and dangerous for women *with child* and for nursing mothers burdened and delayed by the necessity of caring for a baby.

24:20 *In winter . . . on a sabbath.* When inclement weather or religious scruples might tempt them to put off flight.

24:26 *In the wilderness.* Cf. Acts 21:38.

24:28 *Body . . . eagles (vultures).* A carcass attracts vultures with uncanny certainty. With the same certainty the Son of Man will appear to deliver and judge.

24:29 The language used to depict the convulsion of the universe is from the OT: Is 24:21; 34:4; Jl 2:30, 31. Jesus introduces no "novelties" in speaking of the last things; His emphasis is religious and personal, on the return of the *Son of man* (30) and the *gathering of His elect.*

24:30 *The sign of the Son of man* is the appearing of the Son of Man in His *power* and *glory.*

24:32—25:46 THE SIGN OF HIS COMING: YOU MUST BE READY

24:32—25:46 Jesus is not the great forecaster of the future; His words are designed to give His disciples a sure and responsible hope, to make them ready for His coming. Only a third of His words in Matthew's record of His teaching on last things are predictive (24:1-31); the rest are directly and explicitly admonitory. Six parables and a magnificent depiction of the Last Judgment are all directed to the paramount question in all NT teaching on the last things: "What sort of persons ought you to be in your lives of holiness and godliness waiting for and hastening [or "earnestly desiring"] the coming of the day of God?" (2 Ptr 3:11-12)

1) 24:32-35 The Fig Tree

24:32-35 The parable of the fig tree frees the disciples from excited impatience in their hoping; they can await the coming of their Lord as they await the coming of *summer* with patience, knowing that it is in the Creator's hands. His work has begun; the tree is budding, their Lord is near. This they know from His sure, eternal *words.*

24:34 *This generation* can refer to the Jews (Mt 11:16; 12:39, 41, 42, 45; 16:4). For all the severity of God's judgment on Israel, its history shall not end with the destruction of the temple and the fall of Jerusalem; there is a place for Israel in the new and eternal people of God. Or the reference can be one of time; Jesus' contemporaries dare not think of *all these things* as an event in the distant future; the end of Jerusalem ushers in the end, and all men live henceforth under the tension and responsibility of "these last days." (Heb 1:2)

24:35 *My words.* Jesus' words surpass even the words of the Law in their enduring validity (cf. 5:18). Only One who is very God of very God can speak thus of His Word.

2) 24:36-44 The Days of Noah; the Thief

24:36-44 The parables of the *days of Noah* and of the *thief* in the night both stress the complete incalculability of the coming of the Son of Man. The *days of Noah* were deceptively normal days, and the householder does not know the hour of the thief's coming—he knows only the cost of unreadiness. *Therefore you . . . must* be *ready.*

24:36 Cf. Acts 1:6-7.

24:37 *Days of Noah.* Gn 6:5—7:24.

24:40 *One is taken* by the Son of Man when He gathers in His elect (31), *and one is left,* to be eternally separated from God. Cf. John the Baptist's image of the wheat and the chaff, 3:12.

24:43 *Thief.* Cf. 1 Th 5:2; 2 Ptr 3:10; Rv 3:3; 16:15. The suddenness of the coming of the Son of Man, which cuts off all possibility of forecast and calculation, makes the disciples' hope one of perpetual vigilance *(watch).*

3) 24:45-51 The Importance of Faithful Service

24:45-51 The disciple is to be composed and ready; this means that he must be *faithful and wise* in the service of His coming Lord. The reward for faithful service is generous, out of all proportion to the service rendered (47). The penalty for unfaithful folly is a fearful one.

24:45 *Servant . . . over his household* (cf. 49, *beat his fellow servants).* The promise and warning are addressed particularly to leaders in the church.

24:51 *Hypocrites.* The "Christian" hypocrite, whose profession of faith is not reflected in his practice, will be dealt with as severely as the Judaic hypocrite (23:33), "For God shows no partiality." (Ro 2:11)

4) 25:1-13 The Wise and Foolish Maidens

25:1-13 The parable of the wise and foolish maidens makes clear that the disciple, whose life has been made the evening before the festival, dare not merely luxuriate in his hope; he lives by it in responsible readiness. He lives and hopes as a member of the church; but the church cannot hope for him or *be ready* for him. Each man moves toward the end in personal responsibility and individual vigilance. Otherwise he forfeits forever the joy of communion with his Lord.

25:12 *I do not know you.* "You are not Mine." (Cf. 7:23)

25:13 *Watch.* Be on the alert.

5) 25:14-30 The Talents

25:14-30 The parable of the *talents* portrays the Christ entrusting His property and business to His *servants.* Every gift of the Christ imposes its claim on the recipient and asks of him fidelity, whether the gift be large or small. The Christ rewards with the lavishness of grace; the faithful two-talent man receives the same great reward as the faithful five-talent man; both feast with their Lord (see note on 21). The Christ measures a man not by what he has received but by his fidelity in what he has received. Therefore the Law which governs revelation *(to every one who has,* 29, cf. 13:12) also governs ministry, service; and therefore the *one talent,* the free gift of divine grace, dare not be neglected. To neglect it is to desecrate the grace of God.

25:15 *According to his ability.* The gift is seen to be the opportunity of serving the Christ.

25:21 *Joy of your master.* Cf. 23. *Joy* is probably used in the sense (found in Judaic writings) of festive dinner, banquet; the faithful servants enter into the joyous fellowship of the meal with their master. (Cf. 26:29)

26:27 *Invested my money with the bankers.* Even a course which involved minimal effort and imagination would have met with the master's approval. As he gives to "each according to his ability" (15), he is ready to reward accordingly.

6) 25:31-46 The Last Judgment

25:31-46 The great Shepherd who *separates the sheep from the goats* (32) once said: "He who is not with me is against me, and he who does not gather with me scatters" (12:30). That is what determines now, in the judgment; the separation takes place before any deed of man is mentioned. Whether a man has been against Him or for Him has been documented in his deeds; deeds of mercy done or left undone have been man's yea or nay to Christ. The merciful will find mercy in the judgment, as Jesus had promised (5:7)—and mercy it is, for the Judge buries all their failures in forgiving silence and remembers only their deeds of mercy. The unmerciful have committed themselves to the unmerciful enemy of God and share his doom, that *eternal fire* which God did not design for man.

25:32 *All the nations,* to whom the Servant ministered (12:18) and gave hope; who had the Gospel proclaimed to them (24:14); who hated the disciples for the sake of Christ's name. (24:9)

Sheep . . . goats. Cf. Eze 34:17-24.

25:34 *Blessed of my Father.* God's work of *blessing,* begun in His creation (Gn 1:22), continued in history (Gn 12:2), active in the worship and life of His people (Nm 6:24; Eph 1:3), comes to its eternal climax here.

26:1—28:20 CONCLUSION AND CLIMAX

26:1—28:20 The Passion, death, and resurrection of the Messiah complete and crown His ministry. The risen Lord in the perfection of His grace and power gives His disciples their universal and enduring commission as His apostles.

26:1—27:66 Passion and Death

26:1-16 PRELUDE TO THE PASSION

26:1-16 The opening of the Passion story sounds most of the notes heard in that account; the majestic certitude of the Christ who goes of set purpose to His death (2) and shapes the future of the universal Gospel (13); the determined enmity of the leaders of the people (3-5); the devotion of a woman to the dying Christ (6-13); the failure of Jesus' disciples—they all object to the generous gesture of the woman (8), and Judas agrees to betray Him. (14-15)

26:2 *Passover.* See note on 26:26.

You know. Jesus had predicted His death thrice: 16:21; 17:22-23; 20:17-19. Jesus knows that His "hour" is at hand.

Will be delivered up. The passive voice indicates God's action. (Cf. Ro 8:32)

26:6 *Simon the leper,* mentioned only here and Mk 14:3. Apparently he had been healed of his leprosy by Jesus.

26:12 *Ointment . . . burial.* For the anointing of the dead cf. Mk 14:8; Lk 23:56.

26:15 *They paid him.* Judas has become the opposite of a disciple and apostle. He had received from Jesus "without pay" (10:8); he betrays Jesus for pay.

26:17-29 THE LAST PASSOVER, THE NEW PASSOVER

26:17-29 The obedient suffering Servant is in charge of His own history; Jesus determines the place of the *passover* meal (17-19), unmasks His betrayer, and pronounces God's judgment on him (20-25). He makes *bread* and *wine* the vehicles of His self-giving, atoning death and establishes the new *covenant* of the *forgiveness of sins* (26-28). He looks forward confidently to the *new,* eternal fellowship of the meal in His *Father's kingdom* in the world to come. (29)

26:17 *Unleavened Bread,* the term used to designate the Passover (cf. 2) AND the 7-day festival which followed.

26:19 *Prepared the passover.* For the ritual of the Passover meal see Ex 12.

26:23 *Dipped his hand in the dish.* The outrageousness of the betrayal by Judas is underscored; he is violating the sacred bond of table fellowship. (Cf. Ps 41:9; Jn 13:18)

26:24 *As it is written . . . woe to that man.* God can use the wrong of man to carry out His settled purpose *(written);* but that does not excuse man's wrong. (Cf. Ro 3:5-8)

26:25 *You have said so.* Cf. 26:64; 27:11. There is a mysterious reticence in the way Jesus speaks His Yes to the questions of the disciple who betrayed Him, the Jewish council which condemned Him, and the Roman governor who executed Him.

26:26 *As they were eating.* In the course of the meal of the Passover, which commemorated the "passing over" or sparing of Israel when the firstborn of Egypt were slain (Ex 12; 13:3-9), Christ institutes the new Passover based on His self-sacrifice (cf. 1 Co 5:7); on the memorial day of the first covenant He establishes the new *covenant* promised for the new age.

Covenant evokes many OT memories: the Lord's covenant with Israel (Ex 24:6-8); His promise to David (2 Sm 23:5; Ps 89:3, 4, 28), the Servant who is the "covenant to the people" (Is 42:6), the ancient promise of a new covenant to supersede the one which unfaithful Israel had broken (Jer 31:31-34; Eze 16:60; 34:25; 37:26, Is 54:10; 55:3; 61:8). In establishing the covenant, a gracious God takes the initiative to establish fellowship between Himself and estranged man, to create a new order of things where His grace and will prevail. In using the term *covenant* of His death, Jesus marks His dying as God's grace toward man, His deed for man, His gift toward man. God is saying: "I will be your God."

26:30-56 THE STRICKEN SHEPHERD AND THE SCATTERED FLOCK

26:30-56 Jesus knows that He must drink the cup of God's judgment on man's sin alone and unsustained, and He accepts the burden laid on Him. He predicts the defection of His disciples and Peter's denial (30-35). He prays, in a genuinely human agony, for the strength to align His will with the Father's, while His disciples *sleep* (36-46). Strengthened and unwavering (46), He faces the *crowd* come to arrest

Him and the disciple who betrays Him, stays the hand of the disciple who would defend Him with the *sword,* and goes the way marked out for Him by the *scriptures,* while His disciples *forsook him and fled.* (47-56).

26:30 *Hymn.* The singing of the Hallel (Pss 113 to 118) was a regular part of the Passover ritual. Jesus' last hours are worship, filled with hymns, Scripture, and prayer.

26:31 *Strike the shepherd.* Zechariah the prophet had spoken of the death of a Good Shepherd of God's people who was to perish by the judicial action of God (by His "sword," Zch 13:7). The immediate effect of the Shepherd's death was to be a dispersal of the flock, a time of trial and sifting for the people of God; the ultimate effect would be the restoration of a trusting and confessing people of God. (Zch 13: 7-9)

26:36 *Gethsemane,* an olive yard east of Jerusalem.

26:37 *Sons of Zebedee.* James and John.

26:38 *My soul is sorrowful.* Ps 42:5, 11; 43:5.

26:39 *This cup.* Cf. 20:22 note.

26:41 *The spirit is willing.* Cf. Ps 51:12. The *willing spirit* is God's gift to man; it arises from "joy in His salvation." The *flesh* is man in his frailty and unwillingness to accept God's salvation.

26:49 *Kiss.* For the kiss as an expression of honor for a teacher *(Master,* rabbi) cf. Lk 7:45.

26:52 *Perish by the sword.* Jesus' word refers particularly to those who, like the Zealots, attempt to achieve religious ends by miltary-political means.

26:55 *Robber.* The term was also used to designate a political revolutionary, a Zealot, such as Barabbas was (called "robber" in Jn 18:40 and "rebel" in Mk 15:7, cf. Lk 23:19).

26:57-75 THE TRIAL BEFORE CAIAPHAS AND PETER'S DENIAL

26:57-75 Jesus endures in silence the waves of malice that sweep over Him: the *false testimony,* the charge of *blasphemy,* the decision that He must die, and the mockery designed to discredit His Messianic claim. He is the Servant who "opened not his mouth" when the Lord laid on Him "the iniquity of us all" (Is 53:6-7). He endures in silence, and He endures alone; Peter, the "first" of His disciples and apostles (10:2), denies Him—his iniquity, too, becomes part of the burden laid on the one obedient Servant.

26:61 *Destroy the temple.* The charge is a distortion of a word of Jesus recorded in Jn 2:19, where Jesus marked His opponents as the destroyers of the temple and Himself as the Restorer of what they had destroyed. (Cf. Jn 2:21-22)

26:64 *You have said.* Cf. 26:25 note.

Power. Judaic expression for God.

Son of man . . . coming on clouds. Jesus in His "good confession" combines two of the mightiest Messianic utterances of the OT, Ps 110:1 (cf. Mt 22:43-45) and Dn 7:13-14, where the *Son of man* is pictured in the light of the heavenly world, as Judge over the kingdoms of this world and as recipient of a universal and imperishable kingdom.

26:65 *Blasphemy.* Cf. 9:3. Galilee and Jerusalem bring the same charge against the Son of Man who looks to His rightful place at God's right hand. Jesus is to be executed because of His claim to deity.

26:67-68 *Spat . . . struck . . . slapped . . . you Christ.* Cf. Is 50:6, a word concerning the Servant. The mistreatment of Jesus by His judges is to justify their verdict; if He is so defenseless, He cannot be the Messiah, the Son of the Blessed.

27:1-31 THE TRIAL BEFORE PILATE

27:1-31 Jesus' prediction that His people would "deliver him to the Gentiles to be mocked and scourged and crucified" (20:19) is fulfilled. And Jesus' prediction that "the Son of man is to be delivered into the hands of MEN" (17:22) is fulfilled too. Men—Jew, disciple, Gentile—are guilty of His death; and none can evade that guilt. The remorse of Judas and the return of the silver (3-10) cannot clear Judas; his fate is a terrifying prediction of the fate of all who "profaned the blood" of the Son of God (Heb 10:29). The men of Israel cannot evade responsibility by delivering Jesus to Pilate (2, 11-14); the choice between Jesus and Barabbas is their choice and makes Pilate's verdict their verdict (15-23). And no *washing* can sweeten Pilate's *hands,* he *releases Barabbas, scourges Jesus,* and *delivers him to be crucified* (24-26); and it is soldiery under his command that completes the parallel between Jew and Gentile by *mocking* the *King of the Jews* (27-31) just as His own people had mocked Him (26:67-68). The trial of Jesus is a miniature of the guilt of mankind.

27:1-2 Legal tradition demanded that in the case of capital offenses the trial had to extend over two days and the verdict had to be reached in the daytime. This second meeting seems to have been held to meet that requirement. *Took counsel.* Better: "decided."

27:3 *Repented.* The Greek word here is not the usual one for *repent.* Better: "felt remorse"; not the same as the "repentance that leads to salvation." (2 Co 7:10)

27:6 *It is not lawful.* Tainted money could not be brought into the house of the Lord. (Cf. Dt 23:18)

27:9 *Jeremiah.* The passage quoted is basically Zch 11:12-13; reminiscences of Jer 32:6-15; 18:2-3 probably led to the citing of Jeremiah's name. The language of the Zechariah passage is mysterious and the text uncertain; therefore the fulfillment connection is hard to trace. Common to Zechariah and Matthew is the thought that One whom the Lord appointed to be Shepherd over His people is rejected by them and held cheap—*thirty pieces of silver* are the indemnity money to be paid for the killing of a slave. (Ex 21:32)

27:11 *King of the Jews,* a political messianic pretender, a revolutionary and therefore dangerous to Rome.

You have said so. Cf. 26:25, 64.

27:14 *No answer.* Again (cf. 26:63) the Servant suffers silently. (Is 53:7)

27:17 *Barabbas* means "son of Abbas" (cf. 16:17); there is considerable probability in the reading given in RSV note *k, Jesus Barabbas.* There would then be a tragic contrast between the Jesus whom Israel produced (Barabbas) and the *Jesus* the Christ whom God gave to Israel as Savior (1:21); the one was liberated by his people, the other was sent to the cross although said to be innocent. (Cf. 27:19)

27:18 *Out of envy.* Jn 11:47-48 is an eloquent commentary on this statement.

27:19 Three Gentiles attest Jesus' innocence in Matthew: Pilate's wife, Pilate (23-24), and the centurion. (54)

27:25 *On us and on our children.* Those who spin fables about a hereditary curse upon the Jews ignore the fact that it was not God who uttered this imprecation, that the apostles went to the Jews first and offered them forgiveness, and that "the gifts and call of God are irrevocable." (Ro 11:29)

27:27 *Praetorium,* the palace of the Roman governor.

27:27-31 The mockery of Gentile soldiery is parallel to that of Judaic scribes and elders (26:67). Jesus once told His brothers: "The WORLD . . . hates me because I testify of it that its works are evil." (Jn 7:7)

Only here does the Messiah appear with the title and insignia of royalty; thus, by suffering He comes to kingship. (Cf. Ph 2:9)

27:32-66 THE CRUCIFIXION, DEATH, AND BURIAL OF JESUS

27:32-66 Old Israel rejects the King sent to her; the beginning of the history of the new Israel, the Twelve, is a sad chapter of failure. A stranger carries the cross for the Christ (32); a hitherto unknown disciple provides for His burial (57-60); only the devotion of women remains constant (55-56, 61). Jesus dies alone, and He tastes death to the full, "numbered with the transgressors" (38, 44; Is 53:12), forsaken by God (46), fully conscious to the last (34, 50). But the Father attests the Son even now when He gives Him the cup to drink, in catastrophic *darkness* (45), in the rent curtain of the temple, in earthquake, and in the *rising of the saints fallen asleep* (51-53); the mockery under the cross is made to publish once more all that Jesus is and claims to be (39-43); a Gentile centurion is *filled with awe* at this crucified criminal and calls Him *Son of God* (54). The language of the account is rich in reminiscences of the OT; Matthew saw that these things were no mere accident—the drink offered to Jesus (34, 48), the casting of lots for His garments (36), Jesus' crucifixion in the company of transgressors (44)—in all this Scripture is being fulfilled; God's will is being done. Jesus had gone this way in the assurance that it was God's will ("must," 16:21; "is to be," 17:22); that will also was that "He be raised on the third day." No posted guard, no *seal* of Roman security, no *secure sepulchre* can frustrate that will. (62-66)

27:32 *Compelled.* Literally "to requisition, press into service."

27:34 *Wine . . . mingled with gall.* A narcotic to help deaden the pain. Jesus' refusal expresses His will to drink the cup of suffering to the full.

27:39 *Wagging their heads.* Ps 22:7. A gesture of mockery.

27:45 *Sixth . . . until the ninth hour.* Noon till three.

Darkness. Amos had prophesied that the Lord God would "make the sun go down at noon and darken the earth in broad daylight" (Am 8:9) on the day of threatened judgment against His people. Cf. Am 8:2: "The end has come upon my people Israel."

27:46 *Eli.* Ps 22:1. In the hour when He is forsaken, He still calls God *my God.* He is the Servant "who walks in darkness and has no light, yet . . . relies upon his God." (Is 50:10)

27:47 *Calling Elijah.* Elijah was celebrated in Judaic legend as helper in time of need.

27:48 *Vinegar.* Sour wine.

27:50 *Cried with a loud voice.* It was probably for this that Jesus had accepted the sour wine (48). He departed from life consciously; His death was not His fate but His act.

27:51-53. The *torn curtain of the temple,* the shaken *earth,* the *opened tombs,* and the exclamation of the *centurion* mark the significance of the hour. The rending of the *curtain* which divided the Holy of Holies from the Holy Place (Ex 26:33) signifies that God no longer dwells in His house; it is "forsaken and desolate" (23:38). Others take this to signify that the Holy of Holies is now open to all believers (cf. Heb 6:19; 10:19-22). The shaking of the earth is a frequent feature in many of the OT theophanies (appearances of God); here God is manifesting Himself, in the death of the Servant the arm of the Lord is being revealed (Is 53:1); the *saints* proceeding from their *tombs* and *appearing* in the *holy city* indicate that Christ's death is the victory over death, that He is the firstborn from the dead. The exclamation of the *centurion and those who were with him,* Gentiles all, indicates that in His dying the Christ has fulfilled His ministry to the Jew and now goes to all nations to assert His Lordship over all.

27:57 *Joseph . . . a disciple.* John adds that he was a disciple "secretly, for fear of the Jews" (Jn 19:38). This may account for Matthew's previous silence concerning him.

27:62 *Day of Preparation.* The day before the Sabbath, when preparation for the Sabbath was made.

27:66 *Sealing the stone.* The presence of the seal made any violation of the grave an offense against Roman authority. (Cf. Dn 6:17)

28:1-20 The Resurrection

28:1-20 The supreme event of the gospel is economically told. The actual event of the resurrection is, as in all the gospels, veiled in the silence of awe; only the annunciation of the resurrection is dramatically narrated (2-3). Wondrous as the crowning event is, it retains continuity with the previous history of Jesus. There is the same determined opposition by the leadership of His people (11-15), the same devotion inspired in womankind (1), the same genuine humanity of Jesus *(took hold of his feet* 9), the same instability in His disciples *(some doubted,* 17), the same *Galilee* that witnessed the calling of the first disciples (10, 16). Jesus remains the Forgiver and Restorer; the angel calls men who had forfeited their right to discipleship *his disciples* still (7), and Jesus calls men who had forsaken and denied Him His *brethren* (10). The *authority* of Jesus (18) emerges into the full light of Easter, but it is of a piece with His "authority on earth to forgive sins" (9:6); His compassionate authority makes the disciples' apostolate an apostolate to *all nations* (19), no longer confined to the lost sheep of the house of Israel. His authority gives the grace of Baptism and the gift of His teaching to all mankind and promises the abiding power of His presence *always, to the close of the age* (20). One *name* (19) unites the *Son* with the *Father* and the *Spirit;* Jesus' Godhead is apparent now, and in that Godhead He is Servant—His will is to *make disciples* still. (19)

28:19 *Baptizing . . . in the name. In the name of* was a term used in Judaism to indicate that a man was being effectually COMMITTED TO something or someone. E.g., a man circumcised "in the name of the covenant" was committed to the covenant, brought under its blessing and placed under its obligations. A man baptized *in the name of the Father* has God as his Father; baptized *in the name of the Son,* he receives all the benefits of the Son's redeeming act; baptized *in the name of the Spirit,* he receives the life-giving, life-sustaining power and presence of the Spirit. Baptism is the enacted Gospel of the Trinity.

28:20 *Commanded.* Jesus is not a new lawgiver, as Matthew's account of His teaching has shown. His command is given to men baptized in His name, men with whom He is present as their crucified and risen Lord. *Command* calls for what Paul calls "the obedience of faith" (Ro 1:5). For the command contained in the gift of Baptism cf. Ro 6:3-14.

MARK

INTRODUCTION

1 The second gospel begins with the words, "The beginning of the gospel of Jesus Christ, the Son of God." This is too comprehensive and solemn a phrase to be the title of the opening section only, as some have thought, the part which deals with John the Baptist and Jesus' baptism and His temptation, the preparation for Jesus' Messianic ministry. It is designed to be the title to the whole work, and it is a significant one. Mark's book aims to set before the readers the record of the beginning and origin of that Good News which they knew and believed, that powerful and saving Word of God which the Son of God first proclaimed in word and deed (1:14-15), a word which was still the voice of Christ when proclaimed to men by human apostles and evangelists. Mark is answering the question of converts who, once they had heard the basic kerygma (Gospel), naturally and rightly asked, "How did this great Good News that has revolutionized our lives begin? What is its history? Tell us more of the strong Son of God who loved us and gave Himself for us. Recount for us His words and works, which will make clear His will for us who have become His own." Mark is doing what Luke did when he wrote "an orderly account" for Theophilus, in order that he might know the truth concerning *the things of which he had been informed* (Lk 1:3-4). Mark's book is "teaching"; it is the filling in of the outline of the kerygma for Christian readers. This is confirmed by many details in the book itself; for instance, the noun "gospel" occurs seven times in this gospel, while it occurs only four times in Matthew's much longer work and not at all in Luke and John. And it is in Mark's Gospel that Jesus identifies "gospel" so closely with His own person that the two are practically one entity, as when He says, "Whoever loses his life for my sake *and the gospel's* will save it." (Mk 8:35; cf. 10:29)

2 The earliest tradition of the church confirms this view of the gospel as "teaching." Papias, bishop of Hierapolis, writing about A. D. 130 and citing as his authority the "Elder John" (perhaps John the apostle, certainly a man close to the apostolic age), writes concerning the second gospel: "Mark, having become Peter's interpreter, wrote down accurately, though not in order, as many as he remembered of the things said or done by the Lord. For he neither had heard the Lord nor followed Him, but at a later time, as I said, [he followed] Peter, *who delivered his instructions* according to the needs [of the occasion] . . . ." Other early notices locate this preaching of Peter's and Mark's recording of it in Italy, more specifically in Rome. An early prolog to the gospel (one of the so-called Anti-Marcionite prologs) says that Mark wrote his record of Peter's preaching "in the regions of Italy," and Clement of Alexandria reports an early tradition that Mark wrote his gospel in Rome at the request of those who had heard Peter preach there. Since Christianity had been established in Italy and Rome long before Peter ever worked there, both these notices are taken most naturally as referring to a *teaching* activity of Peter in Rome rather than to a strictly missionary activity.

Author of the Gospel

3 Mark (referred to in the New Testament also as John and as John Mark, Acts 13:5, 13; 12:12) was the son of a certain Mary who owned a house in Jerusalem. At the time of Peter's imprisonment, A. D. 44, Jerusalem Christians assembled there for prayer, and it was thither that Peter turned when he was miraculously released from prison. Peter evidently knew the fam-

ily, and since he calls Mark his "son" in 1 Ptr 5:13, we may assume that Mark was converted by him. In A. D. 46 Mark accompanied Paul and Barnabas on the first missionary journey as far as Perga in Pamphylia, whence he returned to Jerusalem (Acts 13:13). Barnabas wished to take his cousin Mark along on the second missionary journey also, but Paul objected so violently that the two missionaries parted ways (Acts 15:37 ff.). Barnabas took Mark with him to Cyprus. Mark was with Paul again during the first Roman imprisonment according to Phmn 24 (A. D. 59—61), and Paul bespeaks a warm welcome for him on the part of the Christians of Colossae (Cl 4:10-11 f.). In 1 Ptr 5:13 Peter includes greetings from his "son" Mark to the Christians of Asia Minor; apparently he had worked there and was known there. Mark was with Peter in Rome at the time when he wrote First Peter in the early sixties. A few years later, at the time of Paul's last imprisonment, he was again in Asia Minor. Paul urges Timothy to bring Mark with him when he comes to Rome (2 Ti 4:11). This is the last New Testament notice of Mark. According to the church historian Eusebius, Mark was the founder of the church at Alexandria in Egypt and its first bishop. He is said to have died a martyr's death there.

4 Early tradition is unanimous in ascribing the second gospel to Mark, the interpreter of Peter. There is one bit of evidence in the gospel itself which also points, although only indirectly, to Mark. Only this gospel records the incident of the young man who ran away naked at the arrest of Jesus (Mk 14:51-52). Since no other convincing reason can be found for the inclusion of this detail, many scholars assume that the young man was Mark himself; the evangelist is thus appending his signature, as it were, to the gospel. It may even be that the house of Mark's mother, Mary, was the house in whose upper room our Lord celebrated the Passover with His disciples on the night in which He was betrayed.

Place and Date of Writing

5 The style and character of the gospel itself, which make it probable that the book was written for Gentile readers, confirm the tradition that Mark wrote his gospel in Rome. The gospel is therefore to be dated in the sixties of the first century, since Peter did not reach Rome until his later years. Some of the early witnesses declare that Mark wrote after the death of Peter. This would necessitate a date after A. D. 64. But since the tradition is not unanimous on this point, there can be no absolute certainty on it.

Characteristics of Mark's Gospel

6 The Gospel According to Mark is a gospel of action. As compared with Matthew, Mark emphasizes the deeds of Jesus. The deeds of Jesus are by no means isolated from His words; the word is Jesus' instrument in His deeds too; He speaks, and it is done. And Mark, besides giving two longer discourses of Jesus (4:1-34; 13:1-37), repeatedly emphasizes the centrality of the word in the ministry of Jesus and the effect of its authority on men, 1:14, 22, 38-39 f.; 2:2, 13; 4:1; 6:1-7; 9:7; 10:1; 11:18; cf. also 8:38. But it is chiefly by His works that Jesus is marked as the Proclaimer and the Bringer of the almighty grace of the kingdom of God, as the anointed King in whom man can trust, the Son of God in whom man can believe.

7 The Gospel According to Mark is Peter's Gospel. Papias' statement that Mark "became Peter's interpreter" can be variously interpreted; but his assertion that Mark's Gospel incorporates the preaching of Peter is certainly confirmed by the character of the gospel itself; it beigns with Peter's call (1:16); it reaches its critical point when Peter in the name of the Twelve confesses the Christ (8:29); it closes with a message from the risen Lord to His disciples *and Peter* (16:7). Peter's house is the center of operations at Capernaum (1:29), the followers of Jesus are called "Simon and those who were with him" (1:36), and Mark's use of an indefinite "they" for the disciples is most naturally understood as reproducing Peter's use of "we" (e.g., 1:21; 6:53). The resemblance of the structure of the gospel to that of Peter's sermon in the house of Cornelius (Acts 10:34-43) points in the same direction.

8 The many vivid and dramatic

touches in the gospel which mark the account as that of an eyewitness also reflect the preaching of Peter and are quite in keeping with what we know of his warm, vivacious, and volatile nature. The expressions, bearing, gestures, and feelings of Jesus are often noted, as is the effect of His words and deeds on the disciples and the multitudes. The narrative frequently drops into the vivid historical present, and Jesus' words are usually given in direct speech. The occasional reproduction of Jesus' words in His own tongue is probably also an echo of Peter's concrete and vivid narrative. (E.g., 5:41; 7:34)

9 The ancient tradition that Mark wrote his gospel for Gentiles, specifically at the request of Roman Christians, is confirmed by the gospel itself. Hebrew and Aramaic expressions are elucidated (3:17; 5:41; 7:11; 15:22), and Jewish customs are explained (7:2-4; 15:42). The evangelist himself quotes the Old Testament explicitly but once (1:2), although his narrative shows by allusion and echo that the narrator is conscious of the Old Testament background of the gospel story (e.g., 9:2-8; cf. Ex 24:12 ff.; 12:1-12; cf. Is 5:1 ff.). Mark reduces Greek money to terms of Roman currency (12:42) and explains an unfamiliar Greek term by means of a Latin one (15:16, *praetorium*); and Latinisms, that is, the direct taking over of Latin terms into the Greek, are more frequent in Mark's language than in that of the other evangelists.

OUTLINE

The Good News of Jesus Christ, the Son of God

I. 1:1-45 Christ's Coming Ushers in Promised Reign of God

II. 2:1—3:6 Christ's Coming Provokes Contradiction: Five Galilean Disputes

III. 3:7—8:30 Christ's Response to Contradiction

IV. 8:31—10:31 Christ Imprints Cross on Life of His Disciples

V. 10:32—13:37 Christ Goes to Jerusalem

VI. 14:1—16:20 Christ's Suffering, Death, and Resurrection

1:1-45 CHRIST'S COMING USHERS IN PROMISED REIGN OF GOD

1:1 *Beginning of the gospel.* This is best taken as the title of the whole gospel. See the Introduction, par. 1.

1:1-13 THE PREPARATION FOR HIS COMING

1:1-13 *John the baptizer* prepares men for Christ's coming by his *baptism of repentance for the forgiveness of sins* and by his announcement of the coming of the *mightier* One with His gift of the *Holy Spirit.* (2-8)

Jesus is prepared for His coming ministry by submitting to John's baptism, an act by which He marks His solidarity with sinful man; by being endowed with the fullnese of the Spirit; by being hailed *from heaven* as the *Son* and Servant of God; by overcoming the temptation of Satan *in the wilderness.* He appears as the embodiment of the new, true Israel, who obeys and triumphs where the old Israel disobeyed and failed.

1:2 *Isaiah the prophet.* Mark introduces the quotation from Isaiah concerning the *voice* (3; Is 40:3) with Malachi's word concerning the messenger (Ml 3:1). For the significance of the prophetic voice cf. Mt 3:1—4:11 note.

Messenger. Malachi had promised God's people that the hoped-for coming of the Lord would not come unheralded; there would be a warning messenger to prepare them before He came to judge and purify. (Ml 3:1-4)

1:4 *John the baptizer.* Cf. Mt 3:1-12 and the notes there for the ministry of John.

1:9-11 *Jesus . . . baptized by John.* Cf. Mt 3:13-17 note.

1:12-13 The temptation. Cf. Mt 4:1-13 note.

1:13 *Tempted by Satan.* This phrase does not imply that the temptation lasted 40 days; the temptation was the significant climax of His 40-day sojourn in the wilderness.

Was with the wild beasts. Only Mark has this feature. It may be merely an indication of the rigors of Jesus' wilderness sojourn; but more probably it signifies that Jesus is the new Man to whom all beasts are subject as they were to Adam (Gn 1:26; 2:19-20), that with the coming of Jesus there has dawned the Messianic age of paradisal peace of which Isaiah spoke (Is 11:6-9), that the covenant of peace promised by Ezekiel is being inaugurated. (Eze 34:25-31)

1:14-45 CHRIST'S COMING IN MIGHT AND MERCY

1:14-45 Jesus ANNOUNCES that the promised and long-awaited (*fulfilled,* 15) *kingdom of God is at hand* and calls men to repentance and faith, bidding them turn to the God who is at this decisive hour turning in might and mercy to them. (14-15)

Jesus ENACTS the good news of God's reign by His sovereign call to discipleship (16-20), His word of authority which *even the unclean spirits* must *obey* (21-28), His healing of the *sick* and the *possessed* (29-34), His cleansing of the *leper* (40-42). Yet, though His *fame spreads* (28, 37, 45), He remains the selfless Son and Servant who works for the glory of God, to whom He *prays* (35), whose law He obeys (44). God shall at His time glorify His Servant-Son, not the demons (24-25, 34), not men who do not as yet understand the significance of His mighty acts. (43-44)

1:14 *Gospel of God.* Both the saving action and His saving proclamation are God's, two aspects or phases of His one royal reign. (Cf. 2 Co 5:18-19, "God RECONCILED . . . entrusting to us the MESSAGE of reconciliation")

1:15 *The time is fulfilled.* The word for *time* implies "decisive time," the great moment foretold by the OT prophets in which God's final offer of His grace and His final summons to accept it and live by it appear in history. For this sense of time cf. Mt 26:18; Lk 19:44; Ro 5:6 ("right time").

Kingdom of God. Cf. Mt 3:2 note.

1:16-20 Calling of disciples. Cf. Mt 4:18-22 note.

1:24 *Holy One of God.* The unclean spirits are confronted by the Bearer of the Holy Spirit (8, 10) and recognize in Him the One destined to destroy them, since no compromise is possible between the Holy and the unclean.

1:27 *New teaching! . . . unclean spirits . . . obey him.* The authority of Jesus' Word establishes itself (teaching, 22); the power to *command* the *unclean spirits* only confirms it. With Jesus word and deed do not fall apart, as is so often the case with men; speech and act are one. (Cf. 2:8-11)

1:32 *At sundown.* The Sabbath ended at sundown, and men could carry their *sick* and *possessed* without fear of violating the Law.

1:40-45 The healing of the leper. Cf. Mt 8:1-4 note.

1:45 *Openly enter a town.* Jesus did not want a fevered "Messianic movement"; He wanted repentant and believing men (15). The mob excitement generated by His presence in a crowded town would have frustrated His purpose.

2:1—3:6 CHRIST'S COMING PROVOKES CONTRADICTION

2:1—3:6 In the account of five disputes in Galilee Mark shows how "religious" man (that is, man who wants to make his own legal righteousness count before God and therefore resists the grace of God) contradicts Christ and the Kingdom. Scribe and Pharisee oppose: the divine forgiveness pronounced by Jesus (2:1-12); Jesus' free fellowship at table with repentant sinners (2:13-17); Jesus the Bridegroom who brings the festal joy of the new age (2:18-22); the Son of Man who is Lord even of the Sabbath (2:23-28); the Healer who saves life on the Sabbath, while they (the jealous guardians of its sanctity) plan to kill on the Sabbath. (3:1-6)

2:1-12 Healing of the paralytic. Cf. Mt 8:23—9:8 note and notes on Mt 9:1, 3, 5, 8.

2:12 *Amazed . . . glorified God . . . "we never saw anything like this!"* Here the uniqueness of Jesus' authority breaks upon men; they see in Him the glory of the God of Israel, the Lord "who forgives . . . iniquity, who heals . . . diseases." (Ps 103:3)

2:13-17 Calling of Levi and eating with sinners. Cf. Mt 9:9-13. See notes on Mt 9:9-17 and 9:10, 14, 15.

2:14 *Levi.* The first gospel calls him Matthew and includes "Matthew the tax collector" in the list of the Twelve (Mt 9:9; 10:3); perhaps Levi came to be known as Matthew ("gift of the Lord") in the Christian community.

2:18-22 Jesus the Bridegroom. Cf. Mt 9:14-17. See notes on Mt 9:9-17 and 9:14, 15.

2:23-28 Plucking grain on the Sabbath. Cf. Mt 12:1-8. See notes on Mt 12:1-21 and 12:3, 4.

2:26 *Abiathar.* The *high priest* in the OT story of *David* and the (sacred) *bread of the Presence* is called Ahimelech (1 Sm 21:1); his son was Abiathar (1 Sm 22:20), closely associated with David. Some important manuscripts omit the reference to Abiathar, as do Matthew and Luke.

2:27-28 *Sabbath was made for man, not man for the sabbath; so the Son of man is lord even of the sabbath.* Jesus saw in the law of God one unified will, that of love (12:28-34). The God who asks love of man is the God who shows love to man—even the rabbis asserted that *the sabbath was made for man* (in order to relax the sabbath-law in cases of dire necessity) but the idea that a man can be *lord . . . of the sabbath* was unheard of in Judaism, and rightly so; Jesus can override the Sabbath only because He is *the Son of man* who brings the love of a forgiving God to man (2:10), who comes to serve and to give His life as a ransom for many

(10:45). The love of God makes Jesus the end of the Law.

3:1-6 *To save life or to kill on the sabbath.* Cf. Mt 12:9-14. See note on Mt 12:1-21. If the Sabbath was made for man and is, as the Lord's Day, the day on which His love is to be manifested, it is the Pharisees, not Jesus, who are violating the Sabbath. (6)

3:5 *Anger* mingled with grief is Jesus' reaction to thsoe who in *their hardness of heart* have no eyes for the divine goodness and mercy revealed to them in the works of Jesus.

3:6 *Herodians,* partisans of the Herods and Roman rule, whose cooperation would be needed *to destroy* Jesus since the Jewish authorities did not have the right to inflict capital punishment. (Jn 18:31)

3:7—8:30 CHRIST'S RESPONSE TO CONTRADICTION

3:7—8:30 Three motifs dominate this section of the gospel. First, the contradicted Christ maintains His will of mercy toward all who will accept the gracious reign of God present in His words and works. He heals, frees men from the power of demons, raises the dead, invites men in great numbers to the fellowship of the common meal, and gives a Gentile woman part in the abundant mercies of the God of Israel. The appointment and sending of the Twelve is the declaration of His mercy to the whole of Israel (12 tribes).

Second, the cleavage between Christ and those who oppose Him becomes ever sharper and deeper. The line of demarcation is drawn between Jesus and His "friends," the scribes and Pharisees, His fellow townsmen, those who are willing to call Him prophet but not to confess Him as the Christ. The death of John the Baptist is prophetic of Jesus' own fate. But even the bitterest opposition cannot make Him swerve from His course as the obedient Son and the Servant Christ. He withdraws before opposition, silences the demons who proclaim Him Son of God, "cannot" do mighty works in the face of His townsmen's unbelief, and refuses to give the sign from heaven that would satisfy arrogant unbelief. He executes judgment only by speaking in parables, which take from the man who has not even what he has.

Third, Christ deepens the communion between Himself and His disciples until they, and they alone, are capable of confessing Him as Christ. He appoints the Twelve to be with Him and gives them a share in His Messianic task and declares His disciples to be His true family. His teaching in parables is for His disciples a deepened revelation of the kingdom of God which equips them for their future task as His apostles. He permits them to witness His victory of death and comes to them across the waters. He evokes from them the confession which He had refused from the demons, the confession of faith which sets them apart from both His enemies and His admirers and binds them wholly to Himself forever, the confession: "You are the Christ."

3:7-12 JESUS WITHDRAWS, HEALS MANY, SILENCES DEMONS

3:7 *Jesus withdrew.* He meets the will to destroy Him (6) with the will to serve as the quiet Servant of God who "will not wrangle or cry aloud." (Mt 12:19-20 f.; 12:15-21)

3:12 *Ordered them not to make him known.* Not the defeated demons in their terror but the men given Him by God shall confess Him before men, in faith. (13-19)

3:13-19 THE APPOINTMENT OF THE TWELVE

3:13 *Called.* Cf. Mt 4:21 note.

3:14 *Appointed,* literally "made"; the apostles are His creation. (Cf. 2 Co 4:5-6)

3:16 *Surnamed Peter.* For the significance of the name cf. Mt 16:18 note.

3:17 *Surnamed Boanerges . . . sons of thunder,* probably because of their impetuous, "stormy" temperament. (9:38; Lk 9:54)

3:18 *Cananaean.* The name which distinguishes this Simon from Simon Peter indicates that he had been a member of the fiercely nationalistic Jewish party, the Zealots. (Cf. Lk 6:15; Acts 1:13)

3:20-30 BY THE PRINCE OF DEMONS HE CASTS OUT DEMONS: BLASPHEMY AGAINST HOLY SPIRIT

3:20-30 For the *Beelzebul* controversy (the deepest cleavage between Jesus and His contemporaries) and the warning concerning the *blasphemy against the Holy Spirit* see Mt 12:22-37 note.

3:20 *They could not even eat. They* are Jesus and His disciples, a particularly clear case of how the "we" of Peter's preaching shines through in Mark's account. See the Introduction, par. 7.

3:21 *His family.* Cf. 31, "his mother . . . brothers." This verse illustrates how Jesus' consuming passion for ministry was misunderstood and misinterpreted even by family and friends.

3:31-35 THE FAMILY OF JESUS

3:31-35 Cf. Mt 12:43-50 note.

3:35 *Sister.* Woman has her place of undiminished honor in the family of God. (Gl 3:28)

4:1-9 THE PARABLE OF THE SOWER

4:1-9 Cf. Mt 13:1-9 note; 13:18-23 note.

4:10-25 THE PURPOSE OF TEACHING IN PARABLES

4:10-12, 21-25 Cf. Mt 13:1-52 note; 13:10-17.

4:13-20 Cf. Mt 13:18-23 note.

4:11 *The secret of the kingdom.* The phrase recalls the vision of Dn 2. The "secret" is the fact that the Kingdom "is at hand" in the person of Jesus (1:15); in His Word and work God is revealing what He had promised through Daniel for "the latter days," the establishment of a kingdom by "the God of heaven," which shall put an end to the kingdoms of this world but shall itself never be destroyed (Dn 2:28, 44-45). See the whole of Dn 2 for a portrayal of the kingdom of God as opposed to earthly kingdoms, coming in unspectacular form ("a stone . . . cut out by no human hand," 34) as a kingdom not of this world but finally and eternally triumphant. To have this secret is God's gift; to have it not is the guilt of refusing God's revelation (cf. 25) and calls forth God's judgment, as Isaiah had pronounced it. (12; cf. Is 6:9-10)

4:13 *Understand this parable . . . understand all the parables?* The key to the parable of the sower is Jesus as the presence of God's kindgom among men. And He is the key to all the parables; the parable of the self-growing seed (26-29) and of the mustard seed (30-32) also tell His story.

4:21-25 If the message of the parable is the story of Jesus Christ, the Son of God (1:1), if it is the Gospel of God (1:14), it must and will emerge from the hiddenness of the parable's veiled utterance and *come to light.* In that coming to light the apostles have a decisive role to play (3:14, "be sent out to preach"); it is therefore of crucial importance that they should have *ears to hear* and *take heed what* they *hear.* The *measure* of obedience to the word which they give will be the measure of the blessing which they will *get* in their ministry; fidelity is all. (Cf. 1 Co 4:1-2)

4:25 *To him who has.* In the Gospel of Matthew Jesus applies this standard to both revelation (Mt 13:12) and ministry (Mt 25:29). Here too both ideas are present.

4:26-29 PARABLE OF SEED GROWING SECRETLY

4:26-29 This parable, only in Mark, conveys both a warning and a word of encouragement to Jesus' disciples. However important their role may be (21-25), they are not to imagine that the Kingdom is their kingdom or its triumph their triumph; the Kingdom remains God's mysteriously creative work. He is "Lord of the harvest" (Mt 9:38). This serves for encouragement also; however slow and unspectacular the "progress" of the Kingdom may be, the outcome is in the sure hands of the Creator. Men may pray, "Thy kingdom come," with patience and confidence.

4:29 *Harvest.* Cf. Mt 9:37; Jn 4:35.

4:30-34 PARABLE OF THE MUSTARD SEED

4:30-34 Cf. Mt 13:31-33 note.

4:33 *As they were able to hear it,* that is, in terms familiar to their experience (sower, seed, mustard seed). The parables speak plainly to those who have not rejected Jesus, the key to the parables.

4:35-41 THE STILLING OF THE STORM

4:35-41 Cf. Mt 8:23—9:8 note and 8:26 note.

The story is told in simple language, and all the details of the account *(other boats, boat was already filling, cushion, said to one another)* leave the impression that the details come from one who experienced the event. The account indicates strongly that Mark "became Peter's interpreter." (Cf. Introduction, par. 7)

4:39 The disciples are made conscious of their frail humanity in the presence of this Lord of the waves. Jesus deepens His communion with the disciples by using His power in the service of compassion for them and by using the event to build up their faith. (40)

5:1-20 THE DEMONIAC OF GERASA

5:1-20 Cf. Mt 8:28-34 note; cf. Mt 8:23—9:8 note. The line of demarcation between Jesus and men is very apparent here, where some want to rid themselves of Him (because He costs them swine) and one man becomes the messenger of His mercy. All marvel; not all respond. (20)

5:1 *Gerasenes.* Both here and in Matthew and Luke the manuscripts fluctuate between Gerasenes, Gergesenes, and Gadarenes.

5:9 *Legion,* the largest unit of the Roman army; then used to indicate any large number. (Cf. Mt 26:53)

5:13 *Drowned in the sea.* Many are offended at the death of the swine here. We had best honor the decision of Him who made both swine and man and gave His life for man.

5:18 *Begged him that he might be with him.* Jesus alone determines who shall be with Him; He calls and appoints. (1:20; 3:14)

5:19 *Go home . . . and tell them.* This contrasts strangely with Jesus' usual command that healed persons tell no one (1:44; 7:36; 8:26). The exception may be due to the fact that the miracle took place in Gentile territory (swine, 11; Decapolis, 20), so that the proclamation of "how much the Lord has done for you" would not impede Jesus' real mission but might serve as preparation for a later mission to the Gentiles in that region.

5:20 *Decapolis.* (Cf. Mt 4:25 note).

5:21-43 JARIUS' DAUGHTER AND THE WOMAN WITH THE FLOW OF BLOOD

5:21-43 Cf. Mt 9:18-34 note; 9:20, 22, 23 notes. In these two mighty acts the majesty of Him whom men dare to contradict is apparent. He is Lord not only over the sea and the demons but over death itself; and His vigilant compassion can hear and answer the unuttered petition of the woman who dared only to touch His garment. He who has eyes to see and ears to hear cannot rank Him with John or Elijah or one of the prophets (8:28); He must be confessed as the Christ. (8:29)

5:33 *Fear and trembling.* Since a woman with a flow of blood was unclean according to the Law, she feared rebuke from the Man whom her touch had defiled. But Jesus, who had touched and healed the unclean leper (1:41), cannot be defiled.

5:40 *They laughed.* This is the only place in the NT where Jesus' presence evokes laughter, just where He manifests Himself as Overcomer of death, which silences laughter.

6:1-6a JESUS REJECTED AT NAZARETH

6:1-6a The men of Nazareth are *astonished* at the *wisdom* and the *mighty works* of Jesus of Nazareth but take *offense* at the *carpenter* whose *mother, brothers,* and *sisters* they know so well. Their *unbelief* makes revelation impossible; He who met every need of man with God's creative power but gave no sign to questioning and demanding unbelief (cf. 8:11-13) *could do no mighty work there.*

6:3 *Son of Mary and brother of James.* The much-debated question whether the brothers of Jesus were children of Joseph and Mary born after Jesus or children of Joseph by a previous marriage or Jesus' cousins will probably never be settled to everyone's satisfaction. The first suggestion (that they were children of Joseph and Mary) seems the most natural.

6:6b-13 THE SENDING OF THE TWELVE

6:6b-13 Cf. Mt 10:1-4; 10:5-15 notes. Jesus draws His disciples closer to Himself by employing them in the extension of His Messianic mission.

6:7 *The twelve.* Cf. 3:13-19.

6:12 *Men should repent. Repent* is shorthand for the message summed up in 1:15.

6:13 *Anointed with oil.* Healing by anointing with oil is mentioned only here and in Ja 5:14 as an act involving the power of God (Lk 10:34 records common medicinal practice). Neither passage explains the significance of the oil; James stresses the power of the accompanying prayer.

6:14-29 THE DEATH OF JOHN THE BAPTIST

6:14-29 Cf. Mt 14:1-12 note. Herod senses that in Jesus the *powers* which he thought he had banished when he executed John are *at work;* the disquieting voice of God calling him to account has not been silenced. The death of John the Baptist, told here and not in its natural place in the sequence of events (cf. 1:14), is prophetic of Jesus' fate (cf. Mk 9:12-13; Mt 17:12-13). Both in the village (1-6) and in the royal court men are turning against Him; the cleavage deepens because of His teaching.

6:30-44 THE RETURN OF THE TWELVE AND THE FEEDING OF THE 5,000

6:30-44 Cf. Mt 14:15-21 note. The contradicted Christ still invites men to Himself by offering them the fellowship of the meal which His *compassion* (34) provides.

6:41 *Blessed.* Jesus speaks the blessing as a Jewish housefather would at his table.

6:45-56 JESUS WALKS ON THE SEA

6:45-56 Cf. Mt 14:22-36.

6:48 *Fourth watch of the night.* Cf. Mt 14:25 note.

6:52 *They did not understand about the loaves.* If their *hearts* had not been dulled by unbelief *(hardened),* they could have known that He who multiplied the *loaves* could come to them, not as a ghost (49) but as a person, and bring peace to them.

6:56 *Fringe of his garment.* Cf. 5:28. The compassion that reached out to the woman is there for all who will follow her example.

7:1-23 THE TRADITION OF THE ELDERS: WHAT DEFILES A MAN

7:1-12 Cf. Mt 15:1-20 note.

7:11 *Corban,* literally "offering." Matthew translates the word *("given to God").* Cf. Mt 15:5-6 note.

7:19 *Thus he declared all foods clean.* Later on the Lord had to remind Peter of this. (Acts 10:9-15)

7:22 *Foolishness* is not only intellectual but moral and religious. Cf. the use of "fool" in Lk 12:20-21 of the man who "lays up treasure for himself, and is not rich toward God."

7:24-30 THE SYROPHOENICIAN WOMAN

7:24-30 Cf. Mt 15:21-28 note.

7:26 *A Greek, a Syrophoenician by birth,* a Greek-speaking inhabitant of Syrophoenicia, a district so called because ancient Phoenicia belonged to the Roman province of Syria and to distinguish it from Libophoenicia around Carthage.

7:31-37 HE HAS DONE ALL THINGS WELL

7:31-37 The mercy of Christ restores the deaf man to health and to the society from which his impediment had shut him out. The response of those who witnessed the act of restoration (37, *done all things well*) recalls the "very good" of creation (Gn 1:31). The coming of the Kingdom is the new creation. (Cf. Is 35:5-6; Mt 11:5)

7:33 *Spat.* Cf. 8:23; Jn 9:33. This feature is found only in cases where communication with the person to be healed is difficult; since spittle was held to have curative powers in Judaism (both by itself and in connection with magical spells), the action indicates to the deaf man the presence of the Healer. The cure is brought about simply by the mighty word of Jesus (34), which eliminates any idea of magic.

8:1-10 THE FEEDING OF THE 4,000

8:1-10 The great gesture of offered fellowship is repeated (cf. 6:30-44). It is difficult to say whether the account of the feeding of 4,000 is intended merely to emphasize by repetition Jesus' will of mercy to the multitudes (cf. the repeated accounts of Sabbath controversies, expulsion of demons, etc.) or has independent significance. Some see such independent significance indicated by the time and locale of this feeding: as the feeding of the 5,000 followed the sending and return of the Twelve (6:30; cf. 6:7) and concludes and crowns the ministry of Jesus in Galilee, the feeding of the 4,000 follows Jesus' wanderings in non-Israelite territory (7:24, 31) and is Jesus' gesture of fellowship toward those Gentile regions. The children of God's household (Israel) are fed first; then the Gentiles partake of His bounty. (7:27-28)

8:10 *Dalmanutha.* Location unknown.

8:11-13 DEMAND FOR A SIGN FROM HEAVEN

8:11-13 For the impiety that lies in the demand for a sign, cf. Mt 12:38-42 note. The "sign of Jonah" of which Jesus speaks in Matthew is not the kind of *sign from heaven* the Pharisees expect. In both gospels Jesus refuses the sign, and the cleavage between Him and Judaic leadership widens. Men who come to Jesus to *argue* and *test* Him cannot find the way to the Christ; Jesus must in sorrow *(sighed deeply)* leave them to the judgment their unbelief invites; they continue their demand for a sign at the cross. (15:32)

8:14-21 THE LEAVEN OF THE PHARISEES AND THE LEAVEN OF HEROD

8:14-21 Cf. Mt 16:5-12 note.

8:15 *Leaven of Herod* (or *Herodians*). Leaven (fermented dough used to make new dough rise) penetrates imperceptibly but irresistibly (cf. Mt. 13:33). The rabbis used the term to designate the evil impulse in man, and that is probably the meaning here. For all their differences, the *Pharisees* in their arrogant self-centered religiosity and Herod, or the Herodians, in their self-seeking political machinations are at one in their impulse of opposition to Jesus Christ (3:6; 12:13). Their example and influence can ruin the disciples, whose hold on Jesus is still a shaky one. (17-21)

8:18 *Eyes . . . ears.* The grace and power of Christ, who gives sight to the blind, hearing to the deaf, and speech to the dumb (7:37; cf. 7:32-36; 8:22-26), has made but slow headway in their unperceptive hearts.

8:22-26 HEALING THE BLIND AT BETHSAIDA

8:23 *Spit.* Cf. 7:33 note; Jn 9:6.

8:27-30 YOU ARE THE CHRIST

8:27-30 Here as always in His relationship to His disciples (cf. call, apostolate) Jesus takes the initiative. He has separated His disciples from those who oppose Him; now He draws the line between disciples who believe in Him and *men* who admire Him and "appreciate" Him and binds them to Himself for better or worse, life or death (cf. 35), and forever.

8:28 *John the Baptist.* Cf. 6:14.

Elijah. Cf. 6:15; Mt 11:14; 17:10; Lk 1:17. "Men" see in Jesus only one who plays a preliminary and preparatory role in the coming of the Kingdom. (Ml 4:5-6)

8:30 *Tell no one.* Cf. Mt 16:20 note.

8:31—10:31 CHRIST IMPRINTS CROSS ON LIFE OF HIS DISCIPLES

8:31—10:31 By His prediction of His Passion (8:31-33), by making the way of the cross the pattern of His disciples' way (8:34—9:1), by going down from the mountain of transfiguration to the contradiction and agony of men (9:2-29), by His teaching that the greatness of the disciple lies in unspectacular ministry to the child (9:30-37), a greatness which is free of narrowhearted exclusiveness (9:38-41) and marked by self-denial (9:42-50)—by these means Christ puts the imprint of His cross on the life of His disciples. They are to go the way of the cross to glory; but they are to go this way within the orders which God has established for this world. Therefore Christ shapes their relationship to marriage, children, and property. (10:1-31)

8:31—9:1 THE WAY OF THE CROSS

8:31—9:1 Jesus predicts His Passion, saying this plainly (8:32). He brands as satanic any will, even Peter's, which would oppose that way. He makes His way to the cross the pattern of the disciple's way; the disciple is to be ready to *lose his life* in the service of Christ in order to *save his life.*

8:32 *Rebuke him.* In Peter's mind the idea of the cross and of the Christ are contradictory; he feels that Jesus is contradicting the confession of 8:29 when He predicts His cross.

8:33 *Seeing his disciples.* Peter has by his rash words endangered the faith of all the disciples; therefore the public and emphatic rebuke of Jesus.

Behind me. The disciple is to follow after Jesus, not to dictate the way of Jesus.

Satan . . . on the side . . . of men. Cf. Mt 16:23 note.

Side of God. God wills the cross; He gives the Son the cup which He drinks. (Cf. 10:38; 14:36)

8:38 *Adulterous.* Unfaithful to the covenant God who was a husband to Israel. (Jer 31:32; Hos 1—3)

9:1 Cf. 9:9; Mt 16:28 note.

9:2-29 THE TRANSFIGURATION

9:2-29 Cf. Mt 17:1-27 note (to 23).

9:2 *After six days.* Since indications of time sequence are rare in Mark, this note is probably intended to link the Transfiguration closely with the confession of Peter in 8:29 and the prediction of 8:31. It provides a commentary on the words "and after three days rise again"—Peter, James, and John have a glimpse of the glory which awaits the Christ beyond the cross.

9:14 *Scribes arguing with them* (the disciples), probably on the basis of their failure to heal the demoniac boy (18, 28), which the scribes would use to discredit their Master.

9:15 *Were greatly amazed.* The reason for their amazement is not stated; perhaps something of the glory of the Transfiguration still lingered about Jesus. Others compare 10:32, where Jesus' resolute devotion to death creates amazement in the disciples.

9:29 *Prayer* and faith are here closely linked. "All things are possible to him who believes" (23), and faith works through prayer.

9:30-50 HE WAS TEACHING HIS DISCIPLES

9:30-50 Jesus teaches His disciples, and His teaching is the cross, His own cross (30-32) and His disciples'; the cross puts an end to the question of who is *the greatest* (34) and makes him great who is *servant of all* (35). The disciple finds his greatness in service to the *child,* the little one who needs his help; in serving the child he serves Christ and God Himself (37). The disciple goes the way of the servant, with no self-seeking motives; this makes him generous and open-hearted toward every recognition of Christ and every slight service rendered to them because of Christ (38-41). This greatness found in service makes the disciple scrupulous toward the *little ones who believe in* Christ, capable of heroic self-sacrifice in their behalf, lest he cause them to sin. They are to become men *salted with fire* (cleansed of self by God's discipline), *salt* that seasons and preserves, and men working together, *at peace with one another.* (42-50)

9:30-32 The second of the three major predictions of the Passion. (Cf. 8:31; 10:32-33)

9:32 *Afraid to ask him.* Cf. 10:32 note; Lk 9:45.

9:37 *One such child . . . receives me.* Cf. Mt 18:1-35 note.

9:38 *In your name,* on Your authority. Cf. Acts 16:18 for the formula.

9:48 *Worm . . . fire.* The language is that of Is 66:24, which describes the place of punishment of those who have rebelled againt the Lord in terms of the place where the refuse of Jerusalem was destroyed, the valley of Hinnom (Gehenna).

9:49 *Salted with fire.* To be acceptable to God, every sacrifice had to be salted with salt (Lv 2:13). So to be an acceptable servant of God and Christ, the disciple must be purified by the fire of self-denial (43-47), which God uses to make him a fit servant. For fire as God's means of purifying His servants cf. Ml 3:2-3. For the apostolic ministry pictured as sacrifice cf. Ph 2:17.

9:50 *Have salt in yourselves.* If they are thus (49) purified for service, they can fulfill their function of being "the salt of the earth." (Mt 5:13)

Peace with one another, instead of vying for greatness. (34)

10:1-31 MARRIAGE, CHILDREN, AND PROPERTY

10:1-31 Cf. Mt 19:1—20:16 notes. The way of the cross does not evade the obligations and temptations of family and money but meets them and deals with them in faith. Marriage is to be the pure communion which God the Creator ordained (1-12). Children are to be received, honored, and imitated as the objects of the love of God the King (13:16). God the only Good can free them from the fatal hold of property, and He will provide for all who renounce the created blessings for His sake and give them *eternal life in the age to come.* (17-31)

(10:1-31, see previous page)

10:31 *First will be last.* The parable of the workers in the vineyard is Jesus' own commentary on this saying. Cf. Mt 20:1-16. Cf. notes at Mt 19:27—20:16 and 19:30.

10:32—13:37 CHRIST GOES TO JERUSALEM

10:32—13:37 The cross pronounces doom on the empty, self-centered piety of Jerusalem (the old Israel) and gives the disciples, the new Israel, their hope of glory. Three phases may be distinguished: (a) Christ binds His disciples to Himself as the Servant Messiah (10:32-52). (b) Christ confronts Jerusalem with His Messianic claim and His call to repentance (11:1—12:37). (c) Christ separates His disciples from the scribes, the teachers of Israel. All three find their conclusion in the discourse of ch. 13, in which Jesus predicts doom for Jerusalem and deliverance for His own.

10:32-52 Christ Binds His Disciples to Himself

10:32-52 Jesus claims His disciples for Himself as the dying Servant Christ. He predicts His death for the third time; Israel's leaders will reject Him, condemn Him to death, and deliver Him to the Gentiles for execution (10:32-34). He is forced to remind His disciples again that participation in His future glory comes only by participation in His suffering, that the measure of all greatness is the self-giving greatness of the Son of Man who serves to the utmost, to the giving of His life for the ransoming of the "many" (13:35-45); and He once more sums up His whole serving and saving ministry in one mighty deed: He opens the eyes of blind Bartimaeus in order that the new, seeing man may follow Him "on the way." (10:46-52)

10:32-45 Cf. Mt 20:17-28 notes.

10:32 *They were amazed . . . afraid.* Cf. 9:32. They were filled with awe at the sight of Him who took His way to the cross in full consciousness of His destiny and its significance for the destiny of mankind.

10:38 *Baptism with which I am baptized.* Cf. Mt 3:13-15 note. The baptism to which Jesus refers is His being plunged into suffering and death. (Cf. Lk 12:50)

10:42 *Supposed to rule,* that is, are recognized as rulers.

10:46-52 Cf. Mt 20:29-34 note. On Jesus as the Servant prophesied in Isaiah cf. Mt 8:17 and 12:18-21 notes.

10:46 *Bartimaeus* means *son of Timaeus.* Cf. Bar-Jona, Mt 16:17.

11:1—12:37 Christ Confronts Jerusalem

11:1—12:37 In deed and word Jesus confronts Jerusalem, the capital and heart of Israel, with His Messianic claim and call to repentance.

11:1-11 THE MESSIANIC ENTRY

11:1-11 Cf. Mt 21:1-11 notes.

11:3 *The Lord has need.* This is the first time in Mark that Jesus calls Himself Lord; this act is a royal requisitioning.

11:10 *Blessed is the kingdom of our father David.* The promise given to David (2 Sm 7:16; Ps 89:3, 4, 20, 21, 27, 28, 29, 35, 36), the long-cherished hope of the Messiah, is being fulfilled. The blessing of His reign *(kingdom)* is about to descend on His people.

11:12-26 THE CALL TO REPENTANCE IN DEED

11:12-26 Cf. Mt 21:12-22. By His cleansing of

the temple (15-18) and His blasting of the fig tree (12-14, 20-26) Jesus pronounces judgment on the self-centered and fruitless piety of Israel and therewith calls His people to repentance.

11:13 *For it was not the season for figs.* These words and the note in 14, "And his disciples heard it" (the curse on the fig tree), indicate that Jesus' action is a symbolic one intended for the instruction of His disciples. Jesus' curse upon the fig tree is not the petulant reaction of one disappointed in hope of refreshment; it is His word of judgment on the fruitless piety of His people. For the image and the idea cf. Mi 7:1-4.

11:16 *Carry anything through the temple,* that is, use the temple courts as a commercial street like any other. "There shall no longer be a trader in the house of the Lord of hosts on that day." (Zch 14:21)

11:25 Cf. Mt 6:12, 14-15 notes.

11:27-33 THE CALL TO REPENTANCE IN WORD: BY WHAT AUTHORITY?

11:27-33 Cf. Mt 21:25, 27. Be refusing to validate His *authority* for the Jewish authorities who have not heeded John the Baptist's call to repentance (his baptism) Jesus once more imposes that call to repentance upon them; if they will not heed that call, they can never know the authority of the Christ and be blessed by it.

11:33 *Neither will I tell you.* They have refused to be told when God spoke to them in John's baptism and in Jesus' word and deed. Now they shall not be told—except by the cross and resurrection of Jesus.

12:1-12 THE CALL TO REPENTANCE IN WORD: THE PARABLE OF THE VINEYARD

12:1-12 Cf. Mt 21:33, 36, 42, 46 notes. The parable of the rebellious tenants presses home Jesus' call to repentance; it calls upon Israel's leaders to give God what is God's, to beware of the fearful fate that awaits them if they disobey, and to realize that they cannot prevent the triumph of the Christ and the rise of a new people of God. Jesus calls in vain. (12)

12:13-34 THE CALL TO REPENTANCE IN WORD: THREE DISPUTES

12:13-34 Cf. Mt 22:15-40. In His disputes with the *Pharisees and Herodians,* with the *Sadducees,* and the *scribes,* Jesus again shows what separates Israel's leading men from the Son whom God has sent to them. The Pharisees (13-17) scruple about *paying taxes to Caesar* but will not give God what is God's—Jesus goes to the cross because He is "on the side of God" (8:33), in order that God's grace and righteousness may prevail. The Sadducees with their rational denial of the *resurrection* (18-27) know neither the *scriptures* nor the *power of God*—Jesus can go to the cross because He knows that the Scriptures direct Him to the cross (9:12) and that the power of the living God will raise Him on the third day and seat Him at God's right hand (12:36). The scribe (28:34) searches amid the manifold commandments of God and cannot for all His searching be sure of the primal will of God—Jesus goes to the cross sure of the will of God; He goes with a whole *love* for God which binds Him in love to man.

12:13 *Herodians.* Cf. Mt 22:16 note.

12:28 *Which commandment is the first?* First in the sense of foremost, most important, most prominent.

12:29-31 Cf. Dt 6:4-5; Lv 19:18.

12:32 *Your are right, Teacher.* The scribe's approval of Jesus' answer is natural enough. The question of the unifying principle of the Law, the commandment which expressed the will underlying all the 613 commandments of the Law, was much discussed in the schools, and answers like that of Jesus were given. But only Jesus wrote the answer with His whole life and death.

12:33 *More than . . . sacrifices.* Cf. 1 Sm 15:22; Hos 6:6.

12:34 *You are not far from the kingdom of God.* One who so grasps the will of God the King is but one step removed from the recognition that in Jesus, the anointed King (the Christ), this will is being fulfilled.

12:35-37 JESUS' MESSIANIC CLAIM: DAVID'S SON AND LORD

12:35-37 Cf. Mt 22:41-46 note; Mk 14:63-64, where Jesus is condemned to die as a blasphemer for making this Messianic claim in the words of Ps 110:1. Here it becomes crystal clear that Jesus is, according to the old saying, "either God or not a good man."

12:38-44 The Scribes and the Poor Widow

12:38-44 Cf. Mt 23:1-39 note. Jesus warns His disciples against the *scribes,* who in their pride and self-seeking introduce a fatal cleavage into their piety and become blind guides to the people for whom they are responsible. They fail both in their lives and in their responsibility and will therefore receive the greater condemnation. The selfless piety of the *poor widow,* who gives *her whole living* to the one good God, loving Him with her whole heart and trusting Him for her future, stands in sharp contrast to that of the scribes—she is, in Jesus' judgment, "not far from the kingdom of God," like the scribe who recognized that the will of God is love. (34)

12:38 *Long robes,* garments which mark them as men of piety and learning.

12:40 *Devour widows' houses,* an extreme case of the "extortion and rapacity" with which Jesus reproaches them in Mt 23:25.

12:41 *The treasury,* trumpet-shaped containers set up in the court of the women in the temple for receiving the contributions of the faithful.

13:1-37 Jesus Predicts Fall of Jerusalem and Deliverance of His Elect

13:1-37 Cf. Mt 24:1-31 note. The fall of the temple is the beginning of the end (1-2). Henceforth all history is to be for Jesus' disciples the *sign* (4) which alerts them to the coming of the *end:* the war-torn history of the world (3-8), the history of the persecuted church and the universal preaching of the *gospel* in the power of the Spirit and in spite of man's failures (9-13), the appearance of the *desolating sacrilege* and the coming of the great tribulation at the fall of Jerusalem, together with the appearance of *false Christs* in those fevered times (14-23)—all constitute the sign which points to the coming of the *Son of man* in *power and glory* to *gather* in *his elect* from all the earth (24-27). The parable of the *fig tree* prepares the disciples to live through that history in calm and patient hope; Jesus' enduring *words* assure them that all this history is in the hands of the Creator whose faithful working they see in the approach of summer year by year (28-31); the parable of the returning master of the house makes their hope a vigilant and responsible expectation of their returning Lord. (32-37)

13:9 *Beaten in synagogues.* Cf. Acts 5:40; 2 Co 11:24.

13:10 *Must . . . be preached.* The same overruling divine will that controls wars and rumors of wars (7) will cause the Gospel to speed and triumph amid disasters.

13:14 *Desolating sacrilege.* Cf. Mt 24:15 note. *Where it ought not to be,* in the holy land and place.

Let the reader understand both the reference to the prophecy of Daniel (Dn 12:11; 9:27) and the warning of Jesus recorded here, which is based on Daniel's word.

13:27 *From the ends of the earth to the ends of heaven.* This seems to be a fusion of two expressions: "from one end of the earth to the other" and "from horizon to horizon."

13:37 *What I say to you I say to all.* The disciples are to transmit this admonition to the church.

14:1—16:20 CHRIST'S SUFFERING, DEATH, AND RESURRECTION

14:1—16:20 Cf. Mt 26—28 notes. Jesus goes alone into His death. His disciples all fail Him; Judas betrays Him (14:10-11, 43-50), the three cannot watch with Him one hour (14:32-42), all flee at His arrest (14:26-31, 43-52), and Peter denies Him (14:66-72). His people reject Him (14:1-2, 43-46, 56-65; 15:1-15); all join in mocking the condemned and dying King of Israel (15:29-32). Gentile (Roman) justice abandons Him to the fury of His people (15:1-15), and Gentile soldiers mock Him (15:16-20). He is forsaken by His God (15:34). He suffers in full and simple humanity; witness the agony in Gethsemane (14:32-42) and His cry from the cross (15:34). And yet He endures with the quiet majesty of the Son of God; He is the Sufferer, and yet He is in charge. He unmasks the betrayer (14:17-21); He gives His dying self to His disciples (14:22-25); He sings the Passover psalms in praise of God the Deliverer at the very hour of His arrest (14:26); He foretells the failure of His disciples (14:27-31); He rebukes His captors (14:48-49), is silent and composed before the Sanhedrin (14:61) and before Pilate (15:4-5), makes no answer to those who mock Him (15:16-20, 29-32), and departs in full consciousness with a loud cry (15:37). His death is His voluntary act; by His shed blood He inaugurates the new covenant (14:23-24), and in His dying He drinks the cup of God's judgment upon the sin of man (15:33-39; cf. 10:38 note; 14:36). The ransom for many is paid. (Cf. 10:45)

His resurrection is enacted forgiveness; the risen Christ restores to His fellowship the disciples, who had failed Him, and Peter, who had denied Him (16:7). He sends His disciples out to *all the world* to preach the Gospel to all creation for the salvation of all men—*all the world* includes the Israel that had rejected Him and killed Him. (16:15, 20)

14:1-11 PRELUDE TO THE PASSION

14:1-11 Cf. Mt 26:1-16 note.

14:1 *Passover.* Cf. Mt 26:26 note.

14:3 *Nard,* an aromatic plant from which a fragrant oil was extracted.

14:12-25 THE LAST PASSOVER, THE NEW PASSOVER

14:12-25 Cf. Mt 26:17-29 note.

14:13 *A man carrying a jar of water.* Since women ordinarily fetched water (cf. Jn 4:28), a man carrying a water jar would be conspicuous.

14:26-52 THE STRICKEN SHEPHERD AND THE SCATTERED FLOCK

14:26-52 Cf. Mt 26:30-56 note.

14:51-52 The story of the young man who ran away is peculiar to Mark; the young man may be Mark himself. See the Introduction, par. 4.

Naked. Cf. Am 2:16, where it is said that "in that day," when God's judgment strikes the sin of His people, "he who is stout of heart among the mighty shall flee away naked." "That day" of judgment has come, and no man can stand before it save One.

14:53-72 THE TRIAL BEFORE CAIAPHAS AND PETER'S DENIAL

14:53-72 Cf. Mt 26:57-75 note.

14:62 *I am.* Cf. 6:50; 13:6. The words are spoken in the usual style of the OT declarations of the Lord (cf. Ex 3:14; Dt 32:39) and may include a claim to deity.

15:1-20 THE TRIAL BEFORE PILATE

15:1-20 Cf. Mt 27:1-31 note.

15:21-47 THE CRUCIFIXION, DEATH, AND BURIAL OF JESUS

15:21-47 Cf. Mt 27:32-66 note.

15:21 *The father of Alexander and Rufus.* Simon and his sons were evidently well known to the church (or churches) for whom Mark wrote. If the Rufus of Ro 16:13 is identical with Simon's son, he was a member of one of the churches in Rome.

15:23 *Mingled with myrrh,* as a narcotic to dull the pain.

15:29 *Aha!* An expression of scornful wonder.

15:43 *Joseph . . . member of the council . . . took courage.* For a member of the council which had condemned Jesus to identify Himself thus with Jesus, publicly and at considerable expense, was an act of great courage. It would seem that Joseph in *looking for the kingdom of God* saw and welcomed its coming in Jesus.

15:44 *Wondered if,* or better, "was surprised that he" was "already dead." The suffering of the crucified was usually prolonged.

16:1-20 THE RESURRECTION

16:1-20 Cf. Mt 28:1-20 note.

16:7 *And Peter.* The special mention of Peter was occasioned by the fact that he had not only fled with the rest but had also denied Jesus in spite of his assurances.

16:8 *Trembling . . . astonishment . . . afraid.* It may be that the book which tells of the "beginning of the gospel of Jesus Christ, the Son of God" (1:1), ended here on this note of astonished fear and awe. This note is a recurrent one in Mark; men are awed and overwhelmed at Jesus' word of authority which even demons must obey (2:12); at the Son of God who stills the storm and walks across the waters (4:41; 6:51); at the Son of Man who has power to heal and to forgive sins on earth (2:12); at Him who conquers death with a word (5:42); at the glory of the transfigured beloved Son (9:6); at the Christ who goes in unshaken majesty toward Jerusalem and the cross (10:32). All this recurs in higher potency at the resurrection; these trembling women know, what every disciple of the Risen One comes to know, that in this Son of God all the compassion and power of God is present, that there is only one thing to do—to fall down before Him and own Him as Lord and God, serve Him, and work out your salvation with fear and trembling, for here in Him God is at work giving men the will and the power to work according to His good pleasure (Ph 2:12-13). It is a solemn close to the gospel; the moment when all choices in life narrow down to one choice is a solemn one. It is the occurrence of that moment, then, that set the Good News going through the world; and it is the recurrence of that moment, ever and again, that keeps it going until the Christ, the Son of God, shall return.

16:9-10 Cf. Jn 20:11-18; Lk 24:10-11.

16:12-13 Cf. Lk 24:13-27.

16:14-18 Cf. Lk 24:36-49; Jn 20:19-23, 26-31; Mt 28:16.

16:15-16 Cf. Mt 28:18-20.

16:19 Cf. Lk 24:50-53; Acts 1:4-14.

LUKE

INTRODUCTION

The third gospel is the most outspokenly "teaching" gospel of them all. This is already obvious from the dedicatory preface (Lk 1:1-4), in which the author promises Theophilus a full and orderly account of things Theophilus to some extent already knows, in order that he may have reliable information concerning the things he has been taught. Luke is not proclaiming the Gospel for the first time to Theophilus and his Gentile readers generally; rather, he intends to expand and fill in the already familiar basic outline of the Gospel message with a full account of what Jesus did and taught (cf. Acts 1:1). This is borne out by the fullness and completeness of his narrative; it is likewise confirmed by the fact that Luke extends his narrative in the Acts of the Apostles to include not only what Jesus "began to do and teach," but also the continued activity of the exalted Lord through His messengers by the power of the Spirit. The words of the preface, "accomplished *among us,*" indicate that Luke had this extension of the account in mind from the very beginning; he is, like Mark, going to tell the beginning of the Gospel of Jesus Christ; but he is going to carry on the account of it to include the triumphant progress of the Gospel from Jerusalem to Rome, the center of the world. He is recording that mighty growth of the Word of the Lord which he and his readers have come to know as the power of God in their own experience. The Spirit of God guided the mind of Luke to see that a man has not come to know the Christ fully until he has come to know also the church which the exalted Christ by His Word and through His messengers creates.

The Gospel According to Luke, with its companion volume, the Acts of the Apostles, is teaching designed for Gentiles. The name Theophilus is best taken as a real name, not merely as a symbolical designation of the Christian reader; the adjective "most excellent" (1:3) would mark him as a man of some standing in society—Paul and Tertullus use the same term in addressed the Roman procurators Felix and Festus (Acts 24:2; 26:25). Luke was following a literary custom of antiquity in dedicating his work to Theophilus. The man to whom the book was dedicated often bore the cost of the publication and the distribution of the book; and this may well have been the case with Theophilus. Since the work follows the contemporary conventions of Greek literature, it would follow that it was designed for Greek readers. And the content of the work confirms this inference.

Author

The ancient church from the second half of the second century onward uniformly ascribes the third gospel and the Acts of the Apostles to Luke, "the beloved physician," Paul's companion on his journeys and his faithful friend in his imprisonment. He was probably a Gentile, for Paul distinguishes him from his Jewish co-workers (Cl 4:10-11, 14). He joined Paul at Troas during the second missionary journey, as the use of the first person plural in Acts 16:11 indicates, accompanied Paul as far as Philippi on that journey, and apparently remained there for the next seven years. He rejoined Paul A. D. 56 when Paul passed through Philippi on his last journey to Jerusalem and was with him continually thereafter. According to 2 Ti 4:11 he was with Paul in his last imprisonment also.

The evidence of the two books themselves confirms the ancient tradition. The gospel and Acts have one author: Both are addressed to Theophilus, and they are markedly alike in language and style; they also show structural similarities. Now, the author of Acts in a number of places speaks in the first person plural (the so-called "we" passages, e. g., Acts 16:11-17; 20:5—21:18; 27:1—28:16), thus indicating that he was an eyewitness of the events recorded. Since these "we" passages are in the same style as the rest of the work and fit naturally into the whole narrative, they can hardly be assigned to another author. This marks the author as a companion of Paul. Of all the known companions of Paul, only Titus and Luke come seriously into consideration; the rest are excluded by the content of the narrative itself or made unlikely by their obscurity. If the ancient church were guessing at the author, it might well have picked Titus, who is more prominent than Luke in the letters of Paul. The tradition which assigns the third gospel and Acts to Luke is therefore in all probability a genuine tradition and is to be trusted.

Scholars have naturally examined the language of Luke to see whether it betrays the physician. The first findings of research in this area greatly exaggerated the medical character of Luke's language. Later investigation has shown that much which had been labeled "medical" was not specifically medical at all but part of the common language of cultured men of the day. But if the language of Luke is not sufficiently medical in character to *prove* that he was a physician, it does confirm the ancient tradition insofar as there is nothing in it which makes it unlikely or impossible that the writer was a physician.

Characteristics of Luke's Gospel

Formally, the work of Luke is obviously the most literary and the most thoroughly Greek of the first three gospels. The preface with its formal structure, its conformity to Greek literary custom, its reference to the work of other writers, and its claim to painstaking and systematic research as the basis of an ordered and articulated account plainly bespeaks an acceptance of the work as a piece of Greek literature. The extensive proportions of the two-book work, its long perspective and broad scope, are in keeping with its announced literary intentions. The language and style have a purity and an elegance which set the work apart from the other gospels. Hebrew and Aramaic words are in general avoided; Latinisms are relatively rare. But the work is in no sense a compromise with Greek thought and spirit, even in style. Especially when the narrative moves on Palestinian soil, as in the gospel and the first 12 chapters of Acts, the style reflects the Semitically colored language of the Septuagint (the Greek translation of the Old Testament). And the gospel, for all its fullness, remains a gospel; it does not become a Greek biography. Likewise, the Acts of the Apostles is sacred history of a unique sort, the history not of heroic men but of the embattled and triumphant Word of the Lord.

The material peculiar to Luke emphasizes the absoluteness and the fullness of the forgiving grace which came into the world in the person of Jesus. Jesus' first Messianic words are "gracious words" (Lk 4:22); they reveal Him as the compassionate Servant of the Lord who brings good news to the poor, sight to the blind, liberty to the oppressed; His coming is the beginning of the great Year of Jubilee, the divinely appointed amnesty for all mankind (Lk 4:16-21). The story of Peter's call makes clear that the summons to discipleship is an act of divine forgiveness (Lk 5:1-11). The story of the sinful woman who anointed Jesus' feet, with its parable of the two debtors, shows how Jesus looked on forgiveness as the source and wellspring of ministering love (Lk 7:36-50). In the parable of the barren fig tree (Lk 13:6-9) Jesus pictures Himself as the Intercessor for a people under the judgment of God. In the moving parables of the prodigal son and the Pharisee and the publican the free and gracious forgiveness of God is put in sharp antithesis to the legalistic harshness and pride of Pharisaic piety (Lk 15:11-32; 18:9-14). The motif is continued in the story of Zacchaeus (Lk 19:1-10); one could inscribe over the whole gospel the Messianic words in which the story culminates: "The Son of man came to seek and to save the lost" (Lk 19:10). It is found in the shadow of the cross—Jesus intercedes for the disciple who will deny Him (Lk 22:31-34)—and on the cross itself; Jesus opens the gates of Paradise to the criminal beside Him (Lk

23:42-43). And the risen Christ sends out His disciples to preach repentance and forgiveness of sins in His name. (Lk 24:47)

The Christ of the third gospel is the Seeker of the lost, the Savior of the lowly. His birth is anounced to the shepherds, whom good Jews suspected and despised (Lk 2:8-20), and He is branded by the righteous in Israel as one who "receives sinners and eats with them" (Lk 15:2). Of a piece with this picture of Jesus as the compassionate and condescending Savior is the special attention paid to women in this gospel, for woman was not highly regarded in Judaism or in the ancient world generally. The infancy story is Mary's story, not Joseph's as in Matthew; and Luke dwells more than the other evangelists on Jesus' relationship to women: Mary and Martha (Lk 10:38-42), the widow of Nain (Lk 7:11-17), the sinful woman (Lk 7:36-50), the women on the *via dolorosa* (Lk 23:27-31)—these are peculiar to Luke's account. And two parables dealing with women are peculiar to Luke also: the parable of the lost coin (Lk 15:8-10) and that of the importunate widow. (Lk 18:1-8)

The third gospel emphasizes the universality of Jesus' grace and Saviorhood. It is richly imbued with Old Testament language and thought, and the portions peculiar to Luke are pronouncedly Palestinian in coloring—no other gospel gives us such sympathetic portraits of the pure Judaic piety which waited for the fulfillment of God's promises as the first chapters of Luke. Yet all that characterizes Jesus' earthly ministry as limited to Israel recedes into the background. Jesus' interpretation of the Law, which occupies so broad a space in Matthew (Mt 5:17-48), has no counterpart in Luke. Luke does not tell of Jesus' dispute with the scribes and Pharisees concerning the tradition of the elders (Mt 15:1-20), nor does he tell the story of the Syrophoenician woman with its emphasis on Israel's prior claim to the Gospel (Mt 15:21-28). His is the universal, missionary outlook; he fits the life of Jesus into world history; the names of Augustus and Tiberius appear only in Luke (Lk 2:1 ff.; 3:1 ff.). His genealogy of Jesus does not stop with Abraham, but goes back to Adam, the father of all mankind (Lk 3:23 to 38), and thus points up the universal significance of the Christ. Little touches here and there keep this motif of universality before the reader; for example, Luke alone records the fact that soldiers, who would be Gentiles, came to be baptized by John (3:14); no other evangelist shows such an interest in Samaritans as Luke (Lk 9:52 ff.; 17:11 ff.; 10:29 ff.); his gospel looks forward to the day when Samaria would receive with joy the Word of God (Acts 8:8, 14), when Peter would be divinely led to preach the Gospel to a Roman centurion (Acts 10), to the time when the Word of the Lord would grow and prevail mightily until it reached "the end of the earth." (Acts 1:8)

Perhaps it is because of Luke's emphasis on the completely gratuitous character of the grace of God in Christ, that Fatherly grace which makes man merciful and sets him free for a love that sees in never-ending ministry its obvious task (Lk 17:7-10), that there is in Luke's Gospel a corresponding emphasis on the radical antithesis between mammon and the kingdom of God. The evangelist who so completely took the measure of God's transfiguring grace had a keen eye also for those elements of Jesus' teaching which warned against the disfiguring power of wealth. The Magnificent of Mary sings of the God who has filled the hungry with good things and has sent the rich away empty (Lk 1:53). Only Luke records the Baptist's admonition, "He who has two coats, let him share with him who has none" (Lk 3:11). Only Luke records the woe upon the rich as the counterpart to the beatitude upon the poor (Lk 6:24). Only Luke tells of Jesus' rebuke to the man who wanted His help in getting his legal rights as heir: "Man, who made me a judge or divider over you?" (Lk 12:14-15). Only Luke has the parables which speak of the false security of the rich (Lk 12:16-21) and of the wrong and right use of riches. (Lk 16:19-31; 16:1-9)

The evangelist who was to write the Gospel of the Holy Spirit (as Acts has aptly been called) naturally emphasizes the activity of the Holy Spirit in the life of the Baptist (Lk 1:15, 17) and in the life and ministry of Jesus (Lk 1:35; 3:22; 4:1, 14, 18;

10:21). The "acceptable year of the Lord" is in Luke's Gospel greeted by a burst of inspired song. Elizabeth, "filled with the Spirit," hails the mother of the Lord (Lk 1:41-42); Zechariah "was filled with the Holy Spirit and prophesied" over the child of his old age, the forerunner of the Lord (Lk 1:67-79). The Holy Spirit was upon Simeon (Lk 2:25) and, "inspired by the Spirit" (Lk 2:27), he hailed the Child in his arms as God's salvation in person (Lk 2:29-32). The Messiah's gift will be the baptism with the Spirit (Lk 3:16); His disciples have the promise of the Spirit for their witness to the world (Lk 12:11, 12; 24:49). The Holy Spirit is the heavenly Father's best gift to His own. (Lk 11:13)

Scholars are inclined to see the influence of Paul in these religious emphases of Luke's Gospel; the emphasis on the absoluteness of God's grace in Christ, on the universality of Christ's redeeming work, and on the Spirit as the mark and the power of the new age is certainly central to Paul's proclamation too. The Lucan antithesis between mammon and the kingdom of God has its counterpart in Paul's antithesis of flesh and Spirit. And since Paul performed his apostolic ministry to the music of prayer and thanksgiving and perpetually admonished his churches to prayer, it may be that Luke's emphasis on prayer owes something to Paul too. He does go beyond the other evangelists in depicting Jesus at prayer (Lk 3:21; 5:16; 6:12; 9:18; 9:28-29; 22:41 ff.; 23:34, 46) and in recording Jesus' teaching on prayer. Jesus, in Luke's Gospel, illustrates the difference between a false, self-righteous piety and the genuine piety of repentance by recounting the *prayers* of the Pharisee and the tax collector (Lk 18:9-14); and two parables of encouragement to prayer are peculiar to Luke. (Lk 11:5-8; 18:1-8)

If Matthew's Gospel is at once the most austere and the most compelling of the gospels, if Mark's is the most vivid and dramatic recital of the deeds of the Christ, Luke's is the warmest and most winning story of them all. It is Luke who has filled the church with the moving music of the New Testament canticles; it is Luke's Nativity story that has most decisively shaped the church's Christmas celebration. And the church's teaching has been immeasurably enriched by the warmth and pathos of such Lucan narratives as those of the widow of Nain, Jesus weeping over Jerusalem, the look of Jesus that called Peter to repentance, Jesus' words to the weeping daughters of Jerusalem, and the story of the walk to Emmaus.

Content of Luke's Gospel

The basic outline of Luke is that of Mark's Gospel. Luke prefaces this Marcan outline with an extensive account of the infancy and youth of both John the Baptist and Jesus, expands the Marcan account by means of two major insertions (Lk 6:20—8:3 between Mk 3:19 and 3:20; and Lk 9:51—18:14 between Mk 9:50 and 10:1) and by considerable additional material in the narrative of the Passion and Resurrection. He rather inexplicably omits the material covered by Mark 6:45 to 8:26. The peculiar quality of Luke's highly original work cannot therefore be very well indicated by an outline, which is consequently kept brief here. An appreciation of the individual accent of the third gospel is best gained (a) by studying the material peculiar to it, and (b) by a study of Luke-Acts as a unified whole.

OUTLINE

1:1-4 Preface

I. 1:5—2:52 John and Jesus: Forerunner and Messiah

II. 3:1-22 The Ministry of John

III. 3:23—9:50 Jesus' Galilean Ministry

IV. 9:51—18:30 Jesus' Travel Ministry

V. 18:31—21:38 Jesus' Last Days in Jerusalem

VI. 22:1—24:53 Jesus' Death, Resurrection, and Ascension

1:1-4 PREFACE

1:1-4 Cf. the Introduction. The preface is done in the manner of a Greek historian and gives an account of the purpose and manner of Luke's work as historian. But the historian is an evangelist concerned with *the things . . . accomplished among us* (1), accomplished BY GOD in fulfillment of His promises.

1:3 *Followed.* The word denotes careful investigation.

1:5—2:52 JOHN AND JESUS: FORERUNNER AND MESSIAH

1:5—2:52 Paul says of the "gospel of God" that it is the Gospel "which he promised beforehand through his prophets in the holy scriptures" (Ro 1:2). All the evangelists bear him out in this. Matthew links his story with that of Abraham and David and sees the way of the Messiah illumined step for step by the Word of the prophets (Mt 1—4). For Mark the Gospel begins "as it is written in Isaiah the prophet" (Mk 1:2). John harks back to the creation (Jn 1:1) and to Moses (Jn 1:17). The first two chapters of Luke, all material peculiar to Luke, also hark back to God's ancient Word. The style, in marked contrast to the finished Greek period of the preface, is the stately and archaic simplicity of OT narrative and the balanced architecture of OT poetry. The material is charged with OT ideas, language, institutions, historical figures. But all serves to point up the fact that the Gospel is the Gospel of God, the fulfillment of His purpose and promise; all points to the great new thing, to the good news (1:19; 2:10) of what God is doing now, in the last days.

1:5-25 ANNUNCIATION OF BIRTH OF JOHN

1:5-25 The *good news* (19) is first spoken amid the sanctities of the Old Covenant (the priesthood and the temple) at the burning of the incense. To an aged priest and his barren wife the angel announces the birth of a son who is to be the vessel of God's grace, the dedicated prophet and Spirit-filled forerunner who shall prepare the hearts of his people for the coming of the Lord. The God with whom nothing is impossible has spoken; before Him the questioning of man must fall silent. Man can only receive, in the total subject of faith, the *words which will be fulfilled in their time.*

1:5 *Herod, king of Judea.* Cf. Mt 2:1 note. Luke uses *Judea* in the wider sense of the whole region occupied by the Jews, all Palestine, not only the southern division. (Cf. 23:5)

Division of Abijah. The 8th of the 24 divisions into which the priests were divided, each class serving one week at a time. (1 Ch 24:10, 19)

1:7 *Barren . . . advanced in years.* Like Abraham and Sarah, to whom the son of the promise was given against all human probabilities. (Gn 18:10-14)

1:10 *Hour of incense.* Incense was offered twice daily, morning and evening (Ex 30:7-8). For *incense* as symbolizing prayer cf. Ps 141:2; Rv 5:8; 8:3-4.

1:13 *Call his name John.* John signifies, "the Lord, the God of the covenant, has been gracious." God Himself, through the angel, gives the significant name. (Cf. Mt 1:21)

1:15 *Great.* John is the only man in the NT (besides our Lord, 1:32) to be called great in a good sense.

Drink no wine. John is to be wholly consecrated to God, like the Nazirite (Nm 6:1-21; Ju 13) of the OT. His sufficiency for the task assigned to him is from God; *he will be filled with the Holy Spirit.* (Cf. Mi 3:8)

1:16 *Turn* is the regular OT term for repentance. (Cf. 1 K 18:37)

1:17 *Spirit and power of Elijah.* Cf. Mt 11:14; 17:13. Through Malachi God had promised to send "Elijah the prophet" before the coming of "the great and terrible day of the Lord," to "turn the hearts" of His people (i.e., lead them to repentance), lest the coming of God find them unprepared and so prove disastrous to them (Ml 4:5-6). Now the great day of the Lord is dawning, and the promised forerunner will appear. His coming is a manifestation of the grace of the Lord. (Cf. 13 note)

Turn the hearts of the fathers to the children. Ml 4:5. The *fathers,* the pious men of old who awaited the fulfillment of God's promises (1:55, 72), will no longer be ashamed of the children who have abandoned the old hope and the old ways.

1:19 *Gabriel.* Cf. Dn 8:16; 9:21.

Stand in the presence of God, as His servant, to carry out His commands. Cf. Gn 41:46, where the phrase "stand in the presence of" is translated "entered the service of."

1:22 *Could not speak,* i.e., to pronounce the blessing which concluded the service.

1:24 *Hid herself.* Zechariah was forbidden to speak (20); Elizabeth voluntarily refrained from speaking of the wondrous promise of God *for five months* until it had become obvious that the words spoken by God's messenger would "be fulfilled in their time." (20)

1:25 *Reproach.* For the reproach, disgrace, of childlessness cf. Gn 30:23; 1 Sm 1:11

1:26-38 ANNUNCIATION OF BIRTH OF JESUS

1:26-38 The annunciation to Mary is narrated in strict parallel to the story of the annunciation to Zechariah (angelic messenger; "troubled" recipient; calming of fear; promise of one who "will be great"; sign given, introduced by "and behold"; assurance of fulfillment); both stories are part of the one Gospel. But there is progression and heightening as well as parallelism. There is in the story of the annunciation to Mary a heightened emphasis on the initiative and the working of God; this is God's Gospel indeed, dominated by Him: here are God's messengers, God's *favor,* God's Word, God's *Spirit,* the *power* of the God with whom nothing is impossible, and above all the grace of God which gives to Israel and mankind the *Son of God* to *reign for ever* on the *throne of . . . David.* God's Gospel is good news "concerning his Son" (Ro 1:3), and it is genuine news of an event on earth, in history. The *Son of the Most High* enters David's line *(his father David,* 32); He comes into the flesh and the world, a world as concrete as Galilee, Nazareth, Joseph, Mary, a mother's womb. The combined supernatural wonder and the earthiness of the whole Gospel are here; and it is this Gospel of peace *on earth* that creates faith: *Let it be to me according to your word.* (38)

1:31 The wording recalls the promise of Immanuel (Is 7:14; cf. Mt 1:18-25 note). The name *Jesus* ("The Lord is salvation") is an unfolding of the meaning of Immanuel ("God with us").

1:32 *His father David.* God implants His Son in *David's* line.

1:32-33 *Throne . . . reign for ever.* For the eternal reign of the Son of David, the Messiah, cf. 2 Sm 7:8-17.

1:35 *Holy Spirit.* Cf. Mt 1:18-25 note.

1:39-56 THE MEETING OF THE TWO MOTHERS: THE MAGNIFICAT

1:39-56 The meeting of the two favored mothers (commonly called the Visitation) pulls together the two stories which have hitherto run parallel but separate. Mary beholds the promised sign (1:36), and experiences more than was promised: she hears from the lips of her inspired kinswoman the Spirit's confirmation of the message of Gabriel concerning herself and her Son, her own blessedness, and her Son's Lordship (39-45). The obedient and submissive faith of her who called herself "the handmaid of the Lord" (1:38) becomes the exultant faith which finds expression in Mary's song, the Magnificat. (46-55)

1:42, 45 *Blessed . . . believed.* Mary is blessed because God has favored her and she has accepted and welcomed His favor in faith. She has heard and kept the Word of God. (11:27-28)

1:44 *Babe . . . leaped for joy.* There is nothing extraordinary in the fact itself that a babe leaps in the womb. But it is significant and a thing of wonder that this babe, the forerunner of the Messiah, leaped at just this moment, when Mary's greeting reached Elizabeth's ears.

1:46-55 The Magnificat, so called from the first word of he song in the Latin Bible ("magnifies"), is the song of the "handmaid of the Lord," a song of faith (cf. 45). She sings of the God who, *holy* and *mighty,* has in mercy condescended to make her the object and instrument of His redeeming work (46-49). The vocabulary of her faith is the vocabulary of the OT, the song of Hannah (1 Sm 2:1-10) and the doxological language of the Psalms and prophets. In the light of God's new revelation the old "prophetic word" is "made more sure" for her (2 Ptr 1:19). She sees in her own history the continuation of the story of the divine *mercy* which *is on those who fear* their *God* and *Savior* (50); more than that, she sees that story drawing to its triumphant close, she sees the dawn of the final fulfillment of all God's promises to His people (55). That final triumph is, for her faith, so certain that she speaks of it (as also many OT prophets did) as already accomplished; God HAS triumphed in His sovereign mercy to *those of low degree,* to the *hungry;* while the *proud,* the *mighty,* and the *rich,* the self-sufficient and self-assertive men who feel no need of His mercy and refuse it, are overridden and destroyed. The blessing promised to *Abraham* (Gn 12:1-3) for all the families of the earth is breaking forth to do its work in all the earth; in the face of God's gracious action all human standards of greatness are inverted, all human greatness melts away.

1:48 *Regarded,* looked upon with favor and acted in love toward. Cf. 9:38, where the father of the afflicted boy asks Jesus "to look upon" his son, i.e., to have mercy on him and heal him.

1:49 *Holy is his name.* He reveals Himself *(name)* in such a way that He makes known the uniqueness of His mighty and merciful Godhead.

1:57-80 BIRTH OF JOHN: THE BENEDICTUS

1:57-80 The story moves on the earth; the sympathetic joy of neighbors and kinsfolk at the arrival of Elizabeth's boy and their kindly aunt-and-uncle officiousness at the naming of the child are homely touches. But this commonplace neighbor-and-relatives atmosphere is only the background and foil to the action of God, which makes men *marvel* and *fear* as they sense the presence of the *hand of the Lord* (63, 65, 66). God has given the child when all hope for children was past; God gives the child its significant name (cf. 1:13); God opens the mouth of Zechariah and gives him the *Holy Spirit* in order that he may *prophesy.* This is God's good news, and glory is given to Him: *Blessed be the Lord God of Israel.* (68)

1:64 *Blessing God.* The content of this blessing, praise, and thanksgiving is given in the Benedictus. (68-79)

1:67 *Prophesied.* Declared and interpreted the will and work of God, present and future.

1:68-79 The Benedictus. "Benedictus" is the first word of Zechariah's song in the Latin Bible and means *blessed.* Like the Magnificat, the Benedictus is couched in the language of the OT, the characteristic speech of the pious who were "looking for the consolation of Israel" (2:25). The first strophe hails the dawn of Messianic salvation (68-75); the second proclaims the role which John is to play, as the *prophet of the Most High,* in this drama of redemption (76-79). Zechariah's prophecy celebrates the fidelity of the *Lord God of Israel,* who has not forgotten *his people* nor *his servant David;* He has made a *promise* and fulfilled it, established a *covenant* and maintained it, sworn an *oath* and kept it. His people can rest secure in the hope that His *tender mercy* will complete what is now begun; they shall be delivered from their enemies and be enabled to *serve* their God *without fear* in *holiness and righteousness.* For God is dealing not only with their enemies but with all that thwarted and corrupted His people's service to Him in the past; He is dealing with their *sins.* He brings *salvation* and *forgiveness;* His people shall see *light* and life and shall worship their God in *peace.* (79)

1:68 *Visited.* He has come to help His people. Cf. Ja 1:27—to "visit orphans and widows in their affliction" means to relieve their affliction, to help them.

1:69 *Horn of salvation.* The horn is a symbol of victorious strength. Cf. 1 Sm 2:10, where "horn" is translated with "power."

1:73 *Oath . . . to . . . Abraham.* Cf. Gn 22:16-18, where the promise is repeated in the form of an oath.

Serve. The Greek word implies religious service, a life lived as worship to God. It was for such service that God had called Israel out of Egypt. (Ex 4:23)

1:78 The *day (or dayspring) . . . from on high* is the coming of the Messiah. Cf. Is 9:1-7 and Mt 4:12-22 note.

1:79 *Peace* has a more comprehensive meaning in Biblical speech than in ordinary English usage, denoting total soundness, health, wholeness (cf. 2:14). The coming of the Messiah will create a world in which all is as God wills it, divinely normal.

1:80 *In the wilderness . . . manifestation.* Since the discovery of the remains of the Essene community at Qumran in the Judean wilderness, there has been much speculation as to whether John may not have been a member of that "order." All that the gospel account tells us is that he grew up in solitude, apart from the corrupting influences of his people, and did not enter the priesthood. He was being preserved and kept for the *day of his manifestation,* the time when God would commission him and install him in his office. (Cf. 3:2)

2:1-20 THE BIRTH OF JESUS

2:1-20 How silently, how silently
The wondrous gift is given.

This story has been so transfigured by Christian legend, song, and art that it is difficult to read it afresh in the simplicity of Luke's narrative. The gift of God IS given "silently." Jesus comes into the world sharing with His people the degradation of foreign, pagan domination. The Roman emperor *Augustus* and the Roman *governor Quirinius* "dictate" the place of His birth. From the beginning "the Son of man has nowhere to lay his head" (9:58). He is bedded in a *manger;* and He is *wrapped* in *swaddling cloths* like any Jewish baby. The news of His birth is proclaimed only to unhonored *shepherds,* for whom His lowliness is to be the *sign* (12, 16) that identifies Him.

The "wondrousness" of the gift is marked by the Word of God, by which the angelic messengers of God interpret the event as God's act for us men and for our savlation. Not the child but the interpretive word has the radiant *glory* and the song of the *heavenly host.* That word is *good news of a great joy,* the fulfillment of God's promise to *David* for *all the people* of God, news of a *Savior,* a Deliverer who brings radical deliverance from man's desperation, the anointed King who has the right and the might *(Lord)* to carry out God's gracious purpose for man, to bring God's *peace* to men who have no claim to it but receive it gratis from His sovereign and spontaneous grace *(is pleased,* 14). Thus God is glorified, in the glory of His grace, and is praised by the tongues of angels (13) and of men. (20)

From this interpretive word fresh light falls on the lowliness of the Christ's beginnings. Not the Romans but God, the Lord of history, dictated the place of Jesus' birth; He is fulfilling His promise of a Deliverer from little *Bethlehem,* the *city of David* (Mi 5:2-4; Mt 2:1-6 notes). God brought the Deliverer down into the depth of man's misery, that He might deliver man by taking up the burden of man's misery Himself. God picked shepherds to be the first recipients of the good news for the poor, that all men may be given ears to hear the good news to the poor.

2:1-2 *Enrolled.* The *enrollment* instituted by Augustus (31 B. C.—A. D. 14) was a census of the whole population designed to enable a complete and equitable taxation. It was made according to families in their native cities. According to documents discovered in Egypt, it was customary to take such a census every 14 years. The exact date of the census mentioned here and the part of *Quirinius* in it remain uncertain.

2:8 *Shepherds,* according to Jewish sources, were among the poor and despised in Palestine. They were suspected of dishonesty. A third-century rabbi expresses surprise at the fact that David can compare God with a shepherd. (Ps 23)

2:14 *God* has His *glory,* is manifested and acknowledged and adored as God, *in the highest,* now when in sending the Savior He creates *peace* (wholeness, health, well-being in every sense) on *earth* purely out of grace (the word translated *pleased* emphasizes the sovereign freedom and spontaneity of His favor).

2:21-40 THE CIRCUMCISION OF JESUS AND THE PRESENTATION IN THE TEMPLE

2:21-40 Jesus is "born under the law" (Gl 4:4); He is incorporated in the people of God by the rite of circumcision (21), which is prescribed by the Law and commits Him to the keeping of the Law (Gn 17:12-14; Lv 12:3; Ro 2:25). The purification of the mother and the presentation of the firstborn Son are carried out *according to the law of Moses.* (22:24)

Here, as He goes the way of obedience to the Law, in His Father's house two prophetic voices bear witness to the Messianic Child. Simeon, moved by the Spirit, recognizes that his time of waiting witness is over; the *consolation of Israel, the Lord's Christ,* has come, and the Lord whose faithful prophet-*servant* he had been will now let him *depart in peace,* his work done. In the language of OT prophecy (Is 40:5; 52:10; 42:6; 49:6, 9; 25:7; 46:13) he hails the Child in his arms as *thy* [Lord's] *salvation* in person, a salvation wrought by the ministry of a Servant Messiah who is to serve and suffer for the salvation of *all peoples,* for the *Gentiles* as well as His *people.* Even Jesus' parents *marveled* at this revelation, which for the first time speaks of the universal mission of Mary's Son (33). Jesus is to be the Servant Messiah who goes through contradiction and suffering (Is 50:5-6) to His ultimate and universal redeeming triumph. He will be a *sign* of God's present gracious working, but a sign *spoken against* (34); men will fail or refuse to see in Him the Lord's salvation, and the ways of men will divide before Him. Some will stumble at Him in unbelief and so *fall* in their unbelief; others will see the saving arm of the Lord revealed in Him as He suffers and dies for the sins of all (Is 53), will repent and believe and find in Him a *rising* to new life (34). None can remain neutral over against Him; the *thoughts* of men's *hearts* will become manifest before Him (35). They will either call the Crucified Lord or will call Him accursed (1 Co 12:3). His mother, blessed among women, cannot be spared the pain of being mother of the Servant (*sword,* 35).

A second prophetic voice confirms the prophecy of Simeon; the venerable *prophetess* Anna speaks of the Christ to all those quiet hopers in Israel who *were looking for the redemption of Jerusalem.* (36-38; Is 52:9)

2:21 *Name given by the angel.* Cf. 1:31 note.

2:22 *Purification . . . present.* Cf. Lv 12:2-8; Ex. 13:2, 12, 15.

2:29-30 Simeon's song is called the Nunc Dimittis after the opening words in the Latin Bible. It is usually sung in the post-Communion liturgy.

2:29 *Servant.* For the prophets as servants cf., e.g., Jer 26:5; 29:19; 35:15; Am 3:7; Zch 1:6.

2:34 *Sign.* Cf. 11:30.

Fall and rising. Cf. Is 8:14-15.

2:40 *Filled with wisdom.* Wisdom, comprehensive insight into the will and work of God, is a characteristic of the Messiah. (Is 11:2)

2:41-52 THE BOY JESUS IN HIS FATHER'S HOUSE

2:41-52 The one recorded incident from Jesus' boyhood shows Him walking the path of obedience. The story begins with His obedience to the Law which established the *Passover* and prescribed its celebration (Ex 12:1-6; 23:15; Dt 16:1-8); it ends with Jesus' obedience to His parents, obedience to the Fourth Commandment, which He later defended so fiercely against the encroachments of tradition (Mt 15:4). In this setting we hear His first words. In these words God is, for the first time in Luke, expressly called Jesus' *Father.* In these words Jesus expresses His high consciousness of His mission and office; His life is to be uniquely a human life wholly lived to God, a life which is in all its parts and in every aspect an act of worship, as man's life ought to be and never had been. He *must be in* His *Father's house,* obedient in the place and for the salvation of all. Here begins the career of obedience "unto death, even death on a cross" (Ph 2:8). Here for the first time Mary has a premonition of the sword that is to pierce her soul. (Cf. 35)

2:41 Cf. Dt 16:1-8; Ex 23:15.

2:44 *Company.* A village or group of villages would make up a caravan for the pilgrimage to Jerusalem. The custom then was probably the same as in modern times, with the women and little children in the lead, followed by the men, while older children stayed with either parent. A 12-year-old would therefore not necessarily be missed until nightfall.

2:48 *Anxiously.* The Greek word thus translated is somewhat stronger, expressing pain. Cf. Acts 20:38, where it is rendered "sorrowing."

2:51 *His mother kept all these things in her heart.* Some scholars see here a hint that Mary herself was Luke's source of information for the events of Jesus' childhood.

2:52 *Wisdom.* Cf. 2:40. The wording is traditional, used in the OT of the growing up of Samson and Samuel. (Ju 13:24; 1 Sm 2:26)

3:1-22 THE MINISTRY OF JOHN THE BAPTIST

3:1-22 Cf. Mt 3:1-17 notes.

3:1-9 THE VOICE IN THE WILDERNESS

3:1-9 Cf. Mt 3:1-10 notes.

3:1-2 In keeping with his markedly universal outlook, Luke connects the history of John with general history, dating the beginning of his ministry by listing the secular and religious authorities of the time.

3:1 *Fifteenth year of . . . Tiberius.* Either A. D. 28/29 or 26/27, depending on whether one dates from the year in which Tiberius succeeded Augustus or from the year when he was associated with Augustus as coruler.

Tetrarch, originally "ruler of the fourth part of a country," then used more loosely to designate any dependent prince with less than royal power and dignity.

3:2 *High-priesthood of Annas and Caiaphas.* Annas was deposed from the high-priesthood in A. D. 15 but continued to have great influence in the Sanhedrin, the Jewish high council. Four of his sons and his son-in-law Caiaphas became high priests. Caiaphas held office from A. D. 18 to 36. Jn 18:13, 24 indicate that Annas and Caiaphas collaborated closely, although Caiaphas alone "was high priest that year." (Jn 11:49)

The word of God came. This is a phrase frequently used in the OT for the calling of a prophet (e.g., Jer 1:4; Hos 1:1; Jon 1:1). The word of the prophet is God's Word, entrusted to the prophet.

3:4-6 Is 40:3-5. Luke quotes Isaiah more fully than the other evangelists to state explicitly the universal significance of the action of God which begins with the ministry of the Baptist (*all flesh,* 6).

3:10-14 JOHN INSTRUCTS THE PENITENT

3:10-14 Luke alone records the words with which John spells out the meaning of "fruits that befit repentance" (8). Those "fruits" are simple acts of social kindliness, beginning at once there in the desolate regions where John baptized, where nights are cold *(coats)* and *food* is not readily obtainable for those who come without adequate provisions (11). Men are not summoned to leave their professions (even the profession of a *tax collector,* which Pharisaic piety looked upon as a dubious one at best, cf. 15:1-2) but to act honestly in their professions. The *soldiers,* probably mercenaries in the service of Herod Antipas, included non-Jews; here is a first fulfillment of the promise that "all flesh" shall see the salvation of God. (6)

3:15-20 PROMISE OF THE MIGHTIER ONE; JOHN SHUT UP IN PRISON

3:15-20 Cf. Mt 3:1 ff.

3:15 *The people were in expectation.* Luke alone records the reaction of the people which occasioned John's witness to the coming Mightier One and his own subservient role.

3:18:20 Luke does not record the execution of John (Mt 14:1-12; Mk 6:17-18); it is presupposed in 9:7-9.

3:21-22 THE BAPTISM OF JESUS

3:21-22 Cf. Mt 3:13-17 notes. Luke's account links Jesus' baptism with that of *all the people,* thus marking the fact that Jesus is making Himself one with His people in their need. The reference to Jesus' *praying* is peculiar to Luke also; Jesus is aligning His will with the will of the Father (cf. 22:42) and submitting to baptism "to fulfil all righteousness." (Cf. Mt 3:13-15 note)

3:23:38 THE GENEALOGY OF JESUS

3:23-38 Cf. Mt 1:1-17 note. As in Matthew, the symmetry of numbers indicates God's control of the history that culminates in the incarnation of the Son of God. There are 77 names in the genealogy, in groupings that are multiples of 7 (21 names from *Jesus* to *Zerubbabel,* 21 names from *Shealtiel* to *Nathan,* 14 names from *David* to *Isaac,* 21 names from *Abraham* to *Adam).* While Matthew's genealogy (from Abraham through David to Jesus) leads up to Him "who will save HIS PEOPLE from their sins" (Mt 1:21), that of Luke leads up to Him who is the Savior of all sons of Adam, all mankind, the One by whom "ALL FLESH shall see the salvation of God" (Lk 3:6; cf. 2:32). Efforts to harmonize the two genealogies have not been altogether successful. A useful suggestion is that Matthew traces the royal line, while Luke traces physical descent.

3:38 *Son of Adam, the son of God.* In Jesus the new creation begins (2 Co 5:17); through faith in Christ Jesus men can all become sons of God again. (Gl 3:26)

4:1-13 THE TEMPTATION OF JESUS

4:1-13 Cf. Mt 4:1-11 note. Two features distinguish Luke's account from that of Mt: (a) Luke inverts the order of the last two temptations, so that the final temptation takes place in *Jerusalem* (9), and Jerusalem is in his gospel the place of Jesus' suffering and death (9:31, 51, 53; cf. 13:22; 13:33-34; 17:11; 18:31; 19:11, 28). Thus the temptation is marked as the beginning of the "trials" of Jesus (22:28, the same word in Greek as "temptation"), which culminate in His Passion and death. (b) The second distinctive feature is related to the first: *The devil . . . departed* from Jesus *until an opportune time;* that final opportune time is the Passion, when "Satan entered into Judas" to betray his Lord (22:3), when Satan sought to sift Jesus' disciples like wheat (22:31), when Jesus greeted His captors with the words: "This is your hour, and the power of darkness" (22:53). Thus Luke marks Jesus' whole career as an unshrinking and victorious confrontation with the power of the Evil One. Cf. also 10:18; 11:18-22; 13:16; Acts 10:38; 26:18. The Son of God goes forth to war.

4:14-30 NAZARETH REJECTS JESUS

4:14-30 Luke sums up Jesus' activity in *Galilee* with *he taught in their synagogues* (15); and it is as Teacher that He confronts His home city *Nazareth.* He teaches as any Jewish teacher might, in the synagog, *on the sabbath,* on the basis of an OT text, standing to read and sitting to teach as custom prescribed. But then He appears as One who teaches *in the power of the Spirit* (14) who had descended upon Him at His baptism (3:22). The beloved Son is not merely another expounder of the prophetic Word; He is the fulfillment of that Word (21). He stands before the men of Nazareth as the Spirit-filled Anointed One of God, with the gift of *good news to the poor, release* for the *captives, sight* for the *blind, liberty* for the *oppressed*—with His appearing the new exodus begins (18). As He proclaims *the acceptable year of the Lord* (19), the great Year of Jubilee when God sets all right again, that is no longer a promise but a reality; the year of the Lord is beginning as men hear it proclaimed by Him. (21)

Men were astonished at His *gracious words,* but they were also offended that Joseph's son, the hometown boy, should assume the authority to speak to them. And when He refused to validate His authority with a sign (23), but pointed to the Scriptures instead, to make plain to them that God's sovereign grace can (and will) be bestowed on Gentile Sidonians and Syrians if Israel will not accept it—when He added His stringent call to repentance to His proffer of the good news (24-27), they were *filled with wrath* (28) and prepared to execute judgment on this blasphemer (29). Already Jesus is the Sign that is spoken against (2:34) who proves to be the fall of many just because God has set Him for the rising of many. Jesus goes toward the cross, and the Gospel will go to the Gentiles.

4:18-19 Is 61:1-2. Significantly, Jesus omits the second half of 61:2, "and the day of vengeance of our God." He offers the free grace of God; God's vengeance will come on all who refuse His grace.

4:19 *The acceptable year.* The background idea is probably that of the Year of Jubilee, every 50th year, a holy year, the "year of liberty" (Eze 46:17), when property reverted to its original owners, debts were remitted, and Israelite slaves were set free (Lv 25:8-24; 27:17-24; Nm 36:4). In this last great Year of Jubilee all captives everywhere shall be set free and all will be made well.

4:25 *Elijah.* Cf. 1 K 17:1, 8-16; 18:1.

4:27 *Elisha.* Cf. 2 K 5:1-14.

4:29 *Throw him down headlong.* This points to stoning, the punishment which the Law prescribed for blasphemy (Lv 24:10-16). The guilty person was thrown down backward from a wall or cliff; and if he survived, heavy stones were cast on him.

4:31-44 THE WORD WITH AUTHORITY

4:31-44 In 4:15 Lk has described Jesus' activity in Galilee as teaching, even though He evidently performed mighty deeds in Capernaum, as 4:23 indicates. The mighty deeds (such as the expulsion of a demon here) are but manifestations of *the word . . . with authority* (32) of the person of Christ. The Word is emphasized throughout this section. Jesus *rebuked* the fever of *Simon's mother-in-law* (39) and *rebuked* the *demons* (41). He owes the *good news of the kingdom of God* to all Israel (43) and goes *preaching in the synagogues of Judea.* (44)

4:31-37 Cf. Mk 1:21-28, esp 1:27 note.

4:38-41 Cf. Mt 8:17 note; Mk 1:32.

4:42-44 Cf. Mk 1:35-38.

5:1-11 THE CALLING OF SIMON PETER AND HIS PARTNERS

5:1-11 Cf. Mt 4:18-22 note. The "word with authority" (4:32) dominates the story. That Word of Jesus, here expressly designated as *word of God,* drew the people to Jesus (1), commandeered Peter's boat (3), creatively produced the great catch of fish contrary to all human likelihood and all fishermen's experience (4-7), removed the fear of Simon Peter when he fell down at Jesus' knees desperately aware of his sinfulness in the presence of this almighty goodness and giving (8), and summoned him to his apostolic ministry (10). That Word produced in Peter and his partners the ready will to leave everything and follow Jesus (11). They were called to renunciation and ministry; but above all, they were called (as Peter later expressed it) to "obtain a blessing." (1 Ptr 3:9)

5:1 *Lake of Gennesaret.* The Sea of Galilee.

5:8 *Lord* represents a higher degree of respect and awe than the *Master* of Peter's first response. (5)

5:9 The word translated *astonished* indicates an awe-filled recognition of how great the distance is between the Holy One of God and sinful man, how undeserved His favor, how intolerable His presence for man on any terms but that of the forgiveness of sins. (Cf. 1:77)

5:12-16 THE LEPER MADE CLEAN

5:12-16 Cf. Mt 8:1-4 notes.

5:17-26 "YOUR SINS ARE FORGIVEN. RISE AND WALK"

5:17-26 Cf. Mt 9:1-8 notes; cf. Mt 8:23—9:8 note.

5:27-39 THE CALLING OF LEVI: THE PHYSICIAN AND THE BRIDEGROOM

5:27-39 Cf. Mt 9:9-17 note.

5:39 The meaning of this verse, only in Lk, remains obscure. Perhaps Jesus is warning those who will not join His disciples in the festive freedom which His forgiving presence brings against clinging to the old ways out of mere attachment to old tradition and pious habit.

6:1-11 TWO SABBATH CONTROVERSIES

6:1-11 Cf. Mt 12:1-14 note. Besides these two Sabbath controversies which he has in common with Mt and Mk, Lk records two others (13:10-17; 14:1-6) peculiar to his gospel.

6:12-16 JESUS APPOINTS 12 APOSTLES

6:12-16 Cf. Mt 10:1-4 note; Mk 3:13-19. The notice that Jesus spent the night before the appointment in prayer (12) occurs only in Lk and marks the solemnity of the act. Jesus is at one with the will of His Father as He begins that extension of His activity through authorized and empowered messengers (9:1) which shall reach "to the end of the earth." (Acts 1:8)

6:17-49 The Sermon on the Plain

6:17-49 Cf. Mt 5:1—7:29 notes. A brief introduction (17-19) indicates that Jesus' ministry has attracted not only a *great crowd of his disciples* but a *great multitude of people,* interested but not yet committed, from among all Jewry (all Judea and Jerusalem) and from regions as far away as Tyre and Sidon to the northwest, where many Jews lived. The time has come to extend His ministry through His *disciples,* and it is they who are addressed in the sermon. (20)

To His disciples, first, the Gospel of God's free royal favor to the *poor* (20-26); second, the imperative of freely giving and forgiving *love* (27-38); and third, the injunction of a ministry *(lead,* 39) which is an expression of their faithful and obedient discipleship. (39-49)

6:20-26 GOOD NEWS TO THE POOR

6:20-26 The good news is proclaimed (as anticipated in the Magnificat, 1:51-53) as the great reversal of the standards and orders of this age in the dawning new age. The *poor,* whose only riches is the *Son of man* (22), whose lot *now* is *hunger,* tears, and dishonor *on account of the Son of man*—they have cause for joy; God is their King and will lead them through the darkness of sorrow and persecution into His perfect *day.* The *rich* and the *full,* who have chosen to live by bread alone (4:4), who live and *laugh* now and enjoy honor in the age for which they live, the age whose short view and selfish standards determine the pattern of their lives—they shall share the fate of the *false prophets* of old, who turned their people from repentance and hope to present enjoyment and perished with their people under the judgment of God.

6:20-21 *Poor . . . hunger . . . weep.* Cf. Mt 5:3-4, 6 notes.

6:22-23 Cf. Mt 5:11 note.

6:22 *Exclude,* i. e., from the community, especially the worshiping community. (Cf. Jn 9:22; 12:42; 16:2)

Cast out your name as evil. Cast out is probably the equivalent of a Hebrew term meaning "to publish abroad" (cf. Dt 22:14, 19). The disciples will be reviled and slandered. (Mt 5:11)

6:23 *In that day,* the day of the Lord (cf. Zph 1:7) when God's judgment will deal with the malice of His enemies and His grace will vindicate and *reward* all who have suffered for His sake.

6:24 *Rich* is not merely an economic designation; the word designates men like the rich man of 16:19-31 whose riches blinded him to the misery of Lazarus and left him no time for Moses and the prophets, or the rich fool of 12:16-21 whose riches shut him up completely with his own concerns, so that he laid up "treasure for himself" and was "not rich toward God." (Cf. Ja 5:1-6)

6:26 *False prophets.* Cf. Mi 2:1-6, 11.

6:27-38 BE SONS OF THE MOST HIGH

6:27-38 The response of the disciples to the love of God shown to them as to the poor, the hungry, the mourners; their response to Him who has given them a hope so sure and strong that they are able to endure dishonor with joy (20-23)—their response is to *love.* "We love because he first loved us" (1 Jn 4:19). This love is to have on it the mark of its divine origin (*sons of the Most High,* 35; *your Father is merciful,* 36). It is love for the *enemies* with no thought for the worthiness of its object (27-28), love that is willing to expose itself to abuse, love simply according to the Golden Rule (29-31), love as different from normal human mutual amiability as God's love is from man's; He is their *Father,* and they derive their capacity for love from Him who *is kind to the ungrateful and the selfish* (32-36). They have found in God the Judge as He is revealed in Jesus the *merciful* God who forgives and gives (cf. 5:1-11); as sons of the Forgiver and Giver they can *forgive* (not *judge* and *condemn*) and can hope for His overwhelmingly generous reward. (37-38)

6:27-30 Cf. Mt 5:38-42 note.

6:31 Cf. Mt 7:12 note.

6:32-36 Cf. Mt 5:43-48 note.

6:35 *Selfish.* This seems rather a mild translation of the Greek word used here, which can mean "evil, bad, base, worthless, vicious," and is used of Satan as the Evil One, e. g., Mt 13:19.

6:37-38 Cf. Mt 7:1-2 note

6:38 *Good measure . . . put into your lap.* The lap is literally the fold of the loose garment as it falls from the chest over the girdle; this pouchlike place was used as a pocket, here for carrying grain (cf. 2 K 4:39). In Is 40:11 the Lord is pictured as carrying a lamb in this fold of the garment.

6:39-49 ONE FULLY TAUGHT WILL BE LIKE HIS TEACHER

6:39-49 The disciples are to become apostles (6:14), representatives of their Lord, called to *lead* the new people of God (39), as He leads; they will have His task of opening the eyes of the *blind* (4:18). If they are not to be blind leaders of the blind (like the scribes and Pharisees who led men to their ruin, Mt 15:14), they must be *fully taught,* in order to be *like* their *teacher* (40). To lead the blind, they need clarity of vision; they can lead men to repentance only as forgiven leaders, as men who have taken the *log* out of their *own eye* by repentance (39-42). They can, moreover, lead men only by being what they proclaim, *good trees* bearing *good fruit, good men* producing good from the treasury of their *hearts* (43-45). In a word, they can fulfill their function by hearing and doing the *words* of their Lord, by taking up His teaching into their mind, heart, and will. Thus their life will be *a house built upon rock,* stable and unshaken when the house *without a foundation* (the house of those who pay only lip service to their Lord, 46) falls in *ruin* under the judgment of their Lord. (46-49)

6:40 *Fully taught,* i. e., completely fitted out, put into perfect working order, as the Greek word suggests.

6:49 *It fell,* an illustration of how the Child in Simeon's arms is "set for the fall . . . of many." (2:34; cf. Is 30:12-13)

7:1-10 HEALING THE CENTURION'S SLAVE

7:1-10 Cf. Mt 8:1-17 note. Peculiar to Lk is the intercession of the Jewish *elders* on behalf of the Gentile *centurion* (3-5). Since the centurion *loves* their *nation* and built them their *synagogue* (5), he is probably one of those Gentiles who were drawn to the monotheism of the synagog and attended the worship services there without, however, submitting to circumcision or obligating themselves to keep the whole Law. Such Gentiles appear frequently in Acts as among the first to accept the Gospel message of Paul, and it is probably for this reason that Lk stresses this feature. Even here Christ appears as the Light of the Gentiles (2:32; for this type of Gentile in Acts, called "devout," "you that fear God," "devout converts to Judaism," "worshiper of God," cf. Acts 10:2; 13:16, 26, 43, 50; 16:14; 17:4, 17; 18:7).

7:11-17 RAISING OF WIDOW'S SON AT NAIN

7:11-17 Recorded by Lk alone. This is the first narrative in which the evangelist calls Jesus *Lord* (13). That divine authority for which distance was no obstacle (6-8) and the grace which reached beyond Israel to help a believing Gentile centurion (9) are here conjoined in Jesus' *compassion* for the *widow* and His word of power to the *only son* lying dead—here is the Lord, "the day" which has dawned "from on high to give light to those . . . in the shadow of death" (1:78-79). Here is cause for holy *fear;* here is reason for *glorifying God;* the long-awaited *prophet* "mighty in deed and word" (24:19) has appeared (16). The prophecy of Zechariah is being fulfilled: "Blessed be the Lord God of Israel, for he has visited and redeemed his people" (1:68). The Gospel preached to the poor is a power; the dead are raised up. (22)

7:13 *Had compassion.* The Greek word used here is used only to designate the compassion of God or of Christ (Mt 9:36; 14:14; 15:32; 18:27; 20:34; Mk 1:41; 9:22; Lk 15:20). The one exception is the compassion of the Good Samaritan. (Lk 10:33)

7:16 *Great prophet.* Cf. Dt 18:15, 18; Acts 3:22-23.

Visited. Cf. 1:68 note.

7:18-30 JOHN'S QUESTION FROM PRISON

7:18-30 Cf. Mt 11:1-15 note.

7:29-30 Peculiar to Lk. Cf. Mt 21:31-32. This is Lk's comment on the people's reaction to John's baptism of repentance.

7:29 *Having been baptized*—perhaps better, "by accepting John's baptism of repentance."

Justified God. They declared that God had dealt righteously with them in dealing with them as sinners and offering them entry into His kingdom by way of repentance and forgiveness. (3:3)

7:30 *The Pharisees and the lawyers,* who sought salvation by way of the Law, *rejected the purpose of God,* "who desires all men to be saved" (1 Ti 2:4), by refusing John's baptism. They sought to establish their own righteousness and "did not submit to God's." (Ro 10:3)

Lawyers, experts in the Mosaic law.

7:31-35 WE PIPED . . . YOU DID NOT DANCE

7:31-35 Cf. Mt 11:16-19 note.

7:34 *Friend of tax collectors and sinners.* This was a stone of stumbling for Pharisee and scribe (cf. 15:1-2 note); they were offended at free forgiveness, whether proclaimed by John (30) or enacted by Jesus. (Cf. 9:21)

7:35 The *wisdom* of God *is justified by all her children.* The new people of God made up of forgiven sinners and accepted outcasts will at the end inherit the Kingdom (cf. Mt 21:31-32), while those who in their self-sufficiency have refused God's grace will perish; thus the *children* of God, created by His wise redemptive counsels, will demonstrate that "the foolishness of God is wiser than men." (1 Co. 1:25)

7:36-50 A MAN HAD TWO DEBTORS: THE SINFUL WOMAN

7:36-50 Recorded only by Lk. Jesus' contemporaries complained that He was "a friend of sinners" (34). Jesus' host, *Simon the Pharisee,* was making the same complaint when he saw Jesus accepting the lavish devotion of a sinful woman (37-38) and concluded that Jesus was no *prophet*—would not a prophet know what *sort of woman* was *touching him* and shrink from such contact with a *sinner,* as every good *Pharisee* did (39)? Jesus' answer to Simon's unspoken objection (which constitutes the heart of the story) proves Him to be a prophet indeed; He sees the sin in Simon's heart and with prophetic authority calls him to repentance. The parable of the *two debtors* (40-43) makes it plain that all men are sinners and all need a "friend of sinners" if they are to have a friend at all. All men are in God's debt, and only divine release from that debt, great or small, can release a man for a life of *love* (42, 47). And then Simon learns that the Prophet who sat at table with him (36) is not only a friend of sinners; He *forgives sins* with divine authority (to the shocked astonishment of Simon's guests, 49) and sends the forgiven sinner, who believed in the Friend of sinners, whose *faith* was active in abundant *love,* with the assurance of salvation *(saved)* and *in peace* (50). Again we hear the "gracious words" of the Anointed of the Lord, and again we sense the contradiction they evoke. (Cf. 4:18-30)

7:39 *A prophet . . . would have known.* Cf. Jn 4:16, 29.

7:41 *For she loved much.* The greatness of her love is evidence of the reality of the forgiveness; she could not have loved much if her *many sins* had not been *forgiven.*

8:1-3 JESUS' COMPANIONS ON HIS TRAVELS

8:1-3 The presence of the *twelve* is noted; they are being trained for their apostolic mission by being witnesses of the *good news of the kingdom of God* proclaimed by Jesus in word and deed. Cf. Mk 3:14: "He appointed twelve, TO BE WITH HIM, and to be sent out to preach." (Cf. also Lk 9:1-2, 6.) The *women* who accompanied Jesus and *provided* for Him and His disciples *out of their means* are examples of those who "loved much" (7:47) because of the forgiving grace which they had experienced (2). Jesus' kindly and respectful attitude toward women is in striking contrast to that of Judaism generally and of the rabbis in particular; He accepts their services, calls woman His "sister" in the household of God (Mt 12:50), and is entirely free of the painful scrupulosity which marked the rabbis' association with womankind—the pure and free association here described would have been unthinkable for them.

8:2 *Mary Magdalene.* Cf. Mt 27:56; 28:1; Jn 20:1.

8:3 *Joanna.* Cf. Lk 24:10.

Chuza, Herod's *steward,* either a manager of some of Herod's properties or a political official in his service. Jesus' influence had extended even to court circles.

Susanna, otherwise unknown.

8:4-15 THE PARABLE OF THE SOWER

8:4-15 Cf. Mt 13:1-9 note; Mt 13:1-52 note.

8:16-21 TAKE HEED HOW YOU HEAR

8:16-21 These words are addressed primarily to the disciples (9) and reinforce the encouragement and warning of the parable of the sower (4-15). The Word of God is an imperiled Word, exposed to the attack of the devil, the power of temptations, and the pressure of both care and pleasure (11-14). But where it is heard and held fast in "an honest and good heart," there it yields bountifully (15). The disciple is to *take heed* that his heart be a good and honest heart ("heart" includes understanding and will). In the good and honest heart the Word is a functioning Word, a *lamp . . . on a stand* that gives *light* (16). The Word has a future and opens up the future; on the lips of the disciple it will make *manifest* the now-hidden presence of the Kingdom, the Messianic glory now veiled by the form of the Servant (17). To *hear* that Word is of crucial importance. Not to "have" it (really have it, hold it fast in a good and honest heart) invokes the judgment of God, who will *take away* the neglected gift. To have it is to enter into the ever-increasing riches of God's future *(will more be given,* 18). For those who *hear and do* the Word the future holds no less a blessing than membership in the family of God *(my mother and my brothers,* 21).

8:22-25 JESUS STILLS THE STORM

8:22-25 Cf. Mt 8:23-27 note. The *disciples* (22) witness the power of Jesus' word *(rebuked the wind and the raging waves,* 24); their *faith,* still weak and wavering, grows stronger as they *marveled* in holy *fear* at Him who *commands even wind and water* (25), evincing the power of God as proclaimed in the OT (Ps 65:7; 89:9; 107:23-29), power employed for their protection. They could learn to say of Jesus what the psalmist said of God: "By dread deeds thou dost answer us with deliverance." (Ps 65:5)

8:26-39 THE GERASENE DEMONIAC

8:26-39 Cf. Mt 8:28-34 notes; Mk 5:1-20 note.

8:40-56 JESUS RAISES JAIRUS' DAUGHTER

8:40-56 Cf. Mt 9:18-26 notes.

9:1-6 THE SENDING OF THE TWELVE

9:1-6 Cf. Mt 9:35—10:42 note. Cf. also Lk 10:1-12, the instruction given to the Seventy. The *twelve,* whose appointment is recorded in 6:13, have been "fully taught" by the words and works of Jesus to be "like their teacher" (6:40). They are *sent out* to be the living extensions of their Lord, with His *authority over all demons* (1; cf. 8:26-33), His authority to *cure diseases* (1) and *to heal* (2; cf. 7:1-10), and *to preach the kingdom of God* (2, 6; cf. 6:20-23; 7:22). Jesus implants in them also His own freedom from care, His certainty that the Father will provide (3-4). His sobering Word (6:22; 7:31-35) has prepared them for the shock of the rejection of the Gospel (5), and His meekness in the face of doubt and opposition has taught them that though they may and must announce the judgment of God on unbelief (5, *a testimony against them*), they are not called on to execute judgment. (Cf. 6:37)

9:5 *Shake off the dust from your feet,* as a sign that they are annulling all connection with them and leaving them to their self-willed fate. Cf. Acts 18:6, where Paul tells those who oppose and revile him as witness to Jesus Christ, "Your blood be upon your heads!"

9:7-9 THE PERPLEXITY OF HEROD

9:7-9 Cf. Mk 6:14-29 note. The mission of the Twelve brought news of Jesus to the court of Herod. The suspicious perplexity of *Herod* Antipas is part of the gathering cloud of opposition which increasingly darkens the way of Jesus from here on (9:22, 23, 31, 44). We hear of his plan to kill Jesus in 13:31; and the words *he sought to see him* (9) point forward to Herod's role in the Passion story. (23:6-12, esp. 8)

9:10-17 THE RETURN OF THE TWELVE AND THE FEEDING OF THE 5,000

9:10 The *apostles,* by the nature of their commission, are required to render an account of their activity. *Bethsaida* lay outside Herod's domain; perhaps that is why Jesus withdrew thither.

9:11-17 For the feeding of the 5,000 cf. Mt 14:15-21 note.

9:11 *Spoke to them of the kingdom of God.* These words, only in Lk, point up the significance of the feeding of the multitudes. Where God reigns, the hungry are fed (6:2) and runaway sons are permitted to eat at the Father's table. (15:23)

9:13 *You give them something to eat.* The *you* is emphatic; Jesus is training the Twelve and challenging their faith.

9:18-27 THE CHRIST OF GOD AND THE CROSS

9:18-27 Cf. Mt 16:1-28 note. The confession to Jesus, to the Christ as the Christ who must suffer and die, Jesus' command that the disciples refrain from proclaiming Him as the Christ, and the imprinting of the cross on the whole life of the disciple—these are common to Mt, Mk, and Lk. Peculiar to Lk and characteristic of him is his reference to Jesus as *praying* (18) at this decisive moment. And Lk alone speaks of taking up one's cross *daily* (23)—the way of the cross is accepted with the daily prayer, "Thy will be done." Lk has no reference to Peter's objection to the cross and Jesus' rebuke. (Mt 16:22-23)

9:28-36 THE TRANSFIGURATION

9:28-36 Cf. Mt 17:1-27 notes. The chief peculiarities of Lk's account are his reference to Jesus' *praying* (28, 29), his indication of the content of the conversation between Jesus and *Moses* and *Elijah* (31), and the designation of Jesus as *my Chosen* by the heavenly voice. (35)

9:31 *Spoke of his departure . . . at Jerusalem.* The departure which Jesus *was to accomplish* at Jerusalem is His dying, which is not a fate that He endures but a deed which He accomplishes, dying freely, of His own will. The Greek word for *departure* is "exodus"; this indicates that Jesus' death will not be defeat but triumph, since it sets His people free. The Servant Messiah will "set at liberty those who are oppressed" (4:18) in the last great Exodus.

9:35 *My Chosen.* This title recalls the Lord's word concerning His Servant who will save His people: "Behold my servant . . . my chosen, in whom my soul delights" (Is 42:1). On the Servant cf. Mt 8:17 note; 12:18-21 note.

9:37-50 IMPERFECT FAITH OF DISCIPLES

9:37-50 Jesus' Galilean ministry is drawing to its close. His disciples have witnessed much, heard much, gone forth to proclaim, confessed the Christ of God—and yet their faith (which the impending Passion will put to so rigorous a test) remains imperfect. They cannot heal the epileptic boy in Jesus' absence (37-43a) and must hear Jesus' disappointed cry of *O faithless and perverse generation* (41); not in them but in Jesus alone is the *majesty of God* made manifest (43). Jesus' second prediction of His Passion (44) leaves them baffled and *afraid;* they cannot yet take in and endure the thought that the *Son of man is to be delivered into the hands of men* (44-45). They cannot yet wholly grasp the thought that the only greatness that matters is Jesus' kind of greatness, the greatness of self-forgetting ministry to the *child,* ministry performed for one who needs it because he needs it (46-48). They have not yet attained to the largeheartedness which can rejoice in any service performed by anyone in Jesus' name and for His glory (49-50; cf. Ph 1:15-18). Accompanied by men still beset by such weaknesses, Jesus "set his face to go to Jerusalem" (51) to suffer and die alone.

9:51—18:30 JESUS' TRAVEL MINISTRY

9:51—18:30 This section contains much material that is peculiar to Luke and characteristic of his gospel, especially the so-called Travel Account. (9:51—18:14)

9:51-56 HOSTILITY IN SAMARIA

9:51-56 The hostility between Jews and *Samaritans* was intense and notorious (cf. Jn 4:9). When a Samaritan *village* expressed this hostility by refusing to *receive* Jesus and His company, *James and John,* those impetuous and fiery "sons of thunder" (Mk 3:17), wished to use their apostolic authority to avenge this insult to their Master by calling down fire on the village, as Elijah had once done (2 K 1:9-16). Jesus lived the love He had taught (6:27-36) and *rebuked* His vengeful disciples as He was wont to rebuke the demons (55; cf., e. g., 4:35, 41). Lk includes more instances of Jesus' concern for Samaritans than the other evangelists (10:29-37; 17:11-19); this incident makes it clear that such concern sprang from pure love, love for the enemy, not from any experience of Samaritan kindness.

9:51 *Set his face.* Cf. Is 50:7.

9:52 *Samaritans,* a people of mixed blood and illegitimate worship, were regarded as unclean and despised by the Jews, and they responded in kind. The concern for these outcasts continues in Acts. (1:8; 8:1-25; 9:31; 15:3)

9:57-62 WHAT IT MEANS TO FOLLOW JESUS

9:57-62 For 9:57-60 cf. Mt 8:18-22 note.

9:62 Only in Lk. He who would follow Jesus must "set his face" steadfastly forward, as Jesus did (9:51); nothing has priority over the *kingdom of God.*

10:1-20 THE SENDING AND THE RETURN OF THE 70 MESSENGERS

10:1-20 The mission of the Seventy (or Seventy-two) is peculiar to Lk. The number 70 (or 72) is the traditional number of the non-Jewish peoples in the world (Gn 10) just as 12 is the number of the tribes of Israel (Mt 10:1-4 note). The choice of this number indicates the ultimate universality of Jesus' saving mission (cf. 2:32) and prepares for the march of the Gospel to the end of the earth in Acts.

10:1-12 Cf. Mt 9:37-38; 10:5-15 note.

10:1 *Two by two,* according to the rule of Dt 19:15, which required two witnesses (cf. 2 Co 13:1). The apostolic church followed the same practice. (Acts 8:14; 13:2; 15:39-40)

10:6 *Son of peace,* one who accepts and welcomes the "peace on earth" which God is giving through His Son to "men with whom he is pleased." (2:14)

10:7-8 *Not go from house to house . . . eat what is set before you.* Cf. 9:4. One believer's house is to be their base of operation (cf. Acts 9:43; 16:15; 17:7; 18:3); and they need not worry about whether the food set before them is "clean" or "unclean" according to Pharisaic standards.

10:13-15 Cf. Mt 11:20-24 note.

10:16 Cf. Mt 10:40-42 note.

10:17-20 The 70 *return with joy.* They had discovered that, poor and "powerless" as they were, they had in the *name* of Jesus (all that Jesus is and signifies for man) a power which even the *demons* could not resist. Jesus confirms them in the joy of their success; their triumph over the hosts of Satan, He tells them, was the carrying out of His own triumph over Satan. Jesus *saw Satan fall . . . from heaven;* since Jesus triumphantly faced him in His temptation, He has freed all men from Satan's power. Satan has lost his place as the accuser of man (cf. Rv 12:7-10). But joy in "success," even success in Jesus' name, can be a treacherous thing for man; it can turn his faith from the power of God toward his own religious prowess. And so Jesus turns the eye of His messengers away from the sight of the scattering hosts of Satan to the cause and grounds of their victory: *Your names are written in heaven.* They have triumphed because God, in bringing them to Jesus, has made them His own, citizens of the city of God, sons and servants of God who find their deepest joy where Jesus found His, in fulfilling the will of their Father in heaven. (Cf. Jn 15:10-11)

10:21-24 JESUS THANKS HIS FATHER

10:21-22 Cf. Mt 11:25-30 note. Peculiar to Lk

and characteristic of him is the notice that Jesus rejoiced *in the Holy Spirit.*

10:23-24 Cf. Mt 13:16 note. Jesus thanks His Father for making the revelation of His power and grace accessible to all by revealing them even "to babes" (21). If the "wise and understanding" let their wisdom blind them to God's revelation, that is their guilt; if the "babes" receive the revelation of God promised by *prophets* and behold the promised King, the Messiah, *desired* by *kings* of old, that is pure grace. They are *blessed,* favored by God.

10:25-37 THE GOOD SAMARITAN

10:25-37 Jesus was not the only Jew who recognized that the beating heart of the *law* is *love,* that love for *God* and love for the *neighbor* constitute the way to *eternal life.* The *lawyer,* skilled in the Law and confident that he was qualified to test Jesus on points of law, recognized it too. His answer to Jesus' counterquestion wins Jesus' full approval (25-28; cf. Mt 22:34-39). But then the gulf which separates the piety of Judaism from that of Jesus becomes apparent. The lawyer recognizes that he, the tester, is being tested when Jesus tells him, *Do this, and you will live* (28). and so he seeks to *justify himself* in his lovelessness. The Law is, after all, not all that clear, he maintains; *neighbor* needs definition. Jesus' reply, the story of the Good Samaritan, makes it plain that the problem is not one of definition. Neighbor is not a generality to be defined but an individual to be met. God, who governs all happenings down to and including the fall of the sparrow (12:6), will "define" neighbor for you by laying him across your road half dead, in need of you. You need not take steps to define and find him; you will have to take steps to avoid him, as the *priest* and the *Levite* did. The Law is clear, and the imperative of love is inescapable; even a *Samaritan* could hear and heed it. In the last analysis the question is not one of mind (who is?) but of will—how can I *prove neighbor* to the man across my path? Five men are confronted by the Law. The lawyer, priest, and Levite evaded it. The Samaritan in the simplicity of his heart obeyed it. Jesus went on to the cross in an unbroken unity of love for God and all His half-dead neighbors and fulfilled it.

10:31-32 *Priest . . . Levite,* both serving in the temple, both in the service of the God whose love offered man communion with Himself and forgiveness in the house where He made His name dwell. They avoided the simple duty of love, perhaps out of fear that the man left half dead might die and so pollute them. (Cf. Lv 21:1)

10:38-42 MARY AND MARTHA

10:38-42 Only in Lk. The story is an illustration in terms of common life of the priority of the Word over bread, which Jesus had asserted in His temptation. (4:4)

10:39 *Sat at the Lord's feet.* Cf. Acts 22:3, where Paul uses the expression to describe his relationship to his teacher Gamaliel. The rabbis refused to teach women the Law; here as always Jesus' attitude toward woman is in striking contrast to that attitude. (cf. 8:1-3 note)

10:42 For the hearing of the Word as the *good portion* cf. 8:15, 21; 11:28.

11:1-13 LORD, TEACH US TO PRAY

11:1 *As John taught his disciples.* Cf. 5:33. The example of John and Jesus' own example of constant prayer, emphasized by Lk, give rise to the disciples' request.

11:2b-4 Cf. Mt 6:9-15 notes. Lk's form of the Lord's Prayer has 5 petitions, as over against the 7 in Mt ("Thy will be done" and "Deliver us from evil" being absent from Lk). This free variation in the form of the prayer as preserved by the inspired evangelists indicates that the Spirit led them to see in Jesus' words a pattern of prayer to be followed rather than a rigid formula to be memorized and repeated; the substance of Jesus' instruction in prayer remains the same.

11:5-8 The parable of the man "bothering" his friend for the loan of *three loaves at midnight* is Jesus' comment on the word "Father" (2), the address of the prayer. "Father" probably reproduces the "Abba" of Jesus' mother tongue; "Abba" was the child's familiar address to his father, with all of a child's confidence and *importunity* (8) in it. Jesus reveals to us a God whom we can bother, who welcomes His children's importunity.

11:9-13 Cf. Mt 7:7-11. The argument is from the less to the greater; if even human fathers, evil though they be at best, can and do give good gifts to their children, how much the more will *the heavenly Father* give the best of all gifts, *the Holy Spirit,* to His own? If men dare hope for that gift, they may confidently expect all good gifts. (Cf. Mt 6:33)

11:14-32 REACTIONS TO JESUS: ADMIRATION, BLASPHEMY, SEEKING A SIGN

11:14-32 Cf. Mt 12:22-45 notes. Jesus casts out a *demon,* and His mighty deed provokes a threefold response. There is, first, astonished admiration: *The people marveled* (14). There is, second, blasphemous contradiction: *He casts out demons by Beelzebul, the prince of demons* (15). There is, third, the reserved skepticism which demands conclusive proof: *Others, to test him, sought from him a sign from heaven.*

Jesus answers the blasphemers by pointing out (17-22) the folly and danger of interpreting His power over the demons as anything but as His overcoming of Satan (the *strong man,* 21) and the coming of the *kingdom of God* (20). Now neutrality is impossible (23); and no one can remain empty who refuses the presence of the Christ—the powers of Satan will fill that vacuum. (24-26)

Jesus answers the sign-seeking skeptics (29-32) with the promise of the *sign of Jonah* (29), a call to repentance, and the threat of *judgment* on those who have refused *something greater* than the revelation given through prophet and king of old (*Jonah, Solomon).*

Jesus' answer to those who respond with nothing stronger than admiration is contained in His reply to the admiring woman (27-28), peculiar to Lk) who called *blessed* the mother of so brilliant a Son. This is no time for admiration; this is the critical hour in which only one thing matters: to *hear and keep the word* which God is in these last days speaking by His Son. (Cf. Heb 1:1-2; 2:3-4)

11:20 *The finger of God* is a symbol of God's irresistible power and unquestionable authority. Pharaoh's magicians recognized the finger of God in the plagues by which the Lord smote Egypt and set His people free (Ex 8:19); and the "tables of stone" which recorded God's will for His covenant people were "written with the finger of God" (Ex 31:18). The psalmist is filled with awe and humble adoration when he beholds the heavens, the work of the "fingers" of God (Ps 8:3-4). God the Deliverer, the Lawgiver, the Creator is at work in this mighty and delivering deed of Jesus.

11:33-36 BE CAREFUL LEST THE LIGHT IN YOU BE DARKNESS

11:33-36 God has not obscured the light of His revelation; Jesus is not *a lamp* set *under a bushel* basket; He is a lamp set on a *stand* for all to *see*. His words and works are clear (33). But as the unsound *eye* deprives the body of the light, though the light is present in all fullness (34), so the unsound eye of unbelief can deprive the whole man of the light which is designed to make man's life *wholly bright*, fully illuminated by the gracious revelation of God. These words are a warning attached to 11:14-32, where the various reactions of men to Jesus' revelatory deed are all examples of the unsound eye that leaves men in darkness.

11:37-54 JESUS' WOE TO THE PHARISEES AND THE LAWYERS

11:37-54 In three woes on the *Pharisees* and three on their theological guides and leaders, the *lawyers* (scribes), Jesus exposes the falsity of the piety that resists Him and plots to entrap Him (53-54). For the substance of Jesus' indictment cf. Mt 23:1-39 note.

11:38 *Not . . . wash before dinner*, as the tradition of the elders prescribed. Cf. Mt 15:2 note on the authority of the tradition.

11:40-41 *He who made.* The God who made man made the whole man, *outside* and *inside*, and so man owes his whole self to God; giving oneself to Him with undivided devotion is the basis of all genuine piety *(alms)* and is a purity which transcends the Pharisaic anxiety about "clean" and "unclean." (Cf. Mt 15:10-20)

11:44 *Walk over them,* and are made unclean by contact with the dead. The Pharisaic piety, displayed and admired, corrupts men's piety.

11:49 *The Wisdom of God said. Wisdom* is the personified wisdom of God (cf. 7:35). They will continue to resist God's counsels (7:30) to their own destruction.

12:1-59 The Disciples in This World

12:1-59 In the presence of a great *multitude* Jesus instructs *his disciples* on the quality of their life in this world as they wait and work in the hope of the world to come. Their life in this world is to be in sharp contrast to the *hypocrisy* of the *Pharisees;* it is the life of the pure in heart (1:34). It is a life animated by a lively hope which keeps them vigilant and faithful, alert and open-eyed to the realities of the world's last days. (35-59)

12:1-34 THE DISCIPLES IN THE WORLD: PURITY OF HEART

12:1-34 To be pure in heart is to will one thing only, to have your heart fixed, whole and undivided, on the supreme *treasure* of your life (34), to *seek* the *kingdom* of God and trust Him wholly (31). To this purity of heart the hypocritical piety of the Pharisees posed an insidious threat; it could work imperceptibly but pervasively, like *leaven,* to corrupt their heart and make them incapable of life in the light (1-3). Purity of heart has in it a holy fear of God, the inescapable Judge, a fear which drives out every fear of men. In the heart of Jesus' *friends* this holy fear coexists with a pure trust in Him who has numbered the *hairs of your head,* so that fear is ever and again swallowed up in fearless faith (4-7). Fearless faith leads to fearless confession in the power of the *Holy Spirit,* that supreme gift of God (cf. 11:13), the Spirit so strong and terrible that men who *blaspheme* Him can no longer hope to be *forgiven.* (4:12)

Purity of heart cannot coexist with *covetousness* (15) and care *(anxious about your life,* 22); both blind a man to God's governance and goodness in his life and give priority to *barns* (18), *food* and *clothing* (23) in his heart, priority over the *kingdom* and the *Father.* Both make man incapable of that largehearted, reckless generosity which provides him with *treasure in the heavens.* (13-34)

12:1 *Pharisees . . . hypocrisy.* Cf. 11:37-54 note; Mt 23:1-39 note. Hypocrisy is the characteristic of the man who attempts to divide his heart between God and self.

12:2-3 *Revealed . . . known,* etc. Hypocrisy cannot succeed; it will be exposed and convicted.

12:4-9 Cf. Mt 10:24-33 note.

12:4 *My friends.* Since they are not only servants (cf. 37) of Christ but His friends, who "know what their Master is doing" (Jn 15:14-15), they are doubly responsible and have full grounds for confident trust in God.

12:10 Cf. Mt 12:31-32 note and Mt 12:22-37 note.

12:12 *Spirit.* Cf. Mt 10:20; Jn 15:26; 16:7-11 (the Spirit as Counselor).

12:13 *Divide the inheritance.* The scribes, or "lawyers," were often called on to adjudicate cases of this sort. Jesus, who came to free men from the clutches of covetousness (15), will not let Himself be used in the service of men's covetings.

12:15 *Life* is God's gift, and no acquisitions of man can either safeguard (20) or prolong it (25).

12:16-21 The rich fool who *lays up treasure for himself* (21) is completely self-centered; he speaks only to himself *(soul,* 19), with no thought for his fellowman or his God. He is the classic case of the man in whom the thorns of the "riches and pleasures of life" have "choked out" the Word of God which bids him love God and his neighbor. (8:7, 14)

12:21 *Rich toward God,* in his relationship to God, the one relationship that counts supremely and endures forever. (Cf. 33)

12:21-31 Cf. Mt 6:19-34 note.

12:32 The *Father* who out of free and sovereign grace *(good pleasure)* gives no less a gift than His *kingdom* can be trusted to provide; the only logical thing to do is to follow in the footsteps of His lavish love.

12:35-59 THE DISCIPLE IN THE WORLD: A LIVELY HOPE

12:35-59 Their lively hope is to make the disciples vigilant and ready, *like men . . . waiting for their master to come home.* The reward for vigilance is astonishingly great—the returning *master* will *serve* His *servants!* But their vigilance must be constant, for the *Son of man* will come as a *thief* in the night; no one knows the *hour* of His coming. His disciples know only how costly an error it will be to miss that hour. (35-40)

Their lively hope is to make them responsible, *faithful and wise stewards* of their *master's household.* The reward is, according to human standards of merit, ridiculously high; the returning master will *set* them *over all his possessions.* The punishment of the *unfaithful* will be correspondingly severe; *to whom much is given, of him will much be required.* (41-48)

Their lively hope is at the same time to be a sober, open-eyed recognition of the seriousness of the present hour. Before that blessed time when they shall sit at their Master's table enjoying the ministry of His love, before the time when they shall be coheirs with Christ (cf. Ro 8:17), there lies the time of fiery trial (49), when the cross (50) shall confront men with a decision and create a *division* which will cut across all ties of kinship (49-53). The vigilant, responsible disciple will, unlike the unheeding *multitudes,* be able *to interpret . . . the present time,* to read the weather signals of God's approaching storm. (54-56)

Their lively hope is therefore held and lived under the shadow of the approaching judgment *(magistrate, judge, officer, prison,* 58). As they live in hope of forgiveness, they live a life that has on it the mark of forgiveness. They forgive and seek forgiveness lest any offended brother stand as their *accuser* on that last and fateful day. (57-59)

12:35 *Loins be girded.* Be ready to serve. (Cf. 37)

12:41-42 *For us or for all?* All disciples are servants; the apostles, for whom Peter is speaking, are servants with a special responsibility as *stewards,* men *set over his household,* all the servants, *to give them their portion of food at the proper time.* What applies to the apostles applies to all who hold positions of ministering leadership. (Cf. 1 Co 4:1-2; Tts 1:7; 1 Ptr 4:7)

12:47-48 *Severe beating . . . light beating.* Responsibility is in proportion to knowledge; to the disciples "it has been given to know the secrets of the kingdom of God" (8:9), and they must face up to their greater responsibility.

12:49 *I came to cast fire upon the earth.* Peculiar to Lk. The *fire* is probably fiery trial, the suffering of those who will take up their cross and follow Jesus and the agonizing conflict and cruel divisions which the Gospel of the Crucified will create. Jesus wishes *that it were already kindled* in order that the result of His work, the new people of God tested and purified by fire, may emerge.

12:50 *A baptism to be baptized with.* For Jesus' suffering and death as a baptism, an immersion into agony, cf. Mk 10:38 note and OT passages like Ps 69:14-15; 144:7.

How I am constrained! The constraint is both His eagerness to fulfill the will of God and that horror of death expressed in Gethsemane.

13:1-35 Repentance, Healing, Parables, Herod's Plan

13:1-9 REPENT, OR YOU WILL ALL PERISH

13:1-9 Recorded by Lk. only. The Pharisees interpreted a disaster which befell a man as an indication that the man involved was being punished by God for some particularly dreadful sin. Thus they could remain aloof and secure in their own sense of righteousness; they did "not know how to interpret the present time" and remained "hypocrites" (12:56). Jesus teaches them "how to interpret the present time." Two recent disasters, the slaughter of the *Galileans* and the construction accident which killed 18 men at the *tower in Siloam* in Jerusalem, are tokens and portents of the judgment of God which impends over *all unless* they *repent.* Roman armies will shed more blood than *Pilate* did, and the collapsing walls of besieged *Jerusalem* will bury not 18 but thousands. All Israel is like a fruitless *fig tree* living under the suspended sentence of *Cut it down!* And yet God's love is still at work to move His people to repentance; the Gardener still digs and nurtures the tree to save it from its doom. "Note then the kindness . . . of God." (Ro 11:22)

13:1 The incident of *Pilate* killing *Galileans* while they were engaged in *sacrifice* is otherwise unknown but is of a piece with known instances of his brutal disregard for the religious feelings of the people whom he governed.

13:4 *Tower in Siloam.* Siloam was a pool which formed part of the water-supply system of Jerusalem; the collapse of the tower probably occurred during construction on the water system.

13:10-17 JESUS FREES A DAUGHTER OF ABRAHAM FROM SATAN'S BONDAGE

13:10-17 ` Recorded by Luke only. "God's kindness is meant to lead" Israel "to repentance" (Ro 2:4). The *ought* (16), the must, of God's merciful will governs the whole life of Jesus (2:49; 4:43; 9:22; 13:33; 17:25; 19:5; 22:37; 24:7, 44). That ought impels Jesus to His deed of mercy toward the *woman* whom demonic power *(spirit of infirmity,* 11) bent and bowed. She must be set free, for she is a *daughter of Abraham;* and God has made a promise "to Abraham and to his posterity for ever" (1:55), a promise of blessing (Gn 12:2). She must be set free *on the sabbath,* for God's blessing rests on the Sabbath (Gn 2:3). She must be set free, for the mercy of God will not allow Satan to usurp His creation forever. And God's kindness does lead some men to repentance; the daughter of Abraham *praised God* (13), and *all the people rejoiced at all the glorious things that were done* by Jesus (17). But His kindness collides with the *hypocrites* whose cloven piety will make a Sabbath exception for their *ox or ass* in order that "life, their life, may go on," but will not permit God to do His work of mercy on the Sabbath in order that His gift of life, life freed from Satan, may go on (15). Thus Jesus woos His people; the example of the *ruler of the synagogue* (14) shows that He woos in vain: "You would not!" (13:34)

13:18-21 MUSTARD SEED AND THE LEAVEN

13:18-21 Cf. Mt 13:31-33 note. Jesus is not discouraged and Israel need not be offended by the littleness of the beginnings of the *kingdom of God;* these little beginnings have in them the promise and pledge of future greatness.

13:22-30 WILL THOSE WHO ARE SAVED BE FEW?

13:22-30 Jesus will not permit anyone to be a spectator at the drama of salvation. He will not allow men to ask theoretical questions like, *Will those who are saved be few?* (23). (Theoretical questions put off repentance and do not lead to faith.) Jesus' answer is therefore not a statement but a command: *Strive* (24). Strive to take up God's call into your heart and will, though it be against the grain and in the face of the majority. Strive now before it is too late, now before the *door* is *shut* forever on men who can claim historical knowledge of Jesus but have not been moved to repentance and faith by Him and cannot be acknowledged by Him (25-28). Strive in fear and trembling lest all the grace of God which made you *first* (the promise to *Abraham* and the living oracles of the *prophets,* 28) prove to be grace given in vain and the *last,* long distant from God (Eph 2:11-22), come from the four corners of the earth to accept the invitation which you have rejected (14:18-24) and sit down to the feast (29-30) which "the Lord of hosts will make for all people." (Is 25:6)

13:31-35 I MUST GO ON MY WAY

13:31-35 We can guess why *Herod* Antipas *wants to kill* Jesus; he who had found the Baptist uncomfortable, a man to be gotten out of the way (3:19-20); 9:7-9), would not be happy with the Man who had come "to cast fire upon the earth" (12:49). We are not told why the *Pharisees* informed Jesus of Herod's plan (31). The center of interest lies in Jesus' response. Not Herod, Jesus declares, but God shall determine the time and place of His death; *today and tomorrow* and on the day following (day by day) He is listening for the striking of God's clock. At God's time he *must* and will finish His course where God wills it, in *Jerusalem.* The city that has heard and *killed* the *prophets,* God's servants, shall hear the voice of God's Son also. Then He will pour out His life and intercede for transgressors. The will of self-sacrificing love that impels Jesus toward Jerusalem finds eloquent expression in His cry of injured love over Jerusalem (34-35; cf. Mt 23:37-39 and note on Mt 23:1-39, last paragraph).

14:1-35 Salt Is Good: the Pharisees and the Multitudes

14:1-35 Jesus sought and found nothing on earth but men. Whether He is talking with *Pharisees* at dinner (1) or summoning *multitudes* (25) to *renounce all* and be His *disciples* (33), He is seeking and saving men. And it is His will to make men *salt* of the earth (34)—whole men of God, men in whom nature and function are one, men who are what they profess and DO what they are, who express their saltness by salting whatever they touch. Moreover, His words to both Pharisees and multitudes make sense only as the words of One who can claim men wholly because He is giving Himself to them wholly; as the healing mercy of God, the inviting voice of God in person.

14:1-24 JESUS AND THE PHARISEES

14:1-6 The healing of the man with dropsy (peculiar to Lk). To the Pharisees, entrenched in their legal piety and keeping a suspiciously watchful eye on the breaker of the *sabbath* (1), Jesus presents the healing mercy of God in His own person; He *heals* the dropsical *man before him* on the Sabbath, on God's Day. For the Pharisees mercy on the Sabbath is the exception (5); for Jesus mercy on all days is the rule (3). They can become good salt only by breaking their stubborn silence (4, 6) and speaking a glad assent to the healing mercy of God present in Jesus. (Cf. 15:31-32)

14:1 *Watching* maliciously, lying in wait to see whether Jesus would violate the Sabbath as He had done before. (6:6 ff.; 13:10 ff.)

14:7-14 Found only in Lk. Jesus is not lecturing on table manners or giving rules on party-giving. The scene before Him offers the material for a *parable* (7) concerning men's faith in God the Exalter (11) and Rewarder (14). Jesus did not exalt Himself; He went the way of obedient ministry into the depths, the way of the merciful Servant, trusting in God to exalt Him at His time and in His way (cf. Ph 2:6-11). He resisted the satanic temptation to greatness (4:5-8) and lavished his power and love on the *poor, the maimed, the lame, the blind* (13). He loved and served men who could not *repay, because* they could not repay (14). He loved with the love of the Most High (6:35). In summoning the Pharisee from his self-seeking and self-interest to this selfless way, Jesus is inviting them to Himself and to a share in His great reward. Thus they can become good salt.

14:11 *Will be humbled . . . be exalted.* The passive voice, as often, indicates divine action. (Cf., e.g., 6:21)

14:14 *The resurrection of the just.* This does not exclude a resurrection of those who "shall awake . . . to shame and everlasting contempt" (Dn 12:2). Jesus is speaking to the hope of the Pharisee, whom He called "just" or "righteous" in contrast to flagrant sinners. (Cf. 15:7; 5:32)

14:15-24 Cf. Mt 22:1-10. The Pharisee shares with Jesus the hope of partaking in God's feast in the future *kingdom of God* (15; cf. 13:29; 22:16). What the Pharisee in his comfortable hope does not see, what his concern for *field, oxen,* and to be *married* (18-20) blinds him to is the fact that the future kingdom is making its claim on him now, that now in the person of Jesus "the kingdom of God is in the midst" of them (17:21). With the coming Jesus God is saying, *Come, for all is now ready* (17). Jesus is God's invitation to the feast; through Him God *compels* men and *fills* His *house* (23) with guests. To evade Him is to be excluded from the great *banquet* of God. (24)

14:21-23 The verses point to the inclusion of the Gentiles, the theme of the Book of Acts. (Cf. 24:47)

14:25-35 JESUS AND THE MULTITUDES

14:25-35 Since Jesus is God's future, the only future that matters (cf. 14:15-24), it is not enough to accompany Him (25), man must come to Him (26). Man must be ready to turn his back on the dearest things this life holds for him: family (26), *life,* and honor (both given up in the criminal's death on the *cross,* 26-27), *all that he has* (33). He must do so with open-eyed sobriety and *count the cost* (28); romantic enthusiasm, illusions about victory without war—these will not do. Only discipleship, only faith in Jesus Christ will make a man *good salt;* only living and active faith will save him from the fate of salt that *has lost its taste. He who has ears to hear, let him hear* (35) the words not of a stern ascetic moralist but of Jesus Christ, the Wisdom of God and the Power of God. (Cf. 1 Co 1:24)

15:1-32 Jesus, the Seeker of the Lost

15:1-32 Once again (cf. 5:29-30) Jesus' free and forgiving association with *sinners* provokes the dissent of the "righteous," *the Pharisees and the scribes* (1-2). In three parables Jesus seeks to open the eyes of the dissenters to the wonder and glory of the history which is taking place before their eyes; it is the beginning of the last chapter of the story of the Lord who has promised to seek and save the lost (Eze 34:16; cf. Lk 19:10). The twin parables of the lost sheep (3-7) and the lost coin (8-10) make it plain: God is in Christ seeking His own; these *sinners* are His creatures, in whom He has an owner's interest (cf. Jn 10:11-17), for whose return He is willing to take trouble, to *seek diligently* (8), at whose recovery He and all His angels rejoice exceedingly (10). There is *joy in heaven* (7) now when Jesus admits sinners to table fellowship with Himself; shall there be murmuring on earth? (1)

This searching question is implicit in the first two parables; it becomes explicit in the third parable (11-32), which tells the same story in the personal terms of father and son, waiting love, repentance and return, free forgiveness, and exuberant joy. The parable of the prodigal son ends with the conversation between the rejoicing father and the angry *elder son,* the righteous who stayed home and *served* and *never disobeyed* his father's *command* (29). In the father's remarkably gentle and winning rebuke (31-32) Jesus is wooing the righteous to speak a joyous assent to His mission—not without pointing to their deep disease, their self-seeking will. In the end the elder son and the prodigal son both suffer from the same disease, self-seeking. The younger son said, *Give me* (12); the elder son said, *You never gave me.* (29)

15:2 *Eats with them.* For the significance of the common meal cf. Mt 14:15-21 note.

15:8-32 Only in Lk.

15:8 *Ten silver coins.* The ten coins probably were part of her dowry and adorned her headdress, a treasured possession.

15:11-32 Only in Lk.

15:13 *Gathered all he had,* i.e., converted it into cash.

15:15-16 *Feed swine . . . no one gave him.* A Jew could hardly sink lower than this: herding the unclean animals and filching their fodder for food.

15:11-32 Only in Lk.

15:13 *Gathered all he had,* i.e., converted it into cash.

15:21 *Called your son.* The father does not allow him to finish his prepared speech of repentance (cf. 19, "treat me as one of your hired servants"); the penitent, returning son is son with full honors (22-23). God's forgiveness is instant and total. (Cf. Mi 7:18-19)

15:33 For the *robe* as a symbol of forgiveness cf. Zch 3:4.

15:29 *Many years I have served you.* The elder son felt that he had been dealt with unfairly. He had worked for the good of the home all his life; the younger brother had squandered everything he had received.

15:31 *You are always with me.* That is what life under the covenant means: constant communion with God.

15:32 *Your brother was dead.* Cf. Eph 2:1-2, "dead through the trespasses and sins in which you once walked."

16:1-31 The Possibilities and Perils of Mammon

16:1-31 *Mammon* is a word from Jesus' mother tongue, Aramaic, and means "possessions." Luke's Gospel is particularly rich in Jesus' teaching on mammon. (See Introduction).This whole chapter is devoted to the subject. Jesus speaks of the possibilities of mammon to His *disciples,* and of the perils of mammon to the *Pharisees, who were lovers of money.* In both cases He speaks of man's use of mammon in view of man's long future; man's use of mammon can lead to the *eternal habitations* (9) or to the eternal *place of torment.* (28)

16:1-13 THE POSSIBILITIES OF MAMMON: THE DISHONEST STEWARD

16:1-13 *Mammon,* property, can serve eternally useful ends if it is used with *shrewdness* (8); the disciples can learn that shrewdness from the example of an unscrupulous rascal like the dishonest steward. Shrewdness is the ability to appraise a situation realistically, to find ways and means to meet the situation, and to employ the means and ways vigorously and consistently toward gaining one's desired end. In this, and in this alone, the steward is exemplary. He knows that his time is short, that he must work with what he has while there still is time; and he does work with it shrewdly and boldly. And so he ensures his future against degradation and want (3). He wins out by giving away what he has while he still has it. This the disciples are to imitate, not the dishonesty but the prudence. They are to know that they are stewards, whose property is entrusted to them for a short time by Another; that they are to work with that property while they can, giving away diliberately and recklessly with an eye to the future and its *eternal habitations* (9). Thus they will provide themselves with "purses that do not grow old, with a treasure in the heavens that does not fail." (1-9; cf. 12:33)

Mammon, Jesus adds (10-13), is but a *very little* thing compared with the *true riches* which are theirs. But in this little thing they can and must demonstrate their faithfulness; in it they can show their singlehearted devotion to their one Master; they can *serve* only one Master, God. But in their prudence learned from Jesus they can make mammon serve God's cause and their own eternal welfare. (10-13)

16:1 *Wasting his goods.* That is what the tax collectors who drew near to Jesus (15:1) and men like the younger son of the parable had done (15:13, 30); they had wasted God's goods. Now, as disciples of Jesus, they still have a little time to use wisely the goods entrusted to them, as Zacchaeus did (19:8) when salvation came to his house. (19:9)

16:8 *The master.* The steward's master, cf. 3, 5; even the man who had suffered from the steward's dishonesty had to admire his *shrewdness* as a "smart operator." *The sons of this world,* the men who live for and by the profits of this age, have a keener eye for shrewdness on their level and in men of their own kind than the Christian has.

Sons of light, the men who derive their being and character from the light that has dawned on the world in Jesus Christ. (1:78-79; 2:32; Acts 26:23)

16:9 *They may receive you.* They are the people helped and won by the disciples' generosity. What was done to them was done to Christ and God (9:48) and receives the gracious reward of life in their *eternal habitations.*

16:14-31 THE PERILS OF MAMMON: THE RICH MAN AND LAZARUS

16:14-31 The *Pharisees,* known not only from the NT but also from Judaic sources as *lovers of money, scoffed* at Jesus (14). They saw no conflict between serving God and mammon (13). When John the Baptist came with the call to repentance and the gift of forgiveness by Baptism, these men did not "justify God" as "the people and the tax collectors" did by accepting God's judgment on their sin and His forgiveness for their sin (7:29 note). They "rejected the purpose of God" by refusing Baptism (7:30) and continued to *justify* themselves *before men* (15) with their hollow and pretentious piety. Jesus tries once more to open their eyes to the reality of their present situation and of their impending future. *God,* He tells them, *knows* them for what they are, for He knows their *hearts* (15). They have heard *the law and the prophets* from childhood on; they have heard *John* the Baptist; they are hearing *the good news of the kingdom of God,* and they see man hazarding all to enter that proclaimed kingdom *(enters it violently,* 16). They know from Jesus' own teaching that the Gospel does not "overthrow the law" but "upholds the law" (17; cf. Ro 3:31). And yet they continue to flout the sanctity of marriage which the Law commands and the Gospel upholds. No word of God has turned them from their self-serving distortion of the Law, from their self-exaltation, their worship of themselves, which makes them an *abomination* (an idol) in the *sight of God.* (15)

The story of the *rich man* and *Lazarus* (19-31) makes terrifyingly clear what is the future of men who attempt to serve both God and mammon. Mammon has made the rich man blind to the need of the neighbor whom God has put at *his gate,* inescapably visible. Mammon has made the rich man deaf to the voice of God in *Moses and the prophets,* which he had. His heart was not fixed in love on God or man; his heart lay where his treasure was *(purple and fine linen . . . feasted sumptuously,* 19). At the great reversal which Mary had hailed in the Magnificat, Lazarus is filled with good things and the rich is sent empty away, into the *place of torment* (cf. 1:51-53). Too late he realizes that the Word of God is more precious than gold, than fine gold. Too late he learns that those who have not heeded the Law and the prophets have made impossible the greater gift of God, the word of one risen from the dead. He and his *brothers* have not really had the gift of the Law and the prophets; "from him who has not, even what he thinks that he has will be taken away." (8:18)

16:20 *Lazarus* is the only person in Jesus' parables who is given a name; the name is therefore significant. It means "God is my help" and indicates that the poor man is not merely destitute but one who is "poor in spirit," wholly dependent on God. (Cf. Mt 5:3 note)

16:21 *Dogs . . . licked his sores.* Since dogs, lean and hungry scavengers of the streets, are regarded as unclean (Mt 7:6), this feature serves to mark the extremity of the poor man's misery.

16:22 *Abraham's bosom,* the place of honor (Jn 13:23) at the great feast in the world to come (Lk 13:28-29; Mt 8:11). God has "exalted those of low degree." (1:52)

16:31 *If some one should rise from the dead.* Perhaps a hint of the coming resurrection of Jesus and the renewed proclamation of the Gospel to Israel, "beginning from Jerusalem" (24:47). Even then no "sign" will be given to those who demand one; Jesus will appear to His disciples—all others will be dependent on the Word.

17:1-19 Service and Healing

17:1-10 THE DISCIPLES' SERVICE: FAITH WORKING THROUGH LOVE

17:1-10 For 1-2 cf. Mt 18:6-9; for 3-4 cf. Mt 18:15, 21-22; for 5-6 cf. Mt 17:20 note. 7-10 is peculiar to Lk.

Jesus lays on *his disciples* (1), who are to be *apostles* of their *Lord,* living extensions of His ministering love, a burden that only *faith* (5) can bear: He asks of them a love which will in holy fear avoid putting *temptations to sin* (or *stumbling blocks,* 1) in the way of *little ones* (2), the weak and wavering brothers, easily shocked, readily mislead. Paul's words in Ro 14:13—15:2 show what loving consideration, what disciplined self-sacrifice this involves. Jesus asks of His disciples a readiness to forgive the penitent brother which knows no limits *(seven times in the day,* 4). He asks of them a servant's (slave's) total devotion which works with no thought of reward, a love which considers a *duty done* the least that love can do (7-10). No wonder that the disciples make the request, *Increase our faith* (5). And Jesus does increase it when He assures them that it is not the power of their believing but the power of the God in whom they believe that achieves the impossible—the firmly rooted *sycamine tree . . . rooted up* (6), bearing patiently with little ones, forgiving without limit.

17:7 No master of a slave is expected to serve his servants; but Jesus will do the unexpected. To those who work in faith and love, with no thought of reward, He gives the reward which none may claim and only He can give: "He will gird himself and have them sit at table, and he will come and serve them." (12:37; cf. Rv 3:20)

17:11-19 THE HEALING OF THE 10 LEPERS

17:11-19 Peculiar to Lk. *Faith* (19) links this third story involving Samaritans (cf. 9:52-55; 10:30-37) with the preceding; as faith is manifested in considerate, self-denying love (17:1-2), in forgiving (17:3-4), and in service to the Lord (17:7-10), so it is in the nature of faith *to . . . give praise to God* (18; cf. Ro 4:20). The common tragedy of leprosy united the Samaritan with nine Jews in their misery; his *faith* unites him with Jesus and makes him a member of the new people of God, while the Jews who accept the gifts of the Messiah but will not believe in Him and *give thanks* to God for Him are excluded. (Cf. Mt 8:11-12)

17:12 *Village.* Judaic interpretation of the Law (Lv 13—14) excluded *lepers* from Jerusalem and walled cities but permitted them to live in segregation in or near unwalled villages.

At a distance, as prescribed in Lv 13:45-46.

17:14 *Show yourselves to the priests.* Cf. Lv 14:2-32.

17:18 *Was no one found?* Jesus laments over the unbelief and ingratitude of His people, represented here by the nine lepers (cf. 19:41-44); He does not revoke the gift of healing. His is the divine love that "risks betrayal." (Luther)

17:20—18:30 The Presence and the Coming of the Kingdom

17:20—18:30 Faith (17:1-19) and hope are inseparable; this section speaks of hope. The units of this section are held together by the idea of the presence and the future coming of the kingdom of God. The question of the *Pharisees* is a question concerning the *when* of the reign of God (17:20-21); Jesus speaks to His disciples of *one of the days of the Son of man,* which is another way of speaking of the Kingdom (17:22-37); the parable of the *widow* and the *judge* encourages continual, unflagging prayer for the coming of the Son of Man in glory (18:1-8); the story of the *Pharisee* and the *publican* points toward the future judgment when the self-righteous *will be humbled* and the penitently humble *will be exalted* (18:9-14); Jesus' welcoming of the *children* speaks of man's entry into the *kingdom* (18:15-17); the *ruler's* question is concerned with *eternal life,* and Jesus' answer concerns entry into the *kingdom of God* (18:18-30). The whole mystery of the Kingdom, present in the person of Jesus, won or lost by man's response to Him now, and coming incalculably and gloriously in the future, is presented here.

17:20-21 PHARISEES' QUESTION CONCERNING THE COMING OF THE KINGDOM

17:20-21 The healing of the 10 lepers (11-19) may have prompted the Pharisees' question. Their rabbis equated the healing of a leper with the resurrection of a dead man; and the resurrection of the dead was a sure *sign* of the arrival of the long-awaited Kingdom. Jesus' answer cuts off all calculation of time and place concerning the future Kingdom and seeks to open their eyes for the beginning of "the acceptable year of the Lord" (4:19), the dawn of the Kingdom in His own words and works now, spoken and done *in the midst* of them (cf. 19:20). The Pharisee felt sure of his place in the Kingdom (14-15) and needed only to be assured of its arrival; Jesus' answer implies that the drawing near of the Kingdom is not a time for observation but for repentance. (Cf. Mt 4:17; Mk 1:15)

17:22-37 THE HOPE OF THE DISCIPLE: THE DAY OF THE SON OF MAN

17:22-37 Jesus' words to His *disciples* are somber and sobering words, full of pastoral concern for them. The *Son of man . . . must suffer* (25) before He can "enter into his glory" (24:26); and His own must follow Him on that path of suffering (cf. Ro 8:17). Therefore their longing for the return of the Son of Man in glory will be intense (22). They must not let that intensity of hope make them credulous toward misleading voices (23); they need no word but the Word of their Lord, and it assures them that *the Son of man . . . in his day* will be as inescapably apparent in His glorious coming as *lightning flashes* to illumine the sky from horizon to horizon (24). They must never lose the intensity of their hope and become so enmeshed in the normal concerns of life that the return of the Son of Man comes upon them unawares and proves their destruction. The *days of Noah* and the *days of Lot* should warn them against that, those "normal" days which ended suddenly in judgment by *flood* and *fire* (26-30). The example of *Lot's wife* warns them of the danger of the one last look backward at the perishing world; no desire for self-preservation dare tempt them to *gain* their *life* and so, at the last moment, *lose it* (31-34). That last moment will bring terribly unexpected divisions; the ties of this world will be sundered forever (35-36). Jesus cuts off all curious questioning; the eagles of God *will be gathered together* for judgment at the time of this world's death *(body,* corpse), which only God knows. (37)

17:26 *Days of Noah.* Cf. Gn 6:5-8; 7:6-24; Mt 24:37-39.

17:28 *Days of Lot.* Cf. Gn 18:20-33; 19:24-25.

17:35 *One . . . taken,* that is, taken to Himself by the Son of Man when He comes to gather His elect. (Cf. Mt 24:31)

18:1-8 THE HOPE OF THE DISCIPLE: PRAY AND NOT LOSE HEART

18:1-8 Peculiar to Lk. As in the case of the dishonest steward (16:1-9), Jesus uses an extreme case to make His point. If even an irreverent and *unrighteous judge* will finally heed the plea of a *widow* who has no money to bribe him and no prestige or influence to sway him, how much the more will not a righteous *God* give ear to the prayers of those whom His love has made His *elect* and *vindicate them speedily?* God will keep faith, Jesus says, with those who long and pray for the day of the Son of Man; and He concludes with the searching question: Will you keep faith?

18:9-30 WILL THE SON OF MAN FIND FAITH ON EARTH?

18:9-30 Will the Son of Man, when He comes, find faith on earth (cf. 8)? He will find faith in men like the crushed and contrite *tax collector* who throws himself unconditionally upon the mercy of God (13); *he who humbles himself* in faith *will be exalted* on that day (14). He will find faith in the childlike who *receive* at God's hand the *kingdom of God* (17), dependent on Him and looking to Him. He will find it in him who has permitted God to do what is *impossible with men* (27)—turn him from serving mammon to serving God (18-27). He will find it in him who has permitted God to do what is *impossible with men* (27)—turn him from serving mammon to serving God (18-27). He will find it in those who, trusting in Jesus' promise of *eternal life,* have *left* all and *followed* Him. (28-30)

18:9-14 Peculiar to Lk. The piety of the *Pharisee* and of the *tax collector* finds expression in their prayers. The Pharisee's righteousness has made him contemptuous and loveless and self-centered; he prays *with himself* and gives thanks that he is *not like other men* (11). The praying tax collector *beats his breast* in desperation, prays the prayer of Ps 51:1, and receives the promise of Ps 51:17: "The sacrifice acceptable to God is a broken spirit; a broken and contrite heart, O God, thou wilt not despise." He goes *down to his house justified* (14). The great promise of the future *(will be exalted)* has restored and renewed him even now.

18:15-17 Cf. Mt 19:13-15 note.

18:18-30 Cf. Mt 19:16-29 note.

18:31—21:38 JESUS' LAST DAYS IN JERUSALEM

18:31-34 THIRD PREDICTION OF THE PASSION

18:31-34 Cf. Mt 20:17-19 note. In this third formal prediction of the Passion (cf. 9:22; 9:44) the accent peculiar to Lk is the fact that Jesus goes to His death in order that *everything that is written . . . by the prophets* may be *accomplished* (31) and that His disciples do not *grasp what was said* (34). Both point forward to Jesus' final instruction to His disciples after His resurrection. (Cf. 24:25-26, 44-47)

18:35-43 THE HEALING OF THE BLIND MAN AT JERICHO

18:35-43 Cf. Mt 20:29-34 note.

19:1-10 ZACCHAEUS: TODAY SALVATION HAS COME TO THIS HOUSE

19:1-10 Peculiar to Lk. In this last incident before Jesus' entry into Jerusalem all that has characterized Lk's account of Jesus' ministry appears in concentrated form. Jesus as *Son of man* is come to do God's own work: *to seek and to save the lost* (cf. Eze 34:16). He is the promised Savior in person (2:11). The lost is the outcast *tax collector,* lost in greed, victim of mammon, forgetful of God's promise and unmindful of His law. The God of *Abraham,* however, has not forgotten His promise (9; cf. 1:54-55, 73; 13:16) and brings His free and undeserved *salvation* (1:69, 71, 77) to the house of this disobedient *son of Abraham;* the joy of the new age is there *(joyfully,* 6; cf. 1:14; 2:10; 10:20; 13:17). This course Jesus *must* (5) follow in obedience to His Father's will (cf. 2:49; 4:43; 9:22; 17:25; 22:37; 24:7, 26, 44; 13:16, 33). His people objected to this free grace of His way at the beginning in Nazareth (4:22-29); and now, with Jerusalem in sight, *all murmured* (7) at His grace to the tax collector. And so this course leads to His rejection by His people, to the cross.

19:1-2 *Jericho . . . chief tax collector.* Jericho was the winter capital of Herod and then of Archelaus, his son; it had a rich export from its balsam groves and was an important customs station. Zacchaeus' post was no doubt a highly remunerative one.

19:8-9 *Salvation* came to Zacchaeus' *house* simply because he *also* was a *son of Abraham* and heir of the promise. This "kindness" of God led him "to repentance" (Ro 2:4), and this repentance manifested itself in his generosity to the poor and the *fourfold* restitution to men whom he had *defrauded,* which was more than the Law required (cf. Lv 6:5; Nm 5:5-7) except for stolen cattle and sheep. (Ex 22:1)

19:11-27 THE PARABLE OF THE POUNDS

19:11-27 Similar to Mt 25:14-30 but not identical. Most striking Lukan feature is the rebellion of the citizens against their king. (14, 27)

As Jesus draws *near to Jerusalem* (11) amid opposition (cf. 19:7) and expectation *(kingdom of God . . . appear immediately,* 11), He speaks a parable which makes plain His purpose as King of the Kingdom and what that purpose means for men. Jesus will not claim or even fight for His kingly power in Jerusalem; He will *receive* it in *a far country* from Another's hand (12; cf. 22:29). Then He will return in *kingly power* and glory to reward and judge. Meanwhile—the chief stress lies on this "meanwhile"—His opponents may still learn to lay aside their fatal enmity before the Final Judgment cuts them down (14, 27). He calls on His people to repent before it is too late (cf. 19:41-44; 23:28-31). Meanwhile those who have acknowledged His royal claim on them are to await His return as faithful workers with what has been entrusted to them, fortified by hope of a splendid reward (17, 19) and sobered by the prospect of being found unfaithful in the King's scrutiny. (20-26)

19:11 *Kingdom . . . appear.* Cf. 17:20-21.

19:12-14 Jesus takes His material from a piece of history that many of His hearers would remember. Upon the death of Herod the Great, Herod's son and principal successor, Archelaus, was confronted by a hostile people. His situation was further complicated by the intrigues of his brother and rival Herod Antipas. He therefore went to Rome to have his claim to the throne confirmed by the emperor Augustus. While he was in Rome, a deputation of Jews arrived petitioning the emperor to do away with Herodian rule altogether and allow the Jews to live according to their own laws.

19:16:18 *Your pound has made.* The good servant claims no credit for his successful trading. The king's *pound* has done the king's work. Cf. Paul's description of his apostolic "success," Ro 15:17-19.

19:17-19 *Ten . . . five cities.* The good servants' reward is wholly at the king's discretion since it is of his grace. Both participate in his reign. (Cf. 22:28-30; Mt 19:28)

19:20 *Napkin,* or "face cloth, handkerchief." The wicked servant kept the money safe but did nothing with it.

19:22 *Condemn you out of your own mouth.* "Judge you by your own standard." The servant's conception of his lord was a false one (as the lord's generous treatment of the faithful servants shows), but he is unfaithful even on the basis of that conception; even though obsessed by fear, he might have performed a safe and slight ministry. (23; cf. Mt 25:17 note)

19:24-26 The action does not seem "equitable" to men. And it is not, since the whole operation is not one of equity but of sheer "unreasonable" grace—being entrusted with the king's property and business is grace (as Paul calls his apostolate, Eph 3:8), the reward given for service, whether great or small, is grace. (Cf. Mt 25:14-30 note)

19:28-40 JESUS ENTERS JERUSALEM

19:28-40 Cf. Mt 21:1-11 note; Mk 11:3, 10 notes.

19:37-38 *Blessed is the King . . . peace . . . glory.* These words recall the message of the angel (2:11) and the song of the heavenly host (2:14) at the birth of the *King,* the Anointed (Christ). The *multitude of the disciples* have *seen* how the *mighty works* of Jesus have fulfilled the angelic promise of peace and joy on earth; His expulsion of demons, His merciful healings, His triumph over death, His forgiving proclamation of the Good News have spelled out that promise in act. They know that He is the promised King who speaks peace to the nations (Zch 9:9; cf. Is 9:6). There is *peace in heaven,* the God who gives His people and mankind such a King wills peace for man. The King may still be King incognito and may still have a journey to go into a far land (12), but God's will shall be done, and He shall have His *glory in the highest,* that is, He shall be known, acknowledged, and adored as the great and good God that He is. The praise of the disciples, like the song of Mary (1:46-55 note) anticipates that final triumph of His great goodness.

19:39-40 The *Pharisees* consider such a Messianic acclamation imprudent (if not foolish) and dangerous; the Roman authorities would not tolerate Messianic pretenders. Jesus' answer is that God's will must be done, that God will raise up witnesses to His anointed King from the *very stones* if men will not witness to Him. For the crying stone as witness cf. Hab 2:11. Jesus' answer could also be rendered to mean: "If my disciples are silenced, the very stones of Jerusalem will *cry out;* the judgment of

God on Jerusalem which will not leave one of Jerusalem's stones upon another (44; 21:6) will be a tragic witness to the fact that those who acclaimed Jesus as King were in the right and those who tried to silence their acclamation were in the wrong." This latter seems the more probable interpretation.

19:41-48 THE GUILT OF JERUSALEM

19:41-48 The King whose coming means peace (38 note) weeps over the city that has refused and is refusing *the things that make for peace,* the city that will not recognize the times of God's gracious *visitation;* the Prince of Peace is forced to predict war, siege, and destruction for the guilty city (41:44). The men of Jerusalem have made the *house of prayer,* God's temple, a *den of robbers* (45-46). In unwearied compassion Jesus continues His mission to Jerusalem, *teaching daily in the temple;* but Jerusalem's authorities respond by seeking *to destroy him.* (47-48)

19:44 *Visitation.* Cf. 1:68 note.

19:46 *Den of robbers.* Cf. Mt 21:13 note and 21:12-22 note.

20:1-8 WHO GAVE YOU THIS AUTHORITY?

20:1-8 Cf. Mt 21:23-27, esp. 21:27 note. To men who have "rejected the purpose of God for themselves" by refusing the gift of repentance and forgiveness which the *baptism of John* offered, to men who have refused to repent (7:30), Jesus "cannot" speak of His *authority.* For His authority is the authority "to forgive sins" (5:24) and "to seek and to save the lost" (19:10), an authority which men who refuse to face up to their sin and their lostness cannot comprehend. Jesus is *preaching the gospel* (1) whose power only the forgiven can know.

20:9-18 THE PARABLE OF THE VINEYARD LET TO TENANTS

20:9-18 Cf. notes on Mt 21:23—22:14; 21:33; 21:36-37; 21:42; and 21:46.

20:18 The saying concerning the destructive effect of the *stone* is based on Is 8:14-15 and Dn 2:34-35, cf. 44-45. The point in both passages is that he who resists the saving purposes of God will be destroyed.

20:19-26 TRIBUTE TO CAESAR

20:19-26 Cf. Mt 22:15-40 note and 22:16, 17, 21 notes.

20:27-40 THE SADDUCEES' QUESTION CONCERNING THE RESURRECTION

20:27-40 Cf. Mt 22:15-40 note and 22:23-33 notes.

20:35 *That age,* used in contrast to "this age" (34), is a Judaic expression used to indicate the world to come.

20:36 *They cannot die any more,* and so there is no need of procreation.

Sons of the resurrection. Their nature and life is determined by the resurrectin and the life of the world to come.

20:41-44 JESUS' MESSIANIC MANIFESTO

20:41-44 Cf. Mt 22:41-46 note.

20:45-47 BEWARE OF THE SCRIBES

20:45-47 For Jesus' indictment of the scribes cf. 11:45-52. For the particular vices of honor-seeking, avarice, and hypocrisy cf. Mt 23:5-7, 12, 25, 28; Mk 12:40; and Mt 23:1-39 note; Mk 12:38-44 note.

21:1-4 THE POOR WIDOW'S GIFT

21:1-4 Cf. Mk 12:38-44 note.

21:5-38 Jesus' Prophecy of the Future

21:5-38 For the whole topic cf. Mt 24:1—25:46 notes; Mk 13:1-37 note; Lk 17:22-37 note and 17:20—18:30 note.

Jesus' words concerning the future and the end are prophecy; "he who prophesies speaks to men for their upbuilding and encouragement and consolation" (1 Co 14:3). Jesus does predict, as the OT prophets did before Him, the nearer and the farther and the farthest future: the destruction of the temple (6), the coming of false prophets and false Christs (8), wars and disasters in the world (10-11), persecution and martyrdom for the church (12-17), the fall of Jerusalem (20-24), the fainting anxiety of the world in the last days and the coming of the Son of Man (25-28). But His predictions are the framework and scaffolding of the structure of His commands, warnings, and promises, which serve to upbuild, encourage, and console His disciples and His church in the last days, that they *may have strength to escape all these things that will take place, and to stand before the Son of man,* sure of their justification and final victory. (36)

21:5-19 BY YOUR ENDURANCE YOU WILL GAIN YOUR LIVES

21:5-19 Jesus predicts the destruction of the temple but refuses to answer the curious question of *when* or to give *the sign* (7) which would enable men to calculate the coming of the disaster. Rather, He uses the occasion to warn His disciples against false and feverish hopes (8) and to safeguard them against panic terror; all disasters are part of God's plan *(must first take place),* and He alone will determine and declare the time of the *end* (9). Even the sufferings of the church are no accident; God will use them for the spreading of His Word *(testimony,* 13), and the Christ will give His own the *mouth and wisdom* which will make their testimony powerful and fruitful (13, 15). They are in God's hand, and no power of their enemies and no treachery of their friends can harm them (12, 15, 16); *not a hair of your head will perish* (18). They can be so confident of God's future that they will have the power to endure the present, even if the present means death, and so *gain* their *lives* forever. (19)

21:5 *Offerings,* votive gifts presented to the temple by princes and private individuals for its adornment.

21:9 *The end will not be at once.* Cf. 2 Th 2:1-2, where Paul calms a feverish excitement of hope to restore the church to confidence and obedience. (13-15; cf. 3:3-13)

21:20-24 THE DESOLATION OF JERUSALEM

21:20-24 Jesus predicts the fall of Jerusalem at the hand of *Gentile armies* (20, 24). His prophetic care for His disciples opens their eyes to see in this event the fulfillment of *all that is written* (22), so that in this respect, too, they can have the OT "prophetic word made more sure" (2 Ptr 1:19). The men who constitute the new Israel need not share in the fate of old Israel; Jesus bids them flee the doomed city and land (21) when the long-foretold *days of vengeance* and the time of God's *wrath* upon His disobedient *people* come (22, 23). The phrase *the times of the Gentiles* (24) points them to their future mission to the Gentiles, portrayed by Lk in Acts (Cf. Acts 28:25-28; Ro 11:11-12; 11:25)

21:20 *Surrounded by armies.* Cf. 19:43.

Desolation. An echo of Dn 9:27; 11:31; 12:11; cf. Mt 24:15 note.

21:22 *Days of vengeance . . . written.* Cf. Dt 32:28-35; Jer 5:29; Hos 9:7.

21:23 *Those . . . with child.* The blessing of motherhood will only intensify their *distress.*

21:24 *Trodden down by the Gentiles.* Cf. Is 63:18-19.

21:25-28 THE COMING OF THE SON OF MAN

21:25-28 Amid the agony of a collapsing world, amid the intolerable *fear* and *foreboding* of men for whom the coming of the *Son of man . . . with power and great glory* signifies destruction, the disciples can *look up and raise* their *heads* in joyous expectation; they know this Son of Man as their Savior who brings their ultimate *redemption.* (Cf. Dn 7:13-14, 17-18)

21:25 *Roaring of the sea.* At creation God set bounds to the sea: "Thus far shall you come, and no farther, and here shall your proud waves be stayed" (Jb 38:11; cf. Ps 65:8). Now God's ancient order disintegrates to make way for His new creation; and the failing of the ancient order is terrifying to men without hope.

21:29-38 ASSURANCE AND ADMONITION

21:29-36 For 29-33 cf. Mt 24:32-35. The *parable* of the *fig tree* and Jesus' assurance concerning His enduring *words* give the disciples' hope a firm basis. They need not fear for God and the coming of His kingdom; they need to live in holy fear lest this world's pleasures and cares *weigh* them *down* and leave them unprepared for the coming of *that day.* Vigilant, unceasing prayer is called for.

21:36 *Stand before,* as your Judge who shall pronounce your acquittal. Cf. Mt 25:34; for the expression cf. Rv 6:17.

21:37-38 A summary of Jesus' activity during His last days in Jerusalem.

22:1–24:53 JESUS' PASSION, DEATH, RESURRECTION, AND ASCENSION

22:1-6 THE PLOT TO DESTROY JESUS

22:1-6 Cf. Mt 26:1-16 note.

22:1 *Unleavened Bread . . . called the Passover.* Strictly speaking these are two separate festivals, the day of Passover and the 7-day feast of Unleavened Bread which directly followed the Passover (Lv 23:4-6). But since the Passover could be celebrated only in Jerusalem (Dt 16:2, 5-6), the two festivals tended to merge for people outside Jerusalem and Palestine, especially for Gentiles like Luke's readers.

22:3 *Satan entered into Judas.* When Satan left Jesus after the temptation, he did so "until an opportune time" (4:13); the opportune time for his final assault on Jesus has now come, and Judas becomes the instrument of the "power of darkness" (22:53). Cf. also 22:31; Jn 6:70-71; 13:2, 27.

22:4 *Officers,* the men in charge of the temple police; the head captain ranked next to the high priest in authority. Cf. 52; Acts 4:1; 5:24, 26.

22:5 *Give him money.* Cf. Mt 26:15 note.

22:7-23 THE LAST SUPPER

22:7-23 Cf. Mt 26:17-29 note.

22:7 *Day of Unleavened Bread.* Cf. 22:1 note.

22:12 *Furnished* with couches on which the participants reclined while eating. The word translated "sat at table" in 14 means literally "reclined."

22:14 *The hour* probably signifies both the hour of the Passover and the climactic hour of Jesus' ministry. (Cf. 22:53; Jn 7:30; 8:20; 12:23, 17; 13:1; 17:1)

22:15-16 *Passover . . . fulfilled in the kingdom of God.* Cf. Mt 26:26 note. All that the Passover signified and the feast of the Passover memorialized will be fully revealed and accomplished in the future, consummated kingdom of God to which Jesus looks forward: God's elective love for His people, His mighty deliverance, His covenant-will of fellowship with man. Jesus is interpreting His death as a divine act of deliverance in these words and preparing His disciples for the Lord's Supper.

22:17 *Cup . . . divide it among yourselves.* The significance of this first cup (cf. 19-20 note), recorded only by Lk, is left somewhat mysterious. The Passover ritual of Jesus' day prescribed individual cups for the participants; Jesus offers His disciples a common cup, to be shared by them all. The context speaks of Jesus' impending Passion ("suffer," 15) and the future "kingdom of God" (16, 18). The first cup, then, signifies that a man receives, as a gift, his share in the coming kingdom; and that He receives it as a gift from Him who is destined (22) to suffer (15), to give His body (19) and His blood (20) in order that God's final covenant (20) may be established.

22:20 *New covenant in my blood.* Cf. Mt 26:26 note. The word *new* recalls especially Jer 31:31-

34 with its emphasis on the forgiveness of sins.
22:22 Cf. Mt 26:24 note.

22:24-38 Jesus Teaching at Table

22:24-38 Lk frequently portrays Jesus teaching at table (cf. 7:36 ff.; 10:38 ff.; 11:37 ff.; 14:1 ff.), and he here records material largely peculiar to him. Each of the three units of Jesus' discourse (24-30; 31-34; 35-38) is related to Jesus' impending Passion.

22:24-30 THE WAY TO GREATNESS

22:24-30 The old *dispute* (cf. 9:46-48) as to who *was* to *be regarded as greatest* breaks out once more. Jesus makes plain once more that greatness is not won by the upward reach for *lordship* and *authority* but on the downward way of self-denying service, following in the footsteps of the King who is among them *as one who serves* (24-27). (Cf. Mt 20:17-28 note.) In the last analysis greatness is not "won" by man at all; it comes to the followers of Jesus as His free gift to them and is a greatness beyond all deserving; table fellowship and coregency with Him in His *kingdom* (28-30). (Cf. Mt 20:20-28)

22:27 *As one who serves.* At the Passover feast the reclining guests were waited on by a servant; on this one night even the poorest Israelite was great and free. Some interpreters think that Jesus actually waited on His disciples at this feast, thus providing a first fulfillment of His promise in 12:37. However that may be, Jesus is referring to His whole life's work as a Servant ministry, to be crowned by His dying as "a ransom for many." (Cf. 37 note; Mt 20:28)

22:28 *My trials.* Here used generally of all the hardships of His way. (Cf. Acts 20:19)

22:29-30 *I assign.* The verb translated *assign* belongs to the same word family as "covenant" (20) and underscores the fact that participation in the festal joy and royal power *(thrones)* of the *kingdom* is Jesus' free gift.

22:31-34 SIMON, I HAVE PRAYED FOR YOU

22:31-34 Satan's last attack on Jesus (cf. 3 note) will be an attack on His disciples too. He will *demand to have* them, as he once "demanded" Job (Jb 1:6-12), and will *sift* them, shake and disturb them, in order to get some of the *wheat* of God's harvest for himself, as he has already gotten Judas (3). *Simon's* confidence in himself (33) is an indication that he is especially vulnerable to Satan's attack; self-confidence and the confidence of faith are two different things. Jesus, Servant to the last, intercedes for him (ther Servant intercedes for transgressors, 23:34 note; cf. Is 53:12). Thus Simon's failure in his denial will not prove to be his final downfall; in repentance *(turned again,* 32) he will replace self-confidence with confidence in his Lord and so find the strength to *strengthen* his *brethren.* (32)

22:32 *Strengthen your brethren.* Cf. the Introduction to 1 Ptr.

22:35-38 BUY A SWORD

22:35-38 Jesus goes to a criminal's death, *reckoned with transgressors* (37; Is 53:12). The disciples will *now* (36) be witnesses to the Crucified, the one declared accursed by Israel's leadership according to their law (cf. Gl 3:13; 1 Co 12:3; Dt 21:23). The old carefree days of the first mission of the Twelve and the Seventy are over (35; 9:3; 10:4). Their mission will become an embattled progress through hostile territory—the martyrdom of Stephen and the execution of James are landmarks on that road (Acts 7; 12:1-2). Jesus' command to provide equipment for the journey and to *buy* a *sword* (even if it means selling one's *mantle* to get it, 36) is probably a figurative way of bidding the disciples brace themselves for this new situation. Jesus' way is not the way of power and warfare (cf. 25-26); and He could hardly have called two swords *enough* (38) if He had planned a Messianic war.

22:37 *Reckoned with transgressors.* Is 53:12. For Jesus as the Servant cf. Mt 12:18-21 note.

22:39-46 JESUS' AGONY OF PRAYER

22:39-46 Cf. Mt 26:30-56 note. The scene in Gethsemane (Lk uses only the more general designation *Mount of Olives)* reveals as hardly another the genuine humanity of the Son of God; and Lk lays special stress on this humanity with his reference to the physical *agony* of Jesus at prayer (44). The appearance of the *angel from heaven, strengthening him* (43) is another "human" touch; it recalls the story of the prophet Elijah at a point when that man of God was wearied and discouraged. (1 K 19:4-8)

22:39 *As was his custom.* Cf. 21:37. Jesus is taking the initiative, confronting his captors in a place where they knew He could be found.

22:40 *Temptation.* Cf. 31-34.

22:47-53 THE ARREST: THIS IS YOUR HOUR

22:47-53 Cf. Mt 26:30-56 note. If Gethsemane lays bare the humanity of Jesus, the arrest reveals the free majesty with which *the Son of man* (48) goes to His death. Touches peculiar to Lk emphasize this majestic freedom. Jesus' reproach to Judas exposes his treachery in all its ugliness (48). In healing the slave of the high priest He continues His ministry as physician (cf. 5:31) and at the same time protects His disciples against reprisals (51). And He makes clear to His captors at what a fearful cost they have made this hour their hour; they have sold themselves to *the power of darkness.* (53; cf. 3 note)

22:54-65 PETER DENIES JESUS

22:54-65 Cf. Mt 26:57-75 note. Lk hardly notices the nocturnal hearing conducted in *the high priest's house* (54; cf. Mt 26:57-68); the mockery recorded in 63-65 presupposes such a hearing and an adverse verdict. Lk concentrates on Peter's denial; Lk alone records that *the Lord turned and looked at Peter* (61). We are not told what all was in that look—reproach, sorrow, appeal—but Peter must have read in that look the unfailing love of the Lord who had interceded for him; his faith did not fail utterly. (32)

22:59 *A Galilean,* recognizable by his dialect. (Mt 26:73)

22:63-65 Cf. Mt 26:67-68 note.

22:66-71 JESUS BEFORE THE COUNCIL

22:66-71 Lk's account of Jesus' hearing before the council is highly condensed, concentrating on the crucial point of Jesus' claim to be the Christ and *Son of God* (67, 70). (Cf. Mt 26:67-68 note)

22:66 *When day came.* For the legal technicality involved cf. Mt 27:1-2 note.

22:67-68 *You will not believe . . . you will not answer.* It was not Jesus' silence but their unbelief and stubbornness which had veiled His Messiahship from their eyes. Cf. 20:1-8 note, where they refused Him an answer; and 20:41-44 note, where they received His Messianic self-attestation (given in terms of Ps 110 and Dn 7, as now, 69) with unbelieving silence.

23:1-56 Jesus Condemned and Crucified

23:1-5 JESUS BROUGHT BEFORE PILATE

23:1-5 Cf. Mt 27:1-31 note for the whole trial before Pilate.

Before the council the charge is religious (22:66-71). Before the Roman governor it is political. The attempt to make Jesus appear politically dangerous employs half-truths; Jesus did indeed claim to be *Christ a king,* but not king in the sense that Pilate was inclined to understand it—He looked to God alone for victory (20:41-45) and quelled His followers' attempt at violence (22:49-51). The accusers do not even shrink from the direct lie *(forbidding . . . tribute to Caesar,* 2; cf. 20:25). Pilate's examination of Jesus (presupposed by Lk here but not recounted, cf. 14) leads him to make the first of three declarations of Jesus' innocence. (4; cf. 14, 22)

23:5 *All Judea,* i.e., all Palestine.

23:6-12 JESUS SENT OVER TO HEROD

23:6-12 Only in Lk. Cf. Acts 4:27

The presence of *Herod in Jerusalem* at Passover time afforded Pilate a chance to evade his responsibility of pronouncing judgment on Jesus. Herod thus becomes the second witness to Jesus' innocence (cf. 15; Dt 19:15). Herod, no longer fearful of Jesus (13:31-33) but still curious (9:7-9), *was hoping to see some sign done by* Jesus. Jesus refused to answer the questions of the man whom He had once dismissed as "that fox" with no power to control His ministry (13:32 note), and He refused, as always, to use His miraculous power to defend or advance Himself *(sign;* cf. 4:4, 11:16, 29). Herod dismissed Him with *contempt;* the *gorgeous apparel* is intended to mock the impotent and captive Messianic pretender.

23:12 *Became friends.* Pilate had acknowledged Herod's jurisdiction over Jesus (7), and Herod had remanded the case to Pilate (11) for final adjudication. This exchange of courtesies ended the *enmity* between the men who had long been jealous rivals for power. One may see beneath the political surface an indication of the "world's" unanimity of opposition to Jesus. (Cf. Jn 7:7; 15:18)

23:13-25 PILATE DELIVERS JESUS UP TO HIS ACCUSERS

23:13-25 Cf. Mt 27:1-31 note. Pilate makes two more attempts to secure Jesus' *release:* the offer of a compromise punishment of flogging *(chastise,* 16) and of the choice between *Barabbas* and Jesus (18-19). But His accusers' *voices prevailed.*

23:18 *Barabbas'* story is briefly told by Lk, as if he could presuppose knowledge of it on the part of his readers. (Cf. Mt 27:15-26; 27:17 note)

23:25 *Jesus he delivered up to their will.* Historians have puzzled over Pilate's evasive and compliant attitude during the trial of Jesus; he had previously demonstrated a brutal disregard for the feeling of his subjects (cf. 13:1). There is some evidence that Pilate's dealings with the high priest Caiaphas had been such that he was not free to resist pressure from that quarter. Others point out that the political situation in Rome had changed drastically just before this time and that Pilate's position had become so insecure that he could ill afford to besmirch an already soiled record with another arbitrary execution. The evidence is only indirect; but Pilate was removed from office in A. D. 37, and Caiaphas was deposed as high priest in the same year, and this lends some plausibility to these conjectures.

23:26-31 THE ROAD TO GOLGOTHA

23:26-31 The incident of the crossbearer *Simon of Cyrene,* which marks the utter forsakenness of Jesus, is common to Mt, Mk, and Lk. Cf. Mt 27:32 note. The story of the wailing *daughters of Jerusalem* is peculiar to Lk. Such wailing was customary; Jesus' words to the women were unique. Jesus had often foretold the fall of Jerusalem, its temple, and its people (11:50-51; 13:34-35; 19:11-27; 20:9-19; 21:20-24). He wept when He entered the city for the last time (19:41-44), and His last words as He left were a last call to repentance in the form of a prediction of Jerusalem's doom.

23:31 Men will prefer annihilation to the fearful judgment of God which confronts them. (Cf. Hos 10:8; Rv 6:16)

They do this. "They" is a Judaic way of referring to God. The RSV translators elsewhere render it by means of the passive voice (cf. 6:38, where "will be put" renders a verb that says literally, "they will put").

Green wood . . . dry. If God's judgment, thought of as a consuming fire (3:9, 16, 17; 17:29), does not spare even God's Son, the green wood not ready for the fire (not ripe for judgment), but delivers Him up thus (cf. Ro 8:32), what will become of those who have refused God's mercy and have in their impenitence become dry wood ripe for judgment?

23:32-38 THE CRUCIFIXION

23:32-38 Cf. Mt 27:32-66 note. Jesus is "reckoned with transgressors" (22:37; Is 53:12). The Servant at the apex of His servanthood, when He "pours out his soul to death" (Is 53:12) as Savior of mankind, is *mocked* for His impotence to save by the *rulers* of His people and by the Roman *soldiers;* there is mockery even in the *inscription* which was hung over Him (cf. Jn 19:19-22). But just here, in the depths, the power of the Servant to save is revealed; His unconquerable love intercedes for transgressors (34; peculiar to Lk) as He "bears the sins of many." (Is. 53:12)

23:33 *Skull,* translation of the Aramaic "Golgotha." Why so called remains obscure.

23:34 *Forgive them.* Cf. Stephen's prayer, Acts 7:60.

They know not what they do. Cf. Acts 3:17; 13:27; 1 Ti 1:13 note.

23:35 *Chosen One,* a designation of the servant. (Is 42:1; cf. 9:35 note)

23:39-43 THE PENITENT CRIMINAL

23:39-43 Jesus' second word from the cross (43) is the word of Him "who justifies the ungodly" (Ro 4:5), for it assigns to the *criminal* (who ceases to justify himself and throws himself unreservedly on His royal mercy, 42) a place in *Paradise,* the abode of the righteous dead. Whosoever is in communion with Jesus *(with me)* has entered the great *today* of "great joy" (2:10-11), of "the acceptable year of the Lord" (4:19-21), of forgiveness and healing (5:36, cf. 17-25), of "salvation" in fulfillment of the promise made to Abraham (19:5, 9). This word is a promise to Israel; the way of faith to Jesus and to justification is still open "to the Jew first" (Ro 1:16; Acts 1—12). The diverse reaction of the two criminals is a prophecy of the course of the Gospel through Israel (and mankind) as a savor of life and a savor of death.

23:40 *Fear God,* basic to repentance, faith, and salvation. (Rv 14:7)

23:42 *Remember me.* To be remembered by the divine mercy is to be helped. (Cf. Ps 106:4, 6; Lk 1:54, 72)

23:44-56 THE DEATH AND BURIAL OF JESUS

23:44-56 The characteristic feature of Lk's account of Jesus' death is the third word which Jesus speaks from the cross in the third gospel (46). As at the beginning of His ministry, at the temptation and in the synagog at Nazareth (4:1-19), so at the close the Scriptures are Jesus' life element. He dies with a prayer from the Psalter on His lips (Ps 31:5). The whole of His unwavering trust in His Father, which made Him the Man of prayer and the Teacher of prayer, lives in this last word. The whole of the psalm should be considered in this connection (perhaps Jesus prayed it through).

23:45 *Sun's light failed.* Cf. Mt 27:45 note.

Curtain of the temple. Cf. Mt 27:51-53 note.

23:47 *Centurion . . . praised God.* Jesus' whole mission was "to the glory of God the Father" (Ph 2:11). Cf 5:8; 7:16; 9:43; 13:13; 17:15; 18:43; 19:8, 37, where Jesus' might and mercy leads men to praise, or glorify, God.

23:48 *Beating their breasts,* as a sign of grief. (Cf. 18:13)

23:49 *Stood at a distance.* Cf. Ps 38:11; 88:8, 18. The echo of the Psalms intensifies the note of Jesus' desolation. His disciples have severed the bond of discipleship; Lk does not call them "disciples" from 22:45 on. Only Jesus' forgiving grace can restore what they have destroyed.

23:53-56 The burial was hasty and provisional only (cf. 56); the Law demanded that an executed criminal be buried "the same day" (Dt 21:22-23), and the *sabbath* began at sunset.

24:1-53 The Resurrection and Ascension

24:1-53 Lk's resurrection story is the indispensable transition to his story of the apostolic mission and church in the Book of Acts. Of Jesus' many post-resurrection appearances (1 Co 15:5-8), he records only appearances that took place in or near Jerusalem; for it is in Jerusalem that the apostolic story begins (48, 49; Acts 1:4). And the story of the risen Christ is the story of the creation of *witnesses* to Him (48; Acts 1:8). Men do not become witnesses on their own initiative but by a divine act; and the whole account is marked by this divine initiative. God leads men from sorrow and unbelief to faith and joy; His messengers, His Son, His Word, and the promise of His Spirit control the course of events.

God creates witnesses; and He makes them witness to facts: the *stone rolled away* (2); the empty tomb (3); a Man who walks on a Palestinian road toward a *village* with a name, interprets the familiar Bible of the Jews, and *breaks bread* (13-30); a Man (no disembodied *spirit)* with *hands* and *feet,* a body of *flesh and bones* to be *seen* and *handled;* a Man who eats *broiled fish;* a Man who has been *crucified,* who spoke *words* to be remembered (14-44)—of such hard stuff the witness of the apostolic Gospel is to be made. It is to be not myth but news.

But faith is not a conclusion drawn by man from bare facts; *repentance and forgiveness of sins* (47) is given to men by the divine revelation which illumines and interprets the facts. *Perplexed* (4), *frightened* (5), *sad* (17), *startled, frightened,* and superstitious (37) people become witnesses in the full Biblical sense by the operation of the word of angels (5) and the *remembered words* of Jesus (8), when Jesus *interprets* and *opens* up the OT Word of God for them (27) and God *opens their eyes* (31), when *the Lord appears* (34) and *opens their minds* through the *scriptures* to the saving significance of His suffering and death (46-47). Then they become witnesses wholly claimed by the Lord to whom they witness, empowered by the Spirit whom He sends (49), with a message designed by God to claim men wholly *(repentance,* 47). The witnessing apostles are the first examples of men who are a new creation in Christ (2 Co 5:17). Through them Jesus can continue all that He "began to do and teach"

(Acts 1:1). While He *blessed them, he parted from them.* (51)

24:1-11(12) THE EMPTY TOMB

24:4 *Two men . . . in dazzling apparel.* Angels. (Cf. Acts 1:10)

24:6 *Remember how he told you.* Cf. 9:22, 44.

24:12 RSV prints this verse in a footnote in agreement with the opinion of most scholars that it was added to the text by copyists on the basis of Jn 20:3-10 and in view of Lk 24:24.

24:13-35 EMMAUS: KNOWN IN THE BREAKING OF THE BREAD

24:13 *Emmaus* ("warm springs"). Location is uncertain.

24:16 *Their eyes were kept.* Cf. 31, "Their eyes were opened." Revelation is given when and where God pleases.

24:18 *Cleopas* is identified by some with the Clopas of Jn 19:25, to whom early tradition assigns considerable importance in the history of the Jerusalem church. He may be one of the "eyewitnesses" referred to in Lk 1:2.

Visitor to Jerusalem, for the celebration of the Passover, which drew visitors from all Palestine and the Dispersion.

24:25 *Slow of heart. Heart* in Biblical usage includes the whole inner man, feeling and willing and understanding.

24:30 *Took the bread . . . broke it.* The Guest takes the position of the father of the house and distributes the bread. The disciples recognize Him in His characteristic role of Giver and Provider (9:16; 22:19); as such He will be with His disciples, present in His Supper, "known . . . in the breaking of the bread." (35)

24:32 *Hearts burn within us.* The phrase describes the warm glow of dawning recognition and nascent faith.

24:34 *The Lord. Lord,* not used in Lk since 22:61, expresses the joyous rigor of their reborn faith. (Cf. Ro 10:9-10)

Appeared to Simon. Cf. 1 Co 15:5 ("Cephas" is the Aramaic form of "Peter").

24:36-49 THE RISEN CHRIST AND HIS WITNESSES

24:44 *While I was still with you.* The resurrection does not reduce Jesus' previous ministry to insignificance but rather lets it be seen in its true significance.

Moses . . . prophets . . . psalms, the three divisions of the OT canon.

24:45 *Opened their minds.* For the contrast (the OT read without insight into its character as witness to Christ) cf. 2 Co 3:14-16.

24:47 *Beginning from Jerusalem.* Jesus' intercession for those who crucified Him has been heard. (23:34)

24:49 *The promise of my Father,* the Holy Spirit. (Cf. Acts 2:16-21, 32-33)

24:50-53 WHILE HE BLESSED THEM, HE PARTED FROM THEM

24:50-53 The story of God's dealings with man is the story of His blessing from creation (Gn 1:22) to the consummation (Mt 25:34). The story of the incarnate Son fitly ends with His parting (and enduring, Acts 3:26) blessing. In the strong assurance of that blessing His disciples *returned to Jerusalem* and the beginning of the worldwide task that awaits them there *with great joy, blessing God* for the blessing which He has bestowed on them: "Blessed be the God and Father of our Lord Jesus Christ, who has blessed us in Christ." (Eph 1:3)

24:50 *Bethany,* village on the Mount of Olives about 2 miles from Jerusalem.

24:53 *In the temple.* The first part of Lk's two-volume story ends where it began (1:9), in the house of God, where He gives His blessing and His people respond with blessing.

JOHN

INTRODUCTION

Occasion and Purpose of the Gospel

1 The central and controlling purpose of the gospel is stated by John himself: "Now Jesus did many other signs in the presence of the disciples, which are not written in this book; but these are written that you may believe that Jesus is the Christ, the Son of God, and that believing you may have life in his name" (Jn 20:30-31). The book is not a missionary appeal; it addresses Christians and seeks to deepen and strengthen their faith in Jesus as the Christ. It does so by recounting and interpreting the words and deeds of Jesus, His "signs," or significant actions. It is therefore, like the first three gospels, "teaching" in the sense of Acts 2:42. Like the other gospels, it no doubt had behind it a long history of oral teaching; it is, as ancient tradition also indicates, the result of John's many years of oral apostolic witness to Christ in the churches of Asia Minor. Some scholars see indications that the book had its origin in the worship life of the church of Asia Minor in such features of the gospel as its simple but exalted style, its dramatic structure, its highly selective way of dealing with the career of Jesus, and its rich use of the solemn "I am" sayings of Jesus. They may well be right.

2 John's teaching did not take place in a vacuum. The church that he taught was in the world, a church in conflict and under temptation. And we can tell from the gospel's particular emphases what some of the conflicts and temptations were. The Gospel of the Crucified was a stumbling block to the Jew and folly to the Greek in John's day as it had been in Paul's (1 Co 1:23). The fierce hatred of the Jews of Asia had pursued Paul (Acts 20:19; 21:27); we find the same embittered Jewish offense at the cross active in Smyrna against Christians a generation after John at the time of the martyrdom of Polycarp. And in the letters to the churches at Smyrna and Philadelphia in Revelation (most probably written within a few years of the time of the Gospel of John) we find references to Jews opposed to the church, "those who say that they are Jews and are not, but are a synagogue of Satan" (Rv 2:9; 3:9; cf. John 8:44). Conflict with the Jews had not ended with the death of Jesus nor with the death of Paul. Rather, according to the witness of the fourth gospel, it persisted in intensified form; the Gospel of John presents the conflict between Jesus and the Jews in even stronger colors than does the Gospel of Matthew. He speaks of the Jews for the most part simply as "Jews." He knows the distinctive coloring of the various Jewish parties, but the distinction between Pharisees and Sadducees is no longer of importance to him or his readers. John speaks of his people simply as of the people who rejected Jesus as their Messiah, and "Jew" is practically equivalent to "unbelieving Jew" (Jn 2:18, 20; 5:10, 16, 18; 6:41, 52; 7:13; 9:22, etc.). The "Jews" are the opponents of Jesus, blind and stubborn in their refusal to recognize Him, persecuting Him with an ever-mounting hatred. They deny that He is the Son of God (Jn 5:18; 8:40-59); they seek His life (Jn 5:18; 8:40, 59; 10:31, 39; 11:8, 50), and in all things they show themselves not as true children of Abraham but as children of the devil (Jn 8:39-44). Jesus predicts that this hatred will persist; they will deem it a service to God if they kill Jesus' disciples (Jn 16:2). The Spirit whom Jesus will send will enable His disciples to continue the struggle He had in His lifetime carried on against His opponents. (Jn 16:2-4, 7-11)

3 This feature of John's Gospel may be due in part to the fact that he devotes so much space to Jesus' ministry in Jerusalem, where opposition to Jesus was

concentrated most strongly. But only in part; it is due chiefly to the fact that the lines have been drawn by Israel's national rejection of her Messiah, that judgment has been executed on Jerusalem and a gulf has been fixed between the ancient people of God and the new Israel, the church. But this does not mean that the fourth gospel has an anti-Semitic bias. John is at one with the other evangelists and with Paul (Ro 9:1-5) in his positive appreciation of what the Jew had by the grace of God received and in his hope that the Jew may still receive of that grace. John's harsh indictment of the Jew is therefore to be construed as a call to repentance addressed to the Jew. It is in the fourth gospel that Jesus declares to the Samaritan woman that "salvation is from the Jews" (Jn 4:22); the Scripture given to the Jews is for the Jesus of John the supreme authority as it is for the Jesus of Matthew (e.g., Jn 10:35). The flock for which the Good Shepherd dies is a flock gathered out of Israel (Jn 10:16); the hour of the Gentiles, the hour for the Greeks who would see Jesus, is yet to come (Jn 10:16; 12:20, 32). Israel's own high priest must declare that Jesus is the One who dies for the whole people (Jn 11:50-51). The title of the Crucified is "King of the Jews" (Jn 19:19). Jesus is "King of Israel" (Jn 1:49), and the gospel still pleads with the Jew to become an "Israelite indeed," an Israelite "in whom is no guile," by acknowledging Israel's King as Nathanael acknowledged Him (Jn 1:47). This motif is so strong that one modern scholar has advanced and defended the theory that the fourth gospel is primarily a missionary appeal addressed to the Jew—an overstatement, of course, but an indication of the tendency of the gospel.

4 Another less direct form of Judaic opposition to Jesus and His church is also combated by the fourth gospel. Some in Israel became disciples of John the Baptist but did not accept his witness to Jesus as the Christ. They continued to exist as a separate group or sect, and apparently their reverent esteem for the Baptist was such that they assigned to him the titles and functions of the Messiah. The incident recorded in Acts 19:1-7 (Paul's encounter with "disciples" who knew only the baptism of John) would seem to indicate that this movement had spread as far as Ephesus, where the fourth gospel was written. This would account for the fact that the fourth gospel emphasizes that the Baptist has his significance and honor in his subordination to Jesus as the Christ: "He was not the light, but came to bear witness to the light" (Jn 1:8); in John's account of him the Baptist will accept no title of honor, but calls himself merely the voice in the wilderness—his whole significance lies in his function as the herald of the Christ (Jn 1:19-23). He must decrease, as the Messiah must increase; and he finds his perfect joy in the Christ's increasing (Jn 3:28-30). He points his disciples to the Lamb of God, who takes away the sin of the world (Jn 1:29-36). But the evangelist is not minded to belittle the true stature of the Baptist; he sees in him "a man sent from God" (Jn 1:6), a valid and mighty witness to the only Son from the Father (Jn 1:14-15). John alone records the witness of the people to John ("Everything that John said about this man was true," Jn 10:41), and he alone records the words with which Jesus Himself places His seal on the Baptist's mission: "You sent to John, and he has borne witness to the truth. . . . He was a burning and shining lamp." (Jn 5:33, 35)

5 The Gospel was a stumbling block to the Jew and foolishness to the Greek. And the Gospel of John is directed also against a Greek perversion of the Gospel, which was in effect a denial of the Gospel. According to the second-century father Irenaeus, the Gospel of John was written to combat the heresy of Cerinthus. This is hardly the whole purpose of the gospel, but John's emphatic declaration that the eternal Son, the Word, "became flesh" (Jn 1:14) does seem to be aimed at one of the tenets of the sect of Cerinthus. For Cerinthus denied that the "heavenly Christ" had been identified with man, the creature of flesh, in any real and lasting way; he maintained that not the Christ but only the man Jesus (in whom the Christ had dwelt guest-fashion from the time of His baptism onward up to the eve of His Passion) had suffered and died. This could also be the historical background to the fact that in the fourth gospel and in it

alone Jesus is hailed at the very beginning of His ministry as the dying Christ, as "the Lamb of God" (Jn 1:29), and is at the end of His ministry worshiped by Thomas as the Crucified. Thomas says, "My Lord and my God," to the Christ who bears on His body the marks of the crucifixion (Jn 20:27-28). Perhaps John's insistence in the opening verses of his gospel that "all things were made through him [the Word], and without him was not anything made that was made" (Jn 1:3) is also pointed at Cerinthus, who maintained that the world was created not by the highest God who sent the heavenly Christ into the world, but by a power which had separated itself from God. The fact that the First Letter of John is patently directed against a heresy like that of Cerinthus lends great plausibility to the suggestion that the gospel, too, has a polemical point aimed at Cerinthus.

Content of the Gospel

6 John begins his gospel with a compressed, thematic statement that contains in essence the message of the whole book (Jn 1:1-18). Everything that follows is really only a fuller and more profound development of this statement, an unfolding of all that is implicit in it. The recital of the words and deeds of Jesus that follows does not pretend to be a complete record of Jesus' activity (Jn 20:30); the words and deeds are freely selected from a much larger mass of material (some of it, no doubt, familiar to John's readers from the other gospels) freely arranged and told in stylized form, with one aim only: to proclaim what Jesus is and signifies; to present Jesus to men as John and his fellow witneses had been led by the Spirit to behold Him, as the very Word of God, the only Son in whom God has uttered His whole will for man, the grace and truth of God in person and enacted in the history of a human life witnessed by men.

7 The movement of the gospel is therefore not so much movement in a straight line as in spiral form, a spiral that rises higher and higher and grows wider and wider but remains always over the same area, the area marked out by the first 18 verses of the gospel. For example, the theme of the cross is already stated in the first unit, 1:10-11: "The world knew him not . . . his own people received him not." It recurs in the witness of the Baptist in 1:29: "Behold, the Lamb of God, who takes away the sin of the world!" This spiral comes around to it again in 3:14: "As Moses lifted up the serpent in the wilderness, so must the Son of man be lifted up," and again and again—in 6:51: "The bread which I shall give for the life of the world is my flesh"; in 8:28: "When you have lifted up the Son of man, then you will know that I am he"; in 10:11: "I am the good shepherd. The good shepherd lays down his life for the sheep"; in 12:24: "Truly, truly, I say to you, unless a grain of wheat falls into the earth and dies, it remains alone; but if it dies, it bears much fruit"; and in 12:31-32: "Now is the judgment of this world, now shall the ruler of this world be cast out; and I, when I am lifted up from the earth, will draw all men to myself," to mention only a few passages. The spiral movement touches the cross again in ch. 13, for the cross is the luminous background of Jesus' action when He washes His disciples feet (13:1-20). The spiral movement of the cross runs through the last discourses of Jesus (e.g., 15:13, 18-21; 16:20). This movement does not cease at the actual crucifixion; it goes on over the narrative of Jesus' appearance to Thomas—Thomas beholds the Crucified (Jn 20:25-29)—and continues over the narrative of Jesus' last conversation with Peter, for Jesus' words, "Feed my sheep" (21:15-19), unmistakably recall the Good Shepherd who lays down His life for the sheep.

OUTLINE

I. 1:1-18 Theme: The Eternal Word of God in the Flesh

II. 1:19—5:54 The Word Is Spoken to All Israel

1:1-18 THEME: THE ETERNAL WORD OF GOD IN THE FLESH

1:1-5 THE ETERNAL WORD

1:1-5 He whom John and his fellow disciples had known as Jesus, the Man in history (cf. 17), was not of this world (8:23). *In the beginning,* before the world began, He *was with God* as God's *Word,* personally united with God as God's speaking, willing, and working, so closely united with God that He must be confessed as *God* (cf. 20:28). He is not creature but Creator of all things; in Him God called into being matter and flesh and called them "very good" (Gn 1:31). The *life* which only God has and can impart (5:26) was in Him and was designed to bless mankind *(light of men,* 4). The powers of evil *(darkness,* 5), mysteriously present and maliciously at work in God's good world, have opposed that life but have not *overcome* Him; He remains God's No to all evil.

1:6-13 THE WORD SPOKEN TO MEN: THE LIGHT OF THE WORLD

1:6-13 As in Mt, Mk, and Lk, the history of the incarnate Word begins with the ministry of John the Baptist, the first master of the fourth evangelist (1:35-40). The great glory of the Baptist—his only glory—is that he was witness to the Word spoken to men, to the Light coming into the world, in order that men might believe in the Light and have life by that Light through him. (6-8)

The coming of the Light revealed how deep and evil was the darkness (cf. 5) that opposed Him. The *world* would not listen to the Word; it would not acknowledge the Light *(knew him not,* 10). His *own people,* prepared for His coming by the voices of prophecy from Moses (cf. 17) to John, loved darkness rather than light and *received him not* (11); their answer to His coming was the cross. But the authority of the Word and the trueness of the Light are not thereby called in question; all who *received him,* all who *believed in his name,* trusted in Him and surrendered themselves to Him as to God's final Word and God's creative Light—they found in Him life from God and with God *(born . . . of God,* 13; *children of God,* 12).

1:14-18 THE WORD GIVEN TO THE DISCIPLES: GRACE AND TRUTH

1:14-18 Simple statement (1:13) gives way to warm personal confession *(us; we,* 14; *we,* 16). The excited cry, "We have found the Messiah" (2:41), with which the disciples first proclaimed Him finds an echo here. They have believed in His name and have found in Him divine *grace* which has gone the whole way to man *(became flesh and dwelt among us,* 14) in man's darkness, the grace of the eternal *Word,* grace in which God's *truth* is present (14); grace that is one with *glory,* the holiness of God manifested in Him who is the *only Son* (14), through whom alone men receive power to become sons of God (12). There is none who can be ranked with Him or compared with Him; not John the Baptist, who himself confessed the towering superiority of the One who came after him (15); not the disciples, who remain only and always the recipients of His grace (16); not Moses for all his dignity as mediator of the Law, for Moses could not give what his word demanded and promised—*grace* and *truth* became a reality only in the Word made flesh *(came through Jesus Christ,* 17). Not any man, for no man *has ever seen God* as the only Son has seen Him; He, the trusted Companion of His Father *(in the bosom,* alone *made him known.* (18)

1:19—4:54 THE WORD IS SPOKEN TO ALL ISRAEL

1:19—4:54 This first section is an unfolding of the thematic words: "He came to his own home" (1:11). All three divisions of the land of Israel (Judea, Samaria, Galilee) are scenes of the revelation.

1:19-34 The Witness of John the Baptist

1:19-34 Cf. 1:6-8; 15. "He . . . came to bear witness to the light" (1:8). In that act of witnessing John himself sees his whole and only function. When questioned by an official delegation from Jerusalem, he disclaims every title or honor that will detract from the Light. He, John, is not the *Christ* (20), not the looked for *Elijah* of the last days (21); not the *prophet* like Moses whom God promised to raise up for His people (21; cf. Dt 18:15). He is only the *voice . . . in the wilderness* (23; Is 40:1 ff.). Only his cry signifies. John's baptism has its whole significance as preparation for the revelation of Him who is to come, the Unknown who can no longer remain unknown (21-28). *He* will bring the last-days baptism with the Spirit, for He is the *Lamb of God,* the sacrifice for the world's sin which God provides. On Him the *Spirit* promised for the Messianic descendant of Jesse (Is 11:2) rests; He is the Eternal, the Son of God. (29-34)

1:35-51 The Call and Confession of the First Disciples

1:35-51 "The Word became flesh and dwelt among us" (1:14). That was John's first statement concerning his discipleship. The story of the beginnings of discipleship is "flesh," down-to-earth history. Natural and normal associations play their part in bringing men within earshot of the Word: a master's word points two disciples to the Lamb of God (36), brother brings brother (40-42), and a man of Bethsaida tells a fellow townsman (43-45). Jesus' first words to His first disciples are simplicity itself: *What do you seek? . . . Come and see.* (38-39)

Yet through this flesh the Word's eternal glory shines: the voice proclaims Him as God's final and universal sacrifice (36). The ancient words of promise inevitably find their goal in Him (45). He knows "what is in man" (cf. 2:25), and this knowledge has a shattering effect on the skeptic Nathanael (47-49). The first five disciples cannot but confess Him as *the Messiah* (41), *the King of Israel, the Son of God.* (49)

And this was but a foretaste and token of the glory they were to behold in Him; greater things awaited them (50). The disciples' first and overwhelming experience of Him was the experience of His grace (cf. 1:16). They turned to Him as to the Lamb of God, God's sufficient answer to their desperate need as members of a sinful world (36; cf. 29). He took the initiative *(What do you seek?* 38) and invited them to His lodgings and received them at His table (see note on v. 39). He bade an undistinguished Philip follow Him (43). When He called Simon *Cephas,* that was grace; for He spoke of a ministry that Simon would be privileged and enabled to perform, a partaking in the Christ's own work of building a new temple (cf. 2:19), a new Israel (cf. Mt 16:16-19). His grace forgave Nathanael his sneer at Nazareth and reached out to fulfill the heart's desire of that guileless Israelite (45-49). His promise of *greater things* is a promise of "grace upon grace." The disciples shall see in the Word become flesh the work of the God who opens heaven and comes down, who seeks, establishes, and maintains fellowship with man in the person of One who calls Himself *the Son of man.* (50-51)

1:39 *About the tenth hour,* 4 p.m., when the main meal of the day was eaten.

2:1-12 First Sign: Jesus Manifests His Glory

2:1-12 Jesus first manifests His glory by giving; the gift speaks anew His Father's blessing on the creation that came into being through Him (1:3), on the creaturely flesh which He has made His own (1:14). Jesus blesses marriage by His presence at the wedding feast and by His giving blesses the wine that makes glad the heart of man. He gives in obedience to the Father, awaiting the hour which He has ordained (4) in sovereign independence of all others, even of His kindly mother (3-4). He gives royally; the gift is lavish in both quantity and quality (6, 10). Jesus' first sign is like the last sign recorded by John in that both are extreme-case signs. As the last sign (ch.11) shows—by Jesus' mastery over death—that there is no limit to His power to give, so the first sign shows that there is no limit to His will to give; even the slightest need (the embarrassment of a host and the dampening of festal pleasure) is enough to evoke His compassionate aid. The disciples are to know how freely and confidently they may ask in His name. (14:13; 15:16)

2:4 *O woman.* There is nothing disrespectful in this form of address.

2:6 *Jewish rites of purification.* Cf. Mk 7:3-4.

2:10 The steward is worldly wise, well versed in the ways of drinkers; but he is an objective witness to the reality of the miracle.

2:11 *Signs,* the miracles in their significance as the revelation of the mind and will of God. (Cf. 6:26)

2:13-22 The Cleansing of the Temple

2:13-22 The disciples, John said, beheld the glory of the incarnate Word as "the glory of the only Son," a glory the Son received "from the Father" in obedient self-subordination to the Father (1:14). The obedient Son is zealous for the honor of His Father's house, the temple. He will not have men attempt to serve God and mammon in its hallowed precincts (13-16; cf. Mt 6:24). He is challenged by the temple authorities: If He is reforming Israel's worship with an assumption of prophetic (or even Messianic) authority, He must authenticate Himself by performing a *sign,* a miraculous demonstration of His authority (18). Jesus, who leaves no believing petition unanswered, refuses as always the sign which will satisfy the demand of the impenitent. He gives the authorities a riddling answer (19), one which even His disciples understood fully only after His resurrection (22). But, though it posed a riddle, it was unmistakably a call to repentance. The course which they are pursuing, Jesus is telling them, will bring the judgment of God on the desecrated temple; the future of the people of God lies, not with the custodians of the temple or even with the temple itself but with the Son whom they will resist, defeat, and kill. He will arise from the dead as the new and living temple, the center and focus for the worship of men (19). The sneer with which *the Jews* answer His call to repentance (20) makes it clear that Jesus knew what was in their hearts when He refused their demand for a sign. The lines are drawn; His people will not receive Him (1:11). But to those who do receive Him He manifests His glory as much in this refusal of a sign as in the doing of a sign. His disciples' faith grows. They see in Him the ultimate meaning of the OT words concerning the Righteous Sufferer (Ps 69:9) and come to know Him as One whose Word has the same unbreakable force as that of their Sacred Scriptures. (22; cf. 10:35)

2:13 *Passover.* It is characteristic of John that he dwells on Jesus' appearances in Jerusalem at the great festivals, concerning which the other gospels are silent, although the words of Jesus in Mt 23:37 and Lk 13:34; 19:41 presuppose a ministry in Jerusalem also.

2:19 *Three days,* the time when observable corruption of a corpse sets in; cf. 11:39, "dead four days."

2:23—3:21 Faith: The Conversation with Nicodemus

2:23—3:21 The eternal Son gives power to become children of God to all who believe in His name (1:12). What is believing? What does faith involve? The brief notice concerning the *many* who *believed . . . when they saw the signs which he did* (2:23)—a faith which Jesus could not accept (2:24)—seems designed to raise this question, and the conversation with Nicodemus (3:1-21) seems designed to answer it. The word *believe* occurs 8 times in these 24 verses (as over against 5 times in the preceding 73 verses).

Believing is more than seeing *signs* and being somehow drawn to Him who performs them. Jesus knows *what is in man* and knows that the stance of the sympathetic spectator is not the stance of faith; He cannot give Himself to the spectator. (2:23-25)

Believing is more than a good man's sincere religious interest in Jesus as a *teacher come from God* (3:1-2); Jesus' brusque disregard of Nicodemus' compliment makes that plain (3:3). To believe is to let God be God *(kingdom of God,* 3:3,5); it is living with and on the miracle, where God is the sole agent. Faith lives on the miracle of a new birth *from above* (3:3,5), birth by the *water* of John's baptism and by the Spirit baptism given by the Son of God (3:5; cf. 1:32-33). Faith cannot ask, as Nicodemus does, *How can this be?* (3:9; cf. 3:4), for man can raise the question of *how* only in the domain of man, the domain of *the flesh;* the *Spirit* is beyond his questioning. Man can find an analogy for the mystery of the Spirit's working in the mysterious ways of God's creation, in the *wind* whose sound he hears and whose reality he feels without being able to explain its coming and going (3:8). The *teacher of Israel* can find the record and reality of the Spirit in the Sacred Scriptures on which he bases his teaching (3:10; cf. e.g., Eze 36:27). The miracle of the prophets (with whom Jesus associates Himself as THE Prophet, *we,* 3:11) can help him toward a believing encounter with the greater miracle of the *Son of man,* the valid witness of *heavenly things . . . who has descended from heaven.* (3:12-13)

The *teacher of Israel* can find in the record of *Moses* (Nm 21:4-9) the miracle of the love of God manifested to a people who had by rebellion against Him (Nm 21:5, 7) forfeited all right to His love—he can find there a similitude for the miracle of the supreme love which will cause the *Son of man* to *be lifted up* to the cross and to the throne of God (3:14; cf. 8:28; 12:32, 34). But this does not exempt him from the total submission of faith; it can but help him to *believe* in the Son of Man and so find *eternal life* in Him (3:15). The miracle of God's love for His people can prepare him for faith in the uncaused, universal love of God for the *world* in rebellion against Him, the love which *gave* the *only Son* for the life of the enemy, the love which wrought salvation and *eternal life* for all (3:16). Faith cannot ask *how* in the face of this miracle; and faith dare not ask for reasons, for faith is the desperate reach for life in the midst of death, in the face of judgment and condemnation (3:18). And judgment is not a far-off event; the judgment is taking place now, in the unbelief of men who *love darkness,* which dooms them and does not want to be *exposed* by the *light* (3:19-20). For unbelief the Last Judgment has moved into the present. But for faith the final miracle takes place; the believer moves from the passivity of being born and being loved to the activity of doing *what is true,* of enacting the truth in *deeds* that have God's hallmark on them, deeds *wrought in God.* (3:21)

3:22-36 The Last Witness of John the Baptist

3:22-36 The Baptist, the witness through whom men come to faith (1:6-8), is a man of faith. He lives on the miracle and therefore knows that all men live on God's giving (27). His disciples' anxiety for their master's honor therefore leaves him unmoved; he is content to play the subordinate role which God has assigned to him (28). He is more than content; he rejoices, as the bridegroom's friend rejoices in the bridegroom's joy, in the fact that the will of God *(must,* 30) has decreed that the increasing Light should reduce to insignificance the burning and shining lamp of the witness to the Light (30; cf. 5:33). No mists of selfish ambition becloud his vision of the Light; he can witness to Him fully because he witnesses freely; the One whom John attests comes *from above,* from God, and is *above all,* high over the witness John, who is and speaks *of the earth* (31); *He* is eye- and ear-witness to the world of God from which He comes (32); possessed of the Spirit in unprecedented fullness. He utters the very *words of God* (34); one with the Father who *loves* Him, He is the Bearer of all God's counsels, the Executor of all God's purposes for men (35). the believing witness to the cruciality of faith when he declares that he who *believes in the Son* attests that God is faithful to His promises (33) and *has* the promised *eternal life* in the Son; whoever will not yield to Him the obedience of faith has willed to remain under the *wrath of God.* (36)

3:22 *He . . . baptized.* Cf. 4:2, where baptizing is restricted to Jesus' disciples. Through them He (Jesus) baptized.

3:33 *Sets his seal to this,* that is, attests, certifies, acknowledges.

3.34 *Not by measure . . . he* (the Father) *gives the Spirit* (to the Son). This distinguishes Jesus from all other recipients of the Spirit (judges, Ju 6:34; kings, 1 Sm 16:13; prophets, Mi 3:8; cf. 1:33).

4:1-42 The Woman of Samaria

4:1-42 Nicodemus, high-minded Pharisee, ruler, and teacher of Israel; John the Baptist, witness, voice, friend of the Bridegroom, a shining lamp in Israel; and third, the *woman of Samaria,* these are an ill-assorted company. For she was alien to Jewry; no good Jew would set his lip to a Samaritan water jar (9). She was walled in by sectarian pride and prejudice (12); hemmed in by a low horizon of physical desires and satisfactions (15); and, living with her sixth man, she had a past and a present that she preferred to be ambiguous about (16-18). And yet she joins that company of witnesses of which John was the first (39). If the story of Nicodemus shows that nothing less than faith will avail, her story makes it plain that nothing more than faith is needed. (4:21-26)

The love of Jesus, which could be brusque with the teacher of Israel, deals gently with this sorry slut of Samaria. Gradually and patiently He leads her to see in Him more than a tired, thirsty, and impertinent Jew (9), to see in Him more than a mysteriously attesting personality who has a gift to give (10-15), a prophet who can divine her secret sins and can point her beyond the competing claims of Mount Gerizim in Samaria and Mount Zion in Jerusalem to a new and true worship in which all men may join, a worship made possible and acceptable by the gift of the Spirit and His revelation of the truth (16-24). He leads her, finally, to a dawning recognition of Him as the Christ whose coming resolves the religious riddles of the past (25-26, 29). He makes her a believer and a witness, and she enjoys a witness's reward; her fellow townsmen come to Jesus, prevail on Him to stay with them, and find in Him the Savior who, though He asserts the primacy of the Jew in God's counsels of salvation (22), excludes no one from salvation, the *Savior of the world.* (28-30, 39-42)

For Jesus this bit of evangelization done in transit on His way to Galilee (3-4) was no little thing. He was doing the will of His Father who seeks worshipers (23), and that was the *food* He lived on (32-34). He, the patient Sower, sees the fields which His disciples shall reap *already white for harvest* and *rejoices* with these *reapers* who *shall reap that for which others* (John the Baptist, Jesus) *have labored* (35-38). The Savior of the world looks down the missionary road that leads through Samaria into the far corners of the world, and His joy is full.

4:43-54 Jesus' second (cf. 2:11) *sign* in Galilee again shows Jesus as the Giver. He is curiously reserved and austere in His giving. He chides the poor father who has ridden 18 miles to get help for his dying son (48). But He holds back and chides, not because He is unwilling to give but because He is minded to give the petitioner more than he asks for. And He does give Him more; He gives him his son, and He gives him a faith in His Word (50) that is independent of signs and wonders, a faith that can endure beyond the crisis which evoked it, a faith that lives and communicates itself to others *(and all his household,* 53).

4:48 *Unless you see signs.* The *you* is plural, "you Galileans." (Cf. 45)

5:1—12:50 THE WORD IS REJECTED BY ISRAEL

5:1—12:50 The thematic word, "His own people received him not" (1:11), is not forgotten in the first four chs. (cf. 2:23-25; 3:11; 3:32; 4:44). But it is chs. 5—12 that this theme is fully developed and becomes a dominant motif of the narratives and discourses in which Jesus reveals Himself amid a hostile and obdurate people.

5:1-47 The Healing at Bethesda on the Sabbath

5:1-18 Jesus brought the grace and truth of God into the life of a hopeless invalid; He did so with characteristically quiet unobtrusiveness *(had withdrawn,* 13). He made clear to the healed man that the whole restorative grace of God had touched his life and that this grace dare not be received in vain *(sin no more,* 14). His deed brought Him into conflict with His people because He had broken the jealously guarded Sabbath in doing it (18). The conflict became a deadly conflict when Jesus pleaded in His defense that He was acting thus in oneness with His Father, the Creator who has been working ceaselessly from creation onward, on weekdays and holy days alike *(is working still,* 17). In the eyes of His people He was defending sacrilege with blasphemy when He called God His Father, making Himself equal with God. (18)

5:19-29 Jesus' reply to this charge is simply the declaration of the mystery of His Sonship. He is not MAKING Himself equal with God when He calls Him Father in this unique sense; His Sonship is enacted in obedience (19) and is lived under the law enunciated by the Baptist: "No one can receive anything except what is GIVEN HIM FROM HEAVEN" (3:27). The initiative is not His own but His Father's; the Father's love for the obedient Son puts all things into the Son's hands (19:20): the eternal issues of life and death (21) and the judgment, which is God's own prerogative (22; cf. Dt 32:35). The Father crowns the Son with His own glory and honor; therefore the Son's Word is the divine two-edged sword of *judgment* and *eternal life* (24), both now and hereafter (25, 28); now, for the underived *life* of God is present now, in the *Son of man,* and is given to man now (cf. 24); the alternative is judgment from the Son of Man now (27); hereafter, for the voice heard now (25) will be heard again at the Last Day to open tombs and to make manifest the judgment which is being enacted now. (28-29)

5:30-37a The Son has witnesses who live and can tell of the truth and selflessness of His Sonship. There is the testimony of *John,* who called Him both Lamb of God (1:29, 36) and Son of God (1:34); His testimony counts, not because it is a man's word but because He was a *lamp* kindled by God Himself; the Jews themselves have, for a time at least, delighted in that *light* (33-35). There is the witness of the *works* which the Father has *granted* Him to *accomplish;* the working Word that gladdens and restores is God's Word spoken for the need of man (36). And the Father's voice has testified to the Son at His baptism. (37; cf. 1:33, 34)

5:37b-47 The Accused now becomes the Accuser of His accusers: "You who are so zealous for God's Sabbath and God's honor," He asserts, "do not even know the God for whom your unenlightened zeal (cf. Ro 10:2) contends. If His *word,* the *scriptures,* had really found a home in your hearts *(abiding in you,* 38) as well as in your searching minds (39), you could recognize the authentic accent of the eternal Word, who has heard and seen God; you would believe Him and find in Him *eternal* life (39, 40). If your selfish love for the *glory* that lives from man to man (44) had not killed in you the *love of God* (42), you would *receive* the Son who unselfishly comes in His *Father's name* (43), doing His will, seeking His glory, not *glory from men* (41). As it is, you can believe only a messiah who is as self-centered as yourselves (43b). The *Moses . . . on whom you set your hope* (45) stands before the Father as your accuser: 'You have not *believed his writings* in their essential import, as witnesses to Me.' " (45-47; cf. 1:45; 3:14)

6:1-71 Feeding the 5,000 in Galilee

6:1-71 The story of the feeding of the 5,000 (Jesus' enacted invitation to fellowship) and its sequel, the story of Jesus' coming to His disciples across the waters (the enactment of Jesus' unconquerable will to fellowship with His own) are familiar to us, as they probably were to John's first readers, from the accounts in the first three gospels. (Cf., e.g., Mt 14:1-33). Peculiar to the fourth gospel (aside from details, such as the reference to the *Passover,* 4) is the emphasis on Jesus' deeds as *signs,* as wondrous acts which point beyond themselves, from the gift to the Giver (cf. 26). John had previously recorded Jesus' mistrust of a "faith" that feeds on signs alone; He could not "trust himself" to such a faith (2:23-25); the sequel to the story of the feeding in John (v. 15) makes plain why He who "knew what is in man" could not give Himself to such a faith; such a faith has room in it for the self-seeking will of man, man who will not be taught and drawn to Jesus by the Father (44-45) but seeks by force to *make* Him King whom only the Father can make both King and Lord (cf. Acts 2:36). The faith which feeds on signs is an appetite that grows by what it feeds on; it cannot rest in the revelation of the given sign but demands another. (26)

Jesus' discourse on the bread of life makes clear the true significance and the real function of the sign (26-71). The sign of the multiplied loaves points beyond itself, beyond the *food which perishes* to *the food which endures to eternal life* (27), beyond any *works of God* (28) which man in his zeal can do to the one *work of God* which God in His grace does, to faith in the *Son of man* whom God has sent, not only to give (34) but to be *the true bread from heaven* that *gives life to the world* (32, 33, 35). Jesus in His person is the *bread of life* (35, 48), eternal life (40, 51); His person is the Word become flesh (cf. 1:14). The *bread which* He *shall give for the life of the world is* His *flesh* (51), the flesh of the Lamb of God (1:29), of the Crucified whose *blood* (53, 55, 56) is shed for the life of the world. Whosoever eats that flesh and drinks that blood (in the sacrament which the dying Son of Man instituted as the perpetual memorial of His death and as the vehicle of its blessing) *has eternal life* and shall be raised up by the Son of Man *at the last day* (54), for he shall be in abiding communion with Him who shares the life of the Father, Source and Creator of all life (57)

At every word which Jesus speaks the sign grows more luminous and points to greater things than God gave to His people through *Moses* (31, 32, 49, 58; cf. 1:17). Inevitably the sign becomes "a sign that is spoken against" (Lk 2:34). The *Jews murmur* when the *son of Joseph* (41) lays claim to divine Sonship and descent from heaven (38-40); they *dispute among themselves* (52) when the grace of the Son of Man and the love of the Father confront them with the incredible gift of eternal life in the flesh and blood of the Son of Man, given "for us Christians to eat and to drink." Even *many of* the *disciples* find the words of Jesus a *hard saying* and *take offense* at them, drawing back and forsaking His fellowship (66) just when they encounter the "greater things" which Jesus had promised, just when they behold the full glory of the Son of Man. (Cf. 1:50-51)

But the sign has not been given and interpreted in vain; it is given in order that men "may believe that Jesus is the Christ, the Son of God, and that believing" they "may have life in his name" (20:30). In *Simon Peter* (68) and the *twelve* (67) there is born a faith that cannot lose its hold on Him who has *the words of eternal life,* even in the face of the diabolical attack which has made *Judas . . . one of the twelve* (71) its victim.

6:4 *The Passover . . . was at hand.* The memorial feast of the Exodus (Ex 12) recalls Moses, the first deliverer of Israel, and the gift of manna (cf. 6:31, 32, 49, 58). The theme announced in 1:17 is being developed.

6:14 *The prophet.* The promised prophet of Dt 18:15, 18-19 and the Messiah were closely associated in Judaic thinking, cf. 6:15 *(king)* and 7:40-41.

6:23 *Tiberias,* a city on the west shore of the Sea of Galilee, founded by Herod Antipas and named for the Roman emperor Tiberius. The Sea of Galilee came to be called after the city. (6:1)

6:27 *God the Father set his seal.* Cf. 3:33 note.

6:31 *He gave them bread from heaven.* Ps. 105:40; cf. 78:24; Neh 9:15.

6:34 *Give us this bread always.* Cf. 4:15.

6:45 *Written in the prophets.* Cf. Jer 31:34; Is 54:13.

6:62 *What if you were to see the Son of man ascending where he was before?* Then they would have all the more reason to take offense, for the Son of Man will ascend to where He was before by going to the cross, to a criminal's death.

6:63 *Spirit . . . flesh . . . words.* When Jesus has ascended where He was before, He will bestow the Spirit on those who believe in Him (7:39). The Spirit will lead those who believe into all truth (16:13); He will enable the believer to apprehend that the *flesh* of Jesus, which in itself is of *no* more *avail* than any human flesh, is the sacrifice of the Lamb of God, given for the life of the world (6:51). The Spirit will recall and confirm in the believer the *words* of Jesus which gave His flesh this significance and power (14:26); thus the Spirit will give *life.*

6:64 *Some . . . that do not believe.* For such neither the witness of the Spirit nor the words of Jesus have any force.

6:69 *The Holy One of God.* The use of this term indicates that Peter is confessing more than the term "Christ" (or "Messiah") commonly connoted. In his confession in Mt 16:16 this "more" is expressed in the words "the Son of the living God." Peter is confessing the deity of his Lord.

6:70 *One of you is a devil.* As one "inspired" by the devil (13:2, 27), *Judas* has become so much a part of the diabolical attack on Jesus (cf. 14:30) as to be identified with him.

7:1—11-54 Jesus and Jerusalem

7:1—11:54 The Word has been rejected in Galilee (ch. 6). Jesus goes from Galilee to Judea in order that the Word may be spoken to the full and for the last time (7:6, 8) to Jerusalem, the heart and center of Israel. The Word of grace and truth is offered to Israel in the person of Him who makes man's body whole (7:23), who promises rivers of living waters (the Spirit) to a parched land, who is the Light of the world (8:12) and brings man freedom from sin and death (8:32, 51), who opens blind eyes (ch. 9) and goes into death as the Good Shepherd who lays down His life for the sheep (10:11, 14), who is the Resurrection and the Life (11:25). The Word is spoken in that Jesus shows His people the "many good works from the Father" (10:32) which declare God's love for the world. It is man's obduracy, not God's intent, that makes these days of bitter and fierce contention; Jerusalem represents the mankind which loved darkness rather than light (cf. 3:19) when the men of Jerusalem impulsively take up stones (8:59; 10:31) and at last deliberately resolve (11:47, 57) to destroy Him who is the Light of mankind.

7:1-13 JESUS GOES TO JERUSALEM: JESUS AND HIS BROTHERS

7:1-13 Jesus' manner of removing from Galilee to Jerusalem illustrates the cleavage between Jesus and His people. His unbelieving (5) brothers cannot understand a Brother who is so wholly one with God that His time is completely in His Father's hands (6, 8) and His whole life is a walking indictment of the world's evil works (7). He goes at God's time (10) and *in private* (10), the quiet way of the Servant and obedient Son, to confront a people as yet wavering and uncertain about Him (12), although within the circles of official Judaism *(the Jews,* 13) the decision has been made against Him. (Cf. 7:25, 32, 44-52)

7:2 *Feast of Tabernacles,* the third of three great annual festivals of Israel, in October, celebrated by constructing booths (tabernacles) of fruit and palm trees to commemorate the years of wandering when Israel dwelt in tents. (Lv 23:40-42)

7:6, 8 *My time.* The time is that of His "glorification" by dying (12:23-24) for the sins of the world. (11:50-52)

7:14-52 CONTROVERSY AT THE FEAST OF TABERNACLES

7:14-52 Jesus forces a decision upon His wavering (12) people. He confronts them with His *teaching* (16): they cannot call it the teaching of a good man (cf. 12), a learned rabbi versed in inherited rabbinical lore, to be *marveled at* (15). His teaching is a divine Word, to be known and recognized as such in obedience to the *will* of God (17), marked by its selfless candor as the Word of the obedient Son *who seeks the glory of him who sent him* (18). Men who have not obeyed the voice of God heard in the *law* given them by *Moses* are ill-prepared to hear God's voice in the teaching of the Son; inevitably, they must join the ranks of those who hate the Son because He testifies that their works are evil (7) and finally *seek to kill* Him. (19)

Jesus confronts them with His *deed* (21) of healing on the Sabbath (cf. ch. 5); that, too, is not something they may merely *marvel at* (21). It is the work of God (cf. 5:17), as much a doing of His will as a circumcision performed on the Sabbath *that the law of Moses may not be broken* (23). Those who *judge with right judgment* (24), a judgment that desires the will of God, are able to look beyond the *appearances* of illegality to the real character of the deed and call it good.

Jesus confronts them with His impending (25, 32) death. That death will not be a successful countermeasure taken by *chief priests and Pharisees* (32) against one who "is leading the people astray" (12). It will be the Son's free act of returning to His Father (33) that will remove Him forever from the pursuit of men (34). The Son's free act will bring the blessing of the *Spirit* on those who have *believed in Him* (39). In that free act of love the Son will be *glorified.* (39)

The result: *there was a division among the people over him* (43). The division runs deep; reactions are as various as the sneer of those who call Jesus possessed (20) or deliberately misunderstand His allusion to His death to be a reference to a proposed trip into the Dispersion, to *teach the Greeks* (35) or the passing inclination of others to suspect that the *authorities* are not, after all, serious in their opposition to *the Christ* (26) and to see in Jesus the promised *prophet* and the expected *Christ* (40, 41)—or the reaction of *many of the people* (31) in whom the dawning recognition of the Christ was not suppressed by their preconceptions concerning Him (27, 41-42), the *many* who *believed in him* (31). Even in the camp of the authorities who sought to kill Him (25) and *sent officers to arrest Him* (32) there is uncertainty and wavering. The *officers,* who returned overawed by Jesus' words (46), and *Nicodemus,* who ventured a timid objection to the illegality of their procedure (51), were shouted down (47-49; 52). But it is clear that the last word has not yet been said.

7:53—8:11 THE WOMAN TAKEN IN ADULTERY

7:53—8:11 The section is in all likelihood a later insertion into the text of the fourth gospel. Many of the ancient manuscripts omit this section, and it is unknown to commentators of the Greek church down to the 11th century. Further doubt is thrown on this section as a part of the fourth gospel by the fact that other manuscripts insert it at Jn 7:36 or Jn 21:24, while still others insert it after Lk 21:38. Besides, the section differs from the fourth gospel in language and style. The story is probably true, a genuine part of the story of Jesus; but is can hardly be a part of the gospel which John wrote.

8:12-59 CONTROVERSY CONTINUED: SON OF GOD AND SONS OF THE DEVIL

8:12-59 The controversy of ch. 7 is continued *(again,* 12). The time and place *(temple,* 20, 59) are the same. But Jesus' interlocutors are no longer "the people" (7:12, 20, 31, 43) but official Judaism *(Pharisees,* 8:13; *the Jews,* 8:31, 48, 52). The center of dispute is the question of fatherhood: Whose Son am I? Whose sons are you? This question becomes the expressly stated point of dispute only in the third major section of the controversy (31-59); but the question is in the air from the beginning and determines Jesus' speech concerning the validity of His witness to Himself, the first formal point of difference between Him and His interlocutors (12:20; note 14, 16, 18, 19), as it does His words concerning His death, the second point of dispute. (21-30; note 23; 26-27; 28, 29)

8:12-20 Jesus witnesses to Himself as *the light of the world* (13). To the *Pharisees'* objection that the unsupported witness of one man *is not true,* Jesus responds that His testimony is valid even on the terms of the Law, on which they take their stand *(your law,* 17; cf. Dt 19:15); the *Father* (from whom He comes and to whom He returns, whom He knows and the Pharisees do not, 14, 19) is the great Second Witness to Him (18). Their blindness toward the Son, born of their enmity toward Him (cf. 20b), blinds them to the Father too. (19)

8:12 *Light of the world.* Jesus is making a Messianic claim (Is 42:6; 49:6; 60:1-3; cf. Mt 5:14, where Jesus calls His disciples, who shall witness to Him, "the light of the world"). There may be an allusion here to the ceremonial of the Feast of Tabernacles (7:2), which included both libations of water (cf. 7:37-38) and a great illumination of the entire temple area.

8:15 *I judge* (i.e., condemn) *no one.* Cf. 3:17.

8:21-30 Jesus speaks of His death, allusively but unmistakably *(I go away,* 21; cf. 22). The leaders of Israel, wilfully blind to the fact that His death is the death of the Lamb of God, a sacrifice *pleasing* to God (29), can only answer with a sneer (22, *will he kill himself?).* They will die *in* their *sins,* the sin of unbelief (24; cf. 16:9). They cannot believe; trapped in their own world *(from below . . . of this world,* 23), they will not accept Jesus' testimony to Himself (25, cf. 21). Too late, when they have *lifted up the Son of man* to the cross (and to glory), they will learn the truth (28), that He is God of God and Light of Light *(I am he,* 28), one with the Father and obedient to Him (28) in life and in death.

8:26 *Much to say . . . and much to judge.* The mission of the Son is to save the world, not to condemn it (3:17); yet, when God's saving intent collides with man's unbelief, judgment results. Jesus can therefore say of Himself, "I judge no one" (8:15), and with equal truth, "For judgment I came into this world." (9:39)

8:28 *I am he.* For Judaic ears, attuned to the OT, these words contain a claim to deity (cf. Is 43:10, 25). For a similar use of this absolute *I am* in this gospel cf. 8:58, 13:19; 18:5-8.

8:31-59 "As he spoke thus, many believed in him" (30). Jesus seeks to exploit this faith (however imperfect it may be and however transitory it may prove to be). He offers to *the Jews who had believed in him* (31) all that He can give to faith: His Word, the truth, the freedom of free sons of God—the full blessing of obedient discipleship (32). As He made His offer to them He reveals more and more fully what His Sonship is: His full communion with the Father, which makes His Word God's Word (38), His free obedience to the One who sent Him (42), His valid witness to God as the free Son unmarred and unenslaved by sin (45-46), His unalloyed devotion to the Father's *honor* (49), His serene confidence that the Father will glorify Him who does not seek His own glory (50, 54)—until He blazes upon them in the glory of eternal Godhead *(I am,* 58). As His self-attestation mounts, the opposition to Him mounts also, and His opponents reveal ever more clearly whose sons *they* are. They claim to be Abraham's free sons (descended from free-born Isaac and not from the slave woman's son Ishmael), but their enslavement to sin gives the lie to their claim that they are free; and their actions belie their claim to kinship with believing and obedient Abraham—*he* never opposed a murderous will to God's truth (41). They have lost title also to the privilege of being sons of God, which the OT conferred upon them (e.g., Ex 4:22-23; Hos 11:1; Is 1:2; Ml 1:6), for they have not acted as sons of God. They do not love Him whom the Father loves (42). Not Abraham's sons, not God's sons—they have in fact become sons of the devil, committed to his will to destroy what is God's and to his primeval (cf. Gn 3) and unceasing denial of the truth (44). They cannot bear to hear the words of Him who speaks God's Word, and so they *seek to kill* (40) Him who has *told them the truth which* He *heard from God.* Whatever faith they may have had has melted away in the fires of this conflict; they who were ready to believe are now prepared to stone. (59)

8:32 *The truth will make you free.* The truth which Jesus reveals—and is (1:17)—will make them free of the enslavement of sin (34), free for God, free to abide forever in the Father's house. (35)

8:33 *Have never been in bondage.* The Egyptian bondage, the Babylonian captivity, and the Roman domination are bondage, to be sure, but Israel has remained Israel through all that and has not become just another pagan people without God and without hope.

Descendants of Abraham. Jesus does not deny their descent from Abraham, but their real kinship with Abraham. (Cf. 39-40)

8:41 *We were not born of fornication.* The *we* is emphatic; perhaps a slur on Jesus' birth is intended; as the virgin's son, He is slandered as illegitimate.

8:44 *A murderer from the beginning.* Cf. Gn 3, where the Tempter's lie brought death into the world.

8:48 *Samaritan.* For the bitterness between Jews and Samaritans cf. 4:9. Just why the Jew should call Jesus a Samaritan is not clear. Perhaps the reason is that the Samaritans, too, cast doubt on the Jews' claim to be the true and only descendants of Abraham.

8:58 *Before Abraham was, I am.* For the force of *I am* cf. 8:28 note.

9:1-41 THE GIFT OF SIGHT AND THE JUDGMENT OF BLINDNESS

9:1-41 The Light of the world (5; cf. 8:12) shines in healing beneficence on man, giving sight (6-7) and creating faith (35-38; cf. 17). But men love darkness (3:19), and the most fervid lovers of darkness are the men who deem themselves already in the light, the Pharisees (13), *the disciples of Moses* (28), jealous guardians of God's *sabbath* (16) and God's honor (24), quick to judge and to *cast out* (16, 34), tyrannizing over the conscience of the common man (22-23), indignant at the suggestion that the light they walk by may be darkness (40, *Are we also blind?).* And so He who proclaims Himself the *light of the world* (5) and is sent to do the gracious *works of* the *God* who loved this dark world (3:16) is compelled by man's unbelief to proclaim: *For judgment I came into this world, that those who do not see may see, and that those who see may become blind* (39). Those who lack the light shall have it as the free gift of the Son of Man; those who refuse the light shall have the darkness which they have loved, as God's judgment on their unbelief; *your guilt remains.* (41)

9:1-4 Jesus imposes on His disciples the rule of "Judge not!" (cf. Mt 7:1); the God whom the Son makes known (1:18) is the God of grace and truth (1:17). It is *the works of him* that Jesus and His disciples must do while it is day, before the night of God's judgment descends (*We* [Jesus and His disciples, as light of the world, cf. Mt 5:14] must work, 4.) The disciples of Moses in their blindness judge and condemn; the disciples of Jesus serve God, who loves the world.

9:7 *Siloam . . . Sent.* The name *Siloam* is derived from the Hebrew word meaning "to send." The *Sent* One is God's Son. He, not some power inherent in the waters of the pool, gives sight to the man born blind.

9:22 *Be put out of the synagog,* i.e., be excommunicated from the fellowship of God's people.

9:34 *You were born in utter sin.* The Pharisees judge; they interpret the man's blindness as a judgment of God on his parents. (Cf. 2)

9:41 *You say, 'We see.'* For the Pharisees' claim to vision, knowledge, and the consequent right and capacity to judge others cf. 16, 24, 28, 29, 34.

10:1-21 JESUS THE DOOR OF THE SHEEP AND THE GOOD SHEPHERD

10:1-21 Jesus is still conversing with the Pharisees (cf. 9:40). Using the familiar picture of Israel as the flock of God (cf., e.g., Eze 34), He accuses the leaders of Israel of being *thieves and robbers,* (8), men who by stealth or violence have despoiled and destroyed God's people (10; cf. Eze 34:1-6). Only through Him will Israel get true shepherds; He is the *door* of the sheepfold through whom the true shepherds, whom the sheep can recognize and trust (3-5), have access to the flock of God; through His guarding and fostering care Israel, no longer "the lost sheep of the house of Israel" (cf. Mt 9:36; 10:5), will be God's protected *(saved,* 9) and tended *(find pasture,* 9) flock. More than that: in Him Israel will get a *shepherd* who deserves the name (11, 14), devoted unto death to His own; no selfish *hireling* (12, 13), He freely lays down His life that *they may have life, and have it abundantly* (10). This Shepherd-King who dies that the flock may live shall be great "to the ends of the earth" (Mi 5:4); such is the compulsion of His love *(must,* 16) that He will join men of all nations to His own in Israel and thus create *one flock,* one new Israel, under one *shepherd* (16), known and obeyed by His flock (14, 16), united with Him in a love like that which unites the Father and the Son (15, 17).—Again there is *division among the Jews* (19). *Again* the charge is made by *many* that *he has a demon* (20); *others* recognize that the charge rings hollow when leveled at one whose word and deed, far from being the expression of demonic hatred for the creation of God, breathes God's own love for God's misled and suffering people. (21)

10:3 *The gatekeeper,* the man who stands guard over the sheepfold at night.

10:6 *This figure Jesus used,* i.e., He spoke to them in this picture language.

10:15 *Knows . . . know.* This knowing is the personal communion of love. (Cf. 17)

10:18 *Of my own accord . . . this charge I have received.* Such is Jesus' love for the Father who loves Him (15) that desire and duty do not conflict in Him; the Father's will and His desire are one.

10:22-42 "IF YOU ARE THE CHRIST, TELL US PLAINLY"

10:22-42 *The Jews,* whether out of uncertainty, as they profess (24), or from the desire to involve Jesus in conflict with Rome, if He proclaims Himself the *Christ,* the King of the Jews (cf. 19:14-15), ask Jesus the Messianic question and demand an unambiguous answer (24). Jesus replies: *I told you* (25). His words in Jerusalem (cf. chs. 5, 7, 8) have blazoned forth the Christ; the *works* which He has done *in* the *Father's name . . . bear witness* to Him as the Healer of men (ch. 5), the Opener of blind eyes (ch. 9), the Christ in whom all God's promises find their Yes (cf. 2 Co 1:20). They do not lack evidence; they lack faith (25-26). They have not listened to the voice of the Good Shepherd and have not followed Him (cf. 27); their unbelief has shut them out from *eternal life,* from the sure protection of the Son's almighty *hand* (28), of God's own hand (29), for the Son and the Father *are one.* (30)

At this *"blasphemy"* (33), the *Jews* take up *stones again to stone him* (31). Jesus points once more to the witness of His *many good works from the Father* (32) and meets the charge of blasphemy with an appeal to His opponents' own Sacred Scriptures (*your law,* 34), that inviolable revelation of the mind and will of God (35). He has not, He asserts, *made* Himself *God* in equating His hand with the hand of God (cf. 29-30). The Father has done that by consecrating Him and sending Him into the world as a *man* (33) among men (36). If the God whose voice they hear in their *law* can address as *gods* the men to whom *the word of God came* (35; Ps 82:6), where is the blasphemy when He who speaks God's Word and is God's Word calls Himself the *Son of God* (36)? His words are pure, and His works are the *works of* His *Father* (37). He cannot but repeat His "blasphemous" claim: *The Father is in me and I am in the Father* (38). The old claim arouses once more the old opposition: *Again they tried to arrest him.* (39)

Jesus *escaped from their hands* (39); His hour has not yet come. But He can no longer await that hour in Jerusalem; He goes *across the Jordan* and remains at the scene of John's baptizing (cf. 1:28). There the witness of John bears belated fruit: *Many believed in him there.* (42)

10:22 *Feast of the Dedication.* This feast, celebrated in October-November, celebrated the cleansing of the temple after it had been desecrated by Antiochus Epiphanes. (1 Mac 4:52-59)

10:35 *Called them gods to whom the word of God came.* The words of Ps 82:6 are addressed to unjust judges who have abused the power entrusted to them by *the word of God* which authorized them. For the bearer of God's Word as "god" cf. Ex 4:16.

11:1-54 THE RAISING OF LAZARUS: JESUS THE RESURRECTION AND THE LIFE

11:1-54 The seventh sign recorded by John is the supreme sign. He who creatively gives wine to make glad the heart of man (ch. 2), who by His Word gives healing to the sick (chs. 4—5), who sets a table in the wilderness and comes to His own across the waters (ch. 6) in token of His will to dwell with man and bless him, who gives sight to the blind (ch. 9)—He now gives life to the dead in token of His will to be the resurrection and the life for man. (11:25-26)

The raising of Lazarus is marked out emphatically as a "sign," as the enacted Word of God which reveals God to man. Jesus is portrayed as solely and sovereignly in charge of the action; the Word of life speaks in this deed. In obedience to His Father's will *he* determines the time and manner of the resurrection of Lazarus. He delays the resurrection of His friend in a way that would appear arbitrary and harsh were it not for the evangelist's express assurance that His love is active in this arbitrary harshness (5); He stays away from Bethany when He is most needed there, *two days* beyond the critical time (6, cf. 21, 32). He goes to Bethany when His going is a going into certain death (8, 16), in the calm certitude which His obedient oneness with His Father gives Him; He knows that the working day of *twelve hours* which His Father has assigned to Him (9-10; cf. 9:4) is not yet over. He restores to life a man who is *four days* dead, when corruption has set in (17, 39), when all human experience cries out, "Too late!" when faith can be only faith in the God "who gives life to the dead and calls into existence the things that do not exist." (Ro 4:17)

The sign is acted doxology; it is done *for the glory of God* (4, cf. 40). In that glory the *Son of God* is *glorified;* He prays at the door of the tomb for the given gift, in order that men may know that the Father has sent Him (42) and may believe that in Him God is giving mankind the resurrection and the life, now, in the hour of His presence among men (25). The enacted Word that glorifies God is spoken to Jerusalem, to the city and the people for whose faith Jesus has been wrestling all this time (chs. 7—10); men of nearby Jerusalem are present to comfort the mourning sisters and hear the cry which speaks eternal life to all who will believe: *Lazarus, come out!* (43; cf. 19, 31)

The Word is being spoken in the flesh; this is the climax of the signs done by *Jesus* (20:30) the Man who loves (3, 5), who is *deeply moved in spirit and troubled* (33, 38), who weeps (35) and prays. (41)

The final sign creates faith in *many of the Jews* (45; cf. 12:11, 17-18); it also brings the opposition of the *chief priests and Pharisees* (47) to a head. Official Judaism fears a Messianic movement that will erupt in violence and bring down on them the intervening arm of Rome to put an end to the last remnants of Israel's national-political existence (48, 50). The *Pharisees* see clearly enough the end which they must pursue; they cannot *let* Jesus *go on thus* (48); *Caiaphas* sees the means to this end: it is *expedient* that Jesus *should die* (50). And so the intention of Israel's leaders to destroy Him, manifest before this, becomes their resolve to destroy Him (53). The decision is made; the actual trial before the council will be a formality, so much a mere formality that John does not even record it in his account of the Passion. (Cf. 18:12-27 note)

11:2 *Who anointed the Lord.* Cf. 12:3. Matthew and Mark also record the anointing (Mt 26:6-13; Mk 14:3-9); only John identifies the woman as *Mary.*

11:8 *Seeking to stone you.* Cf. 8:59: 10:31.

11:16 *Twin* is the translation of the Aramaic word *Thomas.*

11:17 *Four days.* Cf. 39.

11:22 Cf. 41.

11:25 *I am the resurrection.* With the coming of Him in whom is the life that is the light of men (1:3) *the resurrection* is no longer merely a far-off event *at the last day* (24); it is a presently effective reality. *He who believes* in Him "HAS eternal life; he . . . HAS PASSED from death to life." (5:24)

11:48 *Holy place,* the temple.

11:51 *But being high priest that year he prophesied.* Under Roman rule the high priesthood had ceased to be a lifelong office. Caiaphas, *high priest that year,* the year in which Jesus concluded His ministry, is compelled by God to utter more than he intends or knows. Like Balaam of old, he must speak what God puts in his mouth. (Nm 23:12)

11:54 *Ephraim,* a small town NE of Jerusalem; its precise location is not known.

11:55—12:50 The Result of Jesus' Ministry

11:55—12:50 The sign of the resurrection of Lazarus has made Jesus a man of note, sought after by the Passover pilgrims in Jerusalem (11:55-57); Mary's anointing of Him is a token of the devotion He has inspired in His own (12:1-8); a crowd hails the *King of Israel* at His entry into Jerusalem (12:9-19); Greek proselytes present at the Passover seek Him out (12:20-22); even among the authorities there are many who believe in Him, though they cannot find the courage to confess Him (12:42-43). But to Israel as a whole the Word has been spoken in vain: Judas, one of the Twelve will betray Him (12:4-6); the chief priests and Pharisees, the most influential group in Israel, are hardened against Him (11:57; 12:19, 42). Jesus knows that His Passion impends. *The hour has come for the Son of man to be glorified* (23). The seed must fall into the ground and die before it can bear much fruit—life for the world is won by dying (12:23-26). The agony of Gethsemane is already in the air as the Son, to glorify His Father's name, prepares to do battle with the *ruler of this world,* to overcome him by the cross *(I am lifted up from the earth,* 32), and so to draw all men to Himself (27-34). The Light of the world has but a little while to shine (12:35-36); the Word of God, spoken by the Son to save mankind, will on the Last Day judge those who have rejected it in unbelief. (12:44-50)

11:55 *To purify themselces.* An Israelite had to be ritually clean to participate in the Passover (Nm 9:1-14). One who had become unclean had to undergo a purifying ceremony. (Nm 19:11-13; cf. 18:28)

12:11 *Were going away,* i.e., deserting the Jewish faith. For *going away* as a term for abandoning a religious allegiance c.f. 6:67.

12:13 *Hosanna.* Cf. Mt 21:9 note.

12:15 Cf. Mt 21:5 note.

12:20-22 *Philip . . . Andrew.* Both these disciples have Greek names and were probably more familiar than the other disciples with the Greek language and Greek-speaking people of Palestine, such as these *Greeks* probably were.

12:25-26 The way Jesus goes, through death to glory, is to be the way of His disciples too, the way of those who *follow* and serve Him.

12:27 *Now is my soul troubled.* Cf. Jesus' words in Gethsemane, Mt 26:38; Mk 14:34; Lk 22:44.

12:28 *I have glorified it, and I will glorify it again.* God has glorified His name, His revealed self, through the words and deeds of the Son whom He sent into the world (cf. 11:4, 40); He will glorify it again in the death and resurrection of the Son whom He has given to be the Lamb of God, the sacrifice for the sins of the world. (1:29; cf. 13:31-32; 17:1)

12:29 *An angel has spoken to him.* Cf. Acts 23:9.

12:31 *Now is the judgment of this world, now shall the ruler of this world be cast out.* The ruler of this world is the devil, the evil one (14:30; 16:19; cf. 1 Jn 5:19). *Now* in the hour of Jesus' crucifixion (cf. 32-33), it is apparently Jesus who is being judged; but in reality the *world* which hates (3:20; 7:7; 15:18, 23, 24) and seeks to destroy the Son is coming under *judgment.* The world hates and seeks to destroy Him under the leadership and inspiration of the ruler of this world; when he comes to assail Jesus, he finds in Him a human love for God and obedience to God which is proof against His temptation (14:30-31). The Accuser therefore loses his place as the Accuser of mankind when the Son of Man whose love embraces all mankind overcomes him (cf. Rv 12:10); the love and obedience of the Son convict the murderous lord of lies (8:44); HE is judged (16:11), and those who have willed to be ruled by him are judged with him. (16:33; cf. Mt 25:41)

12:33 *By what death he was to die,* that is, crucifixion; for this sense of "lifted up" cf. 8:28.

12:38 *The word spoken by the prophet Isaiah* concerning the Suffering Servant of God who goes through suffering, degradation, and death to exaltation and glory (Is. 52:13—53:12), bearing the sins of many, was an incredible word for the prophet's contemporaries (Is. 53:1).

When the Word became flesh and appeared among men in a servant's form, Isaiah's prophecy concerning the Suffering Servant was *fulfilled;* fulfilled, too, was the prophetic word which pictured His people's unbelief and their rejection of the Servant.

12:39-40 The fearful judgment of obduration once pronounced on God's people by *Isaiah* (Is 6:10) is repeated in the history of Jesus; here too God's judgment locks men up in their unbelief. They would not believe; they are condemned to become men who *could not believe.*

12:43 *Loved the praise of men more than the praise of God.* Cf. 5:44

13:1—17:26 THE WORD IS RECEIVED BY THE DISCIPLES

13:1—17:26 "To all who received him, who believed in his name, he gave power to become children of God" (1:12). The record of Jesus' last meal with His disciples and of His last words to His disciples is the record of His giving, ministering love: *He loved them to the end* (13:1). He enacts His ministering love for His disciples in the footwashing. By identifying the betrayer, He shows them the way His ministering love must go, the way of the cross. Thus He imposes on them His commandment of love (13:2-38). He prepares His disciples for the time when they shall be separated from His bodily presence, by revealing to them what they will gain by His departure: He promises that the Father will send them the Spirit. The Spirit shall be their Counselor in their conflict with the world, lead them into all the truth, and complete the presence of the Christ among them (chs. 14—16). Even when Jesus is praying for His own glorification (17:1-6), His disciples are remembered (17:2b-3), and the bulk of His prayer is intercession for His disciples (17:7-19), for those who shall come to faith through their Word (17:20-23), for all who are His by the Father's giving. (17:24-26)

13:1-30 Farewell Meal, Footwashing, the Betrayer

13:1-30 The first paragraph (1-11), which portrays the act of footwashing, begins and ends with words that connect this act of Jesus with His Passion *(his hour had come,* 1; *he knew who was to betray him,* 11). This menial act is the act of Him who "came . . . to serve, and to give his life as a ransom for many" (Mt 20:28). In His interpretation of the act (12-20) Jesus makes plain how His free gift of Himself *(part in me,* 8) commits His disciples to a life like that of their *Teacher and Lord* (13-14). They can find blessedness in Him (17), believe in Him, their ministering Lord who squanders His service on His betrayer (18-19), and can be credible and valid messengers of Him (20), only in following His example by washing one another's feet. (14-15)

Jesus is *troubled in spirit* (21) at the harsh reality of His Passion, now present in the person of His betrayer. He identifies His betrayer with a word from the Psalter (26; Ps 41:9) and an action (the giving of the morsel dipped in the common bowl, 26) which lay bare the full horror of the betrayer's sin and hint (at the least) that the Betrayed retains unshaken that trust in God of which the psalmist spoke: "By this I know that thou art pleased with me, in that my enemy has not triumphed over me. But thou hast upheld me because of my integrity, and set me in thy presence for ever." (Ps 41:11-12)

13:7 *Afterward you will understand:* "After you have failed Me and denied Me and My forgiving love has restored you, you will realize how completely you are dependent on My Servant ministry to you." (Cf. 21:15-19)

13:10 *He who has bathed does not need to wash, except for his feet.* The forgiven man *(he who has bathed)* can be wholly and forever sure of God's forgiveness. "The Lamb of God TAKES AWAY the sin of the world" (1:29); but in their life with one another the disciples are in danger of forfeiting the divine forgiveness by failing to forgive as they have been forgiven—hence the need for repeated footwashing as a mutual ministry. (14; cf. Mt 18: 21-35)

13:16 *He who is sent.* The Greek word is the same as the word for "apostle." Jesus puts the disciples in mind of their future ministry. (Cf. 20:21)

13:19 *I am he.* For the connotation of deity in this phrase cf. 8:28 note. The fact that Jesus will be betrayed need not shake the disciples' faith in Him as divine; the fact that He foreknows and foretells the betrayal reveals that He goes into death freely; death is His sovereign act, not a fate to which He helplessly submits. (Cf. 10:17-18)

13:23 *One of his disciples, whom Jesus loved.* This is in all probability John, the son of Zebedee, to whom tradition assigns the authorship of the fourth gospel. The beloved disciples appears again in 19:26; 20:2, 3, 4, 8; 21:7, 20-23; in two other passages an unnamed disciple figures, and he is probably to be identified with the beloved disciple. (1:40; 18:15-16)

13:27 *Satan entered into him.* The expression here is stronger than that of 13:2 ("the devil . . . put it into the heart of Judas"); Judas has become completely the instrument of Satan, the murderer from the beginning. (Cf. 8:44)

13:29 *That he should give something to the poor.* Judas was treasurer and almoner for Jesus and the Twelve. (Cf. 12:6)

13:30 *It was night.* The literal fact has symbolic significance; Judas has shut himself out from the Light of the world, and the daylight hours in which Jesus does the works of the Father who sent Him are over. (Cf. 11:9; 12:46)

13:31—14:31 Jesus' Last Words to His Disciples

13:31—14:31 John records two farewell discouses of Jesus; the first (13:31—14:31) is delivered in the room in which the supper was eaten, the second (chs. 15—16) at an unspecified place. In 13:31—14:31 Jesus is bracing His disciples for the shock of His departure and strengthening them for their life and work as His disciples and witnesses after His departure.

This first discourse begins and ends on a note of assured victory. Judas has departed to "do quickly" (at Jesus' behest!) what Satan has impelled him to do (13:27-30). *Now,* Jesus says, . . . *God is glorified* (13:31); *now,* in the Passion of the *Son of man,* God is reaching the goal of all His ways; the glory that He will not give to another shall be His, manifestly and forever. God is glorified; and the *ruler of this world* is defeated; He is *coming* to fight a battle that he has already lost; *he has no power over* the Son who loves and obeys even unto death (14:30-31). The reality and seriousness of Jesus' suffering is not forgotten or evaded; Jesus knows that He goes a way which He must go bitterly alone (13:33); not even the intensest devotion will enable Peter, or any man, to go with Him into the depths (13:36-38). Out of the strength of His own assurance of victory Jesus is able to strengthen His disciples. His death is not the end of all that He has meant for them but the beginning of all that He can mean for them. He gives them a vision of the final fullness of the grace upon grace (1:16) which they shall receive from Him; He will return and take them to Himself, to their place in the Father's house, which He has Himself prepared for them (14:2-3; cf. 14:18-19, 28). They shall live, in the full sense of "living," as the Son lives, possessed of life from the Father (14:28; cf. 5:26), a life victorious over death.

Meanwhile, they shall not be left desolate; their life is not to be only a life of hope. They know their final home, and they know the *way* there, for they know Him by faith who is *the way, and the truth, and the life* (14:6). Knowing Him, they know the Father to whose house they are going (14:7), for Jesus *is in the Father and the Father in* Him (14:11). The love of the Father and the love of the Son will fill their lives (14:23-24). They can believe with a new certitude (14:1) and pray with new confidence (14:13). They can obey the "new commandment" of mutual love (13:34; cf. 14:15, 21) and are empowered to do the *works* that the Christ did in the days of His flesh *(works that I do,* 14:12) and the *greater works* which the Christ at God's right hand will do through them (14:12). Those who do the works of the Christ must expect the opposition which He met. To meet, endure, and overcome that opposition, Christ will give His disciples *the Spirit,* whose mark and gift is *the truth* that sets men free (14:17; cf. 8:32); the Spirit will be in future what the Christ has been heretofore, the *Counselor (another Counselor,* 14:16), the advocate and spokesman for the disciples; He will make the departed and exalted Christ a Christ at hand for them by teaching the disciples all things, by bringing to their remembrance all that Christ has taught them; they will not mourn an absent Teacher; He will be with them in the powerful Word and witness of the Spirit. (14:26-27)

Peace will be theirs; Jesus leaves them peace, not as a gracious wish *(as the world gives,* 14:27) but as His gift, bestowed in a Word that conveys what it expresses (14:27). Their *hearts* need not *be troubled* at His departure; they need not *be afraid* for the future (14:27); they can and should rejoice that Jesus is going to the almighty and gracious Father. (14:28)

13:31 *Glorified.* Cf. 12:28 note.

13:34 *A new commandment.* The commandment enjoining brotherly love is as old as Lv 19:18; but is new because it has received a new depth and new power in Him who loved us and gave Himself for us. (Cf. 1 Jn 2:7-8)

13:36 *You shall follow afterward.* Cf. 21:18-19, where Jesus foretells Peter's martyrdom.

14:2 *Would I have told you that I go to prepare a place for you?* John records no word of Jesus that corresponds word for word to what Jesus refers to here; but 12:26 contains the substance of the promise to which Jesus is referring.

14:12 *Greater works than these will he do.* Jesus' works were done in the shadow of the cross, and His activity was confined to Israel. The disciples' works will be done in the light of the resurrection, in the power of the Spirit sent by the exalted Christ (14:15-17, 25-26), and will embrace the world of the Gentiles too. Cf. Jesus' words concerning His mission to the Greeks after His suffering, death, and resurrection. (12:20-24)

14:17 *For he* (the Spirit) *dwells with you,* now in the words and works of Jesus, on whom the Spirit descended and remained (1:32), to whom the Father gave the Spirit "not by measure" (3:34) but in fullness. *And will be in you,* after Jesus' death, when their worldwide ministry begins. (14:16, 25-26; 16:4-11)

14:22 Judas' question is answered indirectly in the following verses. The world, under the domination of the ruler of this world, cannot love Jesus or keep His Word (23:24), cannot receive the Spirit of truth because it is ruled by the lie and the father of lies. (26, cf. 17)

14:27 *Peace . . . my peace . . . not as the world gives. Peace* was a common form of greeting. On Jesus' lips the word is filled once more with the fullness of meaning which it had in the OT, where the blessing pronounced on God's people by the sons of Aaron culminates in "and give you *peace"* (Nm 6:26), where the promised Messiah bears the significant title, "Prince of *Peace"* (Is 9:6, cf. 7), where the Lord's "covenant of *peace"* with His people ensures that total wholeness, soundness, and health which only God can give (Eze 34:25-31; 37:26-28): "I will be their God, and they shall be my people." (Eze 37:27)

14:28 *The Father is greater than I.* The Son, the Word made flesh, can in His obedient self-subordination speak thus of Himself. Believing man can only echo Thomas' cry: "My Lord and my God!" (20:28)

15:1—16:33 JESUS' LAST WORDS TO HIS DISCIPLES

15:1—16:33 The second farewell discourse (cf.

13:31—14:31 note) has much in common with the first (13:31—14:31). But there is a new emphasis on the fullness and strength of the disciples' union and communion with Jesus: this is expressed most explicitly in the figure of the vine and the branches (15:1-17); but the same motif runs through Jesus' words on their exposure to the world's hatred for His sake (15:18—16:4), on the Spirit whom He will bestow on them (16:5-15), and on the *little while* which must elapse before their reunion with Him shall give them *full joy.* (16:16-33)

15:1-17 UNION WITH JESUS: THE VINE AND THE BRANCHES

15:1-17 The figure of the *vine* and the *branches* emphasizes the vitally organic nature of the disciples' communion with their Teacher and Lord. He initiates that communion (16), and they remain forever dependent on Him; they can *bear fruit* only by virtue of their continuing union with Him (4-5). Jesus' comment on the figure makes clear what the figure in itself cannot express: that their union with Him is conscious, personal union, involving responsibility and God's judgment on infidelity (2, 6), involving the conscious resolve to do His will which finds expression in prayer (7), in keeping His commandment of love, and in sharing the joy of their Lord (11). The *branch* is no mere mystically vegetable appendage to the *vine;* Jesus' disciple is not merely *servant* to His Lord (15), high and honorable as the title servant is—it dignifies Moses and the prophets (Jos 1:2; Am 3:7; Jer 7:25) and Paul bears it proudly (e.g., Ro 1:1). Jesus' disciple is not an ignorant servant (or slave) who obeys because he must; he is a *friend* who acts freely and gladly because he knows what his Master is doing, namely, the will of the Father. (14-15)

15:1 *The true vine.* The vine is an OT figure for Israel (Is 5:7; Jer 2:21; Eze 19:10-14). That vine has, as Jeremiah complained, "turned degenerate and become a wild vine" (Jer 2:21); man now becomes a member of God's people and has a place in God's house (14:2), not by membership in Israel but by being incorporated in the *true vine,* the Son who is all that God's "firstborn" (Ex 4:22), Israel, failed to be.

15:2 *Fruit.* Since the vine is a person and the branches are persons, it seems natural to think of the fruit as persons also, as those who come to faith through the disciples' Word (17:20). Jesus is laying a missionary, apostolic obligation upon His disciples. (Cf. 20:21)

15:3 *You are already made clean.* The word translated as "prunes" in the preceding verse means literally "to make clean."

15:5 *You can do nothing.* Jesus' prediction of Peter's denial (13:37-38) and of His disciples' defection (16:31-33) are concrete exemplifications of the truth of this saying. The disciples "on their own" are failures.

15:18—16:4a THE WORLD'S HATRED

15:18—16:4a The Jesus who loved His own to the end (13:1) has assured His disciples that they can continue in His love as surely as He Himself abides in the Father's love (15:9-10). It is His love for them that forewarns them of the world's hatred and forearms them against it (16:1). Because they are identified with Christ as He is identified with the Father (15:18, 21), because His choice of them has made them alien to the world (19), the world will hate them. As surely as they are servants of this Lord, so surely will they inherit the hatred of the world which persecuted Him and ignored His Word (20; cf. 1:10-11). That hatred will be the satanic hatred of men who have heard and seen and have rejected the words and deeds of Jesus which revealed the Father, the hatred of men who *have sin* (15:22, 24) as their demonic master (cf. 8:34) because they have rejected Him who is God's forgiving grace and truth. The satanic impulse will disguise itself as religious zeal; these men will excommunicate and kill to the greater glory of God (16:2; cf. 2 Co 11: 14-15). But the world's hatred shall not triumph; the light that shines in this darkness of hate shall not be quenched (cf. 1:5). The Spirit's witness and the disciples' inspired witness will continue and shall prevail.

15:18 *World . . . hated me.* Cf. 7:7.

15:20 *The word that I said to you.* Cf. 13:16.

15:24 *They have seen and hated both me and my Father.* They have seen but have not accepted and acknowledged; therefore Jesus can say both: "They have seen," and "They do not know" (15:21). Love opens the eyes of faith; hatred blinds them. (Cf. 16:3)

15:25 *Word . . . written in their law.* Ps 35:19; 69:4. For *law* in the comprehensive sense of "Old Testament" cf. 10:34.

15:26 *The Counselor . . . will bear witness.* This anticipates the theme of 16:4b-15.

15:27 *You also are witnesses.* For the united witness of the Spirit and the disciples cf. Acts 5:32.

16:4b-15 THE COUNSELOR WHOM JESUS SENDS

16:4b-15 *Now* that Jesus is leaving them, the disciples are keenly and sadly aware of their own helplessness; what can they do without Him against the concerted hatred of the world? If they had the wit to ask the right question, *Where are you going?* (5), Jesus would give them the answer that would remove the *sorrow* that *has filled* their *hearts* (6); for Jesus is going to the *Father,* and that is *to* their *advantage,* for He will send (7) the *Counselor* "from the Father" (15:26); and the Counselor's witness will do what no human eloquence or persuasion can do: it will *convince* (8), that is, expose the world's wrong and call the *world* to repentance. The world that hates and crucifies Jesus for the sin of blasphemy (10:33; cf. 8:59; 19:7) is still blind to *sin;* since Jesus has come to be "the Lamb of God, who takes away the sin of the world" (1:29), there is but one sin that shuts a man out from the God who loves the world, the rejection of God's proffered forgiveness: *They do not believe in me* (9). The world that asserts, "We have a law, and by that law he ought to die, because he has made himself the Son of God"

(19:7), is still blind to *righteousness* (8-9); the only righteousness that avails is in Him who dies for the world's sin and goes in triumph *to the Father,* removed from sight but present to faith (10). The world that bullies Pilate into executing *judgment* by crucifying the King who bears witness to the truth (19:12-16; cf. 18-37) does not know what judgment is being executed when this King dies: *The ruler* of this world is judged (11; cf. 12:31 note). The Spirit who witnesses through the witnessing disciples will present the crucified and exalted Christ as God's atonement for man's sin, God's righteousness for unrighteous man, God's judgment on the murderous and lying ruler of this world. Men will behold Him as He really is in that inspired witness, and men will repent.

To the disciples the Counselor will present the Christ in all the fullness of His glory, a glory they are not yet equipped to comprehend (12-15). The gospels, and indeed all the apostolic writings of the NT, witness to the fact that Jesus kept His promise concerning the Counselor, that men who once understood their Lord so ill (cf., e.g., 2:22; 12:16) were guided by the Spirit *into all the truth* (13) and learned to understand Him so well that their written witness to His glory has become the inexhaustible treasure of His church.

16:4 *Because I was with you,* to keep you and guard you. (Cf. 17:12)

16:12 *You cannot bear them now.* Not until men have been broken by their own failure (13:37-38; 16:31-32) and have been restored by Jesus' forgiving grace (cf. 20:17 "my brethren"; 20:19 "Peace be with you"; cf. 21:15-19)—not until then are they ripe for the full revelation of His glory.

16:16-33 A LITTLE WHILE: PASSING SORROW AND LASTING JOY

16:16-33 Jesus sees in one perspective His resurrection and His return in glory at the end of days; the *little while* (16) of which He speaks is both the three days of His entombment and the time until His second coming. Jesus explains to His puzzled (16:17-18) disciples: The approaching time of separation *will* be a time of sorrow, the time of the world's triumphant joy at its apparent victory over the buried and unseen (cf. 16:10) Son of God (20); but it will be only a little while and that little while will not be a time of hopeless sorrow. The disciples' sorrow at the departure of their Lord will be like the sorrow of a *woman in travail,* real and poignant but also sorrow which has a goal and a hope. The agony will be followed, and swallowed up, by *joy* over the new life *born into the world* (21). When their Lord returns (from the grave and in His second coming), the *sorrow* of the disciples will be *turned into joy* which no man can take from them (22). All the questions which have perplexed and troubled them will be answered (23; *you will ask me no questions);* all the desires of their heart will be fulfilled by the *Father* who *loves* them who *have loved* Him and *believed* in Him whom the Father has sent (27). The Son will have given them a sonship that can ask of God with a child's freedom and a child's assurance. The disciples will have the strength and courage to endure the *tribulation* which they must endure *in the world,* for they know that they are held securely by Him who has *overcome the world.* (33)

16:20 *Your sorrow will turn into joy.* Cf. 20:20.

16:23 *Ask . . . ask.* The first *ask* means "ask" in the sense of "ask questions, inquire"; the second *ask* is "ask" in the sense of "request."

16:24 *You have asked nothing in my name.* To ask, make a request, in Jesus' name is to ask on the basis of Jesus' completed mission as the Son sent by the Father. Similarly, the Father will give in Jesus' name (23) when He gives to those who have loved and believed in the Son sent by the Father.

16:32 *You will be scattered . . . and leave me alone.* Cf. Mt 26:31 note.

17:1-26 Jesus' Farewell Prayer

17:1-26 Now that *the* supreme *hour* of His life on earth has come, Jesus prays. He prays for Himself (1-5), asking the Father for the promised gift (cf. 12:28) of the glorification through suffering and death, that His own may have *eternal life* in the knowledge of the *only true God* who so loved the world that He gave His only Son for the world's salvation (cf. 3:16), that thus the obedient son, *Jesus Christ,* may *glorify* the Father and then return to His primordial place of glory with the Father. (5)

He prays for His disciples (6-19), the men whom the Father has given Him (6), who have *received* and *believed the words* (8) from the Father and have kept His *word;* the men in whom the Son achieves the glory (10) that is rightly His as the Savior who consecrates Himself as a Sacrifice (19) for their sins. He prays that the Father may preserve them in an alien (16) and hostile (14) world, may *sanctify them in the truth* (17) of His *word* and so equip them to be apostles of the Son sent to save the world. (18)

He prays also for His future disciples, those who shall come to faith in Him through the Word of His witness (20-26). He asks that they *may all be one* (21), *perfectly one* (23), united with one another as Jesus is united with the Father and united with Jesus and the Father, that there may be an unbroken line of valid witnesses (the Son, the Son's disciples, and the disciples' disciples), witnesses to the Father's love which works in and through them all (21, 23). He prays that all those whom the Father has given Him, all who know the Son and have learned from Him God's name, "Father," *may be with* Him to behold His ancient and eternal glory. (24)

17:9 *I am not praying for the world.* Jesus' prayer for the world's salvation is contained in His prayer for His witnesses (21, 23, "that the world may believe . . . may know").

17:11 *Keep them in thy name,* that is, keep them as what they have become by the revelation given in the Son who has manifested God's name to them.

17:12 *That the scripture might be fulfilled.* Cf. 13:18; Ps 41:9.

17:17 *Sanctify them.* Separate them from all evil and make them Thine own, for service to Thee. (Cf. 18)

17:19 *I consecrate myself.* Cf. 10:36, where the action of consecrating is ascribed to the Father; the Son does freely what He owes as obedience to the Father. (Cf. 10:18 note)

17:25 *O righteous Father.* God is righteous both in His judgment on the world that has rejected Him *(not known thee)* and in His glorification of the obedient Son and of those who believe in Him *(know that thou hast sent me).*

18:1—20:31 THE WORD SPEAKS GOD'S GRACE AND TRUTH

18:1—20:31 In the Passion, death, and resurrection of Jesus His disciples behold His glory, the glory of the Good Shepherd who dies for His flock, the glory of the King whose kingdom is not of this world, the glory of the ministering Lord who on the cross commits His mother to the disciple whom He loves, the glory of the Word made flesh in full human reality, who said, "I thirst." It is the glory of the Savior of the world who cried, "It is finished," the glory of the risen Lord of life who breathed on them with creative breath and gave them the Holy Spirit for their apostolic task, the glory of the Lord and God who overwhelmed the stubborn doubt of Thomas and called them blessed who, without seeing, believe.

18:1-11 Jesus went out to meet the onset of the ruler of this world with a resolute, "rise, let us go hence" (14:30,31). His resolution does not fail Him now when He is confronted by the betrayer in the flesh and sees in the friend who ate His bread (13:18) the incarnation of the will of Satan (cf. 13:2, 27). The quiet majesty with which He takes the initiative, goes to meet His captors, questions them (4, 7), and gives Himself into their hands has a shattering effect on them (6). He loves His own to the end; the Good Shepherd goes freely (cf. 4) into death in order that His flock may live (8-9; cf. 10:11). And He remains to the end the obedient Son who cannot but *drink the cup* of suffering *which the Father has given* Him. (11)

18:9 *The word which He had spoken.* Cf. 17:12.

18:10 Only the fourth gospel identifies the wielder of the sword as *Peter* and gives the name of the high priest's slave, *Malchus.*

18:11 *Drink the cup.* For the cup as a symbol of suffering under the punitive judgment of God cf. Mt 20:22 note; 26:39.

18:12-27 The Hearing Before Annas and Peter's Denial

18:12-27 The most remarkable feature of this part of John's narrative is that it practically omits the story of Jesus' trial before the high council of His people (cf., e.g., Mt 26:57-68). The hearing before Annas (12:13; 19-23) is not a trial, and Jesus' appearance before Caiaphas is just mentioned (24). They are hardly more than the background to the story of Peter's denial (15-18; 25-27). The reason for this omission is not far to seek; John has alrady portrayed the "trial" of Jesus before His own people; the record of chs. 7—12 makes clear that they have in effect tried and condemned Him. See the note on 11:1-54, especially the last paragraph.

18:13 *Annas.* See Lk 3:2 note. John continued to call *Annas the high priest* despite the fact that he had been deposed by the Roman governor in the year 15 (15, 19; cf. 22). The office of high priest was by law a lifelong office, and Annas enjoyed great respect and exerted great influence for many years after he had been deposed.

18:14 Cf. 11:49-51.

18:15 *Another disciple.* See 13:23 note.

18:19 *Questioned Jesus about his disciples.* The question was probably designed to incriminate the disciples, so that they too might be prosecuted. Jesus shields them (20-21), as He had shielded them at His arrest in the garden. (8)

18:27 *The cock crowed.* Cf. 13:38.

18:28—19:16 The Trial Before Pilate

18:28—19:16 The disciples, taught by the Spirit who glorifies the Son (16:14), behold the glory of their Lord in His Passion (see note on 18:1—20:31); they behold there too, and just there, the Light of the world; but the Light shines in darkness, and the darkness struggles fiercely, though unsuccessfully, to overcome the Light (1:5). The nation for whom He dies (11:50-51) is in the forefront of that struggle. The nation whose peculiar glory it is that "to them belong . . . the giving of the law" (Ro 9:4) is punctilious in the observance of the lesser matters of the Law (18:22, 28), but uses the Law to rid itself of the Light of the world that exposes its deeds as evil (3:19; 19:7). "Of their race, according to the flesh, is the Christ" (Ro 9:5); yet they choose *Barabbas* the *robber,* in preference to Him (18:40), and deny the anointed King God gave them (19:15), and will *have no king but Caesar.* (19:15)

But it is not only His nation that seeks to kill the King and quench the Light. Judas, who became their willing tool, may have *the greater sin* (19:11), but the Gentile world, too, takes part in the struggle and shares the guilt. Pilate, representative of the Gentile world, holder of a *power* given him *from above* (19:11), chosen to be custodian of God's wrath upon the wrongdoer (cf. Ro 13:4), will not use that power to protect the Man whose innocence he has thrice attested (18:38; 19:4, 6). The divinely appointed guardian of truth and justice shrugs off his responsibility with a skeptical, "What is truth?" and hands over the incarnate grace and truth of God *to be crucified.* (18:38; 19:16)

The *world* united to overcome the Light, and

Pilate spoke better than he knew when he presented the scourged and thorn-crowned King of the Jews, robed in purple, with the words, *Behold the man!* (19:5). He is indeed THE MAN, not the Jew merely, but the Man on whom the sin of mankind is visited, in whom the hope of the world lies hid.

18:28 *The praetorium,* the headquarters of the Roman governor. *That they might not be defiled,* by entering the dwelling of a Gentile. Defilement would exclude them from the celebration of the *passover.* (Cf. 11:55 note)

18:32 *By what death he was to die.* Jesus' prediction that He would be "lifted up" (8:28; 12:32) is fulfilled by His crucifixion, the Roman form of punishment, not by stoning, the Jewish form of punishment for blasphemers.

18:34 Jesus' question determines whether Pilate's inquiry concerning the "King of the Jews" is prompted, like that of the Magi (Mt 2:2), by a religious interest in Him or is merely formal and official. Pilate's reply both here (35) and later (38) makes clear his indifference toward any Messianic claim (except insofar as it might prove a threat to Roman rule) and to the whole world of "truth" (divine revelation) that Jesus represents. He is not "of the truth."

18:36-37 Jesus declares His kingship in terms which a Gentile can understand. He is no king whose followers fight for Him that He may gain and hold a throne; no Roman governor need suspect Him of seditious intent. His kingship lies on another plane altogether; He is come *to bear witness to the truth* of God that sets men free from the lust for being king or making kings.

19:6 *The officers.* The "officers of the Jews" (18:12, 18) are meant.

19:7 *A law,* particularly the law against blasphemy, Lv 24:16.

Made himself the Son of God. Cf. 10:33.

19:11 *Power . . . given you from above.* Cf. Ro 13:1.

He who delivered me, Judas, the instrument of Satan. (13:2, 27)

19:12 *You are not Caesar's friend.* The emperor Tiberius' chronic suspiciousness (there were many trials for sedition and treason during his reign) and Pilate's far-from-unblemished record as governor made this veiled threat a powerful one.

19:14 *The Pavement . . . Gabbatha.* The Pavement could be either a place paved with stones (conspicuous in a city whose streets were largely unpaved) or a place covered with mosaic. The meaning of the Hebrew term *Gabbatha* is uncertain.

19:14 *Preparation for the Passover . . . sixth hour.* The sixth hour is noon; the Preparation for the Passover is, properly, the "eve of the Passover." On the afternoon of the preparation the paschal lambs were slain; Jesus, the true Lamb (1:29; cf. 1 Co. 5:7), gives the OT shadow its substance by dying at the appointed time. (Cf. 19:36 note)

Behold your King! Pilate speaks more truly than he, by his mocking words, intends.

19:17-42 The Crucifixion, Death, and Burial of Jesus

19:17-42 Jesus dies, as He has lived, fulfilling His Father's will according to the Scriptures (24, 28, 36, 37); He dies a real human death, mindful of the parental ties that bind Him to humanity (25-27), suffering human pain (28, *I thirst)* but He dies as the divine Good Shepherd who lays down His life of His own accord (28, *knowing that all was now finished).*

19:22 *What I have written I have written.* Cf. 19. By God's governance of history the stubbornness of the Roman governor, weary of altercations with a people he does not respect and cannot understand, ensures the proclamation of the truth. Nathanael's confession at the beginning of Jesus' ministry finds a strange echo at its close: "You are the King of Israel!" (1:49)

19:24 *To fulfil the scripture.* Cf. Ps 22:18.

19:26 *The disciple whom he loved.* Cf. 13:23 note.

19:28 *To fulfil the scripture.* Cf. Ps 69:21.

19:29 *Hyssop,* a small bushy plant with aromatic leaves. Since the short stalk of this plant seems to be ill adapted to the purpose of bringing the *vinegar* to the lips of the crucified, some scholars have conjectured that the text has suffered in transmission: *hyssopos* has been mistakenly written for a word of similar appearance *(hyssos)* which means javelin.

19:31 *Preparation.* Cf. 19:14 note.

That sabbath was a high day, since it coincided with the Passover.

Legs . . . broken, to ensure a speedy death.

19:34 *Blood and water.* some see here a symbolism pointing to the Lord's Supper and Baptism.

19:35 *He who saw it,* the beloved disciple of v. 26, eyewitness of the events and author of the gospel. (Cf. 21:24)

You, plural, the readers of the gospel.

19:36 *That the scripture might be fulfilled.* The reference is either to the Passover lamb (Ex 12:46; Nm 9:12) or to Ps 34:19-20, which speaks of God's care for the righteous in delivering him out of his afflictions: "He keeps all his bones; not one of them is broken."

19:37 *Another scripture.* Zch. 12:10

20:1-29 The Risen Lord

20:1-29 The disciples are fully assured of the reality of the resurrection; they are to know: "Because I live, you will live also" (14:19). The silent witness of the empty tomb is enough for one of the two disciples to whom it was granted: *He saw and believed* (8). Mary sees the Good Shepherd who "calls his own sheep by name" (10:3, 14), the familiar *Teacher* (16) but already bound for that world whither she cannot follow now (17). To the ten disciples huddled behind shut doors *for fear of the Jews* (19) He manifests Himself as the crucified Victor (20), bestows on them His *peace* (21), and the *Holy Spirit,* who is to be the power of their apostolate (21, *so I send you).* Doubting *Thomas* cannot remain *faithless*

(27) when he beholds the Crucified with the marks of battle and the tokens of victory on His body; believing, *Thomas* bows before Him: *My Lord and my God!*

20:4 *The other disciple.* Cf. 13:23 note.

20:6-7 The orderly disposition of the *linen cloths* and the *napkin* is evidence that this is not the work of grave robbers. (Cf. 13, 15)

20:9 *For as yet they did not know the scriptures, that he must rise from the dead.* Since their minds were not yet opened to understand the Scriptures (in the sense of Lk 24:45-46) as witnessing to Jesus' resurrection, the faith of the "other disciple" (8) is all the more remarkable.

20:17 *My brethren . . . my Father and your Father . . . my God and your God.* Every word expresses the completeness of the atonement wrought by Jesus: "It is finished" indeed. (19:30)

20:20 *The disciples were glad.* Cf. 16:20, 22.

20:23 Cf. Mt 16:19; 18:18.

20:30-31 Conclusion: the Purpose of the Gospel

20:30-31 Cf. Introduction, Par. 1

21:1-15 AFTERWORD: JESUS, PETER, AND THE BELOVED DISCIPLE

21:1-25 The afterword, whether written by John himself or by followers of John (cf. 24, *we know),* records the risen Christ's third manifestation of Himself to His disciples (14; cf. 20:19, 26). Once more, this time in Galilee and amid the everyday occupations of a fisherman, they behold Him in the glory of His gracious Lordship. He admits His own to the fellowship of the common meal (1:14). His forgiving love thrice restores to his apostolic shepherd's task *Simon,* who had denied Him thrice (15-17) and makes him once more Peter, the rock on whom the Christ will build His church (1:42; cf. Mt 16:18). He appoints for Peter the death by which he is to *glorify God* (18-19). He alone determines the fate of *the disciple whom* He *loved* (20-23). It is this disciple, the apostle determined wholly by his Lord, who witnesses to the Word in the written Word, and the men who have come to faith and have found life through that Word (cf. 20:31) *know* (what millions of readers have come to know with unshakable certainty since) *that his testimony is true.* (24)

21:11 *Large fish, a hundred and fifty-three of them.* The number 153, and indeed the whole story of the catch of fish, have often been interpreted allegorically as indicating the worldwide mission of the apostles. But the text itself contains no hint that it is to be understood allegorically, and the most natural explanation of the number 153 would seem to be that there were 153 fish in the net.

21:19 *By what death he was to glorify God,* that is, by martyrdom. Reliable tradition has it that Peter died a martyr's death, probably by crucifixion, in Rome under Nero.

ACTS

INTRODUCTION

Title of the Work

1 "Acts of the Apostles" can hardly be the title given to the second part of his work by Luke himself. An an indication of the content it is inaccurate. Of the apostles only Peter and Paul are really leading figures. John appears a few times in the early chapters and then disappears; James the son of Zebedee appears only as a martyr, with one short sentence devoted to his execution. On the other hand, men who are not apostles play a considerable role in the narrative—Stephen, Philip, Barnabas, Silas, Agabus. Furthermore, if the title were to be understood in the sense suggested by similar works current in antiquity, such as the Acts of Alexander by Callisthenes or the Acts of Hannibal by Sosylus, it could actually be misleading. It would suggest a narrative of human heroism and achievement. Of course the very term "apostle," as defined by Jesus and used by the apostles themselves, should have excluded that idea, for the apostle is by definition nothing of himself and everything by virtue of the commission given him by his Lord. But would Luke have selected a title which even suggested the idea of human greatness? His book tells the story of men only because and insofar as men are instrumental in the growth and triumph of the Word of the Lord. The Book of Acts is to be thought of as the direct continuation of Luke's Gospel, with the exalted Christ as its dominant figure. (Acts 1:1)

Content of the Acts of the Apostles

2 Luke has himself outlined the structure of his work by inserting summarizing statements at six points in it (Acts 6:7; 9:31; 12:24; 16:5; 19:20; 28:31). Each of the units marks a step in the progress of the Word of the Lord on its way from Jerusalem to Rome. It is probably not accidental that the first five of the summarizing statements alternate in stressing the Word (6:7; 12:24; 19:20) and the church (9:31; 16:5), while the last one (28:31) gives the content (kingdom of God; Lordship of Jesus) which makes the Word a creative power that has built and shall build the church. Where the Word is spoken, even though it be by "defeated" men in prison, there God the King, revealed in Jesus the Lord, is gathering the new people of God, the church, which multiplied despite opposition.

OUTLINE

I. 1:1—6:7 The Word of the Lord in Jerusalem

The Spirit-filled apostolic Word creates and sustains in Jerusalem a church which overcomes internal tensions and triumphs and grows despite outside opposition.

Summarizing statement: "And the word of God increased; and the number of the disciples multiplied greatly in Jerusalem, and a great many of the priests were obedient to the faith." (6:7)

II. 6:8—9:31 The Word of the Lord Triumphs over Persecution

The Word goes to Samaria, and the persecutor Saul becomes the Lord's chosen instrument.

Summarizing statement: "So the church throughout all Judea and Galilee and Samaria had peace and was built up; and walking in the fear of the Lord and in the comfort of the Holy Spirit it was multiplied." (9:31)

III. 9:32—12:25 The Word of the Lord Becomes a Light to the Gentiles (cf. Acts 26:23)

Peter, mighty in deed and word, preached the Gospel to the Roman centurion. The Word goes to Antioch in Syria and creates a predominantly Gentile church there (Barnabas and Saul). Peter is rescued "from the hand of Herod and from all that the Jewish people were expecting"; he is preserved to promote the growth of the Word by championing Gentile freedom from the Law (Acts 15:7-11), while the persecuting king is destroyed.

Summarizing statement: "But the word of God grew and multiplied." (12:24)

IV. 13:1—16:5 The Word of the Lord Unites Jew and Gentile in One, Free Church

Paul's first missionary journey; the Judaistic controversy and its resolution at the Jerusalem Council.

Summarizing statement: "So the churches were strengthened in the faith, and they increased in numbers daily." (16:5)

V. 16:6—19:20 The Word of the Lord Goes in Conflict and Triumph to Macedonia, Achaia, and Asia

The second and third missionary journeys of Paul.

Summarizing statement: "So the word of the Lord grew and prevailed mightily." (19:20)

VI. 19:21—28:31 The Power of the Word of the Lord Made Perfect in Weakness

Paul the prisoner witnesses before "rulers and authorities" (Lk 12:11) and brings his Gospel to Rome.

Summarizing statement: "Preaching the kingdom of God and teaching about the Lord Jesus Christ quite openly and unhindered." (28:31)

Purpose of Acts

3 It may be, as some scholars have supposed, that the purpose of Acts is to make plain to the Roman world that Christianity is no treasonable, subversive movement but is innocent of any politically dangerous intent; its preachers may be "turning the world upside down" (Acts 17:6), but not in any sense that threatens the stability of the empire. It has often been pointed out that Luke repeatedly notes that Roman officials find Christianity politically innocuous (e.g., Acts 18:14-15; 23:29; 25:18-19; 26:32). But that purpose is at most a secondary one. The prime intent of the work is religious. It portrays the impact of the risen and exalted Christ on the wide world. The Christ confronts men

in the inspired Word of the messengers whom He Himself has chosen. He confronts all sorts and conditions of men—Jews, Samaritans, Greeks, Romans, the high and the lowly, the king and the cripple, suave metropolitan philosophers and superstitious, excitable louts of the hinterland. He confronts them all with the gracious claim of His saving Lordship. Whether the response be the submission of faith or the resistance of unbelief or the mockery of skepticism, He is the Lord before whom the ways of men divide, the Christ who is gathering the new people of God from among all the nations of the earth.

4. The book does not pretend to be a history of the first church or even a history of early missions; it would be woefully incomplete as either of the two. It is the continuation of the story of the Christ and can therefore be as selective in recording the facts of history as the Gospel itself. Of all the ways which the Gospel went, Luke selects just one, the high road to Rome. And even that segment of the total history of missions is not fully portrayed. There are, for instance, large gaps in the record of the career of Paul; both his 2-year ministry at Corinth and his 3-year ministry at Ephesus are merely illustrated by means of typical incidents rather than chronicled. The whole work illustrates rather than chronicles the course of the Word that proclaims and presents the Christ. Luke selects incidents and actions that illumine and bring out in clear outline the impact of that Word on men, the tensions and conflicts that ensue when the Word of the Lord is heard, and the triumphant progress of that Word despite tensions and conflicts.

5 If we understand the book thus on its own terms, the ending no longer appears strange or weak. Many have found the ending puzzling and inadequate: Why is the outcome of Paul's trial not told? Either his release or martyrdom would seem to constitute a more fitting conclusion to the work than the one Luke has seen fit to give it. Some scholars have suggested that Luke perhaps intended to add a third volume to his work, one that would round out and conclude the story by recounting Paul's release, his voyage to Spain, and his martyr's death. But there is no real indication that Luke intended such a continuation of his book; neither is the suggestion very plausible that Luke did not record the outcome of Paul's trial because the outcome was martyrdom, and he did not wish to conclude his account of the victorious Gospel on a sad and negative note. To judge from Luke's account of the martyrdom of Stephen (Acts 7:54-60) and from Paul's own attitude toward martyrdom as recorded by Luke (Acts 20:24; 21:13), neither Luke or Paul looked on martyrdom as something negative and depressing.

6 The fact is that the present ending makes sense both as the conclusion of Acts and as the conclusion of the two-part work. It is not merely the end but the conclusion of Acts; the goal pointed to in Acts 1:8 has been reached: the Gospel is being proclaimed in Rome, the capital of the world; it has stepped through the door that opens into all the world. That is the fact that counts; before it any man's fate, even Paul's, pales into insignificance. And the present ending is a meaningful conclusion to the whole work. When Jesus "began to do and to teach" in His own city Nazareth, He offered His people God's free forgiveness on the basis of a word from Isaiah (Lk 4:18-21). He had met with objection and resistance from His own people even then (Lk 4:22-23, 28-30). And He had hinted that the Word they were rejecting would go to the Gentiles (Lk 4:24-27). Jesus' prediction is now being fulfilled; the Jews of Rome are following the course set by the Jews of Galilee and Jerusalem and the cities of Asia and Macedonia and Achaia. They are rejecting the proffered good news of God. The prophet Isaiah is heard once more, this time uttering words of fearful judgment on a people who will not hear (Acts 28:25-27). But God's purposes are being worked out nevertheless: "This salvation of God has been sent to the Gentiles; they will listen." (Acts 28:28)

1:1—6:7 THE WORD OF THE LORD IN JERUSALEM

1:1—6:7 The Spirit-filled apostolic Word, spoken by men under the command and promise of the Lord Jesus (1:8), creates and sustains in Jerusalem a church which overcomes internal tensions and triumphs and grows despite outside opposition.

1:1-11 The Link with Luke, the 40 Days, the Ascension

1:1-11 The first verse clearly marks Acts as the continuation of Luke's Gospel; the gospel is referred to as the *first book, Theophilus* is addressed again as at the beginning of the gospel (Lk 1:1-4), and the words *Jesus began to do and teach* imply that this second volume will recount what Jesus will continue to do and teach by His Spirit through His apostles. This continuity with the gospel is marked also in the account of the 40 days (1:2-5), which harks back to the *passion* (3) and portrays Jesus as continuing His teaching of the *kingdom of God,* the theme of His teaching in the gospel (e.g., 4:43; 8:1; 9:2, 11; 11:20). At the Ascension the *cloud* which receives Jesus recalls the cloud at the Transfiguration in the gospel (Lk 9:34). And the words of the *two men . . .* in *white robes* (10) maintain the link with the gospel history *(Men of Galilee . . . will come in the same way,* 11).

1:4 *The promise of the Father,* the promised Holy Spirit. (Cf. Lk 24:49; Jn 14:16, 26; 15:26)

1:7-8 Jesus turns the thoughts of His disciples away from the idea of a reign in Israel toward a ministry by the power of the Spirit in the wide world.

1:8 *Jerusalem . . . Judea . . . Samaria . . . end of the earth.* These stages of the progress of the Gospel indicate the structure of Acts. (Cf. Introduction)

1:12-14 The Waiting Disciples

1:12-14 The example and teaching of Jesus (cf. Introduction to Luke's Gospel, par. 12) had made of His disciples men of prayer; *with one accord devoted themselves to prayer.* (14)

1:12 *Mount called Olivet,* the Mount of Olives. *A sabbath day's journey,* the distance a pious Jew may travel on the Sabbath, about 800 yards.

1:14 *Mary.* The last mention of the mother of our Lord in the NT.

1:15-26 The Enrollment of Matthias Among the Apostles

1:15-26 When Jesus appointed the 12 apostles (Lk 6:13), He was offering His Messianic grace and laying His Messianic claim to the 12 tribes, to ALL Israel. After Jesus' intercession for the people who crucified Him (Lk 23:34), that offer and claim is to be stated anew. Therefore Judas *must* be replaced (22); God wills that all Israel be confronted with the crucified and risen Christ (cf. 2:36; 3:25-26) and so be offered His forgiveness anew. (Cf. Lk 24:47)

1:16 *Mouth of David,* in the Psalter. Cf. 20 *(book of Psalms).*

1:18-19 Cf. Mt 27:3-10.

1:20 Cf. Ps 69:25; 109:8.

1:22 *The baptism of John* marks the beginning of the Gospel record in all the evangelists.

1:26 *They cast lots.* The casting of lots to determine the will of God is an OT provision; cf., e.g., Lv 16:8-10. This is the last instance of it in the Bible. Notice that it is BEFORE Pentecost.

2:1-13 Pentecost

2:1-13 The church follows in the footsteps of the church's Lord. When Jesus emerged from Nazareth to undertake His public ministry in Israel (Lk 3:23), He was prepared and heralded for that ministry by a manifest, "dramatic" bestowal of the Holy Spirit descending upon Him "in bodily form, as a dove" (Lk 3:22). So His church, emerging from the prayerful quiet of the upper room (Acts 1:13-14), was prepared by a miraculous bestowal of the Spirit, manifested in the power of wind and fire (2:2-3), for a ministry of witness in word (2:14-36, 38-40) and deed. (2:42-47)

2:1 *Pentecost.* The term means "fiftieth" (day) and designates the Feast of Weeks celebrated at the end of the grain harvest seven weeks after the Passover (Lv 23:15; Dt 16:9). This feast of grateful recognition of the goodness of the Creator drew Jewish pilgrims from all over the world to Jerusalem. (Cf. 9-11)

2:2-3 *Like the rush . . . as of fire.* The mysterious and mighty manifestation of the Spirit is recorded in language that is suggestive rather than descriptive.

2:4 *Speak in other tongues.* Cf. 2:6, 8, 11. The curse of Babel is canceled (Gn 11:7, 9); the church is enabled by the Spirit to speak to men of all nations in their own tongues and will become the new people of God gathered out of all nations, God's harvest of a new mankind united in Christ.

2:12-13 The history of the church is the continuation of that of Jesus (cf. 1:1-11 note); again there is "a division among the Jews because of these words" (Jn 10:19-21). Some are led to ask and seek, others mock.

2:14-47 Witness in Word and Deed

2:14-47 "Beginning with . . . scripture he told . . . the good news of Jesus" (Acts 8:35). The words with which Luke describes Philip's witness to the Ethiopian eunuch are an apt characterization of all NT proclamation. (Cf. Jesus' proclamation in Nazareth, Lk 4:16-21.) Peter interprets the Pentecost miracle as the fulfillment of the OT prophecy of Joel which promised the outpouring of the Spirit *upon all flesh* (17) for the last days (Jl 2:28-32). That outpouring would usher in the day of God's final reckoning, the *day of the Lord . . . great and manifest* (20). On that day only he who *calls on the name of the Lord shall be saved* (21). And that Lord, Peter proclaims, is none other than *Jesus of Nazareth,* whom God attested to His people *with mighty works and wonders and signs* (22), whom *God raised up,* vindicated and glorified, though His people *crucified* Him (32, 36). He is the Giver of the Spirit; He is the Lord who will judge; He is the *Lord and Christ* on whose name men must call in order to be saved from *this crooked generation* of men who have rejected Him. (40)

2:15 *The third hour,* about 9 a.m., too early for any but the most dissolute to be *drunk.* The charge is dismissed as the absurdity it is, rather than rebutted.

2:22-36 This part of Peter's sermon is concerned to show that Jesus is the *Lord* of v. 25, that His crucifixion was not an untoward accident but a part of God's *definite plan* for His Servant (23), that God reversed the verdict of men upon Him by raising Him from the dead, as *David* had foreseen and foretold (Ps 16:8-11; Acts 2:25-34), that David's greater Son has indeed been manifested *(made,* 36) as *both Lord and Christ* by God Himself.

2:30 *God had sworn an oath.* Ps 132:11.

2:34 Ps 110:1 is added to the witness of Ps 16 to indicate that Jesus' resurrection signified not only survival but Lordship and the glory of being enthroned with God; Jesus *did* (what could not be said of the speaker of the psalm) . . . *ascend into the heavens,* there to reign and triumph.

2:39 *Whom the Lord our God calls.* When men "call on the name of the Lord" (12), that is the result of God's effectual calling to them.

2:41-47 The operation of the Spirit transformed not only the disciples' crude Galilean speech (7) but their whole inner life, making it a life centered in the apostles' inspired *teaching,* a life of *fellowship* at the Table of their Lord *(breaking of bread)* and of *prayer,* a new life marked by an active communal love (44-45) and a high-hearted *(glad and generous hearts,* 46) adoration of God. Thus their works reinforced the witness of their words; men sensed the presence of the divine among them, *and fear came upon every soul* (43); the whole demeanor of the disciples among their people, whether in the public worship in the *temple* (46) or *in their homes* (46), was such that it won them *favor with all the people* (47), and the Lord used it to win men (47, *added to their number).*

3:1—4:31 Healing the Lame Beggar and Conflict with Authorities

3:1—4:31 The apostles Peter and John did what they as apostles of Christ had to do; they were poor, yet equipped by Christ to make many rich (2 Co 6:10). To the lame beggar at the Beautiful Gate of the temple they gave the riches of Christ's healing compassion, so that *leaping up,* he *walked* (3:8). They spoke—as they had to speak—as witnesses of Christ in Jerusalem (1:8); they dared not let this deed of God's servant Jesus be attributed to their *own power or piety* (3:12). The apostle of Christ must point men away from himself *to the God of Abraham and of Isaac and of Jacob* and *his servant Jesus* (3:13). It was their simple fidelity to the charge given them by their Lord that led to their first collision with the Jewish authorities, not any provocative manifesto issued in the name of the rejected Messiah nor any planned program of opposition to Judaism. In fact the apostles (like their Lord before them) went all the way to seek and find the lost sheep of the house of Israel where they lived. They went to Israel's temple at the appointed hour to pray (3:1), they spoke in the language of Israel's sacred book, in terms of the *God of Abraham and of Isaac and of Jacob* (3:13), in terms of the *servant* whose fate and significance (for Israel and all nations) Isaiah had foretold (3:13, 26), in terms of *Moses'* promise of a *prophet* like himself (Dt 18:15-16, 23), One whose word would spell weal or woe to every soul as it was accepted or rejected, in terms of God's *covenant* with *Abraham* with its promise of blessing for *all the families of the earth* (3:25; Gn 22:18). They spoke of God's amnesty for His people's *wickedness* (3:26). And when they were called to account by the high court of their people (4:5), they spoke simply as the *Holy Spirit* (4:8) prompted them, silent neither concerning the guilt of those who had *crucified Jesus Christ of Nazareth* (4:10) nor concerning the *salvation* (4:12) which God was offering His people, in spite of all, in the name of the Crucified (4:12). Moreover, in the prayer and praise with which the church responded to the persecution at the hands of their fellow Jews there is no trace of any vengeful spirit. These men of the church bow before the Creator and Lord of history (4:23-26), who guides the actions of kings, governors, and nations to do what God's *hand* and *plan had predestined to take place* (4:27-28; cf. Ps 2:1-2). They commit their future to God's almighty hand *(look upon their threats,* 4:29), but they do not pray for revenge; they ask for boldness in their speech and for the gift of healing in their deeds (4:29-30). They go in the meek way of the *servant* Jesus and are confirmed in this course by a renewed outpouring of the Holy Spirit and a clear manifestation of the Spirit's presence among them *(the place . . . was shaken,* 4:31).

If the men of Israel were to suffer the doom of being hardened in their sin, as Isaiah had threatened (cf. Acts 28:26-27), and so leave the Gentiles to inherit the promised salvation of God, the guilt was Israel's, not the apostles' or their Lord's. *They* had spoken God's final offer of salvation to the full, inspired and moved by the Spirit.

3:1 *Hour of prayer . . . the ninth hour.* The hour of prayer coincided with the offering of the two daily sacrifices, early in the morning and at the ninth hour. (3 p.m.)

3:2 *Beautiful,* probably to be identified with an Eastern gate which a contemporary source describes as made of Corinthian bronze and "far exceeding in value those plated with silver and set in gold."

3:11 *Portico called Solomon's.* Cf. Jn 10:23. This portico soon became a regular gathering place for the Christians in the early days at Jerusalem. (Cf. 5:12)

3:14 *Righteous One.* Cf. Is 53:11; Acts 7:52; 22:14; Ja 5:6; 1 Jn 2:1.

3:17 *You acted in ignorance.* Cf. Lk 23:34; 1 Ti 1:13. For the opposite cf. Heb 10:26, "If we sin deliberately after receiving the knowledge of the truth," and Heb 6:4-6 note.

3:25 *Sons of the prophets and of the covenant,* destined to inherit the promise spoken by the prophets and the blessing promised by the covenant. (Cf. 26)

3:26 *To you first, to bless you.* Cf. Ro 1:16.

4:1-2 The *Sadducees,* members of the party in which the priestly aristocracy was most influential, would naturally be in the forefront of opposition to Christianity for two reasons: (1) They sought to remain on good terms with the Romans and therefore looked with suspicion on any Messianic movement which might bring on Roman intervention and put an end to their privileged priestly position (cf. Jn 11:48). (2) They denied the resurrection of the dead in principle (cf. Mt 22:23; Lk 20:27; Acts 23:8). When the Christians proclaimed the resurrection of the dead in Jesus (a Messianic "Pretender" whom the Romans had executed!), they were politically unacceptable and theologically offensive to the Sadducees.

4:1 The *captain of the temple,* an officer in charge of the temple guard (composed of Levites) and responsible for preserving order in the temple. He was second in authority only to the high priest. (Cf. 5:24, 26)

4:6 *Annas* and *Caiaphas.* Although Annas had been deposed from the high priesthood about A. D. 15, he continued to be so influential during the high priesthood of his sons and his son-in-law Caiaphas (cf. Jn 18:13) that he was regarded as a virtual high priest, as here. Cf. Lk 3:2, where his name is coupled with that of Caiaphas in dating the beginning of the Baptist's ministry.

John and *Alexander* cannot be identified.

4:9 *Examined . . . concerning a good deed.* Cf. the words of Jesus in Jn 10:31.

4:11 Cf. Mt 21:42, where Jesus cites Ps 118:22 to interpret His mission and its significance in the same sense.

4:25-26 Ps 2:1-2.

4:27 *Herod.* Cf. Lk 23:6-12.

4:32—6:7 "All the Words of This Life"

4:32—6:7 The angel of the Lord released the imprisoned apostles in order that they might *go and stand in the temple and speak to the people all the words of this Life* (5:20), the new life made possible by the resurrection of Jesus from the dead. Those words by the power of the Spirit create the life of God's new world in the midst of the old; they are words to be lived and words that must be spoken (4:20). In the midst of the old world they can be lived and spoken only amid a constant struggle. (Paul calls on Christians to put on the "armor of light" in order to live "as in the day," Ro 13:12-13.)

The *words of this Life* created in the young church that unanimity of *heart and soul* (4:32) which the Spirit inspires, a unanimity that did not remain sentiment and theory; it expressed itself in the sacrificial giving of *lands and houses* for the needs of the community—*they had everything in common* (4:32). But the church had not only the encouragement of the example of a *Barnabas* (4:36-37), rightly named *Son of encouragement;* the church had to endure the shock of seeing an *Ananias* and a *Sapphira* attempting the fearful blasphemy of lying to the Holy Spirit and of putting His omniscient majesty to the test (5:3, 9). The church had to endure the salutary but shattering experience of the *great fear* that *came upon the whole church and upon all who heard of these things* (5:11) when God's judgment laid the blasphemers dead at their feet (5:1-11). The *words of this Life* become "a fragrance of death" (2 Co 2:16) to those who will not bow before them.

The Word of life had to be spoken; and the apostles spoke it so vigorously that their Sadducee opponents had reason to complain that the apostles had *filled Jerusalem with their teaching* (5:28). The disciples' prayer that God would stretch out His hand to heal and do signs and wonders through the name of His holy Servant Jesus (4:30) was heard. So strongly did God reinforce their words with the many signs and wonders done by the hands of the apostles that the people *held them in high honor* (5:13). But they did not escape renewed persecution; and though officialdom dealt cautiously with them (5:26), the new hearing before the council (5:27) confronted the apostles with Sadducees so *enraged* that they *wanted to kill them* (5:33); only the prudent words of the Pharisaic teacher of the Law, Gamaliel (5:34-39), restrained them so far that they were content, for the time being, with a renewed enjoinder to silence and a flogging (5:40) before releasing the apostles.

Threats and flogging could not silence the inspired witnesses to *Jesus as the Christ* (5:42); but the apostles' devotion to their prime task of *prayer and . . . ministry of the word* (6:4) was impeded, or at least threatened, by an internal dissension concerning the *daily distribution* of support to the widows (6:1); but God gave the church men *full of the Spirit and of wisdom* (6:3) so that *the words of this Life* could be both lived and proclaimed with no confusion of priorities. Luke can look back on the checkered history of the Word in Jerusalem with the calm and confident words: *The word of God increased; and the number of the disciples multiplied greatly.* (6:7)

4:36 *Barnabas,* first mentioned here, is a telling example of the validity of Jesus' law: "To him who has will more be given, and he will have abundance" (Mt 13:12). He has "the words of this Life" and accepts the claim these words make on him, sharing actively in the life of the church. And to him more is given. He takes the initiative in binding Paul (Saul) and the Jerusalem church together (9:27); he is privileged to be the emissary of the Jerusalem church to the new Gentile church in Antioch (11:22-23); he is associated with Paul in administering the charity of Gentile Antioch toward Judaic Jerusalem (11:30; 12:25) and in Paul's first missionary thrust into the Gentile world (Acts 13—15). Paul's mention of him in 1 Co 9:6 shows that he remained throughout his richly blessed ministry the same selfless, generous man whom we meet here, "a good man, full of the Holy Spirit and of faith," as Luke characterizes him in 11:24.

Son of encouragement. How this meaning is derived from the name Barnabas is not clear. It was probably his gift of encouraging speech that earned him the name. (The word translated "exhorted" in 11:23 can also be translated "encouraged.")

5:4 These words show how completely voluntary the sharing of property was. The term "Christian communism," sometimes applied to this aspect of the life of the Jerusalem church, is at best misleading.

5:12 *Solomon's Portico.* Cf. 3:11.

5:17 *Sadducees.* Cf. 4:1-2 note.

5:21 *Senate,* another name for the supreme council (Sanhedrin) composed of high priests, elders, and scribes. (Cf. 4:15)

5:24 *Captain of the temple.* Cf. 4:1 note.

5:26 *Stoned by the people.* Stoning was the punishment appointed for blasphemy (Lv 24:15-16). The people would construe an attack on men so signally distinguished by marks of God's favor (cf. 12) and characterized by sanctity of life as a blasphemous act.

5:30 *Hanging him on a tree.* The OT language (Dt 21:22-23) recalls the fact that one thus executed was considered to be cursed by God. (Cf. 1 Co 12:3)

5:31-32 *We are witnesses . . . and so is the Holy Spirit.* Cf. Jn 15:26-27. Any man with eyes and ears could have been a witness to Jesus' crucifixion; only men endowed with the *Spirit* could testify that the Crucified is *Leader and Savior* in whom God offers *Israel repentance* and *forgiveness of sins.*

5:34 *Gamaliel,* renowned and long-remembered *teacher of the law,* referred to by Paul as his teacher in 22:3. For the differences in teaching and temper (and consequently in their attitude toward Christianity) between Sadducee and Pharisee cf. 23:6-10.

5:36 *Theudas,* otherwise unknown. A Theudas mentioned by the Jewish historian Josephus as a false messiah arose some years after (A. D. 44) the events here recorded by Luke.

5:37 *Judas the Galilean,* leader of a rebellion against Rome when the Roman legate stated Rome's claim to lordship over Israel in drastic terms by ordering a *census* (for purposes of taxation) taken. Judas and his followers found in this an intolerable conflict with God's own lordship over His people. His followers were later known as Zealots. Cf. Lk 6:15; Acts 1:13; for the census cf. Lk 2:1-2 note.

5:41 *Rejoicing . . . suffer dishonor.* Cf. Lk 6:22-23.

6:5 The names indicate that the seven chosen to supervise the charitable work were Hellenists (6:1); one of them was not a born Jew but a convert to Judaism *(proselyte).*

6:7 This is the first of six summarizing statements (cf. 9:31; 12:24; 16:5; 19:20; 28:31) with which Luke indicates the plan, or pattern, of his history. (Cf. Introduction, par. 2)

6:8—9:31 THE WORD OF THE LORD TRIUMPHS OVER PERSECUTION

6:8—9:31 Persecution could not halt the progress of the Word in Jerusalem (cf. 6:7). The Word sped on and triumphed over and through persecution. Neither could persecution halt the march of the Word from Jerusalem to Samaria and the Gentile world. Three men are prominent in that movement: Stephen (6:8—8:2), Philip (8:4-40), and Saul (Paul, 9:1-30). Through Stephen, one of the seven (6:1-6), the line of division between Christianity and Judaism was sharply drawn, and it was through him that persecution broke out, not only on the apostles but on the whole church. The persecution that scattered the church also scattered abroad the Gospel. Philip, another of the seven (6:5), escaped from the jurisdiction of the Jerusalem authorities into Samaria and planted the Gospel there; and it was Philip who baptized an Ethiopian eunuch, excluded from the ancient people of God both because he was a Gentile and because he was a eunuch (Dt 23:1). So the promise of Is 56:3-5 and the prayer of Ps 68:31 were fulfilled in this foreigner, and the universally inclusive character of the new people of God found an unforgettable expression. The third man involved in this stage of the progress of the Word was Saul, the faithful Pharisee and zealous devotee of Judaic tradition (cf. Gl 1:14) who spearheaded the new persecution of the church and carried it beyond Jerusalem to Damascus (9:2). The light that broke on Saul near Damascus, when the Lord laid claim to His chosen instrument (9:15), was destined to break through Saul the persecutor turned Paul the apostle (cf. 13:9 note) on the whole Gentile world. (26:23)

6:8 *Full of grace and power.* Cf. 6:3, 6, 10. The seven were never intended to be narrow specialists in welfare work.

6:9 *Synagogue of the Freedmen.* Jerusalem had literally hundreds of synagogs at this time, some of which were designed to serve special national or linguistic groups. The *Freedmen* were evidently Jewish men who had been Roman captives or sons of such captives and had been liberated. They would naturally be Greek-speaking Jews rather than "Hebrews" (6:1), and the synagog named after them would be one in which the Greek language was used (this would hold also of the synagogs of the *Cyrenians, Alexandrians, those from Cilicia and Asia*—if indeed we are to think of them as separate synagogs; perhaps one synagog served all these Greek-speaking groups). Such men would naturally carry on their dispute with a Greek-speaking Jew like Stephen.

6:11-14 Cf. Lk 23:1-2. Luke points up the parallel between the trial of Stephen and that of Jesus. (Cf. Mt 26:59-66)

7:1-53 Stephen's defense, apparently a mere survey of the history of Israel, is in fact a pointed answer to the charges brought against him (6:11-14). His narrative, based on OT Scriptures, makes plain that the *God of glory* (2; cf. Ps 29, esp. v. 3) works where He wills, independent of any "holy place," including the temple. He performed His mighty acts in distant and "unholy" lands, calling Abraham in *Mesopotamia* (2), making *holy ground* of a spot in the *wilderness of Mount Sinai* when He appeared to Moses (30-33), performing signs and wonders through Moses *in Egypt and at the Red Sea and in the wilderness* (36). All through the decisive, foundation-laying portion of its history Israel had no temple (44); and after Solomon had built a house for Israel's God (47), Isaiah spoke the Word of the Lord which declared that no house could contain the Creator of heaven and earth (48-50; Is 66:1-2). The temple could not be the ultimate expression of God's presence among His people; Judaic zeal for the temple is branded by Scripture itself as fanatical and misplaced, and Israel's fury at any doubt cast on its permanence is not an expression of holy zeal.

The record of Israel is not a record of holy zeal for what is God's; rather it is a record of rebellion and apostasy. The nation which betrayed Joseph (9), rejected and disobeyed Moses (35, 39), turned from the living God to idols (40-43), persecuted the prophets (52), killed the men of God *who announced beforehand the coming of the Righteous One*, the Christ (52), *betrayed and murdered* the Righteous One when He appeared (52), a nation that *did not keep* the Law for which they profess such zeal (53)—how dare they crown their persistent resistance to the Holy Spirit (51) by attempting to silence the Spirit who speaks in Stephen (cf. 6:10)? When they stop their ears to evade the force of Stephen's words, that is of a piece with the fact that they have stopped their ears to the voice of the Law itself, which pointed beyond itself, beyond Moses to the Prophet promised for latter days. (37; cf. 3:22-23; Dt 18:15, 18)

7:42-43 Cf. Amos 5:25-27, quoted freely.

7:56 *Son of man,* Jesus' most characteristic self-designation, occurs some 80 times in the gospels but only here, on the lips of the first martyr, outside the gospels.

7:59-60 Stephen prays to his Lord (Jesus), as Jesus had prayed to the Father. (Cf. Lk 23:46; 23:34)

8:1 *Saul was consenting to his death.* Cf. 22:19-20.

Except the apostles. The apostles probably felt bound to remain in Jerusalem, where their first duty lay; as "Hebrews" (6:1) they had less to fear than men like Stephen and Philip from an outbreak directed primarily at "Hellenists." The men of the NT neither fear martyrdom nor seek it.

Samaria. Cf. 1:8. The second stage of the church's witness as foretold by Jesus is now reached.

8:9-24 *Simon.* Later generations wove many legends about the figure of Simon, but for Luke the point seems to be that this is the first of a series of confrontations between Christianity and the world of pagan *magic.* (9; cf. 13:6-12; 16:16-18; 19:11-20)

8:20 *Obtain the gift of God with money.* The difference between the world of magic with its murky self-seeking and the world of the Gospel is sharply illumined by this statement. Witnesses to the Christ not only receive but also give "without pay." (Mt 10:8)

8:23 *Gall of bitterness . . . bond of iniquity.* To Peter's enlightened vision the man whom blind superstition accepted as "somebody great" (9) and hailed as "that power of God which is called Great" (10) appears as the victim of the bitter poison and enslaving power of sin.

8:27 *Minister,* a court official *in charge of* the queen's treasury. *(Candace* is a title rather than a proper name.) His visit to Jerusalem and his interest in the OT indicate that he was in some sense a proselyte to Judaism.

8:32-33 Cf. Is 53:7-8, a prophecy of Jesus, the Suffering Servant who suffers vicariously for the sins of many.

8:40 *Philip was found at Azotus.* The vagueness of the language reflects the mysteriousness of the Spirit's action. (39)

9:1-19 For the conversion of Saul cf. 22:3-21; 26:9-20; Gl 1:13-17.

9:2 *The Way.* This designation of Christianity is found only in Acts (19:9, 23; 22:4; 24:14, 22) as a name applied by Christians to themselves (cf. 24:14). The origin of the term remains obscure.

9:4 *Persecute me.* Whosoever persecutes the church, the body of Christ, persecutes the Head of the church, Christ.

9:10 *Here I am.* The response implies a willingness to obey the voice heard in the vision. (Cf. Gn 22:1, 7, 11; 1 Sm 3:4; Is 6:8)

9:15 *To carry my name.* Cf. Paul's own words, Ro 15:20.

9:23-25 Cf. 2 Co 11:32-33.

9:31 *Peace . . . built up . . . multiplied.* This calm doxology for triumph through persecution is the second of Luke's six summarizing conclusions marking stages in the progress of the Gospel from Jerusalem to Rome. (Cf. Introduction, par. 2)

9:32—12:25 THE WORD OF THE LORD A LIGHT TO THE GENTILES

9:32—12:25 Luke's record has already made it plain that the living and active Word could not be contained in Jerusalem; it had to break forth and begin its conquering progress through the world, in Samaria and beyond. As subsequent events were to show (e.g., ch. 15), the transition of the Word from the Judaic to the Gentile world would be fraught with the danger to the church that the admission of Gentiles would cause a cleavage between Judaic and Gentile

Christianity. This section of Acts (9:32—12:25) reveals how the Lord of the church moved to avert that danger as He dealt with His servants Peter, Barnabas, and Saul (Paul) and with His new people in Jerusalem. Peter, mighty in word and deed (9:32-43), is divinely taught to overcome his Judaic exclusiveness (10:9-29); as he is moved to bring the Gospel to the Gentile Roman centurion Cornelius he sees the wideness of God's mercy with new eyes and associates freely with men whom he had previously considered unclean (10:34-35); Barnabas the Levite (4:36) is sent by the Jerusalem church to Antioch in Syria, where the Word had called into being a predominantly Gentile church (11:20-21); he rejoiced (11:23) at the grace of God which united Antioch and Jerusalem, Gentile and Jew, in one new people of God. And through Barnabas, that *good man full of the Holy Spirit and of faith* (11:24), Saul is drawn into the work among the Gentiles in Antioch. The bond established between Gentile and Judaic Christians by the sending of Barnabas to Antioch is further strengthened when the Gentile Christians of Antioch are moved to respond to the need of Judaic Christians in Jerusalem and send help by the hand of Barnabas and Saul (11:27-30; 12:25). Palestinian Christians learned that an accommodation with Judaism was not to be hoped for. Judaism spoke a hard no to the Gospel by its approval of Herod's action in executing the apostle James and imprisoning Peter (12:1-3). James is not replaced by a new apostle, as Judas was at the beginning (1:15-26 note); the 12 tribes have heard, but in vain, the witness of the 12 messengers of Jesus. But Peter is rescued *from the hand of Herod and from all that the Jewish people were expecting* (12:11) to continue God's offer of grace to "a disobedient and contrary people" (Ro 10:21; cf. Gl 2:7, 9) and to become the champion of Gentile freedom from the Law (Acts 15:7-11), while the judgment of God strikes the persecuting king. (12:20-23)

9:34 *Jesus Christ heals you.* These words are the perfect brief interpretation of the nature of the mighty deeds wrought by the apostles. (Cf. Ro 15:18-19)

10:1 *Italian Cohort.* A cohort, the tenth part of a legion, numbered 600 men or more, with auxiliary calvary in addition. The name *Italian* indicates that the troops had been mustered in Italy and were probably Roman citizens.

10:2 As often in Acts (10:22, 35; 16:14; 17:4, 17), the words used to describe Cornelius indicate a Gentile who has been drawn to Judaism and has in some sense been "converted" to the Jewish faith. They are frequently the most receptive hearers of the Gospel. The term "worshiper" (18:7) is also found in this sense. Cornelius gave generous help to the Jewish people.

10:4 *Common or unclean.* The two words are synonyms, designating foods prohibited by the Law.

10:25-26 Cf. 3:12; 14:14-15. The apostles are selfless men and consistently refuse to accept any honor due their Lord, in complete antithesis to the human tendency as seen, for instance, in Herod. (12:22)

11:2 *The circumcision party,* those Judaic Christians who insisted that Gentiles could come into the new people of God only via Judaism, i.e., by submitting to circumcision and the law of Moses. (Cf. 15:1, 5; Gl 2:11-12)

11:8 *Common or unclean.* Cf. 10:14 note.

11:17 Cf. 15:7-8.

11:18 *They were silenced,* not necessarily convinced, a hint that the objection advanced by the circumcision party (11:2) would be heard again. (Cf. 15:1, 5)

11:22 The Jerusalem church continues the practice begun in Samaria (8:14-17) of establishing and fostering solidarity between the old and the new churches.

11:26 *For the first time called Christians.* The term "Christian" was first applied to the followers of Jesus by outsiders; in all three NT occurrences the term is either used by outsiders (here and 26:28) or reflects their attitude. (1 Ptr 4:16)

11:28 *Claudius,* Roman emperor A.D. 41—54.

12:1 *Herod the king.* Herod Agrippa I, grandson of Herod the Great, was reared in Rome, where he found friends among members of the Imperial family. Through the favor of various Roman emperors he greatly expanded his territory until it practically equaled that of his grandfather, Herod the Great. At the same time he sought and won the favor of his subjects by presenting himself to them as devotee and champion of Judaism. His willingness to accept divine honors, after the manner of pagan rulers (12:22), indicates that his Judaism was more of the surface than of the substance.

12:3 *Days of Unleavened Bread,* the seven days immediately following and closely associated with the Passover. (Ex 12:8; 13:3-10)

12:12 *John . . . Mark.* Cf. Introduction to Mark's Gospel.

12:17 *James,* the brother of the Lord, appears here as the acknowledged leader of the Jerusalem church. (Cf. Gl 1:19; 2:9, 12; and Introduction to Letter of James)

12:24 The third of Luke's summarizing statements (cf. Introduction, par. 2). In spite of internal tensions and outside persecution, *the word of God grew and multiplied.*

12:25 Cf. 11:27-30.

13:1—16:5 THE WORD OF THE LORD UNITES JEW AND GENTILE

13:1—16:5 Paul's first missionary journey (chs. 13—14), the Judaistic controversy and its resolution at the Jerusalem Council (ch 15). See Introduction to Galatians.

13:2 *Set apart.* The verb used suggests the idea of consecration for a particular task. (Cf. Ro 1:1)

13:5 *John.* Cf. 12:12 note and Introduction to Mark's Gospel.

13:8 *Magician.* Cf. 8:9-24.

That is the meaning of his name. The explanatory note is not clear; Bar-Jesus (6) does not mean "magician," and that meaning can be given to *Elymas* only by indirect and unconvincing ways. Perhaps all that Luke intends to say is that the magician had two names, one Jewish and the other Greek, as Saul (Paul) did. (9)

13:9 *Saul, who is also called Paul.* As a Roman citizen (22:27-28) Saul/Paul no doubt had both a Jewish and a Roman name from his youth. Luke at this point, where the Gospel moves into the larger Roman world, begins to call him by his Roman name and mentions him before Barnabas, whereas hitherto Barnabas has been named first. In the Roman world the initiative lies with Paul.

13:10 *Son of the devil.* The expression is Hebraic, indicating that the magician derives his nature and character as opponent of the Gospel from the devil.

13:15 *Word of exhortation.* Cf. Heb 13:22 note.

13:16 *You that fear God,* proselytes. Cf. 10:2 note.

13:16-41 Paul's first recorded sermon, in the synagog at Pisidian Antioch, reads like an expansion of the summary of the Gospel which Paul himself gives in Ro 1:1-5: "The gospel of God which he promised beforehand through his prophets in the holy scriptures, the gospel concerning his Son, who was descended from David according to the flesh and designated Son of God in power according to the Spirit of holiness by his resurrection from the dead, Jesus Christ our Lord, through whom we have received grace." Paul proclaims the Gospel of God; it is His Word concerning His saving action. "God" is the first word of the sermon (17), and He is the acting subject throughout the history that runs from Abraham *(our fathers,* 17) to Jesus (17-30). He proclaims a Gospel which God "promised beforehand": the record of *this people Israel* (17) is the record of a history which runs toward the fulfillment of God's promise to Israel for all nations (32-33), and the voices of psalmist and prophet "in the holy scriptures" are the abiding interpretative witnesses to God's saving act in the cross and resurrection (33, 34, 35). Paul's Gospel is emphatically God's Gospel "concerning his Son"; Paul's recital of the history of Israel leaps over a thousand years from *David* (22), the recipient of the Messianic promise (2 Sm 7:8-16), to the *Savior, Jesus,* the fulfillment of the promise (23); and *John* the Baptist is assigned a place in that history which is characterized as strictly preliminary (24) and subordinate (25) to that of the Son. The Son, according to Paul's Gospel, is the incarnation and revelation of God's grace. Every man of Israel knew that the OT history of Israel is a record of Israel's persistent failure and God's indomitable grace; that grace overruled even Israel's ultimate failure and crowning disobedience (the rejection of the Son and Savior, 27-28) by raising His Son *from the dead* and raising up witnesses and evangelists to attest to His guilty people the *good news* of the fulfillment of *what God promised to the fathers* (31-32). What the Law could not do, God has done: Israel is free, *freed* by the forgiveness of sins proclaimed in Jesus. Before this incredible miracle of grace Israel must bow in fear and faith. (40-41)

13:39 *Freed.* The original has Paul's word "justified" here; they are "freed" by the acquitting verdict of God. (Cf. Ro 8:3)

13:46 *It was necessary . . . first to you.* The promise was given to Israel (32, 34); the fulfillment in Jesus, Son of David and Son of God, was enacted in Israel (33); Jesus commanded His disciples to preach repentance and forgiveness of sins to all nations, "beginning from Jerusalem" (Lk 24:47-49). For this "necessity" of proclaiming Jesus "to the Jew first" in Paul's own writings cf. Ro 1:16.

13:47 Cf. Is 49:6; Lk 2:32. The word spoken concerning the Servant Messiah is applied by Paul to the servants of the Servant in whom He speaks and acts. (Cf. Ro 15:18; 2 Co 13:3)

13:51 *Shook off the dust from their feet,* as a sign that all communion between them had been ended by their unbelief and enmity. (Cf. 18:6; Mt 10:14)

14:11-12 *"The gods have come down to us" . . . Zeus . . . Hermes. Zeus,* chief god of the Greeks, and *Hermes,* messenger of the gods, were linked in a local cult, and a story retold by the Roman poet Ovid tells how an old couple, Philemon and Baucis, entertained the two gods unawares when they *came down . . . in the likeness of men.* It was this familiar story that led the natives to identify Paul and Barnabas as gods and to attempt to honor them with sacrifice.

14:14 *Tore their garments,* as a sign of grief and horror at the idolatrous action. Cf. Mt 26:65, where the high priest reacts to Jesus' "blasphemy" with the same action.

14:15 *Turn from these vain things to a living God.* For Paul's own summary of his preaching to pagans cf. 1 Th 1:9-10. In Acts 17:21-31 Luke gives a fuller account of Paul's preaching to pagan hearers, when Paul cannot, as in the synagog, presuppose a knowledge of the OT. (Cf. 13:16-41)

14:17 *Not . . . without witness.* Cf. Ro 1:19-20.

14:19 *Stoned Paul.* Cf. 2 Co 11:25.

14:23 *Appointed elders.* Cf. Tts 1:5. The apostolic mission aims, not at a loose, enthusiastic "movement" but at a church solidly rooted and grounded, as is evidenced not only by the appointment of elders but also by Paul's practice of revisiting already evangelized territory (cf., e.g., Acts 15:36; 16:4-5), his ministry by letter, and his frequent employment of emissaries to the churches.

15:1—16:5 For the origin and significance of the tension that led to the Apostolic Council and the resolution of the tension cf. Introduction to Galatians.

15:5 *Circumcise them, and to charge them,* the newly converted Gentiles concerning whose conversion Paul and Baranbas had reported. (3-4)

15:7-9 For Peter's experience cf. 10:1—11:18.

15:10 *Why do you make trial of God by putting a yoke,* etc.? As Peter's experience has shown (7:9) and as the experience of Paul and Barnabas will show (12), God has gone His way of free grace (11) with the Gentiles; no man has the right to experiment with God, to see whether He will go man's way, i.e., the way of *putting a yoke* (of the Law) *upon the neck of the disciples* which God Himself has not imposed. To experiment with God is the way of magic, not of faith.

15:13 *James.* For the position and influence of James, the brother of our Lord, in Judaic Christianity cf. 12:17 and Introduction to Letter of James.

15:15-18 James quotes from the prophet Amos (9:11-12) concerning the inclusion of the Gentiles in the promised Messianic salvation; his use of the plural "prophets" indicates that the sentiment is not only that of Amos. (Cf., e.g., Is 11:9-10; 42:4, 6; 49:6; Jer 12:14-17)

15:20 Cf. 28-29, where the advice of James appears as the official request of Judaic to Gentile Christians.

15:22 *Judas . . . Barsabbas.* Known only from this passage and vv. 27 and 32.

Silas, known also by the Latinized form of his name, Silvanus, becomes prominent in the history of Gentile missions (Acts 15:40 and chs. 16—18; cf. 2 Co 1:19; 1 Th 1:1; 2 Th 1:1), associated both with Paul and Peter (1 Ptr 5:12; cf. Introduction to First Peter).

15:28 *These necessary things.* Cf. Introduction to Galatians, par. 10.

15:37 *John called Mark.* Cf. Introduction to Mark's Gospel.

15:38 *Withdrawn from them in Pamphylia.* Cf. 13:13.

16:1 *Timothy.* Cf. Introduction to First Timothy.

16:3 *Circumcised him because of the Jews . . . in those places.* When, as in the case of the Gentile Titus, circumcision was demanded by men intent on putting the yoke of the Law on the neck of Gentile disciples (Acts 15:10; Gl 2:3-5), Paul would not yield. Here in the case of Timothy, son of a Jewish mother, Paul of his own free will marked his future companion and co-worker as a member of Israel in order not to offend the Jews. Paul's willingness to "become all things to all men" in order that he "might by all means save some" (1 Co 9:22; cf. 19-23) gave him an astonishing flexibility.

16:5 *So the churches,* etc. The fourth of Luke's summarizing statements (cf. 6:7; 9:31; 12:24), coming as it does at the close of a series of events that had in them the seeds of discord and dissolution, is illuminated by words written by the apostle who played so signal a role in those events: "Speaking the truth in love, we are to grow up in every way into him who is the head, into Christ, from whom the whole body, joined and knit together by every joint with which it is supplied, when each part is working properly, makes bodily growth and upbuilds itself in love." (Eph 4:15-16)

16:6—19:20 THE WORD OF THE LORD GOES TO EUROPE AND ASIA MINOR

16:6—19:20 Luke concludes this section with the words: "So the word of the Lord grew and prevailed mightily" (19:20). His language is strong, stronger than that of previous summary statements (cf. 6:7; 9:31; 12:24; 16:5), but not too strong for the facts. The half-dozen years spanned by this portion of the record witnessed the progress of the Word of the Lord through an area far greater than that covered by any previous period—toward the close of this period Paul could write to the Christians of Rome: "From Jerusalem and as far round as Illyricum [in NW. Greece] I have fully preached the gospel of Christ" (Ro 15:19), and he could look to Rome and Spain as the next necessary stage of his missionary travels (Ro 15:23-24, 28). This period saw the crossing of the Gospel from Asia to Europe (16:10-12) and saw it firmly planted in two strategic centers, Ephesus in Asia and Corinth in Europe.

The Word prevailed in the face of opposition and conflict. Whether the opposition came from the synagog (17:5-8, 13; 18:6, 12-17), from Gentile superstition and avarice (16:16-24), from itinerant Jewish exorcists (19:13), or from the indifference of philosophic Athenians (17:23), it succeeded in inflicting on the bearers of the Word beatings, imprisonment, and enforced untimely departure from their chosen field of activity. It did not succeed in hindering the progress of the Word even when it invoked the strong arm of Roman law; Luke's exultant summary is a reading of the facts as the Spirit illumines them and is justified praise of the God who watched over His Word to make it prevail in spite of all opposition, by the guidance of His Spirit (16:6-7), by visions (16:8; 18:9), by the still, small voice that opened the heart of Lydia (16:14), and by the earthquake that shook the prisoners free in the jail at Philippi (16:26) and made the trembling jailer ask the question that is the opened door to the Gospel, "Men, what must I do to be saved?" (16:30)

16:6-10 The Call to Macedonia

16:6-10 God is in charge, even of the itinerary. His Spirit (which is the Spirit of His Son Jesus continuing the work He had begun on earth, 16:7; cf. 1:1) turns His messengers back from the next logical step, the evangelization of the rest of Asia Minor, and calls them to cross over to Europe and preach the Gospel in Macedonia.

16:6 *Phrygia and Galatia,* that is, that part of the Roman province of Galatia which was both a part of the ancient area of Phrygia and a part of Galatia, scene of Paul's labors on the first missionary journey.

Asia, the Roman province of that name in western Asia Minor, whose capital was Ephesus.

16:6-8 The Spirit cuts off the "logical" lines of advance to the west *(Asia)* and the north *(Bithynia)* and leads Paul and his companions to *Troas* in NW. Asia Minor and to Macedonia in northern Greece.

16:10 *We sought to go on into Macedonia.* The change from the third person plural of vv. 6, 7, 8 to *we* indicates that Luke joined Paul's party at Troas. Other "we" sections in Acts besides

16:10-17 are 20:5-16; 21:1-18; 27:1—28:16; they are probably Luke's way of indicating that he was an eyewitness of the events there recorded.

16:11-40 Philippi

16:11-40 Cf. Introduction to Philippians.

16:11 *Neapolis,* the port city of Philippi.

16:12 *A Roman colony.* Cf. Introduction to Philippians, par. 1.

16:13 *Riverside . . . a place of prayer,* an unofficial open-air place of worship for the Jews of Philippi. Paul as usual offers the Gospel "to the Jew first." (Ro 1:16; cf. Acts 13:46 note)

16:14 *A worshiper of God.* A convert to Judaism.

16:21 *Not lawful for us Romans.* As members of a Roman colony (cf. 16:12 note) the Philippians enjoyed and no doubt prided themselves on Roman citizenship.

16:22 *Beat them with rods.* Cf. 2 Co 11:25.

16:31 *Believe in the Lord Jesus.* For the title *Lord* as a summary of all that Jesus signifies for faith cf. Ro 10:9; 1 Co 12:3.

16:37 *Uncondemned,* without the due process of law to which a Roman citizen was entitled. (Cf. Acts 22:24-29)

17:1-9 Thessalonica

17:1-9 Cf. Introductions to Letters to the Thessalonians.

17:4 *Devout Greeks.* Converts to Judaism.

17:7 *Acting against the decrees of Caesar . . . another king, Jesus.* The Jews attempt to make the Gospel of Jesus appear politically dangerous, subversive to the Roman state. (Cf. 18:13; 24:5)

17:9 *Taken security.* Paul's host, Jason, and the rest of his friends were bound under penalty to see to it that the disturbance would not recur.

17:10-15 Beroea

17:10-15 The men of the synagog at Beroea proved more *noble* than those of Thessalonica, i.e., they gave the Gospel a hearing on its own terms, "in accordance with the [OT] scriptures" (cf. 1 Co 15:3-4), with the result that *many of them . . . believed* (12). But again the apostle was forced to leave before the founding of a church in Beroea was really completed.

17:16-34 Athens

17:16-34 "The Greeks seek wisdom" (1 Co 1:22), Paul wrote to the Corinthians some 5 years after his visit to Athens. In this respect the Athenians were the most Greek of the Greeks, and the intellectual vigor which made 5th-century and 4th-century Athens "the eye of Greece" was not yet entirely spent; the intellectual climate of Athens favored philosophy (18), and the *foreigners who lived there* (21) were attracted thither by the cultural atmosphere of Athens *(telling or hearing something new,* 21). But if Athens was the scene of the triumph of human wisdom, it was also the scene of wisdom's signal failure: "The world did not know God through wisdom" (1 Co 1:21) *The city was full of idols* (16), and the *very religious* (22) men of Athens were haunted by the fear that haunts all polytheism, namely, that some god or goddess might have been overlooked and offended; the altar with the *inscription, To an unknown god* (23) testified to this fear and so to the failure of wisdom. It is to this fear and failure that Paul attached in his address (22:31). He points men away from the sorry splendors of their idolatry to the one true God, the almighty Creator whom no *shrines made by man* (24) can contain, the Lord of all history who attests Himself to man by His works (25) and wills to be found by man (27). God has in His long patience *overlooked* (30) man's guilty failure to find Him, but the time of His forbearance is drawing to a close, the *day on which he will judge the world in righteousness* (31) is near; and the Judge is *appointed,* the Man whom He has raised from the dead. For all the difference of approach and method, Paul's proclamation to the Greek is one with his proclamation to the Jew; he is "testifying both to Jews and Greeks of repentance to God and of faith in our Lord Jesus Christ" (Acts 20:21), the Deliverer and Judge of both Jew and Greek. Human wisdom is not easily persuaded of its failure; the mind boggles at the miracle of the resurrection of the dead. *Some mocked,* while others clothe their rejection in a polite request that the matter be discussed further (32). *But some . . . believed* (34), and these "some" (cf. 1 Co 9:22) are the future of the church and of the world.

17:18 *Epicurean and Stoic philosophers* represent the two most widely held philosophic faiths (and faiths they were rather than philosophies, strictly speaking) of late antiquity.

Babbler. This contemptuous term, used literally of birds that pick up seeds, designated a person who picked up scraps of learning and culture and paraded without having made them really his own.

17:19 *Areopagus,* name of a hill near the Acropolis of Athens and of an ancient court which sat there. In Paul's day this court was primarily concerned with matters of education and religion. As a "preacher of foreign divinities" (18) Paul would come under this scrutiny.

17:22 *Religious.* The term used could be used in either a derogatory ("superstitious") or a positive sense ("religious"). Paul's use of it is probably neutral; his subsequent words indicate that he does not intend to be either insulting or laudatory.

17:24 *Does not live in shrines made by man.* Cf. Is 42:5; 66:1-2. (Acts 7:49-50)

17:27 Cf. Ro 1:19-21.

17:28 The quotations are from two Greek poets, Epimenides (cf. Tts 1:12 note) and Aratus. The wise Greeks sensed the presence and working of God, yet did not turn from their idols to respond to Him with thanks and praise. (Ro 1:21)

17:30 *Times of ignorance God overlooked.* Cf. Ro 3:25.

18:1-17 Corinth

18:1-17 Corinth proved to be the farthest reach and the most important evangelization center of the second missionary journey (Acts 15:36—18:22). For the character and subsequent history of the church in Corinth see Introductions to Letters to the Corinthians. Paul was encouraged to extend the time of his ministry there (11) by the fact that he encountered *Aquila* and *Priscilla,* fellow Jews (2) and followers of the same trade (3) who became his "fellow workers in Christ Jesus," deserving of the gratitude of Paul and of "all the churches of the Gentiles" (Ro 16:4). His meeting with them was an encouragement in another respect also: it enabled him to maintain himself by working at his trade (3) and so to "make the gospel free of charge" (1 Co 9:18; cf. 2 Co 11:7-11) to his converts in Corinth. But the decisive encouragement came from the Lord Himself, who appeared to Paul in a vision in the night and promised him fruitful labors and protection against attack (10). The Lord kept both promises; the church grew (cf. 8) despite the hostility of the synagog (6); and the *united attack* of the Jews on Paul before the tribunal of the Roman proconsul Gallio (12-17) failed of its purpose.

18:2 *Claudius . . . commanded all the Jews to leave Rome.* Claudius (Roman emperor A.D. 41—54) virtually commanded the Jews to leave Rome because of their turbulent behavior by banning their assemblies; since this deprived devout Jews of opportunity to worship, they were forced to leave. The action of Claudius probably affected Jewish Christians also, though it is not clear whether Aquila and his wife had been converted in Rome or were won for Christ by Paul in Corinth.

18:3 *Tentmakers.* Tents made out of the felted cloth of goats' hair were produced in Cilicia, Paul's home province.

18:5 *Silas and Timothy arrived from Macedonia.* Cf. 17:15 and 1 Th 3:6.

Was occupied with, or perhaps better, "wholly absorbed in," *preaching.* Timothy's report concerning the fidelity of the Thessalonian church relieved Paul of anxiety over the young congregation, and he could throw himself into the work at Corinth with renewed vigor. (Cf. 1 Th 3:1-8)

18:12 *Gallio . . . proconsul of Achaia.* With headquarters in Corinth, Gallio was proconsul of Achaia either A. D. 51—52 or 52—53.

18:13 *Contrary to the law.* Gallio perceived that the *law* involved was not the Roman law but Jewish law and therefore refused to recognize the charge brought against Paul. (Cf. 14-15)

18:17 The mistreatment of *Sosthenes* was not an official Roman action but an outburst of popular anti-Semitic feeling on the part of bystanders. Some identify this Sosthenes, *the ruler of the synagogue,* with the Sosthenes whom Paul calls "our brother" in 1 Co 1:1; if the two are identical (possible but not certain), one must assume that Sosthenes was later converted and became, like Paul, a member of the church he had once persecuted.

18:18-23 The Return to Antioch

18:18 *Cenchreae,* the eastern seaport of Corinth on the isthmus.

Cut his hair, for he had a vow. For the provisions of the Nazirite vow cf. Nm 6 and Acts 21:23-36. There is nothing to indicate the purpose of the vow, nor is it altogether clear who had taken the vow, Paul or Aquila.

18:22 *The church,* i.e., the Jerusalem church.

Antioch in Syria, Paul's missionary base. (Cf. 13:1-3; 15:35)

18:23 *Galatia and Phrygia.* Cf. 16:6 note.

18:24—19:20 Ephesus

18:24—19:20 For a survey of Paul's ministry at Ephesus cf. Introduction to First Corinthians, pars. 1-6.

18:25 *He knew only the baptism of John,* the baptism of promise, which had been superseded by the baptism of fulfillment "in the name of the Lord Jesus" (19:4-5) and the gift of the Holy Spirit. (19:6)

18:27 *Wished to cross to Achaia.* For an account of Apollos' influence in Achaia, particularly at Corinth, cf. Introduction to First Corinthians, pars. 10-11.

19:2 *Never even heard that there is a Holy Spirit,* that is, that the Holy Spirit has been bestowed upon the new people of God, the church (cf. Jn 7:39). Disciples of John the Baptist (such as these disciples were, 19:1) would have heard of the Holy Spirit (Mt 3:11) if they did not already know of Him from the OT.

19:3 *John's baptism.* Cf. 18:25 note.

19:6 Cf. 8:17; 10:44-45; 11:15.

19:9 *The hall of Tyrannus.* The Greek word for *hall* indicates a place where a school meets, a lecture hall. Tyrannus is otherwise unknown.

19:14 *Sons of a Jewish high priest named Sceva.* There is no record of a Jewish high priest with this name. Sceva is a name of Latin origin; perhaps the high priest in question bore a Hebrew and a Latin name (as Saul/Paul did) and could be identified if his Hebrew name were known.

19:19 *Brought their books together and burned them,* thus publicly renouncing their magical practices. The books were books of magic, for which Ephesus was famous.

19:21—28:31 THE POWER OF THE WORD OF THE LORD

19:21—28:31 As Paul was about to leave Ephesus, he "resolved in the Spirit to . . . go to Jerusalem, saying, 'After I have been there, I *must* also see Rome' " (19:21). The *must* that impelled him toward Jerusalem and to Rome was the *must* of the will of his Lord, who appeared to him in Jerusalem and said, "As you have testified about me at Jerusalem, so you *must* bear witness also at Rome" (23:11). It was a Christlike way that he went; it was a way of love, for he went bringing gifts. "I came to bring to my nation alms and offerings," he said at his trial before Felix (24:17). He attached great importance to these alms and offerings, for he saw in them the concrete expression of what he had written to the Corinthians concerning the members of the body of Christ: "If one member suffers, all suffer together" (1 Co 12:26); in these gifts of Gentile to Jewish Christians he saw the miracle of the unity of the church being enacted. (Ro 15:25-29; cf. 15:7-9)

Paul knew that the way he was going was a dangerous one (Ro 15:31). He knew how much his unbelieving fellow countrymen hated him and how desperately they wanted him out of the way; he had been in "danger from his own people" more than once before (2 Co 11:26). His fears were confirmed at Corinth, where a "plot was made against him by the Jews as he was about to set sail for Syria" (20:3) and Paul was forced to change his itinerary to avoid death. And as he journeyed toward Jerusalem, the Spirit warned him, directly and through the voice of prophecy, that "imprisonment and afflictions" awaited him. (20:22-23; cf. 21:4, 10-11)

And yet he went willingly and resolutely to Jerusalem, for he saw in this bringing of gifts to Jerusalem a piece of the ministry which he had received from the Lord Jesus, "to testify to the gospel of the grace of God" (20:24). To whom did Paul want to testify? To his Jewish Christian brethren surely; the gift from the Gentile churches would speak unmistakably to them of the universal grace of God. But surely also to his Jewish "kinsmen by race" who had not yet obeyed the Gospel. Their hatred of him had not engendered hatred in his heart; his mission to the Gentiles did not mean the end of his love for his kinsmen or the cessation of his efforts on their behalf (Ro 9:1-5; 10:1; 11:13, 14). "I came to bring *to my nation* alms and offerings," Paul said pointedly at his trial (24:17); he evidently hoped that the sight of gifts pouring into Jerusalem from Gentile lands, to which the Jew had hitherto looked in vain for kindness, might open the eyes of at least some to the grace of God and its "inexpressible gift."

Luke marks this way of Paul's as a Christlike way, one of giving, of suffering, of love for his people the Jews. Even externally the life of Paul has on it the imprint of his Lord's life: the time of travels is followed by a time of imprisonment and suffering. The parallelism between the Lord and His apostle is apparent in the story of the arrest and imprisonment of Paul. Like Jesus, he is tried before the Sanhedrin (22:30—23:10; cf. Lk 22:66-70), before the Roman procurator (24:1-23; 25:6-12; cf. Lk 23:1-5, 13-25), and before a Jewish king, Herod Agrippa II (25:23—26:32; cf. Lk 23:6-12). And he resembles Jesus in this too that he tries to the last to bring the men of Jerusalem under the wings of the Christ who can save them (cf. Mt 23:37); even when the Jerusalem mob was screaming for his blood, he once more addressed them in their own tongue, and sought even then to gain a hearing by stressing all that he and they had in common by the grace of God.

Paul appealed to his people in vain. He was imprisoned at Jerusalem, removed to Caesarea when the fury of his people again threatened his life (23:12-35), and imprisoned there for two years under the procurator Felix, who hoped for a bribe from Paul or his friends (24:26), and when that was not forthcoming left Paul in prison at the end of his term, "desiring to do the Jews a favor" (24:27). When even the fair and conscientious Festus, Felix's successor as procurator, wanted to prolong his already long-drawn trial by transferring him for trial to Jerusalem, Paul made use of his privilege as a Roman citizen and appealed to Caesar. (25:11)

"You have appealed to Caesar; to Caesar you shall go," Festus said (25:12). Paul was sent to Rome. The long voyage to Rome with its dangers and disasters, through all which Paul was led safely to the goal set for him by his Lord, is, as it were, an epitome of his whole career as an apostle of Jesus Christ; again the strength of the Lord was made perfect in His apostle's weakness. Jesus' promise that Paul would testify to Him at Rome was fulfilled (23:11); and Jesus' more sweeping promise to the Twelve (1:8), was fulfilled also; the Gospel is being proclaimed in Rome, the capital of the world; it has stepped through the door which opens into all the world, to the ends of the earth. Paul is seen at the close of Acts "preaching the kingdom of God and teaching about the Lord Jesus Christ quite openly and unhindered." (28:31)

19:21-41 Final Conflict in Ephesus: "Great Is Artemis"

19:21-41 Cf. Introduction to First Corinthians, par. 6.

19:24 The *silver shrines of Artemis* were probably sold to the worshipers to be used as votive gifts in the temple of Artemis, one of the seven wonders of the ancient world.

19:26 *Gods made with hands are not gods.* Cf. 17:24-25, 29.

19:31 *Asiarchs,* men of substance and influence, prominent in the cult of emperor worship, known for their loyalty to Rome. The details of the nature of their office are not known.

19:35 *Town clerk,* the principal municipal officer of Ephesus, whom the Roman government would hold responsible for civic disorders. Translators have used terms like "chancellor," "secretary of state," and "mayor" in their attempts to convey the importance of this office.

Temple keeper of the great Artemis, an honorific title of which the Ephesians were evidently proud, found in inscriptions and on coins.

Sacred stone that fell from the sky, probably a meteorite which, from its resemblance to a many-breasted female figure, was identified with the Ephesian mother-goddess Artemis.

19:38-40 *The courts are open, and there are proconsuls,* that is, the regular channels of government provided by Roman rule are sufficient for the redress of any real grievances. Tumultuous proceedings are unnecessary as well as dangerous, since the Romans would take a grave view of them.

20:1-12 Through Greece to Troas

20:3 *There he spent three months.* Paul probably spent much of this time at Corinth, where he wrote his Letter to the Romans. Cf. Introduction to Romans.

20:4 *Sopater . . . Aristarchus,* etc. The men named were probably representatives of the Gentile churches who brought the gifts of the Gentiles to the poor saints of Jerusalem. (Cf. 1 Co 16:3-4)

20:5-6 *Us . . . we.* Cf. 16:10 note. Luke rejoins Paul at Philippi.

20:6 *Days of Unleavened Bread,* the seven days following the Passover and so closely associated with that feast that the two terms are practically interchangeable.

20:8 The presence of *many lights* is noted as accounting for the sleepiness of Eutychus (8); the burning of many oil lamps would create an oppressive atmosphere.

20:13-38 To Miletus: Paul's Farewell to Elders of Ephesus

20:16 *The day of Pentecost.* Cf. 2:1 note.

20:18-35 Luke has recorded addresses of Paul the missionary speaking to Jews in their synagog (13:16-41) and to Gentiles, both the wise (17:22-31) and the foolish (14:15-17). It is only in this farewell address to the elders of Ephesus that Luke presents Paul the pastor speaking to Christians. As he faces these elders for what in all probability is the last time (25), he recalls his missionary ministry among them, a ministry marked by fidelity to his Lord and *humility* toward men amid the *trials* and *tears* of his imperiled life as missionary, how he had resisted the temptation to abridge his Gospel or to restrict his audience for the sake of "success" (18:21). He turns to the future. He himself faces *imprisonment and afflictions,* but that is not what concerns him. What does concern him is that he remain faithful unto death in the ministry his Lord has given him and run true in the course He has set for him (22-24). The future of the church in Ephesus, too, is dark. The new people of God *(flock,* 28) will be beset by both foe and traitor (29-30). The elders must therefore be alert and vigilant in the exercise of their office, as Paul has been in his; he has given them the Word of life fully and faithfully; no man has lost eternal life by any fault of his (26-27, 31). Paul's charge to the elders has been sober and uncompromising (28-31); he gives them the heart and strength to execute it by his promise. He commends them to the Word of divine grace, which has been his own sufficiency all his days, a Word that has power to build them up and to carry them through the dark days ahead into God's bright final future (32). They can live of that grace and hope for that future if they follow Paul's example of self-giving, which has the blessing and promise of the Lord Jesus. (34-35)

20:23 *The Holy Spirit testifies to me,* probably through Christian prophets such as Agabus. (21:10-11)

20:26 *I am innocent of the blood of all of you.* Cf. 18:6.

20:29 *Fierce wolves . . . not sparing the flock.* For the people of God as the *flock* of God, and *wolves* (false prophets and teachers) as enemies of the flock, cf. Mt 7:15.

20:34 *These hands ministered to my necessities.* Cf. 1 Co 4:12; 9:3-18; 2 Co 11:7-11; 12:13; 1 Th 2:3-10; 2 Th 3:7-9.

20:35 *The words of the Lord Jesus.* This word of our Lord is not recorded in the gospels.

21:1-16 From Miletus to Jerusalem

21:4 *Having sought out the disciples, we stayed there.* Passages like this (cf. 8, 16) show the relevance of the admonitions to Christian hospitality in the letters of Paul (Ro 12:13; 1 Ti 3:2; 5:10; Tts 1:8), Peter (1 Ptr 4:9), and Heb 13:2.

21:8 *Philip the evangelist . . . one of the seven.* Cf. 6:5; 8:5-13, 26-40.

21:10 *Agabus.* Cf. 11:28.

21:11 *Took Paul's girdle.* Like the OT prophets, Agabus reinforces his message by symbolic action. (Cf. 1 K 11:29-36; Is 20:2-4; Eze 4:1-17)

21:13 *Breaking my heart,* that is, "trying to break down my resolve." (Cf. 14)

21:17-26 The Request of the Jerusalem Church

21:18 For James as leader of the Jerusalem church cf. 12:17 note.

21:21 *Teach . . . the Jews . . . not to circumcise their children.* The report that reached Jerusalem was a distortion of Paul's teaching regarding Christian freedom from the Law. For Paul's true position concerning circumcision cf. 16:3 note and 1 Co 7:17-19.

21:22-24 Paul is to purge himself of the suspicion that he has become a traitor to the religion of his fathers and to his people by publicly associating himself with *four men . . . under a vow,* a Nazirite vow (cf. 18:18 note), and by paying the considerable *expenses* involved in the sacrificial ceremony of purification.

21:25 *We have sent a letter.* Cf. 15:20, 23-29; 16:4; and Introduction to Galatians.

21:26 Paul's consent to the request of the Jerusalem church is in keeping with what he has written. (1 Co 9:20)

21:27-40 Paul's Arrest in the Temple

21:27 *The seven days* required for the rite of purification for a Nazirite who had incurred defilement. (Cf. Nm 6:9)

Jews from Asia. Paul's break with the synagog at Ephesus (19:9) and his subsequent missionary success (19:10) apparently had made the Jews of Asia especially bitter toward him (cf. 20:19). They were present in Jerusalem for Pentecost. (20:16)

21:28 *Brought Greeks into the temple.* Gentiles were permitted in the outer court of the temple, but for a Gentile to enter the inner precincts was an offense punishable by death.

21:30 *All the city was aroused.* Religious-national feelings ran high at the time of the great festivals. The Roman garrison, quartered in the fortress Antonia adjacent to the temple precincts (cf. 31, 34), was often reinforced on these occasions in expectation of disorders like the one recorded here. (30-35)

21:31 *Tribune,* Roman officer in command of a *cohort,* a division of a legion.

21:36 *"Away with him!"* The crowd raised the same cry concerning Jesus at His trial (Lk 23:18)

21:38 *Egyptian.* The tribune had identified Paul with an Egyptian imposter who had appeared in Jerusalem a few years before. He claimed to be a prophet and promised his followers that the walls of Jerusalem would fall before him and that the Roman power would be overcome. When Roman troops squashed the attempted revolt, the Egyptian disappeared.

The Assassins were Jews whose zeal for the cause of Jewish freedom led them to assassinate Jews suspected of collaboration with the Romans. Men of this type would join in revolts such as the Egyptian fomented.

22:1-21 Paul Speaks for the Last Time to His People

22:1-21 Paul's last words to his people are a monument to his inextinguishable love for Israel (cf. Ro 9:1-5; 10:1-2; 11:13-14). His every word is designed to win the men who had just attempted to kill him (21:31) and would soon cry for his blood again (22:22). He speaks to them in their mother tongue (21:40), not without effect (22:2). His mode of address *(Brethren and fathers,* 22:1) and his first words to them *(I am a Jew,* 22:3) avow his kinship with them. He has been *brought up* in their city, has studied under their revered teacher *Gamaliel, educated according to the strict manner of the law* of the Jewish fathers who are both their fathers and his, *zealous for God* as they *are this day* (3; cf. Ro 10:2). The man through whom the blinded persecutor received his sight and saw his new Lord was *a devout man according to the law, well spoken of by all the Jews who lived there,* in Damascus (12-13); this man, *Ananias,* acted in obedience to *the God of our fathers* and spoke of Christ in terms familiar to the Jews from their OT *(Just One,* 14; cf. Is 53:11). And Paul's own impulse and desire had been to witness to his Lord among the Jews (17-20); it was the overruling word of his Lord that sent him to the Gentiles (21), not some dissatisfaction with or resentment toward his people. The substance of Paul's words, too, is thoroughly Jewish; his appeal to them is the *narrative* of his conversion. The Jew was accustomed from his OT to appeal by narrative; he rightly called the books which we call "historical books" the Former Prophets (Joshua through 2 Kings).

22:22-30 The Result of Paul's Address to His Countrymen

22:22-30 At the word "Gentiles" (21) the prejudice and fury of the mob breaks out anew (22:23; cf. 21:28). The tribune decides to interrogate Paul under torture (24) but is deterred from this course when he discovers that Paul is a Roman citizen (25-29). *Desiring to know the real reason why the Jews accused* Paul, he determines to bring him before the council. (30)

22:24 *Examined by scourging.* This third-degree manner of obtaining evidence was common enough; but to apply it to a Roman citizen was illegal. (Cf. 25-26)

22:25 *Tied him up,* preparatory to scourging. *Uncondemned,* without due process of law. (Cf. 16:37)

22:28 *For a large sum.* The tribune evidently doubted that a man such as he saw before him had the means to purchase Roman citizenship, as he himself had done.

23:1-11 Paul Divides the Council

23:1-11 "With me it is a very small thing that I should be judged . . . by any human court," Paul had written to the Corinthians (1 Co 4:3). The Jewish high court certainly demonstrated that this very human court was not competent to judge an apostle of Jesus Christ. The presiding high priest, Ananias, begins procedings with a gross illegality, exposing himself as the *whitewashed wall* that he is (2-3). The members of the council are hopelessly and violently at variance, *Sadducee* against *Pharisee.* Paul, serenely independent of the judgment of men, utilizes the split between Pharisee and Sadducee to remove himself from the judicature of men incompetent to judge him (6-10). There is only One who is competent to judge the apostle, and His word is one of assurance *(take courage)* and promise. (11)

23:1 *In all good conscience.* Cf. 2 Ti 1:3.

23:4 *You whitewashed wall,* whose fair exterior conceals from the eyes of men the weakness of the structure doomed to the judgment of God. (Cf. Eze 13:10-16)

23:5 Paul's words may be ironic: "I did not recognize as *God's high priest* one who acted in so ungodly and unpriestly a way."

You shall not speak, etc. Cf. Ex 22:28.

23:8 *No resurrection.* Cf. Lk 20:27.

23:12-35 The Plot Against Paul; He Is Sent to Caesarea

23:23 *Third hour of the night,* about 9 p.m.

23:34 *Cilicia,* a Roman province whose inhabitants would come under Roman jurisdiction.

23:35 *Herod's praetorium.* The governor's headquarters *(praetorium)* in Caesarea was situated in a building which had been Herod the Great's palace.

24:1-23 Paul Before Felix the Roman Governor

24:1-23 Paul's first trial before the governor

ends inconclusively (22, *put them off).* Paul answers the second of the two charges brought against him (attempted profanation of the temple, 6) by pointing out that his stay in Jerusalem has been brief *(twelve days,* 11) and peaceable (12). As to the first charge *(ringleader of the sect of the Nazarenes,* i.e., Christians, 5), he admits it freely (14) but insists that he occupies the same religious ground as his opponents *(law . . . prophets,* 14; the hope of Israel, 15), implying that the case is one of a theological difference within Judaism, one which a Roman court is neither willing nor able to adjudicate (cf. Gallio's attitude, 18:13-15). If he has in fact been an *agitator among . . . the Jews* (5), the "agitation" he has provoked is theological, not political. (20-21; cf. 23:6-10)

24:1 *Tertullus,* otherwise unknown.

24:14 *The Way.* Cf. 9:2 note.

24:14-15 *Law . . . prophets . . . hope.* For Paul's attitude toward the OT Scriptures cf. Ro 3:21; 15:4.

24:18 *Jews from Asia.* Cf. 21:27 note.

24:21 *I cried out while standing among them.* Cf. 23:6.

24:24-27 Paul and Felix and Drusilla

24:24-27 Roman and Jewish historians agree in giving *Felix* a bad character; his Jewish wife, *Drusilla,* had left her first husband to marry him. Whatever prompted him to ask Paul to *speak upon faith in Christ Jesus* (24), he could not have expected and certainly did not relish talk of *justice and self-control and future judgment* (25). With a past like his, and with such a wife beside him, it is no wonder he was *alarmed* (25) and cut the interview short.

24:27 *Desiring to do the Jews a favor,* probably to offset the bitterness engendered by his administration, a bitterness so great that the Jews sent a deputation to Rome to bring charges against Felix.

25:1-12 Paul Before Festus: the Appeal to Caesar

25:1-12 The new trial before Festus produces nothing really new; prosecution and defense are the same as in the trial before Felix (6-8; cf. 24:2-21). When Festus is inclined to make a conciliatory gesture to the Jews by shifting the trial to Jerusalem (9), Paul makes use of his privilege as a Roman citizen to lodge an appeal to have his case tried in Rome.

25:13-22 The Arrival of Agrippa

25:13 *Agrippa the king.* Herod Agrippa II, son of Herod Agrippa I (Acts 12:1-4, 20-23), the last of the Herodians, had attained and held his power by his devotion and subservience to Rome; hence his prompt courtesy call on the newly arrived Roman governor. Drusilla, wife of Felix, was his sister, as was *Bernice.* There was scandalous gossip, apparently not unfounded, that his relationship with Bernice was incestuous. Embarrassed by the fact that he had on his hands an appeal case which he did not understand (cf. 26-27), Festus welcomed the opportunity to consult with one "especially familiar with all customs and controversies of the Jews." (26:2)

25:23—26:23 The Hearing Before King Agrippa

25:23—26:23 Paul speaks in defense of his Gospel for the last time on Jewish soil, before the last Jewish king. As in his words to the mob in the temple court (ch. 22), he stresses the continuity between his Judaic past and his present position as an apostle of Jesus Christ; the Gospel he proclaims is the fulfillment of the promise made to his Jewish fathers, the fulfilled content of the hope of the 12 tribes of Israel. That Paul should be accused *for this* Jewish *hope by Jews* (7) is supreme and tragic irony. (4-8)

Paul admits that he had once been as blind to the purpose and working of God in Jesus as his accusers now are (9-11). It was not until "the God who said, 'Let light shine out of darkness,' " had shone in his heart "to give the light of the knowledge of the glory of God in the face of Christ" (2 Co 4:6) that he had ceased to persecute Jesus and begun to proclaim Him to Jew and Gentile. (12-18)

He could not be *disobedient to the heavenly vision* (19) that burst on him near Damascus, no more than he could disobey the voice of God that spoke to him from the OT (22). The threat of death cannot deter him, for he is sure of God's help as he continues Christ's own work in proclaiming *light both to the people* (Israel) *and to the Gentiles.* (19-23)

26:4 *My manner of life from my youth.* Cf. 22:3.

26:6 *On trial for hope in the promise.* Cf. 23:6.

26:9-18 Cf. 9:1-8; 22:4-16.

26:9 *Opposing the name of Jesus,* that is, opposing all that *Jesus* stands for, all that He signifies for those who believe in Him.

26:14 *To kick against the goads,* to resist the divine Driver who is leading you in His way.

26:18 Cf. Cl 1:13.

Sanctified, made God's own, His "saints."

26:22 *What the prophets and Moses said.* Cf. Lk 24:44-47.

26:23 *Light both to the people and to the Gentiles.* Cf. Is 42:7, 16.

26:24-32 The Effect of Paul's Words

26:24-32 Both Festus and the king are, it seems, more deeply affected by Paul's words than they care to be. Both fight their way back into the cooler realm of common sense, Festus by his bluff *you are mad* (24), Agrippa with a feeble joke when confronted by Paul's personal appeal (27-28). Both agree that Paul is innocent. (31-32)

27:1-44 The Stormy Voyage to Rome

27:1 *Augustan Cohort.* A cohort was one tenth of a legion; cohorts stationed in Palestine numbered 760 infantry and 240 cavalry. An Augustan cohort is known to have been stationed in Syria at this time, but the origin and significance of the term *Augustan* is not clear.

27:9 *The fast.* The Day of Atonement, the great annual fast day in Israel (Lv 16), is meant, the modern Yom Kippur. The time is autumn, when travel by sea became dangerous and shipping was normally suspended until spring. (Cf. 12)

27:17 *Undergird the ship.* To prevent the wooden hull from breaking up in rough weather, it was reinforced by ropes passed under the ship and wrapped around it.

Syrtis, sandbanks off the coast of north Africa south of Crete, feared by sailors.

27:24 Cf. 23:11.

27:27 *Adria,* the Adriatic Sea, although its limits are not the same as in modern usage.

28:1-10 Winter in Malta

28:4 *Justice* is probably thought of as a personified power, and the word might therefore well be capitalized.

28:6 *Said that he was a god.* Cf. 14:8-13.

28:11-16 From Malta to Rome

28:15 *Paul thanked God and took courage.* His Lord had fulfilled His promise (23:11); the long-cherished wish that he might see Rome also (19:21; Ro 1:13; 15:22, 29, 32) has been granted; and the fact that Roman Christians have come some 40 miles to meet him is heartwarming assurance that his letter to them has borne fruit; the Roman Christians will not disappoint Paul's hope that he may be "sped on his journey" to Spain by their assistance. (Ro 15:24)

28:17-29 Paul and the Jews of Rome

28:17-29 In Rome Paul brings the Gospel to the Jew first, as has been his consistent practice. He invites the local leaders of the Jews to his quarters and explains to them why he has come to Rome as a prisoner (17:20). He has done nothing against his people (17)—nor has he any charge to bring against the people he still calls *my nation* (19). He is innocent of any offense against Roman law (18). *Because of the hope of Israel,* he is *bound with this chain* (20). This hope is fulfilled in Jesus, proclaimed by Paul. There is implicit in Paul's account a call to repentance and a plea for a fair hearing.

The leaders are willing to give him a hearing (21-22), and on the appointed day Paul confronts them on the basis of their Scriptures with the hope of Israel fulfilled: *the kingdom of God,* God's reign, as actualized and established by *Jesus* (23). And once more Paul learns by experience that "not all who are descended from Israel belong to Israel" (Ro 9:6); *some were convinced . . . while others disbelieved* (24). When Jesus began His ministry in Nazareth, He invited His fellow townsmen to inherit the hope of Israel with words of glad promise from Isaiah (Lk 4:18-19; Is 61:12). Even then the response of His people was such that He hinted that the Good News would pass from them to the Gentiles (Lk 4:23-27). Now it is Paul's bitter duty to dismiss his departing fellow countrymen with a word of Isaiah's of quite another kind: The people who WILL not hear the voice of their God SHALL not hear it (25-27), and the salvation they have refused will go to the Gentiles. (28)

28:28 *To the Gentiles.* Cf. 13:46.

28:30-31 The Word Is Not Bound

28:30-31 Paul remains a prisoner, but Jesus' own message of the *kingdom of God* (cf. 1:3) and Paul's witness to Him as *the Lord,* the royal reign of God in person, sound forth nevertheless *quite openly and unhindered,* and the end of that sounding forth is not yet.

ROMANS

INTRODUCTION

1 It is historically natural and fitting that the Letter to the Romans has always been of special interest and import to Western Christendom. For with this letter Paul is looking westward. The hope of coming to Rome was one he had been cherishing "for many years" at the time of writing (15:23). He had met Aquila and Priscilla as early as the year 50. An edict of Emperor Claudius banishing all Jews from Rome had brought that couple, destined to be so dear and so valuable to him, to Corinth, where Paul was then beginning his work. They could tell him of the church (or, more accurately, churches) in that key city of the empire, its life, its problems, and its possibilities, especially its possibilities as a missionary center for the western part of the Roman Empire. It was this last point that was no doubt of greatest interest to Paul, whose missionary strategy had as its chief object the founding of churches in the key cities of the empire. That strategy had carried him from Antioch to Corinth and Ephesus.

The Occasion of the Letter

2 It was probably in late summer A.D. 55, when Paul was about to conclude his work at Ephesus and was about to return to Jerusalem with the offering gathered among the Gentiles for the poverty-stricken saints of Jerusalem, that he gave expression to his long-cherished hope of going to Rome: "After I have been there, I must also see Rome" (Acts 19:21). He spoke of that hope again when he wrote to the Corinthians from Macedonia a few weeks later: "Our hope is that as your faith increases, our field among you may be greatly enlarged, so that we may preach the gospel in lands beyond you" (2 Co 10:15-16). "Lands beyond you"—this expression coming from a man who had been working his way westward "from Jerusalem and as far round as Illyricum" in northwestern Greece (Ro 15:19) surely points to the West.

3 The letter itself enables us to fix the time of writing fairly closely. Paul is about to conclude his work in the East, so that he no longer has "any room for work in these regions" between Jerusalem and Illyricum (Ro 15:23; cf. 15:19). He is about to go to Jerusalem with the collection gathered in Macedonia and Achaia (Ro 15:25-27; cf. 2 Co 8 and 9). All this points to the close of the so-called third missionary journey and the winter A.D. 55—56.

4 The place of writing is fairly certain also. Paul spent three months in southern Greece at the close of his third missionary journey. He had promised the Corinthians that he would stay with them or "even spend the winter" with them (1 Co 16:6). Corinth would therefore seem to be the most likely place of writing. This is confirmed by three notices in the letter itself. In 16:23 Paul sends greeting from "Erastus, the city treasurer"; Erastus is associated with Corinth in 2 Ti 4:20, and an inscription found at Corinth mentions an Erastus as a city official there. In Ro 16:1 Paul commends to the brethren at Rome a woman named Phoebe, a deaconess of the church at Cenchreae, the eastern harbor town of Corinth (she is probably the bearer of the Letter to the Romans). In Ro 16:23 Paul mentions Gaius as his host and transmits his greetings to the Romans. One Gaius was a member of the church at Corinth (1 Co 1:14); but since Gaius was a very common Roman name, this is not a particularly weighty piece of evidence.

5 The above paragraph assumes that ch. 16 is an original and integral part of the letter. Many scholars doubt this and are inclined to see in this chapter a letter, undoubtedly by Paul (with the possible

exception of vv. 25-27), addressed to the church at Ephesus, which somehow got attached to the Letter to the Romans when the letters of Paul were collected. The arguments for this hypothesis are chiefly the following: (1) The letter seems to come to a close at 15:33 with a benediction such as is common at the close of a Pauline letter. (2) The closing doxology (16:25-27) is placed at various points in the ancient manuscripts; some place it after 14:23, some after 15:33, and some after 16:23. This is thought to indicate that ch. 16 was not a fixed part of the letter in the manuscript tradition. (3) Paul greets 26 people in this chapter; it seems unlikely that Paul had so many friends in Rome, whereas it would be very natural for him to have so many friends in Ephesus, the scene of more than two years' missionary activity. (4) It seems unlikely that Aquila and Priscilla would change their place of residence so often as this chapter, as a part of the Letter to the Romans, would indicate. They have moved from Rome to Corinth, from Corinth to Ephesus, and thence again to Rome (Acts 18:2, 19; Ro 16:3); and a few years later they are once more in Ephesus (2 Ti 4:19). (5) The stern warning of 16:17-20 is not prepared for by anything in the first 15 chapters; the tone of the warning seems to be more brusque and authoritative than Paul's usually tactful way of addressing a church he has not himself founded and does not know personally.

6 These arguments are not conclusive. (1) 15:33 *is* a closing benediction, but a lengthy postscript to the letter is not inherently improbable. (2) The varying position of the doxology points to varying liturgical usage in the churches; they probably did not all read the last chapter or chapters in their public worship. This says nothing about the original length of the letter, for even the manuscripts that place the doxology early contain all 16 chapters of the letter. (3) We have no way of telling how many friends Paul might have had at Rome. It seems unlikely, however, that he would single out some two dozen persons for personal greetings in writing to Ephesus, where he knew and was known by all members of the church; that would be tactless, and Paul was not a tactless man. In a letter to an unknown church it would be natural for him to single out those whom he knew personally for special greetings and thus draw nearer to the church as a whole. (4) The movements of Aquila and Priscilla really present no problem. Travel was relatively easy and safe within the Roman Empire, so that people with business interests could move freely in the pursuit of commercial advantages; and besides, Aquila and Priscilla would probably move with the Gospel. (5) We do not know the historical situation well enough to judge whether the stern warning of 16:17-20 would be probable or improbable in a letter to the Romans. Chapters 12—15 bristle with strong imperatives; Paul tempers the brusqueness of his imperatives there with a tactful reference to the Romans' Christian maturity and capacity for mutual correction (15:14). He likewise tempers the brusqueness of Ro 16:17-20 by acknowledging the Romans' exemplary obedience to the Gospel (16:19). To conclude: it is difficult to explain how a letter to Ephesus got so firmly attached to the Letter to the Romans, and there is not a single outright witness for the omission of the chapter in all the manuscripts that have come down to us. Any hypothesis that separates the last chapter from the rest of the letter must be supported by weightier arguments than those hitherto advanced.

The Purpose of the Letter

7 Paul wrote his Letter to the Romans from Corinth during the winter A.D.55—56. His purpose in writing it is delicately but clearly stated in the letter itself. The letter is to prepare for his visit to Rome. But Rome is not his ultimate goal. It cannot be, for Paul has made it his ambition as apostle to the Gentiles "to preach the gospel, not where Christ has already been named," lest he "build on another man's foundation" (Ro 15:20). The apostle's task is to lay foundations, not to build on foundations already laid by others (1 Co 3:10). The foundation has long since been laid in Rome. Paul's language in the Letter to the Romans indicates that the church there had been in existence for some time; the faith of the Roman

Christians is already being proclaimed "in all the world" (1:8); their obedience is known to all (16:19); Paul has longed for many years to come to them (15:23). Non-Christian sources indicate that there was a church in Rome at least as early as A.D. 49 and probably earlier. Neither Paul or any other early source points to any single outstanding personality as founder of the Roman church; Christianity probably came to Rome through the agency of a number of nameless men such as the "visitors from Rome" who were present in Jerusalem at Pentecost (Acts 2:10) and later returned to Rome, bringing with them the Word of God "sent to Israel, preaching good news of peace by Jesus Christ." (Acts. 10:36)

8 The "visitors from Rome" present at Pentecost were in all probability Jews, and the church at Rome was no doubt strongly Jewish in its beginnings. At the time when Paul wrote to the Romans the church was no longer predominantly Jewish; indeed, Paul speaks of it and to it as a basically Gentile church (1:13-15; cf. 1:5-6; 11:13, 28-31). But there remained in it, no doubt, a strong Jewish-Christian element. The presence of this element helps explain why Paul in this letter expounds his Gospel by setting it in contrast to Judaism (the works of the Law, circumcision, descent from Abraham) and why he speaks at such length (chs. 9—11) of the relationship between the old Israel and the new Israel, the church.

9 Paul plans to spend some time in Rome to enrich and be enriched by his association with the Roman Christians and to proclaim the Gospel there (1:11-13; 15:24). But he is looking beyond Rome to Spain (15:24-28). Paul hopes to be "sped on his way" there by the Romans (15:24). The expression "to be sped on one's way" seems to have become almost technical for the support, both moral and material, given to missionaries by established churches or individual Christians (Acts 20:38; 21:5; 1 Co 16:6, 11; 2 Co 1:16; Tts 3:13; 3 Jn 6). Paul evidently hopes that Rome may become his missionary base in the West, what Syrian Antioch had been for him in the East.

10 This explains why the Letter to the Romans, a letter written merely to *prepare* for his visit to Rome, is so deep and massive a treatment of the Gospel, which Paul proclaims and now intends to proclaim in the West. Everything that we know of Paul's missionary preaching and missionary methods (for example, his practice of revisiting already established churches and his continued contact with them by letter or by means of personal emissaries) makes it clear that he did not aim at creating a vague, emotional, and enthusiastic movement but rather the firmly rooted, grounded, and established church of God in which the Word of Christ dwelt richly. What he looked for and strove for in a church that was to be his base in the West was a full and thorough going common understanding of the Gospel. At his former base in the East this common understanding was something he could presuppose. Antioch had been deeply influenced by Barnabas, and Paul himself had preached and taught at Antioch for a full year before the Holy Spirit sent him forth on his wider mission to the Gentiles (Acts 11:26;13:1-3). What a year's ministry had accomplished in the East, a brief visit and a single letter had to accomplish in the West. That letter had to be a full and rich one.

The Content of the Letter

11 The theme of the letter is announced in 1:16-17; it is the Gospel as the power of God for salvation. This theme is developed in four great movements of thought that unfold the creative power of the Gospel (1:18—15:13). This body of the letter is preceded and followed by sections that make clear paul's relationship of the Romans to the gospel's westward movement. The following outline may serve as a guide:

OUTLINE

I. 1:1-15 Introduction

II. 1:16—15:13 The Gospel That Goes Westward
- A. 1:16—5:21 The Gospel Creates a New Status for Man
  1. 1:16—3:20 The Old Status: Man Under the Revelation of the Wrath of God
  2. 3:21—5:21 The New Status: Man Under the Revelation of the Righteousness of God
- B. 6:1—8:39 The Gospel Creates a New Life in Man.
  1. 6:1-23 Man Is Freed from Sin
  2. 7:1-25 Man Is Freed from the Law
  3. 8:1-39 Man Is Freed from Death
- C. 9:1—11:36 The Gospel Creates a New Israel out of Jew and Gentile
  1. 9:1-29 God's Freedom to Create His Israel as He Wills
  2. 9:30—10:21 God's Justice in Rejecting Ancient Israel
  3. 11:1-36 God's Wisdom in the Creation of His New Israel
- D. 12:1—15:13 The Gospel Creates a New Worship for the New People of God
  1. 12:1—13:14 All Life in the Church and in the World a Spiritual Worship
  2. 14:1—15:13 The Weak and the Strong in Faith United in One Worship for the Glory of God

III. 15:14—16:27 Conclusion
- A. 15:14-33 The Apostle's Plans: From Jerusalem to Rome to Spain
- B. 16:1-16, 21-24 Commendation and Greetings
- C. 16:17-20 The Apostle's Warning
- D. 16:25-27 Concluding Doxology.

1:1-15 INTRODUCTION: GREETINGS, THANKSGIVING, AND PRAYER

1:1-7 GREETINGS: PAUL, THE BEARER OF THE GOSPEL

1:1-7 Paul's greeting follows a common ancient letter form: The sender (1) to the recipients (7a), greetings (7b). But it differs from the ancient form in two points; for one thing the first element (naming of the sender) is greatly expanded, a feature found only in ancient OFFICIAL letters; for another, the whole is given a distinctly Christian character and content. It is Paul's confession to the *grace* (cf. 5) which *called* and consecrated *(set apart,* 1) him to be an accredited and authorized messenger of Christ *(apostle,* 1), bearer of the Gospel which proclaims Him universally *(among all nations,* 5) as *Son of David* and *Son of God in power,* the risen *Lord* (3-4) to whom every knee must bow for His glory *(obedience of faith for the sake of his name,* 5). By virtue of this God-given authority he invokes on the Roman people of God *(called to be saints,* 7) the undeserved recreating favor of God *(grace,* 7) and His *peace* (7), the well-being of divine health which God's fatherly grace revealed in the *Lord Jesus Christ* creates for men. (7)

1:1 *Servant* (or *slave)* expresses Paul's total subjection and devotion to his Lord and at the same time states a high claim; he stands in the succession of men of God of the OT who were permitted to speak His Word and execute His purposes: Moses (Jos 1:2), Joshua (Jos 24:29), David (Ps 78:70), and the prophets (Am 3:7; Jer 7:25; Dn 9:6). Jesus Himself applied the title to His apostles. (Mt 10:24-25; Jn 13:16)

1:2 *Promised . . . prophets . . . holy scriptures.* God's Gospel is the culmination of His revelation, the fulfillment of His promises; therefore Paul cherishes, together with Jesus and all the men of the NT, the ancient OT writings as Holy Scriptures, God's own Word.

1:5 *Grace and apostleship.* Cf. 1 Co 15:10; Eph 3:8; 1 Ti 1:12-14.

Among all the nations. The universal lordship of Christ makes Paul's apostleship universal. Hence his great interest in Rome, that crossroads of the nations, and in lands beyond Rome, like Spain. (Cf. 15:24, 28)

1:7 *God's beloved . . . called . . . saints.* The combination constitutes a good description of what the Bible means by saints; men whom God in His love has called to be His own and serve Him.

Lord is the most comprehensive confession of Jesus in His significance for faith. (Cf. 10:9-13; Ph 2:11)

1:8-15 THE APOSTLE'S THANKSGIVING AND PRAYER

1:8-15 Paul gives thanks for the *faith* (8) of the Roman church. Faith is so essential to the Christian life that he uses the term to designate the whole existence and activity of the Roman Christians. The life of faith in Rome has been so active and effective that it has made worldwide news; and the apostle, dedicated to bringing about "the obedience of faith . . . among all nations" (5) must needs follow and foster the course of that life with his prayers. He prays to God that he may fulfill his long-cherished desire (cf. Acts 19:21) to visit Rome in order to *reap some harvest* (13) of men won for Christ among them and to *strengthen* (and be strengthened by, 12) them for the task of carrying the Gospel to the western regions beyond Rome. (Cf. 15:24)

1:13 *Harvest.* For the metaphor cf. Mt. 9:37-38; 1 Co 3:6-9; 9:10-12.

1:14-15 *I am under obligation . . . I am eager.* Under the grace of God, duty and desire become one in the bearer of the Gospel.

1:16—5:21 THE GOSPEL CREATES A NEW STATUS FOR MAN

1:16—3:20 The Old Status: Man Under the Wrath of God

1:16-17 THEME OF THE LETTER

1:16-17 Paul is eager to preach the Gospel to the men of Rome, his gateway to the West. With that he has reached the point where he must deal at length with that which impels him Romeward and westward. He now states the theme which is to occupy him for the rest of the letter: the Gospel as the *power of God for salvation,* the revelation of the *righteousness of God,* to all believers. He is *not ashamed* of the Gospel, though his missionary experience has taught him that the *Jew* finds the good news of a crucified Messiah offensive and the intellectual Greek finds it foolishness (1 Co 1:23) and knows that he will meet both Jew and Greek again in Rome; for he knows that the Gospel is not a product of Judaic dreams and not a plausible system of thought competing with plausible systems devised by the Greek. He knows that the Gospel is no less than the power of God which can effect the salvation of man, a radical deliverance out of man's desperate situation (cf. Ex 14:13; 15:2). The Gospel is power because in it a revelation takes place; by it God makes Himself known and makes Himself count among men. The Gospel is news of God's action through His Son (cf. 1:3-4), a saving action which gives men the gift of the righteousness of God. Gift it is, for it asks of the hearer only the receptive yes of faith, and it creates that faith in the hearer; it is revealed for faith. And the Gospel has for it the witness of God's prophets, through whom God promised His Gospel beforehand (1:2). In the day when the whole hope of God's people seemed cut off, Habakkuk had uttered the great word which pronounced the unbreakable connection between faith, righteousness, and life: *He who through faith is righteous shall live.* (Hab 2:4)

1:16 *To the Jew first.* To the Jew the promises had been made, and so the good news of their fulfillment comes to him first. Paul was mindful of this as missionary; wherever he came, he preached first in the synagog (Acts 13:14-16, 46), and in his work among the Gentiles he never lost sight of his fellow Jews. (Ro 11:13-14)

1:18-32 THE WRATH OF GOD ON IDOLATRY

1:18-32 The Gospel is the power of God to deliver man out of a desperate situation. It is a desperate situation; for man is under the revelation, the making known and making felt, of the *wrath of God,* God's fearfully destructive reaction to man's *ungodliness and wickedness.* Men *suppress the truth,* the truth of truths, the encountered reality of God and His will for man *(decree,* 32). They know God but will *not honor him as God or give thanks to him* (21). In their folly (22) they seek independence of God but cannot free themselves from Him wholly, and so they exchange *the glory of the immortal God* for gods of their own devising, worshiping and serving *the creature rather than the Creator* (24-25). God is not mocked; He uses the very wickedness of man, that dubious liberty which they sought when they fled from the Creator by suppressing the truth, to punish their ungodliness. God gives men up, judicially, to the wickedness they wanted by giving them more of it than they wanted; He delivers them up to the degradation of their unleashed sensuality (24), to the debasement of sexual perversion (26-27), to the *base mind* which sets man against man and makes men hell to each other in the social order that was designed by God to be their protection and blessing. (28-32)

1:18 *From heaven.* It is as inescapable as the revelation of God's wrath at the end of days (2:5). All days since the coming of God's Son are "last days" (Heb 1:2), and the revelation of wrath in these days is the upbeat of that last dreadful music of damnation.

1:29-31 All the vices listed here have this in common: they rend the fabric of society and make an agony of communal life.

2:1-11 THE WRATH OF GOD THE JUDGE UPON THE MAN WHO JUDGES HIS FELLOWMAN.

2:1-11 Many of Paul's contemporaries, both Jews and Greeks, would concur with his condemnation of the idolatry and immorality of the pagan world and assent to his proclamation of the wrath of God on them. They would thereby exempt themselves from the judgment proclaimed and feel secure in their ethical superiority to the libertine, the pervert, and the antisocial criminal. Paul's aim is to stop every mouth and to make all the world, including the ethical world, accountable to God (3:19); otherwise he cannot bring men to the obedience of faith. As long as a man still has the strength and confidence to judge his fellowman, he is not ready to receive, in the beggary of faith, the radical rescue of the righteousness of God. Paul therefore proceeds to proclaim the judgment of God on these judges of mankind. In assenting to God's judgment on others they are (he tells them) passing judgment on themselves, for they are equally guilty of suppressing the truth when they commit, in refined form perhaps, the wickedness they condemn. No man dare think that he is the one exception to God's judgment; no man dare see in the forbearing kindness of God toward himself a license to continue in his sin; when God's *kindness is meant to lead* him, not to a sense of security but to *repentance* (3-4). The Judge whom the ethical men have been applauding is a righteous and impartial Judge, who will judge men not by the quality of their ethical judgments but by their deeds.

2:10 *The Jew first.* Cf. 1:16. If the Jew misused his priority in the grace of God, he has a priority in punishment, as his own prophets have warned him. (Am 3:2)

The proclamation of the impartial judgment of God on every man according to his works is really one great question addressed to man: "You knew Me; did you honor and thank Me by doing My will?" But God Himself has made a great distinction between the Jew and the rest of mankind. He made His covenant with Israel and gave His law to Israel alone. The one great question therefore breaks down into two questions. Concerning the Gentiles: Did the nations without the Law know God? Can God hold them accountable? Concerning the Jew: He knew God, no doubt; the only question concerning him is, Did he do God's will? Paul deals with these two questions in 2:12-24.

2:12-16 THE QUESTION CONCERNING THE GENTILE

2:12-16 All who sin will perish, each man being judged on the basis of the revelation God has given him. The deed is what counts, whether it is done by a Jew who possesses the Law or by a Gentile who has it not. The deed will decide in the judgment; the deed is the great leveler between Gentile and Jew. And yet the Jew is guided in his action by the written Law, the direct, express Word of God. But, Paul says, God has attested His will to the Gentile too; the finger of God has written on his heart what the Law requires. The deeds of the Gentiles testify to that. So does their conscience. The voice of conscience may be howled down by the voice of mad desire or reasoned out of court by the perverse logic of the base mind. But it is still there; the thoughts which Gentile men think upon their deeds are still *conflicting thoughts,* some for the prosecution, some for the defense. Each Gentile carries about in his heart a secret miniature of the Last Judgment as it were. It will no longer be secret when the Last Judgment comes. On that day God will judge the *secrets of men.* Judgment according to works is clearly not a judgment on the bare, external deed; a man is judged by the deeds with which he has expressed the hidden motions of his heart.

2:16 *According to my gospel.* Over against the idea that the Gospel of free grace is an invitation to continue in sin (6:1; cf. 3:8; Ph 3:18-19) Paul solemnly asserts that "his" Gospel is the Gospel of God, the Gospel of that divine grace which can forgive and overcome sin but cannot compromise with sin. The Christ of "his" Gospel is the Judge of man as surely as He is his Savior (2 Co 5:10). Paul is servant and apostle of the Christ who spoke judgment on salt that loses its saltness (Mt 5:13) and kept His disciples mindful of the fact that a man's life moves on a path that takes him to his Judge. (Mt 5:25-26; 7:1, 16:27)

2:17-24 THE QUESTION CONCERNING THE JEW

2:17-24 The Jew knows God's will and proudly fancies himself the destined teacher and enlightener of mankind. Only he does not keep the Law, which is his pride; he brings disgrace on his God by flouting it.

To sum up: The Gentile is a law to himself; the Jew has and knows the Law. Both, when they sin, suppress the truth; both are without excuse.

2:21-22 Paul's indictment of the Jew is the same as Jesus': "They preach, but do not practice." (Mt 23:3)

2:22 *Abhor idols . . . rob temples.* The Jew expresses his contempt for idols by robbing their temples, but in that act he gives his heart to the idol Mammon.

2:23-24 What Isaiah (52:5) and Ezekiel (36:20) once said of the captive people of God must be said now of the Jew who boasts of the Law but does not obey it. Both provoke the blasphemous taunt: "Where is your God?"

2:25-29 CIRCUMCISION AND THE LAW

2:25-29 Not the mere possession of the Law makes the Jew a Jew. Long before the giving of the Law, God made His covenant with father Abraham and his descendants and set on it the sign and seal of circumcision. In circumcision God incised on the flesh of the Jew His pledge "I will be your God" (cf. Gn 17). Could the Jew, then, thus marked and honored by God, be made to stand on a level with the Gentiles in the judgment? Would not the enduring covenantal sacrament shield him from the wrath of God? Paul replies: Circumcision is the sign both of God's gift and of His claim to the Jews; the covenant puts the Jew under both the promise and the command of God, and he is called on to speak his Amen to the promise by obeying the command (cf. Dt 10:16; Jer 4:4, 6:10). Circumcision is no magic spell, but God's personal dealing with responsible man. If a man breaks the Law, the covenant of God, circumcision cannot save him; it indicts him. The obedient Gentile, uncircumcised though he be, succeeds to the position of the disobedient Jew. More than that, since he has been obedient where the Jew has failed, he is in person the living condemnation of the Jew who with God's law before him and God's mark upon him yet breaks the Law. The true Jew is in fact not an ethnic quantity at all. A line must be drawn between the physical Jew and the Jew in heart whose *praise is . . . from God,* (29), on whom God's good pleasure rests.

2:29 *Praise.* Paul is alluding to the root meaning of the name Judah, from which "Jew" is derived. When Judah was born, his mother cried out, "I will praise the Lord" (Gn 29:35), and Jacob's blessing on his son Judah, the bearer of the Messianic promise, was, "Your brothers shall praise you." (Gn 49:8)

3:1-20 THE JEW'S OBJECTIONS AND PAUL'S REPLIES

3:1-20 Three times the objection to Paul's indictment is heard (1, 5, 9a); Paul's reply follows in each case, in vv. 2-4, 6-8, and 9b-20. This last section with its cluster of quotations from the OT and two summarizing sentences (19-20) rounds off not only the dialog with the Jew but the whole major section which begins at 1:18.

The first Judaic objection is: "If possession of the Law and circumcision does not avail in the Judgment, at the one point where it matters supremely, what advantage DOES the Jew have?" The Jew is asking the question in order to evade the call to repentance that is contained in the proclamation of the wrath and the impartial judgment of God. Paul, seeking by all means to save some (1 Co 9:22), honors the question and deals seriously with it. He concentrates in his reply on the one great advantage of the Jew: he has been *entrusted with the oracles of God* (2). To him God gave Law and Promise; to him he spoke by His servants the prophets and in the last days by His Son (cf. Mt 21:37; Heb 1:1). With these utterances the Jew was entrusted; what God spoke to the children of Abraham was intended for a blessing on all the families of the earth (Gn 12:3; 18:18; 22:17-18; 26:4). Paul's reply meets the uttered objection and anticipates another related objection ("If the blessing is contingent upon our obedience to these oracles, where is our advantage?"). He remembers the faithful remnant in Israel who remained faithful (11:5). The failure of others does not call into question the validity and power of the Word given to Israel. God is still faithful to His given Word. To deny that this Word, present and still speaking, is an advantage is to utter blasphemy, a denial of the bedrock affirmation of OT and NT, the affirmation that God is true, that His Word holds, whatever else may break. Where God's will and man's collide, it is axiomatic for faith that the will of man is false. This faith speaks in the words of the psalmist (4) who will not attempt to conceal or excuse his sin but confesses it freely (Paul's brief quotation is intended to recall the context of Ps 51:3-4) in order that God may be seen to be the righteous God that He is and all men may be still and know that He is God of all men. (Cf. Ps 46:10)

The second objection (5) attaches itself to Paul's previous reply: "If God always *prevails when* He is *judged,* does not the history of our nation, blackened as it is by our unfaithfulness, show forth God's justice, His fidelity to the covenant which we broke—can He still in justice *inflict wrath* on us for what in the last analysis glorifies Him?" Paul replies (6-8) that the Jew's objection proves too much: since God's sovereign control of history overrules the sin of all men, to His glory, every sinner could make this plea and God would have to abdicate as (what both Jew and Christian confess Him to be) Judge of the world. Even Paul, whom the Jew hated and despised as a renegade to the faith of his fathers, whose Gospel seemed to them an open invitation to sin for the greater glory of God, even he would no longer be condemned. Paul pauses to pronounce judgment on those who caricature his Gospel as they do: *Their condemnation is just.* (8)

The third objection is no longer a reasoned one, but irony: "Are we Jews actually worse off?" (This rendering or the one given in RSV note *c* is to be preferred to the one given in the text, as fitting better in this context). Paul's answer (9b-20) is what he has been maintaining all along: All men stand equally guilty before the tribunal of God. But Paul repeats with a difference. (a) Here sin appears as a *power* ruling over men (cf. 5:12, 21; 6:6, 7, 12, 14, etc.). (b) Paul enforces his indictment of man with the witness of the OT, its verdict on man. This is the Jew's Bible speaking to his people; this the Jew cannot evade. His Psalter (Ps 14:1-3; 5:9; 140:3; 10:7; 36:1) and his prophets (Is 59:7-8) combine to *stop* his *mouth* (19). The last sentence of Paul's reply (20) introduces two new thoughts that he will treat more fully later: man's inability to find acceptance before God by way of *works of the law* (man's own effort to win the acquitting verdict of God) and the Law's uncanny effect of man under the domination of sin, that of *the knowledge of sin* (20); through man's confrontation with the Law, sin becomes a powerful reality in man's life. (Cf. ch. 7)

Thus every mouth pleading in man's defense is stopped. The old status of man under sin and wrath is, for man, irrevocable and fixed. If he is to have a new status, he can obtain it only if God, his Judge, creates it, and he can receive it only as His gift, by faith.

3:21—5:21 The New Status: Man Under the Righteousness of God

3:21-31 MAN'S FREE ACQUITTAL

3:21-31 *But now* God has spoken, and all mankind must fall silent. His Word is acquittal, full and free *(as a gift,* 24). This is judicial action, but it is *apart from law* (21), indeed it violates all legal justice. Legal justice can recognize the fact that a man is righteous: only God's righteousness can make a man righteous. God makes man a gift of His acquittal and gives him, effectually, the status of righteousness, lets him stand and count as righteous in His sight. He bestows righteousness on man (cf. Ph 3:9). That is pure grace, gratuitous favor, against all man's deserving. This acquitting and restoring grace is lavish, generous, without reserve. But it is neither sentimental nor arbitrary. It does not simply ignore sin. God deals with sin; in His grace He remains the God of justice. His freely given acquittal has a solid basis in the *redemption* which He Himself has provided *in Christ Jesus.* God's grace was a holy, costly grace. He ransomed men from their ruined past "with the precious blood of Christ" (1 Ptr 1:19). He did not spare His son but "gave him up for us all" (8:32). He restored man to communion with Himself by providing the perfect and availing sacrifice *(expiation,* 25) in His Son. In going the way of grace to the utmost by way of redemption and sacrifice God has asserted His righteousness to the utmost. In passing over sins in the past, He did so with this hour and this act of love and justice in view. When He now justifies the man *who has faith in Jesus* (26), there is no "as if" in that acquitting verdict; it is a serious, executed verdict. All merit of man disappears; all *boasting* of man is silenced. There is now room only for the faith which receives everything from God and gives all glory to God: the believing Greek sheds his sorry wisdom, leaves his idols (1:22-23), and bows down before his God. The believing Jew strips off the filthy rags of his own righteousnes (Is 64:6), drops his high pretensions, and finds the God of Abraham who justifies the ungodly (4:5), a God greater than the God he knew when he worshiped Him as the God of the Law; for if the Law given to the Jew is God's first and last word, God is *God of the Jews only* (29), not the God of all. But He is manifested now in His acquitting Word to all who have faith as the Lord of all, Jew and Gentile alike. The First Commandment, and every other commandment that reveals His will, is made to stand and count in this new revelation made to faith. Men who believe do what the Law requires, what men suppressing the truth have failed to do: they glorify God. (1:21; 4:20)

4:1-25 JUSTIFICATION THROUGH FAITH: THE DECISIVE CASE OF ABRAHAM

4:1-25 *What then shall we say about Abraham?* (1) Paul dare not ignore Abraham if he would win the Jew, for Judaic legend had made of Abraham a "works" hero, one who had kept the Law (revealed to him by special dispensation four centuries before Sinai) perfectly—for the Jew, Abraham was clearly justified by works. Moreover, Paul's loyalty to the OT Scripture (1:2, 17; 3:21) made it imperative that he speak of Abraham; for according to Scripture, God's dealing with Abraham represents the first and basic step in the creation of the people of God; if Paul represents God as acting now, in Christ, in a way that contradicts that first and primal act, he is flouting the authority of God's Word. And the question then is not merely one of formal authority; it is theological. If the Gospel of Paul is God's Gospel, it must remain in harmony with God's earlier revelation of Himself. The case of Abraham will decide whether Paul is proclaiming the mighty acts of the Creator and Redeemer revealed in the OT (as Paul himself avers), or is indeed, as the Athenians once suspected (Acts 17:18), introducing an alien God.

Paul therefore uses the OT itself to demonstrate that Abraham was justified through faith, *apart from works* (1-8); through faith, without circumcision (9-12), through faith, without the Law. (13-15)

WITHOUT WORKS (1:8): In the one place where Genesis speaks of Abraham's righteousness (15:6), it speaks not of Abraham's doing but of his believing. Here God was acting, and Abraham remained passive; God reckoned his faith to him as righteousness. God opened up the future for him and all mankind by forgiving him with that free and total forgiveness of which David sang (Ps 32:1-2) and so of His free grace made him a blessing.

WITHOUT CIRCUMCISION (9-12): The Judaic teachers contended hat the blessing pronounced by Ps 32 applied only to the circumcised, specifically to the Israelites on the Day of Atonement (Lv 16). Paul shows from the OT record that Abraham came under the blessing of Ps 32 before he received circumcision, the sign and seal of his justification. The reckoned righteousness received by faith (Gn 15) and the gift of circumcision are two chapters and (according to the rabbis) 29 years apart. Thus in the case of Abraham faith counted supremely, and all men of faith, not only the circumcised, can claim Abraham as father.

WITHOUT THE LAW (13-15): Where God promises, God is at work, not demanding but giving. Where the law of God demands works of man, there is wrath of God over against the failure of man, and there can be no justification. But where the promise is, God's creative giving deals and does away with man's transgression and unites man with his God. If God's word to Abraham is promise, it must be pure promise, unmixed with and unadulterated by the demands of the Law.

Abraham's faith depended wholly on the promise (20), for he saw the possibility of life and blessing in God alone, in God who gives life to the dead and calls into existence the things that do not exist (17); he saw in himself only death (18-19), and so he gave glory to God alone, the sole Author and Giver of life as He is the sole Author of righteousness.

Abraham's faith is the prototype and exemplar of the Christian's faith (23-25). The Christian sees in Christ's death the hopelessness and inevitable dying of man, sees in His resurrection the divinely given sole possibility of life for man, because it is God's righteousness for man. And the Christian lives by his hold on the redeeming Word of God, the Gospel, which proclaims and gives him Christ as his righteousness and life.

4:2 *Something to boast about.* Thus Abraham would be a refutation of what Paul said in 3:27.

4:5 *Justifies the ungodly.* Perhaps the most pointed formulation of justification in the NT. Forgiveness as pure gift (cf. 3:24) to man under the wrath of God. (Cf. 1:18)

4:13 *Promise . . . that they should inherit the world.* Paul uses the language with which Judaic teachers used to paraphrase God's promises to Abraham.

5:1-11 THE NEW STATUS: PEACE WITHOUT END

5:1-11 Our new status before God is no neutral state. Being justified does not mean merely that we have "gotten off" unpunished. It means *peace* in the full sense given to that word by the OT, that divinely normal state in which we have access to God and His grace, grace as the power that enables us to stand and play our part according to the will of God. Peace fills the present, and it opens up a future that is cause for exultation: *sharing* in the very *glory of God.* That bright prospect makes present *suffering,* too, a cause for rejoicing, for faith can recognize in suffering that same unparalleled love of God that has justified us contrary to all our deserving; and suffering, by tempering us and strengthening us, gives us that sure *hope* which only the Spirit-given knowledge of the love of God can inspire: the reconciling love that sought and found us when we were *still weak* (6), incapable of response; *ungodly* (6) and *sinners* (8), *enemies* (10) of the Christ who died for us—that love assures us that the *wrath of God* (9) which looms up at the end of all men's ways to destroy them does not loom up at the end of our new way; the living Christ, once dead for our salvation, looms up, and He will save us from the wrath to come. *We . . . rejoice in God.* (11)

5:12-21 THE OLD AND THE NEW: ADAM AND CHRIST

5:12-21 From his vantage point of exultant certainty Paul looks back and surveys the ground he has traveled. All that he has said of sin and grace, of Law and Gospel, of man's old status under the judgment of God and his new status under the acquittal of God, he sums up once more in the monumental comparison-and-contrast between Adam and Christ. After stating the first half of the comparison-contrast (12), he inserts two parenthetical thoughts; one (13-14) is designed to support his statement that *all men sinned* in the death-dealing primal sin of Adam, head of the human race, that the sway of death over mankind is due to mankind's solidarity in sin with Adam—what else could explain the unbroken universal sway of death during the period without Law between Adam and Moses?

The other parenthesis (15-17) safeguards the unique glory of Christ against the misunderstanding that Christ and Adam are equal forces in the life of mankind. Three times Paul asserts the positive, vital, creative plus on the side of Christ. Then (19-20) two pithy statements enunciate the comparison-contrast between Adam's trespass and disobedience and Christ's act of righteousness and obedience, both universally effective in their result for all mankind. A brief (20-21) conclusion points up the subordinate and negative role of the Law in the desperate situation created by the sin of Adam and resolved triumphantly by the grace of God. Grace has established a reign whose gift to man is righteousness. That reign means life, unbroken, full, eternal life. That grace, reign, righteousness, life—all are through Jesus Christ, our Lord.

5:12 *Therefore.* Since Christ is the key Figure in the history of God's dealing with man (cf. the frequent use of "through" Christ or "by" Christ in the preceding, 1:5; 1:8; 2:16; 5:1-2), He may be compared to another key figure in that history, Adam.

5:14 *Type.* In Adam was prefigured in black the bright figure of Him who would, like Adam, by His action determine the history of all mankind and be the Beginning, Head, and Representative of a new mankind.

6:1—8:39 THE GOSPEL CREATES A NEW LIFE IN MAN

6:1-23 Man is Freed from Sin

6:1—8:39 The creative force of the gospel as God's power for man's salvation is not exhausted in creating a new status for man; it creates a new life in man, and it is to this aspect of salvation that Paul devotes the next three chapters. His Gospel proclaims the same act which gives man his new status through faith, namely, the death and resurrection of God's Son, as giving man a new life lived in the obedience of faith: for that act of God frees man for obedience. It liberates him from the power of sin (ch. 6, esp. 6:3-4, 11), from the Law (ch. 7, esp. 7:4-6), and from death. (Ch. 8, esp. 8:3-4, 10-11)

6:1-14 FREED FROM SIN BY SHARING IN CHRIST'S DEATH AND RESURRECTION THROUGH BAPTISM

6:1-14 If increasing sin means abounding grace (5:20), a satanic kind of logic might conclude that man might well *continue in sin* (1). But such logic is impossible for the man of faith. For faith knows that man cannot fly in the face of an action of God's. By an action of God's by the death and resurrection of His Son, made ours in our baptism, continuing in sin has become not only reprehensible but impossible, as impossible as reversing the irreversible act of Christ's death and resurrection. That death and resurrection embraced us all and ushers us into a wholly new kind of life, the resurrection-life of Christ, in which there is no room for sinning. Paul's proclamation in vv. 5-10 is but an underscoring of this double statement: (a) the reality of our union with Christ through Baptism; (b) the wholly new quality of our resurrection-life.

Three times he asserts the reality of our union with the dying and resurrected Christ (5, 6, 8). A real death has taken place, a death-and-burial death, as Jesus' was (4); a criminal's death (*crucified,* 6) which destroyed our old, active criminal self (*sinful body,* 6) and set us free for righteousness; a death that opens up a future in which we may live as Christ now lives, His back forever turned to sin, *to God* (10). Our present life gets its character, direction, and purpose from the fact that we shall live with Him who now lives a life beyond death; a life lived wholly to God, now that He has died an atoning death, once for all, to sin. Now, and not until now, Paul utters his first imperatives (11-13). Now that his word has revealed the way trodden by Christ before us and for us, he can bid us enter on that way. And he gives us courage and strength to enter by pronouncing the promise: *Sin will have no dominion over you . . . you are . . . under grace* (14). We enter, not under the compulsion of Law but under the power of enabling grace.

6:15-23 FREED FROM SIN AND ENSLAVED TO RIGHTEOUSNESS THROUGH THE WORD

6:15-23 Being *under grace* does not revive the old wild dream of "continuing in sin." Rather, it forces us to face facts and gives us the power to face them and joy in facing them. One set of facts is grim: the fact that we cannot "take or leave sin"—sin takes us, enslaves us (16), and rewards us with the due reward (wages) of *death* (23). Being *free in regard to righteousness* (20) is the most dubious of dubious liberties. The other set of facts is glorious: God Himself has freed us from that dubious liberty by Himself committing us to His Word (*standard of teaching,* 17) and making us obedient to it. He has made us slaves to Him "whom to serve is perfect liberty." He has caught us up into His work of making God's men of us (*sanctification,* 19-22) and holds out to us His *free gift of . . . eternal life in Christ Jesus our Lord* (23). God's facts are infinitely better than our tawdry dreams.

7:1-25 Man Is Freed from the Law

7:1-25 Paul has drawn a sharp division between the Gospel and the Law (3:28; cf. 3:20). The working and effect of the Law is the opposite of that of the Gospel, negative and destructive. It indicts the Jew (2:17-24) and renders all men accountable to God (3:19). It makes sin a known and experienced reality in man's life (3:20) and therefore "brings wrath" (4:15); it increases the trespass initiated by Adam (5:20). Men can live to God only when grace replaces Law as the impelling power in their lives (6:14). Why does the Law, the Word of God, have this uncanny effect on man, and why must man be liberated from it if he is to be God's saint? Paul answers this question in 7:7-25. Before that he answers another, related question: How is it possible that man be liberated from the Law, that holy, just, and good (7:12) Word of God?

7:1-6 HOW CAN MAN BE FREED FROM THE LAW?

7:1-6 Liberation from the Law is not an arbitrary act of man. It is a liberation on the Law's own terms, by death, which severs legal ties, as the analogy of marriage shows. By God's action we died to the Law *through the body of Christ* (4) and were set free by Him that we might *serve* Him in the *new life* bestowed by His *Spirit.*

7:6 *New life of the Spirit.* This, the first reference to the Spirit, points forward to the theme of ch. 8, "the law of the Spirit of life in Christ Jesus." (8:2)

7:7-25 WHY MUST MAN BE LIBERATED FROM THE LAW?

7:7-25 The Law is *holy* and its commandment is *holy and just and good* (12). But sin, that diabolic power, manifests itself in its true colors (13) by using just that good Word of God to rouse in man the dormant will of opposition to God which destroys him. Paul illustrates this working of the Law (as misused by the power of sin) from both his early life (7-13) and from his experience with the Law as a Christian (14-25). It was contact with the Law, confronting him as the *commandment,* that first gave sin its deadly power in his life (9-11). Paul the Christian, when confronted by the Law, becomes a man rent by an agonizing inner struggle (14-24) from which only Christ can and does release him. (25)

7:7 *Covet* has a wider scope than the English word "covet" commonly indicates, namely, all the self-centered desiring of man which ignores or opposes the will of God.

7:8 *Lies dead.* Is dormant and therefore inactive.

7:11 *Sin . . . deceived me.* The tragic history of the Fall (Gn 3) was reenacted in Paul's life; sin is personified in the role of the Tempter.

7:14 *Sold under sin.* Not the old slavery of preconversion days, where total slave-devotion (6:20) made any other tie impossible; here the claim of sin is offset and opposed by an anterior and superior claim. (15:17)

7:24 *Body of death.* The unceasing encroachment of sin (21-23) threatens ever and again to make the body a "sinful body" (6:6), the expressive instrument of the sinner's revolt against God, and thus to doom it to death.

8:1-39 Man Is Freed from Death

8:1-8 THE ESTABLISHMENT OF THE LAW OF THE SPIRIT OF LIFE

8:1-8 Where sin reigns, there is death (6:16, 21, 23). Where Jesus Christ is Lord, sin is overcome and the Law no longer controls and condemns; there is a new "law," a new and compelling order of things which sets men free from the old dark orders of sin and death. Christ's order is the order of righteousness and life, presented and enforced by the Spirit of life. This new order of the Spirit of life was inaugurated by the sending of Christ. The Law could not break the old order, for it could not overcome the *flesh,* man's innate will of opposition to God. God did overcome it by sending His Son into the flesh, wholly identified with man, to endure a penal and sacrificial *(as a sin offering,* 3; RSV note *i)* death for man's sin. By His death the Spirit, God's own creative and renewing presence, was released for man and creates new possibilities of obedience in man; now the *just requirement of the law* (4) can be fulfilled—there can be a people of God living in love with God and one another where the Spirit is at work. Nothing less than this action of God and this Spirit of God will overcome man's fleshly, deathward bent and give him life and peace under God. The indwelling Spirit (ch. 8) triumphs over indwelling sin. (Ch. 7)

8:1 *Therefore . . . no condemnation . . . in Christ Jesus. Therefore* is the logic of faith, which reasons thus: Whatever I lack and need I find in Christ. If the Law condemns (ch. 7), it follows that there is acquittal *(no condemnation)* in Christ.

8:9-17 THE PRESENT LIFE OF THE CHRISTIAN UNDER THE NEW LAW

8:9-17 Life in the Spirit—and that is what the Christian life is, if it be Christian (9)—is life with a future. The grave is not its goal; the indwelling of the Spirit is the sure pledge that our *mortal bodies* (11) will be raised from death as Jesus' body was.

Life in the Spirit is life with a purpose.—We are bound *(debtors,* 12) to live the new life of freedom under the law of the Spirit of life, on pain of death; we are led by the Spirit to lead the Son's life of obedience to the Father whom we can address with the familiarity of a child's love *(Abba!* 15) by the prompting of the Spirit. As *heirs of God and fellow heirs with Christ* (17) we can go steadfastly down the road of Christ through suffering to glory.

8:15 *Abba.* In Jesus' mother tongue this word was the child's address to its father, the word Jesus Himself (who did not lose a child's dependence and trust in manhood) used to address His Father at the supreme crisis of His life (Mk 14:36; cf. Gl 4:6). The Spirit who brought to remembrance all that Jesus had told His disciples (Jn 14:26) implanted the word in the prayers of the church in its original form.

8:18-39 THE FUTURE OF THE CHRISTIAN UNDER THE LAW

8:18-39 The glory that awaits the suffering fellow heirs of Christ is so great that present sufferings cannot outweigh it (18) nor can Paul describe it. He pictures it by describing the greatness of the longing it evokes. All *creation . . . subjected to futility* by the fall of man (20; cf. Gn 3) and destined to participate in the final *glorious liberty of the children of God* (21) longs for the day when it shall be set free from *its bondage to decay* (21). Men, who possess in the Spirit a foretaste and a pledge of that glory, *groan inwardly* (23) in the intensity of their longing for the day when their sonship shall be freely manifested and fully enjoyed, when their bodies shall be transformed into glorious bodies (Ph 3:21), fit instruments to serve Him whom they can call Abba even now. Even the *Spirit* (26), who prompts the Christian's prayers, joins in the universal longing and *intercedes* for saints in their stammering weakness when they pray, "Thy kingdom come!" That glory is as certain as it is great (28-30). For those who know the unparalleled love of God for them and love Him because He first loved them, for such man a golden chain of unbreakable certitude links all actions of God together, from His first motion of eternal predestining love to the crowning act which will give to His firstborn glorified Son a host of glorified brethren.

Standing on this height, Paul leads all Christendom in a song of triumphant certitude (31-39): He who in the unsparing sanctity of His love gave up His Son for us all will give us no less than all. The Judge of mankind has spoken; no one can reverse His verdict. Christ sits enthroned beside His Father; who dares to raise a voice against His intercession for us? No sufferings, no powers seen or unseen, no aspect or dimension of all creation can henceforth *separate us from the love of God in Christ Jesus our Lord.* (39)

9:1—11:36 THE GOSPEL CREATES A NEW ISRAEL OUT OF JEW AND GENTILE

9:1-29 God's Freedom to Create His Israel as He Wills

9:1—11:36 As surely as the Gospel creates a new status for man before God (chs. 1—5) and creates a new life in man that sets him free to serve God by the power of His Spirit (chs. 6—8), so surely it creates a new Israel, a new people of God in the last days. The new Israel has a continuity with the old; its members can call Abraham "father" (4:12) and walk in the footsteps of his faith (4:12). But there is also a tragic and disturbing discontinuity; there are many Gentile sons of believing Abraham, but few from among the Jews who "follow the examples of the faith" of Abraham (4:12). It is quite natural, then, that when Paul comes to speak of the new Israel, he should do so with constant reference to the old Israel, as he does in chapters 9—11, and should begin with the nature of Israel's election (what makes Israel the people of God, ch. 9) and with the reason for the rejection of old Israel (ch. 10), before turning to the prospect of the new, inclusive Israel *(all Israel,* 11:26), the church of God chosen from among both Jews and Gentiles. (Ch. 11)

9:1-5 PAUL MOURNS FOR ISRAEL

9:1-5 Paul writes no cool and thoughtful essay on "The Problem of the Jew"; he mourns, as all sons of Abraham must, for his *kinsmen by race* (3), as Jesus mourned (Mt 23:37-39; Lk 19:41-42), and he is ready (as once Moses was, Ex 32:32) to lose all for their gain (3), if that were possible. He cannot but mourn as he recalls the greatness of God's gifts to them (4-5), gifts squandered now by Israel's disobedience and unbelief.

9:4 *Israelites,* the sacred name which marks the Jews as elect and favored recipients of the revelation, the grace, and the promises of God. (Cf. Eph 2:12)

Sonship. Cf. Ex 4:22-23; Hos 11:1.

The glory. Cf. Ex 16:7, 10; 24:16; 40:34-35; 1 K 8:10-11.

The giving of the law spelled out for Israel the claim of the covenant.

The covenants, in which God said, "I will be your God," to Abraham (Gn 15:18), to the whole people (Ex 24), to David (2 Sm 23:5). Cf. also the promise of the "new and final covenant" with His people in Jer 31:31-34; Eze 34:25-31.

9:5 *God who is over all.* The reading given in RSV note *n* is to be preferred. (a) The statement of Christ's Godhead is needed to balance the statement *according to the flesh.* (b) It was Jesus' claim to Godhead that led to His people's rejection of Him (cf. Mk 2:7; Jn 5:18; 8:18; 10:33) and led them to execute Him for blasphemy (Mt 26:65-66). (c) The doxology to *God,* which comes in naturally at 1:25, does not seem to fit so well here.

9:6-13 THE WORD OF GOD HAS NOT FAILED

9:6-13 If Israel is cause for mourning, does that mean that the Word of God, which called Israel into being and shaped Israel's history, has failed? If the Word of God can fail, the church has no grounds for faith and hope; for the church lives and dies in the power of God's Word. Paul looks into the history that the Word of God has made and sees there the revelation of God's will which will solve the mystery of unbelieving Israel: *Not all who are descended from Israel belong to Israel* (6). If the physical descendants of Israel have failed; that does not mean that God's Word has failed; God's Word has always made a distinction between the essential Israel and the physical descendants of Israel, as the cases of Isaac and Ishmael (7-9) and Jacob and Esau show (10-13). Paul is saying: "If you would know where Israel, God's people, is, look where God's promise is at work creating Israel." See there how the Word of God in sovereign freedom works: *not the children of the flesh . . . are the children of God, but the children of the promise are reckoned as descendants* (8); God creates His Israel as He wills.

9:14-29 GOD HAS NOT BEEN UNJUST

9:14-29 In emphasizing the fact that the unbelief of physical Israel does not call in question the power of God's Word to Israel, Paul has asserted the free sovereignty of God boldly, to the point of ambiguity. The question can arise: Is not this freedom mere arbitrariness, a tyrannic assertion of His will because it is His will? Is God, after all, unjust? Paul anticipates the question and answers it (a) by pointing to God's revelation of Himself in the OT (for that, and not some abstract notion of "justice," is the only standard to be applied to God's action) and showing there, in God's dealing with faithful Moses and rebellious Pharaoh (15-18), the unquestionably sovereign mercy and judgment of God; (b) by asserting the absolute authority over man which is God's as man's Creator—an authority which He has, moreover, used in the service of His mercy (19-24); (c) by citing the words of Hosea and Isaiah which prefigured and foretold the history of God's undeserved compassion on the Gentiles and His rejection of the mass of Israel. (25-29)

9:15 *To Moses.* The name is emphatic by its position in the Greek. Even Moses, whose innocence amid Israel's apostasy the Lord Himself attested (Ex 32:33), could stand before God and live only on terms of His free mercy.

9:18. This is one side of the argument; that more can and must be said about man's responsibility (and consequent guilt) when confronted by God, is clear from what follows in 9:30—10:21. Paul's argument here is convincing only for those who share with him two convictions (which he can presuppose on the part of Christian readers—and on the part of the Jew, for that matter): (a) the conviction that the OT is the Word of God, an adequate disclosure of His being and will; (b) that God Himself, as disclosed in His Word, is the standard of righteousness.—Paul is illustrating the righteousness of God in His present actions by pointing to God's words and deeds of old and making plain that His actions are all of a piece.

9:19 For the same kind of question, based on similar reasoning, cf. 3:5-8 note.

9:20-21 For the image of the *potter* and the *clay* cf. Is 29:16; 45:9; 64:8; and esp. Jer 18:6.

9:22-24 When a man has bowed before the revelation of Scripture (14-18) and has submitted in obedience to his Creator (19-21), he is enabled to look into God's ways and see in them the logic of God's mercy. How can there be any talk of God's injustice, in the light of His great forbearance and His all-inclusive *(called . . . Jews . . . also . . . Gentiles,* 24) mercy?

9:25 *Hosea.* If the free majesty and boundless reach of God's love is such that He can restore to Himself an Israel which had forfeited every right to be His *beloved people,* it is but a small step in the inclusion of the Gentiles in His people.

9:27-29 *Isaiah.* If the number of Jews included in the ultimate people of God seems pitifully small, still that is what Israel's prophets had foretold. (Is 1:9; cf. 10:22)

9:30—10:21 The tenor of Paul's proclamation thus far (9:1-29) has been: "Be still, and know that I am God" (Ps 46:10). God is free to call His people into being and to form it as He wills. If

Israel has now become a vessel of His wrath, while Gentiles now praise Him for His mercy (cf. 15:9), no one can say that His Word has failed or that His ways have been arbitrary. But there is another equally important aspect to the fall of Israel: Israel's guilty unbelief. And so Paul must point to Israel's guilt and say: "If you will not believe, surely you shall not be established" (Is 7:9). The section 9:30-33 forms a transition from the first theme to the second. It looks backward, emphasizing God's sovereignty: He lays the stone in Zion (33), that is, establishes and reveals the way of salvation; man may stumble over it or be saved by it, but man can neither lay the stone nor question Him who lays it. The section also looks forward to ch. 10 in its emphasis on the necessity of faith (9:32-33) and the guilt of unbelief.

Paul speaks in ch. 10 as the compassionate intercessor for His people, not as their judge (1). He must in love lay bare the guilt of their unenlightened *zeal* (2): When Israel was confronted by the revelation of God's saving righteousness in Christ, it was being summoned to believe, find righteousness, and live. But Israel ignored the proffered righteousness and chose to go its own way and to establish its own righteousness on the basis of the Law, which God superseded by the sending of Christ *(end of the law,* 4). That wrong choice was disobedience *(did not submit,* 3) and unbelief and therefore guilt (cf. 21). The right choice had inevitably to be made; man, whether Jew or Greek, had to choose between Moses' "Do!" and the "It is done" proclaimed in the Gospel (5-13). The right choice could be made; God saw to that: every link in the golden chain which binds men in faith to the Lord has been forged by Him. He has sent His heralds; they have proclaimed Christ, and men have come to faith and called upon His name for their salvation (14-17). The *foolish nation* of the Gentiles has heard and understood; *those who did not seek* (20) the Lord have found Him. If Israel did not *confess* and *believe* (9-10), but disobeyed and contradicted instead (21), the fault is clearly Israel's; they have ignored the outstretched, pleading hands of God.

9:33 *Laying in Zion a stone.* Cf. Is 8:14 and 28:16. Since Zion is the citadel of the anointed king of Israel, the salvation promised is that given in the anointed King, the Messiah. (Cf. 1 Ptr 2:4-6)

10:15 *How beautiful are the feet.* Cf. Is 52:7. As in the days when God took up His kingly power and freed His people from Babylon, so now when His kingdom comes in Christ, His heralds go forth to bring the good news to captive men.

10:18 *Their voice has gone out.* Cf. Ps 19:1-4, which speaks of the heavens that tell the glory of God, of the firmament which proclaims His handiwork, of the ordered times and seasons which proclaim the God who ordered them. Paul is implying: When God, the almighty Creator, wants to be heard, He will be heard. He who has all powers in heaven and on earth at His command can (and does) raise up men to preach His Gospel. That Gospel has been "fully preached" (15:19). The men of Israel have heard it, no doubt of that.

11:1-36 God's Wisdom in the Creation of His New Israel

11:1-36 God is free, and Israel is guilty; chs. 9 and 10 would suffice "to justify the ways of God to man." But it is not Paul's mission to provide a theodicy, to vindicate God; he is an apostle of Jesus Christ (1:1), who knew that there are no limits to the creative possibilities of God (Mt 19:26) and could see in the hopeless spectacle of the lost sheep of Israel the harvest field of God. Paul, His servant, has the mind of Christ. Paul has, moreover, been set apart for the Gospel of God (1:1) and serves the Creator, whose Word has never failed (9:6), whose Word says, "Let light shine out of darkness" (2 Co 4:6; Gn 1:3; cf. Is 9:2). His Word can make light shine even out of Israel's present darkness; His Word has uses for the dead branches cut from the tree of Israel (11:17), for Israel hardened in resistance to God (11:25). For God's almighty love is in that Word. A proclamation of God's Gospel which stops at theodicy would be an incomplete proclamation; beyond God's freedom (ch. 9) and justice (ch. 10) the illimitable wisdom of God opens up prospects for His new people of which an apostle must speak. (Ch. 11)

11:1-10 THE PRESENT STATE OF ISRAEL

11:1-10 The present case of Israel is cause for mourning. The majority of the Israelites are a spectable for tears: men whom God has petrified in their stony resistance to the truth *(hardened,* 7), whose verdict Paul pronounces in terms of Isaiah (8; cf. Is 29:10) and Ps 69:22-23 (9:10). But in that darkness of doom a light shines nevertheless, the light of God's sheer grace, which has preserved a believing *remnant* (5) in Israel. Paul himself is living proof that *God has not rejected his people* (2), His chosen ones. God's Word has reached him and is working through him; while one Israelite fulfills Israel's function of bearing witness to Israel's God, Israel exists; Israel is not rejected (1). And Paul knows that he is not a lone true Israelite (His fellow apostles were all Jews!), no more than *Elijah* was of old, when he felt alone amid an unbelieving nation (2:4; cf. 1 K 19:10, 14). God's assurance to Elijah (1 K 19:18) is an assurance to Paul; he knows that he belongs to a *remnant, chosen by grace* (5), that the history of Israel has not ended in the extinction of Israel.

11:9 *Let their table become a snare and a trap* Ps 69:22 depicts the enemies of the righteous sufferer as feasting in their triumph over him. The righteous sufferer calls on his God to vindicate him: their table, symbol of their triumphant security, is to be their doom.

11:11-16 GOD'S USES FOR ISRAEL

11:11-16 The wisdom of God can make even Israel's *trespass* (11) and Israel's *rejection* (15) serve His saving purposes. Paul has seen with his own eyes how Jewish rejection of the Word of God has served to send that Word of life out among the Gentiles to enrich *(riches for the world,* 12) men of Pisidian Antioch (Acts 13:45-47) and Corinth (Acts 18:5-6). In bringing *reconciliation* to the *world* of the nations (15), God has not forgotten His ancient people, the *first fruits* of His harvest and the *root* (16) of the tree that is the people of God (cf. 17-24); what happens to Gentiles has its effect on Israel also. God is wooing Israel when He makes *Israel jealous* (11, 14). When God receives into His new people those Israelites won by Paul's work among the Gentiles, will that not be His proper work (cf. 4:17) of bringing *life from the dead* (15), a triumph of His creative grace in Christ Jesus?

11:14 *Save some of them.* Paul does not envision a mass conversion of the nation Israel. This is important for the interpretation of "all Israel" in 11:26.

11:17-24 THE TREE AND THE BRANCHES

11:17-24 The new people of God is a fair *olive tree* (17). Cultivating that tree bears witness to the *kindness and the severity of God* (22). His kindness has given the Gentile *(a wild olive tree,* 24) his place and life in that tree; it was an extravagant kindness, one that sovereignly ignored the rules of horticulture (normally and naturally, cultivated branches are engrafted on the wild plant; the reverse is *contrary to nature,* 24). His severity was provoked by *unbelief* (20); God's judgment struck the natural branches because they had, unnaturally, by unbelief, refused life from Him. The Gentile has no cause for smug complacency; rather let him *stand in awe* (20). That same severity can deal unsparingly with him (21), and that same kindness can restore the natural branches, now removed and withered by His judgment (24), to their native tree. The Gentile dare not boast; and the Jew (and all who mourn for him) need not despair.

11:25-27 THE MYSTERY

11:25-27 Paul states in another form what he has already said in the figure of the tree and the branches. This form he calls *mystery,* a prophetic utterance concerning God's hidden counsels, which only God can reveal. There are three elements in this mystery: (1) The hardening of Israel is only partial, and there is still a time of grace for Israel; (2) this time of grace will endure *until the full number of the Gentiles come in,* that is, to the end of this age, when judgment comes; until the end of this age, the coming in of the Gentiles will continue to provoke Israel to jealousy, and God will thus continue to call Israel to repentance; (3) *and so*—by God's wise governance of the history of Gentile and Jew—*all Israel* (the whole of God's people from among Gentiles and Jews) *will be saved.* What the image of the tree and the branches opened up as something possible (23-24), the mystery asserts as an action of God. What God can do, He will do. Under the blessing of His Messianic *(Zion,* 26) deliverance, under the new covenant of forgiveness (27), all God's people, cleansed and restored, will come home to Him.

11:26-27 Paul combines the basic thought of Is 59:20-21 with touches from Ps 14:7 and Ps 53:6; the picture of the new *covenant* contains reminiscences of Jer 31:33-34.

11:28-32 ENEMIES AND BELOVED

11:28-32 Israel as a nation has refused the *gospel,* which offered them righteousness and life; that has made them *enemies* of God (28). As surely as God lifts up His countenance upon the Gentiles who call Jesus Lord, so surely His face is set against the men who persecute His church and say that Jesus is accursed. And yet, no simple scheme of guilt and punishment can enclose the mysterious workings of the Word of God. God is God and not man; His *election,* His *gifts and the call* have their cause and origin in Him alone; they are not generated by the goodness of man and do not evaporate before the badness of man. They remain *irrevocable* so far as His will to give is concerned. The history of man, Gentile and Jew alike, is a history of his disobedience. The disobedience of the Jew was the occasion of mercy shown to the Gentile, but they did not merit that mercy by any previous obedience of their own. *God has consigned all men to disobedience* (32). By strange ways His wisdom has brought all men to that dead end where man must turn and face the wrath of God, must cease to boast, must cease to offer excuses, must throw himself in total surrender on the mercy of Him whose wrath He fears, in order that the passionate Pursuer of His enemies may at last have mercy on them all.

11:33-36 DOXOLOGY

11:33-36 All men end up in beggary (11:32); only God is rich, and only He is wise; no one can give Him counsel (34), and no one can earn His favor (35) in the work that is solely His: the salvation of man. He stands at the beginning as the Creator of all, the Giver of all gifts. He holds the reins of man's sorry history in His wise, almighty hands. He shall bring His creation home, that all may witness to His glory everlastingly.

12:1—15:13 THE GOSPEL CREATES A NEW WORSHIP FOR THE NEW PEOPLE OF GOD

12:1—13:14 All Life in the Church and in the World a Spiritual Worship

12:1-2 THE GOSPEL BASIS

12:1-2 The new people of God are universal, and their worship is total. The whole living man presents his acting self *(bodies)* as a living *sacrifice* to God in a true *(spiritual)* dedication of all his powers, including his intelligence *(prove what is the will of God).* The call to worship is therefore not based on the compulsion of Law but on the inspiration of the Gospel. The Gospel, which sheds abroad in man's heart *the mercies of God,* turns man from conformity to *this* self-seeking and dying *world* and *transforms* him into the true worshiper living his renewed life to God in faith (3-8), love (9-11), and hope. (12-21)

12:3-8 THE RENEWED LIFE A LIFE OF FAITH

12:3-8 Faith that is born of the mercies of God and lives of them spells the end of pride (3) and makes of a man a soberly functioning member of the *one body in Christ,* the new people of God (5). Whether his new worship is by way of the vocal ministries of *prophecy* (6, declaring the will of God to God's people in each new situation) or *teaching* (7, probably instruction in the church's first Bible, the OT) or *exhortation* (8, the warm and winning word that moves men to action according to the will of God) or in the silently winning witness of *service* (7) or generous contribution (8) or giving *aid* (8) or *acts of mercy* (8)—all is done in the knowledge and conviction that they are recipients and stewards of the mercies of God, empowered and circumscribed by Him *(according to the measure of faith . . . assigned,* 3).

12:9-11 THE RENEWED LIFE A LIFE OF LOVE

12:9-11 Faith and love are inseparable; faith is always faith working through love (Gl 5:6). Love animated and informed by faith is holy love; it speaks God's No to *evil,* while holding *fast to what is good* as it dispenses the mercies of God in *brotherly affection* and self-effacing humility (10). Faith, inspired by *the Spirit* (11), knows that all love is a service rendered to *the Lord* (11); no one dare offer Him the unclean ministry of a sentimental love that makes human pride or blurs the line between good and evil with a tear.

12:12-21 THE RENEWED LIFE A LIFE OF HOPE

12:12-21 *Hope* is faith looking forward, rejoicing in the future provided by the mercies of God (cf. 8:19-39). The assurance of that great future gives the believer patience in present tribulation and constancy in prayer (cf. 8:26-27); it gives him the generous largeness of heart which can *contribute to the needs of the saints* (13), can love and bless even the enemy and the persecutors (14), can enter with ready sympathy into other men's laughter and tears (15), can preserve harmony and quell pride (18), can forego vengeance in the assurance that the Lord who reserves vengeance to Himself (19; Dt 32:35) "will vindicate his people and have compassion on his servants" (Dt 32:36). The only "vengeance" open to the man of hope is the vengeance of undeserved love, which heaps *burning coals* of agonizing contrition upon the head of the enemy (20; Pr 25:21-22). Thus Christian hope triumphs by overcoming *evil with good.* To do evil in return for evil is defeat, is to *be overcome by evil* and so to lose all that glorious victory and future which Christ, who overcomes evil with good, has won for us.

13:1-7 THE RENEWED LIFE WITHIN THE ORDERS OF THIS WORLD

13:1-7 Ch. 13 repeats the emphasis of ch. 12 on faith (1-7),love (8-10), and hope (11-14). To faith it is given to recognize in *the governing authorities* (1) an order that *God has appointed* for His good ends and man's benefit (2), to see in Caesar *God's servant* (4) and in Caesar's *sword* (symbol of Caesar's power over life and death) the consecrated instrument of *God's wrath* (5) and to obey *for the sake of conscience* (5), to pay not only *taxes* and *revenue* but also the heart's tribute of *respect* and *honor* to this ambiguous representative of God (7). No area of life, however "secular," is exempted from the claim of total worship.

13:8-10 THE DEBT OF LOVE

13:8-10 Paul's preaching of faith does not overthrow the Law but upholds it (3:31). Believing men are expected to pay what is due, wherever it is due (7). *Love* does not stop at what is due but works unceasingly to pay the debt of love perpetually owed, never marked "paid in full." Where love born of faith, born of the mercies of God, lives and works, the just requirement of the Law has been fulfilled; there is no wrong that the Law must condemn. The will of God, "what is good and acceptable and perfect" is "proved" (12:2), known, and done. (9-10)

13:11-14 LIFE AS IN THE DAY

13:11-14 The summons to pay the debt of love (8-10) is reinforced by a *(Besides this,* 11) hymn of hope (11-14). To know God's *hour* (11; cf. 3:26), His appointed time of final salvation, as the imminent hour that it is, involves acting on that knowledge; means being aroused from *sleep,* from ignorance of and indifference to one's opportunities and duties. The hour when the night of this age of sin and death is far gone and the great day of God's new world of righteousness and life is at hand—that hour is one that challenges the renewed man to resist the still potent forces of darkness and bear militant witness to the reality of the inbreaking day, to live a whole life as in the coming *day* (13) in a bodily witness to the day and its righteousness; renewed man professes his hope in things as concrete and ordinary as his attitude toward sex and alcohol and the peaceable preservation of society (13). Only the renewed man can do this, the man who makes his baptism his daily dress and clothes Himself in the Christ in whom he has been clothed at baptism (cf. Gl 3:27). With *Jesus Christ* for his *Lord* he can turn his back on the old concerns of his *flesh* and live a life launched forward into the eternal day. (14)

14:1—15:13 The Weak and the Strong in Faith United in One Worship

14:1—15:13 Unanimity is essential to the life of the new worshiping people of God. That this unanimity does not involve a monotonous uniformity of faith, Paul has already shown in 12:3-8, where he stressed the individuality of faith in the varied ministries in the church, where "gifts that differ according to the grace given" (12:6) to each believer serve not to disrupt but to maintain and further the unanimity and health of the church. Differences in faith make themselves felt and create tensions in other areas also. Not all are equally strong in faith. To some it is given to see the new life and worship steadily and to see it whole in all its implications for action. They walk through life untroubled by scruples, with a glad and free self-confidence. These are the strong in faith. Others have not the power of faith to appropriate for themselves at once and altogether the liberty for which their Lord has set them free (Gl 5:1); they walk more timidly and circumspectly than the strong, troubled by doubts and inhibitions. These are the weak in faith.

Paul uses differences of conviction concerning food and drink and the observance of holy days to exemplify his teaching here; it may be that in Rome the weak were Judaic Christians, coming from a part in which dietary prescriptions ("clean"and "unclean" foods) and strict Sabbath observance were important for piety; while the Gentiles, not so conditioned by their past, breathed more easily in the free atmosphere of the church—they were the "strong." At any rate these differences were not, for all their external character, a trifling matter; they were a matter of faith, and so a matter of central concern in a community of believers; and the difference in attitude toward foods would affect the common meal, so important in the life of the early church as the symbol and expression of fellowhsip (cf. 1 Co 11). Paul first addresses both groups together (14:1-12), then the strong alone (14:13—15:6), and then again appeals to both. (15:7-13)

14:1-12 TO THE WEAK AND THE STRONG

14:1-12 Paul, characteristically, first espouses the cause of the *weak;* the weak man is to find a real *welcome* in the new people of God; he is not merely to be accepted in order that the strong may argue him out of his misguided *opinions* (1). That would be contempt (3), which has no place in a community of love whose law is: "Outdo one another in showing honor" (12:10). The weak is tempted to *pass judgment* (3) on the brother whose strong freedom looks to the weak dangerously like religious indifference and a disregard of the danger lurking in such freedom. Paul reminds the censorious, worrying weak brother that he has no reason to worry and no right to judge. The strong man in his freedom has been received by God (3) and has a Master who can sustain him in his freedom (4). In fact we all, weak and strong alike, have one Lord, whom we serve in all that we do, to whom we live and die, and each of us is accountable to God Himself for his service to that Master.

14:13—15:6 TO THE STRONG

14:13—15:6 Paul identifies himself with the strong (14:14; 15:1, *we who are strong)* and states their obligation of love both negatively (14:13-23) and positively (15:1-6). Negatively: *Whatever does not proceed from faith is sin* (23)—even the practicing of a freedom of faith without regard for its injurious effect on the weaker brother is sin; for to leave the path of love and to *injure* the *brother* (15), to misuse one's freedom so as to *cause the ruin of one for whom Christ died* (15), to bring disrepute upon his Christian liberty *(your good,* 16) by employing it ruthlessly (16), to *destroy the work of God* in a man, his faith and salvation (20), to make men *stumble* (21) and *fall* (20) by one's own swaggering walk of freedom, to indulge in freedom in such a way that one's conscience becomes uncertain *(doubts,* 23) about it—these are not fruits of faith. Positively: Faith looks to Christ, and the life of faith gets its content and shape from the life of Christ; He *did not please himself* (15:3) but gave Himself so wholly to a life lived for others (the weak who needed Him most) that His righteous countrymen reproached Him for the prodigal liberality of His grace and thereby reproached God for sending His Son to seek the lost. The cry of the psalmist became the cry of the Christ: *The reproaches of those who reproached thee fell on me* (Ps 69:9; 15:3). Christ found the pattern of His life in the OT Scriptures, and the church of the last days that would serve and love in *accord with Christ Jesus* (15:5) can find the pattern and power for its life there too, and so find strength to rise above tensions and difficulties to a life of hope-filled unanimous doxology. (15:4-6)

15:7-13 TO ALL: WELCOME ONE ANOTHER

15:7-13 The *welcome* which binds brother to brother, despite the difficulties and tensions caused by the difference between the weak and strong, is the church's echo of Christ's welcome; that costly welcome (it cost Him His life) revealed God's love to the full, and so glorified Him (7). God's love in Christ spanned greater and graver differences than those which separate vegetarians from those who eat meat; it embraced both Jew (to whom God faithfully kept His promises, 8) and Gentile (in whom God's undeserved and unexpected mercy awakened songs of praise, 9). The fulfillment of the promises made to Israel *(patriarchs,* 8) brought the fulfillment of the promises made for the Gentiles in the OT (9-12). The God who gave these promises and fulfilled them in Jesus Christ is *the God of hope* (13); all men may confidently lay their future in His hands. He can give to both the strong and the weak the *joy and peace* they need for living and worshiping together. Joy and peace can be theirs by *believing,* by receiving from God. Thus, by God's working, by the power of God's Spirit, they can *abound* in hope. They can meet the severest demands made on their love with kindly evenness of mind. (13)

15:14—16:27 CONCLUSION

15:14:33 THE APOSTLE'S PLANS: JERUSALEM, ROME, SPAIN

15:14-33 By his letter Paul has already imparted a generous installment of the "spiritual gift" he had promised to impart to the saints of Rome when he should come to them (1:11). He, "called to be an apostle" (1:1), has set before them once more *by way of reminder* (15:15) what it means to be "called to be saints" (1:7). Now he can disclose to them more fully his plans (cf. 1:10-13) and invite the church, newly strengthened by his spiritual gift, to an active "partnership in the Gospel." (Cf. Ph 1:5)

An apostle's plans are not his own, to make or alter as he pleases; for the apostle is an instrument in the hands of the Trinity: God has given him grace to be a minister of Christ Jesus, and the offering which his priestly ministry presents to God (Gentiles won to the obedience of faith) is *sanctified by the Holy Spirit* (16). Therefore the apostle cannot move westward, to Rome and Spain, until God's business has been finished in the East, until he has *fully preached* the Gospel of God where God wants it preached (19-21), until he has strengthened the tie that binds the new Israel into one by presenting to the *saints at Jerusalem* the Gentiles' *contribution* of love. Only then can he come to Rome in the high-hearted assurance that he comes *in the fulness of the blessing of Christ.* (29)

Paul draws the called saints into the orbit of the called apostle by requesting two services of them. He asks that their prayers accompany him to Jerusalem, where he has cause to fear both the rancor of his inveterate enemies, *the unbelievers in Judea,* and the suspicions of Judaic Christians (31; cf. Acts 21:20-26). He wishes, moreover, *to be sped on* his *journey* (24) by the churches of Rome—this "speeding on," as passages like Ti 3:13-14; 3 Jn 6; 1 Co 16:6, 11; 2 Co 1:16 show, could include a variety of services rendered to a missionary on his travels: e.g., letters of recommendation, guides, information, money. Thus the Gospel creates the apostolic, missionary church.

16:1-16, 21-24 COMMENDATION AND GREETINGS

16:1-16, 21-24 Paul's commendation of Phoebe, deaconess of Cenchreae (1-2), his greetings to members of the Roman church personally known to him (3-16), and the greetings from his coworkers and companions (21-23) give us a revealing glimpse of the energetic and many-sided life of the early church. Some of those named had worked and suffered with Paul in the East (3, 4, 7, 9); all knew him and could tell the Roman Christians what manner of man was soliciting their sympathy and aid for work in the West. The number of women in the list is remarkable, and Paul's characterization of them is no less remarkable; the apostle who enjoined silence on woman in the public worship of the church (1 Co 14:34) obviously was no smug male belittler of womankind. The mobility of the first Christians is documented here too; men and women from all over the Mediterranean world are met in Rome; that mobility is coupled with a sense of churchmanship which is anything but parochial or provincial. Paul can write: *All the churches of Christ greet you* (16)—all the churches know of Paul's plans, all accompany him with their prayers, all bespeak a welcome for him in Rome.

16:5 *The church in their house.* The house-church seems to have been normal for Rome, as it was for most of the early church. Cf. 14 and 15, "the brethren who are with them . . . the saints who are with them."

16:17-20 THE APOSTLE'S WARNING

16:17-20 This note of warning comes unexpectedly and abruptly; if we recall the nature of the early church's service of worship (at which Paul's letters were read, cf. Cl 4:16), the occasion of the warning is clear. The picture of such a service shimmers through here (16-20). The assembled church has heard the apostolic Word; the solemn celebration of the Lord's Supper is about to begin. The assembly expresses its solidarity in the Lord by the exchange of the holy kiss (16; cf. 1 Th 5:26; 2 Co 13:12; esp. 1 Co 16:20-22). Having thus spoken a corporate yea to their Lord, the worshipers speak their inevitable nay to all who deny His Lordship and exclude them from their communion (cf. the anathema of 1 Co 16:22, "accursed"). Here the anathema takes the form of a stern warning against men who, for all their deceptively winning eloquence *(fair and flattering words,* 18), are serving themselves and not the Lord, disrupting the church *(dissensions,* 17) and endangering her faith *(difficulties,* 17; literally "stumbling blocks"), *in opposition to the doctrine . . . taught* in all Christendom (17). No church may tolerate or compromise with them, least of all the Roman church, conspicuous among all Christians by her position and by her record of fidelity (19). *Avoid them* (17), that is the only possible course, the only wise (19) course when confronted by such satanic intrusions into the church; then God will give the victory and resolve all dissensions with His peace. (20)

16:25-27 CONCLUDING DOXOLOGY

16:25-27 Paul began the body of his letter with an affirmation of the power of God at work in the Gospel (1:16); the whole letter has set forth the past and present workings of that power for salvation. Paul closes with a hymn in praise of the God of power. He is a God at hand, able to sustain the Romans in their conspicuous and responsible position, able to strengthen them for the greater tasks which Paul's coming will open up for them. His Word is near them. Paul's Gospel itself is that Word; it can strengthen them because Jesus Christ is preaching in Paul's Gospel. And Jesus Christ is the disclosure of God's *mystery* (25), the revelation of His long counsels of salvation which worked in strange and secret ways for long ages, hidden in the sad and inconspicuous history of His little people in Israel. In Christ that plan is now disclosed and is working on the stage of universal history to the ends of the earth. All nations shall know the

Christ; the *prophetic writings* (26) of the OT are the interpretive witnesses to what the eternal God has revealed in Christ. Thus men will be brought to the obedience of faith. The Romans need not fear; whatever apostolic task they undertake will not be undertaken in vain. They need but bow with Paul in adoration before he God whose wisdom (27) guides all history to His goal, to the glory of His grace. Whatever serves that glory cannot fail.

FIRST

CORINTHIANS

INTRODUCTION

1 Paul wrote his letters to Corinth during the period of his life commonly known as his third missionary journey (A. D. 52—56). The heart of that journey was the nearly 3-year ministry in the great metropolis of Asia Minor, Ephesus; it was preceded by a revisitation of the churches founded on the first missionary journey and followed by a revisitation of the European churches of Macedonia and Achaia founded on the second journey.

2 Paul himself had prepared the way for his ministry in Ephesus by his visit to Ephesus on his return from Corinth to Palestine at the close of the second journey (Acts 18:19-21). The men of the synagog were so much moved by his words that they asked him to stay on. He promised to return to Ephesus and left Aquila and Priscilla there. As their contact with Apollos shows (Acts 18:24-26), they did not remain silent concerning the faith that was in them. Through them the learned and eloquent Apollos became a full-fledged witness to the Christ (Acts 18:26) and thus further prepared the way for Paul. Perhaps the 12 "disciples" who knew only the baptism of John and had not heard of the outpouring of the Holy Spirit in the last days (Acts 19:1-7) had been won by Apollos. Paul baptized them and laid hands on them that they might receive the Holy Spirit. Thus his work at Ephesus began. The beginning was slight, only 12 men, but the foundation was, as always, essentially his own (Ro 15:20), and he built on it with a will.

3 That will generated conflict. Luke's account of Paul's Ephesian ministry is anything but complete. He gives no chronicle of it, but presents it as a series of three conflicts, each of which results in a triumph for the cause of the apostle of Christ. The first conflict was with the synagog (Acts 19:8-10). Paul was here permitted to witness in the synagog for an unusually long period, for 3 months, and with considerable success. The Jews of the province of Asia were therefore particularly bitter against him, and it was they who later instigated the riot in Jerusalem which led to Paul's arrest and imprisonment (Acts 21:27-28). As was inevitable, the break with the synagog came: "Some were stubborn and disbelieved, speaking evil of the Way before the congregation" (Acts 19:9), and Paul withdrew from the synagog to continue his teaching in the school of Tyrannus. He continued there for 2 years, and the conflict with Judaism proved to be a triumph for the Word of the Lord: "All the residents of Asia heard the word of the Lord, both Jews and Greeks." (Acts 19:10)

4 The second conflict generated by the Christ-centered will of Paul was the conflict with magic, for which Ephesus was notorious (Acts 19:11-20). The fact that "God did extraordinary miracles by the hands of Paul" (Acts 19:11) made the superstitious look upon Christianity as a new and more potent kind of magic; but the experience of the Jewish exorcists who sought to use the names of Jesus and Paul in their trade made it plain that Jesus is Lord in personal and august power, a Lord who can defend His name against misuse by those who deem Him a power which they can manipulate and employ. "The name of the Lord Jesus was extolled," and the conscience of believers was quickened—the line between magic and religion was sharply and critically drawn for them by this incident. They confessed their wrong and burned their infamous Ephesian books of charms and incantations, and "the word of the Lord grew and prevailed mightily" (Acts 19:20). The magical word by which men sought power grew impotent before the divine word.

5 The third and most dangerous conflict was the conflict with the commercialized state religion of Ephesus (Acts 19:23-41). The zeal of the silversmith Demetrius and his guild was something less than a purely religious fervor; but the fury of the guild members and of the huge, shouting city mob they aroused is nevertheless an illustration of the demonic power which Paul in his First Letter to the Corinthians describes as at work in the worship of gods that are no gods (1 Co 10:19-20). The fury of that demonic power fell on Paul and the Christians of Ephesus; but the conflict led to a vindication of Paul and his followers, so that Paul could leave Ephesus with an unsullied reputation and with the respect of men like the Asiarchs and the town clerk (the most important city official of Ephesus). This was something Paul valued; soon after he left Ephesus he wrote the words: "We aim at what is honorable not only in the Lord's sight but also in the sight of men." (2 Co 8:21; cf Cl 4:5-6)

6 Luke himself gives a hint that the Ephesian years were filled with difficulties and dangers beyond those noted by him in his account of those years. He records the words of Paul to the elders of Ephesus which speak of the trials that befell him through the plottings of the Jews (Acts 20:19), tells of the plot against Paul's life at Corinth a little later (Acts 20:3), and notes that the Jews of Asia were especially rancorous in their hatred of Paul (Acts 21:17). Paul's letters of this period further fill in the picture of this time as a period of perils. Paul speaks in First Corinthians of the fact that his great opportunity at Ephesus has as its cast shadow the presence of many adversaries (1 Co 15:9), and that he has "fought with beasts at Ephesus" (1 Co 15:32)—whether the expression is to be taken literally or, as is more probable, figuratively, it is a vivid expression of extreme peril. In the opening verses of Second Corinthians Paul gives thanks for an unlooked-for divine deliverance from desperate danger in the province of Asia (2 Co 1:8-10). And when he speaks in his Letter to the Romans of the fact that Aquila and Priscilla have risked their necks for him, he is probably referring to the Ephesian period also. (Ro 16:4)

7 Paul is no bloodless saint on a gold background. He held life dear just because he had committed it wholly to the Christ, and he hoped to live to see his Lord when He returned in glory (1 Co 15:51; 2 Co 5:1-5). While he was ready to sacrifice his life (Acts 20:24), he was not ready to waste it. And so he suffered in a genuinely human way. He feared in the face of perils and was racked by his fears. But in his human frailty, which he never denied but rather asserted (1 Co 2:3-4), he held in faith to the fact that all things that are and that happen are from God the Father and are mediated by the Lord Jesus Christ, so that he saw in everything that befell him God's fatherly dealings with him and the Lordship of Christ exercised over him and through him (1 Co 8:6). He experienced again and again the truth of what his Lord had told him: "My grace is sufficient for you, for my power is made perfect in weakness" (2 Co 12:9). Thus a period marked by perils was for Paul also an exhilarating one; we see him in the letters of this period welcoming suffering as essential to the Christian life and a salutary part of it (Ro 5:3-5; 8:35-39) and boasting of his perils and afflictions as being the glory of his life as an apostle. He is employing high irony when he contrasts the assured complacency of the Corinthians with his own sorry and embattled existence (1 Co 4:8-13), and the only boast he really permits himself over against the boasting of his detractors in Corinth is a glorying in his sufferings (2 Co 11:23-33). He sees in the paradox of "dying, and behold we live" (2 Co 6:9) the apex of his apostolate.

8 It was a perilous period; it was also a strenuous one. The evangelization of Ephesus was also the evangelization of the province of Asia. Whether men like Epaphras, who brought the Gospel to Colossae in the interior, worked under the direct supervision of Paul or not cannot be made out; certainly he and others like him must have consulted Paul frequently in the course of their work, as Epaphras did later on when heresy threatened the inland cities (Cl 1:7-8; 4:12). The sending of Timothy and Erastus to Macedonia (Acts 19:22) indicates that the churches there, too, needed help. But Paul's dealings with

his beloved, brilliant, and wayward child, the church of Corinth, give us the most vivid picture of what Paul meant when he spoke of the daily pressure of "anxiety for all the churches" (2 Co 11:28). If the growth of the Word of the Lord in this period meant conflict, if it meant "fighting without," it also meant for Paul an intense personal and pastoral anxiety; it meant "fear within." (2 Co 7:5)

9 The church of Corinth was a brilliantly endowed church, "enriched . . . with all speech and all knowledge . . . not lacking in any spiritual gift" (1 Co 1:5, 7). Corinth had had the benefit of a much longer ministry by Paul than any of the other Greek cities. Paul was the "father" of the Corinthian Christians: their life in Christ had his unmistakable and ineradicable imprint on it. We can gauge from Acts and from Paul's letters what it meant to have Paul for a father, how rich a heritage this father gave his children. (Cf. 2 Co 12:14)

10 They had also had the benefit of the ministry of Apollos, the eloquent and fervent Alexandrian, powerful in the Scriptures (Acts 18:24). His coming to Corinth with letters of recommendation from Ephesus (Acts 18:27-28) apparently led to a renewed contact with the synagog in Corinth, which had previously broken with Paul (Acts 18:6-8, 28). Perhaps it was Apollos who won for Christ the ruler of the synagog, Sosthenes, whom the crowd had beaten before the tribunal of Gallio (Acts 18:17). Paul includes Sosthenes with himself in the sending of his First Letter to the Corinthians (1 Co 1:1). If this Sosthenes is a Corinthian converted by Apollos, the fact that Paul thus singles him out is significant; Paul is telling the clique-ridden church of Corinth: Here is one who received the Gospel from Apollos and is one with me in all that I am telling you, just as Apollos himself is. (1 Co 3:5-9; 16:12)

11 At the time when Paul wrote his first letter there were in the Corinthian church those who said, "I belong to Cephas" (1 Co 1:12). They professed a special allegiance to Simon Peter, and they used the original Aramaic form of his official name (Cephas). This would indicate that they were Jews who had come to Corinth from one of the eastern Judaic churches which Peter had evangelized. The presence of these Christians from the fields where Peter had worked no doubt meant an enrichment of the church at Corinth; but it also created tensions. The various components of the young church—the original converts of Paul, the converts of Apollos, and the new arrivals from the east—could not as yet, or would not, unite in that free and richly various oneness which Paul described as essential to the life of the church (1 Co 12). Apollos himself had worked in complete harmony with Paul; no shadow of blame attached to him, as every mention of him in the first letter shows. But there were those, converts or admirers of Apollos, who compared this personable, energetic, and brilliant preacher with Paul and found him more to their liking than Paul, the bondman of God who had come to Corinth "in weakness and in much fear and trembling" (1 Co 2:3), who candidly described himself as "unskilled in speaking" (2 Co 11:6), and preached the *crucified* Christ with single-minded insistence (1 Co 2:2). The new arrivals from the east, the Cephas people, quite naturally felt themselves to be the representatives of a maturer, more original kind of Christianity than that of the churches founded by Paul. They had received the Word from Peter, the "first" of the apostles, who had seen the Lord Jesus and had lived with Him; Paul was in their eyes an apostle of not quite equal rank with the Twelve, the child "untimely born" (1 Co 15:8), not really a full member of the apostolic brotherhood. They felt as charter members of an old, honorable club might feel toward newer members, who besides being new would not be members at all if *they* had not generously relaxed the rules a bit.

12 The church was full of tensions and ferment, and the church's outward situation did nothing to improve its inward state. This church lived in Corinth, where all the brilliance of the Greek mind and all the vagaries of the Greek will mingled with an influx of Oriental religiosity to produce a moral climate which even the Greeks found singularly vicious.

13 The Corinthian church had, moreover, never been tried, refined, and unified by persecution. The policy of

noninterference which the Roman proconsul Gallio had enunciated to the Jews (Acts 18:14-16) apparently remained in force with his successors, and while the church no doubt had to endure the social pressures and animosities which any consistent opposition to the prevailing culture and religiosity evoked, it was safe from real persecution. The Christians of Corinth waited for the "revealing of our Lord Jesus Christ" (1 Co 1:7), but they were tempted more than other churches to make themselves comfortable and at home in the world while they waited. They enjoyed security, and they had leisure to speculate about the implications of the Gospel, since they were not called on to affirm the Gospel in action in the face of persecution.

14 Such was the climate of the church life in Corinth. All that was potentially harmful and disruptive in it was crystallized and intensified by the emergence of a fourth group in the congregation. Since Paul never fully describes this group, it is difficult to get a clear picture of these people, and sometimes it is impossible to see where the line between them and the Cephas people, for instance, is being drawn. But the following would seem to be a fair characterization of them: They came from outside the Corinthian church. Paul distinguishes them from those who professed allegiance to himself or to Apollos, the men who had worked at Corinth (1 Co 1:12). His words in 2 Co 11:4 explicitly mark this group as new arrivals in Corinth: "If some one *comes* and preaches another Jesus than the one we preached . . . ." Paul's contemptuous reference in 2 Co 3:1 to "some" who need letters of recommendation makes it probable that they came with such letters from one of the eastern churches (which need not imply that any of the eastern churches was necessarily responsible for the teaching which they developed at Corinth). They were Judaic and proud of it, Hebrews, Israelites, descendants of Abraham (2 Co 11:22). But they were not Judaizers of the sort that had disturbed the churches of Galatia; we hear nothing of circumcision and the reimposition of the Mosaic law in connection with these men. One can imagine that they claimed to be the inheritors of the true Judaic-Christian tradition and for that reason felt themselves uniquely qualified to lead the church beyond the first stages of that tradition into the full riches of knowledge and freedom in Christ.

15 What they brought into Corinth was a brilliant and persuasive kind of liberalism which operated (as liberalism characteristically does) with genuinely Christian slogans and catchwords. If, according to Paul, they preached "another Jesus," *they* no doubt claimed that they were preaching the genuine Jesus; if they proclaimed a "different gospel" and had and imparted a "different spirit," it was Paul who said so, not they; they claimed that their gospel was the true Gospel and their spirit the true Spirit of God (2 Co 11:4). The slogan which they brought with them (or developed in the course of their activities at Corinth) was as Christian as a slogan can be: "I belong to Christ" (1 Co 1:12; 2 Co 10:7). Paul himself uses the phrase to designate the Christian. (1 Co 3:23; cf. Ro 8:9)

16 They exalted the Christ and awaited His return; they treasured His gift of the Spirit and set great store by the gifts given by the Spirit (2 Co 11:4; cf. 1 Co 7:40). But they exalted the Christ as the Giver of knowledge and treasured the gifts of the Spirit primarily as a means to knowledge of God, as the way to wisdom (1 Co 3:18-20; 8:1-3, 10, 11; 13:9). And this knowledge, they claimed, made them free; the knowledge and wisdom they possessed carried them beyond any previous revelation of God, beyond the Old Testament Scriptures, beyond anything contained in the apostolic Word. Before this ultimate knowledge of God, which they claimed to possess, all previous standards became meaningless, all former ties were dissolved, all the old taboos were gone: "All things are lawful for me"—that was their boast (1 Co 6:12; 10:23). It was an intellectually appealing and an intoxicating message they brought; it is not surprising that they attracted followers and deeply influenced the whole church.

17 Their deep influence on the life of the church was also harmful in the extreme. We can trace its beginnings in Paul's reference to a letter (now lost) which he had written to the Corinthians before

our present first letter (1 Co 5:9). In that earlier letter Paul had demanded of the Corinthians that they refuse to have fellowship with "immoral men." This demand was questioned by the church, perhaps even rejected as being unclear and impracticable. (1 Co 5:9-11)

18 Perhaps it was "Chloe's people" (1 Co 1:11) who delivered Paul's earlier letter to Corinth; they would then have seen and could report to Paul how it was received, how the church broke up into factions over the issues involved (1 Co 1—4). It was probably they who reported to Paul the conditions which resulted from this new proclamation of absolute liberty at Corinth; they could tell Paul why his letter was questioned and contradicted: the new teachers were saying that the new knowledge set men free, and at least one Corinthian Christian had drastically used that liberty (1 Co 5:1): Why should not a man be free to "live with" his father's wife (probably his stepmother) after his father's death? What the Old Testament said no longer bound him (Dt 22:30; 27:20), and the authority of Jesus and His apostles had been superseded by the new revelation of the Spirit. The Corinthian church as a whole not only tolerated this immorality but was even "arrogant" about it (1 Co 5:2); these men felt that they were demonstrating their spiritual maturity in tolerating it. The people of Chloe could tell Paul, too, of the breakdown of discipline in the church, how differences between Christian brethren were no longer being settled in the church but were being taken to pagan courts; the preachers of the new freedom had no interest in or taste for the serious and painful business of keeping the church pure by calling erring brethren to repentance (1 Co 6:1-11). Paul has to hammer home the most elementary moral facts in his attempt to pierce the complacency of the people intoxicated by the new freedom. (1 Co 6:9-11)

19 The new liberty preached in Corinth conceded to the Christian man the freedom to associate with prostitutes. The law which demanded sexual purity of them was being put on the same level with the law concerning clean and unclean foods (1 Co 6:12-20)—or at least the satisfaction of sexual desire was being put on the same level with the satisfaction of hunger (1 Co 6:13). The fact that the Apostolic Council had expressly laid the abstaining from immorality on the consciences of the Gentile Christians made no impression in Corinth. (Acts 15:29)

20 Not everyone at Corinth was so completely swept away by the eloquent rationalism of the new teachers or so deeply intoxicated by the liberty they offered that he asked no questions or raised no objections. Men like Stephanas (1 Co 16:15) and Fortunatus and Achaicus (1 Co 16:17) saw that it was high time that Paul be consulted explicitly and at length on the questions raised by the new theology of knowledge and freedom, and they saw to it that he was consulted. The congregation wrote Paul a letter (1 Co 7:1) and laid before him a series of questions on points where it was becoming evident that the teaching of the new teachers was not only different from Paul's but was contradicting it.

21 The first question concerned marriage (1 Co 7). The form that Paul's answer to their question takes makes it tolerably clear what direction the new teachers were taking here. Pursuing their ideal of religious self-fulfillment, they saw in marriage merely an impediment to the religious life and were intent on making the church an association of celibates without regard for the moral dangers involved in this mass imposition of celibacy, without regard for the authority of the Lord Jesus, who had blessed little children and had declared the bond which united man and woman to be inviolable (Mt 19:3-9, 13-15) and made celibacy a gift reserved for those "to whom it is given" (Mt 19:11). They were running counter to the thinking and practice of the apostles also, for the apostles saw in the family and all natural orders primarily vehicles which the grace of God might employ—"You will be saved, *you and your household,*" Paul told the jailer at Philippi (Acts 16:31). But the new teachers not only sought to keep men and women from marriage (the passage on the "unmarried" and the "betrothed" takes cognizance of this, 1 Co 7:25-38); they also apparently permitted men and women to free themselves of their spouses, especially pagan spouses, in order to be "free for the Lord," again in contradiction to the express

command of Jesus (1 Co 7:10-11). Perhaps the license which they conceded with regard to association with harlots (1 Co 6:12-20) is connected with this attitude toward marriage: If a man could not be continent and yet wished to be free of the impediment of marriage, the association with the harlot would be a solution, since "all things are lawful for me." (1 Co 6:12)

22 To the question, "May a Christian eat food that has been offered as a sacrifice to idols?" (1 Co 8—10), the new teachers had a ready and simple answer: "All of us possess knowledge" (1 Co 8:1), which meant, since knowledge gives liberty, that "all things are lawful," including the sacrificial meats consecrated to idols. In their self-centered piety, puffed up as they were by knowledge, they did not consider what harm their freedom might do to the brother whose knowledge was not yet deep and firm enough to make him capable of exercising such freedom. In their complacent self-assurance they did not pause to consider that demonic powers are at work behind all false worship of false gods, though the gods themselves are nothing. They disregarded the warning example of Israel recorded for them in the Old Testament. They flouted the example of the apostles, whose knowledge was as great as theirs, whose wisdom was more profound and certainly more sober and realistic than theirs. Paul has to remind the Corinthians: "Be imitators of me, as I am of Christ." (1 Co 11:1)

23 But it was not only in the family and in private life that the intoxication of the new liberty was working mischief; it infected the worship life of the church too (1 Co 11—14). Women were asserting their newfound liberty by appearing at worship without the veil, which was the badge of their womanliness and their recognition of the place God the Creator and Redeemer (1 Co 11:3, 8) had assigned to them (1 Co 11:2-16). They were also adding to the confusion of an already chaotic public worship by an unwomanly assumption of a teaching authority which neither Jesus nor the apostles had given them (1 Co 14:33-36). But the voice of Jesus, the voice of His apostles, the practice of the churches of God (1 Co 11:16) did not deter the proponents and adherents of the new liberty; they were "disposed to be contentious" nevertheless.

24 This spirit of rampant individualism made the common fellowship meals of the church a scene of feasting and carousing in which the rich disregarded the poor and made of the Lord's Supper, celebrated in connection with the common meal, anything but the *Lord's* Supper. The Supper which commemorated and made effectively present the utter self-giving and self-sacrifice of the Lord Jesus Christ and was designed to unite the Lord's people in the eating of the one loaf and the partaking of the one cup became the scene and the means of man's self-assertion and of division (1 Co 11:17-34). When knowledge is the capstone of the religious structure and love no longer rules (1 Co 13), decency and order are sacrificed, edification is no longer possible, the salutary commands of the apostle are disregarded (1 Co 14:37-38), and the example of the churches of God everywhere means nothing. (1 Co 14:36)

25 All that characterizes the "Christmen" appears in a concentrated and a peculiarly clear form in their denial of the bodily resurrection of the dead (1 Co 15)—their false spirituality, which disregarded and degraded the body and all things natural; their false conception of knowledge, which made them manipulators of ideas; who could disregard the central fact of all history, the bodily resurrection of Jesus Christ from the dead; their false conception of freedom, which moved them to oppose themselves and their ideas not only to Paul but to all the apostles and to the Old Testament witness to Christ as well. In their intoxication of liberty (Paul has to tell them to come to their right mind, to sober up, 1 Co 15:34) they felt free to sacrifice the central fact of the apostolic proclamation to Greek prejudice—to the Greek the idea of a bodily resurrection was particularly offensive, as the reaction of the Stoics and Epicureans at Athens to Paul's preaching of the resurrection shows. (Acts 17:32)

26 It has become abundantly clear by now that when these men said, "We belong to Christ," they were saying it in an exclusive sense, as a fighting slogan. The liberty which their "knowledge" gave them, their "freedom" in the Spirit, necessarily involved a break with the authority of Paul,

who had planted the Word in Corinth; there is some evidence to indicate that they considered Paul superseded and unnecessary to the church at Corinth and claimed that he would not come to Corinth again; Paul's words in 1 Co 4:18-19 hint as much: "Some are arrogant, as though I were not coming to you. But I will come to you soon, if the Lord wills, and I will find out not the talk of these arrogant people but their power." A break with Paul necessarily meant a break with Apollos, who had watered where Paul had planted; and it meant a break with all apostolic authority. Paul's words concerning their arrogance (1 Co 4:18-19) and their contentiousness (1 Co 11:16; 14:38) seem to indicate that they were highly autocratic and contemptuous of any power but their own, a fact confirmed by the bitter irony of Paul's reproach to the Corinthians in 2 Co 11:20-21: "You bear it if a man makes slaves of you, or preys upon you, or takes advantage of you, or puts on airs, or strikes you in the face." They and those who were most completely taken in by them thus constituted a clique in the church; and as a clique produces more cliques by way of reaction, there ensued that sorry and divided state of the church which Paul deals with so powerfully in the first four chapters of his first letter. At Corinth the line between the church (where Christ alone is Lord) and the world (where *men* head movements and command loyalties) was being perilously blurred.

27 Our present first letter is Paul's response to this situation, as he had learned it from Chloe's people, from Stephanas, Fortunatus, and Achaicus, and from the letter of the Corinthian church. If all the problems at Corinth have a common root, all Paul's responses to the various derangements and sins in the church also have a common denominator. The first letter, for all its variety, is one unified answer, one brilliant demonstration of how a genuinely apostolic authority makes itself felt. And the common denominator, the unifying power, is the cross of Jesus Christ seen in its full significance by the light of the resurrection.

28 Paul operates with the slogans of the new leaders, but by relating them all to the cross he gives them a radically different content. If they extolled the Christ as the Giver of knowledge and freedom, Paul exalts Him as the Lord of glory who was crucified by the rulers of this world. If they empty the cross of its power (1 Co 1:17), he is resolved to know nothing but the cross (1 Co 2:2); and he sets the cross squarely in the center of the church again, the cross which with its pure and all-inclusive grace lays a total claim on man, body and soul, for a life lived wholly to God (1 Co 6:19-20). The cross, which pronounces an annihilating judgment on all human greatness and on all human pretenses to wisdom, cuts off all boasting of man and marks as monstrous and unnatural any clustering about great men in schools and factions that give their loyalty to men rather than to Christ.

29 If they boast of possessing the Spirit and foster a spirituality which disregards the body and feeds the religious ego, Paul interprets the Spirit by the cross, by that event in history in which the Son of God suffered in the flesh for men in the flesh, that event in which God spoke His unmistakable yea to the body which He had created. Paul proclaims a Spirit who dwells in the human body and lays a consecrating claim on it (1 Co 6:19). He proclaims a Spirit who enables men to say that *Jesus* is the Lord (that is, Jesus the Crucified whom the Jews call the Accursed because He hung on the tree, 1 Co 12:3, cf. Gl 3:13), a Spirit who gives gifts to the church "for the common good" (1 Co 12:7), whose highest gift is the love which does not seek its own. (1 Co 13)

30 If they boast a knowledge which makes them "wise in this age" (1 Co 3:18), a knowledge which puffs men up (1 Co 8:1) and makes them boast of men and creates cliques clustered about men, Paul proclaims the offensive wisdom of the cross (1 Co 2:6-13), which brings man low, both Jew and Greek, and makes him glory in the Lord alone. Paul proclaims a whole and unabridged grace of God, the grace of the cross, and that grace gives a knowledge which is not primarily *man's* knowing at all, but man's being known by God; it means that a man has a knowledge that matters when God knows him (that is, loves, chooses, and calls him), and man is thus enabled to love God. (1 Co 8:1-3)

31 If they have and exercise a freedom which overrides all authority, exalts the

self of man, and disregards the brother, Paul proclaims the freedom of the Christian man, who is lord of all things because he is the Christ's (1 Co 3:21-22) and in this his freedom comes under the law of Christ and enslaves himself to all men in order that he may by all means save some (1 Co 9:21-22). Paul knows freedom as freedom from sin and self, a being set free for ministry to one's fellowman.

32 These are the basic convictions underlying Paul's full and many-sided treatment of all the questions posed by the situation in Corinth. No outline of the letter can do justice to it. The following may suffice to indicate the scope of the letter.

OUTLINE

I. 1:1—4:21 Factions in the Church

II. 5:1—6:20 Moral Problems
- A. 5:1-13 Incest
- B. 6:1-11 Litigation
- C. 6:12-20 Sexual Immorality

III. 7:1-40 Celibacy and Marriage

IV. 8:1—11:1 The Eating of Meat Offered to Idols

V. 11:2—14:40 Disorders in the Worship Life of the Church
- A. 11:2-16 Woman in the Church
- B. 11:17-34 The Lord's Supper
- C. 12:1—14:40 The Use of Spiritual Gifts

VI. 15:1-58 The Resurrection of the Dead

VII. 16:1-24 Practical and Personal Matters
- A. 16:1-4 Collection for the Saints of Jerusalem
- B. 16:5-9 Paul's Travel Plans
- C. 16:10-12 Timothy and Apollos
- D. 16:13-20 Admonition, Commendations, and Greetings
- E. 16:21-24 Autograph Conclusion

1:1—4:21 FACTIONS IN THE CHURCH

1:1—4:21 The Gospel of the Crucified is the opposite of that wisdom of this world which fosters human greatness and creates factions centering in men. The cross of Christ destroys all human greatness. If men in the Corinthian church seek "wisdom" and create factions, Paul seeks the unity of the church by subjecting all men to the Crucified and decries all parties, including the one called after himself.

1:1-9 Introduction: Greetings and Thanksgiving

1:1-9 The salutation (1-3) follows ancient epistolary practice but has been made thoroughly Christian in all three of its members (sender—recipients—greeting). The sender Paul identifies himself as a *called* and authorized messenger of Christ Jesus; the recipients are characterized as *called to be saints,* separated and sanctified members of God's one holy people; and the greeting invokes on the readers the characteristically NT blessings of God's undeserved, effective favor *(grace)* and that well-being and wholeness which God's favor creates *(peace).*

1:1 *Sosthenes.* Former ruler of the synagog at Corinth (Acts 18:17), probably converted by Apollos. Cf. Introduction, par. 10.

1:1-2 *Called . . . to be an apostle . . . called to be saints.* The parallelism is significant; Paul is already calling on the Corinthians to be "imitators" of himself. (4:16; 11:1)

1:2 *Saints together with all,* etc. Paul even here is warning his readers against that opinionated individualism he so stingingly rebukes in 14:36.

1:4-9 The customary thanksgiving dwells on the richness of the church's endowment. To some this has seemed like a hollow compliment in view of the sorry state of the church as revealed in the following chapters. But Paul is not complimenting the church; he is thanking God, the reality of whose gracious gifts is not made doubtful by the fact that some of the recipients have misused them. *God is faithful,* Paul is saying—"have you been faithful?" (9)

1:7 *Revealing of . . . Jesus Christ,* on the Last Day. (Cf. Cl 3:4)

1:10-17 The Folly of Dissensions

1:10-17 God, who is faithful, has called men "into the fellowship of his Son Jesus Christ OUR Lord" (9). To Him all are subject (as all have been baptized in His name); even the greatest and most brilliant are servants (cf. 3:5). To make little gods of human leaders is to call in question the unique Lordship of the Crucified, to forget what baptism in His name signifies (commitment to Him, incorporation in Him, cf. 12:12-13), to lose sight of the true nature of the *gospel as power.*

1:11 *Chloe's people.* Cf. Introduction, par. 18.

1:12 For the factions in Corinth cf. Introduction, pars. 9-19.

1:13 *Crucified . . . baptized.* For the connection between Christ's death and baptism in His name cf. Ro 6:3-4.

1:14 Paul's irony is not intended to depreciate Baptism, on which he sets the highest value (cf., e.g., 6:11, "washed"; 12:12-13; Ro 6:1-11). Rather, it (like the reference to the Crucified in 13) draws attention away from Paul to his Lord. For the practice of leaving the act of baptism to subordinates of the apostle cf. Acts 10:48.

Crispus. Leader of the synagog in Corinth, converted by Paul. (Acts 18:8)

Gaius. Cf. Ro 16:23. Whether he is to be identified with the Gaius of Acts 19:29 and 20:4 is doubtful.

1:17 *Eloquent* [human] *wisdom* empties the cross of its power because it substitutes an attainment of man (his system persuasively reasoned and rationally accepted) for God's mighty act of deliverance.

1:18—2:5 The Word of the Cross as the Power of God

1:18—2:5 The cross of Christ (17) and the *word of the cross* are God's action for us men and for our salvation (cf. 2 Co 5:18-19); therefore both are the power of God (cf. Ro 1:16-17). This power is not recognized and known by a critical examination of it but by being *saved* and being *called* by it (18, 24). Its divine character is made manifest by the very fact that it does not meet the expectations and demands of men, neither of the *Jews,* who expect to be overwhelmed into salvation by *signs* which make repentance and faith unnecessary, nor by the *Greeks,* who expect to be reasoned and argued into a salvation that they find rationally acceptable (22-23). The Gospel it not "according to man" (Gl 1:11). A man would have made a beginning in Corinth with converts of another kind (1:26-31); God worked in sovereign freedom when He called the Corinthians. He worked as only God can work, creatively *(chose . . . things that are not,* 28; *he is the source of your life,* 30). A man would have chosen a messenger of another kind (2:1-5), not a Paul with his *weakness . . . fear and trembling* (2:3) and his lack of *plausible words of wisdom* (2:4). God's work of rescue has excluded all self-assertion of man *(boast,* 29, 31; cf. Ro 3:27) and has made men's *faith . . . rest* in Him who alone can be its resting place. (2:5)

1:19 Cf. Is 29:14; Ps 33:10.

1:21 *World did not know God through wisdom,* the wisdom, namely, of God, manifested in His creation, which men beheld and "knew" and yet refused to thank and glorify the wise Creator (Ro 1:19-23). For the connection between wisdom and creation in Biblical thought cf. Jb 28:20-28; Pr 8:1, 22-31.

1:22 *Jews* and *Greeks* represent mankind, especially mankind at its "best," the religiously favored and the intellectual elite.

Jews demand signs. Cf. Mt 12:38; 16:1; Jn 4:48; 6:30.

Greeks seek wisdom. Cf. Acts 17:20-21, 31-32; when Paul speaks of God's judgment and the resurrection of Jesus, the Greeks are no longer interested.

1:24 *Called.* For the effectual call of God cf. 1:1-2 and Ro 8:28-30. *Wisdom* (cf. 30) points forward to the theme developed in 2:6 ff. (the Gospel as the wisdom of God).

1:28 *Things that are not.* Cf. Ro 4:17.

1:31 *Let him who boasts.* Cf. Jer 9:23-24.

2:2 *And him crucified.* Cf. Introduction, pars. 27 and 28.

2:4 *Spirit.* Cf. 3:12-13.

2:6-16 The Word of the Cross as the Wisdom of God

2:6-16 The Word of the cross is also a word of *wisdom* (cf. 1:24, 30); indeed it is the only wisdom which gives God's answer to man's predicament and makes final, perfect sense. But only the *mature* (6) can recognize it as such, that is, only those who have experienced its saving power as God's call (1:18, 24). They are those who have accepted the *gifts bestowed* by God (12), who *love him* for His inexpressible favors (9). They have parted ways forever with the *wisdom of this age* and *of the rulers of this age* (6, 8); they in their self-seeking drive have no understanding for God's gracious purposes and collide with them—the rulers of this age *crucified the Lord of glory* (8). For them God's loving wisdom remains a *secret and hidden* thing (7). To those who have experienced the love of God and have responded to His love, He reveals His wisdom *through the Spirit* (10). The Spirit is God's valid (10-11) and only (14) Interpreter. By the power of the Spirit man can leave this age and enter into the new world of God (cf. Heb 6:4-5) where he is free and independent of all the judgments of this age (15); the *mind of Christ,* no less, is his. (16)

2:6 *Rulers of this age . . . doomed to pass away.* The new world of God, prepared by His self-giving love, will pass judgment on and destroy all self-seeking (Mt 20:25) power. (Cf. 13:8, 13)

2:7 *Decreed . . . glorification.* Cf. Ro 8:28-30.

2:9 *It is written.* No such passage is found in our OT. For the thought in the OT cf. Is 52:13; 64:4; 65:17.

2:13 *Interpreting,* etc. The first alternative reading given in RSV note *d* ("interpreting spiritual truths in spiritual language") seems to fit the context better.

2:16 Cf. Is 40:13. The passage 40:1-31 is a mighty hymn on God's sovereign power in the service of His saving love.

3:1—4:7 God's Word and God's Servants

3:1—4:7 Now that Paul has made clear the nature of the Gospel as the power and wisdom of God, he can hope to be understood when he speaks of the place and function of men as proclaimers of that wise and potent Word. Men such as *Paul* and *Apollos* cannot be heads of rival cliques (3:3-4), as the Corinthians would have them be; they are merely *servants* (3.5, 4:1), *God's fellow workers* (3:9), planters and waterers for Him who creatively *gives the growth* (3:6, 9); they are merely *stewards of the mysteries of God,* accountable to God for their stewardship (4:1-5; cf. 3:12-15). The church which they found and foster is not theirs but God's—*God's field, God's building* (3:9), *God's temple* indwelt by *God's Spirit* (3:16-17). If the Corinthians really want to be what they claim to be, *spiritual men,* and no longer *babes in Christ* (3:1), no longer *men of the flesh, ordinary men, merely men* trapped in the wisdom of this age (3:1-4), they must learn so to regard these proclaimers and themselves. They dare not make Paul or Apollos the ultimate focus of their loyalties (3:4), the ground of their boasting, and the occasion of their conceited rivalries (3:21; 4:6). They do not *belong* to Paul or Apollos (3:4); these men are part of God's great gift to them (3:21-22; 4:7). As surely as Christ was crucified for them and they are baptized in His name (2:7-8; 1:13), they *are Christ's* and so belong to God (3:23). Thus they may learn . . . *not to go beyond what is written,* that Word of God which exalts God and silences the pretensions of men. (Cf. the quotations from the OT at 1:19, 31; 2:9, 16; 3:19-20)

3:1 *Men of the flesh. Flesh* designates man in his natural state of alienation from and enmity against God (Ro 8:5-8; note the antithesis to "Spirit"), incapable of communion with God as "unspiritual man" (2:14). Cf. "ordinary men" (3), "merely men" (4). Paul is raising the question whether the Corinthians may not have received the grace of God in vain.

3:13 *Day . . . fire.* The Day is the Day of Judgment; fire is a common symbol of God's judgment, which *will test* the *work done* by the proclaimers of the Word. For God's judgment as a consuming fire cf., e.g., Ml 3:2; 4:1; Mt 3:11-12.

3:15 *Saved . . . only as through fire.* Even the careless workman is not excluded from the forgiving compassion of God. But Paul repeats his warning ("Let each man take care how he builds," 10) in the sternest terms; the careless workman is playing with an eternal fire. For the expression cf. Zch 3:2; Jude 23

3:16-17 *God's temple.* Cf. 6:19; 2 Co 6:16. God's temple, the church, is being destroyed when men substitute the wisdom of this age for the folly of the cross. (18-20)

3:19-20 *It is written.* Jb 5:13; Ps 94:11.

3:21 *All things are yours.* Cf. Ro 8:32, 37-39.

3:23 *You are Christ's,* who has bought you "with a price" (6:20; 7:23; cf. Acts 20:28). Paul is giving the party slogan "I belong to Christ" (1:12; cf. Introduction, pars. 14-15) its true meaning by referring it to Christ crucified.

Christ is God's. God has given "all authority in heaven and on earth" (Mt 28:18; cf. 11:27) to His anointed King, His obedient Son. (Cf. 15:27-28)

4:3 *Judged by your or by any human court.* Cf. 2:15. As a spiritual man (7:40) Paul cannot submit to any judgment based on the standards of the wisdom of this age, such as the Corinthians have passed on him and Apollos. (3:4; 4:6)

4:7 *Who sees anything different in you?* Better, "Who distinguishes you," that is, marks *you* (singular, "any one of you") out as something special? You all have *received* apostles and teachers as gifts from the ascended Christ (Eph 4:7-12); you cannot therefore boast of any one of them as your private claim to distinction.

4:8-21 Be Imitators of Me

4:8-21 Paul, "called . . . to be an apostle of Christ Jesus" (1:1), goes the way of Jesus the Crucified, the way which the wise in this age reject as folly (10; cf. Mt 11:25), the way of weakness, deprivation, dishonor, and death, losing his life for Christ's sake in order to find it in Him (cf. Mt 16:25). With biting irony he indicts the Corinthians, men "called to be saints" (1:2), for leaving the way of their sainthood—Jesus' beatitudes upon the poor, hungry, and persecuted no longer apply to them (cf. Mt 5:3, 6, 10). In their arrogance they are no longer the meek to whom Jesus promised the earth as their inheritance (Mt 5:5), no longer imitators of their meek apostle (12-13) and *father in Christ Jesus* (15). Paul points to their underlying disease, of which their factions are a symptom; they have left the cross behind them in pursuing the mirage of wisdom and power. In calling on them to be *imitators* of himself (16), he is, for all his bitter language, summoning them back as his *beloved children* (14) to the one and enduring source of wisdom and power and life, to the *gospel* (15). *Timothy's* mission to them is to reinforce the apostle's plea that they become once more the "apostolic" church.

4:9 *Last of all . . . men sentenced . . . spectacle*

to the world. Paul seems to envision a sort of procession of doomed men, of which the apostles are the last and saddest lot. The whole world, both *angels and men,* looks uncomprehendingly on their sufferings.

4:13 *Refuse . . . offscouring* are words of abuse expressing profound contempt.

4:15 *Father . . . through the gospel.* Cf. 1:30; Phmn 10.

4:16 *Imitators.* Imitation involves acceptance of the apostolic Word and submission to apostolic authority as well as emulation. (Cf. 11:1; Ph 3:17; 1 Th 1:6; 2 Th 3:7, 9)

4:17 *Timothy.* Cf. 16:10.

Ways, Paul's proclamation and instruction. For *way* in this sense cf. Ps 25:4-5.

4:18-19 *Arrogant . . . arrogant people.* For the arrogance of the men who were opposing and belittling Paul at Corinth cf. 2 Co 10—13, esp. 11:20.

5:1—6:20 MORAL PROBLEMS

5:1—6:20 Cf. Introduction, pars. 16-19. Paul deals with three cases of a gross misuse of Christian liberty.

5:1-13 Incest

5:1-13 Paul jars the Corinthians out of complacent *(arrogant,* 2; *boasting,* 6) misuse of their Christian liberty by calling for immediate and rigorous discipline on the *man . . . living with his father's wife* (1). As the ancient people of God were liberated from bondage in order to serve God (Ex. 4:23), so it is with the new people: the Passover sacrifice of Christ *(our paschal lamb,* 7) has liberated the church for a life of *sincerity and truth* (8). The Christian life is to be a perpetual celebration of liberation from sin, not an indulgence in liberty to sin.

5:1 *Not . . . even among pagans.* Not only the OT law (Dt 22:30; 27:20) but also Greek and Roman law forbade such incestuous unions. The example of Oedipus, who blinded himself when he discovered that he had (unwittingly) married his father's wife, is an expression of the revulsion which even pagans felt.

5:2 *Mourn,* undertake the sad duty of discipline rather than be *arrogant* about their supposed achievement of liberty.

5:3-5 Though the apostle has *already pronounced judgment,* he cannot act alone, for he does not "lord it over" their faith (2 Co 1:24). Apostle and apostolic church act together with the power of Him who is Lord over them both.

5:5 *Deliver this man to Satan.* Cf. 1 Ti 1:20. Excommunication is meant (cf. 13), for the "whole world" outside the church "is in the power of the evil one" (1 Jn 5:19). The intention of the act of excommunication is that the man be ultimately *saved* in the *day* of judgment. The flesh, his opposition to the will of God (cf. 3:1 note), will be destroyed when he realizes whither his sin has brought him; and when he turns in repentance to the *Lord Jesus,* his Judge and his Forgiver, his *spirit* will *be saved.*

5:6 *Little leaven . . . whole lump.* Cf. Mt 13:33; Gl 5:9. This cuts off the plea that the man's offense is "only one" case, or an "exceptional case." The solidarity of the church is such that all members are affected by each member, for better or worse. (Cf. 12:26)

5:7-8 *Unleavened bread* was eaten at the Passover, the feast which commemorated Israel's deliverance from Egyptian bondage. It symbolizes the complete break with the past (Ex 12:8, 14-20; 13:3-10; Dt 16:1-4). So the Christian Passover, in which Christ is the *paschal lamb* that *has been sacrificed,* ushers in a new era in which the *malice and evil* of the past are done away with.

As you really are unleavened, i.e., pure, clean. The Christian is called on to enact in his living what God's redeeming act has made him to be. *Truth* is not only to be known but to be obeyed (Ro 2:8), to be done (Jn 3:21; 1 Jn 1:6); the opposite of truth is "wickedness," "wrong," "walking in darkness."

5:9 *In my letter.* Cf. Introduction, par. 17.

5:11 *Not even to eat.* The bond created by participation in the common meal was strongly felt (cf. Mt 14:15-21 note). Not to eat with a man was to exclude him from fellowship.

5:12 *Judging others . . . those inside the church . . . you are to judge.* God reserves judgment on the world to Himself (Mt 7:1; Ro 12:19); the Christians are to judge those inside the church, in the sense that they confront them with their sin and call them to repentance. (Mt 18:15-18; 1 Co 5:3-5)

5:13 Cf. Dt 17:7; 19:19; 22:21, 24; 24:7.

6:1-11 Litigation

6:1-11 The new people of God have by virtue of their baptism *(washed,* 11) been *sanctified* and *justified in the name of the Lord Jesus Christ and in the Spirit of our God* (11); they belong to Christ (3:22) and are therefore destined to *judge the world* and *angels* with Him (2-3). They belong, as men endowed with God's Spirit, to the new world of God and cannot therefore commit their task of dealing with brothers at variance with one another to the powers of this judged and dying world.

6:7 *Defeat for you,* because it is a decline from the level at which the saints (2) really live as heirs of the future (1-3) in obedience to the Word of Jesus (Mt 5:39-42). Here too they have become "men of the flesh," "ordinary men," "merely men." (3:1, 3, 4)

6:12-20 Sexual Immorality

6:12-20 Cf. Introduction, pars. 16 and 19. Paul quotes a catchword of the proponents of "freedom" at Corinth *(All things are lawful for me,* 12) and a bit of the reasoning with which they defended their position that the spiritual man of knowledge is free to associate with prostitutes: sexual indulgence, they claimed, is on a par with the satisfaction of hunger, a morally indifferent part of life in this passing age (13). Then he exposes their specious catchword and murky reasoning to the light of the cross. The Christ who died for man's sins declared that to indulge in sin is to be *enslaved* to sin (12; Jn 8:34), and from that enslavement His cross has ransomed man *(bought with a price,* 20), with a whole redemption of the whole corporeal person. His grace has laid claim to man's body *(for the Lord,* 13), marked it for resurrection and eternal life (14), made it a member of Himself (15), a temple of the *Holy Spirit* (19), a place of inviolable sanctity—no longer man's to do with as he pleases *(not your own,* 19) but the instrument of his worship (20; cf. Ro 12:1). If the Corinthians *join* this body *to a prostitute* (16), they are desecrating what the cross has made holy; if they indulge in this enslaving freedom, they are denying their "only Master and Lord, Jesus Christ" (Jude 4). The bodily character of this act, far from making the act indifferent, makes it particularly heinous.

7:1-40 CELIBACY AND MARRIAGE

7:1-40 The same depreciation of the body and man's bodily life which found expression in an easy conscience on fornication (6:12-20) gave rise at Corinth to an uneasy conscience concerning marriage and fostered an impulse toward universal celibacy. The church's letter to Paul *(matters about which you wrote,* 1) probably quoted a catchword of the new teaching: *It is well for a man not to touch a woman* (1) and indicated the problems to which the application of this principle had given rise. Married people were conducting ascetic experiments to which they were not always equal (2-5). Some were considering divorce from their spouses, especially pagan spouses, as a way toward a fuller religious life (10-16). The *unmarried and the widows* were being made uncertain regarding their right to marry or remarry (8-9, 25-28, 39-40). Whatever the exact meaning of 36-38 (see note on the passage), it indicates the same uneasiness of conscience regarding marriage as the rest. Paul answers the questions fully, and his answers are as sober and evangelically fair as the assertions of the new teaching were one-sided and legalistic.

Christ, he tells his church, has *bought* men *with a price* (7:23) and has destined them for glory. Their life within the orders of this world (marriage, slavery, commerce) has a provisional, next-to-the-last character, for *the form of this world is passing away* to give place to the new world of God. As redeemed men they are to have a loose hold on the things of this world (29-31) and are to aim always at an *undivided devotion to the Lord* who has bought them (35). That gives celibacy its value and place in the life of the church, one that Paul is the first to appreciate, being himself celibate (7, 8, 26, 38, 40). But celibacy is a gift which only the free grace of God can give (7); man cannot simply claim or take it for himself, much less impose it as a rule on others without regard for their limitations. Moreover, if life in this world has a provisional, preliminary character, it also has a preparatory character; men are to live their present lives in the faith that God's *call* has summoned them to be His own in the place where they are and to serve Him there (17-24). They may not in blind enthusiasm set out blithely to free themselves of the marriage bond which the Word of their redeeming Lord has hallowed (10); and they dare not attempt a self-chosen course of celibate devotion which will plunge them into sin. (2-5; 9, 36)

7:1 *You wrote.* Cf. Introduction, par. 20, and 8:1; 11:2; 12:1; 16:1.

7:4 Even in these down-to-earth words on the physical aspect of marriage it is clear that erotic love is transfigured by that specifically Christian love which does not seek its own (13:4-7); spouses simply exist for each other.

7:10 *The Lord.* Jesus has no specific word on the wife's seeking a divorce, since under Jewish law she could not sue for divorce. But His word on the inviolability of marriage, Mt 19:6, covers the case.

7:11 *If she does.* Better, "If she is already divorced."

Remain single. She is free to remarry only after the death of her husband. (39-40)

7:12 *To the rest,* to those married to pagan spouses.

I . . . not the Lord. Although Paul is emphatic about his apostolic authority (1:1; 7:25; 7:40) and goes so far as to assert that "Christ is speaking in" him (2 Co 13:3; cf. Ro 15:18), he distinguishes carefully between his word and a word uttered by Jesus in the days of His flesh.

7:14 *Unbelieving husband is consecrated through his wife.* Consecration is, as 16 shows, not the same as salvation; the wife's faith does not automatically "save" the unbelieving husband. The thought seems, rather, to be this: When God in His grace called the woman, He called her as she was, in the closest of human associations with an unbeliever; His grace reached her even so and is sufficient for her even so. The pagan husband is, whether he wills and knows it or not, partner in a Christian marriage and is in that respect consecrated by the divine grace which is over that marriage. The Christian wife can and may "remain with God" in that state in which she was called (24). She is not living in an unhallowed union, and the *children* of her marriage are not *unclean* but destined to be part of the holy temple of God (3:16-17) by the grace of Baptism, as she well knew when she brought her children to be baptized.

7:16 Both apostle and the church know that they can only "by all means save SOME." (9:22)

7:17 Paul generalizes from his statement concerning mixed marriage (12-16) and illustrates his *rule* with the examples of circumcision (18-19) and slavery. (21-22)

7:23 Christians, redeemed *with a price,* are "to be judged by no one" (2:15); they would *become slaves of men* if they accepted and acted on the judgment of men concerning the importance and significance of such things as circumcision (18-19) or slavery. (21-22)

7:26 *Present distress,* the time of the "great

tribulation" which precedes the return of Christ. (Cf. 7:29; Mt 24:21, 29; Lk 23:29)

7:31 *The form of this world is passing away,* and the new age, when marriage will be no more, is at hand. (Mt 22:30)

7:36-38 As translated in the RSV, the *any one* of 36 is an engaged man who has determined to keep his relationship to his *betrothed* a purely spiritual one, *to keep her as his betrothed.* (38). Paul's advice to such is the same as that given to the unmarried and the widows, 8-9; marriage is no sin—*he who marries his betrothed does well,* but for him to whom it is given, to *refrain from marriage is better.*

But it is more likely that *any one* of 36 is the father of the girl. The word translated *betrothed* in 36, 37, 38 is in the Greek simply "virgin"; and the word translated *marries* is regularly used for "giving in marriage" by the father. The passage ought then probably be rendered thus: "If any one thinks that he is not behaving properly toward his virgin (daughter, by not allowing her to marry), if she is fully mature and it ought so to be, let him do as he wishes; let them (the daughter and the young man involved) marry—it is no sin. But whoever is firmly established in his heart, being under no necessity but in control of his will and has determined this in his heart, to keep her as his virgin (daughter), he will do well. So that he who gives his virgin in marriage does well, and he who refrains from giving her in marriage will do better."

7:39-40 Apparently an appendage to 10-11, 15. (Cf. 7:11 note)

7:39 *In the Lord,* that is, to a fellow Christian, with a full sense of what Christian marriage involved.

8:1—11:1 THE EATING OF MEAT OFFERED TO IDOLS

8:1—11:1 Cf. Introduction, pars. 16 and 22. *Food offered to idols* (8:1) became a problem for Christians because in sacrifices to pagan deities only a part of the sacrificial animal was actually offered to the deity; the rest was either *sold in the meat market* (10:25) or eaten at festal meals *in an idol's temple* (8:10; cf. 10:27). It was understandable that some Christians were troubled in conscience about partaking of foods thus "contaminated" by close contact with abhorrent idolatry. The men of *knowledge* (8:1), blithely confident in the *liberty* (8:9) which their knowledge gave them, overrode the scruples of these weaker brothers by partaking freely and publicly (8:10) of foods offered to idols. Paul, fair as always, first assents fully to what is true in the claim that knowledge gives liberty (8:1-6; 10:19-20, 27, 29); the Christian knows the exclusive sovereignty of his God and Lord and is forever free from all other gods and lords (8:5-6). Then Paul proceeds to purge knowledge of self-will and pride by pointing out the obligation of love to those who do *not . . . possess this knowledge* as they do (8:7-13)—the weak brother ruined by the strong man's knowledge. He then points to his own apostolic ministry as the example of self-denying, self-giving love which made him, free as he was, the *slave to all* (9:1-23), leading a life that knows harsh self-discipline (9:24-27). This discipline of the Christ whom Paul "imitates" and summons the strong and knowledgeable to imitate (10:31—11:1) is the yoke of the Christ to whose self-giving love they owe their existence (8:6), who died for the brother whom they despise and ruin (8:11), the incarnate Lord *Jesus* (9:1), whose redemptive blessings they know and experience in the Supper of the Lord. (10:16-17; cf. 10:1-4)

This Lord had tempered the boldness of His disciples' faith with holy fear when he taught them to pray (Mt 6:13) and when He bade them watch and pray that they might not enter into temptation on the night in which He was betrayed (Mt 26:41). Paul imitates his Lord in this too. He deepens the knowledge of the knowing *(I want you to know,* 10:1) with the knowledge that he who *thinks that he stands* may, but for the grace of God, yet *fall* (10:12-13), as Israel once fell in spite of all that God had given her (10:1-11). He sobers the knowing in their careless contempt of idols by pointing to the fact that the idol-nonentity becomes a demonic reality when worshiped, a reality with which no worshiper of God can come to terms. (10:14-22)

Then, having laid a foundation of selfless love and reverent fear, Paul can give brief and down-to-earth directions concerning contact with food offered to idols.

These chapters, together with Ro 14—15, are the classic apostolic treatment of the use and misuse of the liberty with which Christ has set us free. (Gl 5:13)

8:1 and 4 Cf. Introduction, par. 16. The words set off by quotation marks in the text are probably slogans used by the new leaders. For the knowledge-love relationship cf. 13:2.

8:2 For the radical reconstruction effected in man's thinking by the Gospel cf. Paul's words of wisdom, 3:18.

8:3 *Is known by him* (God). Real "knowledge" is not an attainment of man but God's gift to man, not so much a knowing as a being-known, that is, being loved, chosen, and called by God. Cf. Mt 11:27, where Jesus describes knowledge of the Father as His free gift to the weary and heavy laden, and Ro 8:29 ("foreknew") note.

8:5 *Lord* was a common title of deity in oriental religions, many of which had become popular in the Roman world, and was used of the deified Roman emperor.

8:6 For the *Father* as Source and Goal of creation and history cf. Ro 11:36. For *Jesus Christ* as Mediator of both creation and salvation cf. Jn 1:3; Cl 1:16-20; Heb 1:13.

8:7 *Accustomed to idols,* as real and influential powers in their life. (Cf. 12:2)

As really offered to an idol. Cf. 10:19-20

8:8 *Food will not commend,* that is, as the second half of the verse shows, the eating of or abstaining from certain foods. Our eating and drinking is done "to the glory of God" (10:31) when it is motivated by love for the brother. (8:13)

8:10 *Encouraged,* literally "built up," the same Greek word as in 8:1. Those who made such reckless use of their liberty as is here described evidently argued that their example "built up" the weaker brother, encouraged him to become equally free; Paul's pastoral insight rejects such rough measures as injurious and destructive—the weak conscience is "defiled" (7), "wounded" (12), and the weak man "falls" and is "destroyed" (13, 11) since he is led to act in violation of his conscience. (Cf. Ro 14:14)

9:1-2 Paul develops further the thought of 8:13. He is as *free* as anybody (cf. 8:9; 9:19) and has "rights" (3, 5, 6, 12, 18) of a special kind as *apostle,* authenticated by his own history *(seen Jesus,* cf. 15:8) and by the existence of the apostolic church which his ministry has produced *(seal).*

9:5 *Accompanied by a wife.* This would increase the burden laid on the churches who supported the apostles.

Cephas, the Aramaic form of Peter's name.

9:6-14. Paul demonstrates his *right* to maintenance by the church from the principle of equity in the occupations of ordinary life (7; cf. 10-12), by the principle laid down by the Law in the OT (8-10, 13), and by an appeal to the command of Jesus. When he waived his right (15), he was waiving indisputable rights.

9:9 *Law.* Dt 25:4. The apostle, who had an ear for the groaning of subhuman creation and knew of a promise and a hope that embraced all creation (Ro 8:18-22), can hardly be thought of as denying God's care for all His creatures, or that oxen are beneath His dignity. But he is saying very dramatically that God's provision for threshing *oxen* embodies a principle of His rule over all creation.

9:12 *Obstacle in the way of the gospel.* The suspicion that the apostle was preaching for gain would be such an obstacle (cf. 1 Th 2:5; Acts 20:33; 3 Jn 7). Even at Corinth Paul had to ward off that suspicion. (2 Co 12:14-18)

9:13 *Temple service.* Nm 18:8-32; Dt 18:1-3. Paul occasionally speaks of his own ministry as "the PRIESTLY service of the gospel." (Ro 15:16)

9:14 *The Lord commanded.* Mt 10:10; Lk 10:7-8.

9:15-18 Paul's talk of *boasting* (15, 16) and *reward* (17, 18) has a strange ring coming from a man who so rigorously excludes all boasting of man from man's relationship to God (1:29; Ro 3:27). It can be understood only in the context of grace; we hear Paul speaking of his *ground for boasting* again in 15:10, when he says: "I worked harder [or more abundantly] than any of them." There his boast is preceded and followed by a thankful acknowledgment of the sole working of God's grace in and through him. So here, boasting and reward are an exultant recognition of the divine grace which has made him not merely an obedient slave with a *necessity . . . laid upon* him (16-17) who can claim no reward for doing what he ought (cf. Lk 17:7-10)—this grace has made him an "imitator" of Christ (11:1), a free son giving freely *(of my own will,* 17; *free of charge,* 18), as the Son gave (Gl 1:4; 2:20; cf. Mt 10:8). Thus he can look to sharing in His master's joy (Mt 25:21). All is of grace, and so Paul's "boasting" is in the last analysis a boasting "of the Lord." (1:31)

9:19-27 "Love builds up" (8:1). Paul's single desire to build the living church not only led him to renounce the financial support that was his due (9:3-18); it also made him a *slave to all* (19), in obedience to the *law of Christ* (cf. Gl 6:2). He became *all things to all men* (22), to the *Jews . . . under the law* (20), to Gentiles *outside the law* (21), to the *weak* Christian brothers (22). He sought and found the Jew where he lived, under the Law, never flouting Judaic sanctities, never belittling the high majesty of the Law or casting doubt on the promises given to Israel or concealing the fact that the Gospel is given "to the Jew first" (Ro 1:16). He sought and found the Gentile where he was, outside the Law, without imposing the Law on him, fighting for the Gentile's freedom from the Law (cf. Gl). Chapters 8—10 of 1 Co are abiding evidence of how he entered sympathetically into the fears and scruples of the weak, dealing gently with them like a nurse or father (1 Th 2:7, 11), shielding them from the offense of the inconsiderate strong. He pursues this course with the intense devotion of an *athlete* in training (24-25), in the knowledge that only he who lives and shares the *gospel . . . may share in its blessings* (23) and in the somber realization that he must yet face the judgment of his Lord (cf. 4:4) and may yet be *disqualified* in the race and lose the prize. (27; cf. Ph 3:14)

10:1-22 Paul remembers what the "wise" and "strong" ignore: that God's grace and gifts put man into a personal and responsible relationship to Him; they do not "insure" man against sin and judgment magically and automatically. Ancient Israel is a warning example; Israel experienced the same wondrously working grace that Christians have experienced in their baptism, Israel had a *supernatural* supper given by the Lord to nurture His presence in the church. And yet Israel fell and provoked the judgment of God (1-10). From Israel's history the new Israel of the last days, the church, may learn: *Let any one who thinks that he stands take heed lest he fall* (12).—Not that the Christians live in sheer terror; they know that the *faithful God* who called them into the fellowship of His Son (cf. 1:9) remains protectively in charge of their embattled lives (13).—But the warning stands; the *worship of idols* stands in complete opposition to the worship of God. The communion with the Crucified ever renewed and nurtured in the *table of the Lord* is total and exclusive and makes any other communion a communion with *demons.* The *Lord* who gives His *body* and *blood* in His *cup* and at His *table* is a jealous Lord (22)—what "strong" man dare fancy that he can challenge His Lordship with impunity? (14-22). (The implication seems to be that any eating of meat offered to idols which concedes reality to the idols does challenge His Lordship.)

10:2 *Baptized into Moses.* To mark the parallel

between Israel and the church, Paul calls the Exodus *(cloud . . . sea,* Ex 13:21; 14:22, 29) a baptism. There in the Exodus (as now in Baptism) God was acting graciously for man's salvation (Ex 14:13; 15:2). In both cases the person of the mediator (Moses, Christ) is of decisive importance, so that baptism is *into* him. That Christ's mediation of salvation lies on a higher level than that of Moses goes without saying. (Cf. Jn 1:17)

10:3-4 The comparison between Israel's manna and water from the Rock *(supernatural food . . . drink)* and the Christian's Supper of the Lord again marks the parallel between Israel and the church and brings the warning of Israel's history close to home.

Rock . . . followed . . . was Christ. In speaking of the *Rock which followed* Paul is employing a bit of Judaic tradition, which deduced from the two accounts of water from the rock (Ex 17:6; Nm 20:11) that the *Rock followed* Israel through the wilderness. In saying that the *Rock was Christ* he is looking back on Israel's history from the vantage point of its culmination in Jesus Christ and is saying: Wherever we find God graciously at work for man, there the Christ is present; all the past history of salvation has Christ as its hidden center—in Him all the spoken and acted "promises of God find their Yes." (2 Co 1:20)

10:5-11 For the record of Israel's sins in the *wilderness* and God's judgment upon them cf. for 10:5 *(overthrown in the wilderness)* Nm 14:29-30; for 10:6 *(desire evil)* Nm 11:4, 34; for 10:7 *(idolaters)* Ex 32:4-6; for 10:8 *(indulge in immorality . . . fell in a single day)* Nm 25:1-18; for 10:9 *(put the Lord to the test . . . serpents)* Nm 21:5-6; for 10:10 *(grumble . . . destroyed)* Nm 16:30-49.

10:10 *Destroyer.* God's destroying angel. (Cf. 1 Ch 21:12, 15)

10:14-22 The Corinthian Christians know how deep and vital a thing *participation* (16) in the divine is, how it dominates and shapes the life of the participants. They know this from the Lord's Supper, in which they encounter and are blessed by the very presence of their incarnate, redeeming Lord *(blood, body,* 16); their common nurture in their common partaking of the one *bread* (in which their one Lord is really and effectively present) creates a common life *(one body,* 17). They know this also from the Scriptures written for their instruction (cf. 11); the priests who according to the Law (Lv 7:6; cf. 1 Co 9:13) *eat the sacrifices* are by that act *partners in the altar* and of the Godhead whose presence the altar signifies; "the Lord is their inheritance" (Dt 18:1-5). From the depth and reality of this participation in the divine they can *judge for* themselves (15) how dangerous and entrapping a participation in the pseudo-divine, the demonic, must be. In partaking of the *cup* and *table of demons,* they are giving the demons power over them (for what a man gives his heart to becomes his god, cf. Mt 6:21; Eph 5:5, Cl 3:5); they *provoke the Lord* who alone is entitled to power over them *to jealousy,* challenging His authority over them. (22)

10:16 *Is it not . . . ?* Paul's use of the rhetorical question shows that he is appealing to a belief commonly held in the church; he is arguing from the real presence of Christ, not about it. (Cf. 11:27-29)

10:20 *To demons.* Cf. Dt 32:17.

10:22 *Provoke . . . to jealousy.* Cf. Dt 32:21.

10:23—11:1 Paul's pastoral wisdom has instilled faith (8:4-6), love (8:7—9:27), and fear (10:1-22)—on that basis he can give succinct advice: Even the weakest of consciences can grow strong enough to eat meat that has come from the idol's temple to the common *market;* the sovereign claim of the Creator (26) is not questioned here. The strong in his strength can forgo his freedom in a situation where another's conscience is involved, with his inner freedom unimpaired. What matters finally is that all life be lived *to the glory of God;* and God is glorified when men become *imitators* of the apostle of Christ and thus of *Christ* Himself, who went the servant's way, *not seeking* His *own advantage, but that of many, that they may be saved,* to the glory of His Father. (Cf. Ph 2:11)

10:23 *All things are lawful.* Cf. 6:12.

10:26 *The earth is the Lord's.* Cf. Ps 24:1; 50:12.

10:28 *Offered in sacrifice.* The expression, different from that used in 8:1, etc., indicates that the informer is convinced to some degree of the reality of the god to whom meat has been offered.

10:30 *I give thanks.* The act of thanksgiving acknowledges the fact that it is God's creation (26) and His gift. (Cf. Ro 14:6; 1 Ti 4:4-5)

11:2—14:40 DISORDERS IN THE WORSHIP LIFE OF THE CHURCH

11:2—14:40 Cf. Introduction, pars. 23 and 24.

11:2-16 Woman in the Church

11:2-16. Cf. Introduction, par. 23. Paul reverts to the question of woman's place in the church in 14:34-36, where he treats the question of her role in the public assemblies of instruction and worship. Here he establishes the basic fact that woman's place in the church dare not involve a denial of her place as God's creature, as woman. Within the pattern of the customs and values of the first church a woman did deny her womanliness if she prayed or prophesied *with her head unveiled* (5, cf. 6). Dropping the *veil* signified that she was flouting the will of Him who has placed an *authority* over her (10 and RSV note *r*); she has her true place in an order of subordination: *God—Christ—man—woman* (3). The fact that Christ, the Son of God, is included in this order makes clear that this "subordination" has nothing servile or degrading about it; Christ is "subordinated" as the freely obeying, loving Son who seeks the glory of His Father and finds the goal and climax of His ministry in laying all that His ministry has won at His Father's feet (15:28; cf. Ph 2:11). Within this order set by God at creation (8-9; cf. Gn 2:21-23) man and woman have their place as Christians (*in the Lord,* 11) and live their lives together, complementing each other—Paul leaves no room for male pride when he assigns headship to the man. (11-12)

That is Paul's main argument, based on the Genesis account of creation and the fact of the incarnate Christ; he closes with an appeal to his readers' "natural" sense of fitness (*nature . . . teach,* 13-15) and to the example of the apostles and the apostolic churches. (16)

11:2 Paul is evidently acknowledging the church's profession of loyalty to him and his teaching *(traditions . . . delivered),* probably quoting from their letter. (Cf. 7:1)

11:3 *Head of,* authority over.

Head of Christ is God. Cf. 3:23 note.

11:6 *Cut off her hair.* Ironic: let her go the whole way in denying her womanliness—if she would "dishonor her head" (5) by removing the badge of her womanliness, let her dishonor it utterly.

11:7 *Glory,* here, in connection with *image,* in the sense of "reflection of the glory." (Gn 1:26)

11:8 Cf. Gn 2:21-23.

11:12 *All things are from God.* The same God who made woman "a helper fit for him" (Gn 2:18) made her also "the mother of all living." (Gn 3:20)

11:17-34 The Lord's Supper

11:17-34 Cf. Introduction, par. 24. The Lord's Supper is the Supper of the Lord of glory crucified for man (2:8); it is the gift of His cross effectually present in the church to enrich and unify the church. To make of it man's supper, a meal wherein the Lord's real and redeeming bodily presence is not recognized, to make of it the scene of man's carousing and the expression of his factious and comtemptuous self-will is to invite the judgment of God on His church.

11:18-19 In the chemistry of God's rule over the church *divisions must* harden into *factions* in order that the false and the *genuine* be *recognized* as they openly confront each other and the truth win out.

11:21-22 The common meal, an expression of fellowship (cf. Acts 2:42, 46) and love, lost that character when each one went *ahead with* the *meal* which he had brought, thus *humiliating those who had nothing.*

Houses to eat in, if physical nurture and enjoyment were the whole purpose of the meal. A common meal during which the Lord's Supper is celebrated has quite another character.

11:23-26 Cf. Mt 26:26-28; Mk 14:22-24; Lk 22:19-20, and the notes there.

11:23 *Received from the Lord.* The significance and sanctity of the Supper do not rest on any intermediate human authority but derive from the Lord Himself.

11:24-25 *In remembrance of me.* Cf. Lk 22:19. *Remembrance* includes a believing recall and a grateful recognition and confession of the divine redemptive action. (Cf. Ps 6:5)

11:26 *You proclaim the Lord's death.* The body and the blood as interpreted by the words of the Lord Himself ("for you") point to the crucified Lord of glory. *Until he comes* points to the risen and returning Lord of glory, an echo of Jesus' word concerning His future fellowship with His disciples in Mt 26:29 and Mk 14:25, when He instituted His Supper.

11:27 *In an unworthy manner.* As 29 makes plain, the "unworthiness" lies in not *discerning the body* in its sanctity and significance for man, eating and acting as if the present Lord were not present but had failed to keep His promise, as if His redemptive death did not signify, as if His "Drink of it, all of you," did not bind all His disciples together. The "unworthiness" is impenitence and unbelief. Cf. the "worthy" of Mt 10:11, 13.

11:32 *Chastened.* The Lord's judgments are disciplinary and corrective, designed to create repentance and to lead men to righteousness and life. (Cf. Heb 12:5-11)

12:1—14:40 The Use of Spiritual Gifts

12:1—14:40 Cf. Introduction, par. 24. The Holy Spirit puts men under the Lordship of Jesus, the Crucified; the gifts which the Spirit bestows are therefore to be the expression of the Lord's self-giving will and are to be used in mutual ministration for the church, the body of Christ, where (as in the human body) no member can be solitary and self-sufficient and all members are necessary (ch. 12). The highest gift of the Spirit is the gift of that indispensable love which sets man free for ministry (ch. 13). No gift of the Spirit is being used rightly when it is used to foster individualism in worship and creates a confusion which does not edify. The God who gave His Son to be the Peace of the world is a God of peace and not of confusion; He would have *all things . . . done decently and in order.* (Ch. 14)

12:1 *Spiritual gifts,* gifts "inspired" by the Holy Spirit (11), apportioned to various individuals in the church "for the common good" (7). For a list of such gifts (not intended to be exhaustive), see 8-10, 28, and cf. Ro 12:6-8.

12:2 *Led astray,* by demonic "spirits" (cf. 10:20). Man is never autonomous; as he is subject either to sin or righteousness (Ro 6:18, 22), so he is inspired either by a spirit that leads him to reject Jesus as the Accursed (cf. Gl 3:13) or by the Spirit, who leads him to confess Jesus as Lord. (3)

12:3 *Jesus is Lord.* This has been appropriately called the church's first creed. To confess Jesus as Lord is to anticipate the universal acclamation that will hail Him Lord at the end of days (Ph 2:9-11) and to enter into the salvation of the last days even now. (Ro 10:9)

12:9 *Faith.* In distinction from the faith which is the common and indispensable possession of all Christians, this is that peculiar "measure of faith" (Ro 12:3), given to some, which enables them "to move mountains" (13:2; Mt 17:20; 21:21). Men with this gift draw their life so wholly from God and can live their life so wholly for God that they dare things deemed impossible.

12:10 *Distinguish between spirits,* whether they are demonic (cf. 2 note) or of God, of Christ or of antichrist. (1 Jn 4:1-3)

Kinds of tongues, glossolalia, a kind of devotional utterance inspired by the Spirit which does not engage the mind of the speaker as prophetic speech does (14:13-19) and remains unintelligible to the hearers unless interpreted to them by one endowed with the gift of *interpretation* (14:6-9). Paul prizes the gift of tongues both for himself and the church (14:5, 18, 39) but is constrained to protest against an exaggerated estimate and an irresponsible, self-centered use of it (ch. 14). It is significant that he mentions this gift last both here and in 2:28.

12:12 *So it is with Christ.* One would expect "with the church"; the fact that Paul says *Christ* shows how close the tie between Christ and His church is.

12:13 *Made to drink,* i. e., "given to drink" (there is no thought of compulsion). The reference is to the Lord's Supper.

12:22-24 *Parts of the body . . . weaker . . . less honorable . . . unpresentable.* Jesus' concern for the "little ones" in His church (Mt 18:5, 10, 14) is reflected in Paul's words here. He is protecting the less brilliantly endowed members of the church against the disregard and contempt of the Corinthian admiration society. The analogy of the body's less honorable members enables Paul to make two points: God, Creator and Redeemer, has put them where they are, and He has made them an indispensable part of the whole organism.

12:28 *Apostles . . . prophets . . . teachers.* Cf. Eph 4:11 note.

12:31 *The higher gifts,* those that especially serve the common good (7), which are a manifestation of love (ch. 13), for the upbuilding of the church. (Ch. 14)

13:1 *Tongues of men and of angels,* the overprized gift at Corinth. (Cf. 12:10 note, 28; ch. 14)

Gong . . . cymbal, sound that signifies nothing.

Love. The question whether Paul is speaking of love for God or for man is beside the point. Both are meant; works like "patient" and "kind" (4) indicate that love for man is included, and the close connection between love and faith and hope (13, cf. 7) shows that love for God is included also. Paul sees the two as a unity, as Jesus did. (Mt 22:34-40; cf. Mt 22:15-40 note)

13:2 *Faith.* Cf. 12:9 note.

13:3 *Body . . . burned.* Even the heroic grace of martyrdom is valueless if it is not an expression of love as Christ's death was, a death "for many."

13:4 *Not jealous.* The word *not* occurs six times (eight times in the Greek) in the enumeration of the qualities of love, an indication that this love runs against the grain of man's normal willing and doing. It is not of this age or this world but a gift from God, an anticipation of the world to come. (Cf. 8-13)

13:7 *Love* is able to bear up under all pressures that threaten to suppress it *(bears, endures)* because it is completely open to God *(believes all things)* and to God's great future for men *(hopes all things).* For the intrinsic connection between love and hope cf. Cl 1:4; Ro 13:8-11; between love and faith, Gl 5:6; 1 Ti 1:5.

13:12 *Dimly,* because the divine reality is apprehended at second hand, by reflection, mediately rather than with the immediacy of *face to face* encounter.

13:13 *Faith, hope, love.* Cf. 7 note. As these three coexist in necessary connection now, so they will *abide,* continue in eternity, together; love is *greatest* because without it even a faith which removes mountains (2) and a hope that expends its life in hope of the world to come (3) is void and valueless.

14:3 *Speaks to men for their upbuilding.* Cf. 12:7, "for the common good." This is the major emphasis of the chapter: 4, 5, 6 ("benefit"), 12, 17, 19 ("instruct"), 25 ("he will worship God"), 26, 31 ("learn . . . be encouraged"). Gifts receive their place and value in accordance with their power to edify all; therefore prophecy (inspired preaching) is superior to the self-edifying (4) gifts of tongues. (5)

14:13-19 The word *mind* occurs four times in seven verses. The letters of Paul witness to the intense intellectual activity which the Spirit produces. Anti-intellectualism will find small comfort in the apostolic Word, which recognizes man's mind as a gift from God.

14:21-25 *In the law. Law* is used for the OT generally. (Cf. Ro 3:19, where Psalms are called "law.") The quotation is from Is 28:11-12; there the prophet threatens the people who have sneered (Is 28:9-10) at the clear prophetic Word: God will speak to them in an unclear fashion *by men of strange tongues* as a punishment on their impenitence and unbelief, "that they may go, and fall backward, and be broken, and snared, and taken" (Is 28:13). Thus the unintelligible language of strange *tongues* becomes a *sign,* a token of God's presence and activity, *for unbelievers,* to harden them judgmentally in their unbelief; while the clear speech of *prophecy* becomes a token of God's present activity *for believers,* to establish and confirm them in their faith. They will not call men *mad* who speak openly for God; they will repent and *worship God.*

14:29 *Weigh what is said.* Cf. 1 Th 5:19-21.

14:32-33. *The spirits of prophets are subject to prophets.* The prophets may not evade responsibility for the unedifying confusion by pleading that inspiration compels them to speak; prophets are not mad dervishes but clear-minded and responsible spokesmen of the God of wholesome order *(peace).*

14:34-35 *Women . . . keep silence.* In 11:3-16 Paul had established the basic rule for the behavior of woman: Even in prayer and prophecy, where she is her most religious and spiritual self, woman is not to forget or deny her created womanliness. This is now applied to woman's behavior *in the churches,* the assemblies or meetings. What the *law says* (Gn 3:16) is upheld by the Gospel: Woman is to be *subordinate* and not assume a function in the church beyond that which her Lord has assigned to her. (Cf. 1 Ti 2:11-12; 1 Ptr 3:1; Eph 5:22-33)

14:36 The church at Corinth is neither the first nor the only church and cannot therefore claim a privileged position on this point; the *word of God* rules all churches equally.

14:37 *Command of the Lord,* since Christ speaks in Paul (2 Co 13:3; Ro 15:18) and his word is God's Word to men. (1 Th 2:13)

14:38 *He is not recognized,* that is, not recognized by Christ as His own. If he continues in disobedience to the apostolic Word, he must expect to hear his Lord say to him on the Last Day: "I never knew you." (Mt 7:23)

15:1-58 THE RESURRECTION OF THE DEAD

15:1-58 Cf. Introduction, par. 25. To the vaporings of *some* who deny the resurrection of Christ by denying the resurrection of the dead in Christ, Paul opposes his trenchant and detailed proclamation of the central significance of the resurrection of Christ and clears the question of the manner of the bodily resurrection of the dead.

15:1-34 Significance of Resurrection of Christ

15:1-34 The resurrection of the dead stands or falls with the firmly attested fact of the resurrection of the Christ who *died for our sins;* Paul marshals the witnesses to the fact (1-11). So firmly established is the link between the two, between the resurrection of the Christ and the resurrection of those who are His, that the reverse is also true: The resurrection of Christ stands or falls with the resurrection of the Christian dead. And if the resurrection of Christ falls, all is lost; the cross is indeed "emptied of its power" (1:17), for no mere martyr's death can assure the forgiveness of sins; what the apostles are proclaiming is nothing and worse than nothing, a lie; what the church believes is nothing; and the church's hope is nothing. Christian suffering and martyrdom have lost all point and purpose (12-19, 29-32). *But in fact Christ has been raised from the dead* (20)—and that fact is the all-controlling fact of all history. As surely as *all men* are, under the judgment of God, in a solidarity of dying *in Adam,* so surely all men are, by God's acquitting judgment, destined to *be made alive,* destined to share in His reign, in His triumph over death, and in His final obeisance to the Father, *that God may be everything to every one* (20-28). And yet the Corinthians have listened to *some* who *have no knowledge of God,* for all their vaunted knowledge and wisdom. In their intoxicated delusion they have admitted into their midst *bad company* that will ruin them morally by tampering with the fact on which the whole Christian life depends. (32-34)

15:3-4 Scholars are generally agreed that these sentences are a quotation from an early Christian catechism.

15:4 *Was raised.* The tense of *raised* in Greek is different from that of the preceding two verbs, being a present perfect, which indicates completed action with enduring results; Paul is emphasizing the fact that the resurrection of Christ is of enduring force and significance.

15:5 *Cephas,* Peter. Cf. 1:12.

15:7 *James,* most likely James the brother of Jesus, prominent in the first church. Cf. Introduction to the Letter of James.

All the apostles, apparently a larger group than the original "twelve" (5), men commissioned by the risen Christ. (Cf. Ro 16:1-16 note)

15:8 *One untimely born.* Paul did not come to apostleship in the normal way, as a disciple of the Lord on earth (cf. Acts 1:21-22); thus he appears as an abnormal and violent birth.

15:11 *Believed,* came to believe, were brought to faith.

15:17 *Still in your sins.* For the same thought stated positively (salvation is by faith in the risen Christ) cf. Ro 10:9.

15:21-22 *Adam . . . Christ.* Cf. Ro 5:12-21 note.

15:23 *First fruits.* Christ is the beginning and the guarantee of the full harvest of the resurrection of the dead.

15:25 *Enemies under his feet.* Cf. Ps 110:1; Mt 22:41-44.

15:27 *All things . . . in subjection.* Cf. Ps 8:6. In the "man" (21) Jesus Christ the psalmist's word concerning man becomes full truth. (Cf. Heb 2:5-9)

15:28 *The Son himself will also be subjected.* Christ's whole Servant ministry and His subsequent exaltation are both "to the glory of God the Father." (Cf. Ph 2:11 note)

15:29 *Baptized on behalf of the dead.* Since baptism on behalf of the dead is not explained or even mentioned elsewhere in the NT, one can only conjecture what Paul is referring to here. Many conjectures have been made, none really satisfactory. One that meets the conditions of Paul's argument is this: A man is moved to accept the faith and be baptized by the pleadings of a dying relative or friend; he receives baptism *on behalf of* (for) *the dead,* i.e., in the hope of meeting the beloved person in the life of the world to come. If there is no resurrection and no life in the world to come, such an action is obviously foolish.

15:31 *By my pride in you.* For Paul's proud delight in his churches as the "crown" of his sufferings and labors, the "seal" of his apostleship in the Lord, cf. 9:2; 2 Co 1:14; 1 Th 2:19-20. Paul can exult in his work and in his converts only as one who has led them into eternal life by implanting in them "Christ . . . the hope of glory." (Cl 1:27, cf. 24)

15:32 *Fought with beasts,* probably a figurative expression for facing extreme danger; Paul had "many adversaries" at Ephesus (16:9), and he is probably referring to an incident in Ephesus when he speaks of a great "affliction" and a "deadly peril" in the province of Asia. (2 Co 1:8-10)

Let us eat, etc. Cf. Is 22:13, where the saying is found in the mouth of desperate and reckless men who have refused God's call to repentance.

15:33 *Bad company,* etc. Paul is quoting from a play by Menander, a popular dramatist.

Good morals. For the moral power of the resurrection cf. Ro 6:4, 12-14.

15:34 *Come to your right mind.* Literally "Sober up!" Only one who is intoxicated on the heady wine of the "new theology" could dream of abandoning the bright sobriety of the resurrection hope.

Knowledge of God. To know God in faith is to know Him as the God "who gives life to the dead." (Ro 4:17)

15:35-58 Manner of Resurrection of the Dead

15:35-58 Those who deny the resurrection of the dead are foolish enough to ask: *How are the dead raised? With what kind of body do they come?* (35). They thereby reveal their ignorance of God (cf. 34), who with His lavish creative power gives each of His creatures its own fit kind of body and beauty; for Him the death of the seed is the occasion for a new *life* (36-41). He can as certainly create a new, *spiritual* body for His new creature, the man in Christ, as He created a physical body for the man in Adam. He can bridge the gulf that separates *flesh and blood* from His future *kingdom,* by clothing *mortal* men with *immortality* (42-53). How can the Corinthians listen to *foolish men* who in their ignorance of God cast to the winds the *victory* over sin and death given them *through* the *Lord Jesus Christ,* that triumphant certainty of life which makes men not theological theorists or debaters but *steadfast, immovable, always abounding in the work of the Lord?* (54-58)

15:38 *God gives it a body.* Paul is arguing not from "nature" but from God the Creator, who can provide body (38), flesh (39), and glory (40) as He wills.

15:44 *Spiritual body. Spiritual* may mean simply "supernatural" (the word is so translated in 10:3-4), or may designate a body which is the perfect dwelling and instrument of the Spirit (cf. 6:19), the kind of body for which those who have "the first fruits of the Spirit" so intensely long. (Ro 8:23)

15:45 *The first . . . Adam.* Cf. Gn 2:7.

The last Adam, Christ.

15:46 *Not the spiritual which is first but the physical.* Paul is arguing against an idea current in Judaism that the first man is an ideal man, the redeemer; Jesus, "the last Adam" (45), the "man from heaven" (47), the *spiritual* man (conceived by the Spirit, endued with the Spirit, working in the power of the Spirit) is the Redeemer, He alone.

15:50 *Flesh and blood cannot inherit the kingdom.* Cf. 53: "This perishable nature must put on the imperishable." Paul stresses both the continuity and the discontinuity between man's present existence and his existence in the world to come. The words "put on" provide the link between the two.

15:54 *Death is swallowed up,* etc. Cf. Is 25:8.

15:55 Cf. Hos 13:14.

15:56 Here Paul establishes the connection between Adam as the author of death for all men and Adam as the source of guilt and sin in all men (cf. Ro 5:12-21 note). It is *sin* that gives *death* power over men, sin is the *sting,* or goad, with which death impels men into his realm; "because of one man's trespass, death reigns over men" (Ro 5:17). The *law* is the *power of sin;* sin (personified) grows powerful when man is confronted by the Law and rebels against the will of God (Ro 7:7-11). Thus the Law comes in "to increase the trespass." (Ro 5:20)

15:58 *Work of the Lord.* Faith in the risen Lord made a worker of Paul (10), and it will make workers of the men of the church.

16:1-24 PRACTICAL AND PERSONAL MATTERS

16:1-4 THE COLLECTION FOR THE SAINTS AT JERUSELAM

16:1-4 For the *contribution for the saints* and what it meant for the apostle cf. Ro 15:25-28; 2 Co 8 and 9; and Introduction to 2 Co, par. 6.

16:4 *Advisable that I should go.* The journey to Jerusalem would be dangerous for Paul. Cf. Ro 15:25, 30-31; Acts 20:22-24; 21:10-12; and the story of Paul's arrest in Jerusalem, which led to his imprisonment in Caesarea and Rome (Acts 20:27—28:31). See also the Introduction to the Captivity Letters (Eph, Ph, Cl, Phmn).

16:5-9 PAUL'S TRAVEL PLANS

16:5 *Visit you.* Cf. 4:18-21; 11:34.

16:8 *Pentecost,* the Hebrew Feast of Weeks. (Ex 34:22; Dt 16:10)

16:9 *Door.* For the figurative sense of *door* as "opportunity" cf. 2 Co 2:12; Cl 4:3.

16:10-12 TIMOTHY AND APOLLOS

16:10 *Timothy . . . put him at ease.* Cf. 4:17 and Introduction to 2 Co. par. 1. The request to put him at ease is accounted for by Timothy's inclination to timidity (2 Ti 1:7) and the tensions that had arisen (and were to increase) between Paul and the Corinthian church.

16:12 *Apollos.* Cf. Introduction, pars. 10 and 11. Both Paul's affectionate tone in speaking of him and Apollos' refusal to come to Corinth at a time when his presence would tend to intensify the factionalism in the church testify to the cordial and harmonious relationship between the two men.

16:13-20 ADMONITION, COMMENDATIONS, AND GREETINGS

16:15-17 *Stephanas . . . Fortunatus . . . Achaicus.* Cf. Introduction, par. 20.

16:18 *Refreshed my spirit as well as yours.* The presence of these three stalwarts refreshed Paul's spirit by bringing him assurance of the church's desire to continue in obedience to their apostle (11:2) and by providing him with accurate, firsthand information. Their presence with Paul in Ephesus refreshes the spirit of the Corinthian church because it assures the faithful that their concerns are known to their father in Christ and will be dealt with.

16:19 *Aquila and Prisca.* Cf. Ro 16:3 note.

16:20 *Holy kiss.* Cf. Ro 16:16; 1 Ptr 5:14. The exchange of the kiss marked the congregation as one family in Christ.

16:21-24 AUTOGRAPH CONCLUSION

16:21 *With my own hand.* For Paul's habit of adding a greeting in his own handwriting to his dictated letters cf. Gl 6:11; Cl 4:18; 2 Th 3:17.

16:22 *Our Lord come!* Paul gives this prayer for the return of the Lord in Aramaic: *Maranatha.* The original language was probably retained in the liturgy of Greek-speaking churches, as were terms like "amen," "hosanna," and "hallelujah."

SECOND

CORINTHIANS

INTRODUCTION

For the history of Paul's previous association with the Corinthian church see the Introduction to First Corinthians.

The Coming of Timothy

1 Paul had in his first letter prepared the church of Corinth for a coming visit by Timothy. That visit was designed by Paul to reinforce and carry further the work which his letter was designed to do, namely, to bring the Corinthians back from their flight out of Christian reality into an intoxicated and enthusiastic individualism, back to the cross, back to where Paul stood: "I urge you . . . be imitators of me. Therefore I sent to you Timothy . . . to remind you of my ways in Christ, as I teach them . . . in every church" (1 Co 4:16-17). What those "ways in Christ" were the immediately preceding context makes plain: Paul ironically contrasts the blissful state of the Corinthians, who have become kings, who are rich and reign, are wise and strong and held in honor, with the apostles' wretched and unfinished state under the cross, men sentenced to death, a spectacle for angels and men to gaze on, fools, weak, in disrepute, hungry, thirsty, ill-clad, homeless, the meekly enduring, toilworn refuse of the world (1 Co 4:8-13). Paul anticipates that Timothy's task will not be a pleasant one and that the reception he will get may be less than amiable (1 Co 16:10-11). Timothy's stay was brief, and since Second Corinthians says nothing of it, we know nothing of its results except what we can infer from the events that followed.

Paul's Intermediate Visit to Corinth

2 Timothy soon returned to Paul, who thus quickly learned how his letter had been received and how things stood at Corinth. What he heard moved him to interrupt his work at Ephesus and to proceed to Corinth at once. This is the second visit, which is implied by 2 Co 13:1-2; 12:21, the "painful visit" to which Paul alludes in 2 Co 2:1. Timothy's report had made clear to Paul that the influence of the new teachers had spread farther and gone deeper than he had realized. There were not only "some" who were arrogant (1 Co 4:18), "some" who denied the central content of the apostolic proclamation (1 Co 15:12); the whole church was infected and endangered—the very existence of the "temple of God" (1 Co 3:17) was being threatened. Immediate action was necessary, drastic action which had to be taken personally. The visit therefore proved to be a painful one for the Corinthians, who were rudely shaken out of their dreaming self-assurance by the home truths which their apostle had to tell them (2 Co 2:2; 13:2); but it was a painful visit for Paul too, for the opposition to him, under the leadership of the men who claimed to be Christ's, proved strong. They must have been bold, intellectually vigorous, and capable men—they were able to face Paul and keep a sizable part of the congregation with them. Just what form Paul's dealings with the church took cannot be clearly made out, but this much is plain: Paul was convinced that fellowship with the new leaders was no longer possible, that a break had to be made (2 Co 13:2); he left Corinth, however, without immediately forcing the issue. He still trusted that the church would come to see the necessity for the break as clearly as he himself saw it and left with the promise that he would return to Corinth when his work in Ephesus was done and would pay the church a double visit, both before and after the proposed revisitation of the Macedonian churches (2 Co 1:15-16). This was of course a change from the travel plans Paul had announced in 1 Co 16:5-6.

The Severe Letter

3 What follows now is the obscurest part of an obscure history. Paul's trust that the church would see the light and would walk in that light was apparently disappointed. There occurred an incident which strained still further the already strained relations between Paul and the church. Paul speaks of one who did an injury which caused him pain (2 Co 2:5), an injury not directly to Paul himself but affecting him. Since Paul does not indicate the nature of the wrong done him, we can only conjecture what it may have been. Perhaps one of the men loyal to Paul suffered violence at the hands of an opponent in the heat of party strife. At any rate, the offense was so flagrant and involved the authority of Paul so immediately that the church could not ignore it and still be in any sense "his" church, still esteem him as apostle and father in Christ. Paul therefore changed his plans once more; instead of going directly to Corinth from Ephesus, he first proceeded northward toward Macedonia by way of Troas. Before leaving Asia he wrote a letter (now lost) to which he refers as a "severe" letter, a letter written "with many tears" (2 Co 2:4). This letter summoned the church to repentance in no uncertain terms: The wrongdoer must be dealt with and disciplined, and the church must return in obedience to its apostle. Paul dispatched the letter by the hand of Titus and instructed Titus to rejoin him at Troas and report on its effect.

The Report of Titus

4 Titus had not yet returned to Troas when Paul arrived there (2 Co 2:12); and so Paul, in an agony of doubt concerning the outcome of Titus' mission, left Troas and proceeded to Macedonia (2 Co 2:13). And God, who comforts the downcast, comforted him by the coming of Titus (2 Co 7:5-6). For Titus brought good news. The church at Corinth had heeded Paul's summons to repentance, had bowed to his authority, had disciplined the offender, who had also repented and asked for forgiveness. The church was ready to forgive him and only awaited Paul's assent to such a course before granting forgiveness. The church thus cleansed and restored by repentance longed to see Paul again, in order that the ties so long strained and endangered might be confirmed and strengthened once more. (2 Co 2:6; 7:7-16)

5 That was the positive side of Titus' report, and Paul welcomed it with that exuberant gratitude with which he received every good gift of God; he did not let the fact that there was another side to the report, a negative one, dampen his joy. Titus' news was not all good. The offender at Corinth had been punished by the "majority" of the congregation only, not by all (2 Co 2:6). There were still those at Corinth who held to the new teachers. Neither Paul's visit nor his severe letter had silenced the men who maliciously misinterpreted his every word and action, for example, his change in his travel plans (2 Co 1:17) or his letters (2 Co 1:13), and sought always to undermine his apostolic authority. It was probably their influence that had brought to a standstill a project which Paul had promoted with such energy and with such good initial success: the collection for the poor saints at Jerusalem.

Occasion of Paul's Second Letter to the Corinthians

6 The unfinished task of the collection for the saints of Jerusalem was the occasion of Paul's fourth letter to the church at Corinth, our present Second Corinthians, but only the occasion. Dear as the success of that undertaking was to Paul's heart and much as he valued the collection as an expression of the unity between the Gentile and the Judaic church, it is not the central concern of his letter. That is rather the reestablishment of a full and pure understanding of his authority as "apostle of Jesus Christ by the will of God." His desire to make clear forever to the Corinthians wherein the glory and power of his ministry lay is the dominant impulse in his writing. This concern dominates the first section (chs. 1—7), which looks to the past, wherein Paul welcomes the penitent advances of the majority of the church, forgives the disciplined wrongdoer and bespeaks the love of the church for him, and appeals for a renewal of the full communion of love which had been characteristic of his

association with the church of Corinth from of old. It dominates the last section of the letter also, where Paul looks forward to his coming visit to Corinth and deals rigorously and definitively with his detractors and their hangers-on (chs. 10—13). And that concern has left its marks also on the chapters (8—9) which deal with the collection; here we see in action that peculiarly divine apostolic authority which seeks nothing for itself, but all for Christ, which will not autocratically lord it over men's faith, but works with men for their joy in Christ (2 Co 1:24). This authority is essentially the vehicle of the potent claim of the grace of the Lord Jesus Christ; therefore it will not command, but need only advise (8:8, 10). It is an expression of the lordship of Christ (8:5), which can expect and claim obedience only because it is centered wholly in God, the Father of the Lord Jesus Christ, in His power (8:5), His gifts and goodness (8:16; 9:7, 8, 11, 12, 15), and has His glory for its goal. (9:13)

Effect of the Letter

7 Paul spent the three winter months A. D. 55—56 in Greece, shortly after the second letter was dispatched to Corinth (Acts 20:2-3), and he there wrote his Letter to the Romans, most likely at Corinth itself. In Romans he looks back over his work in the eastern Mediterranean area as finished and looks westward with serenity and confidence (Ro 15:14-33). No doubt the second letter had done the work it was intended to do, and the reconciliation with Corinth was complete.

Value of the Letter

8 Second Corinthians is certainly one of the most difficult of Paul's letters—which is not to say that it was difficult or obscure for its first readers; they lived in the situation which we must laboriously reconstruct. Since the hints given by the letter itself are not always full enough to permit a complete and accurate reconstruction of the situation, the letter is for us difficult, an angel to be wrestled with if we would receive a blessing. But the blessing is a rich one and worth the wrestling.

9 The letter resembles the Letter to the Galatians in being richly autobiographical; we here see Paul the man in all the human frailty and the human agony which he never attempts to conceal. But Paul the man cannot be separated from Paul the apostle of Jesus Christ by the will of God. And the letter reveals the apostle with a fullness that even Galatians cannot rival. As in Galatians, we see the apostle engaged in battle, here a battle for his very existence as apostle to the Corinthians; and in battle a man shows what he truly is. The battle which Paul wages in this letter reveals him down to the very roots and bases of his apostolic existence. We learn from this revelation that battle must be, and why it must be, in the church of the God and the Prince of peace, that lines must be drawn and where they must be drawn; we learn that Satan is at work even in that which passes for an advanced and superior form of Christianity, that his weapon is always the plausible lie which imitates the truth—one must never forget how very "nice" and very "Christian" the men of the Christ party must have appeared to be. We learn that battle is necessary in the life of the church and can be salutary for its life.

10 We learn also that the necessity of battle need not harden the battler; the church that fights for truth need not lose the love it had at first, as the church at Ephesus did (Rv 2:4); the first seven chapters of this letter are a witness to the fact that the love which "does not rejoice at wrong, but rejoices in the right" (1 Co 13:6) is the only genuine love. Luther had these chapters especially in mind when he wrote of Second Corinthians: "In his first epistle St. Paul dealt severely with the Corinthians on many points and poured sharp wine into their wounds and terrified them; therefore he now . . . also pours oil into their wounds and is wondrously gracious to them."

11 As an apostle, Paul is a "man in Christ," a man whose whole existence and activity is shaped and formed by the single fact of Him in whom God reconciled the world to Himself. There is hardly a more vivid documentation of this lived Christianity than Second Corinthians. No aspect of Paul's life is exempt from Christ; if he says, "Yes, I will come" or "No, I shall not come," he can say it only in the light of

the great Yes which God has spoken to all His promises in Christ (1:20). He can speak of Christian giving only in terms of the grace of our Lord Jesus (8:9). His suffering is the mark of the Christ imprinted on his life.

12 As an apostle Paul is a man in whom Christ speaks; he is the earthen vessel that conveys the treasure of the Christ. Paul is here fighting for his apostolate; that means, he is fighting for the Christ, for the apostolate is nothing less than the power and the presence of Christ among men. Men will find the treasure in this earthen vessel, or they will not find it at all; they will behold the light of the knowledge of the glory of God in the face of Christ in the apostolate, or they will not behold it at all. There is nothing like this letter to bind the church to the apostolic Word of the New Testament. The Reformation's embattled emphasis on *Sola Scriptura* finds powerful justification in this embattled epistle.

13 Through conflict to triumph—Second Corinthians was born of conflict; and the triumph which Christ worked through it is not limited to the restoration of the Corinthian church of the first century. By it the church can triumph still.

OUTLINE

I. 1:1—7:16 Retrospect: Paul's Authority and Ministry in Corinth
- A. 1:1-11 Ministry Under the God of All Comfort
- B. 1:12—2:17 The Ministry of Divine Triumph
- C. 3:1-3 The Ministry Commended by Christ
- D. 3:4—4:6 The Ministry of the New Covenant
- E. 4:7—5:10 The Minsitry of Imparting the Life of Jesus to Men
- F. 5:11—6:10 The Ministry of Reconciliation
- G. 6:11—7:4 The Ministry of God's Exclusive Appeal
- H. 7:5-16 Titus' Report: The Joyful Prospect of Reconciliation

II. 8:1—9:15 The Present: Collection for Saints of Jerusalem
- A. 8:1-7 The Example of the Churches of Macedonia
- B. 8:8-15 You Know the Grace of the Lord Jesus Christ
- C. 8:16—9:5 Commendation of Titus and Two Brothers
- D. 9:6-15 God Loves a Cheerful Giver

III. 10:1—13:14 Prospect: Paul's Impending Visit to Corinth
- A. 10:1-18 Paul's Defense Against the Charges of His Opponents
- B. 11:1—12:21 Paul's "Foolish" Boasting
- C. 13:1-14 Paul's Impending Visit and Conclusion

1:1—7:16 RETROSPECT: PAUL'S AUTHORITY AND MINISTRY IN CORINTH

1:1—7:16 These 7 chapters are actually the thanksgiving with which Paul regularly opens his letters (cf., e.g., 1 Co 1:4-9); it is here, as in 1 Th, executed on a monumental scale, as an awed and grateful retrospective survey of the ministry which God in His grace has assigned to him, a ministry that binds him to the church of Corinth with a bond nothing human dare undo.

1:1-11 Ministry Under the God of All Comfort

1:1-11 The ministry with which God has entrusted him is pure grace, and the grace of God sustains him in it. He designates himself as *apostle . . . by the will of God* (1), that divine will which has made him the vehicle of *grace . . . and peace* to men, and opens with a thanksgiving to the *Father of our Lord Jesus Christ,* who had delivered him from *deadly peril* in the province of Asia, giving him *comfort* in order that he might be able to comfort others in the strength thus given him, the strength, namely, to *rely* solely *on God who raises the dead.* (9)

1:1 *Timothy.* Cf. Introduction, par. 1.

Achaia, the Roman province comprising the southern half of Greece, of which Corinth was the capital. The inclusion of the *saints . . . in the whole of Achaia* in the greeting may indicate that the unsettling tendencies and events in Corinth had affected other churches in the province also.

1:5 *Share . . . in Christ's sufferings.* Cf. Cl 1:24 note.

1:8 *Asia.* The Roman province of Asia is meant. Ephesus was capital of that province, and the events referred to may have occurred there. Cf. 1 Co 16:8-9 ("many adversaries").

1:9 For *God who raises the dead* as object of the faith which despairs of itself and expects everything from His unlimited power cf. Ro 4:17-18.

1:11 Paul involves the church in his ministry; their *prayer* will set off a chain reaction of *blessing granted* and "thanksgiving, to the glory of God" (4:15). The apostle is sent, faith is created, the church exists and functions to the end that He be glorified.

1:12—2:17 The Ministry of Divine Triumph

1:12—2:17 The grace of Paul's apostolic ministry makes his life a life full of agonizing stress; he has had to endure the malice of men who misinterpreted his letters and read all manner of subtleties into his transparent *holiness and . . . sincerity* (1:12-14), men who used his change of plans regarding his forthcoming visit to Corinth to charge him with vacillation and unreliability, whereas he had in fact delayed his coming to Corinth in order to *spare* (1:23) the church. He has relied, not on *earthly wisdom* but on the *grace of God* which leads him to act in love always (1:15—2:4). And that grace has triumphed; Paul stands vindicated as the proclaimer of the Christ who is God's Yes of fulfillment to all His promises. The church over whose disobedience he has travailed has repented; the offending brother has been disciplined, and Paul pleads that they *reaffirm* their *love for him* (2:8; cf. Introduction, par. 3). *Thanks be to God,* Paul breaks out (2:14) even before he has told of his meeting with Titus, who brought him the comforting news (cf. 7:5-16; Introduction, par. 4), *who in Christ always leads us in triumph.* (2:15-17)

1:12 *For.* "I feel confident of your prayers, *for* I have done nothing to forfeit your confidence and concern," Paul says.

1:14 *Understood in part,* a hint that there are some tensions remaining in the relationship of the church to the apostle; with these Paul intends to deal in chs. 10—13. *The day of the Lord Jesus,* when the purposes of every heart will be disclosed (1 Co 4:5), will put an end to all misunderstandings and tensions.

1:15-16 Paul's plans as projected in 1 Co 16:5 did not provide for two visits to Corinth; perhaps Paul had mentioned this double visit in a letter or by messenger. Now circumstances have moved him to change back to his original plan.

1:20 *We utter the Amen through him.* As God has affirmed and fulfilled all His promises IN Christ, so the church speaks its *Amen* in thanksgiving, praise, and prayer THROUGH Him who is the fulfillment of all promises and the ruling Lord of the church.

1:22 *Seal . . . Spirit.* Cf. Eph 1:13.

Guarantee. Literally "down payment," which in ancient times was a sizable portion of the whole.

2:4 *I wrote you . . . with many tears.* Cf. Introduction, par. 3.

2:10 *You forgive . . . I also forgive.* For Paul's apostolic desire that the church be a mature church capable of independent Christian action cf. 1 Co 5:1-5; 2 Co 13:1-10 note.

2:11 *Satan . . . gaining the advantage over us.* Where the church fails in forgiving and restoring love, Satan (the accuser of men before God, cf. Rv 12:10) has gained a victory.

2:14 *Triumph.* Paul is probably thinking of the splendid triumphal processions with which the Caesars and their generals celebrated their victories of human power. Paul's triumph is the triumph of God's grace in Christ.

2:15-16 *Aroma . . . fragrance . . . death . . . life.* What Paul describes in terms of light in 4:6 ("light of the knowledge of the glory of God in the face of Christ"), he here describes as an aroma. That aroma is a reviving and life-giving fragrance to those who accept the Gospel in faith, but a death-dealing fragrance to those who refuse it. The action of the Gospel is not a chemical action "through faith for faith" (Ro 1:17), calling for faith and creating faith. Where it is resisted, the aroma of life becomes the fragrance of *death.*

2:17 *For we are not . . . peddlers of God's word.* Paul dares to answer his question, "Who is sufficient for these things?" (2:16) with a bold, "We are!" because his "sufficiency is from God" (3:5) and his power is the power of His word, which he does not dilute or adulterate as peddlers do their wares. (Cf. 4:2)

Commissioned by God, in the sight of God. As he is aware of the divine SOURCE of his "sufficiency," so he is aware of his responsibility to Him who has given it to him.

3:1-3 The Ministry Commended by Christ

3:1-3 Since his sufficiency is from God (cf. 4), Paul needs no *letters* of men to recommend him in his ministry; the church which his apostolic ministry has by God's grace created stands, open to inspection by all men (2), as his letter of recommendation, *a letter from Christ . . . written . . . with the Spirit of the living God* (3). One thus commended by the Trinity does not need to buttress his authority (as the "Christ-men" apparently did) with letters from men.

3:2 *Your hearts,* where the Word of God has been received and faith created. (Cf. Ro 10:10)

3:4—4:6 The Ministry of the New Covenant

3:4—4:6 God has given Paul his sufficiency as a minister of God's new covenant to exercise a ministry, not of the *written code* of the Law which condemns and kills but a ministry of the *Spirit* which justifies and *gives life,* a ministry not of transient and fading *splendor* (7) (such as Moses' legal ministry was) but of surpassing and enduring glory, which gives him a boldness (12) which Moses could not have and which Israel cannot know until she *turns to the Lord, Christ,* a boldness in the Lord whose *Spirit* gives man freedom to look upon the face of God and carries the apostle (and all who receive his liberating Word) *from one degree of glory to another* (3:18). This boldness brings with it a pure and candid honesty (4:2), for the apostle is no self-seeking, devious proclaimer of himself but of *Jesus Christ as Lord* (5) with himself as *servant* of man, servant to the Servant Jesus *(for Jesus' sake,* 5). He proclaims what can be known only as God's work, His miracle of the new creation, the dawn of the new first day, *the light of the knowledge of the glory of God in the face of Christ.* (4:6)

3:6 *New covenant.* Cf. Jer 31:31-33; Lk 22:20; 1 Co 11:35; Heb 8:8-10; 10:16. In sharp contrast to the demand and compulsion of the old legal covenant, the new covenant is God's free proffer of forgiveness, which inwardly renews man and inspires in him a will that is in harmony with God's will.

3:7 *Splendor . . . could not look at Moses' face.* Cf. Ex 34:29-34.

3:13 *Put a veil over his face.* Cf. Ex 34:33-35.

3:15 *Whenever Moses is read a veil lies over their minds.* As the veil which Moses put over his face concealed from the Israelites the transient character of the old covenant and its orders (12), so now when the Law (Moses) is read they cannot see the real significance of the Law as WITNESS, together with the prophets, to the newly revealed righteousness of God in the Gospel. (Cf. Ro 3:21)

3:16 *When a man turns to the Lord,* that is, comes to Christ, then he recognizes that "Christ is the END OF THE LAW, that every one who has FAITH may be justified." (Ro 10:4)

3:17 *The Lord is the Spirit.* Cf. 6. Since the Lord (Christ) is present among His people, known, and operative by the power of the Spirit, the two are so closely associated in God's working and in the church's experience that Paul can simply identify them in order to emphasize the fact that God's new order of things ("new covenant . . . life," 6; "righteousness . . . splendor," 9; "glory," 18) is experienced by man IN CHRIST. (Cf. 5:17)

3:18 *From one degree of glory,* in this present life with the rich endowment of gifts and blessings bestowed on us by the Spirit, *to another,* in the world to come, where "the Lord Jesus Christ . . . will change our lowly body to be like his glorious body." (Ph 3:20-21)

4:4 *The god of this world.* Since the world is mankind in its opposition to God (cf. Ja 4:4), Satan as the inspirer and leader of that opposition is god of this world. Cf. "the ruler of this world" in Jn 12:31; 14:30; 16:11.

4:6 *Let the light shine.* Cf. Gn 1:3; 2 Co 5:17

4:7—5:10 The Ministry of Imparting the Life of Jesus to Men

4:7—5:10 The glory of the apostolic ministry is solely God's, not man's; therefore the frailty and the sufferings of the men who exercise this ministry, as men who are *afflicted, perplexed, persecuted,* and *struck down* (8-9), take nothing from its glory, for it is just in their weakness that *the transcendent power* of God is manifested (7); in their defeat and dying the new life of Jesus is being released for men (10-12). And so suffering and the prospect of dying do not discourage these ministers of God; they work in the faith that the God who raised Jesus from the dead will raise them also with Jesus (12), in the courageous certitude that the as-yet-unseen glory of the new creation will enfold them in an eternal splendor which far outweighs their present light weight of momentary affliction (17-18), in the knowledge that the Spirit given them by God is His pledge of a new and eternal bodily life (cf. 5:5). They long to be at home with their Lord, clothed with the new body which God will give them; but this longing does not make them weak and inert dreamers—it makes them strong and courageous workers, men who make it their *aim* to please the Christ before whose judgment seat they must all appear to give an account of their working (5:6-10)

4:7 *Earthen vessels.* Vessels of earthenware, fragile and to be valued only for their content, the life-giving Gospel.

4:12 *Death is at work in us,* the persecuted and endangered proclaimers of the Gospel, *but life in you,* the recipients of the Gospel with its lifegiving fragrance. (Cf. 2:14-16)

4:13 *I believed, and so I spoke.* Cf. Ps 116:10.

4:15 *It may increase thanksgiving.* The apostle lives and dies in the pattern set by His Lord, "to the glory of God the Father." (Ph 2:11, cf. 5-11)

4:17 Cf. Ro 8:18.

5:1 *Earthly tent,* the "mortal body" (Ro 6:12), "dead because of sin" (Ro 8:10), which the onslaughts of man can destroy; the *building from God, a house not made with hands* is the body as it is destined to be when God has raised and glorified it (1 Co 15:42-53). This new, glorious body is thought of as prepared and ready for redeemed man *in the heavens,* a new garment ready to be worn in glory.

5:2 Cf. Ro 8:23.

5:3 *Found naked,* in a disembodied state.

5:4 *Unclothed* in death; *further clothed* at the return of the Lord. (Cf. 1 Co 15:51-55)

5:5 *Spirit as a guarantee.* Cf. Eph 1:13-14.

5:8 *Rather be away from the body.* Though Paul shrinks from the thought of the "nakedness" which physical death brings (cf. 5:3), the thought of being *at home with the Lord* (which is "far better," Ph 1:23) overcomes that fear.

5:11—6:10 The Ministry of Reconciliation

5:11—6:10 The apostle works to win (*persuade,* 11) men, but with a high independence over against the praise or blame of men. Whether men esteem him mad (*beside ourselves,* 13) because of the fervor of his commitment to Christ or sane (*in our right mind,* 13) because of his shrewd planning as the wise master builder of the church (cf. 1 Co 3:10)—that is of small moment to him; his "madness" and his "sanity" are both in the service of his apostolic ministry, manifestations of his love for God and for men. His ministry moves between the two poles of *the fear of the Lord* (11), who will judge all men (10), on the one hand, and the compelling impulse of the love of Christ, who died for all men in order that all might live for Him (14-15), on the other hand. Human standards do not apply to this ministry, for it is nothing less than the divinely given ministry of reconciliation; it gets its content and authority from that reconciling act in Christ by which God's new creation has broken victoriously into the present evil world, to make new all things and to make the old world and its standards irrelevant and obsolete. The apostle is nothing less than the ambassador for Christ, who knew no sin but was made by God to be sin (or a sin offering) for sinful man, in order that sinful man might find the righteousness of God in Him (5:16-21). God Himself makes His appeal for reconciliation through the apostle; now, in God's *acceptable time,* in His *day of salvation,* God's appeal is being heard in the ministry which has on it the marks of DIVINE greatness and power. Paul lists nine examples of human hardships and sufferings in which the divine strength is manifested (6:4-5); he gives nine examples of the divine gracious power which appears and works in God's afflicted messengers (6:6-7), and in nine pairs of contrasts he rounds out the picture of the apostolate, humanly insignificant and defeated, divinely significant and triumphant (6:8-9): *dying, and behold we live.* (6:9)

5:11 *Persuade,* that is, seek to persuade, appeal to.

5:12 *Those who pride themselves,* etc. the supporters of the "Christ-men."

5:16 *Regarded Christ from a human point of view.* To Paul the Jew, Jesus the Servant Messiah failed to measure up to his expectation of the King who would glorify His people; and Jesus the Crucified appeared as One accursed by God, cf. 1 Co 12:3; Gl 3:13. Now *(no longer,* 16), with eyes enlightened by the Spirit, he can see Him as the power and the wisdom of God in person, the One in whom God reconciled the world to Himself. (19)

6:1 *Accept the grace of God in vain.* The grace is received in vain, squandered and wasted, when (as in the case of the "Christ-men" and their following) it is made to serve the interests of human pride and self-seeking. (Cf. 2 Co 11:20)

6:2 *At the acceptable time,* etc. Is 49:8.

6:4 *Commend ourselves in every way,* not by obtaining letters of commendation from men (3:1) but by going the way of self-expending *servants of God,* who follow in the footsteps of the Servant Jesus Christ, suffering as He suffered, serving as He served, and "making many rich" (10), as He enriched mankind by His very poverty. (8:9)

6:7 *Weapons . . . for the right hand and for the left,* for both offense and defense.

6:10 *Possessing everything.* In Christ they are heirs of the world (Ro 4:13), of "all things." (Ro 8:32)

6:11—7:4 The Ministry of God's Exclusive Appeal

6:11—7:4 The church lives by perpetual repentance (cf. the first of Luther's 95 Theses). The church at Corinth can be a real church, an apostolic church, the "church of God at Corinth" (1:1) only by heeding the appeal of God spoken through the apostle. Reconciliation with Paul (so freely and generously offered by him, 7:11-13) can take place only as a piece of the church's renewed reconciliation with God. And so Paul reminds the Corinthian church that the appeal of God the Reconciler is an exclusive appeal; reconciliation with God calls for a radical break with all that opposes God. He reminds them that if God is their Father and they are His sons and daughters, it behooves them to *come out* from the world around them, to *touch nothing unclean* (6:17) and to *cleanse* themselves *from every defilement of body and spirit, and make holiness* (their consecration to God) *perfect in the fear of God* (7:1). Paul is once more combating the secularized Christianity with which he had dealt in 1 Co. When they have opened their hearts to God, they can open their hearts to the apostle, who loves them as his *children* (6:13) with the forgiving, reconciling love of God: *You are in our hearts, to die together and to live together.* (7:3)

6:12 *Not restricted by us.* Nothing in Paul, in whom the Holy Spirit works "forbearance, kindness . . . genuine love" (6:6), hinders reconciliation; the Corinthians are restricted, hindered, and impeded by their *own affections,* which are divided between God and what opposes God. (Cf. 14-16)

6:15 *Belial,* literally "Worthlessness," here

used of the embodiment of all "worthlessness," the devil.

6:16 *Temple.* For the church as the temple of God cf. 1 Co 3:16-17.

As God said. The following cento of OT passages (16-18) consists of quotations from Lv 26:11-12; Eze 37:27; Is 52:11; Jer 51:45; Hos 1:10; Is 43:6.

7:2 *We have wronged no one,* etc. Cf. 12:16-17 and chs 10—13 generally. These statements reflect charges brought against Paul by his opponents at Corinth.

7:5-16 Titus' Report: The Joyful Prospect of Reconciliation

7:5-16 Now at last Paul tells what he had been on the verge of telling at 2:13 but could not before he had given thanks to God for His gift, now he tells of his meeting with Titus and of Titus' report of the Corinthians' repentance. And now the note of thanksgiving with which Paul began and which has been the constant undertone in all his portrayal of his apostolate is heard once more full and clear. Paul is comforted (6, 13) and rejoices (9, 13, 16); he cannot say it often enough, all the more so since the Corinthians' repentant behavior has been a source of comfort and joy to Titus also. (7, 13, 15)

7:10 *Godly grief . . . repentance . . . salvation . . . worldly grief produces death.* One is reminded of the contrast between the penitent tears of Peter (Mt 26:75) and the suicidal remorse of Judas. (Mt 17:3-10)

7:11 *What punishment!* Cf. 2:5-11, esp. 2:6.

7:12 Paul is seeking, not punishment for the offender (note how he appeals for a loving treatment of him in 2:7-8) but the building up of the whole church (cf. 13:10). For the probable reconstruction of the event referred to, see Introduction, par. 3.

8:1—9:15 THE PRESENT: COLLECTION FOR SAINTS OF JERUSALEM

8:1—9:15 Paul turns from the retrospective thanksgiving for all that God has given him and the Corinthians in his ministry of reconciliation (chs. 1—7) to the present and the common task which will be the expression and confirmation of the reconciliation between him and his church (chs. 8—9). He closed his account concerning Titus' report with the words: "I rejoice, because I have perfect confidence in you" (7:16). The two chapters in which he gives directions for the completion of the collection are an expression of that confidence, tactful and gentle though his directions are.

8:1-7 The Example of the Churches of Macedonia

8:1-7 Paul holds up the example of the Macedonian churches, who in their poverty and affliction (see Introduction to Philippians) gave *beyond their means* (8:3)—because the grace of God moved them to *give themselves* (8:5) to the Lord and to His apostle. When men give themselves, their money is given too.

8:7 *You excel in everything,* etc. Cf. 1 Co 1:4-7.

8:8-15 You Know the Grace of the Lord Jesus Christ

8:8-15 Paul will not command them; he reminds them instead of what they already know—of the grace of the Lord Jesus Christ, who became poor for the enrichment of men and so provides them with the pattern and the power for their giving. And Paul reminds them of what they have already accomplished; they had set about the gathering of the collection as early as the previous year.

8:13-14 *Equality.* The church is the body of Christ in which all members work together equally for the common good. Cf. 1 Co 12:12-26 with 12:7.

8:15 *As it is written.* Cf. Ex 16:18. As God disposed His gift of bread from heaven for His people, so that no one had superfluity and no one lacked, so His church is to administer its charity.

8:16—9:5 Commendation of Titus and Two Brothers

8:16—9:5 Paul is sending Titus, an eager volunteer (16-17), and two other brothers in charge of the collection to aid the Corinthians in the task which will prove their love and make good Paul's boast concerning them, lest Paul (and the Corinthians themselves) be put to shame when he comes to Corinth with the representatives of the Macedonian churches and finds the Corinthians not ready.

8:18 *The brother.* Neither this brother nor the one mentioned in 22 can be identified.

8:19 *Appointed by the churches.* Cf. 1 Co 16:3-4.

8:23 *The glory of Christ.* In their willing charity the Christ who gave Himself into poverty that men might be rich (8:9) is manifested to men in the glory of His grace.

9:2 *Achaia.* Cf. 1:1 note.

9:5 *An exaction.* That is what a gift given only under pressure would be, not a *willing gift.*

9:6-15 God Loves a Cheerful Giver

9:6-15 Paul reminds the Corinthians that generous giving reaps a great harvest; not only will the God who loves a cheerful giver reward such giving; also, God will be glorified in the thanksgiving of the recipients of the gift. As in the description of his apostolic ministry (chs. 1—7), so here also in the exercise of his ministry (chs. 8—9) Paul's first and last word is in praise of the grace of God. That Gentiles are bound to Jews in such fellowship that Jewish need provokes a Gentile gift, that this gift is the fire which sends up clouds of grateful incense in Jerusalem to the glory of the God who is Lord of Jew and Gentile both, that is grace, grace greater than man's words can tell. *Thanks be to God for his inexpressible gift!* (9:15)

9:7 *God loves a cheerful giver.* Pr 22:8, according to the ancient Greek version (as an addition to the Hebrew text translated in English versions).

9:8 Cf. Ph 4:19.

9:9 Is 55:10. *Righteousness,* God's fidelity to His covenant, is often used of His acts of love and deliverance for His people. Cf. 1 Sm 12:7, where the RSV rightly renders the word as "saving deed."

10:1—13:14 PROSPECT: PAUL'S IMPENDING VISIT TO CORINTH

10:1-18 Paul's Defense Against the Charges of his Opponents

10:1—13:14 Paul has spoken the word of conciliation to the full; he has set before the eyes of the Corinthians all the wondrous grace of God which has united him with them in the past (chs. 1—7). He has enlarged on the task which now unites them in a common effort of love (chs. 8—9). But between Paul and the Corinthians there still falls the shadow of the men who say, "We belong to Christ," in their peculiar and exclusive sense. They stand in the way of full conciliation. And there is no possibility of conciliation with them; they have given no identification of a change of heart. Being what they are, they MUST oppose Paul, for Paul is the opponent of all human greatness, including his own. He is opposed to all factions and all parties in the church, the "Pauline" party included (cf. 1 Co 1:12-13). Paul upholds and affirms all that they have sought to override and supersede—the OT Scriptures, the commands of Jesus, the apostolate as the vehicle of the presence and power of Christ, an earthen vessel perhaps, but the vessel which God Himself has chosen and therefore the only vessel. Paul interprets all the terms which they used as slogans ("freedom," "knowledge," "Spirit," "the lordship of Christ") in a sense radically different from theirs. There is no possibility of compromise here, no prospect of conciliation; and so the message of conciliation must show the hard and cutting edge of its exclusiveness—Paul must unmask them for what they are, satanic messengers who destroy the work of God, and must bid the Corinthians come out from them and be separate from them.

Paul had touched on the attitudes, methods, and accusations of his opponents as early as the first letter (1 Co 4:18-21; 7:40; 14:37), and the anathema on those who have no love for the Lord (1 Co 16:22) is no doubt intended primarily for them. There are indications in the first section of the second letter too that Paul is seeking conciliation in an atmosphere charged with calumny and controversy (cf. e.g., 2 Co 1:12-14; 2:6; 3:1-3; 4:2, 5; 5:11 ff.; 6:3). But it is not until now, when the word for conciliation has been fully spoken, that he meets his adversaries and their charges head on.

10:1-12 THE CHARGES OF PAUL'S OPPONENTS, WITH PAUL'S REPLY

Their charges, as Paul enumerates them, are: Paul is humble when face to face with the Corinthians and bold only when absent; he terrifies them with his letters, but his bodily presence is weak, and his speech is of no account (10:9-10); he acts *in worldly fashion,* blustering when he can and stepping softly when he must. This proves that he is not one who "belongs to Christ" in the sense and to the degree that they, his bold and persuasive opponents, can claim to belong to Him (10:7)

Paul's answer is simply this: Do not force me to demonstrate the authority divinely given me, an authority given for building up the church, not for destruction, an authority which therefore has the patience to wait for repentance and its fruits before it performs the necessary but painful task of destruction by judgment (10:4-6), an authority which my opponents, since they know nothing but themselves and must judge others by their own self-centered standards (10:12), cannot even understand.

10:1 *I, Paul, myself, entreat you.* As the *myself* indicates, the last four chapters of the letter are probably a greatly extended autograph conclusion, such as we find, e.g., in Gl 6:11-18.

By the meekness and gentleness of Christ. The terms of this adjuration already put the humility and unworldly "inconsistency" of Paul in their true light. When he exposes himself thus to the criticism of opponents, "Christ," the gentle and meek, "is speaking in" him. (13:3)

10:13-18 PAUL'S AUTHORITY AS APOSTLE

10:13-18 Over against the self-commendation of his detractors (12, 18) Paul sets the fact that the Lord has "commended" him by building the church at Corinth through him (13-14). Paul has built the church, and he has not thrust himself into another man's field of labor either, as his opponents have done (15). That is the solid and factual vindication of his authority, one that permits him to boast only *of the Lord* (17) and allows him to hope that he will be further vindicated by greater work in a wider field (15-16), as the Corinthians' faith increases and he is free to go on to further labors in the West *(in lands beyond you,* 16). Paul is looking (as his Letter to the Romans makes plain) to Rome and beyond Rome to Spain (see Introduction to Romans).

10:13 *Beyond limit.* This seems to be a hit at the extravagance of the claims with which his opponents had overawed the Corinthians. (Cf. 11:20-21)

11:1—12:21 Paul's "Foolish" Boasting

11:1-4 PAUL'S REASON FOR BOASTING

11:1-4 To defend the church which he has betrothed to Christ and to protect her from the satanic influence of those who proclaim *another Jesus* (4), Paul will play the fool and boast; a holy *jealousy* (2) for the church impels him.

11:2 *Betrothed you to Christ.* For the people of God (the church) as the betrothed, or bride, of God or Christ cf. Hos 2:19-20; Eph 5:26-27.

11:3 *Serpent deceived Eve.* Cf. Gn 3:4

11:4 *Another Jesus.* See Introduction to 1 Co, par. 15.

11:5-6 THE BOAST OF KNOWLEDGE

11:5-6 Though he makes no pretense of rivaling these *superlative apostles* (5) in skilled speech, he will boast of his *knowledge.* (6)

11:6 *Unskilled in speech.* Cf. 1 Co 1:17; 2:4.

Knowledge. For Paul's conception of knowledge in contrast to that of his opponents, cf. 1 Co 8:1-2.

11:7-15 THE BOAST OF SERVING WITHOUT PAY

11:7-15 He will boast, ironically, of that which has been made a reproach to him, of the fact he *preached God's gospel without cost* to his converts (7). He will not let the insinuation of the false apostles (who evidently interpreted his refusal to accept remuneration as an admission that he lacked full apostolic stature) drive him from this policy, which is dictated by his love for the Corinthians.

11:8-9 *Robbed other churches,* by accepting support from them in their poverty. Cf. Paul's words to the Macedonian church at Philippi, Ph 4:15, 18.

11:10 *This boast of mine.* Cf. 1 Co 9:3-6, 12, 15-18.

11:14 *Satan.* For Satan as the enemy or perverter of true Gospel proclamation cf. Ro 16:20 with 16:17-18.

11:15 *Their end will correspond to their deeds.* They will in the end, when God crushes Satan under foot (Ro 16:20) and renders to all men according to their works (Ro 2:6), be punished as they deserve.

11:16-33 THE BOAST OF THE SERVANT OF CHRIST

11:16-33 Though he is too "weak" to assume the arrogant self-seeking demeanor of his opponents, he will boast of all that they dare boast of—and more. He can claim all that they claim in the way of Judaic descent and Judaic prerogative (22). And he is a better *servant of Christ* (23) than they, better because he is marked (as the Servant Christ was) by toil, suffering, and persecution, worn by the daily pressure of his anxious care for all the churches. He *will boast of the things that show* his *weakness* (30), to the glory of his Lord.

11:18 *Worldly things,* such as power and prestige (20) and descent. (22)

11:22 *Hebrews . . .Israelites . . . descendants of Abraham.* Cf. Introduction to 1 Co, par. 14, and Ph 3:4-5. *Hebrews* here probably designates those Jews who were Palestinian born and retained their mother tongue, in contrast to the Jews of the Dispersion, who adopted Greek, the common language of their world. (Cf. Acts 6:5 note)

11:24-25 *Five times . . . three times . . . once,* etc. Paul adopts the style of the inscriptions in which Hellenistic kings and Roman emperors recorded their exploits. Thus his careful enumeration is formally a "boasting" in the "worldly" style, but since the boasting is wholly concerned with his sufferings, it becomes in substance a tribute to the Lord who has deigned to make him His servant (cf. Acts 9:15-16), the Lord for whom it is an honor to suffer.

11:29 *Who is weak,* etc.? On Paul's sympathetic concern for the weak, cf. 1 Co 8 and 9:22; Ro 14:1—15:13 note.

11:32 *Aretas,* a name of a number of kings of the Nabataean Arabs. Aretas IV (9 B. C.—A. D. 40) held *Damascus* in A. D. 39—40.

11:33 *Let down in a basket . . . escaped.* Cf. Acts 9:24-25.

12:1-10 THE BOAST OF VISIONS, REVELATIONS AND A "THORN IN THE FLESH"

12:1-10 He will boast of visions and revelations of the Lord which have been given him; but he again ends by boasting of his weakness, of the affliction (*thorn . . . given me in the flesh,* 7) which his Lord would not take from him even though he prayed for relief repeatedly, in order that his Lord's power might be made perfect in the apostle's weakness. He boasts of his weakness, for in his weakness the power of Christ rests on him, and only thus he is strong.

12:2 *A man in Christ.* Paul after his conversion. Paul is reticent before the mystery of his visionary experiences.

Third heaven. In Judaic tradition, heaven was thought of as consisting of a number of levels, of which the third was the highest.

12:3 *Paradise,* most likely identical with the third heaven of 12:2. This heavenly Paradise was conceived of as the abode of the souls of the righteous awaiting the resurrection. (Cf. Lk 23:43)

12:7 *Thorn . . . in the flesh.* It is certain that some form of affliction is meant; just what form it took we have no way of knowing.

A messenger of Satan. For Satan as the imposer of afflictions (under the overruling control of God) cf. Job 2:6-7; as the one who impedes the apostolic mission cf. 1 Th 2:18.

12:8 *I besought the Lord.* Paul PRAYS to Jesus Christ as naturally as he does to God, strong indication of the deity of our Lord.

12:11-18 THE BOAST OF SIGNS, WONDERS MIGHTY WORKS, SELFLESS SERVICE

12:11-18 Though in his person he is nothing but a fragile vehicle of the power of Christ, Paul is not at all inferior to *these superlative apostles* (11); he can boast of the *signs of a true apostle* (12), *mighty works,* performed in complete selflessness (*in all patience,* 12) as Jesus performed His mighty works, not for Himself but as a gift and blessing for others. In the light of this, the Corinthians cannot give ear to those who interpret his refusal to accept pay as a sign that they were less favored than churches founded by other apostles; neither can they lend credence to the charge that he refused to take pay directly in order to gain it directly, through his helpers and associates; selfless men like *Titus* (18) are the sufficient refutation of that charge. This practice was dictated by fatherly love (14) for them, and he will not depart from it now, even though there are those who misinterpret it as a *wrong* (13) done to the Corinthians.

12:14 *The third time.* Cf. 13:1 and Introduction, par. 2.

12:18 *Urged Titus ... sent the brother.* Cf. 2:13, 8:18.

12:19-21 REASON FOR PAUL'S BOASTING: THE UPBUILDING OF THE CHURCH

12:19-21 Paul's boasting has not been a decline from the high apostolic independence which he had professed earlier (cf. 5:11—6:10 note); he has not been pleading in his own defense before a human court; he has been speaking in *the sight of God . . . in Christ* (19), for his church's edification, in order that they might repent (21) before Paul's visit and spare him and themselves the grief and humiliation of another "painful" visit. (Cf. Introduction, par. 2)

12:21 *Impurity, immorality,* etc. Cf. 6:14—7:1.

13:1-14 Paul's Impending Visit and Conclusion

13:1-10 PAUL'S IMPENDING VISIT

13:1-10 Paul will come and deal unsparingly with those who refuse to repent; they shall have full proof of the POWER of his apostolic authority (1-4). But, characteristically, the apostle who is strong when he is weak implores the Corinthians not to put his authority to the test. His desire is, not to triumph over them but to upbuild them. He therefore prays that they *may not do wrong* (7), in order that he *may seem to have failed* (7), since he is helpless over against the *truth* of the Gospel and its workings in repentant men (8). Nowhere, perhaps, does the selflessness of Paul's apostolic will and the purity of his apostolic love appear in clearer light than here, where he wills not to demonstrate by serverity (10) the power given him by the exalted Christ who speaks in him.

13:1 *Two or three witnesses,* as the Law requires, Dt 19:15; cf. Mt 18:16; 1 Ti 5:19; Heb 10:28.

13:4 *Weakness ... power.* As in his missionary proclamation (1 Co 2:1-2), so in his pastoral care of the church Paul is determined to know nothing except "Jesus Christ and him crucified." He will be only the servant of the Servant Christ, with His weakness and HIS strength.

13:11-14 CONCLUSION: ADMONITION (11), GREETINGS (12-13), BENEDICTION (14)

13:11 This concluding admonition is a summary expression of the will to reconciliation (by way of repentance) which informs the whole letter; the will of God which made Paul an apostle of Christ Jesus (1:1) is a will of *love and peace.*

13:12 *Holy kiss.* Cf. Ro 16:16 note.

13:14 The Trinitarian benediction is a revelation of all that makes obedience to the admonition of v. 11 ("mend your ways," etc.) possible and inescapable. The whole *love of God* which broke in glory upon mankind when the *grace of the Lord Jesus Christ* was manifested in poverty for the enrichment of the world (cf. 8:9), that *love* and *grace,* conveyed by the *Spirit* who unites men with God and with one another (fellowship)—that is the church's resource, alive and working in the apostolic Word; and with it all things are possible.

GALATIANS

INTRODUCTION

The Word of the Lord grows; where it grows, the Lord Jesus Christ is present and at work; and He is always "a sign that is spoken against" (Lk 2:34). Where the Word of the Lord grows, the kingdom of God is present. Jesus once described the presence and working of the Kingdom by comparing it with the working of leaven in dough; where the Kingdom is, there is ferment, disturbance, change, and upheaval. And so it is not surprising and in no way a contradiction of the fact that it is a divine Word if the growth of the Word brings with it tension and rouses conflict, not only between the church and the world but also within the church itself. The first church experienced such tension and conflict when the Word of the Lord began to grow on Gentile soil and the question of the relationship between the converted Gentile and the Christian Jew became an acute question, involving as it did the question of the relationship between the new, universal Gospel and the ancient Law given by God to Israel.

The apostles and the apostolic church knew from the beginning that the Christ is Lord of all and that the Word of the Lord must grow on every soil under heaven. Jesus had made His apostles His witnesses, not only in Jerusalem and all Judea but also in Samaria and to the end of the earth (Acts 1:8). The miracle of Pentecost spelled out in roaring wind, in apportioned flame, and in the gift of a speech that men of every nation could understand as their own the fact that the Spirit was to be poured out on "all flesh," that the Gospel was to go to all men in every tongue, that the promise for the last days, now being fulfilled in the outpouring of the Spirit, was not only to the Jews but also "to all that are far off, every one whom the Lord our God calls to him." (Acts 2:39)

This knowledge did not remain mere theory; nor was it the active possession of only a few. When Samaria received the Word of God preached there by Philip, the Jerusalem apostles acknowledged and welcomed the fellowship of the Samaritans and cemented the fellowship between the church of Samaria and the church of Jerusalem by sending Peter and John there to confer on them the gifts of the Spirit in full measure; and the apostles further extended that fellowship by "preaching the gospel to many villages of the Samaritans" (Acts 8:4-25). Philip was prompted by the angel of the Lord to tell the good news of Jesus to the Ethiopian eunuch and to baptize him, thus bringing into the new people of God one who had been doubly excluded from the ancient people of God both by the fact that he was a Gentile and by the fact that he was a eunuch (Dt 23:1). Thus the promise made for just such men through the prophet was fulfilled (Is 56:3-8). Such incidents were surely not isolated—Luke records typical incidents in his compressed account of how the Word of the Lord grew—nor were they unknown or forgotten in Jerusalem.

Another such incident, the conversion of the Gentile Cornelius and his family and friends (Acts 10:1-48), is characteristic of the attitude of the Palestinian church. The account of Luke marks this incident as a turning point, an epochal event. He tells it very fully, with emphasis on the divine guidance given by visions granted to both Peter and Cornelius; he records the sermon delivered by Peter in the house of Cornelius; and he points to the striking manifestations of the Spirit in these Gentile converts, manifestations at which the Jewish Christians were "amazed." Luke also records the fact that Peter's Jewish reluctance to enter a Gentile house had to be overcome (Acts 10:9-16, 27) and that there were those in Jerusalem who were dubious and critical about the step Peter had taken (Acts 11:1-18). For Peter this incident was of decisive and lasting importance, as his reference to it at the Apostolic Council shows (Acts 15:7-9). That the doubts of the men of Jerusalem were not wholly overcome by Peter's answer to their objections (Acts 11:4-18) is evident from the subsequent course of events. Thus there were present in Judaic Christianity two conflicting impulses, both the will for the inclusion of the Gentiles and a Judaic reluctance to accept the uncircumcised Gentiles as brethren without reservation or limitation.

The beginnings and the seeds of conflict were there. The tension was made acute and brought into the open chiefly by three events: the conversion of Saul, the founding of a predominantly Gentile church at Antioch on the Orontes, and the missionary journey of Paul and Barnabas to Cyprus and the cities of Southern Galatia in Asia Minor. The conversion of the Pharisee and persecutor Saul is marked both in the three accounts of it in Acts (Acts 9:1-19; 22:3-21; 26:9-18) and in Paul's own reference to it in his epistles (Gl 1:15-16; 1 Co 15:8-10; Eph 3:3, 8; 1 Ti 1:12-16) as a creative act of the sovereign grace of God, an act which made Saul God's "chosen instrument" (Acts 9:15). The history of Saul, or Paul, his Roman name by which he was known in his work among the Gentiles and is remembered in the church, shows us how the Lord of history had prepared His chosen instrument. Paul was a Roman citizen (Acts 16:37; 22:25); a citizen of Tarsus in Cilicia, no mean Greek city (Acts 21:39); and a Hebrew of the Hebrews (Ph 3:5). Here was a man whose history had fitted him for the task to which the grace of God had called him. He was enabled by it to become all things to all men; he could, in a world dominated politically by Rome, bring the Gospel to men decisively influenced by Greek culture and speaking the Greek language. And he would be the last man to break ruthlessly with Judaic Christianity, even when the question of the relationship between Gentile and Jew in the church made fellowship between Jew and Gentile agonizingly difficult, for he remained in the highest sense a Hebrew of the Hebrews to the last (cf. Ro 9:1-5). In Paul God gave the church the man whose word and work would inevitably heighten the tensions latent there, and also the man who would work wholeheartedly for a salutary resolution of those tensions.

Paul did not found the Gentile church at Antioch; some unnamed Jews, men of Cyprus and Cyrene, did that, or rather the "hand of the Lord" did it through them (Acts 11:20-21). Paul is not quite the lone genius in pioneering Gentile missions and in establishing Gentile churches free from the Law that some romanticizing accounts make him out to be. Neither was he the first to work for contact and communion between the new Gentile community and the older Judaic churches. The Jerusalem church itself did that by sending Barnabas, that "good man, full of the Holy Spirit and of faith" (Acts 11:24), to Antioch. And it was Barnabas who brought Paul to Antioch (Acts 11:25-26). But the influence of Paul's preaching at Antioch must have been deep and decisive. How great Paul's influence was we can measure by the fact that it was Paul whom the brethren chose to go with Barnabas to bring relief to the brethren in Judea during the famine (Acts 11:27-30), and by the fact that the Spirit chose him for the first organized mission to the Gentiles (Acts 13:1-3). It was no doubt largely due to Paul's influence that the church of Antioch remained a church free of the Law, a church that both cultivated a full and active fellowship with the Judaic church and became the base for mission work to the Gentiles.

On the missionary journey that took Paul and Barnabas to Cyprus and Asia Minor (Acts 13—14) Paul emerges as the leader; Luke now calls him by his Roman name Paul (13:9), and now usually speaks of the two men in the order "Paul and Barnabas," whereas previously he has put the name of Barnabas first. From the time of their meeting with the Roman proconsul Sergius Paulus on Cyprus (Acts 13:6-12), Paul is the central figure in Gentile missions and dominates the rest of Luke's account of how the Word of the Lord grew. The conduct of the mission which Paul undertook jointly with Barnabas is characteristic of the ecumenical outlook of Paul. He sought contact with the synagog everywhere and found a ready acceptance of his good news especially among the "devout converts to Judaism" (Acts 13:43) and those Gentiles whom Luke designates as "men who fear God," Gentiles who without actually being full converts to Judaism still were on the fringes of the synagog, attracted by its pure preachment of the sole God and the high character of its moral teaching. Paul sought contact with the synagog and became a Jew to the Jew in his preaching by emphasizing how all God's previous dealings with Israel, from the time of the patriarchs to John the Baptist, have been leading up to and preparing for the message of Jesus as the Messiah, whom Paul now proclaimed to them (Acts 13:26-41). But at the same time he made it startlingly plain that his Gospel was, as the fulfillment of the promises of God, no mere supplement to the Law, but the end of the Law and the antithesis to it, that the Word of God was now going beyond the confines of Israel into all the world, that through the Savior whom God had brought of David's line *"every one that believes* is freed [literally "justified"] from everything from which you could not be freed by the law of Moses" (Acts 13:39). He threw the doors of the new temple of God wide open to all, to Jew, to proselyte, to Gentile, and gave all men direct access to God, in Christ and simply by faith. He was saying out loud and in so many words what had long been implicit in the miracle of Pentecost, in the evangelization of the Samaritans, and in the conversion of the Ethiopian eunuch, Cornelius, and the Gentiles of Antioch.

As a result there came into the church large numbers of Gentiles, without circumcision, without submitting to the customs of Moses, not by way of Judaism, not as Jewish proselytes, but directly. And these people were, to some extent at least, conscious of the fact that they did not need to come into the church by way of Judaism, that they were full members of the new people of God, just as they were and as God had called them. This was bound to raise questions in the minds of Jewish Christians who had not yet or would not ever grasp the total newness of the New Testament, who could not or would not face all that was implicit in the words of John the Baptist when he said, "God is able *from these stones* to raise up children to Abraham" (Mt 3:9), or all that Jesus had meant when He said, in view of one Gentile's faith, "*Many* will come from east and west and sit at table with Abraham, Isaac, and Jacob in the kingdom of heaven" (Mt 8:11). Not that anyone denied the Gentile the right to membership in the church; the question was rather: *How* was the Gentile to attain such membership? Were all God's ancient ordinances, all the marks and tokens of His covenant with Israel, simply to be discarded by the new and culminating revelation of God in Christ? Was the ancient people of God, the people who claimed Abraham the believer as their father, simply to disappear, lost in the inbreaking wash of Gentile converts? Thus was created the tension in the church which led to the convocation of the Apostolic Church Council and the writing of Paul's Letter to the Galatians.

The Apostolic Council

The immediate occasion of the Apostolic Council was the arrival at Antioch of Jewish Christian men who insisted that Gentile converts must come into the church by way of Judaism; such men are commonly labeled "Judaizers." These Judaizers came to Antioch with the demand that the Gentile Christians be circumcised "according to the custom of Moses" (Acts 15:1; cf. 15:5), and they demanded circumcision as necessary to salvation: "Unless you are circumcised . . . you cannot be saved" (Acts 15:11). This party, or group, had its forerunners in men of the type who had called Peter to account for entering the house of the Gentile Cornelius (Acts 11:1-18). If Gl 2:1-5 refers, as seems most probable, to Paul's visit to Jerusalem A. D. 46 at the time of the famine (his second visit, Acts 11:30; 12:25), men of this sort had already collided with Paul when they demanded that his Greek companion Titus be circumcised. And Paul had stoutly resisted their demands. At least some of them were converted Pharisees (Acts 15:5). They were, then, a group or party within the church and did not, so far as we can see, expressly deny any part of the Gospel as preached by Paul and the rest. In fact they seem to have claimed the support of the Jerusalem church and the Jerusalem apostles for their demands (Acts 15:24); Luke is perhaps tacitly disallowing their claim when he says that they came "down from *Judea*" (Acts 15:1) and not from Jerusalem.

They were so insistent in their demands, argued so stubbornly and so skillfully with Paul and Barnabas, and so unsettled the minds of the Gentile Christians at Antioch (Acts 15:24) as well as elsewhere in Syria and Cilicia (Acts 15:23) that it was decided to carry the matter to the apostles and elders in Jerusalem (Acts 15:2). At the meeting in Jerusalem, which apparently included not only the apostles and elders but also representatives of the "whole church" (Acts 15:22), the voices of Peter and James, the brother of the Lord, were raised decisively in favor of Gentile freedom from the Law (Acts 15:7-11, 13-21). This was quite in keeping with the position they had previously taken over against Paul's Gospel and his apostolate to the Gentiles A. D. 46 (Gl 2:1-10), and the Judaic church followed their leadership in refusing to impose on the Gentiles "a yoke . . . which neither our fathers nor we have been able to bear" (Acts 15:10). But it must be remembered that for Judaic Christianity the question of the freedom of the Gentiles had two facets. The one half of the question, Must a Gentile become a proselyte to Judaism in order to be saved? was answered at once and decisively by the council. But the other half of the question need to be answered also, and that was, What is the relationship between the circumcised, ritually clean Jewish Christian and the uncircumcised, ritually unclean Gentile Christian to be? How are they to live together, and how are they to carry out that act which loomed so large as an expression of Christian fellowship, namely, table fellowship—how are they to eat together? (It should be remembered that the common meal and the celebration of the Lord's Supper were closely connected in the early church.) For the radical Judaizers the answer was of course simple: Let the Gentiles be circumcised and become good Jews. For Jewish men of good will who sought to fulfill the mission to Israel which God had given them (Gl 2:8-9), a mission which made it impossible for them to assume the freedom they had granted to the Gentiles, the answer was anything but simple. And in the light of this fact the words in the letter sent to the churches must be understood, the words, namely, "It has seemed good . . . to us to lay upon you no greater burden than these necessary things: that you abstain from what has been sacrificed to idols and from blood and from what is strangled and from unchastity" (Acts 15:28-29). The "necessary things" requested of the Gentiles are not marked as necessary to salvation and are therefore not a reimposing of the Law upon them; this is a *request* addressed to the Gentiles, a request which asked them to abstain from foods and practices abominable to Jewish feelings, foods and practices which their pagan past and their pagan surroundings made natural and easy for them. It is understandable that abstention from "unchastity" should be included also in the request, when we remember how closely connected unchastity was with pagan worship, pagan festivals, and pagan life generally. The so-called Apostolic Decree is therefore anything but a triumph of Judaic legalism. If a burden of love was laid on the Gentile brethren by it, the Judaic brethren also assumed no light burden in not expecting and asking more. The reception of the letter at Antioch (Acts 15:31) and later on in the province of Galatia (Acts 16:4, 5) shows that the Gentile churches did not view it as a defeat for Gentile freedom: "They rejoiced at the exhortation" (Acts 15:31) and "were strengthened in the faith, and they increased in numbers daily." (Acts 16:5)

The men of the church learned, as the Word of the Lord grew among them, not to use their freedom as an opportunity for the flesh, but through love to "be servants of one another" (Gl 5:13). Thus Christianity was safeguarded against a reimposition of the Law; the very real danger that Christianity might degenerate into a Judaic sect (and so perish with Judaism) was averted. And the unity of the church was preserved; the new Gentile church was kept in contact with the Judaic church, to which it owed the Gospel (cf. Ro 15:27) and was thus kept firmly rooted in the Old Testament Scriptures—a great blessing, for the history of the church has shown how readily alien and corrosive influences beset the Gospel once contact with the Old Testament is lost. To surrender the Old Testament is the first step toward misunderstanding, perverting, and so losing the Gospel of the New Testament.

The Letter of Paul to the Galatians

The struggle was in principle decided by the council at Jerusalem. But that did not mean that the Judaizers were forever silenced or that their influence was completely neutralized. Their claims were decisively rejected by the church at Jerusalem; but they had, apparently, meanwhile gone on to spread their mischief beyond Jerusalem and Antioch in the churches which Paul and Barnabas had established in Southern Galatia on their first missionary journey at Pisidian Antioch, Iconium, Lystra, and Derbe (Acts 13.14). They did so with considerable success, for what they proclaimed was a very plausible sort of substitute and the Gospel which Paul's converts had heard from him. To judge from Paul's polemics against them, they did not in so many words deny any positive teaching that Paul had brought to the Galatians; they acknowledged and proclaimed Jesus as the Messiah, the Son of God, the risen and exalted Lord, the Giver of the Spirit, in whose name is salvation; they did not deny that He would soon return in glory to consummate God's work in grace and judgment. The evidence does not even indicate that they completely ignored or obliterated the cross in its redemptive significance; Paul's repeated and passionate emphasis on the central and all-embracing significance of the cross in his letter does indicate that for them the Messiah of the cross was overshadowed by the Messiah in glory, that the cross of Christ tended to become an episode which His exaltation counterbalanced and reduced to relative insignificance.

They did not, on their own profession, come to destroy Paul's work, but to complete it (Gl 3:3). The coming of the Messiah, in their proclamation, crowned Israel's history and consummated Israel; it did not therefore by any means signify the end of the Law and such sacred ordinances as circumcision and the Sabbath, which God Himself had ordained as the mark and condition of the covenant between Himself and His people forever. The coming of the Christ did not free men from the Law; the Christ confirmed the teaching of the Law and deepened the obedience which it demanded. Salvation by the mediation of the Christ therefore most assuredly included the performance of the works of the Law. A Christian estate based on faith alone, without circumcision and without the Law, was a very rudimentary and unfinished estate; perfection lay in circumcision and in keeping the Law to which it committed a man. Thus a man became a true son of Abraham and the heir of the blessing promised to Abraham, a member of God's true and ancient people. To dispense with the Law would mean moral chaos, or at best a very dubious and dangerous sort of liberty.

Paul, these men insinuated, had not told them all that was necessary for their full salvation. He was, after all, not an apostle of the first rank, not on a par with the original Jerusalem apostles, through whom he had received his apostolate. His failure to insist on the keeping of the Law was a piece of regrettable weakness on his part, due no doubt to his missionary zeal, but regrettable nevertheless; he had sought to gain converts by softening the rigor of the genuine Gospel of God—he had, in other words, sought to "please men." They, the Judaizers, were now come to complete what Paul had left unfinished, to lead them to that Christian perfection which Paul's Gospel could never give them.

Their attack was thus a three-pronged one. It was (a) an attack on the apostolate of Paul, (b) an attack on the Gospel of Paul as omitting essential demands of God, and (c) an attack which pointed up the moral dangers that would result from a proclamation of salvation by mere faith in an absolutely free and forgiving grace of God.

The attack was subtle; it was also, apparently, an organized attack under a single leadership; Paul refers to one personality as particularly responsible for the harm that had been done in the Galatian churches (Gl 5:10). And the attack was ominously successful, understandably enough. For the converted Jew this new form of the Gospel promised a more relaxed relationship with his unconverted fellow Jews; the Gentile converts would be impressed by the authority of the Jerusalem apostles which the new preachers invoked for their cause. And the zeal of these uncompromising extremists no doubt impressed both Gentile and Jew.

Paul probably heard of the activity of these men and of their incipient success while he was still at Antioch on the Orontes. Since he was about to go up to Jerusalem to thresh out the question raised by the Judaizers with the apostles and elders there, he could not go to Galatia in person, as he might have wished (Gl 4:20), to meet the attack and to combat the danger. He met it by writing the Letter to the Galatians, which is therefore to be dated A. D. 48 or 49.

The letter achieved its purpose; the Galatians joined loyally in the gathering of gifts for the poor in Jerusalem (1 Co 16:1), an undertaking close to Paul's heart, as an expression of the unity between Gentile and Judaic Christianity. A certain Gaius of Derbe (in Galatia) was among the representatives of the Gentile churches who accompanied Paul when he took the Gentile offerings to Jerusalem. (Acts 20:4)

The Letter to the Galatians is one of the most personal and autobiographical of the letters of Paul, invaluable for the historical appreciation of his Gospel and his work; it is therefore valuable for the understanding of the growth of the Word of the Lord. We see here that the growth of that Word is genuine human history; the chosen instruments of the Lord are anything but robots—they do their work and the will of the Lord with the passionate intensity of personal involvement. The men who witness to the Christ are laid hold of by the Christ, and their mission becomes flesh of their flesh and bone of their bone.

Scarcely another epistle so emphasizes the "alone" of "by grace alone, through faith alone" as does this fighting exposition of the Gospel according to Paul with its embattled stress on the fact that Law and Gospel confront man with an inescapable, not-to-be-compromised either-or. Paul's Letter to the Romans expounds the same theme more calmly and more fully and has a value of its own; but there is no presentation of the Gospel that can equal this letter in the force with which it presents the inexorable claim of the pure grace of God. Luther, who had to fight Paul's battle over again, said of Galatians: "The Epistle to the Galatians is my own little epistle. I have betrothed myself to it; it is my Catherine of Bora."

It should be remembered that the letter addresses itself to a very earnest, very pious, and very Christian sort of heresy and crushes it with an unqualified anathema. Our easy age, which discusses heresy with ecumenical calm over teacups, can learn from this letter the terrible seriousness with which the all-inclusive Gospel of grace exludes all movements and all men who seek to qualify its grace.

1:1-10 INTRODUCTORY: SALUTATION, REPROACH, AND CURSE

1:1-10 The peculiarly impetuous and passionate character of the letter is apparent from the start. After the salutation Paul, without pausing for the thanksgiving and prayer which usually follow (cf., e.g., Ro 1:8-13), breaks into a severe reproach of the Galatians for deserting the Gospel and an unqualified condemnation of the men who have misled them with what purports to be *another gospel* but is in reality a perversion of the one true Gospel. With that he has already begun the theme that is to occupy him through the first two chapters: the defense of his apostolate. Paul is not, as his opponents claim, a man-pleaser who has diluted the Gospel to achieve a quick and cheap success: he is wholly *a servant of Christ*—neither he nor anyone else has authority to change the Gospel of Jesus Christ.

1:1-5 The salutation touches on all three of the themes of the letter: the divine origin and independence of Paul's apostolate *(not from men nor through man)*, chs. 1—2; the centrality of the cross *(who gave himself for our sins)*, chs.

3—4; and the new life which removes men from "the present evil age," where the compulsion and condemnation of the Law have their necessary place. (Chs. 5—6)

1:2 *All the brethren who are with me.* Paul often associates individuals with himself in the salutation (cf., e.g., 1 Co 1:1; 2 Co 1:1; Ph 1:1; Cl 1:1); only here does he include a group (his co-workers [?], representatives of a congregation or congregations [?]). He is indicating perhaps that what he has to say is not one man's opinion, one apostolic voice. The whole apostolic church is warning them and pleading with them in what follows.

1:11—2:21 PAUL'S DEFENSE OF HIS APOSTOLATE

1:11—2:21 In three stages Paul defends his apostolate against the charge that his authority is secondary and derivative ("from men . . . through man," 1:1): his apostolate is divine grace conferred directly on him (1:11-24), recognized as such by the Jerusalem apostles (2:1-10), independent even over against so powerful a figure as Cephas. (2:11-21)

1:11-24 Paul's Apostolate: Its Origin in God

1:11-24 *The gospel . . . preached by me is not man's gospel* (11); Paul's first word concerning his apostolate is a word concerning the Gospel for which he is "set apart" (Ro 1:1), with which his apostolate is so closely identified that he can on occasion refer to it as "my gospel" (Ro 2:16; 2 Ti 2:8; cf. 2 Co 4:3; 1 Th 1:5). This Gospel, the beating heart of his apostolate, he has not received from man; he did not learn it as he learned the Law and the *traditions of* his *fathers* at the feet of Gamaliel (Acts 22:3). Christ came to Him by *revelation,* by that act of God in which God alone is active to make Himself known and to make Himself count in man's life (12, cf. 16). No man contributed to that, least of all Paul himself; his willing and running were in violent opposition to God's revelation all the way (13-14, cf. 23). Neither did the first *apostles* contribute anything (17): Paul did not meet *Cephas* (Peter) until 3 years later and then only briefly (18). *The churches . . . in Judea* knew him only by hearsay for 14 years—and they gave all the credit for his conversion to God (*glorified God because of me,* 24). Like them, Paul can attribute his conversion and call to the apostolate only to God's eternal counsels, His sovereignly gracious good pleasure, His *grace* that forgave him his rebellious past and empowered him for his future ministry to the Gentiles (15-16). Paul's autobiography is an echo of Jesus' words to Peter: "Flesh and blood has not revealed this to you, but my Father who is in heaven." (Mt 16:17)

1:11 *For.* Paul is saying, "I am a slave of Christ [10], for God has by His revelation made me His slave."

1:13 *Persecuted the church.* Cf. Acts 8:1-2; 9:1-4; 22:4-16; 26:9-18.

1:14 *Traditions of my fathers* are that body of interpretations of (and additions to) the Law which had grown up around the Law and enjoyed a prestige and authority in Judaism practically equal to that of the Law itself. (Cf. Mt 15:2)

1:15 *Set me apart before I was born.* Paul describes God's control of his existence in terms used by the Lord when He called Jeremiah into His service as His prophet. (Cf. Jer 1:5)

Through his grace. Paul always looks on his apostolate as sheer grace. (Cf. Ro 1:5; 1 Co 15:10; Eph 3:2, 7, 8; 1 Ti 1:14)

1:17 *Arabia.* The kingdom of the Nabataean Arabs extended northward to within a short distance south of Damascus.

1:18 *Cephas,* Aramaic form of "Peter." (Cf. Jn 1:42)

1:19 *Apostles except James the Lord's brother.* According to this translation, James is called *apostle.* He would then belong to that larger group (beyond the Twelve) of apostles who were commissioned by the risen Lord (cf. 1 Co 15:7). But the Greek words may also be translated to read: "I saw none of the other apostles, but I did see James, the Lord's brother."

2:1-10 Paul's Apostolate Recognized by the Pillars of the Church

2:1-10 Paul's second visit to Jerusalem raised the very question which the agitators in the Galatian churches were raising: Had Paul, or anyone, the authority to bring Gentiles into the church without circumcision? The question was bound to be raised, for Paul took with him *Titus,* an uncircumcised Gentile convert (1). And the question was raised—not by the Jerusalem apostles but by *false brethren secretly brought in* (4), men of the same stripe as those now subversively active in Galatia. These Paul resisted for the Gentiles' sake, the Gospel's sake, for the truth's sake, for the sake of the *freedom* with which Christ made men free (5). The pillar of the Jerusalem church made common cause with Paul, recognized the *grace* of God *given* to him in his apostolate to the Gentiles, laid no restrictions on his preaching of the Gospel of freedom (*adding nothing to me,* 6), gave him and Barnabas *the right hand of fellowship,* and agreed on a division of labor (9). The only request they made of Paul and Barnabas was that they cement the bond of fellowship between Jewish and Gentile Christians by an active charity (*remember the poor,* 10), a request that Paul met more than halfway.

2:1 *After fourteen years*—14 years after Paul's conversion or after the first visit described in 1:18-19? The whole question of the chronology of Paul's visits to Jerusalem and their relationship to the visits recorded in Acts is a complicated and much-discussed problem whose solution does not contribute much to the understanding of the letter. On the whole it seems best to identify this visit with that of Acts 11:27-30 (rather than with that of Acts 15, as many interpreters do). The revelation referred to in 2:2 would there probably be that given by the prophet Agabus (Acts 11:28): *Barnabas* was with Paul on that visit (Acts 11:30) as well as on that described in Acts 15; and since the visit of Acts 11 was a relief mission (Acts 11:29), the words of the "pillars" to Paul and Barnabas in Gl 2:10 could be rendered, with fidelity to the Greek, as: "They asked us to continue to remember the poor, which very thing I had been eager to do." A private (2:2) discussion concerning the Gospel preached among the Gentiles could well have been held on the occasion of that visit.

2:2 *Run in vain.* Paul knew that if the Jerusalem authorities were not sympathetic to his Gentile mission, his work could be seriously impaired. They had shown a ready and active sympathy with the work done among the Greeks at Antioch (Acts 11:20-26); he hoped for the same sympathy in regard to work further afield. And he was not disappointed in that hope.

2:6 *What they were makes no difference to me.* This seems to conflict with what he has said in 2:2. There Paul obviously set great store by the sympathy and approval of the men of Jerusalem. The point he is making here is that the Gospel, not being a "man's gospel" (1:11), cannot be validated by any man's approval, just as no man, not Paul himself, can alter it and make "another gospel" of it. (1:9)

2:7-9 This administrative measure either did not work out in practice—we find Paul going regularly into the Jewish synagog on his missionary travels (e.g., Acts 13:5, 14) and Peter writing to Gentile churches (1 Ptr)—or, as seems more likely, was never intended as a rigid rule. Paul's road ran westward to the Greek-speaking world; if he encountered Jews on that road, he would inevitably speak the Good News "to the Jew first" (Ro 1:16), and he never forgot his kinsmen even in his mission to the Gentiles. (Ro 11:13-14)

2:9 *Grace.* Cf. 1:15 and the note there.

Pillars. The church is thought of as the structure raised by the Lord Christ (cf. Mt 16:18); in that structure these men are prominent and important.

2:10 *Remember the poor.* For Paul's interest in the collection for the poor in Jerusalem see Ro 15:24-28; 1 Co 16:1-4; 2 Co 8—9; and cf. Acts 24:17.

2:11-21 Paul's Apostolate: Encounter with Peter

2:11-21 Paul illustrates the independence of his apostolate by means of an incident in the history of the church at Antioch. When *Cephas* (Peter) by his behavior there first attested the equality and freedom of the Gentile Christians by eating with them and then denied it by withdrawing from table fellowship with them (12), Paul *opposed him to his face* (11). He spelled out for Peter the meaning of his inconsistent behavior, his *insincerity* (13), his evasion of the *truth of the gospel* (14) which *condemned* him (11). Paul bluntly pointed out to Peter, the "first" of the Twelve, what his actions (whether he was conscious of it or not) were saying. They were saying to the Gentile Christians: Unless you *live like Jews* (14), submitting to the Law, you remain unclean *Gentile sinners* (15) unfit for table fellowship with the Jew. These actions were saying to his fellow Jewish Christians: We have sinned by eating with unclean Gentiles; being *justified by faith in Christ* (16) is not enough to make and keep us clean. With that Peter by his actions was saying: Christ is *an agent of sin* (17), for faith in Him has led us into this sin. This amounts to saying: The *grace of God* (21) and the love of the Son (20) manifested in the death of Christ are ineffectual: Christ *died to no purpose* (21). Our baptism is meaningless: We have not *died to the law* by being *crucified with Christ* (19, 20; cf. Ro 6:3-6) *Christ* does not *live in* us (20). Peter did indeed stand condemned: he was *building up again* the Law, to which he had died with Christ; in thus denying the grace of God he was proving himself *a transgressor* (18) of the Law, which bade him love the Lord his God with all his heart.

Paul's words to Peter constitute the transition to the theme of the second major part of his letter, the either-or of Law or Promise, Law or Gospel. (3:1—4:31)

2:11 *He stood condemned,* by his actions. He had divided the church which God had made one in Christ Jesus. (3:26-28)

2:12 *Came from James,* that is, from Jerusalem, where James soon became the acknowledged leader of the church (see Introduction to the Letter of James). It is not said that James sent them to put an end to the table fellowship between Jewish and Gentile Christians; it is not even said that they remonstrated with Peter, Barnabas, and the rest. The mere presence of representatives of the Jerusalem church was enough to remind Peter of the criticism that his action would provoke in the Jewish-Christian stronghold of Jerusalem (cf. Acts 11:1-3) and to make him waver in his freedom.

He ate with the Gentiles. The common meal was a token and expression of fellowship, deeply felt as such; moreover, the Lord's Supper was celebrated in connection with it. (Cf. 1 Co 11:17-34)

2:15 *Gentile sinners.* The phrase represents the attitude of the pious Law-observing Jew toward nations without the Law.

2:19 *Through the law died to the law.* The Christian, "crucified with Christ" (20) in Baptism (Ro 6:3-11), has died *through the law* since it was Christ's obedience to the Law (a whole love for God and for man) that took Him to the cross; he *died to the law* because in Christ's death the condemnation and curse of the Law (cf. 3:13) was executed on man once for all, and the man in Christ is freed from the Law legally, on the Law's own terms, by dying. (Cf. Ro 7:1-6)

3:1—4:31 PAUL'S DEFENSE OF THE GOSPEL OF FREE GRACE

3:1-14 Three Witnesses to the True Nature of Law and Gsopel

3:1-14 First witness: Paul appeals first to the witness of the *experience* (4) of the Galatians. They owe their conversion to the proclamation of the Crucified; and the cross is God's verdict on mankind, His rejection of all the works of man. It is by *hearing with faith* (not by works which the Law commands and rewards) that they have received the Spirit and witness the miracles done among them. They must be *bewitched* to believe that a progression from the Spirit to *flesh* (circumcision), from Gospel to Law, is an advance and not a retrogression. (1-5)

Second witness: He then meets the Judaizers on their own ground by appealing to the witness of the Old Testament concerning Abraham; Abraham is the father of the people of God as a justified believer, and those who are *men of faith* are his true sons, heirs of the blessing promised to all nations. (6-9; cf. Ro 4)

Third witness: Paul further appeals to the witness of the Law itself. The Law demands deeds and pronounces a *curse* on all who do not obey it fully. *No man,* though, *is justified before God by the law;* all men are under its curse and can be justified only by the faith which looks to Him who took upon Hismelf the curse of the Law in our stead. In Him all men, Gentiles as well as Jews, receive the *blessing of Abraham* and the gift of the *Spirit promised* for the last days of fulfillment *through faith.* (10-14)

3:1 *As crucified.* Cf. 2:21. The cross, as God's crushing verdict on man and as His acquittal of man for Christ's sake, has forever excluded man's performance, the way of the Law, as the way of salvation.

3:3 *Are you now ending,* or "being made complete," alluding to the claim of the Judaizers that Paul had preached an "incomplete" gospel in Galatia, one that needed to be supplemented by their teaching. *Flesh* probably refers to circumcision.

3:6 For a fuller treatment of *Abraham* as father of the whole people of God, of all believers both Gentile and Jew, cf. Ro 4 and the notes there.

Thus. The connecting link in the thought is the answer which the question of 5 expects: "You have received the Spirit because you heard and *believed,* just as Abraham (with whom the history of the people of God begins) also believed and was justified." Therefore you are walking in the footsteps of Abraham, stand before God as he stood, are justified as he was, and are in the truest sense his sons.

Believed God, etc. Cf. Gn 15:6; Ro 4:3.

3:8 Cf. Gn 12:3

3:10 *Cursed be.* Cf. Dt 27:26. Paul cites freely; the *all things written* is implied but not stated in Dt 27:26. But compare Dt 28:15 ("do all his commandments and his statutes"). For the full horror of the *curse* cf. Dt 28:15-68.

3:11 Cf. Hab 2:4; Ro 1:17; and the notes on those passages.

3:12 *Faith . . . does them.* Salvation by grace through faith and salvation by works are mutually exclusive. (Cf. Ro 4:2-5; 9:32; 11:6)

3:13 *A curse for us.* For a similarly drastic statement of the vicarious atonement cf. 2 Co 5:21.

Cursed be every one. Dt 21:22-23 pronounced this curse on the executed criminal. For Paul, the unconverted Pharisee, this had probably been the greatest stumbling block; he had probably joined in the cry, "Jesus be cursed!" (1 Co 12:3), for how could the Crucified, He whom the Law pronounced accursed, be the Christ, the Lord!

3:15-29 The Relationship Between Promise and Law

3:15-18 THE PROMISE OF GOD AS A WILL OR TESTAMENT

3:15-18 The blessing of Abraham and the gift of the Spirit do not come by way of the Law (cf. 3:1-14). But the Law is God's law; it is "holy, and the commandment is holy and just and good" (Ro 7:12), for God's will of love is expressed in the Law (5:14, 23). The Law cannot therefore be merely dismissed; it must be seen in its place and time as it functions in God's overall plan for the salvation of man as God has revealed it. God Himself, not Paul, has assigned to the Law its secondary place. God's first word in the history of His people was the *promise* made to Abraham, not the *law* given through Moses. The promise, this basic and primary word to mankind, is a giving word: "I will bless you, and make your name great, so that you will be a blessing . . . in you all the families of the earth shall be blessed" (Gn 12:2-3). The promise says, "I will give" (Gn 12:7). Now, no one can annul a will *once it has been ratified* (by the testator's death); so also the Law, coming centuries after the promise, cannot be thought of as in any way annulling or even modifying His promise (15-18)—"the gifts and the call of God are irrevocable." (Ro 11:29)

3:15 *A man's will.* As RSV note *g* indicates, the same Greek word is used for both *will* and *covenant;* this suggests the comparison. For the promise as covenant, a gracious, freely giving declaration of God which establishes and regulates a relationship between God and man, cf. Gn 17:2-14.

3:16 *Offspring . . . Christ.* From the vantage point of the fulfillment of the promise, Paul sees that there is but *one* offspring of Abraham in whom the promised blessing is finally realized, *Christ,* "the son of Abraham." (Mt 1:1)

3:17 *Four hundred and thirty years afterward.* Cf. Ex 12:40.

Previously ratified. Because the covenant is God's, it is ratified and in force as soon as it is uttered—unlike a human testator's will which is in force only after the testator's death.

3:18 *By the law . . . no longer by promise. Law* ("You shall") and *promise* ("I, God, will") exclude one another (cf. Ro 4:14). God's demanding words and His giving word are reconciled only in the cross. (13)

3:19-29 THE SUBORDINATE, TEMPORARY FUNCTION OF THE LAW

3:19-29 The function of the Law was not to annul the promise of God; rather, the Law had a negative and temporary function in relation to the promise (19, 22), one limited to the nation Israel (20, see the note below). The Law has subserved the gracious purpose of God's promise; it has performed *a custodian's,* or overseer's, service over God's people until the time of the fulfillment of the promise. Now that the new age of *faith* has come (faith in the *promise*), the Law ceases to perform that function.

3:19 *Added.* Cf. Ro 5:20: "Law came in." The Law came after the promise and is of limited duration, controlling the life of God's people *till the offspring* (Christ) *should come.*

Because of transgressions. The Law brought man's sin out into the open as a violation of God's will (Ro 3:20) and so actually served to "increase the trespass." (Ro 5:20; cf. Ro 7:13)

Ordained by angels. Cf. Dt 33:2-4; Acts 7:53. Jew and Judaizer saw in this a mark of the glory of the Law; Paul sees in it a mark of the inferiority of the Law. When God gave His promise for all nations, He spoke directly to Abraham, the father of the people; He gave His law through *angels* and a human *intermediary,* Moses.

3:20 This obscure verse seems designed to make clear the significance of the *intermediary* in the giving of the Law. An *intermediary implies more than one,* namely, the nation Israel, for whom the Law was designed. The Law is limited both in time (19) and in scope, confined to Israel. It is therefore not the first nor the last nor the prime word of the one God of both Jew and Gentile who will justify both by faith. (Ro 3:29-30)

3:21 *If . . . law . . . could make alive.* The Law could not and did not overthrow the reign of death (cf. Ro 5:12, 17), did not make alive men "dead through ... trespasses and sins" (Eph 2:1; Cl 2:13). The promise, fulfilled in Christ, did.

3:22 *Consigned all things to sin.* God's will and verdict as expressed in *the scripture* imprisoned *all things* under the power of sin; the condemnation covered both man (Ro 3:9-19; 11:32) and man's world. (Gn 3:17-19; Ro 8:20, 22)

3:23-24 Three times in two verses Paul expresses the negative, provisional, subordinate character of the working of the Law, already expressed once in 22 ("consigned . . . to sin"): *confined, restraint, custodian.*

3:25 *Faith* is shorthand for the new age in which by faith men are blessed with Abraham (9), are righteous and live by faith (3:11) in the Christ, are released from the curse by Him, receive the Spirit through faith (3:13-14), and are all sons of God and united in Christ Jesus through faith. (3:27-28)

3:26-29 With the fulfillment of the promise in Christ (cf. 16), the distinctions set up by the custodian Law *(Jew, Greek),* all the distinctions of the "present evil age" (1:4) are done away with (*slave, free, male, female,* 28). The new people of God, all who are *baptized,* stand before God clothed in Christ, as *Abraham's offspring,* heirs *according to the promise* made to Abraham. (Cf. 16)

3:27 *Put on Christ.* We think of clothing as something external, which may or may not express what the clothed person is. Biblical thought generally conceives of clothing as being expressive of the person; one clothed in righteousness, majesty, strength, etc., is righteous, majestic, and strong (cf. e.g., Ps 132:9; 93:1; Is 52:1; 59:17). To put on Christ therefore means that a man is fully and wholly in Him; Christ is His real, true existence. (Cf. 2:20)

3:29 *Christ's . . . offspring . . . heirs.* Cf. 3:16.

4:1-31 Three Aspects of Sonship Confirming the Gospel of Grace

4:1-31 This section has a rather miscellaneous character, but the three units of thought are held together by the idea of sonship. (Cf. 4:7, 19, 31)

4:1-11 SONS AND HEIRS

4:1-11 The position of Israel under the Law was that of son and heir, but a minor heir, a child without liberty, no better than a slave. For the Jew to turn from the Gospel of free grace to the Law and its bondage would mean turning from manhood to childhood, from a freedom which the Father Himself has bestowed to a self-chosen slavery. For the Gentile, a turning from the Gospel to the Law would be practically a return to idolatry—he would be worshiping the outworn and discarded garments of God, not the living God as now revealed in His Son.

4:3 *Elemental spirits of the universe.* Cf. 9, "weak and beggarly elemental spirits." The exact meaning of the word translated as *elemental spirits* (here and in Cl 2:8, 20) is uncertain. The idea of "spirit" is not necessarily included under the term, which basically means simple "element," something rudimentary, as in Heb 5:12 ("first principles"). Whatever the precise meaning of the term may be, Paul's general argument is clear. Paul is pointing up what Israel under the Law and paganism have in common; the Jew under the Law and the Gentile immersed in paganism are both unfree, in contrast to their present freedom in Christ. The Jew under the Law is bound to such elements of the world as "days, and months, and seasons, and years" (cf. 10), subject to physical circumcision, obliged to distinguish between clean and unclean foods, and to offer physical, animal, and cereal offerings. The Gentile in his paganism is enslaved to "weak and beggarly" elemental things—and worse, he is in bondage to gods that "are no gods" (8, Paul does not say this of the Jew under the law of God). But a return to the past is unthinkable for either Jew or Gentile now that they are both free sons of God by God's act in Christ.

4:6 *Abba* is in Jesus' mother tongue the child's familiar and affectionate address to his father; it illustrates the perfect freedom of the Christian's sonship (cf. Ro 8:16-17) and echoes Jesus' own mode of addressing His Father. (Mk 14:36)

4:9 *To know God* and *to be known by God* are two sides of one reality, describing the communion established by God's grace and enjoyed through faith. (Cf. 1 Co 8:2-3)

4:12-20 MY LITTLE CHILDREN!

4:12-20 The Galatians have known what joy it is to be *children* of God in Christ. Paul gave them a new birth with the Gospel of free grace (19). Will they now turn from him whom they once loved so fervently, count him their enemy, and listen to the flattering persuasion of men who woo them now by *making much* of them in order to lord it over them later?

4:12 *Become as I am, for I also have become as you are,* that is, free of the Law. Paul had come to them simply as an apostle of Jesus Christ; he had become "to those outside the law . . . as one outside the law" (1 Co 9:21) and had given them the freedom with which Christ had made him free.

You did me no wrong, when I first came to you in physical weakness.

4:17 *They make much of you.* The Judaizers are wooing them now to win them over; but they want to *shut* them *out* from full membership in the church in order that the Galatians may make much of them, that is, become dependent on them as on the men who can give them all that they need to become true sons of Abraham and members of the people of God—circumcision, the Law.

4:19 *My little children.* Cf. 1 Co 4:15. Paul is like a mother *in travail,* but he does not labor to bring forth children in his own likeness—Paul has no use for Paulinists (cf. 1 Co 1:12-13). His words, his Gospel, are to bring forth Christians, men in whom *Christ* is *formed,* in whom Christ lives. (Cf. 2:20)

4:20 *Change my tone.* Paul has already used a great variety of "tones," ranging from the sharpest denunciation (1:6-9) to warmest appeal (19). If he were *present* with them to hear their questions and to know firsthand their problems, he might find yet another form of speech with which to win them back to the truth.

4:21-31 SONS OF ABRAHAM: ISHMAEL OR ISAAC?

4:21-31 Those who seek to win over the Galatians promise them that they will make the Galatians "sons of Abraham" by incorporating them in Israel (through circumcision, etc.). Paul's reply is: "Abraham had two sons; which son of Abraham will you be, Ishmael or Isaac? If you set store by physical descent from Abraham and want to join his physical descendants, your sonship is that of Ishmael, the son *born according to the flesh,* son of a slave woman who is typical of the covenant of *Mount Sinai* (a covenant which imposed the Law and could no more be God's final redemptive word than the birth of Ishmael could be the fulfillment of the promise to Abraham). That covenant produces slaves; and the slave woman has her counterpart in *Jerusalem,* the enslaved and doomed city of the Jews. True sonship is that of Isaac, born *through promise,* produced by the gracious and creative Word of God, son of the free woman, who is typical of the covenant of freedom and corresponds to the *Jerusalem above* (the redeemed and free people of God). The child of the free woman was persecuted by the child of the slave woman; so also the church is persecuted by Israel. But that does not change the destiny of either one. Those who would be Abraham's sons must go the way of the Gospel and freedom, not the way of enslavement under the Law."

4:21 *The law,* that is, the Book of Genesis, one of the five books of the Law. For the story of Hagar and Ishmael cf. Gn 16 and 21:8-21.

4:23 *Born according to the flesh,* that is, by the devising of man. (Cf. Gn 16:1-4)

4:25 *Hagar is Mount Sinai in Arabia.* The text here is very uncertain. The reading given in RSV note *i* is perhaps to be preferred. In Greek the word for "for" is very similar to the word for Hagar, and this may have led to confusion in copying the text. If we adopt the reading of the note *(For Sinai is a mountain in Arabia),* the sense seems to be: It is right to identify the slavery covenant of Sinai with Hagar, for Mount Sinai is in Arabia, the home of Hagar's slave-children, Ishmael and his descendants.

4:26 *The Jerusalem above,* that is, the second covenant (cf. 24), the new covenant of free sonship. (4:7)

4:27 *It is written.* Cf. Is 54:1. The prophetic Word was addressed to Jerusalem, the destroyed, captive, desolate capital of the deported people of God. The city is compared to a *barren* and deserted wife who is promised the miracle of abundant offspring. This promise finds its fulfilment in the church, the new Israel of God (cf. 6:16) that shall triumph over persecution (cf. 29) and increase marvelously.

4:29 *Persecuted.* Cf. Gn 16:12, where it is said of Ishmael: "He shall be a wild ass of a man, his hand against every man and every man's hand against him; and he shall dwell over against all his kinsmen," and Gn 21:9, which was interpreted by Judaic tradition as indicating Ishmael's hostility toward Isaac.

4:30 *Cast out the slave.* Cf. Gn 21:10-12.

To meet the charge that his Gospel of free grace means a breakdown of morality, Paul depicts the life of freedom, first in general terms (5:1-24) and then by concrete examples. (5:25—6:10)

5:1—6:10 PAUL'S DEFENSE OF THE GOSPEL: LIFE IN FREEDOM

5:1-24 Life in Freedom: General Description

5:1-12 FREEDOM AND THE LAW

5:1-12 Freedom and Law are incompatible. Freedom is not a way which man has chosen, but the way which Christ has established. No man may therefore compromise with it; to return to the way of the Law in however slight a measure (such as submitting to circumcision) is to cancel the Gospel of freedom and lose the Christ who has set us free. (1)

5:3 *Bound to keep the whole law.* Once a man goes the way of the Law, he must go the whole way. (Cf. 3:10; Ja 2:10)

5:6 *Faith working through love.* The parallels to this expression in 1 Co 7:19; Gl 6:15 are instructive. The "new creation" (Gl 6:15) means a life of "faith working through love" (Gl 5:6) and so "keeping the commandments of God." (1 Co 7:19)

5:8 *This persuasion,* that is, to accept circumcision and go the way of the Law does not come from Him who called you, for He called you "in the grace of Christ" (1:6) and not with the demands of the Law.

5:11 *Preach circumcision . . . persecuted.* Paul's opponents evidently accused him of compromising on circumcision on occasion; the incident of Timothy's circumcision (Acts 16:3) shows how far Paul was willing to go in becoming a Jew to the Jews "in order to win Jews" (1 Co 9:20). But Paul's stand over against the demand that Titus be circumcised (2:2-5) shows that he never wavered on the matter where "the truth of the gospel" was involved. Here his answer is simply to point to the fact that he is still being persecuted (by Jews and Judaizers); he could easily have avoided persecution by a little compromise—but did not, since circumcision and the cross are mutually exclusive.

5:12 *Mutilate themselves!* Since in Christ circumcision has become meaningless (6), the act is a mere mutilation of the flesh (cf. Ph 3:2). With bitter irony Paul wishes that the devotees of circumcision (mutilation) would go the whole senseless way and emasculate themselves, as the pagan devotees of the goddess Cybele, for instance, did. The cult of Cybele originated in Pessinus in the Roman province of Galatia and would be familiar to the Galatians.

5:13-24 FREEDOM AND THE SPIRIT

5:13-24 Freedom must not be misinterpreted to mean license; freedom means being set free from self to serve one's fellowman (which is the essence of God's will as expressed in the Law.)

Freedom means walking, conducting oneself, by the power and leading of the Spirit. It means entering that struggle against the flesh and its desires which a man can wage and win only in the power of the Spirit. It means living a life *led by the Spirit,* a life which moves on a level that the Law's threats and condemnation cannot touch. It means that Christ's death to sin (*crucified,* 24) becomes a reality in those *who belong to Christ.*

5:15 *Bite and devour one another.* The bitter factionalism which the proponents of the Law have brought into the churches threatens to destroy them.

5:17 Cf. Ro 7:15-23.

5:25—6:10 Life in Freedom: Concrete Examples

5:25—6:10 Life in freedom means the end of all self-centered pride, the end of provocative self-assertion and envy (5:25-26). It means a life of meek and gentle ministry to the erring, a ministry performed in the consciousness of one's own frailty (6:1-5). It means loving generosity toward those who teach in the church. (6:6)

As the life in the freedom of faith is a life of love (cf. 5:6), so it also is a life of soberly responsible hope. Freedom in Christ does not absolve a man of responsibility for his action; rather it heightens responsibility. Man will reap what he has sown. God will hold him accountable for what he has in his freedom done with the gift of the Spirit.

5:25 *Walk.* The word implies an orderly, disciplined walking, a being guided by the Spirit.

6:2, 5 *Bear one another's burdens . . . . Each man will have to bear his own load.* Christians serve one another, and yet each man remains individually responsible for his own life's work. "Each of us shall give account of himself to God." (Ro 14:12)

6:4 *Reason to boast . . . in his neighbor,* that is, boasting of one's supposed superiority to one's neighbor.

6:6 It may be that Paul's opponents had used Paul's refusal to accept support for himself as a pretext to cover a callous neglect toward the teachers of the church. Paul always insisted on obedience to the Lord's command "that those who proclaim the gospel should get their living by the gospel" (1 Co 9:14; cf. Mt 10:10; Lk 10:7-8), even though he himself made no use of this right. (1 Co 9:14)

6:7 *God is not mocked* with impunity; His justice will deal with those who flout His will.

6:8 *Sows to his own flesh,* that is, expends his energies and life in the kind of activities enumerated in 5:19-21. Similarly, *sows to the Spirit* is illuminated by 5:22.

Corruption, the opposite of *eternal life,* eternal destruction in the judgment of God. The same Greek word is translated "destruction" in 2 Ptr 2:12.

6:10 *Household of faith.* Cf. Mt 10:25, where Jesus calls His disciples "those of his household."

6:11-18 CONCLUSION

6:11-18 The conclusion, written by Paul's own hand (the rest of the letter was dictated), sums up once more the chief thought of the letter, with special emphasis on the selfish motives of the Judaizers and the selfless, Christ-centered motivation of Paul. The letter closes with a plea that he whom suffering has marked as Christ's own may be spared further agony at the hands of the Galatians and with a benediction on all who *walk by this rule* of the Gospel of freedom and are therefore the true *Israel of God,* true sons of Abraham. (Cf. 3:7, 29)

6:11 The *large letters* may be for emphasis. Some think that the "bodily ailment" to which Paul refers in 4:13 may have been a disease of the eyes (cf. 4:14) which left his eyesight permanently impaired, then the large letters would be necessitated by his imperfect vision.

With my own hand. For Paul's habit of dictating his letters and adding a postscript or a greeting in his own handwriting cf. 1 Co 16:21; Cl 4:18; 2 Th 3:17. In Ro 16:22 the secretary, Tertius, adds a greeting of his own.

6:12 *May not be persecuted for the cross of Christ.* By practising circumcision they continue to identify themselves with Judaism and hope to be tolerated as a sect within Judaism. The *cross* rules out *circumcision,* every concession to legalism, for in the cross Christ has redeemed men from the curse and power of the Law. (Cf. 3:13)

6:14 *The world,* in which man's "good showing," his personal glory, counts and is pursued, has ceased to exist for those who believe in the Crucified. They still live in it, as they live in the flesh (2:20), but it does not set standards for them or control their conduct.

6:15 Cf. 5:6; 1 Co 7:19.

6:17 *The marks of Jesus.* In the Greek world devotees or slaves of a deity were marked or tattooed with the sign of their master and so became sacrosanct; Paul calls the scars of his sufferings marks of Jesus which consecrate him to the Lord and should evoke awe and loving consideration for the apostle.

The Captivity Letters

The letters of Paul to the Ephesians, Philippians, Colossians, and Philemon are known as the Captivity Letters because they were all written while Paul was a prisoner, most likely at Rome, in A. D. 59—61. Some scholars date some of the Captivity Letters from Paul's 2-year imprisonment in Caesarea in A. D. 56—58 (cf. Acts 23:11-24, 27). Others date them all from a supposed imprisonment in Ephesus during his ministry there in A. D. 52—55, an imprisonment not mentioned by Luke in Acts but made probable by the troubled character of Paul's Ephesian years. But on the whole the ancient tradition which assigns the Captivity Letters to Rome still seems the most probable.

The Book of Acts tells the moving story of how Paul went up to Jerusalem for the last time bearing gifts from the Gentile churches to the church of Jerusalem, how this Christlike action of ministry to his people in the face of danger and death led to his arrest in Jerusalem, to his 2-year imprisonment in Caesarea, to his appeal to Caesar, and to the perilous voyage which finally brought him to Rome as he had long been hoping (Ro 1:10-11; 15:23, 32; Acts 19:21) and as his Lord had promised (Acts 23:11), but in a way he had not foreseen, as a prisoner (Acts 28:20). He remained a prisoner in Rome for two years, but the terms of his imprisonment were such that he was not reduced to idleness. He had his own rented quarters and his friends, the emissaries of the churches, and his co-workers had free access to him (Acts 28:31); they could cheer him by their presence and inform him personally of the fortunes and misfortunes of his churches. And the matured wisdom and ageless love of the aging apostle were available to them. We see him, at the end of the Book of Acts, "preaching the kingdom of God and teaching about the Lord Jesus Christ quite openly and unhindered." (Acts 28:31)

Paul's imprisonment was therefore not an interruption of his ministry but an exercise of his ministry. Paul himself viewed it as such: he sees in his sufferings an extension, as it were, of "Christ's afflictions" (Cl 1:24) for the sake of His church; he is a "prisoner for Christ Jesus" on behalf of the Gentiles (Eph 3:1), "a prisoner for the Lord" (Eph 4:1); his imprisonment is an imprisonment for the Gospel (Phmn 13); he is an "ambassador in chains" for the Gospel (Eph 6:19-20); and his trial at Rome is for the "defense and confirmation of the gospel" (Ph 1:7). He sees in his sufferings a part of the grace bestowed on him in the gift of his ministry, and so he rejoices in them. (Cl 1:24; Ph 2:17)

Not least among the fruits which grew on that tree of adversity are the Captivity Letters. In them we have Paul's profoundest proclamation of the all-embracing significance of the Christ (Letter to the Colossians) and of the nature and glory of His church (Letter to the Ephesians), a small but impressive record of how the Gospel can transfigure even mean and sordid aspects of human life (Letter to Philemon), and a letter whose dominant note of hopeful joy in the midst of suffering has through the ages helped keep the church a hoping Advent church even under persecution (Letter to the Philippians).

EPHESIANS

INTRODUCTION

The Letter to the Ephesians is linked by the evidence in the letter itself to the Letter to the Colossians and the Letter to Philemon. Tychicus is the bearer of the letter (Eph 6:21) and will give the readers fuller information concerning the imprisoned apostle (Eph 6:22). Since Tychicus is also the bearer of the Letter to the Colossians, and since Onesimus is returning to Colossae with Tychicus (Cl 4:7-9), the three letters (Ephesians, Colossians, Philemon) have a common historical background; they proceed from Paul's Roman captivity and are to be dated somewhere within the two years of that captivity (A. D. 59—61), perhaps in the earlier part of it.

But was the letter really addressed to the church in Ephesus? The earliest manuscripts do not have the words "in Ephesus" in the salutation (1:1), and their witness is confirmed by that of the early church fathers; the RSV translators had good reason for omitting the words from their revision of the text. Moreover, the letter itself nowhere indicates that Paul and the readers whom he is addressing are personally acquainted with one another; there are passages which indicate the very opposite (Eph 1:15; 3:2). When we consider how long Paul ministered in Ephesus and what close ties that ministry established (Acts 20:36-38), the absence of any personal touches in the letter is very striking. Similarly the letter gives no hint that Paul is personally acquainted with the life of the church—there are no concrete details, no reminiscences of former personal contacts. Paul's letters to the Corinthians, written to a church in which he had worked and with which he was intimately acquainted, present a striking contrast to the Letter to the Ephesians in this respect. One can hardly avoid the conclusion that the letter known as the Letter to the Ephesians was not originally addressed to Ephesus, at least not to Ephesus alone.

The best explanation of the historical background of the letter would seem to be the one suggested as early as the 16th century by Beza, Grotius, and Ussher: When Paul sent Tychicus to Colossae, he at the same time sent a general letter designed especially for a group of churches in Asia Minor which had been evangelized under his supervision during his Ephesian ministry, but had for the most part never been personally visited by him, places like Colossae, Hierapolis, and Laodicea. Tychicus would leave a copy with each church in the towns through which he passed on his way to Colossae, and possibly he transmitted copies to towns which did not lie on his route. In the latter case Paul's promise that Tychicus would inform the churches of his estate (Eph 6:21) would be fulfilled when Tychicus visited these churches after having completed his mission to Colossae. Each copy would bear the name of the church addressed. When Paul's letters were later collected and published, probably at Ephesus, the letter naturally came to bear the title "To the Ephesians," since Ephesus was no doubt included in the number of the churches addressed and was the most prominent among them. Some later copyist then probably inserted the words "in Ephesus" in the salutation to bring the text of the letter into harmony with its title. Some scholars are inclined to see in the letter "from Laodicea" referred to in Cl 4:16 the letter we know as Ephesians. It may be; copying was an onerous task in antiquity, and it would be natural and sensible to make one copy do for the two churches, since Colossae and Laodicea lay only 13 miles apart.

The sending of Tychicus to Colossae thus provided the external occasion for the writing of the circular letter now called the Letter to the Ephesians. What Paul's motives in sending such a letter were, we can infer from the apostolic church's missionary practice and from a statement made by Paul toward the end of the letter itself. The apostolic church always sought contact with newly founded churches. John and Peter were sent to Samaria after the evangelist Philip had founded a church there (Acts 8:14). Barnabas was sent to the young church at Antioch (Acts 11:22). Paul took representatives of the Jerusalem church with him on his first two missionary journeys (Barnabas, Mark, Silas); he maintained contact with Jerusalem and Judaic Christianity and sought to express and maintain the unity of the Spirit in the bond of peace by means of the Gentile collection for the Jerusalem saints; and he regularly revisited the churches which he had founded. As Paul surveyed his work in the East from the vantage point of his position in Rome, and saw from the reports of his co-workers the temptations and the dangers to which the young churches were exposed, he might well be moved to do by letter what he could not do in person, to go through his territory once more, "strengthening the churches" (Acts 15:41). That would be one motive for writing to the churches in the East.

The other motive was provided by Paul's peculiar situation. Paul in Rome knew himself to be an ambassador for the Gospel, albeit an ambassador in chains (Eph 6:20). Again the strength of the Lord was being made perfect in weakness. The Gentile churches saw the human weakness of the imprisoned apostle to the Gentiles more clearly than they saw the divine strength which worked through him; they had grown dispirited at the news of his imprisonment (Eph 3:13). Moreover, Paul was facing a crisis in his ambassadorship, one that would ask of him all the boldness he could muster (Eph 6:18-20). Paul therefore did two things in his letter. He asked for the intercessions of the churches, thus removing them from the role of lamenting spectators and making them active participants in his great ambassadorial task. And he held up before them the greatness of that task, the greatness of the church which the mighty divine Word proclaimed by him had created and was sustaining. He had just written to the Colossians how God's acts in the cross of Christ has made a peace which embraces the universe in all its parts and in all its powers (Cl 1:20); he had just written to Philemon and had seen, in applying the power of the Gospel to heal the breach between master and runaway slave, how that peace heals all man's life and removes its ugly rancors. He now spoke of "Christ our peace" (Eph 2:14) to all the scattered and troubled churches and held before them the greatness of the new people of God which God has created by uniting Jew and Gentile, once enemies, in one church; he held up before them the glory of that one, holy church, thus keeping the churches conscious of their high privilege of unity in Christ and of the obligation which the high privilege of membership in the one church involves. If the Letter to the Colossians is the letter of Christ, the Head of the church, the Letter to the Ephesians is the letter of the church, the body of Christ. Its purpose and outreach are as universal as its destination is general.

Content of the Letter

The Letter to the Ephesians consists of two portions, the first being an exposition of what the church is, the second an exhortation concerning all that membership in the church involves. We can sum up the message of the letter in the words of ch. 2, v. 10: "We are his workmanship, created in Christ Jesus for good works . . . that we should walk in them."

Value of the Letter

Paul is here singing hymns in prison, as he once did at Philippi. It is a hymn rich in content, a hymn which sings of the "manifold wisdom of God" and "the unsearchable riches of Christ." One perceptive modern interpreter has compared the letter with the Letter to the Romans; in both letters, he points out, Paul elaborates the theme stated in 1 Co 1:24, "Christ the power of God and the wisdom of God." Whereas Romans stresses the element of power (Ro 1:16), Ephesians emphasizes the wisdom of God. The church that is always prone to forget that it is God's creation and likes to think of itself as a structure of strength which man in *his* wisdom has reared and can in his wisdom control will do well to immerse itself again and again in this hymn from prison and learn from the ambassador in chains an awed humility in the presence of that awful, divine wisdom.

1:1—3:21 THE CHURCH: CREATED IN CHRIST JESUS

1:1-2 Salutation

1:1 On the absence of a place name in the salutation see the Introduction.

1:3-14 Doxology to the Father of Our Lord Jesus Christ

1:3-14 The opening doxology (cf. 2 Co 1:3 ff.; 1 Ptr 1:3 ff.) surveys the whole range of God's redemptive blessings: the eternal purpose of God which *chose* and *destined* men to be His own through Christ, to the *praise of His glorious grace (3-6a); the bestowal of His grace in the redemption wrought by Christ's death and in the proclamation of the mystery of his will* which shall unite all things in Him *for the praise of his glory* (6-12); the ultimate fulfillment of His redemption, the inheritance which the gift of the Holy Spirit guarantees to the church *to the praise of his glory. (13-14)*

The church comes into being by God's will in Christ. Note the constant recurrence of words denoting God's plan and purpose *(purpose, will, mystery of his will, plan, counsel, chose, destined, appointed)* and the red thread of "in Christ" which runs through the whole doxology.

1:3 *In Christ.* Cf. 4, 6, 7, 9, 10, 11, 13. Paul uses this phrase in a wide variety of applications to indicate the unique significance of Christ in God's redeeming purpose, action, and the results of His action in the redeemed community now and in the universe at the end of days (1:10). Christ as the comprehensive Representative of mankind is the place where (or Person through whom) God acts for us men and our salvation; He is therefore the place where (the Person in whom) we receive and enjoy all that God's action has bestowed on man.

1:6 *the Beloved,* Christ, the Son beloved of the Father. (Cf. Mt 3:17; 17:5; Cl 1:13)

1:9 *Mystery* indicates that God's great plan for the salvation of man and the restoration of all things can be known only by God's revelation. (Cf. 3:3-5; Dn 2:27-28 and 2:22)

1:10 *Fulness of time.* The time, determined by God, when His redeeming purpose reaches its full measure in the sending of His Son. (Cf. Mk 1:15; Gl 4:4)

1:13 *Sealed,* marked as God's property and assured of His protection. (Cf. 4:30; 2 Co 1:22)

1:14 *Guarantee,* literally "down payment," "first instalment," which in ancient times was a substantial portion of the whole.

1:15-23 Thanksgiving and Prayer

1:15-23 Paul *gives thanks* for the faith and love of his readers (15-16) and prays that they may be enabled by the Spirit to comprehend all that God has wrought for them (17): the *hope* which God's call has given them (18), the certainty of the *inheritance* which God's call has promised them (18), and the assurance that God's *power* (19) will carry believers safely through the dark present into future glory (14)—the power which He supremely manifested when He *raised* Jesus Christ *from the dead* and made Him Lord of all and Head *over all things for the church,* the *body* of Christ. (20-22)

1:17 *A spirit of wisdom.* Better "the Spirit of . . ."; the Holy Spirit is meant and is characterized by the gifts, *wisdom* and *revelation,* which He bestows. Cf. Ro 8:15 ("Spirit of adoption"), where v. 16 makes plain that the Holy Spirit is meant, and 2 Co 4:13; 2 Ti 1:7; Heb 10:29. For the connection between *Spirit* and *wisdom* cf. 1 Co 12:8; Cl 1:9; Acts 6:3, 10; between *Spirit* and *revelation* cf. 1 Co 2:10, 12; Eph 3:5.

1:18 *Hearts.* The heart in Biblical usage is the seat and organ not only of feeling, as with us, but of the whole inner life of men, including will and mind: "to say in one's heart" means "to think." (Ro 10:6; Ps 14:1)

Inheritance in the saints. The *inheritance* belongs to the future (cf. 1:14; 1 Ptr 1:4, "kept in heaven for you"), but *in the saints* (in the church) the future blessing is by the gift of the Spirit (1:14) already known and enjoyed. (Cf. Heb 6:4-5)

1:21 *Rule, authority, power, dominion.* Names for angelic powers, whether benign or hostile, taken over from Judaism; they are mentioned in order to assert the incomparable superiority of the Lordship of Christ (cf. Ro 8:38-39; 1 Co 15:24; Cl 1:16; 2:10, 15). For the whole thought cf. Heb 1:4-14.

Name. Title of dignity and honor. (Cf. Ph 2:9)

1:22-23 *Head over all things for the church . . . his body. Head* signifies dominion, lordship (not the intellect as with us). Christ's relationship to His church is more than mere power-dominion over it; He is vitally and organically united with His church and functions personally through it. This unique Lordship is expressed by the head-body image. (Cf. 5:23; Cl 1:18, 24)

Fulness, as being completely "filled" by Christ.

Fills all in all. For "fill" in the sense of "dominate," "rule," cf. 4:10 and Jer 23:24, where the ideas of rule and omnipresence are combined.

2:1-10 The Gentiles Have Part in the Redemption

2:1-10 God's universal redemption includes the Gentiles. He has delivered them from death and the dominion of Satan and has raised them to life and glory with the risen and exalted Christ (1-7). All this is unmerited grace, the gift of God received by faith. The church is solely and wholly God's creation, created for good works. (8-10)

2:2 *Walked.* For "walk" as designating "total behavior," "a way of life," cf. v. 10; Ro 6:4; 8:4; 14:5, etc. In Ro 13:13 the word for walk is rightly rendered "conduct ourselves."

Sons of disobedience, disobedient men (cf. 5:6; Cl 3:6). "Son of" is used to designate a man's character or calling ("son of the soil" is a farmer), sometimes his destiny, as in "son of perdition," 2 Th 2:3.

2:3 *We all,* Jews as well as Gentiles. (Cf. Ro 3:9)

2:4 *But God.* Cf. Ro 3:21, "But now . . . ." Salvation is God's "nevertheless" to man's desperate situation under His wrath. This is the first of a series of expressions which underscore the sheer gratuity of salvation (mercy, love, loved, grace, gift, not because of works, created).

2:10 *Workmanship,* what He has made, created; the same word is translated in Ro 1:20 as "the things that have been made."

For good works, etc. Faith (v. 8) is purely receiving, but it is a receiving, and therefore faith is inevitably an active faith which *walks* in the *good works* which God has *prepared* beforehand. Passages like this show how close to each other Paul and James are. (Ja 2:14-26)

2:11-22 The Gentiles Have Part in the Redeemed Community

2:11-22 Christ by the cross has abolished the Law which divided mankind into Jew and Gentile and excluded the Gentile from the *covenants* and *hope* of Israel. Thus He has created and proclaimed *peace,* the end of the ancient *hostility* between Israel and the Gentiles and the union of Jew and Gentile into one reconciled people of God. The Gentiles are incorporated into the people of God, into the family of God, into the living *temple* of God.

2:12 *Covenants of promise.* The covenant expresses God's gracious will to have fellowship with man, to create a bond (where no "natural" bond exists) between Himself and man, to give fallen man a future and a hope. The basic content of the covenant is, "I will be your God," and this gives all forms of the covenant the character of a promise, whether it be the covenant with Abraham (Gn 17:7-8), with Israel (Ex 24:3-11; cf. 19:3-6), with David (2 Sm 23:5), or the covenant as embodied in the person and ministry of the Servant (Is 42:6-7), or the promised new covenant (Is 54:10; 55:3; 61:8; Jer 31:31-34; Eze 16:60; 34:25; 37:26). To this the Gentiles were *strangers,* until Christ established the new covenant in His blood. (Mt 26:28; 1 Co 11:25)

2:16 *In one body.* The *one body* of Christ which hung on the cross under the judgment of God for the sins of all (Gl 3:13; 2 Co 5:21) is the atoning basis for the *one body* which is His church (4:4). Because the love of God comprehended all men in that suffering and dying body, there can now be a church composed of Jew and Gentile, a body of the risen Christ, sharing His exaltation and glory. (2:6)

2:17 *He came and preached,* through His apostles, in whose Word His atoning work lives on effectually.

2:18 *Access in one Spirit to the Father.* Cf. Ro 5:1-2; 8:15-16.

2:20 *Prophets.* The word order and 3:5 ("NOW . . . revealed to his . . . prophets") indicate that New Testament prophets are meant. (Cf. 4:11; Ro 12:6; 1 Co 12:28; 14:1-33)

Cornerstone, which determines the form and function of the various parts and of the whole.

3:1-21 The Apostle's Prayer for the Gentiles

3:1-21 As in 1:15 ff., Paul moves from the recital of the blessings bestowed on the Gentiles to a prayer for his Gentile readers (1). He prays that they may comprehend the full measure of the blessings bestowed on them, that they may know fully the incomprehensible love of the Christ who has redeemed them and may thus be filled with all the fullness of the God who has blessed them (14-19). In a long parenthesis (2-13) he dwells on the grace bestowed on him as apostle to the Gentiles, the high privilege of proclaiming to them their inclusion in the new people of God now realized in Christ Jesus. This grace gloriously transfigures the suffering which his apostolic task entails. The prayer concludes with a doxology to the God who is greater than our thoughts of Him and our prayers to Him: *To him be glory in the church and in Christ Jesus.* (20-21)

3:1 *A prisoner for Christ Jesus.* Cf. 4:1. The man who is an apostle "by the will of God" (1:1) is captured by that gracious will; he serves as the accredited messenger of Christ, not in spite of his sufferings but in and through them; the *prisoner* Paul is "an ambassador in chains." (6:20, cf. 2 Co 4:7-12; 12:9; Cl 1:24-25; 2 Ti 2:9-10)

3:3, 4, 9 *Mystery.* See 1:9 note.

3:5 *Holy apostles.* The apostles are holy because God has "set them apart" for the Gospel. (Ro 1:1)

3:6 *Partakers of the promise.* Cf. 2:12.

3:7 *Minister,* a servant who provides for the needs of others, such as those who wait on tables.

3:9 *God who created.* For the unity of God the Creator and Redeemer see 2 Co 4:6 and Paul's use of "new creation," 2:10, 15; 4:24; Cl 3:10; 2 Co 5:17; Gl 6:15; cf. Ja 1:18.

3:10 *Principalities and powers.* Cf. 1:21 note.

3:13 *Which is your glory.* Through the apostle's suffering Christ is glorified (cf. Ph 1:20; 2 Co 12:9), and therein His body, the church, is glorified.

3:14 *Bow my knees.* The usual posture of prayer was standing (Mt 6:5; Lk 18:11, 13); kneeling indicates unusual fervency and urgency of prayer. (Lk 22:41; Acts 21:5)

Every family . . . is named. The word for *family* denotes both "family" and also larger communal groupings derived from a common ancestor, such as a clan or tribe. Every communal grouping in which concord and peace prevail is in some way a witness to Him who is in the truest sense Father, the God of peace and not of disorder (1 Co 14:33), the God whose plan and purpose it is to unite all things in heaven and on earth into one "family" again. (1:10)

3:18 *With all the saints.* Being "rooted and grounded in love" (17), they are united with the whole company of saints, fellow Christians (cf. 1:1), whose varied gifts and graces work together to give all a full comprehension (*breadth and length,* etc.) of the wondrous workings of the love of Christ. (19)

3:20 "Thou art coming to a King,
Large petitions with thee bring."

3:21 *In the church.* It is an indication of the churchliness of this letter that this is the only doxology in the NT which contains this phrase.

4:1—6:24 THE CHURCH IS CREATED FOR GOOD WORKS

4:1-16 Diversity of Gifts in the Service of Unity

4:1-16 God's call (1) is a call to unity, to the denial of self (2) in the zealous pursuit of unity (3), to the utilization of the varied gifts bestowed by the exalted Christ for the full realization of this unity, that the church may be the mature and perfectly functioning body of Christ, who is its Head. (4-16)

4:3 *Unity of the Spirit.* The unity created and fostered by the Spirit (cf. 4 and 2:18). Vv. 4-6 describe this given unity.

4:4-6 There are seven ones in this description of the unity of the church, seven being the number of completeness and perfection. The first three look to the present: the church is *one body,* alive with the creative vitality of the *one Spirit,* animated by the *one hope* which the Spirit inspires and guarantees (cf. 1:13-14). The next three look to the historical origin of the church; Jew and Gentile came to be united in one church, when they came to *one faith* in *one Lord* (cf. Ro 10:12-13) and were baptized in His name. The last *one* looks to the ultimate origin of the church, the *one God and Father* who has from everlasting blessed us in Christ (1:3). He is *above all* in "the immeasurable greatness of his power" (1:9), works *through all* for the attainment of His gracious purposes (cf. 1:1, "apostle . . . by the will of God"; 3:2, 7), and dwells *in all* whom the Spirit has made a "dwelling place of God." (2:22)

4:8 Cf. Ps 68:18. Paul makes three interpretive changes as he quotes. First, he transfers the Old Testament utterance concerning God to Christ, as is often done in the New Testament in witness to the faith in His deity. Second, he changes from a second-person address to a third-person statement ("Thou didst ascend"; *he ascended*). Third, and this is most striking, he changes the "receiving gifts among men" of the psalm to *he gave gifts to men.* So bold a recasting of the psalm verse is intended to recall (rather then merely quote) the psalm, which does in fact celebrate God the Victor as the Giver of gifts to His people. (Ps 68:5, 6, 9, 10, 20, 35)

4:9-10 There is no domain or power in all the universe which the suffering and exalted Christ has not subdued. When He gives gifts, He gives out of "unsearchable riches" (3:8) and with absolute authority. For the sense of *fill* cf. 1:23.

4:11 *Apostles . . . prophets . . . evangelists . . . pastors and teachers.* A comparison with 1 Co 12:27-28 shows that the list is not intended to be exhaustive. The *apostles,* eye- and ear-witnesses and authorized messengers of Christ, are essential to the establishment of church (cf. 2:20, "foundation of the apostles"); through them Christ speaks and gathers His own (Ro 15:18-19; 2 Co 13:3). *Evangelists* spread the apostolic Word abroad (Acts 8:5-40; cf. 21:8); *prophets* guide and enlighten the church in such matters as missions (Acts 13:1-3) and charity (Acts 11:27-30). *Pastors and teachers* attend to the day-by-day nurture and edification of the churches established by the labors of apostle and evangelist.

4:12 *Saints,* all members of the church. "There is on earth a little holy flock or community of pure saints under one head, Christ. . . . I was brought to it by the Holy Spirit and incorporated into it through the fact that I have heard and still hear God's Word." (Luther)

4:15 *Speaking the truth,* or "living of the truth (or the true faith) in love."

4:15-16 *Grow up . . . into . . . the head . . . Christ, from whom.* The reality (what Christ signifies for the church) breaks the limit of the image *(head, body).*

4:17-24 The Radical Break with the Pagan Past

4:17-24 The new life of truth in love (18) calls for a radical break with the Gentiles' pagan past and their pagan surroundings. It means putting on the *new nature, created after the likeness of God in true righteousness and holiness* and putting off the *old nature which . . . is corrupt through deceitful lusts.*

4:17 *Futility of their minds.* Cf. Ro 1:21; 1 Ptr 1:18. *Mind* is here used in the broad sense of "attitude, way of thinking." The *futility* of the mind, its frustrate purposelessness, is defined in v. 18 in terms of a lack of clear judgment ("darkened in . . . understanding"), a distorted vitality exercised in "ignorance," and moral obtuseness or insensibility ("hardness of heart").

4:21-22 *Taught in him.* This unusual phrase probably refers to the instruction which the readers had received after their baptism, when they had "put on Christ" (Gl 3:27) and were *in him* but had yet to learn what their baptismal confession to Jesus as Lord (Ro 10:9) meant, concretely and in detail, for the conduct of their lives. *The truth* which could displace the futile lies that had filled their former life they found in the words and works of *Jesus,* the historical Man who had lived a life not "alienated from the life of God" (18), a truly human life in communion with the life of God.

4:22 *Deceitful lusts.* They promise man heaven and give him hell.

4:24 *Created.* Cf. 2:9-10. *After the likeness of God.* Cf. Gn 1:26-27.

4:25—5:20 Walk in Love, in the Light, in Wisdom

4:25—5:20 Christians are "created in Christ Jesus for good works, which God prepared beforehand, that we should *walk* in them" (2:10). This "walking" is here considered from three points of view, as a walking *in love* (4:25—5:2); a walking as *children of light* (5:3-14); and a walking *not as unwise men but as wise.* (5:15-20)

4:25—5:2 WALK IN LOVE

4:25—5:2 Men whose lives are bounded by the Holy Trinity live and move in the domain of love. As men *sealed in the Holy Spirit* (4:30), *as beloved children of God* who imitate their Father (5:1), as men brought near to God by the atoning sacrifice of the *Christ* who *gave Himself up* for them (5:2), they must *walk in love* (5:2). The *neighbor* can no longer be the victim of their self-assertion, to be exploited by their *falsehood* (4:25), assaulted by their *anger* (4:26), diminished by their thieving (4:28), degraded by their *evil talk* (4:29; cf. 31). The neighbor has become precious in their eyes, as the human life in which their love has scope to *give* (4:28), to *impart grace* (4:29), to be *kind* and *tenderhearted,* to *forgive* (4:32).

4:26 *Be angry but do not sin.* There is such a thing as righteous anger, but there is the ever-present danger that it may turn into all-too-human spite.

4:27 *Opportunity to the devil,* for whom the wrath of man affords welcome scope.

5:1-2 For a similar combination of ideas (God's love manifested in Christ's self-giving into death) cf. Ro 5:5-10.

5:2 *Fragrant offering and sacrifice.* For the language of sacrifice in a literal sense cf. Ex 29:18, in a figurative sense, Eze 20:41.

5:21—6:9 Be Subject to One Another

5:3-14 WALK AS CHILDREN OF LIGHT

5:3-14 *Children of light,* who have become *light in the Lord* (8), are no longer at home in the murky world of dark, unbridled desire, whether it be sexual desire or the desire for things (3); knowing the love of God (cf. 1-2), they no longer wage the undeclared war against God which is the heart of our evil desires. Neither are they at home in the world of moral *filthiness* (4); they have a clear vision of what is *fitting* in the light and know that God has given them tongues for *thanksgiving* (4). They have a clear vision of God's judgment too; no sophistry can hide the Judge from their eyes (5-6). They can no longer participate in *works of darkness;* they cannot even find a comfortable compromise with them. They must *expose them* (7-11), and so bring men out of the sleep of sin and death into the wakeful day, where *Christ shall give them light.* (12-14)

5:5 *Covetous . . . idolater.* Cf. Mt 6:24.

Kingdom of Christ and of God. One kingdom, one royal reign, is meant; *of Christ* probably accents the present manifestations of the reign, *of God* the future kingdom when Christ "delivers the kingdom to God the Father." (1 Co 15:24)

5:10 *Try to learn.* This describes the intelligent operation of the enlightened Christian conscience which determines what is *pleasing to the Lord* in any given situation.

5:11 The word here translated *exposed* is regularly used in the New Testament of confronting a man with his sin in order to lead him to repentance. Cf. Mt 18:15 ("tell him his fault"); Jn 3:20 ("exposed"); 8:46 ("convicts"); 16:8 ("convince"); 1 Co 14:24 ("convicted"); 1 Ti 5:20 ("rebuke").

5:12 The shamefulness of the deeds of darkness becomes apparent when they are called by their proper name, not kept secret and not concealed by silly talk and levity. (Cf. 4)

5:13 Light not only exposes; it also overcomes darkness. the words of the children of light proclaim not only judgment but also repentance, faith, and forgiveness, and so what is *exposed by the light* becomes *light.*

5:14 These words are probably quoted from a baptismal hymn.

5:15-20 WALK AS WISE MEN

5:15-20 Christians walk wisely in this evil world; their wisdom is to *understand what the will of the Lord is* (15, 17). And the will of the Lord is that the body of Christ do His work while there is still time (16). The only intoxication in their lives is the intoxication of the *Spirit* manifested in the exuberance of song and thanksgiving. (18-20)

5:18 *Do not get drunk.* The common meal, symbol and expression of Christian fellowship, would naturally include *wine.* 1 Co 11:20-22 shows that this admonition was a needed one.

5:19 *Psalms and hymns and spiritual songs.* It is hardly possible to make clear distinctions between the three types of sacred song here enumerated. The adjective *spiritual* probably applies to all and means "inspired by the Holy Spirit."

5:21—6:9 Be Subject to One Another

5:21—6:9 The Christians' reverence for Christ will mold their conduct in the relationship of this age and will make all these relationships channels for the love of Christ. The family and household relationship of spouses, of children and parents, and of slaves and masters will all have on them the mark of the Christ who is Lord of all. In all three cases Paul first addresses the party of whom subjection and self-abnegation is most obviously required *(wife, children, slaves)* and then proceeds to lay the equally demanding yoke of considerate love on the shoulders of the other party to the relationship.

5:26 *Washing of water with the word,* that is, Baptism, which derives its force and significance from the Word of Christ, who commands it and assigns to it its efficacy and significance. (Mt 28:19)

5:31 Cf. Gn 2:24.

5:32 *This mystery . . . a profound one,* known only by God's revelation, appears to be this: Only the man to whom "the mystery of the gospel" (6:19) has been revealed, only he who has come to know the love of Christ for His church, can know and understand how total a communion of love between man and woman the Creator established in marriage. Some translations render *profound mystery* with "great truth."

6:2 Cf. Ex 20:12.

6:5 *Slaves* were considered a part of the family, or household, and so would naturally be included in a table of duties such as this.

6:6 *Eyeservice.* Service rendered only because and so long as the master's eye is on them.

6:10-24 The Armor of God and the Power of Prayer

6:10-24 The church is God's outpost and bridgehead in an alien and still hostile world. The Christians' life is therefore of necessity a life of battle with the powers of Satan. For this battle God prepares them; He gives them knowledge of the unseen and ever-present enemy, gives them strength, and equips them with divine defensive and offensive weapons—His *truth* for their cincture, His *righteousness* for their *breastplate,* His *gospel of peace* for their sandals of agility, *faith* for their shield, the hope of *salvation* for their *helmet,* His *word* for their spiritual *sword* (10-17). These weapons they employ with *prayer,* strengthening their ranks by *supplication* for one another *(all the saints,* 18), extending God's conquest by supplication for their apostle that he may proclaim the Word boldly. (19-20)

6:12 *In the heavenly places.* This phrase is used elsewhere of God (1:3), of Christ (1:20), of Christians exalted with Christ (2:6), of angelic principalities and powers (3:10). Its use here of satanic powers indicates that they are transcendent powers (the extreme opposite of localized and recognizable powers of *flesh and blood*) pressing in on man, terrifyingly omnipresent and conquerable only by divine power and weaponry. Cf. "prince of the power of the air, the spirit." (2:2)

6:13-17 The description of the Christian's weapons is strongly colored by phrases from the Old Testament, which recall the weaponry of the Lord (Is 59:17), the Messiah (Is 11:4-5), and the great Servant of the Lord (Is 49:2). Thus the divine character of the Christian's equipment is stressed.

6:19 *Also for me.* Paul constantly sought the intercessions of the churches, one of the ways by which he made it clear that the apostle does not lord it over the church's faith (2 Co 1:24). Cf. Ro 15:30; 2 Co 1:11; Cl 4:3-4; 2 Th 3:1-2.

6:21-22 See the Introduction.

PHILIPPIANS

INTRODUCTION

The Captivity Letters tell of visitors who came from Paul's churches in the East to see Paul in Rome (cf. Colossians and Philemon). One of these was Epaphroditus, and he came from Philippi in Macedonia, the first church founded by Paul in Europe (Acts 16:11-40). Paul, Silas, Timothy, and Luke had arrived in Philippi early in the second missionary journey (A.D. 49—51). Philippi was a Roman "colony," that is, a settlement of Roman soldiers enjoying Roman citizenship, settled at a strategic point in the system of Roman roads for the security of the empire. Apparently not many Jews were there; neither a regular synagog, only a "place of prayer" (Acts 16:13), probably in the open air, at a riverside. It was there that Paul had begun his work. The Lord opened the ear of a proselyte named Lydia to his words, and we may suppose that the house of this wealthy and generous woman became the meeting place of the church (Acts 16:14—15). Paul knew "conflict" (Ph 1:30) and suffering in Philippi; he had been beaten and imprisoned without the due process of law to which his Roman citizenship entitled him. He had known not only conflict but also that joy in the midst of conflict and suffering which is the characteristic token of the apostolic and Christian existence (Acts 16:25). And he had experienced triumph in conflict and suffering, the triumph of the Lord whose strength is made perfect in weakness and defeat; he was released from prison and vindicated, and he gained the jailer and his household for the Lord. (Acts 16:25-40)

The church which grew, as the Word of the Lord grew, in Philippi was predominantly Gentile. And it was a church which remained especially near and dear to Paul. It was Paul's firstborn in Europe; the faithful and consecrated Luke remained there when Paul continued on his journey and provided spiritual leadership of a high order; the impetuous generosity of Lydia in the first days evidently set the tone of the church's life for the years that followed. We recall how she viewed her baptism as an initiation into a life of giving; she told Paul and his companions, "If you have judged me to be faithful . . . come to my house and stay," and "prevailed" on them to comply with her wish (Acts 16:15). The generosity of the Philippians was so genuinely rooted in Christ and His Gospel that Paul felt free to accept gifts from them; he can call them his "partners" in the proclamation of the Gospel (Ph 1:5; 4:15). They supplied his wants in Thessalonica (Ph 4:16) and again in Corinth (2 Co 11:9), and that too at some sacrifice to themselves; Paul told the Corinthians, "I robbed other churches by accepting support from them in order to serve you" (2 Co 11:8). This same actively generous partnership in the Gospel had moved the Philippians (and the other churches of Macedonia) to contribute to the collection for the Jerusalem saints "beyond their means," even in the midst of a "severe test of affliction" and in the depths of poverty. (2 Co 8:1-5)

The coming of Epaphroditus was another link in the golden chain of Philippi's gracious generosity. Still suffering persecution (Ph 1:29), still poor (Ph 4:19), the men and women of Philippi had nevertheless gathered a gift for Paul, probably under the direction of their "bishops and deacons," whom Paul singles out in the salutation of his letter (and only in this letter, Ph 1:1). They had sent the gift to Paul by the hand of one of their number, Epaphroditus, and had instructed him to remain in Rome with Paul as a minister to his need (Ph 2:25). Epaphroditus had delivered the gift and had performed his task of ministry with such self-forgetting devotion that "he nearly died for the work of Christ, risking his life" to complete the service of the Philippian Christians to their apostle. (Ph 2:30)

Date of Writing

These events help fix the date of Paul's Letter to the Philippians more exactly within the limits of his 2-year imprisonment at Rome (A. D. 59—61). There has been time for a series of communications between Rome and Philippi; news of Paul's imprisonment has reached distant Philippi; the Philippians' gift has been gathered, sent, and received; news of Epaphroditus' illness has reached Philippi and has caused great concern there; and news of this concern has again come to Paul and Epaphroditus at Rome. It has been calculated that this series of communications would require a total of at least five or six months; they probably took considerably longer. Moreover, the letter itself indicates that Paul's long-deferred trial is at last in progress (Ph 1:7), that it has proceeded so far that Paul can with some confidence hope for an early release from imprisonment (Ph 1:25; 2:24), though there is still real danger of an adverse verdict and death. All this points to a date toward the close of the 2-year imprisonment, probably to the early months of A. D. 61.

Paul is about to return Epaphroditus to Philippi (Ph 2:25-30); he sends with him a letter in which he gives his partners in the Gospel news of himself, his trial, and his prospects of release; thanks them for their gift; and excuses and commends their messenger Epaphroditus, who through no fault of his own has been unable to carry out fully the ministry entrusted to him. He notices too with pastoral concern and with kindly evangelical tact their internal troubles, a tendency to self-assertion on the part of some, with its consequent tendency to disunity. He encourages them in the persecution which pressed on them from without; and he warns them with passionate sternness of the dangers which threaten them, alerting them to the threat posed by Judaistic and libertine perverters of the Gospel.

Value of the Letter

Among the Captivity Letters, Colossians and Ephesians show us Paul the fighter for the truth, the thinker and theologian, the great strategist of church unity; the Letter to Philemon shows us Paul the man whose whole life is irradiated by the grace and glory of the Gospel. The Letter to the Philippians with its many and various facets is harder to classify; one modern scholar has brilliantly used this letter as an introduction to the whole thought-world of Paul; he sees in it the characteristic union of Paul the believer, Paul the missionary, and Paul the theologian. Perhaps one might best use the bold joy of faith as the common denominator of its multiplicity, faith as Luther once described it: "Faith is a living, resolute, total confidence in God's grace, a trust so certain that it is willing to die a thousand deaths for its belief. And such a trust in God's grace and such knowledge of God's grace make a man joyous, resolute, and robustly cheerful over against God and all God's creatures." An imprisoned apostle writes to a persecuted church, and the keynote of his letter is: "I rejoice. Do you rejoice?" Where under the sun is anything like this possible except where faith is, where the Holy Spirit breathes His wholesome and creative breath? The whole letter is a good illustration of a word Paul used in Ph 4:5, a word which we are obliged to translate with some such term as "forbearance." But "forbearance" expresses only a part of Paul's meaning; the Greek word which he uses points to a princely quality in man, to that largeness of heart, that spacious generosity, that freedom from the cruelly competitive scrabble of this world which only he possesses whose "commonwealth is in heaven," who is heir to all that is Christ's.

1:1-2 THE SALUTATION

1:1 *Saints* is one of Paul's regular terms for Christians; it marks them as called and claimed by God, to be instruments of His purpose.

For the special mention of *bishops* (overseers)

and *deacons* (their assistants, especially in charitable work) see the Introduction.

1:3-11 THANKSGIVING AND PRAYER

1:3-11 Paul gives thanks for the Philippians' *partnership in the gospel from the first day until now* and emphasizes the personal character of the bond which this partnership has established between himself and them (3-8). He prays that their *love* may grow and increase and that their *knowledge* and *discernment* may keep pace with their love. (9-11)

1:4 *Joy.* The dominant note of the letter. (Cf. 1:18-19, 25; 2:2, 17-18, 28, 29; 3:1; 4:1, 4, 10)

1:5 *Your partnership in the gospel.* They heard and believed it (1:29); suffered for it (1:28-30); lived and witnessed it (2:15; 4:3); and supported its proclamation (Acts 16:14-15; Ph 2:25, 30; 4:10 ff.; 4:15-16). The Gospel entered their life and controlled it.

1:7 *Partakers with me of grace.* Paul always speaks of his apostolate as grace (Ro 1:5; 1 Co 15:9-10; Eph 3:7-8; 1 Ti 1:14). The apostolic church, which is caught up into his apostolic mission and impetus, shares in that grace.

Imprisonment . . . defense and confirmation of the gospel. Apparently Paul's trial is in progress and has afforded him a welcome opportunity to proclaim the Gospel, clear it of misunderstandings and misinterpretations, and thus plant it firmly on Roman soil. (Cf. 1:12, 16)

1:9-11 Paul implores for his partners in the Gospel the kind of life in Christ which he describes in 3:12-16 as his own: a life of continual forward tension, of ever-deepening apprehension of the Christ who made him His own. Such a life will be one of increasing love and growing knowledge and discernment, a life in which "mind and heart according well . . . make one music," in which love, being motivated by knowledge of Jesus Christ, works intelligently toward clearly conceived goals, capable of distinguishing not only between good and bad but also between better and best. Paul's Letter to the Philippians is the classic expression of such an informed and intelligent love.

1:11 *Fruits of righteousness.* Righteousness is "through faith in Christ, the righteousness from God that depends on faith" (3:9; cf. Ro 1:17; 3:21-31; 2 Co 3:9; 5:21). *The fruits of righteousness . . . come through Jesus Christ* just as the righteousness itself does; the new life of the man declared righteous is His creation, the fruit borne by branches that receive their life from the vine. (Jn 15:5-8)

To the glory and praise of God. The life of all servants of God is, like the life of the Servant Christ, a living doxology. (Cf. 2:11; Jn 15:8)

1:12-26 NEWS FROM PRISON

1:12-26 The news is good. Paul's trial has made it clear that he is not what his accusers have charged, a seditious disturber of the Roman peace, but what he himself has always claimed, "a prisoner for Christ." Thus the cause of the Gospel has been advanced through his imprisonment and trial (12, 13). The turn which Paul's case has taken has emboldened his brethren to speak the Word of God without fear; and in this Paul rejoices, even though some of these preachers are motivated by selfish and partisan zeal in their preaching (14-18). Paul is convinced that whatever may befall him, life or death, Christ will be glorified through him. His heart's desire is to depart and be with Christ forever; but the duty which he gladly takes upon hismelf is that he remain in the service of his Lord on earth. And so he looks forward to being released and rejoining his church at Philippi.

1:13 *Praetorian guard,* the soldiery that guarded Paul. They would be struck by the contrast between the charges laid against their prisoner and his deportment and bearing, so completely gracious and noncriminal; and their curiosity would give Paul an opportunity to testify to his cause both before them and, directly or indirectly, also to *all the rest* who might hear of him. The reading of RSV note *c (in the whole praetorium)* would refer to the residence of the Roman governor in a province; a goodly number of scholars are inclined to think that all or some of the Captivity Letters were written by Paul from Ephesus during an otherwise unknown imprisonment there. In that case the reading of the note would be the more likely, since the word is used in this sense in the NT. (Mk 15:16; Jn 18:28, 33; 19:9; etc.)

1:26 *Glory in Christ Jesus, because of my coming.* Paul's coming to the Philippians will further their faith (cf. 25), and it is of the essence of faith to "pour contempt" on all human pride and to glory and boast in Christ alone. (Cf. 1 Co 1:26-31 and 4:7; Gl 6:14)

1:27—2:18 ADMONITION: A LIFE WORTHY OF THE GOSPEL

1:27—2:18 If they are partners in the Gospel, their life must correspond to the Gospel; this will show itself in their unity of spirit (1:27—2:2), in humility and self-effacement (2:3-11), and in their attitude as obedient servants of God. (2:12-18)

1:27-30 Unity of Spirit

1:27-30 Unity of spirit is especially important in the face of the persecution which it is their privilege to endure for Christ. No enemy from without can destroy them; God will destroy their enemies. But they can destroy themselves by disunity.

1:27 *Worthy of,* corresponding to; the kind of life the Gospel of Christ calls for and makes possible. Cf. Eph 4:1; Cl 1:10; 1 Th 2:12; 2 Th 1:5, where the standard and dynamic of the new life is expressed in various terms, all of them in the last analysis corresponding to the *gospel* in the present passage: "calling" (Eph), "the Lord" (Cl), "God, who calls you" (1 Th), "the kingdom of God." (2 Th)

For the faith of the gospel. In their firm and unanimous endurance of opposition their own faith is being tested and purified (cf. 1 Ptr 1:6-7); they are mutually strengthening one another in the faith; and the witness of their suffering for Christ's sake (cf. 29) will propagate the faith in others, as Paul's own suffering has done (30) and continues to do. (1:7, 12, 18)

1:28 *A clear omen.* Cf. 2 Th 1:5-10.

1:29 *Granted to you.* For suffering as grace and privilege cf. Mt 5:10-12; Acts 5:41; 1 Ptr 2:20; 4:12-14.

1:30 *The same conflict,* suffering and imprisonment (cf. Acts 16:19-40; 21:27—28:31). Paul can speak credibly on suffering, for he speaks from experience.

2:1-11 Humility and Self-Effacement

2:1-11 The admonition to humility is closely related to the preceding. The strong and ancient enemies of unity and pride *(conceit)* and *selfishness;* only where they are displaced by *humility* and self-sacrifice is true unity possible. This self-effacing and self-giving humility is theirs in Christ Jesus, who went a way that was the divine way, the very opposite of the way willed by Satan (to be "like God," Gn 3:5), the Servant-Messiah's way of self-giving (Is 52:13—53:12) that took Him to the cross and thus to universal Lordship to the glory of God the Father.

2:1 In the light of 2 Co 13:14, which this verse so strongly resembles, one could paraphrase as follows: "As surely as Christ encourages you in your suffering for His sake, as surely as the love of God impels you, as surely as you participate in the creative and life-giving power of the Spirit—in short, as surely as God's love and compassion are a reality in your lives . . . ." Cf. Ro 12:1, where Paul bases his appeal on "the mercies of God."

2:2 *Complete my joy.* Paul's joy is his confident and resolute yea to the Gospel which proclaims his Lord and extends His Lordship over men; it is his glad amen to the Gospel in its effectual working (1:18-19; 2:17-18) and its effects (1:3; 2:2; 4:1, 10, and here). He rejoices, as he bids the Philippians rejoice, "in the Lord." (3:1; 4:4)

2:2, 5 *Mind* here denotes the whole set and bent of man's will. Cf. Cl 3:1-2, where "seek" and "set your minds" are used as synonyms.

2:5 *Which is yours in Christ Jesus,* that is, by virtue of the fact that Christ Jesus has made you His own (3:12), the fact that you have been incorporated in Him by Baptism and He lives in you; the will of Him who loved you and gave Himself for you has laid claim to your will. (Gl 2:20)

2:5-11 These words are poetry, both in form and content. This and the fact that a number of the expressions used do not occur elsewhere in Paul make it likely that he is quoting an early Christian hymn which both the Philippians and he knew and sang at worship. The successive stanzas adore Christ in His preexistence with God and as God (6), in His humiliation unto death (7-8), in His exaltation and final glory when at His coming the whole universe shall do obeisance before Him. (9-11)

2:6 *In the form of God.* Whatever the precise meaning of these much-discussed words, the general sense is clear from the phrase in which the thought is picked up once more, *equality with God.*

A thing to be grasped, to be used to the full, exploited for His own advantage.

2:7 *Emptied himself.* The phrase probably echoes Is 53:12, "He poured out his soul to death," and describes the Servant's complete self-giving; it is a sort of heading over the whole of 7-8.

2:8 *Death on a cross,* the criminal's death in the sinners' stead.

2:9 *Name* tells not only who He is, to distinguish Him from others, but what He is, His significance for others. The name is Lord (11) in the fullest and completest sense of that word. For the New Testament, no other title so sums up the significance of Jesus as Lord. (Cf. Ro 10:9)

2:12-18 Obedient Servants

2:12-18 The admonitions to unity (1:27-30) and to humility and self-effacement (2:1-11) lead up to and prepare for (*therefore,* 2:12) the admonition to obedient service. As the culminating statement concerning the Servant Jesus Christ in His humiliation was a statement concerning His utter obedience (2:8), so the crowning admonition calls for obedience. First, Paul stresses the quality of that obedience: the *fear* and *trembling* (12) of the servant totally devoted to his Lord and apprehensive of betraying the trust reposed in him and of frustrating the purpose of the God who works in him (13); the complete and unquestioning submission of the servant who is, like Jesus, minded to live by every word that proceeds from the mouth of God (*without grumbling or questioning,* 14; *holding fast the word of life,* 16; cf. Mt 4:4); the servant's active and energetic working in dependence on God (*work . . . for God is at work,* 12-13; *Do . . . that you may be . . . children of God,* 14-15). Second, Paul gives an inspiring picture of the effects of obedient ministry: the obedient, active servants become an extension of the Servant who is the Light of the world (15; cf. Mt 5:14; Lk 2:32; Jn 8:12; 12:35, 46; Is 42:4; 49:4), a light which the opposition and persecution of *a crooked and perverse generation* (15) cannot quench; they shall appear *in the day of Christ* as the crowning glory of the apostle through whom Christ speaks and works (16); the life of the obedient servants, their working faith, becomes a living sacrifice, a spiritual worship offered to God (17; cf. Ro 12:1); and so they come to know the whole joy of faith (cf. 1:20), Jesus' own joy in ministry fulfilled. (Jn 15:11)

2:12-13 *Work out your own salvation . . . for God is at work.* This is the classic expression of the logic of faith and grace; faith is "faith which works through love" (Gl 5:6), not in order to win the favor of God but because it is rich in the possession of His favor and strong by virtue of His grace continually bestowed. (Cf. 3:12; Mt 4:17; 1 Co 15:10; 1 Th 4:7; Cl 1:29; Heb 13:20-21)

2:17 *Libation upon the sacrificial offering.* For the *libation* of wine which accompanied the daily burnt offering cf. Ex 29:38-46; Nm 28:1-10; Jl 1:9. For the imagery of sacrifice applied to the apostolic ministry cf. Ro 15:16.

2:19—3:1 PAUL'S ACTIONS ON THE PHILIPPIANS' BEHALF

2:19—3:1 Paul is sending Timothy, the most selfless and dependable of his co-workers, to the Philippians. He will cheer Paul by a fresh and firsthand report of them and will be genuinely concerned for their welfare. And Paul himself hopes to come to them shortly (2:19-24). He is sending the Philippians' emissary, Epaphroditus, back to Philippi, with thanks to God for sparing his life (which he has risked in serving Paul), with warm commendation of the work which he has done, and with the request that his church receive him and honor him in the Lord (2:25-30). Paul concludes his admonitions with a final call to joy in the Lord. (3:1)

2:19 *In the Lord Jesus.* Paul's will and work are wholly dominated by the Lord whom he serves; he can therefore hope and plan only in communion with Him. (Cf. 24; 1 Co 16:7)

Timothy. See the Introduction to First Timothy, and for Timothy's mission cf. 1 Co 4:17; 1 Th 3:1-2.

2:23 *How it will go with me,* that is, in the trial. (Cf. 1:19-26)

2:25 *Epaphroditus.* Paul calls him *fellow soldier* because he has shared hardship and danger with him. (Cf. 4:8)

3:1 *To write the same thing,* etc. It is difficult to determine whether these words refer to the repeated command to rejoice which precedes them or to the warning which follows. The words *is safe for you* seem to go more naturally with the warning.

3:2—4:1 CHRISTIAN "PERFECTION": WARNING AND INSTRUCTION

3:2—4:1 Paul warns against two perversions of the Gospel, two false ideas of Christian "perfection" (3:12), that of legalistic Judaizers (3:2-11) and that of libertine *enemies of the cross of Christ* (3:17-21), who "pervert the grace of our God into licentiousness" (Jude 4). Between the two warnings he portrays himself, the man in Christ, as the true example of Christian perfection or maturity. (3:15)

3:2-11 Warning Against Judaizers

3:2-11 With a vehemence which is in startling contrast to the cheerful serenity of the rest of the letter, Paul warns against his old and persistent enemies, the Judaizers, who had once created such havoc in the churches of Galatia (see the Introduction to Galatians) and elsewhere and were, apparently, still at work. He turns against them every boast and every claim with which they bolstered their position. They who called the uncircumcised Gentiles unclean *dogs* are themselves unclean scavenger "dogs"; they who insist on works as the way to salvation are themselves *evil-workers,* disturbing the faith and peace of the church. The circumcision of which they boast as the token of the covenant Paul bitterly terms a meaningless mutilation of the flesh; what circumcision once signified, namely, membership in the people of God, is no longer to be found in circumcision but in Christ (3:3). Paul uses himself, the Israelite and former Pharisee, as an example of how all the old Israelite prerogatives and privileges have become meaningless in the presence of Christ and the righteousness which man can find only in Him. Paul here (3:9) gives his sharpest and most eloquent definition of the *righteousness from God,* a dominant motif in his Letter to the Romans.

3:2 *Mutilate the flesh.* This gains added point if it is remembered that such mutilation actually excluded a man from "the assembly of the Lord." (Dt 23:1)

3:3, 4 *Flesh* here signifies what a man "naturally" is by virtue of his descent, birth, and upbringing—as opposed to what God's mighty grace makes possible, gaining and knowing Christ, being found in Christ, having righteousness through Him, sharing His resurrection life (8-11). If Paul were to boast of being a descendant of Benjamin, he would be boasting in the flesh; but he glories in Christ.

3:3 *The true circumcision.* For the church as the true covenant people of God cf. Ro 2:29; 4:16, 23; Gl 3:7; 4:28; 6:16.

Worship God in spirit. Perhaps better with RSV note *e, worship by the Spirit of God.* (Cf. Jn 4:24)

3:5 *A Hebrew born of Hebrews.* Paul's family, though resident in the Greek city Tarsus (Acts 21:39) and distinguished by Roman citizenship (Acts 22:28), remained strictly faithful to the ancient ways of their ancestral religion and retained the Hebrew (Aramaic) language which many Jews living in the Dispersion soon forgot.

3:6 *Blameless.* By the standards that he then applied, which were those of his fellow Jews (cf. Gl 1:14). For Paul's integrity as Jew and Pharisee cf. 2 Ti 1:3.

3:7 *Counted as loss,* because they had led him to oppose Christ in His body, the church.

3:8 *Knowing Christ.* As the sequel shows, this knowing is personal encounter and fellowship with Christ, having Him as Lord of one's life, gaining Him, being found in Him (9), believing in Him, etc. Knowing Christ, or God, and being known by Him come to the same thing. (Cf. 1 Co 8:2-3; 13:12; Gl 4:9)

3:9 *Righteousness of my own . . . righteousness from God.* For the contrast cf. Ro 10:3. For righteousness as God's gift, the whole of the salvation bestowed by Him, cf. Mt 5:6; 6:33; Ro 1:17; 3:21-31; 1 Co 1:30; 2 Co 3:9; 5:21.

3:10-11 For suffering and dying with Christ as

the way and transition to life with Him cf. Ro 8:17; 2 Co 4:10-17; 13:4; 2 Ti 2:11-12; and Jesus' word to His disciples, Mt 16:25.

3:12-16 True Christian Perfection

3:12-16 In a passage which provides the link between his warning against the Judaizers and his warning against the "enemies of the cross of Christ" (3:17-21), both of them people who had arrived and talked of their "perfection," Paul gives a remarkable description of the Christian life as a constant and never-finished straining forward toward that which God's grace holds out to the believer in Christ: *I press on to make it my own, because Christ Jesus has made me his own* (3:12). Paul sees Christian perfection and Christian maturity in just this ever imperfect and ever renewed appropriation of the gift of God in Christ.

3:14 The picture is that of a runner competing for a prize, all tensed and concentrated energy. God's call ushers man "into the fellowship of His Son, Jesus Christ" (1 Co 1:9) a fellowship which grows deeper as it is appropriated and lived and is perfected in the glory of the world to come (cf. 3:21); toward this the whole Christian life moves, toward the full realization of the "hope that belongs to your call." (Eph 4:4)

3:15-16 Revelation is given in increasing measure as it is gratefully received and used, according to Jesus' word, "To him who has will more be given, and he will have abundance." (Mt 13:12)

3:17—4:1 Warning Against the Enemies of the Cross

3:17—4:1 Since Paul describes this group only enough to condemn them, we cannot be absolutely sure of their identity. He had spoken of them to the Philippians often (3:18), and they could readily identify them. Paul is probably pointing to men of the kind whom he had had to deal with at Corinth (see Introduction to Letters to the Corinthians)—the proud, secular, superspiritual men of knowledge who said, "We belong to Christ," and yet emptied the cross of its content, who on the basis of their higher "knowledge" came to terms with sin and made the church at home in the world by conforming it to the world. Paul had put an end to their influence at Corinth, but they apparently continued their activities elsewhere, and not without success. Paul reminds the Philippians (who as Roman "colonists" had their citizenship in the distant and splendid city of Rome) where their true home lies and where their heart should be: *Our commonwealth is in heaven, and from it we await a Savior, the Lord Jesus Christ* (3:20). They cannot boast in the flesh, the things of this world, like the Judaizers, or make this world their real home, like the enemies of the cross. In the pure hope of the Gospel they *stand firm ... in the Lord* (4:1), who is Lord of the future and better world.

3:17 *Imitating me.* For the apostle as object of imitation (which involves a recognition of his authority as emissary and spokesman of Christ) cf. 1 Co 4:16; 11:1; Gl 4:12; 1 Th 1:6; 2 Th 3:7, 9. In Eph 5:1 God Himself is the object of imitation.

3:18 *Enemies of the cross.* A man becomes an enemy of the cross when he ignores God's fearful and costly judgment on human sin in the death of His Son. The cross makes impossible any compromise with sin.

3:19 *Their god is the belly.* They live for the satisfaction of their physical appetites and passions. (Cf. Ro 16:18)

They glory in their shame. They glory in their "freedom," which is actual degrading licentiousness, as in the mark of their superior spirituality. (Cf. 1 Co 5:2, 6; 6:12-13; Jude 4, 8, 10, 13, 16, 18, 19)

3:21 *Change our lowly body.* Cf. Ro 8:23; 1 Co 15:43, 49, 53. Man is redeemed, all of him as he came from the Creator's hand.

4:1 *My ... crown.* When they appear "pure and blameless" before Christ at His coming (1:10), that will be the apostle's crowning glory. (2:16; cf. 1 Th 2:19)

4:2-9 THE WHOLE AND HEALTHY LIFE OF PEACE

4:2-9 The hope for the return of the Lord and the glory of the world to come (3:20-21) does not make the Christian indifferent toward this life and its problems and duties. Rather, the return of the Lord gives life now, with its problems and decisions, its full significance; the light of His coming falls upon the present and fills it, for all its dangers and difficulties, with joy and peace. *Euodia* and *Syntyche,* who have fallen out, are to settle their differences *in the Lord,* whom they have proclaimed together, whose coming will judge all violators of His peace; one whom Paul addresses as *yokefellow* is to help them find their way back to one another—their quarrel is not their individual concern only but concerns the whole church, all *whose names are* inscribed in God's *book of life* (2-3). The whole and undivided church is to *rejoice in the Lord,* whose coming is *at hand,* their high hope is to give them a blithe and princely generosity (*forbearance,* 5) toward all men. Their grateful prayer to God is to be the cure for all anxiety and care. Thus the *peace of God* will guard (*keep,* 7) their *hears* and *minds* more surely and securely than the Roman garrisons keep the Roman peace at Philippi (4-7). They cannot treat this poor present world with indifference or contempt; whatever in it is *just, pure, lovely, gracious,* etc., is deserving of their sympathetic thought. These things cannot be their ultimate norm and standard; they cannot set their minds on earthly things (3:19) in this sense. But the apostolic Gospel which Paul has proclaimed and lived among them, their true and only norm for action (*do,* 9), will equip them for a positive and discerning appreciation of these things, e.g., the Roman sense for the beneficence of law and the veteran's loyalty to his state. And God who is God of peace and not of confusion (1 Co

14:33) will *be with* them as they pursue this course. (8-9)

4:2, 3 *Euodia, Syntyche,* and *Clement* are otherwise unknown. The *true yokefellow* is evidently an especially trusted co-worker of Paul's at Philippi.

4:3 *The book of life* as a symbol of God's elective love (those who names are in it are His elect, objects of His love, enrolled among the citizens of the city of God) is found frequently in both Testaments. (Cf. Ex 32:32-33; Ps 69:28; 138:16; Is 4:3; Dn 12:1; Ml 3:16; Lk 10:20; Heb 12:23; Rv 3:5; 13:8; 17:8; 20:12, 15)

4:5 *Forbearance.* The Greek word is difficult to reproduce in English; it signifies the gracious condescension of a superior, one so sure of his strength and greatness that he is above the competitive scramble that makes men selfish and cruel; such the Christians are as heirs of the world to come, and as such they are to act to all sorts and conditions of men.

4:7 *Passes all understanding.* Surpasses all attempts of human thought and devising to obtain security. *Peace* in Biblical language is often more than cessation of hostilities; it expresses that wholeness which the grace of God creates when it sets all right, the divinely normal order of things. Cf. Paul's usual greeting of "grace and peace" and especially Ro 5:1 ff. in which Paul expands on the idea of "peace with God." *Peace* is seen as similarly active and powerful in Cl 3:15.

4:10-20 THANKS FOR THE PHILIPPIANS' GIFT

4:10-20 Paul expresses his joy at this fresh token of their concern for him; it has supplied, not so much his physical need (Christ has given him strength to rise above that) as his need of their love—they have *shared* his *trouble* (10-14). He appreciates their gift as one more example of their partnership in the Gospel (cf. 1:5, 7) and as a *fragrant offering, a sacrifice acceptable and pleasing to God,* whom they serve in serving him who is apostle by the will of God (cf. Cl 1:1) and servant of His Son (Ph 1:1). He promises them that His God, the rich and generous Rewarder of all who seek Him with no thought of reward, will *supply* their *every need;* their giving will not make them poor but rich. To Him belongs all glory. (15-20)

4:11 *Content,* that is, self-sufficient; only, Paul's sufficiency is from his Lord (13), not from himself.

4:15 *The beginning of the gospel,* when it was first preached among you and proceeded southward from your home, *Macedonia* (Cf. Acts 16:11—17:15)

Partnership with me in giving and receiving. Paul contributed the Word; they contributed to his support. Paul usually refused to take support from churches which he founded (2 Co 11:7; 12:13; 1 Th 2:5-9), although he knew himself to be entitled to it (1 Co 9:7). His motive was the desire to avoid all appearance of self-seeking (1 Th 2:5; 2 Co 12:17-18), to put no "obstacle in the way of the gospel of Christ" (1 Co 9:12). In the case of the Philippians he made an exception, they supported Paul so regularly (cf. v. 16; 2 Co 11:8-9) that Paul can call their relationship a business partnership, using the language of commerce to describe it. The phrase cited above was technical for "in settlement of a mutual account"; in v. 17 *to your credit* could be rendered "credited to your account," and in v. 18 *I have received full payment* is the ancient formula for having "received in full."

4:18 *A fragrant offering.* Cf. Ex 29:18; Lv 1:9; 2:2; 3:5, etc.

4:21-23 CONCLUSION

4:21-23 Paul sends greetings, as at the beginning (1:1) to *every saint,* all members of the church at Philippi, from *the brethren who are with him* (probably his own associates), and from *all the saints* (probably members of the church at Rome) and concludes with the benediction or *grace.*

4:22 *Those of Caesar's hosuehold,* slaves or freedmen of the imperial house, servants at the emperor's court rather than members of his family. Many of them occupied positions of some importance both in Rome and in the provinces of the empire.

COLOSSIANS

INTRODUCTION

Among those who came to Paul and were welcomed by him during his Roman imprisonment was Epaphras. He came from Colossae, a city in Asia Minor some 125 miles east of Ephesus. He brought Paul news of the Gentile church that had been founded there, probably by Epaphras himself (Cl 1:5-8), working under the direction of Paul or at least with Paul's full approval (Cl 1:7). He had good news to bring. He could speak warmly of the Colossian's faith and of their love; the Gospel had grown and borne fruit in Colossae as everywhere (Cl 1:6). But what had brought Epaphras to Rome was his anxiety for the church at Colossae, not his pride in it. The Christians of Colossae and of neighboring Laodicea were still holding to the Gospel which they had received; but that pure loyalty was being threatened and undermined. The church was threatened by a new teaching that was in many ways strikingly similar to the Gospel Epaphras had preached there. Both the new teaching and the Gospel originally preached in Colossae proclaimed a non-national universal religion. Both recognized the great gulf that exists between God and natural man. And both proffered a redemption that would bridge the gulf. But the new teaching was in the last analysis an utter distortion of the Gospel Epaphras had proclaimed. He sensed the difference but could not, perhaps, analyze and define it well enough to be able to oppose it effectively. He therefore appealed to Paul, wise in the ways of Greek and Jew alike, keen in insight, and ready to do battle for the truth. Would Paul help him?

It is difficult to get a clear and consistent picture of the heresy which threatened Colossae, for Paul in his Letter to the Colossians does not so much oppose it argumentatively as overwhelm it by confronting it with the whole riches of the true Gospel of Christ. It seems to have been a religion of self-redemption of the "gnostic" type. Built on a Jewish or Jewish-Christian basis, it was a fusion of Greek and Oriental ideas and combined at least three elements. One of these elements was theosophic, that is, the new teaching claimed to have and to impart an occult, profound knowledge derived from God; Paul speaks contemptuously of a "tradition" and a "philosophy" (Cl 2:8). Another element was ritualistic; stress was laid on circumcision (Cl 2:11); questions of food and drink, festivals, new moons, and sabbaths were deemed important (Cl 2:16). A third element was ascetic; Paul speaks of prescriptions of abstinence ("Do not handle, Do not taste, Do not touch," Cl 2:21) and of a "rigor of devotion," of "self-abasement," and of "severity to the body" (Cl 2:23). We are left to conjecture how these elements were combined into a system.

Paul's references to the "worship of angels" (Cl 2:18) and to "elemental spirits of the universe" (2:8, 20) indicate what was the heart of the danger in this teaching. Other powers besides the Christ were being proclaimed and invoked as mediators between God and man; the ritual and ascetic aspects of this religion probably represent means of placating or of obtaining contact and communion with these powers. What Epaphras, with a sound Christian instinct, surely sensed and what Paul clearly saw was this: *the new teaching called into question and obscured the unique greatness of the Christ and the complete sufficiency of His atonement.* What made this heresy all the more dangerous was the fact that it claimed not to supplant but to supplement the Gospel which the Colossians had received. The new teaching would, so the new teachers claimed, carry the Colossian

Christians beyond their rudimentary Christianity to fullness and perfection; hence Paul's repeated emphasis on the fact that the Colossians are complete and full in the Gospel which they have received, that in the Christ whom they know they can find all the treasures of divine wisdom. (2:2, 3, 9, 10; cf. 1:28)

Value of the Letter

"As for you," Joseph told his brothers, "you meant evil against me; but God meant it for good" (Gn 50:20). The new movement at Colossae meant evil, for it was an attack, all the more vicious because it was not a frontal attack, on the fact that dominates the whole New Testament, the sole Lordship of the Lord Jesus Christ. But God meant it for good; He gave us in Paul's Letter to the Colossians a proclamation of the Lord Jesus Christ in unparalleled fullness and depth. The church that in its creed intones, "God of God, Light of Light, very God of very God, begotten not made, being of one substance with the Father," is indebted not least to this letter.

The Letter to the Colossians is also a striking fulfillment of the promise of Jesus to His disciples, "Every scribe who has been trained for the kingdom of heaven is like a householder who brings out of his treasure what is new and what is old" (Mt 13:52). The apostles of Jesus are not merely disciples of a rabbi, whose sacred duty it is to pass on their master's words unchanged. They are witnesses to Him who has all authority in heaven and on earth, and they have the Spirit as His gift, the Spirit who leads them into all truth and thus glorifies the Christ. At the time of the church's need the Spirit opened up to Paul dimensions of the glory of the Christ which the new people of God had not apprehended so fully before; this strengthened their loyalty to the Gospel.

1:1-14 INTRODUCTION: SALUTATION, THANKSGIVING, AND PRAYER

1:1-14 Paul gives *thanks* for the Colossians' *faith* and *love,* a love inspired and sustained by the *hope laid up for you in heaven.* He assures them that the *gospel* which has produced this in them, which they have heard from *Epaphras,* is the true, universal, powerful, and productive Gospel preached *in the whole world,* proclaiming and conveying the *grace of God in truth* (the Gospel which needs no supplementation by "philosophy" and "human tradition," cf. 2:6-8).

Paul *prays* that they may grow in the *knowledge* of this Gospel, a knowledge of God's gracious *will* (not of empty speculations) which produces a life rich *in every good work, increasing* as it is employed in the service of the *Lord,* the *beloved Son* of God, King of a *kingdom* whose subjects *have redemption, the forgiveness of sins,* now and the hope of an *inheritance* in the bright future world of God *(in light,* 12). Paul prays that God the Father, who has given them their present blessing and their glorious future, may strengthen them to endure with *patience* the pressure of the present and that the lives of the Colossians, lived in the *power* bestowed by Him, may be an unbroken song of thanksgiving to Him.

1:1 For *Timothy* as cosender (hardly coauthor) of letters to churches cf. the salutations of 2 Co, Ph, 1 and 2 Th, Phmn.

1:2 *Saints,* Christians, those whom God has by His call (cf. Ro 1:7; 1 Co 1:2) consecrated for Himself and His purposes.

1:7 *Epaphras.* See the Introduction.

1:9 *Spiritual,* produced by the Holy Spirit.

1:13 Cf. Paul's words to King Agrippa, Acts 26:18.

1:15—2:23 THE SUFFICIENCY OF CHRIST AND THE GOSPEL

1:15-23 The Full Glory of Christ, the Son of God

1:15-23 The mention of God's beloved Son, who is God's redemption and forgiveness in person (1:13-14), leads over to a mighty hymn in praise of Christ in His fully glory as Creator and Redeemer. Paul holds before the eyes of the church all that they have in Him whom Epaphras (1:7) proclaimed to them: He is God's *image,* the perfect manifestation of the *invisible God; the first-born of all creation,* the Mediator of creation, antecedent to and Lord over all created beings, including all angelic powers *(thrones, dominions, principalities, authorities).* As He is Lord of creation, He is also *head* of *the church;* as He is *the first-born of all creation,* He is also *the first-born from the dead,* the Lord in whom all mankind may find life everlasting. *In him all the fulness* of the God who willed man's redemption graciously dwelt; in obedience to that will He went into the depths of a criminal's violent death *(blood of his cross)* to restore man and all man's fallen world to God. He is *in everything . . . pre-eminent;* in His kingdom (1:13) they are secure—no powers of darkness have power to harm them there.

1:15 *Image of the invisible God.* Cf. 2 Co 4:4; Heb 1:3. In Him the invisible God has made Himself known, not only in the Word but in a Person (cf. Heb 1:1-2); He has condescended to men in audible, visible, palpable form (1 Jn 1:1), in the flesh common to all men (Jn 1:14). In the Son men may behold Him who sent Him, the Father. (Jn 12:45; 14:9)

Firstborn of all creation. As v. 16 indicates, this does not put Christ among God's creatures, but asserts His superiority and primacy over them.

1:16 *Created.* For Jesus Christ as Mediator of creation cf. 1 Co 8:6; Jn 1:3; Heb 1:2; Rv 3:14.

Thrones, dominions, etc. Names common to Judaism and the New Testament of angelic or demonic powers that are thought of as in some sense controlling the universe. The false teachers apparently assigned to them power independent of Christ (2:8) and held them to be objects of worship (2:18). Paul, in proclaiming Christ as their Creator, roundly asserts His Lordship over them and so already indicates the irrelevance and wrongness of any angel worship. For the names cf. Ro 8:38; 1 Co 15:24; Eph 1:21; 3:10; Cl 2:10, 15.

Created . . . for him, to serve His gracious purpose of establishing God's reign, challenged by man's sin. Our Lord's miracles document His sovereign control over all creation during His sojourn on earth. As exalted Lord He reigns over all creation (Mt 28:18; Ro 8:39; Rv 5:13), will bring all creation home to God (Ro 8:19-22), and shall receive the homage of universal creation. (Ph 2:10-11)

1:17 *All things hold together.* Cf. Eph 1:22; Heb 1:3.

1:18 *Head of the body, the church.* Cf. Eph 1:22-23 and Cl 2:19. The idea of intimate and vital connection between Christ and His people, the church, is obvious; not so obvious perhaps is the thought that the head is a symbol of power and lordship (cf. 1 Co 11:3, Eph 5:23), the head is even thought of as the source of life and growth. (Eph 4:16; Cl 2:19)

First-born from the dead. Christ's resurrection is THE resurrection, the basis and the beginning of the resurrection of all who are His. Cf. especially 1 Co 15:20-23. Christians have a "living hope" of eternal life "through the resurrection of Jesus Christ from the dead." (1 Ptr 1:3; cf. 1 Co 6:14; 1 Th 4:14)

1:19 *The fulness of God.* The whole grace *(was pleased)* and power of God was at work in Him; the triumph over death (18) is total, the reconciliation (20) complete. There is no need to supplement it in any way: "In him the whole fulness of deity dwells bodily, and you have come to fulness of life in him." (2:9)

1:21-23 This Christ in all His glory is the Colossians' Christ; He is their Reconciler; He will *present* them *holy and blameless* in the judgment, justified. They need not seek Him in any new and mystical ways, for He has come into the *flesh* in real humanity and found them. They need only *continue in the faith* and remain steadfast in the *hope of the gospel,* the old known Gospel, the universal Gospel for all the world proclaimed by Paul who is "apostle of Jesus Christ by the will of God." (1:1)

1:21 *Estranged and hostile.* Cf. Eph 2:12; 4:18; Ro 5:6-10.

1:23 *Gospel . . . preached to every creature,* to the whole world. Cf. 1:6 and Mk 16:15. Paul probably uses *creature* here to indicate that the Gospel preached to man is good news both for man and for man's world. (Cf. v. 20; Ro 8:19-21)

1:24—2:5 The Full Glory of the Gospel

1:24—2:5 The Colossians have this Christ as their Reconciler and Justifier in the Gospel and in it alone (cf. 1:23). The Gospel is therefore infinitely precious; Paul *rejoices* to *suffer* in its behalf as he *toils* with Christ-inspired *energy* to proclaim it. The Gospel is universal in its scope and power, proclaiming the revealed secret of God (*mystery,* 27) far beyond the limits of His ancient people, bestowing the riches of the glory of His grace on the *Gentiles;* it is present and powerful for *every man,* to make *every man mature in Christ.* God did not intend it for a coterie, and no coterie can claim it as its own. The Gospel is complete and sufficient, the sure ground of *hope* (1:27; cf. 1:23), *faith,* and *love* and the source of all *understanding* and *knowledge.* Any pretense of a higher knowledge, beyond the Christ proclaimed in the Gospel, is delusion and deceit, for in Christ *all the treasures of wisdom and knowledge* are to be found. In the power of this Gospel the church can be (what the Colossians now are) an ordered and disciplined army of God.

1:24 *I rejoice in my sufferings,* etc. The difficulty of this passage lies particularly in the phrase *complete what is lacking in Christ's afflictions.* That Christ's redemptive suffering and death need no supplementing is clear from 1:20-21 and 2:9-15 and the whole tenor of the letter, which opposes the idea that the work of Christ needs any supplementation by any human effort ("philosophy," ritual performance, or ascetic rigors). It is clear, moreover, that Paul looks upon his sufferings as suffering in union with Christ, as is all Christian suffering (Ro 8:17), a participation in the afflictions of Him who is persecuted when His church is persecuted (Acts 9:4), that this suffering of his is essential to his "divine office" as proclaimer of Christ (Acts 9:16), is gladly accepted as such (cf. Ph 2:17), and redounds to the benefit of the church (cf. 2 Co 1:5-7; 4:10-12; Eph 3:13). One had, perhaps, best leave open the question whether *what is lacking* refers to the destined afflictions of Christ in His church generally (Mt 24:6; Rv 6:11), a "quota" of suffering to be filled by those who "through many tribulations . . . must enter the kingdom of God" (Acts 14:22), or whether Paul rejoices, more specifically, in the thought that he by his suffering reduces the church's share in the destined tribulations. The essential thought, on either interpretation, remains that suffering for the Gospel's sake is a positive, creative contribution to the life of the church.

1:25 *Divine office.* To speak the *word of God,* to reveal God's mystery—this is God's own work (Dn 2:27-28); man can do so only if God appoints and empowers him (1:1; 1:29). For the apostolic Word as Word of God or of Christ cf. 1 Th 2:13; Ro 15:18; 2 Co 13:3.

1:26-27 *The mystery.* Cf. 2:2; 4:3. From its first occurrence in the Bible onward (Dn 2:28), the word *mystery* has two connotations. First, the *mystery* is a mystery, or secret, because only God can reveal it; but He does reveal it—it is His "open secret" which He wills ultimately to share with all mankind. In the New Testament it is constantly associated, as here in Colossians (1:27; 4:3-4), with verbs like "make known" or "reveal" (cf., e.g., Mt 13:11; Mk 4:11; Ro 16:25-26; Eph 3:3-5). Second, the content of the *mystery* is God's hidden governing of all history toward the establishment of His reign (Dn 2:31-45). This culminates in the sending of His Son, the offense of His cross, and the triumph of His resurrection (Mt 13:11, 16-17; Ro 16:25-26; 1 Co 2:1-2 [RSV note *c*], 7; Eph 1:7-9; 3:3-4, 9; 6:19- 1 Ti 3:16): it will be "fulfilled"; carried to its triumphant conclusion, when God's seventh and last trumpet sounds (Rv 10:7) and "the kingdom of the world has become the kingdom of our Lord and of his Christ." (Rv 11:15)

1:26 *Hidden from ages and generations,* in Israel, the nation entrusted with the oracles of God (Ro 3:2), into whose life, history, and worship the coming Christ cast shadows before Him to prefigure and announce His coming. (2:17)

1:28 *Every man . . . every man . . . every man.* The mystery, the Gospel, the Christ are there for all men, Gentile or Jew. Perhaps Paul is also aiming at the tendency of the errorists to create an exclusive clique within the church.

2:2 *Understanding . . . knowledge.* Cf. 1:9.

2:3 *Are hid.* The *treasures of wisdom* are hidden in the Crucified, overlaid by the offense and foolishness of the cross (1 Co 1:23), but revealed to faith by the Spirit. (1 Co 2:6-13)

2:5 *Good order . . . firmness.* The words have military associations.

2:6-23 The Refutation of the Colossian Heresy

2:6-7 Paul has one weapon of offense: Christ. In the opening admonition (6-7) he bids the Colossians base their whole existence on Him. He is the soil in which they have struck root, from which they continue to draw nourishment and strength. He is the foundation on which the growing structure of their life rests and rises. In Him they have the firmness of faith which Paul rejoiced to behold (*established,* 7; cf. 5), in Him, the Christ whom they know, for whom they continually give thanks to the Father. (1:12)

2:6 *Received Christ Jesus.* The proper object of *received* is the Gospel or "The word of God" (cf. 1 Co 15:1, 3; Gl 1:9, 12; 1 Th 2:13; cf. 4:1 and 2 Th 3:6); but the Gospel is a power (Ro 1:16) which bestows what it proclaims and so to receive the Gospel is to receive Christ Jesus.

Live in him. The word here translated "live" (literally "walk") is used by Paul, in common with the Old Testament and Judaism, with a great variety of modifiers to designate the whole bent and tenor of man's life. Only here does he use the phrase *in him* with it, another indication of the Christ-centeredness of this letter.

2:8-15 Christ is the norm of all teaching (*according to Christ,* 8; cf. 7, "as you were taught"), for in Him God has given them all that is His to give: the *whole fulness of deity* incarnate for us men and for our salvation, *fulness of life* under Him who is Lord over all powers, a life which no *elemental spirits of the universe,* no *rule* or *authority* dare challenge or attack, life as members of the new people of God (*circumcision of Christ,* 11). It is the life of the risen Christ that they share by virtue of their baptism, just as they shared thereby His death. With Christ God has *made* them *alive,* as forgiven men, beyond the reach of their dead past, beyond the accusation of the unfulfilled Law that stood against them as their damning certificate of indebtedness, for in the *cross* God *canceled* that *bond* and published its cancellation. Now that their gulit is gone, the *principalities and powers* have no hold on them; they participate in Christ's *triumph* over them. The Gospel is Christ all the way (*in Him,* four times; *with Him,* twice; circumcision *of Christ*). Any pretentiously speculative theology *(philosophy)* which departs from Him as the all-controlling norm by substituting *human tradition* for divine revelation is *empty deceit,* a pseudo-gospel without content. It cannot lead them to life and freedom; it can only entrap and exploit them *(makes a prey of you).*

2:8 *Philosophy* is used more broadly than in current usage to include what we should call theosophy or (loosely) theology, any comprehensive view of God, man, and the world.

Elemental spirits of the universe, supernatural powers (sometimes identified in ancient thought with the stars) thought of as controlling the universe. But the idea of *spirits* is not necessarily associated with the word in question, and the phrase could be translated "principles of this world"; it would then indicate the earthbound, human character of this theology controlled by crude this-worldly ideas.

2:9-10 *Whole fulness of deity dwells bodily,* in a form in which man can comprehend, know, and love, a form communicable to man so that he receives *fulness of life.*

2:11-12 *Circumcision* was once the prerequisite and mark of membership in the ancient people of God (Gn 17:9-14), the token and seal of God's covenant with Abraham (Ro 4:11). It admitted a man to the blessings of the covenant and committed him to the claims of the covenant (Dt 10:16; Jer 4:4; cf. Dt 30:6; Ro 2:25). Circumcision has been surpassed and superseded by the *circumcision of Christ,* by *baptism,*

God's own act of *putting off* man's *body of the flesh,* that is, his old sinful nature (Cf. Ro 6:6), by *burying and raising* him with Christ, the inclusive Representative of mankind. A return to circumcision now is both meaningless and impious, for it ignores this final and triumphant act of God.

2:16-19 Christ is the only and all-controlling norm of all worship. The foods and festivals of Israel foreshadowed Him and have significance only in that foreshadowing; they cannot now constitute the *substance* of worship—only Christ can do that, for He is the fulfillment of all the promises of God: the clean food for the new Israel, Bread and Water of life (Jn 6:35-51; 7:37), their sabbath rest (Heb 4:9), their Passover (1 Co 5:7-8). He is the Head from whom His body derives its functioning unity and godly growth. The only *self-abasement* that has any validity is self-abasement before Him; any *worship of angels* that obscures Him is human pride in religious disguise. Whoever does not hold fast to Him as *Head* has lost the standard of *judgment* and the right to judge any pious manifestation of true faith; he cannot set himself up as umpire and *disqualify* those who run the course which Christ has laid out for them. (Cf. 1 Co 9:24-27; Ph 3:12-16)

2:18 *Angels,* perhaps to be identified with the "elemental spirits" of 2:8 and 20.

Sensuous mind. Literally "mind of the flesh."

2:20-23 Christ is the only norm for the Christian's relationship to the *world* of creaturely things, things that men *handle, taste,* and *touch. With Christ* the Christian has died to that world and has been raised into the world of God (cf. 3:1); that world can never again be a threat to him or a norm for his conduct, the object of fearfully detailed *regulations* which govern his relationship to them as to powers (*elemental spirits,* 20) that have a decisive influence on him. Such ascetic regulations, *human precepts and doctrines,* are, for all their appearance of wise and strenuous piety (23), a manifestation of the *flesh,* that is, of self-seeking, self-assertive man seeking to do for himself what God in Christ has done for him.

2:22 *Things which all perish as they are used.* This and the phrase *human precepts* indicate that Paul is thinking of the words of Jesus, Mt 15:9, 17.

2:23 The reading of RSV note *e (serving only to indulge the flesh)* seems perferable, since Paul is throughout this section (8-23) stressing the "fleshly" (humanly proud and self-assertive) character of the superior piety of the Colossian errorists ("empty deceit . . . human tradition," 8; "puffed up . . . by his sensuous mind," 18; "human precepts and doctrines," 22).

3:1—4:6 LIFE IN THE ALL-SUFFICIENT CHRIST

3:1—4:6 As Christ is the whole Gsopel and the whole refutation of all distortions of the Gospel (1:15—2:23), so He is the whole basis and power of the new life of those who believe in Him. His name *(Christ, Lord, Lord Jesus, Lord Christ)* occurs 15 times in the 31 verses of this section.

3:1-17 Seek the Things That Are Above, Where Christ Is

3:1-17 The reality of the Christian life is to be seen in Christ; nothing is more real than the fact that Christians have died with Him, have been raised with Him, and share the glory of His life in God. But that glory is as yet a hidden glory; until the Christ *who is* their *life appears,* its glory is a reality to be realized and manifested in a life whose bent and intent (*seek,* 1; *set your minds,* 2) is a militant no to *what is earthly,* to the old world to which the Christian has died; a no to the old world of erotic self-assertion (5) and economic self-assertion (*covetousness,* 5), to the old world of heroic self-assertion (8), the old world of devious self-assertion, the lie (9), the old world in which ethnic, religious, cultural, and social divisions fragment mankind (11). The Christian has *died* to all that (3) in Christ; and this death is realized in his putting *to death* of all that. His resurrection to glory is realized in his enacted yea to God's recreating act (10); his continual putting on (12) of the garment in which God's elective love (12) has clothed him. He speaks his yea to God's love in a life of compassionate, meek, forgiving love (12-14), a life in which the *peace of Christ* (the soundness and health which His reconciliation has produced) controls all relationships (15), where His potent *word* is the indwelling power that produces salutary and grateful song (16), where *everything* is done *in the name of the Lord Jesus*—what the incarnate Lord is, has done, and signifies for man is the source and power of it all. (17)

3:1 *Raised with Christ.* Cf. 2:13. For the thought and particularly the significant combination of the indicative (what God has done) and the imperative (what the believer now should and can do by the grace of God) cf. Ro 6:1-14 and the notes there. Both here and in Eph 2:6 Paul goes one step beyond what he has said in Ro 6 by speaking of the Christian's resurrection as already accomplished (cf. the future tense in Ro 6:8). But Paul can speak in Ro 8:30 of the future glorification of the believer as an accomplished fact ("glorified"), which comes to the same thing.

Seated at the right hand of God, in power and majesty coequal. (Cf. Ps 110:1)

3:4 *Appear with him in glory.* Cf. Ph 3:20-21; 2 Th 1:10.

3:5 *Put to death.* Cf. Ro 6:11.

3:10 *New nature . . . renewed in knowledge after the image,* etc. For the new creation cf. 2 Co 5:17; Gl 6:15; Eph 2:10, 15; 4:24. *In knowledge*—it was the lure of "knowledge" that led man down the path of rebellion against the God who had created him in His image (Gn 3:5-6). That path led him to alienation from God, enmity toward God (1:21), darkened understanding, and a futile mind (Eph 4:17-18). In Christ, the obedient Man, the fearful rebellion of man is ended and its results are healed; man can again know God and be known by Him (1 Co 8:2-3; Gl 4:9); man can find in Christ "all the treasures of wisdom and knowledge." (2:3)

3:11 *Scythians,* natives of the region which is now southern Russia, were reputed in antiquity to be the most *barbarian* of the barbarians.

3:13 *As the Lord has forgiven.* Cf. Jesus' answer to Peter's question on forgiveness, Mt 18:21-35.

3:16 *Word of Christ . . . teach . . . admonish . . . wisdom.* This corresponds exactly to what Paul has described as his own task in 1:28. The apostolic church is to be an "imitator" of the apostle. (Cf. 1 Co 4:16; 11:1; Gl 4:12; Ph 3:17; 1 Th 1:6; 2 Th 3:7, 9)

3:18—4:1 Christ the Lord of the Household

3:18—4:1 The hidden glory of the new life manifests itself in the ordinary household relationships of wife and husband, children and parents, slaves and masters. The glory is hidden; things remain as they were, the old order of subordination and obedience lives on. And yet all is new, for Christ has become Lord over both the obedient and the obeyed.

3:22 *Slaves* were considered a part of the household. Cf. the notes on Paul's Letter to Philemon for the New Testament attitude toward slavery.

4:1 *Masters.* The Greek word is elsewhere translated "lord."

4:2-6 Vigilance in Prayer, Wisdom Toward the World

4:2-6 The new life is a vigilant life of continual *prayer,* particularly prayer for the progress of the apostolic *word,* the proclamation of the *mystery of Christ* (3-4). The new life is itself a proclamation of the mystery to the world (*outsiders,* 5), a witness which calls for the gift of wisdom (5, cf. 1:9-10) and for speech marked by Christian taste and tact (*seasoned with salt,* 6).

4:3 *Door for the word,* that is, a missionary "opening." The Word is thought of as living and actively moving. (Cf. 1:26; 2 Th 3:1)

4:7-18 CONCLUSION: PERSONAL MATTERS

4:7-18 The last paragraphs deal with the sending of Tychicus, bearer of the letter, and the return of the Colossian slave Onesimus; convey greetings; direct an exchange of letters between Colossae and the neighboring town of Laodicea; and charge Archippus to fulfill his ministry. Paul concludes with a greeting written with his own hand, a renewal request for their intercessions, and a brief benediction. These are personal matters, to be sure; but with Paul there is no cleavage between personal and official aspects of his life.

4:7 *Tychicus* of Asia accompanied Paul on his last journey to Jerusalem (Acts 20:4) and was the bearer of the Letter to the Ephesians also (Eph 6:21; see the Introduction to that letter). We catch a glimpse of his later activity as Paul's co-worker in Tts 3:12 and 2 Ti 4:12.

4:9 *Onesimus.* See the Introduction to Philemon. In calling this embezzling runaway slave *the faithful and beloved brother, who is one of yourselves,* Paul is bidding the Colossians put into practice the injunction of 3:13: "As the Lord has forgiven you, so you also must forgive," totally, with no rancorous remembrance of past failings.

4:10 *Aristarchus* of Thessalonica is called *fellow prisoner* (literally "prisoner of war") as one who shares difficulties and dangers with Paul, the soldier (1 Co 9:7; 2 Co 10:3) and prisoner (Eph 3:1; 4:1; Phmn 1, 9) for Christ. He had been seized by the mob at Ephesus (Acts 19:29) and accompanied Paul on the dangerous last voyage to Jerusalem (Acts 20:4) and to Paul's Roman imprisonment (Acts 27:2). He is listed among Paul's fellow workers in Phmn 24 also.

Mark. See the Introduction to Mark's Gospel. Cf. Acts (where he is called John Mark, John, or Mark) 12:12, 25; 13:13; 15:37-39; Phmn 24; 2 Ti 4:11.

4:11 *Jesus . . . Justus.* Known only from this passage. *Of the circumcision,* i.e., Jewish. This implies that Epaphras (12), Luke, and Demas (14) were of Gentile birth.

4:12 *Epaphras.* Cf. 1:7; Phmn 23 and the Introduction.

4:13 *Laodicea and Hierapolis* with Colossae constituted a triangle of neighboring towns in the Lycus valley.

4:14 *Luke.* Mentioned only here and in 2 Ti 4:11 and Phmn 24 in NT. Cf. Introduction to Luke.

Demas. Known only from this passage, 2 Ti 4:10, and Phmn 24.

4:15 *Nympha.* Known only from this passage.

The church in her house. For the house-church (the usual form in the first days of the church) cf. Acts 2:46; Ro 16:5 (the grouping of names in Ro 16:15-16 suggests house-churches also); and Phmn 2.

4:16 For the theory that *the letter from Laodicea* is the work which we know as the Letter to the Ephesians see the Introduction to Ephesians.

4:17 *Archippus,* called "fellow soldier" by Paul in Phmn 2. He may have been Philemon's son. We can only guess as to the exact nature of the *ministry* which he had *received from the Lord.*

4:18 *With my own hand.* Cf. 1 Co 16:21; Gl 6:11; 2 Th 3:17. Paul dictated the body of his letters, Ro 16:22.

FIRST

THESSALONIANS

INTRODUCTION

The Letters to the Thessalonians are part of that history of the growth of the Word of the Lord we commonly designate as Paul's second missionary journey. It took Paul, with his new companions Silas and Timothy, to Europe. The heart of this was the apostle's 18-month ministry in the great commercial center of Corinth. That ministry was preceded by a revisitation of the churches of Syria and Cilicia and of the Galatian churches founded on the first missionary journey; by missionary work in the European cities of Philippi, Thessalonica, and Berea, work again and again cut short by the malice of superstitious avarice or by the plottings of jealous Jews; and by missionary activity at Athens, the great cultural center of Greece. It was followed by a brief exploratory visit to Ephesus which prepared for Paul's long ministry there on his third missionary journey.

The Word of the Lord sped on and triumphed (2 Th 3:1) in Europe, but in its peculiarly divine way. It sped on surely but not without opposition; it triumphed with the inevitable triumph of a work of God, but its history is not the history of an easy and effortless triumph—it is a history marked, rather, by the persecution, suffering, and internal difficulties of the human bearers and the human recipients of the Word. The history of the second missionary journey has left its mark on the Letters to the Thessalonians. Paul's companions on the journey, Silas (Paul calls him by his Roman name Silvanus) and Timothy, join in the sending of both letters. Paul's opening words in the first letter are a commentary on the history that brought him to Thessalonica: "We know, brethren beloved by God, *that he has chosen you;* for our gospel came to you not only in word, but also in power and in the Holy Spirit and with full conviction" (1 Th 1:4-5). Paul knew from his own experience that the existence of the church at Thessalonica was due not to human planning and devising, but to the elective love of God which had become history in Paul's mission to Europe. Paul would recall, as he wrote these words, how he and his companions had been led, uncomprehending but obedient, by God's own hand and by the Spirit of Jesus (Acts 16:7) past the province of Asia, which would have seemed the logical next step on their missionary way, past Mysia, away from Bithynia, to Troas, to receive there the vision which summoned them to Europe (Acts 16:9); he would recall, too, how persecution had pushed him on with illogical haste from Philippi to Thessalonica. When Paul spoke of the elctive love of God to the Thessalonians, he was not uttering a theoretical tenet of his faith; he was uttering what God has woven into the living texture of his faith by a history in which he, Paul, had himself acted and suffered.

Paul bore the badge of suffering, which was the mark of his apostolate, when he came to Thessalonica from Philippi. The Paul and Silvanus who took to "praying and singing hymns to God" in the jail at Philippi after being beaten by the magistrates (Acts 16:24) had learned to see in their sufferings not the defeat but the triumph of the Word of the Lord; and they spoke the Word in Thessalonica with the robust and confident courage of men who know that they are bearers of the Word of God (1 Th 2:13)—and they did not conceal from their Thessalonian hearers that their word would put the imprint of suffering on the church of God in Thessalonica, too (1 Th 1:6; 2:14; 3:3-4; 2 Th 1:4-7). No small part of that suffering was due to the rancor of unbelieving Jews; and this, too, finds expression in the letter. (1 Th 2:14-16)

Paul experienced anew on this journey the power and activity of Satan, who plants weeds where the Lord plants good seed. Forced to leave Thessalonica before his work there was really finished, he tried again and again to return to the young church—"but Satan hindered us," he writes (1 Th 2:18; cf. 3:5). He experienced also the power for order and discipline which God had set into the world in the form of the Roman government (cf. Ro 13:1-7); his Roman citizenship had procured him an honorable release from prison at Philippi (Acts 16:37-39), and the power of Rome was to stand between him and Judaic malice again at Corinth (Acts 18:12-17), when the proconsul Gallio refused to entertain the ambiguous and invidious Jewish charges against him. When Paul spoke to the Thessalonians of the power that restrains the antichristian attack on God and God's people (2 Th 2:6-7), he was writing revelation which God had given him, to be sure; but God had written that revelation into the history and the experience of Paul the apostle, too.

The Founding of the Church at Thessalonica

Thessalonica was the kind of place that Paul usually chose for an intensive and prolonged ministry. It was the capital of the Roman province of Macedonia and the residence of the Roman proconsul, commercially important as a harbor town, and an important communications center lying on the *Via Egnatia,* the road which connected Rome (by way of Dyrrachium) with Byzantium and the East. It was thus naturally fitted to become a missionary center, a point from which the Word of the Lord, once established in men's hearts, might readily "sound forth." (1 Th 1:8)

Paul arrived with his companions Silas and Timothy (one rperesenting the old Jerusalem church; the other, half Jew and half Greek, representing the young church in Galatia) at Thessalonica in A. D. 50 and began his work, as usual, in the synagog. According to Luke (Acts 17:2), Paul's work in the synagog lasted "three sabbaths," and Luke records no further activity in Thessalonica. But Paul's own account of his work as missionary and as pastor of the new church in Thessalonica (1 Th 2:1-12) suggests a more prolonged ministry among the Gentiles after the break with the synagog had taken place (Acts 17:5). This is confirmed by a notice in Paul's Letter to the Philippians, where he recalls that the Philippians *twice* sent money for his needs when he was at Thessalonica (Ph 4:16). Luke's account in Acts is therefore a highly compressed one; he gives an impression of Paul's ministry at Thessalonica by indicating only the initial and the final stages of his work there.

The break with the synagog came early; the ministry among the Gentiles was perhaps prolonged for several months. The congregation at Thessalonica was therefore, as the Letters to the Thessalonians also indicate, predominantly Gentile (1 Th 1:9; 2:14; cf. Acts 17:4). The life of that congregation was from the first a vigorous one marked by the characteristically Christian joy which even severe trials cannot quench, an active faith which documented itself in a far-reaching missionary witness (1 Th 1:3, 7 f.), a brotherly love which Paul can speak of as taught them by God Himself (1 Th 4:9-10), and an intense hope which longed for the return of "Jesus who delivers us from the wrath to come" (1 Th 1:10; cf. 4:13 ff.). Paul says of them (and Paul's generous recognition of what God has wrought in men never degenerates into empty flattery) that they "became an example to all the believers in Macedonia and in Achaia," all Greece (1 Th 1:7). Only, they were still little children in Christ, good and gifted children, but not mature and stable men, when Paul was forced to leave them. (Acts 17:5-10; 1 Th 2:17)

Occasion of the First Letter

Paul proceeded southwest from Thessalonica to Berea; and from there, when Jews from Thessalonica stirred up opposition to him in Berea also (Acts 17:10-13), to Athens. After a brief ministry there, which brought him into contact with the philosophy of the Greeks, he went on to Corinth, where a vision of the Lord bade him remain and work in depth. And remain he did—for almost two years. Meanwhile the church at Thessalonica remained in his thoughts and his prayers, and he was filled with a deep and restless anxiety for the brethren of whom he was "bereft . . . in person not in heart" (1 Th 2:17). Would they stand fast under the persecution which had come upon them? Would they misunderstand his departure and his continued absence from them? In this connection it is well to remember that Paul and his companions were not the only propagandists and pleaders for a cause that traveled the Roman roads in those days; they were part of a numerous and motley troup of philosophers, rhetoricians, propagandists for various foreign and domestic cults, missionaries, charlatans, and quacks who went from town to town, all intent on getting a hearing, all eager for money or fame or both. These usually came and went, never to be heard from again. Paul would in the popular mind be classified with them. And Paul in Thessalonica, A. D. 51, was not yet the apostle Paul as the church has learned to see him since; he was simply a hitherto unknown little Jew who had come and gone, like hundreds of brilliant and persuasive men before him. The church of Thessalonica would of itself not be minded to classify Paul thus; but his enemies would, and they would thus undermine his apostolic authority and with it the faith in the Gospel with which he was identified as apostle.

Paul's anxieties and fears were well founded. And he could not return to Thessalonica, although he attempted to do so more than once, to relieve his anxieties and to do the work that would obviate the dangers which gave rise to them. Satan hindered him (1 Th 2:18); we can only guess as to what form this hindering took. Finally, when he could no longer endure the suspense, he sacrificed the aid and companionship of Timothy (a real sacrifice, for Paul's was a nature that needed the presence of friends and brethren) and sent him to Thessalonica, both to strengthen the faith of the church and to learn firsthand how they fared. (1 Th 3:1-5)

Neither the account in Acts nor Paul's account in his first letter makes it clear whether Timothy first joined Paul at Athens and was sent back to Thessalonica from there or whether Paul, alone at Athens, directed Timothy by letter to revisit Thessalonica before rejoining him at Corinth. At any rate, when Timothy returned from Thessalonica to Paul at Corinth with the good news of the Thessalonians' faith and love and fidelity to Paul (1 Th 3:6), it meant for Paul the release from a long and agonizing tension. He threw himself with new vigor into his work at Corinth (Acts 18:5), and he wrote the letter which we call First Thessalonians. This letter is Paul's response to Timothy's report, a long thanksgiving for the good news which Timothy had brought, a thanksgiving which looks back over the whole history of the Thessalonian church since its founding and is at the same time a vindication of the purity and sanctity of his motives as their apostle and pastor (chs. 1—3). The thanksgiving is followed by a series of admonitions suggested by Timothy's report. Paul is doing by letter what he could not do face to face; he is supplying what is lacking in their faith. (Cf. 1 Th 3:10)

Timothy would have reported that these Christians in a Gentile environment, and in a Greek harbor town at that, where the idea of sexual purity was complete novelty, were having difficulty in maintaining the chastity a life of faith demands; that their past made it difficult for them to shed at once and altogether the unscrupulous craftiness which they had hitherto regarded as normal and prudent; that their fervent hope easily degenerated into an excited and irresponsible enthusiasm which led them to neglect the tasks and duties of daily life; that their imperfect grasp of the hope which the promised return of the Christ gave them made them despondent regarding their kin and brethren who had died before that return; that their hope was not content to be pure hope and leave the times and seasons of fulfillment in God's hands but sought to calculate and predict; that their life as a community bound together by faith and love and hope was not without its frictions and difficulties. To these difficulties Paul's warm and pastoral heart responded with a wisdom and a love that only the Spirit of God can bestow.

The first three chapters give us a

particularly vivid picture of Paul the missionary and pastor at work in a young Gentile church—how the Word of the Lord grows on pagan soil.

The value of the hortatory section may be measured by the fact that these two brief chapters have furnished no less than three Epistles in the ancient church's pericopal system, the Epistle for the Second Sunday in Lent (1 Th 4:1-7) and the Twenty-fifth and Twenty-seventh Sundays After Trinity. (1 Th 4:13-18; 5:1-11)

Few letters offer more sustenance for the hope of God's people than this one; besides the two great sections on the lot of the dead in Christ (4:13-18) and on the times and seasons of the Lord's return (5:1-11), note the fact that practically every major section in the letter ends on the note of the return of the Lord. (1:10; 2:12, 16, 19; 3:13; 5:23)

1:1 SALUTATION

1:1 *Silvanus* and *Timothy,* Paul's co-workers on the second missionary journey and cofounders of the church at Thessalonica. See the Introduction.

1:2—3:13 THANKSGIVING FOR THE WORD OF GOD IN THESSALONICA

1:2—3:13 The first three chapters are an unusual expansion of the thanksgiving with which Paul usually opens his letters. In grateful reminiscence Paul looks back to the time of the founding of the church (1:2—2:12), to the time of persecution (2:13-16), to the time of his separation from the Thessalonians (2:17—3:5), gives thanks for the good news which Timothy's report concerning them has brought (3:6-10), and includes a prayer. (3:11-13)

1:2—2:12 The Founding of the Church at Thessalonica

1:2—2:12 Paul recalls the coming of the Gospel to Thessalonica, the Thessalonians' exemplary reception of the Word, and the missionary impact of their example (1:2-10). He dwells on his own behavior as apostle (courageous, pure in motive, unselfish, and gentle, 2:1-8) and as their pastor—his selfless devotion in supporting himself by the toil of his hands while he tended them with a father's care. (2:9-12)

1:3 *Faith . . . love . . . hope.* For this triad as summary of man's life as a Christian cf. 5:8; 1 Co 13:13; Cl 1:4-5; Heb 10:22-24.

Work of faith. Faith, in Paul as in James, must inevitably manifest itself in deeds, as "faith working through love." (Gl 5:6; cf. Ja 2:14-26)

1:4 *He has chosen you.* Cf. 2 Th 1:13. Paul's experience on the second missionary journey had powerfully brought home to him that God's elective love in its mysterious working brings men to faith. See the Introduction.

1:6 *Imitators of us and of the Lord.* The apostle (with his co-workers) can be the object of imitation only because Christ works through him (Ro 15:18) and speaks in him (2 Co 13:3). For Christ as recipient of the Word cf. Jn 17:8; Rv 1:1. For the apostle as object of imitation cf. 1 Co 4:16; 11:1; Gl 4:12; Ph 3:17; 2 Th 3:7, 9.

1:8 *Word of the Lord sounded forth.* Cf. 2 Th 3:1.

Macedonia and Achaia. The northern and southern halves of Greece, the two provinces into which the Romans had divided Greece.

1:9-10 An instructive summary of Paul's missionary preaching to Gentiles, with its penetrating appeal to the conscience of man *(the wrath to come;* cf. 2 Co 4:2). The triad of faith *(turned to God),* love *(serve),* and hope *(wait for his Son)* is heard again.

2:2 *Suffered . . . at Philippi.* Cf. Acts 16:19-39.

In the face of . . . opposition. Cf. Acts 17:1-8.

2:3 *Error,* illusion, self-deception.

Uncleanness, impure motives.

2:4 *God who tests our hearts.* Paul implicitly compares himself to the prophet Jeremiah, who committed his cause to God when persecuted (Jer 11:20, cf. 18-19). In Gl 1:15 Paul speaks of his call to the apostolate in language taken from Jeremiah's description of his call. (Jer 1:5)

2:5 *Cloak for greed,* that is, noble language that conceals the speaker's intention of getting money out of his hearers. (Cf. Acts 20:33)

2:8 *Share . . . our own selves.* Cf. 2 Co 12:15; Ph 2:17.

2:9 *Worked night and day.* Cf. Acts 18:3; 20:34-35; 1 Co 4:12; 9:6, 12, 14-18.

2:11 *Father.* At the very beginning, in their infancy, he was their gentle nurse (2:7); as they advanced, he became their father, who trained and reared them.

2:12 *Calls.* The present tense is significant. The once-for-all initial call (e.g., Ro 8:30; 1 Co 1:9; Gl 1:6; 1 Th 4:7) which brings man under the reign of God *(kingdom)* and sets him on the road to *glory* is continually renewed in the Word, which becomes his daily nurture. Cf. 5:24; the once-accepted converting Word of God continues to work in the believers. (2:13)

2:13-16 The Time of Persecution

2:13-16 Paul gratefully recalls how the Thessalonians received the apostolic Word as the very *word of God* which it is, how that divine

Word evinced its power in them by enabling them to endure persecutions comparable to those endured by the churches of Judea.

2:14 *From your own countrymen,* Gentiles, since the church at Thessalonica was predominantly Gentile (see the Introduction). Persecution at Thessalonica originated with the Jews, but they succeeded in inflaming the Gentile townsmen and officials against the new Christian community. (Acts 17:5-9)

2:15-16 It would be easy to dismiss these words as an anti-Semitic outburst prompted by the rancor of a Jewish renegade. But it is to be noted (a) that the statement simply takes up Jesus' indictment of His countrymen (*killed . . . the prophets,* cf. Mt 23:37); (b) that it is a straightforward record of what happened in the history of Jesus, the Judaic church, and Paul's missionary work; and (c) that Paul incurred and endured Judaic enmity just because his love for the Jew and his faith in the promises of God compelled him to proclaim the Gospel "to the Jew first" (Ro 1:16; Acts 12—28), a practice which he continued in the face of persistent rejection and persecution. For Paul's unquenchable love for his people cf. Ro 9:1-3; 10:1.

2:16 *Fill up the measure of their sins.* Cf. Gn 15:16. The whole tragedy of Israel is contained in the fact that Paul is forced to describe them in the language the Lord had used of the pagan nation He drove out of Canaan to provide a home for His people.

God's wrath has come upon them. The hardening which has befallen Israel (Ro 11:7-10, 25) is God's judgment on Israel's unbelief and is as such a token and foretaste not only of the fall of Jerusalem but of the final judgment, "the wrath to come." (1:10)

2:17—3:5 The Time of Separation

2:17—3:5 Paul recalls his longing to see the church of Thessalonica again, his repeated attempts to return to them (frustrated by Satan), and finally the sending of Timothy to establish them in their faith and to bring him word concerning their faith.

2:18 The vehemence of Paul's assurance is probably due to the fact that his enemies sought to discredit him by saying that he had left his converts to face persecution alone while he had taken to his heels.

Satan hindered us. What form the satanic opposition took can only be conjectured. One likely suggestion is that Paul could not return to Thessalonica without endangering his former host, Jason, from whom the city authorities had taken security to keep the peace. Any disturbance resulting from Paul's return would put Jason in jeopardy. (Acts 17:9)

2:19 *Crown of boasting,* a mark of honor and distinction of which I can boast or in which I can exult. (Cf. 2 Co 1:14)

3:3-4 Cf. Mt 5:10-12; Acts 14:22. Neither Jesus nor his apostle ever fostered the illusion that the church is an island of tranquillity.

3:5 *The tempter* (Satan, cf. Mt 4:3) *had tempted you* successfully.

3:6-10 Timothy's Good News

3:6-10 Paul rejoices at and gives thanks to God for their steadfastness in faith and love and their loyalty to himself.

3:6 *Brought us the good news.* Paul uses the word commonly used for proclaiming the Gospel; their continued faith and love are God's working, and news of His gracious activity is "gospel."

3:10 *Supply what is lacking in your faith.* This is what Paul does or at least begins to do in chs. 4—5. Here, as in 1:3 ("your work of faith"), Paul is thinking of faith as operative and productive.

3:11-13 Prayer

3:11-13 As is usual in Paul's letters, the long thanksgiving is followed by an intercessory prayer. Paul prays that God and the Lord Jesus may direct his way back to Thessalonica and that the Lord may establish the hearts of the Thessalonian believers in love and hope.

3:11 *Lord Jesus* is the object of prayer, strong evidence for His deity.

3:13 *With all his saints,* literally "holy ones"; probably angels are meant. (Cf. Zch 14:5; Mt 25:31)

4:1—5:22 EXHORTATIONS

4:1-12 Moral Exhortations for Individuals

4:1-12 The admonitions to sexual purity (1-8), to brotherly love (9-10), and to quiet industry (11-12) were probably prompted by Timothy's report.

4:1 *To please God* involves the idea of willing service to Him. (Cf. 1:9; Cl 1:10)

4:2 *Through the Lord Jesus,* on His authority.

4:3 *Unchastity.* Sexual immorality is meant.

4:5 *Heathen who do not know God.* The OT uses this phrase of the heathen, in contrast to Israel (Ps 79:6; Jer 10:25); the "heathen" Thessalonians have become the new Israel of God who know God.

4:8 *Who gives his Spirit to you,* or "into you," that is, "into your hearts" (cf. Eze 36:27). The promise given to ancient Israel has become a reality in the new Israel. With the gift of the Spirit, God gives the power to do what He commands.

4:9 *Taught by God.* Mt 18:32-33, with the preceding parable (23-31), is the best commentary on this phrase.

4:11 *Live quietly.* Cf. 2 Th 3:11-12.

4:12 *Respect of outsiders.* The vitality of the Christian hope excited the curiosity and interest of men (cf. 1 Ptr 3:15), but if the hope made idlers and busybodies of those who held it, it would soon become an object of derision.

4:13-18 Concerning Those Who Are Asleep

4:13 For the occasion and need for this admonition see the Introduction.

4:14 *Jesus . . . rose again . . . through Jesus.* Here, as everywhere in the NT, the resurrection of Jesus is the sole and whole basis for the hope of eternal life. His resurrection is the resurrection of the dead (cf. 1 Co 15:12-22; 2 Co 4:14). He is "the resurrection and the life." (Jn 11:25)

4:15 *By the word of the Lord.* No known word of Jesus corresponds exactly to what Paul is saying here. Paul may be quoting a saying of Jesus not recorded in our gospels, as he does in Acts 20:35.

4:17 *Meet the Lord . . . be with the Lord.* For all the dramatic splendor which marks Paul's portrayal of the Lord's return (16), the Christian hope here remains, as always in the NT, personal, a hope for full communion with our Lord.

4:18 *Comfort one another.* Cf. 5:11. Thus, by being spoken from man to man, the Word of God proclaimed by the apostle continues to work in the believers. (2:13)

5:1-11 The Times and Seasons of the Lord's Return

5:1-11 The coming of the Day of the Lord is as incalculable *(thief)* as it is certain *(travail).* Its coming does not call for a calculating curiosity but vigilance and sobriety; for nothing less than salvation, life with Christ, is at stake.

5:1-2 *Times and the seasons.* Like Jesus (Mt 24:3-4, 36-44; Acts 1:7), Paul will not enter into the question of times and seasons at all; there is a gentle irony in *you . . . know well* (literally "exactly")—the Christian's "exact" knowledge of the Day of the Lord is that its time is unknowable. *For thief in the night* cf. Mt 24:43; Lk 12:39-40; 2 Ptr 3:10; Rv 3:3; 16:15.

5:3 *Travail.* The point of comparison is inevitability.

5:5 *Sons of.* To be "son of" something means that you have your nature and destiny determined by it (cf. Eph 2:2; 5:6; Cl 3:6; 2 Th 2:3), as a child derives its character and place in life from its parents.

5:6-7 Cf. Ro 13:11-14.

5:8 For the whole armor of God cf. Eph 6:13-17.

5:10 *Whether we wake or sleep,* whether we are among the living or the dead at the coming of the day of the Lord. Paul is touching once more on the thought of 4:13-18. For Christ as Lord of the living and the dead by virtue of His atoning death and resurrection cf. Ro 14:8-9.

5:11 See 4:18 and the note there.

5:12-22 Exhortations for Congregational Life

5:12-22 Paul exhorts the congregation to a loving recognition of its leaders *because of their work* (12-13); to a life of loving and patient ministry to one another (14-15); to a worship of continual joy, prayer, and thanksgiving (16-18); to a full but discerning use of the gifts of the Spirit. (19-22)

5:19-20 *Not quench the Spirit...prophesying.* Apparently Paul is inculcating a proper appreciation of both the "enthusiastic" manifestations of the Spirit, such as speaking with tongues, and the more sober and sobering gifts, such as the plain instructive and edifying speech of prophecy. For a fuller treatment see 1 Co 12 and 14.

5:21 *Test everything.* Cf. 1 Co 14:29, where the church is told to "weigh what is said" by the prophets, and 1 Jn 4:1.

5:22 *Every form of evil,* even when it appears in "spiritual" guise.

5:23-28 CONCLUSION

5:23-28 The second half of the letter is rounded out by an intercessory prayer very similar to that of the conclusion of the first half (23-24; cf. 3:11-13). This is followed by a request for the church's intercession, greetings, instruction for the public reading of the letter, and a closing benediction. (25-28)

5:23 *Spirit and soul and body,* the total human being as a unity of his renewed capacity for communion with God *(spirit),* his natural vitality *(soul),* and his physical existence *(body).*

5:24 *Calls.* See note on 2:12.

5:27 We see here the beginnings of the liturgical use of the apostolic letters. Cf. Cl 4:16, where Paul prescribes an exchange of letters between churches. Why Paul should be so emphatic in entreating that all should hear the letter is not apparent; perhaps there was a tendency to break up into cliques. (Cf. 5:13)

5:28 Paul's closing benediction in his epistles always contains the same thought, but the form varies from epistle to epistle.

SECOND

THESSALONIANS

INTRODUCTION

For the history of the Thessalonian church see the Introduction to First Thessalonians. The Second Letter to the Thessalonians was evidently written not long after the first, perhaps a few months later, A. D. 50, at Corinth. According to reports which reached Paul at Corinth (we do not know how; perhaps the church wrote to Paul), the Christians of Thessalonica were still standing firm under persecution (2 Th 1:4), but false notions concerning the "coming of our Lord Jesus Christ and our assembling to meet him" (2 Th 2:1) had gained currency in the church. Those who advocated these notions apparently appealed to some alleged prophetic utterance ("spirit") or teaching or writing of Paul's to support them (2 Th 2:2). The resultant excited, almost hysterical expectation (2 Th 2:2) had led some to abandon their regular occupation and to lead an idle and disorderly life in dependence on the charity of the church (2 Th 3:6-12). Others, it would seem, struck by the high demands of the first letter (the demand that they be found "blameless" at the coming of the Lord, 1 Th 3:13; 5:23), had grown fearful and despondent concerning the coming of the Christ; for them, they felt, it would mean not deliverance but judgment and destruction.

Paul's second letter is his answer to this situation in the church at Thessalonica. It therefore sounds two notes. For those who indulge in overheated fantasies concerning the last times there are sobering words that point to the events which must necessarily precede the coming of the Christ in glory (2 Th 2:1-12). For the despondent and the fearful there is an eloquent and reassuring recognition of the new life which God has worked in them and a comforting emphasis on the certainty of their election by God (2 Th 1:3-12; 2:13-15). Paul turns the church from both excitement and despondency to that sober and responsible activity which is the hallmark of the genuinely Christian hope: The hoping church turns from preoccupation with itself to God; the church must pray, pray "that the word of the Lord may speed on and triumph" (2 Th 3:1); and the hoping church must work—work for its living in sober industriousness and for its own health as the church of God by disciplining and correcting all whose life is a departure from the apostolic Word and example and therefore a denial of the real character of the church. (3:6-15)

Second Thessalonians is an outstanding example of the spiritual tact of the apostle, which enables him to quell the fevered excitement of a hope grown hysterical without quenching the fervor and the life-shaping force of that hope and to instill sobriety without robbing the Christian hope of its intensity, leaving both fear and faith to do their salutary work in man. His emphasis on working industry in this connection (an emphasis which he spelled out in his life too by supporting himself) is a part of the apostolic recognition of the order established by God the Creator and remains one of the great safeguards of Christian sanity over against all falsely spiritual contempt for the gifts and claims of God's created world.

The eschatological teaching is an amplification and an enrichment of what Paul has given the church in the first letter, particularly in ch. 2. The passage renews and explicates the warning of Jesus, who taught His disciples that wheat and weeds must ripen together till the harvest; it reminds the church that the satanic counterthrust is inevitable and constant wherever God's Word grows and God's reign is established, that any shallow ecclesiastical optimism which bows the knee to the idol of Progress and any churchly piety which becomes comfortably at home in this world is a denial of the revelation on which the life of the church is built.

1:1-2 SALUTATION

1:3-12 THANKSGIVING, ASSURANCE, AND PRAYER

1:3-12 Paul gives thanks for the ever-increasing faith and love of the Thessalonians and for their steadfastness under persecution (3-4). The fidelity and righteousness of God, he assures them, make their present suffering His pledge that they shall participate in the final deliverance, when those who do not obey the Gospel and oppress the church shall perish in the judgment of the Lord Jesus (5-10). Paul prays that God, who has called them, may in His grace and power foster and make fruitful the faith which His call has created, to the glory of their Lord, who shares His glory with them. (11-12)

1:5 *Evidence* or "a clean omen" (cf. Ph 1:28), *of the* (future) *righteous judgment.*

Made worthy of the kingdom. For suffering as God's gracious discipline to prepare His own for the glory of the Kingdom cf. Ro 5:2-5; 8:17-18, 28; 2 Co 4:17.

1:7 *Grant rest with us.* Paul too is suffeirng (cf. 3:2) and can therefore speak credibly concerning their suffering.

2:1-17 TWO ADMONITIONS CONCERNING THE DAY OF THE LORD

2:1-12 Be Not Quickly Shaken in Mind

2:1-12 Paul speaks from a pastoral concern. Some utterance of his concerning the imminent character of the coming of the Day of the Lord (cf. 1 Th 5:1-3) had been misinterpreted to mean the Day of the Lord had already come, with the result that the responsible sobriety of Christian hope (1 Th 5:8) had given way to hysterical excitement and irresponsible idleness (cf. 3:11). His words are intended to restore the hope of the church to health and vigor (1-2). What he has to say concerning the great apostasy (rebellion) and the revelation of the man of lawlessness as signs of the coming of the Day of the Lord is no novelty but a repetition of what he had taught during his ministry in Thessalonica (5), a part of the basic instruction which bade his converts "wait for" the coming of God's "Son from heaven" (1 Th 1:10). That instruction, as Paul himself asserted (1 Co 15:11), was the common stock of all apostolic preaching, the proclamation of Christ in His significance "in accordance with the scriptures" (1 Co 15:3-4). The OT speaks of a great counterthrust to the kingdom of God in the last days, a demonic counterkingdom concentrated and incarnated in a historical figure (cf. Eze 38—39); Daniel sees in Antiochus Epiphanes IV, the Seleucid king who sought to stamp out Israel's worship of the God of her fathers and sparked the Maccabean revolt, one such incarnation (Dn 7:23-27; 8:23-25; 11:36-37; cf. 9:27; 12:11). The warning issued by Daniel lived on in Jewry, and the expectation of the counter-Messiah, or Antichrist, was very much alive in Israel in the time between the Testaments. Jesus' parable of the weeds and the wheat takes up this OT expectation of a diabolical counterkingdom which appears in religious guise, hard to distinguish (in its beginnings) from the kingdom of God (Mt 13:24-30, 36-43). And Jesus speaks more explicitly in His discourse on last things of false Christs who will come in His name with marvelous manifestations of power to deceive His elect (Mt 24:5, 23-24). He employs the language of Daniel (Dn 9:27; 11:31; 12:11) to warn His disciples of "the desolating sacrilege" whose shadow shall fall across "the holy place" and empty it of worshipers (Mt 24:15). It was of this aspect of the "word of the Lord" that Paul had spoken and now speaks, as of something familiar to his readers, as John does in 1 Jn 2:18, 4:3. His speech is therefore succinct and allusive, for us somewhat "hard to understand" (2 Ptr 3:16)

Paul first speaks (3-8) of the sequence of the terrible events which must precede the coming of the Day of the Lord. There will be a great *rebellion* headed by and concentrated in a figure who is called *the man of lawlessness,* one who rebels so radically against God that he deifies himself and therefore dooms himself (*son of perdition,* 3). The great counterthrust works in hiddenness and secrecy at first, *as the mystery of lawlessness;* and God's merciful governance of history will raise up a power and a person to restrain it (*what is restraining,* 6; *who now restrains,* 7). But the hour will come when *the lawless one will be revealed* (8), to work openly and freely—and to be judged and destroyed. (8)

Paul then dwells on the satanic character of the lawless one (9-12). First, his great weapon is the satanic lie (cf. Jn 8:44); the Antichrist is pseudo-Christ, a satanic perversion of the Christ of God: he has a *coming* (9), to imitate and oppose the *coming* of Christ (8); *signs and wonders* (9), to imitate and oppose the Christ "attested . . . by God with mighty works and wonders and signs" (Acts 2:22); a *mystery of lawlessness* (7) to imitate the "mystery of Christ" (Eph 3:4; Cl 4:3); a potent and persuasive lie (*pretended signs,* 9; *wicked deception,* 10; *strong delusions . . . what is false,* 11), to imitate and oppose the *truth* (10, 12) of the Gospel of Christ. Second, like all the workings and incarnations of Satan, *the man of lawlessness* cannot escape the sovereign control of God. There is no uneasy balance of power between the satanic and the divine; the man of lawlessness must, unwittingly and unwillingly, serve God's purposes. Through him God executes His judgment, that fearful judgment which delivers up men who will not love the truth to the lie which they desire. Only those become victims of the potent lie who "suppress the truth" (Ro 1:18) and so invoke the wrath of God.

Just wherein Paul saw the first workings of the mystery of lawlessness we cannot say; perhaps in was the deification of the Roman emperor as it had manifested itself in Caligula (A. D. 37—41). Nor do we know just what or whom he had in mind when he spoke of a restraint and a restrainer: perhaps it was the benign power of Roman law and order which made seas and roads safe for the bearers of the Gospel and permitted the Word of the Lord to "speed on and triumph" (3:1). Nor do we know how far he was permitted to look into the future toward the final historical manifestation of the mystery of lawlessness and its judgment. Paul wrote, prophetically, to sober men's hope and to alert men to the realities of the history in which they live. The men of the Lutheran Reformation responded responsibly to that alert when they looked upon the papacy and saw there the marks of the man of lawlessness. A responsible church is called on to do in this our day what they did, with faith and fears, in theirs.

2:2 *By spirit,* an utterance inspired by the Holy Spirit. Perhaps someone with the gift of prophecy interpreted Paul's preaching in a sense not intended by him; if so, Paul is calling on the church to "test" the prophetic utterance. Cf. 1 Th 5:21 and the note there.

Letter purporting to be from us. Cf. 3:17. Perhaps a forged letter is meant. But Paul may be simply warding off a misinterpretation of his first letter.

2:3 *Son of perdition,* doomed to perish. for the idiom "son of," as indicating a man's nature and destiny, cf. 1 Th 5:5; Eph 2:2; and the notes on those passages.

2:4 *Temple of God,* the church (cf. 1 Co 3:16-17; Eph 2:21), where God is known and worshiped. The man of lawlessness is usurper.

2:8 *Slay him with the breath of his mouth.* Cf. Is 11:4.

2:10, 12, 13 *Truth,* the Gospel. (Cf. Gl 2:5, 14; Eph 1:13; Cl 1:5)

2:2 *Truth . . . unrighteousness.* Cf. Ro 2:8.

2:13-17 Stand Firm

2:13-17 The Antichrist and the counterkingdom cannot shake or make questionable the sovereign reign of the triune God; to Him Paul gives thanks for His gracious work in the Thessalonian believers, past (*chose,* 13; *called,* 14), present (*sanctification . . . belief in the truth,* 13), and future (*to be saved,* 13; *obtain the glory,* 14). In the presence of His gracious majesty Paul can bid his readers *stand firm* in the truth which he has transmitted to them (15). With Him Paul intercedes, with the Giver of *eternal comfort and good hope,* the God of *love* and *grace,* to keep His church in Thessalonica strong in heart and steadfast in *every good work and word.* (16-17)

2:15 *Traditions.* For the Gospel (and instruction for conduct derived from it) as *tradition,* received from the Lord and delivered or transmitted to others, cf. 1 Co 11:2, 23; 15:3; 2 Th 3:6; cf. Heb 2:3.

2:16-17 Unlike the prayer in 1 Th 3:11-13, this one contains no request that Paul may be enabled to return to Thessalonica. Paul had meanwhile received the vision which bade him remain in Corinth. (Acts 18:9-11)

3:1-15 EXHORTATIONS TO INTERCESSION AND DISCIPLINE

3:1-15 Paul turns the mind of the church from overexcited, idle hope to the work of the apostolic church; he asks for the church's intercessions on his behalf, now that his work is opposed and threatened by *wicked and evil men;* assures the church once more of the aid and protection of their *faithful Lord* and of his, Paul's, confidence in their obedience; and implores for them the gift of love and steadfast hope. (1-5)

A last *command* deals with the disciplining of brethren who disobey the apostolic *tradition* and ignore the apostle's own *example* by living lives of *idleness* at the expense of others. The church's treatment of them is to remind them, forcefully yet fraternally, that they are by their disobedience excluding themselves from the fellowship which the apostolic Word has created. (6-15)

3:16-18 CONCLUSION: BENEDICTION AND AUTOGRAPH GREETING

3:16-18 Paul dictated his letters (cf. Ro 16:22) and added a final greeting in his own handwriting (1 Co 16:21; Gl 6:11). This autograph conclusion is to serve as a mark of identification should there be any doubt about the genuineness of a letter. (Cf. 2:2)

The Pastoral Letters

The Name "Pastoral"

The name "Pastoral" has been applied since the 18th century to the letters addressed to Timothy and Titus; the title had been applied to First Timothy alone as early as the 13th century by Thomas Aquinas. This designation marks the letters as directed to "pastors" or shepherds of the church and as dealing with the office of the pastor. It is more properly applied to First Timothy and to the Letter to Titus than to Second Timothy. Second Timothy has pastoral elements in it, but is basically a personal letter and in a class by itself. First Timothy and Titus are official letters, addressed not only to the recipient in each case but also to the churches to which these men were being sent, and they cover the whole range of church life: offices in the church, the worship life of the church, the care of souls, and especially the combating of error which threatens the health of the church. The official character of the letters is seen in their form also; the usual Pauline thanksgiving at the beginning is replaced by words which indicate that the content of the letter is a repetition in writing of oral instructions already given—a common feature in official letters (1 Ti 1:3; Tts 1:5). The personal communications usually found at the close of Pauline letters are either absent entirely, as in the Letters to Timothy, or kept extremely brief, as in the Letter to Titus. The style of the letters likewise reflects this "official" character: We have here terse and pointed directions delivered with apostolic authority; the doctrinal background and basis of the directions are given in pointed and pregnant formulations designed to be readily grasped and remembered; some of them are "sure sayings," probably already familiar to the churches. (1 Ti 1:15; 3:1; 4:9; Tts 3:8)

Historical Background of the Pastoral Letters

Since we do not have the help of the Book of Acts for the period in which the writing of the Pastoral Letters falls and must reconstruct the history of this period entirely from hints given in the letters themselves, the order of events must remain somewhat doubtful; even an approximate dating of them is difficult. The following is a probable reconstruction of the course of events:

1. That Paul was released at the end of the 2-year imprisonment recorded in Acts 28:30 (A. D. 61) seems certain; there is really no evidence at all that his first Roman imprisonment ended in martyrdom. Paul apparently did not remain long in Rome after his release; the jealousies and frictions to which he alludes in Philippians (Ph 1:15-17) would make it advisable for him to leave soon.

2. Whether Paul ever carried out his intention of going to Spain (Ro 15:28) must remain doubtful. The Captivity Letters say nothing of an anticipated Spanish voyage, and the Pastoral Letters likewise say nothing of that undertaking. Neither did the Spanish church preserve any tradition which attributed its origin to the missionary work of Paul. On the other hand, Paul's journey to Spain is attested by early and reliable Roman sources like the Letter of Clement of Rome to the Corinthians (I, vv. 5-7), written within a generation after the events (A. D. 96), and the Muratorian Canon (about A. D. 175). The apocryphal Acts of Peter (written about A. D. 200) also refers to the Spanish voyage of Paul; and no one in antiquity seems to have questioned it. If Paul did make the voyage, it was probably soon after his release from imprisonment A. D. 61.

3. Paul intended to revisit his former mission fields in Asia and Macedonia (Phmn 22; Ph 2:24); the Pastoral Letters indicate that he carried out this intention. He returned to the East by way of Crete, where he remained for a time as missionary. He left Titus in charge of the task of consolidating the church there when he himself proceeded eastward. (Tts 1:5)

4. Paul may have touched at Ephesus; if he did, he could not have remained there long. The instructions which he gave Timothy, whom he left in charge at Ephesus, indicate that much work still remained to be done there. (1 Ti 1:3)

5. Paul himself proceeded from Ephesus to Macedonia, and from there he wrote First Timothy. (1 Ti 1:3)

6. Paul wrote the Letter to Titus either from Macedonia just before his departure for Nicopolis or during the journey to Nicopolis, where he planned to spend the winter. There were several prominent cities called Nicopolis; the one referred to in the Letter to Titus is probably Nicopolis in Epirus. Titus was to join Paul in Nicopolis when relieved in Crete by Artemas or Tychicus. (Tts 3:12)

7. During the interval between the writing of the Letter to Titus and Second Timothy Paul visited Troas, Corinth, and Miletus. (2 Ti 4:13, 20)

8. Paul was again arrested (whether in the East or at Rome can hardly be made out) and imprisoned at Rome. This time his imprisonment was much more severe than A. D. 59—61, and he saw no hope of an acquittal. In Second Timothy he summons his "beloved child" to him once more before the end.

9. This second imprisonment in Rome ended in the martyrdom of Paul. It took place under Nero, certainly, but hardly during the great Neronian persecution A. D. 64. Paul would hardly have summoned Timothy, the man to whom he looked for the faithful continuation of his work, to a certain death in Rome; neither would it be like Paul to lament that none of the Roman Christians had stood by him at his first hearing if those Christians were at that time dying for their faith. The writing of Second Timothy and Paul's death must be dated either before the great persecution under Nero, perhaps A. D. 63, or later, perhaps even so late as A. D. 67, the last year of Nero's reign.

FIRST

TIMOTHY

INTRODUCTION

Paul, on his way to Macedonia, has left Timothy at Ephesus with instructions to "charge certain persons not to teach any different doctrine" (1 Ti 1:3). Paul does not describe this "different doctrine" systematically; but from his attacks on it in 1:3-7; 4:1-3, 7; 6:3-5, 20-21 and from the tenor of his instructions for the regulation of the life of the church, it is clear that Timothy must do battle with a form of "Gnosticism," an early stage of that heresy which was to become in its fully developed form the most serious threat to the church in succeeding generations. Gnosticism is not so much a system as a trend or current of thought which produced a great variety of systems, often by combining with some already existing religion. It was therefore present and active as a corrupting force long before the great Christian-Gnostic systems of the second century appeared; we have already seen one example of it in the heresy which threatened the church at Colossae.

Basic to all forms of Gnosticism is a dualistic conception of reality, that is, the view that what is spiritual, nonmaterial, is of itself good and what is material or physical is of itself bad. This view affects man's whole attitude toward the world of created things. The dreary details of Gnostic speculation on the *origin* of the material universe need not concern us here. It may suffice to note:

a. that the world is no longer viewed as God's good creation, as the Scriptures view it (that is, a world which God created, fallen with fallen man but redeemed with man and destined to be transfigured with him, Ro 8:19-22); rather, the created world is viewed as in itself alien and hostile to God because it is matter and not spirit;

b. that man's desperate predicament, his alienation from God, is no longer seen as being due to his sinful rebellion against God, but to the fact that he is entangled in the world of matter;

c. that redemption consists in being freed from the material world in which man dwells and is entangled. This liberation can come about only by knowledge (Greek, *gnosis,* hence the name of the heresy); this knowledge must be imparted to man by revelation from a higher world;

d. the mission of the Savior-God is to impart this knowledge not to all men, but to a select few who will pass it on to those who are "worthy";

e. that those who have knowledge, the "gnostics," must free themselves from the influence of matter by abstaining from certain foods and from marriage. (Sometimes the negative attitude toward things physical and material had the opposite effect and led to a supreme indifference to things physical and material, so that, for instance, the sexual life of man was considered to be morally indifferent.)

Such a trend of thought would lead inevitably to an utter distortion of all that "the glorious gospel of the blessed God" (1 Ti 1:11) proclaimed. God the Creator disappears—all the good gifts of food and drink which He gives are suspected and feared; all the salutary orders which He has established in this world (marriage, family, government) are despised and ignored. The Old Testament, which rings with glad adoration of the God who made the heavens and the earth and blesses man within the orders of this world, must either be ignored or have its obvious sense interpreted away by allegorizing "myths and endless genealogies." The Law becomes the arena of speculation and vain discussions, not the voice of God which calls the sinner to account and condemns him. In terms of this kind of thought, there can be no real incarnation of the Son of

God; for how can the divine, which is spiritual, enter into union with matter, which is of itself evil? And when sin is not recognized as man's guilt, there can be no real redemption either. Where knowledge is made central in the religious life of man and self-redemption by way of ascetic exercise is made the way of salvation, there is no possibility of that pure Christian love that "issues from a pure heart and a good conscience and sincere faith" (1 Ti 1:5). A narrow and sectarian pride takes its place (1 Ti 6:4, 20; cf. 1:3-7). Where the teaching office becomes a wordy, speculative, disputatious purveying of "knowledge" to a select coterie of initiates, it is bound to become corrupted; it appeals to the pride, selfishness, and mercenary instincts of men, and the teacher becomes that ghastly, demon-ridden caricature of the true teacher which Paul has described in 1 Ti 4:1-2.

Timothy's task will be to let the fresh and wholesome winds of "sound doctrine" into the house of God, whose air has been infected by the morbid and infectious mists of this *gnosis.* To the demonic denial of God the Creator and the rejection of His good gifts he must oppose the glorious Gospel of the blessed God "who gives life to all things" (1 Ti 6:13), the God whose every creation still has on it the mark of His primeval "Very good!" (Gn. 1:31) and is even in its fallen state "consecrated by the word of God and prayer" (1 Ti 4:5). To "godless and silly myths" he is to oppose the grateful adoration of the Creator. To the Gnostic misuse of the Law he must oppose the right and lawful use and let the sinner hear the fearful verdict of God in order that he may give ear to God's acquittal in His Gospel. (1:8-11)

To the rarefied and unreal Christ of Gnostic speculation he must oppose "the *man* Christ Jesus" (1 Ti 2:5), the Christ Jesus who really entered into history under Pontius Pilate (1 Ti 6:13) and died a real death on the cross for the sins of all men (1 Ti 2:6). He must present this Christ as the whole content of the truth which the church upholds and guards, the mystery of God "manifested *in the flesh*" (1 Ti 3:16). To Gnostic self-redemption by means of knowledge and ascetic self-manipulation he must oppose redemption as the sole act of the Christ who came into the world, not to impart higher knowledge but "to save sinners" (1 Ti 1:15), the Christ "who gave Himself as a ransom for all" (1 Ti 2:6). To Gnostic exclusiveness he must oppose the all-embracing grace of God, and to their narrow sectarian pride he must oppose the Gospel of universal grace (1 Ti 2:4) and thus make of the church a church which can pray wholeheartedly for *all* men (1 Ti 2:1), a church which lives in the "love that issues from a pure heart and a good conscience and sincere faith." (1 Ti 1)

To the imposing picture of the Gnostic teachers, these brilliant, speculative, disputatious, and mercenary men, he must oppose the picture of the true teacher. He must, first of all, himself *be* that picture; he dare not let himself be drawn down to the level of his opponents and fight demonic fire with fire; he must do battle, "holding faith and a good conscience" (1 Ti 1:19); he must, as a good minister of Jesus Christ, not allow himself to be infected by what he opposes but must continue to be "nourished on the words of faith" (not knowledge) "and of the good doctrine" which he has followed hitherto. He must train himself, athlete-like, in godliness (1 Ti 4:6-7). Thus he will be able to fight the good fight of faith as a "man of God," standing in the succession of Moses and the prophets, singly devoted to God's cause (1 Ti 6:11-12; cf. 6:3-10), taking hold even now of that eternal life which shall be his in fullness at the appearing of the Lord Jesus Christ (1 Ti 6:11-15). He must himself be all that the Gnostic teachers are not; and he is to see to it that the men who oversee the church's life and administer the church's charity, the bishops and deacons, are men of like character. They need not be brilliant men; they must be good men. It is enough if a bishop be "an apt teacher" (1 Ti 3:2); he need not be a brilliant speaker or a captivating personality. The qualifications which Paul sets up for bishops and deacons are singularly sober and down to earth; but the moral standards which he sets up for them are awesomely high (1 Ti 3:1-13). Paul wants men whom the grace of God has "trained," as he puts it in his Letter to Titus (2:11-12), seasoned, selfless, wise, and gracious men whose faith has borne fruit in their homes, in their marital fidelity, and in the training of their children. (1 Ti 3:2, 4, 12)

Timothy had a great piece of work assigned to him. And he was a good man for the task. He was both Jew and Greek (Acts 16:1). He had lived with the Old Testament from childhood (2 Ti 3:15). Prophetic voices had assigned him to this "good warfare" (1 Ti 1:18). God had given him the requisite gifts for it (1 Ti 4:14), and his whole history had been one that fostered those gifts. He had been Paul's almost constant companion for a dozen years (Acts 16:1 ff.). The apostolic "pattern of sound words" (2 Ti 1:13) had become a part of his makeup, and the apostolic example had been constantly before him (2 Ti 3:10, 11, 14). Paul had employed him as his emissary before this, though never for so extended and difficult a mission as this one. When Paul was prevented from returning to Thessalonica, he sent Timothy to the young and troubled church to establish the believers in their faith and to exhort them (1 Th 3:1-2). He had sent Timothy to Corinth during that troubled period when the Corinthians were becoming drunk on the heady wine of the new teaching, to remind them of the apostle's "ways in Christ" (1 Co 4:17; 16:10). He had sent him to Philippi from Rome during the time of his imprisonment and had commended him to the Philippians with the finest tribute that can be paid to a servant of God in the Gospel: "I have no one like him, who will be genuinely anxious for your welfare. They all look after their own interests, not those of Jesus Christ. But Timothy's worth you know, how as a son with a father he has served with me in the gospel." (Ph 2:20-22)

If Paul was a fond father to Timothy, he was not a blind one. He knew his beloved child's weaknesses: Timothy was still young and apparently conscious of it as a handicap (1 Ti 4:12). He was inclined to be timid (cf. 1 Co 16:10-11; 2 Ti 1:7). Besides, his health was not of the best; his stomach troubled him, an ailment not uncommon among sensitive and conscientious young men of God (1 Ti 5:23)

Therefore Paul writes Timothy a letter which sums up once more the oral instructions already given him (1 Ti 1:3). This letter will give his work the sanction and authority of Paul, "an apostle of Christ Jesus by command of God our Savior and of Christ Jesus our hope" (1 Ti 1:1). Paul is in effect telling the church of Ephesus what he had once told the Corinthians: "He is doing the work of the Lord, as I am. So let no one despise him." (1 Co 16:10-11)

1:1-2 SALUTATION

1:1-2 *An apostle.* Paul need not present his apostolic credentials to Timothy, his *true child in the faith,* of course; but the letter is an official one intended also for the church at Ephesus and is to undergird the authority of Timothy. See the Introduction and the note on 6:21

1:3—3:16 THE GNOSTIC HERESY CORRUPTS THE DOCTRINE OF THE CHURCH

1:3 ff. The letter falls into three major sections (I. 1:3—3:16; II. 4:1—6:2; III. 6:3-21). Each section is introduced by an indictment of the Gnostic heresy (1:3-7; 4:1-5; 6:3-10), which is followed by positive instruction on how the evil described in the indictment is to be combated and overcome.

1:3—3:16 Paul does not give a detailed description of the *different doctrine;* but he indicates clearly what its tendency is (which makes his indictment all the more valuable for the church of later days in the necessary task of theological self-examination and self-criticism). The doctrine which Timothy is to combat is, first, speculative, a human search for knowledge, not God's revelation which enters into and shapes men's lives *(training)* and is received and progressively appropriated *in faith,* in a grateful and obedient receiving (1:4). It is, second, loquacious and disputatious, a matter of *vain discussion* (6) which leads nowhere and effects nothing worthwhile, whereas the *charge* (5) received by Paul and by all proclaimers of the Gospel aims at solid, practical goals: *faith* in a God who saves and forgives, the *good conscience* of the forgiven man, the *pure heart* of unalloyed devotion which divine forgiveness can create in man, the *love* which grows on the soil of sincere faith and the good conscience and pure heart which faith gives a man (5). The *different doctrine* is, third, a "different gospel" (cf. Gl 1:6; 2 Co 11:4) and therefore no gospel at all (Gl 1:7); its proponents desire to be *teachers of the law* (7) and want to effect by prohibitions and prescriptions (cf. 4:3; Tts 1:14) what only *the glorious gospel of the blessed God* (11) can create. Paul's indictment (1:3-7) makes clear that there can be no compromise with this different doctrine, which corrupts both Law and Gospel; Timothy must *wage the good warfare* (1:18) of God against it. He will do so by proclaiming the Law as law (1:8-11) and by proclaiming the Gospel with which the apostle has been entrusted, the Gospel of the sheer overflowing grace of our Lord which Paul knows from profoundest personal experience (1:11-17), the Gospel which he commits to Timothy as to one whom the Spirit of God has marked out for this ministry (1:18-20). But since the Gospel is not a theory but a power which produces a life to be lived, Timothy's good warfare will also be concerned with the worship of the church (2:1-15) and with its organization (3:1-13). The Gospel, as the *divine training that is in faith* (1:4), is to produce and form a church which is in its whole life and all its manifestations the *pillar and bulwark of the truth* (3:15), the place where and the means through which there is exhibited for all men to see the creative grace of her incarnate and exalted Lord. (3:16)

1:3-7 The Indictment

1:3-7 See the note on 1:3—3:16 above.

1:4 *Myths and endless genealogies.* Just what these were is impossible to say. Some think of fanciful Judaic elaborations on the Old Testament, others of Gnostic speculations. The adjective *endless* is an indication of the apostle's low opinion of this kind of theological activity, an opinion that comes out plainly in the words "speculations" (4) and "vain discussion." (6)

1:5 *Our charge,* the obligation to proclaim the Gospel, laid on Paul (11) and on Timothy (18), and to be enjoined upon those teaching a different doctrine. (3)

1:7 *Teachers of the law.* Cf. 4:1-3; Tts 1:14.

1:8-20 The True Proclamation of Law and Gospel

1:8-20 Timothy is to combat and overcome the threatening corruption of doctrine by recognizing and proclaiming the true function of the Law, by using the Law *lawfully,* in accordance with its own intent (of opposing and exposing sin and condemning the sinner) and in the light of the *glorious gospel of the blessed God* (8-11), by which God makes men *just,* clear of the compulsion and condemnation of the Law (8). Timothy is to proclaim the Gospel with which Paul has been *entrusted* (11) as the antidote to the corrupted gospel of the false teachers, for Paul's own apostolate is the clearest Gospel of divine grace written into the life of undeserving man (12-17). Timothy can take up *the good warfare* (18) confidently, for God has taken the initiative in his ministry as in Paul's; His Spirit moved men to the *prophetic utterances* which *pointed* to him for this mission (18). He has cause for fear only if he ceases to believe the Gospel which he proclaims or violates his *conscience* by falsifying the Gospel and so *making shipwreck of* his *faith,* as *Hymenaeus and Alexander* have done. (18-20)

1:8 *We know,* etc. Cf. Ro 7:12, 16.

1:9-10 The list of transgressors follows the order of the Decalog, with six instances for the first table of the Law and eight for the second table. Paul gives extreme cases of transgression (e.g., *murderers of fathers* for the Fourth Commandment) to emphasize the negative character of the Law.

1:12-17 Cf. 1 Co 15:9; Gl 1:15; Eph 3:7-8.

1:13 *I had acted ignorantly.* This did not make him guiltless, but he had not placed himself outside the sphere of Jesus' prayer from the cross (Lk 23:34) by deliberate rejection of known and acknowledged truth, as the false teachers are doing, 4:1-2; 6:5. (Cf. Heb 6:4-8; 10:26-31)

1:18 *Prophetic utterances which pointed.* Cf. Acts 13:1-3 for a similar operation of the Spirit in prophecy.

Warfare. Cf. 1 Co 9:7; 2 Ti 2:3-4.

1:20 *Hymenaeus.* Cf. 2 Ti 2:17-18. *Alexander* may be identical with the Alexander mentioned in 2 Ti 4:14-15.

Delivered to Satan, for punishment (cf. Job 2:6). Exclusion from the church, excommunication, is meant, 1 Co 5:3-5, 13. Perhaps the imposing of bodily suffering is also implied. (1 Co 5:5, "destruction of the flesh"; Acts 13:11)

2:1-15 The Divine Training That Is in Faith: Worship

2:1:15 Timothy is to oppose and overcome the corrupting influence of the false teaching by so ordering the worship of the church that its prayers may be an expression of the all-embracing grace of God proclaimed in the Gospel and a recognition of government as a salutary functioning of the law of God (1-7). Prayers are to be said in the peaceable and forgiving spirit which the one Mediator between God and man has enjoined in the Fifth Petition (8). The conduct and demeanor of the worshipers is to be a recognition of the sanctity of the position which the Creator has assigned to woman. (9-15)

2:1 *First of all.* Worship is of supreme importance as the bridge between doctrine and action, the means whereby all life is hallowed so as to become worship. (Cf. Ro 12:1)

All occurs six times in six verses as an emphasis on the universality of the Gospel and as a protest against the sectarian exclusiveness of the Gnostic heresy, which produced an intellectual in-group. The church faces and loves the world.

2:2 *For kings.* Cf. Jer 29:7; 1 Ptr 2:13-17.

2:5 *One mediator.* One only, Christ Jesus, not Moses, not any of the intermediate beings which Gnostic speculation interposed between God and man. Jesus alone has mediated the whole grace of God's new and perfect covenant for all. (Cf. Heb 8:6; 9:15; 12:24)

The man. Cf. Ro 5:12-19; 1 Co 15:21-22, 45-49.

2:6 A clear echo of Jesus' word on His life and death as a vicarious redemption for "many." Paul changes the Hebraic "many" of Mt 20:28 and Mk 10:45 into "all" for Greek ears, since in Hebrew usage "many" can be used for "all." (Cf.

Ro 5:18 with 19, where "all" and "many" are used interchangeably.)

The testimony . . . borne. The redeeming act in Christ and the proclamation of it to men are but two phases, or aspects, of one saving act of God (cf. 2 Co 5:18-19; Eph 1:7-9; 2:13-16 with 17). In 2 Ti 1:10 and Tts 1:2-3 the second phase serves as a shorthand designation for the whole.

2:7 *I am not lying.* Evidently Paul's apostolic authority was being questioned in Ephesus, as it had been earlier, for example, in Galatia. (Cf. Gl 1—2)

2:8 *Lifting holy hands.* The uplifted hand (palm upward) was the common gesture of prayer in antiquity.

Without anger or quarreling. Cf. Mt 6:12; Mk 11:25.

2:9-15 Paul had special occasion to speak of woman's place in the worship of the church; the false teachers were introducing ascetic rigors regarding food and marriage (4:3). Nothing less than the goodness of God's good creation, including marriage, was at stake. Paul is fighting to preserve the divine order, which honors and fosters both man and woman in their individuality, as man, as woman. He points first to creation (13) and the Creator's intention to create woman as "a helper fit" for man (Gn 2:18). Then he points to the Fall, where the very qualities that make woman glorious as "a helper fit" for man (her pliability and openness to suggestion) proved her downfall (Gn 3:1-6). These two facts support the statement which denies the office of public teaching with its exercise of *authority over men* to woman (12). Paul finally (15) points to the sphere where woman's powers and gifts have full and free scope, the rearing of children (one which modern psychology with its discovery of the crucial importance of the first five years of a man's life has exalted); there she may walk in faith, love, and modest holiness toward the salvation which she shares equally with man (cf. Gl 3:28). Whoever sees in this an indication of "male superiority" or "female superiority" is certainly not thinking in terms of "the glorious gospel of the blessed God" (1:11) and has not yet learned to bow in adoration before the Creator, who has made all things well.

2:15 *Will be saved through bearing children.* The Greek preposition here translated *through* is a flexible one; it can indicate not only mediation or agency but also attendant circumstances; Paul uses the same preposition in 2 Co 2:4 to say that he wrote a letter with tears, weeping as he wrote. This seems the more natural sense here too; woman will find salvation by *faith* in the sphere of activity assigned to her by her Creator. The interpretation given in RSV note c *(by the birth of the child,* that is, Christ) is a possible rendering of the Greek but hardly fits the context.

3:1-16 The Divine Training That Is in Faith: Organization

3:1-16 Timothy is to oppose and overcome the corrupting influence of the false teachers by providing for *bishops* and *deacons* whose conduct, example, and influence shall be a living embodiment of the fact that the church is *the pillar and bulwark of the truth,* the truth namely, of the Gospel, which proclaims Christ as the Savior of men by a real incarnation that ties Him to the *flesh,* to the *nations,* and to the *world*—not the Christ of Gnostic speculation, who has no real contact with man. The true Gospel proclaims both His complete manhood and His total Godhead, His humiliation and His exaltation; He is the embodiment of the grace of God which saves man and transforms his life to one of uprightness and godliness. (Cf. Tts 2:11-14)

3:1 *Bishop* means "overseer" of a congregation; the modern "pastor" is closer to it than the sense that bishop has acquired in church language. The kind and quality of the "overseeing" implied may be gathered from the fact that Peter applies the term along with "Shepherd" to Christ Himself (1 Ptr 2:25, well translated as "Guardian" there). The overseer-shepherds derive their authority and character from the chief Shepherd. (1 Ptr 5:1-4)

3:2 *Husband of one wife.* This is aimed not at remarriage after the death of one's spouse but at concubinage and the virtual polygamy of illicit divorce.

Hospitable. The bishop would be called on to receive delegates of other churches and traveling missionaries. (3 Jn 5 ff.)

3:6 *Recent convert . . . conceit . . . condemnation of the devil.* A man still immature in faith would be particularly liable to the besetting sin of the clergy, pride; and the Accuser (Rv 12:10; Zch 3:1; cf. Lk 22:31) would be quick to bring his charge and demand punishment.

3:7 *Reproach and the snare of the devil.* A known tainted past may rise up to discredit the bishop and the community which he represents. He may be driven either to despair or to some rash and wrong action; in either case he proves easy prey to the devil.

3:8 *Deacons* (the word means "servant, one who waits on another," and is a title of honor, cf. Mt 20:26) provided for the poor and the ill in the congregation.

3:9 *The mystery of the faith,* the revealed Gospel, (cf. v. 16). Since Christian charity is care for the whole man, the deacon is not merely a "practical" functionary; he must be a man of Christian spirituality, able to apply the Gospel to man's need in the various areas of life.

3:10 *Also be tested.* Implies that bishops too underwent careful scrutiny before appointment, as 2, 4, 6, 7 imply.

3:11 *The women.* Either the wives of the deacons or, more probably, deaconesses. (Cf. Ro 16:1)

3:13 *Gain a good standing,* literally "a step," which may mean either that in doing God's work of mercy they draw closer to God and so learn to speak the Gospel ever more confidently, or that they grow in stature and influence by the faithful exercise of their office and so, matured and emboldened, advance to the office of bishop.

The two interpretations are not mutually exclusive.

3:15 *One ought to behave.* The *one* is very broad, including Timothy himself (cf. 4:12), teachers (1:3-4), men and women, bishops, deacons, deaconesses in their relationship to one another and to the Father of the house in the household of God.

3:15 *Pillar and bulwark of the truth.* The properly functioning church exhibits and supports the truth by which its members live and move and have their being, the truth being nothing less than the incarnate and exalted Christ Himself. To use another Pauline image, in beholding the body of Christ, the church, men can come to know Christ.

3:16 *The mystery of our religion.* A mystery because only God can reveal it and has in these last days revealed it, for Christ as the mystery in person cf. Cl 1:27, 2:2. The content of the revelation is unfolded in the following six lines, probably an early Christian hymn, pithy and pointed as a message inscribed in stone, a remarkable contrast to the "endless genealogies" (1:4) and "vain discussion" (1:6) of the Gnostics. Six passive verbs describing six mighty acts of God sum up the Gospel which we know from the four gospels and Acts. The Son of God *was manifested in the flesh;* He became the Servant of God and in a human life lived God's will of atoning love for man; that Servant life brought Him under the judgment of God and veiled His Godhead so completely that men standing by His cross could tauntingly demand that He *vindicate* Himself by descending from it. He cried out and died on the cross and left His vindication in His Father's hands. And God did vindicate Him. In the power of the invincible life of the *Spirit,* manifested at His conception (Mt 1:18, 20), His baptism (Mt 3:16), His temptation (Mt 4:1-10), in His proclamation (Lk 4:14, 18), and in His triumph over satanic powers (Mt 12:28)—in that power He rose from the dead (Ro 1:4). *Angels* beheld what no human eye could see; the angels who had hailed His birth (Lk 1:13) set a table in the wilderness for the obedient Son (Mt 4:11), hovered over Him in legions as He walked on earth (Jn 1:51; Mt 26:53). They proclaimed God's vindication of His Son and Servant to the disciples and prepared them for their meeting with the risen Lord (Mt 28:5; Lk 24:4-7). He, the vindicated Son of God in power, sent them out, under His command and empowered by the Spirit, to the *nations* (Mt 28:19; Lk 24:47). There in the alienated and hostile *world* the crowning miracle took place—the nations who had been far off were brought near; they *believed* on the Christ and came into the household of God (Eph 2:19). The Christ lives and reigns; when He was *taken up* from earth, He was enthroned at the right hand of the Father, *in glory.* That is the mystery of our religion. That is why there can and must be a "household of God," a "church of the living God," on earth. That is why worship and ministry can and must be so pure and powerful. That is why Timothy and all who believe on the incarnate Lord must and can wage the good warfare for the truth.

4:1—6:2 THE GNOSTIC HERESY CORRUPTS THE LIFE OF THE CHURCH

4:1—6:2 The appearance of these false teachers is a first fulfillment of the Spirit's warning for the latter days. Their teaching, for all its pretensions to rigorous piety, is a demonic denial of the goodness of God's creation (4:1-5). Timothy is to oppose and overcome this corrupting influence—*take heed to yourself and to your teaching;* let his food be the sound and wholesome food of the Gospel, his exercise to *train . . . in godliness.* Thus nurtured and trained, let him perform his duties soberly, scrupulously, and strenuously, fixing his hope in the living God, using to the full the gift which God has given him, and setting an *example in speech and conduct, in love, in faith, in purity* (4:6-16). His treatment of various age groups and classes in the church is to safeguard the soundness of the life of the church. He is to deal with young and old as with his kinfolk in the household of God (5:1-2). His treatment of widows who receive support from the church is to be both wisely realistic and lovingly respectful (5:3-16). He is to honor the elders who do their work faithfully; he is to deal soberly and conscientiously with those who fail in their duties (5:17-25). He is to remind slaves that their relationship to their masters, particularly Christian masters, is not abrogated by their freedom in Christ, but is hallowed by it; they are to serve all the better for serving freely. (6:1-2)

4:1-5 The Indictment

4:1-5 For a general description of the heresy see the Introduction.

4:1 *The Spirit . . . says.* For prophecies concerning the rise of false prophets and perversions of Christianity cf. Mt 24:11; Mk 13:22; Acts 20:29-30; 2 Th 2:9-10; and for a later date, Rv 13.

Deceitful spirits . . . demons. For the demonic-satanic character of all false religion cf. 1 Co 10:20-21; of perversions of the Gospel particularly, 2 Co 11:3-4, 13-15; 2 Th 2:9-10; 2 Ti 2:26.

4:2 *Consciences . . . seared,* scarred and calloused by compromise with sin (cf. Eph 4:19). The word *seared* can also mean *branded,* that is, marked as slaves of the devil. (Cf. 2 Ti 2:26)

4:3 *Forbid marriage.* For the positive appreciation of marriage which Paul opposes to this cf. 2:15; 3:2; 4-5, 12; and the whole conception of the church as the family of God, 3:15; 5:1-2.

4:4 *Everything . . . good.* Cf. Gn 1:4, 10, 12, 18, 21, 25, 31. To reverse God's own verdict of "very good" is to speak a demonic no to the Creator, now revealed as Savior (1:1; 2:3) to "those who believe." (3)

Received with thanksgiving, from the hand of the Creator, the Father of the household to whom all look for food (Ps 145:15-16), as the man Jesus did. (Mt 15:36; Lk 24:30, etc.)

4:5 *Consecrated by the word of God,* both the word spoken by God at creation (Gn 1:31) and the word of Scripture incorporated in the table prayer.

4:6-16 Take Heed to Yourself and to Your Teaching

4:6 *Brethren.* The picture of family of God still dominates. (Cf. 3:15; 5:1-2)

4:10 *Strive,* like athletes in a contest, continuing the metaphor of training (8). (Cf. 1 Co 9:24-27; 2 Ti 2:5; 4:7-8)

Especially of those who believe, since in them His will to save reaches its goal.

4:12 *Your youth.* Timothy was probably in his thirties; "youth" covered the period when a man was liable to military service, extending to the 40th year.

4:14 Cf. 1:18. The reference is to Timothy's ordination and commissioning. Cf. 2 Ti 1:6, where Paul speaks of himself as having ordained Timothy. Whether the reference is to two different occasions or whether Paul joined the elders in the laying on of hands can hardly be made out.

4:16 Cf. 1 Co 9:22-23.

5:1—6:2 How One Ought to Behave in the Household of God

5:1—6:2 See the analysis of 4:1—6:2 given at 4:1—6:2. The household of God embraces young and old (5:1-2), widows (5:3-16), elders with their special authority and responsibility (5:17-25), and slaves (6:1-2). The idea of the family of God runs through the whole unit, and in the section on the treatment of widows Paul is at pains to safeguard the ties and duties of the natural family (5:4, 8, 16). There is no conflict of interest between membership in the family of God and in the natural family.

5:3-16 Care for the widow was from of old well established in the life of the church. God is celebrated in the OT as "Father of the fatherless and protector of widows" (Ps 68:5, cf. Dt 10:18) and the OT enjoins care and concern for the widow (Dt 24:17; Is 1:17). The first organized charity of the church arose out of concern for the widow (Acts 6:1-6). Paul is here not so much enjoining care for the widow as regulating it; apparently the generosity of the church in this respect had been widely abused, and there was danger of a churchly pauperism. Hence the note of sobriety and caution here: a list (9) to be kept of widows qualified by age, need, and character to receive support from and (perhaps) render service in the church (9-10); in the light of past experience the enrollment of younger widows is discouraged (11-15); and the duty of family members to provide for their own and not shift their obligations over to the church is stressed. (4, 8, 16)

5:5 Cf. Lk 2:37.

5:10 *Brought up children,* both her own and orphaned children.

Washed the feet of the saints. This would be part of the *hospitality* mentioned (cf. Lk 7:44) but adds the note of humble, self-denying service, after the example of Christ (Jn 13:14-17). The *saints* are traveling Christians in need of hospitable ministry.

5:12 *Their first pledge,* not to remarry, made when enrolled in the list of widows.

5:17-25 Since Paul is in this unit not dealing with church offices (as in ch. 3), it would be better to translate the word rendered *elders* with the nontechnical term "older men" (as in 5:1) both in 17 and 19. (In fact, the nontechnical sense would fit Tts 1:5 also, so that the "office" of elder is not necessarily present in the Pastoral Letters at all, although found elsewhere in the NT, Acts 14:23; 1 Ptr 5:1 ff.). Paul is instructing Timothy on how to deal with a group of men whose place in the household of God gave rise to special problems. They enjoyed especial prestige, and leaders and teachers were normally drawn from their ranks (17). They would therefore be open to invidious attack; and in case of wrongdoing on the part of these grave and respected men, disciplinary action would be unusually difficult. Paul therefore insists on the honor due them (17-18) and protection from irresponsible attack (19). He goes on to remind Timothy that the salutary discipline of the erring prescribed by Jesus applies to them too and should be exercised without partiality but with due deliberation and especial care. (20-25)

5:17 *Double honor,* perhaps both esteem and financial support.

5:18 Dt 25:4; Lk 10:7; cf. 1 Co 9:9, 14.

5:19 Cf. Mt 18:15-17; Dt 19:15; 2 Co 13:1.

5:20 *Presence of all.* Cf. Mt 18:17: "Tell it to the church."

5:21 For a similar solemn adjuration cf. 2 Ti 4:1, where the reference to the Last Judgment is more explicit than here. But the reference to the Last Judgment is unmistakable here too: God will "judge the secrets of men by Christ Jesus" (Ro 2:16), who will come to judge "in his glory, and all the angels with him" (Mt 25:31). Timothy is to exercise judgment in the sobering consciousness that he, too, will be judged.

Elect angels, as opposed to fallen angels. (2 Ptr 2:4; Jude 6)

5:22 *Hasty in the laying on of hands,* either in ordination (remembering what may ensue if an unworthy candidate is ordained, cf. 3:10) or as a gesture of forgiveness toward the disciplined sinner (be sure that his repentance is serious and likely to prove lasting).

5:23 A parenthetical remark suggested by the word "pure" (22). Timothy's present practice of total abstinence from wine is not only bad for his health; it may also give the impression that he is seeking purity, as the Gnostics sought it, by abstinence. (Cf. 4:3)

5:24-25 What a man is, good or bad, will out sooner or later; therefore deliberate thoroughness is in order both in testing a man before ordination and in the process of disciplining the errant.

6:1 *May not be defamed.* Cf. Tts 2:10, where the same thought is put positively.

6:3-21 THE GNOSTIC HERESY CORRUPTS ITS TEACHERS

6:3-21 Men who have broken with the *sound words of our Lord Jesus Christ* and *wandered away from the faith* become conceited, ignorantly and morbidly contentious, *depraved in mind and bereft of the truth* which they have spurned. Their self-centered and self-seeking bent manifests itself most obviously in their avarice, which proves their ruin; they have lost the faith and the peace of a good conscience (3-10). Timothy is to oppose and overcome this corrupting influence by being a true *man of God,* combining a militant zeal for God's cause with love and gentleness, finding his whole riches in the *eternal life* to which he has been *called* (11-12); by unalloyed obedience to the *commandment* which his baptism and ordination have imposed on him, in a career of selfless ministry until the return of the Lord Jesus Christ, who will reward and judge His servants (13-16); by faithfully *guarding* the truth which has been *entrusted* to him, remembering that the key to it is not a vaunted *knowledge* but *faith* (20-21). Verses 16-19 are a parenthetic general warning suggested by the example of the corrupt teachers. Not only teachers are exposed to the temptation of avarice; the *rich* are to be admonished to find their true riches in God, in generous deeds, and in the life to come, which is life indeed.

6:3-10 Paul has applied Jesus' simple test for false prophets. ("You will know them by their fruits," their output, Mt 7:16) to the teaching promulgated by the false teachers (1:3-7) and to the life produced in their followers (4:1-5). He now applies the test to the character of the teachers, the person identified with the teaching. There has been some anticipation of this, inevitably, in the preceding indictments. (1:6; 4:2)

6:5 *Bereft of the truth.* They have opposed the truth (2 Ti 3:8), turned away from listening to the truth (2 Ti 4:4), rejected the truth (Tts 1:14). Their guilt becomes their doom; God deprives them of the truth. (Cf. Mt 13:12; Ro 1:28 and 1:18)

6:11 *Man of God.* Cf. 2 Ti 3:17. The phrase is used in the OT to denote bearers of God's Word: Moses, Ps 90 (superscription), Dt 33:1; prophets, 1 Sm 2:27; 1 K 13:1; 2 K 1:9-10; 4:16, etc. Jesus aligned His disciples with the prophets, Mt 5:12.

6:12 *You made the good confession,* at your baptism or your ordination or perhaps both.

6:13 *God who gives life.* Over against the false teaching (4:3) Paul again asserts the majesty of the Creator, as he recalls His goodness in v. 17.

Christ . . . Pontius Pilate . . . good confession. Over against Gnostic myths of a Christ too heavenly to be a real man, Paul asserts the Christ who appeared in history, before a Roman governor. Over against those who flout "the sound words of our Lord Jesus Christ" (6:3) he reminds Timothy that they are the words of One who sealed His testimony with His blood. (Jn 18:37, cf. 36)

6:19 *For the future,* that is, for the world to come. (Cf. Mt 6:19-20; Lk 12:33; 16:9)

6:20 *Contradictions of what is falsely called knowledge,* Gnostic antitheses to the sound teaching of the apostles and their Lord.

6:21 *With you.* The *you* is plural, an indication that the letter is intended for the church as well as for Timothy. See the Introduction.

SECOND

TIMOTHY

INTRODUCTION

Paul writes from prison in Rome. He has been a prisoner for some time: Onesiphorus, a Christian of Ephesus, had already sought him out and visited him in Rome (2 Ti 1:16-17). There has already been one hearing, at which Paul was deserted by all men and yet, with the Lord's help, so successfully defended himself that he "was rescued from the lion's mouth" (2 Ti 4:16-17). But Paul has no hope of ultimate acquittal; he is at the end of his course. And he is virtually alone; only Luke is with him. He longs to see "his beloved child" Timothy once more and bids him come to Rome before the winter makes travel by sea impossible (2 Ti 1:4; 4:9, 21). But he must reckon with the possibility that Timothy may not reach Rome in time; and so he must put in writing all that he hopes to tell Timothy in person if and when he arrives. The letter is thus, as Bengel has put it, Paul's "last will and testament" in which he bids Timothy preserve the apostolic Gospel pure and unchanged, guard it against the increasingly vicious attacks of false teachers, train men to transmit it faithfully, and be ready to take his own share of suffering in the propagation and defense of it. The most personal of the Pastoral Letters is therefore in a sense "official" too; for Paul cannot separate his person from his office. The man who has been "set apart for the gospel of God" (Ro 1:1) remains one with that Gospel in life and in death.

Date of writing: A. D. 65—67.

1:1-2 SALUTATION

1:3-18 PAUL'S APPEAL: REKINDLE THE GIFT WITHIN YOU

1:3-18 Paul introduces his appeal with thanksgiving for the bond of affection which has united him and Timothy, with an expression of his strong desire to see him again, and with a grateful recollection of the sincere faith that dwells in him (3-5). His appeal to Timothy is threefold: to *rekindle the gift of God* within him and so make full proof of the Spirit of *power and love and self-control* dwelling in him (6-7); to continue his task of witnessing to the Lord whom they both serve, to remain unashamedly loyal to the imprisoned apostle and ready to *share in suffering for the gospel* in the assurance that the gracious power of God which has overcome death and has sustained Paul in the faithful discharge of his appointed task will empower him too (8-12); to hold fast and guard the truth which Paul has committed to him, by the power of the Spirit who dwells in him as He dwells in Paul (13-14). Paul concludes his appeal by pointing to the warning example of *all . . . in Asia* who have failed him and to the heartening example of the kind and courageous Onesiphorus. (15-18)

1:3 *Serve with a clear conscience,* perhaps in contrast to the false teachers who have rejected conscience (1 Ti 1:19) and have seared and corrupted consciences. (1 Ti 4:2; Tts 1:15)

As did my fathers. For Paul's insistence on the integrity of his piety as a Pharisee cf. Ph 3:6.

1:5 Cf. Acts 16:1-3. For Timothy's rearing in the faith cf. 3:15.

1:6 *Rekindle.* The gift of God is a spiritual gift (cf. v. 14; 1 Co 12:1). For the Spirit pictured as fire cf. Acts 2:3; 1 Th 5:19; Rv 4:5.

The laying on of my hands. Cf. 1 Ti 4:14.

1:8 *Ashamed.* Cf. Ro 1:16.

1:9 *Gave us in Christ Jesus.* Cf. Eph 1:3-4

1:11 The *preacher* (or "herald") proclaims the Gospel; the *apostle* (commissioned messenger) disseminates it; the *teacher* applies it to daily living as the "divine training that is in faith." (1 Ti 1:4; cf. 1 Ti 2:7)

1:12 *What has been entrusted to me,* the Gospel in its purity and the whole future of the apostolic church. God will have a care for His Word and His people (cf. 2:19). But there is much to be said for the rendering given in RSV note *a: what I have entrusted to him,* i.e., Paul's life, the reference to Paul's suffering, his expectation of death (4:6-8) on the one hand, and the divine triumph over death (1:10) on the other, and the usage of the Greek word translated as *what has been entrusted* combine to favor this translation.

1:15 *Phygelus and Hermogenes* are otherwise unknown; they were probably former co-workers of Paul, from whom he might expect aid and support in time of need.

1:16-18 *Onesiphorus.* Paul's tribute to his energetic and fearless love remains his only but enduring monument. He was apparently dead at the time when Paul wrote. (Cf. 18; 4:19)

1:18 He who found the prisoner will *find* mercy in the judgment (cf. Mt 25:36 and 34). Paul's prayer is for the given gift of Christ, mercy for those whom God's mercy has made merciful. (Mt 5:7)

2:1—4:8 PAUL'S CHARGE: ENTRUST THE WORD TO FAITHFUL MEN

2:1—4:8 The theme of this unit is stated in 2:2: *What you have heard from me . . . entrust to faithful men who will be able to teach others also,* the "apostolic succession" of sound apostolic teaching, the only apostolic succession that the NT knows. These faithful men are not as prominent in what follows as one might expect, although it is clear that they are not forgotten. Cf 2:14 *(remind them);* 2:21 *(if any one purifies himself);* 2:24 *(the Lord's servant);* 3:12 *(all . . . will be persecuted);* 4:8 *(all who have loved his appearing).* The reason for this is not far to seek; in all his letters Paul manifests a strong consciousness of how "personal" the apostolate is; how the grace of the Lord lays claim to and employs the whole person with all his powers, experiences, and actions; how a man must be what he proclaims lest he "put an obstacle in the way of the gospel of Christ" (1 Co 9:12). He therefore speaks freely of himself; and he can say quite without vanity, "Be imitators of me, as I am of Christ" (1 Co 11:1). What holds for the apostle holds for all men entrusted with the apostolic Word of witness. Paul is therefore speaking of the training of *faithful* apostolic *men,* not only when specifically issuing instructions concerning them but also when he speaks of himself (2:8-10; 3:10-11, 14; 4:6-8) and of the man that Timothy ought to be (2:3-13, 15-16, 22-23; 3:14-17; 4:1-2, 5). In all this he is saying to the faithful men entrusted with the Gospel: "Join in imitating me, and mark those who so live as you have an example in us." (Ph 3:17)

2:1-13 Entrust the Truth to Faithful Men

2:1-13 Timothy can train and inspire faithful men only if he is himself faithful, ready to endure hardships and toil with a soldier's single loyalty, an athlete's rigorous self-discipline, and a farmer's strenuous industry (1-7). This he can do in the strength which is to be found in the risen Christ, who has given Paul the courage to suffer imprisonment and disgrace for the sake of God's elect. Timothy is to work and suffer in the faith that union with Christ in suffering and death is the assurance of union with Him in life and glory. (8-13)

2:2 *Heard . . . before many witnesses,* at his ordination or commissioning when he was pledged to the apostolic truth and "made the good confession in the presence of many witnesses." (1 Ti 6:12)

2:7 *Think over.* Paul does not spell out the application of the three pictures for Timothy. The Lord whom he serves will give him the insight he needs. (Cf. Ph 3:15-16)

2:8 Cf. Ro 1:3-4. Both passages are probably a quotation or an echo of an early creed.

2:9 *The word of God is not fettered.* See the notes on 4:10-12 and 4:17.

2:11 *The saying is sure.* Cf. 1 Ti 1:15; 3:1; 4:9; Tts 3:8. What follows is probably a quotation from an early Christian hymn; note the rhythmic language and the parallelism.

Died . . . live. Cf. Ro 6:8.

2:12 *Endure . . . reign.* Cf. Ro 8:17; 1 Ptr 4:17.

Deny. Cf. Mt 10:32-33; Rv 3:5.

2:13 *He remains faithful.* His "overflowing" (1 Ti 1:14) grace breaks the symmetry of the song; He who taught His disciples to pray daily for forgiveness (Mt 6:12) will not *deny himself;* they shall find forgiveness through Him. (Cf. Ro 8:34)

2:14-26 Train Faithful Men to Defend the Truth

2:14-26 Timothy is to warn these faithful men against sinking to the level of their opponents in their defense of the truth; they love disputes about words, but the teacher of the church is not to be a debater (14). Timothy can do this effectively only if he himself is an honest workman of the Lord, not like Hymenaeus and Philetus with their godless, cancerous, and disturbing teaching (15 to 18). He must, moreover, do his work in the believing confidence that God's truth cannot be overcome, that God will protect and vindicate His own (19). If he obeys the imperative of God's elective grace, he will become a pure and precious vessel fit for God's noblest uses. As such he will be able to rise above stupid controversies and create faithful men in his own image (20-23), servants of the Lord who can overcome error with apt teaching, with kindly, forbearing, gentle correction, in the faith and hope that God can grant their opponents repentance and deliver them from the devilish lie which intoxicates and ensnares them. (24-26)

2:14 *Them,* the "faithful men" of v. 2.

Does no good, i.e., does not convert the opponent, while the church *(hearers)* is shaken in the faith.

2:17 *Hymenaeus* is mentioned as a blasphemous teacher, excommunicated by Paul, in 1 Ti 1:20; *Philetus* is otherwise unknown.

2:18 *Holding that the resurrection is past already.* The resurrection of the dead is meant. Their teaching was a distortion of the idea that the Christian participates in Christ's death and resurrection through his baptism (Ro 6:3-11). By making the resurrection a purely inner, spiritual experience they evaded the thought of the resurrection of the body, which was offensive to Greek thinking (Acts 17:32. The Greek depreciated the body and thought of it as the prison of the soul, from which the immortal soul was released by death). Their teaching was therefore a demonic denial of the goodness of God's creation (1 Ti 4:1-5), a blasphemous attack on the Creator. (1 Ti 1:20)

2:19 *Foundation.* The truth on which the church is built (Eph 2:20), thought of as living and working in its witnesses *(those who are his).*

Seal, mark of God's ownership and therefore of His protection. (Cf. Eph 1:13)

"The Lord knows those who are his." Quoted from Nm 16:5, where the RSV translates rightly, "The Lord WILL SHOW who is his," for the Hebrew word "know" bears that dynamic sense. The words were spoken by Moses when one Korah and his companions challenged the leadership of Moses and Aaron. In the ordeal that ensued (Nm 16:5-35), Korah and his company were destroyed when "the earth opened its mouth and swallowed them" (Nm 16:32) because they had "despised he Lord" (Nm 16:30). As in the days of Moses, so now (cf. 3:8) those who despise the Lord and rebel against His apostles will be dealt with by the judgment of God.

"Let every one, etc." This is not a direct quotation of any one OT passage but a sort of summarization of a number of them (cf. Is 52:11; 26:13). The thought that acknowledging the God of the covenant as Lord *(names the name of the Lord)* commits a man to a life of righteousness under the blessings of His covenant is basic to the whole OT.

2:21 *If any one purifies himself,* i.e., obeys the imperative of God's elective grace: "Depart from iniquity." (19)

2:22 *Youthful passions,* in this context not erotic desires but youth's tendency to passionate partisanship, impatient pride, intellectual delight in controversy, etc.

2:24 *The Lord's servant.* Cf. Isaiah's prophecy of the Servant (Is 42:2), fulfilled in Jesus, Mt 12:17-21, esp. v. 19.

2:26 *Escape from,* literally "return to sobriety and so escape from."

Snare of the devil. For the demonic-satanic character of false religion generally cf. 1 Co 10:20-21; of perversions of the Gospel particularly cf. 2 Co 11:3-4, 13-15; 2 Th 2:9-10; 1 Ti 4:1.

3:1-9 There Will Come Times of Stress

3:1-9 Timothy is do to his work in the sobering conviction that times and men will grow worse and that opposition to the truth will increase. The only alleviating feature of this dark future is that the folly of those who oppose the truth will expose itself.

3:1 *In the last days.* Cf. 4:1, 3.

3:5 *Form of religion.* This may include both a correct creed and proper religious observances that have no influence on men's daily life.

3:6-7 This is probably an allusion to current activities of heretical teachers, the exact nature of which escapes us. Perhaps they cultivated the acquaintance of fashionable and flighty women whose "interest in religion" made them perpetually curious about the latest religious fad. (Cf. 4:3)

3:8 Jewish tradition assigned the names *Jannes* and *Jambres* to the Egyptian sorcerers who opposed Moses when he appeared before Pharaoh (Ex 7:11, 22; 8:7). Their opposition to the truth took the form of a counterfeit of the truth.

3:10-17 Continue in What You Have Learned

3:10-17 Timothy is to do his work in the solid assurance that he has the equipment needed for his difficult and dangerous task in the example of Paul, in the apostolic teaching he has received, and in the inspired Scriptures which are able to *instruct* man *for salvation through faith in Christ Jesus.*

3:11 *What befell me at Antioch,* etc. Cf. Acts 13:14-52; 14:1-20; 16:1-5. Timothy's home was in *Lystra,* and the memory of his first experience with the suffering of an apostle would be particularly vivid.

3:15-17. There is hardly another passage which sums up so succinctly and powerfully the convictions of our Lord and His apostles concerning the OT. These are: (1) The OT achieves its true utterance (says what it means) only in living connection with the NT Gospel, as witness to the righteousness of God manifested in Christ Jesus (Ro 3:21). Only the ear of faith *(faith in Christ Jesus)* hears its true utterance; only the believer in Christ Jesus experiences its power to effect God's radical deliverance of man from his desperate situation *(salvation).* (2) The Scriptures have this power because they are the product and the instrument of the Spirit of God *(inspired by God;* cf. 2 Ptr 1:19-21). (3) As such they are *profitable,* useful, performing a function. Being the work of the Spirit, whose creative possibilities begin where man's possibilities end, they can give man what man cannot give himself: *teaching,* knowledge of the will and ways of the God of illimitable power, wisdom, and goodness; *reproof,* the exposure and conviction of sin which make a man cry out, "Woe is me! For I am lost," in the presence of his holy God (Is 6:5); *correction,* the raising up of man to life and ministry where man has failed and totally collapsed (Is 6:6-8); *training in righteousness*—the inspired Word takes man in hand, lays the gentle yoke of his Savior God upon him, puts his reckless life in order, and makes of him a *man of God . . . complete, equipped for every good work.* (17)

4:1-8 Do the Work of an Evangelist

4:1-8 Timothy is to fulfill his ministry strenuously, insistently, courageously in the face of men's indifference to sound teaching and in spite of their itching desire for false teaching;

he is responsible, not to men but to the Christ who will return to judge all men. It is Timothy who must now do the work of an evangelist. Paul's course is run, his fight finished; he looks to the reward that awaits him and all faithful men who look in love for their Lord's appearing, His return to reign.

4:5 *Always be steady,* literally "be sober in all things."

4:6 *Sacrificed.* Cf. Ph 2:17.

4:8 *Crown of righteousness. Righteousness,* the final verdict of the God who "justifies him who has faith in Jesus" (Ro 3:26), is the *crown.* Cf. "crown of life," Ja 1:12.

4:9-22 PAUL'S REQUEST: COME TO ME SOON

4:9-22 *Come to me soon* (9). Paul's longing for his beloved child (cf. 1:4), a longing intensified by loneliness *(Luke alone* of all his co-workers is with him, 11), and his desire to impress on Timothy once more face to face the greatness and the glory of the task which is now his to carry on break forth in the urgent request that Timothy come to him in Rome. So intense is his feeling that he repeats the request in the midst of the greetings at the end: *Do your best to come before winter.* (21)

4:10 *Demas, in love with this present world,* rather than with the future "appearing" (8) of his Lord. Demas is otherwise unknown.

4:10-12 These verses, along with v. 20, provide an instructive commentary on 2:9: "The word of God is not fettered." Paul continues to deploy his workers *(Crescens, Titus, Tychicus)* with his accustomed energy and draws in new forces *(Mark).* Crescens is otherwise unknown; for Titus see the Introduction to the Letter to Titus. For Tychicus see the Introduction to the Captivity Letters and cf. Acts 20:4; Eph 6:21; Cl 4:7; Tts 3:12; perhaps he is to relieve Timothy at *Ephesus.* For Mark see the Introduction to his gospel.

4:13 *Cloak.* Paul's prison was no doubt a cold place.

Books . . . parchments. The first may be documents that would be useful to Paul in his trial; the latter probably were parts of the OT.

4:14 *Alexander.* Both the person and the event referred to are otherwise unknown. Alexander may be identical with the Alexander of 1 Ti 1:20; but the name was a common one, and it is difficult to see why the excommunicated false teacher of 1 Ti 1:20 should be identified as the *coppersmith* here.

4:16 *My first defense.* See the Introduction. Possibly the words refer to the earlier trial of Paul in A. D. 61, in which Paul was acquitted and released for further work in his mission to the Gentiles. (Cf. v. 17)

May it not be charged. Paul prays as Jesus prayed (Lk 23:34) and as Stephen prayed. (Acts 7:60)

4:17 *That all the Gentiles might hear it.* Whether the reference is to Paul's earlier trial or to a first hearing in his present trial, Paul appeared before the tribunal of Caesar as "an ambassador in chains" (Eph 6:20) and presented the cause and claim of Christ to the Gentiles. (Cf. Ph 1:12-18)

Lion's mouth, symbol of deadly peril. (Ps 22:21)

4:18 A reminiscence of the Lord's prayer. (Mt 6:13)

4:19 *Prisca and Aquila.* Cf. Acts 18:2-3, 18, 24-26 (Luke uses the diminutive form of Prisca's name, Priscilla); Ro 16:3-4; 1 Co 16:19.

Onesiphorus. Cf. 1:16-18.

4:20 *Erastus.* Cf. Acts 19:22; the Erastus of Ro 16:23, called "the city treasurer," is hardly the same person.

Trophimus. Cf. Acts 20:4; 21:29.

4:21 *Before winter,* when travel by sea was suspended (cf. Acts 27:12; 28:11). If Timothy waits until shipping is resumed in the spring, he will not find Paul alive.

Eubulus . . . Pudens . . . Linus . . . Claudia and all the brethren. Probably members of the church at Rome. Linus appears as second bishop of Rome (after Peter) in ancient lists. The others are otherwise unknown. If they were among those who failed Paul at his first defense (16), Paul's mention of them here (as brethren!) is evidence that Paul could forgive completely, as his Lord did when He called the disciples who had failed Him "my brethren." (Mt 28:10)

4:22 *Grace be with you.* The *you* is plural; Paul is greeting the church at Ephesus, perhaps more particularly the "faithful men" (2:2) to whom Timothy is to entrust the apostolic teaching. *Grace* is the apostle's last word.

TITUS

INTRODUCTION

The Letter to Titus is quite similar to First Timothy in its occasion, purpose, and content and can therefore be treated rather briefly here. Paul had worked for a while as missionary on the island of Crete together with Titus, the prudent, able, and tactful Gentile companion who had rendered him such valuable services at the time when the relationship between the Corinthian church and Paul had been strained to the breaking point (2 Co 2:13; 7:6 ff.; 8:6; 12:18). At his departure from Crete Paul left Titus in charge of the task of consolidating and organizing the newly created Christian communities. His task resembled that of Timothy at Ephesus in that the faith and life of the church were being endangered by the rise of false teachers of a Gnostic type, more pronouncedly Judaic in their teaching than those at Ephesus (Tts 1:14; 3:9). The situation was further complicated in Crete, however, by the fact that in these newly founded Christian communities solid organization was lacking and the pagan environment was particularly vicious (1:5, 12, 13). Whereas Timothy was to restore order in established churches, Titus had to *establish* order in young churches. It was a task which called for all his courage, wisdom, and tact. Paul wrote to Titus to encourage him in his task of organizing and edifying the churches and, not least, to give Titus' presence and work in Crete the sanction and support of his own apostolic authority. This last intention of the letter is evident in the salutation of the letter, which dwells on Paul's apostolate (1:1-3), and in the closing greeting, "Grace be with you *all*" (3:15), which shows that the letter addressed to Titus is intended for the ear of the churches also.

Time and place of writing: about A. D. 63 in Macedonia or en route to Nicopolis.

1:1-4 SALUTATION

1:1-4 The salutation is unusually detailed; like that of Paul's Letter to the Romans, written to a church which did not know the apostle personally, it dwells on the nature and function of the *apostle,* his place in the eternal counsels of God the Savior (the age-old promise now fulfilled, manifested and proclaimed) *to further* the *faith, knowledge,* and *hope of God's elect.* For the purpose of this full exposition of the apostolate see the Introduction.

1:2-3 *Promised . . . manifested.* Cf. 2 Ti 1:9-10; Eph 3:5.

1:5-16 AMEND WHAT IS DEFECTIVE

1:5-16 Titus is to supply the immature churches with sober and responsible leadership by appointing *elders* (5) to oversee *(bishop,* 7) the life of the church; they are to be men of unimpeachable character *(blameless,* 6), exemplary in their family life (6), and fitted by their disciplined and gracious maturity to function as *God's steward* (7), firmly grounded in *sound doctrine,* able to instruct the faithful and confute the contradictor (9). This last quality is especially important in Crete, where the church is exposed to the pernicious teachings of men who *profess to know God (gnosis),* but *deny him by their deeds* (16), insubordinate, loquacious, deceitful, mercenary men of Jewish-Christian background *(circumcision party,* 10) who purvey speculative theology *(myths,* 14) and impose human commands of abstinence in the name of higher knowledge and higher purity. These men *must be silenced* (11), for their teaching reveals their ignorance of God and the impurity of their minds. (15-16)

1:5 *Elders* designates the leaders according to the age group from which they are drawn; *bishop* (7) describes them according to their function, that of being overseers. (Cf. Acts 20:28)

1:6-9 Cf. 1 Ti 3:1-7 and the notes there.

1:10-16 The description of the false teachers is very similar to those of 1 Ti 1:3-11; 4:1-11; 6:3-10; 2 Ti 2:14-18, which help toward the understanding of what is very briefly indicated here; the peculiarity of the situation in Crete sets this passage off from the others (12). For a general description of the Gnostic heresy see the Introduction to First Timothy.

1:12 *A prophet of their own.* The quotation was commonly attributed to the sixth-century poet and religious reformer Epimenides, himself a Cretan and so a valid witness to their national character, which had a bad reputation in antiquity generally.

1:13 *Rebuke . . . that they may be sound in the faith.* The aim of rebuke is to free men of error and to restore their faith to health. Cf. Mt 18:15: "You have gained your brother."

1:14 *Jewish myths,* probably allegorical interpretations of the Old Testament in support of Gnostic speculation.

1:14-15 *Reject the truth . . . all things are pure.* The truth which these men reject is that enunciated by Jesus when He rejected Judaic tradition (Mk 7:6-8) and "declared all foods clean." (Mk 7:19)

1:15 *To the pure,* etc. This echoes Jesus' teaching concerning what defiles a man (Mk 7:18-23). The pure man is the new man in Christ who receives with thanksgiving everything created by God and enjoys it with a clear conscience (cf. 1 Ti 4:4-5; Ro 14:14, 20). The *corrupt and unbelieving* men cannot feel at home in God's good creation because they know neither their Savior nor their Creator. (Cf. v. 16)

2:1—3:8a SOUND DOCTRINE AND SOUND LIVING

2:1-15 The Training Grace of God in Daily Life

2:1-15 Titus is to let *sound doctrine* (1) make sound the whole life of man. He is to instruct men of all ages and classes by word and example (7-8) in that wholesome conduct of life which God's universal grace in Christ has made possible; the life of the redeemed people of God is to be a living preachment of that enabling grace; even the life of the slave may adorn the doctrine of God our Savior. (10)

2:10 *Adorn the doctrine,* as a fruitful tree adorns the soil on which it grows.

2:11-14 This is the pithiest and most comprehensive statement on the grace of God to be found in the Pauline letters. It looks back to God's spontaneous act *(appeared,* 11) of love in Jesus Christ, His act of universal radical deliverance *(salvation)* for the redemption of mankind (14). It looks to the future, to the fulfillment of the *blessed hope* given by that redemption (13). But the chief emphasis is on the present. God's saving grace is a *training* grace (12) which makes man's life sound in every respect. Under the benign sway of this grace (cf. Ro 6:14) man's relationship to himself is one of self-control *(sober,* 12); to his fellowman, one of justice *(upright,* 12); and to his God, one of piety *(godly,* 12). God's grace fulfills His ancient intention and promise of a people redeemed and purified for a life of service to Him. (14; cf. Ps 130:8; Eze 37:23)

2:15 *Reprove,* that is, call to repentance. The new life of the new people of God does not "come naturally," but is a life of constant repentance, as Luther declared in the first of his Ninety-five Theses.

3:1-8a Reborn for Obedience, Courtesy, Good Deeds

3:1-8a Sound doctrine produces sound civic life. Members of God's new people are to be obedient to governmental authority, active and energetic in the pursuit of the civic good, showing all men that gentle and winning Christian courtesy which has been engendered in them by the *goodness and loving kindness of God our Savior* (4). His saving, justifying, renewing work (5-7) equips believers for their profession: *good deeds.* (8)

3:2 *Gentle.* The word translated *gentle* suggests the graciousness of a superior, one who is above the pressure of cruel competitiveness; it is a gentleness born of strength.

Courtesy is a good rendering here for a word elsewhere rendered as "meekness" (Ja 1:21; 3:13). It is the considerate and kindly attitude of one who knows that it is God who makes the decisions and confidently leaves the ultimate decisions to Him.

3:3-7 This second passage on the redeeming love of God (cf. 2:11-14) with its emphasis on the complete absence of merit or deserving on the part of the redeemed serves to counteract cold Christian smugness toward non-Christians. We dare not despise non-Christians or write them off as being of no consequence; to do so would be to deny the mercy of Him who did not write us off.

3:5-7 God's saving act is detailed in the order in which the Christian has experienced it. In Baptism he has been buried with Christ and has risen to new life with Him; the blessings of the cross and resurrection are his by this *washing of regeneration* (Ro 6:3-14). In Baptism he has received the Holy Spirit, who leads him into all truth and glorifies for him the Christ into whose name he has been baptized (Jn 16:13-14). Under the Spirit's tutelage he realizes ever more fully what it means to be justified by grace, to have a present unburdened by past guilt, and to live in the resilient *hope of eternal life.* For a similar sequence cf. 1 Co 6:11.

3:8b-11 THE EXCLUSION OF UNSOUND TEACHING

3:8b-11 Men who live and work in the wholesome light of *excellent and profitable* (8) sound teaching have neither taste nor time for endless, useless, and morbid theological debate. They do their duty toward the man who makes propaganda for his error and gathers followers for it *(factious,* 10). They confront him with the truth and call him to repentance *(admonishing,* 10). If he refuses repeated admonition, they must exclude him from the church, for he has condemned himself by persisting in his sinful perversion of the truth and has excluded himself from their fellowship. (11)

3:8b *Who have believed,* that is, have come to faith and are believers.

3:9 *Genealogies.* Cf. 1 Ti 1:4. These probably refer to speculative and fanciful interpretations of Old Testament history. They are *unprofitable and futile* because they do not employ the inspired Scriptures for the purpose for which they were given, to "instruct" men "for salvation through faith in Christ Jesus." (2 Ti 3:15-17)

3:10 *Factious,* creator and leader of a faction, one of those "who create dissensions and difficulties, in opposition to the doctrine which you have been taught" (Ro 16:17). The Greek word has given us the term "heretic," and these verses are the classical definition of the heretic.

Once or twice. The procedure is to be that prescribed by Jesus, Mt 18:15-17.

3:11 *Perverted and sinful . . . self-condemned.* Since he has both turned aside from the true course and has refused the admonition that would restore him, he stands condemned by his own actions and must be left to the judgment of God (Cf. 1 Co 5:5, 12-13)

3:12-15 CONCLUSION: INSTRUCTIONS, GREETINGS, BENEDICTION

3:12-15 Titus is to rejoin Paul in Nicopolis when Artemas or Tychicus comes to relieve him (12). He is to help Zenas and Apollos, the bearers of this letter, on their way (13). The Cretan Christians, too, are to do their part in supporting these missionaries (14). Paul and his coworkers send greetings to Titus and all believers in Crete.

3:12 *Artemas.* Otherwise unknown.

Tychicus. Cf. Acts 20:4; Eph 6:21; Cl 4:7-9; 2 Ti 4:12.

Nicopolis, probably in Epirus. See the Introduction to the Pastoral Letters.

3:13 *Zenas the lawyer.* Probably a converted Jewish scribe.

Apollos. Cf. Acts 18:24-28; 1 Co 1:12; 3:4-6, 22; 16:12.

3:15 *With you all.* At least the substance of this letter is intended for all the Christians in Crete.

PHILEMON

INTRODUCTION

During his 2-year imprisonment in Rome Paul "welcomed all who came to him" (Acts 28:30). Among the many who sought out Paul was one disreputable character, and Paul "welcomed" him too, the slave Onesimus. Onesimus had run away from his master Philemon of Colossae, lining his pockets for the journey with his master's goods, as was the usual practice with runaway slaves (Phmn 18). Somehow he reached Rome, and somehow he came into contact with Paul. Paul's welcome for poor Onesimus must have been a warm one, for he converted the young runaway and became very fond of him. Paul would gladly have kept Onesimus with him, for he was now living up to his name (Onesimus means "useful") in his devoted service to Paul. Since the slave's master Philemon was also a convert of Paul's, bound to him by a sacred and enduring tie, he might have made bold to do so. But Paul honored all human ties, including the tie which bound slave to master, as hallowed in Christ (Cl 3:22 ff.; Eph 6:5 ff.). He therefore sent Onesimus back to Colossae with Tychicus, the bearer of his Letter to the Colossians (Cl 4:7-9), and wrote a letter to his master in which he bespoke for the runaway a kindly and forgiving reception. We can measure the strength of the bond between the apostle and his converts by the confidence with which Paul makes his request of Philemon, a request all the more remarkable in the light of the fact that captured runaways were usually very harshly dealt with. Paul goes even farther: he hints that he would like to have Onesimus back for his own service. (13, 14, 20, 21)

Brief and personal though it is, the Letter to Philemon affords two valuable Christian insights. First, there is no line of cleavage between the official Paul, the apostle, and the person Paul; for both, life has one content and one meaning: "For me to live is Christ." Luther portrays Paul as being a "Christ" to Onesimus, "pleading the cause of the runaway as Christ has pleaded ours. For we are all His Onesimi, if we believe it." A man who believes and knows that he has come back to God as God's runaway slave and has been welcomed as a son, such a man can write the Gospel into life's minutiae as naturally and gracefully as Paul does in this letter.

Second, the Letter to Philemon illustrates the apostolic and Christian attitude toward social problems. Paul does not plead for Onesimus' liberation. There is nothing like a movement to free slaves, even Christian slaves of Christian masters, either here or elsewhere in the New Testament. But a Gospel which can say to the master of a runaway slave that he is to receive him back "for ever, no longer as a slave, but more than a slave, as a beloved brother" (Phmn 15-16), has overcome the evil of slavery from within and has therefore already rung the knell of slavery.

1-3 GREETINGS

1:3 *Timothy* had been with Paul during his 3-year ministry in Ephesus and no doubt was acquainted with many Christians of the province of Asia, such as *Philemon,* his wife, *Apphia,* and his son *Archippus,* who had a special ministry at Colossae (Cl 14:17) and so is singled out as *fellow soldier* of the apostle.

4-7 THANKSGIVING AND PRAYER

4-7 Paul gives thanks for Philemon's faith and love and prays that they may continue their effectual witness. Philemon seems to have recently distinguished himself by a work of love which *refreshed the hearts of the saints.* Paul is about to request another such refreshment of heart for himself. (20)

6 The *knowledge* which Philemon's love born of faith is to promote may be the knowledge which his witness produces or increases in others. The thought might, however, also be that Philemon's own knowledge is deepened as his faith is demonstrated and exercised in love.

8-20 PAUL'S PLEA FOR HIS CHILD ONESIMUS

8-20 Paul appeals to Philemon to receive Onesimus again, now more than a slave to him, a beloved brother forever. Paul lets Philemon know how greatly he cherishes this child of his imprisonment and hints pretty broadly that he would like to have him back in his own service; after all, Paul argues, Philemon owes him more than the gift of a slave could repay—as Paul's convert he owes his very life and self to Paul. (19)

10 Cf. 1 Co 4:15: "I became your father in Christ Jesus through the gospel."

14 *Your goodness* here means the generous action of making Paul a gift of the "useful" Onesimus.

16 Onesimus has become a *beloved brother* to his master *both in the flesh,* that is, in his legal-human position as a slave, and *in the Lord,* as fellow member in the church, the body of Christ. These words are a concrete application of what Paul has taught the churches in Cl 3:11; 3:22—4:1; and Eph 6:5-9; cf. 1 Ti 6:1-2; Tts 2:9-14.

17 Philemon is Paul's "beloved fellow worker" (v. 1), "his brother" (v. 7), and his *partner* (v. 17; cf. Ph 1:5). In v. 19 Paul speaks of him as owing his very existence to Paul. So strong is the bond created by the Gospel.

19 The language here is that of a formal IOU. This is probably a touch of humor. Paul hardly had the means to compensate Philemon for the loss which he had sustained through Onesimus. But the second half of the verse is serious truth clothed in the language of familiar friendship; since Philemon was once "dead in trespasses" (Cl 2:13) and came "to fulness of life" in Christ (Cl 2:10) through Paul's proclamation of the Gospel, he owes himself, the true self that will live forever, to Paul.

21-25 CONCLUDING GREETINGS

21-25 Paul bespeaks Philemon's hospitality for the time of his release and return to Colossae, transmits the greetings of his visitors and fellow workers at Rome, and closes with a benediction.

22 *To be granted to you,* that is, by being released from imprisonment and so becoming free to revisit the churches of Asia.

23-24 The names mentioned here all occur in Cl 4:10-14. The term *fellow prisoner* means literally "fellow prisoner-of-war." It is used figuratively to indicate that Epaphras is voluntarily sharing his hardships as a soldier of Christ.

HEBREWS

INTRODUCTION

1 The Letter to the Hebrews is surely a part of the story of how the Word of the Lord grew and prevailed. Here if anywhere in the New Testament we are made conscious of the fact that God's speaking is a mighty onward movement, an impetus of revelation designed to carry man with it from glory to glory. And here it is impressed on us that if a man resists that impetus, he does so at his own deadly peril; we are warned that stagnation and retrogression invite the destroying judgment of God. But the letter is itself also the proof that God does not abandon the weak and sickly stragglers of His flock; He sends forth His Word and heals them.

Destination of the Letter.

2 The title "To the Hebrews" is not part of the original letter, but was probably added in the second century when the New Testament letters were gathered into a collection. Moreover, there is no salutation which would identify the readers. The destination of the letter must therefore be inferred from the letter itself. It is not so personal as a letter of Paul's. It is more on the order of a sermon (cf. 13:22, "my word of exhortation"), and it is more literary, with its high stylistic finish and strictly unified theme. Still, it is not merely an essay in letter form, but a genuine letter. It grows out of a personal relationship between the author and his readers. The author has lived among the people whom he is now addressing; and though he is at the time of writing separated from them, he hopes to be restored to them soon (13:18-19, 23). The content of the letter indicates that the readers were Jewish Christians, so that the title given by the men of the second century is not unfitting.

3 Many modern scholars are inclined to see in the readers not Jewish Christians in danger of relapsing into Judaism, but Gentile Christians (or Christians in general) in danger of lapsing into irreligion. And they have often argued their case with considerable ingenuity. But it is difficult to see why the letter should in that case be from beginning to end one great and emphatic exposition of the superiority of the New Testament revelation over that of the Old Testament. Why should an appeal to *Gentile* Christians in danger of apostasy take just this form? Jewish Christians seem to be more likely recipients of the letter.

4 Where these Jewish Christians lived cannot be definitely made out. Italy is the most likely place, and within Italy, Rome. The letter contains greetings to the church from "those who come from Italy" (13:24), evidently from members of the Jewish Christian church who are now with the author and are sending greetings to their home church. This is confirmed by the fact that Hebrews is first quoted and alluded to by Roman writers, namely, Clement of Rome and Hermas. The readers have their own assembly (10:25), but are also connected with a larger group, as the words "greet *all* your leaders and *all* the saints" (13:24) indicate. It has therefore been very plausibly suggested that the recipients were one of the house churches to which Paul refers in Romans. (16:5, 14-15)

Occasion and Purpose of the Letter

5 These Christians had in the past given evidence of their faith and love (6:10). They had stoutly endured persecution themselves and had courageously aided others under persecution (10:32-34). Their believing courage had not failed them in times of crisis; but it was failing them in the longdrawn, unending struggle with sin (12:4). They were growing dispirited and slack (12:12); the continuous pressure of public contempt, particularly

the contempt of their fellow Jews (13:13), had revived in them the old temptation to be offended at the weakness of the Christ they believed in, at His shameful death, and at the fact that the Christ did not fulfill their Judaic expectation and "remain for ever" on earth (cf. Jn 12:34) but was removed from sight in the heavens. They had ceased to progress in their faith (5:11-14) and were neglecting the public assembly of the church which could strengthen them in their faith (10:25). Some had perhaps already apostatized (6:4-8); all were in danger of falling away (3:12) and reverting to Judaism (13:9-14). Judaism with its fixed and venerable institutions, its visible and splendid center in the Jerusalem temple and its cultus, its security and exemption from persecution as a lawful religion under Roman law must have had for them an almost overwhelming fascination.

6 The letter is therefore basically just what its author calls it, a "word of exhortation" (13:22), an appeal to "hold fast the confession . . . without wavering" (10:23; cf. 10:38; 3:14). The author points his readers to Jesus and urges them to look to Jesus, "the pioneer and perfecter of our faith, who for the joy that was set before him endured the cross, despising the shame, and is seated at the right hand of the throne of God" (12:2). They are to consider Him with the eyes of faith and find in Him the strength to overcome their weariness and faintheartedness (12:3). The whole long and detailed exposition of the high priesthood of Christ is anything but a merely informative theological treatise. It is wholly pastoral and practical in its aim and intent. The author is a leader like the leaders whom he describes in his letter (13:17); he is keeping watch not over the theology of his people but over their souls as one who will have to give an account of his leadership.

The Author of the Letter

7 The letter does not name its author, and there is no consistent tradition in the early church concerning its authorship. In the East the letter was regarded either as directly written by Paul or as in some sense owing its origin to Paul. Origen of Alexandria reflects this tradition; he says of the letter: "Its thoughts are the thoughts of the apostle, but the language and composition that of one who recalled from memory and, as it were, made notes of what was said by the master. . . . Men of old times handed it down as Paul's. But who wrote the epistle God only knows certainly." The Western church did not attribute the letter to Paul; Tertullian of Carthage assigned it to Barnabas, while in Rome and elsewhere the letter was anonymous.

8 The fact that the author counts himself and his readers among those who received the Word of salvation at second hand from those who had heard the Lord is conclusive evidence that the author is not Paul (2:3), for Paul appeals repeatedly to the fact that he has seen the Lord and has received the Gospel directly from Him (1 Co 9:1; 1 Co 15:8; Gl 1:11-12). The general character of the theology of the letter and the author's acquaintance with Paul's companion Timothy (13:23) point to someone who moved in the circle of Paul's friends and co-workers. The characteristics of the letter itself further limit the possibilities: they indicate that the author was in all probability a Greek-speaking Jewish Christian, thoroughly at home in the Old Testament in its Greek translation, and intimately acquainted with the whole worship and cultus of the Jews, a man capable, moreover, of the most finished and literary Greek in the New Testament. Barnabas, the Levite from Cyprus (Acts 4:36) and companion of Paul would be a not unlikely candidate for authorship. Whether Tertullian attributed the letter to him on the basis of a genuine tradition or was making a plausible conjecture, cannot be determined. Apollos, whom Luther suggested as the possible author, is even more likely. He was associated with Paul, though not in any sense a "disciple" of Paul, and Luke in the Book of Acts describes him as a Jew, a native of that great center of learning and rhetoric, Alexandria, an eloquent man, well versed in the Scriptures, and fervent in spirit (Acts 18:24-25), all characteristics that we find reflected in Hebrews.

9 Luther's conjecture remains the most reasonable of all the ancient and modern

conjectures, which have attributed the letter to a great variety of authors—Luke, Clement of Rome, Silvanus, Aquila and Priscilla, Priscilla alone, etc. But Origen's word still holds: "Who wrote the epistle God only knows certainly." More important than the man's name is the kind of man he was; he was an earnest teacher of the church, deeply conscious of his responsibility for the church, whom the Holy Spirit moved to employ all his resources of language and learning in order to restore to health and strength the weak and faltering church.

Date of the Letter

10 Since Hebrews is quoted by Clement of Rome in his letter to the Corinthians of A. D. 96, the letter must be earlier than that date. There is no evidence which enables us to determine exactly how much earlier it was written. Timothy is still alive at the time of writing (13:23), but since he was a young man when Paul first took him as his companion in A. D. 49 (Acts 16:1-3), he may have lived to the end of the first century or beyond. The readers have been converted by personal disciples of the Lord (2:3), and considerable time has elapsed since their conversion: they have had time for development and growth (5:12). Some of their first leaders are now dead (13:7). They have endured one persecution (probably the Neronian persecution A. D. 64) and are apparently facing another (10:36). All this points to the latter half of the first century. Since the author dwells on the fact that the old system of priesthood and sacrifice was destined to be superseded by a greater and more perfect priesthood and sacrifice, it would seem strange that he does not mention the fall of Jerusalem (which put an end forever to the old cultus) if that event had taken place. The argument from silence is strong in this case, and a dating before A. D. 70, probably shortly before, seems very probable. But it should be said that many scholars today are not inclined to attach much weight to this argument; they argue that the author is thinking not of the Jerusalem temple and its cultus, but of the cultus as he knows it from the Old Testament, and date the letter somewhere in the eighties.

Characteristics of the Letter

11 The purpose of the letter is practical, like that of every book of the New Testament; its aim is to strengthen faith and hope, to inculcate stout patience and a joyous holding fast to the Christian confession. The message which provides the basis for the exhortation and the impetus and power for its fulfillment has three primary characteristics. It is founded on the Old Testament; it is centered in Christ; and it is marked by an intense consciousness of the fact that all days since the coming of the Christ are last days.

12 The message is, first, founded on the Old Testament. It is to a large extent an interpretation and exposition of Old Testament Scriptures. It has been likened to a Christian sermon or a series of sermons on selected psalms (2, 8, 95, 110). The letter therefore contains high testimony to the inspiration and authority of the Old Testament Scriptures. In the first verse the whole Old Testament is designated as the very voice of God speaking to men, and throughout the letter words which men of God spoke of old are presented as spoken by God Himself (e. g., 1:5, 6, 13; 5:5) or by Christ (e.g., 2:11-13; 10:5) or by the Holy Spirit. (3:7; 10:15)

13 The author's characteristic use of the Old Testament is that which has been termed the typological use, that is, he sees in the history and the institutions of the Old Covenant events, persons, and actions which are typical, foreshadowings and prefigurings of that which was to become full reality in the New Covenant. In one sense the whole epistle is a set of variations on a theme from Paul: "These [the Old Testament sacral institutions] are only a shadow of what is to come; but the substance belongs to Christ" (Cl 2:17). Thus Melchizedek, both priest and king, is divinely designed to point beyond himself to the great High Priest Jesus Christ (7:1—10:18). The fate of God's people in the wilderness, their failure to attain to the promised Sabbath rest, points beyond itself to the eternal Sabbath rest which awaits the New Testament people of God (3:7—4:13). This view and use of the Old Testament never degenerates into mere

allegory; that is, the Old Testament figures are never merely symbols of eternal truths, as in the allegorizing interpretation of the Jewish philosopher Philo; rather, the Old Testament history is always taken seriously as history. As such, as history, it points beyond itself to the last days. This use of Scripture is therefore an eloquent expression of the faith that God is Lord of all history, shaping it for His purposes and leading it toward His great redemptive goal. The Old Testament is therefore of abiding value and enduring significance for the people of God in the last days, for it enables them to see the whole sweep and direction of the mighty redeeming arm of God.

14 The message is, second, centered in Christ. Christ, the Son of God, dominates the whole, and Christ colors every part of the whole. He stands at the beginning of history as the Son through whom God created the world; He stands at the end of all history as the divinely appointed "heir of all things" (1:2). He dominates all history and rules the whole world, "upholding the universe by his word of power" (1:3). He is God's ultimate and definitive Word to man (1:2), and His high-priestly ministry is God's ultimate deed for man—a whole, assured, eternal deliverance from sin. That high-priestly, atoning ministry spans the whole of Jesus' existence: His entry into mankind, His sacrificial suffering and death, His entering into the heavenly Holy of Holies, His presentation of His sacrifice at the throne of God, and His return in glory to the waiting people of God are all high-priestly acts. (E. g., 2:17-18; 4:14; 9:11-14, 28)

15 His high-priestly ministry marks Him as full partaker in the Godhead and as completely one with man. Indeed, no letter of the New Testament is so full of the humanity of Jesus as Hebrews. Since He is both Son of God and a Priest fully one with man, His priesthood and His sacrifice have a real and eternal significance and top and supersede every other priestly ministration. The impress of the incarnate Christ is upon His people; His history of suffering and triumph is their history; His obedience and fidelity to the Father make possible their faithful obedience to God. His entering into the Holy Place gives them access to the throne of God.

16 The message is, third, marked by the consciousness that the days since God spoke in His Son are "these last days" (1:2). Christ has appeared "at the end of the age to put away sin by the sacrifice of himself" (9:26). It is the beginning of the end; the new world of God has become a reality in the midst of the old, and men "have tasted . . . the powers of the age to come" (6:5) even now. What former ages had possessed in an imperfect form, a form which itself pointed to a fuller realization, is now a present blessing — a better covenant (7:22), better sacrifices (9:23), a better possession (10:34), and a better hope (7:19). Men still hope, and the full realization of all that Christ has wrought is still to come. But the Day is drawing near (10:25) when all that is now a sure hope shall be fully realized. This "last days" character of Jesus' work, its eschatological character, gives it a final, once-for-all character and makes the decision of faith one of terrible urgency; eternal issues are being decided now, in faith or unbelief. Man is confronted by an eternal and inescapable either-or. Seen in this eschatological light, the sternness of the warnings in 6:4-8 and 10:26-31, warnings which at first glance seem to preclude the possibility of a second repentance, is not strange. (These warnings seemed to Luther to be "hard knots" and made him dubious about the letter.) God has spoken His last Word, and the time is short; men must not be left under the delusion that they can coolly and deliberately sin and then repent in order to sin again. Such sinning is the last step on the way toward apostasy; it is the expression of an "evil, unbelieving heart" (3:12) which cannot find the way to repentance because it has deliberately cut itself off from God, the Giver of repentance.

17 The pastoral intent of the writer (cf. par. 6) dictates the structure of his letter; instruction alternates with words of admonition, warning, and appeal. The statements which expound the surpassing significance of Jesus the Son as God's last Word to man are followed by imperatives which summon men to heed that Word.

OUTLINE

I. 1:1—4:13 God's Ultimate Word, Spoken by a Son
  A. 1:1-14 Instruction: The Son Superior to Angels
  B. 2:1-4 Admonition: Do Not Neglect Such a Great Salvation
  C. 2:5-18 Instruction: The Son Made Lower than the Angels
  D. 3:1-6 Instruction: Jesus Worthy of More Glory than Moses
  E. 3:7—4:13 Warning: Harden Not Your Hearts

II. 4:14—10:18 Jesus, the Ultimate High Priest
  A. 4:14—5:10 Instruction: Jesus a True High Priest
  B. 5:11—6:20 Warning and Encouragement
  C. 7:1—10:18 Instruction: Jesus the High Priest

III. 10:19—12:29 Exhortation and Warning
  A. 10:19-25 Exhortation: Draw Near with a True Heart
  B. 10:26-31 Warning: Judgment on Apostasy
  C. 10:32-39 Exhortation: Do Not Throw Away Confidence
  D. 11:1—12:2 Exhortation: Run the Race
  E. 12:3-29 Exhortation to Faith and Fear

IV. 13:1-25 Concluding Admonitions and Close
  A. 13:1-6 True Love and False
  B. 13:7-19 Concerning Leaders in the Church
  C. 13:20-25 Close

1:1—4:13 GOD'S ULTIMATE WORD, SPOKEN BY A SON

1:1—4:13 God has spoken His ultimate Word in His Son, who surpasses all previous mediators of divine revelation (prophets, angels, Moses); therefore give heed to that Word of salvation.

1:1-14 Instruction: The Son Superior to Angels

1:1-14 God has climaxed His ancient Word of promise *(prophets,* 1) by His final Word *spoken* in *these last days by a Son* (2). The unique importance of this Word is revealed in the unique greatness of its Bearer, God's Son. SEVEN WEIGHTY STATEMENTS expound the Son's greatness (2-4). He is seen at the end of God's ways as *heir,* Owner, and Ruler of the universe (2). He is seen at the beginning of God's ways, in creation, as partaking in the Creator's action (2). To behold His glory is to see the *glory of God* going forth into the world. To know Him is to know God's *nature* (3). The Son's *word of power* is God's own Word, *upholding the universe* (3). The Son's work, *purification for sins,* is God's proper work (3; cf. Eze 36:25-33). The Son is enthroned in honor on God's own throne *(right hand of the Majesty on high,* 3). His *name,* expressing all that He is and signifies for man, marks Him as *superior to angels,* who declared God's law. (4; cf. 2:2)

SEVEN OT QUOTATIONS (5-13) cite the witness of God's ancient Word concerning the surpassing greatness of the Son. In two passages God speaks of David's son and Lord as HIS Son (5; cf. Ps 2:7; 2 Sm 7:14). Two passages point up the angels' inferiority to the Son (6:7; cf. Dt 32:43; Ps 97:7). Two passages again hail the Son as the incarnation of God's kingdom, eternally enthroned in the Creator's unchanging Majesty (8-12; cf. Ps 45:6-7; Ps 102:25-27). The seven quotations, like the seven statements, reach their climax in the words of Ps 110:1, which set the King at God's right hand and promise Him victory (13; cf. 3). Angels cannot compete with Him; they can only *serve* His gracious purpose of *salvation.* (14)

1:2 *A Son.* The prophets were true messengers of God, but servants, each entrusted with a portion of the message which was to be fully and finally expressed in the sending of One who was Son in the full sense. (Cf. Mt 21:37; Mk 12:6)

Heir of all things . . . created the world. Paul has the two thoughts in inverse order: "All things were created through him and for him" (Cl 1:16). Cf. also Jn 1:3 and Mt 28:18. Sonship and heirship go together. (Cf. Ps 2:7-8)

1:3 *Bears the very stamp of his nature,* as a coin reproduces the pattern of the die which stamped it.

1:5-13 The author's use of the OT will appear audacious, or even arbitrary, to anyone who does not share his convictions that: (a) the whole OT is the voice of God; (b) Jesus Christ is very God; (c) the whole OT testifies to Him. (Cf. Introduction, pars. 12 and 13; Jn 5:39; Acts 10:43; 2 Co 1:19-20; 2 Ti 3:15)

1:5a Ps 2:7, where God addresses the king on David's throne in words whose full meaning becomes real and apparent in the Son of David, the Son of God.

1:5b 2 Sm 7:14. God's promise to David (through the prophet Nathan) concerning David's successors, a promise fully fulfilled in Jesus Christ.

1:6 Words which in their original setting (Dt 32:43) called upon the *angels* to worship the Lord God of Israel as the Avenger and Savior of His people are here applied to the incarnate Son of God, "that all may honor the Son, even as they honor the Father" (Jn 5:23). The OT is quoted according to the Septuagint (an ancient Greek translation of the OT), which differs from the one reproduced in English versions. Recent discoveries indicate that this reading may well be the original one.

1:7 Ps 104:4 God's *angels* ("messengers") appear in various forms, fulfill their service, and vanish. God's Son endures unchanged. (1:8-10)

1:8-9 In Ps 45:6-7 the anointed king of God's people is, as God's vice-regent and executor of His righteousness on earth, called *God* (or his reign is marked as divine, cf. RSV note *a*): being under the favor of God, his reign is destined to endure. This ancient promise found its final Yes in Jesus Christ. (Cf. 2 Co 1:20)

1:10 Ps 102:25-27. Ps 102 is entitled "A prayer of one afflicted, when he is faint and pours out his complaints before the LORD." The psalmist, his existence shattered, can find grounds for hope only in the God who endures when all else passes away. He will arise and have pity on His people, so that all "nations will fear the name of the LORD, and all the kings of the earth" will bow before His glory (Ps 102:12-15). In Jesus Christ God did arise and help and lead all peoples to worship Him; and the words of Ps 102 are fitly applied to the Son.

1:13 Ps 110:1. God addresses His anointed king. It was with the words of this psalm that Jesus Himself had stated His Messianic claim most powerfully. (Cf. Mt 22:41-46 note)

Stool for thy feet, symbol of conquest. (Cf. Jos 10:24)

1:14 *Ministering spirits.* The angels who worship (6) the Son are sent forth to *serve* man, with whom the Son has identified Himself and to whom He has given salvation.

2:1-4 Admonition: Do Not Neglect Such a Great Salvation

2:1-4 Even the Law, *declared by angels,* imposed fearful penalties on *every transgression or disobedience;* how much the more does God's final Word of *salvation* confront its hearers with a dreadful alternative for those who *neglect* it; for they are rejecting the Word of Christ, the attestation of His apostles, the witness of the *God* who does *wonders,* the working of His *Spirit.*

2:1 *Drift away.* Cf. Introduction, pars. 5 and 6.

2:2 *Declared by angels.* Cf. Acts 7:53; Gl 3:19.

Just retribution. Cf. 10:29, which echoes the language of Nm 15:30-31; 35:30; Dt 17:2-7.

2:5-18 Instruction: The Son Made Lower than the Angels

2:5-18 The fact that the Son *was made lower than the angels* (9) takes nothing from His glory and does not call in question His superiority to the angels; rather, it is the essential part of His glory. If in His humiliation He is subjected to the *suffering of death,* He *tastes death for every one* (9) in order that all men may share in the *glory and honor* which *the grace of God* has designed for man (6, 9). He partakes of man's *nature, in flesh and blood,* and dies man's *death* (14) in order to deliver men from the tyranny of the lord of death, *the devil* (14-15). He *suffered* and was *tempted* as One who was destined thereby to become *a merciful and faithful high priest to God . . . to make expiation for the sins of the people* (17). Vicariously and victoriously He has "made purification for sins" (1:3) and therefore is enthroned as Son of God in glory (1:3) and brings the *many sons* of God *to glory.* (2:10)

2:5 *For* points back to 1:14. God's Word (Ps 8, quoted in vv. 6-8) has destined man, not angels, to have dominion in *the world to come;* therefore the Son identifies Himself with man, and the angels are sent forth to serve man.

2:6 *Testified somewhere.* Only here in Hebrews is an OT word introduced as spoken by a man; the vagueness of the reference seems designed to play down the human aspect of its authorship.

2:6-8 The words of Ps 8:4-6 recall Gn 1:26, where the Creator gives man dominion over His creation; they point forward to the "world to come" in which that dominion will be fully restored to man. In this world *(as it is)* that perfect dominion is not a visible reality but an object of faith and hope.

2:9 *We see Jesus.* In Jesus (marked as man by the use of His human name alone) the believed destiny of man is a reality; He who died *for every one* has risen and has entered into the honor, glory, and dominion designed for man.

2:10 *He* is God, Lord of history and creation *(for whom and by whom all things exist). It was fitting,* in harmony with His revealed nature as holy and righteous God, that He should *bring* men *to glory* and *salvation,* not by overlooking their sin but by dealing with it. He dealt with man's sin by giving His Son as the *pioneer* of man's salvation, who opens the way and leads the way to salvation. The Son becomes the *perfect pioneer* by *suffering* for man's sin (and dying for man's sin, cf. 14).

2:11 The Son's act of suffering and dying to make "purification for sins" (1:3) is a sacrificial, priestly act (cf. 17); therefore the principle of priesthood applies to Him: priest *(he who sanctifies)* and people *(those who are sanctified)* are both of *one origin,* both are human. (Cf. 5:1, 8-10)

2:11b-13 The three OT passages all emphasize the Son's solidarity with the men for whom He performs His priestly service. Ps 22:22 pictures the righteous Sufferer (the prototype and prediction of the suffering Christ, cf. Mt 27:35, 39, 43, 46; Jn 19:28) as calling men His *brethren* (11). The other two are words of the prophet Isaiah (Is 8:17-18). The prophet had proclaimed the will and Word of the Lord to his people and their king in vain. The prophet binds up his testimony and seals his teaching among his disciples, trusting in God to vindicate His servant the prophet as the bearer of His Word. He and the disciples *(children)* given Him by God will meanwhile stand as living witnesses while "the LORD . . . is hiding his face" from His people (Is 8:17). Even so Jesus met the unbelief and the rejection with which His people responded to Him. He *put* His *trust* in God, as a man can do it, thanked God for the men God had given Him, for His disciples and the church created by their witness (cf. 2:3). Thus He entered fully into His brotherhood with man.

2:14 *The devil has the power of death* because He can accuse sinful man (cf. Rv 12:9-10). When the Son enters mankind and confronts Satan with a human righteousness which the devil cannot accuse, the accuser is "destroyed" and man is set free.

2:17 *High priest.* Cf. 11 note. Here the author states the theme that is to dominate the whole central section of his epistle, 4:14—10:18.

The "admonition" portion of this section is touched on lightly in the verse (3:1) which introduces the next instruction, probably because the admonition based on the high priesthood of the Son is to be developed so fully in 10:19 ff.

3:1-6 Instruction: Jesus Worthy of More Glory than Moses

3:1-6 Jesus is *apostle,* the authorized Messenger or Envoy of God who speaks and acts in His name; He is *high priest* who with intercession and sacrifice represents man before God. As such He can be compared with *Moses,* who delivered God's people from bondage in Egypt (cf. 2:15) as God's spokesman and agent (Ex 3:10-12; 4:10-17) and more than once stood before God as a priestly intercessor for his people (Ex 32:11-14, 30-32; Nm 14:13-19). Both, too, were *faithful* in their service *in God's house* (God's people, His household). Yet Jesus is *worthy of . . . much more glory than Moses.* Whereas Moses served as *servant,* Jesus was faithful *as a Son,* Lord *over God's house as He is Creator of the house (builder).* Whereas Moses' service pointed beyond itself to a greater future *(to testify to the things that were to be spoken later),* Jesus' Word and work ushers in God's final great Today (cf. 3:7, 13, 15; 4:7). The house over which He is Lord in the last days is made up of men of all nations whose *confidence, pride, and hope* is fixed on Him, not on Moses.

3:1 *Apostle* is used as a title of Jesus only here in the NT. But cf. Jn 20:21, where the verb ("sent") used to describe Jesus' own mission is the one from which the noun "apostle" is derived.

3:4 *Builder . . . is God.* As "Builder" of the people of God, Jesus is entitled to divine honor, just as He is as Creator of the world. (1:2)

3:5 *Moses was faithful.* Cf. Nm 12:17: "My servant Moses . . . entrusted with all my house."

3:7—4:13 Warning: Harden Not Your Hearts

3:7—4:13 Where God builds and blesses His house, when He gives His people an apostle and high priest, the members of His household are tempted to desecrate the gift and so lose it. So it was of old when Israel *left Egypt under the leadership of Moses* (3:16); men hardened their hearts and put God to the test in the wilderness (3:8-9). In their disobedience and *unbelief* (3:19) they provoked God to wrath, forfeited the *rest* He had promised and provided in the Promised Land, and *fell in the wilderness* (3:17-18). So it may be now in the days of "Jesus, the apostle and high priest" of the Christian faith ("our confession," 3:2). Therefore the *Holy Spirit's* warning as recorded in Ps 95 (3:7-11) must be heeded now: *Take care* and *exhort one another,* for the *unbelieving heart and the deceitfulness of sin* threaten still to drive men into apostasy *from the living God.* (3:12-14)

The *promise of entering* God's *rest remains* (4:1). The unbelief of the men under Moses' leadership destroyed them but did not nullify the promise. The rest which God created by His resting on the seventh day of creation endures; it *remains a sabbath rest for the people of God* (4:9). The promise was not exhausted when *Joshua,* Moses' successor, brought the people into the rest of the Promised Land. God repeated the promise to the people *through* David, in the Psalter, *long afterward* (4:7) and opened up the prospect of a rest greater than Canaan could give. The history of God's promise is cause for salutary *fear* (4:1) and spurs His people on to *strive to enter that rest* (4:11) which Jesus, the Son greater than the servants Moses and Joshua, gives to those *who have believed* (4:3). The promise is forfeited, now as then, when it meets the *same sort of disobedience* and destroys the disobedient (4:11), for the promise is the live and effective *word of God,* trenchant, penetrating, discerning, exposing him who hears it to the inescapable scrutiny of his Judge *(with whom we have to do,* 4:12-13).

3:7-11 Ps 95:7-11. The first half of the psalm is a call to worship the Savior, King, Creator, and Shepherd of Israel (Ps 95:1-6), expressing Israel's "confidence and pride" in her hope (Heb 3:6). The second half, quoted here, is a stern warning that worship without obedience is in vain.

3:8-9 *Rebellion . . . put me to the test.* For the history alluded to here and recalled more explicitly below (16-19) cf. Ex 17:1-7; Nm 14:1-23.

3:12 *Fall away.* The ultimate outrage of conscience which we call apostasy (6:6) is meant. (Cf. Introduction, par. 16)

4:2 *Good news . . . message . . . faith.* The terms in which the story of Israel's hardness of heart and rebellion is told emphasize the parallel between Israel and the NT people of God. The word for *good news* is the verb for "gospeling," evangelizing.

4:3 *We who have believed enter.* "We who have come to faith are in process of entering." For Christians, entry into God's rest is not ONLY future; they taste "the powers of the age to come" (6.5) even now.

4:3-6 *His works were finished . . . God rested . . . it remains for some to enter it* (God's rest). God's movement in creation (from works to rest) is the pattern for His movement in redemption. As He gave men "dominion over the WORKS" of His hands (Ps 8:6), He will give them part in His everlasting Sabbath rest. (Cf. 10)

4:14—10:18 JESUS, THE ULTIMATE HIGH PRIEST

4:14—5:10 Instruction: Jesus a True High Priest

4:14—5:10 There is cause for holy fear in the presence of God's enduring promise (cf. 4:1); but there is even stronger cause for *confidence* (4:16). In *Jesus, the Son of God,* we have a *great high priest,* sympathetic with us in *our weaknesses* (14-15). Through His priestly intercession the awesome throne of God has become the *throne of grace* for us, source of divine *mercy* and *grace to help in time of need.* (16)

Jesus is a true high priest, being a man acting *on behalf of men,* clothed in our humanity, learning a human *obedience* by suffering (5:1-3, 7-9). He has also that other qualification for true priesthood, divine appointment. He is *called, appointed* by God (5:4-6), *designated by God a high priest after the order of Melchizedek.* (5:10)

5:3 *Sacrifice for his own sins.* Cf. Lv 9:7; 16:6-9. This trait of the OT priesthood is noted not because Jesus' priesthood has anything corresponding to it, but merely to illustrate the humanity of priesthood.

5:4 *As Aaron was.* Ex 28:1.

5:5 *Christ . . . appointed.* The word spoken in Ps 2:7 to the anointed king found its ultimate fulfillment when uttered by the voice from heaven at Jesus' baptism, where the Son of God became one with mankind under the wrath of God in order "to fulfill all righteousness." (Mt 3:13-17)

5:6 *In another place.* Ps 110:4. The same divine word which designated the King as representative of God's victorious power on earth (Ps 110:1; cf. Heb 1:13 note) marked Him out as the Priest who represents man before God. (Cf. 10)

5:7 *Loud cries and tears.* The reference is to Jesus' praying in Gethsemane (Mt 26:36-46) and the human cries wrung from Him by the burden of priestly office, such as those recorded in Mt 17:17 and Jn 12:27.

His godly fear, the humbly submissive reverence which led him to conclude His *prayers and supplications* with, "Nevertheless, not as I will, but as thou wilt." (Mt 26:39)

5:8 *Learned obedience.* One "learns" obedience (makes it one's own) by concrete acts of obedience. This the Son did, by obeying even where obedience meant taking the cup of suffering which man's sin had mixed.

5:9 *Made perfect.* Cf. 2:10. That is, perfectly qualified to be the *source of salvation* to all who obediently confess Him (cf. 4:14) as their High Priest.

5:10 *Melchizedek.* The author indicates the theme he will develop fully in 7:1—10:18.

5:11—6:20 Warning and Encouragement

5:11—6:20 The author has reached the point where he would develop fully the major theme of his letter: Jesus the High Priest after the order of Melchizedek (5:10). His next words (5:11—6:20) show that he feels what many a leader of a less-than-perfect flock has felt. He looks at the PRESENT state of his charges and feels a disappointed dissatisfaction at their stagnant immaturity. They have not advanced as they should and cling to a bottle-fed infancy when they should be advancing to the solid food of maturity. (5:11-14)

His resolve to lead them on to maturity is therefore beset by a crippling fear for their FUTURE. He sees them drifting with the current which sweeps toward *apostasy* (6:6), to that dread extremity of impenitence from which there is no hope of return. (6:1-8)

But then he recalls their PAST and the past (and present) fruitfulness of their love and thus gains the assurance that the God who has begun His good work in them will carry it through to completion (cf. Ph 1:6). The sure promise of God, made doubly sure by His assuring oath, still holds for them and can realize the full assurance of hope. This Godward look gives him the strength to continue his task of keeping watch over these wavering souls, not "sadly" but "joyfully." (9:20; cf. 13:17)

5:12 *You need milk.* This, like the preceding *you need some one to teach you,* etc., is not merely an objective analysis of the readers' state but an indictment and a reproach. The author does not propose to take them back to the ABC's of Christianity but wills to carry them "on to maturity." (6:1)

5:13 *Word of righteousness* may mean the Gospel. But this meaning hardly fits in with the clause that follows, *for he is a child;* the Gospel is accessible to babes (Mt 11:25). And in 6:1-2 the author concedes that his readers do know the elementary doctrines of Christ. Another possible rendering, "normal, right, mature speech," is therefore preferable. By persisting in childish ways when childhood is past, a man loses his capacity for grasping and expressing the Gospel for the mature, such as is expressed in the doctrine of the priesthood of Jesus.

5:14 *Faculties trained by practice to distinguish.* Cf. Ro 12:2, where Paul describes the growth to Christian maturity as a constant "proving" (a testing and discerning) of what is the will of God.

6:1-2 The readers are to *leave the elementary doctrine,* not in the sense of abandoning it but (as the use of *foundation* shows) of building upon it, using it as the basis for progress. The elementary doctrine is described by six terms arranged in pairs. The first pair speaks of the beginning of the Christian life, the response to missionary preaching (cf. Acts 20:21), which bids men turn *(repentance)* from the evil works of their past, when they "were dead in trespasses" (Cl 2:13), to the God who forgives and renews *(faith).* The next pair speaks of their initiation into the Christian life by the Sacrament of Baptism *(ablutions),* and by the reception of the Spirit, which was often accompanied by *the laying on of hands* (cf. Acts 8:14-18; 19:1-6). The third pair points to the goal of the new life *(resurrection of the dead, and eternal judgment);* it reads like a paraphrase of the early creed which Paul cites in Ro 10:9: "If you confess with your lips that Jesus is Lord and believe in your heart that God raised him from the dead, you will be saved" (from death and the judgment).

6:2 *Ablutions.* The word is similar to but not identical with the word regularly used for Christian Baptism; that, and the fact that it is used in the plural, indicates that the *instruction* pointed up the distinctiveness of Christian Baptism as over against the baptism of John (cf. Acts 19:1-4) or the various ablutions known in Judaism. (Cf. 9:10; Mk 7:4)

6:3 *If God permits.* God's grace CAN do the "impossible" (4); but to "PRESUME upon the riches of his kindness and forbearance and patience" is perilous in the extreme and invites His judgment. (Ro 2:4-5)

6:4-6 For the nature and peril of *apostasy* (6) cf. 10:26-31 and Introduction, par. 16.

6:6 *Crucify . . . on their own account.* Men who have fully known and THEN rejected the blessings won for them by the Crucified have made common cause with those who rejected the Son of God, crucified Him, and uttered mockeries under His cross *(contempt).*

6:10 *God is not so unjust.* God's merciful justice gives to him who has (uses and values) God's previous gifts (Mt 13:12). God is the faithful vinedresser who prunes "every branch that does bear fruit . . . that it may bear more fruit." (Jn 15:2)

Work . . . love . . . in serving the saints. Cf. 10:32-34.

6:12-13 God's *promise to Abraham,* supported by oath, serves as the classic example of encouragement to those who like him endure in *faith and patience* to *inherit the promises.* In the record of Gn 22:16-17 the "unchangeable character of his purpose" (6:17) is clearly seen.

6:18-20 *The hope set before us* (the hoped-for blessing) serves as *anchor of the soul,* holding it firm and steady, lest it "drift away" (2:1) into lethargy and apostasy. The *hope* is Jesus Himself (cf. Cl 1:27), our *high priest* who has entered into the Holy of Holies (God's presence) as our *forerunner* to bring us there too. With the mention of the eternal *high priest . . . after the order of Melchizedek* the author returns to his main theme.

6:19 *Behind the curtain* which separated the *inner shrine* (Holy of Holies) from the rest of the sanctuary. There only the high priest went, and he only once a year. (Lv 16:2, 12; Heb 9:3, 6-7, 25)

7:1—10:18 Instruction: Jesus the High Priest

7:1—10:17 Jesus is the true High Priest (4:1 to 5:10); more than that, He is Priest of a higher order. His *priestly office* (ch. 7), the better *sanctuary* in which He ministers (ch. 8), and the final and perfect *sacrifice* which He offers (9:1—10:18)—all mark Him out as the ultimate High Priest, the Mediator who has established God's new and final covenant, His new and ultimate order of things in which the Law is superseded and God's grace holds free and final sway (7:22; 8:6, 7, 8, 10, 13; 9:15; 10:16, 28; cf. 12:24; 13:20). The whole section, so richly elaborated, is designed to overcome the Judaic tendency to take offense at Jesus at the two points where offense was likeliest and strongest: (1) His "shameful" death on the cross and His present hiddenness (cf. Introduction, pars. 5 and 6); (2) the fact that His life and priestly ministry signified the "end of the law" (cf. Ro 10:4), that law which the Jews revered as the inviolable and eternal Word of God.

7:1-28 INSTRUCTION: MELCHIZEDEK AND AARON, PRIESTHOOD OF PROMISE AND LAW

7:1-28 Jesus is the High Priest of a higher order, not that of Aaron and Levi, established and regulated by the Law, but that of Melchizedek, established by the promise of God to endure forever. His priesthood supersedes and antiquates the legal Levitical priesthood.

7:1-10 The eternal priesthood of the Messiah is foretold and promised in Ps 110:4 (cf. Heb 5:6, 10; 6:20). It is foreshadowed in Gn 14:17-20, in the figure of the priest-king Melchizedek and in the story of his meeting with Abraham. Both what is said and what is left unsaid of Melchizedek in the sacred record mark him as *resembling the Son of God . . . a priest for ever* (3) and as being thus distinct from and superior to those priests who are *descendants of Levi* and derive their authority from the Law. (5)

7:1-3 According to the record, Melchizedek, type (cf. Introduction, par. 13) of Jesus the

Messianic Priest, bears SIGNIFICANT NAMES: His titles, *king of righteousness* and *king of peace* suggest the Messiah to whom eternal priesthood is promised in Ps 110:4 Cf. the Messianic designations, "the LORD our righteousness," Jer 23:6, and "Prince of Peace," Is 9:6. The OT record generally and its prescriptions for priesthood particularly emphasize *genealogy*. There is a SIGNIFICANT SILENCE, however, concerning Melchizedek's descent. He confronts us in Genesis as one who, singularly, has no recorded *beginning of days nor end of life*. Unlike the priests under the Law, he stands in no succession and has no successors but continues in unique and eternal majesty *a priest for ever*.

7:4-10 And he performs SIGNIFICANT ACTIONS: Melchizedek receives tithes from Abraham and *blesses* Abraham. Both are priestly actions; they show that Melchizedek functions as priest even to Abraham, the recipient of the *promises*. Even Abraham, "called the friend of God" (Ja 2:23; cf. Is 41:8; 2 Ch 20:7), needs the mediation and blessing of this eternal priesthood, the priesthood of the "Son of God, a priest for ever" (3), of Him in whom "all the promises of God find their Yes" (2 Co 1:20). Even Abraham, destined by the promise to "inherit the world" (Ro 4:13), acknowledges the surpassing greatness of this priesthood by paying tithes to Melchizedek. Just as Melchizedek's act of blessing marks him as *superior* (7) to Abraham, so Abraham's act of giving him a *tithe of the spoils* (4) is an acknowledgement of Melchizedek's superiority. *See how great he is!* His is the greatness of *our Lord* (14), the Christ, a greatness not derived from *a commandment in the law* and not dependent on the *genealogy* which the Law prescribes but inherent in his person by "the power of an indestructible life" (16). He is not, like the *descendants of Levi . . . a mortal* man (8) clothed for a time only in the dignity and power of priesthood; *he lives,* and his life and his priesthood are one; both are everlasting.

7:11-28 The eternal priesthood of Christ as foreshadowed in Melchizedek is acknowledged as superior by Abraham, the "patriarch" (4) and the ancestor of Levi, the tribe of the priesthood; Levi himself, present in his ancestor Abraham, thus acknowledges the superiority of Christ's priesthood (9-10). All this marks the priesthood of the Law as merely preliminary to Christ's ultimate priesthood. The promise pointed, not to Levi, the tribe designated by the *Law of Moses* as the priestly tribe, but to the tribe of *Judah* (14) from which our Lord was to spring. *Another priest* arises by virtue of God's potent promise, and with His coming the old order passes; the *former commandment,* which established the Levitical priesthood, is *set aside* (18); the introduction of *a better hope* (19) which really effects what priesthood is designed to effect, that is, enable men to *draw near to God*, makes clear the *weaknesss* and *uselessness* of the old legal order in comparison with the new, how much *better* is the new *covenant* ensured by the ultimate High Priest Jesus Christ. (22)

This new hope and new priesthood is God's promise at work, promise in its purest form, the *oath* of God (20; cf. 6:13-14). In His oath God commits His life to the blessing of man (cf. Gn 22:15-18). His oath (Ps 110:4) gives man the everlasting Priest, always alive *to make intercession* (23-25), the sinless Son who *offered up himself* in sacrifice once for all (27) and thus was *made perfect* as priest, capable of interceding for sinful man *for ever.* (26-28)

8:1-13 INSTRUCTION: JESUS' PRIESTLY MINISTRY IN THE TRUE SANCTUARY, THE HEAVENS, MEDIATING THE NEW AND BETTER COVENANT

The Son's priesthood is of another order than that of the Levitical priesthood and superior to it, as both the promise (Ps 110:4) and prefiguration (Gn 14:17-20) and their fulfillment (7:15-16) show. This superiority is manifest also in the place of His priestly ministration, *heaven* (1), the *true tent* (or *tabernacle),* the *heavenly sanctuary* of which the earthly sanctuary where the descendants of Levi serve is but a *copy and shadow* (5). In that earthly sanctuary the sons of Levi serve and die (cf. 7:23); *in heaven* the Son is *a minister* (2) who lives and reigns *(seated at the right hand,* 1; cf. 1:13), made perfect in His priesthood forever (7:28). As the appearance of the Son as ultimate Priest ushers in a whole new divine order of things (7:12, 18-19), so His ministry in the new heavenly sanctuary involves a new order of things, the promised new and better covenant (7-13). No longer is man thrust into the presence of God by a commandment of the Law; he is drawn near to God under this new priesthood in the new sanctuary by the inner impulse of a renewed mind and heart in which God is known (acknowledged and adored) and His law is inscribed; the reluctance and resistance of sinful man is overcome by God's creatively renewing forgiveness of sin. (12)

8:2 *Sanctuary and the true tent.* The question of the PLACE of Christ's priestly ministry was an important one for Jewish Christians. The old order to which they were accustomed was visible and impressive; the Holy City with its temple, to which the priests repaired in a continued rhythm of prescribed duties, that lodestone which drew Jews from all over the world for the celebration of the great festivals—ancient, venerable, and celebrated in the songs of Israel—what was there in the new order to replace and surpass it? The answer of Hebrews is: If the Christ, the new High Priest, is invisible, that is because He is in the true sanctuary, in heaven; if He does not appear in the earthly sanctuary, that is because He is too great for that priesthood and its sanctuary. (4)

8:4 *If he were on earth, etc.* The sanctuary in which Christ ministers MUST be in heaven; there is, as it were, no room for Him and His ministry within the old shadow-order of the Levitical priesthood on earth.

9:1—10:18 INSTRUCTION: ULTIMATE ATONING SACRIFICE OF CHRIST

9:1—10:18 *But when Christ appeared* (9:11)—

with this mighty adversative clause comparable to Paul's "BUT now" in Ro 3:21 or his "BUT God" in Eph 2:4, Hebrews introduces the climax of its argument concerning the last days, the supreme Word of God spoken by a Son (cf. 1:2), the ultimate High Priest. It has already been declared that the High Priest of the promise holds a higher and more enduring office than was ever given by the Law to the sons of Levi (ch. 7); that He ministers in a greater SANCTUARY than the Law could prescribe or men could erect (ch. 8). Now, the latter proclaims that He offers a better and everlasting SACRIFICE (9:1—10:18), *his own blood,* Himself, and thus secures for man what the old order never secured, *an eternal redemption* (9:12). Again and again the author asserts the supremacy of Christ's ultimate atoning sacrifice: The old order itself points beyond its own limitations to the unlimited possibilities of God in the future. Even at the high point in the ancient sacrificial system, the ritual of the Day of Atonement (Lv 16), the fact that only *the high priest . . . and he but once a year* entered the Holy of Holies amounts to a confession that the way into the sanctuary was not yet so wholly and freely accessible as it was to become *when Christ appeared as a high priest of the good things that have come* (9:11), with the sacrifice which alone could *perfect* the conscience of sinful man and set him unafraid before his God. That sacrifice is Christ's self-offering *(his own blood,* not that of *goats and bulls,* 9:13); by the death of Christ the testament (covenant) of God takes effect validly and forever, just as a human testator's will, or testament, takes effect at the testator's death (9:15-17). What the shedding of blood in the ancient rites of purification and the sprinkling of blood at the establishment of the covenant at Sinai (18-22)—what that signified and symbolized is full and glorious reality now; with this *shedding of blood* there IS forgiveness of sins (9:22). Christ's offering of Himself is unique and unrepeatable—there can be no return to the old and no expectation of anything more. When Christ shall come again, He shall return as Savior, as One whose sacrificial dealing with sin is complete, over and done with (9:28). *The shadow of good things to come* which the Law had (10:1) gives way to the *realities* (10:1) present in Christ, the *high priest of good things that have come* (9:11). Those ancient sacrifices *continually offered year after year* testified, by the very fact that they were repeated, to their own insufficiency; they could not put away sin effectively and forever, as Christ's *sacrifice of himself* (9:26) has done (cf. 10:4). Christ's personal, voluntary offering of His whole self to God (10:5-10) is the unique (10:11-14) final sacrifice (10:15-18). In that sacrifice the ancient promise of the new covenant has been utterly fulfilled. The forgiveness of sin, the goal of all sacrifice, has been attained. There need no longer be and there can *no longer* be *any offering for sin.* (10:18)

9:4 *Altar of incense.* According to Ex. 30:6, the altar of incense seems to have been located outside the Holy of Holies, in the Holy Place. Perhaps the author is already thinking of the once-a-year ritual of the Day of Atonement (7; cf. Lv 16), when an offering of incense was made in the Holy of Holies (Lv 16:12), in contrast to the daily offering of incense in the Holy Place, and so is led to locate the incense altar within the Holy of Holies.

Manna. Cf. Ex 16:33.

Aaron's rod. Cf. Nm 17:1-11.

9:5 *We cannot now speak in detail.* The author, writing "briefly" (13:22), will not linger over the symbolic significance of the sanctuary furnishings but presses on to what is most significant for his theme, the once-a-year ritual of the Day of Atonement. (6-7; cf. Lv 16)

9:8 *The Holy Spirit indicates,* in the OT Word, which He inspired.

9:9 *Symbolic for the present age.* The full significance of the OT arrangements, which reveal the limitations of the old order, can be grasped only now when Christ has "opened the new and living way" into the very presence of God. (10:19)

9:10 *The time of reformation,* the time of Christ's high priesthood, when the Law's "shadow of good things to come" is replaced by "the true form of these realities" (10:1; cf. Cl 2:17), "the good things that have come" (9:11), when the merely ritual cleansing provided by *regulations for the body* is replaced by the internal "purification for sins" (1:3) which can "perfect the conscience" (9:9) and give man true access to God.

9:11 *Not made with hands . . . not of this creation.* Not of human manufacture and therefore not limited by the external character of created materials. For the idea of a true sanctuary *not made with hands* see the words of Jesus, Mk 14:58; Jn 2:19-21; and of Stephen, Acts 7:48; cf. Is 66:1-2.

9:13 Cf. Lv 16:6-7, 15-16; Nm 19:1-22.

9:14 *Through the eternal Spirit,* as the sinless Son of God (cf. Ro 1:4) and the Servant of God who does His atoning work in the power of the Spirit of God (Is 42:1; Is 53). The Spirit at work in Christ's sacrifice there reveals "the depths of God." (1 Co 2:10)

9:15-16 *Covenant . . . will . . . death.* The same Greek word is used for both *covenant* and *will,* and the author makes use of this to show how the *death* (blood) of Christ is essential to the establishment of the *new covenant* of the forgiveness of sins. (Cf. 22)

9:19-20 Cf. Ex 24:6-8.

9:22 *Almost everything.* For exceptions permitted by the Law cf. Lv 5:11 and Nm 16:46; 31:22 f.; 31:50.

Shedding of blood . . . forgiveness. Cf. Lv 17:11.

9:24 *Heaven itself.* Cf. 8:1.

9:26 *Sacrifice of himself.* Cf. 7:27. This statement sums up the superiority of Christ's sacrifice as a total self-offering, the oblation of His life ("own blood," 9:12; "body," 10:10) and the devotion of His will. (10:4-9)

9:27 Christ's sacrifice has the once-for-all finality of a man's *death* and *judgment,* with the amazing difference that His death leads to deliverance from judgment ("save," 28).

10:5-7 Ps 40:6-8 according to the Septuagint (ancient Greek translation), which differs from the Hebrew but conveys the essestial point that total self-devotion is the ultimate, essential sacrifice.

10:16-17 Cf. Jer 31:33-34. The significance of the promise of the new covenant has been dwelt on in 8:6-13.

10:19—12:29 EXHORTATION AND WARNING

10:19—12:29 The instruction of 4:14—10:18 has been eloquently rich and full; the exhortation is correspondingly vigorous, urgent—and filled with a deadly serious concern. The author evinces himself as one who has heard attentively the witness to Jesus which brought God's "great salvation" to him and as inspired by the Spirit who lived and worked in that witness (2:3-4); by that Spirit Jesus lives and works in his words. Jesus planted both confident faith and holy fear in His disciples when He told them, "To him who has will more be given, and he will have in abundance; but from him who has not, even what he has will be taken away" (Mt 13:12). That same combination of faith and fear lives in the author's heart, and he implants it in the hearts of his readers too. He invites them to draw near to God wholeheartedly and actively by the "new and living way" which their High Priest has consecrated for them (10:19-25) and at the same time warns them against "not having," not possessing and using, God's ultimate gift, repeating his earlier (6:1-8) warning against apostasy (10:26-31; cf. Introduction, par. 16). He bids them recall the believing steadfastness of their former days when the light of God's salvation first broke upon them, for their encouragement he calls the roll of ancient men of faith and bids his readers look to Jesus, the Pioneer and Perfecter of their faith, and so to run with perseverance the race they must run, cheered on by the great cloud of witnesses who ran the race before them (10:32—12:3). He teaches them to see even in their present sufferings the hand of the God who gives, the Father who disciplines every child whom He receives as His own (12:4-11). He urges them to repent of their past slackness and to grow strong again before (again the note of holy fear is sounded) the time for repentance be forever past. The final splendor of God's gracious speaking is more awesome than were the terrors of Mount Sinai when the Law was given (12:18-24). To refuse Him who is speaking NOW is to ignore the final warning spoken from heaven itself and invites the judgment of Him who—though He gives to all who will receive and have the gift a kingdom that cannot be shaken—will prove a consuming fire to all who will not offer Him the acceptable worship which is His due. (12:25-29)

10:19-25 Exhortation: Draw Near with a True Heart

10:19-25 The *true heart* (22) is the heart of one whose eye is fixed on Jesus the *great priest* (19-21) and can therefore *draw near* to God in confident *faith* (22) and unwavering *hope* (23), living a life of responsible *love* (24) in the fellowship of the worshiping church.

10:20 *Curtain . . . his flesh.* The curtain is the curtain which divides the Holy Place from the Holy of Holies (9:3). Jesus has opened up the way into the innermost sanctuary, into the very presence of God, through the curtain of His human life and body (flesh) destroyed in sacrifice for the sinner's sake.

10:21 *Over the house of God.* Cf. 3:6.

10:22 *Draw near,* for worship and service.

Hearts sprinkled . . . bodies washed. The OT ceremonial washings (cf. 9:13-14; Ex 30:20; Lv 16:4) furnish the picture for the effectual sanctification of the whole man in Baptism.

10:25 *The Day,* of the return of Christ and judgment. (Cf. 1 Co 3:13)

10:26-31 Warning: Judgment on Apostasy

10:26-31 Cf. Introduction, par. 16, and 6:4-8. The harsh warnings on apostasy are the negative counterpart to the warm and winning invitation of 19-25, prepared for, however, by the mention of the "Day" in 25.

10:26 *There no longer remains a sacrifice for sins.* The apostate has *deliberately* and against better *knowledge* rejected the one, final sacrifice provided by God (29). (Cf. 2 Ptr 2:20-21)

10:28-29 For the aggravated offense of sinning against God's ultimate "great salvation" cf. 2:1-3.

10:28 Cf. Dt 17:2-6; also Nm 15:30.

10:29 *Spurned . . . profaned . . . outraged.* All three verbs emphasize the deliberate (26) character of apostasy against knowledge of the truth.

Outraged the Spirit. Cf. Mt 12:31-32 note; Mk 3:28-30.

10:30 *Vengeance is mine.* Dt 32:35-36.

10:32-39 Exhortation: Do Not Throw Away Confidence

10:32-39 Again, as in 6:9-10, the author looks to his readers' past and finds there a joyous stamina of faith (32-34) which is encouraging to him and can be an incentive to them. *Therefore do not throw away your confidence* (35). The light that shone on them at their conversion (32) has illumined dark days for them; in that light they can still endure, *do the will of God and receive what is promised* (36). In the *little while* before their Lord's return (37), they need not be among the number of the apostates who *shrink back and are destroyed;* they can stand in the ranks *of those who have faith* and live (38-39) by God's promise.

10:37-38 Hab 2:3-4 is quoted according to the Septuagint (ancient Greek version most commonly used in the Greek-speaking church). This differs considerably from the Hebrew as translated in English versions, but the cardinal point (the unbreakable connection between faith, righteousness, and life, 38) is not affected thereby.

11:1—12:2 Exhortation: Run the Race

11:1—12:2 When Moses led Israel into the Promised Land, he set before them "life and death, blessing and curse" and bade them choose life (Dt 30:19-20). The same choice confronts the wandering people of God in the last days; and the choice-of-life is faith (10:39). The whole record of God's dealing with man in the OT, from creation onward, is one long demonstration of the crucial necessity of "having faith." Only by faith can man live by the invisible realities of God and enter upon God's future (11:1). The record of the men of old shows that man can live only by faith in the sunlight of God's favor (11:2). Only by faith, indeed, can man live in God's world as God's creature at all, for only faith can know that the world is God's creation and the theater of His royal rule over His creation (11:3); only the invisible sway of God's Word makes it possible to "draw near" to God; to live in His world without heeding His Word is a "shrinking back" from Him that leads to destruction (cf. 10:39). Three men are singled out from the generation before the Flood: *Abel* (4), *Enoch* (5), and *Noah* (7). *By faith* each of them *received divine approval.* (4, 5, 7; cf. 2)

The OT record of the patriarchs is a record of their faith. *By faith Abraham obeyed* (8) when God called him and entered into God's invisible future (cf. 13-16) on the pilgrimage whose goal is the eternal *city* of God (9-10). *By faith* Abraham dared to sacrifice the son of the promise when God *tested* him (17); and his faith was not put to shame (19). *Isaac* and *Jacob* invoked the future which they saw and knew only *by faith* (20, 21) upon their sons and sons' sons when they blessed them.

The record of the Exodus, the heart of the faith by which Israel was to live for centuries, is a record of faith (22-29). *Joseph* would not seek immortality for his body in the skill of Egyptian embalmers; he committed himself to the unseen, hoped-for future deliverance of his people (21) by giving *directions* that his body be joined to his believing people's pilgrimage. Five times (23, 24, 27, 28, 29) the career of *Moses* is characterized as a career of faith. *By faith* God's *people crossed the Red Sea as if on dry land* (29) when the visible superiority of the *Egyptians* perished. The story of Israel's entry into the Land of Promise is the story of faith, whether it be the faith of a great leader like Joshua capturing *Jericho* (30) or of a pagan harlot like *Rahab* (31). There is not time to call the entire roll, to tell the whole story of the power of faith as shown in mighty heroic acts (32-35) or in the enduring of hardships and death (35-38). And God has kept all these ranks of faithful men poised and waiting for the final fulfillment of His promises till now! He has done us the honor of joining us to them that all might be *made perfect* together. (39-40)

11:1 *Assurance of things hoped for,* inner certainty concerning them.

11:3 *Things which do not appear,* the will, Word, and working of God, which cannot be rationally or empirically demonstrated.

11:4 *He is still speaking.* He lives on and speaks in the pages of the OT, and his witness is an incentive to all subsequent believers. He is one in that "great cloud of witnesses" of which 12:1 speaks.

11:5 *Enoch.* Cf. Gn 5:21-24, esp. 24.

11:6 *Rewards those who seek him.* Cf. Am 5:4, 6.

11:7 *Noah . . . took heed.* Gn 6:13-22.

He *condemned the world.* His faithful obedience to God's Word (Gn 6:22) was a living indictment of the heedlessness of the doomed world round about him (cf. Gn 6:5-7). For this use of "condemn" cf. Mt 12:41-42.

11:8 *Obeyed when . . . called.* Cf. Gn 12:1-8.

11:11 *Sarah . . . power to conceive.* Cf. Gn 17:19; 18:11-14; 21:2.

11:12 *Stars of heaven . . . grains of sand.* Cf. Gn 15:5-6; 22:17; 32:12.

11:13 *What was promised,* that is, the final last-days fulfillment of the promise. (Cf. 33)

Strangers and exiles. Cf. Gn 23:4, where Abraham so describes himself when negotiating for the purchase of a burial plot for Sarah—his possession of the Promised Land was still one of "the things hoped for" when he had no room in it even to bury his dead!

11:16 *Their God,* "the God of Abraham . . . Isaac . . . Jacob." (Ex 3:6, 15; 4:5)

11:17 *Abraham . . . was tested.* Cf. Gn 22:1-10.

11:18 *Descendants be named.* Cf. Gn 21:12.

11:19 Cf. Ro 4:17.

From the dead . . . he did receive him back. Since the Word of God determines what a man is, Isaac, as designated for sacrifice by God's command, was already among the dead.

11:20 *Isaac invoked future blessings.* Cf. Gn 27:27-29, 39-40.

11:21 *Jacob . . . blessed . . . sons of Joseph.* Cf. Gn 48:8-22.

Bowing . . . over the head of his staff. The phrase is taken from Gn 47:31, following the Greek translation (Septuagint).

11:22 *Joseph.* Cf. Gn 50:24-25; Ex 13:19.

11:23 *Was hid . . . by his parents.* Cf. Ex 2:2 and 1:22. Their faith could not abandon a child born under the promises of God.

11:25 *Fleeting pleasures of sin.* The sin would have been the one that so much exercises the author's concern, namely, the apostasy; cf. 6:1-8 notes and 10:26-31.

11:26 *Suffered for the Christ.* Suffering for the sake of the future promised to God's people is suffering for the Christ; the Christ IS the future of His people.

11:27 *Not . . . afraid of the anger of the king.* These words make it clear that Moses' second departure from Egypt (rather than his first fearful departure in Ex 2:15) with his people is meant, when he told the panicking Israelites,

"Fear not, stand firm, and see the salvation of the LORD." (Ex. 14:13)

11:28 *Kept the Passover.* Cf. Ex 12:21-28, 29-30.

11:29 *Crossed the Red Sea.* Cf. Ex 14:21-31.

11:30-31 *Walls of Jericho fell down . . . Rahab.* Cf. Jos 2:1-21; 6:22-25.

11:32 *Gideon.* Cf. Ju 6—8.

Barak. Cf. Ju 4—5.

Samson. Cf. Ju 13—16.

Jephthah. Cf. Ju 11—12.

David. Cf. 1 Sm 16—30; 2 Sm 1—24; 1 K 1—2:11.

Samuel. Cf. 1 Sm 1—12; 16:1-13.

11:33 *Conquered kingdoms.* E.g., Gideon overcame the Midianites against overwhelming odds; Jephthah defeated the Ammonites; David conquered the Philistines.

Enforced justice. Cf. what is said of David's reign in 2 Sm 8:15.

Received promises. Cf., e.g., God's promise to Gideon, Ju 6:16: "I will be with you, and you shall smite the Midianites as one man."

Stopped the mouths of lions. Cf. Dn 6.

11:34 *Quenched raging fire.* Cf. the three men in the fiery furnace, Dn 3:25.

Escaped the edge of the sword. Cf. Ps 144:10; 1 Sm 18:11.

Won strength out of weakness. Cf. Ju 16:28.

Became mighty in war. Cf. 1 Sm 17.

Put foreign armies to flight. This may refer either to exploits of great leaders, such as those referred to in 11:32, or to the victories over foreign power recorded in the apocryphal books 1 and 2 Mac.

11:35 *Women received their dead by resurrection.* Cf. 1 K 17:17-24; 2 K 4:25-37.

11:35-38 offer examples of great endurance sustained by faith. Some of the examples were probably suggested by cases of heroic suffering by the faithful during the Maccabean revolt recorded in 1 and 2 Mac.

11:37 *Sawn in two.* According to Judaic tradition, Isaiah suffered this fate under the wicked king Manasseh, who "shed very much innocent blood." (2 K 21:16)

11:38 *The world was not worthy.* They were too good for the wicked "world" (men without God and opposed to His will) which persecuted them and made wandering outlaws (cf. 11:37) of them.

11:39 *Well attested by their faith.* Cf. 11:1—12:2 note.

11:40 *Something better,* namely, the new and better covenant with all the blessings that full forgiveness entails. (Cf. 8:6, 8-12)

12:1 *Lay aside every weight,* anything that would weigh down, encumber, and slow down the runner in his course. Faith involves renunciation.

Sin which clings so closely, like an encumbering garment which slows the runner's stride.

12:2 *The joy . . . set before him.* For the *joy* of Jesus, His delight in fulfilling His Father's will and delivering man, cf. Jn 15:11; 17:13; see also Jn 4:35-38.

Is seated, in triumphant majesty. Cf. 1:3; 10:12; Ps 110:1.

12:3-29 Exhortation to Faith and Fear

12:3-29. The double note of confident faith and holy fear runs through the close and climax of the last long exhortation, which began at 10:19. There are many grounds for the triumphant certainty of faith. There is Jesus, who has run our race and fought our fight before us and for us, one with us in His manhood (note the use of the human name alone, Jesus, 2) who faced the *hostility* of the *sinners,* to whom He ministered, and was obedient *to the point of shedding blood* (4), unshaken to the end in His "assurance of things hoped for" and His "conviction of things not seen" (11:1; cf. 12:2). There is the God whom, through Jesus, we know as Father, who *addresses* us *as sons* (5) and bids us accept discipline and chastisement from His fatherly hand (5-6; Pr 3:11-12) as the sure token of our sonship (7-8). His discipline and chastisement are a better thing than what our less wise and sometimes arbitrary *(at their pleasure,* 10) fathers could give us, and they bear better fruit: life (9) and the *peaceful fruit of righteousness to those who have been trained by* them (11). From Him we can seek and find new strength for *drooping hands* and *weak knees* (12); when we grow weary, strength to help one another along straightened paths, strength to heal the lagging *lame* and help them on their way in *peace* and *holiness* (14). The prospect that greets the marchers is a splendid and heartening one: no longer the terrors that accompanied the giving of the Law on Sinai (18-21) but the festal triumph of the gathered people of God in *the city of the living God,* assembled with *angels* and archangels and all the company of heaven around *Jesus, the mediator of the new covenant* by virtue of His *sprinkled blood* (24), inheritors at last of *a kingdom that cannot be shaken.* (28)

But we are not yet what we then shall be, *just men made perfect* (23), and we still have need of the salutary discipline of holy fear. We need the Word that warns us of the danger of growing *weary or fainthearted* (3), that will not let us forget God's Word to His sons regarding their chastisement (5-11). We need the Word that wakens us to our responsibility toward our fellows, lest they and we both *fail to obtain the grace of God* (15). We need the warning against growing bitter and resentful under the benign pressure of God's hand, lest the "root of bitterness" grow up into a spreading noxious weed which troubles and defiles (15). We need to be reminded of the tragic instance of *Esau,* lest we like him take the cash and let the credit go, forfeiting the blessing that we shall one day seek in vain *with tears* (16-17). We need to be reminded that in *the city of the living God* which is the goal of our journeying there is *a judge who is God of all* (23), whose scrutiny no one and nothing can escape. We dare not forget that He *who is speaking* to us now and is warning us from heaven (25) is the omnipotent

Lord of the future, whom we dare not refuse, least of all now when He is poised for that last act of His which *will shake not only the earth but also the heaven.* Our gratitude *for receiving a kingdom that cannot be shaken* (28) is real gratitude only if we look to the great Giver *with reverence and awe* (28). *Thus,* as men impelled by faith and hallowed by fear, we can *offer acceptable worship.* (28)

But the somber note of fear does not drown out the glad note of faith. Even when we are confronted with the ultimate terror of God as a *consuming fire,* we are permitted to remember that He remains *our God* (29) and are reminded that He becomes consuming fire only when we in our self-will will not let Him be our God.

12:5-6 Pr 3:11-12.

12:9 *Father of spirits.* God is so called in contrast to human, physical fathers, to indicate the surpassing character of His Fatherhood.

12:12 *Drooping hands . . . weak knees,* both signs of the exhausted runner. (Cf. 12:1)

12:13 *Make straight paths.* The picture is changed from that of a runner in a race to that of the pilgrim people of God marching over difficult terrain, where the *lame* would sustain injury unless their fellow marchers cared for them.

12:14 *Strive for peace with all men.* Peace within the fellowship of the church is meant. Where there is discord, there cannot be that care for one another which is enjoined in the following.

12:15 *"Root of bitterness."* The phrase is taken from the Greek version of Dt 29:18. The Hebrew text has "a root bearing poisonous and bitter fruit" (RSV). Dt 29:18 warns against apostasy.

12:16 *Esau . . . sold his birthright.* Cf. Gn 25:29-34.

12:17 *He was rejected.* Gn 27:30-40.

He found no chance to repent. Another rendering of the Greek is possible and indeed probable. The "no chance to repent" could refer to the fact that Isaac could not withdraw the blessing once he had bestowed it on Jacob (Gn 27:37, cf. 35) and the whole might be rendered: "He found no chance to change his father's decision."

Tears Gn 27:34, 38.

12:18 *What may be touched,* i.e., a physical place like Sinai. For the terrors of Sinai cf. Ex 19:12-22; 20:18-21; Dt 4:11-12; 5:22-27.

12:20 Cf. Ex 19:12-13.

12:21 *"I tremble with fear."* Cf. Dt 9:19, where, however, Moses' fear is occasioned by his discovery of the golden calf and the people's apostasy. Cf. Acts 7:32 for a similar phrase describing Moses in his encounter with God.

12:23 *Assembly of the first-born* probably refers to angels, created before man and occupying a place of honor in the "city of the living God, the heavenly Jerusalem." (22)

12:24 *Mediator of a new covenant.* Cf. 8:6; 9:15.

Sprinkled blood that speaks more graciously. The well-known hymn verse is an apt commentary:

Abel's blood for vengeance (Gn 4:10)
Pleaded to the skies;
But the blood of Jesus
For our pardon cries.

12:25 *They did not escape,* that is, the people Israel, Ex 19:21, 24. For the thought cf. 2:1-4.

12:26 Cf. Hg 2:6, where the words refer to God's last coming to glorify His abode.

12:29 *Fire* is a common Biblical symbol of divine judgment in both the OT and the NT. Cf., e.g., Am 1:, 7, 10, 12, 14; 2:2, 5, 7:4; Mt 3:10-11.

13:1-25 CONCLUDING ADMONITIONS AND CLOSE

13:1-6 True Love and False

13:1-6 The first set of admonitions encourages the readers to *continue* in true *love:* love for brothers in the family of God, both the known and near and those from afar *(hospitality);* actively sympathetic love for the prisoner and the persecuted *(ill-treated);* pure conjugal love *(marriage).* The threat of God's judgment upon those who violate the sanctity of wedded love (4) provides the transition to the warning against false love, *love of money,* which is mistrust and unbelief toward Him who has promised His help.

13:2 *Hospitality,* not merely cordial sociability but a ministry of love to traveling, persecuted, and missionary fellow Christians. (Cf. 3 Jn 8; Ro 12:13)

Entertained angels, as Abraham and Lot did. (Gn 18:1-8; 19:1-3)

13:3 *In prison . . . ill-treated.* Cf. 6:10; 10:32-34.

Since you also are in the body, and therefore yourselves liable to suffering.

13:15 *"I will never . . . forsake you."* The promise of God which sustained Joshua when he led the wandering people of God into Canaan (Jos 1:5; Dt 31:6-8) will sustain God's people on their last journey to their eternal city. (Cf. 13:14)

13:6 Cf. Ps 118:6, expressing the confident boast of the man who though "pushed hard" by his enemies (13) and "sorely chastened" by the Lord (18), found in Him his strength and song and salvation. (14)

13:7-19 Concerning Leaders in the Church

13:7-19 Three admonitions concern *leaders* in the church. The first and longest (7-16) deals with the leaders, now dead (7), who *spoke . . . the word of God* to them. The second (17) concerns their present leaders in their pastoral function as men *keeping watch over* their *souls.* The third takes the form of a request by the author of the letter for the intercession of the church. (18-19)

13:7-16 The leaders are to honor the memory of the *leaders* who first taught them *the word of God* (cf. 2:3) by following in the footsteps *(imitate,* 7) of their *faith;* for their faith, like their teaching, was centered and fixed in Christ. Christ abides unchanged. His first witnesses may die, and *diverse and strange teachings* may attempt to distort Him or becloud His glory; yet He remains the *same for ever* (8). In Him they will continue to find the *grace* which will keep the *heart* strong and firm in faith (9); in Him they will find the strength they need, not in *foods* (as the authors of the diverse and strange teachings apparently claim). These foods were apparently connected with the old order of the Law and its cultus which "made nothing perfect" (7:19; 9:9-10) and therefore never *benefited their adherents* (9) as the grace of God in Christ can benefit His adherents now. That old order had sacrifices in which people and priests had the *right to eat* (10) of the sacrificial animal. But that was never the procedure in the case of the *sacrifice for sin* (11) on the Day of Atonement, where the *bodies of those animals* were *burned outside the camp* (11; cf. Lv 16:27). And the once-for-all sacrifice of *Jesus* was such a sacrifice for sin, for He suffered on the Day of Atonement *in order to sanctify the people through his own blood* and was consumed by the fire of suffering *outside the gate* of Jerusalem (12). The *altar* on which Christ's blood was offered offers His adherents *grace,* not food; those who cling to the old order and will not in faith recognize the new *(those who serve the tent,* or *tabernacle,* 10) *have no right to eat* (10) there; for they seek food, not grace. No new teaching can force Jesus back into the old and doomed Jerusalem, back into the old order of unprofitable foods. Men must continue to seek Him where He is to be found, in the new *city which is to come* (14), the new Jerusalem (cf. 12:22-24). For the Christian Jew that meant a painful break with the past and with the majority of his people, who will *abuse* him as a renegade to the faith and the God of his fathers (13). But he need not fear that his worship life has become poorer because he has broken with the splendid cultus of old Israel. There is left him a true *sacrifice . . . pleasing to God* (15-16), sacrifice that his OT itself approved (Ps 50:14, 12; Hos 14:2; cf. Ps 51:15-17): the sacrifice of praise to God and beneficence to man. (15:16; cf. Ja 1:27; 1 Ptr 2:5)

13:7 *Life,* that is, their mode of life, their fidelity to their Lord which made the *outcome* of their life a triumphant one, perhaps a martyr's death.

13:17 *To give account.* Cf. 1 Ptr 5:2-4.

Of no advantage to you. A leader hampered by the disobedience of his people, doing his pastoral duty *sadly,* cannot give his people the full benefit of his leadership.

13:18 *A clear conscience.* Only a leader with a clear conscience can lay a justified claim to the intercessions of his people. (Cf. 2 Co 1:11-12)

13:20-25 Close

13:20-25 The author's own intercession for his readers (20-21), an appeal to *bear with* his *word of exhortation* (22), news concerning his own and Timothy's coming to them (23), greetings (24), and a brief benediction (25) conclude the letter.

13:20-21 The intercession invokes the *God* who has created and bestowed *peace* (that perfect health and soundness in the relationship between God and man which He desires) by the death and resurrection of His Son. *Through Jesus Christ* and His covenant sacrifice He has created His people; through Him, the *great shepherd,* He will preserve His people, equipping them for all that is *pleasing in his sight.*

13:20 *Shepherd . . . covenant.* Cf. Eze 37:24-27.

13:22 *Word of exhortation* would be for Jewish-Christian ears the equivalent of "sermon." Cf. Acts 13:15, where the term is so used in the synagog.

Briefly. The letter is brief in comparison with the extended discourse and discussion which his presence (19, 23) with them would make possible.

13:23 The mention of *Timothy,* long an associate of Paul, suggests that the author, too, was associated with Paul. The fact that Timothy is mentioned alone, with no reference to the man with whom he was identified lifelong so closely, indicates that Paul was no longer among the living.

13:24 *Those . . . from Italy.* Cf. Introduction, par. 4.

JAMES

INTRODUCTION

The Letter of James is addressed to Jewish Christians. The words of the salutation, "To the twelve tribes in the Dispersion" (1:1), in themselves do not necessarily mark the readers as Jewish, since the New Testament constantly appropriates the titles and attributes of Israel for the New Testament people of God (cf. Gl 6:16; Ph 3:3; 1 Ptr 1:1, 17; 2:9-10; Rv 7:4 ff.; 14:1); but these words are part of the generally Judaic coloring of the letter. The situation presupposed among the Christians addressed in the letter—that of a poor, tired, oppressed, and persecuted church—corresponds to what we know of the Jerusalem church of Acts 1—12; and what held for Jerusalem very probably held for other Jewish churches in Palestine and in the Dispersion also. The sins which the letter particularly deals with are the sins of Judaism in their Christianized form; the problem of sexual license, for instance, which looms so large in Gentile Christianity and is constantly dealt with in letters addressed to Gentile churches, is not touched on here, while the prime sin of Israel under the leadership of scribe and Pharisee, that of cleavage between profession and practice (Mt 23:3), which evoked Jesus' most stringent polemics, is scored heavily by James. The place of worship is called by the same names as the Jewish synagog (2:2), a practice which was long observed in Judaic Christianity but was never frequent elsewhere in Christendom. The author takes all his examples from the Old Testament (Abraham, Rahab, Job, the prophets, Elijah), and this tells us something about the readers as well as the author.

Date of the Letter

The letter is apparently addressed to Judaic Christians of the early days, during the period covered by Acts 1—12. The church is still firmly enmeshed in Judaism, a part of historic Israel, so much so that one modern scholar has argued that the letter is addressed to *all* Israel, stressing all that Christians and Jews have in common, and is intended to be a missionary appeal, by way of admonition and a call to repentance, to all Jews. Although this theory amounts to an overstatement of the case and can hardly be accepted in the form in which it is advanced, it does call attention to the essentially Judaic character of the persons addressed, and it recognizes the fact that there are portions in the letter which address the readers particularly as members of historic Israel (4:1 ff.) and passages which are apostrophes directed to the Judaic world around the church rather than admonitions spoken directly to the church (4:13-17; 5:1-6). Judaism has not yet definitely expelled the new community. Furthermore, there is no indication in the letter of the tensions and difficulties which arose when Gentiles came into the church in large numbers, those tensions which gave rise to the Apostolic Council (Acts 15) and occasioned Paul's Letter to the Galatians. A date prior to Paul's first missionary journey is therefore most probable, about A. D. 45; and the phrase "twelve tribes of the Dispersion" is intended to designate the new people of God at a time when it consisted primarily of converted Jews.

Author of the Letter

The only indications of authorship in the letter are the name James in the salutation and the general tone and character of its content. If we ask which of the various men named James in the New Testament could expect to be recognized and identified when he calls himself simply "James, a servant of God and of the Lord

Jesus Christ" (1:1) and could speak with such massive authority to Judaic Christianity as he does in this writing, the most probable answer is: James, the brother of the Lord. (The much-debated question whether the brethren of the Lord were His cousins, half brothers, or full brothers need not detain us here; the last alternative, that they were the children of Joseph and Mary, would seem to be the most probable; that they were his half brothers is possible; the theory that makes them his cousins is beset by almost insuperable difficulties.)

This James had, like his brothers, refused to accept his brother as the Christ during His lifetime (Jn 7:5). It was not apparently until the risen Lord appeared to him that his doubts were overcome and he became the servant of Him whom he henceforth called "the Lord Jesus Christ" (cf. 1 Co 15:7; Acts 1:14). Active in the life of the church from the beginning, he seems to have confined his work to Jerusalem. Possibly he undertook missionary journeys within Palestine, like his brothers (1 Co 9:5). At any rate, it was in Jerusalem that he became and remained prominent. As early as A. D. 44 he was the acknowledged leader of the Jerusalem church, as Peter's words in Acts 12:17 show. About to leave Jerusalem after his deliverance from jail, Peter bids the people assembled in Mary's house tell of his release and departure "to James and to the brethren." At the Apostolic Council the voice of James is the final and decisive voice in the discussion (Acts 15:13-29). When Paul at the end of his third missionary journey reports to the Jerusalem church and brings the gifts of the Gentile church to the saints at Jerusalem, he reports to James (Acts 21:18). The picture we have of James in Acts is confirmed by what we find in the letters of Paul; Paul can refer to him simply as "James" and reckon on being understood (1 Co 15:7); he practically ranks him with the apostles in Gl 1:19, and even mentions him before Peter and John as one of the "pillars" of the church (Gl 2:9). James is, for Paul, so integral a part of the life of the Jerusalem church that he can describe Jerusalem Christians who came to Antioch by saying, "Certain men came *from James*" (Gl 2:12). Jude can in his letter identify himself to his readers by calling himself "brother of James." (Jude 1)

A later Jewish-Christian tradition preserved for us by Eusebius (*HE* II, 23, 4) pictures James as a paragon of Judaic piety in the sense that he was deeply interested in and devoted to the ritual side of that piety; but none of the New Testament notices of him confirms this. He is, according to the New Testament, a Christian Jew devoted to his mission to Israel and therefore faithful to the temple and to the Law so long as the temple stands and there is an Israel that will hear him. Reliable tradition has it that he was faithful to his people to the end and died a martyr's death A. D. 66. So strongly had his piety and his love for his people impressed men that even pious Jews called him the Just and saw in the Jewish wars and the fall of Jerusalem God's righteous visitation on Israel for putting this righteous man to death.

Occasion of the Letter

The Epistle of James shows that the author is acquainted with the situation of his readers, but none of the references is so specific that it enables us to point to any particular event or set of circumstances as the immediate occasion for writing. Still, it is probably not accidental that the epistle opens with a summons to find cause for joy in "various trials" (1:2) and closes with an admonition to restore the brother who "wanders from the truth" (5:19). The "twelve tribes" are under the twin pressures of poverty and persecution; they are tempted to grow depressed, bitter, and impatient—depressed at the fate of the doomed people of which they remained a part, a fate which loomed ever more clearly and more terribly against the stormy skies of Palestine; bitter at the fact that they were offering the grace of God in vain to this doomed people; and impatient for the "times of refreshing" and the establishing of all things (Acts 3:19-21) which the resurrection of Jesus Christ from the dead had promised and assured.

They were tempted, in this apathetic slackening of their energies, this declension in their Christian stamina, to relapse and accommodate their life to the life of the world which pressed on them from every side and sought to put its mark and impress on them. For them accommodation to the "world" meant, of course, accommodation to the Judaism from which they had escaped. Judaism with its distorted piety, its encrusted and inactive faith, its superficial and fruitless hearing of the Word, its arrogant and quarrelsome "wisdom," its ready response to the seduction of wealth, its mad thirst for liberty. The danger of apostasy was for members of this church anything but remote and theoretical; it was immediate and real. (5:19-20)

In such a situation, in a church beset from without and within, faced with the necessity of constant correction and discipline, it is small wonder that the love of many grew cold, that the church was troubled by inner dissensions, that men were ready to speak against and to judge one another, that the spontaneous mutual ministrations of the first glad days were in danger of lapsing and being forgotten.

Content of the Letter

To these Judaic churches in this characteristically Judaic situation the leader of Judaic Christianity addressed a thoroughly Judaic letter, or rather a homily in letter form; for the letter is a letter chiefly in form—and even the letter form is not complete; the personal conclusion, characteristic of Paul's letters, is absent here. A phrase like *"Listen,* my beloved brethren" (2:5) shows that we have to do with a writing that is simply the extension of the spoken "implanted word"; and the whole style of the letter bears this out. The leader and teacher whose word is the vehicle of the will of God to the Jerusalem church is speaking to the Judaic churches in Judea, Samaria, Galilee, Syria, Cilicia—perhaps the letter went even farther afield than that.

The "miscellaneous" character of James' admonitions has often been exaggerated, sometimes in the interest of theories concerning the origin of the book. This miscellaneous character is more apparent than real, being due to the Semitic habit of thought which sets down related thoughts side by side without explicitly coordinating them or subordinating one to the other as we are accustomed to do. James' call to repentance breaks down on closer investigation into six rather massive units, each of which again usually has two aspects.

1:1 SALUTATION

1:1 James begins with an obeisance to *God and . . . the Lord Jesus Christ;* he stands in the same relation to both; he is *servant,* totally devoted to both in the obedience of faith. And he speaks to the new Israel, the *twelve tribes* of the new age who have not yet reached their eternal home but live as scattered exiles in this world *(in the Dispersion;* cf. 1 Ptr 1:1; Ph 3:20). He speaks as the servants of the Lord, the prophets (Am 3:7), spoke of old to God's people, and their message is also his, the call to repentance: "Turn" (cf., e.g., Jer 25:5). This turning is both a turning from evil and a turning to the Lord who makes repentance possible (Lm 5:21) and bestows His forgiveness and blessing on the penitent. (Jl 2:12-14)

Twelve tribes. For the NT church as the new Israel cf. Gl 6:16; Ph 3:3; 1 Ptr 1:1, 17; 2:9-10; Rv 7:4 ff.; 14:1.

1:2-27 TURN TO GOD, THE GIVER OF PERFECT GIFTS

1:2-18 Turn to the God Who Perfects You by Trial

1:2-18 Turn from your folly (5), from your wavering double-mindedness (6-8), your doubt of God's goodness, your Judaic fatalism which attributes man's sin to God. (13-15)

Turn to your God and find in Him the power to speak a glad assent to the trials which He sends you (2); find in Him the tried and tested faith which gives steadfastness (3) and perfection (4); find in Him, by the prayer of faith, the wisdom which will enable you to bear your trials (5), a wisdom which enables the poor man to see in his poverty his exaltation (9) and gives to the rich man the power to see his greatness elsewhere than in himself and his riches (10-11). Turn to God and find in Him the unchanging Giver of all good gifts, the Giver of the supreme gift of new birth by His Word, a rebirth which is the beginning and pledge of creation's rebirth (18). Thus empowered, endure your trials manfully and joyfully and receive from Him the crown of life. (12)

1:2 *Joy.* Cf. 5:10-12.

1:3 *Faith.* When Christians are put to the test, faith is being tested. Faith is of central importance for James. (Cf. ch. 2)

1:5 *Wisdom* in the Scriptures is a gift of God (charismatic), centered in God and practical, having to do with management of life. One might describe it as the ability to see God steadily and see Him whole, in all aspects of one's life, even in trial and suffering, as here.

Ask . . . given. Cf. Mt 7:7.

1:10-11 Cf. Is 40:6-8, where the contrast to man in his frailty and transience is the "word of our God" which "will stand for ever." The Word of God plays a significant part in this chapter, 1:18, 21, 22, 23, 25 ("perfect law").

1:12 *Crown of life.* Life, eternal life in a glory bestowed by God, is the crown.

1:13 Trial and temptation lie close together; God's testing of faith can be the occasion of the temptation to refuse God's loving discipline and to depart from Him. *"I am tempted by God."* The rabbis attributed to God the creation of the evil impulse in man (for which the Law was given as the cure), and the Qumran sect held a similar view. James' warning would be particularly relevant to Jewish Christians. (Cf. 16, "Do not be deceived.")

1:14-15 *Own desire.* Man is responsible for the uncanny sequence that leads with the inevitability of conception, gestation, and birth to *death.*

1:17 *Father of lights,* Creator (cf. Jb 38:28). God ordained the lights to "be for signs and for seasons" (Gn 1:14, 18); they are the most certain thing in creation, yet even they undergo *variation* and *change;* God's giving, His will of grace, is more certain than the most certain of His creations.

1:18 James is referring to the supreme gift of God to His new 12 tribes, namely, new birth, new life. 1 Ptr 1:3 connects this gift explicitly with "the resurrection of Jesus Christ from the dead"; and the resurrection of the "Lord of glory" (2:1) constitutes the unspoken presupposition of James' word.

Word of truth, the Gospel. (Cf. 1 Ptr 1:22-25; Eph 1:13; Cl 1:5)

1:19-27 Turn to the God Who Implanted His Word Among You

1:19-27 Turn from the pride which breaks out in self-assertive speech before it has heard the good Giver out, turn from the anger which resents His judgment on man's sins (19), from the filthiness and wickedness which insulates a man against the wholesome fires of God's judgment and against the life-giving warmth of His grace (21). Turn from speaking to hearing, from self-assertive anger to the meekness which hears God out on His terms (19-21), turn to God and receive from His Word the righteousness which God alone can work (20), receive it in a repentance which strips off the filth and wickedness of self and in its naked helplessness receives from God salvation of the soul. (21)

When you have so heard the Word in repentance and faith, turn from the self-deception which thinks that God's Word is a word to be contemplated, that a man may hear God's Word without being moved by it (22, 26); turn from such mere and forgetful hearing of His Word (22, 24, 25) to a persevering and vital hearing of it, turn to a doing of the Word which God's great gift has made for you a perfect law of liberty, a law which sets you free for God and for your fellowmen (25), that law which leads man to a pure and undefiled worship of God, which hallows his speaking, makes his deeds deeds of mercy, and sets him apart from the defilement and the doom of this dark world. (26-27)

1:19 *Know this,* that God is the generous (1:5), unchangingly sure Giver of every good gift (1:17) and that His supreme gift of new life comes to man by His Word (1:18). Therefore the hearing (and doing) of this Word is of such critical importance.

1:20 *Righteousness of God.* Since a meek hearing does "work" this righteousness, and since the Word is one which does God's own work of saving men's souls (21), the righteousness of God can hardly be anything but His redeeming righteousness of which both the OT (e.g., 1 Sm 12:7, where the word for righteousness is translated "saving deeds") and St. Paul (Ro 3:21) speak. Cf. also Jesus' beatitude on those who hunger and thirst for righteousness. (Mt 5:6)

1:25 *Perfect law . . . of liberty.* This description of God's Word is in a series with the life-giving "word of truth" (18) and the "implanted word which is able to save" (21). It is therefore best taken as signifying the Gospel in its transforming and formative impact on man's life.

1:26-27 *Religious . . . religion.* The word used stresses the manifestations or exercise of religion, religion in action, and might be rendered "a worshiper . . . worship."

1:27 *Pure and undefiled.* James uses the language of OT cultic worship to describe the new worship in Spirit and truth, as Paul does, Ro 12:1; cf. 1 Ptr 2:5.

Visit orphans and widows. Visit is not mere sociability but active sympathy and assistance. *Orphans and widows,* those who are most in need of help and least capable of repaying, are especially objects of God's love.

2:1-13 Turn from a partiality which fawns on the rich and dishonors the poor (1-3), for that is for you a cleavage of yourself and a transgression of your Lord's command of "Judge not" (4); it involves an impious judgment on the poor and a false and unrealistic judgment on the rich (5-7)

Turn from the pious self-justification which pleads the law of love to excuse partiality toward the rich (8); free yourselves of the last traces of the Judaic theory of compensation, which seeks to offset the transgression of one commandment with the fulfillment of another (9-11); turn from the mercilessness which you can conceal from yourselves but will not be able to conceal from God in the Judgment. (12-13)

Turn to the Lord Jesus Christ, who will bestow the glory of the kingdom of God on the poor and has made the poor rich even now as heirs of the Kingdom (1, 5), who lifts those who believe in Him above the petty difference between rich and poor. Rise in faith to the vision which sees men, both poor and rich, with the eyes of God, the poor as heirs of God, the rich as the oppressors of the people of God and the blasphemers of the holy name pronounced on the believer at his baptism (5-7). Return to a real and repentant confrontation with the will of God—see in the law of love the royal law which gives meaning to all the commandments and includes them all; and remember that you will be judged under the law of liberty, that law which sets you free for God and for your fellowman; remember that only a faith whose work is mercy can hope for mercy in the merciful judgment of God. (8-13)

2:1-26 TURN TO THE TRUE AND ACTIVE FAITH

2:1-13 Turn: Break with Partiality Toward the Rich

2:1 *Faith of,* perhaps better, "faith in." As Jesus Christ is on a par with God, He is like God the object of faith. As God in the OT is called "King of glory" and "God of glory" (Ps 24:7; 29:3), so *Lord of glory* is a title of deity applied to Jesus.

2:4 *Made distinctions among yourselves.* Better, "are at odds with yourself, waver in your own mind." The Christian assembly as a whole is contradicting its own deepest convictions of faith when it fails to look on the poor with the eyes of God.

2:5 *Poor . . . kingdom.* Cf. Mt 5:3; 1 Co 1:26-29.

2:6 *The rich. Rich* is not a purely economic designation (cf. 1:10; 5:1-6). The rich man whom James condemns is the man who seeks to secure his existence by means of secular guarantees with no thought for God or man, like the rich fool of Jesus' parable (Lk 12:15-21), "who lays up treasure for himself, and is not rich toward God."

2:7 *Name . . . invoked over you.* An allusion probably to baptism in the name of Jesus Christ, and the phrase could also be rendered: "That honorable name which was pronounced over you." The persecutors of the church met the confession "Jesus is Lord" with the anathema "Jesus be cursed!" (Cf. 1 Co 12:3)

2:8 *Royal law,* the law as interpreted by Jesus, who is the kingdom of God in person. (Cf. Mt 22:34-40)

2:12 *Law of liberty.* Cf. 1:25 and the note there.

2:13 *Mercy triumphs over judgment.* Cf. Mt 5:7, where Jesus promises mercy in the Judgment to the merciful, and Mt 25:31-46, which is Jesus' commentary to the beatitude on the merciful.

2:14-26 Turn from Mere Profession to an Active Faith

2:14-26 Turn from a merely verbal faith, for a faith that exhausts itself in words is as useless as a charity that exhausts itself in gracious phrases (14-16); turn from a faith that is in reality no faith at all, but dead (17) and unable to save. (14)

Turn: Cease trying to excuse yourselves with a pious sophistry which makes an impossible cleavage between faith and works by distributing them as several gifts, faith to one man, works to another (18); this reduces faith to a merely intellectual grasp of truths about God—demons have that kind of faith, and they know that it cannot save them; they shudder at the judgment that is to come upon them. (19)

Turn from this delusion about your barren faith, a faith as impotent and inactive as a corpse (20, 26). Turn to that faith which is a living faith and must needs evince itself in works (18), a faith which justifies because it is a faith that commits a man wholly to his God and is therefore a working faith, such a faith as Abraham's was: he was ready to give to God the best gift God had given him, his son. Abraham's faith was active in his works and found its fullest expression in works (21-22). In the fact that believing Abraham showed in deed that he held God dearer than God's dearest gift there was seen the full meaning of the words, *Abraham believed God, and it was reckoned to him as righteousness* (23). Abraham, the believing friend of God, was friend in word and deed, and so one can even say that man is justified by works and not by faith alone, for faith is never alone, as even the example of Rahab shows: Hers was a simple and unfinished faith, and yet this believing woman, with her stained and ruined past, acted out her faith in works, and she too was thus justified by works as one whose faith made her the doer of the will of God. (25)

Turn to the faith which is the creation of the God who is God of the living and not of the dead, a faith that is a body animated by a living soul, not a corpse. (26)

2:18 *You . . . I.* One person . . . another person. *Show you my faith.* Note that James does not say "Show you my works"; he is interested in faith.

2:19 *You do well.* Ironic.

The demons believe—and shudder. Cf. Mt 8:28-29.

2:21 *Offered his son.* Gn 22:1-19.

2:22 This and v. 26 are James' carefully measured statements on faith as working faith. Statements like 19 and 24 are more in the nature of argumentative "shockers" designed to shatter the complacency of those who argue for a workless faith.

Completed, in the sense that an apple tree is completed when it produces what God intended and created it to produce, apples. One modern translator renders, "Found its highest expression in" instead of *was completed.*

2:23 Gn 15:6; Is 41:8; 2 Ch 20:7.

Fulfilled. Not in the sense that a prediction proved true, for Gn 15:6 is not a prediction; rather, the Word of God which imputed righteousness to Abraham's faith documented itself in deeds and so found its full expression when he feared God and obeyed His voice. (Gn 22:12, 18)

2:25 *Rahab the harlot.* Rahab's sinful past is not glossed over, as it was in Judaic legends concerning her. For the story of Rahab cf. Jos 2:1-24; 6:1-25. For her faith cf. particularly Jos 2:8-11.

At the time of the Reformation the place of James in the church's canon (the collection of sacred books which are authoritative for the faith of the church) was again questioned, not only by Luther but also by Roman Catholic scholars such as Erasmus and Cajetan. Luther's objection to James is based chiefly on the section Ja 2:14-26, which to Luther seemed to be in irreconcilable conflict with Paul and the Gospel of salvation by grace through faith without the works of the law. But James' words on faith and works are not aimed at Paul; neither do they really contradict Paul's teaching. The idea that faith is merely the certainty that God is one (2:19) has nothing to do with Paul; neither was Paul the first to see in Abraham the exemplar of saving faith—the rabbis had done that before him, as had Jesus Himself (Mt 8:11, Jn 8:56). The polemics of James *may* be directed at a watered-down and distorted version of Paul's Gospel, such as might have been reported in Jerusalem from Antioch when Paul was preaching there (Acts 11:25-26). But it is more likely that James is combating not a doctrine but a practical threat to faith that came to his readers from their Judaic past and surroundings. Jesus had said of the teachers of Judaism that they professed without practicing (Mt 23:3)—what would be more natural than a recurrence of this Judaic fault in a Christianized form in Judaic Christianity? It should be noted, moreover, that the bold but monumentally simple argument of James would be pitifully weak, if not malicious, as a refutation of Paul's teaching. And the James whom we know from his letter is neither weak intellectually nor malicious morally. James is not attacking Paul.

Neither does James, at bottom, contradict Paul. Both Paul and James are moved to speak by love. Paul emphasizes the fact that our salvation is wholly God's grace and entirely His doing and that faith is therefore first and foremost pure receiving. Paul will leave no desperate sinner outside God's call of grace. James emphasizes the fact that faith is union and communion with God and commits us wholly, with all our thoughts and all our doing, to God; James will allow no brother to destroy his faith and himself by making of faith an intellectual acceptance of doctrinal propositions and emptying it of love and works. Paul speaks to the sinner's desperation; James speaks to Christian complacency. When James is speaking to the repentant sinner, he makes no mention of works but bids such a one in his desperation draw near to God, in the assurance that God will draw near to him like the father of the returning prodigal son (Ja 4:8). James describes man's redemption as a new birth from God, solely by the will and Word of God (Ja 1:18); and he describes God's love for man as God's sole and sovereign choice, as God's election (Ja 2:5). Paul, on the other hand, can combine his own characteristic emphasis with that of James in a single sentence: "By grace you have been saved through faith; and this is not your own doing, it is the gift of God—not because of works, lest any man should boast. For we are his workmanship, *created in Christ Jesus for good works,* which God prepared beforehand, that we should walk in them." (Eph 2:8-10)

The same Luther who objected so strenuously to James' conception of justification by faith has given us a description of faith which would delight the heart of James: "Faith is a divine work in us, which transforms us and gives us a new birth from God (Jn 1:13) and kills the old Adam . . . Oh, it is a living, busy, active, and mighty thing, this faith; it cannot but be ever doing good. Faith does not ask if there are good works to be done, but has done them before one can ask and is ever a-doing. But whoever does not do such works is a man without faith; he goes groping about in search of faith and good works and knows neither what faith nor what good works are." And the first of Luther's theses, which makes repentance the beating heart of the Christian existence, might serve as a title to the Letter of James. The presence of this letter in the canon is a perpetual reminder to the church not to misconstrue Paul by making him the advocate of a lazy and workless faith, a reminder to hear and be guided by the real Paul, the Paul who entreats us "not to accept the grace of God in vain." (2 Co 6:1)

Turn from the blithe self-assurance which presses boldly into the teaching office, unmindful of the fearful responsibility imposed on human frailty by that office (1-2); consider what a struggle is involved in the control of the tongue (2), what fearful power for evil this small member wields, how fierce and untamable this ruthless evil, this very embodiment of the godless world, is (3-6). Turn from the delusion that any man can tame this evil—man is lord of creation but is not master of his tongue (7-8). Turn from that unnatural cleavage of the soul which makes the tongue the means by which men both bless God and curse man, the creature made in the image of God (9-12). Since *no man* can tame the tongue, turn to Him who alone can overcome the evil in man. (This is implicit in *no human being can tame the tongue:* the positive side of the call to repentance is really expressed in 3:13-18.)

3:1-18 TURN, TEACHERS IN THE CHURCH, TO GOD-GIVEN WISDOM

3:1-12 Turn from Your Sinful Selves to God

3:1 *With greater strictness.* Cf. Lk 12:48.

3:2-5 The three images used to illustrate the power of the tongue *(bit, rudder, small fire)* all stress slight cause and great effect; the third (fire) adds the huge destructiveness of the effect. The tongue is thought of as the expressive instrument of the will.

3:6 *Unrighteous world.* The world, with its contempt for the poor whom God has chosen (2:5) and its ruthless and insatiable passions which drive it into opposition to God (4:1-4), defiles the Christian from without (1:27); the tongue, the instrument of communication with the world, defiles *(staining)* from within. (Cf. Mt 15:11, 18-20)

Set on fire by hell. Since *hell (Gehenna)* in Biblical usage is the place of punishment (not the abode of Satan), the thought here seems to be that the tongue is so evil that the fires of the future judgment already envelop it. (Cf. Lk 16:24)

3:9 *The likeness of God* (Gn 1:27) is referred to in Gn 9:6 to justify capital punishment for murder. James' use of the idea here reflects Jesus' teaching that the commandment "You shall not kill" is violated when the tongue is used to injure one's fellowmen. (Mt 5:21-22)

3:12 Cf. Mt 7:16 for the same image.

3:13-18 Turn from Earthly Wisdom to God

3:13-18 Turn from a wisdom which in its selfish bitterness creates divisions and produces every vile practice and thus gives the lie to the truth which God has given you in His Word of truth (13:16). Turn from a wisdom that is earthly, unspiritual, and devilish (15). Turn to God, who gives true wisdom and understanding, who alone can save man from his fruitless and arrogant wisdom and give him true wisdom characterized by meekness and productive of good (13), a wisdom whose purity attests its divine origin, an active and graciously productive wisdom that goes its way in the certitude and candor of faith (17). Turn in the strength of this wisdom to a life devoted to the making of peace, as teachers who by their words and deeds plant seeds which grow and ripen into righteousness. (18)

3:13 Wisdom, like faith, must have *works* if it be genuine.

The *meekness of wisdom.* Meekness is essential to the conception of wisdom. Meekness is closely related to "the fear of the Lord," which the OT declares to be the beginning of wisdom (Ps 111:10; cf. Pr 1:7; Jb 28:28). Jesus' beatitude on the meek is practically a quotation from Ps 37 (Mt 5:5; Ps 37:11), and Ps 37 is a portrait of meekness. Meekness is centered in God; the meek man trusts in the Lord and does good (Ps 37:3), delights in the Lord (4), commits his way to the Lord and trusts His way (5), is still before the Lord and waits patiently for Him (7), knowing that the steps of a man are from the Lord (23), and takes refuge in Him (40). Jesus called Himself meek (Mt. 11:29) and entered Jerusalem as the meek King promised by Zechariah (Mt 21:5; Zch 9:9). In meekness man receives the Word that has power to save his soul (Ja 1:21), and in meekness he receives wisdom from above, as God's gift (Ja 1:5). Meekness is therefore the extreme opposite of the harsh egoism that is characteristic of human wisdom. (Ja 3:14, 16)

3:14 *False to the truth.* A jealously selfish and ambitious wisdom contradicts the Word of truth, the Gospel, to which the Christian owes his new life (1:18), and is a wandering from the truth, which brings death to the soul. (5:20)

3:15 *From above,* coming to men as God's good gift. (Cf. 1:17)

3:17 The word translated *gentle* is used to describe the free, generous graciousness of a superior, such as a prince or king or God. *Open to reason* might perhaps better be rendered as "compliant," having a ready ear for the pleas of men. The seven adjectives sound like a description of the Christ of the gospels, who is "the wisdom of God." (1 Co 1:24)

3:18 Cf. Dn 12:3; Is 32:16-17

4:1-12 TURN TO GOD, THE GIVER OF THE SPIRIT AND ALL GRACE

4:1-10 Turn from Assimilation to the World to God

4:1-10 Turn from the world's passionate wars and fierce fightings (1-2). Turn from the world's worldly, self-centered, and therefore fruitless prayers (3). Turn from your friendship with the world which is infidelity to God and enmity against Him, and turn from the devil, the author of all enmity against God (4, 7). Turn from your impurity and double-mindedness, from your secular laughter and your worldly joys. (8-9)

Turn to the God who has made His Spirit to dwell in you and yearns jealously for that Spirit—you dare not receive the grace of God in vain (5). Turn to God, who opposes the proud but gives grace to the humble, who will welcome all who penitently draw near to Him (6, 8). Turn to the God who exalts those who speak a resolute no to the devil and thus submit to God and humble themselves before Him. (7, 10)

4:4 *Unfaithful creatures,* literally "adulteresses." (Cf. Hos 1—3; Mt 12:39; 16:4; Mk 8:38)

4:5 *Yearns jealously.* God, who gave the Spirit, desires the fruits of the Spirit, "love, joy, peace, patience, kindness, goodness, faithfulness, gentleness, self control." (Gl 5:22)

Scripture. The quotation cannot be identified.

4:6 *More grace.* God's promise is greater than His threat.

Gives grace to the humble. Pr. 3:34.

4:7 The best commentary on this verse is the account of the temptation of our Lord, Mt 4:1-11.

4:8 *Double mind,* divided between God and the world.

4:10 *Humble yourselves.* Cf. Mt 18:4; 23:12; Lk 14:11; 18:14; Ph 2:8-9.

4:11-12 Turn from the World's Evil-Speaking

4:11-12 Turn from that refined form of murder (cf. 2), the malicious word against your brother (11). Turn from your quarrel with God, which is what your words against your brother come to; for when you condemn your brother, you condemn God's law, which demands of you a whole and unbroken love for your brother (11). Turn in fear to Him who has power to destroy, the one Lawgiver and Judge whose office you dare not usurp (12). Turn in faith and hope to Him who is able to *save* as well as to destroy. (12)

4:12 *Who are you . . . ?* Mt 7:1-5; Ro 2:1; 14:4.

4:13—5:6 TURN FROM THE WORLD IN ITS HAUGHTY SELF-ASSURANCE

4:13—5:6 This section does not address the church directly but rather addresses itself indirectly to the world in the midst of which the church lives, just as the OT prophets do with the "nations" round about Israel. Note that (a) the address "brethren," found in every other section of the epistle, does not occur here; (b) the brusque and peremptory expression *come now* (4:13 and 5:1) occurs only in this section. The warning to the world is, of course significant to the church in the world; the church lives in the midst of the world, is threatened by the world, and can be infected by the world. Also, the church is thus kept aware of the fact that God's call to repentance is a universal call, as universal as the grace of God, with whom nothing is impossible, not even the conversion of the ungodly rich. But because it is the world that is primarily addressed here, the positive aspects of the command to "turn" are here only implicit.

4:13-17 Turn from the World's Self-Assurance in Planning

4:13-17 Turn from the secular self-assurance of the trader, who lays his plans under the delusion that man is lord of his tomorrows, forgetting the frailty and transience of all human life and forgetting Him who is Lord of the morrow (13-17). Turn to the Lord who rules all life and all its tomorrows and learn to say *"If the Lord wills"* in all your planning (15), for to know the Lord and not to live constantly under His Lordship is sin. (17)

4:15 This is another example of the meekness of which James speaks in 3:13. See note there.

4:17 The reader can no longer plead ignorance; he has been warned.

5:1-6 Turn from the World's Accumulation of Wealth

5:1-6 Turn from the world's callous and brutal pursuit of riches, its heaping up of possessions beyond any conceivable need, its fat and wanton luxury; for the rich live luxuriously under the very shadow of judgment, unmindful of the fact that the last days are already upon them, that the slaughter-day of judgment (Jer 12:3) is imminent, that day on which their treacherously gotten and unused wealth will rise up to witness against them. They employ the Law to kill the righteous man, as they used it to condemn and kill the Righteous One, and they find in the patient submission of the righteous the assurance that all is well.

5:1 *Rich.* Cf. 2:6, where the antithesis to the rich are those "rich in faith" (2:5), and the note there.

5:3 *Evidence against you,* in the Final Judgment. (Cf. 8-9)

For the last days, literally "in the last days." All days since the coming of Christ, the Lord of glory, are "last days." (Heb 1:2)

5:4 *Lord of hosts.* This title, expressive of the high majesty and the illimitable power of the God who has rank on rank of powers at His disposal, is frequently used by the prophets in threats of judgment (cf., e.g., Am 4:13; 6:14; 9:5; Nah 2:13; 3:5); for the *Lord of hosts,* as Judge of those "who oppress the hireling in his wages" cf. Ml 3:5.

5:6 *The righteous man.* There may be a reference to Jesus as the Righteous One here. (a) "Righteous One" occurs as a Messianic designation of Jesus in Acts 3:14; 7:52; 22:14 (all in an early Palestinian setting) and in Is 53:10 as a designation of the Suffering Servant who by His vicarious death makes "many to be accounted righteous." (b) The death of the righteous is accomplished by legal means *(condemned);* it is judicial murder. (c) The second half of the verse would then be read as a question: "Does He not resist you?" (i.e., as your Judge). This would give point to the "therefore" of v. 7. "Therefore," James would be saying, "since the Righteous One has suffered before you and for you and God has highly exalted Him, therefore endure patiently until He returns as Deliverer (8) and Judge. (9)

5:7-20 TURN TO THE RETURNING LORD

5:7-12 Rest in the Lord, Wait Patiently for Him

5:7-12 Turn from the impatience of the wavering heart (7-8). Renounce all grumbling against the brother; all our attempts to have the last word now show that we have forgotten Him who will come to have the last word soon (9). Renounce all swearing; when we invoke the presence of the Lord on some of our words, we show that we have forgotten the coming Lord who is the remembering witness of our every word. (12)

Turn to the patience of the farmer who waits but knows why he must wait and what he waits for—the precious harvest which crowns his year with festal joy (7-9). Turn to the comforting knowledge of the Lord's ways given you in the Scriptures, to the example of the prophets who spoke the Word of the Lord as you are speaking it now, who suffered for that speaking as you are suffering now, who suffered with a patient endurance which you must emulate; for you know from the example of Job what the purpose of the Lord in all man's suffering is; you know Him as the compassionate and merciful Lord (10-11), and you know that steadfastness under His Lordship brings a great reward (11). Turn to that speaking which always has the end in view, so that your every word to your brother is a word of love and your simple yes and no is an oath spoken in the presence of Him who comes to judge and to reward. (9, 12)

5:7 *The Lord.* Jesus Christ, so also in 8. In both cases the word for coming is that regularly used in the NT of our Lord's second coming.

The early and the late rain. The early rain in autumn and the late rain in spring were both essential to the success of agriculture. The early rain prepares the ground for plowing and seeding; the late rain helps mature the grain. The OT praises God as the Giver of both. (Dt 11:14; Jer 5:24; Jl 2:23)

5:10 Cf. Mt 5:11-12

5:11 *Job.* Cf. Jb 1:21-22; 42:10-17.

5:12 Cf. Mt 5:34-37.

5:13-20 Let Your Whole Life Be Attuned to His Coming

5:13-20 Turn: Let every aspect of your life, your suffering and your joy, be hallowed by the Word of God and by prayer. (13)

Turn: Let the life of the church be one of ministering love to the sick, a love which deals with suffering man in the believing confidence that forgiveness and healing are THERE by God's giving, there for the reaching hand of the prayer of faith; faith can pray as Elijah prayed. (14-18)

Turn: Let the love of the seeking Shepherd live in you, that love which pursues the brother who has wandered from the truth and brings him back, back from death to life, from sin to the forgiveness of sins. (19-20)

5:14 *Elders of the church,* probably the officials called by that name, men whose experience with affliction and prayer gave them the Christian stamina necessary for intercession on behalf of men oppressed by both illness and the consciousness of their sins. For the office of elder cf. Acts 11:30; 14:23; 15:2; 4, 6, 22-23; 16:4; 20:17, 28; 21:18; 1 Ti 5:17-18; Tts 1:5-9; 1 Ptr 5:1-4.

5:14 *Anointing him with oil in the name of the Lord.* For the use of oil in the treatment of illness cf. Is 1:6; Eze 16:9; Mk 6:13. Probably medical treatment is all that is meant; such treatment is undertaken in the name of the Lord, at His command and invoking His aid. Another possibility is suggested by Lk 7:46, where it is implied that anointing the head with oil is a way of welcoming a guest. Then the anointing would be an assurance to the sick man that he is not separated from the church whose assembly (2:2) he cannot attend for common prayer and praise and participation in the Supper of the Lord: he is one with them and all members suffer with him (cf. 1 Co 12:26). In any case it is the prayer of faith, not the oil in itself, that restores the sick man, because it effectively invokes the aid of the Lord. (15)

5:16 *Prayer of a righteous man.* Cf. 15, "prayer of faith." Righteousness and faith are closely linked for James, as they are for Paul.

5:17 *Elijah.* Cf. 1 K 17:1; 18:1, 42-45; Lk 4:25.

5:20 *Cover a multitude of sins,* that is, bring about forgiveness for the erring brother's sins. For this sense of cover cf. Ro 4:7 (Ps 32:1-2). For the authority to pronounce God's forgiveness to the penitent sinner cf. Mt 18:15, 18; Lk 17:3. We have reason to feel that one of the two coordinated thoughts *(save, cover)* should be subordinated: "Will save his soul from death by covering a multitude of sins"; cf. 5:10, where SUFFERING and patience amounts to what we should call PATIENCE amid suffering. The interpretation frequently suggested that the one who brings back an erring brother thereby secures the forgiveness of his OWN sin can hardly stand, for it is without parallel in the NT.

FIRST

PETER

INTRODUCTION

It is because the Word of the Lord comes from God to man as a pure gift and as creative grace that it lives and grows from man to man. On the night in which He was betrayed Jesus foretold the failure of His disciples. Satan, He said, would sift them like wheat in the hope and to the intent that they might prove chaff to be burned in the unquenchable fire. On that occasion Jesus gave Peter, who was to fail most signally, a special proof of His love: "Simon, Simon," He said, "I have prayed for you that your faith may not fail" (Lk 22:31-32). That forgiving love of Jesus laid the divine claim of grace on Peter even then, on the principle that he who is forgiven much shall love much (Lk 7:47). Jesus went on to say, "And when you have turned again, strengthen your brethren" (Lk 22:32). Because he had failed and had been forgiven, because he knew both the fragility of man's resolves and the strength of divine grace, Peter was fitted for the task of strengthening his brethren. We find him doing this in his letters as the strengthener of persecuted brethren (1 Ptr) and as the strengthener and warner of brethren whose hold on the Christian hope is growing weak. (2 Ptr)

Occasion of the First Letter of Peter

This letter is addressed to the Christians of five provinces of Asia Minor. Peter calls them "exiles of the Dispersion" (1:1), a term which suggests "the dispersion of the Jews" and might naturally be thought to imply Jewish Christian readers, especially since Peter was primarily the apostle to the circumcised (Gl 2:7-9). But the letter itself shows that the readers have a Gentile background (e.g., 1:14; 2:9-10; 4:3-4); they are therefore "exiles of the Dispersion" in a figurative sense, strangers and sojourners on this earth (1:17; 2:11), dispersed in an unbelieving world. There is nothing to indicate that Peter and his readers knew each other personally.

The Christians addressed are undergoing some form of persecution (3:16-17) and are perhaps being threatened by an even severer form of persecution (4:12-19). They are being slandered, ridiculed, and suspected of disloyalty to the state (4:14, 16; 4:4; cf. 2:13-17); but there is nothing to indicate a full-scale official persecution. We hear nothing of a demand for emperor worship, for instance; nor is there any hint of confiscation of property, imprisonment, or martyr's death. Yet it is a time of severe trial; they are going through a "fiery ordeal" (4:12), perhaps the first great ordeal they have been called on to endure, since they are finding it "strange" (4:12). And Peter writes to them out of the riches of the grace which he has himself experienced, out of the fullness of the glorious hope which Christ has implanted in him, to encourage them in steadfast endurance in the strength of that grace and for the sake of that hope. He writes to admonish them to a life which befits the great salvation that is in store for them. He writes in order to make these afflicted men see once more the full eternal dimensions of the true grace of God in order that they may stand fast in it. (5:12)

Place and Time of Writing: Silvanus' Part in the Letter

Peter sends greetings to his readers from her "who is at Babylon, who is likewise chosen" (5:13). This no doubt refers to a church (the Greek word for church is feminine), and the church referred to is in all probability the church at Rome. Christianity seems to have taken over this name for Rome from late Judaism. Babylon had been branded by Old Testament prophecy as the embodiment of world power at enmity with God and His people.

Peter is, in using this name for Rome, reminding his readers that the hostile world which now has power to impose the fiery ordeal on the scattered and homeless people of God is doomed to destruction under the judgment of God. The letter was thus written at Rome.

The place of writing helps fix the time of writing. There is no reason to doubt that Peter did reach Rome and did die a martyr's death there. But Peter did not reach Rome until the latter years of his life, after Israel had been called to repentance and had been called in vain. Since the persecution to which the letter refers does not seem to be an official one like that under Nero and since Peter can still call for solid loyalty to the state (2:13-17), a date before the Neronian persecution of A. D. 64 is probable.

As for the circumstances which prompted Peter to write to Gentile churches, some of which had their origin in Paul's missionary labors, one can only guess. A recent commentator on First Peter has made a suggestion which is probable and attractive, to the effect that Peter may have written at Paul's suggestion. Paul, about to leave for Spain in A. D. 61 or 62, having heard of the situation of the churches of northern Asia Minor, laid it on Peter's heart to write to them a circular letter, just as Paul himself had written somewhat earlier to a group of churches in Asia Minor (Letter to the Ephesians). This receives some confirmation from the fact that Silvanus, Paul's longtime companion, had a part in the writing of the letter. Peter's words, "By [or "through"] Silvanus, a faithful brother as I regard him, I have written briefly to you" (5:12), probably indicate that he was more than merely a secretary to Peter. Perhaps he acted as translator; Peter as a Galilean would know Greek but was doubtless more at home in Aramaic. Or perhaps Silvanus worked more freely, carrying out Peter's general instructions as to content and submitting his work to Peter's supervision, a practice not uncommon in ancient letter writing. Silas as the trusted companion of Paul and a man endowed with the gift of prophecy (Acts 15:32) may have been called into the consultation between Peter and Paul when the letter was planned and was thus acquainted with its purpose and content from the outset.

Special Value of the Letter

First Peter is often and rightly called the Letter of Hope. Hope in the full Christian sense of a serene and confident dependence on God, hope based on the unshakable certainty of the resurrection of the dead which is begun and guaranteed in the resurrection of Jesus Christ, hope as a mighty energizing power for the whole life of men in the church is certainly a dominant note of the letter. But such convenient catchword summaries are necessarily oversimplifications and can serve to conceal from the student the variety and riches of the letter. These qualities of variety and richness have been noted by many students. Erasmus called it "an epistle sparse in words, crammed with content." The comprehensiveness of the letter is taken into account by those scholars who have suggested that the section 1:3—4:11 represents a baptismal homily, or address, which laid before the newly converted all that their new life in the church conferred on them as God's gift and all that it asked of them as the response of faith and hope to that gift. Others have taken the whole letter as a record of an early Christian service of worship, beginning with an address to the newly baptized converts (1:3—4:11) and concluding with an address to the whole church (4:12—5:11). A modern New Testament scholar makes the penetrating comment that the compressed fullness of the letter marks it as the production of a *worker* who knows how to utilize his time; he sees in the "luminous" power of Peter's sentences the hallmark of that composed and settled intellectual strength which results from a life of constant prayer. Luther included First Peter in his list of the prime and capital books of the New Testament. Anyone looking for a key book which will unlock for him the meaning of the whole New Testament would do well to give his days and nights to this letter.

1:1-2 SALUTATION

1:1-2 The salutation follows the ancient letter form (sender, recipients, greetings) but is crammed with specifically Christian content. The sender presents himself as *apostle*—eyewitness (5:1) and called and authorized representative—*of Jesus Christ,* in whom Christ Himself speaks (Mt 10:40; 2 Co 13:3). The recipients are marked as under the abundant blessing of the triune God *(Father, Spirit, Jesus Christ).* And the greeting, familiar to us from the letters of Paul, invokes on the readers an ever-increasing measure of the free, undeserved favor of God *(grace)* and of that sound and healthy well-being which God's grace creates *(peace,* cf. 5:14).

1:1 *Exiles of the Dispersion.* The term *dispersion* was applied from the Babylonian Captivity onward to the Jews living scattered abroad in the world, far from their homeland (cf. Jn 7:35). In the NT the term (cf. Ja 1:1) and the idea are applied to Christians living in this world, far from their true and eternal home. (Cf. 1:17; 2:11; 2 Co 5:6; Ph 3:20; Cl 3:1-4 and 2:20)

Pontus, Galatia, etc. The letter is designed to circulate in a series of Roman provinces, beginning at Pontus, south of the Black Sea, moving southward to Galatia and *Cappadocia,* then westward to *Asia* and northward to *Bithynia.*

1:2 *Chosen and destined.* Literally "FORE-chosen and PRE-destined." The uncaused, free elective love of God, antecedent to man's history and independent of man's deserts or efforts, is the strongest possible assurance and comfort amid trials. (Cf. Ro 8:28-39)

Sanctifed by the Spirit. Sanctified belongs to the same word-family as "holy" (cf. 1:16). The Holy Spirit consecrates, sets apart, men for God and empowers them to lead lives of *obedience* to His will as revealed in His Son. (Cf. Ro 8:2-4)

Sprinkling with his blood. The once-for-all atoning sacrifice of Christ (1:18-19) avails constantly to restore the Christian to communion and fellowship with God whenever he fails in his obedience (cf. 1 Jn 1:8-9; 2:1-2). *Sprinkling with . . . blood* recalls Ex 24:7-8, the establishment of God's covenant with His people and their response: "We will be obedient." The new covenant is established by the blood of Christ (Mt 26:28) and evokes the obedience of faith.

1:3-12 THE EXULTATION OF HOPE

1:3-12 The opening doxology rings with the high confidence of triumph over death which fills the whole NT. By God's great mercy Christians have been born anew to a living hope through the resurrection of Jesus Christ from the dead, to a sure and eternal inheritance in Christ (3-5), who has accomplished the salvation which the prophets promised and desired (10-12). No suffering can dim this joyous hope or quench their love for Christ or shake their faith in Him. (6-9)

1:3 *Born anew.* For the new life in Christ as a new birth cf. 1:23; Jn 3:3, 7, 8; Ja 1:18; 1 Jn 2:29; 3:9; 4:7; 5:1, 4, 18.

1:4 *Inheritance.* Israel's inheritance was the promised land of Canaan (Dt 4:21; 19:14; Jos 1:6; Jer 3:19), a good land but, because of the sins of Israel, defiled by idolatry, withered by drought, and overrun by invaders. The new land of promise, the new heavens and earth, will be forever exempt from all that.

1:5 *Guarded.* The living, valid hope of the Christian is doubly safeguarded; the inheritance is kept safe for them in heaven (4) and those who hope are guarded by God as with a strong body of soldiery. For the military term cf. 2 Co 11:32; for the thought, Ph 4:7.

Salvation. The final, ultimate deliverance. (Cf. 1:9; 2:2; Ro 13:11; 1 Th 5:8, 9; Heb 9:28)

1:6 *Suffer . . . trials.* For the difficulties and dangers besetting the Christians addressed cf. the Introduction.

1:7 *Redound to praise and glory and honor,* primarily of God. Cf. 4:11; Eph 1:6, 12, 14; Ph 2:11, but with the suggestion (since the recipient of the praise and glory and honor is not specified) that the believers too participate in them (Cf. 4:13-14; 5:1, 4, 10)

Revelation of Jesus Christ, at His second coming. (Cf. 1:13; 4:13; 1 Co 1:7; 2 Th 1:7)

1:10 *The prophets.* For the OT prophets as belonging to the "not-yet" of the time before the coming of Christ cf. Mt 13:17. This passage attests strongly the unity of the OT and the NT; one revelation, one Spirit, one Christ bind them together.

1:11 *What . . . time.* Cf. Dn 12:6 ff.

The Spirit of Christ. As the Christ, before His incarnation, was Mediator of creation (Jn 1:3; Cl 1:16; Heb 1:2), so He was active also in the inspiration of the prophets who foretold His coming. For the activity of the preexistent Christ cf. also 1 Co 10:4, 11; Eph 1:3-5.

Sufferings of Christ and . . . glory. Cf. especially Is 52:13—53:12. The idea of *sufferings* and *subsequent glory* is also suggested by the fact that in many Messianic promises the figure of the future Deliverer appears against a dark background of judgment and misery: Is 9:1-7; 11:1 ("stump" of Jesse; cf. the threats of the preceding ch.); Mi 5:1-4. Cf. Lk 24:25-26.

1:12 *Angels long to look.* For the angels' interest and activity in God's redeeming activity cf. Heb 1:14 and the manifold ministrations of the angels in Revelation.

Through the Holy Spirit. The inspiration of those who proclaim the fulfillment corresponds to the inspiration of the prophets who predicted the grace (10) to come in Christ.

1:13—4:6 THE MINISTRY OF HOPE

1:13—4:6 God's gift of a living hope claims the Christians wholly; every aspect of their existence is colored and shaped by it. The living hope becomes a lived hope. It claims them as children (1:13—2:3), as the new people of God (2:4-10), as men who have become aliens and exiles in this world. (2:11—4:6)

1:13—2:3 Living Hope: Ministry of Obedient Children

1:13—2:3 God's gift of a new birth to a living hope makes them children of God who obey and serve Him in the sober and alert vigilance of that hope (1:13-14). Their conduct reflects the holiness of the Father who gave them life by His call (1:15-16). They honor their Father in lives of holy fear for they know the fearful cost of the redemption which a righteous God has provided; it cost the life of the Lamb of God (1:17-21). Since they owe their new life to the living Word of God, their lives express God's will of love which the Word reveals: in obedience to it they love their brethren (1:22-25). They make the Word the constant nurture of their lives and grow in stature as sons of God destined for salvation. (2:1-3)

1:13 *Gird up,* as men gird up their robes in preparation for vigorous action. (Cf. Lk 12:35)

Grace. the substance of the prophetic promise (10) is also the object of their hope.

Revelation of Jesus Christ. Cf. v. 7.

1:14 *Children.* The conception of Christians as children of God colors this whole section. Cf. 1:17 ("Father"); 1:23 ("born anew"); 2:2 ("newborn babes"); the contrast with their old life is expressed in like terms (1:18, "ways inherited from your fathers").

Ignorance, their pagan past. (Cf. Acts 17:30; Eph 4:18)

1:15-16 Holiness is God's gift; His effective call sets men apart for Himself; makes them His "called saints," literally His "called holy ones" (cf. Ro 1:7; 1 Co 1:2); this given holiness claims from men and makes possible for men a holy life, a life lived to God; they are "sanctified" (made holy) "for obedience" (1:2). Thus the just requirement of the Law (1:16; Lv 22:44-45) is fulfilled in those who walk according to the Spirit. (Ro 8:4)

1:17-19 *Father . . . fear.* The great mercy (3) of the Father is His infinite and costly condescension, the condescension of Him who remains the impartial Judge who spared not His own Son but delivered Him up for us all (Ro 8:32), made Him the Ransom for many (18; cf. Mt 20:28), and provided the atoning sacrifice (19). He is therefore to be served with fear (17); just because His grace is so lavish and costly a grace, man dare not desecrate it by misprizing or squandering it (cf. Ph 2:12). "There is forgiveness with thee, that thou mayest be feared." (Ps 130:4)

Invoke as Father. Probably referring to the Lord's Prayer. (Mt 6:9; cf. Ro 8:15; Gl 4:6)

Fear implies reverential awe and, above all, obedience. Cf. Gn 22:12, 18; 2 Co 5:11; 7:1, 15.

Lamb without blemish or spot. Suggests the Passover lamb (Ex 12:5) by whose blood Israel was delivered from the judgment of God when the firstborn of Egypt perished. (Ex 12:12-13; cf. 1 Co 5:7)

1:21 *Your faith and hope are in God,* based on divine reality and therefore certain. God has chosen and destined them (2), has given them new birth (3), is guarding them with His power (5), has provided the liberating ransom (18) and the atoning sacrifice (18) which He predestined from everlasting and manifested at the end of time (20), has *raised* Christ from the dead and glorified Him (21). In obeying Christ (2), in loving Him and believing in Him (8), in heeding the prophetic Word inspired by the Spirit of Christ (12), in hoping for the grace that comes at the revelation of Jesus Christ (13), they are fixing their *faith and hope . . . in God.* They come to the Father through Him. (Cf. Jn 14:6)

1:22—2:3 The readers love Christ and believe in Him without having seen or seeing Him (8); their faith has come from what they heard, the *good news* (25) which effectually bestows what it announces. That living *truth* (22), heard and heeded, has purified them, made them fit for converse and communion with God. Since this is personal communion, it involves responsibility. The living Word produces living men who love one another as *brethren* having one merciful Father (22) and grow in stature as sons of God by the nurture of *pure spiritual milk* (2:2); the Word of God that gave them life sustains their life. It is noteworthy that the first concrete applications of the demand "You shall be holy" (15) are love (cf. 1 Co 13:13) and growth— "The Christian life is not a having become but a becoming" (Luther; cf. Ph 3:12-15). The emphasis on brotherly love and growing maturity prepares for the idea of the corporate priesthood of the whole people in 2:4-10.

1:24 Cf. Is 40:6-9. The Word that sustained Israel when, buried in the Babylonian Captivity, her future hung solely on the creative Word of God with no human and earthly probabilities to guarantee it—that Word is fitly applied to the church of exiles (1:1, 17; 2:11) which lives on a future made certain only by the Word of God.

Flesh. Man (including man in his most impressive and powerful manifestations, cf. Is 31:1-3) in his frailty and transience.

1:25 *The Lord.* The OT passage has "our God"; Peter is applying the passage to Christ and His good news.

2:2 *Salvation.* As in 1:5 and 9, ultimate salvation. Growth continues until the day when they shall be acknowledged and proclaimed by God as His sons. (Mt 5:9)

2:3 Cf. Ps 34:8, which is again quoted at 3:10-12. *Lord,* the OT designation for the covenant God of Israel is here, as often, applied to Jesus (cf. v. 4)—strong witness to His deity.

2:4-10 Living Hope: Ministry of the New People of God

2:4-10 By being joined to Christ, the living Stone to whom Scripture points as the Rock of salvation for all who believe and the Stone over which unbelief stumbles and falls—by being joined to Him they become living stones in a new and better temple, priests who offer acceptable sacrifices of praise to the God who has called them out of darkness into His marvelous light, to be His own people, a holy nation of kingly priests to serve and glorify Him.

2:4-5 These verses state the theme of the passage; the thought of v. 4 is further developed in vv. 6-8, that of v. 5 in vv. 9-10.

2:5 *Spiritual house . . . spiritual sacrifices.* The Holy Spirit produces the new habitation of God (cf. Eph 2:22) and makes possible the new and acceptable sacrifices, for He lives and works in the OT Word (1:11) and in the NT Gospel (1:12) and so sanctifies (1:2) men for obedience to Jesus Christ.

2:6 The quotation (Is 28:16) reinforces the idea of v. 4, "in God's sight chosen and precious." In Isaiah God opposes His way of deliverance to that of the unscrupulous and worldly rulers of Jerusalem, who have made lies their refuge and have taken shelter in falsehood and hope to escape destruction by shrewd political alliances (Is 28:14-15). His way is the way of divine justice and righteousness (Is 28:17) and calls for faith (Is 28:16; cf. 7:9; 30:15). That way is ultimately Christ, God's final No to the wisdom and power of men. (1 Co 1:18-25)

2:7 The line of demarcation between God's people and the world is no longer national or racial but is drawn between faith and unbelief. Ps 118:22 elaborates the idea of "rejected by men" in v. 4. Ps 118 celebrates the steadfast love of the Lord who has given victory and deliverance against all human probabilities (10-14) to His king and people. The triumph is His and His alone (23-24; cf. 5-9). Jesus had used these words to express to the leaders of Israel His confidence that God would vindicate Him and lead Him to victory despite their rejection of Him (Mt 21:42). Peter now saw fulfilled in the Gentile churches of Asia Minor the prediction Jesus had made on that occasion: "The kingdom of God will be taken away from you and given to a nation producing the fruits of it." (Mt 21:43)

2:8 Cf. Is 8:14-15. In Isaiah it is the God of Israel Himself who becomes "a stone of offense and a rock of stumbling to both houses of Israel" when they refuse to go the way of faith (cf. Is 7:9) and of obedience in holy fear to which He has summoned them. In Christ Israel and all men are once more, and finally, confronted by the covenant God who asks of them only faith but can accept nothing less than faith. (Cf. Ro 9:32-33)

Disobey the word. Christ is accepted or rejected in the inspired Word that brings Him into men's lives (1:12, 25). *As they were destined to do:* Even in his revolt against God man does not escape the all-encompassing governance of God.

2:9 Cf. Ex 19:5-6; Dt 7:6; Is 43:21; 45:4-6; 61:6. All the glory that was Israel's, all that God by His covenant intended Israel to be, has now passed to the Israel of God (Gl 6:16) composed of men of all nations: the new people is elect and special, its function mediatorial (priests) and doxological.

2:10 The words which Hosea had used (Hos 2:23; cf. 1:10) in an amazing promise of mercy to a people who had forfeited every right to be called God's people Israel (Hos 1:2-9), is used by Peter as it is by Paul (Ro 9:25) to proclaim God's mercy to the Gentiles.

2:11—4:6 Living Hope: Ministry of Aliens in This World

2:11—4:6 Their new position as God's priestly and special people sets them apart as aliens and exiles in this world. They are therefore called on to live amid an alien and hostile mankind in such a way that their life is a witness which silences slander and can lead men to glorify God (2:11-12). This applies to their every social relationship, as subjects to civil authorities (2:13-17); as servants, especially where servitude involves undeserved suffering meekly borne after the example of Christ (2:18-25); as spouses (3:1-7); as members of the Christian community united in love and humility (3:8). As heirs of God's blessing their function in the world is to bless, not to return evil for evil (3:9-12). Though the witness and ministry of blessing involves them in undeserved suffering, no harm can come to them if they take Christ for their Lord, their example, and their Savior and with Him pass through suffering to glory (3:13-22), for by suffering they can learn to speak Christ's triumphant No to the flesh and His whole Yes to the will of God. (4:1-6)

2:11 *Exiles.* Cf. 1:1, 17. *Aliens and exiles* are under close scrutiny in the land of their exile.

Wage war. For sin as a militant power cf. Ro 7:23.

2:12 *Day of visitation,* the day when God turns their hearts to Himself. On that day they will thank God for the *good deeds* which played a part in bringing about their conversion (cf. Mt 5:16). For *visitation* in the sense of God's gracious approach to man cf. Lk 19:44. For the verb "visit" in the same sense cf. Lk 1:68; 7:16.

2:13-14 Cf. Ro 13:1-7; Tts 3:1.

2:18-25 *Servants.* House slaves are meant. The equality and honor accorded the slave in the Christian community was in striking contrast to the position of the slave in the Gentile community, where he was generally esteemed a thing rather than a person. The slave's witness was therefore especially important, and the demand laid on him is a staggeringly high one. The motivation is correspondingly profound and rich: they are to find the model and the power for their conduct in Christ, the Suffering Servant (22, 24; cf. Is 53), who died to make them whole men, and in the Good Shepherd and Guardian of their souls (25), who has set their futile (cf. 1:18) lives in order.

3:6 Cf. Gn 18:12, where the word for *lord* is translated as "husband" in the RSV.

3:7 *The weaker sex.* In common parlance this phrase has come to have a derogatory sense. But it is human male pride that made it depreciatory, not Peter. He uses it to commend woman to man's love and care; the second half of the verse makes clear how high a place he assigns to woman, as does the NT generally. (Cf. Gl 3:28; Cl 3:11, 19)

3:9 *Evil for evil,* etc. Cf. 2:23; Lk 6:27-28; Ro 12: 14, 17.

Obtain a blessing. Gl 3:9, 29; Gn 12:2.

3:10-12 Cf. Ps 34:12-16. Peter quotes from the third section of Ps 34, an admonition to "depart from evil, and do good; seek peace, and pursue it." The admonition is based on the experience of the goodness of the Lord (v. 8; cf. 1 Ptr 2:3) which the psalm celebrates with the joyfulness that characterizes the letter of Peter. (Ps 34:1-10)

3:15 *The hope that is in you.* The buoyancy of the Christian hope must have made a deep impression on the men of late antiquity, which was marked by a deep hopelessness. The golden age lay in the past, not the future. The Roman poet Horace, even when called on to celebrate the glories of the new age ushered in by Augustus, never quite managed to grow warm about the future: "Our parents' age, worse than that of our grandfathers, has produced us, inferior to them and destined to bring forth an even more vicious progeny," he wrote, damning four generations in three short lines.

3:18-22 The main drift of this much-debated passage is clear. As in 2:21-25, Peter appeals to the example of Christ (18 ff.) to enforce and establish what he has said in 13-17. The suffering, triumphant, and exalted Christ is the basis for his triumphant question in v. 13, for the beatitude on those who "suffer for righteousness' sake" which echoes Jesus' own words (14a, cf. Mt 5:10), for the commands to endure sufferings untroubled and unafraid (14b), with Christ enthroned in the temple of their hearts, persisting amid suffering in their witness to the hope that inspires them, maintaining a clear conscience in behavior that can silence the slanders of those who revile them (14b-16). When Peter in summary says, *It is better to suffer for doing right, if that should be God's will, than for doing wrong* (17), he is not stating an abstract and general principle; he is proclaiming Christ the Lord (cf. 15). Concerning Him, the supreme Zealot "for what is right" (13), the great Sufferer "for righteousness' sake" (14, 17), Peter makes three major statements. The first statement is clear (18): Christ's suffering and death was vicarious *(the righteous for the unrighteous)* and atoning *(bring us to God)*. The third statement (22) is also clear: The risen Christ *has gone into heaven;* He is enthroned at the *right hand of God* with all powers in subjection to Himself. But what does the second statement signify (19-21)? *He went and preached to the spirits in prison* (19)—what sort of "preaching" is meant, and who are the *spirits in prison?*

Many, perhaps most, interpreters see in the *spirits in prison* a reference to men who have died, specifically those who perished in the Flood (20), supreme examples of disobedience to God's call, and interpret the preaching as a saving proclamation of the Gospel. The second statement as a whole would then assert the universal efficacy of Christ's atoning death and resurrection. But grave difficulties beset this view of the passage: It is difficult to find parallels to the spirits (without modifiers) in the sense of the spirits of the departed dead. If the preaching was a saving proclamation, one would expect to hear that the spirits, or some of them, were saved by it; but of this the text says nothing. The context speaks only of the saving of *a few,* Noah and his family (20). It seems preferable therefore to take *spirits* in the well-documented sense of supernatural evil powers. (Cf. Mt 8:16; 12:45; Mk 9:20; Lk 9:39; 10:20; 11:26; Acts 16:18.) The word translated *preached* in itself means simply "proclaimed"; it is most commonly used in the NT of Gospel proclamation, but occurs also of the proclamation of the Law (Acts 15:21; Ro 2:21; Gl 5:11), or in a general sense (Rv 5:2). The second statement then would assert the triumph of Christ over the demonic powers to whom He proclaimed their defeat and deposition (cf. Cl 2:15). This gives a natural and climactic sequence: atonement, triumph, enthronement.

3:18 *Once for all.* This emphasizes both the everlasting efficacy of His sacrificial death (cf. Heb 9:26, 28; 10:10, 14) and the fact that "death no longer has dominion over him." (Ro 6:9-10)

Flesh . . . spirit, cf. Ro 1:4. In the *flesh,* in full and suffering humanity, He went to His death and endured the infliction of it upon Himself in all its bitterness. The *spirit,* which he committed to His Father's hands, was kept safely there. (Lk 23:46; cf. 2 Ti 1:12)

3:19 The phrase translated *in which* could as well be rendered "in the course of which," referring not to *spirit* alone but to the whole of His Passion, death, and quickening. The proclamation to the spirits then took place between His death and resurrection, as it is stated in the Apostles' Creed.

3:20 *Who . . . did not obey.* This may refer to the fallen angels of Gn 6:1-4. In the structure of Genesis they constitute the third and final example of that ever-increasing "wickedness of man" (Gn 6:5) which led to the judgment of the Flood, the first being Cain (Gn 4:1-16) and the second, Lamech (Gn 4:23-24; cf. 2 Ptr 2:4-5; Jude 6). Jewish tradition made much of the incident as indicating the origin of demonic powers.

3:20-21 These verses are formally a digression from the main theme; but the digression serves the general purpose of the admonition to endure suffering (a) by pointing up the seriousness of the hour, comparable to the *days of Noah* in which *few* were saved when the disobedient perished (cf. our Lord's last-days admonition, Mt 24:37-39; Lk 17:26-27) and (b) by offering the comfort of *baptism, which . . . now saves* (as the ark once saved), giving men part in the *resurrection of Jesus Christ.* (Cf. Ro 6:3-5)

3:21 *Appeal to God for a clear conscience.* The candidate for baptism undergoes baptism in the hope and assurance that God will thereby forgive him all his trespasses. (Cl 2:12-13)

3:22 *Authorities . . . powers,* names for supernatural powers whether good or evil, angelic or demonic. Here evil powers seem to be meant. (Cf. v. 19)

4:1-6 This section is parallel to the preceding

(3:13-22), but the thought shifts from the Christ on the cross to the Christ of Gethsemane, who spoke a whole Yes to *the will of God* (2) which presented to Him the cup of suffering and death, although His whole manhood *(flesh,* 1) cried out for preservation and life (Mt 26:42). Peter bids his readers *arm* themselves with that *same thought* (1), to let the mind of the Christ who died for them be their mind, to think His thought, to will His will. They are to arm themselves, for this is a fighting matter, a struggle against the grain. The way they are to go is against their Gentile past, and the past is hard to shake (3), it is a minority way, with the suasion of the masses against it and exposed to the *abuse* of the majority (4). And it is, apparently, a discredited way; those among them who heard the good news of the living hope have died like all other men. The final futility of death came to them as it came to the discredited Messiah in whom they hoped; like Him, they were *judged in the flesh like men* (6). But the resurrection of Jesus Christ triumphantly gives the lie to all that. He lives enthroned at the right hand of God (3:22), *ready to judge the living and the dead* (4:5). Those who have abused the Christ in abusing the Christian hope *will give account to him* (5); those who have hoped in Him and have armed themselves with His thought shall *live,* as He lives (cf. 3:18), *in the spirit like God.* (6)

4:1 *Whoever has suffered,* etc. The only way to have done with sin is the way of suffering, which Christ has gone *for us* (the reading given in RSV note *i* should probably be adopted). Cf. Ro 6:2, 7. Communion with Him takes the Christian, too, down the road of suffering.

4:6 This verse seems designed to answer the question with which Paul deals in 1 Th 4:13-18, the question which oppressed some early Christians: "What of those who have died before our Lord's return—will they have part in the promised glory?" As 1 Co 15 shows, there were those who presumed to say no to that question.

4:7—5:11 THE SOBRIETY OF HOPE

4:7—5:11 The living hope is exuberant, attended by an "unutterable and exalted joy" (1:8). But it is not a witless intoxication; the command, "Be sober," is heard as early as 1:13. And this aspect of hope is particularly prominent in the closing admonitions of the letter (cf. 4:7; 5:8). The approaching end of all things calls for a sober vigilance in prayer, a life of love and mutual ministry, to the glory of God through Jesus Christ (4:7-11). It alerts Christians to see in their sufferings both a sharing in the suffering of Christ (and therefore a guarantee of their future participation in His glory) and also the sign and dawn of the approaching Last Judgment (4:12-19). It calls for a sober and responsible congregational life: the elders are to exercise their shepherd's office with a pure zeal, conscious of their responsibility to the Chief Shepherd who is about to be manifested. The church is to submit obediently to the elders. All are to be clothed in humility (5:1-5). It calls on all to submit to the governance of God and to trust in His care, to be vigilant and firm in resisting the devil in the assurance that suffering is the normal lot of God's people and that the God of all grace will sustain them and in due time exalt them. (5:6-11)

4:7-8 *End . . . prayers . . . love.* The prayer, "Thy kingdom come," or "Maranatha" ("Our Lord, come!" 1 Co 16:22; Rv 22:20), and the prayer, "Thy will be done" (love), belong together. For the connection between expectation of the end and love cf. Ro 13:8-11; Heb 10:23-25; and 1 Co 13:8-13.

4:8 *Love covers a multitude of sins.* Love proves *unfailing* in the face of the brother's sins; it can forgive 70 times 7 times (Mt 18:22). He who prays the second petition of the Lord's Prayer cannot but pray the fifth petition too, both halves of it. (Cf. Ja 5:20)

4:9 *Hospitality,* a much-needed service rendered to traveling Christians and missionaries. (Cf. 3 Jn 5-8; Ro 12:13; 1 Ti 3:2; 5:10; Heb 13:2)

4:10 *Good stewards.* This removes all pride and therefore all harshness from Christian ministrations. Cf. 1 Co 4:7, and for the whole question of the gifts of the Spirit and the responsible employment of them for the benefit of the church, Ro 12:3-8 and 1 Co 12—14.

4:11 *Renders service.* The word is used particularly of supplying the physical needs of the poor in the church. Cf. Acts 6:1 ff., where the RSV renders it as "daily distribution."

Glorified . . . glory. In the active love of the church the future glory of God (when every knee shall bow in adoration before Him) is anticipated; He is, in the church, to be even now what He shall one day be manifestly and universally, "all in all." (Cf. Eph 4:6)

4:12 *Surprised . . . strange.* For suffering as the normal and inevitable lot of the church in this age cf. Lk 6:22-23, 26; Acts 14:22; 1 Th 3:4.

Ordeal . . . comes. What was before a possibility (3:13 ff.) is now an actuality. (Various conjectures have been made to explain this shift from possibility to actuality. The most probable is that Peter, having closed his letter with a doxology and an "Amen" at 4:11, was moved to add a postscript when he received news from Asia Minor that the situation there had worsened and the to-be-expected *fiery ordeal* had begun.)

4:13 *Rejoice.* Cf. Mt 5:11-12; Acts 5:41; Ja 1:2 ff.

Share Christ's sufferings. Cf. Ro 8:17; 2 Co 1:5; Ph 3:8-11; Cl 1:24; 2 Ti 2:12.

His glory is revealed. Cf. 1:7, 13; 5:1.

4:14 *Spirit of glory. Spirit* should be capitalized; the Holy Spirit is characterized by the gift which He bestows *(glory;* cf. "Spirit of sonship," (Ro 8:15). The Spirit is the beginning and guarantee of the blessings of the world to come (cf. 2 Co 1:22; 5:5; Eph 1:14); those who "have become partakers of the Holy Spirit and have tasted . . . the powers of the age to come" (Heb 6:4-5)—they have a foretaste of the future glory amid the sufferings of this age.

4:16 *As a Christian.* It is curious that the term

which has become the commonest designation for followers of Christ occurs only three times in the NT. The name was first applied to disciples of Jesus in Antioch (Acts 11:26), is found in the mouth of the skeptical king Herod Agrippa II (Acts 26:28), and here in 1 Ptr, and seems to be the name applied to the church by hostile outsiders. Originally it may have been a term of mockery.

4:17 If the church undergoes a fiery ordeal (12), that is an indication that the end of all things is at hand (7); for the judgment which overtakes the *household of God,* the church (cf. 1 Ti 3:15), is the last preliminary to the Last Judgment (cf. Jer 25:29; Eze 9:6). This thought has a double value for the church: (a) It assures the church that her suffering is not blind chance but has a meaningful place in God's activity (cf. note on v. 12); (b) it warns the members of the church that to seek to escape suffering by renouncing the faith is fatally senseless; they will escape present suffering only to find certain doom.

4:18 *Where will . . . appear?* What will become of him? The verse is a quotation from Pr 11:31 in the form given by the ancient Greek translation of the OT (Septuagint), which differs from the present Hebrew text as translated in the RSV. For the thought cf. Lk 23:31.

4:19 *Entrust their souls to a faithful Creator.* As Jesus did on the cross (Lk 23:46; cf. 1 Ptr 2:23). A *faithful* God will not betray His trust, and He who willed and created the life of man has the will and the power to preserve it.

5:1 *Elders.* As the context shows ("tend the flock," 2) a general designation for officials exercising pastoral care. (Cf. Acts 20:17, 28)

Fellow elder . . . witness . . . partaker in the glory. Although Peter in quiet humility joins the ranks of the elders and does not stand on his dignity as apostle, he cannot be silent concerning the grace given him as *witness of the sufferings of Christ.* Some see in the phrase *partaker in the glory . . . to be revealed* an allusion to Peter's presence at the Transfiguration (Mt 17:1-8), where he was eyewitness to "honor and glory from God the Father" (2 Ptr 1:17) that was to be Christ's beyond the cross and was a *partaker* in it in the sense that he had a firsthand experience of it. This has considerable probability.

5:2 *Tend.* For a picture of all that a shepherd's care involved cf. Is 40:11 and Eze 34:1-6, 11-16; the latter is also the background and prototype of our Lord's words in Jn 10:1-16.

Flock of God. Cf. Eze 34:31.

5:3 *Examples.* For the idea of leadership by example and the related idea of imitation cf. 1 Co 4:16; 11:1; Ph 3:17; 1 Th 1:6; 2 Th 3:7-9; 1 Ti 4:12; Tts 2:7.

5:4 *Chief Shepherd,* Christ the Good Shepherd. (Jn 10:11, 14; cf. Heb 13:20)

Unfading crown, unlike the festal crown or the Greek athlete's crown of victory, which was of leaves or flowers that soon withered away.

5:5 *Clothe yourselves . . . with humility,* as Jesus did (Jn 13:4) to Peter's dismay. (Jn 13:6-8; cf. 12-20)

God opposes . . . Cf. Pr 3:34; Ja 4:6.

5:6 *Humble . . . exalt.* The quotation from Proverbs in 5:5 connects the two ideas of humility toward one another (5) and humility before God.

Mighty hand. The mighty hand of God which once delivered His people out of the house of bondage in Egypt (Dt 9:26, 29; 26:8) is still mighty to save, and He will lead His people home in the last great Exodus, in spite of all diabolic opposition. (8)

5:7-9 Humility toward God is not an abject groveling before Him but profound and grateful trust in Him (7); it does not reduce man to fatalistic apathy but gives him power and courage for vigilant and heroic action. (8-9)

5:7 *Cast . . . on him.* Cf. Ps 55:22; Mt 6:25-32; Lk 12:22-31.

5:8 *Prowls around like a roaring lion.* The threat posed by the devil is not underestimated: he is everywhere, powerful, bent on destruction.

5:10 *Little while . . . eternal glory.* Cf. Ro 8:18; 2 Co 4:16.

5:12-14 CONCLUSION

5:12-14 The conclusion takes gracious notice of Silvanus' help in the composition of the letter, sums up its purport in one pithy statement, conveys the greetings of the church at Rome (Babylon) and of Mark, enjoins the kiss of love, and bestows the benediction of peace.

5:12 *Silvanus* is the Latinized form of Silas, prominent member of the early Jerusalem church, prophetically endowed (Acts 15:38), entrusted with an important mission (Acts 15:22-23), thereupon companion and co-worker of Paul. (Acts 15:40—18:5; 2 Co 1:19; 1 Th 1:1; 2 Th 1:1)

5:13 *She who is at Babylon . . . likewise chosen.* The church at Rome. See the Introduction.

5:13 *My son Mark.* Mark the evangelist, called *son* because converted by Peter. (Cf. 1 Co 4:15; Phmn 10)

5:14 *The kiss of love,* elsewhere called the "holy kiss" (Ro 16:16; 1 Co 16:20; 2 Co 13:12; 1 Th 5:26), later became a regular part of the Communion liturgy. The origin of the practice is not known; it probably derives from the exchange of kisses between members of a family frequently mentioned in the OT and expresses the family solidarity of the "household of God."

SECOND

PETER

INTRODUCTION

The historical contours of the First Letter of Peter are tolerably distinct; we can answer with considerable assurance most of the questions that historical inquiry raises concerning it. The second letter, however, is wrapped in mystery, and the reconstruction of its historical background is beset at almost every point with perplexing uncertainties. While the first letter's place in the canon has always been an assured one, that of the second letter has been disputed, with the weakest historical attestation of any book in the New Testament. There are some faint indications that the letter was known and used in the church before the time of Origen (A. D. 185 to 254), who uses the letter and considers it apostolic, but is aware of the fact that its place in the canon is in dispute. The authenticity of the first letter, though questioned by modern critical scholarship, is actually quite solidly established by the external and internal evidence, whereas the authenticity of the second letter was questioned even in the early church and is denied by the great majority of scholars today. The circle of readers for whom the first letter was intended is clearly defined by the letter itself; the address of the second letter is very general: "To those who have obtained a faith of equal standing with ours" (1:1), and leaves the location of the readers uncertain. The words, "This is now the *second letter* that I have written to you, beloved" (3:1), make it likely but not certain that its destination is the same as that of the first letter. Concerning the time and place of writing of the second letter we can only say that it must be dated toward the close of Peter's life and that it was therefore probably written from Rome. We can see what sort of tendencies and difficulties occasioned the second letter, but we cannot fix them as to place and time with any precision.

Content of the Second Letter of Peter

If all else is uncertain, there is no uncertainty about the intent and the message of the letter. Like the First Letter of Peter, it is written in the service of Christian hope. The letter has, to be sure, often been called the Epistle of Knowledge, and "knowledge" is a prominent motif in the letter; but knowledge is not being emphasized and imparted for its own sake, but for the purpose of strengthening the Christian hope and defending it against the attack of error and to preserve it from the corrosion of doubt (cf. 1:3 with 1:8 and 11; 3:17-18). If the first letter is designed to keep hope alive and strong in men under the stress of persecution, the second letter is designed to maintain hope pure and strong in men whose hope is threatened by false teaching and is in danger of being weakened by doubt.

1:1-2 SALUTATION

1:1 *Faith of equal standing with ours.* If the letter is addressed to Gentiles, *ours* may refer to Jewish Christians. Cf. Acts 15:9, where Peter says that God "made no distinction between us [Jews] and them [the Gentiles], but cleansed their hearts by FAITH." Otherwise *ours* would refer to the apostles; the faith of those who believed the apostolic Word is as valid as the faith of the eye- and ear-witness. (Vv. 16-18)

Righteousness of our God. His saving righteousness, revealed in the Gospel to every one who has faith, Jew and Greek. (Ro 1:16)

1:2 *Grace and peace.* Cf. 1 Ptr 1:2.

Knowledge, not merely intellectual apprehension but a knowing that involves the whole man and is a communion between the knower and the known. (Cf. 1:3, 8, 9; 2:20; Cl 1:9-10)

1:3-11 THE GREATNESS OF THE CHRISTIAN HOPE

1:3-11 The Christian hope bestows a great gift; the great and precious promises of our God and Savior Jesus Christ call men into communion with Him and into the glory and excellence of His eternal kingdom (3-4); cf. v. 11. The Christian hope makes a great claim on men; the possession of this hope calls for a life of strenuous sanctification. (5-11)

1:4 For the *promises* of God as the motivation and means of a new life see 2 Co 7:1 (cf. 6:16-18). In the divine promise the Word of promise and the blessing promised are one, for the Word effectually imparts what it says.

Corruption . . . in the world because of passion. Cf. 1 Jn 2:16.

1:5 *Make every effort.* Cf. 1:3, "His divine power has granted us all things." (In the Greek *every* and *all* are expressed by the same word.) This is the logic of the Gospel: God's free and all-sufficient giving motivates and makes possible the wholehearted *effort* of man's response to it. Paul's words in Ph 2:12-13 are perhaps the classic expression of it: "Therefore [since Christ has gone the way of the servant for us to the cross] . . . WORK OUT your own salvation . . . for God is at WORK in you, both to will and to work for his good pleasure."

1:5-7 *Supplement your faith. Supplement,* as the fruit of a tree "supplements" the tree. But the translation is somewhat misleading. The word means "furnish" or "provide," and there is a preposition ("in") with *faith;* it would be preferable to render: "In your faith provide virtue" (i.e., let your faith provide, or produce, virtue) and continue the whole series (5-7) in the same way. The whole series describes, in chain-reaction form, the flowering and fruitage of faith; the qualities selected for emphasis are all in antithesis to the characteristics of the false teachers who pervert the way of truth (ch. 2) and deny the heart of the Christian hope (3:3-4): *virtue* is set over against their wrongdoing (2:13); true living *knowledge* which gives *grace and peace* and all that *pertains to life and godliness* (1:2-3) is set over against their brutish ignorance (2:12); *self-control* is set over against their greed and licentiousness (2:2, 3, 10, 12, 13, 14, etc.); *godliness* over against their brash and blasphemous impiety (2:1, 10, 12); *brotherly affection* and *love,* over against their self-seeking propagation of destructive heresies (2:1), their ruthless exploitation of the church. (2:3, 14, 18)

1:8-9 *The knowledge of our Lord Jesus Christ* is living, personal knowledge of Him; one possesses it by using it, acting on it, living it; otherwise it is lost. "To him who has will more be given, and he will have in abundance; but from him who has not, even what he has will be taken away." (Mt 13:12; cf. Cl 1:9-10)

Was cleansed, through Baptism.

1:10 God's *call,* which brings the eternal love of His *election* into man's life, is *confirmed* when it does not remain an idea or something learned from the catechism but is allowed to do its proper work and produces a life "worthy of the calling." (Eph 4:1)

1:12—2:22 THE CERTAINTY OF THE CHRISTIAN HOPE

1:12-21 The Christian Hope and the Prophetic Word

1:12-21 The Christian hope is guided and sustained by the inspired OT prophetic Word, now made sure by the apostolic witness to the majesty of Christ, the fulfillment of prophecy.

1:12 *Therefore,* since their life can be effective and fruitful now (8) and can lead to the eternal kingdom (11) and if *the truth that* they *have* remains their constant and ever-increasing possession.

Remind. Cf. Ro 15:15; 1 Jn 2:21; Jude 5.

1:14 *Our Lord . . . showed me.* Jn 21:18-19.

1:15 *These things:* All that the apostolic witness has given to the church: the knowledge of God and of Jesus our Lord (2), the precious and very great promises (4) that enable men to become partakers of the divine nature (4) and to enter into the eternal kingdom of our Lord and Savior Jesus Christ. (11)

1:16-21 "These things" (15) are invaluable and indispensable and must be preserved, not because the apostles were great religious geniuses who clothed their dreams and aspirations in *cleverly devised myths* but because it was given them to be *eyewitnesses* of great acts of God (16). In the Transfiguration (17-18) they beheld the *majesty of our Lord Jesus Christ* (16), the anticipation of that *power, honor and glory* (17) which would be His as the Father's gift at His second *coming* (16); there they heard the *voice* of the *Majestic Glory* and learned the full intent of God's word to His anointed King (*my beloved Son,* 17; cf. Ps 2:7) and the full significance of His word concerning His Spirit-filled Servant (*with whom I am well pleased,* 17; cf. Is 42:1); there in the Lord Jesus Christ, in God's Son and Servant, they saw God's Word accomplishing that which He purposed and prospering in the thing for which He sent it (Is 55:11). Now the apostles have the *prophetic word,* on which their hope of the final and universal triumph of the Son and Servant depends, *made more sure,* buttressed by fact and fulfillment (19). This Word is their gift to the church; this Word is a *lamp* unto men's feet and a light for their path by which they can confidently walk in dark places until the great *day dawns* whose light makes lamps superfluous, the time when the light within them *(morning star . . . in your hearts)* will answer to the light that falls upon them from without and prophecies, their service done, will pass away. (1 Co 13:8)

God is His own interpreter and makes plain what His Word intends; when men twist the

Scriptures (cf. 3:16) and impose their *own interpretation* (20), they do so to their own destruction (3:16), for they darken God's lamp and lay unholy hands on the handiwork of the *Holy Spirit,* who *moved* men to utter what their own *impulse* never prompted; under His inspiration the prophets spoke *from God* (21); they could say: "Thus says the Lord."

1:17-18 Transfiguration. Mt 17:1-8; Mk 9:2-8; Lk 9:28-36; the *mountain* is called *holy* because it was the scene of revelation. (Cf. Gn 28:16-17)

1:19 For the OT as the book of the NT church's hope cf. Ro 15:4.

2:1-22 The Christian Hope and False Teachers

2:1-22 The Christian hope need not be shaken by the godless false teachers who shall come, for the church is forewarned of their coming, knows that their condemnation is sure, and is assured that *the Lord knows how to rescue the godly from trial.* (9)

To understand the violence of the language, the sternness of the strictures, and the severity of the threats of this section, one must bear in mind how plausible an imitation of Christianity the proclamation of these false teachers must have seemed to many, especially to the *unsteady souls* (14) of men recently converted from paganism (18). They operated in *false words* (3), with great and legitimate catchwords of Christianity like *freedom* (19), a conception close to the heart of the Gospel (cf. Jn 8:32, 36; Ro 8:2, 21; 2 Co 3:17; Gl 4:26, 31; 5:1). How readily this idea of freedom lent itself to distortion and falsification can be seen from warnings like Gl 5:13 and 1 Ptr 2:16. The gift of liberation from sin (Ro 6:18, 22) easily became the license to sin (Ro 6:1; cf. 3:8). And for recently converted pagans the prospect of slipping back, with a good conscience, into the easy vices of their past must have been enticing (14, 18) indeed. The danger was acute; the church needed to be told in no uncertain terms that these teachings were wholly vicious and that any compromise with these teachers was impossible.

2:1 *False prophets . . . among the people,* Israel, Dt 13:1-5. (Cf. Mt 7:15; 24:4-5, 11, 24; Acts 20:28-31)

False teachers among you. Cf. Mt 7:15; 24:4-5, 11, 24; Acts 20:28-31; 2 Ti 3:1-9.

Denying the Master who bought them. Cf. Jude 4. They may call Him "Lord, Lord," but their lives are a contradiction of His will and Word. (Cf. Lk 6:46)

Bought them. Cf. especially 1 Co 6:19-20 for the idea that Christ's redeeming act obligates to a pure life. Cf. also 1 Co 7:23; Gl 3:13; Rv 5:9; 14:3-4. The purchase idea is akin to that of ransom and redemption. (Mt 20:28; 1 Ptr 1:18-19)

2:2 *Way of truth . . . reviled.* Outsiders, who cannot distinguish between true Christianity and false, judge the way of truth by the lives of these men and their followers and condemn it.

2:3 *Condemnation . . . destruction.* The Word of God which condemns them and threatens their destruction is thought of as an active, vigilant power waiting to pounce on them.

2:4-10a Three OT examples (*angels* who *sinned,* 4; *a flood,* 5; *Sodom and Gomorrah,* 6) support the thesis that *the Lord knows how . . . to keep the unrighteous under punishment until the day of judgment* (9), while the examples of *Noah* (5) and *Lot* (7) offer proof for the comforting assurance that *the Lord knows how to rescue the godly from trial* (9). Cf. Jude 6-8.

2:4 *Hell* (RSV note *f: Tartarus*). The term *Tartarus* is borrowed from the Greeks, who used it to designate a subterranean place where divine punishment was visited on the wicked dead.

Angels. Cf. Gn 6:1-4; Jude 6; 1 Ptr 3:19-20.

2:5 *Noah, a herald of righteousness.* Noah proclaimed righteousness by "walking with God" (Gn 6:9), obedient to His will and Word (Gn 6:22), in the midst of a generation whose every thought "was only evil continually" (Gn 6:5). Jewish tradition elaborated on Noah as proclaimer of righteousness.

Flood. Gn 6:5—8:12.

2:6 *Sodom and Gomorrah.* Gn 19.

2:9 *Keep . . . under punishment until the day of judgment.* Cf. 4. For the thought that the wicked dead suffer punishment prior to the Last Judgment cf. Lk 16:23-28.

2:10a *Authority,* that of the Lord and Master, Jesus Christ.

2:10b-11 Jude 8-9 goes into more detail on this. These emancipated, licentious, greedy, lying, and proud men rush in where angels fear to tread; men hardened in sin lose their awe for God's judgment and are insensitive to Jesus' warning, "Judge not." (Mt 7:1)

2:12 This emphasis on the brutish, *animal* character of the false teachers has a special point in the light of the fact that many of the libertine errorists who arose in the church laid claim to a special "spirituality."

2:13 *Revel in the daytime.* Even pagan public opinion frowned on this.

Blots and blemishes on the Christian community, in whose common meals they still share (*carousing with you;* cf. 1 Co 11:20-22, 33-34).

2:14 *Accursed children!* Literally "children of the curse," "accursed ones"; cf. Mt 25:41. Cf. "children of the promise," Ro 9:8; Gl 4:28; "children of wrath," Eph 2:3; "children of light," Eph 5:8.

2:15-16 *Balaam.* Jude 11; Nm 22—24.

Ass. Nm 22:21-32.

2:17 *Waterless springs,* unproductive of good.

Mists driven, unstable and unreliable.

Nether gloom . . . reserved. Cf. vv. 4 and 9.

2:19 *Slaves . . . enslaved.* For the enslavement to sin see Jn 8:34; Ro 6:16, 20; cf. Gn 4:7.

2:20-21 *Last state . . . worse . . . than the first.* The sin against the light, apostasy in the face of known and acknowledged truth, has unforeseeable consequences. One of Jesus' sternest parables is a warning against this sin. (Mt 12:42-45; cf. also Heb 10:26, 31)

2:21 *Holy commandment.* For *commandment* as expressing the whole of the Christian proclamation, with the emphasis on the fact that it claims man for Christ, cf. 3:2; 1 Ti 6:14; Mt 28:20 ("all that I have commanded you"); and Paul's use of "law" in Ro 8:2 ("law of the Spirit of life in Christ Jesus") and "charge" in 1 Ti 1:5. James' "law of liberty" (1:25) is similar.

2:22 *The dog.* Pr 26:11.

The scoffers who say, "Where is the promise of his coming?" simply ignore the fact that the God who once judged the world by water can and will judge the world by fire.

3:1-18 THE DELAYED FULFILLMENT OF THE CHRISTIAN HOPE

3:1-7 "Where Is the Promise of His Coming?"

3:1 *Sincere,* pure, a mind inaccessible to the alien influences and sinful desires which slacken or frustrate obedience to the commandment of the Lord and Savior. (2)

Reminder. Cf. 1:12-15.

3:2 *Commandment,* in the same comprehensive sense as in 2:21.

3:3 *In the last days.* For the thought that opposition to the truth is itself a sign of the last days cf. 1 Ti 4:1-2; 1 Jn 2:18.

Scoffers . . . following their own passions. This emphasis on passions indicates that the scoffers are identical with, or at least related to, the false teachers of ch. 2. Paul had to combat the same combination of libertinistic "freedom" and the denial of the Christian hope (1 Co 6 and 15): Hope and purity live together. (1 Jn 3:3)

3:4 *Where is . . . ?* What has become of it? It has not been fulfilled.

Coming. Cf. 1:16.

Fathers, the first Christian generation.

All things have continued. The argument from the regularity and continuity of the created order is met with the reference to God's Word, which created and controls that order. (5-6)

3:5 *Out of water and by means of water.* The thought of this difficult phrase seems to be an echo of the creation account in Genesis. The earth emerged from the waters (Gn 1:2) when God separated the upper and nether waters by means of the firmament (Gn 1:6-8) and gathered the nether waters together into one place. (Gn 1:9-10; cf. Ps 24:2)

3:7 *Fire . . . judgment.* Cf. 10-12. *Fire* is frequently used in the OT Scriptures as a symbol of God's punitive and destructive wrath, sometimes in connection with His final judgment, e.g., Zph 1:18; 3:8; Ml 4:1. The *fire of judgment* is here pictured as destroying not the world but *ungodly men.* This should be kept in mind for the interpretation of 10-12.

3:8-10 "The Lord Is Not Slow About His Promise

3:8-10 The church is to see in the Lord's delay a missionary command: the delay is the forbearance of the God who wills the salvation of man and would have all men come to repentance.

3:8 *With the Lord.* To speak of "delay" in connection with the Lord's coming is to impose human standards on the Lord, to try to fit Him into categories which are not His (Ps 90:4). A genuinely Christian hope will not seek to master God thus; it will not be curious about the Lord's timetable but will be concerned about His purpose. (9)

3:9 The Lord's purpose is clear; He would have *all* men *reach repentance* and live; and that gives the waiting and hoping church its direction and goal—and its solemn responsibility, in the face of which the question of the time of His coming fades into insignificance. (Cf. 11, 12, 15)

3:10 *Like a thief.* With this image, emphasizing the "unexpectedness" and suddenness (Mk 13:36; Lk 21:34) of His coming, Jesus cut off all attempts at calculating the time of His return (Mt 24:43; cf. 36). It is echoed by Paul (1 Th 5:2) and John. (Rv 3:3; 16:15)

3:10 *Will be burned up.* If this is the correct text, the total annihilation of the present world is meant, while the rest of the NT speaks rather of a restoration of creation (e.g., Ro 8:19-22). But the best attested text is the very difficult "will be found," which may mean that *the earth and the works* of man that both adorn and disfigure the earth will be exposed to the fire of God's judgment, be refined and purified, and emerge as God's "new heavens and a new earth" (13). The universe will pass through fearful convulsions (*dissolved,* 10, "melt," 12) as Jesus foretold (Mt 24:29). But God's goal for His creation, over which He once spoke His "very good" (Gn 1:3; 1 Ti 4:4), is not extinction but restoration and transfiguration.

3:11-18 "What Sort of Persons Ought You to Be"

3:11-18 The church is to see in the Lord's delay a summons to a life of sanctified, tense, and vigilant expectancy, a life characterized by growth in grace and knowledge of our Lord and Savior Jesus Christ.

3:11 *What sort of persons.* This is the center of gravity in all the NT teaching of last things from John the Baptist and Jesus onward.

3:12 *Hastening the coming of the day,* by living a life and proclaiming the truth which will enable men to reach repentance. (9)

Elements, the various parts of which the world is composed.

3:13 *Heavens and earth* indicate the continuity of the world to come with God's first creation (Gn 1:1), our world. The otherness of the coming world is expressed by *new,* a word characteristic of the new quality of all that pertains to the world to come. Cf. Mt 26:29; 2 Co 5:17; Eph 4:24; Heb 10:10; Rv 2:17; 3:12; 5:9; 14:3; 21:1-2, 5; for the whole expression cf. Is 65:17; 66:22; Rv 21:1.

Righteousness dwells. In the world to come

God's will shall be done on earth as it is in heaven. All the ruin and frustration with which man's sin has disfigured God's good world will have passed away. (Cf. Ro 8:19-22)

3:15 *Forbearance . . . salvation.* Cf. 9; Ro 2:4. *So also . . . Paul wrote.* Characteristic words of Paul on the urgency of the last days are Ro 13:12-14; 1 Co 7:29-31; 1 Th 5:1-11.

Wisdom. Cf. 1 Co 3:10; also 1 Co 2:6; 3:18.

3:16-17 *Some things . . . hard to understand.* Paul's critics at Corinth conceded that his letters were "weighty and strong" (2 Co 10:10) but apparently asserted that the Gospel was "veiled" by the rich profundity of his thought and language (2 Co 4:3). Paul himself complains that men have maliciously misinterpreted his bold language on the free grace of God (Ro 3:8; cf. 6:1), and it is probable that the false teachers of ch. 2 did the same thing and are here alluded to as *the ignorant and unstable* (cf. 2:12, 17); certainly the designation *lawless men* fits them.

3:18 *Day of eternity,* the day of the Lord (10) which ushers in eternity. The church asserts and proclaims the still-hidden divine glory of its Lord even now.

THE RELATIONSHIP BETWEEN 2 PETER AND JUDE

The relationship between 2 Peter and the Letter of Jude is usually considered one of the strong arguments against the authenticity of 2 Peter. The Letter of Jude and the second chapter of 2 Peter are so similar in language and thought that there is obviously a historical connection between the two; they can hardly have originated altogether independently of each other. Most scholars today argue that 2 Peter is the later of the two documents and has incorporated the Letter of Jude. The arguments used to prove the dependence of 2 Peter on Jude cannot be discussed in detail here. But it should be noted that this theory of borrowing on the part of a second-century writer leaves a good many unanswered questions. For example, if Jude is the earlier document and 2 Peter the later, why is it that Jude's account of the false teachers is the darker and more sinister of the two? In Jude the false teachers are compared not only to Balaam, but also to Cain and Korah—why should a second-century writer, engaged in so desperate a struggle against such a dangerous heresy that he must invoke the name of Peter in order to combat it, tone down the indictment of Jude? Note also that Jude twice (4 and 17) refers to an older apostolic writing which predicts the errorists who at Jude's time are present in the church. 2 Peter answers to that document; it predicts future errorists (2:1, 3) whose coming and working Jude notes as present in his time. It would seem to follow that Jude knew and prized as apostolic a document which must have been very similar to the second chapter of our 2 Peter. If 2 Peter is not apostolic but later than Jude, the original apostolic document referred to by Jude (4 and 17) must have been lost early without leaving a trace.

FIRST

JOHN

INTRODUCTION

The Gospel of John was to some degree polemical. It was probably not directly occasioned by false teaching, but some characteristic accents and features of the gospel are most readily understood as John's answer to a false teaching which perverted the true Gospel. The First Letter of John is wholly and vigorously polemical. It is aimed at false teachers, and although the letter never enters into a detailed refutation of their error, much less a full presentation of their teaching, the general character of the heresy can be ascertained with tolerable accuracy from hints given in the letter.

The false teachers had arisen in the church: "They went out from us," John writes, "but they were not of us; for if they had been of us, they would have continued with us; but they went out, that it might be plain that they all are not of us" (1 Jn 2:19). At the time when John wrote, they had separated themselves from the church—or had been expelled by the church: "You are of God, and have overcome them," John tells the church (1 Jn 4:4). They had apparently constituted themselves as a separate community, and they continued to make vigorous propaganda for their cause (cf. 2 Jn 7, 10) and still constituted a threat to the church. (1 Jn 2:27; 3:7)

They were a real threat, for they were very "religious" men. They were "spiritual" men and claimed the prophetic authority of the Holy Spirit for their teaching (1 Jn 4:1). They propagated a high and solemn sort of piety which claimed immediate communion with God and operated with slogans like "I know Him," "I abide in Him," "I am in the light" (1 Jn 2:4, 6, 9), and "I love God" (1 Jn 4:20). They probably felt themselves and professed themselves to be a new elite in Christendom, the "advanced" type of Christian. John is probably referring to them in his second letter when he speaks of those who "go ahead" and do not abide in the doctrine of Christ (2 Jn 9). It was no wonder that they deceived many and that many who remained in the church were perhaps not fully convinced that the church had been in the right when it separated itself from them. Or there might well have been some who were still secretly attracted to this brilliant new theology.

They deceived many, these new teachers. But they could not deceive the heart of John, for his heart was in fellowship with the Father and with His Son Jesus (1 Jn 1:3). The eyes that had seen the Word of life in the flesh (1 Jn 1:1) saw these men for what they were. They are, in John's clear vision of them, not prophets of God but false prophets (1 Jn 4:1); their words are inspired not by the Spirit of truth but by the spirit of error (1 Jn 4:6); they are not the Christ's, but the very embodiment of the Antichrist of the last days (1 Jn 2:18), impelled and informed by the spirit of the Antichrist (1 Jn 2:22; 4:3), who inspires the lie.

What was this lie? They denied not the deity but the full humanity of the Christ. They denied that Jesus, the man in history, was the Christ, the Son of God (1 Jn 2:22; cf. 4:3; 4:15; 5:5); they denied that Jesus was the Christ who had come "in the flesh" (1 Jn 4:2; cf. 2 Jn 7). We get a hint of how far this denial went in the words of John which state positively the significance of the Christ who came in the flesh: "This is he who came by water and blood, Jesus Christ, not with the water only but with the water and the blood" (1 Jn 5:6). These words are in themselves somewhat obscure; but they become clearer against the background of the heresy which they combat. That heresy was most probably the heresy of Cerinthus and his followers, of which Irenaeus has left us a description (*Adv. haer.*, I, 26, 1). Cerinthus, according to Irenaeus, taught that Jesus was a man among men, a superior man but still merely man, the son of Joseph and Mary; at His baptism the "heavenly Christ" descended on Him in the form of a dove and enabled Him to reveal the hitherto unknown God and to perform miracles; at His Passion, however, the "heavenly Christ" again left Jesus, and only Jesus the man suffered and died. In other words, the Christ came "by water" (the baptism of Jesus). The cross of Jesus, the shed blood of the Son of God, which the apostolic witness celebrated as the crown and culmination of the ministry of Christ, was thus ignored or relegated to the background. The blood of Jesus, the Son of God, was no longer the blood which "cleanses us from all sin." (1 Jn 1:7)

Where the cross is not taken seriously, sin is no longer taken seriously either. Men whose proud piety centers in their assumed *knowledge* of God and ignores the cross in which God has revealed Himself as both the Judge of sinful man and the Forgiver of sinners can think of sin as something that need not concern them; they can deceive themselves and say that they have no sin; they can say, "We have not sinned," and thus make a liar of God, who has in the cross declared that all men have sinned (1 Jn 1:8, 10) and has in the cross given His Son as the "expiation . . . for the sins of the whole world" (1 Jn 2:2). Such a piety can be comfortable in this world; the offense of the cross is gone, and the lives of Christians are no longer a walking indictment of the sins of the world. The world, which does not recognize the children of God, but rather hates them (1 Jn 3:1, 13), can come to terms with these men and with the Christ whom they proclaim: "They are of the world, therefore what they say is of the world, and the world listens to them." (1 Jn 4:5)

Over against these men John asserts, with all the concentrated power that this inspired Son of Thunder can command, the full reality of the incarnation, the fact that life and communion with God are to be found in Jesus, the Christ who came and died for man's sin in the flesh, or they will not be found at all; that any claim to know and love God which does not produce a life of righteousness and love is a blank lie; that the child of God cannot ever, without denying himself and his God, be at home in the world which is in the power of the Evil One. The letter is controversial and polemical, but it is not merely or one-sidedly polemical. John meets the danger which threatens the church by a powerfully positive restatement of what the Christian life really is, a passionate appeal to recognize in action the full measure of the gift and the full extent of the claim of that grace of God which has given man fellowship with the Father and the Son.

First John is a letter written to Christians, to men whose faith is being endangered by heresy and is being tried by temptation. Although the usual letter forms (salutation, close, etc.) are missing, it is nevertheless a genuine letter written for a specific situation by a father in Christ to his "children," and it is pervaded by an intense personal and pastoral concern for these "children." In its white-hot passion for the truth, for a Christian Gospel and a Christian life that is genuine, whole, and uncompromised, it remains a tonic and bracing word for the church always. It summons a church grown easy and comfortable to bethink itself penitently of the basic facts and the basic laws of its existence. Nowhere is black so black and white so white as in this letter; the antithesis of truth-lie, Christ-Antichrist, God-devil leaves the church no possibility of doubt as to where she must stand. And the letter likewise leaves no doubt that the church *can* stand where she must stand; the greatness of God's enabling gift is lettered out in pithy statements which are as profound as they are brief and pointed. Perhaps no New Testament book of like compass has furnished so many brief sayings, sayings that Christian men can lay up in their hearts, to live by and to die on, as this First Letter of John. (E.g., 1:5, 8; 2:2, 9-11, 15-17, 23; 3:1-2; 4:1-3, 7-12, 19; 5:3-5, 11-12)

Style of the Letter

The utterances of the letter do not move forward step for step in a straight line but circle, spiral fashion, around three great themes, with a continued enrichment of the thought at each turn. Consequently, there is considerable overlapping, both in the major divisions and in the subdivisions; no formal outline is a wholly satisfactory guide to the content of the letter. It is, in the last analysis, best appropriated by giving oneself to its movement with energetic sympathy and without too much concern for grasping it structurally. But as a first introduction to the letter the outline used in these notes may prove useful. It is adapted from the work of an English and a German scholar who, working independently of each other, arrived at the same analysis of the content. According to it, the letter begins with a statement of the revelation which God has given in His Son (1:1-4) and then proceeds to apply three tests to the Christian life as it is lived in the light of this revelation. This revelation furnishes three STANDARDS according to which Christian life is tested: (1) "God is light" (1:5); (2) "We are God's children now" (3:2); and (3) "God is love" (4:8). According to these standards three TESTS are applied to the Christian life: The test of righteousness, the test of love, and the test of true belief. All three of them occur in each of the three major divisions of the letter.

1:1-4 THE REVELATION

1:1-4 God has spoken His ultimate Word, the *word of eternal life,* in the audible, visible, palpable historical reality of His incarnate Son. With that Word He has admitted man to fellowship with Himself and has placed men into *fellowship* with one another. This revelation lives and works on in the spoken and written word of the first witnesses to the incarnation.

For the whole paragraph cf. Jn 1:1-18.

1:4 *Our joy may be complete.* Cf. Jn 15:11. The joy of the apostolic witnesses, like that of the Son Himself, is made full when God's will is done, the will that none be lost from the fellowship which He has created. (Cf. Jn 17:12-13)

1:5—5:12 THE TESTS OF THE CHRISTIAN LIFE

1:5—2:27 The First Standard

1:5—2:27 *God is light and in him is no darkness at all* (1:5). Fellowship with God means walking in the light (1:7); test yourselves to know whether you are walking in the light.

1:5—2:6 THE TEST OF RIGHTEOUSNESS

1:5—2:6 Walking in the light means facing the fact of your *sins* (which are exposed by the light), confessing your sins, and receiving forgiveness by the atoning death *(blood)* of Christ. Only thus is fellowship with God a genuine fellowship.

1:5 *Light . . . darkness.* Men who live in an electrically lighted world and know little of the uncertainties and terrors of darkness cannot appreciate this image as the ancients did. For John, Jesus Christ *is* the Light, cf. 2:8, and Jn 1:4, 5, 7-9; 3:19-21; 8:12; 9:5; 12:35, 36, 46; when he says that God is *light,* he is pointing to God as manifested in His only Son, the Giver of grace, truth, life, and sonship. The light both blesses freely and obligates, men are called upon to believe in the light, walk in the light, and become "sons of light" (Jn 12:36); that is, their whole nature and all their action is to be determined by the light. *Darkness* is similarly not merely a state but a power, waging a battle against the light (Jn 1:5), doomed (1 Jn 2:8) but not yet annihilated, blinding men (Jn 2:11) and claiming their love and loyalty. (Jn 3:19)

1:7-8 The *light* which overcomes man's sins necessarily exposes sin. (Cf. Jn 3:20)

1:7 *Blood,* of the Lamb of God, the final sacrifice for sin. (Jn 1:29; 1 Jn 5:6)

1:9 *Faithful and just.* God is *faithful* in that He holds to His promises, to which He has spoken His Yea in Jesus Christ (2 Co 1:19-20). He is *just* in that He does not overlook sin but has dealt with it righteously and effectually in the atoning death of Jesus, His Son. (Cf. Ro 3:24-26)

1:10 *Make him a liar.* When God gave His Son for the world's life, the Sacrifice for the WORLD'S sin (Jn 3:16; 1:29), He declared all men guilty. (Cf. 2:2)

2:1 *Advocate.* Cf. Ro 8:34 for Christ as Intercessor at the right hand of God.

2:2 *Expiation.* The rendering of the KJV, "propitiation," is preferable in that it keeps alive the essential thought that sin is personal rebellion against God and invokes His wrath, which is averted by the sacrifice that God Himself in His great love provides. (4:10)

2:3-6 "Walking in the light" means keeping God's commandments, keeping His *word* in *love* and walking as Christ walked.

2:4 *"I know him,"* like "I abide in him" (cf. 6), is apparently one of the slogans of the false teachers. John points out that knowledge of God without obedience is a self-contradiction, a lie.

2:5 *Love for God is perfected.* His love for God finds full and adequate expression, reaches its goal.

2:6 *Way in which he walked,* namely, Jesus

Christ, who could say "I do know him [the Father] . . . and I keep his word." (Jn 8:55)

2:7-17 THE TEST OF LOVE

2:7-17 The exposition of the test of love follows the scheme of Jesus' twin commandment of love (cf. Mt 22:34-40), love for neighbor (*brother,* 7-11) and love for God (15-17). The latter commandment is preceded by a brief reminder of all that motivates and enables the readers to love God with all their hearts: the forgiveness of sins, knowledge of the eternal Christ and of the Father who sent Him, victory over the Evil One in the power of the Word of God. (12-14)

2:7-8 *Old commandment . . . new commandment.* The *commandment* of love is *old;* it goes back to Christ (Jn 13:34), and the readers have known it as long as they have known Christ. And yet it is *new,* for Christ not only restored the Law's old commandment of love; by His self-giving love He has created a new situation, with new possibilities of obedience and fulfillment: as the commandment is fully realized and done *(true) in him,* so it can become a live reality in those who know Him. With the coming of Christ, the *light,* the new world of God has become a reality in the midst of the old *(already shining),* and the abiding reality of this new world is love. (Cf. 1 Co 13:8, 13)

2:10 *No cause for stumbling.* Cf. 11, the effect of darkness. If the rendering of RSV note *c (in him there is no cause for stumbling)* is adopted, the meaning would be: He who loves his brother will be a living witness to his faith, not an obstacle or offense to the faith of others.

2:12-17 Walking in the light means loving the *Father,* not the dying and doomed *world* separated from Him by its *lust* and *pride.*

2:12-15 With an effective monotony of repetition John brings home to his readers the unshakable Gospel certainties which are the motive and basis of their love for God. The *children* are the church as a whole. (John repeatedly addresses his readers as "little children" or "children," 2:1, 28; 3:18; 4:4; 5:21). They can and should love God with all their heart because their *sins are forgiven* for Christ's sake (12); the evil they have done, being forgiven, no longer blocks their way to the light (cf. Jn 3:20), and they know God as their way to the light and their forgiving *Father* (13). The *fathers,* backbone of the church, mature Christians with settled convictions, know *him who is from the beginning,* the "word of life" (1:1), who brought them into their enduring fellowship of love with God (1:3). The *young men,* the hope and future of the church, have won a victory over the *evil one* in the years when victory is most difficult; they know that they have found the strength for that victory in the *word of the God,* who first loved them in order that they might love Him. (4:10, 19)

2:15 *Do not love the world.* As 16 makes plain, the "way of the world" (its lust, greed, and pride) is meant. For the absolute opposition between "world" and God cf. Ja 4:4.

2:16 *Pride of life,* or "pride in one's possessions." (The word here translated "life" can also mean "means of livelihood" and is rendered as "goods" in 3:17). The rich farmer of Jesus' parable (Lk 12:16-21), the "rich" of Ja 5:1-6, and all the devotees of conspicuous consumption suggest themselves as illustrations.

2:18-27 THE TEST OF TRUE BELIEF

2:18-27 Walking in the light means holding to the Christ revealed from the beginning as the incarnate Christ, *Jesus* (22); it means rejecting the lie of the Antichrist, who, in denying the incarnate Son, denies the Father too.

2:18 *The last hour.* For the appearance of pseudochristian and antichristian powers as a mark of the beginning of the end cf. Mt 24:5, 11, 24; 1 Ti 4:1; 2 Ti 3:1; 2 Ptr 3:3; Jude 18.

Antichrist . . . many antichrists. Cf. 22, "the antichrist"; 4:3, "the spirit of antichrist . . . ." John does not say whether he identifies the many antichristian teachers with THE Antichrist of whom the church has been warned (cf. 2 Th 2) or sees in them precursors of the Antichrist. The important thing is that the church recognize and reject their antichristian teaching.

2:19 For a summary of the origins and character of the false teachers see the Introduction.

2:20 *Anointed* (cf. 27), endowed with the Holy Spirit, who leads into all truth (Jn 16:13). For anointing in this sense cf. 2 Co 1:21.

The Holy One, Christ. Cf. Mk 1:24; Lk 4:34; Jn 6:69; Rv 3:7.

You all know. The *all* is emphatic, rejecting the claim to special knowledge put forward by the false teachers. (4)

2:22 *Jesus,* asserting the full manhood of Christ. (Cf. 4:2; 2 Jn 7; Jn 1:14)

2:25 Cf. Jn 17:1-3.

2:27 Cf. 20 and note there.

2:28—4:6 The Second Standard

2:28—4:6 *We are God's children now* (3:2). Fellowship with God means being God's children; test yourselves to know whether you are born of God.

2:28—3:10 THE TEST OF RIGHTEOUSNESS

2:28—3:10 The Son of God, through whom you have become children of God, *appeared to take away sins* (3:5), *to destroy the works of the devil* (3:8); being *born of God* therefore means a radical antagonism to the evil (*who has sinned from the beginning,* 3:8), and a total aversion from sin (3:9). Those who sin are *children of the devil,* not *children of God.* (3:10)

2:28-29 These verses form the transition from *abide in Him* (28; cf. 2:24, 27) to the idea of the following section that being born of God means doing *right.*

2:28 *When he appears.* The thought of the imminent return of Christ adds urgency to the repeated appeal to *abide in Him.*

3:1 *Know,* in the full sense of "recognize,

acknowledge, be in harmony with"; cf. 3:13, where the world's attitude is called "hate," and Jn 16:2-3.

3:2 *Shall be like him,* like Christ, sons in freedom and glory. (Cf. Jn 12:26; 8:18, 21, 29; Ph 3:21; Cl 3:4)

3:3 *Hopes . . . purifies himself.* This unbreakable connection between hope and purity of life, between the confidence in the returning Christ that looks to Him for everything and the resolute self-committal that devotes everything to Him, is the hallmark of all NT teaching on hope, from John the Baptist to John the prophet on Patmos.

3:4-10 Nowhere is the test of righteousness more rigorously applied than here. In the light of misleading and plausible false teaching (*let no one deceive you,* 7) which dodges and minimizes the seriousness of sin, John makes two major assertions and draws the inescapable inferences from them. First, *sin is lawlessness,* violation of the holy will of God (4). God took sin so seriously that He sent His sinless Son into death *to take away sins;* to cancel the guilt and take away the power of sin (5). Faith in Him (*abides in him . . . seen . . . known him,* 6) cannot coexist with sinning. Second, *sin is of the devil* (8), is diabolical revolt and enmity against God. God sent His Son into death to liberate men from their diabolical imprisonment in revolt (8) and to make them His obedient sons (9). To sin is to deny God as your Father and to recommit yourself to the paternity and tyranny of the devil. Sin is sin, and righteousness is righteousness in fact and act (7, 10), and nothing and no one can make sin innocent or righteousness a matter of indifference. (Cf. Ro 3:31; 8:4)

3:4 Cf. 5:17.

3:8 Cf. Jn 8:44.

3:9 *God's nature,* literally "seed"; the indwelling Spirit is probably meant as the presence and power of God.

3:9 *He cannot sin.* Cf. Ro 6:2. This statement seems to be a flat contradiction of 1:7-10. Both statements deal with sin, not abstractly and in general but in relationship to the atoning work of Christ (1:7, "blood"; 3:5, 8). Both are fighting words directed against the attempt to minimize sin, either by denying the presence of it or by trying to make it smell sweeter by another name. The relationship between the two statements might be stated thus: Unless sin is faced for what it is, as the hideous abnormality described in 3:4-10, there can be no genuine confession of sins as demanded in 1:7-10. Where sin is accepted as "normal," there is no confession and absolution, no fellowship with God and man, no church. (1:6-7)

3:10 *Nor he who does not love his brother.* Transition to the next unit, 3:11-24, the test of *love.*

3:11-24 THE TEST OF LOVE

3:11-24 The Son of God *laid down his life for us* (16); thereby He laid upon all sons of God His commandment that they *should love one another* (11). To believe in the name of God's Son and to love one another as sons of God, these two cannot be separated from each other. To hate, as Cain hated, is to be a murderer and a child of the devil and to abide in death. To love, as Christ loved, in deed and in truth, is to be a child of God, with a child's confidence before God, the assurance of being heard by Him.

3:11 *Message.* The commandment is so organically connected with the Gospel message that it can be called by the same name. Cf. 23, where "commandment" is used to cover both faith and love.

3:12 *Cain.* Gn 4:7-8 *Why? . . . his own deeds were evil.* It is characteristic of the evildoer that he hates the light and all who walk in the light. (Cf. 13 and Jn 3:20)

3:14 Cf. Jn 5:24. *Because* introduces the reason why *we know,* not why *we have passed out of death.*

3:15 *Hates . . . murderer.* Cf. Mt 5:21-22.

3:19-20 *By this,* by loving in deed and truth (18) and so having God's love abiding in us (17), *we shall* know that *the truth* which sets men free from sin and self (cf. Jn 8:32) has sway over us and determines our actions. Then the accusation of our consciences (*hearts,* 19, 20) will fall silent before the testimony of our deeds and, much more, before the mightier testimony of our God, whose love lives in our hearts. In that love He is mightier (*greater*) than our faltering human hearts; that love is the awesome love of the God who forgives (Ps 130:4), the love of Him who says, "I will not execute my fierce anger . . . FOR I am God and not man, the Holy One in your midst" (Hos 11:9), the love whose measure our hearts cannot take (Ro 5:6-8)

3:20 *He knows everything.* Cf. Mt 25:31-45, where the Son of Man, as divine Judge, knows and values deeds of love which those who did them would not dare to plead in their own behalf.

3:24 *The Spirit.* The mention of the Spirit serves a twofold function. It makes clear that our assured consciousness of God's love in our lives is not our own subjective mood-making but God's own work; and it provides a transition to 4:1-6, with its antithesis between "the Spirit of God and . . . the spirit of antichrist." (2, 3)

4:1-6 THE TEST OF TRUE BELIEF

4:1-6 God's final revelation has been the Word made flesh (4:2; cf. 1:1-4; Jn 1:14). This revelation has drawn the line of division between the children of God and the world. Christ and Antichrist, true prophecy and false prophecy, the Spirit of truth and the spirit of error, the Spirit of God and the spirit of Antichrist, these confront one another in absolute antithesis. The test of true belief is therefore clear and simple; whether or not a man believes the final Word of God as God has spoken it, as the Word spoken *in the flesh* (4:2), determines whether a man is a child of God. (Cf. 2:18-27)

4:1 *Test the spirits.* Since both true and *false prophets* claim the inspiration of the Spirit for their utterances, the church must weigh and test their utterances, especially where errorists lay claim to a higher "spirituality" as they did and do. (Cf. 1 Th 5:19-21; 1 Co 12:10; 14:29; 1 Ti 4:1)

4:3 *Jesus,* the human historical figure, "flesh."

4:4 *Have overcome them,* since the Son of God has "overcome the world" (Jn 16:33) and the prince of this world. (3:8; cf. Jn 12:31; 14:30; 16:11)

4:5 *Of the world.* They partake of the nature of the world in its estrangement from and opposition to God, think its thoughts, and speak its language; they are in tune with the times. (Cf. Jn 15:19)

4:7—5:12 The Third Standard

4:7—5:12 *God is love* (4:8). The three tests (of righteousness, love, and true belief) recur in this section but not in the same order as in the first and second. Rather, the idea that all three are related and inseparable is stressed; therefore the three tests in this section interlock and overlap. The test of love is clearly seen in 4:7-12, 16-21; the test of righteousness in 5:1-5; the test of true belief in 4:13-15; 5:6-12.

4:7-12 THE TEST OF LOVE (Cf. 2:7-17; 3:11-24)

4:7 *Love one another.* The emphasis here, as throughout the letter, is on the mutual love of brothers within the church. This emphasis is dictated by the situation of the church; a church which has passed through a life-or-death struggle for the truth and has been hurt and shaken by the departure from its ranks of men once cherished as brothers in the faith (2:19) is in grave danger of settling into cold distrust, abandoning the love which it had at first (Rv 2:4; cf. Mt 24:12). It is clear that this fraternal love is not thought of as excluding universal love; if it did, the love of God for the world (9) could not serve as the exemplar and source of this love. Cf. also Jn 13:35, where the love of the disciples for one another is portrayed as their witness to all men.

4:12 *No man has ever seen God.* This thought comes in somewhat abruptly here; its place in the argument is made clear in 20.

4:13-15 THE TEST OF TRUE BELIEF (Cf. 2:18-27; 4:1-6)

4:13 *Spirit.* For the connection between the Spirit and true belief cf. 4:1-2 and Jn 14:26; 15:26-27; 16:7-15; note the designation "Spirit of truth," Jn 14:17; 15:26; 16:13; 1 Jn 4:6; 5:6.

4:16-21 THE TEST OF LOVE

4:16 *So we know and believe.* The unbreakable connection between true belief and love is indicated here.

4:17 *As he is.* He who believes in Jesus is like Him in that God abides in him and he in God (15); therefore he need not fear the Judgment.

4:18 *Fear* is here not the wholesome fear of mingled awe and obedience (e.g., Ph 2:12), but abject terror at the impending judgment. For *punishment* in connection with the Last Judgment cf. Mt 25:46.

4:21 *Commandment . . . love.* The organic connection between love and righteousness (5:1-5) is indicated.

5:1-5 THE TEST OF RIGHTEOUSNESS (Cf. 2:18-27; 4:1-6)

5:1-2 *Believes . . . loves . . . obey his commandments.* Here the interconnection of true belief, love, and righteousness is made clear.

5:3 *Commandments are not burdensome.* Cf. Mt 11:30. Not because they are easy to fulfill, but because the child of God has been given the power to fulfill them. (4)

5:4-5 *Whatever is born of God.* Referring both to Jesus Christ and to all who become children of God by *faith* in Him (Cf. 5). By faith in Him they enter into His victory over the *world* (Jn 16:33), over the spell cast by the world's lust and pride (2:16), and over the Evil One who rules in the world. (5:19)

5:5 Again the close connection between righteousness and true belief *(believes)* is indicated.

5:6-12 THE TEST OF TRUE BELIEF

5:6 *By water and blood.* For the connection between this statement and the heresy of Cerinthus see the Introduction. The Son of God has overcome the world by identifying Himself with man in the whole compass of His mission, from His baptism *(water),* the beginning of His public ministry, to His death on the cross *(blood);* therefore His resurrection is the resurrection of man, eternal life for man.

5:7 *Spirit is the truth.* Just as Jesus can speak of Himself as the truth (Jn 14:6), so the Spirit who glorifies Him (Jn 16:14) by His witness can be called the truth.

5:8 *Three witnesses, the Spirit, the water, and the blood.* The historical facts as interpreted by the Spirit; this describes the four gospels and for that matter the whole of the NT witness to Jesus, the Son of God. *And these three agree.* The Spirit works with the facts and holds men to the facts; there is no Christian "spirituality" which can ignore them. (Cf. 4:2-3)

5:9 *Testimony of men,* according to the law that demands "two or three witnesses." (Dt 19:15)

5:10 *Has the testimony in himself,* by the operation of the Spirit, concerning whom Jesus gave the promise, "He will be in you." (Jn 14:17)

5:13-21 CONCLUSION

5:13-21 Like the gospel (Jn 20:31), 1 John closes with a statement of purpose (13), which is followed by a postscript. (14-21; cf. Jn 21)

5:14-17 These verses reiterate the assurance of 3:21-22 that prayer is heard. The assurance here is even stronger (15) and is directed specifically to intercession for an erring brother. But the assurance and promise is restricted to intercessions *for those whose sin is not mortal* (16). *Mortal sin* is not defined, but the context of the letter suggests that the sin of the false teachers and their followers is meant. The question would naturally arise in the church: May we still intercede for those who have gone out from us, for men who have broken our sacred fellowship, who have resisted the witness of the Spirit (5:7), despised the blood that atones for us (5:6; cf. Heb 10:29), given themselves to the spirit of Antichrist and error (4:3-4)? Is prayer for them still a prayer according to God's will (5:14)? Is not their sin the unforgivable blasphemy against the Spirit of which Jesus warned (Mt 12:31), and have they not removed themselves from the sphere and power of Christian intercession for the sinner, which always presupposes that repentance is still possible, as it is necessary? John's answer is marked by great reserve; he will not command such intercession. But he does not forbid it and gives no simple rule to be mechanically applied (and misused); each renewed Christian mind must in each case "provide what is the will of God, what is good and acceptable and perfect." (Ro 12:2)

5:18-21 Amid the doubt which successful heresy can raise and amid the hurt which the departure of men who once were brothers in the faith inflicts on men whose faith lives in love, even amid these the church can remain unshaken and unafraid. For the church is certain that those born of God will be preserved from *sin* and the *evil one* (18), certain that there can be no compromise between the church and the world (19), certain that in the Son of God she has the true revelation of God and eternal life, for Jesus Christ *is the true God and eternal life*—any worship which excludes Him is idolatry. (20-21)

SECOND

JOHN

INTRODUCTION

The Second Letter of John is addressed by one who calls himself simply "the elder" to "the elect lady and her children" (v. 1). This is probably a figurative way of addressing a church (the word for church is feminine in Greek), rather than a literal address to some Christian woman and her children. The very broad statement of the salutation, "whom I love in the truth, and not only I but also all who know the truth" (v. 1) is more suitable to a church than to an individual. The expression in v. 4, "I rejoiced greatly to find some of your children following the truth," is most naturally understood of a church, some of whose members had resisted the inroads of the heresy which was then ravaging the church of Asia Minor. The greeting of v. 13, "The children of your elect sister greet you," also seems to be more naturally taken as a greeting from a sister church in whose midst the elder is writing. And finally, the content of the letter (the renewal of the commandment of love and a stern warning against false teachers) seems eminently suitable as a message to a church. Besides, if the "elect lady" is an individual, why is she not named, as Gaius is named in Third John?

The letter was occasioned by the activity of false teachers, most probably the same group that John dealt with in his first letter. There is the same emphasis on the commandment of love (5-6), the same emphasis on the reality of the incarnation of the Son of God (His "coming . . . in the flesh," 7), the same designation of the false teaching as deceit and the work of the "antichrist" (7), the same insistence on the fact that no one can know the Father except through the incarnate Son (9). The letter contains one of the sternest warnings in the New Testament against participating in or furthering the activities of those who pervert the Gospel (10-11). It is this furthering of the work of the false teachers that is referred to, of course, in the words, "Do not receive him into the house or give him any greeting" (10); evangelists were dependent on the hospitality of Christians as they moved from place to place, as Third John shows; they had no missionary fund to draw on.

The second letter is probably to be dated about the same time as the first. The designation "elder" would seem to indicate that John had outlived his generation and had become the grand old man of the church in Asia Minor.

1 *The elder.* See Introduction. Some scholars identify the author of 1 and 2 Jn, who calls himself *the elder* (as well as the unnamed author of 1 Jn) with a rather shadowy figure, the elder John, referred to by Papias, a second-century church father of Hierapolis in Asia Minor. But the identification is highly uncertain, and the very existence of this second (elder) John is questionable.

Truth is used in the comprehensive and dynamic sense familiar to us from the fourth gospel (e.g., Jn 1:17; 8:32; 14:6) and 1 Jn (e.g., 1:6, 8; 3:19) both here and in 2 and 4. Truth is, practically, all that Jesus Christ is, does, and signifies for man; truth is therefore not only known but followed (4) and done. (Jn 3:21; 1 Jn 1:6)

4:11 The letter to Ephesus (Rv 2:1-7), the church which in its honest zeal for purity of teaching "abandoned the love it had at first," illustrated the necessity of combining the commandment of love with the warning against false teaching.

7 Cf. 1 Jn 2:22.

8 *What you have worked for.* The elder is concerned lest all the God-given energies with

which they have "worked out their salvation with fear and trembling" (Ph 2:12) should have been expended in vain, that all the "toil and patient endurance" (Rv 2:2) with which they have combated error and clung to the truth should fail of the *full reward* which is promised to the faithful. (Cf. Rv 2:7, 10-11, 26-28; 3:5, 12, 21)

9 *Who goes ahead.* Progress *in the doctrine of Christ* is essential (cf. 1 Ptr 2:2); a supposed "progress" beyond Him who is God's final and definitive Word (Heb 1:1) is fatal pride and deadly error.

12 *Joy.* Cf. 1 Jn 1:4; Jn 15:11.

THIRD

JOHN

INTRODUCTION

The Third Letter of John gives us another glimpse into the apostolic activity of John in his latter years. If the first and second letters dealt with heresy, the third letter deals with a missionary problem. The recipient of the letter, "the beloved Gaius," had distinguished himself by his loyal support of some traveling evangelists (5-8). These evangelists had meanwhile reported to their home church, probably at Ephesus, and had there testified to the love which Gaius had shown them (6). He had done so in the face of grave difficulties; a certain Diotrephes had sought, and was at the time of writing still seeking, to put himself in control of the church to which Gaius belonged and had refused to welcome the missionary brethren. He went even farther than that and sought to stop those who wished to receive the missionaries and "put them out of the church" (9-10). In so doing he was consciously opposing the elder himself. (9)

Content of Third John

John in his letter warmly commends Gaius, who has by his support of the missionaries shown himself as a "fellow worker in the truth" (8); at the same time he commends to Gaius the bearer of the letter, Demetrius, who is probably the leader of a group of evangelists (12). Since a letter to the church dominated by Diotrephes has not had the desired effect, John promises to come himself and to deal with Diotrephes and to put an end to his malicious "prating." (9-10)

When the Lord called Paul to be His apostle, He said, "I will show him how much he must suffer for the sake of my name" (Acts 9:16). What the Lord said of Paul held for all the apostles; they remained servants and sufferers to the end. John never became his serene highness, the lord of the church of Asia; he remained the apostle of the Crucified, with no power but that of the Word with which he was entrusted, the contradictable Word of the Gospel. He lived and worked "in honor and dishonor, in ill repute and good repute" (2 Co 6:8). The New Testament has preserved the record of the apostle's dishonor too; these things are written for the apostolic church and for our learning.

The third letter probably dates from the same period as the first and second letters. Some scholars think that the letter to the church referred to in v. 9 may be our Second John. This cannot be either proved or disproved.

1 *Gaius* was a very common Roman name. This Gaius cannot be identified with others of the same name mentioned in the NT. (Acts 19:29; 20:4; Ro 16:23; 1 Co 1:14)

3 *The truth of your life,* literally "your truth." He *follows the truth* so wholeheartedly that his life has become a document in which the truth is inscribed for all men to read.

6 *Send . . . on their journey.* The term seems to have become almost technical as a designation for the furtherance and support of missionaries. (Acts 15:3; Ro 15:24; 1 Co 16:6; Tts 3:13)

12 *Demetrius.* See the Introduction.

From the truth itself. This probably means that some Christian prophet, impelled by the Spirit of *truth,* marked Demetrius out for his missionary task. Cf. Acts 13:2, where the Holy Spirit so designates Barnabas and Saul.

15 *Friends.* Found only here as an expression of Christian solidarity ("brothers" being the common term): perhaps a reminiscence of Jesus' use of "friends." (Jn 15:13-15; cf. Lk 12:4)

JUDE

INTRODUCTION

The author, "Jude, a servant of Jesus Christ and brother of James" (1), is probably the brother of our Lord, mentioned together with James in Mk 6:3 and Mt 13:55. James, the brother of our Lord and head of the Jerusalem church, was probably the only James (after the early death of the apostle James, the son of Zebedee) prominent enough to serve as identification; and the brothers of Jesus, James and Jude, are the only *pair* of brothers bearing those names that we know from New Testament times. Jude can hardly be the apostle of that name; aside from the fact that he does not designate himself as apostle, the manner in which he speaks of the apostles in v. 17 makes it clear that he does not claim to be one of them. One may wonder why he does not call himself "brother of Jesus"; but the brothers of Jesus remembered their Brother's word: "Whoever does the will of my Father in heaven is my brother" (Mt 12:50); they knew that faith alone establishes the tie which binds a man to Jesus and makes him an obedient son of God.

The Letter of Jude was occasioned by the appearance and activity of men who answered Paul's question, "Are we to continue in sin that grace may abound?" (Ro 6:1) in a way that was the very opposite of Paul's. They saw in the freedom which Christ had won for men not a liberation from sin but the liberty to sin. They perverted the free grace of God into licentiousness, thus denying their Master and Lord (4), who bade men follow Him in purity of heart. Moreover, they proclaimed this ungodly liberty quite openly, even arrogantly (8, 13, 16, 19). Far from breaking with the church, they carried on their propaganda within it; having "gained admission secretly" (4), they joined in the fellowship of the common meal (12) and created divisions *within* the church with their teachings (19). For teachers they evidently were, or claimed to be; Jude calls them clouds, from which men expect water (12); the church evidently was led to expect refreshment and life from their words. Jude does not deign to enter into a discussion of whatever system of teaching these men may have used to support their distorted conception of Christian liberty; he speaks of their "dreamings" (8), which would seem to indicate that they were speculative in their theology, or perhaps appealed to a special revelation by visions to support their claims. Jude centers his attack on the impiety of these "ungodly persons" (4); he is following the guidance of Jesus, who told His disciples, "You will know them by their fruits" (Mt 7:16). He points to the evil fruits of this bad tree; the vehemence with which he does so is an indication that these were persuasive and impressive men, all the more dangerous to the church because they would not break with the church whose Lord they denied (4). Jude therefore insists that the church break with them. He rouses holy fear in his readers as he calls on them to do battle for "the faith," for all that their Lord and His apostle had given them (3). They are to avoid all contact and compromise with the false teachers lest they fall under the fearful judgment of God which they know so well from their Old Testament; for that judgment will surely destroy these destroyers of the church of God (5-7; cf. 13-15). Even the attempt to save those brethren who are wavering between the new error and the old truth is to be made in this holy fear: "Have mercy with fear." (23)

But fear is not Jude's only resource; he also instills the high confidence of faith. His readers know from the ancient word of Enoch and from the apostolic Word of these last days (14-15; 17-18) that these arrogant, contentious, and mercenary blasphemers are doomed; they will perish in their pride (4, 11, 14-15). And, above all, the church is secure in the love of God which will preserve her for "Jesus Christ" (1) when He returns. And so the letter closes with a doxology filled with exuberant confidence of hope. (24-25)

Jesus gave His disciples only one simple test by which to distinguish false prophets from true prophets: "You will know them by their fruits" (Mt 7:16). The test seems almost absurdly simple when one considers the history of error in the church, error in its ever-new and plausible disguises. But this little, powerful Letter of Jude is living proof that Jesus' confidence in His followers was not misplaced. Endowed with the Spirit of Jesus, Jude rightly saw and soundly declared that what these ungodly men were producing as the newest theology in A.D. 70—80 was not a fruit of the Spirit. The church was greatly aided by Jude's word in her second-century struggle with the Gnostic heresy. Our own century is evidence that the impulse to pervert the grace of God into licentiousness is a perennial plant which must be eradicated ever and again. The church will find in Jude an honest gardener to help her in this painful but necessary task.

1:2 THE SALUTATION: ASSURANCE IN THE FACE OF THREATENING EVIL

1:2 There is a strong note of assurance in both the description of the persons addressed (1) and the greeting (2). The struggle to which Jude calls them (3) need not terrify them. The eternal love of God has effectually reached them in His call (cf. Ro 8:28-30); it is now their safe abode, and by it they will be *kept for Jesus Christ,* that is, for the day when He returns to judge mankind and to gather in His own. Compare Paul's prayer in 1 Th 3:11-13 and 5:23-24.

1 The description of the persons addressed is so general that we can do little more than guess who the readers were or where they were situated. According to Paul (1 Co 9:5) the brothers of Jesus were active in missionary work, and we may imagine that the persons addressed are a congregation or a group of congregations founded by Jude himself; he knows their situation and feels a pastoral responsibility for them.

2 "To him who has will more be given" (Mt 13:12). The *mercy, peace, and love* of God which is theirs as men called by Him will be theirs in increasing measure. "But from him who has not, even what he has will be taken away" (Mt 13:12); they can lose these blessings if they will not face and fight the evil that has crept into the midst. It is this evil that Jude unmasks and describes in the body of his letter.

3-4 THE EVIL UNMASKED

The evil is a radical one, a threat to the very roots of the Christian existence: *our common salvation, the faith which was once for all delivered to the saints, the grace of our God, our only Master and Lord, Jesus Christ.* The danger is all the greater for being as yet an unperceived danger; it has crept into the church *secretly* in a Christian guise.

3 No Christian teacher has a natural taste for controversy; he is forced into it by his concern and responsibility for *our common salvation.*

The *faith . . . delivered to the saints* is the creed which contains and conveys the interpreted facts that are the substance of belief. We may think of such early catechetical summaries of apostolic teaching as the one cited by Paul in 1 Co 15:3-11 and the materials which we now have in the four gospels. That the OT too constituted an integral and authoritative part of this *faith* is shown by the Letter of Jude itself and by the whole NT. Since God's act in Christ is His final Word (Heb 1:1-2), the *faith* is delivered *once for all;* there is no going beyond it. (Cf. 2 Jn 9)

4 *Long ago . . . designated,* by ancient prophecy (14-15) and the predictions of the apostles. (17)

5-16 THE EVIL DESCRIBED AND JUDGED

5-7 Jude draws on the faith once for all delivered to the saints, on the OT, to remind his readers of God's unsparing judgment on unbelief and disobedience such as confronts the church in the teaching of these ungodly persons (4). The judgment strikes and dooms all evil, whether it be the unbelief of Israel in the wilderness (5), the disobedience of angels (6), or the flagrant and perverse immorality of Sodom and Gomorrah. (7)

5 Cf. Nm 14, especially v. 11, for the unbelief of the people. For a similar use of Israel's infidelity as a warning to the church cf. 1 Co 10:1-13; Heb 3:7—4:11.

6 For the mysterious story of the angels who *left their proper dwelling* see Gn 6:1-4.

7 See Gn 19. Gn 19:5 is the background of our ugly word "sodomy."

8-13 Undeterred by these warnings from the past (*yet,* v. 8), these godless persons go their arrogant way, defying all authority (8), unwilling to leave judgment to God, as even the archangel Michael did (9), but arrogating it to themselves (10). There is to the eye of faith something bestial in the way they rush into their own destruction (10), pursuing the way of the killer Cain, the mercenary prophet Balaam, and the rebel Korah (11). Such they are to the forewarned eye of faith. On the surface they do not look so horrible as all that; they take part in the fellowship of the church's *love feasts,* the common meal sometimes associated with the celebration of the Lord's Supper (12), as all good churchmen do. But this deceptive appearance need deceive no one: their participation in the common meal, designed to be an expression of selfless mutual love, is just another coarse expression of their self-centered arrogance, of a piece with their demeanor as teachers who promise much but give nothing, like waterless *clouds* (12) that give no rain, *trees* that yield no fruit (12) or *stars* (13) that give the sailor no guidance. Inconstant as waves of the sea, shameless in their shame, they invite the judgment of God. (13)

8 The false teachers *defile the flesh* by their sexual license. For a similar example of "spiritual" emancipation (based on the false idea that Spirit and flesh have nothing to do with each other) and for Paul's judgment upon it cf. 1 Co 6:12-20. They *reject authority* when they deny Jesus Christ as their only Master and Lord (cf. 4). They are willing to accept Christ as Liberator and Giver of the Spirit but will not accept Him as the Lord who said, "TEACH them to observe all that I have commanded you" (Mt 28:20). In so doing they withdraw from the authority of His apostles (cf. 17) and of the OT too. They *revile the glorious ones,* the angels, messengers and ministers of God, guardians and preservers of God's order in the world. Perhaps Jude is recalling the word of Jesus in Mt 18:10, where He speaks of the angels of the "little ones" (those who need the help and guidance of the church) as having constant access to God; this word is part of Jesus' warning to those who despise these little ones and cause them to sin (cf. Mt 18:5-9). When the false teachers try to mislead unwary, simple Christians, they are flouting the authority of the angels whom God has given for their protection.

9 The false teachers have less awe for the judgment of God than the angels themselves. Even the archangel Michael, in his contention with the devil, remembered the word of God which said, "Vengeance is mine, I will repay, says the Lord" (Ro 12:19: Dt 32:35). The phrase *The Lord rebuke you* occurs in Zch 3:2 as a rebuke to Satan when he brings his accusation against Joshua the high priest. The story of Michael's contention with Satan for the body of Moses is, according to the witness of early church fathers, taken from a work called Assumption of Moses written about A.D. 30, now imperfectly preserved. According to it, Michael was charged with the burial of Moses; Satan claimed the body on the ground that Moses was a murderer, having slain an Egyptian (Ex 2:12). Michael left the judgment to God, who intervened on Moses' behalf.

11 *The way of Cain,* the murderer of his brother, appears in 1 Jn 3:12 as the very antithesis of the way enjoined by Jesus ("that we should love one another," 1 Jn 3:11). It is therefore a fitting description of the conduct of men who deny our only Master and Lord, Jesus Christ (4), and are blemishes on the love feasts of the followers of Jesus.

Balaam, the prophet hired by Balak to curse Israel (Nm 22—24), who for the sake of gain attempted to go against his own inspired convictions, is the prototype of men who claim special revelation ("dreamings," 8) and act from mercenary motives (16). It was also the counsel of Balaam which misled Israel into licentious idolatry. (Nm 31:16; 25:1-2; Rv 2:14)

Korah is a striking OT example of those who reject authority (8). He headed a rebellion against the authority of Moses and Aaron and was destroyed by the judgment of God. (Nm 16:1-35)

12 *Twice dead,* because, once rescued from death by the Gospel (cf. Eph 2:1-10), they have returned to the old way of sin and death (cf. 2 Ptr 2:21). For *uprooted* as a picture of God's judgment cf. Mt 15:13.

14-16 They have the prophetic word of Enoch against them, these sensual, self-seeking, loud-mouthed men who can never get all they want and all that they think they deserve, for all their brash pushing and contriving. The Lord will convict and condemn them when He appears for judgment.

14-15 The words of Enoch are quoted from the apocryphal Book of Enoch (1:9); its language is echoed also in v. 6. Jude's use of apocryphal books, like Enoch and Assumption of Moses, has troubled some men in both the ancient and the modern church. Unnecessarily, it would seem. The fact that an inspired author uses a story from the Assumption to illustrate a point and cites from Enoch a statement on the divine judgment which echoes many OT passages does not necessarily mean that he regards the whole books, with all their strange and bizarre features, as authoritative and inspired. Paul quotes even pagan writers with approval (e.g., Menander in 1 Co 15:33 and Epimenides in Tts 1:12) to make a point.

17-23 THE DEFENSE AGAINST THE EVIL

17-23 The men called by God and kept for Jesus Christ (1) are not without defense. They have the apostolic Word and face the evil forewarned and open-eyed (17-18); they have the *faith* once and for all delivered to them as the firm foundation on which their house of life may be built (20); they have the Spirit to inform their prayers (20); they have the love of God to sustain them in the bright hope of the return of their Lord, the hope of eternal life (21). Thus furnished for defense, they need not fall prey to the sectarian divisions produced by worldly, unspiritual men (19); they can even take the offensive and undo, in pure mercy and holy fear, at least some of the evil these ungodly persons have produced. (22-23)

17-18 The *predictions of the apostles* quoted in the following verse are not found in exactly that form in any of the apostolic writings. The quotation reflects such passages as Acts 20:29-30; 1 Ti 4:1 ff.; 2 Ti 3:1 ff.; 2 Ptr 3:3; cf. 1 Jn 2:18-23; 4:1-3.

19-21 The *most holy faith* is inviolable: no one dare lay profane hands on it, for the whole majesty of the Trinity is contained in it *(Spirit, God, Lord Jesus Christ).*

20 Pray in the Holy Spirit. Cf. Ro 8:15-16, 26-27; Eph 6:18.

21 For *mercy* in the Last Judgment cf. 2 Ti 1:18, Ja 2:13. Jesus promised mercy in the Judgment to the merciful (Mt 5:7; cf. 25:31-45). The latter part of the verse therefore leads directly to the admonition of vv. 22-23, to deal mercifully with those entangled in the lies of the libertine teachers.

23 The *fire* from which the faithful Christians are to snatch their erring brothers is the fire of God's judgment that is threatening to destroy them (cf. Am 4:11; Zch 3:2). *The garment spotted by the flesh* is a strong expression to indicate that even the slightest contact, even an apparently external contact, is to be avoided.

24-25 DOXOLOGY: CONFIDENCE OF VICTORY OVER EVIL

24-25 The closing doxology repeats and intensifies the note of assurance with which the letter began. The church has good reason to fear (cf. 23); she has no reason to despair. There is One who has the power to bring her safely and triumphantly through all the temptations that beset her into His glorious presence at the Judgment, the Savior God whose eternal glory, majesty, dominion, and authority are all in the service of His mercy, which shall pronounce her blameless on that day. She shall hear Jesus Christ her Lord say, "Come unto Me!"

REVELATION

INTRODUCTION

Occasion and Purpose

Revelation is, in form, a letter addressed to seven churches in the Roman province of Asia (Rv 1:4), complete with salutation and closing benediction (Rv 1:4; 22:21). The situation which called forth the writing is made clear by the writing itself: the churches are being troubled by false teachers (Rv 2:6, 14-15), slandered and harassed by Jews, the "synagogue of Satan" (Rv 2:9; 3:9), and are undergoing a persecution (Rv 1:9) which has already cost the lives of some faithful witnesses (Rv 2:13; 6:9-10) but has not yet reached its height (Rv 6:11). To these churches John, himself in banishment on the island of Patmos "on account of the word of God and the testimony of Jesus" (Rv 1:9), writes the account of the visions given to him there, the record of "the revelation of Jesus Christ, which God gave him to show to his servants" (Rv 1:1). He writes in order to strengthen them in their trials, both internal and external, to hold before them the greatness and the certitude of their hope in Christ, and to assure them of their victory, with Christ, over all the powers of evil now let loose on the world and, to all appearances, destined to triumph on earth. The book is thoroughly practical, like all the books of the New Testament, designed to be read in the worship services of the churches, as the first of the seven beatitudes which the book pronounces shows: "Blessed is he who reads aloud the words of the prophecy, and blessed are those who hear, and who keep what is written therein; for the time is near." (Rv 1:3)

Time and Place of Writing

Irenaeus' statement (*Adv. Haer.* V, 30, 3) that Revelation was written toward the close of the reign of the emperor Domitian (A. D. 81—96) gives us the most probable date for the book, A. D. 95 or 96. Domitian was the first Roman emperor to make an issue of emperor worship; and since the emperor cult was propagated with great zeal in the province of Asia, the collision between the emperor, who laid claim to men's worship as "Lord and God," and those who would call no one Lord but Jesus and would worship Him alone proved to be inevitable in Asia. That John should have been banished from Ephesus to Patmos, off the coast of Asia, "on account of the word of God and the testimony of Jesus" (Rv 1:9), that Antipas should have died a martyr's death at Pergamum in Asia (Rv 2:13), that the souls of men who had been slain for the witness they had borne should cry aloud for vindication (Rv 6:9-10)—all this fits in naturally with the historical situation in Asia in the latter years of Domitian's reign. The payment of divine honors to the emperor was made the test of loyalty; the Christian had to refuse, and that refusal made him liable to the penalty of death. The visions given to John made it unmistakably plain to the churches why the Christian had to refuse and die; and these visions wrote out in letters of gold and fire the promise that such dying was not defeat but triumph, a triumph which man shared with the Lamb that was slain, with Him who is King of kings and Lord of lords, whose people go His way through death to victory and royal reign.

The Literary Form of the Book

Revelation, with its visions of riders, trumpets, and bowls, of dragon and beasts, its use of number symbolism, and its mysterious and suggestive style generally, strikes the modern reader as strange and bizarre, and he is inclined to agree with Luther when he says, "My spirit cannot adapt itself to this book." Much in the book that puzzles us today was familiar to John's first readers; much that we can gain access to only by laborious study and by a gradual process of sympathetic immersion into this alien world spoke directly to them. They had been familiarized with the imagery of John's vision by a form of Judaic religious literature known as "apocalyptic." Apocalyptic elaborated certain elements or aspects of Old Testament prophecy found in such passages and books as Isaiah 24—27, Zechariah 9—14, Ezekiel, Joel, and Daniel. It sought to interpret all history on the basis of purported visionary experiences of the author. It was especially interested in eschatology, that is, in the end of history and the ushering in of the world to come. It utilized pictures, allegories, and symbols (which soon became traditional); numbers, colors, and stars were in these images endowed with a profound significance. Books of this type were the book of Enoch, the Book of Jubilees, Fourth Esdras, and Assumption of Moses.

Formally, Revelation belongs to this class; apocalyptic, as it were, furnished the familiar vocabulary of its speech. But Revelation is set apart from the general run of apocalyptic literature by profound differences. Apocalyptic itself drew heavily on the Old Testament; John draws even more heavily. No other New Testament book can compare with it in the number of allusions to the Old Testament; Revelation is saturated with the Old Testament. In fact, it is the Old Testament itself and not apocalyptic that constitutes the immediate background and the richest source for Revelation. Revelation is at bottom much more deeply akin to the Old Testament than it is to the apocalyptic which it resembles so strongly on the formal side. Other differences are equally striking. Apocalyptic works are generally pseudonymous; that is, they claim some great figure from Israel's past, such as Enoch, as author; and the past course of history as known to the actual author is made a prediction in the mouth of the purported author. John, however, writes in his own name. Apocalyptic has speculative interests and seeks to calculate the times and seasons of the world's last days and the world's end. John has no such speculative interest; he does not aim to satisfy men's curiosity but to give them hope and courage, and he does not attempt to calculate the approach of the end. "I come quickly" is the burden of the revelation of Christ as given to John. The visions of apocalyptic betray their origin; they are the fantasies of men. The visions of John have on them the stamp of genuine visionary experience; they are not products of the study. If apocalyptic may be termed literary meditation on prophetic themes, Revelation is genuine prophecy, a prophecy which uses apocalyptic motifs and forms insofar and only insofar as they are legitimate explications of Old Testament prophetic themes and are germane to its own thoroughly Christ-centered proclamation. The Lord in speaking through John speaks in the tongues of men; but He does not think the thoughts of men.

The peculiar advantage or virtue of utterance in this form lies not in the precision and clarity with which the utterance can be made, but in the power with which the thing said can be brought to bear on the whole man—on his mind, his imagination, his feelings, his will. His whole inner life is caught up in the moving terror and splendor of these visions; and the course and bent of his life are determined by them as they could hardly be determined by any other kind of communication. But just this characteristic of the book has given rise to widely divergent interpretations of the book; men have attempted, usually in a one-sided fashion, to be more precise in their interpretation of the book than the book itself by its very nature can be. One group of interpreters has fixed on the fact that the visions have their occasion and basis in real historical events and interprets the book wholly in terms of what had already happened at the time of writing; they see no real prediction anywhere in it, but merely an interpretation of past events in the guise of prediction. This, of course, ignores the prophetic claim of the book itself. Others refer everything but the content of the first three chapters to the very end of time, to the period immediately preceding the advent of Christ, and think of it as still awaiting fulfillment. This ignores the fact that for the author himself all time since the ascension of Christ is the time immediately preceding the advent of Christ and makes the book largely irrelevant for the very people for whom it was first written. Others again see in the visions a more or less detailed predictive portrayal of the successive events of universal history or of the history of the church to the end of time; here again one must ask how such a series of predictions was to be of any aid and comfort to the troubled churches of Asia A. D. 95. Still others renounce all attempts to relate the message of the book *directly* to history and see in the visions rather the enunciation of general principles which will hold good throughout history. But the book itself, with its life-and-death involvement in the crisis of A. D. 95, is anything but the enunciation of abstract principles.

Each of these attempts to interpret the book is, in its one-sidedness, a falsification. A true interpretation will, with the first group, look for the roots of the work in the history contemporary with it, for the book was obviously written for the church's encouragement and strengthening at a certain time and place. It will, with the second group, recognize the fact that the prophecy embraces all time between the now of the church and the return of the Lord of the church. It will, with the third group, take seriously the relevance of the book to all history; but it will, with the last group, be inclined to see in it not a blueprint of history but a divine light that strikes history and illumines where it strikes, a pointing finger of God to guide men through history and judgment to the end. If the book is so viewed and so taken to heart, its value for the church and the individual will not depend on the completeness of one's comprehension of every detail of its imagery.

Value of the Book

To men sitting in the quiet of their studies and to the church at peace in the world the Revelation to John presents difficulties and often brings perplexities. Others in the church have used the book to feed their fevered dreams. But the book did not originate as a book to be coolly pondered or as food to feed the dreams of idle men. It is the cry of victory raised for the cause of Christ when His cause seemed doomed—what was this pitifully weak assembly of nobodies to oppose the might of Rome? This book took the word of Jesus, His beatitude upon the persecuted, with absolute seriousness and wrote it into the history of the church when it was clearly becoming a bloody history: "Rejoice and be glad, for your reward is great in heaven!" And so it has happened again and again in the history of the church that when all secular securities were swept away and all human guarantees of triumph were lost, men turned to this book. They turned to this book, which looks with the same unperturbed clarity of vision on the face of Satan and on the face of God and His Anointed and sees written in both the triumph of God and His Christ. Men have turned to this book and have found the strength not only to endure but to sing. The doxologies of the Book of Revelation have echoed in the church most mightily just when men as men could find no cause for songs of praise.

Content of the Revelation to John

Revelation is a carefully constructed and elaborately articulated whole in which the number seven is the dominant unit. An outline such as the following, which views the whole work as a series of seven visions, therefore commends itself as probable. It also seems to be clear that there is a major break between the third and fourth set of visions. This break is constituted not so much by a change of theme as by a change in the vantage point from which the theme is viewed and treated. Important for the understanding of the whole is the observation that each of the units (with the possible exception of the first) spans the whole period between the present and the return of the Lord Jesus, so that we have a set of parallel presentations of the same basic fact and truth, cumulative in effect as each presentation brings in a new aspect of the same basic theme. There is progression in the sense that the end of all things is portrayed with increasing fullness as the visions progress (return of the Lord, last judgment, the new world of God). We have here the same "spiral" thought pattern that is characteristic of the Gospel and the First Letter of John.

OUTLINE

I. 1:1-8 Introduction

II. 1:9—11:19 First Three Visions: The Church and the Powers of This World

A. 1:9—3:22 First Vision: the Seven Letters

B. 4:1—7:17 Second Vision: The Seven Seals

C. 8:1—11:19 Third Vision: The Seven Trumpets

III. 12:1—22:5 Last Four Visions: Christ and the Powers of Darkness

A. 12:1—14:20 Fourth Vision: Anti-Trinity and Christ

B. 15:1—16:21 Fifth Vision: The Seven Bowls

C. 17:1—19:10 Sixth Vision: The Fate of Babylon, the Anti-Church

D. 19:11—22:5 Seventh Vision: Judgment and Renewal

IV. 22:6-21 Conclusion

1:1-8 INTRODUCTION

1:1-8 The introduction to the visions consists of three parts: a title to the whole book (1-3), an epistolary salutation (4-5a), and a threefold statement of praise, promise, and assurance concerning *Jesus Christ* and His *God and Father.* (5b-8)

1:1-3 The title indicates the source of the *revelation (Jesus Christ, God,* 1) how the revelation is mediated *(angel, servant John, all that he saw,* 1, 2), and how it is to be received *(keep what is written,* 3). There is a strong stress on the last-days urgency of the message of the book *(must soon take place,* 1; *time is near,* 3).

1:1 *Of Jesus Christ, which God gave him.* For Jesus as both Recipient and Giver of revelation cf. Mt 11:25-27; Jn 3:35; 5:20-24, 26-27; 7:16; 8:28; 12:48-49; 16:15; 17:1-8.

Servants, a common OT title of the prophets; cf. 1:3 ("prophecy"); 10:7; 11:18.

1:2 *Word of God* unites this prophet's witness with that of the OT prophets (so richly reflected in his words); testimony of Jesus Christ marks his word as part of the Word of God spoken "in these last days by a Son" (Heb 1:2); and all that he saw refers to the peculiar visionary form in which the word was given to him.

1:3 *Blessed,* the first of seven beatitudes in Rv. (Cf. 14:13; 16:15; 19:9; 20:6; 22:7; 22:14)

Reads aloud, in the worship service, where the letter is to be heard by the assembled faithful. (Cf. Cl 4:16)

Keep. Prophecy is not designed to satisfy curiosity; it opens up the future in order that men may know and obey the will of God which shapes that future. Only those who hear in faith and hope will read this book profitably. Cf. 1, "to show to his SERVANTS."

1:4-5a The salutation has the form familiar to us from the letters of Paul (cf. Ro 1:1-7; Gl 1:1-3). The whole book is a letter, a personal, purposeful, practical word to the church.

1:4 *Asia,* the Roman province in western Asia Minor is meant.

Seven spirits, the one Holy Spirit as given to and active in the seven churches. (Cf. 2:7, 11, etc.)

1:5 The *faithful witness* refers to the Christ who became incarnate and died (Jn 18:37); the *firstborn of the dead,* to the Risen One; and the *ruler of kings,* to the exalted Christ at the right hand of God.

1:5b-8 The salutation opens out into a doxology to the Christ who died and rose and rules (cf. 5a), whose *love* has *freed* men *from* their *sins* and so has created the new Israel, the royal priestly people of God (5b-6; cf. Ex 19:6; Is 61:6). The promise speaks of the return of Christ as the Son of Man to judge and reign (Dn 7:13, *coming with the clouds;* cf. Zch 12:10). The word of assurance (8) is spoken by the *Lord God* Himself; however dreadful "what soon must take place" (1) may prove to be, nothing escapes His control who is the Beginning and the End of all things *(Alpha . . . Omega);* the kings and priests of God may stand firm in the assurance that they are in the hands of *the Almighty.*

1:8 *Alpha . . . Omega,* the first and last letters of the Greek alphabet.

1:9—11:19 FIRST THREE VISIONS THE CHURCH AND THE POWERS OF THIS WORLD

1:9—11:19 Rv is a word of prophecy (1:3), a revelatory word. In this word God makes

Himself known and makes Himself count in the life and history of His people. He gives men eyes to see (in the present and in the future) what the eye of man cannot see and hearts that can conquer where victory seems impossible. He gives men eyes and hearts to see and believe the reign of God and His Anointed where that reign is anything but a transparent and palpable reality. Thus He enables men to believe "in hope against hope." (Ro 4:18)

1:9—3:22 First Vision: The Seven Letters

1:9—3:22 Christ, Victor over death and Lord of the church, appears to His prophet in blazing divine majesty, overwhelms him, restores him, and commissions him to write to the seven churches in His name (1:9-20). In the seven letters the church, under the blessing, power, and judgment of the exalted Christ, is asked to do the impossible in an intolerable situation (perversion of the Gospel from within, persecution to the death from without). Christ places on His church the inexorable claim of His grace: No compromise! No compromise with falsehood or with lovelessness, no compromise over against the satanic *(synagogue of Satan,* 2:9; *Satan's throne,* 2:13; 3:9; *deep things of Satan,* 2:24), no compromise with compromisers (*Nicolaitans,* 2:6, 15), no compromise with sloth, indifference, or lukewarmness. He *who conquers* (2:11), and he alone, has the great promises of the Lord of the church. (Chs. 2—3)

1:9-20 THE PROPHET'S INAUGURAL VISION

1:9 *Patmos,* a small island off the SW coast of Asia Minor, 30 miles south of Samos, used as a place of banishment by the Roman emperors.

1:10 *In the Spirit,* for this term for inspiration cf. Mt 22:43, where it is used of the inspired psalmist.

1:11 *Seven churches.* The seven cities mentioned all lay on a Roman road which ran northward from *Ephesus* through *Smyrna* to *Pergamum* and then turned inland and southward to *Thyatira, Sardis, Philadelphia, Laodicea;* all were assize towns and centers in which the cult of the emperor was fostered. What the Spirit said to these *seven churches* could be readily transmitted to other churches in the area. The *seven* are thought of as representative of the whole church; note the recurrent phrase, "What the Spirit says to the churches," 2:7, 11, etc.

1:12 *Lampstands.* Cf. 20 note.

1:13-16 The appearance of the exalted Christ is described in terms taken from OT descriptions of the *son of man* (Dn 7:13), of a mysterious heavenly figure in Dn 10 who reveals the future to Daniel (Dn 10:5-6), and of God Himself (cf. Dn 7:9; Eze 1:24, 26-27). Thus there is a strong stress on the deity of Christ, in close connection with the emphasis on the humanity which took Him into man's death. (18)

1:16 *Seven stars,* symbol of universal sovereignty, found on Imperial Roman coins.

1:17 *Fell . . . as though dead.* The APPEARANCE of Christ expresses His majesty and purity. His searching eye and inescapable tread, His overwhelming and piercing word of judgment; before it the prophet collapses, as Isaiah did in the presence of the Lord of hosts. (Is 6:5; cf Eze 1:28; Dn 10:7-9; Ju 6:22-23)

1:17-18 *Fear not.* In the WORDS of Christ His divine, eternal power *(the first and the last, living one)* is seen to be in the service of His love. He who in love *died* for men (cf. 1:5, "blood") lives *for evermore* to release men from the power of *Death.*

1:18 *Keys of,* authority over. (Cf. Mt 16:19)

Hades, the realm of the dead. (Cf. Mt 16:18)

1:19 *What is* refers to the contents of chs. 2—3; *what is to take place hereafter,* to the succeeding visions.

1:20 *Mystery,* what can be known only by divine revelation. (Cf. 17:6-7)

Stars . . . lampstands . . . angels . . . churches. Both the stars and the lampstands signify the church. The seven stars, symbol of universal dominion, point to the angels, the church as a divine reality, as it is in God's eyes and therefore really is and eternally shall be. The lampstands point to the churches as a historical reality, functioning on earth at a certain time and place as the light of the world (Mt 5:14; Ph 2:15-16). These two aspects of the church cannot be separated; when Christ addresses the church in Ephesus, for instance, He speaks to the "angel of the church" (2:1). His words of recognition, rebuke, correction, threat, and promise addressed to the angel of the church are telling the church to be in its human actions what the church by divine action is, somewhat as we rebuke and encourage with the words, "Be yourself." The close connection between angel and lampstand is seen very clearly in 2:5: If the angel will not repent, the lampstand will be removed.

2:1-7 THE LETTER TO EPHESUS

2:1-7 The seven letters all have the same structure. (a) After the command to write, Christ designates and describes Himself as the Author of the letter; the self-designation usually picks up some feature from the inaugural vision of 1:9-20. (b) The Lord of the church addresses the church in words of diagnosis (praise and rebuke) and exhortation. (c) The summons to vigilant hearing *(He who has an ear,* 7) either precedes or follows. (d) The word of promise given *to him who conquers,* to the repentant and obedient church.

2:1 *Ephesus,* capital of the province of Asia and its greatest city, of outstanding political, commercial, religious, and cultural importance. Paul's extended and successful ministry there is sketched in bold strokes in Acts 19:1—20:1; cf. also Paul's farewell words to the elders of Ephesus in Acts 20:17-35.

Stars . . . lampstands. Cf. 1:12, 13-16, 20 notes.

2:2-6 The church is unreservedly praised for

its unwearied zeal in contending "for the faith which was once for all delivered to the saints" (Jude 3) but is called on to *repent* of its decline in *love,* a failing that threatens the very existence of the church (5). The bitterness of necessary controversy has embittered its heart; the church has forgotten that "love . . . is not irritable or resentful . . . bears all things, believes all things, endures all things." (1 Co 13:5-7)

2:2 *Apostles,* true witnesses to the Lord Christ. (Cf. 2 Co 11:13-15)

2:6 *Works of the Nicolaitans.* There can and must be a hatred of evil *works,* without hatred of the men who do them. The *Nicolaitans* (cf. 2:14-15) advocated and defended a compromise with the paganism that surrounded the church in the public festivals of the city and in many social and civic associations. For the Gentile reaction of hurt surprise at the fact that Christians abstained from such associations cf. 1 Ptr 4:3-4; the temptation to compromise for the sake of peace and public approval must have been strong.

2:7 To *conquer* is to obey the Lord of the church who speaks to the church by His Spirit and to return in the power of the Spirit to a love like that of Jesus Christ, in whom a faithful witness to the truth and a self-expending love were perfectly united (cf. 1:5-6). The Christian's victory is a partaking in His victory *(I will grant).*

Eat of the tree of life, find that true eternal life which man's sin had forfeited (Gn 2:9; 3:22-24) and return to a life of unbroken fellowship with God in *paradise.* (Cf. 22:2, 14, 19)

2:8-11 THE LETTER TO SMYRNA

2:8-11 For the structure of the letter cf. 2:1-7 note.

2:8 *Smyrna,* an ancient and famous city 40 miles north of Ephesus, a great commercial center proud of its emperor cult, with a considerable Jewish population.

First and . . . last, etc. Cf. 1:17-18. The eternal Lord of life and Victor over death speaks with authority to the persecuted church facing death, urging faithfulness unto death and promising the crown of life. (10)

2:9 *Poverty . . . rich.* Cf. Ja 2:5.

Jews . . . synagogue of Satan. By committing themselves to the satanic lie *(slander)* and to the murderous satanic will they have forfeited their right to be called the people of God (cf. Jn 8:44). Jewish opposition to the church persisted in Smyrna; Jews took a leading part in the martyrdom of Polycarp, bishop of Smyrna, in A. D. 155.

2:10 *Ten days,* a relatively short period of time (Gn 24:55; Dn 1:12, 14); the main emphasis is on the fact that the time of *tribulation* is measured and controlled by God.

2:11 *Second death,* the final eternal separation from God and His life, described in 20:14 and 21:8 as eternal torment in "the lake of fire." (Cf. Mt 10:28)

2:12-17 THE LETTER TO PERGAMUM

2:12-17 For the structure of the letter cf. 2:1-7 note.

2:12-13 *Pergamum,* to the north of Smyrna, a city renowned for the rich variety of its pagan cults, a strong center of the Imperial cult (worship of the Roman emperor). Here, where the satanic power that lurks behind every idol (1 Co 10:19-20) was so powerfully entrenched *(Satan's throne . . . where Satan dwells),* the decision of the church for the Lord Jesus and against all other "lords" (1 Co 8:5-6) was particularly difficult and dangerous. The church had already experienced the shock of martyrdom *(Antipas . . . my faithful one . . . was killed)* and was in especial need of the powerful *words of him who has the sharp two-edged sword,* His recognition (13), His warning (14-16), and His promise (17). *My faith,* faith in Me as Lord *(name).*

2:14-15 *Balaam* once brought about the fall of God's people by enticing them into the lascivious worship of Baal of Peor (Nm 31:15-16; cf. Nm 25:1-3); the *Nicolaitans* with their *teaching* (cf. 2:6 note) posed a similar threat to God's people now. For the history of Israel as warning and introduction for the new people of God cf. 1 Co 10:1-22.

2:17 *Hidden manna . . . new name.* Those who have in fidelity to Christ refused to compromise with satanic pagan idolatry by eating food sacrificed to idols (14) will be fed with food from heaven by Christ Himself in the world to come; those who have held fast to His name (13) will receive from Him a *new name,* that is, a new eternal status and being in the world to come. For the sense of *new name* cf. Is 62:1-4.

Hidden, invisible to unbelief, known to faith but not yet seen. "Hope that is seen is not hope. For who hopes for what he sees? But if we hope for what we do not see, we wait for it with patience." (Ro 8:24-25)

White stone. The image is probably that of an amulet engraved with a divine name which assures the wearer of safety and well-being. (Cf. 3:12)

Which no one knows except him who receives it. Only by the grace of God, through His Spirit, does man come "to know the love of Christ which surpasses knowledge." (Eph 3:14-19).

2:18-29 THE LETTER TO THYATIRA

2:18-29 For the structure of the letter cf. 2:1-7 note.

2:18 *Thyatira,* the smallest of the seven cities addressed, lay to the SE of Pergamum. The church receives high praise for its living and flourishing faith (19) but is sternly rebuked and warned for its tolerance of a false "prophetess" whose seductive teaching leads men to compromise with licentious paganism surrounding them. (20-23)

Son of God . . . eyes . . . feet. The church is confronted with the high majesty of the Judge (cf. Jn 5:25-29). The scrutiny of His fiery eye "searches mind and heart" (23); and He advances toward judgment on *feet . . . like burnished bronze,* feet that no power can resist or stay.

2:20 *Jezebel.* The name of King Ahab's Tyrian queen, who corrupted the religion of Israel with "the harlotries and the sorceries" of her native gods Baal and Astarte (2 K 9:22; 1 K 16:31-32; 18:19), is fittingly applied to the *prophetess* who, like the Nicolaitans (2:6, 15) was corrupting the life of the new people of God.

2:22-23 *Sickbed,* condign punishment for the bed of *adultery.*

Those who commit adultery with her are those who have come under the spell of her beguiling doctrine but are not yet completely carried away by it; for them repentance is still possible. *Her children* are those who have absorbed her teaching so completely that they are wholly like her, immoral and impenitent (cf. 21); them the Judge will *strike . . . dead* in their guilt.

2:24 *Deep things of Satan.* The adherents of the prophetess spoke of their peculiar "enlightened" tenets (which distinguished them from simple and decent God-fearing folk) as the *deep things* of God; the prophet John fearlessly calls them by their right name.

2:26 *My works,* the good works which Christ both commands and enables them to do.

2:26-27 In language taken from Ps 2:8-9 Christ promises the faithful a part in His own eternal Messianic reign. (Cf. 3:21)

2:28 *The morning star,* probably Venus, which symbolized worldwide dominion.

3:1-6 THE LETTER TO SARDIS

3:1-6 For the structure of the letter cf. 2:1-7 note.

3:1 *Sardis,* an ancient Lydian city south of Thyatira with a long and brilliant past, important in Roman times as an industrial center, seat of a Roman provincial court, and site of a temple for emperor worship. The church seems to have been untroubled by persecution and not tested by internal struggle. Its besetting sin was religious and moral apathy.

3:1-2 *Seven spirits . . . seven stars.* Christ not only has dominion over the churches *(stars* 1:16, 20), He has the fullness of the creative power of the Spirit (cf. 1:4) as His gift to the churches. He can therefore bid the *dead* church of Sardis *awake and strengthen what . . . is on the point of death,* for He gives what He commands by His gift of the Spirit.

Dead . . . works. Cf. Ja 2:26

Not . . . perfect. Literally "not fulfilled." God has created the church "for good works" which He Himself "prepared beforehand, that we should walk in them" (Eph 2:10). Good works not done are like prophecy unfulfilled.; God's purpose for man is being thwarted, His grace is being received in vain. (2 Co 6:1)

3:3 *Remember,* recall and relive.

I will come like a thief. Cf. Jesus' word concerning His final coming, Mt 24:43, echoed once more in Rv 16:15.

3:4 *Soiled their garments,* by infidelity to their Lord.

3:5 *White garments* symbolize vindication and victory. (Cf. 6:11)

Book of life, in which the names of the citizens of the city of God are enrolled. (Cf. Ex 32:32-33; Ps 69:28; Dn 12:1; Lk 10:20; Ph 4:3; Heb 12:23)

I will confess his name. An echo of Jesus' words, Mt 10:32.

3:7-13 THE LETTER TO PHILADELPHIA

3:7-13 For the structure of the letter cf. 2:1-7 note.

3:7-13 To *Philadelphia,* the church which despite its *little power* in means and prestige has been faithful (8) and enduring in obedience to the Word of the Lord (10), the *holy* and faithful *(true)* Lord promises missionary opportunity and triumph (8-9) and preservation in the coming universal *hour of trial* (10). *He who conquers* (12) shall have his enduring place of honor in the living *temple of . . . God;* God will acknowledge him as His own *(name of my God),* enroll Him among the citizens of the *new Jerusalem,* the *city of . . . God; he shall share in the glory of Christ the Conqueror (my . . . new name)*—all this as the free gift of the Christ who with Messianic authority *(key of David,* 7) *opens* the kingdom of heaven to all believers.

3:7 *Philadelphia,* SE of Sardis, strategically located and situated in a fruitful land, was a rich and commercially important city. The church there was neither rich nor "important"—but faithful.

Key, symbol of authority (cf. Mt 16:19 note: Is 22:22), here of the authority to admit or exclude men from the Kingdom.

3:8 *Open door,* of missionary opportunity (cf. 1 Co 16:9; 2 Co 2:12). Others take it of the door to the Kingdom (cf. 7 and 12); but the promise of the conversion of the hostile Jews (9) seems rather to suggest missionary success.

3:9 *Synagogue of Satan.* Cf. 2:9 note.

3:10 *Hour of trial . . . coming on the whole world.* The following visions depict this hour of trial (seals, 4:1—8:1; trumpets, 8:2—11:21; bowls, 15:1—16:21) as growing ever more intense. Visions such as 7:1-17 depict the preservation of the faithful.

3:12 *Pillar in the temple.* Perhaps an allusion to a custom of Philadelphia, where citizens who had deserved well of the state had pillars set up in their honor in a local temple.

3:14-22 THE LETTER TO LAODICEA

3:14-22 For the structure of the letter cf. 2:1-7 note.

3:14 *Laodicea,* SE of Philadelphia, was a rich city renowned as a center of commerce, banking, and cloth manufacture, seat of a medical school. The church there seems to have taken color from its environment and to have become self-satisfied, secure in itself, "lukewarm" Laodicea had forgotten what Philadelphia remembered, that the Kingdom is promised to the poor in spirit. (Mt 5:3)

3:18 *Buy,* in the sense of Is 55:1-2, "without money and without price." Cf. the gracious assurance of v. 20 and the lavish promise of 21.

The threat of 16 ("spew you out") is to make them receptive for the promise of 19-21.

3:18 *Gold . . . garments . . . salve,* alluding to the banking, manufacture, and medicine which had made Laodicea rich—and "lukewarm." The Laodiceans had spent their money "for that which is not bread" and their "labor for that which does not satisfy." (Is 55:2)

3:19 *Zealous,* the opposite of "lukewarm." (16)

3:20 *Hears my voice and opens the door.* This is a pictorial explanation of "repent" (19); *hears* includes the idea of "obeys."

3:20-21 *Eat with him . . . sit with me on my throne.* Both the picture of the common meal and that of the shared reign emphasize the completeness of personal communion with Christ, what it means to be "forever with the Lord."

4:1—7:17 Second Vision: The Seven Seals

4:1—7:17 The vision of the seven seals tells the church that compromise is neither necessary nor possible. The evils that sweep around the church (including the satanic thrust into the church) are no wild chance, no irrational vagaries of fate, no secular uncertainties with which men may come to terms. No, in all this God, the *one seated on the throne* (4:2), is reigning (ch. 4); in all this Christ, the slain Lamb, is opening the seals of God's book, executing His counsels (ch. 5). Though the riders of ruin go forth, though the martyrs cry, though the structure of the universe topples till men grow desperate in the face of God's judgment (ch. 6)—nevertheless the preservation of the church and the eternal vindication of God's saints are sure, for they are part of God's royal will (ch. 7). "Your God reigns," the prophet proclaims to the church; "unite your will with His."

4:1-11 ONE SEATED ON THE THRONE

4:1-11 God, the omnipotent Creator, is manifested in splendor, receiving the adoration of the whole creation, over which He rules.

4:1 *After this.* The visions turn from the interpretation of the present (chs. 2—3) to the future of the world and the church.

4:2 *Throne.* For the throne as symbol of God's reign cf. Ps 11:4-6; 29:10; 47:8; 80:1; 99:1; 103:19-22; Is 6:1; Eze 1:26; Dn 7:9.

4:3 *Rainbow* recalls God's covenant of compassionate forbearance with every living creature after the Flood (Gn 9:13-16). The God who sits enthroned on high, the dread Judge of Sinai (cf. Ex 19:16), separated from men by the "sea of glass" (6), is nevertheless a God of grace. (Cf. Eze 1:28)

4:4 *Twenty-four elders* probably represent the people of God as they are in God's intent, in Christ, made alive, raised up, and seated in heavenly places (Eph 2:6), glorified (Ro 8:30) in God's presence *(white garments, golden crowns).* Others think of them as a superior class of angels especially close to God, familiar with His counsels (cf. 5:5; 7:13). But multiples of twelve usually refer to the people of God. (Cf. 7:4-8; 21:12, 14)

4:5 *Fire . . . seven spirits.* Cf. 1:4. The fostering warmth, the light, and the constant motion of fire make it an apt symbol of the genial Spirit through whom God communicates to man.

4:6 *Sea of glass.* Cf. v. 3 note; 15:2; Ps 104:3; Eze 1:22.

4:6-8 *Four living creatures* combines features of the seraphim of Is 6:2 and the cherubim of Eze 1:5, 18. They represent nature in the service of the Almighty; the lordly power of the *lion,* the solid strength of the *ox,* the skill and intelligence of *man,* the tireless speed of the *eagle* are at His disposal. Man thus appears twice in this vision, among the creatures and as a member of the people of God, created AND redeemed.

4:10-11 *Cast their crowns,* to indicate that their *glory and honor and power* is theirs purely as a gift from God, their Creator and Lord.

4:11 *To receive glory.* God receives His glory when man acknowledges Him as God and adores Him, "gives glory to God."

5:1-14 THE SLAIN LAMB AND THE SEALED SCROLL

5:1-14 The counsels of God are a sealed book, an unknown and dreadful secret for sinful man and his fallen world. The prophet weeps when the strong angel's challenge goes unanswered and the world is left without a future and a hope. There is hope in One only, in the slain and triumphant Messiah; He can take the book and reveal and execute the counsels of God. His appearance evoked a triple chorus of adoration from the living creatures and elders, from myriads of angels, and from every creature in God's world. The last song, that of the creatures, unites praise for the Lamb with praise for God the Enthroned, thus marking the Lamb as in majesty coequal with God and linking ch. 5 closely with ch. 4.

5:1 For the *scroll* as a symbol of God's counsels cf. Eze 2:9—3:3; Rv 10:2-11.

5:5 *Lion . . . Root of David.* Both are OT designations for the Messiah who was to come. *Lion* stresses His conquering power (Gn 49:8-10); *Root of David* speaks of the lowly and unpromising beginnings of One who shall triumph solely in the power of the Spirit of the Lord. (Is 11:1-2; cf. 3:10)

5:6 *Lamb . . . slain.* Cf. Is 53:7; Jn 1:29, 35 notes. The atoning sacrifice of Christ's death is the key to all the counsels of God.

Seven horns, symbol of all-encompassing power.

Seven eyes . . . seven spirits, symbols of the penetrating insight of Him who "shall not," like human rulers, judge merely "by what his eyes see" and of that "wisdom and understanding . . . counsel and might . . . knowledge and fear of the Lord" with which He shall establish God's rule of righteousness and restore the peace of Paradise on earth. (Is 11:2-9)

5:8 *Incense . . . prayers.* Cf. Ps 141:2. The suffering church is assured that the *prayers of the saints,* Christians, are heard before the throne of God and the Lamb.

5:9 *Ransom,* set free by payment, redeemed. (Cf. Mt 20:28 note)

5:12 *To receive power,* etc. (Cf. 4:11 note)

5:13 *Every creature.* All creation, which shall share in the glory of redeemed man, anticipates that hour of "glorious liberty" in this song. (Cf. Ro 8:19-21)

6:1-17 SIX SEALS OPENED

6:1-17 The opening of the seals is not merely the revelation of God's purposes but also the execution of them. What follows now, after the Lamb's decisive act and the universal exultation which it evoked, is disturbing: not an immediate triumph of God and the Lamb but the usual sequence of disasters that make human history. At the opening of the first seal the Antichrist, opponent and imitator of Christ, rides forth, *conquering and to conquer* (2). At the breaking of the second seal the red horse of war rides forth *to take peace from the earth* and to bring death (3-4). The opening of the third seal ushers in a season of scarcity (5-6). And the fourth seal signifies the triumph of the rider on the pale horse, *Death* (7-8). All this is marked as being under God's control, to be sure; God's *living creatures* utter the command that lets these fearful riders range (1, 3, 5, 7), and the power they have *was given* them by the Lord God Almighty (2, 4, 8). But this is not God's final victory. It is therefore no wonder that at the opening of the fifth seal the martyrs are heard crying out to God for vindication, asking that the God for whom they have died hallow His name by rendering judgment in their favor. They are given an anticipatory vindication in the white robe of glory but are given to know that the End is not yet (9-11). The End is in view at the opening of the sixth seal, when a convulsed universe heralds a judgment of God so terrible that men, even the greatest and mightiest, call on the mountains to fall on them and cover them; extinction is preferable to facing the wrath of God and the Lamb. (12-17)

6:2 *White horse.* The crowned victorious *rider* on the white horse RESEMBLES the victorious Christ as portrayed in 19:11-21, superfically at least. But his weapon is the *bow,* which in Eze 39:3 is the weapon of God, the great enemy of the people of God in the last days (Eze 38—39). Moreover, he appears in a series of sinister figures. The figure is best understood, therefore, as the Antichrist, both opponent and imitator of Christ. On this understanding we find in the first four seals the same sequence as in the words of Jesus concerning the last days in Mt 24:5-10—(1) misleading by false Christs; (2) wars; (3) famines; (4) death (by persecution in Mt 24:9, which is taken up in the fifth seal here). Others take the first rider to be Christ Himself, or the victorious Gospel (cf. Mk 13:10); still others think of a triumphant militarism such as that of the Parthians, an Eastern people who had inflicted a memorable defeat on Roman forces in A.D. 62. But the interpretation given above seems to fit the text and context best. For the figure of Antichrist cf. ch. 12. For the deceptive and misleading appearance of the antichristian power cf. "the synagogue of Satan" (2:9; 3:9), "throne of Satan" (2:13), and "the deep things of Satan." (3:24)

6:6 A *denarius* represents a day's wage for a laborer (cf. Mt 20:2); a *quart of wheat* is a day's ration for a man. A day's work would just keep a man alive on wheat; if he bought the cheaper *barley,* he would have something for his family also, but hardly enough. The inflationary price of food has been estimated as being 8 to 16 times normal prices.

Do not harm oil and wine. The luxuries of life are available—for those who can afford them; the small man is hardest hit, as is usual in times of dearth.

6:8 *Death* is the power to which all men must succumb in this age; *Hades* is the realm or kingdom of death, to which unbelieving men are committed while those who die in the Lord (14:13) are delivered from it. (Cf. Mt 16:18 note)

A fourth of the earth. The judgments of God depicted in the vision of the seven seals are still partial and preliminary, designed to call men to repentance. (Cf. 8:7, 9, 11, 12, "a third"; 3:20)

6:9 *Under the altar.* The slaying of God's witnesses has not been mere senseless butchery; their dying had a meaning and purpose, as a sacrifice offered to their God. (Cf. Ph 2:17; 2 Ti 4:6)

6:10 The honor of their *Sovereign Lord* is at stake in their death, and so they commit their cause to Him "who judges justly," as Christ did. (1 Ptr 2:23)

6:16 *Wrath of the Lamb.* He who in His great love was slain and by His blood did ransom men for God (5:9) will at the End appear as Judge of all who have despised and rejected His love.

7:1-17 INTERLUDE: THE NUMBERED SAINTS AND THE REDEEMED MULTITUDE

7:1-17 "The great day of their wrath has come, and who can stand before it?" (6:17) is the frantic question to which desperate men can find no answer. The prophet is given a twofold answer. First, the vision of the 144,000 members of the completed people of God, numbered by God and marked as His everlasting own by His seal, assures him and the church that nothing and no one can pluck God's elect from His hand—THEY shall be able to stand (1-8). Second, the vision of the innumerable multitude from among all nations assures him and the church that the grace of God which has cleansed them by the blood of the Lamb will bring them safely out of the last great tribulation which still awaits them (cf. 6:11) and enable them to stand before their Judge unafraid; more than that, His grace will bring them into a new life of enraptured adoration, a life of perpetual worship *(serve,* 15) before the throne in the temple of God, a life of consummated salvation in which the agonies of their present creaturely life are no more: no hunger, no thirst, no blasting heat, no tears any more, but fulfilled life in the shelter of God's presence and under the everlasting kindly care of their Good Shepherd (9-17). Now the seventh seal can be opened (8-1) and God's winds of judgment can be let loose upon the earth (7:1-3). God's people can endure to the end.

7:1 For the *four winds* as instruments of God's judgment cf. Jer 49:36.

7:2 *Rising of the sun,* a quarter of good omen. Paradise lay in the east (Gn 2:8), and in Judaic tradition the Messiah was expected to come from the east.

The *seal* marks them as God's property and under His protection; the *living God* is the acting God, no inert idol but mighty to save. For God's sealing as His act of protecting His own faithful ones amid judgment cf. Eze 9:4.

7:4 The number 12 is the number of the people of God, once the 12 tribes of Israel, now made up of men from every nation. The number 10 is the number of the rounded whole (10 Egyptian plagues, 10 commandments, etc.). 144,000 expresses the full number of the people of God under His watchful providence.

7:9 The innumerable *great multitude* is the same as the numbered tribes of Israel, seen from another point of view. While the 144,000 stresses the certainty of God's elective purpose, the innumerable *multitude* expresses the overwhelming greatness of His ultimate triumph.

Palm branches were carried by the festal crowds at the Feast of Booths (or Tabernacles), the feast of ingathering and thanksgiving for the harvest, the feast that commemorated the time when Israel dwelt in booths when God brought them up out of Egypt (Lv 23:33-43). Zch 14:16 contains a special promise that the Gentiles should one day partake in it.

7:10 *Salvation,* the accomplished deliverance of the Exodus of the last days (cf. 9 and Ex 15:1-2), is solely the act of God in Christ. (Cf. Eph 2:8-10)

7:14 *The great tribulation,* well known from the OT (Dn 1 2:1) and the words of Jesus. (Mt 24:21)

7:16-17 the language and thought of the OT, always a major influence in Rv, are especially prominent here. (Cf. Is 49:9-10; Ps 121:6; Eze 34:23; Ps 23; Is 25:8)

8:1—11:19 Third Vision: The Seven Trumpets

8:1—11:19 The opening of the seventh seal introduces, not the expected End but a new series of visions which surveys once more the time from the Now of the church to the End (11:15-19). The church must be prepared to remain uncompromisingly steadfast amid even sterner visitations than the vision of the seals had foretold. What the church trembles at now is but the beginning of the travail which precedes the world's rebirth (cf. Mt 24:8). The seals are followed by the trumpet blasts of God, judgmental visitations which warn mankind and call on men to repent (cf. 9:20-21). These visitations first strike man's world—the earth, the sea, the living waters, sun and moon and stars; they are still partial *(a third,* 8:7, 9, etc.), but under their impact the solid comfort of man's creaturely existence grows fragile and uncertain (ch. 8). These are followed by visitations in which the demonic, uncanny character of the powers employed by God becomes apparent, visitations which make increasingly plain the helplessness of man (locusts from the bottomless pit and innumerable troops of infernal calvary, 9:1-19). The church is not permitted to hope for "better times," for man is pictured as remaining impenitent and obdurate over against God's trumpet calls (9:20-21). Before the seventh trumpet (as before the seventh seal, ch. 7) there is an interlude (chs. 10—11) which assures the church that amid all this God's purposes are ripening fast; there shall be no more delay and the salutary, steadying voice of prophecy shall still be heard (ch. 10). The pseudo-church may be abandoned to its fate, but God's protecting hand will be over the true church (11:1-2), and the church's witness will continue in martyr-triumph (11:3 ff.). The beast from the abyss (11:7, announcing the theme of chs. 12—14) shall gain no lasting victory (11:11-12). At the sound of the seventh trumpet a song is heard in heaven which already celebrates the triumph of the Lord and His Christ (11:14-18). This song announces the themes of the second half of Rv (chs. 12—22): God and His Christ have become kings over the world with a reign that no satanic powers can long contest (chs. 12—14). The time has come to judge the dead (ch. 20), to reward the saints (chs. 21—22), and to destroy the enemies of God who destroy the earth (chs. 17—19). God's ultimate grace of the covenant and His ultimate judgment are in view. (11:19)

8:1-12 THE FIRST FOUR TRUMPETS

8:2 *Stand before,* an OT expression for "are in the service of."

Trumpets were in the Biblical world more means of signaling than a musical instrument, used in the temple worship, in warfare, sounded at the accession of kings. The prophets spoke of the trumpet blast which would herald the coming of the Day of the Lord (Jl 2:1, Zph 1:16), and the NT speaks of the trumpet which shall herald the return of Christ and the resurrection of the dead (Mt 24:31; 1 Co 15:52; 1 Th 4:16). Here the trumpets speak of God's becoming King and the coming of the End.

8:3-5 *Prayers of all the saints* are welcomed and sped on to God by God's angels. When the saints pray, "Thy kingdom come," they pray for judgment on all that opposes the coming of God's kingdom; hence the *peals of thunder, etc.*

8:7 *Hail . . . on the earth* recalls seventh plague on Egypt, Ex 9:23 ff.

8:9 *Sea became blood.* Cf. the first Egyptian plague, Ex 7:20 ff.

8:11 *Wormwood,* bitter and poisonous. (Cf. Jer 9:15)

8:12 Cf. the ninth Egyptian plague, Ex 10:21-23.

8:13—9:21 THE FIFTH AND SIXTH TRUMPETS

8:13 *Eagle.* For the eagle (or vulture) as a bird of ill omen cf. Hos 8:1.

9:1-3 The prophet sees a bright object *(star)* descended from heaven; on closer view this bright object is seen to be one of God's bright ministers *(he);* similarly the *smoke* from the *bottomless pit* is seen to be a dark swarm of *locusts.*

9:1 *Bottomless pit,* cf. 11; 20:1, 3. The wrath of God removes the barrier which His long-suffering patience has placed between the dark infernal world and man; man is exposed to powers he can no longer explain away as "the usual course of history" or "natural catastrophes." Man is made to feel his helplessness before the wrath of God.

9:3 *Locusts.* Cf. the eighth Egyptian plague, Ex 10:1-20, and Jl 1—2, which show how fearful a thing even a plague of natural locusts could be.

9:4 *Seal of God.* Cf. 7:3-4.

9:4-11 Three things distinguish these infernal locusts from the familiar locusts: (a) they attack, not vegetation but men, inflicting a pain like that of the bite of a *scorpion,* so intense that those smitten long for death; (b) their grotesquely horrible appearance; (c) their leader, the *angel of the bottomless pit, Abaddon,* the Destroyer.

9:5 *Five months,* the life-span of the locust.

The poisonous bite of the *scorpion* was proverbial (cf. 1 K 12:11; Eze 2:6). The scorpion is associated with "the power of the enemy" (Satan) in the word of Jesus, Lk 10:19.

9:11 *Abaddon* was in the OT a name for the PLACE of destruction, often associated with Sheol, the realm of the dead (cf. Jb 26:6; 28:22; Pr 15:11; Ps 88:11). Here it is a personal power of destruction.

9:12-19 The *troops of cavalry,* 200 million strong, are even more pronouncedly supernatural-demonic than the locusts, and their power of destruction greater *(killed,* 18). The only link with history is the mention of the *Euphrates* (14). Israel had experienced destructive judgments of God from beyond the great river (cf. Is 8:5-8), and in the Roman world men trembled for the security of the empire when they looked to the east.

9:20-21 God in His wrath has powers at His disposal which are so uncannily overwhelming that man can only throw himself on His mercy in repentance. This man refuses to do; he clings to his ungodliness (idolatry, 20) and his unrighteousness (21) in spite of all. (Cf. Ro 1:18)

9:20 *Works of their hands,* idols which their hands have made. (Cf. Hos 14:3)

10:1—11:19 INTERLUDE: ASSURANCE FOR THE CHURCH

10:1—11:13 Whatever the difficulties in interpreting the details of this vision, the main points of God's assurance to the church are plain: the oath sworn by the mighty angel assures the church that "the Lord is not slow about his promise as some count slowness" (2 Ptr 3:9), that He will fulfill all that He has promised (10:1-3). The bitter scroll eaten by the prophet is the renewal of his prophetic commission and assures the church that she shall not lack the guidance of the prophetic Word in the time of the third great woe (10:8-11). The vision of the measured temple assures the true church of God's protection and warns the church against compromise: the false church will perish (11:1-2). The church's task and destiny in the last days is pictured in the career of the two witnesses who call mankind to repentance *(sackcloth,* 11:3) with all the power of an Elijah and a Moses, in their defeat by the beast from the bottomless pit, in their triumphant ascent into heaven. (11:3-13)

10:1 The *rainbow* indicates that the *mighty angel,* for all his blinding majesty and terrifying voice, is a messenger of the covenant God of mercy. (Cf. 4:3 note)

10:4 *Seal up what the seven thunders have said.* For the seven thunders as a manifestation of "the God of glory" cf. Ps 29. God remains sovereignly free in His revelation; the prophet is permitted to record not everything but what the church needs to know, and what the church needs to know is contained in the angel's oath, 5-7.

10:7 *The mystery of God* is God's whole purpose for the world, to be known only by His revelation as it interprets His royal reign in history, moving toward His gracious goal. (Cf. Dn 2)

Announced, literally "told as good news." The *trumpet* of the *seventh angel* ushers in the third woe (8-11; cf. 11:14) for the impenitent but brings the good news of God's fulfilled purpose to the faithful.

10:8-11 For the taking and eating of the scroll as descriptive of the prophet's inspiration cf. Eze 2:8—3:3; Jer 15:16. The prophet can only receive the word from God; but once he has received it, it becomes a part of him. The receiving of the word is *sweet,* for the prophet is thus admitted into personal communion with God; it is *bitter* because the prophet is compelled to pronounce judgment on a rebellious world and the unfaithful church.

10:8 The *scroll* is *open* because the Lamb has opened the seals of God's book (ch. 5), and His secret has become an "open secret" since the coming of Christ.

10:9 The *scroll* is *little* as contrasted to the scroll in the hand of God in ch. 5, which contained the whole counsel of God; its content is confined to God's FINAL action in dealing with "Peoples and nations and tongues and kings" (11), either the material of 11:1-13, or all of ch. 11, or more probably the remainder of Rv.

11:1-2 The *temple* is not the Jerusalem temple, destroyed 26 years before the writing of Rv, but signifies the church (cf. 1 Co 3:16; 2 Co 6:16). The *measuring* of the temple marks it off as God's property, sacrosanct and protected. The *court outside the temple* is the false or apostate church abandoned by God, as the ancient temple was when Israel went after false gods. (Cf. Is 63:10-19)

Forty-two months (cf. 1,260 days, 3), the 3½ years of the terrible reign of Antiochus IV (168 to 165 B. C.), when the temple was desecrated, became the measure for the duration of a period of oppression and affliction in Judaic tradition. (Cf. Dn 7:25; 12:7)

11:3 *Sackcloth,* sign of penitential mourning (cf. Jon 3:5-10; Mt 11:21). They preach repentance.

11:4 *Two olive trees . . . two lampstands.* The imagery is freely adapted from Zch 4:3, 11-14 (where the reference is to the political and the priestly leader of God's people) and marks the two witnesses as authorized representatives of God, active in His service, *stand before.* (Cf. 8:2 note)

11:5-6 The power of the two witnesses (the witnessing church) is portrayed in terms that recall the mighty deeds of Elijah (2 K 1:10, 12; K 17:1) and Moses. (Ex 7:17, 19)

11:7 The *beast,* Antichrist, or the antichristian power. (Cf. ch. 13)

11:8 *Great city,* apparently the same as the "holy city" of v. 2, the apostate people of God which has (like the Jerusalem that *crucified* the *Lord* Jesus) become the enemy of God and must therefore be called by names like *Sodom* and *Egypt,* typical opponents of the divine will.

Allegorically, or "spiritually"; that is, those enlightened by the Spirit know its true name and nature.

11:9 The refusal of burial adds degradation to defeat. (Cf. Jer 8:2; 22:18-19)

11:13 *Gave glory to . . . God,* by confessing their sin (cf. Jos 7:10; Jn 9:24). Here, in the word of assurance to the church, it becomes clear that there will be exceptions to the general rule of man's impenitence (cf. 9:20-21); through His witnessing church God will "by all means save some." (1 Co 9:22)

11:14-18 The *third woe* is not pictured at all; the *voices in heaven* and the *twenty-four elders* in their songs anticipate the outcome of that final woe; the manifest, uncontested, and eternal reign of the *Lord and of his Christ,* when divine judgment and grace have done their work.

11:17 *Who art and who wast.* There is no longer any need to say "who art to come." The promise of His coming has been fulfilled, the prayer of the church has been answered.

11:19 *Temple . . . opened . . . ark of his covenant . . . seen.* God is no longer hidden from men's eyes in the Holy of Holies enthroned unseen upon the *ark. His covenant* promise ("I will be your God") is forever fulfilled, and those that love Him see Him face to face.

12:1—22:7 To see and grasp fully the futility of any attempt at compromise, the church must be given eyes to see the satanic background of history, to look into the depths beneath the apparently solid surface, solid only to the unwarned, unrepentant, unexpectant eye. The deeper reality of history is the irreconcilable conflict between God and Satan, between God's kingdom and the satanic counter-kingdom. This history, hinted at in the first half of Rv (2:9; 3:9; 2:13, 24; 9:1, 11; 11:7), is the subject of the second half.

12:1—22:5 LAST FOUR VISIONS: CHRIST AND THE POWERS OF DARKNESS

12:1—14:20 Fourth Vision: Anti-Trinity and Christ

12:1—14:20 The birth of the Messianic Child and the history of His persecuted church are nothing less than the final working out of the primal struggle that began with the fall of man in Gn 3. This history is the history of the assault of the enemy, furious but futile, on the Messiah and the Messianic people of God. (Ch. 12)

Satan is the imitator of God (cf. 2 Co 11:3-4, 13-15); he constitutes himself an anti-trinity (dragon, first beast, second beast) in opposition to the Father, Son, and Spirit. The satanic will becomes incarnate in historical powers which threaten to make the world too small for the people of God; Jesus' promise that the meek shall inherit the earth seems an uncertain word over against the might of these overwhelming and seductive powers. (Ch. 13)

But the ultimate triumph of Christ and His church is not called into question. The 144,000 faithful who have His Father's name inscribed on their brows sing their new song of victory on Mount Zion. Somber angelic voices call all men to repentance as they proclaim an eternal Gospel, announce the fall of Babylon (the anti-church, cf. ch. 17), and pronounce a curse on all who submit to the beast (the Antichrist). The golden-crowned Son of Man is seen reaping His ripened harvest and executing the bloody judgment of His vintage on the earth. (Ch. 14)

12:1, 3 The word *portent,* occurring here for the first time in Rv, marks the beginning of a new series of visions.

Woman symbolizes the people of God from whom the Messiah sprang; her splendor *(sun, moon, stars)* is from the heavenly world, God's gift to her. (By contrast, the anti-church Babylon, pictured as a harlot, has her ornaments from the lower world, the earth and the sea, 17:4). The *twelve stars* recall the 12 tribes. (Cf. 7:4-8)

12:2 *Pangs of birth.* Cf. Mi 5:3.

12:3-4 *Dragon,* "that ancient serpent . . . Devil and Satan" (9), killer of men and father of the lie (Jn 8:44), is the inveterate opponent by nature of the Messianic Child whose coming means God's grace and truth for men (Jn 1:17); he is poised to destroy Him. The *ten horns* indicate his great power, the *seven diadems* his claim to royalty as "ruler of this world." (Jn 14:30)

12:4 *Swept down a third of the stars.* His terrible power has made inroads even on the heavenly world (cf. Dn 8:10). These fallen stars are the dragon's angels. (7)

12:5 The verse is practically a quotation of Ps

2:7-9 and definitely identifies the Child as the Messiah. The whole victorious career of the Messiah is summed up in the words *was caught up to God and to his throne;* Jesus similarly sums up His whole life's work in its triumphant conclusion: "I go to the Father." (Jn 16:10)

12:6 The Christ is at the right hand of God; the church is still in *the wilderness,* on earth far from her true and lasting home, like Israel far from Canaan. There God provides for her, as He did for Israel, until the time of affliction (1,260 days, cf. 11:1-2 note) is past. (The story of the woman is continued in 12:13-17.)

12:7-12 The church lives, imperilled and apparently helpless, in the wilderness; but God's saints can look forward confidently to ultimate victory and security and can face the prospect of martyrdom (11) and the last wrathful attack of the devil with serenity, for they know they face a defeated enemy. The decisive battle has been fought. Satan has lost his place as *accuser* of men before God (10), for the *blood* of the Lamb has atoned for man's guilt. The great and decisive reality now is, not the devil's short season of wrath but *the salvation and the power and kingdom of our God and the authority of his Christ.*

12:10 *Accuser.* He has no power over man because man has found in the man Jesus (who comprehends all men in Himself by His love) a love for God and an obedience to Him which the seducer could not destroy even in death. Jesus could say concerning him as He went to the cross: "He has no power over me." (Jn 14:30)

Our brethren. For the bond that unites angels and men, created by one God to serve Him as sons, cf. 22:8-9.

12:13-17 The church's position in the world wears a double aspect. She knows in faith that victory is hers; she HAS conquered by the blood of the Lamb (cf. 11). On the other hand, she knows of Satan's great wrath and has good cause for fear. The prophet's word of assurance to her is that the dragon cannot harm her, the God who led His ancient people safely through the sea and nourished them with manna in the wilderness will deliver her from the flood and will feed her.

12:14 *Time, and times, and half a time.* Still another way of expressing the 3½ years or 1,260 days. (Cf. Dn 7:25; Rv 11:1-2 note)

12:17 *The rest of her offspring.* The church appears as both inviolable and under attack. Therefore she is represented both by the *woman* and by *the rest of her offspring,* those whom Jesus claims as His brothers. (Heb. 2:11; cf. Ro 8:29)

13:1-18 As Satan is anti-God, so he has his anti-Christ, a world power in which his opposition to God becomes incarnate (the first *beast,* 1-10). As the Holy Spirit witnesses to Christ and glorifies Him (cf. Jn 15:36; 16:14), so there is a satanic anti-Spirit to witness to the Antichrist and to glorify him. *(Another beast,* 11-18)

13:1 *Beast rising out of the sea.* As the prophet looked out over the sea from Patmos (cf. 1:9), he looked toward Rome. Rome, the great world power with its deified emperor making a totalitarian claim on the loyalties of men, was the hostile world power confronting men in A. D. 96 and is the model for the beast as portrayed by the prophet. Its characteristic features reappear in subsequent history.

Ten horns, etc., point up the impressive, organized power of the Roman state.

Blasphemous name, e.g., the title favored by the emperor Domitian, "Lord and God."

13:2 Features that characterize successive world powers in Dn 7:1-6 are combined to characterize this world power.

13:3 *Mortal wound . . . healed.* The Antichrist is an imitation of the real Christ; he has apparently triumphed over death, like the slain Lamb. (Cf. 1:18; 5:6)

13:5 *Was given . . . was allowed.* Cf. 7, 14, 15. The use of the passive voice indicates that God remains in control of this wild satanic rebellion and sets limits to it *(forty-two months,* cf. 11:1-2 note). The reign of Antichrist is limited; He "who sits upon the throne and the Lamb" shall have "honor and glory and might for ever and ever." (5:13)

13:7 *War on the saints.* Cf. "on the rest of her offspring," 12:17 note.

13:8 *Book of life.* Cf. 3:5 note. Those *written . . . in the book of life* are God's elect, whom nothing and no one can separate from the love of God in Christ Jesus. (Cf. Ro 8:28-39)

13:10 Cf. Jer 15:1-2. The church's mission is to suffer and die (cf. 6:11), not to offer violent resistance *(slays with the sword).* But the allusion to Jer 15:1-2 indicates that another reading suggested by some ancient authorities may be preferable. That reading is: "If any one is TO BE SLAIN with the sword, with the sword he must be slain," repeating the idea of the first half of the verse.

13:11 *Beast . . . out of the earth.* When the prophet on Patmos looked landward, he looked toward Asia Minor, where the cult of the deified Roman emperor had its most avid practitioners and propagandists. There the anti-Spirit is doing his work of glorifying the Antichrist.

Lamb . . . dragon. Cf. Jesus' description of the false prophet, Mt 7:15. However "religious" he may sound, this spirit is unmistakably the spirit of the *dragon,* Satan.

13:14-15 *Allowed.* The anti-Spirit too remains under God's overruling control. (Cf. 13:5 note)

13:16-17 With his *mark* the beast claims men as completely as God makes men His own by His seal (7:3); by means of economic sanctions *(buy or sell),* he seeks to make men dependent on himself for their existence.

13:18 *Number of the beast* (666 or 616). Much ingenuity has been expended on the deciphering of this cryptic number, but no one solution has won general acceptance. It was probably used as a precautionary measure to prevent an utterance which could be construed as treasonable from falling into hostile Roman hands. The threefold six may indicate a threefold falling short of seven, the number of perfection; the anti-trinity is branded as a sorry imitation of the Trinity.

14:1-20 In God's mysterious governance of history the enemy has been "allowed to make war on the saints and to conquer them" (13:7); but the enemy's victory is as hollow as his claim to deity is false. Once more, just when the anti-trinity appears invincible, the suffering and dying church is assured of triumph: God's elect appear singing the new song that only they can know, the pure in heart, the redeemed who have not compromised with the satanic lie (1-5). Once more the church hears angelic voices announcing the impending judgment on all who have exchanged the truth of God for the lie of Babylon and the beast (6-11). Once more the church is permitted to behold the fearful alternative to the final harvest-home: the final vintage and the treading of the winepress of the wrath of God. (17-20)

14:1 *Mount Zion.* All that God has promised concerning His Anointed will come true; He WILL set His Anointed on His holy hill, in triumph over His enemies. (Ps 2:1-6)

His . . . and his Father's name written on their foreheads, not the mark of the beast. (Cf. 13:16; 14:9)

14:4 *Chaste* (virgins). For the virgin as a symbol of unsullied fidelity cf. 2 Co 11:2-3 and the contrast to the "impure passion" inspired by Babylon, 14:8, called "harlot" in 17:1, 5.

14:6-7 The fact that God still calls to men, His creatures, warning them not to repeat the sin of Adam by overleaping the boundary between creature and Creator (Gn 3), that is *gospel.*

14:8 *Babylon.* Cf. chs. 18—19.

14:10 *In the presence of . . . angels and . . . the Lamb.* This underscores the justice of their punishment; neither the angels through whom God warned and wooed them (6 ff.) nor the Lamb once slain for them will intercede for them.

14:13 *Henceforth,* from now and when they are being more and more sorely tried.

Their deeds follow them. They will be remembered in the judgment, when the books of men's lives lie opened before the Judge. (22:12; cf. Mt 25:31-46)

14:14 *One like a son of man,* Christ. (Cf. 1:13)

14:15 *Harvest.* For the harvest as the ingathering of God's people cf. Mt 9:37; Jn 4:35.

14:30 *Blood flowed.* The monstrous river of blood points to the monstrosity of the sin which provoked God's judgment on it.

15:1—16:21 Fifth Vision: The Seven Bowls

15:1—16:21 The mounting impiety of the world under satanic domination and the uttermost straits of the church call for the last judgmental blows of God within history before the Last Judgment, which concludes all history. These blows are represented by the outpouring of the seven bowls of wrath. For all their parallelism with the seven seals (chs. 4—7) and the seven trumpets (chs. 8—11), the bowls have a character of their own. They are related to the content of chs. 12—14 (15:2, 16:2, 10, 13, dragon, beast, false prophet = second beast) and 16:13, 19 points forward to the next unit (judgment on Babylon and the two beasts, chs. 17—19). Above all, these blows of God are characterized as climactic. There is a climactic stress on the fact that God's judgments are in the service of His redemptive will (15:3-8) and a climactic stress on the justice of God's judgmental action (15:3-4; 16:5-7). And the reaction of men is climactic; no longer are they merely desperate (6:15-17) or impenitent (9:20-21); they now cursed the God of heaven (16:9, 11, 21). A heavenly voice speaks a climactic word: *"It is done!"* (16:17)

15:1 *Another portent.* Cf. 12:1, 3. The birth of the Messiah, the dragon's attack on the Messianic Child, and the bowls of wrath are portents of the world's last days.

15:2-4 God had delivered His people from Egypt by acts of judgment on their oppressors. God's final deliverance is pictured in colors taken from that event, the Exodus. As of old, His people stand by the sea, victorious and free, and the *song of Moses* (Ex 15) is taken up into the *song of the Lamb,* which praises God the Deliverer, now revealed as the Deliverer not only of Israel but of *all nations.*

15:5 *Temple . . . opened.* The ministers of God's judgment proceed from the place where God wills to be graciously present among His people (Ex 40:34-38); His judgments subserve His mercy.

15:8 *Smoke . . . glory of God.* Cf. Is 6:4.

16:9 *Give him glory.* Cf. 11:13 note.

16:12-16 Only the assembling of the armies of the *kings of the whole world . . .* for *battle* is told here; the battle is pictured in 19:19-21.

16:12 *Euphrates.* Cf. 9:12-19 note.

16:13 *Like frogs.* The sense is obscure.

16:14 *The great day.* Cf. 6:17 "great day . . . of wrath."

16:15 *I am coming like a thief.* The voice of Christ (cf. Mt 24:43; Lk 12:39; Rv 3:3) is heard unexpectedly in warning. Even when His return is near, it will not seem near; the huge armies arrayed against God would rather seem to indicate that victory and the End are still far off. Hence His call to vigilance.

16:16 *Armageddon.* This *Hebrew* name can be rendered "hill of assembly" (cf. Is 14:13-14) or "His (God's) fruitful mountain," referring to Mount Zion, from which help comes for God's people (Jl 2:32; 3:16-17, 21). Some translate "Mountain of Megiddo," referring to Mount Carmel—the city Megiddo, lying six miles from the base of the mountain, had been the scene of the victory won against fearful odds over the Canaanites by Deborah and Barak (Ju 5:19). The idea would then be that God's final victory would be similarly unexpected and astonishing. But since Mount Carmel is nowhere else identified by reference to Mediggo, this interpretation, too, remains uncertain.

17:1—19:10 Sixth Vision: The Fate of Babylon, the Anti-Church

17:1—19:10 The announced theme of this vision is "the judgment of the great harlot"

(17:1). In 17:1-18 the nature of this antichristian power, especially the connection between the harlot and the beast, is described and God's intention to destroy the harlot is announced. The next section (18:1-24) predicts and describes the judgment: Heavenly voices are heard proclaiming the doom of Babylon and bidding God's people to escape from her doom (1-8); kings, merchants, and shipmasters are heard lamenting the fall of the mighty and luxurious city (9-20); and a mighty angel is seen hurling a huge stone into the sea, an action symbolizing the overthrow of the city "drunk with the blood of the saints and . . . martyrs of Jesus" (21-24). The final section (19:1-10) brings the response of God's saints, a *great multitude in heaven,* to the overthrow of the persecuting power: a triple hallelujah of praise to the God who has by His judgment delivered them and invited them to the pure marriage supper of the Lamb.

17:1-18 THE HARLOT AND THE BEAST

17:1-18 The church has been (12:1 ff.) and will again be (19:7-8; 21:2, 9) pictured as a woman; the anti-church, too, appears under the figure of a woman, but a woman who is the extreme opposite of both personifications of the church. The woman of ch. 12 is adorned with ornaments of heaven (sun, moon, stars); the harlot is bedizened with ornaments taken from the earth and sea *(purple, scarlet, gold, jewels, pearls).* The woman becomes the mother of the Messiah for the world's salvation (12:5). The harlot is like Babylon, the ancient enemy of God's people who dominated the world and corrupted what it dominated; she is *mother of harlots and of earth's abominations* (17:5). The bride is bound to Christ, in fellowship with God; the woman seated on the beast is a harlot, without ties or loyalties, alienated from God and persecutor of God's people. The woman has only God for her Protector in the wilderness (12:6) and the bride belongs to the unseen Christ who has been taken up to the throne of God (12:5); the harlot has wealth, luxury, and the visible and palpable power of the beast and the kings of the earth for her support.

That power is an uncanny imitation of God and Christ, with a mysteriously persistent vitality *(was, and is not, and is to ascend,* 8; cf. 1:4,17-18) which casts a spell on men (8, 13). But it is a power massed in opposition to the Lamb (14) and so is doomed to *go to perdition* (8, 11). The beast and its subservient powers will in the end carry out God's purpose and fulfill His *words* (17); they *will hate the harlot* (as irrationally as they once were infatuated by her) and destroy her.

17:1 *Many waters.* This feature, taken from the situation of ancient Babylon, is interpreted allegorically in 15 as peoples, multitudes, tongues.

17:2 The *kings of the earth* have purchased her favors by submitting to her rule (cf. 13) and have been corrupted by her.

17:3 *Blasphemous names.* Cf. 13:1 note.

Heads . . . horns. Cf. 9, 10, 12.

17:4 *Cup . . . of abominations.* Perhaps a contrast to the "cup of blessing" (1 Co 10:16) of the Lord's Supper is implied.

17:5 *Name of mystery.* Cf. 7. Only the eye enlightened by God's revelation can see this opulent, voluptuous, and powerful figure for what she is: enemy of the people of God *(Babylon)* and corrupter of mankind *(mother of harlots,* etc.)

17:6 *Drunk with the blood.* She revels in bloodshed; Christians would remember how the emperor Nero had made his massacre of Christians in A. D. 64 a "circus entertainment," as a Roman historian calls it.

I marveled greatly. He had expected to see judgment (1), not this voluptuous and mighty figure, sure of herself. (Cf. 18:7)

17:7-18 The *mystery of the woman, and of the beast* remains something of a mystery. Rome *(seven mountains,* 9; *great city,* 18), a succession of Roman emperors *(seven kings,* 10), and kings who had become subjects of the Roman Empire *(ten kings,* 12-13) constitute the background and furnish the colors for the prophecy. So much is clear. Not so clear is the utterance of 11; the *eighth* seems to point to the return of a Roman emperor who has already appeared in history but will reappear. Perhaps the figure of Nero is the historical point of contact here. Nero had embodied the persecuting power of Rome to a terrible degree. He had died in mysterious circumstances, and popular belief held that he was hidden somewhere in the East and would one day return. The persecuting power which Nero represented will appear again, in more terrible form, for the eighth is "abnormal," breaking the limits of "normal history," which can be structured in a scheme of sevens. This is the final concentration of the antichristian power doomed to go to perdition (11). The harlot Babylon is both dependent on this power (3) and destroyed by it (16). The anti-church has its seeds of destruction within itself. The point of 12 remains obscure.

17:17 The *words of God* are the real, enduring, and decisive power in history. (Cf. Is 40:6-8)

18:1-24 "FALLEN, FALLEN IS BABYLON THE GREAT!"

18:1-24 Cf. the paraphrase at 17:1—19:10. The judgment on Babylon is the most broadly depicted; men needed full assurance that the great city, despite all its appearance of solid permanence, could not endure.

18:2 *Dwelling place of demons.* Demons were thought to haunt desolate places. Cf. the demoniacs "who lived among the tombs." (Mk 5:3)

18:4 *Another voice,* that of Christ, since He refers to *my people* and is distinguished from God. (5, 8)

19:1-10 "HALLEUJAH! FOR THE . . . ALMIGHTY REIGNS"

19:1-10 Cf. the paraphrase at 17:1—19:10.

19:7 *Bride.* Cf. 21:2, 9. The church is here described under a new figure, since the church's union and communion with the Lamb (cf. 9) is to be stressed.

19:8 *It was granted her to be clothed with fine linen . . . the righteous deeds of the saints.* All that the church has, including righteous deeds, is the gift and work of God (Cf. Ph 2:12-13 note). Therefore the dead are in the last judgment "judged . . . by what they had done." (20:12)

19:10 *Worship.* Overwhelmed by the greatness of the revelation which the angel (9) has mediated (cf. 17:1), the prophet offers to give him divine honor. The angel's refusal shows how the line between the Author of revelation and the agents of revelation is carefully safeguarded.

For the testimony of Jesus is the spirit of prophecy. The angel is fellow servant of other (human) witnesses. Jesus speaks by them through the Spirit of truth. (Cf. Jn 14:26; 16:14)

19:11—22:5 Seventh Vision: Judgment and Renewal

19:11-22:5 The satanic opponents of Christ appeared in the order: dragon, first and second beast, the harlot Babylon. They are judged and destroyed in the opposite order: Babylon (chs. 17—18), first and second beast (19:11-21), the dragon (20:1-10). When the dead have been judged and the "last enemy" (1 Co 15:26), death, has been destroyed (20:11-15), then the new world of God appears, the new heaven and new earth, the new Jerusalem, full of splendor, light, and life, wherein God's communion with His own is fully and forever consummated. (21:1—22:5)

19:11-21 CHRIST TRIUMPHANT OVER THE TWO BEASTS

19:11-21 The true Rider on the white horse (whose gruesome parody appeared at the opening of the first seal, 6:2) now appears. Four names express the fullness of His saving significance. He is *Faithful and True* (11), the Fulfiller of all the promises of God. He *has a name . . . which no one knows but himself,* expressing the mystery of His oneness with God, which makes His presence the very presence of God among men (12). He is called *The Word of God* (13), God's uttered light, life, grace, and truth for men (cf. Jn 1:4, 14). His name is *King of kings and Lord of lords* (16), before whom no Antichrist or antichristian emperors can stand. (17:21)

19:12 *Eyes are like a flame.* Cf. 1:13-16 note.

Many diadems. He is Lord of all.

19:13 *Robe dipped in blood.* He is marked as Victor from the outset. Cf. Is 63:1-6, which is again echoed in 15 ("tread the wine press").

19:14 *The armies of heaven* appear, not as armed for battle but in the robes of victory; so sure is the outcome of the battle.

19:15 *Mouth . . . sharp sword . . . rod of iron.* Echoes of Messianic prophecies. (Is 11:4; Ps 1:8)

Tread the wine press. Cf. Is 63:1-6. "The Father . . . has given all judgment to the Son." (Jn 5:22)

19:17-18 The angel's invitation to this *great supper of God* is the grim counterpart to the beatitude on those "invited to the marriage supper of the Lamb." (9)

19:19 *Armies gathered.* The attack planned in 16:12-16 is now to be executed.

19:20 *The beast was captured.* That is the whole description of the battle; the attack was doomed to failure.

False prophet describes the second beast according to his activity as spokesman for the first beast. (Cf. 13:11 ff.)

Lake of fire, the place of eternal punishment. Cf. Mt 25:41 and the description of Gehenna, Mk 9:43, 47-48.

20:1-10 THE OVERTHROW OF THE DRAGON

20:1-10 The overthrow of the dragon is accomplished in two stages. The first stage, the binding of Satan for 1,000 years (1-3), corresponds to the defeat of Satan at the birth of the Messiah (12:7-9). The 1,000 years are the era of the hidden but real reign of Christ, the time of His hidden triumph (hidden under the cross) and the time of the hidden triumph of His church, hidden under martyrdom but in reality a life and reign with Christ (4-6). The hidden triumph becomes a manifest triumph at the end of the 1,000 years, when Satan is permitted to make his last desperate assault and is consigned to everlasting torment in the lake of fire.

20:1 *Bottomless pit.* Cf. 9:1, 11; 11:7; 17:8.

20:2 *Bound him.* Cf. Jesus' word concerning the binding of the "strong man" (Satan) by His (Jesus') coming and the manifestation of that victory in His power over the demons, Mt 12:28-29. Jesus speaks also of Satan as fallen (Lk 10:17-19), cast out (Jn 12:31-32), and judged (Jn 16:11) by His, Jesus', faithful and mighty ministry.

20:3 *Deceive the nations no more.* Since the truth of God has appeared in Jesus (Jn 1:17) to unmask and overcome the satanic lie (Jn 8:44), no one NEED be deceived by him any more; only those who have "refused to love the truth" are condemned to be subject to the "strong delusions" of Satan, to "believe what is false" (2 Th 2:9-11). Cf. also 19:20, where it is said that those who "had received the mark of the beast," i.e., submitted to him, were deceived by the "signs" worked by the "false prophet."

20:4 *Thrones . . . judgment.* The language echoes Dn 7:9, 22, 26-27 and recalls the substance of Daniel's vision: "the Ancient of Days came, and judgment was given for the saints of the Most High, and the time came when the saints received the kingdom." (Dn 7:22)

The souls (cf. 6:9 "souls of those . . . slain," etc.) are those who have lost their life for Christ's sake and now find it in a life and reign with Christ, according to His promise. (Mt 16:25; Jn 12:25-26)

20:5 *The rest of the dead,* those resurrected for judgment. (Cf. 12)

The first resurrection. Their life and reign with Christ NOW is an anticipation of the resurrection and the life of the world to come. Cf. Jn 5:24-25; 12:26, 32; and Jn 11:23-26, where

Jesus directs Martha's thoughts away from "the resurrection at the last day" and turns them to Himself as the present resurrection and life.

20:6 *The second death,* defined in 14 as the eternal torment of "the lake of fire."

They shall reign. It is probably significant that the words "on earth" contained in the promise to the priestly people in 5:10 are not repeated here. This reign during the 1,000 years is not yet the ultimate reign on earth, the new earth of the world to come.

20:8 *Gog* appears in Eze 38—39 as the last great enemy of the people of God, destroyed by God in battle. *Magog* is, in Eze, his land; whether the term is here used in the same way ("Gog and his land, his people") or whether Magog is also a personal name, can hardly be made out.

20:9 *Camp of the saints and beloved ciy* (cf. 21:2, 9) both designate God's people, the church.

Fire came . . . consumed. Again (cf. 19:20) there is really no battle. The already defeated foe (20:1-3) is destroyed.

20:11-15 THE LAST JUDGMENT

20:11 *Throne,* symbol of judgment. (Cf. 4 and Mt 19:28)

Earth and sky fled away. The present heaven and earth, marred by man's sin (Ro 8:20-22), cannot stand before the Judge as they are. They must disappear in their present form ("The FORM of this world is passing away," 1 Co 7:31) to make way for the new, transfigured heaven and earth. (21:1)

20:12 *Books . . . book of life.* Both the book of life and the books which record men's deeds *(what they had done)* are significant in the Judgment. Man is saved and acquitted solely by the grace of God, which has chosen him freely and inscribed his name in the book of life; but the book of each man's life will show whether a man has really received that grace and has not received it in vain, whether God's gracious Word has by its power brought forth fruit for God. This same double emphasis on God's free grace and man's responsibility under that grace appears in Jesus' portrayal of the Last Judgment, Mt 25:31-46 ("Come, O blessed of my Father, inherit the kingdom PREPARED FOR YOU," and "You DID it to me"; cf. Ph 2:12-13).

20:14 *Lake of fire.* Cf. Mt 25:41: "the eternal fire PREPARED FOR THE DEVIL and his angels." When man opposes God, he makes the devil's doom his own.

21:1—22:5 THE NEW WORLD OF GOD

21:1—22:5 The new world of God is restored creation *(new heaven and a new earth,* 1). And it is consummated communion between God and man; therefore it is a *holy city,* a new city of God, *Jerusalem,* united with the *Lamb* as His *Bride* (2, 9). There God dwells with men and shall be their everlasting Comforter (4). The promise made to the Messiah, "I will be his father, and he shall be my son" (2 Sm 7:14), will be fulfilled for all who dwell in the holy city (7). The appointments and dimensions of the new Jerusalem are twelve and multiples of twelve; the city is the perfect embodiment of the community-creating will of God who chose *the twelve tribes* of Israel and of the Lamb who appointed the *twelve apostles* (12, 14). There is *no temple in the city* (symbol and embodiment of God's communion with His people), for the city has more than the temple—the immediate presence of the *Lord God the Almighty and the Lamb* (22). The new community of God embraces all *nations* (24-26); men of all nations shall *worship* Him together, *see his face,* and bear His *name* upon their brows (22:3-4). And all *shall reign* with Him *for ever and ever* (22:5). All that is sad and ugly and false is banished from this city (21:4, 8, 27; 22:3); the new world in which righteousness dwells is full of brilliant beauty (gems!), full of *light* (21:23,24,25), God's own light (22:5), full of life *(water of life,* 21:6; 22:1; *tree of life,* 22:2), and perfect health. (22:2)

21:1 *The sea was no more.* The ancient world dreaded the sea for its violence and treachery (cf. Ps 107:23-28; Is 57:20; Eze 28:8). That God should be Lord even over this untamable element was cause for special awe and wonder (Ps 46:1-3). The dread of a world turned against man will disappear in God's new world.

21:16 *Length and breadth and height are equal,* like that of the Holy of Holies in the temple (1 K 6:20). The whole city has become the innermost sanctuary of God's dwelling.

21:17 *Man's measure, that is, an angel's.* Since the angel is a "fellow servant" of men (19:10; 22:9), he measures with the same standard. Why this should be expressly mentioned here remains obscure.

21:24, 26 All that is bright and best of creation returns home to the Creator, to His glory.

22:6-21 Conclusion

22:6-21 The book closes, as it began (1:4-5), as a letter, a personal urgent word of Christ to His church; the concluding benediction is one commonly used by Paul in his letters (e.g., 1 Co 16:23; 2 Co 13:13; 2 Th 3:18). Three times Jesus' urgent word is heard: *I am coming soon* (7, 12, 20). He comes, the Revealer, whose Word must be heard and heeded (7). He comes, the Recompense, the First and Last who has spoken the first word of grace and will speak the last word of judgment (12-13). He comes, Jesus the incarnate Christ *(root and offspring of David),* the Dawn of salvation *(morning star)* in whom His people have already tasted the powers of the world to come (16). Three times the word of longing response is heard, *Come.* The Spirit-filled church *(Spirit and the Bride,* 17) cries, *Come;* the prophet John prays, *Amen. Come, Lord Jesus* (20); and every one who hears the prophetic word is bidden to join in that prayer (17). When the church, endowed with "eternal comfort and good hope" (2 Th 2:16) through the grace of the Lord Jesus, has become the longing church, the purpose of Rv has been accomplished. The longing church can in the vitality of her hope live in obedience to the Word of God, without adding thereto or taking therefrom (7, 18-19); can in holy fear recognize the fearful alternatives to her appointed way and shun them (11, 15); can live a life of continual repentance by washing her robes (14) and drinking of the freely given waters of life (17) and so come at last to the tree of life and enter the holy city by the gates. (14)

22:7 Cf. 1:3.

22:8-9 Cf. 19:10 note.

22:11 *Let the evildoer,* etc. The issues are clear, by the light of the revelation given; a man may and must choose his way. No one can plead ignorance. The beatitude of 14 and the invitation of 17b make it clear that repentance is still possible; the *filthy* can become clean and the water of life is available without price for the *evil* man who turns from his ways.

22:15 *Dogs* were considered unclean animals; the OT uses the term *dog* of a sodomite. (Dt 23:18)

22:16 *Root and . . . offspring of David.* Cf. Is 11:1.

Star. Cf. Nm 24:17.

22:18-19 Cf Dt 4:2; 13:1; 29:20.

Appendix I
OLD TESTAMENT CHRONOLOGY

DATE (B.C.)	EVENT
c. 2100	Patriarchs in Canaan
c. 1700	Israelites in Egypt
c. 1447	Exodus from Egypt
1406	Joshua as leader
	Conquest
	Division of kingdom
1376	Elders of Israel
1366	Oppression by Mesopotamians
1358	Othniel—deliverance and rest forty years
1318	Oppression by Moab
1301	Ehud—deliverance and peace for 80 years
1221	Oppression by Canaanites
1201	Deborah and Barak—deliverance and 40-year peace
1161	Oppression by Midianites
1154	Gideon—deliverance and 40-year peace
1114	Abimelech—king for three years
1111-1105	Jephthah—6-year rule ending oppression
	Samson's judgeship about 20 years during this period
1066	(?) Eli
1046	(?) Samuel
1026	(?) Saul anointed Israel's first king.
1011	David
971	Solomon
931	Division of the Kingdom into Israel (North) and Judah (South)

	KINGS OF ISRAEL	KINGS OF JUDAH
931	*Jeroboam Dynasty*	
	Jeroboam	Rehoboam (931)
	Nadab	Abijah (913)
909	*Baasha Dynasty*	
	Baasha	Asa (910)
	Elah	
	(Zimri)	
885	*Omri Dynasty*	
	Omri	
	Ahab	Jehoshaphet (872)
	Ahaziah	
	Joram	Jehoram (848)
841	*Jehu Dynasty*	Ahaziah (841)
	Jehu	Athaliah (841)
		Joash (835)
	Jehoahaz	Amaziah (796)
	Jehoash	Uzziah (791)
	Jeroboam II	
	Zechariah	Jotham (750)

752	*Last Kings*	
	Shallum	
	Menahem	
	Pekahiah	Ahaz (735)
	Pekah	
	Hoshea	Hezekiah (728)
722	Fall of Samaria to Assyrians	
		Manasseh (696)
		Amon (642)
		Josiah (640)
		Jehoahaz (609)
		Jehoiakim (608)
		Jehoiachin (597)
		Zedekiah (597)
586	Fall of Jerusalem to Babylonian King Nebuchadnezzar	
539	Edict of Persian King Cyrus and return of the Jews	
522	Zerubbabel	
	Haggai,	
	Zechariah	
515	Jerusalem Temple completed	
457	Ezra	
444	Nehemiah	
331	Egypt conquered and Alexandria founded	
323	Alexander's death at age of 33	
320—198	Ptolemies gain control of Palestine	
198—143	Seleucids in control of Palestine	
175—164	Antiochus IV became Syrian king	
168—143	Maccabean Revolt, ending in independence for Jews	
142—63	Palestine under rule of Maccabean (Hasmonean) family	
63	Pompey assumes control of Palestine for Rome	
40	Herod made king of Palestine	

Appendix II
NEW TESTAMENT CHRONOLOGY *

DATE (A.D.)	EVENT
30	Pentecost; Birthday of the New Testament Church
32	Death of Stephen and Conversion of St. Paul
43	Founding of Gentile Church at Antioch; Paul Summoned to Antioch by Barnabas
44	Death of James the Son of Zebedee
c. 45	EPISTLE OF ST. JAMES
46—48	St. Paul's First Missionary Journey
48	EPISTLE TO THE GALATIANS
49	Apostolic Council
49—51	St. Paul's Second Missionary Journey
50 (early)	1 THESSALONIANS; 50 (summer) 2 THESSALONIANS
52—56	St. Paul's Third Missionary Journey
55 (spring)	1 CORINTHIANS; 55 (summer or fall) 2 CORINTHIANS
56 (early)	ROMANS
56—58	St. Paul's Caesarean Imprisonment
58—59	St. Paul's Voyage to Rome
59—61	St. Paul's Roman Imprisonment
59—61	COLOSSIANS, PHILEMON, EPHESIANS, PHILIPPIANS (The Captivity Letters)
50—60	GOSPEL ACCORDING TO ST. MATTHEW
c. 60	GOSPEL ACCORDING TO ST. MARK
62—63	1 TIMOTHY
63	TITUS
64	Fire in Rome. Neronian Persecution
65—67	2 TIMOTHY
61—62	1 PETER
62 (?)	2 PETER
65—69	GOSPEL ACCORDING TO ST. LUKE. THE BOOK OF ACTS
60—70	JUDE
65—70	HEBREWS
70	Fall of Jerusalem
90—100	GOSPEL ACCORDING TO ST. JOHN 1, 2, 3 JOHN
95	REVELATION OF ST. JOHN

* From *The Word of the Lord Grows,* © 1961, Concordia Publishing House, pp. ix-x.

Appendix III
THE KINGS AND PROPHETS OF ISRAEL *

REIGN (B.C.)	KING	PROPHET †	
931—910	Jeroboam	Ahijah	
910—909	Nadab		
909—886	Baasha		
886—885	Elah		
885	Zimri		
885—874	Omri		
874—853	Ahab	Elijah	
		"	Micaiah
853—852	Ahaziah	"	Elisha
852—841	Jehoram	"	"
			"
			"
841—814	Jehu		"
			"
814—798	Jehoahaz		"
798—782	Jehoash		"
			Jonah
793—753	Jeroboam II	*Amos*	"
		Hosea	
753	Zachariah	"	
752	Shallum	"	
752—741	Menahem	"	
741—739	Pekahiah	"	
739—731	Pekah		
		Oded	
731—722	Hoshea		
	Fall of Samaria 722		

* From *The Books of the Old Testament,* © 1977, Concordia Publishing House, pp. 122-23.
†Italics represent authors of Old Testament books by that name.

Appendix IV
THE KINGS AND PROPHETS OF JUDAH *

REIGN (B.C.)	KING	PROPHET †		
931—913	Rehoboam	Shemaiah		
913—910	Abijah			
910—869	Asa	Azariah		
		Hanani		
		Jehu		
872—848	Jehoshaphat	Jahaziel		
		Eliezer		
848—841	Jehoram	*Obadiah*		
841	Ahaziah			
841—835	Athaliah	(Jehoiada)		
835—796	Joash	Zechariah		
		Joel		
796—767	Amaziah			
791—740	Uzziah			
		Isaiah		
750—732	Jotham	"	*Micah*	
735—716	Ahaz			
		"		
728—687	Hezekiah	"	*Nahum*	
696—642	Manasseh		"	
642—640	Amon		*Habakkuk*	
640—609	Josiah	*Zephaniah*		
			Huldah	
		Jeremiah		
		(Lamentations)		
609	Jehoahaz	"		
608—597	Jehoiakim	"	*Daniel*	
597	Jehoiachin	"	"	*Ezekiel*
597—586	Zedekiah	"	"	"
	Fall of Jerusalem	"	"	"
	586 B.C.	"	"	"
	Restoration—536 B.C.		"	

After the Restoration *Haggai/Zechariah* 520, *Malachi* 400 B.C.

* From *The Books of the Old Testament,* © 1977, Concordia Publishing House, pp. 122-23.
†Italics represent authors of Old Testament books by that name.

Appendix V
OVERVIEW OF OLD TESTAMENT MESSIANIC PROPHECY *

The entire Old Testament is a development of the one theme that the Son of God will come to earth to redeem the *world* from sin. The first assertion of this is made when God tells the serpent in the presence of Adam and Eve that the seed of the woman will bruise the serpent's, or rather the devil's, head. Thereafter the prophecies become more and more explicit. God chose the *Hebrew people,* descendants of Abraham, for this specific purpose. Out of them came the Messiah, the One through whom all the peoples of the earth should be blessed. Thus the Hebrew people are the center of Old Testament history, the ones with whom God makes His *covenant.* Through Jacob, the grandson of Abraham, God narrowed the Messianic prophecy to the *tribe of Judah.* Four hundred years later God said through Moses that it would be "another Prophet" like unto him. The whole system of Jewish sacrifices also pointed to the coming sacrifice which the Messiah was to bring for the sins of the world.

One thousand years after God spoke to Abraham, He narrowed the prophecy still more by saying that from the tribe of Judah it would be the *family of David.* From that time on to the close of the Old Testament, the central interest is in David's family. The first form that God's covenant promise to David took was the promise of an *eternal throne* for David and his family. Then came a long line of prophets, explaining that the promises to the Davidic family of an everlasting dynasty would find their culmination in One Great King, who Himself would live forever and establish an *everlasting kingdom.* The *Psalms of David* abound in hints and prophecies of the coming King: His deity, His humiliation and suffering, His resurrection, His eternal priesthood, His conquering might, His endless universal righteous reign, and the immortal bliss of His redeemed people.

Two hundred years later *Joel* paints a beautiful picture of the Gospel age when by the Holy Spirit people from every nation would be brought to God. About this time *Jonah* was sent on his errand of mercy to Nineveh. Earlier *Obadiah* had prophesied the doom of Edom because it opposed Israel, God's chosen people. *Amos,* when the throne of David was falling and when it looked as if God's promises were coming to naught, insisted that the kingdom would be revived and yet be supreme in the world. *Hosea,* about the same time, in the days of Israel's apostasy (adultery), was certain a remnant of Israel would remain true and God would be acknowledged by Gentiles also.

Isaiah, three hundred years after David, when David's kingdom lay low, prophesied that the family of David would persist and a Wonderful Child would be born who would inherit the throne of David. As Jehovah's Servant, He would endure severe humiliation and suffering for man, and then live and rule forever. *Micah,* contemporary with Isaiah, said the Wonderful Child would be born in Bethlehem.

About a hundred years later *Nahum* comforted God's people by announcing the doom of Nineveh. *Zephaniah* announced judgment on a number of idolatrous nations but promised a remnant of Judah would be hid by God and saved. *Habakkuk* was certain Jehovah's glory would yet cover the earth, though all seemed dark at that time. *Jeremiah,* while David's kingdom was falling and God's people were being scattered, announced that God's promises are irrevocable. Therefore the covenant with David could not be broken and

God would yet accomplish through the family of David what He said He would through the Righteous Branch to be born into that family.

Ezekiel, in a foreign land, justified to the captive people the ways of God in permitting the captivity and saw visions of a reborn nation, an ideal King and an ideal temple, symbolizing the Savior and the New Testament church. *Daniel,* contemporary with Ezekiel, counselor to the kings of Babylon and Persia, predicted the course of empires from his days to the time when the "Anointed One," the Prince, would appear. *Haggai* and *Zechariah,* back again in Jerusalem, urged the people to rebuild the temple and pointed forward to the far grander House of God (New Testament church) to be built by the coming Davidic King, the "desire of nations." Zechariah abounded in specific Messianic prophecies. *Malachi* closed the Old Testament by stating that the Messiah would be ushered in by a prophet like Elijah.

The Old Testament: Book by Book

GENESIS: Creation; flood; Abraham; Isaac; Jacob; Joseph.
EXODUS: Israel called out of Egypt and consecrated.
LEVITICUS: Sacrifices; priesthood; purifications; festivals.
NUMBERS: Israel's journey from Sinai to Moab.
DEUTERONOMY: Moses' farewell rehearsal of Jewish laws and history.
JOSHUA: The conquest and division of Canaan.
JUDGES: Alternate oppressions and deliverances in first years in Canaan.
RUTH: Beginning of Messianic family of David: Boaz-Ruth-Obed-Jesse.
1 SAMUEL: Israel under Samuel, Saul, and David.
2 SAMUEL: The reign of David.
1 KINGS: The reign of Solomon and division of the kingdom.
2 KINGS: History of the kingdoms of Israel and Judah.
1 CHRONICLES: The reign of David.
2 CHRONICLES: History of the Southern Kingdom (Judah).
EZRA: Return from the Captivity; building the temple; reforms.
NEHEMIAH: Rebuilding the walls of Jerusalem.
ESTHER: Escape of Jews, by God's providence, from extermination.
JOB: Enduring suffering under critical analysis in the hope of a Redeemer.
PSALMS: National hymnbook of God's people (150 psalms).
PROVERBS: Collection of moral and religious maxims.
ECCLESIASTES: Vanity of earthly life without fear of God.
SONG OF SOLOMON: Wedded love as symbol of God's love for the church.
ISAIAH: Messianic prophet: Jehovah is Salvation.
JEREMIAH: God's final effort to save Jerusalem, by this martyr prophet.
LAMENTATIONS: A dirge over desolation of Jerusalem.
EZEKIEL: "They shall know that I am God." Justifies God's action upon Judah.
DANIEL: The kingdoms of the world and the kingdom of God.
HOSEA: Apostasy from God is spiritual adultery.
JOEL: Locust plague; repentance; Gospel age of Holy Spirit.
AMOS: Judgments on Gentile nations and Israel. David's house will rule.

OBADIAH: Edom doomed because of opposition to Israel.

JONAH: God's mercy knows no boundaries (Nineveh).

MICAH: Bethlehem the birthplace of the Messiah for all people.

NAHUM: Destructive vengeance on Nineveh.

HABAKKUK: Judah invaded; Chaldea doomed; just shall live by faith.

ZEPHANIAH: Searching judgments of God. The remnant "hid by God."

HAGGAI: "Build ye the house of the Lord."

ZECHARIAH: The house of the Lord and its glorious future in the New Testament church.

MALACHI: Final message to a disobedient people (Elijah—John the Baptist).

* From *The Books of the Old Testament,* © 1977 Concordia Publishing House, pp. 124-27.

Appendix VI
MESSIANIC PROPHECY *

Prophecies of a Kingly Messiah

Ps. 2:6-8; Ps. 68:18; Ps. 118:22; Is. 9:6, 7; Is. 32:1-3; Is. 42:1-4; Jer. 23:5; Dan. 2:44; Dan. 7:13, 14; Micah 5:2; Zech. 6:12, 13; Zech. 9:9, 10; Mal. 3:1.

Prophecies of a Suffering Messiah

Ps. 22:18; Ps. 69:21; Is. 50:6; Is. 52:14; Is. 53:1-10; Dan. 9:26; Zech. 11:12; Zech. 12:10; Zech 13:7

Prophecies		Fulfillment
Gen. 3:15	Would be the "Seed of a Woman"	Gal. 4:4
Gen. 18:18	Promised Seed of Abraham	Acts 3:25
Gen. 17:19	Promised Seed of Isaac	Matt. 1:2
Num. 24:17	Promised Seed of Jacob	Luke 3:34
Gen. 49:10	Will Descend from the Tribe of Judah	Luke 3:33
Is. 9:7	The Heir to the Throne of David	Matt. 1:1
Micah 5:2	Place of Birth	Matt. 2:1
Dan. 9:25	Time of Birth	Luke 2:1, 2
Is. 7:14	Born of a Virgin	Matt. 1:18
Jer. 31:15	Massacre of Infants	Matt. 2:16
Hos. 11:1	Flight into Egypt	Matt. 2:14
Is. 9:1, 2	Ministry in Galilee	Matt. 4:12-16
Deut. 18:15	As a Prophet	John 6:14
Ps. 110:4	As a Priest, like Melchizedek	Heb. 6:20
Is. 53:3	His Rejection by the People	John 1:11
Is. 11:2	Some of His Characteristics	Luke 2:52
Zech. 9:9	His Triumphal Entry	John 12:13, 14
Ps. 41:9	Betrayed by a Friend	Mark 14:10
Zech. 11:12	Sold for Thirty Pieces of Silver	Matt. 26:15
Zech. 11:13	Money to be Returned for a Potter's Field	Matt. 27:6, 7
Ps. 109:7, 8	Judas' Office to be Taken by Another	Acts 1:18-20
Ps. 27:12	False Witnesses Accuse Him	Matt. 26:60, 61
Is. 53:7	Silent When Accused	Matt. 26:62, 63
Is. 50:6	Smitten and Spat Upon	Mark 14:65
Ps. 69:4	Was Hated Without a Cause	John 15:23-25
Is. 53:4, 5	Suffered Vicariously	Matt. 8:16, 17
Is. 53:12	Crucified with Sinners	Matt. 27:38
Ps. 22:16	Hands and Feet Pierced	John 20:27
Ps. 22:6-8	Mocked and Insulted	Matt. 27:39, 40
Ps. 69:21	Given Gall and Vinegar	John 19:29
Ps. 22:8	Hears Prophetic Words Repeated in Mockery	Matt. 27:43
Ps. 109:4	Prays for His Enemies	Luke 23:34
Zech. 12:10	His Side to Be Pierced	John 19:34
Ps. 22:18	Soldiers Cast Lots for His Coat	Mark 15:24

Ps. 34:20	Not a Bone to Be Broken	John 19:33
Is. 53:9	To be Buried with the Rich	Matt. 27:57-60
Ps. 16:10	His Resurrection	Matt. 28:9
Ps. 68:18	His Ascension	Luke 24:50, 51

* From *The Books of the Old Testament,* © 1977 Concordia Publishing House, pp. 128-29.

Appendix VII
CONTENT SUMMARY OF THE SYNOPTIC GOSPELS *

No.	Incident	Location Matt.	Mark	Luke
	1. The Infancy Narratives			
1.	Genealogy	1:1-17	—	(3:23-38)
2.	The birth of Christ	18-25	—	(2:1-20)
3.	Visit of the Wise Men	2:1-12	—	—
4.	Flight and return	13-23	—	—
5.	Luke's prologue	—	—	1:1-4
6.	Promise of John's birth	—	—	5-25
7.	The Annunciation	—	—	26-38
8.	The Visitation	—	—	39-56
9.	The birth of John	—	—	57-80
10.	The birth of Christ	—	—	2:1-20
11.	The Circumcision	—	—	21-40
12.	The 12 year-old Christ	—	—	41-52
	2. The Galilean Period			
13.	The Mission of John	3:1-12	1:1-8	3:1-20
14.	The introduction of Jesus	13—4:11	9-13	21—4:13
15.	The first preaching tour in Galilee	12-25	14-39	14—5:11
16.	The Sermon on the Mount	5:1—7:29	—	—
17.	The second preaching tour with many miracles	8:1—9:34	1:40—2:22	5:12-39
18.	The first commission of the disciples	9:35—11:1	—	—
19.	Christ and the Baptist	11:2-19	—	(7:18-35)
20.	Further Galilean ministry	20—12:21	23—3:19	6:1 16
21.	The Sermon on the Plain	—	—	17-49
22.	Miracles and conflict in Galilee	22-50	20-35	7:1—8:3
23.	Parables of the Kingdom	13:1-52	4:1-34	4-18
24.	Four miracles	(8:23—9:26)	4:35—5:43	19-56
25.	Christ rejected, sends out the 12 a second time	53-58	6:1-13	9:1-6
26.	Herod and the Baptist	14:1-12	14-29	7-9
27.	Another series of miracles, chiefly to the north of Galilee	13—16:12	30—8:26	10-17
28.	Confession and Transfiguration	13—17:21	27—9:29	18—43a
29.	Brief discourses on brotherhood	22—18:35	30-50	43b-50

3. Luke's Travel Narrative

30. Christ journeys north and east of Galilee, tells parables, performs many miracles	—	—	51— 18:14

4. The Judean Ministry

31. Marriage and divorce	19:1-15	10:1-16	15-17
32. The rich young man, Bartimaeus, Zacchaeus	16— 20:34	17-52	18— 19:27
33. The entry into Jerusalem, conflict	21:1-27	11:1-33	28— 20:8
34. A series of parables and questions	28— 24:3	12:1— 13:4	9— 21:7
35. The discourse on the last times	4— 25:46	5-37	8-38
36. Plotting against Jesus	26:1-19	14:1-16	22:1-13
37. The Last Supper	20-29	17-25	14-38
38. In Gethsemane	30-56	26-52	39-53
39. Christ on trial	57— 27:31	53— 15:20	54— 23:25
40. The crucifixion and burial	32-66	21-47	26-56
41. The Resurrection	28:1-10	16:1-8	24:1-12

5. The Postresurrection Narratives

42. Mark's account, appearance to women mission command, special powers promised	—	9-20	—
43. The bribing of the soldiers	11-15	—	—
44. The command to baptize	16-20	—	—
45. The Emmaus disciples	—	—	13-35
46. His appearance in Jerusalem	—	—	36-49
47. The Ascension	—	—	50-53